# the Next EXIT®

*Congratulations...*

on your purchase of the 2009 edition of the
**most complete interstate highway services guide
ever printed!** ®

## the Next EXIT ®

will save time, money and frustration.
This travel tool will help you find services along the
*USA Interstate Highways*
like nothing you have ever used.

PO Box 888
Garden City, UT  84028

**www.theNextEXIT.com**

# the Next Exit®
# USER GUIDE

Copyright 2009 - The Next Exit®

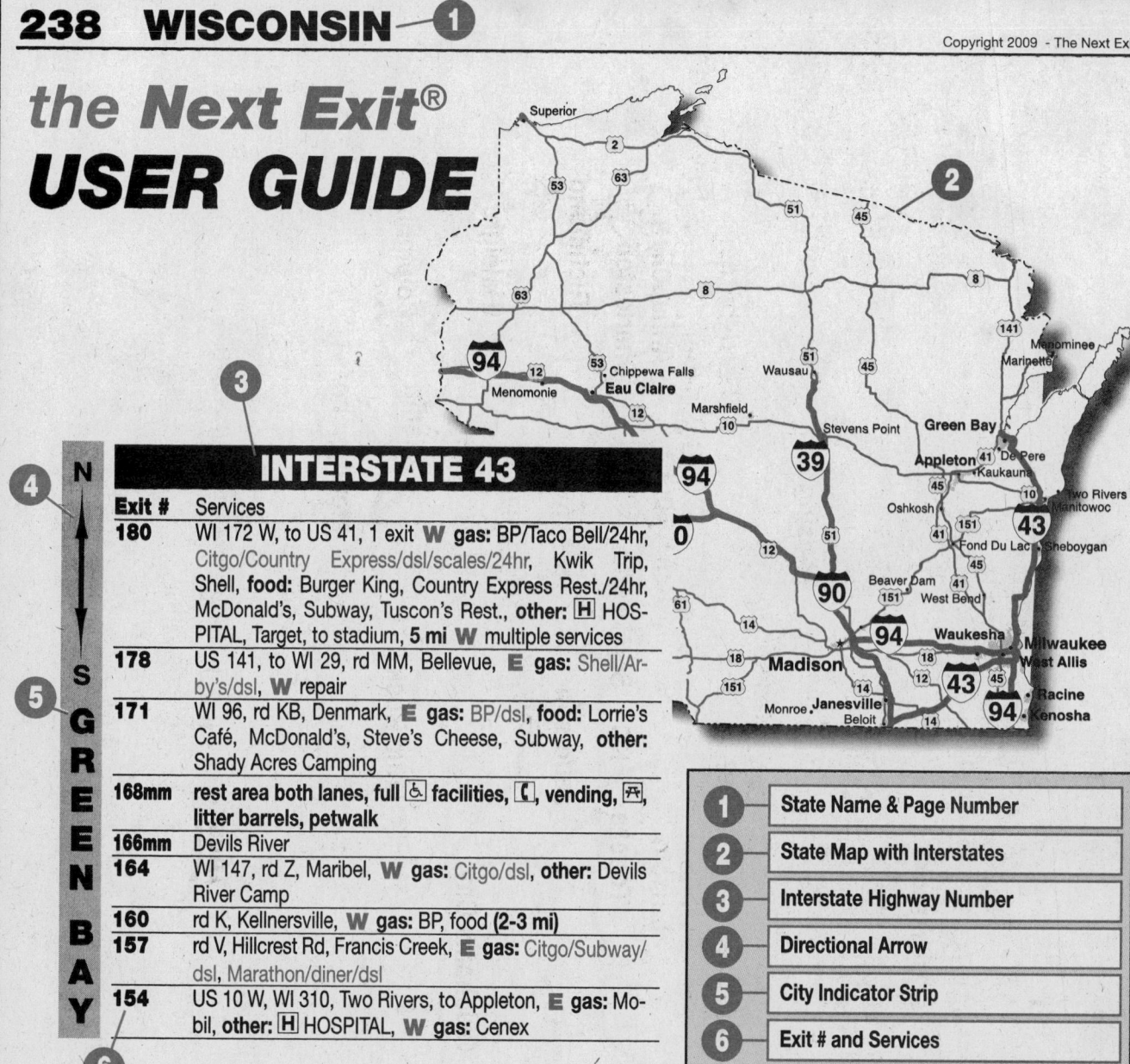

**the Next EXIT® USER GUIDE**

## INTERSTATE 43  ③

| Exit # | Services |
|--------|----------|
| **180** | WI 172 W, to US 41, 1 exit **W** gas: BP/Taco Bell/24hr, Citgo/Country Express/dsl/scales/24hr, Kwik Trip, Shell, **food:** Burger King, Country Express Rest./24hr, McDonald's, Subway, Tuscon's Rest., **other:** H HOS-PITAL, Target, to stadium, **5 mi W** multiple services |
| **178** | US 141, to WI 29, rd MM, Bellevue, **E** gas: Shell/Arby's/dsl, **W** repair |
| **171** | WI 96, rd KB, Denmark, **E** gas: BP/dsl, **food:** Lorrie's Café, McDonald's, Steve's Cheese, Subway, **other:** Shady Acres Camping |
| **168mm** | rest area both lanes, full ♿ facilities, 📞, vending, 🚲, litter barrels, petwalk |
| **166mm** | Devils River |
| **164** | WI 147, rd Z, Maribel, **W** gas: Citgo/dsl, **other:** Devils River Camp |
| **160** | rd K, Kellnersville, **W** gas: BP, food **(2-3 mi)** |
| **157** | rd V, Hillcrest Rd, Francis Creek, **E** gas: Citgo/Subway/dsl, Marathon/diner/dsl |
| **154** | US 10 W, WI 310, Two Rivers, to Appleton, **E** gas: Mobil, **other:** H HOSPITAL, **W** gas: Cenex |

④ N ↕ S
**GREEN BAY**

⑤

⑥

| | |
|---|---|
| **①** | State Name & Page Number |
| **②** | State Map with Interstates |
| **③** | Interstate Highway Number |
| **④** | Directional Arrow |
| **⑤** | City Indicator Strip |
| **⑥** | Exit # and Services |

## Exit #

Most states number exits by the nearest mile marker(mm). A few states use consecutive numbers, in which case mile markers are given in ( ). Mile markers are the little green vertical signs beside the interstate at one mile intervals which indicate distance from the southern or western border of a state. Odd numbered interstates run north/south, even numbered run east/west.

## Services

Services are listed alphabetically by category...**gas, food, lodging, other** services including camping. "H HOSPITAL" indicates an exit from which a hospital may be accessed, but it may not be close to the exit. Services located away from the exit may be referred to by "access to," or "to...," and a distance may be given. A directional notation is also given, such as **N, S, E** or **W**

## Directional Arrows

Follow exits DOWN the page if traveling from North to South or East to West, UP the page if traveling South to North or West to East.

# TABLE OF CONTENTS

## Abbreviations & Symbols used in *the Next EXIT* ®

| | | | |
|---|---|---|---|
| AFB | Air Force Base | NP | National Park |
| B&B | Bed&Breakfast | NRA | Nat Rec Area |
| Bfd | Battlefield | pk | park |
| Ctr | Center | pkwy | parkway |
| Coll | College | rest. | restaurant |
| Cyn | canyon | nb | northbound |
| dsl | diesel | sb | southbound |
| $ | Dollar | eb | eastbound |
| Mem | Memorial | wb | westbound |
| Mkt | Market | SP | state park |
| Mtn | Mountain | SF | state forest |
| mm | mile marker | Sprs | springs |
| N | north side of exit | st | street, state |
| S | south side of exit | sta | station |
| E | east side of exit | TPK | Turnpike |
| W | west side of exit | USPO | Post Office |
| NM | National Monument | vet | veterinarian |
| NHS | Nat Hist Site | whse | warehouse |
| NWR | Nat Wildlife Reserve | @ | truckstop (full service) |
| NF | National Forest | red print | RV accessible |
| H | Hospital | ♿ | Handicapped accessible |
| ✈ | Airport | ☎ | Telephone |
| ⛱ | Picnic Tables | | |

For Trans Canada Highway (TCH) information and more,
please visit us on the web at *www.thenextexit.com*

TABLE OF CONTENTS

# Christmas Pictures...

by Mark Watson - Winter-2008

Traveling during the Holidays is a completely American thing to do. Even when the economy isn't great, people find a way to be with family at this wonderful time of the year. The airlines are busy and highways are jammed with travelers trying to get to their loved ones, either from near or far. You can tell when a vehicle is headed home for Christmas. With windows filled to the brim with packages and dirty snow clinging to their bumpers, the drivers push on relentlessly, as if their pursuit of happiness somehow depends on getting there a few moments sooner. In all of the bustle, someone finally asks, "Did you remember to bring the camera?" and the answer after a momentary pause, "of course."

"Show and tell" after Christmas vacation makes sense to teachers. Sharing with classmates what Santa Claus brought extends the season of good feelings and allows children to settle back into school again after the Holidays. Christmas means different things to many people and these days the emphasis is more on "things", but it wasn't that way the year I was in third grade at Thornwell Elementary.

By 1959, several of my older siblings had left our South Carolina farm to attend college in the west. The country was a lot larger in those days. When the subject of Christmas came up the task of getting everyone home dominated the talk of my parents and I knew that money was an issue. Christmas in our home had always been mostly about being together, and the extra financial strain of helping family members get home would be a factor this year. Being able to enjoy each other's company and Mama's holiday cooking was the main thing though, so the plans were laid.

We began to look forward to their coming, some from as far away as Southern California. Not much shopping was done, but many preparations were made as our expectations mounted. One Sunday night several weeks before the Big Day we were riding home from church listening, as always, to our local radio station, with the sounds of Christmas filling the car. A song ended and the announcer's deep voice said that the next selection, "I'll Be Home For Christmas," had been requested by someone on the other side of the country. I'll never forget how Mama looked at Daddy when the man on the radio gave out the name of my brother. Long distance phone calls were rare back then, but somehow he had gotten a message through, knowing that we would hear and be thrilled. He would not have been disappointed.

The older children arrived and we were together for what was becoming a rare occasion. There were lots of trips to town to see friends, and Mama cooked. There were nights when the talk and laughter lasted till early morning, and Mama baked. Finally someone suggested that we make some fruitcake and we all pitched in to produce, under her direction, the best icebox fruitcake in the world, which, like Christmas, didn't last long enough either. Once again our home overflowed with the happy sounds of family, complete and with no one missing. Christmas came and went too fast that year. Like so many good things we anticipate, it was over before we were ready.

Then the good-byes were said, the older ones departed and those of us still at home prepared to return to school. Santa Claus surely brought me something that year, for even in those times my parents would not have let Christmas morning come without a surprise under the tree. It would have been something practical and useful, but not especially exciting to share with my third grade friends during "show and tell."

The first day back at school featured little boys and girls marching alphabetically to the front of the class with BB guns, skates, dolls and jump ropes. I sat quietly through each presentation, hoping that I might be overlooked altogether, only a little comforted by knowing that I was a "W." When my turn finally came, the buzzing undertone of voices hushed as I walked to the front of the room with nothing in my hands. Turning my back to the blackboard, I saw 33 questioning faces. Then I reached into my back pocket and withdrew four snapshots. Holding them high for everyone to see, I explained in a high, nervous voice how Santa Claus had gone all the way to California just to deliver my older brothers and sister home to me for Christmas, and here were the very pictures of these important people. Not much was said as I returned to my seat and everybody began comparing those photos with new bicycles and other tangible gifts. I sat down and kind, old Mrs. Smith cleared her throat and thanked me for sharing my special Christmas with the class.

It would be 20 years before our family had another Christmas like that, as we scattered across many lands. When we did gather again, the feelings were the same, only now the house was bursting with grandchildren, and Mama baked and cooked. We talked and laughed and visited until the early morning hours and shared our memories of Christmases past. As we reminisced, I could not recall most of the gifts I had received through the years, but I could never forget the photographs of that third grade Christmas. Realizing at last what they really represented, when it came time to take the pictures that year, I stood very still and smiled for the camera.

**MOBILE** (left vertical margin)

E ↕ W (left vertical margin)

## INTERSTATE 10

| Exit # | Services |
|---|---|
| **66.5mm** | Alabama/Florida state line |
| **66mm** | Welcome Ctr full ♿ facilities, 📞, vending, 🛎 litter barrels, petwalk |
| **53** | rd 64, Wilcox Rd, **N gas**: BP/Oasis/Stuckeys/Subway/Chester's/dsl/scales/24hr/@, **other**: Styx RV Park, fireworks, **S gas**: Chevron/dsl, Outpost/dsl, **other**: Hilltop RV Park (1.5 mi), Wilderness RV Park, fireworks |
| **44** | AL 59, Loxley, **N gas**: Loves/Arby's/dsl/scales/24hr, **S gas**: Chevron/dsl, Exxon/DQ/dsl, RaceWay, **food**: Hardee's, McDonald's, Waffle House, **lodging**: Bay Inn, Loxley Motel (3mi), WindChase Inn, **other**: to Gulf SP |
| **38** | AL 181, Malbis, **N food**: Chick-fil-A, Cracker Barrel, Logan's Roadhouse, McDonald's, Moe's SW Grill, Olive Garden, Panera Bread, Ruby Tuesday, Russo's Rest., Ryan's, Starbucks, Stix Asian, Wendy's, **lodging**: Comfort Suites, Country Inn&Suites, Holiday Inn Express, La Quinta, **other**: Barnes&Noble, Belk, Best Buy, Dillards, $Tree, Goodyear/auto, Michael's, Old Navy, Petsmart, Ross, Tuesday Morning, Walgreens, World Mkt, **S gas**: Chevron/dsl, Shell/LA Subs, Texaco/dsl, **food**: Burger King, Don Carlos, **lodging**: Malbis Motel (1mi), **other**: Honda, Lowes Whse, Sam's Club, Toyota/Scion |
| **35** | US 90, US 98, **N gas**: Shell, Summit, **food**: Beef O'Brady's, China Fun, **lodging**: Fairfield Inn, **other**: Bass Pro Shop, Circuit City, JC Penney, Kohl's, Rite Aid, USPO, **S gas**: Exxon/dsl, Shell, **food**: Arby's, Burger King, Checker's, Dolive Bay, Domino's, El Rancho Mexican, Firehouse Subs, Grand Buffet, Hooters, IHOP, Krystal, Longhorn Steaks, McAlister's Deli, McDonald's, O'Charley's, Papa John's, Pizza Hut, S China Rest., Starbucks, Subway, Taco Bell, Waffle House, Wendy's, Zaxby's, **lodging**: Comfort Suites, Eastern Shore Motel, Hampton Inn, Hilton Garden, Homewood Suites, Microtel, **other**: Ⓗ HOSPITAL, BooksAMillion, GNC, Goody's, Home Depot, Office Depot, Steinmart, TJ Maxx |
| **30** | US 90/98, Battleship Pkwy, same as 27 |
| **29mm** | tunnel begins wb |
| **28mm** | tunnel begins eb |
| **27** | US 90/98, Battleship Pkwy, Gov't St, **S food**: Capt's Table Seafood, Felix's Fish Camp, Oysterella's Rest., **lodging**: Best Western, **other**: to USS Alabama |
| **26b** | Water St, Mobile, downtown, **N lodging**: Hampton Inn, Radisson, Ramada, Renaissance, to Visitors Ctr |
| **26a** | Canal St (from eb), same as 26b |
| **25b** | Virginia St, Mobile, **N gas**: Shell/dsl |
| **25a** | Texas St (from wb, no return) |
| **24** | Broad St, to Duval St, Mobile, **N gas**: Chevron |
| **23** | Michigan Ave, **N gas**: Exxon, **other**: $General |
| **22b** | AL 163, Dauphin Island Pkwy, **N gas**: BP, **lodging**: PortCity Inn, **other**: Family$, **S gas**: Circle K/dsl, Exxon/Subway/24hr, Shell/dsl, **food**: Checker's, Gone Fishin Rest., Kim's Palace, Waffle House, **other**: $General |
| **20** | I-65 N, to Montgomery |
| **17** | AL 193, Tillmans Corner, to Dauphin Island, **N gas**: Chevron/24hr, **food**: Boiling Pot, Firehouse Subs, Golden Corral, IHOP, Ruby Tuesday, Ryan's, Zaxby's, **other**: Ⓗ HOSPITAL, Big 10 Tire, Lowes Whse, Radio Shack, Turning Wheel RV Ctr, Walmart SuperCtr |
| **15b a** | US 90, Tillmans Corner, to Mobile, **N gas**: Chevron/24hr, RaceWay, Shell, **food**: Arby's, Azteca's Mexican, Burger King, Checker's, CiCi's, Domino's, Godfather's, KFC, Hooters, McDonald's, Papa John's, Pizza Hut, Popeye's, Russell's BBQ, Sonny's BBQ, Subway, Taco Bell, Waffle House, **lodging**: Baymont Inn, Comfort Suites, Day's Inn, Econolodge, Hampton Inn, Holiday |

## INTERSTATE 10 CONT'D

**15b a** Continued
Inn, InTown Suites, Knight's Inn, La Quinta, Motel 6, Red Roof Inn, Rodeway Inn, Super 8, Wingate Inn, **other:** AutoZone, Big Lots, CarQuest, $General, $Tree, Family$, Firestone/auto, O'Reilly Parts, Rite Aid, Sears Essentials, Walgreens, USPO, vet, **S gas:** Chevron/24hr, RaceWay/dsl, Shell/dsl/24hr, **food:** Hardee's, Waffle House, **other:** B&R RV Ctr, Jonnys RV Ctr, Peterbilt, auto repair, tires, transmissions

**13** to Theodore, **N gas:** BP, Citgo, Pilot/Wendy's/dsl/24hr, Shell/Subway, Texaco/McDonald's, **food:** Church's, Waffle House, **other:** Advance Parts, Family$, Food World, Greyhound Prk, Rite Aid, **S gas:** Chevron/dsl, **other:** I-10 Kamping, Paynes RV Park(4mi), Bellingraf Gardens

**10** rd 39, Bayou La Batre, Dawes, **N other:** Kenworth/Volvo

**4** AL 188 E, to Grand Bay, **N gas:** BP, Citgo/dsl, Energize/Blimpie, Shell/Stuckey's, TA/BP/Buckhorn Rest./dsl/scales/24hr/@, **food:** Subway, Waffle House, **S gas:** Chevron/24hr, **food:** Hardee's, **other:** Trav-L-Kamp

**1mm** Welcome Ctr eb, full ♿ facilities, info, 🕿, 🍴, litter barrels, petwalk, RV dump

**0mm** Alabama/Mississippi state line

## INTERSTATE 20

**Exit #** Services
**215mm** Alabama/Georgia state line, Central/Eastern time zone
**213mm** Welcome Ctr wb, full ♿ facilities, info, 🕿, vending, 🍴, litter barrels, petwalk, RV dump, 24hr security
**210** AL 49, Abernathy, **N** fireworks, **S** fireworks
**209mm** Tallapoosa River
**208mm** weigh sta wb
**205** AL 46, to Heflin, **N gas:** BP/dsl/rest., **food:** 205 Cafe, **other:** RV Camping, tires, **S gas:** Shell/dsl/24hr, **other:** Truck Repair
**199** AL 9, Heflin, **N gas:** Texaco/Subway/dsl/24hr, **food:** Hardee's, Pop's Charburgers, **lodging:** Howard Johnson, **other:** Ford, USPO, **S gas:** Chevron, SuperMart, **food:** Huddle House
**198mm** Talladega Nat Forest eastern boundary
**191** US 431, to US 78
**188** to US 78, to Anniston, **N gas:** Shell/KFC, Texaco/Subway, **food:** Cracker Barrel, IHOP, LoneStar Steaks, Los Mexicano, Sonny's BBQ, Waffle House, Wendy's, Zaxby's, **lodging:** Country Inn&Suites, Hampton Inn, Holiday Inn Express, Jameson Inn, Sleep Inn, Wingate Inn, **other:** Camping World RV Ctr, Harley-Davidson, Honda, Lowes Whse, Nissan, O'Reilly Parts, **S food:** Arby's, Longhorn Steaks, Mexico Lindo Grill, Olive Garden, **other:** Best Buy, Home Depot, Kohl's, Old Navy, PetsMart, Ross, Target, TJ Maxx
**185** AL 21, to Anniston, **N gas:** BP/dsl, Chevron/24hr, Shell, **food:** Applebee's, Arby's, Burger King, Capt D's, CiCi's, China Luck, Domino's, Garfield's Rest., HappyStar Buffet, Hardee's, Jack's rest., Krystal, Logan's Roadhouse, McAlister's, McDonald's, O'Charley's, Pizza Hut, Red Lobster, Shoney's, Sonic, Starbucks, Taco Bell, Waffle House, Western Sizzlin, **lodging:** Day's Inn, Liberty Inn

**185** Continued
Oxford Inn, Red Carpet Inn, **other:** BooksAMillion, Dillards, $General, Firestone/auto, FoodMax, Goody's, JC Penney, Sears/auto, mall, to Ft McClellan, **S gas:** Exxon, Kangaroo/dsl/scales, Shell/Subway/dsl, Texaco, **food:** Chick-fil-A, El Poblano Mexican, Outback Steaks, Waffle House, Wendy's, **lodging:** Baymont Inn, Comfort Inn, Econolodge, Motel 6, Travelodge, **other:** ⒽHOSPITAL, Goodyear/auto, Walmart SuperCtr/gas

**179** to Munford, Coldwater, **S gas:** Chevron **food:** China King, Jack's Rest., **other:** Rite Aid, **N gas:** Texaco/dsl, **other:** Anniston Army Depot

**173** AL 5, Eastaboga, **S gas:** Shell, **food:** DQ/Stuckey's, **other:** to Speedway/Hall of Fame

**168** AL 77, to Talladega, **N gas:** Citgo, QV/Domino's, Super 77, **food:** Jack's Rest., KFC/Taco Bell, Waffle House, **S gas:** Chevron/Subway/dsl, Shell/dsl/scales, Texaco/Burger King, **food:** McDonald's, Rana's Mexican, **lodging:** Comfort Inn, Day's Inn, McCaig Motel, **other:** to Speedway, Hall of Fame

**165** Embry Cross Roads, **N gas:** Hi-Tech Fuel, **S gas:** Chevron/Huddle House/dsl, TrkStp/rest./dsl/scales/24hr, **lodging:** McCaig Motel/rest.

**164mm** Coosa River

**162** US 78, Riverside, **N other:** Safe Harbor Camping, **S gas:** Marathon, Texaco/dsl, **food:** Budsy's Steaks, **lodging:** Best Value Inn

**158** US 231, Pell City, **N gas:** Exxon/dsl, **food:** Arby's, Cracker Barrel, Golden Rule BBQ, Jade Garden Chinese, Krystal, Legacy Steaks, Wendy's, **lodging:** Hampton Inn, Holiday Inn Express, **other:** City Tire, $Tree, Home Depot, Radio Shack, Walgreens, Walmart SuperCtr/gas, **S gas:** BP, Chevron, Putts/dsl, **food:** Burger King, Hardee's, Jack's Rest., KFC, McDonald's, Pizza Hut, Subway, Taco Bell, Waffle House, **lodging:** Quality Inn, **other:** ⒽHOSPITAL, AutoZone, Chevrolet/Pontiac, Chrysler/Dodge/Jeep, CVS Drug, Ford/Lincoln/Mercury, Fred's Drug, RV Camping

**156** US 78 E, to Pell City, **S gas:** Chevron/dsl/24hr, Exxon/dsl/24hr, Shell

**153** US 78, Chula Vista

**152** Cook Springs

**147** Brompton, **N gas:** Citgo, **S gas:** Chevron/dsl, **other:** Suncoast RV Ctr/LP

**144** US 411, Leeds, **N gas:** BP/dsl, Raceway, Shell/Subway, **food:** Arby's, Burger King, Cracker Barrel, Krystal, Milo's Café, Pizza Hut, Ruby Tuesday, Waffle House, Wendy's, **lodging:** Best Western, Comfort Inn, **other:** $Tree, Food Giant, RV camping, **S gas:** Chevron, RaceWay, **food:** Capt D's, Chick-fil-A, Guadalajara Jalisco Mexican, Hardee's, KFC, McDonald's, Papa John's, Santa Fe Steaks, Taco Bell, Waffle House, **lodging:** Day's Inn, **other:** Advance Parts, AutoZone, $General, Lowes Whse, NAPA, O'Reilly Parts, Radio Shack, Walgreens, Walmart SuperCtr/Subway

**140** US 78, Leeds, **S gas:** Chevron, Exxon, Shell(1mi), **lodging:** Best Value Inn, **other:** Bass Pro Shop

**139mm** Cahaba River

**136** I-459 S, to Montgomery, Tuscaloosa

**135** US 78, Old Leeds Rd, **N other:** B'ham Racetrack

**133** US 78, to Kilgore Memorial Dr, (wb return at 132), **N gas:** Chevron, Exxon/dsl/24hr, **food:** Golden Rule BBQ,

## INTERSTATE 20 CONT'D

E ↕ W

**133** Continued
Hamburger Heaven, Jack's Rest., Krystal, Waffle House, **lodging:** Comfort Inn, Eastwood Hotel, Siesta, same as 132, **S gas:** BP, **food:** Arby's, China Buffet, El Mexicano, Gus' Hotdogs, McDonald's, Subway, **lodging:** Best Western, Hampton Inn, Holiday Inn Express, Quality Inn, **other:** $Tree, Ford, Graham Tire, Sam's Club/gas, Walmart

**132b a** US 78, Crestwood Blvd, **N gas:** Exxon, **food:** Barnhill's Buffet, Krystal, Villa Fiesta, Waffle House, **other:** Chevrolet, O'Reilly Parts, SuperPetz, **S gas:** BP, Crown/24hr, Shell/24hr, **food:** Arby's, Capt D's, China Garden, Denny's, Emperor House, Hooters, IHOP, KFC, LJ Silver/Taco Bell, Logan's Roadhouse, McDonald's, New China Buffet, Olive Garden, Pizza Hut, Red Lobster, Ryan's, Wendy's, **lodging:** Comfort Inn, Delux Inn, Economy Lodge, Park Inn, USA Lodge, **other:** H HOSPITAL, Circuit City, Home Depot, K-Mart, Office Depot, Radio Shack, Sears/auto, TJ Maxx, Waldenbooks, mall

**130b** US 11, 1st Ave, **N gas:** BP, Chevron/24hr, Conoco/dsl, Crown, **lodging:** Bama Motel, **other:** AutoZone, Southern Foods, **S food:** McDonald's, Pacific Seafood, **lodging:** Relax Inn, Sky Inn

**130a** I-59 N, to Gadsden

**I-59 S and I-20 W run together from Birminghan to Meridian, MS**

**129** Airport Blvd, **N lodging:** Sheraton, **other:** ✈ **S gas:** BP, Shell, **food:** Hardee's, Taqueira, **lodging:** Best Inn, Holiday Inn

**128** AL 79, Tallapoosa St, **N gas:** Kangaroo/Subway/dsl, Exxon/dsl

**126b** 31st St, **N gas:** Citgo, Shell, **food:** McDonald's

**126a** US 31, US 280, 26th St, Carraway Blvd, **N gas:** Phillips 66, **food:** Church's, KFC, Rally's

**125b** 22nd St, **N lodging:** Sheraton

**125a** 17th St, Civic Ctr

**124b a** I-65, S to Montgomery, N to Nashville

**123** US 78, Arkadelphia Rd, **N gas:** Chevron/24hr, Jet-Pep, Pilot/Wendy's/dsl/24hr, Shell, **food:** Popeye's, **lodging:** Day's Inn, **other:** transmissions, **S other:** H HOSPITAL, to Legion Field

**121** Bush Blvd (from wb, no return), Ensley, **N gas:** BP, Exxon, **food:** Wings&Waffles

**120** AL 269, 20th St, Ensley Ave, **N food:** KFC, **other:** GMC/Pontiac, Breeze RV, **S gas:** BP, **other:** H HOSPITAL, Chevrolet, Chrysler/Jeep, Hyundai, Toyota

**119b** Ave I (from wb)

**119a** Scrushy Pkwy, Gary Ave, **N gas:** BP, Chevron/dsl, **food:** Burger King, Fairfield Seafood, McDonald's, Seafood Express, Subway, Taco Bell, **other:** Family$, Food Fair, **S gas:** Mobil, Texaco, **food:** Omelet Shoppe, **other:** H HOSPITAL

**118** AL 56, Valley Rd, Fairfield, **N other:** NAPA, **S food:** Papa John's, **lodging:** Inn At Fairfield, **other:** Home Depot, Radio Shack, Sears, Winn-Dixie

**115** Allison-Bonnett Memorial Dr, **N gas:** BP/dsl, Phillips 66, RaceWay, Shell/dsl, **food:** Church's, Guadalajara Grill, Hardee's, Subway, **other:** Advance Parts, O'Reilly Parts

**113** 18th Ave, to Hueytown, **S gas:** Chevron/dsl, **food:** McDonald's

**112** 18th St, 19th St, Bessemer, **N gas:** Citgo, RaceWay, Shell, **food:** Jack's Rest., **other:** OK Tire/repair, **S gas:**

B E S S E M E R

**112** Continued
Chevron, **food:** Arby's, Burger King, Krystal, McDonald's, **other:** Lowe's Whse

**110** AL Adventure Pkwy

**108** US 11, AL 5 N, Academy Dr, **N gas:** Exxon, **food:** Applebee's, Cracker Barrel, Golden Rule BBQ, Santa Fe Steaks, Waffle House, **lodging:** Best Western, Comfort Inn, Country Inn&Suites, Courtyard, Fairfield Inn, Holiday Inn Express, Jameson Inn, **other:** Chevrolet, Chrysler/Jeep/Dodge, **S gas:** BP, Citgo/Church's/dsl, **food:** Burger King, Little Caesar's, McDonald's, Milo's Burgers, Ruby Tuesday, Sonic, Wendy's, Zaxby's, **lodging:** Days Inn, Hampton Inn, Scottish Inn, **other:** H HOSPITAL, Big 10 Tire, $Tree, Ford, Goody's, Radio Shack, Walmart SuperCtr, Winn-Dixie, to civic ctr

**106** I-459 N, to Montgomery

**104** Rock Mt Lake, **S gas:** ⊕FLYING J/Conoco/dsl/LP/rest./24hr

**100** to Abernant, **N gas:** Citgo, **other:** McCalla Camping, **S gas:** BP, Exxon, Petro/Chevron/dsl/rest./scales/24hr/@, **other:** $General, Tannehill SP (3mi)

**97** US 11 S, AL 5 S, to W Blocton, **S gas:** BP/KFC/dsl, Exxon/Subway/dsl, Shell/dsl, **food:** Jack's Rest.

**89** Mercedes Dr, **N lodging:** Baymont Inn, **S other:** Mercedes Auto Plant

**86** Vance, to Brookwood, **N gas:** BP/dsl, Shell/dsl/rest./24hr

**85mm** rest area both lanes, full ♿ facilities, 🚻, vending, 🍽, litter barrels, petwalk, RV dump

**79** US 11, University Blvd, Coaling, **S gas:** Chevron/dsl

**77** Cottondale, **N gas:** Chevron/McDonald's, TA/BP/Subway/Taco Bell/dsl/@, Wilco/Wendy's/dsl/scales/24hr, **food:** Arby's, Pizza Hut, Ruby Tuesday, **lodging:** Hampton Inn, Microtel, **other:** Blue Beacon, SpeedCo, USPO, **S** Chevrolet

**76** US 11, E Tuscaloosa, Cottondale, **N gas:** Citgo, Exxon, Shell/dsl, **food:** Burger King, Cracker Barrel, Waffle House, **lodging:** Comfort Inn, Howard Johnson, Western Motel, **other:** transmissions, **S gas:** Pilot/Subway/dsl/scales/24hr, Texaco/dsl, **lodging:** Sleep Inn

**73** US 82, McFarland Blvd, Tuscaloosa, **N gas:** BP/dsl, Chevron/dsl, Exxon, RaceWay, Shell/dsl, **food:** Arby's, Buffalo Wild Wings, Burger King, Capt D's, Chick-fil-A, Jason's Deli, Krystal, Los Calientes, Moe's SW Grill, Olive Garden, Popeye's, Red Lobster, Waffle House, **lodging:** Best Western, Best Value Inn, Comfort Suites, Guest Lodge, Masters Inn, **other:** Aamco, Advance

**TUSCALOOSA E ⟷ W**

## INTERSTATE 20 CONT'D

| | |
|---|---|
| 73 | Continued<br>Parts, Big 10 Tire, Bruno's Foods, $General, Firestone, Goodyear/auto, OK Tire, Old Navy, SteinMart, U-Haul, mall, **S gas:** Exxon, Shell, **food:** Checker's, Chili's, Grand Buffet, Guthries, Hardees, KFC, Logan's Road-house, McDonald's, Pizza Hut, Sonic, Subway, Taco Bell, Taco Casa, Wendy's, **lodging:** Country Inn&Suites, Days Inn, Econolodge, La Quinta, Motel 6, Quality Inn, Ramada Inn, Super 8, **other:** BooksAMillion, Chrysler/Dodge/Jeep, Dillard's, $Tree, FoodWorld, Goody's, Michael's, NAPA, Office Depot, Rite Aid, Sam's Club/gas, TJ Maxx, Walmart SuperCtr |
| 71b | I-359, Al 69 N, to Tuscaloosa, **N other:** H HOSPITAL, U of AL, to Stillman Coll |
| 71a | AL 69 S, to Moundville, **N gas:** Chevron, MapCo, Parade, Shell/dsl, **food:** Arby's, Hooters, IHOP, LoneStar Steaks, OutBack Steaks, Pizza Hut, Ryan's, Waffle House, Wendy's, Zaxby's, **lodging:** Courtyard, Fairfield Inn, Hilton Garden, Jameson Inn, **other:** Advance Parts, Goodyear/auto, K-Mart, Lowes Whse, Mazda/VW, O'Reilly Parts, to Mound SM |
| 68 | Northfort-Tuscaloosa Western Bypass |
| 64mm | Black Warrior River |
| 62 | Fosters, **N gas:** BP, Chevron/dsl |
| 52 | US 11, US 43, Knoxville, **N gas:** Exxon/dsl, **other:** Knox Hill Camping |
| 45 | AL 37, Union, **S gas:** BP/dsl/rest./24hr, Chevron/Subway, **food:** Hardee's, **other:** Greene Co Greyhound Park |
| 40 | AL 14, Eutaw, **N other:** to Tom Bevill Lock/Dam, **S gas:** BP, H HOSPITAL |
| 39mm | rest area wb, full ♿ facilities, 🚻, vending, 🏕, litter barrels, petwalk, RV dump |
| 38mm | rest area eb, full ♿ facilities, 🚻, vending, 🏕, litter barrels, petwalk, RV dump |
| 32 | Boligee, **N gas:** BP/dsl/rest./24hr, **S gas:** Chevron/Subway/24hr |
| 27mm | Tombigbee River, Tenn-Tom Waterway |
| 23 | Epes, to Gainesville |
| 17 | AL 28, Livingston, **S gas:** BP/dsl/24hr, Chevron/Subway/24hr, Shell/dsl, **food:** Burger King, Pizza Hut, **lodging:** Comfort Inn, Western Inn, **other:** repair/24hr |
| 8 | AL 17, York, **S gas:** BP/dsl/rest./scales/@, **lodging:** Day's Inn/Briar Patch Rest. |
| 1 | to US 80 E, Cuba, **N gas:** Rocking Chair Trkstp/Rest./dsl/, **S gas:** Chevron, Dixie |
| .5mm | Welcome Ctr eb, full ♿ facilities, 🚻, vending, 🏕, litter barrels, petwalk, RV dump |
| | I-20 E and I-59 N run together from Meridian, MS to B'ham |
| 0mm | Alabama/Mississippi state line |

## INTERSTATE 22 (FUTURE)

| Exit # | Services |
|---|---|
| 85 | US 78 (I-22 future continues eb, local traffic only) |
| 81 | rd 45, W Jefferson |
| 78 | Dora, Sumiton |
| 72 | rd 61, Cordova |
| 70 | rd 22, Cordova, Parish |

**E ⟷ W**

| | |
|---|---|
| 65 | Bevill Industrial Pkwy, Jasper, H HOSPITAL, Chevrolet, to walker Co Lake |
| 63 | AL 269, Jasper, Parish, **N gas:** Chevron/deli/dsl |
| 61 | AL 69, Jasper, Tuscaloosa, **N gas:** 69 Superstop(1mi) |
| 57 | AL 118 E, Jasper, **N gas:** Chevron, Exxon, **food:** BBQ |
| 52 | AL 118, Carbon Hill, **S lodging:** Shadowbrook Inn |
| 46 | rd 11, Carbon Hill, Nauvoo, **S gas:** Shell |
| 39 | AL 13, Natural Bridge, Eldridge |
| 34 | AL 233, Glen Allen, Natural Bridge, no serivces |
| 30 | AL 129, Brilliant, Winfield, **S gas:** Shell/deli/dsl, Texaco/deli/dsl |
| 26 | AL 44, Brilliant, Guin, H HOSPITAL |
| 22 | rd 45 |
| 16 | US 43, US 278, Hamilton, Guin, **S gas:** Shell/deli/dsl |
| 14 | Hamilton, **N gas:** Woco/dsl, **food:** Huddle House, **lodging:** Keywest Inn |
| 11 | AL 17, Hamilton, Sulligent, **N gas:** Citgo/dsl, **other:** H HOSPITAL |
| 7 | Hamilton, Weston, H HOSPITAL |
| 3 | rd 3 |
| 0mm | Alabama/Mississippi State Line |

## INTERSTATE 59

**N ⟷ S · FT PAYNE · GADSDEN**

| Exit # | Services |
|---|---|
| 241.5mm | Alabama/Georgia state line, Central/Eastern time zone |
| 241mm | Welcome Ctr sb, full ♿ facilities, 🚻, vending, 🏕, litter barrels, petwalk, RV dump |
| 239 | to US 11, Sulphur Springs Rd, **E other:** Sequoyah Caverns Camping (4mi) |
| 231 | AL 40, AL 117, Hammondville, Valley Head, **E other:** Sequoyah Caverns Camping (5mi), **W gas:** Victory Fuel |
| 222 | US 11, to Ft Payne, **E gas:** Shell, **other:** Chevrolet, **1 mi E food:** Arby's, Hardee's, Jack's Rest., KFC, Krystal, Pizza Hut, Subway, Western Sizzlin, **lodging:** Rodeway Inn, **other:** $General, Foodland/gas, **W gas:** Jetpep/dsl, **food:** Waffle King |
| 218 | AL 35, Ft Payne, **E food:** Asian Palace, Capt D's, Catfish 1, Fillin Station, Golden Rule BBQ, McDonald's, New China, Papa John's, Quizno's, Taco Bell, Wendy's, Zaxby's, **other:** Advance Parts, AutoZone, Big Lots, Buick/Pontiac/GMC, Chrysler/Dodge, Curves, $General, O'Reilly Parts, **W gas:** Chevron, Kangaroo/dsl, Victory Fuel, **food:** Burger King, Cracker Barrel, Domino's, Hardee's, Ryan's, Ruby Tuesday, Santa Fe Steaks, Subway, Waffle House, **lodging:** Day's Inn, Econolodge, Hampton Inn, Holiday Inn Express, **other:** H HOSPITAL, $Tree, Ford/Lincoln/Mercury, GNC, Goody's, Kia, K-Mart, Lowes Whse, Radio Shack, Walgreens, Walmart SuperCtr/gas |
| 205 | AL 68, Collinsville, **E gas:** Chevron, **food:** Jack's Rest., Smokin' Joe's Rest., **lodging:** Howard Johnson, **other:** to Little River Canyon, Weiss Lake, **W gas:** BP/dsl, Shell |
| 188 | AL 211, to US 11, Gadsden, **E gas:** Jet-Pep, **other:** Noccalula Falls RV Park, **W gas:** Jet-Pep/dsl |
| 183 | US 431, US 278, Gadsden, **E gas:** Jet-Pep/dsl, Shell, Texaco, **food:** Waffle House, Wendy's, **lodging:** Days Inn, Econolodge, Rodeway Inn, **other:** st police, **W gas:** Chevron/24hr, Exxon, Jet-Pep, **food:** KFC/Taco Bell, Krystal, Jumbo Buffet, McDonald's, Pizza Hut, Subway, **lodging:** Super Value |
| 182 | I-759, to Gadsden |

## INTERSTATE 59 CONT'D

N
↕
S

| | |
|---|---|
| **181** | AL 77, Rainbow City, to Gadsden, **E** gas: Petro/rest./ dsl/scales/24hr/@, **food:** Austin's Rest., **lodging:** Day's Inn, **W** gas: Citgo, Kangaroo/dsl, Pure/dsl, Texaco, **food:** Arby's, Cracker Barrel, DQ, Hardee's, Los Arcos, Ruby Tuesday, Santa Fe Grill, Subway, Waffle House, **lodging:** Best Western, Comfort Suites, Fairfield Inn, Holiday Inn Express, **other:** $General, $Tree, O'Reilly Parts, Radio Shack, Walmart SuperCtr |
| **174** | to Steele, **W** gas: Clean Fuels/dsl, JetPep/dsl |
| **168mm** | rest area sb, full ♿ facilities, 🚻, vending, 🛆, litter barrels, petwalk, RV dump |
| **166** | US 231, Whitney, to Ashville, **E** gas: Chevron/dsl, Discount/gas, **W** gas: Texaco/dsl, **food:** Jack's Rest., Huddle House, Subway |
| **165mm** | rest area nb, full ♿ facilities, 🚻, vending, 🛆, litter barrels, petwalk, RV dump |
| **156** | AL 23, to US 11, Springville, to St Clair Springs, **W** gas: Horizon, **food:** Azteca's Mexican, China Stix, Waffle House, **other:** Walmart SuperCtr/Subway |
| **154** | AL 174, Springville, to Odenville, **W** gas: Chevron/24hr, Exxon, Shell/dsl, Texaco/Subway/Dominos, **food:** Jack's Rest., McDonald's, Seafood Mkt Rest, Smokin BBQ |
| **148** | to US 11, Argo, **E** gas: BP |
| **143** | Mt Olive Church Rd, Deerfoot Pkwy |
| **141** | to Trussville, Pinson, **E** gas: BP/dsl, Shell/Subway/ dsl, Texaco/dsl, **food:** Applebee's, Arby's, Cracker Barrel, LoneStar Steaks, McDonald's, Papa Johns, Pizza Hut, Taco Bell, Waffle House, Wendy's, **lodging:** Comfort Inn, Holiday Inn Express, Jameson Inn, **other:** Curves, Harley-Davidson, **W** gas: Chevron/24hr, Shell, **food:** Arby's, Buffalo Wild Wings, Burger King, Chick-fil-A, Costa's BBQ, Costa's Italian, DQ, East Buffet, Frontera Grill Mexican, Krystal, Milo's Burgers, Moe's SW Grill, Palace Chinese, Ruby Tuesday, Whataburger, Zaxby's, **other:** Aldi Foods, CVS Drug, $Tree, GNC, Goody's, K-Mart, Kohl's, Marshall's, Office Depot, Petsmart, Radio Shack, Sam's Club/gas, Walgreens, Walmart SuperCtr, vet |
| **137** | I-459 S, to Montgomery, Tuscaloosa |
| **134** | to AL 75, Roebuck Pkwy, **W** gas: Chevron, Exxon, Mobil, Shell, **food:** Arby's, Azteca Mexican, Burger King, Chick-fil-A, Krystal, McDonald's, Milo's Burgers, O'Brien's Seafood, O'Charley's, Rally's, Ruby Tuesday, Starbucks, Steak&Ale, Subway, Taco Bell, Waffle House, Yoshiko Japanese, **other:** 🏥 HOSPITAL, Aldi Foods, CVS Drug, Dodge, Firestone/auto, Ford, Goodyear/auto, Honda, Hyundai, Jo-Ann Fabrics, Lincoln/Mercury, NTB, O'Reilly Parts, VW, Walgreens, Walmart SuperCtr/gas |
| **133** | 4th St, to US 11 (from nb), **W** food: Papa John's, **other:** $General, Food World, Goody's, Rite Aid, Suzuki, USPO, same as 134 |
| **132** | US 11 N, 1st Ave, **E** same as 131, **W** gas: Chevron/24hr, Shell, **food:** Krispy Kreme, **other:** Westwood Parts, **other:** city park |
| **131** | 77th Ave (from nb), **E** gas: Exxon, **food:** Church's, **other:** CVS Drug, O'Reilly Parts, U-Haul, same as 132, **W** gas: Texaco |
| **130** | I-20, E to Atlanta, W to Tuscaloosa |
| **I-59** | S and I-20 W run together from Birmingham to Mississippi. See Alabama Interstate 20. |

E ← W
ATHENS
DECATUR

## INTERSTATE 65

| Exit # | Services |
|---|---|
| **366mm** | Alabama/Tennessee state line |
| **365** | AL 53, to Ardmore, **E** gas: William's Service, **lodging:** Budget Inn |
| **364mm** | Welcome Ctr sb, full ♿ facilities, info, 🚻, vending, 🛆, litter barrels, petwalk, RV dump |
| **361** | Elkmont, **W** gas: BP/dsl/rest., HQ/dsl/rest., William's Service/dsl/rest., **food:** Sonny G's BBQ, **other:** antiques, repair |
| **354** | US 31 S, to Athens, **W** gas: Chevron, Texaco/dsl, **food:** Capt. D's, China Dragon, Jack's Rest., Little Caesars, McDonald's, Subway, **lodging:** Budget Inn, Mark Hotel, **other:** 🏥 HOSPITAL, Advance Parts, CVS Drug, $General, K-Mart, Northgate RV Park, Piddly Wiggly, Rite Aid, Walgreens |
| **351** | US 72, to Athens, Huntsville, **E** gas: Exxon, RaceWay, Shell/Subway, Texaco/dsl, **food:** Burger King, Clark's Rest., Cracker Barrel, Lawler's BBQ, McDonald's, Waffle House, Wendy's, **lodging:** Comfort Inn, Country Hearth Inn, Hampton Inn, Quality Inn, **other:** Russell Stover, vet, **W** gas: BP, Chevron/24hr, **food:** Applebee's, Arby's, Bojangles, Burger King, Catfish Cabin, Casa Blanca Mexican, Chick-fil-A, Hardee's, Krystal, Logan's Roadhouse, Papa John's, Pizza Hut, Ruby Tuesday, Shoney's, Sonic, Starbucks, Taco Bell, Zaxby's, **lodging:** Best Western, Day's Inn, Holiday Inn Express, Sleep Inn, Super 8, **other:** 🏥 HOSPITAL, Chevrolet, Chrysler/Jeep, $General, Big 10 Tire, Ford/Lincoln/Mercury, Goodyear/auto, Lowe's Whse, O'Reilly Parts, Radio Shack, Staples, Walmart SuperCtr/gas, to Joe Wheeler SP |
| **340b** | I-565, to Huntsville, to Alabama Space & Rocket Ctr |
| **340a** | AL 20, to Decatur, **W** gas: Chevron/dsl, RaceWay, 2 mi **W** lodging: Courtyard, Hampton Inn, Holiday Inn |
| **337mm** | Tennessee River |
| **334** | AL 67, Priceville, to Decatur, **E** gas: BP/dsl, RaceWay/ dsl, **food:** JW's Steaks, **lodging:** Day's Inn, Super 8, **other:** $General, **W** gas: Chevron, Pilot/Subway/Wendy's/dsl/scales/24hr, **food:** Burger King, DQ, Hardee's, Krystal, Libby's Diner, McDonald's/playplace, Smokehouse BBQ, Waffle House, **lodging:** Comfort Inn, **other:** 🏥 HOSPITAL, Andy's RV Ctr (1mi), Hood RV Ctr |
| **328** | AL 36, Hartselle, **W** gas: BP, Cowboys/dsl, Shell, **food:** Huddle House, **lodging:** Country Hearth Inn |
| **325** | Thompson Rd, to Hartselle |
| **322** | AL 55, to US 31, to Falkville, Eva, **E** gas: BP/dsl/rest., **W** gas: Chevron, Loves/McDonald's/Subway/scales/ dsl/24hr, **other:** $General |

## INTERSTATE 65 CONT'D

**318** US 31, to Lacon, **E gas:** BP/DQ/Stuckey's, **lodging:** Lacon Motel

**310** AL 157, Cullman, West Point, **E gas:** BP, Chevron, Conoco/Subway/dsl, Exxon, Shell/dsl/24hr, Texaco/Wendy's/dsl, **food:** Arby's, Backyard Burger, Baxter's Steaks, Burger King, Cracker Barrel, Denny's, KFC, LJ Silver/Taco Bell, McDonald's, Ruby Tuesday, Waffle House, **lodging:** Best Western, Comfort Inn, Hampton Inn, Holiday Inn Express, Sleep Inn, **other:** H HOSPITAL, Ford/Lincoln/Mercury, Pontiac/Buick/GMC, **W gas:** BP, Exxon/dsl, **lodging:** Super 8, **other:** Cullman Camping (2mi)

**308** US 278, Cullman, **E lodging:** Day's Inn, **W gas:** Chevron/24hr, **other:** flea mkt

**304** AL 69 N, Good Hope, to Cullman, **E gas:** Chevron/dsl, Exxon/dsl, Shell/dsl/rest/scales, Texaco/dsl, **food:** Hardee's, Jack's Rest., Waffle House, **lodging:** Econolodge, **other:** H HOSPITAL, Good Hope Camping, dsl repair, **W gas:** JetPep/dsl, to Smith Lake, **other:** $General

**301mm** rest area both lanes, full ♿ facilities, 📞, vending, 🚻 litter barrels, petwalk, RV dump

**299** AL 69 S, to Jasper, **E other:** Millican RV Ctr, **E gas:** BP/dsl, Dodge City/Conoco/dsl/rest./scales/24hr, Texaco/dsl, Shell/McDonald's/dsl, **food:** Jack's Rest., **other:** CarQuest, $General, repair/tires

**291** AL 91, to Arkadelphia, **E gas:** Conoco/dsl, **food:** Nan's Cafe, **other:** Country View RV Park(1mi), **W gas:** Shell/dsl/rest./24hr/@, **food:** Southern Sunrise Cafe

**291mm** Warrior River

**289** to Blount Springs, **W gas:** BP/DQ/Stuckey's, **other:** to Rickwood Caverns SP

**287** US 31 N, to Blount Springs, **E gas:** Citgo/dsl, Conoco/dsl

**284** US 31 S, AL 160 E, Hayden, Corner, **E gas:** Conoco/dsl, Shell/dsl, **W** tires

**282** AL 140, Warrior, **E gas:** Chevron/Subway/24hr, Exxon/McDonald's, FuelZ/dsl, **food:** Hardee's, Pizza Hut, Taco Bell, **W gas:** BP/dsl

**281** US 31, to Warrior, **E other:** Chevrolet

**280** to US 31, to Warrior, **E other:** Chevrolet

**279mm** Warrior River

**275** to US 31, Morris

**272** Mt Olive Rd, **E gas:** Chevron/24hr, Shell, Texaco/dsl, **food:** Jack's Rest., **other:** $General

**271** Fieldstown Rd, **E gas:** BP/Circle K, Chevron/24hr, RaceWay, Shell, **food:** Arby's, Buffet Garden, Chik-fil-A, DQ, Guthrie's Diner, Habenero's Mexican, Jim'n Nick's BBQ, KFC, Little Caesar's, LJ Silver/Taco Bell, McDonald's, Milo's Burgers, Pasquales Pizza, Pizza Hut, Ruby Tuesday, Ryan's, Shoney's, Subway, Waffle House, Wendy's, Zaxby's, **lodging:** Microtel, **other:** Advance Parts, AutoZone, $Tree, Goody's, Kia/Subaru, Napa, Walgreens, Walmart SuperCtr/gas, **W gas:** Shell, **food:** Cracker Barrel, **lodging:** Best Western

**267** Walkers Chapel Rd, to Fultondale, **E gas:** Chevron/dsl, Jetpep, Shell/Subway/dsl, **food:** Burger King, Chilli's, China One, Domino's, Fullmoon BBQ, Jack's Rest., Logan's Roadhouse, O'Charley's, Outback Steaks, Taco Bell, Waffle House, Whataburger, Zaxby's, **lodging:** Comfort Suites, Fairfield Inn, Hampton Inn, Holiday Inn Express, La Quinta, **other:** AAA, Best Buy, Books A

**267** Continued
Million, CVS Drug, $General, JC Penny, Lowe's Whse, O'Reilly Parts, Rite Aid, Ross, Target, Volvo Trucks, Winn-Dixie, USPO, **W gas:** Chevron/dsl

**266** US 31, Fultondale, **E gas:** Chevron/24hr, **lodging:** Day's Inn, Super 8

**264** 41st Ave, **W gas:** ⚡FLYING J/CountryMkt/dsl/LP/scales/24hr/@

**263** 33rd Ave, **E gas:** Chevron/dsl, **lodging:** Apex Motel, **W gas:** Exxon, **other:** Colonial RV Ctr

**262b a** 16th St, Finley Ave, **E gas:** Bama/dsl, BP, Shell/dsl/scales, **W gas:** Chevron/24hr, Citgo/dsl/24hr, Conoco/scales/dsl, **food:** Capt D's, McDonald's, Popeye's

**261b a** I-20/59, E to Gadsden, W to Tuscaloosa

**260b a** 3th Ave N, **E gas:** BP, Shell, Texaco, **food:** Mrs Winner's, **lodging:** Tourway Inn, **other:** Buick, Chevrolet, Chrysler/Jeep, Nissan, **W gas:** Chevron, **other:** to Legion Field

**259b a** University Blvd, 4th Ave, 5th Ave, **E gas:** Chevron/dsl, **food:** Waffle House, **other:** H HOSPITAL, **W gas:** Chevron, **other:** Goodyear

**258** Green Springs Ave, **E gas:** Chevron, Shell, **food:** Exotic Wings

**256b a** Oxmoor Rd, **E gas:** Exxon, Mobil/dsl, Shell, **food:** Acapulco Grill, Burger King, Capt. D's, Domino's, KFC, Krystal, Lovoy's Italian, McDonald's, Purple Onion, Qdoba Mexican, Rally's, Zaxby's, **lodging:** Howard Johnson, **other:** Aldi Foods, AutoZone, CVS Drug, $Tree, Firestone/auto, Food World, Goodyear/auto, K-Mart, Office Depot, Publix, Walmart Mkt, **W gas:** Chevron/24hr, Texaco/dsl, **food:** Hamburger Heaven, Hardee's, Jim & Nick's BBQ, **lodging:** Econolodge, Comfort Inn, Country Hearth Inn, Microtel, Motel 6, Quality Inn, Super 8, **other:** Batteries+, vet

**255** Lakeshore Dr, **E gas:** BP/Circle K, **other:** H HOSPITAL, to Samford U, **W gas:** Chevron, **food:** Alladin's Grill, Arby's, Capt D's, Chili's, Chick-fil-A, Costas BBQ, Dragon Chinese, Hooters, IHOP, Landry's Seafood, Loco's Deli, LoneStar Steaks, McAlister's Deli, Milo's Burger, Moe's SW Grill, Mr. Wang's, O'Charley's, Outback Steaks, Subway, Taco Bell, Taco Casa, Wendy's, **lodging:** Best Western, Drury Inn, Hampton Inn, Hilton Garden, Holiday Inn, La Quinta, Residence Inn, Studio+, TownePlace Suites, **other:** BooksAMillion, Bruno's Foods, $Tree, IHOP, Lowe's Whse, Old Navy, Radio Shack, Sam's Club/gas, SuperPetz, Walmart SuperCtr, mall

**254** Alford Ave, Shades Crest Rd, **W gas:** Chevron, **other:** vet, **E gas:** BP, Shell

**252** US 31, Montgomery Hwy, **E gas:** BP, Chevron, Shell, Texaco/dsl, **food:** Arby's, Backyard Burger, Bruster's, Capt D's, ChuckeCheese, Hardee's, Milo's, Sol Azteca Mexican, **lodging:** Baymont Inn, Quality Inn, Vestavia Hotel, **other:** H HOSPITAL, Aamco, Big 10 Tire, GMC/Saturn, Lincoln/Mercury, Tuesday Morning, NAPA, Volvo, vet, **W gas:** BP, Chevron, Exxon, Shell, **food:** Burger King, Chick-fil-A, Full Moon BBQ, Golden Rule BBQ, Habanero's Mexican, Krispy Kreme, Krystal, McAlister's Deli, McDonald's, Outback Steaks, Papa John's, Salvatori's Pizza, Schlotsky's, Starbucks, Steakout, Subway, Waffle House, **lodging:** Day's Inn, **other:** Advance Parts, Acura, BooksAMillion, Bruno's Food, Buick, Chevrolet, Chrysler/Jeep, $Tree, Firestone, Goodyear/auto, Honda, Mr. Transmissions, Nissan, Pontiac, Publix, Rite Aid, Staples, TJ Maxx

## INTERSTATE 65 CONT'D

**N ↑↓ S**

**250** I-459, to US 280

**247** Al 17, Valleydale Rd, **E gas:** BP, **W gas:** Citgo, Mobil, RaceWay, Shell, **food:** Arby's, IHOP, Milo's Burgers, Papa John's, RagTime Café, Sonic, Subway, Waffle House, Zapata's Mexican, **lodging:** Comfort Suites, La Quinta, Oaktree Lodge, **other:** O'Reilly Parts, Rite Aid, Publix, Walgreens, vet

**246** AL 119, Cahaba Valley Rd, **E other:** to Oak Mtn SP, **W gas:** BP/dsl, Kangaroo/Subway/dsl, RaceWay, Shell, **food:** Applebee's, Arby's, Capt D's, Chick-fil-A, Cracker Barrel, DQ, Golden Corral, Hooters, KFC, Krystal, Margarita Grill, McDonald's, McCalister's Deli, Mkt Cafe, O'Charley's, Pizza Hut, Purple Onion, Ruby Tuesday, Shoney's, Sonic, Taco Bell, Two Pesos Mexican, TX Roadhouse, Waffle House, Wendy's, Whataburger, **lodging:** Best Western, Comfort Inn, Hampton Inn, Holiday Inn Express, Quality Inn, Ramada Ltd, Sleep Inn, Travelodge, ValuePlace, **other:** H HOSPITAL, Advance Parts, Curves, Ezell's Fishcamp, Firestone/auto, Harley-Davidson, Mazda, Walmart SuperCtr/gas

**242** Pelham, **E gas:** Chevron/dsl/24hr, Exxon/dsl, Shell, **other:** CVS Drug, Publix, **W lodging:** Shelby Motel (2mi), **other:** Good Sam Camping (1mi)

**238** US 31, Alabaster, Saginaw, **E food:** Arby's, Buffalo Wild Wings, Chick-fil-A, Coldstone Creamery, DQ, Full Moon Cafe, Habanero's Mexican, Jim'n Nick's BBQ, Longhorn Steaks, Moe's SW Grill, O'Charly's, Olive Garden, Quizno's, Ruby Tuesday, Salsarita's Mexican, Starbucks, Subway, Taco Bell, **lodging:** Candlewood Suites, **other:** Belk, Best Buy, Books-A-Million, GNC, JC Penney, Lowes Whse, Old Navy, Petsmart, Radio Shack, Ross, Target, TJ Maxx, Walmart SuperCtr/dsl, **W gas:** Cannon, Chevron/dsl, Shell/dsl, **food:** Waffle House, Whataburger, 2 mi **W lodging:** Shelby Motel, **other:** H HOSPITAL

**234** **E gas:** BP/Subway/dsl, **W gas:** Chevron/dsl/24hr, Shell/dsl, **other:** GMC/Pontiac, Cahaba RV Ctr

**231** US 31, Saginaw, **E gas:** BP/dsl, GasBoy, Shell, **food:** Capt D's, Cracker Barrel, Fish Mkt, Golden Rule BBQ, Los Potrillos Mexican, McDonald's, Taco Bell, Waffle House, Yoe Wok Chinese, **lodging:** Hampton Inn, Holiday Inn Express, **other:** Burton RV Ctr, $Tree, Radio Shack, Rolling Hills RV Ctr, Walmart SuperCtr/Subway/gas, **W food:** Donna's Café

**228** AL 25, to Calera, **E gas:** Citgo/dsl, Shell/dsl, **lodging:** Best Value Inn, Day's Inn, **W gas:** Chevron/dsl, **food:** Hardee's(1mi), **other:** $General, to Brierfield Works SP

**227mm** Buxahatchie Creek

**219** Union Grove, Thorsby, **E gas:** Chevron/dsl/24hr, Exxon/Subway/dsl, **food:** Peach Queen Camping, **W gas:** Shell, **food:** Jack's Rest., Smokey Hollow Rest.

**213mm** rest area both lanes, full ♿ facilities, 🛢 vending, 🏕 litter barrels, petwalk, RV dump

**212** AL 145, Clanton, **W gas:** Chevron/dsl, **other:** Toyota/Scion, **E gas:** Texaco/Subway, Headco/dsl, **other:** H HOSPITAL, One Big Peach

**208** Clanton, **W gas:** Love's/Arby's/dsl/24hr **E gas:** Exxon/dsl/24hr, **food:** Shoney's, **lodging:** Guesthouse Inn, **other:** Heaton Pecans

**205** US 31, AL 22, to Clanton, **E gas:** BP, Shell/dsl, Texaco/dsl, **food:** McDonald's, Waffle House, Whataburger,

---

**C L A N T O N**

**205** Continued **lodging:** Best Western, Day's Inn, Holiday Inn Exress, Scottish Inn, **other:** Peach Park, to Confed Mem Park, **W gas:** BP/dsl, Chevron/dsl/24hr, **food:** Burger King, Capt D's, Hardee's, KFC, New China Buffet, Subway, Taco Bell, **lodging:** Key West Inn, **other:** Durbin Farms Mkt, Walmart SuperCtr/gas (2mi), 2 mi west Boomerang's Grill, San Marcos Mexican, Wendy's, Zaxby's, **other:** $General, Walmart SuperCtr/gas

**200** to Verbena, **E gas:** Texaco/dsl, **W gas:** Shell/DQ/Stuckey's/dsl, **other:** RV camping

**195** Worlds Largest Confederate Flag

**186** US 31, Pine Level, **E other:** Confederate Mem Park (13mi), **W gas:** BP/dsl, Chevron/24hr, Citgo, Conoco/Subway/dsl, **lodging:** Pine Motel, **other:** H HOSPITAL

**181** AL 14, to Prattville, **E gas:** Chevron/dsl/24hr, Entec/dsl, **W gas:** Exxon, QV, Texaco/DQ/dsl, **food:** Cracker Barrel, El Torito, Ruby Tuesday, Subway, Waffle House, **lodging:** Best Western, Comfort Inn, La Quinta, Super 8, **other:** H HOSPITAL

**M I L L B R O O K**

**179** US 82 W, Millbrook, **E gas:** Chevron/dsl, **food:** Asian Grill, **lodging:** County Inn&Suites, Key West Inn, Sleep Inn, **other:** K&K RV Park, 0-2 mi **W gas:** Exxon/Subway/24hr, Jet-Pep, RaceWay, Shell, USA/dsl, **food:** A&W/KFC, Applebee's, Bruster's, Burger King, Capt. D's, Casitas Mexican, Chick-fil-A, Cobbs Ford Grill, Hardee's, Jim'n Nick's BBQ, Krystal, Logan's Roadhouse, Longhorn Steaks, Lowe's, McCalister's Deli, McDonald's, Mexico Topico, Moe's SW Grill, O'Charley's, Outback Steaks, Ryan's, Sonic, Steak'n Shake, Yellow Mushroom, Waffle House, **lodging:** Courtyard, Days Inn, Econolodge, Hampton Inn, Holiday Inn, Jameson Inn, **other:** AutoZone, Bass Pro Shops, Belk, Best Buy, BigLots, Big 10 Tire, Books A million, Chevrolet, Circuit City, CVS Drug, $General, $Tree, Ford, GNC, Goody's, Home Depot, JC Penny, Lowe's Whse, Michael's, Office Depot, Ross, Target, Target, TJ Maxx, Walmart SuperCtr, vet

**176** AL 143 N (from nb, no return), Millbrook, Coosada

**173** AL 152, North Blvd, to US 231

**172mm** Alabama River

**172** Clay St, Herron St, **E lodging:** Embassy Suites, **W gas:** Chevron/dsl

**171** I-85 N, Day St

**170** Fairview Ave, **E gas:** Citgo/Subway, Gas Depot, **food:** China King, Church's, McDonald's, **other:** Advance Parts, AutoZone, CVS Drug, O'Reilly Parts, Rite Aid, **W gas:** Exxon, **other:** Calhoun Foods, Family$

## INTERSTATE 65 CONT'D

**N ↑ S**

**169** Edgemont Ave (from sb), **E** gas: Liberty, **other:** carwash

**168** US 80 E, US 82, South Blvd, **E** gas: BP/dsl, Entec/dsl, Kangaroo/dsl, TA/dsl/rest./24hr/@, **food:** Arby's, Capt D's, KFC, McDonald's, Popeye's, Pizza Hut, Taco Bell, Waffle House, **lodging:** Best Inn, Economy Inn, Travel Inn, **other:** H HOSPITAL, Family$, **W** gas: Chevron/dsl, Shell/Subway/dsl, Speedy/dsl, **food:** DQ, Hardee's, Wendy's, **lodging:** Airport Inn, Comfort Inn, Econolodge, Inn South, Peddler's Inn, Ramada Inn

**167** US 80 W, to Selma

**164** US 31, Hope Hull, **E** gas: BP/24hr, Petro+, Saveway/dsl/scales/24hr, **lodging:** Lakeside Hotel, **other:** MC RV Park, **W** gas: BP/Burger King, Chevron/24hr, Liberty/Subway, **food:** Waffle House, **lodging:** Best Western, Hampton Inn, Motel 6, **other:** auto repair

**158** to US 31, **E** gas: BP/DQ/Stuckey's **W** gas: ◆FLYING J /CountryMkt/dsl/scales/24hr

**151** AL 97, to Letohatchee, **W** gas: BP, PaceCar/dsl

**142** AL 185, to Ft Deposit, **E** gas: Shell/dsl/24hr, USA/dsl, **food:** Priester's Pecans, **W** gas: Chevron/24hr

**133mm** rest areas both lanes, full & facilities, ℂ, vending, ☕, litter barrels, petwalk, RV dump

**130** AL10 E, AL 185, to Greenville, **E** gas: Chevron/dsl/24hr, Citgo, Shell/24hr, USA/dsl, **food:** Arby's, Capt D's, China Town Buffet, Hardee's, KFC, McDonald's, Pizza Hut, Russell Stover, Waffle House, Wendy's, **lodging:** Best Value, Day's Inn, **other:** Advance Parts, CVS Drug, $General, Goody's, Russell Stover, Super Foods, to Sherling Lake Park, **W** gas: Phillips 66/Subway/dsl, QV, Texaco/dsl, **food:** Bates Turkey Rest., Burger King, Cracker Barrel, El Rodeo Mexican, Hook's BBQ, Krystal, Ruby Tuesday, Shoney's, Taco Bell/TCBY, Tomatoes Etc., The Border, **lodging:** Best Western, Comfort Inn, Hampton Inn, Holidy Inn Express, Jameson Inn, **other:** Chevrolet, Chrysler/Dodge/Jeep, Walmart SuperCtr/gas, Winn-Dixie

**128** AL 10, to Greenville, **E** gas: Shell/Smokehouse/dsl, **other:** H HOSPITAL, **W** gas: BP

**114** AL 106, to Georgiana, **W** gas: BP, Chevron/24hr, **other:** auto repair

**107** rd 7, to Garland

**101** to Owassa, **E** gas: BP/dsl, **W** gas: Exxon/dsl, **other:** Owassa RV Park

**96** AL 83, to Evergreen, **E** gas: Chevron/24hr, Shell, **food:** Burger King, Hardee's, KFC/Taco Bell, McDonald's, **other:** H HOSPITAL, **W** gas: Citgo/Chester's/Subway/dsl, **food:** Black Angus Rest., Pizza Hut, Waffle House, **lodging:** Best Value Inn, Comfort Inn, Day's Inn

**93** US 84, to Evergreen, **E** gas: Shell/dsl, USA/dsl, **other:** PineCrest RV Park, **W** gas: BP/dsl

**89mm** rest area sb,full & facilities, ℂ, vending, ☕, litter barrels, petwalk, RV dump

**85mm** rest area nb, full & facilities, ℂ, vending, ☕, litter barrels, petwalk, RV dump

**83** AL 6, to Lenox, **E** gas: Exxon/dsl/LP, **other:** Sunshine RV Park (4mi)

**77** AL 41, to Range, Brewton, Repton, **E** gas: BP, **W** gas: Citgo/dsl, Shell/Stuckey's/dsl, **food:** Old Timer's Cafe, Ranch House Rest.

**69** AL 113, to Flomaton, **E** gas: BP/Subway/dsl, Shell/dsl/scales24hr, **other:** dsl repair, **W** gas: Minute Stop/dsl/24hr, **food:** Huddle House

**GREENVILLE EVERGREEN**

**A T M O R E**

**57** AL 21, to Atmore, **E** gas: Exxon/BBQ/dsl, Shell/dsl, **food:** Creek Family Rest., **lodging:** Best Western, **other:** Indian Bingo, **W** gas: BP/dsl, **other:** to Kelley SP

**54** Escambia Cty Rd 1, **E** gas: BP/Subway/dsl, Citgo/dsl, **other:** to Creek Indian Res

**45** to Perdido, **W** gas: Chevron/dsl

**37** AL 287, Gulf Shores Pkwy, to Bay Minette, **E** gas: BP

**34** to AL 59, to Bay Minette, Stockton, **other:** H HOSPITAL

**31** AL 225, to Stockton, **E** other: to Blakeley SP, Confederate Mem Bfd, **W** gas: Shell/dsl

**29mm** Tensaw River

**28mm** Middle River

**25mm** Mobile River

**22** Creola, **E** marine ctr, RV Park, truck repair

**19** US 43, to Satsuma, **E** gas: Chevron/dsl/24hr, Pilot/Arby's/dsl/scales/24hr, **food:** McDonald's, Pintoli's Italian, Waffle House, **W** gas: BP/dsl, **other:** I-65 RV Park (1.5mi)

**15** AL 41, **E** gas: Chevron, **food:** China Chef, Godfather's Pizza, **other:** Family$, Food World, **W** gas: Circle K/gas, Shell/Subway/dsl, **other:** $General

**13** AL 158, AL 213, to Saraland, **E** gas: Shell/dsl/24hr, **food:** Ruby Tuesday, Waffle House, Wintzell's Oyster House, **lodging:** Comfort Suites, Day's Inn, Holiday Inn Express, **other:** Walmart SuperCtr, **W** gas: Exxon/Subway/Pizza Inn, **lodging:** Hampton Inn, **other:** to Chickasabogue Campground

**10** W Lee St, **E** gas: Minute Stop, Parade/dsl, Shell/Subway, **lodging:** Best Inn

**9** I-165 S, to Mobile, to I-10 E

**8b a** US 45, to Prichard, **E** gas: Chevron/24hr, Shell/dsl, **food:** Church's, **other:** Family$, Tiger Foods, **W** gas: BP/24hr, Conoco/dsl, 1st Stop, Pride Trkstp/dsl/scales, RaceWay, **food:** Burger King, Domino's, Golden Egg Café, McDonald's, **other:** vet

**5b** US 98, Moffett Rd, **E** gas: Exxon/dsl, Texaco, **food:** Burger King, Church's, DQ, McDonald's, Saucy Q BBQ, **other:** Advance Parts, Big 10 Tire, **W** gas: MinuteStop/dsl, **food:** Hardee's, **lodging:** Super 8

**5a** Spring Hill Ave, **E** gas: Chevron, Shell/dsl, **food:** KFC, McDonald's, **other:** H HOSPITAL, AutoZone, Big 10 Tire, CarQuest, Family$, Tiger Foods, **W** gas: Exxon, Shell/dsl, **food:** Starbucks, Waffle House, Zaxby's, **lodging:** Extended Stay America, Wingate Inn

**4** Dauphin St, **E** gas: BP/dsl, Shell, Summit Gas/dsl, **food:** Checker's, Chick-fil-A, Cracker Barrel, Godfather's, Krystal, McDonald's, Popeye's, Subway, Taco Bell, TCBY, Waffle House, Wendy's, **lodging:** Comfort Inn, Comfort Suites, Red Roof Inn, RodeWay Inn, **other:** Cadillac/Pontiac/GMC, $General, FoodWorld, Hyundai, Lowe's Whse, Mercedes, Mr Transmission, Rite Aid, Subaru, Tuesday Morning, Walmart SuperCtr, same as 3 & 5a, **W** other: H HOSPITAL

**3** Airport Blvd, **E** gas: BP, **food:** Burger King, Cane's, Golden China, Logan's Roadhouse, Macaroni Grill, Morrison's Cafeteria, Piccadilly's, Wendy's, **lodging:** Marriott, **other:** H HOSPITAL, Acura/Jaguar/Infiniti, Barnes&Noble, Belk, Best Buy, BooksAMillion, Dillard's, $Tree, Firestone/auto, Ford, Goodyear/auto, Goody's, Harley-Davidson, Honda, Mitsubishi, Nissan, Old Navy, Saab, Sam's Club/gas, Saturn, Sears/auto, Staples, mall, **W** gas: Mystik, Shell, **food:** American Café, Arby's, Burger King, Carrabba's,

**M O B I L E**

## INTERSTATE 65 CONT'D

**3** Continued

Subs, Honeybaked Ham, Hooters, IHOP, JR's Smoke-house, LoneStar Steaks, Los Rancheros Mexican, Marble Slab, McDonald's, Moe's SW Grill, O'Charley's, Olive Garden, Panera Bread, Pizza Hut, Popeye's, Quizno's, Red Lobster, Ruby Tuesday, S China Seafood, Starbucks, Subway, Taco Bell, Waffle House, Wanfu, Wings Grill, **lodging:** Airport Inn, Ashberry Suites, Best Inn, Best Value Inn, Courtyard, Day's Inn, Drury Inn, Econolodge, Fairfield Inn, Family Inn, Hampton Inn, Hilton Garden, InTowne Suites, La Quinta, Motel 6, Quality Inn, Ramada Inn Residence Inn, **other:** BooksaMillion, Circuit City, $General, Fresh Mkt Foods, Home Depot, Jo-Ann Fabrics, Michael's, Office Depot, PepBoys, Petsmart, Radio Shack, Ross, Stein-Mart, TJ Maxx, U-Haul, Walgreens, to USAL

**1b a** US 90, Government Blvd, **E gas:** Chevron, Raceway, **food:** McAlister's Deli, Steak'n Shake, **lodging:** Howard Johnson, **other:** Audi/VW, BMW, Buick/Isuzu/Volvo, Chevrolet, Chrysler/Jeep, Dodge, Honda, Isuzu, Kia, Lexus, Lincoln/Mercury, Mazda, Toyota, **W gas:** Shell/dsl, **food:** Waffle House, **lodging:** Rest Inn

**0mm** I-10, E to Pensacola, W to New Orleans, I-65 begins/ends on I-10, exit 20

## INTERSTATE 85

| Exit # | Services |
|---|---|
| 80mm | Alabama/Georgia state line, Chattahoochee River |
| 79 | US 29, to Lanett, **E gas:** Big Cat/dsl, BP/dsl, Lo-Bucks/24hr, **food:** Arby's, Burger King, Capt D's, Chuck's BBQ, KFC, Krystal, McDonald's, Pizza Hut, San Marcos Mexican, Subway, Taco Bell, Waffle House/24hr, Wendy's, **other:** H HOSPITAL, Advance Parts, $General, $Tree, Walmart SuperCtr/gas, transmissions, to West Point Lake, **W gas:** Jetpep, Petro, QV, **food:** Domino's, Ocean Breeze, Sonic, **lodging:** Day's Inn, Econolodge, **other:** AutoZone, CVS Drug, Kroger, O'Reilly Parts, Parts+, vet |
| 78.5mm | Welcome Ctr sb, full ♿ facilities, ☏, vending, ⛱, litter barrels, petwalk |
| 77 | AL 208, to Huguley, **E gas:** Spectrum, Jet Pep/dsl, **food:** Waffle House, Waffle King, **lodging:** Holiday Inn Express, **other:** Chevrolet, Chrysler/Dodge/Ford/Lincoln/Mercury, **W** fireworks |
| 76mm | Eastern/Central time zone |
| 70 | AL 388, to Cusseta **E gas:** BP, Shell/Country Pride/Subway/dsl/scales/24hr/@, **W** fireworks |
| 66 | Andrews Rd, to US 29 |
| 64 | US 29, to Opelika, **E gas:** BP, **lodging:** Guesthouse Inn, **W gas:** Tiger/dsl |
| 62 | US 280/431, to Opelika, **E gas:** Chevron, Eagle/dsl, Liberty Gas, Spectrum/Church's/dsl, **food:** Burger King, Durango Mexican, McDonald's, Subway, Wok'n Roll Rest., Yang's Buffet, **lodging:** Day's Inn, Econolodge, GuestHouse Inn, Holiday Inn, Knight's Inn, Motel 6, **other:** Lakeside RV Park (4.5mi), **W gas:** Jet Pep, Shell, **food:** Capt. D's, Cracker Barrel, Sizzlin Steaks, Thai Rest., Waffle House, **lodging:** Comfort Inn, Travelodge, **other:** Chevrolet, Chrysler/Dodge, Ford, Harley Davidson, Jeep, USA Stores/famous brands |
| 60 | AL 51, AL 169, to Opelika, **E gas:** BP/dsl, Raceway, **food:** Hardee's, **other:** $General, **W gas:** Shell/dsl, **food:** Wendy's(1.5 mi), **other:** H HOSPITAL |

| | |
|---|---|
| **58** | US 280 W, to Opelika, **E lodging:** Hampton Inn, **other:** Kohl's, golf, museum, **W gas:** BP, Chevron/Subway, Liberty Gas, **food:** Arby's, Buffalo Wild Wings, Chick-fil-A, DQ, Golden Corral, Jim Bob's, Moe's SW Grill, Logan's Roadhouse, Longhorn Steaks, O'Charley's, Olive Garden, Outback Steaks, Quizno's, Sonic, Starbucks, Taco Bell, **other:** H HOSPITAL, Best Buy, Books-A-Million, Home Depot, Kroger/gas, Lowe's Whse, Office Depot, Ross, Target, TJ Maxx |
| **57** | Glenn Ave, **W gas:** Exxon, QV, **food:** Shakey's Pizza, Waffle House, **lodging:** Hilton Garden, Plaza Hotel, University Motel, **other:** Sam's Club/gas |
| **51** | US 29, to Auburn, **E gas:** BP/dsl/24hr, **lodging:** Hampton Inn, **other:** Leisure Time RV Park, to Chewacla SP, **W gas:** Chevron/Subway, Raceway, **food:** Arby's, Burger King, Carino's Italian, Firehouse Subs, Golden Rule BBQ, Guthrie's Rest., Hooters, Krystal, Little Caesar's, McDonald's, Panda Chinese, Philly Connection, Pizza Hut, Ruby Tuesday, Santa Fe Steaks, Sonic, Taco Bell, Waffle House, Wendy's, Zaxby's, **lodging:** Best Western, Comfort Inn, Econolodge, Holiday Inn Express, Microtel, Sleep Inn, **other:** Advance Parts, Ford/Lincoln/Mercury, Nissan, Toyota, Walmart SuperCtr/gas, to Auburn U, tires/repair, vet |
| **44mm** | **rest area both lanes, full ♿ facilities, ☏, vending, ⛱ litter barrels, petwalk, RV dump, 24hr security** |
| **42** | US 80, AL 186 E, Wire Rd, **E other:** to Tuskegee NF, dsl repair/tires, **W gas:** Torch 85/rest./dsl/24hr |
| **38** | AL 81, to Tuskegee, **E** to Tuskegee NHS |
| **32** | AL 49 N, to Tuskegee, **E gas:** BP/dsl |
| **26** | AL 229 N, to Tallassee, **E gas:** Shell/Guthrie's/dsl, **W** H HOSPITAL |
| **22** | US 80, to Shorter, **E gas:** BP/dsl, Chevron/Petro/dsl/rest., Exxon/dsl, **lodging:** Day's Inn, **other:** to Macon Co Greyhound Pk, Windrift RV Park |
| **16** | Waugh, to Cecil, **E gas:** BP/Subway/dsl, **other:** auto repair |
| **11** | US 80, to Mt Meigs, **E gas:** Exxon/Subway/dsl, Liberty/dsl, **food:** Anthony's Rest., Burger King, Cracker Barrel, Jose's Grill, Sommer's Grill, Waffle House, **lodging:** Comfort Inn, Holiday Inn Express, Sleep Inn, **other:** Bruno's Foods, Home Depot, Walmart SuperCtr, **W gas:** Chevron/dsl/24hr |
| **9** | AL 271, to AL 110, to Auburn U/Montgomery, **E food:** Applebee's, Arby's, BoneFish Grill, Champp's Grill, Chick-fil-A, Chili's, Guthrie's, Ixtapa Mexican, McDonald's, Moe's SW Grill, Panera Bread, Red Robin, Red Star |

N ↕ S

L A N E T T N ↕ S O P E L I K A

A U B U R N

## INTERSTATE 85

**N ↑ S**

| | |
|---|---|
| 9 | Continued |
| | Grill, Ruby Tuesday, Sonic, Starbucks, Subway, Texas Roadhouse, Wendy's, Whataburger, **lodging:** Hampton Inn, **other:** BooksAMillion, Costco/gas, Dillard's, Kohl's, Petsmart, Ross, Target, World Mkt, **W** H HOSPITAL |
| 6 | US 80, US 231, AL 21, East Blvd, **E gas:** Chevron/24hr, Exxon/dsl/24hr, RaceWay, **food:** Apple Pie Grill, Arby's, Burger King, Carrabba's, Chick-fil-A, Cuco's Mexican, Golden Corral, Hooters, Jason's Deli, KFC, McDonald's, Ming's Chinese, O'Charley's, Olive Garden, Piccadilly's, Popeye's, Roadhouse Grill, Schlotsky's, Shogun Japanese, Starbucks, Subway, Taco Bell, Up The Creek Grill, Waffle House, Wendy's, Wings Grill, Zaxby's, **lodging:** Best Inn, Comfort Inn, Country Inn&Suites, Courtyard, Extended Stay America, Fairfield Inn, Hampton Inn, La Quinta, Quality Inn, Ramada Inn, Residence Inn, SpringHill Suites, Studio+, TownePlace Suites, Wingate Inn, **other:** Acura, Barnes& Noble, Books-a-Million, $General, Fresh Mkt Foods, Home Depot, Honda, Lowe's Whse, Marshall's, Michael's, Pontiac/Cadillac, Radio Shack, Walmart SuperCtr, USPO, **W gas:** BP, Citgo, Liberty Gas/dsl, Shell, Texaco, **food:** Burger King, Capt D's, Church's, Dreamland BBQ, KFC, Krystal, LoneStar Steaks, McDonald's, Outback Steaks, Red Lobster, Shoney's, Waffle House, **lodging:** Best Western, Comfort Suites, Drury Inn, Econolodge, Lexington Hotel, Motel 6, **other:** Audi, BMW, Buick, Cadillac, Chevrolet, Chrysler/Jeep, Ford, Hyundai, Isuzu, Kia, Lexus, Mazda, Mercedes, Mitsubishi, Nissan, Sam's Club/gas, Toyota, VW, to Gunter AFB, **1 mi W food:** Buffet City, Capt D's, Hardee's, IHOP, Ruby Tuesday, **other:** JC Penney, Sears/auto, mall |
| 4 | Perry Hill Rd, **E other:** Bruno's Foods, Rite Aid, **W gas:** Cannon Gas, Chevron/24hr, **food:** Hardee's, Subway, **lodging:** Hilton Garden, Homewood Suites, **other:** $General, Express Oil Change |
| 3 | Ann St, **E gas:** BP/dsl, Chevron, **food:** Arby's, Capt D's, Domino's, Down the St Cafe, Hardee's, KFC, Krystal, McDonald's, Taco Bell, Waffle House, Wendy's, **lodging:** Day's Inn, **other:** Big 10 Tire, **W gas:** Entec, Exxon, PaceCar, **lodging:** Stay Lodge, **food:** Chick-fil-A, Cici's Pizza, Popeye's, **other:** $Tree, Office Depot, Radio Shack, Ross, Walmart SuperCtr/gas |
| 2 | Forest Ave, **E** CVS Drug, **W** H HOSPITAL |
| 1 | Court St, Union St, downtown, **E gas:** BP/dsl, Exxon, **W** to Ala St U |
| 0mm | I-85 begins/ends on I-65, exit 171 in Montgomery |

## INTERSTATE 459 Birmingham

**N ↑ S**

| Exit # | Services |
|---|---|
| 33b a | I-59, N to Gadsden, S to Birmingham |
| 32 | US 11, Trussville, **N gas:** BP/24hr, **lodging:** Best Inn(3mi), **S gas:** Chevron/dsl/24hr, RaceWay/24hr, Shell/Wendy's/dsl, **food:** A&W/KFC, Arby's, Beef'o Brady's, Chili's, Coldstone Creamery, Habanero's Rest., Hooters, Jack's Rest., Jim& Nick's BBQ, John's City Diner, Logan's Roadhouse, McDonald's, Quizno's, Red Robin, Starbucks, Waffle House, **lodging:** Courtyard, Hampton Inn, **other:** Belk, |

| | |
|---|---|
| 32 | Continued |
| | Best Buy, Big 10 Tires, BooksAMillion, Buick/GMC/Pontiac, Circuit City, Harley-Davidson, Home Depot, JC Penney, Lowes Whse, Mazda, Michael's, Old Navy, Staples, Target, TJ Maxx |
| 31 | Derby Parkway, **W other:** Birmingham Race Course |
| 29 | I-20, E to Atlanta, W to Birmingham |
| 27 | Grants Mill Rd, **S gas:** Exxon/dsl, **other:** BMW/Lexus, Cadillac |
| 23 | Liberty Parkway, **S food:** Billy's Grill, DQ, **lodging:** Hilton Garden |
| 19 | US 280, Mt Brook, Childersburg, **N gas:** Chevron, **food:** Flemings Rest., Village Tavern, **other:** Barnes&Noble, **0-3 mi S gas:** BP/Circle K, Exxon, **food:** Arby's, Buffalo Wild Wings, Burger King, Carraba's, Chili's, Cracker Barrel, Edgar's Rest., Full Moon BBQ, Hooters, IHOP, Jason's Deli, Joe's Crabshack, Japanese, Logan's Roadhouse, LongHorn Steaks, McDonald's, Outback Steaks, Papa John's, Pizza Hut, Ralph&Kacoos, Ruby Tuesday, Schlotzky's, Shogun Japanese, Taco Bell, TGIFriday, Wendy's, **lodging:** Candlewood Suites, Courtyard, Drury Inn, Fairfield Inn, Hampton Inn, Hilton, Holiday Inn Express, Homestead Suites, Homewood Suites, Hyatt Place, La Quinta, Marriott, Residence Inn, Sheraton, Studio Inn, Wingate, **other:** Best Buy, Fresh Mkt Foods, Home Depot, Kohl's, Michael's, NTB, PetCo, Ross, Walmart SuperCtr |
| 17 | Acton Rd, **N gas:** Shell/dsl/24hr, **food:** Krystal, McDonald's |
| 15b a | I-65, N to Birmingham, S to Montgomery |
| 13 | US 31, Hoover, Pelham, **N gas:** BP, Chevron, Exxon, Shell, **food:** Burger King, Chick-fil-A, Fish Mkt Rest., Full Moon Cafe, Golden Rule BBQ, Habanero's, Krispy Kreme, Krystal, McDonald's, Outback Steaks, Quizno's, Starbucks, Subway, **lodging:** Day's Inn, **other:** Acura/Honda, BooksAMillion, Buick, Cadillac, Chevrolet, Chrysler/Jeep, $Tree, Firestone, Goodyear, Kia, Mitsubishi, Nissan, Pontiac, Rite Aid, Staples, TJ Maxx, Toyota, vet, **S gas:** Jet-Pep, Shell/dsl/24hr, **food:** CA Pizza Kitchen, Chipotle Mexican, China Buffet, Guthrie's, Jim&Nicks BBQ, McDonald's, Moe's SW Grill, Olive Garden, Pizza Hut, Taco Bell, Ted's MT Grill, Top China, Wendy's, **lodging:** Best Western, Courtyard, Hyatt Place, Hotel, **other:** Belk, Best Buy, Bruno's Foods, Costco/gas, CVS Drug, Goody's, Hancock Fabrics, Home Depot, Infiniti, JC Penney, Macy's, Marshall's, Mercedes, Michael's, NTB, Office Depot, Petsmart, Sam's Club, Sears, Tuesday Morning, Walmart (1mi), mall |
| 10 | AL 150, Waverly, **N gas:** Chevron (1mi), Shell (1mi), **lodging:** Renaissance Motel(6mi), **S gas:** BP/dsl/24hr, Exxon, **food:** Hyatt Place, Mei China, **other:** Ford, GNC, Walgreens, Publix/deli |
| 6 | AL 52, to Bessemer, **N gas:** BP/dsl, **S gas:** BP, Shell, Texaco/Taco Bell, **food:** Arby's, China Wok, Domino's, McDonald's, Pizza Hut, Quizno's, San Antonio Grill, Subway, Waffle House, Wendy's, **lodging:** Sleep Inn, **other:** Cherokee Beach RV Park, $General, CVS Drug, TrueValue, Winn-Dixie |
| 1 | AL 18, Bessemer, **N gas:** Exxon, Shell/dsl, **other:** Target, **S gas:** BP/dsl, **food:** China King, McDonald's, Momma's Rest., Subway, **other:** Advance Parts, CVS Drug, FoodWorld/drug, to Tannehill SP |
| 0mm | I-459 begins/ends on I-20/59, exit 106 |

## INTERSTATE 8

I-8 (15)

| Exit # | Services |
|---|---|
| 178b a | I-10, I-8 begins/ends on I-10, exit 199, E to Tucson, W to Phoenix |
| 174 | Trekell Rd, to Casa Grande, **2-4 mi** **N** other: **H** HOSPITAL, gas, food, lodging |
| 172 | Thornton Rd, to Casa Grande, **2-4 mi** **N** gas, food, lodging, **S** other: Francisco Grande Resort |
| 171mm | Santa Cruz River |
| 169 | Bianco Rd |
| 167 | Montgomery Rd, **S** Francisco Grande Golf Club |
| 163mm | Santa Rosa Wash |
| 161 | Stanfield Rd |
| 151 | AZ 84 E, Maricopa Rd, to Stanfield, **S** Harrah's Casino (14mi), **S** gas: Gas'n Go, Pullman Trkstp/dsl, other: Saguaro RV Park |
| 150mm | picnic area wb, 🔁, litter barrels |
| 149mm | picnic area eb, 🔁, litter barrels |
| 144 | Vekol Rd |
| 140 | Freeman Rd |
| 119 | Butterfield Trail, to AZ 85, I-10, Gila Bend, **N** gas: Shell/dsl/scales/RV Park/24hr, **food**: American/Mexican Rest., **lodging**: America's Choice Inn, **other**: Augie's RV camping, **3 mi** **N** gas: Shell/Subway/Noble Roman's/dsl, **food**: DQ, Little Italy, Space Age Rest., **lodging**: Best Western, Travelodge, Yucca Motel |
| 117mm | Sand Tank Wash |
| 115 | AZ 85, to Gila Bend, **1-2 mi** **N** gas: Loves/Taco Bell/dsl/scales/24hr, Circle K/gas, Texaco/dsl, **food**: Burger King, McDonald's, **lodging**: Best Western, El Coronado Motel, Yucca Motel, **other**: **H** HOSPITAL, Goodyear/auto, NAPA, Wheel Inn RV park |
| 111 | Citrus Valley Rd |
| 106 | Paloma Rd |
| 102 | Painted Rock Rd |
| 87 | Sentinel, Hyder, **N** gas: Sentinel Gen Store/dsl |
| 85mm | rest area wb, full ♿ facilities, 🚻, 🔁, litter barrels, vending, petwalk |
| 84mm | rest area eb, full ♿ facilities, 🚻, 🔁, litter barrels, litter barrels, vending, petwalk |
| 78 | Spot Rd |
| 73 | Aztec, **4 mi** **S** Oasis RV Park/dump |
| 67 | Dateland, **S** gas: Exxon/24hr, other: Oasis RV Park/dump |
| 56mm | rest area both lanes, full ♿ facilities, 🚻, 🔁, litter barrels, vending, petwalk |

| | |
|---|---|
| 54 | Ave 52 E, Mohawk Valley |
| 42 | Ave 40 E, to Tacna, **N** gas: Chevron/dsl/24hr, **lodging**: Chaparral Motel |
| 37 | Ave 36 E, to Roll |
| 30 | Ave 29 E, Wellton, **N** gas: Circle K/gas, other: Tier Drop RV Park, **S** gas: Chevron, **food**: Jack-in-the-Box, Shooter's Cantina, **lodging**: Microtel, **other**: Coyote Wash Foods |
| 24mm | Ligurta Wash |
| 23mm | Red Top Wash |
| 22mm | parking area both lanes |
| 21 | Dome Valley, **N** other: Ligurta Sta RV park, Yuma Proving Ground (16mi) |
| 17mm | insp sta eb |
| 15mm | Fortuna Wash |
| 14 | Foothills Blvd, **N** other: Sundance RV Park, **S** food: Domino's, other: Ace Hardware, FootHills RV Park, The Grocery Store/gas/dsl, auto/RV care/lube ctr |
| 12 | Fortuna Rd, to US 95 N, **N** gas: Chevron/24hr, Valero/Barney's/dsl/scales/24hr, **food**: Day Breakers Cafe, Jack-in-the-Box, Pizza Hut, **lodging**: Courtesy Inn, |

Left margin: E ↑ W | GILA BEND

Right margin (of map column): WELLTON

**AZ**

## INTERSTATE 8 CONT'D

**E ← W**

**Y U M A**

| | |
|---|---|
| 12 | Continued **other:** Caravan RV Park, Oasis RV Park, **S gas:** Shell/Burger King/dsl, SP/dsl, **food:** Applebees, A&W/KFC, Checkers, Debois Pizza, DQ, Subway, **lodging:** Microtel, **other:** Big O Tire, $General, Family$, Fry's Foods, Radio Shack |
| 9 | 32nd St(no EZ wb return), to Yuma, **S other:** Sun Vista RV Park, Walmart Super Ctr |
| 7 | Araby Rd, **S gas:** Circle K/dsl, **S gas:** Chevron/Jack-in-the-Box/dsl, Circle K/dsl, **other:** RV World, Sun Vista RV Park, to AZWU |
| 3 | AZ 280 S, Ave 3E, **S gas:** Loves/Chester's/Subway/dsl/scales/24hr, **lodging:** Candlewood Suites, Holiday Inn Express, **other:** Harley-Davidson, to Marine Corp Air Sta |
| 2 | US 95, 16th St, Yuma, **N gas:** 76/Circle K, **food:** Arnie's Cafe, Chili's, ChuckeCheese, Cracker Barrel, Del Taco, Denny's, Famous Dave's BBQ, In-n-Out, Jamba Juice, Logans Roadhouse, Mimi's Cafe, Panda Express, Red Lobster, Subway, **lodging:** Best Western, Day's Inn, Fairfield Inn, Hampton Inn, Holiday Inn, La Fuente Inn, Holiday Inn, Motel 6, OakTree Inn, Shilo Inn/rest., SpringHill Suites, TownePlace Suites, Wingate Inn, **other:** Best Buy, Circuit City, Dillards, JC Penney, Jo-Ann Fabrics, Kohl's, Old Navy, Petsmart, Ross, Sam's Club/gas, Target, auto/tire repair, **2 mi S on Pacific Ave food:** Mr. Lu's Chinese, Peter Piper Pizza, Subway, Wienerschnitzel, **other:** Big O Tire, NAPA, Kia, Walmart SuperCtr/gas, **S gas:** Arco/dsl/24hr, Chevron/Blimpie/dsl, Shell, Valero, **food:** Applebee's, Burger King, Carl's Jr, Chretin's Mexican, IHOP, Jack-in-the-Box, McDonald's, Golden Corral, Outback Steaks, Texas Roadhouse, Wendy's, Village Inn Pizza, **lodging:** Comfort Inn, Interstate 8 Inn, Motel 6, Super 8, **other:** H HOSPITAL, BigLots, Big O Tires, Family$, Home Depot, KIA, Radio Shack, Staples, U-Haul |
| 1.5mm | weigh sta both lanes |
| 1 | Giss Pkwy, Yuma, **N other:** to Yuma Terr Prison SP, S on 4th Ave **S gas:** Chevron, Circle K/gas, **food:** Jack-in-the-Box, Yuma Landing Rest., **lodging:** Best Western |
| 0mm | Arizona/California state line, Colorado River, Mountain/Pacific time zone |

## INTERSTATE 10

**E ← W**

| Exit # | Services |
|---|---|
| 391mm | Arizona/New Mexico state line |
| 390 | Cavot Rd |
| 389mm | rest area both lanes, full ♿ facilities, Ⓒ, 🎋, litter barrels, vending, petwalk |
| 383mm | weigh sta eb, weigh/insp sta wb |
| 382 | Portal Rd, San Simon |
| 381mm | San Simon River |
| 378 | Lp 10, San Simon |

**WILCOX**

| | |
|---|---|
| 366 | Lp 10, Bowie Rd, **N gas:** Shell/Subway/dsl/24hr, **S other:** Alaskan RV park |
| 362 | Lp 10, Bowie Rd, **N gas:** lodging, camping, **S** to Ft Bowie NHS |
| 355 | US 191 N, to Safford, **N** to Roper Lake SP |
| 352 | US 191 N, to Safford, same as 355 |
| 344 | Lp 10, to Willcox |
| 340 | AZ 186, to Rex Allen Dr, **N gas:** TA/Shell/Popeye's/Subway/dsl/scales/24hr/@, **lodging:** Super 8, **other:** Magic Circle RV Park, Stout's CiderMill, **S gas:** Chevron/dsl/24hr, Circle K, Texaco, **food:** Burger King, KFC/Taco Bell, McDonald's, Pizza Hut, Plaza Rest., Salsa Fiesta, **lodging:** Best Western, Day's Inn, Motel 6, **other:** H HOSPITAL, Ace Hardware, Autozone, Beall's, Big O Tire, $General, Food City, Radio Shack, Safeway, Grande Vista RV Park, to Chiricahua NM |
| 336 | AZ 186, Willcox, **S gas:** Chevron/dsl/LP, 1-3 mi **S lodging:** Desert Inn Motel, **other:** Ft Willcox RV Park |
| 331 | US 191 S, to Sunsites, Douglas, **S other:** to Cochise Stronghold |
| 322 | Johnson Rd, **S gas:** Shell/DQ/dsl/gifts |
| 320mm | rest area both lanes, full ♿ facilities, Ⓒ, 🎋, litter barrels, vending, petwalk |
| 318 | Triangle T Rd, to Dragoon, **S** lodging, camping |
| 312 | Sibyl Rd |
| 309mm | Adams Peak Wash |
| 306 | AZ 80, Pomerene Rd, Benson, **S gas:** Shell/dsl, Mobil, **food:** G&F Pizza Palace, **other:** Pato Blanco RV Park, San Pedro RV Park |
| 305mm | San Pedro River |
| 304 | Ocotillo St, Benson, **N food:** Denny's, Jack-in-the-Box, **lodging:** Day's Inn, Super 8, **other:** Benson RV Park, KOA, Red Barn RV Park, **S gas:** Chevron, Texaco, **food:** Apple Farm Rest., Country Folks Rest., Galleano's Rest., Magaly's Mexican, Plaza Rest., Wendy's, **lodging:** Best Western, QuarterHorse Inn, **other:** H HOSPITAL, Ace Hardware, Alco, Dillon RV Ctr, $General, Family$, NAPA, Radio Shack, Safeway, San Pedro RV Park, Walmart SuperCtr |
| 303 | US 80, to Tombstone, Bisbee, **1 mi S gas:** Shell/dsl, **food:** Beijing Chinese, Reb's Rest., Ruiz Mexican, Shoot Out Steaks, Wendy's, **other:** NAPA, Safeway, auto/dsl/repair, to Douglas NHL |
| 302 | AZ 90 S, to Ft Huachuca, Benson, **S gas:** Gas City/A&W/Pizza Hut/TCBY/dsl, Shell/Subway/dsl, **food:** KFC/Taco Bell, McDonald's, **lodging:** Holiday Inn Express, Motel 6, **other:** Cochise Terrace RV Park, Ft Huachuca NHS, Walmart SuperCtr |
| 301 | ranch exit eb |
| 299 | Skyline Rd |
| 297 | Mescal Rd, J-6 Ranch Rd, **N gas:** QuickPic/dsl/deli/24hr |
| 292 | Empirita Rd |
| 289 | Marsh Station Rd |
| 288mm | Cienega Creek |
| 281 | AZ 83 S, to Patagonia |

**BENSON**

## INTERSTATE 10 CONT'D

**E ↕ W**

**279** Vail/Wentworth Rd, **N gas:** QuikMart/gas, **food:** Montgomery's Grill, **other:** to Colossal Caves

**275** Houghton Rd, **N other:** to Saguaro NP, camping, **S** to fairgrounds

**273** Rita Rd, **N gas:** Rita Ranch, (2mi), **S** fairgrounds

**270** Kolb Rd, **N lodging:** La Quinta(9mi), **S other:** Voyager RV Resort

**269** Wilmot Rd, **N gas:** Chevron/A&W/dsl, **lodging:** Travel Inn, **S gas:** Shell/Quizno's

**268** Craycroft Rd, **N gas:** TTT/dsl/rest./scales/24hr, Circle K, Spirit/dsl, **other:** Crazy Horse RV Park, **S** dsl repair

**267** Valencia Rd, **N gas:** Arco/Jack-in-the-Box, **other:** Pima Air Museum, **S** ✈

**265** Alvernon Way, Davis-Monthan AFB

**264b a** Palo Verde Rd, **N gas:** Chevron/Wendy's/dsl, **food:** Brooklyn's Grill, Carl's Jr, Denny's, Waffle House, **lodging:** Crossland Suites, Day's Inn, Fairfield Inn, Holiday Inn, Red Roof Inn, **other:** Freedom RV Ctr, **S gas:** QuikMart/gas, **food:** Arby's, McDonald's, **lodging:** Ramada Inn, Studio 6, **other:** Beaudry RV Ctr/resort, Camping World RV Resort, Holiday Rambler RV Ctr, La Mesa RV Ctr, Factory Outlet/famous brands

**263b** Kino Pkwy N

**263a** Kino Pkwy S, **S gas:** Shamrock, **food:** Fry's Foods, **other:** AutoZone, Radio Shack, to Tucson Intn'l ✈

**262** Benson Hwy, Park Ave, **S gas:** Arco/24hr, Chevron, **food:** Country Folks, KFC, McDonald's, Waffle House, **lodging:** Best Value, Howard Johnson, Motel 6, Quality Inn, Western Inn, **other:** 7-11, Volvo

**261** 6th/4th Ave, **N gas:** GasCo, **food:** Happy Iguana, Little Caesar's, **lodging:** Econolodge, **other:** Discount Tire, Food City, 99¢ Store, **S gas:** Shell, **food:** Church's, El Indio, Jack-in-the-Box, LJ Silver, **lodging:** Lazy 8 Motel, **other:** Family$, Spanish Trail

**260** I-19 S, to Nogales

**259** 22nd St, Starr Pass Blvd, **N gas:** Circle K/dsl, **S food:** Kettle, Waffle House, **lodging:** Knight's Inn, La Quinta, Motel 6, Super 8, Travel Inn

**258** Congress St, Broadway St, **N gas:** Circle K/gas, **food:** Garcia's Rest., **lodging:** Inn Suites, **S food:** Carl's Jr, Whataburger, **lodging:** Days Inn, Howard Johnson, Motel 6, Ramada Ltd, River Park Inn, Travelodge

**257a** St Mary's Rd, **N gas:** 76, **other:** Ⓗ HOSPITAL, **S gas:** Arco, Shell/24hr, **food:** Burger King, Denny's, Furr's Cafeteria, **lodging:** Ramada Ltd., **other:** Pim Comm Coll

**257** Speedway Blvd, **N lodging:** Best Western, **other:** Ⓗ HOSPITAL, Victory Motorcycles, Old Town Tucson, museum, U of AZ, **S gas:** Arco/dsl/24hr

**256** Grant Rd, **N food:** Sonic, dsl/transmission repair, **S gas:** Circle K, Shamrock, **food:** Del Taco, IHOP, Las Cazuelita's, Subway, Waffle House, **lodging:** Baymont Inn, Comfort Inn, Hampton Inn, Holiday Inn Express, Quality Inn, Super 8, **other:** dsl/transmission repair

**255** AZ 77 N, to Miracle Mile

**TUCSON**

**254** Prince Rd, **N other:** U-Haul, tires, **S other:** Prince of Tucson RV Park, golf

**252** El Camino del Cerro, Ruthrauff Rd, **N gas:** Arco/24hr, **other:** Ruthrauff RV Ctr, **S gas:** Shell/Jack-in-the-Box

**251** Sunset Rd

**250** Orange Grove Rd, **N gas:** Arco/24hr, Circle K, **food:** Domino's, Subway, Wendy's, **other:** RV Central, on Thornydal **N food:** El Chalito, Little Caesar's, Quizno's, Weinerschnitzel, **other:** Big O Tire, Costco/gas, Home Depot, Parts+

**248** Ina Rd, **N gas:** Chevron/dsl, Circle K, Conoco, QuikMart/dsl, **food:** Arby's, Carl's Jr, DQ, Donut Wheel, Eegee's Cafe, El Pollo Loco, Hooters, Jack-in-the-Box, LJ Silver, McDonald's, Old Father Rest., Peter Piper's Pizza, Pizza Hut, Rubio's Grill, Starbucks, Taco Bell, Waffle House, **lodging:** InTown Suites, Motel 6, Old Father Inn, **other:** BigLots, CarQuest, CVS Drug, Discount Tire, Fry's Foods, Goodyear/auto, JiffyLube, Lowe's Whse, 99¢ Store, Office Depot, PepBoys, Radio Shack, Target, U-Haul, Walgreens, **S gas:** Circle K, **food:** Denny's, **lodging:** Comfort Inn, Red Roof Inn, Travelodge

**246** Cortaro Rd, **N gas:** Circle K/Arby's/dsl, **food:** IHOP, Wendy's, **S gas:** Shell/dsl, **food:** Burger King, Chili's, Cracker Barrel, Eegee's Rest., HotDog Heaven, In-n-Out, KFC, McDonald's, Panda Express, Starbucks, Subway, Taco Bell, Texas Roadhouse, **lodging:** Best Western, Day's Inn, Holiday Inn Express, La Quinta, Super 8, **other:** Ace Hardware, Batteries+, Checker Parts, Kohl's, USPO, Walmart SuperCtr, access to RV camping

**242** Avra Valley Rd, **S other:** Saguaro NP (13mi), RV camping, ✈

**240** Tangerine Rd, to Rillito, **S** A-A RV Park, **S** USPO

**236** Marana, **S gas:** Chevron/dsl/LP, Circle K/gas, **other:** Sun RV Park, auto repair

**232** Pinal Air Park Rd, **S** Pinal Air Park

**228mm** wb pulloff, to frontage rd

**226** Red Rock, **S** USPO

**219** Picacho Peak Rd, **N gas:** Mobil/DQ/dsl, Shell/dsl, **S other:** Ostrich Ranch, Pichaco Peak RV Park, to Picacho Peak SP

**212** Picacho (from wb), **N gas:** Premium Gas/tires, **other:** USPO **S** Picacho Camping

## INTERSTATE 10 CONT'D

**211b** AZ 87 N, AZ 84 W, to Coolidge

**211a** Picacho(from eb), **S other:** Picacho RV Park, state prison

**208** Sunshine Blvd, to Eloy, **N gas:** Pilot/Subway/dsl/scales/24hr, dsl repair, **S gas:** ⊕FLYING J/Conoco/Cookery/dsl/scales/24hr, **other:** Blue Beacon

**203** Toltec Rd, to Eloy, **N gas:** Chevron/McDonald's/24hr, Circle K/dsl, **food:** Carl's Jr, El Zarape Mexican, **lodging:** Best Value Inn, Red Roof Inn, **other:** Desert Valley RV Park, dsl/tire repair, **S gas:** TA/A&W/Taco Bell/dsl/24hr/@, **food:** Pizza Hut, **other:** truckwash

**200** Sunland Gin Rd, Arizona City, **N gas:** Petro/Iron Skillet/dsl/scales/24hr/@, Pride/Subway/dsl/24hr, **food:** Burger King, Eva's Mexican, **lodging:** Day's Inn, **other:** Blue Beacon, Eagle Truckwash, Las Colinas RV Park, **S gas:** Loves/Arby's/Baskin-Robbins/dsl/24hr, **food:** Golden 9 Rest., Starbucks, **lodging:** Motel 6, **other:** Speedco Lube

**199** I-8 W, to Yuma, San Diego

**198** AZ 84, to Eloy, Casa Grande, **N** Robson Ranch Rest./Golf, **S food:** Wendy's, **other:** Casa Grande Outlets/famous brands, Buena Tierra RV Pk

**194** AZ 287, Florence Blvd, to Casa Grande, **N other:** Dillards, JC Penney, Kohl's, Petsmart, Staples, Sunscape RV Park(7mi), Target, 0-2 mi **S gas:** Arco/dsl/24hr, Chevron/DQ, **food:** Burger King, Cracker Barrel, Del Taco, Denny's, Golden Corral, IHOP, LJ Silver, Panda Express, Taco Bell, **lodging:** Best Western, Comfort Inn, Mainstay Suites, Super 8, **other:** Ⓗ HOSPITAL, CVS Drug, Palm Creek RV/golf resort, Walmart SuperCtr

**190** McCartney Rd, **N other:** to Central AZ Coll

**185** AZ 387, to Coolidge, Florence, **S other:** hwy patrol, RV camping

**183mm** rest area wb, full ♿ facilities, 🅲, 🚻, litter barrels, vending, petwalk

**181mm** rest area eb, full ♿ facilities, 🅲, 🚻, litter barrels, vending, petwalk

**175** AZ 587 N, Casa Blanca Rd, **S gas:** Shell/dsl

**173mm** Gila River

**167** Riggs Rd, to Sun Lake, **N** Akimel Crafts

**164** AZ 347 S, Queen Creek Rd, to Maricopa, **N other:** to Chandler ✈

**162b a** Wild Horse Pass Rd, Sundust Rd, **N gas:** Loves/Arby's/dsl/scales/24hr, **other:** Beaudry RV Ctr, **S other:** Firebird Sports Park, Gila River Casino

**160** Chandler Blvd, to Chandler, **N gas:** Chevron, Circle K, Mobil, **food:** Burger King, Denny's, Marie Callender's, Village Inn, Whataburger/24hr, **lodging:** Hampton Inn, Homewood Suites, Motel 6, Radisson, Red Roof Inn, Super 8, **other:** Big O Tire, Harley-Davidson, to Compadre Stadium, to Williams AFB, **S gas:** Chevron, 7-11, Water&Ice/dsl, **food:** Applebees, Arriba Mexican, Chili's, Cracker Barrel, Del Taco, Hong Kong Buffet, Hooters, Wendy's, **lodging:** Holiday Inn Express, Extended Stay

**160** Continued

America, InTown Suites, La Quinta, **other:** Ⓗ HOSPITAL, AutoZone, Brakes+, CVS Drug, Discount Tire, Kohl's

**159** Ray Rd, **N gas:** Circle K, Shell/dsl, **food:** Buca Italian, Carrabba's, Charleston's Rest., El Pollo Loco, 5&Diner, Fleming's Steaks, In-n-Out, Jilly's Rest., McDonald's, Outback Steaks, Red Lobster, Roy's Cafe, Rumbi Grill, Tomaso's Italian, TGI Fridays, **lodging:** Courtyard, **other:** Borders Books, Ford, Home Depot, Lexus, Lowe's Whse, Mercedes, Petsmart, Sam's Club, **S gas:** Circle K/dsl, **food:** Boston Mkt, Cafe Rio, IHOP/24hr, Jack-in-the-Box, Macaroni Grill, Mimi's Café, On-the-Border, Peter Piper Pizza, Pizza Hut, Subway, Sweet Tomatoes, Wendy's, **lodging:** Extended Stay America, **other:** URGENT CARE, Albertson's/Osco/24hr, Barnes&Noble, Best Buy, Jo-Ann Fabrics, Michael's, Old Navy, Ross, SteinMart, Target

**158** Warner Rd, **N gas:** Circle K, QT, **food:** Port of Subs, **S gas:** Arco/24hr, Circle K/dsl, **food:** Burger King, Chuck-eCheese, DQ, Macayo's, Malaya Mexican, McDonald's, Mello's Pizza, Panda Garden, Quizno's, Ruffino's Italian, **other:** Ace Hardware, Basha's Foods, Big O Tire, Goodyear/auto

**157** Elliot Rd, **N gas:** Chevron, Shell/Circle K, **food:** Applebee's, Arby's, Baja Fresh, Burger King, Chili's, Coco's, Country Harvest Buffet, Fuddrucker's, Gelato BBQ, Guam Cuisine, HoneyBear's BBQ, Kobe Japanese, Kyoto Japanese, Mi Amigos Mexican, Olive Garden, Panda Express, Red Robin Rest., Sooper Salad, Sonic, Subway, Taco Bell, Village Inn Rest., Wendy's, **lodging:** Country Inn&Suites, **other:** Cadillac/GMC, Circuit City, Costco/gas, Discount Tire, Dodge, $Tree, Fiddlesticks Funpark, Ford/Lincoln/Mercury, Honda, Nissan, PetsMart, Saturn, Savers, Staples, Toyota, U-Haul, Walmart, **S gas:** Mobil/dsl, Shell/Circle K, **food:** Baskin-Robbins, Burrito Co, China Star, KFC, McDonald's, Sub Factory, **lodging:** Clarion, Grace Inn, **other:** Checker Parts, Safeway, Walgreens

**155** Baseline Rd, Guadalupe, **N gas:** Mobil, Shell/Circle K/Popeye's/dsl, **food:** Carl's Jr, ClaimJumper, El Pollo Loco, 5& Diner, Joe's Crabshack, McDonald's, Rainforest Cafe, Waffle House, Wendy's, **lodging:** Best Western, Candlewood Studios, Holiday Inn Express, InnSuites, Ramada Ltd, Residence Inn, SpringHill Suites, TownePlace Suites, **other:** AutoZone, AZ Mills Factory Shops, CVS Drug, JC Penney Outlet, Marshall's, Pro Auto Parts, Ross, **S gas:** Arco, QT, 7-11, **food:** Aunt Chilada's Mexican, China Town, Denny's, Sonic, Subway, **lodging:** Homestead Village, Motel 6, **other:** Fry's Electronics, Fry's Foods

**154** US 60 E, AZ 360, Superstition Frwy, to Mesa, **N other:** to Camping World(off Mesa Dr)

**153b a** AZ 143 N, Broadway Rd E, on University **N food:** Denny's, **lodging:** Courtyard, Fairfield Inn, Hilton, Homestead Suites, La Quinta, Sheraton, Sleep Inn, **other:** to

# INTERSTATE 10 CONT'D

| | |
|---|---|
| **153b a** | Continued<br>Diablo Stadium, **N gas:** Chevron, Shell/Circle K/Taco Bell/24hr, **food:** Del Taco, George&Dragon, Papa John's, Pizza Hut, Port of Subs, Ranch House Rest., Taco Bell, Whataburger, **lodging:** Hampton Inn, **other:** Staples |
| **152** | 40th St, **N gas:** Shell/dsl, **other:** U Phoenix, **S gas:** Shell/Circle K, **food:** Burger King |
| **151mm** | Salt River |
| **151b a** | 28th St, 32nd St, University Ave, **N food:** Waffle House, **lodging:** Extended Stay America, Hilton Garden, Holiday Inn Express, Radisson, **other:** AZSU, U Phoenix, **S gas:** Circle K, **food:** McDonald's |
| **150b** | 24th St E(from wb), **N** Air Nat Guard, **lodging:** Motel 6, **S lodging:** Best Western/rest. |
| **150a** | I-17 N, to Flagstaff |
| **149** | Buckeye Rd, **N other:** Sky Harbor ✈ |
| **148** | Washington St, Jefferson St, **N gas:** Chevron, Shell, Tiemco/dsl, **food:** Carl's Jr, Mandy's Fish'n Chips, McDonald's, Rally's, **lodging:** Motel 6, Sterling Hotel, **other:** to Sky Harbor ✈, **S gas:** Circle K, **other:** Ⓗ HOSPITAL |
| **147b a** | AZ 51 N, AZ 202 E, to Squaw Peak Pkwy |
| **146** | 16th St, **N gas:** Circle K/Shell, **food:** KFC, **S gas:** Circle K, **food:** Antonio's Rest., Church's, Tradicione's, **other:** Ranch Mkt |
| **145** | 7th St, **N food:** McDonald's, **other:** Safeway Foods, Walgreens, **S gas:** Circle K, Shell, **other:** Ⓗ HOSPITAL, to America West Arena |
| **144** | 7th Ave, Amtrak, central bus dist |
| **143c** | 19th Ave, US 60 |
| **143b a** | I-17, N to Flagstaff, S to Phoenix |
| **142** | 27th Ave (from eb, no return), **N lodging:** Comfort Inn |
| **141** | 35th Ave, **N food:** Jack-in-the-Box, Rita's Mexican, **S gas:** Shell/Circle K |
| **140** | 43rd Ave, **N gas:** Circle K/dsl, 7-11, Shell, **food:** Filberto's Mexican, Pizza Hut, Salsita's Mexican, Subway, **other:** AutoZone, Fry's Foods, 99¢ Store, Radio Shack, Walgreens |
| **139** | 51st Ave, **N gas:** Chevron/dsl, Circle K, **food:** Burger King, Domino's, El Pollo Loco, McDonald's, Sonic, Waffle House, **lodging:** Budget Inn, CrossLand Suites, Day's Inn, Holiday Inn, InTowne Suites, La Quinta, Motel 6, Red Roof Inn, Travelodge, **other:** Discount Tire, Food City, 7-11, **S gas:** DZ/dsl, QT/dsl/scales, **food:** Carl's Jr, IHOP, Taco Bell, **lodging:** Hampton Inn, Phoenix West Inn, Super 8, Travelers Inn |
| **138** | 59th Ave, **N gas:** Circle K, Shamrock, **food:** Armando's Mexican/24hr, Subway, **other:** AutoZone, Checker Parts, Family$, 7-11, Walgreens, **S gas:** Liberty/Wendy's/dsl/24hr, **food:** Waffle House, Whataburger/24hr, **other:** Blue Beacon/scales |
| **137** | 67th Ave, **N gas:** QT, Circle K/dsl, Shell/dsl, **food:** Church's, **S gas:** ✈FLYING J/Conoco/CountryMkt/dsl/LP/24hr/@ |
| **136** | 75th Ave, **N gas:** Chevron, Circle K/gas, **food:** A&W, Del Taco, Denny's, Starbucks, Whataburger, Taco Bell/Pizza Hut, Taco Del Mar, Texas Roadhouse, Whataburger, **other:** Ford, Home Depot, Lowe's Whse, Petsmart, Staples, Walmart SuperCtr, **S gas:** Arco/24hr |
| **135** | 83rd Ave, **N gas:** Circle K, QT, **food:** Arby's, Burger King, Jack-in-the-Box, Waffle House, **lodging:** Econolodge, Premier Inn, **other:** Sam's Club |
| **134** | 91st Ave, Tolleson |
| **133b** | Lp 101 N |
| **133a** | 99th Ave, **N gas:** Chevron/dsl, **food:** Baja Fresh, Carrabba's, ClaimJumper, Ichiban Rest., Island's Burgers, McDonald's, Subway, Village Inn, **other:** Best Buy, Borders Books, Circuit City, Costco/gas, GNC, Marshall's, Old Navy, PetCo, **S food:** Pilot/Wendy's/Subway/dsl/scales/24hr/@, **other:** CarMax |
| **132** | 107th Ave (from eb), **N other:** Walgreens, **S other:** Earnheart RV Ctr, Dodge, Hyundai, Kia, Mazda, Mitsubishi, Nissan, Saturn, Subaru |
| **131** | Avondale Blvd., to Cashion, **N gas:** Mobil, **S lodging:** Hilton Garden, Homewood Suites, **other:** to Phoenix International Raceway |
| **129** | Dysart Rd, to Avondale, **N gas:** Chevron, Shell/Circle K/dsl, **food:** Big Apple Rest., Carino's Italian, Chick-fil-A, In-n-Out, Jack-in-the-Box/24hr, Mimi's Cafe, NY Pizza, Panda Express, Papa Murphy's, Quizno's, Taco Bell, **lodging:** Wingate Inn, **other:** AutoZone, Discount Tire, $Tree, Jo-Ann Fabrics, Fry's Foods, Kohl's, Lowe's Whse, Petsmart, Walmart SuperCtr, **S gas:** QT, **food:** A&W/LJ Silver, Black Bear Diner, Del Taco, Gandolfo's, Golden Corral, KFC, McDonald's, Peter Piper Pizza, Subway, Waffle House, Whataburger, **lodging:** Best Value Inn, Super 8, **other:** Brakemasters, Chevrolet, Chrysler/Dodge/Jeep, Food City, Home Depot, Sam's Club, Suzuki, Walgreens |
| **128** | Litchfield Rd, **N gas:** Mobil/Blimpie/dsl, **food:** Applebee's, Black Angus Steaks, Carl's Jr, Chili's, Chipotle Mexican, Cracker Barrel, Denny's, El Paso BBQ, Fazoli's, Macaroni Grill, Macavo's Mexican, McDonald's, McGrath's Fishouse, On the Border, Starbucks, Subway, TGIFriday, Wendy's, **lodging:** Hampton Inn, Holiday Inn Express, Residence Inn, **other:** Ⓗ HOSPITAL, Barnes&Noble, Best Buy, Michael's, Ross, Target, |

AZ

## INTERSTATE 10 CONT'D

**128** Continued
Wigwam Resort/rest(3mi), to Luke AFB, **S gas:** Mobil, **food:** Arby's, Burger King, JB's, Schlotsky's, Taco Bell, **lodging:** Best Western, **other:** AutoZone, Fry's Food/drug, Goodyear/auto, 99¢ Store, Osco Drug, Pontiac/GMC, Radio Shack

**126** PebbleCreek Pkwy, to Estrella Park, **S food:** Bro's Pizza, Its a Grind, Jack-in-the-Box, Subway, **lodging:** Comfort Suites, **other:** Safeway Foods/gas, Walgreens, Walmart SuperCtr

**125mm** Roosevelt Canal

**124** Cotton Lane, to AZ 303, **N** st prison, **S other:** Pheonix RV Park

**121** Jackrabbit Trail, **N gas:** Chevron/dsl, **S gas:** Circle K

**120** Verrado Way

**117** Watson Rd, **S food:** Jack-in-the-Box, Palermo's Pizza, Peter Piper Pizza, Subway, Wendy's, **other:** Fry's Foods/gas, Lowes Whse, Petsmart, Walgreens, Walmart SuperCtr, vet

**114** Miller Rd, to Buckeye, **S gas:** Loves/Chester Fried/Subway/dsl/scales/24hr, **food:** Burger King, **lodging:** Day's Inn, **other:** Leaf Verde RV Park

**112** AZ 85, to I-8, Gila Bend, **S** Subway (3mi)

**109** Sun Valley Pkwy, Palo Verde Rd

**104mm** Hassayampa River

**103** 339th Ave, **S gas:** TA/Shell/Subway/dsl/LP/scales/24hr/@, **food:** Country Fair Rest. **other:** truckwash

**98** Wintersburg Rd

**97mm** Coyote Wash

**95.5mm** Old Camp Wash

**94** 411th Ave, Tonopah, **S gas:** Chevron/dsl, Mobil/dsl, Shell/Chester's/Noble Roman's/Subway/dsl/LP/24hr, **food:** Tonopah Joe's Rest., **lodging:** Mineral Wells Motel, **other:** USPO, tires/repair, Saddle Mtn RV Park, playground

**86mm** rest area both lanes, full ♿ facilities, ☎, ⛱, litter barrels, petwalk, vending

**81** Salome Rd, Harquahala Valley Rd

**69** Ave 75E

**53** Hovatter Rd

**52mm** rest area both lanes, full ♿ facilities, ☎, ⛱,, vending, litter barrels, petwalk

**45** Vicksburg Rd, **N gas:** Zip TC/HotStuff/dsl/24hr, **S gas:** Valero/dsl/rest./scales/24hr, **other:** Jobski's dsl Repair/towing, RV Park, tires, wildlife refuge

**31** US 60 E, to Wickenburg, **12 mi N other:** food, camping

**26** Gold Nugget Rd

**19** Quartzsite, to US 95, Yuma, **N gas:** Chevron/dsl, Park Place TC/subs/dsl, Shell/dsl, **food:** Taco Mio, **other:** Beall's, CarQuest, Family$, Radio Shack, Roadrunner Foods, RV camping

**18mm** Tyson Wash

---

**17** US 95, AZ 95, Quartzsite, **N gas:** Mobil/Burger King/LP, Pilot/DQ/Subway/dsl/scales/24hr, **food:** Best Mexican, Carl's Jr, McDonald's, Quarter Yacht Grill, **other:** RV camping, tires/repair, **S gas:** Loves/Chester's/Subway/dsl/24hr, **lodging:** Super 8, **other:** Desert Gardens RV Park

**11** Dome Rock Rd

**5** Tom Wells Rd, **N gas:** Texaco/SunMart/Quizno's/dsl

**4.5mm** rest area both lanes, full ♿ facilities, ☎, ⛱, , vending, litter barrels, petwalk

**3.5mm** eb AZ Port of Entry, wb weigh sta

**1** Ehrenberg, to Parker, **N other:** River Breeze RV Resort, **S gas:** ♦FLYING J/Wendy's/Cookery/dsl/LP/scales24hr/@, **lodging:** Best Western

**0mm** Colorado River, Arizona/California state line, Mountain/Pacific time zone

## INTERSTATE 15

| Exit # | Services |
|---|---|
| 29.5mm | Arizona/Utah state line |
| 27 | Black Rock Rd |
| 21mm | turnout sb |
| 18 | Cedar Pocket, **S other:** Virgin River Canyon RA/camping, parking area |
| 16mm | truck parking both lanes |
| 15mm | truck parking nb |
| 14mm | truck parking nb |
| 10mm | truck parking nb |
| 9 | Farm Rd |
| 8.5mm | Virgin River |
| 8 | Littlefield, Beaver Dam, **E other:** RV park, **1 mi W** gas/dsl, food, lodging, camping |
| 0mm | Arizona/Nevada state line, Pacific/Mountain time zone |

## INTERSTATE 17

| Exit # | Services |
|---|---|
| 341 | McConnell Dr, I-17 begins/ends, **N gas:** Chevron, Conoco/dsl, Exxon/Wendy's/dsl, Gasser/dsl, Giant/dsl, Mobil, Circle K, **food:** Arby's, Blimpie, Burger King, Buster's Rest., Carl's Jr, Cilantro's Mexican, Chili's, China Garden, Coco's, DQ, Del Taco, Denny's, Domino's, Fazoli's, IHOP, Jack-in-the-Box, Fuddrucker's, Furr's Café, KFC, McDonald's, Olive Garden, Perkins, Pizza Hut, Quizno's, Red Lobster, Roma Pizza, Sizzler, Souper Salad, Strombolli's, Subway, Taco Bell, TCBY, Village Inn Rest., **lodging:** AZ Motel, AmeriSuites, Comfort Inn, Crystal Inn, Day's Inn, Econolodge, Embassy Suites, Fairfield Inn, Hampton Inn, Hilton, La Quinta, Motel 6, Quality Inn, Ramada Ltd, Rodeway Inn, Sleep Inn, **other:** Barnes&Noble, Basha's Foods, CarQuest, Checker Parts, Discount Tire, Hastings Books, Jo-Ann Crafts, K-Mart, Michael's, Osco Drug, Safeway, Staples, Target, Walgreen, Walmart |
| 340b a | I-40, E to Gallup, W to Kingman |
| 339 | Lake Mary Rd(from nb), Mormon Lake, **E gas:** Circle K/dsl, **lodging:** AZ Mtn Inn, access to same as 341 |

E W PHOENIX TONOPAH

QUARTZSITE N S N S FLAGSTAFF

## INTERSTATE 17 CONT'D

**N ↕ S**

**SEDONA**

**337** AZ 89A S, to Sedona, Ft Tuthill RA, Oak Creek Canyon

**333** Kachina Blvd, Mountainaire Rd, **E food:** Mountainaire Rest.(2mi), **lodging:** Sled Dog B&B, **W gas:** Conoco/Subway/dsl

**331** Kelly Canyon Rd

**328** Newman Park Rd

**326** Willard Springs Rd

**322** Pinewood Rd, to Munds Park, **E gas:** Chevron/dsl, Woody's/dsl, **food:** Lone Pine Rest., **other:** Motel in the Pines/RV camp, USPO, **W gas:** Exxon/dsl, **other:** Munds RV Park, auto/RV repair

**322mm** Munds Canyon

**320** Schnebly Hill Rd

**317** Fox Ranch Rd

**316mm** Woods Canyon

**315** Rocky Park Rd

**313mm** scenic view sb, litter barrels

**306** Stoneman Lake Rd

**300mm** runaway truck ramp sb

**298** AZ 179, to Sedona, Oak Creek Canyon, **7-15 mi W food:** Burger King, Cowboy Club Rest., Joey's Bistro, Taco Bell, **lodging:** Belrock Inn, Hilton Garden, La Quinta, Quality Inn, Radisson/cafe, Wildflower Inn

**297mm** rest area both lanes, full ♿ facilities, 🕿, 🍴, litter barrels, vending, petwalk

**293mm** Dry Beaver Creek

**293** Cornville Rd, McGuireville Rd, to Rimrock, **E gas:** ExpressFuel, **food:** Tunes Rest., **W gas:** 76/dsl, **food:** Crusty's Cafe

**289** Middle Verde Rd, Camp Verde, **E gas:** Mobil/dsl, **food:** Rockets Café, Sonic, **lodging:** Cliff Castle Lodge/casino/rest., **other:** to Montezuma Castle NM, **W other:** Distant Drums RV Park

**288mm** Verde River

**287** AZ 260, to AZ 89A, Cottonwood, Payson, **E gas:** Arco, Chevron, Shell/Noble Roamn's/Subway/dsl/RVdump/LP/24hr, **food:** A&W/KFC, Burger King, Coldstone Creamery, DQ, Denny's, Los Betos Mexican, McDonald's, Quizno's, Starbucks, Taco Bell, **lodging:** Comfort Inn, Day's Inn, Super 8, **other:** Territorial RV Park(1mi), Trails End RV Park, Zane Grane RV Park, **W gas:** Chevron/Wendy's/dsl/24hr, **other:** to Jerome SP, RV camping

**CAMP VERDE**

**285** Camp Verde, Gen Crook Tr, **3 mi E food:** Rio Verde Mexican, **lodging:** Territorial Town Inn, **other:** Zane Gray RV Park(9mi), Trail End RV Park, to Ft Verde SP

**281mm** safety pullout area nb

**278** AZ 169, Cherry Rd, to Prescott

**269mm** Ash Creek

**268** Dugas Rd, Orme Rd

**265.5mm** Agua Fria River

**262b a** AZ 69 N, Cordes Jct Rd, to Prescott, **E gas:** Chevron/McDonald's/24hr, Shell/Noble Roman's/Chester's/dsl/24hr, **food:** CJ's Diner, McDonald's, **lodging:** Cordes Jct Motel/RV Park

**17** Cave • Creek

**10** Phoenix • • Scottsdale Tempe • Mesa • Sun Lakes

**10** • Sacaton

**8** Casa Grande

**10**

**10**

**AZ**

**BLACK CANYON CITY**

**262mm** Big Bug Creek

**259** Bloody Basin Rd, to Crown King, Horsethief Basin RA

**256** Badger Springs Rd

**252** Sunset Point, **W** scenic view/rest area both lanes, full ♿ facilities, 🕿, 🍴, litter barrels, vending

**248** Bumble Bee, **A other:** Horsethief Basin RA

**244** Squaw Valley Rd, Black Canyon City, **E food:** Kid Chileean BBQ/Steaks, **other:** KOA, **W gas**

**243.5mm** Agua Fria River

**242** Rock Springs, Black Canyon City, **E** KOA, **W gas:** Chevron/dsl/24hr, Shell, **food:** Byler's Kitchen, Rock Springs Café, **lodging:** Bradshaw Mtn RV Resort, Mtn Breeze Motel

**239.5mm** Little Squaw Creek

**239mm** Moore's Gulch

**236** Table Mesa Rd

**232** New River, **E food:** RoadRunner Rest., **other:** Curves, vet

**231.5mm** New River

**229** Anthem Way, Desert Hills Rd, **E gas:** Mobil/dsl, **food:** Auntie Anne's, McDonald's, Native Newyorker Rest., Pizza Hut, Quizno's, Rosati's Pizza, Starbucks, Subway, Taco Del Mar, **other:** Ace Hardware, CVS Drug, Osco Drug, Safeway, **W gas:** Chevron/dsl, Mobil/dsl, **food:** Del Taco, Denny's, **lodging:** Hampton Inn, **other:** Anthem Outlets/famous brands/food court, Brake Masters, Discount Tire, U-haul, Walmart SuperCtr

**227** Daisy Mtn Dr, **E gas:** Circle K, **food:** Jack-in-the-Box, Subway, **other:** CVS Drug, Fry's Foods

**227mm** Dead Man Wash

**225** Pioneer Rd, **W other:** Pioneer RV Park, museum

**223** AZ 74, Carefree Hwy, to Wickenburg, **E gas:** Chevron, **food:** Applebees, AZool Grill, It's-a-Grind, McDonald's, Rays Pizza, Subway, **other:** Albertson's/Osco, Home Depot, Kohl's, **W other:** Lake Pleasant Park, camping

**219mm** Skunk Creek

**218** Happy Valley Rd, **E gas:** Shell, **food:** Applebees, Bajio, Carl's Jr, Coldstone Creamery, Jack-in-the-Box, Logan's Roadhouse, Panda Express, Quizno's, Rays Pizza, Red Robin, Shane's Ribshack, Starbucks, TGIFriday, Tilly's Grill, **other:** Barnes&Noble, Circuit City, Lowe's Whse, Old Navy, PetCo, Staples, Steinmart, TJ Maxx, Walmart SuperCtr, World Mkt

**AZ**

N ↑ S

S C O T T S D A L E

## INTERSTATE 17 CONT'D

**217**    Pinnacle Peak Rd, E Phoenix RV Park

**215a**   Rose Garden Ln, same as 215b

**215b**   Deer Valley Rd, E **gas:** Exxon/dsl, Shell/Circle K, **food:** Arby's, Armando's Mexican, Jack-in-the-Box, McDonald's, Sonic, Taco Bell, Wendy's, **other:** RV Ctr, W **gas:** Arco, Circle K, **food:** Black Angus, Cracker Barrel, Denny's, El Patron Mexican, Times Square Italian, **lodging:** Best Western, Country Inn&Suites, Extended Stay America, **other:** H HOSPITAL, NAPA, Target, U-Haul

**214c**   AZ 101 loop

**214b**   Yorkshire Dr, W **food:** In-n-Out, Jack-in-the-Box, **lodging:** Budget Suites, **other:** H HOSPITAL, Costco/gas, W **on 27th Ave gas:** 7-11, **food:** 5&Diner, Jack-in-the-Box, Wendy's, **other:** Michael's, Petsmart, Target

**214a**   Union Hills Dr, E **gas:** Circle K/dsl, Shamrock, W **lodging:** Park Plaza Hotel, Sleep Inn, Studio 6

**212b a**   Bell Rd, Scottsdale, to Sun City, E **gas:** Chevron/dsl, Exxon, Mobil, QT, 76/dsl, **food:** Black Bear Diner, Burger Mania, Caramba Mexican, IHOP/24hr, Jack-in-the-Box, LJ Silver, McDonald's, Papa John's, Quizno's, Waffle House, **lodging:** Best Western, Comfort Inn, Fairfield Inn, Motel 6, **other:** Big O Tire, Checker Parts, Chevrolet, Chrysler/Jeep/Dodge, Ford/Lexus/Isuzu, Kohl's, Lincoln/Mercury, Nissan/Infiniti, Pontiac/Buick/GMC, Sam's Club/gas, Toyota, U-Haul, Walmart SuperCtr, W **gas:** Chevron, **food:** Applebee's, Denny's, Good Egg Rest., HomeTown Buffet, Hooters, Sizzler, **lodging:** Red Roof Inn, **other:** Fry's Foods

**211**    Greenway Rd, E **lodging:** Embassy Suites, La Quinta, **other:** 7-11

**210**    Thunderbird Rd, E **gas:** Circle K, **food:** Asian Cafe, Pizza Hut/Taco Bell, Wendy's, **other:** Home Depot, Jiffy Lube, Osco Drug, Walgreen, W **gas:** QT, **food:** Fazoli's, McDonald's, Quizno's, **other:** Best Buy, Fry's Electronics, Lowe's Whse

**209**    Cactus Rd, E **gas:** Chevron/24hr, 7-11, **food:** Cousins Subs, China Harvest, Don Pedro's Mexican, **lodging:** Ramada Inn, **other:** Firestone, Food City

**208**    Peoria Ave, E **food:** Fajita's, LoneStar Steaks, Pappadeaux, TGIFriday, **lodging:** AmeriSuites, Candlewood Suites, Comfort Suites, Crowne Plaza, Extended Stay America, Homewood Suites, W **food:** Black Angus, Burger King, China Chan, Chipotle Mexican, El Torito, Fatburger, Island Burger, Lonestar Steaks, Mimi's Cafe, Old Country Buffet, Olive Garden, Pappadeux's, Peter Piper Pizza, Red Lobster, Ruby Tuesday, Samauri Sam's, Sizzler, Souper Salad, Starbucks, Subway, TGI Fridays, Wendy's, Whataburger, **lodging:** Premier Inn, Sheraton, **other:** Barnes&Noble, Brake Master, Circuit City, Dillard's, Firestone/auto, JC Penney, Macy's, Michael's, Old Navy, PetCo, Ross, Sears/auto, Staples, Trader Joe's, mall

**208.5mm**   Arizona Canal

---

P H O E N I X

**207**    Dunlap Ave, E **gas:** Shell/dsl, **food:** Blimpie, Fajitas, Fuddrucker's, Lonestar Steaks, Outback Steaks, Sweet Tomato, **lodging:** Budget Lodge, Comfort Suites, Courtyard, Mainstay Suites, Sheraton, Sierra Suites, SpringHill Suites, TownPlace Suites, **other:** Aamco, Firestone, Sun City RV Ctr, mall, W **gas:** Chevron, **food:** Bobby Q's BBQ, Denny's, Schlotsky's, Subway, **other:** U-Haul, repair

**206**    Northern Ave, E **gas:** Circle K, Shell/dsl, **food:** Boston Mkt, Burger King, Del Taco, Denny's/24hr, El Pollo Loco, Los Compadres Mexican, Marie Callender's, McDonald's, Mr. Sushi, Papa John's, Pizza Hut, Starbucks, Subway, **lodging:** Best Western, **other:** Albertson's, Checker Parts, USPO, Walgreens, W **gas:** Arco, QT, **food:** DQ, Village Inn Rest., **lodging:** Motel 6, Residence Inn, Super 8, **other:** K-Mart, vet

**205**    Glendale Ave, E **other:** Ace Hardware, vet, W **gas:** Circle K/dsl, **food:** Jack-in-the-Box, **other:** Checker Parts, 7-11, Walgreens, to Luke AFB

**204**    Bethany Home Rd, E **gas:** Arco/24hr, Shell/Church's/dsl, **food:** McDonald's, Subway, Samauri Sam's, Whataburger, **other:** H HOSPITAL, BigLots, Circle K, vet, W **gas:** Shell, Valero, **food:** Burger King, Great Dragon, Lazy Lou's, **other:** Food City, Jiffy Lube, Savers

**203**    Camelback Rd, E **gas:** Arco/24hr, Circle K, **food:** Blimpie, Burger King, Church's, Denny's/24hr, Pepe's Taco Villa, Pizza Hut, **other:** Buick, Checker Parts, Chrysler/Jeep/Dodge, Discount Tire, Firestone/auto, KIA, NAPA, Walgreens, W **gas:** QT, **food:** DQ, Jack-in-the-Box, McDonald's, Taco Bell, TacoMex, **lodging:** Comfort Inn, **other:** AutoZone, Chevrolet, Circle K, to Grand Canyon U

**202**    Indian School Rd, E **gas:** Arco/24hr, **food:** Domino's, Federico's Mexican, Pizza Hut, Subway, **other:** Ace Hardware, CVS Drug, Food City, Skyline RV Ctr, W **gas:** Circle K, Red Dog/dsl/LP, Shell, Valero, **food:** JB's, Subway, Wendy's, **lodging:** Motel 6, **other:** 7-11, auto repair

**201**    Thomas Rd, E **gas:** Chevron/McDonald's, **food:** Arby's, Big Burrito, Denny's, Jack-in-the-Box, Roman's Pizza, Starbucks, **lodging:** Day's Inn, La Quinta, **other:** Circle K, W **gas:** QT, **food:** Carl's Jr, Subway, **other:** NAPA

**200b**   McDowell Rd, Van Buren, E **other:** Goodyear, W **lodging:** Travelodge

**200a**   I-10, W to LA, E to Phoenix

**199b**   Jefferson St (from sb), Adams St(from nb), Van Buren St(from nb), E **gas:** Circle K/76/24hr, **food:** Jack-in-the-Box, McDonald's, **other:** Suzuki, to st capitol, W **gas:** Circle K/76, **food:** La Canasta Mexican, Salsita's Mexican, **other:** Penny Pincher Parts, PepBoys

**199a**   Grant St

**198**    Buckeye Rd(from nb)

**197**    US 60, 19th Ave, Durango St, E **food:** Jack-in-the-Box, Whataburger/24hr, to St Capitol

**196**    7th St, Central Ave, W **gas:** DZ/dsl

## INTERSTATE 17 CONT'D

| | |
|---|---|
| 195b | 7th St, Central Ave, **E gas:** Big Tiger/24hr, Circle K, Trailside Gas/dsl/24hr, **food:** McDonald's, Taco Bell, **lodging:** EZ 8 Motel/rest., **other:** H HOSPITAL |
| 195a | 16th St (no EZ return from sb), **E food:** Burger King, **other:** Checker Parts, Food City, to Sky Harbor ✈ |
| 194 | I-10 W to AZ 151, to Sky Harbor ✈ |
| I-17 | begins/ends on I-10, exit 150a |

## INTERSTATE 19

| Exit # | Services |
|---|---|
| **I-19** uses kilometers (km) | |
| 101b a | I-10, E to El Paso, W to Phoenix, I-19 begins/ends on I-10, exit 260 |
| 99 | AZ 86, Ajo Way, **E gas:** Conoco, 76/Circle K, **food:** Hamburger Stand, Pizza Hut, Subway, Taco Bell, **other:** Fry's Foods, GNC, Goodyear/auto, U-Haul, Walgreens, auto repair, vet, **W gas:** Chevron/dsl/24hr, Conoco/dsl, Circle K, **food:** Burger King, Domino's, **other:** H HOSPITAL, Food City, Jiffy Lube, to Old Tucson, museum |
| 98 | Irvington Rd, **E gas:** Arco/24hr, **other:** Fry's Foods, **W gas:** Chevron, **food:** China Olive Buffet, McDonald's, Olive Garden, Panda Express, Starbucks, Subway, **other:** Food City, Home Depot, Marshall's, Petsmart, Ross, Target |
| 95b a | Valencia Rd, **E gas:** Conoco, **food:** Church's, Donut Wheel, Jack-in-the-Box, McDonald's, Peter Piper Pizza, Sonic, Whataburger, Yokohama RiceBowl, **other:** Aamco, AutoZone, Brake Masters, Checker Parts, Food City, Jiffy Lube, USPO, **W gas:** Chevron/dsl, 76/Circle K, **food:** Applebee's, Arby's, Burger King, Carl's Jr, Chili's, Chuey's Cafe, Denny's, Dunkin Donuts, Golden Corral, IHOP, Papa John's, Pizza Hut, Taco Bell, Wendy's, **other:** Big O Tire, CVS Drug, Lowe's Whse, 99¢ Store, Radio Shack, Walgreens, Walmart SuperCtr, repair, transmissions |
| 92 | San Xavier Rd, **W other:** to San Xavier Mission |
| 91.5km | Santa Cruz River |
| 87 | Papago Rd, emergency phones sb |
| 80 | Pima Mine Rd, **E food:** Agave Rest., Diamond Casino |
| 75 | Helmut Peak Rd, to Sahuarita, **E gas:** Shell, **other:** Fry's Foods/drug, USPO |
| 69 | US 89 N, Duval Mine Rd., Green Valley, **E food:** Denny's, Pizza Hut, Popeye's, Quizno's, Siagon Flavor, Subway, **other:** Basha's Food, Radio Shack, Walgreens, Walmart SuperCtr, **W gas:** Circle K/gas, Texaco/DQ/dsl, **food:** Burger King, Domino's, Manuel's Rest., Rigoberto's Mexican, Taco Bell/TCBY, **lodging:** Holiday Inn Express, **other:** Big O Tire, Ford/Lincoln/Mercury/Hyundai, Green Valley RV Resort, Safeway/gas, Titan Missile Museum |
| 65 | Esperanza Blvd, to Green Valley, **W gas:** Shell/repair, **A gas:** Texaco/dsl, **food:** AZ Family Rest., China View, |

| | |
|---|---|
| 65 | Continued Dona's Rest., La Placita Mexican, **lodging:** Baymont Inn, Best Western, **other:** Ace Hardware, Family$, Walgreens |
| 63 | Continental Rd, Green Valley, **E food:** Quail Valley Rest., **other:** golf, USPO, **2 mi E other:** San Ignacio Golf Club/rest., **W gas:** Chevron, Shell (2mi), **food:** China Vic, HotStuff Pizza, KFC, McDonald's, Starbucks, Trivettie's Rest., **other:** CVS Drug, Parts+, Safeway, TrueValue, Walgreens, to Madera Cyn RA |
| 56 | Canoa Rd, **A lodging:** San Ignacio Inn |
| 54km | **rest area both lanes, full ♿ facilities, 📞, 🚻, litter barrels, vending, petwalk** |
| 48 | Arivaca Rd, Amado, **2-3 mi E lodging:** Amado Inn, **other:** Mtn View RV Park, Rex Ranch Resort, **W gas:** Amado Plaza, **food:** Cow Palace Rest., Longhorn Grill, **other:** Amado Mkt |
| 42 | Agua Linda Rd, to Amado, **E other:** Mtn View RV Park |
| 40 | Chavez Siding Rd, Tubac, **3-5 mi E gas:** Tubac Mkt/dsl/deli, **other:** Tubac Golf Resort |
| 34 | Tubac, **E gas:** Tubac Mkt/dsl, **food:** Artists Palate, Knob hill Rest., Montura Rest., **other:** Tubac Golf Resort, USPO, to Tubac Presidio SP |
| 29 | Carmen, Tumacacori, **E gas:** food, lodging, **other:** to Tumacacori Nat Hist Park |
| 25 | Palo Parado Rd |
| 22 | Pec Canyon Rd |
| 17 | Rio Rico Dr, Calabasas Rd, **W gas:** Chevron, **food:** La Placita, **other:** IGA Foods, USPO |
| 12 | AZ 289, to Ruby Rd, **E gas:** Pilot/Wendy's/dsl/24hr, **W other:** to Pena Blanca Lake RA |
| 8 | US 89, AZ 82 (exits left from sb, no return), Nogales, **0-3 mi E gas:** Circle K/gas **food:** Denny's, **lodging:** Americana Motel, Best Western, Day's Inn, **other:** H HOSPITAL, Goodyear/auto, U-Haul, Mi Casa RV Park |
| 4 | AZ 189 S, Mariposa Rd, Nogales, **E gas:** Chevron, FasTrip, Jumpin' Jack Gas, 76, **food:** Arby's, Bella Mia Rest., ChinaStar, Denny's, DQ, HomeTown Buffet, Jack-in-the-Box, KFC, McDonald's, Mesquite Grill, Shakey's, Sonic, Taco Bell, Yokohama Rest., **lodging:** Motel 6, Super 8, **other:** Batteries+, BigLots, Chevrolet, $Tree, |

**N**
**S**
**E**
**W**

## INTERSTATE 19 CONT'D

| | |
|---|---|
| **4** | Continued |
| | Ford/Lincoln/Mercury, Home Depot, JC Penney, K-Mart, NAPA, Pontiac/Buick/GMC, Radio Shack, Ross, Safeway, Walgreens, Walmart SuperCtr (N Grand Ave), **W gas:** Valero/dsl, **food:** Carl's Jr, IHOP, **lodging:** Candlewood Suites, Holiday Inn Express, **other:** Chrysler/Dodge/Jeep |
| **1b** | Western Ave, Nogales |
| **1a** | International St |
| **0km** | I-19 begins/ends in Nogales, Arizona/Mexico Border, **1/2 mi**...gas: Circle K/gas, Jumpin'Jack/dsl, **food:** Burger King, Church's, Domino's, Jack-in-the-Box, McDonald's, Noble Roman's, Peter Piper Pizza, Subway, **other:** AutoZone, CarQuest, Checker Parts, Family$, Food City, NAPA, Parts+, PepBoys, Walgreens, museum |

## INTERSTATE 40

| Exit # | Services |
|---|---|
| **359.5mm** | Arizona/New Mexico state line |
| **359** | Grants Rd, to Lupton, **N Welcome Ctr/rest area both lanes,full &#9855; facilities, &#9750;, &#127869;, litter barrels, petwalk, gas:** Speedy's/dsl/rest./24hr/@, **other:** Tee Pee Trading Post/rest., YellowHorse Indian Gifts |
| **357** | AZ 12 N, Lupton, to Window Rock, **N other:** Shirley's Trading Post, USPO, **S other:** Scotty's RV/dsl Repair |
| **354** | Hawthorne Rd |
| **351** | Allentown Rd, **N other:** Chee's Indian Store, Indian City Gifts |
| **348** | St Anselm Rd, Houck, **N gas:** Chevron, **other:** Ft Courage Food/gifts |
| **347.5mm** | Black Creek |
| **346** | Pine Springs Rd |
| **345mm** | Box Canyon |
| **344mm** | Querino Wash |
| **343** | Querino Rd |
| **341** | Ortega Rd, Cedar Point, **N gas:** Armco/gas/gifts |
| **340.5mm** | insp/weigh sta both lanes |
| **339** | US 191 S, to St Johns, **S gas:** Conoco/dsl, **other:** USPO |
| **333** | US 191 N, Chambers, **N gas:** Chevron/dsl, **other:** to Hubbell Trading Post NHS, RV camping, **S gas:** Mobil/dsl, **lodging:** Chieftain Inn/rest. |
| **330** | McCarrell Rd |
| **325** | Navajo, **S gas:** Shell/Subway/Navajo Trading Post/dsl/24hr |
| **323mm** | Crazy Creek |
| **320** | Pinta Rd |
| **316mm** | Dead River |
| **311** | Painted Desert, **N gas:** Chevron, **other:** Petrified Forest NP, Painted Desert |
| **303** | Adamana Rd, **N** Stewarts/gifts, **S gas:** Painted Desert Indian Ctr/gas |
| **302.5mm** | Big Lithodendron Wash |

**CHAMBERS**

| | |
|---|---|
| **301mm** | Little Lithodendron Wash |
| **300** | Goodwater |
| **299mm** | Twin Wash |
| **294** | Sun Valley Rd, **N** Root 66 RV camping, **S other:** Knife City |
| **292** | AZ 77 N, to Keams Canyon, **N gas:** Conoco/Burger King/dsl/24hr/@, **other:** dsl repair, **S other:** museum |
| **289** | Lp 40, Holbrook, **N gas:** Chevron/dsl, Mustang/dsl, **food:** Alberto's Mexican, Denny's, Jerry's Rest., Mesa Rest., **lodging:** Best Inn, Best Western, Comfort Inn, Day's Inn, Econolodge, Motel 6, Ramada Ltd, Sahara Inn, Super 8, Travelodge, **other:** Alley's Tire/Lube, KOA, OK Camping, same as 286 |
| **286** | Navajo Blvd, Holbrook, **N gas:** Mobil/dsl, Circle K, **food:** Alberto's Mexican, Burger King, Hilltop Cafe, KFC, McDonald's, Pizza Hut, Taco Bell, **lodging:** Comfort Inn, Holiday Inn Express, **other:** Checker Parts, $General, KOA, OK RV Park, **S gas:** Chevron/dsl/repair, MiniMart/gas, Mustang/dsl, 76/repair, Super Fuels, Woody's/dsl, **food:** DQ, Rte 66 Cafe, **lodging:** Best Value, El Rancho Motel, **other:** &#9882; HOSPITAL, Ford/Lincoln/Mercury, Chrysler/Jeep/Dodge, museum, rockshops, transmissions |
| **285** | US 180 E, AZ 77 S, Holbrook, **1 mi S gas:** Mustang Gas, Pacific Pride/dsl, **food:** Butterfield Steaks, Wayside Mexican, **lodging:** Best Western, Star Inn, Wigwam Motel, **other:** Safeway, RV repair, rest area/picnic tables/litter barrels, to Petrified Forest NP |
| **284mm** | Leroux Wash |
| **283** | Perkins Valley Rd, Golf Course Rd, **S gas:** Texaco/Country Host Rest./dsl/24hr/@ |
| **280** | Hunt Rd, Geronimo Rd, **N other:** Geronimo Trading Post |
| **277** | Lp 40, Joseph City, **N gas:** Love's/Chester's/Subway/scales/dsl/24hr, **S other:** to Cholla Lake CP, RV camping |
| **274** | Lp 40, Joseph City, **N gas:** food, lodging, RV camping |
| **269** | Jackrabbit Rd |
| **264** | Hibbard Rd |
| **257** | AZ 87 N, to Second Mesa, **N other:** to Homolovi Ruins SP, camping, **S other:** SW Indian Ctr |
| **256.5mm** | Little Colorado River |
| **255** | Lp 40, Winslow, **N gas:** Winslow Fuel/dsl, **lodging:** Holiday Inn Express, **other:** RV Park, **S gas:** &#8853;FLYING J/CountryMkt/dsl/LP/scales/RV Dump/24hr, **food:** Sonic, **lodging:** Comfort Inn (2mi), **other:** Chevrolet, Chrysler/Jeep |
| **253** | N Park Dr, Winslow, **N gas:** Chevron, Texaco/SenorD's/dsl/RV dump/scales/24hr/@, **food:** Arby's, Capt Tony's Pizza, Denny's, Pizza Hut, **other:** Checker Parts, $General, Ford, Jiffy Lube, Walmart SuperCtr, **S food:** Alfonso's Mexican, Dominos, KFC, McDonald's, Subway, Taco Bell, **lodging:** Comfort Inn, Econolodge, Motel 6, **other:** &#9882; HOSPITAL, Basha's Foods, Family$, NAPA, Safeway |
| **252** | AZ 87 S, Winslow, **S gas:** Shell/dsl, **food:** Almost Home Buffet, **lodging:** Day's Inn, Rest Inn, Super 8, The lodge, **other:** NAPACare, Old Trails Museum, dsl repair |

**HOLBROOK**

**WINSLOW**

## INTERSTATE 40 CONT'D

| | |
|---|---|
| **245** | AZ 99, Leupp Corner |
| **239** | Meteor City Rd, Red Gap Ranch Rd, **S other:** Meteor City Trading Post, to Meteor Crater |
| **235mm** | **rest area both lanes, full** 🚻 **facilities,** ☕, 🏕, **litter barrels, petwalk** |
| **233** | Meteor Crater Rd, **S gas:** Mobil/Subway/Meteor Crater RV Park, **other:** to Meteor Crater NL |
| **230** | Two Guns |
| **229.5mm** | Canyon Diablo |
| **225** | Buffalo Range Rd |
| **219** | Twin Arrows |
| **218.5mm** | Padre Canyon |
| **211** | Winona, **N gas:** Shell/dsl/repair |
| **207** | Cosnino Rd |
| **204** | to Walnut Canyon NM |
| **201** | US 89, to Flagstaff, **N gas:** Conoco/dsl, Express/dsl, 76/repair, Shell, **food:** Arby's, Burger King, Del Taco, Jack-in-the-Box, Los Altos Tacos, McDonald's, Pizza Hut, Quizno's, Ruby Tuesday, Sizzler, Taco Bell/LJ Silver, Wendy's, Village Inn Rest., **lodging:** Best Western, Day's Inn, Hampton Inn, Howard Johnson, Luxury Inn, Super 8, Travelodge, **other:** 🏥 HOSPITAL, Aamco, Big O Tire, Checker's Parts, CVS Drug, Dillard's, Family$, Flagstaff RV Ctr/LP, Goodyear/auto, Honda/Isuzu/Mazda, JC Penney, KOA, PitStop Lube, Safeway, Sears/auto, Toyota, mall, **S gas:** Mobil/dsl, **lodging:** Residence Inn |
| **198** | Butler Ave, Flagstaff, **N gas:** Chevron, Conoco/dsl, Shell, Mustang Gas, **food:** Burger King, Country Host Rest., Cracker Barrel, Denny's, Hogs Rest., McDonald's, Outback Steaks, Starbucks, Sonic, Taco Bell, **lodging:** Econolodge, Flagstaff Inn, Holiday Inn Express, Howard Johnson, Motel 6, Quality Inn, Ramada Ltd, Super 8, Travelodge, **other:** NAPA, Sam's Club, **1 mi N on Rte 66 gas:** Carter/dsl, **food:** China Star, Dog Haus Cafe, Kachina Mexican, KFC, Salsa Brava Mexican, Subway, **lodging:** Americana Inn, Best Value, Best Western, Red Rose Inn, Relax Inn, Royal Inn, 66 Motel, Travelodge, Timberline Motel, Western Hills Motel, **other:** Albertson's, Auto Value Parts, AutoZone, Buick/Pontiac, Firestone, Fry's Foods/dsl, Nissan/Subaru, PepBoys, U-Haul, **S gas:** Mobil, Sinclair/Little America/dsl/motel/@, **food:** Black Bart's Steaks/RV Park, vet |
| **197.5mm** | Rio de Flag |
| **195b** | US 89A N, McConnell Dr, Flagstaff, **N gas:** Chevron/dsl, Conoco/dsl, Gasser/dsl, Giant/dsl, Mobil, Circle K, Shell, Texaco/Wendy's/dsl, **food:** Arby's, August Moon Chinese, Baskin-Robbins, Bella Donna Italian, Blimpie, Buffalo Wild Wings, Burger King, Buster's Rest., Carl's Jr, Casa Bonita, Chili's, China Garden, Coco's, Coldstone, DQ, Del Taco, Denny's, Domino's, Fazoli's, Garcia'a Mexican, IHOP, Jack-in-the-Box, KFC, Mandarin Buffet, McDonald's, Olive Garden, Picazzo's Pizza, Peter Piper Pizza, Pizza Hut, Quizno's, Red Lobster, Roma Pizza, Sizzler, Starbucks, Strombolli's, Subway, Taco Bell, TCBY, Village Inn Rest., **lodging:** AZ Motel, |

| | |
|---|---|
| **195b** | **Continued** AutoLodge, AmeriSuites, Best Value, Budget Inn, Comfort Inn, Crystal Inn, Day's Inn, Drury Inn, Econolodge, Embassy Suites, Fairfield Inn, Hampton Inn, Hilton Garden, La Quinta, Motel 6, Quality Inn, Ramada Ltd, Rodeway Inn, Sleep Inn, Super 8, **other:** 🏥 HOSPITAL, Barnes&Noble, Basha's Foods, Hastings Books, Jiffy Lube, Jo-Ann Crafts, Kohl's, Michael's, Staples, Target, Walgreen, Walmart |
| **195a** | I-17 S, AZ 89A S, to Phoenix |
| **192** | Flagstaff Ranch Rd |
| **191** | Lp 40, to Grand Canyon, Flagstaff, 5 mi **N gas:** Chevron, **food:** DQ, **lodging:** Best Western, Budget Host, Comfort Inn, Day's Inn, Econolodge, Radisson, Super 8, Travelodge, **S other:** Woody Mtn Camping |
| **190** | A-1 Mountain Rd |
| **189.5mm** | Arizona Divide, elevation 7335 |
| **185** | Transwestern Rd, Bellemont, **N gas:** Pilot/McDonald's/Subway/dsl/scales/24hr, **lodging:** Best Value, **S other:** Harley-Davidson/Roadside Grill |
| **183mm** | **rest area wb, full** 🚻 **facilities,** ☕, 🏕, **vending, weather info, petwalk** |
| **182mm** | **rest area eb, full** 🚻 **facilities,** ☕, 🏕, **litter barrels, vending, weather info, petwalk** |
| **178** | Parks Rd, **N food:** Mustang/dsl/24hr, **food:** Rack&Bull Café, **other:** Ponderosa Forest RV Park |
| **171** | Pittman Valley Rd, Deer Farm Rd, **S lodging:** Quality Inn/grill |
| **167** | Garland Prairie Rd, Circle Pines Rd, **N other:** KOA |
| **165** | AZ 64, to Williams, to Grand Canyon, **N gas:** Texaco(8mi), Shell/dsl(4mi), **other:** KOA, **S lodging:** Super 8(4mi), **other:** RV Ctr |
| **163** | Williams, **N gas:** Chevron/Subway/dsl, **lodging:** Fairfield Inn, **other:** Cyn Gateway RV Park, to Grand Canyon, **S gas:** Mobil/dsl, Circle K, 76/dsl/repair, **food:** Buckle's Rest., Jack-in-the-Box, McDonald's, Pancho McGillicuddy's Mexican, Pine Country Rest., Pizza Hut, Rod's Steaks, Rosa's Cantina, **lodging:** Budget Host, Downtowner Motel, Econolodge, El Rancho Motel, Gateway Motel, Holiday Inn, Howard Johnson Express, Motel 6, Mountainview Motel, Knight's Inn, Rancho Motel, Rodeway Inn, Rte 66 Inn, Travelodge, **other:** CarQuest, USPO, same as 161 |

**AZ**

**WILLIAMS** E ← → W

## INTERSTATE 40 CONT'D

**161** Lp 40, Golf Course Dr, Williams, **N** RV camping, **1-3 mi S gas:** Chevron/dsl, Circle K, Mobil, 76, Shell, **food:** Cruiser's Cafe 66, DQ, Denny's, Jessica's Rest., Old Smokey Rest., Pizza Factory, Ralberto's Mexican, **lodging:** Best Western, Best Value, Budget Host, Canyon Country Inn, Day's Inn, Highlander Motel, Motel 6, Westerner Motel, **other:** Ⓗ HOSPITAL, NAPA, Family$, Safeway, Railside RV Ranch, to Grand Canyon Railway

**157** Devil Dog Rd

**155.5mm** safety pullout wb, litter barrels

**151** Welch Rd

**149** Monte Carlo Rd, **N other:** Monte Carlo Truck Repair

**148** County Line Rd

**146** AZ 89, to Prescott, Ash Fork, **N gas:** Mobil/dsl, Mustang, **food:** Ranch House Cafe, **lodging:** Ash Fork Inn

**144** Ash Fork, **N lodging:** Ash Fork Inn/rest., **other:** Grand Canyon RV Park, USPO, **S gas:** Chevron/Piccadilly's/dsl, Texaco/dsl/RV Park, **other:** auto repair

**139** Crookton Rd, to Rte 66

**132mm** weigh sta both lanes

**123** Lp 40, to Rte 66, Seligman, **N gas:** Mustang/dsl, Shell/dsl, **lodging:** 66 Motel, **other:** KOA (1mi), to Grand Canyon Caverns, USPO, **S gas:** Chevron/Subway/dsl/24hr

**121** Lp 40, to Rte 66, Seligman, **N gas:** Chevron/A&W, **food:** Lilo's Rest. (2mi), 66 Cafe (1mi), **lodging:** Canyon Lodge

**109** Anvil Rock Rd

**108mm** Markham Wash

**103** Jolly Rd

**96** Cross Mountain Rd

**91** Fort Rock Rd

**87** Willows Ranch Rd

**86mm** Willow Creek

**79** Silver Springs Rd

**75.5mm** Big Sandy Wash

**73.5mm** Peacock Wash

**71** US 93 S, to Wickenburg, Phoenix

**66** Blake Ranch Rd, **N gas:** Petro/Mobil/Iron Skillet/Noble Roman's/dsl/rest./scales/24hr/@, **other:** Blake Ranch RV Park, Blue Beacon, SpeedCo Lube

**60mm** Frees Wash

**59** DW Ranch Rd, Hualapai Mtn Rd, **N gas:** Love's/Chester Fried/Subway/dsl/24hr, **other:** truckwash

**57mm** Rattlesnake Wash

**KINGMAN**

**53** AZ 66, Andy Devine Ave, to Kingman, **N gas:** Chevron, /@ **FLYING J**/Conoco/Cookery/dsl/LP/scales/24hr/@, Mobil/dsl, Terrible's/dsl, Texaco, **food:** Arby's, Burger King, Denny's, Jack-in-the-Box, McDonald's, Pizza Hut, Taco Bell, **lodging:** Day's Inn, Econolodge, First Value Inn, Motel 6, Silver Queen Motel, Super 8, Travelodge, **other:** Basha's Foods, Goodyear/auto, Harley-Davidson, K-Mart, KOA(1mi), TireWorld, dsl/tire repair, **S gas:** 76/dsl, Shell/repair, **food:** ABC Rest., JB's, Lo's

**KINGMAN**

**53** Continued

Chinese, Sonic, **lodging:** Best Value Inn, Best Western, Comfort Inn, Day's Inn, High Desert Inn, Holiday Inn Express, Lido Motel, Relax Inn, Rodeway Inn, Rte 66 Motel, **other:** Chrysler/Jeep/Dodge, NAPA, Sunrise RV Park, Uptown Drug

**51** Stockton Hill Rd, Kingman, **N gas:** Arco/24hr, Chevron, 76/Circle K, **food:** Chili's, Cracker Barrel, Del Taco, Golden Corral, IHOP, In-n-Out, KFC, Papa John's, Sonic, Subway, Taco Bell/24hr, Whataburger, **lodging:** Hampton Inn, **other:** Ⓗ HOSPITAL, AutoZone, Big Lots, Brake Master's, Checker Parts, Chevrolet/Buick/Pontiac/Cadillac, $General, Ford/Lincoln/Mercury, Home Depot, Honda, Hyundai, Nissan, Oil Can Henry's, Smith's Foods/dsl, Staples, Superior Tire, TrueValue, Toyota, Walgreens, Walmart SuperCtr, KOA(2mi), vet, **S gas:** Circle K, **food:** Alfonso's Mexican, DQ, Kingman Co Steaks, Little Caesar's, Pizza Hut, **other:** CarQuest, Family$, Hastings Books, JC Penney, Radio Shack, Safeway

**48** US 93 N, Beale St, Kingman, **N gas:** Chevron/dsl, Express Stop, Mobil/dsl/RV dump, 93 Fuel, USA/Subway/dsl/24hr, Shell/dsl/24hr, TA/76/Country Pride/Popeye's/dsl/24hr, Woody's, **food:** Chan Chinese, Lotta Lou's Cafe, Wendy's, **lodging:** Frontier Motel, Knights Inn, **other:** Best Tire, auto/RV repair, truckwash, **S gas:** Chevron/dsl/24hr, **food:** Calico's Rest., Carl's Jr, Quizno's, Roadrunner Cafe, **lodging:** AZ Inn, Motel 6, Quality Inn(1mi), **other:** CarQuest, Ft Beale RV Park, museum

**46.5mm** Holy Moses Wash

**44** AZ 66, Oatman Hwy, McConnico, to Rte 66, **S gas:** Crazy Fred's Fuel/dsl/café, **other:** truckwash

**40.5mm** Griffith Wash

**37** Griffith Rd

**35mm** Black Rock Wash

**32mm** Walnut Creek

**28** Old Trails Rd

**26** Proving Ground Rd, **S other:** Ford Proving Grounds

**25** Alamo Rd, to Yucca, **N gas:** Micromart/dsl/diner, **other:** USPO, **S** auto repair, towing

**YUCCA**

**23mm** rest area both lanes, full ♿ facilities, 🚻, 🍴, litter barrels, vending, petwalk

**21mm** Flat Top Wash

**20** Santa Fe Ranch Rd

**18.5mm** Illavar Wash

**15mm** Buck Mtn Wash

**13.5mm** Franconia Wash

**13** Franconia Rd

**9** AZ 95 S, to Lake Havasu City, Parker, London Br, **S gas:** Chevron/Burger King/dsl, Pilot/Wendy's/dsl/scales, **other:** Prospectors RV Resort

**4mm** weigh sta both lanes

**2** Needle Mtn Rd

**1** Topock Rd, to Bullhead City, Oatman, **N gas:** food, camping, to Havasu NWR

**0mm** Arizona/California state line, Colorado River, Mountain/Pacific time zone

**E / W**

**LITTLE ROCK**

## INTERSTATE 30

| Exit # | Services |
|---|---|
| **143b a** | I-40, E to Memphis, W to Ft Smith, I-30 begins/ends on I-40, exit 153b |
| **142** | 15th St, **S** gas: Super Stop/dsl |
| **141b** | US 70, Broadway St, downtown, **N** gas: Exxon, US Fuel/dsl, **other:** AllTel Arena, Kroger, U-Haul, **S** gas: Citgo, Valero, **food:** Arby's, KFC/LJ Silver, McDonald's, Popeye's, Taco Bell, Wendy's |
| **141mm** | Arkansas River |
| **141a** | AR 10, Cantrell Rd, Markham St, wb only, to downtown |
| **140** | 9th St, 6th St, downtown, **N** gas: Exxon, Phillips 66, Shell, Texaco, **food:** Pizza Hut, **lodging:** Best Western, Holiday Inn, **S** gas: Phillips 66, **food:** Waffle House, **lodging:** Comfort Inn |
| **139b** | I-630, downtown |
| **139a** | AR 365, Roosevelt Rd, **N** gas: Exxon, **other:** AutoZone, **S** gas: Shell, **other:** Family$, Kroger, NAPA |
| **138b** | I-530 S, US 167 S, US 65 S, to Pine Bluff |
| **138a** | I-440 E, to Memphis, airport |
| **135** | W 65th St, **N** gas: Express, Exxon/dsl, Shell/dsl, **lodging:** Executive Inn, **S** lodging: Rodeway Inn |
| **134** | Scott Hamilton Dr, **S** gas: Exxon/dsl, **food:** Waffle House, **lodging:** Best Value Inn, Motel 6 |
| **133** | Geyer Springs Rd, **N** gas: Exxon, Hess, **food:** Church's, Sim's BBQ, Sonic, Subway, **S** gas: Conoco, Exxon, Phillips 66, Shell, Total, **food:** Arby's, Backyard Burgers, Blimpie, Burger King, Dixie Café, El Chico, KFC, Little Ceasars, Mazzio's, McDonald's, Panda Chinese, Pizza Inn, Rallys, Taco Bell, TCBY, Waffle House, Wendy's, **lodging:** Best Western, Hampton Inn, Rest Inn, Super 8, **other:** Advance Parts, Family$, Goodyear/auto, Harvest Foods, Kroger/gas, Radio Shack, Walgreen |
| **132** | US 70, University Ave, **N** gas: SuperStop, Valero, **lodging:** Best Value, **other:** Chevrolet, Dodge, **S** food: Luigi's Pizza |
| **131** | McDaniel Dr, **N** other: U-Haul, **S** lodging: Knight's Inn, Super 7 Inn, **other:** Crain RV Ctr, Firestone |
| **130** | AR 338, Baseline Rd, Mabelvale, **N** gas: Express/dsl, **other:** Harley-Davidson, **S** gas: Phillips 66, Shell, **food:** Applebee's, China Buffet, Dixie Cafe, McDonald's, Pizza Hut, Popey's, Ryan's, Sonic, Taco Bueno, Wendy's, **other:** $Tree, GNC, Walmart SuperCtr |
| **129** | I-430 N |
| **128** | Otter Creek Rd, Mabelvale West, **S** gas: Exxon, **lodging:** La Quinta/rest., **other:** [H] HOSPITAL, Goodyear |

**LITTLE ROCK**

| | |
|---|---|
| **126** | AR 111, County Line Rd, to Alexander, **N** gas: Shell/dsl, US Fuel, **S** gas: Express/dsl, **other:** Hyundai, Moix RV Ctr |
| **123** | AR 183, Reynolds Rd, to Bryant, Bauxite, **N** gas: Phillips 66, Shell/Blimpie, **food:** A&W/LJ Silver, Arby's, Backyard Burgers, Burger King, Catfish Barn, Cracker Barrel, De-Light China, Dominos, Firehouse Subs, KFC, Pizza Hut, Quizno's, Ruby Tuesday, Waffle House, **lodging:** Best Value, Comfort Inn, Holiday Inn Express, Vista Inn, **other:** AutoZone, $Tree, Harvest Foods, Radio Shack, Walmart SuperCtr/gas, **S** gas: Conoco/dsl, Exxon/dsl, Phillips 66/dsl, **food:** Bryant Cafe, Chick-fil-A, Little Caesar's, McDonald's, Sonic, Subway, Taco Bell, Wendy's, **lodging:** Super 8, **other:** $General, Foster's Foods, Isuzu, Lowe's Whse, USPO |
| **121** | Alcoa Rd, **N** gas: Pilot/Subway/dsl/scales/24hr/@, Texaco/dsl, **food:** McDonald's, **other:** Buick/Pontiac/GMC, Chrysler/Dodge/Jeep, **S** food: Chili's, Moe's SW Grill, Subway, **other:** Buick/Chevrolet/GMC, Kohls, Target |
| **118** | Congo Rd, **N** gas: Shell/dsl, **food:** Applebee's, Brown's Rest, CiCi's, Dixie Café, Santa Fe Grill, Weng's Chinese, **lodging:** Relax Inn, **other:** Buick/Pontiac/GMC, Curves, Home Depot, **S** gas: Citgo, Exxon, Shell, Valero, **food:** Arby's, Backyard Burger, Burger King, Colton's Steaks, DQ, La Hacienda Mexican, Sonic, Taco Bell, TCBY, Waffle House, Wendy's, Western Sizzlin, **lodging:** Best Western, Day's Inn, Econolodge, Ramada Inn, **other:** Advance Parts, Family$, Ford/Lincoln/Mercury/Kia, GMC, GNC, Hastings Books, JC Penney, Kroger, RV City, USPO, Walmart SuperCtr/gas |
| **117** | US 64, AR 5, AR 35, **N** gas: Conoco/dsl, Shell, **food:** Bo's BBQ, Denny's, IHOP, Pizza Hut, Santa Fe Grill, |

**AR**

E ← W

M A L V E R N

A R K A D E L P H I A

## INTERSTATE 30 CONT'D

**117** Continued
Waffle House, Weng's Chinese, **lodging:** Best Inn, Best Western, Econolodge, Ramada Inn, Relax Inn, **other:** Home Depot, **S other:** Ⓗ HOSPITAL, **S on Military...gas:** Exxon, Shell, **food:** Arby's, Burger King, Colton's Steaks, IHOP, McDonald's, Quizno's, Taco Bell, Wendy's, Western Sizzlin, **lodging:** Days Inn, **other:** AutoZone, Firestone, Kroger, O'Reilly Parts, Radio Shack, Suzuki

**116** Sevier St, **N gas:** Citgo, Shell/dsl, **food:** Hunan Chinese, **lodging:** Troutt Motel, **S gas:** BP, Shell, US Fuel/dsl, **lodging:** Capri Inn

**114** US 67 S, Benton

**113mm** insp sta both lanes

**111** US 70 W, Hot Springs, **N lodging:** Cloud 9 RV Park, to Hot Springs NP

**106** Old Military Rd, **N gas:** Fina/JJ's Rest./dsl/scales/@, **S** JB'S RV Park

**99** US 270 E, Malvern, **N** Ⓗ HOSPITAL

**98b a** US 270, Malvern, Hot Springs, **N food:** Hungry Fisherman Rest., **lodging:** Super 8, **S gas:** Fina/dsl, Shell/dsl, Valero, **food:** Burger King, Great Wall Buffet, McDonald's, Pizza Hut, Pizza Pro, Sonic, Subway, Taco Bell, TCBY, Wendy's, Waffle House, **lodging:** Comfort Inn, Economy Inn, Executive Inn, Holiday Inn Express, **other:** Ⓗ HOSPITAL, Advance Parts, AutoZone, Buick/Pontiac/GMC, Chevrolet, Chrysler/Dodge/Jeep, Curves, $General, $Tree, Ford/Lincoln/Mercury, GNC, O'Reilly Parts, Radio Shack, USPO, Walmart SuperCtr/gas, tires/repair

**97** AR 84, AR 171, **N other:** Lake Catherine SP, RV camping

**93mm** **rest area (both lanes exit left), full** ♿ **facilities,** 🅲, 🏠, **litter barrels, vending, petwalk**

**91** AR 84, Social Hill, **S other:** Social Hill Country Store/RV Park

**83** AR 283, Friendship, **S gas:** Shell/dsl

**78** AR 7, Caddo Valley, **N gas:** Fina/dsl/24hr, Valero/dsl, Shell/dsl, **food:** Cracker Barrel, **other:** Arkadelphia RV Park, to Hot Springs NP, **S gas:** Exxon/Subway/dsl, Phillips 66/Stuckey's, Shell/dsl, **food:** McDonald's, Subway, Taco Bell, TaMolly's Mexican, Waffle House, Wendy's, **lodging:** Best Value, Best Western, Comfort Inn, Day's Inn, Hampton Inn, Quality Inn, Super 8, **other:** De Gray SP

**73** AR 8, AR 26, AR 51, Arkadelphia, **N gas:** Citgo/dsl, Shell, **food:** Domino's, Great Wall Buffet, McDonald's, Western Sizzlin, **other:** $Tree, Walmart SuperCtr, to Crater of Diamond SP, **S gas:** Exxon/dsl, Shell, **food:** Andy's Rest., Burger King, Cancun Mexican, Mazzio's, Subway, Taco Tico, **other:** Ⓗ HOSPITAL, AutoZone, Brookshire Foods, Fred's Drug, JC Penney, O'Reilly Parts, USPO, Walgreen, repair

**69** AR 26 E, Gum Springs

**63** AR 53, Gurdon, **N gas:** Citgo/dsl/rest., **lodging:** Best Value Inn, **S gas:** Shell/dsl/rest., **other:** to White Oak Lake SP

**56mm** **rest area both lanes, full** ♿**facilities,** 🏠, **vending, litter barrels, vending, petwalk**

**54** AR 51, Gurdon, Okolona

**46** AR 19, Prescott, **N gas:** Fina/dsl, **other:** Crater of

H O P E

E ← W

M E M P H I S

**46** Continued
Diamonds SP (31mi), **S gas:** Love's/Hardee's/dsl/24hr/scales, **food:** Trucker's Rest., **other:** repair

**44** AR 24, Prescott, **N gas:** TA/Country Fair/Subway/Taco Bell/dsl/24hr/@, **S gas:** Norman's 44 Trkstp/dsl/rest./scales/@, **lodging:** Econolodge, **other:** Ⓗ HOSPITAL, truckwash, to S Ark U

**36** AR 299, to Emmet, **S gas:** Citgo

**31** AR 29, Hope, **N gas:** Shell/dsl, **food:** Uncle Henry's Smokehouse, **lodging:** Econolodge, Relax Inn, Village Inn/RV park, **other:** carwash, st police, **S gas:** Exxon/dsl, Shamrock, Shell, Valero/dsl, **food:** Andy's Rest., KFC, **lodging:** Best Value, Economy Inn,. **other:** Ⓗ HOSPITAL

**30** AR 4, Hope, **N gas:** Valero, **food:** Dos Loco Gringos, Western Sizzlin, **lodging:** Best Western, Holiday Inn Express, Super 8, **other:** Walmart SuperCtr/gas, Millwood SP, Old Washington SP, **S gas:** Exxon/Baskin-Robbins/Wendy's, Shell, **food:** Amigo Juan Mexican, Burger King, McDonald's, Pizza Hut, Sheba's Rest., Taco Bell, **lodging:** Day's Inn, **other:** Ⓗ HOSPITAL, Advance Parts, Brookshire's/gas, Buick/Pontiac/GMC/Chevrolet, Chrysler/Jeep/Dodge, $Tree, Ford/Lincoln/Mercury, Radio Shack, Super 1 Foods/gas, Old Washington Hist SP, Walgreen

**26mm** weigh sta both lanes

**18** rd 355, Fulton

**17mm** Red River

**12** US 67 (from EB), Fulton

**7mm** **Welcome Ctr eb, full** ♿ **facilities, info,** 🅲, 🏠, **litter barrels, vending, petwalk**

**7** AR 108, Mandeville, **N gas:** ⊕FLYING J/Conoco/Cookery/dsl/LP/24hr/@, **food:** J&R BBQ, **lodging:** Texarkana RV Park, **other:** truckwash

**2** US 67, AR 245, Texarkana, **N gas:** Circle K/dsl, Road-Runner/dsl, **S gas:** BP/dsl, **food:** T-Town Diner

**1** US 71, Jefferson Ave, Texarkana, **N** KOA, **S lodging:** Country Host Inn

**0mm** Arkansas/Texas state line

## INTERSTATE 40

| Exit # | Services |
|---|---|
| **285mm** | Arkansas/Tennessee state line, Mississippi River |
| **284mm** | weigh sta wb |
| **281** | AR 131, S to Mound City |
| **280** | Club Rd, Southland Dr, **N gas:** Pilot/Subway/Wendy's/scales/dsl, **other:** Goodyear, **S gas:** ⊕FLYING J/Conoco/LP/dsl/rest., Petro/Iron Skillet/dsl/rest./24hr/@, Pilot/Subway/dsl/@, **food:** KFC/Taco Bell, McDonald's, Waffle House, **lodging:** Best Western, Deluxe Inn, Express Inn, Super 8, **other:** Blue Beacon, SpeedCo Lube |
| **279b** | I-55 S (from eb) |
| **279a** | Ingram Blvd, **N food:** Margarita's Mexican, **lodging:** Comfort Inn, Day's Inn, Homegate Inn, Red Roof Inn, Rodeway Inn, **other:** Ford, Greyhound Park, U-Haul, **S gas:** Citgo/dsl, **food:** Perkins, Waffle House, **lodging:** Best Value, Econolodge, Hampshire Inn, Hampton Inn, Holiday Inn, Motel 6, Relax Inn, same as 280 |
| **278** | AR 77, 7th St, Missouri St, **N gas:** Citgo/24hr, **S on 7th St...food:** BBQ, Cracker Barrel, KFC, Pizza Inn, TCBY, **lodging:** Quality Inn, **other:** Ⓗ HOSPITAL, Sawyers |

## INTERSTATE 40 CONT'D

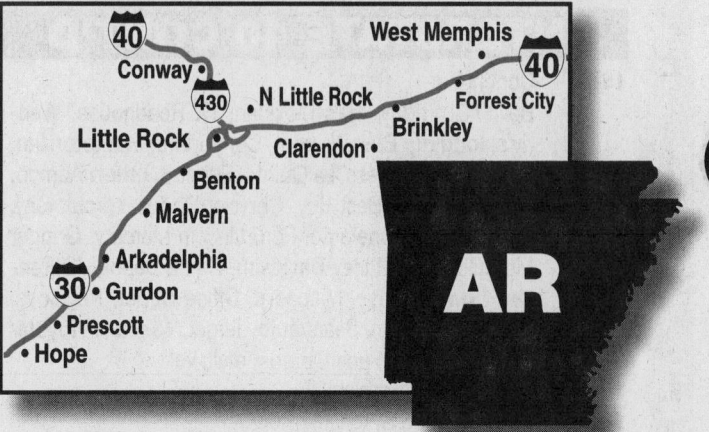

**E ↕ W**

**278** Continued
RV Park, Sears, **S on Missouri St gas:** Citgo/dsl, Exxon, Mapco, Phillips 66/dsl, **food:** Bonanza, Burger King, Domino's, Howard's Doughnut, Krystal, Lenny's Subs, Mrs Winner's, Pizza Hut, Popeye's, Subway, Taco Bell, Wendy's, **lodging:** Hampton Inn, Ramada Ltd, **other:** $Tree, Goodyear/auto, Walgreens

**277** I-55 N, to Jonesboro

**276** AR 77, Rich Rd, to Missouri St(from eb only), **S food:** Applebee's, Bonanza, Burger King, Krystal, McDonald's, Popeye's, Shoney's, Wendy's, **lodging:** Ramada Ltd, **other:** Kroger, Walmart SuperCtr, same as 278

**275** AR 118, Airport Rd, **S gas:** Horizon, **food:** DQ, Huddle House, Pizza Hut, **other:** URGENT CARE, city park

**275mm** Welcome Ctr wb, full ♿ facilities, info, 📞, ⛱, litter barrels, petwalk

**274mm** weigh sta eb

**271** AR 147, to Blue Lake, **S gas:** BP/dsl, Exxon/Chester Fried, **other:** to Horseshoe Lake, RV camping

**265** US 79, AR 218, to Hughes, **S food:** Bole's Foods

**260** AR 149, to Earle, **N gas:** TA/BP/Country Pride/Burger King/Taco Bell/dsl/scales/24hr/@, Dairy King/Subway/Gas, Valero/dsl, **lodging:** Super 8, **other:** Shell Lake Camping, **S gas:** Shell, **other:** dsl repair

**256** AR 75, to Parkin, **N gas:** MapCo/Stuckey's/dsl/rest., **other:** to Parkin SP (12mi)

**247** AR 38 E, to Widener

**245mm** St Francis River

**243mm** rest area wb, full ♿ facilities, 📞, vending, ⛱, litter barrels, petwalk

**242** AR 284, Crowley's Ridge Rd, **N other:** to Village Creek SP, camping, Ⓗ HOSPITAL

**241b a** AR 1, Forrest City, **N gas:** BP/dsl, Phillips 66/Popeye's/dsl, **food:** Denny's, HoHo Chinese, Wendy's, **lodging:** Best Value Inn, Day's Inn, Econolodge, Hampton Inn, Holiday Inn, Super 8, **other:** Buick/Chevrolet/Pontiac, Dodge, Ford/Lincoln/Mercury, st police, **S gas:** Citgo, Exxon, Shell, **food:** Bonanza, Burger King, Dragon China, KFC, McDonald's, Mrs Winners, Old South Pancakes, Pizza Hut, Subway, Taco Bell, Waffle House, **lodging:** Best Western, **other:** Advance Parts, $General, $Tree, Food Giant, Sav-A-Lot, Walmart SuperCtr/gas

**239** to Wynne, Marianna

**235mm** rest area eb, full ♿ facilities, 📞, vending, ⛱, litter barrels, petwalk

**234mm** L'Anguille River

**233** AR 261, Palestine, **N gas:** Love's/Chester's/Subway/dsl/scales/24hr, **lodging:** Rest Inn, **S gas:** BP/BBQ/dsl, **food:** Head's Cafe

**221** AR 78, Wheatley, **N gas:** Exxon/dsl/repair, **lodging:** Super 8, **S gas:** BP/dsl, MapCo/Subway/dsl

**216** US 49, AR 17, Brinkley, **N gas:** Exxon/dsl, Citgo, Shell, KFC/dsl, **food:** Western Sizzlin, **lodging:** Baymont Inn, Best Inn, Day's Inn/RV park, Econolodge, **other:** dsl repair, **S gas:** Exxon/dsl, MapCo/dsl/24hr, Phillips 66, Valero, **food:** Laura's Diner, McDonald's, Pizza Hut, Sonic, Subway, Taco Bell, Waffle House, **lodging:** Best Value, Best Western, Heritage Inn/RV Park, **other:**

**FORREST CITY**

---

**216** Continued
Chrysler/Dodge/Jeep, $General, Family$, Kroger, MapCo, O'Reilly Parts, Walmart

**205mm** Cache River

**202** AR 33, to Biscoe

**200mm** White River

**199mm** rest areas both lanes, full ♿ facilities, vending, ⛱, litter barrels, no phones

**193** AR 11, to Hazen, **N gas:** Exxon/Chester Fried, **S gas:** Shell/dsl/24hr, T-rix/dsl/RV Park, **food:** Subway, **lodging:** Super 8, Travel Inn

**183** AR 13, Carlisle, **S gas:** Conoco/dsl, Exxon/dsl, Phillips 66/dsl, **food:** Nick's BBQ, Pizza 'N More, Sonic, **lodging:** Best Value, Carlisle Motel, **other:** $General

**175** AR 31, Lonoke, **N gas:** Phillips 66, Valero/dsl, **food:** McDonald's, **lodging:** Day's Inn, Economy Inn, Holiday Inn Express, Super 8, **S gas:** Shell/Subway, **food:** KFC/Taco Bell, Pizza Hut, Sonic, **lodging:** Perry's Motel/rest., **other:** Chevrolet, Harvest Foods, Walmart

**169.5** insp sta both lanes

**169** AR 15, Remington Rd

**165** Kerr Rd

**161** AR 391, Galloway, **N gas:** Love's/Chester's/dsl/24hr, **other:** Camping World RV Ctr, Freightliner, **S gas:** Petro/Mobil/Iron Skillet/dsl/scales/24hr/@, Pilot/Subway/Chester's/dsl/scales/24hr/@, IA-80 TruckOMat/dsl/scales, **lodging:** Galloway Inn, **other:** Blue Beacon, River City RV Ctr

**159** I-440 W, to ✈

**157** AR 161, to US 70, **N gas:** Exxon/dsl, **S gas:** Flash/dsl, Hess, Super S Stop, Shell/dsl, **food:** Burger King, KFC/Taco Bell, McDonald's, Sonic, Subway, Waffle House, **lodging:** Best Value Inn, Comfort Inn, Day's Inn, Red Roof Inn, Rest Inn, Super 8

**156** Springhill Dr, **N gas:** Phillips 66, **food:** Burger King, Cracker Barrel, Red Lobster, **lodging:** Fairfield Inn, Holiday Inn Express, Residence Inn

**155** US 67 N, US 167, to Jacksonville (exits left from eb), Little Rock AFB, **1 mi on US 167/McCain Blvd N gas:** Phillips 66, Shell, **food:** Applebee's, Arby's, Burger King, Carino's Italian, Chili's, ChuckeCheese, CiCi's Pizza, Denny's, El Porton Mexican, Golden Corral, Hooters, IHOP, Jason's Deli, Kanpai Japanese, McDonald's, Lonestar Steaks, Luby's, Montana Steaks, Outback Steaks, Pizza Hut, Rally's, Red Lobster, Roadhouse Grill, Ryan's, Sonic, Shorty's BBQ, Starbucks, Subway, Taco

**LONOKE   LITTLE ROCK**

## INTERSTATE 40 CONT'D

**E** ↕ **W**

**AR**

**LITTLE ROCK**

**155** Continued
Bell, TGI Friday, Tia's Mexican, TX Roadhouse, Wendy's, **lodging:** Best Western, Comfort Inn, Hampton Inn, Holiday Inn Express, La Quinta, Super 8, **other:** Aamco, Barnes&Noble, Best Buy, Chrysler/Dodge, Circuit City, Dillard's, Firestone/auto, Ford/Lincoln/Mercury, Gander Mtn, Goody's, Harley-Davidson, Home Depot, JC Penney, Lowe's Whse, Michael's, Office Depot, PepBoys, PetsMart, Saturn, Sears/auto, Target, TJ Maxx, Toyota/Scion, Walmart SuperCtr/gas, mall, vet

**154** to Lakewood(from eb)

**153b** I-30 W, US 65 S, to Little Rock

**153a** AR 107 N, JFK Blvd, **N gas:** Exxon, Express, Shell, **food:** Schlotsky's, **lodging:** Travelodge, **S gas:** Exxon, **food:** Royal Buffet, Waffle House, **lodging:** Country Inn Suites, Hampton Inn, Holiday Inn, Howard Johnson, Motel 6, **other:** H HOSPITAL, USPO

**152** AR 365, AR 176, Camp Pike Rd, Levy, **N on Camp Robinson Rd N gas:** Exxon, EZ Mart, Phillips 66, Shell, **food:** Burger King, EggRoll Express, KFC/Taco Bell, Little Caesars, Mexico Chiquito, McDonald's, Pizza Hut, Rally's, Sonic, Subway, US Pizza, Wendy's, **other:** AutoZone, Fred's Drug, O'Reilly Parts, Walmart **S gas:** Phillips 66, Shell, **food:** Cancun Mexican, Chicken King, Church's, **other:** H HOSPITAL, Chevrolet, Family$, Kroger, Radio Shack, Sav-A-Lot

**150** AR 176, Burns Park, Camp Robinson, **S other:** info, camping

**148** AR 100, Crystal Hill Rd, **N gas:** Shell, **S** KOA

**147** I-430 S, to Texarkana

**142** AR 365, to Morgan, **N gas:** Phillips 66, Valero/dsl, **lodging:** Day's Inn, **other:** Auto Value Parts, Trails End RV Park, **S gas:** Shell/dsl, **food:** KFC/Taco Bell, McDonald's, Razorback Pizza, Smokeshack BBQ, Subway, Waffle House, **lodging:** Comfort Suites, Quality Inn, **other:** antiques

**135** AR 365, AR 89, Mayflower, **N gas:** Hess, **other:** Mayflower RV Ctr (1mi), **S gas:** Exxon/dsl, Valero, **food:** Glory B's Rest., Sonic, **other:** $General

**134mm** insp sta both lanes

**CONWAY**

**129** US 65B, AR 286, Conway, **N gas:** Citgo, **S gas:** Citgo, Exxon, MapCo, Shell, **food:** Arby's, Smitty's BBQ, Sonic, Subway, Wendy's, **lodging:** Budget Inn, Continental Motel, **other:** HOSPITAL, Chrysler/Dodge/Jeep, Honda, Toyota/Scion, st police, to Toad Suck State Park

**127** US 64, Conway, **N gas:** BP, Exxon, **food:** Annie's Rest, Arby's, Chick-fil-A, Chili's, Denny's, Starbucks, Subway, Waffle House, **lodging:** Best Value, Best Western, Comfort Suites, Day's Inn, Economy Inn, Hampton Inn, Hilton Garden, **other:** Belk, Best Buy, Chevrolet, Ford/Mercury, GMC/Buick/Pontiac, Goodyear/auto, Home Depot, Honda, Hyundai, Kohl's, Moix RV Ctr, NAPA, Nissan, Old Navy, O'Reilly Parts, Petsmart, Radio Shack, Target, TJ Maxx, repair/transmissions, to Lester Flatt Park, **S gas:** RaceWay, Shell/Subway/dsl, Valero/dsl, **food:** Burger King, Church's, Colton's Steaks, Hardee's, LJ Silver, Mazzio's, McDonald's, Pizza Inn, Popeye's, Quizno's, Rally's, TCBY, Taco Bell, Wendy's, Western Sizzlin, **lodging:** Kings Inn, **other:** AutoZone, BigLots,

**CONWAY**

**127** Continued
CarQuest, Family$, Fred's Drugs, Goodyear/auto, Hancock Fabrics, Kroger/gas, Radio Shack, Sav-a-Lot Foods, Walgreens

**125** US 65, Conway, **N gas:** Conoco/dsl, Exxon/Subway/dsl, Phillips 66/dsl, Shell/dsl/24hr, **food:** Acapulco Mexican, China Town, Cracker Barrel, El Chico, La Hacienda Mexican, MktPlace Grill, McDonald's, **lodging:** Quality Inn, **other:** JC Penney, Office Depot, Sears, **S gas:** Citgo, Fina, Mobil/dsl, **food:** Backyard Burger, Burger King, CiCi's, Dixie Cafe, Fazoli's, Firehouse Subs, Hart's Seafood, IHOP, McAlister's Deli, New China, Outback Steaks, Ryan's, Salsa'a Grill, Sonic, Starbucks, Subway, Village Inn Rest., Waffle House, Wendy's, **lodging:** Candlewood Suites, Holiday Inn Express, Howard Johnson, Motel 6, Stacy Motel, Super 8, **other:** H HOSPITAL, Advance Parts, $General, $Tree, Hastings Books, Kelly Tire, Lowes Whse, Walmart SuperCtr/gas

**124** AR 25 N, to Conway, **S gas:** Hess/dsl, Shell/dsl, **food:** DQ, KFC, Mazzio's, Popeye's, **other:** HOSPITAL, U-Haul

**120mm** Cadron River

**117** to Menifee

**MORRILTON**

**112** AR 92, Plumerville, **N gas:** Exxon, **S gas:** Country Store/dsl, **other:** USPO

**108** AR 9, Morrilton, **S gas:** Phillips 66/24hr, Murphy USA, Shell/dsl/24hr, **food:** Bonanza, KFC, Mkt Place Café, McDonald's, Pizza Hut, Pizza Pro, Sonic, Subway, TCBY, Waffle House, Wendy's, **lodging:** Super 8, **other:** H HOSPITAL, Buick/Chevrolet/Pontiac, $General, Ford/Lincoln/Mercury, Goodyear, GMC, Kroger, Radio AR 9 Shack, Walmart SuperCtr/gas, to Petit Jean SP (21mi), RV camping, vet

**107** AR 95, Morrilton, **N gas:** Shell/dsl, **lodging:** Scottish Inn, KOA, **S gas:** Love's/Subway/dsl/24hr, Shell, **food:** Mom&Pop's Waffles, Morrilton Drive Inn, Wendy's(2 mi), **lodging:** Day's Inn, **other:** CarQuest

**101** Blackwell, **N gas:** Blackwell TrkStp/Valero/dsl/diner/scales/24hr, **other:** Utility Trailer Sales

**94** AR 105, Atkins, **N gas:** Exxon/dsl/24hr, Shell/McDonald's/dsl, **food:** Angelina's Mexican, KFC/Taco Bell, Pizza Meister, Sonic, **other:** $General, repair, **S** Saxton Foods

**88** Pottsville, **S food:** Pottsville Country Cafe, **other:** truck repair/wash

**RUSSELLVILLE**

**84** US 64, AR 331, Russellville, **N gas:** ✈FLYING J/Conoco/Country Mkt/dsl/LP/24hr/@, Shell/dsl, **other:** Ivys Cove RV Retreat, trucklube, **S gas:** Phillips 66, Pilot/Subway/Wendy's/dsl/24hr/scales/@, **food:** CiCi's, Hardee's, Hunan Chinese, McDonald's, Sonic, Waffle House, **lodging:** Comfort Inn, Ramada Inn, **other:** HOSPITAL, AutoZone, Belk, Chevrolet, Chrysler/Dodge/Jeep, $Tree, Firestone, JC Penney, K-Mart, Lowes Whse, Nissan, Staples, Toyota, USPO

**83** AK 326, Weir Rd, **S gas:** Phillips 66, **food:** AlDente's Italian, DQ, Popeye's, Ryan's, Starbucks, Subway, Taco Bueno, **other:** Walmart SuperCtr/gas

**81** AR 7, Russellville, **N gas:** SuperStop/dsl, **food:** Burger Boy, **lodging:** Days Inn, Motel 6, **other:** Outdoor RV Ctr/Park, **S gas:** Exxon/dsl/24hr, Phillips 66/dsl/24hr, Shell/24hr, **food:** Arby's, Burger King, Colton's Steaks, Cracker Barrel, Dixie Café, Dos Rios, La Huerta Mexican, New China, Pizza Inn, Ruby Tuesday, Subway,

## INTERSTATE 40 CONT'D

**E**
↕
**W**

**81** Continued
Waffle House, **lodging:** Best Value, Best Western, Day's Inn, Fairfield Inn, Hampton Inn, Holiday Inn, La Quinta, Super 8, **other:** antiques, Russell RV Ctr, to Lake Dardanelle SP, RV camping

**80mm** Dardanelle Reservoir

**78** US 64, Russellville, **S food:** Fat Daddy's BBQ, **other:** Darrell's Mkt, Mission RV Park, to Lake Dardanelle SP

**74** AR 333, London

**72mm** rest area wb, full 🔣 facilities, 📞, 🚻, litter barrels, vending, petwalk

**70mm** overlook wb lane, litter barrels

**68mm** rest area eb, full 🔣 facilities, 📞, 🚻, litter barrels, vending, petwalk

**67** AR 315, Knoxville, **S gas:** Citgo, Knoxville Mkt, **food:** JC's Cafe, **other:** USPO

**64** US 64, Clarksville, Lamar, **A gas:** Valero/Pizza Pro/dsl, **lodging:** Dad's Dream RV Park

**58** AR 21, AR 103, Clarksville, **N gas:** Phillips 66, Shell/dsl, **food:** Bienvenidos Mexican, Emerald Dragon Chinese, KFC, Mazzio's, McDonald's, Pizza Hut, Sonic, Taco Bell, Waffle House, Wendy's, **lodging:** Best Western, Comfort Inn, Economy Inn, Super 8, **other:** HOSPITAL, Chevrolet/Pontiac/GMC, **S gas:** Shell/dsl/rest./24hr, **food:** Arby's, South Park Rest., **other:** Chrysler/Dodge/Jeep, $Tree, Ford/Lincoln/Mercury, Walmart SuperCtr/dsl

**57** AR 109, Clarksville, **N gas:** Conoco/dsl, **food:** Subway, **other:** Family$, Harvest Foods/drug, **S gas:** Shell/pizza/subsdsl, **other:** auto repair

**55** US 64, AR 109, Clarksville, **N gas:** Citgo/dsl, **food:** Catfish House, Crosswoods Rest, Hardee's, Kountry Kitchen, **lodging:** Day's Inn, Hampton Inn, Holiday Inn Express, **S gas:** Exxon/dsl, **food:** Western Sizzlin, **other:** st police

**47** AR 164, Coal Hill

**41** AR 186, Altus, **S food:** Wiederkehr Rest., **other:** Pine Ridge RV Park, winery

**37** AR 219, Ozark, **S gas:** Love's/Subway/dsl/24hr, Shell/McDonald's/dsl, **food:** KFC/Taco Bell, **lodging:** Day's Inn, **other:** HOSPITAL

**36mm** rest area both lanes, full 🔣 facilities, 📞, 🚻, litter barrels, petwalk

**35** AR 23, Ozark, **3 mi S gas:** 23 One Stop, **food:** Hardee's, **lodging:** Ozark Inn, Oxford Inn, **other:** HOSPITAL, Aux Arc Park(5mi), to Mt Magazine SP (20 mi)

**24** AR 215, Mulberry, **S** Vine Prairie Park

**20** Dyer, **N gas:** Conoco/dsl, **other:** Freightliner/Western Star, **S gas:** Phillips 66/dsl, Shell/dsl, **lodging:** Mill Creek Inn

**13** US 71 N, to Fayetteville, **N gas:** Phillips 66/dsl, Shell, **food:** Burger King, China Fun, Cracker Barrel, Dairy Queen, KFC, La Fiesta Mexican, Mazzio's, Subway, Taco Bell, **lodging:** Comfort Inn, Meadors Inn, **other:** Crabtree RV Ctr/Park, Curves, $General, KOA (2mi), O'Reilly Parts, to U of AR, Lake Ft Smith SP, **S gas:** Citgo/dsl, Shamrock, **food:** Braum's, Geno's Pizza, McDonald's, Sonic, **lodging:** Day's Inn, **other:** C&H Tires, Coleman Drug, CV's Foods, Harp's Foods, NAPA/lube/repair, Walmart SuperCtr/gas/auto

**C L A R K S V I L L E**

**O Z A R K**

Missouri/Arkansas Border
• Bentonville
• Rogers
• Springdale
• Fayetteville
540
Ozark
Van Buren
Fort Smith
Clarksville
40 Atkins
Russellville
Conway
430
N Little Rock
Little Rock
Blytheville
Osceda
55
West Memphis
40 Forrest City

AR

**V A N B U R E N**

**N** ↕ **S**

**12** I-540 N, to Fayetteville, **N other:** to Lake Ft Smith SP

**9mm** weigh sta both lanes

**7** I-540 S, US 71 S, to Ft Smith, Van Buren, **S** H HOSPITAL

**5** AR 59, Van Buren, **N gas:** Phillips 66, **food:** Arby's, Art's BBQ, Burger King, Capt D's, Chili's, China Buffet, Domino's, Firehouse Subs, La Fiesta Mexican, McDonald's, Popeye's, Santa Fe Café, Starbucks, **lodging:** Best Western, Hampton Inn, **other:** Advance Parts, $Tree, Radio Shack, Lowe's Whse, NAPA, Walmart SuperCtr/gas, USPO, tires, **S gas:** Shell/dsl/24hr, **food:** Braum's, Big Jake's Steaks, El Torrito Mexican, Gino's Hamburgers, Homerun Pizza, KFC/Taco Bell, Rick's Ribs, Sonic, Subway, Waffle House, Wendy's, **lodging:** Holiday Inn Express, Motel 6, Sleep Inn, Super 8, **other:** CV's Foods, $General, Firestone, Grizzle Tire, Overland RV Park, Outdoor RV Ctr, Walgreen, dsl repair

**3** Lee Creek Rd, **N gas:** Shell, **other:** Park Ridge Camping

**2.5mm** Welcome Ctr eb, full 🔣 facilities, info, 📞, 🚻, litter barrels, vending, petwalk

**1** to Ft Smith (from wb), Dora

**0mm** Arkansas/Oklahoma state line

## INTERSTATE 55

| Exit # | Services |
| --- | --- |
| **72mm** | Arkansas/Missouri state line |
| **72** | State Line Rd, weigh sta sb |
| **71** | AR 150, Yarbro |
| **68mm** | Welcome Ctr sb, full 🔣 facilities, info, 📞, 🚻, litter barrels, petwalk |

**67** AR 18, Blytheville, **E gas:** Phillips 66/dsl, **food:** Burger King, Capt D's, Skinny's Diner, Zaxby's, **lodging:** Day's Inn, Travelodge, **other:** $Tree, Lowe's Whse, Walmart SuperCtr, **W gas:** BP/dsl, Citgo/dsl, Shell, **food:** El Acupulco Mexican, Geatwall Chinese, Grecian Steaks, Hardee's, La Cabana, Mazzio's, McDonald's, Olympia Steaks, Pizza Inn, Red Apple Rest., Sonic, Starbucks, Subway, Taco Bell, Wendy's, **lodging:** Comfort Inn, Hampton Inn, Holiday Inn, Super 8, **other:** H HOSPITAL, Advance Parts, AutoZone, Family$, Ford/Lincoln/Mercury, Fred's Drug, JC Penney

**63** US 61, to Blytheville, **E gas:** BP/dsl, **other:** Shearins RV Park(2mi), **W gas:** Dodge's Store/dsl, Exxon/Chester Fried/dsl, Shell/McDonald's/dsl/24hr, **lodging:** Best Western, Garden Inn, Relax Inn, Royal Inn (2mi), **other:** Chevrolet, Nissan

**B L Y T H E V I L L E**

**N ↕ S** *(left margin: KEISER · MARION · WEST MEMPHIS)*

**AR**

## INTERSTATE 55 CONT'D

| | |
|---|---|
| 57 | AR 148, Burdette, **E** other: NE AR Coll |
| 53 | AR 158, Victoria, Luxora |
| 48 | AR 140, to Osceola, **E** gas: Mobil/dsl, Shell/dsl, other: Cotton Inn Rest., Huddle House, lodging: Days Inn, Deerfield Inn, Fairview Inn, Plum Point Inn, 3 mi **E** food: McDonald's, Pizza Inn, Sonic, Subway, other: H HOSPITAL |
| 45mm | rest area nb, full ♿ facilities, 🅿 litter barrels, petwalk |
| 44 | AR 181, Keiser |
| 41 | AR 14, Marie, **E** other: to Hampson SP/museum |
| 36 | AR 181, to Wilson, Bassett |
| 35mm | rest area sb, full ♿ facilities, 🅿 litter barrels, ℂ, petwalk |
| 34 | AR 118, Joiner |
| 23b a | US 63, AR 77, to Marked Tree, Jonesboro, ASU, **E** gas: Citgo/chicken/pizza |
| 21 | AR 42, Turrell, **W** gas: Exxon/rest./dsl/scales/24hr |
| 17 | AR 50, to Jericho |
| 14 | rd 4, to Jericho, **E** gas: Citgo/scales/dsl/24hr, other: flea market, **W** gas: Citgo/Stuckey's, other: Chevrolet, KOA |
| 10 | US 64 W, Marion, **E** gas: Citgo/Subway/scales, Mapco/dsl, Shell/McDonald's/dsl, food: KFC/Taco Bell, Tops BBQ, lodging: Hallmarc Inn, other: $General, Market Place Foods, **W** gas: BP/dsl, JP Mkt, Shell, food: Colton's Grill, Wendy's, Zaxby's, lodging: Best Western, Journey Inn, other: AutoZone, to Parkin SP(23mi) |
| 9mm | weigh sta/truck parking both lanes |
| 8 | I-40 W, to Little Rock |
| 278 | AR 77, 7th St, Missouri St, **E** gas: Citgo/24hr, **W** on 7th St...food: BBQ, Cracker Barrel, KFC, Pizza Inn, TCBY, lodging: Quality Inn, other: HOSPITAL, Sawyers RV Park, Sears, **W** on Missouri St...gas: Citgo/dsl, Exxon, Mapco, Phillips 66/dsl, food: Bonanza, Burger King, Domino's, Howard's Doughnut, Krystal, Lenny's Subs, Mrs Winner's, Pizza Hut, Popeye's, Subway, Taco Bell, Walgreen, Wendy's, lodging: Hampton Inn, Ramada Ltd, other: $Tree, Goodyear/auto, Walgreens |
| 279b | I-40 E, to Memphis |
| 279a | Ingram Blvd, **E** food: Margarita's Mexican, lodging: Comfort Inn, Day's Inn, Homegate Inn, Red Roof Inn, Rodeway Inn, other: Ford, Greyhound Park, U-Haul, **W** gas: Citgo/dsl, food: Perkins, Waffle House, lodging: Best Value, Econolodge, Hampshire Inn, Hampton Inn, Holiday Inn, Motel 6, Relax Inn, same as 280 |
| 4 | King Dr, Southland Dr, **E** gas: ♦FLYING J/Conoco/LP/scales/RV dump/dsl/rest., Petro/Iron Skillet/dsl/rest./24hr/@, Pilot/Subway/dsl/scales/@, food: KFC/Taco Bell, McDonald's, Waffle House, lodging: Best Western, Deluxe Inn, Express Inn, Super 8, other: Blue Beacon, SpeedCo Lube, **W** gas: Citgo, food: Poncho's Mexican, lodging: Sunset Inn, other: Goodyear |
| 3b a | US 70, Broadway Blvd, AR 131, Mound City Rd (exits left from nb), **W** lodging: Budget Inn |
| 2mm | weigh sta nb |
| 1 | Bridgeport Rd |
| 0mm | Arkansas/Tennessee state line, Mississippi River |

## INTERSTATE 430 - LITTLE ROCK

| Exit # | Services |
|---|---|
| 13b a | I-40. I-430 begins/ends on I-40, exit 147. |
| 12 | AR 100, Maumelle, **W** gas: Citgo, other: NAPA |
| 10mm | Arkansas River |
| 9 | AR 10, Cantrell Rd., **W** Pinnacle Mtn SP |
| 8 | Rodney Parham Rd, **E** gas: Conoco, Shell, food: El Chico, Firehouse Subs, McCalister's Grill, McDonald's, Mt. Fuji Japanese, lodging: La Quinta, other: Kroger, USA Drug, **W** gas: Exxon, food: Black Angus Steaks, Burger King, Chili's, ChuckeCheese, CiCi's, Dixie Café, Dominos, El Acapulco Mexican, Franke's Café, LoneStar Steaks, Olive Garden, Small's Ribs, Wendy's, other: Audi, Cadillac, Firestone, Harvest Foods, JiffyLube, K-Mart, Radio Shack, USA Drug, Waldenbooks, Wild Oats Mkt |
| 6 | I-630, Kanis Rd, Markham St, to downtown, **E** lodging: Comfort Inn, Motel 6, SpringHill Suites, **W** gas: Exxon, Texaco, food: Denny's, Rega's Grill, Waffle House, Wendy's, lodging: AmeriSuites, Courtyard, Embassy Suites, Extended Stay America, Holiday Inn, La Quinta, Ramada Ltd |
| 5 | Kanis Rd, Shackleford Rd, **E** food: Cracker Barrel, lodging: Candlewood Suites, Comfort Inn, Motel 6, SpringHill Suites, other: JC Penny, **W** gas: Exxon, Shell, food: Denny's IHOP, Jason's Deli, Julie's Rest., Krispy Kreme, Lenny's Subs, Waffle House, lodging: Comfort Inn, Courtyard, Embassy Suites, Hampton Inn, Holiday Inn Select, La Quinta, Residence Inn, Studio+, Wingate Inn, other: H HOSPITAL, Lexus |
| 4 | AR 300, Col Glenn Rd, **E** food: Subway, Wendy's, lodging: Holiday Inn Express, other: Toyota/Scion, **W** gas: Valero/Burger King/dsl, other: Jaguar, Kia, Land Rover, Mazda, Nissan |
| 1 | AR 5, Stagecoach Rd, **E** food: Our Place Grill, **W** food: Jordan's BBQ |
| 0mm | I-30. I-430 begins/ends on I-30, exit 129. |

## INTERSTATE 440 - LITTLE ROCK

| Exit # | Services |
|---|---|
| 11 | I-40. |
| 10 | US 70, **W** other: Peterbuilt |
| 8 | Faulkner Lake Rd, **W** gas: BP/mart |
| 7 | US 165, to England, **S** museum |
| 6mm | Arkansas River |
| 5 | Fourche Dam Pike, LR Riverport, **N** gas: Exxon, Shell, food: McDonald's, lodging: Travelodge, **S** gas: Fina/dsl/@, Total/dsl |
| 4 | Lindsey Rd |
| 3 | Bankhead Dr, **N** lodging: Comfort Inn, other: LR Airport, **S** gas: Conoco, food: Waffle House, lodging: Day's Inn, Holiday Inn, Holiday Inn Express |
| 1 | AR 365, Confederate Blvd |
| 0mm | I-440 begins/ends on I-30, exit 138. |

## INTERSTATE 540 - FAYETTEVILLE

| Exit # | Services |
|---|---|
| 93 | US 71B, Bentonville, I-540 begins/ends on US 71 N. |
| 88 | AR 72, Bentonville, Pea Ridge, **E** gas: Conoco, food: River Grille, lodging: Courtyard, Simmon's Suites, **W** gas: Shell, food: Hot Dog Alley, Smokin' Joe's Ribs |

## INTERSTATE 540 CONT'D - FAYETTEVILLE

**N ↑ S**

**B E N T O N V I L L E   F A Y E T T E V I L L E**

**86** US 62, AR 102, Bentonville, Rogers, **E** lodging: Towne-Place Suites, **other:** Harley-Davidson, Sam's Club/gas, Walmart Mkt/gas, Pea Ridge NMP, **W** gas: Phillips 66/McDonald's/dsl, Shell/dsl, **food:** Arby's, Sonic, Subway, Taco Bell, **lodging:** Value Place Inn, **other:** Buick/GMC/Pontiac, Walmart Visitor Ctr

**85** US 71B, AR 12, Bentonville, Rogers, **E** gas: BP/dsl, Citgo/dsl, **food:** Abuelo's, Applebee's, Arby's, Atlanta Bread, Carino's Italian, Chick-fil-A, Chili's, CiCi's, Colton's Steaks, Copeland's Rest., Dixie Café, Dixie Cafe, Famous Dave's, IHOP, KFC, King Buffet, McDonald's, O'Charley's, Oscar's Rest., On-the-Border, Outback Steaks, Quizno's, Red Robin, Sonic, Starbucks, **lodging:** AmeriSuites, Candlewood Suites, Country Inn&Suites, Fairfield Inn, Hampton Inn, Hartland Lodge, Homewood Suites, Mainstay Suites, Regency Inn, Residence Inn, **other:** Barnes&Noble, Belk, Firestone/auto, Honda, Kohl's, Lowe's Whse, Office Depot, Old Navy, PetCo, Staples, Beaver Lake SP, Prairie Creek SP, **W** gas: Exxon, Phillips 66, **food:** Bojangles, Braum's, Brioso-Brazilian, Denny's, Krispy Kreme, Lin's Chinese, Mama Fu's Asian, McCallister's Deli, Moe's Grill, Simon's Pancakes, Shogun Japanese, Taco Bueno, Village Inn, Waffle House, Zaxby's, **lodging:** Amerisuites, Best Western, Clarion, Comfort Inn, Comfort Suites, Day's Inn, Hilton Garden, Holiday Inn Express, La Quinta(1mi), Sleep Inn, SpringHill Suites, Super 8, **other:** Ⓗ HOSPITAL, Buick/GMC/Pontiac, Honda, Hyundai, Nissan, Toyota/Scion

**83** AR 94 E, Pinnacle Hills Pkwy, **E** food: Hillbilly Smokehouse, Rib House, **lodging:** Best Value (3mi), Ramada Inn (3mi), **other:** Ⓗ HOSPITAL, Best Buy, Dillards, Home Depot, Horse Shoe Bend Park, **W** food: Plaza Rest., Subway, **lodging:** Embassy Suites, Holiday Inn, Staybridge Suites

**81** Pleasant Grove Rd, **E** food: Backyard Burger, Chick-fil-A, Golden Corral, Mad Pizza, McDonald's, Starbucks, Subway, Taco Bueno, **lodging:** Super 8, **other:** Curves, Sportsman's Whse, Walgreens, Walmart SuperCtr/gas, **W** Green Country RV Park

**78** AR 264, Lowell, Cave Sprgs, Rogers, **E** gas: Kum&Go, Phillips 66/dsl, **food:** Arby's, Dominos, DQ, KFC, Mazzio's Pizza, McDonald's, Sonic, Starbucks, Subway, Taco Bell, **other:** Ramada, **other:** New Hope RV Ctr

**76** Wagon Wheel Rd, **E** to Hickory Creek Park

**73** Elm Springs Rd, **E** gas: Kum&Go, Valero/dsl, **food:** AQ Chicken House (3mi), Eureka Pizza, Western Sizzlin(2mi), **lodging:** Magnolia Gardens Inn(3mi), Value Place Inn, **other:** Chevrolet, Goodyear

**72mm** weigh sta nb

**72** US 412, Springdale, Siloam Springs, **E** gas: Citgo, Exxon, Phillips 66/Subway, **food:** Applebee's, Armadillo Grill, Braum's, Chilis, Denny's, Maria's Mexican, McDonald's, Sizzler, Sonic, Taco Bell, Waffle House, Wendy's, **lodging:** Best Western, Comfort Inn, Day's Inn, DoubleTree Hotel, Executive Inn, Extended Stay America, Fairfield Inn, Hampton Inn, Hartland Inn, Holiday Inn, La Quinta, Residence Inn, Sleep Inn, Springdale Motel, Super 8, **other:** Kenworth/Volvo Trucks, Lowe's Whse, Office Depot, **W** gas: Pilot/Burger King/dsl/24hr/scales/@, **food:** Cracker Barrel, Jose's Mexican, KFC, **other:** Big Lots,

---

Missouri/Arkansas Border

Bentonville • Rogers • Springdale • Fayetteville — 540

Ozark, Van Buren, Fort Smith — 40 — Clarksville, Atkins, Russellville, Conway — 430 — Little Rock

**AR**

---

**F A R M I N G T O N**

**72** Continued
Buick/Pontiac/GMC/Jeep, Fred's$, Layman's Harware, Melon RV Ctr

**71mm** weigh sta sb

**69** Johnson, 1-2 mi **E** food: Chick-fil-A, Eureka Pizza, Fire Mtn Grill, Hooter's, Inn at the Mill Rest, James Rest, Shogun Japanese, **lodging:** Inn at the Mill, **W** Ⓗ HOSPITAL

**67** US 71B, Fayetteville, Ⓗ HOSPITAL

**66** AR 112, **E** gas: BP/dsl, **lodging:** Day's Inn (2mi), **W** Acura/Chevrolet/Hummer/Honda/Toyota

**65** Porter Rd

**64** AR 16 W, AR 112 E, Wedington Dr, **E** food: AQ Chicken House (3mi), Eureka Pizza (2mi), **W** gas: Citgo/McDonald's/dsl, Phillips 66, **food:** Boar's Nest BBQ, Guido's Pizza, IHOP, Sonic, Subway, Taco Bell, **lodging:** Country Inn Suites, Holiday Inn Express, Quality Inn, **other:** Harp's Food/gas, vet

**62** US 62, AR 180, Farmington, **E** gas: Conoco, Shell, **food:** Arby's, Braum's, Burger King, Charlie's Chicken, Hardee's, JD China, KFC, McDonald's, Mexico Viejo, Sonic, Taco Bell, Taiwan Chinese, Waffle House, Wendy's, **lodging:** Best Western, Red Roof Inn, **other:** USA Drug, **W** food: Braum's, Denny's, Firehouse Subs, Papa Murphy's, Pavilion Buffet, Ruby Tuesday, **lodging:** Clarion, Comfort Inn, Hampton Inn, Quality Inn, Regency 7 Motel, Super 8, Value Place Inn, **other:** AutoZone, $Tree, Lowes Whse, Walmart SuperCtr/gas

**61** US 71, to Boston Mtn Scenic Lp, sb only

**60** AR 112, AR 265, Razorback Rd, **E** to U of AR

**58** Greenland, **W** gas: Phillips 66/McDonalds/dsl/scales, **food:** Sonic

**56** **E** gas: BP, **W** other: Acura, Chevrolet, Honda, Sam's Club/gas, Toyota

**53** AR 170, West Fork, **E** other: Winn Creek RV Resort (4mi), **W** to Devils Den SP

**45** AR 74, Winslow, **W** to Devils Den SP

**41mm** Bobby Hopper Tunnel

**34** AR 282, to US 71, Chester, **W** Chester Mercantile/gas, USPO

**29** AR 282, to US 71, Mountainburg, **1 mi** **E** gas: BP/dsl/rest/scales, **other:** to Lake Ft Smith SP

**24** AR 282, to US 71, Rudy, **A** gas: Shell/dsl, **food:** Red Hog BBQ, **other:** KOA, Boston Mtns Scenic Lp

**21** Collum Ln

**20** to US 71, **E** gas: Shell, **food:** KFC, Taco Bell, **lodging:** Comfort Inn, Day's Inn

## INTERSTATE 5

**N ↑↓ S**

**CA**

| Exit # | Services |
|---|---|
| 797mm | California/Oregon state line |
| 796 | Hilt, **W gas:** State Line Service/café/gas |
| 793 | Bailey Hill Rd |
| 791mm | inspection sta sb |
| 790 | Hornbrook Hwy, Ditch Creek Rd |
| 789 | A28, to Hornbrook, Henley, **E gas:** Chevron/dsl/LP, **other:** Blue Heron RV Park, 🄲, to Iron Gate RA |
| 786 | **CA 96, Klamath River Hwy, W rest area both lanes, full ♿ facilities, info,** 🄲, 🛆, **litter barrels, petwalk, to Klamath River RA** |
| 782mm | Anderson Summit, elev 3067 |
| 780mm | vista point sb |
| 779mm | Shasta River |
| 776 | Yreka, Montague, **E lodging:** Holiday Inn Express, **other:** Yreka RV Park, **W gas:** USA/dsl, **food:** Casa Ramos Mexican, Ket Rest., Puerto Vallarta, **lodging:** Mtn View Motel, Super 8, **other:** Curves, Goodyear, Ray's Foods |
| 775 | Miner St, Central Yreka, **W gas:** Chevron/24hr, Texaco/dsl, Valero/dsl, **food:** China Dragon, Denny's, Grandma's House, KFC, RoundTable Pizza, **lodging:** Best Western, Budget Inn, Econolodge, Klamath Motel, Relax Inn, Rodeway Inn, Yreka Motel, **other:** H HOSPITAL, CarQuest, Chevrolet/Cadilac/Pontiac, Clayton Tire, Honda, PriceLess Foods, Radio Shack, Rite Aid, USPO, museum |
| 773 | CA 3, to Ft Jones, Etna, **E gas:** CFN/dsl, **other:** Schwab Tire, Trailer Haven RV Park, **W gas:** Shell/dsl, **food:** BlackBear Diner, Burger King, Carl's Jr, Jeanne's Seafood, Linda's Cafe, McDonald's, Papa Murphy's, Subway, Taco Bell, **lodging:** Baymont Inn, Comfort Inn, Motel 6, **other:** H HOSPITAL, $Tree, Ford/Lincoln/Mercury, JC Penney, NAPA, Raley's Foods, Schuck's Parts, Walmart, CHP, **1 mi W gas:** Valero, **food:** BBQ Express, KFC, Yreka Pizza, **lodging:** Relax Inn, **other:** PriceLess Foods, Rite Aid, transmissions |
| 770 | Shamrock Rd, Easy St, **W gas:** Beacon, Fuel 24/7/dsl, **other:** RV camping |
| 766 | A12, to Gazelle, Grenada, **E gas:** 76/dsl, **W gas:** Texaco/dsl, **other:** RV camping |
| 759 | Louie Rd |
| 753 | **Weed Airport Rd, W rest area both lanes, full ♿ facilities,** 🛆, **litter barrels,** 🄲, **petwalk** |
| 751 | Stewart Springs Rd, Edgewood, **E lodging:** Lake Shasta RA/RV camp (2mi), **W other:** RV camp (7mi) |
| 748 | to US 97, to Klamath Falls, Weed, **E gas:** Chevron/24hr, Shell/dsl, Spirit/dsl, **food:** Ellie's Espresso, Pizza Factory, Sabor Latino, **lodging:** Hi-Lo Motel/rest., Motel 6, Summit Inn, Townhouse Motel, **other:** NAPA, Ray's Foods, golf, RV camping, Weed Repair |
| 747 | Central Weed, **E same as 748, other:** auto repair, **W** Coll of Siskiyou |
| 745 | S Weed Blvd, **E gas:** CFN, Chevron/dsl/24hr, Shell/dsl/24hr, Travel Plaza/Subway/dsl/scales/24hr, **food:** Burger King, Dos Amigos Mexican, McDonald's, Silva's Rest., Taco Bell, **lodging:** Comfort Inn, Quality Inn, SisQ Inn, **other:** Friendly RV Park |
| 743 | Summit Dr, Truck Village Dr, **E gas:** CFN/dsl |
| 742mm | Black Butte Summit, elev 3912 |

**YREKA**  **WEED**

**MT SHASTA DUNSMUIR**  **LAKEHEAD**

| | |
|---|---|
| 741 | Abrams Lake Rd, **E other:** Schwab Tire, **W lodging:** Abrams Lake RV Park |
| 740 | Mt Shasta City (from sb), **E gas:** Pacific Pride/dsl/LP, **lodging:** Cold Creek Inn |
| 738 | Central Mt Shasta, **E gas:** 76/dsl, Chevron/dsl, Shell/dsl/LP, Spirit/dsl, **food:** BlackBear Diner, Burger King, KFC/Taco Bell, RoundTable Pizza, Subway, **lodging:** Best Western/Treehouse Rest., Travel Inn, **other:** H HOSPITAL, Do It Hardware, NAPA, Ray's Foods, Rite Aid, Schuck's Parts, USPO, visitors info, **W lodging:** Mt Shasta Resort/rest., Lake Siskiyou RV Park |
| 737 | Mt Shasta City (from nb), same as 738 |
| 736 | CA 89, to McCloud, to Reno, **E food:** Casa Ramos, Jade Garden, Lilly's Rest., **lodging:** Strawberry Inn, Swiss Holiday Lodge, **other:** McCloud RV Park |
| 735mm | weigh sta sb |
| 734 | Mott Rd, to Dunsmuir |
| 732 | Dunsmuir Ave, Siskiyou Ave, **E food:** Penny's Diner, **lodging:** Oak Tree Inn, **W gas:** Chevron/Subway/dsl, **lodging:** Acorn Inn, Cedar Lodge |
| 730 | Central Dunsmuir, **E food:** Cornerstone Cafe, Pizza Factory, **lodging:** Brown Trout Cafe, Burger Barn, Cave Springs Lodge, Hot Dog Depot, Travelodge, **other:** NAPA, USPO, **W gas:** Chevron/Subway/dsl/LP, **lodging:** Cave Springs Motel, **other:** city park |
| 729 | Dunsmuir (from nb), **E gas:** Manfredi's/deli/dsl, **food:** Burger Barn, Cornerstone, Pizza Factory, **lodging:** Dunsmuir Lodge |
| 728 | Crag View Dr, Dunsmuir, Railroad Park Rd, **W other:** Railroad Park Motel/RV Park |
| 727 | (from nb) Crag View dr |
| 726 | Soda Creek Rd, to Pacific Crest Trail |
| 724 | Castella, **W gas:** Chevron/dsl, **other:** RV camping, Castle Crags SP |
| 723mm | vista point nb |
| 723 | Sweetbrier Ave |
| 721 | Conant Rd |
| 720 | Flume Creek Rd |
| 718 | Sims Rd, **W other:** RV camping |
| 714 | Gibson Rd |
| 712 | Pollard Flat, **E gas:** Exxon/dsl/LP/24hr, **food:** Pollard Flat USA Rest. |
| 710 | Slate Creek Rd, La Moine |
| 707 | Delta Rd, Dog Creek Rd, to Vollmers |
| 705mm | **rest area sb, full ♿ facilities,** 🄲, **litter barrels,** 🛆 |
| 704 | Riverview Dr, **E food:** Klondike Diner, **lodging:** Lakehead Camping |
| 702 | Antlers Rd, Lakeshore Dr, to Lakehead, **E gas:** Shell/Subway/dsl/24hr, **lodging:** Antlers RV Park, Lakehead Camping, Neu Lodge Motel, **other:** USPO, auto repair, **W lodging:** Shasta Lake Motel/RV, Lakeshore Villa RV Park |
| 698 | Salt Creek Rd, Gilman Rd, **W lodging:** Salt Creek Lodge/RV Park, Trail In RV Park |
| 695 | Shasta Caverns Rd, to O'Brien, **W** O'brien Mtn Lodge & Camping |
| 694mm | **rest area nb, full ♿ facilities,** 🄲, 🛆, **litter barrels, petwalk** |
| 693 | (from sb)Packers Bay Rd |
| 692 | Turntable Bay Rd |

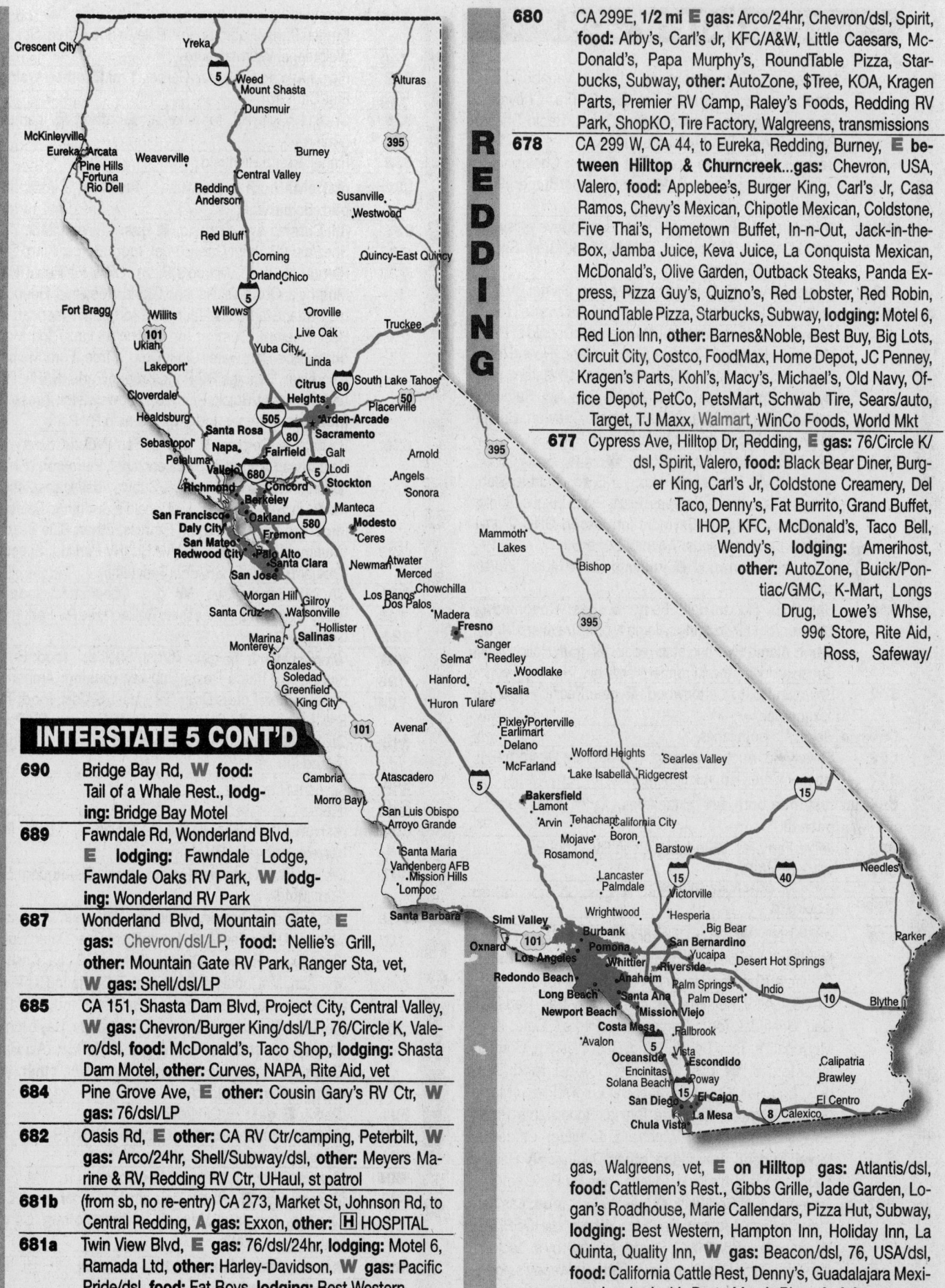

**680** CA 299E, 1/2 mi E gas: Arco/24hr, Chevron/dsl, Spirit, **food:** Arby's, Carl's Jr, KFC/A&W, Little Caesars, McDonald's, Papa Murphy's, RoundTable Pizza, Starbucks, Subway, **other:** AutoZone, $Tree, KOA, Kragen Parts, Premier RV Camp, Raley's Foods, Redding RV Park, ShopKO, Tire Factory, Walgreens, transmissions

**678** CA 299 W, CA 44, to Eureka, Redding, Burney, E **between Hilltop & Churncreek**...**gas:** Chevron, USA, Valero, **food:** Applebee's, Burger King, Carl's Jr, Casa Ramos, Chevy's Mexican, Chipotle Mexican, Coldstone, Five Thai's, Hometown Buffet, In-n-Out, Jack-in-the-Box, Jamba Juice, Keva Juice, La Conquista Mexican, McDonald's, Olive Garden, Outback Steaks, Panda Express, Pizza Guy's, Quizno's, Red Lobster, Red Robin, RoundTable Pizza, Starbucks, Subway, **lodging:** Motel 6, Red Lion Inn, **other:** Barnes&Noble, Best Buy, Big Lots, Circuit City, Costco, FoodMax, Home Depot, JC Penney, Kragen's Parts, Kohl's, Macy's, Michael's, Old Navy, Office Depot, PetCo, PetsMart, Schwab Tire, Sears/auto, Target, TJ Maxx, Walmart, WinCo Foods, World Mkt

**677** Cypress Ave, Hilltop Dr, Redding, E **gas:** 76/Circle K/dsl, Spirit, Valero, **food:** Black Bear Diner, Burger King, Carl's Jr, Coldstone Creamery, Del Taco, Denny's, Fat Burrito, Grand Buffet, IHOP, KFC, McDonald's, Taco Bell, Wendy's, **lodging:** Amerihost, **other:** AutoZone, Buick/Pontiac/GMC, K-Mart, Longs Drug, Lowe's Whse, 99¢ Store, Rite Aid, Ross, Safeway/

## INTERSTATE 5 CONT'D

N ↑ ↓ S

**690** Bridge Bay Rd, W **food:** Tail of a Whale Rest., **lodging:** Bridge Bay Motel

**689** Fawndale Rd, Wonderland Blvd, E **lodging:** Fawndale Lodge, Fawndale Oaks RV Park, W **lodging:** Wonderland RV Park

**687** Wonderland Blvd, Mountain Gate, E **gas:** Chevron/dsl/LP, **food:** Nellie's Grill, **other:** Mountain Gate RV Park, Ranger Sta, vet, W **gas:** Shell/dsl/LP

**685** CA 151, Shasta Dam Blvd, Project City, Central Valley, W **gas:** Chevron/Burger King/dsl/LP, 76/Circle K, Valero/dsl, **food:** McDonald's, Taco Shop, **lodging:** Shasta Dam Motel, **other:** Curves, NAPA, Rite Aid, vet

**684** Pine Grove Ave, E **other:** Cousin Gary's RV Ctr, W **gas:** 76/dsl/LP

**682** Oasis Rd, E **other:** CA RV Ctr/camping, Peterbilt, W **gas:** Arco/24hr, Shell/Subway/dsl, **other:** Meyers Marine & RV, Redding RV Ctr, UHaul, st patrol

**681b** (from sb, no re-entry) CA 273, Market St, Johnson Rd, to Central Redding, A **gas:** Exxon, **other:** H HOSPITAL

**681a** Twin View Blvd, E **gas:** 76/dsl/24hr, **lodging:** Motel 6, Ramada Ltd, **other:** Harley-Davidson, W **gas:** Pacific Pride/dsl, **food:** Fat Boys, **lodging:** Best Western

gas, Walgreens, vet, E **on Hilltop gas:** Atlantis/dsl, **food:** Cattlemen's Rest., Gibbs Grille, Jade Garden, Logan's Roadhouse, Marie Callendars, Pizza Hut, Subway, **lodging:** Best Western, Hampton Inn, Holiday Inn, La Quinta, Quality Inn, W **gas:** Beacon/dsl, 76, USA/dsl, **food:** California Cattle Rest., Denny's, Guadalajara Mexican, Lumberjack's Rest., Mary's Pizza, **lodging:**

## INTERSTATE 5 CONT'D

**N ↑ S**

**CA**

**A N D E R S O N**

**677** Continued
Holiday Inn, Howard Johnson, Motel 6, Vagabond Inn, **other:** Aamco, America's Tire, Big O Tire, Chevrolet, Ford, Honda, Kia, Nissan, Office Depot, Radio Shack, Raley's Foods, Toyota/Subaru, U-Haul

**675** Bechelli Lane, Churn Creek Rd, **E gas:** Chevron/dsl, Valero, **lodging:** Super 8, **W gas:** Texaco/Burger King/dsl, **lodging:** Hilton Garden

**673** Knighton Rd, **E gas:** TA/Pizza Hut/Popeye's/dsl/LP/scales/24hr/@, **W other:** JGW RV Park (3mi), Sacramento River RV Park (3mi)

**670** Riverside Ave, **E** Gaia Hotel, **W other:** Gamel RV Ctr

**668** Balls Ferry Rd, Anderson, **E gas:** USA, Valero/dsl, **food:** A&W, Burger King, Mariachi Mexican, McDonald's, Papa Murphy's, Peacock Chinese, Perko's Rest., RoundTable Pizza, Subway, Taco Bell, **lodging:** Best Western, Valley Inn, **other:** $Tree, GNC, NAPA, Rite Aid, Safeway, Schwab Tire, **W gas:** AFG/food/gas, Chevron, Sarco/dsl, **food:** Giant Burger, **other:** Kragen Parts

**667** CA 273, Factory Outlet Blvd, **W gas:** Shell/dsl/LP, **food:** Arby's, Jack-in-the-Box, LJ Silver, Marble Slab, Mary's Pizza, Panda Express, Pizza Pasta Luigi's, Sonic, Starbucks, **lodging:** Baymont Inn, **other:** GNC, Prime Outlets/famous brands, Walmart SuperCtr

**665** (from sb) Cottonwood, **E lodging:** Alamo Motel, Travelers Motel

**664** Gas Point Rd, to Balls Ferry, **E gas:** Cottonwood, Chevron/dsl/LP, **lodging:** Alamo Motel, Travelers Motel, **other:** Alamo RV Park, auto repair, **W gas:** Holiday/dsl, Sunshine/dsl, **other:** Frontier Hardware, Holiday Foods

**662** Bowman Rd, to Cottonwood, **E gas:** Pacific Pride/dsl, Texaco/dsl

**660mm** weigh sta both lanes

**659** Snively Rd, Auction Yard Rd, (Sunset Hills Dr. from nb)

**657** Hooker Creek Rd, Auction Yard Rd

**656mm** rest area both, full ♿ facilities, 🚻, 🅿, litter barrels, petwalk

**653** Jellys Ferry Rd, **E lodging:** Bend RV Park/LP

**652** Wilcox Golf Rd

**R E D   B L U F F**

**651** CA 36W (from sb), Red Bluff, **A gas:** Chevron, **other:** Ford, same as 650

**650** Adobe Rd, **W gas:** Chevron/dsl, **food:** Casa Ramos Mexican, Starbucks, **lodging:** Hampton Inn, **other:** Chevrolet/Cadillac, Home Depot, Hwy Patrol

**649** CA 33, CA 99, Red Bluff, **E gas:** Liberty Gas, Red Bluff Gas, Shell/dsl, **food:** Burger King, Perko's Cafe, KFC, McDonald's, Taco Bell, **lodging:** Best Western, Comfort Inn, Motel 6, **W gas:** Gas4Less, USA/dsl, **food:** Denny's, Egg Roll King, Los Mariachi, Luigi's Pizza, Maple Garden Chinese, Riverside Dining, RoundTable Pizza, Shari's/24hr, Subway, Winchell's, **lodging:** Cinderella Motel, Super 8, Travelodge, **other:** Durango RV Resort, Foodmaxx, Long's Drug, River's Edge RV Park, vet

**647a b** Diamond Ave, Red Bluff, **E gas:** Valero, **food:** Las Palmas Mexican, **lodging:** Day's Inn, **other:** 🅷 HOSPITAL, **W gas:** Arco/dsl/24hr, USA/dsl, **food:** Arby's, Jack-in-the-Box, Pizza Hut, Starbucks, Subway, Wendy's, **lodging:** American Inn, Triangle Motel, **other:** $Tree, GNC,

**C O R N I N G**

**647a b** Continued
Kragen Parts, Radio Shack, Raley's Food/drug, Staples, Walgreens, Walmart/auto

**642** Flores Ave, to Proberta, Gerber, **1 mi E other:** Walmart Dist Ctr

**636** CA 811, Gyle Rd, to Tehama, **E other:** RV camping (7mi)

**633** Finnell Rd, to Richfield

**632mm** rest area both lanes, full ♿ facilities, 🚻, 🅿, litter barrels, petwalk

**631** A9, Corning Ave, Corning, **E gas:** Chevron/24hr, 7-11, Shell/dsl/LP, Spirit Gas, 76/dsl, **food:** Burger King, Casa Ramos Mexican, Marco's Pizza, Olive Pit Rest., Papa Murphy's, Quizno's, Rancho Grande Mexican, RoundTable Pizza, Starbucks, Taco Bell, **lodging:** American Inn, Best Western, Comfort Inn, Economy Inn, 7 Inn Motel, **other:** Ace Hardware, Clark Drug, $Tree, Ford/Mercury, Goodyear, Heritage RV Park, Kragen Parts, NAPA, Pontiac/Chevrolet/Buick, Rite Aid, Safeway/24hr, Tires+, **W food:** Giant Burger, **lodging:** Corning RV Park

**630** South Ave, Corning, **E gas:** ⊕FLYING J/Country Mkt Rest./dsl/LP/RV dump/scales/24hr, Petro/Iron Skillet/dsl/rest./scales/@, TA/Arby's/Subway/dsl/scales/24hr/@, **food:** Jack-in-the-Box, McDonald's, **lodging:** California Inn, Day's Inn, Holiday Inn Express, **other:** Blue Beacon, Country Mkt, Goodyear, Olive Hut/RV Parking, SpeedCo Lube, Woodson Br SRA/RV Park (6mi)

**628** CA 99W, Liberal Ave, **W gas:** Chevron/dsl, **lodging:** Ramada/rest./casino, **other:** Rolling Hills RV Park

**621** CA 7

**619** CA 32, Orland, **E gas:** 76/dsl, Shell/dsl, **food:** Burger King, Berry Patch Rest., Subway, **lodging:** Amberlight Motel, **other:** Longs Drug, **W gas:** USA/dsl, **food:** Taco Bell, **lodging:** Old Orchard RV Park, Parkway RV Park

**618** CA 16, **E gas:** USA/dsl, **food:** Pizza Factory, **lodging:** Orland Inn

**614** CA 27

**610** Artois

**608mm** rest area both lanes, full ♿ facilities, 🚻, 🅿, litter barrels, petwalk, RV dump

**607** CA 39, Blue Gum Rd, Bayliss, **2 mi E lodging:** Blue Gum Motel

**O R O V I L L E**

**603** CA 162, to Oroville, Willows, **E gas:** Arco/24hr, Chevron/24hr, Shell/dsl, **food:** BlackBear Diner, Burger King, Casa Ramos, Denny's/24hr, KFC, La Cascada Mexican, McDonald's, Papa Murphy's, RoundTable Pizza, Starbucks, Subway, Taco Bell/24hr, **lodging:** Baymont Inn, Holiday Inn Express, Travelodge, Day's Inn/RV parking, Super 8, Motel 6, **other:** 🅷 HOSPITAL, Radio Shack, CHP, **W food:** Nancy's Café/24hr, **other:** Walmart, RV Park (8mi), ✉

**601** CA 57, **E gas:** 76/CFN/dsl

**595** Rd 68, to Princeton, **E** to Sacramento NWR

**591** Delevan Rd

**588** Maxwell (from sb), access to camping

**586** Maxwell Rd, **E other:** Delavan NWR, **W gas:** CFN, Chevron, **lodging:** Maxwell Inn/rest., **other:** Country Mkt, Maxwell Parts

**583** rest area both lanes, full ♿ facilities, 🚻, 🅿, litter barrels, petwalk

## INTERSTATE 5 CONT'D

N ↕ S

**578**    CA 20, Colusa, **W gas:** Orv's/dsl/rest., Shell/dsl, **other:** Ⓗ HOSPITAL, hwy patrol

**577**    Williams, **E gas:** Shell/Baskin-Robbins/Togo's/dsl/24hr, **food:** Carl's Jr, Straw Hat Pizza, Subway, Taco Bell, **lodging:** Holiday Inn Express, **W gas:** CFN/dsl, Chevron/dsl/24hr, 76, Shell/dsl, **food:** Burger King, Casa Lupe Mexican, Denny's, Granzella's Rest., McDonald's/RV parking, Williams Chinese Rest., **lodging:** Comfort Inn, Granzella's Inn, Motel 6, StageStop Motel, **other:** Ⓗ HOSPITAL, NAPA, U-Haul, USPO, ValuRite Drug, camping, hwy patrol

**575**    Husted Rd, to Williams

**569**    Hahn Rd, to Grimes

**567**    frontage rd (from nb), to Arbuckle, **E food:** El Jaliscience Mexican, **W gas:** CFN, Chevron/dsl

**566**    to College City, Arbuckle, **E gas:** Shell/dsl, **other:** Ace Hardware, USPO, **W gas:** J&J/grill/dsl

**559**    Yolo/Colusa County Line Rd

**557mm** rest area both lanes, full ♿ facilities, 🚻, 🅿, litter barrels, petwalk

**D U N N I G A N   D A V I S**

**556**    E4, Dunnigan, **E gas:** Chevron/dsl/24hr, Valero/dsl/LP, **food:** Bill&Kathy's Rest., Jack-in-the-Box, **lodging:** Best Value Inn, Best Western, **other:** USPO, **W gas:** Shell, **lodging:** Camper's RV Park/golf (1mi)

**554**    rd 8, **E gas:** Pilot/Wendy's/scales/dsl/24hr, **other:** Oasis Grill, **lodging:** Hacienda Motel, **other:** HappyTime RV Park, **W gas:** United/dsl

**553**    I-505 (from sb), to San Francisco, callboxes begin sb

**548**    Zamora, **E gas:** Shell/dsl

**542**    Yolo, **1 mi E** gas

**541**    CA 16W, Woodland, **3 mi W other:** Ⓗ HOSPITAL

**540**    West St, **W food:** Denny's

**538**    CA 113 N, E St, Woodland, **W gas:** Chevron/dsl, **food:** Denny's, **lodging:** Best Western, **other:** Woodland Opera House (1mi)

**537**    CA 113 S, Main St, to Davis, **E other:** Chevrolet/Buick/Pontiac, same as 536, **W gas:** Valero, **food:** Denny's, McDonald's, Rafael's Rest., Sonic, Taco Bell, Wendy's, **lodging:** Day's Inn, Motel 6, Quality Inn, **other:** Food 4 Less

**536**    rd 102, **E on Main St...gas:** Arco, Shell, **food:** Applebee's, Burger King, Coldstone Creamery, Jack-in-the-Box, RoundTable Pizza, Quizno's, Subway, **lodging:** Hampton Inn, Holiday Inn Express, **other:** America's Tire, Home Depot, Main St Mkt, Staples, Walmart, museum, same as 537, **W gas:** Chevron, **food:** In-n-Out, **other:** Best Buy, Costco/gas, Michaels, Target

**531**    rd 22, **W** Sacramento

**530mm** Sacramento River

**529mm** rest area sb, full ♿ facilities, 🚻, 🅿, litter barrels, petwalk

**528**    Airport Rd, **E gas:** Arco, **other:** ✈, food, lodging

**525b**    CA 99, to CA 70, to Marysville, Yuba City

**525a**    Del Paso Rd, **E gas:** Chevron, **food:** A&W/KFC, IHOP, In-n-Out, Jack-in-the-box, Jamba Juice, Malabar Rest., Panera Bread, Panda Express, Sizzler, Starbucks, Taco Bell, Wienerschnitzel, **lodging:** Hampton Inn, Holiday Inn Express, Homewood Suites, **other:** Rite Aid, Safeway/gas, **W food:** Subway, **lodging:** Sheraton, **other:** Walgreens

**S A C R A M E N T O**

**524**    Arena Blvd, **E other:** Arco Arena, **W food:** Round Table Pizza, Starbucks, **other:** Bel-Air Food&Drug/gas

**522**    I-80, E to Reno, W to San Francisco

**521 b a**    Garden Hwy, West El Camino, **W gas:** Shell/dsl, **food:** Baja Fresh, Burger King, Carl's Jr, Jack-in-the-Box, Jamba Juice, Togo's, **lodging:** Courtyard, Hilton Garden, Homestead Village, Residence Inn, Springhill Suites

**520**    Richards Blvd, **E gas:** Chevron/dsl/24hr, **food:** Hungry Hunter Rest., Lyon's Rest./24hr, Memphis BBQ, McDonald's, Monterey Rest., Rusty Duck Rest., **lodging:** Governor's Inn, Hawthorn Suites, Ramada Inn, **W gas:** Shell, Valero, **food:** Coyote Jct Mexican, **lodging:** Best Western/rest., Comfort Suites, Days Inn, La Quinta, Motel 6, Super 8

**519b**    J St, Old Sacramento, **E food:** Denny's, **lodging:** Holiday Inn, Vagabond Inn, **W lodging:** Embassy Suites, **other:** Railroad Museum

**519a**    Q St , downtown, Sacramento, **W lodging:** Embassy Suites, to st capitol

**518**    US 50, CA 99, Broadway, **E** services downtown

**516**    Sutterville Rd, **E gas:** Land Park/dsl, **other:** Wm Land Park, zoo

**515**    Fruitridge Rd, Seamas Rd

**514**    43rd Ave, Riverside Blvd (from sb), **E gas:** 76/repair

**513**    Florin Rd, **E gas:** Arco/24hr, Chevron/24hr, Shell/repair, **food:** Rosalinda's Mexican, RoundTable Pizza, Sizzling Wok, **other:** Bel Air Foods, Kragen Parts, Longs Drug, **W food:** Burger King, JimBoy's Tacos, Shari's, Starbucks, Subway, **other:** Marshall's, Nugget Foods, Radio Shack, Rite Aid

**512**    CA 160, Pocket Rd, Meadowview Rd, to Freeport, **E gas:** Shell/dsl/24hr, **food:** IHOP, McDonald's, Togo's, Wendy's, **other:** Home Depot, Staples

**508**    Laguna Blvd, **E gas:** Chevron/McDonald's/dsl, 76/Circle K/dsl/LP, Shell, **food:** A&W/KFC, Starbucks, Subway, Wendy's, **lodging:** Extended Stay America, Hampton Inn, **other:** Big O Tire

**506**    Elk Grove Blvd, **E gas:** Arco/dsl, Chevron/dsl, Shell, **food:** Carl's Jr, Lyla's Mexican, Pete's Grill, Port City Java, Quizno's, Stone Lake Buffet, **lodging:** Comfort Suites, **other:** AAA

**504**    Hood Franklin Rd

**498**    Twin Cities Rd, to Walnut Grove

**493**    Walnut Grove Rd, Thornton, **E gas:** CFN/dsl, 76/Subway/dsl

**490**    Peltier Rd

Copyright 2009 - The Next Exit®

## INTERSTATE 5 CONT'D

**487** Turner Rd

**485** CA 12, Lodi, **E** gas: Arco/dsl/24hr, Chevron/Subway/dsl/LP/@, *FLYING J*/Country Mkt Rest./dsl/scales/24hr/@, Shell/Wendy's/dsl, 76/Rocky's Rest./dsl/scales/24hr/@, **food:** Burger King, Carl's Jr, McDonald's, Starbucks, Taco Bell, **lodging:** Best Western, Microtel, **other:** Blue Beacon, Flag City RV Resort, Profleet Trucklube, **W other:** Tower Park Marina Camping (5mi)

**481** Eight Mile Rd, **E** camping, **W** gas: Chevron, **food:** Del Taco, Hawaiian BBQ, Jack-in-the-Box, Jamba Juice, MooMoo's Burgers, Panda Express, Panera Bread, Qdoba Mexican, Sonic, Starbucks, Strings Italian, Subway, Wendy's, **other:** AAA, Borders Books, Jo-Ann, KOA, Kohl's, Lowes Whse, Office Depot, PetsMart, Ross, Target

**478** Hammer Lane, Stockton, **E** gas: Arco/24hr, 76/Circle K/dsl, **food:** Adalberto's Mexican, Carl's Jr, KFC, Little Caesar's, Shirason Japanese, Subway, **other:** Auto Parts Express, S-mart Foods, **W** gas: QuikStop, Valero, **food:** Burger King, Fugi Express, Jack-in-the-Box, Mexico Lindo, Taco Bell, **lodging:** Vagabond Inn

**477** Benjamin Holt Dr, Stockton, **E** gas: Arco, Chevron/dsl/24hr, **food:** Pizza Guys, **lodging:** Motel 6, **other:** Quikstop, **W food:** McDonald's, Lyon's/24hr, StrawHat Pizza, Subway/TCBY, Wong's Chinese, **other:** Ace Hardware, 7-11

**476** March Lane, Stockton, **E** gas: Citgo/7-11, **food:** Applebee's, Arroyo's Mexican, Black Angus, Carl's Jr, Denny's, El Torito, Jack-in-the-Box, McDonald's, Marie Callender, Red Lobster, StrawHat Pizza, Taco Bell, Wendy's, **lodging:** Comfort Inn, Stockton Brand, **other:** Longs Drug, Marshall's, Smart Foods, **1/2 mi E food:** Burger King, Outback Steaks, Quizno's, Wienerschnitzel, **other:** $Tree, Office Depot, Target, **W** gas: 76/dsl/24hr, 7-11, **food:** Carrow's Rest., In-n-Out, Italian Cuisine, Krispy Kreme, Starbucks, RoundTable Pizza, Old Spaghetti Factory, Wong's Chinese, **lodging:** Extended Stay America, La Quinta, Quality Inn, Super 8, **other:** Home Depot

**475** Alpine Ave, Country Club Blvd, same as 474 b

**474b** Country Club Blvd (from nb), **W** gas: Citgo/7-11, USA/Subway/dsl, Safeway/gas, **other:** Big Lots

**474a** Monte Diablo Ave, **W other:** Aamco

**473** Pershing Ave (from nb), **W** gas: Arco, **lodging:** BestValue

**472** CA 4 E, to CA 99, Fresno Ave, downtown

**471** CA 4 W, Charter Way, **E** gas: Arco/dsl, Chevron/24hr, Shell/24hr, **food:** Burger King, Denny's, McDonald's, Quizno's, **lodging:** Best Western, Motel 6, **other:** Checker Parts, Kragen Parts, transmissions, **W** gas: 76/dsl/rest./scales/24hr, Valero, **food:** Jack-in-the-Box, Taco Bell, **lodging:** Motel 6

**470** 8th St, Stockton, **W** gas: CA Stop/dsl, Shell/Subway/dsl, **food:** Boquita Mexican, **lodging:** Econolodge

**469** Downing Ave, **W food:** Jalapeños Mexican, Mtn Mike's Pizza, Subway, **other:** Food4Less/gas

**468** French Camp, **E** gas: 76/Togo's/dsl/@, **other:** Pan Pacific RV Ctr, **W other:** H HOSPITAL

**467b** Mathews Rd, **E** gas: Exxon/CFN/dsl, **other:** RV Ctr, tires/repair, **W other:** H HOSPITAL

**467a** El Dorado St (from nb)

**465** Roth Rd, Sharpe Depot, **E** **other:** Freightliner, Kenworth, truck repair

**463** Lathrop Rd, **E** gas: Chevron/24hr, Joe's Trkstp/Subway/dsl, TowerMart/dsl, Valero/dsl, **food:** Country Kitchen, Starbucks, **lodging:** Best Western, Comfort Inn, Day's Inn, **other:** SaveMart Foods, **W other:** Dos Reis CP, RV camping

**462** Louise Ave, **E** gas: Arco/24hr, 76, **food:** A&W/KFC, Carl's Jr, Denny's, Jack-in-the-Box, McDonald's, Mtn Mikes Pizza, Quizno's, Taco Bell, Valarta Mexican, **lodging:** Hampton Inn, Holiday Inn Express, **other:** Mossdale CP

**461** CA 120, to Sonora, Manteca, **E** **other:** Oakwood Lake Resort Camping, to Yosemite

**460** Mossdale Rd, **E** gas: Arco/dsl, **W** **food:** fruit stand/deli

**458b** I-205, to Oakland (from sb, no return)

**458a** 11th St, to Tracy, Defense Depot, **2 mi W** gas: gas/dsl/food

**457** Kasson Rd, to Tracy, **W** gas: Valley Pacific/dsl

**452** CA 33 S, Vernalis

**449b a** CA 132, to Modesto, **W** **other:** The Orchard Campground

**446** I-580 (from nb, exits left, no return)

**445mm** Westley Rest Area both lanes, full ♿ facilities, ⊞ litter barrels, ☎, RV dump, petwalk

**441** Ingram Creek, Howard Rd, Westley, **E** gas: Beacon, Chevron/dsl/24hr, Joe's Trvl Plaza/Quizno's/dsl/scales/@, Westley TruckStp/dsl, **food:** Carl's Jr, McDonald's, Subway, **lodging:** Best Value Inn, Day's Inn, Econolodge, Holiday Inn Express, Super 8, **W** gas: Shell/dsl/24hr, **food:** Ingram Creek Rest., fruits, **other:** truck repair

**434** Sperry Ave, Del Puerto, Patterson, **E** gas: Arco/24hr, 76/Subway/dsl, **food:** Denny's, Jack-in-the-Box, KFC/A&W, LJ Silver, Quizno's, Starbucks, Wendy's, **lodging:** Best Western, **other:** Kit Fox RV Park

**430mm** vista point nb

**428** Fink Rd, Crow's Landing

**423** Stuhr Rd, Newman, **5 mi E** food, lodging, **other:** H HOSPITAL, RV camping

**422mm** vista point sb

**418** CA 140E, Gustine, **E** gas: 76/dsl, Shell/dsl

**409** weigh sta both lanes

**407** CA 33, Santa Nella, **E** gas: Andersen's Gas, Arco/Subway/24hr, Pilot/Del Taco/dsl/24hr/@, TA/76/Popeyes/dsl/rest./24hr/@, **food:** Carl's Jr, Wendy's, **lodging:** Best Western/Andersen's, Holiday Inn Express, **W** gas: Chevron/24hr, Rotten Robbie/dsl/scales, Shell/Jack-in-the-Box/dsl, Valero/dsl, **food:** Denny's, McDonald's, Quizno's, Starbucks, Taco Bell, **lodging:** Motel 6, Ramada Inn, **other:** Santa Nella RV Park

**403b a** CA 152, Los Banos, **6 mi E** **other:** H HOSPITAL, **W** gas: Petro/dsl/24hr (1mi), **other:** San Luis RV Park

**391** CA 165N, Mercy Springs Rd, **W** gas: Shell

**386mm** rest area both lanes, full ♿ facilities, ☎, ⊞, litter barrels, petwalk

**385** Nees Ave, to Firebaugh, **W** gas: Chevron/CFN/Subway/dsl/scales

## INTERSTATE 5 CONT'D

| N ↕ S | | |
|---|---|---|

**379** Shields Ave, to Mendota

**372** Russell Ave

**368** Panoche Rd, **W** gas: Chevron/McDonald's, Mobil/Taco Bell/dsl, 76/dsl, Shell/dsl/burgers/@, **food:** Apricot Rest., Foster's Freeze, **lodging:** Best Western/Apricot Inn, **other:** Palms Mkt

**365** Manning Ave, to San Joaquin

**357** Kamm Ave

**349** CA 33 N, Derrick Ave

**337** CA 33 S, CA 145 N, to Coalinga

**334** CA 198, to Lemoore, Huron, **E** gas: Shell/Subway/dsl/24hr, **lodging:** Harris Ranch Inn/rest., **W** gas: Chevron, Mobil/dsl, 76/Circle K, **food:** Burger King, Carl's Jr, Cazuela's Mexican, Denny's, McDonald's, Oriental Express Chinese, Red Robin Rest., Taco Bell, **lodging:** Best Western, Motel 6, Travelodge, **other:** Ⓗ HOSPITAL

**325** Jayne Ave, to Coalinga, **E** gas: Arco/24hr, **lodging:** Almond Tree RV Park, **other:** Ⓗ HOSPITAL

**320mm** rest area both lanes, full ♿ facilities, 📞, 🏕, litter barrels, petwalk

**319** CA 269, Lassen Ave, to Avenal, **W** gas: Hillcrest TP/Valero/dsl/rest.

**309** CA 41, Kettleman City, **E** gas: CFN/dsl, Chevron/McDonald's, Exxon/Subway/dsl, Mobil/dsl/24hr, KwikServ/Quizno's/dsl, Shell/dsl, Valero/dsl, **food:** Carl's Jr, In-n-Out, Jack-in-the-Box, Mike's Roadhouse Café, Pizza Hut/Taco Bell, **lodging:** Best Western, Super 8, **other:** Travelers RV Park

**305** Utica Ave

**288** Twisselman Rd

**278** CA 46, Lost Hills, **E** gas: Texaco/Subway/dsl, **other:** to Kern NWR, **W** gas: Arco/24hr, Beacon/dsl, Chevron/dsl/24hr, Loves/Arby's/dsl, Mobil/McDonald's/, Pilot/Wendy's/dsl/24hr/@, 76/24hr, Shell, **food:** Carl's Jr, Denny's, Jack-in-the-Box, **lodging:** Day's Inn, Motel 6, **other:** KOA

**268** Lerdo Hwy, to Shafter

**263** 7th Standard Rd, Rowlee Rd, to Buttonwillow

**259mm** Buttonwillow Rest Area both lanes, full ♿ facilities, 📞, 🏕, litter barrels, petwalk

**257** CA 58, to Bakersfield, Buttonwillow, **E** gas: Arco/24hr, Bruce's/dsl/scales/@, Chevron/dsl/24hr, Mobil/dsl, TA/76/Taco Bell/dsl/24hr/@, Shell/dsl, **food:** Carl's Jr, Denny's, McDonald's, Starbucks, Subway, Taste of India, Tita's Mexican, Willow Ranch Rest., Zippy Freeze, **lodging:** Homeland Inn, Motel 6, Super 8, Willow Inn, **other:** Roger's Produce/gifts, tires/truckwash, **W** gas: Exxon/dsl

**253** Stockdale Hwy, **E** gas: Shell/dsl/24hr, 76/24hr, **food:** IHOP, Jack-in-the-Box, **lodging:** Best Inn, Best Western, **W** other: Tule Elk St Reserve

**246** CA 43, to Taft, Maricopa, **other:** to Buena Vista RA

**244** CA 119, to Pumpkin Center, **E** gas: Mobil/dsl, **W** gas: Chevron/dsl

**239** CA 223, Bear Mtn Blvd, to Arvin, **W** other: to Buena Vista RA, RV camping

**234** Old River Rd

**228** Copus Rd

**225** CA 166, to Mettler, **2-3 mi** **E** gas/dsl, food

**221** I-5 and CA 99 (from nb, exits left, no return)

**219b a** Laval Rd, Wheeler Ridge, **E** gas: Chevron/Subway, TA/dsl/rest./scales/@, **food:** Burger King, Pizza Hut, Taco Bell, **other:** Blue Beacon, repair, **W** gas: Petro/Mobil/Iron Sillet/Subway/dsl/scales/24hr/@, **food:** In-n-Out, McDonald's, Panda Express, Starbucks, Wendy's, **lodging:** Best Western

**218** truck weigh sta sb

**215** Grapevine, **E** gas: Mobil, **food:** Denny's, Jack-in-the-Box, RanchHouse Rest., **W** gas: 76/dsl, Shell/dsl, **food:** Don Pedro's Mexican, **lodging:** Ramda Ltd.

**210** Ft Tejon Rd, **W** other: to Ft Tejon Hist SP, towing/repair

**209mm** brake check area nb

**207** Lebec Rd, **W** other: USPO, CHP, antiques, towing

**206mm** rest areas both lanes, full ♿ facilities, 📞, vending, 🏕, litter barrels, petwalk

**205** Frazier Mtn Park Rd, **W** gas: Arco, Chevron/Subway/dsl/24hr, ⊕FLYING J/dsl/LP/rest./24hr/@, Shell/Quizno's/dsl, **food:** Jack-in-the-Box, Los Pinos Mexican, Noble Roman's, **lodging:** BestRest Inn, **other:** Auto Parts+, towing/repair/radiators/transmissions, to Mt Pinos RA

**204** Tejon Pass, elev 4144, truck brake insp sb

**202** Gorman Rd, to Hungry Valley, **E** gas: Chevron/dsl/LP, 76, **food:** Carl's Jr, Sizzler, **lodging:** Econolodge, **W** gas: Mobil, **food:** McDonald's, **other:** auto repair

**199** CA 138 E (from sb), Lancaster Rd, to Palmdale

**198b a** Quail Lake Rd, CA 138 E (from nb)

**195** Smokey Bear Rd, Pyramid Lake, **W** other: Pyramid Lake RV Park

**191** Vista del Lago Rd, **W** other: visitors ctr

**186mm** brake inspection area sb, motorist callboxes begin sb

**183** Templin Hwy, **W** other: Ranger Sta, RV camping

**176b a** Lake Hughes Rd, Parker Rd, Castaic, **E** gas: Citgo/7-11, Castaic Trkstp/dsl/rest./24hr/@, Pilot/Wendy's/dsl/24hr/scales, Shell, **food:** Burger King, Café Mike, Carl's Jr, Del Taco, Denny's, Domino's, El Pollo Loco, Foster Freeze, McDonald's, Starbucks, Subway, Vinny's Pizza, Zorba's Rest., **lodging:** Castaic Inn, Comfort Inn, Day's Inn, Rodeway Inn, **other:** Benny's Tire, Kragen Parts, Ralph's Food, Rite Aid, vet, to Castaic Lake, **W** gas: Mobil, 76/Circle K/Pizza Hut/Taco Bell/repair, **food:** Jack-in-the-Box, Las Rosas, Lollie's Rest., **lodging:** Comfort Suites, **other:** Walgreens, auto repair

**N** ↑↓ **S**

**CA**

**SANTA CLARITA · SYLMAR · ARLETA**

## INTERSTATE 5 CONT'D

| | |
|---|---|
| **173** | Hasley Canyon Rd, **W food:** Ameci Pizza/pasta, Coldstone Creamery, Subway, **other:** Ralph's Foods |
| **172** | CA 126 W, to Ventura |
| **171mm** | weigh sta nb |
| **171** | Rye Canyon Rd (from sb), **W gas:** Chevron, Shell, **food:** Del Taco, Jack-in-the-Box, Jimmy Deans, Tommy's Burgers, **other:** funpark |
| **170** | CA 126 E, Magic Mtn Pkwy, Saugus, **E food:** Denny's, **lodging:** Best Western/rest., Holiday Inn Express, **W gas:** Chevron, **food:** El Torito, Hamburger Hamlet, Marie Callender's, Red Lobster, Rio Rio Grill, Wendy's, **lodging:** Hilton Garden, **other:** Six Flags of CA |
| **169** | Valencia Blvd, **E** Shell/dsl, **W** Albertson's |
| **168** | McBean Pkwy, **E other:** H HOSPITAL, **W food:** Baskin-Robbins, Chili's, ChuckeCheese, ClaimJumper Rest., Indian Cuisine, Jamba Juice, Macaroni Grill, Starbucks, Subway, Wood Ranch BBQ, **other:** Circuit City, Marshall's, Michael's, Old Navy, Staples, Vons Foods, WorldMkt |
| **167** | Lyons Ave, Pico Canyon Rd, **E gas:** Chevron/24hr, 76/Circle K, Shell/dsl, **food:** Burger King, Wendy's, **other:** Chevrolet, **W gas:** Arco/24hr, Mobil/Blimpie, Shell, **food:** Carl's Jr, Chuy's Chinese, Coco's, Del Taco, Denny's, Foster's Freeze, El Pollo Loco, Fortune Express Chinese, IHOP, In-n-Out, Jack-in-the-Box, McDonald's, Outback Steaks, Taco Bell, Yamato Japanese, **lodging:** Comfort Inn, Extended Stay America, Fairfield Inn, Hampton Inn, La Quinta, Residence Inn, **other:** Camping World RV Service, GNC, Jiffy Lube, PetsMart, Ralph's Foods, SteinMart, Walmart/auto |
| **166** | Calgrove Blvd |
| **162** | CA 14 N, to Palmdale |
| **161b** | Balboa Blvd (from sb) |
| **160a** | I-210, to San Fernando, Pasadena |
| **159** | Roxford St, Sylmar, **E gas:** Chevron/dsl, Mobil/dsl, **food:** Denny's/24hr, McDonald's, **lodging:** Good Nite Inn, Motel 6 |
| **158** | I-405 S (from sb, no return) |
| **157b a** | SF Mission Blvd, Brand Blvd, **E gas:** Chevron, Mobil/dsl, 76, **food:** Carl's Jr, Carnita's Mexican, In-n-Out, Pollo Gordo, Popeye's, Winchell's, **other:** H HOSPITAL, AutoZone, Rite Aid |
| **156b** | CA 118 |
| **156a** | Paxton St, Brand Ave (from nb), **E gas:** Shell/dsl/24hr |
| **155b** | Van Nuys Blvd (no EZ nb return), **E gas:** Vale, **food:** Jack-in-the-Box, KFC/LJ Silver, McDonald's, Pizza Hut, Popeye's, **other:** AutoZone, USPO, **W food:** Domino's, **other:** auto repair |
| **155a** | Terra Bella St (from nb), **E gas:** Thrifty |
| **154** | Osborne St, to Arleta, **E gas:** Arco/24hr, Chevron/dsl, 76, **food:** El Pollo Loco, Papa's Tacos, Peter Piper Pizza, **other:** BigLots, Food4Less, Target, **W gas:** Mobil/Burger King, **other:** 7-11 |
| **153b** | CA 170 (from sb), to Hollywood |
| **152a** | Sheldon St, **E food:** Big Jim's Rest., **other:** Big O Parts, H HOSPITAL, auto repair |
| **152** | Lankershim Blvd, Tuxford, **E gas:** Superfine/dsl/scales |
| **151** | Penrose St |

**SUN VALLEY · LOS ANGELES AREA**

| | |
|---|---|
| **150b** | Sunland Blvd, Sun Valley, **E gas:** Mobil, 76, **food:** Acapulco Rest., Carl's Jr, El Pollo Loco, Good Fortune Chinese, Quizno's, Subway, Taco Bell, Town Café, **lodging:** Economy Inn, **other:** Ralph's Foods, 7-11, **W gas:** Exxon, Shell, **food:** Dimion's Rest., McDonald's |
| **150a** | GlenOaks Blvd (from nb), **E gas:** Superior/dsl, **lodging:** Willows Motel |
| **149** | Hollywood Way, **W gas:** Shell/dsl, **other:** U-Haul, ✈ |
| **148** | Buena Vista St, **W gas:** Exxon/dsl, **food:** Jack-in-the-Box, **lodging:** Quality Inn, Ramada Inn |
| **147** | Scott Rd, to Burbank, **E gas:** Sevan/dsl, **W food:** Krispy Kreme, Outback Steaks, Panda Express, Starbucks, Wendy's, **lodging:** Courtyard, Extended Stay America, **other:** Best Buy, Lowe's Whse, Marshall's, Michael's, Staples, Target |
| **146b** | Burbank Blvd, **E gas:** 76/repair, **food:** Carl's Jr, ChuckeCheese, El Pollo Loco, Harry's Rest., Hooters, IHOP, In-n-Out, Marie Callender, McDonald's, Popeye's, Pizza Hut, Quizno's, Shakey's Pizza, Starbuck's, Subway, Taco Bell, Tommy's Burgers, Wienerschnitzel, Yoshinoya, **lodging:** Holiday Inn, **other:** Barnes&Noble, Circuit City, CVS Drug, K-Mart, Macy's, Office Depot, Old Navy, Ralph's Foods, Ross, Sears, Von's Foods, **W gas:** Chevron, **food:** Subway |
| **146a** | Olive Ave, Verdugo, **E food:** Black Angus, Brewhouse Rest., **lodging:** Holiday Inn, **other:** Radio Shack, Sears, USPO, **W other:** Chevrolet, 7-11, H HOSPITAL |
| **145b** | Alameda Ave, **E gas:** Chevron, **food:** Starbucks, Togo's/Baskin-Robbins, **other:** CarMax, CVS Drug, Home Depot, Ralph's Foods, Walgreen, **W gas:** Arco, Shell, **lodging:** Burbank Inn, **other:** U-Haul |
| **145a** | Western Ave, **W other:** Gene Autrey Museum |
| **144b a** | CA 134, Ventura Fwy, Glendale, Pasadena |
| **142** | Colorado St |
| **141a** | Los Feliz Blvd, **E other:** H HOSPITAL, **W other:** Griffith Park, zoo |
| **140b** | Glendale Blvd, **E gas:** GasMart, 76, **food:** Starbucks, Subway, **other:** auto repair, **W gas:** Valero |
| **140a** | Fletcher Dr (from sb) |
| **139b a** | CA 2, Glendale Fwy |
| **138** | Stadium Way, Figueroa St, **E food:** IHOP, McDonald's, **other:** Home Depot, **W other:** to Dodger Stadium |
| **137b a** | CA 2, Glendale Fwy |
| **136b** | Broadway St (from sb), **W gas:** 76 |
| **136a** | Main St, **E gas:** Chevron/24hr, 76, **food:** Chinatown Express, Jack-in-the-Box, McDonald's, Mr Pizza, **other:** H HOSPITAL, Parts+ |
| **135c** | I-10 W (from nb), Mission Rd (from sb), **E gas:** 76, **food:** McDonald's, **lodging:** Howard Johnson, **other:** H HOSPITAL |
| **135b** | Cesar Chavez Ave, **W other:** H HOSPITAL |
| **135a** | 4th St, Soto St |
| **134b** | Ca 60 E (from sb), Soto St (from nb) |
| **134a** | CA 60 W, Santa Monica Fwy |
| **133** | Euclid Ave (from sb), Grand Vista (from nb), **E gas:** Arco, USA/dsl, **W gas:** Mobil, Shell, **other:** H HOSPITAL |
| **132** | Calzona St, Indiana St, **E gas:** Arco/dsl |
| **131** | bIndiana St (from nb), **E gas:** Arco/dsl, Valero/dsl |
| **131a** | Olympic Blvd, **E food:** McDonald's, **W food:** Jack-in-the-Box, King Taco, **other:** H HOSPITAL |

**N** ↕ **S**

**LOS ANGELES AREA**

# INTERSTATE 5 CONT'D

**130c b** I-710, to Long Beach, Eastern Ave, **E** **food:** McDonald's

**130a** Triggs St (from sb), **E** **other:** outlet mall, **W** **food:** Denny's/24hr, **lodging:** Destiny Inn

**129** Atlantic Blvd N, Eastern Ave (from sb), **E** **food:** Carl's Jr, Starbucks, **lodging:** Wyndham Garden, **other:** Hyundai, outlet mall/famous brands, **W** **food:** Denny's, Steven's Steaks

**128b** Washington Blvd, Commerce, **E** **gas:** Chevron/dsl/repair/24hr, **food:** McDonald's, **lodging:** Crowne Plaza Hotel/casino, Wyndham Hotel, **other:** Firestone, Office Depot, Old Navy, mall, **W** **gas:** Arco, **food:** Starbucks

**128a** Garfield Blvd, **E** **lodging:** Commerce/Hotel/casino, **other:** Home Depot, Office Depot, **W** **gas:** 76

**126b** Slauson Ave, Montebello, **E** **gas:** Shell, Valero/dsl, **food:** Burger King, Ozzie's Diner, Quizno's, Starbucks, **lodging:** Best Star Inn, Best Western, Super 8, **W** **gas:** Arco, **food:** Denny's, **lodging:** Best Value, Ramada Inn

**126a** Paramount Blvd, Downey, **E** **gas:** Shell/Jack-in-the-Box/dsl

**125** CA 19 S, Lakewood Blvd, Rosemead Blvd, **E** **gas:** Mobil, Thrifty, **food:** Foster's Freeze, Sam's Burgers, Starbucks, Taco Bell, **W** **food:** McDonald's, China Wok, Chris & Pitt's BBQ, Subway, **other:** Ford/Lincoln/Mercury, Ralph's Foods

**124** I-605

**123** Florence Ave, to Downey, **E** **gas:** Mobil, **W** **other:** Chevrolet, Honda, auto repair

**122** Imperial Hwy, Pioneer Blvd, **E** **gas:** Chevron, **food:** Cold Stone Creamery, IHOP, Jack-in-the-Box, King Buffet, McDonald's, Plum Wok Rest, Subway, Togo's, Wendy's, **lodging:** Best Western, **other:** Audi/Porsche, BMW, Firestone/auto, Payless Foods, Rite Aid, Target, **W** **gas:** Citgo/7-11, Shell, **food:** Denny's, HongKong Express, Panda King, Rally's, Sizzler, Tacos Mexico, Wienerschnitzel, **lodging:** Comfort Inn, Keystone Motel, Rodeway Inn, Vistaland Motel, **other:** Ford, Walmart

**121** San Antonio Dr, to Norwalk Blvd, **E** **food:** IHOP, McDonald's, Outback Steaks, Starbucks, **lodging:** Marriott, **W** **gas:** 76, **other:** auto repair

**120b** Firestone Blvd (exits left from nb)

**120a** Rosecrans Ave, **E** **gas:** Valero/dsl, **food:** Burger King, Casa Adelita Mexican, Jim's Burgers, KFC, Pizza Hut/Taco Bell, Taco Joe, **other:** H HOSPITAL, BigSaver Foods, **W** **gas:** Arco/24hr, **food:** El Pollo Loco, **lodging:** Saddleback Inn, **other:** El Monte RV Ctr, Nissan, Stier's RV Ctr, Tuneup Masters

**119** Carmenita Rd, Buena Park, **E** **gas:** 76/dsl, **food:** Jack-in-the-Box, **lodging:** Motel 6, **other:** Ford Trucks, Lowe's Whse, **W** **gas:** Arco/24hr, **food:** Carl's Jr, **lodging:** Budget Inn, Dynasty Suites

**118** Valley View Blvd, **E** **gas:** Arco/dsl/24hr, **food:** Carl's Jr, Elephant Bar Rest, In-n-Out, Northwoods Rest, Red Robin, Subway, **lodging:** Extended Stay America, Holiday Inn Select, Residence Inn, **other:** Staples, **W** **gas:** Chevron, **food:** Denny's, El Pollo Loco, Four Seasons Buffet, Starbucks, **other:** Thompson's RV Ctr, to Camping World

**117** Artesia Blvd, Knott Ave, **E** **gas:** 76/24hr, Shell/Subway/dsl/24hr, **lodging:** Extended Stay America, **other:** Carmax, **W** **gas:** Cardlock/dsl, **other:** Chevrolet, Chrysler,

**LOS ANGELES AREA**

**117** Continued Knotts Berry Farm, to Camping World RV Service/supplies

**116** CA 39, Beach Blvd, **E** **gas:** Chevron, **other:** H HOSPITAL, Acura, BMW, Buick/Pontiac/GMC, CarMax, Honda, Hyundai, Nissan, Toyota, VW, **W** **gas:** Chevron, Valero, **food:** Arby's, Black Angus, Denny's, Fuddruckers, Karuta Japanese, KFC, Outback Steaks, Pizza Hut, Subway, Wendy's, **lodging:** Hampton Inn, Holiday Inn, Red Roof Inn, **other:** Sater Bro's, Target, to Knotts Berry Farm

**115** Manchester (from nb)

**114b** CA 91 E, Riverside Fwy, **W** to ✈

**114a** Magnolia Ave, Orangethorpe Ave, **E** **gas:** Mobil/dsl, **food:** Burger King, Burger Town, Taco Bell, **other:** Harley-Davidson

**113c** CA 91 W (from nb)

**113b a** Brookhurst St, LaPalma, **E** **gas:** Chevron/24hr, **food:** Subway, **W** **gas:** Mobil/dsl, **food:** Carl's Jr., Quizno's, **other:** Home Depot, Staples

**112** Euclid St, **E** **gas:** Mobil, 7-11, **food:** Chris&Pitt's BBQ, Marie Callender's, McDonald's, Subway, **other:** Kings Drug, Old Navy, Ross, Walmart, **W** **gas:** Arco, 76, **food:** Arby's, Burger King, Denny's, **other:** Chevrolet, Radio Shack, SavOn Drug

**111** Lincoln Ave, to Anaheim, **E** **gas:** Shell/dsl, **food:** El Triunfo Mexican, La Casa Garcia Mexican, Starbuck's, Subway, **other:** vet, **W** **other:** Discount Auto Repair, Ford

**110b** Ball Rd (from sb), **E** **gas:** Arco, Chevron/dsl, Citgo/7-11, Shell, **food:** Big's Pizza, Burger King, El Pollo Loco, McDonald's, Shakey's Pizza, Taco Bell, Subway, **lodging:** Anaheim Motel, Astoria Inn, Best Inn, Courtesy Lodge, Day's Inn, Holiday Inn, Traveler's World RV Park, **other:** laundry, **W** **gas:** Arco/24hr, Shell/dsl, **food:** Paris Rest., Spaghetti Sta, **lodging:** Best Western, Budget Inn, Day's Inn, Roadway Inn, Sheraton, Super 8, **other:** Camping World RV Service/supplies

**110a** Harbor Blvd, **E** **gas:** Shell, **lodging:** Day's Inn, Menage Inn, **W** to Disneyland, **food:** Acapulco Mexican, Captain Kidd's, Dennys, IHOP, McDonald's, Millie's Rest., Mimi's Cafe, Tony Roma, **lodging:** Anaheim Resort, Best Inn, Best Western, Camelot Inn, Carousel Inn, Castle Inn Suites, Desert Inn, Fairfield Inn, Howard Johnson, ParkVue Inn, Ramada Inn, Saga Inn, Tropicana Inn, same as 109

**109** Katella Ave, Disney Way, **E** **gas:** Arco, 76/repair, **food:** CA Country Café, Denny's, El Torito, McDonald's, Ming Delight, Mr Stox Dining, **lodging:** Angel Inn, Ramada

## INTERSTATE 5 CONT'D

**109** Continued
Inn, Travelodge, **W gas:** 7-11, **food:** Del Taco, Flakey Jake's, Subway, Thai&Thai, **lodging:** Arena Inn, Comfort Inn, Desert Palms Suites, Extended Stay America, Hilton, Holiday Inn Express, Marriott, Peacock Suites, Portofino Inn, Radisson, Red Roof Inn, Residence Inn, Staybridge Suites, Super 8, to Disneyland

**107c** St Coll Blvd, City Drive, **E lodging:** Hilton Suites, **W lodging:** Doubletree Hotel

**107b a** CA 57 N, Chapman Ave, **E gas:** Mobil, **food:** Burger King, Del Taco, Denny's, **lodging:** Hilton Suites, Motel 6, Ramada Inn, **other:** H HOSPITAL, to Edison Field, **W food:** Krispy Kreme, Wendy's, **lodging:** Ayer's Inn, Country Inn/café, DoubleTree, **other:** H HOSPITAL, Best Buy

**106** CA 22 W (from nb), Garden Grove Fwy, Bristol St

**105b** N Broadway, Main St, **E gas:** 76, **food:** Carl's Jr, FoodCourt, Jamba Juice, Polly's Café, Rubio's Grill, Starbucks, **lodging:** Red Roof Inn, **other:** Barnes&Noble, BMW, Macy's, Nordstrom's, SavOn Drug, Bowers Museum, mall, **W lodging:** Golden West Motel, Travel Inn

**105a** 17th St, **E gas:** 76/dsl/24hr, **food:** Hometown Buffet, IHOP, McDonald's, **lodging:** Grand Courtyard Inn, **other:** Chevrolet, CVS Drug, Food4Less, same as 104b, **W gas:** B&L Gas, Chevron, **food:** Marisco's Seafood, Norm's Rest., YumYum Doughnuts, **other:** 7-11

**104b** Santa Ana Blvd, Grand Ave, **E on Grand food:** Denny's, Hawaiian BBQ, Marie Callender, McDonald's, Popeye's, RoundTable Pizza, Starbucks, Subway, Taco Bell/Pizza Hut, Tacos Mexico, **other:** Big O Tire, CVS Drug, $Tree, Food4Less, Goodyear, Target, vet, **W other:** KIA

**104a** (103c from nb), 4th St, 1st St, to CA 55 N, **E gas:** Chevron, Shell, **food:** Del Taco

**103b** CA 55 S, to Newport Beach

**103a** CA 55 N (from nb), to Riverside

**102** Newport Ave (from sb), **W gas:** Arco

**101b** Red Hill Ave, **E gas:** Mobil/dsl, Shell/repair, **food:** Del Taco, Denny's, Starbucks, Subway, Wendy's, **lodging:** Key Inn, **other:** Drug Emporium/24hr, U-Haul, **W gas:** Arco/24hr, Chevron/24hr, Valero/dsl, **food:** Burger King, Pizza Shack, Roderick's, Taco Bell, **other:** Goodyear, 7-11, Stater Bros Foods

**101a** Tustin Ranch Rd, **E food:** McDonald's, **other:** Acura, Buick, Cadillac, Chevrolet, Costco, Dodge, Ford/Lincoln/Mercury, Infiniti, Lexus, Mazda, Nissan, Pontiac, Sears Essentials, Toyota

**100** Jamboree Rd, **E gas:** Shell, **food:** Black Angus, Buca Italian, Burger King, CA Pizza, Chick-fil-A, El Pollo Loco, In-n-Out, Macaroni Grill, On the Border, Panda Express, Pick-up Sticks, Quizno's, Red Robin, Taco Rosa, **other:** AAA, Barnes&Noble, Best Buy, Circuit City, Costco, Loehmann's, Lowe's Whse, Old Navy, PetsMart, Ralph's Foods, Rite Aid, Ross, Target

**99** Culver Dr, **E gas:** Shell/24hr, **other:** vet

**97** Jeffrey Rd, **E gas:** Arco, **food:** Baskin-Robbins, Daphne's Greek, Fatburger, Juice-it-Up, Quizno's, Starbucks, **other:** Albertson's, Kohl's, **W other:** Ranch Mkt Foods

**96** Sand Canyon Ave, Old Towne, **W gas:** 76/Circle K, **food:** Denny's, Jack-in-the-Box, Knollwood Burgers, Tiajuana's Rest., **lodging:** La Quinta, **other:** H HOSPITAL, Traveland USA RV Park, Irvine RV Ctr

**95** CA 133, Laguna Fwy, N to Riverside, S Laguna Beach

**94b** Alton Pkwy, **E gas:** Shell/Subway, **food:** Carl's Jr, Quizno's, Starbucks, Taco Bell, **food:** Homestead Suites, **W food:** Cheesecake Factory, Corner Bakery, Dave&Buster's, Ling&Louie's, Panda Express, PF Chang's, Wahoo's, Yardhouse Grill, **lodging:** DoubleTree, **other:** Barnes&Noble, Macy's, Nordstroms, Target

**94a** I-405 N (from nb)

**92b** Bake Pkwy, same as 92a

**92a** Lake Forest Dr, Laguna Hills, **E gas:** Chevron/24hr, Shell/dsl, **food:** Black Angus, Burger King, Del Taco, Jack-in-the-Box, McDonald's, Mimi's Café, Panera Bread, Pit BBQ, Pizza Hut, RoundTable Pizza, Subway, Taco Bell, The Hat, **lodging:** Best Western, **other:** America's Tire, Audi/Jeep, Chevrolet, Ford/Lincoln/Mercury, GMC/Kia, Honda, Isuzu, Jaguar, Mazda, Mercedes/Suzuki, PepBoys, Staples, Subaru, Toyota, VW, **W gas:** Chevron/24hr, Shell, **food:** Carl's Jr, Coco's, Del Taco, McDonald's, Quizno's, **lodging:** Comfort Inn, Courtyard, Quality Suites, Travelodge, **other:** AZ Leather, Best Buy, BMW/Mini, Books Etc, JC Penney

**91** El Toro Rd, **E gas:** Chevron/dsl, Shell/dsl, USA, **food:** Arby's, Asia Buffet, Bakers Square, Carino's Italian, Carl's Jr, Coldstone Creamery, Denny's, Flamebroiler, Fuddrucker's, Jack-in-the-Box, Jamba Juice, Johnny Rockets, KFC, McDonald's, MegaBurger, Oeeshi Japanese, Quizno's, Red Lobster, Scarantino's Rest., Sizzler, Starbucks, Subway, Wendy's, **other:** CVS Drug, Home Depot, House of Fabrics, K-Mart, 99¢ Store, Office Depot, PetCo, Ralph's Foods, SavOn Drug, Staples, **W gas:** Chevron/dsl/24hr, Shell/24hr, 76/Circle K, **food:** BJ's Rest., CA Pizza, Carrows, El Torito, In-n-Out, Island Burgers, Kings FishHouse, KooRooRoo Kitchen, LoneStar Steaks, Nami Seafood Buffet, Pizza Hut, **other:** H HOSPITAL, Dalton's Books, Circuit City, Firestone/auto, JC Penney, Longs Drugs, Macy's, Marshall's, Sears/auto, Trader Joe's, Walgreens, USPO, mall

**90** Alicia Pkwy, Mission Viejo, **E gas:** Chevron/24hr, 76/dsl, **food:** Carl's Jr, Del Taco, Denny's, Little Caesar's, Subway, Wendy's, Winchell's, **other:** Albertson's, America's Tire, Buick/Pontiac/Mazda, CVS Drug, Kragen Parts, Target, **W gas:** Chevron, 76/dsl, **food:** Carl's Jr, It's a Grind, Manhattan Grill, Togo's, Wendy's, **other:** AAA, Big Lots, Buick/Pontiac, Mazda

**89** La Paz Rd, Mission Viejo, **E gas:** Arco/24hr, UltraMar, **food:** KFC/Pizza Hut, Starbucks, Taco Bell, **other:** Albertson's, **W gas:** 76, **food:** Claim Jumper Rest., DQ, Hot Off the Grill, Jack-in-the-Box, Krispy Kreme, La Salsa, McDonald's, Outback Steaks, Quizno's, Spasso's Italian, Wienerschnitzel, Yamato Japanese, **lodging:** Holiday Inn, **other:** Best Buy, Borders Books&Café, Curves, Goodyear/auto, Jo-Ann Fabrics, Just Tires, PetCo, 7-11, to Laguna Niguel Pk

**87** Oso Pkwy, Pacific Park Dr, **E gas:** Chevron/repair, 76/repair, **food:** Carl's Jr, Starbucks, Subway, **lodging:** Fairfield Inn

**LOS ANGELES AREA**

**LAGUNA HILLS**

**MISSION VIEJO**

## INTERSTATE 5 CONT'D

**N↑S** **CAPISTRANO** | **SAN CLEMENTE**

**86** Crown Valley Pkwy, E gas: Arco, Chevron, 76, food: Coco's, El Torito, Islands Grill, Versachee Italian, other: H HOSPITAL, Macy's, mall, vet, W gas: Chevron/dsl, other: Aamco, Costco

**85b** Avery Pkwy, E gas: Shell/dsl, food: Carrow's, Del Taco, Jack-in-the-Box, Mongolian BBQ, Quizno's, Starbucks, other: Acura, America's Tire/auto, Infiniti/Audi, Land Rover/Jaguar, Lexus, Parts+, Saab, World Mkt, W gas: Mobil, Shell/dsl/24hr, food: A's Burgers, Carl's Jr, In-n-Out, lodging: Best Value Laguna Inn, other: Costco, Firestone/auto, GMC/Cadillac, Hyundai, Mercedes

**85a** CA 73 N (toll)

**83** Junipero Serra Rd, to San Juan Capistrano, W gas: Shell, Spirit/dsl

**82** CA 74, Ortego Hwy, E gas: Chevron/dsl, 76, food: Bravo Burgers, Denny's, lodging: Best Western, other: W gas: Chevron/24hr, food: Arby's, Carl's Jr, Del Taco, Jack-in-the-Box, Marie Callender's, McDonald's, Sizzler, Subway, Taco Bell, Walnut Grove Rest., lodging: Mission Inn, other: Ralph's Foods, TruValue, San Juan Capistrano

**81** Camino Capistrano, E other: Peugeot/VW, W gas: Chevron, food: Baskin-Robbins, Domino's, El Adobe Rest., Eng's Chinese, Harry's Rest., KFC, Pick-up-Stix, Pizza Hut, Ricardo's Mexican, Ruby's Cafe, Starbucks, other: Goodyear, Harley-Davidson, PetCo, Radio Shack, Rite Aid, San Juan Capistrano (1mi), SP

**79** CA 1, Pacific Coast Hwy, Capistrano Bch, Capistrano, 1 mi W gas: Arco/24hr, 76, food: A's Burgers, Cario's Mexican, Carl's Jr, Del Taco, Denny's, Jack-in-the-Box, JuiceStop, McDonald's, Subway, lodging: Dana Point Inn, DoubleTree, Harbor Inn, Holiday Inn Express, other: Chevrolet, Chrysler/Jeep, Honda, Nissan, Saturn, Toyota, USPO, vet

**78** Camino de Estrella, San Clemente, E gas: 76/dsl, food: Bakers Square, Carl's Jr, China Well, Coldstone Creamery, JuiceStop, Melting Pot, RoundTable Pizza, Rubio's Grill, Subway, Wahoo's Fish Taco, other: H HOSPITAL, CVS Drug, Ralph's Foods, Stater Bros Foods, Trader Joe's, W gas: Arco/dsl, food: Las Golondrienas, other: Big Lots, Kragen Parts, Sears Essentials

**77** Ave Vista Hermosa

**76** Ave Pico, E gas: Mobil, food: Buono Pizza, Carrow's, Golden Spoon, Juice it Up, McDonald's, other: Albertson's, GNC, W gas: Chevron, Shell/dsl, food: BurgerStop, Del Taco, Denny's/24hr, Pick-up-Stix, Pizza Hut, Subway, Waffle Lady, lodging: Country Plaza Inn, other: Curves, 99¢ Store, Staples, Tuesday Morning, USPO, tires/repair

**75** Ave Palizada, Ave Presidio, W gas: Arco, Valero, food: Antoine's Café, Baskin-Robbins, Coffee Bean, KFC, Mr. Pete's Burgers, Ricardo's Mexican, Subway, Starbucks, lodging: Holiday Inn, other: Albertson's, Ford

**74** El Camino Real, E gas: Chevron/dsl/24hr, food: El Mariachi Rest., lodging: San Clemente Inn, Shorehouse Landing, same as 75, W gas: Exxon, 76, food: Fat-Burger, KFC, LoveBurger, Pizza Hut/Taco Bell, Taste Of China, Tommy's Rest./24hr, other: Kragen Parts, Radio Shack, Ralph's Foods, 7-11

**OCEANSIDE** | **ESCONDIDO**

**73** Ave Calafia, Ave Magdalena, E gas: Chevron, 76, Shell, food: El Mariachi Rest., Jack-in-the-Box, Molly Bloom's Cafe, Pipes Cafe, Sugar Shack Cafe, lodging: Budget Inn, Calafia Beach Motel, C-Vu Inn, Hampton Inn, LaVista Inn, San Clemente Motel, Travelodge, other: San-O Tire, 7-11, W to San Clemente SP

**72** Cristianitos Ave, E food: Carl's Jr., lodging: Comfort Suites, Carmelo Motel, other: San Mateo RV Park/dump, W other: to San Clemente SP

**71** Basilone Rd, W other: San Onofre St Beach

**67mm** weigh sta both lanes

**66mm** viewpoint sb

**62** Las Pulgas Rd

**59mm** Aliso Creek rest area both lanes, full ♿ facilities, 🚻, vending, ☎, litter barrels, petwalk, RV dump

**54c** Oceanside Harbor Dr, W gas: Chevron, Mobil, food: Burger King (1mi), Del Taco, Denny's/24hr, lodging: Comfort Inn, Sandman Hotel, Travelodge, The Bridge Motel, other: to Camp Pendleton

**54b** Hill St (from sb), to Oceanside, W gas: Mobil, food: Carrow's Rest., lodging: Comfort Inn

**54a** Ca 76 E, Coast Hwy

**53** Mission Ave, Oceanside, E gas: Arco/24hr, Mobil/dsl, 76/LP, food: Arby's, Armando's Tacos, Burger King, China Star, El Charrito Mexican, Jack-in-the-Box, KFC, McDonald's, Mission Donuts, Pizza Hut, lodging: Econolodge, Quality Inn, Ramada Ltd, other: CarQuest, NAPA, PepBoys, Valu+ Foods, W food: Panda Express, Wendy's, other: 99¢ Store, Office Depot

**52** Oceanside Blvd, E gas: Arco, food: Alberto's Mexican, Cosina Italiana, Domino's, IHOP, McDonald's, Papa John's, Pizza Hut, Rosarita's Café, Starbucks, Subway, Taco Bell, Weinerschnitzel, other: Boney's Foods, CVS Drug, Longs Drug, Ralph's Food, Von's Food, CHP, W lodging: Oceanside Inn

**51c** Cassidy St (from sb), W gas: Citgo/7-11, Mobil, 76, other: H HOSPITAL

**51b** CA 78, Vista Way, Escondido, E gas: Chevron/dsl/24hr, 76, Shell, food: Applebee's, Boston Mkt, Burger King, Chili's, ChuckeCheese, Finnigan's Grill, Fuddrucker's, Golden Taipei, Hooters, Macaroni Grill, McDonald's, Mimi's Café, Olive Garden, QuikWok, Rubio's, Spoon's Grill, Starbucks, Wendy's, West Buffet, lodging: Holiday Inn Express, other: Best Buy, CVS Drug, $Tree, JC Penney, Macy's, Marshall's, Michael's, PetCo, Saturn, Sears/auto, Staples, Stater Bros Foods, Steinmart,

Copyright 2009 - The Next Exit®

## INTERSTATE 5 CONT'D

| | |
|---|---|
| **51b** | Continued<br>Target, Tuesday Morning, Walmart/auto, World Mkt, **W** **food:** Hunter Steaks |
| **51a** | Las Flores Dr |
| **50** | Elm Ave, Carlsbad Village Dr, **E** **gas:** Shell/24hr, **food:** Lotus Thai Bistro, **W** **gas:** Carlsbad/LP, Chevron/repair/24hr, 76, Valero, **food:** Al's Cafe, Carl's Jr, Denny's/24hr, Jack-in-the-Box, KFC/Taco Bell, Mikko Japanese, **lodging:** Motel 6, **other:** Albertson's |
| **49** | Tamarack Ave, **E** **gas:** Chevron/24hr, Exxon/dsl, **food:** Village Kitchen, **lodging:** Carlsbad Lodge, Super 8, Travel Inn, **other:** GNC, Rite Aid, Von's Foods, **W** **gas:** Arco, 76/repair/24hr |
| **48** | Cannon Rd, Car Country Carlsbad, **E** **other:** Acura, Buick, Chevrolet/Cadillac, Ford, Honda, Isuzu, Lexus, Lincoln/Mercury, Mazda, Mercedes, Toyota, VW |
| **47** | Carlsbad Blvd, Palomar Airport Rd, **E** **gas:** Chevron, Mobil/dsl, Citgo/7-11, **food:** Carl's Jr, Islands Burgers, Panda Express, Pat&Oscar's Rest., Subway, Strauss Brewery Rest., Taco Bell, TGIFriday, **lodging:** Holiday Inn, Motel 6, **other:** Costco, Flower Fields/Carlsbad Ranch, Ford, Jiffy Lube, outlet mall, **W** **gas:** Shell/dsl, **food:** ClaimJumper Rest., In-n-Out, Marie Callender's, McDonald's, Sammy's Pizza, **lodging:** Hilton Garden, **other:** S Carlsbad St Bch |
| **45** | Poinsettia Lane, **W** **gas:** Chevron, **food:** Benihana, El Pollo Loco, Golden Spoon, Jack-in-the-Box, Pick-Up Sticks, Starbucks, Subway, **lodging:** La Quinta, Motel 6, Quality Inn, Ramada, **other:** Ralph's Foods, Rite Aid, Volvo/Porsche |
| **44** | La Costa Ave, **E** vista point, **W** **gas:** Chevron/dsl |
| **43** | Leucadia Blvd, **E** **lodging:** Howard Johnson, **W** **gas:** Shell/service |
| **41b** | Encinitas Blvd, **E** **gas:** Chevron, Exxon, O'Brien Sta., **food:** Coco's, Del Taco, Oggi's Pizza, **other:** Albertson's, CVS Drug, NAPA, to Quail Botanical Gardens, vet, **W** **gas:** Shell, **food:** Denny's, Wendy's, **lodging:** Best Western/rest., Day's Inn, **other:** PetCo |
| **41a** | Santa Fe Dr, to Encinitas, **E** **gas:** Shell, **food:** Carl's Jr, El Nopalito, Papa Tonie's Pizza, **other:** 7-11, **W** **food:** Today's Pizza, **other:** Ⓗ HOSPITAL, Rite Aid, Von's Foods, vet |
| **40** | Birmingham Dr, **E** **gas:** Chevron, Valero, **food:** Mandarin City, **lodging:** Comfort Inn, **W** **gas:** Arco/24hr |
| **39mm** | viewpoint sb |
| **39** | Manchester Ave, **E** **gas:** 76, **other:** to MiraCosta College |
| **37** | Lomas Santa Fe Dr, Solana Bch, **E** **food:** Baskin-Robbins, Pizza Nova, Samurai Rest., **other:** Ross, Von's Foods, We-R-Fabrics, **W** **gas:** Arco, Mobil, **food:** Carl's Jr, Denny's, Jamba Juice, Panda Express, Panera Bread, RoundTable Pizza, Starbucks, Togo's, **other:** CVS Drug, Discount Tire, Henry's Foods, Marshall's, Staples |
| **36** | Via de La Valle, Del Mar, **E** **gas:** Chevron, Mobil, **food:** Aliya Bistro, Burger King, Chevy's Mexican, Coffee Bean, McDonald's, Milton's Deli, Paradise Grill, Pasta Pronto, Papachino's Italian, Silver Skillet, Taste of Thai, **other:** Albertson's/SavOn, PetCo, Radio Shack, **W** **gas:** Arco/24hr, Shell/dsl, **food:** Denny's, FishMkt Rest., Red Tracton's Rest., **lodging:** Hilton, **other:** racetrack |
| **34** | Del Mar Heights Rd, **E** **gas:** Shell/dsl, **W** **gas:** 7-11, **food:** Elijah's Rest., Jack-in-the-Box, Mexican Grill, **other:** Longs Drug, Von's Foods |
| **33** | Carmel Mtn Rd, **E** **gas:** Arco, Shell/repair, **food:** Taco Bell, Tio Leo's Mexican, **lodging:** DoubleTree Hotel, Hampton Inn, Marriott |
| **32** | CA 56 E, Carmel Valley Rd |
| **31** | I-805 (from sb) |
| **29** | Genesee Ave, **E** **other:** Ⓗ HOSPITAL |
| **28b** | La Jolla Village Dr, **E** **food:** Italian Bistro, **lodging:** Embassy Suites, Hyatt, Marriott, **other:** Ⓗ HOSPITAL, to LDS Temple, **W** **gas:** Mobil/dsl, **food:** BJ's Grill, CA Pizza, Coldstone Creamery, Domino's, Elijah's Deli, El Torito, Flame Broiler, Islands Burgers, RockBottom Café, Rubio's Grill, TGIFriday, Trader Joe's, **lodging:** Sheraton, **other:** Ⓗ HOSPITAL, CVS Drug, Marshall's, PetsMart, Radio Shack, Ralph's Foods, Ross, Whole Foods |
| **28a** | Nobel Dr (from nb), **E** **lodging:** Hyatt, **other:** LDS Temple, **W** same as 28b |
| **27** | Gilman Dr, La Jolla Colony Dr |
| **26b** | CA 52 E, Ardath Rd (from nb) |
| **26a** | Ardath Rd (from nb) |
| **23b** | CA 274, Balboa Ave, **1 mi E** **gas:** Shell, **food:** Del Taco, **other:** Albertson's, **W** **gas:** Mobil, 76/repair, 7-11, **food:** McDonald's, In-n-Out, Rubio's Grill, Wienerschnitzel, **lodging:** Days Inn, Holiday Inn Express, Mission Bay Inn, San Diego Motel, **other:** Ⓗ HOSPITAL, Discount Tire, Express Tire, Ford, Nissan, Toyota, Mission Bay Pk |
| **23a** | Grand Ave, Garnet Ave, **W** **other:** Cadillac |
| **22** | Clairemont Dr, Mission Bay Dr, **E** **gas:** Arco, Shell, **food:** Carl's Jr, HomeTown Buffet, Jack-in-the-Box, KFC, McDonald's, Subway, **lodging:** Best Western, **other:** Chevrolet/VW, Rite Aid, **W** to Sea World Dr |
| **21** | Sea World Dr, Tecolote Dr, **E** **gas:** Shell, **lodging:** Seaside Motel, **other:** Circle K, Firestone, PetCo, **W** **lodging:** Hilton, **other:** Old Town SP, Seaworld |
| **20** | I-8, W to Nimitz Blvd, E to El Centro, CA 209 S (from sb), to Rosecrans St |
| **19** | Old Town Ave, **E** **gas:** Arco/24hr, Shell, **lodging:** Courtyard, La Quinta |
| **18b** | Washington St, **E** **lodging:** Comfort Inn |
| **18a** | Pacific Hwy Viaduct, Kettner St |
| **17b** | India St, Front St, Sassafras St, **E** **gas:** Mobil, Rte 66 Gas, **W** **other:** ✈, civic ctr |
| **17a** | Hawthorn St, Front St, **W** **gas:** Exxon/dsl, **lodging:** Holiday Inn, Motel 6, Radisson, **other:** Ⓗ HOSPITAL |
| **16b** | 6th Ave, downtown |
| **16a** | CA 163 N, 10th St, **E** **other:** AeroSpace Museum, **W** **gas:** Shell, **food:** Del Taco, Jack-in-the-Box, McDonald's, **lodging:** Days Inn, Downtown Lodge, El Cortez Motel, Holiday Inn, Marriott, **other:** Ⓗ HOSPITAL |
| **15c b** | CA 94 E (from nb), Pershing Dr, B St, civic ctr |
| **15a** | CA 94 E, J St, Imperial Ave (from sb), |
| **14b** | Cesar Chavez Pkwy |
| **14a** | CA 75, to Coronado, **W** toll rd to Coronado |
| **13b** | National Ave SD, 28th St, **E** **food:** Little Caesar's, Starbucks, Subway, **other:** AutoZone, **W** **gas:** Shell, **food:** Burger King, Del Taco, El Pollo Loco |
| **13a** | CA 15 N, to Riverside |
| **12** | Main St, National City |

## INTERSTATE 5 CONT'D

**N ↕ S**

**SAN DIEGO AREA**

| | |
|---|---|
| 11b | 8th St, National City, **E gas:** Arco, Shell/24hr, **food:** Jack-in-the-Box, **lodging:** Holiday Inn, Howard Johnson, Ramada Inn, Super 8, Value Inn, **W gas:** Chevron/dsl |
| 11a | Harbor Dr, Civic Center Dr |
| 10 | Bay Marina, 24th St, Mile of Cars Way, 1/2 mi **E food:** Denny's, In-n-Out |
| 9 | CA 54 E |
| 8b | E St, Chula Vista, **E lodging:** Motel 6, **W food:** Anthony's Fish Grotto, **lodging:** GoodNite Inn |
| 8a | H St |
| 7b | J St (from sb) |
| 7a | L St, **E gas:** 7-11, 76, Shell/dsl, **food:** Mandarin Chinese, **lodging:** Best Western, **other:** AutoZone, NAPA, Parts+, Office Depot |
| 6 | Palomar St, **E gas:** Arco, **food:** China King, Del Taco, DQ, HomeTown Buffet, KFC, Little Caesar, McDonald's, Subway, **lodging:** Palomar Inn, **other:** Food4Less, Office Depot, 7-11, **E on Broadway…food:** Jack-in-the-Box, KFC, Panda Express, Quizno's, Yoshinoya, **other:** Costco/gas, Michael's, Ross, Target, Walmart |
| 5b | Main St, to Imperial Beach, **E gas:** Arco, **food:** AZ Chinese |
| 5a | CA 75 (from sb), Palm Ave, to Imperial Beach, **E gas:** Arco, **food:** Armando's Mexican, Papa John's, Wahshing Chinese, **other:** Discount Tire, 7-11, Soto's Transmissions, **W gas:** Arco, 7-11, Shell/repair/24hr, Thrifty, **food:** Boll Weevil Diner, Burger King, Carl's Jr, Carrow's, Coldstone Creamery, El Chile Mexican, Los Pancho's Tacos, McDonald's, Rally's, Red Hawk Steaks, Roberto's Mexican, Subway, Taco Bell, Wienerschnitzel, **lodging:** Super 8, Travelodge, **other:** AutoZone, CVS Drug, Home Depot, Jiffy Lube, 99¢ Store, Von's Foods |
| 4 | Coronado Ave (from sb), **E gas:** Chevron/service, Shell/service, **food:** Denny's, Taco Bell, **lodging:** EZ 8 Motel, **other:** 7-11, **W gas:** Shell/dsl, **lodging:** Day's Inn, **other:** to Border Field SP |
| 3 | CA 905, Tocayo Ave, **W gas:** 7-11 |
| 2 | Dairy Mart Rd, **E gas:** Arco/24hr, Circle K, **food:** Burger King, Carl's Jr, Coco's, KFC, McDonald's, Roberto's Mexican, **lodging:** Americana Inn, Best Value, Super 8, Valli-Hi Motel, **other:** CarQuest, Radio Shack, Pacifica RV Resort |
| 1b | Via de San Ysidro, **E gas:** Chevron, Exxon, Mobil, 76, **other:** Max's Foods, NAPA, **W gas:** Chevron, **food:** Denny's, KFC, **lodging:** Economy Inn, Knights/RV park, Motel 6 |
| 1a | I-805 N (from nb), Camino de la Plaza (from sb), **E food:** Burger King, El Pollo Loco, Jack-in-the-Box, KFC, McDonald's, Subway, **lodging:** Flamingo Motel, Gateway Inn, Holiday Motel, Travelodge, **other:** AutoZone, **W food:** Achiato Mexican, Gingling House Chinese, IHOP, Iron Wok, McDonald's, Pizza Hut/Taco Bell, Sunrise Buffet, **other:** Baja Duty-Free, K-Mart, Ross, Marshall's, factory outlet, border parking |
| 0 | US/Mexico Border, California state line, customs, I-5 begins/ends |

## INTERSTATE 8

**YUMA E ↕ W**

**EL CENTRO**

| Exit # | Services |
|---|---|
| 172.5mm | California/Arizona state line, Colorado River, Pacific/Mountain time zone |
| 172 | 4th Ave, Yuma, **N** Ft Yuma Casino, **S gas:** Chevron, Circle K, **food:** Jack-in-the-Box, Yuma Landing Rest., **lodging:** Best Western, **other:** Rivers Edge RV Park, to Yuma SP |
| 170 | Winterhaven Dr, **S** Rivers Edge RV Park |
| 166 | CA 186, Algodones Rd, Andrade, **S** to Mexico |
| 165mm | CA Insp/weigh Sta |
| 164 | Sidewinder Rd, **N** st patrol, **S gas:** Shell/LP, **other:** Pilot Knob RV Park |
| 159 | CA 34, Ogilby Rd, to Blythe |
| 156 | Grays Well Rd, **N** Imperial Dunes RA |
| 155mm | **rest area both lanes (exits left), portapotties, 🚻, litter barrels, petwalk** |
| 151 | Gordons Well |
| 146 | Brock Research Ctr Rd |
| 143 | CA 98, to Calexico, Midway Well |
| 131 | CA 115, VanDerLinden Rd, to Holtville, 5 mi **N** gas, food, lodging, RV camping |
| 128 | Bonds Corner Rd |
| 125 | Orchard Rd, Holtville, 4 mi **N** gas/dsl, food |
| 120 | Bowker Rd |
| 118b a | CA 111, to Calexico, 1 mi **N gas:** Shell/dsl/café/scales, **other:** RV park, tires/truckwash |
| 116 | Dogwood Rd, **S food:** Arby's, Carino's, Chili's, Chuck-eCheese, Denny's, Famous Dave's BBQ, Jack-in-the-Box, Starbucks, Taco Bell, **lodging:** Fairfield Inn, **other:** Best Buy, Dillard's, JC Penney, Macy's, Marshall's, Old Navy, Ross, Sears/auto, Staples, mall |
| 115 | CA 86, 4th St, El Centro, **N gas:** Arco/24hr, Chevron, Citgo/7-11/dsl, Shell/dsl, **food:** Carl's Jr, China Express, Exotic Thai, Jack-in-the-Box, Mexicali Taco, McDonald's, **lodging:** Holiday Inn Express, Motel 6, **other:** El Sol Foods, Firestone/auto, Goodyear/auto, Ford/Lincoln/Mercury, U-Haul, radiators, **S gas:** On the Go/Subway, **food:** Dudley's, IHOP, In-n-Out, Millie's Kitchen, Taco Bell, **lodging:** Best Western, Comfort Inn, Rodeway Inn, **other:** AutoZone, Buick/Cadillac/Pontiac, Chevrolet, Chrysler/Dodge/Jeep, Home Depot, Honda, Lucky Foods, Desert Trails RV Park |
| 114 | Imperial Ave, El Centro, **N gas:** Chevron/service, Citgo/7-11/dsl, Shell, USA/dsl, **food:** Del Taco, Denny's, |

**CA**

E ↑
↓
W

## INTERSTATE 8 CONT'D

**114** Continued
Domino's, KFC, McDonald's, Pizza Hut, Scribble's Rest, TasteeFreez Burgers, **lodging:** Howard Johnson, Laguna Inn, Ramada Inn, Vacation Inn/RV Park, **other:** Kragen Parts, st patrol, **1-3 mi N gas:** Arco/24hr, **food:** Applebee's, Burger King, Carl's Jr, Carrow's, Church's, Domino's, El Pollo Loco, Farmer Boys, Golden Corral, Jack-in-the-Box, Little Caesars, Papa John's, Pizza Hut, Popeye's, Quizno's, Rally's, Sizzler, Sonic, Starbucks, Subway, Taco Bell, Wendy's, **lodging:** Day's Inn, Super Star Inn, **other:** Aamco, America's Tire, BigLots, Costco/gas, Food4Less, Goodyear/auto, K-Mart, Kragen Parts, Lowe's Whse, PepBoys, Rite Aid, Sears/auto, Staples, Target, Toyota, Von's Foods, Walgreens, Walmart SuperCtr Winston Tire

**111** Forrester Rd, to Westmorland

**108mm** Sunbeam Rest Area both lanes, full ♿ facilities, 📞, 🚾, litter barrels, petwalk, RV dump

**107** Drew Rd, Seeley, **N** Sunbeam RV Park, **S** Rio Bend RV Park

**101** Dunaway Rd, Imperial Valley, elev 0 ft, **N** st prison

**89** Imperial Hwy, CA 98, Ocotillo, **N food:** Old Hwy Cafe, USPO, **S gas:** Texaco/dsl, **food:** Desert Kitchen, **other:** auto repair, RV camping, museum

**87** CA 98 (from eb), to Calexico

**81mm** runaway truck ramp, eb

**80** Mountain Springs Rd

**77** **N** phone, towing

**75mm** brake insp area eb, 📞

**73** Jacumba, **S gas:** Shell/Subway/dsl/towing/24hr, Valero/dsl, **other:** RV camping

**65** CA 94, Boulevard, to Campo, **S gas:** MtnTop/dsl, **food:** Salsa Linda, **lodging:** Lux Inn, **other:** auto repair, to McCain Valley RA

**63mm** Tecate Divide, elev 4140 ft

**62mm** Crestwood Summit, elev 4190 ft

**61** Crestwood Rd, Live Oak Springs, **S gas:** Golden Acorn Trkstp/casino/dsl, **food:** Country Broiler Rest., **lodging:** Live Oak Sprs Country Inn, **other:** Outdoor World RV Camp, info

**54** Kitchen Creek Rd, Cameron Station, **S** food, RV camping

**51** rd 1, Buckman Spgs Rd, to Lake Morena, **S** gas/dsl/LP, food, lodging, RV camping, Lake Morena CP (7mi), Potrero CP (19mi), **rest area both lanes, full** ♿ **facilities,** 📞, 🚾, **litter barrels, petwalk, RV dump**

**48** inp sta, wb

**47** rd 1, Sunrise Hwy, Laguna Summit, elev 4055 ft, **N** to Laguna Mtn RA

**45** Pine Valley, Julian, **N food:** Frosty Burger, Major's Diner, El Rancho Grande Diner, **lodging:** Pine Valley Inn, **other:** Curves, Mtn SuperMkt, to Cuyamaca Rancho SP, vet

**44mm** Pine Valley Creek

**42mm** elev 4000 ft

**40** CA 79, Japatul Rd, Descanso, **N food:** Descanso Rest., **other:** to Cuyamaca Rancho SP

**37mm** vista point eb, elev 3000 ft

**36** E Willows, **N** Alpine Sprs RV Park, Viejas Indian Res, casino

**E L C A J O N**

**33** W Willows Rd, to Alpine, **N** Alpine Sprs RV Park, Viejas Outlets/famous brands, casino, same as 36, **S** ranger sta

**31mm** elev 2000 ft

**30** Tavern Rd, to Alpine, **N gas:** Chevron/dsl, Valero, **S gas:** 76/Circle K, Shell, **food:** Breadbasket Rest., Carl's Jr, China Flavor, La Carreta Mexican, Mediterranean Grill, Subway, **lodging:** Ayer's Inn, **other:** Alpine Mkt Foods, Radio Shack, Rite Aid, TrueValue, city park

**27** Dunbar Lane, Harbison Canyon, **N other:** RV camping, Flinn Sprgs CP

**25mm** elev 1000 ft

**24mm** no services, 📞

**23** Lake Jennings Pk Rd, Lakeside, **N gas:** Arco/Jack-in-the-Box/dsl/24hr, to Lake Jennings CP, **other:** RV camping, **S gas:** 7-11, **food:** Burger King, Karla's Mexican, Marechiaro's Pizza

**22** Los Coches Rd, Lakeside, **N gas:** Eagle/dsl/LP, 7-11, Valero, **food:** Laposta Mexican, Las Cazuela's, Pizza Pan, **other:** RV camping/dump, **S gas:** Shell/dsl, **food:** Denny's, Giant Pizza, McDonald's, Panda Express, Subway, Taco Bell, **other:** Radio Shack, Von's Foods, Walmart/auto

**20b** Greenfield Dr, to Crest, **N gas:** Chevron/dsl, Exxon/dsl/24hr, **food:** Jack-in-the-Box, Janet's Café, McDonald's, Panchos Taco, **other:** H HOSPITAL, Albertson's, Curves, Ford, 99¢ Store, RV camping, 7-11, auto repair, st patrol, **S gas:** Mobil/LP

**20a** E Main St (from wb, no EZ return), **N lodging:** Embasadora Motel, Fabulous 7 Motel, HP Inn, **other:** Ford, Vactioner RV Park, **S gas:** Arco, **other:** Cadillac

**19** 2nd St, CA 54, El Cajon, **N gas:** Arco/24hr, Chevron, Exxon/dsl, **food:** Mariachio's Pizza, Rosanna Grilled Panini, **other:** CVS Drug, Parts+, Von's Foods, **S gas:** 76, Gas Depot, Shell, **food:** A&W/KFC, Arby's, Boll Weevil Rest., Burger King, Carl's Jr, DQ, Estrada's Mexican, IHOP, Jack-in-the-Box, KFC, McDonald's, Pizza Hut, Subway, Taco Bell, Taco Shop/24hr, Tyler's Rest., **other:** Firestone/auto, Jiffy Lube, PetCo, Ralph's Foods, Radio Shack, Rite Aid, Walgreens

**18** Mollison Ave, El Cajon, **N gas:** Chevron, **food:** Denny's, **lodging:** Best Western, Days Inn, **S gas:** Arco/24hr, KwikTrip/dsl, **food:** Taco Bell, **lodging:** Super 8, Valley Motel

**17c** Magnolia Ave, CA 67 (from wb), to Santee, **N food:** Del Taco, Jack-in-the-Box, LJ Silver, Panda Express, **other:** Arco, Food4Less, Target, mall, **S gas:** Shell/service, **food:** Red Brick Pizza, Wienerschnitzel, **lodging:** Motel 6, Northgate Motel, Rodeway Inn, **other:** Nudo's Drug

**17b** CA 67 (from eb), same as 17 a&c

**17a** Johnson Ave (from eb), **N food:** Applebee's, Boston Mkt, Burger King, Jamba Juice, KFC, LJ Silver, On the Border, Rubio's, Sizzler, Subway, **other:** Albertson's, Best Buy, Border's Books, Chevrolet, $Tree, Home Depot, Honda, JC Penney, K-Mart, Long Drug, Macy's, Marshall's, Michael's, Office Depot, PetsMart, Rite Aid, Sears/auto, Walmart, mall, **S other:** Aamco, Isuzu, Saturn

**16** Main St, **N gas:** Arco/24hr, **food:** Denny's/24hr, 7-11, Sombrero Mexican, **lodging:** Relax Inn, **S gas:** 76/RV Dump, Chevron, **other:** Nissan, brakes/transmissions

## INTERSTATE 8 CONT'D

**E ← → W  EL CAJON   SAN DIEGO AREA**

**15** El Cajon Blvd (from eb), **N lodging:** Quality Inn, **S gas:** Mobil/dsl, Shell, **food:** BBQ, **other:** Chrysler

**14c** Severin Dr, Fuerte Dr (from wb), **N gas:** Arco/24hr, Mobil, **food:** Anthony's Fish Rest., Charcoal House Rest., La Casa Blanca, **lodging:** Holiday Inn Express, **S food:** Brigantine Seafood Rest.

**14b a** CA 125, to CA 94

**13b** Jackson Dr, Grossmont Blvd, **N gas:** Chevron, **food:** Arby's, BJ's Grill, Casa de Pico, Chili's, ClaimJumper, Fuddrucker's, Jamba Juice, McDonald's, Panda Express, Panera Bread, Red Lobster, Rubio's, **other:** Barnes&Noble, Chrysler/Jeep/Dodge, Dodge, Kragen Parts, Long's Drug, Macy's, 7-11, Staples, Target, Walmart, mall, **S food:** Honeybaked Ham, Jack-in-the-Box, **other:** Circuit City, Discount Tire, Firestone/auto, Ford, Hyundai, Ralph's Foods, Ross, VW

**13a** Spring St (from eb), El Cajon Blvd (from wb), **N other:** Dodge/Kia, Jeep, **S food:** La Salsa Mexican, **lodging:** La Mesa Lodge, **other:** 99¢ Store

**12** Fletcher Pkwy, to La Mesa, **N gas:** Shell, **food:** Baker's Square, Carl's Jr., Chipotle Mexican, McDonald's, **lodging:** EZ 8 Motel, Holiday Inn, **other:** Costco, 7-11, **S food:** La Salsa Mexican, **lodging:** Motel 6, **other:** Chevrolet, San Diego RV Resort

**11** 70th St, Lake Murray Blvd, **N gas:** Shell, **food:** Subway, **other:** truck/RV repair, **S gas:** Shell/dsl/repair, **food:** Aiken's Deli, Denny's, Marie Callender's, **other:** H HOSPITAL

**10** College Ave, **N gas:** Chevron/dsl, **other:** Windmill Farms Mkt, **S other:** H HOSPITAL, to San Diego St U

**9** Waring Rd, **N food:** Nicolosi's Italian, **lodging:** Days Inn, Quality Inn

**8** Fairmont Ave (7 from eb), to Mission Gorge Rd, **N gas:** Arco/24hr, Mobil/dsl, Valero/dsl, **food:** Arby's, Burger King, Carl's Jr, Chili's, El Pollo Loco, Jack-in-the-Box, El Pollo Loco, KFC, McDonald's, Rally's, Starbucks, Subway, Szechuan Chinese, **lodging:** Super 8, **other:** H HOSPITAL, Aamco, Discount Tire, Home Depot, Honda, Longs Drugs, NAPA, Radio Shack, Rite Aid, Toyota, Tuesday Morning, Von's Foods

**7b a** I-15 N, CA 15 S, to 40th St

**6b** I-805, N to LA, S to Chula Vista

**6a** Texas St, Qualcomm Way, **N food:** Dave&Buster's, same as 5

**5** Mission Ctr Rd, **N gas:** Chevron, **food:** Chevy's Mexican, Fuddrucker's, Hooters, In-n-Out, King's Fishouse, Mimi's Cafe, On The Border, Outback Steaks, Pick-Up Sticks, Taco Bell, **lodging:** Marriott, **other:** Best Buy, Borders Books&Café, Chevrolet, Ford, Lincoln/Mercury, Macy's, Marshall's, Michael's, Nordstrom Rack, Old Navy, Macy's, Staples, Target, mall, **S gas:** Arco/24hr, **food:** Benihana, Denny's, El Torito, Fugi Japanese Steaks, Todai Rest., Wendy's, **lodging:** Comfort Inn, Hilton, La Quinta, Radisson, Ramada Ltd, Red Lion Inn, Sheraton, **other:** Chrysler, Dodge, GMC/Pontiac, Hummer, Mazda, Subaru

**4c b** CA 163, Cabrillo Frwy, **S** to downtown, zoo

**4a** Hotel Circle Dr (from eb), CA 163 (from wb)

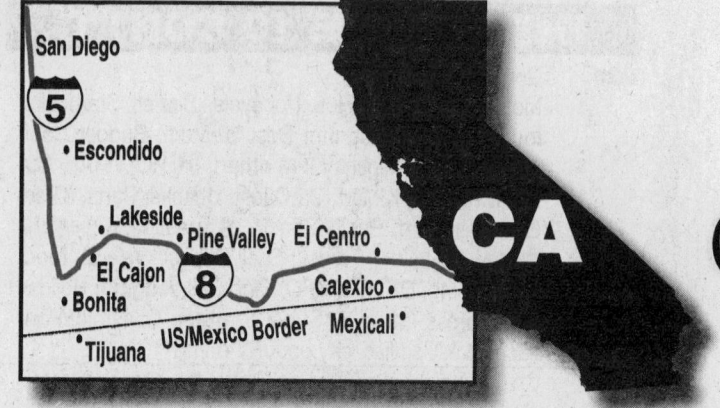

**3a** Hotel Circle, Taylor St, **N gas:** Chevron, **food:** DW Ranch Rest., Hunter Steaks, Kelly's Steaks, **lodging:** Comfort Suites, Crowne Plaza, Handlery Hotel, Motel 6, Town&Country Motel, **other:** AAA, cinema, golf, **S gas:** Chevron, **food:** Adam's Cafe, Albie's Rest., Ricky's Rest., Tickled Trout, Valley Kitchen, **lodging:** Best Western, Comfort Inn, Days Inn, DoubleTree Inn, Extended Stay America, Hawthorn Suites, Hilton, Holiday Inn, Howard Johnson, King's Inn/rest., Mission Valley Hotel, Quality Resort, Ramada Inn, Residence Inn, Super 8, Travelodge, Vagabond Inn

**2c** Morena Blvd (from wb)

**2b** I-5, N to LA, S to San Diego

**2a** Rosecrans St (from wb), CA 209, **S gas:** Chevron, **food:** Burger King, Del Taco, In-n-Out, McDonald's, Perry's Café, Rally's, **lodging:** Best Western, Day's Inn, Holiday Inn, Howard Johnson, Quality Inn, Super 8, **other:** Chrysler/Jeep, Circuit City, Goodyear/auto, House of Fabrics, Staples, SaveOn Drug

**1** W Mission Bay Blvd, Sports Arena Blvd (from wb), **N** to SeaWorld, **S gas:** Arco, **food:** Arby's, Denny's, Jack-in-the-Box, McDonald's, Souplantation, Taco Shop, Wendy's, **lodging:** Holiday Inn Express, Premier Inn, **other:** Curves, Home Depot, U-Haul

**0mm** I-8 begins/ends on Sunset Cliffs Blvd, **N** Mission Bay Park, 1/4 mi **W gas:** Exxon, Shell, **food:** Jack-in-the-Box, Kaiserhof Cafe

## INTERSTATE 10

| Exit # | Services |
|---|---|
| **245mm** | California/Arizona state line, Colorado River, *Pacific/Mountain time zone* |
| **244mm** | inspection sta wb |
| **243** | Riviera Dr, **S other:** Riviera RV Camp |
| **241** | US 95, Intake Blvd, Blythe, **N gas:** Mobil/dsl, **food:** Lalo's Mexican, Steaks'n Cakes Rest., Sunset Grille, **lodging:** Best Western, Days Inn, Desert Winds Motel, Travelers Inn Express, **other:** Burton's RV Park, auto/RV repair/24hr, to Needles, **S** McIntyre Park |
| **240** | 7th St, **N gas:** Chevron/service, EZ Mart, **food:** Blimpie, Foster's Freeze, Starbucks, **lodging:** Astro Motel, Blue Line Motel, Blythe Inn, Budget Inn, Comfort Suites, Dunes Motel, **other:** Albertson's, AutoZone, Chrysler/Dodge/Jeep, Ford, Rite Aid, RV repair/LP |
| **239** | Lovekin Blvd, Blythe, **N gas:** Mobil/Subs/dsl, Shell/Quizno's, **food:** Carl's Jr, Del Taco, Domino's, El Ranchito Mexican, Jack-in-the-Box, La Casita Dos Mexican, |

## INTERSTATE 10 CONT'D

**E ↕ W**

**239** Continued
McDonald's, Pizza Hut, Popeye's, Sizzler, Starbucks, **lodging:** Best Value Inn, Best Western, Budget Host, Hampton Inn, Regency Inn, **other:** H HOSPITAL, Ace Hardware, Big K Mart, CarQuest, Checker Parts, $Tree, Goodyear/auto, Radio Shack, **S gas:** Arco/dsl/24hr, Chevron/dsl/24hr, 76/dsl, Shell/DQ/dsl, Valero, **food:** Burger King, Denny's, KFC, Taco Bell, **lodging:** Holiday Inn Express, Motel 6, Super 8, **other:** Chevrolet/Pontiac/Buick/Cadillac, city park/RV dump

**236** CA 78, Neighbours Blvd, to Ripley, **N gas:** Valero/service, **S** to Cibola NWR

**232** Mesa Dr, **N gas:** 76/dsl/rest./24hr/@, Valero/dsl

**231** weigh sta wb

**222mm** Wileys Well Rd, **N** rest area both lanes, full ♿ facilities, 🚻, 🏕, litter barrels, petwalk, **S** to st prison

**217** Ford Dry Lake Rd

**201** Corn Springs Rd

**192** CA 177, Rice Rd, to Lake Tamarisk, **N gas:** gas/repair/24hr, **food:** Desert Ctr Cafe, **other:** camping

**189** Eagle Mtn Rd

**182** Red Cloud Rd

**177** Hayfield Rd

**173** Chiriaco Summit, **N gas:** Chevron/Foster's Freez/dsl/24hr, **food:** Chiriaco Rest, **other:** Patton Museum, truck/tire repair

**168** to Twentynine Palms, to Mecca, Joshua Tree NM

**162** frontage rd

**159mm** Cactus City Rest Area both lanes, full ♿ facilities, 🏕 litter barrels, petwalk

**147mm** 0 ft elevation

**146** Dillon Rd, to CA 86, to CA 111 S, Coachella, **N gas:** Chevron/24hr, Loves/Carl's Jr/dsl/24hr/@, **S gas:** TA/Arby's/Arco/Taco Bell/dsl/24hr/@, Shell/Jack-in-the-Box, **other:** Spotlight Casino

**145** (from eb), CA 86 S

**144** CA 111 N, CA 86 S, Indio, **N food:** Nuevo Paraiso Rest., **lodging:** Holiday Inn Express, **other:** Classic RV Park, Fantasy Sprgs Casino/Hotel/Cafe

**143** Jackson St, Indio, **N** RV Park, **S** Circle K

**142** Monroe St, Central Indio, **N other:** RV camping, **S gas:** Circle K, 76, Shell/dsl/LP, **food:** Marisco's Mexican, Mexicali Cafe, **lodging:** Quality Inn

**139** Jefferson St, Indio Blvd, **N other:** Shadow Hills RV Resort, hwy patrol

**137** Washington St, Country Club Dr, to Indian Wells, **N gas:** Arco/24hr, Chevron, **food:** Burger King, Burger Time, Coco's, Del Taco, Mario's Italian, Starbucks, **lodging:** Comfort Suites, Motel 6, **other:** Buick/Pontiac/GMC, Ford/Lincoln/Mercury, Giant RV Ctr, Honda, Toyota/Scion, Rite Aid, Stater Bro's, Walgreens, **S gas:** Mobil/dsl, 76/Circle K, **food:** Carl's Jr, China Wok, La Tacita Mexican, Lili's Chinese, Pizza Hut, Quizno's, Subway, Togo's, Wendy's, **lodging:** Embassy Suites, **other:** Goodyear/auto

**134** Cook St, to Indian Wells, **S gas:** Arco, Mobil, **food:** Applebees, Jack-in-the-Box, Starbucks, **lodging:** Courtyard, Hampton Inn, Hilton/Homewood Suites, Residence Inn

**I N D I O**

**131** Monterey Ave, Thousand Palms, **N gas:** Arco/24hr, **food:** Jack-in-the-Box, **S food:** Del Taco, El Pollo Loco, IHOP, McDonald's, Panda Express, Quizno's, Starbucks, Subway, Taco Bell, **other:** America's Tire, Costco/gas, Home Depot, PetsMart, Sam's Club/gas, Walmart SuperCtr

**130** Ramon Rd, Bob Hope Dr, **N gas:** Chevron/24hr, ⊕FLYING J/dsl/LP/rest./24hr, Mobil/dsl, Valero, **food:** Carl's Jr, Casa de Pasta, Del Taco, Denny's, Guerro Mexican, In-n-Out, McDonald's, **lodging:** Red Roof Inn, **other:** truckwash, **S food:** Sage Grill, Steak House, **other:** H HOSPITAL, Agua Caliente Casino/rest.

**126** Date Palm Dr, Rancho Mirage, **S gas:** Arco/24hr, Mobil, Valero, **food:** Domino's

**123** Gene Autry Tr, Palm Dr, to Desert Hot Sprgs, **N gas:** Arco, Chevron/Jack-in-the-Box, **other:** Caliente Springs Camping, **3 mi S** to Gene Autry Trail

**120** Indian Ave, to N Palm Sprgs, **N gas:** 76/Circle K, Shell, **food:** Denny's, **lodging:** Motel 6, **S gas:** Chevron, Pilot/DQ/Wendy's/dsl/24hr, **food:** Jack-in-the-Box, **other:** H HOSPITAL, Bud's Tire

**117** CA 62, to Yucca Valley, Twentynine Palms, to Joshua Tree NM

**114** Whitewater, many windmills

**113mm** rest area both lanes, full ♿ facilities, 🚻, 🏕, litter barrels

**112** CA 111 (from eb), to Palm Springs

**110** Hugeen-Lehmann

**106** Main St, to Cabazon, **N gas:** Shell/dsl, **food:** Burger King, Spanky's BBQ, Wheel Inn Rest., **S gas:** Arco/dsl/24hr

**104** Cabazon, same as 103

**103** Fields Rd, **N gas:** Chevron, TC/A&W/dsl, **food:** McDonald's, Ruby's Diner, **other:** Hadley Fruit Orchards, Premium Outlets/famous brands, Morongo Reservation/casino

**102.5mm** Banning weigh sta both lanes

**102** Ramsey St (from wb)

**101** Hargrave St, Banning, **N gas:** 76/Church's, Shell/dsl/LP, Valero, **lodging:** Country Inn, **other:** tires

**100** CA 243, 8th St, Banning, **N gas:** Chevron, **food:** Ahloo Chinese, IHOP, Jack-in-the-Box, **other:** Rite Aid, **S other:** RV camping

**99** 22nd St, to Ramsey St, **N gas:** Arco/24hr, Shell, **food:** Carl's Jr, Carrow's, Chelo's Tacos, Del Taco, KFC, McDonald's, Pepe's Mexican, Pizza Hut, Sizzler, Starbucks, Subway, Wall Chinese, **lodging:** Day's Inn, Super 8, Travelodge, **other:** Chrysler/Jeep/Dodge, Ford, Goodyear/auto

**98** Sunset Ave, Banning, **N gas:** Chevron/dsl, **food:** Domino's, Gramma's Kitchen, Gus Jr #7 Burger, **other:** Ace Hardware, AutoZone, BigLots, Chevrolet/Buick/Pontiac/GMC, Radio Shack, Ray's RV Ctr, Rio Ranch Mkt, Rite Aid, vet

**96** Highland Springs Ave, **N gas:** Arco/24hr, Chevron, Valero/dsl, **food:** Applebee's, Burger King, Denny's, Farmhouse Rest., Jack-in-the-Box, Orchid, Papa John's, Pizza Run, Subway, Wendy's, **lodging:** Hampton Inn, **other:** H HOSPITAL, Ace Hardware, Food4Less, Kragen Parts, NAPA, Radio Shack, Stater Bros Foods, Walgreens, **S gas:** Mobil, **food:** Baskin-Robbins, Carl's

**P A L M S P R I N G S**

**B A N N I N G**

# INTERSTATE 10 CONT'D

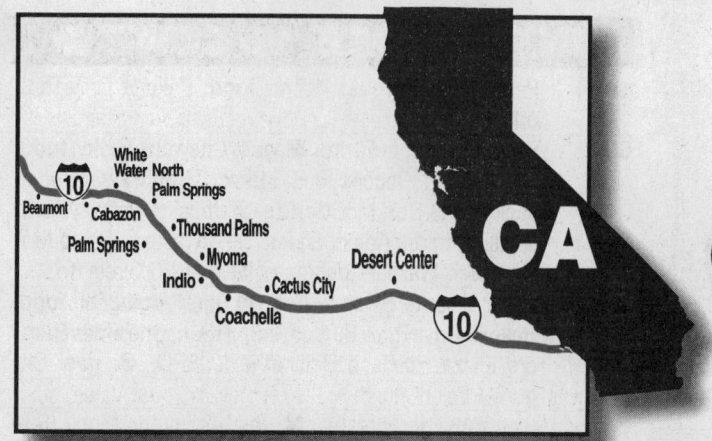

| | |
|---|---|
| **BEAUMONT** | |

**96** Continued
Jr, Chili's, McDonald's, **other:** Albertson's, Best Buy, BK RV Ctr, Home Depot, K-Mart, Kohls, Rite Aid, Ross, Staples, Walmart SuperCtr, hwy patrol

**95** Pennsylvania Ave, Beaumont, **N gas:** Circle K, **food:** ABC Rest., Rusty Lantern Rest., **lodging:** Windsor Motel, **other:** Miller RV Ctr, Tom's RV Ctr

**94** CA 79, Beaumont, **N gas:** 76, Thrifty Gas, **food:** Baker's DriveThru, McDonald's, El Rancho Steaks, Popeye's, YumYum Donuts/24hr, **lodging:** Best Western, Best Value Inn, **other:** Auto Value, NAPA, **S food:** Del Taco, Denny's, **other:** RV camping

**93** CA 60 W, to Riverside

**92** San Timoteo Canyon Rd, Oak Valley Pkwy, **N lodging:** Holiday Inn Express, **other:** Rite Aid, golf, **S** golf

**91mm** rest area wb, full ♿ facilities, 📞 🏕, litter barrels, petwalk

**90** Cherry Valley Blvd, truck/tire repair

**89** Singleton Rd (from wb), to Calimesa

**88** Calimesa Blvd, **N gas:** Arco/24hr, Chevron/dsl, Shell, **food:** Best Wok, Burger King, McDonald's, Subway, Taco Bell, **lodging:** Calimesa Inn, **other:** Stater Bros Foods, **S food:** Big Boy, Jack-in-the-Box

**87** County Line Rd, to Yucaipa, **N gas:** FasTrip/gas, Shell/dsl, **food:** Baker's DriveThru, Del Taco, **other:** auto repair/tires

**86mm** Wildwood Rest Area eb, full ♿ facilities, 📞 🏕, litter barrels, petwalk

**85** Live Oak Canyon Rd, Oak Glen

**83** Yucaipa Blvd, **N gas:** Arco/dsl/24hr, Chevron, **food:** Baker's DriveThru

**82** Wabash Ave (from wb)

**81** Redlands Blvd, Ford St, **S gas:** 76

**80** Cypress Ave, University St, **N** Ⓗ HOSPITAL, to U of Redlands

**79b a** CA 38, 6th St, Orange St, Redlands, **N gas:** Chevron, **food:** Redland Rest., **lodging:** Budget Inn, Stardust Motel, **other:** Goodyear, Stater Bros Foods, **S gas:** 76, Shell, **food:** Chipotle Mexican, Denny's, Open Kitchen Chinese, Rubio's, Togo's, Trader Joe's, Starbucks, **other:** Albertson's, Buick/GMC, Kragen Parts, Lincoln/Mercury, NAPA, Office Depot, Von's Foods

**77c** (77b from wb) Tennessee St, **N food:** Shakey's Pizza, **other:** Home Depot, **S gas:** Shell, **food:** Arby's, Bakers DriveThru, Burger King, Carl's Jr, Coco's, El Pollo Loco, Papa John's, Subway, Taco Bell, **lodging:** Best Western, Comfort Suites, Dynasty Suites, **other:** Ford, Tri-City Mall, USPO

**77b** (77c from wb) CA 30, to Highlands, **S** to Tri-City Mall

**77a** Alabama St, **N food:** Chili's, Chick-fil-A, Denny's, Famous Dave's BBQ, Hawaiian BBQ, Jamba Juice, Macaroni Grill, Mr. Tortilla, Red Robin, Starbucks, **lodging:** Courtyard, Red Lands Motel, Super 8, TownePlace Suites, **other:** Barnes&Noble, Ford, JC Penney, Jo-Ann Superstore, Marshall's, Michael's, PetCo, Target, VW, U-Haul, **S gas:** Arco, Chevron, Flagg, Shell, **food:** Comfort Suites, Del Taco, IHOP, McDonald's, Nick's Burgers, Quizno's, Slim's BBQ, Starbucks, Zabella's Mexican,

| | |
|---|---|
| **SAN BERNADINO** | |

**77a** Continued
**lodging:** Best Western, Country Inn&Suites, GoodNite Inn, **other:** Aamco, Chief Parts, Chevrolet, Goodyear/auto, Hyundai, K-Mart, Longs Drug, Nissan, PepBoys, Pic'n Sav Foods, Ross, Toyota, Tri-City Mall

**76** California St, **N other:** funpark, museum, **S gas:** Arco/24hr, Shell/LP/24hr, **food:** Applebee's, Jack-in-the-Box, Jose's Mexican, Panda Express, Subway, Weinerschnitzel, Wendy's, **other:** Food4Less, Just Tires, Radio Shack, Walmart/auto, RV camping

**75** Mountain View Ave, Loma Linda, **N gas:** Valero/dsl, **S food:** Domino's, FarmerBoys Burgers, Lupe's Mexican, Subway

**74** Tippecanoe Ave, Anderson St, **N gas:** Thrifty Gas, **food:** Chipotle Mexican, Denny's, Elephant Bar Rest., El Pollo Loco, In-n-Out, Jack-in-the-Box, Jamba Juice, Pick-Up Stix, Starbucks, Wendy's, **lodging:** American Inn, Fairfield Inn, Residence Inn, **other:** Costco/gas, Sam's Club, Staples, **S gas:** 76/dsl, **food:** Baker's DriveThru, Del Taco, HomeTown Buffet, KFC, Napoli Italian, Taco Bell, Wienerschnitzel, **other:** Audi, Harley-Davidson, Honda, Jaguar, Porsche, Saab, Saturn, transmissions, to Loma Linda U

**73b a** Waterman Ave, **N gas:** 76, Shell/dsl/24hr, **food:** Baja Fresh, Black Angus, Chili's, ChuckeCheese, ClaimJumper, Coco's, Crabby Bob's, El Torito, Guadala-Harry's Diner, IHOP/24hr, King Buffet, Lotus Garden Chinese, Mimi's Café, Olive Garden, Outback Steaks, Panda Express, Pat&Oscar's, Red Lobster, Sizzler, Starbucks, TGIFriday, Togo's, Yamazato Japanese, **lodging:** Best Western, Comfort Inn, Hilton, La Quinta, Quality Inn, Super 8, **other:** Best Buy, Circuit City, Home Depot, Office Depot, PetsMart, **S gas:** Arco/24hr, Beacon/dsl/rest., **food:** Baker's Driv-Thru, Burger King, Gus Jr Burger #8, McDonald's, Popeye's, Starbucks, Taco Bell, **lodging:** Motel 6, **other:** Camping World RV Service/supplies, La Mesa RV Ctr

**72** I-215, CA 91

**71** Mt Vernon Ave, Sperry Ave, **N gas:** Arco/24hr, **food:** Peppersteak Rest., **lodging:** Colony Inn, **other:** brake/muffler, repair

**70b** 9th St, **N gas:** Mobil, **food:** Baskin-Robbins, Burger King, Denny's, KFC, McDonald's, P&G's Burgers, Subway, Taco Bell, **lodging:** Hampton Inn, **other:** Parts+, Stater Bros Foods

**70a** Rancho Ave, **N food:** Del Taco, Jack-in-the-Box, KFC/Taco Bell, Wienerschnitzel

CA

S A N B E R N A D I N O

## INTERSTATE 10 CONT'D

**69** Pepper Dr, **N gas:** Valero, **food:** Baker's DriveThru, **other:** Ford

**68** Riverside Ave, to Rialto, **N gas:** Chevron, Thrifty, **food:** Burger King, Coco's, El Pollo Loco, HomeTown Buffet, Jack-in-the-Box, McDonald's, Starbucks, Subway, Taco Joe's, **lodging:** American Inn, Best Western, Rialto Motel, **other:** Walmart, dsl repair, **S gas:** 76/Circle K

**66** Cedar Ave, to Bloomington, **N gas:** Arco/24hr, **food:** Baker's DriveThru, Burger King, DQ, FarmerBoys Burgers, Pizza Hut/Taco Bell, **other:** USPO, **S gas:** Citgo/7-11

**64** Sierra Ave, to Fontana, **N gas:** Arco/24hr, Mobil, Texaco, **food:** Applebee's, Arby's, Billy J's Rest., Burger King, ChuckeyCheese, DQ, Denny's, Del Taco, El Giro Mexican, In-n-Out, Jack-in-the-Box, KFC, McDonald's, Millie's Kitchen, Papa John's, Pizza Hut/Taco Bell, Popeye's, Sizzler, Subway, 3 Hermanos, Wendy's, Wienerschnitzel, **lodging:** Comfort Inn, Econolodge, Guest House Inn, Motel 6, **other:** H HOSPITAL, Aamco, Albertson's, BigLots, Chevrolet, $Tree, Food4Less, Goodyear/auto, Honda/GMC, Kia, KidsRUs, K-Mart, Kragen Parts, Mazda, Nissan, PepBoys, Pic'n Sav Foods, Radio Shack, Rite Aid, SavOn Drug, Stater Bros Foods, Winston Tire, **S food:** China Buffet, Circle K/24hr, Fosters Freeze, Nogales Burgers, **other:** Ross, Target

**63** Citrus Ave, **N gas:** Beacon/gas, 76, **food:** Baker's Drive Thru, Taqueria Mexican, **other:** Ford

**61** Cherry Ave, **N gas:** Arco/24hr, Chevron/Taco Bell/dsl, Trucktown Trkstp/dsl/24hr/@, **food:** Carl's Jr, **lodging:** Circle Inn Motel, **other:** Ford Trucks, **S gas:** North American Trkstp/dsl, 3 Sisters Trkstp/dsl/@, 76/Circle K, **food:** Farmer Boy's Rest., Mariscos Mexican, **other:** Peterbilt

**59** Etiwanda Ave, Valley Blvd

**58b a** I-15, N to Barstow, S to San Diego

**57** Milliken Ave, **N gas:** Arco, Chevron, Mobil/Subway/dsl, 76/Del Taco/dsl, Shell/dsl, **food:** Baja Fresh, Burger King, Carl's Jr, Coco's, CoffeeBean, Cucina Italian, Dave&Buster's, Del Taco, Denny's, Fazoli's, FoodCourt, In-n-Out, Jack-in-the-Box, McDonald's, NY Grill, Outback Steaks, RainForest Café, Rubio's Rest., Tokyo Wako Japanese, Wendy's, Wienerschnitzel, Wolfgang Puck Café, **lodging:** AmeriSuites, Ayers Suites, Country Suites, Hampton Inn, **other:** America's Tire, Carmax, JC Penney, Jo-Ann Crafts, Sam's Club, mall, **S gas:** TA/76/Subway/Taco Bell/dsl/rest./24hr/@, **other:** RV Ctr

**56** Haven Ave, Rancho Cucamonga, **N gas:** Mobil, Benihana, **food:** Black Angus, Crabby Bob's Seafood, El Torito, Quizno's, Tony Roma, **lodging:** Best Western, Extended Stay America, Hilton, Holiday Inn, La Quinta, **S food:** Panda Chinese, TGIFriday, **lodging:** Fairfield Inn

**55b a** Holt Blvd, to Archibald Ave, **N gas:** Arco, Mobil/dsl, **food:** Baker's Drive-thru, Weinerschnitzel

**54** Vineyard Ave, **N gas:** 76/Circle K, Shell, **food:** Del Taco, Carl's Jr, One-Dollar Chinese, Pizza Hut/Taco Bell, Popeye's, Quizno's, Rocky's Foods, Sizzler, **other:** AutoZone, Chief Parts, Ralph's Foods, Rite Aid, Stater Bros Foods, **S gas:** Arco/24hr, Mobil, Shell, USA Gas, **food:** Circle K, Cowboy Bugers, Denny's, In-n-Out, Marie

**54** Continued

Calender, Michael J's Rest., Rosa's Italian, Spires Rest., Yoshinoya Japanese, Wendy's, **lodging:** Ayers Suites, Best Western, Comfort Inn, Country Suites, Countryside Suites, DoubleTree Inn, Express Inn, GoodNite Inn, Ramada Ltd, Red Roof Inn, Residence Inn, Sheraton, Super 8, **other:** Chevrolet/Cadillac

**53** San Bernardino Ave, 4th St, to Ontario, **N gas:** Arco, Chevron, Circle K, Shell, **food:** Baskin-Robbins, Burger King, Carl's Jr, Del Taco, Jack-in-the-Box, Popeye's, Sizzler, Taco Bell/24hr, **lodging:** Motel 6, Quality Inn, **other:** Chief Parts, K-Mart, Radio Shack, Ralph's Foods, Rite Aid, **S gas:** Arco/24hr, 76, **food:** Alfredo's Mexican, Denny's, KFC, McDonald's, Pizza Hut, YumYum Donuts, **lodging:** CA Inn, Travelodge, West Coast Inn

**51** CA 83, Euclid Ave, to Ontario, Upland, **N food:** Coco's Rest., **other:** H HOSPITAL

**50** Mountain Ave, to Mt Baldy, **N gas:** Arco, Chevron, Mobil, Shell/dsl, **food:** BBQ, Carrow's, Denny's, El Burrito, El Torito, Green Burrito, Happy Wok Chinese, Mimi's Café, Mi Taco, Subway, Trader Joe's, Wendy's, **lodging:** Super 8, **other:** Home Depot, Longs Drug, Staples, **S gas:** 76/dsl, **food:** Baskin-Robbins, Carl's Jr, Cold Stone Creamery, El Gran Burrito, Mary's Mexican, Quizno's, **other:** Rite Aid, USPO

**49** Central Ave, to Montclair, **N gas:** Chevron, Mobil, Shell/24hr, 7-11, **food:** Burger King, Carl's Jr., El Pollo Loco, Incredible Pizza, Island Burger, KFC, McDonald's, Quizno's, Subway, Tom's Burgers, **other:** Best Buy, Borders Books, Circuit City, Firestone/auto, Goodyear/auto, Hi-Lo Auto Supply, JC Penney, Just Tires, Macy's, Office Depot, PepBoys, Ross, Sears/auto, mall, same as 48, **S gas:** 76, **food:** Jack-in-the-Box, LJ Silver, Subway, Wienerschnitzel, **other:** Acura, Costco/gas, Honda, Infiniti, K-Mart, Macy's, Nissan, Target

**48** Monte Vista, **N gas:** Shell, **food:** Acapulco Mexican, Applebee's, Chilis, Black Angus, Elephant Rest., Olive Garden, Red Lobster, Tony Roma, **other:** H HOSPITAL, Lens Crafters, Nordstrom's, Macy's, mall, same as 49

**47** Indian Hill Blvd, to Claremont, **N gas:** Mobil, **food:** Bakers Square, **lodging:** Claremont Lodge, Howard Johnson, **S gas:** Chevron/McDonald's, 76/dsl, **food:** Burger King, Carl's Jr, Charo Chicken, Denny's, In-n-Out, RoundTable Pizza, 7-11, Starbucks, Wienerschnitzel, **lodging:** Ramada Inn, **other:** Albertson's, America's Tire, AutoZone, Ford, Kia, Radio Shack, Toyota

**46** Towne Ave, **N gas:** Citgo/7-11, Puma/Subway/dsl, **food:** Jack-in-the-Box, Subway

**45b** Garey Ave, to Pomona, **N gas:** Delta, **other:** H HOSPITAL, vet, **S gas:** Chevron, Shell/dsl, **food:** Del Taco

**45** White Ave, Garey Ave, to Pomona

**44** (43 from eb)Dudley St, Fairplex Dr, **N gas:** Arco/dsl, **food:** Coppacabana Rest., Denny's, **lodging:** LemonTree Motel, Sheraton, **S gas:** Chevron/24hr, **food:** McDonald's

**42b** CA 71 S (from eb), to Corona

**42a** I-210 W, CA 57 S

**41** Kellogg Dr, **S** to Cal Poly Inst

**40** Via Verde

## INTERSTATE 10 CONT'D

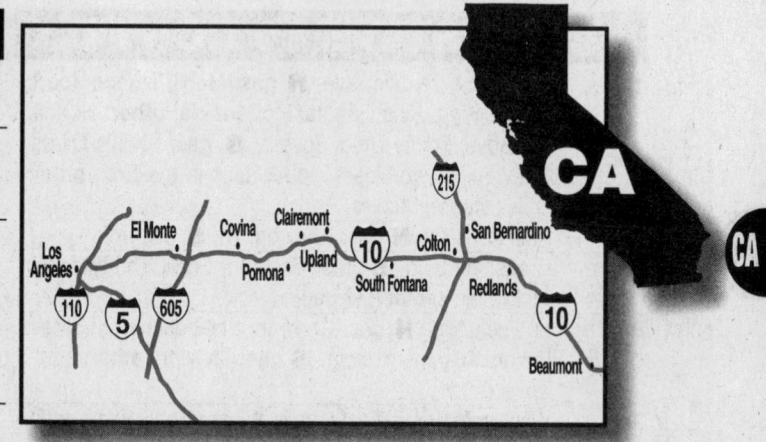

**E ↕ W**

**L O S A N G E L E S A R E A**

| | |
|---|---|
| **38b** | Holt Ave, to Covina, **N** **food:** Blake's Steaks/seafood, **lodging:** Embassy Suites |
| **38a** | Grand Ave, **N** **gas:** Arco/dsl, **food:** Baily's Rest, Denny's, Japanese/Mongolian/Thai Rest., **lodging:** Best Western |
| **37b** | Barranca St, Grand Ave, **N** **gas:** Shell/repair, **food:** BJ's Rest., Chili's, Dockside Grill, El Torito, Hooters, Marie Callender, Mariposa Mexican, Woodpit BBQ, **lodging:** Best Western, Hampton Inn, Holiday Inn, **other:** Circuit City, Old Navy, Target, **S** **food:** In-n-Out, McDonald's, **lodging:** Courtyard, 5 Star Inn |
| **37a** | Citrus Ave, to Covina, **N** **gas:** Chevron, **food:** Burger King, Carl's Jr, Del Taco, IHOP, Jack-in-the-Box, TGI-Friday, Winchell's, **other:** Acura, Buick, GMC, Honda, Lincoln/Mercury, Longs Drug, Marshall's, Mazda, Office Depot, Old Navy, Ralph's Foods, Ross, Target, Volvo/VW, **S** **gas:** 76/autocare, **food:** Classic Burger, Trader Joe's, **other:** Ⓗ HOSPITAL, Cadillac |
| **36** | CA 39, Azusa Ave, to Covina, **N** **gas:** Arco/24hr, 76, **food:** Black Angus, Brazillian BBQ, Imperio Rest., McDonald's, Papa John's, Quizno's, Red Lobster, Subway, **lodging:** El Dorado Motel, **other:** Chrysler/Jeep/Dodge, Circuit City, Stater Bro's, **S** **gas:** Mobil, Shell, **food:** Carrow's, **other:** Honda, Hummer, Toyota |
| **35** | Vincent Ave, Glendora Ave, **N** **gas:** Chevron/24hr, **food:** KFC, Pizza Hut, Wienerschnitzel, **S** **gas:** 76, **food:** Applebee's, Baja Fresh, Chevy's Mexican, Elephant Rest., Grand Buffet, Pizza Hut, Quizno's, Red Robin, Sakura Japanese, Starbucks, Subway, Weinerschnitzel, **other:** Barnes&Noble, Best Buy, Big O Tire, JC Penney, Macy's, Macy's, Sears/auto, mall |
| **34** | Pacific Ave, **N** **gas:** 76, **S** **gas:** Mobil, Shell, **food:** La Posada Mexican, **other:** Ⓗ HOSPITAL, Discount Tire, K-Mart, Goodyear/auto, JC Penney, Jo-Ann Fabrics, Sears, mall, same as 35 |
| **33** | Puente Ave, **N** **gas:** Chevron, **food:** A&W/LJ Silver, China Palace, Denny's, Farmer Boy's, Guadalajara Grill, McDonald's, Panda Express, Quizno's, Sizzler, Starbucks, **lodging:** Courtyard, Motel 6, **other:** Home Depot, Staples, Walmart, **S** **gas:** Valero/dsl, **lodging:** Regency Inn, **food:** Jack-in-the-Box, **other:** Harley-Davidson, Saturn, U-Haul |
| **32b** | Francisquito Ave, to La Puente, **N** **gas:** V&G, **food:** Papa John's, **other:** hwy patrol, **S** **gas:** Chevron, **food:** Carl's Jr, In-n-Out, Wienerschnitzel, **lodging:** Grand Park Inn |
| **32a** | Baldwin Pk Blvd, **N** **gas:** Arco, Chevron/McDonald's, Shell, USA, **food:** Burger King, IHOP, Jack-in-the-Box, Pizza Hut/Taco Bell, Seven Mares Rest., **other:** Ⓗ HOSPITAL, CVS Drug, Food4Less, Target, **S** **food:** In-n-Out, **other:** Altman's RV Ctr |
| **31c** | (31b from wb)Frazier St, **N** **food:** 7-11, **lodging:** Angel Motel |
| **31b a** | (31a from wb) I-605 N/S, to Long Beach |
| **30** | Garvey Ave, **S** Prena Gas |
| **29b** | Valley Blvd, Peck Rd, **N** **gas:** Chevron, **food:** Burger King, Carl's Jr., Denny's, KFC, Shakey's Pizza, Yoshinoya, **lodging:** Motel 6, **other:** Ford, Dodge, Goodyear/auto, Honda, K-Mart, Nissan, Toyota/Scion/Lexus, |

**L O S A N G E L E S A R E A**

| | |
|---|---|
| **29b** | Continued **S** **gas:** 76/dsl, Shell, **food:** Christina'a Seafood, Del Taco, **other:** Pontiac/GMC |
| **29a** | S Peck Rd (from eb) |
| **28** | Santa Anita Ave, to El Monte, **N** **other:** Chevrolet, Hyundai, **S** **gas:** 76, **food:** 7-11 |
| **27** | Baldwin Avenue, Temple City Blvd, **S** **gas:** Arco/24hr, **food:** Denny's, Edward's Steaks, same as 27b a |
| **26b** | CA 19, Rosemead Blvd, Pasadena, **N** **food:** Denny's, IHOP, Subway, **lodging:** Ramona Inn, Rosemead Inn, **other:** Goodyear/auto, Office Depot, Radio Shack, Target, **S** **food:** Jack-in-the-Box, Quizno's, Starbucks |
| **26a** | Walnut Grove Ave |
| **25b** | San Gabriel Blvd, **N** **gas:** Arco, Mobil, Shell/autocare, **food:** Carl's Jr, Popeye's, Taco Bell/Pizza Hut, Wienerschnitzel, **lodging:** Budget Inn, **other:** AutoZone, San Gabriel Foods, **S** **gas:** Citgo/7-11 |
| **25a** | Del Mar Ave, to San Gabriel, **N** **gas:** 76, **other:** auto repair, **S** **gas:** Arco, Chevron/dsl, **lodging:** Best Value |
| **24** | New Ave, to Monterey Park, **N** **gas:** Mobil, to Mission San Gabriel |
| **23b** | Garfield Ave, to Alhambra, **S** **gas:** Shell/dsl, SoCal, **lodging:** Grand Inn, **other:** Ⓗ HOSPITAL |
| **23a** | Atlantic Blvd, Monterey Park, **N** **gas:** Mobil, **food:** Del Taco, Pizza Hut, Popeye's, **other:** Ⓗ HOSPITAL, **S** **lodging:** Best Western, **other:** Ralph's Foods, auto repair |
| **22** | Fremont Ave, **N** Ⓗ HOSPITAL, tuneup, **S** 7-11 |
| **21** | I-710, Long Beach Fwy, Eastern Ave (from wb) |
| **20b a** | Eastern Ave, City Terrace Dr, **S** **gas:** Chevron/service, Mobil, **food:** Burger King, McDonald's |
| **19c** | Soto St (from wb), **N** **gas:** Shell, Soto Gas, **food:** Burger King, **other:** Ⓗ HOSPITAL, **S** **gas:** Mobil, Pronto |
| **19b** | I-5 (from wb), US 101 S, **N** to Burbank, S to San Diego |
| **19a** | State St, **N** Ⓗ HOSPITAL |
| **17** | I-5 N |
| **16b** | I-5 S (from eb) |
| **16a** | Santa Fe Ave, San Mateo St, **S** **gas:** Shell, **other:** Hertz Trucks, industrial area |
| **15b** | Alameda St, **N** **food:** Jack-in-the-Box, to downtown, **S** industrial area |
| **15a** | Central Ave, **N** **gas:** Shell/repair |
| **14b** | San Pedro Blvd, **S** industrial |
| **14a** | LA Blvd, **N** conv ctr, **S** **other:** Kragen Parts, Radio Shack, Rite Aid |
| **13** | I-110, Harbor Fwy |

## INTERSTATE 10 CONT'D

**E** ← **W** **LOS ANGELES AREA** **N** ↑ **S** **CA**

**12** Hoover St, Vermont Ave, **N gas:** Mobil, Texaco, **food:** Burger King, King Donuts, McDonald's, **other:** Honda, PepBoys, Thrifty Drug, Toyota, **S gas:** Amin's Oil/dsl Chevron, Valero/dieses, **food:** Jack-in-the-Box, **other:** Office Depot, Staples

**10** Arlington Ave, **N gas:** Chevron, 76, **S** Chevron

**9** Crenshaw Blvd, **S gas:** Chevron, Shell, Thrifty, **food:** McDonald's, **other:** U-Haul

**8** La Brea Ave, **N gas:** Chevron, Shell/dsl/repair, **other:** Walgreen, transmissions, **S gas:** Chevron, **other:** Auto-Zone

**7b** Washington Blvd, Fairfax Ave, **S gas:** Mobil, same as 8

**7a** La Cienega Blvd, Venice Ave (from wb), **N gas:** Chevron/24h, Mobil, **food:** Carl's Jr., Del Taco, **other:** Firestone/auto, **S food:** Subway, **other:** Aamco

**6** Robertson Blvd, Culver City, **N gas:** Chevron, Mobil, **food:** Domino's, Taco Bell, **other:** EZ Lube, Goodyear, museum, **S food:** Del Taco, Albertson's, **other:** Ross, SavOn Drug, Ross

**5** National Blvd, **N gas:** 76, United Oil, **food:** Papa John's, Starbucks, Subway, **other:** Rite Aid, Von's Foods, **S gas:** Arco, **food:** KFC

**4** Overland Ave, **S gas:** Mobil, **food:** Winchell's

**3b a** I-405, N to Sacramento, S to Long Beach

**2c b** Bundy Dr, **N gas:** Chevron, Shell/dsl, **food:** Eddy's Café, Pizza Hut, Taco Bell, **other:** U-haul

**2a** Centinela Ave, to Santa Monica, **N food:** Taco Bell, **S food:** McDonald's, Trader Joe's, **lodging:** Santa Monica Hotel

**1c** 20th St (from wb), Cloverfield Blvd, 26th St (from wb), **N gas:** Arco, Shell/repair, **other:** [H] HOSPITAL

**1b** Lincoln Blvd, CA 1 S, **N food:** Denny's, **food:** Norm's Rest., **lodging:** Holiday Inn, **other:** Brake Masters, Jo-Ann Fabrics, Macy's, Sears, Vons Foods, auto repair, transmissions, **S gas:** Chevron/24hr, Exxon, **food:** Jack-in-the-Box, **other:** EZ Lube, Firestone/auto, U-Haul

**1a** 4th, 5th, (from wb), **N other:** Macy's, Sears, mall

**0** Santa Monica Blvd, to beaches, I-10 begins/ends on CA 1.

## INTERSTATE 15

| Exit # | Services |
|---|---|
| 298 | California/Nevada state line, facilities located at state line, Nevada side |
| 291 | Yates Well Rd |
| 286 | Nipton Rd, **E** E Mojave Nat Scenic Area, to Searchlight |
| 281 | Bailey Rd |
| 276mm | brake check area for trucks, nb |
| 272 | Cima Rd, **E** gas, food |
| 270mm | **Valley Wells Rest Area both lanes, full** ♿ **facilities,** [C], 🚻 **, litter barrels, petwalk** |
| 265 | Halloran Summit Rd, **E gas:** Hilltop Gas/dsl, **other:** towing/tires/repair |
| 259 | Halloran Springs Rd |
| 248 | to Baker (from sb), same as 246 |
| 246 | CA 127, Kel-Baker Rd, Baker, to Death Valley, **W gas:** Arco/24hr, Mobil/dsl, 76/dsl, Shell/Jack-in-the-Box/dsl, Valero/A&W/Pizza Hut/Subway/TCBY, Valero/DQ/dsl, |

**BAKER** **BARSTOW**

**246** Continued
**food:** Alien Fresh Jerky, Arby's, Big Boy Rest., Burger King, Coco's Rest., Del Taco, Denny's, Mad Greek Café, Starbucks, **lodging:** BunBoy Motel, Royal Hawaiian Motel, **other:** Baker Auto Parts, Baker Mkt Foods, Country Store, World's Largest Thermometer, repair

**245** to Baker (from nb), same as 246

**239** Zzyzx Rd

**233** Rasor Rd, **E gas:** Rasor Rest Sta/gas/dsl/towing/24hr

**230** Basin Rd

**221** Afton Rd, to Dunn, **W** market

**217mm** rest area both lanes, full ♿ facilities, [C], 🚻, litter barrels, petwalk

**213** Field Rd

**206** Harvard Rd, to Newberry Springs, **W other:** Rock-a-Hoola WaterPark/resort (1mi)

**198** Minneola Rd, **E gas:** Mobil

**197mm** agricultural insp sta sb

**196** Yermo Rd, Yermo

**194** Calico Rd

**191** Ghost Town Rd, **E gas:** Arco/24hr, Mohsen Oil Trkstp/dsl/24hr, **food:** Jack-in-the-Box, Peggy Sue's 50s Diner, **lodging:** OakTree Inn, **W gas:** Clink's #2/Shell/dsl/24hr, 76, **food:** Jenny Rose' Rest., **other:** Calico GhostTown (3mi), KOA, to USMC Logistics

**189** Ft Irwin Rd

**186** CA 58 W, to Bakersfield, **W food:** Hacienda Colima, Idle Spur Steaks

**184** E Main, Barstow, Montera Rd (from eb), to I-40, **E food:** Doughnut Star Chinese, Imenez's Mexican, Krissy's Café, McDonald's, Panda Express, Pizza Hut, Popeye's, Quizno's, Starbucks, Straw Hat Pizza, Tom's Burgers, **lodging:** Best Western, Travelodge, **other:** Pic'n Sav, mall, **S of I-40...gas:** Arco/24hr, **other:** Walmart/auto/gas, **W gas:** Chevron, Circle K/TCBY, Shell/dsl, Thrifty Gas, Valero, **food:** Arby's, Burger King, Carl's Jr, Carrow's Rest., China Gourmet, Coco's, Del Taco, Gallardo's Mexican, Jack-in-the-Box, KFC, LJ Silver, Ruby's Rest., Sizzler, Taco Bell, Weinerschnitzel, **lodging:** AstroBudget Motel, Best Motel, Budget Inn, California Inn, Day's Inn, Desert Inn, Econolodge, Economy Inn, Quality Inn, Ramada Inn, Rodeway Inn, Super 8, **other:** AutoZone, Food 4 Less, Goodyear, Kragen Parts, Radio Shack, U-Haul/LP, Von's Foods, tires

**184a** I-40 E (from nb), I-40 begins/ends

**183** CA 247, Barstow Rd, **E gas:** 76, Valero/gas, **food:** Pizza Hut, Jimenez Mexican, **other:** Rite Aid, **W gas:** Chevron/24hr, **other:** [H] HOSPITAL, Food4Less, TrueValue, Mojave River Valley Museum, st patrol,

**181** L St, W Main, Barstow, **W gas:** ATC/Mrs. B's Diner/dsl/rest., Chevron, Thrifty, **food:** BunBoy Rest., Pizza Palace, Robertiroz Mexican, **lodging:** Best Value Inn, Holiday Inn Express, **other:** Home Depot, NAPA, tires/towing

**179** CA 58, to Bakersfield

**178** Lenwood, to Barstow, **E gas:** Chevron/dsl, ⊕ **FLYING J**/CountryMkt/dsl/24hr/@, Shell/24hr, 76/dsl, Valero/Circle K, **food:** Arby's, Baja Fresh, Baskin-Robbins, Big Boy, Burger King, Carl's Jr, Del Taco, Denny's, El Pollo Loco, FoodCourt, Hana Grill, In-n-Out, Jack-in-the-Box, KFC, Panda Express, Quigley's, Starbucks, Subway,

## INTERSTATE 15 CONT'D

**N ↕ S**

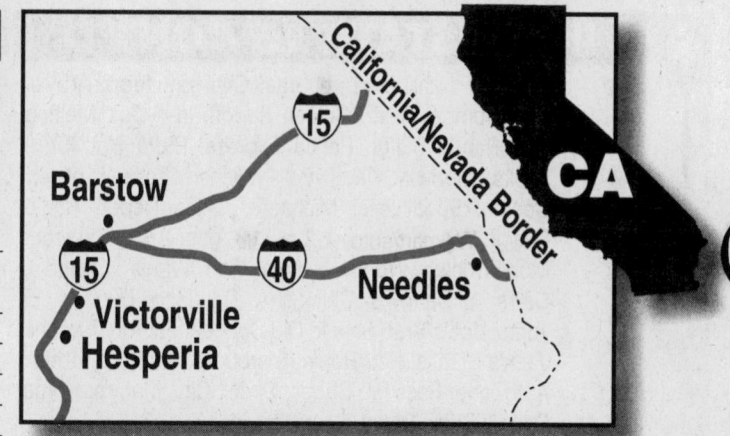

| | |
|---|---|
| **178** | Continued |
| | Taco Bell, Tommy's Burgers, **lodging:** Hampton Inn, Holiday Inn Express, **other:** Blue Beacon, Tanger Outlet/famous brands, **W gas:** Pilot/DQ/dsl/scales/24hr/@, TA/Subway/dsl/truckwash/scales/24hr/@, **food:** McDonald's, **lodging:** Red Roof Inn, **other:** Firestone, truck repair |
| **175** | Outlet Ctr Dr, Sidewinder Rd, **4 mi E other:** factory outlets |
| **169** | Hodge Rd |
| **165** | Wild Wash Rd |
| **161** | Dale Evans Pkwy, to Apple Valley |
| **157** | Stoddard Wells Rd, to Bell Mtn |
| **154** | Stoddard Wells Rd, to Bell Mtn, **E food:** Taco Chon, **other:** RV Camping, **W gas:** Mobil, 76, **food:** Denny's, **lodging:** Howard Johnson, Motel 6, Queens Motel |
| **153.5mm** | Mojave River |
| **153b** | E St |
| **153a** | CA 18 E, D St, to Apple Valley, **E gas:** 76, **other:** **H** HOSPITAL, Cooper Tire, **W gas:** Arco/24hr |
| **151b** | Mojave Dr, Victorville, **E gas:** 76/dsl/24hr, **lodging:** Budget Inn, **W gas:** Valero, **lodging:** Sunset Inn, **other:** transmissions |
| **151a** | La Paz Dr, Roy Rogers Dr, **E gas:** Chevron, Shell/A&W/TCBY, USA/dsl, **food:** Bravo Burgers, China Palace, DQ, HomeTown Buffet, IHOP, Jack-in-the-Box, McDonald's, Wendy's, Yum Yum Donuts, **lodging:** New Corral Motel, **other:** Asian Mkt, Costco/gas, Food4Less/24hr, Goodyear/auto, Harley-Davidson, Honda, Jo-Ann Fabrics, 99¢ Store, Pic'n Sav Foods, Rite Aid, Toyota, Winston Tire, same as 144, **W gas:** Arco/24hr, **food:** Carl's Jr, Dominos, Hawaiian BBQ, Papa Johns, Quizno's, Starbucks, **other:** Home Depot, Honda, Kia, Nissan, Pontiac/GMC, Stater Bros |
| **150** | CA 18 W, Palmdale Rd, Victorville, **E food:** All-Star Buffet, Baker's Drive-Thru, Burger King, Carl's Jr, Denny's, Don's Rest., El Pollo Loco, Goody's Rest., Jack-in-the-Box, KFC, Richie's Diner, Starbucks, **lodging:** Green Tree, Red Roof Inn, **other:** Autozone, Cadillac/GMC, Chrysler/Jeep, Dodge, PepBoys, **W gas:** Shell, Thrifty, Valero, **food:** Andrew's Rest., Cask&Cleaver, Coco's, Del Taco, Los Domingos Mexican, LJ Silver, McDonald's, Pina's Mexican, Pizza Hut, Subway, Taco Bell, Tom's #2 Rest., **lodging:** Ambassador Inn, Budget Inn, Days Inn, Ramada Inn, **other:** **H** HOSPITAL, Aamco, AutoZone, Buick/Pontiac, Chevrolet/Hyundai, Chrysler/Jeep, Ford/Lincoln/Mercury, Honda/Toyota, Kamper's Korner RV, Kia, Nissan, Ralph's Foods, Target, Town&Country Tire, mall |
| **147** | Bear Valley Rd, to Lucerne Valley, **E gas:** Arco/24hr, Chevron, Citgo/7-11, Mobil, 76/Circle K, Shell, **food:** A&W, Arby's, Baker's Drive-Thru, Burger King, Carl's Jr, Del Taco, Dragon Express, Golden Gate Chinese, Hogi Yogi, Incredible Pizza, John's Pizza, KFC, LJ Silver, Los Toritos Mexican, Marie Callender's, McDonald's, NY Deli, Panda Express, Quizno's, Red Robin, Panda Express, Pizza Palace, Popeye's, Shakey's Pizza, Stein'n Steer, Straw Hat Pizza, TNT Café, Wienerschnitzel, Winchell's, **lodging:** American Inn, Comfort Suites, Day's Inn, Econolodge, Hilton Garden, La Quinta, Red Roof Inn, Super 8, Travelodge, **other:** America's Tire, |

**VICTORVILLE**

| | |
|---|---|
| **147** | Continued |
| | AutoZone, Circuit City, Firestone/auto, Home Depot, Jiffy Lube, Kragen Parts, Michael's, Range RV, Staples, Walmart/auto, funpark, **W gas:** Chevron, Valero, **food:** Applebee's, Archibald's Drive-Thru, Baja Fresh Grill, Carinos, Chili's, ChuckeCheese, Cold Stone Creamery, El Pollo Loco, El Tio Pepe Mexican, Farmer Boy's Rest., Greenhouse Café, Jack-in-the-Box, Mimi's Cafe, Olive Garden, On-the-Border, Outback Steaks, Red Lobster, RoadHouse Grill, Starbucks, Subway, Tony Roma, 2 Guys Grill, Wendy's, **lodging:** Hawthorn Suites, **other:** Barnes&Noble, Best Buy, Circuit City, CVS Drug, JC Penney, Kohl's, Lowe's Whse, Range RV Ctr, Sears/auto, Stater Bro's, Vallarta Foods, mall |
| **143** | Main St, to Hesperia, Phelan, **E gas:** Shell/A&W/Popeyes/dsl, Valero/DQ/pizza, **food:** Burger King, Denny's, IHOP, In-n-Out, Jack-in-the-Box, **lodging:** SpringHill Suites, **W gas:** Arco/24hr, 76/Big Boy/dsl, **food:** Baker's Drive-thru, **lodging:** Holiday Inn Express, RV camping |
| **141** | US 395, to Adelanto, **W gas:** Pilot/Wendy's/dsl/scales/24hr, **food:** Newt's Outpost Café, **other:** repair |
| **138** | Oak Hill Rd, **E gas:** Shell/dsl, **food:** Summit Inn/café, **W other:** RV camping, LP |
| **132** | Cajon Summit, elevation 4260, brake check sb |
| **131** | CA 138, to Palmdale, Silverwood Lake, **E gas:** Chevron/McDonald's/24hr, **other:** repair, **W gas:** 76/Circle K/Del Taco/LP, Shell/Subway/dsl, **lodging:** Best Western |
| **131mm** | weigh sta both lanes, elevation 3000 |
| **129** | Cleghorn Rd |
| **124** | Kenwood Ave |
| **123** | I-215 S, to San Bernardino, **E gas:** Arco/24hr, to Glen Helen Park |
| **122** | Glen Helen Parkway |
| **119** | Sierra Ave, **W gas:** Arco/Jack-in-the-Box/dsl/24hr, Chevron/McDonald's/dsl, Shell/Del Taco/dsl/@, **other:** to Lytle Creek RA |
| **116** | Summit Ave, **E gas:** Arco, Chevron, 7-11, Shell/Del Taco, Valero/dsl, **food:** Chili's, Hawaiian BBQ, Jack-in-the-Box, Panera Bread, Quizno's, Roundtable Pizza, Starbucks, Subway, Taco Bell, Wendy's, **other:** CVS Drug, GNC, Kohl's, Marshall's, Michale's, PetsMart, Ross, Staples, Stater Bro's, Target |
| **115b a** | CA 210, Highland Ave, **E** to Lake Arrowhead |
| **113** | Base Line Rd, **E gas:** USA, **food:** Denny's, Jack-in-the-Box, Logans Roadhouse, Pizza Hut, Quiznos, Rosa Maria's, Starbucks, **lodging:** Comfort Inn |

## INTERSTATE 15 CONT'D

**N↕S**

**CA**

**O N T A R I O**

**112** CA 66, Foothill Blvd, **E gas:** Chevron, **food:** Arby's, ClaimJumper Rest., Golden Spoon, In-n-Out, Melting Pot, Panda Buffet, Panda Express, Pizza Hut, Starbucks, Subway, Taco Bell, Wienerschnitzel, **other:** Costco, Food4Less, Michael's, Office Depot, Radio Shack, Walmart/auto, **1-2 mi W gas:** Arco, Chevron, Mobil/Subway, **food:** Buffalo Wild Wings, Carino's, Carl's Jr, Carrow's, Chick-fil-A, Del Taco, Denny's, El Torito, Joe's Crab Shack, Old Spagetti Factory, Omaha Jack's Steaks, Red Robin, Starbucks, Wendy's, **other:** AutoZone, Bass Pro Shops, Circuit City, Macy's, Home Depot, Office Depot, Sears Grand

**110** 4th St, **E gas:** Arco/dsl, **W gas:** Arco/24hr, Mobil/Subway/dsl, 76/dsl, **food:** Applebee's, BJ's Rest., Boston's, Cali Grill, Carl's Jr, Chevy's Mexican, Chipotle, Coco's, Dave&Buster's, Del Taco, El Pollo Loco, Fazoli's, Fuddruckers, Jack-in-the-Box, KFC, Krispy Kreme, McDonald's, Mi Casa Mexican, NY Grill, Olive Garden, Outback Steaks, Quizno's, Rain Forest Cafe, Red Lobster, Rubio's, Starbucks, Subway, TokyoWako, Wendy's, Wienerschnitzel, **lodging:** AmeriSuites, Ayre's Suites, Courtyard, Hampton Inn, Hilton Garden, Homewood Suites, TownePlace Suites, **other:** America's Tire, Big O Tire, Costco/gas, JC Penney, Ontario Mills Mall, Sam's Club, Staples, Target

**109b a** I-10, E to San Bernardino, W to LA

**108** Jurupa St, **E food:** Starbucks, **other:** Affordable RV, BMW, Buick, Chrysler/Jeep/Dodge, GMC/Pontiac, Honda, Lexus, Mazda, Mitsubishi, Nissan, Saturn, Toyota, Volvo, VW, **W gas:** Arco/24hr, **food:** Carl's Jr, **other:** Ford, Kia, Lincoln/Mercury, Scandia funpark

**106** CA 60, E to Riverside, W to LA

**104** new exit

**103** Limonite Ave, **E other:** Lowes Whse, Michael's, PetCo, Ross, **W gas:** Ralph's, **food:** Applebees, Coldstone Creamery, El Grande Burrito, Quizno's, Red Brick Pizza, Wendy's, **other:** Best Buy, GNC, Home Depot, Kohl's, PetsMart, Staples, Target, TJ Maxx, Von's Foods

**100** 6th St, Norco Dr, Old Town Norco, **E gas:** Chevron/24hr, Exxon/dsl, **food:** Jack-in-the-Box, McDonald's, **other:** Rite Aid, **W gas:** Arco/24hr, Valero, **food:** Norco's Burgers, Starbucks, Weinerschnitzel, **lodging:** Guesthouse Inn, **other:** Brake Masters, Jiffy Lube, USPO, vet

**98** 2nd St, **W gas:** 76/dsl, Shell/dsl, Spirit, Texaco, Thrifty, **food:** Burger King, Chipotle Mexican, Del Taco, Denny's, Domino's, Fazoli's, In-n-Out, Little Caesar's, Marie Callender, Miguel's Jr, Pizza Hut, Polly's Cafe, Sizzler, **lodging:** Howard Johnson Express, **other:** America's Tire, AutoZone, Big O Tire, Chrysler, Dodge, Ford, Jeep, Mazda, Mitsubishi, Pontiac, Norco RV, 7-11, Staples, Stater Bro's, Target

**97** Yuma Dr, Hidden Valley Pkwy, **E food:** Baja Fresh, Chick-fil-A, **other:** Kohl's, Stater Bro's, **W gas:** Chevron, 76/dsl, Shell/dsl, **food:** Alberto's Mexican, Arby's, Carl's Jr, Jamba Juice, Jack-in-the-Box, McDonald's, Papa John's, Pizza Hut, Quizno's, Rodrigo's Mexican, Rubio's, Starbucks, Wendy's, **lodging:** Hampton Inn, **other:** Albertson's, Big Lots, Kragen Parts, SavOn Drug, Staples, Winston Tire, Walgreens

**96b a** CA 91, to Riverside, beaches

**95** Magnolia Ave, **E gas:** Chevron/dsl, **food:** Islands Grill, Jack-in-the-Box, **other:** Lowe's Whse, Office Depot, **W gas:** Mobil, Shell, **food:** A&W/LJ Silver, Burger King, Carl's Jr, Coco's, El Tapatio Mexican, Little Caesar's, Lotus Garden, McDonald's, Pizza Palace, Sizzler, Subway, Zendejas Mexican, **lodging:** Holiday Inn Express, **other:** CVS Drug, $Tree, Kragen Parts, Ralph's Foods, Rite Aid, Stater Bros Foods

**93** Ontario Ave, to El Cerrito, **E gas:** Shell, **food:** Starbucks, **W gas:** Arco/24hr, Chevron/24hr, 76, **food:** Denny's, In-n-Out, Jack-in-the-Box, McDonald's, Miguel's Mexican, Quizno's, Tommy's Burgers, Wienerschnitzel, **other:** Albertson's, Home Depot, Long's Drug, Radio Shack, Sam's Club, USPO, Walmart/auto

**92** El Cerrito Rd

**91** Cajalco Rd, **E food:** Chick-fil-A, Chili's, Jamba Juice, King's Fish House, Macaroni Grill, On-the-Border, Panera Bread, Starbucks, Wendy's, **other:** Barnes&Noble, Best Buy, Kohl's, Marshall's, Michael's, Old Navy, PetCo, Ross, Staples, Target, **W gas:** Mobil, **food:** Golden Spoon, Jack-in-the-Box, NY Pizza, Subway, **other:** Stater Bros

**90** Weirick Rd, **E food:** Salsa-Mar, TGI Friday, **other:** 7 Oaks Gen Store

**88** Temescal Cyn Rd, Glen Ivy, **E gas:** Shell, **W gas:** Arco/dsl/24hr, **food:** Carl's Jr, Tom's Farms/BBQ

**85** Indian Truck Trail

**81** Lake St

**78** Nichols Rd, **W gas:** Arco/24hr, **other:** VF Outlet/famous brands, auto repair

**L A K E   E L S I N O R E**

**77** CA 74, Central Ave, Lake Elsinore, **E gas:** Arco/24hr, Chevron, Mobil, **food:** Archibald's, Burger King, Chili's, Coffee Bean, Coldstone Creamery, Del Taco, Douglas Burgers, Panda Express, Taco Del Mar, Wendy's, **other:** Costco/gas, Lowes Whse, PetsMart, Staples, **W food:** El Pollo Loco, Farmer Boys, Golden Chopsticks, Starbucks, **other:** Home Depot, 99¢ Store, PetCo, Target, Walgreens

**75** Main St, Lake Elsinore, **W gas:** 76, **lodging:** Elsinore Motel, **other:** Circle K, tires/repair

**73** Railroad Cyn Rd, to Lake Elsinore, **E gas:** 76/Circle K, **food:** Denny's, El Pollo Loco, In-n-Out, KFC, Papa John's, Peony Chinese, Quizno's, Starbucks, Wienerschnitzel, **other:** GNC, Jiffy Lube, Kragen Parts, Von's Foods, Walmart/auto, **W gas:** Arco, Chevron, Mobil/dsl, **food:** Cafe China, Carl's Jr, Coco's, Del Taco, Don Ruben Mexican, McDonald's, Pizza Hut, Sizzler, Subway, Taco Bell, **lodging:** Lake View Inn, Quality Inn, **other:** Albertson's, AutoZone, Big O Tire, Buick/Pontiac/GMC, Chevrolet, CVS Drug, Express Tire/auto, Firestone, Ford, NAPA, Radio Shack, Rite Aid, SavOn Drug, 7-11, Stater Bros Foods, vet

**71** Bundy Cyn Rd, **W gas:** Arco/24hr, **food:** Jack-in-the-Box

**69** Baxter Rd, **E food:** Pizza Factory

**68** Clinton Keith Rd, **E gas:** Chevron, USA, **food:** McDonald's, Starbucks, Wienerschnitzel, **other:** Ⓗ HOSPITAL, Albertsons/Sav-on, **W gas:** Arco, 7-11, **food:** Charro Chicken, China Panda, Del Taco, Jack-in-the-Box, Olivera's Rest., Starbucks, **other:** Stater Bro's

**65** California Oaks Rd, Kalmia St, **E gas:** Chevron, Mobil/dsl, 76/Circle K, Shell/dsl, **food:** Burger King, Carl's Jr,

## INTERSTATE 15 CONT'D

**N ↕ S**

**T E M E C U L A**

**65** Continued
Chili's, Craziano's, DQ, KFC, Papa John's, Starbucks, **lodging:** Comfort Inn, **other:** Albertson's, AutoZone, Kragen Parts, Radio Shack, Rite Aid, Target, Walgreens, **W gas:** Arco/24hr, Chevron, **food:** Applebee's, Carrow's, Chick-fil-A, Farmer Boys, Jack-in-the-Box, Sizzlin Steer, **other:** America's Tire, Giant RV Ctr, Kohl's, Lowe's Whse, Office Depot, PetCo, fun ctr

**64** Murrieta Hot Springs Rd, to I-215, **E gas:** Citgo/7-11, Shell/dsl, **food:** Carl's Jr, El Pollo Loco, Fazoli's, Richie's Diner, Sizzler, Starbucks, Wendy's, **other:** Ralph's Foods, Rite Aid, Ross, Sam's Club/gas, Walgreens, **W gas:** Citgo, Shell/Popeyes/dsl, **food:** Arby's, Chuy's, Coldstone Creamery, Denny's, IHOP, McDonald's, MegaToms, Panda Express, Quizno's, Starbucks, Subway, Wienerschnitzel, **other:** Best Buy, Big Lots, Home Depot, 99¢ Store, PetsMart, Staples, Walmart/auto

**63** I-215 N (from nb), to Riverside

**61** CA 79 N, Winchester Rd, **E gas:** Chevron, Mobil, **food:** Alberto's Mexican, Anthony's Ristorante, Baja Fresh, Burger King, Carino's, Carl's Jr, Coldstone Creamery, El Torito, Harry's Grill, Islander Grill, Macaroni Grill, McDonald's, Mimi's Café, On-the-Border, Outback Steaks, Panda Express, Roadhouse Grill, Shogun Chinese, Souplantation, Starbucks, Taco Bell, TGIFriday, Togo's, Yellow Basket Hamburgers, **other:** America Tire, AutoZone, Barnes&Noble, Big O Tire, Circuit City, Costco/gas, Food4Less, Dodge, Ford, Express Tire, Honda/Acura, Jo-Ann Fabrics, K-Mart, Kragen Parts, Longs Drug, Lowe's Whse, Macy's, PepBoys, PetCo, Sears/auto, Toyota, TJ Maxx, VW, WinCo Foods, World Mkt, **W gas:** Arco/24hr, Chevron/dsl, **food:** Arby's, Banzai Japanese, Blue Marlin Rest., CA Burgers, ChungKing Chinese, Del Taco, El Pollo Loco, Farmer Boys, Guadalahara Mexican, Hooters, Hungry Hunter, In-n-Out, Jack-in-the-Box, Richie's Diner, Sizzler, Starbucks, Super China, Tony Roma's, Wendy's, **lodging:** Best Western, Comfort Inn, Extended Stay America, Fairfield Inn, Holiday Inn Express, **other:** Hyundai, NAPA, VW, st patrol, tires/repair

**59** Rancho California Rd, **E gas:** Arco, Mobil/dsl, Shell/dsl, **food:** Black Angus, Chili's, ClaimJumper, Del Taco, Marie Callender's, Pizza Hut, Round Table Pizza, Rubio's, Texas Loosey's, Starbucks, **lodging:** Embassy Suites, **other:** Big Lots, CVS Drug, Michael's, Orchard's Foods, Target, Von's Foods, **W gas:** Chevron/repair, 76/Circle K/dsl, **food:** Denny's, Domino's, KFC, McDonald's, Mexico Chiquito's, OldTown Donuts, Penfold's Mexican, Rick's Burgers, Rosa's Café, **lodging:** Hampton Inn, Motel 6, Rancho California Inn, Rodeway Inn, **other:** USPO

**58** CA 79 S, to Indio, Temecula, **E gas:** Arco, Mobil, Valero/Circle K/dsl, **food:** Carl's Jr, Del Taco, In-n-Out, Starbucks, Temecula Pizza, other, America's Tire, Longs Drug, 7-11, **W gas:** Arco, Shell/dsl/24hr, **food:** Alberto's Mexican, Country Jct Rest., Wienerschnitzel, **lodging:** Ramada Inn, **other:** Express Tire, Firestone, Harley-Davidson, RV service

**55mm** check sta nb

**E S C O N D I D O**

**54** Rainbow Valley Blvd, **2 mi E** gas, food, **W** CA Insp Sta

**51** Mission Rd, to Fallbrook, **W H** HOSPITAL

**46** CA 76, to Oceanside, Pala, **W gas:** Mobil, **lodging:** Comfort Inn, Pala Mesa Resort, **other:** RV camp

**44mm** San Luis Rey River

**43** Old Hwy 395

**41** Gopher Canyon Rd, Old Castle Rd, **1 mi E lodging:** Welk Resort, **other:** RV camping, gas

**37** Deer Springs Rd, Mountain Meadow Rd, **W gas:** Arco/24hr

**34** Centre City Pkwy (from sb)

**33** El Norte Pkwy, **E gas:** Arco/24hr, Shell/dsl, **food:** Arby's, DQ, IHOP, Taco Bell, **lodging:** Best Western, **other:** Goodyear, RV Resort, **W gas:** 76/dsl, Circle K, **food:** Jack-in-the-Box, Wendy's, **other:** Longs Drug, Von's Foods

**32** CA 78, to Oceanside

**31** Valley Pkwy, **E gas:** Arco/24hr, **food:** Baja Fresh, Chili's, ChuckeCheese, McDonald's, Olive Garden, Panda Express, Subway, Uno Grill, **other:** **H** HOSPITAL, Barnes&Noble, Circuit City, Michael's, PetCo, mall, **W gas:** Express, **food:** Applebee's, Boston Mkt, Burger King, Carl's Jr, Chipotle Mexican, Coco's, Del Taco, Jamba Juice, La Salsa, Panera Bread, Starbucks, Subway, Wendy's, **lodging:** Comfort Inn, Holiday Inn Express, **other:** Home Depot, 7-11, Staples, Target, TJ Maxx, World Mkt

**30** 9th Ave, Auto Parkway, **E gas:** AAA, Infiniti, Mercedes, same as 31

**29** Felicita Rd

**28** Centre City Pkwy (from nb, no return), **E food:** Center City Café, **lodging:** Palms Inn

**27** Via Rancho Pkwy, to Escondido, **E gas:** Chevron/24hr, Shell, **food:** FoodCourt, Macaroni Grill, On-the-Border, Orami Grill, Panera Bread, Red Robin, **other:** JC Penney, Macy's, Nordstrom's, Sears/auto, Wild Animal Zoo, mall, **W gas:** Shell/Subway/dsl, **food:** Big Daddy's Steaks, CA Coffee, McDonald's, Starbucks

**26** W Bernardo Dr, to Highland Valley Rd, Palmerado Rd

**24** Rancho Bernardo Rd, to Lake Poway, **E gas:** Arco/24hr, Mobil, **food:** Domino's, **lodging:** Hilton Garden, **other:** Von's Foods, **W gas:** 76/Circle K, Shell/repair, **food:** Elephant Bar Rest., Hooters, **lodging:** Holiday Inn, Rodeway Inn

## INTERSTATE 15 CONT'D

**23** Continued
Carl's Jr, Coco's, Denny's, El Torito, Hunan Chinese, Jack-in-the-Box, Quizno's, Rubio's Grill, 7-11, Taco Bell, **other:** CVS Drug, Express Tire, Firestone/auto

**22** Camino del Norte

**21** Carmel Mtn Rd, **E gas:** Chevron, Shell, Texaco, **food:** Baskin-Robbins, Boston Mkt, Cafe Luna, CA Pizza Kitchen, Carl's Jr, Chevy's Mexican, ClaimJumper, El Pollo Loco, In-n-Out, Islands Burgers, JambaJuice, Marie Callender, McDonald's, Olive Garden, Oscar's Rest., Quizno's, Rubio's Grill, Subway, Taco Bell, TGIFriday's, Wendy's, **lodging:** Residence Inn, **other:** Barnes&Noble, Borders Books, Circuit City, Costco, EZ Lube, GNC, Home Depot, Marshall's, Michael's, PetCo, Ralph's Foods, Rite Aid, Ross, Sears Essentials, Staples, Trader Joes, USPO, **W gas:** Chevron, **food:** Jack-in-the-Box, Starbucks, **other:** Albertson's, Big O Tire, Office Depot, 7-11

**19** CA 56 W, Ted Williams Pkwy

**18** Rancho Penasquitos Blvd, Poway Rd, **E gas:** Arco/24hr, **W gas:** Exxon/dsl, Mobil/dsl, 76/dsl, **food:** Burger King, IHOP, McDonald's, Mi Ranchito Mexican, Starbucks, Subway, Taco Bell, **lodging:** La Quinta, **other:** 7-11

**17** Mercy Rd, Scripps Poway Pkwy, **E gas:** USA/dsl, **food:** Chili's, Fish Grille, Wendy's, **lodging:** Residence Inn, Springhill Suites, **W gas:** Chevron, **food:** KFC, Starbucks

**16** Mira Mesa Blvd, to Lake Miramar, **E food:** Chuck-eCheese, Denny's, Filippi's Pizza, Golden Crown Chinese, Lucio's Mexican, Shozen BBQ, Wendy's, **lodging:** Holiday Inn Express, Quality Suites, **other:** Medco Drug, USPO, **W gas:** Arco/24hr, Shell, **food:** Applebee's, Arby's, Buca Italian, Burger King, Café China, In-n-Out, Islands Burgers, Jack-in-the-Box, Jamba Juice, Little Caesar's, McDonald's, Mimi's Café, On the Border, Oscar's Burgers, Panera Bread, Ralph's, Rubio's Grill, Starbucks, Subway, Wendy's, **other:** Albertson's, Barnes&Noble, Best Buy, Home Depot, Longs Drug, Old Navy, Ralph's Foods, Rite Aid, Ross, USPO

**15** Carroll Canyon Rd, to Miramar College, **E food:** Carl's Jr

**14** Pomerado Rd, Miramar Rd, **W gas:** Arco/dsl, Chevron, Mobil, Shell/24hr, **food:** Carl's Jr, Chin's Rest., Keith's Rest., Pizza Hut, Subway, **lodging:** Best Western, Budget Inn, Holiday Inn Select, **other:** Aamco, Audi/Porsche/VW, Land Rover

**13** Miramar Way, US Naval Air Station

**12** CA 163 S (from sb), to San Diego

**11** to CA 52

**10** Clairemont Mesa Blvd, **W food:** Carl's Jr, Giovanni's Pizza, Jack-in-the-Box, La Salsa, McDonald's, Mr Chick Rest., Panda Express, Subway, Sunny Donuts, Taco Bell, Togo's, Wendy's

**9** CA 274, Balboa Ave

**8** Aero Dr, **W gas:** Arco/24hr, Shell, **food:** Jack-in-the-Box, McDonald's, Papa John's, Sizzler, Starbucks, Submarina, Taco Bell, **lodging:** Holiday Inn, **other:** $Tree, Fry's Electronics, Radio Shack, Von's Foods, Walmart/auto

---

**7b** Friars Rd W, **W food:** Dragon Chinese, IHOP, Islands Hamburgers, Little Fish Mkt, McDonald's, Oggi's Pizza, Subway, **other:** Costco, Lowes Whse, San Diego Station

**7a** Friars Rd E

**6b** I-8, E to El Centro, W to beaches

**6a** Adams Ave, downtown

**5b** El Cajon Blvd, **E gas:** Chevron/dsl, **other:** KIA, **W gas:** Mobil

**5a** University Ave, **E gas:** Chevron/dsl

**3** I-805, N to I-5, S to San Ysidro

**2b** (2c from nb)CA 94 W, downtown

**2a** Market St, downtown

**1c** National Ave, Ocean View Blvd

**1b** (from sb) I-5 S, to Chula Vista

**1a** (from sb) I-5 N. I-15 begins/ends on I-5

## INTERSTATE 40

| Exit # | Services |
|---|---|
| 155 | California/Arizona state line, Colorado River, *Pacific/Mountain time zone* |
| 153 | Park Moabi Rd, to Rte 66, **N** boating, camping |
| 149mm | insp both lanes |
| 148 | 5 Mile Rd, to Topock, Rte 66 (from eb) |
| 144 | US 95 S, E Broadway, Needles, **N gas:** Chevron/dsl, Mobil, Shell/dsl, **food:** Domino's, **other:** Basha's Foods, Laundry, Rite Aid, U-Haul, **S lodging:** Best Value, **other:** tires/repair |
| 142 | J St, Needles, **N gas:** 76/24hr, Valero, **food:** Jack-in-the-Box, McDonald's, **lodging:** Travelers Inn, **other:** NAPA, **S food:** Denny's, **lodging:** Day's Inn, Motel 6, **other:** H HOSPITAL, st patrol |
| 141 | W Broadway, River Rd, Needles, **N food:** KFC, **lodging:** Best Motel, Desert Mirage Inn, River Valley Motel, **other:** Goodyear/auto, KOA (1mi), tire/dsl repair, **S gas:** Arco/24hr, Chevron/dsl/24hr, Mobil/dsl, Shell/DQ/24hr, **food:** Carl's Jr, China Garden, Taco Bell, Wagon Wheel Rest., **lodging:** Best Western, Budget Inn, Needles Inn, Relax Inn, **other:** Chevrolet/Cadillac/Buick/GMC, auto/RV/tire/repair |
| 139 | River Rd Cutoff (from eb), **N** rec area, Hist Rte 66, **other:** KOA, Desert View RV Park |
| 133 | US 95 N, to Searchlight, to Rte 66 |
| 120 | Water Rd |
| 115 | Mountain Springs Rd, High Springs Summit, elev 2770 |
| 107 | Goffs Rd, **N** gas/dsl/food, Hist Rte 66 |
| 106mm | rest area both lanes, full ♿ facilities, 🚻, ⛽, litter barrels, petwalk |
| 100 | Essex Rd, Essex, **N** to Providence Mtn SP, Mitchell Caverns |
| 78 | Kelbaker Rd, to Amboy, E Mojave Nat Preserve, Kelso, **S** Hist Rte 66, **other:** RV camping (14mi) |
| 50 | Ludlow, **N gas:** 76/DQ/24hr, **S gas:** Chevron, **food:** Coffee Shop, **lodging:** Ludlow Motel |
| 33 | Hector Rd, to Hist Rte 66 |
| 28mm | rest area both lanes, full ♿ facilities, 🚻, ⛽, litter barrels, petwalk |
| 23 | Ft Cady Rd, **N gas:** Texaco/dsl/24hr, **S lodging:** Newberry Mtn RV Park |
| 18 | Newberry Springs, **N other:** Calico/dsl, **S gas:** Chevron/Kelly's Grill/LP |
| 12 | Barstow-Daggett Airport, **N** ✈ |
| 7 | Daggett, **N other:** RV camping (2mi), to Calico Ghost Town |

N ↕ S   CA   SAN DIEGO AREA   NEEDLES

## INTERSTATE 40 CONT'D

| | |
|---|---|
| **5** | Nebo St (from eb), to Hist Rte 66 |
| **2** | USMC Logistics Base, **N lodging:** Pennywise Inn |
| **1** | E Main St, Montara Rd, Barstow, **N gas:** Chevron, Barstow Fuel/dsl, Shell/repair, **food:** Burger King, Krissy's Café, Mega Tom's Burger, McDonald's, Panda Express, Quizno's, Starbucks, Straw Hat Pizza, Tom's Burgers, **lodging:** Best Western, Gateway Motel, **other:** Pic'n Sav Foods, **N 1 mi...gas:** Arco/24hr, Chevron, 76/Circle K/Subway/TCBY, Shell, **food:** Arby's, Burger King, Carl's Jr, Carrow's Rest., China Gourmet, Coco's, Del Taco, Denny's, FireHouse Italian, Golden Dragon, IHOP, Jack-in-the-Box, KFC, LJ Silver, Sizzler, Taco Bell, **lodging:** AstroBudget Motel, Best Motel, Budget Inn, Comfort Inn, Day's Inn, Desert Inn, Econolodge, Economy Inn, Executive Inn, Quality Inn, Ramada Inn, Super 8, **other:** AutoZone, Kragen Parts, Radio Shack, U-Haul/LP, Von's Foods, **S gas:** Arco/24hr, **other:** Walmart/McDonald's/auto/gas |
| **0mm** | I-40 begins/ends on I-15 in Barstow |

## INTERSTATE 80

| Exit # | Services |
|---|---|
| **208** | California/Nevada state line |
| **201** | Farad |
| **199** | Floristan |
| **194** | Hirschdale Rd, **N** to Boca Dam, Stampede Dam |
| **191mm** | (from wb), weigh sta., inspection sta. |
| **190** | Overland Trail |
| **188** | CA 89 N, CA 267, to N Shore Lake Tahoe, **N other:** USFS, **S** same as 186 |
| **186** | Central Truckee (no eb return), **S gas:** Beacon, 76, **food:** Burger Mee, Casa Baeza Mexican, El Toro Bravo Mexican, Wagontrain Café, **lodging:** Hilltop Lodge, Truckee Hotel |
| **185** | CA 89 S, to N Lake Tahoe, **N food:** DQ, Jiffy's Pizza, Nick'n Willy's Pizza, Panda Express, Port of Subs, RoundTable Pizza, Starbucks, Zano's Pizza, **other:** H HOSPITAL, URGENT CARE, Ace Hardware, GNC, NAPA, New Moon Natural Foods, Radio Shack, Rite Aid, Safeway, 7-11, hwy patrol, **S gas:** Shell/dsl, **food:** Cheesesteak, KFC, McDonald's, Mongolian BBQ, Pizzaria, Subway, **other:** Longs Drugs, Savemart Foods, auto repair, to Squaw Valley, RV camping |
| **184** | Donner Pass Rd, Truckee, **N gas:** Shell/dsl, **food:** La bamba Mexican, Pizza Shack, Smokey's Kitchen, **lodging:** Sunset Inn, **other:** factory outlet/famous brands, **S gas:** Chevron/dsl/24hr, 76, **food:** Taco Bell, **lodging:** Holiday Inn Express, **other:** chain service, to Donner SP, RV camp/dump |
| **181mm** | vista point both lanes |
| **180** | Donner Lake (from wb), **S lodging:** Donner Lake Village Resort |
| **177mm** | **Donner Summit, elev 7239, rest area both lanes, full &#9855; facilities, view area, [C, 🏞, litter barrels, petwalk** |
| **176** | Castle Park, Boreal Ridge Rd, **S lodging:** Boreal Inn/rest., **other:** Pacific Crest Trailhead, skiing |
| **174** | Soda Springs, Norden, **S gas:** Beacon/LP/dsl, **food:** Summit Rest., **lodging:** Donner Summit Lodge, **other:** chain services |

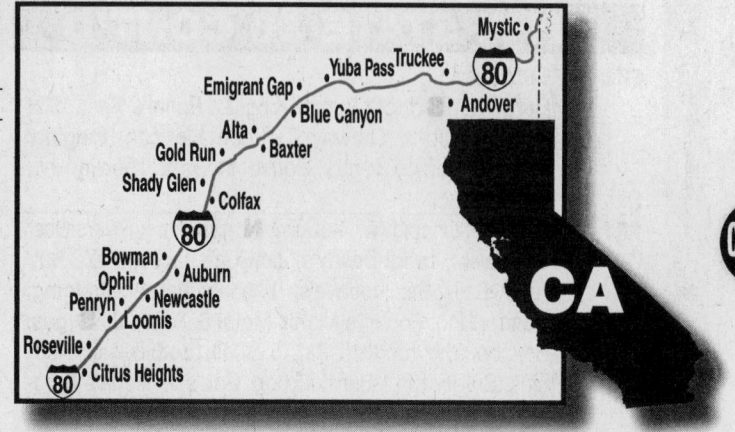

| | |
|---|---|
| **171** | Kingvale, **S gas:** Shell |
| **168** | Rainbow Rd, to Big Bend, **S lodging:** Rainbow Lodge/rest., **other:** RV camping |
| **166** | Big Bend (from eb) |
| **165** | Cisco Grove, **N other:** RV camp/dump, skiing, snowmobiling, **S gas:** Valero/24hr, **other:** chain services |
| **164** | Eagle Lakes Rd |
| **161** | CA 20 W, to Nevada City, Grass Valley |
| **160** | Yuba Gap, **S other:** snowpark, phone, picnic tables, boating, camping, skiing |
| **158** | Laing Rd, **S lodging:** Rancho Sierra Inn/café |
| **157mm** | brake check area, wb |
| **158a** | Emigrant Gap (from eb), **S lodging:** Rancho Sierra Inn/café |
| **156** | Nyack Rd, Emigrant Gap, **S gas:** Shell/Burger King/dsl, **food:** Nyack Café |
| **156mm** | brake check area |
| **155** | Blue Canyon |
| **150** | Drum Forebay |
| **148b** | Baxter, **N other:** RV camping, chainup services, food, phone |
| **148a** | Crystal Springs |
| **146** | Alta |
| **145** | Dutch Flat, **N food:** Monte Vista Rest., **S gas:** Tesoro/dsl, **other:** RV camping, chainup services, hwy patrol |
| **144** | Gold Run (from wb), **N** gas/dsl, food, [C, chainup |
| **143mm** | **rest area both lanes, full &#9855; facilities, [C, 🏞, litter barrels, petwalk** |
| **143** | Magra Rd, Gold Run, **N** chainup services |
| **140** | Magra Rd, Rollins Lake Rd, Secret Town Rd |
| **139** | Rollins Lake Road (from wb), RV camping |
| **135** | CA 174, to Grass Valley, Colfax, **N gas:** 76/dsl, **food:** McDonald's, Pizza Factory, Starbucks, Taco Bell, TJ's Roadhouse, **lodging:** Colfax Motel, **other:** Best Hardware, Curves, One Buck Store, Sierra Mkt Foods, NAPA, **S gas:** Chevron/dsl, Valero/dsl, **food:** Drooling Dog BBQ, Shang Garden Chinese, Subway |
| **133** | Canyon Way, to Colfax, **S other:** Chevrolet, Plaza Tire |
| **131** | Cross Rd, to Weimar |
| **130** | W Paoli Lane, to Weimar, **S gas:** Weimar Store/dsl |
| **129** | Heather Glen, elev 2000 ft |
| **128** | Applegate, **N gas:** Applegate Gas/dsl/LP, **other:** chainup services |
| **125** | Clipper Gap, Meadow Vista |
| **124** | Dry Creek Rd |
| **123** | Bell Rd |

**BARSTOW**

**E ↕ W TRUCKEE**

**COLFAX**

**E ↕ W** — **AUBURN** — **NEW CASTLE**

## INTERSTATE 80 CONT'D

**122** Continued
ing/dump, **S food:** Burger King, La Ponte's Rest., Sizzler, Starbucks, Subway, TioPepe Mexican, **lodging:** Best Western, Country Squire Inn/rest., Quality Inn, same as 121

**121** (from eb) Lincolnway, Auburn, **N gas:** Arco, Flyers Gas/dsl, Valero, **food:** Denny's, JimBoy's Tacos, Pizza Hut/Taco Bell/24hr, Popeye's, Wienerschnitzel, **lodging:** Comfort Inn, Foothills Motel, Motel 6, Super 8, **S gas:** Beacon, Chevron/dsl/24hr, 76, Shell, **food:** Baskin-Robbins, Burger King, Burrito Shop, Carl's Jr, Ikeda's Burgers, Jack-in-the-Box, KFC, LaBonte's Rest., McDonald's, Pete's Cafe, Sierra Grill, Sizzler, Smoothie King, Starbucks, Subway, TioPepe Mexican, **lodging:** Best Western, Quality Inn, **other:** Raley's Foods

**120** Russell Ave (from wb), to Lincolnway from eb, same as 121

**119c** Elm Ave, Auburn, **N gas:** 76/dsl, Shell, **food:** Foster's, **lodging:** Holiday Inn, **other:** Grocery Outlet, Longs Drug, Rite Aid, SaveMart Foods, Staples

**119b** CA 49, to Grass Valley, Auburn, **N gas:** 76, Shell, **food:** In-n-Out, Marie Callender's, **lodging:** Holiday Inn, **other:** Staples

**119a** Maple St, Nevada St, Old Town Auburn, **S gas:** Valero, **food:** Mary Belle's, Tiopete Mexican

**118** Ophir Rd (from wb)

**116** CA 193, to Lincoln, **S other:** truck repair

**115** Indian Hill Rd, Newcastle, **N other:** transmissions, **S gas:** Arco, Flyers/dsl, **food:** Denny's, CHP

**112** Penryn, **N gas:** 76/dsl/LP, Valero/Subway/dsl, **food:** Houston's Steaks, L'Omelet Cafe

**110** Horseshoe Bar Rd, to Loomis, **N food:** Burger King, Quizno's, RoundTable Pizza, Starbucks, Taco Bell, **other:** Raley's Food

**109** Sierra College Blvd, **N gas:** Chevron/McDonald's/dsl, 7-11, **food:** Carl's Jr, **other:** Camping World RV Service/supplies, Gamel RV Ctr, Harley Davidson, antiques

**108** Rocklin Rd, **N gas:** Rocklin Gas, **food:** A&W/KFC, Arby's, Baskin-Robbins, China Gourmet, Denny's, Golden Dragon, Jack-in-the-Box, Jamba Juice, KFC, Papa Murphy's, RoundTable Pizza, Starbucks, Subway, Taco Bell, **lodging:** Days Inn, Heritage Inn, Howard Johnson, **other:** GNC, Land Rover, Longs Drug, Porsche, Radio Shack, Safeway, **S gas:** Arco/24hr, **food:** Casa Bella, **lodging:** Rocklin Park Hotel

**106** CA 65, to Lincoln, Marysville, **1 mi N on Stanford Ranch Rd...gas:** Shell, **food:** Applebee's, Buca Italian, Carl's Jr, Cheesecake Factory, IHOP, Jack-in-the-Box, McDonald's, On-the-Border, Red Robin, Subway, **lodging:** Comfort Suites, **other:** AutoZone, Barnes&Noble, Best Buy, Costco, JC Penney, Macy's, Marshall's, Nordstrom's, Old Navy, Ross

**105b** Taylor Rd, to Rocklin (from eb), **N food:** Cattlemen's Rest., **other:** Albertson's (1mi), **S gas:** Chevron, 76/Burger King, **food:** Islands Burgers, Paradise Grill, Sierra Mtn Dining, Tahoe Joe's, **lodging:** Courtyard, Fairfield Inn, Hilton Garden, Holiday Inn Express, Larkspur Suites, Residence Inn, **other:** H HOSPITAL, SaveMart

**105a** Atlantic St, Eureka Rd, **S gas:** Joe's Mkt/Sonic, 76, Shell/Circle K, **food:** Brookfield's Rest., Black Angus,

**CITRUS HEIGHTS**

**105a** Continued
Carver's Steaks, In-n-Out, Panda Express, Supermex Rest., Taco Bell, Tahoe Joe's, Wendy's, **lodging:** Marriott, **other:** America'sTire, Buick/GMC, Carmax, Chevrolet, Ford, Home Depot, Hyundai, Lexus, Nissan, PetsMart, Sam's Club, Saturn, Subaru, Toyota/scion, VW, Walmart, mall

**103b a** Douglas Blvd, **N gas:** Arco/24hr, Chevron, 76, **food:** Burger King, Carolina's Mexican, Jack-in-the-Box, McDonald's, Starbucks, **lodging:** Best Western, Extended Stay America, Heritage Inn, Residence Inn, **other:** H HOSPITAL, Ace Hardware, BigLots, Big O Tire, BrakeMasters, $Tree, Firestone, Goodyear, Kragen Parts, Radio Shack, Trader Joe's, **S gas:** Shell, **food:** Carl's Jr, Carrow's, Del Taco, Denny's, Outback Steaks, Subway, Togo's, **lodging:** Hampton Inn, Orchid Suites, **other:** Lincoln/Mercury, Office Depot, Rite Aid, Ross, Target

**102** Riverside Ave, Auburn Blvd, to Roseville, **N gas:** Arco/24hr, Chevron/dsl, **food:** Starbucks, Subway, **other:** vet, **S gas:** 76, Shell, Tower, Valero/dsl, **food:** Asiana China, Back 40 Rest., Baskin-Robbins, Big Joe's BBQ, CA Burgers, Charlie's Rest., DQ, Jack-in-the-Box, **other:** AutoZone, BMW Motorcycles, $World, K-Mart, NAPA, Schwab Tire, Village RV Ctr, transmissions

**100** Antelope Rd, to Citrus Heights, **N gas:** 76, **food:** Carl's Jr, Giant Pizza, KFC, McDonald's, Popeye's, Round Table Pizza, Subway, Taco Bell, Wendy's, **other:** $Tree, Raley's Foods, Rite Aid, 7-11, vet

**100mm** weigh sta both lanes

**98** Greenback Lane, Elkhorn Blvd, Orangevale, Citrus Heights, **N gas:** 76/service, **food:** Carl's Jr, McDonald's, Pizza Hut, Subway, Taco Bell, **other:** Longs Drug, Radio Shack, Safeway

**96** Madison Ave, **N gas:** Chevron, Valero, **food:** Brookfield's Rest., Denny's, El Zarape Mexican, Jack-in-the-Box, Starbucks, **lodging:** Motel 6, Super 8, **other:** funpark, to McClellan AFB, **S gas:** Arco/24hr, 76, Shell/repair, **food:** Boston Mkt, Burger King, Chipotle Mexican, El Pollo Loco, IHOP, In-N-Out, Jack-in-the-Box, McDonald's, Panda Express, Starbucks, Subway, **lodging:** Holiday Inn, La Quinta, **other:** Acura, Chevrolet, Ford/Isuzu, Office Depot, PepBoys, Schwab Tire, 7-11, Target, Walgreens

**95** CA 99 S

**94b** Auburn Blvd

**94a** Watt Ave, **N gas:** 76, **lodging:** Day's Inn, Mote 6, **other:** Firestone, McClellan AFB, **S gas:** Arco/24hr, Chevron, Shell, **food:** CheeseSteak, China Taste, Denny's, Jimboy's Tacos, Quizno's, Starbucks, Subway, Wendy's, **lodging:** Great Western Inn

**93** Longview Dr

**92** Winters St

**91** Raley Blvd, Marysville Blvd, to Rio Linda, **N gas:** Arco/24hr, Chevron/dsl/24hr, **S other:** Mkt Basket Foods, Valley Tires, USPO

**90** Norwood Ave, **N gas:** Arco/Jack-in-the-Box/24hr, Valero, **food:** McDonald's, Quizno's, RoundTable Pizza, Starbucks, Subway, **other:** Rite Aid, Viva Foods

**89** Northgate Blvd, Sacramento, **N other:** Fry's Electronics, **S gas:** Arco, Circle K/gas, Shell, **food:** Carl's Jr,

E ↕ W

S A C R A M E N T O

## INTERSTATE 80 CONT'D

**89** Continued
Classic Burgers, Domino's, El Pollo Loco, IHOP, KFC, LJ Silver, McDonald's/playplace, Subway, Taco Bell, **lodging:** Extended Stay America, Quality Inn, **other:** BigLots, $Tree, Foodsco Foods, Goodyear/auto, Kragen Parts, PepBoys, Schwab Tire

**88** Truxel Rd, **N gas:** Chevron, Shell/dsl, **food:** Applebee's, BJ's Rest, Carino's Italian, Chili's, Chipotle Mexican, Del Taco, Famous BBQ, Hooters, In-n-Out, Just Juice, Logan's Roadhouse, Mimi's Cafe, On the Border, Panera Bread, Pei Wei asian diner, Qdoba, Quizno's, Sonic, Starbucks, TGI Friday's, **lodging:** Staybridge Suites, **other:** Arco Arena, Barnes&Noble, Best Buy, BevMo, Home Depot, Michael's, Old Navy, PetsMart, Raley's Depot, Ross, Sam's Club/gas, Staples, Target, Walmart, World Mkt, mall

**86** I-5, N to Redding, S to Sacramento, to CA 99 N

**85** W El Camino, **N gas:** Chevron/Subway/dsl/24hr, 49er Trkstp/Silver Skillet/dsl/scales/24hr/@, **food:** Burger King, **lodging:** Fairfield Inn, Super 8

**83** Reed Ave, **N gas:** 76, **food:** Jack-in-the-Box, Los Amigo's, Quizno's, Panda Express, Starbucks, Subway, TCBY, **lodging:** Extended Stay America, **other:** Ford Trucks, dsl repair, **S gas:** Arco/24hr, Shell/McDonald's/dsl, **other:** Walmart Super Ctr

**82** US 50 E, W Sacramento

**81** Enterprise Blvd, W Capitol Ave, W Sacramento, **N gas:** Chevron/dsl/24hr, Valero/dsl, **food:** Eppie's Rest/24hr, **lodging:** Granada Inn, **S gas:** 7-11/gas, **food:** Denny's, Quizno's, Starbucks, Subway, **other:** KOA

**78** Rd 32A, E Chiles Rd, **S** Produce Mkt

**75** Mace Blvd, **N gas:** Arco, **S gas:** Chevron/24hr, 76, Spirit/dsl, Valero/dsl, **food:** Burger King, McDonald's, Mtn Mikes Pizza, Subway, Taco Bell/24hr, Wendy's, **lodging:** Howard Johnson, Motel 6, **other:** Chevrolet/Toyota, Chrysler/Jeep, Ford/Mercury/Nissan, Honda, La Mesa RV Ctr, Mazda/VW, Nugget Mkt Foods, Pontiac/Buick/GMC, Schwab Tire, Toyota/Scion, to Mace Ranch

**73** Olive Dr (from wb, no EZ return)

**72b a** Richards Blvd, Davis, **N gas:** Shell/24hr, **food:** Caffe Italia, In-n-Out, Redrum Burger, **lodging:** University Park Inn, **other:** NAPA, **S gas:** Chevron, **food:** Applebee's, Del Taco, IHOP, KFC, RoundTable Pizza, Wendy's, **lodging:** Comfort Suites, Holiday Inn Express, **other:** Jiffy Lube, Kragen Parts

**71** to UC Davis

**70** CA 113 N, to Woodland, **N H** HOSPITAL

**69** Kidwell Rd

**67** Pedrick Rd, **N gas:** Chevron/dsl, 76/LP, **other:** produce

**66b** Milk Farm Rd (from wb)

**66a** CA 113 S, Currey Rd, to Dixon, **S gas:** Arco, CFN/dsl, 76/Popeye's/dsl, Shell/dsl, **food:** Cattlemen's Rest., Jack-in-the-Box, Taco Del Mar, Wendy's, **other:** Walmart SuperCtr

**64** Pitt School Rd, to Dixon, **S gas:** Chevron/24hr, Valero/24hr, **food:** Arby's, Burger King, Cenario's Pizza, Chevy's Mexican, China Doll, Denny's, Domino's, IHOP/24hr, Mary's Pizza, McDonald's, Pizza Hut, Solano Bakery, Starbucks, Subway, Taco Bell, **lodging:**

**64** Continued
Best Western, Microtel, **other:** Ford, Kragen Parts, Radio Shack, Safeway/dsl

**63** Dixon Ave, Midway Rd, **N gas:** Truck Stp/dsl, **S gas:** Chevron/LP/lube, USA/24hr, **food:** Carl's Jr, KFC/A&W, Perla Del Mar, **lodging:** Super 8, **other:** Dixon Fruit Mkt, $Heaven, Food Market, RV Dump

**60** Midway Rd, Lewis Rd, Elmyra, **N** RV camping

**59** Meridian Rd, Weber Rd

**57** Leisure Town Rd, **N H** HOSPITAL, **S gas:** KwikStop/dsl, Valero, **food:** Black Oak Rest., Jack-in-the-Box, SplitFire Rest., Vaca Joe's, **lodging:** Best Value, Extended Stay America, Fairfield Inn, Holiday Inn Express, Motel 6, Residence Inn, Vaca Valley Inn, **other:** Chevrolet, Chrysler/Dodge/Jeep, Harley-Davidson, Home Depot, Honda, Kohl's, Mazda, Nissan, Toyota, VW

**56** I-505 N, to Winters,

**55** Nut Tree Pkwy, Monte Vista Dr, Allison Dr, **N gas:** Citgo/7-11, 76/Circle K, Shell, Valero, **food:** Arby's, Burger King, Denny's, Hisui Japanese, IHOP, McDonald's, Murillo's Mexican, Nations Burger, Panera Bread, Pelayo's Mexican, Taco Bell, Wendy's, **lodging:** Best Western, Royal Motel, Super 8, **other:** **H** HOSPITAL, Best Buy, Big O Tire, Borders, Firestone/auto, Goodyear/auto, Lowes Whse, Nugget Foods, Old Navy, U-Haul, transmissions, **S gas:** Arco/24hr, Chevron/24hr, **food:** Applebee's, Baja Fresh Mexican, BJ's Grill, Black Oak Rest., Carl's Jr, Chevy's Mexican, Chili's, Fresh Choice Cafe, In-n-Out, Jack-in-the-Box, KFC, Mel's Cafe, Popeyes, Quizno's, Starbucks, Tahoe Joe's Rest., TGIFridays, Togo's, **lodging:** Courtyard, Fairfield Inn, Residence Inn, **other:** Goodyear, Home Depot, Michael's, Old Navy, Pontiac/GMC, Ross, Safeway, Sam's Club, Staples, Target, Toyota, Vacaville Stores/famous brands, Walmart/auto

**54b** Mason St, Peabody Rd, **N gas:** Chevron, Valero, **food:** A&W/LJ Silver, **lodging:** Hampton Inn, **other:** NAPA, Schwab Tire, **S gas:** USA Gas, **food:** Domino's, Solano's Bakery, Wok'n Roll Chinese, **other:** Costco/gas, Ford/Mercury, Goodyear/auto, 7-11

**54a** Davis St, **N gas:** Chevron/McDonald's, **food:** Outback Steaks, **lodging:** Hampton Inn **S gas:** QuikStop, **other:** WinCo Foods, repair

**53** Merchant St, Alamo Dr, **N gas:** Chevron, Shell/dsl, Valero, **food:** Baldo's Mexican, Bakers Square, Lyon's/24hr, RoundTable Pizza, Subway, Tin Tin Buffet, **lodging:**

V A C A V I L L E

Copyright 2009 - The Next Exit®

## INTERSTATE 80 CONT'D

**E** ↕ **W**

**CA**

**FAIRFIELD**

**VALLEJO**

| | |
|---|---|
| **53** | Continued<br>Alamo Inn, **other:** Big Lots, vet, **S gas:** 76, **food:** Jack-in-the-Box, KFC, McDonald's, Pizza Hut, Port Subs, Starbucks, **other:** Radio Shack |
| **52** | Cherry Glen Rd (from wb) |
| **51b** | Pena Adobe Rd, **S lodging:** Ranch Hotel |
| **51a** | Lagoon Valley Rd, Cherry Glen |
| **48** | N Texas St, Fairfield, **S gas:** Arco/24hr, Chevron, Shell, **food:** Burger King, RoundTable Pizza, Pollo Loco, **lodging:** EZ 8 Motel, **other:** Long's Drugs, Raley's Foods |
| **47** | Waterman Blvd, **N food:** Dynasty Chinese, Hungry Hunter Rest., RoundTable Pizza, Strings Italian, **other:** Buick/Pontiac/GMC, Chevrolet/Cadillac, Safeway, to Austin's Place, **S** to Travis AFB, museum |
| **45** | Travis Blvd, Fairfield, **N gas:** Arco/24hr, Chevron/24hr, Shell/dsl, **food:** Burger King, ChuckeCheese, Denny's, In-n-Out, Peking Rest., Subway, Taco Bell, **lodging:** Courtyard, Holiday Inn, Motel 6, **other:** Raley's Foods, Harley-Davidson, Ford, Hyundai, Nissan, CHP, **S gas:** Shell, **food:** Applebee's, Baja Fresh Mexican, Blue Frog Grill, Carino's Italian, Chevy's Mexican, Coldstone Creamery, FreshChoice Rest., Gordito's Mexican, Great Wall Chinese, Jamba Juice, Marie Callender's, Mimi's Café, Olive Garden, Panda Express, Red Lobster, Starbucks, Subway, **lodging:** Hilton Garden, **other:** H HOSPITAL, Barnes&Noble, Best Buy, Circuit City, Firestone/auto, JC Penney, Macy's, Michael's, Old Navy, Ross, Sears/auto, Trader Joe's, WorldMkt, mall |
| **44** | W Texas St, same as 46, Fairfield, **N gas:** Shell/dsl, **food:** ChuckeCheese, Gordito's Mexican, **lodging:** Extended Stay America, **other:** Mazda/Subaru, Suzuki, **S gas:** Valero, **food:** Baldo's Mexican, McDonald's, Paleyo's Mexican, Scenario's Pizza, **lodging:** Travelodge, **other:** Acura/Honda, Chrysler/Jeep/Dodge, FoodMaxx, Home Depot, Hyundai, Infiniti, Mitsubishi, Nissan, Target, Toyota, Volvo, Walgreens |
| **43** | CA 12 E, Abernathy Rd, Suisun City, **S other:** Budweiser Plant, Walmart |
| **42mm** | weigh sta both lanes, phone |
| **41** | Suisan Valley Rd, **S gas:** Arco/24hr, Chevron, 76/Circle K/dsl/24hr, Shell/dsl, Valero, **food:** Arby's, Bravo's Pizza, Burger King, Carl's Jr, Denny's, Jack-in-the-Box, McDonald's, Starbucks, Subway, Taco Bell, Wendy's, **lodging:** Best Western, Comfort Suites, Days Inn, Fairfield Inn, Holiday Inn Express, **other:** Camping World RV Service, Ray's RV Ctr, Scandia FunCtr |
| **40** | I-680 (from wb) |
| **39b** | Green Valley Rd, I-680 (from eb), **N food:** Applebees, Happy Garden Chinese, RoundTable Pizza, Sticky Rice Bistro, Subway, **other:** Costco/gas, Longs Drug, Radio Shack, Safeway, TJ Maxx, **S gas:** Arco, **other:** Saturn |
| **39a** | Red Top Rd, **N gas:** 76/Circle K/24hr, **food:** Jack-in-the-Box |
| **36** | American Canyon Rd |
| **34mm** | rest area wb, full ♿ facilities, info, 📞, 🍴, litter barrels, petwalk, vista parking |
| **33b a** | CA 37, to San Rafael, Columbus Pkwy, **N gas:** Chevron, **food:** Carls Jr., **lodging:** Courtyard, **S** same as 32 |

| | |
|---|---|
| **32** | Redwood St, to Vallejo, **N gas:** 76, **food:** Denny's, Panda Garden, **lodging:** Best Value Inn, Motel 6, **other:** H HOSPITAL, **S gas:** Arco, BonFair, Shell, **food:** Applebee's, Black Angus, Chevy's Mexican, Chinese Cuisine, Coldstone Creamery, IHOP, Jamba Juice, Little Caesar's, Lyon's Rest., McDonald's, Mtn Mike's Pizza, Olive Garden, Panda Express, Quizno's, Red Lobster, Starbucks, Subway, Taco Bell, Wendy's, **lodging:** Comfort Inn, Ramada Inn, **other:** AutoZone, Best Buy, Buick/GMC, Costco/gas, Hancock Fabrics, Home Depot, Honda, Longs Drug, Michael's, PepBoys, Radio Shack, Ross, Safeway, Toyota |
| **31b** | Tennessee St, to Vallejo, **S gas:** 76, Valero, **food:** Jack-in-the-Box, Pacifica Pizza, Pizza Guys, **lodging:** Great Western Inn, Quality Inn, **other:** USPO |
| **31a** | Solano Ave, Springs Rd, **N food:** Burger King, Church's, El Rey Mexican, Taco Bell, **lodging:** Deluxe Inn, Relax Inn, **other:** Ford, Albertson's, Rite Aid, U-Haul, **S gas:** Chemco, Chevron, Grand Gas, QuikStop, **food:** DQ, India Garden, Pizza Hut, Starbucks, Subway, **lodging:** Islander Motel, **other:** Kragen Parts, Walgreens |
| **30c** | Georgia St, Central Vallejo, **N gas:** Safeway, **other:** Ford, **S gas:** Shell/Starbucks/dsl, **food:** Coconut Grove, McDonald's, **lodging:** California Motel |
| **30b** | Benicia Rd (from wb), **S gas:** Shell/dsl, **food:** McDonald's, Starbucks |
| **30a** | I-780, to Martinez |
| **29b** | Magazine St, Vallejo, **N gas:** 76/dsl, **food:** Starbucks, **lodging:** Budget Inn, El Rancho, 7 Motel, **other:** Tradewinds RV Park, **S food:** McDonald's, **lodging:** Travel Inn, **other:** 7-11 |
| **29a** | CA 29, Maritime Academy Dr, Vallejo, **N gas:** Chevron/24hr, 5 Star Gas, **food:** Subway, **lodging:** Motel 6, Vallejo Inn |
| **28mm** | toll plaza, pay toll from eb |
| **27** | Pomona Rd, Crockett, **N food:** seafood rest. |
| **26** | Cummings Skyway, to CA 4 (from wb), to Martinez |
| **24** | Willow Ave, to Rodeo, **N food:** Straw Hat Pizza, Subway, **other:** Curves, NAPA, Safeway/24hr, USPO, **S gas:** 76/Circle K/dsl, **food:** Burger King, Mazatlan, Starbucks |
| **23** | CA 4, to Stockton, Hercules, **N gas:** Shell, **food:** Jack-in-the-Box, Starbucks, **other:** Radio Shack, on Sycamore **N food:** Burgerama, McDonald's, RoundTable Pizza, Subway, Taco Bell, **other:** Albertson's, Home Depot, Rite Aid, USPO |
| **22** | Pinole Valley Rd, **S gas:** Arco/24hr, Chevron/dsl, **food:** China House, Jack-in-the-Box, Papa John's, Red Onion Rest., Subway, **other:** 7-11 |
| **21** | Appian Way, **N gas:** Beacon, **food:** McDonald's, **other:** Kragen Parts, Longs Drug, Safeway, **S gas:** Valero/dsl, **food:** Burger King, Carl's Jr, HomeTown Buffet, HotDog Sta, KFC, Krispy Kreme, In n' Out, LJ Silver, Panda Express, RoundTable Pizza, Sizzler, Starbucks, Subway, Taco Bell, Wendy's, **lodging:** Day's Inn, Motel 6, **other:** Albertson's, Autozone, Best Buy, Goodyear/auto, K-Mart, Radio Shack |
| **20** | Richmond Pkwy, to I-580 W, **N gas:** Chevron, **food:** McDonald's, IHOP, Subway, **other:** Barnes&Noble, Chrysler/Jeep, Circuit City, Ford, Ross, **S gas:** Chevron, Shell/dsl, **food:** Applebee's, Chuck Steak, In-n-Out, Krispy Kreme, Outback Steaks, Panda Express, |

## INTERSTATE 80 CONT'D

**E** → **W**
**RICHMOND**
**BERKELEY**

| | |
|---|---|
| 20 | Continued<br>Round Table Pizza, **other:** FoodMaxx, GoodGuys, Kinko's, Kragen Parts, Old Navy, Michael's, Staples, Target |
| 19b | Hilltop Dr, to Richmond, **N gas:** Chevron, **food:** Chevy's Mexican, Olive Garden, Red Lobster, Subway, Tokyo Rest., **lodging:** Courtyard, Extended Stay America, **other:** Albertson's, Buick/Pontiac, Chevrolet, Firestone, JC Penney, Jo-Ann Fabrics, Macy's, Nissan, Sears/auto, mall, **S gas:** Hilltop Fuel/Bobby's BBQ/dsl |
| 19a | El Portal Dr, to San Pablo, **S gas:** Shell, **food:** McDonalds, KFC, **other:** Raley's Foods |
| 18 | San Pablo Dam Rd, **N gas:** 76, 7-11, **food:** Burger King, Denny's, Jack-in-the-Box, KFC, Long's Burgers, McDonald's, Nations Burgers, Quizno's, Taco Bell, **lodging:** Holiday Inn Express, **other:** Ⓗ HOSPITAL, Albertson's, K-Mart, Longs Drug, **S other:** CamperLand RV Ctr |
| 17 | Macdonald Ave (from eb), McBryde Ave (from wb), Richmond, **N gas:** Arco/24hr, Citgo/7-11, **food:** Burger King, Church's, KFC, Taco Bell, **S gas:** Chevron/24hr, **food:** Bakers Square, Wendy's, **other:** Albertson's, Safeway, auto repair |
| 16 | San Pablo Ave, to Richmond, San Pablo, **S gas:** Chevron, 76, **food:** Subway, Wendy's, **other:** Safeway |
| 15 | Cutting Blvd, Potrero St, to I-580 Br (from wb), to El Cerrito, **N gas:** Arco, **S gas:** Chevron, 76/dsl, **food:** Carrow's Rest., Church's, Denny's, IHOP, Jack-in-the-Box, McDonald's, **lodging:** Super 8, **other:** $Tree, FoodsCo Foods, Home Depot, Honda, PepBoys, Radio Shack, Staples, Target, Walgreens |
| 14b | Carlson Blvd, El Cerrito, **N gas:** 76, **lodging:** 40 Flags Motel, **S lodging:** Best Value |
| 14a | Central Ave, El Cerrito, **S gas:** 76, Valero, **food:** Burger King, KFC, Nations Burgers, **other:** Branch Mkt Foods, mall |
| 13 | to I-580 (from eb), Albany |
| 12 | Gilman St, to Berkeley, **N** Golden Gate Fields Racetrack |
| 11 | University Ave, to Berkeley, **S gas:** 76, Beacon, **other:** to UC Berkeley |
| 10 | CA 13, to Ashby Ave |
| 9 | Powell St, Emeryville, **N gas:** Shell, **food:** Chevy's Mexican, **lodging:** Holiday Inn, **S gas:** Beacon, **food:** Burger King, Denny's, Jamba Juice, Lyon's Rest., Starbucks, Trader Joe's, **lodging:** Courtyard, Day's Inn, Sheraton, Wyndham Suites, **other:** Borders Books, Circuit City, Emery Bay Mkt, Good Guys, Jo-Ann Fabrics, Old Navy, Ross |
| 8c b | Oakland, to I-880, I-580 |
| 8a | W Grand Ave, Maritime St |
| 7mm | toll plaza wb |
| 5mm | SF Bay |
| 4a | Treasure Island (exits left) |
| 2c b | Fremont St, Harrison St, Embarcadero (from wb) |
| 2a | 4th st (from eb), **S gas:** Shell |
| 1 | 9th St Civic Ctr, downtown SF |
| 1b a | I-80 begins/ends on US 101 in SF |

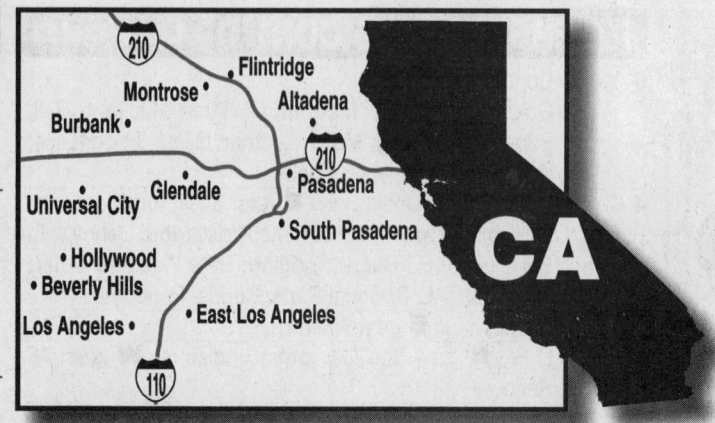

## INTERSTATE 110 - Los Angeles

**LOS ANGELES AREA**

| Exit # | Services |
|---|---|
| 21 | I-110 begins/ends on I-10. |
| 20c | Adams Blvd, **E other:** Chevron, Nissan, Office Depot, LA Convention Ctr. |
| 20b | 37th St, Exposition Blvd, **E** repair, **W gas:** Chevron/McDonald's, **lodging:** Radisson |
| 20a | MLK Blvd, Expo Park, **W gas:** Chevron, **food:** McDonald's, Subway |
| 19b | Vernon Ave, **E gas:** Mobil, **W gas:** 76/24hr, Shell, **food:** Burger King, Jack-in-the-Box, **other:** Ralph's Foods |
| 18b | Slauson Ave, **E gas:** Mobil, **W gas:** 76 |
| 18a | Gage Blvd, **E gas:** Arco, **food:** Church's |
| 17 | Florence Ave, **E gas:** Mobil, **food:** Jack-in-the-Box, **W gas:** Arco, Chevron, Shell/24hr, **food:** Burger King, McDonald's, Pizza Hut |
| 16 | Manchester Ave, **E gas:** Arco, **food:** McDonald's, **other:** AutoZone, **W gas:** 76/Circle K, **food:** Church's, Jack-in-the-Box, Tom's Burgers, Popeye's, **other:** Ralph's Foods |
| 15 | Century Blvd, **E gas:** Arco, Shell/Subway, **food:** Burger King, **W gas:** 76 |
| 14b | Imperial Hwy, **W gas:** Petro Zone, **food:** McDonald's, Jack-in-the-Box |
| 14a | I-105 |
| 13 | El Segundo Blvd, **E food:** Pizza Hut, Taco Bell, **W food:** Denny's |
| 12 | Rosecrans Ave, **E gas:** Arco/24hr, Prena, SC Fuels, **W gas:** Chevron/McDonald's, Mobil, **food:** Jack-in-the-Box, KFC, Popeye's, Subway, **other:** Chief Parts, 7-11 |
| 11 | Redondo Beach Blvd, **E food:** McDonald's, **W gas:** Mobil, **other:** Ⓗ HOSPITAL |
| 10b a | CA 91, 190th St, **W food:** Carl's Jr, Jack-in-the-Box, Krispy Kreme, McDonald's, Taco Bell/Pizza Hut, **other:** Albertson's, Food4Less, Sam's Club |
| 9 | I-405, San Diego Fwy |
| 8 | Torrance Blvd, Del Amo, **E food:** Baskin-Robbins, Burger King, Chile Verde, Panda Bowl, **other:** K-mart, **W gas:** Mobil, Shell/dsl |
| 7b | Carson St, **E food:** KFC, **lodging:** Cali Inn, **W gas:** Mobil, Shell, **food:** Bakers Square, Hong Kong Garden, In-n-Out, Jack-in-the-Box, **other:** Ⓗ HOSPITAL, Carson Drug, Kragen Parts, Radio Shack |
| 5 | Sepulveda Blvd, **E food:** McDonald's, **other:** Albertson's, Home Depot, Staples, Target, **W gas:** Arco/24hr, Chevron, Mobil, Shell, **food:** Burger King, Carl's Jr, |

## INTERSTATE 110 CONT'D - Los Angeles

| | |
|---|---|
| 5 | Continued<br>Golden Ox Burger, McDonald's, Pizza Hut/Taco Bell, Popeye's, **lodging:** Motel 6, **other:** $Tree, Food4Less, K-Mart, Rite Aid, Von's Foods |
| 4 | CA 1, Pacific Coast Hwy, **E gas:** Shell, **food:** Jack-in-the-Box, **W gas:** Chevron, Mobil/dsl, **food:** Denny's, El Pollo Loco, EZ Burger, **lodging:** Best Western, **other:** H HOSPITAL, Discount Parts, Honda, PepBoys |
| 3b | Anaheim St, **E gas:** Shell |
| 3a | C St, **E gas:** Shell/dsl, **other:** radiators, **W gas:** 76 Refinery |
| 1b | Channel St |
| 1a | CA 47, Gaffey Ave |
| 0mm | I-110 begins/ends |

## INTERSTATE 205 - Tracy

| Exit # | Services |
|---|---|
| 12 | I-205 begins wb, ends eb, accesses I-5 nb |
| 9 | MacArthur Dr, Tracy, **S** gas Chevron/Jack-in-the-Box/Subway/dsl, **other:** Prime Outlet Ctr/famous brands |
| 8 | Tracy Blvd, Tracy, **N gas:** Chevron, Shell/dsl, Tracy Trkstp/Mean Gene's Burger/dsl/24hr, **food:** Denny's/24hr, **lodging:** Holiday Inn Express, Motel 6, **S gas:** Arco/24hr, **food:** American Diner, Arby's, Burger King, In-n-Out, McDonald's, Nations Burgers, Subway, Tracy Buffet, Wendy's, **lodging:** Best Western, Microtel, Quality Inn, **other:** H HOSPITAL, FoodMaxx, Kragen Parts, Longs Drugs, Walgreens, CHP |
| 6 | Grant Line Rd, Antioch, **N gas:** Chevron, **food:** Applebee's, Burger King, Chevy's Mexican, Golden Corral, Hometown Buffet, IHOP, Jamba Juice, Olive Garden, Panda Express, Quizno's, Sonic, Starbucks, Strings Italian, Taco Bell, Texas Roadhouse, Wienerschnitzel/TasteeFreeze, **lodging:** Extended Stay America, Fairfield Inn, Hampton Inn, **other:** America's Tire, Barnes&Noble, Chevrolet, Costco/gas, Ford, Home Depot, Hyundai, JC Penney, Michael's, Nissan, Ross, Schwab Tire, Sears/auto, Staples, Target, Toyota, Walmart/McDonald's/auto, World Mkt, mall, **S gas:** Arco/24hr, Citgo/7-11, Shell/dsl, Valero, **food:** Carl's Jr, Chili's, Hawaian BBQ, KFC/A&W, Mtn Mike's Pizza, NYPD Pizza, Orchard Rest., Taco Del Mar, **other:** Cadillac/Pontiac/GMC, Rite Aid, Tracy Marine |
| 4 | 11th St (from eb), to Tracy, Defense Depot |
| 2 | Mtn House Pkwy, to I-580 E |
| 0mm | I-205 begins eb/ends wb, accesses I-580 wb. |

## INTERSTATE 210 - Pasadena

| Exit # | Services |
|---|---|
| 63 | I-15 N to Barstow, S to San Diego |
| 62 | Day Creek Blvd, **S gas:** Arco/dsl, Shell, **food:** Jack-in-the-Box, Pizza Factory, Starbucks, Wendy's, **other:** Ralph's Foods |
| 60 | Mileken Ave, **S gas:** Mobil, **food:** Taco Bell, **other:** Albertsons, CVS Drug, Kragen Parts |
| 59 | Haven Ave, **N gas:** 76, 7-11, Mobil, **food:** Del Taco, Dominos, Jack-in-the-Box, **other:** Walgreens |
| 58 | Archibald Ave, **S other:** Stater Bros |
| 57 | Carnelion St, **S gas:** 76, **food:** El Ranchero Mexican, |

| | |
|---|---|
| 57 | Continued<br>Papa John's, **other:** Radio Shack, Rite Aid, Vons Foods, Walgreens |
| 56 | Campus Ave, **S food:** Carl's Jr, Chick-fil-A, IHOP, Jamba Juice, Quizno's, Starbucks, **other:** Albertsons, Home Depot, Kohl's, Office Depot, PetsMart, Target |
| 54 | Mtn Ave, Mount Balde |
| 52 | Baseline Rd |
| 50 | Towne Ave |
| 48 | Fruit St, LaVerne, **S gas:** 76, **other:** U of LaVerne |
| 47 | Foothill Blvd, LaVerne, **N food:** Denny's, **S gas:** Chevron, Shell |
| 46 | San Dimas Ave, , **N** San Dimas Canyon CP |
| 45 | CA 57 S, Lone Hill Ave, Santa Ana, **S gas:** Chevron, **food:** Baja Fresh, Blimpie, Coco's, In-n-Out, Wendy's, **other:** Chevrolet, Dodge, Ford, Home Depot, Hyundai, Kohl's, Sam's Club, Toyota, Walmart/auto |
| 43 | Sunflower Ave |
| 42 | Grand Ave, to Glendora, **A gas:** 76, Valero, **food:** Denny's, **other:** H HOSPITAL |
| 41 | Citrus Ave, to Covina |
| 40 | Ca 39, Azuza Ave, **N gas:** Arco/24hr, Chevron, Shell/Subway/Del Taco, **food:** Jack-in-the-Box, **lodging:** Super 8, **S gas:** 76, **food:** In-n-Out, **lodging:** Azuza Inn |
| 39 | Vernon Ave (from wb), same as 38 |
| 38 | Irwindale, **N gas:** Arco, **food:** Carl's Jr, Denny's, FarmerBoys Rest., McDonald's, Shanghai Buffet, Taco Bell, **other:** Costco/gas |
| 36b | Mt Olive Dr |
| 36a | I-605 S |
| 35b a | Mountain Ave, **N gas:** Chevron **food:** Old Spaghetti Factory, Tommy's Hamburgers, Weinerschnitzel, **lodging:** Oak Park Motel, **other:** BMW/Mini, Buick, Chevrolet, Ford/Lincoln/Mercury, Honda, Infiniti, Isuzu, Mazda, Mitsubishi, Nissan, Saturn, Staples, Subaru, Target, Walgreens, **S food:** IHOP, Panda Express, **other:** Home Depot, Ross, Walmart |
| 34 | Myrtle Ave, **S gas:** Chevron, 76, **food:** Jack-in-the-Box |
| 33 | Huntington Dr, Monrovia, **N gas:** Shell, **food:** Acapulco Rest., Applebee's, Black Angus, Burger King, Chili's, ChuckeCheese, Leroy's Rest., McDonald's, Mimi's, Panda Express, Quizno's, RoundTable Pizza, Rubio's, Trader Joe's, **lodging:** Courtyard, **other:** GNC, Marshall's, Office Depot, Rite Aid, tires, **S food:** Baja Fresh, BJ's Grill, ClaimJumper, Daphne's Rest., Derby Rest., Gold Dragon, Macaroni Grill, Olive Garden, Outback Steaks, Red Lobster, Starbucks, Subway, Taisho Rest., Togo's, Tokyo Woko, Tony Roma, **lodging:** Embassy Suites, Extended Stay America, Hampton Inn, Holiday Inn, Homestead Suites, OakTree Inn, Residence Inn |
| 32 | Santa Anita Ave, Arcadia, **N gas:** Arco, **food:** McDonald's, **other:** Von's Foods, **S gas:** Chevron, **food:** In-n-Out, **other:** carwash |
| 31 | Baldwin Ave, to Sierra Madre |
| 30b a | Rosemead Blvd, **N gas:** Arco, 76, **S gas:** 76, **food:** Coco's, Jack-in-the-Box, **other:** Big-O Tires |
| 29b a | San Gabriel Blvd, Madre St, **N gas:** Arco, 76, **food:** El Torito, **lodging:** Panda Inn, **other:** Ralph's Foods, Ross, **S gas:** 76, **food:** Jack-in-the-Box, **lodging:** Best |

## INTERSTATE 210 CONT'D - Pasadena

**PASADENA E ↑ W SAN FERNANDO  N ↑ S**

| | |
|---|---|
| **29b a** | Continued<br> Western, Holiday Inn Express, Quality Inn, **other:** Buick/Chevrolet/Pontiac/GMC, Cadillac, Circuit City, Hyundai, Jiffy Lube, Staples, Target, Toyota |
| **28** | Altadena Dr, Sierra Madre, **S gas:** Chevron, Mobil, **other:** Just Tires, Office Depot |
| **27** | Hill Ave |
| **26** | Lake Ave, **N gas:** Mobil |
| **25b** | CA 134, to Ventura |
| **25a** | Del Mar Blvd, CA Blvd, CO Blvd  (exits left from eb) |
| **24** | Mountain St |
| **23** | Lincoln Ave, **S lodging:** Lincoln Motel, **other:** auto repair |
| **22b** | Arroyo Blvd, **N food:** Jack-in-the-Box, **S** to Rose Bowl |
| **22a** | Berkshire Ave, Oak Grove Dr |
| **21** | Gould Ave, **S gas:** Arco, **food:** Dominos, McDonald's, RoundTable Pizza, Trader Joes, **other:** Firestone, Just Tires, Ralph's Foods |
| **20** | CA 2, Angeles Crest Hwy |
| **19** | CA 2, Glendale Fwy, **S other:** H HOSPITAL |
| **18** | Ocean View Blvd, to Montrose |
| **17b a** | Pennsylvania Ave, La Crescenta, **N gas:** Mobil, Shell, **food:** Quizno's, Wienerschnitzel, **other:** Nissan, Office Depot, Toyota, Von's Foods, **S other:** Gardenia Mkt/deli |
| **16** | Lowell Ave |
| **14** | La Tuna Cyn Rd |
| **11** | Sunland Blvd, Tujunga, **N gas:** 76, **food:** Coco's, Sizzler, **other:** Ralph's Foods, Rite Aid, 7-11 |
| **9** | Wheatland Ave, **N other:** food mkt |
| **8** | Osborne St, Lakeview Terrace, **N food:** Ranch Side Cafe, **other:** 7-11 |
| **6a** | Paxton St |
| **6b** | CA 118 |
| **5** | Maclay St, to San Fernando, **S gas:** Chevron, 76, **food:** El Pollo Loco, KFC, McDonald's, Peter Piper Pizza, Quizno's, Taco Bell, **other:** Home Depot, Office Depot, Radio Shack, Sam's Club |
| **4** | Hubbard St, **N gas:** Chevron, **food:** Denny's, **other:** Radio Shack, Rite Aid, **S gas:** Mobil/dsl, Shell, **food:** El Caporal Mexican, Jack-in-the-Box, Shakey's Pizza, Subway, **other:** Vons Foods |
| **3** | Polk St, **S gas:** Arco, Chevron/24hr, **food:** KFC, **other:** 7-11 |
| **2** | Roxford St, **N** H HOSPITAL, **S lodging:** Country Side Inn |
| **1c** | Yarnell St |
| **1b a** | I-210 begins/ends on I-5, exit 160. |

## INTERSTATE 215 - Riverside

| Exit # | Services |
|---|---|
| **55** | I-215 begins/ends on I-15. |
| **54** | Devore, **E gas:** Devore Minimart/dsl, Petra |
| **50** | Palm Ave, Kendall Dr, **E gas:** 7-11/gas, Mobil/Subway/dsl, **food:** Burger King, Popeye's, Starbucks, **W food:** Denny's |
| **48** | University Pkwy, **E gas:** Chevron, 76/Circle K, **food:** Alberto's, Baskin-Robbins/Togo's, Carl's Jr, Del Taco, Dominos, IHOP, KFC, Little Ceasars, McDonald's, Papa John's, Starbucks, Weinerschnitzel, **other:** Ralph's Foods, Staples, **W gas:** Arco/24hr, Shell/dsl/LP, **food:** |

**SAN BERNARDINO**

| | |
|---|---|
| **48** | Continued<br>Jack-in-the-Box, Pizza Hut/Taco Bell, Zendejas Mexican, **lodging:** Day's Inn, Motel 6, **other:** Lowe's Whse, Walmart/Subway |
| **46c b** | 27th St, **E** golf, **W** golf |
| **46a** | CA 30 W, Highland Ave |
| **45b** | Muscupiade Dr, **E gas:** Shell, Thrifty, **food:** Jack-in-the-Box, **other:** Chevrolet, Home Depot, SavOn Foods, Stater Bros |
| **45a** | CA 30 E, Highlands |
| **44b** | Baseline Rd |
| **44a** | CA 66 W, 5th St, **E lodging:** Econolodge |
| **43** | 2nd St, Civic Ctr, **E gas:** Arco, Chevron, **food:** China Hut, Del Taco, Denny's, In-n-Out, LJ Silver, Pizza Hut/Taco Bell, **lodging:** Radisson, **other:** Ford, Food4Less, JC Penney, Kelly Tire, Marshall's, mall |
| **42b** | Mill St, **E food:** Carl's Jr, Dell Taco, Jack-in-the-Box, McDonald's, **other:** Suzuki/Honda, **W gas:** Shell, **food:** Yum-yum Donuts |
| **42a** | Inland Ctr Dr, **E food:** Carl's Jr, Del Taco, Gottschalk's, Jack-in-the-Box, **other:** Macy's, Sears/auto, mall, **W food:** Alice's Rest. |
| **41** | Orange Show Rd, **E gas:** Arco, Chevron, Exxon, **food:** Denny's, Pancho Villa Mexican, **lodging:** Guest House Inn, Knight's Inn, **other:** BigLots, Chevrolet, Dodge, Firestone, Gottschalk's, Kelly Tire, Macy's, Mazda, Radio Shack, Subaru, 99¢ Store, Target, **W other:** Cadillac, Giant RV, Isuzu, Jeep, Kia, Mitsubishi, Nissan, Toyota, Volvo, VW |
| **40b a** | I-10, E to Palm Springs, W to LA |
| **39** | Washington St, Mt Vernon Ave, **E gas:** Arco/24hr, 5 Points, **food:** Arby's, Baker's Drive-Thru, Siquios Mexican, Taco Joe's, Starbucks, **lodging:** Colton Inn, **other:** BigLots, $Tree, Goodyear, Jiffy Lube, **W food:** Burger King, Carl's Jr, Del Taco, Denny's, El Pollo Loco, Jack-in-the-Box, McDonald's, Quizno's, Sassy Steer, Starbucks, Subway, Taco Bell, Zendejas Mexican, **lodging:** Red Tile Inn, **other:** GNC, 99¢ Store, Radio Shack, Ross, Walmart/auto, multiple RV dealers |
| **38** | Barton Rd, **E gas:** Arco, Shell/Circle K, **other:** AutoZone, **W food:** Dorothy's Burgers |
| **37** | La Cadena Dr, **E gas:** Shell/dsl/24hr, **food:** Jack-in-the-Box, YumYum Rest., **lodging:** Holiday Inn Express |
| **36** | Center St, to Highgrove, **W gas:** Valero |

**CA**

## INTERSTATE 215 CONT'D - Riverside

| | |
|---|---|
| **35** | Columbia Ave, **E** gas: Arco, **W** other: Circle K |
| **34b a** | CA 91, CA 60, Riverside, to beach cities |
| **33** | Blaine St, 3rd St, **E** gas: 76, Shell, Valero, food: Bakers Drive-Thru, Jack-in-the-Box, Starbucks |
| **32** | University Ave, Riverside, **W** gas: Arco, Mobil, Shell, food: Baker's Drive-Thru, BK Subs, Carl's Jr, Coco's, Del Taco, Denny's, Domino's, Green Burrito, Gus Jr, IHOP, Jilberto's Tacos, Papa John's, Quizno's, Santana's Mexican, Shakey's Pizza, Starbucks, Taco Bell, Togo's, Wienerschnitzel, Winchell's, lodging: Comfort Inn, Courtyard, Dynasty Suites, Motel 6, Super 8, other: Kragen Parts, Rite Aid |
| **31** | MLK Blvd, El Cerrito |
| **30b** | Central Ave, Watkins Dr |
| **30a** | Fair Isle Dr, Box Springs |
| **29** | CA 60 E, to Indio, **E** on Day St...gas: Arco/24hr, Shell/Del Taco/dsl, food: Applebees, Baker's Drive-Thru, Café Chinese, Carl's Jr, HomeTown Buffet, McDonald's, Mimi's Cafe, Panda Express, Red Robin, Starbucks, Subway, Wendy's, Wienerschnitzel, other: Best Buy, Circuit City, Costco/gas, Home Depot, JC Penney, Jo-Ann Fabrics, Lowes, Macy's, Old Navy, PetCo, Ralph's Foods, Sam's Club/gas, Sears/auto, Staples, Target, Walmart, WinCo Foods, mall |
| **28** | Eucalyptus Ave, Eastridge Ave, **E** on Day St...other: Sam's Club/gas, Walmart, same as 29 |
| **27b** | Alessandro Blvd, **E** gas: Arco/24hr, 76/dsl, other: Big O Tire, auto repair, **E** gas: Chevron |
| **27a** | Cactus Air Blvd, **E** gas: Chevron, Circle K/76/dsl, food: Carl's Jr, Richie's Burgers |
| **25** | Van Buren Blvd, **E** other: March Field Museum, **W** other: Riverside Nat Cen. |
| **23** | Oleander Ave |
| **22** | Ramona Expswy, 1 mi **E** on Perris Blvd...gas: Arco/24hr, Mobil, Shell/Subway/dsl, food: Taco Bell, other: Albertson's, Walmart/auto, **W** gas: 76/Circle K, food: Jack-in-the-Box |
| **19** | Nuevo Rd, **E** gas: Arco/24hr, Mobil, 76, food: Burger King, Carl's Jr, China Buffet, Del Taco, El Pollo Loco, IHOP, Jenny's Rest., McDonald's, Pizza Hut, Sizzler, Starbucks, Taco Bell, other: Albertsons, AutoZone, Food4Less, GNC, Kragen Parts, Radio Shack, Rite Aid, Stater Bros Foods, Walmart |
| **17** | CA 74 W, 4th St, to Perris, Lake Elsinore, **E** gas: Shell/24hr, **W** gas: Chevron, food: Del Taco, Denny's, Jack-in-the-Box, Jimenez Mexican, Little Caesar's, Nick's Burgers, Popeye's, lodging: Day's Inn, other: Autozone, CarQuest, Chrysler/Dodge/Jeep, USPO |
| **15** | CA 74 E, Hemet, **E** other: motel, Ford/Lincoln/Mercury |
| **14** | Ethanac Rd, **E** food: KFC/Taco Bell, other: Richardson's RV/Marine, **W** gas: Exxon/dsl |
| **12** | McCall Blvd, Sun City, **E** gas: Valero, food: Wendy's, lodging: Best Value, Super 8, other: [H] HOSPITAL, **W** gas: Chevron/dsl, 76, Valero, food: Burger King, Coco's, McDonald's, Santana's Mexican, other: Stater Bros Foods, Walgreens |
| **10** | Newport Rd, Quail Valley, **E** gas: Shell/Del Taco/dsl, food: Cathay Chinese, Coldstone Creamery, Jack-in-the-Box, Subway, Taco Bell, other: AutoZone, GNC, |

**R I V E R S I D E** N ↕ S

**P E R R I S**

---

| | |
|---|---|
| **10** | Continued |
| | Ralph's Foods, Ross, Target, **W** gas: Arco/24hr, Mobil, 76/Circle K, food: Yellow Basket Cafe |
| **7** | Scott Rd, **E** gas: 7-11, food: Del Taco, Subway, other: Albertson's/SavOn, Curves |
| **4** | Clinton Keith Rd |
| **2** | Los Alamos, **E** gas: Shell, food: CA Grill, Carnita's Mexican, Mama Rosa's Pizza, Peony Chinese, Taco Bell, **W** gas: Mobil/McDonald's, food: ChuckeCheese, City Deli/bakery, Jack-in-the-Box, Mongolian BBQ, Subway, other: CVS Drug, Radio Shack, Stater Bros Foods |
| **1** | Murrieta Hot Springs, **E** food: Carl's Jr, Del Taco, Domino's, Sizzler, other: Ralph's Foods, Rite Aid, Ross, Sam's Club/gas, USPO, Weston's Mkt |
| **0mm** | I-215 begins/ends on I-15. |

## INTERSTATE 280 - Bay Area

| Exit # | Services |
|---|---|
| **58** | 4th St, I-280 begins/ends, downtown |
| **57** | 6th St, to I-80, downtown |
| **56** | Mariposa St, downtown |
| **55** | Army St, Port of SF |
| **54** | US 101 S, Alemany Blvd, Mission St, **E** gas: Shell |
| **52** | San Jose Ave, Bosworth St (from nb, no return) |
| **51** | Geneva Ave |
| **50** | CA 1, 19th Ave, **W** gas: Chevron, other: to Bay Bridge, SFSU |
| **49** | Daly City, **E** gas: Olympian, 76/dsl/LP, **W** gas: Arco, food: Carl's Jr, Domino's, IHOP, In-n-Out, Krispy Kreme, McDonald's, Val's Rest., lodging: Hampton Inn |
| **48** | Serramonte Blvd, Daly City (from sb), **E** other: Chevrolet, **W** gas: Olympian, 76, food: Boston Mkt, Daiso Japanese, Elephant Bar Rest., McDonald's, Starbucks, other: Macy's, Circuit City, Longs Drugs, Office Depot, PetsMart, Ross, Target |
| **47b** | CA 1, Mission St, Pacifica, **E** gas: Chevron, Silver/gas, food: Hawaiian BBQ, RoundTable Pizza, Sizzler, other: [H] HOSPITAL, Chrysler/Jeep/Dodge, Drug Barn, Ford, Fresh Choice Foods, Home Depot, Infiniti, Isuzu, Jo-Ann Fabrics, Lexus, Mitsubishi, Nissan, Nordstrom's, PetCo, Saturn, Target, mall |
| **46** | Hickey Blvd, Colma, **E** gas: Chevron/dsl/24hr, Shell, **W** gas: Shell/dsl/24hr, food: Celia's Rest., Moonstar, Outback Steaks, Sizzler, other: 7-11 |
| **45** | Avalon Dr, Westborough, **W** gas: Arco/24hr, Valero/dsl, food: Denny's, McDonald's, other: Walgreens/24hr, Skyline Coll |
| **43b** | I-380 E, to US 101, to San Francisco ✈ |
| **43a** | San Bruno Ave, Sneath Lane, **E** food: Baskin-Robbins, Carl's Jr, Extreme Pizza, Jamba Juice, Pasta Pomodoro, Taco Bell, other: Longs Drugs, Mollie Stones Mkt, **W** gas: Chevron, 76, food: Baker's Square, other: 7-11 |
| **42** | Crystal Springs, county park |
| **41** | CA 35 N, Skyline Blvd (from wb, no EZ return), to Pacifica, 1 mi **W** gas: Chevron |
| **40** | Millbrae Ave, Millbrae, **E** gas: Chevron |
| **39** | Trousdale Dr, to Burlingame, **E** [H] HOSPITAL |
| **36** | Black Mtn Rd, Hayne Rd, **W** golf, vista point |
| **36** | **Crystal Springs rest area wb, full [&] facilities, [C], [⚐], litter barrels, petwalk** |
| **35** | CA 35, CA 92W (from eb), to Half Moon Bay |

**E** ↕ **W**

**S A N   F R A N C I S C O**

CA

## INTERSTATE 280 CONT'D - Bay Area

**E / W** (San Jose direction)

| Exit | Services |
|---|---|
| 34 | Bunker Hill Dr |
| 33 | CA 92, to Half Moon Bay, San Mateo |
| 32mm | vista point both lanes |
| 29 | Edgewood Rd, Canada Rd, to San Carlos, **E other:** H HOSPITAL |
| 27 | Farm Hill Blvd, **E other:** Cañada Coll, phone |
| 25 | CA 84, Woodside Rd, Redwood City, **1 mi W gas:** Chevron/dsl, **other:** USPO |
| 24 | Sand Hill Rd, Menlo Park, **1 mi E gas:** Shell, **food:** Starbucks, **other:** Longs Drug, Safeway |
| 22 | Alpine Rd, Portola Valley, **E other:** H HOSPITAL, **W gas:** Chevron, Shell/autocare, **food:** Red Lotus Cafe, RoundTable Pizza, **other:** Curves |
| 20 | Page Mill Rd, to Palo Alto, **E** H HOSPITAL, to Stanford U |
| 16 | El Monte Rd, Moody Rd |
| 15 | Magdalena Ave |
| 13 | Foothill Expswy, Grant Rd, **E gas:** Chevron/24hr, **food:** Trader Joe's, **other:** Rite Aid, **W other:** to Rancho San Antonio CP |
| 12b a | CA 85, N to Mtn View, S to Gilroy |
| 11 | Saratoga, Cupertino, Sunnyvale, **E gas:** Chevron, **food:** Carl's Jr, **lodging:** Cupertino Inn, **other:** Goodyear, Michael's, Rite Aid, repair, **W gas:** Alliance, Chevron, 76, **food:** BJ's Brewhouse, Mandarin Gourmet, Outback Steaks, **lodging:** Cypress Hotel, **other:** Apple Computer Hdqrts, Target |
| 10 | Wolfe Rd, **E gas:** Arco/24hr, **food:** Starbucks, **lodging:** Courtyard, Hilton Garden, **other:** Ranch Mkt, **W gas:** 76, **food:** Alexander Steaks, CA Pizza Kitchen, TGIFriday, **other:** FreshChoice Foods, JC Penney, Jiffy Lube, Sears/auto, Vallco Fashion Park, RV Ctr |
| 9 | Lawrence Expswy, Stevens Creek Blvd (from eb), **N food:** McDonalds, Mtn Mikes Pizza, Panda Express, Quizno's, Starbucks, **other:** Rite Aid, Safeway, Marshall's, **S gas:** Rotten Robbie gas, 76, **food:** IHOP, Subway, **lodging:** Wellsley Inn, Woodcrest Hotel |
| 7 | Saratoga Ave, **N gas:** Arco/24hr, Chevron/24hr, **food:** Black Angus, Burger King, Garden City Rest., Happi House, Harry's Hofbrau, McDonald's, Taco Bell, **lodging:** TownePlace Suites, **other:** Cost+, Goodyear, Jiffy Lube, Lion Foods, PepBoys, 7-11, Toyota, **S gas:** 76, Shell, Valero, **food:** Applebee's, Baskin Robbins, Tony Roma's, **lodging:** MoorPark Hotel |
| 5c | Winchester Blvd, Campbell Ave (from eb) |
| 5b | CA 17 S, to Santa Cruz, I-880 N, to San Jose |
| 5a | Leigh Ave, Bascom Ave |
| 4 | Meridian St (from eb), **N other:** Big O Tire, Foodmaxx, **S gas:** Chevron, 76, **food:** KFC, Taco Bell, Wienerschnitzel |
| 3b | Bird Ave, Race St |
| 3a | CA 87, **N lodging:** Hilton, Holiday Inn, Hotel Sainte Claire, Marriott |
| 2 | 7th St to CA 82, **N** convention center |
| 1 | 10th St 11th St, **N other:** 7-11, **other:** to San Jose St U |
| 0mm | I-280 begins/ends on US 101. |

**SAN JOSE**

## INTERSTATE 405 - Los Angeles

**N / S LOS ANGELES AREA**

| Exit # | Services |
|---|---|
| 73 | I-5, N to Sacramento, I-5, N to Sacramento |
| 72 | Rinaldi St, Sepulveda, **E gas:** Chevron, 76, **food:** Arby's, Presidente McDonald's, Mexican, Subway, **other:** H HOSPITAL, Toyota, **W gas:** Shell, **lodging:** Best Value |
| 71 | CA 118 W, Simi Valley |
| 70 | Devonshire St, Granada Hills, **E gas:** Arco, Mobil, 76, **food:** Holiday Burger, Millie's Rest., Papa John's, Quizno's, Safari Room Rest., Starbucks, Subway, **other:** Discount Tire, Kwik Serve, Nissan, Ralph's Foods, Rite Aid, Von's Foods, USPO |
| 69 | Nordhoff St, **E gas:** Mobil/dsl, **other:** 7-11/24hr, Vallarta Foods, Walgreen, **W gas:** Arco, 76, **food:** Jack-in-the-Box, Pizza Hut |
| 68 | Roscoe Blvd, to Panorama City, **E gas:** Exxon, 76, **food:** Burger King, Denny's, Jack-in-the-Box, McDonald's, Panda Express, Quizno's, Taco Bell, Yoshinoya, **lodging:** Holiday Inn Express, **other:** AutoZone, Ford/Lincoln/Mercury/Jaguar/Starbucks, Saturn, **W gas:** Chevron/dsl, Shell/dsl, **food:** Tommy's Burgers, **lodging:** Motel 6 |
| 66 | Sherman Blvd, Reseda, **E gas:** Chevron, Mobil/LP, **food:** Ameci Pizza, KFC, McDonald's, Starbucks, **other:** BigLots, CVS Drug, Jon's Foods, **W gas:** 76/dsl/24hr, **food:** Taco Bell, **other:** H HOSPITAL, USPO |
| 65 | Victory Blvd, Van Nuys, **E on Sepulveda...food:** Carl's Jr, El Pollo Loco, Jack-in-the-Box, Subway, Wendy's, **other:** CVS Drug, El Monte RV Ctr, Costco/gas, Office Depot, PepBoys, Staples, **W on Victory...gas:** Arco/24hr, **other:** H HOSPITAL |
| 64 | Burbank Blvd, **E gas:** Chevron, Shell, **food:** Denny's, **lodging:** Best Western, **other:** Target |
| 63b | US 101, Ventura Fwy |
| 63a | Ventura Blvd (from nb), **E gas:** Mobil, **food:** Denny's, El Pollo Loco, **other:** Food Mkt, mall, **W gas:** Chevron, 76, **food:** Corner Bakery Cafe, IHOP, McDonald's, **lodging:** Best West Inn, Courtyard, **other:** Rite Aid |
| 63a | Valley Vista Blvd (from sb) |
| 61 | Mulholland Dr |
| 59 | Sepulveda Blvd, **W** to Getty Ctr |
| 57 | Sunset Blvd, Morega Dr, **E gas:** Chevron/24hr, 76/dsl, **other:** to UCLA, **W lodging:** Luxe Hotel |

## INTERSTATE 405 CONT'D - Los Angeles

| | |
|---|---|
| **56** | Waterford St, Montana Ave (from nb) |
| **55c b** | Wilshire Blvd, **E** downtown, **W** gas: Mobil, other: H HOSPITAL, 7-11 |
| **55a** | CA 2, Santa Monica Blvd, **E** gas: Chevron, Mobil, Thrifty, food: Chinese Cuisine, Jack-in-the-Box, Jamba Juice, Quizno's, Starbucks, Winchell's, Yoshinoya, Zankau Chicken, lodging: Travelodge, other: Firestone, 7-11, LDS Temple, Staples, vet, **W** gas: Chevron, 76/24hr, food: Subway, lodging: Holiday Inn |
| **54** | Olympic Blvd, Peco Blvd (from sb), **E** food: Pazzo Pizzaria, Subway, other: 7-11, **W** food: Panda Express, Starbucks, other: Best Buy, Marshall's, other: USPO |
| **53** | I-10, Santa Monica Fwy |
| **52** | Venice Blvd, **E** gas: Chevron/service, Shell/dsl, food: Carl's Jr, Subway, lodging: Ramada, other: 7-11, **W** gas: SP/dsl, food: FatBurger, other: services on Sepulveda |
| **51** | Culver Blvd, Washington Blvd, **E** food: Dear John's Café, Taco Bell, other: Chevrolet, **W** gas: 76/repair |
| **50b** | CA 90, Slauson Ave, to Marina del Rey, **E** gas: Arco/24hr, food: Del Taco, Shakey's Pizza, other: Circuit City, Firestone/auto, Goodyear/auto, JC Penny, Office Depot, Old Navy, Macy's, Pic'n Sav Foods, transmissions, **W** gas: 76, food: Denny's, other: Albertson's |
| **50a** | Jefferson Blvd (from sb), **E** food: Coco's, Jack-in-the-Box, other: Rite Aid, **W** to Los Angeles ✈ |
| **49** | Howard Hughes Pkwy, to Centinela Ave, **E** gas: Mobil/dsl, food: Sizzler, lodging: Ramada Inn, Sheraton, other: Ford, JC Penney, Macy's, Saturn, mall, **W** gas: Chevron, food: Dinah's Rest., Islands Burgers, On the Border, Subway, lodging: Extended Stay America, Radisson, other: CVS Drug, Howard Hughes Ctr, mall |
| **48** | La Tijera Blvd, **E** gas: Mobil, food: Burger King, ChuckeCheese, El Pollo Loco, Jamba Juice, KFC, McDonald's, Subway, TGIFriday, lodging: Best Western, other: CVS Drug, EZ Lube, 99¢ Store, Ross, Von's Foods, **W** gas: Chevron/dsl/24hr, 76/Circle K, food: Buggy Whip Rest., Subway, Wendy's, other: USPO |
| **47** | CA 42, Manchester Ave, to Inglewood, **E** gas: 76/Circle K/dsl/24hr, food: Carl's Jr, Subway, lodging: Best Western, Economy Inn, other: 7-11, **W** gas: Arco, Mobil, Shell, 76, food: Arby's, Burger King, Jack-in-the-Box, Louis Burgers, lodging: Day's Inn, other: CarMax, Chrysler/Jeep/Dodge, Home Depot, Hyundai |
| **46** | Century Blvd, **E** gas: 76, food: Burger King, Casa Gamino Mexican, Flower Drum Chinese, Rally's, Subway, lodging: Best Western, Comfort Inn, Motel 6, Tiboli Hotel, other: AutoZone, **W** gas: Arco/24hr, Chevron/dsl, 76/Circle K, Shell, food: Carl's Jr, Denny's, McDonald's, Taco Bell, lodging: Hampton Inn, Hilton, Holiday Inn, Marriott, Quality Hotel, Travelodge, Westin Hotel |
| **45** | I-105, Imperial Hwy, **E** gas: Arco, Mobil/dsl, Shell, food: BBQ, El Pollo Loco, El Tarasco Mexican, Jack-in-the-Box, McDonald's, other: J&S Trasmissions, **W** food: Proud Bird Rest. (1mi) |
| **44** | El Segundo Blvd, to El Segundo, **E** gas: Chevron/24hr, Thrifty, food: Burger King, Christy's Donuts, Jack-in-the-Box, Jase Burgers, Rally's, Subway, lodging: |

| | |
|---|---|
| **44** | Continued El Segundo Inn, **W** food: Denny's, Chappie's Rest, lodging: Ramada Inn |
| **43b a** | Rosecrans Ave, to Manhattan Beach, **E** gas: 76, Mobil/dsl, Shell, food: Del Taco, Denny's, El Pollo Loco, Pizza Hut, Starbucks, Subway, other: Albertson's, Best Buy, Circuit City, CVS Drug, Food4Less, Ford, Home Depot, Marshall's, Michael's, Office Depot, Ross, **W** gas: Thrifty, food: Carl's Jr, China Chef, Chipotle Mexican, Luigi's Rest., McDonald's, Qdoba Mexican, Robeks Juice, Sansai Japanese, Starbucks, lodging: Ayres Hotel, other: Chevrolet/Pontiac/GMC, Costco/gas, Staples, VW |
| **42b** | Inglewood Ave, **E** gas: Arco, food: Del Taco, Denny's, Domino's, Hong Kong Express, In-n-Out, Quizno's, Wok Wok Chinese, Yoshinoya, other: CVS Drug, Marshall's, PetCo, Von's Foods, **W** gas: Arco, 76, Shell/dsl/24hr, food: La Salsa Mexican, Leo's Mexican, other: Drug Emporium, Goodyear/auto |
| **42a** | CA 107, Hawthorne Blvd, **E** food: Jack-in-the-Box, Little Caesars, McDonald's, Panda Express, Papa John's, Spires Rest, Taco Bell, Wienerschnitzel, Wendy's, lodging: Best Western, Day's Inn, Holiday Inn, other: CVS Drug, Kragen Parts, 99¢ Store, Radio Shack, vet, **W** gas: Arco/24hr, Chevron/dsl, Thrifty, food: Boston Mkt, Marie Callendar's, Sizzler, Subway, Taco Bell, Yoshinoya, other: AutoZone, Macy's |
| **40b** | Redondo Beach Blvd (no EZ sb return), Hermosa Beach, **E** gas: Arco/24hr, Prena, Thrifty, food: ChuckeCheese, Jack-in-the-Box, other: golf, **W** food: Boston Mkt, Pizza Hut, other: CVS Drug, Nordstrom's, U-Haul |
| **40a** | CA 91 E, Artesia Blvd, to Torrance, **W** gas: Chevron, other: Carl's Jr., Starbucks, other: Winchell's |
| **39** | Crenshaw Blvd, to Torrance, **E** gas: Arco/24hr, food: Burger King, McDonald's, other: Ralph's Foods, **W** gas: Mobil/dsl, Shell/Subway/dsl, other: Jiffy Lube |
| **38b** | Western Ave, to Torrance, **E** gas: Arco, Chevron, 76/dsl, food: Del Taco, Denny's, Papa John's, Starbucks, Wendy's, Yorgo's Burgers, lodging: Dynasty Inn, other: Albertson's, GNC, Toyota, **W** gas: Mobil, food: Mill's Rest., lodging: Courtyard, other: Lexus |
| **38a** | Normandie Ave, to Gardena, **E** lodging: Comfort Inn, **W** gas: Shell/dsl, food: Carl's Jr, Chile Verde Mexican, Quizno's, Starbucks, Subway, Taco Bell/Pizza Hut, Wienerschnitzel, lodging: Extended Stay America, other: Goodyear, Office Depot, Walmart |
| **37b** | Vermont Ave (from sb), **W** lodging: Holiday Inn, other: hwy patrol |
| **37a** | I-110, Harbor Fwy |
| **36** | Main St (from nb) |
| **36mm** | weigh sta both lanes |
| **35** | Avalon Blvd, to Carson, **E** gas: Arco/24hr, Chevron, Mobil, Shell, food: Chili's, ChuckeCheese, Denny's, FoodCourt, Jack-in-the-Box, McDonald's, Pizza Hut, Quizno's, Shakey's Pizza, Sizzler, Subway, Tony Roma, lodging: Quality Inn, other: America's Tire, Firestone, Goodyear/auto, Ikea, JC Penney, PepBoys, Sears/auto, mall, **W** gas: Arco/24hr, Mobil, Shell, food: Carl's Jr, El Charro, IHOP, other: Chrysler/Dodge/Jeep, Ford/Lincoln/Mercury, Isuzu, Kia, Ralph's Foods, USPO |

N S

CA

HAWTHORNE

TORRANCE

CARSON

## INTERSTATE 405 CONT'D - Los Angeles

**34** Carson St, to Carson, **E food:** Del Taco, **lodging:** Comfort Inn, **W gas:** Mobil, 76/dsl/24hr, **food:** Carl's Jr, El Charro, IHOP, Jack-in-the-Box, Subway, **lodging:** Hilton

**33b** Wilmington Ave, **E gas:** Arco/service, **food:** Carson Burgers, **W gas:** Chevron/repair/24hr, Shell/Subway/Taco Bell/dsl, **food:** Del Taco, **other:** Chevrolet/Hyundai, Toyota

**33a** Alameda St

**32d** Santa Fe Ave (from nb), **E gas:** Arco/24hr, **W gas:** Chevron/24hr, Shell

**32c b** I-710, Long Beach Fwy

**32a** Pacific Ave (from sb)

**30b** Long Beach Blvd, **E gas:** 76, **W gas:** Mobil, **other:** H HOSPITAL, Toyota

**30a** Atlantic Blvd, **E gas:** Chevron/dsl, Shell/Subway/dsl, **food:** Arby's, Black Angus, Denny's/24hr, El Patio, El Torito, Jack-in-the-Box, **other:** Mercedes, Staples, Target, Walgreen, **W other:** H HOSPITAL, Chrysler/Jeep, Nissan

**29c** Orange Ave (from sb), **W other:** Dodge/Pontiac/GMC

**29b a** Cherry Ave, to Signal Hill, **E gas:** Mobil/dsl, **food:** Fantastic Burgers, **other:** Ford, auto repair, **W food:** John's Burgers, Charley Brown's Steaks/Lobster, Rib Café, **other:** BMW, Dodge, Firestone, Nissan

**27** CA 19, Lakewood Blvd, **E lodging:** Marriott, **W gas:** Chevron, Shell/24hr, **food:** Spires Rest., Taco Bell, **lodging:** Holiday Inn, Residence Inn, **other:** H HOSPITAL, Ford, Goodyear/auto, Kia

**26b** Bellflower Blvd, **E gas:** Chevron, 76, **food:** Burger King, Carl's Jr, KFC, **other:** Chevrolet, Ford, K-Mart, Lowe's Whse, **W gas:** Mobil/dsl, 76, **food:** FishTale Rest., Hof's Rest., McDonald's, Quizno's, Wendy's, **other:** H HOSPITAL, Borders Books, Circuit City, Goodyear/auto, Rite Aid/24hr, SavOn Drug, Sears, Target

**26a** Woodruff Ave (from nb)

**25** Palo Verde Ave, **W gas:** 76, **food:** Del Taco, Dr Wi Donuts, Pizza Hut/Taco Bell, Subway

**24b** Studebaker Rd

**24a** I-605 N

**23** CA 22 W, 7th St, to Long Beach

**22** Seal Beach Blvd, Los Alamitos Blvd, **E gas:** Chevron/repair/24hr, Mobil, 76, **food:** Carl's Jr, KFC, Panda Chinese, Spagatini Grill, Winchell's, **other:** Albertson's, Goodyear/auto, Ralph's Foods, Rite Aid, Target, Winston Tire

**21** CA 22 E, Garden Grove Fwy, Valley View St, **E gas:** Mobil, Shell/dsl, **food:** Coco's, DQ, Maxwell's Seafood Rest., Sizzler, **other:** Chevrolet, Ford, Rite Aid, Von's Foods

**19** Westminster Ave, to Springdale St, **E gas:** Arco/24hr, Chevron/dsl, 76/Circle K, Thrifty, 7-11/24hr, **food:** Café Westminster, Carl's Jr, In-n-Out, KFC, La Casa Brita, McDonald's, Taco Bell, Yoshinoya, **lodging:** Motel 6, Travelodge, **other:** Albertson's, America's Tire, Home Depot, Kragen Parts, Radio Shack, Rite Aid, **W gas:** Chevron/dsl/24hr, Shell/dsl/24hr, **food:** Pizza Hut, Subway, **lodging:** Best Western, Day's Inn

**18** Bolsa Ave, Golden West St, **E food:** Pizza Hut, Popeye's, **W gas:** Chevron, Mobil, 76, Shell, **food:** , Coco's, El Torito, IHOP, Jack-in-the-Box, **other:** Best Buy, JC Penney, Jo-Ann Fabrics, Jon's Foods, Macy's, Sears/auto, mall

**16** CA 39, Beach Blvd, to Huntington Bch, **E gas:** Shell, **food:** Hof's Rest., Jack-in-the-Box, Mei's Chinese, **lodging:** BeachWest Inn, Princess Inn, Super 8, Westminster Inn, **other:** H HOSPITAL, Buick/Pontiac/GMC, K-Mart, PepBoys, Toyota, **W gas:** Arco, Mobil/service, 76, **food:** Arby's, Burger King, Diedrich's Coffee, El Torito, Jack-in-the-Box, Macaroni Grill, Marie Callender's, Popeye's, Starbucks, **lodging:** Holiday Inn, **other:** Barnes&Noble, Chevrolet, Chrysler/Jeep, Circuit City, Dodge, Ford/Lincoln/Mercury, Just Tires, Marshall's, Mitsubishi, Subaru, Target, VW

**15 b a** Magnolia St, Warner Ave, **E gas:** Shell, **food:** Del Taco, Sizzler, **other:** **W gas:** Chevron, Mobil, **food:** Bullwinkle's Rest., Carrow's, Magnolia Café, Tommy's Burgers, **lodging:** Ramada Inn, **other:** IGA Foods, SavOn Drug

**14** Brookhurst Ave, Fountain Valley, **E gas:** Arco/24hr, Chevron, Thrifty, **food:** Alberto's Mexican, Coco's, Del Taco, **lodging:** Courtyard, Residence Inn, **other:** Thompson's RV Ctr, **W gas:** Chevron/service/24hr, Shell/dsl, **food:** Black Angus, Stix Chinese, Wendy's, **other:** Albertson's, Office Depot

**12** Euclid Ave, **E food:** CA Noodle Factory, Cancun Fresh, Carl's Jr, Coffee Bean, George's Burgers, Panda Express, Pita Fresh Grill, Quizno's, Starbuck's, Souplantation, Taco Bell, Z Pizza, **other:** H HOSPITAL, Costco/gas, Fry's Electronics, Office Depot, PetsMart, Staples, Tire Whse

**11b** Harbor Blvd, to Costa Mesa, **E food:** Hooters, **lodging:** La Quinta, **W gas:** Arco, Chevron, Mobil, Shell/dsl, 7-11, **food:** Burger King, Denny's, Domino's, El Pollo Loco, IHOP, Jack-in-the-Box, KFC, LJ Silver, McDonald's, Subway, **lodging:** Costa Mesa Inn, Motel 6, Super 8, Vagabond Inn, **other:** Albertson's, Big O Tire, Cadillac, Chevrolet, Dodge/Acura, Ford/Lincoln/Mercury, Honda, Infiniti, JustTires, Mazda, Pontiac/Buick, Radio Shack, Rite Aid, Target, Von's Foods, Winchell's

**11a** Fairview Rd, **E other:** Barnes&Noble, Best Buy, Marshall's, Nordstrom's, Old Navy, **W gas:** Chevron, 76, Shell, **food:** Del Taco, Jack-in-the-Box, Round Table Pizza, Taco Bell, **other:** CVS Drug, Kragen Parts, Stater Bro's

**10** CA 73, to CA 55 S (from sb), Corona del Mar, Newport Beach

**9b** Bristol St, **E gas:** Chevron/dsl, Shell/24hr, **food:** Bloomingdale's, Blue Water Grill, Carrow's, Chicago Pizza, Chick-fil-A, China Olive, Chipotle Mexican, Claim Jumper Rest., Clubhouse Cafe, Greek Island Grill,

**C O S T A   M E S A**

## INTERSTATE 405 CONT'D - Los Angeles

| Exit | Services |
|------|----------|
| 9b | Continued<br>In-n-Out, Jack-in-the-Box, Macaroni Grill, Maggiano's Rest., Magic Wok, McDonald's, Morton's Steaks, Pat & Oscar's, Pizza Hut, Red Robin, Scott Seafood, South Coast Rest, Starbucks, Ztejas Rest, **lodging:** Marriott Suites, Westin Hotel, **other:** BigLots, CVS Drug, Firestone/auto, Goodyear/auto, Macy's, Michael's, Nordstrom's, Office Depot, PetCo, Radio Shack, Rite Aid, Ross, Target, Sears/auto, Staples, Target, TJ Maxx, Von's Foods, World Mkt, mall, **W gas:** Chevron, 76/dsl, **food:** Del Taco/24hr, El Pollo Loco, McDonald's, Subway, Wahoo Taco, **lodging:** Hilton, Holiday Inn, **other:** PepBoys, 7-11, vet |
| 9a | CA 55, Costa Mesa Fwy, to Newport Bch, Riverside |
| 8 | MacArthur Blvd, **E gas:** Chevron, Mobil/Subway, **food:** Agora Rest, Carl's Jr, Juice it Up, McDonald's, Quizno's, Russel's Seafood, Starbucks, Taco Factory, **lodging:** Crowne Plaza Hotel, Holiday Inn, **other: W gas:** Chevron, **food:** El Torito, Gulliver's Ribs, IHOP, **lodging:** Atrium Hotel, Hilton, to ✈ |
| 7 | Jamboree Rd, Irvine, **E lodging:** Courtyard, Hyatt, Residence Inn, **food:** Soup Plantation, **E on Main St... gas:** Shell, **food:** Burger King, JambaJuice, **other:** Jiffy Lube, Ralph's Foods, **W food:** California Pizza Kitchen, El Torrito, Daily Grill, FatBurger, Gulliver's, Houston's, IHOP, Inka Grill, Jack Shrimp, Melting Pot Rest, Ruth's Chris Steaks, Subway, Taleo Mexico, Wahoo's Taco, **lodging:** Marriott |
| 5 | Culver Dr, **W gas:** Alfie's Gas, Chevron/dsl, **food:** Carl's Jr, Subway, **other:** Ace Hardware, Rite Aid, Wholesome foods Mkt |
| 4 | Jeffrey Rd, University Dr, **E gas:** Chevron, Circle K/gas, **food:** Baja Fresh, Cofee Bean, El Cholo Cantina, El Pollo Loco, Golden Spoon, Juice It Up, McDonald's, NY Pizza, Peiwei Asian, Pomodoro Italian, Starbucks, Stix Chinese, Togo's, **other:** Ace Hardware, CVS Drug, Gelson's Mkt, Office Depot, Ralph's Foods, SavOn Drug, H HOSPITAL, **W gas:** Mobil/dsl, **food:** IHOP, Korean BBQ, **other:** Ralph's Foods, vet |
| 3 | Sand Canyon Ave, **E H** HOSPITAL, **W gas:** Arco/dsl, **lodging:** Juice It Up, Lucca Cafe, Red Brick Pizza, **other:** Albertsons, Starbucks, CVS Drug |
| 2 | CA 133, to Laguna Beach, **E other:** DoubleTree Inn |
| 1c | Irvine Center Dr, **E food:** Dave & Buster's, Chang's Chinese Bistro, **other:** Barnes&Noble, **W food:** Burger King |
| 1b | Bake Pkwy, **W** Toyota |
| 1a | Lake Forest |
| 0mm | I-405 begins/ends on I-5, exit 132. |

## INTERSTATE 505 - Winters

| Exit # | Services |
|--------|----------|
| 33 | I-5. I-505 begins/ends on I-5. |
| 31 | CA 12A |
| 28 | CA 14, Zamora |
| 24 | CA 19 |
| 21 | CA 16, to Esparto, Woodland, **W gas:** Guy's Food/fuel |
| 17 | CA 27 |
| 15 | CA 29A |

| 11 | CA 128 W, Russell Blvd, **W gas:** Chevron/24hr, Interstate/dsl, **food:** RoundTable Pizza, Subway, **other:** Lorenzo Mkt |
| 10 | Putah Creek Rd, no crossover same as 11 |
| 6 | Allendale Rd |
| 3 | Midway Rd, **E other:** RV camping |
| 1c | Vaca Valley Pkwy |
| 1b | I-80 E. I-505 begins/ends on I-80. |

## INTERSTATE 580 - Bay Area

| Exit # | Services |
|--------|----------|
| 79 | I-580 begins/ends, accesses I-5 sb. |
| 76b a | CA 132, Chrisman Rd, to Modesto, **E gas:** 76/dsl, **other:** RV camping (5mi) |
| 72 | Corral Hollow Rd |
| 67 | Patterson Pass Rd, **W gas:** 76/dsl/24hr |
| 65 | I-205 (from eb), to Tracy |
| 63 | Grant Line Rd, to Byron |
| 59 | N Flynn Rd, Altamont Pass, elev 1009, **S** Brake Check Area, many wind-turbines |
| 57 | N Greenville Rd, Laughlin Rd, Altamont Pass Rd, to Livermore Lab, **S gas:** Chevron/Subway/dsl, **lodging:** Best Western, La Quinta, **other:** Harley-Davidson |
| 56mm | weigh sta both lanes |
| 55 | Vasco Rd, to Brentwood, **N gas:** Arco, Chevron, Quik-Stop/dsl, 76, Shell/dsl/deli, **food:** A&W/KFC, McDonald's, **S gas:** Citgo/7-11, Valero/dsl, **food:** Blimpie, Jack-in-the-Box, Taco Bell, **lodging:** Quality Inn |
| 54 | CA 84, 1st St, Springtown Blvd, Livermore, **N gas:** Chevron, **lodging:** DoubleTree Hotel, Holiday Inn, Motel 6, Springtown Inn, **other:** 7-11, **S gas:** Shell, 76/24hr, Valero/Circle K, **food:** Applebee's, Arby's, Burger King, Chevy's Mexican, Chili's, Crazy Buffet, IHOP, Italian Express, McDonald's, Panda Express, Starbucks, Subway, Taco Bell, Togo's, **other:** America's Tire, Longs Drug, Lowe's Whse, Office Depot, Radio Shack, Ross, Safeway/gas, Target |
| 52 | N Livermore Ave, **S gas:** Chevron/Jack-in-the-Box, Citgo/7-11, **food:** Baja Fresh, Coldstone Creamery, In-n-Out, Popeye's, Quizno's, String's Italian, **lodging:** Hawthorn Suites, **other:** Home Depot, Honda, Schwab Tire, Walmart/auto |
| 51 | Portola Ave, Livermore (no EZ eb return) |
| 50 | Airway Blvd, Collier Canyon Rd, Livermore, **N gas:** Shell/dsl, **food:** Baskin-Robbins, Wendy's, **lodging:** Courtyard, Hampton Inn, Hilton Garden, Holiday Inn Express, Residence Inn, **other:** Costco Whse/gas, **S food:** Cattlemen's Rest., Chicago Pizza, Starbucks, **lodging:** Extended Stay America, **other:** Chrysler/Jeep, Ford/Lincoln/Mercury, Mazda, 7-11 |
| 48 | El Charro Rd, O'Fallon Rd |
| 47 | Santa Rita Rd, Tassajara Rd, **N other:** Buick/Pontiac/GMC, Saab, Safeway Foods, Saturn, **S gas:** Shell, **food:** Bakers Square, Korea Garden, McDonald's, Quizno's, Subway, Taco Bell, TGI Friday, Thai Quisine, **other:** Acura, BMW, Cadillac, GMC, Hummer, Infiniti, Lexus, Long's Drug, MiniCooper, Mitsubishi, Rose Pavilion, Saab, Saturn, Trader Joe's, Volvo |
| 46 | Hacienda Dr, Pleasanton, **N gas:** Shell, **food:** Applebee's, Black Angus, Fuddruckers, Macaroni Grill, Mimi's Cafe, On-the-Border, Papa John's, Woks Up, |

## INTERSTATE 580 CONT'D - Bay Area

**E ← → W**

**PLEASANTON**

| | |
|---|---|
| 46 | Continued **lodging:** AmeriSuites, **other:** Barnes&Noble, Best Buy, Ford, Old Navy, TJ Maxx, **S food:** Red Robin, **other:** H HOSPITAL, Borders Books, Kohl's, Staples, Walmart/auto |
| 45 | Hopyard Rd, Pleasanton, **N gas:** 76/Circle K, Minimart, Shell/dsl, **lodging:** Hilton, Holiday Inn Express, **other:** America's Tire, Dodge, El Monte RV Ctr, Goodyear, Honda, Nissan, Office Depot, Pak'n Sav, RV Ctr, U-Haul, Toyota, **S gas:** Chevron, Shell/dsl, **food:** Arby's, Burger King, Chef India, Chevy's Mexican, Chili's, Denny's, El Balazo, In-n-Out, Nations Burgers, Pleasant Asian, Starbucks, Taco Bell, **lodging:** Candlewood Suites, Courtyard, Hilton, Larkspur Landing, Marriott, Motel 6, Sheraton, Super 8, **other:** Home Depot, Mercedes |
| 44b | I-680, N to San Ramon, S to San Jose |
| 44a | Foothills Rd, San Ramon Rd, **N gas:** Chevron, Shell, 76, Valero, **food:** Baskin-Robbins, Burger King, Carl's Jr, Casa Orozzo, China Wall, Hooters, KFC, McDonald's, Outback Steaks, Popeye's, RoundTable Pizza, Starbucks, Subway, Wendy's, **lodging:** Radisson, **other:** Big Lots, Buick, Chevrolet, Chrysler/Jeep, $Tree, Ford, Honda, Isuzu, Jo-Ann Fabrics, Kragen Parts, Long's Drug, Michael's, PetCo, Rite Aid, Ross, Target, **S food:** Cheesecake Factory, **lodging:** Crowne Plaza, Residence Inn, Sheraton, **other:** JC Penney, Macy's, Nordstrom's, mall |
| 39 | Eden Canyon Rd, Palomares Rd, **S other:** rodeo park |
| 37 | Center St, Crow Canyon Rd, same as 35, **S gas:** Arco/24hr, Chevron/dsl/, 76, Quikstop, **food:** McDonald's, Starbucks, Subway, **lodging:** Econolodge |
| 35 | Redwood Rd (from eb), Castro Valley, **N gas:** Arco, Chevron, 76/dsl, Shell/dsl, **food:** KFC, McDonald's, Quizno's, RoundTable Pizza, Sizzler, Taco Bell, Wendy's, **other:** Comfort Suites, Holiday Inn Express, **other:** Longs Drug, NAPA, Rite Aid, Safeway |
| 34 | I-238 W, to I-880, CA 238, **W off I-238 food:** Jack-in-the Box, **other:** Dodge/Jeep |
| 33 | 164th Ave, Miramar Ave, **E gas:** Chevron/dsl, **lodging:** Budget Inn, Fairmont Inn |
| 32b | 150th Ave, Fairmont, **E other:** H HOSPITAL, **W gas:** Shell, 76, Valero, **food:** Denny's, RoundTable Pizza, Tito's Cafe, **other:** Macy's, Pepboys, Target |
| 32a | Grand Ave (from sb), Dutton Ave, **W gas:** Coast, **other:** Rite Aid |
| 30 | 106th Ave, Foothill Blvd, MacArthur Blvd, **W gas:** Arco, **food:** Church's |
| 29 | 98th Ave, Golf Links Rd, **E gas:** Shell, **W gas:** 76 |
| 27b | Keller Ave, Mtn Blvd, **E** repair |
| 27a | Edwards Ave (from sb, no EZ return), **E** US Naval Hospital |
| 26a | CA 13, Warren Fwy, to Berkeley (from eb) |
| 26b | Seminary Rd, **E** Observatory/Planetarium, **W gas:** Arco/24hr |
| 25b a | High St, to MacArthur Blvd, **E gas:** 76, **food:** Subway, **other:** Albertson's, Kragen Parts, 7-11, **W gas:** 76, **other:** Walgreens |
| 24 | 35th Ave (no EZ sb return), **E gas:** 76, **food:** Taco Bell, **W gas:** Chevron, QuikStop, 76 |
| 23 | Coolidge Ave, Fruitvale, **E gas:** Shell/24hr, **food:** McDonald's, **other:** Longs Drug, Farmer Joe's, **W gas:** 76 |

**OAKLAND AREA**

| | |
|---|---|
| 22 | Park Blvd, **E** Shell, **W** Arco, Quikstop, **other:** H HOSPITAL |
| 21b | Grand Ave, Lake Shore, **E gas:** Chevron, 76/24hr, 7-11, **food:** Domino's, KFC, Subway, **other:** Albertson's, Long's Drug, Lucky Foods, **W gas:** Chevron/dsl/24hr |
| 21a | Harrison St, Oakland Ave, **E gas:** Quikstop |
| 19d c | CA 24 E, I-980 W, to Oakland |
| 19b | West St, San Pablo Ave, **E lodging:** Extended Stay America, **other:** Best Buy, Home Depot, Jo-Ann Fabrics, Michael's, Office Depot |
| 19a | I-80 W |
| 18c | Market St, to San Pablo Ave, downtown |
| 18b | Powell St, Emeryville, **E gas:** 76, **food:** Burger King, Denny's, Lyon's Rest., Starbucks, Trader Joe's, **lodging:** Courtyard, Day's Inn, Sheraton, Woodfin Suites, **other:** Barnes&Noble, Borders, Circuit City, Jo-Ann Fabrics, Old Navy, Ross, **W gas:** Shell, **food:** Chevy's Mexican, **lodging:** Hilton Garden, Holiday Inn |
| 18a | CA 13, Ashby Ave, Bay St, same as 18b |
| 17 | University Ave, Berkeley, **E gas:** 76, University Gas, **food:** Brennan's Cafe, **lodging:** Best Western, **other:** Toyota |
| 16 | Gilman St, **E gas:** Chevron, **other:** Walgreens, Golden Gate Fields |
| 13 | Albany St, Buchanan St (from eb) |
| 12 | Central Ave (from eb), El Cerrito, **E gas:** Shell, **W** Costco/gas |
| 11 | Bayview Ave, Carlson Blvd, **E gas:** 76 |
| 10b | Regatta Blvd, **E gas:** Golden Gate/dsl, **W food:** Cafe Teatro, Quizno's, **other:** Long's Drug |
| 10a | S 23rd St, Marina Bay Pkwy, **E gas:** Stop and Save/dsl |
| 9 | Harbour Way, Cutting Blvd, **E gas:** Arco, **food:** El Caballo Mexican, **W** Burger King |
| 8 | Canal Blvd, Garrard Blvd, **W gas:** Chevron/dsl, **lodging:** Quality Inn |
| 7b | Castro St, to I-80 E, Point Richmond, downtown industrial |
| 7a | Western Drive (from wb), Point Molate |
| 5mm | Richmond-San Rafael Toll Bridge |
| 2a | Francis Drake Blvd, to US 101 S, **E lodging:** Extended Stay Deluxe, **other:** BMW, Saab |
| 1b | Francisco Blvd, San Rafael, **E gas:** Beacon, Circle K, Valero, **food:** Burger King, Picante Cafe, Subway, **lodging:** Days Inn, **other:** Circuit City, Dodge/Isuzu, Ford, Home Depot, Mazda, Tires, **W food:** Wendy's, **other:** Best Buy, Borders Books, USPO, to San Quentin |
| 1a | US 101 N to San Rafael, I-580 begins/ends on US 101. |

## INTERSTATE 605 - Los Angeles

**N ↕ S**

**CA**

**L O S   A N G E L E S   A R E A**

| Exit # | Services |
|---|---|
| 25 | Huntington Dr. I-605 begins/ends. |
| 24 | I-210 |
| 23 | Live Oak Ave, Arrow Hwy, **E** Santa Fe Dam, **W** Irwindale Speedway |
| 22 | Lower Azusa Rd, LA St |
| 21 | Ramona Blvd, **E gas:** Mobil, **food:** Del Taco/24hr |
| 20 | I-10, E to San Bernardino, W to LA |
| 19 | Valley Blvd, to Industry, **E gas:** Chevron/Subway, 76, **food:** McDonald's, Taco King, **lodging:** Valley Inn |
| 18 | CA 60, Pamona Fwy |
| 17 | Peck Rd, **E gas:** Shell, **W other:** Ford Trucks |
| 16 | Beverly Blvd, RoseHills Rd |
| 15 | Whittier Blvd, **E gas:** Arco, 76, **food:** Carl's Jr, Taco Bell, **lodging:** GoodNite Inn, **other:** 7-11, **W gas:** Chevron, **other:** Buick, Chrysler/Dodge, Ford, GMC, Honda, Isuzu, Jeep, Kia, Pontiac, Saturn, Toyota, Volvo |
| 14 | Washington Blvd, to Pico Rivera, **E other:** Firestone/auto |
| 13 | Slauson Ave, **W gas:** Arco, Mobil, **food:** Denny's, **lodging:** Motel 6, **other:** Jeep, Kia, Nissan, **E** Ⓗ HOSPITAL |
| 12 | Telegraph Rd, to Santa Fe Springs, **W gas:** Chevron, **food:** Del Taco, Jack-in-the-Box, KFC, Taco Bell, **other:** st patrol, **W gas:** Arco/dsl |
| 11 | I-5 |
| 10 | Florence Ave, to Downey, **E gas:** Mobil, **other:** Cadillac, Chevrolet, Honda |
| 9 | Firestone Blvd, **E gas:** 76, **food:** ChuckeCheese, KFC, McDonald's, Norm's Burgers, Sam's Burgers, **lodging:** Best Western, **other:** BMW, Costco, Food4Less, Staples, VW/Audi, **W gas:** Arco, Chevron/repair, 76/dsl, **food:** Starbucks, **other:** Dodge, Office Depot, Target |
| 8 | I-105, Imperial Hwy, **E gas:** 76, **food:** KFC, McDonald's, Pizza Hut/Taco Bell, **other:** Food4Less, SavOn Drug, **W gas:** Arco |
| 7 | Rosecrans Ave, to Norwalk, **E gas:** Chevron, Mobil, **food:** Del Taco, McDonald's, **W food:** Carrow's Rest, **lodging:** Motel 6 |
| 6 | Alondra Blvd, **E gas:** Citgo/7-11, Chevron, **food:** A&W, Alondra's Mexican, KFC, **lodging:** Spires Rest., **other:** Home Depot, SavOn Drug, Staples, **W gas:** Shell/Subway/24hr |
| 5 | CA 91 |
| 4 | South St, **E other:** Macy's, Nordstrom's, Sears/auto, mall, **W gas:** Shell/service, UltraMar, **other:** Buick/GMC/Pontiac, Chrysler, Daewoo, Dodge, Ford, Honda, Hyundai, Infiniti, Isuzu, Saturn, Toyota, Volvo |
| 3 | Del Amo Blvd, to Cerritos, **E food:** Del Taco, Duke's Burgers, **other:** Ralph's Foods, **W gas:** Mobil |
| 2 | Carson St, **E gas:** Arco, 76, Shell, **food:** Jack-in-the-Box, KFC, Little Caesar's, McDonald's, Popeye's, Sky Burgers, Spike's Rest., Taco Bell/Pizza Hut, Wienerschnitzel, **lodging:** Lakewood Inn, **other:** Chief Parts, Kragen Parts, **W gas:** Chevron/dsl, Mobil/Subway/dsl, **food:** Denny's, Del Taco, El Pollo Loco, El Torito, FoodCourt, In-n-Out, Jack-in-the-Box, Leucille's BBQ, Roadhouse Grill, Starbucks, TGIFriday, Zen's Buffet, **other:** America's Tire, Barnes&Noble, GNC, Lowe's |

| Exit # | Services |
|---|---|
| 2 | Continued Whse, Michael's, Old Navy, Radio Shack, Ross, Staples, Sam's Club/gas, Walmart/auto |
| 1 | Katella Ave, Willow St, **E gas:** Shell, **food:** Burger King, McDonald's, **other:** Ⓗ HOSPITAL |
| 0mm | I-605 begins/ends on I-405. |

## INTERSTATE 680 - Bay Area

**N ↕ S**

**C O N C O R D**

| Exit # | Services |
|---|---|
| 71b a | I-80 E, to Sacramento, W to Oakland, I-680 begins/ends on I-80. |
| 70 | Green Valley Rd (from eb), Cordelia, **N other:** Costco, Longs Drug, Safeway |
| 69 | Gold Hill Rd, **W gas:** TowerMart/dsl |
| 65 | Marshview Rd |
| 63 | Parish Rd |
| 61 | Lake Herman Rd, **E gas:** Arco/Jack-in-the-Box/dsl, **W gas:** Gas City/dsl, Shell/Carl's Jr/dsl/24hr, **other:** vista point |
| 60 | Bayshore Rd, industrial park |
| 58 | I-780, to Benicia, toll plaza |
| 56 | Marina Vista, to Martinez |
| 55mm | Martinez-Benicia Toll Br |
| 54 | Pacheco Blvd, Arthur Rd, Concord, **W gas:** 76, Shell/dsl |
| 53 | CA 4 E to Pittsburg, W to Richmond, |
| 52 | CA 4 E, Concord, Pacheco, **E food:** Peppermill Coffeeshop, Taco Bell, **lodging:** Holiday Inn, **other:** Ford, Hyundai, Infiniti/VW, Toyota, USPO, **W gas:** Chevron/24hr, Grand Gas, Shell/24hr, 7-11, **food:** Burger King, Carrow's, Denny's, KFC, McDonald's, **other:** Barnes&Noble, Firestone, Goodyear/auto, K-Mart, Kragen Parts, Longs Drug, Marshall's, Target |
| 51 | Willow Pass Rd, Taylor Blvd, **E food:** Benihana Rest., Buffet City, Claim Jumper, Denny's, Elephant Bar Rest., El Torito, Fuddruckers, Grissini Italian, JJ North's Buffet, Krispy Kreme, Marie Callender's, Panera Bread, Red Lobster, Sizzler, Tony Roma, **lodging:** Hilton, **other:** Circuit City, Cost+, Office Depot, Old Navy, Willows Shopping Ctr, **W food:** Baja Fresh, Red Robin, Tahoe Joe's, **other:** Firestone, JC Penney, Macy's, Sears/auto |
| 50 | CA 242 (from nb), to Concord |
| 49 | Gregory Lane, to Pleasant Hill, **E gas:** Valero/dsl, **food:** Country Waffles, Hawaiian BBQ, Panda Express, Starbucks, **lodging:** Extended Stay America, **other:** Jo-Ann Fabrics, Kohl's, Office Depot, **W food:** Boston Mkt, Jack-in-the-Box, Lyon's Rest., Nations Burgers, Pizza Hut, **lodging:** Courtyard, Summerfield Suites, Sun Valley Inn, **other:** Borders, Rite Aid, Safeway Foods, Staples |
| 48 | Oak Park Blvd, Geary Rd, **E gas:** Chevron, 7-11, **food:** Subway, **lodging:** Embassy Suites, Renaissance Inn, **other:** Best Buy, **W gas:** Chevron, **food:** Black Angus, Burger King, Curry House, Primavera Pasta, Quizno's, Starbucks, Sweet Tomatos, Wendy's, Yan's China Bistro, **lodging:** Courtyard, Holiday Inn, **other:** Mazda/Subaru, Nissan, Staples, Volvo, Walgreens |
| 47 | N Main St, to Walnut Creek, **E gas:** Chevron/Subway, Shell, USA, **food:** Black Diamond Brewery/rest., Fuddrucker's, Jack-in-the-Box, Taco Bell, Vino Ristorante, **lodging:** Marriott, Motel 6, Walnut Cr Motel, **other:** Cadillac, Chrysler/Jeep, Harley-Davidson, Mercedes, Target, **W gas:** 76/dsl/24hr, 7-11, **food:** Domino's, **other:** Honda, NAPA |

## INTERSTATE 680 CONT'D - Bay Area

**N ↕ S**

| | |
|---|---|
| **46b** | Ygnacio Rd |
| **46a** | CA 24, to Lafayette, Oakland |
| **45** | S Main St, Walnut Creek, **E** **H** HOSPITAL |
| **43** | Livorna Rd |
| **42b a** | Stone Valley Rd, Alamo, **W gas:** Chevron, Shell/dsl, 7-11, **food:** Papa Murphy's, Starbucks, Subway, Taco Bell, **other:** Curves, Longs Drugs, Rite Aid, Safeway |
| **41** | El Pintado Rd, Danville |
| **40** | El Cerro Blvd |
| **39** | Diablo Rd, Danville, **E gas:** 76/24hr, **food:** Chinese Cuisine, Taco Bell, **other:** Mt Diablo SP (12mi), **W gas:** 76 |
| **38** | Sycamore Valley Rd, **E gas:** Shell, **food:** Denny's, **lodging:** Best Western, **W gas:** 76/dsl, Valero/dsl |

**SAN RAMON**

| | |
|---|---|
| **36** | Crow Canyon Rd, San Ramon, **E gas:** Shell, **food:** Burger King, Carl's Jr, Chili's, Max's Diner, O'Zachary's Rest., **lodging:** Extended Stay America, **other:** **H** HOSPITAL, Albertson's, Marshall's, Office Depot, Rite Aid, USPO, **W gas:** Chevron/repair/24hr, 76, Shell/autocare, Valero, **food:** Boston Mkt, Chipotle Mexican, Giuseppe's Italian, In-n-Out, McDonald's, Quizno's, Taco Bell, TGI-Friday, **lodging:** Sierra Suites, **other:** Harley-Davidson, Longs Drug, Safeway, vet |
| **34** | Bollinger Canyon Rd, **E gas:** Valero, **food:** Izzy's Pizza, Subway, **lodging:** Marriott, Residence Inn, **other:** Borders Books, Target, Whole Foods, **W gas:** Chevron/Foodini's, **food:** Applebee's, Chevy's Mexican, Marie Callender's, **lodging:** Courtyard, Homestead Village |
| **31** | Alcosta Blvd, to Dublin, **E gas:** 76, **other:** 7-11, **W gas:** Chevron, Shell/dsl, **food:** ChuckeCheese, DQ, Mike's Pizza, McDonalds, Papa Murphy's, Starbucks, Subway, Taco Bell, **other:** Albertson's, Walgreens |
| **30** | I-580, W to Oakland, E to Tracy |
| **29** | Stoneridge, Dublin, **E lodging:** Crowne Plaza, Hilton, **W food:** Black Angus, Taco Bell, **other:** Chrysler/Jeep, Cost+, Honda, Macy's, Nordstrom's, Sears, mall |
| **26** | Bernal Ave, Pleasanton, **E gas:** Shell/Jack-in-the-Box, **food:** Lindo's Mexican |
| **25** | Sunol Blvd, Pleasanton |

**FREMONT**

| | |
|---|---|
| **21b a** | CA 84, Calvaras Rd, Sunol, W to Dumbarton Bridge |
| **20** | Andrade Rd, Sheridan Rd(from sb), **E gas:** Sunol Super Stp/dsl |
| **19mm** | weigh sta nb |
| **19** | Sheridan Rd (from nb) |
| **18** | Vargas Rd |
| **16** | CA 238, Mission Blvd, to Hayward, **E gas:** Shell, **food:** McDonald's, **W** **H** HOSPITAL |
| **15** | Washington Blvd, Irvington Dist, **E gas:** QuikStop |
| **14** | Durham Rd, to Auto Mall Pkwy, **W gas:** 76/Circle K/Subway/24hr, Shell/Jack-in-the-Box, **other:** Fry's Electronics, Home Depot, Walmart |
| **12** | CA 262, Mission Blvd, to I-880, Warm Springs Dist, **W gas:** 76, Valero, **food:** Burger King, Carl's Jr, Denny's, KFC, RoundTable Pizza, Starbucks, Subway, Taco Bell, **lodging:** Extended Stay America, **other:** GNC, Longs Drug, Radio Shack, Ross, Safeway, 7-11, Walgreens |
| **10** | Scott Creek Rd |
| **9** | Jacklin Rd, **E other:** Bonfare Mkt, **W gas:** Shell |
| **8** | CA 237, Calaveras Blvd, Milpitas, **E gas:** Shell/repair, 76, **food:** Domino's, Flames CoffeeShop, RoadTable |

**SAN JOSE**

| | |
|---|---|
| **8** | Continued |
| | Pizza, Sizzler, Subway, **lodging:** Exectuive Inn, **other:** Oceans SuperMkt, 7-11, **W gas:** Shell, **food:** El Torito, Giorgio's Italian, It's a Grind, Lyon's Rest., McDonald's, Red Lobster, **lodging:** Embassy Suites, Extended Stay America, **other:** Albertson's, Longs Drug, Safeway, Staples |
| **6** | Landess Ave, Montague Expswy, **E gas:** Arco, Chevron, 76, **food:** Burger King, Jack-in-the-Box, McDonald's, Taco Bell, Togo's, Wienerschnitzel, **other:** Albertson's, Firestone, Radio Shack, Rite Aid, Target, Walgreens |
| **5** | Capitol Ave, Hostetter Ave, **E gas:** Shell, **food:** Carl's Jr, Popeye's, **other:** SaveMart Foods, **W gas:** Valero, **other:** Jiffy Lube |
| **4** | Berryessa Rd, **E gas:** Arco/24hr, USA, Valero/repair, **food:** Denny's, Lee's Sandwiches, McDonald's, Taco Bell, **other:** AutoZone, Longs Drug, Safeway |
| **2b** | McKee Rd, **E gas:** 76, Chevron, Shell, **food:** Burger King, HomeTown Buffet, Pizza Hut, Quizno's, Starbucks, Togo's, Wienerschnitzel, **other:** $Tree, PaknSave Foods, Ross, Target, Walgreens, **W gas:** World Gas, **food:** Baskin-Robbins, Foster's Freeze, Lee's Sandwiches, McDonald's, RoundTable Pizza, Yum Yum Doughnut, Wendy's, **other:** **H** HOSPITAL, Kohl's |
| **2a** | Alum Rock Ave, **E gas:** Shell/dsl/24hr, **food:** Jack-in-the-Box, Taco Bell, **W gas:** Chevron, 76/24hr, **food:** Carl's Jr |
| **1d** | Capitol Expswy |
| **1c** | King Rd, Jackson Ave (from nb), **E gas:** L&D Gas, Shell, **food:** El Gallo Giro, Jamba Juice, Kings Burger, Panda Express, Starbucks, Super Buffet, Taco Bell, **other:** Target, Walgreens |
| **1b** | US 101, to LA, SF |
| **1a** | (exits left from sb) I-680 begins/ends on I-280. |

## INTERSTATE 710 - Los Angeles

**E ↕ W**

| Exit # | Services |
|---|---|
| **23** | I-710 begins/ends on Valley Blvd, **E gas:** Arco |
| **22b a** | I-10 |
| **20c** | Chavez Ave |
| **20b** | CA 60, Pamona Fwy, **W gas:** Shell, **E food:** King Taco, Monterrey Hill Rest. |
| **20a** | 3rd St |
| **19** | Whittier Blvd, Olympic Blvd, **W gas:** Shell, **food:** McDonald's |
| **17b** | Washington Blvd, Commerce, **W gas:** Commerce Trkstp/dsl/rest. |
| **17a** | Bandini Blvd, Atlantic Blvd, industrial |

## INTERSTATE 710 CONT'D - Los Angeles

| | |
|---|---|
| **15** | Florence Ave, **E food:** IHOP, KFC, McDonald's, Taco Bell, **other:** Food4Less, Ralph's Foods, Rite Aid, Kragen Parts, ToysRUs, **W** truck repair |
| **13** | CA 42, Firestone Blvd, **E gas:** Arco, **food:** Burger King, Denny's, Krispy Kreme, McDonald's, Panda Express, Starbucks, Subway, **lodging:** Guesthouse Inn, **other:** El Super Foods, Ford, Jeep, Kia, Nissan, Radio Shack, Sam's Club, Target |
| **12b a** | Imperial Hwy, **E gas:** Shell/Subway/dsl, **food:** Carl's Jr., El Pollo Loco, Tacos Mexico, **W gas:** Chevron/dsl, 76, Shell, **food:** Casa Corona, LJ Silver/KFC, Panda Express, Starbucks, Subway, Taco Bell/Pizza Hut, Winchell's, Wienerschnitzel, **other:** AutoZone, Manny's Tires, Radio Shack, Walgreen |
| **11b a** | I-105 |
| **10** | Rosecrans Ave |
| **9b a** | Alondra Ave, **E** Home Depot |
| **8b a** | CA 91 |
| **7b a** | Long Beach Blvd, **E gas:** Mobil/repair, 76, **food:** El Ranchito Mexican, McDonald's, Taco Bell, **W gas:** Arco/24hr, **food:** Chano's Mexican, Jack-in-the-Box, Quizno's, **lodging:** Day's Inn, Luxury Inn |
| **6** | Del Amo Blvd |
| **4** | I-405, San Diego Freeway |
| **3b a** | Willow St, **E gas:** Chevron, **food:** Baskin-Robbins, Chee Chinese, Dominos, Pizza Hut, **other:** Walgreen, **W gas:** Arco, Mobil, 76, **food:** KFC, Popeye's, **other:** AutoZone, Ralph's Foods |
| **2** | CA 1, Pacific Coast Hwy, **E gas:** Arco/mart, Chevron, LB Fuel, Valero/dsl, **food:** Burger Express, Hong Kong Empress, **other:** auto repair, **W gas:** 76/service, Shell/Carl's Jr/dsl, PCH Trkstp/dsl, Xpress Minimart, **food:** Golden Star Rest., Jack-in-the-Box, McDonald's, Tom's Burgers, Winchell's, **lodging:** Hyland Motel, SeaBreeze Motel |
| **1d** | Anaheim St, **W gas:** Speedy Fuel, **other:** dsl repair |
| **1c** | Ahjoreline Dr, Piers B, C, D, E, Pico Ave |
| **1b** | Pico Ave, Piers F-J, Queen Mary |
| **1a** | Harbor Scenic Dr, Piers S, T, Terminal Island, **E lodging:** Hilton |
| **0mm** | I-710 begins/ends in Long Beach |

## INTERSTATE 780 - Vallejo

| Exit # | Services |
|---|---|
| **7** | I-780 begins/ends on I-680. |
| **6** | E 5th St, Benicia, **N gas:** Fast&Easy, **S gas:** Citgo/7-11, Valero/dsl, **food:** China Garden, **other:** Big O Tire, repair, vet |
| **5** | E 2nd St, Central Benicia, **N gas:** Valero, **lodging:** Best Western, **S food:** McDonald's, Pappa's Rest. |
| **4** | Southampton Rd, Benicia, **N food:** Asian Bistro, Burger King, Coldstone Creamery, Country Waffles, Jamba Juice, Rickshaw Express, RoundTable Pizza, Starbucks, Subway, **other:** Ace Hardware, Radio Shack, Raley's Foods, vet |
| **3b** | Military West |
| **3a** | Columbus Pkwy, **N gas:** Shell, **food:** Burger King, Napoli Pizza, Subway, **other:** Jiffy Lube, Longs Drugs, **S** to Benicia RA |

| | |
|---|---|
| **1d** | Glen Cove Pkwy, **N** Hwy Patrol, **S food:** Baskin-Robbins, Subway, Taco Bell, **other:** Safeway |
| **1c** | Cedar St |
| **1b a** | I-780 begins/ends on I-80. |

## INTERSTATE 805 - San Diego

| Exit # | Services |
|---|---|
| **28mm** | I-5 (from nb). I-805 begins/ends on I-5. |
| **27.5** | CA 56 E (from nb) |
| **27** | Sorrento Valley Rd, Mira Mesa Blvd |
| **26** | Vista Sorrento Pkwy, **E gas:** Mobil/dsl, Shell, **food:** Chili's, Jamba Juice, McDonald's, Starbucks, **lodging:** Country Inn, Courtyard, Holiday Inn Express, **other:** Staples |
| **25b a** | La Jolla Village Dr, Miramar Rd, **1 mi E gas:** 76/dsl, **other:** Discount Tire, Firestone, **W food:** Coast Cafe, Cozymel's Cantina, Donovan's Grill, Harry's Grill, Miami Grill, PF Chang's, **lodging:** Embassy Suites, Marriott, **other:** H HOSPITAL, Macy's, Nordstom's, Sears, mall |
| **24** | Governor Dr |
| **23** | CA 52 |
| **22** | Clairemont Mesa Blvd, **E gas:** Chevron, Mega/Subway/dsl, Shell, **food:** Arby's, Burger King, Carl's Jr, Coco's, Godfather Rest., McDonald's, Players Grill, Quizno's, Rubio's Grill, Souplantation, Starbucks, Tommy's Burgers, **other:** Food4Less, Ford, Jiffy Lube, Ranch Mkt, Sears Essentials, Walmart, **W gas:** Arco/24hr, **food:** Joe's Pizza, Mr. Bon's Rest., VIP Oriental Buffet, **lodging:** Best Western, CA Suites, Motel 6 |
| **21** | CA 274, Balboa Ave, **E gas:** Arco, Chevron, Exxon/dsl, 76, Shell, **food:** Applebee's, Islands Burger, Jack-in-the-Box, **other:** Albertson's/SavOn, Balboa AutoCare, Chevrolet, Dodge, Saturn |
| **20** | CA 163 N, to Escondido |
| **20a** | Mesa College Dr, Kearney Villa Rd, **W** H HOSPITAL |
| **18** | Murray Ridge Rd, to Phyllis Place |
| **17b** | I-8, E to El Centro, W to beaches |
| **16** | El Cajon Blvd, **E gas:** Arco/24hr, Ultra, **food: other:** Pancho Villa Mkt, **W gas:** North Park Gas, 76, **food:** Carl's Jr, Jack-in-the-Box, Starbucks, Subway, Wendy's |
| **15** | University Ave, **E gas:** Chevron, **food:** Subway, **other:** Radio Shack, **W gas:** Exxon, Thrifty/dsl, **food:** Starbucks, **other:** CVS Drug, Walgreens |
| **14** | CA 15 N, 40th St, to I-15 |
| **13b** | Home Ave, MLK Ave |
| **13a** | CA 94 |
| **12b** | Market St |
| **12a** | Imperial Ave, **E gas:** Exxon, Homeland Gas/dsl, **W food:** Domino's, KFC/LJ Silver, Sizzler, Starbucks, **other:** Home Depot, 99¢ Store |
| **11b** | 47th St |
| **11a** | 43rd St, **W food:** Giant Pizza, Jack-in-the-Box, **other:** AutoZone, CVS Drug, Northgate Mkt |
| **10** | Plaza Blvd, National City, **E food:** Chow King, DQ, Dragon Garden Chinese, McDonald's, Pizza Hut, Popeye's, Starbucks, Winchell's, **other:** H HOSPITAL, AutoZone, Firestone/auto, Ralph's Foods, Walgreens, Well's Drug, vet, **W gas:** Thrifty Gas, **food:** Family House Rest., IHOP, Sizzler, **lodging:** Comfort Inn, Stardust Inn, **other:** Big Lots, CVS Drug, Discount Tire, Jo-Ann Fabrics |

## INTERSTATE 805 CONT'D - San Diego

**9** Sweetwater Rd, **E** **food:** Applebee's, Outback Steaks, **other:** JC Penney, 7-11, **W** **gas:** Chevron/dsl, **food:** Ben's Rest., Carl's Jr, Denny's, Hanaoka Japanese, La Placita Mexican, L&L BBQ, Pizza Hut, Starbucks, Subway, Taco Bell, **other:** Circuit City, Curves, Goodyear, Longs Drug, Staples

**8** CA 54

**7c** E St, Bonita Rd, **E** **on Bonita Plaza Rd...food:** Applebee's, **food:** Outback Steaks, Pat&Oscar's Rest., **other:** JC Penney, Macy's, mall, **W** **gas:** Chevron, Shell, **food:** Burger King, Denny's, Love's Rest., **lodging:** La Quinta, Ramada Inn, **other:** RV Park

**7b a** H St, **E** **gas:** Carmalor Gas, **food:** China China, Coldstone Creamery, Jack-in-the-Box, Subway, Taco Bell, **other:** Longs Drug, Marshall's, Vons Foods, mall, RV camping

**6** L St, Telegraph Canyon Rd, **E** **gas:** Canyon Fuel/dsl, **food:** Mandarin Canyon, McDonald's, Starbucks, Subway, **other:** H HOSPITAL, Rite Aid, Olympic Training Ctr, RV camping, **W** **gas:** Thrify, **other:** 7-11

**4** Orange Ave, **E** Olympic Training Ctr

**3** Main St, Otay Valley Rd, **E** **gas:** Shell, **food:** Panda Express, Souplantation, **other:** Chevrolet, Chrysler/Jeep/Dodge, Ford, Kohl's, PetsMart, Scion, Staples, Toyota, **W** **lodging:** Holiday Inn Express

**2** Palm Ave, **E** **gas:** Arco/24hr, Chevron/24hr, **food:** Carl's Jr, Hometown Buffet, Starbucks, Subway, Taco Bell, **other:** Big O Tires, Home Depot, Radio Shack, USPO, Von's Foods, Walmart, **W** **gas:** 76/dsl, **food:** KFC, McDonald's

**1b** CA 905, **E** Brown Field Airport, Otay Mesa Border Crossing

**1a** San Ysidro Blvd, **E** **gas:** Arco, Shell, **lodging:** Travelodge, Factory2U, Kragen Parts, Longs Drug, 99¢ Store, U-Haul, **W** **gas:** Chevron, Exxon, Mobil, 76, **food:** Denny's, McDonald's, Si Senor Mexican, **lodging:** Motel 6

**0mm** I805 begins/ends on I-5.

## INTERSTATE 880 - Bay Area

| Exit # | Services |
|---|---|
| **46b a** | I-80 W (exits left). I-80 E/580 W. |
| **44** | 7th St, Grand Ave, downtown |
| **42b a** | Broadway St, **E** **food:** KFC, **lodging:** Marriott, **W** to Jack London Square |
| **41a** | Oak St, Lakeside Dr, downtown, **W** **gas:** Shell/dsl |
| **40** | 5th Ave, Embarcadero, **W** **lodging:** Executive Inn, Homewood Suites, Motel 6 |
| **39b a** | 29th Ave, 23rd Ave, to Fruitvale, **E** **gas:** Shell, **food:** Boston Mkt, Burger King, DonutStar, Starbucks, **other:** Albertson's, AutoZone, Big Lots, GNC, Office Depot, Radio Shack, **W** **gas:** 7-11 |
| **38** | High St, to Alameda, **E** **lodging:** Coliseum Motel, $Inn, **other:** El Monte RV Ctr, **W** **gas:** Shell/dsl, **food:** McDonald's, **other:** Home Depot |
| **37** | 66th Ave, Zhone Way, **E** coliseum |
| **36** | Hegenberger Rd, **E** **gas:** Arco/24hr, Shell/dsl, **food:** Burger King, Denny's, Jack-in-the-Box/24hr, McDonald's, Sam's Hofbrau, Taco Bell, **lodging:** Comfort Inn, Day's Inn/rest., Fairfield Inn, Motel 6, Quality Inn, **other:** |

**36 Continued** Pak'n Save Foods, GMC/Volvo, Freightliner, AutoParts Club, **W** **gas:** Chevron, 76/Circle K/dsl, Super Stop/dsl, **food:** Carrows Rest., Francesco's Rest., Green Garden Buffet, Hegen Burger, In-n-Out, Jamba Juice, Panda Express, Quizno's, Starbucks, Subway, **lodging:** Courtyard, Hilton, Park Plaza Motel, Ramada Inn, **other:** Goodyear, Harley-Davidson, Lexus, Walmart, to Oakland ✈

**35** 98th Ave, **W** ✈

**34** Davis St, **W** **gas:** Shell/Burger King, **food:** Starbucks, Togo's, **other:** Costco/gas, Home Depot, Office Depot, Walmart

**33b a** Marina Blvd, **E** **gas:** Valero, **food:** Jack-in-the-Box, La Salsa Mexican, Starbucks, **other:** H HOSPITAL, Firestone/auto, Ford, Honda, Hyundai, Kia, Marshall's, Nissan, Nordstrom's, Old Navy, KIA, **W** **gas:** Flyers/dsl, **food:** A&W/KFC, DairyBelle, Denny's, Mtn Mike's Pizza, **other:** USPO

**32** Washington Ave(from nb), Lewelling Blvd (from sb), **W** **gas:** Arco, 76, TechCo, **food:** Chili Palace, Hometown Buffet, Jack-in-the-Box, McDonald's, Papa Murphy's, Subway, **other:** Big Lots, Big O Tire, GNC, Longs Drug, 99Cent Store, Radio Shack, Safeway/24hr, SavMax Foods, SP Parts, Walgreens/24hr

**31** I-238 (from sb), to I-580, Castro Valley

**30** Hesperian Blvd, **E** **gas:** 76, **food:** Bakers Square, KFC, Mr Pizza, Starbucks, Western Superburger, **other:** House of Fabrics, Kragen Parts, Target, Wheelworks Repair, **W** **gas:** Arco, Chevron, 76, **food:** Black Angus, Carrow's Rest., KFC, McDonald's, Taco Bell, **lodging:** Hilton Garden, Vagabond Inn, **other:** Albertson's, Kragen Parts, Radio Shack

**29** A St, San Lorenzo, **E** **gas:** 76/Circle K, **food:** McDonald's, **lodging:** Best Western, **other:** Costco, tires/repair, **W** **gas:** 76/Circle K, **food:** Burger King, Carrow's, Hawaiian BBQ, Jamba Juice, McDonald's, Starbucks, Subway, **lodging:** Day's Inn, Heritage Inn, La Quinta, MainStay Suites, Pheonix Lodge, **other:** $Tree, Target

**28** Winton Ave, **W** **gas:** Chevron, Valero/dsl, **food:** Applebee's, Coldstone Creamery, Elephant Bar Rest., Marie Calendar's, Panda Express, Panera Bread, **other:** Firestone, JC Penney, Jo-Ann Fabrics, Macy's, Old Navy, Ross, Sears/auto, mall

**27** CA 92, Jackson St, **E** **gas:** Valero/24hr, **food:** Asian Wok, Nations Burgers, Popeye's, Subway, Taco Bell, **other:** Albertson's/Sav-On, Grocery Outlet, Longs Drug, Radio Shack, Rite Aid, Safeway, **W** San Mateo Br

Copyright 2009 - The Next Exit®

## INTERSTATE 880 CONT'D - Bay Area

**26** Tennyson Rd, **E gas:** All American/dsl, 76, Shell, **food:** Jack-in-the-Box, KFC, **other:** Kragen Parts, Walgreens, **W gas:** 76, **other:** H HOSPITAL

**25** Industrial Pkwy(from sb), **E gas:** Valero, **W lodging:** Pheonix Lodge

**24** Whipple Rd, Dyer St, **E gas:** Chevron/24hr, 76, **food:** Country Waffles, Denny's, Hawaiian BBQ, McDonald's, Panda Express, Quizno's, Starbucks, Taco Bell, Taco Del Mar, **lodging:** Best Value Inn, Motel 6, Super 8, **other:** Circuit City, FoodMaxx, Home Depot, PepBoys, Target, **W gas:** QuikStop/24hr, 76, Shell, **food:** Applebee's, Burger King, Chevy's Mexican, Chili's, FreshChoice, Fuddrucker's, In-n-Out, IHOP, Jamba Juice, Krispy Kreme, La Salsa Mexican, Pasta Pormadora, Texas Roadhouse, TGIFriday, Togo's, Tony Roma's, **lodging:** Extended Stay America, Holiday Inn Express, **other:** Albertson's/SavOn, Best Buy, Borders Books, Lowe's, Michael's, PetCo, RadioShack, Walmart/auto

**23** Alvarado-Niles Rd, (same as 24) **E gas:** Shell, **lodging:** Crowne Plaza, **other:** 7-11, **W gas:** Shell, **other:** Walmart/auto

**22** Alvarado Blvd, Fremont Blvd, **E food:** Phoenix Garden Chinese, Subway, **lodging:** Motel 6, **other:** Albertson's/SavOn

**21** CA 84 W, Decoto Rd to Dumbarton Br, **E gas:** Citgo/7-11, **food:** McDonald's, **other:** Walgreens

**19** CA 84 E, Thornton Ave, Newark, **E other:** Chevrolet, U-Haul, **W gas:** Chevron/dsl/24hr, Shell, **food:** Bakers Square, Carl's Jr, KFC, Mtn Mike's Pizza, Taco Bell, **other:** Big Lots, Home Depot, 7-11

**17** Mowry Ave, Fremont, **E gas:** Chevron/dsl, QuikStop, 76/Circle K, Valero, **food:** Applebee's, Burger King, Denny's, Hawaiian BBQ, Jerico's Steaks, KFC, Olive Garden, Starbucks, Subway, **lodging:** Best Western, Extended Stay Deluxe, Residence Inn, **other:** H HOSPITAL, Albertson's, Cost+, Jo-Ann Fabrics, **W gas:** 76, **food:** Arby's, Bombay Garden, El Burro Mexican, FreshChoice Rest., HomeTown Buffet, Jack-in-the-Box, Lyon's Rest., McDonald's, Red Robin, Sizzler, Subway, Taco Bell, TK Noodles, **lodging:** EZ 8 Motel, Holiday Inn Express, Homewood Suites, Motel 6, Towneplace Suites, Woodfin Suites, **other:** $Tree, Firestone, Ford, Goodyear/auto, Hancock Fabrics, JC Penney, Jiffy Lube, Macy's, Marshall's, Sears/auto, Staples, Target, mall

**16** Stevenson Blvd, **E gas:** Shell, **food:** Jack-in-the-Box, Outback Steaks, **other:** 7-11, **W gas:** Chevron, **food:** Chevy's Mexican, ChuckeCheese, Sizzler, Togo's, **lodging:** Hilton, **other:** Cadillac, FoodMaxx, Ford, Harley-Davidson, Nissan, Pontiac/GMC, PepBoys, Saturn, Tuesday Morning, Walmart

**15** Auto Mall Pkwy, **E gas:** Arco, Chevron, **food:** Subway, **W gas:** Shell/dsl, **food:** Chipotle Mexican, Claim Jumper, In-n-Out, Jamba Juice, Panera Bread, PF Chang's, Quizno's, Rubio's, Starbucks, Subway, Wendy's, **lodging:** Hawthorn Suites, **other:** BMW, Circuit City, Costco/gas, Dodge/Isuzu, Honda, Jo-Ann Fabrics, Kia, Kohl's, Lexus, Lowes Whse, Mercedes, Office Depot,

**15** Continued
Old Navy, Radio Shack, Staples, Toyota

**14mm** weigh sta both lanes

**13** Fremont Blvd, Irving Dist, **W gas:** Valero, **food:** McDonald's, SmartBrew, **lodging:** GoodNite Inn, Homestead Village, La Quinta, Marriott, **other:** Chrysler, Dodge, Honda, Lexus, Mercedes, Toyota,

**13b** Warren St (from sb), **W lodging:** Amerisuites, Courtyard, Hampton Inn

**13a** Gateway Blvd (from nb), **E lodging:** Holiday Inn Express

**12** Mission Blvd, **E** to I-680, **gas:** 76, Valero, **food:** Carl's Jr, Denny's, Jack-in-the-Box, KFC, Togo's, **lodging:** Holiday Inn Express, Quality Inn, **other:** Longs Drugs, Safeway, 7-11, Walgreens

**10** Dixon Landing Rd, **E gas:** Chevron, **food:** Starbucks, **lodging:** Residence Inn, **other:** 7-11

**8b** CA 237, Alviso Rd, Calaveras Rd, to McCarthy Rd,, Milpitas, **E gas:** Arco, 76, **food:** Chili's, Denny's, Marie Callender's, RoundTable Pizza, **lodging:** Best Western, Inns of America, Travelodge, **other:** Albertson's, Big Lots, Kragen Parts, SaveMart Foods, 7-11, Walgreens, **W on McCarthy Rd gas:** Chevron, **food:** Applebee's, Black Angus, HomeTown Buffet, In-n-Out, Macaroni Grill, McDonald's, On the Border, Red Robin, Taco Bell, **lodging:** Candlewood Suites, Crowne Plaza, Hampton Inn, Hawthorn Suites, Hilton Garden, Homestead Suites, Staybridge Suites, **other:** Best Buy, Borders Books, Chevrolet, Michael's, Ranch Mkt Foods, Ross, Walmart/auto

**8a** Great Mall Parkway, Tasman Dr, **E** mall

**7** Montague Expswy, **E gas:** 76, Shell/dsl, Valero, **food:** Jack-in-the-Box, **lodging:** Sleep Inn, **other:** U-Haul, auto repair, **W gas:** Chevron/dsl, **food:** Dave&Buster's, **lodging:** Beverly Heritage Hotel, Sheraton

**5** Brokaw Rd, **W other:** Ford Trucks, CHP

**4d** Gish Rd (nb only), **W other:** auto/dsl repair/transmissions

**4c b** US 101, N to San Francisco, S to LA

**4a** 1st St, **E gas:** 76, Shell/repair, **food:** Subway, **W gas:** 76, **food:** Cathay Chinese, Denny's/24hr, Gengi Japanese, McDonald's, **lodging:** Clarion, Day's Inn, Executive Inn, EZ 8 Motel, Holiday Inn Express, Homestead Suites, Radisson, Vagabond Inn, Wyndham Garden

**3** Coleman St, **E gas:** Valero/dsl, **W** ✈

**2** CA 82, The Alameda, **W gas:** Shell/repair, **food:** Cozy Rest., **lodging:** Best Western, Santa Clara Inn, St. Francis Hotel, Valley Inn, **other:** Safeway, Santa Clara U

**1d** Bascom Ave, to Santa Clara, **W gas:** Rotten Robbie/dsl, Valero, **food:** Burger King, Normandy House

**1c** Stevens Creek Blvd, San Carlos St, **E gas:** Valero/dsl, Valley/dsl, **lodging:** Valley Park Hotel, **other:** H HOSPITAL, **W gas:** 76, **food:** Arby's, Burger King, Cheesecake Factory, Jack-in-the-Box, **lodging:** Studio's Inn, **other:** Audi/VW, Best Buy, Chevrolet, Firestone/auto, Goodyear/auto, Isuzu, Lexus, Longs Drugs, Macy's, Mitsubishi, Nordstrom's, Safeway, Subaru, mall

**1b** I-280. I-880 begins/ends on I-280

**1a** Ca 17 to Santa Cruz.

## INTERSTATE 25

N ← → S

FT COLLINS

| Exit # | Services |
|---|---|
| 299 | Colorado/Wyoming state line |
| 296 | point of interest both lanes |
| 293 | to Carr, Norfolk |
| 288 | Buckeye Rd |
| 281 | Owl Canyon Rd, **E** KOA Campground |
| 278 | CO 1 S, to Wellington, **W** gas: Kum&Go, Loaf'N Jug/Blimpie, Shell, food: Burger King, Subway, Taco Bell, lodging: Comfort Inn, other: Main St Mkt/drugs, USPO |
| 271 | Mountain Vista Dr, **W** Budweiser Brewery |
| 269b a | CO 14, to US 87, Ft Collins, **E** food: Gambler's Steaks, McDonald's, lodging: Mulberry Inn, **W** gas: Conoco, Phillips 66/dsl, Denny's, Waffle House, lodging: Comfort Inn, Day's Inn, Econolodge, La Quinta, Motel 6, Plaza Inn, Ramada Inn, Sleep Inn, Super 8, other: RV Service, U-Haul, truck repair, vet, to CO St U, **2mi** **W** gas: Shamrock, DQ, Papa John's, Qdoba Mexican, other: Home Depot, Radio Shack, Walmart SuperCtr |
| 268 | Prospect Rd, to Ft Collins, **W** other: **H** HOSPITAL, **Welcome Ctr, rest area both lanes, full ♿ facilities, litter barrels, ⛱, petwalk** |
| 267mm | weigh sta both lanes |
| 266mm | st patrol |
| 265 | CO 68 W, Timnath, **E** Walmart SuperCtr, **W** gas: Shell/dsl, **2-3 mi** **W** food: Austin's Grill, Carrabba's, Golden Corral, Hunan Chinese, IHOP, Macaroni Grill, Outback Steaks, Papa John's, Quizno's, Subway, Texas Road |

| | |
|---|---|
| 265 | *Continued* house, Village Inn Rest., lodging: Courtyard, Hampton Inn, Marriott, Residence Inn, Safeway/gas, Sam's Club |
| 262 | CO 392 E, to Windsor, **E** gas: Conoco/dsl, Phillips 66/Subway/dsl, food: Arby's, GoodTimes Burgers, Taco John's, lodging: AmericInn, Super 8, **W** other: Powder River RV Ctr |
| 259 | Crossroads Blvd, **E** gas: Phillips 66/dsl, Carl's Jr, Qdoba Mexican, Subway, lodging: Candlewood Suites, Embassy Suites, Holiday Inn Express, **W** food: Hooters, other: BMW, Chevrolet, Chrysler/Dodge/Jeep, GMC/Pontiac, Harley-Davidson, Subaru, to airport |
| 257b a | US 34, to Loveland, **E** gas: gas/deli, food: Biaggi Italian, BoneFish Grill, Costa Vida, Culver's, On-the-Border, PF Changs', Red Robin, Rock Bottom Rest., Spicy Pickle, Starbucks, other: Barnes&Noble, Best Buy, Macy's, **W** gas: Conoco/dsl, food: Arby's (2mi), Blackeyed Pea, Carino's Italian, Chick-fil-A, Chili's, Chipotle Mexican, Cracker Barrel, Hooters, IHOP, KFC/Taco Bell, LoneStar Steaks, McDonald's, Mimi's Cafe, Noodles&Co, Old Chicago, Panera Bread, Quizno's, Subway, Taco John's, Waffle House, Wendy's, lodging: Best Western, Comfort Inn, Fairfield Inn, Hampton Inn, Holiday Inn Express, Residence Inn, Super 8 (2mi), other: **H** HOSPITAL, JoAnn Fabrics, Loveland Outlets/famous brands, Marshall's, PetsMart, Ross, Sportsman's Whse, Staples, Target, RV camping, museum, to Rocky Mtn NP |
| 255 | CO 402 W, to Loveland |
| 254 | to CO 60 W, to Campion, **E** gas: Johnson's Corner/ |

**N ↑ ↓ S**

**CO**

## INTERSTATE 25 CONT'D

**254** Continued
Sinclair/dsl/café/motel/24hr, **lodging:** Budget Host, **other:** RV camping/service

**252** CO 60 E, to Johnstown, Milliken, **W gas:** Loaf'N Jug/Subway

**250** CO 56 W, to Berthoud, **W** Berthoud B&B, to Carter Lake

**245** to Mead

**243** CO 66, to Longmont, Platteville, **E gas:** Conoco/dsl, Boulder Gas/Gyros/dsl, **food:** Red Rooster Rest., **other:** Big John's RV Ctr, Camping World/K&C RV Ctr, tires, **W** to Rocky Mtn NP, to Estes Park

**241mm** St Vrain River

**240** CO 119, to Longmont, **E gas:** Phillips 66/dsl, Carl's Jr, Del Taco, Qdoba, Quizno's, Starbucks, Wendy's, **lodging:** Best Western, Value Place Inn, **other:** Kia, Lexus, Toyota/Scion, **W gas:** Conoco/Subway/dsl/scales/24hr, Shell/dsl, **food:** Arby's, Burger King, McDonald's, Taco Bell, Waffle House, **lodging:** Best Value Inn, Comfort Inn, Day's Inn, 1st Inn, Super 8, **other:** H HOSPITAL, Del Camino RV Ctr, Valley Camper RV Ctr, museum, to Barbour Ponds SP

**237** new exit

**235** CO 52, Dacono, **E other:** Ford, **W gas:** Conoco/McDonald's/dsl/LP, **food:** Pepper Jacks, **other:** Harley-Davidson, to Eldora Ski Area

**232** to Erie

**229** CO 7, to Lafayette, Brighton, **E food:** Chick-fil-A, Famous Dave's BBQ, Goodtimes Burgers, Gunther Toody's, Heidi's, La Fogata, Starbucks, Village Inn, **other:** Costco/gas, Circuit City, Home Depot, PetsMart, Sears Grand

**228** E-470, tollway, to Limon

**226** **W food:** Mimi's Cafe, Red Robin, Starbucks, **other:** JC Penney, Macy's, SuperTarget

**225** 136th Ave, **W food:** Big Burrito, Carl's Jr, Starbucks, Subway, **other:** Lowes Whse, Walmart SuperCtr/McDonald's

**223** CO 128, 120th Ave, to Broomfield, **E gas:** Conoco, Shamrock/dsl, Applebee's, Burger King, Chipotle Mexican, Chick-fil-A, Coldstone Creamery, Damon's, Fazoli's, Fuddrucker's, Krispy Kreme, LoneStar Steaks, McDonald's, Panda Express, Pizza Hut, Olive Garden, Outback Steaks, Sonic, TGI Friday, **lodging:** Hampton Inn, Radisson, Ramada Inn, Sleep Inn, **other:** Albertson's, Barnes&Noble, Big Lots, Big O Tire, Brakes+, CarQuest, Checker's Parts, Discount Tire, GNC, Michael's, PetCo, SuperTarget, Tires+, Walgreens, vet, **W gas:** Conoco/dsl, Shell/Circle K/Popeye's/dsl, Shamrock, **food:** Chili's, Cracker Barrel, DQ, Hooters, Jade City Chinese, Laguna's Mexican, Perkins, Starbucks, Subway, Village Inn Rest., Wendy's, **lodging:** Comfort Suites, Extended Stay America, Fairfield Inn, La Quinta, Savannah Suites, Super 8

**221** 104th Ave, to Northglenn, **E gas:** Conoco, Phillips 66, **food:** Burger King, DQ, Denny's, IHOP, Old Chicago, Sonic, Subway, Taco Bell/Pizza Hut, Texas Roadhouse, **other:** H HOSPITAL, AutoZone, Gander Mtn, Gordman's, Home Depot, King's Sooper's, **W gas:** Conoco, 7-11, Shell/dsl, **food:** Applebee's, Blackeyed Pea, Cinzinetti's Italian, GoodTimes Burger, Gunther Toody's, Hop's Grill, Mandarin Garden, McDonald's, Quizno's,

**221** Continued
Red Lobster, Taco Bell, **lodging:** Best Value Inn, **other:** Best Buy, Borders Books, Dodge, Firestone/auto, Ford, Goodyear/auto, Jo-Ann Fabrics, Lowe's Whse, Marshall's, Office Depot, Old Navy, Ross, Subaru, mall

**220** Thornton Pkwy, **E food:** Golden Corral, Starbucks, Taco Del Mar, **other:** H HOSPITAL, GNC, Sam's Club/gas, Tires+, Walmart Super Ctr, Thornton Civic Ctr, **W gas:** Conoco, Shamrock, Western/gas

**219** 84th Ave, to Federal Way, **E gas:** Conoco, Shamrock, **food:** Arby's, Goodtimes Grill, Quizno's, Starbucks, Subway, Taco Bell, Waffle House, **lodging:** Crossland Suites, **other:** Walgreens, **W gas:** Econogas, Shamrock/dsl, **food:** Burger King, DQ, El Jimador, Pizza Hut, Popeye's, Santiago's Mexican, Village Inn Rest., **lodging:** Motel 6, **other:** H HOSPITAL, AutoZone, CarQuest, Discount Tire, Sav-A-Lot, Sportsman's Whse, vet

**217** US 36 W (exits left from nb), to Boulder, **W food:** Subway, **other:** Chevrolet, Toyota

**216b a** I-76 E, to I-270 E

**215** 58th Ave, **E food:** Burger King, McDonald's, Steak Escape, Taco John's, Wendy's, **lodging:** Comfort Inn, **W gas:** Conoco/dsl, Shamrock/dsl/LP, **lodging:** Super 8

**214c** 48th Ave, **E** coliseum, ⌕, **W food:** Village Inn Rest., **lodging:** Holiday Inn, Quality Inn

**214b a** I-70, E to Limon, W to Grand Junction

**213** Park Ave, W 38th Ave, 23rd St, downtown, **E gas:** Conoco, 7-11, Shell, **food:** Denny's, Domino's, McDonald's, Starbucks, Quizno's, **lodging:** La Quinta, **other:** Goodyear, **W lodging:** Regency Inn, Town&Country Motel

**212c** 20th St, downtown, Denver, **W food:** Pagliacci's Italian

**212b a** Speer Blvd, **E** downtown, museum, **W gas:** Conoco, Shell, **lodging:** Ramada Inn, Residence Inn, Super 8, Travel Inn

**211** 23rd Ave, **E** funpark

**210c** CO 33 (from nb)

**210b** US 40 W, Colfax Ave, **W food:** Denny's, KFC, **lodging:** Ramada Inn/rest., Red Lion Inn, **other:** Mile High Stadium

**210a** US 40 E, Colfax Ave, **E** civic center, downtown, U-Haul

**209c** 8th Ave, **E lodging:** Motel 7, **other:** Bob's Auto Parts

**209b** 6th Ave W, US 6, **W lodging:** Day's Inn

**209a** 6th Ave E, downtown, Denver

**208** CO 26, Alameda Ave (from sb), **E gas:** Shamrock/dsl, **food:** Burger King, Denny's, **other:** Home Depot, same as 207b **E gas:** Conoco

**207b** US 85 S, Santa Fe Dr, same as 208

**207 a** Broadway, Lincoln St, **E food:** Griff's Burgers, **other:** USPO

**206b** Washington St, Emerson St, **E other:** WildOats Mkt/café, **W other:** H HOSPITAL

**206a** Downing St (from nb)

**205b a** University Blvd, **W** to U of Denver

**204** CO 2, Colorado Blvd, **E gas:** Conoco, Shamrock, 7-11, Shell, Sinclair, **food:** Arby's, Asian Grill, Black Eyed Pea, Boston Mkt, GoodTimes Grill, Hooters, KFC, Lazy Dog Café, McDonald's, Noodles&Co, Pizza Hut, Starbucks, Subway, Taco Bell, Village Inn Rest., Wild Oats Cafe, **lodging:** Cherry Creek, Day's Inn, Fairfield Inn, Hampton Inn, Lowes Denver, Ramada, **other:** AAA, Barnes&Noble, Best Buy, Chevrolet/Buick, Circuit City,

**THORNTON**

**BRIGHTON**

**DENVER AREA**

**N ↑ S**

**CHERRY HILLS**

## INTERSTATE 25 CONT'D

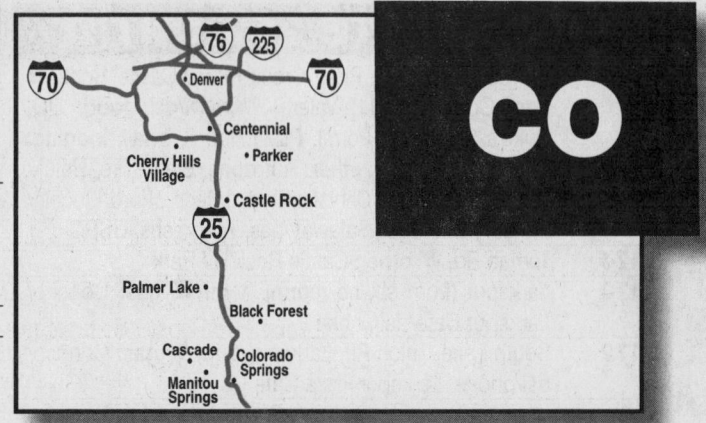

CO

**204** Continued
Mercedes/BMW. Ross, Safeway Foods, VW, Walgreens, **W gas:** Conoco, **food:** A&W/KFC, Dave&Buster's, Denny's, McDonald's, Perkins, **lodging:** La Quinta

**203** Evans Ave, **E gas:** Conoco, **food:** Big Papa's BBQ, Breakfast Inn, McDonald's, Palace Chinese, Quiznos, **lodging:** Rockies Inn, **other:** AutoZone, Discount Tire, NAPA, Walgreens, **W lodging:** Cameron Motel, **other:** Ford

**202** Yale Ave, **W gas:** Shamrock

**201** US 285, CO 30, Hampden Ave, to Englewood, Aurora, **E gas:** Conoco/Circle K/LP, Phillips 66, Shamrock, Sinclair, **food:** Ajuuai Rest, Applebee's, Boston Mkt, Chicago Grill, Chili's, Domino's, Einstein Bro's, McDonald's, Mexican Grill, Noodles&Co, NY Deli, Old Chicago, Onthe-Border, Qdoba, Starbucks, Subway, **lodging:** Embassy Suites, Marriott, Sheraton, TownePlace Suites, **other:** Discount Tire, King's Sooper Foods, Walgreens, Whole Food Mkt, vet, **W gas:** Conoco, **food:** Aurelio's Pizza, Burger King, Starbucks, **other:** Safeway

**200** I-225 N, to I-70

**199** CO 88, Belleview Ave, to Littleton, **E gas:** Sinclair, **food:** Chipotle Mexican, Harvest Rest., Off Belleview Grill, Pancake House, Panera Bread, Sandwiches+, Starbucks, Tosh's Hacienda Rest., Wendy's, **lodging:** Amerisuites, Hyatt Regency, Marriott, Wyndham, **W gas:** Conoco, Shamrock, **food:** McDonald's, Pappadeaux Café, Paradise Valley Grill, Pizza Hut, Taco Bell, **lodging:** Day's Inn, Extended Stay America, Holiday Inn Express, HomeStead Village, Ramada, Super 8, Wellesley Inn

**198** Orchard Rd, **E food:** Del Frisco's Steaks, Shepler's, **W gas:** Shell/Circle K, Quizno's, **lodging:** Hotel Denver Tech, **other:** Ⓗ HOSPITAL

**197** Arapahoe Blvd, **E gas:** Conoco, Shell/Circle K, **food:** A&W, Arby's, Bro's BBQ, Burger King, Carlos Miguel's, Del Taco, Dickie's BBQ, El Parral, Gunther Toody's Rest., Hoong's Palace, KFC, Mr. Panda, Outback Steaks, Pat's Cheesesteak, Pizza Hut, Sonic, Subway, Wendy's, **lodging:** Candlewood Suites, Courtyard, Homestead Suites, Sleep Inn, **other:** Big A Parts, Buick, Cadillac, Chrysler, Discount Tire, Ford, GMC, Home Depot, Honda, Hyundai, Jeep, Lowe's Whse, Mazda, Nissan, Pontiac, Scion, Subaru, Target, Toyota, USPO, Walmart SuperCtr, **W gas:** Phillips 66, Shamrock, Shell, **food:** Arby's, Blackeyed Pea, Boston Mkt, Chipotle Mexican, DQ, Einstein Bro's, Elephant Bar rest., Jamba Juice, KFC, Macaroni Grill, McDonald's, Mongolian BBQ, Papa John's, Qdoba, Quizno's, Red Robin, Souper Salad, Sushi Moon, Taco Bell, **lodging:** Residence Inn, Wingate Inn, **other:** Albertson's, Barnes&Noble, Brakes+, Curves, Firestone/auto, Goodyear/auto, Office Depot, Sav-On

**196** Dry Creek Rd, **E food:** IHOP, Landry's Seafood, Maggiano's Italian, Trail Dust Steaks, **lodging:** Best Western, Bradford Suites, Country Inn Suites, Days Inn, Holiday Inn Express, Homestead Suites, La Quinta, Quality Inn, Ramada Ltd, Studio+, **W lodging:** Drury Inn

**195** County Line Rd, **E lodging:** Courtyard, Residence Inn, **W gas:** Conoco, **food:** Buffalo Wild Wings, Burger King, California Pizza Kitchen, Champ's Rest., Chick-fil-A, Fleming's Rest., PF Changs, Red Robin, Rock

**195** Continued
Bottm Brewery/Cafe, Starbucks, Thai Basil, **lodging:** AmeriSuites, **other:** Barnes&Noble, Best Buy, Borders, Costco/gas, Dillard's, Home Depot, JC Penney, JoAnn Fabrics, Michaels, Nordstrom's, PetsMart

**194** CO 470 W, CO 470 E (tollway), **1 exit W on Quebec...**
**food:** Arby's, ClaimJumper, Country Buffet, LoneStar Steaks, McDonald's, TGIFriday, **lodging:** AmeriSuites, Comfort Suites, Fairfield Inn, **other:** Barnes&Noble, Circuit City, Firestone, Home Depot, PepBoys, Sam's Club, Walmart/auto/gas

**193** Lincoln Ave, to Parker, **E gas:** Shamrock, **food:** Carraba's, PanAsia Bistro, Hacienda Colorado, **lodging:** Candlewood Suites, Extended Stay America, Hilton Garden, **W gas:** Conoco/dsl, **food:** Chipotle Grill, Chili's, Heidi's, McDonald's, Pizza Hut/Taco Bell, Starbucks, Subway, **lodging:** Marriott, **other:** Ⓗ HOSPITAL, Discount Tire, Safeway

**191** no services

**190** Surrey Ridge

**188** Castle Pines Pkwy, **W gas:** Conoco, Shell/Circle K/Popeye's/24hr, **food:** Cafe De France, La Dolce Vita, Little Italy, Starbucks, Subway, Wendy's, **other:** Big O Tires, Discount Tire, King's Sooper/dsl, Safeway, vet

**187** Happy Canyon Rd, **services 2 mi W**

**C A S T L E   R O C K**

**184** Founders Pkwy, Meadows Pkwy, to Castle Rock, **E gas:** Conoco/dsl, Shell/dsl, **food:** A&W/KFC, Applebee's, Carl's Jr., Chipotle Mexican, Goodtimes Grill, Qdoba, Quizno's, Outback Steaks, Red Robin, Sonic, Starbucks, Subway, Taco Bell, Wendy's, **other:** Discount Tire, GNC, Goodyear, Grease Monkey, Home Depot, King's Sooper/24hr, Kohl's, Office Depot, PetsMart, Radio Shack, Target, Walgreens, Walmart SuperCtr, **W gas:** Conoco/Blimpie/Loaf'N Jug/dsl, **food:** Arby's, Blackeyed Pea, Chili's, Food Court, IHOP, McDonald's, Rockyard Café, **lodging:** Best Western, Comfort Suites, Day's Inn, Hampton Inn, **other:** Castle Rock Outlet/famous brands, Lowes Whse, Midas

**183** US 85 N (from nb), Sedalia, Littleton

**182** CO 86, Castle Rock, Franktown, **E gas:** Conoco, Phillips 66/dsl, Western, **food:** El Meson Mexican, Little Caesar's, Sapporo Japanese, **other:** st patrol, **W gas:** Shamrock, Shell/dsl, **food:** Burger King, KFC, Maragrita's Mexican, McDonald's, Shari's/24hr, Taco Bell, Village Inn Rest., Waffle House, Wendy's, **lodging:** Comfort Inn, Holiday Inn Express, Quality Inn, Super 8, **other:** Chrysler/Dodge/Jeep, NAPA

**N S LARKSPUR COLORADO SPRINGS**

## INTERSTATE 25 CONT'D

**181** CO 86, Wilcox St, Plum Creek Pkwy, Castle Rock, **E gas:** Conoco, 7-11, Valero, Western/dsl **food:** DQ, Duke's Steaks, El Porral, Pizza Hut, Subway, **lodging:** Castle Rock Motel, **other:** Autozone, Big O Tire, Buick/GMC, Chevrolet, Chrysler/Dodge/Jeep, Ford/Lincoln/Mercury, Hummer, Safeway/gas, Walgreens, USPO

**174** Tomah Rd, **W other:** Castle Rock RV Park

**173** Larkspur (from sb, no return), **1 mi W gas:** Conoco/Larkspur Cafe/dsl/phone

**172** South Lake Gulch Rd, Larkspur, **2 mi W gas:** Conoco/dsl/phone, Larkspur Pizza Cafe

**171mm** rest area both lanes, full ♿ facilities, 📞, 🏞, litter barrels, petwalk

**167** Greenland

**163** County Line Rd

**162.5mm** Monument Hill, elev 7352

**162mm** weigh sta both lanes

**161** CO 105, Woodmoor Dr, **E gas:** Conoco, **food:** Margarita's Mexican, **other:** vet, **W gas:** Conoco/Circle K/dsl, 7-11, **food:** Arby's, Casa Viejo, Domino's, McDonald's, Pizza Hut, Rosie's Diner, Starbucks, Subway, Taco Bell, Village Inn Rest., **other:** Big O Tire, Curves, Radio Shack, Safeway, USPO

**158** Baptist Rd, **E gas:** Shell/Circle K/Popeye's/dsl/24hr, **food:** Asian Garden, Carl's Jr, Chili's, Jackson Creek Chinese, Nick&Willy's, Papa Murphy's, Rotelli's, Subway, Texas Roadhouse, **other:** Checker Parts, Home Depot, King's Sooper/24hr, Kohl's, PetsMart, Staples, Walmart SuperCtr, **W gas:** Shamrock/dsl/scales

**156b** N Entrance to USAF Academy, **W** visitors center

**156a** Gleneagle Dr, **E** mining museum

**153** InterQuest Pkwy, **E lodging:** Hampton Inn, Residence Inn

**152** scenic overlook on sb

**151** Briargate Pkwy, **E gas:** Conoco, **food:** Biaggi's, California Pizza Kitchen, Champp's, Colorado Steaks, Panera Bread, PF Changs, Qdoba, Starbucks, Ted's MT Grill, **lodging:** Hilton Garden, Homewood Suites, **other:** to Black Forest

**150b a** CO 83, Academy Blvd, **E gas:** Conoco, Shamrock/dsl, Shell/dsl, **food:** Applebee's, Blimpie, Boston Mkt, Buca Italian, Buffalo Wild Wings, Burger King, Chipotle Mexican, Country Buffet, Cracker Barrel, Denny's, Egg&I Café, Elephant Bar Rest., Extreme Pizza, Famous Daves, Fat Burger, Fazoli's, IHOP, Jason's Deli, KFC, McDonald's, Mimi's Café, Olive Garden, On-the-Border, Panera Bread, Pizza Hut, Qdoba, Quizno's, Salt Grass Steaks, Schlotsky's Starbucks, Subway, Village Inn Rest., Wendy's, **lodging:** Best Western, Comfort Suites, Day's Inn, Drury Inn, Sleep Inn, Super 8, **other:** Advance Parts, Barnes&Noble, Best Buy, Big O Tire, Borders Books, Checker Parts, Circuit City, Dillard's, $Tree, Firestone/auto, Home Depot, King's Sooper, Marshall's, NAPA, Office Depot, PepBoys, Sam's Club, Sears/auto, Steinmart, USPO, Walmart SuperCtr, Whole Foods Mkt, mall, to Peterson AFB, **W** S Entrance to USAF Academy

**149** Woodmen Rd, **E gas:** Loaf'n Jug/Subway/dsl, **food:** Carl's Jr, Carraba's, **other:** Nissan, **W gas:** Shell/Circle K, **food:** Old Chicago Pizza, Hooters, Outback Steaks, TGIFriday, Zio's Italian, **lodging:** Comfort Inn, Embassy

**149** Continued
Suites, Fairfield Inn, Hampton Inn, Holiday Inn Express, Microtel, Staybridge Suites

**148b a** Corporate Ctr Dr (exits left from sb), Nevada Ave, **E other:** Harley-Davidson, K&C RV Ctr, **W food:** New South Wales Rest. **lodging:** Bradford Suites, Extended Stay America, Marriott

**147** Rockrimmon Blvd, **W gas:** Shell, **lodging:** Wyndham, to Rodeo Hall of Fame

**146** Garden of the Gods Rd, **E gas:** Conoco, Shell/dsl, **food:** Carl's Jr, Denny's, McDonald's, **lodging:** Econolodge, La Quinta, **other:** Aamco, **W gas:** Conoco, Phillips 66, 7-11, Shamrock, **food:** Applebee's, Arby's, Blackeyed Pea, Del Taco, Quizno's, Ranch Steaks, Souper Salad, Sonic, Starbucks, Subway, Taco Bell, Village Inn Rest., Wendy's, **lodging:** AmeriSuites, Day's Inn, Hyatt Place, Quality Inn, Super 8, **other:** Curves, Discount Tire, to Garden of Gods

**145** CO 38 E, Fillmore St, **E gas:** 7-11, Shamrock, **food:** Burger King, DQ, **lodging:** Budget Host, **other:** H HOSPITAL, Advance Parts, Firestone, **W gas:** Conoco/dsl, Loaf'N Jug, Shell/Circle K/dsl, **food:** Howard's BBQ, Waffle House, **lodging:** Best Western, Central Inn, Motel 6

**144** Fontanero St

**143** Uintah St, **E gas:** 7-11, **other:** Uintah Fine Arts Ctr

**142** Bijou St, Bus Dist, **E other:** Firestone/auto, **W gas:** 7-11, **food:** Denny's, **lodging:** Clarion

**141** US 24 W, Cimarron St, to Manitou Springs, **W gas:** Conoco, Phillips 66, **food:** Arby's, Burger King, Capt D's, La Castia Mexican, McDonald's, Papa John's, Popeye's, Sonic, Subway, Taco John's, Texas Roadhouse, Waffle House, **lodging:** Express Inn, Holiday Inn Express, **other:** Acura, AutoZone, Brakes+, Buick/GMC/Pontiac, Chevrolet, Chrysler, Discount Tire, Dodge, Ford, Gateway RV Ctr, Grease Monkey, Hyundai, Just Brakes, Infiniti, Isuzu, Lexus, Lincoln/Mercury, Mazda, Mercedes, NAPA, Nissan, Office Depot, Porsche, Radio Shack, Saturn, Subaru/Saab/VW, Suzuki, Toyota, Volvo, Walmart, to Pikes Peak,

**140b** US 85 S, Tejon St, **E other:** Tires 4 Less, **W gas:** Conoco, **other:** Chrysler/Jeep, access to same as 141

**140a** Nevada Ave, **E lodging:** Chateau Motel, Howard Johnson, Nevada Motel, Samaritan's Inn, **other:** Tire King, **W gas:** BP, Citgo/7-11, Shamrock, **food:** Burger King, China Kitchen, KFC, McDonald's, Subway, Taco Bell, Taco Express, Wendy's, **lodging:** Chief Motel, Cheyenne Motel, Econolodge, **other:** Big O Tire, Checker Parts, Sears, USPO, Walgreens, access to auto dealers at 141

**139** US 24 E, to Lyman, Peterson AFB

**138** CO 29, Circle Dr, **E gas:** Conoco, Shell/Circle K/dsl, McDonald's, **lodging:** Crowne Plaza, Day's Inn, Super 8, **other:** Kohl's, airport, zoo, **W gas:** 7-11, **food:** Arby's, Burger King, Carrabba's, Carl's Jr, Chili's, ChuckeCheese, Denny's, Fazoli's, Outback Steaks, Papa John's, Village Inn Rest., Subway, **lodging:** Best Western, Comfort Inn, DoubleTree Hotel, Fairfield Inn, Hampton Inn, Holiday Inn, La Quinta, Residence Inn, Wingate Inn, **other:** Batteries+, GNC, PetCo, Radio Shack, Target

**135** CO 83, Academy Blvd, **E** to Cheyenne Mtn SP, to 🚂, **W** Ft Carson

**CO**

**COLORADO SPRINGS**

## INTERSTATE 25 CONT'D

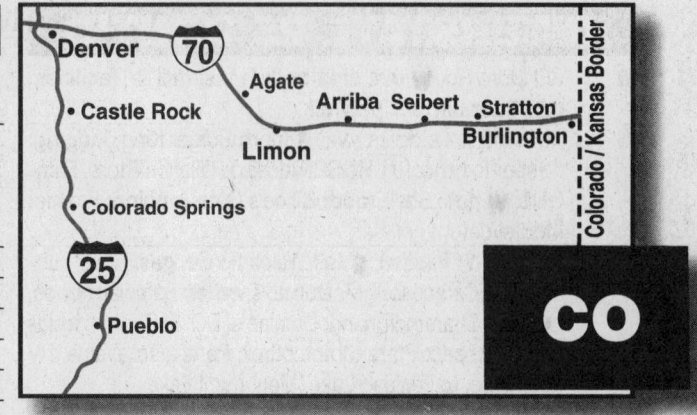

| | |
|---|---|
| **132** | CO 16, Wide Field Security, **E gas:** Loves/Subway/dsl, **other:** Camping World RV SuperCtr, KOA |
| **128** | to US 85 N, Fountain, Security, **E gas:** Citgo/7-11, Loaf'N Jug/Subway/dsl, Texaco, **food:** Grand China, **lodging:** Ute Motel, **other:** USPO, **W gas:** Tomahawk/ Shell/dsl/rest./24hr/@, **lodging:** Fountain Inn, Super 8 |
| **125** | Ray Nixon Rd |
| **123** | no services |
| **122** | to Pikes Peak Meadows, **W** Pikes Peak Intn'l Raceway |
| **119** | Midway |
| **116** | county line rd |
| **115mm** | rest area nb, full H facilities, C, litter barrels, petwalk |
| **114** | Young Hollow |
| **112mm** | rest area sb, full H facilities, C, litter barrels, petwalk |
| **110** | Pinon, **W gas:** Sinclair/dsl/repair, **lodging:** Pinon Tree Inn |
| **108** | Bragdon, **E gas:** racetrack, **W** KOA |
| **106** | Porter Draw |
| **104** | Eden, **W food:** Buffalo Wild Wings, Carino's, Chili's, **other:** Best Buy, Kohl's, PetCo |
| **102** | Eagleridge Blvd, **E gas:** Loaf'N Jug, **food:** Burger King, Texas Roadhouse, **other:** Big O Tire, Home Depot, Sam's Club/gas, **W gas:** Shell/Blimpie/dsl, **food:** Bel-lissimo Rest., Cactus Flower Mexican, Cracker Barrel, IHOP, Starbucks, Village Inn Rest., **lodging:** Comfort Inn, Econolodge, La Quinta, Ramada, Wingate Inn, **other:** Tires+, Harley-Davidson, frontage rds access 101 |
| **101** | US 50 W, Pueblo, **E gas:** Conoco, Capt D's, Denny's, 3 Margarita's Mexican, Souper Salad, Ruby Tuesday, **lodging:** Sleep Inn, **other:** Barnes&Noble, Circuit City, Dillards, JC Penney, Ross, Sears/auto, Target, Walmart SuperCtr, U-Haul, mall, **W gas:** Loaf'N Jug, Phillips 66, 7-11, Shamrock/dsl, **food:** Angelo's Pizza, Applebee's, Arby's, Blackeyed Pea, Boston Mkt, Burger King, Carl's Jr, Coldstone Creamery, Country Kitchen, DQ, Domino's, Fazoli's, Giacomo's Rest., Golden Corral, McDonald's, Olive Garden, Papa John's, Papa Murphy's, Popeye's, Quizno's, Red Lobster, Starbucks, Subway, SW Grill, Taco Bell, Wendy's, **lodging:** Days Inn, Motel 6, Pueblo Hotel, Quality Inn, Super 8, **other:** Aamco, Advance Parts, Albertson's/gas, AutoZone, Batteries+, Brakes+, Checker Parts, Chevrolet, Discount Tire, Dodge, Ford, Goodyear/auto, Honda, KIA, K-Mart, Lincoln/Mercury, Lowe's Whse, PetsMart, Staples, Toyota, Walgreens, frontage rds access 102 |
| **100b** | 29th St, Pueblo, **E food:** Country Buffet, KFC, Mongolian Grill, Panda Buffet, **other:** $Tree, King's Sooper Foods, Peerless Tires, mall, **W gas:** Phillips 66/dsl, **food:** Sonic, **lodging:** USA Motel, **other:** Grease Monkey, Safeway foods |
| **100a** | US 50 E, to La Junta, **E gas:** Loaf'N Jug, Phillips 66, **food:** KFC, McDonald's, Wendy's, **lodging:** Value Stay Inn, **other:** Big R Foods, Goodyear, Walgreens |
| **99b a** | Santa Fe Ave, 13th St, downtown, **W food:** Taco Bell, Wendy's, **lodging:** Guesthouse Inn, Travelers Motel, **other:** H HOSPITAL, Chevrolet, Chrysler/Jeep, Ford/ Subaru, Honda, Mazda, Nissan, Pontiac, Saturn, VW |
| **98b** | CO 96, 1st St, Union Ave Hist Dist, Pueblo, **W gas:** Loaf'N Jug, **food:** Carl's Jr, **lodging:** Marriott |
| **98a** | US 50E bus, to La Junta, **W gas:** Phillips 66/dsl, **food:** Sonic |
| **97b** | Abriendo Ave, **W gas:** Texaco |
| **97a** | Central Ave, **W gas:** Shamrock |
| **96** | Indiana Ave, **W other:** H HOSPITAL, Cobra Automotive |
| **95** | Illinois Ave (from sb), **W** to dogtrack |
| **94** | CO 45 N, Pueblo Blvd, **W gas:** Loaf'N Jug, Western/ dsl, **food:** Pizza Hut/Taco Bell, **lodging:** Hampton Inn, Microtel, **other:** Lowes Whse, RV camping, fairgrounds/ racetrack, to Lake Pueblo SP |
| **91** | Stem Beach |
| **88** | Burnt Mill Rd |
| **87** | Verde Rd |
| **83** | no services |
| **77** | Hatchet Ranch Rd, Cedarwood |
| **74** | CO 165 W, Colo City, **E gas:** Shamrock/deli/dsl/24hr, **other:** KOA, **W gas:** Shell/Subway/Noble Roman's/dsl, **food:** Los Cuervo's, Max's Rest., **lodging:** Days Inn/ rest., **rest area both lanes, full** facilities, C, **vending,** litter barrels, petwalk |
| **71** | Graneros Rd, access to Columbia House |
| **67** | to Apache |
| **64** | Lascar Rd |
| **60** | Huerfano |
| **59** | Butte Rd |
| **56** | Redrock Rd |
| **55** | Airport Rd |
| **52** | CO 69 W, to Alamosa, Walsenburg, **W gas:** Phillips 66/A&W/dsl/24hr, Western Gas, **food:** Andy's BBQ, Alpine Rose Café (2mi), Carl's Jr (2mi), George's Rest., Pizza Hut, Rambler Rest., Subway (2mi), **lodging:** Best Western, Budget Host, Country Host RV Park, to Great Sand Dunes NM, San Luis Valley |
| **50** | CO 10 E, to La Junta, **W** H HOSPITAL, tourist info |
| **49** | Lp 25, to US 160 W, Walsenburg, **1 mi W gas:** Loaf'N Jug, **food:** Carl's Jr. **lodging:** Knight's Inn (4mi), Lathrop SP, to Cuchara Ski Valley |
| **42** | Rouse Rd, to Pryor |
| **41** | Rugby Rd |
| **34** | Aguilar, **E gas:** Cenex/dsl/rest. |
| **30** | Aguilar Rd, **W** truck/tire repair |
| **27** | Ludlow, **W** Ludlow Memorial |
| **23** | Hoehne Rd |

## INTERSTATE 25 CONT'D

| | |
|---|---|
| **18** | El Moro Rd, **W rest area both lanes, full** ♿ **facilities,** ⛲, **litter barrels, petwalk** |
| **15** | US 350 E, Goddard Ave, **E food:** Burger King, **lodging:** Super 8, **other:** H HOSPITAL, Big R Ranch Store, Family$, **W gas:** Shell, **food:** B Lee's Café, **lodging:** Frontier Motel/café |
| **14b a** | CO 12 W, Trinidad, **E** CO Welcome Ctr, **gas:** Shell/Subway, KFC/Taco Bell, McDonald's, **other:** Safeway Foods, **W gas:** Shamrock, **food:** Domino's, DQ, El Captan, **lodging:** Prospect Plaza Motel, **other:** Parts+, TrueValue, RV camping, to Trinidad Lake, Monument Lake |
| **13b** | Main St, Trinidad, **E gas:** Shell, **food:** McDonald's, Sonic, **lodging:** Tinidad Hotel, **other:** CarQuest, Safeway |
| **13a** | Santa Fe Trail, Trinidad, **E lodging:** Best Western, **other:** RV camping |
| **11** | Starkville, **E gas:** Shell/Wendy's/dsl/24hr, weigh/check sta, **food:** Bob & Earl's Rest, Taquila's Mexican, **lodging:** Budget Host, Budget Summit Inn/RV Park, Holiday Inn, **other:** Bigg's RV Park, to Santa Fe Trail, **W food:** Country Kitchen, **lodging:** La Quinta, Quality Inn, **other:** Big O Tire, Checker Parts, Chevrolet/Buick, Grease Monkey, Walmart SuperCtr/gas |
| **8** | Springcreek |
| **6** | Gallinas |
| **2** | Wootten |
| **1mm** | scenic area pulloff nb |
| **0mm** | Colorado/New Mexico state line, Raton Pass, elev 7834, |

## INTERSTATE 70

| Exit # | Services |
|---|---|
| **450mm** | Colorado/Kansas state line |
| **438** | US 24, Rose Ave, Burlington, **N gas:** Conoco, **other:** H HOSPITAL, Buick/GMC/Pontiac, CarQuest, Chevrolet, Family$, Ford/Lincoln/Mercury, Goodyear, Safeway Foods, **S gas:** Shell/Renaldo's Mexican/dsl/24hr, **other:** Bonny SRA, RV Camping, truck repair |
| **437.5mm** | Welcome Ctr wb, **full** ♿ **facilities, info,** 🕻, ⛲, **litter barrels, petwalk, historical site** |
| **437** | US 385, Burlington, **N gas:** Conoco/dsl/24hr, On the Go/dsl, **food:** Arby's, Burger King, McDonald's, Pizza Hut, Route Steaks, Subway, **lodging:** Best Value, Burlington Inn, Chaparral Motel, Comfort Inn, Western Motel, **other:** H HOSPITAL, Alco, to Bonny St RA |
| **429** | Bethune |
| **419** | CO 57, Stratton, **N gas:** Cenex/dsl, Conoco/dsl, **lodging:** Best Western/rest., Claremont Inn/café, **other:** Marshall Ash Village Camping, auto museum |
| **412** | Vona, 1/2 mi **N** gas, phone |
| **405** | CO 59, Seibert, **N** Shady Grove Camping, **S gas:** Conoco/dsl, **other:** tire repair |
| **395** | Flagler, **N gas:** Loaf&Jug/subs/dsl, **lodging:** I-70 Diner, **lodging:** Little England Motel, **other:** Flagler SWA, NAPA, RV camping, **S gas:** Cenex/dsl **other:** golf |
| **383** | Arriba, **N gas:** DJ/dsl/café, motel, **S rest area both lanes full** ♿ **facilities,** ⛲, **litter barrels, point of interest, petwalk, RV camping** |
| **376** | Bovina |
| **371** | Genoa, **N** point of interest, gas, food, 🕻, **S** H HOSPITAL |

| | |
|---|---|
| **363** | US 24, US 40, US 287, to CO 71, to Hugo, Limon, **13 mi** **S** H HOSPITAL |
| **361** | CO 71, Limon, **N other:** Ace Hardware, Chrysler/Dodge/Jeep, **S gas:** Conoco/dsl/24hr, Phillips 66/Wendy's/dsl/24hr, **food:** Golden China, Pizza Hut, **lodging:** 1st Inn Gold, Travel Inn, **other:** Alco, KOA, st patrol, RV camping |
| **360.5mm** | weigh/check sta both lanes |
| **359** | to US 24, CO 71, Limon, **N gas:** ✈ FLYING J/dsl/Country Mkt/scales/LP/24hr, **other:** dsl repair, RV camping, **S gas:** Phillips 66, TA/Shell/Subway/Country Fair/dsl/scales/24hr/@, Valero/dsl/24hr, **food:** Arby's, Denny's, McDonald's, Oscar's Grill, **lodging:** Best Western, Comfort Inn, Econolodge, Holiday Inn Express, Inn Suites, Super 8, TS Inn, **other:** camping |
| **354** | no services |
| **352** | CO 86 W, to Kiowa |
| **348** | to Cedar Point |
| **340** | Agate, **1/4 mi S** gas/dsl, phone |
| **336** | to Lowland |
| **332mm** | **rest area wb, full** ♿ **facilities, info,** 🕻, ⛲, **litter barrels, vending, petwalk** |
| **328** | to Deer Trail, **N gas:** Phillips/dsl, **S gas:** Shell/dsl, **other:** USPO |
| **325mm** | East Bijou Creek |
| **323.5mm** | Middle Bijou Creek |
| **322** | to Peoria |
| **316** | US 36 E, Byers, **N gas:** Sinclair, **food:** Longhorn rest., **lodging:** Budget Host, **other:** Thriftway Foods/Drug, **S gas:** Tri Valley/gas, **food:** Country Burger Rest., **lodging:** Lazy 8 Motel (1mi), **other:** USPO |
| **310** | Strasburg, **N gas:** Conoco/dsl/24hr, Ray's gas/24hr, **food:** Corona Mexican, Pizza Shop, **lodging:** Strasburg Inn, **other:** KOA, NAPA, Parts+, Western Hardware, repair, RV camping, USPO |
| **306mm** | Kiowa , Bennett, **N rest area both lanes, full** ♿ **facilities,** 🕻, ⛲, **litter barrels, petwalk** |
| **305** | Kiowa (from eb) |
| **304** | CO 79 N, Bennett, **N gas:** Conoco/Hotstuff Pizza/dsl **food:** China Kitchen, Subway, **other:** Kings Sooper Foods/dsl, USPO, **N other:** Ace Hardware |
| **299** | CO 36, Manila Rd |
| **295** | Lp 70, Watkins, **N gas:** Shell/Tomahawk/dsl/rest./24hr/@, **food:** Biscuit's Cafe, Lulu's Steakhouse, **lodging:** Country Manor Motel, **other:** USPO |
| **292** | CO 36, Airpark Rd |
| **289** | E-470 Tollway, 120th Ave, CO Springs |
| **288** | US 287, US 40, Lp 70, Colfax Ave  (exits left from wb) |
| **286** | CO 32, Tower Rd, **N food:** Chili's, Chipotle Mexican, Del Taco, Starbucks, Wendy's, **other:** Best Buy, Checker Parts, Brakes+, Home Depot, Office Depot, PetCo, Walmart Super Ctr/Subway |
| **285** | Airport Blvd, **N** Denver Int Airport, **S gas:** ✈ FLYING J/Conoco/dsl/rest./24hr, Texaco/McDonald's/dsl, **lodging:** Comfort Inn, Crystal Inn, **other:** Harley-Davidson |
| **284** | I-225 N  (from eb) |
| **283** | Chambers Rd, **N gas:** Conoco, Shell/Circle K, **food:** A&W/KFC, Applebees, Cantina Margarita, Chicago Grill, Montana Grill, Outback Steaks, Pizza Hut, Qdoba, Quizno's, Sonic, Subway, Taco Bell/LJ Silver, Ted's MT Grill, Wendy's, **lodging:** Cambria Suites, Country Inn&Suites, Crowne Plaza, Hilton Garden, Homewood Suites, Hyatt |

# INTERSTATE 70 CONT'D

**283** Continued
Place, Marriott, Residence Inn, Sleep Inn, Stonebridge Suites, **other:** Tires+, U-haul, **S gas:** Shamrock, **food:** Burger King, **lodging:** Crossland Suites, **other:** America East RV Ctr

**282** I-225 S, to Colorado Springs

**281** Peoria St, **N gas:** Conoco, Phillips 66, 7-11, **food:** Burger King, Del Taco, Domino's, GoodTimes Burgers, McDonald's, Peoria Grill, Pizza Patron, Quizno's, Subway, **lodging:** Drury Inn, Timbers Motel, **other:** Big O Tire, Family$, **S gas:** Conoco/dsl, Shamrock/dsl, **food:** Bennett's BBQ, Chester's Grill, Church's, Denny's, KFC, Old Santa Fe Grill, Pizza Hut/Taco Bell, Real Mina's Mexican, Subway, Waffle House, Wendy's, **lodging:** Motel 6, Quality Inn, Star Motel, Stay Inn, **other:** Curves, Goodyear/auto, auto/RV repair, vet

**280** Havana St, **N lodging:** Embassy Suites

**279** I-270 W, US 36 W (from wb), to Ft Collins, Boulder

**278** CO 35, Quebec St, **N gas:** Sapp Bros/Sinclair/Subway/dsl/@, TA/dsl/rest./24hr/@, **food:** Del Taco, Jim&Nick's BBQ, Olive Garden, Qdoba, Red Lobster, TGIFriday, Wahoo's, **lodging:** Comfort Inn, Studio Suites, **other:** Bass Pro Shops, Border's Books, Circuit City, JC Penney, Macys, Old Navy, Super Target, mall, **S food:** Arby's, Country Buffet, Mariposa Mexican, McDonald's, IHOP, Panda Express, Panera Bread, Sonic, Subway, **lodging:** Courtyard, DoubleTree Hotel, Guesthouse Inn, Red Lion Inn, Renaissance Inn, **other:** GNC, Home Depot, Office Depot, Radio Shack, Ross, Sam's Club, Walmart/gas

**277** to Dahlia St, Holly St, Monaco St, frontage rd

**276b** US 6 E, US 85 N, CO 2, Colorado Blvd, **S gas:** Conoco/Subway/dsl, **food:** Carl's Jr, KT'S BBQ, Potrillo's Mexican, Starbucks

**276a** Vasquez Ave, **N gas:** Pilot/Wendy's/dsl/scales/24hr, **lodging:** Colonial Motel, Western Inn, **other:** Blue Beacon, Ford/Mack Trucks, **S gas:** 7-11, **food:** Burger King

**275c** York St (from eb), **N lodging:** Colonial Motel

**275b** CO 265, Brighton Blvd, Coliseum, **N gas:** 7-11

**275a** Washington St, **N food:** Pizza Hut, **S gas:** Conoco, **food:** McDonald's, Quizno's, Subway

**274b a** I-25, N to Cheyenne, S to Colorado Springs

**273** Pecos St, **N gas:** Safeway, **S gas:** Conoco, Phillips 66/dsl, Circle K, **lodging:** Discount Hotel, **other:** transmissions

**272** US 287, Federal Blvd, **N gas:** Sinclair, **food:** Burger King, Goodtimes Burgers, Hamburger Stand, Loco Pollo, McCoy's Rest., McDonald's, Pizza Hut, Subway, Taco Bell, Village Inn Rest., Wendy's, **lodging:** Motel 6, **other:** K-Mart, **S gas:** Amoco, Conoco, 7-11, **food:** Popeye's, **lodging:** Howard Johnson/Las Palmeras Mexican

**271b** Lowell Blvd, Tennyson St (from wb)

**271a** CO 95, **S** Wild Chipmunk Amusement Park

**270** Sheridan Blvd, **S gas:** Shamrock, **food:** Arby's, Oriental Rest., Sunrise Café, **other:** Target, U-Haul, funpark, mall

**269b** I-76 E (from eb), to Ft Morgan, Ft Collins

**269a** CO 121, Wadsworth Blvd, **N gas:** Conoco, LuckyMart/dsl, 7-11/gas, **food:** Alimos Verdes Mexican, Applebee's, Bennet's BBQ, Chipotle Pexican, Coldstone Creamery, Country Buffet, Fazoli's, Gunther Toody's Diner, IHOP,

**269a** Continued
LoneStar Steaks, McDonald's/playplace, Ruby Tuesday, Starbucks, Taco Bell, TX Roadhouse, **other:** Advance Parts, Brakes+, Costco/gas, Discount Tire, Home Depot, Lowes Whse, Office Depot, PetsMart, Radio Shack, Sam's Club, Tires+, Waldenbooks, mall

**267** CO 391, Kipling St, Wheat Ridge, **N gas:** Conoco, Shell/Carl's Jr/Circle K/dsl, **food:** Burger King, Denny's, Einstein Bro.'s, Furr's Dining, Qdoba, Quizno's, Subway, **lodging:** American Inn, Motel 6, **other:** Chevrolet/Cadillac, Chrysler/Jeep, GNC, 7-11, Target, **S gas:** Conoco/Circle K, **food:** Pizza Hut/Taco Bell, Village Inn Rest., **lodging:** Comfort Inn, Holiday Inn Express, Interstate Inn, Motel 6, Ramada, **other:** Ketelesen RV Ctr

**266** CO 72, W 44th Ave, Ward Rd, Wheat Ridge, **N gas:** Conoco/dsl/transmissions, Phillips 66/dsl, **S gas:** Shamrock/dsl, TA/rest./scales/dsl/24hr/@, **lodging:** Howard Johnson

**265** CO 58 W (from wb), to Golden, Central City

**264** Youngfield St, W 32nd Ave, **N gas:** Conoco/Circle K, **food:** GoodTimes Burgers, Marie's Country Cafe, **lodging:** La Quinta, **S gas:** Conoco, Abrusci's Italian, Chili's, DQ, McDonald's, Old Chicago Pizza, Pizza Hut/Taco Bell, Starbucks, Subway, **other:** Camping World RV Ctr/service, Casey's RV Ctr, King's Sooper/24hr, PetsMart, Radio Shack, Walgreens, Walmart

**263** Denver West Blvd, **N lodging:** Marriott/rest., **S food:** Keg Steaks, Macaroni Grill, McGrath's Fishouse, Qdoba, **other:** Barnes&Noble, Best Buy, Office Depot, Wild Oats Mkt, same as 262

**262** US 40 E, W Colfax, Lakewood, **N gas:** Sinclair, **food:** Arby's, Jack-in-the-Box, **lodging:** Hampton Inn, **other:** CO RV Ctr, Dodge, Home Depot, Honda, Hyundai, Kohl's, NAPA, PetCo, U-Haul, transmissions, **S gas:** Shell/Circle K/dsl/LP, **food:** Cipotle Mexican, Daybreak Rest., Hops Brewery, Keg Steaks, Macaroni Grill, McGrath's Fishouse, Mimi's Cafe, On-the-Border, Outback Steaks, Pei Wei Asian, Qdoba, Quizno's, Wendy's, **lodging:** Courtyard, Day's Inn/rest., Holiday Inn, Residence Inn, **other:** Barnes&Noble, Best Buy, Borders Books, Chevrolet, Lexus, Old Navy, Target, Toyota, Wild Oats Mkt, mall, same as 263

**261** US 6 E (from eb), W 6th Ave, to Denver

**260** CO 470, to Colo Springs

**259** CO 26, Golden, **N gas:** Conoco, **lodging:** Hampton Inn (2mi), **other:** Heritage Sq Funpark, **S** Music Hall, to Red Rock Park

**CO**

**E / W** (arrows)

**IDAHO SPRINGS**

## INTERSTATE 70 CONT'D

| | |
|---|---|
| **257mm** | runaway truck ramp eb |
| **256** | Lookout Mtn, **N** to Buffalo Bill's Grave |
| **254** | Genesee, Lookout Mtn, **N** to Buffalo Bill's Grave, **S gas:** Conoco/Genesee Store, LP, **food:** Buffalo Moon, Chart House Rest., Christie's Rest., Guido's Pizza, **other:** vet |
| **253** | Chief Hosa, **S** RV Camping, [C] |
| **252** | (251 from eb), CO 74, Evergreen Pkwy, **S gas:** Conoco, **food:** Burger King, El Rancho Rest., McDonald's, Qdoba, Starbucks, Subway, **lodging:** Quality Suites, **other:** Big O Tire, Home Depot, Jiffy Lube, King's Sooper/deli, Walmart SuperCtr/auto |
| **248** | (247 from eb), Beaver Brook, Floyd Hill, **S** antiques |
| **244** | US 6, to CO 119, to Golden, Central City, Eldora Ski Area |
| **243** | Hidden Valley |
| **242mm** | tunnel |
| **241b a** | rd 314, Idaho Springs West, **N gas:** Conoco/McDonald's/dsl, Sinclair, Shell/dsl, Western, **food:** AJ's Cafe, Buffalo Rest., JC Sweet's, King's Derby Rest., Marion's Rest., Starbucks, Subway, Wildfire Motel, **lodging:** H&H Motel, Heritage Inn, Idaho Springs Hotel, JC Motel, Marion's Rest., Peoriana Motel, 6&40 Motel/rest., The Lodge, **other:** CarQuest, Radio Shack, Safeway, USPO |
| **240** | CO 103, Mt Evans, **N gas:** Shell, Sinclair, **food:** 2 Bros Deli, Beaujo's Pizza, Buffalo Restaurant, Paco's, Picci Pizza, Jiggie's Cafe, Subway, Tommy Knocker Grill, West Winds Tavern, same as 241, **S** to Mt Evans |
| **239** | Idaho Springs, **S other:** camping |
| **238** | Fall River Rd, to St Mary's Glacier |
| **235** | Dumont (from wb) |
| **234** | Downeyville, Dumont, **N gas:** Conoco/Subway/dsl, **food:** Burger King, Starbucks, **other:** ski rentals, weigh sta both lanes |
| **233** | Lawson (from eb) |
| **232** | US 40 W, to Empire, **N** to Berthoud Pass, Winterpark/Silver Creek ski areas |
| **228** | Georgetown, **S gas:** Conoco/Subway/dsl, Phillips 66/dsl, Shamrock/dsl, **food:** Happy Cooker, Mountaineer's Cafe, New Peking Garden, **lodging:** Georgetown Lodge, Super 8, **other:** visitors ctr |
| **226.5mm** | scenic overlook eb |
| **226** | Georgetown, Silver Plume Hist Dist, **N other:** Buckley Bros Mkt, repair |
| **221** | Bakerville |
| **220mm** | Arapahoe NF eastern boundary |
| **218** | no services |
| **216** | US 6 W, Loveland Valley, Loveland Basin, ski areas |
| **214mm** | Eisenhower/Johnson Tunnel, elev 11013 |
| **213mm** | parking area eb |
| **205** | US 6 E, CO 9 N, Dillon, Silverthorne, **N gas:** Conoco/dsl, 7-11, Sav-O-Mat, Shell/dsl, **food:** China Gourmet, Mtn Lyon Café, Murphy's Cafe, Old Chicago Grill, Old Dillon Inn Mexican, Quizno's, Village Inn Rest., Wendy's/24hr, **lodging:** Day's Inn, 1st Interstate Inn, La Quinta, Luxury Suites, Quality Inn, Silver Inn, **other:** CarQuest, Chevrolet/Cadillac/Buick, Ford/Mercury, Old Navy, Silverthorn Outlets/famous brands, Target, True Value, **S gas:** Phillips 66, Shamrock, Tesoro, **food:** Arby's, Bamboo Garden, Blue Moon Deli, Burger King, Coldstone, Dan |

**FRISCO**

**VAIL**

**AVON**

| | |
|---|---|
| **205** | Continued |
| | Brewery Rest., DQ, JJ Chinese, McDonald's, Nick & Willy's Pizza, Pizza Hut, Red Mtn Grill, Ruby Tuesday, SweetPeas, Starbucks, Subway, **lodging:** Comfort Suites, Super 8, **other:** Borders Books, City Mkt Foods, Dillon Stores/famous brands, vet |
| **203.5mm** | scenic overlook both lanes, [C] |
| **203** | CO 9 S, to Breckenridge, Frisco, **S gas:** Conoco/Wendy's/dsl, 7-11, Shell, Valero/dsl, **food:** A&W, Back Country Brewery/rest., BBQ, KFC, Mexican Bar & Grill, Ore House Steaks, Pizza Hut, Q 4 You BBQ, Starbucks, Subway, Taco Bell, **lodging:** Best Western, Holiday Inn, Ramada Ltd, Summit Inn, **other:** Big O Tire, Discout tire, NAPA, Radio Shack, Safeway, Walmart/Mcdonald's/drugs, vet, to Breckenridge Ski Area, Tiger Run RV Resort (6mi) |
| **201** | Main St, Frisco, **S gas:** Conoco, Loaf N' Jug, **food:** Brewery Rest., Fiesta Mexican, KFC, Pizza Hut, Spruce Inn Steakhouse, **lodging:** Bighorn Reservations, Frisco Lodge, Pearl Head Lodge, Snowshoe Motel, Skyvue Motel, Woodbridge Inn, **other:** RV camping, to Breckenridge Ski Area |
| **198** | Officers Gulch, emergency callbox |
| **196mm** | scenic area |
| **195** | CO 91 S, to Leadville, **1 mi S gas:** Conoco/dsl, **food:** Quizno's, Starbucks, Tucker's Tavern, **lodging:** Copper Lodging, **other:** to Copper Mtn Ski Resort |
| **190** | **S** rest area both lanes, full [&] facilities, [C], [picnic], **litter barrels** |
| **189mm** | Vail Pass Summit, elev 10662 ft, parking area both lanes |
| **180** | Vail East Entrance, [C], **services 3-4 mi S** |
| **176** | Vail, **S other:** [H] HOSPITAL, ski info/lodging |
| **173** | Vail Ski Area, **N gas:** Phillips 66, Shell/dsl, **food:** Bagali's Italian, DQ, Domino's, May Palace Chinese, McDonald's, Subway, Taco Bell, Wendy's, **lodging:** Holiday Inn, **other:** City Mkt Foods/deli, Safeway Food/Drug, **S gas:** Conoco/dsl/LP, **lodging:** Black Bear Inn, Marriott/Streamside Hotel, The Roost Lodge |
| **171** | US 6 W, US 24 E, to Minturn, Leadville, **N food:** Leadville Café, **other:** Ski Cooper ski area, **2.5 mi S gas:** Phillips 66, **food:** Child Wild Steaks, Minturn Steaks, **lodging:** Minturn Inn |
| **169** | Eaglevale, from wb, no return |
| **168** | William J. Post Blvd, **S food:** McDonald's, **other:** Home Depot, Walmart SuperCtr |
| **167** | Avon, **N gas:** Conoco/dsl, Phillips 66, **food:** Pizza Hut, **other:** Goodyear, **S food:** Burger King, Denny's, Domino's, Fiesta Mexican, Outback Steaks, Quizno's, Starbucks, Subway, **lodging:** Avon Ctr Lodge, Christie Lodge, Comfort Inn, Seasons Hotel, Sheraton, Westin, **other:** City Mkt/drugs, GNC, Office Depot, to Beaver Creek/Arrowhead Ski, Office Depot, ski info/lodging |
| **163** | Edwards, **S** rest area both lanes, full [&] facilities, [C], [picnic], **litter barrel, RV dump, gas:** Conoco, Shell/Wendy's/dsl, Fiesta Cantina, Frides Cafe, Gashaus Rest., Gore Range Brewery, Marble Slab Creamery, Marko's Pizza, Moe's SW Grill, Smiling Moose, Subway, Starbucks, **lodging:** Riverwalk Inn, **other:** to Arrowhead Ski Area, USPO |
| **162mm** | scenic area both lanes |

## INTERSTATE 70 CONT'D

**E A G L E**

E ↕ W

**G L E N W O O D   S P R I N G S**

| | |
|---|---|
| **159mm** | Eagle River |
| **157** | CO 131 N, Wolcott, **N** to gas, [L], to Steamboat Ski Area |
| **147** | Eagle, **N gas:** Shamrock/dsl, **food:** Burger King, Dominos, Mi Pueblo Mexican, **lodging:** AmericInn, Comfort Inn, Holiday Inn Express, **other:** City Mkt Foods, **S gas:** Conoco/pizza, Sinclair/dsl, **food:** Eagle Diner, Pazzo's Pizzaria, Smiling Moose, Subway, Wendy's, Gourmet China, **lodging:** Best Western, Silverleaf Suites, **other:** Costco/gas (3mi), Curves, **rest area both lanes, full** 🚻 **facilities, info** |
| **140** | Gypsum, **S gas:** Conoco, Phillips 66/dsl, **food:** Columbine Mkt Deli, Mexican-American Café, **other:** auto/truck repair, airport, **3 mi S** River Dance Resort camping |
| **134mm** | Colorado River |
| **133** | Dotsero, **N other:** Access to Riverdance RV Camping (3mi) |
| **129** | **Bair Ranch, S rest area both lanes, full** 🚻 **facilities,** 🏕, **litter barrels, petwalk** |
| **128.5mm** | parking area eb |
| **127mm** | tunnel wb |
| **125mm** | tunnel |
| **125** | to Hanging Lake (no return eb) |
| **123** | Shoshone (no return eb) |
| **122.5mm** | exit to river (no return eb) |
| **121** | **to Hanging Lake, Grizzly Creek, S rest area both lanes, full** 🚻 **facilities,** 🏕, **litter barrels,** |
| **119** | **No Name, rest area both lanes, full** 🚻 **facilities, RV camping, rafting** |
| **118mm** | tunnel |
| **116** | CO 82 E, to Aspen, Glenwood Springs, **N gas:** Conoco/dsl, Shell/dsl, **food:** BB's Wings, Fiesta Guadalajara, KFC, Pizza Hut, Qdoba, Subway, Tequila Rest., Village Inn Rest., **lodging:** AmericInn, Best Western, Glenwood Inn, Hampton Inn, Holiday Inn Express, Hotel Colorado, Ramada Inn, Silver Spruce Motel, Starlight Motel, **other:** Land Rover, Mazda, Nissan, Saab, Suzuki, Toyota, Volvo, Hot Springs Bath, funpark, **0-2 mi S gas:** Conoco, Phillips 66/dsl, Shamrock, Shell, Sinclair, **food:** Arby's, China Town, Domino's, McDonald's, Pizza Hut, Subway, Taco Bell, Tai Pei Japanese, Wendy's, **lodging:** Caravan Inn, Cedar Lodge, Frontier Lodge, Hotel Denver, **other:** 🏥 HOSPITAL, Alpine Tire, City Mkt Foods, Harley-Davidson, Honda, NAPA, Office Depot, Rite Aid, Safeway Foods, 7-11, Subaru/Nissan, Walmart, USPO, city park, to Ski Sunlight |
| **115mm** | **rest area eb, full** 🚻 **facilities,** 🏕, **litter barrels** |
| **114** | W Glenwood Springs, **N gas:** Phillips 66, 7-11, Shell, **food:** Burger King, CharBurger, Dos Hombres Mexican, Oasis Mexican, Ocean Pearl Chinese, **lodging:** Affordable Inn, Best Value Inn, Ponderosa Motel, Red Mtn Inn, Rodeway Inn, **other:** Big O Tire, Checker Parts, CarQuest, Chrysler/Dodge, Ford, JC Penney, K-Mart, Radio Shack, mall, **S gas:** Conoco/dsl, **food:** Chili's, DQ, **lodging:** Glenwood Suites, Quality Inn, **other:** Audi/VW, Lowes Whse, PetCo, Target |
| **111** | South Canyon |
| **109** | Canyon Creek |

**R I F L E**

| | |
|---|---|
| **108mm** | parking area both lanes |
| **105** | New Castle, **N gas:** Conoco/dsl, Kum&Go/dsl, **food:** Hong's Garden, New Castle Diner, Subway, **lodging:** Rodeway Inn, **other:** City Mkt Foods/deli, Elk Creek Campground (4mi), KOA (4mi), **S other:** Best Hardware |
| **97** | Silt, **N gas:** Conoco/dsl/24hr, Kum&Go, Phillips 66/dsl, **other:** auto repair, to Harvey Gap SP, **S lodging:** Holiday Inn Express, **other:** Heron's Nest RV Park |
| **94** | Garfield County Airport Rd |
| **90** | CO 13 N, Rifle, **N rest area both lanes, full** 🚻 **facilities,** [L], 🏕, **litter barrels, RV dump, NF Info, gas:** Conoco, Kum&Go/gas, Phillips 66/dsl, Shell, **lodging:** Winchester Motel (1mi), **other:** 🏥 HOSPITAL, USPO, **S gas:** Kum&Go, Phillips 66/dsl, **food:** Burger King, Dominos, Little Caesar's, McDonald's/playplace, Rib City Grill, Starbucks, Subway, Sonic, Taco Bell/LJ Silver, **lodging:** La Quinta, Red River Inn/rest., Rusty Cannon Motel, **other:** 🏥 HOSPITAL, Big O Tire, Checker Parts, Radio Shack, Walmart SuperCtr |
| **87** | to CO 13, West Rifle |
| **81** | Rulison |
| **75** | Parachute, **N rest area both lanes, full** 🚻 **facilities, info,** [L], 🏕, **litter barrels, petwalk, gas:** Sinclair/dsl, Shell/dsl/24hr, **food:** El Tapatio Mexican, Hong's Garden Chinese, Outlaws Rest., Subway, **lodging:** Super 8, **other:** NAPA, Radio Shack, USPO, vet, **S gas:** Conoco/Wendy's/dsl, Phillips 66, **lodging:** Candlewood Suites, Holiday Inn Express, **other:** Family$, Good Sam RV Park (4mi) |
| **63mm** | Colorado River |
| **62** | De Beque, **N gas:** CFN Fuel, **other:** Canyon Lake Campground, food, lodging, [L], auto repair |
| **50mm** | parking area eastbound, Colorado River, tunnel begins eastbound |
| **49mm** | Plateau Creek |
| **49** | CO 65 S, to CO 330 E, to Grand Mesa, Powderhorn Ski Area |
| **47** | Island Acres St RA, **N** CO River SP, RV camping, **S gas:** Conoco/rest./dsl |
| **46** | Cameo |
| **44** | Lp 70 W, to Palisade, **3 mi S** gas, food, lodging |
| **43.5mm** | Colorado River |
| **42** | US 6, Palisade, **1 mi S** Fruitstand/store, gas, lodging, **other:** wineries |
| **37** | to US 6, to US 50 S, Clifton, Grand Jct, **0-1 mi S gas:** Conoco/dsl, Shamrock/dsl, Sinclair, **food:** Burger King, |

## INTERSTATE 70 CONT'D

**E / W / GRAND JUNCTION / FRUITA**

| | |
|---|---|
| 37 | Continued |
| | Dos Hombres Mexican, KFC, Little Caesar's, McDonald's/playplace, Papa Murphy's, Pizza Hut, Qdoba, Sonic, Starbucks, Subway, Taco Bell, Teahouse Chinese, The Diner, Wendy's, **lodging:** Best Western, **other:** Ace Harware, AutoZone, Broomes RV Ctr, Checker Parts, City Mkt Food/gas, Family$, Murdoch's Store, USPO, Walgreens, Walmart SuperCtr (2mi), repair |
| 31 | Horizon Dr, Grand Jct, **N gas:** Shamrock, Shell/dsl, **food:** Coco's, Diorio's Pizza, Pepper's Rest., Village Inn Rest., Wendy's, **lodging:** Best Value Inn, Comfort Inn, Courtyard, Grand Vista Hotel, Holiday Inn, La Quinta, Motel 6, Ramada Inn, Residence Inn, **other:** Harley-Davidson, USPO, Zarlingo's Repair, airport, **S gas:** Conoco/Subway/dsl, Phillips 66/dsl, **food:** Applebees, Burger King/playland, Denny's, Good Pastures Rest., Nick & Willy's Pizza, Pizza Hut, Starbucks, Taco Bell, **lodging:** Affordable Inn, Best Western, Country Inn, Doubletree Hotel, Mesa Inn, Quality Inn, Super 8, **other:** H HOSPITAL, Safeway Food/drug/gas, golf, visitors ctr, to Mesa St Coll, CO NM |
| 28 | Redlands Pkwy, 24 rd, **N** camping, **0-2 mi S** same as 26 |
| 26 | US 6, US 50, Grand Jct, **N other:** Hyundai, Jct W RV Park, **0-4 mi S gas:** Conoco/A&W/dsl **food:** Bear Rock Cafe, Black Bear Diner, Boston's Cafe, Burger King, Carino's Italian, Carl's JR., Chick-fil-A, Chili's, Chipotle Mexican, Coldstone Creamery, ChuckeCheese, Famous Dave's BBQ, Genghis Grill, Golden Corral, IHOP, McDonald's/playplace, Olive Garden, Outback Steaks, Panchero's Mexican, Papa Murphy's, Red Lobster, Red Robin, Starbucks, Taco Bell, Wendy's **lodging:** Holiday Inn Express, Westgate Inn, **other:** AutoZone, Barnes&Noble, Best Buy, Big O Tire, Borders Books, Cameron's RV Ctr, Chrysler/Dodge, $Tree, Ford/Lincoln/Merury, Home Depot, Honda, JC Penney, Kohl's, Lowes Whse, Michael's, Mobile City RV Park, Nissan, Office Depot, Old Navy, PetCo, PetsMart, Ross, Sam's Club/gas, Scott RV Ctr, Sears/auto, Sportsman's Whse, Subaru, Toyota, Walmart SuperCtr, mall |
| 19 | US 6, CO 340, Fruita, **N gas:** Conoco/dsl, **food:** Burger King, Munchie's Burgers/Pizza, **lodging:** Balanced Rock Motel, **other:** H HOSPITAL, City Mkt Foods/deli/24hr, USPO, **S Welcome Ctr both lanes, full** 🚻 **facilities,** 🚻 **, litter barrels, RV dump, petwalk, gas:** Conoco/Subway/dsl/24hr, Shell/Wendy's/dsl/24hr, **food:** Chinese-American Rest., McDonald's/playplace, Rib City Grill, Taco Bell, **lodging:** Comfort Inn, La Quinta, Super 8, **other:** CO Mon Trading Co, Peterbilt, camping, dinosaur museum, to CO NM |
| 17mm | Colorado River |
| 15 | CO 139 N, to Loma, Rangely, **N** to Highline Lake SP, gas/dsl, phone |
| 14.5mm | weigh/check sta both lanes, phones |
| 11 | Mack, **2-3 mi N** gas/dsl, food |
| 2 | Rabbit Valley, to Dinosaur Quarry Trail |
| 0mm | Colorado/Utah state line |

## INTERSTATE 76

**E / W / STERLING / FT MORGAN**

| Exit # | Services |
|---|---|
| 184mm | Colorado/Nebraska state line |
| 180 | US 385, Julesburg, **N gas:** ⊕ *FLYING J*/dsl/LP/rest./24hr, Shell, **food:** Subway, **lodging:** Budget Host, **other:** H HOSPITAL, **Welcome Ctr/rest area both lanes, full** 🚻 **facilities, info, RV dump, S gas:** Conoco/dsl |
| 172 | Ovid, **2 mi N** gas, food |
| 165 | CO 59, to Haxtun, Sedgwick, **N** Lucy's Cafe/gas |
| 155 | Red Lion Rd |
| 149 | CO 55, to Fleming, Crook, **S gas:** Sinclair/dsl/café |
| 141 | Proctor |
| 134 | Iliff |
| 125 | US 6, Sterling, **N gas:** Cenex/dsl, **lodging:** Best Western, 1st Interstate Inn, **other:** H HOSPITAL, N Sterling SP, museum, st patrol, **rest area both lanes. full** 🚻 **facilities,** 🚻 **, litter barrels, petwalk, vending, RV dump, 0-3 mi N gas:** Sinclair, **food:** Arby's, Burger King, KFC, McDonald's, Pizza Hut, Sonic, Taco John's, Village Inn, Wendy's, **other:** Chrysler/Jeep/Dodge, Checker Parts, $Tree, Home Depot, NAPA, Walgreens, Walmart SuperCtr/gas, tires **S gas:** Phillips 66/Quizno's/dsl, **food:** Country Kitchen, **lodging:** Comfort Inn, Ramada Inn, Super 8, Travelodge, **other:** Jellystone Camping |
| 115 | CO 63, Atwood, **N gas:** Sinclair/dsl, **other:** H HOSPITAL, **S food:** Steakhouse |
| 102 | Merino |
| 95 | Hillrose |
| 92 | to US 6 E, to US 34, CO 71 S |
| 90b a | CO 71 N, to US 34, Brush, **N gas:** Tomahawk Trkstp/Shell/rest./dsl/24hr, **food:** China Buffet, Pizza Hut, Wendy's, **lodging:** Econolodge, **S gas:** Conoco/dsl, **food:** McDonald's, Subway, **lodging:** Microtel |
| 89 | Hospital Rd, **S** H HOSPITAL, golf |
| 86 | Dodd Bridge Rd |
| 82 | Barlow Rd, **N gas:** Conoco/dsl, **food:** Maverick's Grill, **lodging:** Comfort Inn, Rodeway Inn, **S gas:** Phillips 66/dsl/scales, **food:** Burger King, Quizno's, **other:** $Tree, Walmart SuperCtr/Subway/dsl |
| 80 | CO 52, Ft Morgan, **N other:** City Park, Golf, RV Camping, **S gas:** Conoco/dsl/24hr, Shell/dsl, **food:** Arby's, DQ, McDonald's, Sonic, Subway, Taco John's, **lodging:** Best Western/rest., Central Motel, Day's Inn, Super 8, **other:** H HOSPITAL, AutoZone, Rite Aid |
| 79 | CO 144, to Weldona, no WB return |
| 75 | US 34 E, to Ft Morgan, st patrol |
| 74.5mm | weigh sta both lanes |
| 73 | Long Bridge Rd |
| 66b | US 34 W (from wb), to Greeley |
| 66a | CO 39, CO 52, to Goodrich, **N gas:** Phillips 66, **other:** to Jackson Lake SP, **S gas:** Sinclair/cafe/dsl, **other: rest area both lanes, full** 🚻 **facilities,** 🚻 **, litter barrels, petwalk,** 📞 **, vending** |
| 64 | Wiggins (from eb) |
| 60 | to CO 144 E, to Orchard |
| 57 | rd 91 |
| 49 | Painter Rd (from wb) |

## INTERSTATE 76 CONT'D

| | |
|---|---|
| **48** | to Roggen, **N gas:** Phillips 66/dsl, **S other:** USPO |
| **39** | Keenesburg, **S gas:** Phillips 66/dsl, **food:** Rooster's Rest., **lodging:** Keene Motel |
| **34** | Kersey Rd |
| **31** | CO 52, Hudson, **N gas:** Love's/Subway/Carls Jr/scales/24hr/dsl, **S gas:** Conoco/dsl, Phillips 66/dsl, **food:** El Faro Mexican, Pepper Pod Rest., **other:** RV camping, USPO |
| **25** | CO 7, Lochbuie, **N gas:** Shell/dsl |
| **22** | Bromley Lane, **N gas:** Shamrock/dsl, **food:** Wendy's, **other:** Kohl's, Home Depot, Lowe's Whse, Target, **other:** H HOSPITAL, **2-4 mi N food:** Applebee's, Arby's, Kings Sooper/gas, Starbucks, Village Inn, **lodging:** Brighton Inn, Comfort Inn, **S** Barr Lake SP |
| **21** | 144th Ave, **N food:** Chili's, Heidi's Deli, Quizno's, Taco Bell, **other:** $Tree, GNC, Home Depot, Kohl's, PetsMart, Super Target |
| **20** | 136th Ave, **N** Barr Lake RV Park, same as 21 |
| **18** | E-470 tollway, to Limon  (from wb) |
| **16** | CO 2 W, Sable Blvd, Commerce City, **N gas:** Shell/Tomahawk Trkstp/Blimpie/dsl/24hr/@, to Denver Airport |
| **12** | US 85 N, to Brighton, Greeley |
| **11** | 96th Ave, **N** dsl repair, **S** GMC Trucks |
| **10** | 88th Ave, **N gas:** Phillips 66/Blimpie/dsl, **lodging:** Holiday Inn Express, Super 8, **S** flea mkt |
| **9** | US 6 W, US 85 S  (wb returns st 10), Commerce City, **S gas:** Shell/dsl, **other:** GMC/Freightliner, transmissions, st patrol |
| **8** | CO 224, 74th Ave (no EZ eb return), **1 mi N** NAPA, **S gas:** Shamrock/dsl |
| **6b a** | I-270 E, to Limon, to ✈, to I-25 N, to ✈ |
| **5** | I-25, N to Ft Collins, S to Colo Springs |
| **4** | Pecos St |
| **3** | US 287, Federal Blvd, **N gas:** Shamrock/dsl, **S food:** Taco House |
| **1b** | CO 95, Sheridan Blvd |
| **1a** | CO 121, Wadsworth Blvd, **N gas:** Conoco, LuckyMart/dsl, 7-11/gas, **food:** Alimos Verdes Mexican, Applebee's, Bennet's BBQ, Chipotle Pexican, Coldstone Creamery, Country Buffet, Fazoli's, Gunther Toody's Diner, IHOP, LoneStar Steaks, McDonald's/playplace, Ruby Tuesday, Starbucks, Taco Bell, TX Roadhouse, **other:** Advance Parts, Brakes+, Costco/gas, Discount Tire, Home Depot, Lowe's Whse, Office Depot, PetsMart, Radio Shack, Sam's Club, Tires+, Waldenbooks, mall |
| **0mm** | I-76 begins/ends on I-70, exit 269b. |

## INTERSTATE 225

| Exit # | Services |
|---|---|
| **12b a** | I-70, W to Denver, E to Limon |
| **10** | US 40, US 287, Colfax Ave, **E gas:** Conoco/dsl, 7-11, **food:** Arby's, Del Taco, KFC, McDonald's, Pizza Hut/Taco Bell, **other:** Aamco, Advance Parts, Chevrolet, K-Mart, RV camping, **W gas:** Conoco, Phillips 66 |

| | |
|---|---|
| **9** | Co 30, 6th Ave, **E gas:** Conoco, **food:** Denny's, **lodging:** Super 8, **W gas:** Phillips 66/dsl, **other:** H HOSPITAL |
| **8** | Alameda Ave, **E gas:** Conoco, Valero, **food:** Benny's Cafe, Chili's, Coldstone, Macaroni Grill, Mimi's Cafe, Panda Express, Starbucks, Tgi Friday, **other:** Atlanta Bread, Barnes&Noble, Foley's, JC Penney, NAPA, Old Navy, Ross, Sears/auto, Target, mall, **W gas:** Conoco/mart, Shell/repair |
| **7** | Mississippi Ave, Alameda Ave, **E food:** Arby's, Burger King, Cici's, Chubby's Mexican, ChuckeCheese, Denny's, DQ, Fazoli's, Schlotsky's, Sonic, Subway, **lodging:** Best Western, Hampton Inn, La Quinta, **other:** Best Buy, Burlington Coats, Circuit City, Home Depot, JoAnn Fabrics, Sam's Club/gas, Tires +, Walmart, **W food:** IHOP, McDonald's, Senor Rics, Vietnam House, Waffle House, **other:** AutoZone, Curves, 7-11, Office Depot |
| **5** | Iliff Ave, **E gas:** 7-11, **food:** Applebee's, Boston Mkt, Carrabba's, Fuddrucker's, Japanese Steaks, Joe's Crabshack, Outback Steaks, Rosie's Diner, Ruby Tuesday, Sweet Tomato, Texas Roadhouse, **lodging:** Comfort Inn, Crestwood Suites, Fairfield Inn, Homestead Suites, Motel 6, **W gas:** Phillips 66, **food:** Dragon's Boat, Subway, **lodging:** DoubleTree |
| **4** | CO 83, Parker Rd, **E lodging:** Radisson, **other:** Cherry Creek SP, **W gas:** Phillips 66/dsl, **food:** DQ, Denny's, Lonestar Steaks, Pizza Hut, Popeyes, Starbucks, Subway, Taco Bell, Wendy's, **other:** $Tree, Kings Sooper |
| **2b** | no services |
| **2** | DTC Blvd, Tamarac St, **W gas:** Conoco, 7-11, **food:** La Fogata Mexican, Quizno's, Sonic |
| **0mm** | I-225 begins/ends on I-25, exit 200. |

## INTERSTATE 270

| Exit # | Services |
|---|---|
| **4** | I-70 |
| **3** | **N gas:** TA/Popeye's/Quizno's/Pizza Hut/dsl24hr/@, **S gas:** Sapp Bros/Sinclair/Subway/dsl/@ |
| **2b a** | US 85, CO 2, Vasquez Ave, **N gas:** Conoco, **food:** Arby's, Carls Jr, Chipotle Mexican, GoodTimes Grill, KFC, McDonald's, Pizza Inn, Taco Bell, Taco John's, Wendy's, **other:** Walgreens, Walmart Super Ctr |
| **1b** | York St |
| **1a** | I-76 E, to Ft Morgan |
| **1c** | I-25 S, to Denver |

**E** ↕ **W**

**CT**

## INTERSTATE 84

| Exit # | Services |
|---|---|
| **98mm** | Connecticut/Massachusetts state line |
| **74** (97) | CT 171, Holland, **S food:** Traveler's Book Rest., **other:** RV camping |
| **95mm** | weigh sta wb |
| **73** (95) | CT 190, Stafford Springs, **N other:** camping (seasonal), motor speedway, st police |
| **72** (93) | CT 89, Westford, **N lodging:** Ashford Motel, camping (seasonal), phone |
| **71** (88) | Ruby Rd, **N** Citgo, **S gas:** TA/Shell/Burger King/Country Fried/dsl/scales/24hr/@, **lodging:** Econolodge |
| **70** (86) | CT 32, Willington, **N gas:** H HOSPITAL, **S gas:** Mobil/dsl, Sunoco/dsl, **other:** RV Camping |
| **85mm** | rest area both lanes, full ♿ facilities, info, 🅲, vending, ⛽ litter barrels, petwalk, campers, RV dump |
| **69** (83) | CT 74, to US 44, Willington, **S** gas, food, 🅲, RV camping, st police |
| **68** (81) | CT 195, Tolland, **N gas:** Gulf/dsl, Mobil, **food:** Papa T's Rest., Subway, **other:** NAPA, RV camping, **S gas:** Citgo, **other:** Big Y Foods, |
| **67** (77) | CT 31, Rockville, **N gas:** Mobil, Shell, **food:** Burger King, China Taste, McDonald's, Subway, Theo's Rest., Tim Horton, **other:** H HOSPITAL, **S** Nathan Hale Mon |
| **66** (76) | Tunnel Rd, Vernon |
| **65** (75) | CT 30, Vernon Ctr, **N gas:** Mobil/24hr, Shell, **food:** ChowderTown, KFC, Vernon Diner, **lodging:** Comfort Inn, Howard Johnson Express, **other:** CarQuest, Vernon Drug |
| **64** (74) | Vernon Ctr, Vernon Ctr, **N gas:** Mobil/24hr, Sunoco, **food:** Acqua Oyster Bar, Angellino's Italian, Anthony's Pizza, D'Angelo's, Denny's, Dunkin Donuts, Friendly's, McDonald's, 99 Rest., Taco Bell, **lodging:** Holiday Inn Express, **other:** Advance Parts, AutoZone, CVS Drug, Firestone, GNC, Goodyear/auto, K-Mart, PriceChopper, Radio Shack, Staples, Stop&Shop, TJ Maxx, TownFair Tire, **S lodging:** Quality Inn |
| **63** (72) | CT 30, CT 83, Manchester, **S** Windsor, **N gas:** Shell, **food:** Macaroni Grill, McDonald's, HomeTown Buffet, Outback Steaks, TGIFriday, Uno Pizzaria, **lodging:** Courtyard, **other:** Barnes&Noble, Best Buy, Circuit City, JC Penney, Michael's, Office Depot, Sears/auto, Walgreens, Walmart, same as 62, **S gas:** Getty, Gulf, Shell/24hr, Xtra, **food:** Century Buffet, Panera Bread, Roy Roger's, **lodging:** Best Value Inn, Extended Stay America, Super 8, **other:** H HOSPITAL, Big Y Mkt, Chrysler, Ford/Kia, Kohl's, Lincoln/Mercury/Mazda, Rite Aid, Subaru, Toyota |
| **62** (71) | Buckland St, **N gas:** Exxon/dsl/24hr, **food:** Boston Mkt, Bugaboo Creek Steaks, Chili's, Friendly's, Hooters, John Harvard's Brewhouse, Olive Garden, Taco Bell, **other:** Borders Books, Firestone/auto, Home Depot, Jo-Ann Fabrics, Lowes Whse, Sam's Club, mall, same as 63, **S gas:** Citgo/dsl, Xtra, **food:** Burger King, Carraba's, ChuckeCheese, Dunkin Donuts, Golden Dragon, McDonald's, Subway, Wendy's, **other:** Buick, Honda, USPO |
| **61** (70) | I-291 W, to Windsor |
| **60** (69) | US 6, US 44, Burnside Ave (from eb), no faciites |
| **59** (68) | I-384 E, Manchester |
| **58** (67) | Roberts St, Burnside Ave, **N food:** Margarita's Grill, **lodging:** Days Inn, Holiday Inn, **S other:** vet |

**VERNON**

**WINDSOR**

| | |
|---|---|
| **57** (66) | CT 15 S, to I-91 S, Charter Oak Br |
| **56** (65) | Governor St, E Hartford, **S** ✈ |
| **55** (64) | CT 2 E, New London, downtown |
| **54** (63) | Old State House, **N other:** Ford/Isuzu, Lincoln/Mercury, **S lodging:** Marriott, Sheraton |
| **53** (62) | CT Blvd  (from eb) |
| **52** (61) | W Main St  (from eb), downtown |
| **51** (60) | I-91 N, to Springfield |
| **50** (59.8) | to I-91 S  (from wb) |
| **48** (59.5) | Asylum St , downtown, **N lodging:** Crowne Plaza, **S lodging:** Hilton, Holiday Inn Express, Residence Inn, **other:** H HOSPITAL |
| **47** (59) | Sigourney St, downtown, **N** Hartford Seminary, Mark Twain House |
| **46** (58) | Sisson St, downtown, UConn Law School |
| **45** (57) | Flatbush Ave  (exits left from wb), **N** Shaw's Foods |
| **44** (56.5) | Prospect Ave, **N gas:** Exxon, Shell, **food:** Burger King, D'angelo's, Gold Roc Diner/24hr, HomeTown Buffet, McDonald's, **other:** Shaw's Foods/Osco Drug |
| **43** (56) | Park Rd, W Hartford, **N** to St Joseph Coll |
| **42** (55) | Trout Brk Dr  (exits left from wb), to Elmwood |
| **41** (54) | S Main St, American School for the Deaf |
| **40** (53) | CT 71, New Britain Ave, **S gas:** Shell, Sunoco, **food:** California Pizza, Dunkin Donuts, Olive Garden, Red Robin, Starbucks, Wendy's, **lodging:** Courtyard, **other:** Barnes&Noble, Best Buy, Borders, JC Penney, Office Depot, Old Navy, Radio Shack, Sears/auto, Target, mall |
| **39a** (52) | CT 9 S, to New Britain, Newington, **S** H HOSPITAL |
| **39** (51.5) | CT 4, Farmington, **N** H HOSPITAL |
| **38** (51) | US 6 W  (from wb), Bristol, **N gas:** Shell |
| **37** (50) | Fienemann Rd, to US 6 W, **N gas:** Shell, **food:** Subway, **lodging:** Marriott |
| **36** (49) | Slater Rd (exits left from eb), **S** H HOSPITAL |
| **35** (48) | CT 72, to CT 9  (exits left from wb), New Britain, **S** H HOSPITAL |
| **34** (47) | CT 372, Crooked St, **N gas:** Citgo, Sunoco, **food:** Applebee's, Friendly's, Imperial Buffet, LJ Silver/Taco Bell, McDonald's, Starbucks, Wendy's, **lodging:** Plainville Inn, **other:** Big Y Mkt, Ford, Kohl's, Lowe's Whse, Old Navy, VW |
| **33** (46) | CT 72 W, to Bristol |
| **32** (45) | Ct 10, Queen St, Southington, **N gas:** Cumberland Farms, Exxon, Shell/dsl, Bertucci's, Burger King, Chili's, D'angelo's, Denny's, Dunkin Donuts, JD's Rest., KFC, McDonald's, Outback Steaks, Puerto Valarta, Randy's Pizza, Ruby Tuesday, Starbucks, Subway, Taco Bell, **lodging:** Motel 6, **other:** H HOSPITAL, CVS Drug, $Tree, Shaw's Foods, Staples, TJ Maxx, TownFair Tire, **S gas:** Hess, Mobil, Sunoco, **food:** Blimpie, Brannigan's Ribs, Friendly's, Ponderosa, Subway, Wendy's, Wood'n Tap Grill, **lodging:** Holiday Inn Express, Howard Johnson, Travelers Inn, **other:** Chevrolet, Jaguar, Firestone, PriceChopper Foods, Walmart |
| **31** (44) | CT 229, West St, **N gas:** Mobil, Sunoco/dsl/24hr, **S gas:** Citgo, Gulf, **food:** Dunkin Donuts, Giovanni's Pizza, Subway, Valentino's Pizzaria, **lodging:** Residence Inn |
| **30** (43) | Marion Ave, W Main, Southington, **N** ski area, **S gas:** Mobil/repair, **other:** H HOSPITAL |
| **29** (42) | CT 10, Milldale (exits left from wb) |

**HARTFORD**

**SOUTHINGTON**

**CT**

**M A R I O N**

**E ↕ W**

## INTERSTATE 84 CONT'D

**41.5mm** rest area eb, full ♿ facilities, info, 🕿, ⛱, litter barrels, petwalk

**28 (41)** CT 322, Marion, **S gas:** Mobil, Sams Gas, TA/Pizza Hut/Popeye's/dsl/scales/24hr/@, **food:** Blimpie, Burger King, DQ, Dunkin Donuts, Manor Inn Rest., Milldale Diner, **lodging:** Comfort Suites, Milldale Inn, **other:** Home Depot, radiators, USPO

**27 (40)** I-691 E, to Meriden

**26 (38)** CT 70, to Cheshire, **N food:** Silver Diner, **lodging:** CT Grand Hotel

**25a (37)** Austin Rd (from eb), **N lodging:** CT Grand Hotel, **other:** Costco/gas

**25 (36)** Scott Rd, E Main St, **N gas:** Exxon, Gulf/dsl, Dunkin Donuts, **S gas:** Mobil, **food:** Burger King, Friendly's, McDonald's, Nino's Rest., **lodging:** Ramada Inn, Super 8, **other:** BJ's Whse, Cadillac, Chevrolet, CVS Drug, Super Stop&Shop

**24** Harper's Ferry (from eb), **S gas:** Gulf, Shell/24hr

**24** Harper's Ferry (from eb), Gulf, Shell/24hr

**23 (33.5)** CT 69, Hamilton Ave, **N gas:** Citgo, **food:** Bertucci's, Chili's, HomeTown Buffet, McDonald's, Ruby Tuedsay, TGIFriday's, **other:** H HOSPITAL, Barnes&Noble, JC Penney, Macy's, Sears/auto, Shaw's Foods, Walgreens, mall, **S gas:** Shell, **food:** Dunkin Donuts

**22 (33)** Baldwin St, Waterbury, **N gas:** McDonald's, **lodging:** Courtyard, **other:** H HOSPITAL, same as 23

**21 (33)** Meadow St, Banks St, **N gas:** Citgo, **other:** 7-11, Shaw's Foods, **S gas:** Sunoco/dsl/24hr, **other:** Home Depot, PetsMart

**S O U T H B U R Y**

**20 (32)** CT 8 N (exits left from eb), to Torrington, **N gas:** Shell, **food:** Burger King, McDonald's

**19 (32)** CT 8 S (exits left from wb), to Bridgeport

**18 (32)** W Main, Highland Ave, **N food:** Lena's Deli, **lodging:** Hampton Inn, **other:** H HOSPITAL, CVS Drug

**17 (30)** CT 63, CT 64, to Watertown, Naugatuck, **N food:** Maggie McFly's Rest., **S gas:** Mobil/dsl, **food:** Maples Rest.

**16 (25)** CT 188, to Middlebury, **N gas:** Mobil, **food:** Patty's Pantry Deli, **lodging:** Crowne Plaza

**15 (22)** US 6 E, CT 67, Southbury, **N gas:** Shell, **food:** Dunkin Donuts, Friendly's, McDonald's, **lodging:** Heritage Inn, **other:** K-Mart, Stop&Shop, to Kettletown SP, **S gas:** Mobil

**14 (20)** CT 172, to S Britain, **N gas:** Mobil/24hr, **food:** Maggie McFly's, Miranda's Pizza, **other:** st police

**20mm** motorist callboxes begin eb, end wb

**13 (19)** River Rd (from eb), to Southbury

**11 (16)** CT 34, to New Haven

**10 (15)** US 6 W, Newtown, **S gas:** Mobil/dsl, Shell/24hr, **food:** Blue Colony Diner/24hr, Pizza Palace, **other:** H HOSPITAL

**9 (11)** CT 25, to Hawleyville, **S lodging:** Best Western, Hillside Inn, Microtel

**8 (8)** Newtown Rd, **N gas:** Global, Mobil/dsl, **food:** Outback Steaks, **other:** Lowes Whse, **lodging:** Wellesley Inn, **S gas:** BP, Shell, Sunoco, **food:** Bertucci's Italian, Boston Mkt, Burger King, Chili's, Denny's, Dunkin Donuts, Friendly's, Ichiro Steaks, McDonald's, Subway, Taco Bell, Union Buffet, **lodging:** Best Western, Hampton Inn, Holiday Inn/rest., Quality Inn, **other:** Buick/Pontiac, Chrysler/Jeep/Kia, Goodyear/auto, Marshall's, Radio Shack, Staples, Stop&Shop, Target, Walmart

**7 (7)** US 7N/202E, to Brookfield, (exits left from eb), New Milford, **1 exit N on Federal Rd...food:** Applebee's, **lodging:** Best Inn, **other:** Borders Books, Circuit City, Ford, Harley-Davidson, Home Depot, mall

**6 (6)** CT 37 (from wb), New Fairfield, **N gas:** Shell, **food:** McDonald's, **other:** H HOSPITAL, to Squantz Pond SP

**CT**

**E ← → W**

## INTERSTATE 84 CONT'D

**5** (5) CT 37, CT 39, CT 53, Danbury, **N gas:** Exxon, Shell, **lodging:** Best Value Inn, **S gas:** Mobil, **food:** Dunkin Donuts, Taco Bell, **other:** H HOSPITAL, to Putnam SP

**4** (4) US 6 W/202 W, Lake Ave, **N gas:** Gulf/dsl, Shell/dsl, Xtra, **food:** Dunkin Donuts, McDonald's, **lodging:** Ethan Allen Hotel, Maron Hotel, Super 8, **other:** CVS Drug, Goodyear/auto, Stop&Shop, **S gas:** Sunoco, **food:** Chuck's Steaks, **lodging:** Residence Inn, to mall

**3** (3) US 7 S (exits left from wb), to Norwalk, **S gas:** Exxon, **food:** Coldstone Creamery, Olive Garden, Red Lobster, **other:** Barnes&Noble, JC Penney, Macy's, Sears/auto, mall

**2b a** (1) US 6, US 202, Mill Plain Rd, **N gas:** Exxon/dsl, **food:** Desert Moon Café, Starbucks, **lodging:** Comfort Suites, Hilton Garden, **other:** Eckerd, Staples, **S Welcome Ctr/ weigh sta, full** ♿ **facilities, info,** 🅿 **litter barrels, pet- walk, to Old Ridgebury, lodging:** Sheraton

**1** (0) Saw Mill Rd, **N lodging:** Comfort Suites (2mi), Danbury Motel, Hilton Garden

**0mm** Connecticut/New York state line

## INTERSTATE 91

**N ← → S**

**HAZARDVILLE**

| Exit # | Services |
|---|---|
| **58mm** | Connecticut/Massachusetts state line |

**49** (57) US 5, to Longmeadow, MA, **E gas:** Pride, Valero, Friendly's, McDonald's, **lodging:** Crowne Plaza, **other:** Acme Auto Repair, **W food:** Cloverleaf Café

**48** (56) CT 220, Elm St, **E gas:** Mobil, **food:** Arby's, Burger King, Denny's, Dunkin Donuts, Friendly's, McDonald's, Oyama Japanese, Outback Steaks, Panera Bread, Ruby Tuesday, TGIFriday, Wendy's, **other:** AutoZone, Best Buy, Costco/gas, Circuit City, $Tree, JC Penny, Macy's, Home Depot, Honda, Kohl's, Nissan, Radio Shack, Sears/auto, Target, same as 47

**47** (55) CT 190, to Hazardville, **E gas:** Mobil, **food:** Bickford's, D'angelo, Domino's, Dunkin Donuts, Hazard Grille, KFC, McDonald's, 99 Rest., Olive Garden, Pizza Hut, Quiz- no's, Red Robin, Starbucks, Taco Bell, **lodging:** Hamp- ton Inn, Motel 6, Red Roof Inn, **other:** H HOSPITAL, Advance Parts, AutoZone, Barnes&Noble, Big Y Foods, CVS Drug, $Tree, Ford, Marshall's, Michael's, NAPA, Office Depot, PetCo, Rite Aid, Shaw's Foods, Staples, Stop&Shop Foods, Walgreen, mall, same as 48

**46** (53) US 5, King St, to Enfield, **E gas:** Mobil, **food:** Astro's Rest., **W lodging:** Super 8

**45** (51) CT 140, Warehouse Point, **E gas:** Shell/Dunkin Donuts, **food:** Blimpie, Burger King, Cracker Barrel, Friendly's, Green Tea China, Sofia's Pizza, Starbucks, **lodging:** Comfort Inn, **other:** Big Y Foods, Walmart, to Trolley Museum, **W gas:** Sunoco/dsl/24hr, **lodging:** Clarion, **other:** Advance Parts

**44** (50) US 5 S, to E Windsor, **E gas:** Sunoco/dsl, **food:** Dunkin Donuts, E Windsor Rest., KFC, Wendy's, Taco Bell, **lodging:** Holiday Inn Express

**49mm** Connecticut River

**42** (48) CT 159, Windsor Locks, **E** Longview RV Ctr, **W** same as 41

**41** (47) Center St (exits with 39), **W food:** Ad Pizzaria, **lodging:** Beverly Hills Suites

**40** (46.5) CT 20, **W** Old New-Gate Prison, ☞

**39** (46) Kennedy Rd (exits with 41), Community Rd, **W gas:** Shell/dsl/24hr, **food:** Chili's, **other:** $Tree, GNC, PetCo, Radio Shack, Stop&Shop Foods, Target

**WINDSOR AREA**

**ROCKY HILL**

**38** (45) CT 75, to Poquonock, Windsor Area, **E gas:** Mobil/dsl, **food:** Buffalo Wild Wings, China Sea, Domino's, Dunkin Donuts, Quizno's, Subway, **other:** to Ellsworth Home- stead, Price Chopper Foods, **W lodging:** Courtyard, Hilton Garden, Marriott

**37** (44) CT 305, Bloomfield Ave, Windsor Ctr, **E gas:** Mobil/dsl, **food:** McDonald's, **W gas:** Sunoco, **lodging:** Residence Inn

**36** (43) CT 178, Park Ave, to W Hartford

**35b** (41) CT 218, to Bloomfield, to S Windsor, **E** gas/dsl, food

**35a** I-291 E, to Manchester

**34** (40) CT 159, Windsor Ave, **E gas:** Shell/dsl, **W gas:** Citgo/ dsl, **lodging:** Flamingo Inn, **other:** H HOSPITAL

**33** (39) Jennings Rd, Weston St, **E other:** Buick/Pontiac/GMC, Saturn, repair, **W gas:** Mobil/Subway, Sunoco/dsl, **food:** Burger King, Dunkin Donuts, McDonald's, Quizno's, **lodging:** Motel 6, Super 8, **other:** Cadillac, CarMax, Honda, Hyundai, Jaguar, Nissan, Subaru, Toyota/Scion

**32b** (38) Trumbull St (exits left from nb), **W** to downtown, **lodging:** Crowne Plaza, Hilton, **other:** H HOSPITAL, Goodyear

**32a** (exit 30 from sb), I-84 W

**29b** (37) I-84 E, Hartford

**29a** (36.5) US 5 N, CT 15 N (exits left from nb), **W** downtown, **other:** H HOSPITAL, capitol, civic ctr

**28** (36) US 5, CT 15 S (from nb), **W food:** Burger King, Wendy's

**27** (35) Brainerd Rd, Airport Rd, **E gas:** Mercury/Dunkin Do- nuts/Subway/dsl, Shell/dsl, **food:** McDonald's, **lodging:** Day's Inn, Holiday Inn Express, **other:** Ford Trucks, to Regional Mkt

**26** (33.5) Marsh St, **E** Silas Deane House, Webb House, CT MVD

**25** (33) CT 3, Glastonbury, Wethersfield

**24** (32) CT 99, Rocky Hill, Wethersfield, **E gas:** Phillips 66, Sunoco, **food:** Chuck's Steaks, Dakota Steaks, Dunkin Donuts, McDonald's, On-the-Border, Rockyhill Pizza, Subway, Tim Horton, **lodging:** Hampton Inn, Howard Johnson, **other:** Aldi Foods, Kohl's, **W gas:** Mobil, Shell, Valero/dsl, **food:** Burger King, D'angelo's, Denny's, Dunkin Donuts, Friendly's, Giovanni's Pizza, HomeTown Buffet, Humphrey's Grill, McDonald's, Mihng Chinese, Quizno's, Red Lobster, Saki Japanese, Sapporo Japa- nese, Starbucks, Townline Diner, Wendy's, Wood-n-Tap Grill, **lodging:** Best Western, Motel 6, **other:** Curves, CVS Drug, $Tree, Goodyear/auto, Marshalls, Office De- pot, Radio Shack, Stop&Shop, TJMaxx, TownFair Tire, True Value, Walgreens, Walmart/Subway

**23** (29) to CT 3, West St, Rocky Hill, Vet Home, **E lodging:** Mar- riott, **other:** H HOSPITAL, to Dinosaur SP, **W gas:** Cit- go/dsl, Mobil, **food:** Angelo's Pizza, D'angelo's, Dunkin Donuts, Subway, **lodging:** Residence Inn, **other:** IGA Foods

**22** (27) CT 9, to New Britain, Middletown

**21** (26) CT 372, to Berlin, Cromwell, **E gas:** Sunoco/dsl/repair, Wooster St Pizza, **lodging:** Comfort Inn, Crowne Plaza, **other:** Krauszer's Foods, **W gas:** Citgo/Subway/dsl, Mobil/dsl, **food:** Blimpie, Burger King, Chili's, Cromwell Diner/24hr, Dunkin Donuts, McDonald's, Oyama Japa- nese, Slice Heaven Pizza, **lodging:** Courtyard, Holiday Inn, Super 8, **other:** A&P, Curves, Firestone/auto, Price Rite Foods, Walmart/drug

**20** (23) Country Club Rd, Middle St

**22mm** **rest area/weigh sta nb, full** ♿ **facilities, info,** 🕿, 🅿, **litter barrels, vending, RV dump, petwalk**

**19** (21) Baldwin Ave (from sb)

## INTERSTATE 91 CONT'D

**N ↕ S**

**18** (20.5) I-691 W, to Marion, access to same as 16 & 17, ski area

**17** (20) CT 15 N (from sb), to I-691, CT 66 E, Meriden, **W gas:** BP, Getty, **lodging:** Best Western, Extended Stay America, Residence Inn

**16** (19) CT 15, E Main St, **E gas:** Gulf/dsl, Mobil, Valero, **food:** American Steaks, Gianni's Rest., NY Pizza, Olympos Diner, Subway, Zorba's Rest., **lodging:** Candlewood Suites, Hampton Inn, Sheraton, The Meridan Inn, **other:** Family$, Ford, Lowe's Whse, Volvo, **W gas:** BP/dsl, Getty/dsl, Gulf/repair, **food:** Boston Mkt, Burger King, Dominos, Dunkin Donuts, Friendly's, Great Wall Chinese, KFC, McDonald's, Subway, Taco Bell, Tim Horton, Wendy's, **lodging:** Comfort Inn, **other:** H HOSPITAL, CarQuest, CVS Drug, Hancock's Drug, Walgreens

**15** (16) CT 68, to Durham, **E golf, W lodging:** Courtyard, Fairfield Inn, Homewood Suites

**15mm** rest area sb, full ♿ facilities, info, 🕿, ⌷, litter barrels, petwalk

**14** (12) CT 150 (no EZ return), Woodhouse Ave, Wallingford

**13** (10) US 5 (exits left from nb), Wallingford, **2 mi W on US 5** services, to Wharton Brook SP

**12** (9) US 5, Washington Ave, **E gas:** Shell, Sunoco, Valero, **food:** Boston Mkt, Burger King, D'angelo, Dunkin Donuts, Friendly's, Jade City Chinese, McDonald's, Quizno's, Rustic Oak Rest., Starbucks, Subway, Wendy's, **other:** CVS Drug, Stop&Shop Food, Walgreens, **W gas:** Getty, Gulf/dsl, Mobil, **food:** Arby's, Athena II Diner, Blimpie, Greatwall Chinese, Outback Steaks, Thai Cuisine, **lodging:** Holiday Inn/Harry's Grill, **other:** BigY Foods/drug, CarQuest, vet

**11** (7) CT 22 (from nb), North Haven, same as 12

**10** (6) CT 40, to Cheshire, Hamden

**9** (5) Montowese Ave, **W gas:** Berkshire/dsl, Sunoco, **food:** Coldstone Creamery, Dunkin Donuts, Friendly's, McDonald's, Panera Bread, Subway, **other:** Barnes&Noble, BJ's Whse/gas, Circuit City, Home Depot, Michael's, PetCo, PetsMart, Staples, Target, TJMaxx

**8** (4) CT 17, CT 80, Middletown Ave, **E gas:** Citgo, Global/dsl, 7-11/gas, Shell, Splash/dsl, Sunoco/24hr, **food:** Burger King, Dominos, Dunkin Donuts, Exit 8 Diner, KFC, McDonald's, Taco Bell/Pizza Hut, **lodging:** Day's Inn, **other:** Advance Parts, Lowe's Whse, Walgreens, vet, Walmart SuperCtr/Subway, **W gas:** Mobil/dsl, Splash/dsl

**7** (3) Ferry St (from sb), Fair Haven, **W gas:** Hess

**6** (2.5) Willow St (exits left from nb), Blatchley Ave, **E gas:** New Star Diner

**5** (2) US 5 (from nb), State St, Fair Haven, **E food:** New Star Diner

**4** (1.5) State St (from sb), downtown

**3** (1) Trumbull St, downtown, **W** Peabody Museum

**2** (.5) Hamilton St, downtown, New Haven

**1** (.3) CT 34W (from sb), New Haven, **W** H HOSPITAL, downtown

**0mm** I-91 begins/ends on I-95, exit 48.

## INTERSTATE 95

| Exit # | Services |
|---|---|
| **112mm** | Connecticut/Rhode Island state line |
| **106mm** | Welcome Ctr/rest area sb, full H facilities, 🕿, ⌷, litter barrels, petwalk, vending |
| **100mm** | scenic overlook nb |

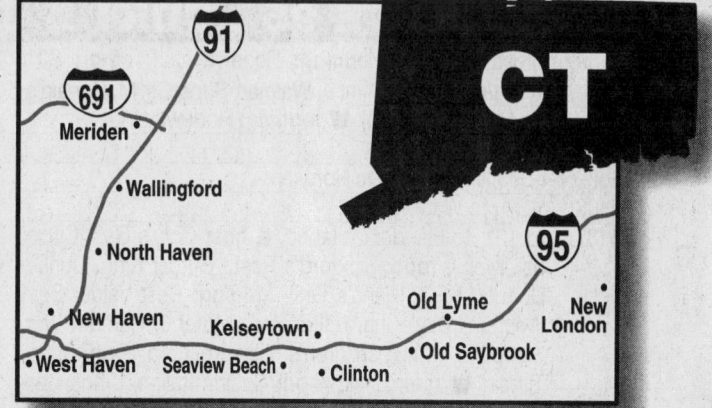

**94.5mm** Thames River

**N ↕ S**

**93** (111) CT 216, Clarks Falls, **E gas:** Shell/repair, to Burlingame SP, **W gas:** Mobil/dsl, Shell/Stuckey's/Roy Rogers/dsl/scales/24hr, Republic/Citgo/dsl/rest./@, **food:** McDonald's, Tim Horton, **lodging:** Stardust Motel

**92** (107) CT 2, CT 49 (no EZ nb return), Pawcatuck, **E gas:** Shell, **other:** H HOSPITAL, **W lodging:** Cedar Park Suites, **other:** FoxWoods (8mi), KOA

**91** (103) CT 234, N Main St, to Stonington, **E other:** H HOSPITAL

**90** (101) CT 27, Mystic, **E gas:** Mobil/Domino's/dsl, **food:** Bickford's, Friendly's, GoFish Rest., Jamm's Seafood, McDonald's, Peking Tokyo, Quizno's, Starbucks, Steak Loft, **lodging:** Econolodge, Hilton, Holiday Inn Express, Howard Johnson, Hyatt Place, **other:** Curves, Mystic Outlet Shops, aquarium, **W gas:** Shell/Subway/Dunkin Donuts/dsl, **food:** Ground Round, Pizza Grille, Starbucks, **lodging:** Best Western, Comfort Inn, Day's Inn, Hampton Inn, Residence Inn, **other:** Chevrolet, Chrysler/Dodge, Ford, RV camping, True Value

**89** (99) CT 215, Allyn St, **W** camping (seasonal)

**89mm** weigh sta both lanes

**88** (98) CT 117, to Noank, **E** ✈, **W food:** Octagon Steaks, Starbucks, Tim Horton, **lodging:** Marriott

**87** (97) Sharp Hwy (exits left from sb), Groton, **E lodging:** Hampton Inn, **other:** to Griswold SP, ✈

**86** (96) rd 184 (exits left from nb), Groton, **E food:** Applebees, 99 Rest., **lodging:** Hampton Inn, Knight's Inn, Quality Inn, **W gas:** Cory's Gas, Hess, Mobil, Shell/dsl, **food:** Chinese Kitchen, Domino's, Dunkin Donuts, Flanagan's Diner, Groton Rest., KFC, Taco Bell, **lodging:** Best Western, Super 8, **other:** Advance Parts, $Tree, Honda, Kohl's, Mitsubishi, Stop'n Shop, to US Sub Base

**85** (95) US 1 N, Groton, downtown, **E gas:** Citgo/dsl, **other:** NAPA

**84** (94) CT 32 (from sb), New London, downtown

**83** (92) CT 32, New London, **E** to Long Island Ferry

**82a** (90.5) frontage rd, New London, **E food:** Pizza Hut, **other:** AutoZone, Goodyear, Staples, TownFair Tire, TownTown Foods, same as 82, **W food:** Chili's, ChuckeCheese, Outback Steaks, Subway, **lodging:** Holiday Inn, SpringHill Suites, **other:** Marshall's, ShopRite Foods, same as 82

**82** (90) New London, **W gas:** Mobil, **food:** Charley's Rest., Coldstone Creamery, FoodCourt, Olive Garden, Panera Bread, Ruby Tuesday, Subway, Wendy's, **lodging:** Fairfield Suites, Holiday Inn, **other:** Best Buy, Borders Books, Home Depot, JC Penney, Macy's, Marshall's, Michael's, PetCo, Sears/auto, Target, mall

## INTERSTATE 95 - CONT'D

**N / S**

**81 (89.5)** Cross Road, **W lodging:** Rodeway Inn, **other:** BJ's Whse/gas, Lowes Whse, Walmart SuperCtr/McDonald's

**80 (89.3)** Oil Mill Rd (from sb), **W lodging:** Rodeway Inn

**78mm** Connecticut River

**76 (89)** I-395 N (from nb), to Norwich

**75 (88)** US 1, to Waterford

**74 (87)** rd 161, to Flanders, Niantic, **E gas:** Cory's Gas, Citgo/dsl, Mobil, **food:** Bickford's Rest., Burger King, Dunkin Donuts, KFC, Illiano's Grill, **lodging:** Best Value, Best Western, Day's Inn, Hilltop Inn, Motel 6, Ramada Inn, Sleep Inn, **other:** Children's Museum, Ford, Stop&Shop, Tires+, **W gas:** Shell, **food:** Cusina Italian, Kings Garden Chinese, McDonald's, Shack Rest., Smokey's BBQ, Yummy yummy Pizza, **other:** Curves, IGA Foods, Rite Aid, True Value, RV camping, vet

**74mm** **rest area sb, full ♿ facilities, st police**

**73 (86)** Society Rd

**72 (84)** to Rocky Neck SP, **2 mi E** food, lodging, RV camping, to Rocky Neck SP

**71 (83)** 4 Mile Rd, River Rd, to Rocky Neck SP, beaches, **1 mi E** camping (seasonal)

**70 (80)** US 1, CT 156, Old Lyme, **W gas:** Shell/dsl, **lodging:** Bee & Thistle Inn, Old Lyme Inn/dining, Subway, **other:** A&P, Old Lyme Drug, Griswold Museum

**69 (77)** US 1, CT 9 N, to Hartford, **W food:** Saybrook Fish House, Vinnie's Fishouse, **lodging:** Comfort Inn

**68 (76.5)** US 1 S, Old Saybrook, **E gas:** Citgo/dsl, Mobil, **food:** Cloud 9 Deli, Bellasera Italian, Pat's Country Kitchen, Subway, **other:** Ford, **W lodging:** Liberty Inn, **other:** Chevrolet/Nissan, Kia, NAPA, Pontiac/Buick/GMC, Toyota/Scion, antiques

**67 (76)** CT 154, Elm St (no EZ sb return), Old Saybrook, **E food:** Pasta Vita Itaian, same as 68

**66mm** **service area both lanes, Mobil/dsl, McDonald's, atm**

**66 (75)** to US 1, Spencer Plain Rd, **E gas:** Citgo/dsl/24hr, **food:** Aleia's Rest, Atlantic Seafood, Blue Crab Steaks, Brick Oven Pizza, Cuckoo's Mexican, DQ, Dunkin Donuts, Luigi's Italian, Sal's Pizza, Stella D'Oro Italian, **lodging:** Day's Inn, Heritage Inn, Sandpiper Motel, Sabrook Motel, Super 8, **other:** Benny's Mkt, transmissions, vet

**65 (73)** rd 153, Westbrook, **E gas:** Mobil, Valero, **food:** Denny's, Fiore's Pizza, Subway, Westbook Deli, **lodging:** Sandpiper Hotel, **other:** Honda, Old Navy, Tanger Factory Stores/famous brands, Walgreens

**64 (70)** rd 145, Horse Hill Rd, Clinton

**63 (68)** CT 81, Clinton, **E gas:** Shell, **1 mi E on US 1...gas:** Shell/dsl/LP, Sunoco/dsl, **food:** Chips Rest., Friendly's, McDonald's, **other:** CVS Drug, vet, **W food:** Coldstone Creamery, Dunkin Dounits, **other:** Clinton Crossing Premium Outlets/famous brands, PetCo

**62 (67)** E to Hammonasset SP, RV camping, beaches

**61 (64)** CT 79, Madison, **E gas:** Gulf, Shell, Sunoco, **food:** Cafe Allegre, Starbucks, Subway, Village Pizza, **other:** CVS Drug, Stop&Shop, USPO

**61mm** East River

**60 (63.5)** Mungertown Rd (from sb, no return), **E** food, lodging

**59 (60)** rd 146, Goose Lane, Guilford, **E gas:** Citgo, Mobil/24hr, Shell/DQ/dsl, **food:** Dunkin Donuts, First & Last Rest., First Garden Chinese, Nick & Tony's Pizza, McDonald's, Pasta Avest Pizza, Shoreline Diner, The Whole Enchilada, Wendy's, **lodging:** Comfort Inn, Tower Motel, **other:** Chevrolet/Pontiac, NAPA, **W** URGENT CARE, st police

**58 (59)** CT 77, Guilford, on US 1 **E food:** Getty, Hess, Mobil, Sunoco, **other:** CVS Drug, to Whitfield Museum, **W** st police

**57 (58)** US 1, Guilford, **W other:** Land Rover, Saab

**56 (55)** rd 146, to Stony Creek, **E lodging:** Rodeway Inn, **W gas:** Mobil, TA/Popeye's/Starbucks/Subway/dsl/rest./24hr/scales/@, Sunoco, Dunkin Donuts, Friendly's, Humphrey's Rest., USS Chowderpot, **lodging:** Best Western, Best Value, **other:** Freightliner, Stop&Shop Foods

**55 (54)** US 1, **E gas:** Branford, Global, Thornton/dsl, **food:** Campania Ristorante, D'amato's Seafood, Lynn's Rest., Marco Pizzaria, Rita's Custard, Hole in the wall Deli, **lodging:** Holiday Inn Express, Motel 6, **other:** Ford, Walgreens, vet, **W gas:** Exxon/dsl, Mobil/Dunkin Donuts/dsl, **food:** Brother's Deli, Chuck's Margarita Grill, Gourmet Wok, Parthenon Diner/24hr, Su Casa Mexican, **lodging:** Day's Inn

**54 (53)** Cedar St, Branford, **E gas:** Citgo/repair, Mobil, **food:** Branford Townhouse Rest., Dragon East Chinese, Dunkin Donuts, La Luna Ristorante, **other:** Hyundai, Staples, Subaru, **W** Krauszer's Foods

**52mm** **service area both lanes, Mobil/dsl/24hr, McDonald's, atm**

**52 (50)** rd 100, North High St, **E other:** to Trolley Museum, **W** st police

**51 (49.5)** US 1, Easthaven, **E gas:** Shell, Sunoco, **food:** Boston Mkt, Chili's, Friendly's, KFC, McDonald's, **lodging:** Quality Inn, **other:** Chevrolet, Lexus, Rite Aid, TJ Maxx, **W food:** Dunkin Donuts, King China, Wendy's, **other:** AutoZone, CarMax, Home Depot, USPO

**50 (49)** Woodward Ave (from nb), **E other:** US Naval/Marine Reserve, Ft Nathan Hale

**49 (48.5)** Stiles St (from nb)

**48 (48)** I-91 N, to Hartford

**47 (47.5)** CT 34, New Haven, **W gas:** Mobil/dsl, **lodging:** Omni Hotel, **other:** Ⓗ HOSPITAL

**46 (47)** Long Wharf Dr, Sargent Dr, **E food:** Leon's Rest., **W gas:** Mobil/dsl, Brazi Italian, Dunkin Donuts, **lodging:** La Quinta

**45 (46.5)** CT 10 (from sb), Blvd, same as 44, **W gas:** Getty, **food:** DQ, Dunkin Donuts, McDonald's

**44 (46)** CT 10 (from nb), Kimberly Ave, **E lodging:** Super 8, **W gas:** Getty, **food:** DQ, Dunkin Donuts, McDonald's, Wendy's, same as 45

**43 (45)** CT 122, 1st Ave (no EZ return), West Haven, **W gas:** First Fuel/dsl, **food:** China Sea, **other:** Ⓗ HOSPITAL, to U of New Haven

**42 (44)** CT 162, Saw Mill Rd, **E gas:** Mobil, **food:** Pizza Hut, **lodging:** Econolodge, **W gas:** Shell, Mobil, 7-11, **food:** American Steaks, D'angelo's, Denny's, Dunkin Donuts, Friendly's, Pizza Hut, Subway, TX Roadhouse, **lodging:** Best Western, Hampton Inn, **other:** Staples, Walmart

**41 (42)** Marsh Hill Rd, to Orange

**41mm** **service area both lanes, gas:** Mobil/dsl, McDonald's

**40 (40)** Old Gate Lane, Woodmont Rd, **E gas:** Citgo/dsl, Pilot/Wendy's/dsl/scales/24hr, Shell, Sunoco, **food:** Cracker Barrel, D'angelo's, Duchess Rest., Dunkin Donuts, Gipper's Rest., **lodging:** Hilton Garden, Hyatt Place, Mayflower Hotel, Milford Inn, Quality Inn, **other:** Blue Beacon, Lowe's Whse

**39 (39)** US 1, to Milford, **E gas:** Cumberland Farms/dsl, **food:** Athenian Diner, Chicago Grill, Friendly's, Hooters, **lodging:** Howard Johnson, Super 8, **other:** Firestone/auto, Mazda/Volvo, Walgreens, **W on US 1...gas:** Mobil, **food:** Arby's, Boston Mkt, Buffalo Wild Wings, Burger King,

**CT**

**OLD SAYBROOK**

**MADISON**

**BRANFORD**

**NEW HAVEN**

## INTERSTATE 95 - CONT'D

**39 (39)** Continued
Chili's, Dunkin Donuts, Honey-Baked Ham, KFC, Krispy Kreme, Moe's SW Grill, McDonald's, Starbucks, Subway, Taco Bell, Wendy's, **other:** Acura, Barnes & Noble, Borders Books, Chrysler/Jeep, Macy's, JC Penney, Jo-Anne Fabrics, Macy's, Marshall's, Michael's, Old Navy, PetCo, Rite Aid, Sears/auto, Staples, Stop&Shop Food, Target, TownFair Tire, USPO, Walmart, mall

**38 (38)** CT 15, Merritt Pkwy, Cross Pkwy

**37 (37.5)** High St ( from nb), **E gas:** Gulf, Sunoco, USA Fuel, **food:** Kimberly Diner, **other:** 7-11, Toyota/Scion

**36** Plains Rd, **E gas:** Mobil, **lodging:** Hampton Inn

**35 (37)** Bic Dr, School House Rd, **E gas:** Citgo, **food:** Armellino's Italian, McDonald's, Pizza Hut, Subway, Taco Bell, Wendy's, **lodging:** Fairfield Inn, **other:** AutoZone, Buick, Chevrolet, Chrysler/Jeep, Dennis Parts, Dodge, Ford/Lincoln/Mercury, Honda, Kia, K-Mart, Land Rover, Pontiac/Nissan, Stop&Shop Foods, Subaru, Walgreens, **W lodging:** Red Roof Inn, SpringHill Suites

**34 (34)** US 1, Milford, **E food:** Dunkin Donuts, McDonald's, Pizza Hut, Taco Bell, **lodging:** Devon Motel

**33 (33.5)** US 1 (from nb, no EZ return), CT 110, Ferry Blvd, **E gas:** Shell/dsl, Sunoco, **food:** Harborside Grill, Margarita Grill, **other:** BJ's Whse, PetCo, Staples, **W food:** McDonalds, 99 Rest., Pepino's Italian, Subway, **other:** Home Depot, Marshall's, Shaw's Foods, Stop&Shop Foods, Walmart

**32 (33)** W Broad St, Stratford, **E gas:** Mobil, **food:** Subway, **W gas:** Gulf, **food:** Dunkin Donuts

**31 (32)** South Ave, Honeyspot Rd, **E gas:** Gulf/Dunkin Donuts, **lodging:** Comfort Suites, **W gas:** Citgo/dsl, **other:** NAPA, TownFair Tire

**30 (31.5)** Lordship Blvd, Surf Ave, **E gas:** Shell/24hr, **food:** Dunkin Donuts, **lodging:** Ramada/rest., **other:** Harley-Davidson, **W gas:** Massey/dsl

**29 (31)** rd 130, Stratford Ave, Seaview Ave, **W H HOSPITAL**

**28 (30)** CT 113, E Main St, Pembrook St

**27 (29.5)** Lafayette Blvd, downtown, **W food:** Dunkin Donuts, Subway, **other:** **H HOSPITAL**, Barnum Museum

**27a (29)** CT 25, CT 8, to Waterbury

**26 (28)** Wordin Ave, downtown

**25 (27)** CT 130 (from sb, no EZ return), State St, Commerce Dr, Fairfield Ave, **E gas:** Getty/dsl, **other:** Stop&Shop, USPO, **W gas:** Gulf, **food:** McDonald's, **other:** transmissions

**24 (26.5)** Black Rock Tpk, **E food:** Blackrock Oyster Bar, D'Angelo, Starbucks, Subway, **lodging:** Best Western, **other:** Audi, Lexus, Mercedes, Pontiac, Porsche, Staples, **other:** BJ's Whse, Staples, USPO, **W gas:** Getty, Gulf, **other:** Firestone/Auto, Ford/Nissan

**23 (26)** US 1, Kings Hwy, **E gas:** Sunoco/dsl, **food:** Ziggy's Grill, **other:** Home Depot

**22 (24)** Round Hill Rd, N Benson Rd

**23.5mm** service area both lanes, **gas:** Mobil/dsl, **food:** FoodCourt (sb), McDonald's/24

**21 (23)** Mill Plain Rd, **E gas:** Citgo, Mobil, Shell, Sunoco, **food:** Avellino's Italian, DQ, Domino's, Starbucks, Subway, Wilson's BBQ, **other:** Borders Books, Hemlock Hardware, Rite Aid

**20 (22)** Bronson Rd (from sb)

**19 (21)** US 1, Center St, **E** Southport Brewing/rest., **W gas:** Getty, Shell/Dunkin Donuts/dsl, **food:** Athena Diner, Friendly's, **other:** TownFair Tire, Walgreens

**18 (20)** to Westport, **E** Sherwood Island SP, beaches, **1 mi on US 1 W gas:** Citgo, Exxon, Gulf, Mobil, **food:** Arbys, Bertucci's Italian, Carvel Ice Cream, Cedar Brook Café, Chef's Table, McDonald's, Sakura Japanese, Sherwood Diner, Starbucks, Swanky Frank's Sandwiches, Subway, Westport Pancakes, **other:** Barnes & Noble, Cadillac/Pontiac/GMC, Toyota/Scion, Shaw's Foods, Volvo, Walgreens, st police, vet

**17 (18)** CT 33, rd 136, Westport, **W other:** FastStop Mart

**16 (17)** E Norwalk, **E gas:** Citgo, Mobil, Shell/dsl, Sunoco, **food:** Baskin-Robbins/Dunkin Donuts, Eastside Café, Penny's Diner, Subway, **other:** Rite Aid

**15 (16)** US 7, to Danbury, Norwalk, **E gas:** Shell, **W gas:** Getty

**14 (15)** US 1, CT Ave, S Norwalk, **E** st police, **W gas:** BP/dsl, C Gas, Shell, Sunoco, **food:** Angela Mia's Café, Burger King, Dunkin Donuts, Post Road Diner, Silver Star Diner, **other:** **H HOSPITAL**, Barnes&Noble, Best Buy, Circuit City, Home Depot, Kohl's, Old Navy, Radio Shack, ShopRite Foods, Shoprite Foods, Stop&Shop, TJ Maxx, TownFair Tire, same as 13

**13 (13)** US 1 (no EZ return), Post Rd, Norwalk, **W gas:** Exxon, Mobil, Shell/24hr, **food:** American Steaks, Bertucci's, Burger King, Driftwood Diner, Duchess Rest., Dunkin Donuts, Friendly's, KFC, Matsuri Japanese, McDonald's, Pasta Fair Rest., Wendy's, **lodging:** DoubleTree Hotel, **other:** Costco, Home Depot, Kohl's, Land Rover, Old Navy, PetsMart, Radio Shack, ShopRite Foods, Staples, TownFair Tire, Walmart, vet, same as 14

**12.5mm** service area nb...**gas:** Mobil/dsl, **food:** McDonald's

**12 (12)** rd 136, Tokeneke Rd (from nb, no return), **W food:** deli

**11 (11)** US 1, Darien, **E gas:** BP, **food:** Chuck's Steaks, **other:** Chevrolet, Jaguar, Nissan, vet, **W gas:** Exxon, **lodging:** Howard Johnson, **other:** BMW

**10 (10)** Noroton, **W gas:** Getty, Shell

**9.5mm** service area sb...**gas:** Mobil/dsl, **food:** McDonald's

**9 (9)** US 1, rd 106, Glenbrook, **W gas:** Gulf, **food:** Dunkin Donuts, McDonald's, **other:** Aamco, AutoZone, Firestone, Toyota, cat vet

**8 (8)** Atlantic Ave, Elm St, **E** Uhaul, **W gas:** Sunoco, **lodging:** Marriott, **other:** **H HOSPITAL**

**7 (7)** CT 137, Atlantic Ave, **W lodging:** Marriott, **food:** Kona Grill, Mitchell's Fish mkt, PF Chang's, **other:** Barnes & Noble, mall, USPO, same as 8

**6 (6)** Harvard Ave, West Ave, **E gas:** Exxon, Shell, **food:** City Limits Diner, **lodging:** La Quinta, **other:** Advance Parts, Subaru, USPO, **W gas:** Shell/24hr, **lodging:** Super 8, **other:** **H HOSPITAL**

**N** ← S ↓ N ← S

**CT**

**N** P U T N A M / H O P E V I L L E

## INTERSTATE 95 - CONT'D

**5 (5)** US 1, Riverside, Old Greenwich, **W** gas: Getty, Mobil, Balducci's Italian, Boston Mkt, Corner Deli, McDonald's, Taco Bell, **other:** CVS Drug, Staples, Walgreens, tires

**4 (4)** Indian Field Rd, Cos Cob, **W** other: Bush-Holley House Museum

**3 (3)** Arch St, Greenwich, **E** Bruce Museum, **W** gas: Mobil, **other:** H HOSPITAL, Lexus, Saab

**2mm** weigh sta nb

**2 (1)** Delavan Ave, Byram

**0mm** Connecticut/New York state line

## INTERSTATE 395

| Exit # | Services |
|---|---|
| **55.5mm** | Connecticut/Massachusetts state line |
| **100 (54)** | E Thompson, to Wilsonville |
| **99 (50)** | rd 200, N Grosvenor Dale, **E W** Thompson Lake Camping (seasonal) |
| **98 (49)** | to CT 12 (from nb, exits left), Grosvenor Dale, same as 99 |
| **97 (47)** | US 44, to E Putnam, **E** food: Dunkin Donuts, Empire Buffet, McDonald's/playplace, Subway, Wendy's, **other:** Advance Parts, $Tree, GNC, Radio Shack, Sears Essentials, Stop&Shop Foods/gas, TJ Maxx, **W** gas: Shell/dsl/repair/24hr, Sunoco, **other:** Walmart |
| **96 (46)** | to CT 12, Putnam, **W** lodging: King's Inn, **other:** H HOSPITAL |
| **95 (45)** | Kennedy Dr, to Putnam, **E** Ford/Mercury, **W** H HOSPITAL |
| **94 (43)** | Ballouville, **W** food: Gold Eagle Rest., **lodging:** Holiday Inn Express |
| **93 (41)** | CT 101, to Dayville, **E** gas: Shell/dsl, **food:** Burger King, China Garden, Dunkin Donuts, Subway, Zip's Diner, **other:** Wibberley Tire, **W** gas: Xtra/dsl/24hr, **food:** Dunkin Donuts, McDonald's, Mozzarella's Grill, **other:** Lowe's Whse, Michael's, Target, Staples, Super Stop & Shop, city park |
| **92 (39)** | to S Killingly, **W** food: Giant Pizza, **other:** Bonneville Drug, st police |
| **91 (38)** | US 6 W, to Danielson, to Quinebaug Valley Coll |
| **90 (36)** | to US 6 E (from nb), to Providence |
| **35mm** | rest area both lanes, full ♿ facilities, gas: Mobil/dsl |
| **89 (32)** | CT 14, to Sterling, Central Village, **E** gas: Gulf, **other:** Chevrolet/Dodge/Jeep, RV camping, **W** gas: 7-11/dsl, Shell/Dunkin Donuts/dsl, **food:** Music Lady Cafe, Subway, **lodging:** Plainfield Motel, **other:** transmissions |
| **88 (30)** | CT 14A to Plainfield, **E** RV camping (seasonal), **W** gas: Mobil |
| **87 (28)** | Lathrop Rd, to Plainfield, **E** gas: Shell/Tim Horton's/Domino's/dsl, **food:** Dunkin Donuts, HongKong Star Chinese, Subway, Wendy's, **lodging:** Holiday Inn Express, Quality Inn, **other:** Big Y Foods, Ford, Hyundai, Mazda, Radio Shack, **W** gas: Citgo, Sunoco/dsl, **food:** Bakers Dozen Cafe, McDonald's, O'Connor's Steaks/Pizza, Paradise Rest., **other:** Advance Parts, CVS Drug |
| **86 (24)** | rd 201, Hopeville, **E** Hopeville Pond SP, RV camping |
| **85 (23)** | CT 164, CT 138, to Pachaug, Preston, **E** other: Curves, $Tree, RV camping, **W** lodging: AmericInn |
| **84 (21)** | CT 12, Jewett City, **E** food: Ruby Tuesday, **other:** Ford, Home Depot, Kohl's, Walmart SuperCtr, **W** gas: Gulf/dsl, Mobil/dsl, Shell/dsl, **food:** McDonald's, **other:** Val-U Foods |

**N** O R W I C H T O W N

**E** ↕ **W**

| **83a (20)** | CT 169 (from nb), Lisbon, **E** RV camping |
|---|---|
| **83 (18)** | rd 97, Taftville, **E** gas: Getty/dsl, **other:** camping, repair, **W** gas: 7-11/gas |
| **82 (14)** | to CT 2 W, CT 32 N, Norwichtown, **E** food: Friendly's, **other:** tires, **W** gas: Chucky's/dsl, Citgo/dsl, Lukoil/Dunkin Donutsdsl, Shell/dsl, **food:** Illiano's Grill, McDonald's, Mona Lisa's Rest., Subway, **lodging:** Courtyard, Rosemont Suites, **other:** Ace Hardware |
| **81 (14)** | CT 2 E, CT 32 S, Norwich, **E** H HOSPITAL, to Mohegan Coll |
| **80 (12)** | CT 82, Norwich, **E** gas: Mobil, Shell, Xtra, **food:** Burger King, Chinese Buffet, Dominic's Pizza, Dunkin Donuts, Friendly's, KFC/Taco Bell, McDonald's, 99 Rest., Papa Gino's, Subway, Tim Horton, Wendy's, **other:** Brooks Drug, Jo-Ann Fabrics, Radio Shack, ShopRite Foods, Staples, TownFair Tire, **W** lodging: Hampton Inn, Holiday Inn, **other:** Big Y Foods, Walmart |
| **79a (10)** | CT 2A E, to Ledyard, **E** to Pequot Res |
| **8.5mm** | nb st police, ☎, sb Mobil/dsl, **rest area, full** ♿ **facilities** |
| **79 (6)** | rd 163, to Uncasville, Montville, **1 mi E** gas: Mobil/dsl, **food:** Dunkin Donuts, Friendly Pizza, McDonald's, Subway, **other:** Beit Bro's Foods, Rite Aid, auto repair |
| **78 (5)** | CT 32 (from sb, exits left), to New London, RI Beaches |
| **77 (2)** | CT 85, to I-95 N, Colchester, **1/2 mi E** gas: Shell/dsl, Dunkin Donuts, **lodging:** Oakdell Motel |
| **0mm** | I-95. I-395 begins/ends on I-95, exit 76. |

## INTERSTATE 691

| Exit # | Services |
|---|---|
| **I-691 begins/ends on I-91** | |
| **12 (12)** | Preston Ave |
| **11 (11)** | I-91 N, to Hartford |
| **10 (11)** | I-91 S, to New Haven, CT 15 S, **W** Cross Pkwy |
| **8 (10)** | US 5, Broad St, **N** gas: Citgo, Cumberland, Shell/dsl, **food:** Broad St Pizza, Chinese Gourmet, DQ |
| **7 (9)** | downtown, Meriden (from wb), **S** gas: Citgo |
| **6 (8)** | Lewis Ave (from wb, no EZ return), to CT 71, **N** food: Ruby Tuesday, **other:** H HOSPITAL, Best Buy, Borders Books, Circuit City, Macy's, JC Penney, Macy's, Sears/auto, Target, mall, **S** 7-11/gas |
| **5 (7)** | CT 71, to Chamberlain Hill (from eb, no EZ return), **N** other: H HOSPITAL, Best Buy, Target, mall, **S** gas: 7-11/gas, **food:** McDonald's, Subway |
| **4 (4)** | CT 322, W Main St (no re-entry from eb), **1 mi N** gas: Exxon, **food:** Arbys, Dominique's Pizza, McDonald's, Subway, **N** gas: Sunoco, **food:** Dunkin Donuts, **other:** H HOSPITAL |
| **3mm** | Quinnipiac River |
| **3 (1)** | CT 10, to Cheshire, Southington, **N** gas: Sunoco, **food:** Sam's Clams Rest. |
| **2 (0)** | I-84 E, to Hartford |
| **1 (0)** | I-84 W, to Waterbury |
| **I-691 begins/ends on I-84** | |

## INTERSTATE 95

| Exit # | Services |
|---|---|
| 23mm | Delaware/Pennsylvania state line, motorist callboxes for 23 miles sb |
| 11 (22) | I-495 S, DE 92, Naamans Rd, **E food:** China Star, **other:** Burlington Coats, $General, Goodyear/auto, Jo-Ann Fabrics, K-Mart, Sav-A-lot Foods, WaWa, **W gas:** Gulf/dsl, **food:** Crossroads Rest, KFC/Taco Bell, Quizno's, **lodging:** Holiday Inn Select, **other:** Home Depot, Radio Shack, Rite Aid |
| 10 (21) | Harvey Rd (no nb return) |
| 9 (19) | DE 3, to Marsh Rd, **E** to Bellevue SP, st police, **W food:** Lamberti's Cafe, Starbucks, **other:** museum |
| 8b a (17) | US 202, Concord Pike, to Wilmington, **E other:** Home Depot, **W gas:** Cumberland Farms, **food:** Arby's, Dunkin Donuts, 5 Guys Burgers, Golden Castle Diner, McDonald's, Taco Bell, **lodging:** Best Western, Quality Inn, **other:** H HOSPITAL |
| 7b a (16) | DE 52, Delaware Ave |
| 6 (15) | DE 4, MLK Blvd, **E food:** McDonald's, **other:** Fresh Grocer Foods, Rite Aid, **W gas:** BP |
| 5c (12) | I-495 N, to Wilmington, to DE Mem Bridge |
| 5b a (11) | DE 141, to US 202, to New Castle, Newport, **E lodging:** Quality Inn |
| 4b a (8) | DE 1, DE 7, to Christiana, **E food:** Don Pablo, FoodCourt, Houlihan's, Ruby Tuesday, **other:** Circuit City, Costco, JC Penney, Macy's, Michael's, Nordstrom's, mall, **W food:** Applebees, Bugaboo Steaks, Cheeseburger Paradise, Chili's, Dunkin Donuts, Michael's Rest., Old Country Buffet, Olive Garden, Quizno's, Red Lobster, **lodging:** Country Inn&Suites, Courtyard, Day's Inn, Fairfield Inn, Hilton, Red Roof Inn, **other:** H HOSPITAL, Best Buy, Borders Books, Home Depot, Office Depot, PetsMart, TJ Maxx, casino/racetrack |
| 3b a (6) | DE 273, to Newark, Dover, **E gas:** BP/24hr, Exxon/dsl, Bertucci's, Bob Evans, Boston Mkt, Famous Dave's BBQ, Red Robin, Olive Grill Italian, Shell Hammer's Grille, Wendy's, **lodging:** Ramada Inn, Residence Inn, Staybridge Suites, TownePlace Suites, **other:** Acme Foods, Boscov's, Jo-Ann Fabrics, Old Navy, Staples, **W gas:** Getty, Shell, **food:** Denny's, Dunkin Donuts, Pizza Hut, **lodging:** Econolodge, Hampton Inn, Holiday Inn Express, **other:** 7-11 |
| 5mm | service area both lanes (exits left from both lanes), info, gas: Sunoco, Big Boy, Roy Rogers, Sbarro's, Starbucks |
| 1b a (3) | DE 896, to Newark, to U of DE, Middletown, **W gas:** Exxon, Gulf/dsl, Shell/dsl/24hr, Sunoco, **food:** Boston Mkt, College Town Cafe, China Garden, Dunkin Donuts, Friendly's, Mario's Pizza, Matilda's Rest, McDonald's, TGIFriday, **lodging:** Courtyard (3mi), Embassy Suites, Homewood Suites, Howard Johnson, Quality Inn, Sleep Inn |
| 1mm | toll booth, st police |
| 0mm | Delaware/Maryland state line, motorist callboxes for 23 |

## INTERSTATE 295 - Wilmington

| Exit # | Services |
|---|---|
| 15mm | Delaware/New Jersey state line, Delaware River, Delaware Memorial Bridge |
| 14.5mm | toll plaza |
| 14 | DE 9, New Castle Ave, to Wilmington, **E gas:** BP/24hr, Citgo, Giovanni's Cafe, **other:** Advance Parts, Family$, Firestone/auto, Harley-Davidson/rest., Rite Aid, SuperFresh Foods, **W gas:** Gulf, Shell, **food:** Dunkin Donuts, McDonald's, **lodging:** Motel 6, Rodeway Inn, SuperLodge |

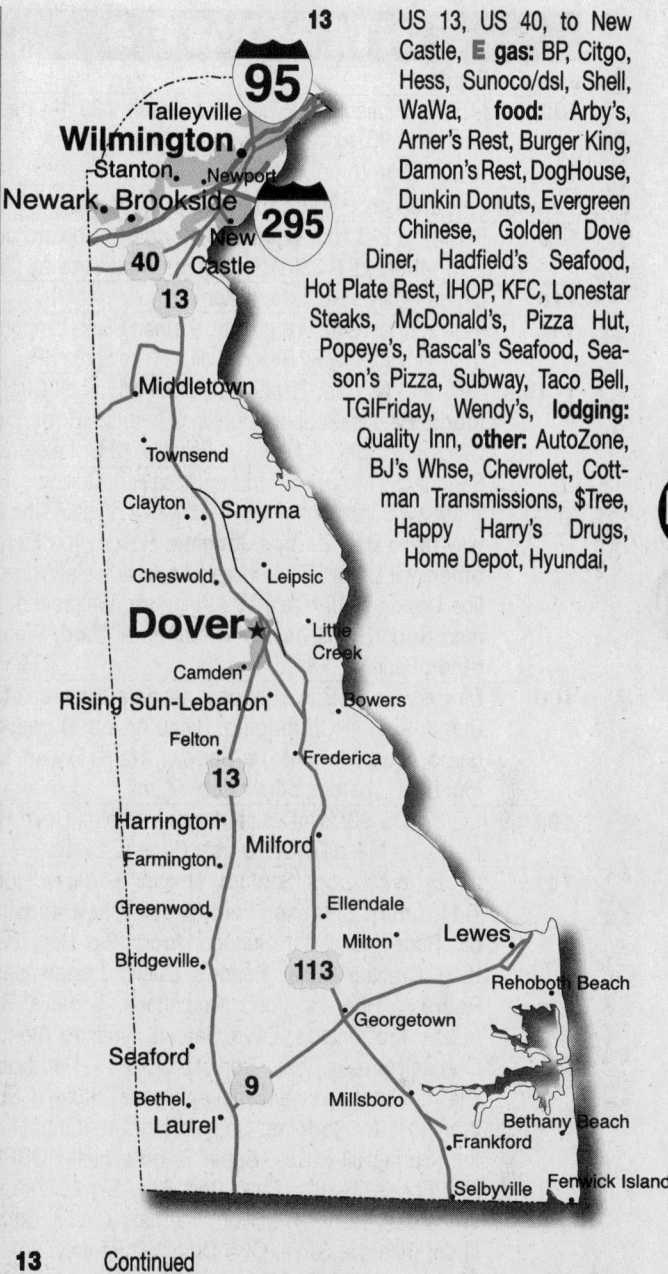

**13** US 13, US 40, to New Castle, **E gas:** BP, Citgo, Hess, Sunoco/dsl, Shell, WaWa, **food:** Arby's, Arner's Rest, Burger King, Damon's Rest, DogHouse, Dunkin Donuts, Evergreen Chinese, Golden Dove Diner, Hadfield's Seafood, Hot Plate Rest, IHOP, KFC, Lonestar Steaks, McDonald's, Pizza Hut, Popeye's, Rascal's Seafood, Season's Pizza, Subway, Taco Bell, TGIFriday, Wendy's, **lodging:** Quality Inn, **other:** AutoZone, BJ's Whse, Chevrolet, Cottman Transmissions, $Tree, Happy Harry's Drugs, Home Depot, Hyundai,

| 13 | Continued Kia, Mazda, Nissan, PathMark Foods, PepBoys, Radio Shack, Ross, Sav-A-Lot, 7-11, Staples, Toyota/Scion, repair, **W gas:** Shell, WaWa, **food:** Dunkin Donuts, **lodging:** Clarion, **other:** Ford Trucks, Lowes Whse |
|---|---|
| 12 | I-495, US 202, N to Wilmington |
| I-295 | begins/ends on I-95 |

## INTERSTATE 495

| Exit # | Services |
|---|---|
| 11mm | I-95 N. I-495 begins/ends on I-95. |
| 5 (10) | US 13, Phila Pike, Claymont, **W gas:** Sunoco, **food:** Arby's, Boston Mkt, Claymont Steaks, Jake's, McDonald's, |
| 4 (5) | US 13, rd 3, Edgemoor Rd, to Fox Point Park |
| 3 (4) | 12th St |
| 2 (3) | rd 9A, Terminal Ave, Port of Wilmington |
| 1 (1) | US 13, **E gas:** Shell, WaWa, **food:** Dunkin Donuts, **lodging:** Clarion, **other:** Ford Trucks, Kia, Lowes Whse |
| 0mm | I-95 S. I-495 begins/ends on I-95. |

Copyright 2009 - The Next Exit®

## INTERSTATE 4

| Exit # | Services |
|---|---|
| 132 | I-95, S to Miami, N to Jacksonville, FL 400. I-4 begins/ends on I-95, exit 260b |
| 129 | to US 92 (from eb, exits left) |
| 126mm | rest area eb, 🚻, litter barrels, no security |
| 118 | FL 44, to DeLand, **N gas:** BP, **lodging:** Howard Johnson, **other:** Ⓗ HOSPITAL, **S gas:** Citgo/Subway (2mi) |
| 116 | Orange Camp Rd, Lake Helen |
| 114 | FL 472, to DeLand, Orange City, **N other:** Clark Campground (1mi), Orange City RV Resort (1mi), to Blue Sprgs SP |
| 111b a | Deltona, **N gas:** Hess/dsl, RaceTrac, Shell/Circle K, **food:** Baskin-Robbins/Dunkin Donuts, Bob Evans, Chick-fil-A, Chili's, Denny's, Fazoli's, KFC, Lelo's BBQ, Panchero's Mexican, Perkins, Pizza Hut, Quizno's, Ruby Tuesday, Sonic, Sonny's BBQ, Steak'n Shake/24hr, Subway, Taco Bell, Zaxby's, **lodging:** Holiday Inn Express, **other:** Ⓗ HOSPITAL, Home Depot, Lowe's Whse, Office Depot, Publix/deli, Tire Kingdom, Walgreens, Walmart SuperCtr, **S gas:** Chevron/repair, **food:** Wendy's, **other:** Family$, Walgreens |
| 108 | Dirksen Dr, DeBary, Deltona, **N gas:** Chevron, **food:** Burger King, IHOP, **lodging:** Hampton Inn, **S gas:** Kangaroo, **food:** McDonald's, Subway, Waffle House, **lodging:** Best Western, **other:** Publix (2mi) |
| 104 | US 17, US 92, Sanford, **N food:** Captains Cove Rest., **other:** La Mesa RV Ctr, **S gas:** Citgo/Subway |
| 101c | rd 46, to Mt Dora, Sanford, **N gas:** BP/Pizza Hut/dsl, 7-11, **other:** Chevrolet, Ford, **S gas:** Chevron/dsl, Mobil, RaceTrac, 7-11, Sunoco, **food:** Big Boy, Burger King, Cracker Barrel, Denny's, Dunkin Donuts/Baskin-Robbins, Hooters, Joe's Crabshack, Logan's Roadhouse, McDonald's, Olive Garden, Orlando Alehouse, Outback Steaks, Pollo Tropical, Quizno's, Red Lobster, Rte 46 Smokehouse, Smokey Bones, Steak'n Shake, Waffle House, **lodging:** Comfort Inn, Day's Inn, Holiday Inn, SpringHill Suites, Super 8, **other:** Ⓗ HOSPITAL, Aldi Foods, Beall's, Belk, Best Buy, Big 10 Tire, BJ's Whse/gas, Books-A-Million, Carmax, Circuit City, Dillards, Dillard's, $Tree, CVS Drug, JC Penney, Jo-Anne, Macy's, Marshall's, Michael's, Old Navy, Ross, Sears/auto, Target, Tire Kingdom, Toyota/Scion, Walmart SuperCtr, World Mkt, mall |
| 101a b | rd 46a, FL 417 (toll), FL 46, Sanford, Heathrow, **N food:** Applebees, Crisper's, FishBones, Moes SW Grill, Ruth's Chris Steaks, **lodging:** Hampton Inn, Marriott, **other:** Chevrolet, Walgreens, **S gas:** Chevron, Sunoco, **food:** Olive Garden, Cracker Barrel, McDonald's, Outback Steaks, Red Lobster, Waffle House, **lodging:** Comfort Inn, Days Inn, Super 8, **other:** Acura, Books-A-Million, Dillards, Harley-Davidson, Honda, JC Penny, Macy's, Sam's Club/gas, Sears, Toyota |
| 98 | Lake Mary Blvd, Heathrow, **N gas:** Shell, **food:** Mario's Pizza, Panera Bread, Stonewood Grill, **lodging:** Courtyard, Hyatt Place, **other:** CVS Drug, Walgreens, Winn-Dixie, **S gas:** BP/24hr, Chevron/24hr, Citgo, Mobil/dsl, 7-11, **food:** Arby's, Bob Evans, Boston Mkt, Burger King, Checkers, Chick-fil-A, Chili's, Chipotle Mexican, Chop Stix, Cuban Cafe, Dunkin Donuts/Baskin-Robbins, Firehouse Subs, Frank&Naomi's, KFC, Krystal, Longhorn |

| | |
|---|---|
| 98 | **Continued**<br>Steaks, Macaroni Grill, McDonald's, Papa John's, Papa Joe's Pizza, Pizza Hut, Quizno's, Starbucks, Steak'n Shake, Subway, Taco Bell, Taste of China, TGIFriday, Tropical Smoothie, Uno, Wendy's, WingZone, **lodging:** Candlewood Suites, Extended Stay America, Hilton Garden, Homestead Suites, Homewood Suites, La Quinta, **other:** Advance Parts, Albertson's, Gander Mtn, Goodyear, Home Depot, K-Mart, PestMart, Publix, Staples, Target, Tires+, TJ Maxx, USPO, mall, vet |
| 95mm | rest areas both lanes, full ♿ facilities, 🄲, vending, 🚻, litter barrels, petwalk, 24hr security |
| 94 | FL 434, to Winter Springs, Longwood, **N gas:** Hess/dsl, Mobil, 7-11, **food:** Burger King, Imperial Dynasty, Kobe Japanese, Melting Pot Rest., Miami Subs, Panera Bread, Papa Joe's Pizza, Quizno's, Starbucks, Wendy's, **lodging:** Comfort Inn, **other:** CVS Drug, **S food:** Bonefish Grill, Boston Mkt, Calipso Grill, Carmela's Rest., Crisper's, **lodging:** Candlewood Suites, **other:** Ⓗ HOSPITAL, 7-11 |
| 92 | FL 436, Altamonte Springs, **N gas:** Medallion, 7-11, Shell/Circle K/dsl, **food:** Boston Mkt, Checker's, Chick-fil-A, Chipotle Mexican, ChuckeCheese, Cracker Barrel, Dominos, Golden City Chinese, Kobe Japanese, LongHorn Steaks, McDonald's, Olive Garden, Perkins, Pollo Tropical, Popeye's, Red Lobster, Steak&Ale, Sweet Tomatoes, Taco Bell, TGIFriday, WingHouse, **lodging:** Day's Inn, Hampton Inn, Hotel Altamonte, Quality Suites, Ramada, SpringHill Suites, **other:** Best Buy, CVS Drug, Family$, Firestone/auto, Goodyear/auto, Tire Kingdom, U-Haul, Walgreens, **S gas:** BP, Citgo, Hess, Mobil, **food:** Bahama Breeze, Burger King, Chili's, Denny's, Dunkin Donuts, Elephant Bar, Five Guys Burgers, Moe's SW Grill, Jason's Deli, Mimi's Cafe, Orlando Alehouse, Panda Express, Pizza Hut, Shane's Ribshack, Straud's Seafood, Chili's, Denny's, Steak'n Shake, Subway, **lodging:** Embassy Suites, Hilton, Homestead Suites, **other:** Ⓗ HOSPITAL, Advance Parts, Albertsons, Barnes & Noble, CVS Drug, Dillards, JC Penny, Marshall's, Michael's, Office Depot, PetCo, Publix, Ross, Sears/auto, TJMaxx, vet |
| 90b a | FL 414, Maitland Blvd, **N gas:** 7-11/gas, **food:** Applebee's, Chick-fil-A, Oak Grill, Wendy's, **lodging:** Extended Stay, Extended Stay Deluxe, Courtyard, Sheraton, **S** Maitland Art Ctr |
| 88 | FL 423, Lee Rd, **N gas:** 7-11/gas, Texaco, **food:** Arby's, Burger King, China One, Del Frisco, IHOP, Little Caesars, LJ Silver/Taco Bell, McDonald's, Quizno's, Shell's Seafood, Taco Bell, **lodging:** Comfort Inn, Countryside Inn, InTown Inn, La Quinta, Motel 6, **other:** Aamco, Firestone, Home Depot, Infinity, Land Rover, Tires+, VW, **S gas:** Chevron/dsl, Mobil/dsl, Sunoco, **food:** Denny's, **other:** BMW |
| 87 | FL 426, Fairbanks Ave (no eb re-entry), **N gas:** Hess/Blimpie/Godfather's/dsl, **1mi S gas:** Chevron, **food:** Burger King, Steak'n Shake, Subway, Wendy's |
| 86 | Par Ave (from eb, no re-entry), **S gas:** Shell/Circle K |
| 85 | Princeton St, **S gas:** Chevron, 7-11, **other:** Ⓗ HOSPITAL |
| 84 | FL 50, Colonial Dr (from wb), Ivanhoe Blvd, **N lodging:** Crowne Plaza, **S lodging:** Sheraton |
| 83b | US 17, US 92, FL 50, Amelia St (from eb), **N lodging:** Crowne Plaza |

**E ↕ W**

**FL**

**SANFORD**

**HEATHROW**

**ALTAMOMTE SPRINGS**

## INTERSTATE 4 CONT'D

**E ↕ W**

**O R L A N D O**

| | | |
|---|---|---|
| **83a** | FL 526 (from eb), Robinson St, **N** lodging: Marriott |
| **83** | South St (from wb), downtown |
| **82c** | Anderson St E, Church St Sta Hist Dist, downtown |
| **82b** | Gore Ave (from wb), **S** H HOSPITAL, downtown |
| **82a** | FL 408 (toll), to FL 526 |
| **81b c** | Kaley Ave, **S gas:** Citgo, Sunoco, **other:** H HOSPITAL |
| **81a** | Michigan St (from wb), **N gas:** Citgo/dsl |
| **80b a** | US 17, US 441 S, US 92 W, **S gas:** Citgo, Chevron, RaceTrac, Shell, Sunoco, **food:** Checkers, Gyros, McDonald's, Subway, **lodging:** Day's Inn, **other:** AutoZone, Goodyear/auto, SavAlot Foods |
| **79** | FL 423, 33rd St, John Young Pkwy, **N lodging:** Ramada Inn, **other:** Harley-Davidson, **S gas:** RaceTrac, 7-11, **food:** IHOP, KFC, McDonald's, **lodging:** Days Inn |
| **78** | Conroy Rd, **N gas:** 7-11, **S food:** BJ's Rest., Bloomingdale's, Elephant Bar Rest., Green's Grill, Krispy Kreme, McDonald's, Mimi's Cafe, Moe's SW Grill, Olive Garden, Panda Express, Polo Tropical, TGIFriday, Village Tavern, Waffle Shop, Wendy's, Zaxby's, **other:** Circuit City, Home Depot, Macy's, Marshall's, Mercedes, Old Navy, PetCo, Super Target, mall |
| **77** | FL 527, FL TPK (toll) |
| **75b a** | FL 435, International Dr (exits left from both lanes), **N gas:** Mobil, **food:** Cracker Barrel, Denny's, TGIFriday, **lodging:** Days Inn, DoubleTree Motel, Fairfield Inn, Holiday Inn, Hyatt Place, **other:** to Universal Studios, **S gas:** Chevron, 7-11, **food:** Bamboo Rest., Black Angus Steaks, Denny's, Great Western Steaks, IHOP, Ponderosa, Red Lobster, Steak&Ale, Sizzler, **lodging:** Best Western, Clarion, Court of Flags Hotel, Econolodge, Hampton Inn, Hilton Garden, Holiday Inn Express, Homewood Suites, Howard Johnson, International Gateway Inn, Knight's Inn, Lakefront Inn, Las Palmas Hotel, Motel 6, Rodeway Inn, Sheraton, Super 8, multiple hotels & resorts, **other:** Bass Pro Shops, Belz Outlet/famous Brands, Books A Million, Office Depot, Walgreens |
| **74b** | Universal Studios (from wb) |

**O R L A N D O**

**74a** FL 482, Sand Lake Rd, **N gas:** Chevron, 7-11, **food:** Alexander's Rest., Chick-fil-A, McDonald's, Timpano Italian, Wendy's, multiple restaurants, **lodging:** Comfort Suites, **other:** K-Mart, Publix, Whole Food Mkt, Walgreens, Walmart Superctr, **S gas:** BP, Chevron, Mobil, 7-11, Shell/Circle K, **food:** Buffalo Wild Wings, Burger King, Cattleman's Steaks, Charley's Steaks, Checker's, Chili's, Cici's, Denny's, Don Pablos, Friendly's, Golden Corral, IHOP, Italianni's, Kobe Japanese, Lobster Feast, McDonald's, Olive Garden, Perkins, Pizza Hut, Ponderosa, Popeye's, TGIFriday, Tony Roma, Uno, Vito's Chophouse, Wendy's, Wild Bean Cafe, **lodging:** Best Western, Castle Hotel, Courtyard, Comfort Inn, Crowne Plaza, Econolodge, Embassy Suites, Fairfield Inn, Fishbones, Hampton Inn, Holiday Inn, Howard Johnson, Hyatt Place, Knights Inn, La Quinta, Marriott, Masters Inn, Microtel, Peabody Hotel, Quality Inn, Radisson Inn, Ramada Inn, Red Roof Inn, Residence Inn, Rodeway Inn, Staybridge Suites, Wyndham Garden, **other:** H HOSPITAL, Harley-Davidson, Ripley's Believe-it-or-not!, Stouffer Resort, Walgreens, RV Park

**E
W
ORLANDO
ORLANDO**

FL

## INTERSTATE 4 CONT'D

**72** FL 528 E (toll, no eb re-entry), to Cape Canaveral, **S** to ✈

**71** Central FL Pkwy (from eb no re-entry), **S gas:** Chevron, **food:** Wendy's, **lodging:** Hilton Garden, Renaissance Resort, Residence Inn, to SeaWorld

**68** FL 535, Lake Buena Vista, **N gas:** Chevron/24hr, 7-11, Shell/Circle K/dsl, **food:** AleHouse, Black Angus Steaks, Buffalo Wild Wings, Burger King, Cici's, Chevy's Mexican, Chili's, China Buffet, Crossroads Dining, Denny's, Domino's, Dragon Buffet, Flipper's Pizzaria, Fortune Chinese, Fuddrucker's, Giordano's, Havana's Cuisine, Hooters, IHOP, Joe's Crabshack, Jonnie's Rest., Kobe Japanese, Macaroni Grill, McDonald's, Olive Garden, Perkins, Pizza Hut, Qdoba Mexican, Quizno's, Red Lobster, Shoney's, Sizzler, Steak'n Shake, Subway, Taco Bell, TGIFriday, Uno, Vallarta Mexican, Willy's Rest., **lodging:** Comfort Inn, Country Inn&Suites, Courtyard, Doubletree, Embassy Suites, Extended Stay Deluxe, Hampton Inn, Hawthorn Suites, Hilton, Holiday Inn Express, Homewood Suites, Hotel Orlando, Hyatt Hotel, Quality Inn, Radisson, Residence Inn, Sheraton, SpringHill Suites, StayBridge Suites, **other:** Gooding's Foods, USPO, Walgreens, **S gas:** Chevron, 7-11, Shell, **food:** Bahama Breeze, Carrabba's, Chick-fil-A, Cici's Pizza, Dunkin Donuts, Golden Corral, Landry's Seafood, LoneStar Steaks, Panera Bread, Starbucks, Wendy's, **lodging:** Blue Heron Resort, Buena Vista Suites, Courtyard, Fairfield Inn, Holiday Inn Resort, Marriott Village, Residence Inn, Sheraton, SpringHill Suites, **other:** CVS Drug, Orlando Premium Outlets, Super Mkt Foods, Walgreens

**67** Fl 536, to Epcot (wb only), **N** DisneyWorld, **1 mi S gas:** 7-11, **food:** Ponderosa, **lodging:** Buena Vista, Marriott, **other:** CVS Drug, Prime Outlet, to airport, multiple resorts

**65** Osceola Pkwy, to FL 417 (toll), **N** to DisneyWorld, Epcot, Animal Kingdom, and Wide World of Sports

**64b a** US 192, FL 536, to FL 417 (toll), to Kissimmee, **N gas:** 7-11, to DisneyWorld, MGM, **S gas:** Mobil/dsl, RaceTrac, 7-11, **food:** Arbys, Bob Evans, Boston Lobster Feast, Burger King, Cattleman's Steakhouse, Charlie's Rest., Chili's, Chinese Buffet, Cici's Pizza, Cracker Barrel, Denny's, Domino's, Golden Corral, IHOP, Joe's Crabshack, Kabuki Japanese, KFC, Kobe Japanese, Logans Roadhouse, Longhorn Steaks, Macaroni Grill, McDonald's, Nemo's Steaks, Ocean 11 Rest., Olive Garden, Orange World, Pacino's Italian, Papa John's, Perkins, Pizza Hut, Ponderosa, Quizno's, Red Lobster, Ruby Tuesday, Shoney's, Sizzlin Grill, Starbucks, Subway, Taco Bell, TGIFriday, Uno Pizzaria, Waffle House, Wendy's, **lodging:** Comfort Suites, Days Inn, Econolodge, Holiday Inn, Howard Johnson, Masters Inn, Mona Lisa Motel, Motel 6, Old Towne Suites, Orlando Resort, Parkway Resort, Quality Suites, Radisson, Red Roof Inn, Rodeway Inn, Sun Inn, Super 8, Seralago Hotel, Travelodge, **other:** Ace Hardware, Camping World RV Service/supplies (3mi), CVS Drug, Harley-Davidson, Publix, Walgreens, USPO, factory outlet/famous brands

**62** FL 417 (toll, from eb), World Dr, **N** to DisneyWorld, **S** Celebration, to airport

**60** Fl 429 N (toll), Apopka

---

**LAKELAND**

**58** FL 532, to Kissimmee, **N gas:** BP, 7-11, **food:** Chili's, China One, McDonald's, Pizzaria, Subway, **other:** Publix, Walgreens, **S** Dunkin Donuts (1mi)

**55** US 27, to Haines City, **N gas:** 7-11, Sunoco, **food:** Burger King, Cracker Barrel, Denny's, McDonald's, Waffle House, Wendy's, **lodging:** Fairfield Inn, Hampton Inn, Super 8, **other:** Ford, FL CampInn (5mi), **S gas:** BP/dsl, Exxon, Marathon, RaceWay/24hr, 7-11, Shell/dsl/service, **food:** Bob Evans, Grand China, GreenLeaf Chinese, Perkins/24hr, Quizno's, Subway, **lodging:** Microtel, Quality Inn, Southgate Inn, **other:** H HOSPITAL, Belk, Best Buy, Books A Million, Deer Creek RV Resort, $Tree, JC Penny, KOA, Michael's, PetsMart, Ross, Staples, Target, Theme World RV Park, to Cypress Gardens

**48** rd 557, to Winter Haven, Lake Alfred, **S gas:** BP/dsl

**46mm** rest area both lanes, full ♿ facilities, 𝄐, vending, 🚻, litter barrels, petwalk, 24hr security

**44** FL 559, to Auburndale, **S gas:** BP/dsl/scales/24hr, Loves/Arby's/dsl/scales/24hr, **other:** fruit

**41** FL 570 W toll, Auburndale, Lakeland

**38** FL 33, to Lakeland, Polk City

**33** rd 582, to FL 33, Lakeland, **N gas:** BP, Exxon/24hr, 7-11, **food:** Applebee's, Cracker Barrel, Five Guys Burger, Starbucks, Wendy's, **lodging:** Crestwood Suites, Country Inn & Suites, Days Inn, Hampton Inn, La Quinta, Quality Inn, Ramada, Sleep Inn, **other:** BMW, CVS Drug, Publix, **S gas:** BP/dsl, **food:** Waffle House, **lodging:** ValuePlace, **other:** H HOSPITAL, Harley-Davidson, Lakeland RV Resort, Nissan

**32** US 98, Lakeland, **N gas:** BP/dsl, Chevron, Murphy USA, 7-11, **food:** Beef O'Brady's, Chili's, ChuckeCheese, Cici's Pizza, Domino's, DQ, Dunkin Donuts, Golden Corral, Hooters, IHOP, KFC, Ling's Buffet, McDonald's, Olive Garden, Outback Steaks, Palaca Garden, Panera Bread, Pizza Hut, Red Lobster, Smokey Bones BBQ, Sonic, Sonny's BBQ, Steak'n Shake/24hr, Subway, TGIFriday, Wendy's, Whataburger, Zaxby's, **lodging:** Comfort Inn, La Quinta, Royalty Inn, **other:** Aldi Foods, Barnes&Noble, Belk, Best Buy, Circuit City, CVS Drug, Dillard's, $General, Firestone/auto, Goodyear/auto, JoAnn Fabrics, Lowes Whse, Macy's, Michael's, PepBoys, RV World, Sam's Club/gas, Sears, Staples, Target, Tire Kingdom, Tires+, Walgreens, Walmart SuperCtr (2mi), vet, **S gas:** BP, RaceTrac, 7-11, Sunoco/dsl, **food:** Bob Evans, Burger King, Cassie's Cafe, Denny's, LJ Silver, McDonald's, Popeye's, Waffle House, **lodging:** Holiday Inn, Howard Johnson, Motel 6, **other:** H HOSPITAL, AutoZone, Beall's, Chrysler/Dodge, Family$, Home Depot, U-Haul

**31** FL 539, to Kathleen, Lakeland, **N gas:** Shell, **food:** Romeo's Pizza, Wendy's, **other:** Publix, **S** hist dist

**28** FL 546, to US 92, Memorial Blvd, Lakeland

**27** FL 570 E toll, Lakeland

**25** County Line Rd, **S gas:** Citgo/dsl, Shell/Circle K/Subway, **food:** McDonald's, Wendy's, **lodging:** Fairfield Inn, **other:** FL Air Museum

**22** FL 553, Park Rd, Plant City, **N other:** Chevrolet, **S gas:** Shell/Circle K/Subway, **food:** Arby's, Burger King, Denny's, Popeye's, **lodging:** Comfort Inn, Holiday Inn Express, **other:** RV Sales

## INTERSTATE 4 CONT'D

**21**   FL 39, Alexander St, to Zephyrhills, Plant City, **S gas:** BP/dsl, Citgo, Shell, **lodging:** Day's Inn, Red Rose Inn/rest.

**19**   FL 566, to Thonotosassa, **N gas:** BP, **S gas:** RaceTrac, **food:** Applebee's, BuddyFreddy's Rest., Carraba's, Lin's Express, Little Caesars, McDonald's, Mi Casa, OutBack Steaks, Sonny's BBQ, Starbucks, Subway, Waffle House, **other:** H HOSPITAL, $General, Publix

**17**   Branch Forbes Rd, **N gas:** Marathon, Sunoco, **other:** Dinosaur World, **S gas:** BP, Citgo, Shell/Circle K/Subway/dsl, **other:** Advance Parts, AutoZone

**14**   McIntosh Rd, **N gas:** BP/dsl, **other:** Longview RV Ctr, Windward RV Park (2mi), **S gas:** 7-11/dsl, **food:** Burger King, McDonald's/playplace, **other:** Bates RV Ctr, East Tampa RV Park

**12mm**   weigh sta, both lanes

**10**   rd 579, Mango, Thonotosassa, **N gas:** ⊕FLYING J/CountryMkt/dsl/LP/scales/24hr, Sunoco, TA/Arby's/Popeye's/dsl/scales/24hr/@, **food:** Bob Evans, Cracker Barrel, **lodging:** Country Inn Suites, Hampton Inn, **other:** Camping World RV Service/supplies, Ford/Lincoln/Mercury, Hillsboro River SP, Lazy Day's RV Ctr, Rally RV Park, **S gas:** Shell/Circle K/dsl, Hardee's, Subway, Wendy's, **lodging:** Masters Inn

**9**   I-75, N to Ocala, S to Naples

**7**   US 92W, to US 301, Hillsborough Ave, **N on US 92... gas:** Citgo/rest./scales/dsl, **food:** Waffle House, **other:** Motel 6, **other:** Hard Rock Hotel/casino, **S gas:** BP, Citgo, Hess, **food:** WingHouse, **lodging:** Holiday Inn Express, La Quinta, Red Roof Inn, **other:** FL Expo Fair

**6**   Orient Rd (from eb)

**5**   FL 574, MLK Blvd, **N food:** McDonald's, **S gas:** BP, Sunoco, **food:** Subway, Wendy's, **lodging:** Holiday Inn Express, Masters Inn, **other:** Kenworth

**3**   US 41, 50th St, Columbus Dr (exits left from eb), **N gas:** Shell, **lodging:** Day's Inn, Motel 29, **other:** Busch Gardens, **S gas:** Marathon, Sunoco/dsl, **food:** Checker's, Church's, KFC, McDonald's, Salem's Subs, Subway, Taco Bell, **lodging:** Howard Johnson, **other:** Advance Parts, Family$

**1**   FL 585, 22nd, 21st St, Port of Tampa, **S gas:** BP/24hr, **food:** Burger King, Columbia Rest., McDonald's, **other:** museum

**0mm**   I-4 begins/ends on I-275, exit 45b.

## INTERSTATE 10

| Exit # | Services |
|---|---|
| **363mm** | I-10 begins/ends on I-95, exit 351b. |

**362**   Stockton St, to Riverside, **S gas:** BP, Gate, **other:** H HOSPITAL

**361**   US 17 S (from wb), downtown

**360**   FL 129, McDuff Ave, **S gas:** BP, Chevron, Popeye's

**359**   Lenox Ave, Edgewood Ave (from wb)

**358**   FL 111, Cassat Ave, **N gas:** Hess/Blimpie/dsl, Shell/Subway/dsl, **food:** Burger King, McDonald's, Wendy's, **other:** AutoZone, **S gas:** BP, RaceWay/24hr, **food:** Domino's, Dunkin Donuts, Taco Bell, **other:** Advance Parts, Discount Tire, Lowes Whse, Walgreens

**357**   FL 103, Lane Ave, **N gas:** Hess/dsl, **food:** Andy's Sandwiches, **lodging:** Day's Inn, Ramada Ltd, **S gas:** BP, Shell/dsl, Applebee's, Bono's BBQ, Cross Creek Steaks, Hardee's, KFC, Lee's Drive-In, Linda's Seafood, McDonald's, Piccadilly's, **lodging:** Budget Inn, Diamond Inn, **other:** Home Depot, Office Depot, Pep Boys

**356**   I-295, N to Savannah, S to St Augustine

**355**   Marietta, **N gas:** Gate/dsl/24hr, Exxon, **S gas:** Hess/Blimpie/dsl, Shell/dsl

**351**   FL 115, Chaffee Rd, to Cecil Fields, **N gas:** Kangaroo/dsl/24hr, **other:** Rivers RV Ctr, **S gas:** Chevron, KwikChek/gas, Shell/Subway/dsl/24hr, **food:** Cracker Barrel, Fastboys Wings, King Wok, McDonald's, Quizno's, Wendy's, **lodging:** Best Western, Hampton Inn, Holiday Inn Express, **other:** Family$, Winn-Dixie

**349**   new exit/no services

**343**   US 301, to Starke, Baldwin, **S gas:** BP, Chevron, Pilot/Subway/dsl/scales/24hr/@, TA/Shell/Arby's/dsl/scales/rest./24hr/@, **food:** Burger King, McDonald's, Waffle House, **lodging:** Best Western, **other:** NAPA

**336**   FL 228, to Maxville, Macclenny, **N food:** Starbucks, **other:** H HOSPITAL, Walmart SuperCtr/Subway, fireworks

**335**   FL 121, to Lake Butler, Macclenny, **N gas:** BP/dsl, Citgo, **food:** China Dragon, Domino's, Hardee's, KFC, McDonald's, Pier 6, Pizza Hut, Subway, Taco Bell, Waffle House, Wendy's, Woody's BBQ, Zaxby's, **lodging:** American Inn, **other:** H HOSPITAL, Advance Parts, AutoZone, Curves, $General, $Tree, Food Lion, Radio Shack, Walgreens, Winn-Dixie, **S gas:** RaceWay, Exxon/dsl, Burger King, China Buffet, Down Home Cafe, **lodging:** Econolodge, Travelodge

**333**   rd 125, Glen Saint Mary, **N gas:** Citgo/dsl/24hr

**327**   rd 229, to Raiford, Sanderson, **1 mi N** gas

**324**   US 90, to Olustee, Sanderson, **S gas:** Citgo/dsl, to Olustee Bfd

**318mm**   rest area both lanes, full 🚹 facilities, 🎟 vending, 🍴, litter barrels, petwalk, 24hr security

**303**   US 441, to Fargo, Lake City, **N gas:** Chevron/dsl/24hr, **other:** KOA (1mi), Oaks'n Pines RV Park, **S gas:** SuperTest/dsl, Shell/dsl, **food:** Huddle House, **lodging:** Day's Inn, **other:** H HOSPITAL

**301**   US 41, to Lake City, **N gas:** Exxon/dsl, **other:** Kelly's RV Park (6mi), to Stephen Foster Ctr, **S other:** H HOSPITAL

**296b a**   I-75, N to Valdosta, S to Tampa

## INTERSTATE 10 CONT'D

**E ↕ W**

**LEE**

**TALLAHASSEE**

| | |
|---|---|
| **294mm** | rest area both lanes, full ♿ facilities, 🚻, vending, 🏕, litter barrels, petwalk, 24hr security |
| **292** | rd 137, to Wellborn |
| **283** | US 129, to Live Oak, **N gas:** Penn/dsl, to Boys Ranch, **S gas:** BP, Chevron, Shell/dsl, Texaco, **food:** China Buffet, Huddle House, Krystal, McDonald's, Subway, Taco Bell, Waffle House, Wendy's, **lodging:** Best Western, Econolodge, Holiday Inn Express, **other:** Ⓗ HOSPITAL, $Tree, Lowe's Whse, Walmart SuperCtr/gas |
| **275** | US 90, Live Oak, **N** to Suwannee River SP, **S other:** Ⓗ HOSPITAL |
| **271mm** | weigh sta both lanes |
| **269mm** | Suwannee River |
| **265mm** | rest areas both lanes, full ♿ facilities, 🚻, vending, 🏕, litter barrels, petwalk, 24hr security |
| **264mm** | weigh sta both lanes |
| **262** | rd 255, Lee, **N gas:** Exxon/dsl, **other:** to Suwannee River SP, **S gas:** Jimmy's/Citgo/Rest./dsl/24hr, Love's/Arby's/dsl/scales/24hr |
| **258** | FL 53, **N gas:** Shell/Burger King/dsl/24hr, Mobil/DQ/Subway/Wendy's/dsl/scales/24hr, **food:** Denny's, Waffle House, **lodging:** Day's Inn, Holiday Inn Express, Super 8, **other:** Ⓗ HOSPITAL, **S lodging:** Deerwood Inn, **other:** Jellystone Camping, Madison Camping |
| **251** | FL 14, to Madison, **N gas:** Mobil/Arby's/24hr, **other:** Ⓗ HOSPITAL |
| **241** | US 221, Greenville, **N gas:** Mobil/DQ |
| **234mm** | rest area both lanes, full ♿ facilities, 🚻, 🏕, litter barrels, petwalk, 24hr security |
| **233** | rd 257, Aucilla, **N gas:** Shell/dsl |
| **225** | US 19, to Monticello, **S gas:** BP, Chevron/McDonald's, Exxon/Wendy's, Mobil/Arby's/dsl, **food:** Huddle House, **lodging:** Day's Inn, Super 8, **other:** KOA, dogtrack |
| **217** | FL 59, Lloyd, **S gas:** BP/dsl/rest./scales/24hr, Shell/Subway/dsl, **lodging:** Quality Inn |
| **209b a** | US 90, Tallahassee, **S gas:** Circle K/dsl, Shell/Subway/dsl, **food:** Cross Creek Grill, Paulina's Pizza, Waffle House, **lodging:** Best Western, Country Inn&Suites, **other:** Publix, Tallahassee RV Park, car museum |
| **203** | FL 61, US 319, Tallahassee, **N gas:** BP/dsl, Shell/Circle K, USA Gas, **food:** Applebee's, Bonefish Grill, Firehouse Subs, Great Wall Chinese, Hungry Howie's, KFC, McDonald's, Moe's SW Grill Popeye's, Starbucks, Subway, Taco Bell, TCBY, Waffle House, Wendy's, **lodging:** Motel 6, **other:** Albertson's, BooksAMillion, CVS Drug, Discount Tire, Fresh Mkt Foods, GNC, Publix, Radio Shack, Sav-On, SteinMart, SuperLube, TJ Maxx, Walgreens, Walmart SuperCtr (3mi), **S gas:** Citgo, **food:** Boston Mkt, Carraba's, Chick-fil-A, Osaka Japanese, Outback Steaks, Quizno's, Steak'n Shake, Ted's MT Grill, TGI-Friday, Village Inn, Zaxby's, **lodging:** Cabot Lodge, Courtyard, Hampton Inn, Hilton Garden, Residence Inn, Studio+, **other:** Ⓗ HOSPITAL, Advance Parts, Home Depot, Infiniti, Office Depot, PetsMart, vet |
| **199** | US 27, Tallahassee, **N gas:** BP/dsl, Chevron/dsl, McKenzie/dsl, **food:** Burger King, Dominos, Pizza Hut, Taco Bell, Waffle House, **lodging:** Comfort Inn, Country |

**TALLAHASSEE**

**QUINCY**

| | |
|---|---|
| **199** | Continued |
| | Inn&Suites, Days Inn, Fairfield Inn, Holiday Inn, Microtel, Quality Inn, Sunshine State Inn, **other:** Big Oak RV Park (2mi), **S gas:** BP/24hr, Chevron/dsl, Shell, USA, Arby's, Boston Mkt, Burger King, Chick-fil-A, China Buffet, ChuckeCheese, Cracker Barrel, Crystal River Seafood, DQ, Firehouse Subs, Golden Corral, Hooters, Julie's Rest., KFC, Krispy Kreme, Longhorn Steaks, Los Compadres Mexican, McDonald's, On-the-Border, Papa John's, Qdoba Mexican, Quizno's, Red Lobster, Shoney's, Sonny's BBQ, Starbucks, Subway, TCBY, Whataburger, Wendy's, Zaxby's, **lodging:** Best Value Inn, Cabot Lodge, Econolodge, Howard Johnson, La Quinta, Ramada Inn, Red Roof Inn, Rodeway Inn, Super 8, Wingate Inn, **other:** Albertson's/Sav-On, AutoZone, Barnes&Noble, Big 10 Tire, CVS Drug, $Tree, Goody's, Old Navy, Publix, Ross, Staples, Sun Tire, Tire Kingdom, Tuffy Auto, Walgreens, mall, vet |
| **196** | FL 263, Tallahassee, **S gas:** BP, Chevron/dsl, Shell/dsl, Stop'n Save Gas, **food:** Applebee's, Firehouse Subs, KFC, Sonic, Steak'n Shake, Subway, Waffle House, Wendy's, Zaxby's, **lodging:** Sleep Inn, **other:** Aamco, Chrysler/Jeep/Dodge, Harley-Davidson, Home Depot, Lowe's Whse, Mazda, Walgreens, Walmart SuperCtr |
| **194mm** | rest area both lanes, full ♿ facilities, 🚻, vending, 🏕, litter barrels, petwalk, 24hr security |
| **192** | US 90, to Tallahassee, Quincy, **N gas:** BP, ⊕FLYING J/Conoco/dsl/LP/scales/24hr, **lodging:** Comfort Inn, Howard Johnson, **S gas:** Pilot/Subway/dsl/scales/24hr, **food:** Waffle House, **lodging:** Best Western, **other:** Lakeside RV Park (4mi) |
| **181** | FL 267, Quincy, **N other:** Ⓗ HOSPITAL, Walmart Super Ctr/gas, **S gas:** BP/dsl, Pure, **lodging:** Hampton Inn, Holiday Inn Express, Parkway Inn, to Lake Talquin SP |
| **174** | FL 12, to Greensboro, **N gas:** BP, Shell/Burger King/dsl, **other:** Beaver Lake RV Park |
| **166** | rd 270A, Chattahoochee, **N** to Lake Seminole, to Torreya SP, **S gas:** Shell/dsl, **other:** KOA (1mi) |
| **161mm** | rest area both lanes, full ♿ facilities, 🚻, vending, 🏕, litter barrels, petwalk, 24hr security |
| **160mm** | Apalachicola River, central/eastern time zone |
| **158** | rd 286, Sneads, **N** Lake Seminole, to Three Rivers SP |
| **155mm** | weigh sta both lanes |
| **152** | FL 69, to Grand Ridge, **N gas:** BP, Exxon, **lodging:** Durdens Inn |
| **142** | FL 71, to Marianna, Oakdale, **N gas:** Pilot/Arby's/dsl/scales/24hr, **food:** Burger King, Firehouse Subs, KFC, LJ Silver, Pizza Hut, PoFolks, Ruby Tuesday, San Marco's Mexican, Sonny's BBQ, Waffle House, **lodging:** Comfort Inn, Country Inn&Suites, Hampton Inn, Holiday Inn Express, Microtel, Quality Inn, Super 8, **other:** Ⓗ HOSPITAL, $Tree, Lowes Whse, Radio Shack, Walmart SuperCtr/dsl, to FL Caverns SP (8mi), **S gas:** Chevron/dsl, Sunoco/dsl, TA/BP/dsl/rest./scales/24hr/@, **food:** McDonald's, **lodging:** Best Value Inn, **other:** camping |
| **136** | FL 276, to Marianna, **N other:** to FL Caverns SP (8mi) |
| **133mm** | rest area both lanes, full ♿ facilities, 🚻, 🏕, litter barrels, petwalk, 24hr security |
| **130** | US 231, Cottondale, **N gas:** BP/dsl, Chevron, **food:** Hardee's, Subway, **other:** Big Rig RV Park, **S gas:** RaceWay |

## INTERSTATE 10 CONT'D

**E ← → W**

**BONIFAY**

**120** FL 77, to Panama City, Chipley, **N gas:** BP/dsl, Exxon/Burger King, Petro/Domino's, **food:** Arby's, Hardee's, JJ's Kitchen, KFC, New Star Chinese, McDonald's, Pizza Hut, Sonic, Taco Bell, Waffle House, Wendy's, **lodging:** Comfort Inn, Day's Inn/rest., Executive Inn, Holiday Inn Express, Super 8, **other:** [H] HOSPITAL, CVS Drug, $Tree, Save-a-Lot Foods, Walmart SuperCtr/gas, **S** Falling Water SRA

**112** FL 79, Bonifay, **N gas:** Chevron, Exxon/dsl, Tom Thumb/dsl, **food:** Blitch's Rest., Burger King, Hardee's, McDonald's, Pizza Hut, Simbo's Rest, Subway, Waffle House, **lodging:** Bonifay Inn, Economy Inn, Tivoli Inn, **other:** [H] HOSPITAL, Fred's Drug

**104** rd 279, Caryville

**96** FL 81, Ponce de Leon, **N** to Ponce de Leon SRA, Vortex Spring Camping, **S gas:** BP/dsl/24hr, 87 Depot/Subway/dsl, Exxon/dsl, **other:** Ponce de Leon Motel, **rest area both lanes, full [&] facilities, [C], [A], litter barrels, petwalk, 24hr security**

**85** US 331, De Funiak Springs, **N gas:** Chevron/24hr, **food:** Arby's, Beef O'Brady's, Burger King, LaRumba Mexican, McLain's Steaks, Pizza Hut, Sonic, Subway, Waffle House, **lodging:** Best Value Inn, Sundown Inn, Super 8, Travelodge, **other:** [H] HOSPITAL, $General, Lowes Whse, Walgreens, Walmart SuperCtr/gas, Winn-Dixie, winery, **S gas:** BP, 87 Depot/dsl, Emerald Express/dsl, **food:** KFC, McDonald's, Whataburger, **lodging:** Best Western, **other:** [H] HOSPITAL

**70** FL 285, to Ft Walton Bch, Eglin AFB, **N gas:** RaceWay, **S gas:** Shell/Subway/dsl/scales/24hr, **lodging:** Rodeway Inn, **other:** repair

**60mm** **rest area both lanes, full [&] facilities, [C], vending, [A], litter barrels, petwalk, 24hr security**

**CRESTVIEW**

**56** FL 85, Crestview, Eglin AFB, **N gas:** BP/dsl, Mobil, Shell/dsl, **food:** Applebee's, Asian Garden, Beef O'Brady's, Burger King, Capt D's, Firehouse Subs, Lee's Chicken, McDonald's, Ryan's, Sonic, Starbucks, Taco Bell, **lodging:** Country Inn&Suites, Econolodge, **other:** [H] HOSPITAL, Advance Parts, AutoZone, Big Lots, $General, Lowes Whse, Publix, Walgreens, Walmart SuperCtr, **S gas:** Exxon, Tom Thumb/dsl, **food:** Arby's, Coach-n-Four Steaks, Cracker Barrel, Hardee's, Hooters, LaRumba Mexican, Tokyo Rest., Waffle House, Wendy's, Whataburger, **lodging:** Comfort Inn, Day's Inn, Hampton Inn, Holiday Inn Express, Jameson Inn, Quality Inn, Super 8, **other:** Buick/Pontiac/GMC, Chrysler/Dodge/Jeep, Ford/Mercury, museum, RV camping

**45** rd 189, to US 90, Holt, **N gas:** Chevron (1mi), **other:** to Blackwater River SP, Cozy Corner RV Park, Eagle Landing RV Park, **S** River's Edge RV Park (1mi)

**31** FL 87, to Ft Walton Beach, Milton, **N gas:** Exxon/Quizno's/dsl/24hr, **food:** Waffle House, **lodging:** Holiday Inn Express, **other:** Blackwater River SP, Gulf Pines Camping, KOA, **S gas:** BP, Shell/dsl, **lodging:** Comfort Inn, Red Carpet Inn

**31mm** **rest area both lanes, full [&] facilities, [C], [A], litter barrels, petwalk, 24hr security**

**PENSACOLA**

**28** rd 89, Milton, **N** [H] HOSPITAL, **S** Cedar Lakes RV Camping (2mi

**27mm** Blackwater River

**26** rd 191, Bagdad, Milton, **N gas:** Shel/Circle K/dsl, **other:** [H] HOSPITAL, **S gas:** Chevron/DQ/Stuckey's, **other:** Pelican Palms RV Park

**22** N FL 281, Avalon Blvd, **N gas:** BP/dsl, Tom Thumb, **food:** McDonald's, Oval Office Cafe, **S gas:** Shell/Subway/dsl, Waffle House, **lodging:** Red Roof Inn, **other:** By the Bay RV Park (3mi)

**18mm** Escambia Bay

**17** US 90, Pensacola, **N gas:** BP/dsl, **S gas:** Exxon, **food:** DQ, **lodging:** Ramada Inn/rest.

**14mm** truck inspection sta

**13** FL 291, to US 90, Pensacola, **N gas:** BP, Exxon, Shell/dsl, **food:** Arby's, Barnhill's Buffet, Capt D's, Denny's, La Hacienda Mexican, McDonald's, Starbucks, Subway, Taco Bell, Waffle House, **lodging:** Best Value Inn, Comfort Inn, Holiday Inn, La Quinta, Motel 6, Villager Inn, **other:** CVS Drug, Food World/24hr, Walgreens, **S food:** ChuckeCheese, Fazoli's, Honeybaked Ham, Los Rancheros Mexican, O'Charley's, Steak&Ale, Waffle House, Wendy's, Whataburger, **lodging:** Clarion, Courtyard, Extended Stay America, Fairfield Inn, Hampton Inn, Motel 6, Red Roof Inn, Residence Inn, TownePlace Suites, **other:** [H] HOSPITAL, Belk, Big 10 Tire, BooksaMillion, Circuit City, $General, Firestone/auto, JC Penney, JoAnn Fabrics, Pepboys, PetsMart, Sears/auto, TJ Maxx, Tuesday Morning, U-Haul, mall

**12** I-110, to Pensacola, Hist Dist, Islands Nat Seashore

**10b a** US 29, Pensacola, **N gas:** BP, Fleet/dsl/scales, **food:** Church's, Hardee's, Ryan's, Sonic, Waffle House, **other:** Advance Parts, AutoZone, Carpenter's RV Ctr, $Tree, GNC, Office Depot, O'Reilly Parts, Radio Shack, Tires+, Walmart SuperCtr/gas, **S gas:** RaceWay, Shell, **food:** Burger King, Capt D's, Founaris Bro's Rest., IHOP, Las Palma's Mexican, McDonald's, Ruby Tuesday, Smokey's BBQ, Wendy's, Whataburger, **lodging:** Best Value Inn, Day's Inn, Econolodge, Executive Inn, Howard Johnson, Hospitality Inn, Luxury Suites, Motel 6, Palm Court, Ramada Inn, Travelodge, **other:** Chevrolet, Ford, Harley-Davidson, Jeep, KIA, Leisure Tyme RV Ctr, Lincoln/Mercury, NAPA, Saturn, Suzuki/Toyota

**7b a** Fl 297, Pine Forest Rd, **N gas:** Chevron, **food:** Beef O'Brady's, Starbucks, Wendy's, **lodging:** Best Western, Comfort Inn, Garden Inn, Value Place,

## INTERSTATE 10 CONT'D

**7b a** Continued
**other:** Albertson's/gas, Tall Oaks Camping, **S gas:** BP, Citgo, Burger King, Carnley's Diner, Cracker Barrel, Hardee's, McDonald's, Ruby Tuesday, Sonny's BBQ, Subway, Waffle House, **lodging:** Country Inn&Suites, Holiday Inn Express, Microtel, Quality Inn, Sleep Inn, **other:** Food World/24hr, Big Lagoon SRA (12mi), museum

**5** US 90 A, **N gas:** BP, Fleet/Shell/Subway/dsl, **other:** Albertson's/gas, Walgreens, **S** Leisure Lakes Camping

**4mm** Welcome Ctr eb, full ♿ facilities, info, 📞, vending, 🚻, litter barrels, petwalk, 24hr security

**3mm** weigh sta both lanes

**1mm** inspection sta eb

**0mm** Florida/Alabama state line, Perdido River

## INTERSTATE 75

**Exit #** Services

**471mm** Florida/Georgia state line., Motorist callboxes begin sb.

**469mm** Welcome Ctr sb, full ♿ facilities, info, 📞, vending, 🚻, litter barrels, petwalk

**467** FL 143, Jennings, **E gas:** Chevron, Fastrac, **other:** Budget Lodge, **W gas:** Exxon/dsl, **food:** Jennings House, **lodging:** N Florida Inn, Scottish Inn, **other:** Jennings Camping

**460** FL 6, Jasper, **E gas:** BP/Burger King, Indian River Fruit/gas, Penn Oil/Huddle House/dsl, **lodging:** Day's Inn, **W gas:** Fastrac, Shell/dsl, **food:** Sheffield's Catfish, **lodging:** Scottish Inn, **other:** Suwanee River SP

**451** US 129, Jasper, Live Oak, **E gas:** Mobil/DQ/Subway/dsl, **W gas:** BP/Cowboys BBQ/dsl, **other:** Suwanee Music Park (4mi), to FL Boys Ranch

**448mm** weigh sta both lanes

**446mm** insp sta both lanes

**443mm** Historic Suwanee River

**439** to FL 136, White Springs, Live Oak, **E gas:** Fastrac, Gate/dsl, Shell/dsl, **food:** Kitchen, McDonald's, **lodging:** Scottish Inn, **other:** Kelly RV Park (5mi), Lee's Camping (3mi), Suwanee RV Camping (4mi), to S Foster Ctr, **W lodging:** Best Value Inn

**435** I-10, E to Jacksonville, W to Tallahassee

**427** US 90, to Live Oak, Lake City, **E gas:** BP, Chevron/dsl/24hr, Exxon, Gas'n Go/Subway, Murphy USA, Shell, **food:** Applebee's, Arby's, Burger King, Cazbor's Grille, Cedar River Seafood, Coolwater Grille, Cracker Barrel, Domino's, Elliano's Coffee, El Potro, Hardee's, IHOP, Ken's BBQ, KFC, Krystal, McDonald's, Moe's SW Grill, Ole Times Buffet, Pizza Hut, Red Lobster, Ruby Tuesday, Sonny's BBQ, Starbucks, Steak&Shake, Subway, Taco Bell, TX Roadhouse, Waffle House, Wendy's, Zaxby's, **lodging:** Best Inn, Cypress Inn, Day's Inn, Driftwood Inn, Holiday Inn, Howard Johnson, Jameson Inn, Knight's Inn, Piney Woods Motel, Ramada Ltd, Rodeway Inn, Scottish Inn, **other:** Ⓗ HOSPITAL, Advance Parts, AutoZone, Belk, CVS Drug, Ford/Lincoln/Mercury, Goody's, Home Depot, JC Penney, Lowe's Whse, Publix, Radio Shack, Tire Kingdom, Walgreens, Walmart SuperCtr, In&Out RV Park, mall, **W gas:** BP, Chevron, Citgo, Shell, **food:** Bob Evans, Shoney's, Subway, Waffle House, **lodging:** Best Western, Comfort Suites,

**427** Continued
Country Inn&Suites, Econolodge, Fairfield Inn, Gateway Inn, Hampton Inn, Motel 6, Quality Inn, Red Roof Inn, Travelodge, White Swan Inn, **other:** Chevrolet/Mazda, Chrysler/Dodge, vet

**423** FL 47, to Ft White, Lake City, **E gas:** Shell/dsl, **other:** Mack Trucks/Volvo, **W gas:** BP/dsl, Exxon/dsl, **food:** Little Caesar's, Subway, **lodging:** Motel 8, Super 8, **other:** Casey Jones Camping, Freightliner, Never Dunn (6mi), USPO

**414** US 41, US 441, to Lake City, High Springs, **E gas:** Chevron/dsl/24hr, Pitstop/gas, Texaco, **lodging:** Traveler's Inn, Travelodge, **W gas:** BP/dsl, Shell/dsl, **food:** Huddle House, Subway, **lodging:** Econolodge, **other:** antiques, tires, to O'Leno SP

**413mm** rest areas both lanes, full ♿ facilities, 📞, vending, 🚻, litter barrels, petwalk

**409mm** Santa Fe River

**404** rd 236, to High Springs, **E gas:** Chevron/fruits/gifts, Citgo/dsl, Sunoco, **W** High Sprs Camping

**399** US 441, to High Sprs, Alachua, **E gas:** BP, **food:** Dominos, McDonald's, Moe's SW Grill, Pizza Hut, Sonny's BBQ, Subway, Waffle House, **lodging:** Econolodge, Quality Inn, **other:** Advance Parts, Family$, FoodLion, Hitchcock's Foods, Traveler's Campground (1mi), **W gas:** Chevron, Citgo/Taco Bell/dsl, Exxon/Wendy's, **food:** Kazbor's Grille, KFC, **lodging:** Day's Inn, Royal Inn

**390** FL 222, to Gainesville, **E gas:** Chevron/dsl, Exxon/McDonald's/dsl, Kangaroo/dsl, **food:** Burger King, La Fiesta Mexican, Pomodoro Cafe, Sonnys BBQ, Wendy's, **other:** Publix, Walgreens, **W gas:** BP/DQ/dsl, **lodging:** Best Western, **other:** Harley-Davidson, Jeep/Mercedes, auto repair, vet

**387** FL 26, to Newberry, Gainesville, **E gas:** BP, Chevron, Sunoco, Shell/dsl, **food:** Bono's BBQ, Boston Mkt, Buffet City, Burger King, Dunkin Donuts, FoodCourt, LJ Silver, Macaroni Grill, McAlister's Deli, McDonald's, Perkins, Red Lobster, Ruby Tuesday, Starbucks, Subway, Wendy's, **lodging:** La Quinta, **other:** Ⓗ HOSPITAL, Belk, BooksAMillion, Borders Books, Dillard's, JC Penney, Macy's, Office Depot, PetCo, Sears/auto, Steinmart, to UFL, mall, **W gas:** BP, Chevron/dsl, Exxon/dsl, Mobil/dsl/LP, **food:** El Nortino's Mexican, KFC, Krystal, Macaroni Grill, Moe's SW Grill, Napolatanos Rest., Taco Bell, Waffle House, Whataburger, **lodging:** Clarion, Day's Inn, Econolodge, Fairfield Inn, **other:** Advance Parts, Circuit City, $Tree, Goodyear/auto, Home Depot, JoAnn Fabrics, K-Mart, PepBoys, Publix, TJ Maxx, Walgreens, Winn-Dixie, tires/repair, vet

**384** FL 24, to Archer, Gainesville, **E gas:** BP, Chevron/dsl/24hr, Citgo, Exxon/dsl, Shell, **food:** Arby's, Atlanta Bread, BoneFish Grill, Burger King, Capt D's, Checker's, Chick-fil-A, Chili's, Chipotle Mexican, CiCi's Pizza, Coldstone Creamery, DQ, Firehouse Subs, Gainesville Alehouse, Hooters, KFC, McAlister's Deli, McDonald's, Moe's SW Grill, Olive Garden, On-the-Border, OutBack Steaks, Panera Bread, Papa John's, Pizza Hut, Shoney's, Sonny's BBQ, Starbucks, Steak'n Shake, Subway, Taco Bell, TX Roadhouse, TGIFriday, Zaxby's, **lodging:** Cabot Lodge, Comfort Inn, Courtyard, Extended Stay America, Hampton Inn, Motel 6, Red Roof Inn,

## INTERSTATE 75 CONT'D

**N / S**

**384** Continued
Sleep Inn. Spring Hill Suites, Super 8, **other:** Albertson's, Barnes&Noble, Best Buy, CarQuest, CVS Drug, Firestone/auto, GNC, Goody's, Kohls, Lowe's Whse, Michael's, Old Navy, PetsMart, Publix, Radio Shack, Ross, Target, Walmart, **W gas:** Mobil/dsl, **food:** Cracker Barrel, **lodging:** Country Inn&Suites, Holiday Inn Express, **other:** Sunshine RV Park, to Bear Museum

**382** FL 121, to Williston, Gainesville, **E gas:** Citgo/dsl/24hr, Mobil/dsl, **food:** First Wok, McDonalds, Subway, **lodging:** Travelodge, **other:** Publix, **W gas:** BP/dsl, Chevron/dsl/24hr, Kangaroo/dsl, **food:** 43rd St Deli, **lodging:** Quality Inn, Rodeway Inn, **other:** Fred Bear Museum

**381mm** rest areas both lanes, full ♿ facilities, 🚻 vending, 🍴 litter barrels, petwalk, 24hr security

**374** rd 234, Micanopy, **E gas:** BP, Chevron/dsl, **other:** antiques, fruit, to Paynes Prairie SP, **W gas:** Micanopy/repair, Texaco, **lodging:** Knight's Inn

**368** rd 318, Orange Lake, **E gas:** Chevron, Jim's/BBQ, Petro/Mobil/dsl/scales/24hr/@, Wendy's, **other:** Grand Lake RV Park (3mi), **W** Ocala N RV Camping

**358** FL 326, **E gas:** BP/FL Citrus Ctr/dsl, Mobil/McDonald's/dsl, Pilot/Arby's/dsl/scales/24hr, Pilot/Wendy's/dsl/24hr, **other:** Freightliner, auto/truck repair, **W gas:** Chevron/dsl, **food:** DQ

**354** US 27, to Silver Springs, Ocala, **E gas:** BP/24hr, RaceTrac, **food:** Burger King, Rascal's BBQ, **lodging:** Golden Palms Inn, **W gas:** BP/dsl, Chevron, Texaco, **food:** Barbazon's Grill, Blanca's Cafe, Waffle House, **lodging:** Budget Host, Comfort Suites, Day's Inn, Howard Johnson, Ramada, **other:** Ace Hardware, $General, Nelson's Trailers, Oaktree Village Camping, Publix, Walgreens, Winn-Dixie

**352** FL 40, to Silver Springs, Ocala, **E gas:** BP/dsl, Chevron, Citgo, RaceTrac/24hr, **food:** Dunkin Donuts, McDonald's, Pizza Hut/Taco Bell, Subway, Wendy's, Whataburger/24hr, **lodging:** Day's Inn/café, Economy Inn, GS RV Park, Motor Inn/RV, Quality Inn, **other:** park, fruits, **W gas:** Shell/dsl, Texaco, **food:** Denny's, Golden Coast Buffet, Waffle House, **lodging:** Red Roof Inn, Super 8, Travelodge, **other:** Gander Mtn, Holiday Trav-L Park, vet

**350** FL 200 , to Hernando, Ocala, **E gas:** BP, Chevron, Citgo/repair, Kangaroo, RaceWay, Texaco/dsl, **food:** Applebee's, Arby's, Backyard Burger, Bob Evans, Boston Mkt, Burger King, Carrabba's, Checkers, Chick-fil-A, Chili's, ChuckeCheese, Cici's Pizza, Crisper's, Coldstone Creamery, Domino's, El Toreo Mexican, Fazoli's, Firehouse Subs, Flipside Cafe, Golden Corral, Grand Buffet, Hooters, Krystal, Lee's Chicken, Little Caesars, Logan's Roadhouse, McDonald's, Olive Garden, Outback Steaks, Papa John's, Panera Bread, Perkins, PetsMart, Pizza Hut, Red Lobster, Roadhouse Grill, Ruby Tuesday, Smoothie King, Starbucks, Sonic, Sonny's BBQ, Subway, Taco Bell, Wendy's, Whataburger, Zaxby's, **lodging:** Country Inn Suites, Hampton Inn, Hilton, La Quinta, **other:** Ⓗ HOSPITAL, Acura, Advance Parts, Aldi Foods, Belk, Best Buy, Buick, Chevrolet/Nissan, Circuit City, CVS Drug, Discount Tire, Dodge,

**350** Continued
$General, Goodyear/auto, Home Depot, JC Penney, JoAnn Fabrics, Kia, K-Mart, Kohl's, Lowe's Whse, Macy's, Michael's, Office Depot, PepBoys, PetsMart, Publix, Ross, Sears, Staples, Steinmart, Suzuki, Target, Tire Kingdom, TJ Maxx, Toyota, Walgreens, Walmart SuperCtr, fruits, mall, **W gas:** BP/24hr, Chevron/24hr, Shell, **food:** Bonefish Grill, Burger King, Cracker Barrel, Dunkin Donuts, KFC, Mimi's Cafe, Panera Bread, Stabucks, Steak'n Shake/24hr, Waffle House, **lodging:** Best Western, Courtyard, Fairfield Inn, Holiday Inn, Homewood Suites, Residence Inn, **other:** Barnes&Noble, BMW/posrche, Cadillac, Camper Village RV Park, Dillards, Kohl's, Ocala RV Park, Old Navy, PetCo, Pontiac, Sam's Club/gas, Tires+, Walgreens, vet

**346mm** rest area both lanes, full ♿ facilities, 🚻 vending, 🍴 litter barrels, petwalk, 24hr security

**341** FL 484, to Belleview, **E gas:** Chevron/fruit/24hr, Citgo/Dunkin Donuts, Exxon/dsl, Shell, **food:** Cracker Barrel, Sonny's BBQ, Zaxby's, **lodging:** Microtel, Sleep Inn, **other:** FL Citrus Ctr, museums, **W gas:** BP/repair, Pilot/Arby's/DQ/dsl/scales/24hr, **food:** McDonald's, Waffle House, **other:** Ocala Ranch RV Park, outlets

**338mm** weigh sta both lanes

**329** FL 44, to Inverness, Wildwood, **E gas:** Gate/Steak'n Shake/dsl, Mobil/dsl, Sunoco, **food:** Burger King, Denny's, DQ, McDonald's, Waffle House, Wendy's, **other:** FL Citrus Ctr, Three Flags RV Resort (1mi), KOA, **W gas:** Citgo/dsl/repair/24hr, Pilot/dsl/24hr/scales, TA/BP/Pizza Hut/Subway/Popeye's/scales/dsl/24hr/@, **food:** IHOP, KFC, **lodging:** Day's Inn/rest., Economy Inn, Super 8, Wildwood Inn, **other:** truckwash, truck repair

**328** FL TPK (from sb), to Orlando

**321** rd 470, to Sumterville, Lake Panasoffkee, **E gas:** Spirit/deli/scales/dsl/rest./24hr, **other:** Coleman Correctional, **W gas:** BP/Hardee's/Subway/dsl, Chevron/7-11, **other:** Countryside RV Park (1mi), Turtleback RV Resort (1mi)

**314** FL 48, to Bushnell, **E gas:** BP/dsl, Citgo, Murphy USA, Shell/Circle K/Subway, **food:** Four-Season Chinese, KFC/Taco Bell, Little Caesars, McDonald's, Wendy's, **lodging:** Rodeway Inn, **other:** BlueBerry Hill RV Camp, Red Barn RV Camp, The Oaks Camp (1mi), Walmart SuperCtr, to Dade Bfd HS, **W gas:** Shell/dsl, Sunoco/dsl, **food:** Beef O'Brady's, Sonny's BBQ, Waffle House, **lodging:** Microtel, **other:** Flagship RV Ctr

## INTERSTATE 75 CONT'D

**309** rd 476, to Webster, **E** Breezy Oaks RV Park (1mi), Sumter Oaks RV Park (1mi)

**307mm** rest areas both lanes, full ♿ facilities, 🔌, coffee, vending, 🍴, litter barrels, petwalk, 24hr security

**301** US 98, FL 50, to Dade City, **E** **gas:** BP, RaceTrac, Sunoco, **food:** Arbys, Beef O'Brady's, Cracker Barrel, Denny's, McDonald's, Quinzo's, Waffle House, Wendy's, **lodging:** Day's Inn, Holiday Inn Express, **other:** Ⓗ HOSPITAL (10mi), Advance Parts, Curves, $General, Tall Pines RV Park, Winn-Dixie, USPO, **W** **gas:** Chevron/Subway/dsl, **food:** Burger King, **lodging:** Best Western, Hampton Inn, Microtel

**293** rd 41, to Dade City, **E** **gas:** Citgo (2mi), **other:** to Sertoma Youth Ranch, **W** **other:** Travelers Rest Resort RV Park

**285** FL 52, to Dade City, New Port Richey, **E** **gas:** ⊕FLYING J/Country Mkt/dsl/LP/scales/24hr, **other:** Ⓗ HOSPITAL, **W** **gas:** Citgo/dsl/scales/24hr, **food:** Waffle House

**279** FL 54, to Land O' Lakes, Zephyrhills, **E** **gas:** Hess/Blimpie/Godfather's/Dunkin Donuts/dsl, RaceTrac, Shell, **food:** Applebee's, Burger King, Gona China, Papa's John's, Pizza Hut/Taco Bell, Sonny's BBQ, Subway, Waffle House, Wendy's, **other:** Ace Hardware, Advance Parts, Beall's, Ford, Happy Days RV Camping (9mi), Kia, Leasure Days RV Park (7mi), Nissan, Publix, Ralph's RV Camping (7mi), Toyota/Scion, Walgreens, **W** **gas:** BP, 7-11, Shell/Circle K/dsl, **food:** Beef O'Brady's, Buffalo's, DQ, Cracker Barrel, McDonald's, Outback Steaks, Remington's Steaks, Shanghai Chinese, SW Cafe, **lodging:** Best Western, Comfort Inn, Holiday Inn Express, Sleep Inn, **other:** Best Buy, CVS Drug, $Tree, Encore RV Camping, Goodyear/auto, Honda, Hyundai, Mazda, Michael's, PetsMart, Quail Run RV Camping, Ross, SweetBay Foods, TJ Maxx, USPO

**278mm** rest areas both lanes, full ♿ facilities, 🔌, vending, 🍴, litter barrels, petwalk, 24hr security

**275** FL 56

**274** I-275 (from sb), to Tampa, St Petersburg

**270** rd 581, Bruce B Downs Blvd, **E** **gas:** Citgo/7-11, Hess/Blimpie/Godfather's/dsl, Mobil, Shell/Taco Bell/dsl, **food:** Boston Mkt, Burger King, Chick-fil-A, Chili's, Coldstone Creamery, DQ, Golden China, KFC, Liang's Asian Bistro, Macaroni Grill, McDonald's, Moe's SW Grill, Panera Bread, Papa John's, Quizno's, Ruby Tuesday, Selmon's Cafe, Starbucks, Subway, **lodging:** Holiday Inn Express, Wingate Inn, **other:** Circuit City, Home Depot, Kauffman's Tire, Michael's, Panera Bread, Publix, Walgreens, **W** **gas:** Citgo/7-11, **food:** McDonald's, Olive Garden, Red Lobster, Stonewood Grill, **other:** BJ's Whse, Lowe's Whse

**266** rd 582A, Fletcher Ave, **W** **gas:** Shell/Circle K/dsl, **food:** Baskin Robbins/Dunkin Donuts, Bob Evans, Lenny's Subs, Starbucks, Wendy's, **lodging:** Courtyard, Extended Stay America, Fairfield Inn, Hampton Inn, Hilton Garden, La Quinta, Residence Inn, Sleep Inn, **other:** Ⓗ HOSPITAL

**265** FL 582, Fowler Ave, Temple Terrace, **E** **other:** Happy Traveler RV Park, flea mkt, **W** **gas:** BP, Chevron/dsl,

**265** Continued **food:** IHOP, **lodging:** Ramada Inn, **other:** NAPA Auto Care, UHaul

**261** I-4, W to Tampa, E to Orlando

**260b a** FL 574, to Mango, Tampa, **E** **gas:** Chevron/24hr, Citgo, Shell/Circle K/Subway/24hr, **food:** Dunkin Donuts/Baskin-Robbins, China Wok, Quizno's, Waffle House, **other:** SweetBay Foods, Walgreens, **W** **gas:** BP, Mystik, **lodging:** Crowne Plaza Hotel, Hilton Garden, Residence Inn

**257** FL 60, Brandon, **E** **gas:** Citgo, Mobil, **food:** Arby's, Brandon Ale House, Boston Mkt, Buddy Freddy, Cheescake Factory, Chili's, China Buffet, ChuckeCheese, Cody's Roadhouse, Denny's, DQ, Dunkin Donuts, Firehouse Subs, Fuego Steaks, Hungry Howie's, Kabuki Japanese, Macaroni Grill, Moe's SW Grill, Olive Garden, Outback Steaks, Panda Express, Panera Bread, Papa John's, Picadilly's, Red Lobster, Smokey Bones BBQ, Subway, Village Inn, Waffle House, Wendy's, **lodging:** Holiday Inn Express, HomeStead Suites, La Quinta, **other:** Ⓗ HOSPITAL, Aamco, Advance Parts, Barnes&Noble, Best Buy, Books A Million, Curves, CVS Drug, Dillard's, $General, Firestone/auto, JC Penney, Jo-Ann Fabrics, Kia, Kohl's, K-Mart, Macy's, Marshall's, Michael's, Office Depot, PepBoys, PetCo, Radio Shack, Ross, Sam's Club, Sears/auto, Staples, Target, Tires+, TJ Maxx, Tuffy Auto, Uhaul, mall, **E on Causeway Blvd**- **gas:** Hess, **food:** Buca Italian, Longhorn Steaks, McDonald's, Quizno's, Starbucks, Steak'n Shake, **other:** Cadillac, Costco/gas, JoAnne, Kohl's, PetsMart, Publix, Saturn, Walmart SuperCtr, **W** **gas:** Citgo, Marathon, Shell, **food:** Beef O'Brady's, Bob Evans, Burger King, Hooters, McDonald's, Sonny's BBQ, Subway, Sweet Tomatoes, Wendy's, **lodging:** Best Western, Comfort Inn, Country Inn & Suites, Courtyard, Day's Inn, Embassy Suites, Fairfield Inn, Homewood Suites, La Quinta, Red Roof Inn, **other:** Buick/Pontiac/GMC, Chevrolet, Chrysler/Dodge/Jeep, Circuit City, Harley-Davidson, Home Depot, Honda, KIA, Mazda, Mitsubishi/Hyundai/Suzuki, Nissan, Office Depot, Toyota/Scion, VW

**256** FL 618 W (toll), to Tampa

**254** US 301, Riverview, **E** **gas:** RaceTrac, **food:** Steak'n Shake, **other:** CVS Drug, Home Depot, Super Target, **W** **gas:** Circle K, 7-11/dsl, Shell, **food:** Subway, **lodging:** Hilton Garden

**250** Gibsonton Dr, Riverview, **E** **gas:** RaceWay, 7-11, **food:** Burger King, DQ, Little Caesars, McDonald's, New China, Pizza Hut, Quizno's, Ruby Tuesday, Subway, Taco Bell, Wendy's, **other:** Alafia River RV Resort, Beall's, CVS Drug, Family$, Hidden River RV Resort (4mi), Lowe's Whse, Winn-Dixie, USPO, **W** **gas:** BP, Murphy USA, **other:** Walmart SuperCtr

**246** FL 672, Big Bend Rd, Apollo Bch, **E** **gas:** Hess/dsl, 7-11, **food:** Applebees, Beef O'Brady's, Buffalo Wild Wings, China Taste, CiCi's Pizza, East Coast Pizza, Five Guys Burgers, Little Caesars, McDonald's, Panera Bread, Papa John's, Sonic, Starbucks, Subway, Qdoba, Quizno's, Village Inn Rest., Vocelli, **other:** Ace Hardware, Advance Parts, Beall's, Goodyear/auto, Publix, Sweetbay Foods, **W** **gas:** Chevron, 7-11

**240b a** FL 674, Sun City Ctr, Ruskin, **E** **Visitors Ctr, gas:** Shell, **food:** Beef O' Brady's, Bob Evans, Burger King,

## INTERSTATE 75 CONT'D

**N ↕ S**

**240b a** Continued
Checker's, Denny's, King Buffet, Pizza Hut, Sonny's BBQ, Taco Bell, Wendy's, **lodging:** Comfort Inn, **other:** H HOSPITAL, Beall's, GNC, Home Depot, Radio Shack, SweetBay Foods, SunLake RV Resort (1mi), to Little Manatee River SP, **W gas:** Circle K/dsl, Hess/dsl, Race-Trac, **food:** China Wok, Domino's, KFC, McDonald's, Ozzie's Buffet, Subway, **lodging:** Holiday Inn Express, **other:** CVS Drug, NAPA, auto repair

**237mm** rest area both lanes, full ♿ facilities, 🚹 vending, 🍴, litter barrels, petwalk, 24hr security

**229** rd 683, Moccasin Wallow Rd, to Parrish, **E** Little Manatee Sprs SRA (10mi), **W other:** Circle K, Fiesta Grove RV Park (3mi), Frog Creek RV Park (3mi), Terra Ceia RV Village (2mi), Winterset RV Park (3mi)

**228** I-275 N, to St Petersburg

**B R A D E N T O N**

**224** US 301, to Bradenton, Ellenton, **E gas:** BP, Chevron/24hr, RaceWay, Shell/dsl, **food:** Applebee's, Checker's, Kings Wok, Hungry Howie's, McDonald's, Ruby Tuesday, Sonic, Wendy's, Woody's River Grill, **lodging:** Hampton Inn, Sleep Inn, **other:** Ace Hardware, Beall's, $Tree, Just Brakes, K-Mart, Publix, Walgreens, USPO, Prime Outlets/famous brands, **W gas:** Pilot/dsl, **food:** Anna Maria's, Crabtrap Seafood, Waffle House, **lodging:** GuestHouse Inn, Ramada Ltd

**220b a** FL 64, to Zolfo Springs, Bradenton, **E** Lake Manatee SRA, **W gas:** BP/dsl, Citgo/dsl/24hr, RaceTrac, Shell/Circle K/dsl, **food:** Burger King, Cracker Barrel, Dunkin Donuts, Friendly's, KFC/LJ Silver, McDonald's, Sonny's BBQ, Subway, Waffle House, Wendy's, **lodging:** Budget Inn, Comfort Inn, Day's Inn, Econolodge, Holiday Inn Express, Motel 6, **other:** H HOSPITAL, Dream RV Ctr, Encore RV Resort (1mi), Harley-Davidson, Walmart SuperCtr

**217b a** FL 70, to Arcadia, **E gas:** Hess/Blimpie/Godfather's/dsl/24hr, **food:** Crisper's Salads, **other:** Goodyear/auto, Sweetbay Foods, **W gas:** BP/dsl/LP, Circle K, 7-11/dsl, Shell/Circle K, Applebee's, Arby's, Bob Evans, Chick-fil-A, Hungry Howie's, LJ Silver, McDonald's, Papa John's, Starbucks, Subway, Taco Bell, **other:** Beall's, CVS Drug, Lowe's Whse, Macy's, Publix, Tire Kingdom, Tires+, HorseShoe RV Park, Pleasant Lake RV Resort, Publix, vet

**S A R A S O T A**

**213** University Parkway, to Sarasota, **E gas:** Mobil/dsl, **food:** Broken Egg Rest., Chili's, Monty's Pizza, Pizza Hut, **lodging:** Fairfield Inn, Holiday Inn, **other:** GNC, Publix, Walgreens, **W food:** Altanta Bread, Bellacino's, BoneFish Grill, Carrabba's, Five Guys Burgers, Moe's SW Grill, Ruby Tuesday, Starbucks, Stonewood Grill, Wendy's, **lodging:** Comfort Suites, **other:** Beall's, Best Buy, BJ's Whse, Circuit City, CVS Drug, Fresh Mkt Foods, Home Depot, Kohl's, Michael's, Ringling Museum, Staples, Super Target

**210** FL 780, Fruitville Rd, Sarasota, **1 mi E other:** Sun'n Fun RV Park (1mi), **W gas:** BP/dsl/LP, Mobil/dsl, Race-Trac, **food:** Shell, Applebee's, Bob Evans, Burger King, Checker's, Chick-fil-A, Dunkin Donuts, Rest, KFC, Longhorn Steaks, McDonald's, Perkins, Quizno's, Subway, Taco Bell, Wings'n Weenies, **lodging:** AmericInn, Homewood Suites (2mi), **other:** Advance Parts, $Tree,

**S A R A S O T A**

**210** Continued
Curves, CVS Drug, GNC, Lowe's Whse, Publix, Radio Shack, Sam's Club, Target, Winn-Dixie

**207** FL 758, Sarasota, **W gas:** BP, Shell/Subway, **food:** Arby's, Chili's, Bella Cucina Italian, Grand China Buffet, Grand China, Italian Buffet, MadFish Grill, McDonald's, Panera Bread, Pizza Hut, Sarasota Alehouse, Steak'n Shake, Sugar&Spice, Taco Bell, Tuesday Morning, **lodging:** Hampton Inn, **other:** H HOSPITAL, Beall's, $Tree, Goodyear/auto, Home Depot, Publix, Selby Botanical Gardens (8mi), Tuesday Morning, Walgreens, Walmart, vet

**205** FL 72, to Arcadia, Sarasota, **E** Myakka River SP (9mi), **W gas:** BP/dsl, Exxon/dsl, Mobil, 7-11/dsl, **food:** Applebee's, Burger King, Chick-fil-A, Dunkin Donuts, Firehouse Subs, Gecko's Grill, McDonald's, Quizno's, Starbucks, Subway, Waffle House, Wendy's, Wings & Weenies, **lodging:** Comfort Inn, Country Inn & Suites, Days Inn, **other:** Beall's, BMW, CVS Drug, Jaguar, Land Rover, Lexus, Mercedes, Publix, Tire Kingdom, USPO, Walgreens, Windward Isle RV Park, vet

**200** FL 681 S (from sb), to Venice, Osprey, Gulf Bchs

**195** Laurel Rd, Nokomis, **E gas:** BP/dsl, **other:** Stay'n Play RV Park (1mi), USPO, **W other:** Encore RV Park (2mi), Scherer SP (6mi)

**V E N I C E**

**193** Jaracanda Blvd, Venice, **W gas:** Citgo/Subway/dsl/24hr, Hess/Blimpie/Godfather's/dsl, RaceTrac, **food:** Cracker Barrel, McDonald's, Ping's Chinese, Waffle House, **lodging:** Best Western, Holiday Inn Express, **other:** H HOSPITAL, CVS Drug, Publix

**191** rd 777, Venice Rd, to Inglewood, **W other:** Encore RV Park (3mi), Venice Campground (1mi), to Myakka SF (9mi)

**182** Sumter Blvd, to North Port, **2mi W gas:** Hess/Quizno's, **other:** Publix

**179** Toledo Blade Blvd, North Port, **1-2 mi W gas:** Shell, **food:** Quizno's, **other:** Publix

**170** rd 769, to Arcadia, Port Charlotte, **E gas:** Murphy USA, RaceTrac, 7-11/dsl, **food:** Applebees, **lodging:** Hampton Inn, Holiday Inn Express, **other:** Lettuce Lake Camping (7mi), Riverside Camping (5mi), Walmart SuperCtr, **W gas:** Hess/dsl, Chevron/dsl, 7-11/Subway/DQ/dsl, Shell/Circle K, **food:** Brick House Pizza, Burger King, Cracker Barrel, Domino's, DQ, McDonald's, Quizno's, Taco Bell/Pizza Hut, Waffle House, Wendy's, **lodging:** Country Inn & Suites, La Quinta, **other:** H HOSPITAL,

N ↕ S

FL

FT MYERS

CAPE CORAL

## INTERSTATE 75 CONT'D

**170** Continued
Ace Hardware, Advance Parts, Beall's, Curves, CVS Drug, $General, GNC, Publix, USPO, Walgreens, Winn-Dixie

**167** rd 776, Port Charlotte

**164** US 17, Punta Gorda, Arcadia, **E gas:** Chevron/dsl, RaceWay, Shell/dsl/24hr, **food:** King House Chinese, Subway, **other:** $General, KOA (2mi), Winn-Dixie, **W gas:** Shell/Circle K, **food:** Fisherman's Village Rest. (2mi), **lodging:** Best Western (2mi), **other:** H HOSPITAL, vet

**161** FL 768, Punta Gorda, **E rest area both lanes, full ⠿ facilities, ☏, vending, ▥ litter barrels, petwalk, 24hr security,** Waters Edge RV Park (2mi), **W gas:** BP/DQ/Subway/dsl, Murphy USA, Pilot/Arby's/dsl/scales/24hr, Sunoco/Quizno's, **food:** Burger King, McDonald's, Paradise Cafe, Pizza Hut, Waffle House, Wendy's, **lodging:** Day's Inn, Motel 6, **other:** Encore RV Park (2mi), Walmart SuperCtr

**160mm** weigh sta both lanes

**158** rd 762, **E** Babcock-Wells Wildlife Mgt Area, **W** Tamiami RV Camping (12mi)

**143** FL 78, to Cape Coral, N Ft Myers, **E gas:** Marathon/dsl, **W gas:** RaceTrac/dsl/24hr, **food:** AZ Pizza, **lodging:** Encore RV Camping

**141** FL 80, Palm Bch Blvd, Ft Myers, **E gas:** Citgo, Sunoco, Cracker Barrel, Waffle House, **lodging:** Comfort Inn, ValuePlace, **W gas:** Citgo, Hess/dsl, 7-11, **food:** Hardee's, Juicy Lucy's Burgers, Papa John's, Perkins, Pizza Hut, Sonny's BBQ, Subway, Taco Bell, **other:** Beall's, BigLots, CVS Drug, $General, Martin's Tire/auto, North Trail RV Ctr, Publix, Radio Shack

**139** Luckett Rd, Ft Myers, **E other:** Cypress Woods RV Resort, Mark's RV Ctr, **W gas:** Pilot/Subway/dsl/scales/24hr/@, **other:** Camping World RV Service/supplies, Lazy J's RV Park

**138** FL 82, to Lehigh Acres, Ft Myers, **E food:** Subway, **W gas:** Citgo/dsl, Sunoco

**136** FL 884, Colonial Blvd, Ft Myers, **E lodging:** Candlewood Suites, **food:** Five Guys Burgers, Starbucks, **other:** Best Buy, Books-A-Million, Home Depot, PetCo, Ross, Staples, Target, **W gas:** BP, Marathon/Subway, Murphy USA, Shell/Circle K/dsl, **food:** Applebees, Bob Evans, Chick-fil-A, Golden Corral, McDonald's, Steak'n Shake, **other:** H HOSPITAL, Beall's, Honda, Kohl's, Lowe's Whse, Tire Choice/auto, Walmart SuperCtr

**131** Daniels Pkwy, to Cape Coral, **E rest area both lanes, full ⠿facilities, ☏, vending, ▥ litter barrels, petwalk, 24hr security, gas:** BP/Subway/dsl, **food:** Cracker Barrel, Starbucks, **lodging:** AmericInn, Comfort Inn, WynStar Inn, airport, **W gas:** Chevron/dsl, Hess/Krispy Kreme/dsl, RaceTrac/24hr, 7-11/24hr, Shell/Circle K/24hr, **food:** Arby's, Bella Rica Italian, Burger King, DQ, Denny's, J. Daniels Grill, McDonald's, New China, Taco Bell, Uno Pizzaria, Waffle House, Wendy's, **lodging:** Best Western, Comfort Suites, Country Inn Suites, Econolodge, Hampton Inn, La Quinta, SpringHill Suites, **other:** H HOSPITAL, American RV Ctr, CVS Drug, Publix, Tire Choice/auto

ESTERO

NAPLES

**128** Alico Rd, San Carlos Park, **E gas:** 7-11, **food:** Chick-fil-A, Firepit Grill, Gators Grill, Miller's Alehouse, McDonald's, Moe's SW Grill, Outback Steaks, Red Robin, **lodging:** Courtyard, Hilton Garden, Holiday Inn, Homewood Suites, Residence Inn, **other:** Bass Pro Shop, Belk, Best Buy, Borders, Costco/gas, $Tree, JC Penney, JoAnn, Marshall's, PetCo, Ross, Staples, Super Target, **W gas:** Hess/Dunkin Donuts/dsl, Site/Subway/dsl

**123** rd 850, Corkscrew Rd, Estero, **E gas:** BP/dsl, Chevron/dsl, **food:** McDonald's, Perkins, Subway, **other:** CVS Drug, Germaine Arena, Johnson Tire/auto, Miramar Outlet/famous brands, Publix, **W gas:** 7-11, Shell, Sunoco/Subway/Dunkin Donuts, **food:** Applebee's, Arby's, Arizona Pizza, Ruby Tuesday, **lodging:** Embassy Suites, Hampton Inn, **other:** Chevrolet, Lowe's Whse, Tire Choice/auto, Koreshan St HS (2mi), Woodsmoke RV Park (4mi)

**116** Bonita Bch Rd, Bonita Springs, **E gas:** Chevron/dsl, Mobil, **other:** Publix, Tire Choice, **W gas:** BP/McDonald's/24hr, Hess/Blimpie/dsl/24hr, **food:** Subway, Waffle House, **lodging:** Best Western, **other:** Advance Parts, Albertson's/gas, CVS Drug, Home Depot, Imperial Bonita RV Park, Publix, Tire Choice/auto, Walgreens

**111** rd 846, Immokalee Rd, Naples Park, **E gas:** 7-11, **food:** Bob Evans, Chili's, Panera Bread, Pizza Hut, Starbucks, **lodging:** Hampton Inn, **other:** Staples, Super Target, World Mkt, **W gas:** Shell/Circle K/dsl, **food:** CiCi's Pizza, Jasons Deli, McDonald's, **other:** H HOSPITAL, Publix, TrueValue, Walmart SuperCtr, to Delnor-Wiggins SP

**107** rd 896, Pinebridge Rd, Naples, **E gas:** BP/McDonald's/dsl/24hr, **food:** China Garden, Clubhouse Cafe, Coldstone Creamery, Giovanni Ristorante, Starbucks, Subway, **other:** H HOSPITAL, Publix, Walgreens, vet, **W gas:** Chevron/dsl24hr, RaceTrac, Shell/dsl/24hr, **food:** Bajio Grill, Burger King, Figaro's Pizza, Five Guys Burgers, Hooters, IHOP, Perkins, Roman Oven, Waffle House, **lodging:** Best Western, Hawthorn Suites, Spinnaker Inn, **other:** Goodyear/auto, Harley-Davidson, Johnson Tire/auto, Nissan, vet

**105** rd 886, to Golden Gate Pkwy, Golden Gate, **E food:** Subway, **W gas:** to airport, zoo

**101** rd 951, to FL 84, to Naples, **E gas:** BP/Subway, **lodging:** Fairfield Inn, Springhill Suites, **W gas:** BP/Cafe/dsl, Circle K, Shell/dsl/24hr, **food:** Cracker Barrel, McDonald's, Mr V's, Subway, Taco Bell, Waffle House, **lodging:** Comfort Inn, Holiday Inn Express, La Quinta, Super 8, **other:** Club Naples RV Ctr, Endless Summer RV Park (3mi), KOA

**100mm** toll plaza from eb

**80** FL 29, to Everglade City, Immokalee, **W other:** Big Cypress NR, Everglades NP, Smallwoods Store

**71mm** Big Cypress Nat Preserve, hiking, no security

**63mm** **W rest area both lanes, full ⠿ facilities, ☏, vending, ▥ litter barrels, petwalk, 24hr security**

**49** Gov't Rd, Snake Rd, Big Cypress Indian Reservation, **E gas:** Miccosukee Service Plaza/deli/dsl, **other:** museum, swamp safari

**41mm** rec area eb, ▥ litter barrels

## INTERSTATE 75 CONT'D

**N ↕ S**

**WESTON · MIAMI · MIAMI**

| | |
|---|---|
| 38mm | rec area wb, 🏕, litter barrels |
| 35mm | W rest area both lanes, full ♿ facilities, ☏, vending, 🏕, litter barrels, petwalk, 24hr security |
| 32mm | rec area both lanes, 🏕, litter barrels |
| 26mm | toll plaza wb, motorist callboxes begin/end |
| 23 | Us 27, FL 25ddx Miami, South Bay |
| 22 | NW 196th, Glades Pkwy, W other: Publix, same as 21 |
| 21 | FL 84 W (from nb), Indian Trace, W gas: Chevron (1mi), Citgo/dsl, food: Mamma Nostra, Papa John's |
| 19 | I-595 E, FL 869 (toll), Sawgrass Expswy |
| 15 | Royal Palm Blvd, Weston, Bonaventure, W gas: Exxon, Mobil, food: Flanigan's Rest, Iltoscano Rest., La Granja, Lucille's Cafe, Offerdahl's Grill, Pollo Tropical, Ristorante, Quizno's, Subway, The Catch Rest., Wendy's, lodging: Courtyard, Hawthorn Suites, Residence Inn, other: Ⓗ HOSPITAL, Tires+, USPO |
| 13b a | Griffin Rd, E gas: Shell/dsl, food: Burger King, Outback Steaks, Waffle House/24hr, other: Goodyear/auto, Infiniti, Publix, W gas: 7-11, Tom Thumb/gas, food: Chili's, Mayer's Rest., McDonald's, Ultimate Burrito, other: Home Depot, Honda, Hyundai, Nissan/Volvo, Office Depot, Publix, Toyota/Scion, Walgreens |
| 11b a | Sheridan St, E gas: Chevron, food: Cracker Barrel, Wendy's, lodging: Hampton Inn, Holiday Inn Express, other: Ⓗ HOSPITAL (3mi), BMW, Lincoln/Mercury, W gas: Shell, food: Applebees, Bistro 555, China One, Coldstone Creamery, El Mariachi, Little Caesars, McDonald's, Original Pancake House, Roasters'n Toasters, Rotelli Cafe, Starbucks, Subway, TGIFriday, Original Pancake House, other: GNC, Lowe's Whse, Publix, Walgreens |
| 9b a | FL 820, Pine Blvd, Hollywood Blvd, E gas: BP, Shell, food: Boston Mkt, Brio Italian, Brimstone Woodfire Grill, Chili's, Jason's Deli, Latin-American Grill, Macaroni Grill, McDonald's, Starbucks, Village Tavern, Wendys, other: Barnes&Noble, BJ's Whse/gas, Dodge, JC Penney, Macy's, Mercedes, Walgreens, USPO, W gas: BP, Exxon, Shell, food: KFC/Taco Bell, Las Vegas Cuban, McDonald's, Panda Express, Quizno's, Starbucks, Sweet Tomatoes, other: Acura, Advance Parts, Buick, Costco/gas, Lexus, Pontiac/GMC, Publix, Staples, Tires+, USPO, Walgreens, Winn-Dixie |
| 7b a | Miramar Pkwy, E gas: Chevron, food: Brushetta Italian, Dunkin Donuts, La Carreta, McDonald's, Pollo Tropical, Sal's Italian, Subway, Wendy's, lodging: Courtyard, Hilton Garden, Residence Inn, Wingate Inn, other: Publix, Walgreens, USPO, W gas: Shell, food: Chick-fil-A, Chili's, McDonald's, Panera Bread, Quizno's, Starbucks, other: Ⓗ HOSPITAL, CVS Drug, Home Depot, Marshall's, Office Depot, Ross, SuperTarget, Walgreens, Winn-Dixie |
| 5 | to FL 821 (from sb), FL TPK (toll) |
| 4 | FL 860, NW 186th, Miami Gardens Dr, E gas: BP/24hr, Chevron/24hr, food: Carrabba's, McDonald's, Subway, other: CVS Drug, GNC, Publix/deli, Sedenos Foods |
| 2 | NW 138th, Graham Dairy Rd, W gas: Mobil/dsl, Shell, food: China Casa, Little Caesars, McDonald's, Starbucks, Subway, Wendy's, other: Ⓗ HOSPITAL, GNC, Publix, Walgreens |
| 1b a | I-75 begins/ends on FL 826, Palmetto Expswy, multiple services on FL 826. |

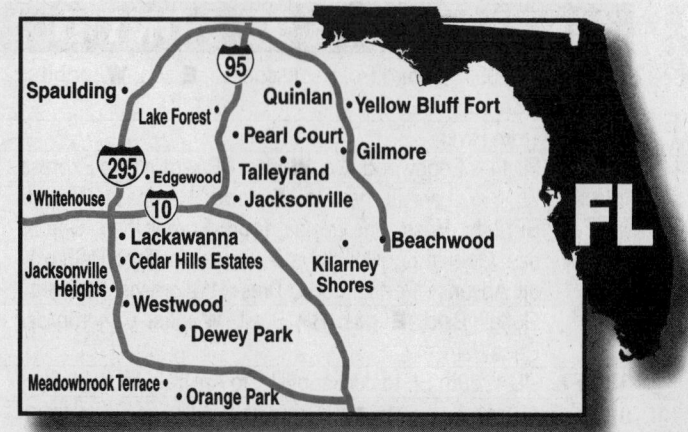

## INTERSTATE 95

**N ↕ S**

**JACKSONVILLE**

| Exit # | Services |
|---|---|
| 382mm | Florida/Georgia state line, St Marys River, motorist callboxes begin/end. |
| 381mm | inspection sta both lanes |
| 380 | US 17, to Yulee, Kingsland, E Osprey RV Park, W gas: Shell/24hr, lodging: Day's Inn |
| 378mm | Welcome Ctr sb, full ♿ facilities, ☏, vending, 🏕, litter barrels, petwalk, 24hr security |
| 376mm | weigh sta both lanes |
| 373 | FL 200, FL A1A, to Yulee, Callahan, Fernandina Bch, E gas: Flash/Krystal, Sunoco, food: Burger King, KFC/Pizza Hut, DQ, McDonald's, Wendy's, lodging: Comfort Inn, Country Inn&Suites, Hampton Inn (3mi), Nassau Holiday Motel (3mi), other: Lofton Creek Camping (3mi), to Ft Clinch SP (16mi), W gas: BP/Domino's/Subway/dsl, Exxon/dsl |
| 366 | Pecan Park Rd, W Flea&Farmer's Mkt, Pecan Park RV Camping |
| 363b a | Duval Rd, E gas: Mobil, food: Arby's, Boston's, Chick-fil-A, Chili's, Coldstone Creamery, Cracker Barrel, 5 Guys Burgers, Green Papaya, Hardee's, Jasmine's Bistro, McDonald's, Panda Express, Panera Bread, Red Lobster, Starbucks, Sticky Fingers, other: Best Buy, Discount Tire, $Tree, Gander Mtn, GNC, Goodyear/auto, Lowes Whse, Michael's, Old Navy, PetsMart, Ross, Walmart SuperCtr, W gas: BP, Exxon, Shell/dsl, Sunoco/Subway, food: Denny's, Longhorn Steaks, Millhouse Steaks, Ruby Tuesday, Waffle House, Wendy's, Zaxby's, lodging: Airport Inn, Best Western, Comfort Suites, Country Hearth Inn, Fairfield Inn, Hampton Inn, Hilton Garden, Holiday Inn, Microtel, Red Roof Inn, Residence Inn, Rodeway Inn, Springhill Suites, Travelodge, Wingate Inn, other: RV Ctr |
| 362b a | I-295 S, FL 9A, to Blount Island, Jacksonville |
| 360 | FL 104, Dunn Ave, Busch Dr, E gas: Gate/dsl, food: Applebee's, Hardee's, Waffle House, lodging: Executive Inn, other: Sam's Club/gas, USPO, W gas: BP, Hess, Shell, food: Arby's, Bono's BBQ, Burger King, Capt D's, Chan's Chinese, Checker's, CiCi's, KFC, Krystal, McDonald's, New Century Buffet, New China, Pizza Hut, Popeye's, Shoney's, Sonny's BBQ, Subway, Taco Bell, Wendy's, lodging: Best Value Inn, Best Western, La Quinta, Motel 6, other: Aamco, Advance Parts, BigLots, CVS Drug, $Tree, Family$, Office Depot, PepBoys, Publix, Radio Shack, Tire Kingdom, Tires+, Walgreens |

## INTERSTATE 95 CONT'D

**N ↑ S**

**JACKSONVILLE**

**358b a** FL 105, Broward Rd, Heckscher Dr, E zoo, W **lodging:** USA Inn

**357mm** Trout River

**357** FL 111, Edgewood Ave, W **gas:** BP/repair, Gas Express

**356b a** FL 115, Lem Turner Rd, E **food:** Hardee's, W **gas:** BP/24hr, Hess, Shell/repair, **food:** Burger King, Checker's, Golden EggRoll, Krystal, Popeye's, Taco Bell, **other:** Advance Parts, Foods, Tires+, Walgreens, flea mkt

**355** Golfair Blvd, E **gas:** BP, Shell, W **gas:** Chevron/dsl, RaceWay

**354b a** US 1, 20th St, to Jacksonville, to AmTrak, MLK Pkwy

**353d** FL 114, to 8th St, E **food:** McDonald's, **other:** H HOSPITAL, Walgreens

**353c** US 23 N, Kings Rd, downtown

**353b** US 90A, Union St, Sports Complex, downtown

**353a** Church St, Myrtle Ave, Forsythe St, downtown

**352c** Monroe St (from nb), downtown

**352b a** Myrtle Ave (from nb), downtown

**351d** Stockton St, H HOSPITAL, downtown

**351c** Margaret St, downtown

**351b** I-10 W, to Tallahassee

**351a** Park St, College St, H HOSPITAL, to downtown

**351mm** St Johns River

**350b** FL 13, San Marco Blvd, E H HOSPITAL,

**350a** Prudential Dr, Main St, Riverside Ave (from nb), to downtown, E **gas:** BP, **lodging:** Extended Stay America, Hampton Inn, Wyndham, W **food:** Panera Bread, **lodging:** Hilton Garden

**349** US 90 E (from sb), to beaches, downtown, W **lodging:** Super 8

**348** US 1 S (from sb), Philips Hwy, W **lodging:** Scottish Inn, Super 8, **other:** Volvo

**347** US 1A, FL 126, Emerson St, E **gas:** Chevron, Shell, **food:** Hot Wok, **other:** Advance Parts, Family$, O'Reilly Parts, W **gas:** BP/dsl, Gate/dsl, Hess/dsl, **food:** McDonald's, Taco Bell, **lodging:** Emerson Inn, **other:** Chevrolet, Goodyear/auto

**346b a** FL 109, University Blvd, E **gas:** BP, Exxon/dsl, Hess/dsl, Shell, **food:** Capt D's, Checkers, DQ, El Potro Mexican, Family$, Firehouse Subs, Happy Garden Chinese, Huddle House, Korean BBQ, Krystal, Mi Tierra, Papa John's, Pizza Hut, Subway, Ying's Chinese, **other:** H HOSPITAL, Ace Hardware, CVS Drug, Firestone/auto, NAPA, Tire Kingdom, Tires+, Sun Tire, Winn-Dixie, W **gas:** BP/dsl, Chevron, RaceTrac, **food:** Arby's, Burger King, Dunkin Donuts/Baskin Robbins, KFC, McDonald's, Sonny's BBQ, Taco Bell, Wendy's, **lodging:** Comfort Lodge, Day's Inn, Ramada Inn, **other:** U-Haul, auto repair

**345** FL 109, University Blvd (from nb), E **gas:** Chevron, Gate/dsl/24hr, Hess/Blimpie/Godfather's Pizza/dsl, **food:** Bono's BBQ, Schnitzel House, **other:** H HOSPITAL

**344** FL 202, Butler Blvd, E **gas:** Gate, **food:** Dave&Buster's, **lodging:** Best Western, Candlewood Suites, Econolodge, Holiday Inn Express, Homestead Suites, Howard Johnson, Marriott, Radisson, **other:** H HOSPITAL, USPO, W **gas:** BP/dsl, Shell, **food:** Applebee's, Chick-fil-A, Cracker Barrel, Dunkin Donuts, Hardee's, Latin Cuisine, McDonald's, Quizno's, Sonic, Starbucks, Waffle House,

**ST AUGUSTINE**

**344** Continued

Wendy's, Whataburger/24hr, Zaxby's, **lodging:** Courtyard, Extended Stay America, Fairfield Inn, Jameson Inn, La Quinta, Microtel, Red Roof Inn, Wingate Inn

**341** FL 152, Baymeadows Rd, E **gas:** BP/dsl, Gate/dsl, Shell/dsl, **food:** Arby's, Buffalo Wild Wings, Chili's, Hardee's, Omaha Steaks, Quizno's, Starbucks, Waffle House, **lodging:** Comfort Suites, Embassy Suites, Holiday Inn, HomeStead Suites, **other:** Publix, Tires+, Winn-Dixie, W **gas:** Exxon/dsl, Gate, Kangaroo, **food:** Burger King, Chicago Pizzaria, Denny's, Firehouse Subs, Gator's Seafood, IHOP, KFC, Larry's Subs, McDonald's, Red Chilies, Red Lobster, Starbucks, Steak-Out, Taco Bell, Wendy's, Woody's BBQ, **lodging:** Best Inn, Homewood Suites, La Quinta, Quality Inn, Residence Inn, Sheraton, Studio 6, Sun Suites, **other:** BJ's Whse/gas, Discount Tire, $Tree, Harley-Davidson, Lowe's Whse, Office Depot

**340** FL 115, Southside Blvd (from nb), E on FL 115...**gas:** Kangaroo/dsl, **food:** Five Guys Burgers, Longhorn Steaks, **other:** Borders, Circuit City, Home Depot, Michael's, PetsMart, Target, same as 339

**339** US 1, Philips Hwy, E **gas:** Kangaroo/dsl, **food:** Arby's, Bono's BBQ, Buca Italian, Burger King, Chick-fil-A, McDonald's, Olive Garden, Ruby Tuesday, Starbucks, Taco Bell, Waffle House, **other:** Belk, Best Buy, Chevrolet, Dillard's, Ford, JC Penney, Kia, Sears/auto, Tire Kingdom, Toyota, mall, W **gas:** BP/dsl, **food:** Steak&Shake

**337** I-295 N, to rd 9a, Orange Park, Jax Beaches

**335** Old St Augustine Rd, E **gas:** Chevron, Gate/dsl, Shell, **food:** Applebees, McDonald's, Panera Bread, Starbucks, **lodging:** Courtyard, Hampton Inn, **other:** H HOSPITAL, Walgreens, Kohl's, Publix

**331mm** rest area both lanes, full ♿ facilities, 📞 vending, 🍴, litter barrels, petwalk, 24hr security

**329** rd 210, E **gas:** Pilot/McDonald's/dsl/scales/24hr, Sunoco/fruit, TA/Shell/Subway/dsl/rest./scales/@, **food:** Waffle House, W **gas:** BP/Subway/dsl, Mobil/dsl, Shell, **food:** Burger King, Cherry's Grill, China Wok, Domino's, Firehouse Subs, Jenk's Pizza, Larry's Subs, Starbucks, Subway, Tropical Smoothie, **other:** CVS Drug, Winn-Dixie, USPO, fireworks

**323** International Golf Pkwy, E **gas:** BP/Sbarro's/dsl, Shell/Subway/dsl, **lodging:** Comfort Suites, W **food:** Cino's Pizza, King Wok, Village Grill/Subs, **lodging:** Renaissance Resort, **other:** Publix, World Golf Village, vet

**318** FL 16, Green Cove Sprgs, St Augustine, E **gas:** BP/DQ, Gate/dsl/fruit, Kangaroo/dsl, Shell, **food:** Burger King, McDonald's, Huddle House, Subway, **lodging:** Comfort Inn, Econolodge, Ford, Quality Inn, **other:** Camping World RV Ctr, Cadillac, Gander Mtn, Lincoln/Mercury, Prime Outlets, W **gas:** Exxon, RaceTrac, **food:** Cracker Barrel, Denny's, IHOP, KFC, Ruby Tuesday, Shoney's, Sonny's BBQ, Taco Bell, Wendy's, **lodging:** Best Western, Day's Inn, Hampton Inn, Ramada Ltd, Scottish Inn, Super 8, Wingate Inn, **other:** Harley-Davidson, St Augustine Premium Outlets Ctr, Premium Outlets/Famous Brands, RV camping, funpark

**311** FL 207, St Augustine, E **gas:** BP/dsl, Chevron/24hr, Hess/Subway/dsl, Indian River Fruit/gas, **other:** H HOSPITAL, Indian Forest RV Park (2mi), KOA (7mi), St

## INTERSTATE 95 CONT'D

**N ↑ S**

**P A L M  C O A S T**

**323** Continued
Johns RV Park, flea mkt, to Anastasia SP, fruit/fireworks, **W gas:** Mobil/dsl, **lodging:** Quality Inn

**305** FL 206, to Hastings, Crescent Beach, **E gas:** ⊕**FLYING J**/Country Mkt/dsl/scales/LP/24hr, **other:** Gore RV Ctr, to Ft Matanzas NM, truck repair

**302mm** rest areas both lanes, full ♿ facilities, 🚽, vending, 🍽 litter barrels, petwalk, 24hr security

**298** US 1, to St Augustine, **E gas:** BP/dsl, Indian River Fruit/gas, Sunoco, **other:** to Faver-Dykes SP, **W gas:** Mobil/DQ/dsl, Sunrise/gas, **food:** Waffle House

**289** to FL A1A (toll br), to Palm Coast, **E gas:** Kangaroo/dsl, RaceTrac, Shell, **food:** Beef o' Brady's, Cracker Barrel, Denny's, Grand Hong Kong, KFC, Lucky Buffet, Chinese, McDonald's, Pizza Hut, Starbucks, Taco Bell, Wendy's, **lodging:** Best Western, Courtyard, Microtel, Sleep Inn, **other:** CVS Drug, Publix, Staples, Walgreens, **W gas:** Chevron, Shell, Kangaroo, **food:** Baskin-Robbins/Dunkin Donuts, Bob Evans, Brusters, Golden Corral, Honey Baked Ham, Outback Steaks, Perkins, Ruby Tuesday, Sonny's BBQ, Steak'n Shake/24hr, Taco Bell, **other:** Advance Parts, Beall's, Belk, CVS Drug, Ford, Home Depot, Lowe's Whse, Tire Kingdom, Walgreens, Walmart SuperCtr, Winn-Dixie, USPO

**286mm** weigh sta both lanes, 🚽

**284** FL 100, to Bunnell, Flagler Beach, **E gas:** Chevron/dsl/24hr, Citgo, Shell, **food:** Burger King, Domino's, McDonald's, Oriental Garden, Subway, Woody's BBQ, **lodging:** Hampton Inn, Holiday Inn Express, **other:** Ace Hardware, Russell Stover's, Winn-Dixie, vet, **W gas:** BP/dsl, **lodging:** Hilton Garden, **other:** Ⓗ HOSPITAL, Chevrolet, Chrysler/Dodge/Jeep

**278** Old Dixie Hwy, **E gas:** 7-11, **other:** Publix, Bulow RV Park (3mi), to Tomoka SP, **W gas:** BP/dsl, **food:** Luigi's Pizza, Rodeo Mexican, **lodging:** Country Hearth Inn, **other:** Holiday Travel Park

**273** US 1, **E gas:** Chevron, Mobil/Wendy's/dsl, RaceTrac, **food:** McDonald's, Saddle Jack's Grill, Waffle House, **lodging:** Comfort Suites, Econolodge, **other:** fruit/fireworks, RV Ctr, **W gas:** Exxon/Burger King, Loves/Arby's/dsl/scales/24hr, **food:** DQ, Houligan's, **lodging:** Days Inn, Daytona Hotel, Ormond Inn, Scottish Inn, Super 8, **other:** Encore RV Park, Harley-Davidson

**268** FL 40, Ormond Beach, **E gas:** Chevron/dsl, Shell, **food:** Applebee's, Boston Mkt, Chili's, Chick-fil-A, Denny's/24hr, Dustin's BBQ, Krispy Kreme, Papa John's, Quizno's, Royal Dynasty, Starbucks, Steak'n Shake, Subway, Taco Bell, Takeya Japanese, Waffle House, Wendy's, Wok&Roll, **lodging:** Sleep Inn, **other:** Ⓗ HOSPITAL, Beall's, Discount Tire, K-Mart, Lowe's Whse, Publix, Ross, Pomok SP, USPO, vet, Walmart SuperCtr, **W gas:** BP, Mobil/dsl, 7-11/gas, Texaco, **food:** Cracker Barrel, Domino's, Legends Grill, McDonald's, **lodging:** Hampton Inn, Jameson Inn, **other:** Walgreens

**O R M O N D  B E A C H**

**265** LPGA Blvd, Holly Hill, Daytona Beach, **E gas:** 7-11, Shell/dsl, **food:** Wendy's, Subway (2mi), **other:** CVS Drug, **W lodging:** Hampton Inn, **other:** Chrysler/Dodge, Ford, Kia, Mazda, Nissan

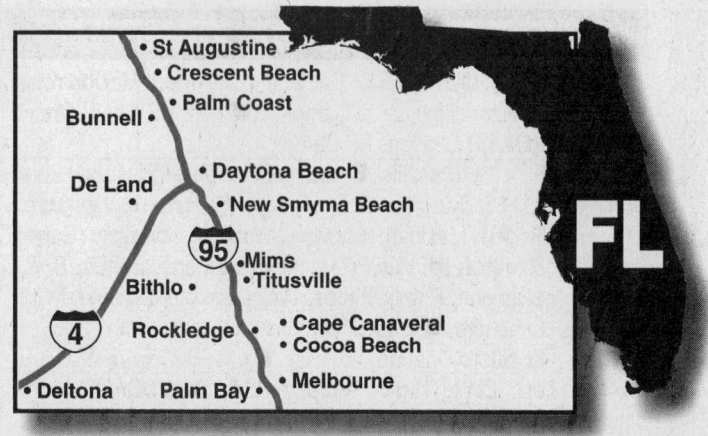

**D A Y T O N A  B E A C H**

**261b a** US 92, to DeLand, Daytona Bch, **E gas:** Hess/Blimpie/dsl, Mobil, RaceWay/24hr, 7-11/gas, Shell/dsl, **food:** Bob Evans, Buca Italian, Burger King, Cancun Rest., Carrabba's, Checker's, Chick-fil-A, Chilli's, China Buffet, Chipotle Mexican, Cracker Barrel, Daytona Ale House, Denny's, Fazoli's, Friendly's, Honey Baked Ham, Hooters, Jimmy John's, KFC, Krystal, Longhorn Steaks, McDonald's, Olive Garden, Panera Bread, Picadilly, Pizzaria Uno, Quizno's, Red Lobster, Ruby Tuesday, Sonny's BBQ, Smoothie King, Sonny's BBQ, Sorrento's, Subway, Taco Bell, Tijuana Flats, Tuesday Morning, Waffle House, Winghouse, **lodging:** Comfort Suites, Courtyard, Hampton Inn, Hilton Garden, Holiday Inn Express, Homewood Suites, La Quinta, Quality Inn, Ramada Inn, Residence Inn, **other:** Ⓗ HOSPITAL, Barnes&Noble, Beall's, Best Buy, Circuit City, Dillard's, Firestone/auto, Home Depot, JC Penney, Jo-Anne Fabrics, K-Mart, Macy's, Marshall's, Michael's, Office Depot, Old Navy, PepBoys, PetCo, PestMart, Ross, Sears/auto, Staples, SteinMart, Target, TJMaxx, World Mkt, mall, to Daytona Racetrack, **W gas:** BP/dsl, Sunoco, **food:** IHOP, McDonald's, **lodging:** Day's Inn, Super 8, **other:** KOA, RV camping, flea mkt

**260b a** I-4, to Orlando, FL 400 E, to S Daytona, **E gas:** Chevron/dsl

**256** FL 421, to Port Orange, **E gas:** BP, Circle K/gas, Shell, **food:** Applebee's, Bob Evans, Chick-fil-A, Chili's, Denny's/24hr, Dustin's BBQ, Firehouse Subs, Marble Slab Creamery, Monterey Grill, Panera Bread, Papa John's, Quizno's, Smoothie King, Sonny's BBQ, Tijuana Flats, Tropical Smoothie, **lodging:** Country Inn & Suites, Day's Inn, La Quinta, **other:** Holiday Camp RV Park, Home Depot, Lowe's Whse, Super Target, Walgreens, Walmart SuperCtr (1mi), vet, **W gas:** 7-11, Hess, Texaco, **food:** McDonald's, Subway, Wendy's, **other:** Kohls, Publix, Walgreens

**249b a** FL 44, to De Land, New Smyrna Beach, **E gas:** Shell/dsl/fruit, **other:** New Smyrna RV Camp (3mi), **W gas:** Chevron/dsl

**244** FL 442, to Edgewater, **E gas:** BP/dsl/24hr, **other:** truck repair

**231** rd 5A, Scottsmoor, **E gas:** BP/Stuckey's/dsl, **other:** Crystal Lake RV Park

**227mm** rest area sb, full ♿ facilities, 🚽, vending, 🍽 litter barrels, petwalk, 24hr security

**225mm** rest area nb, full ♿ facilities, 🚽, vending, 🍽 litter barrels, petwalk, 24hr security

## INTERSTATE 95 CONT'D

**223** FL 46, Mims, **E** gas: Chevron (2mi), food: McDonald's, other: Willow Lakes Camping, **W** gas: BP, Shell, other: KOA/LP, Seasons RV Camp

**220** FL 406, Titusville, **E** gas: BP/dsl, Shell/dsl, food: Beef 'O' Brady's, 1st Wok, Kelsey's Pizzaria, McDonald's, Rodeo Mexican, Subway, Wendy's, lodging: Super 8, other: H HOSPITAL, Advance Parts, Beall's, Belk, $General, Publix, Tires+, Walgreens, to Canaveral Nt'l Seashore, **W** gas: Chevron/dsl

**215** FL 50, to Orlando, Titusville, **E** gas: BP/KFC/Pizza Hut/dsl, Circle K/gas, Murphy USA, Shell/DQ/dsl, food: Burger King, Denny's, Durango Steaks, McDonald's, Panda Express, Quizno's, Sonny's BBQ, Taco Bell, Waffle House, Wendy's, Whistle Jct, lodging: Best Western, Ramada Inn, other: Aldi Foods, Ford/Mercury, GNC, Hame Depot, Lowe's Whse, PetCo, Radio Shack, Staples, Target, Tire Kingdom, Walmart SuperCtr, to Kennedy Space Ctr, **W** food: Cracker Barrel, IHOP, lodging: Comfort Inn, Day's Inn, Fairfield Inn, Hampton Inn, other: Christmas RV Park (8mi), Great Outdoors RV Camp

**212** FL 407, to FL 528 toll (no re-entry sb)

**208** Port St John

**205** FL 528 (toll 528), to Cape Canaveral & Cape Port AFS

**202** FL 524, Cocoa, **E** gas: Shell/dsl, other: Museum of History & Science, **W** gas: BP/dsl, lodging: Day's Inn, Ramada Inn/rest., Super 8

**201** FL 520, to Cocoa Bch, Cocoa, **E** gas: BP/dsl, Chevron, Pilot/Subway/scales/dsl/24hr, food: IHOP, Waffle House, lodging: Best Western, Motel 6, other: H HOSPITAL, Sams Club/gas, fireworks, **W** gas: Chevron/dsl, Shell/Burger King, Sunoco/dsl, food: McDonald's, lodging: Holiday Inn Express, other: Sun Coast RV Ctr

**195** FL 519, Fiske Blvd, **E** gas: 7-11, Shell/dsl (1mi), food: Ruby Tuesday, lodging: Swiss Inn, other: H HOSPITAL, Lowe's Whse, Space Coast RV Park

**191** rd 509, to Satellite Beach, **E** gas: BP, Citgo/7-11, Hess/dsl, food: Bob Evans, Denny's, McDonald's, Perkins, Sonny's BBQ, Tropical Smoothie, Uno, Wendy's, lodging: Hampton Inn, Holiday Inn, other: CVS Drug, Goodyear/auto, UHaul, to Patrick AFB, **W** gas: Chevron/dsl, Murphy USA, food: Asian Wok, Burger King, Chili's, Cracker Barrel, Longhorn Steaks, Mimi's Cafe, Starbucks, Steak&Shake, Subway, lodging: La Quinta, other: Belk, $Tree, Kohl's, Office Depot, PetCo, Ross, SuperTarget, Walmart SuperCtr/McDonald's, World Mkt

**183** FL 518, Melbourne, Indian Harbour Beach, **E** gas: BP, Chevron/Baskin Robbins/Dunkin Donuts/dsl, RaceTrac/24hr, 7-11, other: art museum, **W** Flea Mkt

**180** US 192, to Melbourne, **E** gas: BP/dsl, Circle K/gas, Mobil/dsl, 7-11/gas, Sunoco/dsl, food: Denny's, IHOP, Waffle House, lodging: Budget Inn, Days Inn, Fairfield Inn, Hampton Inn, Holiday Inn Express, Howard Johnson, York Inn, other: H HOSPITAL, Sam's Club/gas, Saturn, vet

**176** rd 516, to Palm Bay, **E** gas: BP/dsl, Murphy USA, 7-11/gas, food: Baskin Robbins/Dunkin Donuts, Bob Evans, Chick-fil-A, Cracker Barrel, Denny's, Golden Corral, Starbucks, lodging: Jameson Inn, other: Aldi Foods, BJ's Whse/gas, Chevrolet, $Tree, GNC, Harley-Davidson,

**176** Continued
Office Depot, Walmart SuperCtr, Walgreens, **W** gas: 7-11/gas, Shell, food: Ranchero's Mexican, Subway, Wendy's, other: Curves, CVS Drug, Publix, Walgreens

**173** FL 514, to Palm Bay, **E** gas: Shell/dsl, Sunoco/dsl, other: H HOSPITAL, Ford, Subaru, truck/RV repair, **W** gas: BP/dsl, Hess, Shell, food: Arby's, Baskin-Robbins, Burger King, IHOP, McDonald's/playplace, Panda Express, Sonny's BBQ, Subway, Taco Bell, TX Roadhouse, Waffle House, Wendy's, Woody's BBQ, lodging: Comfort Suites, Motel 6, other: Advance Parts, BigLots, CVS Drug, $General, Gatto's Tire/repair, Home Depot, Lowe's, Publix, Tire Kingdom, USPO, Walgreens, Walmart SuperCtr

**168mm** rest areas both lanes, full & facilities, C, vending, litter barrels, petwalk, 24hr security

**156** rd 512, to Sebastian, Fellsmere, **E** gas: BP/DQ/Stuckey's/dsl, Chevron/McDonald's, other: H HOSPITAL, Encore RV Park, Sebastian Inlet SRA, Vero Bch RV Park (8mi), **W** other: Marsh Landing Camping, St Sebastian SP

**147** FL 60, Osceola Blvd, **E** gas: Citgo/dsl/24hr, Mobil/dsl, Sunoco, Texaco, TA/BP/Popeye's/Subway/dsl/24hr/scales/@, 7-11/gas, Valero/dsl, food: IHOP, Mrs. B's Rest., Quizno's, Sloane's Rest., Waffle House, Wendy's, lodging: Best Western, Days Inn, Howard Johnson, Travelodge, other: H HOSPITAL, NAPA, USPO, vet, **W** food: Cracker Barrel, McDonald's, Steak'n Shake, lodging: Country Inn&Suites, Hampton Inn, Holiday Inn Express, other: Vero Bch Outlets/famous brands

**138** FL 614, Indrio Rd, 3 mi **E** other: Oceanographic Institute

**133mm** rest areas both lanes, full & facilities, C, vending, litter barrels, petwalk, 24hr security

**131b a** FL 68, Orange Ave, **E** to Ft Pierce SP, **W** gas: ⊕FLYING J/CountryMkt/dsl/LP/scales/24hr, other: Blue Beacon

**129** FL 70, to Okeechobee, **E** gas: Hess/dsl, Mystik/dsl, Murphy USA, RaceTrac, Sunoco/dsl, food: Applebee's, Sonic, Gator's Rest., Golden Corral, Waffle House, other: H HOSPITAL, Advance Parts, $General, $Tree, Firestone/auto, Home Depot, Radio Shack, Walgreens, Walmart SuperCtr, truck tires, **W** gas: Chevron, Citgo/scales/dsl, Exxon, Mobil/Dunkin Donuts/Subway, Pilot/Arby's/dsl/24hr/@, Pilot/McDonald's/dsl/scales/24hr, Shell/dsl, food: Burger King, Cracker Barrel, LJ Silver, KFC, McDonald's, Mi Rancho Mexican, Red Lobster, Steak'n Shake, Waffle House, Wendy's, lodging: Best Western, Comfort Suites, Day's Inn, Fairfield Inn, Hampton Inn, Holiday Inn Express, La Quinta, Motel 6, Quality Inn, Rodeway Inn, Sleep Inn, Treasure Coast Inn, other: Treasure Coast RV Park, to FL TPK, UF R&E Ctr

**126** rd 712, Midway Rd, services 3-5 mi **E**

**121** St Lucie West Blvd, **E** gas: BP/Dunkin Donuts, Chevron/24hr, Murphy USA, 7-11/gas, Shell/Subway/dsl, food: Arbys, Bob Evans, Burger King, Chili's, Coldstone, Crisper's Rest., Duffy's Grill, Friendly's, McDonald's, Morelli's, Outback Steaks, Quizno's, Red Ginger Asian, Ruby Tuesday, TGI Friday, Wendy's, lodging: Hampton Inn, Holiday Inn Express, Residence Inn, SpringHill Suites, other: Circuit City, Curves, Outdoor Resorts Camping (2mi), PetCo, Publix/deli, Steinmart,

## INTERSTATE 95 CONT'D

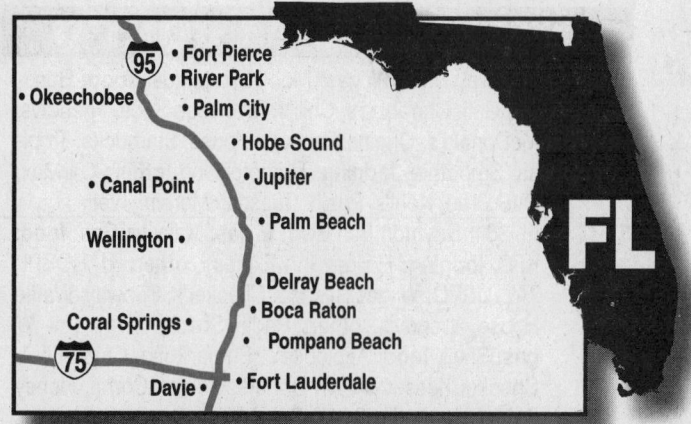

**N ↑ S**

**PALM CITY**

**121** Continued
Radio Shack, Tires+, Tire Kingdom, USPO, Walgreens, Walmart SuperCtr, **W gas:** Mobil/dsl, **lodging:** Hilton Garden, MainStay Suites, Sheraton, **other:** PGA Village

**120** new exit

**118** Gatlin Blvd, to Port St Lucie, **E gas:** BP/dsl/LP, Chevron/dsl, Sunoco, Dunkin Donuts, Subway, **other:** Home Depot, Sam's Club/gas, Walgreens, Walmart SuperCtr, **W food:** Longhorn Steaks, McDonald's, Olive Garden, **other:** Michaels, Old Navy, PetsMart, Publix, Target, TJ Maxx

**113mm** new exit

**110** FL 714, to Stuart, Palm City, **E** H HOSPITAL

**106mm** rest areas both lanes, full ♿ facilities, 🅲 vending, 🍴 litter barrels, petwalk, 24hr security

**102** FL 713, to Stuart, Palm City

**101** FL 76, to Stuart, Indiantown, **E gas:** Chevron/24hr, Sunoco/dsl, **food:** Baskin-Robbins/Dunkin Donuts, Cracker Barrel, McDonald's, Wendy's, **lodging:** Courtyard, Holiday Inn Express, **other:** H HOSPITAL, RV camping, **W gas:** Shell/DQ/Stuckey's/deli/dsl

**96** rd 708, to Hobe Sound, **E** Dickinson SP (11mi), RV camping

**87b a** FL 706, to Okeechobee, Jupiter, **E gas:** Citgo, Mobil, Shell, **food:** Applebee's, Cheeseburgers & More, China Dragon, Duffy's Rest., Dunkin Donuts, Gator's Rest., IHOP, KFC, McDonald's, Pollo Tropical, Sonny's BBQ, Starbucks, Subway, Taco Bell, Tomato Pie, **lodging:** Comfort Inn, Fairfield Inn, **other:** H HOSPITAL, URGENT CARE, Advance Parts, Books-A-Million, Dodge/Mazda, GNC, Home Depot, PepBoys, Publix, Tire Kingdom, Walgreens, Winn-Dixie, to Dickinson SP, hist sites, museum, vet, **W gas:** Sunoco, **other:** info, RV camping, to FL TPK

**83** Donald Ross Rd, **E gas:** Shell, **lodging:** Homewood Suites, **other:** stadium

**79c** FL 809 S (from sb), **W** to FL TPK, same services as 79b

**79a b** FL 786, PGA Blvd, **E gas:** Shell, **food:** Chili's, TGIFriday, **lodging:** Hampton Inn, Marriott, **other:** H HOSPITAL, Best Buy, Michael's, Publix, **W gas:** Shell/dsl/24hr, **food:** Abbey Rd Grill, Cantina Laredo, Field Of Greens Cafe, Outback Steaks, **lodging:** DoubleTree Hotel, Embassy Suites, **other:** Publix

**77** Northlake Blvd, to W Palm Bch, **E gas:** Hess, Shell/dsl, Texaco, **food:** Applebee's, Arby's, Burger King, Checker's, Chick-fil-A, McDonald's, Panera Bread, Pollo Tropical, Quarter Deck Rest., Starbucks, Taco Bell, **other:** H HOSPITAL, Buick/Pontiac/GMC, Chevrolet, Chrysler/Jeep/Dodge, Costco, CVS Drug, $Tree, Ford, Gander Mtn, Home Depot, Hyundai, K-Mart, Lincoln/Mercury, Lowe's Whse, PepBoys, Ross, Staples, Subaru, Target, VW, Walgreens, **W gas:** BP, Chevron, Mobil/dsl, Shell, Sunoco, **food:** Duffy's Grill, Gator's Rest., Papa John's, Pizza Hut, Wendy's, **lodging:** Inn of America, **other:** Advance Parts, Albertson's, CVS Drug, Radio Shack, Publix, Winn-Dixie

**76** FL 708, Blue Heron Blvd, **E gas:** BP/dsl, Shell/dsl, **food:** Wendy's, **lodging:** Travelodge, **other:** Honda, Kia, Nissan, Walgreens, **W gas:** BP, Cumberland Farms, RaceTrac, Texaco/dsl, **food:** Burger King, Denny's, McDonald's, Quizno's, **lodging:** Super 8

**W PALM BEACH**

**PALM BEACH**

**74** FL 702, 45th St, **E food:** Burger King, Hong Kong Cafe, IHOP, **lodging:** Day's Inn, **other:** H HOSPITAL, Cadillac, Walgreens, **W gas:** RaceTrac, Sunoco, **food:** Cracker Barrel, McDonald's, Pollo Tropical, Subway, Taco Bell, Wendy's, **lodging:** Courtyard, Extended Stay Deluxe, Holiday Inn Express, Homewood Suites, Inn Town Suites, Red Roof Inn, Residence Inn, Springhill Suites, **other:** Curves, Goodyear, Harley-Davidson, Palm Beach RV Ctr, Sams Club/gas, Goodyear/auto, Walmart SuperCtr

**71** Lake Blvd, Palm Beach, **E gas:** BP, **food:** McDonald's, **lodging:** Best Western, Hawthorn Suites, **other:** H HOSPITAL, Best Buy, Dillard's, Firestone/auto, JC Penney, Macy's, Sears/auto, Target, mall, **W gas:** Texaco/dsl, **food:** Carrabba's, Chick-fil-A, Chipotle Mexican, Hooters, Manzo Italian, PA BBQ, Picadilly's, Rain Dancer Steaks, Red Lobster, Sweet Tomatoes, **lodging:** Comfort Inn, La Quinta, **other:** Walgreens, vet

**70b a** FL 704, Okeechobee Blvd, **E gas:** Exxon, **lodging:** Marriott, **other:** museum, **W gas:** Chevron/dsl, Exxon/dsl, Hess, Shell, Texaco, **food:** Checkers, McDonald's, Nick's Diner, Pizza Hut, Pollo Tropical, Shell's Rest., **other:** BMW, Chevrolet, Circuit City, Lincoln/Mercury, Old Navy, PetsMart, Staples

**69** Belvedere Rd, **W on Australian Ave gas:** BP, Shell, **food:** Burger King, Denny's, IHOP, Wendy's, **lodging:** Best Western, Courtyard, Crowne Plaza, Doubletree, Hampton Inn, Hilton Garden, Holiday Inn/rest., Motel 6, Studio 6, **other:** to airport

**68** US 98, Southern Blvd, **E gas:** Texaco, **other:** CVS Drug, Publix, **W lodging:** Hilton

**66** Forest Hill Blvd, **E** Havana Cafe, **W gas:** Sunoco, **food:** Amigo's Mexican, Palm Spring Pizza,

**64** 10th Ave N, **W gas:** Citgo, Shell/dsl/24hr, **food:** China Empire, Dunkin Donuts, Flanigans Grill, McDonald's, Wendy's, **other:** CarQuest, $General, Family$, Ford, Goodyear, President Foods, Urgent Care, vet

**63** 6th Ave S, **W** H HOSPITAL

**61** FL 812, Lantana Rd, **E gas:** Shell, **food:** Dominos, KFC, McDonald's, Quizno's, Reggin's Crabhouse, Subway, **lodging:** Motel 6, **other:** Ace Hardware, Beall's, CVS Drug, $General, Publix, 7-11, **W food:** Rosalita's Café, **other:** H HOSPITAL, Costco/gas

**60** Hypoluxo Rd, **E gas:** BP, Mobil/dsl, Shell/dsl, **food:** Popeye's, Taco Bell, Wendy's, **lodging:** Best Western, Comfort Inn, Super 8, **other:** Sam's Club, Tires+, Tire Kingdom, **W gas:** Chevron/dsl, **other:** Advance Parts

## INTERSTATE 95 CONT'D

**N ↕ S**

**PALM BEACH**

**59** Gateway Blvd, **W gas:** Mobil/Blimpie/dsl, **food:** Bonefish Grill, Carrabba's, Chili's, Firehouse Subs, Friendlys, McDonald's, Original Pancake House, Starbucks, Tropical Smoothie, **lodging:** Hampton Inn, **other:** CarMax, CVS Drug, Kohl's, Publix, Tuesday Morning, vet

**57** FL 804, Boynton Bch Blvd, **E gas:** Majestic Gas, **food:** KFC, **lodging:** Holiday Inn Express, **other:** H HOSPITAL, USPO, **W gas:** Texaco, Checker's, Subway, Waffle House, Wendy's, **other:** Radio Shack, 7-11, 1mi **W gas:** Shell, **food:** Applebee's, Burger King, Chick-Fil-A, ChuckeCheese, Dunkin Donuts, Golden Corral, Honey Baked Ham, Jim Smith Subs, KFC, Sonic, Starbucks, Steak'n Shake, TGIFriday, **other:** Barnes&Noble, BJ's Whse/gas, Office Depot, Old Navy, Publix, Steinmart, TJ Maxx, Walmart SuperCtr, USPO

**56** Woolbright Rd, **E gas:** Shell/24hr, McDonald's, **other:** H HOSPITAL, 7-11, **W gas:** RaceTrac/24hr, **food:** Burger King, Cracker Barrel, Dunkin Donuts, Quizno's, **other:** Advance Parts, Home Depot, Lowe's Whse, Staples

**52b a** FL 806, Atlantic Ave, **W gas:** Chevron, Shell/dsl, **food:** Burger King, McDonald's, Sandwich Man, **other:** H HOSPITAL, Aamco, Publix, Tires+, Walgreens, vet

**51** rd 782, Linton Blvd, **E gas:** Shell, **food:** Applebees, Arby's, Chipotle Mexican, DQ, KFC, Lucille's BBQ, McDonald's, Outback Steaks, Pollo Tropical, Steak'n Shake, Subway, Taco Bell, Wendy's, **other:** Chevrolet, Ford, Home Depot, Mercedes, Nissan, PetsMart, Publix, Ross, Staples, Target, Tire Kingdom, **W gas:** Shell, **other:** H HOSPITAL, Family$, Winn-Dixie, auto repair

**50** Congress Ave, **W gas:** NeXStore/gas, **lodging:** Hilton Garden, Homestead Motel

**48b a** FL 794, Yamato Rd, **E gas:** Mobil, **food:** Panera Bread, **other:** CVS Drug, vet, **W gas:** Chevron/dsl, **food:** Blue Fin, Dunkin Donuts, Jimmy John's, McDonald's, Quizno's, Sal's Italian, Starbucks, Subway, Wendy's, **lodging:** DoubleTree, Embassy Suites, Hampton Inn, SpringHill Suites, TownePlace Suites

**45** FL 808, Glades Rd, **E food:** Alexander's Rest, Jamba Juice, McCormick and Schmick's, Mon Ami Cafe, Subway, **lodging:** Fairfield Inn, **other:** Barnes&Noble, Circuit City, Jamba Juice, PF Chang's, Whole-Foods Mkt, museum, **W gas:** BP, **food:** Abe&Louie's, Brewzzi Cafe, Cheesecake Factory, Chili's, Chipotle Mexican, Houston Rest., Maggiano's Italian, Mario's Italian, Moe's SW Grill, Quizno's, Starbucks, **lodging:** Courtyard, Holiday Inn, Marriott, Renaissance/grill, **other:** Macy's, Nordstrom, Sears/auto

**44** Palmetto Park Rd, **E gas:** Sunoco, **food:** Denny's, Dunkin Donuts, Red's BBQ, Subway, Tomasso's Pizza, **other:** K-Mart, Publix, museums, **W food:** McDonald's (2mi)

**42b a** FL 810, Hillsboro Blvd, **E gas:** BP, Shell/dsl, **food:** McDonald's, Popeye's, Wendy's, **lodging:** Hampton Inn, Hilton, La Quinta, **other:** Advance Parts, **W gas:** Chevron, Mobil/dsl, **food:** Boston Mkt, Checker's, Denny's, **lodging:** La Quinta, **other:** CVS Drug, Home Depot, Walgreens

**41** FL 869 (toll), SW 10th, to I-75, **E gas:** Mobil, **food:** Cracker Barrel, **lodging:** Extended Stay America, **W lodging:** Best Western, Comfort Suites,

**POMPANO BEACH**

**39** FL 834, Sample Rd, **E gas:** BP, Hess, Marathon, Shell/dsl, **other:** H HOSPITAL, 7-11, UHaul, **W gas:** Chevron, Mobil/dsl, Sunoco/dsl, **food:** Arby's, Checker's, IHOP, McDonald's, Miami Subs, Subway, **other:** CarMax, Costco/gas, CVS Drug, Family$, Seabra Foods, 7-11, vet

**38b a** Copans Rd, **E food:** McDonald's, Subway, **other:** Land Rover, Mercedes, PepBoys, Porche/Audi, Walmart, **W gas:** BP, Chevron, **other:** Harley-Davidson, Home Depot, NAPA

**36b a** FL 814, Atlantic Blvd, to Pompano Beach, **E gas:** RaceTrac, **food:** KFC/Pizza Hut/Taco Bell, Miami Subs, **1 mi W gas:** BP, Mobil/dsl, Murphy USA, Burger King, Dunkin Donuts, Golden Corral, KFC/LJ Silver, McDonald's, Pollo Tropical, Popeye's, Wendy's, **other:** Advance Parts, Chevrolet, CVS Drug, $Tree Radio Shack, Walmart SuperCtr, Winn-Dixie, USPO, to FL TPK, Power Line Rd has multiple services

**33b a** Cypress Creek Rd, **E gas:** BP, Hess, **lodging:** Extended Stay America, Hampton Inn, Westin Hotel, **W gas:** Hess, Shell/repair, **food:** Arby's, Burger King, Chili's, Hooters, Jamba Juice, Longhorn Steaks, McDonald's, Moonlite Diner, Quizno's, Steak&Ale, Subway, Sweet Tomatoes, Wendy's, **lodging:** Courtyard, Extended Stay Deluxe, La Quinta, Marriott, Sheraton Suites, **other:** GNC, Jaguar, Office Depot, Tires+

**32** FL 870, Commercial Blvd, Lauderdale by the Sea, Lauderhill, **E food:** Subway, **W gas:** BP, Circle K, Mobil, Shell, Sunoco/dsl, **food:** Burger King, Dunkin Donuts, KFC, McDonald's, Miami Subs, Waffle House, **lodging:** El Palacio, Red Roof Inn, University Inn, **other:** Advance Parts, BJ's Whse, Larrys Tires/Repair

**FT LAUDERDALE**

**31b a** FL 816, Oakland Park Blvd, **E gas:** Chevron, Mobil/24hr, **food:** Burger King, CC's Fishcamp, Denny's, Dunkin Donuts, Little Caesars, McDonald's, Miami Subs, Subway, Wendy's, **other:** K-Mart, Lowe's Whse, Publix, Radio Shack, Walgreens, **W gas:** BP/dsl, Citgo, RaceTrac, Shell, Texaco, **food:** Burger King, Dunkin Donuts/Baskin-Robbins, IHOP, KFC, **lodging:** Day's Inn, **other:** $General, Home Depot, Toyota, USPO, vet

**29b a** FL 838, Sunrise Blvd, **E gas:** Shell, Sunoco/dsl, **food:** Burger King, Popeye's, **other:** Advance Parts, Family$, Winn-Dixie, **W gas:** Citgo, Shell, Sunoco, **food:** Capt Crabs, Church's, McDonald's, Subway, **other:** H HOSPITAL, Walgreens

**27** FL 842, Broward Blvd, Ft Lauderdale, **E H HOSPITAL**

**26** I-595 (from sb), FL 736, Davie Blvd, **W to** ✈

**25** FL 84, **E gas:** Marathon, RaceTrac/24hr, 7-11, Shell/dsl, Sunoco, Texaco, Valero, **food:** Dunkin Donuts, Li'l Red's BBQ, McDonald's, Subway, Wendy's, **lodging:** Best Western, Candlewood Suites, Hampton Inn, Holiday Inn Express, Motel 6, Sky Motel, **other:** BigLots, Firestone/auto, Radio Shack, U-Haul, Winn-Dixie, **W lodging:** Ramada Inn, Red Carpet Inn, Rodeway Inn, **other:** Ford Trucks

**24** I-595 (from nb), to I-75, **E to** ✈

**23** FL 818, Griffin Rd, **E lodging:** Hilton, Sheraton, **W gas:** BP, Citgo/dsl, **food:** Subway, Tropical Acres, **lodging:** Courtyard, **other:** Bass Pro Shops

## INTERSTATE 95 CONT'D

**22** FL 848, Stirling Rd, Cooper City, **E** gas: Mobil, food: AleHouse Grill, Burger King, Dave&Buster's, Quizno's, McDonald's, Moonlite Diner, Quizno's, Red Lobster, Sweet Tomatoes, Taco Bell, TGIFriday, Wendy's, lodging: Comfort Inn, Hampton Inn, Hilton Garden, La Quinta, SpringHill Suites, other: Advance Parts, Barnes&Noble, BigLots, BJ's Whse, CVS Drug, GNC, Home Depot, K-Mart, Marshall's, Michael's, Old Navy, PetsMart, Ross, to Lloyd SP, **W** food: Las Vegas Cuban, Mr M's Sandwiches, Subway, lodging: Best Western, other: Circle K, CVS Drug, PepBoys, Tire Kingdom, Walgreens

**21** FL 822, Sheridan St, **E** gas: BP, Citgo, Cumberland Farms/gas, same as 22, **W** gas: Shell, food: Denny's, lodging: Day's Inn, Holiday Inn

**20** FL 820, Hollywood Blvd, **E** gas: Shell, IHOP, Miami Subs, lodging: Hollywood Gateway Inn, other: Goodyear/auto, Office Depot, vet, **W** gas: BP, Chevron, food: Boston Mkt, Dunkin Donuts, Firehouse Subs, McDonald's, Offerdahl's Grill, Quizno's, Taco Bell, Starbucks, Subway, Wendy's, other: Ⓗ HOSPITAL, Publix, Target, Walgreens

**19** FL 824, Pembroke Rd, **E** gas: Shell, **W** gas: Shell

**18** FL 858, Hallandale Bch Blvd, **E** gas: Exxon, 7-11, Shell, Ugas/E85, food: Burger King, Denny's, Dunkin Donuts, Fat Lou's, IHOP, KFC, Little Caesar's, McDonald's, Miami Subs, Pollo Tropical, Subway, Wendy's, Won Ton Garden, lodging: Best Western, other: Ⓗ HOSPITAL, Family$, Goodyear/auto, Office Depot, Tire Kingdom, Walgreens, Winn-Dixie, vet, **W** gas: BP, RaceTrac, other: Advance Parts

**16** Ives Dairy Rd, **E** Ⓗ HOSPITAL, mall, **W** gas: BP, Subway

**14** FL 860, Miami Gardens Dr, N Miami Beach, **E** Ⓗ HOSPITAL, Oleta River SRA, **W** gas: BP, Chevron, Citgo, Marathon/dsl, food: Subway

**12c** US 441, FL 826, FL TPK, FL 9, **E** gas: BP, Chevron, Hess, 7-11, Ugas/dsl, Valero, food: Burger King, Dunkin Donuts/Baskin-Robbins, Wendy's lodging: Holiday Inn, other: Ⓗ HOSPITAL

**12b** US 441 (from nb), same as 12c

**12a** FL 868 (from nb), FL TPK N

**11** NW 151st (from nb), **W** gas: Sunoco, food: McDonald's, other: Advance Parts, Winn-Dixie, services on US 441 N

**10b** FL 916, NW 135th, Opa-Locka Blvd, **W** gas: Chevron, Liberty, Mobil, food: Checker's, Subway

**10a** NW 125th, N Miami, Bal Harbour, **W** gas: Shell, food: Wendy's

**9** NW 119th (from nb), **W** gas: BP/McDonald's, food: KFC, other: AutoZone, Family$, Walgreens, Winn-Dixie

**8b** FL 932, NW 103rd, **E** gas: Shell, Texaco, other: 7-11, **W** gas: Chevron, Marathon, Sunoco, food: Baskin-Robbins/Dunkin Donuts, Bravo Foods

**8a** NW 95th, **E** gas: BP, **W** gas: Mobil, food: McDonald's, other: Ⓗ HOSPITAL, Advance Parts, Walgreens

**7** FL 934, NW 81st, NW 79th, **E** gas: Chevron/dsl, Citgo/dsl, **W** gas: Texaco, food: Cafe China, Checker's, other: Lincoln/Mercury

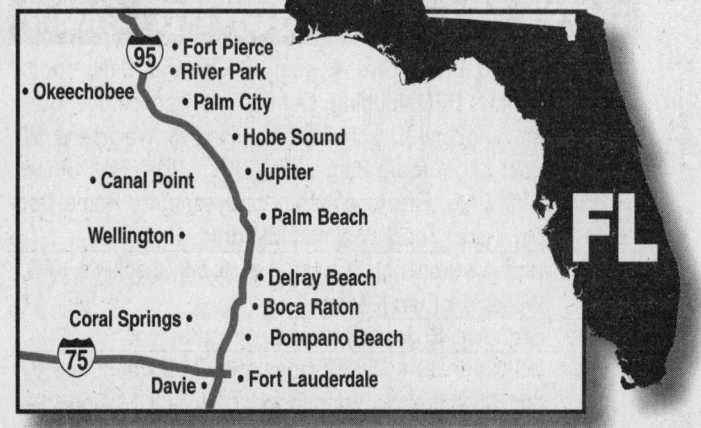

**6b** NW 69th (from sb)

**6a** FL 944, NW 62nd, NW 54th, **W** food: McDonald's, Subway, other: Family$, Jorge&Jerry's Foods, Walgreens

**4b a** I-195 E, FL 112 W (toll), Miami Beach, **E** downtown, **W** ✈

**3b** NW 8th St (from sb)

**3a** FL 836 W (toll) (exits left from nb), **W** Ⓗ HOSPITAL, to ✈

**2d** I-395 E (exits left from sb), to Miami Beach

**2c** NW 8th, NW 14th (from sb), Miami Ave, **E** Port of Miami

**2b** NW 2nd (from nb), downtown Miami

**2a** US 1 (exits left from sb), Biscayne Blvd, downtown Miami

**1b** US 41, SW 7th, SW 8th, Brickell Ave, **E** gas: Chevron, Citgo, food: McDonald's, Subway, lodging: Extended Stay America, Hampton Inn, Holiday Inn Express, other: CVS Drug, GNC, Publix, **W** gas: Shell, food: Papa John's

**1a** SW 25th (from sb), downtown, to Rickenbacker Causeway, **E** lodging: Hampton Inn, other: museum, to Baggs SRA

**0mm** I-95 begins/ends on US 1, **1 mi S** gas: Citgo, Quizno's

## INTERSTATE 275 - TAMPA

| Exit # | Services |
|---|---|
| **59mm** | I-275 begins/ends on I-75, exit 274. |
| **53** | Bearss Ave, **E** gas: Citgo/dsl, other: Carmax, **W** gas: BP, CC's/dsl, Chevron/dsl, RaceTrac, Shell, food: Burger King, McDonald's, Perkins, Quizno's, Subway, lodging: Quality Inn, other: BigLots, CVS Drug, GNC, Ross |
| **52** | Fletcher Ave, **E** gas: BP, Citgo, Hess, RaceTrac, Sunoco, Texaco, food: Arby's, DQ, Golden Dynasty, Hoho, Krystal, Little Caesars, McDonald's, Popeye's, lodging: Day's Inn, other: Ⓗ HOSPITAL, Tire Kingdom, Toyota, auto repair, **W** gas: BP, Chevron, Citgo, lodging: Super 8, other: Beall's, Cadillac, Family$, Jaguar, Saturn, Sweetbay Foods |
| **51** | FL 582, Fowler Ave, **E** gas: Citgo/dsl, GK, Shell/Circle K, food: A&W/LJ Silver, Burger King, Chili's, China Buffet, Chipotle Mexican, City Mkt, Denny's, Dunkin Donuts, Jason's Deli, Longhorn Steaks, McDonald's, Pizza Hut, Quizno's, Steak'n Shake, Subway, Taco Bell, TGIFriday's, Waffle House, Wendy's, lodging: Clarion, Howard Johnson, other: Advance parts, CarQuest, CVS Drug, Dillards, Family$, Macy's, Office Depot, Sears/auto, Walgreens, **W** lodging: Economy Inn, Motel 6, Rodeway Inn, other: BMW |

## INTERSTATE 275 CONT'D - TAMPA

| | |
|---|---|
| **50** | FL 580, Busch Blvd, **E gas:** BP, Chevron, Citgo, **food:** Sonny's BBQ, **lodging:** Comfort Inn, Econolodge, **other:** AutoZone, Busch Gardens, Famliy$, Walgreens, **W gas:** Citgo, **food:** Burger King, KFC, Pizza Hut, **other:** CVS Drug, Firestone/auto, Goodyear/auto, Home Depot, Radio Shack, Walmart Mkt/drug |
| **49** | Bird Ave (from nb), **W gas:** Shell **food:** Checker's, KFC, Wendy's, **other:** K-Mart |
| **48** | Sligh Ave, **E gas:** BP, Sunoco, **W other:** zoo |
| **47b a** | US 92, to US 41 S, Hillsborough Ave, **E gas:** Circle K/gas, Shell, Texaco, Valero, **food:** Checkers, McDonald's, Popeye's, Subway, Wendy's, **other:** Advance Parts, **W gas:** BP, Shell/Circle K, **food:** Starbucks, **lodging:** Dutch Motel |
| **46b** | FL 574, MLK Blvd, **E gas:** BP, Shell, **other:** Advance Parts, Sweetbay Foods, Walgreens, **W gas:** Marathon, **food:** McDonald's, **other:** H HOSPITAL |
| **46a** | Floribraska Ave |
| **45b** | I-4 E, to Orlando, I-75 |
| **45a** | Jefferson St, downtown E |
| **44** | Ashley Dr, Tampa St, downtown W |
| **42** | Howard Ave, Armenia Ave, **W gas:** Texaco/dsl, **food:** Popeye's |
| **41c** | Himes Ave (from sb), **W** RJ Stadium |
| **41b a** | US 92, Dale Mabry Blvd, **E gas:** BP, Marathon, Mobil/dsl, Shell/Circle K, **food:** Alexander's Rest., Burger King, Carrabba's, Chick-Fil-A, Don Pan Cuban, Donatello Italian, Giordano's Italian, Honey Baked Ham, IHOP, PeiWei Asian, Perkins, Pizza Hut, Ruby Tuesday, Shells Rest., Starbucks, Village Inn, **lodging:** Best Western, Courtyard, **other:** Barnes & Noble, Borders, CVS Drug, Office Depot, PetsMartto MacDill AFB, **W gas:** BP, **food:** Burger King, Chili's, China 1, Crazy Buffet, Denny's, Longhorn Steaks, Macaroni Grill, McDonald's, Quizno's, Smoothie King, Sonic, Sonny's BBQ, Subway, Sweet Tomatoes, Tia's TexMex, Tijuana Iguana, Wendy's, **lodging:** Day's Inn, Howard Johnson, **other:** Best Buy, Circuit City, Dodge/Chrysler/Jeep, Home Depot, K-Mart, PetsMart, Staples, SweetBay Foods, Target, Walmart, Whole Foods Mkt |
| **40b** | Lois Ave, **W gas:** Marathon, **food:** Charlies Rest., **lodging:** DoubleTree Hotel, Sheraton |
| **40a** | FL 587, Westshore Blvd, **E gas:** Chevron, Citgo, Shell, **food:** Chipotle Mexican, Maggiano's Rest., Panera Bread, PF Chang's, Starbucks, Steak&Ale, Taco Bell, Waffle House, **lodging:** Embassy Suites, Ramada Inn, Wyndam, **other:** Goodyear, JC Penney, Macy's, Old Navy, PetCo, Sears/auto, Walgreens, **W gas:** Shell/Subway, **food:** West Shore Rest., **lodging:** Marriott, Quorum Hotel, SpringHill Suites |
| **39b a** | FL 60 W, **W food:** Outback Steaks, **other:** to airport |
| **32** | Fl 687 S, 4th St N, to US 92 (no sb reentry), no faciletes |
| **31b a** | 9th St N, MLK St N (exits left from sb), info, airport |
| **30** | FL 686, Roosevelt Blvd, **2mi W food:** Quaker Steak & Lube, **lodging:** Wingate Inn |

| | |
|---|---|
| **28** | FL 694 W, Gandy Blvd, Indian Shores, **1-2mi W food:** Bob Evans, Godfather's Pizza, **lodging:** La Quinta, **other:** Robert's RV Resort |
| **26b a** | 54th Ave N, **E gas:** Cracker Barrel, **lodging:** Comfort Inn, Holiday Inn Express, **W gas:** Citgo, RaceTrac, **food:** Waffle House, **lodging:** Day's Inn, **other:** H HOSPITAL, Harley-Davidson, NAPA |
| **25** | 38th Ave N, to beaches, **E food:** McDonald's, **W gas:** Citgo/dsl, **food:** Burger King, Hardee's |
| **24** | 22nd Ave N, **E gas:** Mobil, 7-11, **other:** Sunken Garden, **W gas:** Citgo/dsl, RaceTrac, **other:** Home Depot, Lowe's Whse |
| **23b** | FL 595, 5th Ave N, **E** H HOSPITAL |
| **23a** | I-375, **E** The Pier, Waterfront, downtown |
| **22** | I-175 E, Tropicana Fields, **W** H HOSPITAL |
| **21** | 28th St S, downtown |
| **20** | 31st Ave (from nb), downtown |
| **19** | 22nd Ave S, Gulfport, **W gas:** Chevron, Citgo, Shell, **food:** Church's, Cici's Pizza, KFC, Quizno's, **other:** Family$, PriceBuster Foods |
| **18** | 26th Ave S (from nb) |
| **17** | FL 682 W, 54th Ave S, Pinellas Bayway, services **W on US 19 (34th St)...gas:** 7-11, Sunoco, **food:** Bob Evans, Burger King, Denny's, McDonald's, Papa John's, Pizza Hut, Ponderosa, Subway, Taco Bell, Wendy's, **lodging:** Bayway Inn, Crystal Inn, **other:** Beall's, CVS Drug, GNC, K-Mart, Publix, to Ft DeSoto Pk, St Pete Beach, |
| **16** | Pinellas Point Dr, Skyway Lane, to Maximo Park, **E lodging:** Holiday Inn resort, **W** marina |
| **16mm** | toll plaza sb |
| **13mm** | N Skyway Fishing Pier, **W** rest area both lanes, full facilities, vending, litter barrels, petwalk |
| **10mm** | Tampa Bay |
| **7mm** | **S Skyway Fishing Pier, E** rest area both lanes, full facilities, vending, litter barrels, petwalk |
| **6mm** | toll plaza nb |
| **5** | US 19, Palmetto, Bradenton |
| **2** | US 41 last nb exit before toll, Palmetto, Bradenton, **E other:** Terra Ceia Village Campground, Circle K, Fiesta Grove RV Resort, Frog Creek Campground, Winterset RV Resort, **W gas:** BP/DQ/Subway/dsl |
| **0mm** | I-275 begins/ends on I-75, exit 228. |

## INTERSTATE 295 - JACKSONVILLE

| Exit # | Services |
|---|---|
| **35b a** | I-95, S to Jacksonville, N to Savannah. I-295 begins/ends on I-95, exit 362b. |
| **33** | Duval Rd, **W** ✈ |
| **32** | FL 115, Lem Turner Rd, **E food:** China Wok, Cross Creek Steak, Larry's Subs, McDonald's (1mi), Subway, Wendy's, **other:** Home Depot, Radio Shack, Walmart SuperCtr, **W other:** Flamingo Lake RV Resort, Lakeside Cabins/RV Park |
| **30** | FL 104, Dunn Ave, **E gas:** Gate/dsl, Shell/24hr (1mi), **food:** McDonald's (1mi), **W other:** Big Tree RV Park |

## INTERSTATE 295 CONT'D - JACKSONVILLE

**N ↕ S**

**JACKSONVILLE**

**28b a**   US 1, US 23, to Callahan, Jacksonville, **E** gas: Kangaroo/gas, **W** gas: BP/DQ/dsl, Chevron/Subway/dsl, RaceTrac/24hr, auto repair

**25**   Pritchard Rd, **W** gas: Kangaroo/Subway/dsl/deli/24hr

**22**   Commonwealth Ave, **E** gas: Sprint/dsl, **food:** Burger King, Hardee's, Waffle House, **lodging:** Holiday Inn, **other:** dogtrack, **W** food: Wendy's, **lodging:** Comfort Suites, Country Inn & Suites

**21b a**   I-10, W to Tallahassee, E to Jacksonville

**19**   FL 228, Normandy Blvd, **E** gas: BP/dsl/24hr, Murphy USA, **food:** Arby's, Burger King, El Potro, Firehouse Subs, Golden Corral, Hot Wok, McDonald's, Papa John's, Sonic, Wendy's, **other:** CVS Drug, $Tree, Food Lion, Radio Shack, Walgreens, Walmart SuperCtr, st patrol, **W** gas: BP, Hess/dsl, QuickStop, RaceTrac, Shell, **food:** China Wok, Famous Amos, Golden China, Hardee's, Hungry Howie's Pizza, KFC/A&W, McDonald's, Pizza Hut, Popeye's, Subway, Whataburger, **other:** Advance Parts, Curves, CVS Drug, Family$, K-Mart, Publix, Winn-Dixie

**17**   FL 208, Wilson Blvd, **E** gas: BP/Subway/dsl, Hess/dsl, **food:** China Wok, Hardee's, McDonald's (1mi), **other:** Advance Parts, $General, Food Lion, **W** gas: Kangaroo

**16**   FL 134, 103rd St, Cecil Field, **E** gas: BP, Gate/dsl, Hess, **food:** Applebee's, Arby's, Capt D's, Firehouse Subs, McDonald's, Papa John's, Popeye's, Red Apple Asian, Shoney's, Sonic, Wendy's, Ying's Chinese, **lodging:** Hospitality Inn, **other:** Advance Parts, $General, GNC, NAPA, Tires+, Walmart SuperCtr, **W** gas: BP, Chevron, Exxon/dsl, Hess, Kangaroo, Shell, **food:** Burger King, DQ, Dragon Garden Chinese, El Chaparral Mexican, Mexican, Hot Wok, IHOP, KFC, McDonald's, Mi Toro Mexican, Pizza Hut, Subway, Taco Bell, **other:** Aamco, AutoZone, Family$, Food Lion, Goodyear/auto, Publix, SavRite Foods, Sun Tires, Walgreens, vet

**12**   FL 21, Blanding Blvd, **E** gas: BP, RaceWay, Texaco, Burger King, Larry's Subs, McDonald's, Pizza Hut, Subway, Sunrise Cafe, **other:** Acura, Best Buy, Buick/Pontiac, Cadillac, CVS Drug, $General, Dodge, Ford, Honda, Office Depot, PetsMart, Saturn, U-Haul, **W** gas: BP, Kangaroo/dsl, Shell, Applebee's, Arby's, Buffalo's, Burger King, Carrabba's, Chick-fil-A, Chili's, China Buffet, ChuckeCheese, Denny's, El Potro, Honey Baked Ham, Hooters, Ichiro Japanese, KFC, Kyodai Steaks, Longhorn Steaks, Maggie Moo's, Olive Garden, Outback Steaks, Panera Bread, Papa John's, Quizno's, Red Lobster, Ruby Tuesday, Smokey Bones, Sonic, Starbucks, Steak&Shake, Subway, Taco Bell, Ted's MT Grill, TGIFriday, Thai Garden, **lodging:** Country Inn, Hampton Inn, La Quinta; Motel 6, Red Roof Inn, Suburban Lodge, Super 8, **other:** H HOSPITAL, Belk, Books A Million, Circuit City, Dillard's, Discount Tire, $Tree, Food Lion, Goodyear/auto, Home Depot, JC Penny, JoAnn Fabrics, Michael's,

**12**   Continued
Old Navy, O'Reilly Parts, Publix, Sam's Club/gas, Sears/auto, Target, TJMaxx, Toyota, Walgreens, mall

**10**   US 17, FL 15, Roosevelt Blvd, Orange Park, **E** lodging: Best Western, **W** gas: BP, Chevron/dsl/24hr, Hess, RaceWay, **food:** Aaron's Pizza, Cracker Barrel, Krystal, McDonald's, Sam's Seafood, Ramirez Rest., Subway, Waffle House, Wendy's, **lodging:** Comfort Inn, Courtyard, Day's Inn, Econolodge, Fairfield Inn, Hilton Garden, Holiday Inn, Howard Johnson, Rodeway Inn, **other:** H HOSPITAL, Chrysler/Jeep, $General, Harley-Davidson, Honda, Nissan, Sun Tire, VW

**7mm**   St Johns River, Buckman Br

**5b a**   FL 13, San Jose Blvd, **E** gas: Chevron/DQ/dsl, Hess, **food:** Arby's, Bob Evans, Bono's BBQ, Boston Mkt, Carrabba's, Domino's, Famous Amos, Fastboy's Wings, Firehouse Subs, Krystal, Mi Torro Mexican, Outback Steaks, Popeye's, Smoothie King, Starbucks, St. John's Seafood, Steak'n Shake, Subway, Tijuana Flats, Village Inn, Wendy's, Woody's BBQ, **lodging:** La Quinta, Ramada Inn, **other:** Aamco, Ace Hardware, Advance Parts, CVS Drug, Firestone/auto, Goodyear/auto, K-Mart, Office Depot, PepBoys, Publix, Sun Tire, Target, Tire Kingdom, Walgreens, auto repair, **W** gas: BP, Citgo, Shell (1mi), **food:** Brooklyn Pizza, Bruster's, Chili's, Chipotle Mexican, Golden China, Golden Corral, Hardees, Kan-Ki Japanese, Krispy Kreme, Lee's Chicken, Mamafu's, McDonald's, Moe's SW Grill, Osaka Grill, Panera Bread, Papa John's, Pizza Hut, Subway, Taco Bell, **other:** Ace Hardware, Advance Parts, Barnes&Noble, BooksAMillion, Fresh Mkt, Friendly$, Goodyear/auto, Marshall's, Michael's, NAPA, PetCo, Publix, Radio Shack, Staples, SteinMart, Tire Kingdom, TJMaxx, U-Haul, Walmart SuperCtr, Winn-Dixie, World Mkt

**3**   Old St Augustine Rd, **E** gas: BP, Shell, **food:** Burger King, China Garden, Little Caesars, Little China, McDonald's, Pizza Hut, Taco Bell, Wendy's, **lodging:** Holiday Inn Express, **other:** CVS Drug, $General, Family$, Food Lion, Publix/deli, Winn-Dixie, **W** gas: Gate/dsl, Kangaroo/dsl, **food:** Firehouse Subs, KFC/Pizza Hut, Rosy's Mexican, Subway, **other:** Lowe's Whse, Walgreens, vet

**61 a b**   I-295 begins/ends on I-95, exit 337

## INTERSTATE 16

| Exit # | Services |
|---|---|
| 167b a | W Broad, Montgomery St, Savannah, **N gas:** BP/dsl, Chevron, Enmark, **lodging:** Comfort Suites, Courtyard, Econolodge (1mi), Hampton Inn (1mi), Howard Johnson, Quality Inn, Sheraton, **S food:** Burger King, KFC, Popeye's, Wendy's, I-16 begins/ends in Savannah. |
| 166 | US 17, Gwinnet St, Savannah |
| 165 | GA 204, 37th St (from eb), to Ft Pulaski NM, Savannah College |
| 164b a | I-516, US 80, US 17, GA 21 |
| 162 | Chatham Pkwy, **S gas:** Shell/dsl, **food:** Kan Pai Japanese, Larry's Subs, Sunrise Rest., **other:** Acura, Kia, Lexus, Toyota, vet |
| 160 | GA 307, Dean Forest Rd, **N gas:** Shell/dsl, Pilot/Subway/dsl/scales, **food:** Ronnie's Rest., Waffle House |
| 157b a | I-95, S to Jacksonville, N to Florence |
| 155 | Pooler Pkwy |
| 152 | GA 17, to Bloomingdale |
| 148 | Old River Rd, to US 80 |
| 144mm | weigh sta both lanes |
| 143 | US 280, to US 80, **S gas:** BP, El Cheapo/dsl/café/@ |
| 137 | GA 119, to Pembroke, Ft Stewart |
| 132 | Ash Branch Church Rd |
| 127 | GA 67, to Pembroke, Ft Stewart, **N gas:** El Cheapo/dsl, Shell/dsl, **food:** Morgan Creek Rest., **other:** antiques, **S gas:** Chevron/dsl/24hr |
| 116 | US 25/301, to Statesboro, **N gas:** Chevron/dsl/rest/scales/24hr, **food:** to GA S U, **S gas:** Sunoco/rest/dsl, **lodging:** Motel |
| 111 | Pulaski-Excelsior Rd, **S gas:** Citgo/cafe/dsl, **food:** Grady's Grill, **other:** Brookwood RV Park, truck lube |
| 104 | GA 22, GA 121, Metter, **N gas:** BP/dsl/scales/24hr, Chevron/dsl, Exxon, Pure, Shell/dsl, **food:** Burger King, Crabby Joes, DQ, Hardee's, Huddle House, Jomax BBQ, KFC/Taco Bell, Krispy Chic, McDonald's, Subway, Village Pizza, Waffle House, Western Steer, Zaxby's, **lodging:** American Inn, Econolodge, Comfort Inn, Scottish Inn, Holiday Inn Express, **other:** H HOSPITAL, Chevrolet, Rite Aid, to Smith SP, RV camping, **S gas:** Marathon/dsl, Phillips 66/dsl, **other:** Ford |
| 101mm | Canoochee River |
| 98 | GA 57, to Stillmore, **S gas:** BP/dsl/24hr, Chevron/dsl, **other:** to Altahama SP |
| 90 | US 1, to Swainsboro, **N gas:** BP, Ed's Trkstp/Pure/dsl/rest., Marathon/Gary's Subs/dsl, **other:** tires |
| 88mm | Ohoopee River |
| 84 | GA 297, to Vidalia, **N** truck sales |
| 78 | US 221, GA 56, to Swainsboro, **N gas:** BP/dsl (1mi) |
| 71 | GA 15, GA 78, to Soperton, **N gas:** Chevron/dsl |
| 67 | GA 29, to Soperton, **S gas:** Chevron/dsl, Marathon/dsl, **food:** Huddle House |
| 58 | GA 199, Old River Rd, East Dublin |
| 56mm | Oconee River |
| 54 | GA 19, to Dublin, **S gas:** Chevron |
| 51 | US 441, US 319, to Dublin, **N gas:** BP/Stuckey's/Subway/dsl, Flash Foods/gas, Neighbor's/dsl, Pilot/dsl/scales, Shell/24hr, **food:** Arby's, Buffalo's Café, Burger King, KFC, McDonald's, Pizza Hut, Ruby Tuesday, Shoney's, Taco Bell/TCBY, Waffle House/24hr, Wendy's, |

| Exit # | Services |
|---|---|
| 51 | Continued **lodging:** Comfort Inn, Day's Inn, Econolodge, Executive Inn, Hampton Inn, Holiday Inn Express, Jameson Inn, Super 8, **other:** H HOSPITAL, Ace Hardware, Jeep/Dodge, Steve's RV, **S gas:** Chevron, **food:** Cracker Barrel, **lodging:** La Quinta, **other:** Pinetucky Camping (2mi), antiques, to Little Ocmulgee SP |
| 49 | GA 257, to Dublin, Dexter, **N gas:** Chevron, **other:** H HOSPITAL, **S gas:** Love's/Chester's/Subway/dsl/scales/24hr, **other:** auto/dsl repair |
| 46mm | rest area wb, full H facilities, litter barrels, vending, petwalk, RV dump |
| 44mm | rest area eb, full H facilities, litter barrels, vending, petwalk, RV dump |
| 42 | GA 338, to Dudley |
| 39 | GA 26, to Cochran, Montrose |
| 32 | GA 112, Allentown, **S gas:** Chevron/dsl |
| 27 | GA 358, to Danville |
| 24 | GA 96, to Jeffersonville, **N gas:** Marathon/dsl, **S gas:** BP/dsl/24hr, **food:** Huddle House/24hr, **lodging:** Best Value, **other:** to Robins AFB, museum |
| 18 | Bullard Rd, to Jeffersonville, Bullard |
| 12 | Sgoda Rd, Huber, **N gas:** Marathon/dsl |
| 6 | US 23, US 129A, East Blvd, Ocmulgee, **N gas:** BP, **food:** DQ, **lodging:** Day's Inn (2mi), **other:** to airport, GA Forestry Ctr, **S gas:** Chevron/Huddle House/dsl, Friendly Gus, Subway |
| 2 | US 80, GA 87, MLK Jr Blvd, **N other:** H HOSPITAL, Ocmulgee NM, conv ctr, **S gas:** Marathon/dsl, Saf-T-Oil/dsl, **food:** Willow Rest., to Hist Dist |
| 1b | GA 22, to US 129, GA 49, 2nd St (from wb), **N other:** coliseum, **S lodging:** Ramada, **other:** H HOSPITAL |
| 1a | US 23, Gray Hwy (from eb), **N gas:** BP, Flash/dsl, Marathon, Shell, **food:** Arby's, Burger King, China Buffet, DQ, Fincher's BBQ, Golden Corral, Hong Kong Express, Huddle House, Isuzu, Krispy Kreme, McDonald's, Old Time Buffet, Papa John's, Popeye's, Subway, Taco Bell, Wendy's, **other:** H HOSPITAL, CVS Drug, Kroger, O'Reilly Parts, Radio Shack, U-Haul, Walgreens, transmissions, **S gas:** BP, Conoco/dsl, Exxon, Marathon/dsl, Spectrum, **food:** Burger King, Checker's, KFC, Krystal, Pizza Hut, Waffle House, Wendy's, Zaxby's, **lodging:** Scottish Inn, **other:** Hyundai, Pontiac, Staples, Tires+ |
| 0mm | I-75, S to Valdosta, N to Atlanta. I-16 begins/ends on I-75, exit 165 in Macon. |

## INTERSTATE 20

| Exit # | Services |
|---|---|
| 202mm | Georgia/South Carolina state line, Savannah River |
| 201mm | Welcome Ctr wb, full facilities, vending, litter barrels, petwalk |
| 200 | GA 104, Riverwatch Pkwy, Augusta, **N gas:** Pilot/Wendy's/dsl/24hr, **food:** Waffle House, **lodging:** Baymont Inn, Candlewood Suites, Courtyard, Jameson Inn, Microtel, Sleep Inn, Value Place |
| 199 | GA 28, Washington Rd, Augusta, **N gas:** BP, Raceway/24hr, Shell/Circle K, Sprint Gas, **food:** Applebees, A&W, Burger King, CA Dreaming, Capt D's, Checker's, Chick-fil-A, DQ, Damon's, Denny's, Dunkin Donuts, Fujiyama Japanese, Huddle House, KFC, King Buffet, Krystal, Longhorn Steaks, McDonald's, Ole Mexican, |

## INTERSTATE 20

**199** Continued
Piccadilly, Pizza Hut, Quizno's, Rhinehart's Seafood, Starbucks, Sonic, Subway, Waffle House, Wild Wing Cafe, **lodging:** Augusta Inn, Best Value Inn, Clarion, Fairfield Inn, Hampton Inn, Holiday Inn, Homewood Suites, La Quinta, Masters Inn, National Inn, Scottish Inn, Sunset Inn, **other:** AutoZone, Buick/GMC/Pontiac, BMW/Infiniti, Chrysler/Jeep, Chevrolet, Goodyear/auto, Hancock Fabrics, Hyundai, Jaguar, Land Rover, Lexus, Lincoln/Mercury, Lowe's Whse, Mazda, Mercedes, NAPA, Nissan, Suzuki, Toyota, Tuesday Morning, **S gas:** 76/Circle K, Shell/Circle K/dsl, **food:** Arby's, Blimpie, Bojangles, BoneFish Grill, Cane's Chicken, Carrabba's, China Rest., Church's, Domino's, Famous Dave's BBQ, Hardee's, Hooters, Krispy Kreme, LoneStar Café, LJ Silver, McDonald's, Olive Garden, Outback Steaks, Peking Chinese, Red Lobster, Shangri-La Chinese, Sonic, Subway, Taco Bell, T-Bonz Steaks, TGIFriday, Thai Jong Rest., Vallarta Mexican, Waffle House, Wendy's, **lodging:** Amerihost, Country Inn&Suites, Econolodge, Fairfield Inn, Knight's Inn, Ramada Inn, Rodeway Inn, Westbank Inn, **other:** Aamco, BooksAMillion, Dillard's, $General, Eckerd, Firestone, Fred's Drug, Goodyear/auto, Kroger/gas, PepBoys, SteinMart, Tire Kingdom, Walgreens

**196b** GA 232 W, **N gas:** Enmark, Raceway, **food:** Arby's, Bojangles, Burger King, Checker's, Golden Corral, Krystal, Ruby Tuesday, Ryan's, Salsa's Grill, Waffle House, Wendy's, **lodging:** Travel Inn, **other:** $Tree, GNC, Home Depot, Lowes Whse, O'Reilly Parts, Sam's Club, Tire Kingdom, Tires+, Walgreens, Walmart SuperCtr

**196a** I-520, Bobby Jones Fwy, **S gas:** BP, **food:** Backyard Burger, Chili's, Logan's Roadhouse, Macaroni Grill, O'Charley's, Sticky Fingers, Waffle House, **lodging:** DoubleTree Hotel, **other:** H HOSPITAL, Best Buy, Border's, Circuit City, Office Depot, Target, Tires+, to ✈

**195** Wheeler Rd, **N gas:** Sprint Gas, 0-2 mi **S gas:** BP/dsl, Shell/Circle K/Blimpie/24hr, **food:** Chili's, O'Charley's, Sonic, Waffle House, **lodging:** Candlewood Suites, Day's Inn, **other:** H HOSPITAL, Harley-Davidson, Rite Aid

**194** GA 383, Belair Rd, to Evans, **N gas:** Citgo, Shell/Circle K/Blimpie/dsl, Sprint Gas, **food:** Burger King, Poeye's,

**194** Continued
Sun Kwong Chinese, Waffle House, Wendy's, **lodging:** GA Inn, **other:** Food Lion, Funsville Park, **S gas:** BP/DQ/Stuckey's/dsl, Pilot/Subway/dsl/24hr, **food:** A&W/KFC, Cracker Barrel, Huddle House, Waffle House, **lodging:** Best Suites, Best Value Inn, Best Western, Comfort Inn, Econolodge, Hampton Inn, Holiday Inn, Motel 6, Quality Inn, Red Roof Inn, Super 8, Wingate Inn, **other:** Goodyear/auto

**190** GA 388, to Grovetown, **N gas:** BP/dsl, Waffle House, 2 mi **S gas:** Shell, **food:** KFC, McDonald's, Subway

**189mm** weigh sta both lanes

**183** US 221, to Harlem, Appling, **N gas:** Shell (2mi), **other:** Travel Country RV Ctr, **S gas:** BP/dsl

**182mm** rest area both lanes, full ♿ facilities, 🚻 vending, 🛈 litter barrels, RV dump, petwalk

**175** GA 150, **N gas:** Chevron/USA Trkstp/dsl/rest./24hr, **lodging:** Day's Inn, **other:** to Mistletoe SP

**172** US 78, GA 17, Thomson, **N gas:** BP/dsl, Chevron/dsl, Loves/Subway/dsl/scales/24hr, **food:** Waffle House, **other:** Chrysler/Dodge/Jeep, Ford/Mercury,

**THOMSON**　**E**　**W**

**GA**

**MADISON**

## INTERSTATE 20 CONT'D

**172** Continued
GMC/Pontiac, **S gas:** BP/DQ/dsl/24hr, M&A, Raceway/dsl, 76/Blimpie/Circle K, Shell, **food:** Amigo's Mexican, Arby's, Burger King, Checker's, Domino's, Krystal, LJ Silver, Lucky Rest., McDonald's, Mingwah Chinese, Pappa's BBQ, Pizza Hut, Taco Bell, Waffle House, Wendy's, Zaxby's, **lodging:** Best Western, Econolodge, Holiday Inn Express, Scottish Inn, **other:** H HOSPITAL, Advance Parts, AutoZone, Buick/Cadillac/Chevrolet, CVS Drug, Family$, Food Lion, K-Mart, Lowes Whse, Walmart SuperCtr/gas  (2mi)

**165** GA 80, Camak

**160** E Cadley Rd, Norwood

**154** US 278, GA 12, Barnett

**148** GA 22, Crawfordville, **N gas:** BP/dsl, **other:** to Stephens SP, **S gas:** Pure/rest./dsl

**138** GA 77, GA 15, Siloam, **N gas:** ⊕ FLYING J/Country Mkt/dsl/LP/scales/24hr, **S gas:** BP/dsl, Metro/dsl, **other:** H HOSPITAL

**130** GA 44, Greensboro, weigh sta, **N gas:** BP/dsl/24hr, Exxon/Subway, **food:** McDonald's, Pizza Hut, Subway, Waffle House, Wendy's, Zaxby's, **lodging:** Jameson Inn, Microtel, Thrift Court, **other:** H HOSPITAL, Buick/Chevrolet/Pontiac, $General, **S gas:** Chevron/dsl/24hr, **food:** Arby's, **lodging:** Hampton Inn, Holiday Inn Express, **other:** Home Depot

**121** to Lake Oconee, Buckhead, **S gas:** Chevron, **other:** Museum of Art (3mi)

**114** US 441, US 129, to Madison, **N gas:** Chevron/Subway, Citgo, Pilot/dsl/scales/24hr, RaceTrac, **food:** Arby's, Burger King, Chick-fil-A, Cracker Barrel, Domino's, KFC, Krystal, McDonald's, Pizza Hut, Sancho's Mexican, Starbucks, Waffle House, Wendy's, Zaxby's, **lodging:** Comfort Inn, Day's Inn, Hampton Inn, Holiday Inn, **other:** H HOSPITAL, Advance Parts, AutoZone, Buick/Chevrolet/GMC/Pontiac, $General, Ingles Foods/gas, Lowes Whse, Rite Aid, Walmart SuperCtr, **S gas:** Flash, TA/BP/Popeye's/dsl/@, Shell, Texaco, **food:** Waffle House, **lodging:** Best Value Inn, Red Roof Inn, Super 8, Wingate Inn, **other:** RV camping

**113** GA 83, Madison, **N gas:** BP, **other:** H HOSPITAL, st patrol, **S gas:** Liberty/gas

**108mm** rest area wb, full H facilities, [C, [�⚡],litter barrels, vending, RV dump, petwalk

**105** Rutledge, Newborn, **N gas:** BP/dsl, Yesterday Café, **other:** Hard Labor Creek SP

**103mm** rest area eb, full H facilities, [C, [⚡], litter barrels, vending, RV dump, petwalk

**101** US 278

**98** GA 11, to Monroe, Monticello, **4 mi N food:** Blue Willow Inn/rest., Log Cabin Rest., Sycamore Grill, **S gas:** BP/Blimpie/dsl, Chevron/dsl, Citgo

**95mm** Alcovy River

**93** GA 142, Hazelbrand Rd, **S gas:** Citgo, Phillips 66/dsl, **food:** Sonic, Waffle House, **lodging:** Quality Inn, **other:** H HOSPITAL, Ingles Foods, Walmart SuperCtr/Subway

**92** Alcovy Rd, **N gas:** Chevron/dsl, Circle K/dsl, **food:** Waffle House, **lodging:** Baymont Inn, Best Value Inn, Cornerstone Lodge, Day's Inn, Super 8, **0-2 mi S gas:**

**COVINGTON**　**CONYERS**

**92** Continued
Shell, Chick-fil-A, Dunkin Donuts, Krystal, McDonald's, Pizza Hut, Wendy's, **other:** H HOSPITAL

**90** US 278, GA 81, Covington, **S gas:** Citgo, Pure, QT, Raceway, **food:** Applebees, Arby's, Baskin-Robbins/Dunkin Donuts, Bojangles, Capt D's, Checker's, Chick-fil-A, Church's, DQ, Hong Kong Buffet, KFC, Longhorn Steaks, Nagano Japanese, Papa John's, Pizza Hut/Taco Bell, Popeye's, Royal Palace Chinese, Sunset Grill, Waffle House, Zaxby's, **lodging:** Holiday Inn Express, **other:** Aamco, Advance Parts, Big Lots, Chevrolet, $General, Food Depot, Goody's, Ingles Foods, K-Mart, Kroger/gas, O'Reilly Parts, Rite Aid

**88** Almon Rd, to Porterdale, **N gas:** Chevron/dsl, **S gas:** BP/Blimpie, Liberty, **food:** McDonald's, Subway (2mi), **other:** Riverside Estates RV Camp, transmissions/repair

**84** GA 162, Salem Rd, to Pace, **N gas:** BJ's Whse/gas, QuickSpot/dsl, **other:** Suzuki, Turning Wheel RV Ctr, **S gas:** Chevron/24hr, Phillips 66, QT, RaceWay, **food:** Baskin-Robbins, Burger King, Chick-fil-A, Dunkin Donuts, Hardee's, House Of Min, Los Bravos Mexican, McDonald's, Quizno's, Rib Tickling BBQ, Subway, Taco Bell, Waffle House, **other:** Advance Parts, Big 10 Tire, $General, Eckerd, Family$, Food Depot, Ingles/gas, Medicine Shoppe, O'Reilly Parts, Rite Aid, tires/repair

**83mm** parking area wb

**82** GA 138, GA 20, Conyers, **N gas:** BJ's Gas, QT, **food:** Applebees, Chili's, ChuckeCheese, Cracker Barrel, Don Pablo, Golden Corral, IHOP, O'Charley's, Outback Steaks, Red Lobster, Roadhouse Grill, Sonic, Subway, Up-the-Creek, **lodging:** Conyers Inn, Country Hearth Inn, Country Inn&Suites, Days Inn, Hampton Inn, Jameson Inn, La Quinta, **other:** Belk, Circuit City, Ford/Hyundai, Goody's, Home Depot, Kohl's, Michael's, NAPA, Office Depot, Old Navy, PetsMart, Staples, Tires+, U-Haul, Walmart SuperCtr, **S gas:** Chevron/24hr, Shell/dsl, **food:** Arby's, Blimpie, King, Capt D's, Checker's, Chick-fil-A, CiCi's, City Buffet, Folk's Rest., Grand Buffet, Hooters, Huddle House, KFC, King Buffet, Krystal/24hr, LJ Silver, McDonald's, Moe's SW Grill, Oaks Family Rest., Papa John's, Piccadilly's, Pizza Hut, Popeye's, Red Tomato, RolyPoly Sandwiches, Ruby Tuesday, Ryan's, Sonny's BBQ, Starbucks, Taco Bell, TCBY, Waffle House, Wendy's, **lodging:** InTown Inn, Microtel, Suburban Lodge, **other:** Big Lots, Big 10 Tire, Cub Foods, Dodge, $General, Eckerd, Firestone/auto, Food Depot, GNC, Goodyear/auto, Honda, Jo-Ann Fabrics, Kroger/gas/24hr, NTB, PepBoys, Publix, Radio Shack, Rite Aid, Target, TJ Maxx, Toyota, USPO, mall

**80** West Ave, Conyers, **N gas:** Chevron, Shell/dsl, **food:** DQ, Domino's, Mrs Winner's, Subway, Waffle House, **lodging:** Richfield Lodge, **other:** Chevrolet, Conyers Drug, Family$, Harley-Davidson, Piggly Wiggly, **S gas:** Exxon/dsl/24hr, Texaco, **food:** Longhorn Steaks, McDonald's, **lodging:** Comfort Inn, **other:** Chrysler/Dodge/Jeep, JustBrakes, Kia, Mitsubishi, Nissan, Suncoast RV Ctr, vet

**79mm** parking area eb

**78** Sigman Rd, **N gas:** Circle K/gas, **food:** Waffle House, **S other:** Buick/GMC/Mazda/Pontiac, Crown RV Ctr, st police

## INTERSTATE 20 CONT'D

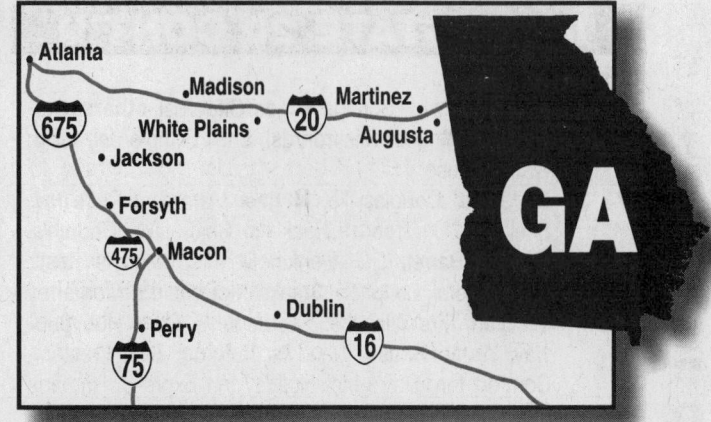

**E ↕ W**

**L I T H O N I A**

**75** US 278, GA 124, Turner Hill Rd, **N gas:** BP/dsl, Citgo/dsl/24hr, **S food:** Applebee's, Arizona's, Atlanta Steaks, Barnacle's Seafood, Buffalo Wild Wings, Bugaboo Steaks, Chick-fil-A, Chili's, Firehouse Subs, Grand China, KFC/Pizza Hut/Taco Bell, McDonald's, Olive Garden, Panera Bread, Ruby Tuesday, Smokey Bones BBQ, Steak n'Shake, Wendy's, Zaxby's, **lodging:** Comfort Inn, Fairfield Inn, Hilton Garden, Holiday Inn Express, Hyatt Place, **other:** Best Buy, Borders Books, Curves, Dillard's, Eckerd, JC Penney, Kohl's, Macy's, Marshall's, Rite Aid, Ross, Sam's Club/gas, Sears/auto, Staples, Target, Tires+, World Mkt, mall

**74** GA 124, Lithonia, **N gas:** Chevron/24hr, Shell/24, Texaco, **food:** Capt D's, KFC/Taco Bell, McDonald's, Pizza Hut, SoulFood Rest., Subway, Waffle House, Wendy's, **other:** Advance Parts, CVS Drug, **S gas:** Citgo/dsl/24hr, **food:** Da-Bomb Wings/Seafood, DQ, Dudley's Rest., Krystal/24hr, Waffle House, **lodging:** Econolodge, Microtel, **other:** $General

**71** Hillandale Dr, Farrington Rd, Panola Rd, **N gas:** QT/dsl, **food:** Burger King, Checker's, KFC, McDonald's, Mrs. Winner's, Popeye's, Waffle House, **lodging:** Holiday Inn Express, Motel 6, Super 8, **other:** Family$, **S gas:** BP/dsl/24hr, Citgo, Shell, **food:** IHOP, New China, Popeye's, Ruby Tuesday, Starbucks, Subway, Taco Bell/LJ Silver, Wendy's, **lodging:** Red Roof Inn, **other:** Lowes Whse, NAPA, Publix, Radio Shack, Walgreens, Walmart SuperCtr/gas

**68** Wesley Chapel Rd, Snapfinger Rd, **N food:** Blimpie, Capt D's, Checker's, Chick-fil-A, China Buffet, Church's, KFC, Popeye's, Subway, Taco Bell, Waffle House, Wendy's, **lodging:** Economy Inn, **other:** CVS Drug, Ford, Home Depot, Kroger, NTB, **S gas:** Chevron/dsl/24hr, Mobil, Shell/dsl, Texaco, **food:** Dragon Chinese, JJ's Fish& Chicken, McDonald's, Popeye's, **lodging:** Super Inn

**67b a** I-285, S to Macon, N to Greenville

**66** Columbia Dr (from eb, no return), **N gas:** Chevron

**65** GA 155, Candler Rd, to Decatur, **N gas:** BP/24hr, Chevron, Citgo, Marathon, **food:** Pizza Hut, Popeye's, Red Lobster, Supreme Fish Delight, Wendy's, **lodging:** Econolodge, Motel 6, **other:** CVS Drug, U-Haul, **S gas:** BP, Chevron/24hr, Marathon, Shell/dsl, Stop&Go, **food:** Baskin-Robbins/Dunkin Donuts, Burger King, Checker's, China Café, Church's, DQ, Homebox Rest., KFC/Pizza Hut, McDonald's, Picadilly's, Taco Bell, **lodging:** Sunset Lodge, **other:** Big Lots, Firestone/auto, Kroger, Macy's, mall

**63** Gresham Rd, **N gas:** Chevron, Citgo/dsl, **other:** Walmart SuperCtr/Subway, **S gas:** BP/24hr/dsl, Citgo, Phillips 66, Shell, **food:** Church's, **other:** auto repair

**62** Flat Shoals Rd (from eb, no return), **N gas:** Exxon

**61b** GA 260, Glenwood Ave, **N gas:** BP, Chevron, Texaco/dsl, **food:** KFC, Wild Bean Cafe

**61a** Maynard Terrace (from eb, no return)

**60b a** US 23, Moreland Ave, **N gas:** Exxon, **lodging:** Atlanta Motel, **S gas:** Phillips 66/dsl, Shell, **food:** Checker's, Krystal, LJ Silver, McDonald's, Mrs Winner's, Wendy's

**59b** Memorial Dr, Glenwood Ave (from eb)

**59a** Cyclorama, **N gas:** Chevron/dsl, Shell **food: other:** Confederate Ave Complex, MLK Site, **S gas:** BP

**A T L A N T A   A R E A**

**58b** Hill St (from wb, no return), **N gas:** Shell, **food:** Mrs. Winners

**58a** Capitol St (from wb, no return), downtown, **N** to GA Dome, **S** Holiday Inn

**57** I-75/85

**56b** Windsor St (from eb), to Turner Field

**56a** US 19, US 29, McDaniel St (eb only), **N gas:** Chevron

**55b** Lee St (from wb), Ft McPherson, **S gas:** BP, **food:** Church's, Popeye's, Taco Bell

**55a** Ashby St, **S gas:** BP, Exxon/dsl, **food:** Church's, Popeye's, Stop 1 Food Court, Taco Bell, **other:** CVS Drug, Family$, Sav-a-Lot Foods, Sears, mall

**54** Langhorn St (from wb), to Cascade Rd

**53** MLK Dr, to GA 139, **N gas:** Chevron/24hr, Shell/dsl/24hr, **S gas:** BP, Right Stuf Gas, **other:** auto repair

**52b a** GA 280, Holmes Dr, High Tower Rd, **S gas:** Chevron, Exxon/dsl, **food:** Church's, McDonald's, Wendy's, **other:** AutoZone, CVS Drug

**51b a** I-285, S to Montgomery, N to Chattanooga

**49** GA 70, Fulton Ind Blvd, **N gas:** Citgo/dsl/24hr, Shell, **food:** Capt D's, DQ, Subway, Wendy's, **lodging:** Best Value Inn, Fulton Inn, In Home Suites, Moseley Motel, **S gas:** BP/dsl, Chevron, Citgo/dsl, Shell, **food:** Grand Buffet, McDonald's, Waffle House, **lodging:** Super 8, Travelodge

**48mm** Chattahoochee River

**47** Six Flags Pkwy (from wb), **N gas:** BP, **lodging:** Royal Inn, **S lodging:** Howard Johnson, Sleep Inn, Wingate Inn, **other:** Six Flags Funpark

**46b a** Riverside Parkway, **N gas:** Citgo/Church's, Marathon, QT, **food:** Hong Kong Buffet, Waffle House, **lodging:** Baymont Inn, **S gas:** Pure, **food:** Wendy's, **lodging:** Howard Johnson, Sleep Inn, Wingate Inn, **other:** Six Flags Funpark

**44** GA 6, Thornton Rd, to Lithia Springs, **N gas:** BP/24hr, QT, RaceTrac, Shell, **food:** Burger King, Chick-fil-A, El Pollo Loco, Golden Dragon Chinese, IHOP, KFC, Krystal, McDonald's, Ruby Tuesday, Shoney's, Sonic, Subway, Taco Bell, Waffle House, Wendy's, Zaxby's, **lodging:** Budget Inn, Comfort Inn, $General, Knight's Inn, Suburban Lodge, **other:** [H] HOSPITAL, Carmax, Chevrolet, Ford, Harley-Davidson, Home Depot, Honda, Kroger/gas, Mazda, Nissan, Office Depot, Saturn, Tires+, VW, Walgreens, **S food:** Cracker Barrel, La Fiesta Mexican, Wendy's, **lodging:** Country Inn&Suites, Courtyard, Fairfield Inn, Hampton Inn, Hilton Garden, Motel 6, SpringHill Suites, **other:** Buick/GMC, Chrysler/Jeep, Dodge, Toyota, Walmart SuperCtr, to Sweetwater Creek SP

**GA**

## INTERSTATE 20 CONT'D

| | |
|---|---|
| **42mm** | weigh sta eb |
| **41** | Lee Rd, to Lithia Springs, **N gas:** Citgo/dsl, **other:** transmissions, **S gas:** Chevron/dsl, Shell/Blimpie/dsl, **food:** Waffle House |
| **37** | GA 92, to Douglasville, **N gas:** Marathon, RaceTrac, Shell/dsl/24hr, **food:** Checker's, Chick-fil-A, Church's, Cracker Barrel, DQ, Dunkin Donuts, Kenny's Rest., KFC, Krystal, Longhorn Steaks, McDonald's, Monterrey Mexican, Mrs Winner's, Papa John's, Pizza Hut, Subway, Waffle House, Wendy's, **lodging:** Best Western, Comfort Inn, Day's Inn, Holiday Inn Express, Ramada Ltd, Royal Inn, Super 8, **other:** H HOSPITAL, Advance Parts, AutoZone, Big Lots, CVS Drug, Family$, Fred's Drug, Kroger/24hr, NAPA, O'Reilly Parts, Tires+, Walgreens, **S gas:** QT, Waffle House, **other:** Aamco |
| **36** | Chapel Hill Rd, **N** H HOSPITAL, **S gas:** QT/24hr, Shell/dsl **food:** Applebee's, Arby's, Asia Buffet, Blimpie, Carraba's, Chaunce's Rest., China Garden, Coldstone Creamery, Joe's Crabshack, Johnny's Subs, McDonald's, Logan's Roadhouse, O'Charley's, Olive Garden, Outback Steaks, Panda Express, Provino's Italian, Quaker Steak&Lube, Taste Of Thai, Texas Roadhouse, TGIFriday, Waffle House, **lodging:** Hampton Inn, **other:** Belk, Borders, Circuit City, Dillard's, Discount Tire, Firestone/auto, Goody's, JC Penney, Kohl's, Macy's, Marshall's, Michael's, Old Navy, PetsMart, Rite Aid, Ross, Sears/auto, Target, mall |
| **34** | GA 5, to Douglasville, **N gas:** RaceTrac, Texaco, **food:** Hooters, Ryan's, Waffle House, Williamson Bro's BBQ, Zaxby's, **lodging:** Holiday Inn Express, La Quinta, Sleep Inn, **other:** $Tree, Honda/Isuzu, Sam's Club, Walmart SuperCtr, **S gas:** Chevron/24hr, Circle K, Shell, **food:** Applebee's, Atlanta Bread, Bruster's, Buffalo Wild Wings, Burger King, Chili's, Chick-fil-A, ChuckeCheese, CiCi's, DQ, Dunkin Donuts, El Rodeo Mexican, Fiesta Mexican, Folk's Rest., Golden Buddah, Golden Corral, IHOP, KFC, Krystal, LJ Silver, McDonald's, Moe's SW Grill, Papa John's, Pizza Hut, Quizno's, Red Lobster, Ruby Tuesday, Seabreeze Seafood, Sonic, Sonny's BBQ, Subway, Taco Bell, Taco Mac, Waffle House, Wendy's, **lodging:** InTown Suites, **other:** Advance Parts, Best Buy, Big 10 Tire, Eckerd, GNC, Goodyear/auto, Home Depot, Jo-Ann Crafts, K-Mart, Kroger, Lowes Whse, Office Depot, PetCo, Publix, Radio Shack, Tuesday Morning, U-Haul, USPO, Walgreens |
| **30** | Post Rd, **S gas:** Shell/dsl |
| **26** | Liberty Rd, Villa Rica, **N gas:** Shell/dsl, Swifty/dsl, **food:** China Wok, Mex-Grill, Subway, Waffle House, **other:** H HOSPITAL, Publix, Walgreens, **S gas:** Chevron, Wilco/Hess/Subway/Godfather's Pizza/dsl/scales/24hr/@, **lodging:** American Inn |
| **24** | GA 101, GA 61, Villa Rica, **N gas:** Citgo, RaceTrac, Shell/dsl, **food:** Arby's, Chick-fil-A, Hardee's, KFC/Taco Bell, Krystal, McDonald's, Pizza Hut, Romero's Mexican, Subway, Waffle House, Wendy's, **lodging:** Comfort Inn, Days Inn, Hometowne Lodge, Super 8, **other:** H HOSPITAL, AutoZone, CVS Drug, Ingles Foods, Piggly Wiggly, Rite Aid, **S gas:** QT, Shell/dsl, **food:** Burger King, Capt D's, Domino's, El Ranchito Mexican, O'Charley's, |

| | |
|---|---|
| **24** | Continued |
| | Papa John's, Philly Connection, Waffle House, Zaxby's, **other:** Chevrolet, $Tree, Home Depot, GNC, Walmart SuperCtr/Subway, to W GA Coll |
| **21mm** | Little Tallapoosa River |
| **19** | GA 113, Temple, **N gas:** ⊕ *FLYING J*/Conoco/Country Mkt/dsl/24hr, Pilot/Subway/Wendy's/dsl/24hr/@, Texaco, **food:** Fortune Star Chinese, Hardee's, McDonald's, Waffle House, **other:** Truck-o-Mat/scales |
| **15mm** | weigh sta wb |
| **11** | US 27, Bremen, Bowdon, **N gas:** Bremen Express/dsl, SuperMart/dsl, Texaco, **food:** Arby's, Capt D's, Checker's, Chopsticks Chinese, Cracker Barrel, Juanito's, KFC, McDonald's, Papa John's, Pizza Hut, Quizno's, Subway, Waffle House, Wendy's, Zaxby's, **lodging:** Day's Inn, Holiday Inn Express, Hampton Inn, Quality Inn, **other:** H HOSPITAL, Advance Parts, $General, Ford, Ingles Foods, Walmart SuperCtr/gas (1mi), **S gas:** BP/dsl, Kangaroo, Waffle House, John Tanner SP |
| **9** | Waco Rd, **N** Love's/Subway/dsl |
| **5** | GA 100, Tallapoosa, **N gas:** Citgo/dsl/24hr, Exxon/dsl/24hr, Waffle House **other:** Big Oak RV park, **S gas:** Noble Trk-Stp/dsl/24hr/@, Pilot/KFC/Taco Bell/dsl/scales/24hr, Shell/Subway, **food:** DQ, Huddle House, Janet's Diner, **lodging:** Comfort Inn, **other:** to John Tanner SP |
| **1mm** | **Welcome Ctr eb, full** ♿ **facilities,** 📞 **, vending,** 🛉 **, litter barrels, petwalk** |
| **0mm** | Georgia/Alabama state line, Eastern/Central time zone |

## INTERSTATE 59

| Exit # | Services |
|---|---|
| **I-59** | begins/ends on I-24, exit 167. For I-24, turn to Tennessee Interstate 24. |
| **20mm** | I-24, W to Nashville, E to Chattanooga |
| **17** | Slygo Rd, to New England, **W gas:** Midnite/dsl, **other:** KOA (2mi) |
| **11** | GA 136, Trenton, **E gas:** Chevron/dsl, Exxon/dsl, Kangaroo, **food:** Asian Garden, Hardee's, McDonald's, Pizza Hut, Subway, **lodging:** Days Inn, **other:** Advance Parts, CVS Drug, Family$, Ingles, O'Reilly Parts, to Cloudland Canyon SP, **W gas:** BP, Citgo, **food:** Huddle House, Krystal, Little Caesar's, Taco Bell, Wendy's, **other:** BiLo, $General, Food Lion |
| **4** | Rising Fawn, **E gas:** Citgo/24hr, **W gas:** BP/dsl/24hr, Pilot/Chester Fried/Subway/dsl/24hr, **other:** camping |
| **0mm** | Georgia/Alabama state line, eastern/central time zone |

## INTERSTATE 75

| Exit # | Services |
|---|---|
| **355mm** | Georgia/Tennessee state line |
| **354mm** | Chickamauga Creek |
| **353** | GA 146, Rossville, **E gas:** BP/24hr, Chevron, **lodging:** Knight's Inn, **W gas:** BP/Subway/dsl, Shell, **other:** antiques |
| **352mm** | **Welcome Ctr sb, full** ♿ **facilities,** 📞 **, info, vending,** 🛉 **, litter barrels, petwalk** |
| **350** | GA 2, Bfd Pkwy, to Ft Oglethorpe, **E gas:** BP/dsl, Kangaroo, **lodging:** Hometown Inn, **W gas:** RaceTrac/24hr, Shell, **other:** H HOSPITAL, 1-3 mi **W gas:** Conoco/dsl/rest., **food:** BBQ Corral, Fazoli's (3mi), O'Charly's (3mi), Taco Bell (3mi), Zaxby's (3mi), **other:** KOA, Walmart SuperCtr (3mi), to Chickamauga NP |

*(left margin, top to bottom)* E ← W — D O U G L A S V I L L E — V I L L A R I C A

TEMPLE — N ↑ S — T R E N T O N — N ↑ S

GA

## INTERSTATE 75 CONT'D

**N ↕ S**

**DALTON**

**348** GA 151, Ringgold, **E gas:** BP/Subway/dsl, Conoco, Shell/dsl, **food:** Cracker Barrel, Hardee's, Krystal/24hr, KFC, Los Reyes Mexican, McDonald's, Pizza Hut, Ruby Tuesday, Taco Bell, Waffle House, **lodging:** Day's Inn, Holiday Inn Express, Red Roof Inn, Super 8, **other:** Advance Parts, CVS Drug, Chevrolet, Chrysler/Jeep, Family$, Ingles, RV camping, North GA RV Ctr, **W gas:** BP, Kangaroo, Shell, **food:** Domino's, Wendy's, **lodging:** Comfort Inn, **other:** Food Lion, Ford, Northgate RV Ctr, Peterbilt

**345** US 41, US 76, Ringgold, **E gas:** BP, **W gas:** Chevron, Cochran's/Exxon/dsl/rest./24hr/@, Kangaroo/Subway/dsl, **food:** Waffle House

**343mm** weigh sta both lanes

**341** GA 201, to Varnell, Tunnel Hill, **W gas:** Chevron, Shell, **other:** carpet outlets

**336** US 41, US 76, Dalton, Rocky Face, **E gas:** Chevron/Blimpie, RaceTrac, Shell, **food:** Waffle House, **lodging:** Econolodge, Stay Lodge, **other:** Ⓗ HOSPITAL, Checker Parts, Home Depot, Walmart SuperCtr/gas, **W gas:** BP/dsl, Exxon, **food:** Denny's, Los Pablos Mexican, Wendy's, **lodging:** Best Western/rest., Motel 6, Royal Inn, Super 8, carpet outlets

**333** GA 52, Dalton, **E gas:** BP/dsl, Chevron/24hr, Kangaroo, RaceTrac/dsl, **food:** Applebee's, A&W/LJ Silver, Burger King, Capt D's, Chick-fil-A, CiCi's, Cracker Barrel, Dairy Queen, Fuddrucker's, IHOP, Jimmy's Rest., KFC, Lizzi's Deli, Longhorn Steaks, McDonald's, O'Charley's, Outback Steaks, Pizza Hut, Schlotsky's, Shoney's, Sonic, Steak'n Shake, Taco Bell, Waffle House, Wendy's, **lodging:** Best Inn, Days Inn, Hampton Inn, Travelodge, **other:** Chevrolet, Chrysler/Jeep, Ford, Harley-Davidson, Isuzu, K-Mart, Kroger, Mr Transmission, Tanger Outlets/famous brands, Walgreen, **W food:** Chili's, Red Lobster, **lodging:** Comfort Inn, Courtyard, Country Inn Suites, Holiday Inn, Jameson Inn, Quality Inn, Ramada, Wingate Inn, **other:** NW GA Trade/Conv Ctr

**328** GA 3, to US 41, **E gas:** BP/dsl, Pilot/Arby's/dsl/scales/24hr, **food:** Antonio's Mexican, Waffle House, Wendy's, **lodging:** Super 8, **W** carpet outlets

**326** Carbondale Rd, **E gas:** Chevron/dsl, Pilot/McDonalds/Subway/dsl/scales, **W gas:** BP, Exxon

**320** GA 136, to Lafayette, Resaca, **E gas:** ⚡FLYING J/Cookery/dsl/LP/rest./24hr/@, **other:** truckwash, truck repair/parts

**319mm** Oostanaula River, rest area sb, full ♿ facilities, 🅲, vending, 🅿 litter barrels, petwalk

**RESACA**

**318** US 41, Resaca, **E gas:** Hess/Wilco/DQ/Wendy's/dsl/24hr, **food:** Hardee's, **lodging:** Knight's Inn, **W gas:** Shell/dsl, **lodging:** Best Inn, Budget Inn, Duffy's Motel, Smith Motel, Super 8

**317** GA 225, to Chatsworth, **E** New Echota HS, Vann House HS, **W lodging:** Express Inn

**315** GA 156, Redbud Rd, to Calhoun, **E gas:** Citgo/dsl, Kangaroo, **food:** Waffle House, **other:** Food Lion, KOA (2mi), antiques, **W gas:** BP/dsl, Liberty/Subway, Shell, **food:** Arby's, Shoney's, **lodging:** Ramada Ltd, **other:** Ⓗ HOSPITAL, Eckerd

**CALHOUN**

**312** GA 53, to Calhoun, **E gas:** Shell/dsl, **food:** Cracker Barrel, Longhorn Steaks, **lodging:** Country Inn, Preferred Inn, Quality Inn, **other:** Prime Outlets/famous brands, **W gas:** BP/Arby's, Chevron/dsl, Kangaroo, RaceWay, **food:** BJ's Rest., Bojangles, Burger King, Capt D's, Checker's, Chick-fil-A, China Cook, DQ, Domino's, Eastern Cafe, Fire Mtn Grill, Gondola Pizza, Huddle House, IHOP, KFC, Krystal/24hr, Little Caesar's, Lizzi's Seafood, LJ Silver/A&W, McDonald's, Papa's Pizza, Pizza Hut, Ruby Tuesday, Subway, Taco Bell, Zaxby's, **lodging:** Comfort Inn, Guest Inn, Hampton Inn, Holiday Inn Express, Jameson Inn, Royal Inn, **other:** Advance Parts, AutoZone, Chrysler/Jeep/Dodge, CVS Drug, $General, GNC, Goodyear/auto, Goody's, Home Depot, Ingles, Kroger/Starbucks/gas, Office Depot, Walmart SuperCtr/gas

**308mm** rest area nb, full Ⓗ facilities, 🅲, 🅿, litter barrels, vending, petwalk

**ADAIRSVILLE**

**306** GA 140, Adairsville, **E gas:** Cowboy's/dsl, Patty's/Citgo/dsl/24hr/@, QT/dsl/scales/24hrs, Shell, **food:** Cracker Barrel, Huddle House, Wendy's, **W gas:** All American/dsl/scales, BP/dsl, Chevron, Exxon/dsl, **food:** Burger King, Hardee's, McDonald's, Taco Bell, Waffle House, Zaxby's, **lodging:** Best Western, Comfort Inn, Ramada Ltd, **other:** Harvest Moon RV Park

**296** Cassville-White Rd, **E gas:** Food & Fuel, Pilot/McDonald's/Subway/dsl/scales/@, Pure, TA/Burger King/Pizza Hut/Popeye's/Taco Bell/dsl/scales/24hr/@, Texaco/24hr, **lodging:** Sleep Inn, **W gas:** Chevron, Citgo/dsl, Shell, **food:** Waffle House/24hr, **lodging:** Best Inn, Budget Host/rest., Howard Johnson, Red Carpet Inn, **other:** KOA

**293** US 411, to White, **E gas:** BP/dsl, Texaco, **lodging:** Scottish Inn, **W gas:** Chevron/dsl, Citgo/dsl/24hr, Horizon/Backyard Burger/Pizza Hut/dsl, Roman's Steaks, Tom's Place Rest., Waffle House, **lodging:** Courtesy Inn, Holiday Inn/AJ's Cafe, **other:** RV camping, mineral museum, st patrol

**290** GA 20, to Rome, **E gas:** Chevron/Subway/dsl, Exxon/dsl, Kangaroo/dsl, **food:** Arby's, Fruit Jar Cafe, McDonald's, Wendy's, **lodging:** Best Western, Comfort Inn, Country Inn Suites, Econolodge, Motel 6, Ramada Ltd, Super 8, **W gas:** BP, Shell, **food:** Cracker Barrel, Pappas Pizza House, Pruitt's BBQ, Shoney's, Waffle House, **lodging:** Day's Inn, Hampton Inn, **other:** Ⓗ HOSPITAL, RV camping (7mi), Walmart SuperCtr/gas (1.5mi)

**288** GA 113, Cartersville, **2 mi W gas:** BP/dsl, Exxon/dsl, **food:** Applebee's, Burger King, Chick-fil-A, Krystal/24hr, Mrs Winner's, Pizza Hut, Red Lobster, Subway, Waffle

## INTERSTATE 75 CONT'D

**N** ↕ **S**

**ACWORTH**

**288** Continued
House, **lodging:** Knight's Inn, Quality Inn, **other:** Kroger, to Etowah Indian Mounds (6mi)

**286mm** Etowah River

**285** Emerson, **E gas:** Texaco/24hr, **lodging:** Red Top Mtn Lodge, **other:** to Allatoona Dam, to Red Top Mtn SP

**283** Emerson Allatoona Rd, Allatoona Landing Resort, camping

**280mm** Allatoona Lake

**278** Glade Rd, to Acworth, **E gas:** BP/dsl, Shell, **lodging:** Best Value, **other:** McKinney Camping (3mi), to Glade Marina, **W gas:** Chevron, Petro, Shell, **food:** Bojangles, County Café, Hong Kong Chinese, KFC, Krystal, Papa John's, Pizza Hut, Subway, Taco Bell, Waffle House, **lodging:** Best Inn, **other:** AutoZone, BigLots, Eckerd, Ingles/cafe, K-Mart, NAPA, Radio Shack

**277** GA 92, **E gas:** BP, RaceTrac, **food:** Hardee's, Shoney's, Waffle House, **lodging:** Comfort Suites, Holiday Inn Express, Ramada Ltd, **W gas:** Chevron/dsl, Shell/DQ/dsl, **food:** Bamboo Garden, Domino's, McDonald's, Ricardo's Mexican, Sonic, Waffle House, Wendy's, Zaxby's, **lodging:** Best Western, Day's Inn, Econolodge, Super 8, **other:** Advance Parts, CVS Drug, Goodyear/auto, Publix, Walgreen

**273** Wade Green Rd, **E gas:** BP, Pure, RaceTrac, **food:** Arby's, Burger King, China King, Dunkin Donuts, Las Palmas Mexican, McDonald's, Mrs Winners, Pizza Hut/Taco Bell, Subway, Waffle House, **lodging:** Travelodge, **other:** BigLots, Eckerd, Goodyear/auto, Publix, **W gas:** Shell, Texaco/dsl, **food:** BBQ Street, Coldstone, Hunan Chinese, Johnny's Pizza/Subs, Starbucks, Wendy's, **other:** Kroger/gas, Walgreen

**271** Chastain Rd, to I-575 N, **E gas:** Chevron, **food:** Brewsters, Cracker Barrel, Dunkin Donuts, Firehouse Subs, Los Reyes, McAlister's Deli, O'Charley's, Panda Express, Sidelines Grille, ToGo's/Baskin Robbins, Zaxby's, Zucca Pizza, **lodging:** Best Western, Comfort Inn, Extended Stay America, Fairfield Inn, Residence Inn, Suburban Lodge, Super 8, **other:** Circuit City, Goodyear/auto, Outlets Ltd Mall, Walmart/auto, funpark, **W gas:** Citgo, Swifty Save Gas/Blimpie, Shell/dsl, **food:** Arby's, Mellow Mushroom, Mrs Winners, Quizno's, Waffle House/24hr, Wendy's, **lodging:** Country Inn Suites, SpringHill Suites, Sun Suites, **other:** museum

**MARIETTA**

**269** to US 41, to Marietta, **E gas:** Chevron/24hr, Shell, Texaco/dsl, **food:** Applebee's, Burger King, Fuddrucker's, Longhorn Steaks, McDonald's, New China, Olive Garden, Pizza Hut, Provino's, Red Lobster, Shogun Japanese, Smokey Bones, Starbucks, Subway, Waffle House, **lodging:** Comfort Inn, Econolodge, Holiday Inn Express, La Quinta, Red Roof Inn, Super 8, **other:** Barnes&Noble, Big 10 Tire, Firestone/auto, Home Depot, Macy's, Marshall's, Publix, Sears/auto, TJ Maxx, mall, **W gas:** BP, Exxon, **food:** Bahama Breeze, Bailey's Grill, Bugaboo, Carrabbas, Copelands Grill, Creek Steaks, Chick-fil-A, Chili's, ChuckeCheese, Coldstone, Golden Corral, Joe's Crabshack, Macaroni Grill, On-the-Border, Outback Steaks, Rafferty's, Starbucks, Steak'n Shake, Sweet Tomato, TGIFriday, Willy's Mexican, **lodging:** Day's Inn, Hampton Inn, Hilton Garden, Quality Inn, Wingate Inn, **other:** Best Buy, Borders, Buick/Pontiac/

**MARIETTA**

**269** Continued
GMC, CarMax, Chevrolet, Circuit City, Costco/gas, Ford/Lincoln/Mercury, Goodyear/auto, Jo-Anne Fabrics, Kia/Toyota, Nissan, Mitsubishi, NTB, Office Depot, Old Navy, PetsMart, Target, mall, to Kennesaw Mtn NP

**268** I-575 N, GA 5 N, to Canton

**267b a** GA 5 N, to US 41, Marietta

**265** GA120, N Marietta Pkwy, **W gas:** Chevron, Shell/dsl, **food:** Arbys, Bojangles, Chick-fil-A, KFC, **lodging:** Days Inn, Sun Inn, Suburban Lodge, Travelers Motel

**263** GA 120, to Roswell, **E gas:** Chevron/dsl/24hr, QT, Texaco/24hr, **W gas:** Exxon/dsl, RaceTrac, **food:** Applebee's, Capt D's, China Kitchen, DQ, Hardee's, Haveli Rest., Piccadilly's, Subway, **lodging:** Best Western, Crowne Plaza, Fairfield Inn, Hampton Inn, Marietta Motel, Ramada Ltd, Regency Inn, Super 8, Wyndham Garden, **other:** U-Haul

**261** GA 280, Delk Rd, to Dobbins AFB, **E gas:** Exxon, RaceTrac, Shell/McDonald's/24hr, **food:** CC Cafeteria, China Wok, Hardee's, KFC/Taco Bell, Murphy's Deli, Ruby Tuesday, Spaghetti Whse, **lodging:** Budget Inn, Courtyard, Drury Inn, Motel 6, Scottish Inn, Sleep Inn, Super 8, Travelers Inn, **other:** Publix, **W gas:** BP, Chevron/24hr, **food:** Cracker Barrel, D&B Rest., Waffle House, **lodging:** Best Inn, Comfort Inn, Days Inn, Fairfield Inn, Holiday Inn, La Quinta, Quality Inn, Wingate Inn

**SMYRNA**

**260** Windy Hill Rd, to Smyrna, **E gas:** BP, **food:** Boston Mkt, Famous Dave's, Fuddrucker's, Houston's Rest., Jersey Mike's Subs, NY Pizza, Pappasito's Cantina, Pappadeaux Seafood, Philly Cafe, Salgrosso Brazilian, Schlotsky's, Starbucks, Subway, TGIFriday, **lodging:** Econolodge, Extended Stay Deluxe, Hilton Garden, Hyatt, Marriott, Studio Lodge, **other:** CVS Drug, **W gas:** Chevron, Citgo, Shell, **food:** Arby's, Chick-fil-A, Fatburger, Halftime Grill, McDonald's, Panda Express, Popeye's, Starbucks, Waffle House, Wendy's, **lodging:** Best Western, Country Inn Suites, Courtyard, Day's Inn, DoubleTree, Hilton, Masters Inn, Red Roof Inn, **other:** H HOSPITAL, Target

**259b a** I-285, W to Birmingham, E to Greenville, Montgomery

**258** Cumberland Pkwy, **W food:** Doc Green's Rest., Hooters, Moe's SW Grill, Shane's Ribshack, Subway

**257mm** Chattahoochee River

**256** to US 41, Northside Pkwy

**255** US 41, W Paces Ferry Rd, **E gas:** Chevron, Shell/dsl, **food:** Blue Ridge Grill, Caribou Coffee, Chick-fil-A, Houston's Rest., McDonald's/playplace, OK Café/24hr, Pero's Pizza, Starbucks, Steak'n Shake, Taco Bell, Willy's Rest., **other:** H HOSPITAL, Ace Hardware, CVS Drug, Publix, **W gas:** Exxon/24hr

**254** Moores Mill Rd

**252b** Howell Mill Rd, **E gas:** Shell, **food:** Chick-fil-A, Domino's, McDonald's, Willy's Grill, **other:** Goodyear, Publix, Rite Aid, USPO, **W gas:** Shell, **food:** Arby's, Arthur's Italian, Chin Chin Chinese, Einstein Bro's, Kayson's, KFC/Pizza Hut, Mexican, Rest., Piccadilly, Sensational Subs, Starbucks, Subway, Taco Bell, US BBQ, Waffle House, Wendy's, **lodging:** Budget Inn, Holiday Inn, **other:** Ace Hardware, Firestrone/auto, GNC, Just Brakes, Kroger, Office Depot, PetsMart, Ross, TJ Maxx, Walmart Super Ctr

## INTERSTATE 75 CONT'D

**N ↕ S**

**AUGUSTA**

**252a** US 41, Northside Dr, **E gas:** H HOSPITAL, **W gas:** Shell, **food:** Krystal/24hr, Little Zio's, McDonald's, Waffle House, **lodging:** Day's Inn

**251** I-85 N, to Greenville

**250** Techwood Dr (from sb), 10th St, 14th St, **E lodging:** Travelodge

**249d** 10th St, Spring St (from nb), **E gas:** BP, Chevron/24hr, **food:** Checker's, Domino's, Pizza Hut, The Varsity, **lodging:** Fairfield Inn, Regency Suites, Renaissance Hotel, Residence Inn, **W food:** McDonald's, **lodging:** Courtyard, Comfort Inn, **other:** H HOSPITAL, to GA Tech

**249c** Williams St (from sb), downtown, to GA Dome

**249b** Pine St, Peachtree St (from nb), downtown, **W lodging:** Hilton, Marriott

**249a** Courtland St (from sb), downtown, **W lodging:** Hilton, Marriott, **other:** GA St U

**248d** Piedmont Ave, Butler St (from sb), downtown, **W lodging:** Courtyard, Fairfield Inn, Radisson, **other:** H HOSPITAL, Ford, MLK NHS

**248c** GA 10 E, Intn'l Blvd, downtown, **W lodging:** Hilton, Holiday Inn, Marriott Marquis, Radisson

**248b** Edgewood Ave (from nb), **W other:** H HOSPITAL, downtown, hotels

**248a** MLK Dr (from sb), **W** st capitol, to Underground Atlanta

**247** I-20, E to Augusta, W to Birmingham

**246** Georgia Ave, Fulton St, **E lodging:** Comfort Inn, Country Inn& Suites, Holiday Inn, **other:** stadium, **W gas:** BP, **food:** KFC, **other:** to Coliseum, GSU

**245** Ormond St, Abernathy Blvd, **E lodging:** Comfort Inn, Country Inn& Suites, **other:** stadium, **W** st capitol

**244** University Ave, **E gas:** Chevron, Exxon, **other:** NAPA, **W food:** Mrs Winner's

**243** GA 166, Lakewood Fwy, to East Point

**242** I-85 S, to airport

**241** Cleveland Ave, **E gas:** BP, Chevron, **food:** Checker's, Church's, McDonald's, Subway, **lodging:** Palace Inn, **other:** Advance Parts, K-Mart, **W gas:** Shell, Marathon, Phillips 66, Texaco, **food:** Blimpie, Burger King, Krystal/24hr, Mrs Winners, **lodging:** American Inn, Day's Inn, **other:** CVS Drug, Kroger

**239** US 19, US 41, **E gas:** Chevron/dsl, **food:** Waffle House, **other:** USPO, **W gas:** Texaco, **food:** IHOP, McDonald's, Wendy's, **lodging:** Best Western, to airport

**238b a** I-285 around Atlanta

**237a** GA 85 S (from sb), **W food:** Denny's, **lodging:** Burger King, McDonald's, Waffle House, **lodging:** Day's Inn, Day's Lodge

**237** GA 331, Forest Parkway, **E gas:** Chevron, Exxon, Happy Store/gas, Shell, **food:** Burger King, McDonald's, Waffle House, **lodging:** Econolodge, Motel 6, Rodeway Inn, **other:** Farmer's Mkt, Chevrolet, **W lodging:** Day's Inn, Ramada Ltd

**235** US 19, US 41, GA 3, Jonesboro, **E gas:** Chevron/dsl, Exxon/Subway/dsl, Phillips 66, Shell (1mi), Valero, **food:** Waffle House, **lodging:** Super 8, Travelodge, **other:** Atlanta RV Ctr, **W gas:** FuelMart/dsl, Marathon, RaceTrac/dsl, Shell, Texaco, **food:** Checker's, Dunkin Donuts, Folks Rest., Johnny's Pizza, KFC, Krystal, McDonald's, Red Lobster, Waffle House, **lodging:** Best Value,

**MORROW**

**235** Continued
Comfort Inn, Day's Inn, Econolodge, Holiday Inn Express, **other:** H HOSPITAL, $General, Dodge, Office Depot

**233** GA 54, Morrow, **E gas:** BP, Chevron, Citgo, Conoco/dsl, Phillips 66/dsl, **food:** Cracker Barrel, Krystal/24hr, Mrs Winner's, Taco Bell, Waffle House, Walter's Cafe, Wendy's, **lodging:** Best Western, Days Inn, Drury Inn, Fairfield Inn, Red Roof Inn, **other:** Walmart SuperCtr/gas, **W gas:** Exxon/24hr, RaceTrac, Shell/dsl, **food:** China Café, Indian Cuisine, Japanese Rest., KFC, McDonald's, Pizza Hut, Shoney's, Subway, Waffle House, **lodging:** Hampton Inn, Quality Inn, **other:** Acura/Cadillac, Best Buy, Chevrolet, Harley-Davidson, HobbyLobby, JiffyLube, Kroger, Mazda, Nissan, TJ Maxx, Toyota, mall

**231** Mt Zion Blvd, **E gas:** QT, **other:** Chrysler/Dodge/Jeep, Ford, Honda, **W gas:** Chevron, Citgo, Conoco, Exxon/dsl, Texaco/dsl, **food:** Arby's, Blimpie, Brewster's, Chick-fil-A, Chili's, Del Taco, Longhorn Steaks, McDonald's, Mo-Joe's, Mrs Winner's, On-the-Border, Papa John's, Pizza Hut, Steak'n Shake, Subway, TGIFriday, Waffle House, Wendy's, **lodging:** Country Inn&Suites, Extended Stay America, Howard Johnson Express, Sleep Inn, Sun Suites, **other:** Best Buy, Circuit City, Goody's, Home Depot, Michael's, NTB, Old Navy, Publix, Target

**JONESBORO**

**228** GA 54, GA 138, Jonesboro, **W gas:** Exxon, Raceway/24hr, **food:** Applebee's, Arby's, Broadway Diner, Burger King, Chick-fil-A, ChinChin Chinese, CiCi's, DQ, Folk's Rest., Frontera Mexican, Golden Corral, Honeybaked Ham, IHOP, KFC, Krystal, LJ Silver, McDonald's, Piccadilly's, Philly Connection, Shoney's, Subway, Taco Bell, Taco Mac, Tokyo Seafood, Waffle House, Wendy's, **lodging:** Best Western, Day's Inn, Comfort Inn, Holiday Inn, La Quinta, Hampton Inn, Motel 6, Red Roof Inn, **other:** H HOSPITAL, GNC, Goodyear, K-Mart, Kroger, Lowes Whse, Office Depot, Tires+, **W gas:** BP/24hr, Chevron, PaceCar/dsl, Sunoco/Wendy's, **food:** Ranchero's Mexican, Waffle House, **other:** CarMax, Chrysler/Jeep, CVS Drug, Kohl's

**227** I-675 N, to I-285 E (from nb)

**224** Hudson Bridge Rd, **E gas:** BP, Citgo/24hr, Phillips 66, Texaco/dsl, **food:** Buckhead Steaks, Chick-fil-A, China Wok, DQ, Dunkin Donuts, McDonald's, Outback Steaks, Subway, Waffle House, Wendy's, **lodging:** AmeriHost Inn, Microtel, **other:** H HOSPITAL, **W gas:** Phillips 66, QT, **food:** Domino's, Southern Skillet, Subway, Teddy's Diner/24hr, **lodging:** Super 8, **other:** Kroger, Walgreen, Walmart SuperCtr

## INTERSTATE 75 CONT'D

**222** Jodeco Rd, **E gas:** BP, Citgo/24hr, Texaco, **food:** Hardee's, Waffle House, **W gas:** BP, Chevron/dsl, **food:** Blimpie, **other:** Atlanta So. RV Camping, KOA

**221** Jonesboro Rd, **E gas:** BP, Citgo/dsl, **W food:** Burger King, Chili's, Cici's Pizza, Golden Corral, Hooter's, Logan's Roadhouse, Longhorn Steaks, McDonald's, O'Charley's, Red Lobster, Subway, Truit's Grill, Wendy's, Woody's BBQ, **other:** Belk, Best Buy, Books-A-Million, BJ's Whse/gas, Home Depot, Marshall's, Radio Shack, Ross, Sam's Club/gas, Staples, Target, flea market, KOA

**218** GA 20, GA 81, McDonough, **E gas:** BP, Murphy USA, Phillips 66, QT, Texaco, **food:** Applebee's, Arby's, Burger King, China Star, Cracker Barrel, DQ, KFC, IHOP, McDonald's, Mrs Winner's, Pizza Hut, Ruby Tuesday, Ryan's, Taco Bell, Waffle House, Wendy's, Zaxby's, **lodging:** Best Inn, Budget Inn, Economy Inn, Hampton Inn, Super 8, **other:** Lowe's Whse, Walmart SuperCtr, **W gas:** Citgo/dsl, Shell/24hr, **food:** DQ, Joey's Grill, Subway, Waffle House, **lodging:** Comfort Inn, Econolodge, Holiday Inn Express, Master's Inn, **other:** Toyota

**216** GA 155, McDonough, Blacksville, **E gas:** Shell, Sunoco/Backyard Burger, Texaco/dsl, **food:** Blimpie, **lodging:** Best Value, Budget Inn, Day's Inn, Roadway Inn, **other:** Buick/Pontiac, **W gas:** BP/dsl, Chevron, Citgo/dsl/24hr, Mystik/dsl, **food:** Da Vinci's Pizza, El Arriero, Krystal, Milan's Pizza, Subway, UMI Steaks, Waffle House, **lodging:** Country Inn&Suites, Quality Inn, Sleep Inn

**212** to US 23, Locust Grove, **E gas:** BP/McDonald's/dsl, Chevron/Burger King, Citgo/dsl, Exxon/dsl, Liberty Gas/Subway, Shell/dsl, **food:** Country Steaks, Denny's, Huddle House, KFC/Pizza Hut/Taco Bell, Sunrise China, Waffle House, Wendy's, Zaxby's, **lodging:** Econolodge, Executive Inn, Ramada Ltd, Red Roof Inn, **other:** Ingles/gas, Napa, Tanger Outlet/famous brands, **W gas:** Chevron/dsl, Citgo/DQ/dsl, Exxon/dsl, **lodging:** Scottish Inn, Sundown Lodge, Super 8

**205** GA 16, to Griffin, Jackson, **E gas:** BP, **lodging:** Simmon's BBQ, **other:** Forest Glen RV Park, **W gas:** BP, Chevron/dsl´

**201** GA 36, to Jackson, Barnesville, **E gas:** Love's/McDonald's/dsl/grill/scales/24hr, TA/Subway/Taco Bell/dsl/scales/24hr/@, Wilco/Hess/DQ/Stuckey's/Wendy's/dsl/scales/24hr/@, **other:** Blue Beacon, **W gas:** BP/dsl, ✈FLYING J/Conoco/Cookery/dsl/LP/24hr/@, **other:** Sagon RV Ctr, Speedco Lube

**198** Highfalls Rd, **E gas:** Exxon (1mi), **lodging:** High Falls Lodge, **other:** High Falls SP, **W** High Falls RV Park

**193** Johnstonville Rd, **E gas:** BP

**190mm** weigh sta both lanes

**188** GA 42, **E gas:** Shell/24hr, **lodging:** Best Western, Budget Inn, **other:** to Indian Spings SP, RV camping

**187** GA 83, Forsyth, **E lodging:** Econolodge, New Forsyth Inn, Regency Inn, **W gas:** BP, Citgo/dsl, Marathon, Shell, **food:** Burger King, Capt D's, China Inn, DQ, Hardee's, McDonald's, Pizza Hut, Subway, Taco Bell, Waffle House, Wendy's, **lodging:** Day's Inn, Tradewinds Motel, **other:** Advance Parts, CVS Drug, Family$, Freshway Foods, Walmart

**186** Tift College Dr, Juliette Rd, Forsyth, **E** Jarrell Plantation HS, KOA, **W gas:** BP/dsl, Chevron, Marathon, **food:** Waffle House, **lodging:** Holiday Inn/rest., Holiday Inn Express, Super 8, **other:** H HOSPITAL, Chrysler/Dodge, CVS Drug, Ingles/Deli

**185** GA 18, **E** Forsyth RV Park, **W gas:** BP/Stuckeys/24hr, Shell/dsl, **food:** Shoney's, **lodging:** Comfort Inn, **other:** Ford, st patrol

**181** Rumble Rd, to Smarr, **E gas:** BP/dsl/24hr, Shell/dsl/24hr

**179mm** rest area sb, full ♿ facilities, ☏, vending, 🍴 litter barrels, petwalk

**177** I-475 S around Macon (from sb)

**175** Pate Rd, Bolingbroke (from nb, no re-entry)

**172** Bass Rd, **E food:** Pig in a Pit BBQ, McDonald's, Quizno's, Starbucks, **other:** Bass Pro Shop, funpark, **W gas:** Citgo/dsl/24hr, **other:** to Museum of Arts&Sciences

**171** US 23, to GA 87, Riverside Dr, **E gas:** BP, Marathon/dsl, Shell, **food:** Jock&Jill's Grill, **other:** Acura, KIA, Lincoln/Mercury, Mercedes, Volvo, **W food:** Backyard Burger, Cracker Barrel, Hooters, **other:** Lexus, Toyota, same as 169 W

**169** to US 23, Arkwright Dr, **E gas:** Shell/24hr, **food:** Carrabba's, Logan's Roadhouse, Outback Steaks, Waffle House, Wager's Grill, **lodging:** Comfort Inn, Courtyard, Fairfield Inn, Hampton Inn, Holiday Inn, La Quinta, Red Roof Inn, Residence Inn, Super 8, **other:** Buick/Cadillac/GMC/Saturn, **W gas:** BP/dsl, Chevron/24hr, Marathon/dsl, **food:** Arby's, Backyard Burger, Burger King, Chick-fil-A, Chili's, Cheddar's, Cracker Barrel, Dunkin Donuts, El Azteca Mexican, 5 Guys Burgers, Giuseppi's Italian, Hooters, KFC, Krystal, Longhorn Steaks, Mandarin Chinese, McDonald's, Mikata Japanese, Papa John's, Papoulis' Gyros, Panera Bread, Pizza Hut, Shoki Japanese, Starbucks, Steak'n Shake, Steve B's Pizza, Subway, Taco Bell, Waffle House, **lodging:** Best Inn, Extended Stay Deluxe, Holiday Hotel, Macon Hotel, Quality Inn, Travelodge, Wingate Inn, **other:** H HOSPITAL, Ace Hardware, Barnes&Noble, Chrysler/Jeep/Dodge, $Tree, GNC, K-Mart, Kroger, Mazda, Pontiac, Publix, Radio Shack, same as 167

**167** GA 247, Pierce Ave, **E lodging:** Days Inn, **W gas:** BP/dsl, Chevron, Conoco, Exxon, Marathon/Subway/dsl, Shell, **food:** Applebee's, CJ's Grill, Loco's Deli, Pier 97 Seafood, Pizza Hut, Red Lobster, San Marcos Mexican, S&S Cafeteria, Shogun Japanese, SteakOut Rest., Waffle House, Wendy's, **lodging:** Best Western/rest., Comfort Inn, Holiday Inn Express, Howard Johnson, Motel 6, **other:** Eckerd, ExperTire, Goodyear/auto

**165** I-16 E, to Savannah

**164** US 41, GA 19, Forsyth Ave, Macon, **E food:** Sid's Rest., **other:** hist dist, **W gas:** BP, Citgo, **other:** H HOSPITAL, museum

**163** GA 74 W, Mercer U Dr, **E lodging:** Hilton Garden, **other:** to Mercer U, **W gas:** Citgo, Marathon/dsl

**162** US 80, GA 22, Eisenhower Pkwy, **W gas:** BP, Chevron/24hr, Lo-lo Gas, **food:** Burger King, Capt D's, Checker's, IHOP, Krispy Kreme, Krystal, LJ Silver, McDonald's, Mrs Winners, Subway, Taco Bell, Wendy's, **other:** $Tree, Office Depot, O'Reilly Parts, PepBoys, SavAlot Foods, Walgreens

(left margin labels: N S, GA, MCDONOUGH, BARNESVILLE, FORSYTH, MACON)

## INTERSTATE 75 CONT'D

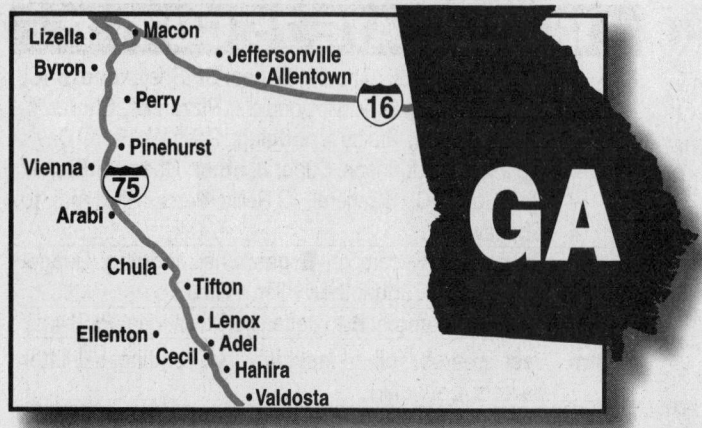

**N ↕ S**

**BYRON**

| | |
|---|---|
| **160** | US 41, GA 247, Pio Nono Ave, **E** gas: Flash/dsl, Race-Way/Dunkin Donuts, **food:** Waffle House, **lodging:** Best Inn, **W** gas: BP, Enmark/dsl, **food:** Advance Parts, Arby's, DQ, KFC, King Buffet, McDonald's, Subway, Waffle House, **other:** Advance Parts, $General, Goodyear/auto, NAPA, O'Reilly Parts, Roses, USPO, same as 162 |
| **156** | I-475 N around Macon (from nb) |
| **155** | Hartley Br Rd, **E** gas: BP/KFC/dsl/24hr, **food:** Wendy's, **other:** Curves, Kroger/gas, **W** gas: Citgo/dsl, Exxon, **food:** McDonald's, Subway, Waffle House, Zaxby's, **lodging:** Best Value, **other:** CVS Drug |
| **149** | GA 49, Byron, **E** gas: Chevron/dsl, Marathon/dsl, Shell/24hr, **food:** Burger King, Denny's, Krystal, McDonald's, Pizza Hut, Subway, Waffle House, Wendy's, Zaxby's, **lodging:** Best Western, Comfort Inn & Suites, Holiday Inn Express, Super 8, **other:** Campers Inn RV Ctr, Mid-State RV Ctr, Peach Stores/famous brands, antiques, **W** gas: BP, Citgo/dsl/24hr, Exxon, Flash/dsl, Marathon, RaceWay, **food:** DQ, Huddle House, Waffle House, **lodging:** Econolodge, Passport Inn, Quality Inn, **other:** Advance Parts, Camping World RV Ctr, CarQuest, Chevrolet, $General, Family$, Ford, Suncoast RV Ctr |

**PERRY**

| | |
|---|---|
| **146** | GA 247, to Centerville, **E** gas: Exxon, Flash/dsl, Shell, **food:** Subway, Waffle House, **lodging:** Econolodge, Knights Inn, **other:** H HOSPITAL, to Robins AFB, museum, **W** gas: Pilot/Arby's/dsl/24hr |
| **144** | Russel Pkwy, **E** Robins AFB, aviation museum |
| **142** | GA 96, Housers Mill Rd, **E** gas: Chevron/dsl, **other:** Ponderosa RV Park |
| **138** | Thompson Rd, **E** gas: Texaco/Chester's/dsl, **other:** H HOSPITAL, **W** ✈ |
| **136** | US 341, Perry, **E** gas: BP, Flash, Shell, **food:** Arby's, Burger King, Capt D's, Chick-fil-A, Hong Kong Buffet, KFC, Krystal, Longhorn Steaks, McDonald's, Pizza Hut, Red Lobster, Sonny's BBQ, Subway, Taco Bell, Waffle House, Wendy's, Zaxby's, **lodging:** Best Inn, Great Inn, Hampton Inn, Howard Johnson, Jameson Inn, Super 8, **other:** H HOSPITAL, Ace Hardware, Advance Parts, $Tree, GNC, Kroger, NAPA, Radio Shack, Rite Aid, Walmart SuperCtr, **W** gas: Chevron/dsl, RaceWay/24hr, **food:** Applebee's, Green Derby Rest., **lodging:** Ashburn Inn, Comfort Inn, Econolodge, Holiday Inn, Knight's Inn, Passport Inn, Quality Inn, **other:** Ford, Crossroads Camping |
| **135** | US 41, GA 127, Perry, **E** gas: BP/dsl, Exxon, Flash, Marathon, Shell, **food:** Cracker Barrel, Subway, Waffle House, **lodging:** Best Western, Red Carpet Inn, Relax Inn, Rodeway Inn, Travelodge, **other:** Chrysler, Jeep/Dodge, GA Nat Fair, **W** other: Fair Harbor RV Park, st Patrol |
| **134** | South Perry Pkwy, **W** gas: Texaco/dsl, **lodging:** Microtel, **other:** Chevrolet/Buick/Pontiac/GMC, Priester's Pecans |
| **127** | GA 26, Henderson, **E** Twin Oaks Camping, **W** gas: Chevron |
| **122** | GA 230, Unadilla, **E** gas: Chevron/dsl, Colonial/dsl, **other:** Chevrolet/Ford, **W** lodging: Red Carpet Inn, **other:** Bleakley RV Ctr |

**UNADILLA**

**CORDELE**

**WENONA**

| | |
|---|---|
| **121** | US 41, Unadilla, **E** gas: BP, Borum/repair, Flash/DQ/dsl, Shell, **food:** Country Boys BBQ, Don Ponchos Mexican, Subway, **lodging:** Economy Inn, Scottish Inn, **other:** $General, Piggly Wiggly, Southern Trails RV Resort, **W** gas: Citgo/dsl/rest./scales/24hr, **lodging:** Regency Inn |
| **118mm** | rest area sb, full ♿ facilities, 🚻, vending, 🏕 litter barrels, petwalk, RV dump |
| **117** | to US 41, Pinehurst, **W** gas: BP/Pinehurst/cafe/dsl/scales/24hr |
| **112** | GA 27, Vienna, **W** gas: BP/dsl, Marathon |
| **109** | GA 215, Vienna, **E** gas: Pilot/McDonalds/dsl/scales/24hrs, **W** gas: Citgo/dsl, El Cheapo, Shell/Subway/dsl/E85, **food:** Huddle House, **lodging:** Executive Inn, **other:** H HOSPITAL, antiques |
| **108mm** | rest area nb, full ♿ facilities, 🚻, vending, 🏕 litter barrels, petwalk, RV dump |
| **104** | Farmers Mkt Rd, Cordele |
| **102** | GA 257, Cordele, **W** food: Pecan House, **other:** H HOSPITAL |
| **101** | US 280, GA 90, Cordele, **E** gas: Exxon/dsl, Pilot/Arby's/dsl/scales/24hr, Shell, **food:** Denny's, Golden Corral, Waffle House, **lodging:** Day's Inn, Fairfield Inn, Ramada Inn, **other:** Ford/Lincoln/Mercury, st patrol, **W** gas: BP/dsl, Danfair, Liberty, RaceWay/24hr, Bob Evans, Burger King, Capt D's, Compadres Mexican, Cracker Barrel, Cutter's Steaks, DQ, Hardee's, KFC/Pizza Hut/Taco Bell, Krystal/24hr, McDonald's, Shoney's, Sonic, Subway, Super China, Taco Bell, TJ's Rest., Wendy's, Zaxby's, **lodging:** Ashburn Inn, Athens 8 Motel, Best Western, Comfort Inn, Deluxe Inn, Econolodge, Hampton Inn, Holiday Inn Express, Premier Inn, Travelodge, **other:** Advance Parts, AutoZone, Belk, $General, $Tree, Goody's, Harvey's Foods, Home Depot, NAPA, O'Reilly Parts, Radio Shack, Walgreens, Walmart SuperCtr, to Veterans Mem SP, J Carter HS |
| **99** | GA 300, GA/FL Pkwy, **W** food: Waffle House, **lodging:** Country Inn&Suites, **other:** to Chehaw SP |
| **97** | to GA 33, Wenona, **E** other: Cornel RV Park, dsl repair, **W** gas: TA/BP/Popeye's/Pizza Hut/dsl/scales/24hr/@, **other:** KOA, truckwash |
| **92** | Arabi, **E** gas: Chevron/Plantation House, **W** gas: BP/dsl, **other:** Southern Gates RV Park |
| **85mm** | rest area nb, full ♿ facilities, 🚻, vending, 🏕 litter barrels, petwalk |
| **84** | GA 159, Ashburn, **E** gas: Shell/dsl, **W** gas: Chevron/dsl/24hr, **food:** DQ, Subway, **lodging:** Ashburn Inn/RV Park |

**N ↑↓ S**

**T I F T O N**

**GA**

## INTERSTATE 75 CONT'D

**82** GA 107, GA 112, Ashburn, **W gas:** BP, Shell, **food:** KFC, Huddle House/24hr, McDonald's, Pizza Hut, Shoney's, Waffle House, Zaxby's, **lodging:** Best Western, Day's Inn, Howard Johnson, Super 8, **other:** Chevrolet/Buick/Pontiac/GMC, $General, O'Reilly Parts, Rite Aid, to Chehaw SP

**80** Bussey Rd, Sycamore, **E gas:** Shell, **lodging:** Budget Inn, **W gas:** Citgo, **other:** Allen's Tires

**78** GA 32, Sycamore, **E** to Jefferson Davis Mem Pk (14mi)

**76mm** rest area sb, full ♿ facilities, 📞, vending, 🛉 litter barrels, petwalk

**75** Inaha Rd, **W gas:** BP/Stuckey's

**71** Willis Still Rd, Sunsweet, **W gas:** BP/dsl

**69** Chula-Brookfield Rd, **E gas:** Phillips 66, **lodging:** Carpet Inn, **other:** antiques

**66** Brighton Rd

**64** US 41, Tifton, **E gas:** BP/dsl, **other:** Ⓗ HOSPITAL, $General, Harvey's Foods, **W gas:** Petro

**63b** 8th St, Tifton, **E gas:** Bob's, Flash, **food:** KFC, Los Compadres, **lodging:** Budget Inn, **other:** Goody's, same as 63a, **W food:** Pit Stop BBQ

**63a** 2nd St, Tifton, **E gas:** BP, Chevron, **food:** Asahi Xpress, Arby's, Burger King, Checker's, El Cazador Mexican, Krystal, McDonald's, Pizza Hut, Red Lobster, Taco Bell, Waffle House, **lodging:** Econolodge, Super 8, **other:** Advance Parts, Belk, Buick/Pontiac/Cadillac/GMC, $Tree, JC Penney, **W gas:** West Side/Cafe/dsl, **food:** TX Jack's Grill, **lodging:** Quality Inn, Travelodge

**62** US 82, to US 319, Tifton, **E gas:** Citgo, Flash/dsl, **food:** Applebee's, Charles Seafood, Chili's, Country Buffet, Cracker Barrel, DQ, Golden Corral, Red Lobster, Sonic, Waffle House, Zaxby's, **lodging:** Comfort Inn, Courtyard, Country Inn & Suites, Fairfield Inn, Hampton Inn, Microtel, **other:** Advance Parts, $Tree, Family$, Ford/Lincoln/Mercury, Pecan Outlet, Staples, **W gas:** BP, Chevron/Burger King, EZ Mart, Murphy USA, RaceWay/24hr, Shell/dsl, **food:** Burger King, Capt D's, Chick-fil-A, Cici's Pizza, $General, Little Caesars, Loco's Grill, Longhorn Steaks, McDonald's, Old Mexico, Moe's SW Grill, Quizno's, Ruby Tuesday, Shoney's, Sonny's BBQ, Subway, Starbucks, Waffle House, Wendy's, **lodging:** Day's Inn, Hilton Garden, Holiday Inn, Ramada Ltd, Rodeway Inn, **other:** Chevrolet, Chrysler/Dodge, $General, Honda, Lowe's Whse, Radio Shack, Toyota, Walmart SuperCtr

**61** Omega Rd, **W gas:** Petro USA/Stuckey's/Waffle King/dsl/24hr, **lodging:** Motel 6, **other:** Harley-Davidson, Pines RV Park, **E** Nissan

**60** Central Ave, Tifton, **E gas:** Chevron, **food:** Dragon 1 Chinese, **W gas:** Pilot/Subway/Steak'n Shake/dsl/scales/24hr, **other:** Amy's RV Camping, Blue Beacon

**59** Southwell Blvd, to US 41, Tifton, **E gas:** Loves/Hardees/dsl/24hr

**55** to Eldorado, Omega, **E gas:** Chevron/Magnolia Plantation, **W gas:** Pure/dsl

**49** Kinard Br Rd, Lenox, **E gas:** Dixie/dsl, **lodging:** Knight's Inn, **W gas:** BP/dsl/24hr

**47mm** rest area both lanes, full ♿ facilities, 📞, vending, 🛉 litter barrels, petwalk

---

**A D E L**

**V A L D O S T A**

**V A L D O S T A**

**45** Barneyville Rd, **E lodging:** Relax Inn

**41** Rountree Br Rd, **E gas:** Citgo, **W** to Reed Bingham SP

**39** GA 37, Adel, Moultrie, **E gas:** Shell/McDonald's/dsl, Texaco, **food:** DQ, Hardee's, Subway, Waffle House, **lodging:** Budget Lodge, Scottish Inn, Super 8, **other:** Family$, Rite Aid, Winn-Dixie, **W gas:** BP, Citgo/Huddle House/dsl/@, **food:** Burger King, Capt D's, IHOP, Mama's Table, Taco Bell, Wendy's, Western Sizzlin, **lodging:** Day's Inn, Hampton Inn, **other:** Factory Stores/famous brands, to Reed Bingham SP

**37** Adel

**32** Old Coffee Rd, Cecil, **W gas:** Chevron

**29** US 41 N, GA 122, Hahira, Sheriff's Boys Ranch, **E food:** Subway, **other:** NAPA, **W gas:** Big Foot TC/Apple Valley/dsl, BP/Blimpie/TCBY/dsl, **lodging:** Knights Inn

**23mm** weigh sta both lanes

**22** US 41 S, to Valdosta, **E gas:** BP, Shell/Subway/dsl, **food:** Waffle House, **lodging:** Hawthorn Suites, **other:** Ⓗ HOSPITAL, Chevrolet/Mazda, Dodge/Jeep, Lincoln/Mercury, golf, **W gas:** Citgo/Burger King/DQ/Stuckey's, **lodging:** Day's Inn

**18** GA 133, Valdosta, **E gas:** Big Foot/dsl, Exxon, Flash, Phillips 66, Texaco/dsl, **food:** Applebee's, Arby's, Atl. Bread Co, Beijing Cafe, Brusters, Burger King, Chick-fil-A, Chili's, Cracker Barrel, Cici's Pizza, Crystal River Seafood, Denny's, El Potro Mexican, El Toreo, Fazoli's, Hooters, KFC, Krystal, Little Caesar's, Longhorn Steaks, McCalister's Deli, McDonald's, Ole Times BBQ, Outback Steaks, Quizno's, Red Lobster, Ruby Tuesday, Sonny's BBQ, Starbucks, Steak'n Shake, Taco Bell, TX Roadhouse, Waffle House, Wendy's, **lodging:** Comfort Suites, Country Inn&Suites, Courtyard, Hampton Inn, Hilton Garden, InnTown Suites, Jameson Inn, Jolly Inn, La Quinta, Lee's Grill, Quality Inn, Rodeway Inn, **other:** Belk, Best Buy, Books A Million, $Tree, Goody's, Home Depot, JC Penney, Kohl's, Lowe's Whse, Michaels, Office Depot, Old Navy, PetsMart, Publix, Ross, Sears/auto, Target, TJ Maxx, Walgreens, mall, **W gas:** BP/dsl, RaceWay, Shell, **lodging:** Best Western, Econolodge, Sleep Inn, **other:** RiverPark Camping, Toyota

**16** US 84, US 221, GA 94, Valdosta, **E gas:** Big Foot/dsl, BP/dsl, Chevron, Citgo/Stuckey's/dsl, Danfair Express, Shell/dsl, **food:** Aligatou Japanese, Burger King, IHOP, McDonald's, Old South BBQ, Pizza Hut, Shoney's, Sonic, Waffle House, Wendy's, **lodging:** Day's Inn, Guesthouse Inn, Hampton Inn, Holiday Inn, Motel 6, New Valdosta Inn, Quality Inn, Ramada Ltd, Super 8, Wingate Inn, **other:** Sam's Club/gas, Walmart Super Ctr/Subway, to Okefenokee SP, **W gas:** Shell/Dee Dee's Rest./dsl/24hr, **food:** Austin's Steaks, **lodging:** Comfort Inn, Knight's Inn

**13** Old Clyattville Rd, Valdosta, **W** Wild Adventures Park

**11** GA 31, Valdosta, **E gas:** Pilot/Subway/dsl/24hr/@, Wilco/Hess/Stuckey's/dsl/scales/24hr, **food:** Waffle House, **lodging:** Travelers Inn, **W gas:** BP

**5** GA 376, to Lake Park, **E gas:** Chevron, Flash/Krystal/dsl, RaceWay, Shell, **food:** Chick-fil-A, Domino's, FarmHouse Rest., Hardee's, Lin's Garden Chinese, Shoney's, Sonic, Sonny's BBQ, Subway, Waffle House, **lodging:** Guesthouse Inn, Quality Inn, **other:** Eagles Roost RV Park, Family$, Preferred Outlets/famous brands, Travel Country RV Ctr, Winn-Dixie, USPO, **W gas:** Citgo/dsl,

## INTERSTATE 75 CONT'D

**N ↕ S**

| 5 | Continued |
| | Shell/dsl, **food:** Cracker Barrel, McDonald's, Pizza Hut, Taco Bell, Wendy's, **lodging:** Day's Inn, Hampton Inn, Super 8, Travelodge, **other:** KOA, SunCoast RV Ctr |
| 3mm | Welcome Ctr nb, full ♿ facilities, 📞, vending, 🍽, litter barrels, petwalk |
| 2 | Lake Park, Bellville, **E** gas: Mobil/DQ, SpeedCo, Shell/dsl, TA/BP/Arby's/dsl/rest./scales/24hr/@, **W** gas: ⊕FLYING J/Conoco/dsl/LP/rest./scales/24hr, **other:** lube/tires/wash |
| 0mm | Georgia/Florida state line |

## INTERSTATE 85

**N ↕ S** 
**LAVONIA**
**COMMERCE**

| Exit # | Services |
|---|---|
| 179mm | Georgia/South Carolina state line, Lake Hartwell, Tugaloo River |
| 177 | GA 77 S, to Hartwell, **E** gas: BP/gifts/dsl, **food:** Dad's Grill, **other:** to Hart SP, Tugaloo SP |
| 176mm | Welcome Ctr sb, full ♿ facilities, 📞, info, 🍽, litter barrels, vending, petwalk |
| 173 | GA 17, to Lavonia, **E** gas: RaceTrac/24hr, **food:** Domino's, La Cabana Mexican, McDonald's, Subway, Taco Bell, Waffle House, **lodging:** Best Western, Sleep Inn, **other:** $General, Lavonia Foods, Rite Aid, **W** gas: Chevron/dsl, Exxon/dsl, **food:** Burger King, Hardee's, Pizza Hut, Shoney's Inn/rest., Wendy's, Zaxby's, **lodging:** Holiday Inn Express, Super 8, **other:** Chrysler/Dodge/Jeep, Ford, to Tugaloo SP |
| 171mm | weigh sta nb |
| 169mm | weigh sta sb |
| 166 | GA 106, to Carnesville, Toccoa, **E** gas: Wilco/Hess/DQ/Wendy's/dsl/scales/24hr, **W** gas: Echo Trkstp/Chevron/Country Kitchen/dsl/rest./scales/24hr, **other:** truck repair |
| 164 | GA 320, to Carnesville |
| 160mm | rest area nb, full ♿ facilities, 📞, vending, 🍽, litter barrels, petwalk |
| 160 | GA 51, to Homer, **E** gas: Shell/Subway/dsl/24hr, **other:** Sterling RV Ctr, **W** gas: ⊕FLYING J/Country Mkt/dsl/24hr, Petro/Pizza Hut/dsl/scales/24hr/@, **other:** Blue Beacon |
| 154 | GA 63, Martin Br Rd |
| 149 | US 441, GA 15, to Commerce, Homer, **E** gas: Chevron, Shell, TA/76/dsl/rest./24hr/@, **food:** Capt D's, Chinese Chef, Grand China, Joy's, Longhorn Steaks, Outback Steaks, Papa Jack's, Pizza Hut/Taco Bell, Shoney's, Sonny's BBQ, Waffle House, Zaxby's, **lodging:** Admiral Benbow Inn, Day's Inn, Hampton Inn, Scottish Inn, **other:** Ⓗ HOSPITAL, $Tree, Goody's, KOA, Radio Shack, Tanger Outlet/famous brands, Walmart SuperCtr/gas, **W** gas: BP/dsl, Chevron, Citgo, RaceTrac/dsl, Texaco, **food:** Applebee's, Arby's, Burger King, Checker's, Chick-fil-A, Cracker Barrel, DQ, Denny's, KFC, Krystal, La Fiesta, La Hacienda, McDonald's, Pizza Hut, Ruby Tuesday, Ryan's, Sonic, Starbucks, Subway, Wendy's, **lodging:** Best Western, Comfort Inn, $Wise Inn, Holiday Inn Express, Howard Johnson, Jameson Inn, Red Roof Inn, Super 8, **other:** Buick/Pontiac/GMC, Home Depot, Tanger Outlet/famous brands, tires |

**JEFFERSON**

| 147 | GA 98, to Commerce, **E** gas: Citgo/dsl, ⊕FLYING J/cafe/dsl/24hr/, FuelMart/dsl, **other:** Ⓗ HOSPITAL **W** other: Cody's Fuel |
| 140 | GA 82, Dry Pond Rd, **W** Freightliner/RV & Truck Repair |
| 137 | US 129, GA 11 to Jefferson, **E** gas: BP, RaceTrac, Shell, **food:** Arby's, El Jinete Mexican, McDonald's, Waffle House, Zaxby's, **lodging:** Comfort Inn, **other:** museum, **W** gas: QT/dsl/24hr, **food:** Burger King, Waffle House, Wendy's, **other:** flea mkt |
| 129 | GA 53, to Braselton, **E** gas: Chevron/dsl, Shell/Golden Pantry/dsl, **food:** La Hacienda Mexican, Waffle House, **lodging:** Best Western, **W** gas: Pilot/McDonald's/dsl/scales/24hr, **food:** Cracker Barrel, Dominos, Hickory Wind BBQ, Wendy's, Zaxby's, **other:** $Store |
| 126 | GA 211, to Chestnut Mtn, **E** gas: Shell/dsl, **food:** Subway, Waffle House, **W** gas: BP/dsl, **food:** Blimpie, Chateau Elan Winery/rest., China Garden, Papa John's, **lodging:** Holiday Inn Express, **other:** Publix, vet |
| 120 | to GA 124, Hamilton Mill Rd, **E** gas: BP, QT/dsl, **food:** Arby's, Buffalo's Café, Burger King, Caprese Rest., Dos Copas Mexican, McDonald's, Moe's SW Grill, Rib Shack, Starbucks, Subway, Wendy's, Zaxby's, **other:** Home Depot, Kohl's, Publix/Deli, auto repair, vet, **W** gas: Chevron, Shell/Huddle House/dsl, **food:** Barbarito's, Beaner's Coffee, Chick-fil-A, Chili's, Log Cabin BBQ, **other:** CVS Drug, Walmart SuperCtr/gas |
| 115 | GA 20, to Buford Dam, **E** gas: QT, **W** gas: QT/dsl, **food:** Arby's, Artuzzi's Italian, Bruster's, Buffalo's Cafe, Burger King, Chick-fil-A, Chili's, ChuckeCheese, Einstein's Bagels, 5 Guy's Burgers, Kani House, Krispy Kreme, Longhorn Steaks, Liu's Buffet, Macaroni Grill, McDonald's, Mimi's Cafe, Moe's SW Grill, O'Charley's, Olive Garden, On-the-Border, Panda Express, PF Chang's, Quizno's, Red Lobster, Shogun Japanese, Starbucks, Steak n' Shake, Subway, Taxco Mexican, Ted's MT Grill, TGIFriday, Waffle House, Wendy's, **lodging:** Country Inn&Suites, Hampton Inn, SpringHill Suites, Wingate Inn, **other:** Belk, Best Buy, Borders Books, Circuit City, Costco/gas, Dillard's, $Tree, JC Penney, Lowes Whse, Macy's, Mazda, Michael's, Nissan, Nordstrom's, PetCo, Ross, Sam's Club, Staples, Target, TJ Maxx, Toyota/Scion, Walmart SuperCtr, Mall of GA, to Lake Lanier Islands |
| 113 | I-985 N (from nb), to Gainesville |
| 111 | GA 317, to Suwanee, **E** gas: BP, Phillips 66/dsl, Sim's, **food:** Applebee's, Arby's, Blimpie, Burger King, Checker's, Chick-fil-A, Cracker Barrel, Mrs Winner's, Oriental |

**GA**

**SUWANEE N ↕ S DULUTH**

**GA**

## INTERSTATE 85 CONT'D

**111** Continued
Garden, Outback Steaks, Philly Connection, Pizza Hut, Subway, Taco Bell/Pizza Hut, Waffle House, Wendy's, **lodging:** Admiral Benbow Inn, Best Western, Comfort Inn, Courtyard, Days Inn, Fairfield Inn, Holiday Inn, Red Roof Inn, Sun Suites, **other:** CVS Drug, GNC, Kauffman Tire, **W gas:** Chevron/dsl/24hr, RaceTrac, Shell, **food:** A&W/KFC, Atlanta Bread, CiCi's Pizza, Kacey's Rest., McDonald's, Moe's SW Grill, Shane's Ribshack, Sonic, Wild Wing Cafe, **lodging:** Motel 6, Super 8, **other:** $Tree, Office Depot, Radio Shack, Tires +, Walmart SuperCtr/gas, flea mkt

**109** Old Peachtree Rd, **E gas:** QT/dsl/24hr, **food:** McDonald's, **lodging:** Hampton Inn, **other:** $World, Publix, **W food:** Bistro's Sandwich Cafe, Califonia Dreaming, China Delight, Magnolia Cafe, Sidelines Grille, Subway, Waffle House, **lodging:** Hilton Garden, Holiday Inn, **other:** Home Depot

**108** Sugarloaf Pkwy, **E lodging:** Hampton Inn, **W food:** Chick-fil-A, **lodging:** Hilton Garden, Holiday Inn, **other:** Gwinnett Civic Ctr

**107** GA 120, to GA 316 E, Athens, **E gas:** Shell, **food:** Burger King, Carino's, Jillian's, Zaxby's, **other:** Bass Pro Shop, Books-a-Million, Burlington Coats, Discount Tire, Eckerd, Food Ct, Mercedes, Nieman-Marcus, Ross, Saks 5th Ave, Sears, Suburban Tire, **W gas:** BP, Chevron, **food:** Carrabba's, China Gate, McDonald's, Roadhouse Grill, Subway, **lodging:** La Quinta, Suburban Lodge

**106** Boggs Rd (from sb, no return), Duluth, **W gas:** QT/dsl/24hr

**104** Pleasant Hill Rd, **E gas:** Chevron/24hr, Circle K, Sim's, **food:** Bahama Breeze, Blue Marlin, Burger King, Chick-fil-A, East Pearl, GA Diner, Grand Buffet, Ida's Pizza Kitchen, Joe's Crabshack, Krispy Kreme, La Pantera Rosa, Macaroni Grill, McDonald's, Moe's SW Grill, Popeye's, Starbucks, Subway, TGIFriday, Waffle House, Wendy's, **lodging:** Candlewood Suites, Comfort Suites, Hampton Inn Suites, Holiday Inn Express, Marriott, Residence Inn, Sun Suites, **other:** Best Buy, $General, Eckerd, Goodyear/auto, Home Depot, Old Time Pottery, Publix, Walgreens, **W gas:** BP/dsl, Chevron, Murphy USA/dsl, RaceTrac, **food:** Applebee's, Arby's, Bruster's, Burger King, Checker's, Chili's, Chipotle Mexican, Golden China, Hooters, IHOP, KFC, McDonald's, Olive Garden, On the Border, Panda Express, Pizza Hut, Red Lobster, Ryan's, Starbucks, Steak'n Shake, Subway, Taco Bell, Waffle House, Wendy's, **lodging:** Courtyard, Day's Inn, Extended Stay America, Hyatt Place, InTown Suites, Quality Inn, Wingate Inn, **other:** Barnes&Noble, Batteries+, BMW, Chevrolet, Dodge, Eckerd, Firestone/auto, Ford/Lincoln/Mercury, Fry's Electronics, Goodyear/auto, Honda, Jo-Ann Fabrics, KIA, Macy's, Marshall's, Mazda/Hyundai, Mitsubishi, Nissan, PetCo, Sears/auto, Staples, Target, TJ Maxx, Toyota, Walmart Super Ctr, mall

**103** Steve Reynolds Blvd (from nb, no return), **W gas:** QT, Shell, **food:** Dave&Buster's, La Fiesta Mexican, Waffle House, **other:** Circuit City, Costco Whse, Goody's, Kohl's, Sam's Club

**102** GA 378, Beaver Ruin Rd, **E gas:** Shell/dsl, QT, **W gas:** Citgo

**ATLANTA AREA**

**101** Lilburn Rd, **E gas:** QT/dsl, Shell/dsl/24hr, **food:** Blimpie, Bojangles, Bruster's, Burger King, Hong Kong Buffet, Manhattan Pizza, McDonald's/playplace, Quizno's, Starbucks, Krystal, KFC, Taco Bell, Waffle House, **lodging:** Guesthouse Inn, InTown Suites, **W gas:** Chevron/24hr, QT, **food:** Arby's, El Indo Mexican, El Taco Veloz, Little Caeser's, Mrs Winner's, Papa John's, Pizza Plaza, Waffle House, Wendy's, **lodging:** Knight's Inn, Red Roof Inn, **other:** CarMax, Chrysler/Jeep, CVS Drug, Little Giant Mkt, Lowe's Whse

**99** GA 140, Jimmy Carter Blvd, **E gas:** Phillips 66/dsl, Shell, **food:** Checker's, Chick-fil-A, Cracker Barrel, Denny's, Don Taco, KFC, McDonald's, Papa John's, Pizza Hut/Taco Bell, Waffle House, Wendy's, **lodging:** Best Western, Comfort Inn, Courtyard, La Quinta, Motel 6, **other:** Advance Parts, Aldi Foods, CVS Drug, Family$, Goodyear, Office Depot, U-Haul, Walgreens, **W gas:** Chevron/24hr, Citgo, QT/dsl/24hr, **food:** Barnacle's Grill, Five Guys Cafe, Hong Kong Buffet, Hooters, Pappadeaux Steak/seafood, Sonic, Waffle House, Wendy's, **lodging:** Days Inn, Drury Inn, Country Inn Suites, Microtel, **other:** AutoZone, Big 10 Tire, BJ's Whse/gas (3mi), CarQuest, NTB, O'Reilly Parts, PepBoys

**96** Pleasantdale Rd, Northcrest Rd, **E food:** Burger King, Pleasantdale Chinese, **lodging:** Peachtree Inn, **W gas:** Exxon/dsl, QT/dsl, **food:** Waffle House, **lodging:** US Economy Lodge

**95** I-285

**94** Chamblee-Tucker Rd, **E gas:** Shell, Texaco, **lodging:** Masters Inn, **W gas:** QT/dsl, Shell, **food:** DQ, Waffle House, **lodging:** Motel 6, Super 8, **other:** to Mercer U

**93** Shallowford Rd, to Doraville, **E gas:** Shell, **food:** Blimpie, Collard Green Cafe, El Salvador, Hop Shing Chinese, **other:** Publix, U-Haul, **W gas:** Circle K, Shell/dsl, **lodging:** Quality Inn

**91** US 23, GA 155, Clairmont Rd, **E gas:** Chevron, Shell, **food:** Grand Buffet, IHOP, Mo's Pizza, Popeye's, **other:** Brakes&More/repair, IGA Foods, **W gas:** BP, **food:** Donnie's, McDonald's, Roadhouse Grill, Waffle House, **lodging:** Marriott, Wingate Inn, **other:** NTB, Sam's Club/gas

**89** GA 42, N Druid Hills, **E gas:** Chevron/Subway/dsl, QT/dsl/24hr, Shell, **food:** Arby's, Boston Mkt, Burger King, Chick-fil-A, Einstein Bro's, Lettuce Souperise, McDonald's, Moe's SW Grill, Panera Bread, Picadilly's, Starbucks, Taco Bell, TCBY, **lodging:** Courtyard, Homestead Suites, **other:** $Tree, Firestone/auto, Target, **W gas:** Chevron, Exxon, Shell, **food:** Atlanta Diner, Dunkin Donuts, HoneyBaked Ham, Krystal, Waffle House, **lodging:** DoubleTree, Hampton Inn, Red Roof Inn, **other:** CVS Drug, Just Brakes, vet

**88** Lenox Rd, GA 400 N, Cheshire Br Rd (from sb), **E gas:** Shell, **lodging:** La Quinta

**87** GA 400 N (from nb)

**86** GA 13 S, Peachtree St, **E gas:** BP, **food:** Denny's, Wendy's, **lodging:** Intown Inn, La Quinta, **other:** Brake-O

**85** I-75 N, to Marietta, Chattanooga

**84** Techwood Dr, 14th St, **E gas:** BP, Shell, **food:** CheeseSteaks, La Bamba Mexican, Thai Cuisine, VVV Ristorante Italiano, **lodging:** Best Western, Hampton Inn, Marriott, Sheraton, Travelodge, **other:** Woodruff Arts Ctr, **W food:** Blimpie, **lodging:** Courtyard, Knight's Inn, **other:** CVS Drug, Dillard's, Office Depot, to Georgia Tech

**249d** 10th St, Spring St (from nb), **E gas:** BP, Chevron/24hr, Shell, **food:** Checker's, Domino's, Pizza Hut, Varsity

## INTERSTATE 85 CONT'D

**249d** Continued
Drive-In, **lodging:** Fairfield Inn, Marriott, Regency Suites, Renaissance Hotel, Residence Inn, Wyndham Hotel, **other:** Publix, to Mitchell House, **W food:** McDonald's, **lodging:** Courtyard, **other:** H HOSPITAL, CVS Drug, to GA Tech

**249c** Williams St (from sb), downtown, to GA Dome

**249b** Pine St, Peachtree St (from nb), downtown, **E lodging:** Reniassance Inn, **other:** H HOSPITAL, to midtown, **W** downtown, hotels

**249a** Courtland St (from sb), downtown, **W lodging:** Hilton, Marriott, **other:** GA St U

**248d** Piedmont Ave, Butler St (from sb), downtown, **W lodging:** Courtyard, Fairfield Inn, Radisson, **other:** H HOSPITAL, Ford, MLK NHS

**248c** GA 10 E, Intn'l Blvd, downtown, **W lodging:** Hilton, Holiday Inn, Marriott Marquis, Radisson

**248b** Edgewood Ave (from nb), **W other:** H HOSPITAL, downtown, hotels

**248a** MLK Dr (from sb), **W** st capitol, to Underground Atlanta

**247** I-20, E to Augusta, W to Birmingham

**246** Georgia Ave, Fulton St, **E lodging:** Hampton Inn, Holiday Inn Express, **other:** to Turner Stadium, **W food:** KFC, **other:** to Coliseum, GSU

**245** Ormond St, Abernathy Blvd, **E lodging:** Comfort Inn, Country Inn Suites, Hampton Inn, Holiday Inn Express, **other:** Turner Stadium, **W** st capitol

**244** University Ave, **E gas:** Chevron, Exxon, **food:** Wendy's, **other:** NAPA, **W gas:** Amoco, **food:** Mrs Winner's, **other:** Ford Trucks

**243** GA 166, Lakewood Fwy, to East Point

**77** I-75 S

**76** Cleveland Ave, **E gas:** Citgo/dsl, Marathon, Phillips 66/Blimpie, **food:** Arby's, Burger King, Krystal, Mrs Winner's, McDonald's, **other:** H HOSPITAL, BigLots, CVS Drug, $Tree, Kroger, Radio Shack, **W gas:** Shell/dsl, Texaco/dsl, **food:** Chick-fil-A, Church's, KFC, **other:** Chevrolet, CVS Drug, Honda, O'Reilly Parts

**75** Sylvan Rd, **E gas:** Citgo, Phillips 66, Shell/dsl, **food:** Chick-fil-A, City Garden Chinese, IHOP, McDonald's, Wendy's, **lodging:** InnCity Suites

**74** Loop Rd, Aviation Commercial Center

**73b a** Virginia Ave, **E gas:** Citgo/dsl, **food:** Hambone's BBQ, Jonny's Pizza, Landmark Diner, Magnolia Grill, Malone's Grill, McDonald's, Pizza Hut, Ruby Tuesday, Schlotsky's, Spondivit's Rest., Waffle House, Wendy's, Willy's Mexican, **lodging:** Courtyard, Drury Inn, Hilton, Renaissance Hotel, Red Roof Inn, Residence Inn, **W gas:** Chevron/Subway/24hr, Shell, **food:** Arby's, Blimpie, Happy Buddah Chinese, Harsfield's Grill, KFC/A&W, La Fiesta Mexican, Steak&Ale, Waffle House, **lodging:** Comfort Inn, Crowne Plaza, DoubleTree, Econolodge, Fairfield Inn, Hampton Inn, Holiday Inn, Hyatt Place, Wellesley Inn

**72** Camp Creek Pkwy

**71** Riverdale Rd, Atlanta Airport, **E food:** Ruby Tuesday, **lodging:** Courtyard, Fairfield Inn, Microtel, Hampton Inn, Holiday Inn, Hyatt Place, La Quinta, Sheraton/grill, Sleep Inn, Springhill Suites, Super 8, **W gas:** Chevron, **food:** Joe's Rest., **lodging:** Day's Inn, Embassy Suites, Hilton Garden, Holiday Inn Express, Marriott, Westin Hotel

**69** GA 279, **E gas:** Chevron/24hr, **food:** Denny's, Waffle House, **lodging:** Atlanta So. Hotel, La Quinta, Motel 6, Quality Inn, Radisson, **other:** CVS Drug, Goodyear/auto, **W gas:** BP, Citgo, Conoco/dsl, Exxon/dsl, RaceTrac, Texaco, **food:** Arby's, Blimpie, Burger King, Cajun Crabhouse, Checker's, Church's, El Ranchero Mexican, KFC, Krystal, Longhorn Steaks, McDonald's, Pizza Hut, Red Lobster, ShowCase Eatery, Steak&Ale, Subway, Taco Bell, Wendy's, **lodging:** Baymont Inn, Day's Inn, Fairfield Inn, Red Roof Inn, **other:** Advance Parts, AutoZone, Cottman Transmissions, Family$, Kroger, Radio Shack, Target, U-Haul

**68** I-285 Atlanta Perimeter

**66** Flat Shoals Rd, **W gas:** BP, Chevron/dsl, Mobil/dsl, Shell/Blimpie, **food:** Supreme Fish Delight, Waffle House, **lodging:** Motel 6

**64** GA 138, to Union City, **E gas:** BP/Blimpie/dsl, RaceTrac, **food:** Waffle House, **lodging:** Econolodge, Super 8, **other:** Buick/Pontiac/GMC, Chevrolet, Chrysler, Dodge, Ford, Honda, Kia/Nissan, Infiniti, Saturn, Toyota, VW, **W gas:** Chevron, QT, Shell, **food:** Arby's, Burger King, Capt D's, Cracker Barrel, IHOP, KFC, Krystal, McDonald's, Papa John's, Pizza Hut, Shoney's, Sonic, Subway, Taco Bell, Wendy's, **lodging:** Best Western, Comfort Inn, Country Hearth Inn, Holiday Inn Express, **other:** Aamco, BigLots, Chevrolet, $Tree, Eckerd, Firestone, Goodyear/auto, Ingles, Kroger, NTB, O'Reilly Parts, PepBoys, Sears/auto, Walgreens, Walmart SuperCtr, mall

**61** GA 74, to Fairburn, **E gas:** BP/dsl/scales, RaceTrac, Shell, **food:** Cafe 74, Chick-fil-A, McDonald's, Waffle House, Wendy's, Zaxby's, **lodging:** Hampton Inn, Holiday Inn Express, Sleep Inn, Wingate Inn, **W gas:** Citgo/dsl, Marathon, Phillips 66/Blimpie/dsl, **lodging:** Efficiency Motel

**56** Collinsworth Rd, **W gas:** BP, Marathon/dsl, **food:** Frank's Rest., **other:** South Oaks Camping

**51** GA 154, to Sharpsburg, **E gas:** Phillips 66/Blimpie/dsl, Summit/dsl, Hardee's, Wendy's (mi), **W gas:** Chevron/dsl, Shell/dsl, **food:** Waffle House

**47** GA 34, to Newnan, **E gas:** BP, Chevron/dsl, Citgo/Subway, HotSpot/dsl, QT, Shell, **food:** Applebee's, Arby's, Capt. D's, Chinchin Chinese, Dunkin Donuts, Hooters, LongHorn Steaks, Moe's SW Grill, Panda Express, Peg-Leg Polly's, Red Lobster, Ruby Tuesday, Sprayberry's BBQ, Steak'n Shake, Texas Roadhouse, Waffle House, Wendy's, **lodging:** Hampton Inn, Jameson Inn, Springhill Suites, **other:** Belk, Circuit City, Goodyear, Goody's, Home Depot, Kohl's, Lowe's Whse, Ross,

N ↕ S ATLANTA AREA

Left margin (bottom): ATLANTA AREA

ATLANTA AREA

Right margin (bottom): FAIRBURN N

Right margin tab: GA

Copyright 2009 - The Next Exit®

## INTERSTATE 85 CONT'D

**NEWNAN** N ↕ S

**MOUNTVILLE** N ↕ S

| | |
|---|---|
| 47 | Continued |
| | Walmart SuperCtr, **W gas:** Phillips 66, RaceTrac, Bugaboo Creek Steaks, Burger King, Chick-fil-A, Chili's, Cracker Barrel, Golden Corral, IHOP, KFC, O'Charley's, Panera Bread, Shane's BBQ, TGI Friday, Waffle House, Zaxby's, **lodging:** Best Western, Comfort Inn, Day's Inn, Holiday Inn Express, La Quinta, Motel 6, **other:** Ⓗ HOSPITAL, BJ's Whse, Chevrolet, Mazda/Jeep/Hyundai, Michael's, Office Depot, Old Navy, Pontiac/Buick/GMC, Publix, Target, Tires+, TJ Maxx, Toyota |
| 41 | US 27/29, Newnan, **E gas:** Pilot/Subway/Wendy's/dsl/scales/24hr, **W gas:** BP/dsl/24hr, Chevron, Phillips 66, **food:** Huddle House, McDonald's, Waffle House, **lodging:** Day's Inn, Howard Johnson, Super 8 |
| 35 | US 29, to Grantville, **W gas:** BP/dsl, Phillips 66/dsl |
| 28 | GA 54, GA 100, to Hogansville, **E gas:** Shell/dsl, **W gas:** BP/dsl, Chevron/dsl, SBS, **food:** China Cafe, Dos Compadres, Intnat'l Cafe, McDonald's, Roger's BBQ, Subway, Waffle House, Wendy's, **lodging:** Econolodge, Garden Inn, **other:** Ingles |
| 23mm | Beech Creek |
| 22mm | weigh sta both lanes |
| 21 | I-185 S, to Columbus |
| 18 | GA 109, to Mountville, **E gas:** Chevron/Domino's/dsl, **lodging:** Quality Inn, **other:** to FDR SP, Little White House HS, **W gas:** BP/dsl, RaceTrac, Shell/Church's/dsl, Spectrum/dsl, Summit/dsl, **food:** Applebee's, Burger King, Conestoga Steaks, Cracker Barrel, Juanito's Mexican, Longhorn Steaks, Los Nopales, Moe's SW Grill, Ryan's, Subway, Waffle House, Wendy's, Zaxby's, **lodging:** Best Western, Comfort Inn, Jameson Inn, Super 8, **other:** Belk, Chrysler/Dodge/Jeep, Ford/Lincoln/Mercury, Home Depot, Honda, Hoofer's RV Park (3mi), JC Penney, mall |
| 14 | US 27, to La Grange, **W gas:** BP/24hr, Pure, Shell, **lodging:** Hampton Inn |
| 13 | GA 219, to La Grange, **E gas:** Shell/dsl/scales/24hr/@, **food:** Waffle House, **lodging:** Day's Inn, **other:** truckwash, **W gas:** BP/dsl, Pilot/Subway/dsl/scales/24hr, **food:** Arbys, McDonald's, **other:** Ⓗ HOSPITAL |
| 10mm | Long Cane Creek |
| 2 | GA 18, to West Point, **E gas:** BP, Shell/dsl/24hr, **lodging:** Travelodge, **W food:** KFC (1.5mi), **other:** to West Point Lake, camping |
| .5mm | Welcome Ctr nb, full ♿ facilities, 🚽, 🏕, litter barrels, vending, petwalk |
| 0mm | Georgia/Alabama state line, Chattahoochee River |

## INTERSTATE 95

| Exit # | Services |
|---|---|
| 113mm | Georgia/South Carolina state line, Savannah River |
| 111mm | Welcome Ctr/weigh sta sb, full ♿ facilities, 🚽, info, vending, 🏕, litter barrels, petwalk |
| 109 | GA 21, to Savannah, Pt Wentworth, Rincon, **E gas:** Enmark/dsl, Pilot/McDonald's/Subway/dsl/scales/24hr, **food:** Waffle House, **lodging:** Country Inn&Suites, Hampton Inn, Mulberry Grove Inn, Wingate Inn, **other:** Peterbilt, **W gas:** Shell/Circle K/Quizno's/dsl, **food:** Island Grill, Wendy's, Zaxby's, **lodging:** Comfort Suites, Day's Inn, Holiday Inn Express, Quality Inn, Ramada Ltd, Sleep Inn, Super 8, **other:** CVS Drug, FoodLion, Green Piece RV Park (5mi), Whispering Pines RV Park (3mi) |

## INTERSTATE 95 CONT'D

**SAVANNAH**

| | |
|---|---|
| 107mm | Augustine Creek |
| 106 | Jimmy DeLoach Pkwy |
| 104 | Savannah Airport, **E gas:** BP, Shell/dsl, **food:** Sneed's Grill, Waffle House, **lodging:** Cambria Suites, Candlewood Suites, Comfort Suites, Country Inn&Suites, Fairfield Inn, Hampton Inn, Hawthorn Suites, Hilton Garden, Sheraton, Springhill Suites, Staybridge Suites, Towneplace Suites, Wingate Inn, **other:** to airport, **W gas:** Shell/Subway, **food:** Arby's, Cheddar's, Chick-fil-A, Hilliard's Rest., Longhorn Steaks, Ruby Tuesday, Sonic, Zaxby's Café, **lodging:** Red Roof Inn, **other:** Home Depot, Sam's Club/gas, Walmart SuperCtr/McDonald's/gas |
| 102 | US 80, to Garden City, **E gas:** BP, Enmark/dsl, Flash/dsl, **food:** Angel's Pizza, Cracker Barrel, Huddle House, KFC, Krystal, Masato Japanese, McDonald's, Nagano Japanese, Peking Chinese, Pizza Hut/Taco Bell, Quizno's, Waffle House, **lodging:** Best Western, Jameson Inn, Microtel, Ramada Ltd, Travelodge, **other:** Camping World RV Ctr, Food Lion, Family$, to Ft Pulaski NM, museum, **W gas:** BP, Gate/Subway/dsl, Shell, Texaco, **food:** Burger King, Domino's, Don's BBQ, El Potro Mexican, Hardee's, Italian Pizza, Mihn Zing Chinese, Wendy's, Western Sizzlin, **lodging:** Econolodge, Holiday Inn, La Quinta, Magnolia Inn, Quality Inn, Sleep Inn, **other:** NAPA, auto repair |
| 99b a | I-16, W to Macon, E to Savannah |
| 94 | GA 204, to Savannah, Pembroke, **E gas:** BP/dsl, El Cheapo, Exxon, 76/Circle K, Shell/dsl, **food:** Applebees, Cracker Barrel, Denny's, Hardee's, Hoolihan's, McDonald's, Perkins, Ruby Tuesday, Shoney's, Sonic, **lodging:** Baymont Inn, Best Value Inn, Best Western, Clarion, Comfort Suites, Country Inn&Suites, Day's Inn, Fairfield Inn, Hampton Inn, Holiday Inn Express, Howard Johnson, La Quinta, Quality Inn, Ramda Inn, Red Roof Inn, Rodeway Inn, Sans Boutique Hotel, Sleep Inn, Spring-Hill Suites, Super 8, Wingate Inn, **other:** Ⓗ HOSPITAL, Factory Stores/Famous Brands, GNC, Walmart SuperCtr/gas (2mi), **W gas:** Chevron/dsl/24hr (2mi), Shell, **food:** El Potro Mexican, Hooters, JT's Grill, Shellhouse Rest, Subway, Waffle House, **lodging:** Country Hearth Inn, Econolodge, Microtel, Travelodge, **other:** Harley-Davidson, Bellaire Woods RV Park (2mi) |
| 91mm | Ogeechee River |
| 90 | GA 144, Old Clyde Rd, to Ft Stewart, Richmond Hill SP, **E gas:** Chevron, Exxon, **other:** Kroger/deli, **W gas:** Love's/McDonald's/dsl/scales/24hr, Shell/dsl, **other:** Gore's RV Ctr |
| 87 | US 17, to Coastal Hwy, Richmond Hill, **E gas:** BP/Subway, Chevron/dsl/24hr, Citgo, RaceWay, **food:** China 1, Denny's/24hr, Domino's, Smokehouse Grill, Southern Image Rest., Steamer's Rest., Subway, Waffle House, **lodging:** Day's Inn, Motel 6, Royal Inn, Scottish Inn, Travelodge, **W gas:** El Cheapo, Exxon/McDonald's/dsl, TA/BP/LJSilver/Pizza Hut/Popeye's/dsl/24hr/@, Shell/dsl, **food:** Arby's, Burger King, KFC/Taco Bell, Waffle House, Wendy's, **lodging:** Best Western, Comfort Suites, Econolodge, Hampton Inn, Holiday Inn, Knight's Inn, **other:** KOA |
| 85mm | Elbow Swamp |
| 80mm | Jerico River |
| 76 | US 84, GA 38, to Midway, Sunbury, **E** hist sites, **W gas:** BP/dsl, El Cheapo/dsl/scales, **food:** Holton's Seafood, |

## INTERSTATE 95 CONT'D

| | |
|---|---|
| **76** | Continued<br>Huddle House, **other:** Ⓗ HOSPITAL, museum |
| **67** | US 17, Coastal Hwy, to S Newport, **E gas:** Chevron/<br>Subway/dsl, Citgo/dsl, El Cheapo, Shell/McDonald's,<br>**food:** Jones BBQ, **other:** Harris Neck NWR, Newport<br>Camping (2mi), **W gas:** BP |
| **58** | GA 99, GA 57, Townsend Rd, Eulonia, **E gas:** BP/dsl,<br>Citgo, **lodging:** Eulonia Lodge, **other:** $General, USPO,<br>**W gas:** Chevron/dsl/24hr, Citgo, Shell/Stuckey's/dsl,<br>**food:** Huddle House, **lodging:** Day's Inn, Knight's Inn,<br>**other:** McIntosh Lake RV Park, Lake Harmony RV<br>Camp |
| **55mm** | weigh sta both lanes, phone |
| **49** | GA 251, to Darien, **E gas:** Chevron/dsl/24hr, Mobil/dsl,<br>**food:** DQ, McDonald's, Waffle House, **lodging:** King<br>George Motel, **other:** Ford, Inland Harbor RV Park, Tall<br>Pines RV Park, **W gas:** BP, El Cheapo/Larry's Subs/dsl/<br>scales, Shell/dsl, **food:** Burger King, Huddle House,<br>KFC/Pizza Hut/Taco Bell, Ruby Tuesday, Smokey Joe's<br>BBQ, TCBY, Wendy's, **lodging:** Clean Stay USA, Com-<br>fort Inn, Hampton Inn, Quality Inn, Super 8, **other:** Pre-<br>ferred Outlets/famous brands, flea mkt |
| **47mm** | Darien River |
| **46.5mm** | Butler River |
| **46mm** | Champney River |
| **45mm** | Altamaha River |
| **42** | GA 99, **E** to Hofwyl Plantation HS |
| **41mm** | rest area sb, full ♿ facilities, 🕾, info, vending, 🚻,<br>litter barrels, petwalk |
| **38** | GA 25, to US 17, N Golden Isles Pkwy, Brunswick, **E**<br>**gas:** RaceTrac, **food:** Millhouse Steaks, **lodging:** Country<br>Inn&Suites, Embassy Suites (2mi), Fairfield Inn, Holiday<br>Inn, Microtel, St James Suites, **other:** Ⓗ HOSPITAL, Nis-<br>san, **W gas:** BP, Chevron, Flash, Shell/dsl, **food:** China<br>Town, Denny's, Huddle House/24hr, La Fuente Mexican,<br>Waffle House, **lodging:** Courtyard, Econolodge, Guest<br>Cottage Motel, Hampton Inn, Quality Inn, **other:** $Gen-<br>eral, Harley Davidson, Harvey's Foods, Toyota |
| **36b a** | US 25, US 341, to Jesup, Brunswick, **E gas:** Chevron/<br>dsl/24hr, Exxon/dsl, RaceWay, **food:** Burger King, Crack-<br>er Barrel, IHOP, KFC, Krystal/24hr, McDonald's, Pizza<br>Hut, Shoney's, Starbucks, Taco Bell, Wendy's, **lodging:**<br>Day's Inn, Hampton Inn, Knight's Inn, La Quinta, Motel 6,<br>Ramada Inn, Red Roof Inn, **other:** Newcastle RV Ctr, **W**<br>**gas:** BP, Mobil/dsl, Parker's/dsl, Sunoco, **food:** Beef'o<br>Brady's, Capt Joe's Seafood, Huddle House/24hr, Larry's<br>Subs, Sonny's BBQ, Subway, Waffle House, **lodging:**<br>Best Western, Clarion, Clean Stay USA, Rodeway Inn,<br>Sleep Inn, Super 8, **other:** Advance Parts, CVS Drug,<br>$General, Family$, Fred's Drug, Winn-Dixie |
| **33mm** | Turtle River |
| **30mm** | S Brunswick River |
| **29** | US 17, US 82, GA 520, S GA Pkwy, Brunswick, **E gas:**<br>Citgo/Church's/dsl, Exxon, Mobil, Pilot/Steak'n Shake/<br>Subway/dsl/scales/24hr, Sunoco/Backyard Burger,<br>**food:** GA BBQ, Huddle House, Krystal, McDonald's,<br>Whataburger, **other:** Blue Beacon, SpeedCo Lube,<br>**W gas:** ✈FLYING J/Conoco/Country Mkt/dsl/LP/<br>scales/24hr, Goasis/Burger King/Subway/dsl/24hr, Mo-<br>bil, **food:** Waffle House, **lodging:** GuestHouse Inn, |

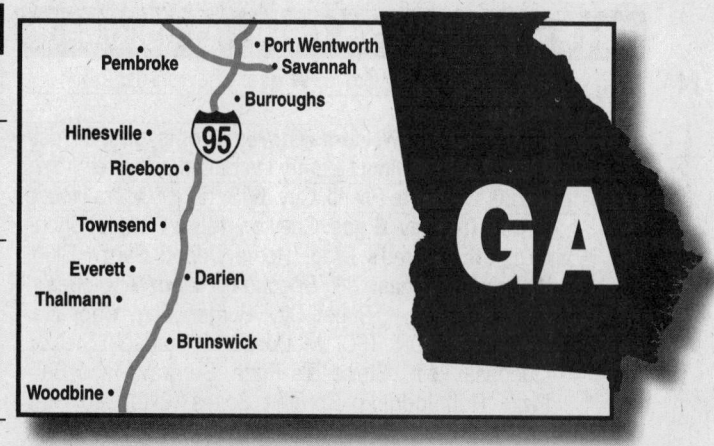

| | |
|---|---|
| **29** | Continued<br>Microtel, Super 8, **other:** $General, Golden Isles Camp-<br>ing, TA Truck Service |
| **27.5mm** | Little Satilla River |
| **26** | Dover Bluff Rd, **E gas:** Mobil/Stuckey's/dsl |
| **21mm** | White Oak Creek |
| **19mm** | Canoe Swamp |
| **15mm** | Satilla River |
| **14** | GA 25, to Woodbine, **W food:** Chevron/Sunshine/dsl/<br>rest./24hr, Jack's BBQ, **lodging:** Stardust Motel (3mi) |
| **7** | Harrietts Bluff Rd, **E gas:** Exxon/dsl, Shell/Subway,<br>**food:** Huddle House, **W gas:** BP/dsl |
| **6.5mm** | Crooked River |
| **6** | Laurel Island Pkwy, **E gas:** Cisco/BP/Arby's/dsl/scales/24hr |
| **3** | GA 40, to St Marys, **E gas:** El Cheapo, Exxon/Krys-<br>tal, Shell/Subway, **food:** Applebee's, Bonzai, Burger<br>King, Chick-fil-A, China Wok, Hong Kong Buffet, KFC,<br>McDonald's, Pablo's Mexican, Ruby Tuesday, Shon-<br>ey's, Sonny's BBQ, Taco Bell, Waffle House, Wendy's,<br>Zaxby's, **lodging:** Best Western, Comfort Inn, Country<br>Inn&Suites, Day's Inn, 4Star Inn, Hampton Inn, Haw-<br>thorn Suites, Holiday Inn Express, Magnolia Inn, Micro-<br>tel, Quality Inn, Sleep Inn, **other:** Ⓗ HOSPITAL, Chevro-<br>let/Buick, Chrysler/Dodge/Jeep, CVS Drug, $Tree, Ford/<br>Mercury, Kia, K-Mart, Lowes Whse, Publix, Winn-Dixie,<br>to Submarine Base, **W gas:** Citgo, Flash/dsl, Petro/<br>Quizno's/Church's/dsl/scales/24hr/@, **food:** Cracker<br>Barrel, IHOP, Oasis Grill, Waffle House, **lodging:** Clean<br>Stay USA, Days Inn, Econolodge, Jameson Inn, La<br>Quinta, Ramada Inn |
| **1** | St Marys Rd, **E Welcome Ctr nb, full ♿ facilities, 🕾,**<br>**vending, 🚻, litter barrels, petwalk, gas:** Cisco/Blimp-<br>ie/DQ/LJ Silver/Mrs Winners/Pizza Hut/dsl, Shell/dsl,<br>**food:** to Cumberland Is Nat Seashore, **W gas:** BP/dsl,<br>Chevron/dsl, Wilco/Hess/Wendy's/dsl/scales, Jack's<br>BBQ, **other:** GS RV Park, KOA |
| **0mm** | Georgia/Florida state line, St Marys River |

## INTERSTATE 185 COLUMBUS

| Exit # | Services |
|---|---|
| **48** | I-85. I-185 begins/ends on I-85. |
| **46** | Big Springs Rd, **E** BP, **W gas:** Shell |
| **42** | US 27, Pine Mountain, **E gas:** BP, Shell/dsl, **food:**<br>Waffle House, **other:** to Callaway Gardens, Little White<br>House HS |
| **34** | GA 18, to West Point, **E gas:** Shell/dsl/24hr |
| **30** | Hopewell Church Rd, Whitesville, **W gas:** BP/dsl |
| **25** | GA 116, to Hamilton, **W** RV camping |

### INTERSTATE 185 CONT'D COLUMBUS

| | |
|---|---|
| 19 | GA 315, Mulberry Grove, **W** gas: Chevron/dsl/24hr |
| 14 | Smith Rd |
| 12 | Williams Rd, **W** **Welcome Ctr/rest rooms, gas:** BP/dsl/cafe, Shell, **lodging:** Country Inn Suites, Microtel |
| 10 | US 80, GA 22, to Phenix City, **W** Springer Opera House |
| 8 | Airport Thruway, **E** gas: Chevron, **food:** Blimpie, Shoney's, **other:** Fred's Drug, Home Depot, Sam's Club, Walmart, **W** gas: BP, Spectrum, **food:** Applebee's, Backyard Burger, Buffet City, Burger King, Capt D's, Hardee's, IHOP, KFC, McDonald's, Outback Steaks, Quepasa Rest., Stevie B's Pizza, Subway, Taco Bell/Pizza Hut, **lodging:** Comfort Suites, Extended Stay America, Hampton Inn, Sheraton, **other:** K-Mart |
| 7 | 45th St, Manchester Expswy, **E** gas: Chevron, **food:** Applebee's, Burger King, Carino's Italian, Krystal, Ruby Tuesday, WildFish Grill, **lodging:** Courtyard, La Quinta, Super 8, **other:** Best Buy, Chevrolet/Cadillac, Dillard's, K-Mart, Macy's, mall, **W** gas: BP, Chevron, Spectrum, Texaco, **food:** A&W/KFC, Arby's, China Express, Crystal River Seafood, Golden Corral, Logan's Roadhouse, Lucky China, McDonald's, Pizza Hut, Ryan's, Sonic, Subway, Waffle House, Wendy's, **lodging:** Fairfield Inn, Holiday Inn, Shogun Japanese, Sleep Inn, **other:** [H] HOSPITAL, Vet, Advance Parts, $General, tires, transmissions |
| 6 | GA 22, Macon Rd, **E** gas: Chevron, Spectrum, **food:** Brewster's, Burger King, China Buffet, KFC, Taco Bell, Waffle House, **lodging:** Best Western, Comfort Inn, Day's Inn, **other:** Eckerd, Ford, Kia, Nissan, U-Haul, Walgreens, **W** gas: BP, Chevron, **food:** American Deli, Capt D's, ChuckeCheese, Cici's Pizza, Country BBQ, Denny's, Firehouse Subs, Longhorn Steaks, McDonald's, Schlotzky's, **lodging:** Efficiency Lodge, La Quinta, **other:** CVS Drug, Firestone/auto, Freds Drug, GNC, Goodyear, Hancock Fabrics, Honda, Publix, Radio Shack |
| 4 | Buena Vista Rd, **E** gas: BP, Solo, **food:** Arby's, Burger King, Capt D's, Chef Lee Chinese, Checker's, Church's, Krystal, McDonald's, Pizza Hut, Taco Bell, Waffle House, Zaxby's, **other:** AutoZone, $Tree, Firestone/auto, Goodyear/auto, Rainbow Foods, Walmart/Subway/drugs, Winn-Dixie, repair, **W** gas: Chevron, Spectrum |
| 3 | St Marys Rd, **W** gas: BP, FuelTech, **food:** DQ, Hardee's, KFC, **other:** Ace Hardware, $General, Piggly Wiggly |
| 1b a | US 27, US 280, Victory Dr, **1-3 mi W** gas: RaceWay/24hr, **food:** Burger King, Denny's, KFC, McDonald's, Popeye's, Subway, Valarta Mexican, Wendy's, **lodging:** Econolodge, Colony Inn, Day's Inn, Motel 6, Advance Parts, I-185 begins/ends. |

### INTERSTATE 285 ATLANTA

| Exit # | Services |
|---|---|
| 62 | GA 279, S Fulton Hwy, Old Nat Hwy, **N** gas: Chevron, Texaco, **food:** City Cafe, **lodging:** Econolodge, **S** gas: Chevron, Exxon, Shell, **food:** Blimpie, Burger King, Checker's, China Cafeteria, Church's, El Nopal Mexican, KFC/Pizza Hut, Krystal, Longhorn Steaks, McDonald's, Mrs Winner's, Popeye's, Subway, Taco Bell, Waffle House, Wendy's, **lodging:** Clarion, Comfort Inn, Day's Inn, Howard Johnson, Motel 6, Quality Inn, **other:** AutoZone, Cottman Transmissions, Curves, Family$, NAPA, U-Haul |
| 61 | I-85, N to Atlanta, S to Montgomery, **Services 1 mi** **N** GA I-85, exit 71. **E** food: Ruby Tuesday, lodging: Comfort Suites, Courtyard, GA Conv Ctr, Microtel, Hampton Inn, Sheraton/grill, Sleep Inn, Sumner Suites, Super 8, Wingate Inn, **W** food: lodging: Comfort Inn, Day's Inn, Embassy Suites, Marriott, Quality Inn, Ramada, Super 8, Travelodge, Westin Hotel |
| 60 | GA 139, Riverdale Rd, **N** lodging: Microtel (2mi), Wingate Inn (2mi), **S** gas: BP, Exxon, QT, Shell/dsl, **food:** Blimpie, Checker's, China Café, Church's, KFC/LJ Silver, McDonald's, Papa John's, Wendy's, **lodging:** Best Western, Country Inn&Suites, Day's Inn, Ramada Inn, **other:** Advance Parts, $General, Family$, U-Haul, Wayfield Foods |
| 59 | Clark Howell Hwy, **N** air cargo |
| 58 | I-75, N to Atlanta, S to Macon (from eb), to US 19, US 41, to Hapeville, **S** gas: BP, Chevron/24hr, **food:** Bojangles, Philly Connection, Subway, Waffle House, Wendy's, **lodging:** Home Lodge Motel |
| 55 | GA 54, Jonesboro Rd, **N** lodging: Super 8, **S** gas: BP, Citgo/dsl, Phillips 66, Shell/dsl, **food:** Alondra's Mexican/Chinese, Capt D's, Church's, DaiLai Vietnamese, Golden Gate Chinese, LJ Silver, McDonald's, Subway, Taco Bell, **other:** Home Depot, repair |
| 53 | US 23, Moreland Ave, to Ft Gillem, **N** gas: BP, Citgo, Conoco/dsl, **S** gas: Citgo, Shell, TA/dsl/24hr/@, **food:** Popeye's, Wendy's, **lodging:** Economy Inn |
| 52 | I-675, S to Macon |
| 51 | Bouldercrest Rd, **N** gas: BP, Pilot/Wendy's/dsl/24hr, **food:** A&W/LJ Silver, Hardee's, KFC/Pizza Hut, WK Wings, **lodging:** DeKalb Inn, **other:** Family$, Wayfield Foods, **S** gas: Chevron/dsl |
| 48 | GA 155, Flat Shoals Rd, Candler Rd, **N** gas: BP, Chevron, Marathon, Shell/dsl, Stop'n Go, **food:** Arby's, Burger King, Checker's, DQ, KFC/Pizza Hut, McDonald's, Subway, Taco Bell, Waffle King, WK Wings, **lodging:** Country Hearth Inn, Gulf American Inn, **other:** BigLots, Macy's, Pep Boys, **S** gas: QT, Phillips 66, **food:** Sonic |
| 46b a | I-20, E to Augusta, W to Atlanta |
| 44 | GA 260, Glenwood Rd, **E** gas: Marathon, Super 8, **lodging:** Old English Inn, **W** gas: Citgo, Shell, **food:** Church's, Mrs Winner's, **lodging:** Glenwood Inn |
| 43 | US 278, Covington Hwy, **E** gas: Chevron/Subway/24hr, Citgo/dsl, **food:** Waffle House, **other:** U-Haul, **W** gas: BP/24hr, QT, Shell/dsl, **food:** Blimpie, Checker's, KFC/Taco Bell, Mrs Winner's, Wendy's, **lodging:** Best Inn, **other:** Advance Parts, Family$, Firestone/auto |
| 42 | (from nb), Marta Station |
| 41 | GA 10, Memorial Dr, Avondale Estates, **E** gas: Citgo, QT, Shell/dsl, **food:** Applebee's, Arby's, Burger King, Church's, DQ, McDonald's, Pancake House, Pizza Hut, Super China, Waffle House, Wendy's, **lodging:** Savannah Suites, Suburban Lodge, **other:** Advance Parts, AutoZone, Big 10 Tire, $General, Firestone/auto, Office Depot, Radio Shack, U-Haul |
| 40 | Church St, to Clarkston, **E** gas: Chevron, Shell/dsl, Texaco, **W** gas: other: [H] HOSPITAL |
| 39b a | US 78, to Athens, Decatu |
| 38 | US 29, Lawrenceville Hwy, **E** gas: Phillips 66, Shell, **food:** Waffle House, **lodging:** Knight's Inn, Super 8, **other:** [H] HOSPITAL, **W** gas: BP, USA, **food:** Waffle House, **lodging:** Masters Inn, Motel 6 |
| 37 | GA 236, to LaVista, Tucker, **E** gas: Chevron, Circle K, **food:** Checker's, Chili's, Folks Rest., IHOP, O'Charley's, |

## INTERSTATE 285 ATLANTA

**ATLANTA AREA**

**37** Continued
Olive Garden, Picadilly's, Schlotsky's, Steak&Ale, Waffle House, **lodging:** Comfort Suites, Country Inn Suites, **other:** Firestone, Target, **W gas:** BP/repair, Citgo/dsl, Shell, **food:** Arby's, Blackeyed Pea, Blue Ribbon Grill, Capt D's, City Cafe, Domino's, DQ, Fuddrucker's, Jason's Deli, McDonald's, Panera Bread, Philly Connection, Pizza Hut, Red Lobster, Taco Bell, Wendy's, **lodging:** Courtyard, Fairfield Inn, Holiday Inn, Magnolia Motel, Quality Inn, Radisson, **other:** Best Buy, $Tree, Goodyear/auto, JC Penney, Kroger, Macy's, Michael's, Office Depot, Publix, TJ Maxx, mall

**34** Chamblee-Tucker Rd, **E gas:** Chevron, Citgo, Phillips 66, Shell, **food:** Arby's/Mrs Winner's, China Star, KFC/Taco Bell, Moe's SW Grill, S&S Cafeteria, Taco Bell, **lodging:** Day's Inn, **other:** Ace Hardware, Advance Parts, Eckerd, Goodyear, Kroger, **W gas:** BP, Citgo, **food:** Little Cuba, LoneStar Steaks, McDonald's, Subway, Waffle House, **other:** BigLots, $Tree

**33b a** I-85, N to Greenville, S to Atlanta

**32** US 23, Buford Hwy, to Doraville, **E gas:** BP/24hr, **food:** Baldino's Subs, Burger King/playland, Checker's, Chick-fil-A, El Pescador, Krystal, Wendy's, **other:** Big 10 Tire, Firestone/auto, Goodyear/auto, K-Mart, 99¢ Store, **Wgas:** Citgo, Shell, **food:** First China, McDonald's, Monterrey Mexican, Waffle House, **lodging:** Holiday Inn

**31b a** GA 141, Peachtree Ind, to Chamblee, **W gas:** Citgo, Shell, Texaco, **food:** Arby's, Chick-fil-A, Dunkin Donuts, McDonald's, Piccadilly, Pizza Hut, Waffle House, Wendy's, **other:** Acura, Advance Parts, Audi/VW, Buick/Pontiac/GMC, Chevrolet, Chrysler/Jeep/Dodge, CVS Drug, Dodge, Firestone, Ford, Honda, Hyundai, Kia, Lexus, Mazda, Porsche, Saab, Toyota, VW

**30** Chamblee-Dunwoody Rd, N Shallowford Rd, to N Peachtree Rd, **N gas:** BP, Chevron, **food:** Bagel&Co., Burger King, Garcia's Mexican, Guthrie's, Lucky China, Maggie's Creamery, McDonald's, Quizno's, Starbucks, Subway, Waffle House, **other:** Kroger, **S gas:** Exxon/Blimpie/Arby's, Mobil, Phillips 66/dsl, Shell, **food:** Bombay Grill, City Café, La Botana Mexican, Mad Italian Rest., Olde Mill Steaks, Papa John's, Taco Bell, Wendy's, Wild Ginger Thai, **lodging:** Holiday Inn Select, Residence Inn

**29** Ashford-Dunwoody Rd, **N gas:** BP, Exxon/Subway, **food:** Applebee's, Brio Tuscan, Bloomingdale's, CA Pizza Kitchen, Denny's, Food Court, Garrison's Broiler, Goldfish, Houlihan's, Jason's Deli, J. Alexander's, Maggiano's Italian, McDonald's, McCormick & Shmick's, PF Chang's, Schlotsky's, **lodging:** Crowne Plaza, Fairfield Inn, **other:** Barnes&Noble, Best Buy, Border's, Dillard's, Firestone/auto, Goodyear/auto, Macey's, Marshall's, Old Navy, Walmart SuperCtr, USPO, mall, **S gas:** Chevron, **food:** Arby's, **lodging:** Hilton Garden

**28** Peachtree-Dunwoody Rd (no EZ return wb), **N food:** Arby's, Chequer's Grill, Fuddrucker's, Sweet Tomatos, **lodging:** Comfort Suites, Courtyard, Extended Stay America, Extended Stay Deluxe, Fairfield Inn, Hampton Inn, Hilton Suites, Holiday Inn Express, Homestead Suites, La Quinta, Marriott, Microtel, Residence Inn, Westin, **other:** Costco/gas, Home Depot, PetsMart, Publix, Rite Aid, Ross, Target, TJ Maxx, mall, **S H HOSPITAL**

**27** US 19 N, GA 400, **2 mi N** LDS Temple

**ATLANTA AREA**

**26** Glenridge Dr (from eb), Johnson Ferry Rd

**25** US 19 S, Roswell Rd, Sandy Springs, **N gas:** BP, Chevron, Exxon, Shell/dsl, **food:** American Pie Rest., Applebee's, Arby's, Boston Mkt, Burger King, Caribbean Cafe, Chicago Pizza, Chick-fil-A, Chipotle Mexican, Domino's, Dunkin Donuts, El Azteca Mexican, El Toro Mexican, IHOP, KFC/Pizza Hut, Landmark Diner, La Rumba Cafe, Longhorn Steaks, Madarin House, McDonald's, Mellow Mushroom Cafe, Noodles Cafe, Panera Bread, Rumi's Kitchen, Ruth's Chris Steaks, Starbucks, Steak'n Shake, Subway, Taco Bell, Waffle House, Wendy's, **lodging:** Comfort Inn, Hampton Inn, Homestead Suites, **other:** H HOSPITAL, CVS Drug, DeKalb Tire, $Tree, Hancock Fabrics, Marshall's, NAPA AutoCare, Office Depot, PepBoys, Publix, Target, Toyota, Whole Foods Mkt, **S gas:** Chevron/24hr, Shell, **food:** El Taco Veloz, Frankie's Grill, Kobe Steaks, Mama's Café, **lodging:** Day's Inn/rest., **other:** Kroger/gas (1.5mi)

**24** Riverside Dr

**22** New Northside Dr, to Powers Ferry Rd, **N gas:** Shell, **S gas:** BP, Chevron/24hr, **food:** McDonald's, Waffle House, Wendy's, **lodging:** Candlewood Suites, Crowne Plaza, Hawthorn Suites, Homestead Suites, **other:** CVS Drug

**21** (from wb), **N gas:** Shell, **food:** HillTop Café, Homestead Village, **other:** BMW/Mini

**20** I-75, N to Chattanooga, S to Atlanta (from wb), to US 41 N

**19** US 41, Cobb Pkwy, to Dobbins AFB, **N gas:** BP, Chevron/24hr, Citgo, Shell, **food:** Arby's, BBQ, Bruster's, Carrabba's, ChuckeCheese, Denny's, Dunkin Donuts, Hardee's, IHOP, Jade Palace, Joe's Crabshack, KFC, McDonald's, Olive Garden, Papa John's, Pizza Hut, Red Lobster, Steak'n Shake, Subway, Sunny's BBQ, The Border Mexican, Waffle House, Wendy's, Wingate Inn, **lodging:** Hilton, Holiday Inn Express, **other:** Best Buy, Cadillac, Buick/Pontiac/Subaru, Chevrolet/Saab, Circuit City, Eckerd, Honda, Hyundai, Lexus, Marshall's, Michael's, Office Depot, PetsMart, Ross, Target, Walgreen, **S gas:** Chevron/24hr, **food:** Buffalo's Café, Cheese Factory, Chipotle Mexican, Chick-fil-A, El Toro Mexican, Hooters, Jason's Deli, Johnny Rocket's, Longhorn Steaks, Maggiano's Italian, Malone's Grill, Olde Mill Steaks, PF Chang, Pizza Hut, Ruby Tuesday, Schlotsky's, **lodging:** Courtyard, Homewood Suites, Renaissance Motel, Sheraton Suites, Stouffer Waverly Hotel, Sumner Suites, **other:** A&P, Barnes&Noble, Circuit City, Costco/gas, JC Penney, Macy's, Sears/auto, USPO, mall

**18** Paces Ferry Rd, to Vinings, **N food:** Panera Bread, **lodging:** Fairfield Inn, La Quinta, **S gas:** QT/24hr, **food:**

**ATLANTA AREA**

**GA**

## INTERSTATE 285 CONT'D ATLANTA

**18** Continued
Chick-fil-A, Subway, Willy's Grill, **lodging:** Extended Stay Deluxe, Hampton Inn, Wyndham, **other:** Eckerd, Goodyear/auto, Home Depot, Publix

**16** S Atlanta Rd, to Smyrna, **N food:** Five Guys Burgers, Waffle House, Zio's Italian, **lodging:** Holiday Inn Express, **other:** H HOSPITAL, **S gas:** Pilot/Wendy's/dsl/scales/24hr, Shell/dsl, Texaco, **other:** Kroger

**15** GA 280, S Cobb Dr, **E lodging:** Microtel, **other:** U-Haul, **W gas:** BP/dsl, RaceTrac, Shell, **food:** Arby's/Mrs Winners, Checker's, Chick-fil-A, China Buffet, IHOP, Krystal/24hr, McDonald's, Subway, Taco Bell, Wendy's, Zaxby's, **lodging:** AmeriHost, Comfort Inn, Country Inn Suites, Knight's Inn, Sun Suites, **other:** H HOSPITAL

**14mm** Chattahoochee River

**13** Bolton Rd (from nb)

**12** US 78, US 278, Bankhead Hwy, **E gas:** Citgo/dsl, Petro/Iron Skillet/dsl/rest./scales/24hr/@, Shell/dsl/24hr, **food:** Mrs Winner's, **other:** Blue Beacon, **W gas:** BP, Marathon

**10b a** I-20, W to Birmingham, E to Atlanta (exits left from nb), **W** to Six Flags

**9** GA 139, MLK Dr, to Adamsville, **E gas:** Phillips 66, Shell, **food:** Mrs Winner's, **other:** Family$, Wayfield Foods, **W gas:** Chevron, Shell, **food:** Checker's, Church's, Golden House Chinese, KFC/Taco Bell, McDonald's

**7** Cascade Rd, **E gas:** Marathon, **food:** Papa John's, **other:** Kroger, **W gas:** BP, Phillips 66, **food:** Applebee's, China Express, KFC, McDonald's, Moe's SW Grill, Mrs Winner's, Pizza Hut, Quizno's, Starbucks, Subway, Up the Creek, Wendy's, **other:** H HOSPITAL, Eckerd, GNC, Home Depot, Publix, Radio Shack, Tires+

**5b a** GA 166, Lakewood Fwy, **E gas:** Chevron, Shell, **food:** Blimpie, Burger King, Capt D's, Checker's, IHOP, KFC, Taco Bell, Wendy's, **other:** Goodyear, Firestone, Kroger, Macy's, mall, **W gas:** BP, Citgo/dsl, RaceWay, Shell/dsl/24hr, **food:** Church's, KFC, Mrs Winner's, Wendy's, **lodging:** Deluxe Inn, **other:** VET, AutoZone, CVS Drug, Family$

**2** Camp Creek Pkwy, to airport, **E gas:** BP, Exxon, Texaco, **food:** Checker's, McDonald's, Mrs Winner's, **lodging:** Comfort Suites, **W gas: food:** American Deli, Brewster's, Carino's, Chick-fil-A, Jason's Deli, LongHorn Steaks, Panda Express, Red Lobster, Ruby Tuesday, Wendys, **other:** Barnes&Noble, BJ's Whse/gas, Circuit City, Lowes Whse, Marshall's, Old Navy, PetsMart, Publix, Ross, Staples, Target, Walgreens

**1** Washington Rd, **E gas:** Texaco/dsl, **W gas:** Chevron, **lodging:** Regency Inn

## INTERSTATE 475 MACON

| Exit # | Services |
|---|---|
| 16mm | I-475 begins/ends on I-75, exit 177. |
| 15 | US 41, Bolingbroke, **1 mi E gas:** Exxon/dsl/LP, Marathon/dsl |
| 9 | Zebulon Rd, **E gas:** Citgo, Shell/Pizza Hut/Taco Bell/24hr, **food:** Buffalo's Café, Chick-fil-A, Hong Kong Rest., Krystal, Margarita's Mexican, McAlister's Deli, McDonald's, NU Wiener's, Papa John's, Subway, Taki Japanese, Waffle House, Wendy's, **lodging:** Baymont Inn, Fairfield Inn, Sleep Inn, **other:** H HOSPITAL, GNC, Kohl's, Kroger, Krystal, Lowe's Whse, Radio Shack, |

**MACON / CANTON**

**9** Continued
Walgreens, Walmart SuperCtr/dsl, USPO, **W gas:** Marathon, Polly's Café, **other:** Advance Parts, CVS Drug

**8mm** **rest area nb, full** facilities, , **vending,** litter barrels, petwalk

**5** GA 74, Macon, **E gas:** RaceWay, **food:** Waffle House, **other:** Harley-Davidson/Suzuki, to Mercer U, **W gas:** Flash/Subway, Texaco/Church's/dsl, **food:** Capt D's, Wok&Roll Chinese, **lodging:** Howard Johnson, **other:** $General, Food Lion, Tires+, vet, to Lake Tobesofkee

**3** US 80, Macon, **E gas:** Marathon/dsl, Raceway, Spectrum/Subway, China Buffet, Cracker Barrel, JL's BBQ, McDonald's, Waffle House, **lodging:** Best Western, Comfort Inn, Day's Inn, Discovery Inn, Economy Inn, Hampton Inn, Holiday Inn, Motel 6, Quality Inn, Red Carpet Inn, Rodeway Inn, Super 8, Travelodge, Villager Inn, **other:** Walmart SuperCtr/gas, **1 mi E gas:** Stop n' Shop, **food:** Applebee's, Chick-fil-A, Cici's, DQ, Golden Corral, KFC, Krystal, Ryan's, Sonny's BBQ, Taco Bell, **other:** Best Buy, BooksAMillion, Chrysler, CVS Drug, Dillard's, Goody's, Home Depot, Jo-Ann Fabrics, Kroger, Lowe's Whse, Marchall's, Michael's, Nissan, Old Navy, PetsMart, Sam's Club/gas, Target, Toyota, mall, **W gas:** Marathon/dsl, Shell, **food:** Burger King, **lodging:** Econolodge, Knight's Inn

**0mm** I-475 begins/ends on I-75, exit 156.

## INTERSTATE 575

| Exit # | Services |
|---|---|
| 30mm | I-575 begins/ends on GA 5/515. |
| 27 | GA 5, Howell Br, to Ball Ground |
| 24 | Airport Dr |
| 20 | GA 5, to Canton, **E gas:** BP, **food:** Casey's rest., Chick-fil-A, Hooters, Ryan's, Stevi B's Pizza, Waffle Wouse, Wendy's, **lodging:** Comfort Inn, Homestead Inn, **other:** Chevrolet, Toyota, Walmart SuperCtr, **W gas:** Citgo, RaceTrac, **food:** Applebee's, Arby's, Cracker Barrel, Longhorn Steaks, McDonald's, O'Charley's, Outback Steaks, Panda Express, Red Lobster, Starbucks, Subway, Waffle House, Zaxby's, **lodging:** Holiday Inn Express, **other:** Belk, Goody's, Home Depot, Michaels, Publix, Radio Shack, Ross |
| 19 | GA 20 E, Canton |
| 17 | GA 140, to Roswell (from sb), Canton |
| 16 | GA 20, GA 140, **E gas:** Pure, **W gas:** Citgo, Shell, **food:** BBQ, Burger King, KFC, Mandarin House, LJ Silver, Papa John's, Taco Bell, Waffle House, **other:** $General, K-Mart |
| 14 | Holly Springs, **E gas:** Citgo/dsl, **food:** Domino's, Pizza Hut, **lodging:** Pinecrest Motel, **W gas:** BP, Chevron, RaceTrac, Shell, **food:** Subway, Viva Mexico, Wendy's, Zaxby's, **other:** Kroger, Publix, Walgreens |
| 11 | Sixes Rd, **E gas:** Chevron, QT, **W gas:** Citgo |
| 8 | Towne Lake Pkwy, to Woodstock, **E gas:** Citgo, Shell, **food:** McDonald's, Waffle House, Waffle King/24hr, **other:** Ford, Hyundai, **W gas:** Phillips 66 |
| 7 | GA 92, Woodstock, **E gas:** Chevron, QT, Shell, **food:** Arby's, Burger King, Capt D's, Checker's, Chick-fil-A, DQ, Firehouse Subs, Folk's Kitchen, KFC, McDonald's, Moe's SW Grill, Mrs Winner's, O'Charley's, Resturante Mexico, Ruby Tuesday, Subway, Taco Bell, Waffle House, Wendy's, **lodging:** Comfort Suites, Hampton Inn, Suburban Lodge, **other:** Big 10 Tire, Camping World, |

## INTERSTATE 575 CONT'D

**7** Continued
CVS Drug, Firestone/auto, Goodyear/auto, Ingles, Just Brakes, **W gas:** BP, **food:** Caribou Coffee, IHOP, Mi Casa Mexican, Schlotzky's, Steak'n Shake, Taco Mac, **other:** Atlanta Bread, Big Lots, BJ's Whse/gas, Discout Tire, Honda, Home Depot, Kohl's, Lowe's Whse, Office Depot, Old Navy, Target

**4** Bells Ferry Rd, **W gas:** QT/24hr, Shell/dsl, **food:** Arby's, Burger King, Ralph's Grill, Subway, Waffle House, **other:** Eckerd

**3** Chastain Rd, to I-75 N, **W gas:** Chevron, Citgo, Shell, **food:** Arby's, Cracker Barrel, Mrs. Winner's, Los Reyes, O'Charley's, Panda Express, Sidelines Grill, Subway, ToGo's/Baskin Robbins, Waffle House, Wendy's, **lodging:** Best Western, Comfort Inn, Country Inn&Suites, Fairfield Inn, Residence Inn, Springhill Suites, Suburban Inn, **other:** to Kennesaw St Coll

**1** Barrett Pkwy, to I-75 N, US 41, **E gas:** Chevron, Murphy USA/dsl, QT, **food:** Barnacle's Cafe, Buffalo Wild Wings, Burger King, Fuddruckers, KFC, Moe's SW Grill, Quizno's, Starbucks, Texas Roadhouse, Waffle House, Wendy's, Zaxby's, **other:** Atlanta Bread, Barnes&Noble, CVS Drug, $Tree, Firestone, Publix, Ross, SteinMart, Walmart SuperCtr/dsl, **W gas:** Shell, Texaco, **food:** Applebee's, Fuddrucker's, McDonald's, Olive Garden, Provino's Italian, Red Lobster, Smokey Bones, Starbucks, Waffle House, **lodging:** Comfort Inn, Crestwood Suites, Day's Inn, Holiday Inn Express, La Quinta, Ramada Ltd, Red Roof Inn, **other:** Big 10 Tire, Firestone/auto, Home Depot, Marshall's, Michael's, TJ Maxx, mall

**0mm** I-575 begins/ends on I-75, exit 268.

## INTERSTATE 675

| Exit # | Services |
| --- | --- |
| **10mm** | I-285 W, to Atlanta Airport, E to Augusta. I-675 begins/ends on I-285, exit 52. |
| **7** | Anvil Block Rd, Ft Gillem, **E gas:** BP, **food:** Subway, **W gas:** Exxon |
| **5** | Forest Pkwy, **E gas:** Texaco/dsl, **W gas:** QT/dsl/scales, McDonald's, Waffle House |
| **2** | US 23, GA 42, **E gas:** BP, Texaco, **food:** Horizon/Backyard Burger, Mo-Joe's Café, **W gas:** Chevron/dsl, Citgo, **food:** Teapot Chinese, Waffle House, **other:** Eckerd, Family$, Food Depot, Goodyear/auto, USPO |

**1** GA 138, to I-75 N, Stockbridge, **E gas:** Chevron/24hr, Citgo/dsl, Exxon, Marathon, Shell, **food:** A&W/LJ Silver, Arby's, Blimpie, Burger King, Capt D's, Checker's, DQ, Golden Corral, KFC, King Buffet, McDonald's, Papa John's, Pizza Hut, Popeye's, Ryan's, Taco Bell, Waffle House, Wendy's, Zaxby's, **lodging:** Best Value, Comfort Inn, Holiday Inn Express, Magnolia Inn, Motel 6, Stockbridge Inn, Suburban Lodge, **other:** Advance Parts, Aldi Foods, BigLots, Cub Foods, CVS Drug, $Tree, Eckerd, Goodyear, Ingles Foods, NAPA, Radio Shack, Walmart SuperCtr/gas, USPO, **W gas:** Exxon, Raceway/24hr, **food:** Applebee's, Arby's, Broadway Diner, Burger King, Chick-fil-A, ChinChin Chinese, CiCi's, DQ, Folk's Rest., Frontera Mexican, Golden Corral, Honeybaked Ham, IHOP, KFC, Krystal, LJ Silver, McDonald's, Piccadilly's, Philly Connection, Shoney's, Subway, Taco Bell, Taco Mac, Tokyo Seafood, Waffle House, Wendy's, **lodging:** Best Western, Day's Inn, Comfort Inn, Holiday Inn, La Quinta, Hampton Inn, Motel 6, Red Roof Inn,

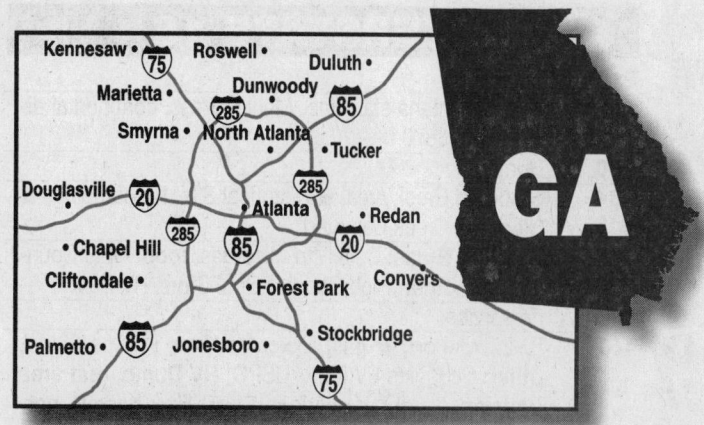

**1** Continued
**other:** H HOSPITAL, GNC, Goodyear, K-Mart, Kroger, Lowes Whse, Office Depot, Tires+

**I-675** begins/ends on I-75, exit 227.

## INTERSTATE 985 - GAINESVILLE

| Exit # | Services |
| --- | --- |
| **I-985** | begins/ends on US 23, 25mm . |

**24** to US 129 N, GA 369 W, Gainesville, **N other:** H HOSPITAL, GA Mtn Ctr, **S gas:** BP/Subway/dsl, Chevron/dsl, Citgo, **food:** Double B Burger, Rabbit Trail Cafe,

**22** GA 11, Gainesville, **N gas:** BP/dsl, Citgo, QT/24hr, **food:** Burger King, McDonald's, **lodging:** Best Western/rest., **S gas:** Chevron, Shell/dsl, **food:** Waffle House, **lodging:** Motel 6

**20** GA 60, GA 53, Gainesville, **N gas** Citgo/dsl, **food:** El Manarca, McDonald's, Mrs Winners, **lodging:** Best Value Inn, Hampton Inn, **S gas:** Kangaroo, **food:** Subway, Waffle House

**16** GA 53, Oakwood, **N gas:** BP, Citgo, **food:** Arby's, Baskin-Robbins/Dunkin Donuts, Burger King, DQ, El Sombrero Mexican, Hardee's, KFC, McDonald's, Pizza Hut, Subway, Taco Bell, Waffle House, Zaxby's, **lodging:** Admiral Benbow Inn, Country Inn Suites, Jameson Inn, **other:** Chrysler/Jeep, CVS Drug, Food Lion, RV Ctr, Sam's Club, **S gas:** Citgo/dsl, QT/dsl, **food:** Checker's, Krystal, Mrs Winners, Sonny's BBQ, Waffle House, Wendy's, **lodging:** Comfort Inn, **other:** AutoZone, Goodyear/auto, Publix, Walgreens

**12** Spout Springs Rd, Flowery Branch, **N gas:** Exxon/dsl, **S gas:** BP/Subway, Chevron/dsl, **food:** Burger&Shake, China Garden, CrossRoads Grill, Domino's, El Sombrero Mexican, TCBY, Thai Dish, **other:** Eckerd, Publix

**8** GA 347, Friendship Rd, Lake Lanier, **N gas:** BP, Chevron, Shell, Texaco, **food:** Backyard Burger, Blimpie, Burger King, China Garden, Huddle House, McDonald's, Sonia's Mexican, Subway, 3rd Coast, Waffle House, Wendy's, Vinny's NY Grill, Zaxby's, **other:** Advance parts, Publix, **S** Harley Davidson, Camper City RV Ctr

**4** US 23 S, GA 20, Buford, **N gas:** QT, Shell, **food:** Arby's, Burger King, Capt D's, Checker's, Golden Buddah, Golden Corral, Huddle House, IHOP, KFC, McDonald's, Saigon Bangkok, Taco Bell, Wendy's, Zaxby's, **lodging:** Days Inn, Holiday Inn Express, **other:** Ace Hardware, Buick/Pontiac/GMC, Dodge/Jeep, Home Depot, KIA, Tuesday Morning, **S gas:** BP, Chevron, Citgo, Texaco, **food:** Ryan's, Sonny's BBQ, Waffle House, **other:** $Tree, Expert Tire, Honda, Lowes Whse, Walmart SuperCtr

**0mm** I-985 begins/ends on I-85.

## INTERSTATE 15

| Exit # | Services |
|---|---|
| 196mm | Idaho/Montana state line, Monida Pass, continental divide, elev 6870 |
| 190 | Humphrey |
| 184 | Stoddard Creek Area, **E** Historical Site, RV camping, **W** Stoddard Creek Camping |
| 180 | Spencer, **E** gas: Opal Mtn Mine/gas, food: Opal Country Café, other: High Country Opal Store, RV Park |
| 172 | no services |
| 167 | ID 22, Dubois, **E** gas: Exxon/dsl/24hr, Phillips 66/dsl, other: Scoggins RV Park, USPO, **RV Dump, rest area both lanes, full 🚻 facilities, 🟦, 🏕, litter barrels, petwalk, W** to Craters NM, Nez Pearce Tr |
| 150 | Hamer, **E** other: Ron's Tire, USPO, Camus NWR, food, phone |
| 143 | ID 33, ID 28, to Mud Lake, Rexburg, **W** Sacajawea Hist Bywy, weigh sta both lanes |
| 142mm | roadside parking, hist site |
| 135 | ID 48, Roberts, **E** gas: Tesoro/dsl/LP, other: Roberts Mkt, **W** Western Wings RV Park |
| 128 | Osgood Area, **E** gas, camping (6mi) |
| 119 | US 20 E, to Rexburg, Idaho Falls, E on Lindsay gas: Sinclair/dsl, food: Chili's, Denny's, Outback Steaks, Sandpiper Rest., Smitty's Rest., lodging: Best Western, Comfort Inn, Day's Inn, Guesthouse Inn, LeRitz Hotel, Microtel, Motel 6, Red Lion Hotel, Shilo Inn/rest., Super 8, other: KOA, LDS Temple, RV Park, **W** lodging: Microtel |
| 118 | US 20, Broadway St, Idaho Falls, **E** gas: Phillips 66/dsl, food: Applebees, Arctic Circle, Brownstone Rest., Domino's, Jalisco Mexican, Mini's Rest., Olive Garden, Quizno's, Ruby River, Sherry's Rest., Starbucks, Wendy's, lodging: AmeriTel, Fairfield Inn, Hilton Garden, other: 🄷 HOSPITAL, American RV, Buick/GMC, Ford, Harley-Davidson, Subaru, LDS Temple, Walmart SuperCtr/Subway, tires, **W** gas: Chevron/dsl, Exxon, ⊕**FLYING J**, Maverik, Phillips 66/dsl, food: Arby's, Burger King, DQ, Jack-in-the-Box, Little Caesar's, McDonald's, O'Brady's, Papa Murphy's, Pizza Hut, Subway, lodging: Comfort Inn, Motel 6, Motel West/rest., other: Albertson's, AutoZone, Checker Parts, Rite Aid, Walgreens |
| 116 | no facilites |
| 113 | US 26, to Idaho Falls, Jackson, **E** gas: Chevron/A&W/dsl, Sinclair/Dad's/dsl/24hr/@, Exxon/dsl, other: 🄷 HOSPITAL, Jack's Tires, Peterbilt, Sunnyside RV Park, Targhee RV Park |
| 108 | Shelley, Firth Area, 1 mi **E** other: RV Park/dump |
| 101mm | **rest area both lanes, full 🄷 facilities, 🟦, 🏕, litter barrels, petwalk, geological site** |
| 98 | Rose-Firth Area |
| 94.5mm | Snake River |
| 93 | US 26, ID 39, Blackfoot, **E** gas: Chevron/24hr, ⊕**FLYING J**/dsl/LP/24hr, Maverik, food: Arby's, Arctic Circle, Domino's, Homestead Rest., Italiano's, KFC, Little Caesar's, McDonald's, Papa Murphy's, Pizza Hut, Roberto's Mexican, Sonic, Subway, Taco Bell, Taco Time, Wendy's, Wingers, lodging: Best Western, Super 8, other: Albertson's, Auto Zone, Checker Parts, Chrysler/Dodge, Kesler's Foods, Radio Shack, RiteAid, Sav-On, Schwab Tire, Walmart SuperCtr, **W** Phillips 66, Riverside Boot/saddleshop (4mi) |
| 90.5mm | Blackfoot River |
| 89 | US 91, S Blackfoot, **2 mi E** lodging: Y Motel |

| Exit # | Services |
|---|---|
| 80 | Ft Hall, **W** gas: Sinclair/dsl/rest./casino, **other:** Shoshone Bannock Tribal Museum |
| 72 | I-86 W, to Twin Falls |
| 71 | Pocatello Creek Rd, Pocatello, **E** gas: Chevron/Burger King, Phillips 66/dsl, Shell/dsl/24hr, food: Applebee's, Jack-in-the Box, Perkins, Sandpiper Rest., Subway, lodging: AmeriTel, Best Western, Comfort Inn, Holiday Inn, Red Lion Inn, Super 8, other: 🄷 HOSPITAL, KOA (1mi), **W** gas: Exxon, Maverik/dsl, food: Arby's, Bamboo Garden, Butterber's, Changs Garden Chinese, DQ, Golden Corral, Jamba Juice, KFC, McDonald's, Papa Kelsey's Pizza, Papa Murphy's, Pier 49 Pizza, Pizza Hut, Schlotsky's, Senor Iguana's Mexican, SF Pizza, Sizzler, Skipper's, Taco Bell, Taco Time, TCBY, Wendy's, Winger's, other: Albertson's, AutoZone, CarQuest, Checker Parts, Chevrolet, Ford, Fred Meyer, Grease Monkey, Harley Davidson, Honda, Jeep, JoAnn Fabrics, Radio Shack, RiteAid, Subaru, Toyota, Walgreens, WinCo Foods |
| 69 | Clark St, Pocatello, **E** gas: Maverik/dsl, Shell/Blimpie/dsl, Sinclair/Arctic Circle/dsl, lodging: Hampton Inn, TownPlace Suites, **W** other: 🄷 HOSPITAL, to ID St U, museum |
| 67 | US 30/91, 5th St, Pocatello, **E** gas: Exxon/24hr, **1-2 mi W** gas: Phillips 66/dsl, Shell, Sinclair/dsl, food: Elmer's Dining, 5th St Bagels, Goody's Deli, Jimmy John's, McDonald's, Pizza Hut, Poppa Cafe, Subway, Taco Bell, lodging: Best Western, Econolodge, Thunderbird Motel, other: 🄷 HOSPITAL, Albertson's, Cowboy RV Park, Old Fort Hall, info, museum, zoo |
| 63 | Portneuf Area, **W** other: to Mink Creek RA, RV camp/dump |
| 59mm | **rest area/weigh sta both lanes, full 🄷 facilities, 🟦, 🏕, litter barrel, vending, petwalk, hist site** |
| 58 | Inkom (from sb), **1/2 mi W** gas: Sinclair/dsl/café, other: Pebble Creek Ski Area, USPO, repair |
| 57 | Inkom (from nb), same as 58 |
| 47 | US 30, to Lava Hot Springs, McCammon, **E** gas: Chevron/A&W/Taco Time/dsl, ⊕**FLYING J**/dsl/LP/RV Dump/rest./24hr, food: Subway, other: to Lava Hot Springs RA, McCammon RV Park |
| 44 | Lp 15, Jenson Rd, McCammon, **E** access to food |
| 40 | Arimo, **E** gas: Sinclair/dsl/deli, other: USPO |
| 36 | US 91, Virginia |
| 31 | ID 40, to Downey, Preston, **E** gas: Shell/Flags West/dsl/motel/café/24hr/@, other: Downata Hot Springs RV camping (6mi) |
| 25mm | **rest area sb, full 🄷 facilities, 🟦, 🏕, litter barrels, petwalk** |
| 24.5mm | Malad Summit, elev 5574 |
| 22 | to Devil Creek Reservoir, **E** RV camping |
| 17 | ID 36, to Weston, to Preston |
| 13 | ID 38, Malad City, **W** gas: Chevron/Burger King, Phillips 66/dsl/café, Texaco/dsl, food: Me&Lou's Rest., Subway, lodging: Village Inn Motel, other: 🄷 HOSPITAL, 3R's Tire, TrueValue, pioneer museum, repair, RV dump |
| 7mm | **Welcome Ctr nb, full 🚻 facilities, 🟦, info, 🏕, litter barrels, vending, petwalk** |
| 3 | to Samaria, Woodruff |
| 0mm | Idaho/Utah state line |

## INTERSTATE 84

| Exit # | Services |
|---|---|
| 275mm | Idaho/Utah state line |
| 270mm | **rest area both lanes, full 🚻 facilities, geological site, 🟦, 🏕, litter barrels, petwalk** |

*(left margin, top to bottom): E ↕ W  DUBOIS · IDAHO FALLS · BLACKFOOT*

*(right margin, top to bottom): POCATELLO · INKOM*

*(left side tab): ID*

**B
U
R
L
E
Y**

| | |
|---|---|
| 208 | Continued |
| | Shell/Taco Bell, Sinclair, **food:** Arby's, Burger King, Garibaldi Mexican, Jack-in-the-Box, JB's, Little Caesar's, McDonald's, Morey's Steaks, Perkins, Wendy's, **lodging:** Best Western, Budget Motel, Fairfield Inn, **other:** Ⓗ HOSPITAL, Cal Store, Radio Shack, Walmart SuperCtr/dsl, to Snake River RA, **1 mi** Ⓢ **gas:** Sinclair/dsl, **food:** Guadalajara Mexican, KFC, **other:** Buick/Pontiac/GMC, CarQuest, Checker Parts, Chrysler/Dodge/Jeep, Commercial Tire, NAPA, Stoke's Foods |
| 201 | ID 25, Kasota Rd, to Paul |
| 194 | ID 25, to Hazelton, Ⓢ **gas:** Sinclair/dsl/café, **other:** RV camping |
| 188 | Valley Rd, to Eden |
| 182 | ID 50, to Kimberly, Twin Falls, Ⓝ **gas:** Sinclair/dsl, **other:** Gary's RV Ctr/park/dump, Ⓢ **gas:** Shell/Blimpie/Taco Bell/dsl/24hr, **lodging:** Amber Inn, **other:** Ⓗ HOSPITAL, to Shoshone Falls scenic attraction |
| 173 | US 93, Twin Falls, Ⓝ **gas:** ⓕFLYING J//Thad's/dsl/24hr/@, **lodging:** Day's Inn, **other:** KOA (1mi), Blue Beacon/24hr, to Sun Valley, **5 mi** Ⓢ **gas:** Chevron/dsl, Exxon, Phillips 66, Sinclair, **food:** Applebee's, Arby's, Arctic Circle, Aztlan Mexican, Blimpie, Burger King, Carino's Italian, Chili's, Coldstone Creamery, DQ, Elmer's, Fiesta, Golden Corral, Hart's Cafe, Idaho Joe's, IHOP, Jack-in-the-Box, Jaker's Rest., JB's, KFC, Mandarin Chinese, McDonald's, Outback Steaks, Perkins, Quizno's, Shari's, Sizzler, Subway, Taco Bell, Taste Of Thai, Tomato's Grill, Wok In Grill, **lodging:** Best American Inn, Best Western, Comfort Inn, Hampton Inn, Holiday Inn Express, Motel 6, Red Lion, Shilo Inn, Super 8, Weston Inn, **other:** Ⓗ HOSPITAL, AutoZone, Barnes&Noble, Buick, Chevrolet/Pontiac/Cadillac, Costco/gas, Dell, $Tree, Ford, Goodyear, Hastings, Home Depot, Honda, JC Penney, Lowe's Whse, Macy's, Michael's, Mitsubishi, Nissan, Old Navy, PetsMart, Schuck's Parts, Schwab Tire, ShopKO, Sportsman's Whse, Target, Tuesday Morning, WinCo Foods, Coll of S ID |
| 171mm | rest area/weigh sta eb, full ♿ facilities, Ⓒ vending, ⛽ litter barrels, petwalk |

**J
E
R
O
M
E**

| | |
|---|---|
| 168 | ID 79, to Jerome, Ⓝ **gas:** Chevron/dsl, Shell/Wendy's/dsl, Sinclair/dsl, **food:** Burger King, McDonald's, Pizza Hut, Sonic, **lodging:** Best Western, Crest Motel, **other:** AutoZone, Brockman RV Ctr, Walmart SuperCtr/gas, **2 mi** Ⓝ **food:** DQ, **lodging:** Holiday Motel, **other:** Ⓗ HOSPITAL, Chevrolet, Ⓢ **food:** Subway, **other:** ID RV Ctr/marine |
| 165 | ID 25, Jerome, Ⓝ **gas:** Sinclair/dsl, **lodging:** Holiday Motel (1mi), **other:** Ⓗ HOSPITAL, RV camping/dump |
| 157 | ID 46, Wendell, Ⓝ **food:** Subway, **1 mi** Ⓝ **other:** Ⓗ HOSPITAL, Intermountain RV Park, Ⓢ **gas:** Sinclair/dsl, **food:** Farmhouse Rest. |
| 155 | ID 46, to Wendell, Ⓝ Intermountain RV Camp/ctr |
| 147 | to Tuttle, Ⓢ **other:** to Malad Gorge SP, High Adventure RV Park/cafe |
| 146mm | Malad River |
| 141 | US 26, to US 30, Gooding, Ⓝ Ⓗ HOSPITAL, Ⓢ **gas:** Phillips 66/dsl/café, Stinker/Sinclair/dsl/24hr, **lodging:** Amber Inn, Hagerman Inn (9mi), Y Inn Motel, **other:** RV camping |
| 137 | Lp 84, to US 30, to Pioneer Road, Bliss, **2 mi** Ⓢ **gas:** Sinclair/Stinker/dsl/24hr, **other:** camping |

## INTERSTATE 84 CONT'D

**E** ⬍ **W**

**D
E
C
L
O**

| | |
|---|---|
| 263 | Juniper Rd |
| 257mm | Sweetzer Summit, elev 5530 |
| 254 | Sweetzer Rd |
| 245 | Sublett Rd, to Malta, Ⓝ **gas:** Sinclair/dsl/café, **other:** camping |
| 237 | Idahome Rd |
| 234mm | Raft River |
| 229mm | rest area/weigh sta both lanes, full Ⓗ facilities, Ⓒ ⛽, litter barrels, petwalk |
| 228 | ID 81, Yale Rd, to Declo |
| 222 | I-86, US 30, E to Pocatello |
| 216 | ID 77, ID 25, to Declo, Ⓝ **gas:** Phillips 66/FoodCourt/dsl, **other:** Ⓗ HOSPITAL, Village of Trees RV Park, to Walcott SP, Ⓢ **gas:** Shell/Jake's Café/dsl |
| 215mm | Snake River |
| 211 | ID 24, Heyburn, Burley, Ⓝ **gas:** Chevron/A&W/dsl, Sinclair/dsl/café, **lodging:** Tops Motel, Wayside Cafe, **other:** Ⓗ HOSPITAL, Country RV Village/park, Ⓢ **gas:** Love's/Carl's Jr./dsl/scales/24hr, **other:** Riverside RV Park, truck repair |
| 208 | ID 27, Burley, Ⓝ **gas:** Phillips 66/dsl, Conner's Cafe, **lodging:** Super 8, Ⓢ **gas:** Chevron/Subway/dsl/24hr, |

# 132    IDAHO

Copyright 2009 - The Next Exit®

## INTERSTATE 84 CONT'D

**133mm** rest area both lanes, full ♿ facilities, info, 🌲 litter barrels, petwalk, 📞

**129** King Hill

**128mm** Snake River

**125** Paradise Valley

**122mm** Snake River

**121** Glenns Ferry, **1 mi S gas:** Shell/dsl, Sinclair, **lodging:** Redford Motel, **other:** Carmela Winery/rest., to 3 Island SP, Trails West RV camp/dump

**120** Glenns Ferry (from eb), same as 121

**114** ID 78 (from wb), to Hammett, **1 mi S** access to gas/dsl, to Bruneau Dunes SP

**112** to ID 78, Hammett, **1 mi S** gas/dsl, food, to Bruneau Dunes SP

**99** ID 51, ID 67, to Mountain Home, **2 mi S lodging:** Maple Cove Motel, camping

**95** US 20, Mountain Home, **N gas:** Chevron/KFC/dsl/24hr, Pilot/Arby's/dsl/scales/24hr, **food:** AJ's Rest., Jack-in-the-Box, Subway, **lodging:** Best Western, Hampton Inn, Sleep Inn, **S food:** Golden Crown Chinese, McDonald's, Wendy's, **lodging:** Hilander Motel (1mi), Towne Ctr Motel (1mi), **other:** Ⓗ HOSPITAL, Curves, Walmart SuperCtr/gas, to Mtn Home RV Park

**90** to ID 51, ID 67, W Mountain Home, **S gas:** Chevron/Burger King/dsl/24hr, **food:** McDonald's (4mi), **lodging:** to Hilander Motel (4mi), Maple Cove Motel (4mi), Towne Ctr Motel (4mi), **other:** to Mtn Home RV Park

**74** Simco Rd

**71** Orchard, Mayfield, **S gas:** Sinclair/dsl/StageStop Motel/rest./24hr, **other:** phone, truckwash

**66mm** weigh sta both lanes

**64** Blacks Creek, Kuna, historical site

**62mm** rest area both lanes, full ♿ facilities, OR Trail info, 📞, 🌲, litter barrels, vending, petwalk

**59 b a** S Eisenman Rd, Memory Rd

**57** ID 21, Gowen Rd, to Idaho City, **N food:** Jack-in-the-Box, McDonald's, Perkins, Subway, Taco Del Mar, Tulley's Coffee, **lodging:** Best Western, **other:** Albertson's/gas, GNC, to Micron, **S gas:** Chevron/24hr, **food:** Burger King, FoodCourt, **other:** Boise Stores/famous brands, ID Ice World

**54** US 20/26, Broadway Ave, Boise, **N gas:** Chevron/dsl/24hr, ⊕FLYING J/Conoco/Arby's/dsl/LP/24hr/@, Shell/dsl, **food:** Chili's, Jack-in-the-Box, Port Of Subs, Subway, Wendy's, **lodging:** Courtyard (3mi), **other:** Ⓗ HOSPITAL, Big O Tire, Dowdie's Automotive, Goodyear/auto, Jo-Ann Fabrics, Radio Shack, ShopKO, to Boise St U, **S gas:** TA/Tesoro/Taco Bell/Subway/dsl/rest./24hr/@, **lodging:** Shilo Inn, **other:** Kenworth, Mtn View RV Park

**53** Vista Ave, Boise, **N gas:** Citgo/7-11, Shell/dsl, Texaco/dsl, **food:** Pizza Hut, **lodging:** Cambria Suites, Comfort Suites, Extended Stay America, Fairfield Inn, Hampton Inn, Holiday Inn/rest., Holiday Inn Express, Super 8, **other:** Parts'n Stuff, museums, st capitol, st police, zoo, **S gas:** Chevron/McDonald's/24hr, **food:** Denny's, Kopper Kitchen, **lodging:** Best Western, Comfort Inn, InnAmerica, Motel 6, Sleep Inn

**52** Orchard St, Boise, **N gas:** Shell/dsl/24hr, **other:** Mazda/Nissan, GMC, **1-2 mi N food:** Burger King, Jack-in-the-Box, McDonald's, Raedean's Rest., Round Table Pizza, Wendy's, **other:** Albertson's/gas, Walgreens

**50b a** Cole Rd, Overland Rd, **N gas:** Chevron/24hr, Shell, **food:** Eddie's Rest., McDonald's, Outback Steaks, Pizza Hut, Subway, Taco Bell, Taco Time, **lodging:** Harrison Hotel, **other:** Ace Hardware, LDS Temple, Pontiac/Buick, transmissions, **S gas:** ⊕FLYING J/Conoco/dsl/24hr, Phillips 66/dsl, **food:** A&W/KFC, Burger King, Carino's, Carl's Jr, Casa Mexico, Chuck-a-Rama, Cracker Barrel, Fuddruckers, Jamba Juice, KFC, McGrath's FishHouse, On the Border, Pollo Rey Mexican, Port Of Subs, Yen Ching Chinese, **lodging:** AmeriTel, Hilton Garden, Homewood Suites, Oxford Suites, **other:** Commercial Tire, CostCo/gas, Goodyear, Lowe's Whse, Schwab Tire, Walmart SuperCtr

**49** I-184 (exits left from eb), to W Boise, **N lodging:** Rodeway Inn, National 9 Inn, **other:** Ⓗ HOSPITAL

**46** ID 55, Eagle, **N gas:** Chevron/McDonald's/dsl/24hr, Shell/dsl, **food:** Del Taco, IHOP, Subway, **lodging:** Comfort Suites, Hampton Inn, Holiday Inn Express, SpringHill Suites (5mi), **other:** Ⓗ HOSPITAL, **S gas:** Shell/Jack-in-the-Box/dsl, **food:** Chicago Connection, NY NY Deli, Quizno's, Sakana Japanese, Subway, Taco Bell, **lodging:** Candlewood Suites, Courtyard, Marriott, **other:** RV Park/playground (3mi),

**44** ID 69, Meridian, **N gas:** Chevron/dsl/24hr, Sinclair, **food:** A&W/KFC, Blimpie, China Wok, DQ, Jack-in-the-Box, Mason's Grill, McDonald's, Mongolian Express, Pizza Hut, Quizno's, Shari's/24hr, Starbucks, Subway, Taco Bell, Taco Time, Tony Roma, Wendy's, Wong's Chinese, **lodging:** Best Western, Motel 6, **other:** Bodily RV Ctr, Home Depot, Schwab Tire, WinCo Foods, **S gas:** Shell/dsl/24hr, **food:** JB's, **lodging:** Mr Sandman Motel, **other:** Bodily RV, Ford, Schuck's Parts, Uhaul, waterpark

**38** Garrity Blvd, Nampa, **N gas:** Chevron/dsl, **food:** Port of Subs, Taco Del Mar, **lodging:** Hampton Inn, **other:** Cadillac, Chevrolet/Pontiac/Buick/GMC, Chrysler/Dodge/Jeep, Ford, KIA, Nissan, Sam's Club, Swiss Village Cheese, Toyota/Scion, Walmart SuperCtr, **S gas:** Phillips 66/dsl, Shell/Taco Time/dsl/24hr, **food:** McDonald's, Megabites, **lodging:** Holiday Inn Express, **other:** Ⓗ HOSPITAL, Garrity RV Park, JC Penney

**36** Franklin Blvd, Nampa, **N gas:** Maverik, **food:** Elmer's Rest., Jack-in-the-Box, Noodles Rest., **lodging:** Shilo Inn/rest., **other:** Nelson's RV Ctr, **S gas:** Chevron/dsl/24hr, Shell/A&W/Taco Bell/dsl/RV dump/24hr, **lodging:** Sleep Inn, **other:** Ⓗ HOSPITAL, Freightliner, Mason Cr RV Park, 7th Heaven RV Ctr

**35** ID 55, Nampa, **S gas:** Shell/dsl, **food:** Denny's/24hr, **lodging:** Days Inn, Shilo Inn, Super 8, **1 mi S food:** Burger King, McDonald's, Pizza Hut, Taco Time, El Tanampa Mexican, **other:** Ⓗ HOSPITAL

**33b a** ID 55 S, Midland Blvd, Marcine, **S food:** Applebees, Arby's, Carl's Jr, Golden Corral, IHOP, Jade Garden, Jalapeno's Mexican, Olive Garden, Outback Steaks, Red Robin, Shari's Rest., Taco Bell, **other:** Best Buy, Big Lots, Big O Tire, Costco/gas, $Tree, Grocery Outlet, Home Depot, JoAnne Fabrics, K-Mart, Kohl's, Lowes Whse, Michael's, Old Navy, PetCo, Ross, ShopKO, Staples, Target, U-Haul, WinCo Foods, World Mkt

**29** US 20/26, Franklin Rd, Caldwell, **N gas:** ⊕FLYING J/Conoco/Country Mkt/dsl/LP/rest./scales/24hr/@, **other:** Ambassador RV camping, **S gas:** Sage/Sinclair/cafe/dsl/24hr, **food:** Perkins/24hr, **lodging:** Best Western, La Quinta

**28** 10th Ave, Caldwell, **N gas:** Maverik/gas, **lodging:** I-84 Motel, **other:** Harley-Davidson, **S gas:** Chevron/24hr, Shell, **food:** Carl's Jr, Domino's, Fiesta Mexican,

## INTERSTATE 84 CONT'D

**28** Continued
Jack-in-the-Box, KFC, Mr V's Rest., Papa Murphy's, Pizza Hut, Subway, Wendy's, **lodging:** Sundowner Motel, **other:** H HOSPITAL, AutoZone, Paul's Food/Drug, Walgreens, tires

**27** ID 19, to Wilder, **1 mi** S **gas:** Tesoro/dsl/24hr

**26.5mm** Boise River

**26** US 20/26, to Notus, **N other:** Caldwell Campground, S **gas:** Sinclair/dsl

**25** ID 44, Middleton, **N gas:** Shell/dsl, **food:** Bud's Burgers/shakes, S Insp sta eb

**17** Sand Hollow, **N food:** Sand Hollow Café, **other:** Country Corners RV Park

**13** Black Canyon Jct, S **gas:** Sinclair/dsl/motel/rest./scales/24hr, phone

**9** US 30, to New Plymouth

**3** US 95, Fruitland, **N gas:** Shell/A&W/dsl, **5 mi N other:** Neat Retreat RV Park, to Hell's Cyn RA

**1mm** Welcome Ctr eb, full ♿ facilities, info, 📞, 🏔, litter barrels, petwalk

**0mm** Snake River, Idaho/Oregon state line

## INTERSTATE 86

**Exit #** Services

**63b a** I-15, N to Butte, S to SLC. I-86 begins/ends on I-15, exit 72.

**61** US 91, Yellowstone Ave, Pocatello, **N gas:** Exxon, Loaf'n Jug, Shell/dsl, **food:** Arby's, Arctic Circle, Burger King, Chapala Mexican, Johnny B Goode's Diner, Lei's BBQ, Papa Murphy's, Pizza Hut, Red Lobster, Subway, Wendy's, **lodging:** Motel 6, Ramada Inn, **other:** Budget RV Park, Checker Parts, $Tree, Family $, Smith's Foods/dsl, S **gas:** ♿FLYING J/dsl/24hr, Phillips 66/dsl, **food:** Del Taco, Denny's, Green Tea Grill, IHOP, Me&Lou's Rest., McDonald's, Red Lobster, Starbucks, Texas Roadhouse, **other:** Costco/gas, Dillard's, Ford, Home Depot, JC Penney, K-Mart, Lowe's Whse, Macy's, Michael's, PetCo, Ross, Schwab Tire, Sears, ShopKO, Sportsman's Whse, TJ Maxx, Walgreens, Walmart SuperCtr, dsl repair, mall

**58.5mm** Portneuf River

**58** US 30, W Pocatello, **N** RV dump, S **gas:** Stinker/dsl

**56** N Pocatello Air Terminal, S **gas:** Sinclair/dsl/24hr

**52** Arbon Valley, S **gas:** Sinclair/Bannock Peak/dsl, **other:** casino

**51mm** Bannock Creek

**49** Rainbow Rd

**44** no services

**40** ID 39, American Falls, **N gas:** Phillips 66/dsl, Sinclair, **food:** Pizza Hut, Sagebrush Rest., Tres Hermanos Mexican, **lodging:** American Motel, **other:** H HOSPITAL, Chevrolet/GMC, NAPA, Schwab Tire, to Am Falls RA, RV Park/dump, S **lodging:** Hillview Motel

**36** ID 37, to Rockland, American Falls, **2 mi N gas:** Shell/dsl/24hr, **lodging:** Falls Motel, **other:** H HOSPITAL, **2 mi** S Indian Springs RV Resort

**33** Neeley Area

**31mm** rest area wb, full ♿ facilities, 📞, 🏔, litter barrel, petwalk, vending, hist site

**28** **N other:** to Massacre Rock SP, Register Rock Hist Site, RV camping/dump

**21** Coldwater Area

**19mm** rest area eb, full ♿ facilities, 📞, 🏔, litter barrel, petwalk, vending, hist site

**15** Raft River Area, S **gas:** Sinclair, phone

**1** I-84 E, to Ogden. I-86 begins/ends on I-84, exit 222.

## INTERSTATE 90

**Exit #** Services

**74mm** Idaho/Montana state line, Pacific/Central time zone Lookout Pass elev 4680

**73mm** scenic area/hist site wb

**72mm** scenic area/hist site eb

**71mm** runaway truck ramp wb

**70mm** runaway truck ramp wb

**69** Lp 90, Mullan, **N gas:** gas/dsl/24hr, **lodging:** Lookout Motel (1mi), **other:** USPO, museum

**68** Lp 90 (from eb), Mullan, same as 69

**67** Morning District,

**66** Gold Creek (from eb)

**65** Compressor District

**64** Golconda District

**62** ID 4, Wallace, S **gas:** Exxon, **food:** Pizza Factory, Smokehouse BBQ, **lodging:** Brooks Hotel, Stardust Motel, **other:** H HOSPITAL, Accelerated Parts, Depot RV Park, Harvest Foods, TrueValue, museum, repair

**61** Lp 90, Wallace, S **gas:** Conoco/dsl, **food:** Wallace Sta Rest./gifts, **lodging:** Brooks Hotel/rest., Molly B-Damm Inn, Wallace Inn, **other:** auto repair, info ctr, same as 62

**60** Lp 90, Silverton, S **lodging:** Molly B-Damm Inn, **other:** RV camping

**57** Lp 90, Osburn, S **gas:** Shell/dsl/24hr, **other:** Blue Anchor RV Park, auto repair, USPO

**54** Big Creek, **N other:** Elk Creek Store/repair, hist site, rv dump

**51** Lp 90, Division St, Kellogg, **N gas:** Conoco/dsl, **food:** Broken Wheel Rest., **lodging:** Trail Motel, **other:** H HOSPITAL, Buick/Cadillac/Chevrolet/GMC/Pontiac, Chrysler/Dodge/Jeep, Schwab Tire, Stein's Foods, Sunnyside Drug, S **food:** In Cahoots Cafe, Moose Creek Grill, **other:** USPO, auto repair, museum

**50** Hill St (from eb), Kellogg, **N lodging:** Trail Motel, **other:** Ace Hardware, NAPA, Stein's Foods, Sunnyside Drug, S **gas:** Conoco/dsl **other:** Gary's Drug, Silver Mtn Ski/summer resort/rec area, Yoke's Foods, museum

**49** Bunker Ave, **N gas:** Conoco/dsl, **food:** McDonald's, Sam's Drive-In, Subway, **lodging:** Silverhorn Motel/rest., **other:** H HOSPITAL, S **food:** Noah's Canteen, Silver Mtn rest., **lodging:** Baymont Inn, Morning Star

## INTERSTATE 90 CONT'D

**49** Continued
Lodge, **other:** museum, RV dump

**48** Smelterville, **N gas:** Silver Valley Car/trkstp/motel/café, **S food:** Boat Rest., **other:** Tire Factory, Walmart SuperCtr

**45** Pinehurst, **S gas:** Chevron/dsl, Conoco/dsl/24hr, **other:** By-the-way Camping, Harvest Foods, NAPA, KOA, RV Park/dump, True Value Hardware

**43** Kingston, **N gas:** Shell/dsl/24hr, **food:** Snakepit Café, **lodging:** Enaville Resort, RV camping, **S gas:** Exxon/dsl/rv dump, USPO

**40** Cataldo, **N food:** Mission Inn Rest., USPO, **S** RV Park

**39.5mm** Coeur d' Alene River

**39** Cataldo Mission, **S other:** Old Mission SP, Nat Hist Landmark

**34** ID 3, to St Maries, Rose Lake, **S gas:** Conoco/dsl, Rose Lake/dsl, **food:** Rose Lake Cafe, **other:** White Pines Scenic Rte

**32mm** chainup area/weigh sta wb

**31.5mm** Idaho Panhandle NF, eastern boundary, 4th of July Creek

**28** 4th of July Pass Rec. Area, elev 3069, Mullan Tree HS, ski area, snowmobile area, turnout both lanes

**24mm** chainup eb, removal wb

**22** ID 97, to St Maries, L Coeur d' Alene Scenic ByWay, Wolf Lodge District, Harrison, **1 mi N** Wolf Lodge Campground, **S other:** A-Ok RV Park, Squaw Bay Resort (7mi)

**20.5mm** Lake Coeur d' Alene

**17** Mullan Trail Rd

**15** Lp 90, Sherman Ave, Coeur d' Alene, **N other:** forest info, Lake Coeur D' Alene RA/HS, **S gas:** Shell, Tesoro/dsl, Texaco, **food:** Michael D's Eatery, Willie's Rest., **lodging:** Bates Motel, BudgetSaver Motel, Cedar Motel, El Rancho Motel, Holiday Motel, Japan House Suites, La Quinta, Lake Drive Motel, Monte Vista Motel, State Motel, **other:** Peterson's Foods/24hr, NAPA, tourist info

**14** 15th St, Coeur d' Alene, **S gas:** TAJ Mart, **other:** Jordon's Grocery

**13** 4th St, Coeur d' Alene, **N gas:** A&D/dsl, **food:** Baskin-Robbins, Carl's Jr, DQ, Davis Donuts, Denny's, Fiesta Mexican, Godfather's, IHOP, KFC, Little Caesar's, Panda Express, Wendy's, **lodging:** Comfort Inn, **other:** AutoZone, Big Lots, Costco/gas (1mi), Hastings Books, NAPA, Radio Shack, Schuck's Parts, Schwab Tire, Tire Factory, same as 12, **S gas:** Exxon/dsl, **food:** Subway, Thai Bamboo

**12** US 95, to Sandpoint, Moscow, **N gas:** Exxon/dsl, Holiday/dsl, Mobil, **food:** Applebees, Arby's, Burger King, Cafe Chulo Mexican, Casa de Oro, Chili's, Dragon House Chinese, JB's Rest., McDonald's, Olive Garden, Panda Express, Perkins, Pizza Hut, Pizza Shoppe, Red Lobster, Skipper's, Taco Bell, **lodging:** Best Western, Guesthouse Inn, La Quinta, Motel 6, Shilo Suites, Super 8, **other:** Alton's Tires, AutoZone, Best Buy, Borders Books, Buick/Pontiac/GMC, Cadillac/Isuzu, Dodge, $Tree, Ford/Lincoln/Mercury, Fred Meyer, GNC, Grocery Outlet, Harley-Davidson, Home Depot, JC Penney, Kia, K-Mart, Kohl's, Mazda, Michael's, Office Depot, PetCo, Ross, Safeway/gas, Schuck's Parts, Sears/auto, Super 1 Foods, Target, TJ Maxx, Toyota, Tuesday Morning, U-haul, Walgreens, radiators, **S gas:** Shell, **food:** Jack-in-the-Box, Papa John's, Qdoba Mexican, Quizno's, Schlotsky's, Shari's, Starbucks, **lodging:** AmeriTel, **other:** H HOSPITAL, Albertson's/gas, Rite Aid, ShopKO/drugs, Staples, same as 13

**11** Northwest Blvd, **N gas:** Conoco/Taco Time/dsl, **other:** Lowes Whse, **S gas:** Texaco/dsl, **food:** Azteca Mexican, Cold Stone Creamery, Joey's BBQ, Outback Steaks, Pizza Smizza, Red Robin, SF Sourdough, Starbucks, Subway, **lodging:** Day's Inn, Holiday Inn Express, **other:** H HOSPITAL, Honda, Kohl's, Riverwalk RV Park

**8.5mm** Welcome Ctr/weigh sta eb, rest area both lanes, full ♿ facilities, 🅲, 🚻, info litter barrels, petwalk

**7** ID 41, to Rathdrum, Spirit Lake, **N gas:** Exxon/dsl, **food:** Del Taco, Jamba Juice, La Cocina Mexican, Noodle Express, Papa Murphy's, Quizno's, Sonic, Starbucks, Subway, Wendy's, **other:** Radio Shack, Subaru, Walmart SuperCtr/gas, Couer d'Alene RV Park, **S gas:** Chevron/dsl/24hr, **food:** A&W/KFC, Capone's Grill, DQ, **lodging:** Comfort Inn, **other:** truck repair

**6** Seltice Way, **N gas:** 7-11, **food:** La Cabana Mexican, Pizza Hut, **other:** AutoZone, Chevrolet, Hyundai, NAPA, Nissan, Subaru, Super 1 Foods/24hr, Walgreens, vet, **S gas:** Conoco/dsl/LP, **food:** Arby's/Taco John's, Big Cheese Pizza, Denny's, Hot Rod Café, McDonald's, Subway, Taco Bell, Wingers, **other:** Ace Hardware, Alton's Tire, Curves, Schuck's Parts, USPO

**5** Lp 90, Spokane St, Treaty Rock HS, **N gas:** Shell/dsl, **food:** Domino's, Golden Dragon Chinese, Hunter's Steaks, Rob's Seafood/burgers, WhiteHouse Grill, **other:** AutoZone, CarQuest, Mazda, Schwab Tire, Seltice RV Ctr, **S gas:** 76/dsl, **food:** MillTown Grill, **lodging:** Red Lion Inn

**2** Pleasant View Rd, **N gas:** ⊛FLYING J/Conoco/dsl/rest./LP/scales/24hr, Shell/dsl, **food:** McDonald's, Toro Viejo Mexican, **lodging:** Howard Johnson, **other:** Suntree RV Park, **S gas:** Shell/Subway/dsl/24hr, **food:** Zip's Drive-in, **lodging:** Riverbend Inn, Sleep Inn, **other:** GNC, North Idaho Outlets/famous brands, dogtrack

**0mm** Idaho/Washington state line

## INTERSTATE 184 - BOISE

| Exit # | Services |
|---|---|
| **6mm** | I-184 begins/ends on 13th St, downtown, **gas:** Shell, **food:** PF Chang's, **lodging:** Hampton Inn, Safari Inn, **other:** Harley-Davidson, Office Depot, USPO |
| **5** | River St (from eb), **W gas:** Chevron, **food:** McDonald's, **other:** Ford/Mercury |
| **4.5mm** | Boise River |
| **3** | Fairview Ave, to US 20/26 E, **W food:** McDonald's, **lodging:** Budget Inn, DoubleTree Inn, Econolodge, **other:** Commercial Tire |
| **2** | Curtis Rd, to Garden City, **E lodging:** Rodeway Inn, **other:** H HOSPITAL |
| **1b a** | Cole Rd, Franklin Rd, **E gas:** Chevron/Subway, **lodging:** Harrison Hotel, **other:** Acura/Honda, Buick/Pontiac, Dodge, Jaguar, Land Rover, Volvo, **W gas:** Maverik, Sinclair, **food:** Burger King, Carl's Jr, Cheesecake Factory, Chili's, Hooters, Jack-in-the-Box, LoneStar Steaks, Old Chicago Pizza, Perkins, Quizno's, Red Robin, Sizzler, Shari's, Starbucks, TGI Friday, Wendy's, Yang Sheng Chinese, **lodging:** Ameritel, Residence Inn, **other:** Best Buy, Borders, Cabela's, Circuit City, Dillard's, JC Penney, Macy's, Michael's, Office Depot, Old Navy, PetCo, Ross, Saturn, Sears/auto, Target, TJ Maxx, mall, vet |
| **0mm** | I-184 begins/ends on I-84, exit 49. |

# INTERSTATE 24

| Exit # | Services |
|---|---|
| 38mm | Illinois/Kentucky state line, Ohio River |
| 37 | US 45, Metropolis, **N** rest area both lanes, full ♿ facilities, info, vending, 🎪 litter barrels, petwalk, Citgo/dsl, **S gas:** BP/Quizno's/dsl, Shell/dsl/24hr, **food:** Buggy BBQ, Huddle House, KFC (2mi), McDonald's, Pizza Hut, Ponderosa, Stoner's Steaks, Waffle Hut, **lodging:** Best Inn, Best Western, Comfort Inn, Day Plaza Inn, Day's Inn/rest. (2mi), Holiday Inn Express, Metropolis Inn, Super 8, **other:** Ⓗ HOSPITAL, Buick/Cadillac/Pontiac, Chrysler/Jeep/Dodge, O'Reilly Parts, to Riverboat Casino, Ft Massac SP, camping |
| 27 | to New Columbia, Big Bay |
| 16 | IL 146, Vienna, **N lodging:** Budget Inn/rest., **S gas:** BP/dsl, Citgo, Gas&Go/dsl, **food:** DQ, Jumbo Grill, McDonald's, Subway, **lodging:** Budget Inn, Limited Inn |
| 14 | US 45, Vienna, **S gas:** Casey's, Citgo, **other:** camping |
| 7 | to Goreville, Tunnel Hill, **N gas:** Citgo/dsl, **other:** winery, **S other:** to Ferne Clyffe SP, camping |
| 1 | I-57, N to Chicago, S to Memphis. I-24 begins/ends on I-57, exit 44. |

# INTERSTATE 39

| Exit # | Services |
|---|---|
| | I-39 and I-90 run together into Wisconsin. See Illinois Interstate 90. |
| 122b a | US 20 E, Harrison Ave, to Belvidere, **W gas:** Road Ranger/Subway, **food:** Arby's, Bergner's, Burger King, DQ, Franchesco's Rest., Taco Bell, TGIFriday, **other:** Barnes & Noble, Chevrolet, Collier RV Ctr, Harley-Davidson, Hilander Foods/gas, Macey's, Menard's, Sears/auto, Tires+, mall, last nb exit before toll rd |
| 119 | US 20 W, Alpine Rd, to Rockford |
| 116.5mm | Kishwaukee River |
| 115 | Baxter Rd, **E gas:** Shell/scales/dsl/24hr/@ |
| 111 | IL 72, to Monroe Center, **E gas:** BP/Sunrise Family Rest./dsl/24hr, Marathon (1mi) |
| 104 | IL 64, to Oregon, Sycamore, **W** Grubsteakers Rest. (2mi) |
| 99 | IL 38, to De Kalb, Rochelle, **0-2 mi W gas:** BP/dsl, Petro/Iron Skillet/scales/dsl/rest./RV Dump/@, Road Ranger/Subway/scales/dsl/24hr, Shell/24hr, **food:** Arby's, China Wok, Culvers, DQ, McDonald's, Pizza Hut, Sunrise Rest., Taco Bell, Wendy's, **lodging:** Colonnade Motel, Comfort Inn, Lincoln Hwy Hotel, US Express, Super 8, **other:** Ⓗ HOSPITAL, Blue Beacon, Curves, $General, Radio Shack, Sullivan's Foods |
| 97a b | I-88 tollway, to Moline, Rock Island, Chicago |
| 93 | Steward |
| 87 | US 30, to Sterling, Rock Falls, **E** to Shabbona Lake SP, **W** Jellystone Camping (16mi) |
| 84.5mm | rest area both lanes, full ♿ facilities, 🛢️, 🎪, litter barrels, vending, petwalk |
| 82 | Paw Paw, **3 mi E** Casey's, **W** Many wind turbines |
| 72 | US 34, to Mendota, Earlville, **W gas:** BP/Buster's Buffet/scales/dsl/24hr, Road Ranger/dsl/24hr, **food:** McDonald's, Ziggie's Rest., **lodging:** Comfort Inn, Super 8, **other:** HOSPITAL |
| 67.5mm | Little Vermilion River |
| 66 | US 52, Troy Grove, **E** KOA (1mi) |
| 62.5mm | Tomahawk Creek |
| 59b a | I-80, E to Chicago, W to Des Moines |
| 57 | US 6, to Peru, La Salle, **1-2 mi W gas:** Casey's, Shell/24hr, **food:** Hardee's, **lodging:** Daniels Motel |
| 56mm | Illinois River, Abraham Lincoln Mem Bridge |

**Left margin (I-24):** E ↕ W / VIENNA

**Left margin (I-39):** ROCKFORD / N ↕ S

**Right margin (I-39):** P E R U

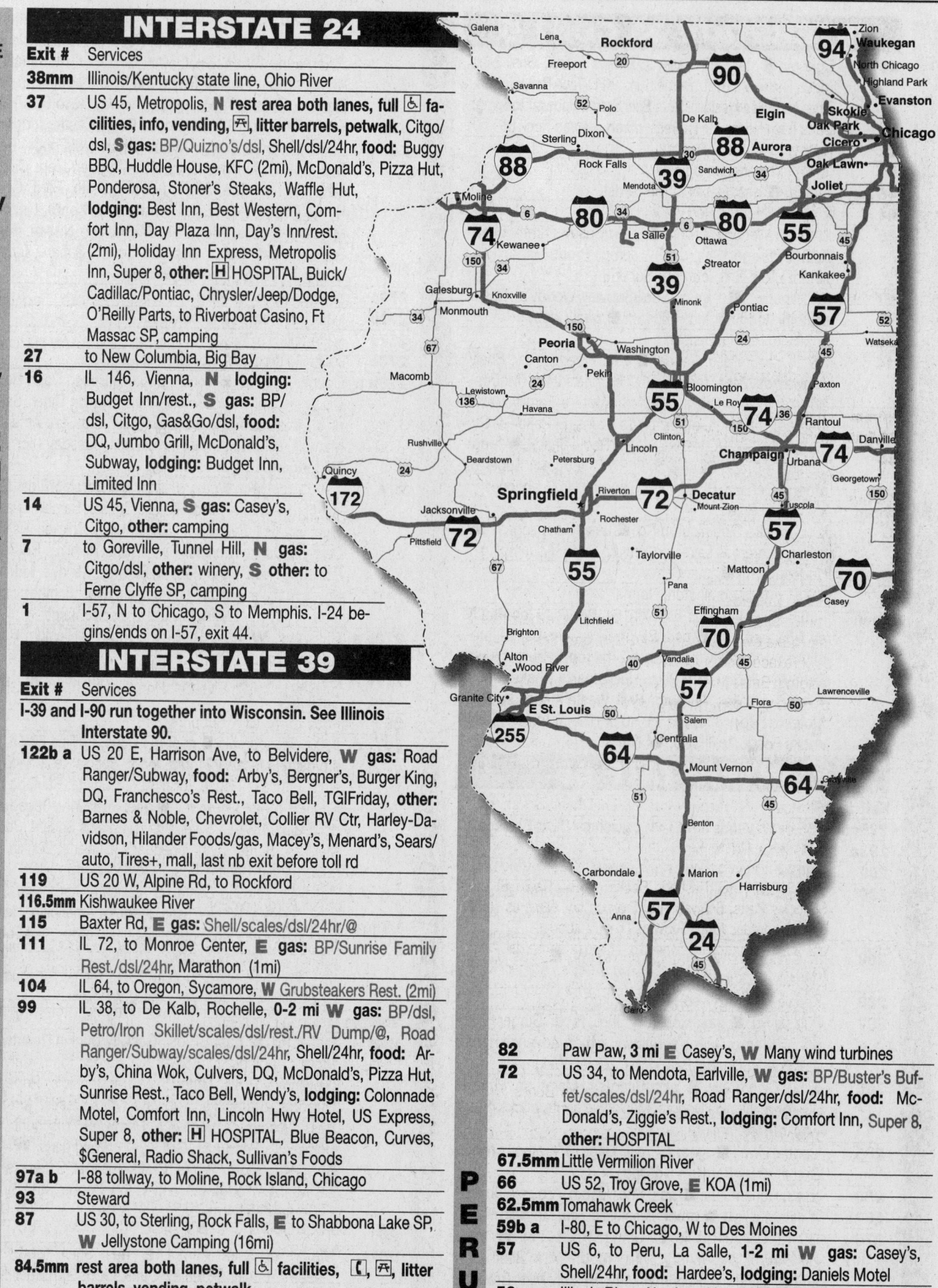

## INTERSTATE 39 CONT'D

**54** Oglesby, **E gas:** BP, Casey's, Phillips 66/dsl, Shell/24hr, **food:** Delaney's Rest., Burger King, KFC/Taco Bell, McDonald's, Mr. Salsa Mexican, Root Beer Stand, Subway, **lodging:** Day's Inn, Holiday Inn Express, **other:** Starved Rock SP

**52** IL 251, to La Salle, Peru

**51** IL 71, to Hennepin, Oglesby

**48** Tonica, **E gas:** Casey's, Tonica/dsl

**41** IL 18, to Streator, Henry

**35** IL 17, to Wenona, Lacon, **E gas:** Casey's (2mi), Shell/Subway/Burger King/dsl/RV dump, **food:** Pizza Hut, Wright Bro's Grill, **lodging:** Super 8

**27** to Minonk, **E gas:** Shell/Subway/Woody's Rest./dsl/24hr, **lodging:** Motel 6, **1 mi E gas:** Casey's

**22** IL 116, to Peoria, Benson

**14** US 24, to El Paso, Peoria, **E gas:** Freedom/dsl, Shell/Subway/dsl/24hr, **food:** DQ, Hardee's/24hr, McDonald's/playplace, Oriental Buffet, Woody's Family Rest., **lodging:** Day's Inn, **other:** Doc's Drugs, El Paso RV Ctr, Ford, IGA Foods/Chesters, NAPA, Radio Shack, **W food:** Monical's Pizza, Olive Branch Rest., **lodging:** Super 8, **other:** $General, Hickory Hill Camping (4mi), antiques

**9mm** Mackinaw River

**8** IL 251, Lake Bloomington Rd, **E** Lake Bloomington, **W other:** Evergreen Lake, to Comlara Park, RV camping

**5** Hudson, **1 mi E gas:** Casey's

**2** US 51 bus, Bloomington, Normal

**0mm** I-39 begins/ends on I-55, exit 164, **Services located N on I-55, exit 165. E gas:** BP/Circle K/24hr, FS/dsl, Mobil/Arby's/dsl, QIK-n-EZ, Shell/24hr, **food:** Burger King, Denny's, McDonald's, Pizza Hut, Steak'n Shake, Uncle Tom's Pancakes, **lodging:** Best Western, Holiday Inn, Motel 6, Super 8, **other:** H HOSPITAL, $General, Schnucks Foods, to Ill St U, **W** NAPA

## INTERSTATE 55

| Exit # | Services |
|---|---|
| **295mm** | I-55 begins/ends on US 41, Lakeshore Dr, in Chicago. |
| **293a** | to Cermak Rd (from nb) |
| **292** | I-90/94, W to Chicago, E to Indiana |
| **290** | Damen Ave, Ashland Ave (no EZ nb return), **E gas:** Marathon, **food:** Burger King, Popeye's, Subway, White Castle, **other:** $Tree, Dominick's Foods, GNC, Target |
| **289** | to California Ave (no EZ nb return), **E gas:** Citgo, Speedway/Subway/dsl, |
| **288** | Kedzie Ave, (from sb) **E gas:** Citgo |
| **287** | Pulaski Rd, **E gas:** Mobil/dsl, Shell, **food:** Burger King, Krispy Kreme, Quizno's, Subway, **other:** Advance Parts, Aldi Foods, Dodge, Pete's Mkt, Target, Walgreens |
| **286** | IL 50, Cicero Ave, **E gas:** Citgo/dsl, Marathon, Phillips 66, **food:** Dunkin Donuts, McDonald's, Starbucks, Subway, **other:** Family$ |
| **285** | Central Ave, **E gas:** BP/dsl, Citgo, Marathon, **food:** Burger King, Donald's HotDogs |
| **283** | IL 43, Harlem Ave, **E gas:** Shell, **food:** Arby's, Subway |
| **282b a** | IL 171, 1st Ave, **W other:** Brookfield Zoo, Mayfield Park |
| **279b** | US 12, US 20, US 45, La Grange Rd, **1-2 mi W gas:** BP/24hr, Clark, Mobil, Shell, **food:** Al's Beef, Applebee's, Arby's, Beef'n Brandy, Boston Mkt, Brown's Chicken, Burger King, Dino's Pizza, Dunkin Donuts, |

**279b Continued**
Jimmy John's, KFC, Komb's Rest., Ledo's Pizza, LJ Silver, Lone Star Steaks, Main St. Pizza, McDonald's, Nancy's Pizza, NoNo's Pizza, Old Country Buffet, Panda Express, Pizza Hut, Popeye's, Subway, Taco Bell, Taco Taco, Time Out Grill, Wendy's, White Castle, **lodging:** Holiday Inn, La Grange Motel, **other:** Aldi Foods, Best Buy, Buick, Cadillac, Chevrolet, Chrysler/Jeep, Circuit City, Discount Tire, $Tree, Firestone/auto, Ford, GNC, Home Depot, Honda, Jo-Ann Fabrics, Kohl's, Lincoln/Mercury, Mazda, Menard's, Mitsubishi, Nissan, Pep-Boys, Pontiac, Sam's Club/gas, Saturn, Subaru, Target/drugs, Toyota/Scion, VW, Walmart

**279a** La Grange Rd, to I-294 toll, S to Indiana

**277b** I-294 toll (from nb), S to Indiana

**277a** I-294 toll, N to Wisconsin

**276c** Joliet Rd (from nb), no facilites

**276b a** County Line Rd, **E food:** Bobak's Buffet, Capri Rest., Ciazzi's Cafe, Max&Erma's, Moon Dance Diner, Salerno's Pizza, Subway, **lodging:** Extended Stay America, Marriott, **other:** Farmer's Fresh Mkt, Tuesday Morning, **W lodging:** SpringHill Suites

**274** IL 83, Kingery Rd, **E gas:** Shell/24hr, **W gas:** Mobil/dsl, Phillips 66, Shell/24hr, **food:** Bakers Square, Barnelli's Pasta, Blueberry Hill Pancakes, Burger King, Chicken Basket, Denny's, Dunkin Donuts, Patio Rest., Portillo's HotDogs, Potbelly's Rest., Senor Tequila, Subway, Wendy's, **lodging:** Holiday Inn, La Quinta, Red Roof Inn, Super 8, **other:** Firestone, Ford/KIA, K-Mart, Michael's, Staples, Target

**273b a** Cass Ave, **W gas:** Shell/24hr, **food:** Millenium Rest., Rosati's Pizza

**271b a** Lemont Rd, **E** Extended Stay America, **W gas:** Shell/24hr

**269** I-355 toll N, to W Suburbs

**267** IL 53, Bolingbrook, **E gas:** BP, Citgo, Phillips 66/55 Trk-stp/dsl/rest./scales/24hr/@, **food:** Bono's Rest., McDonald's, Pancake House, **lodging:** La Quinta, Ramada Ltd, Super 8, **other:** Chevrolet, **W gas:** Shell/24hr, Speedway/dsl, **food:** A&W/LJ Silver, Arby's, Baker's Square, Buco's Mexican, Burger King, Cheddar's, Culver's, Dunkin Donuts, Family Square Rest., Golden Corral, IHOP, KFC, Popeye's, Rancho Santa Fe Mexican, Starbucks, Subway, Wendy's, White Castle, **lodging:** AmericInn, Hampton Inn, Holiday Inn, SpringHill Suites, **other:** Aldi Foods, Camping World RV Supplies, CarQuest, $General, Fiesta Mkt, Food-4-Less/gas, Just Tires, Menard's, Murray's Parts, NAPA, U-Haul, Walgreens, Walmart

**266mm** weigh sta both lanes

**263** Weber Rd, **E gas:** BP/dsl, GasCity/Dunkin Donuts/dsl, **food:** Applebee's, A&W/KFC, Burger King, Culver's, Giovanny's Pizza, Little China, McDonald's, Popeye's, Quizno's, Starbucks, Subway, White Castle, **lodging:** Best Western, **other:** Ace Hardware, Discount Tire, Dominick's Food/gas, GNC, 7-11, Walgreens, **W gas:** Shell/24hr, **food:** Arby's, Cracker Barrel, Salerno's Pizza, Wendy's, **lodging:** Comfort Inn, Country&Inn Suites, Extended Stay America

**261** IL 126 (from sb), to Plainfield

**257** US 30, to Joliet, Aurora, **E gas:** Shell, **food:** Applebee's, Baskin Robbin's/DunkinDonuts, Burger King, ChuckeCheese, Diamand's Rest., Hooters, KFC,

## INTERSTATE 55 CONT'D

**N** ↕ **S**

**JOLIET**

**257** Continued
LoneStar Steaks, McDonald's, Old Country Buffet, Outback Steaks, Pizza Hut, Red Lobster, Steak'n Shake/24hr, Subway, Taco Bell/LJ Silver, Texas Roadhouse, TGIFriday, Wendy's, **lodging:** Comfort Inn, Fairfield Inn, Hampton Inn, Holiday Inn Express, Motel 6, Super 8, **other:** Aldi Foods, Barnes& Noble, Best Buy, Circuit City, Discount Tire, Gander Mtn, Home Depot, Honda, JC Penney, K-Mart, Macy's, NTB, Old Navy, PetsMart, Sears/auto, Target, mall, **W gas:** BP/dsl/24hr, I-55/Clark/dsl/scales/24hr

**253b a** US 52, Jefferson St, Joliet, **E gas:** Citgo/dsl, Phillips 66, Shell/24hr, **food:** KFC/Pizza Hut, McDonald's, **lodging:** Best Budget Inn, Best Western, Elk's Motel, Joliette Inn, Wingate Inn, **other:** HOSPITAL, Ford/Suzuki, Harley-Davidson, Rick's RV Ctr, **W gas:** BP/dsl/24hr, **food:** Baba's Rest., Burger King, Casa Maya, DQ, Louis Rest., Subway (1mi), **other:** H HOSPITAL, Chrysler/ Jeep, Goodyear, Jewel-Osco/gas, White Inn

**251** IL 59 (from nb), to Shorewood, access to same as 253 W

**250b a** I-80, W to Iowa, E to Toledo

**248** US 6, Joliet, **E gas:** Citgo/dsl/24hr, Speedway/dsl, **food:** Ivo's Grill, Quizno's, Taco Burrito King, **lodging:** Manor Motel, **other:** Radio Shack, **W gas:** BP/McDonald's, **food:** Lone Star Rest. (2mi), **other:** to Ill/Mich Tr

**247** Bluff Rd

**245mm** Des Plaines River

**245** Arsenal Rd, **E other:** Exxon/Mobil Refinery

**241** to Wilmington

**241mm** Kankakee River

**240** Lorenzo Rd, **E gas:** Valero/dsl, **W gas:** Clark/dsl/ rest./24hr, Mobil, **food:** R Rest., **lodging:** Motel 55

**238** IL 129 S, to Wilmington, Braidwood

**236** IL 113, Coal City, **E food:** Good Table Rest., **other:** Chrysler/Dodge/Jeep, Fossil Rock Camping, **W gas:** Shell, **3 mi W gas:** BP, Citgo, Mobil/dsl/24hr, **food:** Agizio's, McDonald's, Subway

**233** Reed Rd, **E gas:** Marathon, **food:** Antonia's Italian, **lodging:** Sun Motel, **W other:** antiques

**227** IL 53, Gardner, **E gas:** Casey's, Gardner Haus Rest., **W gas:** BP/dsl/24hr

**DWIGHT**

**220** IL 47, Dwight, **E gas:** BP/Burger King/dsl/24hr, Casey's, Marathon/Circle K/dsl/24hr, **food:** Arby's, Dwight Chinese Rest., McDonald's, Pete's Rest., Subway, **lodging:** Classic Motel, Super 8

**217** IL 17, Dwight, **E gas:** Casey's, Shell/50's Rest./Circle K/dsl/24hr, **food:** DQ, Java Drive Thru, Rte 66 Rest., **other:** Chrysler/Dodge/Jeep, Family$, NAPA

**213mm** Mazon River

**209** Odell, **E gas:** BP, **food:** Wishing Well Café

**201** IL 23, Pontiac, **1-3 mi E food:** DQ, **other:** Pontiac RV Ctr, 4H RV Camp (seasonal)

**198mm** Vermilion River

**197** IL 116, Pontiac, **E gas:** BP/dsl/24hr, Shell, Thornton's/ dsl, **food:** Arby's, Baby Bull's Rest., Burger King, Family Table Rest., KFC, McDonald's, Subway, Taco Bell, Wendy's, **lodging:** Comfort Inn, Fiesta Motel (1mi), Holiday Inn Express, Super 8, **other:** H HOSPITAL, Aldi Foods, AutoZone, Cadillac, Chevrolet/Buick, $Tree, Lincoln/

**197** Continued
Mercury/Dodge, Walmart SuperCtr, st police, **W gas:** Citgo

**193mm** rest area both lanes, full ♿ facilities, 📞, 🍴, litter barrels, vending, petwalk

**187** US 24, Chenoa, **E gas:** Casey's, Phillips 66/McDonald's, Shell/Subway/dsl/24hr, **food:** Chenoa Family Rest., Super 8, **other:** Chevrolet

**279mm** Des Plaines River

**178** Lexington, Lexington, **E gas:** BP/McDonalds/dsl, Freedom/dsl, **W** Chevrolet

**178mm** Mackinaw River

**171** Towanda, **E gas:** FastStop

**167** Lp 55 S Veterans Pkwy, to Normal, **0-2 mi E gas:** Marathon/Circle K, **food:** Baker's Square, Bob Evans, Carlos O'Kelly's, Chili's, Cold Stone, Fazoli's, Logan's Roadhouse, Lonestar Steaks, McDonald's, Monical's Pizza, Hardee's, Outback Steaks, Panera Bread, Pizza Hut, Quizno's, Starbucks, Steak & Shake, Taco Bell, **lodging:** Candlewood Suites, Comfort Suites, Courtyard, Days Inn, Hampton Inn, Holiday Inn Express, Signature Inn, Super8, **other:** H HOSPITAL, Aldi Foods, Best Buy, Borders Books, $Tree, Gordman's, Home Depot, Honda, Jewel-Osco, Kroger, Meijer/dsl, Menard's, Mitsubishi, Office Depot, PetCo, Pontiac/Buick, Sam's Club/gas, Saturn, Target, TJ Maxx, Walgreens, Walmart SuperCtr/ gas, World Mkt, mall, to 📧

**BLOOMINGTON**

**165b a** US 51B, to Bloomington, **E gas:** BP/Circle K/24hr, FS/dsl, Mobil/Arby's/dsl, QIK-n-EZ, Shell/24hr, **food:** Burger King, Denny's, McDonald's, Pizza Hut, Steak'n Shake, Uncle Tom's Pancakes, **lodging:** Best Western, Motel 6, Super 8, **other:** H HOSPITAL, $General, Schnuks Foods, to Ill St U, **W** NAPA

**164** I-39, US 51, N to Peru

**163** I-74 W, to Peoria

**160b a** US 150, IL 9, Market St, Bloomington, **E gas:** BP/ Circle K, Freedom/dsl, Pilot/Wendy's/dsl/scales/24hr, Shell, EnergyMart/dsl, TA/dsl/rest./scales/24hr/@, **food:** Arby's, Burger King, Cracker Barrel, Culver's, KFC, McDonald's/playplace, Popeye's, Subway, Taco Bell, **lodging:** Best Inn, Comfort Inn, Days Inn, Econolodge, Hawthorn Suites, La Quinta, Quality Suites, **other:** H HOSPITAL, Advance Parts, Blue Beacon, Family$, Morforless Foods, **W gas:** Marathon/Circle K, **food:** Bob Evan's, Greatwall Chinese, Steak'n Shake/24hr, **lodging:** Comfort Suites, Country Inn&Suites, Fairfield Inn,

Copyright 2009 - The Next Exit®

## INTERSTATE 55 CONT'D

**N ↕ S**

**LINCOLN**

**SPRINGFIELD**

**160b a** Continued
Holiday Inn Express, Ramada Ltd, **other:** Aldi Foods, $tree, F&F/dsl, Radio Shack, Walmart SuperCtr/gas

**157b** Lp 55 **E**, Veterans Pkwy, Bloomington, **N gas:** Clark/24hr, FS, **food:** CJ's Rest., Froggy's Pad Rest., **lodging:** Parkway Inn/rest., Roadway Inn, Sunset Inn, **other:** **H** HOSPITAL, to ✈

**157a** I-74 E, to Indianapolis, US 51 to Decatur

**154** Shirley

**149** **W** rest area both lanes, full ♿ facilities, [C, 🚻], litter barrels, vending, playground, petwalk

**145** US 136, **E** RV Ctr, **W gas:** Dixie/Stuckey's/scales/dsl/rest./24hr, Shell, **food:** McDonald's, Subway, **lodging:** Super 8

**140** Atlanta, **E** RV camping, **W gas:** Casey's, FS/dsl, **food:** Country-Aire Rest., **lodging:** Best Value, **other:** NAPA

**133** Lp 55, Lincoln, **2 mi E gas:** Citgo, **lodging:** Budget Inn, **other:** **H** HOSPITAL, Camp-A-While Camping

**127** I-155 N, to Peoria

**126** IL 10, IL 121 S, Lincoln, **E gas:** Shell, Thornton/dsl/24hr, **food:** Burger King, Clubhouse Steaks, Cracker Barrel, Culver's, KFC/Taco Bell, LJ Silver, McDonald's, Pizza Hut, Rusty's Grill, Steak'n Shake, Wendy's, **lodging:** Comfort Inn, Crossroads Motel, Holiday Inn Express, Super 8, **other:** **H** HOSPITAL, Aldi Foods, AutoZone, $General, Goody's, Ford/Lincoln/Mercury, Kroger, Radio Shack, Russell Stover, Walmart SuperCtr

**123** Lp 55, to Lincoln, **E lodging:** Lincoln Inn, **other:** HOSPITAL

**119** Broadwell

**115** Elkhart

**109** Williamsville, **E gas:** Casey's, **food:** Huddle House, **W gas:** Love's/McDonalds/scales/dsl/24hr, New Salem HS

**107mm** weigh sta sb

**105** Lp 55, to Sherman, **W gas:** Casey's, **food:** Cancun Mexican, DQ, Subway, **other:** to Prairie Capitol Conv Ctr, Riverside Park Campground, hist sites, repair

**103mm** rest area sb, full ♿ facilities, [C, 🚻], litter barrels, vending, petwalk

**102mm** Sangamon River

**102mm** rest area nb, full ♿ facilities, [C, 🚻], litter barrels, vending, petwalk

**100b** IL 54, Sangamon Ave, Springfield, **W gas:** BP/Circle K/24hr, Shell/dsl, Speedway/dsl, **food:** Arby's, Burger King, Culver's, Hickory River BBQ, International Buffet, McDonald's, Parkway Cafe, Ryan's, Sonic, Steak'n Shake, Subway, Taco Bell, Wendy's, Wings Etc., Xochimilco Mexican, **lodging:** Northfield Suites, Ramada Ltd, **other:** Harley-Davidson, Lowe's Whse, Menard's, Walmart SuperCtr/gas, to Vet Mem

**100a** Il 54, E to Clinton, **E gas:** Road Ranger/Stuckey's/dsl, **food:** Star Cafe/24hr **other:** Kenworth/Ryder/Volvo Trucks, truckwash

**98b** I-72, IL 97, Springfield, **W gas:** BP/Circle K/24hr, Shell/dsl/24hr, **food:** Arby's, McDonald's, Starbucks, Subway, Wendy's **lodging:** Best Western, **other:** **H** HOSPITAL, Ford, K-Mart, Walgreens, to Capitol Complex

**98a** I-72, US 36 E, to Decatur

---

**SPRINGFIELD**

**LITCHFIELD**

**96b a** IL 29 N, S Grand Ave, Springfield, **W gas:** Road Ranger/dsl/24hr, **food:** Burger King, Godfather's, Mike's Rest., Popeye's, **lodging:** Quest Inn, Red Roof Inn, Super 8, **other:** Advance Parts, AutoZone, Buick, Freightliner, Hyundai, Isuzu, JC Penney, O'Reilly Parts, Pontiac/GMC, Shop'n Save, Volvo, museum

**94** Stevenson Dr, Springfield, **E** KOA (7mi), **W gas:** BP/Circle K/Quizno's, Mobil/Subway/dsl, **food:** Antonio's Pizza, Applebee's, Arby's, Bob Evans, Carlos O'Kelley's, Cheddar's, Cici's Pizza, Denny's, Hardees, Hooters, IHOP, La fiesta Mexican, LJ Silver, Maverick Steaks, McDonald's, Outback Steaks, Panera Bread, Papa John's, Pizza Hut, Quizno's, Red Lobster, Smokey Bones BBQ, Steak'n Shake, Taco Bell, Taipan Chinese, **lodging:** Comfort Suites, Crowne Plaza, Day's Inn/rest., Drury Inn, Hampton Inn, Hilton Garden, Holiday Inn Express, Microtel, PearTree Inn, Signature Inn, Stevenson Inn, **other:** BigLots, CVS Drug, Jo-Ann Fabrics, Radio Shack, ShopKO, USPO, Walgreens

**92b a** I-72 W, US 36 W, 6th St, Springfield, **W gas:** Road Ranger, Thornton's, **food:** Arby's, Bellacino's Rest., Burger King, DQ, Jimmy John's, KFC, McDonald's/playplace, New China, Pizza Hut, Sgt. Pepper's Cafe', Subway, Taco Bell, **lodging:** Route 66, Super 8, Travelodge/rest., **other:** **H** HOSPITAL, AutoZone, Mazda/Lincoln/Mercury, Walgreens, Walmart SuperCtr

**90** Toronto Rd, **E gas:** Quik-n-EZ/dsl, Shell/Circle K, **food:** Antonio's Pizza, Cracker Barrel, HenHouse, China Express, McDonald's, Subway, Taco Bell, Wendy's, **lodging:** Baymont Inn, Motel 6, Ramada Ltd, **other:** **H** HOSPITAL

**89mm** Lake Springfield

**88** E Lake Dr, Chatham, **E other:** to Lincoln Mem Garden/Nature Ctr, st police, **W** KOA

**83** Glenarm, **W** JJ RV Park/LP (4mi)

**82** IL 104, to Pawnee, **E** to Sangchris Lake SP, **W gas:** Mobil/Auburn Trvl Ctr/Subway/scales/dsl/rest./24hr/@, **other:** antiques/crafts

**80** Hist 66, Divernon, **W gas:** Marathon/Quizno's/dsl, **food:** Bearden's Rest., **other:** antiques

**72** Farmersville, **W gas:** Citgo/dsl/24hr, Shell/24hr, Subway/TCBY, **lodging:** Art's Motel/rest.

**65mm** rest area both lanes, full ♿ facilities, [C, 🚻], litter barrels, vending, playground, petwalk

**63** IL 48, IL 127, to Raymond

**60** IL 108, to Carlinville, **E other:** Kamper Kampanion RV Park, truck parts, **W gas:** Shell/dsl/LP/café, **lodging:** Best Western, **other:** antiques, to Blackburn Coll

**56mm** weigh sta nb

**52** IL 16, Hist 66, Litchfield, **E gas:** BP/24hr, Casey's, Citgo/Jack-in-the-Box/dsl, Phillips 66/dsl, Shell/24hr, **food:** Arby's, Ariston Café, Burger King, China Town, DQ, Denny's, Domino's, El Rancherito, Jubelt's Rest., KFC, LJ Silver/A&W, Maverick Steaks, McDonald's/playplace, Pizza Hut, Ponderosa, Ruby Tuesday, Subway, Taco Bell, Wendy's, **lodging:** Baymont Inn, Best Value Inn, Comfort Inn, Hampton Inn, Holiday Inn Express, Super 8, **other:** **H** HOSPITAL, Aldi Foods, Chevrolet/Pontiac, Chrysler/Jeep/Dodge, Dodge, $General, $Tree, Firestone/auto, Ford/Mercury, Goodyear/auto, IGA Foods, NAPA, Rainmaker Camping (8mi), Walgreens, Walmart SuperCtr/gas, **W** st police

## INTERSTATE 55 CONT'D

**N ↕ S**

**44**   IL 138, to Benld, Mt Olive, **E** gas: Citgo/dsl, **food:** Crossroads Diner, **lodging:** Budget 10 Motel, **other:** Mother Jones Mon.

**41**   to Staunton, **E** Country Classic Cars, **W** gas: Casey's, **food:** DQ, RJ's Rest., Schweppes Rest., Subway, **lodging:** Super 8, **other:** HOSPITAL

**37**   Livingston, New Douglas, **W** gas: BP/dsl/24hr, **food:** Country Inn, Gasperoni's Café

**33**   IL 4, to Staunton, Worden, **W** Gas & Tires

**30**   IL 140, Hamel, **E** Innkeeper Motel, **W** gas: Shell, **food:** Scotty's Rest., **other:** NAPA

**28mm**   rest area both lanes, full ♿ facilities, 🚻, 🏕, litter barrels, vending, petwalk

**23**   IL 143, Edwardsville, **E** gas: Phillips 66/dsl, **other:** repair, **W** Red Barn Camping (apr-oct)

**20b**   I-270 W, to Kansas City

**20a**   I-70 E, to Indianapolis

**I-55 S and I-70 W run together 18 mi**

**18**   IL 162, to Troy, **E** gas: Phillips 66/dsl, Pilot/Arby's/dsl/scales/24hr, TA/BP/Country Pride/dsl/scales/24hr/@, ZX Gas, **food:** Burger King, China King, DQ, Dominos, Imo's Pizza, Jack-in-the-Box, KFC, Little Caesar's, McDonald's/playplace, Pizza Man, Pizza Hut, Randy's Rest., Subway, **other:** H HOSPITAL, Ace Hardware, $General, NAPA Autocare, Speedco, SuperValu Foods, USPO, **W** gas: Phillips 66/dsl/24hr, **food:** China Garden, Cracker Barrel, Krieger's Grill, Taco Bell, **lodging:** Congress Motel, Holiday Inn Express, Red Roof Inn, Super 8, **other:** Freightliner

**17**   US 40 E, to Troy, to St Jacob

**15b a**   IL 159, Maryville, Collinsville, **E** gas: Phillips 66/dsl, Shell, ZX Gas, **food:** Sharkey's Rest., Steak-Out, Wing Wah Chinese, **other:** Chevrolet, $General, Ford/Lincoln/Mercury, **W** gas: Fast Stop, **lodging:** Econolodge

**14mm**   weigh sta sb

**11**   IL 157, Collinsville, **E** gas: Casey's, **food:** A&W/LJ Silver, Denny's, Han's Buffet, McDonald's/playplace, Penn Sta Subs, Qdoba Mexican, St. Lewis Bread Co, Waffle House, **lodging:** Best Western, **other:** Home Depot, Midas, Radio Shack, Walgreens, Walmart SuperCtr, **W** gas: Motomart/dsl/24hr, **food:** Applebee's, Arby's, Bandana's BBQ, Bob Evans, Burger King, Culvers, DQ, Pizza Hut, Ponderosa, Ruby Tuesday, Steak'n Shake, White Castle/24hr, Zapata Mexican, **lodging:** Comfort Inn, Days Inn, Drury Inn, Extended Stay Suites, Fairfield Inn, Hampton Inn, Holiday Inn/rest., Super 8, **other:** Buick/Pontiac/GMC, Chrysler/Dodge/Jeep, st police

**10**   I-255, S to Memphis, N to I-270

**9**   Black Lane (from nb, no return), **E** Fairmount RaceTrack

**6**   IL 111, Great River Rd, Fairmont City, **E** gas: Phillips 66, **lodging:** Rainbo Motel, Royal Budget Inn, Cahokia Mounds SP, **W** Horseshoe SP

**5mm**   motorist callboxes begin at 1/2 mi intervals nb

**4b a**   IL 203, Granite City, **E** gas: Phillips 66/dsl/24hr, **lodging:** Western Inn, **W** gas: Gateway/Pizza Hut/Taco Bell/dsl/24hr/@, **food:** Burger King, **other:** Gateway Int Raceway

**3**   Exchange Ave

**2**   I-64 E, IL 3 N, St Clair Ave

**COLLINSVILLE**

**2b**   3rd St

**2a**   M L King Bridge, to downtown E St Louis

**1**   IL 3, to Sauget (from sb)

**I-55 N and I-70 E run together 18 mi**

**0mm**   Illinois/Missouri state line, Mississippi River

## INTERSTATE 57

**N ↕ S**

**CHICAGO**

| Exit # | Services |
| --- | --- |
| **358mm** | I-94 E to Indiana, I-57 begins/ends on I-94, exit 63 in Chicago. |

**357**   IL 1, Halsted St, **E** gas: BP, Mobil, **other:** auto repair, 🍴 gas: Clark, Marathon, **food:** McDonald's, **other:** Walgreens

**355**   111th St, Monterey Ave, **W** gas: BP, Citgo

**354**   119th St, **W** gas: Citgo, **other:** Target

**353**   127th St, Burr Oak Ave, **E** gas: Citgo, Shell/Subway, **food:** Burger King, Dillinger's, McDonald's, Wendy's, **lodging:** Holiday Inn Express, Plaza Inn, Heritage Inn, **other:** H HOSPITAL, Ace Hardware, Family$, Walgreens, **W** gas: BP, Phillips 66, **other:** JJ Fish&Chicken

**352mm**   Calumet Sag Channel

**350**   IL 83, 147th St, Sibley Blvd, **E** gas: Citgo, Marathon/dsl, **food:** McDonald's, **W** gas: Gas Shop, **other:** Curves, USPO

**348**   US 6, 159th St, **E** gas: Marathon/dsl, **food:** Burger King, Dunkin Donuts/Baskin-Robbins, McDonald's, Subway, Taco Bell, White Castle, **lodging:** Comfort Inn, **other:** Big Lots, $Tree, Family$, Radio Shack, U-Haul, Walgreens, **W** gas: Citgo/dsl, Mobil/dsl

**346**   167th St, Cicero Ave, to IL 50, **E** gas: BP, Citgo/dsl, **food:** Applebee's, Baskin Robbins/Dunkin Donuts, Harold's Chicken, Panda Express, Quizno's, Shark's Fish&Chicken, Starbucks, Subway, Wendy's, **lodging:** Oak Forest, Walmart SuperCtr, **W** gas: Shell

**345b a**   I-80, W to Iowa, E to Indiana, to I-294 N toll to Wisconsin

**342a**   Vollmer Rd, **E** gas: Shell/24hr, **other:** H HOSPITAL

**340b a**   US 30, Lincoln Hwy, Matteson, **E** gas: BP/24hr, Citgo/dsl, Shell, **food:** A&W/LJ Silver, Applebee's, Bakers Square, Burger King, ChuckeCheese, Cracker Barrel, Dominick's, Empire Buffet, Fuddrucker's, IHOP, Jimmy John's, JN Michael's Grill, KFC, Knock Outs Grill, McDonald's, Nino's Pizza, Old Country Buffet, Olive Garden, Panda Express, Panera Bread, Peppy's Mexican, Pizza Hut, Red Lobster, Starbucks, Subway, Taco Bell, Wendy's, White Castle, **lodging:** Country Inn&Suites, Days Inn, Holiday Inn/rest., La Quinta, **other:** Best Buy,

Copyright 2009 - The Next Exit®

## INTERSTATE 57 CONT'D

**N ↕ S**

**B R A D L E Y**

**K A N K A K E E**

**340b a** Continued

Border's, Dodge, Dominick's Foods, Goodyear/auto, Home Depot, Isuzu, JC Penney, K-Mart, Marshall's, Menard's, NTB, Old Navy, Pep Boys, Sam's Club/gas, Sears/auto, Target, Walgreens, Walmart, mall, **W other:** Buick, Chevrolet, Ford, GMC, Honda, Isuzu, Kia, Mitsubishi, Pontiac, VW

**339** Sauk Trail, to Richton Park, **E gas:** Citgo, **food:** McDonald's, **other:** Walgreens

**335** Monee, **E gas:** BP/Subway/dsl, Petro/dsl/rest./24hr/@, Pilot/McDonald's/dsl/scales/24hr/@, **food:** Burger King, Quizno's, Schoops Rest., **lodging:** Best Western, Country Host Motel, Holiday Inn Express, Super 8, **other:** Blue Beacon

**332mm** Prairie View Rest Area both lanes, full 🚻 facilities, info, 🄲, vending, 🛉, litter barrels, petwalk

**330mm** weigh sta both lanes

**327** to Peotone, **E gas:** Casey's, Shell/Circle K/24hr, **food:** Bierstede German, McDonald's

**322** Manteno, **E gas:** BP/McDonald's/24hr, Phillips 66/Subway, **food:** Huddle House, KFC/Pizza Hut/Taco Bell, Monical's Pizza, Wendy's, **lodging:** Country Inn&Suites, Howard Johnson, **other:** Curves, Harley-Davidson, **W gas:** GasCity/dsl

**315** IL 50, Bradley, **E gas:** F&F, Shell/Burger King/Circle K/24hr, **food:** Armenises Rest., Cracker Barrel, Lone-Star Steaks, Old Country Buffet, Pizza Hut, Red Lobster, Ruby Tuesday, TGIFriday, White Castle, **lodging:** Fairfield Inn, Hampton Inn, Holiday Inn Express, Lee's Inn, **other:** Barnes&Noble, JC Penney, Marshall's, Michael's, Sears/auto, Staples, Target, mall, **W gas:** BP/dsl, Speedway/dsl, **food:** Applebee's, Arby's, Bakers Square, Coyote Canyon Steaks, Denny's, El Campesino Mexican, Hong Kong Buffet, IHOP, LJ Silver, McDonald's, Oberweis Ice Cream, Starbucks, Steak'n Shake, Subway, Taco Bell, Tacos Del Norte, VIP Rest., Wendy's, **lodging:** Motel 6, Quality Inn, Super 8, **other:** Aldi Foods, Buick/Nissan, Chevrolet/RV Ctr, $Tree, Honda, Hyundai, Jo-Ann Fabrics, K-Mart, Lowe's Whse, Menard's, Nissan, Walmart, to Kankakee River SP

**312** IL 17, Kankakee, **E other:** Chrysler/Dodge, Twin River's Camping, **W gas:** BP, Marathon, Shell/Circle K/24hr, **food:** McDonald's, PoorBoy Rest., Subway, Uncle Johnni's Rest., Wendy's, **lodging:** Best Value Inn, **other:** �H HOSPITAL, Advance Parts, Walgreens, auto repair

**310.5mm** Kankakee River

**308** US 45, US 52, to Kankakee, **E** KOA (3mi), **W gas:** Gas City/Dunkin Donuts/Subway/dsl, Homestead Italian Steaks, **lodging:** Economy Inn, Fairview Motel, Hilton Garden, **other:** Walmart SuperCtr, ✈

**302** Chebanse, **W** truck repair

**297** Clifton, **W gas:** Phillips 66/DQ/dsl, **food:** CharGrilled Cheeseburgers

**293** IL 116, Ashkum, **E gas:** BP/Noble Roman/dsl **W food:** Loft Rest., **other:** st police, tires

**283** US 24, IL 54, Gilman, **E gas:** Apollo/rest./dsl/scales/24hr@, BP/diner/dsl/24hr, K&H Truck Plaza/dsl/scales/24hr/@, Shell, **food:** Burger King, DQ, McDonald's, Monical's Pizza, **lodging:** Budget Host, Super 8,

**283** Continued

Travel Inn, **W gas:** BP/Subway/dsl, **other:** R&R RV Ctr

**280** IL 54, Onarga, **E gas:** Casey's (1mi), Phillips 66, **other:** camping, **W** other Lake Arrowhead RV camping

**272** to Roberts, Buckley

**268.5mm** rest area both lanes, full 🚻 facilities, vending, 🄲, 🛉, litter barrels, petwalk

**261** IL 9, Paxton, **E gas:** Casey's, Phillips 66 (1mi), **food:** Hardee's, Monical's Pizza, Pizza Hut, Subway, **other:** Chevrolet/Pontiac/Buick/GMC, **W gas:** BP, Marathon, **food:** Country Garden Rest., **lodging:** Paxton Inn

**250** US 136, Rantoul, **E gas:** BP/rest./24hr, Phillips 66 (1mi), **food:** Arby's, KFC/Taco Bell, LJ Silver, McDonald's, Monical's, Red Wheel Rest., **lodging:** Best Western, Day's Inn/rest., Rantoul Motel, Super 8, **other:** NAPA, Walmart SuperCtr, camping, vet, to Chanute AFB

**240** Market St, **E gas:** Road Ranger/McDonald's/dsl/scales, **other:** D&W Lake Camping, Kenworth, truck/tire repair

**238** Olympian Dr, to Champaign, **W gas:** Mobil/dsl, **food:** DQ, **lodging:** Microtel, **other:** RV/dsl repair

**237b a** I-74, W to Peoria, E to Urbana

**235b** I-72 W, to Decatur

**235a** University Ave, to Champaign, **E** �H HOSPITAL, U of Ill

**232** Curtis Rd, new exit

**229** to Savoy, Monticello, **E gas:** Marathon/dsl/24hr

**221.5mm** rest area both lanes, full 🚻 facilities, 🄲, 🛉, litter barrels, vending, petwalk

**220** US 45, Pesotum, **W gas:** Citgo, st police

**212** US 36, Tuscola, **E gas:** FuelMart/dsl, **W gas:** BP/24hr, Marathon, Road Ranger/dsl/scales, **food:** Amish Buffet, Burger King, DQ, Denny's, McDonald's, Monical's Pizza, Pizza Hut, Subway, Tuscany Steaks, **lodging:** Cooper Motel, Holiday Inn Express, Super 8, **other:** Chevrolet/Pontiac/Buick/GMC, Ford, IGA Foods, Pamida, Radio Shack, Tanger Outlets/Famous Brands, camping

**203** IL 133, Arcola, **E gas:** Citgo/dsl/24hr, **other:** CampALot, **W gas:** Shell/Subway/dsl/24hr, Sunrise Gas, **food:** DQ, Flower Patch B&B, Hen House, Monical's Pizza, **lodging:** Arcola Inn, Budget Inn, Comfort Inn, **other:** Country Charm Amish, $General, NAPA, Rockome Gardens, Arcola Camping

**192** IL 18, new exit

**190b a** IL 16, to Mattoon, **E gas:** BP/dsl, **other:** �H HOSPITAL, to E IL U, Fox Ridge SP, **W gas:** Marathon/Subway, **food:** Alamo Steaks, Buffalo Wild Wings, Cody's Roadhouse, Cracker Barrel, Don Sol Mexican, El Vaquero Mexican, Jumbo Buffet, McDonald's/playplace, QQ Buffet, Quizno's, Stadium Grill, Steak'n Shake/24hr, Taco Bell, Wendy's, **lodging:** Baymont Inn, Budget Inn, Comfort Suites, Hampton Inn, Holiday Inn Express, Ramada Inn/rest., Super 8, **other:** Aldi Foods, Big Lots, CVS Drug, $General, Home Depot, JC Penney, Sears, Staples, Walgreen, Walmart SuperCtr/dsl, mall

**184** US 45, IL 121, to Mattoon, **E gas:** Marathon/pizza/dsl, **W gas:** Marathon/dsl, Subway, **food:** McDonald's, **lodging:** Budget Inn, US Grant Motel (2mi), **other:** to Lake Shelbyville

**177** US 45, Neoga, **E gas:** Depot/Subway/dsl, **W gas:** Casey's (1mi), Marathon/rest./dsl

**166.5mm** rest area both lanes, full 🚻 facilities, vending, 🄲, 🛉, litter barrels, petwalk

**C H A M P A I G N**

**M A T T O O N**

## INTERSTATE 57 CONT'D

**N ↕ S**

**EFFINGHAM**

**163** I-70 E, to Indianapolis

**I-57 S and I-70 W run together 6 mi**

**162** US 45, Effingham, **E gas:** Motomart, **other:** Harley-Davidson, **W gas:** Marathon/Subway/dsl, Pilot/McDonald's/dsl/scales/24hr/@, **food:** Tuscany Rest., **other:** Crossroads RV Ctr, truck repair, Camp Lakewood (2mi), truck repair

**160** IL 33, IL 32, Effingham, **E gas:** BP/dsl, **food:** LoneStar Steaks, Pizza Hut, **lodging:** Comfort Inn, Fairfield inn, Hampton Inn, **other:** H HOSPITAL, Aldi Foods, $General, K-Mart, Kroger, Midas, Walgreens, vet, **W gas:** BP/Quizno's, Citgo, ⊕FLYING J/CountryMkt/dsl/scales/24hr/@, Marathon, TA/Popeye's/Sbarro's/dsl/rest./@, **food:** A&W, Arby's, Burger King, Cracker Barrel, Denny's, El Rancherito Mexican, KFC, LJ Silver, McDonald's, Ponderosa, Quizno's, Ryan's, Ruby Tuesday, Starbucks, Steak'n Shake, Subway, Taco Bell, TGIFriday, Wendy's, **lodging:** Best Inn, Country Inn Suites, Hilton Garden, Holiday Inn Express, Keller Hotel, Motel 6, Ramada Ltd, Super 8, Travelodge, **other:** Blue Beacon, $Tree, Ford/Lincoln/Mercury, Kohl's, Menard's, Radio Shack, Walmart SuperCtr/gas

**159** US 40, Effingham, **E gas:** BP/dsl/24hr, Marathon/dsl, **food:** China Buffet, Culver's, Domino's, Hardee's/24hr, Little Caesars, Niemerg's Rest., Papa John's, Subway, **lodging:** Comfort Suites, Crossroads Inn, Econolodge, Howard Johnson, Rodeway Inn, **other:** AutoZone, Family$, Firestone, O'Reilly Parts, SavALot Foods, Walgreens, tires/repair, **W gas:** Petro/Mobil/Iron Skillet/dsl/rest./24hr/@, **lodging:** Best Western, **other:** Blue Beacon, Truck-O-Mat/scales/wash

**I-57 N and I-70 E run together 6 mi**

**157** I-70 W, to St Louis

**151** Watson, 5 mi **E** Percival Springs RV Park

**150mm** Little Wabash River

**145** Edgewood, **E gas:** Marathon

**135** IL 185, Farina, **E gas:** BP/Subway/dsl, **other:** Ford

**127** to Kinmundy, Patoka

**SALEM**

**116** US 50, Salem, **E gas:** Huck's, Motomart/dsl/24hr, Shell/Circle K, **food:** Burger King, Domino's, KFC, La Cabana Mexican, LJ Silver, McDonald's, Pizza Hut, Subway, Taco Bell, Village Garden, Wendy's, **other:** AutoZone, Chrysler/Dodge/Jeep, Forbes SP (17mi), NAPA, O'Reilly Parts, Pontiac/GMC, to Forbes SP, **W gas:** Marathon/dsl, **food:** Applebee's, Arby's, Denny's, **lodging:** Comfort Inn, Salem Inn, Super 8, **other:** Carlisle Lake (23mi), Chevrolet/Buick, $Tree, Ford, Salem Tires, Walmart SuperCtr/gas

**114mm** rest area both lanes, full ♿ facilities, 🅲, 🆇, litter barrels, vending, petwalk, playground

**109** IL 161, to Centralia, **W gas:** Biggie's General Store/cafe/dsl

**103** Dix, **E gas:** Phillips 66/dsl, **lodging:** Red Carpet Inn, **other:** camping

**96** I-64 W, to St Louis

**95** Mt Vernon, **I-64 and I-57 run together 5 mi. E gas:** BP/dsl/24hr, Hucks, Phillips 66, **food:** Capt D's, El Rancherito Mexican, Fazoli's, Hardee's, Jade Garden, KFC, LJ Silver, McDonald's, Papa John's, Pasta House, Pizza Hut, Steak'n Shake/24hr, Subway, Taco Bell,

**MT VERNON**

**95** Continued
Wendy's, **lodging:** Best Value Inn, Budget Inn, Comfort Suites, Drury Inn, Motel 6, Super 8, Thrifty Inn, **other:** H HOSPITAL, Aldi Foods, AutoZone, Chevrolet, CVS Drug, $Tree, Ford, Goodys, Harley-Davidson, JC Penney, K-Mart, Kroger/gas, O'Reilly Parts, Radio Shack, Sears, Walgreens, **W gas:** Hucks/dsl/scales/rest./24hr, Marathon/Circle K, Pilot/Denny's/dsl/scales/24hr, Shell/Circle K/24hr, TA/Citgo/Popeye's/dsl/24hr/@, **food:** Applebee's, Arby's, Bob Evans, Burger King, Chili's, Cracker Barrel, LoneStar Steaks, McDonald's/playplace, Quizno's, Ryan's, Sonic, Stonewolf Steakhouse, Subway, **lodging:** Day's Inn, Fairfield Inn, Hampton Inn, Holiday Inn, Quality Inn, **other:** Cadillac/Pontiac/Buick/GMC, Freightliner, Lowe's Whse, NAPA, Outlet Mall, Pontiac/Buick/GMC, Quality Times RV Ctr, Staples, Toyota, Walmart SuperCtr, camping, truckwash

**92** I-64 E, to Louisville

**83** Ina, **E gas:** Lakeview/dsl/deli/24hr, Love's/McDonald's/scales, **other:** Sherwood Camping (2mi), **W** to Rend Lake Coll

**79mm** rest area sb, full ♿ facilities, info, vending, 🅲, 🆇, litter barrels, petwalk, playground

**77** IL 154, to Whittington, **E gas:** Shell/24hr, **food:** Giddy's Grill, **other:** Holiday Trav-L Park, **W lodging:** Seasons at Rend Lake Lodge/rest., **other:** to Rend Lake, golf, Wayne Fitzgerrell SP

**74mm** rest area nb, full ♿ facilities, vending, 🅲, 🆇, litter barrels, petwalk, playground

**BENTON**

**71** IL 14, Benton, **E gas:** Phillips 66, Shell, **food:** Arby's, Hardee's, KFC/Taco Bell, Pizza Hut, Wendy's, **lodging:** Day's Inn/rest., Gray Plaza Motel, Super 8, **other:** H HOSPITAL, AutoZone, KOA (1.5mi), O'Rielly Parts, Plaza Tire, **W gas:** BP/Burger King/dsl, Shell/dsl/24hr, **food:** Applebee's, Burger King, McDonald's, Subway, **other:** CVS Drug, Walmart SuperCtr/dsl, to Rend Lake

**65** IL 149, W Frankfort, **E gas:** GasForLess, Shell/dsl, **food:** China Garden, Hardee's, KFC, LJ Silver, Mike's Drive-In, Pancake House/24hr, Sonic, Subway, **lodging:** Gray Plaza Motel, **other:** H HOSPITAL, CarQuest, $General, MadPricer Foods, NAPA, **W gas:** Casey's, **food:** Burger King, EEE Rest, McDonald's, **lodging:** Best Value Inn, **other:** Chevrolet/Pontiac, Chrysler/Dodge, CVS Drug, $Tree, K-Mart, VF Factory Stores

**59** to Herrin, Johnston City, **E gas:** BP/dsl, Shell/dsl/24hr, **food:** DQ, Hardee's, McDonald's, Subway, **other:** NAPA, camping (2mi), **W other:** H HOSPITAL, camping (4mi)

## INTERSTATE 57 CONT'D

**N ↑ S   M A R I O N**

| | |
|---|---|
| **54b a** | IL 13, Marion, **E gas:** Phillips 66/24hr, **food:** Arby's, Fazoli's, Hardee's, KFC, LJ Silver, Papa John's, Pizza Hut, Quizno's, Subway, Tequila's Mexican, Wendy's, **lodging:** Day's Inn, **other:** Aldi Foods, Advance Parts, AutoZone, Chevrolet/Cadillac, Family$, Ford/Lincoln/Mercury/Hyundai, Kroger/gas, Plaza Tire, Radio Shack, SavALot Foods, USPO, **W gas:** BP/dsl/rest/scales/24hr/@, Phillips 66, **food:** 17th Street Grill, Applebee's, Asian Bistro, Backyard Burger, Bob Evans, Burger King, McDonald's, O'Charley's, Rock'n Roll Buffet, Red Lobster, Ryan's, Sonic, Steak'n Shake, Taco Bell, **lodging:** Best Inn, Drury Inn, Fairfield Inn, Hampton Inn, Motel 6, Super 8, **other:** Buick/GMC/Pontiac/Mercedes, Chrysler/Dodge/Jeep, Dillard's, Harley-Davidson, Home Depot, Kia, Mitsubishi, Sam's Club/gas, Sears, Target, Walmart SuperCtr, mall |
| **53** | Main St, Marion, **E gas:** Shell/dsl, **food:** DQ, **lodging:** Motel Marion/camping, **other:** H HOSPITAL, NAPA, **W gas:** Motomart/24hr, **food:** Cracker Barrel, HideOut Steaks, **lodging:** Comfort Inn, Comfort Suites, Holiday Inn Express |
| **47mm** | weigh sta both lanes |
| **45** | IL 148, **1 mi E gas:** King Tut's Food/dsl/24hr, **lodging:** Lake Tree Inn, **other:** camping, dsl repair |
| **44** | I-24 E to Nashville |
| **40** | Goreville Rd, **E other:** Ferne Clyffe SP, camping, scenic overlook |
| **36** | Lick Creek Rd, **W other:** vineyards |
| **32mm** | **Trail of Tears Rest Area both lanes, full** ♿ **facilities, info,** 🕿, 🅿, **litter barrels, vending, petwalk, playground** |
| **30** | IL 146, Anna, Vienna, **W gas:** Shell/dsl/rest./24hr, **other:** H HOSPITAL, auto/tire repair |
| **25** | US 51 N (from nb, exits left), to Carbondale |
| **24** | Dongola Rd, **W gas:** BP/dsl |
| **18** | Ullin Rd, **W gas:** Citgo/dsl/24hr, **food:** EEE BBQ, **lodging:** Best Western, **other:** st police |
| **8** | Mounds Rd, to Mound City, **E other:** K&K AutoTruck/dsl/repair |
| **1** | IL 3, to US 51, Cairo, **E lodging:** Belvedere Motel (2mi), Day's Inn, **other:** $General, Mound City Nat Cem (4mi), camping, **W** camping |
| **0mm** | Illinois/Missouri state line, Mississippi River |

## INTERSTATE 64

| Exit # | Services |
|---|---|
| **131.5mm** | Illinois/Indiana state line, Wabash River |
| **131mm** | **Skeeter Mtn Welcome Ctr wb, full** ♿ **facilities,** 🕿, **vending,** 🅿, **litter barrels, petwalk** |
| **130** | IL 1, to Grayville, **N gas:** Casey's (2mi), Shell/dsl/24hr, **food:** Subway, **lodging:** Best Western/rest., Super 8, **other:** museum, Beall Woods St Park |
| **124mm** | Little Wabash River |
| **117** | Burnt Prairie, **S gas:** Marathon/dsl, **food:** ChuckWagon Charlie's Café, **other:** antiques |
| **110** | US 45, Mill Shoals |
| **100** | IL 242, to Wayne City, **N gas:** Marathon/dsl |
| **89** | to Belle Rive, Bluford |
| **86mm** | **rest area wb, full** ♿ **facilities,** 🕿, **vending,** 🅿, **litter barrels, petwalk** |

**M t V E R N O N      N E W   B A D E N**

| | |
|---|---|
| **82.5mm** | **rest area eb, full** ♿ **facilities,** 🕿, **vending,** 🅿, **litter barrels, petwalk** |
| **80** | IL 37, to Mt Vernon, **2 mi N gas:** BP/Burger King/dsl/24hr, Hucks/dsl/24hr, **lodging:** Royal Inn, **other:** $General, camping |
| **78** | I-57, S to Memphis, N to Chicago |
| **95 [157]** | Mt Vernon, I-64 and I-57 run together 5 mi. **N gas:** BP/dsl/24hr, Hucks, Phillips 66, **food:** Capt D's, El Rancherito Mexican, Fazoli's, Hardee's, Jade Garden, KFC, LJ Silver, McDonald's, Papa John's, Pasta House, Pizza Hut, Steak'n Shake/24hr, Subway, Taco Bell, Wendy's, **lodging:** Best Value Inn, Budget Inn, Comfort Suites, Drury Inn, Motel 6, Super 8, Thrifty Inn, **other:** H HOSPITAL, Aldi Foods, AutoZone, Chevrolet, CVS Drug, $Tree, Ford, Goodys, Harley-Davidson, JC Penney, K-Mart, Kroger/gas, O'Reilly Parts, Radio Shack, Sears, Walgreens, **S gas:** Hucks/dsl/scales/rest./24hr, Marathon/Circle K, Pilot/Denny's/dsl/scales/24hr, Shell/Circle K/24hr, TA/Citgo/Popeye's/dsl/24hr/@, **food:** Applebee's, Arby's, Bob Evans, Burger King, Chili's, Cracker Barrel, LoneStar Steaks, McDonald's/playplace, Quizno's, Ryan's, Sonic, Stonewolf Steakhouse, Subway, **lodging:** Day's Inn, Fairfield Inn, Hampton Inn, Holiday Inn, Quality Inn, **other:** Cadillac/Pontiac/Buick/GMC, Freightliner, Lowe's Whse, NAPA, Outlet Mall, Pontiac/Buick/GMC, Quality Times RV Ctr, Staples, Toyota, Walmart SuperCtr, camping, truckwash |
| **73** | I-57, N to Chicago, S to Memphis |
| **69** | Woodlawn |
| **61** | US 51, to Centralia, Richview, **S** access to gas, food |
| **50** | IL 127, to Nashville, **N** to Carlyle Lake, **S gas:** BP/24hr (3mi), Citgo/dsl/24hr, Conoco/dsl/rest., Shell/dsl/24hr, **food:** McDonald's, Subway (3mi), **lodging:** Best Western, Little Nashville Inn/rest., **other:** HOSPITAL |
| **41** | IL 177, Okawville, **S gas:** Phillips 66/Burger King/dsl/24hr, **food:** DQ, Hen House/24hr, Golfer's Steakhouse, Subway, **lodging:** Original Springs Motel, Super 8, **other:** truck repair |
| **37mm** | Kaskaskia River |
| **34** | to Albers, **3 mi N gas:** Casey's |
| **27** | IL 161, New Baden, **N gas:** Shell/dsl/24hr, **food:** Good Ol' Days Rest., McDonald's, Outside Inn Rest., Subway, **other:** Chevrolet |
| **25mm** | **rest area both lanes, full** ♿ **facilities, info,** 🕿, **vending,** 🅿, **litter barrels, petwalk** |
| **23** | IL 4, to Mascoutah, **3 mi N food:** Hardee's, McDonald's, **S** ✈ |
| **19b a** | US 50, IL 158, **N gas:** Motomart/24hr, **food:** Schiappa's Italian, Subway, **lodging:** Comfort Inn, **S gas:** Citgo/dsl, **other:** H HOSPITAL, to Scott AFB |
| **18mm** | weigh sta eb |
| **16** | to O'Fallon, Shiloh, **N food:** Denny's, **S food:** Applebee's, Arby's, Buffalo Wild Wings, Cafe Avanti, Coldstone Creamery, Cracker Barrel, 54th St. Grille, Golden Corral, Johnny Rocket's, Qdoba Mexican, Quizno's, St. Louis Bread Co., Texas Roadhouse, **lodging:** Drury Inn, Holiday Inn Express, **other:** Dierbergs's Foods, Radio Shack, Target |
| **15mm** | motorist callbox every 1/2 mile wb |
| **14** | O'Fallon, **N gas:** QT, Shell/24hr, **food:** IHOP, Japanese Garden, Steak'n Shake/24hr, Subway, **lodging:** |

**E ↕ W**

IL

## INTERSTATE 64 CONT'D

**E** ↕ **W**

**14** Continued
Baymont Inn, Extended Stay America, Howard Johnson, Sleep Inn, **other:** Chevrolet, Ford, O'Reilly Parts, Saab/Cadillac, **S food:** Chevy's Mexican, Culver's, DQ, Emperor's Wok, Grand Buffet, Hardee's, Jack-in-the-Box, KFC, Lion's Choice, LoneStar Steaks, McDonald's, O'Charley's, Papa Murphy's, Pepper's Rest., Taco Bell, **lodging:** Candlewood Suites, Courtyard, Econolodge, Quality Inn, Ramada Ltd, **other:** BMW, Harley-Davidson, Home Depot, Honda, Hyundai, Kia, Lion's Choice, Mazda, Mitsubishi, Nissan, Sam's Club/gas, Subaru, Suzuki, Toyota/Scion, VW, Walmart SuperCtr

**12** IL 159, to Collinsville, **N gas:** Shell, **food:** Applebee's, Bob Evans, Carlos O'Kelly's, Ginger Buffet, Houlihan's, Joe's Crabshack, Lotawalla Creek Grill, Olive Garden, Red Lobster, TGIFriday, **lodging:** Best Western, Comfort Inn, Drury Inn, Fairfield Inn, Hampton Inn, Ramada Inn/rest., Sheraton, Super 8, **other:** Circuit City, Gordman's, Michael's, **S gas:** BP/24hr, Motomart/dsl/24hr, **food:** Boston Mkt, Burger King, Capt D's, Casa Gallardo, Chili's, Denny's, Domino's, Fazoli's, Hardee's, IHOP, Krispy Kreme, Longhorn Steaks, LJ Silver, McDonald's, Old Country Buffet, Outback Steaks, Ponderosa, Popeye's, Quizno's, Rally's, Red Robin, Ruby Tuesday, Russell Stover, Smokey Bones BBQ, Steak'n Shake, St. Louis Bread, Taco Bell, White Castle, **other:** Aamco, Advance Parts, AutoTire, Barnes&Noble, Best Buy, Borders, Dillard's, $Tree, JC Penney, K-Mart, Kohl's, Lowes Whse, Macy's, Marshall's, Office Depot, Old Navy, PetCo, Schnuck's Foods, TJ Maxx, Walgreens, mall

**9** IL 157, to Caseyville, **N gas:** BP/24hr, Phillips 66/Subway/repair, **food:** Hardee's, Wendy's, **lodging:** Western Inn, **S gas:** BP/dsl/repair, **food:** Cracker Barrel, DQ, Domino's, McDonald's, Pizza Hut/Taco Bell, **lodging:** Day's Inn, Econolodge, Motel 6, Quality Inn

**7** I-255, S to Memphis, N to Chicago

**6** IL 111, Kingshighway, **N gas:** BP, Mobil/24hr, Shell, **food:** Church's, Popeye's

**5.5mm** motorist callbox every 1/2 mi eb

**52** 5th St

**41** 5th St, Baugh

**3** I-55 N, I-70 E, IL 3 N, to St Clair Ave, to stockyards

**2b a** 3rd St, **S** gas

**1** IL 3 S, 13th St, E St Louis, **N** Casino Queen

**0mm** Illinois/Missouri state line, Mississippi River

## INTERSTATE 70

**E** ↕ **W**

| Exit # | Services |
|---|---|
| **156mm** | Illinois/Indiana state line |
| **154** | US 40 W |
| **151mm** | weigh sta wb |
| **149mm** | rest area wb, full ♿ facilities, info, ☏, ⛲, vending, litter barrels, petwalk, camping |
| **147** | IL 1, Marshall, **N gas:** Jerry's Rest., **S gas:** Casey's (1mi), Jiffy/dsl/24hr, Marathon/Arby's/dsl, **food:** McDonald's, Pizza Hut, Sam's Steaks, Subway, Wendy's, **lodging:** Lincoln Motel (2mi), Relax Inn, Super 8, **other:** Walmart SuperCtr, Lincoln Trail SP, antiques, camping |
| **136** | to Martinsville, **S gas:** Fast Stop/dsl/24hr |

Map showing Illinois interstate routes with labels: 55, 70 (Effingham), Alton, Vandalia, 57, St Louis, Salem, 64, Nashville, Mt Vernon, 64, 55. State of Illinois outline with "IL" label.

**C A S E Y**

| | |
|---|---|
| **134.5mm** | N Fork Embarras River |
| **129** | IL 49, Casey, **N other:** RV service, KOA (seasonal), **S gas:** BP/Subway/dsl, Casey's, Fast Stop, Marathon/Circle K/dsl, **food:** DQ, Hardee's, McDonald's, Pizza Hut, **lodging:** Comfort Inn, **other:** IGA Foods |
| **119** | IL 130, Greenup, **S gas:** Casey's, Jimmy's/Subway, Marathon, **food:** DQ, **lodging:** Budget Host, 5 Star Motel, **other:** $General, camping, hist sites |
| **105** | Montrose, **N other:** Spring Creek Camping (1mi), **S gas:** BP/dsl, Marathon/dsl/24hr, **lodging:** Fairview Inn |
| **98** | I-57, N to Chicago |
| **I-70 and I-57 run together 6 mi. See Interstate 57, exits 159-162** | |
| **92** | I-57, S to Mt Vernon |
| **91mm** | Little Wabash River |
| **87mm** | rest area both lanes, full ♿ facilities, info, ☏, vending, ⛲, litter barrels, playground, petwalk, RV dump |
| **82** | IL 128, Altamont, **N gas:** Casey's, Jimmy's/Subway/dsl/24hr, Marathon, **food:** Dairy Bar, McDonald's, **lodging:** Altamont Motel/rest., Knight's Inn, **S food:** Longhorn Rest., **lodging:** Super 8 |
| **76** | US 40, St Elmo, **N gas:** Casey's, **lodging:** Waldorf Motel, **other:** Timberline Camping (2mi) |
| **71mm** | weigh sta eb |
| **68** | US 40, Brownstown, **N other:** Okaw Valley Kamping, **S** truck repair |
| **63.5mm** | Kaskaskia River |

**V A N D A L I A**

| | |
|---|---|
| **63** | US 51, Vandalia, **N food:** Chuck Wagon Cafe, LJ Silver, **lodging:** Day's Inn, **S gas:** BP/Burger King/24hr, Casey's, Marathon, Shell/dsl, **food:** Arby's, China Buffet, DQ, McDonald's, Pizza Hut, Quizno's, Rancho Nuevo Mexican, Sonic, Subway, Wendy's, **lodging:** Jay's Inn, Travelodge, **other:** Ⓗ HOSPITAL, Aldi Foods, Harmons Foods, hist site |
| **61** | US 40, Vandalia, **N gas:** Fast Stop/dsl/scales/24hr, **S gas:** Murphy USA/dsl, **food:** KFC/Taco Bell, Los Amigos Mexican, Ponderosa, **lodging:** Holiday Inn Express, Ramada Ltd, **other:** AutoZone, $Box, Walmart SuperCtr |
| **52** | US 40, Mulberry Grove, **N gas:** Jimmy's/dsl, **other:** Timber Trail Camp-In (2mi), tires, **S** Cedar Brook Camping (1mi) |
| **45** | IL 127, Greenville, **N gas:** Jimmy's/Domino's/dsl, Shell/dsl/24hr, **food:** KFC/Taco Bell, Lu-Bob's Rest., Red Apple Rest., Mabry's Rest., McDonald's, **lodging:** Budget Host, Econolodge, Super 8, 2 Acre Motel, |

## INTERSTATE 70 CONT'D

**E ↕ W  DECATUR**

| | |
|---|---|
| **45** | Continued |
| | **other:** H HOSPITAL, Ford/Mercury, **S food:** Hacienda Mexican, **lodging:** Sleep Inn, **other:** RV Service, to Carlyle Lake |
| **41** | US 40 E, to Greenville |
| **36** | US 40 E, Pocahontas, **S gas:** BP/dsl/24hr, Phillips 66/dsl/24hr, **lodging:** Lighthouse Lodge, Powhatan Motel/rest., Tahoe Motel, **other:** truck/tire repair |
| **30** | US 40, IL 143, to Highland, **S gas:** Shell/dsl/24hr, **food:** Blue Springs Café, **other:** H HOSPITAL, Tomahawk RV Park (7mi) |
| **26.5mm** | Silver Lake rest area both lanes, full ♿ facilities, 🚻, 🅿, litter barrels, vending, petwalk |
| **24** | IL 143, Marine, **4 mi S food:** Ponderosa, **lodging:** Holiday Inn Express, **other:** H HOSPITAL |
| **21** | IL 4, Lebanon |
| **15b a** | I-55, N to Chicago, S to St Louis, I-270 W to Kansas City |
| | I-70 and I-55 run together 18 mi. See Interstate 55 exits 1-18. |
| **0mm** | Illinois/Missouri state line, Mississippi River |

## INTERSTATE 72

**E ↕ W  DECATUR**

| Exit # | Services |
|---|---|
| **183mm** | 1 mi E on University...**food:** Arby's, Burger King, Garcia's Pizza, La Bamba's Mexican, McDonald's, Monical's Pizza, Pizza Hut, Sonic, Subway, Taffy's Rest, Texas Roadhouse, Village Inn, **other:** Advance Parts, Aldi Foods, AutoZone, CVS Drug, Firestone/auto, County Mkt Foods, Schnuck's Foods/24hr |
| **182b a** | I-57, N to Chicago, S to Memphis, to I-74 |
| **176** | IL 47, to Mahomet |
| **172** | IL 10, Lodge, Seymour |
| **169** | White Heath Rd |
| **166** | IL 105 W, Market St, **N** Ford/Mercury, **S gas:** Mobil/dsl, **food:** Red Wheel Rest., **lodging:** Best Western, Foster Inn, **other:** vet |
| **165mm** | Sangamon River |
| **164** | Bridge St, **1 mi S gas:** Mobil, **food:** Best Wok, Hardee's, McDonald's, Monical's Pizza, Subway, **other:** H HOSPITAL, $General, Chevrolet/Buick/Pontiac, Chrysler/Dodge/Jeep |
| **156** | IL 48, to Weldon, Cisco, **S** Friends Creek Camping (may-oct) (3mi) |
| **153mm** | rest area both lanes, full ♿ facilities, 🚻, 🅿, litter barrels, vending, petwalk |
| **152mm** | Friends Creek |
| **150** | Argenta |
| **144** | IL 48, Oreana, **S gas:** Pilot/McDonald's/Subway/dsl/scales/24hr, **lodging:** Sleep Inn, **other:** H HOSPITAL, Dodge, Honda, Hyundai, Mitsubishi |
| **141b a** | US 51 S, Decatur, **N gas:** Shell/Circle K, **food:** Applebee's, Cheddar's, Cracker Barrel, HomeTown Buffet, McDonald's, O'Charley's, Pizza Hut, Red Lobster, Steak'n Shake, Subway, Taco Bell, Texas Roadhouse, **lodging:** Baymont Inn, Comfort Inn, Country Inn&Suites, Fairfield Inn, Hampton Inn, Holiday Inn Express, Ramada Ltd, **other:** Advance Parts, Bergner's, Best Buy, Buick/GMC, $Tree, Harley Davidson, JC Penney, Lowe's Whse, Kohl's, Mitsubishi/Hyundai/Honda, Menard's, PetsMart, Sears/auto, Staples, mall, **S food:** Arby's, |

**DECATUR  SPRINGFIELD**

| | |
|---|---|
| **141b a** | Continued |
| | Burger King, El Rodeo Mexican, Monical's Pizza, Panera Bread, Quizno's, **other:** Circuit City, Jo-Ann Fabrics, PetCo, Radio Shack, Sam's Club, Walgreens, Walmart SuperCtr |
| **138** | IL 121, Decatur, **S** HOSPITAL |
| **133b a** | US 36 E, US 51, Decatur, **S gas:** Phillips 66/Subway/dsl, **lodging:** Day's Inn, Decatur Hotel/rest. |
| **128** | Niantic |
| **122** | to Mt Auburn, Illiopolis, **S gas:** Fastop |
| **114** | Buffalo, Mechanicsburg |
| **108** | Riverton, Dawson |
| **107mm** | Sangamon River |
| **104** | Camp Butler, **2 mi N lodging:** Best Rest Inn, Best Western, Park View Motel, **food:** Chesapeake Seafood, Starbucks, **other:** golf |
| **103b a** | I-55, N to Chicago, S to St Louis, Il 97, to Springfield |
| | I-72 and I-55 run together 6 mi. See Interstate 55 exits 92-98 |
| **93** | IL 4, Springfield, **N gas:** Hucks, Thorntons, **food:** Applebee's, Arby's, Bakers Square, Buffet King, Burger King, Chili's, China Buffet, Corky's BBQ, Denny's, Grand Buffet, Huck's, LoneStar Steaks, Longhorn Steaks, Maverick Rest., McDonald's, Oberweis Ice Cream, Old Country Buffet, Olive Garden, Panera Bread, Pasta House, Perkins, Popeye's, Qdoba Mexican, Sonic, Starbucks, Taco Bell, TGIFriday, **lodging:** Comfort Inn, Courtyard, Fairfield Inn, Sleep Inn, **other:** Barnes&Noble, Best Buy, Circuit City, Curves, Discount Tire, Gordman's, Jo-Ann Crafts, K-Mart, Kohl's, Lowe's Whse, Menard's, Michael's, Office Depot, Old Navy, PetsMart, Sam's Club/gas, Sears/auto, ShopKO, Staples, Target, TJ Maxx, Walgreens, Walmart/auto, vet, **S gas:** Meijer/dsl, **food:** Bob Evans, O'Charley's, Steak'n Shake, **lodging:** Hampton Inn, Staybridge Suites, **other:** Cadillac, Chevrolet, Chrysler/Dodge/Jeep, Ford, Honda, Saturn, Funpark |
| **91** | Wabash Ave, to Springfield, **N food:** Buffalo Wild Wings, Coz's Pizza, Culver's, **other:** Nissan, **S** Colman RV SuperCtr |
| **82** | New Berlin, **S gas:** Phillips 66/The Plaza Rest./dsl |
| **76** | IL 123, to Ashland, Alexander |
| **68** | to IL 104, to Jacksonville, **2 mi N gas:** BP, **other:** H HOSPITAL |
| **64** | US 67, to Jacksonville, **N gas:** Clark/Quizno's/dsl, **lodging:** Comfort Inn, Econolodge, Holiday Inn Express, **other:** Hopper RV Ctr, Walgreens, **2 mi N gas:** BP/dsl, **food:** Classic Diner, DQ, McDonald's, Subway, **lodging:** Super 8, **other:** H HOSPITAL, Harpers Food/gas |
| **60** | to US 67 N, to Jacksonville, **6 mi N** H HOSPITAL, gas, food, lodging |
| **52** | to IL 106, Winchester, **N** golf, **2 mi S** gas, food, lodging |
| **46** | IL 100, to Bluffs |
| **42mm** | Illinois River |
| **35** | US 54, IL 107, to Pittsfield, Griggsville, **4 mi N** gas, food, lodging, **S other:** HOSPITAL, Pine Lakes Camping (6mi), st police |
| **31** | to Pittsfield, New Salem, **5 mi S** H HOSPITAL, gas, food, lodging, camping |
| **20** | IL 106, Barry, **S gas:** Phillips 66/dsl/24hr, Shell/dsl/24hr, **food:** Ice House, Wendy's, **other:** Truckload Foods, antiques, winery |

## INTERSTATE 72 CONT'D

| | |
|---|---|
| **10** | IL 96, to Payson, Hull |
| **4a** | I-172, N to Quincy |
| **1** | IL 106, to Hull, no faciities |
| **0mm** | **Illinois/Missouri state line, Mississippi River. Exits 157 & 156 are in Missouri.** |
| **157** | to Hannibal, MO 179, **S gas:** Ayerco, BP, Phillips 66, Shell, **food:** Mark Twain Dinette, **lodging:** Hannibal Inn, Hotel Clemens, Super 7 Motel, Travelodge |
| **156** | US 61, New London, Palmyra. I-72 begins/ends in Hannibal, MO on US 61., **N gas:** BP, Conoco/dsl, **food:** Burger King, Country Kitchen, Golden Corral, Hardee's, Hunan Chinese, LJ Silver, McDonalds, Papa Johns, Pizza Hut, Sonic, Taco Bell, **other:** Aldi Foods, Big Lots, $General, Ford, Goody's, Kroger, Radio Shack, TrueValue, Walmart SuperCtr/gas, **0-2 mi S gas:** Ayerco/Joe's Diner, Shell/dsl, **food:** Cassano's Subs, DQ, Hardee's, KFC, Wendy's, **lodging:** Comfort Inn, Days Inn, Econolodge, Hannibal Inn, Holiday Inn Express, Mark Twain Motel, Super 8, **other:** AutoZone, County Mkt Foods, Injun Joe's RV Camp, Walgreens |

## INTERSTATE 74

| Exit # | Services |
|---|---|
| **221mm** | Illinois/Indiana state line, Central/Eastern Time Zone |
| **220** | Lynch Rd, Danville, **N gas:** BP/dsl, Marathon (1mi), **food:** Big Boy, **lodging:** Best Western, Comfort Inn, Danville Inn, Fairfield Inn, Holiday Inn Express, Sleep Inn, Super 8 |
| **216** | Bowman Ave, Danville, **N gas:** Freedom, Mobil/dsl/24hr, Phillips 66/dsl, **food:** Godfather's, KFC |
| **215b a** | US 150, IL 1, Gilbert St, Danville, **N gas:** BP, Citgo/dsl, Harper, Speedway, Phillips 66, **food:** Arby's, Baskin-Robbins/Dunkin Donuts, Danville Rest., La Potosina, LJ Silver, McDonald's, Pizza Hut, Steak'n Shake, Subway, Taco Bell, **lodging:** Best Western, Day's Inn, **other:** H HOSPITAL, Aldi Foods, Ford/Lincoln/Mercury, **S gas:** Casey's/dsl, Speedway/dsl/24hr, **food:** Burger King, Green Jade Chinese, Monical's Pizza, **other:** AutoZone, Big R, Pontiac/GMC, $General, Family$, Harley-Davidson, Forest Glen Preserve Camping (11mi), NAPA, Toyota |
| **214** | G St, Tilton |
| **210** | US 150, MLK Dr, **2 mi N gas:** Marathon, **food:** Little Nugget Steaks, **other:** H HOSPITAL, to Kickapoo SP, camping, **S food:** PossumTrot Rest. |
| **208mm** | **Welcome Ctr wb, full facilities, info, litter barrels, vending, petwalk** |
| **206** | Oakwood, **N gas:** Marathon/dsl/rest./scales/24hr, **S gas:** Phillips 66/Subway/dsl, Mobil/Oakwood/rest./dsl, Casey's (1mi), **food:** McDonald's, Oaks Grill |
| **200** | IL 49 N, to Rankin, **N camping** |
| **197** | IL 49 S, Ogden, **S gas:** Phillips 66/dsl, **food:** Billy Bud's Steaks, Godfather's Pizza |
| **192** | St Joseph, **S food:** DQ, **other:** antiques |
| **185** | IL 130, University Ave |
| **184** | US 45, Cunningham Ave, Urbana, **N food:** A&W, **lodging:** Park Inn, **other:** Farm&Fleet, Toyota, VW, **S gas:** Freedom/dsl/24hr, Marathon/Circle K/Subway, Speedway/dsl, Shell, **food:** Cracker Barrel, Domino's, Hickory River, Longhorn Steaks, Ned Kelly's Steaks, |

| | |
|---|---|
| **184** | Continued Steak'n Shake/24hr, **lodging:** Best Value Inn, Best Western, Eastland Suites, Motel 6, Travelers Stay, **other:** Auto Park, $General, Family$, Firestone/auto, NAPA, Sav-A-Lot |
| **183** | Lincoln Ave, Urbana, **S gas:** Marathon/Circle K/Quizno's, Mobil/dsl, Speedway/dsl, **food:** Seasons Rest., Urbana Garden Rest., **lodging:** Holiday Inn/rest., Holiday Inn Express, Ramada Ltd, Sleep Inn, Super 8, **other:** H HOSPITAL, Harley-Davidson, to U of IL |
| **182** | Neil St, Champaign, **N food:** Alexander Steaks, Bob Evans, Chevy's Mexican, FoodCourt, Gordman's, McDonald's, Olive Garden, Panera Bread, Subway, Taco Bell, Za's Italian, **lodging:** Baymont Inn, Comfort Inn, La Quinta, Red Roof Inn, Super 8, **other:** Barnes&Noble, Chevrolet/Cadillac, Chrysler/Dodge/Jeep, Hancock Fabrics, JC Penney, Kohl's, Macy's, Mercedes/Volvo, Office Depot, Sears/auto, TJ Maxx, mall, same as 181, **S gas:** Mobil, **other:** JoAnn Fabrics |
| **181** | Prospect Ave, Champaign, **N gas:** Meijer/dsl/24hr, **food:** Applebee's, Best Wok, Boston's, Buffalo Wild Wings, Burger King, Cheddar's, Chili's, China Town, Culver's, Fazoli's, HomeTown Buffet, LoneStar Steaks, McCalister's Deli, O'Charley's, Outback Steaks, Pen Sta Subs, Red Lobster, Ruby Tuesday, Ryan's, Steak'n Shake/24hr, Subway, Wendy's, **lodging:** Country Inn&Suites, Courtyard, Drury Inn, Extended Stay America, Fairfield Inn, Wingate Inn, **other:** Advance Parts, Best Buy, Borders Books, Circuit City, $Tree, Hyundai/Kia, Lowe's Whse, Menard's, Michael's, Mitsubishi, Old Navy, PetsMart, Sam's Club/gas, Staples, Target, Tires+, Walmart SuperCtr/dsl, same as 182, **S gas:** Freedom/dsl, Marathon/Circle K, Mobil/Jimmy John's, **food:** Arby's, Dos Reales Mexican, Dunkin Donuts, Great Wall Chinese, KFC, LJ Silver, Real Hacienda Mexican, **lodging:** Day's Inn, Econolodge, **other:** CarX, $General, Home Depot, JoAnn Fabrics, NAPA, Tire Barn, RV/dsl repair, Walgreens |
| **179b a** | I-57, N to Chicago, S to Memphis |
| **174** | Lake of the Woods Rd, Prairieview Rd, **N gas:** BP/dsl, Casey's, Mobil/dsl, **food:** Hideaway Woods Cafe, **other:** Tin Cup Camping, Lake of the Woods SP, **S gas:** Marathon/Subway/dsl, **food:** McDonald's |
| **172** | IL 47, Mahomet, **N other:** R&S RV Sales, **S gas:** BP, Mobil/dsl, Shell/Domino's/dsl, **food:** Arby's, DQ, Esmerelda's, HenHouse Rest., Los Zarapes, Monical's Pizza, Subway, Taco Loco, The Wok, **lodging:** Heritage Inn, **other:** Ace Hardware, Curves, CVS Drug, IGA Foods, NAPA, vet |

## INTERSTATE 74 CONT'D

**E ↕ W**

**B L O O M I N G T O N**

**IL**

| | |
|---|---|
| **166** | Mansfield, **S gas:** BP, **food:** Mansfield Rest. |
| **159** | IL 54, Farmer City, **S gas:** Casey's, Huck's/Quizno's/dsl, **food:** Farmer City Cafe, **lodging:** Budget Motel, Day's Inn, **other:** NAPA, to Clinton Lake RA |
| **156mm** | rest area both lanes, full ♿ facilities, 🚻, 🏕, litter larrels, vending, playground, petwalk |
| **152** | US 136, to Heyworth |
| **149** | Le Roy, **N gas:** Freedom, Love's/Arby's/dsl/scales/24hr, **food:** Jac's Cafe, KFC, McDonald's, Roma Ralph's Pizza, Subway, **other:** Doc's Drug, $General, IGA Foods, NAPA, True Value, to Moraine View SP, **S gas:** Shell/Woody's Rest./dsl/scales/24hr, **lodging:** Super 8, **other:** Clinton Lake, camping |
| **142** | Downs, **N gas:** BP/Pizza/Subs/dsl/24hr, **other:** USPO |
| **135** | US 51, Bloomington, **N gas:** BP/dsl, Huck's, Mobil/dsl, **food:** McDonald's, **other:** Ⓗ HOSPITAL, to IL St U, **S gas:** Marathon/dsl |
| **134b** [157] | Veterans Pkwy, Bloomington, **N gas:** Clark/24hr, FS, **other:** 🛫 |
| **134a** | I-55, N to Chicago, S to St Louis, I-74 E |
| **160b a** [55] | **I-74 and I-55 run together 6 mi. N gas:** BP/Circle K, Freedom/dsl, Pilot/Wendy's/dsl/scales/24hr, Shell, EnergyMart/dsl, TA/dsl/rest./scales/24hr/@, **food:** Arby's, Burger King, Cracker Barrel, Culver's, KFC, McDonald's/playplace, Popeye's, Subway, Taco Bell, **lodging:** Best Inn, Comfort Inn, Days Inn, Econolodge, Hawthorn Suites, La Quinta, Quality Suites, **other:** Ⓗ HOSPITAL, Advance Parts, Blue Beacon, Family$, Morforless Foods, **S gas:** Marathon/Circle K, **food:** Bob Evan's, Greatwall Chinese, Steak'n Shake/24hr, **lodging:** Comfort Suites, Country Inn&Suites, Fairfield Inn, Holiday Inn Express, Ramada Ltd, **other:** Aldi Foods, $tree, F&F/dsl, Radio Shack, Walmart SuperCtr/gas |
| **127** [163] | I-55, N to Chicago, S to St Louis, I-74 W to Peoria |
| **125** | US 150, to Bloomington, Mitsubishi Motorway |
| **123mm** | weigh sta wb |
| **122mm** | weigh sta eb |
| **120** | Carlock, **N gas:** BP/dsl/repair, **S** Kamp Komfort Camping (Apr-Oct) |
| **114.5mm** | rest area both lanes, full ♿ facilities, vending, 🚻, 🏕, litter barrels, petwalk |
| **113.5mm** | Mackinaw River |
| **112** | IL 117, Goodfield, **N gas:** Shell/Subway/dsl, **food:** Busy Corner Rest., **other:** to Timberline RA, Jellystone Camping (1mi), Eureka Coll, Reagan Home |
| **102b a** | Morton, **N gas:** BP/rest/dsl, Casey's, Mobil/Arby's/dsl/scales/24hr, **food:** Burger King, Pizza Ranch, Cracker Barrel, Culver's, Ruby Tuesday, Steak'n Shake, Subway, Taco Bell, **lodging:** Best Western, Comfort Inn, Day's Inn, Quality Inn, Travelodge, **other:** Freightliner, Walmart SuperCtr, **S gas:** Circle K/gas, Shell/Subway/dsl/24hr, **food:** China Dragon, KFC, La Fiesta, Lin's Buffet, McDonald's, Monical's Pizza, Quizno's, **other:** Buick/GMC, Chrysler/Dodge/Jeep, CVS Drug, $Tree, Ford, K-Mart, Kroger |
| **101** | I-155 S, to Lincoln |
| **99** | I-474 W, 🛫 |
| **98** | Pinecrest Dr |
| **96** | 95c (from eb), US 150, IL 8, E Washington St, E Peoria, |

**P E O R I A**

| | |
|---|---|
| **96** | Continued **N gas:** Fast Stop, **food:** Monical's Pizza, **lodging:** Super 8, **other:** O'Reilly Parts |
| **95b** | IL 116, to Metamora, **N gas:** Shell/dsl, **food:** Burger King, **lodging:** Hampton Inn, Paradise Hotel, **other:** casino |
| **95a** | N Main St, Peoria, **S gas:** BP/24hr, **food:** A&W/LJ Silver, Bob Evans, China Buffet, Godfather's Pizza, Hardee's, Subway, **lodging:** Holiday Inn Express, Motel 6, **other:** Aldi Foods, Advance Parts, Curves, CVS Drug, $General, Goodyear/auto, Kohls, Kroger, Walgreens, transmissions/auto repair |
| **94** | IL 40, RiverFront Dr, **S gas:** Hucks/Godfather's/24hr, **food:** Applebee's, Arby's, Buffalo Wild Wings, Chili's, Culver's, Logan's Roadhouse, Lorena'a Mexican, Ming's Rest., Panera Bread, Papa John's, Quizno's, Shlotzky's, Steak'n Shake, Texas Roadhouse, **lodging:** Embassy Suites, **other:** Lowe's Whse, PetsMart, Radio Shack, Walmart SuperCtr |
| **93.5mm** | Illinois River |
| **93b** | US 24, IL 29, Peoria, **N gas:** BP, **S** civic ctr |
| **93a** | Jefferson St, Peoria, **S food:** Chicago Grill, **lodging:** Holiday Inn, Mark Twain Hotel, **other:** to civic ctr |
| **92** | Glendale Ave, Peoria, **S other:** Ⓗ HOSPITAL, downtown |
| **92a** | IL 40 N, Knoxville Ave, Peoria, **S lodging:** Holiday Inn, **other:** Ⓗ HOSPITAL |
| **91** | University St, Peoria |
| **90** | Gale Ave, Peoria, **S gas:** Marathon, **food:** Mikey's Pizza, **other:** to Bradley U |
| **89** | US 150, War Memorial Dr, Peoria, **N on War Memorial... gas:** BP/Circle K, **food:** Arby's, Avanti's Rest., Baskin-Robbins/Dunkin Donuts, Beef O'Brady's, Bob Evans, Cheddar's, Chevy's Mexican, ChuckeCheese, Hometown Buffet, IHOP, Krispy Kreme, Lonestar Steaks, Louie's Rest., McDonald's, Perkins/24hr, Pizza Hut, Red Lobster, Ruby Tuesday, Schlotsky's, Starbucks, Steak'n Shake, Subway, Wendy's, **lodging:** Baymont Inn, Best Western, Comfort Suites, Courtyard, Extended Stay America, Heritage Inn, Ramada, Red Roof Inn, Residence Inn, Sleep Inn, Springhill Suites, Super 8, **other:** AutoZone, Barnes&Noble, Best Buy, Chevrolet, Circuit City, Cub Foods, $Tree, Firestone, JC Penney, Lowe's Whse, Macy's, PetsMart, Pontiac/Cadillac, Sears/auto, Target, Tires+, U-Haul, Walmart, Walgreens, mall, vet |
| **88** | to US 50, War Memorial Dr, same as ex 89 |
| **87b a** | I-474 E, IL 6, N to Chillicothe, **E** 🛫 |
| **82** | Edwards Rd, Kickapoo, **N gas:** Mobil/dsl/service, Shell/Subway/dsl, **food:** Jubilee Café, **other:** craft mall, to Jubilee Coll SP, **S other:** USPO, Wildlife Prairie SP |
| **75** | Brimfield, Oak Hill, **N gas:** Casey's |
| **71** | to IL 78, to Canton, Elmwood |
| **62mm** | rest area both lanes, full ♿ facilities, 🚻, 🏕, litter barrels, vending, petwalk |
| **61.5mm** | Spoon River |
| **54** | IL 97, Lewistown, **N other:** TravL Park Camping (1mi), **S gas:** Mobil/dsl (2mi) |
| **51** | Knoxville, **S gas:** BP/dsl, Phillips 66/Charlie's Subs/dsl/scales, **food:** Hardee's/24hr, McDonald's, **lodging:** Super 8 |
| **48b a** | E Galesburg, Galesburg, **N lodging:** Best Western, **other:** Harley-Davidson, **S gas:** Beck's, BP/Circle K, Mobil/dsl, Phillips 66, **food:** DQ, KFC, Hardee's, |

## INTERSTATE 74 CONT'D

**E ↕ W**

**M O L I N E**

**B E T T E N D O R F**

**48b a** Continued
Jalisco Mexican, McDonald's, Pizza Hut, Subway, Taco Bell, **lodging:** Holiday Inn Express, **other:** Econo Foods, Family$, Firestone, Goodyear, HyVee Foods/gas, Save-A-Lot Foods, Walgreens, to Sandburg Birthplace, Lincoln-Douglas Debates

**46b a** US 34, to Monmouth, **N other:** Nichol's dsl Service, **S other:** HOSPITAL, **1 mi S food:** Buffalo Wild Wings, **other:** Menard's, Walmart SuperCtr

**32** IL 17, Woodhull, **N gas:** BP/dsl, Shell/dsl/scales, **food:** Homestead Rest., Subway, **S other:** Shady Lakes Camping (8mi)

**30mm** rest area wb, full ♿ facilities, vending, ⛱ litter barrels, 🚻 playground, petwalk, RV dump

**28mm** rest area eb, full ♿ facilities, vending, ⛱ litter barrels, 🚻 playground, petwalk, RV dump

**24** IL 81, Andover, **N gas:** Casey's (2mi), camping

**14mm** I-80, E to Chicago, I-80/I-280 W to Des Moines

**8mm** weigh sta wb

**6mm** weigh sta eb

**5b** US 6, Moline, **S gas:** Star Gas/dsl, **food:** McDonald's, Montana Jack's, **lodging:** Country Inn&Suites, Econolodge, Hampton Inn, Holiday Inn, La Quinta, Motel 6, Quality Inn, **other:** ✈

**5a** I-280 W, US 6 W, to Des Moines

**4b a** IL 5, John Deere Rd, Moline, **N gas:** BP, Phillips 66, Star Gas, **food:** Applebee's, Burger King, Carlos O'Kelly's, Culver's, Hungy Hobo, Panera Bread, Ryan's, Shoney's, Starbucks, Steak'n Shake, Subway, Wendy's, **other:** Cadillac, Curves, $Tree, Lowe's Whse, Radio Shack, Ryan's, Staples, Tires+, Toyota/Scion, Volvo, Walmart SuperCtr, **S gas:** BP, **food:** Arby's, Denny's, Dillard's, Garfield's Rest., Gordman's Rest., IHOP, Los Agaves Mexican, LJ Silver/A&W, Miss Mamie's, New Mandarin Chinese, Osaka Japanese, Taco Bell, Wendy's, **lodging:** Best Western, Comfort Inn, Fairfield Inn, Super 8, **other:** Best Buy, Chevrolet, $General, Firestone/auto, Ford/Lincoln/Mercury, Goodyear/auto, Hancock Fabrics, JC Penney, Old Navy, PetCo, Pontiac/Buick/GMC, Sears/auto, Von Maure, Walgeeens, Younkers, mall

**3** 23rd Ave, Moline, **N lodging:** Economy Inn

**2** 7th Ave, Moline, **S gas:** Cenex, **other:** to civic ctr, riverfront

**1** 3rd Ave (from eb), Moline, **S gas:** Cenex, **lodging:** Stony Creek Inn

**0mm** Illinois/Iowa state line, Mississippi River. **Exits 4-1 are in Iowa.**

**4** US 67, Grant St, State St, Bettendorf, **N gas:** BP, Phillips 66/dsl, Shell, **food:** Ross' Rest./24hr, Subway, **lodging:** Traveler Motel, Twin Bridges Motel, **other:** CarQuest, **S food:** Village Inn Rest., **lodging:** City Ctr Motel, **other:** $General

**3** Middle Rd, Locust St, Bettendorf, **S gas:** BP, **food:** Bennigan's, China Taste, Grinders Rest., McDonald's, Starbucks, Subway, **lodging:** Holiday Inn, **other:** HOSPITAL, Home Depot, Marshall's, Schnuck's Foods, Walgreens

**2** US 6 W, Spruce Hills Dr, Bettendorf, **N gas:** BP/dsl, Phillips 66, **food:** Domino's, Old Chicago Pizza,

**2** Continued
**lodging:** Courtyard, Heartland Inn, Ramada Inn, The Lodge Hotel/rest., **other:** U-Haul, **S food:** Applebee's, Burger King, Godfather's, KFC, Panera Bread, Red Lobster, Subway, **lodging:** Day's Inn, Fairfield Inn, La Quinta, **other:** Buick/Pontiac/GMC/Cadillac, Kohl's, Gander Mtn, Gordman's, Kohl's, Lowe's Whse, Sam's Club/gas, st patrol

**1** 53rd St, Hamilton, **N gas:** BP, **food:** Biaggi's Italian, Chili's, Granite City Rest., Red Robin, Ruby Tuesday, TX Roadhouse, **lodging:** Hampton Inn, Staybridge Suites, **other:** HOSPITAL, Borders Books, Harley-Davidson, HyVee Foods, Michael's, Old Navy, TJ Maxx, Walgreens, **S gas:** Phillips 66, **food:** Arby's, Azteca Mexican, China Cafe, DQ, Dynasty Buffet, El Sembrador Mexican, Golden Corral, Hungry Hobo, IHOP, Noodles & Co., Qdoba Mexican, Quizno's, Sonic, Starbucks, Steak'n Shake, Subway, TGIFriday's, Village Inn Rest., Taco Bell, Wendy's, **lodging:** Sleep Inn, **other:** Best Buy, Staples, Target, Walmart SuperCtr/gas

**0mm** I-74 begins/ends on I-80, exit 298. **Exits 1-4 are in Iowa.**

## INTERSTATE 80

**E ↕ W**

| Exit # | Services |
|---|---|
| **163mm** | Illinois/Indiana state line |

**161** US 6, IL 83, Torrence Ave, **N gas:** BP, **food:** Arby's, Burger King, Chili's, Culver's, Dixie Kitchen, Hooters, IHOP, Liang's Garden, New China Buffet, Old Country Buffet, Olive Garden, Rib House, Taco-Burrito's, Wendy's, **lodging:** Comfort Suites, Day's Inn, Extended Stay America, Holiday Inn Express, Howard Johnson Express, Red Roof Inn, Sleep Inn, Super 8, **other:** Best Buy, CarEx, Chrysler/Jeep, $General, Fannie May Candies, Firestone/auto, Home Depot, JustTires, K-Mart, PepBoys, Radio Shack, Ultra Foods, Walmart Super Ctr, **S gas:** Gas for Less, Marathon, Mobil, **food:** China Chef, Burger King, DQ, Dunkin Donuts, Golden Crown Rest., Jonny's K's Cafe, McDonald's/playplace, Mr. Gyro's, Popolono's Italian, Quizno's, Subway, Tuesday Morning, **other:** Auto Clinic, Chevrolet, PetsMart, Saab, Sam's Club, SunRise Foods, Walgreens, vet

**160b** I-94 W, to Chicago, tollway begins wb, ends eb

**160a** IL 394 S, to Danville

**159mm** Oasis, **gas:** Mobil/dsl, **food:** Auntie Annie's, McDonald's, Panda Express, Starbucks, Subway

## INTERSTATE 80 CONT'D

**E ↕ W CHICAGO AREA**

**157** IL 1, Halsted St, **N gas:** Citgo/dsl, Marathon/dsl, **food:** Burger King, Maxwell St Grill, **lodging:** Chicago Southland Hotel, Chicago Park Hotel, Comfort Inn, Econolodge, Hilton Garden, Holiday Inn Express, Regency Inn, **S gas:** Speedway, **food:** Applebee's, Arby's, Boston Mkt, Chili's, Dunkin Donuts, Fannie May Candies, KFC, McDonald's, Panda Express, Popeye's, Quizno's, Starbucks, Subway, Taco Bell, Washington Square Rest., Wendy's, **lodging:** Homewood Hotel, Super 8, **other:** Best Buy, Chevrolet, Discount Tire, $Tree, Firestone/auto, Goodyear/auto, Home Depot, Jewel-Osco, Jo-Ann Fabrics, K-Mart, Menard's, Office Depot, PepBoys, PetCo, Target, TJ Maxx

**156** Dixie Hwy (from eb, no return), **S gas:** Mobil, **food:** Leona's Rest., **other:** golf

**155** I-294 N, Tri-State Tollway, toll plaza

**154** Kedzie Ave (from eb, no return), **N gas:** Speedway, **S** Ⓗ HOSPITAL

**151b a** I-57 (exits left from both directions), N to Chicago, S to Memphis

**148b a** IL 43, Harlem Ave, **N gas:** Speedway/dsl, **food:** Al's Beef, Buffalo Wild Wings, Burger King, Chicago Café, Cracker Barrel, Culver's, Eggi Grill, Papa John's, Papa Luigi's, Quizno's, Wendy's, **lodging:** Comfort Suites, Fairfield Inn, Hampton Inn, Holiday Inn Select, La Quinta, Sleep Inn, Wingate Inn, **S food:** Arby's, Taco Bell, TGIFriday, **other:** Best Buy, Carmax, Kohl's, Michael's, PetsMart, SuperTarget, World Music Theatre, Windy City Camping

**147.5mm** weigh sta wb

**145b a** US 45, 96th Ave, **N food:** Arrenello's Pizza, Arby's, Blackberry's Pancakes, Dunkin Donuts, Quizno's, Silverstar Chinese, Tokyo Steaks, TX Roadhouse, **lodging:** Country Inn Suites, Hilton Garden, **0-3 mi S gas:** BP, Clark, Shell/Circle K/dsl/24hr, **food:** Beggar's Pizza, Burger King, DQ, Denny's, McDonald's, Mindy's Ribs, Morgan's Grill, Rising Sun Chinese, Stoney Pt Grill, Subway, White Castle, Wendy's, **lodging:** Super 8, **other:** Timber View Ctr, Windy City Camping

**143mm** weigh sta eb

**140** SW Hwy, I 355 N Tollway, US 6 S

**137** US 30, New Lenox, **N food:** Williamson's Rest., **other:** K-Mart, **S gas:** Speedway/dsl, **food:** Beggar's Pizza, Burger King, KFC, McDonald's/playplace, Paisono's Pizza, Papa Joe's/LJ Silver, Pizza Hut, Subway, Taco Bell, **other:** Ace Harware, Goodyear/auto, Jewel-Osco/dsl, Walgreens, vet

**134** Briggs St, **N gas:** Speedway, **other:** Ⓗ HOSPITAL, Martin Camping, **S gas:** Citgo/dsl, Valero/dsl, **other:** EZ Lube

**133** Richards St

**132b a** US 52, IL 53, Chicago St

**131.5mm** Des Plaines River

**131** US 6, Meadow Ave, **N** to Riverboat Casino

**130b a** IL 7, Larkin Ave, **N gas:** Citgo/dsl, Clark, Marathon/24hr, Shell/24hr, Speedway, **food:** A&W/KFC, Bellagio Pizzaria, Bob Evans, Burger King, Dunkin Donuts/Baskin-Robbins, DQ, Quizno's, Steak'n Shake, Subway, Taco Bell, Wendy's, White Castle, Yu's Garden, **lodging:**

**JOLIET**

**130b a** Continued
Budget Inn, Comfort Inn, Motel 6, Holiday Inn, Red Roof Inn, Super 8, **other:** Ⓗ HOSPITAL, Chevrolet/Cadillac, Discount Tire, Ford, Goodyear/auto, K-Mart, Radio Shack, Sam's Club/gas, White Hen, Walmart, to Coll of St Francis, vet, **S** auto repair

**127** Houbolt Rd, to Joliet, **N gas:** BP/deli, 7-11, **food:** Burger King, Cracker Barrel, Arby's, Heros Sports Grill, McDonald's, Split-Second Deli, **lodging:** Fairfield Inn, Hampton Inn, Ramada Ltd, **other:** Riverboat Casino

**126b a** I-55, N to Chicago, S to St Louis

**125.5mm** Du Page River

**122** Minooka, **N gas:** Citgo/dsl/24hr, **S gas:** BP/24hr, Pilot/Arby's/scales/dsl/24hr, **food:** DQ, McDonald's/playplace, Subway, Wendy's, **other:** SuperValu Foods

**119mm** rest area wb, full ♿ facilities, vending, Ⓒ, 🖼, litter barrels, playground, petwalk

**117mm** rest area eb, full ♿ facilities, vending, Ⓒ, 🖼, litter barrels, playground, petwalk

**112** IL 47, Morris, **N gas:** BP/Quizno's/scales/dsl/24hr/@, Citgo/dsl, **food:** Bellacino's, Chili's, **lodging:** Comfort Inn, Day's Inn, Holiday Inn Express, **other:** Curves, $General, Menard's, **S gas:** BP, Mobil, Phillips 66, Shell/24hr, **food:** Burger King, Culver's, KFC/LJ Silver, Maria's Ristorante, McDonald's, Morris Diner, Pizza Hut, Subway, Taco Bell, Wendy's, **lodging:** Park Motel, Sherwood Oaks Motel, Super 8, **other:** Aldi Foods, AutoZone, Big R Store, Chevrolet/Buick/Cadillac, Fisher Parts, Ford, Jewel-Osco, Morris Drug, Pontiac/GMC, Radio Shack, Walgreens, Walmart SuperCtr, to Stratton SP, transmissions/repair

**105** to Seneca

**97** to Marseilles, **S gas:** Marathon/Boz Dogs/dsl, **food:** Taco Time, **other:** Four Star Camping, Glenwood Camping (2mi), Prairie Lakes Resort/rest., to Illini SP, RV camping

**93** IL 71, Ottawa, **N gas:** Mobil/24hr, Shell/dsl/24hr, **other:** Skydive Chicago RV Park (2mi), **S food:** Hank's Farm Rest., **other:** Ⓗ HOSPITAL

**92.5mm** Fox River

**90** IL 23, Ottawa, **N gas:** BP/Subway, **food:** Arby's, Cracker Barrel, Quizno's, Taco Bell, **lodging:** Hampton Inn, Holiday Inn Express, **other:** F&F, Ford/Lincoln/Mercury/Kia, Honda, Toyota, Walmart SuperCtr, **S gas:** BP/dsl/LP, Thornton's/dsl **food:** China Inn, Country Kitchen, Dunkin Donuts, Hardee's, KFC/LJ Silver, Starbucks, **lodging:** Budget Inn, Comfort Inn, Sands Motel (2mi), Super 8, Surrey Motel, **other:** HOSPITAL, Aldi Foods, $Tree, Harley-Davidson, Kroger, Radio Shack, USPO

**81** IL 178, Utica, **N gas:** Love's/McDonald's/Subway/scales/dsl/24hr, **other:** Hickory Hollow Camping, KOA (2mi), **S gas:** Shell/Jimmy Johns/dsl, **food:** Duffy's Tavern (2mi), **lodging:** Starved Rock Inn, **other:** to Starved Rock SP

**79b a** I-39, US 51, N to Rockford, S to Bloomington

**77.5mm** Little Vermilion River

**77** IL 351, La Salle, **S gas:** FS/24hr, ⊛FLYING J/Country Mkt/dsl/scales/24hr, **food:** UpTown Grill, **lodging:** Daniels Motel, **other:** st police

**75** IL 251, Peru, **N gas:** BP, Crazy D's/scales/dsl, Shell/dsl/rest./24hr, **food:** Arby's, McDonald's, Pinecone Rest.,

**OTTAWA**

## INTERSTATE 80 CONT'D

**75** Continued
Quizno's, Starbucks, Taco Bell/TCBY, **lodging:** Baymont Inn, Econolodge, Kings Inn, Super 8, **other:** Kohl's, Walmart/SuperCtr, **S gas:** BP, **food:** Applebee's, Culver's, DQ, Dunkin Donuts, IHOP, Master Stir Fry, Pizza Hut, Red Lobster, Steak'n Shake, Subway, Wendy's, **lodging:** Fairfield Inn, La Quinta, **other:** HOSPITAL, AutoZone, BigLots, Buick/Pontiac/GMC, Chevrolet/Nissan/Mercedes, Chrysler/Jeep, Goodyear/auto, Home Depot, HyVee Food/gas, JC Penney, Jo-Ann Fabrics, K-Mart, Marshall's, Menard's, Mitsubishi, Sears/auto, Staples, Target, Toyota/Scion, Walgreens, mall

**73** Plank Rd, **N gas:** Sapp Bros/scales/dsl/@, **food:** Apple Barrel Rest., Burger King/playland, **other:** Kenworth, Volvo Trucks, camping

**70** IL 89, to Ladd, **N gas:** Casey's, **S gas:** BP (3mi), **other:** H HOSPITAL

**61** I-180, to Hennepin

**56** IL 26, Princeton, **N gas:** Road Ranger/Stuckey's/scales/dsl/@, **lodging:** Super 8, **S gas:** Phillips 66, Shell/dsl, **food:** Beck's, Big Apple Rest., Burger King, Country Kitchen, Culver's, KFC, McDonald's, Pizza Hut (1mi), Taco Bell, Wendy's, **lodging:** Day's Inn, Econolodge, Princeton Motel, **other:** HOSPITAL, AutoZone, Chevrolet/Pontiac/Buick/Cadillac, $General, O'Reilly Parts, Pennzoil, Sullivan's Food/gas, Walmart SuperCtr, antiques, vet

**51.5mm** rest area both lanes, full ♿ facilities, 🚻, 🛢, litter barrels, vending, playground, petwalk, RV dump

**45** IL 40, **N lodging:** Day's Inn/Crossroads Rest., **other:** to Ronald Reagan Birthplace (21mi), **S other:** Hennepin Canal SP, camping

**44mm** Hennepin Canal

**33** IL 78, to Kewanee, Annawan, **N gas:** Shabbona RV Ctr/Camp (3mi), **S gas:** Cenex, Mobil/dsl, **food:** Olympic Flame Rest., Phoenix Grill, **lodging:** US Express, **other:** to Johnson-Sauk Tr SP

**27** to US 6, Atkinson, **N gas:** Casey's, Mobil/dsl/rest./24hr

**19** IL 82, Geneseo, **N gas:** BP, Phillips 66/dsl/24hr, Shell, **food:** Culvers, DQ, Hardee's, Happy Joe's Pizza, Genny Dogs, McDonald's, Pizza Hut, Quizno's, Subway, Trapper's Creek, **lodging:** Amerihost, Deck Motel/diner, Super 8 (1mi), **other:** H HOSPITAL, $General, Ford, Jewel-Osco, Walmart/drugs, vet, **S food:** KFC

**10** I-74, I-280, W to Moline, E to Peoria

**9** US 6, to Geneseo, **N food:** Lavender Crest Winery/Cafe, **S other:** Niabi Zoo

**7** Colona, **N gas:** Shell/dsl, **food:** Country Fixins Rest.

**5mm** Rock River

**4a** IL 5, IL 92, W to Silvis, **S other:** to Quad City Downs, Lundeen's Camping

**4b** I-88, IL 92, E to Rock Falls

**2mm** weigh sta both lanes

**1.5mm** Welcome Ctr eb, full ♿ facilities, info, 🚻, 🛢, litter barrels, petwalk, scenic overlook

**1** IL 84, 20th St, Great River Rd, E Moline, **N gas:** BP/diesel, Git-Go, **food:** Brothers Rest., **other:** auto repair, camping, The Great River Rd, **3 mi S gas:** BP, **other:** camping

**0mm** Illinois/Iowa state line, Mississippi River

## INTERSTATE 88

| Exit # | Services |
|---|---|
| **139.5mm** | I-88 begins/ends on I-290. |
| **139** | I-294, S to Indiana, N to Milwaukee |
| **138mm** | toll plaza |

**137** IL 83 N, Cermak Rd, **N food:** Clubhouse rest., Ditkas Rest., McDonald's, **lodging:** Marriott, Renaissance Inn, **other:** Macy's, Nieman-Marcus

**136** IL 83 S, Midwest Rd (from eb), **N gas:** Shell, **food:** Bennigan's, Burger King, Denny's, Dunkin Donuts, Giordano's rest., Jamba Juice, McDonalds, Noodles & Co, Quizno's, Starbucks, Tin Fish, Vic's Steaks, Subway, **lodging:** Holiday Inn, La Quinta, **other:** Costco/gas, Home Depot, Nordstrom's, Old Navy, TJ Maxx, Walgreens, World Mkt

**134** Highland Ave (no EZ wb return), **N food:** Baker's Square, Bouna Beef, Brio Grille, Buca Italian, Burger King, Capital Grille, Champps Grill, Cheeseburger Paradise, Cici's, Claimjumper Rest., Fuddruckers, Grill Room, Hooters, Joe's Crab Shack, Kyoto, Magnum's, McCormick & Schmick's, Olive Garden, Panera Bread, PF Chang's Chinese, Parker's Grill, Potbelly's, Qdoba, Red Lobster, Rockbottom Brewery, Ruby Tuesday, Starbucks, Taylor Brewing Co, TGIFriday, Tortilo's Hotdogs, **lodging:** Amerisuites, Comfort Inn, Embassy Suites, Holiday Inn Express, Homestead Studios, Hyatt Place, Marriott, Red Roof Inn, Westin Hotel, **other:** H HOSPITAL, Best Buy, Circuit City, Firestone/auto, Fry's Electronics, Home Depot, JC Penny, Kohl's, PetsMart, Vonmaur, mall, **S food:** Parkers Ocean Grill

**132** I-355 N (from wb)

**131** I-355 S (from eb)

**130** IL 53 (from wb), **1mi N gas:** BP, Mobil, **food:** McDonald's, **other:** Walmart

**127** Naperville Rd, **N food:** Mullen's Grill, **lodging:** Hilton, Wyndam, **S food:** Buona Beef, Maggiano's, McDonald's, Panera Bread, Pizza Hut, TGIFriday, Wendy's, **lodging:** Best Western, Courtyard, Day's Inn, Exel Inn, Fairfield Inn, Hampton Inn, Holiday Inn Select, **other:** Ford, Jeep, Kia, K-Mart, Office Depot, Radio Shack, Subaru

**125** Winfield Rd, **N gas:** BP, Mobil, **other:** H HOSPITAL, Walgreen, **S food:** Arby's, Al's Italian, Atlanta bread, Buffalo Wild Wings, California Pizza, Chipotle Mexican, Cold Stone Creamery, GoRoma, Max&Erma's, McDonald's, Potbelly's, Red Robin, Rockbottom Brewery,

## INTERSTATE 88 CONT'D

**E↕W**

| | |
|---|---|
| **125** | Continued<br>Starbucks, StirCrazy Grill, **lodging:** Springhill Suites, **other:** SuperTarget, Walgreens |
| **123** | IL 59, **N food:** Riva Steaks/Seafood, **other:** Carmax, **S gas:** BP, Mobil/dsl, Speedway, **food:** Cracker Barrel, Danny's Grill, Dunkin Donuts/Baskin Robbins, Jimmy John's, Lee's Garden, Starbucks, Steak'n Shake, Subway, TX Roadhouse, Wendy's, **lodging:** Extended Stay America, Fairfield Inn, Red Roof Inn, Sleep Inn, SpringHill Suites, Towneplace Suites, **other:** White Hen Pantry |
| **119** | Farnsworth Ave, **N gas:** BP, Shell, **food:** Papa Bear Rest., Quizno's, Starbucks, **lodging:** Fox Valley Inn, Motel 6, **other:** Firestone/auto, Premium Outlets/Famous Brands, **S gas:** Marathon, Phillips 66/dsl, Shell, Speedway, **food:** Dunkin Donuts/Baskin-Robbins, Goody's Drive-Thru, Little Caesars, McDonald's, Mike & Denise's Pizza, Subway, Taco Bell, **other:** AutoZone, Family$, Goodyear, Walgreens, White Hen Pantry |
| **118mm** | toll plaza |
| **117** | IL 31, IL 56, to Aurora, Batavia, **N gas:** Citgo/dsl, Marathon, **food:** A&W, Tastee Freez, **S gas:** Mobil, Thornton's, **food:** Culver's, Denny's, KFC, LJ Silver, McDonald's, Popeye's, Quizno's, Taco Bell, Togo's/Baskin-Robbins/Dunkin Donuts, White Castle, **lodging:** Baymont Inn, **other:** HOSPITAL, AutoZone, Cermac Foods, Firestone, GNC, Jewel/Osco, Murray's Parts, Radio Shack, U-Haul, Walgreens |
| **115** | Orchard Rd, **N other:** Chrysler/Dodge/Jeep, Ford/Lincoln/Mercury, Isuzu, JC Penny, Michaels, NTB, Nissan, PetCo, Pontiac, Saturn, Subaru, Target, **S gas:** 7-11, **food:** A&W/KFC, Chili's, Coldstone, IHOP, Jimmy John's, Panera Bread, Papa Saverio's, Pizza Hut, Quizno's, Starbucks, Wendy's, **lodging:** Hampton Inn, Holiday Inn, **other:** CVS Drug, Discount Tire, Home Depot, Lowe's Whse |
| **114** | IL 56W, to US 30 (from wb, no EZ return), to Sugar Grove |
| **109** | IL 47, Elburn |
| **94** | Peace Rd, to IL 38, **N H** HOSPITAL |
| **93mm** | Dekalb Oasis/24hr both lanes, Dekalb Oasis/24hr both lanes, **gas:** Mobil/dsl, **food:** McDonald's, Panda Express, Subway |
| **93mm** | toll plaza |
| **92** | IL 38, IL 23, Annie Glidden Rd, to DeKalb, **N lodging:** Super 8, **2-3 mi N gas:** BP, Road Ranger/dsl, Marathon, Shell, **food:** Baker's Square, Burger King, Chipotle Mexican, El Burrito Loco, Happy Wok Chinese, Jct Rest., Lukulo's Rest., McDonald's, Papa John's, Potbelly, Pizza Hut, Pizza Villa, Quizno's, Rammy's Subs, Starbucks, Subway, Taco Bell, Tom & Jerry's, Topper's Pizza, Vinny's Pizza, Wendy's, Yen Ching Chinese, **lodging:** Baymont Inn, Best Western, Travelodge, **other:** $General, Ford, Illini Tire, Schnuck's Food/Drug, to N IL U |
| **91mm** | toll plaza |
| **78** | I-39, US 51, S to Bloomington, N to Rockford |
| **76** | IL 251, Rochelle, **N gas:** BP, Casey's, Shell, **other:** HOSPITAL, Dodge, Ford/Mercury, GMC |
| **55** | IL 26, Dixon, **N gas:** BP/Subway/scales/dsl, **food:** Panda Chinese, Pizza Hut, **lodging:** Comfort Inn, |

**DEKALB**

| | |
|---|---|
| **55** | Continued<br>Quality Inn, Super 8, **other:** Walmart/Super Ctr/gas, **1-2 mi N food:** Culver's, Hardee's, **other:** H HOSPITAL, to Ronald Reagan Birthplace, to John Deere HS, to St Parks |
| **54mm** | toll plaza |
| **44** | US 30 (last free exit eb), **N** gas, food, lodging, camping |
| **41** | IL 40, to Sterling, Rock Falls, **1-2 mi N gas:** Marathon, Mobil/24hr, Shell/deli, **food:** Arby's, Arthur's Deli, Burger King, Candlelight Rest., Culver's, El Tapatio Mexican, First Wok Chinese, Hardee's, KFC, McDonald's/playplace, Pizza Hut, Red Apple Rest., Subway, **lodging:** All Seasons Motel, Candlelight Inn, Country Inn Suites, Holiday Inn, Super 8, **other:** H HOSPITAL, AutoZone, Country Mkt Foods, Curves, $General, Goodyear/auto, Harley-Davidson, O'Reilly Parts, Sav-A-Lot, Walgreens, Walmart |
| **36** | to US 30, Rock Falls, Sterling |
| **26** | IL 78, to Prophetstown, Morrison, **N other:** to Morrison-Rockwood SP, **S gas:** Conoco/dsl (3mi) |
| **18** | to Albany, Erie |
| **10** | to Port Byron, Hillsdale, **S gas:** Phillips 66/dsl, Shell/Mama J's Rest./scales/dsl/24hr |
| **6** | IL 92 E, to Joslin, **N food:** Jammerz Roadhouse (2mi), **S other:** Sunset Lake Camping (1mi) |
| **2** | Former IL 2 |
| **1b a** | I-80, W to Des Moines, E to Chicago |
| **0mm** | I-88 begins/ends on I-80, exit 4b. IL 5, IL 92, W to Silvis, to Quad City Downs, Lundeen's Camping |

## INTERSTATE 90

**E↕W**

| Exit # | Services |
|---|---|
| **0mm** | Illinois/Indiana state line, Chicago Skyway Toll Rd begins/ends |
| **1mm** | US 12, US 20, 106th St, Indianapolis Blvd, **N gas:** Citgo, Mobil, Shell/dsl, **other:** casino, **S food:** Burger King, KFC, McDonald's, **other:** Aldi Foods, Jewel-Osco, auto repair |
| **2.5mm** | **gas:** Skyway Oasis, **food:** McDonald's, **other:** toll plaza |
| **3mm** | 87th St (from wb) |
| **4mm** | 79th St, services along 79th St and Stoney Island Ave |
| **5.5mm** | 73rd St (from wb) |
| **6mm** | State St (from wb), **S gas:** Citgo |
| **7mm** | I-94 N (mile markers decrease to IN state line), |
| | **I-90 E and I-94 E run together. See Interstate 94 - exits 43b-59a** |
| **84** | I-94 W Lawrence Ave, **N gas:** BP |
| **83b a** | Foster Ave (from wb), **N gas:** BP, **food:** Checker's, Dunkin Donuts, **other:** Firestone/auto, Goodyear/auto, Walgreen |
| **82c** | Austin Ave, to Foster Ave |
| **82b** | Byrn-Mawr (from wb) |
| **82a** | Nagle Ave |
| **81b** | Sayre Ave (from wb) |
| **81a** | IL 43, Harlem Ave, **S gas:** BP, Shell |
| **80** | Canfield Rd (from wb), **N other:** Walgreen |
| **79b a** | IL 171 S, Cumberland Ave, **N gas:** 7-11, Marathon, **food:** Hooters, McDonald's, Outback Steaks, Starbucks, **lodging:** Holiday Inn, Marriott, SpringHill Suites, Westin Hotel, **other:** Dominick's Foods, **S food:** Bennigan's, **lodging:** Ramada, Renaissance |

**CHICAGO AREA**

# INTERSTATE 90 CONT'D

**E / W**

**CHICAGO AREA**

| | |
|---|---|
| **0mm** | River Road Plaza, **N food:** McDonald's, **lodging:** Marriott, Westin Hotel, **S** Hyatt (mile markers increase to Rockford) |
| **1mm** | I-294, I-190 W, to O'Hare ✈ |
| **2mm** | IL 72, Lee St (from wb), **N lodging:** Extended Stay America, Quality Inn, Wyndham, **S food:** McDonald's, **lodging:** Best Western, Holiday Inn Express, Holiday Inn Select, Sheraton Gateway, Studio+ |
| **5mm** | Des Plaines Oasis both lanes...**gas:** Mobil/dsl/24hr, **food:** McDonald's/24hr, Panda Express, Starbucks, Subway |
| **6mm** | Elmhurst Rd (from wb), **S gas:** Marathon, McDonald's/playplace, **lodging:** Best Western, Comfort Inn, Day's Inn, La Quinta, Microtel |
| **7.5mm** | Arlington Hts Rd, **N** on Algonqui **gas:** Shell, **food:** Arby's, Baja Fresh, Birch River Grill, Buona Beef, Chicago Pizza, Chili's, Chipotle Mexican, Denny's, Honey Baked Ham, Magnum Steaks, McDonald's, Panda Express, Pappadeaux Rest., Potbelly's, Steak'n Shake, Subway, Yanni's Greek Rest., **lodging:** AmeriSuites, Courtyard, DoubleTree, Motel 6, Radisson, Red Roof Inn, Jameson Suites, Sheraton, **other:** Lowe's Whse, Meijer, NTB, Sam's Club, Staples, Walmart, vet, **S lodging:** Sheraton |
| **11mm** | I-290, IL 53, **N lodging:** Embassy Suites, Holiday Inn, Renaissance Inn, **other:** mall, **S lodging:** Amerisuites, Extended Stay America, Residence Inn |
| **13mm** | Roselle Rd (from wb), **N** Medieval Times, **S lodging:** Extended Stay America, **other:** BMW/Mini |
| **16mm** | Barrington Rd (from wb), **N lodging:** Hilton Garden, **1 mi S lodging:** Hampton Inn, Hyatt Place, **other:** U-Haul |
| **19mm** | IL 59, **N food:** Buffalo Wild Wings, **lodging:** Marriott, **other:** Cabela's, Michael's, PetsMart, Target, to Poplar Creek Music Theatre |
| **21mm** | Beverly Rd (from wb) |
| **22mm** | IL 25, **N food:** Milk Pail Rest., **lodging:** Day's Inn, **S gas:** BP, Citgo, Shell, Speedway/dsl, **food:** Arby's, Baker Hill Pancakes, Subway, Wendy's, **other:** Ⓗ HOSPITAL, NAPA |
| **24mm** | IL 31 N, **N gas:** BP, Thornton's/dsl, **food:** Alexander's Rest., Dunkin Donuts/Baskin-Robbins, **lodging:** Courtyard, Hampton Inn, Holiday Inn, Quality Inn, Super 8, TownePlace Suites |
| **25mm** | toll plaza, Ⓒ |
| **27mm** | Randall Rd, **N food:** Jimmy's Charhouse, **food:** Big Sammy's Hot Dogs, Henessey Rest., Jimmy John's, Panera Bread, Pizza & Pub, Starbucks, **lodging:** Comfort Inn, Country Inn Suites, **S Ⓗ** HOSPITAL |
| **32mm** | IL 47 (from wb), to Woodstock, **N other:** Prime Outlets/famous brands, Chevrolet |
| **37mm** | US 20, Marengo, **N gas:** Mobil/Arrowhead Rest/Chester's/dsl/scales/24hr/@, Road Ranger/dsl/scales, TA/BP/Burger King/Popeye's/scales/dsl/rest./24hr/@, **food:** McDonald's, Wendy's, **lodging:** Super 8, **other:** Trav-L Park, museums, to Prime Outlets at exit 32 (6mi) |
| **41mm** | Marengo-Hampshire toll plaza, Ⓒ |
| **53mm** | Genoa Rd, to Belvidere, **N food:** Applebee's, Arby's, Quizno's, Rosatis, Starbucks, Thai Basil, **other:** Walmart SuperCtr/gas, camping |
| **55mm** | Belvidere Oasis both lanes...**gas:** Mobil/dsl/24hr, **food:** Food Court, McDonald's/24hr, Starbucks, Subway, Taco Bell, Ⓒ |

**ROCKFORD**

| | |
|---|---|
| **56mm** | toll plaza |
| **60.5mm** | Kishwaukee River |
| **61mm** | I-39 S, US 20, US 51, to Rockford, **S** funpark |
| **63mm** | US 20, State St, **N gas:** Mobil, Phillips 66/Subway/dsl, **food:** Cracker Barrel, **lodging:** Baymont Inn, Clocktower Resort, Exel Inn, **S gas:** Road Ranger/dsl, Mobil/dsl, **food:** Applebee's, Atlanta Bread Co, Burger King, Caribou Coffee, Cheddar's, Chili's, Damon's, Denny's, Don Pablo, Dos Reales, Gerry's Pizza, Giovanni's Rest., Hong Kong Buffet, IHOP, KFC, Lino's Pizza, LoneStar Steaks, Machine Shed Rest., McDonald's, Old Chicago Grill, Old Country Buffet, Olive Garden, Outback Steaks, Panda Express, Panino's Drive-Thru, Perkins, PotBelly, Quizno's, Red Lobster, Red Robin, Ruby Tuesday, Starbucks, Steak'n Shake, Subway, Taco Bell, ThunderBay Grille, Tom & Jerry's, Tumbleweed Grill, Tuesday Morning, TX Roadhouse, Uncle Nick's, Wendy's, **lodging:** Candlewood Suites, Comfort Inn, Courtyard, Extended Stay America, Fairfield Inn, Hampton Inn, Hilton Garden, Holiday Inn, Motel 6, Quality Suites, Radisson, Red Roof Inn, Residence Inn, Sleep Inn, Staybridge Suites, Studio+, Super 8, **other:** Ⓗ HOSPITAL, Advance Parts, Aldi Foods, Barnes&Noble, Best Buy, Borders Books, Buick/Pontiac/GMC, Circuit City, Dodge, $Tree, Hancock Fabrics, Home Depot, Jo-Ann Fabrics, K-Mart, Kohl's, Lexus, Lowe's Whse, Marshalls, Michael's, Office Depot, Old Time Pottery, Old Navy, PepBoys, PetsMart, Radio Shack, Sam's Club, Saturn, Target/drug, TJ Maxx, Toyota/Scion, Walgreens, Walmart SuperCtr, World Mkt |
| **66mm** | E Riverside Blvd, Loves Park, **1-2 mi S gas:** BP/24hr, Mobil/dsl, Phillips 66/dsl, Road Ranger/Subway/dsl, Shell, **food:** Arby's, Basil Café, BeefARoo, Burger King, Culver's, DQ, Happy Joe's Pizza, KFC, McDonald's, Sam's Ristorante, Subway, Thai Cuisine, Wendy's, **lodging:** Day's Inn, Holiday Inn Express, **other:** Audi/Honda/Jaguar/Mercedes, Autoworks, Farm&Fleet, Walgreens, to Rock Cut SP, funpark |
| **70mm** | Il 173, new exit |
| **75.5mm** | tollbooth, Ⓒ (mile markers decrease from W to E to Chicago) |
| **3** | Rockton Rd, **S gas:** Love's/Hardee's/dsl/scales/24hr |
| **1.5mm** | Welcome Ctr/rest area eb, full ♿ facilities, info, 🏕, litter barrels, Ⓒ, petwalk, playground, RV dump |
| **1** | US 51 N, IL 75 W, S Beloit, **S gas:** Road Ranger/McDonald's/dsl, **S gas:** BP/dsl, Road Ranger/Beef a Roo/Subway/scales/dsl/24hr, ✦ FLYING J/Country Mkt/ |

## INTERSTATE 90 CONT'D

| | |
|---|---|
| **1** | Continued<br>scales/dsl/24hr, **lodging:** Best Western, Knight's Inn, **other:** Ford/Lincoln/Mercury, GMC, Pearl Lake camping (2mi) |
| **0mm** | Illinois/Wisconsin state line |

## INTERSTATE 94

| Exit # | Services |
|---|---|
| **77mm** | Illinois/Indiana state line |
| **161** | US 6, IL 83, Torrence Ave |
| **I-94 and I-80 run together 3 mi. See Interstate 80 exit 161.** | |
| **74b** [160] | I-80/I-294 W |
| **74a** | IL 394 S to Danville |
| **73b a** | US 6,159th St, **N** food: Fuddrucker's, Outback Steaks, **other:** Chevrolet, Honda, Lincoln/Mercury, Nissan/Hyundai, Target, Tire Barn, Toyota, **S** gas: Marathon, **food:** Fannie May Candies, Subway, **lodging:** Cherry Lane Motel, **other:** Aldi Foods, Buick/Pontiac, Ford, Stanfa Tire/auto |
| **71b a** | Sibley Blvd, **N** gas: Citgo, Mobil/dsl, **food:** McDonald's, Nicky's Gyros, Popeye's, Subway, **lodging:** Baymont Inn, **other:** Dominick's Foods, **S** gas: BP, Shell, **food:** Dusty's Buffet, Wendy's, White Castle |
| **70b a** | Dolton |
| **69** | Beaubien Woods (from eb), Forest Preserve |
| **68b a** | 130th St |
| **66b** | 115th St, **S** food: McDonald's |
| **66a** | 111th Ave, **S** gas: BP, Shell, **other:** Firestone |
| **65** | 103rd Ave, Stony Island Ave |
| **63** | I-57 S |
| **62** | **N** gas: Citgo, Mobil, **food:** Subway |
| **61b** | 87th St, **N** gas: BP, Shell, **food:** Burger King, McDonald's, **S** other: Best Buy, Home Depot, Jewel-Osco, Marshall's |
| **61a** | 83rd St (from eb), **N** gas: Shell, **other:** st police |
| **60c** | 79th St, **N** gas: BP, Mobil, Shell, **other:** Walgreens, **S** gas: Citgo/dsl, **food:** Church's |
| **60b** | 76th St, **N** gas: BP, Mobil, Shell, **other:** Walgreen/24hr, **S** food: KFC, Popeye's |
| **60a** | 75th St (from eb), **N** gas: BP, Mobil, Shell, **S** food: KFC, Pizza Hut, Popeye's, **other:** Walgreens |
| **59c** | 71st St, **N** gas: Citgo, **S** food: McDonald's |
| **59a** | I-90 E, to Indiana Toll Rd |
| **58b** | 63rd St (from eb), **N** gas: Citgo, **S** gas: Mobil |
| **58a** | I-94 divides into local and express, 59th St, **S** gas: BP |
| **57b** | Garfield Blvd, **N** food: Checker's, Popeye's, Subway, **other:** Trak Auto, Walgreens, **S** gas: Mobil, Shell/24hr, **food:** Wendy's, **other:** H HOSPITAL |
| **57a** | 51st St, **N** food: McDonald's |
| **56b** | 47th St (from eb) |
| **56a** | 43rd St, **S** gas: Citgo/dsl, Econo/dsl |
| **55b** | Pershing Rd |
| **55a** | 35th St, **S** to New Comiskey Park |
| **54** | 31st St |
| **53c** | I-55, Stevenson Pkwy, N to downtown, Lakeshore Dr |
| **53b** | I-55, Stevenson Pkwy, S to St Louis |
| **52c** | 18th St, **N** other: Dominick's Foods |
| **52b** | Roosevelt Rd, Taylor St (from wb), **N** gas: Citgo |
| **52a** | Taylor St, Roosevelt Rd (from eb), **N** gas: Citgo |
| **51h-i** | I-290 W, to W Suburbs |

**CHICAGO AREA**

| | |
|---|---|
| **51g** | E Jackson Blvd, downtown |
| **51f** | W Adams St, downtown |
| **51e** | Monroe St (from eb), downtown, **S** lodging: Quality Inn, **other:** Walgreens |
| **51d** | Madison St (from eb), downtown, **S** lodging: Crowne Plaza, **other:** Dominick's Foods, Walgreens |
| **51c** | E Washington Blvd, downtown |
| **51b** | W Randolph St, downtown |
| **51a** | Lake St (from wb) |
| **50b** | E Ohio St, downtown, **S** gas: Marathon |
| **50a** | Ogden Ave |
| **49a b** | Augusta Blvd, Division St, **N** other: Lexus, Mercedes, **S** gas: BP, Shell, **food:** Pizza Hut |
| **48b** | IL 64, North Ave, **N** gas: BP, **other:** Home Depot, **S** gas: Valero |
| **48a** | Armitage Ave, **N** other: Best Buy, Kohl's, **S** gas: Shell, **other:** Jaguar, Land Rover, Volvo |
| **47c b** | Damen Ave, **N** gas: Citgo, car/vanwash |
| **47a** | Western Ave, Fullerton Ave, **N** gas: Citgo, **food:** Burger King, Dunkin Donuts, Popeye's, Starbucks, Subway, **other:** Circuit City, Costco/gas, Cub Foods, Home Depot, Jo-Ann Fabrics, Pepboys, PetsMart, Staples, Target, **S** gas: Marathon |
| **46b a** | Diversey Ave, California Ave, **N** gas: Citgo, **S** food: IHOP/24hr, Popeye's |
| **45c** | Belmont Ave, **N** food: Wendy's |
| **45b** | Kimball Ave, **N** gas: Marathon/dsl, **S** gas: Valero, **food:** Dunkin Donuts, Pizza Hut, Subway, **other:** Delray Farms Foods, Radio Shack, Walgreens |
| **45a** | Addison St (from eb) |
| **44b** | Pulaski Ave, Irving Park Rd, **N** gas: BP, Mobil |
| **44a** | IL 19, Keeler Ave, Irving Park Rd, **N** gas: BP, Shell/24hr, **other:** to Wrigley Field |
| **43c** | Montrose Ave |
| **43b** | I-90 W |
| **43a** | Wilson Ave |
| **42** | W Foster Ave (from wb), **S** gas: Citgo, Marathon |
| **41mm** | Chicago River, N Branch |
| **41c** | IL 50 S, to Cicero, to I-90 W |
| **41b a** | US 14, Peterson Ave, **N** other: Whole Foods Mkt |
| **39b a** | Touhy Ave, **N** gas: BP/dsl, Shell, **other:** Cassidy Tire, Toyota/Scion, **S** gas: BP, Citgo, Shell, **food:** Baja Fresh, Baskin-Robbins/Dunkin Donuts, Buffalo Wild Wings, Burger King, Chili's, Chipotle Mexican, ChuckeCheese, Jack's Rest./24hr, McDonald's, Noodles&Co, Outback Steaks, Quizno's, Sander's Rest., Starbucks, Subway, **lodging:** Holiday Inn, **other:** Barnes&Noble, Best Buy, Circuit City, GNC, Jewel-Osco, Lee's Auto Parts, Nissan, Office Depot, PepBoys, PetCo, Radio Shack, Walgreens, Walmart, vet |
| **37b a** | IL 58, Dempster St |
| **35** | Old Orchard Rd, **N** gas: BP, Shell, **food:** Bloomingdale's, California Pizza Kitchen, Cheese Factory, McCormick&Schmick's Seafood, **other:** HOSPITAL, Nissan, mall, **S** food: Ruby Tuesday, **lodging:** Extended Stay America, Hampton Inn |
| **34c b** | E Lake Ave, **N** gas: BP, **food:** Omaha Steaks, Panda Express, Starbucks, **other:** Borders Books, GNC, **S** gas: BP, Shell, **food:** DQ |

**CHICAGO AREA**

## INTERSTATE 94 CONT'D

E ↕ W

| | |
|---|---|
| **34a** | US 41 S, Skokie Rd (from eb) |
| **33b a** | Willow Rd, **S** **gas:** BP, Shell, **food:** Starbucks, **other:** Dominick's Foods, Walgreens |
| **31E** | Tower Rd, **S** **other:** BMW, Carmax, Chrysler/Dodge/ Jeep, Infiniti, Mercedes, Toyota/Scion, vet |
| **30b a** | Dundee Rd (from wb, no EZ return), **S** **gas:** Citgo, Marathon, **food:** Barnaby's Rest., Morton's Steaks, Potbelly's, Ruth's Chris Steaks, Starbucks, **lodging:** Renaissance |
| **29** | US 41, to Waukegan, to Tri-state tollway |
| **50mm** | IL 43, Waukegan Rd, **N** **gas:** BP, Shell, **food:** Baja Fresh, Old Country Buffet, **lodging:** Red Roof Inn, Embassy Suites, **other:** Best Buy, Borders Books, Home Depot, Jewel-Osco, NTB, Steinmart, TJ Maxx |
| **53mm** | I-294 S, Lake-Cook Rd (from sb), **E** **food:** J-Alexander's Rest., **lodging:** Hyatt |
| **53.5mm** | Deerfield Rd toll plaza, [¢] |
| **54mm** | Deerfield Rd (from nb), **W** **gas:** Mobil, **lodging:** Marriott Suites |
| **56mm** | IL 22, Half Day Rd, **E** **lodging:** La Quinta |
| **59mm** | IL 60, Town Line Rd, **E** [H] HOSPITAL, **W** **lodging:** Hilton Garden, Residence Inn |
| **60mm** | **Lake Forest Oasis both lanes...E** **gas:** Mobil/dsl, **food:** KFC, McDonald's, Panda Express, Starbucks, Subway, Taco Bell, **other:** info |
| **62mm** | IL 176, Rockland Rd (no nb re-entry), **E** **other:** Harley-Davidson, to Lamb's Farm |
| **64mm** | IL 137, Buckley Rd, **E** **other:** to VA [H] HOSPITAL, Chicago Med School |
| **67mm** | IL 120 E, Belvidere Rd (no nb re-entry), **E** [H] HOSPITAL |
| **68mm** | IL 21, Milwaukee Ave (from eb, no sb re-entry), **E** **food:** Papa John's, **other:** [H] HOSPITAL, Six Flags |
| **70mm** | IL 132, Grand Ave, **E** **gas:** Speedway/dsl, **food:** Baskin-Robbins/Dunkin Donuts, Burger King, ChuckeCheese, Cracker Barrel, Culver's, Golden Corral, Ichibahn, IHOP, Joe's Crabshack, Jimmy John's, Krispy Kreme, McDonald's, Moe's SW Grill, Monkey Dish Grill, Oberweiss, Old Chicago Red Hots, Olive Garden, Outback Steaks, Subway, **lodging:** Comfort Suites, Country Inn&Suites, Grand Hotel, Extended Stay America, Hampton Inn, La Quinta, **other:** Six Flags Park, **W** **gas:** Shell, **food:** Applebee's, Bakers Square, Boston Mkt, Chicago Grill, Chili's, Denny's, LoneStar Steaks, Max&Erma's, McDonald's, Noodles&Co, Panda Express, Panera Bread, Pizza Hut, Potbelly's, Quizno's, Red Lobster, Ruby Tuesday, Starbucks, Steak'n Shake, Taco Bell, TGIFriday, Wendy's, White Castle, **lodging:** Comfort Inn, Fairfield Inn, Holiday Inn, **other:** AutoZone, Bass Pro Shops, Borders, Buick/GMC/Pontiac, Circuit City, Dodge, Dominick's Foods, Firestone/auto, Gurnee Mills Outlet Mall/famous brands, Home Depot, Honda, Hyundai, JC Penney, Jewel-Osco, Kohl's, Menard's, Michaels, Nissan, Old Navy, PetsMart, Radio Shack, Sam's Club, Saturn, Sears/auto, Target/drugs, TJ Maxx, VW, Walgreens, Walmart/drugs, World Mkt |
| **73mm** | Waukegan toll plaza, Waukegan toll plaza, [¢] |
| **76mm** | IL 173 (from nb, no return), Rosecrans Ave, **E** to IL Beach SP |
| **1b** | US 41 S, to Waukegan, **E** **other:** Sky Harbor RV Ctr |

C H I C A G O  A R E A

| | |
|---|---|
| **1a** | Russell Rd, **W** **gas:** Citgo/dsl/scales/24hr, TA/Country Pride/dsl/scales/24hr/@, **other:** Peterbilt |
| **0mm** | Illinois/Wisconsin state line |

## INTERSTATE 255 - ST LOUIS

| Exit # | Services |
|---|---|
| **I-255** | begins/ends on I-270, exit 7. |
| **30** | I-270, W to Kansas City, E to Indianapolis |
| **29** | IL 162, to Glen Carbon, to Pontoon Beach, Granite City |
| **26** | Horseshoe Lake Rd, **E** st police |
| **25b a** | I-55/I-70, W to St Louis, E to Chicago, Indianapolis |
| **24** | Collinsville Rd, **E** **gas:** BP/24hr, **food:** Jack-in-the-Box, **other:** Shop'n Save, **W** Fairmount Racetrack |
| **20** | I-64, US 50, W to St Louis, E to Louisville, services **1 mi** E off I-64, exit 9. |
| **19** | State St, E St Louis, **E** **gas:** Clark, **lodging:** Western Inn, **other:** Holten SP |
| **17b a** | IL 15, E St Louis, to Belleville, Centreville, **E** ⊕ FLYING J/CountryMkt/dsl/scales/24hr |
| **15** | Mousette Lane, **E** [H] HOSPITAL, **W** **other:** GMC/Volvo Trucks |
| **13** | IL 157, to Cahokia, **E** **gas:** Casey's, **W** **gas:** BP/24hr, QT, **food:** Burger King, Capt D's, China Express, DQ, Domino's, Hardee's, KFC, McDonald's, Pizza Hut, Ponderosa, Popeye's, Rally's, Taco Bell, **lodging:** Holiday Inn Express, **other:** Advance Parts, Aldi Foods, AutoZone, CarQuest, $General, GMC/Pontiac, Goodyear/auto, Schnuck's, Walgreen, Walmart/drugs, Cahokia RV Parque (2mi) |
| **10** | IL 3 N, to Cahokia, E St Louis, **W** **gas:** Shell |
| **9** | to Dupo |
| **6** | IL 3 S, to Columbia, **E** **gas:** Citgo, Shell/24hr, **other:** Chevrolet |
| **4mm** | Missouri/Illinois state line, Mississippi River |
| **3** | Koch Rd |
| **2** | MO 231, Telegraph Rd, **N** **gas:** Shell, **food:** Hardee's, McDonald's, Pizza Hut/Taco Bell, Steak'n Shake, **other:** Dierberg's Foods, $Tree, Walmart SuperCtr, Jefferson Barracks Nat Cem, **S** **gas:** CFM/dsl, **food:** DQ |
| **1d c** | US 50, US 61, US 67, Lindbergh Blvd, Lemay Ferry Rd, accesses same as I-55 exit 197 E, **N** **gas:** Phillips 66, **food:** Arby's, ChuckeCheese, Dillard's, Honey Baked Ham, Hooters, KFC, Krispy Kreme, Macaroni Grill, Noodle's & Co, Qdoba Mexican, Quizno's, Station Subs, Steak'n Shake, St Louis Bread Co, Subway, Tucker's Place, **other:** Advance Parts, Best Buy, Border's Book, Circuit City, Costco/gas, Dillard's, Discount Tire, |

N ↕ S

E A S T  S T  L O U I S

**N**
**↕**
**S**

**E**
**↕**
**W**

**IL**

**C
H
I
C
A
G
O

A
R
E
A**

## INTERSTATE 255 CONT'D - ST LOUIS

| | |
|---|---|
| **1d c** | Continued |
| | Dodge, Ford, Home Depot, JC Penny, Kia, K-Mart, Macy's, Marshall's, NTB, Sears/auto, Tuesday Morning, mall, **S** gas: Phillips 66, **food:** Jack-in-the-Box, McDonald's, Rich & Charlie's Italian, White Castle, **other:** BigLots, $General, Firestone, Old Navy, PetsMart, Sam's Club/gas, Walgreens |
| **1b a** | I-55 S to Memphis, N to St Louis. I-255 begins/ends on I-55, exit 196. |

## INTERSTATE 270 - ST LOUIS

### See Missouri Interstate 270 (St Louis)

## INTERSTATE 294 - CHICAGO

| Exit # | Services |
|---|---|
| **I-294** | begins/ends on I-94, exit 74. Numbering descends from west to east. |
| **I-294 & I-80 run together 5 mi. See Interstate 80 exits 155-160** | |
| **160b** | I-94 W, to Chicago, tollway begins wb, ends eb |
| **160a** | IL 394 S, to Danville |
| **159mm** | Oasis, **gas:** Mobil/dsl, **food:** Burger King, TCBY |
| **157** | IL 1, Halsted St, **N** gas: Citgo/dsl, Clark, Marathon/dsl, **food:** Burger King, Yellow Ribbon Rest., **lodging:** Best Western, Comfort Inn, Econolodge, Hilton Garden, Holiday Inn Express, Motel 6, Park Inn, **S** gas: Shell, Speedway, **food:** Applebee's, Arby's, Boston Mkt, Dunkin Donuts, Fannie May Candies, KFC, McDonald's, Popeye's, Shooter's Buffet, Subway, Taco Bell, Washington Square Rest., Wendy's, **lodging:** Rodeway Inn, Super 8, Villager Lodge, **other:** Chevrolet, $Tree, Firestone/auto, Goodyear/auto, Home Depot, Jewel-Osco, K-Mart, PepBoys, Target |
| **156** | Dixie Hwy (from eb), **S** golf |
| **155** | I-294 N, Tri-State Tollway, toll plaza |
| **5mm** | I-80 W, access to I-57 |
| **5.5mm** | 167th St, toll booth, **C** |
| **6mm** | US 6, 159th St, **E** gas: BP, Citgo, Mobil, Shell, **other:** Aldi Foods, AutoZone, Walgreen, **W** gas: Clark, Marathon, **food:** Burger King, Dunkin Donuts/Baskin-Robbins, Hung's Garden Chinese, KFC/Pizza Hut, Popeye's, Taco Bell, USA Rest., White Castle, **lodging:** Holiday Inn Express, **other:** Firestone/auto, Radio Shack, U-Haul, Walgreen |
| **11mm** | Cal Sag Channel |
| **12mm** | IL 50, Cicero Ave, **E** gas: Citgo/7-11, Speedway, **food:** Onion Field Rest., **W** gas: BP, Gas City/Subway/dsl/24hr, **food:** Boston Mkt, IHOP, Pizza Hut, Pizzaria Uno, Popeye's, Portillo's Dogs, Quizno's, Starbucks, **lodging:** Baymont Inn, Hampton Inn, **other:** Best Buy, Dominick's Foods, NTB, PepBoys, Sears/auto |
| **18mm** | US 12/20, 95th St, **E** gas: Clark, **food:** Bennigan's, McDonald's, Papa John's, **other:** H HOSPITAL, Buick, Honda, Mazda, Sears/auto, mall, **W** gas: Citgo/7-11, Shell, Speedway/dsl, **food:** Arby's, Burger King, Denny's, George's Rest., Quizno's, Schoop's Burgers, Wendy's, **lodging:** Exel Inn, **other:** H HOSPITAL, Jewel-Osco, Walgreen |
| **20mm** | toll booth, **C** |

**C
H
I
C
A
G
O

A
R
E
A**

**E
↕
W

P
E
O
R
I
A**

| | |
|---|---|
| **22mm** | 75th St, Willow Springs Rd |
| **23mm** | I-55, Wolf Rd, to Hawthorne Park |
| **25mm** | Hinsdale Oasis both lanes, **gas:** Mobil/dsl, **food:** Baskin-Robbins, Wendy's/24hr |
| **28mm** | US 34, Ogden Ave, **E** zoo, **W** gas: BP, Shell/deli, **food:** Dunkin Donuts, McDonald's, Starbucks, **other:** H HOSPITAL, Audi/Porsche, Firestone/auto, LandRover, Maserati, Rolls-Royce/Bentley/Ferrari/Lotus, Wild Oats Mkt |
| **28.5mm** | Cermak Rd (from sb, no return) |
| **29mm** | I-88 tollway |
| **30mm** | toll booth, **C** |
| **31mm** | IL 38, Roosevelt Rd (no EZ nb return), **E** gas: Citgo/dsl, **lodging:** Hillside Manor Motel |
| **32mm** | I-290 W, to Rockford (from nb) |
| **34mm** | I-290 (from sb), to Rockford |
| **38mm** | O'Hare Oasis both lanes, **gas:** Mobil/dsl, **food:** Burger King, TCBY |
| **39mm** | IL 19 W (from sb), Irving Park Rd, **E** gas: Clark, Marathon/dsl, **other:** 7-11, Walgreen, **1 mi E** gas: BP/repair, Clark, **food:** DQ, Dunkin Donuts, McDonald's, Subway, Wendy's, **lodging:** Comfort Suites, **other:** Aldi Foods, **W** lodging: Candlewood Suites, Day's Inn, Hampton Inn, Howard Johnson, Sheraton |
| **40mm** | I-190 W, **E** services from I-90, exit 79...gas: Mobil, **food:** McDonald's, **lodging:** Courtyard, Doubletree, Embassy Suites, Holiday Inn, Hotel Softel, Hyatt, Marriott, Radisson, Rosemont Suites, Westin |
| **41mm** | toll booth, **C** |
| **42mm** | Touhy Ave, **W** gas: Mobil/service, **food:** Tiffany's Rest., **lodging:** Comfort Inn |
| **43mm** | Des Plaines River |
| **44mm** | Dempster St (from nb, no return), **E** H HOSPITAL, **W** food: Dunkin Donuts, Subway |
| **46mm** | IL 58, Golf Rd, **E** gas: Citgo/dsl, Shell, **food:** Omega Rest., Senoya Oriental, **other:** Best Buy, CVS Drug, Golf Mill Mall, Target, auto repair |
| **49mm** | Willow Rd, **W** food: TGIFriday, **lodging:** Baymont Inn, Doubletree Suites, Courtyard, Fairfield Inn, Motel 6, **1 mi W on Milwaukee...gas:** BP, **food:** Burger King, Denny's, McDonald's, **lodging:** Wingate Inn |
| **53mm** | Lake Cook Rd (no nb re-entry), **E** Hyatt, **lodging:** Embassy Suites |
| **I-294** | begins/ends on I-94. |

## INTERSTATE 474 - PEORIA

| Exit # | Services |
|---|---|
| **15** | I-74, E to Bloomington, W to Peoria |
| **9** | IL 29, E Peoria, to Pekin, **N** gas: Shell/Arby's, Thornton's, **food:** Driftwood Pizza, DQ, Pizza Hut, Taco John's, **lodging:** Ragon Motel, **other:** Riverboat Casino (6mi), **S** gas: Casey's, Shell/Subway/dsl, **food:** Denny's, KFC, McDonald's, **other:** Chrysler/Jeep/Dodge, Toyota |
| **8mm** | Illinois River |
| **6b a** | US 24, Adams St, Bartonville, **S** gas: BP/dsl, Shell/24hr, **food:** Hardee's, KFC, McDonald's, Tyroni's Café |
| **5** | Airport Rd, **S** gas: Phillips 66 |
| **3a** | to IL 116, Farmington, **S** Wildlife Prairie Park |
| **0b a** | I-74, W to Moline, E to Peoria. I-474 begins/ends on I-74, exit 87. |

# INTERSTATE 64

| Exit # | Services |
|---|---|
| **124mm** | Indiana/Kentucky state line, Ohio River |
| **123** | IN 62 E, New Albany, **N gas:** BP/Circle K/24hr, Sunoco, **food:** DQ, **other:** Firestone/auto, Goodyear/auto, Sav-a-Lot Foods, **S gas:** Circle K/gas, Marathon/dsl/24hr, **food:** Lancaster's Deli, Subway, Waffle House, **lodging:** Hampton Inn, Holiday Inn Express, **other:** [H] HOSPITAL |
| **121** | I-265 E, to I-65 (exits left from eb), **N** access to [H] HOSPITAL |
| **119** | US 150 W, to Greenville, 1/2 mi **N gas:** Marathon, **food:** Bean St Cafe, Beef'O Brady's, China Cafe, Domino's, DQ, El Nopal, Los Indios, Papa John's, Sam's Family Rest., Subway, Taco Bell, Tumbleweed Grill, **other:** Curves, Huber Winery, Rite Aid, Walgreens |
| **118** | IN 62, IN 64W, to Georgetown, **N gas:** Marathon/dsl/24hr, Shell/Circle K, **food:** Korner Kitchen, McDonald's, **lodging:** Motel 6, **other:** Mr. Hardware, Thriftway Foods, vet, **S gas:** Marathon/dsl |
| **115mm** | Welcome Ctr wb, full &♿ facilities, vending, [♨], [🏕], litter barrels |
| **113** | to Lanesville |
| **105** | IN 135, to Corydon, **N gas:** Marathon/dsl, Shell/24hr, **food:** Big Boy, **S gas:** BP/dsl, Chevron, **food:** Arby's, Beef'O Brady's, Burger King, Cracker Barrel, Culver's, DQ, El Nopal Mexican, Hong Kong Buffet, Lee's Chicken, LJ Silver, McDonald's, O'Charley's, Papa John's, Pizza Hut, Quizno's, Ryan's, Subway, Taco Bell, Waffle House, Wendy's, White Castle, **lodging:** Baymont Inn, Hampton Inn, Holiday Inn Express, Super 8, **other:** AutoZone, BigO Tire, Chevrolet/Pontiac/Buick, CVS Drug, $Tree, Ford/Mercury, Pontiac, Radio Shack, Walgreens, Walmart SuperCtr, RV camping |
| **100mm** | Blue River |
| **97mm** | parking area both lanes |
| **92** | IN 66, Carefree, **N** Marengo Caves, **S gas:** Marathon/dsl/rest./24hr, Pilot/Subway/dsl/scales/24, **food:** Country Style Rest., **lodging:** Day's Inn, **other:** to Wyandotte Caves, Harrison Crawford SF, auto/truck repair |
| **88mm** | Hoosier Nat Forest eastern boundary |
| **86** | IN 37, to Sulphur, **N** to Patoka Lake, **S** gas, food, [♨], scenic route |
| **79** | IN 37, to Tell City, St Croix, **S** to Hoosier NF, Rec. Facilities, [♨], to OH River Br |
| **76mm** | Anderson River |
| **72** | IN 145, to Birdseye, **N** to Patoka Lake, **S** gas, [♨], St Meinrad Coll |

| | |
|---|---|
| **63** | IN 162, to Ferdinand, **N gas:** Sunoco/dsl, **food:** Wendy's, **lodging:** Comfort Inn, **other:** Ferdinand SF, **S** (8mi)Lake Rudolph RV Camping |
| **58mm** | rest areas both lanes, full ♿ facilities, info, vending, [🏕], litter barrels, [♨] |
| **57** | US 231, to Dale, Huntingburg, **N** [H] HOSPITAL, **S gas:** Shell/dsl/24hr, **food:** Denny's, **lodging:** Baymont Inn, Motel 6, **other:** Lincoln Boyhood Home, Lincoln SP |
| **54** | IN 161, to Holland, Tennyson |
| **39** | IN 61, Lynnville, **N gas:** Fast Fuel |
| **32mm** | Wabash & Erie Canal |
| **29b a** | I-164 S, IN 57 S, to Evansville, **N gas:** Sunoco/Sunny's Subs/dsl/24hr |
| **25b a** | US 41, to Evansville, **N gas:** 🅙FLYING J/CountryMkt/dsl/24hr/scales/@, Pilot/Wendy's/dsl/24hr, Pilot/Subway/dsl/24hr, **lodging:** Quality Inn, **other:** |

**N E W   A L B A N Y   N ↑ ↓ S**

## INTERSTATE 64 CONT'D

**25b a** Continued
Blue Beacon, truck repair/lube, **S gas:** BP/motel, **food:** Arby's, Denny's, McDonald's, Stoll's Rest., Triple Dragon Buffet, **lodging:** Best Western, Comfort Inn, Holiday Inn Express, Super 8, **other:** Freightliner, st police, to U S IN

**18** IN 65, to Cynthiana, **S gas:** Motomart/dsl/24hr

**12** IN 165, Poseyville, **S** gas, dsl, food, **other:** Chevrolet, New Harmonie Hist Area/SP

**7mm** **Black River Welcome Ctr eb, full ♿ facilities, 📞 🏕, litter barrels, petwalk**

**5mm** Black River

**44** IN 69 S, New Harmony, Griffin, **1 mi N** gas/dsl, food, motel, antiques, USPO, **S** Harmony St Park

**2mm** Big Bayou River

**0mm** Indiana/Illinois state line, Wabash River

## INTERSTATE 65

| Exit # | Services |
|---|---|
| **262** | I-90, W to Chicago, E to Ohio, I-65 begins/ends on US 12, US 20. |
| **26** | 115th Ave, to Gary, **E** Mack/Volvo Trucks, **W gas:** Marathon |
| **259b a** | I-94/80, US 6W |
| **258** | US 6, Ridge Rd, **E gas:** Marathon/dsl, Speedway/dsl, **food:** Country Lounge Diner, Diner's Choice Rest., **W gas:** Citgo, Glen Park Gas, Phillips 66 |

**255** 61st Ave, Merrillville, **E gas:** Marathon, Speedway/dsl/24hr, Thornton, **food:** Arby's, Cracker Barrel, McDonald's, Pizza Hut/Taco Bell, Wendy's, **lodging:** Comfort Inn, $Inn, Lee's Inn, **other:** Chevrolet, Menard's, I-65 Repair, **1 mi W gas:** Shell, **food:** Burger King, Subway, **other:** Ⓗ HOSPITAL

**253b** US 30 W, Merrillville, **W gas:** Meijer/dsl/24hr, Mobil/dsl, Shell, Speedway/dsl, **food:** Abuelo's Mexican, Applebee's, Caribou Coffee, Denny's, Dunkin Donuts, Fannie May Candies, Golden Corral, Hooters, House of Kobe, Jonnie's Rest., KFC, LoneStar Steaks, Oriental Buffet, Outback Steaks, Panera Bread, Pepe's Mexican, Pizza Hut, Portillo's Hot Dogs, Starbucks, Steak'n Shake, Subway, Texas Corral Steaks, TJ Maloney's Grill, Wendy's, White Castle, **lodging:** Courtyard, Deluxe Inn, Fairfield Inn, Hampton Inn, Holiday Inn Express, Radisson, Red Roof Inn, Residence Inn, **other:** Aldi Foods, Aamco, CarEx, CarQuest, Celebration Sta, $Tree, Discount Tire, Firestone, Ford, Goodyear/auto, Hyundai/Mitsubishi, Jo-Ann Fabrics, K-Mart, Lincoln/Mercury, Mazda, Midas, NTB, Saturn, Subaru, Toyota, U-Haul, Walgreens, RV Ctr, transmissions

**253a** US 30 E, **E gas:** BP/dsl/24hr, Speedway/dsl, **food:** Arby's, Bakers Square, Bob Evans, Boston Mkt, Chili's, Chipotle Mexican, ChuckeCheese, DQ, Don Pablo, Great China Buffet, Heavenly Ham, Jimmy John's, Joe's Crabshack, KFC/LJ Silver, Longhorn Steaks, McDonald's, Old Country Buffet, Olive Garden, Popeye's, Potbelly, Pizzaria Uno, Popeye's, Quizno's, Red Lobster, Red Robin, Ruby Tuesday, Starbucks, Subway, Taco Bell, TGIFriday, Tuesday Morning, Uno Pizzaria, Wendy's, **lodging:** Day's Inn, Candlewood Suites, Country Inn Suites, Extended Stay America, Holiday Inn,

**253a** Continued
Knight's Inn, La Quinta, Motel 6, Super 8, **other:** Audi, Barnes&Noble, Best Buy, Carmax, Circuit City, Costco/gas, Dodge, Firestone/auto, Home Depot, JC Penney, Kia, Kohl's, Lowe's Whse, Macey's, Michael's, Nissan, Office Depot, Old Navy, PetCo, Sam's Club/gas, Sears/auto, Target, TJ Maxx, Tire Barn, Toyota, VW, Walmart SuperCtr, mall, vet

**247** US 231, Crown Point, **W gas:** Mobil/24hr, **other:** Ⓗ HOSPITAL, Vietnam Vet Mem

**241mm** weigh sta sb

**240** IN 2, Lowell, **E gas:** ✈ FLYING J/Cookery/dsl/24hr/@, Mobil/Burger King, Pilot/McDonalds/scales/dsl/24hr, **lodging:** Super 8, **other:** truck wash, **W** st police

**234mm** Kankakee River

**231mm** **rest area both lanes, full ♿ facilities, 📞, info, 🏕, litter barrels, vending, petwalk**

**230** IN 10, Roselawn, **E gas:** Gas City/The Diner/scales/dsl/rest./24hr, **W gas:** Family Express, Marathon/Subway, **food:** China Wok, **other:** CarQuest, CVS Drug, $General, Fagen Drug, IGA Foods, TrueValue, Lake Holiday Camping, USPO

**220** IN 14 Winamac, **W other:** Fair Oaks Farms Store

**215** IN 114, Rensselaer, **E gas:** Family Express/dsl/24hr, **food:** Arby's, KFC, L&G Rest., McDonald's, **lodging:** Holiday Inn Express, Knight's Inn, **other:** HOSPITAL, **W gas:** Grandma's/rest./dsl, Marathon/Trail Tree Rest./dsl/24hr, **food:** Burger King, **lodging:** Economy Inn, **other:** tires/repair/towing/24hr

**212mm** Iroquois River

**205** US 231 Remington, **E gas:** Crazy D's/Pop's Kitchen/scales/rest/dsl, BP/dsl, **food:** Vienna Beef, **other:** HOSPITAL, to St Joseph's Coll

**201** US 24/231, Remington, **W gas:** Family Espress/dsl, Petro/Marathon/Iron Skillet/dsl/scales/24hr/@, Pilot/Subway/scales/dsl/24hr, **food:** KFC, McDonald's, **lodging:** Sunset Inn, Super 8 **E other:** Caboose Lake RV

**196mm** **rest area both lanes, full ♿ facilities, vending, 📞, info, 🏕, litter barrels, petwalk**

**193** US 231, to Chalmers, **E gas:** BP/Wayfara Rest./DQ/Stuckey's, **food:** DQ

**188** IN 18, to Brookston, Fowler

**178** IN 43, W Lafayette, **E gas:** GA/Taco Bell, Phillips 66/Subway/dsl, **food:** McDonald's, **lodging:** Rodeway Inn, **other:** to Tippecanoe Bfd, museum, st police, **W** to Purdue U

**176mm** Wabash River

**175** IN 25, Lafayette, **E gas:** Family Express/24hr, **W other:** Ⓗ HOSPITAL, **gas:** Marathon (1mi)

**172** IN 26, Lafayette, **E gas:** Meijer/dsl/24hr, **food:** Cracker Barrel, DQ, Rodeo Rest., Starbucks, Steak'n Shake, White Castle, **lodging:** Baymont Inn, Comfort Inn, Holiday Inn Express, Lee's Inn, Microtel, Motel 6, Quality Inn, TownePlace Suites, **other:** Curves, **W gas:** BP/dsl/24hr, Shell, Speedway/dsl, **food:** Arby's, Bob Evans, Burger King, Chick-fil-A, Chili's, ChuckeCheese, Cici's Pizza, Country Cafe, Culvers, Denny's, Don Pablo, Fazoli's, Golden Corral, Gordman's, Grindstone Charlie's, Hour Time Rest., Hunan House, IHOP, KFC, Krispy Kreme, Logan's Roadhouse, McDonald's, McCalister', Mt Jack's, Nanking Rest., Olive Garden,

N
↕
S

L E B A N O N

## INTERSTATE 65 CONT'D

**172** Continued
Outback Steaks, Pizza Hut, Quizno's, Spageddie's, Steak'n Shake, Subway, Taco Bell, TGIFriday, **lodging:** Best Western, Fairfield Inn, Hampton Inn, Homewood Suites, Knight's Inn, Quality Inn, Ramada Inn, Red Roof Inn, Signature Inn, Super 8, **other:** H HOSPITAL, Aamco, Buick/Cadillac/Nissan, CVS Drug, $Tree, Firestone/auto, Home Depot, Jo-Ann Fabrics, Lowe's Whse, Marsh Foods, Sam's Club/gas, Sportsman's Whse, Target, TJ Maxx, Walmart SuperCtr, vet, USPO, to Purdue U

**168** IN 38, IN 25 S, Dayton, **E gas:** BP/Piccadilly's/24hr, Mobil/dsl

**158** IN 28, to Frankfort, **E gas:** BP/dsl/24hr, Phillips 66, **other:** Harley-Davidson, **2 mi W lodging:** Lincoln Lodge Motel, **other:** H HOSPITAL, camping

**150mm** rest area sb, full ♿ facilities, info, 🏛 litter barrels, 🚽 vending, petwalk

**148mm** rest area nb, full ♿ facilities, info, 🏛 litter barrels, 🚽 vending, petwalk

**146** IN 47, Thorntown, **W** camping

**141** US 52 W (exits left from sb), Lafayette Ave, **E H** HOSPITAL

**140** IN 32, Lebanon, **E gas:** BP, **food:** Denny's, McDonald's, White Castle, **lodging:** Comfort Inn, **other:** HOSPITAL, AutoZone, Goodyear/auto, **W gas:** McClure/dsl, **food:** Arby's, Flapjacks Pancakes, KFC, Ponderosa, Steak'n Shake, Subway, **lodging:** Day's Inn, Hoilday Inn Express, Lee's Inn, Super 8, **other:** truckwash

**139** IN 39, Lebanon, **E gas:** GA, **food:** Hardee's, Wendy's, **W gas:** ⊕FLYING J/Country Mkt/dsl/LP/scales/24hr, **lodging:** Quality Inn, **other:** HOSPITAL, Homemade Chocolates

**138** to US 52, Lebanon, **E gas:** Citgo/dsl, **other:** Chevrolet, Ford

**133** IN 267, Whitestown

**130** IN 334, Zionsville, **E gas:** CF/Subway/dsl, Citgo, Marathon/Starbucks/Stuckey's/dsl/24hr, **food:** Burger King, **other:** CVS Drug, **W gas:** TA/BP/Popeye's/scales/dsl/24hr/@

**129** I-865 E, to I-465 E, US 52 E (from sb)

**126mm** Fishback Creek

**124** 71st St, **1 mi E gas:** BP, **food:** Bob Evans, Hardee's, Steak'n Shake, **lodging:** Courtyard, Hampton Inn, Residence Inn, Wingate Inn, **W** Eagle Creek Park

**123** I-465, **S** to 🛫

**121** Lafayette Rd, **E gas:** GA, Speedway/dsl, **lodging:** Lee's Inn, **W gas:** BP, Shell/Circle K/24hr, **food:** Applebee's, Arby's, Church's, Fazoli's, King Wok, Papa John's, Sizzling Wok, Subway, TCBY, Wendy's, **lodging:** Travelodge **other:** HOSPITAL, Batteries+, Chrysler/Jeep, Discount Tire, Family$, Firestone/auto, Kia, NAPA, Nissan, Macey's, PepBoys, Save-a-Lot Foods, Sears/auto, Speedway Parts, Tire Barn, Toyota/Scion, Walmart SuperCtr, mall, transmissions, vet, same as 119

**119** 38th St (no nb return), **W gas:** Speedway, **food:** Arby's, ChuckeCheese, Cici's Pizza, KFC/Taco Bell, La Bamba Mexican, McDonald's, New Taste Buffet, Pizza Hut, Popeye's, Red Lobster, Starbucks, Taco Bell, **other:** Aldi Foods, Chevrolet, Dodge/Hyundai, Ford, Honda, K-Mart, NAPA, Office Depot, Tires+, mall, same as 121

I N D I A N A P O L I S   A R E A

**117.5mm** White River

**117** MLK St (from sb), **W gas:** Marathon/dsl

**116** 29th St, 30th St (from nb), Marian Coll

**115** 21st St, **E gas:** Shell/Circle K, **other:** H HOSPITAL, **W** museums, zoo

**114** MLK St, West St, downtown

**113** US 31, IN 37, Meridian St, to downtown, **E other:** H HOSPITAL

**112a** I-70 E, to Columbus

**111** Market St, Michigan St, Ohio St, **E food:** Hardee's, **W other:** City Market, to Market Square Arena, museum

**110b** I-70 W, to St Louis

**110a** Prospect St, Morris St, E St

**109** Raymond St, **E H** HOSPITAL, **W gas:** Speedway, **food:** White Castle, **other:** CVS Drug, Safeway

**107** Keystone Ave, **E gas:** Mystik, **lodging:** Best Value, **other:** H HOSPITAL, **W gas:** Phillips 66/dsl, Speedway, Valero, **food:** Burger King, Denny's, Great Wall Chinese, McDonald's, Starbucks, Subway, Walmart Mkt, Wendy's, **lodging:** Holiday Inn Express, **other:** $General, U of Indianapolis

**106** I-465 and I-74

**103** Southport Rd, **E gas:** BP/McDonald's/24hr, Shell/Circle K, **food:** Arby's, Azteca Mexican, Bubbaz Grill, Chick-fil-A, Hardees, El Puerto, Longhorn Steaks, Noble Roman, O'Charley's, Panda Express, Panera Bread, Pen Sta Subs, Pizzaria Uno, Qdoba, Quizno's, Starbucks, Taco Bell, **other:** Aldi Foods, Firestone/auto, Harley-Davidson, Home Depot, Kohl's, Meanard's, Meijer/dsl/24hr, Radio Shack, Staples, Target, **W gas:** Circle K/gas, 7-11, Speedway/dsl/24hr, **food:** Beef & Brew, Bob Evans, Burger King, Carrabba's, Cheeseburger Paradise, Cracker Barrel, Damon's, KFC, McDonald's, Starbucks, Steak'n Shake, TX Roadhouse, Waffle House, Wendy's, **lodging:** Comfort Suites, Best Western, Country Inn Suites, Courtyard, $Inn, Fairfield Inn, Hampton Inn, Jameson Inn, Quality Inn, Super 8, **other:** H HOSPITAL

**101** CountyLine Rd, **W food:** Buffalo Wild Wings, Quizno's, Subway, **lodging:** Hilton Garden, Holiday Inn Express, **other:** H HOSPITAL, Gander Mtn, Kroger, Walmart SuperCtr/gas

**99** Greenwood, **E gas:** Road Ranger/Subway/scales/dsl/24hr, **W gas:** Marathon, 7-11/gas, Shell/Circle K, **food:** Arby's, Bob Evans, Byrd's Cafeteria, Denny's, McDonald's, Noble Roman's, Starbucks, Subway, Taco Bell, Waffle House, White Castle, **lodging:** Comfort Inn, InTown Suites, Lee's Inn, Red Carpet Inn,

## INTERSTATE 65 CONT'D

**N ↑ S**

**99** Continued
Red Roof Inn, **other:** Ⓗ HOSPITAL, Camping World RV Ctr, Sam's Club

**95** Whiteland, **E gas:** ✈FLYING J/CountryMkt/scales/dsl/24hr/@, Marathon/dsl, **other:** tires, **W gas:** Pilot/Arby's/dsl/24hr/@, Pilot/McDonald's/dsl/scales/24hr/@, **other:** Family RV Ctr

**90** IN 44, Franklin, **W gas:** BP/Circle K, **food:** Burger King, Don&Dona's (2mi), McDonald's, Subway, Waffle House, **lodging:** Comfort Inn, Howard Johnson, Quality Inn, Super 7 Inn/rest., Super 8, **other:** Ⓗ HOSPITAL, golf

**85mm** Sugar Creek

**82mm** Big Blue River

**80** IN 252, to Flat Rock, Edinburgh, **W gas:** Marathon/dsl, Shell/dsl

**76b a** US 31, Taylorsville, **E gas:** Shell/Circle K/dsl, Speedway/dsl, **food:** A&W/KFC, Burger King, Waffle House, **lodging:** Red Roof Inn, **other:** HOSPITAL, Chevrolet/Buick/Cadillac/GMC, Toyota, **W gas:** Marathon, Thornton/café/dsl, **food:** Arby's, Cracker Barrel, Hardee's, Max&Erma's, McDonald's, Mexico Viejo, Montana Mikes, Ruby Tuesday, Snappy Tomato Pizza, Subway, Taco Bell, **lodging:** Best Western, Hampton Inn, Hilton Garden, Holiday Inn Express, **other:** Goodyear, Harley-Davidson, Premium Outlets/famous brands, antiques, repair

**73mm** rest area both lanes, full ♿ facilities, 📞, vending, info, 🚻, litter barrels, petwalk

**68mm** Driftwood River

**68** IN 46, Columbus, **E gas:** BP/Circle K/dsl/24hr, Shell, Speedway/dsl, **food:** Burger King, Dimitri's Rest., McDonald's, Snappy Tomato Pizza, Starbucks, Subway, **lodging:** Comfort Inn, Holiday Inn/rest., Sleep Inn, Super 8, **other:** HOSPITAL, Nissan, Sam's Club/gas, Walmart SuperCtr, **W gas:** Marathon, Swifty, **food:** Arby's, Bob Evans, Denny's, KFC, Max's Grill, Noble Roman's, Subway, Taco Bell, Tuesday Morning, Wendy's, **lodging:** Day's Inn, Knight's Inn, Travelodge, **other:** CVS Drug, $General, Jay-C Foods, Tuesday Morning, to Brown Co SP

**64** IN 58, Walesboro, **W gas:** Marathon/Kathy's Express/dsl, **other:** to RV camping

**55** IN 11, to Jonesville, Seymour

**54mm** White River

**51mm** weigh sta both lanes

**50b a** US 50, Seymour, **E gas:** Marathon/Circle K/dsl, Swifty, TA/BP/Country Pride/dsl/24hr/@, **food:** McDonald's, Waffle House, **lodging:** Allstate Inn, Day's Inn, Econolodge, Motel 6, Super 8, **other:** Seymour Shops/famous brands, **W gas:** Shell/Circle K/dsl, Speedway/dsl, Sunoco/dsl, **food:** Applebee's, Arby's, Buffet China, Burger King, Chapala Mexican, Chili's, Cracker Barrel, Dominos, Grand China, Hardee's, KFC, LJ Silver, Max & Erma's, McDonalds, Papa John's, Pizza Hut, Rally's, Ryan's, Santa Fe Mexican, Starbucks, Steak'n Shake, Subway, Taco Bell, Tumbleweed Grill, Wendy's, **lodging:** Hampton Inn, Holiday Inn/rest., Knight's Inn, Lee's Inn, Quality Inn, **other:** Ⓗ HOSPITAL, AutoZone, BigLots, Chevrolet/Buick/Pontiac/GMC, CVS Drug, $General, Ford/Lincoln/Mercury, GNC, Goody's, Home Depot, Jay C Foods, JC Penney, O'Reilly Parts, Radio Shack, Russell Stover Candies, Staples, Walmart SuperCtr/gas, st police

**COLUMBUS   SEYMOUR**

**41** IN 250, Uniontown, **E** tires, **W gas:** UnionTown/dsl/rest./24hr, **other:** auto/truck repair

**36** US 31, Crothersville, **E gas:** Shell, **W gas:** Marathon

**34a b** IN 256, Austin, **E gas:** BP/Circle K, **other:** to Hardy Lake, Clifty Falls SP, **W gas:** Fuelmart/scales/dsl, **food:** A&W

**29b a** IN 56, to Salem, Scottsburg, **E gas:** Marathon, MotoMart, Speedway/dsl, Swifty, **food:** Burger King, Cracker Barrel, Oriental Inn, Papa John's, Ponderosa, Sonic, Subway, Taco Bell, **lodging:** Holiday Inn Express, Mariann Motel/rest., **other:** HOSPITAL, Ace Hardware, Advance Parts, AutoZone, CVS Drug, Family$, **W gas:** Marathon, Shell/Circle K, **food:** Arby's, Domino's, LJ Silver, McDonald's, Pizza Hut, Roadhouse USA, Waffle House, Wendy's, **lodging:** Days Inn, Hampton Inn, Super 8, **other:** Big O Tire, Jellystone Camping (4mi), Walmart SuperCtr/gas

**22mm** rest area both lanes, full ♿ facilities, info, 📞, 🚻, litter barrels, vending, petwalk

**19** IN 160, Henryville, **E gas:** Shell/Circle K/24hr, Sprint/Subway/dsl, **food:** Schuler's Rest.

**16** Memphis Rd, Memphis, **E gas:** BP, Love's/Subway/McDonald's/Scales/dsl/24hr, **W gas:** Pilot/Arby's/scales/dsl/24hr/@, **other:** Customers 1st RV Ctr.

**9** IN 311, to New Albany, Sellersburg, **E gas:** BP, Chevron, Five Star Gas, Shell/Circle K, Swifty, **food:** Arby's, Cracker Barrel, DQ, Quizno's, Waffle House, **lodging:** Ramada Ltd, **other:** Carmerica Tires/service, Ford, O'Reilly Parts, st police, **W gas:** Marathon/Circle K, **food:** Burger King, McDonald's, Taco Bell, **lodging:** Comfort Inn, **other:** city park

**7** IN 60, Hamburg, **E gas:** BP/dsl/24hr, **W food:** KFC/Pizza Hut, **lodging:** Day's Inn

**6b a** I-265 W, to I-64 W, IN 265 E, New Albany

**5** Veterans Parkway, **E gas:** Ⓗ HOSPITAL, **W gas:** Speedway/dsl, **food:** Asian Buffet, Cheddars, Chick-fil-A, DQ, Famous Dave's BBQ, IHOP, Kensai Japanese, Longhorn Steaks, McCalisters Deli, Moe's SW Grill, Olive Garden, Panera Bread, Papa Murphy's, Ruben's Mexican, Ruby Tuesday, Sonic, Subway, Taco Bell, **other:** Bass Pro Shop, Best Buy, Chevrolet, Lowe's Whse, Old Navy, PetsMart, Sams Club, Staples, Target, Tuesday Morning, Walmart SuperCtr/Subway/gas

**4** US 31 N, IN 131 S, Clarksville, New Albany, **E gas:** Thornton/Dunkin Donuts/dsl, **food:** White Castle, **other:** Raben Tire, **W gas:** Speedway/dsl, **food:** Applebee's, Arby's, Big Boy, Bob Evans, Burger King, Capt D's, ChuckeCheese, Denny's, Don Pablo, Fazoli's, Golden Corral, Honey Baked Cafe, Hooters, Iguana Rest., La Frontera Mexican, Logan's Roadhouse, LJ Silver, McDonald's, Mr Gatti's, O'Charley's, Outback Steaks, Papa John's, Pizza Hut, Rally's, Red Lobster, Steak'n Shake/24hr, TX Roadhouse, Tuesday Morning, Wendy's, **lodging:** Best Western, Colonial Motel, Hampton Inn, **other:** AutoZone, Big K-mart, BigLots, Buick/Pontiac/GMC, Circuit City, Dillard's, $Tree, Firestone/auto, Ford, Goodyear, Hancock Fabrics, Home Depot, Honda, JC Penney, Kia, K-Mart, Kroger/gas, Mazda, Office Depot, O'Reilly Parts, PepBoys, Scion/Toyota, Sears/auto, Suzuki, Toyota, USPO, Walgreens, mall

**SCOTTSBURG   CLARKSVILLE**

**IN**

# INDIANA 159

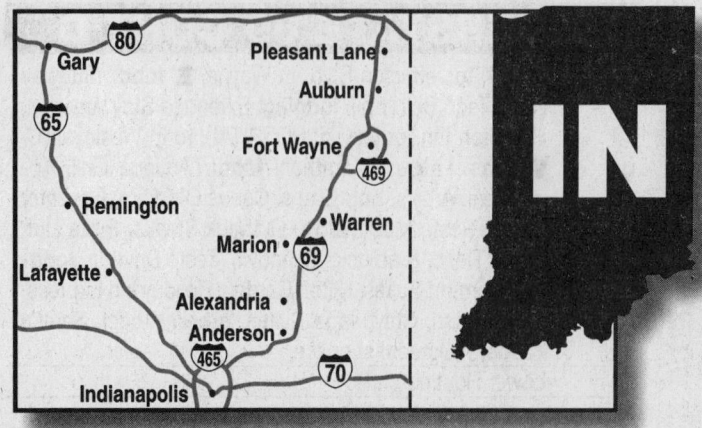

## INTERSTATE 65 CONT'D

| | | |
|---|---|---|
| **N** | **2** | Eastern Blvd, Clarksville, **E** **lodging:** Best Inn, Comfort Inn, Day's Inn, Motel 6, Super 8, **other:** HOSPITAL, U-Haul, **W** **gas:** BP, Shell, **lodging:** Best Inn, Holiday Inn, **other:** Camping World/Stinnet RV Ctr |
| ↑↓ | **1** | US 31 S, IN 62, Stansifer Ave, **E** **gas:** Thornton, **food:** DQ, **other:** H HOSPITAL, Advance Parts, Walgreens, info ctr, **W** **lodging:** Holiday Inn, **other:** Camping World/Stinnett RV Ctr |
| **S** | **0** | Jeffersonville, **E** **gas:** Thornton, **food:** Hardee's, Mc-Donald's, Waffle House, **other:** H HOSPITAL, Chrysler/Jeep, Hyundai, Nissan, Walgreens, to Falls of OH SP |
| | **0mm** | Indiana/Kentucky state line, Ohio River |

## INTERSTATE 69

| | | |
|---|---|---|
| **N** | **Exit #** | **Services** |
| | **158mm** | Indiana/Michigan state line |
| ↑↓ | **157** | Lake George Rd, to IN 120, Fremont, Lake James, **E** **gas:** Petro/Mobil/dsl/24hr/@, **lodging:** Lake George Inn, **other:** Freightliner, **W** **gas:** Pilot/Wendy's/dsl/scales/24hr, Shell/Subway/dsl/24hr, **food:** McDonald's, Red Arrow Rest., **other:** Jellystone Camping (5mi), Outlet Shops/Famous Brands, fireworks |
| **S** | **156** | I-80/90 Toll Rd, E to Toledo, W to Chicago |
| | **154** | IN 127, to IN 120, IN 727, Fremont, Orland, **E** **food:** Applebee's (2mi), Bennigans (2mi), Ruby Tuesday, **lodging:** Hampton Inn, Super 8, Travelers Inn, **other:** Oak Hill RV camp, golf, **W** **gas:** Marathon/dsl, **lodging:** Budgeteer Motel, Holiday Inn Express, **other:** Prime Outlets/Famous Brands, to Pokagon SP, Jellystone Camping (4mi) |
| | **150** | rd 200 W, to Lake James, Crooked Lake, **E** **gas:** BP/dsl, **W** **gas:** Marathon, Shell, **other:** Marine Ctr |
| | **148** | US 20, to Angola, Lagrange, **E** **gas:** Citgo/Subway/dsl, GA, Speedway/dsl, **food:** McDonald's, Wendy's (1mi), **other:** HOSPITAL, **other:** Circle B RV Prk |
| | **145mm** | Pigeon Creek |
| | **144mm** | rest area sb, full & facilities, info, 📞, ⛽, litter barrels, vending, petwalk |
| | **140** | IN 4, to Hamilton, Ashley, Hudson, **1 mi** **W** **gas:** BP/Ashley Deli/dsl |
| | **134** | US 6, to Waterloo, Kendallville, **W** **gas:** BP/dsl, Marathon/dsl/24hr, **food:** Morning Star Rest |
| **A** **U** **B** **U** **R** **N** | **129** | IN 8, to Garrett, Auburn, **E** **gas:** Citgo, GA, Lassus, Marathon/dsl/24hr, Speedway/dsl, **food:** Applebee's, Arby's/24hr, Ard's Rest., Bob Evans, Burger King, DQ, Fazoli's, KFC, McDonald's, Papa Murphy's, Pizza Hut, Ponderosa, Starbucks, Steak'n Shake, Subway, Taco Bell, TCBY, Wendy's, Zesto Drive-In, **lodging:** Best Western, Comfort Suites, Days Inn, Holiday Inn Express, La Quinta, Super 8, **other:** HOSPITAL, Ace Hardware, Advance Parts, AutoZone, Chevrolet/Pontiac/Buick/RV Ctr, Chrysler/Jeep/Dodge, CVS Drug, Davis RV Ctr, $General, $Tree, Ford, GMC, Kroger, Radio Shack, Staples, Walmart SuperCtr, museum, **W** **gas:** Marathon, **food:** Buffalo Wild Wings, Cracker Barrel, FireMtn Grill, Sonic, **other:** Home Depot |
| | **126** | IN 11-A, to Garrett, Auburn, **E** Kruse Auction Park, **W** KOA |
| | **116** | IN 1 N, Dupont Rd, **E** **gas:** Citgo/Burger King, **food:** Arby's, Culver's, **lodging:** Comfort Suites, **other:** H HOSPITAL, **W** **gas:** Lassus/Elmo's Pizza, |

| | |
|---|---|
| **116** | Continued Speedway/dsl, **food:** Bandito's Mexican, Bob Evans, Ground Level Coffee, Laguna Grill, Mancino's Grinders, RolyPoly, Trolley Grill, **lodging:** AmericInn, Sleep Inn, **other:** H HOSPITAL |
| **115** | I-469, US 30 E |
| **112b a** | Coldwater Rd, **E** **gas:** BP/dsl/24hr, Marathon, Sunoco, **food:** Arby's, 's, Carlos O'Kelly's, Chili's, DeBrand's Chocolate, Hall's Factory Rest., Hunan Chinese, IHOP, LoneStar Steaks, Papa John's, Ponderosa, Quizno's, Rally's, Red Lobster, Red River Steaks, Steak'n Shake, Taco Bell, Wendy's, **lodging:** Hyatt Place, Marriott, **other:** Hyundai, Jo-Ann Fabrics, NAPA, U-Haul, Walmart SuperCtr, **W** DQ (1mi) |
| **111b a** | US 27 S, IN 3 N, **E** **gas:** Shell, **food:** Arby's, Cap'n Cork, ChuckeCheese, Don Pablo, DQ, Fazoli's, Golden Corral, Hall's Rest., **lodging:** Candlewood Suites, Residence Inn, **other:** Discount Tire, Ford, Honda, Infiniti, Nissan, Pontiac/GMC, Toyota, **W** **gas:** Lassus/dsl, Marathon, Meijer/dsl/24hr, **food:** Applebee's, Burger King, Cracker Barrel, IHOP, KFC, Logan's Roadhouse, McDonald's, Mega Wraps, O'Charley's, Quizno's, Starbucks, Subway, Taco Bell, Teriyaki Express, Texas Roadhouse, **lodging:** Baymont Inn, Best Value Inn, Courtyard, County Inn&Suites, Day's Inn, Guesthouse Motel, Hampton Inn, Signature Inn, Studio+, **other:** CVS Drug, Gander Mtn, Home Depot, Lowe's Whse, Sam's Club/gas, VW |
| **109b a** | US 33, Goshen Rd, Ft Wayne, **E** **gas:** BP, Citgo/Subway/dsl/scales, Marathon, **food:** McDonald's, Pointe Rest., **lodging:** Best Inn, Country Hearth Inn, Knight's Inn, Motel 6, Quality Inn, Red Roof Inn, Travel Inn, **other:** HOSPITAL, Blue Beacon, NAPA, to Children's Zoo |
| **105b a** | IN 14 W, Ft Wayne, **E** **gas:** Lassus, Shell/Subway/dsl, Speedway/LP, **food:** Arby's, Bob Evans, Chick-fil-A, El Patron Mexican, Flat Top Grill, Great Wall Buffet, Krispy Kreme, Logan's Roadhouse, O'Charley's, Papa Murphy's, Smokey Bones BBQ, Starbucks, Steak'n Shake, Wendy's, **lodging:** Klopfenstein Suites, **other:** HOSPITAL, Acura, Audi/Porsche, Barnes&Noble, Best Buy, Big Lots, BMW, Cadillac, Chevrolet, Chrysler/Jeep, Dodge, Harley-Davidson, Hummer, KIA, Kohl's, Lexus, Lowe's Whse, Mazda, Meijer/dsl/24hr, NAPA, Old Navy, PetsMart, Pontiac/Buick/GMC, Saab, Saturn, Staples, Subaru, Toyota/Scion, Tuesday Morning, Volvo, Walmart SuperCtr/gas, to St Francis U, **W** **food:** Bandito's, **other:** Corvette Museum |

The letters **F T W A Y N E** appear vertically in the left margin beside exits 109b a and 105b a.

**FT WAYNE N ↕ S**

## INTERSTATE 69 CONT'D

| | |
|---|---|
| **102** | US 24, to Jefferson Blvd, Ft Wayne, **E** **food:** Subway (1mi), Taco Bell (1mi), **lodging:** Extended Stay America, Hampton Inn, **other:** H HOSPITAL, to In Wesleyan U, **W** **gas:** Lassus, Marathon, **food:** Antigua Grill, Applebee's, Arby's, Bob Evans, Carlos O'Kelly's, Coventry Tavern Rest., McDonald's, Outback Steaks, Pizza Hut, Sara's Rest., Starbucks, Wendy's, Zesto Drive-In, **lodging:** Comfort Suites, Hilton Garden, Holiday Inn Express, Luxbury Inn, Staybridge Suites, **other:** Kroger, Scott's Foods, Walgreen, st police |
| **99** | Lower Huntington Rd |
| **96b a** | I-469, US 24 E, US 33 S, **E** to ✈ |
| **93mm** | **rest area sb, full** ♿ **facilities, info,** 🚻 **, vending,** ⛽ **, litter barrels, pet walk** |
| **89mm** | **rest area nb, full** ♿ **facilities, info,** 🚻 **, vending,** ⛽ **, litter barrels, pet walk** |
| **86** | US 224, to Huntington, Markle, **E** **gas:** Marathon/24hr (1mi), Sunoco/Subway, **food:** DQ, Huddle House, Vinatelli's, **lodging:** Guesthouse Inn, Super 8, **other:** H HOSPITAL, **W** repair/tires, to Huntington Reservoir |
| **80mm** | weigh sta sb/parking area nb |
| **78** | IN 5, to Warren, Huntington, **E** **gas:** Sunoco/dsl, **lodging:** Huggy Bear Motel, **W** **gas:** Crazy D's/dsl/24hr, Marathon/Subway/dsl/24hr, **food:** McDonald's, Ugalde's Rest., **lodging:** Comfort Inn, Motel 6, **other:** H HOSPITAL, RV Camping, fireworks, to Salmonie Reservoir |
| **76mm** | Salamonie River |
| **73** | IN 218, to Warren |
| **64** | IN 18, to Marion, Montpelier, **W** **gas:** BP/Subway/dsl, Marathon/dsl, **food:** Arby's, **lodging:** Days Inn, **other:** H HOSPITAL, Harley-Davidson, Jeep/Chrysler, **E** **gas:** Love's/McDonalds/dsl/scales/24hr |
| **60mm** | Walnut Creek |
| **59** | US 35 N, IN 22, to Upland, **E** **gas:** Valero/Subway, **food:** Burger King, China 1, Cracker Barrel, E Chicago Pizza, Taste of Texas, **lodging:** B&B, Best Western, Super 8, **other:** Mar-Brook Camping, Taylor U, **W** **gas:** Marathon/dsl/24hr, McClure Trkstp/dsl/24hr, Shell/dsl, **food:** KFC/Taco Bell, Starbucks, **lodging:** Holiday Inn Express, **other:** Smitty's Truckwash, to IN Wesleyan |
| **55** | IN 26, to Fairmount |
| **50mm** | **rest area both lanes, full** ♿ **facilities, info,** 🚻 **,** ⛽ **, litter barrels, vending, pet walk** |
| **45** | US 35 S, IN 28, to Alexandria, Albany, **E** **gas:** Petro/Shell/Iron Skillet/Taco Bell/dsl/scales/24hr/@, **other:** RV Camping |
| **41** | IN 332, to Muncie, Frankton, **E** **gas:** BP/dsl, Citgo/dsl, **other:** H HOSPITAL, to Ball St U |
| **34** | IN 67, to IN 32, Chesterfield, Daleville, **E** **gas:** Pilot/Subway/dsl/scales/24hr, Shell, **food:** Arby's, Taco Bell, White Castle, **lodging:** Budget Inn, **other:** H HOSPITAL, **W** **gas:** GA/dsl, Pilot/Cafe/dsl/24hr, **food:** McDonald's, Subway, 3rd Generation Pizza, Wendy's, **lodging:** Best Value Inn, **other:** flea mkt |
| **26** | IN 9, IN 109, to Anderson, **E** **gas:** Meijer/dsl/24hr, **food:** Culver's, KFC/A&W, Ryan's, **lodging:** Deluxe Inn, Hampton Inn, Quality Inn, **other:** **W** **gas:** BP, GA, Marathon, Speedway, **food:** Applebee's, Arby's, |

**ANDERSON / INDIANAPOLIS AREA**

| | |
|---|---|
| **26** | Continued
Bob Evans, Burger King, China Buffet, Cracker Barrel, Fazoli's, Great Wall Chinese, IHOP, La Charreada Mexican, LoneStar Steaks, McDonald's, Noble Roman's, Panera Bread, Penn Sta. Subs, Perkins, Pizza Hut, Olive Garden, Red Lobster, Ritter's, Ruby Tuesday, Starbucks, Steak'n Shake, Subway, Taco Bell, Waffle House, Wendy's, White Castle, Wings Etc., **lodging:** Baymont Inn, Best Inn, Comfort Inn, Days Inn, Fairfield Inn, Garden Inn, Lee's Inn, Motel 6, Rose Carpet Inn, **other:** HOSPITAL, Aldi Foods, Cadillac/GMC, Curves, Freightliner, Kohl's, Old Navy, O'Rielly Parts, Payless Foods, Radio Shack, Target, Tire Barn, Toyota, Walmart SuperCtr, to Anderson U, to Mounds SP |
| **22** | IN 9, IN 67, to Anderson, **W** **gas:** GA, **food:** Skyline Chili, **lodging:** Anderson Country Inn (1mi), **other:** H HOSPITAL, st police |
| **19** | IN 38, Pendleton, **E** **gas:** Marathon, **food:** Burger King, McDonald's, Subway |
| **14** | IN 13, to Lapel, **E** **gas:** BP, **W** **gas:** Pilot/Subway/dsl/scales/24hr, **other:** camping |
| **10** | IN 238, to Noblesville, Fortville, **W** **other:** JC Penney |
| **5** | IN 37 N, 116th St, to Noblesville, Fishers, **E** **gas:** BP/Wild Bean Cafe, **W** **gas:** Shell/autocare, Speedway, **food:** A&W/KFC, Greek Pizzaria, Handel's Ice Cream, Hawg Wild BBQ, McAlister's Deli, McDonald's, O'Charley's, Qdoba Mexican, Quizno's, Starbucks, Station Rest., Steak'n Shake, Subway, Wendy's, **lodging:** Hampton Inn, **other:** Target |
| **3** | 96th St, **E** **gas:** Meijer/dsl/24hr, Shell, VP/dsl, **food:** Applebee's, Cracker Barrel, Donato's Pizza, Golden Wok Chinese, McDonald's, New China, Noble Roman's, Panera Bread, Pizza Shop, Qdoba Mexican, Ruby Tuesday, Steak'n Shake, **lodging:** Hilton Garden, Holiday Inn, Holiday Inn Express, Hotel Indigo, Studio 6, **other:** Kohl's, Marsh Food/gas, PepBoys, PetCo, Radio Shack, Staples, Tuesday morning, Walmart SuperCtr/gas, **W** **gas:** Marathon, **food:** Arby's, Bob Evans, Burger King, Cheeseburger Paradise, Culver's, Journey Rest., Panda Express, Peterson's Steaks/seafood, Quizno's, Starbucks, Taco Bell, **lodging:** Comfort Suites, Residence Inn, SpringHill Suites, Staybridge Suites, **other:** Aldi Foods, $Tree, Home Depot, NAPA, Sam's Club/gas |
| **1** | 82nd St, Castleton, **E** **food:** Pizza Hut, **lodging:** Country Inn&Suites, Drury Inn, Extended Stay America, Hilton, Super 8, **other:** H HOSPITAL, Lowe's Whse, **W** **gas:** Speedway, **food:** Applebee's, Arby's, Burger King, Cancun Mexican, Charleston's Rest., Denny's, Fazoli's, Hooters, IHOP, KFC/A&W, Loonlake Lodge Rest., McDonald's, Olive Garden, Penn Sta. Subs, Rally's, Red Lobster, Skyline Chili, Starbucks, Steak'n Shake, Taco Bell, Tuscany Grill, Wendy's, **lodging:** Best Western, Candlewood Suites, Day's Inn, Hampton Inn, Red Roof Inn, **other:** Aamco, Best Buy, Discount Tire, $Tree, Goodyear/auto, Indy Tires, Sears/auto, Tire Barn, mall |
| **0mm** | I-465 around Indianapolis. I-69 begins/ends on I-465, exit 37, at Indianapolis. |

## INTERSTATE 70

| Exit # | Services |
|---|---|
| **156.5mm** | Indiana/Ohio state line, weigh sta |

## INTERSTATE 70 CONT'D

**E W RICHMOND**

**156b a** US 40 E, Richmond, **N gas:** FuelMart/dsl, Petro/Marathon/Pizza Hut/dsl/rest./24hr/@, Swifty, **lodging:** Fairfield Inn, **other:** Blue Beacon, **S gas:** BP/White Castle, Shell, Speedway, **food:** A&W/LJ Silver, Applebee's, Big Boy, Bob Evans, Buffalo Wings Cafe, Burger King, Chili's, Cici's Pizza, Cracker Barrel, Domino's, Fazoli's, Golden Corral, Hacienda Mexican, Jade House Chinese, KFC, McDonald's, MCL Cafeteria, O'Charley's, Pizza Hut, Red Lobster, Ruby Tuesday, Ryan's, Steak'n Shake, Subway, Super China, Taco Bell, TCBY, Texas Roadhouse, **lodging:** Best Western, Day's Inn, Hampton Inn, Holiday Inn, Lee's Inn, Motel 6, **other:** AAA, Advance Parts, Aldi Foods, BigLots, Chevrolet/Cadillac, Chrysler/Jeep, Curves, Dillards, $General, Expert Tire, Ford/Lincoln/Mercury, Goody's, Goodyear/auto, Hastings Books, JC Penney, Kroger, Lowes Whse, Midas, Sav-a-Lot Foods, Sears/auto, Target, Tires+, Toyota/Scion, Tuffy, U-Haul, Walgreens, Walmart SuperCtr/gas

**153** IN 227, to Whitewater, Richmond, **2 mi N** Grandpa's Farm RV Park (seasonal)

**151b a** US 27, to Chester, Richmond, **N food:** Fricker's Rest., **other:** Best Buy RV Ctr, Dodge, Honda, KOA, **S gas:** Meijer/dsl/24hr Shell, **food:** Bob Evans, Burger King, Carver's Rest., McDonald's, Pizza Hut, Subway, Taco Bell, Wendy's, **lodging:** Comfort Inn, Super 8, **other:** H HOSPITAL, Harley-Davidson

**149b a** US 35, IN 38, to Muncie, **N** Love's/Hardee's/dsl/scales/24hr, **S gas:** Shell/Quizno's/dsl, **other:** Best Buy RV Ctr, Raper's RV service Ctr

**148mm** weigh sta wb

**145** Centerville, **N gas:** BP/DQ/Stuckey's, **lodging:** Super 8, **other:** Goodyear/truck repair, **S** Warm Glow Candles

**145mm** Nolands Fork Creek

**144mm** rest area both lanes, full ♿ facilities, info, vending, 📞, 🍴, litter barrels, petwalk

**141mm** Greens Fork River

**137** IN 1, to Hagerstown, Connersville, **N** Amish Cheese, **S gas:** Crazy D's/dsl/rest./24hr, GA/mart/24hr, Shell/mart/24hr, **food:** Burger King, McDonald's

**131** Wilbur Wright Rd, New Lisbon, **S gas:** Marathon/KFC/Taco Bell/dsl/scales/24hr/@, **other:** New Lisbon RV park

**126mm** Flatrock River

**123** IN 3, to New Castle, Spiceland, **N lodging:** All American Inn (3mi), Best Value Inn, Best Western (3mi), Holiday Inn Express (3mi), Super 8, **other:** H HOSPITAL, Irwin RV Park (1mi), **S gas:** ⊘FLYING J/CountyMkt/dsl/scales/LP/24hr

**117mm** Big Blue River

**115** IN 109, to Knightstown, Wilkinson, **N gas:** GA/Gas Grill/dsl/scales/24hr, **food:** Burger King, **other:** Jellystone Camping

**107mm** rest area both lanes, full ♿ facilities, vending, 📞, 🍴, litter barrels, petwalk

**104** IN 9, Greenfield, Maxwell, **N gas:** GA/mart, **S gas:** GA, Murphy USA, Shell/Circle K, Sunoco/White Castle, Swifty/mart, **food:** Applebee's, Arby's, Bamboo Garden, Bob Evans, Burger King, Cracker Barrel, Culver's, Domino's, El Rodeo Mexican, Hardee's, KFC, McDonald's, Mi Casa Mexican, MT Mike's Steaks,

**INDIANAPOLIS AREA**

**104** Continued
O'Charley's, Papa Murphy's, Penn Sta. Subs, Pizza Hut, Ponderosa, Quizno's, Ritter's Custard, Starbucks, Steak'n Shake, Subway, Taco Bell, Wendy's, **lodging:** Comfort Inn, $Inn, Hampton Inn, Holiday Inn Express, Quality Inn, Super 8, **other:** Advance Parts, Aldi Foods, Autozone, Big Lots, Big O Tire, CVS Drug, $General, $Tree, GNC, Home Depot, Kroger, Marsh Foods, Radio Shack, Walmart SuperCtr

**96** Mt Comfort Rd, **N gas:** GA/mart, Pilot/Pizza Hut/dsl/scales/24hr, **food:** Burger King, Subway, Wendy's, **other:** Heartland RV Park (2mi), **S gas:** Shell/mart, **food:** McDonald's, **other:** KOA (seasonal), Mt Comfort RV Ctr

**91** Post Rd, to Ft Harrison, **N gas:** Marathon/7-11, Swifty, **food:** Cracker Barrel, Denny's, Joe's Crabshack, Outback Steaks, Steak'n Shake, Wendy's, **lodging:** InTown Suites, La Quinta, **other:** Lowe's Whse, st police, **S gas:** Admiral, BP/mart, Shell/mart, Speedway, **food:** Hardee's, KFC/Taco Bell, Little China, Waffle House, **lodging:** Days Inn, Super 8, **other:** CVS Drug, Family$, Home Depot, Marsh Foods

**90** I-465 (from wb)

**89** Shadeland Ave, I-465 (from eb), **N gas:** Marathon, **food:** Bob Evans, **lodging:** Comfort Inn, Comfort Suites, Hampton Inn, Motel 6, **other:** Toyota, U-Haul, **S gas:** Admiral Gas, Circle K/Quizno's, Marathon, Shell/24hr, Speedway/dsl, **food:** Arby's, Burger King, Blimpie, 4Seasons Diner, Lincoln's Rest., McDonald's, Noble Roman's, Papagalo's Italian, Penn Sta. Subs, Rally's, Red Lobster, Starbucks, Texas Roadhouse, Wendy's, **lodging:** Always Inn, Day's Inn, Fairfield Inn, Holiday Inn/Damon's, Knight's Inn, La Quinta, Marriott, Quality Inn, **other:** Aamco, Buick, CVS Drug, Chevrolet, Dodge, Honda, KIA, Mitsubishi, Nissan

**87** Emerson Ave, **N gas:** BP/McDonald's, Speedway, **S gas:** Shell, **other:** H HOSPITAL

**85b a** Rural St, Keystone Ave, **N** fairgrounds, **S gas:** Marathon

**83b (112)** I-65 N, to Chicago

**83a (111)** Michigan St, Market St, downtown, **S food:** Hardee's

**80 (110a)** I-65 S, to Louisville

**79b** Illinois St, McCarty St, downtown

**79a** West St, **N lodging:** Comfort Inn, **other:** H HOSPITAL, to Union Sta, Govt Ctr, RCA Dome, zoo

**78** Harding St, to downtown, **S gas:** Marathon, **food:** Wendy's

IN

## INTERSTATE 70 CONT'D

**E** ↕ **W**

| | |
|---|---|
| **77** | Holt Rd, **S gas:** Shell, **food:** McDonald's, **other:** Ford Trucks |
| **75** | Airport Expswy, to Raymond St (no EZ wb return), **N gas:** Marathon, Speedway/dsl, **food:** Cracker Barrel, Denny's, Indy's Rest., Waffle House, **lodging:** Adam's Mark, Candlewood Suites, Courtyard, Econolodge, Extended Stay Deluxe, Fairfield Inn, Holiday Inn, Hyatt Place, La Quinta, Quality Inn, Ramada, Residence Inn, **other:** NAPA, to ✈ |
| **73b a** | I-465 N/S, I-74 E/W (from wb) |
| **69** | (only from eb)to I-74 E, to I-465 S |
| **68** | Six Points Rd |
| **66** | IN 267, to Plainfield, Mooresville, **N gas:** BP/24hr, Shell/Circle K, Speedway/dsl, Thornton's/dsl, **food:** Arby's, Bob Evans, Burger King, Coachman Rest., Cracker Barrel, Denny's, Golden Corral, Hog Heaven BBQ, McDonald's, Steak'n Shake, Subway, Wendy's, White Castle, Wood Fire Grill, **lodging:** Baymont Inn, Cambria Suites, Comfort Inn, Day's Inn, Hampton Inn, Holiday Inn Express, Homewood Suites, Motel 6, Ramada Ltd, Staybridge Suites, Super 8, Value Place Inn, Wingate Inn, **other:** Chateau Thomas Winery, Harley-Davidson |
| **65mm** | **rest area both lanes, full** ♿ **facilities, info, vending,** 🚻, 🎇, **litter barrels, petwalk** |
| **59** | IN 39, to Belleville, **N gas:** Marathon/mart, **other:** Ⓗ HOSPITAL, **S gas:** TA/Country Pride/dsl/rest./24hr/@ |
| **51** | rd 1100W, **S gas:** Koger's/Sunoco/dsl/rest./24hr, **other:** repair/towing/24hr |
| **41** | US 231, to Greencastle, Cloverdale, **S gas:** BP/dsl, Casey's (2mi), Marathon/scales/dsl/24hr, **food:** Arby's, Chicago's Pizza, Cloverdale Rest., KFC, McDonald's, Subway, Taco Bell, Wendy's, **lodging:** Best Value Inn, Colverdale Inn, Day's Inn, Holiday Inn Express, Motel 6, Super 8, **other:** Discount Tire, Value Mkt Foods, to Lieber SRA |
| **37** | IN 243, to Putnamville, **S gas:** Marathon/dsl/mart, **other:** to Lieber SRA |
| **23** | IN 59, to Brazil, **N gas:** Pilot/McDonald's/Subway/scales/dsl/mart/24hr, **other:** Ⓗ HOSPITAL, **S gas:** AM Best/Shell/Brazil Grill/dsl/scales/24hr/@, BP/Rally's/dsl/mart, Roadranger/Subway/scales/dsl, **food:** Burger King, Jerry's Rest., **lodging:** Howard Johnson Express |
| **15mm** | Honey Creek |
| **11** | IN 46, Terre Haute, **N gas:** Pilot/Arby's/scales/dsl/mart/24hr, Thornton/dsl, **food:** Burger King, McDonald's, **other:** ✈, S KOA |
| **7** | US 41, US 150, Terre Haute, **N gas:** Marathon/dsl, Thornton's/dsl, **food:** Applebee's, Beef o'Brady's, Bob Evans, Cracker Barrel, China Buffet, Fazoli's, IHOP, LoneStar Steaks, Pizza Hut, Quizno's, Real Hacienda Mexican, Sam's Steaks, Starbucks, Steak'n Shake, TX Roadhouse, Tumbleweed SW Grill, **lodging:** Best Western, Comfort Suites, Drury Inn, Econolodge, Fairfield Inn, PearTree Inn, Ramada Ltd., Super 8, **other:** AutoZone, **S gas:** Speedway/dsl, Thornton's/mart, **food:** Arby's, Buffalo Wild Wings, Burger King, Cheeseburger Paradise, Coldstone Creamery, Crazy Buffet, DQ, Denny's, Garfield's Rest., Golden Corral, Hardee's, KFC, Little Caesar's, Los Tres Caminos, |

**TERRE HAUTE**

| | |
|---|---|
| **7** | Continued LJ Silver, McDonald's, Olive Garden, Outback Steaks, Panera Bread, Papa John's, Penn Sta. Subs, Rally's, Red Lobster, Ruby Tuesday, Ryan's, Starbucks, Subway, Taco Bell, TGIFriday, Wendy's, **lodging:** Hampton Inn, Holiday Inn, Knight's Inn, SpringHill Suites, **other:** HOSPITAL, Aldi Foods, Big Lots, BooksAMillion, Buick/Cadillac/GMC/Pontiac, Burlington Coats, Chevrolet/Hyundai/Nissan, Circuit City, Curves, Dodge, $Tree, Gander Mtn., Goodys, Goodyear/auto, Harley-Davidson, Jo-Ann Crafts, K-Mart/gas, Kohl's, Kroger/gas, Lowes Whse, Macy's, NAPA, Old Navy, PetCo, Sam's Club/gas, Saturn, Sears/auto, Staples, Tire Barn, TJ Maxx, Tuesday Morning, Walgreens, Walmart SuperCtr |
| **5.5mm** | Wabash River |
| **3** | Darwin Rd, W Terre Haute, **N** to St Mary of-the-Woods Coll |
| **1.5mm** | **Welcome Ctr eb, full** ♿ **facilities, info,** 🎇, **litter barrels,** 🚻, **vending, petwalk** |
| **1** | US 40 E (from eb, exits left), to Terre Haute, W Terre Haute |
| **.5mm** | weigh sta, eb only |
| **0mm** | Indiana/Illinois state line |

## INTERSTATE 74

**E** ↕ **W**

| Exit # | Services |
|---|---|
| **171.5mm** | Indiana/Ohio state line |
| **171mm** | weigh sta wb |
| **169** | US 52 W, to Brookville |
| **168.5mm** | Whitewater River |
| **164** | IN 1, St Leon, **N gas:** Exxon, Shell/dsl, **S gas:** BP/dsl |
| **156** | IN 101, to Sunman, Milan, **S gas:** Exxon/dsl |
| **152mm** | **rest area both lanes, full** ♿ **facilities,** 🚻, 🎇, **litter barrels, vending, petwalk** |
| **149** | IN 229, to Oldenburg, Batesville, **N gas:** Shell/dsl/24hr, Sunoco, **food:** Acapulco Mexican, China Wok, McDonald's, Starbucks, Subway, Wendy's, **lodging:** Hampton Inn, **other:** $General, Kroger/gas, Pamida, **S gas:** BP, **food:** Arby's, DQ, KFC/Taco Bell, La Rosa's Pizza, Skyline Chili, Waffle House, **lodging:** Comfort Inn, **other:** Ⓗ HOSPITAL, CVS Drug |
| **143** | to IN 46, New Point, **N gas:** Petro/Marathon/Iron Skillet/dsl/rest./24hr/@, **S gas:** Marathon |
| **134b a** | IN 3, to Rushville, Greensburg, **S gas:** BP/dsl, Marathon/DQ/Subway, Shell/24hr, Speedway, **food:** A&W, Arby's, Big Boy, Burger King, Chili's, El Reparo Mexican, El Tapatio Mexican, Great Wall Buffet, KFC, McDonald's, Papa John's, Prime Time Grill, Subway, Taco Bell, Waffle House, Wendy's, **lodging:** Fairfield Inn, Lee's Inn, Holiday Inn Express, **other:** Advance Parts, Aldi Foods, AutoZone, Big O Tire, Chevrolet/Cadillac, Chrysler, CVS Drug, $General, Ford/Mercury, Goody's, Radio Shack, Staples, Walmart SuperCtr, Walgreens |
| **132** | US 421 (from eb), to Greensburg |
| **130mm** | Clifty Creek |
| **123** | Saint Paul, **S** camping |
| **119** | IN 244 E, to Milroy |
| **116** | IN 44, to Shelbyville, Rushville, **N gas:** Bigfoot/dsl, **S gas:** BP, Marathon, Shell/24hr, Swifty, **food:** Applebee's, Arby's, Bellacino's, Bob Evans, Burger King, China Buffet, Denny's, Golden Corral (1mi), King's Buffet, |

## INTERSTATE 74 CONT'D

**116** Continued
LJ Silver, McDonald's, Papa John's, Pizza Hut, Subway, Taco Bell, Wendy's, **lodging:** Lee's Inn, **other:** HOSPITAL, Ace Hardware, Advance Parts, Aldi Foods, Big Lots, Chevrolet, CVS Drug, $General, Ford/Lincoln/Mercury, GNC, Goody's, Kroger/gas, Marsh Foods, NAPA, Radio Shack, Walgreens, Walmart SuperCtr/gas

**115mm** Little Blue River

**113mm** Big Blue River

**113** IN 9, to Shelbyville, **N gas:** BP, GA, **food:** Cracker Barrel, Wendy's, **S gas:** BP, Shell, **food:** El Emparador Mexican, McDonald's, Santa Fe Steaks, Waffle House, **lodging:** Best Western, Comfort Inn, Day's Inn, Hampton Inn, Super 8, **other:** HOSPITAL, Buick/GMC, Chrysler, Ford/Lincoln/Mercury

**109** Fairland Rd, **N gas:** Pilot/McDonald's/dsl/scales/24hr, **other:** Indiana Downs, **S other:** Brownie's Marine

**103** London Rd, to Boggstown

**102mm** Big Sugar Creek

**101** Pleasant View Rd, **N gas:** Marathon

**99** Acton Rd

**96** Post Rd, **N gas:** Marathon/Subway/dsl/24hr, **food:** McDonald's, **S gas:** Shell/dsl, **food:** Wendy's, **other:** Chevrolet

**94b a** I-465/I-74 W, I-465 N, US 421 N

**I-74 and I-465 run together 21 miles. See I-465, exits 2-16, and 52-53.**

**73b** I-465 N, access to same services as 16a on I-465

**73a** I-465 S, I-74 E

**71mm** Eagle Creek

**68** new exit

**66** IN 267, Brownsburg, **N gas:** Citgo/dsl, Shell, **food:** Applebee's, Asia Wok, Hardee's, Ritters Custard, Steak'n Shake, Subway, Trip's Grill, **lodging:** Hampton Inn, Holiday Inn Express, **other:** Big O Tire, **S gas:** BP/dsl, Speedway/dsl, **food:** Arby's, Blimpie, Bob Evans, Burger King, China's Best, McDonald's, Papa Murphy's, Quizno's, Starbucks, Taco Bell, Wendy's, White Castle, Wing Etc., **lodging:** Comfort Suites, Super 8, **other:** CVS Drug, $Tree, Ford, Kohl's, Kroger/gas, K-Mart, Lowe's Whse, Radio Shack, Walmart SuperCtr

**61** to Pittsboro, **S gas:** Loves/Godfathers/Subway/dsl/scales/24hr

**58** IN 39, to Lebanon, Lizton, **S H HOSPITAL**

**57mm** **rest area both lanes, full & facilities, [, 🎪, litter barrels, vending, petwalk**

**52** IN 75, to Advance, Jamestown, **2 mi S** gas, food, camping

**39** IN 32, to Crawfordsville, **S gas:** Pilot/Subway/dsl/scales/24hr

**34** US 231, to Linden, **S gas:** BP, CTP/dsl/scales/24hr, GA, Marathon/dsl, **food:** Burger King, KFC, McDonald's, Vickery's Cafe (1mi), **lodging:** Comfort Inn, Day's Inn, Holiday Inn, Ramada Ltd., Super 8, **other:** H HOSPITAL, KOA (1mi), Sugar Creek Campground (4mi)

**25** IN 25, to Wingate, Waynetown

**22mm** **rest area both lanes, full & facilities, [, 🎪, litter barrels, vending, petwalk**

**19mm** weigh sta eb/parking area wb

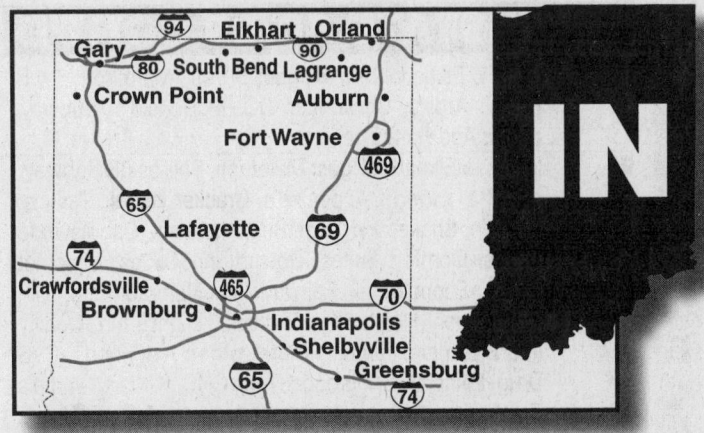

**15** US 41, to Attica, Veedersburg, **1/2 mi S gas:** Marathon/Subway/dsl, **food:** Apple Tree Diner, **other:** to Turkey Run SP, camping

**8** Covington, **N gas:** Shell, **food:** Maple Corner Rest. (1mi), **other:** fireworks

**7mm** Wabash River

**4** IN 63, to Newport, **N gas:** BP/Wendy's, Pilot/Arby's/dsl/scales/24hr, **food:** Beefhouse Rest.

**1mm** **Welcome Ctr eb, full & facilities, info, [, 🎪, litter barrels, vending, petwalk**

**0mm** Indiana/Illinois state line, Eastern/Central Time Zone

## INTERSTATE 80/90

| Exit # | Services |
| --- | --- |
| **157mm** | Indiana/Ohio state line |
| **153mm** | toll plaza, litter barrels |
| **146mm** | TP both lanes, Mobil/dsl, DQ, McDonald's, playground |

**144** I-69, US 27, Angola, Ft Wayne, **N gas:** Petro/Mobil/dsl/LP/@, Pilot/Wendy's/dsl/scales, Shell/Subway/dsl, **food:** McDonald's, Red Arrow Rest., **lodging:** Redwood Lodge, Lake George Inn, **other:** Freightliner/Western Star/truck repair, **S gas:** Marathon/dsl/24hr, **lodging:** Holiday Inn Express, **other:** Outlet Shops/famous brands, **services on IN 120 E lodging:** Hampton Inn, Super 8, Traveler's Inn, **other:** golf/rest, **W** to Pokagon SP, Jellystone Camping (5mi)

**131.5mm** Fawn River

**126mm** TP both lanes, Mobil/dsl, Fazoli's, Hardee's, gifts, RV dump

**121** IN 9, to Lagrange, Howe, **N gas:** Golden Buddha, **lodging:** Best Value Inn, Best Western, Hampton Inn, Travel Inn, **other:** H HOSPITAL (4mi), **2 mi N gas:** Speedway/dsl, **food:** Applebee's, Burger King KFC, King Dragon, Little Caesar's, McDonald's, Pizza Hut, Savory Rest., Subway, Taco Bell, Wendy's, **lodging:** Regency Inn, **other:** $Tree, Ford, GNC, K-Mart, Kroger, Radio Shack, Walgreens, Walmart SuperCtr/gas, **S gas:** Valero, **lodging:** Holiday Inn Express, Super 8, **other:** H HOSPITAL (8mi)

**120mm** Fawn River

**108mm** trucks only rest area both lanes

**107** US 131, IN 13, to Middlebury, Constantine, **N gas:** Marathon/dsl, **food:** Country Table Rest. (2mi), **lodging:** Patchwork Quilt B&B, Plaza Motel, **1 mi S gas:** BP/Blimpie/dsl, **food:** Yup's DairyLand, **other:** Eby's Pines RV Park, KOA (apr-nov)

**101** IN 15, to Goshen, Bristol, **1 mi S gas:** Speedway/dsl, **food:** River Inn Rest., **other:** Eby's Pines Camping (3mi)

## INTERSTATE 80/90 CONT'D

**E W ELKHART SOUTH BEND** (left vertical tab)

**96**   rd 1, E Elkhart, **2 mi S gas:** BP/dsl, Marathon, 7-11, **food:** Arby's, China Star, DQ, McDonald's, Subway, **other:** Ace Hardware

**92**   IN 19, to Elkhart, **N gas:** Marathon, Phillips 66/Subway/dsl, 7-11, **food:** Applebee's, Cracker Barrel, Perkins, Steak'n Shake, **lodging:** Best Western, Candlewood Suites, Comfort Suites, Country Inn&Suites, Diplomat Motel, Econolodge, Fairway Inn, Hampton Inn, Hilton Garden, Holiday Inn Express, Knight's Inn, Quality Inn, Sleep Inn, Turnpike Motel, **other:** Aldi Foods, CVS Drug, Elkhart Campground (1mi), GNC, K-Mart, Martin's Foods, Tiara RV Ctr, tires, transmissions, **0-2 mi S gas:** Marathon/dsl, Shell, **food:** Arby's, Blimpie, Bob Evans, Burger King, Callahan's Rest., Chicago Grill, CiCi's Pizza, Culver's, Da Vinci's Pizza, DQ, KFC, LJ Silver, Matterhorn Rest., McDonald's, North Garden Buffet, Olive Garden, Pizza Hut, Red Lobster, Ryan's, Taco Bell, Texas Roadhouse, Wendy's, Wings Etc., **lodging:** Budget Inn, Day's Inn, Jameson Inn, Ramada Inn, Red Roof Inn, Super 8, **other:** H HOSPITAL, Ace Hardware, AutoZone, CarQuest, $Tree, Family$, Lowes Whse, Menard's, Michiana RV Ctr, Radio Shack, Walmart SuperCtr, truck/RV repair

**91mm**   Christiana Creek

**90mm**   TP eb, George Craig TP wb, BP/dsl, Burger King, Pizza Hut, Starbucks, Z Mkt, RV Dump, USPO

**83**   to Mishawaka, **N gas:** BP/dsl, Marathon/Blimpie, Phillips 66/Subway/dsl, **other:** CVS Drug, $Tree, Marshall's, Martin's Foods/gas, Menard's, Walgreens, **1-2 mi N on IN 23 W food:** Applebee's, Famous Dave's BBQ, King's Buffet, Olive Garden, Pizza Hut, Quizno's, Wendy's, **lodging:** Country Inn&Suites, Fairfield Inn, Hampton Inn, Holiday Inn Express, Super 8, **other:** Best Buy, JC Penney, Kroger, Macy's, Michael's, Sears/auto, Target, KOA (mar-nov), mall, **2 mi S on Grape Rd & Main St (off IN 23W)...gas:** Meijer/dsl/24hr, **food:** Arby's, Bob Evans, Buffalo Wild Wings, Burger King, Carraba's, Chick-fil-A, Chili's, Chipotle Mexican, Del Taco, Houlihan's, Hooters, Jimmy John's, Krispy Kreme, Logan's Roadhouse, Mancino's Pizza, Max&Erma's, McDonald's, Outback Steaks, Panera Bread, Papa Vino's Italian, Red Lobster, Ryan's, Starbucks, Steak'n Shake, Subway, Taste of Asia, Texas L&C, TGIFriday, **lodging:** Comfort Inn, Courtyard, Extended Stay America, Hyatt Place Hotel, Residence Inn, SpringHill Suites, Studio+, **other:** Aldi Foods, Barnes&Noble, Borders, Buick/GMC/Pontiac, Chrysler, Circuit City, Discount Tire, Home Depot, Honda, Hyundai, Jo-Ann Fabrics, Kohl's, Lexus, Lowes Whse, Mercedes, Nissan, Old Navy, Sam's Club, TJ Maxx, Walmart SuperCtr

**77**   US 33, US 31B, IN 933, South Bend, **N gas:** Admiral, Mobil/dsl, **food:** Arby's, Burger King, DQ, Eleni's Rest., Fazoli's, J-Willy's Grill, KFC, Marco's Pizza, McDonald's, Papa John's, Ponderosa, Starbucks, Steak&Ale, Steak&Shake, Subway, **lodging:** Comfort Suites, Day's Inn, Hampton Inn, Motel 6, Waterford Lodge, **other:** AutoZone, BMW, Mazda, NAPA, O'Reilly Parts, Radio Shack, TrueValue, Walgreens, **2 mi N on frtge rd gas:** Meijer/dsl/24hr, Phillips 66, **food:** Applebees,

**SOUTH BEND** (left vertical tab)

**IN** (circle tab)

---

**SOUTH BEND PORTAGE GARY AREA** (right vertical tabs)

**77**   Continued
Burger King, McDonald's, Sonic, **other:** Aldi Foods, $Tree, Walmart SuperCtr, **S gas:** Marathon, Phillips 66/dsl, **food:** Bob Evans, Denny's, King Gyro's, Mikados Japanese, Pancake House, Perkins, Taco Bell, Wendy's, **lodging:** Best Value Inn, Hilton Garden, Holiday Inn Express, Howard Johnson, Jameson Inn, Knight's Inn, Quality Inn, St Marys Inn, **other:** H HOSPITAL, vet, to Notre Dame

**76mm**   St Joseph River

**72**   US 31, to Niles, South Bend, **N gas:** Pilot/Subway/dsl/scales/24hr, Speedway/Subway/dsl, **lodging:** Super 8, **2 mi S on US 20 food:** 4 Seasons Rest., McDonald's, Ponderosa, Taco Bell, Wendy's, **lodging:** Day's Inn, Quality Inn, **other:** RV Ctr, to Potato Creek SP (20mi), ✈, st police

**62mm**   Eastern Time Zone/Central Time Zone

**56mm**   **Rockne travel plaza both lanes, BP/dsl, DQ, McDonald's, ℂ, RV dump, litter barrel**

**49**   IN 39, to La Porte, **N lodging:** Hampton Inn, **S lodging:** Best Value Inn, Cassidy Inn & RV, **3 mi S gas:** Mobil/dsl, **lodging:** Blue Heron Motel, Holiday Inn Express, Super 8

**39**   US 421, to Michigan City, Westville, **5 mi N lodging:** Hampton Inn, Holiday Inn, Knight's Inn, **other:** Premium Outlets/famous brands, **S** Purdue U North Cent

**38mm**   **trucks only rest area both lanes, litter barrels**

**31**   IN 49, to Chesterton, Valparaiso, **N lodging:** Best Western, Hilton Garden, Super 8 (3mi), **other:** Sand Creek RV Park (4mi, Apr-Oct), to IN Dunes Nat Lakeshore, **S lodging:** Hampton Inn (8mi), **other:** Yellow Brick Rd Museum/gifts

**24mm**   toll plaza

**23**   Portage, Port of Indiana, **0-2 mi N gas:** Marathon, Shell, **food:** Mark's Grill, **lodging:** Day's Inn, Comfort Inn, Country Inn&Suites, Holiday Inn Express, $Inn, Ramada Inn, Super 8, **S gas:** BP, Clark, Marathon, **food:** Burger King, Cici's Pizza, Dunkin Donuts, DQ, First Wok Chinese, Jimmy John's, KFC, McDonald's, Starbucks, Subway, Wendy's, **other:** Advance Parts, Ace Hardware, $General, Family$, GNC, Town&Country Mkt/24hr, USPO, Walgreens

**22mm**   **TP both lanes, info, gas: BP/dsl, food: Fazoli's, Hardee's, other: playground, scales**

**21mm**   **I-90 and I-80 run together eb, separate wb. I-80 runs with I-94 wb. For I-80 exits 1 through 15, see Indiana Interstate 94.**

**21**   I-94 E to Detroit, I-80/94 W, US 6, IN 51, Lake Station, **S gas:** ⚙FLYING J/Cookery/dsl/scales/24hr/@, Road Ranger/Subway/dsl/scales, TA/BP/Popeye's/dsl/scales/24hr/@, **food:** McDonald's, **other:** Blue Beacon

**17**   I-65 S, US 12, US 20, Dunes Hwy, to Indianapolis

**14b**   IN 53, to Gary, Broadway, **S gas:** Citgo, **food:**

**14a**   Grant St, to Gary, **S H HOSPITAL**

**10**   IN 912, Cline Ave, to Gary, **N** ✈, casino

**5**   US 41, Calumet Ave, to Hammond, **S gas:** Nice'n Easy, RaceCo, Speedway/dsl, **food:** Arby's, Aurelio's Pizza, Dunkin Donuts, Johnel's Rest., KFC, McDonald's, Subway, Taco Bell, White Castle, **lodging:** Quality Inn, Ramada Inn, Super 8, **other:** Aldi Foods, AutoZone, Murray's Parts, Walgreens

## INTERSTATE 80/90 CONT'D

| | |
|---|---|
| **3** | IN 912, Cline Ave, to Hammond, to Gary Reg ✈, **S gas:** BP |
| **1.5mm** | toll plaza |
| **1mm** | US 12, US 20, 106th St, Indianapolis Blvd, **N gas:** Citgo, Mobil, Shell/dsl, **other:** casino, **S food:** Burger King, KFC, McDonald's, **other:** Aldi Foods, Jewel-Osco, auto repair |
| **0mm** | Indiana/Illinois state line |

## INTERSTATE 94

| Exit # | Services |
|---|---|
| **46mm** | Indiana/Michigan state line |
| **43mm** | **Welcome Ctr wb, full ♿ facilities, info, ⌷, ⊞, litter barrels, vending, petwalk** |
| **40b a** | US 20, US 35, to Michigan City, **N food:** McDonald's (3mi), **other:** Ⓗ HOSPITAL, **S gas:** Speedway/dsl |
| **34b a** | US 421, to Michigan City, **N gas:** BP/dsl, Citgo/dsl, Meijer/dsl/24hr, Speedway/White Castle/dsl, Xpress/gas, **food:** Applebee's, Arby's, Baker's Square, Bob Evans, Buffalo Wings, Burger King, Chili's, Culver's, Denny's, El Bracero Mexican, IHOP, KFC, LJ Silver, McDonald's, New China, Pizza Hut/Taco Bell, Popeye's, Quizno's, Red Lobster, Ryan's, Schoop's Rest., Starbucks, Steak'n Shake, Subway, Texas Corral, Wendy's, **lodging:** Comfort Inn, Country Inn Suites, Hampton Inn, Holiday Inn, Knight's Inn, Milan Inn, Red Roof Inn, Super 8, **other:** Ⓗ HOSPITAL, Aldi Foods, AutoZone, BigLots, $Tree, Fanny May Candies, Ford/Lincoln/Mercury, JC Penney, Jo-Ann Fabrics, Lowe's Whse, Meijer, Parts+, Radio Shack, Sears/auto, Walgreens, Walmart/auto, **S gas:** Gas City/Subway, **other:** Buick/Pontiac/GMC, Harley-Davidson |
| **29mm** | weigh sta both lanes |
| **26b a** | IN 49, Chesterton, **N** to IN Dunes SP, **S gas:** BP/White Castle, Shell/24hr, Speedway/dsl, **food:** Applebee's, A&W/KFC, Arby's, Burger King, China Chef, Cold Stone Creamery, Dunkin Donuts, El Salto Mexican, LJ Silver, McDonald's, Pizza Hut, Quizno's, Schoops Rest., Subway, Sunrise Rest., Taco Bell, Wendy's, **lodging:** Best Western, Econolodge, Hilton Garden (3mi), Super 8, **other:** Advance Parts, Curves, Jewel-Osco, K-Mart, Sand Cr Camping (5mi), Walgreens, to Valparaiso |
| **22b a** | US 20, Burns Harbor, **N gas:** Steel City Express/scales/dsl, TA/Subway/Buckhorn Rest./scales/dsl/rest./24hr/@, **other:** Blue Beacon, **S gas:** Mobil, Pilot/McDonald's/Subway/dsl/scales/24hr, **other:** Camp-Land RV Ctr, Chevrolet, Chrysler/Dodge/Jeep, Ford/Mercury, Toyota/Scion, fireworks |
| **19** | IN 249, to Port of IN, Portage, **N gas:** Family Express/dsl, **food:** Hooters, Longhorn Steaks, **lodging:** Country Inn Suites, **other:** Bass Pro Shops, **S gas:** Marathon/24hr, Shell, **food:** Denny's, Ryan's Rest., **lodging:** Best Value, Day's Inn, Dollar Inn, Hampton Inn, Super 8, **2 mi S food:** Burger King, Subway, Wendy's |
| **16** | access to I-80/90 toll road E, I-90 toll road W, IN 51N, Ripley St, same as 15b&a |

**I-94/I-80 run together wb**

| | |
|---|---|
| **15b** | US 6W, IN 51, **N gas:** BP, ⊘FLYING J/Cookery/dsl/scales/24hr/@, Road Ranger/Subway/dsl/scales/24hr, TA/BP/Popeye's/dsl/scales/24hr/@, **food:** McDonald's, **other:** Blue Beacon, **N on US 20 gas:** Dunes/scales/dsl repair, Marathon, **food:** Bayside Grill, Ponderosa, **other:** Parts+ |
| **15a** | US 6E, IN 51S, to US 20, **S gas:** Mobil/dsl, Road Ranger/Subway/scales/dsl, Shell, **food:** Burger King, DQ, Papa John's, LJ Silver, Reuben's Café, Wendy's, **other:** Ace Hardware, Walgreens |
| **13** | Central Ave (from eb) |
| **12b** | I-65 N, to Gary and toll road |
| **12a** | I-65 S (from wb), to Indianapolis |
| **11** | I-65 S (from eb) |
| **10b a** | IN 53, Broadway, **N gas:** Citgo, Clark, **food:** JJ Fish, **S gas:** Gas Depot, Mobil, **food:** DQ, Rally's |
| **9** | Grant St, **N gas:** Clark, **food:** Chicago Hotdogs, **other:** Country Mkt Foods, Save-a-Lot Foods, Walgreens, **S gas:** Citgo, ⊘FLYING J/Cookery/scales/dsl/LP/24hr/@, Steel City/dsl/scales/rest./24hr, **food:** A&W/KFC, Burger King, Church's, Dunkin Donuts, J&J Fish, McDonald's, Subway, **other:** Aldi Foods, AutoZone, CarX, $Tree, Fagen Drug, Firestone/auto, Midas |
| **6** | BurrSt, **N gas:** BP/24hr, Pilot/Subway/dsl/scales/24hr/@, TA/Pizza Hut/Taco Bell/dsl/scales/24hr/@, **food:** J&J Fish & Chicken, Philly's Steaks, Rico's Pizza, **other:** SpeedCo, **S gas:** Citgo/dsl/24hr |
| **5** | IN 912, Cline Ave, **S gas:** BP, Clark, Marathon, Shell, Speedway/Subway, **food:** Arby's, DQ, Jedi's Garden Rest., KFC, McDonald's, Pizza Hut, Popeye's, White Castle, **lodging:** Hammond Inn, Motel 6, Super 8, **other:** $Tree, Fannie May Candies, K-Mart, Radio Shack |
| **3** | Kennedy Ave, **N gas:** Clark, Mobil/dsl, Speedway, **food:** Burger King, Domino's, McDonald's, **other:** AutoCare, Walgreens, **S gas:** Citgo, **food:** Cholie's Pizza, Cracker Barrel, Doggy Dog Grill, DQ, Firehouse Gyros, Squigi's Pizza, Subway, Wendy's, **lodging:** Courtyard, Fairfield Inn, Residence Inn, **other:** IN Welcome Ctr, Radio Shack, visitors ctr |
| **2** | US 41S, IN 152N, Indianapolis Blvd, **N gas:** Gas Stop, Luke, SavAStop, Shell, **food:** Arby's, Dunkin Donuts/Baskin-Robbins, House Of Pizza, Papa John's, Ralley's, Schoop's Burgers, Wheel Rest., Woodmar Rest., |

*Left margin (I-80/90 section): E ↕ W E ↕ W*

*Left margin (lower): P O R T A G E*

*Right margin: G A R Y A R E A*

*Right edge tab: IN*

**E ↕ W**

**INDIANAPOLIS AREA**

**IN**

## INTERSTATE 94 CONT'D

**2**　Continued
**other:** CarX, Goodyear, Midas, vet, **S gas:** Pilot/scales/dsl/24hr, **lodging:** AmeriHost, **other:** Cabela's

**1**　US 41N, Calumet Ave, **N gas:** BP/dsl, Gas Mart/dsl, **food:** Barton's Pizza, Dunkin Donuts/Baskin-Robbins, Subway, **other:** Walgreens, **S gas:** BP, Mobil/dsl, Marathon, Shell, **food:** Arby's, Boston Mkt, Burger King, Canton House Chinese, Dunkin Donuts/Baskin-Robbins, Edwardo's Pizza, Fortune House, Munster Gyros, Quizno's, Taco Bell, Wendy's, **other:** CVS Drug, $Jct, Radio Shack, Staples, Target

**0mm**　Indiana/Illinois state line

## INTERSTATE 465 - INDIANAPOLIS

**Exit #**　Services

**I-465**　loops around Indianapolis. Exit numbers begin/end on I-65, exit 108.

**53b a**　I-65 N to Indianapolis, S to Louisville

**52**　Emerson Ave, **N gas:** Marathon, Shell/Circle K, 24hr, Speedway, **food:** Burger King, Domino's, KFC, LJ Silver, Subway, Taco Bell, **lodging:** Motel 6, **other:** Ⓗ HOSPITAL, CVS Drug, Family$, **S gas:** Speedway/dsl, **food:** Arby's, Bamboo House, China Buffet, Egg Roll, El Puerto, Fazoli's, Fujiyama, Hardee's, McDonald's, Papa John's, Pizza Hut, Ponderosa, Rally's, RibHouse, Steak'n Shake, Subway, White Castle/24hr, Wendy's, **lodging:** Holiday Inn, Red Roof Inn, Super 8, **other:** Advance Parts, AutoZone, Curves, Goodyear/auto, K-Mart, Marsh Foods, NAPA, Radio Shack, Walgreens, Walmart SuperCtr, vet

**I-74 W and I-465 S run together around S Indianapolis 21 miles**

**49**　I-74 E, US 421 S

**48**　Shadeland Ave (from nb)

**47**　US 52 E, Brookville Rd, **E gas:** Shell, **food:** Burger King

**46**　US 40, Washington St, **E gas:** Marathon, **food:** Arby's, Blueberry Hill Pancakes, China Buffet, Italian Graden, Steak'n Shake, Subway, **other:** Ford, Osco Drug, Target, **W gas:** Thornton's, **food:** Applebee's, Burger King, Bob Evans, Fazoli's, McDonald's, Pizza Hut, Pi's Chinese, Wendy's, **lodging:** Signature Inn, **other:** K-Mart, PepBoys, Pontiac/GM/Mazda, Suzuki

**44b**　I-70 E, to Columbus

**44a**　I-70 W, to Indianapolis

**42**　US 36, IN 67 N, Pendleton Pike, **E food:** Hardee's, Papa's Rest., Popeye's, **lodging:** Knight's Inn, Ramada Inn, **W gas:** Speedway, Thornton's, **food:** A&W/KFC, Arby's, Denny's, Domino's, LJ Silver, Los Ranchero's, McDonald's, Pizza Hut/Taco Bell, Subway, Waffle House, White Castle, **other:** Ⓗ HOSPITAL, Advance Parts, CVS Drug, Family$, K-Mart/gas, O'Reilly Parts

**40**　56th St, Shadeland Ave, **E gas:** Marathon, to Ft Harrison

**37b a**　I-69, N to Ft Wayne, IN 37, **W other:** Ⓗ HOSPITAL, services on frontage rds

**35**　Allisonville Rd, **N food:** Applebee's, Hardee's, LJ Silver, McDonald's, MCL Cafeteria, Outback Steaks, Smokey Bones BBQ, **lodging:** Courtyard, **other:** Best Buy, Firestone/auto, Kohl's, mall, **S gas:** Shell, Speedway/dsl, **food:** ChuckeCheese, Papa John's, Perkins/24hr, White Castle, **lodging:** Jameson Inn, **other:** Circuit City, PetsMart, TJ Maxx, Trader Joe's, **S on 82nd food:** China Buffet, Panera Bread, **other:** Marsh Foods

**33**　IN 431, Keystone Ave, **N gas:** BP/McDonald's, Marathon/dsl, Shell, **food:** Arby's, Bob Evans, Burger King, Subway, **lodging:** Motel 6, **other:** BMW/Mini, Ford, Infiniti, KIA, Toyota/Scion, **S food:** Cooker, Keystone Grill, **lodging:** AmeriSuites, Marriott, Sheraton, Westin Suites, **other:** Champ's, Kohl's, mall

**31**　US 31, Meridian St, **N lodging:** Courtyard, Signature Inn, Wyndham Garden, **other:** Ⓗ HOSPITAL, Cadillac, **S gas:** Marathon, Shell/dsl, **food:** Arby's, McDonald's

**27**　US 421 N, Michigan Rd, **N gas:** Speedway/dsl, **food:** Applebee's, McDonald's, Subway, **lodging:** Country Inn& Suites, Red Roof Inn, **other:** Chevrolet, Marshalls, Pontiac/GMC, Target, **S gas:** BP, Marathon, Shell, Sunoco, **food:** Arby's, Bob Evans, Boston Mkt, Burger King, Chic-fil-a, China Buffet, Denny's, IHOP, Max&Erma's, O'Charley's, Outback Steaks, Pizza Hut, Qdoba Mexican, Rally's, Ruby Tuesday, Schlosky's, Steak'n Shake, Subway, Taco Bell, Texas Roadhouse, Wendy's, White Castle, Yen Ching Rest., **lodging:** Best Western, Comfort Inn, $Inn, Drury Inn, Embassy Suites, Extended Stay America, Fairfield Inn, Holiday Inn Select, HomeGate Inn, InTown Suites, La Quinta, Microtel, Quality Inn, Residence Inn, Signature Inn, Super 8, Wellesley Inn, **other:** Aamco, Aldi Foods, Costco/gas, Cub Foods, CVS Drug, Discount Tire, $General, $Tree, Firestone, Lowe's Whse, Office Depot, PepBoys, Radio Shack, Staples, Walmart SuperCtr

**25**　I-465 W

**23**　86th St, **E gas:** Shell/24hr, Speedway, **food:** Atlanta Bread, Arby's, Burger King, Chili's, Macaroni Grill, Longhorn Steaks, Quizno's, Traders Mill Grill, Wendy's, **lodging:** Fairfield Inn, Homestead Suites, Intown Suites, **other:** Ⓗ HOSPITAL, Big O Tires, Marsh Foods, Michaels, Old Navy

**21**　71st St, **E gas:** BP, **food:** Bob Evans, Hardee's, LePeep Rest, Max&Erma's, McDonald's, Quizno's, Starbucks, Steak'n Shake, Subway, **lodging:** Clarion Inn, Courtyard, Hampton Inn, Wingate Inn, **W food:** Bob Evans, Wendy's **lodging:** Residence Inn, Wingate Inn

**20**　I-65, N to Chicago, S to Indianapolis

**19**　56th St (from nb), **E gas:** Citgo/7-11, Speedway/dsl

**17**　38th St, **E gas:** BP, Marathon, Shell/24hr, **food:** Costa Brava, DQ, Golden Corral, Hooters, LJ Silver, Olive Garden, Ponderosa, Steak&Shake, Subway, White Castle, **lodging:** Day's Inn, Red Carpet Inn, **other:** AutoZone, CVS Drug, $Tree, Family$, Ford, Home Depot, Kroger/gas, O'Reilly Parts, Walgreens, **W food:** Arby's,

## INTERSTATE 465 CONT'D - INDIANAPOLIS

**17**   Continued
Burger King, Chili's, Cracker Barrel, Don Pablo, McDonald's, Pizza Hut/Taco Bell, Ruby Tuesday, TGIFriday, **lodging:** Ramada Ltd, Jameson Inn, **other:** Marsh Foods, Target

**I-74 W and I-465 S run together around S Indianapolis 21 miles**

**16b**   I-74 W, to Peoria

**16a**   US 136, to Speedway, **N gas:** Bigfoot, BP, Shell, **food:** Applebee's, Arby's, Blimpie, Buffalo Wild Wings, Burger King, Circle K/gas, Denny's, Hardee's, KFC, LJ Silver, McDonald's, Subway, Taco Bell, Wendy's, White Castle, **lodging:** $Inn, Motel 6, Red Roof, Super 8, **other:** $General, Firestone, Kroger, Marsh Foods, **S lodging:** Clarion

**14b a**   10th St, **N food:** Peking Chinese, Penn Station, Pizza Hut, Wendy's, **other:** HOSPITAL, Lowe's Whse, **S gas:** GA/Subway, Shell, Speedway/24hr, **food:** Arby's, Fazoli's, Hardee's, McDonald's, Taco Bell, **other:** CVS Drug

**13b a**   US 36, Rockville Rd, **N gas:** Marathon/Burger King, **lodging:** Comfort Inn, Sleep Inn, Wingate Inn, **other:** Sam's Club, **S gas:** Speedway/dsl/24hr, **food:** Bob Evans, **lodging:** Best Western

**12b a**   US 40 E, Washington St, **N food:** Burger King, China Buffet, Church's, Fazoli's, McDonald's, Papa John's, Taco Bell, White Castle, **other:** Ace Hardware, Advance Parts, AutoZone, CVS Drug, $Tree, Family$, Kroger/gas, Speedway Parts, U-Haul, Walgreens, transmissions, vet, **S gas:** Marathon/Circle K, Phillips 66/Noble Roman's/dsl, Thornton/24hr, **food:** Arby's, Hardee's, KFC, LJ Silver, McDonald's, Pizza Hut, Steak'n Shake, **lodging:** $Inn, **other:** Aamco, Goodyear, K-Mart, Sav-A-Lot Foods, TireBarn

**11b a**   Airport Expressway, **E gas:** Marathon, **food:** Denny's, Indy's Rest., Waffle House, **lodging:** Adam's Mark Hotel, Amerisuites, Courtyard, Day's Inn, Extended Stay Deluxe, Fairfield Inn, La Quinta, Quality Inn, Ramada Inn, Residence Inn, **W lodging:** Holiday Inn Select, Radisson

**9b a**   I-70, E to Indianapolis, W to Terre Haute

**8**   IN 67 S, Kentucky Ave, **E H** HOSPITAL, **W gas:** BP/McDonald's/dsl, Marathon, Swifty, Speedway, Shell, Subway, **food:** Big Boy, Burger King, Culver's, Damon's, Denny's, Hardee's, KFC, **lodging:** Country Inn&Suites

**7**   Mann Rd (from wb), **N H** HOSPITAL

**4**   IN 37 S, Harding St, **N gas:** Mr Fuel/dsl, Pilot/Subway/dsl/scales/24hr/@, **food:** Omelette Shoppe, **lodging:** Best Inn, Econolodge, **other:** **H** HOSPITAL, Blue Beacon, **S gas:** ⚡FLYING J/Conoco/dsl/LP/rest./scales/24hr/@, Marathon, **food:** Hardeeï¿½s, McDonald's, Taco Bell, White Castle, **lodging:** Knight's Inn, **other:** Freightliner, SpeedCo, Truck'o Mat/scales

**2b a**   US 31, IN 37, **N gas:** BP/24hr, **food:** Arby's, CiCi's, Domino's, DQ, Golden Wok, KFC, King Gyro's, LJ Silver, McDonald's, MCL Cafeteria, Old Country Buffet,

**2b a**   Continued
Pizza Hut, Steak&Ale, Steak'n Shake, White Castle, **other:** Aldi Foods, AutoTire, AutoWorks, AutoZone, Chrysler/Jeep, Dodge, $General, Family$, Firestone, Ford, Goodyear, Hancock Fabrics, Jo-Ann Fabrics, Jiffy Lube, Kroger/gas, Lincoln/Mercury, Office Depot, Osco Drug, Radio Shack, Save-A-Lot, Target, U-Haul, **S gas:** Speedway, **food:** Bob Evans, Denny's, 8Lucky Buffet, McDonald's, Red Lobster, Taco Bell, Wendy's, **lodging:** Best Value Inn, Comfort Inn, Day's Inn, Holiday Inn Express, Super 8, Travelodge, **other:** CVS Drug

**53b a**   I-65 N to Indianapolis, S to Louisville

**I-465**   **loops around Indianapolis. Exit numbers begin/end on I-65, exit 108.**

## INTERSTATE 469 - FT WAYNE

| Exit # | Services |
|---|---|
| **31c b a** | I-69, US 27 S., Auburn Road. I-469 begins/ends. |
| **29.15mm** | St Joseph River |
| **29b a** | Maplecrest Rd, **W gas:** BP/DQ/Subway/dsl, **food:** Mozzarelli's Pizza, Sonic, **other:** Marsh Foods |
| **25** | IN 37, to Ft Wayne, **W gas:** Meijer/dsl/24hr, **food:** Antonio's Pizza, Applebee's, Bob Evans, Buffalo Wild Wings, Cracker Barrel, Golden Corral, HoneyBee Chinese, McDonald's, Steak'n Shake, Subway, Wendy's, Uno Pizzaria, **other:** Discount Tire, Kohls, Marshall's, Office Depot, Walgreens, Walmart SuperCtr/gas |
| **21** | US 24 E |
| **19b a** | US 30 E, to Ft Wayne, **E gas:** Sunoco/Taco Bell/dsl, **other:** truck/tire repair, **W gas:** Citgo/dsl/mart, **food:** Garno's Italian, Golden Gate Chinese, Mancino's Grinders, Richard's Rest., Zesto Drive-In, **lodging:** Holiday Inn Express, **other:** Curves, $General |
| **17** | Minnich Rd |
| **15** | Tillman Rd |
| **13** | Marion Center Rd |
| **11** | US 27, US 33 S, to Decatur, Ft Wayne, **E gas:** BP/Subway/dsl |
| **10.5mm** | St Marys River |
| **9** | Winchester Rd |
| **6** | IN 1, to Bluffton, Ft Wayne, **W to** ✈ |
| **2** | Indianapolis Rd, **W to** ✈ |
| **1** | Lafayette Ctr Rd |

**N↕S**

**F T W A Y N E**

**I N D I A N A P O L I S   A R E A**

**IN**

## INTERSTATE 29

**N ↕ S**

**S I O U X   C I T Y**

| Exit # | Services |
|---|---|
| 152mm | Iowa/South Dakota state line, Big Sioux River |
| 151 | IA 12 N, Riverside Blvd, **E gas:** Casey's, **other:** $General, Fareway Foods, Riverside Prk, to Stone SP, Pecaut Nature Ctr |
| 149 | Hamilton Blvd, **E gas:** Conoco, **food:** Horizon Rest, **lodging:** Quality Inn, **other:** JiffyLube, tires, to Briar Cliff Coll, **W** Iowa Welcome Ctr sb, full facilities, Riverboat Museum |
| 148 | US 77 S, to S Sioux City, Nebraska, **W gas:** Conoco/dsl, **food:** DQ, La Fiesta Mexican, McDonald's, Pizza Hut, Taco Bell, **lodging:** Marina Inn, Regency Inn, **other:** Advance Parts, O'Reilly Parts |
| 147b | US 20 bus, Sioux City, **E gas:** Heritage Gas, **food:** Arby's, Burger King, Chili's, Famous Dave's, Hardee's, IHOP, KFC, Perkins/24hr, **lodging:** Best Western, Clarion, Holiday Inn/rest, Marina Inn, **other:** H HOSPITAL, Chevrolet, Staples, USPO, Walgreen |
| 147a | Floyd Blvd, **E gas:** Shamrock, **other:** Home Depot, **W** to Riverboat Casino |
| 146.5mm | Floyd River |
| 144b | I-129 W, US 20 W, US 75 S |
| 144a | US 20 E, US 75 N, to Ft Dodge, **1 mi E on Lakeport Rd gas:** Casey's, Shell, **food:** Buffalo Wild Wings, Burger King, ChuckeCheese, Coyote Canyon Steaks, Garfield's Rest, Gordman's, Hardee's, HuHot Chinese, Jimmy John's, KFC, LJ Silver/A&W, McDonald's, Olive Garden, Outback Steaks, Pizza Hut, Red Lobster, Red Robin, Starbucks, Tuesday Morning, Village Inn, **lodging:** Comfort Inn, Fairfield Inn, Hampton Inn, Holiday Inn Express, **other:** Barnes&Noble, Best Buy, Buick/Honda/Isuzu, Hy-Vee Foods/gas/24hr, JC Penny, JiffyLube, Jo-Ann Fabrics/crafts, Kohls, Lowe's Whse, Michael's, Old Navy, PetsMart, Sears/auto, Target, Younkers, mall |
| 143 | US 75 N, Singing Hills Blvd, **E gas:** Cenex/dsl, Shell/dsl/motel/café/24hr/@, **food:** China Buffet, Culver's, KFC, McDonald's, Pizza Hut, Quizno's, Taco John's, **lodging:** AmericInn, Baymont Inn, Day's Inn, Haven Motel, **other:** Caddilac/Pontiac/GMC, Lincoln/Mercury, Sam's Club/gas, Toyota/Scion, Walmart SuperCtr/gas, Sgt Floyd Mon, **W gas:** BP/dsl/motel/café/24hr/@, **food:** Wendy's, **lodging:** Super 8, **other:** Kenworth/Peterbilt, truckwash/repair |
| 141 | D38, Sioux Gateway ✈, **E gas:** Phillips 66/dsl, Shell/dsl, **food:** Aggies Ranch, China Taste, DQ, Godfather's, Pizza Ranch, Subway, **lodging:** Econolodge, **other:** Curves, mall, **W lodging:** Motel 6, **other:** ✈, museum |
| 139mm | rest area both lanes, full ♿ facilities, 📞 info, 🍽, litter barrels, RV dump, wireless internet |
| 135 | Port Neal Landing |
| 134 | Salix, **E** gas, **W** camping |
| 132mm | weigh sta sb, rest area nb, 🍽, litter barrels |
| 127 | IA 141, Sloan, **E gas:** Shell/dsl, **food:** B&R Pizza, **lodging:** Rip Van Winkle Motel, WinnaVegas Inn, **3 mi W gas:** Heritage Express, **other:** to Winnebago Indian Res/casino |
| 120 | to Whiting, **W** camping |
| 112 | IA 175, Onawa, **E gas:** Conoco/Subway/dsl/@, |

**COUNCIL BLUFFS**

| | |
|---|---|
| 112 | Continued<br>Phillips 66/dsl, **food:** DQ, Janz Rest., McDonald's, Michael's Rest., Pizza Hut, **lodging:** Super 8, **other:** H HOSPITAL, NAPA, On-Ur-Wa RV Park, Pamida, **2 mi W other:** KOA, Lewis&Clark SP, Keel Boat Exhibit |
| 110mm | rest area both lanes, full ♿ facilities, 📞 info, 🍽, litter barrels, petwalk, RV dump, wireless internet |
| 105 | E60, Blencoe |
| 96mm | Little Sioux River |
| 95 | IA 301, Little Sioux, **E** gas, **other:** Loess Hills SF (9mi), **W** Woodland RV Camp |
| 92mm | Soldier River |
| 91.5mm | rest area both lanes, litter barrels |
| 89 | IA 127, Mondamin, **1 mi E gas:** Jiffy Mart/dsl |
| 82 | F50, Modale, **1 mi W gas:** Cenex/dsl |
| 79mm | rest area both lanes, full ♿ facilities, info, 📞, 🍽, litter barrels, RV dump, wireless internet |
| 75 | US 30, Missouri Valley, **E Iowa Welcome Ctr (5mi), gas:** Shell/dsl/24hr, **food:** Arby's, McDonald's, Penny's Diner, Subway, **lodging:** Oaktree Inn, **other:** H HOSPITAL (2mi), to Steamboat Exhibit, **W gas:** BP/dsl, Phillips 66/rest/dsl, **food:** Burger King, Taco John's, **lodging:** Day's Inn, Rath Inn, Super 8, **other:** Chevrolet/Pontiac/Buick, Chrysler/Jeep/Dodge |
| 73.5mm | weigh sta both lanes |
| 72.5mm | Boyer River |
| 72 | IA 362, Loveland, **E gas:** Conoco/dsl, **W** to Wilson Island SP (6mi) |
| 71 | I-680 E, to Des Moines, **I-29 S & I-680 W run together 10 mi.** |
| 66 | Honey Creek, **W gas:** Sinclair/dsl, **food:** Iowa Feed&Grain Co Rest. |
| 61b | I-680 W, to N Omaha, **I-29 N & I-680 E run together 10 mi, W** Mormon Trail Ctr |
| 61a | IA 988, to Crescent, **E gas:** Phillips 66/dsl, **other:** to ski area |
| 56 | IA 192 S (sb only, exits left), Council Bluffs, **E lodging:** Super 7 Inn, **other:** H HOSPITAL |
| 55 | N 25th, Council Bluffs, **E gas:** Pump'n Munch/dsl, Sinclair/24hr |
| 54b | N 35th St (from nb), Council Bluffs, **E on Broadway...gas:** Bucky's Express, Phillips 66/dsl, Sinclair, **food:** Arby's, Burger King, Popeye's, Sonic, Wendy's, **lodging:** Quality Inn |
| 54a | G Ave (from sb), Council Bluffs |
| 53b | I-480 W, US 6, to Omaha |
| 53a | 9th Ave, S 37th Ave, Council Bluffs, **E gas:** Shell, Valero, **food:** Red Onion Cafe, **lodging:** Day's Inn, **W other:** Harrah's Casino/hotel, RiverBoat Casino, camping |
| 52 | Nebraska Ave, **E gas:** Phillips 66/dsl, **food:** Quaker Steak, Ruby Tuesday, **lodging:** Comfort Suites, SpringHill Suites, **other:** Bass Pro Shop, **W lodging:** AmeriStar Hotel/casino, Hampton Inn, Holiday Inn, **other:** RiverBoat Casino |
| 51 | I-80 W, to Omaha |
| I-29 and I-80 run together 3 miles | |
| 3 | IA 192 N, Council Bluffs, **E** to Hist Dodge House, **W gas:** Cenex, Phillips 66/dsl, Shell/dsl, TA/Pizza Hut/dsl/24hr/scales/@, **food:** Applebee's, Beijing Chinese, Burger King, Cracker Barrel, DQ, Fazoli's, Golden Corral, Hardee's, Huhot Mongolian, La Mesa Mexican, |

Copyright 2009 - The Next Exit®

## INTERSTATE 29 CONT'D

N
↕
S

| | |
|---|---|
| **3** | Continued<br>LJ Silver, McDonald's, Old River Pizza, Perkins, Red Lobster, Subway, Taco Bell, **lodging:** Day's Inn, Fairfield Inn, Motel 6, Settle Inn, **other:** Advance Parts, Aldi Foods, Chrysler/Jeep/Suzuki, Best Buy, Buick/Pontiac, Ford, Gordman's, Home Depot, Kia, Kohl's, Mazda, Menards, Outdoor Recreation RV, Sam's Club/gas, Subaru/Hyundai, Target, U-Haul, Walmart SuperCtr, truck/dsl repair |
| **1b** | S 24th St, Council Bluffs, **E** **gas:** BP, Conoco, Pilot/Arby's/scales/dsl/24hr, Sapp Bros/Shell/Burger King/dsl/rest., **food:** Famous Dave's BBQ, Hooters, Quaker Steak, Ruby Tuesday, Sleep Inn, **lodging:** American Inn, Best Western, Country Inn&Suites, SpringHill Suites, Super 8, **other:** Bass Pro Shop, Blue Beacon, Camping World RV Ctr, Goodyear, Peterbilt, SpeedCo, casino, **W** **Welcome Ctr, full facilities, other:** JC Penny, PetCo, ShopKO |
| **48** | I-80 E (from nb), to Des Moines, **E** **H** HOSPITAL |
| **47** | US 275, IA 92, Lake Manawa, **E** **gas:** Phillips 66, **other:** Iowa School for the Deaf, **W** **gas:** Ampride, **other:** Kohls, Target |
| **42** | IA 370, to Bellevue, **W** **other:** K&B Saddlery, to Offutt AFB, camping |
| **38mm** | **rest area both lanes, full ♿ facilities, 📞, info, 🏞, litter barrels, RV dump, petwalk, wireless internet** |
| **35** | US 34 E, to Glenwood, **E** **lodging:** Western Inn (4mi), **other:** RV Park, **W** **gas:** BP/dsl, **lodging:** Bluff View Motel, **other:** Ford, Harley Davidson |
| **32** | US 34 W, Pacific Jct, to Plattsmouth |
| **24** | L31, to Tabor, Bartlett |
| **20** | IA 145, Thurman |
| **15** | J26, Percival, **1-2 mi** **E** **gas:** BP/dsl |
| **11.5mm** | weigh sta nb |

| | |
|---|---|
| **10** | IA 2, to Nebraska City, Sidney, **E** to Waubonsie SP (5mi), **W** **gas:** BP/Sapp/rest./dsl/scales/24hr, Phillips 66/dsl, Shell/Subway/Crossroads Cafe/dsl/scales/24hr, **food:** Wendy's, **lodging:** Best Value, Super 8, **other:** to Arbor Lodge SP, Victorian Acres Camping (4mi), tire repair |
| **1** | IA 333, Hamburg, **1 mi** **E** **gas:** Casey's/dsl, **food:** Pizza Hut, **lodging:** Hamburg Motel, **other:** **H** HOSPITAL, Soda Fountain |
| **0mm** | Iowa/Missouri state line |

## INTERSTATE 35

N
↕
S

| Exit # | Services |
|---|---|
| **219mm** | Iowa/Minnesota state line |
| **214** | rd 105, to Northwood, Lake Mills, **W** Welcome Ctr both lanes, full ♿ facilities, 🏞 litter barrels, vending, petwalk, RV dump, **gas:** BP/Burger King/dsl, **lodging:** Country Inn Suites, Royal Motel (7mi), **other:** casino |
| **212mm** | weigh sta sb, rest area nb, 🏞, litter barrels |
| **208** | rd A38, to Joice, Kensett, **W** windmills |
| **203** | IA 9, to Manly, Forest City, to Pilot Knob SP |
| **202mm** | Winnebago River |
| **197** | rd B20, **8 mi** **E** Lime Creek Nature Ctr |
| **196mm** | rest area both lanes, 🏞, litter barrels |
| **194** | US 18, to Mason City, Clear Lake, **E** **gas:** BP/dsl, **other:** **H** HOSPITAL (8mi), Chevrolet, Freightliner, truck repair, **W** **gas:** Casey's, Pilot/Subway/dsl/scales, Kum&Go, Shell/Wendy's/dsl, **food:** Arby's, Burger King, Culver's, Denny's, DQ, KFC/Taco Bell, McDonald's, Perkins/24hr, Pizza Hut, Rice House Chinese, Subway, **lodging:** AmericInn, Best Western/rest., Budget Inn, Microtel |
| **193** | rd B35, to Mason City, Emery, **E** **gas:** Kum&Go/dsl, **lodging:** Super 8, **other:** truckwash, **W** **other:** Ford, to Clear Lake SP |
| **190** | US 18, rd 27 E, to Mason City |

IA

## INTERSTATE 35 CONT'D

**N ↕ S**

| Exit | Description |
|---|---|
| 188 | rd B43, to Burchinal |
| 182 | rd B60, to Rockwell, Swaledale |
| 180 | rd B65, to Thornton, **2 mi W other:** camping |
| 176 | rd C13, to Sheffield, Belmond |
| 170 | rd C25, to Alexander |
| 165 | IA 3, **E gas:** Shell/dsl/rest., **lodging:** AmericInn (9mi), Hampton Motel (9mi), **other:** 🄷 HOSPITAL (7mi) |
| 159 | rd C47, Dows, **W rest area both lanes, full** ♿ **facilities info,** 🅲, 🚻, **litter barrels, petwalk, vending, RV dump, wireless internet** |
| 155mm | Iowa River |
| 151 | rd R75, to Woolstock |
| 147 | rd D20, to US 20 E |
| 144 | rd D25, Williams, **E gas:** Phillips 66/dsl/Boondocks Motel&Cafe/@, **lodging:** Best Western, **other:** RV camping, **W gas:** ♦*FLYING J*/Conoco/dsl/rest./scales/24hr/@ |
| 142b a | US 20, to Webster City, Ft Dodge |
| 139 | rd D41, to Kamrar |
| 133 | IA 175, to Jewell, Eldora, **W gas:** Kum&Go/Subway/dsl, Prarie Land |
| 128 | rd D65, to Stanhope, Randall, **5 mi W** Little Wall Lake Pk |
| 124 | rd 115, Story City, **W gas:** Casey's, Kum&Go/dsl/24hr, **food:** DQ, Godfather's, Happy Chef/24hr, McDonald's, Pizza Ranch, Subway, **lodging:** Comfort Inn, Super 8, Viking Motel/rest, **other:** Ford, Gookin RV Ctr, VF Factory Stores/famous brands, Whispering Oaks Camping |
| 123 | rd E18, to Roland, McCallsburg |
| 120mm | **rest area nb, full** ♿ **facilities, info,** 🅲, 🚻, **litter barrels, vending, wireless internet, RV dump/scenic prairie area sb** |
| 119mm | **rest area sb, full** ♿ **facilities,** 🅲, 🚻, **litter barrels, vending, wireless internet, RV dump** |
| 116 | rd E29, to Story, **2 mi W** Story Co Conservation Ctr |
| 113 | 13th St, Ames, **W gas:** BP/Arby's/dsl, Kum&Go/Burger King/dsl, **food:** Buford's Steaks, Starlite Village Rest., **lodging:** Holiday Inn Express, Quality Inn, **other:** 🄷 HOSPITAL, Harley-Davidson, to USDA Vet Labs, ISU |
| 111b a | US 30, to Nevada, Ames, **E** Twin Acres Campground (11mi), **W gas:** Kum&Go/DQ/Subway/dsl, Shell/dsl/rest./@, **food:** Azteca Mexican, **lodging:** AmericInn, Comfort Inn, Country Inn Suites, Fairfield Inn, Hampton Inn, Heartland Inn, Microtel, Super 8, **other:** to IA St U |
| 109mm | S Skunk River |
| 106mm | weigh sta both lanes |
| 102 | IA 210, to Slater, **3 mi W food:** DQ, Subway |
| 96 | to Elkhart, **W** to Big Creek SP (11mi), Saylorville Lake |
| 94mm | **rest area both lanes, full** ♿ **facilities, info,** 🅲, 🚻, **litter barrels, vending, petwalk, wireless internet** |
| 92 | 1st St, Ankeny, **W gas:** Kum&Go, QT, **food:** Ankeny Diner, Applebee's, Arby's, Burger King, Cazador Mexican, Fazoli's, Guadalajara Mexican, KFC, Quizno's, Subway, Village Inn Rest., **lodging:** Best Western/rest., Day's Inn, Fairfield Inn, Heartland Inn, Super 8, **other:** 🄷 HOSPITAL, Goodyear/auto, O'Reilly Parts, Staples, Tires+, auto repair |
| 90 | IA 160, Ankeny, **E food:** Chip's Diner, Outback Steaks, **lodging:** AmericInn, Comfort Inn, Country Inn Suites, Holiday Inn Express, **other:** Buick/GMC/Pontiac, **W** |

**DES MOINES**

**AMES**

| Exit | Description |
|---|---|
| 90 | Continued **gas:** Casey's/dsl, Phillips 66, **food:** B-bops Rest., Burger King, Chili's, China Buffet, Culver's, El Charro, IHOP, McDonald's, Panera Bread, Starbucks, Wendy's, **other:** Big O Tires, Chevrolet, Ford, GNC, Home Depot, Kohl's, Micheal's, Radio Shack, Sportsman's Whse, Target, TJ Maxx, Walgreen, Walmart SuperCtr, to Saylorville Lake (5mi) |
| 89 | Corporate Woods Dr, **W lodging:** Value Place |
| 87b a | I-235, I-35 and I-80 |

**I-35 and I-80 run together 14 mi around NW Des Moines. See Iowa Interstate 89, exits 124-136.**

| Exit | Description |
|---|---|
| 72c | University Ave, **E gas:** Kum&Go/Burger King, QT, **food:** Biaggi's Rest., Boston's, Caribou Coffee, Cracker Barrel, El Rodeo Mexican, Wendy's, **lodging:** Best Western, Country Inn&Suites, La Quinta, **other:** 🄷 HOSPITAL, Granite City Food, Walgreens, **W gas:** BP/MaidRite, **food:** Applebee's, Bakers Square, Cheddar's, Chili's, Huhot Mongaolian, Jason's Deli, Macaroni Grill, McDonald's, Mi Mexico, Outback Steaks, Qdoba Mexican, RockBottom Rest./brewery, **lodging:** Chase Suites, Courtyard, Heartland Inn, Ramada Inn, Sheraton, Wildwood Lodge, **other:** Barnes&Noble, Best Buy, Borders, K-Mart, Kohl's, Lowe's Whse, Marshall's, Office Depot, PetsMart, SteinMart, Target, World Mkt |
| 72b | I-80 W |
| 72a | I-235 E, to Des Moines |
| 70 | Civic Pkwy, Mills, **E gas:** Kum&Go/McDonald's, **food:** Firecreek Grill, Legend's Grill, Quizno's, **other:** HyVee Foods/gas, Walgreens, **W food:** Applebees, BoneFish Grill, Buffalo Wild Wings, Caribou Coffee, Champp's Grill, Cheesecake Factory, Cusina Italiana, Fleming's Rest., Fuddruckers, Iron Wok, Joe's Crabshack, Johnny's Italian Steaks, Joseph's Steaks, Mimi's Cafe, O'Charly's, On-the-Border, Panera Bread, PF Chang's, Quizno's, Red Robin, **lodging:** Courtyard, Drury Inn, Hilton Garden, Holiday Inn, Residence Inn, **other:** Best Buy, Costco/gas, Dillards, Kohl's, Lowe's Whse, PetCo, Scheel's Sports, Target, TJ Maxx, Walmart SuperCtr |
| 69b a | Grand Ave, W Des Moines |
| 68.5mm | Racoon River |
| 68 | IA 5, **7 mi E** to 🛬, to Walnut Woods SP |
| 65 | G14, to Norwalk, Cumming, **14 mi W** John Wayne Birthplace, Madison Co Museum |
| 61mm | North River |
| 56 | IA 92, to Indianola, Winterset, **W gas:** Kum&Go/cafe/dsl, Shamrock/dsl, **food:** Hitchin Post Grill |
| 56mm | Middle River |
| 53mm | **rest area nb, litter barrels** |
| 52 | G50, St Charles, St Marys, **W gas:** Kum&Go, **other, 14 mi:** John Wayne Birthplace, museum |
| 51mm | **rest area sb, litter barrels** |
| 47 | rd G64, to Truro, **W gas:** Kum&Go (1mi) |
| 45.5mm | South River |
| 43 | rd 207, New Virginia, **E gas:** Kum&Go/Subway/dsl |
| 36 | rd 152, to US 69, **3 mi E lodging:** Blue Haven Motel, Evergreen Inn, **W** st patrol |
| 34 | Clay St, Osceola, **W gas:** Kum&Go, **food:** Maid-Rite Cafe, **other:** Lakeside Casino Resort/camping |
| 33 | US 34, Osceola, **E gas:** Casey's/dsl, Shell/rest., **food:** Family Table Rest., McDonald's, Pizza Hut, Subway, |

## INTERSTATE 35 CONT'D

**33** Continued
**lodging:** Regal Inn, Day's Inn, Super 8, **other:** H HOSPITAL, Ford, Chrysler/Dodge/Jeep, Hy-Vee Foods, O'Reilly Parts, Pamida, st patrol, tires, **W gas:** BP/Arby's/dsl, **food:** KFC/Taco Bell, **lodging:** AmericInn, **other:** Walmart SuperCtr

**32mm** rest area both lanes, full & facilities, C, ⊞, litter barrels, vending, petwalk, RV dump, wireless internet

**31mm** weigh sta nb, parking area sb

**29** rd H45

**22** rd J14, Van Wert

**18** rd J20, to Grand River

**12** rd 2, Decatur City, Leon, **E gas:** Shell/dsl/rest, **food:** Country Corner Rest., **5 mi E lodging:** Little River Motel, **other:** H HOSPITAL

**7.5mm** Grand River

**7mm** Welcome Ctr nb/rest area sb, full & facilities, info, C, ⊞, litter barrels, vending, petwalk, RV dump, wireless internet

**4** US 69, to Davis City, Lamoni, **E** to 9 Eagles SP (10mi), **W gas:** Casey's (2mi), **food:** Pizza Hut (2mi), QC Rest, Subway (2mi), **lodging:** Chief Lamoni Motel, Super 8, **other:** CarQuest, auto/truck repair, antiques, IA Welcome Ctr

**0mm** Iowa/Missouri state line

## INTERSTATE 80

**Exit #** Services

**307mm** Iowa/Illinois state line, Mississippi River

**306** US 67, to Le Claire, **N** Welcome Ctr wb (no trucks), full & facilities, ⊞, litter barrels, C, petwalk, **gas:** Phillips 66/dsl, **food:** McDonald's, Subway, **lodging:** Comfort Inn, Holiday Inn, Super 8, **other:** Slagle Foods, **1 mi N gas:** BP, **food:** A&W (2mi), **other:** Buffalo Bill Museum, **S gas:** BP/dsl

**301** Middle Rd, to Bettendorf

**300mm** rest area both lanes, full & facilities, C, ⊞, litter barrels, vending, petwalk, RV dump

**298** I-74 E, to Peoria, **S other:** to H HOSPITAL, st patrol

**295b a** US 61, Brady St, to Davenport, **N gas:** BP, **other:** Hummer, to Scott CP, **0-2 mi S gas:** BP, Phillips 66, Shell, **food:** Burger King, Cracker Barrel, Happy Joe's, Hardee's, McDonald's, Royal Wok, ThunderBay Grille, Village Inn Rest., **lodging:** AmericInn, Best Western/rest., Baymont Inn, Casa Loma Suites, Clarion, Country Inn&Suites, Day's Inn, Heartland Inn, Motel 6, Residence Inn, Super 8, Travelodge, **other:** AutoZone, CarQuest, Meneards, Radio Shack, Sears/auto, Toyota, US Adventures RV Ctr, Von Mar, mall, vet

**292** IA 130 W, Northwest Blvd, **N gas:** ✈FLYING J/Phillips 66/Cookery/dsl/LP/rest./scales/24hr, **lodging:** Comfort Inn, **other:** Interstate RV Park (1mi), Farm&Fleet, Peterbilt, truckwash, **S gas:** BP/McDonald's, Sinclair, **food:** Machine Shed Rest., **lodging:** Econolodge

**290** I-280 E, to Rock Island

**284** Y40, to Walcott, **N gas:** Pilot/Arby's/dsl/24hr/scales, TA/IA 80/BP/DQ/Wendy's/dsl/scales/24hr/@, **food:**

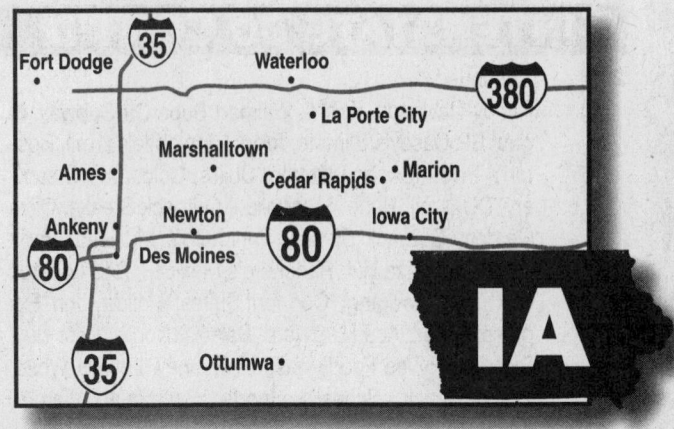

**284** Continued
Gramma's Rest., **lodging:** Comfort Inn, Walcott Motel, **other:** Blue Beacon, IA 80 Trucking Museum, SpeedCo Lube, tires, **S gas:** Pilot/Subway/dsl/24hr, **food:** McDonald's, **lodging:** Day's Inn, **other:** Cheyenne RV Ctr, Walcott CB

**280** Y30, to Stockton, New Liberty

**277** Durant, **2 mi S** food

**271** US 6 W, IA 38 S, to Wilton

**270mm** rest area both lanes, full & facilities, info, C, ⊞, litter barrels, vending, petwalk, RV dump, wireless internet

**268mm** parking areas

**267** IA 38 N, to Tipton, **N gas:** Kum&Go, **other:** Cedar River Camping

**266mm** Cedar River

**265** to Atalissa, **S gas:** Diesel Depot/Blues BBQ/Chesterfried/dsl/scales/24hr

**259** to West Liberty, Springdale, **S gas:** BP/dsl/24hr, **lodging:** Econolodge, **other:** KOA

**254** X30, West Branch, **N gas:** BP/Quizno's, Casey's, **other:** Jack&Jill Foods, USPO, Hoover NHS, **S gas:** Kum&Go, **food:** McDonald's, **lodging:** Presidential Inn, **other:** Chrysler/Dodge/Jeep

**249** Herbert Hoover Hwy, **N** winery (2mi), **S** golf

**246** IA 1, Dodge St, **N gas:** BP/A&W/Subway/dsl, **lodging:** Quality Inn, **S gas:** Sinclair, **food:** Bob's Pizza, **lodging:** Travelodge

**244** Dubuque St, Iowa City, **N** Coralville Lake, **S** H HOSPITAL, to Old Capitol, museum

**242** to Coralville, **N food:** River City Grille, **lodging:** Hampton Inn, Holiday Inn, **S gas:** BP, Conoco, Kum&Go, **food:** Arby's, Big Tenn, Burger King, Cancun Mexican, Edge Rest., Hardee's, IA Riverpower Rest., KFC, LJ Silver, LoneStar Steaks, McDonald's, Milio's Sandwiches, Mondo's Cafe, Old Chicago Grill, Papa John's, Peking Buffet, Perkins/24hr, Slugger's Grill, Sonic, Taco Bell, Taco John's, **lodging:** Baymont Inn, Best Western, Comfort Inn, Days Inn, Fairfield Inn, Marriott, Motel 6, Super 8, **other:** H HOSPITAL, Walgreens, vet

**240** IA 965, to US 6, Coralville, N Liberty, **N gas:** Phillips 66/dsl, **food:** Buffalo Wild Wings, Culver's, McDonald's, Steak'n Shake, TX Roadhouse, Village Inn Rest., Wendy's, **lodging:** AmericInn, Country Inn&Suites, Suburban Lodge, **other:** Colony Country Camping (3mi),

## INTERSTATE 80 CONT'D

E ↑ ↓ W

**240** Continued
Harley-Davidson, Kohl's, Walmart SuperCtr/Subway, **S gas:** BP, Casey's/Blimpie, **food:** Applebee's (1mi), Boston's Pizza, Caribou Coffee, Chili's, Coldstone Creamery, DQ (1mi), Huhot Mongolian, Outback Steaks, Olive Garden, Outback Steaks, Panchero's Mexican, Papa Murphy's, Pizza Hut, Ranchero's Mexican, Red Lobster, Starbucks, **lodging:** Comfort Suites, Holiday Inn Express, **other:** Ace Hardware, Barnes&Noble, Best Buy, Dillard's, HyVee Foods/gas, JC Penney, Lowe's Whse, Radio Shack, Scheel's Sports, Sears/auto, Target, Tires+, U-Haul, Younkers, mall

**239b** I-380 N, US 218 N, to Cedar Rapids
**239a** US 218 S
**237** Tiffin, **1 mi N food:** Jon's Rest., L&J BBQ
**236mm** rest area both lanes, full ♿ facilities, 🕿, 🌲, litter barrels, vending, RV dump, petwalk, wireless internet
**230** W38, to Oxford, **N other:** Sleepy Hollow Camping, Kalona Museum
**225** US 151 N, W21 S, **N** to Amana Colonies, **lodging:** Heritage Inn, **S Welcome Ctr, gas:** BP, Casey's, **food:** Colony Village Rest., MaidRite Cafe, Little Amana Rest./Winery, 7 Villages Rest., Ox Yoke Rest., **lodging:** Econolodge, Holiday Inn, Super 8
**220** IA 149 S, V77 N, to Williamsburg, **N gas:** BP, Casey's/dsl, **food:** Arby's, McDonald's, Subway, **lodging:** Best Western, Crest Motel, Super 8, **other:** GNC, Old Navy, factory outlets/famous brands, **S lodging:** Day's Inn
**216** to Marengo, **N gas:** Kum&Go/Subway/dsl, **lodging:** Sudbury Court Motel (7mi), **other:** H HOSPITAL
**211** to Ladora, Millersburg, **S** Lake IA Park (5mi)
**208mm** rest area both lanes, full ♿ facilities, 🕿, vending, 🌲, litter barrels, petwalk, wireless internet, RV dump
**205** to Victor
**201** IA 21, to Deep River, **N gas:** Phillips 66/SS/dsl/24hr, **food:** Nick's Rest., **lodging:** Sleep Inn, **S gas:** Kwik-Star/Pinecone Rest./dsl/scales/24hr/@, truck repair
**197** to Brooklyn, **N gas:** BP/diner/dsl, **other:** RV camping
**191** US 63, to Montezuma, **N gas:** Sinclair/dsl, **S** to Fun Valley Ski Area (13mi)
**182** IA 146, to Grinnell, **N gas:** Casey's (1mi), Kum&Go/Subway/dsl, **food:** KFC, Taco Bell, **lodging:** Best Western, Comfort Inn, Country Inn, Day's Inn, Super 8, **other:** H HOSPITAL (4mi), Chrysler/Dodge/Jeep (1mi), $General, Hyvee Foods, Walmart SuperCtr (1mi), vet, **S** Fun Valley Ski Area (16mi)
**180mm** rest area both lanes, full ♿ facilities, 🕿, vending, weather info, 🌲, litter barrels, petwalk, playground, RV dump (eb) wireless internet
**179** IA 124, to Oakland Acres, Lynnville
**175mm** N Skunk River
**173** IA 224, Kellogg, **N gas:** Phillips 66/Best Burger/dsl/rest./24hr, **other:** Kellogg RV Park, Rock Creek SP (9mi), **S** Lake Pla-mor Camping, Pella Museum **other:** camping
**168** SE Beltline Dr, to Newton, **1 mi N gas:** Casey's/dsl, **food:** Arby's, Taco John's, **lodging:** Mid-Iowa Motel,

**NEWTON**

**168** Continued
**other:** $Tree, Chrysler/Jeep/Dodge, Radio Shack, Rolling Acres Camping, Walmart SuperCtr/gas, **S gas:** Cenex/dsl, Love's/McDonald's/scales/dsl, **lodging:** AmericInn, **other:** Iowa Speedway
**164** US 6, IA 14, Newton, **N gas:** Casey's, Phillips 66/Subway/dsl, **food:** Country Kitchen, Culver's, KFC/Taco Bell, Okoboji Grill, Perkins/24hr, Pizza Ranch, Senor Tequila Mexican, **lodging:** Day's Inn, Econolodge, Quality Inn, Super 8, **other:** H HOSPITAL, museum, **S lodging:** Newton Inn/rest., **other:** Chevrolet/Cadillac, Ford/Lincoln/Mercury, to Lake Red Rock
**159** F48, to Jasper, Baxter
**155** IA 117, Colfax, **N gas:** BP/McDonald's, **lodging:** Comfort Inn, Microtel, **other:** Pitstop RV Camping, truck repair, **S gas:** Casey's, Kum&Go/Subway/dsl/24hr
**153mm** S Skunk River
**151** weigh sta wb
**149** Mitchellville
**148mm** rest area both lanes, full ♿ facilities, 🕿, 🌲, litter barrels, petwalk, vending, RV dump, wireless internet
**143** Altoona, Bondurant, **N food:** Quizno's (1mi), **S gas:** Casey's, **lodging:** Holiday Inn Express, **other:** HyVee Foods (2mi)

**DES MOINES**

**142b a** US 65, Hubble Ave, Des Moines, **S gas:** BP, Bosselman/Pilot/Sinclair/dsl/rest./24hr/@, Git'n Go, **food:** Big Steer Rest., Burger King, Culver's, Godfather's, KFC/Taco Bell, McDonald's/playpalce, Pizza Hut, Subway, Taco John's, **lodging:** Adventureland Inn, Heartland Inn, Motel 6, Regency Inn, Settle Inn, **other:** Blue Beacon, Freightliner, Peterbilt, camping, casino
**141** US 6 W, US 65 S, Pleasant Hill, Des Moines
**137b a** I-35 N, I-235 S, to Des Moines
**I-80 W and I-35 S run together 14 mi.**
**136** US 69, E 14th St, Camp Sunnyside, **N gas:** BP/dsl, Casey's/Phillips 66, **food:** Bonanza, Country Kitchen, **lodging:** Bavarian Inn, Motel 6, Red Roof Inn, Rodeway Inn, **other:** Volvo/GMC, antiques, **0-1 mi S gas:** Phillips 66, Star Gas, QT/Burger King/dsl/scales/24hr, **food:** Arby's, Fazoli's, McDonald's, Papa Murphy's, Subway, Taco Bell, Taco John's, Village Inn Rest., **lodging:** Baymont Inn, Travelodge, **other:** Advance Parts, Aldi Foods, CarQuest, $General, Family$, Tires+, TruckLube
**135** IA 415, 2nd Ave, Polk City, **N other:** Harley-Davidson, antiques, **S gas:** Git'n Go, QT, Shell, **other:** H HOSPITAL, Earl's Tire, Goodyear, NAPA Auto Care, USPO (2mi), st patrol
**133mm** Des Moines River
**131** IA 28 S, NW 58th St, **N gas:** QT, **food:** Chopsticks, Greenbriar Rest., NorthEnd Diner, Pagliai's Pizza, Panera Bread, Quizno's, Sonic, Starbucks, Subway, **lodging:** Best Inn, **other:** Acura, Goodyear/auto, HyVee Food, Infiniti, VW/Audi, vet, **S gas:** BP/dsl/24hr, Phillips 66, QT, **food:** Arby's, Daytona's Grill, Famous Dave's BBQ, KFC, McDonald's, Perkins, Popeye's, Shangrila Buffet, Village Inn Rest., Wendy's, **lodging:** Day's Inn, Econolodge, Holiday Inn, Quality Inn, Ramada, Super 8, **other:** H HOSPITAL, Best Buy, Chevrolet, Chrysler,

**IA**

## INTERSTATE 80 CONT'D

E ↕ W

**D E S   M O I N E S**

| | |
|---|---|
| **131** | Continued<br>$Tree, Ford/Lincoln/Mercury, NAPA Autocare, Nissan, Office Depot, Toyota/Scion, mall, vet |
| **129** | NW 86th St, Camp Dodge, **N** **gas:** Kum&Go, **food:** Burger King, Coldstone Creamery, Legends Grill, Maid-Rite Cafe, McDonald's, Okoboji Grill, Old Castle Diner, Panchero's Mexican, Planet Sub, Starbucks, TX Roadhouse, Village Inn Rest., **lodging:** Hilton Garden, Stoney Creek Inn, TownePlace Suites, **other:** Dahl's Foods, **S** **gas:** BP, Casey's, **food:** Arby's, B-Bops Burgers, Culver's, Friedrich's Coffee, Happy Joe's Pizza, Papa Murphy's, Torroco Grill, **lodging:** Microtel, **other:** Walgreens |
| **127** | IA 141 W, Grimes, **N** **gas:** BP/dsl, Phillips 66/dsl, **food:** MaidRite Cafe, Subway, **lodging:** AmericInn (3mi), to Saylorville Lake, **S** **food:** Quizno's, **other:** Home Depot, Radio Shack, Target |
| **126** | Douglas Ave, Urbandale, **N** **gas:** Pilot/Grandma Max's/Subway/dsl/24hr/scales/@, **S** **gas:** Kum&Go/dsl, **food:** Dragon China, **lodging:** Day's Inn, Econolodge, Extended Stay America |
| **125** | US 6, Hickman Rd, **N** **gas:** ⊕FLYING J/Conoco/Cookery/dsl/LP/24hr/@, **other:** Dodge/Jeep, Menards, to Living History Farms, **S** **food:** IA Machine Shed Rest., **lodging:** Clyde Hotel, Comfort Suites, Sleep Inn, **other:** GMC, Goodyear, Honda, Hyundai |
| **124** | (72c from I-35 nb), University Ave, **N** **gas:** Kum&Go/Burger King, QT, **food:** Biaggi's Rest., Boston's, Caribou Coffee, Cracker Barrel, El Rodeo Mexican, Wendy's, **lodging:** Best Western, Country Inn&Suites, La Quinta, **other:** Ⓗ HOSPITAL, Granite City Food, Walgreens, **S** **gas:** BP/MaidRite, **food:** Applebee's, Bakers Square, Cheddar's, Chili's, Huhot Mongolian, Jason's Deli, Macaroni Grill, McDonald's, Mi Mexico, Outback Steaks, Qdoba Mexican, RockBottom Rest./brewery, **lodging:** Chase Suites, Courtyard, Heartland Inn, Ramada Inn, Sheraton, Wildwood Lodge, **other:** Barnes&Noble, Best Buy, Borders, K-Mart, Kohl's, Lowe's Whse, Marshall's, Office Depot, PetsMart, SteinMart, Target, World Mkt |
| **I-80 E and I-35 N run together 14 mi** | |
| **123b a** | I-80/I-35 N, I-35 S to Kansas City, I-235 to Des Moines |
| **122** | (from eb) 60th St, W Des Moines |
| **121** | 74th St, W Des Moines, **N** **food:** Biaggi's Rest., Panera Bread, **lodging:** Hampton Inn, Staybridge Suites, **other:** Granite City Foods, HyVee Food/gas, Walgreens, **S** **gas:** Kum&Go/Subway, **food:** Arby's, Burger King, CK's, Culver's, McDonald's, Perkins, Quizno's, Taco John's, **lodging:** Candlewood Suites, Fairfield Inn, Marriott, Motel 6, SpringHill Suites, vet |
| **119mm** | rest area both lanes, full Ⓐ **facilities, info, vending,** Ⓒ, Ⓣ, **petwalk, RV dump, Wireless Internet** |
| **117** | R22, Booneville, Waukee, **N** **food:** Organic Farm Rest., **other:** Timberline Camping (2mi), **S** **gas:** Kum&Go/24hr, **food:** Rube's Steaks, Waveland Rest. (2mi) |
| **115mm** | weigh sta eb |
| **113** | R16, Van Meter, **1 mi** **S** **gas:** Casey's, **other:** Feller Museum, Veteran's Cemetary |

| | |
|---|---|
| **112mm** | N Racoon River |
| **111mm** | Middle Racoon River |
| **110** | US 169, to Adel, DeSoto, **N** Aircraft Supermkt, John Wayne Birthplace, camping (6mi), **S** **gas:** Casey's, Kum&Go/dsl, **lodging:** Countryside Inn, Edgetowner Motel |
| **106** | F90, P58 |
| **104** | P57, Earlham, **S** **gas:** Casey's (2mi), **food:** Master Griller (2mi) |
| **100** | US 6, to Redfield, Dexter |
| **97** | P48, to Dexter, **N** **gas:** Casey's (2mi), camping |
| **93** | P28, Stuart, **N** **gas:** BP/dsl/24hr, Casey's/dsl/scales, Kum&Go, **food:** Burger King, McDonald's/playplace, Subway, **lodging:** AmericInn, Super 8, **other:** Chevrolet, $General, Hometown Foods, **S** **gas:** Phillips 66/dsl, **food:** Country Kitchen, **lodging:** Edgetowner Motel, **other:** NAPA |
| **88** | P20, Menlo |
| **86** | IA 25, to Greenfield, Guthrie Ctr, **S** **other:** Ⓗ HOSPITAL (13mi), to Preston/Spring Brook SP |
| **85mm** | Middle River |
| **83** | N77, Casey, **1 mi** **N** **gas:** Kum&Go, **other:** camping |
| **80.5mm** | **rest area both lanes, full** Ⓐ **facilities,** Ⓒ, Ⓣ, **litter barrels, vending, petwalk, RV dump, wireless internet** |
| **76** | IA 925, N54, Adair, **N** **gas:** Casey's/dsl, Kum&Go/Subway/dsl, **food:** Happy Chef, Smiley's Steaks, **lodging:** Adair Budget Inn, Super 8, **other:** camping |
| **75** | G30, to Adair |
| **70** | IA 148 S, Anita, **S** to Lake Anita SP (6mi) |
| **64** | N28, to Wiota |
| **61mm** | E Nishnabotna River |
| **60** | US 6, US 71, to Atlantic, Lorah, **S** **gas:** Phillips 66/Country Cafe/dsl/24hr, **lodging:** Day's Inn |
| **57** | N16, to Atlantic, **S** Ⓗ HOSPITAL (7mi) |
| **54** | IA 173, to Elk Horn, **6 mi** **N** **Welcome Ctr/Wireless Internet, lodging:** AmericInn, **other:** Windmill Museum, gas, food (7mi) |
| **51** | M56, to Marne |
| **46** | M47, Walnut, **N** **gas:** BP/McDonald's/24hr, **food:** Villager Buffet, **lodging:** Super 8, to Prairie Rose SP (8mi), **S** **gas:** Kum&Go/dsl/24hr, **food:** Aunt B's Kitchen, **lodging:** Red Carpet Inn, repair |
| **44mm** | **weigh sta, wb/parking area eb** |
| **40** | US 59, to Harlan, Avoca, **N** **gas:** Phillip 66/Taco John's/Maidrite/dsl/24hr/scales, **food:** Subway, **lodging:** |

Copyright 2009 - The Next Exit®

## INTERSTATE 80 CONT'D

**E ↕ W**

| | |
|---|---|
| 40 | Continued |
| | Motel 6, **other:** H HOSPITAL (12mi), truckwash, **S gas:** Shell/dsl (1mi), **food:** Embers Rest., **lodging:** Avoca Motel, Capri Motel (1mi), **other:** Avoca Foods, Nishna Museum |
| 39.5mm | **W Nishnabotna River** |
| 34 | M16, Shelby, **N gas:** Shell/Cornstalk Cafe/dsl, **food:** DQ, **lodging:** Shelby Country Inn/RV Park, **S other:** dsl/tire repair |
| 32mm | **rest area both lanes, parking only** |
| 29 | L66, to Minden, **S gas:** Phillips 66/A&W, **lodging:** Mid-Town Motel (2mi), **other:** winery (4mi) |
| 27 | I-680 W, to N Omaha |
| 23 | IA 244, L55, Neola, **S gas:** Kum&Go/dsl, **other:** to Arrowhead Park, camping |
| 20mm | **Welcome Ctr eb/rest area wb, full ♿ facilities,** 🚻, 🅿, **litter barrels, vending, petwalk, RV dump, Wireless Internet** |
| 17 | G30, Underwood, **N gas:** Phillips 66/Subway/dsl/24hr, **lodging:** Underwood Motel, **other:** truck/tire repair |
| 8 | US 6, Council Bluffs, **N gas:** Phillips 66/dsl (1mi) |
| 5 | Madison Ave, Council Bluffs, **N gas:** BP, **food:** Burger King, FoodCourt, Great Wall Chinese, KFC, McDonald's, Panera Bread, Pizza Hut, Skeeter Barn's Steaks, Subway, **lodging:** Heartland Inn, **other:** Barnes&Noble, Dillard's, HyVee Food/drug, JC Penney, Old Navy, Sears/auto, Target, Walgreens, mall, **S gas:** Cenex/dsl, Phillips 66, **food:** DQ, Valentino's Rest., Village Inn Rest., **lodging:** Western Inn, **other:** TruValue |
| 4 | I-29 S, to Kansas City |
| 3 | IA 192 N, Council Bluffs, **N** to Hist Dodge House, **S gas:** Cenex, Phillips 66/dsl, Shell/dsl, TA/Pizza Hut/dsl/24hr/scales/@, **food:** Applebee's, Beijing Chinese, Burger King, Cracker Barrel, DQ, Fazoli's, Golden Corral, Hardee's, Huhot Mongolian, La Mesa Mexican, LJ Silver, McDonald's, Old River Pizza, Perkins, Red Lobster, Subway, Taco Bell, **lodging:** Day's Inn, Fairfield Inn, Motel 6, Settle Inn, **other:** Advance Parts, Aldi Foods, Chrysler/Jeep/Suzuki, Best Buy, Buick/Pontiac, Ford, Gordman's, Home Depot, Kia, Kohl's, Mazda, Menards, Outdoor Recreation RV, Sam's Club/gas, Subaru/Hyundai, Target, U-Haul, Walmart SuperCtr, truck/dsl repair |
| 1b | S 24th St, Council Bluffs, **N gas:** BP, Conoco, Pilot/Arby's/scales/dsl/24hr, Sapp Bros/Shell/Burger King/dsl/rest., **food:** Famous Dave's BBQ, Hooters, Quaker Steak, Ruby Tuesday, Sleep Inn, **lodging:** American Inn, Best Western, Country Inn&Suites, SpringHill Suites, Super 8, **other:** Bass Pro Shop, Blue Beacon, Camping World RV Ctr, Goodyear, Peterbilt, SpeedCo, casino, **S Welcome Ctr, full facilities, other:** JC Penny, PetCo, ShopKO |
| 1a | I-29 N, to Sioux City |
| 0mm | Iowa/Nebraska state line, Missouri River |

## INTERSTATE 235 - DES MOINES

| Exit # | Services |
|---|---|
| 15 | I-80, E to Davenport |
| 13 | US 6, E Euclid Ave, **E gas:** Casey's, **food:** Burger |

**C O U N C I L   B L U F F S**

**IA**

---

**N ↕ S**

| | |
|---|---|
| 13 | Continued |
| | King Dragon House Chinese, Papa John's, Perkins, **other:** $Tree, Hancock Fabrics, HyVee Foods/drug, Walgreen, **W gas:** QT, **other:** Great Outdoor RV Ctr, NAPA |
| 11 | Guthrie Ave, **W other:** CarQuest |
| 10a b | IA 163 W, E University Ave, Easton Dr |
| 9 | US 65/69, E 14th, E 15th, **N other:** Walgreen, **S food:** McDonald's, Quizno's, **other:** H HOSPITAL, st capitol, zoo |
| 8b | E 6th St, Penn Ave (from wb), **N** H HOSPITAL |
| 8a | 3rd St, 5th Ave, **N lodging:** Holiday Inn, **other:** H HOSPITAL, **S lodging:** Embassy Suites, Marriott, Quality Inn, **other:** Conv Ctr |
| 7 | Keo Way |
| 6 | MLK Blvd/31st St, Drake U, Governor's Mansion, **S** ✈ |
| 5b | 42nd St, Science & Art Ctr, **N gas:** Git'n Go, **food:** Papa John's, **other:** Curves |
| 5a | 56th St (from wb), **N** golf |
| 4 | IA 28, 63rd St, to Windsor Heights, **S** Hist Valley Jct, zoo |
| 3 | 8th St, W Des Moines, **N gas:** Kum&Go, **food:** B-Bop's Café, Burger King, **other:** HyVee Foods, PetCo, Sam's Club/gas, Sears AutoCtr, Walmart SuperCtr, **S gas:** BP, Kum&Go, **food:** Coach's Corner Grill, Garcia's Mexican, Jimmy's American Café, **lodging:** Best Western |
| 2 | 22nd St, 24th St, W Des Moines, **N gas:** BP, Phillips 66/dsl, **food:** ChuckeCheese, Culver's, Famous Dave's BBQ, Gordman's, Hardee's, Hooters, LoneStar Steaks, McDonald's, Old Country Buffet, Taco Bell, Village Inn Rest., Zachary's Grill, **lodging:** Studio+, **other:** Firestone/auto, Goodyear/auto, Gordman's, Hancock Fabrics, Michael's, Office Depot, Walgreen |
| 1b | Valley West Dr, W Des Moines, **N gas:** BP/dsl, **food:** Olive Garden, Red Lobster, TGI Friday's, **other:** HyVee Foods, JC Penney, SteinMart, Target, Younker's, mall |
| 0mm | I-235 begins/ends on I-80, exit 123. |

## INTERSTATE 280 - DAVENPORT

| Exit # | Services |
|---|---|
| 18b a | I-74, US 6, Moline, **S gas:** Star Gas/dsl, **food:** McDonald's, Montana Jack's, **lodging:** Country Inn&Suites, Econolodge, Hampton Inn, Holiday Inn, La Quinta, Motel 6, Quality Inn, **other:** ✈ |
| 15 | Airport Rd, Milan, **N food:** (1mi) MaidRite Café, Subway, **other:** Buick/Chevrolet, Firestone |
| 11b a | IL 92, to Andalusia, Rock Island, **S** KOA Camping |
| 9.5mm | Iowa/Illinois state line, Mississippi River |
| 8 | rd 22, Rockingham Rd, to Buffalo |
| 6 | US 61, W River Dr, to Muscatine, **W** gas, camping |
| 4 | Locust St, rd F65, 160th St, **E** H HOSPITAL, to Palmer Coll, St Ambrose U, **W gas:** Star Gas/Subway/dsl |
| 1 | US 6 E, IA 927, Kimberly Rd, to Walcott, **E** lodging, transmissions |
| 0mm | I-280 begins/ends on I-80, exit 290. |

**D E S   M O I N E S**

**E ↕ W**

N ↕ S

KANSAS CITY AREA

OLATHE

## INTERSTATE 35

| Exit # | Services |
|---|---|
| **235mm** | Kansas/Missouri state line |
| **235** | Cambridge Circle |
| **234b a** | US 169, Rainbow Blvd, **E gas:** QT, Shell, **food:** Applebee's, Arby's, Burger King, McDonald's, Rosedale BBQ, Sonic, Wendy's, **lodging:** Best Western, Day's Inn, **other:** KU MED CTR, **W food:** KFC, LJ Silver |
| **233a** | SW Blvd, Mission Rd |
| **233b** | 37th Ave (from sb) |
| **232b** | US 69 N, **E gas:** QT, Phillips 66, **food:** McDonald's, Taco Bell |
| **232a** | Lamar Ave, **E gas:** QT |
| **231b a** | I-635 (exits left from nb) |
| **230** | Antioch Rd (from sb) **E gas:** QT |
| **229** | Johnson Dr, **E gas:** Phillips 66, **food:** Arby's, Chili's, Papa John's, **other:** GNC, Home Depot, Marshall's, Old Navy, PetsMart, Walgreen, **W gas:** Phillips 66/dsl, **other:** Walnut Grove RV Park |
| **228b** | US 56 E, US 69, Shawnee Mission Pkwy, **W food:** Burger King, Denny's, LJ Silver, Perkins, Pizza Hut, Steak'n Shake, Taco Bell, Wendy's |
| **228a** | 67th St, **E gas:** QT, Shell, **food:** Burger King, Denny's, Winstead's Rest., **lodging:** Comfort Inn, Drury Inn, Fairfield Inn, HomeStead Village, Quality Inn, **other:** BMW, CarMax, K-Mart, VW, **W gas:** Phillips 66, **other:** Jaguar, Land Rover, Mercedes, Porsche |
| **227** | 75th St, **E gas:** Circle K, Conoco, QT, **food:** KFC, McDonald's, Perkins, **lodging:** Extended Stay America, Wellesley Inn, **other:** H HOSPITAL, Acura, JC Penney, Walmart, **W gas:** Citgo/7-11, QT/dsl, Shell, **food:** FireMtn Grill, Ryan's, Sonic, Subway, Taco Bell, Wendy's, **lodging:** Hampton Inn |
| **225b** | US 69 S (from sb), Overland Pkwy |
| **225a** | 87th St, **E food:** Arby's, Green Mill Rest., Tippen's Rest., Wendy's, **lodging:** Holiday Inn, **other:** Gomer's Foods, **W gas:** BP, Shell, **food:** Kahn Chinese, Long-Branch Steaks, Mary's Place Gyros, Taco Bell, |

| Exit # | Services |
|---|---|
| **225a** | Continued Zarda BBQ, **other:** NTB, museum |
| **224** | 95th St, **E gas:** Phillips 66, Shell, **food:** Applebee's, Burger King, China Buffet, Chipotle Mexican, Cielio's Italian, Denny's, Holiday Ham Café, Houlihan's, KFC, McDonald's, Mimi's Café, Ming Palace, Mongolian BBQ, Old Chicago Pizza, On the Border, Outback Steaks, Pizza Hut, Ponderosa, Rainforest Cafe, Ruby Tuesday, Santa Fe Café, Steak&Ale, Taco Bell, TGIFriday, **lodging:** Comfort Inn, Day's Inn, Extended Stay America, Holiday Inn, La Quinta, Motel 6, Radisson, Super 8, **other:** H HOSPITAL, Advance Parts, Best Buy, CircuitCity, Dillard's, Firestone, HyVee Foods, JC Penney, Nordstrom's, Sam's Club/gas, SteinMart, mall, **W other:** Costco/gas |
| **222b a** | I-435 W & E |
| **220** | 119th St, **E gas:** Conoco, Phillips 66, Shell, **food:** A&W, Burger King, Carrabba's, Chevy's Mexican, China Café, Cracker Barrel, IHOP, Deli, Jimmy John's, Joe's Crabshack, La Mesa Mexican, LJ Silver, Machine Shed Rest., McDonald's, Rio Bravo Cantina, Ruby Tuesday, Schlotsky's, Souper Salad, Steak'n Shake, Subway, Tres Hombres Mexican, Wendy's, Zio's Italian, **lodging:** Comfort Suites, Fairfield Inn, Hampton Inn, Residence Inn, Value Place Hotel, **other:** Aamco, Best Buy, Barnes&Noble, Borders Books, Dodge, GNC, Goodyear/auto, Home Depot, Honda, Hyundai, Mazda, Old Navy, Radio Shack, Target, U-Haul, transmissions, **W** Bass Pro Shop |
| **218** | 135th, Santa Fe St, Olathe, **E gas:** QT, Shell/dsl, **food:** Backyard Burger, Burger King, Corona Garden Mexican, McDonlad's, Perkins, **other:** Ace Hardware, BigLots, Ford, K-Mart, Osco Drug, **W gas:** BP, Phillips 66, QT, **food:** Denny's, McDonald's, Ponderosa, Waffle House, Wendy's, **lodging:** Day's Inn, **other:** Chevrolet, Chrysler/Jeep, Kia, Mazda, Nissan, Pontiac/Buick/GMC, Saturn, Suzuki, Subaru, Toyota |
| **217** | Old Hwy 56 (from sb), same as 215 |

## INTERSTATE 35 CONT'D

**N ↕ S**

**215** US 169 S, KS 7, Olathe, **E gas:** Phillips 66/24hr, QT/dsl, **food:** Chipotle Mexican, FireMtn Grill, IHOP, Outback Steaks, Panera Bread, Red Robin, **food:** Candlewood Suites, **other:** Aldi Foods, Home Depot, Target, **W gas:** Presto, Shell/dsl/scales/24hr, **food:** Applebee's, Burger King, Chili's, 54th St Grill, FoodCourt, Red Lobster, McDonald's, Taco Bell, Waffle House, Wendy's, **lodging:** Econolodge, Holiday Inn, Microtel, Sleep Inn, **other:** H HOSPITAL, Chrysler/Jeep, Dillard's, Marshalls, mall

**213mm** weigh sta both lanes

**210** US 56 W, Gardner, **W gas:** Phillips 66/dsl, **food:** Arby's, KFC, McDonald's, Mr Goodcents Subs, Pizza Hut, Sonic, Subway, Taco Bell, Waffle House, **lodging:** Super 8, **other:** Walmart SuperCtr

**207** US 56 E, Gardner Rd, **E** Olathe RV Ctr, **W gas:** Conoco/dsl, Shell/dsl

**202** Edgerton

**198** KS 33, to Wellsville, **W gas:** Conoco

**193** Tennessee Rd, Baldwin

**187** KS 68, Ottawa, **W gas:** BP/dsl, Casey's, **food:** DQ, **other:** Buick/GMC/Pontiac, RV Ctr

**185** 15th St, Ottawa

**183** US 59, Ottawa, **W gas:** BP, Conoco/dsl, Ottawa Gas, Phillips 66/dsl, **food:** Applebee's, Burger King, DQ, KFC, LJ Silver, McDonald's, Old 56 Rest, Pizza Hut, Sirloin Stockade, Taco Bell, Wendy's, **lodging:** Best Western, Comfort Inn, Econolodge, Super 8, Travelodge, **other:** H HOSPITAL, Advance Parts, Chrysler/Dodge/Jeep, CountryMart Foods, $General, $Tree, Walmart SuperCtr/gas

**182b a** US 50, Eisenhower Rd, Ottawa

**176** Homewood, **W** RV camping

**175mm** rest area both lanes, full ♿ facilities, 🚻, 🏪, litter barrels, vending, petwalk, RV dump, wireless internet

**170** KS 273, Williamsburg, **W gas:** Sinclair/café/dsl

**162** KS 31 S, Waverly

**160** KS 31 N, Melvern

**155** US 75, Burlington, Melvern Lake, **E gas:** BP/Subway/dsl, TA/Shell/Wendy's/dsl/scales/24hr/@, **food:** Beto Jct Rest., **lodging:** Wyatt Earp Inn

**148** KS 131, Lebo, **E gas:** Casey's, **lodging:** Universal Inn, **W** to Melvern Lake

**141** KS 130, Neosho Rapids, **E** NWR (8mi)

**138** County Rd U, **W** antiques

**135** County Rd R1, **W** RV camping/🚻

**133** US 50 W, 6th Ave, Emporia, **1-3 mi E gas:** Casey's, **food:** McDonald's, Pizza Hut, **lodging:** Budget Host

**131** KS 57, KS 99, Burlingame Rd, **E gas:** Conoco/dsl, **food:** Hardee's, Mr Goodcents Subs, **other:** Dillon's Food

**130** KS 99, Merchant St, **E gas:** Phillips 66/dsl, **food:** Subway, **other:** Emporia St U, Lyon Co Museum

**128** Industrial Rd, **E gas:** Conoco, Finish Line, **food:** Bruff's Steaks, Burger King, Gambino's Pizza, Mazzio's, Pizza Hut, Subway, **lodging:** Econolodge, Travelodge, Motel 6, **other:** H HOSPITAL, Aldi Foods, CarQuest, Dillon's Food, $General, Family$, Goodyear/auto, Hastings Book, JC Penney, Walgreen, **W gas:** Phillips 66/Wendy's/dsl, Shell, **food:** Applebee's, Golden Corral, KFC, McDonald's, MT Mike's Steaks, Planet Sub, Starbucks, Taco Bell, Village Inn Rest., **lodging:** Candlewood Suites, Comfort Inn, Fairfield Inn, Holiday Inn Express,

**128** Continued **other:** Radio Shack, Staples, Walmart SuperCtr

**127c** KS Tpk, I-335 N, to Topeka

**127b a** US 50, KS 57, Newton, **E gas:** Conoco/dsl, ⊕ *FLYING J* /Conoco/Country Mkt/dsl/scales/rest./24hr/@, Phillips 66/dsl, Shell, **food:** Arby's, China Buffet, Papa John's, **lodging:** Best Value, Best Western/rest., Day's Inn, Rodeway Inn, **other:** Chevrolet/Pontiac/Buick, Chrysler/Dodge/Jeep/Toyota, Ford/Lincoln/Mercury/Nissan, Napa, PriceChopper Foods, tires, **W** Emporia RV Park

**127mm** I-35 and I-335 KS Tpk, toll plaza,

**I-35 S and KS Tpk S run together.**

**125mm** Cottonwood River

**111** Cattle Pens

**97.5mm** **Matfield Green Service Area (both lanes exit left), Phillips 66/dsl, McDonald's**

**92** KS 177, Cassoday, **E gas:** Fuel'n Service, 🚻

**76** US 77, El Dorado N, **E** El Dorado SP, **3 mi E gas:** Casey's, **food:** Pizza Hut, Taco Bell, **other:** Dillon's Foods/gas, city park

**71** KS 254, KS 196, El Dorado, **E gas:** Conoco/dsl, Phillips 66, **food:** Arbys, Cajun Shack, Freddy's Rest., KFC, Kountry Kettle, LJ Silver, McDonald's, Pizza Hut, Sonic, Spangles, Taco Tico, **lodging:** Best Western, Heritage Inn, Holiday Inn Express, Sunset Inn, Super 8, H HOSPITAL, **other:** H HOSPITAL, Bumper Parts, Deer Grove RV Park, $General, Ford/Lincoln/Mercury, KS Oil Museum, O'Reilly Parts, Pontiac/Buick/Cadillac, Radio Shack, Walmart SuperCtr/Subway

**65mm** **Towanda Service Area (both lanes exit left), Phillips 66/dsl, McDonald's**

**62mm** Whitewater River

**57** 21st St, Andover, **W** golf, 🚻

**53** KS 96, Wichita, **1 mi W on Kellogg gas:** Conoco/Wendy's, **food:** Burger King, McDonald's, Taco Bell, **other:** Acura, Lowe's Whse, Walmart SuperCtr

**50** US 54, Kellogg Ave, **E** McConnell AFB, **W food:** Italian Garden, **lodging:** Comfort Inn, Clubhouse Inn, Day's Inn, Fairfield Inn, Hampton Inn, Marriott, Motel 6, Residence Inn, Studio+, Super 8, **other:** VA H HOSPITAL, **E on Kellogg Ave gas:** Conoco/dsl, **food:** Bejing Bistro, Burger King, IHOP, McDonald's, Pizza Hut, Sonic, Subway, Taco Bell, **other:** Acura, Buick/Infiniti, CarMax, Lowe's Whse, Mazda, PepBoys, Porsche/Jaguar, Sears Grand, Sportsman's Whse, VW, Walmart SuperCtr, **W on Kellogg Ave food:** Arby's, Green Mill Rest., LJ Silver, McDonald's, Old Chicago Pizza, Pizza Hut, Red Lobster, Souper Salad, Steak&Ale, **lodging:** Econolodge, Garden Inn, Wichita Inn, **other:** Advance Parts, Barnes & Noble, Chevrolet/Cadillac, Chrysler/Dodge/Jeep, Dillard's, Firestone/auto, Ford, Hancock Fabrics, Honda, JC Penney, Kia, Lincoln/Mercury, Mitsubishi, Pontiac/GMC/Hyundai, Radio Shack, Sears/auto, Subaru/Isuzu, Target, TJ Maxx, Toyota/Scion, mall

**45** KS 15, Wichita, **E** Boeing Plant

**44.5mm** Arkansas River

**42** 47th St, I-135, to I-235, Wichita, **E gas:** Conoco, **lodging:** Comfort Inn, Day's Inn, Holiday Inn Express, **W gas:** Phillips 66, **food:** Applebee's, Braum's, Burger King, Carlos O'Kelly's, Godfather's, KFC, LJ Silver, McDonald's, New China Rest., Papa John's, Pizza Hut, Quizno's, Spangles Rest., Subway, Taco Bell, Taco Tico, **lodging:** Best Western, Heritage Inn, Red Carpet Inn,

## INTERSTATE 35 CONT'D

| | |
|---|---|
| **42** | Continued<br>Value Place, **other:** Checker's Foods, Dillon's Foods/dsl, K-Mart, O'Reilly Parts, Radio Shack |
| **39** | US 81, Haysville, **W lodging:** Haysville Inn |
| **33** | KS 53, Mulvane, **E** Mulvane Hist Museum, **W** Wyldewood Winery |
| **26mm** | **Belle Plaine Service Area (both lanes exit left), gas:** Phillips 66/dsl, **food:** McDonald's |
| **19** | US 160, Wellington, **3 mi W food:** Penny's Diner, **lodging:** OakTree Inn, Sunshine Inn, **other:** RV camping |
| **17mm** | toll plaza, I-35N and KS TPK N run together |
| **I-35 N and KS TPK N run together.** | |
| **4** | US 166, to US 81, South Haven, **E gas:** Cenex/dsl, **food:** Picadilly's, **lodging:** Economy Inn/rest., **W** Oasis RV Park |
| **1.5mm** | weigh sta nb |
| **0mm** | Kansas/Oklahoma state line |

## INTERSTATE 70

| Exit # | Services |
|---|---|
| **423b** | 3rd St, James St |
| **423a** | 5th St |
| **422d c** | Central Ave, service rd |
| **422b a** | US 69 N, US 169 S |
| **421b** | I-670 |
| **421a** | **S** railroad yard |
| **420b a** | US 69 S, 18th St Expswy |
| **419** | 38th St, Park Dr, access to 10 motels |
| **418b** | I-635 N (eb only), **N food:** McDonald's, Taco Bell, Wendy's, Dillard's, **other:** JC Penney, mall |
| **418a** | I-635 S |
| **417** | 57th St |
| **415a** | KS 32 E (from eb) |
| **415b** | to US 40 W, State Ave, Kansas City, **N on US 40 gas:** Conoco, Phillips 66/dsl, **food:** Arby's, KFC, Papa John's, Perkins, McDonald's, Taco Bell, **lodging:** Gables Motel, **other:** Advance Parts, Chevrolet, Lowe's Whse, Toyota |
| **414mm** | vehicle insp sta. wb, parking area both lanes, [C] |
| **414** | 78th St, **N gas:** QT, **food:** Wendy's, **lodging:** Days Inn, **N on US 40...gas:** Shell, **food:** Arby's, Burger King, DQ, Sonic, Subway, **other:** [H] HOSPITAL, Chevrolet, $Tree, O'Reilly Parts, Price Chopper Foods, Tires+, Walgreens, **S gas:** BP, **lodging:** American Motel, Comfort Inn |
| **411b** | I-435 N, access to Woodlands Racetrack, to KCI ✈ |
| **411a** | I-435 S |
| **410** | 110th St, **N** Cabela's, KS Speedway, Russel Stover Candies, last free exit wb before KS TPK |
| **225mm** | I-70 W and KS TPK run together |
| **224** | KS 7, to US 73, Bonner Springs, Leavenworth, **N gas:** Roadstar/dsl, QT, **food:** KFC/Taco Bell, Mazzio's, Subway, Waffle House, Wendy's, **lodging:** Holiday Inn Express, Super 8, **other:** museum, **S gas:** BP, **food:** Arby's, McDonald's, Mr. Goodcents, Quizno's, **other:** $General, Ford, PriceChopper Foods, Radio Shack, Walmart SuperCtr |
| **217mm** | toll booth |
| **209mm** | **Lawrence Service Area (both lanes exit left), full facilities,** Conoco/dsl, McDonald's |
| **204** | US 24, US 59, to E Lawrence, **S gas:** Presto/dsl, **food:** Burger King, Sonic, Woody's Gas, **lodging:** Motel 6, |

| | |
|---|---|
| **204** | Continued<br>SpringHill Suites (1mi), **other:** O'Reilly Parts |
| **203mm** | Kansas River |
| **202** | US 59 S, to W Lawrence, **S on US 40 gas:** BP, Conoco/dsl, Phillips 66/dsl, **food:** Burger King, Domino's, McDonald's, Panda Garden, Taco Bell, **lodging:** Baymont Inn, Best Value, Econolodge, Hallmark Inn, Hampton Inn, Holiday Inn, Quality Inn, **other:** [H] HOSPITAL, Advance Parts, Carquest, Firestone/auto, to Clinton Lake SP, to U of KS |
| **197** | KS 10, Lecompton, Lawrence, **N** Perry Lake SP, **S** Clinton Lake SP, |
| **188mm** | **Topeka Service Area, full facilities,** Conoco/dsl, Taco Bueno, Hardee's |
| **183** | I-70 W (from wb), to Denver |
| **367mm** | toll plaza |
| **366** | I-470 W, to Wichita, **I-70 E and KS TPK E run together** |
| **365** | 21st St, Rice Rd, access to Shawnee Lake RA |
| **364b** | US 40 E, Carnahan Ave, to Lake Shawnee |
| **364a** | California Ave, **0-1 mi S gas:** BP/dsl, Phillips 66/dsl, **food:** Arby's, Burger King, Domino's, McDonald's, Pizza Hut, Rosa's Mexican, Subway, Tacos El Mexicano, **other:** AutoZone, Dillon's Food/gas, $General, Family$, Pricechopper, Walgreens |
| **363** | Adams St, downtown |
| **362c** | 10th Ave (from wb), **N lodging:** Ramada Inn, Red Carpet Inn, **S gas:** BP, **other:** st capitol |
| **362b a** | to 8th Ave, downtown, **N lodging:** Capitol Center Inn, Ramada Inn, **other:** to St Capitol, **S gas:** BP |
| **361b** | 3rd St, Monroe St |
| **361a** | 1st Ave, **S** Ryder |
| **359** | MacVicar Ave |
| **358b a** | Gage Blvd, **S food:** McDonald's, Wendy's, **other:** [H] HOSPITAL |
| **357b a** | Fairlawn Rd, 6th Ave, **S gas:** Conoco, Phillips 66, **lodging:** Best Western, Holiday Inn/rest., Motel 6, **other:** $General, repair, zoo-rain forest |
| **356b a** | Wanamaker Rd, **N food:** Carino's, Red Robin, **lodging:** Hyatt Place, **other:** KS Museum of History, **S gas:** BP, Conoco, Phillips 66/dsl, **food:** Applebees, Boston Mkt, Buffalo Wild Wings, Burger King, Chili's, Chipotle Mexican, CiCi's Pizza, Coldstone Creamery, Coyote Canyon Café, Cracker Barrel, Denny's, Freddy's Custard, Golden Corral, Huhot Chinese, Jason's Deli, Hooters, IHOP, Longhorn Steaks, McDonald's, Mike's Subs, Mr. Goodcents, Old Chicago, Olive Garden, On the Border, Panda Buffet, Panera Bread, Papa Johns, Perkins, Pizza Hut, Red Lobster, Rib Crib, Ruby Tuesday, Sonic, Spangles, |

## INTERSTATE 70 CONT'D

**E** ↕ **W** TOPEKA

**356b a** Continued
Starbucks, Steak'n Shake, Taco Bell, Taco John's, TX Roadhouse, Timberline Steaks, Wendy's, **lodging:** Baymont Inn, Candlewood Suites, Clubhouse Inn, Comfort Inn, Country Inn&Suites, Courtyard, Day's Inn, Fairfield Inn, Hampton Inn, Motel 6, Holiday Inn Express, Quality Inn, Residence Inn, Sleep Inn, Super 8, ValuePlace, **other:** Barnes&Noble, Best Buy, Dillard's, Home Depot, JC Penney, K-Mart, Kohl's, Lowes Whse, Macy's, Office Depot, PetCo, Radio Shack, Sam's Club, Suzuki, Target, TJ Maxx, Tuesday Morning, Walmart SuperCtr, mall

**355** I-470 E, to VA MED CTR, Topeka, air museum, **1 mi S** same as 356

**353** KS 4, to Auburn Rd

**351** frontage rd (from eb), Mission Creek

**350** Valencia Rd

**347** West Union Rd

**346** Carlson Rd, to Rossville, Willard

**343** frontage rd

**342** Eskridge Rd, Keene Rd, access to Lake Wabaunsee

**341** KS 30, Maple Hill, **S gas:** 24-7/dsl/café

**338** Vera Rd

**336mm** rest area (exits left from both lanes), full ♿ facilities, 🚻, 🛆, litter barrels, RV dump, wireless internet, petwalk

**335** Snokomo Rd, Skyline Mill Creek Scenic Drive, Paxico

**333** KS 138, Paxico, **N** Mill Creek RV Camping, Winery/gas

**332** Spring Creek Rd

**330** KS 185, to McFarland

**329mm** weigh sta both lanes

**328** KS 99, to Alma, **N** Gas-N-Shop, **S** Wabaunsee Co Museum

**324** Wabaunsee Rd, **N** Grandma Horners Store & Factory

**322** Tallgrass Rd

**318** frontage rd

**316** Deep Creek Rd

**313** KS 177, to Manhattan, 8 mi **N gas:** Phillips 66, **food:** Applebee's, Chili's, McDonald's, Village Inn Rest., **lodging:** Best Western, Comfort Inn, Fairfield Inn, Hampton Inn, Motel 6, Super 8, **other:** Jeep, Nissan, Sears/auto, to KSU

**311** Moritz Rd

**310mm** rest area both lanes, full ♿ facilities, 🚻, 🛆, litter barrels, petwalk

**307** McDowell Creek Rd, scenic river rd to Manhattan

**304** Humboldt Creek Rd

**303** KS 18 E, to Ogden, Manhattan, **N other:** to KSU

**301** Marshall Field, **N other:** Cavalry Museum, Custer's House, KS Terr Capitol, to Ft Riley

**300** US 40, KS 57, Council Grove, **N lodging:** Dreamland Motel, **S** hist church

**299** Flinthills Blvd, to Jct City, Ft Riley, **N gas:** BP/dsl, Phillips 66, **food:** Stacy's Rest., **lodging:** Econolodge, Great Western Inn, Red Carpet Inn, Super 8

**298** Chestnut St, to Jct City, Ft Riley, **N gas:** Shell/Burger King/dsl/24hr, **food:** Arby's, Cracker Barrel, Family Buffet, Mr. Goodcents Subs, Taco Bell, **lodging:** Best Western, Candlewood Suites, Courtyard, Holiday Inn Express, Quality Inn, **other:** Alco, Curves, $General, $Tree, Goody's, Walmart SuperCtr

**296** US 40, Washington St, Junction City, **N gas:** BP, Casey's, Cenex/dsl, Shell/dsl/24hr, **food:** Casa Agave

JCT CITY

**296** Continued
Mexican, Church's, DQ, Denny's, McDonald's, Peking Chinese, Pizza Hut, Sirloin Stockade, Sonic, Subway, **lodging:** Comfort Inn, Day's Inn, Ramada Ltd, ValuePlace Hotel, **other:** Cadillac, Chevrolet, Food4Less/24hr, Haas Tire, Harley Davidson, Jeep, Pontiac

**295** US 77, KS 18, Marysville, to Milford Lake, **N gas:** Phillips 66/Sapp Bro's/A&W/dsl/24hr, **lodging:** Motel 6, **other:** Ⓗ HOSPITAL, truckwash, **S** RV Ctr

**294mm** rest area both lanes, full ♿ facilities, 🚻, 🛆, litter barrels, RV dump, petwalk

**290** Milford Lake Rd

**286** KS 206, Chapman, **S gas:** Cenex/dsl, **other:** KS Auto Racing Museum, **1 mi S gas:** Casey's

**281** KS 43, to Enterprise, **N gas:** Shell/dsl, **other:** 4 Seasons RV Ctr/Park

**277** Jeep Rd

**275** KS 15, to Clay Ctr, Abilene, **N food:** DQ, **lodging:** Brookville Motel/rest., Holiday Inn Express, **S gas:** BP/dsl, Phillips 66, **food:** Burger King, Joe Snuffy's Rest., Kuntz's Drive Inn, M&R Grill, McDonald's, Pizza Hut, Sonic, Subway, **lodging:** Best Value, Budget Inn, Super 8, **other:** Ⓗ HOSPITAL, Alco/gas, AutoZone, Chevrolet/Pontiac/Buick, CountryMart Foods, $General, Ford, Chrysler, Country Mart Foods, Jeep/Dodge, O'Reilly Parts, Radio Shack, Ricco Drug, to Eisenhower Museum

**272** Fair Rd, to Talmage, **S** Russell Stover Candy

**266** KS 221, Solomon

**265mm** rest area both lanes, full ♿ facilities, 🚻, 🛆, litter barrels, vending, petwalk

**264mm** Solomon River

**260** Niles Rd, New Cambria

**253mm** Saline River

**253** Ohio St, **S gas:** ⊕FLYING J/Conoco/Country Mkt/dsl/LP/scales/24hr, **other:** Ⓗ HOSPITAL, Harley-Davidson, Kenworth

**252** KS 143, Salina, **N gas:** Petro/Shell/Wendy's/Pizza Hut/dsl/24hr, Valero/Subway/dsl/rest./24hr **food:** Bayard's Café, IHOP, McDonald's, Ponderosa, **lodging:** Best Inn, Day's Inn, Holiday Inn Express, Motel 6, Salina Inn, Super 8, **other:** Blue Beacon, Freightliner, KOA, **S gas:** Bosselman/Pilot/Sinclair/rest./scales/dsl/24hr/@, Fuel Stop, **lodging:** Best Western, Econolodge

**250b a** I-135, US 81, N to Concordia, S to Wichita

**249** Halstead Rd, to Trenton

**244** Hedville, **N** Sundowner West RV Park, **S gas:** Cenex/dsl, **other:** Rolling Hills Park

**238** to Brookville, Glendale, Tescott

**233** to Beverly, Juniata

**225** KS 156, to Ellsworth, **S gas:** Elkhorn Corner/Pizza/dsl, **other:** Ft Harker Museum, Ft Larned HS

**224mm** rest area both lanes, full ♿ facilities, 🚻, 🛆, litter barrels, petwalk, RV dump

**221** KS 14 N, to Lincoln

**219** KS 14 S, to Ellsworth, **S gas:** Conoco/dsl

**216** to Vesper

**209** to Sylvan Grove

**206** KS 232, Wilson, **N gas:** Travel Shoppe/rest., **other:** RV Park, Wilson Lake (6mi), winery

**199** KS 231, Dorrance, **N** to Wilson Lake, **S** gas/food

**193** Bunker Hill Rd, **N gas:** Conoco/Quizno's/dsl/rest/24hr, to Wilson Lake

**189** US 40 bus, Pioneer Rd, Russell

ABILENE · SALINA

## INTERSTATE 70 CONT'D

**E ← → W**

**187mm** rest area both lanes, full &#9855; facilities, [C], [π], litter barrels, RV dump, petwalk

**184** US 281, Russell, **N** gas: Phillips 66/Mesquite Grill/dsl, 24/7/dsl, food: A&W, Meridy's Rest., McDonald's, Pizza Hut, Sonic, Subway, lodging: AmericInn, Day's Inn, Russell's Inn, Super 8, other: [H] HOSPITAL, Alco, CarQuest, $General, JJJ RV Park, Fossil Creek RV Park, st patrol, vet

**180** Balta Rd, to Russell

**175** KS 257, Gorham, **1 mi N** gas, food, [C]

**172** Walker Ave

**168** KS 255, to Victoria, **S** gas: Ampride/dsl, to Cathedral of the Plains

**163** Toulon Ave

**161** Commerce Parkway

**159** US 183, Hays, **N** gas: Valero/dsl/24hr, food: Applebee's, Carlos O'Kelly's, Golden Corral, IHOP, Red Sun Buffet, Subway, lodging: Best Western, Butterfield Inn, Comfort Inn, Hampton Inn, Sleep Inn, other: Chrysler/Dodge/Jeep, Ford/Lincoln/Mercury, Harley-Davidson, Home Depot, Radio Shack, Toyota, Walmart SuperCtr, **S** gas: BP/24hr, Conoco/dsl/24hr, Love's, Phillips 66/dsl, food: A&W, Arby's, Burger King, China Garden, Imperial Garden, KFC, LJ Silver, Lucky Buffet, McDonald's, MT Mike's Steaks, Papa John's, Pizza Hut, Sonic, Subway, Taco Bell, Taco Express, Taco Grande, Vagabond Rest., Village Inn Rest., Wendy's, Whiskey Creek Grill, lodging: Baymont Inn, Comfort Inn, Day's Inn, Econolodge, Holiday Inn, Motel 6, Quality Inn, Super 8, other: [H] HOSPITAL, Ace Hardware, Advance Parts, Chevrolet, Chrysler, Curves, Dillon's Foods/gas, Firestone/auto, Hastings Books, JC Penney, NAPA, Tires 4 Less, Walgreens, mall, st patrol

**157** US 183 S byp, to Hays, **S** other: museum, to Ft Hays St U

**153** Yocemento Ave

**145** KS 247 S, Ellis, **S** gas: Casey's, Phillips 66/DQ/Subway/dsl/24hr, lodging: Ellis House Inn, other: to Chrysler Museum, Railroad Museum, RV camping, USPO

**140** Riga Rd

**135** KS 147, Ogallah, **N** gas: Schreiner/dsl/café/24hr, **S** to Cedar Bluff SP (13mi)

**132mm** rest area both lanes, full &#9855; facilities, [π], litter barrels, petwalk, RV dump

**128** US 283 N, WaKeeney, **N** gas: Sinclair/dsl/24hr, lodging: Budget Host, Super 8, other: [H] HOSPITAL

**127** US 283 S, WaKeeney, **N** food: DQ, Frisky Biscuit Cafe, Jade Garden Rest., McDonald's, Pizza Hut, lodging: Best Western, KS Kountry Inn, **S** gas: BP/Real Country Cafe/dsl/rest./24hr, Conoco/Subway/dsl, lodging: Econolodge, other: KOA, antiques, auto repair

**120** Voda Rd

**115** KS 198 N, Banner Rd, Collyer

**107** KS 212, Castle Rock Rd, Quinter, **N** gas: Sinclair/dsl, lodging: Budget Host/rest., other: [H] HOSPITAL, Sunflower Campground, auto repair, **S** gas: 1st Stop/dsl/24hr, food: DQ

**99** KS 211, Park, **1 mi N** gas: Sinclair/dsl

**97mm** rest area both lanes, full &#9855; facilities, [π], litter barrels, vending, petwalk, RV dump

**95** KS 23 N, to Hoxie

**93** KS 23, Grainfield, **N** gas: Sinclair/dsl

**85** KS 216, Grinnell, **N** gas (.5 mi)

**79** Campus Rd

**76** US 40, to Oakley, **S** gas: TA/Shell/Subway/Buckhorn Rest./scales/dsl/24hr/@, lodging: Econolodge, 1st Interstate Inn, other: [H] HOSPITAL, Blue Beacon, Fick Museum

**70** US 83, to Oakley, **N** lodging: Free Breakfast Inn, **S** gas: Phillips 66/dsl, Sinclair/dsl, food: Colonial Steaks, other: [H] HOSPITAL, Hi-Plains RV Park, Prairie Dog Town, Fick Museum

**62** rd K, Mingo, **S** gas: gas/dsl/ [C]

**54** Country Club Dr, Colby, **1 mi N** gas: Bosselman's/Pilot/Wendy's/dsl/scales/24hr, lodging: Country Club Motel, other: [H] HOSPITAL, Bourquins RV camping

**53** KS 25, Colby, **N** gas: Conoco/DQ/dsl, 24-7/dsl, food: Arby's, Burger King, China Buffet, DQ, McDonald's, MT Mike's Steaks, Pizza Hut, Sonic, Subway, Taco John's, lodging: Day's Inn, Holiday Inn Express, Motel 6, Quality Inn, Super 8, other: [H] HOSPITAL, Dillon's Foods/gas, $General, Ford/Lincoln/Mercury, Haas Tire, Prairie Art Museum, Quilt Cabin, Radio Shack, Walmart Super Ctr, dsl repair, trucklube/wash, **S** gas: Petro/Phillips 66/scales/dsl, food: Baskin-Robbins, Chester's, City Limits Steaks, Quizno's, Starbucks, Village Inn Rest., lodging: Comfort Inn, Crown Inn, other: Buick/Cadillac/Chevrolet/Pontiac, Chrysler/Dodge/Jeep, outlets, truck wash

**48.5mm** rest area both lanes, full &#9855; facilities, [C], [π], litter barrels, RV park/dump, vending, petwalk

**45** US 24 E, Levant

**36** KS 184, Brewster, **N** gas: Fuel Depot/dsl/24hr

**35.5mm** Mountain/Central time zone

**27** KS 253, Edson

**19** US 24, Goodland, **N** gas: Sinclair, food: Pizza Hut, other: KOA, High Plains Museum

**17** US 24, KS 27, Goodland, **N** gas: Cenex, Conoco, Phillips 66/dsl, food: DQ, El Reynaldo's, McDonald's, Steakhouse Diner, Subway, Taco John's, Wendy's, lodging: Best Value Inn, Comfort Inn, Howard Johnson, Super 8, other: [H] HOSPITAL, Carquest, Buick/Chevrolet/Pontiac, Firestone/auto, Radio Shack, Walmart SuperCtr, **S** gas: Valero/deli/scales/dsl, lodging: Holiday Inn Express, other: Mid-America Camping

**12** rd 14, Caruso

**9** rd 11, Ruleton

**7.5mm** Welcome Ctr eb/rest area wb, full &#9855; facilities, info, [C], [π], litter barrels, petwalk, vending, wireless internet, RV dump

**1** KS 267, Kanorado

## INTERSTATE 70 CONT'D

| .5mm | weigh sta eb |
| 0mm | Kansas/Colorado State Line |

## INTERSTATE 135 - WICHITA

**N ↑ S** | **SALINA** | **McPHERSON**

| Exit # | Services |
|---|---|
| 95b a | I-70, E to KS City, W to Denver. I-135 begins/ends on I-70, exit 250. US 81 continues nb. |
| 93 | KS 140, State St, Salina |
| 92 | Crawford St, **E gas:** KwikShop, Phillips 66/dsl, Shell, Sinclair, 24-7/dsl, **food:** Arby's, Braum's, Guiterra's Rest., McDonald's, Russell's Rest., Spangles, Taco Bell, Subway, Western Sizzlin, **lodging:** Best Western, Comfort Inn, Fairfield Inn, Holiday Inn, Rodeway Inn, **other:** Advance Parts, Dillan's Foods, O'Reilly Parts, Radio Shack, Walgreens, **W gas:** Cenex/dsl, **lodging:** Quality Inn |
| 90 | Magnolia Rd, **E gas:** Phillips 66/dsl, Shell/24hr, **food:** Carlos O'Kelly's, Chili's, Cici's, Coyote Canyon Café, Domino's, Fazoli's, Hong Kong Buffet, IHOP, McDonald's, Mr Goodcents Subs, Papa Murphy's, Potrillo's Mexican, Quizno's, Schlotsky's, Sonic, Subway, Taco Tico, **lodging:** Best Value Inn, Candlewood Suites, **other:** Advance Parts, AutoZone, Buick/Subaru, Dillard's, Dillon's Foods/dsl, $General, $Tree, Goody's, Honda, JC Penney, Jo-Ann Fabrics, Old Navy, O'Reilly Parts, PetCo, Sears, Toyota, Tuesday Morning, mall, **W gas:** Cenex/dsl |
| 89 | Schilling Rd, **E gas:** KwikShop/dsl, **food:** Applebee's, Burger King, Pizza Hut, Popeye's, Red Lobster, Taco Bueno, Tucson's Steaks, Wendy's, **lodging:** Country Inn&Suites, Courtyard, Hampton Inn, **other:** Cadillac/Chevrolet, Lowe's Whse, Sam's Club/gas, Target, Walmart SuperCtr, **W gas:** Casey's, **lodging:** Baymont Inn, Comfort Inn, Super 8 |
| 88 | Waterwell RD, **E other:** Ford/Lincoln/Mercury, Nissan |
| 86 | KS 104, Mentor, Smolan |
| 82 | KS 4, Falun Rd, Assaria, **E other:** RV Camping |
| 78 | KS 4 W, Lindsborg, **E other:** Sandz Gallery/Museum |
| 72 | US 81, Lindsborg, **4 mi E other:** McPherson St Fishing Lake, Maxwell WR, **W other:** H HOSPITAL, gas, food, lodging, [C], camping, museum |
| 68mm | rest areas (both lanes exit left), full & facilities, [C], 📶, litter barrels petwalk, RV dump |
| 65 | Pawnee Rd |
| 60 | US 56, McPherson, Marion, **W gas:** Midway/dsl, **food:** Applebee's, Arby's, Braum's, Golden Dragon Chinse, KFC/LJ Silver, Krehbiels BBQ, La Fiesta Mexican, McDonald's, MT Mike's, Pizza Hut, Subway, Taco Bell, Taco Tico, **lodging:** Best Value Inn, Best Western, Days Inn, Holiday Inn Express, Red Coach Inn, **other:** H HOSPITAL, AutoZone, Chrysler/Dodge/Jeep, $General, Walmart SuperCtr |
| 58 | US 81, KS 61, to Hutchinson, McPherson |
| 54 | Elyria |
| 48 | KS 260 E, Moundridge, **2 mi W** gas, food, [C] |
| 46 | KS 260 W, Moundridge, **2 mi W** gas, food, [C] |
| 40 | Lincoln Blvd, Hesston, **E food:** Aggie Grill, **lodging:** AmericInn, **W gas:** Cenex/dsl, **food:** El Sarito Grill, Lincoln Perk Coffee, Pizza Hut, Sonic, Subway, **lodging:** Best Value Inn |
| 34 | N Newton, Avalene, KS 15, **E other:** RV camping, **W food:** Subway, **other:** Kaufman Museum |

**NEWTON** | **WICHITA**

| 33 | US 50 E, to Peabody (from nb) |
| 31 | 1st St, Broadway St, **E gas:** Cenex, Conoco/dsl, Shamrock, **food:** Applebee's, CJ's Rest., KFC, **lodging:** Best Value Inn, Day's Inn, 1st Inn, **other:** Chevrolet/Cadillac, Chrysler/Dodge/Jeep, Ford/Lincoln/Mercury, **W food:** Braum's, MT Mike's, **lodging:** Best Western/rest. |
| 30 | US 50 W, KS 15 (exits left from nb), to Hutchinson, Newton, **W gas:** Cenex, KwikShop/dsl, **food:** Arby's, Papa Murphy's, Pizza Hut, Quizno's, Sonic, Subway, **other:** H HOSPITAL, AutoZone, Dillon's Foods, $Tree, Walmart SuperCtr |
| 28 | SE 36th St, **W gas:** Shell, **food:** Burger King, **other:** Chisholm Trail Outlets/famous brands |
| 25 | KS 196, to Whitewater, El Dorado |
| 23mm | rest areas both lanes, full & facilities, [C], 📶, litter barrels, vending, petwalk, RV dump |
| 22 | 125th St |
| 19 | 101st St, **W other:** RV camping |
| 17 | 85th St, **E** Valley Ctr, KS Coliseum |
| 16 | 77th St, **E lodging:** Sleep Inn, **other:** Wichita Greyhound Park |
| 14 | 61st St, **E gas:** QT/dsl, Valero, **food:** Applebee's, Chopstix, Cracker Barrel, Pizza Hut, Spangles Rest., Subway, Taco Bell, Wendy's, **lodging:** Comfort Inn, **other:** Chevrolet, TrueValue, vet, **W gas:** Phillips 66/dsl, **food:** KFC, McDonald's, **lodging:** Super 8, **other:** Goodyear/auto |
| 13 | 53rd St, **E** Freightliner, Harley-Davidson, MAC, **W gas:** Phillips 66/dsl, **food:** Country Kitchen, **lodging:** Best Western, Day's Inn |
| 11b | I-235 W, KS 96, to Hutchinson |
| 11a | KS 254, to El Dorado |
| 10b | 29th St, Hydraulic Ave |
| 10a | KS 96 E |
| 9 | 21st St, **E food:** Sonic, **other:** Wichita St U |
| 8 | 13th St |
| 7a | downtown |
| 7b | 8th St, 9th St, Central Ave., **E** School of Medicine |
| 6b | 1st St, 2nd St, **E** AutoZone, **W** Chevrolet, Chrysler/Jeep |
| 5b | US 54, US 400, Kellogg Ave, **E gas:** QT, Valero, **food:** Chipotle Meixcan, McDonald's, Spangles, Subway |
| 5a | Lincoln St, **E food:** DQ, **W gas:** QT |
| 4 | Harry St, **1 mi E gas:** QT, **food:** Church's, Denny's, McDonald's, Spangles Rest., Subway, Wendy's, **W gas:** Don's/dsl |
| 3 | Pawnee Ave, **E gas:** QT, **W gas:** Phillips 66, Shell, **food:** Burger King, Church's, Papa John's, Pizza Hut, Spangles, **lodging:** Pawnee Inn, **other:** AutoZone, Checker's Foods, $General |
| 2 | Hydraulic Ave, **E gas:** QT, **W food:** McDonald's, Subway |
| 2mm | Arkansas River |
| 1c | I-235 N, **2 mi W** Hilton |
| 1b a | US 81 S, 47th St, **E gas:** Conoco, **lodging:** Comfort Inn, Day's Inn, Holiday Inn Express, **W gas:** Phillips 66, **food:** Applebee's, Braum's, Burger King, Carlos O'Kelly's, Godfather's, Hog Wild BBQ, KFC, LJ Silver, McDonald's, New China Buffet, Papa John's, Pizza Hut, Quizno's, Spangles Rest., Subway, Taco Bell, Taco Tico, **lodging:** Best Western, Heritage Inn, Red Carpet Inn, Value Place, **other:** Checker's Foods, Curves, Dillon's Foods/dsl, $General, Home Depot, K-Mart, O'Reilly's Parts, Radio Shack |
| 0mm | I-135 begins/ends on I-35, exit 42 |

## INTERSTATE 24

E ↕ W

| Exit # | Services |
|---|---|
| 93.5mm | Kentucky/Tennessee state line |
| 93mm | **Welcome Ctr wb, full ♿ facilities, 🚻, 🏕 litter barrels, vending, petwalk** |
| 91.5mm | Big West Fork Red River |
| 89 | KY 115, to Oak Grove, **N** to Jeff Davis Mon St HS, **S gas:** Pilot/McDonald's/dsl/scales/24hr/@, Shell/dsl |
| 86 | US 41A, to Ft Campbell, Pennyrile Pkwy, Hopkinsville, **N gas:** Chevron/Taco Tico/dsl/24hr, **S gas:** BP/dsl/24hr, ⊕FLYING J/Country Mkt/dsl/scales/LP/24hr/@, Pilot/Subway/Wendy's/dsl/scales/24hr, **food:** McDonald's, Waffle House, **lodging:** Comfort Inn, Day's Inn, Holiday Inn Express |
| 79mm | Little River |
| 73 | KY 117, to Gracey, Newstead |
| 65 | US 68, KY 80, to Cadiz, **S gas:** BP/dsl, Chevron/dsl, Shell/dsl/24hr, **food:** Cracker Barrel, KFC, McDonald's, Taco Bell, Wendy's, **lodging:** Holiday Inn Express, Knight's Inn, 7 Inn, Super 8, **other:** Ⓗ HOSPITAL, Candy's RV Ctr, Chevrolet, antiques, golf, to NRA's |
| 56 | KY 139, to Cadiz, Princeton, **S gas:** Chevron/dsl, **other:** Nat Rec Areas |
| 47mm | Lake Barkley |
| 45 | KY 293, to Princeton, Saratoga, **N other:** classic car museum, **S gas:** Chevron/dsl, **food:** Farmhouse Rest., **other:** Mineral Mound SP, RV Camping, to KY St Penitentiary |
| 42 | to W KY Pkwy eb |
| 40 | US 62, US 641, Kuttawa, Eddyville, **N lodging:** Country Hearth Inn, Regency Inn, Relax Inn, **other:** camping, **S gas:** BP/Wendy's/dsl/24hr, Huck's/Quizno's/dsl/scales/24hr/@, Shell, **food:** Huddle House, SW grill, **lodging:** Day's Inn, Hampton Inn, **other:** W KY Factory Outlet, to Lake Barkley, KY Lake Rec Areas, camping |
| 36mm | weigh sta both lanes, 🚻 |
| 34mm | Cumberland River |
| 31 | KY 453, to Grand Rivers, Smithland, **N gas:** BP/dsl, **lodging:** Microtel, **S gas:** Cheers/dsl, **food:** Miss Scarlett's, Patti's Rest., **lodging:** Best Western, Grand |

| Exit # | Services |
|---|---|
| 31 | **Continued** Rivers Resort (3mi), Lighthouse Landing Resort, **other:** Exit 31 RV Park, NRA's |
| 29mm | Tennessee River |
| 27 | US 62, to KY Dam, Calvert City, **N gas:** BP, Shell/dsl, **food:** Cracker Barrel, DQ, McDonald's, Waffle House, Willow Pond Rest., **lodging:** Foxfire Motel, KY Dam Motel, Super 8, **other:** Cypress Lakes Camp, Freightliner, KOA, **S gas:** Love's/Arby's/dsl/scales/rest./24hr |
| 25b a | to Calvert City, Carroll/Purchase Pkwy, services **1 mi** N |
| 16 | US 68, to Paducah, **S gas:** BP/Southern Pride/Subway/dsl/scales/24hr/@, Roadside, **food:** Subway, **other:** Stuckey's, flea mkt |
| 11 | rd 1954, Husband Rd, to Paducah, **N gas:** Exxon/dsl, **lodging:** Best Western, **5 mi N food:** Burger King, Wendy's, Waffle House, **lodging:** Economy Inn, Executive Inn, Hickory House Inn, Travel Inn, **other:** Duck Creek RV Park, **S other:** Harley-Davidson |
| 7 | US 45, US 62, to Paducah, **N gas:** BP/dsl, **food:** Burger King, Taco Bell, **other:** Ⓗ HOSPITAL, **S Welcome Ctr both lanes, full ♿ facilities, 🚻 vending, 🏕 litter barrels, petwalk, gas:** BP/dsl, Shell/dsl, **food:** Arby's, Backyard Burger, McDonald's, Popeye's, Sonic, Waffle House, **other:** K-Mart |
| 4 | US 60, to Paducah, **N gas:** BP, Shell/dsl/24hr, **food:** Applebee's, Bob Evans, Burger King, McDonald's, O'Charley's, Outback Steaks, Rafferty's, **lodging:** Courtyard, Day's Inn/rest., Drury Inn, Hampton Inn, Holiday Inn Express, Residence Inn, Westowne Inn, **other:** Hancock Fabrics, Toyota/Scion, **S gas:** BP, Petro Mart, Shell, **food:** Arby's, Capt D's, Chong's Chinese, ChuckeCheese, Cracker Barrel, Dominos, El Chico's, Fazoli's, Hardee's/24hr, IHOP, Logan's Roadhouse, Los Amigos, Olive Garden, Pasta House, Pizza Hut, Red Lobster, Ryan's, Steak'n Shake, Subway, Taco Bell, TX Roadhouse, TGIFriday, Tuesday Morning, Wendy's, **lodging:** Comfort Suites, Country Inn, Drury Suites, Hampton Inn, Motel 6, PearTree Inn, Thrifty Inn, Travelodge, **other:** AAA, Advance Parts, Aldi Foods, BooksAMillion, |

PADUCAH

**E ↕ W**

**G R A Y S O N**

KY

## INTERSTATE 24 CONT'D

**4** Continued
Circuit City, Dillard's, Gander Mtn, Goody's, Goodyear, Home Depot, JC Penney, Kohl's, Lowe's Whse, Michaels, Office Depot, Old Navy, PetsMart, Sam's Club/gas, Sears/auto, TJ Maxx, Walmart SuperCtr/gas, World Mkt, mall

**3** KY 305, to Paducah, **N gas:** BP/dsl/scales, Citgo/dsl/24hr, **food:** Trimble's Rest, **lodging:** Best Value, Comfort Inn/rest., Ramada Ltd, **S gas:** Cheers/dsl, Pilot/Subway/dsl/scales/24hr, **food:** Yu's Kitchen, Waffle Hut, **lodging:** Baymont Inn, **other:** Fern Lake Camping, antiques

**0mm** Kentucky/Illinois state line, Ohio River

## INTERSTATE 64

| Exit # | Services |
|---|---|
| **192mm** | Kentucky/West Virginia state line, Big Sandy River |

**191** US 23, to Ashland, **1-2 mi N gas:** Exxon, GoMart, Marathon/Subway/dsl, Speedway, **food:** Arby's, McDonald's, Waffle House, Wendy's, **lodging:** Ramada Ltd, **other:** H HOSPITAL, Rite Aid, Foodland Foods

**185** KY 180, Cannonsburg, **1-3 mi N gas:** BP/dsl, Chevron/McDonald's, **food:** Arby's, Bob Evan's, Burger King, DQ, Subway, Wendy's, **lodging:** Day's Inn, Fairfield Inn, Hampton Inn, Holiday Inn Express, Knight's Inn, **other:** st police, **S gas:** ⊕FLYING J/CountryMkt/dsl/LP/scales/24hr, **other:** Hidden Valley Camping

**181** 181 US 60, to Princess, **N gas:** BP/dsl, **S gas:** Marathon

**179** rd 67, Industrial Parkway

**174mm** rest areas wb, full 🚻 facilities, 🛢, vending, 🍴 litter barrels, petwalk

**173mm** rest areas wb, full 🚻 facilities, 🛢, vending, 🍴 litter barrels, petwalk

**172** rd 1, rd 7, Grayson, **N gas:** Texaco/dsl/24hr, Superquik/dsl/24hr, **food:** A&W/LJ Silver, Huddle House, KFC, LJ Silver, Pizza Hut, Shoney's, Subway, **lodging:** Day's Inn, Holiday Inn Express, Quality Inn, **other:** Chrysler/Jeep, $General, $Tree, Ford, K-Mart, SaveALot Foods, **S gas:** BP, Chevron/Quizno's, Exxon/Hardees, Marathon, Speedway, Pilot/Wendy's/dsl/24hr, Speedway, **food:** Arby's, Biscuit World, China House, DQ, Little Caesar's, McDonald's, Papa John's, Taco Bell, **lodging:** Super 8, **other:** Advance Parts, AutoZone, $General, Family$, Rite Aid

**161** US 60, to Olive Hill, **N gas:** BP, **other:** to Carter Caves SP, camping, **S gas:** Marathon/dsl/24hr, **lodging:** Spanish Manor Motel

**156** rd 2, to KY 59, to Olive Hill, **S gas:** BP, **food:** DQ

**148mm** weigh sta both lanes

**141mm** rest areas both lanes, full 🚻 facilities, 🛢, vending, 🍴, litter barrels, petwalk

**137** KY 32, to Morehead, **N gas:** BP/DQ/dsl, **food:** CiCi's Pizza, Huddle House, Reno's Roadhouse, **other:** Big Lots, Curves, Kroger/dsl, Lowes Whse, Walmart SuperCtr, **S gas:** BP, Chevron/McDonald's/dsl/24hr, Marathon, **food:** China Buffet, Domino's, Hardee's, KFC, Lee's Chicken, McDonald's, Ponderosa, Shoney's, **lodging:** Day's Inn, Hampton Inn, Holiday Inn Express, Knights Inn, Mtn Lodge Motel, Quality Inn, Super 8,

**W I N C H E S T E R**

**137** Continued
**other:** H HOSPITAL, Ace Hardware, Buick/Pontiac, $General, Food Lion, Goody's, Radio Shack, st police

**133** rd 801, to Sharkey, Farmers, **S gas:** BP/Subway/dsl, **lodging:** Comfort Inn

**123** US 60, to Salt Lick, Owingsville, **N gas:** Chevron/dsl

**121** KY 36, to Owingsville, **N gas:** BP/dsl, Exxon, Marathon, Marathon/dsl, **food:** DQ, McDonald's, Subway, **lodging:** Super 8, **other:** $General, Family$

**113** US 60, to Mt Sterling, **N gas:** Chevron/dsl, **S gas:** Pilot/McDonald's/Subway/scales/dsl/24hr

**110** US 460, KY 11, Mt Sterling, **N gas:** Chevron/dsl/24hr, Shell/Krystal/dsl, **food:** Cracker Barrel, **lodging:** Fairfield Inn, Ramada Ltd, **other:** golf, **S gas:** BP/dsl, Exxon/Subway, Marathon/Huddle House, Speedway/dsl, **food:** Applebee's, Arby's, Burger King, El Camino, KFC, LJ Silver, McDonald's, Pizza Hut, Wendy's, **lodging:** Budget Inn, Day's Inn/rest., **other:** H HOSPITAL, Family$, O'Reilly Parts, **S on KY 686 gas:** Fastlane, **food:** Hardee's, Little Caesar's, Peking Buffet, Pizza Hut, Taco Bell, **other:** Advance Parts, Chevrolet, Chrysler/Dodge/Jeep, Ford, JC Penney, Lowe's Whse, Walmart SuperCtr

**108mm** rest area wb, full 🚻 facilities, 🛢, vending, 🍴, litter barrels, petwalk

**101** US 60

**98.5mm** rest area eb, full 🚻 facilities, 🛢, vending, 🍴, litter barrels, petwalk

**98** KY 402 (from eb)

**96b a** KY 627, to Winchester, Paris, **N gas:** BP/dsl, Marathon/96 Truck Plaza/dsl/rest./scales/, **S lodging:** Day's Inn, Hampton Inn, Quality Inn, **other:** Chevrolet/Buick/Pontiac

**94** KY 1958, Van Meter Rd, Winchester, **N gas:** Chevron/dsl/24hr, Shell/scales/dsl, **lodging:** Best Value Inn, Holiday Inn Express, **other:** flea mkt, **S gas:** BP/dsl, Chevron, Shell, Speedway/dsl, **food:** Applebee's, Arby's, Cantuckee Diner, Capt D's, Domino's, DQ, El Camino, Fazoli's, Golden Corral, Great Wall Chinese, Hardee's, Jade Garden Chinese, KFC, Little Caesar's, McDonald's, Mi Finca Mexican, Papa John's, Pizza Hut, Quizno's, Rally's, Sonic, Subway, Taco Bell, Taste Of China, Waffle House, Wendy's, **lodging:** Best Western, **other:** H HOSPITAL, Advance Parts, AutoZone, Chrysler/Dodge/Jeep, $General, Ford/Mercury, Goody's, K-Mart, Lowe's Whse, Office Depot, O'Reilly Parts, Radio Shack, Rite Aid, SaveAlot Foods, Walgreens, Walmart SuperCtr, to Ft Boonesborough Camping

**87** KY 859, Blue Grass Sta

**81** I-75 S, to Knoxville

**I-64 and I-75 run together 7 mi. See Kentucky Interstate 75 exits 113-115.**

**75** I-75 N, to Cincinnati, access to KY Horse Park

**69** US 62 E, to Georgetown, **N** antiques (mi), **S** Equus Run Vineyards (2mi)

**65** US 421, Midway, **S** antiques

**60mm** rest area both lanes, full 🚻 facilities, litter barrels, petwalk, vending

**58** US 60 to Frankfort, **N gas:** Chevron/dsl, Marathon, Shell, Speedway, **food:** Arby's, Capt. D's, Cattleman's Roadhouse, KFC, McDonald's, Waffle House, White Castle, **lodging:** Best Western, Bluegrass Inn, Fairfield Inn, **other:** Chevrolet/Cadillac/Nissan/Pontiac

## INTERSTATE 64 CONT'D

**E** ↕ **W**

**58** Continued
Chrysler/Jeep/Dodge, $General, $Tree, Ford/Lincoln/ Mercury, Honda, Kohl's, Kroger, Toyota/Scion, to KY St Capitol, KYSU, to Viet Vets Mem, transmissions

**55mm** Kentucky River

**53b a** US 127, Frankfort, **N gas:** Chevron/24hr, Marathon, Shell/24hr, Speedway, **food:** A&W/LJ Silver, Applebee's, Beef O'Brady's, Big Boy, Burger King, Capt D's, Carino's Italian, Chili's, DQ, Fazoli's, Hardee's, KFC, Longhorn Steaks, McDonald's, O'Charley's, Panera Bread, Pizza Hut, Qdoba Mexican, Rio Grande Mexican, Shoney's, Starbucks, Steak'n Shake, Subway, Taco Bell, Taco John's, Wendy's, **lodging:** Best Value Inn, Hampton Inn, Holiday Inn Express, **other:** Ⓗ HOSPITAL, Advance Parts, Big-O Tire, Family$, Goodyear/auto, Goody's, JC Penney, K-Mart, Kroger/gas/24hr, Lowe's Whse, Office Depot, Radio Shack, Rite Aid, Walgreens, Walmart SuperCtr, Ancient Age Tour, to KY St Capitol, st police, vet

**48** KY 151, to US 127 S, **S gas:** BP/dsl, Shell/Subway

**43** KY 395, Waddy, **N gas:** ⊕FLYING J/Conoco/Country Mkt/dsl/LP/scales/24hr, **S gas:** Auto/Truck Plaza/Chester Fried/dsl/scales/24hr

**38.5mm** weigh sta both lanes

**35** KY 53, Shelbyville, **N gas:** BP/dsl, Chevron/dsl, **food:** Cracker Barrel, McDonald's (1mi), Waffle House, **other:** Chevrolet, Ford/Mercury, Kroger/gas/deli, Lake Shelby Camping (3mi), **S gas:** Chevron/White Castle/dsl, Shell/ dsl, **lodging:** Holiday Inn Express, **other:** golf

**32b a** KY 55, Shelbyville, **1-3 mi N gas:** Shell, **food:** Arby's, Asian Buffet, DQ, Finefresh BBQ, KFC, McDonald's, Quizno's, Subway, Waffle House, Wendy's, **lodging:** Country Hearth Inn, Day's Inn, **other:** Ⓗ HOSPITAL, AutoZone, Buick/Pontiac/GMC, $Tree, Lowes Whse, Rolling Hills Camping (16mi), Walgreens, Walmart SuperCtr/gas, **S food:** Cattleman's Roadhouse, **lodging:** Ramada, **other:** Taylorsville Lake SP

**28mm** rest area eb, full ♿ facilities, info, Ⓒ, 🏕, litter barrels, vending, petwalk

**28** KY 1848, Veechdale Rd, Simpsonville, **N gas:** Pilot/ Wendy's/dsl/scales/24hr, **food:** DQ, **other:** golf, **S gas:** Chevron/dsl

**19b a** I-265, Gene Snyder Fwy, **N** to Tom Sawyer SP

**17** S Blankenbaker, **N gas:** Circle K/gas, **lodging:** Staybridge Suites, **other:** Harley-Davidson, **S gas:** BP/Subway, Chevron, Marathon, Thornton's/dsl, **food:** Arby's, BackYard Burger, Burger King, Cracker Barrel, HomeTown Buffet, KFC/A&W, King Buffet, Kingfish Rest., McDonald's, Penn Sta., Ruby Tuesday, Taco Bell/LJ Silver, Waffle House, Wendy's, **lodging:** Candlewood Suites, Comfort Suites, Country Inn&Suites, Hampton Inn, Hilton Garden, Holiday Inn Express, Homestead Suites, Jameson Inn, Microtel, Sleep Inn, Super 8, Wingate Inn, **other:** Lexus, Sam's Club/gas

**15** Hurstbourne Pkwy, Louisville, **N gas:** BP/Circle K/dsl, **food:** Amerigo Italian, Arby's, Bob Evans, Bonefish Grill, Carrabba's, Chili's, Fazoli's, Great Harvest, Jimmy John's, Macaroni Grill, McDonald's, Mimi's Cafe, Olive Garden, Panera Bread, Papa John's, Qdoba, Sichuan-Garden, Starbucks, Skyline Chili, Subway, TGIFriday, Waffle House, **lodging:** Baymont Inn, Courtyard, Days Inn, Drury Inn, Holiday Inn, Hyatt, Red Roof Inn, **other:**

**S** **H** **E** **L** **B** **Y** **V** **I** **L** **L** **E**

**L** **O** **U** **I** **S** **V** **I** **L** **L** **E**

**15** Continued
Barnes&Noble, Kroger/gas, Lowe's Whse, Walgreens, **S gas:** Marathon, Meijer/dsl/24hr, **food:** Applebee's, BD BBQ, Buca Rest., Burger King, China Star, ChuckeCheese, Coldstone Creamery, DQ, Famous Daves, Home Run Burgers, Jumbo Grill, Longhorn Steaks, Lonestar Steaks, McAlister's Deli, Mercedes Grill, Moe's SW Grill, O'Charley's, Old Chicago, Picadilly, Qdoba, Quizno's, Smokey Bones BBQ, Starbucks, Steak'n Shake, Taco Bell, Tumbleweeds Mexican, Wendy's, White Castle, **lodging:** Clarion, Marriott, Red Carpet Inn, **other:** Autozone, Borders, Cadillac, Carmax, Chevrolet/ Subaru, $Tree, Home Depot, Hancock Fabrics, Honda, Infiniti, Kroger/gas, Michael's, Office Depot, Pontiac/ GMC, Radio Shack, Staples, Subaru, Target, VW, Walgreens, Walmart/drugs

**12b** I-264 E, Watterson Expswy, **1 exit N** on US 60...**gas:** Chevron, **food:** Alexander's Rest., Arby's, Big Boy, BJ's Rest., CA Pizza, Cheesecake Factory, Cosina Italian, Fox&Hound, Jay Alexandar's, Logan's Roadhouse, McDonald's, Outback Steaks, Panera Bread, Taco Bell, Wendy's, **other:** Acura, Best Buy, Circuit City, Dillard's, Ford/Lincoln/Mercury, Goodyear/auto, JC Penney, Kia, Kohl's, Macy's, Staples, SteinMart, Towery's AutoCare, Vonmaur, Whole Foods Mkt, mall

**12a** I-264 W, access to Ⓗ HOSPITAL

**10** Cannons Lane

**8** Grinstead Dr, Louisville, **S gas, food:** KT Cafe, Jim Porter's Rest.

**7** US 42, US 62, Mellwood Ave, Story Ave

**6** I-71 N (from eb), to Cincinnati

**5a** I-65, S to Nashville, N to Indianapolis

**5b** 3rd St, Louisville, **N food:** Joe's CrabShack, McDonald's, **S lodging:** Galt House Hotel, Marriott, **food:** Kingfish Rest., **other:** Ⓗ HOSPITAL

**4** 9th St Roy Wilkins Ave, **S** KY Art Ctr, science museum, downtown

**3** US 150 E, to 22nd St, **S gas:** BP/Circle K, Chevron, **food:** DQ, McDonald's, Subway, **other:**

**1** I-264 E, to Shively, **S** ✈, zoo

**0mm** Kentucky/Indiana state line, Ohio River

## INTERSTATE 65

| Exit # | Services |
|---|---|
| **138mm** | Kentucky/Indiana state line, Ohio River |
| **137** | I-64 W, I-71 N, I-64 E, **W** to Galt House, downtown |
| **136c** | Jefferson St, Louisville, **E other:** Ⓗ HOSPITAL, Walgreens, **W gas:** Shell, **food:** McDonald's, Subway, |

KY

**N**
**S**

**L O U I S V I L L E**

**KY**

## INTERSTATE 65 CONT'D

**136c** Continued
White Castle, **lodging:** Courtyard, Fairfield Inn, Hampton Inn, Hyatt, Marriott, Springhill Suites, **other:** Tires+

**136b** Broadway St, Chestnut St (from nb), **E other:** H HOSPITAL, NAPA, Walgreens, **W gas:** Shell, Thornton's, **food:** McDonald's, Rally's, Subway, White Castle, **lodging:** Courtyard, Fairfield Inn, Hampton Inn, Hyatt, Marriott, Springhill Suites, **other:** Tires+, same as 136c

**135** W St Catherine, **E gas:** Shell

**134b a** KY 61, Jackson St, Woodbine St, **W gas:** BP/Circle K, **lodging:** Day's Inn, Quality Inn, **other:** Harley-Davidson

**133b** US 60A, Eastern Pkwy, Taylor Blvd, **E food:** Denny's, Papa John's, Pizza Mia, Snappy Tomato Pizza, Subway, **W gas:** Shell, **food:** Cracker Barrel, McDonald's, **lodging:** Country Hearth Inn, **other:** U of Louisville, Churchill Downs, museum

**133b** Crittenden Dr (132 from sb), **W food:** Arby's, Burger King, Cracker Barrel, Hall of Fame Cafe', **lodging:** Country Inn& Suites, Hilton Garden, Holiday Inn, Ramada Inn, Super 8 **E food:** Denny's, same as 133

**131b a** I-264, Watterson Expswy, **W** Cardinal Stadium, Expo Center, ✈

**130** KY 61, Preston Hwy, **E on KY 61...gas:** BP/Circle K, Speedway/dsl, Thornton, **food:** Blimpie, Bob Evans, Burger King, Domino's, Fazoli's, KFC, Little Caesar's, McDonald's, Papa John's, Popeyes, Rally's, Royal Garden Buffet, Subway, Taco Bell, Waffle House, Wendy's, **lodging:** Econolodge, Red Roof Inn, Super 8, **other:** Aamco, Ace Hardware, AutoZone, Big O Tire, BigLots, Chevrolet/KIA, Chrysler, Cox Drug, $General, Dodge, Ford, O'Reilly's Parts, PepBoys, Radio Shack, Sav-A-lot Foods, Staples, Tires+, U-Haul

**128** KY 1631, Fern Valley Rd, **E gas:** FiveStar, Marathon/Circle K, Thornton/dsl, **food:** Arby's, Big Boy, El Nopal Mexican, Hardee's, Indi's Rest., McDonald's, Outback Steaks, Shoney's, Subway, Taco Bell, Waffle House, White Castle, Wendy's, **lodging:** Comfort Suites, Days Inn, Holiday Inn, InTown Suites, Jameson Inn, **other:** Cottman Transmissions, Lincoln/Mercury, NAPA Care, Sam's Club/gas, Walgreens, **W** UPS Depot

**127** KY 1065, outer loop, **E** TX Roadhouse, **W food:** McDonald's, to Motor Speedway,

**125b a** I-265 E, KY 841, Gene Snyder Fwy

**121** KY 1526, Brooks Rd, **E gas:** BP, Marathon, **food:** Arby's, Burger King, Cracker Barrel, McDonald's, Tumbleweed Grill, **lodging:** Fairfield Inn, Holiday Inn Express, Ramada, **other:** H HOSPITAL, Tinker's RV Ctr, **W gas:** BP/dsl, Pilot/Subway/Taco Bell/dsl/24hr/scales, Shell/dsl, **food:** Waffle House, **lodging:** Baymont Inn, Comfort Inn, Econolodge, Hampton Inn, Quality Inn

**117** KY 44, Shepherdsville, **E gas:** Shell/dsl, **food:** Denny's, Kitchen Rest., **lodging:** Best Western/rest., Day's Inn, **other:** KOA (2mi), **W gas:** Marathon, Speedway/dsl, **food:** Arby's, China Buffet, DQ, El Nopal, Fazoli's, LJ Silver, KFC, McDonald's/playplace, Mr Gatti's, Papa John's, Quizno's, Rio's Steaks, Sonic, Subway, Taco Bell, Waffle House, Wendy's, White Castle, **lodging:** Country Inn&Suites, Motel 6, Sleep Inn, Super 8, **other:** Ace Hardware, Advance Parts, BigLots, $General, Family$, Kroger/gas, Lowe's Whse, NAPA Autocare, Radio Shack, Rite Aid, Sav-a-Lot

**116.5mm** Salt River

**116** KY 480, KY 61, **E gas:** Love's/Subway/Chester's/dsl/scales/24hr, Shell/dsl, **other:** House of Quilts, **W gas:** Chevron/dsl, **other:** Grandma's RV Park

**114mm** rest area sb, full ♿ facilities, ☏ vending, 🍴 litter barrels, petwalk

**112** KY 245, Clermont, **E gas:** Shell/dsl, **other:** Jim Beam Outpost, Bernheim Forest, to My Old Kentucky Home SP

**105** 105 KY 61, Lebanon Jct, **W gas:** Pilot/McDonald's/Subway/dsl/scales/24hr/@, 105 QuikStop/dsl, **food:** Hog-Wild BBQ

**102** KY 313, to KY 434, Radcliff, **W** to Patton Museum

**94** US 62, Elizabethtown, **E gas:** BP/dsl, Marathon/dsl, **food:** Denny's, Waffle House, White Castle, **lodging:** Comfort Inn, Day's Inn, Super 8, **other:** KOA (1mi), **W gas:** BP/dsl, Speedway/dsl, **food:** Arby's, Burger King, Cracker Barrel, Chalupa's Mexican, Heavenly Ham, Hungry Howie's, KFC/Taco Bell, McDonald's, Ruby Tuesday, Ryan's, Shoney's, Stone Hearth, Subway, TX Outlaw Steaks, TX Roadhouse, Wendy's, **lodging:** Baymont Inn, Best Western, Comfort Inn, Country Hearth Inn, Fairfield Inn, Hampton Inn, Holiday Inn Express, Fairfield Inn, La Quinta, Motel 6, Ramada Inn, **other:** H HOSPITAL, Advance Parts, AutoZone, Curves, $General, $Tree, Family$, Kroger/gas, Skagg's RV Ctr, True Value, Walgreens, USPO, st police

**93** to Bardstown, to BG Pky, **E** to My Old KY Home SP, Maker's Mark Distillery

**91** US 31 W, KY 61, WK Pkwy, Elizabethtown, **E gas:** Marathon/dsl, **food:** LJ Silver, **lodging:** Bluegrass Inn, Budget Motel, Commonwealth Lodge, **other:** to Lincoln B'Place, **W gas:** Doug's/dsl, **food:** Jerry's Rest./24hr, **lodging:** KY Cardinal Inn, Roadside Inn, **other:** H HOSPITAL

**90mm** weigh sta both lanes

**86** KY 222, Glendale, **E gas:** Pilot/McDonalds/dsl/scales/24hr, **other:** Glendale Camping, **W gas:** Petro/dsl/rest./scales/24hr/@, **lodging:** Economy Inn, Glendale Inn, **other:** Blue Beacon

**83mm** Nolin River

**81** KY 84, Sonora, **E gas:** BP, Marathon/dsl, Pilot/Subway/dsl/scales/24hr, **other:** Blue Beacon, to Lincoln B'Place, **W gas:** Shell

**76** KY 224, Upton, **E gas:** Chevron/dsl, **W** to Nolin Lake

**75mm** eastern/central time zone

**71** KY 728, Bonnieville

**65** US 31 W, Munfordville, **E gas:** BP/Subway/dsl, Killman/dsl, **food:** DQ, King Buffet, Pizza Hut, McDonald's, Sonic, **lodging:** Super 8, **other:** Advance Parts, $General, Family$, Pamida, **W gas:** Chevron/dsl/24hr, Shell, **food:** Mazatlan Mexican, to Nolin Lake

**61mm** rest area both lanes, full ♿ facilities, info, ☏, 🍴, litter barrels, vending, petwalk Green River

**58** KY 218, Horse Cave, **E gas:** Love's/McDonald's/dsl/scale/24hr, **other:** H HOSPITAL, **W gas:** Chevron/Pizza/dsl, Marathon/dsl/repair, **food:** Aunt Bee's Rest./24hr, **lodging:** Country Hearth Inn, Hampton Inn, **other:** KOA, to Mammoth Cave NP

**53** KY 70, KY 90, Cave City, **E gas:** BP/dsl, JR's, Marathon/dsl, Chevron, Shell, **food:** Cracker Barrel, El Mazatlan Mexican, KFC, LJ Silver/A&W, McDonald's, Pizza Hut/Taco Bell, Subway, Wendy's, **lodging:** Best Western, Comfort Inn, Day's Inn/rest., Econolodge,

**E L I Z A B E T H T O W N**

Copyright 2009 - The Next Exit®

## INTERSTATE 65 CONT'D

**N ↕ S**

**BOWLING GREEN**

**53** Continued
Knight's Inn, Masters Inn, Super 8, **other:** Ⓗ HOSPITAL, Barren River Lake SP (24mi), **W gas:** Marathon/dsl, **food:** Watermill Rest., **other:** Onyx Cave, Mammoth Cave NP, Jellystone Camping, Singing Hills Camping

**48** KY 255, Park City, **E gas:** Shell/dsl/24hr, **other:** Park Mammoth Resort (1 1/2mi), tire repair, **W** Diamond Caverns Resort, to Mammoth Cave NP

**43** Nunn Cumberland Pky, to Barren River Lake SP

**39mm** rest area nb, full ♿ facilities, Ⓒ, vending, 🍴, litter barrels, petwalk

**38** KY 101, Smiths Grove, **W gas:** BP/scales/dsl, Bestway Pizza, Marathon/Subway/dsl, Shell, **food:** McDonald's, Wendy's, **lodging:** Bryce Motel, **other:** $General, IGA Foods, 7 Springs Park, antiques

**36** US 68, KY 80, Oakland, no nb return

**30mm** rest area sb, full ♿ facilities, Ⓒ, vending, 🍴, litter barrels, petwalk

**28** rd 446, to US 31 W, Bowling Green, **W gas:** BP, Shell/24hr, **food:** Hardee's, Jerry's Rest., Wendy's, **lodging:** Continental Inn, Country Hearth Inn, Super 8, Value Lodge, **other:** Ⓗ HOSPITAL, Corvette Museum, 3 mi **W** to WKYU

**26** rd 234, Bowling Green

**22** US 231, Bowling Green, **E gas:** Keystop Gas, Scott/dsl, Shell, **food:** Cracker Barrel, Culver's, Denny's, Domino's, Godfather's, Hardee's, Ryan's, Sonic, Subway, Waffle House, Zaxby's, **lodging:** Best Value, Comfort Inn, Day's Inn, Econolodge, Fairfield Inn, Hometowne Suites, La Quinta, Microtel, Quality Inn, Ramada/rest., Sleep Inn, **other:** URGENT CARE, Camping World RV Supply, $General, Gander Mtn, Harley-Davidson, IGA Foods, USPO, **W gas:** Chevron/dsl, Marathon, RaceWay, Shell/dsl, Speedway/dsl, **food:** Applebee's, Arby's, Baymont Inn, Beijing Chinese, Bob Evans, Bruster's, Buffalo Wild Wings, Burger King, Capt D's, ChuckeCheese, Chick-fil-A, Double-Dog's Chowhouse, KFC, Krystal, Kyoto Steaks, Logan's Roadhouse, LoneStar Steaks, Longhorn Steaks, McDonald's, Moe's SW Grill, MT Grille, O'Charley's, Outback Steaks, Panera Bread, Pizza Hut, Rafferty's, Red Lobster, Ruby Tuesday, Santa Fe Steaks, Shogun Japanese, Shoney's, Smokey Bones BBQ, Sonic, Starbucks, Steak'n Shake, Subway, Taco Bell, TGIFriday, Toots Rest., Waffle House, Wendy's, White Castle, **lodging:** Candlewood Suites, Courtyard, Drury Inn, Hampton Inn, Hilton Garden, Holiday Inn, Motel 6, News Inn, Red Roof Inn, Rodeway Inn, **other:** Ⓗ HOSPITAL, Advance Parts, Barnes&Noble, Best Buy, Buick/GMC, BMW/Mercedes, Cadillac, Chevrolet, Chrysler/Jeep, Curves, CVS Drug, Dillard's, $General, Ford/Lincoln/Mercury, Goodyear, Home Depot, Honda, Hyundai, JC Penney, K-Mart, KOA, KIA, Kohls, Kroger/gas/24hr, Lowe's, Nissan, Office Depot, Old Navy, PetCo, Pontiac, Sam's Club/gas, Saturn, Scotty's Parts, Sears, Target, Toyota, U-Haul, Walmart SuperCtr, mall, vet

**20** WH Natcher Toll Rd, to Bowling Green, access to W KY U, KY st police

**6** KY 100, Franklin, **E gas:** BP/dsl/24hr, Shell/dsl/24hr/@, **W gas:** Pilot/Subway/dsl/scales/24hr/, Pilot/Wendy's/dsl/scales/24hr/, **lodging:** Budget Inn, Day's Inn, **other:** Ⓗ HOSPITAL, Bluegrass RV Park, Petrolube,

**FRANKLIN**

**6** Continued
SpeedCo, truck & tires/repair, truckwash

**4mm** weigh sta nb

**2** US 31 W, to Franklin, **E gas:** ⊕FLYING J/Conoco/Country Mkt/dsl/LP/rest./24hr, Keystop/Marathon/Burger King/dsl/24hr, **W gas:** BP/dsl, **food:** Cracker Barrel, McDonald's, Waffle House, **lodging:** Best Western, Comfort Inn, Econolodge, Hampton Inn, Holiday Inn Express, Super 8, **other:** Ⓗ HOSPITAL

**1mm** Welcome Ctr nb, full ♿ facilities, Ⓒ, vending, 🍴, litter barrels, petwalk

**0mm** Kentucky/Tennessee state line

## INTERSTATE 71

| Exit # | Services |
|---|---|
| | Kentucky/Ohio state line, Ohio River |
| | **I-71 and I-75 run together 19 miles. Exits 175-192. See Kentucky Interstate 75, exits 175-192** |
| **77** [173] | I-75 S, to Lexington |
| **75mm** | weigh sta sb |
| **72** | KY 14, to Verona, **E gas:** BP/dsl, Chevron/dsl, **other:** Oak Creek Camping (5mi) |
| **62** | US 127, to Glencoe, **E gas:** 62 TrkPlaza/rest./dsl, **W gas:** BP/dsl/rest., **lodging:** 127 Motel |
| **57** | KY 35, to Sparta, **E gas:** Marathon/dsl, **other:** Sparta RV Park (3mi), **W gas:** BP/dsl, **lodging:** Ramada Ltd, **other:** KY Speedway |
| **55** | KY 1039, **W gas:** Love's/McDonald's/Subway/scales/dsl/24hr, **other:** KY Speedway |
| **44** | KY 227, to Indian Hills, **W gas:** BP/dsl, Chevron/dsl/24hr, Marathon, Shell, **food:** Arby's, Burger King, Hometown Pizza, KFC, LJ Silver, McDonald's, New China, Sonic, Subway, Taco Bell, Waffle House, **lodging:** Best Western, Comfort Inn, Day's Inn, Hampton Inn, Holiday Inn Express, Super 8, **other:** Ⓗ HOSPITAL, AutoZone, Chevrolet, Chrysler/Jeep/Dodge, Ford/Mercury, $General, Kroger/gas, Radio Shack, Rite Aid, Sav-a-Lot Foods, Walmart SuperCtr/gas, Carroll Butler SP, flea mkt |
| **43.5mm** | Kentucky River |
| **43** | KY 389, to KY 55, English |
| **34** | US 421, Campbellsburg, **W gas:** BP/Subway/dsl, Marathon/dsl, **other:** st police |
| **28** | KY 153, KY 146, to US 42, Pendleton, **E gas:** BP, Marathon/dsl, Pilot/Subway/dsl/scales/24hr/@, **W gas:** Pilot/McDonald's/scales/dsl/24hr |
| **22** | KY 53, La Grange, **E gas:** BP/dsl, Speedway/Rally's, **food:** Applebees, Burger King, Jumbo Buffet, Papa John's, Ponderosa, Subway, Waffle House, |

**N S LOUISVILLE**

## INTERSTATE 71 CONT'D

| | |
|---|---|
| 22 | Continued Wendy's, **lodging:** Best Western-Ashbury, Holiday Inn Express, **other:** H HOSPITAL, Big O Tire, $General, Kroger/gas, Radio Shack, Walgreens, Walmart SuperCtr, **W gas:** Chevron/dsl/24hr, Shell/dsl, Swifty, **food:** Arby's, Cracker Barrel, Domino's, DQ, El Torasco, Hometown Pizza, KFC, LJ Silver, McDonald's, Taco Bell, **lodging:** Comfort Suites, Super 8, **other:** Advance Parts, Chevrolet/Pontiac/Buick, Curves, NAPA, Rite Aid, Sav-a-Lot, tires, flea mkt, USPO |
| 18 | KY 393, Buckner, **W gas:** Marathon/dsl, **food:** Subway |
| 17 | KY 146, Buckner, **E other:** Ford, **W gas:** Shell/dsl, Thornton's/dsl/24hr, **other:** USPO, st police |
| 14 | KY 329, Crestwood, Pewee Valley, Brownsboro, **E gas:** Chevron/24hr, Shell, **2 mi E food:** DQ, Hometown Pizza, Sonic, Starbucks, Subway |
| 13mm | **rest area both lanes, full & facilities, C vending, litter barrels, petwalk** |
| 9b a | I-265, KY 841, Gene Snyder Fwy, **E** to Sawyer SP |
| 5 | I-264, Watterson Expswy (exits left from sb), **E** to Sawyer SP |
| 2 | Zorn Ave, **E** VA H HOSPITAL, **W gas:** Chevron, **food:** KingFish Rest., **lodging:** Ramada Inn, **other:** Art Museum |
| 1b | I-65, S to Nashville, N to Indianapolis |

## INTERSTATE 75

**N S COVINGTON**

| Exit # | Services |
|---|---|
| 193mm | Kentucky/Ohio state line, Ohio River |
| 192 | 5th St (from nb), Covington, **E gas:** BP, Shell, Speedway, **food:** Big Boy, Burger King, GoldStar Chili, McDonald's, Skyline Chili, Subway, Taco Bell, Waffle House, White Castle, **lodging:** Courtyard, Extended Stay America, Holiday Inn, Radisson, **other:** Ford/Lincoln/Mercury, Lexus/Toyota, Subaru/VW, Riverboat Casino, **W lodging:** Hampton Inn |
| 191 | 12th St, Covington, **E other:** H HOSPITAL, Dodge, museum, same as 192 |
| 189 | KY 1072 (from sb), Kyles Lane, **W gas:** BP/dsl, Marathon/dsl, Shell/dsl, Speedway, **food:** Big Boy, Reality Coffeehouse, Skyline Chili, Substation II Subs, **lodging:** Day's Inn, Ramada Inn, same as 188 |
| 188 | US 25, US 42, Dixie Hwy, **E gas:** Sunoco, **food:** Subway, Tuesday Morning, **other:** GNC, Kroger, **W food:** Pizza Hut, **lodging:** Day's Inn, Ramada, USA Hotel, **other:** $Tree, SteinMart, Walgreens, same as 189 |
| 186 | KY 371, Buttermilk Pike, Covington, **E gas:** BP/dsl, Marathon, Texco/DQ, **food:** Graeter's Ice Cream, Montgomery Inn, Oriental Wok, Papa John's, **lodging:** Drawbridge Inn/rest., Super 8, **W gas:** BP, Shell, Sunoco/dsl, **food:** Arby's, Bonefish Grill, Burger King, Chipotle Mexican, Domino's, Dunkin Donuts/Baskin-Robbins, Empire Buffet, GoldStar Chili, La Rosa's Pizza, LJ Silver, McDonald's, Outback Steaks, Pizza Hut, Rema's Diner, Skyline Chili, Staples, Subway, **other:** Home Depot, Remke Foods, Walgreens |
| 185 | I-275 E and W, **W** to ✈ |
| 184 | KY 236, Donaldson Rd, to Erlanger, **E gas:** BP/deli, Marathon, **food:** Double Dragon Chinese, **W gas:** Marathon, Speedway/dsl, Sunoco/Subway/dsl, **food:** Southern Kitchen Rest., Waffle House, **lodging:** Airport Inn, |

**F L O R E N C E**

| | |
|---|---|
| 184 | Continued Comfort Inn, Day's Inn, Econolodge, **other:** Goodyear/auto |
| 182 | KY 1017, Turfway Rd, **E gas:** BP, Shell, **food:** Big Boy, Lee's Chicken, McDonald's, New Wok, Ryan's, 3 Amigo's Mexican, **lodging:** Comfort Inn, Courtyard, Ivy Inn, Rodeway Inn, **other:** Big Lots, Office Depot, Remke Foods, funpark, **W gas:** Meijer/dsl/24hr, **food:** Applebee's, CiCi's Pizza, Cracker Barrel, Dynasty Buffet, Famous Dave's BBQ, Karlo's Italian, Longhorn Steaks, O'Charley's, Rafferty's, Steak'n Shake, Tumbleweeds Grill, Wendy's, **lodging:** Extended Stay America, Hampton Inn, Hilton, Hyatt Place, La Quinta, Red Roof Inn, Studio+, **other:** H HOSPITAL, Best Buy, Biggs Foods, Home Depot, Kohl's, Lowe's Whse, Michaels, PetsMart, Sam's Club, Target, Turfway Park Racing |
| 181 | KY 18, Florence, **E gas:** Speedway, TA/Sunoco/Pizza Hut/Popeye's/dsl/rest./24hr/@, **food:** Goodfellow's Dining, Waffle House, **lodging:** Best Value Inn, Best Western, **other:** Chevrolet, **W gas:** BP/dsl, Chevron, Shell, Speedway, **food:** Cheddars, Hooters, IHOP, Fazoli's, Hooters, La Rosa's, Logan's Roadhouse, LoneStar Steaks, Macaroni Grill, MiYoshi, Panera Bread, Quizno's, **lodging:** Microtel, Stay Lodge, **other:** URGENT CARE, Buick, Chrysler/Jeep, $Tree, Dodge, Ford, Honda, JC Penney, K-Mart, Lincoln/Mercury, Mazda, Nissan, Saturn, Sears/auto, Staples, Tire Discounters, Toyota/Scion, TJ Maxx, Walmart SuperCtr, vet |
| 180a | Mall Rd (from sb), **W food:** Chipotle Mexican, ChuckeCheese, GoldStar Chili, Hardee's, Olive Garden, Pizza Hut, Skyline Chili, Smokey Bones BBQ, Subway, Taco Bell, **other:** AAA, Barnes&Noble, $General, Jo-Ann Fabrics, Kroger/24hr, Macey's, Michael's, PepBoys, Sears/auto, Staples, mall, same as 180 |
| 180 | US 42, US 127, Florence, Union, **E gas:** BP/dsl, Shell, Speedway/dsl, **food:** Big Boy, Bob Evans, Burger King, Camino Real, Capt D's, Dragon Buffet, Dunkin Donuts, Mai Thai, McDonald's, Pen Sta Subs, Pizza Hut, Quality Inn, Rally's, Red Lobster, Subway, Wendy's, **lodging:** Quality Inn, Knight's Inn, Motel 6, Super 8, **other:** Cadillac, Chevron, funpark, **W gas:** Shell/dsl/24hr, Speedway, **food:** Acapulco Mexican, Arby's, Burger King, DQ, KFC, LJ Silver, Perkins/24hr, Ponderosa, Waffle House, White Castle, Kroger/deli, **lodging:** Travelodge, **other:** Circuit City, PepBoys, Tire Discounters, Walgreens |
| 178 | KY 536, Mt Zion Rd, **E gas:** BP/Rally's/dsl, Mobil, Shell/dsl, Sunoco/dsl, **food:** GoldStar Chili, Hometown Pizza, Jersey Mike's Subs, Margarita's Mexican, Rally's, Steak'n Shake, Subway, **other:** Goodyear/auto, Kroger |
| 177mm | **Welcome Ctr sb/rest area nb, full & facilities, C, vending, litter barrels, RV dump** |
| 175 | KY 338, Richwood, **E gas:** TA/BP/Country Pride/Taco Bell/dsl/rest./@, Pilot/Subway/dsl/@, **food:** Arby's, Burger King, White Castle/24hr, **lodging:** Holiday Inn Express, **other:** RV Park, **W gas:** BP, Pilot/Subway/dsl/scales/24hr, Shell/dsl, **food:** GoldStar Chili, McDonald's, Pen Sta Subs, Skyline Chili, Waffle House, Wendy's, **lodging:** Econolodge, Ivy Lodge, **other:** to Big Bone Lick SP |
| 173 | I-71 S, to Louisville |
| 171 | KY 14, KY 16, to Verona, Walton, **E gas:** BP/dsl, Citgo/DQ, **food:** Waffle House, **W gas:** FLYING J/dsl/rest./24hr/scales@ **other:** Blue Beacon, Delightful Days RV Ctr, Oak Creek Camping (1mi), to Big Bone Lick SP |

**N ↑ ↓ S**

## INTERSTATE 75 CONT'D

**168mm** weigh sta sb

**166** KY 491, Crittenden, **E gas:** BP, Citgo/dsl, Marathon/A&W/Taco Bell/dsl, **food:** McDonald's, **other:** Chrysler/Dodge, KOA (2mi), **W gas:** Chevron, Shell/Subway/dsl, **food:** Burger King, Country Bumpkins Rest., Green Acres Rest.

**159** KY 22, to Owenton, Dry Ridge, **E gas:** BP, Marathon/DQ, Shell/dsl, **food:** Arby's/24hr, Burger King, Happy Dragon Chinese, KFC/Taco Bell, LJ Silver, McDonald's, Pizza Hut, Subway, Waffle House, Wendy's, **lodging:** Country Inn Suites, Dry Ridge Inn, Microtel, Super 8, **other:** H HOSPITAL, $General, Radio Shack, Walmart SuperCtr, **W gas:** Speedway/dsl, Sunoco/dsl, **food:** Country Grill, Cracker Barrel, Shoney's, **lodging:** Hampton Inn, Holiday Inn Express, **other:** Camper Village, Dry Ridge Outlets/famous brands, Sav-A-Lot, Toyota, Tire Discounters

**156** Barnes Rd, no facilites

**154** KY 36, Williamstown, **E gas:** Citgo/dsl/LP, Shell/dsl, **food:** Red Carpet Rest., **lodging:** Knight's Inn, **other:** H HOSPITAL, to Kincaid Lake SP, **W gas:** Marathon/dsl, **food:** El Jalisco Mexican, **lodging:** Best Value, Cedar Valley Resorts, Day's Inn

**144** KY 330, to Owenton, Corinth, **E gas:** Marathon/dsl, Noble's Trk Plaza/dsl/rest., **W gas:** BP, **food:** Donna's Diner, **other:** Three Springs Camping

**136** KY 32, to Sadieville, **W gas:** Marathon

**130.5mm** weigh sta nb

**129** KY 620, Delaplain Rd, **E gas:** Pilot/Wendy's/dsl/scales/24hr/@, **food:** Waffle House, **lodging:** Day's Inn, Motel 6, **W gas:** Pilot/McDonald's/dsl/scales/24hr/@, Shell/24hr

**127mm** rest area both lanes, full ♿ facilities, 🆒 vending, ⛽ litter barrels, petwalk

**126** US 62, to US 460, Georgetown, **E gas:** Standard, **food:** Applebee's, Big Boy, Golden Corral, Gold Star Chili, McDonald's, Mi Mexico, O'Charley's, Papa John's, Starbucks, **other:** Kohl's, Lowe's Whse, Valvoline, Walmart SuperCtr/gas/dsl, **W gas:** BP, Marathon, Shell/Subway/24hr, Speedway/A&W/dsl, **food:** Cracker Barrel, Fazoli's, KFC, Ruby Tuesday, Waffle House, Wendy's, **lodging:** Best Western, Comfort Suites, Country Inn&Suites, Econolodge, Fairfield Inn, Hampton Inn, Hilton Garden, Microtel, Quality Inn, Super 8, **other:** H HOSPITAL, Chevrolet/Pontiac/Buick, Ford, Dodge/Jeep, K-Mart/Little Caesar's, Outlets/famous brands, to Georgetown Coll, same as 125

**125** US 460 (from nb), Georgetown, **E gas:** BP/dsl, Marathon, Shell, **food:** FatKat Pizza, **lodging:** Econolodge, Super 8, **W gas:** Swifty, **food:** China Buffet, DQ, LJ Silver, Taco Bell, Wendy's, **other:** Outlets/famous brands, Radio Shack, same as 126

**120** rd 1973, to Ironworks Pike, KY Horse Park, **E** KY Horse Park Camping, **W gas:** AM Best TruckPlaza, Citgo/Stuckey's/dsl/pizza/24hr, **other:** H HOSPITAL

**118** I-64 W, to Frankfort, Louisville

**115** KY 922, Lexington, **E gas:** Shell/Subway/24hr, **food:** Cracker Barrel, McDonald's, Waffle House, **lodging:** Knight's Inn, La Quinta, Sheraton, **other:** SaddleHorse Museum (4mi), **W gas:** Chevron/dsl, **food:** Denny's, Post Rest., Happy Dragon Chinese, **lodging:** Embassy Suites, Holiday Inn, Marriott/rest., Residence Inn, **other:** Rite Aid, museum

**GEORGETOWN**

**LEXINGTON**

**113** US 27, US 68, to Paris, Lexington, **E gas:** Marathon, Speedway, **food:** Waffle House, **lodging:** Ramada Inn, **W gas:** Chevron/dsl/24hr, Shell, **food:** Fazoli's, **lodging:** Day's Inn, Red Roof Inn, **1 mi W food:** Burger King, Capt D's, Hardee's/24hr, Penn Sta., **lodging:** Catalina Motel, **other:** Advance Parts, Bluegrass RV Ctr, Chevrolet, Chrysler/Jeep, Kroger/deli, Northside RV Ctr, Walmart SuperCtr, to UKY, Rupp Arena

**111** I-64 E, to Huntington, WV

**110** US 60, Lexington, **W gas:** Shell, Speedway/dsl, Thornton/Subway/24hr, **food:** Arby's, Bob Evans, Cracker Barrel, Hardee's, International Buffet, McDonald's, Waffle House, Wendy's, **lodging:** Baymont Inn, Best Western, BlueGrass Suites, Comfort Inn, Country Inn&Suites, Hampton Inn, HoJo's, Holiday Inn Express, Knight's Inn, Microtel, Motel 6, Quality Inn, Ramada Ltd, Signature Inn, Super 8, Wilson Inn

**108** Man O War Blvd, **E gas:** Chevron, **W gas:** BP, Citgo/dsl, Meijer/dsl/24hr, Shell/KFC/Wendy's/24hr, Speedway, **food:** Applebee's, Arby's, Backyard Burger, Burger King, Carrabba's, Chick-fil-A, Chipotle Mexican, Damon's, Don Pablo, Fazoli's, Fire Mtn Grill, GoldStar Chili, Harry's Grill, Logan's Roadhouse, Max&Erma's, McDonald's, Outback Steaks, Pizza Hut, Rafferty's, Ruby Tuesday, Starbucks, Steak'n Shake, Taco Bell, TGIFriday, Waffle House, **lodging:** Courtyard, Hilton Garden, Homewood Suites, Sleep Inn, **other:** H HOSPITAL, Audi, Barnes&Noble, Circuit City, Goody's, Kohl's, Old Navy, Radio Shack, Target, Walgreen

**104** KY 418, Lexington, **E gas:** Exxon/Arby's/dsl/24hr, Shell/Hardees, **food:** Waffle House, **lodging:** Comfort Suites, Day's Inn, Econolodge, Holiday Inn, Red Roof Inn, **W gas:** BP/dsl, Chevron, Speedway/Subway, **food:** Wendy's, **other:** H HOSPITAL, **4 mi W food:** Hooters, KFC, Texas Roadhouse

**99** US 25 N, US 421 N

**98mm** Kentucky River

**97** US 25 S, US 421 S, **E gas:** Marathon/Huddle House/dsl/24hr, flea mkt, **W** RV camping (2mi)

**95** KY 627, to Boonesboro, Winchester, **E gas:** BP/dsl, Love's/Arby's/dsl/24hr, **food:** Hall's Diner (6mi), McDonald's, **other:** Ft Boonesborough SP, camping, **W gas:** Shell/dsl/24hr

**90** US 25, US 421, Richmond, **E gas:** Shell, **food:** Cracker Barrel, **lodging:** Knight's Inn, La Quinta, Motel 6, Red Roof Inn, **W gas:** BP, Exxon/Arby's/dsl, Marathon, Shell, **food:** Big Boy, DQ, Hardee's, Pizza Hut, Subway,

**KY**

## INTERSTATE 75 CONT'D

**N ↑ S**

**90** Continued
Super 8, **other:** $General, NTB, Pennzoil, antiques

**87** KY 876, Richmond, **E gas:** BP/dsl, Chevron/24hr, Marathon, Shell/dsl/24hr, Speedway/dsl, **food:** Burger King, Casa Fiesta Mexican, DQ, Fazoli's, Fong's Chinese, Hardee's, Hooters, KFC, King Buffet, Krystal/24hr, Little Caesar's, LJ Silver/A&W, McDonald's, Pizza Hut, Qdoba Mexican, Quizno's, Rally's, Subway, Taco Bell, Waffle House, Wendy's, **lodging:** Best Western, Econolodge, Quality Qtrs Inn, **other:** Ⓗ HOSPITAL, BigLots, $General, Goodyear/auto, Suzuki, to EKU, **W gas:** BP/dsl, Marathon/Circle K, **food:** Bob Evans, Ryan's, Starbucks, Steak'n Shake/24hr, **lodging:** Comfort Suites, Hampton Inn, Holiday Inn Express, Jameson Inn

**B E R E A**

**77** KY 595, Berea, **E food:** Artisan Cafe, **other:** Ⓗ HOSPITAL, Artisan Ctr, to Berea Coll, **W gas:** BP/Subway/24hr, Shell, **food:** Huddle House, La Casa Real, **lodging:** Country Inn&Suites, Day's Inn, Holiday Inn Express

**76** 76 KY 21, Berea, **E gas:** BP, Marathon/Circle K, Shell/Burger King, Speedway/dsl, **food:** Arby's, Cracker Barrel, Dinner Bell Rest., Hong Kong Buffet, KFC, Little Caesar's, LJ Silver, Mariachi Mexican, Mario's Pizza, McDonald's, Papa John's, Pizza Hut, Subway, Taco Bell, WanPen Chinese/Thai, Wendy's, **lodging:** Holiday Motel, Knight's Inn, Super 8, **other:** Ⓗ HOSPITAL, $General, Ford, Radio Shack, Walmart SuperCtr, tires, **W gas:** BP, Chevron/24hr, Marathon, Shell/dsl, **food:** Lee's Chicken, Pantry Family Rest., **lodging:** Comfort Inn, Econolodge, Fairfield Inn, **other:** Chrysler/Dodge/Jeep, Oh! Kentucky Camping, Walnut Meadow Camping

**62** US 25, to KY 461, Renfro Valley, **E gas:** Derby City/rest./dsl, Shell/24hr, **food:** Hardee's, Waffle House, **lodging:** Heritage Inn, Renfro Valley Inn, **other:** KOA (2mi), **W gas:** BP/Blimpie/24hr, Chevron/Wendy's/24hr, Shell/24hr, Marathon/Taco Tico, **food:** Arby's, DQ, Denny's, Godfather's/Subway, KFC, McDonald's, The Steakhouse, **lodging:** Day's Inn, Econolodge, **other:** Ⓗ HOSPITAL, Rite Aid, to Big South Fork NRA, Lake Cumberland

**59** US 25, to Livingston, Mt Vernon, **E gas:** BP, Shell/dsl, TravelCtr/dsl, **food:** Jean's Rest., Pizza Hut, **lodging:** Kastle Inn/rest., **other:** Nicely Camping, **W gas:** BP, **lodging:** Super Sleep Inn

**51mm** Rockcastle River

**49** KY 909, to US 25, Livingston, **W gas:** 49er/dsl/24hr

**41** KY 80, to Somerset, London, **E gas:** Speedway, **food:** Arby's, Azteca Mexican, Burger King, China Town, DQ, KFC, McDonald's, Pizza Hut, Sonic, **lodging:** Carrington Inn, Days Inn, Red Roof Inn, Sleep Inn, Super 8, **other:** Ⓗ HOSPITAL, Advance Parts, AutoZone, CVS Drug, $General, Kroger/deli, Parsley's Tire/repair, Pontiac/GMC, st police, **W gas:** BP/dsl/24hr, Chevron/McDonald's, Clark/dsl, Marathon, Shell/24hr, **food:** Chris's Buffet, Cracker Barrel, LJ Silver, Shiloh Roadhouse, Taco Bell, Waffle House, **lodging:** Budget Host, Hampton Inn, **other:** Westgate RV Camping

**38** KY 192, London, **E gas:** BP/dsl, Marathon, Shell/Quizno's/dsl, Speedway/dsl, **food:** Big Boy, Burger King, Capt D's, El Dorado Mexican, Fazoli's, Fiesta Mexican, Golden Corral, Great Wall Chinese, Hardee's, Huddle House, King Buffet, Krystal, McDonald's,

**38** Continued
O'Malley's, Pizza Hut, Ruby Tuesday, Taco Bell, **lodging:** Comfort Suites, Hampton Inn, Holiday Inn Express, Ramada Ltd, **other:** Ⓗ HOSPITAL, Advance Parts, E Kentucky RV Ctr, Goody's, Kroger, Office Depot, Peterbilt, USPO, Walmart SuperCtr, ✈, camping, toll rd to Manchester/Hazard, to Levi Jackson SP, **W** to Laurel River Lake RA

**34mm** weigh sta both lanes, truck haven

**30.5mm** Laurel River

**C O R B I N**

**29** US 25, US 25E, Corbin, **E gas:** BP, Marathon/dsl/scales/24hr/@, Pilot/McDonald's/Subway/dsl/scales//24hr, **food:** Burger King, David's Steaks, Huddle House, Shoney's, Waffle King, **lodging:** Super 8, **other:** Blue Beacon, Lowes Whse, Walmart SuperCtr/gas, to Cumberland Gap NP, **W gas:** BP/Krystal/dsl, Love's/Hardee's/dsl, Marathon, Shell/dsl/24hr, **food:** Cracker Barrel, Sonny's BBQ, **lodging:** Baymont Inn, Comfort Suites, Fairfield Inn, Hampton Inn, Knight's Inn, **other:** KOA, tires/repair, to Laurel River Lake RA

**25** US 25W, Corbin, **E gas:** Speedway/dsl, **food:** Buckner's Grill, Burger King, McDonald's, O'Malley's, Tuscany Garden, Wendy's, **lodging:** Country Inn&Suites, Day's Inn, Holiday Inn Express, Landmark Inn, **other:** Ⓗ HOSPITAL, auto repair/tires, **W gas:** BP/dsl, Shell/24hr, **food:** Arby's, China Garden, El Dorado Mexican, Subway, Waffle House, **lodging:** Best Western, **other:** to Cumberland Falls SP

**15** US 25W, to Williamsburg, Goldbug, **W gas:** Shell, Xpress, **other:** Cumberland Falls SP

**14.5mm** Cumberland River

**W I L L I A M S B U R G**

**11** KY 92, Williamsburg, **E gas:** BP/dsl, Exxon/dsl, Shell, **food:** Arby's, El Dorado Mexican, Hardee's, KFC, McDonald's, Pizza Hut, Quizno's, Sonic, Subway, Taco Bell, TCBY, **lodging:** Cumberland Inn, Scottish Inn. Super 8 **other:** AutoZone, Chevrolet, Chrysler/Dodge/Jeep, $General, Firestone, Ford, mufflers/transmissions, museum, **W gas:** Shell/dsl, Pilot/Wendy's/dsl/scales, **food:** Burger King, Huddle House, Krystal, LJ Silver, **lodging:** Day's Inn, Williamsburg Motel/RV Park, **other:** Walmart SuperCtr, to Big South Fork NRA

**1.5mm** Welcome Ctr nb, full ♿ facilities, 🕻 vending, 🍴 litter barrels, petwalk

**0mm** Kentucky/Tennessee state line

## INTERSTATE 275 - CINCINNATI

| Exit # | Services |
|---|---|
| **84** | Louisville, I-75, I-71, N to Cincinnati, S to Lexington |
| **83** | US 25, US 42, US 127, **S gas:** Shell, Speedway, **food:** Carrabba's, Max&Erma's, Panera Bread, TGIFriday, Wendy's, **other:** Dillards |
| **82** | rd1303, Turkeyfoot Rd, **S** Ⓗ HOSPITAL |
| **80** | KY 17, Independence, **N gas:** Mobil, Speedway, **food:** Big Boy, Bob Evans, Burger King, Snappy Pizza, Texas Roadhouse, Wendy's, **other:** Tire Discounters, Walmart SuperCtr |
| **78** | KY 16, Taylor Mill Rd, **N gas:** Speedway, **other:** Kroger/gas, **S gas:** BP/dsl, **food:** McDonald's, KFC, Taco Bell |
| **77** | KY 9, Maysville, Wilder, **S gas:** Mobil, Shell, **food:** DQ, Waffle House |
| **74a** | Alexandria, to US 27, (exits left from sb) |
| **74b** | I-471 N, Newport, Cincinnati, **N** Ⓗ HOSPITAL |
| **73mm** | OH/KY state line, OH River |

## INTERSTATE 275 CONT'D - CINCINNATI

**72** Kellogg Ave, **S gas:** Marathon, ✈

**71** US 52

**69** 5 mile rd, **W gas:** BP/dsl, **food:** Big Boy, IHOP, La Rosa Mexican, McDonald's, TGIFriday, Wendy's, **other:** H HOSPITAL

**65** OH 125, Beechmont Ave, Amelia, **E gas:** Marathon, Shell, Sunoco, **food:** Arby's, China Bistro, Hooters, Red Lobster, Wendy's, **lodging:** Motel 6, **other:** Ford, Lowe's Whse, Walgreen, **W gas:** BP, Speedway, Marathon, **food:** Big Boy, McDonald's, Best Western, Bob Evans, Tony Roma, **lodging:** Best Western, Days Inn, Red Roof Inn, **other:** Home Depot

**63b a** OH 32, Betavia, Newtown, **E gas:** BP, Meijer, Shell, Thornton's, **food:** Cheeseburger Paradise, Bob Evans, Burger King, Fazolie's, Max & Erma's, McDonalds, Perkins, Pizza Hut, **lodging:** Comfort Inn, Fairfield Inn, Holiday Inn, **other:** Best Buy, Big's Foods, Circuit City, Dillards, Kohl's, Sears/auto, **W gas:** Speedway, **food:** Big Boy, La Rosa Mexican, Roy Rogers, **lodging:** Comfort Inn, Fairfield Inn, Hampton Inn, Holiday Inn

**59** Milford Pkwy, **S gas:** Mobil, **food:** Buffalo Wings, Cracker Barrel, Goldstar Chili, Red Robin, Ruby Texas Roadhouse, Tuesday, Wendy's, **lodging:** Homewood Suites, **other:** Chryler/Jeep, Office Depot, Target

**57** OH 14 W, Forbes Rd, Broadway Ave, **N gas:** Meijer (1mi), **food:** Arby's, Burger King, Dunkin Donuts, IHOP, Taco Bell, White Castle, **other:** K-Mart, Lowe's Whse, **S gas:** BP, Exxon, **food:** Bob Evans, Cazadora Mexican, Charlie Basil's, **lodging:** Holiday Inn Express, Roadhouse Grill, **other:** H HOSPITAL, Kroger

**54** Wards Corner Rd, **N gas:** BP, Mobil, **food:** Perkins, **lodging:** Hilton Garden, **other:** Lowe's Whse, **S gas:** Mobil, **food:** Big Boy, Dominos, Hilton, Subway

**53mm** Little Miami River

**52** Loveland, Indian Hill, **1 mi N gas:** Circle K, Marathon, Shell, Speedway, **food:** Arby's, Burger King, Taco Bell, Skyline Chili, Starbucks, Wendy's

**50** US 22, OH 3, Montgomery, **N food:** Chili's, DQ, Pizzaria, Starbucks, **S gas:** BP/dsl, Shell, **food:** Goldstar Chili, La Rosa's, McDonald's, Skyline Chili, Wendy's, **other:** H HOSPITAL

**49** I-71 N to Columbus, S to Cincinnati

**47** Reed Hartman Hwy, Blue Ash, **S food:** Goldstar Chili, McDonald's, Starbucks, **lodging:** Amerisuites, Comfort Suites, Doubletree

**46** US 42, Mason, **N gas:** BP, **food:** Perkins, McDonald's, Taco Bell, Wendy's, White Castle, **lodging:** Holiday Inn, Motel 6, **other:** CVS Drug, **S gas:** Marathon, Shell, Speedway, **food:** Arby's, Schezwan House, Waffle House, **lodging:** Days Inn, **other:** Goodyear, Tire Discounters

**44** Mosteller Rd, **S lodging:** Homewood Suites

**43b a** I-75, N to Dayton, S to Cincinnati

**42** OH 747, Springdale, Glendale

**41** OH 4, Springfield Pk, **N gas:** Shell, Sunoco, **food:** Bahama Breeze, Carlo's Bistro, Pappadeaux, **lodging:** Baymont Inn, Ramda Inn, **S gas:** BP, Shell, **food:** Applebee's, Big Boy, DQ, Penn Station Subs, Perkins, Ponderosa, Rosita's Mexican, White Castle,

**41** Continued Wok'n Roll, **lodging:** Extended Stay, Howard Johnson, Super 8, Holiday Inn Express, **other:** Dillard's, Sears

**39** Winton Rd, Winton Woods, **N food:** BP, Meijer, **food:** Bob Evans, Chipotle Mexican, Golden Corral, IHOP, McDonald's, Old Spagetti Factory, Panera Bread, Red Lobster, Roadhouse Grill, Ruby Tuesday, Ryan's, Steak'n Shake, **lodging:** Hampton Inn, **other:** Biggs Foods, Home Depot, K-Mart, Kohl's, Outdoor World, **S gas:** Marathon, Mobil, Shell, **food:** Big Boy, Cracker Barrel, Fiesta Brava Mexican, Fuddrucker's, Popeye's, Skyline Chili, Subway, Wendy's, **lodging:** AmeriSuites, Lee's Inn, **other:** Goodyear, Jo-Ann Fabrics, Kroger/gas, Tires+, Walmart SuperCtr

**36** US 127, Hamilton, Mt Healthy, **N gas:** Citgo, Speedway, **food:** Skyline Chili, Wendy's, **S gas:** Sunoco, **food:** Arby's, Big Boy, La Rosa's Pizza, McDonald's, Pizza Hut/Taco Bell, Subway, **other:** Advance Parts, $General

**33** US 27, US 126, Colerain Ave, **N gas:** BP, Speedway, **food:** Burger King, Skyline Chili, Steak'n Shake, Wendy's, **other:** Colerain RV Ctr, Walmart, **S gas:** Shell, **food:** Arby's, Big Boy, Bob Evans, Cici's Pizza, KFC, LJ Silver, McDonald's, Olive Garden, Outback Steaks, Pizza Hut, Red Lobster, TGIFriday, White Castle, **lodging:** Red Carpet Inn, **other:** Isuzu, Kia, Macy's, Walgreen

**31** Ronald Reagan Hwy, Blue Rock Rd

**28** I-74, US 52, E to Cincinnati, W to Indianapolis

**21** Kilby Rd

**16** US 50, Greendale, Lawrenceburg, **W gas:** Ameristop/dsl, Marathon/dsl, Shell/Circle K/Subway, **food:** Buffalo's, Burger King, McDonald's, **lodging:** Comfort Inn, Holiday Inn Express, Quality Inn, Riverside Inn, **other:** Chevrolet/Pontiac/GMC, Chrysler/Dodge/Jeep, Tire Discounters, Walgreens

**14mm** Ohio River, Kentucky/Indiana state line

**11** to KY 20, Petersburg

**8b a** KY 237, Hebron, **N gas:** BP/DQ/dsl, Mobil/dsl, **food:** Arby's, El Mariachi, Nicky's Pizzaria, Wendy's, **S gas:** Marathon, Mobil/dsl, Shell/Subway, **food:** Burger King, Goldstar Chili, McDonald's, Waffle House

**4a b** KY 212, KY 20, **N gas:** ValAir Gas, **lodging:** Country Inn&Suites, Hampton Inn, Marriott, Sheraton, **S** H HOSPITAL, ✈

**2** Mineola Pike, **N gas:** Mobil/dsl, **food:** Subway, **lodging:** Baymont Inn, Holiday Inn, **S lodging:** Courtyard Inn, Residence Inn

**E** ↕ **W**

**S L I D E L L**

## INTERSTATE 10

| Exit # | Services |
|---|---|
| **274mm** | Louisiana/Mississippi state line, Pearl River |
| **272mm** | West Pearl River |
| **270mm** | Welcome Ctr wb, full ♿ facilities, info, 📞, 🧺, litter barrels, petwalk, RV dump |
| **267b** | I-12 W, to Baton Rouge |
| **267a** | I-59 N, to Meridian |
| **266** | US 190, Slidell, **N gas:** Magnolia, Shell/dsl, TA/Mobil/dsl/rest./24hr/@, **food:** Arby's, Cane's Rest., China Wok, CiCi's, Denny's, KFC, Los Tres Amigos, McDonald's, Pizza Hut, Quizno's, Shoney's, Taco Bell, Wendy's, **lodging:** Best Value Inn, Best Western, Day's Inn, Deluxe Motel, Motel 6, **other:** Ⓗ HOSPITAL, Harley-Davidson, Office Depot, PepBoys, Radio Shack, Rouses Foods, Schwegmann Foods, U-Haul, **S gas:** Chevron/Subway/dsl/24hr, RaceTrac, **food:** Applebee's, Big Easy Diner, Cracker Barrel, McAlister's, Deli, Osaka Grill, Outback Steaks, Ruby Tuesday, Sonic, Starbucks, Texas Roadhouse, Waffle House, **lodging:** Best Inn, La Quinta, Ramada Inn, Value Inn, **other:** Ⓗ HOSPITAL, Lowes Whse, Walmart SuperCtr/gas, auto repair/transmissions, casino, vet |
| **265** | new exit |
| **263** | LA 433, Slidell, **N gas:** BP, Exxon, Shell, **food:** Ray's Rest., Waffle House, **lodging:** Comfort Inn, Hampton Inn, Super 8, **other:** Chevrolet/Cadillac, Mitsubishi, **S gas:** Fleet/Subway/scales/dsl, Texaco/dsl, **food:** McDonald's, Wendy's, **lodging:** Holiday Inn, **other:** Pinecrest RV Park, Chrysler/Dodge/Jeep, Ford/Lincoln/Mercury, Honda, Isuzu, Mazda, Nissan, Pontiac/Buick/GMC, Saturn, Toyota, Slidell Factory Outlet/famous brands, KOA (1mi) |
| **261** | Oak Harbor Blvd, Eden Isles, **N gas:** Exxon/dsl, **food:** Marina Cafe, Waffle House, **lodging:** Sleep Inn, **S gas:** Shell/Subway/dsl |
| **255mm** | Lake Pontchartrain |
| **254** | US 11, to Northshore, Irish Bayou, **S gas:** BP |
| **251** | Bayou Sauvage NWR, **S** swamp tours |
| **248** | Michoud Blvd |
| **246b a** | I-510 S, LA 47 N, S to Chalmette, N to Little Woods, **S** 6 Flags of NO |
| **245** | Bullard Ave, **N gas:** Chevron, Shell, **lodging:** Comfort Suites, Holiday Inn Express, **other:** Honda, **S gas:** Shell, **food:** IHOP, McDonald's, **lodging:** Motel 6, Quarter Hotel, **other:** Ⓗ HOSPITAL, Chrysler/Jeep, Ford, Home Depot, Nissan, Tire Kingdom, Toyota/Scion, Walgreens |
| **244** | Read Blvd, **N food:** McDonald's, **S gas:** EZ Mart/dsl, **food:** Popeye's, **lodging:** Best Western, Best Value Inn, Day's Inn, **other:** KIA |
| **242** | Crowder Blvd, **N gas:** Chevron **S gas:** Crowder Ctr |
| **241** | Morrison Rd, **N gas:** EZ Mart |
| **240b a** | US 90 E, Chef Hwy, Downman Rd, **N lodging:** Super 8, **other:** Chevrolet, U-Haul, **S gas:** Chevron, DZ |
| **239b a** | Louisa St, Almonaster Blvd, **N gas:** Chevron, Fastpay, **food:** Burger King, McDonald's, Popeye's, Rally's, **other:** Goodyear, Home Depot, Walgreens, Winn-Dixie, **S gas:** Day&Night/dsl |

**N E W   O R L E A N S   A R E A**

| | |
|---|---|
| **238b** | I-610 W (from wb) |
| **237** | Elysian Fields Ave, **N gas:** BP/Marti Gras/Subway/dsl, **other:** Lowe's Whse |
| **236c** | St. Bernard Ave |
| **236b** | LA 39, N Claiborne Ave |
| **236a** | Esplanade Ave, downtown |
| **235a** | Orleans Ave, to Vieux Carre, French Qtr, **S lodging:** Days Inn, Holiday Inn, Marriott, Sheraton |
| **235b** | Poydras St, **N** Ⓗ HOSPITAL, **S** to Superdome, downtown |
| **234a** | US 90A, Claiborne Ave, to Westbank, Superdome |
| **232** | US 61, Airline Hwy, Tulane Ave, **N food:** Burger King, S on Carolton **gas:** Exxon, Shell, **food:** KFC, McDonald's, Popeye's, Rallys, **other:** Family$, Pepboys, USPO, vet, to Xavier U |
| **231b** | Florida Blvd, WestEnd |
| **231a** | Metairie Rd |
| **230** | I-610 E (from eb), to Slidell |
| **229** | Bonnabel Blvd |
| **228** | Causeway Blvd, **N gas:** Exxon, Shell, **food:** PF Chang's, **lodging:** Best Western, Hampton Inn, Ramada Ltd, **other:** Borders Books, Dillard's, Old Navy, **S gas:** DZ, Exxon, **food:** IHOP, **lodging:** Days Inn, Extended Stay America, La Quinta, Quality Hotel, Residence Inn, Sheraton |
| **226** | Clearview Pkwy, Huey Long Br, **N gas:** Chevron, Exxon, **food:** Hooters, Popeye's, Taco Bell, **lodging:** Sleep Inn, **other:** Cadillac, Lincoln/Mercury, Sears/auto, Target, Tire Kingdom, **S gas:** Chevron, Danny&Clyde, **food:** Beijing Chinese, Burger King, Piccadilly's, Smoothie King, Subway, **lodging:** Shoney's Inn/rest., Sun Suites, **other:** Ⓗ HOSPITAL, Buick/GMC/Pontiac, Firestone |
| **225** | Veterans Blvd, **N gas:** Chevron, DZ, Shell, **food:** Burger King, Cuco's Mexican, Denny's, McDonald's, Subway, Taco Bell, **lodging:** La Quinta, **other:** Honda, Radio Shack, Rouse's Foods, **S gas:** Shell, **food:** Casa Garcia, Louisiana Purchase, N O Burgers, O'Henry's, Piccadilly's, Popeye's, Tiffin Pancakes, Wendy's, **lodging:** Sheraton, **other:** Acura, Best Buy, BigLots, Chevrolet, $General, Home Depot, K-Mart, Lexus, Nissan, Office Depot, PepBoys, PetsMart, TJ Maxx, Toyota, VW, Walgreens, Walmart/auto, vet |
| **224** | Power Blvd (from wb) |
| **223b a** | LA 49, Williams Blvd, **N gas:** DZ/dsl, Exxon, Shell, **food:** Big Daddy's Seafood, Burger King, Cane's Chicken, Fisherman's Cove, Hibachi House, IHOP, Pizza Hut, Popeye's, Rally's, Subway, Taco Bell, Wendy's, **lodging:** Fairfield Inn, **other:** AutoZone, Family$, Ford, Office Depot, PetCo, Rite Aid, Tuesday Morning, Walmart Mkt, **S gas:** Exxon/dsl, Shell, **food:** Brick Oven, Denny's, Jazz Seafood/steaks, KFC/LJ Silver, McDonald's, Pizza Connection, Quizno's, Sonic, Subway, Taco Tico, Trough's Seafood, **lodging:** Airline Inn, Comfort Inn, Contempra Inn, Extended Stay America, La Quinta, New Orleans Hotel, Park Plaza Inn, Radisson, Travelodge, **other:** Circuit City, CVS Drug, $General, Firestone/auto, Goodyear, NAPA, Radio Shack, Toyota/Scion, U-Haul, mall |
| **221** | Loyola Dr, **N gas:** Circle K, Exxon/dsl, Loyola, Shell/dsl, **food:** Church's, McDonald's, Popeye's, Rally's, Starbucks, Taco Bell, **other:** Advance Parts, Sam's Club/gas, **S gas:** DZ, **food:** Rick's Café, **lodging:** Motel 6, **other:** Family$, 🚂, info |

**LA**

## INTERSTATE 10 CONT'D

**E ↕ W**

| | |
|---|---|
| **220** | I-310 S, to Houma |
| **214mm** | Lake Pontchartrain |
| **210** | I-55N (from wb) |
| **209** | I-55 N, US 51, to Jackson, **N gas:** Shell/Huddle House/casino/dsl, **lodging:** Comfort Inn, **S gas:** Circle K/dsl, Pilot/Subway/dsl/24hr/scales/@, Shell/dsl, **food:** Bully's Seafood, McDonald's, Shoney's, Waffle House, Wendy's, **lodging:** Best Western, Day's Inn, Hampton Inn, Quality Inn |
| **207mm** | weigh sta both lanes |
| **206** | LA 3188 S, La Place, **S gas:** Shell, Texaco/dsl, **food:** McDonald's, **lodging:** Millet Motel, **other:** Ⓗ HOSPITAL |
| **194** | LA 641 S, to Gramercy, **3-5 mi S gas:** Chevron, Taylors/dsl, **food:** Golden Grove Rest, Popeye's, **other:** Ⓗ HOSPITAL, **11-15 mi S** plantations |
| **187** | US 61, N to Sorrento, S to Gramercy |
| **182** | LA 22, Sorrento, **N gas:** Chevron/Popeye's/dsl, Texaco/dsl, **S gas:** Chevron/Subway/dsl, SJ/dsl, **food:** Coffeehouse, Lafitte's Café, McDonald's, Waffle House |

**G O N Z A L E S**

| | |
|---|---|
| **179** | LA 44, Gonzales, **N gas:** Chevron/dsl, **1 mi N other:** Buick/Pontiac/GMC, $General, Fred's Drug, Walgreens, **3 mi S food:** Cabin Fine Cajun Food, Pelican Point Café, **other:** Vesta RV Park |
| **177** | LA 30, Gonzales, **N gas:** Freedom/dsl, **food:** Burger King, Jack-in-the-Box, McDonald's, Outback Steaks, Taco Bell, Waffle House, **lodging:** Best Inn, Best Western, Budget Inn, Highland Inn, Holiday Inn, Western Inn, **other:** Ⓗ HOSPITAL, **S gas:** Chevron, Shell/dsl, **food:** Chili's, Cracker Barrel, Popeye's, Starbucks, Subway, Wendy's, **lodging:** Holiday Inn Express, Supreme Inn, **other:** Bass Pro Shops, Tanger/famous brands, Vesta RV Park |
| **173** | LA 73, to Geismar, Prairieville, **N gas:** Shell/dsl, **S gas:** Exxon/TCBY/dsl, Mobil/McDonald's/dsl, **food:** Burger King, DeAngelo's Pizza, Godfather's Pizza, Popeye's, Sonic, Subway, **other:** Curves, Twin Lakes RV Park (1mi) |
| **166** | LA 42, LA 427, Highland Rd, Perkins Rd, **N gas:** Chevron/Church's/dsl, Exxon/dsl, **food:** Las Palmas |

## INTERSTATE 10 CONT'D

**E ↕ W**

**166** Continued
Mexican, Popeye's, Ruffino's Rest., Sonic, Waffle House, **lodging:** Royal Motel (4mi), **other:** Home Depot, funpark, **S gas:** Shell/BBQ, Texaco/dsl, **food:** Subway

**163** Siegen Lane, **N gas:** Chevron/24hr, RaceTrac, Shell, **food:** Arby's, Burger King, Cane's Chicken, Chick-fil-A, CiCi's Coffee, CiCi's Pizza, Corky's BBQ, Galo's Mexican, Hooter's, IHOP, McAlister's, McDonald's, Olive Garden, Pizza Hut/Taco Bell, Shoney's, Subway, Waffle House, Whataburger, **lodging:** Days Inn, Hampton Inn, Holiday Inn Express, Microtel, Motel 6, **other:** Advance Parts, Big Lots, $Tree, Firestone/auto, Harley-Davidson, Honda, Hummer, Office Depot, PetCo, Radio Shack, Ross, Saab, Saturn, Target, **S food:** Backyard Burger, Chili's, ChuckeCheese, Honeybaked Ham, Joe's Crab-shack, Sicily's, Subway, Texas Roadhouse, Wendy's, **lodging:** Courtyard, Residence Inn, **other:** BooksAMillion, Kohl's, Lowe's Whse, Old Navy, PetsMart, Sam's Club/gas, TJ Maxx, Walmart SuperCtr

**162** Bluebonnet Rd, **N gas:** Chevron/dsl, **food:** Cadillac Cafe, Primo's Steaks, **lodging:** Quality Suites, **S gas:** RaceWay, **food:** Burger King, Cheesecake Bistro, Copeland's Bistro, J Alexander's, King Buffet, Logan's Roadhouse, Ralph&Kacoo's, **lodging:** AmeriSuites, **other:** Best Buy, Dillard's, JC Penney, Macy's, Sears/auto, Mall of LA, World Mkt

**160** LA 3064, Essen Lane, **S gas:** Exxon, RaceTrac, **food:** Burger King, Copeland's Bistro, Domino's, India's Rest., McDonald's, Mr. Gaddy's, Piccadilly's, Popeye's, Starbucks, Subway, Taco Bell, Time's Grill, Wendy's, **lodging:** Fairfield Inn, Springhill Suites, **other:** H HOSPITAL, Albertson's/gas, $General, Firestone, Tire Kingdom, Walgreens

**159** I-12 E to Hammond

**158** College Dr, Baton Rouge, **N gas:** Ride USA, **food:** Alabasha Café, Cane's Chicken, CiCi's, Hooters, Izzo's Grill, Jason's Deli, Macaroni Grill, Mansurs Rest., Melting Pot, O'Charley's, On-the-Border, Ruby Tuesday, Starbucks, Waffle House, Wendy's, **lodging:** Best Western, Chase Suites, Extended Stay America, Homewood Suites, Marriott, **other:** H HOSPITAL, Barnes&Noble, **S gas:** Chevron/24hr, Exxon, Shell, **food:** Casa Maria Mexican, Chili's, China Border, Gino's Pizza, Great Wall Chinese, IHOP, McDonald's, Marina's Mexican, Ninfa's Mexican, Quizno's, Ruth's Chris Steaks, Seminola Grill, Starbucks, Taco Bell, **lodging:** Cambria Suites, Comfort Inn, Embassy Suites, Hampton Inn, Holiday Inn Express, Holiday Inn Select, **other:** Albertson's, AutoZone, $Tree, Office Depot, Radio Shack, Rite Aid, Sav-On Foods, Walgreens, Walmart SuperCtr

**157b** Acadian Thwy, **N gas:** Chevron, Shell, **food:** Mastizo's Grill, Rib's Rest., **lodging:** La Quinta, University Inn, **other:** H HOSPITAL, **S gas:** Shell, **food:** Outback Steaks, **lodging:** Courtyard, **other:** CVS Drug

**157a** Perkins Rd (from eb), same as 157b

**156b** Dalrymple Dr, **S** to LSU

**156a** Washington St

**155c** Louise St (from wb)

**155b** I-110 N, to Baton Rouge bus dist, ✈

**155a** LA 30, Nicholson Dr, Baton Rouge, **N** Sheraton, **S** to LSU

**154mm** Mississippi River

**153** LA 1, Port Allen, **N gas:** Chevron, Shell, **food:** Church's, Sonic, **other:** AutoZone, Family$, **S gas:** Chevron, LA 1S Truck Plaza/BP/dsl, RaceTrac, **food:** Waffle House, **lodging:** Port Allen Inn, **other:** Walmart SuperCtr

**151** LA 415, to US 190, **N gas:** Cash's Trk Plaza/dsl/scales, Chevron, Exxon/dsl, Gold Mine/casino/dsl, RaceTrac, **food:** Burger King, Domino's, KFC/Taco Bell, McDonald's, Popeye's, Shoney's, Waffle House, **lodging:** Best Western, Comfort Inn, Days Inn, Quality Inn, **S gas:** Love's/Arby's/dsl/scales/24hr, Shell/dsl/24hr, **lodging:** Audubon Inn, Motel 6, Super 8

**139** LA 77, Grosse Tete, **N gas:** Shell/Subway/dsl, **other:** Chevrolet, casino, **S gas:** Tiger/Conoco/dsl/rest./@

**135** LA 3000, to Ramah, **N gas:** Ramah/bait

**127** LA 975, to Whiskey Bay

**126.5mm** Pilot Channel of Whiskey Bay

**122mm** Atchafalaya River

**121** Butte La Rose, **visitors ctr/rest area, both lanes, full facilities**, 🚻, **litter barrels, vending, petwalk, tourist info, S food:** Lazy Cajun Grill (2mi), **other:** Frenchman's Wilderness Camground (.5mi)

**115** LA 347, to Cecilia, Henderson, **N gas:** BP/dsl, Exxon/dsl/24hr, Texaco/dsl, **food:** Boudin's Rest., Landry's Seafood, **lodging:** Holiday Inn Express, **other:** casinos, **S gas:** Chevron/dsl, Citgo/dsl, Exxon/Subway/dsl, Shell/McDonald's, Valero, **food:** Popeye's, Waffle House

**109** LA 328, to Breaux Bridge, **N gas:** Shell/dsl, Texaco/grill/dsl/24hr, **food:** Tinata's Mexican, **other:** Campers ULT, casino, **S gas:** Chevron/Popeye's, Mapco, Mobil/Domino's/dsl, Pilot/Arby's/dsl/scales/24hr, **food:** Burger King, Crazy Bout Cajun, McDonald's, Pizza Hut, Sonic, Taco Bell, Waffle House, Wendy's, **lodging:** Sona Inn, Super 8, **other:** AutoZone, Chevrolet, $General, Family$, Ford, Walgreens, Walmart SuperCtr

**108mm** weigh sta both lanes

**104** Louisiana Ave, **S other:** JC Penney, Office Depot, PetCo, Ross, Target,

**103b** I-49 N, to Opelousas

**103a** US 167 S, to Lafayette, **S gas:** Chevron/dsl/24hr, RaceTrac, Shell/dsl, **food:** Checker's, KFC, McDonald's, Pizza Hut, Popeye's, Shoney's, Subway, Taco Bell, Waffle House, Wendy's, **lodging:** Baymont Inn, Econolodge, Fairfield Inn, Hawthorn Suites, Holiday Inn, Howard Johnson, Jameson Inn, La Quinta, Quality Inn, Royal Inn, Super 8, TravelHost Inn, **other:** H HOSPITAL, Albertson's/gas, CVS Drug, Home Depot, Rite Aid, Super 1 Foods/gas, Walmart SuperCtr/gas, transmissions

**101** LA 182, to Lafayette, **N gas:** Chevron/McDonald's, TA/Arby's/dsl/scales/24hr/@, Ride USA/dsl, **food:** Burger King, Waffle House, Whataburger, **lodging:** Red Roof Inn, **other:** Honda Motorcycles, **S gas:** Exxon, RaceTrac, Shell/dsl, **food:** Cracker Barrel, **lodging:** Best Value, Best Western, Day's Inn, Drury Inn, Hilton Garden (2mi), St Francis Motel, **other:** H HOSPITAL, Family$, Hyundai, Isuzu/Kia, O'Reilly Parts

**100** Ambassador Caffery Pkwy, **N gas:** Exxon/Subway/dsl/24hr, **other:** Curves, Gauthier's RV Ctr,

## INTERSTATE 10 CONT'D

**E ← → W**

**100** Continued
**S** gas: Chevron/24hr, RaceTrac/24hr, Shell/dsl, food: Burger King, McDonald's, Pizza Hut/Taco Bell, Sonic, Waffle House, Wendy's, lodging: Ambassador Inn, Hampton Inn, Sleep Inn, Microtel, other: H HOSPITAL, Goodyear, Peterbilt

**97** LA 93, to Scott, **S** gas: Chevron/McDonald's, Shell/Church's/dsl/24hr, food: Fezzo's Seafood, lodging: Holiday Inn Express, Howard Johnson, other: Harley-Davidson, KOA

**92** LA 95, to Duson, **N** gas: Texaco/dsl/casino/RV dump/scales/24hr, **S** gas: BP/Subway/dsl, Chevron/dsl, Exxon/casino/dsl, lodging: Super 8, other: Frog City RV Park

**87** LA 35, to Rayne, **N** gas: Chevron/dsl, Exxon/Subway/dsl/24hr, food: Burger King, McDonald's, lodging: Days Inn, other: $General, RV camping, **S** gas: Frog City/Citgo/dsl, Mobil/dsl/24hr, Valero/dsl, food: Candyland Ice Cream, DQ, Gabe's Café, Popeye's, lodging: The Frog City Inn, other: H HOSPITAL, Advance Parts, CVS Drug, Family$, O'Reilly Parts, Shop Rite/gas, Walgreens, Winn-Dixie

**82** LA 1111, to E Crowley, **S** gas: Chevron/dsl, Murphy USA/gas, food: Chili's, Wendy's, other: H HOSPITAL, $Tree, GNC, Lowes Whse, Radio Shack, Walgreens, Walmart SuperCtr

**80** LA 13, to Crowley, **N** gas: Conoco/Exit 80/dsl/rest./24hr, food: Fezzo's Seafood/steaks, Waffle House, lodging: Crowley Inn, Days Inn, La Quinta, **S** gas: Chevron, Exxon/24hr, RaceWay, Shamrock/dsl, Tobacco+, food: Burger King, Cajun Way, China Dragon, DQ, El Dorado Mexican, Golden Seafood, KFC McDonald's, Mr Gatti's, Pizza Hut, PJ's Grill, Popeye's, Sonic, Subway, Taco Bell, other: AutoZone, Chrysler/Dodge/Jeep, $General, Ford/Mercury/Nissan, Nissan, O'Reilly Parts, Radio Shack, Rite Aid, U-Haul, Winn-Dixie

**76** LA 91, to Iota, **S** gas: Petro/Mobil/Subway/dsl/scales/24hr

**72** Egan, **N** food: Cajun Haven RV Park

**67.5mm** rest areas both lanes full ♿ facilities, 📞, 🧺, litter barrels, petwalk, RV dump

**65** LA 97, to Jennings, **N** gas: Spur/dsl (1.5mi), **S** gas: Shell/dsl/casino, lodging: Day's Inn, other: to SW LA St School

**64** LA 26, to Jennings, **N** Boudreaux Inn, Budget Inn, **S** gas: Chevron, Exxon/dsl, EZ Mart, Jennings Trvl Ctr/dsl, Valero, food: Burger King, General Wok Chinese, McDonald's, Mr Gatti's, Pizza Hut, Popeye's, Shoney's, Sonic, Subway, Taco Bell, Waffle House, Walker's Cajun Rest., Wendy's, lodging: Comfort Inn, Holiday Inn, other: H HOSPITAL, AutoZone, Chrysler/Jeep/Dodge, $General, O'Reilly Parts, Rite Aid, Walgreens, Walmart SuperCtr/gas

**59** LA 395, to Roanoke

**54** LA 99, Welsh, **S** gas: Circle R, Conoco/dsl, Exxon/dsl/24hr, food: DQ, Perky's Pizza

**48** LA 101, Lacassine, **S** gas: Exxon

**44** US 165, to Alexandria, **N** other: Quiet Oaks RV Park (10mi), **S** Coushatta Resort/casino, Wood-n Treasures RV Park

**43** LA 383, to Iowa, **N** gas: Exxon/Pit Grill/dsl/24hr, Loves/Hardee's/dsl/24hr, food: Burger King, lodging: Howard Johnson Express, other: United RV Ctr, **S** gas: Citgo/dsl, Conoco/dsl, Shell, Valero, food: Fausto's Chicken, McDonald's, Subway, other: $General, I-10 Outlet/famous brands, RV park

**36** LA 397, to Creole, Cameron, **N** Jean Lafitte RV Park (2mi), Jellystone Camping, **S** gas: Citgo/dsl, Conoco/dsl/RV dump/24hr, lodging: Sunrise Inn (2mi), other: casino, RV Camping, truckwash

**34** I-210 W, to Lake Charles

**33** US 171 N, **N** gas: Citgo, Exxon/dsl, food: Burger King, Church's, Pink Pig BBQ, Subway, Taco Bell, lodging: Best Western, Lake Charles Inn, La Quinta, other: AutoZone, CVS Drug, Family$, O'Reilly Parts, Walgreens, to Sam Houston Jones SP, **S** lodging: Holiday Inn Express, Motel 6, Treasure Inn

**32** Opelousas St, **N** gas: Exxon, **S** lodging: Holiday Inn Express, Motel 6, Treasure Inn

**31b** US 90 E, Shattuck St, to LA 14, **N** gas: Shell/dsl, **S** gas: PakCo Gas

**31a** US 90 bus, Enterprise Blvd, **S** gas: BP/dsl/24hr, food: Popeye's

**30b** downtown

**30a** LA 385, N Lakeshore Dr, Ryan St, **N** gas: Exxon, food: Waffle House, lodging: Days Inn, LakeView Inn, **S** food: Montana's Smokehouse, lodging: Best Inn, Harrah's Hotel/casino, Lakeview Motel

**29** LA 385, (from eb), **N** gas: Chevron, food: Steamboat Bills Rest., Thai Kitchen, Waffle House, lodging: Lakeview Motel, Travel Inn/rest., **S** lodging: Best Suites, other: Players Island Casino/hotel

**28mm** Calcasieu Bayou, Lake Charles

**27** LA 378, to Westlake, **N** gas: Conoco, Shell, food: Burger King, McDonald's, Subway, other: Bumper Parts, to Sam Houston Jones SP, **S** lodging: Inn at the Isle, other: Riverboat Casinos

**26** US 90 W, Southern Rd, Columbia, **N** gas: Circle K/gas

**25** I-210 E, to Lake Charles

**23** LA 108, to Sulphur, **N** gas: Circle K/gas, Exxon, food: Burger King, Chili's, McDonald's, Popeye's, Subway, Taco Bell, Wendy's, lodging: Quality Inn, other: $General, Lowe's Whse, Radio Shack, Walgreens, Walmart SuperCtr/gas, **S** gas: Chevron/Jack-in-the-Box/dsl, Citgo/dsl, food: Cracker Barrel, Waffle House, Winner's Choice, lodging: Best Western, Days Inn, Crossland

## INTERSTATE 10 CONT'D

**23** Continued
Suites, Holiday Inn Express, Super 8, **other:** Goodyear, casino, tires

**21** LA 3077, Arizona St, **N gas:** Conoco/dsl, Exxon, Shell, **food:** Boiling Point Cajun, China Taste, KFC, **other:** CVS Drug, $General, Ford, Kroger/gas, NAPA, Walgreens, vet, **S gas:** Citgo/dsl, Valero/dsl/casino, **other:** Ⓗ HOSPITAL, Hidden Ponds RV Park

**20** LA 27, to Sulphur, **N gas:** Bayou gas, Chevron, Circle K, Citgo, **food:** Bonanza, Burger King, Casa Ole Mexican, Cajun Charlie's, Checker's, Hollier's Cajun, Hong Kong Chinese, McDonald's, Mr Gatti's, Pitt Grill Cajun, Popeye's, Subway, Taco Bell, Wendy's, **lodging:** Best Value Inn, Econolodge, Hampton Inn, **other:** Brookshire Foods/gas, Family$, Firestone/auto, Goodyear/auto, Jiffy Lube, **S gas:** Pilot/dsl, Shell/dsl, **food:** Navroskey's Burgers, Pizza Hut, Sonic, Waffle House, **lodging:** Candlewood Suites, Fairfield Inn, La Quinta, Microtel, Wingate Inn, **other:** Ⓗ HOSPITAL, casino, to Creole Nature Trail

**8** LA 108, Vinton, **N gas:** Citgo/dsl, Exxon/dsl, **food:** Cajun Cowboy's Rest., **other:** V RV Park

**7** LA 3063, Vinton, **N gas:** Exxon/dsl/Delta Cafe, **food:** Burger King, Sonic, Subway, **N gas:** Loves/Arby's/dsl/scales/24hr

**4** US 90, LA 109, Toomey, **N gas:** Chevron/dsl/casino, Spirit/dsl/casino, **other:** casinos, truck repair, **S gas:** Exxon/dsl, Shell/dsl, **food:** TX Pelican Rest., **other:** RV Park

**2.5mm** weigh sta both lanes

**1.5mm** Welcome Ctr eb, full ♿ facilities, 📞, 🚻, litter barrels, petwalk

**1** (from wb), Sabine River Turnaround

**0mm** Louisiana/Texas state line, Sabine River

## INTERSTATE 12

| Exit # | Services |
| --- | --- |
| **85c** | I-10 E, to Biloxi. I-12 begins/ends on I-10, exit 267. |
| **85b** | I-59 N, to Hattiesburg |
| **85a** | I-10 W, to New Orleans |
| **83** | US 11, to Slidell, **N gas:** Chevron/dsl/24hr, Exxon/dsl, **food:** Burger King, McDonald's, Waffle House, **other:** $General, Lishmann's Foods, **S gas:** Ride USA/dsl, Shell, **other:** Ⓗ HOSPITAL |
| **80** | Airport Dr, North Shore Blvd, **N gas:** Kangaroo/Krystal, **food:** IHOP, Quizno's, Sonic, **other:** Circuit City, PetsMart, Ross, Target, **S gas:** Chevron/24hr, Shell/dsl, **food:** Burger King, Chili's, ChuckeCheese, McDonald's, Olive Garden, Pizza Hut/Taco Bell, Starbucks, Subway, Wendy's, **other:** Best Buy, Dillard's, $Tree, Goodyear/auto, Home Depot, JC Penney, Marshall's, Office Depot, Sam's Club/gas, Sears/auto, Walmart SuperCtr, mall |
| **74** | LA 434, to Lacombe, **N gas:** Chevron/Subway/dsl, **other:** HOSTPITAL, **S** Big Branch Marsh NWR |
| **65** | LA 59, to Mandeville, **N gas:** Chevron/dsl, Danny&Clyde's/cafe, Shell, **food:** Sonic, Waffle House, **S gas:** Kangaroo/Burger King/dsl, Texaco/Domino's/dsl, **other:** Winn-Dixie, to Fontainebleau SP, camping, USPO, vet |

**63b a** US 190, Covington, Mandeville, **N gas:** Chevron, Exxon, RaceTrac, Shell/Circle K, **food:** Acme Oyster House, Applebee's, Burger King, Cane's Rest., Chick-fil-A, Copeland's Grill, 4 Seasons Chinese, Honeybaked Ham, IHOP, KFC, McAlister's Deli, Osake Japanese, Outback Steaks, Piccadilly's, Quizno's, Sonic, Starbucks, Subway, TGIFriday, Waffle House, Wendy's, **lodging:** Best Western, Comfort Inn, Courtyard, Hampton Inn, Holiday Inn, Super 8, **other:** Albertson's, BooksAMillion, Chevrolet, Circuit City, GNC, Home Depot, Hyundai, Lowes Whse, Nissan, Office Depot, Toyota, Walmart SuperCtr, **S other:** Ⓗ HOSPITAL, Chrysler, st police, to New Orleans via toll causeway

**60mm** rest area both lanes, full handicapped facilities, 🚻, litter barrels, vending, petwalk

**59** LA 21, to Covington, Madisonville, **N gas:** Chevron/dsl, Kangaroo, Shell, **food:** Bistro Italia, Coldstone Creamery, Isabella's Pizza, McDonald's, Subway, Wow Cafe, **lodging:** La Quinta, **other:** Ⓗ HOSPITAL, Walgreens, **S gas:** Texaco, **food:** Chick-fil-A, Domino's, Longhorn Steaks, Moe's SW Grill, Quizno's, Taco Bell, Wendy's **other:** Belk, Best Buy, JC Penney, Marshall's, Ross, Target, World Mkt, Fairview Riverside SP

**57** LA 1077, to Goodbee, Madisonville, **S** Family RV Park, to Fairview Riverside SP

**47** LA 445, to Robert, **1-3 mi N other:** Jellystone Camping, to Global Wildlife Ctr

**42** LA 3158, to 🛧, **N gas:** Chevron/dsl/24hr, **lodging:** Friendly Inn, **other:** Truckwash, **S other:** Ⓗ HOSPITAL, Berryland RV Ctr

**40** US 51, to Hammond, **N gas:** RaceTrac, Shell/Circle K/24hr, **food:** Burger King, China Garden, Church's, Coldstone Creamery, IHOP, McDonald's, Pizza Hut, Quizno's, Ryan's, Taco Bell, Wendy's, **lodging:** Best Western, Supreme Inn, **other:** Dillard's, Harley Davidson, Rite Aid, Sears/auto, U-Haul, Walgreens, mall, **S gas:** Petro/Mobil/Subway/dsl/scales/24hr/@, Pilot/Arby's/dsl/scales/24hr, Shell, **food:** Waffle House, **lodging:** Colonial Inn, Days Inn, **other:** Ⓗ HOSPITAL, Blue Beacon, $General, KOA, SpeedCo

**38b a** I-55, N to Jackson, S to New Orleans

**37mm** weigh sta both lanes

**35** Pumpkin Ctr, Baptist, **N gas:** Exxon/dsl, **other:** Camping World RV Service/Supplies, Dixie RV Ctr, Punkin RV Park (2mi), **S gas:** Chevron/24hr

**32** LA 43, to Albany, **N gas:** Chevron/Subway, Exxon/dsl, **S gas:** Citgo/dsl, **other:** to Tickfaw SP

**29** LA 441, to Holden, **N** gas/dsl, **other:** Berryland Campers, RV RestStop (1mi), st police

**22** LA 63, to Frost, Livingston, **N gas:** Chevron/dsl, Conoco/dsl, Mobil, **food:** Subway, Wayne's BBQ, **other:** Family$, **S other:** Lakeside RV Park (1mi)

**19** to Satsuma

**15** LA 447, to Walker, **N gas:** Murphy Express, Shell/Subway/24hr, Texaco, **food:** Burger King, Domino's, Jack-in-the-Box, La Fleur's Seafood, McDonald's, Popeye's, Sherwood PoBoy's, Sonic, Taco Bell, Waffle House, Wendy's, **lodging:** La Quinta, **other:** AutoZone, $Tree, Walmart SuperCtr, Winn-Dixie, vet, **S gas:** Chevron/dsl, **other:** Family RV Ctr

## INTERSTATE 12 CONT'D

| | |
|---|---|
| 12 | LA 1036, Juban Rd |
| 10 | LA 3002, to Denham Springs, **N gas:** Chevron, Circle K, RaceTrac, Shell/Circle K/dsl, **food:** Arby's, Burger King, Cactus Café, Cane's Rest., Chili's, Chinese Inn, Crawford's Cajun, Don's Rest., Fernando's Mexican, IHOP, McDonald's, Popeye's, Ryan's, Sonic, Starbucks, Subway, Waffle House, Wendy's, **lodging:** Best Western, Hampton Inn, HomeGate Inn, **other:** Advance Parts, $General, Home Depot, PetCo, Radio Shack, Rite Aid, Tire Kingdom, Walmart SuperCtr, **S gas:** Pilot/Subway/dsl/scales/24hr, Shell, **food:** Backyard Burger, Fish Co Rest., Piccadilly's, Shoney's, **lodging:** Day's Inn, Highland Inn, **other:** Bass Pro Shop, Dodge/Isuzu, Ford, KOA |
| 8.5mm | Amite River |
| 7 | O'Neal Lane, **N gas:** Mobil, **lodging:** Comfort Suites, **other:** [H] HOSPITAL, Night's RV Park, Office Depot, Toyota/Scion, **S gas:** BP, Chevron/24hr, RaceTrac, **food:** Burger King, Las Palmas Mexican, LoneStar Steaks, McDonald's, Pizza Hut/Taco Bell, Popeye's, Sonic, Subway, Waffle House, Wendy's, **other:** [H] HOSPITAL, AutoZone, $Tree, Radio Shack, Walgreens, Walmart SuperCtr |
| 6 | Millerville Rd, **N gas:** Chevron/dsl/24hr, **food:** Chick-fil-A, Chili's, **other:** Best Buy, Lowes Whse, Office Depot, PetsMart, Super Target, **S gas:** Texaco/dsl, **other:** Ace Hardware |
| 4 | Sherwood Forest Blvd, **N gas:** Exxon, Shell/dsl, **food:** Burger King, Jack-in-the-Box, McDonald's, Popeye's, Sonic, Subway, Taco Bell, Waffle House, **lodging:** Crossland Suites, Red Roof Inn, Super 8, **other:** Goodyear/auto, Rite Aid, **S gas:** RaceTrac, Shell/24hr, **food:** Cane's Rest., Picadilly's, Pizza Hut, Podnuh's BBQ, Schlotzky's, Sherwood PoBoys, **lodging:** Calloway Inn, **other:** Harley-Davidson |
| 2b | US 61 N, **N gas:** B-Quik, Chevron, **food:** Applebee's, Cracker Barrel, McDonald's, Pizza Hut/Taco Bell, Shoney's, Subway, Taste of China, **lodging:** Days Inn, Holiday Inn, Microtel, Motel 6, Ramada Inn, Sleep Inn, **other:** Albertson's/gas, Dodge, Ford/Lincoln/Mercury, Hyundai, Marshall's, Michael's, Nissan, PepBoys, SteinMart, Toyota, Walgreens, Walmart Mkt, transmissions |
| 2a | US 61 S, **S gas:** Chevron, Circle K/gas, Exxon/dsl, **food:** McDonald's, Waffle House, **lodging:** Deluxe Inn, **other:** Cadillac/Volvo, Home Depot, Jubilee/dsl, Mitsubishi |
| 1b | LA 1068, to LA 73, Essen Lane, **N gas:** Shell/Circle K/dsl, **food:** Cane's Rest., McDonald's, **other:** [H] HOSPITAL, Family$, Hancock Fabrics, Hi-Nabor Foods, Radio Shack |
| 1a | I-10 (from wb). I-12 begins/ends on I-10, exit 159 in Baton Rouge |

## INTERSTATE 20

| Exit # | Services |
|---|---|
| 189mm | Louisiana/Mississippi state line, Mississippi River |
| 187mm | weigh sta both lanes |
| 186 | US 80, Delta, **S gas:** Chevron/Subway/dsl/24hr |
| 184mm | rest area both lanes, full [&] facilities, [C], [A], litter barrels, petwalk, RV dump |

| | |
|---|---|
| 182 | LA 602, Mound |
| 173 | LA 602, Richmond, **S other:** Ford |
| 171 | US 65, Tallulah, **N gas:** Chevron/Subway/dsl, Kangaroo/dsl, Shell/dsl, **food:** KFC, McDonald's, Wendy's, **lodging:** Day's Inn, Super 8, **other:** [H] HOSPITAL, **S gas:** Conoco/dsl/scales, Love's/Arby's/dsl/scales/24hr, TA/dsl/rest./scales/24hr/@, Texaco |
| 164mm | Tensas River |
| 157 | LA 577, Waverly, **N gas:** Tiger Trkstp/dsl/rest./24hr, to Tensas River NWR, **S** Chevron/Subway/dsl/24hr, Shell/dsl |
| 155mm | Bayou Macon |
| 153 | LA 17, Delhi, **N gas:** Chevron/Subway/dsl, Texaco/dsl, **food:** Burger King, Boomer's rest., China Garden, DQ, Pizza Hut, Sonic, **other:** [H] HOSPITAL, Brookshire's Foods, $General, Fred's Drugs, **S gas:** Valero/dsl, **lodging:** Best Western, Executive Inn |
| 148 | LA 609, Dunn |
| 145 | LA 183, rd 202, Holly Ridge |
| 141 | LA 583, Bee Bayou Rd |
| 138 | LA 137, Rayville, **N gas:** BP, Pilot/Wendy's/dsl/scales/24hr, **food:** Dragon Buffet, McDonald's, Sonic, **lodging:** Day's Inn, **other:** [H] HOSPITAL, AutoZone, Chevrolet/Pontiac/Buick, $General, Family$, Firestone, Walmart SuperCtr, **S gas:** Chevron/Subway/dsl/24hr, Exxon/Circle K/dsl, RaceWay, **food:** Big John's Rest., Popeye's, Waffle House, **lodging:** Super 8 |
| 135mm | Beouf River |
| 132 | LA 133, Start, **N gas:** Exxon/dsl |
| 128mm | Lafourche Bayou |
| 124 | LA 594, Millhaven, **N gas:** EZ Mart/dsl, **other:** st police, to Arsage Wildlife Area |
| 120 | Garrett Rd, Pecanland Mall Dr, **N gas:** Chevron/dsl, Shell, **food:** Applebee's, Copeland's Rest., Eastern Empire Chinese, Hawg Wild BBQ, IHOP, McAlister's, O'Charleys, Olive Garden, Red Lobster, Sonic, Subway, **lodging:** Courtyard, Residence Inn, **other:** Belk, Dillard's, Firestone/auto, Home Depot, JC Penney, Kohl's, PetCo, Ross, Sears/auto, Target, mall, **S gas:** Kangaroo/dsl, **lodging:** Best Western, Day's Inn, **other:** Freightliner, Harley-Davidson, Hope's RV Ctr, Lowes Whse, Pecanland RV Park, Sam's Club/gas, Shilo RV Camp |
| 118b a | US 165, **N lodging:** Holiday Inn, La Quinta, **other:** Chrysler/Dodge, Goodyear, Home Depot, KIA, |

**LA**

## INTERSTATE 20 CONT'D

**E ↕ W MONROE RUSTON** (left margin direction markers)

**118b a** Continued
Nissan, to NE LA U, **S gas:** Chevron, Exxon, Shell/Circle K, **food:** Burger King, Capt D's, Church's, KFC, McDonald's, Popeye's, Sonic, Subway, Wendy's, **lodging:** Comfort Suites, Hampton Inn, Motel 6, Ramada Ltd

**117b** LA 594, Texas Ave, **N** gas/dsl

**117a** Hall St, Monroe, **N** [H] HOSPITAL, Civic Ctr, **S food:** Popeye's

**116b** US 165 bus, LA 15, Jackson St, **N** [H] HOSPITAL

**116a** 5th St, Monroe

**115** LA 34, Mill St, **N gas:** Chevron, **S other:** Clay's RV Service

**114** LA 617, Thomas Rd, **N gas:** Raceway, **food:** Bennigan's, Burger King, Cane's BBQ, Capt D's, Chick-fil-A, El Chico, Grandy's, KFC, McAlister's Deli, McDonald's, Pizza Hut, Popeye's, Subway, Taco Bell, TCBY, Wendy's, **lodging:** Shoney's Inn/rest., Super 8, Wingate Inn, **other:** [H] HOSPITAL, Big Lots, Office Depot, Walgreens, Walmart SuperCtr/gas, **S gas:** Chevron, Exxon/Circle K/dsl, **food:** Chili's, China Garden, Cracker Barrel, Hooters, Logan's Roadhouse, LoneStar Steaks, Mohawk Seafood, Nicky's Mexican, Outback Steaks, Peking Chinese, Pizza Hut, Sonic, Waffle House, **lodging:** Best Western, Fairfield Inn, Jameson Inn, Red Roof Inn, **other:** Firestone, Radio Shack

**113** Downing Pines Rd, **N lodging:** Hilton Garden, Holiday Inn Express, **other:** Chrysler/Dodge/Jeep

**112** Well Rd, **N gas:** Conoco, Shell/Circle K/dsl/24hr, Texaco/dsl, **food:** Domino's, McDonald's, Sonic, Taco Bell, Waffle House, **other:** Walgreens, **S gas:** Pilot/Subway/Wendy's/dsl/scales/24hr, **other:** Pavilion RV Park

**108** LA 546, to US 80, Cheniere, **N gas:** Shell/dsl

**107** Camp Rd, rd 25, Cheniere, **N** RV Park

**103** US 80, Calhoun, **N gas:** Chevron/dsl/rest., **food:** Johnny's Pizza (1mi), **lodging:** Avant Motel

**101** LA 151, to Calhoun, **S gas:** Citgo/Subway/dsl, Exxon, **food:** Huddle House/24hr, Sonic

**97mm** rest area wb, full [access] facilities, [phone], [picnic], litter barrels, petwalk, RV dump

**95mm** rest area eb, full [access] facilities, [phone], [picnic], litter barrels, petwalk, RV dump

**93** LA 145, Choudrant, **S gas:** Chevron, **other:** Jimmy Davis St Park, camping

**86** LA 33, Ruston, **N gas:** RaceWay, Shell/Circle K/Quizno's/dsl, **food:** Cajun Cafe, Cane's Chicken, Chili's, Hot Rod BBQ, Log Cabin Grill, Ryan's, Sonic, Z Buffet, **lodging:** Comfort Inn, Day's Inn, **other:** Buick/GMC, Cadillac/Chevrolet/Pontiac, Chrysler/Dodge/Jeep, Firestone, Ford/Lincoln/Mercury, Fred's Drug, Lowes Whse, Toyota, Walmart SuperCtr/gas, **S gas:** gas/dsl, **lodging:** Fairfield Inn, Holiday Inn Express

**85** US 167, Ruston, **N gas:** Chevron/Subway, Exxon, Shell/Circle K, **food:** Applebees, Burger King, Capt D's, Huddle House, McDonald's, Peking Chinese, Wendy's, **lodging:** Budget Lodge, Hampton Inn, Howard Johnson, Relax Inn, **other:** $General, Goody's, Office Depot, Radio Shack, Super 1 Foods, TrueValue, **S gas:** BP/dsl, Valero/dsl, **food:** Pizza Hut, **lodging:** Best Value Inn, Sleep Inn, **other:** [H] HOSPITAL, Advance Parts

**84** LA 544, Ruston, **N gas:** Mobil/dsl, **S gas:** Chevron, Exxon, **food:** Domino's, Johnny's Pizza, Pizza Inn, Quizno's, Sam Miguel Cantina, Starbucks, Subway, TCBY, Waffle House, **lodging:** Super 8, Travel Inn, **other:** Curves

---

**M I N D E N** (right margin direction marker)

**81** LA 141, Grambling, **S gas:** Chevron/Church's/dsl/24hr, Exxon, **other:** to Grambling St U

**78** LA 563, Industry, **S gas:** Texaco/dsl

**77** LA 507, Simsboro

**69** LA 151, Arcadia, **S gas:** BP/dsl, Citgo, Exxon, Shell, **food:** Country Cottage Rest., McDonald's, Sonic, Subway, **lodging:** Day's Inn, **other:** Bonnie& Clyde RV Park, Brookshire Foods, $General, Factory Stores/famous brands, Fred's Drugs

**67** LA 9, Arcadia, **N** to Lake Claiborne SP, **S gas:** Shell/dsl

**61** LA 154, Gibsland, **N** to Lake Claibourne SP

**58mm** rest area both lanes, full [access] facilities, [phone], [picnic], litter barrels, petwalk, RV dump

**55** US 80, Ada, Taylor

**52** LA 532, to US 80, Dubberly, **N gas:** Exxon/Mom's Diner/dsl/scales/24hr, Valero/dsl, **S gas:** Clark/dsl

**49** LA 531, Minden, **N gas:** Loves/Arby's/dsl/scales/24hr, Minden TrkStp/Shell/dsl/rest./24hr/@, QuickDraw/Subway/dsl, **food:** Pizza Hut (3mi), Taco Bell (3mi), **other:** Walmart SuperCtr/gas (3mi)

**47** US 371 S, LA 159 N, Minden, **N gas:** Chevron/dsl, Citgo/dsl, Mobil/dsl, **food:** Golden Biscuit, **lodging:** Best Western, Exacta Inn/rest., Holiday Inn Express, Southern Inn, **other:** [H] HOSPITAL, **S** B&B, to Lake Bistineau SP, camping

**44** US 371 N, Cotton Valley, **N gas:** Chevron, Exxon/Huddle House/dsl, **food:** Crawfish Hole #2, Nicky's Cantina, **lodging:** Minden Motel (2mi), **other:** Family$

**38** Goodwill Rd, Ammo Plant, **S gas:** BP/Rainbow Diner/dsl/24hr, **other:** Interstate RV Park

**33** LA 157, Fillmore, **N gas:** Texaco, **other:** Hilltop Camping (2mi), Johnny's Rest., (6mi), **S gas:** Exxon, Pilot/Arby's/dsl/scales/24hr, **food:** Waffle House, **other:** $General, Family$, USPO, Lake Bistineau SP

**26** I-220, Shreveport, **1 mi N gas:** Raceway, **other:** Casino

**23** Industrial Dr, **N gas:** Exxon/Subway, Shell/Circle K, Texaco/Popeye's/24hr, **food:** Barnhill's Buffet, Burger King, McDonald's, Sue's Country Kitchen, Taco Bell, Wendy's, **lodging:** Ramada Inn, **other:** O'Reilly Parts, st police, **S gas:** Chevron/dsl, Mobil/dsl, **lodging:** Econolodge, **other:** Southern RV Ctr

**22** Airline Dr, **N gas:** Chevron/McDonald's/dsl, Citgo/dsl, Shell/Circle K, **food:** Applebee's, Arby's, Backyard Burger, Burger King, Chili's, ChuckeCheese, DQ, IHOP, Little Caesar's, Luby's, Pizza Hut, Popeye's, Red Lobster, Sonic, Starbucks, Taco Bell, Waffle House, **lodging:** Best Western, Crossland Suites, Rodeway Inn, Super 8, **other:** Albertson's/gas, Big Lots, Books-A-Million, CVS Drug, Dillard's, Firestone/auto, Goodyear/auto, JC Penney, K-Mart, Michael's, Office Depot, Old Navy, PepBoys, Sears/auto, Walgreens, mall, **S gas:** Exxon/dsl, Texaco/dsl/24hr, **food:** Capt John's, Church's, Darrell's Rest., Outback Steaks, Quizno's, **lodging:** Microtel, Quality Inn, Red Carpet Inn, Super 8, **other:** [H] HOSPITAL, AutoZone, Super1 Foods, to Barksdale AFB

**21** LA 72, to US 71 S, Old Minden Rd, **N gas:** Circle K, Exxon, Valero, **food:** Burger King, El Chico, McDonald's, Podnah's BBQ, Ralph&Kacoo's, RJ's Rest., Shoney's, Subway, Texas Roadhouse, Whataburger, **lodging:** Budgetel, Hampton Inn, Holiday Inn, La Quinta, Residence Inn, **other:** Audi/Mazda, Advance Parts, AutoZone, $General, O'Reilly Parts, VW, USPO, **S gas:** RaceWay, **food:** Waffle House, Wendy's, **lodging:** Day's Inn, Motel 6

**LA** (left margin tab)

## INTERSTATE 20 CONT'D

| Exit | Services |
|---|---|
| 20c | (from wb) to US 71 S, to Barksdale Blvd |
| 20b | LA 3, Benton Rd, same as 21 |
| 20a | Hamilton Rd, Isle of Capri Blvd, **N gas:** Circle K, Texaco/24hr, **lodging:** Comfort Inn, **S gas:** Exxon, **lodging:** Best Value Inn, **other:** casino |
| 19b | Traffic St, Shreveport, downtown, **N other:** Bass Pro Shop, Chevrolet, casino |
| 19a | US 71 N, LA 1 N, Spring St, Shreveport, **N food:** Don's Seafood, **lodging:** Best Western, Hilton, Holiday Inn |
| 18b-d | Fairfield Ave (from wb), downtown Shreveport, **S** H HOSPITAL |
| 18a | Line Ave, Common St (from eb), downtown, **S gas:** Citgo, **other:** H HOSPITAL |
| 17b | I-49 S, to Alexandria |
| 17a | Lakeshore Dr, Linwood Ave |
| 16b | US 79/80, Greenwood Rd, **N** H HOSPITAL, **S gas:** Citgo/dsl, **food:** El Chico, **lodging:** Travelodge |
| 16a | US 171, Hearne Ave, **N gas:** Citgo/dsl, **food:** Subway, **other:** H HOSPITAL, **S gas:** Raceway, Texaco/dsl, **food:** KFC, **lodging:** Cajun Inn |
| 14 | Jewella Ave, Shreveport, **N gas:** Citgo/dsl, Texaco/dsl/24hr, Valero, **food:** Burger King, China Hat, Church's, McDonald's, Popeye's, Subway, Sonic, Whataburger, **other:** Advance Parts, AutoZone, County Mkt Foods, Family$, O'Reilly Parts, Rite Aid, Super 1 Foods, Walgreens |
| 13 | Monkhouse Dr, Shreveport, **N food:** Bro's Cafe, **lodging:** Best Value Inn, Day's Inn, Guesthouse Inn, Residence Inn, **S gas:** Chevron, Citgo, Exxon/Subway/dsl, **food:** Waffle House, **lodging:** Best Western, Candlewood Suites, Hampton Inn, Holiday Inn Express, Regency Inn, Super 8, **other:** to ✈ |
| 11 | I-220 E, LA 3132 E, to I-49 S |
| 10 | Pines Rd, **N gas:** BP/dsl, **food:** DQ, Pizza Hut, Popeye's, Subway, **S gas:** Exxon/dsl, Shell/Quizno's, **food:** Becca's Cafe, Burger King, CiCi's Pizza, Cracker Barrel, Domino's, Dragon Chinese, Grandy's, IHOP, KFC, Nicky's Cantina, Sonic, Starbucks, Subway, Taco Bell, Waffle House, Wendy's, Whataburger, **lodging:** Comfort Suites, Courtyard, Fairfield Inn, La Quinta, Hilton Garden, Holiday Inn, Jameson Inn, **other:** Chrysler/Dodge, CVS, $Tree, $General, Family$, GNC, Home Depot, KOA, Kroger, O'Reilly Parts, Radio Shack, Rite Aid, USPO, Walgreens, Walmart SuperCtr/gas |
| 8 | US 80, LA 526 E, **N lodging:** Motel 6, **other:** Freightliner, **S gas:** Chevron/dsl, Citgo/dsl, Petro/Mobil/dsl/rest./scales/@, **food:** Wendy's, **other:** Blue Beacon, Camper's RV Ctr/park |
| 5 | US 79 N, US 80, to Greenwood, **N gas:** TA/Country Fried/Subway/dsl/scales/24hr/@, Texaco/dsl, **lodging:** Country Inn, Mid Continent Motel |
| 3 | US 79 S, LA 169, Mooringsport, **S gas:** ✦FLYING J/Conoco/dsl/LP/rest./scales/24hr, Love's/Arby's/dsl/scales/24hr, **food:** Sonic, **other:** SpeedCo |
| 2mm | Welcome Ctr eb, full ♿ facilities, 📞, 🏕, litter barrels, petwalk, RV dump |
| 1mm | weigh sta both lanes |
| 0mm | Louisiana/Texas state line |

## INTERSTATE 49

| Exit # | Services |
|---|---|
| | I-49 begins/ends in Shreveport on I-20, exit 17. |
| 206 | I-20, E to Monroe, W to Dallas |
| 205 | King's Hwy, **E food:** Cane's, McDonald's, Piccadilly's, **other:** Dillard's, Sears/auto, mall, **W gas:** Valero/dsl, |

| Exit | Services |
|---|---|
| 205 | Continued **food:** Burger King, LJ Silver, Subway, Taco Bell, **other:** H HOSPITAL |
| 203 | Hollywood Ave, Pierremont Rd |
| 202 | LA 511, E 70th St, **E gas:** RaceWay, **W gas:** Circle K, **food:** SC Chicken |
| 201 | LA 3132, to Dallas, Texarkana |
| 199 | LA 526, Bert Kouns Loop, **E gas:** Chevron/Arby's/dsl/24hr, Exxon/Circle K, **food:** Burger King, KFC, Taco Bell, Wendy's, **lodging:** Comfort Inn, **other:** Home Depot, **W gas:** RaceWay, Shell/dsl, **food:** McDonald's, Sonic, Starbucks, **other:** Brookshire Foods |
| 196 | Southern Loop |
| 196mm | Bayou Pierre |
| 191 | LA 16, LA 3276, to Stonewall |
| 186 | LA 175, to Frierson, Kingston, **W gas:** Relay Sta./Exxon/rest./casino/dsl/scales |
| 177 | LA 509, to Carmel, **E gas:** Texaco/Eagles Trkstp/casino/dsl/rest. |
| 172 | US 84, to Grand Bayou, Mansfield, **W** New Rockdale RV Prk, Civil War Site |
| 169 | Asseff Rd |
| 162 | US 371, LA 177, to Evelyn, Pleasant Hill |
| 155 | LA 174, to Ajax, Lake End, **W gas:** Spaulding/dsl, **other:** Country Livin' RV Pk |
| 148 | LA 485, Powhatan, Allen |
| 142 | LA 547, Posey Rd |
| 138 | LA 6, to Natchitoches, **E gas:** Exxon/Subway, French Mkt Express, RaceWay, **food:** Popeye's, Shoney's, Wendy's, **lodging:** Best Western, Holiday Inn Express, Super 8 (5mi), Travel Express Inn, **other:** H HOSPITAL, Walmart SuperCtr (5mi), **W gas:** Chevron/dsl, Exxon, Texaco/dsl, **food:** Burger King, El Giro, Huddle House, McDonald's, **lodging:** Country Hearth Inn, Econolodge, Hampton Inn, **other:** Nakatosh RV Park, to Kisatchie NF |
| 132 | LA 478, rd 620 |
| 127 | LA 120, to Cypress, Flora, **E gas:** Texaco, **other:** to Cane River Plantations |
| 119 | LA 119, to Derry, Cloutierville, **E** to Cane River Plantations |
| 113 | LA 490, to Chopin |
| 107 | to Lena, **E** USPO |
| 103 | LA 8 W, to Flatwoods, **E gas:** Shell/dsl, **other:** to Cotile Lake, RV camping |
| 99 | LA 8, LA 1200, to Boyce, Colfax, **6 mi W** Cotile Lake RV camp |

## INTERSTATE 49 CONT'D

| | |
|---|---|
| **98** | LA 1 (from nb), to Boyce |
| **94** | rd 23, to Rapides Sta Rd, **E** gas: Rapides/dsl **W** **LA Welcome Ctr, full** ♿ **facilites, littler barrels, petwalk,** 🚻**, vending, other:** I-49 RV Ctr |
| **90** | LA 498, Air Base Rd, **W** gas: Chevron/dsl/24hr, Exxon/dsl, Mobil/dsl, Texaco/BBQ/dsl, **food:** Burger King, Cracker Barrel, McDonald's, **lodging:** La Quinta, Super 8, Travel Express Inn |
| **86** | US 71, US 165, MacArthur Dr, **0-2 mi W** **gas:** Chevron, Conoco/dsl, Exxon, Mobil, Shell/Circle K, Texaco, **food:** Applebee's, Arby's, Burger King, Cane's, Cajun Landing Rest., Church's, DQ, Fire Mtn Grill, Little Caesar's, Outlaw's BBQ, Popeye's, Schlotzsky's, Shoney's, Sonic, Subway, Taco Bell, **lodging:** Alexandria Inn, Best Western, Comfort Inn, Days Inn, Econolodge, Guesthouse Inn, Holiday Inn Express, Motel 6, Quality Inn, Ramada Ltd, Sai Hotel, Super 8, Value Place Inn, **other:** Advance Parts, AutoZone, BigLots, Checker's, $General, Family$, Kroger, O'Reilly Parts, Saturn, Rite Aid, Super 1 Foods |
| **85b** | Monroe St, Medical Ctr Dr (from nb), **E** 🅷 HOSPITAL |
| **85a** | LA 1, 10th St, MLK Dr, downtown |
| **84** | US 167 N, LA 28, LA 1, Pineville Expswy (no ez return nb) |
| **83** | Broadway Ave, **E** gas, **1 mi W food:** Wendy's, **other:** BooksAMillion, Harley-Davidson, Lowe's Whse, Sam's Club/gas, Target, Walmart SuperCtr |
| **81** | US 71 N, LA 3250, Sugarhouse Rd, MacArthur Dr (from sb), **W** same as 80 and 83 |
| **80** | US 71 S, US 167, MacArthur Dr, Alexandria, **0-3 mi W gas:** Chevron/dsl, Exxon, Mobil, Shell, **food:** Burger King, Capt D's, Carino's Italian, Chili's, KFC, Logan's Roadhouse, McDonald's, Outback Steaks, Pizza Hut, Popeye's, Sonic, Subway, Taco Bell, **lodging:** Best Western, Day's Inn, Hampton Inn, Holiday Inn, Super 8, **other:** Albertson's/gas, Dillard's, Dodge, $General, Ford, Hyundai, JC Penney, PetsMart, Sam's Club/gas, U-Haul, mall |
| **73** | LA 3265, rd 22, to Woodworth, **E** dsl repair, **W** gas: Exxon/Blimpie/dsl, **other:** LA Conf Ctr, to Indian Creek RA, RV camping |
| **66** | LA 112, to Lecompte, **E** gas: Chevron/Burger King/dsl, **food:** Lea's Lunch, **W** gas: Exxon/dsl, **other:** museum |
| **61** | US 167, to Meeker, Turkey Creek, **E** to Loyd Hall Plantation (3mi) |
| **56** | LA 181, Cheneyville |
| **53** | LA 115, to Bunkie, **E** gas: Sammy's/Chevron/dsl/casino/24hr |
| **46** | LA 106, to St Landry, **W** to Chicot SP |
| **40** | LA 29, to Ville Platte, **E** gas: Exxon/Cafe Mangeur/casino/dsl |
| **35mm** | **E** rest area/rec area both lanes, full ♿ **facilities,** 🚻**, litter barrels, vending, petwalk, RV dump** |
| **27** | LA 10, to Lebeau |
| **25** | LA 103, to Washington, Port Barre, **W** gas: Citgo, Mobil, **other:** Family$ |
| **23** | US 167 N, LA 744, to Ville Platte, **E** gas: Chevron/Subway/Stuckey's/dsl, Texaco/dsl/casino |
| **19b a** | US 190, to Opelousas, **E** Evangeline Downs Racetrack, **W** gas: Exxon/dsl, Mobil, RaceTrac/dsl, **other:** 🅷 HOSPITAL, Lowes Whse, USPO |
| **18** | LA 31, to Cresswell Lane, **E** food: Casa Ole's, **lodging:** Holiday Inn, **other:** Chrysler/Dodge/Jeep/Isuzu, $Tree, Home Depot, Little Caesar's, Radio Shack, |

Side label: **N ↕ S** **ALEXANDRIA**

---

| | |
|---|---|
| **18** | Continued Walmart SuperCtr/dsl, **W** gas: Chevron/dsl/24hr, Shell, Valero, **food:** Burger King, Cresswell Lane, Domino's, Hacienda Mexican, King Buffet, McDonald's, Mr Gatti's, Pizza Hut, Popeye's, Subway, Taco Bell, Wendy's, **lodging:** Day's Inn, **other:** Buick/Cadillac/GMC/Pontiac, CVS Drug, Family$, Goody's, Nissan, Piggly Wiggly, Walgreens, repair |
| **17** | Judson Walsh Dr, **E** gas: Texaco/dsl, **W** other: Goodyear/auto |
| **15** | LA 3233, Harry Guilbeau Rd, **W** lodging: Best Value Inn, **other:** 🅷 HOSPITAL, Toyota, RV Ctr |
| **11** | LA 93, to Grand Coteau, Sunset, **E** gas: Citgo/rest./dsl/24hr, Exxon/Popeye's/dsl, **food:** Beau Chere Rest., **W** food: Subway, **other:** $General, Family$, Janise's Foods |
| **7** | LA 182, **W** Primeaux RV Ctr |
| **4** | LA 726, Carencro, **W** gas: Chevron/Popeye's/dsl, Texaco/Subway/dsl, **food:** Burger King, McDonald's, **lodging:** Economy Inn, **other:** Mack, Kenworth |
| **2** | LA 98, Gloria Switch Rd, **E** gas: Chevron/dsl/deli, **food:** Chili's, IHOP, Prejean's Rest., Wendy's, **other:** Stevens RV Ctr, Lowes Whse, **W** gas: Shell/Church's/dsl, **food:** Domino's, Picante Mexican, Subway |
| **1b** | Pont Des Mouton Rd, **E** gas: Exxon/dsl, Texaco/Subway/dsl, **food:** Burger King, **lodging:** Motel 6, Plantation Inn, **other:** st police, **W** Ford |
| **1a** | I-10, W to Lake Charles, E to Baton Rouge, US 167 S gas: Chevron/dsl/24hr, RaceTrac, Shell/dsl, **food:** Checker's, KFC, McDonald's, Pizza Hut, Popeye's, Shoney's, Subway, Taco Bell, Waffle House, Wendy's, **lodging:** Baymont Inn, Econolodge, Fairfield Inn, Hawthorn Suites, Holiday Inn, Howard Johnson, Jameson Inn, La Quinta, Quality Inn, Royal Inn, Super 8, TravelHost Inn, **other:** 🅷 HOSPITAL, Albertson's/gas, CVS Drug, Home Depot, Rite Aid, Super 1 Foods/gas, Walmart SuperCtr/gas, transmissions |

I-49 begins/ends on I-10, exit 103.

Side label: **C A R E N C R O** **N ↕ S**

## INTERSTATE 55

| Exit # | Services |
|---|---|
| **66mm** | Louisiana/Mississippi state line |
| **65mm** | **Welcome Ctr sb, full** ♿ **facilities, tourist info,** 📞**,** 🚻**, litter barrels, petwalk** |
| **64mm** | weigh sta nb |
| **61** | LA 38, Kentwood, **E** gas: BP/dsl, Chevron/dsl, Texaco, **food:** Jam Chicken, Kentwood Seafood Rest., Popeye's, Sonic, **other:** 🅷 HOSPITAL, AutoZone, Brown Drug, $General, Family$, Ford/Mercury, IGA Foods, Super$, **W** gas: Exxon/Subway/dsl, Kangaroo/dsl, **other:** Chevrolet, Chrysler/Jeep/Dodge |
| **58.5mm** | weigh sta sb |
| **57** | LA 440, Tangipahoa, **E** to Camp Moore Confederate Site |
| **53** | LA 10, to Greensburg, Fluker, **W** 🅷 HOSPITAL |
| **50** | LA 1048, Roseland, **E** gas: Chevron/dsl/24hr |
| **46** | LA 16, Amite, **E** gas: Exxon/dsl, RaceTrac/dsl, Shell, **food:** Burger King, Domino's, Hot Wok, KFC, McDonald's, Popeye's, Sonic, Subway, Waffle House, Wendy's, **lodging:** Comfort Inn, **other:** 🅷 HOSPITAL, AutoZone, Fred's Drugs, O'Reilly Parts, Walmart SuperCtr/dsl, Winn-Dixie, **W** gas: Amite Trkstp/rest./dsl (2mi), **food:** Ardillo's, **lodging:** Colonial Inn, **other:** Ford, RV Camping |
| **40** | LA 40, Independence, **E** gas: Conoco, **other:** 🅷 HOSPITAL, Sweetwater Camping (7mi), **W** Indian Cr Camping (2mi) |

Side label: **N ↕ S** **A M I T E**

Side tab: **LA**

## INTERSTATE 55 CONT'D

| 36 | LA 442, Tickfaw, **E gas:** Chevron/dsl/24hr, **other:** camping, to Global Wildlife Ctr (15mi) |
|---|---|
| 32 | LA 3234, Wardline Rd, **E gas:** Kangaroo/dsl, **food:** Burger King, McDonald's, Sonic, Subway, Wendy's, **lodging:** Best Western, **other:** Tony's Tire |
| 31 | US 190, Hammond, **E gas:** Chevron/dsl, Exxon/dsl, Shell/dsl/scales/24hr, **food:** Adobe's Mexican, Applebee's, Buffalo Wild Wings, Burger King, Cane's, Casa Garcia, Chili's, China One, Cici's, Cracker Barrel, KFC, McDonald's, Picadilly's, Pizza Hut, Quizno's, Sonic, Subway, Taco Bell, Waffle House, Wendy's, **lodging:** Comfort Inn, Hampton Inn, Super 8, The Inn, **other:** H HOSPITAL, Advance Parts, Albertson's, AutoZone, Big Lots, BooksAMillion, Chrysler/Jeep/Buick/Dodge, CVS Drug, $General, $Tree, Family$, Goody's, Lowe's Whse, Office Depot, Radio Shack, Sav-A-Lot Foods, Tuesday Morning, Walgreens/24hr, Walmart SuperCtr/gas, Winn-Dixie, transmissions/repair |
| 29b a | I-12, W to Baton Rouge, E to Slidell |
| 28 | US 51 N, Hammond, **E gas:** Exxon, RaceTrac, **food:** Don's Seafood Rest., **lodging:** Landmark Inn/park, Quality Inn, Rockwood Inn, **other:** H HOSPITAL, Mitchell RV Ctr, Toyota/Scion, dsl repair |
| 26 | LA 22, to Springfield, Ponchatoula, **E gas:** Chevron/dsl, Exxon/dsl, Shell, **food:** Burger King, China King, KFC, McDonald's/playplace, Popeye's, Sonic, Subway, Waffle House, Wendy's, **lodging:** Microtel, **other:** AutoZone, Curves, CVS Drug, $General, Family$, Ford, O'Reilly Parts, Walgreens, Winn-Dixie, **W gas:** Exxon/Domino's/dsl, **other:** Tickfaw SP |
| 23 | US 51, Ponchatoula |
| 22 | frontage rd (from sb) |
| 15 | Manchac, **E food:** Middendorf Café, **other:** C, swamp tours |
| 7 | Ruddock |
| 1 | US 51, to I-10, Baton Rouge, La Place, **S gas:** Circle K/dsl, Pilot/Subway/dsl/24hr/scales/@, Shell/dsl, **food:** Bully's Seafood, McDonald's, Shoney's, Waffle House, Wendy's, **lodging:** Best Western, Day's Inn, Hampton Inn, Quality Inn |
| I-55 | begins/ends on I-10, exit 209. |

## INTERSTATE 59

| Exit # | Services |
|---|---|
| 11 | Pearl River Turnaround. Callboxes begin sb. |
| 5b | Honey Island Swamp |
| 5a | LA 41, Pearl River, **E gas:** Chevron/gifts |
| 3 | US 11 S, LA 1090, Pearl River, **W gas:** Shell/Subway/dsl, 1 mi **W** Chevron/dsl/24hr, **food:** D&K Rest. |
| 1.5mm | Welcome Ctr sb, full ♿ facilities, info, C, ⚏, litter barrels, petwalk, RV dump |
| 1c b | I-10, E to Bay St Louis, W to New Orleans |
| 1a | I-12 W, to Hammond. I-59 begins/ends on I-10/I-12. |

## INTERSTATE 220 - SHREVEPORT

| Exit # | Services |
|---|---|
| | I-220 begins/ends on I-20, exit 26. |
| 17b | I-20, W to Shreveport, E to Monroe |
| 17a | US 79, US 80, **N gas:** RaceWay, Shell/Circle K, **food:** Waffle House, **lodging:** SpringHill Suites, **other:** |

| 17a | Continued<br>LA Downs Racetrack/casino, **S gas:** Chevron/Huddle House/dsl, **food:** 1 Eyed Jack's |
|---|---|
| 15 | Shed Rd |
| 13 | Swan Lake Rd |
| 12 | LA 3105, Airline Dr, **N gas:** Shell/Circle K, **food:** Chick-fil-A, Domino's, McAlister's Deli, Quizno's, Starbucks, Subway, **other:** H HOSPITAL, Belk, Best Buy, PetsMart, Ross, Target, Walgreens, **S gas:** Exxon/dsl, Shell/Circle K/Subway, Valero/dsl, **food:** Applebee's, Burger King, Capt D's, CiCi's, McDonald's, Moe's SW Grill, Nicky's Rest., Ruby Tuesday, Ryan's, Sonic, Taco Bell, Trejo's Mexican, Wendy's, **lodging:** Best Western, **other:** $Tree, Home Depot, Lowes Whse, Radio Shack, Walmart SuperCtr/gas |
| 11 | LA 3, Bossier City, **N other:** H HOSPITAL, Buick/GMC/Pontiac, Ford, Lexus/Toyota, Maplewood RV Park (3mi), Suzuki, **S gas:** Chevron/dsl/24hr, **other:** Chrysler/Dodge/Jeep, Nissan |
| 7b a | US 71, LA 1, Shreveport, **N gas:** Citgo, Exxon/dsl, **food:** Domino's, Sonic, Subway, Whataburger/24hr, **other:** Brookshire Foods/gas, Curves, $General, Walgreens, **S gas:** Chevron/24hr, RaceWay, Texaco/dsl/24hr, **food:** Burger King, Church's, KFC, McDonald's, Podnuh's BBQ, Popeye's, Sammy's Rest., Taco Bell, Wendy's, **other:** Advance Parts, AutoZone, CVS Drug, Family$, O'Reilly Parts, Radio Shack, Rite Aid, repair/transmissions |
| 5 | LA 173, Blanchard Rd, **S gas:** Citgo |
| 2 | Lakeshore Dr |
| 1a | Jefferson Paige Rd, **S lodging:** Best Value Inn, Best Western, Day's Inn, Residence Inn, Super 8 |
| 1b c | I-20, E to Shreveport, W to Dallas. |
| | I-220 begins/ends on I-20, exit 11. |

## INTERSTATE 220 - NEW ORLEANS

| Exit # | Services |
|---|---|
| | I-610 begins/ends on I-10 |
| 4 | Franklin Ave (from eb) |
| 3 | Elysian fields, **N** H HOSPITAL, **S gas:** Gas4Less, Shell, **food:** Burger King, McDonald's |
| 2b | US 90, N Broad St, New Orleans St (from wb) |
| 2c | Paris Ave (from wb, no return), **S gas:** Shell/24hr, Spur, **food:** Popeye's |
| 2a | St Bernard Ave (from eb), to LSU School of Dentistry, auto racetrack |
| 1a | Canal Blvd |
| 1b | I-10, to New Orleans |
| | I-610 begins/ends on I-10 |

(side margin) N ↕ S  H A M M O N D

(side margin) N ↕ S

(side margin) S H R E V E P O R T

(side margin) LA

Copyright 2009 - The Next Exit®

## INTERSTATE 95

| Exit # | Services |
|---|---|
| **305mm** | US/Canada border, Maine state line, US Customs. I-95 begins/ends., US Customs |
| **305** | US 2, to Houlton, **E** other: Houlton ✈, DFA Duty Free Shop |
| **303mm** | Meduxnekeag River |
| **302** | US 1, Houlton, **E** gas: Irving/dsl/24hr, **food:** Burger King, KFC, McDonald's, Pizza Hut, Tang's Chinese, **other:** H HOSPITAL, IGA Foods, Rite Aid, **W** rest area both lanes, full ♿ facilities, ℂ, 🛉, litter barrels, petwalk, gas: Citgo/Subway/dsl, Exxon/dsl/LP, Irving/dsl/scales/@, **food:** Tim Horton, York's DairyBar, **lodging:** Ivey's Motel, Shiretown Motel/rest., **other:** Chevrolet/Pontiac/Buick, Family$, Ford/Lincoln/Mercury, Shop'n Save, Walmart |
| **301mm** | B Stream |
| **291** | US 2, to Smyrna, **E** lodging: Brookside Motel/rest. |
| **286** | Oakfield Rd, to ME 11, Eagle Lake, Ashland, **W** gas: Irving/dsl, Valero/dsl, **food:** A Place To Eat, **other:** UPSO |
| **277mm** | Mattawamkeag River, W Branch |
| **276** | ME 159, Island Falls, **E** gas: Porter's/rest., Dysarts Fuel, **other:** Bishop's Mkt, **W** to Baxter SP (N entrance), RV camping |
| **264** | to ME 11, Sherman, **E** gas: Shell/dsl/LP/rest., **W** gas: Irving/dsl, **lodging:** Katahdin Valley Motel, **other:** to Baxter SP (N entrance) |
| **259** | Benedicta (from nb, no re-entry) |
| **252mm** | scenic view Mt Katahdin, nb |
| **247mm** | Salmon Stream |
| **244** | ME 157, to Medway, E Millinocket, **W** gas: Irving/dsl, **lodging:** Gateway Inn, **other:** H HOSPITAL, Pine Grove Camping (4mi), USPO, vet, to Baxter SP (S entrance), city park |
| **244mm** | Penobscot River |
| **243mm** | rest area both lanes, full ♿ facilities, ℂ, 🛉, litter barrels, petwalk |
| **227** | to US 2, ME 6, Lincoln, 4 mi **E** H HOSPITAL, gas, food, lodging, RV camping |
| **219mm** | Piscataquis River |
| **217** | ME 6, Howland, **E** gas: Irving/95 Diner/dsl, **food:** Jim & Jill's Grill, **other:** 95er Towing/repair, LP, camping |
| **201mm** | Birch Stream |
| **199** | ME 16 (no nb re-entry), to LaGrange |
| **199mm** | weigh sta both lanes |
| **197** | ME 43, to Old Town, **E** gas/dsl |
| **196mm** | Pushaw Stream |
| **193** | Stillwater Ave, to Old Town, **E** gas: Citgo/dsl, Irving/dsl, Mobil/dsl, **food:** Burger King, Dunkin Donuts, Governor's Rest., McDonald's/playplace, Subway, Wendy's, **lodging:** Best Western, **other:** $Tree, IGA Foods, mall |
| **191** | Kelly Rd, to Orono, 2-3 mi **E** gas, food, lodging, camping |
| **187** | Hogan Rd, Bangor Mall Blvd, to Bangor, **E** gas: Citgo, **food:** Denny's, **lodging:** Courtyard, Hilton Garden, **other:** H HOSPITAL, Audi/VW, Chevrolet/Cadillac, Chrysler/Dodge, Firestone/auto, Ford, GMC/Isuzu, Honda/Nissan/Volvo, Jeep, Mitsubishi/Hyundai/Mercedes/Saab/Subaru, Saturn, Sam's Club/gas, **W** gas: Citgo/dsl, Exxon/dsl, |
| **187** | Continued **food:** Applebee's, Arby's, Bugaboo Creek Café, Burger King, Chicago Grill, Chili's, China Wall, Happy China, House of Pizza, KFC, McDonald's, Miguel's Mexican, 99 Rest., Olive Garden, Oriental Buffet, Pizza Hut, Starbucks, Subway, TX Roadhouse, **lodging:** Bangor Motel, Comfort Inn, Country Inn, Hampton Inn, **other:** Advance Parts, Best Buy, Borders Books, Circuit City, $Tree, Goodyear/auto, Harley-Davidson, Hannaford Foods, Home Depot, JC Penney, Jo-Ann Fabrics, K-Mart, Kohl's, Lincoln/Mercury/Kia, LL Bean, Macy's, Mr. Quick's Lube, Office Depot, Old Navy, PetCo, Sears/auto, Shaw's Foods, Staples, Target, VIP Parts, Walmart, mall |
| **186** | Stillwater Ave, same as 187 |
| **185** | ME 15, to Broadway, Bangor, **E** gas: Irving, **food:** Tri-City Pizza, **other:** H HOSPITAL, **W** gas: Exxon, Mobil, **food:** Amato's, BoBo Chinese, China Light, DQ, Governor's Rest., KFC, McDonald's, Pizza Hut, Starbucks, Subway, Tim Horton, **other:** Hannaford Foods, Rite Aid, TJ Maxx, Walgreens |
| **184** | ME 222, Union St, to Ohio St, Bangor, **E** gas: Citgo, Exxon, **other:** Rite Aid, **W** gas: Exxon, Gulf, Mobil/dsl, **food:** Burger King, Capt Nick's Rest., Dunkin Donuts, McDonald's, Nicky's Rest., Quizno's, Wendy's, **lodging:** Sheraton, **other:** Hannaford Foods, Marshall's, Staples |
| **183** | US 2, ME 2, Hammond St, Bangor, **E** gas: Exxon, **food:** Papa Gambino's Pizza, **other:** Corner Store, NAPA, TrueValue, **W** ✈ |
| **182b** | US 2, ME 100 W, **W** gas: Irving/Subway/dsl, Mobil/dsl, **food:** Dunkin Donuts, Ground Round, **lodging:** Day's Inn, Econolodge, Fairfield Inn, Holiday Inn, Howard Johnson, Motel 6, Ramada Inn, Super 8, Travelodge, **other:** RV camping, VIP Parts/service |
| **182a** | I-395, to US 2, US 1A, Bangor, downtown |
| **180** | Cold Brook Rd, to Hampden, **E** Citgo, **W** gas: Citgo/dsl/24hr/@, **lodging:** Best Western, **other:** dsl repair |
| **178mm** | rest area sb, full ♿ facilities, info, ℂ, vending, 🛉, litter barrels, petwalk |
| **177mm** | Soudabscook Stream |
| **176mm** | rest area nb, full ♿ facilities, info, ℂ, vending, 🛉, litter barrels, petwalk |
| **174** | ME 69, to Carmel, **E** gas: Citgo/dsl, **W** RV camping |
| **167** | ME 69, ME 143, to Etna |
| **161** | ME 7, to E Newport, Plymouth, **E** LP, **W** RV camping |
| **159** | Ridge Rd (from sb), to Plymouth, Newport |
| **157** | to US 2, ME 7, ME 11, Newport, **E** H HOSPITAL, **W** gas: Irving/dsl/24hr, Mobil/dsl, **food:** Burger King, China Way, Dunkin Donuts, McDonald's, Pando Italian, Pizza House, Quizno's, Sawyers Dairybar, Subway, Tim Horton, **lodging:** Lovley's Motel, **other:** Auto Value Parts, CarQuest, Chrysler/Jeep, GMC, NAPA, Radio Shack, Rite Aid, Shop'n Save, Walmart SuperCtr |
| **151mm** | Sebasticook River |
| **150** | Somerset Ave, Pittsfield, **E** gas: Mobil, **food:** Subway, **lodging:** Pittsfield Motel, **other:** H HOSPITAL, CarQuest, Chevrolet, Family$, Rite Aid, Shop'n Save Foods |
| **147mm** | rest area both lanes, full ♿ facilities, ℂ, 🛉, litter barrels, petwalk |

ME

HOULTON N↕S

BANGOR

BANGOR

NEWPORT

**130** Continued
**lodging:** Best Western, Comfort Inn, Holiday Inn, **other:** Ⓗ HOSPITAL, Advance Parts, Audi/VW, Hannaford Foods, Home Depot, JC Penney, K-Mart, Mazda, Mr Paperback, Radio Shack, Staples, VIP Parts/service, Walmart SuperCtr

**129mm** Messalonskee Stream

**127** ME 11, ME 137, Waterville, Oakland, **E gas:** Citgo/Burger King, Irving/dsl/24hr, Mobil, Xpress Stop, **food:** Applebee's, DQ, Dunkin Donuts, Grand Asian Buffet, McDonald's, Papa John's, Pizza Hut, Quizno's, Subway, Weathervane Seafood, **lodging:** Budget Host, Econolodge, Hampton Inn, **other:** Ⓗ HOSPITAL, Buick/Chevrolet/Pontiac, Chrysler/Dodge/Jeep, Marden's, Shaw's Foods/Osco Drug, Toyota/Scion, **W gas:** Shell, **other:** Aubuchon Hardware, CarQuest, Ford/Lincoln/Mercury

### WATERVILLE

# INTERSTATE 95 CONT'D

**138** Hinckley Rd, Clinton, **W gas:** ME Country Store/dsl

**134mm** Kennebec River

**133** US 201, Fairfield, **E food:** Purple Cow Pancakes

**132** ME 139, Fairfield, **E gas:** Gene's/deli, **W gas:** Pilot/Subway/dsl/scales/24hr

**130** ME 104, Main St, Waterville, **E gas:** Mobil, **food:** Arby's, Friendly's, Governor's Rest., McDonald's, Ruby Tuesday, Starbucks, Subway, Tim Horton, Wendy's,

**N ↕ S**

**AUGUSTA**

## INTERSTATE 95 CONT'D

| | |
|---|---|
| **120** | Lyons Rd, Sidney |
| **117mm** | rest area both lanes, full ♿ facilities, 🕻, vending, ⊞, litter barrels, petwalk |
| **113** | rd 3, new exit |
| **112** | ME 27, ME 8, ME 11, Augusta, **E gas:** Citgo, Lukoil, **food:** Ground Round, Longhorn Steaks, Olive Garden, Panera Bread, Sam's Italian, Red Robin, Ruby Tuesday, **lodging:** Holiday Inn, **other:** Barnes&Noble, Circuit City, GNC, Home Depot, Kohl's, Michael's, Old Navy, Radio Shack, Sam's Club, Staples, Walmart SuperCtr, **W gas:** Irving/dsl/24hr, **food:** Great Wall Chinese, KFC/Taco Bell, 99 Rest., Wendy's, **lodging:** Comfort Inn, Fairfield Inn, **other:** Advance Parts |
| **109** | US 202, ME 11, ME 17, ME 100, Augusta, **E gas:** Getty, Irving/dsl, Mobil, **food:** Applebees, Arby's, Burger King, Capital Buffet, Damon's, Domino's, DQ, Dunkin Donuts, Friendly's, KFC, McDonald's, Pizza Hut, Subway, Tim Horton, Wendy's, **lodging:** Best Western, **other:** Best Buy, BigLots, $Tree, Family$, Lowes Whse, PetsMart, Radio Shack, Shaw's Foods/Osco Drug, Staples, Target, U-Haul, VIP Parts, USPO, **W gas:** Lukoil, Valero, **food:** Margarita's Mexican, **lodging:** Econolodge, Motel 6, Quality Inn, Super 8, **other:** CarQuest, Chrysler/Jeep/Nissan/Subaru, Dodge/Hyundai, Hannaford Foods, KIA, PetCo, Sears/auto, Subaru, TJ Maxx, Toyota/Scion |
| **103** | to I-295 S, ME 9, ME 126, to Gardiner, (from sb) |
| **102** | to I-295 S, rd 9, rd 106, (from nb) |
| **98mm** | toll plaza |
| **97mm** | service plaza nb, Mobil/dsl, Burger King, atm, gifts |
| **86** | to ME 9, Sabattus, new exit |
| **84mm** | Sabattus Creek |
| **83mm** | service plaza sb, Mobil/dsl, Burger King, atm, gifts |
| **80** | ME 196, Lewiston, **W on ME 196 gas:** Gendron's/dsl, Getty, Mobil, Shell, Sunoco, **food:** Burger King, Cathay Hut Chinese, D'angelo's, Dunkin Donuts, Governor's Rest., KFC/Taco Bell, McDonald's, Papa John's, Sam's Italian, Wendy's, **lodging:** Chalet Motel, Motel 6, Ramada Inn, Super 8, **other:** Ⓗ HOSPITAL, $Tree, NAPA, Rite Aid |
| **78mm** | Androscoggin River |
| **75** | US 202, rd 4, rd 100, to Auburn, **E gas:** Irving/dsl, Mobil/Subway/dsl, **lodging:** Dunkin Donuts, Fireside Inn/grill, **other:** Whited RV Ctr, **W** Ⓗ HOSPITAL |
| **71mm** | Royal River |
| **66mm** | toll plaza |
| **63** | US 202, rd 115, rd 4, to ME 26, Gray, **E gas:** Gulf, Mobil, Shell, Sunoco, **food:** China Gray, Dunkin Donuts, Subway, McDonald's, **other:** NAPA, TrueValue |
| **59mm** | service plaza both lanes, Mobil/dsl, Chicago Pizza, Starbucks, atm, gifts |
| **55mm** | Piscataqua River |
| **53** | to ME 26, ME100 W, N Portland, **E gas:** Irving/Subway/dsl, **food:** Bernie's Rest., Dunkin Donuts, **other:** Ⓗ HOSPITAL, Hannaford Foods |
| **52** | to I-295, US 1, Freeport |
| **48** | ME 25, to Portland, **E gas:** Citgo, **food:** Applebee's, Full Belly Deli, Little Caesar's, Quizno's, Subway, |

**LEWISTON**

**ME**

**PORTLAND**

| | |
|---|---|
| **48** | Continued **lodging:** Rodeway Inn, **other:** BJ's Whse/gas, Chevrolet, Firestone, Jo-Ann Fabrics, Lowes Whse, Radio Shack, **W gas:** Citgo/Subway, Irving, **food:** Amato's, Buffalo Wings, Dunkin Donuts, Denny's, Friendly's, KFC, McDonald's, Panera Bread, Pizza Hut, Ruby Tuesday, Tim Horton, Verillo's Rest., Wendy's, **lodging:** Holiday Inn, Howard Johnson, Motel 6, Super 8, Travelodge, **other:** CarQuest, Chrysler/Dodge/Jeep, Ford, Harley-Davidson, Home Depot, Hyundai, JC Penney, Lexus/Toyota/Scion, NAPA, Shaw's Foods/Osco Drug, Tire Whse, VIP Parts/service |
| **47** | to ME 25, Rand Rd |
| **47mm** | Stroudwater River |
| **46** | to ME 22, Congress St, same as 45 |
| **45** | to US 1, Maine Mall Rd, S Portland, **E gas:** Citgo, Sunoco, **food:** Burger King, Bugaboo Creek Steaks, Chicago Grill, Chili's, ChuckeCheese, Dunkin Donuts, Friendly's, Great Wall Chinese, IHOP, Imperial China, LoneStar Steaks, Macaroni Grill, McDonald's, Old Country Buffet, Olive Garden, On the Border, Panera Bread, Pizza Hut, Pizza+, Ruby Tuesday, Tim Horton, Weathervane Seafood, Wendy's, **lodging:** Comfort Inn, Courtyard, Day's Inn, Econolodge, Fairfield Inn, Hampton Inn, Homewood Suites, Wyndham, **other:** Best Buy, Borders Books, $Tree, Macy's, Hannaford Foods, Honda, JC Penney, Macy's, Marshall's, Michael's, Nissan, Office Depot, PetCo, Sears/auto, Staples, Subaru, TJ Maxx, mall, **W food:** Applebee's, Starbucks, **lodging:** Holiday Inn Express, Marriott, **other:** Old Navy, Target |
| **44** | I-295 N (from nb), to S Portland, Scarborough, **1 mi E on ME 114 gas:** Citgo/Domino's, **food:** Dunkin Donuts, Quizno's, Shogun Japanese, Subway, **lodging:** Residence Inn, TownePlace Suites, **other:** Ⓗ HOSPITAL, Lowes Whse, NAPA, Sam's Club, Shaw's Foods/Osco Drug, VIP Parts/service, Walmart |
| **42mm** | Nonesuch River |
| **42** | to US 1, **E other:** Cabela's, Scarborough Downs Racetrack (seasonal) |
| **36** | I-195 E, to Saco, Old Orchard Beach, **E lodging:** Hampton Inn, **other:** KOA |
| **35mm** | **E lodging:** Holiday Inn Express/Saco Hotel Conference Ctr |
| **33mm** | Saco River |
| **32** | ME 111, to Biddeford, **E gas:** Irving/Subway/dsl, **food:** Amato's Sandwiches, Ruby Tuesday, Wendy's, **lodging:** Best Value Inn, Comfort Suites, **other:** Ⓗ HOSPITAL, AutoZone, Shaw's Foods, VIP Parts, Walmart SuperCtr, **W food:** Applebees, Longhorn Steaks, Olive Garden, Panera Bread, **other:** Best Buy, Home Depot, Kohl's, Lowes Whse, Old Navy, PetsMart, Staples, Target, TJ Maxx, Townfair Tire |
| **25mm** | Kennebunk River |
| **25** | ME 35, Kennebunk Beach, **E lodging:** Turnpike Motel |
| **24mm** | service plaza both lanes, **SB** Mobil/dsl, Burger King, Popeye's, Sbarro's, Starbucks, gifts, **NB** Mobil/dsl, Burger King, Popeye's, atm, gifts |
| **19.5mm** | Merriland River |

**BIDDEFORD**

## INTERSTATE 95 CONT'D

| | |
|---|---|
| **19** | ME 9, ME 109, to Wells, Sanford, **W** to Sanford RA |
| **7mm** | Maine Tpk begins/ends, toll booth |
| **7** | ME 91, to US 1, The Yorks, **E** gas: Gulf, Irving/dsl, Mobil/dsl, Shell, **food:** Ruby's Pizza, Wildcat Pizza, **lodging:** Best Western, Econolodge, Microtel, **other:** H HOSPITAL, Chrysler/Dodge/Jeep, Curves, Ford, Hannaford Foods, Rite Aid, TrueValue, last exit before toll rd nb |
| **5.5mm** | weigh sta nb |
| **5mm** | York River |
| **4mm** | weigh sta sb |
| **3mm** | Welcome Ctr nb, full 🦽 facilities, info, 📞, vending, 🚻, litter barrels, petwalk |
| **2** | (2 & 3 from nb), US 1, to Kittery, **E** on US 1 gas: Irving/dsl/scales, 7-11/dsl, **food:** Burger King, Clam Hut Diner, DQ, McDonald's, Subway, Sunrise Grill, Tasty Thai, Weathervane Seafood Rest., **lodging:** Blue Roof Motel, Coachman Inn, Kittery Motel, **other:** Outlets/Famous Brands |
| **1** | ME 103 (from nb, no re-entry), to Kittery |
| **0mm** | Maine/New Hampshire state line, Piscataqua River |

## INTERSTATE 295 - PORTLAND

| Exit # | Services |
|---|---|
| **74.5mm** | Androscoggin River |
| **51** | ME 9, ME 126, to Gardiner, Litchfield, TOLL PLAZA, **W** gas, last free nb exit |
| **49** | US 201, to Gardiner, **E** gas/dsl, **W** gas, RV camping |
| **43** | ME 197, to Richmond, **E** gas: Citgo/dsl |
| **37** | ME 125, Bowdoinham |
| **31** | ME 196, to Lisbon, Topsham, **E** gas: Irving/Subway, Gibbs/dsl, **food:** Arby's, McDonald's, 99 Rest., Romeo's Pizza, Ruby Tuesday, Starbuck's, Wendy's, **lodging:** Best Buy, Double Discount Parts, Hannaford Foods, Home Depot, Jo-Ann Fabrics, PetCo, Radio Shack, Rite Aid, Target, Tire Whse, VIP Parts/service, **E** gas: Express Stop |
| **28** | US 1, Bath, **1 mi E** on US 1...gas: Citgo, Irving/dsl, Mobil/dsl, Shell, **food:** Amato's, Dunkin Donuts, McDonald's, Thai House, **lodging:** Comfort Inn, Econolodge, Fairfield Inn, Travelers Inn, **other:** H HOSPITAL, Chevrolet/Mazda, Ford |
| **24** | to Freeport (from nb), facilities **1 mi** E on US 1 |
| **22** | ME 125, to Pownal, **E** on US 1...gas: Exxon, **food:** Arby's, Azure Cafe, Friendly's, Jameson Rest., McDonald's, Sam's Italian, Starbucks, Taco Bell, **other:** LL Bean, USPO, outlets/famous brands, **W** to Bradbury Mtn SP |
| **20** | Desert Rd, Freeport, **E** gas: Citgo, **food:** Antonia's Pizza, Buck's BBQ, Dunkin Donuts, Friendly's, Subway, Thai Garden Rest., **lodging:** Coastline Inn, Comfort Inn, Dutch Lighthouse Motel, Econolodge, Hampton Inn, Holiday Inn Express, Super 8, **other:** Shaw's Foods, outlets/famous brands, RV camping |

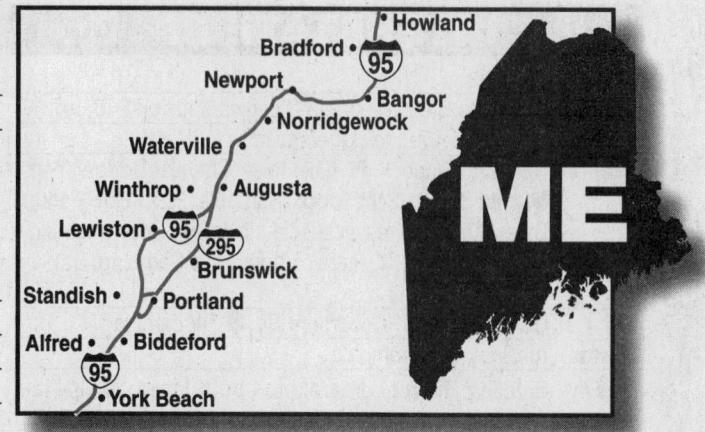

| | |
|---|---|
| **17** | US 1, Yarmouth, **E** rest area both lanes, full 🦽 facilities, info, **food:** Day's Takeout, Muddy Rudder Rest., **lodging:** Best Western, **other:** Ford, Delorme Mapping, **W** gas: Citgo/dsl, Clipper Mart, **food:** Bill's Pizza, Dunkin Donuts, McDonald's, Old World Pizza, Pat's Pizza, **lodging:** Casco Bay Inn, **other:** Ace Hardware, Hannaford Foods, NAPA, VIP Parts/service, vet |
| **15** | US 1, to Cumberland, Yarmouth, **W** gas: Exxon, Mobil, **food:** 233 Grill, **lodging:** Brookside Motel, **other:** Rite Aid |
| **11** | to I-95, ME Tpk |
| **I-295 begins/ends on I-95, exit 103.** | |
| **10** | US 1, to Falmouth, **E** gas: Exxon/dsl, Gulf/dsl, **food:** Dunkin Donuts, Finches Rest., McDonald's, Yummy Pizza, Subway, **other:** Audi/VW, Mazda, Radio Shack, Rite Aid, Saab, Shaw's Foods, Walmart |
| **9mm** | Presumpscot River |
| **9** | US 1 S, ME 26, to Baxter Blvd |
| **8** | ME 26 S, Washington Ave, **E** other: U-Haul |
| **7** | US 1A, Franklin St, **E** other: AAA, CarQuest, NAPA |
| **6b a** | US 1, Forest Ave, **E** gas: Mobil, **other:** H HOSPITAL, Firestone/auto, USPO, **W** food: Arby's, Burger King, Leonardo's Pizza, Pizza Hut, Stavro's Pizza, Subway, **other:** CVS Drug, Hannaford Foods |
| **5b a** | ME 22, Congress St, **E** food: Amato Cafe, Denny's, D'Angelo Sandwiches, McDonald's, Subway, **lodging:** La Quinta, **other:** H HOSPITAL, Sullivan Tire, **W** gas: Citgo/Dunkin Donuts, Mobil/dsl, **food:** Ananias Italian, **lodging:** Clarion |
| **3mm** | Fore River |
| **4** | US 1 S, to Main St, to S Portland, US 1 S, **E** services on US 1 |
| **3** | ME 9, to Westbrook St, no sb return, **W** gas: Irving/dsl, Mobil/dsl, **food:** Costa Vida Mexican, Eggspectation, Olive Garden, Outback Steaks, Ricetta's Pizza, Subway, Wild Willy's Burger, **other:** Chevrolet, Home Depot |
| **2** | to US 1 S, S Portland, **services E** on US 1 gas: Irving/dsl, Mobil, 7-11/gas, **food:** Dunkin Donuts, Governor's Rest., Mexico Lindo, Tony Roma's, Yankee Grill, **lodging:** Best Western, Howard Johnson, Knight's Inn, Quality Inn, **other:** Discount Tire |
| **1** | to I-95, to US 1, multiple services E on US 1, same as 2 |
| **I-295 begins/ends on I-95, exit 44.** | |

**H A N C O C K** E ↕ W

## INTERSTATE 68

| Exit # | Services |
|---|---|
| 82c | I-70 W, to Breezewood. I-68 begins/ends on I-70, exit 1. |
| 82b | I-70 E, US 40 E, to Hagerstown |
| 82a | US 522, Hancock, **N** Chevrolet, Chrysler/Dodge/Jeep, **S** gas: Sheetz/24hr, food: Hardee's, Pizza Hut, Park'n Dine, Subway, Weaver's Rest., lodging: Best Value Inn, Super 8, other: $General, Happy Hills Camping, Sav-a-Lot Foods |
| 77 | US 40, MD 144, Woodmont Rd, **S** RV camping |
| 75mm | runaway truck ramp eb |
| 74mm | **Sideling Hill rest area/exhibit both lanes, full ♿ facilities, vending, 1269 ft** |
| 74 | US 40, Mountain Rd (no return from eb) |
| 73mm | Sideling Hill Creek |
| 72mm | truck ramp wb |
| 72 | US 40, High Germany Rd, Swain Rd, **S** gas: BP/dsl |
| 68 | Orleans Rd, **N** gas: Exxon/dsl |
| 67mm | Town Hill, Town Hill, elevation 940 ft |
| 64 | MV Smith Rd, **S** to Green Ridge SF HQ, scenic overlook, 🍴, 1040 ft |
| 62 | US 40, 15 Mile Creek Rd, **N** Billmeyer Wildlife Mgt Area |
| 58.7mm | Polish Mtn, elevation 1246 ft |
| 57mm | Town Creek |
| 56mm | Flintstone Creek |
| 56 | MD 144, National Pike, Flintstone, **S** gas: Flintstone Petroleum |
| 52 | MD 144, Pleasant Valley Rd, National Pike |
| 50 | Pleasant Valley Rd, **N** food: Lakeside Grill, Signature's Grill, lodging: Rocky Gap Lodge/golf/rest., other: to Rocky Gap SP |
| 47 | US 220 N, MD 144, Dehaven Rd (from wb), Old National Pike, Bedford, same as 46 |
| 46 | US 220 N, Dehaven Rd, Baltimore Pike, Naves Crossroads, **N** lodging: Cumberland Motel, other: Advance Parts, Foodland, vet, **S** food: Puccini's Rest. |
| 45 | Hillcrest Dr, **S** gas: BP/dsl |
| 44 | US 40A, Baltimore Ave, Willow Brook Rd, to Allegany Comm Coll, to Allegany Comm Coll |
| 43d | Maryland Ave (from eb), **N** Ⓗ HOSPITAL, USPO, **S** gas: Liberty/dsl, food: Chick-fil-A, Papa John's, Quizno's, ThaiChai Quisine, other: AutoZone, Martin's Foods/gas |
| 43c | (from wb), same as 43b |
| 43b | Maryland Ave, **N** food: McDonald's, lodging: Holiday Inn, **S** gas: Citgo/dsl, food: Pizza Hut/Taco Bell, Roy Rogers, Wendy's, other: AutoZone |
| 43a | to WV 28A, Beall St, Industrial Blvd, to Cumberland, **N** gas: Sheetz |
| 42 | US 220 S, Greene St, Ridgedale |
| 41 | Seton Dr (from wb) |
| 41mm | Haystack Mtn, elev 1240 ft |
| 40 | US 220 S, to US 40A, Vocke Rd, La Vale, **N** gas: BP/dsl, Exxon/repair, Sunoco, food: Arby's, Asian Garden, Bob Evans, Burger King, D'Atri Rest., DQ, Denny's, Gehaufe's Rest., KFC, LJ Silver, McDonald's, Pizza Hut, Ruby Tuesday, Subway, Texas Grill, Wendy's, lodging: Comfort Inn, Slumberland Motel, Super 8, other: Ⓗ HOSPITAL, Advance Parts, CVS Drug, $General, Ford, Harley-Davidson, Jo-Ann Fabrics, Lowes Whse, |

**C U M B E R L A N D** E ↕ W

| | |
|---|---|
| 40 | Continued Mr Tire, Staples, st police, **S** food: Applebees, Dragon China Buffet, CiCi's Pizza, LaVale Diner, Ponderosa, lodging: Red Roof Inn, other: BonTon, $Tree, Goody's, JC Penney, Kohl's, Martin's Foods/gas, Sears/auto, Walmart SuperCtr, mall |
| 39 | US 40A (from wb), same as 40 |
| 34 | MD 36, to Westernport, Frostburg, **N** gas: BP, Sheetz, food: Burger King, Fox's Pizza, McDonald's, Peking House, Pizza Hut, Subway, Taco Del Mar, lodging: Day's Inn, Hampton Inn, other: Ⓗ HOSPITAL, CarQuest, $General, Family$, Food Lion, Rite Aid, **S** to Dans Mtn SP |
| 33 | Midlothian Rd, to Frostburg, **N** Ⓗ HOSPITAL, **S** to Dans Mt SP |
| 31mm | weigh sta eb |
| 30mm | Big Savage Mtn, elevation 2800 ft |
| 29 | MD 546, Finzel, **N** food: Hen House Rest., other: Mason-Dixon Camping (4mi/seasonal), **S** Savage River Lodge Rest. |
| 25.8mm | eastern continental divide, elevation 2610 ft |
| 24 | Lower New Germany Rd, to US 40A, **S** to New Germany SP, to Savage River SF |
| 23mm | Meadow Mtn, elevation 2780 ft |
| 22 | US 219 N, to Meyersdale, **N** gas: BP/dsl/24hr, Pilot/Arby's/dsl/scales/24hr, food: Burger King, Penn Alps Rest., Subway, lodging: Elliott House Inn, other: $Discount, $General, Foodland, TrueValue Hardware, Hilltop Fruit Mkt, NAPA, Rite Aid, **S** gas: BP/dsl, lodging: Comfort Inn, other: New Germany SP, Savage River SF |
| 20mm | Casselman River |
| 19 | MD 495, to US 40A, Grantsville, **N** gas: Exxon/dsl, Sunoco/dsl, food: Parkside Grill, lodging: Casselman Motel/rest., other: Beachy's Drug, CarQuest, Chevrolet, USPO |
| 15mm | Mt Negro, elevation 2740 ft |
| 14mm | Keyser's Ridge, elevation 2880 ft |
| 14b a | US 219, US 40 W, Oakland, **N** gas: Citgo/dsl, BP/Ridge/dsl/rest., food: McDonald's, repair |
| 6mm | **Welcome Ctr eb, full ♿ facilities, info, 🍴, 🌲, litter barrels, vending, petwalk** |
| 4.5mm | Bear Creek |
| 4mm | Youghiogheny River |
| 4 | MD 42, Friendsville, **N** gas: BP/dsl, Citgo/dsl, food: Jubilee Junction Rest., Old Mill Rest., lodging: Yough Valley Motel, other: S&S Mkt, USPO, **S** lodging: Sunset Inn, other: to Deep Creek Lake SP, camping |
| 0mm | Maryland/West Virginia state line |

## INTERSTATE 70

| Exit # | Services |
|---|---|
| | I-70 begins/ends in Baltimore at Cooks Lane. |
| 94 | Security Blvd N, **S** gas: Shell |
| 91b a | I-695, **N** off exit 17 gas: Exxon, Sunoco, food: Burger King, 5 Guys Burgers, McDonald's, Panera Bread, Popeye's, Quizno's, lodging: Best Western, other: Best Buy, Ford, Macy's, Old Navy, Sears/auto, SuperFresh Foods, mall, **S** gas: BP/repair, Shell, food: Dunkin Donuts, Subway, Wendy's, lodging: Day's Inn, Motel 6, Quality Inn, other: Chevrolet, Mitsubishi, Nissan, |
| 87b a | US 29 (exits left from wb)to MD 99, Columbia, **2 mi S** on US 40...gas: BP/dsl, Shell, Sunoco, Texaco, |

MD

## INTERSTATE 70 CONT'D

**BALTIMORE E ⟷ W**

**87b a** Continued
**food:** Boston Mkt, Burger King, Checker's, Crab Shanty, Domino's, Dunkin Donuts, Jerry's Subs, McDonald's, Oriental Rest., Papa John's, Qdoba Mexican, Quizno's, Subway, **other:** Acura/Infiniti, Advance Parts, Cadillac/Chevrolet, Carmax, Curves, Ford, Giant Foods, Home Depot, Honda, Mar's Foods, Mr Tire, NAPA, Nissan, Rite Aid, Safeway Foods, 7-11, SuperFresh Food, Saturn, Walmart

**83** US 40, Marriottsville (no EZ wb return), **2 mi S lodging:** Turf Valley Hotel/Country Club/rest.

**82** US 40 E (from eb), same as 83

**80** MD 32, Sykesville, **N** golf, **S gas:** Citgo, **food:** Subway

**79mm** weigh/insp sta wb, **C**

**76** MD 97, Olney, **S gas:** Citgo

**73** MD 94, Woodbine, **N gas:** Shell, **food:** Baskin Robbins, China Yee, Dunkin Donuts, Harvest Chicken, McDonald's, Pizza Hut, Subway, **other:** $Tree, Food Lion, Ramblin Pines RV Park (6mi), **S gas:** BP/dsl, Citgo

**68** MD 27, Mt Airy, **N gas:** BP/Blimpie/dsl/24hr, 7-11, Shell, **food:** Arby's, Burger King, China Taste, Domino's, KFC/Taco Bell, Ledo's Pizza, McDonald's, Papa John's, Pizza Hut, Subway, TCBY, **other:** Ace Hardware, Food Lion, Goodyear, Mr Tire, Radio Shack, Rite Aid, Safeway, SuperFresh Foods, Walmart/auto, vet, **S gas:** Exxon/dsl/24hr, Shell, **food:** 4 Seasons Rest., **lodging:** Budget Inn

**66mm** truckers parking area eb

**64mm** weigh/insp sta eb

**62** MD 75, Libertytown, **N gas:** Shell, **food:** Baskin Robbins, Domino's, Dunkin Donuts, McDonald's, Morgan's Grill, **other:** Food Lion, vet, New Market Hist Dist

**59** MD 144

**57mm** Monocacy River

**56** MD 144, **N gas:** Citgo, Sheetz, **food:** Beijing, Burger King, JR's Pizza, McDonald's, Roy Rogers, Taco Bell, Waffle House, Wendy's, **other:** $General, to Hist Dist **S other:** Triangle RV Ctr,

**55** South St, **1 mi N gas:** Citgo, Pacific Pride, Sheetz

**54** Market St, to I-270, **N gas:** Costco/gas, **lodging:** Travelodge, **S gas:** Exxon/dsl, Lowest Price, 7-11, Sheetz/24hr, Shell/24hr, SouStates/dsl, **food:** Arby's, Bob Evans, Burger King, Checker's, Cracker Barrel, El Paso Cantina, Jerry's Rest., KFC, Longhorn Steaks, McDonald's, Papa John's, Peking Gourmet, Popeye's, Roy Rogers, Ruby Tuesday, Subway, Waffle House, Wendy's, **lodging:** Days Inn, Econolodge, Fairfield Inn, Hampton Inn, Holiday Inn Express, Sleep Inn, **other:** Aamco, Audi, Best Buy, Buick, Chrysler,

**FREDERICK**

**54** Continued
Circuit City, CVS Drug, Ford/Lincoln/Mercury/Isuzu, Home Depot, Honda, Hyundai, JC Penney, Kohl's, Lowes Whse, Michael's, Nissan, Ross, Sam's Club, Saturn, Sears/auto, Staples, Tires+, Volvo, Walmart SuperCtr, mall

**53b a** I-270 S, US 15 N, US 40 W, to Frederick

**52b a** US 15 S, US 340 W, Leesburg

**49** US 40A (no EZ wb return), Braddock Heights, **N** on US 40 **gas:** Chevron, Citgo/dsl, Exxon/dsl, Freestate/dsl, GetGo, Shell, Sunoco, **food:** Arby's, Bob Evans, Boston Mkt, Burger King, Casarico Mexican, Denny's, Fritchie's Rest., Ground Round, Hunter's Rest., McDonald's, Miyako Japanese, Mtn View Diner, Outback Steaks, Pizza Hut, Popeye's, Red Horse Rest., Red Lobster, Roy Rogers, Starbucks, Subway, Taco Bell, Wendy's, **lodging:** Comfort Inn, Holiday Inn, **other:** **H** HOSPITAL, Advance Parts, CVS Drug, Ford/Subaru, Giant Eagle Foods, Home Depot, JC Penney, Jo-Ann Fabrics, K-Mart, Merchant Tire, Mr. Tire, PepBoys, 7-11, Toyota, Weis Foods, st police, **S** to Washington Mon SP, camping

**48** US 40 E, US 340 (from eb, no return), **1 mi N** same as 49

**42** MD 17, Myersville, **N gas:** Exxon, Sunoco/dsl/24hr, **food:** Burger King, McDonald's, **other:** to Gambrill SP (6mi), Greenbrier SP (4mi), **S gas:** BP/dsl

**39mm** rest area both lanes, full & facilities, **C**, vending, ☕, litter barrels, petwalk

**35** MD 66, to Boonsboro, **S gas:** Sheetz (1mi), **other:** to Greenbrier SP, camping

**32b a** US 40, Hagerstown, **1-3 mi N gas:** BP/Blimpie, Exxon/24hr, 7-11, Sunoco, **food:** Bob Evans, Cancun Cantina, Denny's, DQ, Dunkin Donuts, Hong Kong Chinese, Ledo's Pizza, McDonald's, Pacific Ocean Buffet, Pizza Hut, Popeye's, Quizno's, Subway, Super Buffet, TX Roadhouse, **lodging:** Clarion, Comfort Suites, Day's Inn, Hampton Inn, Holiday Inn/rest., Sheraton, Super 8, **other:** **H** HOSPITAL, Chevrolet/Cadillac,

**MD**

## INTERSTATE 70 CONT'D

| | | |
|---|---|---|
| 54 | | Continued<br>Chrysler/Dodge, CVS Drug, $Tree, Goodyear/auto, Martin's Foods, Mercedes, Nissan, Subaru, Suzuki, Toyota/Scion, Weis Foods, **S other:** Buick/GMC/Pontiac, Honda, Kia, VW |
| 29b a | | MD 65, to Sharpsburg, **N gas:** Exxon/dsl/24hr, Sheetz/24hr, Sunoco/dsl/24hr, Shell, **food:** FoodCourt, Longhorn Steaks, Pizza Hut, Starbucks, Subway, TCBY, **other:** H HOSPITAL, Prime Outlets/famous brands, st police, **S gas:** Shell/Blimpie/dsl/24hr, **food:** Burger King, Cracker Barrel, McDonald's, Waffle House, Wendy's, **lodging:** Sleep Inn, **other:** Safari Camping, to Antietam Bfd |
| 28 | | MD 632, Hagerstown, **2 mi N gas:** Shell, **food:** Bob Evan's, Burger King, Chick-fil-A, Domino's, Fazoli's, Pizza Hut, Roy Rogers, Shoney's, Western Sizzlin, **lodging:** Country Inn&Suites, **other:** Advance Parts, AutoZone, Food Lion, **S** Jellystone Camping |
| 26 | | I-81, N to Harrisburg, S to Martinsburg |
| 24 | | MD 63, Huyett, **N gas:** Pilot/Subway/dsl/24hr, Sheetz (2mi), **S other:** KOA (2mi), C&O Canal |
| 18 | | MD 68 E, Clear Spring, **N gas:** BP, Chevron, **food:** McDonald's, **S gas:** Exxon/dsl, **food:** Wendy Hill Café |
| 12 | | MD 56, Indian Springs, **S gas:** Exxon/dsl, **other:** Ft Frederick SP |
| 9 | | US 40 E (from eb, exits left), Indian Springs |
| 5 | | MD 615 (no immediate wb return), **N** Log Cabin Rest. (2mi) |
| 3 | | MD 144, Hancock (exits left from wb), **S gas:** ACT/Exxon/dsl, BP/dsl/rest./24hr, **food:** Hardee's, Park'n Dine, Pizza Hut, Subway, Weaver's Rest., **lodging:** Best Value Inn, Hilltop Inn, Super 8, **other:** Ford, NAPA, repair |
| 1b | | US 522 (exits left from eb), Hancock, **N** Chevrolet, Chrysler/Dodge/Jeep, **S gas:** Citgo/dsl, PitStop, Sheetz/dsl, **food:** Hardee's, Lockhouse Rest., Pizza Hut, Subway, Weaver's Rest., **lodging:** Best Value Inn, Super 8, **other:** $General, Sav-a-Lot Foods, Happy Hills Camp, NAPA |
| 1a | | I-68 W, US 40, W to Cumberland |
| 0mm | | Maryland/Pennsylvania state line, Mason-Dixon Line |

## INTERSTATE 81

| Exit # | Services |
|---|---|
| 12mm | Maryland/Pennsylvania state line |
| 10b a | Showalter Rd, **E** to ✈ |
| 9 | Maugans Ave, **E gas:** BP, Sheetz, Shell/Domino's/dsl, **food:** McDonald's, Pizza Hut, Taco Bell, Waffle House, **lodging:** Hampton Inn, **other:** AutoZone, Curves, CVS Drug, $General, Martin's Foods/gas **W food:** Burger King, **lodging:** Microtel, **other:** GMC Trucks, Kenworth, U-haul, Volvo |
| 7b a | MD 58, Hagerstown, same as 6 |
| 6b a | US 40, Hagerstown, **E gas:** Liberty, Shell, **lodging:** Days Inn, Quality Inn, **other:** H HOSPITAL, **W food:** Arby's, Chipotle Mexican, IHOP, KFC, McDonald's, Panera Bread, Uno, Ryan's, Starbucks, Subway, TGIFriday, Wendy's, **other:** Best Buy, Borders Books, Circuit City, $Tree, Home Depot, Marshall's, PetsMart, Walmart SuperCtr |

---

| 5 | | Halfway Blvd, **E gas:** AC&T/dsl/rest., **food:** Bob Evans, Bonton Rest., Boston Mkt., Buffalo Wild Wings, Burger King, Chick-fil-A, ChuckeCheese, CiCi's Pizza, Denny's, Garfield's Rest., McDonald's, Olive Garden, Orchid Garden, Outback Steaks, Popeye's, Red Lobster, Roy Rogers, Ruby Tuesday, Sakura Steaks, Shoney's, Taco Bell, Wendy's, **lodging:** Country Inn&Suites, Holiday Inn Express, Homewood Suites, Motel 6, Plaza Hotel, SpringHill Suites, **other:** BonTon, CVS Drug, $Tree, Ford/Lincoln/Mercury, Hyundai, JC Penney, K-Mart, Kohl's, Lowes Whse, Macy's, Martin's Foods/gas, Michael's, Office Depot, Old Navy, PetCo, Sam's Club/gas, Sears/auto, Staples, Target, mall, **W gas:** AC&T, Exxon |
|---|---|---|
| 4 | | I-70, E to Frederick, W to Hancock, to I-68 |
| 2 | | US 11, Williamsport, **E gas:** AC&T/dsl, **food:** Burger King, **W gas:** Exxon/dsl, Sunoco/dsl/24hr, **food:** China 88, McDonald's, Waffle House, **lodging:** Red Roof Inn, **other:** KOA (4mi) |
| 1 | | MD 63, MD 68, Williamsport, **E gas:** Bowman/dsl, **other:** Jellystone, KOA, to Antietam Bfd, **W gas:** Citgo, **other:** NAPA |
| 0mm | | Maryland/West Virginia state line, Potomac River |

## INTERSTATE 83

| Exit # | Services |
|---|---|
| 38mm | Maryland/Pennsylvania state line, Mason-Dixon Line |
| 37 | to Freeland |
| 36 | MD 439, Bel Air, **W gas:** Sub-Shop, **food:** Maryland Line Inn Grill, **other:** Holiday Travel Park (5mi), Morris Meadows Camping (5mi) |
| 35mm | weigh/insp sta sb |
| 33 | MD 45, Parkton, **E** USPO |
| 31 | Middletown Rd, to Parkton, golf |
| 27 | MD 137, Mt Carmel, Hereford, **E gas:** Exxon/dsl, **food:** Subway, **other:** Graul's Foods, Hereford Drug, Mt Carmel Drug, NAPA, USPO, vet |
| 24 | Belfast Rd, to Butler, Sparks |
| 20 | Shawan Rd, Hunt Valley, **E gas:** BP, Exxon/dsl, **food:** Burger King, Caribou Coffee, Carmine's Pizza, Carrabba's, Chipotle Mexican, McDonald's, Noodles&Co, Outback Steaks, Quizno's, Panera Bread, Subway, Wendy's, Wong's Kitchen, **lodging:** Chase Suites, Courtyard, Embassy Suites, Hampton Inn, Hunt Valley Marriott, Ramada Ltd, **other:** Giant Foods, Goodyear/auto, Sears/auto, 7-11, Wegman's Foods, mall, vet |
| 18 | Warren Rd (from nb, no return), Cockeysville, **E gas:** Exxon, **lodging:** Residence Inn, multiple services E on York Rd |
| 17 | Padonia Rd, Deereco Rd, **E gas:** BP/dsl, Hess, Shell, Texaco, **food:** Applebees, Bob Evans, Chili's, Macaroni Grill, Wendy's, **lodging:** Day's Hotel, Extended Stay America, **other:** Audi/VW, Chevrolet, Goodyear/auto, Mar's Foods, Mr Tire, Porsche, Shopper's Foods, Subaru, Target, USPO, multiple services E on York Rd |
| 16b a | Timonium Rd, **E gas:** BP, Petro/Subway, Sunoco/dsl, **food:** Baja Fresh, McDonald's, Steak&Ale, **lodging:** Crowne Plaza, Red Roof Inn, **other:** Infiniti/Nissan, Rite Aid |
| 14 | I-695 N |
| 13 | I-695 S, Falls Rd, H HOSPITAL, st police |
| 12 | Ruxton Rd (from nb, no return) |
| 10b a | Northern Parkway, **E gas:** Exxon, Shell, **other:** H HOSPITAL |

Side markers: **E W** (I-70), **HAGERSTOWN** (left), **N S** (left bottom), MD

**HAGERSTOWN** (right top), **N S** (right), **BALTIMORE** (right bottom)

## INTERSTATE 83 CONT'D

**N ↕ S**

| | |
|---|---|
| **9b a** | Cold Spring Lane |
| **8** | MD 25 N (from nb), Falls Rd |
| **7b a** | 28th St, **E** **H** HOSPITAL, **W** Baltimore Zoo |
| **6** | US 1, US 40T, North Ave, downtown |
| **5** | MD Ave (from sb), downtown |
| **3** | Chase St, Gilford St, downtown |
| **2** | Pleasant St (from sb), downtown |
| **1** | Fayette St, I-83 begins/ends, downtown Baltimore |

## INTERSTATE 95

**N ↕ S**

| Exit # | Services |
|---|---|
| **110mm** | Maryland/Delaware state line |
| **109b a** | MD 279, to Elkton, Newark, **E** **gas:** Petro/Iron Skillet/dsl/24hr/@, Shell/dsl, **food:** Cracker Barrel, KFC/Taco Bell, McDonald's, Waffle House, **lodging:** Days Inn, Elkton Lodge, Hampton Inn, Hawthorn Inn, Knight's Inn, Motel 6, **other:** **H** HOSPITAL, Blue Beacon, **W** **gas:** TA/Subway/dsl/24hr/@, 7-11, **other:** to U of DE |
| **100** | MD 272, to North East, Rising Sun, **E** **gas:** ⊕ *FLYING J* /dsl/rest./LP/24hr, Sunoco, **food:** Burger King, Dunkin Donuts, Empire Rest., Frank's Pizza, McDonald's, Starbucks, Wendy's, **lodging:** Comfort Inn, Holiday Inn Express, **other:** $Tree, Food Lion, Rite Aid, Walgreens, Walmart/auto, museum, st police, to Elk Neck SP, **W** **gas:** Citgo, **lodging:** Best Western, **other:** zoo |
| **96mm** | Chesapeake House service area (exits left from both lanes), Exxon/dsl, Sunoco/dsl, Burger King, Popeye's, Quizno's, Starbucks, gifts |
| **93** | MD 275, to Rising Sun, US 222, to Perryville, **E** **gas:** Exxon/dsl, Pilot/Subway/dsl/scales/24hr, **food:** Denny's, KFC/Taco Bell, **lodging:** Ramada Inn, **other:** **H** HOSPITAL, Perryville Outlets/famous brands, Riverview Camping |
| **92mm** | weigh sta/toll booth |
| **91.5mm** | Susquehanna River |
| **89** | MD 155, to Havre de Grace (last nb exit before toll), **1-3 mi E** **food:** Burger King, McDonald's, MacGregor's Rest., Waffle House, **lodging:** Best Budget Inn, Super 8, Van Divers B&B, **other:** **H** HOSPITAL, **W** to Susquehanna SP |
| **85** | MD 22, to Aberdeen, **E** **gas:** BP/dsl, 7-11, Royal Farms, **food:** Applebees, Arby's, Bob Evans, Burger King, Durango's, Dunkin Donuts, Family Buffet, Fast Eddie's, Japan House, KFC, Little Caesar's, Mamie's Cafe, McDonald's, Olive Tree Italian, Papa John's, Pizza Hut, Quizno's, Rita's Ice Cream, Subway, Taco Bell, Wendy's, **lodging:** Clarion, Day's Inn, Holiday Inn, La Quinta, Red Roof Inn, Super 8, Travelodge, **other:** Cadillac/GMC/Pontiac, $Express, $General, $Tree, GNC, Home Depot, Klein's Foods, Mars Foods, Radio Shack, Rite Aid, Target, Walgreens, museum |
| **81mm** | **MD House service area (exits left from both lanes),** Exxon/dsl, Sunoco/dsl, Big Boy, Phillips Seafood, Roy Rogers, Sbarro's, Starbucks, TCBY, gifts |
| **80** | MD 543, to Riverside, Churchville, **E** **gas:** BP/Burger King, 7-11, Sunoco, Texaco/dsl, **food:** Arby's, China Moon, Cracker Barrel, Don's Crabs, McDonald's, Pizza Hut, Riverside Pizzaria, Ruby Tuesday, Waffle House, **lodging:** Country Inn&Suites, Extended Stay America, |

**A B E R D E E N**

| | |
|---|---|
| **80** | **Continued** SpringHill Suites, Wingate Inn, **other:** Bar Harbor RV Park (4mi), Klein's Foods, Rite Aid |
| **77b a** | MD 24, to Edgewood, Bel Air, **E** **gas:** Citgo/dsl, Exxon/dsl, Royal Farms/dsl, **food:** Burger King, Charlie's Subs, Denny's/24hr, Giovanni's Rest., McDonald's, My 3 Sons Rest., Vitali's Rest., Waffle House, **lodging:** Best Western, Day's Inn, Hampton Inn, Holiday Inn Express, La Quinta, Ramada Inn, Sleep Inn, **W** **gas:** Exxon/dsl, Wawa, **food:** Chick-fil-A, KFC/Taco Bell, McDonald's, Subway, **other:** **H** HOSPITAL, BJ's Whse, Lowes Whse, Target, Walmart/drugs, Weis Foods |
| **74** | MD 152, Joppatowne, **E** **gas:** BP/dsl, Citgo/dsl, Exxon/dsl, Sheetz, **food:** Friendly's, KFC, Venitian Palace, Wendy's, **lodging:** Edgewood Motel, Super 8, **other:** **H** HOSPITAL, Toyota (1mi), **W** **gas:** Royal Farms |
| **70mm** | Big Gunpowder Falls |
| **67b a** | MD 43, to White Marsh Blvd, US 1, US 40, **E on MD 7 gas:** BP/dsl, Shell, Texaco, **food:** Chick-fil-A, 5 Guys Burgers, McDonald's, Noodles&Co, Panera Bread, Qdoba Mexian, Starbucks, Subway, **other:** Best Buy, Carmax, Chevrolet, Lowes Whse, Nissan, Target, **W on White Marsh Blvd...gas:** Exxon/dsl, 7-11, **food:** Bertucci's, Boscoe's, Buffalo Wild Wings, Chili's, Don Pablo, Fuddrucker's, Lin's Chinese, McDonald's, Olive Garden, PF Chang's, Red Brick Sta., Ruby Tuesday, Taco Bell, TGIFriday, Wendy's, **lodging:** Fairfield Inn, Hampton Inn, Hilton Garden, Residence Inn, **other:** Barnes&Noble, Giant Foods, GNC, Macy's, JC Penney, Macy's, Old Navy, Sears/auto, Staples, USPO, mall, to Gunpowder SP |
| **64b a** | I-695 (exits left), E to Essex, W to Towson |
| **62** | to I-895 (from sb) |
| **61** | US 40, Pulaski Hwy, **E** **gas:** BP, Shell/dsl, **food:** McDonald's |
| **60** | Moravia Rd, **E** **gas:** Citgo/dsl, Shell, **food:** Burger King, **other:** GMC/Pontiac, KIA, K-Mart, Suzuki |
| **59** | Eastern Ave, **W** **gas:** BP/dsl/24hr, Enroy Gas/dsl, Exxon, Royal Farms, **food:** Broadway Diner, Subway, Wendy's, **other:** **H** HOSPITAL, Home Depot, Shopper's Foods |
| **58** | Dundalk Ave, (from nb), **E** **gas:** Citgo, Sunoco/dsl |
| **57** | O'Donnell St, Boston St, **E** **gas:** TA/Buckhorn/Subway/dsl/scales/@, **food:** A&W, McDonald's, KFC, Sbarro's, **lodging:** Best Western, Rodeway Inn |
| **56** | Keith Ave |
| **56mm** | McHenry Tunnel, toll plaza (north side of tunnel) |

**MD**

**N ↑ S**

**B A L T I M O R E**

**MD**

### INTERSTATE 95 CONT'D

| | |
|---|---|
| 54 | MD 2 S, to Hanover St, **W** downtown, **H** HOSPITAL |
| 53 | I-395 N, to MLK, **W** downtown, Oriole Park |
| 52 | Russell St N, **W** **H** HOSPITAL |
| 51 | Washington Blvd |
| 50.5mm | inspection sta nb |
| 50 | Caton Ave, **E** **gas:** Citgo, Hess/dsl, Shell/24hr, Texaco, **food:** Caton House, McDonald's, **lodging:** Quality Inn, **other:** Aldi Foods, Toyota/Scion, **W** **H** HOSPITAL |
| 49b a | I-695, E to Key Bridge, Glen Burnie, W to Towson, to I-70, to I-83 |
| 47b a | I-195, to MD 166, to BWI ✈, to Baltimore |
| 46 | I-895, to Harbor Tunnel Thruway |
| 43 | MD 100, to Glen Burnie, **1 mi E** on US 1 **gas:** Exxon/Wendy's, **lodging:** Best Western |
| 41b a | MD 175, to Columbia, **E** **gas:** Exxon/dsl, Shell, **food:** Arby's, Burger King, Frank's Diner, McDonald's, Panda Express, Starbucks, **lodging:** Comfort Suites, Fairfield Inn, Holiday Inn, Red Roof Inn, Super 8, **W** **gas:** Crown Gas, Exxon, **food:** Applebees, Bob Evans, Fat Burger, Houlihan's, McDonald's, Mimi's Cafe, Olive Garden, On the Border, TGIFriday, **lodging:** Homewood Suites, Studio+, **other:** **H** HOSPITAL, Best Buy, Costco/gas, Lowes Whse, Office Depot, Royal Farms, to Johns Hopkins U, Loyola U |
| 38b a | MD 32, to Ft Meade, **2 mi E** on US 1 **gas:** BP, Royal Farms, **food:** Burger King, McDonald's, Taco Bell, **lodging:** Comfort Inn, Extended Stay America, **other:** to BWI ✈, **E** **other:** **H** HOSPITAL |
| 37mm | **Welcome Ctr both lanes, full** ♿ **facilities, info,** ☏**, vending,** ⛽ **litter barrels, petwalk, RV Dump** |
| 35b a | MD 216, to Laurel, **E** **gas:** Exxon, Shell/dsl, **food:** McDonald's, Red Hot&Blue BBQ, Subway, **lodging:** Quality Inn, **other:** Weis Food/drug |
| 34mm | Patuxent River |
| 33b a | MD 198, to Laurel, **E** **gas:** Exxon, **other:** **H** HOSPITAL, **W** **gas:** Exxon/Blimpie, Shell, **food:** McDonald's, Outback Steaks, Starbucks, **lodging:** Holiday Inn |
| 29 | MD 212, to Beltsville, **W** **gas:** Exxon/Blimpie/dsl, **food:** Baskin-Robbins, Danny's Subs, KFC, McDonald's, Taco Bell, Wendy's, **lodging:** Fairfield Inn, Sheraton, **other:** Cherry Hill Park, CVS Drug, Giant Foods |
| 27 | I-495 S around Washington |
| 25b a | US 1, Baltimore Ave, to Laurel, College Park, **E** **gas:** BP, Chevron, Exxon/dsl, 7-11, Shell/24hr, **food:** Arby's, Burger King, Dickey's BBQ, Domino's, El Mexicano, Jerry's Subs, KFC, McDonald's, Papa John's, Pizza Hut, Potbelly's, Quizno's, Taco Bell, 3 Bro's Rest., Wendy's, **lodging:** Holiday Inn, **other:** Advance Parts, Circuit City, Costco, Cottman Transmissions, CVS Drug, PetCo, Radio Shack, Rite Aid, US Agri Library, **W** **gas:** BP/24hr, Shell, **food:** Dunkin Donuts, China Buffet, College Park Diner, IHOP, Pizza Hut, Yung's Express, **lodging:** Comfort Inn, Day's Inn, Econolodge, Hampton Inn, Howard Johnson, Ramada Ltd, Super 8, **other:** Dick's RV Ctr, GNC, Home Depot, Honda, Hyundai, Shoppers Foods, VW, vet, to U of MD |
| 23 | MD 201, Kenilworth Ave, **E** **food:** Starbucks, **lodging:** Marriott/rest., **1 mi W** on Greenbelt **gas:** Shell, **food:** Atlanta Bread, Boston Mkt, Checker's, Chipotle Mexican, KFC, McDonald's, Popeye's, Silver Diner, TGIFriday's, Wendy's, **lodging:** Courtyard, Hilton Garden, |

**W A S H I N G T O N D C A R E A**

| | |
|---|---|
| 23 | Continued |
| | Residence Inn, **other:** Cadillac, CVS Drug, Giant Food/drug, Jo-Ann Fabrics, Marshall's, Staples, Target |
| 22 | Baltimore-Washington Pkwy, **E** to NASA |
| 20b a | MD 450, Annapolis Rd, Lanham, **E** **gas:** Sunoco, **food:** Burger King, Jerry's Rest., McDonald's, Pizza Hut, Red Lobster, **lodging:** Best Western, Day's Inn/rest., Red Roof Inn, **other:** Ford/Kia, **W** **gas:** BP, Chevron/dsl, Liberty, 7-11, Shell, Sunoco/24hr, Texaco, **food:** Bojangles, Dunkin Donuts, KFC, Pap Pohn's, Popeye's, Quizno's, Wendy's, **lodging:** Sheraton, **other:** **H** HOSPITAL, Aamco, Advance Parts, Chevrolet, Chrysler/Dodge/Jeep, CVS Drug, $Value, Foodway Foods, Just-Tires, Lincoln/Mercury, Lowes Whse, Office Depot, Radio Shack, Shoppers Foods, Staples |
| 19b a | US 50, to Annapolis, Washington |
| 17 | MD 202, Landover Rd, to Upper Marlboro, **E** **food:** Jasper's Rest., Outback Steaks, Ruby Tuesday's, **lodging:** Holiday Inn Express, Radisson, **other:** FedEx Center, **W** **other:** Sears/auto |
| 16 | Arena Dr, **W** to Arena |
| 15 | MD 214, Central Ave, **E** **lodging:** Extended Stay America, Hampton Inn/rest., **food:** ChuckeCheese, Golden Corral, **other:** Circuit City, FedEx Center, to Six Flags, **W** **gas:** Exxon/dsl, Liberty, Shell, Texaco, **food:** A&W/LJ Silver, Checker's, KFC, IHOP, Jerry's Subs, McDonald's, Panda Express, Pizza Hut, Taco Bell, Wendy's, **lodging:** Comfort Inn, **other:** Family$, Goodyear, Home Depot, NTB, U-Haul |
| 13 | Ritchie-Marlboro Rd, Capitol Hgts, **W** **food:** Chick-fil-A |
| 11 | MD 4, Pennsylvania Ave, to Upper Marlboro, **W** **gas:** BP, Exxon, Sunoco, **food:** Applebees, Arby's, 5 Guy's Burgers, IHOP, Ledo's Pizza, LJ Silver, Old Country Buffet, Pizza Hut, Starbucks, Subway, Taco Bell, Wendy's, **other:** CVS Drug, $Tree, Hancock Fabrics, JC Penney, Marshall's, PetCo, Shopper's Foods, Staples, Target, st police |
| 9 | MD 337, to Allentown Rd, **E** **gas:** Shell/repair, Texaco, **food:** Arby's, Bojangle's, Checker's, Dunkin Donuts, McDonald's, Popeye's, **lodging:** Days Inn, Quality Inn, Ramada Inn, Super 8, **other:** **H** HOSPITAL, Advance Parts, Family$, U-Haul, to Andrews AFB |
| 7 | MD 5, Branch Ave, to Silver Hill, **E** **gas:** Exxon, Getty, Sunoco, **food:** Wendy's, **lodging:** Motel 6, **W** **gas:** Shell/Subway/dsl, **other:** **H** HOSPITAL, Buick/GMC/Pontiac, Dodge, Ford, KIA, Lincoln/Mercury, Nissan, VW |
| 4b a | MD 414, St Barnabas Rd, Marlow Hgts, **E** **gas:** Citgo/dsl, Exxon, Shell, Sunoco, **food:** Bojangles, Burger King, Checker's, KFC, McDonald's, Outback Steaks, Pizza Hut, Starbucks, Wendy's, **lodging:** Red Roof Inn, **other:** Aldi Foods, $Tree, Home Depot, K-Mart, Old Navy, PetsMart, Safeway, 7-11, Staples, **W** **gas:** Exxon/dsl, Shell/autocare, **food:** McDonald's, Subway, **other:** Family$ |
| 3b a | MD 210, Indian Head Hwy, to Forest Hgts, **E** **gas:** Chevron, Shell, **food:** Danny's Burgers, Dunkin Donuts, La Hacienda, Pizza Hut, Ranch House Rest., Taco Bell, **lodging:** Comfort Inn, Lexington Hotel, **other:** Advance Parts, Aldi Foods, Shopper's Foods, USPO, **W** **gas:** BP/dsl/24hr, Exxon, Lowest Price, Shell, Texaco, **food:** Burger King, McDonald's, Papa John's, Popeye's, Subway, **food:** CVS Drug, Family$, Giant Foods, Goodyear/auto, Radio Shack, Rite Aid, 7-11 |
| 2b a | I-295, N to Washingon |
| 0mm | Maryland/Virginia state line, Potomac River, Woodrow Wilson Bridge |

## INTERSTATE 97

| Exit # | Services |
|---|---|
| 17 | I-695. I-97 begins/ends on I-695. |
| 16 | MD 648, Ferndale, Glen Burnie, **E gas:** BP, Shell, **food:** Hong Kong Cafe, KFC, McDonald's, Quizno's, Rita's Ice Cream, Wendy's, **other:** $General, Giant Foods, **W gas:** Citgo |
| 15b a | MD 176 W, Dorsey Rd, Aviation Blvd, **E gas:** BP, Shell, **food:** KFC, Wendy's, **W gas:** Royal Farms/dsl, 7-11, **other:** to BWI, st police |
| 14b a | MD 100, Ellicott City, Gibson Island |
| 13b a | MD 174, Quarterfield Rd, **E gas:** AP/dsl, 7-11, Texaco, **food:** The Grill, **other:** WaWa, **W gas:** Shell/dsl, **food:** Chick-fil-A, Quizno's, **other:** Kohl's, Lowes Whse, Rite Aid, Sam's Club/gas, Shoppers Foods, Walmart SuperCtr |
| 12 | MD 3, New Cut Rd, Glen Burnie, **E on Veterans Hwy...gas:** WaWa, **food:** Domino's, KFC/Taco Bell, McDonald's, Wendy's, **other:** CVS Drug, vet, **E gas:** Exxon/24hr, Sunoco, **food:** Burger King, Fortune Cooky, Pizza Hut, **other:** H HOSPITAL, Ace Hardware, Giant Foods, Goodyear/auto, Target, Walgreens |
| 10b a | Benfield Blvd, Severna Park, **E gas:** Citgo, Exxon/dsl, Royal Farms, **food:** Baskin-Robins/Dunkin Donuts, Hella's Rest., **lodging:** White Gables Motel, **other:** KOA, access to same as 12 |
| 7 | MD 3, MD 32, Bowie, Odenton, **E** motel |
| 5 | MD 178 (no EZ sb return), Crownsville |
| 0mm | I-97 begins/ends on US 50/301. |

## INTERSTATE 270 - ROCKVILLE

| Exit # | Services |
|---|---|
| 32 | I-270 begins/ends on I-70, exit 53. |
| 31b a | MD 85, **N gas:** Exxon/dsl, Lowest Price, 7-11, Sheetz/24hr, Shell/24hr, SouStates/dsl, **food:** Arby's, Bob Evans, Burger King, Checker's, Cracker Barrel, El Paso Cantina, Jerry's Rest., KFC, Longhorn Steaks, McDonald's, Papa John's, Peking Gourmet, Popeye's, Roy Rogers, Ruby Tuesday, Subway, Waffle House, Wendy's, **lodging:** Days Inn, Econolodge, Fairfield Inn, Hampton Inn, Holiday Inn Express, Sleep Inn, **other:** Aamco, Audi, Best Buy, Buick, Chrysler, Circuit City, CVS Drug, Ford/Lincoln/Mercury/Isuzu, Home Depot, Hyundai, JC Penney, Kohl's, Lowes Whse, Michael's, Nissan, Ross, Sam's Club, Saturn, Sears/auto, Staples, Tires+, Volvo, Walmart SuperCtr, mall, **S gas:** BP/Blimpie, **food:** Chipotle Mexican, Cracker Barrel, IHOP, Macaroni Grill, McDonald's, Mediterranean Grill, Panda Express, Quizno's, Smoothie King, Starbucks, TGIFriday, **lodging:** Comfort Inn, Courtyard, Extended Stay America, Fairfield Inn, Hampton Inn, Hilton Garden, MainStay Suites, Residence Inn, **other:** Honda, Toyota |
| 30mm | Monocacy River |
| 28mm | viewpoint wb |
| 26 | MD 80, Urbana, **N gas:** Exxon, 7-11, **food:** Dunkin Donuts, Foster's Grill, Mangia Ebevi, McDonald's, Waffle House |
| 22 | MD 109, to Barnesville, Hyattstown, **S food:** Hyattstown Deli, **other:** Food+ |
| 21mm | weigh/insp sta both lanes |
| 18 | MD 121, to Clarksburg, Boyds, **N** Little Bennett Pk, camping, gas, **S** Blackhill Pk |
| 16 | MD 27, Father Hurley Blvd, to Damascus, **N gas:** Exxon, Free State, Sunoco, **W** Express/dsl, **food:** Applebees, Bob Evans, Burger King, McDonald's, Starbucks, |

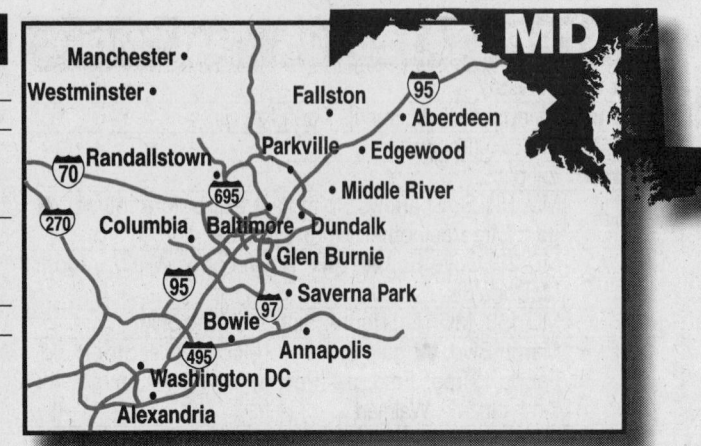

| | |
|---|---|
| 16 | Continued<br>Subway, **lodging:** Extended Stay America, Hampton Inn, **other:** Best Buy, Borders Books, Giant Foods, Home Depot, Kohl's, Michael's, PepBoys, TJ Maxx, Target, Walmart, World Mkt, **S gas:** BP, Exxon, 7-11, **food:** Baja Fresh, Burger King, CA Tortilla, Carrabba's, Chick-fil-A, Coldstone Creamery, 5 Guys Burgers, IHOP, McDonald's, Red Robin, Longhorn Steaks, Panera Bread, Pizza Hut, Ruby Tuesday, Subway, Taco Bell, Wendy's, **lodging:** Fairfield Inn, **other:** Giant Foods, NAPA, Office Depot, PetCo, Rite Aid, same as 15 |
| 15b a | MD 118, to MD 355, **S other:** Honda, same as 16 |
| 13b a | Middlebrook Rd (from wb) |
| 11b a | MD 124, Quince Orchard Rd, **N gas:** Exxon, **food:** Boston Mkt, Panera Bread, Starbucks, Subway, **lodging:** Hilton, Holiday Inn, TownePlace Suites, Wyndham Garden, **other:** Acura, Costco, CVS Drugs, Ford, Hyundai, JC Penney, Lord&Taylor, Macy's, Mazda, NAPA, Nissan, Sam's Club, Sears/auto, Tires+, Toyota, mall, **S gas:** Shell/dsl, **food:** Chevy's Mexican, CiCi's Pizza, Jerry's Subs, Mangaire Italian, Rita's Ice Cream, Starbucks, **lodging:** Motel 6, **other:** Advance Parts, Chevrolet, Circuit City, Giant Foods, Jo-Ann Fabrics, McGruder's Foods, Rite Aid, Staples, Seneca Creek SP |
| 10 | MD 117, Clopper Rd (from wb), same as 11 |
| 9b a | I-370, to Gaithersburg, Sam Eig Hwy, **S on Washington Blvd gas:** Chevron, **food:** Joe's Crabshack, Macaroni Grill, Pizza Hut, Red Rock Grill, Subway, Uncle Julio's, **lodging:** Courtyard, **other:** Barnes&Noble, Kohl's, Target, Weis Mkt |
| 8 | Shady Grove Rd, **N lodging:** Chase Suite Hotel, Sheraton, **S lodging:** Marriott, Quality Suites, Residence Inn, Sleep Inn, SpringHill Suites, **other:** H HOSPITAL |
| 6b a | MD 28, W Montgomery Ave, **N other:** H HOSPITAL, **S lodging:** Best Western |
| 5b a | MD 189, Falls Rd |
| 4b a | Montrose Rd, **N** gas, **S other:** Harris Teeter, st police |
| 2 | I-270/I-270 spur diverges eb, converges wb |
| 1 | MD 187, Old Georgetown Rd, **S gas:** Exxon, **food:** Hamburger Hamlet, **other:** H HOSPITAL, Giant Foods, GNC |
| 1b a | (I-270 spur) Democracy Blvd, **E lodging:** Marriott, **W gas:** Exxon/Shell/dsl, **other:** Macy's, Nordstrom's, Sears, mall |
| 0mm | I-270 begins/ends on I-495, exit 35. |

## INTERSTATE 495 - DC

See Virginia Interstate 495 (DC)

**N ↑↓ S**

**B A L T I M O R E**

## INTERSTATE 695 - BALTIMORE

| Exit # | Services |
|---|---|
| 48mm | Patapsco River, Francis Scott Key Br |
| 44 | MD 695 (from nb) |
| 43mm | toll plaza |
| 42 | MD 151 S, Sparrows Point (last exit before toll sb), **E gas:** Citgo/dsl, **other:** North Point SP |
| 41 | MD 20, Cove Rd, **W gas:** Royal Farms, WaWa, **food:** McDonald's |
| 40 | MD 150, MD 151, North Point Blvd, (nb only) |
| 39 | Merritt Blvd, **W gas:** BP, **food:** McDonald's, **other:** Aldi Foods, $Tree, Ford, JC Penney, Mr Tire, Sears/auto, 7-11, Suzuki, Walmart |
| 38b a | MD 150, Eastern Blvd, to Baltimore, **E gas:** Royal Farms, **W food:** Applebees, Burger King, Checker's, Dunkin Donuts, **other:** Chevrolet/Nissan, Sears/auto, Staples, Walgreens, mall |
| 36 | MD 702 S (exits left from sb), Essex |
| 35 | US 40, **N gas:** WaWa/gas, Sunoco, **food:** Arby's, DQ, Dunkin Donuts, Grand Buffet, Longhorn Steaks, Panda Express, Panera Bread, **other:** Aldi Foods, Best Buy, Circuit City, Harley-Davidson, Home Depot, NTB, Office Depot, PetCo, Sam's Club/gas, U-Haul, Walmart, same as 34 |
| 34 | MD 7, Philadelphia Rd, **N food:** McDonald's, Quizno's, Wendy's, **lodging:** La Quinta, **other:** H HOSPITAL, $General, $Tree, Giant Foods, Goodyear/auto, Marshall's, **S gas:** Exxon, **other:** Walgreens, same as 35 |
| 33b a | I-95, N to Philadelphia, S to Baltimore |
| 32b a | US 1, Bel Air, **N gas:** Exxon, **food:** Arby's, Bob Evan's, Burger King, Denny's, Golden Corral, IHOP, McDonald's, Taco Bell, **other:** BJ's Whse, Curves, Giant Foods, GMC/Pontiac, K-Mart, Mr Tire/auto, 7-11, Toyota/Scion, vet, **S gas:** Getty, Texaco, **food:** Carrabba's, Dunkin Donuts, McDonald's, Mr Crab, Subway, Szechuan Taste, **other:** Goodyear/auto |
| 31c | MD 43 E (from eb) |
| 31b a | MD 147, Harford Rd, **N gas:** BP/24hr, Carroll, 7-11, Shell/dsl, **food:** Dunkin Donuts, Wendy's, **other:** CVS Drug, Chrysler/Jeep, Honda, Mar's Foods, VW, Walgreens |
| 30b a | MD 41, Perring Pkwy, **N gas:** Shell, **food:** Burger King, Checker's, Chick-fil-A, McDonald's, Popeye's, Quizno's, **other:** Chevrolet, Ford, Giant Foods, Home Depot, JoAnn Fabrics, K-Mart, NTB, Office Depot, Ross, Safeway Foods, Shopper's Foods |
| 29b | MD 542, Loch Raven Blvd, **S gas:** BP, Hess, Royal Farms, Texaco, **food:** Bel-Loch Diner, Hooters, Pizza Hut, Subway, **lodging:** Comfort Inn, Ramada Inn, Welcome Inn |
| 29a | Cromwell Bridge Rd, **S lodging:** Holiday Inn |
| 28 | Providence Rd, **S gas:** Citgo, **other:** Royal Farms |
| 27b a | MD 146, Dulaney Valley Rd, **N** Hampton NHS, **S gas:** Exxon, **food:** Bahama Breeze, Burger King, Rainforest Cafe, **lodging:** Sheraton, **other:** Barnes&Noble, Macy's, SuperFresh Food, mall |
| 26b a | MD 45, York Rd, Towson, **N gas:** BP, Exxon/dsl, Ocean, **food:** Dunkin Donuts, Friendly's, PepperMill Rest., Pizza Hut, Subway, **other:** Rite Aid, **S gas:** Exxon, Texaco, **food:** McDonald's, **other:** CVS Drug, Ford, Honda, Lexus, Saturn |
| 25 | MD 139, Charles St, **S** H HOSPITAL |
| 24 | I-83 N, to York |
| 23b | Falls Rd, , **N gas:** Exxon/dsl |
| 23a | I-83 S, MD 25 N, Baltimore |
| 22 | Greenspring Ave |
| 21 | to Stevenson Rd, Park Hghts Rd |
| 20 | MD 140, Reisterstown Rd, Pikesville, **N gas:** Exxon/7-11/dsl, **other:** Barnes&Noble, **S gas:** BP, Shell, Sunoco/Subway, **food:** McDonald's, Olive Branch Italian, **lodging:** Hilton, Ramada Inn, **other:** Target |
| 19 | I-795, NW Expswy |
| 18b a | MD 26, Randallstown, Lochearn, **E gas:** Texaco, **W gas:** BP, Exxon/dsl Shell, **food:** Burger King, Dunkin Donuts, Subway, Taco Bell, **other:** H HOSPITAL, Firestone/auto, Giant Foods, 7-11, Walgreens |
| 17 | MD 122, Security Blvd, **E gas:** BP/repair, Shell, **food:** Dunkin Donuts, Subway, Wendy's, **lodging:** Day's Inn, Motel 6, Quality Inn, **other:** Chevrolet, Mitsubishi, Nissan, **W gas:** Exxon, Sunoco, **food:** Burger King, 5 Guys Burgers, McDonald's, Panera Bread, Popeye's, Quizno's, **lodging:** Best Western, **other:** Best Buy, Ford, Macy's, Old Navy, Sears/auto, SuperFresh Foods, mall |
| 16b a | I-70, E to Baltimore, W to Frederick |
| 15b a | US 40, Ellicott City, Baltimore, **E gas:** BP, **food:** Burger King, Checker's, Chick-fil-A, ChuckeCheese, KFC, IHOP, McDonald's, Panda Express, Quizno's, **lodging:** Day's Inn, Comfort Inn, **other:** CVS Drug, Dodge, $Tree, Lowes Whse, Rite Aid, Ross, Safeway Foods/gas, Sam's Club/gas, U-Haul, Walgreens, **W gas:** BP/dsl, Exxon, Shell, Texaco, **food:** Bob Evan's, McDonald's, Popeye's, Taco Bell, TT Diner, **other:** Circuit City, Firestone/auto, Giant Foods, Goodyear, Home Depot, NTB, Staples, Toyota/Scion, Walmart |
| 14 | Edmondson Ave, **E gas:** Sunoco, **other:** Royal Farms, **W gas:** CF, **food:** Papa John's |
| 13 | MD 144, Frederick Rd, Catonsville, **W gas:** BP, Cisco, Texaco, **food:** Dunkin Donuts, McDonald's/24hr, Subway, **other:** 7-11 |
| 12c b | MD 372 E, Wilkens, **E** H HOSPITAL |
| 11b a | I-95, N to Baltimore, S to Washington |
| 10 | US 1 Washington Blvd (from wb only), **E gas:** Royal Farms, **food:** 3 Bro's Pizza, Quizno's, Wendy's, **lodging:** Beltway Motel/rest., **other:** Goodyear/auto, Home Depot, Office Depot, PetCo, Walmart SuperCtr **W gas:** Exxon, **food:** Burger King |
| 9 | Hollins Ferry Rd, Lansdowne, **E gas:** BP, Sunoco/dsl, **other:** Royal Farms |
| 8 | MD 168, Nursery Rd, **N gas:** Exxon, Shell, **food:** Burger King, KFC, McDonald's, Taco Bell, Wendy's, **lodging:** Motel 6, **S gas:** BP, Citgo, **food:** Snyder's Rest. |
| 7b a | MD 295, **N** to Baltimore, **S** BWI ✈ |
| 6b a | Camp Mead Rd (from nb) |
| 5 | MD 648, Ferndale, gas, food, lodging |
| 4b a | I-97 S, to Annapolis |
| 3b a | MD 2 N, Brooklyn Park, **S gas:** Exxon, Hess, Shell, **food:** Bennigan's, Bob Evan's, BoneFish Grill, Checker's, Chick-fil-A, ChuckeCheese, Denny's, Hunan Rest., KFC, Krispy Kreme, McDonald's, Panera Bread, Pizza Hut, Qdoba, Quizno's, Starbucks, Subway, Taco Bell, **lodging:** Day's Inn, Hampton Inn, Holiday Inn, **other:** Advance Parts, Aldi Foods, Best Buy, $Tree, Giant Foods, Just Tires, K-Mart, Lowes Whse, Mar's Foods, Office Depot, PetCo, Target, Walgreens |
| 2 | MD 10, Glen Burnie |
| 1 | MD 174, Hawkins Point Rd, **S gas:** Citgo/deli/dsl |

**MD**

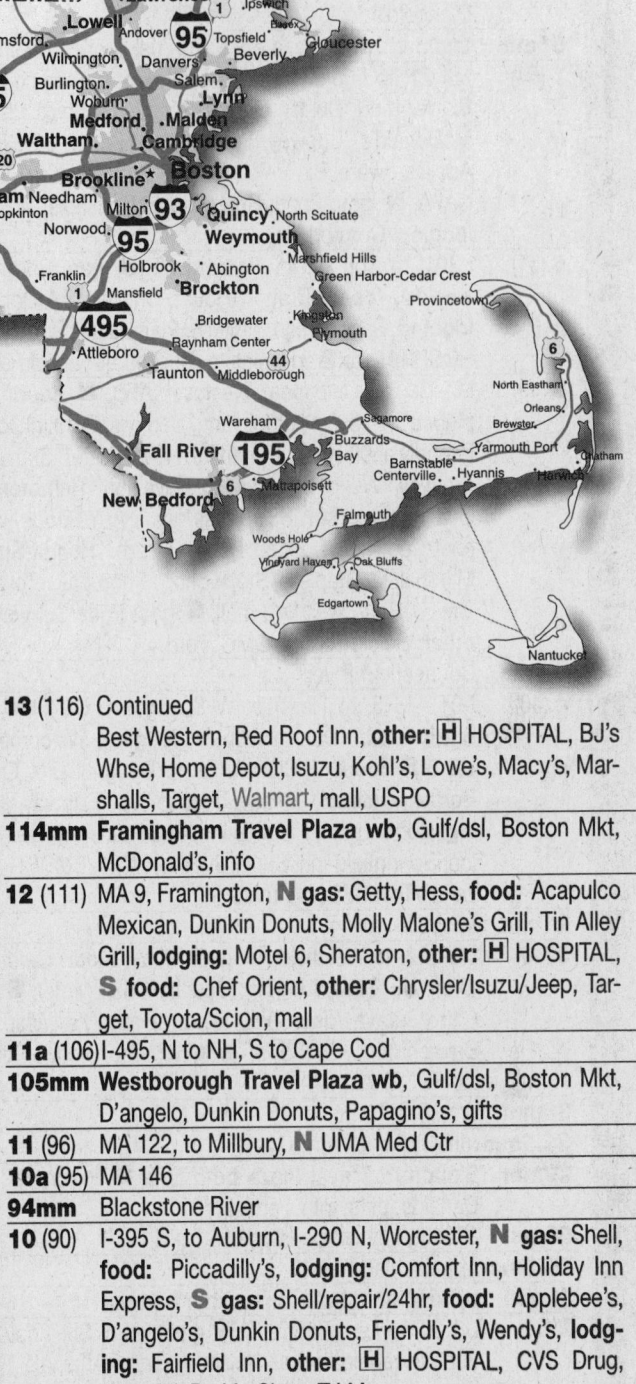

## INTERSTATE 84

| Exit # | Services |
|---|---|
| **4** (11) | I-84 begins/ends on I-90, Exit 9. |
| **3b a** (9) | US 20, Sturbridge, **E gas:** BeeVee, Citgo, **food:** Applebees, Cracker Barrel, Pizzaria Uno, Subway, Wendy's, **lodging:** Comfort Inn, Publick House, **other:** Marshall's, Old Navy, Staples, Stop&Shop, Walmart **W gas:** Citgo, Cumberland Farms, Mobil/dsl, **food:** Burger King, Friendly's, McDonald's, Piccadilly's, Sturbridge Pizza House, **lodging:** Best Value Inn, Best Western, Econolodge, Hampton Inn, Holiday Inn Express, Sturbridge Host Motel, Super 8, **other:** H HOSPITAL, USPO, st police |
| **2** (5) | MA 131, to Old Sturbridge Village, Sturbridge, **S** Day's Inn, RV camping |
| **4mm** | picnic area wb, litter barrels |
| **1** (2.5) | Mashapaug Rd, to Southbridge, **E gas:** Mobil/dsl/24hr, Pilot/deli/dsl/rest./scales/24hr/@, Shell/dsl/24hr, **food:** Boston Pizza, Roy Rogers, Sbarro's, **lodging:** Quality Inn |
| **2mm** | weigh sta wb |
| **.5mm** | picnic area eb |
| **0mm** | Massachusetts/Connecticut state line |

## INTERSTATE 90

| Exit # | Services |
|---|---|
| **137mm** | I-90 begins/ends on I-93, exit 20 in Boston. |
| **25** | to I-93, to downtown Boston |
| **24** | to I-93, to downtown Boston |
| **22** (134) | Presidential Ctr, downtown |
| **20** (132) | MA 28, Alston, Brighton, Cambridge, **N lodging:** Courtyard, Doubletree Inn, **other:** H HOSPITAL, **S gas:** Sunoco |
| **131mm** | toll plaza |
| **19** (130) | MA Ave (from eb), **N food:** IHOP, McDonald's, **lodging:** Day's Inn |
| **17** (128) | Centre St, Newton, **N lodging:** Sheraton, **other:** Cadillac, Chevrolet, Honda, Nissan |
| **16** (125) | MA 16, W Newton, **S gas:** Mobil/repair |
| **15** (124) | I-95, **N gas:** Marriott |
| **123mm** | toll plaza |
| **14** (122) | MA 30, Weston |
| **117mm** | Natick Travel Plaza eb, Gulf/dsl, McDonald's, Dunkin Donuts, info |
| **13** (116) | MA 30, Natick, **S gas:** Getty, Gulf, Shell, **food:** Bickford's, Boston Mkt, Bugaboo Creek Steaks, Burger King, Harvard's Steaks, Lotus Flower Chinese, McDonald's, Papagino's, Panera Bread, Quizno's, **lodging:** |

**E W STURBRIDGE** / **E W** / **BOSTON AREA**

| Exit # | Services |
|---|---|
| **13** (116) | Continued Best Western, Red Roof Inn, **other:** H HOSPITAL, BJ's Whse, Home Depot, Isuzu, Kohl's, Lowe's, Macy's, Marshalls, Target, Walmart, mall, USPO |
| **114mm** | Framingham Travel Plaza wb, Gulf/dsl, Boston Mkt, McDonald's, info |
| **12** (111) | MA 9, Framington, **N gas:** Getty, Hess, **food:** Acapulco Mexican, Dunkin Donuts, Molly Malone's Grill, Tin Alley Grill, **lodging:** Motel 6, Sheraton, **other:** H HOSPITAL, **S food:** Chef Orient, **other:** Chrysler/Isuzu/Jeep, Target, Toyota/Scion, mall |
| **11a** (106) | I-495, N to NH, S to Cape Cod |
| **105mm** | Westborough Travel Plaza wb, Gulf/dsl, Boston Mkt, D'angelo, Dunkin Donuts, Papagino's, gifts |
| **11** (96) | MA 122, to Millbury, **N** UMA Med Ctr |
| **10a** (95) | MA 146 |
| **94mm** | Blackstone River |
| **10** (90) | I-395 S, to Auburn, I-290 N, Worcester, **N gas:** Shell, **food:** Piccadilly's, **lodging:** Comfort Inn, Holiday Inn Express, **S gas:** Shell/repair/24hr, **food:** Applebee's, D'angelo's, Dunkin Donuts, Friendly's, Wendy's, **lodging:** Fairfield Inn, **other:** H HOSPITAL, CVS Drug, Hyundai, Park'n Shop, TJ Maxx |
| **84mm** | Charlton Travel Plaza wb, Exxon/dsl, McDonald's, **info** |
| **80mm** | Charlton Travel Plaza eb, Exxon/dsl, McDonald's, **info**, st police |
| **79mm** | toll plaza |
| **9mm** (78) | I-84, to Hartford, NYC, Sturbridge, access to H HOSPITAL |
| **67mm** | Quaboag River |
| **8** (62) | MA 32, to US 20, Palmer, **S on MA 32...gas:** Citgo, Getty, Shell/dsl, **food:** McDonald's, Oriental Express, Subway, **other:** H HOSPITAL, Big Y Foods, Brooks Drug, Buick/Chevrolet/Pontiac, repair/transmissions |
| **58mm** | Chicopee River |

**MA**

## INTERSTATE 90 CONT'D

**E** ↕ **W** **SPRINGFIELD** **PITTSFIELD**

| | |
|---|---|
| **56mm** | **Ludlow Travel Plaza wb**, Exxon/dsl, Boston Mkt, D'angelo's |
| **55mm** | **Ludlow Travel Plaza eb**, Exxon/dsl, McDonald's |
| **7** (54) | MA 21, to Ludlow, **N gas:** Gulf, Mobil, Sunoco, **food:** Burger King, Dunkin Donuts, Friendly's, Joy's Pizzaria, McDonald's, Subway, Wendy's, **other:** H HOSPITAL, Ace Hardware, Big Y Foods, CVS Drug, Jo-Ann Fabrics, NAPA, **N gas:** Pride, Shell, **food:** Domino's, Wendy's, **lodging:** Comfort Inn |
| **6** (51) | I-291, to Springfield, Hartford CT, **N gas:** Pride/Subway/dsl, **food:** Dragon House Chinese, McDonald's, **lodging:** Econolodge, Motel 6, Plantation Inn, **other:** H HOSPITAL, to Bradley Int ✈, Basketball Hall of Fame |
| **5** (49) | MA 33, to Chicopee, Westover AFB, **N food:** Applebee's, Arby's, Burger King, Denny's, Dunkin Donuts, Friendly's, 99 Rest., Pizza Hut, Royal Buffet, Starbucks, Subway, Wendy's, **lodging:** Days Inn, Hampton Inn, Quality Inn, **other:** BJ's Whse/gas, Big Y Foods, Chevrolet/Cadillac, Dodge, Home Depot, Honda/Subaru, Marshall's, Staples, Stop&Shop Food/gas, TownFair Tire, U-Haul, Walmart, mall, **S gas:** Pride/Subway/dsl, **other:** Buick/Pontiac/GMC, Ford |
| **46mm** | Connecticut River |
| **4** (46) | I-91, US 5, to Holyoke, W Springfield, **US 5 N gas:** Shell, **food:** Dunkin Donuts, **lodging:** Welcome Inn, **US 5 S food:** B'Shara's Rest., Dougnut Dip, On the Border, Outback Steaks, Piccadilly's, Subway, **lodging:** Comfort Inn, Knight's Inn, Red Roof Inn, Residence Inn, Springfield Inn, Super 8, **other:** AAA, BMW, Honda/Lexus/Toyota/Scion, mall |
| **41mm** | st police wb |
| **3** (40) | US 202, to Westfield, **N gas:** Mobil, **food:** Cafe Santorini, NE Pizza, **lodging:** Country Court Motel, **S gas:** Citgo/Subway/dsl, Shell, **food:** Friendly's, Whip City Brewery/rest., Wendy's, **lodging:** Econolodge, **other:** H HOSPITAL, repair |
| **36mm** | Westfield River |
| **35.5mm** | runaway truck ramp eb |
| **29mm** | **Blandford Travel Plaza both lane S** Exxon/dsl, McDonalds, gifts, info, vending |
| **20mm** | 1724 ft, highest point on MA Tpk |
| **14.5mm** | Appalachian Trail |
| **12mm** | **parking area both lanes, litter barrels** |
| **2** (11) | US 20, to Lee, Pittsfield, **N gas:** Citgo, Shell/dsl/24hr, Sunoco/repair, **food:** Arizona Pizza, Athena's Rest., Dunkin Donuts, Friendly's, McDonald's, Red Apple Chinese, **lodging:** Pilgrim Inn, Sunset Motel, Super 8, **other:** Brooks Drug, PriceChopper Foods, **S gas:** Lee/dsl, JFS, **food:** Orient Taste, Subway, Villa Pizza, **other:** Prime Outlets/famous brands |
| **10.5mm** | Hoosatonic River |
| **8mm** | **Lee Travel Plaza both lanes**, Exxon/dsl, McDonald's, TCBY, **atm, bank, info, vending** |
| **4mm** | toll booth, C |
| **1** (2) | MA 41 (from wb, no return), to MA 102, W Stockbridge, the Berkshires, **N lodging:** Pleasant Valley Motel, **other:** to Bousquet Ski Area |
| **0mm** | Massachusetts/New York state line |

## INTERSTATE 91

**N** ↕ **S** **GREENFIELD**

| Exit # | Services |
|---|---|
| **55mm** | Massachusetts/Vermont state line, callboxes begin/end |
| **54mm** | parking area both lanes, 🏕 |
| **28** (51) | US 5, MA 10, Bernardston, **E food:** Bella Notte Ristorante, **lodging:** Fox Inn, **W gas:** Sunoco, **food:** Antonio's Ristorante, Four-leaf Clover Rest., **other:** Country Corner Store, RV camping, USPO |
| **27** (45) | MA 2 E, Greenfield, **US 5 E gas:** Gulf, Magic Fuel, Sunoco, **food:** Burger King, Denny's Pantry, Friendly's, McDonald's, Subway, **other:** H HOSPITAL, AutoZone, Bond Parts, Buick/Pontiac/GMC, CVS Drug, Honda |
| **26** (43) | MA 2 W, MA 2A E, Greenfield, **E gas:** Planet/dsl, Shell/dsl, **food:** Applebee's, China Gourmet, Dunkin Donuts, Herm's, **lodging:** GreenField Inn, Hampton Inn, **other:** H HOSPITAL, Chevrolet, Ford/Lincoln/Mercury, **W gas:** Exxon/24hr, Irving, **food:** Bickford's, Friendly's, KFC/Taco Bell/Pizza Hut, McDonald's, 99 Rest., **lodging:** Hampton Inn, Super 8, **other:** Big Y Foods, BJ's Whse, $Tree, Family$, Home Depot, Hyundai, Staples, to Mohawk Tr |
| **39mm** | Deerfield River |
| **37mm** | weigh sta both lanes |
| **25** (36) | MA 116 (from sb), S Deerfield, hist dist, camping, same as 24 |
| **24** (35) | US 5, MA 10, MA 116, Deerfield (no EZ return), **E gas:** Irving/Subway/Dunkin Donuts, **food:** Chandler's Rest., New Golden China, Wolfy's Rest., **lodging:** Red Roof Inn, **other:** Yankee Candle Co, **W gas:** Exxon/diner/dsl, **food:** 24hr Diner, **lodging:** Whatley Inn |
| **34.5mm** | parking area nb |
| **23** (34) | US 5 (from sb), **E other:** Rainbow Motel/camping |
| **22** (30) | US 5, MA 10 (from nb), N Hatfield, **W** Diamond RV Ctr |
| **21** (28) | US 5, MA 10, Hatfield, **W gas:** Sunoco, **food:** Subway, **lodging:** Scottish Inn, **other:** Long View RV Ctr, st police |
| **20** (26) | US 5, MA 9, MA 10 (from sb), Northampton, **W gas:** Hess/dsl, Pride/Dunkin Donuts, **food:** Bickford's, Burger King, D'angelo's, McDonald's, Papagino's Italian, **other:** H HOSPITAL, Chevrolet/VW, CVS Drug, Firestone/auto, Ford, Honda, NAPA, Pontiac/GMC/Cadillac, Radio Shack, Stop&Shop, Subaru, Toyota/Scion, Townfair Tire, VW, Walmart/Subway |
| **19** (25) | MA 9, to Amherst, Northampton, **E gas:** Getty, Shell, **food:** Butterfly Asian, **lodging:** Comfort Inn, Hampton Inn, Holiday Inn, **other:** H HOSPITAL, to Elwell SP |
| **18** (22) | US 5, Northampton, **E food:** Montana Steaks, **lodging:** Clarion, **W gas:** Shell/Dunkin Donuts/24hr, **lodging:** Quality Inn, Northampton Hotel, **other:** to Smith Coll |
| **18mm** | scenic area both lanes |
| **17b a** (16) | MA 141, S Hadley, **E gas:** Mobil/dsl, Shell/dsl, **food:** Dunkin Donuts, Real China, Subway, **lodging:** Super 8, **other:** Rite Aid, Walgreens, **W** to Mt Tom Ski Area |
| **16** (14) | US 202, Holyoke, **E gas:** Mobil, Shell, **food:** Burger King, Denny's, Dunkin Donuts, Friendly's, Golden Chopsticks, McDonald's, Yankee Pedlar Inn, **other:** H HOSPITAL, Walgreens, to Heritage SP, **W** Soldier's Home |
| **15** (12) | to US 5, Ingleside, **E gas:** Shell, **food:** Chicago Grill, Cracker Barrel, Friendly's, McDonald's, Red Robin, Ruby Tuesday, **lodging:** Holiday Inn, **other:** H HOSPITAL, Barnes&Noble, Best Buy, Borders Books, |

**MA**

**SPRINGFIELD**

**15** (12)   Continued
Circuit City, Macy's, JC Penney, Old Navy, PetCo, Sears/auto, Target, mall, **W lodging:** Homewood Suites

**14** (11)   to US 5, to I-90 (Mass Tpk), E to Boston, W to Albany, **E** **H** HOSPITAL

**13b a** (9)   US 5 N, W Springfield, **E food:** B'Shara's Rest., Dougnut Dip, On the Border, Outback Steaks, Piccadilly's, Subway, **lodging:** Comfort Inn, Knight's Inn, Red Roof Inn, Residence Inn, Springfield Inn, Super 8, **other:** AAA, BMW, Honda/Lexus/Toyota/Scion, mall, **W gas:** Mobil/dsl, Pride/dsl, Sunoco, **food:** Arby's, Bertucci's, Burger King, Cal's Grill, Carrabba's, Chili's, D'angelo's, Friendly's, HomeTown Buffet, KFC, Longhorn Steaks, McDonald's, 99 Rest., Old Country Buffet, Panera Bread, Pizza Hut, Tokyo Cuisine, **lodging:** Bel Air Inn, Candlewood Suites, Clarion, Day's Inn, Econolodge, Hampton Inn, Quality Inn, Red Carpet Inn, **other:** Chrysler/Jeep, Costco, GNC Nutrition, Home Depot, Kohl's, Lincoln/Mercury, Mazda, Michael's, Nissan/Subaru, Stop&Shop Foods, Staples, TownFair Tire

**12** (8.5)   I-391 N, to Chicopee

**11** (8)   Burney Ave (from sb), **E gas:** Mobil, **other:** **H** HOSPITAL

**10** (7.5)   Main St (from nb), Springfield, **E gas:** Mobil

**9** (7)   US 20 W, MA 20A E (from nb), **E food:** McDonald's

**8** (6.5)   I-291, US 20 E, to I-90, **E** downtown, **food:** Hooters, **lodging:** Holiday Inn, **other:** **H** HOSPITAL,

**7** (6)   Columbus Ave (from sb), **E lodging:** Marriott, Sheraton, **W gas:** Pride/Subway/dsl, **other:** to Basketball Hall of Fame

**6** (5.5)   Springfield Ctr (from nb), **W gas:** Pride/Dunkin Donuts/Subway/dsl

**5** (5)   Broad St, **E gas:** Mobil/dsl, Shell/dsl, **W gas:** Sunoco/dsl, **food:** Chicago Grill, **lodging:** Hilton Garden, **other:** Buick/GMC, same as 4

**4** (4.5)   MA 83, Broad St, Main St, **E other:** Hyundai, Saturn, **W food:** Chicago Grill, **lodging:** Hilton Garden, same as 5

**3** (4)   US 5 N, to MA 57, Columbus Ave, W Springfield, **E gas:** Sunoco, **other:** Cadillac, Saturn, **W** Chevrolet

**2** (3.5)   MA 83 S (from nb), to E Longmeadow, **E food:** Friendly's

**1** (3)   US 5 S (from sb)

**0mm**   Massachusetts/Connecticut state line, callboxes begin/end

## INTERSTATE 93

| Exit # | Services |
|---|---|
| **47mm** | Massachusetts/New Hampshire state line, callboxes begin/end |
| **48** (46) | MA 213 E, to Methuen, **E** **H** HOSPITAL |
| **47** (45) | Pelham St, Methuen, **E gas:** Sunoco/24hr, **food:** Dunkin Donuts, McDonald's, Outback Steaks, **W gas:** Getty, **food:** Fireside Rest., **lodging:** Day's Hotel/rest., Guesthouse Inn, **other:** Chrysler/Jeep |
| **46** (44) | MA 110, MA 113, to Lawrence, **E gas:** Getty, Mobil, Shell, **food:** Burger King, Dunkin Donuts, McDonald's/24hr, PapaGino's, Pizza Hut/KFC, MktBasket Foods, Taco Bell, **other:** **H** HOSPITAL, $Tree, Rite Aid, **W gas:** Citgo/dsl, Global, **food:** Dunkin Donuts, Jackson's Rest., Millhouse Rest. |
| **45** (43) | Andover St, River Rd, to Lawrence, **E lodging:** Comfort Suites, Courtyard, Wyndham, **W gas:** Mobil/Dunkin Donuts, **food:** Chateu Italian, Chili's, **lodging:** |

**METHUEN**

**BOSTON AREA**

**45** (43)   Continued
La Quinta, Residence Inn, Springhill Suites

**44b a** (40)   I-495, to Lowell, Lawrence, **E** **H** HOSPITAL

**43** (39)   MA 133, N Tewksbury, **E gas:** Mobil/Dunkin Donuts/24hr

**42** (38)   Dascomb Rd, East St, Tewksbury

**41** (35)   MA 125, Andover, st police

**40** (34)   MA 62, Wilmington

**39** (33)   Concord St, **E** Shriners Auditorium

**38** (31)   MA 129, Reading, **W gas:** Mobil/Dunkin Donuts/dsl, **food:** Burger King, 99 Rest.

**37c** (30)   Commerce Way, Atlantic Ave, **W food:** Starbucks, **lodging:** Red Roof, Residence Inn, **other:** PetCo, Target

**37b a** (29)   I-95, S to Waltham, N to Peabody

**36** (28)   Montvale Ave, **E gas:** Mobil, **lodging:** Courtyard, **W gas:** Citgo/dsl, Exxon/24hr, Lukoil, **food:** Bickford's/24hr, Dunkin Donuts, McDonald's, Polcari's Italian, Spud's Rest., Wendy's, **lodging:** Best Western, Comfort Inn, **other:** **H** HOSPITAL

**35** (27)   Winchester Highlands, Melrose, **E** **H** HOSPITAL (no EZ return to sb)

**34** (26)   MA 28 N (from nb, no EZ return), Stoneham, **E gas:** Mobil, **food:** Friendly's, **other:** **H** HOSPITAL

**33** (25)   MA 28, Fellsway West, Winchester, **E** **H** HOSPITAL

**32** (23)   MA 60, Salem Ave, Medford Square, **W lodging:** AmeriSuites, **other:** **H** HOSPITAL, to Tufts U

**31** (22)   MA 16 E, to Revere (no EZ return sb), **E gas:** Shell, **food:** Bertucci's, Friendly's, McDonald's, Subway, **lodging:** Howard Johnson Rest., **other:** CVS Drug, Lincoln/Mercury, Marshall's, Kohl's, Shaw's Foods, Stop&Shop Foods, mall, st police, **W gas:** Fred's Gas, Mr. C/dsl, **food:** Avellino's Italian, Burger King, Dunkin Donuts, Pizza Hut, **other:** AutoZone, KIA, Mitsubishi, Staples

**30** (21)   MA 28, MA 38, Mystic Ave, Somerville, **W gas:** Mr. C's Gas, **food:** Burger King, **other:** AutoZone, Lincoln/Mercury

**29** (20)   MA 28 (from nb), Somerville, **E food:** Dunkin Donuts, 99 Rest., **lodging:** La Quinta, **other:** Circuit City, Home Depot, K-Mart, Staples, TJ Maxx, mall, **W** same as 30, **gas:** Gulf, Hess, **lodging:** Holiday Inn, **other:** Radio Shack, Stop&Shop

**28** (19)   Sullivans Square, Charles Town, downtown

**27**   US 1 N (from nb)

**26** (18.5)   MA 28 N, Storrow Dr, North Sta, downtown

**25**   Haymarket Sq, Gov't Center

**24** (18)   Callahan Tunnel, **E** ✈

**23** (17.5)   High St, Congress St, **W lodging:** Marriott

**MA**

## INTERSTATE 93 CONT'D

**22** (17)  Atlantic Ave, Northern Ave, South Sta, Boston World Trade Ctr

**21** (16.5)  Kneeland St, ChinaTown

**20** (16)  I-90 W, to Mass Tpk

**19** (15.5)  Albany St (from sb), **W** **gas:** Mobil/dsl, **other:** H HOSPITAL

**18** (15)  Mass Ave, to Roxbury, **W** H HOSPITAL

**17** (14.5)  E Berkeley (from nb), **E** New Boston Food Mkt

**16** (14)  S Hampton St, Andrew Square, **W** **gas:** Shell/24hr, **food:** Bickford's, **lodging:** Holiday Inn Express, **other:** Home Depot, K-Mart/Little Caesar's, Marshall's, Old Navy

**15** (13)  Columbia Rd, Everett Square, **E** **lodging:** DoubleTree Motel, **other:** JFK Library, to UMA, **W** **gas:** Shell

**14** (12.5)  Morissey Blvd, **E** JFK Library, **W** **gas:** Shell, **food:** D'angelo's, **lodging:** Howard Johnson, Ramada Inn, **other:** Stop&Shop Foods

**13** (12)  Freeport St, to Dorchester, **W** **gas:** Citgo/7-11, **food:** Boston Mkt, **other:** CVS Drug, Dodge, Toyota

**12** (11.5)  MA 3A S (from sb, no EZ return), Quincy, **E** **gas:** Shell, **food:** Café Pacific, Domino's, **lodging:** Best Western, **W** **gas:** Boston Mkt, Citgo/7-11, Exxon, Shell, Sunoco, **food:** Arby's, Bickford's, Ground Round, PapaGino's, Wendy's, **other:** AutoZone, CVS Drug, Ford/Lincoln/Mercury, Pontiac/GMC, Staples, Walgreen

**11b a** (11)  to MA 203, Granite Ave, Ashmont, **W** **food:** McDonald's

**10** (10)  Squantum Ave (from sb), Milton, **W** H HOSPITAL

**9** (9)  Adams St, Bryant Ave, to N Quincy, **W** **gas:** Shell/repair

**8** (8)  Brook Pkwy, to Quincy, Furnace, **E** **gas:** Global, Gulf/dsl, Mobil, **other:** Home Depot, Saturn

**7** (7)  MA 3 S, to Cape Cod (exits left from sb), Braintree, **E** **lodging:** Marriott

**6** (6)  MA 37, to Holbrook, Braintree, **E** **gas:** Mobil/24hr, **food:** Boardwalk Café, D'angelo's, Pizzaria Uno, TGI Friday, **lodging:** Sheraton/café, **other:** Circuit City, Firestone/auto, Lord&Taylor, Macy's, Sears/auto, mall, **W** **gas:** Sunoco, **food:** Ascari Café, **lodging:** Candlewood Suites, Extended Stay America, Hampton Inn, Holiday Inn Express, **other:** Barnes&Noble, Ford, Nissan, VW

**5b a** (4)  MA 28 S, to Randolph, Milton, **E** **gas:** Citgo, Mobil/dsl, Shell/repair/24hr, **food:** D'angelo's, Domino's, Dunkin Donuts/Baskin-Robbins/Togo's, Friendly's, IHOP, Lombardo's Rest., Picadilly's Pub, Sal's Calzone Rest., Wong's Chinese, **lodging:** Holiday Inn/rest.

**4** (3)  MA 24 S (exits left from sb), to Brockton

**3** (2)  MA 138 N, to Ponkapoag Trail, Houghtons Pond

**2b a** (1)  MA 138 S, to Stoughton, Milton, **E** golf, **W** **gas:** Mobil, Shell/dsl, Sunoco, **food:** Baskin-Robbins, Dunkin Donuts

**1** (0)  I-95 N, S to Providence. I-93 begins/ends on I-95, exit 12.

## INTERSTATE 95

| Exit # | Services |
|---|---|
| **89.5mm** | **Massachusetts/New Hampshire state line, Welcome Ctr/rest area sb, full &#9855; facilities, &#127860; litter barrels** |
| **60** (89) | MA 286, to Salisbury, beaches, **E** **gas:** Mobil/dsl, **food:** Capt. Hook's, Dunkin Donuts, Lena's Seafood Rest., **other:** camping (seasonal) |

**59** (88)  I-495 S (from sb)

**58b a** (78)  rd 110, to I-495 S, to Amesbury, Salisbury, **E** **gas:** Sunoco/Subway/dsl, **food:** China Buffet, Niko's Place, Sylvan St Grille, Winner's Circle Rest., **other:** Chrysler/Jeep/Dodge, U-Haul, radiators, **W** **gas:** Best Choice/Domino's/dsl, Irving Gas, Mobil, **food:** Acapulco's Mexican, Burger King, Dunkin Donuts, Friendly's, McDonald's, PapaGino's, **lodging:** Fairfield Inn, **other:** Chevrolet/VW, Stop&Shop Foods

**86mm**  Merrimac River

**57** (85)  MA 113, to W Newbury, **E** **gas:** Mobil/24hr, Shell/repair/24hr, Sunoco, **food:** China One, d'Angelo's, Dunkin Donuts, Giuseppe's Italian, McDonald's, PapaGino's, Wendy's, White Hen Pantry/deli, **other:** H HOSPITAL, Brook's Drug, GNC, K-Mart, Marshall's, MktBasket Foods, Radio Shack, Shaw's Foods, Walgreens

**56** (78)  Scotland Rd, to Newbury, **E** st police

**55** (77)  Central St, to Byfield, **E** **food:** Gen Store Eatery, Village Diner, **W** **gas:** Prime/dsl/repair

**54b a** (76)  MA 133, E to Rowley, W to Groveland

**75mm**  weigh sta both lanes

**53b a** (74)  MA 97, S to Topsfield, N to Georgetown

**52** (73)  Topsfield Rd, to Topsfield, Boxford

**51** (72)  Endicott Rd, to Topsfield, Middleton

**50** (71)  US 1, to MA 62, Topsfield, **E** **gas:** Exxon/24hr, Mobil/24hr, **other:** Honda, **W** **food:** Quizno's, **lodging:** Sheraton, **other:** CVS Drug, Hyundai, Staples, Stop&Shop, st police

**49** (70)  MA 62 (from nb), Danvers, Middleton, **W** same as 50

**48** (69)  Hobart St (from sb), **W** **food:** Italian Rest., **lodging:** Comfort Inn, Extended Stay America, Motel 6, **other:** Home Depot, Honda, KIA

**47b a** (68)  MA 114, to Middleton, Peabody, **E** **gas:** Gulf, Sunoco, **food:** Dunkin Donuts, McDonald's, Outback, PapaGino's, Quizno's, **other:** Chevrolet/Buick/Pontiac, Dodge, Infiniti, Lexus, Lowe's Whse, Mazda, Mitsubishi, NTB, PetsMart, Quizno's, Subaru, Toyota/Scion, Walmart, **W** **gas:** Hess, **food:** Chili's, TGIFriday, **lodging:** Motel 6, Residence Inn, TownePlace Suites, **other:** BigLots, Circuit City, Costco, Dodge, Home Depot, LandRover, Mini, NAPA, Pontiac/Hyundai

**46** (67)  to US 1, **W** **gas:** Best, Gulf/dsl, Shell, Sunoco, **food:** Burger King, **other:** Auto Parts+

**45** (66)  MA 128 N, to Peabody

**44b a** (65)  US 1 N, MA 129, **E** **gas:** Shell, **W** **gas:** Best/gas, Citgo, Gulf, Sunoco, **food:** Bennigan's, Bertucci's, Burger King, Carrabba's, Dunkin Donuts, Wendy's, **lodging:** Carriage House Hotel, Hampton Inn, Homewood Suites, SpringHill Suites, **other:** H HOSPITAL

**43** (63)  Walnut St, Lynnfield, **E** to Saugus Iron Works NHS (3mi), **W** **lodging:** Sheraton, **other:** golf

**42** (62)  Salem St, Montrose, **E** **gas:** Prime, Sunoco, **food:** Sub Stop, **W** **lodging:** Sheraton

**41** (60)  Main St, Lynnfield Ctr, **E** **gas:** Shell

**40** (59)  MA 129, Wakefield Ctr, N Reading, **E** **gas:** Exxon, **food:** HoneyDew Doughnuts, **other:** VET, **W** **gas:** Gulf, **other:** Chevrolet, dsl repair

**39** (58)  North Ave, Reading, **E** **gas:** Citgo, **lodging:** Best Western, **other:** Curves, Mazda/Isuzu/Volvo/Saab, **W** **gas:** Shell/dsl/24hr, **food:** BearRock Cafe, Chili's, Fuddrucker's, Macaroni Grill, Starbucks, **other:** H HOSPITAL, Ford, Home Depot, Staples

*(left margin, top to bottom:)* N · S · BOSTON AREA · N · S

*(right margin, top to bottom:)* AMESBURY · PEABODY

*(left side tab:)* MA

## INTERSTATE 95 CONT'D

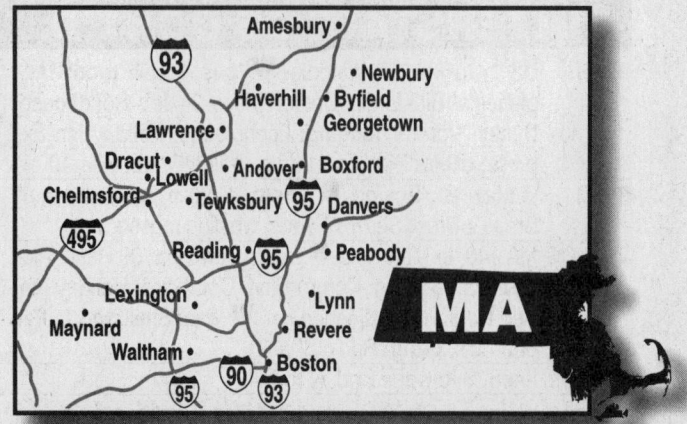

**38b a** (57) MA 28, to Reading, **E gas:** Gulf, Hess/dsl, **food:** Baja Fresh, Boston Mkt, Burger King, China Moon, d'Angelo's/ PapaGino's, Dunkin Donuts, 99 Rest., Subway, **other:** AutoZone, CVS Drug, Ford, GNC, Marshalls, Radio Shack, Shaw's Foods, Walgreens, **W gas:** Exxon, Mobil, Shell, Sunoco, **food:** Burger King, Domino's, Dunkin Donuts, Harrow's Rest., McDonald's, Starbucks

**37b a** (56) I-93, N to Manchester, S to Boston

**36** (55) Washington St, to Winchester, **E gas:** Lukoil, **food:** Dunkin Donuts, FarEast Chinese, The Bistro, **lodging:** Woburn Plaza Motel, **other:** BJ's Whse, Buick/Pontiac/ GMC, Hogan Tire, Jaguar, Mitsubishi, Nissan, Staples, Toyota, **W gas:** Mobil, Sunoco, **food:** China Pearl, d'Angelo's, Joe's Grill, McDonald's, 99 Rest., On the Border, Panera Bread, PapaGino's, Pizza Hut, Pizzaria Uno, TGIFriday, McDonald's, **lodging:** Courtyard, Fairfield Inn, Hampton Inn, Red Roof Inn, **other:** CVS Drug, Kohl's, Lowe's Whse, Mkt Basket Foods, NTB, Office Depot, TJ Maxx, USPO, mall

**35** (54) MA 38, to Woburn, **E lodging:** Holiday Inn, **other:** H H HOSPITAL, **W gas:** Mobil/dsl, **food:** Applebee's, Dunkin Donuts, **lodging:** Extended Stay Deluxe, **other:** Stop&Shop Foods

**34** (53) Winn St, Woburn

**33b a** (52) US 3 S, MA 3A N, to Winchester, **E food:** Bickford's Grille, Café Escadrille, ChuckeCheese, Outback Steaks, Panera Bread, Paparazzi's, **other:** H HOSPITAL, CVS Drug, Honda, Marshalls, Michael's, Roach Bro's Foods, **W gas:** Citgo, Hess, **lodging:** Marriott, **other:** H HOSPITAL, Audi/Porsche, repair

**32b a** (51) US 3 N, MA 2A S, to Lowell, **E gas:** Shell, **lodging:** Hilton Garden, **other:** Circuit City, **W food:** Boston Mkt, Burger King, Cheesecake Factory, Chili's, d'Angelo's, Macaroni Grill, McDonald's, Pizzaria Uno, TCBY, **lodging:** Candlewood Suites, Homestead Suites, **other:** Barnes&Noble, Dodge, Kohl's, Macy's, Sears/auto, Staples, mall

**31b a** (48) MA 4, MA 225, Lexington, **E gas:** Gulf, Mobil/repair, Shell, **food:** Alexander's Pizza, Starbucks, **other:** Walgreens, **W gas:** Exxon/24hr, Shell/24hr, **food:** d'Angelo's, Friendly's, Lexington Cafe, McDonald's, **lodging:** Bedford Motel, Best Western, Quality Inn, **other:** VET, Curves, Staples

**30b a** (47) MA 2A, Lexington, **E gas:** Shell, **other:** H HOSPITAL, **W lodging:** Sheraton, **other:** to MinuteMan NP, Hanscom AFB

**46.5mm** travel plaza nb, Mobil/dsl/24hr, HoneyDew Doughnuts, McDonald's, gifts

**29b a** (46) MA 2 W, Cambridge

**28b a** (45) Trapelo Rd, Belmont, **E gas:** Exxon/dsl, Mobil/dsl, Shell, **food:** Boston Mkt, Dunkin Donuts, Friendly's, McDonald's, Panera Bread, PapaGino's, **other:** Osco Drugs, Shaw's Foods

**27b a** (44) Totten Pond Rd, Waltham, **E gas:** Shell, **food:** Naked Fish Rest., **lodging:** Best Western, Courtyard, Hilton Garden, Holiday Inn Express, Homestead Suites, Westin Hotel, **W food:** Bertucci's Rest., Pizzaria Uno, **lodging:** DoubleTree/rest., **other:** Costco, Home Depot

**26** (43) US 20, to MA 117, to Waltham, **E gas:** Sunoco/dsl, **W gas:** Mobil

**25** (42) I-90, MA Tpk

**24** (41) MA 30, Newton, Wayland, **E gas:** Mobil, **lodging:** Marriott

**23** (40) Recreation Rd (from nb), to MA Tpk

**22b a** (39) Grove St, **E lodging:** Holiday Inn Express, **other:** golf

**38.5mm** travel plaza sb, Mobil/dsl, McDonald's, gifts

**21b a** (38) MA 16, Newton, Wellesley, **E H HOSPITAL, W gas:** Sunoco, **food:** Paparazzi, Starbucks

**20b a** (36) MA 9, Brookline, Framingham

**19** (35) Highland Ave, Newton, Needham, **E gas:** Gulf, Hess, **food:** d'Angelo's, Dunkin Donuts, Ground Round, Mandarin Cuisine, McDonald's, Mighty Subs, **lodging:** Sheraton/rest., **other:** PetCo, Staples, **W food:** Bickford's, **other:** Chevrolet, Ford

**18** (34) Great Plain Ave, W Roxbury

**33.5mm** parking area sb, litter barrels

**17** (33) MA 135, Needham, Wellesley

**32mm** truck turnout sb

**16b a** (31) MA 109, High St, Dedham, **W gas:** Mobil/dsl

**15b a** (29) US 1, MA 128, **E gas:** Gulf, **food:** Bickford's, Bugaboo Steaks, Chili's, Joe's Grill, Krispy Kreme, Panera Bread, PapaGino's, TGIFriday, Vinny T's Rest., **lodging:** Comfort Inn, Fairfield Inn, Holiday Inn, Residence Inn, **other:** VET, Best Buy, BJ's Whse, CVS Drug, Lincoln/Mercury, Nissan, NTB, PepBoys, Speedy Repair, Star Foods, Volvo, **W gas:** Shell/dsl/24hr, **food:** Burger King, Dunkin Donuts, Jade Chinese, McDonald's, **lodging:** Budget Motel, **other:** Aamco, Audi, Buick, Chrysler/Jeep, Hyundai, Mercedes, Pontiac

**14** (28) East St, Canton St, **E lodging:** Hilton

**27mm** rest area sb, full facilities, litter barrels

**13** (26.5) University Ave

**12** (26) I-93 N, to Braintree, Boston, motorist callboxes end nb

**11b a** (23) Neponset St, to Canton, **E gas:** Citgo/repair, Sunoco/repair, **food:** Dunkin Donuts

**22.5mm** Neponset River

**10** (20) Coney St (from sb, no EZ return), to US 1, Sharon, Walpole, **1 mi W on US 1...gas:** Citgo, Mobil, **food:** Caldo's Rest., Dunkin Donuts, Friendly's, IHOP, McDonald's, 99 Rest., Old Country Buffet, Outback Steaks, PapaGino's, Pizza Hut, Starbucks, Taco Bell, TGIFriday, **lodging:** Courtyard, Residence Inn, Sheraton, **other:** Acura, Advance Parts, Barnes&Noble, Brook's Drug, CVS Drug, Home Depot, Kohl's, Lexus, Old Navy, Staples, Stop&Shop Foods, VW, Walgreens, mall

## INTERSTATE 95 CONT'D

**9** (19)  US 1, to MA 27, Walpole, **W gas:** Mobil, **food:** Applebee's, Bickford's, Boston View, Clyde's Roadhouse, Dunkin Donuts, **lodging:** Econolodge, Holiday Inn Express, **other:** BigY Food/drug, Walmart, same as 10

**8** (16)  S Main St, Sharon, **E food:** Dunkin Donuts, **other:** Brook's Drug, Shaw's Foods, whaling museum

**7b a** (13)  MA 140, to Mansfield, **E food:** Domino's, 99 Rest., Piccadilly's, **lodging:** Comfort Inn, Courtyard, Holiday Inn, Red Roof Inn, Residence Inn. **W gas:** Shell, **food:** PapaGino's, **other:** Radio Shack

**6b a** (12)  I-495, S to Cape Cod, N to NH

**10mm**  Welcome Ctr/rest area nb, full ♿ facilities, info, ☏, 🍴, litter barrels, petwalk

**9mm**  truck parking area sb

**5** (7)  MA 152, Attleboro, **E H** HOSPITAL, **W gas:** Gulf/dsl, **food:** Bill's Pizza, Piccadilly Rest., Wendy's, **other:** Radio Shack, Shaw's Foods/Osco Drug

**4** (6)  I-295 S, to Woonsocket

**3** (4)  MA 123, to Attleboro, **E gas:** Shell/dsl, **other:** **H** HOSPITAL, zoo

**2.5mm**  parking area/weigh sta both lanes, no restrooms, litter barrels, motorist callboxes

**2b a** (1)  US 1A, Newport Ave, Attleboro, **E gas:** Mobil/dsl, Shell, Sunoco, **food:** Honeydew Doughnuts, McDonald's, Olive Garden, Spumoni's Italian, **other:** Home Depot, K-Mart, Shaw's Foods, **W gas:** Getty/dsl

**1** (.5)  US 1 (from sb), **E lodging:** Day's Inn, **other:** Brooks Drug, Volvo

**0mm**  Massachusetts/Rhode Island state line

## INTERSTATE 195

| Exit # | Services |
|---|---|
| **22** (41) | I-495 N, MA 25 S, to Cape Cod. I-195 begins/ends on I-495, exit 1. |
| **21** (39) | MA 28, to Wareham, **N gas:** Maxi/dsl/24hr, **food:** Longhorn Steaks, Pomodore's Italian, Qdoba Mexican, Red Robin, **other:** Best Buy, Borders Books, JC Penny, LL Bean, Lowe's Whse, Michaels, Old Navy, PetCo, Staples, Target, **S gas:** Gateway Gas/dsl, Mobil, **other:** **H** HOSPITAL, **other:** NAPA, repair |
| **37mm** | rest area eb, info, ☏, 🍴, litter barrels, petwalk, boat ramp |
| **36mm** | Sippican River |
| **20** (35) | MA 105, to Marion, **S** RV camping (seasonal) |
| **19b a** (31) | to Mattapoisett, **S gas:** Mobil, **food:** Nick's Pizza, **other:** USPO |
| **18** (26) | MA 240 S, to Fairhaven, **1 mi S gas:** Citgo/7-11, Lukoil, **food:** Blimpie, Burger King, Chicago Grill, Dunkin Donuts, Great Wall Chinese, McDonald's, 99 Rest., PapaGino's, Papa John's, Pasta House, Peking Palace, Pizza Hut, Subway, Taco Bell, Wendy's, **lodging:** Hampton Inn, **other:** AutoZone, Curves, $Tree, GMC/Buick/Pontiac, GNC, K-Mart, Marshalls, Mazda, Radio Shack, Shaw's Foods, Staples, Stop$Shop, TownFair Tire, Walgreens, Walmart |
| **25.5mm** | Acushnet River |
| **17** (24) | Coggeshall St, New Bedford, **N gas:** Petro, 7-11/gas, Sunoco, **food:** Dunkin Donuts, EndZone Café, McDonald's, same as 16 |

**16** (23)  Washburn St (from eb), **N gas:** Sunoco, **food:** McDonald's, Papa John's

**15** (22)  MA 18 S, New Bedford, **S** Whaling Museum, hist dist, to downtown,

**14** (21)  Penniman St (from eb), New Bedford, downtown

**13b a** (20)  MA 140, **N** ✉, **S gas:** Buttonwood/dsl, Sunoco, **food:** Dunkin Donuts, Quizno's, **other:** **H** HOSPITAL, Buttonwood Park/zoo, CVS Drug, Honda, Shaw's Foods, Walgreens, VW

**12b a** (19)  N Dartmouth, **S gas:** Hess, Mobil/dsl, **food:** Burger King, D'angelo's, Dunkin Donuts, Friendly's, IHOP, McDonald's, 99 Rest., Old Country Buffet, Olive Garden, Panera Bread, PapaGino's, Peking Garden, Quizno's, Ruby Tuesday, Subway, Taco Bell, TX Roadhouse, Wendy's, **lodging:** Comfort Inn, Residence Inn, **other:** Barnes&Noble, Best Buy, BJ's Whse, Chevrolet, Circuit City, Curves, Firestone/auto, JC Penney, Kohl's, Lowe's Whse, Macy's, Old Navy, Saturn, Sears/auto, Stop&Shop Food/gas, TJ Maxx, TownFair Tire, Toyota/Scion, Walmart, USPO, mall, st police

**11b a** (17)  Reed Rd, to Dartmouth, **2 mi S gas:** Shell/24hr

**10** (16)  MA 88 S, to US 6, Westport, **S gas:** Irving, Rte 6 Gas, Valero/dsl, **lodging:** Hampton Inn

**9** (15.5)  MA 24 N (from nb), Stanford Rd, Westport, **S gas:** Rte 6 Gas, **food:** LePage's Seafood, White's Rest., **lodging:** Hampton Inn

**8b a** (15)  MA 24 S, Fall River, Westport, **N gas:** Crosson Gas, **food:** Papa John's, **S food:** Dunkin Donuts, Subway

**7** (14)  MA 81 S, Plymouth Ave, Fall River, **N gas:** Getty, Hess, **food:** Boston Mkt, Burger King, D'angelo's Rest., Dunkin Donuts, Honeydew Doughnuts, KFC, 99 Rest., Subway, Wendy's, **other:** **H** HOSPITAL, Buick/Pontiac, CVS Drug, **S gas:** Shell, **food:** Applebee's, McDonald's, **other:** Goodyear/auto, Walgreens

**6** (13.5)  Pleasant St, Fall River, downtown

**5** (13)  MA 79, MA 138, to Taunton, **S gas:** Exxon, Lukoil, **food:** Honeydew Doughnuts, Papa John's, **lodging:** Day's Inn

**12mm**  Assonet Bay

**4b a** (10)  MA 103, to Swansea, Somerset, **N gas:** Getty, **food:** Rogers Rest., **other:** auto repair, **S gas:** Shell/24hr, **food:** Jillian's Cafe, **lodging:** Quality Inn, Swansea Motel

**3** (8)  US 6, to MA 118, Swansea, Rehoboth, **N gas:** Citgo/dsl, Hess, **food:** Burger King, Dunkin Donuts, Friendly's, McDonald's, Ponderosa, Thai Taste, Tim Horton, Wendy's, **other:** BigLots, CarQuest, $Tree, Firestone/auto, Jo-Anne, Macy's, Marshall's, NAPA, Old Navy, Price Rite Foods, Seabra Foods, Sears/auto, mall, **S gas:** Gulf/24hr, **food:** Anthony's Seafood, **lodging:** Swansea Motel

**6mm**  rest area eb, full ♿ facilities, ☏, 🍴, litter barrels, petwalk

**5.5mm**  parking area wb

**2** (5)  MA 136, to Newport, **S gas:** Mobil/24hr, Shell/24hr, **food:** Cathay Pearl Chinese, Dunkin Donuts, McDonald's, Michael's Rest., Subway

**3mm**  weigh sta both lanes

**1** (1)  MA 114A, to Seekonk, **N gas:** Citgo, Exxon/dsl, Shell/24hr, **food:** Dunkin Donuts, Honeydew Doughnuts, Newport Creamery, 99 Rest., Tony's Pizza, **lodging:** Motel 6, **other:** vet, **S gas:** Hess, Mobil/24hr, Sunoco/dsl, **food:** Applebee's, BigLots, Bugaboo

## INTERSTATE 195 CONT'D

N ↕ S

**1** (1)   Continued
Creek Steaks, Burger King, Chili's, Darling's Rest., Dunkin Donuts, Friendly's, McDonald's, Old Country Buffet, Outback Steaks, Panera Bread, PapaGino's, Subway, Taco Bell, TGIFriday, Tuesday Morning, Wendy's, Vinny T's Rest., **lodging:** Best Western, Comfort Inn, Extended Stay America, Hampton Inn, Knight's Inn, Mary's Motel, Ramada Inn/rest., Town'n Country Motel, **other:** Acura, Best Buy, BigLots, Bob's Stores, Circuit City, Daewoo, $Tree, Firestone/Auto, GNC, Home Depot, Jiffy Lube, Kohl's, Lowe's Whse, Michael's, PepBoys, PetCo, Sam's Club, Staples, Stop&Shop Foods, Target, TJMaxx, TownFair Tire, Volvo, Walmart/drug

**0mm**   Massachusetts/Rhode Island state line, **Exits 8-1 are in RI.**

**8** (5)   US 1A N, Pawtucket, **S gas:** Mobil/dsl, **food:** Subway, **other:** CVS Drug

**7** (4)   US 6 E, CT 114 S, to Barrington, Seekonk

**6** (3)   Broadway Ave, **N gas:** Speedy AutoService, **S gas:** Shell, Sunoco/dsl

**5** (2.5)   RI 103 E, Warren Ave

**4** (2)   US 44 E, RI 103 E, Taunton Ave, Warren Ave, **N gas:** Sunoco

**3** (1.5)   Gano St, **S lodging:** Radisson

**2** (1)   US 44 W, Wickenden St, India Pt, downtown, **N gas:** Shell/dsl

**1** (.5)   Providence, downtown

**0mm**   **I-195 begins/ends on I-95, exit 20 in Providence, RI, Exits 1-8 are in RI.**

## INTERSTATE 290

E ↔ W

WORCESTER

**Exit #**   Services

**26b a** (20)   I-495. I-290 begins/ends on I-495, exit 25.

**25b a** (17)   Solomon Pond Mall Rd, to Berlin, **N food:** Bertucci's, TGIFriday, **food:** Olive Garden, **lodging:** Comfort Inn, Residence Inn, **other:** Best Buy, Borders Books, JC Penney, Sears/auto, Target, mall, **S** Solomon Pond Grill

**24** (15)   Church St, Northborough

**23b a** (13)   MA 140, Boylston, **N gas:** Citgo/dsl, Mobil, **food:** Dunkin Donuts, Other Place Rest.

**22** (11)   Main St, Worchester, **N gas:** Exxon/24hr, Shell, **food:** Bickford's, Friendly's, McDonald's, Wendy's, **other:** Ⓗ HOSPITAL

**21** (10)   Plantation St (from eb), **N lodging:** Best Western, **other:** Lowe's Whse, Staples, Stop&Shop, Target

**20** (8)   MA 70, Lincoln St, Burncoat St, **N gas:** Charter/24hr, Exxon/Subway/24hr, Shell, Sunoco, **food:** Bickford's, Denny's, Dunkin Donuts, Friendly's, McDonald's, Papa Gino's, Taco Bell, Wendy's, **lodging:** Day's Inn, Econolodge, Holiday Inn, **other:** Auto Palace, CVS Drug, Radio Shack, Shaw's Food/24hr, Walgreen

**19** (7)   I-190 N, MA 12

**18**   MA 9, Framington, Ware, Worcester ✈, **N** Ⓗ HOSPITAL

**16**   Central St, Worcester, **N food:** 99 Rest., **lodging:** Crowne Plaza, Hampton Inn, mall

**14**   MA 122, Barre, Worcester, downtown

**13**   MA 122A, Vernon St, Worcester, downtown

**12**   MA 146 S, to Millbury

**11**   Southbridge St, College Square, **N gas:** Shell/dsl, **food:** Wendy's, **S gas:** Getty

**10**   MA 12 N (from wb), Hope Ave

**9**   Auburn St, to Auburn, **E gas:** Shell, **food:** Arby's, Bickford's, Wendy's, McDonald's, **lodging:** Baymont Inn, Comfort Inn, Holiday Inn Express, **other:** Acura, AutoZone, Firestone, Sears/auto, Shaw's Foods, Staples, mall

**8**   MA 12 S (from sb), Webster, **W gas:** Shell, **lodging:** Best Western

**7**   I-90, E to Boston, W to Springfield.

**I-290 begins/ends on I-90.**

## INTERSTATE 395

N ↕ S

**Exit #**   Services

**I-395 begins/ends on I-90, exit 10.**

**7** (12)   to I-90 (MA Tpk), MA 12, **E gas:** Shell, **food:** Piccadilly's, **lodging:** Comfort Inn, Holiday Inn Express

**6b a** (11)   US 20, **E gas:** Gulf, **food:** Dunkin Donuts, KFC, **other:** Honda, Saab/VW, TCI Tires, truck repair, **W gas:** Shell, **food:** Chuck's Steakhouse, Friendly's, **lodging:** Fairfield Inn, Hampton Inn, **other:** BJ's Whse, Buick/Pontiac/GMC/Cadillac, Ford/Mercury, Home Depot, Mitsubishi, Nissan, TJ Maxx, transmissions

**5** (8)   Depot Rd, N Oxford

**4b a** (6)   Sutton Ave, to Oxford, **W gas:** Mobil/24hr, **food:** Dunkin Donuts, McDonald's, NE Pizza, Subway, **other:** Cahill's Tire/Repair, Cumberland Farms, CVS Drug

**3** (4)   Cudworth Rd, to N Webster, S Oxford

**2** (3)   MA 16, to Webster, **E** Subaru, **W gas:** Exxon/24hr, Getty, Hi-Lo Gas, Sunoco, **food:** Burger King, D'angelo, Dunkin Donuts, Empire Wok, Friendly's, Honey Dew Donuts, KFC/Taco Bell, McDonald's, Papa Gino's, **other:** Ⓗ HOSPITAL, Advance Parts, Auto Repair, Consumer Parts, CVS Drug, Ford, PriceChopper Foods, Rite Aid, Walgreen

**1** (1)   MA 193, to Webster, **E** Ⓗ HOSPITAL, **W gas:** Citgo/dsl, **food:** Golden Greek Rest., Wind Tiki Chinese, **other:** Goodyear/auto

**0mm**   Massachusetts/Connecticut state line

## INTERSTATE 495

**Exit #**   Services

**I-495**   begins/ends on I-95, exit 59.

**55** (119)   MA 110 (from nb, no return), to I-95 S, **E gas:** Best Choice/Domino's/dsl, Irving, **food:** Acupulco Mexican, Burger King, Dunkin Donuts, Friendly's, McDonald's, **lodging:** Fairfield Inn, **other:** Chevrolet/VW,

MA

## INTERSTATE 495 CONT'D

N ↕ S

**55** (119) Continued
Stop&Shop, **W gas:** Gulf, **food:** Amesbury Pizza, **other:** Curves, NAPA

**54** (118) MA 150, to Amesbury, **W** RV camping

**53** (115) Broad St, Merrimac, **W gas:** Gulf, **food:** Dunkin Donuts

**114mm** parking area sb, **[C**, restrooms, **[A]**, litter barrels (6AM-8PM)

**52** (111) MA 110, to Haverhill, **E [H]** HOSPITAL, **W gas:** Lukoil, Mobil/dsl, **food:** Dunkin Donuts, King's Roast Beef

**110mm** parking area nb, **[C**, **[A]**, litter barrels

**51** (109) MA 125, to Haverhill, **E gas:** Citgo, Mobil, **food:** Bros Pizza, China King, **other:** **[H]** HOSPITAL, Family$, **W food:** Dunkin Donuts, Friendly's, Longhorn Steaks, Lucky Corner Chinese, McDonald's, Starbucks, Wendy's

**50** (107) MA 97, to Haverhill, **E [H]** HOSPITAL, **W** Ford, Lowe's Whse, Target

**49** (106) MA 110, to Haverhill, **E gas:** Gulf, Sunoco/24hr, **food:** A1 Deli, Athens Pizza, Dunkin Donuts, McDonald's, Oriental Garden, 99 Rest., PapaGino's, **lodging:** Best Western, Comfort Inn, **other:** Chevrolet/Pontiac/Buick, CVS Drug, MktBasket Foods, Walgreens

**105.8mm** Merrimac River

**48** (105.5) MA 125, to Bradford, **E gas:** BJ's Whse/gas

**47** (105) MA 213, to Methuen, **1-2 mi W food:** Applebees, Bugaboo Steaks, Burger King, ChuckeCheese, McDonald's, Starbucks, TGIFriday, Wendy's, **other:** Borders Books, Home Depot, Marshalls, Old Navy, Walmart, Methuen Mall, Stop&Shop Foods, Target

**46** (104) MA 110, **E gas:** Pleasant Valley Gas, Sunoco/24hr, **gas:** Capalini's Italian, **other:** Lincoln/Mercury, **W [H]** HOSPITAL

**45** (103) Marston St, to Lawrence, **W other:** Chevrolet, Honda, Kia

**44** (102) Merrimac St, to Lawrence

**43** (101) Mass Ave

**42** (100) MA 114, **E gas:** Exxon, Gulf, Mobil, **food:** Boston Mkt, Dunkin Donuts, Friendly's, Lee Chin Cninese, Pizza Hut, **lodging:** Holiday Inn Express, **other:** MktBasket Foods, PetCo, Walgreens, **W gas:** Gas-N-Go, **food:** Denny's, Dunkin Donuts, Pizza Hut, Subway, Taco Bell, Wendy's, **other:** **[H]** HOSPITAL, Rite Aid, Save-A-Lot Foods, VIP Parts/service

**41** (99) MA 28, to Andover, **E food:** Dunkin Donuts, **other:** Chevrolet

**40b a** (98) I-93, N to Methuen, S to Boston

**39** (94) MA 133, to Dracut, **E gas:** Hess, **food:** Longhorn Steaks, McDonald's, **lodging:** Extended Stay America, **W gas:** Mobil/dsl, **food:** Cracker Barrel, Wendy's, **lodging:** Fairfield Inn, Holiday Inn/rest., Residence Inn

**38** (93) MA 38, to Lowell, **E gas:** Shell/dsl, **food:** Applebee's, Burger King, Dunkin Donuts, El Pollo Loco, IHOP, Jade East, 99 Rest., Waffle House, **lodging:** Motel 6, **other:** Home Depot, Honda/VW, Walmart, **W gas:**

CHELMSFORD

**38** (93) Continued
Citgo, Mobil, Sunoco, USA/dsl, **food:** Dunkin Donuts, Milan Pizza, McDonald's, Wendy's, **other:** Chevrolet/Pontiac/Buick/GMC, CVS Drug, Hannaford Foods, Marshalls, Saturn, Sears Essentials, Staples

**37** (91) Woburn St, to S Lowell, **W gas:** Exxon/Dunkin Donuts/Subway

**35c** (90) to Lowell SP, Lowell ConX, **1 mi W food:** Burger King, McDonald's, Outback Steaks, Wendy's, **lodging:** Courtyard, **other:** Shop&Save, Walgreens

**35b a** (89) US 3, S to Burlington, N to Nashua, NH

**34** (88) MA 4, Chelmsford, **E gas:** Mobil, Sunoco, **food:** Dunkin Donuts, Jimmy's Pizza, Papagino's Italian, Skip's Rest., **lodging:** Radisson, CVS Drug, Walgreens, **W gas:** Shell, **food:** Moonstone's Rest., **lodging:** Best Western

**33** MA 4, N Chelmsford (from nb)

**88mm** motorist aid call boxes begin sb

**87mm** **rest area both lanes, full [&]** facilities, **[C**, **[A]**, litter barrels, vending, petwalk, (8AM-8PM)

**32** (83) Boston Rd, to MA 225, **E gas:** Exxon/24hr, Gulf/service, Mobil/24hr, **food:** Applebee's, Burger King, Chili's, D'angelo's, Dunkin Donuts, McDonald's, Starbucks, Westford Grill, **lodging:** Hampton Inn, Residence Inn, **other:** CVS Drug, MktBasket Foods, Radio Shack, Rite Aid, Walgreens, to Nashoba Valley Ski Area

**31** (80) MA 119, to Groton, **E gas:** Gulf, Mobil/dsl/24hr, Shell, **food:** Dunkin Donuts, Ken's Café, **other:** CVS Drug, vet

**30** (78) MA 110, to Littleton, **1 mi E gas:** Shell, **food:** USPO, **W gas:** Citgo/dsl, Shell, Sunoco/dsl, **other:** **[H]** HOSPITAL, RV camping, vet

**29b a** (77) MA 2, to Leominster, **E** to Walden Pond St Reserve

**28** (75) MA 111, to Boxborough, Harvard, **E gas:** Exxon/Dunkin Donuts, **lodging:** Holiday Inn

**27** (70) MA 117, to Bolton, **E gas:** Mobil/dsl, **food:** Subway, **W food:** Bolton Pizza, **other:** Curves, vet

**26** (68) MA 62, to Berlin, **E gas:** Exxon/Dunkin Donuts, **lodging:** Holiday Inn Express, **W gas:** Shell/dsl, **other:** Berlin Farms Cafe

**66mm** Assabet River

**25b** (64) I-290, to Worcester

**25a** to MA 85, Marlboro, **1 mi E gas:** Gulf, Mobil/dsl, **food:** Burger King, Checkerboards Rest., D'angelo's, Domino's, Honeydew Donuts, 99 Rest., Piccadilly's, **other:** CVS Drug, Family$, GMC, Hannaford Foods, Stop&Shop, TJ Maxx, Walgreens

**24b a** (63) US 20, to Northboro, Marlboro, **E gas:** Gulf/repair, Mobil, **food:** Allora Rest., D'angelo's, Dunkin Donuts, Lake Williams Pizza, **lodging:** Holiday Inn, **W gas:** Exxon, Shell, **food:** Boston Mkt, China Taste, Longhorn Steaks, McDonald's/playplace, 99 Rest., Panera Bread, PapaGino's, Quizno's, Starbucks, Subway, Tandoori Grill, Wendy's, **lodging:** Best Western, Courtyard, Embassy Suites, Hampton Inn, Homestead Suites, **other:** $Tree, GNC, Hannaford Foods

MARLBORO

MA

## INTERSTATE 495 CONT'D

**N** ↕ **S**

**23c** (60)  Simrano Dr, Marlboro

**23b a** (59)  MA 9, to Shrewsbury, Framingham, **E gas:** Exxon/dsl, Gulf, **food:** Wendy's, **lodging:** Red Roof Inn, **W gas:** Mobil/dsl/24hr, Shell, **food:** Bertucci's, Burger King, Chateau Rest., D'angelo's, Dunkin Donuts, Friendly's, McDonald's, Piccadilly's, Ruby Tuesday, **lodging:** Doubletree Inn, Extended Stay America, Extended Stay Deluxe, Residence Inn, **other:** H HOSPITAL, Chrysler/Jeep, Marshall's, Mitsubishi, Pontiac/Buick/GMC, Staples, Stop&Shop, VW

**22** (58)  I-90, MA TPK, E to Boston, W to Albany

**21b a** (54)  MA 135, to Hopkinton, Upton, **E gas:** Gulf, Mobil, **food:** Dino's Pizza, Dynasty Chinese, Golden Spoon Rest.

**20** (50)  MA 85, to Milford, **W gas:** Gulf/dsl/LP, Mobil/dsl, **food:** 99 Rest., Pizza 85/deli, TGIFriday, Wendy's, **lodging:** Baymont Inn, Comfort Inn, Courtyard/rest, Day's Inn, Fairfield Inn, Holiday Inn Express, **other:** H HOSPITAL, Best Buy, Lowe's Whse, Staples, Stop&Shop, Target, TJ Maxx

**19** (48)  MA 109, to Milford, **W gas:** Mobil/dsl/24hr, Shell, **food:** Alamo Mexican, Applebee's, Bugaboo Cr Steaks, Burger King, D'angelo, Dunkin Donuts, Friendly's, KFC/Pizza Hut, Maria Italian, McDonald's/playplace, PapaGino's, Subway, **lodging:** La Quinta, Sheraton, **other:** AutoZone, CVS Drug, Hannaford Foods, Jo-Ann Fabrics, K-Mart, Kohl's, Radio Shack, Rite Aid

**18** (46)  MA 126, to Bellingham, **E food:** Chili's, Coldstone Creamery, McDonald's, **other:** Barnes&Noble, MktBasket Foods, Old Navy, Staples, Walmart/Subway, Whole Foods Mkt, **W gas:** Hess, Mobil/24hr, Sunoco/dsl, **food:** DQ, Dunkin Donuts, Outback Steaks, Pizzaria Uno, **other:** Home Depot, PetsMart

**17** (44)  MA 140, to Franklin, Bellingham, **E gas:** Mobil/dsl, Shell, Sunoco, **food:** Applebee's, Asian Cuisine, Burger King, D'angelo's, Dunkin Donuts, KFC, Longhorn Steaks, Panera Bread, PapaGino's, Subway, Taco Bell, **other:** AutoZone, Buick/GMC, Curves, CVS Drug, GNC, Marshalls, Radio Shack, Stop&Shop, **W** H HOSPITAL, BJ's Whse/gas, **food:** 99 Rest., Piccadilly's, **lodging:** Residence Inn

**16** (42)  King St, to Franklin, **E gas:** Sunoco/24hr, **food:** Dunkin Donuts, Franklin Deli, Joe's Grill, King St Cafe, McDonald's, **lodging:** Hampton Inn, **other:** Spruce Pond Creamery, **W lodging:** Hawthorn Inn

**15** (39)  MA 1A, to Plainville, Wrentham, **E gas:** Mobil, **other:** H HOSPITAL, **W gas:** Mobil/dsl, **food:** Chicago Grill, Cracker Barrel, Dunkin Donuts, Friendly's, Ruby Tuesday, Uno Pizzaria, **other:** Premium Outlets/famous brands

**14b a** (37)  US 1, to N Attleboro, **E gas:** Interstate/D'angelo's/PapaGino's/dsl, **food:** Luciano's Rest., **lodging:** Arbor Motel, **other:** Bass Pro Shops (4mi), **W gas:** Mobil, **food:** Chili's, Dunkin Donuts, Panera Bread, **other:** Macdonald's RV Ctr, Stop&Shop, Lowe's, NTB, Target, TJ Maxx, vet

**13** (32)  I-95, N to Boston, S to Providence, access to H HOSPITAL

**12** (30)  MA 140, to Mansfield, **E food:** Bertucci's Italian, Honeydew Doughnuts, Longhorn Steaks, Qdoba Mexican, TGIFriday, Wendy's, **other:** Best Buy,

**12** (30)  Continued
Borders Books, Home Depot, LL Bean, Michael's, PetCo, Kohl's, Shaw's Foods, Staples, Wildharvest Food

**11** (29)  MA 140 S (from sb, no EZ return), **1 mi W gas:** Gulf, **food:** Dunkin Donuts, Mandarin Chinese, McDonald's, Subway, **other:** $Tree

**10** (26)  MA 123, to Norton, **E food:** Dunkin Donuts, **other:** QuickStop, **W** H HOSPITAL

**9** (24)  Bay St, to Taunton, **E food:** Chateau Rest., **W food:** Dunkin Donuts, Jaybo Cafe, Quizno's, Ruby Tuesday's, Wendy's, **lodging:** Holiday Inn, **other:** BJ's Whse

**8** (22)  MA 138, to Raynham, **E gas:** Hess, Mobil/dsl, **food:** Honeydew Donuts, Yummyhouse Rest., **W gas:** Citgo/dsl, Exxon/dsl, Irving/dsl, Shell/dsl/repair, **food:** Cape Cod Cafe, China Garden, D'angelo, Dunkin Doughnuts, Honeydew Donuts, La Casa Mia Rest., Lucky Corner Chinese, McDonald's, Pepperoni's Pizza, Quizno's, Subway, **other:** H HOSPITAL, CVS Drug, Mkt Basket Foods, USPO, vet

**7b a** (19)  MA 24, to Fall River, Boston, **1/2 mi E food:** Burger King

**18mm**  weigh sta both lanes

**17.5mm**  Taunton River

**6** (15)  US 44, to Middleboro, **E gas:** Super/dsl, **food:** Burger King, Dunkin Donuts, Fireside Grille, Friendly's, Hong Kong Taste, PapaGino's, Subway, **W gas:** Mobil/dsl, **lodging:** Dunkin Donuts, Fairfield Inn, Holiday Inn Express, **other:** Crossroads RV Ctr

**M I D D L E B O R O**

**5** (14)  MA 18, to Lakeville, **E food:** Burger King, Dunkin Donuts, Fireside Grille, Friendly's, PapaGino's, **other:** CVS Drug, Kelly's Tire, Stop&Shop Food, **W other:** Massasoit SP, RV camping (seasonal)

**4** (12)  MA 105, to Middleboro, **E gas:** Exxon/dsl/24hr, Shell/24hr, Sunoco/24hr, **food:** DQ, Dunkin Donuts, McDonald's, **lodging:** Day's Inn, **other:** AutoZone, Chevrolet, Rite Aid

**10.5mm**  parking area eb

**10mm**  parking area both lanes

**3** (8)  MA 28, to Rock Village, S Middleboro, **E gas:** Citgo/dsl, **other:** Buds RV's, Fred's Repair, **W gas:** Mobil/Dunkin Doughnuts/Subway/dsl, **food:** Chicken House Rest

**2** (3)  MA 58, W Wareham, **E other:** to Myles Standish SF, **W gas:** 7-11/gas

**2mm**  Weweantic River

**1** (0)  I-495 begins/ends on I-195, MA 25 S.

Copyright 2009 - The Next Exit®

**PORT HURON**

**N ↕ S**

**LAPEER**

**DAVISON**

MI

## INTERSTATE 69

| Exit # | Services |
|---|---|
| 199 | Lp 69 (from eb, no return), to Port Huron, **S gas**: Mobil/dsl, **other**: AutoZone, K-Mart, Sam's Club/gas |
| | **I-69 E and I-94 E run together into Port Huron. See Michigan 94 exits 274-275mm.** |
| 198 | I-94, to Detroit and Canada |
| 196 | Wadhams Rd, **N gas**: BP, Marathon, Speedy Q/dsl, Shell/Wendy's, **food**: Hungry Howie's, McDonald's, Peking Kitchen, Subway, **other**: Carter's Foods, Wadham's Drugs, KOA (1mi), **S golf** |
| 194 | Taylor Rd, **N** Good L's CP, RV camping |
| 189 | Wales Center Rd, to Goodells, **S golf** |
| 184 | MI 19, to Emmett, **N gas**: Citgo/dsl/scales/rest./24hr, **other**: repair, **S gas**: Marathon/dsl/24hr |
| 180 | Riley Center Rd, **N** KOA |
| 176 | Capac Rd, **N gas**: BP/McDonald's/dsl, **food**: Subway (2mi) |
| **174mm** | **rest area wb, full ♿ facilities, 🚻, ☕, litter barrels, vending, petwalk** |
| 168 | MI 53, Imlay City, **N gas**: BP/dsl/24hr, Speedway/dsl, **food**: Big Boy, Big Joe's Pizza, Burger King, DQ, Hungry Howie's, Jet's Pizza, Little Caesar's, Lucky's Steaks, McDonald's, New China, Taco Bell, Wah Wong Chinese, Wendy's/Tim Horton, **lodging**: Day's Inn, M53 Motel, **other**: AutoZone, Chevrolet/Pontiac, Chrysler/Dodge/Jeep, Discount Drug, $Discount, Ford, GNC, IGA Foods, Kroger, NAPA, Pamida, Radio Shack, **S camping** |
| 163 | Lake Pleasant Rd, to Attica |
| **160mm** | **rest area eb, full ♿ facilities, 🚻, ☕, litter barrels, vending, petwalk** |
| 159 | Wilder Rd |
| **158mm** | Flint River |
| 155 | MI 24, Lapeer, **1 mi N gas**: BP, Clark/dsl, FS, Meijer/dsl/24hr, Speedy Q, **food**: Apple Tree Rest., Arby's, Blind Fish Rest., Brian's Rest., Burger King, Coffee Tree Cafe, DQ, Farmhouse Rest., Hot'n Now, Jet's Pizza, KFC, Little Caesar's, McDonald's, Mr Pita, Nick's Rest., Subway, Taco Bell, Tim Horton, Wah Wong Chinese, Wendy's, **lodging**: Best Western, Fairfield Inn, **other**: ⊞ HOSPITAL, AutoZone, Curves, $Tree, Home Depot, K-Mart, Kroger, Murray's Parts, Office Depot, Radio Shack, SavALot, st police, vet, **S gas**: Mobil/dsl, **other**: Buick/Pontiac |
| 153 | Lake Nepessing Rd, **S** to Thumb Correctional, camping, golf |
| 149 | Elba Rd, **S other**: Country Mkt, Torzwski CP, RV/truck repair |
| 145 | MI 15, Davison, **N gas**: Marathon, Shell/dsl, Speedway, **food**: Apollo Rest., Applebee's, Arby's, Big Boy, Big John's Rest., Burger King, Chee Kong Chinese, Country Sun Rest., Hungry Howie's, Italia Gardens, KFC, Little Caesar's, McDonald's, Senor Lucky, Subway, Taco Bell, Tim Horton, **lodging**: Comfort Inn, **other**: AutoValue Parts, GNC, Pontiac/Buick/GMC, Radio Shack, Rite Aid/24hr, Walgreens, repair, **S gas**: Mobil/dsl |
| 143 | Irish Rd, **N gas**: Speedway/dsl, **S gas**: Meijer/dsl, Shell/McDonald's/24hr, **other**: Meijer, 7-11 |
| 141 | Belsay Rd, Flint, **N gas**: 1 stop, Shell/Wendy's/dsl/24hr, **food**: Country Kitchen, Dominos, McDonald's, |

**FLINT**

| | |
|---|---|
| 141 | Continued Taco Bell, **other**: Harley-Davidson, K-Mart, Kroger, Walmart SuperCtr/Subway/auto, **S gas**: Sunoco/A&W/LJ Silver/dsl |
| 139 | Center Rd, Flint, **N gas**: Speedway/dsl, **food**: Applebee's, Boston Mkt, Coney Island, Cottage Pizza, Empire Wok, Halo Burger, Moykong Chinese, Old Country Buffet, Ponderosa, Quizno's, Starbucks, Subway, Tim Horton, **lodging**: Best Inn, **other**: Aldi Foods, Discount Tire, Family$, Home Depot, JC Penney, Jo-Ann Fabrics, Lowe's Whse, Old Navy, Staples, VG Foods, mall, **S gas**: Meijer/dsl/24hr, **food**: Bob Evans, Coney Island, DQ, Firkin & Fox Rest., McDonald's, Mancino's/SaLoupes, Subway, Walli's Rest., **lodging**: Super 8, **other**: Belle Tire, $Tree, Hungry Howies, Meijer, Office Depot, Saab, Target, TJ Maxx, vet |
| 138 | MI 54, Dort Hwy, **N gas**: BP/24hr, Speedway/dsl, Sunoco/dsl, **food**: Big John's Rest., KFC, Little Caesar's, YaYa's Chicken, **other**: ⊞ HOSPITAL, $General, KanRock Tires, Rite Aid, Walgreens, **S gas**: Marathon, Speedway, Sunoco, **food**: Arby's, Big John's Steaks, Burger King, Carl's BBQ, China Empress, Coney Island, El Potrero, KFC, McDonald's, Subway, Taco Bell, **lodging**: Genessee Inn, Travel Inn, **other**: Aamco, Advance Parts, AutoZone, BigLots, Cadillac/Pontiac, $General, Family$, Goodyear, K-Mart, Rite Aid, 7-11, U-Haul, Walgreen |
| 137 | I-475, UAW Fwy, to Detroit, Saginaw |
| 136 | Saginaw St, Flint, **N gas**: Sunoco, **other**: ⊞ HOSPITAL, U MI at Flint, **S other**: ExpertTire, GMC |
| 135 | Hammerberg Rd, industrial area |
| 133b a | I-75, S to Detroit, N to Saginaw, US 23 S to Ann Arbor |
| 131 | MI 121, to Bristol Rd, **1/2 mi N** on **Miller Rd gas**: Speedway, **food**: Chili's, ChuckeCheese, Golden Moon Chinese, Halo Burger, LJ Silver, Logan's Roadhouse, Old Country Buffet, Outback Steaks, Ruby Tuesday, Subway, Taco Bell, Valley Diner, **other**: Best Buy, BigLots, Borders Books, Circuit City, Discount Tire, $Tree, Firestone/auto, Gander Mtn, JC Penney, Jo-Ann Fabrics, Macy's, Michael's, Sears/auto, TJ Maxx, mall |
| 129 | Miller Rd, **S gas**: Marathon, **food**: Arby's, Burger King, McDonald's, Wendy's, **other**: Kroger/gas |
| 128 | Morrish Rd, **S gas**: Admiral/24hr, BP/dsl/24hr, **other**: Sports Creek Horse Racing |
| **126mm** | **rest area eb, full ♿ facilities, info, 🚻, ☕, litter barrels, petwalk** |
| 123 | MI 13, to Saginaw, Lennon, **N gas**: Speedway/dsl |
| 118 | MI 71, to Corunna, Durand, **N** st police, **S gas**: Shell/dsl, Sunoco, **food**: McDonald's, Subway, Wendy's, **lodging**: Quality Inn, Sunset Motel (1.5), **other**: Ace Hardware, Carter's Foods, Chevrolet/Pontiac, Family$, Rite Aid, golf |
| **115mm** | Shiawassee River |
| 113 | Bancroft, **S gas**: BP/dsl, **other**: RV camping |
| 105 | MI 52, to Owosso, Perry, **S gas**: Citgo, Mobil, 7-11/gas, Sunoco/Subway/dsl, **food**: Burger King, Café Sports, McDonald's, Taco Bell, **lodging**: Heb's Inn, **other**: Family$, Ford, IGA Foods, Rite Aid, RV camping, truck repair (1mi) |
| **101mm** | **rest area wb, full ♿ facilities, 🚻, ☕, litter barrels, petwalk** |
| **98.5mm** | Looking Glass River |

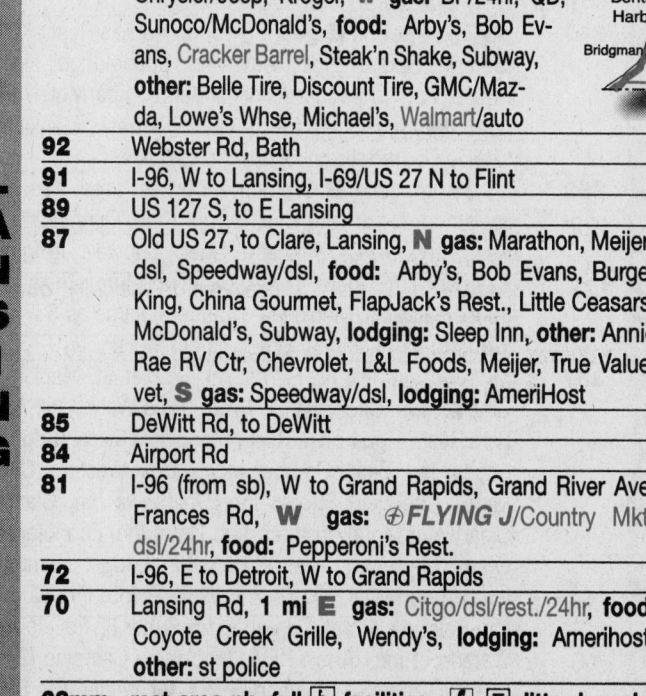

N ↑ ↓ S

**L A N S I N G**

## INTERSTATE 69 CONT'D

| | |
|---|---|
| **98** | Woodbury Rd, to Laingsburg, Shaftsburg, **S** RV camping |
| **95** | I-496, to Lansing |
| **94** | Lp 69, Marsh Rd, to E Lansing, Okemos, **S** **gas:** Admiral/dsl, Speedway/DQ/dsl, **food:** McDonald's, **other:** Gillett RV Ctr, SavALot |
| **93b a** | MI 43, Lp 69, Saginaw Hwy, to Grand Ledge, **E** **gas:** Meijer/dsl/24hr, **food:** Bennigan's, Burger King, Denny's, McDonald's, North Pine Grill, TGIFriday, **lodging:** Best Western, Fairfield Inn, Hampton Inn, Holiday Inn, Motel 6, Quality Suites, Red Roof Inn, Residence Inn, **other:** H HOSPITAL, 1 mi **E** **gas:** Shell, Speedway/dsl, **food:** Carrabba's, Outback Steaks, **other:** Chrysler/Jeep, Kroger, **W** **gas:** BP/24hr, QD, Sunoco/McDonald's, **food:** Arby's, Bob Evans, Cracker Barrel, Steak'n Shake, Subway, **other:** Belle Tire, Discount Tire, GMC/Mazda, Lowe's Whse, Michael's, Walmart/auto |
| **92** | Webster Rd, Bath |
| **91** | I-96, W to Lansing, I-69/US 27 N to Flint |
| **89** | US 127 S, to E Lansing |
| **87** | Old US 27, to Clare, Lansing, **N** **gas:** Marathon, Meijer/dsl, Speedway/dsl, **food:** Arby's, Bob Evans, Burger King, China Gourmet, FlapJack's Rest., Little Ceasars, McDonald's, Subway, **lodging:** Sleep Inn, **other:** Annie Rae RV Ctr, Chevrolet, L&L Foods, Meijer, True Value, vet, **S** **gas:** Speedway/dsl, **lodging:** AmeriHost |
| **85** | DeWitt Rd, to DeWitt |
| **84** | Airport Rd |
| **81** | I-96 (from sb), W to Grand Rapids, Grand River Ave, Frances Rd, **W** **gas:** ✈FLYING J/Country Mkt/dsl/24hr, **food:** Pepperoni's Rest. |
| **72** | I-96, E to Detroit, W to Grand Rapids |
| **70** | Lansing Rd, 1 mi **E** **gas:** Citgo/dsl/rest./24hr, **food:** Coyote Creek Grille, Wendy's, **lodging:** Amerihost, **other:** st police |
| **68mm** | rest area nb, full ♿ facilities, 📞, 🦺, litter barrels, vending, petwalk |
| **66** | MI 100, to Grand Ledge, Potterville, **W** **gas:** BP, Shell/Subway, **food:** McDonald's, to Fox Co Park |
| **61** | Lansing Rd, **E** **food:** Applebee's, **lodging:** Comfort Inn, Crestview Motel, **other:** AutoZone, |

**M A R S H A L L**

| | |
|---|---|
| **61** | Continued Chevrolet/Buick/Pontiac/GMC, Chrysler/Jeep/Dodge, $Tree, Walmart SuperCtr/Subway/24hr, **W** **gas:** Speedway, QD, **food:** Arby's, Big Boy, Blimpie, Burger King, KFC, Little Caesar's, McDonald's, Pizza Hut, Taco Bell, Top Chinese, Wendy's, **other:** H HOSPITAL, Advance Parts, CarQuest, Family$, Ford/Mercury, Geldhof Tire/auto, Jo-Ann Fabrics, Radio Shack, TrueValue |
| **60** | MI 50, Charlotte, **E** **gas:** Meijer/dsl/24hr, **lodging:** Holiday Inn Express, **W** **gas:** Admiral, **lodging:** Super 8, **other:** H HOSPITAL, RV camping |
| **57** | Lp 69, Cochran Rd, to Charlotte, **E** RV camping |
| **51** | Ainger Rd, 1 mi **E** access to gas, food, RV camping |
| **48** | MI 78, to Bellevue, Olivet, 1 mi **E** **gas:** Citgo/Subway, **other:** to Olivet Coll |
| **42** | N Drive N, Turkeyville Rd, **W** **food:** Cornwell's Rest. (1mi) |
| **41mm** | rest area sb, full ♿ facilities, 📞, 🦺, litter barrels, petwalk |
| **38** | I-94, E to Detroit, W to Chicago |
| **36** | Michigan Ave, to Marshall, **E** **gas:** Admiral, Marathon, Shell/Subway, **food:** Applebee's, Arby's, Beaner's, Burger King, Little Caesar, McDonald's, Pizza Hut, |

MI

## INTERSTATE 69 CONT'D

**N ↕ S**

**36** Continued
Taco Bell, Schuler's Rest., Wendy's, Yin Hai Chinese, **lodging:** AmeriHost, **other:** Ⓗ HOSPITAL, AutoZone, Chevrolet, $General, $Tree, Felpausch Foods, GNC, K-Mart, NAPA, Radio Shack, Rite Aid, Sav-a-Lot Foods, **W lodging:** Arbor Inn, **other:** Chrysler/Dodge/Jeep

**32** F Drive S, **E gas:** Shell (3/4 mi) **food:** Moonraker Rest. (3mi), **W other:** RV Camping

**25** MI 60, to Three Rivers, Jackson, **E gas:** BP/dsl, Citgo/Te-Kon/Norma's/dsl/scales/24hr, Sunoco/dsl, **food:** McDonald's, **other:** NAPA Truck Care, RV camping

**23** Tekonsha, **E gas:** Citgo, **W** access to RV camping

**16** Jonesville Rd, **W** Waffle Farm Camping (2mi)

**13** US 12, to Quincy, Coldwater, **E gas:** Meijer/dsl/24hr, Speedway/dsl, **food:** Applebee's, Bob Evans, Grand Buffet, Subway, **lodging:** Hampton Inn, Red Roof Inn, **other:** Aldi Foods, AutoZone, BigLots, Chevrolet/Cadillac, $Tree, GNC, Home Depot, N Country RV Ctr, Radio Shack, SavALot, Walmart SuperCtr, **W gas:** BP/24hr, Citgo, Speedway/dsl, **food:** Arby's, Benedict's Steaks, Big Boy, Burger King, Coldwater Garden Rest., KFC, Little Caesar's, McDonald's, Pizza Hut, Ponderosa, Subway, Taco Bell, Wendy's, **lodging:** Cadet Motel, Comfort Inn, Holiday Inn Express, Super 8, **other:** Ⓗ HOSPITAL, Advance Parts, Ford/Lincoln/Mercury, Rite Aid, Walgreens, st police

**10** Lp 69, Fenn Rd, to Coldwater

**8mm** weigh sta nb

**6mm** **Welcome Ctr nb, full** ♿ **facilities,** Ⓒ, ⛽, **litter barrels, vending, petwalk**

**3** Copeland Rd, Kinderhook, **W gas:** BP, **food:** camping

**0mm** Michigan/Indiana state line

## INTERSTATE 75

| Exit # | Services |
|---|---|
| **395mm** | US/Canada Border, Michigan state line, I-75 begins/ends at toll bridge to Canada |

**394** Easterday Ave, **E gas:** Citgo/dsl, **food:** McDonald's, **lodging:** Holiday Inn Express, **other:** to Lake Superior St U, **W** Welcome Ctr/rest area, info, **gas:** Admiral/dsl, Holiday/dsl/currency exchange, **lodging:** Ramada Inn (2mi)

**392** 3 Mile Rd, Sault Ste Marie, **E gas:** Admiral/dsl, BP/dsl, Holiday/dsl, Shell, USA/dsl/24hr, **food:** Abner's Rest., Ang-Gio's Rest., Applebee's, Arby's, Burger King, Country Kitchen, DQ, Great Wall Chinese, Jeff's Café, KFC, Little Caesar's, McDonald's, Pizza Hut, Quizno's, Studebaker's Rest., Subway, Taco Bell, Wendy's, **lodging:** Best Value, Best Western, Comfort Inn, Day's Inn, Hampton Inn, Park Inn, Plaza Motel, Quality Inn, Skyline Motel, Super 8, **other:** Ⓗ HOSPITAL, Advance Parts, Auto Value Parts, BigLots, Buick/Cadillac, Chevrolet/Pontiac, $Tree, Family$, Glen's Mkt, JC Penney, Jo-Ann Fabrics, K-Mart, NAPA, Radio Shack, Sav-A-Lot, Walgreens, Walmart/Subway, st police, Soo Locks Boat Tours

**389mm** **rest area nb, full** ♿ **facilities, info,** Ⓒ, ⛽, **litter barrels, petwalk**

**386** MI 28, **E lodging:** Cedar Log Motel/rest., **W** to Brimley SP

**379** Gaines Hwy, **E** to Barbeau Area, Clear Lake Camping

**378** MI 80, Kinross, **E gas:** BP/dsl, **food:** Frank&Jim's Diner, **other:** RV West Camping, to Kinross Correctional, ✈, golf

**373** MI 48, Rudyard, **2 mi W** gas/dsl, food, lodging

**359** MI 134, to Drummond Island

**352** MI 123, to Moran, Newberry

**348** H63, to Sault Reservation, St Ignace, **0-2 mi E gas:** Spirit Gas, **food:** Dockside Steaks, Hillside Rest., **lodging:** Bear Cove Inn, Best Value, Birchwood Motel, Budget Host, Comfort Inn, Cedars Motel, Days Inn, Evergreen Motel, Holiday Inn Express, Kewadin Inn, North Bay Inn, NorthernAire Motel, Pines Motel, Quality Inn, Royale Inn, Tradewinds Motel, **other:** Tiki RV Park, st police, to Mackinac Trail, casino, **W** Castle Rock Gifts

**346mm** **rest area/scenic turnout sb, full** ♿ **facilities,** ⛽, **litter barrels, petwalk**

**345** Portage St (from sb), St Ignace

**344b** US 2 W, **W gas:** BP/dsl/rest./24hr, Holiday/dsl, Shell/dsl/24hr, **food:** Big Boy, Burger King, McDonald's, Subway, Suzy's Pasties, **lodging:** 4 Star Motel, Quality Inn, Sunset Motel, Super 8, **other:** Ford, KOA

**344a** Lp 75, St Ignace, **0-2 mi E gas:** Shell, **food:** BC Pizza, Flame Rest., Galley Rest., Mackinac Grille, Marina Rest., Northern Lights Rest., Pizza Guy's, **lodging:** Aurora Borealis Motel, Bentley's Cafe, Boardwalk Inn, Colonial House, Comfort Inn, Days Inn, Econolodge, Holiday Inn Express, Moran Bay Motel, Normandy Motel, Quality Inn, Thunderbird Motel, Village Inn/rest., Voyager Motel, **other:** Ⓗ HOSPITAL, Ace Hardware, Bay Drug, Family$, Glen's Mkt, Radio Shack, TrueValue, USPO, to Island Ferrys, Straits SP, KOA, st police, **E** KOA

**343mm** toll booth to toll bridge, **E** Welcome Ctr nb, full ♿ facilities, Ⓒ, ⛽, litter barrels, **W** museum

**341mm** toll bridge, Lake Huron, Lake Michiganc

**339** US 23, Jamet St, **E gas:** BP, **food:** Audie's Rest., KFC, **lodging:** Budget Host, Days Inn, Econolodge, LightHouse View Motel, Parkside Motel, Riviera Motel, Super 8, **W gas:** Shell, **food:** Darrow's Rest., Mackinaw Cookie Co, **lodging:** Holiday Inn Express

**338** US 23 (from sb), **E** Welcome Ctr/rest area, **gas:** BP, Marathon, **food:** Big Boy, Burger King, Cunningham's Rest., DQ, KFC, Pancake Chef, Subway, **lodging:** Baymont Inn, Chalet Motel, Courtyard Inn, **other:** IGA Foods/supplies, Mackinaw Outfitters, same as 337, **W lodging:** Ft Mackinaw Motel, Vindel Motel

**337** MI 108 (from nb, no EZ return), Nicolet St, Mackinaw City, **E gas:** Citgo/dsl/LP, **food:** Blue Water Grill, Embers Rest., Lighthouse Rest., Mancino's Pizza, **lodging:** Anchor Inn, BeachComber Motel, Best Western, Capri Motel, Cherokee Shores Inn, Chippewa Inn, Clarion, Clearwater Motel, Comfort Inn, Day's Inn, Econolodge, Grand Mackinaw Resort, Hamilton Lodge, Hampton Inn, Huron Motel, Nicolet Inn, NorthPointe Inn, Quality Inn, Rainbow Motel, Ramada Ltd, Super 8, Travelodge, Waterfront Inn, **other:** KOA, Mackinaw Camping (2mi), Old Mill Creek SP, to Island Ferrys, **W** Wilderness SP

**336** US 31 S (from sb), to Petoskey

**328mm** **rest area sb, full** ♿ **facilities, info,** Ⓒ, ⛽, **litter barrels, petwalk**

**326** C66, to Cheboygan, **E gas:** Marathon, **other:** Ⓗ HOSPITAL, Sea Shell City/gifts, **other:** st police

**SAULT STE MARIE**

**MACKINAW CITY**

**MI**

## INTERSTATE 75 CONT'D

**N ⇅ S**

**322** C64, to Cheboygan, **E** **H** HOSPITAL, LP, ✈, st police

**317mm** rest area/scenic turnout nb, full ♿ facilities, info, 🚻, 🔥, litter barrels, petwalk

**313** MI 27 N, Topinabee, **E** **lodging:** Johnson Motel, Indian River RV Resort/Camping

**311mm** Indian River

**310** MI 33, MI 68, **E** **lodging:** Holiday Inn Express, **other:** Jellystone Park (3mi), **W** **gas:** BP/dsl, Ken's Gas, Shell/McDonald's/24hr, **food:** Burger King, DQ, Paula's Cafe, Subway, **lodging:** Coach House Motel, **other:** Ken's Mkt, to Indian River Trading Post/RV Resort, to Burt Lake SP

**301** C58, Wolverine, **E** **gas:** Marathon/dsl, **food:** Whistle Stop Rest., **other:** Elkwood Campground (5mi), **W** **other:** Sturgin River Campground (3mi)

**297mm** Sturgeon River

**290** Vanderbilt, **E** **gas:** BP/dsl/LP/RV dump, Spirit Gas, **other:** Village Mkt Foods, auto repair, **W** **gas:** Mobil/dsl

**287mm** rest area sb, full ♿ facilities, info, 🚻, 🔥, litter barrels

**282** MI 32, Gaylord, **E** **gas:** Amoco/dsl, Citgo, Clark, Holiday/24hr, Mobil, Speedway/dsl, **food:** Arby's, Burger King, DQ, KFC, La Senorita Mexican, McDonald's, Quizno's, Subway, TCBY, Wendy's, **lodging:** Baymont Inn, Best Western, Comfort Inn, Quality Inn, Red Roof Inn, **other:** **H** HOSPITAL, Advance Parts, Glen's Foods, Harley-Davidson, Rite Aid, st police, **W** **gas:** BP, Citgo/dsl, Marathon/dsl, Mobil/dsl, Shell/dsl, **food:** Applebee's, BC Pizza, Big Boy, Bob Evans, China 1, Little Caesar's, Mama Leone's Rest., Mancino's Pizza, Pizza Hut, Ponderosa, Ruby Tuesday, Spicy Bob's Italian, Taco Bell, **lodging:** Day's Inn, Gaylord Travel Inn, Hampton Inn, Holiday Inn Express, **other:** BigLots, Burnside RV Ctr, Chrysler/Dodge/Jeep, Dayton Tire, $Tree, GNC, Home Depot, K-Mart, Lowe's Whse, Radio Shack, Save-A-Lot Foods, Walmart SuperCtr/Subway, RV camping, transmissions, tires

**279mm** *45th Parallel halfway between the equator and north pole*

**279** Old US 27, Gaylord, **E** **gas:** Marathon/Subway/dsl, Mobil/dsl, Shell, **food:** Burger King, Mama Leone's, **lodging:** Gaylord Inn, **other:** Chevrolet, Chrysler/Jeep/Nissan, Ford/Lincoln/Mercury, Pontiac/Buick/GMC, RV Ctr, st police, **W** **lodging:** Bennthums Inn, Marsh Ridge Motel (2mi), KOA (3mi)

**277mm** rest area nb, full ♿ facilities, info, 🚻, 🔥, litter barrels, petwalk

**270** Waters, **E** **gas:** BP/dsl, **food:** Hilltop Rest., **W** lodging, Waters Inn, **other:** IGA/gas, RV repair, Waters RV Ctr, USPO, to Otsego Lake SP

**264** Lewiston, Frederic, **W** access to food, lodging, camping

**262mm** rest area sb, full ♿ facilities, 🚻, 🔥, litter barrels, petwalk

**259** MI 93, **E** Hartwick Pines SP, **2-4 mi W** **lodging:** Fay's Motel, North Country Lodge, Pointe North Motel, River Country Motel, Woodland Motel, **other:** Chevrolet/Pontiac/Cadillac, Chrysler/Dodge/Jeep, Curves, Timberly Village RV Park, auto repair

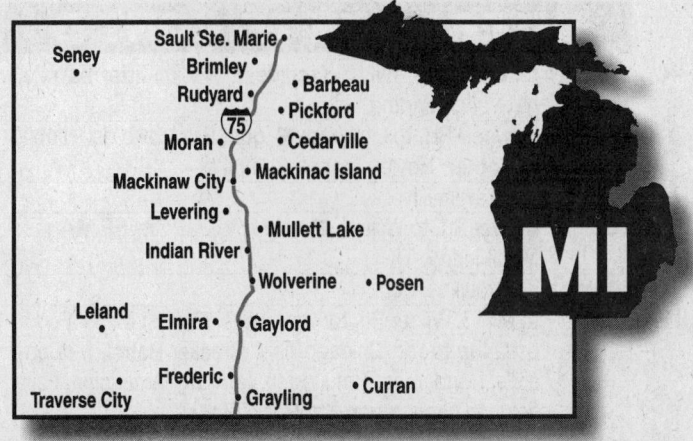

**GAYLORD** (vertical label, left margin)

**GRAYLING** (vertical label, right column)

**256** (from sb), to MI 72, Grayling, access to same as 254

**254** MI 72 (exits left from nb, no return), Grayling, **1 mi W** **gas:** Admiral Gas/dsl, BP, Citgo/7-11, Clark, Shell, Speedway, Valero, **food:** Big Boy, Burger King, DQ, KFC, McDonald's, Moose Rest., Pizza Hut, Subway, Taco Bell, Wendy's, **lodging:** Day's Inn, Ramada, **other:** **H** HOSPITAL, Ace Hardware, Auto Value Parts, $General, Family$, Ford/Lincoln/Mercury, Glen's Foods/24hr, K-Mart, NAPA, Rite Aid, Save-a-Lot Foods

**251mm** rest area nb, full ♿ facilities, info, 🚻, 🔥, litter barrels, petwalk, vending

**251** 4 Mile Rd, **E** Jellystone RV Park (5mi), skiing, **W** **gas:** Marathon/Arby's/dsl/scales/RV Dump/24hr, **lodging:** Super 8

**249** US 127 S (from sb), to Clare

**244** MI 18, Roscommon, **3.5 mi E** **gas:** BP, **food:** McDonald's, **W** **gas:** Valero/dsl, **other:** N Higgins Lake SP, camping, museum

**239** MI 18, Roscommon, S Higgins Lake SP, **E** **other:** gas, food, lodging, camping

**235mm** rest area sb, full ♿ facilities, 🚻, info, 🔥, litter barrels, petwalk, vending

**227** MI 55 W, rd F97, to Houghton Lake, **5 mi W** food

**222** Old 76, to St Helen, **5 mi E** food, lodging, camping

**215** MI 55 E, West Branch, **E** **gas:** Citgo/dsl, **food:** Willow Tree Rest. (2mi), **other:** **H** HOSPITAL

**212** MI 55, West Branch, **E** **gas:** Marathon/7-11, Shell/Subway, **food:** Applebee's, Arby's, Big Boy, Burger King, Lumberjack Rest., McDonald's, Ponderosa, Taco Bell, Wendy's, **lodging:** Quality Inn/rest., Super 8, **other:** **H** HOSPITAL, Home Depot, Tanger Outlet/famous brands, Walmart SuperCtr/Subway/gas, st police, **W** **gas:** BP/dsl

**210mm** rest area nb, full ♿ facilities, info, 🚻, 🔥, litter barrels, petwalk, vending

**202** MI 33, to Rose City, Alger, **E** **gas:** BP/Narski's Mkt/jerky, Mobil/dsl/jerky outlet (1/2mi), Shell/Subway, **other:** camping

**201mm** rest area sb, full ♿ facilities, 🚻, 🔥, litter barrels, petwalk, vending

**195** Sterling Rd, to Sterling, **6 mi E** gas, camping

**190** MI 61, to Standish, **E** **other:** **H** HOSPITAL, Standish Correctional, **W** **gas:** Marathon, Mobil/jerky

**188** US 23, to Standish, **2-3 mi E** gas, food, camping

**181** Pinconning Rd, **E** **gas:** Mobil, Shell/McDonald's/dsl, **food:** Cheesehouse Diner, **lodging:** Pinconning Inn (2mi), **other:** Pinconning Camping, **W** **gas:** Sunoco/pizza/dsl/24hr

MI

## INTERSTATE 75 CONT'D

**N** ↕ **S**

**SAGINAW**

| | |
|---|---|
| **175mm** | rest area nb, full ♿ facilities, 🚻, ⛽, litter barrels, petwalk, vending |
| **173** | Linwood Rd, to Linwood, **E gas:** BP/Arby's/dsl, Mobil/dsl, **other:** Hoyle's Marina Camping |
| **171mm** | Kawkawlin River |
| **168** | Beaver Rd, to Willard, **E other:** to Bay City SP, **W gas:** Mobil/jerky |
| **166mm** | Kawkawlin River |
| **164** | to MI 13, Wilder Rd, to Kawkawlin, **E gas:** Meijer Food/dsl/24hr, **food:** Chicago Grill, Cracker Barrel, McDonald's, Ponderosa, Tim Horton, **lodging:** AmericInn, Fairfield Inn (3mi), **other:** KanRock Tire |
| **162b a** | US 10, MI 25, to Midland, **E** Ⓗ HOSPITAL |
| **160** | MI 84, Delta, **E gas:** Mobil/Subway/dsl, Shell, **W gas:** Citgo/7-11, Speedway, **food:** Berger's Rest., Burger King, KFC/Taco Bell, McDonald's, **lodging:** Econolodge, **other:** RV World Super Ctr, to Saginaw Valley Coll |
| **158mm** | rest area sb, full ♿ facilities, 🚻, ⛽, litter barrels, vending, petwalk |
| **155** | I-675 S, to downtown Saginaw, **4 mi W food:** OutBack Steaks, **lodging:** Hampton Inn, Super 8 |
| **154** | to Zilwaukee |
| **153mm** | Saginaw River |
| **153** | MI 13 E Bay City Rd, Saginaw, **2-3 mi W** lodging |
| **151** | MI 81, to Reese, Caro, **E gas:** Sunoco/Burger King/dsl, **other:** GMC/Volvo Trucks, **W gas:** ⊕FLYING J/Wendy's/dsl/LP/24hr |
| **150** | I-675 N, to downtown Saginaw, **6 mi W food:** OutBack Steaks, **lodging:** Hampton Inn, Super 8 |
| **149b a** | MI 46, Holland Ave, to Saginaw, **W gas:** Admiral, Marathon, Speedway/dsl, Sunoco, **food:** Arby's, Big John's Steaks, Burger King, McDonald's, Subway, Taco Bell, Texan Rest., **lodging:** Best Western, Motel 6, Super 7 Inn, **other:** Ⓗ HOSPITAL, Advance Parts, Save-A-Lot Foods, USPO |
| **144b a** | Bridgeport, **E gas:** Marathon/Subway/dsl, Shell/Blimpie, Speedway/dsl/24hr, **food:** Bavarian Rest., **other:** Jellystone Camping (9mi), **W gas:** Mobil, TA/Country Pride/dsl/scales/24hr/@, **food:** Arby's, Big Boy, Cracker Barrel, Little Caesar's, McDonald's, Peking City, Subway, Taco Bell, Wendy's, **lodging:** Baymont Inn, Knight's Inn, **other:** Curves, Family$, Kroger, st police |
| **143mm** | Cass River |
| **136** | MI 54, MI 83, Birch Run, **E gas:** Mejier, Mobil/dsl/24hr, **food:** Dixie Rest., Exit Rest., Halo Burger, KFC, Subway, **lodging:** Best Western, Comfort Inn, Hampton Inn, Holiday Inn Express, Super 8, **other:** CarQuest, Dixie Speedway, General RV ctr, **W gas:** Marathon, 7-11/gas, Sunoco/dsl, **food:** A&W, Arby's, Applebee's, Big Boy, Bob Evans, Culver's, DQ, Little Caesar's, McDonald's, Quizno's, Starbucks, Taco Bell, Tony's Rest., Uno Pizzaria, Victor & Merek's Pizza, Wendy's, **lodging:** Country Inn Suites, **other:** Birch Run Drugs, Chevrolet/Buick/Suzuki, Old Navy, Prime Outlet/famous brands |
| **131** | MI 57, to Montrose, **E gas:** Mobil/dsl, Shell, Sunoco, **food:** Arby's, Big John's Steaks, Burger King, DQ, KFC, McDonald's, Subway, Taco Bell, Twins Pizza, Wendy's, **other:** AutoZone, Chevrolet, Chrysler/Dodge/Jeep, Ford, KanRock Tire, K-Mart, **W gas:** BP/dsl, |

**MI**

| | |
|---|---|
| **131** | Continued Mobil/dsl, **food:** Big Boy, **other:** Walmart SuperCtr/gas |
| **129mm** | rest area both lanes, full ♿ facilities, 🚻, ⛽, litter barrels, vending, petwalk |
| **126** | to Mt Morris, **E gas:** B&B/Burger King/dsl/24hr, **W gas:** BP/dsl, carwash |
| **125** | I-475 S, UAW Fwy, to Flint |
| **122** | Pierson Rd, to Flint, **E gas:** BP, Marathon/dsl, **food:** McDonald's, Papa's Coney's, Subway, **lodging:** Econolodge, **other:** Goodyear, Kroger/gas, Murray's Parts, **W gas:** Citgo, Meijer/dsl/24hr, Shell/dsl, **food:** A&W/KFC, Arby's, Big John's Steaks, Bob Evans, Burger King, Cantonese Buffet, Cottage Pizza, Cracker Barrel, Denny's, Halo Burger, LJ Silver, Pizza Hut, Red Lobster, Taco Bell, Tim Horton, Wendy's, YaYa Chicken, **lodging:** Baymont Inn, Great Western Inn, **other:** Discount Tire, $Tree, Home Depot |
| **118** | MI 21, Corunna Rd, **E gas:** Sunoco, **food:** Badawest Lebanese, Big John's Steaks, Burger King, Halo Burger, Hungry Howie's, Little Caesar's, Starbucks, Taco Bell, Wingfong Chinese, YaYa Chicken, Wing Fong Chinese, **other:** Ⓗ HOSPITAL, Advance Parts, $General, Kroger/gas, Rite Aid, 7-11, **W gas:** BP/dsl, Citgo, Mobil, Shell/Wendy's, Speedway, Valero, **food:** A&W/KFC, Big Eazy Grill, Burger King, Domino's, Fazoli's, Happy Valley Rest., Krispy Kreme, McDonald's, Subway, White Castle, **lodging:** Economy Motel, **other:** Aldi Foods, AutoZone, Buick, CarQuest, $General, GMC, Home Depot, Kroger/gas, Lincoln/Mercury, Lowe's Whse, Rite Aid, Sam's Club/gas, VG's Foods, Walgreens, Walmart SuperCtr/auto, st police |
| **117b** | Miller Rd, to Flint, **E gas:** Speedway/dsl, Sunoco/dsl, **food:** Applebee's, Arby's, Cottage Pizza, Don Pablo, Fuddrucker's, KFC, LoneStar Steaks, McDonald's, Papa John's, Qdoba, Subway, West Side Diner, **lodging:** Comfort Inn, Motel 6, Sleep Inn, **other:** Belle Tire, K-Mart, **W gas:** BP, Marathon, **food:** BD's BBQ, Bob Evans, Chili's, ChuckeCheese, Coney Island, Famous Dave's, Fire Mtn Grill, Golden Moon, Honey Baked Ham, Hooters, Italia Garden, Logan's Roadhouse, Moe's SW Grill, Old Country Buffet, Olive Garden, Outback Steaks, Pizza Hut, Rib City, Quizno's, Red Robin, Salvatori's Ristorante, Starbucks, Subway, Taco Bell, **lodging:** Red Roof Inn, Super 8, **other:** Barnes & Noble, Best Buy, BigLots, Borders Books, Circuit City, Discount Tire, Dodge, Gander Mtn, Goodyear, JC Penney, Jo-Ann Fabrics, Macy's, Office Depot, Old Navy, PetCo, Radio Shack, Ross, Sears/auto, Target, U-Haul, Valley Tire, mall, vet |
| **117a** | I-69, E to Lansing, W to Port Huron |
| **116** | MI 121, Bristol Rd, **E gas:** Citgo, Speedway/dsl, **food:** Coney Island, KFC, McDonald's, **lodging:** Day's Inn, Rodeway Inn, **other:** AutoZone, **W gas:** Mobil/dsl, **other:** ✈ |
| **115** | US 23 (from sb), **W on Hill Rd gas:** Citgo, Meijer/dsl/24hr, Mobil, **food:** Hill St Grill, Maxie's Rest., McDonald's, Redwood Lodge, Turkey Farm Deli, **lodging:** AmericInn, Courtyard, Holiday Inn, Residence Inn |
| **111** | I-475 N (from nb), UAW Fwy, to Flint |
| **109** | MI 54, Dort Hwy (no EZ return to sb), **1-2 mi E gas:** Marathon/dsl, **food:** Big Boy, Brick St Grill, Damon's, Starbucks, Wendy's |

**FLINT**

## INTERSTATE 75 CONT'D

**N ↑↓ S**

**108** Holly Rd, to Grand Blanc, **E gas:** Sunoco/dsl, **food:** Big Apple Bagels, Da Edoardo Ristorante, Quizno's, **lodging:** Comfort Inn, Holiday Inn Express, **other:** BMW/Mercedes/Toyota, **W gas:** BP/McDonald's./dsl, **food:** Arby's, **other:** H HOSPITAL

**106** Dixie Hwy (exits left from sb, no nb return), Saginaw Rd, to Grand Blanc

**101** Grange Hall Rd, Ortonville, **E gas:** Sunoco, **other:** Holly RA, Jellystone Park, st police, **W gas:** Mobil/dsl, **other:** to Seven Lakes/Groveland Oaks SP, RV camping

**98** E Holly Rd, **E gas:** Mobil/Subway/dsl/24hr, **other:** Ford, golf

**96mm** rest area both lanes, full & facilities, ⊞ litter barrels, info, ℂ, vending, petwalk

**95mm** rest area both lanes, full & facilities, ⊞ litter barrels, info, ℂ, vending, petwalk

**93** US 24, Dixie Hwy, Waterford, **E gas:** BP/dsl, **other:** Dodge, Kroger/gas (2mi), Saturn, **1-3 mi W gas:** Speedway, **food:** Big Boy, McDonald's, Subway, Taco Bell, Wendy's, **other:** Chrysler/Jeep, Walgreens, to Pontiac Lake RA

**91** MI 15, Davison, Clarkston, **E gas:** Sunoco/dsl, **food:** Bullfrog's (5mi), Subway (5mi), **other:** camping, **W gas:** Shell/dsl, **food:** Brioni Grill, Clarkston Grill, DQ, Mesquite Creek Café, **other:** H HOSPITAL, Rite Aid (2mi)

**89** Sashabaw Rd, **E gas:** Shell/dsl, **food:** Culvers, Ruby Tuesday, **other:** county park, **W gas:** BP/24hr, Citgo, **food:** Caribou Coffee, Chicken Shack, Coney Island, E Ocean Chinese, Guido's Pizza, Hong Kong Chinese, Hungry Howie's, Little Caesars, Marble Slab, McDonald's, Nina's Cafe, Quizno's, Subway, Renderonis Pizza, Rio Wraps, Wendy's, **other:** CVS Drug, GNC, Kroger, vet

**86mm** weigh sta sb, parking area nb

**84b a** Baldwin Ave, **E gas:** Shell/24hr, Sunoco/dsl, **food:** Arby's, Big Boy, Joe's Crabshack, Longhorn Steaks, Olive Garden, Wendy's, **other:** Best Buy, Costco/gas, Discount Tire, $Castle, Kohl's, Michael's, Old Navy, PetCo, World Mkt, **W gas:** Mobil/24hr, **food:** Chili's, Jimmy John's, Kerry's Coney Island, Max&Erma's, McDonald's, On-the-Border, Oriental Buffet, Quizno's, Rainforest Cafe, Starbucks, Steak'n Shake/24hr, Subway, **other:** Holiday Inn Express, **other:** Bass Pro Shops, Best Buy, Borders Books, Circuit City, Great Lakes Crossing Outlet/famous brands, Marshall's, TJ Maxx, USPO

**83b a** Joslyn Rd, **E gas:** Meijer/dsl/24hr, **food:** Applebee's, Montana's Grill, Olive Garden, **other:** Belle Tire, Home Depot, Jo-Ann Fabrics, Sam's Club/gas, Target, **W gas:** Sunoco

**81** MI 24, Pontiac (no EZ return), **E** The Palace Arena, **1 mi E gas:** BP/24hr

**79** University Dr, **E gas:** BP, **food:** Coney Island, Jimmy John's, Rio Wraps, Subway, **W gas:** Mobil, Speedway/dsl, **food:** A&W/KFC, Arby's, Burger King, Lelli's Steaks, Mtn Jack's Rest., McDonald's, Taco Bell, Wendy's/Tim Horton, **lodging:** Candlewood Suites, Comfort Suites, Courtyard, Extended Stay America, Extended Stay Deluxe, Fairfield Inn, Hampton Inn, Hilton, Holiday Inn, Hyatt, Motel 6, Staybridge Suites, Wingate Inn, **other:** H HOSPITAL, GM

**DETROIT AREA**

**78** Chrysler Dr, **E other:** Chrysler, Chrysler Museum, Oakland Tech Ctr

**77b a** MI 59, to Pontiac, **2 mi on Adams E other:** Walmart/auto, **1 mi W on Opdyke...gas:** Fastrack/Tubby's/dsl, Shell

**75** Square Lake Rd (exits left from nb), to Pontiac, **W** H HOSPITAL, St Mary's Coll

**74** Adams Rd

**72** Crooks Rd, to Troy, **W food:** Bangkok Bisrto, Coney Island, Nobana Japanese, Quizno's, Red Robin, Starbucks, **lodging:** Embassy Suites, Hilton

**69** Big Beaver Rd, **E food:** Champp's Grill, Shula's Steaks, TGIFriday's, **lodging:** Drury Inn, Marriott, **other: W gas:** BP, **food:** Benihana, Maggiano's Italian, Melting Pot Rest., Morton's Steaks, Ruth's Chris Steaks, **other:** mall

**67** Rochester Rd, to Stevenson Hwy, **E gas:** Marathon, Shell, **food:** Arby's, Burger King, Caribou Coffee, Coney Island, Hooter's, Hungry Howies, Mr Pita, Orchid Rest., Panera Bread, Pizza Hut/Taco Bell, Qdoba, Ram's Horn Rest., Tubby's Grill, **other:** Discount Tire, Nordstrom's, Office Depot, PetsMart, Radio Shack, transmissions, **W food:** Mtn Jack's Steaks, **lodging:** Holiday Inn, Red Roof Inn, **other:** tires

**65b a** 14 Mile Rd, Madison Heights, **E gas:** Marathon/dsl, Mobil, Shell, **food:** Azteca Mexican, Blimpie, Bob Evans, Burger King, Chili's, Krispy Kreme, Logan's Roadhouse, McDonald's, Panera Bread, Starbucks, Steak'n Shake, Taco Bell, **lodging:** Motel 6, Red Roof Inn, **other:** Belle Tire, Borders Books, Circuit City, Dodge, Ford, Home Depot, JC Penney, Lowe's Whse, Macy's, NAPA, Office Depot, Radio Shack, Sam's Club, Sears/auto, TJ Maxx, World Mkt, mall, **W gas:** Marathon/Dunkin Donuts, Mobil, Speedway, **food:** Antonis Kitchen, Applebee's, Big Fish Seafood, Caribou Coffee, Coney Island, McDonald's, Outback Steaks, Quizno's, **lodging:** Best Western, Courtyard, Econolodge, Extended Stay America, Fairfield Inn, Hampton Inn, Residence Inn, **other:** Chevrolet, Costco/gas, Value Ctr Foods

**63** 12 Mile Rd, **E gas:** Clark, Marathon, **food:** Bellacino's Italian, Blimpie, Green Lantern Rest., Marinelli's Pizza, McDonald's, Red Lobster, Sero's Rest., Starbucks, TX Roadhouse, Tim Horton, **other:** Curves, Home Depot, K-Mart/foods, Lowe's Whse, Radio Shack, auto repair, vet, **W gas:** Marathon/Dunkin Donuts, Speedway, **other:** Chevrolet, Costco/gas

## INTERSTATE 75 CONT'D

**N** ↕ **S**

**DETROIT AREA**

| | |
|---|---|
| **62** | 11 Mile Rd, **E** gas: Mobil, **food:** Boodles Rest., Cottage Pizza, Jets Pizza, **other:** Advance Parts, CVS Drug, 7-11, Walgreens, repair/tires, vet, **W** gas: BP, Marathon/dsl, Mobil, **food:** KFC, Taco Bell, Tim Horton, Tubby's Subs, **other:** Belle Tire |
| **61** | I-696 E, to Port Huron, W to Lansing, to Hazel Park Raceway |
| **60** | 9 Mile Rd, John R St, **E food:** Burger King, Checkers, China 1 Buffet, DQ, Hardee's, McDonald's, Subway, Taco Bell, **lodging:** Days Hotel, **other:** Family$, Kroger, Rite Aid, transmissions, **W** gas: Mobil, **food:** Tubby's Subs, Wendy's, **other:** Hasting's Parts, repair |
| **59** | MI 102, 8 Mile Rd, **3 mi W** st fairgrounds |
| **58** | 7 Mile Rd, **W** gas: BP/dsl |
| **57** | McNichols Rd, **E** gas: Citgo, **food:** Coney Island |
| **56b a** | Davison Fwy |
| **55** | Holbrook Ave, Caniff St, **E** gas: Mobil/dsl **W food:** Coney Island |
| **54** | E Grand Blvd, Clay Ave, **W** gas: BP/dsl, **food:** Coney Island |
| **53b** | I-94, Ford Fwy, to Port Huron, Chicago |
| **53a** | Warren Ave, **E** gas: Mobil, Shell, **W** gas: BP |
| **52** | Mack Ave, **E** gas: Shell, **food:** McDonald's |
| **51c** | I-375 to civic center, tunnel to Canada, downtown |
| **51b** | MI 3 (exits left from nb), Gratiot Ave, downtown |
| **50** | Grand River Ave, downtown |
| **49b** | MI 10, Lodge Fwy, downtown |
| **49a** | Rosa Parks Blvd, **E** Tiger Stadium, **W** gas: Mobil, **other:** Firestone |
| **48** | I-96 begins/ends |
| **47b** | Porter St, **E** bridge to Canada, DutyFree/24hr |
| **47a** | MI 3, Clark Ave, **E** gas: Mobil, **W** gas: Marathon |
| **46** | Livernois Ave, to Hist Ft Wayne, **E** gas: Marathon, **food:** KFC/Taco Bell |
| **45** | Fort St, Springwells Ave, **E** gas: BP/dsl, **W** gas: Mobil, **food:** McDonald's |
| **43b a** | MI 85, Fort St, to Schaefer Hwy, **E** gas: BP Sunoco, **W** gas: Marathon Refinery, **other:** to River Rouge Ford Plant |
| **42** | Outer Dr, **W** gas: BP/Subway/dsl, Mobil/dsl |
| **41** | MI 39, Southfield Rd, to Lincoln Park, **E food:** A&W, Bangkok Star Rest., Bill's Place Rest., Tim Horton, **other:** Walgreens, **W** gas: Marathon, **food:** Dunkin Donuts, **lodging:** Sleep Inn, **other:** Buick, Kroger, Rite Aid |
| **40** | Dix Hwy, **E** gas: Marathon, Meijer, Welcome, **food:** Coney Island Diner, Ponderosa, **other:** CVS Drug, Farmer Jack's, 7-11, **W** gas: Mobil, **food:** Big Boy, Burger King, DQ, Dunkin Donuts, LJ Silver, McDonald's, Pizza Hut, Quizno's, Rally's, Taco Bell, **other:** Belle Tire, Family$, Firestone, CVS Drug, Foodland, Sears/auto |
| **37** | Allen Rd, North Line Rd, to Wyandotte, **E** gas: BP, Marathon, Shell, **food:** Anita's Pizza, Chicken Shack, **lodging:** Holiday Inn, **other:** H HOSPITAL, Sam's Club/gas, **W** gas: Mobil, Sunoco, **food:** Arby's, Burger King, K-Bob House, Mallie's Grill, McDonald's, Wendy's, **lodging:** Best Value Inn, Comfort Suites, La Quinta |
| **36** | Eureka Rd, **E** gas: BP, **food:** Amigo's Mexican, Bob Evans, Denny's, Fire Mtn Grill, Orleans Steaks, **lodging:** Ramada Inn, Super 8, **other:** Vet, **W** gas: |

| | |
|---|---|
| **36** | Continued Meijer/dsl/24hr, Mobil/dsl, **food:** Baker's Square, Big Boy, Culver's, Famous Dave's BBQ, Fuddrucker's, Hooters, KFC/Taco Bell, Mongolian BBQ, Mtn Jack's Steaks, Ruby Tuesday, Subway, Texas Roadhouse, Wendy's, **lodging:** Red Roof Inn, **other:** MEDICAL CTR, Belle Tire, Best Buy, Borders Books, CVS Drug, Discount Tire, Home Depot, JC Penney, Kohl's, Macy's, Staples, mall |
| **35** | US 24, Telegraph Rd, (from nb, exits left) |
| **34b** | Sibley Rd, Riverview, **W** gas: Sunoco/Dunkin Donuts/Subway, **other:** RV Ctr |
| **34a** | to US 24 (from sb), Telegraph Rd |
| **32** | West Rd, to Trenton, Woodhaven, **E** gas: Detroiter/Citgo/dsl/rest., Meijer/dsl/24hr, Speedway/dsl, **food:** Applebees, Bob Evans, Burger King, White Castle, Dunkin Donuts, Panera Bread, Pizza Hut, Quizno's, Steak'n Shake, Subway, Taco Bell, **other:** Chevrolet, Discount Tire, Firestone/auto, Ford, Home Depot, K-Mart, Kroger, Michael's, Office Depot, Radio Shack, Target, Walmart/auto, **W** gas: BP/24hr, Shell, **food:** Andy's Pizza, Domino's, Millie's Rest., McDonald's, **lodging:** Best Western/rest., Knight's Inn, Holiday Inn Express, **other:** SavOn Drug |
| **29** | Gilbralter Rd, to Flat Rock, Lake Erie Metropark, **E** gas: FasTrack/dsl, **food:** McDonald's, **other:** H HOSPITAL, **W** gas: Marathon, **lodging:** Sleep Inn, **other:** Ford, st police |
| **28** | rd 85 (from nb), Fort St, **E** H HOSPITAL |
| **27** | N Huron River Dr, to Rockwood, **E** gas: Marathon/Subway/dsl, **food:** Benito's Pizza, Famous Coney Island, Huron River Rest., Ocean Duck Chinese, **other:** Curves, FoodTown Foods, Rite Aid, **W** gas: Speedway/dsl, **food:** Riverfront Rest. |
| **26** | S Huron River Dr, to S Rockwood, **E** gas: Sunoco/dsl, **food:** Dixie Café, **other:** USPO |
| **21** | Newport Rd, to Newport, **E** gas: BP/Taco Bell/24hr, **W** gas: Marathon/Burger King/dsl/24hr |
| **20** | I-275 N, to Flint |
| **18** | Nadeau Rd, **W** gas: Pilot/Arby's/dsl/24hr/@, **other:** H HOSPITAL, RV camping |
| **15** | MI 50, Dixie Hwy, to Monroe, **E** gas: Shell, **food:** Bob Evans, Burger King, Red Lobster, **lodging:** Best Value Inn, Best Western, Hampton Inn, Travel Inn, **other:** to Sterling SP, **W** gas: Pilot/Subway/dsl/24hr/@, TA/BP/Popéye's/Quizno's/Pizza Hut/dsl/24hr/@, **food:** Big Boy, Cracker Barrel, Denny's, McDonald's, Wendy's, **lodging:** Holiday Inn Express, Knight's Inn, **other:** H HOSPITAL, to Viet Vet Mem |
| **14** | Elm Ave, to Monroe |
| **13** | Front St, Monroe |
| **11** | La Plaisance Rd, to Bolles Harbor, **W** gas: Marathon/Taco Bell/dsl, Speedway, **food:** Burger King, McDonald's, Wendy's, **lodging:** AmeriHost, Comfort Inn, Harbor Town RV Resort, **other:** Outlet Mall/famous brands, st police |
| **10mm** | Welcome Ctr nb, full ♿ facilities, 🕿 info, 🌲 litter barrels, vending, petwalk |
| **9** | S Otter Creek Rd, to La Salle, **W** antiques |
| **7mm** | weigh sta both lanes |
| **6** | Luna Pier, **E** gas: Sunoco/dsl, **food:** Ganders Rest., Super 8 |
| **5** | to Erie, Temperance |
| **2** | Summit St |
| **0mm** | Michigan/Ohio state line |

**MONROE**

MI

## INTERSTATE 94

E ← → W
**PORT HURON**

| Exit # | Services |
|---|---|
| **275mm** | I-69/I-94 begin/end on MI 25, **Pinegrove Ave in Port Huron...gas:** BP/24hr, Citgo, Speedway, **food:** Chicken Shack, Jet's Pizza, McDonald's, Tim Horton, Wendy's, White Castle, **lodging:** Day's Inn, Holiday Inn Express, **other:** Buick/Pontiac, Can-Am DutyFree, Family$, Ford, Honda, Rite Aid, tollbridge to Canada |
| **274.5mm** | Black River |
| **274** | Water St, Port Huron, **N Welcome Ctr/rest area, full facilities** (only from wb), **food:** Cracker Barrel, **lodging:** Best Western, **S gas:** SpeedyQ/dsl, Speedway/dsl, **food:** Bob Evans, **lodging:** Comfort Inn, Fairfield Inn, Hampton Inn, **other:** Lake Port SP, RV camping |
| **271** | I-69 E and I-94 E run together eb, Lp I-69, **S gas:** Mobil, **food:** Arby's, McDonalds, KFC, Quay St Grill, Wendy's, **other:** Kroger/gas, K-Mart, Sam's Club, to Port Huron |
| **269** | Dove St, Range Rd, **N gas:** Speedway/dsl/24hr, **lodging:** AmeriHost |
| **266** | Gratiot Rd, Marysville, **S gas:** Admiral, BP/dsl/scales/24hr, Marathon/scales/dsl, Meijer, Speedway, **food:** Arby's, Big Boy, Burger King, KFC, 4 Star Rest., Little Caesars Mancino's Pizza, McDonald's, Mr Pita, Pelican Café, Pizza Hut, Taco Bell, Tim Horton, **lodging:** Super 8, **other:** H HOSPITAL, AutoZone, Curves, Rite Aid, Wally's Foods |
| **262** | Wadhams Rd, **N** camping, **S gas:** Marathon/dsl/showers/24hr, Mobil/dsl |
| **257** | St Clair, Richmond, **S gas:** BP/dsl, **other:** st police |
| **255mm** | **rest area eb, full** ♿ **facilities,** [C], **info,** ⊞ **litter barrels, petwalk** |
| **251mm** | **rest area wb, full** ♿ **facilities,** [C], **info,** ⊞ **litter barrels, petwalk** |
| **248** | 26 Mile Rd, to Marine City, **N food:** McDonald's (2mi), **S gas:** Mejier, 7-11/gas, Speedy Q (1mi) |
| **247mm** | Salt River |
| **247** | MI 19 (no eb return), New Haven |
| **243** | MI 29, MI 3, Utica, New Baltimore, **N gas:** BP, Marathon/dsl, Meijer/dsl/24hr, Sunoco/dsl, **food:** Applebee's, Arby's, Burger King, Chophouse, Cold Stone, Coney Island, Dimitri's Rest., Empire Buffet, Gus Coney Island, McDonald's, Outback Steaks, Panera Bread, Papa Romano's Pizza, Ruby Tuesday, Subway, Starbucks, TX Roadhouse, Wendy's, White Castle, **lodging:** Chesterfield Motel, **other:** Belle Tire, Best Buy, Discount Tire, GNC, Home Depot, Jo-Ann Fabrics, K-Mart, Kohl's, Lowe's Whse, Michael's, PetCo, Radio Shack, Rite Aid, Staples, Target, TJ Maxx, Walgreen, **S gas:** Marathon/dsl/24hr, 7-11/gas, Speedway/dsl/24hr, **food:** Big Boy, Buscemis Pizza, Hot'n Now Burgers, Taco Bell, **lodging:** LodgeKeeper, **other:** Chevrolet |
| **241** | 21 Mile Rd, Selfridge, **N gas:** Marathon/dsl, Shell, **food:** China King, Hungry Howie's, Quizno's, Subway, **other:** Advance Parts, CVS Drug, same as 240 |
| **240** | to MI 59, **N gas:** 7-11/gas, Marathon, Speedway, **food:** Arby's, Bob Evans, Coney Island, McDonald's, O'Charley's, Taco Bell, Tim Horton, **lodging:** Best Western, **other:** $General, Ford, Walmart SuperCtr |
| **237** | N River Rd, Mt Clemens, **N gas:** BP/dsl, Mobil/Subway/dsl, **food:** McDonald's, **lodging:** Quality Inn, **other:** H HOSPITAL, General RV Ctr, Gibralter Trade Ctr |

**DETROIT AREA**

| Exit # | Services |
|---|---|
| **236.5mm** | Clinton River |
| **236** | Metro Parkway, **S food:** Big Apple Bagels, Little Caesars, McDonald's, Subway, **other:** H HOSPITAL, Curves, CVS Drug, GNC, Kroger |
| **235** | Shook Rd (from wb) |
| **234b a** | Harper Rd, 15 Mile Rd, **N gas:** BP/McDonald's, Marathon/dsl, SpeedyQ, Sunoco/dsl/24hr, **food:** Sorrento Pizza, **other:** vet, **S gas:** FL Gas, **food:** China Moon, Subway, Winners Grill |
| **232** | Little Mack Ave (from wb only), **N gas:** Marathon, 7-11/gas, Sunoco, **food:** Arby's, Burger King, Chili's, Cold Stone, Del Taco, Denny's, Hooters, Longhorn Steaks, McDonald's, Panera Bread, Pizza Hut, Red Robin, Sea Breeze Diner, Tim Horton, Woody's Grill, **lodging:** Days Inn, Eastin Hotel, Holiday Inn Express, Red Roof Inn, Super 8, Victory Inn, **other:** Belle Tire, Firestone, JC Penny, Sam's Club, Sears/Auto, Staples, **S gas:** Marathon, Meijer/dsl/24hr, Speedway/dsl, **food:** Cracker Barrel, IHOP, **lodging:** Baymont Inn, Gelato Roama Pizza, **other:** Circuit City, Family$, Home Depot, Jo-Ann Fabrics, PetsMart, same as 231 |
| **231** | (from eb), MI 3, Gratiot Ave, **N gas:** Shell, Speedway, Sunoco, **food:** Applebee's, Arby's, Big Boy, Bob Evans, ChuckeCheese, Denny's, Famous Dave's, Logan's Raodhouse, McDonald's, Pizza Hut, Starbucks, TX Roadhouse, **lodging:** Best Western, Day's Inn, Econolodge, Extended Stay America, Microtel, **other:** Best Buy, Discount Tire, Firestone/auto, Honda/Acura, Kia, Nissan, Sam's Club/gas, Target, Toyota, U-Haul, mall |
| **230** | 12 Mile Rd, **N gas:** American Gas, Mobil/dsl, **food:** BD's Mongolian, Burger King, Jimmy John's, Krispy Kreme, Outback Steaks, **other:** CVS Drug, $Tree, Hyundai/Suzuki, Lincoln/Mercury, Marshall's, Mitsubishi, NAPA, Walmart/Subway, mall, **S gas:** Marathon |
| **229** | I-696 W, Reuther Fwy, to 11 Mile Rd, **N gas:** BP, **S gas:** BP/dsl, Speedway, **other:** 7-11 |
| **228** | 10 Mile Rd, **N gas:** BP/24hr, Mobil, Shell, **food:** Eastwind Chinese, Coney Island, Jet's Pizza, **other:** CVS Drug |
| **227** | 9 Mile Rd, **N gas:** Mobil/dsl, Speedway/dsl, Sunoco, **food:** McDonald's, Papa John's, Subway, Taco Bell/Pizza Hut, Wendy's, **other:** Aldi Foods, CVS $Tree, Drug, Fresh Choice Foods, Office Depot, Pete & Franks Mkt, True Value, **S gas:** Mobil/dsl, **lodging:** Shore Pointe Motel, **other:** BMW, Cadillac, Mercedes |
| **225** | MI 102, Vernier Rd, 8 Mile Rd, **S gas:** BP/Subway, Mobil, Sunoco/dsl, **food:** Coney Island, KFC, Taco Bell, Wendy's, **other:** Kroger, Walgreen |

## INTERSTATE 94 CONT'D

**E** ↕ **W**

**DETROIT AREA**

| | |
|---|---|
| **224b** | Allard Ave, Eastwood Ave |
| **224a** | Moross Rd, **S** **gas:** Shell, **other:** Family Foods, **other:** Ⓗ HOSPITAL |
| **223** | Cadieux Rd, **S** **gas:** BP/Subway, Mobil, Shell, Sunoco, **food:** McDonald's, Taco Bell, Tubby's Subs, Wendy's, White Castle, **other:** Rite Aid |
| **222b** | Harper Ave (from eb), **S** **other:** Family$, Hastings Auto |
| **222a** | Chalmers Ave, Outer Dr, **N** **gas:** BP/Subway/dsl, Marathon, **food:** Coney Island, KFC, Little Caesars, White Castle, **other:** Family$ |
| **220b** | Conner Ave, **N** **gas:** BP, Sunoco |
| **220a** | French Rd, **S** **gas:** Marathon |
| **219** | MI 3, Gratiot Ave, **N** **gas:** Marathon/Subway, Speedy, **food:** Coney Island, KFC, McDonald's, **other:** Family$, **S** **gas:** GasMart, **food:** Burger King |
| **218** | MI 53, Van Dyke Ave, **N** **gas:** BP, Mobil/dsl |
| **217b** | Mt Elliott Ave, **S** **gas:** Marathon, Sunoco/dsl, **food:** Young's BBQ |
| **217a** | E Grand Blvd, Chene St, **S** **gas:** Marathon |
| **216b** | Russell St (from eb), to downtown |
| **216a** | I-75, Chrysler Fwy, to tunnel to Canada |
| **215c** | MI 1, Woodward Ave, John R St |
| **215b** | MI 10 N, Lodge Fwy |
| **215a** | MI 10 S, tunnel to Canada, downtown |
| **214b** | Trumbull Ave, to Ford Ⓗ HOSPITAL |
| **214a** | (from wb) Grand River Ave |
| **213b** | I-96 W to Lansing, E to Canada, bridge to Canada, to Tiger Stadium |
| **213a** | W Grand (exits left from eb) |
| **212b** | Warren Ave (from eb) |
| **212a** | Livernois Ave, **S** **gas:** Marathon/Subway/dsl, Sunoco |
| **211b** | Cecil Ave (from wb), Central Ave |
| **211a** | Lonyo Rd, **S** Ford |
| **210** | US 12, Michigan Ave, Wyoming Ave, **N** **gas:** Mobil, **S** **gas:** BP/dsl, Citgo/dsl, Sunoco/dsl, **food:** YumYum Donuts |
| **209** | Rotunda Dr (from wb) |
| **208** | Greenfield Rd, Schaefer Rd, **N** **gas:** Mobil, **other:** 7-11, **S** River Rouge Ford Plant |
| **207mm** | Rouge River |
| **206** | Oakwood Blvd, Melvindale, **N** **gas:** Marathon, **food:** Applebee's, Carino's, Coney Island, Chili's, Cold Stone, Little Caesars, Longhorn Steaks, Moe's SW Grill, On-the-Border, Panera Bread, Starbucks, Subway, **other:** Best Buy, Ford Plant, GNC, Home Depot, Jo-Ann Fabrics, Lowe's Whse, Meijer, Michaels, Old Navy, PetCo, Staples, Target, TJ Maxx, UPS, World Mkt, Greenfield Village Museum, **S** **gas:** BP, **food:** Burger King, Coney Island, McDonald's, O'Henry's, Sabina's, Subway, **lodging:** Best Western, Holiday Inn Express, **other:** Belle Tire, Big A Parts, Curves, CVS Drug, $General, Rite Aid, 7-11 |
| **205mm** | Largest Uniroyal Tire in the World |
| **204b a** | MI 39, Southfield Fwy, Pelham Rd, **N** **gas:** Marathon, Mobil, Valero/dsl, **food:** Ponderosa Steaks, **other:** 7-11, to Greenfield Village, **S** **gas:** Marathon, **other:** Walgreen |
| **202b a** | US 24, Telegraph Rd, **N** **gas:** Clark, Shell, Sunoco, **food:** Burger King, Checkers, Dunkin Donuts, Jet's Pizza, KFC, McDonald's, Pizza Hut, Ram's Horn Rest., Subway, Taco Bell, Wendy's, **lodging:** Casa Bianca Motel, **other:** Advance Parts, Aldi Foods, Rite Aid, |
| **202b a** | Continued Walgreen, **S** **gas:** BP, Citgo, Marathon/dsl, **food:** Burger King, Hungry Howie's, Leon's Rest., Marina's Pizza, Old Country Buffet, Pizza Hut, Popeye's, Quizno's, Subway, Super China, Yum Yum Donuts, **lodging:** Comfort Inn, **other:** AutoZone, Curves, Family$, Radio Shack, Rite Aid, U-Haul, Walgreens, Walmart, st police |
| **200** | Ecorse Rd, (no ez eb return), to Taylor, **N** **gas:** Marathon/scales/dsl, **S** **gas:** Rich, Speedy/dsl, **food:** Danny's Pizza, Norms Subs |
| **199** | Middle Belt Rd, **S** **gas:** BP/dsl/24hr, **food:** Denny's, McDonald's, Wendy's, **lodging:** Day's Inn, Howard Johnson, Super 8 |
| **198** | Merriman Rd, **N** **food:** Bob Evans, **lodging:** Baymont Inn, Best Value, Best Western, Clarion, Comfort Inn, Courtyard, Crowne Plaza Hotel, Doubletree Inn, Econolodge, Extended Stay America, Fairfield Inn, Hampton Inn, Hilton Garden, Holiday Inn, Howard Johnson, Marriott, Metropolitan Motel, Motel 6, PearTree Inn, Ramada Inn, Sheraton, **S** Wayne Co ✈ |
| **197** | Vining Rd |
| **196** | Wayne Rd, Romulus, **N** **gas:** Shell, **food:** McDonald's, **S** **gas:** Mobil/dsl, **food:** Burger King, Subway |
| **194b a** | I-275, N to Flint, S to Toledo |
| **192** | Haggerty Rd, **N** **gas:** BP, Mobil/24hr, Travel&Truck Plaza/dsl (2mi), **food:** Burger King (2mi), Subway, **S** Lower Huron Metro Park |
| **190** | Belleville Rd, to Belleville, **N** **gas:** BP/24hr, Meijer/dsl/24hr, Marathon, **food:** Applebee's, Arby's, Big Boy, Cracker Barrel, McDonald's, O'Charley's, Quizno's, Taco Bell, Tim Horton, Wendy's, **lodging:** Hampton Inn, Holiday Inn Express, Red Roof Inn, **other:** Camping World RV Service/supplies, CVS Drug, $Tree, Firestone/auto, Ford, Meijer, Michal's RV Ctr, U-Haul, Walgreens, Walmart, **S** **gas:** Shell, **food:** Burger King, China City, Dimitri's Kitchen, Dos Pesos Mexican, Subway, **lodging:** Comfort Inn, Super 8, **other:** USPO |
| **189mm** | rest area wb, full ♿ facilities, info, 📞, 🏪, litter barrels, vending, petwalk |
| **187** | Rawsonville Rd, **S** **gas:** Mobil/dsl, Speedway/dsl, **food:** Burger King, Denny's, KFC, Little Caesar's, LoneStar Steaks, Maria's Pizza, McDonald's, Pizza Hut, Tim Horton, Wendy's, **other:** $General, $Tree, GNC, K-Mart, KOA (3mi), Radio Shack |
| **185** | US 12, Michigan Ave (from eb, exits left, no return), to frontage rds, ✈ |
| **184mm** | Ford Lake |
| **183** | US 12, Huron St, Ypsilanti, **N** **gas:** Marathon/dsl, **other:** to E MI U, **S** **food:** Baker's Square, McDonald's, Primo Coffee, **lodging:** Marriott, **other:** Ⓗ HOSPITAL, Chevrolet/Pontiac/Buick/GMC, st police |
| **181b a** | US 12 W, Michigan Ave, Ypsilanti, **N** **gas:** Meijer/dsl/24hr, Rich, Speedway, **food:** Burger King, Taco Bell/Pizza Hut, Tim Horton/Wendy's, **other:** Ⓗ HOSPITAL, Aamco, BigLots, $Tree, 7-11, Sheena's Food/24hr, Radio Shack, Walmart, **S** **gas:** Shell, **food:** Domino's, Harvest Moon Rest., McDonald's, Subway |
| **180b a** | US 23, to Toledo, Flint |
| **177** | State St, **N** **gas:** BP/24hr, Mobil, Shell, **food:** Bennigan's, Burger King, CA Pizza, Damon's, Graham's Steaks, Los Tres Mexican, Macaroni Grill, |

**MI**

## INTERSTATE 94 CONT'D

**E**
↕
**W**

**A N N   A R B O R**

**177** Continued
Max&Erma's, Olive Garden, Wendy's, **lodging:** Best Value, Crowne Plaza Hotel, Comfort Inn, Courtyard, Fairfield Inn, Hampton Inn, Hilton, Holiday Inn Express, Motel 6, Red Roof Inn, Sheraton, **other:** Firestone, JC Penney, Mitsubishi, Sears/auto, VW, World Mkt, mall, to UMI, **S gas:** Citgo/Subway, **food:** Coney Island, McDonald's, Pizza Hut/Taco Bell, **lodging:** Motel 6, **other:** U-Haul

**175** Ann Arbor-Saline Rd, **N gas:** Shell, **food:** Applebee's, Coney Island, Moe's SW Grill, Old Country Buffet, Panera Bread, Subway, **lodging:** Candlewood Suites, **other:** Office Depot, mall, to UMI Stadium, **S gas:** Meijer/dsl/24hr, **food:** Big Boy, Jet's Pizza, Joe's Crabshack, McDonald's, Outback Steaks, TGIFriday, **other:** Best Buy, Jo-Ann Fabrics, Kohl's, Meijer, Target

**172** Jackson Ave, to Ann Arbor, **N gas:** BP, Marathon, Shell, Sunoco, **food:** Boston Mkt, Burger King, Holiday's Rest., KFC, LJ Silver, Marathon, McDonald's, Quarter Rest., Quizno's, Starbucks, Subway, Taco Bell, Zingerman's Roadhouse, **other:** H HOSPITAL, CVS Drug, $Tree, Discount Tire, Goodyear, K-Mart, Kroger, Rite Aid, Staples, TJ Maxx, Walgreens, mall, **S lodging:** Best Western, Super 8, **other:** Chevrolet/Pontiac/Cadillac, Ford

**171** MI 14 (from eb, exits left), to Ann Arbor, to Flint by US 23

**169** Zeeb Rd, **N gas:** BP/dsl/24hr, **food:** Grand Pies Co, Metzger's Rest., McDonald's, **S gas:** Citgo/dsl, Meijer/dsl, **food:** Arby's, Burger King, Panera Bread, Pizza Hut, Subway, Taco Bell, Wendy's, Westside Grill, **other:** Harley-Davidson, Lowe's Whse, Meijer

**167** Baker Rd, Dexter, **N gas:** Pilot/Subway/scales/dsl/24hr, **S gas:** Pilot/Arby's/dsl/scales/24hr, TA/BP/Popeye's/dsl/rest./scales/24hr/@, **food:** Reddeman Farms Rest. (4mi), McDonald's, **other:** Blue Beacon

**162** Jackson Rd, Fletcher Rd, **S gas:** Clark/dsl/24hr, **food:** Stiver's Rest.

**161mm** rest area eb, full ♿ facilities, ☏, 🛉, litter barrels, vending, petwalk

**159** MI 52, Chelsea, **N gas:** Mobil/dsl, Rich Gas, Sunoco/dsl, **food:** Big Boy, Chelsea Grill, China Garden, Coney Island, Hungry Howie's, KFC/Taco Bell, Little Caesar's, Main St Coney Island, McDonald's, Subway, Wendy's, **lodging:** Comfort Inn, Holiday Inn Express, **other:** H HOSPITAL, Chelsea Drug, Chevrolet/Buick, Chrysler/Dodge/Jeep, Country Mkt Foods/drug, Curves, CVS Drug, Ford, Pamida, Travel Land RV Ctr, vet

**J A C K S O N**

**157** Jackson Rd, Pierce Rd, **N** Gerald Eddy Geology Ctr

**156** Kalmbach Rd, **N** to Waterloo RA

**153** Clear Lake Rd, **N gas:** Marathon/dsl

**151.5mm** weigh sta both lanes

**150** to Grass Lake, **S gas:** Mobil/Subway, **other:** Apple Creek Campground

**150mm** rest area wb, full ♿ facilities, ☏, 🛉, litter barrels, vending, petwalk

**147** Race Rd, **N** Hideaway RV Camp, to Waterloo RA, camping, **S** lodging

**145** Sargent Rd, **S gas:** BP/dsl, Mobil/145 Rest/dsl/scales/rest./24hr, **food:** McDonald's, Wendy's, **lodging:** Colonial Inn

**144** Lp 94 (from wb), to Jackson

**142** US 127 S, to Hudson, **3 mi S gas:** Meijer/dsl/24hr, Speedway, **food:** Domino's, McDonald's, Wendy's, **other:** Advance Parts, Kroger, Parts+, Rite Aid, to MI Speedway

**141** Elm Rd, **N lodging:** Travelodge, **other:** Chevrolet/Dodge/Honda/Hyundai, Ford, **S**

**139** MI 106, Cooper St, to Jackson, **N** st police/prison, **S gas:** Citgo/Subway, **other:** H HOSPITAL

**138** US 127 N, MI 50, to Lansing, Jackson, **N food:** Red Lobster, **lodging:** Baymont Inn, Comfort Inn, Fairfield Inn, Hampton Inn, Holiday Inn, Jackson Inn, **other:** vet, **S gas:** Clark, Marathon, Rich Gas, Shell/24hr, **food:** Arby's, Big Boy, Bob Evans, Dunkin Donuts, Fazoli's, Ground Round, KFC, LJ Silver, Los Tres Amigos, McDonald's, Old Country Buffet, Outback Steaks, Panera Bread, Papa John's, Pizza Hut, Quizno's, Starbucks, Subway, **lodging:** Country Hearth Inn, Motel 6, **other:** Advance Parts, AutoZone, Best Buy, Circuit City, Discount Tire, Home Depot, Kohl's, Kroger, Lowe's Whse, Michael's, Sears/auto, Target, TJ Maxx, Walgreens

**137** Airport Rd, **N gas:** Meijer/dsl/24hr, Shell/Taco Bell/24hr, 7-11, **food:** Burger King, Denny's, Hudson's Rest., McDonald's, Steak'n Shake/24hr, Subway, Wendy's, **other:** Bumper Parts, Meijer, **S gas:** BP/24hr, **food:** Cracker Barrel, Culvers, Olive Garden, LoneStar Steaks, **lodging:** Country Inn&Suites, **other:** K-Mart, Sam's Club/gas

**136** Lp 94, MI 60, to Jackson

**135mm** rest area eb, full ♿ facilities, ☏, 🛉, litter barrels, vending, petwalk

**133** Dearing Rd, Spring Arbor, **S** to Spring Arbor U

**130** Parma, **S gas:** Citgo/dsl/rest./24hr

**128** Michigan Ave, **N gas:** BP/Burger King/scales/dsl/24hr, Marathon/dsl/24hr, **other:** RV camping

**127** Concord Rd, **N** St Julian's Winery

**124** MI 99, to Eaton Rapids, **S** lodging

**121** 28 Mile Rd, to Albion, **N gas:** Mobil, **food:** Arby's, **lodging:** Best Western, **S gas:** FT/dsl/24hr, Marathon, Speedway/dsl/24hr, **food:** Albion Garden, Burger King, Frosty Dan's, Full Moon Rest., KFC, La Casa Mexican, McDonald's, Pizza Hut, **lodging:** Super 9, **other:** H HOSPITAL, AutoZone, Chevrolet/Pontiac/Buick, $General, Family$, Felpausch Foods, Ford/Mercury, Pamida, RV camping

**119** 26 Mile Rd

**115** 22.5 Mile Rd, **N gas:** Citgo/115 Rest./dsl/24hr

**MI**

**MARSHALL** E ↕ W

## INTERSTATE 94 CONT'D

| | |
|---|---|
| **113mm** | rest area wb, full ♿ facilities, [C], [⊼], litter barrels, vending, petwalk |
| **112** | Partello Rd, **S** gas: Loves/Hardee's/scales/dsl/24hr, **food:** Schuler's Rest. |
| **110** | Old US 27, Marshall, **N** gas: Shell/Subway/dsl/24hr, **food:** Country Kitchen/24hr, **S** gas: Citgo/KFC/dsl, **food:** Denny's, Pizza Hut (2mi), Schuler's Rest. (2mi), **lodging:** Hampton Inn, Holiday Inn Express, **other:** Ⓗ HOSPITAL, sheriff |
| **108** | I-69, US 27, N to Lansing, S to Ft Wayne |
| **104** | 11 Mile Rd, Michigan Ave, **N** gas: Pilot/scales/dsl/24hr, Sunoco/Te-Khi Trkstp/rest./scales/24hr/@, **S** gas: Citgo/Subway/dsl/24hr, **lodging:** Quality Inn/rest. |
| **103** | Lp 94 (from wb, no return), to Battle Creek, **N** Ⓗ HOSPITAL |
| **102mm** | Kalamazoo River |
| **100** | Beadle Lake Rd, **N** food: Moonraker Rest., **S** gas: Citgo/dsl, **other:** Binder Park Zoo |
| **98b** | I-194 N, to Battle Creek |
| **98a** | MI 66, to Sturgis, **S** gas: Citgo/Blimpie/dsl, Meijer/dsl/24hr, **food:** Chili's, Don Pablo, McDonald's, Ruby Tuesday, Schlotsky's, Starbucks, Steak'n Shake, **lodging:** Holiday Inn, **other:** Best Buy, Discount Tire, Kohl's, Lowe's Whse, Meijer, Michael's, PetCo, Sam's Club/gas, Staples, TJ Maxx, Walgreens, Walmart SuperCtr, same as 97 |
| **97** | Capital Ave, to Battle Creek, **N** gas: BP/24hr, Marathon, **food:** Arby's, LoneStar Steaks, Lux Cafe, McDonald's, Red Lobster, **lodging:** Comfort Inn, Knight's Inn, **S** gas: Citgo, Shell/24hr, Sunoco/Subway/24hr, **food:** Applebee's, Bob Evans, Burger King, Canton Buffet, Cici's Pizza, Cocina Mexicana, Coney Island, Cracker Barrel, Denny's, Don Pablo, Fazoli's, Godfather's Pizza, Old Country Buffet, Pizza Hut, Quizno's, Taco Bell, Tuesday Morning, Wendy's, **lodging:** Baymont Inn, Best Western, Day's Inn, Fairfield Inn, Hampton Inn, Motel 6, Ramada Inn, Super 8, **other:** Apple Valley Foods, Best Buy, Borders Books, $Tree, Firestone/auto, Goodyear/auto, Harley-Davidson, JC Penney, Macy's, Marshall Fields, Sears/auto, Target, mall, vet |
| **96mm** | rest area eb, full ♿ facilities, [C], [⊼], litter barrels, vending, petwalk |
| **95** | Helmer Rd, **N** gas: Citgo/dsl, **other:** st police, **2 mi N** gas: Meijer/dsl/24hr, **food:** Big Boy |
| **92** | Lp 94, to Battle Creek, Springfield, **N** gas: Citgo/Arlene's Trkstp/dsl/rest./24hr, Shell/24hr, **other:** RV camping, to Ft Custer RA |
| **88** | Climax, **N** Galesburg Speedway |
| **85** | 35th St, Galesburg, **N** gas: Shell/Subway/dsl/24hr, **food:** McDonald's, Subway, **other:** Galesburg Speedway, to Ft Custer RA, River Oaks CP, **S** other: Colebrook CP, Scottsville CP, Winery Tours, RV camping |
| **85mm** | rest area wb, full ♿ facilities, [C], [⊼], litter barrels, vending, petwalk |
| **81** | Lp 94 (from wb), to Kalamazoo |
| **80** | Cork St, Sprinkle Rd, to Kalamazoo, **N** gas: Citgo/dsl, Double Express, Speedway/dsl, **food:** Arby's, Burger King, Chicken Coop, Denny's, Godfather's, Hana East Asian, Perkins, Taco Bell, **lodging:** Best Western, |

**KALAMAZOO**

| | |
|---|---|
| **80** | Continued: Clarion Hotel, Fairfield Inn, Holiday Inn Express, Red Roof Inn, vet, **S** gas: BP/dsl/24hr, Speedway/dsl, **food:** Derk's Rest., Hometown Diner, Horizon Inn, McDonald's, Subway/24hr, Wendy's, **lodging:** Comfort Inn, Econolodge, Horizon Inn, Motel 6 |
| **78** | Portage Rd, Kilgore Rd, **N** gas: BP/Circle K, **food:** China Hut, Cottage Pizza, Uncle Earnie Pancakes, **lodging:** Hampton Inn, **other:** Ⓗ HOSPITAL, **S** gas: Shell/24hr, Speedway, **food:** Angelo's Italian, Bravo Rest., Brewster's, Callahan's Rest., Fat Tony's, McDonald's, Pizza King, Quizno's, Taco Bell, Theo&Stacy's Rest., Subway, **lodging:** Country Inn Suites, Lee's Inn, **other:** AutoValue Parts, museum |
| **76b a** | Westnedge Ave, **N** gas: Admiral, Meijer/dsl/24hr, Speedway/dsl, **food:** Arby's, Beaners, BD BBQ, Hooters, IHOP, Kazoopie's, Lee's Chicken, Mancino's Eatery, Outback Steaks, Papa John's, Pappy's Mexican, Pizza Hut, Root Beer Stand, Steak'n Shake, Stirmax Asian, Subway, Taco Bell, Theo & Stacy's Rest., **other:** BigLots, Discount Tire, Gander Mtn, Goodyear/auto, Lowe's Whse, Meijer, Midas, Office Depot, Rite Aid, **S** gas: Shell/24hr, **food:** Antique Kitchen, Applebee's, Bilbo's Pizza, Bob Evans, Burger King, Carrabba's, Chili's, ChuckeCheese, Cold Stone, Culvers, Empire Chinese, Fazoli's, Heavenly Ham, Jimmy Johns, KFC, Krispy Kreme, Little Caesar's, LJ Silver, Logan's Roadhouse, MacKenzie's Bakery, McDonald's, Noodles & Co, Old Country Buffet, Olive Garden, Panchero's Mexican, Panera Bread, Pizza Hut, Qdoba Mexican, Red Lobster, Red Robin, Schlotsky's, Subway, Taco Bell, TX Roadhouse, Wendy's, **lodging:** Holiday Motel, **other:** AutoZone, Barnes&Noble, Belle Tire, Best Buy, Cadillac/Pontiac/Nissan, Circuit City, $Tree, Fannie Mae Candies, Firestone/auto, Harding's Foods, Home Depot, JC Penney, Jo-Ann Fabrics, K-Mart, Kohl's, MktPlace Foods, Michael's, Old Navy, PepBoys, Pontiac/Cadillac, Radio Shack, Sam's Club, Sears/auto, Target, Walgreens, WorldMkt, mall |
| **75** | Oakland Dr |
| **74b a** | US 131, to Kalamazoo, **N** to W MI U, Kalamazoo Coll |
| **72** | Oshtemo, **N** gas: Citgo/dsl, Speedway/dsl, **food:** Arby's, Burger King, Culver's, McDonald's, Taco Bell, Wendy's, **lodging:** Hampton Inn, **other:** NAPA, Saturn, **S** food: Cracker Barrel, **lodging:** Fairfield Inn, Towne Place Suites |
| **66** | Mattawan, **N** gas: Speedway/Subway/dsl/24hr, **food:** Main St Grill, Mancino's Italian, **other:** Freightliner, Rossman Auto/towing, **S** gas: Shell |
| **60** | MI 40, Paw Paw, **N** gas: BP/24hr, Speedway/dsl/24hr, **food:** Arby's, Big Boy, Burger King, Chicken Coop, Gallagher's Eatery, McDonald's, Pizza Hut, Root Beer Stand, Subway, Taco Bell, Wendy's, **lodging:** Econolodge, Comfort Inn, Super 8, **other:** Ⓗ HOSPITAL, Advance Parts, Chrysler/Dodge/Jeep, Curves, Felpausch Foods, St Julian Winery, Warner Winery |
| **56** | MI 51, to Decatur, **N** st police, **S** gas: Citgo/dsl, Marathon/dsl/24hr |
| **52** | Lawrence, **N** food: Waffle House of America |
| **46** | Hartford, **N** gas: Shell/dsl/24hr, **food:** McDonald's, Panel Room Rest. |

MI

## INTERSTATE 94 CONT'D

| | |
|---|---|
| **42mm** | rest area wb, full ♿ facilities, 🕿, ⛱, litter barrels, vending, petwalk |
| **41** | MI 140, to Niles, Watervliet, **N** gas: BP/24hr, Citgo, Marathon, Wesco, food: Burger King, Chicken Coop, Frosty Boy, Rookies, Subway, Taco Bell, Waffle House, lodging: Ramada, other: Ⓗ HOSPITAL, Curves, camping |
| **39** | Millburg, Coloma, Deer Forest, 0-1 mi **N** gas: BP/dsl, Marathon, Speedway, Westco/dsl, food: Diggins Rest., Friendly Grill, McDonald's, Pizza Hut, Subway, other: Ace hardware, Family$, Holiday RV Ctr, Krenek RV Ctr, True Value, **S** gas: NAPA Auto Care |
| **36mm** | rest area eb, full ♿ facilities, 🕿, ⛱, litter barrels, vending, petwalk |
| **34** | I-196 N, US 31 N, to Holland, Grand Rapids |
| **33** | Lp I-94, to Benton Harbor, 2-4 mi 🛬, sheriff's dept |
| **30** | Napier Ave, Benton Harbor, **N** gas: ✈FLYING J/Wendy's/dsl/24hr/@, Shell/24hr, food: Hot'n'Now (1mi), lodging: Super 8, other: Ⓗ HOSPITAL, Blue Beacon, **S** Chrysler/Dodge/Honda |
| **29** | Pipestone Rd, Benton Harbor, **N** gas: Meijer/dsl/24hr, food: Applebee's, Asian Buffet, Burger King, Hacienda Mexican, Hardee's, IHOP, McDonald's, Pizza Hut, Sophia's Pancake House, Steak'n Shake, Super Buffet, Texas Corral, lodging: Best Western, Courtyard, Motel 6, Red Roof Inn, other: Aldi Foods, Best Buy, $Tree, Home Depot, JC Penney, Lowe's Whse, Meijer, Radio Shack, Sears/auto, Staples, Walgreens, Walmart SuperCtr/Subway, **S** gas: Mobil/dsl/24hr, food: Bob Evans, lodging: Comfort Suites, Holiday Inn Express |
| **28** | US 31 S, MI 139 N, Scottdale Rd, to Niles, **N** gas: Citgo/dsl, Marathon/dsl, food: Bejing House, Burger King, Capozio's Pizza, Chicken Coop, Country Kitchen, DQ, Henry's Burgers, KFC, Pizza Hut, Subway, Taco Bell, lodging: Economy Inn, Executive Inn/rest., other: Ⓗ HOSPITAL, AutoZone, BigLots, Chevrolet, $Tree, Family$, M&W Tire, Midas, NAPA, Office Depot, Old Navy, Rite Aid, Target, TJ Maxx, radiators/repair/transmissions, st police, vet, **S** lodging: Best Value |
| **27mm** | St Joseph River |
| **27** | MI 63, Niles Ave, to St Joseph, **N** gas: BP/24hr, food: Nye's Apple Barn, **S** food: Panera Bread, other: Goodyear |
| **23** | Red Arrow Hwy, Stevensville, **N** gas: Admiral, BP, Marathon/dsl, Mobil, Shell/dsl/24hr, food: Big Boy, Burger King, Cracker Barrel, Culver's, DQ, Fireside Inn Rest., LJ Silver, McDonald's, Papa John's, Popeye's, Quizno's, Subway, Tony's Rest., lodging: Baymont Inn, Candlewood Suites, Comfort Suites, Park Inn, Ray's Motel, other: Curves, Walgreen, **S** food: Five O'Clock Grill, lodging: Hampton Inn |
| **22** | John Beers Rd, Stevensville, **N** to Grand Mere SP, **S** gas: Marathon/dsl, food: Pizza Hut |
| **16** | Bridgman, **N** gas: BP/A&W/dsl/24hr, other: to Warren Dunes SP, **S** gas: JR's Trvl Ctr/dsl/24hr, food: McDonald's, lodging: Bridgman Inn, 1/2 mi **S** food: Olympus Rest., Pizza Hut, Roma Pizza, Sammies Rest., Subway, other: Chevrolet/Buick, vet |

| | |
|---|---|
| **12** | Sawyer, **N** gas: Citgo/scales/dsl/rest./24hr, food: Chubby's Diner, **S** gas: TA/Burger King/Country Pride/Popeye's/Taco Bell/scales/dsl/24hr/@, food: Pizza Hut, lodging: Super 8, other: USPO |
| **6** | Lakeside, Union Pier, **N** other: St Julian's Winery, antiques, **S** RV camping |
| **4b a** | US 12, to Three Oaks, New Buffalo, **N** food: Pizza Hut, st police |
| **2.5mm** | weigh sta both lanes |
| **1** | MI 239, to Grand Beach, New Buffalo, **N** gas: Shell/Quizno's, food: Hana's Rest. (1mi), McDonald's, Wheel Inn Rest., lodging: Best Western, Holiday Inn Express, Rodeway Inn, other: $General, **S** gas: New Buffalo/rest./dsl/24hr, food: Wendy's, lodging: Obrien's Inn |
| **.5mm** | Welcome Ctr eb, full ♿ facilities, info, 🕿, ⛱, litter barrels, vending, petwalk |
| **0mm** | Michigan/Indiana state line |

## INTERSTATE 96

| Exit # | Services |
|---|---|
| I-96 begins/ends on I-75, exit 48 in Detroit. | |
| **191** | I-75, **N** to Flint, **S** to Toledo, US 12, to MLK Blvd, to Michigan Ave |
| **190b** | Warren Ave, **N** gas: BP/dsl, **S** gas: Marathon |
| **190a** | I-94 E to Port Huron |
| **189** | W Grand Blvd, Tireman Rd, **N** gas: BP/Subway, Mobil |
| **188b** | Joy Rd, **N** food: Church's |
| **188a** | Livernois, **N** gas: Mobil, Shell, food: Burger King, KFC, McDonald's, Wendy's |
| **187** | Grand River Ave (from eb) |
| **186b** | Davison Ave, I-96 local and I-96 express divide, no exits from express |
| **186a** | Wyoming Ave |
| **185** | Schaefer Hwy, to Grand River Ave, **N** gas: BP/24hr, Mobil, food: Coney Island, McDonald's, other: CVS Drug, **S** gas: Sunoco |
| **184** | Greenfield Rd |
| **183** | MI 39, Southfield Fwy, exit from expswy and local |
| **182** | Evergreen Rd |
| **180** | Outer Dr, **N** gas: BP/dsl/lube |
| **180mm** | I-96 local/express unite/divide |
| **179** | US 24, Telegraph Rd, **N** gas: BP, Marathon/dsl, food: Arby's, China King, Dunkin Donuts/Baskin-Robbins, McDonald's, Subway, Taco Bell, White Castle, other: Chevrolet, Dodge, Family$, Goodyear, Rite Aid, **S** gas: BP, Marathon/dsl |

## INTERSTATE 96 CONT'D

E ↑↓ W

| | |
|---|---|
| 178 | Beech Daly Rd, **N** gas |
| 177 | Inkster Rd, **N** gas: BP/Tim Horton, food: Panda Chinese, Subway, lodging: Super 8, other: $General, Hancock Fabrics, 7-11 |
| 176 | Middlebelt Rd, **N** food: Bob Evans, IHOP, Olive Garden, lodging: Comfort Inn, **S** food: Logan's Roadhouse, lodging: Crossland Studios, other: Costco/gas, Home Depot, Marshall's, Meijer, Michael's, PetCo, Target, Walgreens, Walmart SuperCtr |
| 175 | Merriman Rd, **N** gas: Mobil, Speedway/dsl, **S** gas: Sunoco, food: Blimpie |
| 174 | Farmington Rd, **N** gas: Mobil/dsl, Sunoco, food: Looney Baker, **S** gas: BP, food: KFC |
| 173b | Levan Rd, **N** Ⓗ HOSPITAL, to Madonna U |
| 173a | Newburgh Rd |
| 171mm | I-275 and I-96 run together 9 miles |
| 170 | 6 Mile Rd, **N** food: Big Boy, CA Pizza Kitchen, Coney Island, Ground Round, Jimmy John's, Louie's Grill, Max&Erma's, Panera Bread, Red Robin, lodging: Best Western, Courtyard, Marriott, Radisson, other: Ⓗ HOSPITAL, Busch's Fresh Foods, Murray Parts, Rite Aid, Walgreens, mall, **S** gas: BP, Mobil, food: Applebee's, Baja Fresh, Brann's Steaks, Buca Italian, Caribou Coffee, Charlie's Grill, Chi Burger, Cold Stone, Claddagh Rest., Flemings, McDonald's, Mitchell's Fishmarket, Noodles & Co, Panchero's, Papa Vino's, PF Chang, Potbelly, lodging: Fairfield Inn, Residence Inn, TownePlace Suites, other: Barnes&Noble, CVS Drug, Office Depot |
| 169b a | 7 Mile Rd, **N** food: Doc's Grill, lodging: Embassy Suites, **S** food: Alexander's Rest., Bahama Breeze Rest., Champp's Rest., Gaucho Steaks, Macaroni Grill, lodging: AmeriSuites, other: Home Depot |
| 167 | 8 Mile Rd, to Northville, **S** gas: Meijer/dsl/24hr, Speedway/dsl, food: Benihana, Big Boy, Chili's, McDonald's, Koney Island, On-the-Border, Quizno's, Starbucks, Taco Bell, Uno Pizzaria, Zoup, lodging: Country Inn Suites, Extended Stay America, Hampton Inn, Holiday Inn Express, Sheraton, other: Best Buy, Costco/gas, Firestone, Home Depot, Kohl's, Meijer, Target, Trader Joe's, to Maybury SP |
| 165 | I-696, I-275, MI 5, Grand River Ave. |
| | I-275 and I-96 run together 9 miles |
| 163 | I-696 (from eb) |
| 162 | Novi Rd, to Walled Lake, Novi, **N** gas: BP, food: Buffalo Wild Wings, Carrabba's, ChuckeCheese, Denny's, Oaks Grill, Red Lobster, Subway, lodging: Crowne Plaza, Hotel Baronette, Residence Inn, other: Ⓗ HOSPITAL, Circuit City, Gander Mtn, JC Penney, Jo-Ann Fabrics, Kohl's, Kroger, Michael's, PetCo, Sears/auto, WorldMkt, mall, **S** gas: Mobil, food: Baja Fresh, Big Boy, Bonefish Grill, Boston Mkt, Coney Island, Famous Dave's, Kim's Chinese, Melting Pot Rest., Olive Garden, Red Robin, Steve & Rocky's, TGIFriday, Wendy's, lodging: Courtyard, Wyndham Garden, other: Borders Books, Discount Tire, Old Navy, TJ Maxx, auto repair, vet |
| 161mm | rest area eb, full ♿ facilities, Ⓒ, vending, ⛐ litter barrels, petwalk |
| 160 | Beck Rd, 12 Mile Rd, **S** food: Coney Island other: Ⓗ HOSPITAL, Home Depot, Kroger, Staples, to Maybury SP |

| | |
|---|---|
| 159 | Wixom Rd, Walled Lake, **N** gas: Marathon/dsl, food: Wendy's, lodging: Baymont Inn, other: to Proud Lake RA, **S** gas: Meijer/dsl/24hr, Mobil, Shell, Valero, food: Arby's, Baskin-Robbins/Dunkin Donuts, Burger King, KFC/A&W, McDonald's, Stinger's Grill, Taco Bell, lodging: Comfort Suites, other: General RV Ctr, Lincoln/Mercury, Meijer |
| 155b a | to Milford, New Hudson, **N** Ford, to RV camping, to Lion Oaks CP, **S** gas: Mobil, Sunoco, food: Applebee's, Arby's, Chili's, Cold Stone, Coney Island, Jet's Pizza, McDonald's, Quizno's, Starbucks, Subway, Wendy's, other: Chevrolet, Discount Tire, Lowe's Whse, Walmart SuperCtr |
| 153 | Kent Lake Rd, **N** Kensington Metropark, **S** gas: Mobil |
| 151 | Kensington Rd, **N** Kensington Metropark, **S** Island Lake RA, food, lodging |
| 150 | Pleasant Valley Rd (no return wb), **S** Ⓒ |
| 148b a | US 23, N to Flint, S to Ann Arbor |
| 147 | Spencer Rd, **N** gas: Mobil, other: st police, **S** to Brighton St RA |
| 145 | Grand River Ave, to Brighton, **N** gas: BP, Shell/dsl, food: Arby's, Cracker Barrel, Outback Steaks, Pizza Hut, lodging: Courtyard, Homewood Suites, other: Cadillac/GMC, $General, Ford/Mercury, Honda, **S** gas: Clark/Subway/dsl, food: Big Boy, Burger King, Chili's, Coney Island, DQ, KFC, Lil Chef, Little Caesar's, LoneStar Steaks, McDonald's, Panera Bread, Red Robin, Taco Bell, Wendy's, lodging: Holiday Inn Express, other: AAA, Best Buy, Bob's Tire, Borders Books, Home Depot, Honda, Jo-Ann Etc., Marshall's, Mazda, Meijer/dsl, Michael's, Radio Shack, Rite Aid, PetsMart, Sears, Staples, Target, USPO, mall, to Brighton Ski Area |
| 141 | Lp 96 (from wb, no EZ return), to Howell, **N** gas: Shell, Sunoco/dsl, food: Applebee's, Bob Evans, Little Caesar's, McDonald's, Mesquite Jct, TW's Italian, lodging: Grandview Inn, other: Chevrolet, Kohl's, **S** gas: Speedway, food: Arby's, Big Boy, Taco Bell, Wendy's |
| 141mm | rest area wb, full ♿ facilities, Ⓒ, vending, ⛐, litter barrels, petwalk |
| 137 | D19, to Pinckney, Howell, **N** gas: Mobil, Shell/dsl, Speedway/dsl, Sunoco/Blimpie/Baskin-Robbins/Dunkin Donuts/dsl, food: Coney Island, lodging: Kensington Inn, other: Ⓗ HOSPITAL, Parts+, Spartan Tire, **S** food: Country Kitchen, lodging: Best Western |
| 135mm | rest area eb, full ♿ facilities, vending, Ⓒ, ⛐, litter barrels, petwalk |
| 133 | MI 59, Highland Rd, **N** gas: 7-11, Sunoco/McDonald's/dsl, food: Arby's, Castaway Cafe (1mi), HoneyTree Grille, lodging: Baymont, other: Tanger Outlets/famous brands |
| 129 | Fowlerville Rd, Fowlerville, **N** gas: BP/rest./24hr, Shell/dsl, Sunoco/dsl, food: A&W/KFC, Big Boy, CO Coffee, Fowlerville Rest., McDonald's, Taco Bell/Pizza Hut, Wendy's, lodging: Best Western, **S** gas: Mobil, food: Quizno's, Subway, other: Chrysler/Dodge/Jeep, other: Ford |
| 126mm | weigh sta both lanes |
| 122 | MI 43, MI 52, Webberville, **N** gas: Mobil/dsl/24hr, food: Angel's Café, McDonald's, other: MI Brewing Co |
| 117 | to Dansville, Williamston, 0-3 mi **N** gas: Admiral, Marathon/subs/dsl, food: Jersey's Giant Subs, Spag's Grill, **S** gas: Sunoco/dsl, food: Subway |

MI

## INTERSTATE 96 CONT'D

**E ↕ W**

**L A N S I N G**

| | |
|---|---|
| **111mm** | rest area wb, full ♿ facilities, 📞, 🍽, litter barrels, vending, petwalk |
| **110** | Okemos, Mason, **N** gas: BP/Dunkin Donuts/24hr, Marathon, Sunoco, food: Applebee's, Arby's, Backyard BBQ, Big Boy, Big John's Steaks, Cracker Barrel, Dunkin Donuts, Gilbert&Blake's Seafood, Grand Traverse, Little Caesar's, McDonald's, Panchero's Mexican, Sheshiang Garden, Starbucks, Stillwater Grill, Subway, Taco Bell, lodging: Comfort Inn, Fairfield Inn, Hampton Inn, Holiday Inn Express, other: 7-11, to stadium |
| **106b a** | I-496, US 127, to Jackson, Lansing, **N** St Police |
| **104** | Lp 96, Cedar St, to Holt, Lansing, **N** gas: Admiral, Speedway, food: Aldaco's Mexican, Applebee's, Barley's Grill, Beaner's, Blimpie, Bob Evans, Boston Mkt., China King, Cici's Pizza, Coney Island, Finley's Rest., Hooters, Jet's Pizza, KFC, Legend's Grill, LJ Silver, Los Tres Amigos, Mr Taco, New China, Pizza Hut, Steak'n Shake, Texas Roadhouse, Wendy's, White Castle/Church's, Zeus Rest., lodging: Day's Inn, Econolodge, Governors Inn, Regent Inn, Super 8, other: Ⓗ HOSPITAL, Aldi Foods, Belle Tire, Cadillac, Chevrolet, Chrysler/Jeep, Discount Tire, Dodge, Family$, GMC, Harley-Davidson, Hyundai, Kia/Suzuki, Lexus, Lincoln/Mercury, Meijer/dsl/24hr, Mitsubishi, Radio Shack, Saab, Sam's Club/gas, Target, Toyota, Walgreen, **S** gas: Marathon, Speedway/24hr, food: Buffalo's SW Café, Burger King, China East Buffet, Dairy Dan, Flapjack's Rest., Hungry Howie, Kang's Buffet, McDonald's, Ponderosa, Sir Pizza, Subway, lodging: Holiday Inn, other: AutoZone, Budget Tire, CarQuest, Family$, Kroger, L&L Foods, Lowe's Whse |
| **101** | MI 99, MLK Blvd, to Eaton Rapids, 0-3 mi **N** gas: Meijer/dsl/24hr, QD, food: Arby's, **S** gas: Speedway/Subway/dsl/24hr, Sunoco/dsl, food: Coach's Grill, McDonald's, Wendy's |
| **98b a** | Lansing Rd, to Lansing, **N** food: Arby's, Wendy's, lodging: AmeriHost, **S** gas: Citgo/dsl/Windmill Rest./24hr, Don's Trkstp, food: Coyote Creek Grill |
| **97** | I-69, US 27 S, S to Ft Wayne, N to Lansing |
| **95** | I-496, to Lansing |
| **93b a** | MI 43, Lp 69, Saginaw Hwy, to Grand Ledge, 0-1 mi **N** gas: Meijer/dsl/24hr, Shell, Speedway/dsl, food: Bennigan's, Burger King, Carrabba's, Denny's, Dolly's Pizza, Fine China, Frank's Grill, Jet's Pizza, McDonald's, Outback Steaks, Red Robin, Roxy's Grill, TGIFriday, Subway, lodging: Best Western, Fairfield Inn, Hampton Inn, Holiday Inn, Motel 6, Quality Suites, Red Roof Inn, Residence Inn, other: Ⓗ HOSPITAL, NAPA, Kohl's, Kroger, Walgreens, **S** gas: BP/24hr, QD, Sunoco/McDonald's, food: Arby's, Art's Pizza, Beaner's, Bob Evans, Cracker Barrel, Steak'n Shake, Subway, lodging: SpringHill Suites, other: Belle Tire, Discount Tire, Gander Mtn, GMC/Mazda, Lowe's Whse, Michael's, Walmart/auto |
| **92mm** | Grand River |
| **91** | I-69 N, US 27 N (from wb), to Flint, **S** gas: ♦FLYING J /Country Mkt/dsl/24hr |
| **90** | Grand River Ave, to ✈ |
| **89** | I-69 N, US 27 N (from eb), to Flint |
| **87mm** | rest area eb, full ♿ facilities, 📞, 🍽, litter barrels, vending, petwalk |

**G R A N D   R A P I D S**

| | |
|---|---|
| **86** | MI 100, Wright Rd, to Grand Ledge, **S** gas: Mobil/McDonald's/dsl, Speedway/Subway/24hr |
| **84** | to Eagle, Westphalia |
| **79mm** | rest area wb, full ♿ facilities, info, 📞, 🍽, litter barrels, vending, petwalk |
| **77** | Lp 96, Grand River Ave, Portland, **N** gas: BP/24hr, Marathon/dsl, Shell/Burger King, Speedway/dsl, food: Arby's, China Star, Little Caesar's, Hungry Howie's, McDonald's, Subway, Two Rivers Rest., Wendy's, lodging: Best Western, other: Family$, Ford, Rite Aid, Tom's Foods, **S** food: Wendy's, other: Ford |
| **76** | Kent St, Portland |
| **76mm** | Grand River |
| **73** | to Lyons-Muir, Grand River Ave |
| **69mm** | weigh sta both lanes |
| **67** | MI 66, to Ionia, Battle Creek, **N** gas: Meijer/dsl/24hr (4mi), Pilot/Subway/dsl/scales/24hr, food: Corner Landing Grill, lodging: AmeriHost (6mi), Midway Motel, Super 8, other: Ⓗ HOSPITAL, Meijer, Walmart SuperCtr (4mi), RV camping, st police |
| **64** | to Lake Odessa, Saranac, **N** Ionia St RA, **S** I-96 Speedway |
| **63mm** | rest area eb, full ♿ facilities, 📞, 🍽, litter barrels, petwalk, vending |
| **59** | Clarksville |
| **52** | MI 50, to Lowell, **N** gas: Mobil/Subway/dsl, other: fairgrounds, **S** gas: Marathon/Noble Roman's/dsl (2mi), other: RV camping |
| **46** | rd 6, to rd 37 |
| **46mm** | Thornapple River |
| **44** | 36 St, **S** ✈ |
| **43b a** | MI 11, 28th St, Cascade, **N** gas: Marathon/dsl, Meijer/dsl/24hr, food: Big Boy, Brann's Steaks, Burger King, Culver's, Macaroni Grill, Panera Bread, Pizza Hut, Quizno's, Sundance Grill, Subway, Wendy's, lodging: Baymont Inn, Best Western, Country Inn Suites, Crowne Plaza Hotel, Holiday Inn Express, Howard Johnson, other: Audi/Subaru/Porsche, Meijer, Mercedes/Volvo/VW, Walmart, **S** gas: BP, Citgo, Shell, Speedway/dsl, food: Applebee's, Arby's, Arnie's Rest., Bob Evans, Burger King, Carabba's, Carlos O'Kelley's, Cantina Mexican, Chili's, ChuckeCheese, Cold Stone, Denny's, Don Pablo, Grand Rapids Brewery, Honey Baked Ham, Hooters, IHOP, Jimmy Johns, Moe's SW Grill, Noodles & Co, Olive Garden, Panera Bread, Perkins, Smokey Bones, Subway, lodging: Comfort Inn, Days Inn, |

## INTERSTATE 96 CONT'D

**43b a** Continued
Extended Stay America, Fairfield Inn, Hampton Inn, Hilton, Holiday Inn, Homewood Suites, Knight's Inn, Motel 6, Quality Inn, Ramada, Red Roof Inn, Sleep Inn, Springhill Suites, **other:** Acura/Audi/Subaru, Barnes&Noble, Belle Tire, CarQuest, Circuit City, Costco/gas, $Tree, Ford, Fresh Mkt Foods, Gander Mtn, Home Depot, Jo-Ann Fabrics, Lentz Automotive, Lowe's Whse, Nissan, Old Navy, PetsMart, Sam's Club/gas, Staples, Target, TJ Maxx, U-Haul

**40b a** Cascade Rd, **N gas:** Forrest Hills Fuel, Marathon/dsl, **food:** Beaners Rest., Blimpie, China Garden, Forrest Hills Rest., Little Bangkok, Subway, **other:** 7-11/24hr, vet, **S gas:** Shell/Quizno's/dsl, Speedway/dsl, **food:** Jimmy John's, Zoup, **other:** H HOSPITAL, Keystone Drug

**39** MI 21 (from eb), to Flint

**38** E Beltline Ave, to MI 21, MI 37, MI 44, **N gas:** BP, Meijer/dsl, **food:** O'Charley's, **other:** Meijer, RV camping, **S food:** Uno Pizzaria, **lodging:** Country Inn Suites, **other:** H HOSPITAL

**37** I-196 (from wb, exits left), Gerald Ford Fwy, to Grand Rapids

**36** Leonard St, **1-2 mi S food:** Arby's, McDonald's (24hr), **other:** sheriff's dept

**33** Plainfield Ave, MI 44 Connector, **N gas:** BP, Meijer/dsl/24hr, Speedway, **food:** Arby's, Beaners, Big Apple Bagel, Blimpie, Buddy's Pizza, Cheers Grill, Fred's Pizza, Golden Dragon, KFC, Little Caesar's, Little Caesars, LJ Silver, McDonald's, Oriental Forrest., Papa Ramano's Pizza, Pizza Hut, Russ' Rest., Taco Bell, Wendy's, **lodging:** Grand Inn, Lazy T Motel, **other:** AutoZone, Belle Tire, BigLots, CarQuest, Chevrolet, Chrysler/Jeep, Discount Tire, Dodge, Firestone, Ford, Lincoln/Mercury, Lowe's, Mitsubishi, Goodyear/auto, K-Mart, Meijer, Midas, NAPA, Nissan/VW, NTB, Jeep, Radio Shack, Save-a-Lot Foods, Toyota, U-Haul, Walgreens, transmissions, vet, **S gas:** BP/24hr, **food:** Breakfast Nook, Denny's

**31mm** Grand River

**31b a** US 131, N to Cadillac, S to Kalamazoo, **1 mi N gas:** BP, **food:** McDonald's

**30b a** Alpine Ave, Grand Rapids, **N gas:** Marathon, 7-11/gas, **food:** Applebee's, Buffalo Wild Wings, Checkers, ChuckeCheese, Cold Stone, Culvers, El Burroti Mexican, Fire Mtn Grill, First Wok, IHOP, Jimmy John's, Logan's Roadhouse, McDonald's, Old Country Buffet, Olive Garden, Outback Steaks, Panera Bread, Peppino's Pizza, Perkins, Qdoba, Quizno's, Russ' Rest., Ryan's, Starbucks, Steak'n Shake, Subway, Taco Bell, TGIFriday, Tuesday Morning, Zoup, **lodging:** Hampton Inn, SpringHill Suites, **other:** Aldi Foods, AutoZone, Belle Tire, Best Buy, CarQuest, Circuit City, Discount Tire, $Tree, Ford/Kia, Kohl's, Marshall's, Michael's, NAPA, PepBoys, Radio Shack, Sam's Club/gas, Schuler Books, Target, TJ Maxx, Walgreens, Walmart SuperCtr/auto, **S gas:** Admiral/dsl, Marathon, Meijer/dsl/24hr, Speedway/dsl, **food:** Arby's, Burger King, Casa De Martina, Fazoli's, KFC, LJ Silver, McDonald's, Papa John's, Pizza Hut, Ponderosa, Wendy's, **lodging:** Motel 6, **other:** Goodyear/auto, Home Depot, Jo-Ann Fabrics, Meijer, Midas, Tuffy Auto, U-Haul

**28** Walker Ave, **S gas:** Meijer/dsl/24hr, **food:** Bob Evans, McDonald's, **lodging:** Baymont Inn, Quality In

**26** Fruit Ridge Ave, **N gas:** Citgo/dsl, **S gas:** Citgo/deli/dsl

**25mm** rest area eb, full ♿ facilities, 📞, 🏞, litter barrels, petwalk

**25** 8th Ave, 4 Mile Rd (from wb), **S gas:** Marathon/dsl, **lodging:** Wayside Motel

**24** 8th Ave, 4 Mile Rd (from eb), **S gas:** Marathon/dsl, **lodging:** Wayside Motel

**23** Marne, **N other:** tires, **S food:** Depot Café, Rinaldi's Café, **other:** USPO, Ernie's Mkt, fairgrounds/raceway

**19** Lamont, Coopersville, **N food, S food:** Sam's Joint Rest., **other:** LP

**16** B-35, Eastmanville, **N gas:** BP/Subway/dsl, Speedway/dsl/24hr, Shell/Burger King/dsl, **food:** Arby's, Little Caesar's, McDonald's, Taco Bell, **lodging:** AmeriHost, Rodeway Inn, **other:** Chevrolet/Poniac/Buick, Curves, Family Fare, Fun 'N Sun RV Ctr, Jeep/Dodge, Rite Aid, **S gas:** Pacific Pride/dsl, **other:** RV camping

**10** B-31 (exits left from eb), Nunica, **N food:** Turk's Rest., **S gas:** Marathon, **other:** RV camping, golf course/rest.

**9** MI 104 (from wb, exits left), to Grand Haven, Spring Lake, **S gas:** Marathon, **other:** to Grand Haven SP

**8mm** rest area wb, full ♿ facilities, 📞, 🏞, litter barrels, vending, petwalk

**5** Fruitport (from wb, no return)

**4** Airline Rd, **N other:** race track, **S gas:** Speedway/dsl, Wesco/dsl, **food:** Burger Crest Diner, Dairy Bar, McDonald's, Subway, Village Inn, **other:** Grover Drug, NAPA, Orchard Mkt Foods, Pleasure Island Water Park (5mi), USPO, to PJ Hoffmaster SP

**1c** Hile Rd (from eb), **S other:** racetrack

**1b a** US 31, to Ludington, Grand Haven, **N lodging:** Alpine Motel, Bel-aire Motel, Haven Motel, **other:** All Seasons RV Ctr, **2 mi N on Sherman Blvd gas:** Citgo/dsl, Westco/dsl, **food:** Applebee's, Arby's, Fazoli's, McDonald's, Old Country Buffet, Pizza Ranch, Red Wok, Ruby Tuesday, Subway, Wendy's, **lodging:** Comfort Inn/rest., **other:** H HOSPITAL, Circuit City, Lowe's Whse, PetsMart, Radio Shack, Sam's Club, Staples, Target, Walmart SuperCtr/gas, **S lodging:** AmeriHost, **other:** ✈, racetrack

**I-96 begins/ends on US 31 at Muskegon.**

## INTERSTATE 196 - GRAND RAPIDS

| Exit # | Services |
| --- | --- |
| **81mm** | I-196 begins/ends on I-96, 37mm in E Grand Rapids. |
| **79** | Fuller Ave, **N** sheriff, **S gas:** Shell/dsl, Speedway/dsl, **food:** Buddy's Pizza/Dogs, Checkers, Elbow Room, KFC, Subway, Taco Bell, Wendy's, **other:** HOSTIPAL, Ace Hardware, Family Foods, Walgreens |
| **78** | College Ave, **S gas:** Marathon/Circle K, **food:** McDonald's, **other:** H HOSPITAL, Rite Aid, ford museum |
| **77c** | Ottawa Ave, downtown, **S** Gerald R Ford Museum |
| **77b a** | US 131, S to Kalamazoo, N to Cadillac |
| **76** | MI 45 E, Lane Ave, **S food:** El Ganadero Mexican, **other:** Gerald R Ford Museum, John Ball Park&Zoo, Parts Plus |
| **75** | MI 45 W, Lake Michigan Dr, **N** to Grand Valley St U |
| **74mm** | Grand River |
| **73** | Market Ave, **N** to Vanandel Arena |
| **72** | Lp 196, Chicago Dr E (from eb) |

(Side bars: E W, GRAND RAPIDS, MUSKEGON, E W, MI)

## INTERSTATE 196 CONT'D - GRAND RAPIDS

E ↕ W

**70** MI 11 (exits left from wb), Grandville, Walker, **S gas:** BP/Subway/dsl, Shell/repair, **lodging:** Day's Inn, **other:** USPO, vet

**69b a** Chicago Dr, **N gas:** Meijer/dsl/24hr, **food:** China City, Culver's, KFC, McDonald's, Papa John's, Peppino's Pizza, Perkins, Subway, Taco Bell, **other:** Aldi Foods, AutoZone, BigLots, $General, $Tree, Meijer, Radio Shack, Save-a-Lot Foods, 7-11, Target, **S gas:** Admiral, Speedway/24 hr, **food:** Adobe Mexican, Arby's, Burger King, Dunkin Donuts/Baskin-Robbins, Little Caesar's, Pizza Hut, Russ' Rest., Wendy's, **lodging:** Best Western, Holiday Inn Express, **other:** NAPA

**67** 44th St, **N gas:** Mobil/dsl, **food:** Burger King, Cracker Barrel, Panera Bread, Steak'n Shake, **lodging:** Comfort Suites, **other:** AAA, Honda, Walmart/auto, **S food:** Famous Dave's, Logan's Roadhouse, Quizno's, Ritter's Custard, Starbucks, Wendy's, **lodging:** Residence Inn (2mi), **other:** Circuit City, Discount Tire, Gander Mtn., Lowe's Whse, PetsMart, World Mkt

**64** MI 6 E, to Lansing (exits left from wb)

**62** 32nd Ave, to Hudsonville, **N gas:** BP/dsl/24hr, Citgo/dsl, **food:** Arby's, Burger King, Maurizio's Pizza, McDonald's, Village Grill, **lodging:** Quality Inn, **other:** Chevrolet, camping, **S gas:** Mobil/Subway/dsl/24hr, **food:** Rainbow Grill, **lodging:** Super 8, **other:** Harley-Davidson, Harvest Foods

**58mm** rest area eb, full ♿ facilities, 🚹, ⛽, litter barrels, vending, petwalk

**55** Byron Rd, Zeeland, **N gas:** 7-11, **food:** Blimpie, McDonald's, **other:** Curves, 3-5 mi **N** H HOSPITAL, to Holland SP

**52** 16th St, Adams St, **2 mi N gas:** Meijer/dsl/24hr, **food:** Wendy's, **lodging:** Best Inn, Econolodge, **other:** H HOSPITAL, Meijer, **S gas:** Mobil/Subway/dsl, **food:** Burger King

**49** MI 40, to Allegan, **N gas:** BP/McDonald's/dsl, **lodging:** Residence Inn, **S gas:** Tulip City/Marathon/dsl/scales/24hr, **food:** Rock Island Rest.

**44** US 31 N (from eb), to Holland, **3-5 mi N lodging:** Country Inn, **other:** H HOSPITAL, gas, food

**43mm** rest area wb, full ♿ facilities, info, 🚹, ⛽, litter barrels, vending, petwalk

**41** rd A-2, Douglas, Saugatuck, **N gas:** Marathon/dsl, Shell/Subway/dsl, **food:** Babaloo's Pizza, Burger King, Spectators Grill, **lodging:** Best Western (1mi), Hootin Motel, Timberline Motel (3mi), **other:** $General, NAPA, Saugatuck RV Resort, to Saugatuck SP, **S food:** Ravine's Rest (1mi), **food:** Belvedere Inn, **lodging:** Shang-rai-la Motel, **other:** Red Barn Gifts

**38mm** Kalamazoo River

**36** rd A-2, Ganges, **N gas:** Shell, **lodging:** AmericInn

**34** MI 89, to Fennville, **N** to West Side CP, **S gas:** Shell/24hr, **other:** Cranes Pie Pantry (4mi, seasonal), Lyons Fruits, Winery Tours

**30** rd A-2, Glenn, Ganges, **N** to Westside Cty Park

**25mm** rest area eb, full ♿ facilities, 🚹, ⛽, litter barrels, vending, petwalk

**26** 109th Ave, to Pullman

**22** N Shore Dr, **N food:** Tello's Ristorante, **other:** to Kal Haven Trail SP, Cousin's RV Camping/rest.

B E N T O N   H A R B O R

N ↕ S

**20** rd A-2, Phoenix Rd, **N gas:** BP/dsl, Marathon/dsl, **food:** Arby's, Checkers, China Buffet, Taco Bell, **lodging:** SouthHaven Motel, **other:** H HOSPITAL, AutoZone, Walgreens, st police, **S gas:** Shell, **food:** Big Boy, McDonald's, Sherman's Dairybar, Wendy's, **lodging:** Comfort Suites, Hampton Inn, Holiday Inn Express, Ramada, **other:** $General, Walmart SuperCtr/gas/dsl

**18** MI 140, MI 43, to Watervliet, **0-2 mi N gas:** BP, Shell/dsl/24hr, Xpress/dsl, **food:** Burger King, 50's Drive Inn, McDonald's, Pizza Hut, **lodging:** Great Lakes Inn, LakeBluff Motel, **other:** AutoValue Parts, Buick/Pontiac/Cadillac/GMC, Chevrolet, Chrysler/Dodge/Jeep, Ford, Village Mkt Foods

**13** to Covert, **N** to Van Buren SP, RV camping

**7** MI 63, to Benton Harbor, **N food:** DiMaggio's Pizza, Vitale's Mkt/subs, **other:** RV camping

**4** to Coloma, Riverside, **S gas:** Marathon/dsl, **other:** KOA

**2mm** Paw Paw River

**1** Red Arrow Hwy, **N** Ross Field ✈

**0mm** I-94, E to Detroit, W to Chicago

I-196 begins/ends on I-94, exit 34 at Benton Harbor.

## INTERSTATE 275 - LIVONIA

**Exit #** Services

I-275 and I-96 run together 9 miles. See Michigan Interstate 96 exits 165-170.

**29** I-96 E, to Detroit, MI 14 W, to Ann Arbor

**28** Ann Arbor Rd, Plymouth, **E gas:** BP/Dunkin Donuts/24hr, Shell, **food:** Atlantis Rest., Denny's, Little Caesars, **lodging:** Days Inn, Red Roof Inn, **W food:** Bennigan's, Burger King, McDonald's, Steak&Ale, **lodging:** Comfort Inn, **other:** Cadillac, CVS Drug, Dodge, K-Mart, Lincoln/Mercury, vet

**25** MI 153, Ford Rd, Garden City, **W gas:** BP, Shell, Speedway, Valero, **food:** Applebee's, Arby's, BD Mongolian BBQ, Bob Evans, Boston Mkt., Bowery Grille, Buffalo Wild Wings, Carraba's, Chili's, ChuckeCheese, Coney Island, Dunkin Donuts/Baskin-Robbins, Hunan Empire Chinese, KFC, Little Caesar's, Outback Steaks, Panera Bread, Quizno's, Roman Forum Rest., Subway, TGIFriday, Tim Horton, TX Corral, Wendy's, White Castle/Church's, **lodging:** Extended Stay America, Fairfield Inn, La Quinta, Motel 6, **other:** Discount Tire, Firestone, Lowe's, PetCo, Richardson Drug, Target, Walgreens, vet

MI

## INTERSTATE 275 CONT'D - LIVONIA

N ↑↓ S

| | |
|---|---|
| 23 | rest area nb, full ♿ facilities, 📞 info, ⛱ litter barrels |
| 22 | US 12, Michigan Ave, to Wayne, **E gas:** BP/24hr, Marathon, Shell, Valero/dsl, **food:** Arby's, Jonathan's Rest., McDonald's, Subway, Wendy's, **lodging:** Day's Inn, Fellows Cr Motel, Holiday Inn Express, Super 8, Willo Acres Motel, **W gas:** Marathon/dsl, 7-11, **food:** Dunkin Donuts, McDonald's |
| 20 | Ecorse Rd, to Romulus, **E gas:** 7-11, **W gas:** Mobil/Burger King/scales/dsl/24hr |
| 17 | I-94 E to Detroit, W to Ann Arbor, **E** ⛽ |
| 15 | Eureka Rd, **E gas:** Shell, ⛽ |
| 13 | Sibley Rd, New Boston, **W gas:** Fusion/Subway/dsl, **food:** LC's Chicken, **other:** to Lower Huron Metro Park |
| 11 | S Huron Rd, **1 mi W gas:** Sunoco/Burger King/dsl, **food:** Jacob's Rest, **other:** RV LP (1mi) |
| 8 | Will Carleton Rd, to Flat Rock |
| 5 | Carleton, South Rockwood, **W** food |
| 4mm | rest area sb, full ♿ facilities, 📞, ⛱ litter barrels |
| 2 | US 24, to Telegraph Rd, **W gas:** Marathon/dsl, lodging |
| 0mm | I-275 begins/ends on I-75, exit 20. |

## INTERSTATE 475 - FLINT

N ↑↓ S

| Exit # | Services |
|---|---|
| 17.5mm | I-475 begins/ends on I-75, exit 125. |
| 15 | Clio Rd, **W gas:** BP, **other:** Chevrolet |
| 13 | Saginaw St, **E gas:** BP, **food:** McDonald's, Papa John's, Taco Bell, **other:** Advanced Parts, Family$, Kroger/gas, **W gas:** Marathon, Sunoco, **food:** Burger King, KFC, Little Caesar's |
| 11 | Carpenter Rd |
| 10 | Pierson Rd |
| 9 | rd 54, Dort Hwy, Stewart Ave, **E gas:** Citgo, **food:** McDonald's |
| 8mm | Flint River |
| 8b | Davison Rd, Hamilton Ave |
| 8a | Longway Blvd, **W food:** China 1 Buffet, **lodging:** Holiday Inn Express, **other:** Ⓗ HOSPITAL, USPO |
| 7 | rd 21, Court St, downtown Flint |
| 6 | I-69, W to Lansing, E to Port Huron |
| 5 | Atherton Rd (from sb), **E gas:** Citgo, Marathon, **other:** Curves |
| 4 | Hemphill Rd, Bristol Rd, **E gas:** Sunoco, **food:** Benitos Pizza, McDonald's, New China, **other:** Rite Aid, **W gas:** Speedway, **food:** Little Caesars, Ole Time Burgers, Tim Horton, Wendy's, **other:** Family$, Kroger/gas |
| 2 | Hill Rd, **E gas:** Speedway, **food:** Applebee's, Bob Evans, **lodging:** Wingate Inn, **other:** Ford, vet, **W gas:** Sunoco/Tim Horton, **food:** Arby's, Bangkok Peppers, Blimpie, Burger St Grill, Little Caesars, Pizza Hut, Wendy's, **lodging:** Courtyard, Holiday Inn, Residence Inn, **other:** Rite Aid |
| 0mm | I-475 begins/ends on I-75, exit 111. |

E ↔ W

## INTERSTATE 696 - DETROIT

| Exit # | Services |
|---|---|
| | I-696 begins/ends on I-94. |
| 28 | I-94 E to Port Huron, W to Detroit, 11 Mile Rd, **E gas:** BP/dsl, Speedway, 7-11 |
| 27 | MI 3, Gratiot Ave, **N gas:** BP, **food:** National Coney Island, **other:** Costco/gas, **S gas:** BP, Mobil/McDonald's, **food:** White Castle, **other:** Goodyear/auto |
| 26 | MI 97, Groesbeck Ave, Roseville, **N gas:** Mobil/dsl, **S gas:** Marathon, **food:** Wendy's |
| 24 | Hoover Rd, Schoenherr Rd, **N gas:** Sunoco, **food:** Burger King, KFC, **S gas:** BP, Mobil, **food:**'s, Subway, Taco Bell, Tim Horton, **lodging:** Holiday Inn Express, **other:** CVS Drug, Kroger, Marshall's |
| 23 | MI 53, Van Dyke Ave, **N gas:** BP, **food:** Arby's, Coney Island, Dunkin Donuts, McDonald's, **lodging:** Baymont Inn, **other:** Cadillac/Pontiac/GMC, Dodge, Jo-Ann Fabrics, radiators, **S gas:** BP/24hr, **food:** Burger King, **other:** Chevrolet, Ford, Toyota, USPO |
| 22 | Mound Rd |
| 20 | Ryan Rd, Dequindre Rd, **N gas:** Marathon, **food:** IHOP, **lodging:** Knight's Inn, Red Roof Inn, **S food:** Bob Evans, McDonald's, **lodging:** Comfort Suites, Ramada Ltd, **other:** Rite Aid, transmissions |
| 19 | Couzens St, 10 Mile Rd, **S** Hazel Park Racetrack |
| 18 | I-75 N to Flint, S to Detroit |
| 17 | Campbell Ave, Hilton Ave, Bermuda, Mohawk, **S gas:** Marathon/dsl |
| 16 | MI 1, Woodward Ave, Main St, **N food:** Burger King, **other:** zoo |
| 14 | Coolidge Rd, 10 Mile Rd, **S gas:** Mobil, Speedway, **food:** Dunkin Donuts, **food:** Jade Palace Chinese, Little Caesar's, LJ Silver, Pizza Hut, Subway, Taco Bell, Wendy's, **other:** CVS Drug, Jo-Ann Fabrics |
| 13 | Greenfield Rd, **S gas:** Mobil, Sunoco, **food:** Dunkin Donuts, **other:** Ford |
| 12 | MI 39, Southfield Rd, 11 Mile Rd, **S gas:** Shell |
| 11 | Evergreen Rd, **S lodging:** Residence Inn |
| 10 | US 24, Telegraph Rd, **N gas:** BP, Marathon, **food:** Denny's, Seoul Garden Korean, **lodging:** Hampton Inn, Embassy Suites, **other:** Belle Tire, Best Buy, Chevrolet, Chrysler/Jeep, Circuit City, Dodge, $General, Farmer Jack's, Ford, Honda/Nissan/Isuzu, Hyundai, Jo-Ann Fabrics, K-Mart, Lexus, Lincoln/Mercury, Office Depot, Pontiac/Buick, USPO, mall, **S gas:** Mobil, **lodging:** Courtyard, Hilton, Holiday Inn, Marriott |
| 8 | MI 10, Lodge Fwy |
| 5 | Orchard Lake Rd, Farmington Hills, **N gas:** Marathon, Mobil, Shell, **food:** Arby's, Hong Hua Chinese, Roberto's Rest., Ruby Tuesday, Starbucks, Steak&Ale, Steamer's Seafood, Subway, Wendy's, **lodging:** Comfort Inn, **other:** Discount Tire, to St Mary's Coll |
| 1 | (from wb), I-96 W, I-275 S, to MI 5, Grand River Ave |

MI

## INTERSTATE 35

| Exit # | Services |
|---|---|
| 260mm | I-35 begins/ends on MN 61 in Duluth. |
| 259 | MN 61, London Rd, to Two Harbors, North Shore, **W gas:** Holiday/dsl, ICO/dsl, Spur/dsl, **food:** Blackwoods Grill, Burger King, KFC, McDonald's, Perkins, Pizza Hut, Subway, Taco John's, Wendy's, **lodging:** Edgewater Inn, **other:** vet |
| 258 | 21st Ave E (from nb), to U of MN at Duluth, same as 259 |
| 256b | Mesaba Ave, Superior St, **E gas:** ICO/DQ, **food:** Caribou Coffee, Grandma's Grill, Little Angie's Cantina, Red Lobster, Timberlodge Steaks, Tradewinds Rest., **lodging:** Canal Park Inn, Comfort Suites, Hampton Inn, Hawthorn Suites, Lake Superior Inn, **W lodging:** Holiday Inn, Radisson, Sheraton |
| 256a | Michigan St, **E** waterfront, **W** H HOSPITAL, downtown |
| 255a | US 53 N, downtown, mall, **W other:** Kia |
| 255b | I-535 spur, to Wisconsin |
| 254 | 27th Ave W, **W gas:** Holiday/Burger King/dsl, Spur/dsl, **food:** Embers Grill, Quizno's, Subway, **lodging:** Motel 6 |
| 253b | 40th Ave W, **W gas:** BP/dsl/24hr, **food:** Perkins/24hr, **lodging:** Comfort Inn, Super 8 |

| | |
|---|---|
| 253a | US 2 E, US 53, to Wisconsin |
| 252 | Central Ave, W Duluth, **W gas:** Conoco/dsl, Holiday/dsl/24hr, **food:** Coffee Express, Giant Panda, KFC, McDonald's, Pizza Hut, Sammy's Café, Subway, **other:** Advance Parts, Checker Parts, Falk's Drug, K-Mart, Super 1 Foods, Walgreen, vet |
| 251b | MN 23 S, Grand Ave, **E lodging:** Holiday Inn Express |
| 251a | Cody St, **E lodging:** Allyndale Motel, **other:** zoo |
| 250 | US 2 W (from sb), to Grand Rapids, 1/2 mi **W gas:** Holiday/dsl, Mobil/dsl/LP, **food:** Blackwoods Grill, Wok-n-Grill, **lodging:** AmericInn |
| 249 | Boundary Ave, Skyline Pkwy, **E gas:** Holiday/McDonald's/dsl, **lodging:** Country Inn Suites, Sundown Motel (1mi), **other:** to ski area, **W** rest area both lanes, full ♿ facilities, info, 🚻, 🏕, litter barrels, vending, **gas:** Phillips 66/dsl/24hr, **food:** Blackwoods Grill, Country Kitchen, **lodging:** AmericInn, Red Roof Inn |
| 246 | rd 13, Midway Rd, Nopeming, **W gas:** Armor/dsl, **food:** Dry Dock Rest. |
| 245 | rd 61, **E food:** Buffalo House Rest./camping |
| 242 | rd 1, Esko, Thomson, **E gas:** BP |
| 239.5mm | St Louis River |
| 239 | MN 45, to Cloquet, Scanlon, **E other:** Jay Cooke SP, KOA (May-Oct), **W gas:** Holiday, **food:** Pantry Rest., |

## INTERSTATE 35 CONT'D

**N** ↕ **S**

| | |
|---|---|
| **239** | **Continued** **lodging:** Golden Gate Motel, Seasons Motel, **other:** H HOSPITAL, Chevrolet, Pontiac/Buick, camping, dsl repair |
| **237** | MN 33, Cloquet, **1 mi W gas:** BP/24hr, Spur, **food:** Applebee's, Arby's, Country Kitchen, DQ, McDonald's, Papa John's, Perkins/24hr, Pizza Hut, Subway, Taco Bell, Taco John's, Wendy's, **lodging:** AmericInn, Super 8, **other:** H HOSPITAL, Chrysler/Jeep/Ford, Family$, NAPA, Super 1 Foods, Walmart SuperCtr/gas, White Drug |
| **236mm** | weigh sta both lanes |
| **235** | MN 210, to Cromwell, Carlton, **E gas:** BP/dsl/rest., Armor Fuel, Spur/dsl/24hr, **food:** Spirit Rest, **lodging:** AmericInn, Royal Pines Motel, **other:** to Jay Cooke SP, **W other:** Black Bear Casino/Hotel/rest. |
| **235mm** | Big Otter Creek |
| **233mm** | Little Otter Creek |
| **227** | rd 4, Mahtowa, **E** camping, **W** TJ's Country Store/gas (2 mi) |
| **226mm** | rest area nb, full 🚻 facilities, 🅲, 🏞, litter barrels, vending, petwalk |
| **220** | rd 6, Barnum, **E** camping, **W gas:** BP/dsl/café/24hr, **lodging:** Northwoods Motel, **other:** Munger Tr |
| **219mm** | Moose Horn River |
| **218mm** | Moose Horn River |
| **216** | MN 27 (from sb, no EZ return), Moose Lake, **1-2 mi W gas:** BP, Cenex, Holiday/dsl, Spur, The Little Store, **food:** Art's Café, Blue Bear Cafe, DQ, **lodging:** AmericInn (4mi), Moose Lake Motel, **other:** H HOSPITAL, CarQuest, Chevrolet/Buick/Pontiac, Ford, Super Valu Foods, 1918 Museum, to Munger Trail |
| **214** | rd 73 (no EZ return from nb), **E other:** Alco, Moose Lake SP (2mi), camping, **W gas:** Conoco/Subway/dsl, **lodging:** AmericInn, **2 mi W lodging:** Moose Lake Motel, **other:** H HOSPITAL, Munger Trail, Red Fox Camping |
| **209** | rd 46, Sturgeon Lake, Sturgeon Lake **E gas:** Phillips 66, **W lodging:** Sturgeon Lake Motel, **food:** Ernie's Rest. (seasonal), **other:** camping (3mi) |
| **209mm** | rest area sb, full 🚻 facilities, 🅲, 🏞, litter barrels, vending, petwalk |
| **206.5mm** | Willow River |
| **205** | rd 43, Willow River, **W gas:** BP/dsl, **other:** camping (2mi), laundry |
| **198.5mm** | Kettle River |
| **198mm** | rest area nb, full 🚻 facilities, 🅲, 🏞, litter barrels, vending, petwalk |
| **195** | rd 18, rd 23 E, to Askov, **E gas:** Shell/cafe/dsl, **food:** Banning Jct Cafe, Lucille's Cafe (4mi), **lodging:** North Country Inn, **other:** to Banning SP, camping, **W** camping |
| **191** | MN 23, rd 61, Sandstone, **E gas:** BP/dsl/LP, Victory/dsl, **lodging:** Sandstone 61 Motel (2mi), **other:** Family Drug |
| **184mm** | Grindstone River |
| **183** | MN 48, Hinckley, **E gas:** Holiday/Hardee's/dsl, Marathon/Tobie's Rest./dsl, **food:** Burger King, DQ, Subway, Taco Bell, **lodging:** Day's Inn, Grand Northern Inn, **other:** Chevrolet, casino, flea mkt, to St Croix SP (15mi), **W gas:** Mobil/24hr, Phillips 66/White Castle/dsl, **food:** Cassidy's Rest., **lodging:** Travelodge, **other:** Fire Museum, laundromat |

**H I N C K L E Y**

**MN**

**P I N E C I T Y**

| | |
|---|---|
| **180** | MN 23 W, rd 61, to Mora |
| **175** | rd 14, Beroun |
| **171** | rd 11, Pine City, **E gas:** SA/dsl, **food:** McDonald's, **other:** Ace Hardware, Chrysler/Dodge/Jeep, **W** camping |
| **170mm** | Snake River |
| **169** | MN 324, rd 7, Pine City, **E gas:** Holiday/dsl, Pump-n-Munch/dsl, **food:** Billy's Grill, Domino's, DQ, KFC, Pizza Hut, Red Shed Rest., Subway, **other:** Ford/Mercury, Radio Shack, Walmart SuperCtr, camping, **W** to NW Co Fur Post HS |
| **165** | MN 70, to Grantsburg, Rock Creek, **E gas:** Rock Creek/dsl, **lodging:** Chalet Motel, **other:** camping, **W gas:** BP/dsl/café |
| **159** | MN 361, rd 1, Rush City, **E gas:** Holiday/Burger King/dsl, **food:** Kooly's Subs, **other:** H HOSPITAL, Rush City Foods, **W** camping (2mi) |
| **154mm** | rest area nb, full 🚻 facilities, 🅲, 🏞, litter barrels, vending, petwalk |
| **152** | rd 10, Harris, **2 mi E** gas/dsl |
| **147** | MN 95, to Cambridge, North Branch, **E gas:** Casey's, Conoco/dsl, Holiday/dsl, **food:** DQ, Domino's, KFC/Taco Bell, McDonald's, Oak Inn Rest, Perkins, Pizza Hut, Subway, **lodging:** AmericInn, Budget Host, **other:** CarQuest, Fisk Tire, NAPA, Radio Shack, SuperValu Foods, to Wild River SP (14mi), vet, **W food:** Applebee's, Burger King, Denny's, **other:** Chevrolet, Chrysler/Dodge/Jeep, Ford, Tanger Outlet/famous brands |
| **143** | rd 17, new exit |
| **139** | rd 19, Stacy, **E gas:** BP, Phillips 66, **food:** Pizza Man, Rustic Rest., Stacy Grill, Subway, **other:** city park, **W gas:** Marathon |
| **135** | US 61 S, rd 22, Wyoming, **E gas:** BP/dsl, Casey's, **food:** Cornerstone Café, DQ, Joe's Pizza, Subway, Tasty Asia, **other:** H HOSPITAL, Ace Hardware, CarQuest, IGA Foods, **W gas:** Shell/dsl, **food:** McDonald's, Village Inn Rest., **other:** camping (10mi), golf |
| **132** | US 8 (from nb), to Taylors Falls |
| **131** | rd 2, Forest Lake, **E gas:** BP/24hr, Holiday/dsl, SA/dsl, **food:** Applebee's, Arby's, Burger King, China Buffet, Cheung Sing Chinese, Culvers, KFC, McDonald's, Papa John's, Perkins, Quack's Cafe, Subway, Sbarro, Taco Bell, White Castle, **lodging:** AmericInn, **other:** H HOSPITAL, AutoValue Parts, Champion Auto, Checker Parts, Kennedy Transmissions, Rainbow Foods/24hr, Target, Tires+, Walgreen, Walmart, RV/Auto repair, **W gas:** Holiday/dsl, **food:** Famous Dave's BBQ, Papa Murphy's, Quizno's, Starbucks, Wendy's, **lodging:** Country Inn Suites, **other:** Buick/Pontiac, Chevrolet/Cadillac, Chrysler/Dodge/Jeep, Cub Foods, Ford, GNC, Home Depot, Jiffy Lube |
| **131mm** | rest area sb, full 🚻 facilities, 🅲, 🏞, litter barrels, vending, petwalk |
| **129** | MN 97, rd 23, **E** camping (6mi), **W gas:** BP/dsl, **other:** Coates RV Ctr, Gander Mtn., camping (1mi) |
| **128mm** | weigh sta both lanes |
| **127** | I-35W, S to Minneapolis. See I-35W. |
| **123** | rd 14, Centerville, **E food:** Dunn Bro's Coffee, **other:** Otter Lake RV Ctr, **W gas:** Marathon, Mobil/dsl, Shell, **food:** DQ, Embers Rest., Sagers Grill, WiseGuys Pizza, **other:** auto repair |
| **120** | rd J (from nb, no return) |

**F O R E S T L A K E**

## INTERSTATE 35 CONT'D

**N** ↑↓ **S**

**S T P A U L**

| | |
|---|---|
| **117** | MN 96, **E gas:** Marathon, SA/dsl, **food:** Burger King, Casa Lupita, **lodging:** AmericInn, **other:** Goodyear/auto, NAPA, **W gas:** BP, PDQ, **food:** Applebee's, Arby's/Sbarro's, Caribou Coffee, Culver's, McDonald's, Subway, **other:** Cub Foods, Tires+, USPO, Walgreen |
| **115** | rd E, **E gas:** BP, Conoco, SA/dsl, **food:** Jimmy's Rest., Perkins, **lodging:** Country Inn Suites, Holiday Inn Express, **W food:** Dunn Bros Coffee, KFC/Pizza Hut, Major's Cafe, McDonald's, Panera Bread, Papa Murphy's, Wendy's, **other:** Festival Foods, GNC, Radio Shack, Target, Walmart/auto |
| **114** | I-694 E (exits left from sb) |
| **113** | I-694 W |
| **112** | Little Canada Rd, **E gas:** BP, **W gas:** Sinclair, **food:** Porterhouse Rest |
| **111a/b** | MN 36 E, to Stillwater/MN 36 W, to Minneapolis |
| **110b** | Roselawn Ave |
| **110a** | Wheelock Pkwy, **E gas:** BP, Marathon, **food:** Subway, **W gas:** Sinclair/dsl |
| **109** | Maryland Ave, **E gas:** Marathon, SA/dsl, **W food:** Wendy's, **other:** K-Mart |
| **108** | Pennsylvania Ave, downtown |
| **107c** | University Ave, downtown, **E gas:** Conoco, **W other:** H HOSPITAL, to st capitol |
| **107b a** | I-94, W to Minneapolis, E to St Paul. I-35 and I-94 run together. |
| **106c** | 11th St (from nb), Marion St, downtown |
| **106b** | Kellogg Blvd (from nb), downtown, **E food:** Eagle St. Grill, Subway, **lodging:** Holiday Inn, **other:** H HOSPITAL |
| **106a** | Grand Ave, **E** H HOSPITAL |
| **105** | St Clair Ave |
| **104c** | Victoria St, Jefferson Ave |
| **104b** | Ayd Mill Rd (from nb) |
| **104a** | Randolph Ave |
| **103b** | MN 5, W 7th St, **E food:** Burger King, **W gas:** SA/dsl, **other:** USPO |
| **103a** | Shepard Rd (from nb) |
| **102mm** | Mississippi River |
| **102** | MN 13, Sibley Hwy, **W gas:** BP, Holiday/Subway |
| **101b a** | MN 110 W, **E food:** Caribou Coffee, Ziggy's Deli, **W gas:** SA |
| **99b a** | I-494 W/I-494 E |
| **98** | Lone Oak Rd, **E lodging:** Homestead Suites, Microtel, **other:** Sam's Club/gas, USPO, **W gas:** Marathon, **food:** Joe Senser's Grill, Magic Thai Café, **lodging:** Hampton Inn, Residence Inn |
| **97b** | Yankee Doodle Rd, **E gas:** Holiday, SA/dsl, **food:** Applebee's, Arby's, Blimpie, Burger King, Cattle Co Rest., Coldstone Creamery, Chili's, Culver's, DQ, Don Pablo, Houlihan's, Jake's Grill, Jimmy John's, KFC, McDonald's, New China Buffet, Noodles & Co, Old Chicago Pizza, Panera Bread, Perkins, Pizza Hut, Pizza Man, Pot Belly, Red Robin, Taco Bell, **lodging:** Residence Inn, Springhill Suites, TownePlace Suites, **other:** Barnes&Noble, Best Buy, Byerly's Foods, Cash Mart, Checker Parts, GNC, Home Depot, Michael's, Office Depot, Old Navy, Pets-Mart, Rainbow Foods, Tires+, TJ Maxx, Walgreen, **W gas:** BP, SA/dsl, **lodging:** Boston Mkt, Dragon Palace Chinese, Loro Mexican, Starbucks, Steak Bones Grill, |

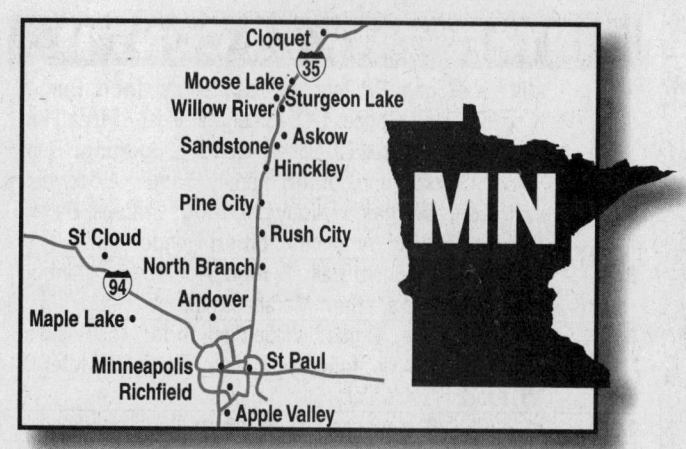

| | |
|---|---|
| **97b** | Continued **lodging:** Best Western, Extended Stay America, **other:** Italian Pie Shoppe |
| **97a** | Pilot Knob Rd, same as 97b, **E gas:** Holiday, **food:** Caribou Coffee, Chilli's, McDonald's, Wendy's, **lodging:** SpringHill Suites, TownePlace Suites, **other:** Firestone, Goodyear, Kennedy Transmissions, Kohl's, Walmart, mall, **W gas:** BP, SA/dsl, **lodging:** Best Western |
| **94** | rd 30, Diffley Rd, to Eagan, **E gas:** Shell/dsl, **other:** CVS Drug, **W gas:** Sinclair, **other:** Tires+ |
| **93** | rd 32, Cliff Rd, **E gas:** Holiday, **food:** Bonfire Grill, Subway, **other:** Ace Hardware, **W gas:** Holiday/dsl, Marathon/dsl, **food:** Baker's Square, Burger King, Boston Mkt, Burger King, DQ, Dolittle's Grill, Greenmill Rest., Hong Wong Chinese, KFC, McDonald's, Quizno's, Starbucks, Taco Bell, Wendy's, **lodging:** Hilton Garden, Holiday Inn Express, Staybridge Suites, **other:** Checker Parts, Cub Foods, Radio Shack, Target, USPO, Walgreen |
| **92** | MN 77, Cedar Ave, **E** Zoo, **1 m W** access to Cliff Rd services |
| **90** | rd 11, **E gas:** KwikTrip, **food:** Subway, **other:** Valley Natural Foods, **W gas:** SA/dsl |
| **88b** | rd 42, Crystal Lake Rd, **E food:** Chianti Grill, Ciatti's Grill, Tuesday Morning, **other:** PetsMart, **W gas:** BP, PDQ, **food:** Arby's/Sbarro's, BBQ, Burger King, Ground Round, McDonald's, Old Country Buffet, Roadhouse Grill, Taco Bell/Pizza Hut, **lodging:** Country Inn, Days Inn, Fairfield Inn, Hampton Inn, Holiday Inn, **other:** H HOSPITAL, Home Depot, USPO, **1/2 mi W gas:** Holiday/dsl, SA, Sinclair, **food:** Applebee's, Bakers Square, Buca Italian, Camaranh Bay, Champp's Grill, Chili's, IHOP, KFC, Kings Buffet, Macaroni Grill, Maya Mexican, Olive Garden, Outback Steaks, Panera Bread, Papa John's, Qdoba Mexican, Red Lobster, Starbucks, Wendy's, **lodging:** InTown Suites, **other:** Barnes&Noble, Best Buy, Chevrolet, Circuit City, Cub Foods, Discount Tire, Goodyear/auto, JC Penney, K-Mart, Kohl's, Macy's, Michael's, PetCo, Rainbow Foods, Sears/auto, Target, Tires+, Walgreen, mall |
| **88a** | I-35W (from nb), N to Minneapolis. See I-35W. |
| **87** | Crystal Lake Rd (from nb), **W gas:** KwikTrip, **other:** Buick, Ford/Lincoln/Mercury, Honda/Nissan, Saturn, Toyota, Beaver Mtn Ski Area |
| **86** | rd 46, **E gas:** KwikTrip, SA/dsl, **food:** KFC, Starbucks, **other:** Harley-Davidson, **W other:** O'Reilly Parts |

**MN**

4e=r4

## INTERSTATE 35 CONT'D

**N ↕ S**

**FARIBAULT**

| Exit | Services |
|------|----------|
| 85 | MN 50, **E** gas: BP/24hr, F&F/dsl, SA/dsl, **food:** Burger King, Caribou Coffee, DQ, Greenmill Rest., Pizza Hut, Subway, Taco Bell/LJ Silver, Wendy's, **lodging:** Best Value, Comfort Inn, **other:** Family Foods, Goodyear, Walgreen, **W** gas: Holiday/dsl, **food:** Cracker Barrel, Perkins, **lodging:** AmericInn, **other:** Gander Mtn. |
| 84 | 185th St W, Orchard Trail, **E** food: Applebee's, Caribou Coffee, Quizno's, **other:** Marshalls, Target |
| 81 | rd 70, Lakeville, **E** gas: Holiday/dsl, **food:** McDonald's, Subway, Tacoville, **lodging:** Holiday Inn/rest, Motel 6, **W** food: Harry's Cafe |
| 76 | rd 2, Elko, **E** gas: gas/dsl, **E** other: Elko Speedway |
| 76mm | rest area sb, full ♿ facilities, 🚻, 🛖, litter barrels, vending, petwalk |
| 69 | MN 19, to Northfield, 6-8 mi **E** gas: KwikTrip, **food:** Applebee's, Subway, Taco Bell, **lodging:** AmericInn, College City Motel, Country Inn Suites, Super 8, **other:** Ⓗ HOSPITAL, Carleton Coll, St Olaf Coll, **W** gas: Sunoco/dsl/rest/scales |
| 68mm | rest area nb, full ♿ facilities, 🚻, 🛖, litter barrels, vending, petwalk |
| 66 | rd 1, to Dundas, 1 mi **W** food: Boonie's Grill |
| 59 | MN 21, Faribault, **E** gas: BP/Pinecone/dsl/rest/scael/24hr., **food:** Hardee's, **lodging:** AmericInn, Best Value Inn, Day's Inn, 2 mi **E** gas: Mobil, SA, **food:** Arbys, A&W, Burger King, Cloud 9 Grill, DQ, Hardee's, KFC, Pizza Hut, Taco John's, **lodging:** Galaxie Inn, Lyndale Motel, **other:** Checker Parts, Ford/Lincoln/Mercury, vet, **W** other: Harley-Davidson, camping |
| 56 | MN 60, Faribault, **E** gas: BP, Hy-Vee Gas/dsl, KwikTrip, **food:** Arby's, Burger King, Great China Buffet, Hardee's, KFC, Perkins, Pizza Hut, Quizno's, Starbucks, Subway, Taco John's, **other:** Ⓗ HOSPITAL, Auto Value Parts, Buick/Pontiac, Checker Parts, Chevrolet, Chrysler/Jeep, Dodge, Family$, Goodyear/auto, Hy-Vee Foods, JC Penney, Jo-Ann Fabrics, Tires+, Walmart SuperCtr, mall, **W** gas: Petro/dsl, **food:** DQ, Happy Chef/24hr, **lodging:** Select Inn, **other:** Sakatah Lake SP, camping |
| 55 | (from nb, no return), 1 mi **E** gas: SA/dsl, KwikTrip, Mobil/dsl, **food:** A&W, Broaster Rest., Burger King, DQ, KFC, Pizza Hut, Quizno's, Southern China Cafe, Subway, Taco John's, **lodging:** AmericInn, Budget Inn, Galaxie Inn, **other:** Ford/Mercury |
| 48 | rd 12, rd 23, Medford, **W** food: McDonald's, **other:** Outlet Mall/famous brands |
| 45 | rd 9, Clinton Falls, **W** gas: KwikTrip/dsl, **food:** Caribou Coffee, Famous Daves BBQ, 43rd St Grill, Sbarros, Sportsman's Grille, Subway, TimberLodge Steaks, Wendy's, **lodging:** Comfort Inn, Holiday Inn, **other:** Cabela's Sporting Goods, Russell-Stover Candies, museum |
| 43 | rd 34, 26th St, Airport Rd, Owatonna |
| 42b a | US 14 W, rd 45, to Waseca, Owatonna, **E** food: Kernel Rest., **lodging:** Budget Host, **other:** AutoZone, Cash-Wise Foods, Chrysler/Dodge/Jeep, Ford/Lincoln/Mercury, **W** gas: BP/dsl/scales, KwikTrip/dsl, **food:** Culver's, Dunn Bros Coffee, Eastwind Buffet, Happy Chef, McDonald's, Perkins, **lodging:** Best Budget Inn, Owatonna Hotel, Super 8, **other:** $Tree, GNC, Kohls, Lowe's Whse, Radio Shack, Walmart SuperCtr/gas/dsl |

**OWATONNA**

**ALBERT LEA**

**N ↕ S**

| Exit | Services |
|------|----------|
| 41 | Bridge St, Owatonna, **E** gas: Holiday/dsl, **food:** Applebee's, Arby's, Burger King, DQ, KFC, Papa Murphy's, Quizno's, Starbucks, Subway, Taco Bell, **lodging:** AmericInn, Country Inn Suites, **other:** Ⓗ HOSPITAL, **W** gas: F&F/dsl, **lodging:** Microtel, **other:** Target |
| 40 | US 14 E, US 218, Owatonna, 1 mi **E** on rd 6 gas: Star/dsl, **food:** El Tequila Mexican, Godfather's, Taco John's, **lodging:** Oakdale Motel, **other:** Ⓗ HOSPITAL, Chevrolet/Pontiac/Buick, Curves, Hy-Vee Foods/24hr, Sterling Drug, TrueValue Hardware, Walgreen, WholesaleTire |
| 38mm | Turtle Creek |
| 35mm | rest area both lanes, full ♿ facilities, 🚻, 🛖, litter barrels, vending, petwalk |
| 34.5mm | Straight River |
| 32 | rd 4, Hope, 1/2 mi **E** camping, 1 mi **W** gas, food |
| 26 | MN 30, to Blooming Prairie, Ellendale, **E** gas: Conoco/dsl/rest., **W** gas: BP/pizza/dsl |
| 22 | rd 35, to Hartland, Geneva, 1 mi **E** gas, food |
| 18 | MN 251, to Hollandale, Clarks Grove, **W** gas: BP/dsl/LP, **other:** camping |
| 17mm | weigh sta, both lanes |
| 13b a | I-90, W to Sioux Falls, E to Austin, **W** Ⓗ HOSPITAL |
| 12 | US 65 S (from sb), Lp 35, Albert Lea, same as 11 |
| 11 | rd 46, Albert Lea, **E** gas: Love's/Wendy's/dsl/scales/24hr, TA/Shell/Coldstone/Pizza Hut/dsl/scales/24hr/@, **food:** Trails Rest., **lodging:** Comfort Inn, **other:** KOA (may-oct/6mi), dsl repair, **W** gas: KwikTrip, Shell/dsl, **food:** Burger King, Casa Zamora Mexican, China Buffet, Green Mill Rest, McDonald's, Perkins, Pizza Hut, Starbucks, Subway, Taco John's, Trumble's Rest., Wendy's, **lodging:** Country Inn Suites, Countryside Inn, Day's Inn, Ramada, Super 8, **other:** Ⓗ HOSPITAL, AutoZone, Buick/Pontiac/Cadillac/Honda, CarQuest, $Tree, Ford, Home Depot, Jeep, Mazda, NAPA, Nissan/VW, Radio Shack, Toyota, Volvo, Walmart SprCtr/gas/dsl, to Myre-Big Island SP |
| 9mm | Albert Lea Lake |
| 8 | US 65, Lp 35 US 65, Lp 35, Albert Lea, 2 mi **W** gas: Freeborn City Co-op/dsl, **food:** DQ, Hardee's |
| 5 | rd 13, to Glenville, Twin Lakes, 3 mi **W** camping |
| 2 | rd 5 |
| 1mm | Welcome Ctr nb, full ♿ facilities, 🚻, 🛖, litter barrels, vending, petwalk |
| 0mm | Minnesota/Iowa state line |

## INTERSTATE 35 - WEST

| Exit # | Services |
|--------|----------|
| 41mm | I-35W begins/ends on I-35, exit 127. |
| 36 | rd 23, **E** gas: BP/dsl, **W** gas: Phillips 66/dsl, **food:** Caribou Coffee, DQ, McDonald's, Miller's Grill, Subway, Taco Palace, **other:** Discount Tire, Kohl's, Super Target |
| 33 | rd 17, Lexington Ave, **E** gas: BP, 1 mi **E** food: Burger King, McDonald's, **W** food: Applebee's, Arby's, Coldstone's, Green Mill Rest., Joey's Seafood, Quizno's, Taco Bell/LJ Silvers, Wendy's, **other:** Cub Foods, GNC, Home Depot, Michael's, Radio Shack, Walgreen, Walmart |
| 329 | 5th Ave NE, to Lexington, Circle Pines, **W** Nat Sports Ctr |
| 31b | Lake Dr, **E** gas: Shell/dsl |
| 31a | rd J, 85th Ave NE (no EZ return to nb) |
| 30 | US 10 W, MN 118, to MN 65 |
| 29 | rd I |

## INTERSTATE 35 CONT'D - WEST

| | |
|---|---|
| **28c b** | rd 10, rd H, **W gas:** BP, **food:** Best Steaks, Jake's Café, KFC, McDonald's, Mermaid Café, Perkins, Pizza Hut/Taco Bell, RJ Riches Rest., Subway, Saturn, **lodging:** AmericInn, Day's Inn, **other:** carwash |
| **28a** | MN 96 |
| **27b a** | I-694 E and W |
| **26** | rd E2, **W gas:** Phillips 66/dsl |
| **25b** | MN 88, to Roseville (no EZ return to sb), **E gas:** SA/dsl, **lodging:** Courtyard, Fairfield Inn, Residence Inn, **W gas:** Mobil, PDQ, **food:** Barley John's, Godfather's, Jake's Café, Main Event Rest., McDonald's, Perkins/24hr, Subway |
| **25** | ard D (from nb), same as 25b |
| **24** | rd C, **E food:** Burger King, **lodging:** Holiday Inn, **W lodging:** Comfort Inn, **other:** Chevrolet/Pontiac/GMC, Chrysler/Dodge/Jeep, Volvo |
| **23b** | Cleveland Ave, MN 36, **E food:** India Palace Rest., Joe Senser's Rest., **lodging:** Day's Inn, Motel 6, Radisson, Super 8 |
| **23a** | MN 280, Industrial Blvd (from sb) |
| **22** | MN 280, Industrial Blvd (from nb), **E lodging:** Sheraton |
| **21b** | ard 88, Broadway St, Stinson Blvd, **E** Ford Trucks, **W food:** Burger King, Country Kitchen, Cousins Subs, McDonald's, Pizza Hut/Taco Bell, **other:** Home Depot, Old Navy, Rainbow Foods/24hr, Target |
| **19** | E Hennepin (from nb) |
| **18** | US 52, 4th St SE, University Ave, to U of MN, **E gas:** BP |
| **17c** | 11th St, Washington Ave, **E lodging:** Holiday Inn, **W gas:** Mobil, **other:** H HOSPITAL, Goodyear, to Metrodome |
| **17b** | I-94 W (from sb) |
| **17a** | MN 55, Hiawatha |
| **16b a** | I-94 (from nb), E to St Paul, W to St Cloud, to MN 65 |
| **153** | 1st St (from nb), Lake St, **E food:** McDonald's, Taco Bell, **other:** W H HOSPITAL |
| **143** | 5th St, 36th St |
| **134** | 6th St |
| **13mm** | Minnehaha Creek |
| **12b** | Diamond Lake Rd |
| **12a** | 60th St (from sb), **W gas:** Mobil, **other:** Cub Foods |
| **11b** | MN 62 E, to ✈ |
| **11a** | Lyndale Ave (from sb), **E gas:** Shell |
| **10b** | MN 62 W, 58th St |
| **10a** | rd 53, 66th St |
| **9c** | 76th St (from sb) |
| **9b a** | I-494, MN 5, to ✈ |
| **8** | 82nd St, **E other:** BMW, **W food:** Red Lobster, Wendy's, **other:** Best Buy, Chevrolet, Infiniti, Kia, Kohl's, Saturn, Suzuki, Toyota |
| **7b** | 90th St |
| **7a** | 94th St, **E gas:** BP, Goodyear/auto, **W lodging:** Holiday Inn |
| **6** | rd 1, 98th St, **E gas:** Holiday, Sinclair, **food:** Bakers Square, Burger King, Coldstone, Jimmy John's, New China, Starbucks, Wendy's, **other:** Bloomington Drug, Coldstone, Checker Parts, Festival Foods, Ford, Radio Shack, Walgreen, **W gas:** SA/dsl, **food:** Denny's |
| **5** | 106th St |
| **5mm** | Minnesota River |

| | |
|---|---|
| **4b** | 113th St, Black Dog Rd |
| **4a** | Cliff Rd, **E** Dodge, **W** VW |
| **3b a** | MN 13, Shakopee, Canterbury Downs, **E lodging:** Select Inn |
| **2** | Burnsville Pkwy, **E gas:** Amstar, Marathon, **food:** Bumpers Grill, **other:** AAA, mall, **W gas:** Holiday, **food:** Gourmet Chinese, Hooters, Perkins, TimberLodge Steaks, **lodging:** Best Value Inn, LivInn, Prime Rate Motel, Red Roof Inn, **other:** Best Buy, Goodyear/auto, vet |
| **1** | rd 42, Crystal Lake Rd. **See Minnesota Interstate 35, exit 88b.** |
| **0mm** | I-35W begins/ends on I-35, exit 88a. |

## INTERSTATE 90

| Exit # | Services |
|---|---|
| **277mm** | Minnesota/Wisconsin state line, Mississippi River |
| **275** | US 14, US 61, to MN 16, La Crescent, **N Welcome Ctr wb, full** ♿ **facilities, info,** 🕿, ⛾, **litter barrels, vending, petwalk, S gas:** Kwik Trip (1mi) |
| **272b a** | Dresbach |
| **270** | Dakota |
| **269** | US 14, US 61, to Winona (from wb), **N** to OL Kipp SP/camping |
| **266** | rd 12, Nodine, **N other:** Great River Bluff SP, camping, **S gas:** BP/Subway/dsl/24hr/@ |
| **261mm** | weigh sta both lanes |
| **257** | MN 76, to Houston, Ridgeway, Witoka, **N** gas, **S** camping |
| **252** | MN 43 N, to Winona, **7 mi N food:** Taco Bell, **lodging:** Express Inn, Holiday Inn, Quality Inn, **other:** H HOSPITAL |
| **249** | MN 43 S, to Rushford, **N other:** Peterbilt Trucks/repair |
| **244mm** | **rest area eb, full** ♿ **facilities,** 🕿, ⛾, **litter barrels, vending, petwalk** |
| **242** | rd 29, Lewiston |
| **233** | MN 74, to Chatfield, St Charles, **N gas:** Kwik Trip/LP/24hr (2mi), **food:** A&W (2mi), Pizza Factory, Subway (2mi), **other:** Whitewater SP, **S gas:** BP/dsl, **food:** Amish Ovens Rest./bakery, **other:** RV dump/LP |
| **229** | rd 10, Dover |
| **224** | MN 42, rd 7, Eyota, **N gas:** KwikTrip/dsl (3mi) |
| **222mm** | **rest area wb, full** ♿ **facilities,** 🕿, ⛾, **litter barrels, vending, petwalk** |
| **218** | US 52, to Rochester, **8 mi N food:** Old Country Buffet, **lodging:** Hampton Inn, Holiday Inn, Motel 6, Sleep Inn, **other:** Brookside RV Park, **S gas:** BP/dsl, **other:** KOA (Mar-Oct) (1mi) |

## INTERSTATE 90 CONT'D

**E ↕ W**

**AUSTIN**

**209b a** US 63, MN 30, to Rochester, Stewartville, 8-10 mi **N** lodging: Comfort Inn, Day's Inn, Econolodge, Hampton Inn, Holiday Inn, Super 8, **1 mi S** gas: KwikTrip, food: DQ, Subway, lodging: AmericInn

**205** rd 6

**202mm** rest area eb, full ♿ facilities, 🚽, 🪑, litter barrels, vending, petwalk

**193** MN 16, Dexter, **S** gas: BP/Oasis Grill/dsl, Windmill/Phillips 66/Pinecone Rest./dsl/24hr, food: Windmill Rest.

**189** rd 13, to Elkton

**187** rd 20, **S** Beaver Trails Camping

**183** MN 56, to Rose Creek, Brownsdale, **S** gas: Freeborn City Co-op/dsl/LP

**181** 28th St NE

**180b a** US 218, 21st St NE, to Austin, Oakland Place, **S** gas: Shell, lodging: Austin Motel

**179** 11th Dr NE, to Austin, **N** gas: BP/dsl/rest./24hr

**178b** 6th St NE, to Austin, downtown

**178a** 4th St NW, **N** food: Culver's, Perkins, Torge's Grill, lodging: AmericInn, Day's Inn, Holiday Inn other: AutoValue Parts, Chevrolet/Pontiac/GMC, vet, **S** gas: BP, KwikTrip/Subway, food: A&W, Burger King, other: Ⓗ HOSPITAL

**177** US 218 N, to Owatonna, Austin, Mapleview, **N** gas: Holiday, food: Applebee's, Arby's, KFC/LJ Silver, King Buffet, Quizno's, Wendy's, Yonkers, other: Aldi Foods, Cashwise Food/gas/24hr, $Tree, Hy-Vee Foods/gas, JC Penney, K-Mart, O'Reilly Parts, Radio Shack, ShopKO, Staples, Target, Walmart SuperCtr/gas, mall, **S** gas: Sinclair/McDonald's/dsl, food: Hardee's, lodging: Super 8

**175** MN 105, rd 46, to Oakland Rd, **N** gas: Mileage/dsl, food: Sportts Grill, lodging: Countryside Inn, **S** gas: BP, Shell/dsl, other: Chrysler/Dodge/Jeep, Ford/Mercury, camping, vet

**171mm** rest area wb, full ♿ facilities, 🚽, 🪑, litter barrels, petwalk

**166** rd 46, Oakland Rd, **N** other: KOA/LP, golf (par3)

**163** rd 26, Hayward, **S** gas: Shell (4mi), Freeborn County Co-op, food: Pizza Hut (4mi), Trails Rest. (4mi), other: Myre-Big Island SP, camping

**161.5mm** rest area eb, full ♿ facilities, 🚽, 🪑, litter barrels, petwalk

**ALBERT LEA**

**159b a** I-35, N to Twin Cities, S to Des Moines

**157** rd 22, Albert Lea, **S** gas: Hy-Vee Foods/gas/24hr, Shell, food: Applebee's, Arby's, DQ, Herberger's, McDonald's, Pizza Ranch, lodging: AmericInn, Holiday Inn Express, other: Ⓗ HOSPITAL, Ace Hardware, Chevrolet, Famliy$, Harley-Davidson, Radio Shack, ShopKO, mall

**154** MN 13, to US 69, to Manchester, Albert Lea, **N** gas: SA/dsl, **3 mi S** lodging: BelAire Motel

**146** MN 109, to Wells, Alden, **S** gas: BP/dsl/rest., Co-Op Gas, food: Tailfins Malt Shop

**138** MN 22, to Wells, Keister, **S** camping

**134** MN 253, rd 21, to Bricelyn, MN Lake

**128** MN 254, rd 17, to Frost

**119** US 169, to Winnebago, Blue Earth, **S** gas: Shell/dsl, Sinclair/dsl, food: Country Kitchen, DQ, McDonald's, Pizza Hut, Subway, lodging: AmericInn, Budget Inn,

**119** Continued Super 8, other: Ⓗ HOSPITAL, Walmart/drugs, Jolly Green Giant, camping

**119mm** rest area both lanes, full ♿ facilities, 🚽, 🪑, litter barrels, petwalk, playground

**113** rd 1, Guckeen

**107** MN 262, rd 53, to East Chain, Granada, **S** other: Flying Goose Camping (May-Oct) (1mi), gas/dsl

**FAIRMONT**

**102** MN 15, to Madelia, Fairmont, **S** gas: Walmart SuperCtr, **0-2 mi S** gas: BP, Cenex/dsl, Phillips 66/dsl, SA/dsl/24hr, food: Burger King, China Buffet, Green Mill Rest., KFC, McDonald's, Perkins, Pizza Ranch, Ranch Family Rest., Starbucks, Subway, Taco John's, Wendy's, Wok'n Grill, lodging: Budget Inn, Comfort Inn, Holiday Inn, Super 8, other: Ⓗ HOSPITAL, Ace Hardware, CarQuest, Chrysler/Dodge/Jeep, Cty Mkt Foods, $Tree, Ford, Freightliner, Goodyear, Hy-Vee Foods, JC Penny, K-Mart, NAPA, Pontiac/Buick/GMC, Radio Shack, Sears, ShopKO, Walgreens, USPO, camping, repair

**99** rd 39, Fairmont, **S** lodging: Highland Court Motel (2mi)

**93** MN 263, rd 27, Welcome, **1/2 mi S** gas: Cenex, camping

**87** MN 4, Sherburn, **1 mi S** gas: Cenex, other: camping

**80** rd 29, Alpha

**73** US 71, Jackson, **N** gas: SA/dsl, food: Burger King/TCBY, lodging: Econolodge, Super 8, other: KOA, to Kilen Woods SP, **S** gas: BP/DQ, food: Embers Rest., Pizza Ranch, Subway, lodging: AmericInn, Budget Host, Earth Inn, Prairie Winds Motel, other: Ⓗ HOSPITAL, Ace Hardware, Family$, Gordy's Foods, Chevrolet/Buick/Pontiac, Chrysler/Dodge/Jeep, to Spirit Lake

**72.5mm** W Fork Des Moines River

**72mm** rest area wb, full ♿ facilities, 🚽, 🪑, litter barrels, vending, petwalk

**69mm** rest area eb, full ♿ facilities, 🚽, 🪑, litter barrels, vending, petwalk

**64** MN 86, Lakefield, **N** Ⓗ HOSPITAL, gas/dsl, food, camping, to Kilen SP (12mi)

**57** rd 9, to Heron Lake, Spafford

**50** MN 264, rd 1, to Brewster, Round Lake, **S** camping

**47** rd 3 (from eb), no return

**46mm** weigh sta eb

**WORTHINGTON**

**45** MN 60, Worthington, **N** gas: BP/Blueline Cafe/dsl/scales, **S** gas: Casey's, Shell/dsl/24hr, food: McDonald's, other: camping

**43** US 59, Worthington, **N** gas: Mobil/dsl, lodging: Travelodge, **S** gas: Casey's, Cenex/dsl, Shell, food: Arby's, Burger King, Country Kitchen, DQ, Godfather's, Ground Round, Happy Chef, Hardee's, KFC, McDonald's, Perkins/24hr, Pizza Hut, Subway, Taco John's, lodging: AmericInn, Budget Inn, Day's Inn, Holiday Inn Express, other: Ⓗ HOSPITAL, County Mkt Foods/24hr, Farm and Fleet, Hy-Vee Foods, Chevrolet/Pontiac/Buick/Cadillac, $General, Family$, Ford, JC Penney, O'Reilly Parts, Radio Shack, ShopKO, Walgreens, Walmart SuperCtr/gas

**42** MN 266, rd 25, to Reading, **S** lodging: Days Inn, Super 8

**33** rd 13, to Wilmont, Rushmore

**26** MN 91, Adrian, **S** gas: Cenex/dsl, Kum & Go/Subway/dsl, Minimart/cafe, food: Bullpin Grill, Countryside Steaks, other: Adrian Camping

**25mm** rest area wb, full ♿ facilities, 🚽, 🪑, litter barrels, petwalk

MN

## INTERSTATE 90 CONT'D

**E ↕ W**

| | |
|---|---|
| 24mm | rest area eb, full &#9855; facilities, &#9742;, &#9851;, litter barrels, petwalk |
| 18 | rd 3, Kanaranzi, Magnolia, **N** camping |
| 12 | US 75, Luverne, **N gas:** Casey's, FuelTime/dsl, Phillips 66/dsl, Shell/dsl, Sinclair, **food:** China Rest., ChitChat's Grill, McDonald's, Subway, Taco John's, Tasty Drive-In, **lodging:** Comfort Inn, Cozy Rest Motel (1mi), Hillcrest Motel (2mi), Sunrise Motel, **other:** &#9412; HOSPITAL, Ace Hardware, Casey's Store, Chevrolet/Pontiac/Buick/GMC, Chrysler/Dodge/Jeep, $General, Glen's Foods, Macy's, truckwash, to Blue Mounds SP, Pipestone NM, **S food:** Magnolia Steaks, **lodging:** Super 8, **other:** Pamida |
| 5 | rd 6, Beaver Creek, **N gas:** Shell/dsl |
| 3 | rd 4, Beaver Creek |
| 1 | MN 23, rd 17, to Jasper, **N other:** to Pipestone NM, access to gas/dsl |
| 0mm | Minnesota/South Dakota state line, **Welcome Ctr/weigh sta eb, full** &#9855; **facilities, info,** &#9742;, &#9851;, **litter barrels** |

## INTERSTATE 94

**E ↕ W**

| Exit # | Services |
|---|---|
| 259mm | Minnesota/Wisconsin state line, St Croix River |
| 258 | MN 95 N, to Stillwater, Hastings, Lakeland, **N food:** Bungalow Grill |
| 257mm | weigh sta wb, **Welcome Ctr wb, full** &#9855; **facilities,** &#9742;, &#9851;, **litter barrels, vending, petwalk** |
| 253 | rd 15, Manning Ave, **N other:** StoneRidge Golf, **S** to Afton Alps SP, ski area |
| 251 | rd 19, Keats Ave, Woodbury Dr, **S gas:** KwikTrip, SA/dsl, **food:** Applebee's, Arby's, Boston's Rest., Burger King, Caribou Coffee, Chili's, Chipotle Mexican, Dino's Rest., Outback Steaks, Ray J's Grill, Subway, **lodging:** Extended Stay America, Holiday Inn Express, **other:** $Tree, Gander Mtn, Hancock Fabrics, Michael's, Sam's Club, Sportsman's Whse, Tuesday Morning, Walmart/auto, outlet mall/famous brands |
| 250 | rd 13, Radio Dr, Inwood Ave, **N food:** Buffalo Wild Wings, Caribou Coffee, Machine Shed Rest., Milio's Rest., Red Lobster, Olive Garden, **lodging:** Hilton Garden, Wild Wood Lodge, **other:** Best Buy, **S gas:** Holiday, **food:** Champp's, Quizno's, Starbucks, Sunsets Grill, Taco Bell, TGIFriday, Veitnam Rest., Wendy's, **other:** Borders Books/Café, Circuit City, Cub Foods, GNC, Hepner's Auto Ctr, Home Depot, JC Penney, Jo-Ann Crafts, LandsEnd Inlet, Old Navy, PetsMart, Tires+, World Mkt, vet |
| 249 | I-694 N & I-494 S |
| 247 | MN 120, Century Ave, **N food:** Denny's, Olympus Grill, **lodging:** AmericInn, Live Inn, **other:** Harley-Davidson, Saturn, **S gas:** SA, Sinclair, **food:** GreenMill Rest., **lodging:** Country Inn/rest., **other:** Chevrolet |
| 246c b | McKnight Ave, **N** 3M |
| 246a | Ruth St (from eb, no return), **N food:** Culvers's, Perkins, **other:** Firestone/auto, Michael's, TJ Maxx |
| 245 | White Bear Ave, **N gas:** SA/Subway, Gas4Less, **food:** Subway, **lodging:** La Quinta, Super 8, **other:** Walgreens, **S gas:** BP, Marathon, **food:** Arby's, Davanni's Pizza/subs, KFC/Pizza Hut, McDonald's, Papa John's, Sonic, Taco Bell, **other:** Byerly's Foods, Chrysler, Curves, Family$, O'Reilly Parts, Target |

| | |
|---|---|
| 244 | US 10 E, US 61 S, Mounds/Kellogg |
| 243 | US 61, Mounds Blvd, **S** River Centre |
| 242d | US 52 S, MN 3, 6th St, **N gas:** Holiday, **food:** Subway |
| 242c | 7th St, **S gas:** SA |
| 242b a | I-35E N, US 10 W, I-35E S (from eb) |
| 241c | I-35E S (from wb) |
| 241b | 10th St, 5th St, to downtown |
| 241a | 12th St, Marion St, Kellogg Blvd, **N lodging:** Best Western Kelly Inn, **other:** Sears, **S gas:** BP, Holiday, SA, **lodging:** Savoy Inn, **other:** &#9412; HOSPITAL, st capitol |
| 240 | Dale Ave |
| 239b a | Lexington Pkwy, Hamline Ave, **N gas:** BP, SA, **food:** Chevy's Mexican, Hardee's/24hr, **other:** &#9412; HOSPITAL, Cub Foods, K-Mart, Target, **S gas:** Holiday |
| 238 | Snelling Ave, **N food:** Applebee's, McDonald's, Perkins, **lodging:** Sheraton, **other:** CVS Drug, Jo-Ann Fabrics, Rainbow Foods, Walgreens, same as 239 |
| 237 | Cretin Ave, Vandalia Ave, to downtown |
| 236 | MN 280, University Ave, to downtown |
| 235b | Huron Blvd |
| 235mm | Mississippi River |
| 235a | Riverside Ave, 25th Ave, **N gas:** Winner, **food:** Starbucks, **S food:** Perkins, Taco Bell |
| 234c | Cedar Ave, downtown |
| 234b a | MN 55, Hiawatha Ave, 5th St, **N lodging:** Holiday Inn, **other:** to downtown |
| 233b | I-35W N, I-35W S (exits left from wb) |
| 233a | 11th St (from wb), **N** downtown |
| 231b | Hennepin Ave, Lyndale Ave, to downtown |
| 231a | I-394, US 12 W, to downtown |
| 230 | US 52, MN 55, 4th St, 7th St, Olson Hwy, **N** Metrodome, **S** &#9412; HOSPITAL, Int Mkt Square |
| 229 | W Broadway, Washington Ave, **N gas:** Holiday, **S gas:** Winner, **food:** Buger King, Little Caesar's, KFC, McDonald's, Subway, Taco Bell, Wendy's, **other:** Cub Foods, Walgreens |
| 228 | Dowling Ave N |
| 226 | 53rd Ave N, 49th Ave N |
| 225 | I-694 E, MN 252 N, to Minneapolis |
| 34 | to MN 100, Shingle Creek Pkwy, **N food:** Barnacle Bill's, Denny's, Oak City Rest., **lodging:** AmericInn, Comfort Inn, Country Inn&Suites, Crowne Plaza, Days Inn, Extended Stay America, Motel 6, Super 8, **S food:** C1 Buffet, Familia Mexican, King Buffet, Panera Bread, **other:** Best Buy, Kohl's, PepBoys, Target, Tires+ |

## INTERSTATE 94 CONT'D

**E ↕ W**

**33** rd 152, Brooklyn Blvd, **N gas:** SA, Shell, **food:** Culver's, Subway, **other:** Chevrolet, Dodge, Honda, Mazda, **S gas:** BP, **food:** Arby's, 50's Grill, Taco Bell, **other:** Family$, Sun Foods, Walgreens

**31** rd 81, Lakeland Ave, **N gas:** SA, Shell, **food:** Beach House Grille, Wendy's, **lodging:** Grand Rios, Ramada Inn, **S lodging:** Best Value Inn, Budget Host

**30** Boone Ave, **N lodging:** La Quinta, Northland Inn/rest., **S other:** Discount Tire, Home Depot

**29b a** US 169, to Hopkins, Osseo

**28** rd 61, Hemlock Lane, **N on Elm Creek food:** Arby's/ Sbarro's, Benihana, Biaggi's Italian, Boston's Grill, Champp's Grill, ChuckeCheese, Granite City Rest., Ground Round, Joe's Crabshack, Olive Garden, Panera Bread, Pittsburgh Blue, Potbelly's, Qdoba, Red Lobster, Starbucks, TimberLodge Steaks, TGI Fridays, **lodging:** Courtyard, Hampton Inn, Holiday Inn, Staybridge Suites, **other:** Best Buy, Border's, Jo-Ann Fabrics, Kohl's, Old Navy, World Mkt, **S gas:** BP, **food:** Perkins/24hr, **lodging:** Select Inn

**216** I-94 W and I-494

**215** rd 109, Weaver Lake Rd, **N gas:** SA/dsl, **food:** Bakers Square, Bella Sera, Broadway Pizza, Bucadibeppo, Burger King, Cattle Co Steaks, ChuckeCheese, DQ, Don Pablo, El Rodeo Mexican, Famous Dave's BBQ, Houlihan's, J Cousineau's Rest., KFC, Krispy Kreme, McDonald's, Old Country Buffet, Papa John's, Pizza Hut, Ricky Shawl's, Starbucks, Subway, Taco Bell, Timberlodge Steaks, Wendy's, **other:** Barnes&Noble, Byerly's Foods, Cub Foods, Gander Mtn, GNC, Goodyear/auto, JC Penney, K-Mart, Michael's, PetCo, Tires+, USPO, Walgreens, mall, same as 28, **S food:** Applebee's, Fuddrucker's

**214mm** rest area eb, full ♿ facilities, 📞, 🏕, litter barrels

**213** rd 30, 95th Ave N, Maple Grove, **N gas:** SA/dsl, **food:** Chipotle Mexican, Subway, **other:** H HOSPITAL, Home Depot, Target, **S gas:** Holiday/dsl, **food:** Culver's, McDonald's, Orient Buffet, Quizno's, **other:** Goodyear/auto, Menard's, Rainbow Foods, Sam's Club, Walgreens, Walmart SuperCtr, KOA (2mi)

**207** MN 101, to Elk River, Rogers, **N gas:** SA/dsl, TA/dsl/ scales/24hr/@, **food:** Applebee's, Arby's, Burger King, Culver's, Denny's, Domino's, DQ, Maynard's, McDonald's, Subway, Taco Bell, Wendy's, **lodging:** Hampton Inn, Super 8, **other:** Best Buy, Cabela's, Camping World, Cub Foods, Discount Tire, Goodyear/auto, Kohl's, Lowes Whse, NAPA, Target, Tires+, Walgreens, vet, **S gas:** BP/ dsl, Sinclair/dsl, Holiday, **food:** Black Bear Rest., BoBo Asia, Cottage Grill, Guadalahara Mexican, **lodging:** AmericInn, **other:** Chevrolet, Curves, CVS Drug

**205.5mm** Crow River

**205** MN 241, rd 36, St Michael, **S gas:** SA/dsl

**202** rd 37, Albertville, **N gas:** Hacks/dsl, **S gas:** BP, Sunoco

**201** rd 19 (from eb), Albertville, St Michael, **N food:** Burger King, Michael B's Grill, Perkins, **lodging:** Country Inn&Suites, **other:** Albertville Outlets/famous brands, Old Navy, **S gas:** Casey's, Mobil, **food:** Caribou Coffee, China Dragon, Culver's, Major's Cafe, Papa Murphy's, Rancho Grande Mexican, Space Aliens Grill, Subway, **other:** Ace Hardware, Coburn's Foods, Goodyear/auto

---

**195** rd 75, Monticello, **N gas:** Cruiser's/dsl, Marathon/dsl, **food:** Caribou Coffee, **other:** H HOSPITAL, Home Depot, Target

**193** MN 25, to Buffalo, Monticello, Big Lake, **N gas:** Holiday/dsl, **food:** Burger King, Caribou Coffee, Guadalajara Mexican, KFC, Papa Murphy's, Perkins, Quizno's, Rancho Grande Mexican, Taco Bell, **lodging:** AmericInn, **other:** AutoValue Parts, Cub Foods, K-Mart, Radio Shack, USPO, **S gas:** SA/dsl, Holiday/dsl, Shell, **food:** Applebee's, Arby's, Chatter's Rest., China Buffet, Culver's, D'Angelo's Pizza, DQ, McDonald's, Subway, Taco John's, **lodging:** Best Western, Day's Inn, Select Inn, **other:** Buick/GMC/Pontiac, Checker Parts, Chevrolet, Ford/Mercury, Chrysler/Dodge/Jeep, Goodyear/auto, KIA, Suzuki, Walmart SuperCtr, vet, Lake Maria SP

**187mm** rest area eb, full ♿ facilities, 📞, 🏕, litter barrels, vending, petwalk

**183** rd 8, to Silver Creek, Hasty, Maple Lake, **S gas:** BP/dsl/ rest./scales/24hr/@, **other:** to Lake Maria SP, camping

**178** MN 24, to Annandale, Clearwater, **N gas:** Holiday/ Petro/dsl/scales/24hr/@, **food:** DQ, Burger King, Keith's Rest., Subway, **lodging:** Best Value Inn, Best Western, **other:** KOA (1mi), Coburn's Foods, **S other:** RV Camping (1mi)

**178mm** rest area wb, full ♿ facilities, 📞, 🏕, litter barrels, petwalk, vending

**173** Opportunity Dr., **N** Good Sam RV Park (May-Oct) (5mi)

**171** rd 7, rd 75, St Augusta, **N gas:** Cenex, MacDaddy's, Pilot/dsl/scales/24hr, **food:** McDonald's, RJ's Grill, Subway, **lodging:** AmericInn, Holiday Inn Express, Travelodge, **other:** H HOSPITAL, Goodyear/auto, **S other:** Pleasureland RV Ctr

**167b a** MN 15, to St Cloud, Kimball, **4 mi N gas:** Holiday, SA/ dsl, **food:** Applebee's, Arby's, Bonanza, Buffalo Wild Wings, Burger King, Chipotle Mexican, IHOP, Little Caesar's, McDonald's, Noodles&Co, Old Chicago Pizza, Olive Garden, Panchero's Mexican, Perkins, Pizza Hut, Taco Bell, Starbucks, TGIFriday's, TimberLodge Steaks, Wendy's, **lodging:** Comfort Inn, Country Inn&Suites, Days Inn, Fairfield Inn, Hampton Inn, Holiday Inn, Homewood Suites, Super 8, **other:** H HOSPITAL, Barnes&Noble, Best Buy, CashWise Foods, Circuit City, JC Penney, Kohl's, K-Mart, Macy's, Office Depot, Old Navy, Sam's Club, Scheel's Sports, Sears/auto, ShopKO, Sportsman's Whse, Target, **S gas:** Shell/dsl (2mi)

**164** MN 23, to St Cloud, Rockville, **4-6 mi N gas:** BP, **food:** Culver's, IHOP, KFC, Space Aliens Rest., Taco Bell, **lodging:** Motel 6, **other:** Gander Mtn, Hyundai, Menard's, PetsMart, Toyota/Scion

**162.5mm** Sauk River

**160** rd 2, to Cold Spring, St Joseph, **N gas:** Holiday, **lodging:** Super 8, **other:** Coll of St Benedict

**158** rd 75 (from eb exits left), to St Cloud, **3 mi N** same as 160

**156** rd 159, St Joseph, **N** St Johns U

**153** rd 9, Avon, **N gas:** Shell/dsl, Tesoro/McDonald's/dsl, **food:** Subway, **lodging:** Budget Host, **other:** Dhalin's Foods, TrueValue, USPO, **S other:** El Rancho Manana Camping (10mi), auto parts

**152mm** rest area both lanes, full ♿ facilities, 📞, 🏕, litter barrels, vending, petwalk

**ST CLOUD**

**MN**

## INTERSTATE 94 CONT'D

**E ↕ W**

**147** MN 238, rd 10, Albany, **N gas:** Holiday/dsl/24hr, Shell/A&W/Subway/dsl, **food:** DQ, Godfather's, Hillcrest Rest., **lodging:** Country Inn&Suites, **other:** H HOSPITAL, Amby's Foods, **S other:** Chrysler/Dodge/Jeep

**140** rd 11, Freeport, **N gas:** Cenex/dsl, Freeport/dsl, **food:** Ackie's Pioneer Rest., Charlie's Café, **other:** Corner Store Foods, USPO, vet

**137** MN 237, rd 65, New Munich

**137mm** Sauk River

**135** rd 13, Melrose, **N gas:** Mobil/dsl/repair, Tesoro/Subway/dsl/24hr, **food:** Burger King, Gundy's Rest., **other:** H HOSPITAL, Ernie's Foods, NAPA, **S gas:** Casey's/dsl, **food:** DQ, El Portal Mexican, **lodging:** Super 8, **other:** Save Foods, vet

**132.5mm** Sauk River

**131** MN 4, to Paynesville, Meire Grove

**128mm** Sauk River

**127** US 71, MN 28, Sauk Centre, **N gas:** Casey's, Holiday/dsl, **food:** DQ, Hardee's, McDonald's, Pizza Hut, Subway, **lodging:** AmericInn, Best Value Inn, Palm's Motel, **other:** H HOSPITAL, Coborn's Foods, Ford/Mercury, Lewis Ctr/rest area, Walmart SuperCtr, **S gas:** BP/dsl/café/scales/24hr/@, **other:** Buick/Chevrolet/Chrysler/Dodge/Jeep/Pontiac, Freightliner

**124** Sinclair Lewis Ave (from eb), Sauk Centre

**119** rd 46, West Union

**114** MN 127, rd 3, to Westport, Osakis, **3 mi N** gas, food, lodging

**105mm** rest area wb, full & facilities, ℭ, ⚲, litter barrels, vending, petwalk

**A L E X A N D R I A**

**103** MN 29, to Glenwood, Alexandria, **N gas:** F&F/dsl, Holiday, Tesoro, **food:** Burger King, Caribou Coffee, Country Kitchen, Culver's, Dolittle's Café, Hardee's, KFC, McDonald's, Perkins, Pizza Hut, Subway, Taco Bell, Wendy's, Whiskey Creek, **lodging:** AmericInn, Day's Inn, Super 8, **other:** H HOSPITAL, Cadillac/Chevrolet/Mazda, County Mkt Foods, Goodyear/auto, Jeep, K-Mart, Menard's, Target, Walmart SuperCtr, **S gas:** Holiday/dsl, **food:** Rudy's Grill, **lodging:** Country Inn&Suites, Holiday Inn, **other:** Alexandria RV Ctr, Buick/GMC/Pontiac

**100** MN 27, **N lodging:** L Motel/RV Park, Skyline Motel, **other:** H HOSPITAL, **S** camping

**100mm** Lake Latoka

**99mm** rest area eb, full & facilities, ℭ, ⚲, litter barrels, vending, petwalk

**97** MN 114, rd 40, to Lowry, Garfield

**90** rd 7, Brandon, **2-3 mi N** gas, food, **lodging:** Lake Country Motel (1mi), **S** camping, ski area

**82** MN 79, rd 41, to Erdahl, Evansville, **2 mi N gas:** BP/dsl, Spur, **food:** Kramer's Rest., **S other:** H HOSPITAL, camping

**77** MN 78, rd 10, to Barrett, Ashby, **N** gas/dsl, food, camping, **S** camping

**69mm** rest area wb, full & facilities, ℭ, ⚲, litter barrels, petwalk, vending

**67** rd 35, Dalton, **N** camping, **S** camping

**61** US 59 S, rd 82, to Elbow Lake, **N gas:** Tesoro/dsl/café/LP/24hr, **other:** H HOSPITAL, Pine Plaza RV Ctr, camping (4mi), **S** camping

**60mm** rest area eb, full & facilities, ℭ, ⚲, litter barrels, petwalk, vending

**F E R G U S   F A L L S**

**57** MN 210, rd 25, Fergus Falls, **N** H HOSPITAL

**55** rd 1, to Wendell, Fergus Falls

**54** MN 210, Lincoln Ave, Fergus Falls, **N gas:** Cenex/dsl, F&F/dsl, Holiday, Tesoro/dsl, **food:** Applebee's, Arby's, Burger King, Burger Time, Debbie's Kitchen, Godfather's, Hunan Buffet, KFC, McDonald's, Papa Murphy's, Perkin's, Pizza Hut, Pizza Ranch, Speedway Grill, Subway, **lodging:** AmericInn, Best Western, Comfort Inn, Day's Inn, Motel 7, Super 8, **other:** H HOSPITAL, Advance Parts, Chrysler/Dodge/Jeep, $Tree, Ford/Lincoln/Mercury, GMC/Pontiac, Herbergers, Home Depot, K-Mart, NAPA, Parts+, Radio Shack, SunMart Foods, Target, Tires+, Toyota, mall, **S food:** Mabel Murphy's Rest., **other:** Walmart/drugs

**50** rd 88, rd 52, to US 59, to Fergus Falls, Elizabeth

**38** rd 88, Rothsay, **S gas:** Tesoro/dsl/café/24hr, **lodging:** Comfort Zone Inn, **other:** Tires

**32** MN 108, rd 30, to Pelican Rapids, Lawndale, **19 mi N** Maplewood SP

**24** MN 34, Barnesville, **N food:** Renee's Drive-in, **1 mi S** gas: Cenex/dsl, Tesoro/dsl, **food:** DQ, **lodging:** motel

**22** MN 9, Barnesville, **1 mi S gas:** Cenex/dsl, Tesoro/dsl, **food:** DQ, **lodging:** motel

**15** rd 10, Downer

**8mm** Buffalo River

**6** MN 336, rd 11, to US 10, Dilworth

**5mm** Red River weigh sta eb

**M O O R H E A D**

**2** rd 52, Moorhead, **1-2 mi N gas:** Holiday/dsl, **food:** Perkins, Pizza Ranch, **lodging:** Travelodge, **other:** H HOSPITAL, KOA, Menard's, Target, **S other:** antiques

**2mm** Welcome Ctr eb, full & facilities, info, ℭ, ⚲, litter barrels, vending

**1b** 20th St, Moorhead (from eb, no return)

**1a** US 75, Moorhead, **N gas:** Clark, **food:** Blimpie, Burger King, Papa Murphy's, Qdoba Mexican, Starbucks, Village Inn, **lodging:** Courtyard, **other:** Curves, SunMart Foods, **S gas:** Bud's, Casey's, Orton's Gas, **food:** Panchero's Grill, Snapdragon Rest., Subway, **lodging:** AmericInn, Grand Inn, Super 8, **other:** CVS Drug, GMC, KIA, Loopy's $Store, TrueValue

**0mm** Minnesota/North Dakota state line, Red River

## INTERSTATE 494/694

| Exit # | Services |
|---|---|
| | **I-494/I-694 loops around Minneapolis/St Paul.** |
| 71 | rd 31, Pilot Knob Rd, **N lodging:** Courtyard, Fairfield Inn, **S lodging:** Best Western, Crowne Plaza, **food:** LoneOak Café |
| 70 | I-35E, N to St Paul, S to Albert Lea |
| 69 | MN 149, MN 55, Dodd Rd, **N food:** Ziggy's Deli, **S food:** Caribou Coffee, McDonald's, Subway, **lodging:** Budget Host, Country Inn&Suites, |
| 67 | MN 3, Roberts St, **1 mi N gas:** BP, Mobil, Holiday, **food:** Acre's Rest., Arby's/Sbarro's, Baker's Square, Buffalo Wings, Burger King, Chipotle Mexican, ChuckeCheese, Culver's, Grand Buffet, KFC, Old Country Buffet, Pizza Hut, Taco Bell, Timber Lodge Steaks, White Castle, **other:** Aamco, Best Buy, Buick/Pontiac, Checker Parts, Chevrolet, Cub Foods, Dodge, Ford, Jo-Ann Fabrics, Kia, K-Mart, Lincoln/Mercury, Mazda, NAPA, Nissan, Rainbow Foods/24hr, Saturn, Target, Tires+, Toyota, VW, Walmart, **S gas:** PDQ |
| 66 | US 52, **S gas:** SA, **food:** Old World Pizza, Outback Steaks, **lodging:** Country Inn&Suites, Microtel |
| 65 | 7th Ave, 5th Ave |
| 64b a | MN 56, Concord St, **N gas:** Conoco/dsl, **lodging:** Best Western Drovers, **other:** Ford Trucks, Goodyear, Peterbilt, **S gas:** EZ Stop, **other:** Chrysler/Jeep/Dodge, Parts+ |
| 63mm | Mississippi River |
| 63c | Maxwell Ave |
| 63b a | US 10, US 61, to St Paul, Hastings, **S gas:** BP, SA, **food:** Burger King, Subway, **lodging:** Boyd's Motel, **other:** NAPA |
| 60 | Lake Rd, **E gas:** SA/dsl, **W lodging:** Country Inn&Suites |
| 59 | Valley Creek Rd, **E gas:** BP/repair, SA/dsl/LP, **food:** America's Burger, Applebees, Broadway Pizza, Chipotle Mexican, DQ, Old Country Buffet, Papa Murphy's, Perkins, Potbelly's Rest., Yang's Chinese, **lodging:** Red Roof Inn, **other:** Barnes&Noble, Kohl's, Marshall's, Office Depot, PetCo, Rainbow Foods, Target, Walgreens, USPO, **W gas:** PBQ, **food:** Bonfire Rest., Burger King, McDonald's, Pizza Hut, Subway, **lodging:** Hampton Inn, **other:** H HOSPITAL, Ace Hardware, Goodyear |
| 58c | Tamarack Rd, **E food:** Paisano's Cafe, Woodbury's Cafe, **lodging:** Sheraton |
| 58b a | I-94, E to Madison, W to St Paul. **I-494 S begins/ends, I-694 N begins/ends** |
| 57 | rd 10, 10th St N, **E gas:** SA **food:** IHOP, Quizno's, **lodging:** Wingate Inn, **W gas:** Holiday, **food:** Burger King, Hunan Buffet, KFC, **other:** $Tree, K-Mart, Rainbow Foods/24hr, mall, vet |
| 55 | MN 5, **E other:** Target, **W gas:** Holiday/dsl, **food:** Subway, **other:** Menard's, st patrol |
| 52b a | MN 36, N St Paul, to Stillwater, **W gas:** F&F/dsl |
| 51 | MN 120, **E gas:** BP, SA/dsl, **food:** Jethro's, Starbucks, **W gas:** Kellie's Corner/gas |
| 50 | White Bear Ave, **E gas:** SA, **other:** K-Mart, Sam's Club/gas, **W gas:** BP, Shell, **food:** Acupulco Chicken, Arby's, Bakers Square, Buffalo Wild Wings, Caribou Coffee, Chili's, Denny's, Great Moon Buffet, IHOP, Jake's Grill, |

| 50 | Continued |
|---|---|
| | Jimmy John's, KFC, McDonald's, Noodles&Co, North China, Old Country Buffet, Outback Steaks, Peiwei Asian, Perkins/24hr, Red Lobster, Taco Bell, TGI Friday, Wendy's, **lodging:** Emerald Inn, **other:** Aamco, Best Buy, Circuit City, Goodyear/auto, JC Penney, Jo-Ann Fabrics, Kohl's, Macy's, Marshall's, Michael's, PetCo, Sears/auto, Tires+, Tuesday Morning, Walgreens, mall |
| 48 | US 61 (from wb), **E other:** Acura, Chrysler/Dodge/Jeep, Ford, Honda, Hyundai, Isuzu/Subaru, Lincoln/Mercury, Saturn, **W food:** Chili's, Gulden's Rest., McDonald's, Olive Garden, **lodging:** Best Western, **other:** H HOSPITAL, Audi/Porsche, Lexus, Mercedes, Toyota, Venburg Tire, Volvo |
| 47 | I-35E, N to Duluth |
| 46 | I-35E, US 10, S to St Paul |
| 45 | rd 49, Rice St, **N gas:** Gas+, Marathon/dsl, **food:** Papa John's, Subway, Taco Bell, **other:** Checker Parts, **S gas:** Marathon/dsl, **food:** A&W, Burger King, Caribou Coffee, Taco John's, **other:** Kath Parts |
| 43b | Victoria St, **S** Bill's Foods |
| 43a | Lexington Ave, **N food:** Greenmill Rest., Red Robin, **lodging:** Hampton Inn, Hilton Garden, **S gas:** Exxon, Sinclair, **food:** Blue Fox Grill, Burger King, Davanni's Pizza, Papa Murphy's, Perkins, Subway, Wendy's, **lodging:** Holiday Inn, Super 8, **other:** Cub Foods, Goodyear/auto, Target, transmissions |
| 42b | US 10 W (from wb), to Anoka |
| 42a | MN 51, Snelling Ave, **1 mi S gas:** Shell, **food:** Flaherty's Grill, Lindey's Steaks, McDonald's, **lodging:** Country Inn&Suites, Holiday Inn |
| 41b a | I-35W, S to Minneapolis, N to Duluth |
| 40 | Long Lake Rd, 10th St NW |
| 39 | Silver Lake Rd, **N gas:** BP, Sinclair, **food:** Champps, McDonald's, **other:** Ford, **S food:** Culver's, Wendy's, |
| 38b a | MN 65, Central Ave, **N gas:** Holiday/dsl, **food:** Crabhouse, Subway, **S gas:** SA, SuperStop, **food:** A&W/KFC, Applebee's, Arby's, Asia Rest., Buffalo Wild Wings, Cousins Subs, Denny's, Flameburger Rest., La Casita Mexican, McDonald's, Papa John's, Ricky's, Taco Bell, Wendy's, White Castle, **lodging:** Starlite Motel, **other:** Advance Parts, Discount Tire, GNC, Radio Shack, Target, Tires+ |
| 37 | rd 47, University Ave, **N gas:** Holiday, SA/dsl, **food:** Burger King, McDonald's, Papa Murphy's Pizza, Zantigo's Rest., **other:** Cub Foods, CVS Drug, Goodyear, Home Depot, PetsMart, Walgreens, **S gas:** Bona Bros/repair, Shell |
| 36 | E River Rd |
| 35mm | **I-494 W begins/ends, I-694 E begins/ends** |
| 35c | MN 252, **N gas:** Holiday, SA |
| 35b a | I-94 E to Minneapolis |
| 34 | to MN 100, Shingle Creek Pkwy, **N food:** Barnacle Bill's, Denny's, Oak City Rest., **lodging:** AmericInn, Comfort Inn, Country Inn&Suites, Crowne Plaza, Days Inn, Extended Stay America, Motel 6, Super 8, **S food:** C1 Buffet, Familia Mexican, King Buffet, Panera Bread, **other:** Best Buy, Kohl's, PepBoys, Target, Tires+ |
| 33 | rd 152, Brooklyn Blvd, **N gas:** SA, Shell, **food:** Culver's, Subway, **other:** Chevrolet, Dodge, Honda, Mazda, **S gas:** BP, **food:** Arby's, 50's Grill, Taco Bell, **other:** Family$, Sun Foods, Walgreens |

MN

## INTERSTATE 494/694 CONT'D

**E ↕ W MINNEAPOLIS**

| Exit | Description |
|---|---|
| 31 | rd 81, Lakeland Ave, **N** gas: SA, Shell, **food:** Beach House Grille, Wendy's, **lodging:** Grand Rios, Ramada Inn, **S lodging:** Best Value Inn, Budget Host |
| 30 | Boone Ave, **N lodging:** La Quinta, Northland Inn/rest., **S** other: Discount Tire, Home Depot |
| 29b a | US 169, to Hopkins, Osseo |
| 28 | rd 61, Hemlock Lane, **N on Elm Creek** food: Arby's/Sbarro's, Benihana, Biaggi's Italian, Boston's Grill, Champp's Grill, ChuckeCheese, Granite City Rest., Ground Round, Joe's Crabshack, Olive Garden, Panera Bread, Pittsburgh Blue, Potbelly's, Qdoba, Red Lobster, Starbucks, TimberLodge Steaks, TGI Fridays, **lodging:** Courtyard, Hampton Inn, Holiday Inn, Staybridge Suites, **other:** Best Buy, Border's, Jo-Ann Fabrics, Kohl's, Old Navy, World Mkt, **S** gas: BP, **food:** Perkins/24hr, **lodging:** Select Inn |
| 27 | I-94 W to St Cloud, I-94/694 E to Minneapolis |
| 26 | rd 10, Bass Lake Rd, **E** gas: Conoco, **food:** Culver's, McDonald's, **lodging:** Extended Stay America, **other:** mall, **W** gas: BP, Sinclair/LP, **lodging:** Hilton Garden |
| 23 | rd 9, Rockford Rd, **E** gas: BP, Holiday, **food:** Chili's, **other:** Checker Parts, Lincoln/Mercury, Old Navy, Radio Shack, Rainbow Foods/24hr, Target, Walgreen, **W** gas: Conoco, PDQ, **food:** Caribou Coffee, Cousins Subs, DQ, LeAnn Chin Chinese, Starbucks, Subway, TGIFriday |
| 22 | MN 55, **E** gas: Holiday/dsl, **food:** Denny's, Green Mill Rest., McDonald's, **lodging:** Best Western Kelly, Radisson, Red Roof Inn, **W** gas: Holiday/dsl, **food:** Arby's, Burger King, Davanni's Rest., Grandma's Grill, Mulligan's Grill, New Dynasty Chinese, Perkins, **lodging:** Comfort Inn, Day's Inn, Holiday Inn, **other:** Goodyear/auto, Tires+ |
| 21 | rd 6, **E** gas: BP/KwikTrip, **other:** Discount Tire, Home Depot |
| 20 | Carlson Pkwy, **E** gas: Holiday/dsl, **food:** Subway, **W** food: Italianni's Rest., **lodging:** Country Inn Suites |
| 19b a | I-394 E, US 12 W, to Minneapolis, **1 mi E** off of I-394 **food:** Applebee's, Byerly's Rest., Godfather's, Uno Pizza, Wendy's, **other:** Best Buy, Borders Books, Circuit City, Ford, JC Penney, Jo-Ann Fabrics, Marshall Field, Mazda, Mercedes/BMW, Saab, Sears/auto, Target, Tires+, mall, **1/2 mi W** gas: BP, **food:** Bankok Bowl, BBQ,'s, Pizza Hut, **other:** ,Chevrolet, Lexus, Mitsubishi, Nissan |
| 17b a | Minnetonka Blvd, **W** gas: Mobil, **food:** Dunn Bros Coffee |
| 16b a | MN 7, **1 mi W** food: Davanni's Rest., Famous Dave's BBQ, Hopkins House Rest., Lund's Rest., McDonald's, Perkins, Subway, Taco Bell |
| 13 | MN 62, rd 62 |
| 12 | Valleyview Rd, rd 39 (from sb) |
| 11c | MN 5 W, **N lodging:** Extended Stay America, **other:** Land Rover, **S** other: Chevrolet |
| 11b a | US 169 S, US 212 W, **N** food: Don Pablo, **lodging:** AmeriSuites, Courtyard, Fairfield Inn, Hampton Inn, Residence Inn, **S** gas: Phillips 66, **food:** Hop's Grill, **lodging:** Homestead Suites, SpringHill Suites, TownePlace Suites, **other:** Cub Foods, Office Depot |
| 10 | US 169 N, to rd 18 |
| 8 | rd 28 (from wb, no return), E Bush Lake Rd |
| 7b a | MN 100, rd 34, Normandale Blvd, **N** gas: Shell/dsl, **food:** Burger King, Chili's, DQ, Embers Rest., Subway, |

**S MINNEAPOLIS**

| Exit | Description |
|---|---|
| 7b a | Continued TGIFriday, **lodging:** Days Inn, Radisson, Sheraton, **S lodging:** Country Inn Suites, Crowne Plaza, Hilton Garden, Holiday Inn, La Quinta, Staybridge Inn |
| 6b | rd 17, France Ave, **N** gas: Mobil, **food:** Cattle Co Rest., ChuckeCheese, Fuddrucker's, Hot Wok, Macaroni Grill, McDonald's, Perkins, Quizno's, **lodging:** Best Western, Park Plaza Hotel, **other:** [H] HOSPITAL, Circuit City, Michael's, Office Depot, Old Navy, World Mkt, **S** food: Denny's, Joe Senser's Grill, Olive Garden, **lodging:** Hampton Inn, **other:** Buick/Pontiac/GMC, Ford, Mercedes, Nissan, Toyota/Scion |
| 6a | Penn Ave (no EZ eb return), **N lodging:** Residence Inn, **other:** Best Buy, Buick, Hyundai, Isuzu, **S** food: Applebee's, Atlantic Buffet, Herburger's, Starbucks, Steak&Ale, Subway, **lodging:** Embassy Suites, **other:** Chevrolet, Chrysler/Pymouth/Jeep, Dodge, Kohl's, Rainbow Foods, Target, TJ Maxx |
| 5b a | I-35W, S to Albert Lea, N to Minneapolis |
| 4b | Lyndale Ave, **N** gas: BP, Conoco, **food:** Boston Mkt, DQ, **lodging:** Candlewood Suites, Hampton Inn, **other:** Best Buy, Borders, Honda, Lands End, Mitsubishi, Radio Shack, Tires+, **S** gas: Phillips 66, **lodging:** Extended Stay America, **other:** Acura, Home Depot, Lincoln/Mercury, Mazda, Subaru |
| 4a | MN 52, Nicollet Ave, **N** gas: SA/dsl, **food:** Burger King, Ember's, Rest, Jumbo Chinese, **lodging:** Candlewood Suites, **other:** Honda, **S** gas: Mobil, Shell, **food:** Kwik Mart, Big Boy, McDonald's, **lodging:** La Quinta, **other:** Home Depot, Sam's Club |
| 3 | Portland Ave, 12th Ave, **N** gas: Phillips 66, Sinclair, PDQ Mart, **food:** Arby's, **lodging:** AmericInn, **S** gas: BP, **food:** Denny's, Outback Steaks, Subway, **lodging:** Comfort Inn/rest., Holiday Inn Express, Microtel, Quality Inn, Residence Inn, Travelodge, **other:** Walgreens, Walmart |
| 2c b | MN 77, **N lodging:** Motel 6, **S** gas: BP, SA, **lodging:** AmeriSuites, Best Western, Courtyard, Embassy Suites, Exel Inn, Fairfield Inn, Grand Motel, Marriott, Sheraton, **other:** Nordstrom's, Sears, Mall of America |
| 2a | 24th Ave, same as 2c b |
| 1b | 34th Ave, Nat Cemetary, **S lodging:** Embassy Suites, Hilton, Holiday Inn |
| 1a | MN 5 E, ✈ |
| 0mm | Minnesota River. I-494/I-694 loops around Minneapolis/St Paul. |

MN

## INTERSTATE 10

| Exit # | Services |
|---|---|
| 77mm | Mississippi/Alabama state line, weigh sta wb |
| 75 | Franklin Creek Rd |
| 74.5mm | **Welcome Ctr wb, full** ♿ **facilities,** 🕻, 🛆, **litter barrels, petwalk, RV dump, weigh sta eb** |
| 74mm | Escatawpa River |
| 69 | MS 63, to E Moss Point, **N gas:** Texaco/Domino's/dsl/24hr, **food:** Waffle House, **lodging:** Deluxe Inn, Econolodge, La Quinta, **S gas:** Chevron/dsl, Cone/dsl, Exxon/Subway/24hr, Shell, **food:** Barnhill's Buffet, Burger King, Cracker Barrel, Hardee's, KFC, McDonald's, Pizza Hut, Ruby Tuesday, S&S Steaks, Waffle House, Wendy's, **lodging:** Best Western, Comfort Inn, Day's Inn, Hampton Inn, Holiday Inn Express, Quality Inn, Shular Inn, **other:** Ⓗ HOSPITAL |
| 68 | MS 613, to Moss Point, Pascagoula, **N gas:** BP, Chevron/dsl, **food:** Coco Loco, **lodging:** Super 8, **S gas:** BP/dsl, **other:** Ⓗ HOSPITAL |
| 64mm | Pascagoula River |
| 63.5mm | **rest area both lanes, full** ♿ **facilities,** 🕻, 🛆, **litter barrels, petwalk, RV dump, 24hr security** |
| 61 | to Gautier, **N other:** MS Nat Golf Course, **1-3 mi S gas:** BP/dsl, **lodging:** Best Western, Suburban Lodge, **other:** Shephard Camping, Sandhill Crane WR |
| 57 | MS 57, to Vancleave, **N gas:** Shell/dsl, **food:** Shed BBQ, **other:** Journey's End Camping, tires, **S gas:** Exxon, **other:** Ⓗ HOSPITAL |
| 50 | MS 609 S, Ocean Springs, **N gas:** Texaco/Domino's/dsl, **food:** Waffle House, **lodging:** Best Western, Comfort Inn, Country Inn&Suites, Ramada Ltd, Red Carpet Inn, Scottish Inn, Super 8, **other:** Martin Lake Camping, **S gas:** BP/dsl, Chevron/McDonald's, Exxon, Fleet/dsl/scales, **food:** Denny's, Waffle House, Wendy's, **lodging:** Day's Inn, Hampton Inn, Holiday Inn Express, Howard Johnson, Quality Inn, **other:** $General, Nat. Seashore, vet |
| 46b a | I-110, MS 15 N, to Biloxi, **N gas:** Chevron, Kangaroo/dsl, **food:** Beef O'Brady's, Chili's, CiCi's Pizza, Outback Steaks, Ruby Tuesday, Strami's Italian, Sonic, Subway, Toro Japanese, Waffle House, Wendy's, Whataburger, **lodging:** Quality Inn, Regency Inn, Travel Inn, Wingate Inn, **other:** Lowes Whse, Radio Shack, Tire Kingdom, Walmart SuperCtr, **S** Ⓗ HOSPITAL, to beaches |
| 44 | Cedar Lake Rd, to Biloxi, **N gas:** Pilot/Subway/dsl/scales/24hr, **other:** Chevrolet, **S gas:** Chevron/dsl, Shell/dsl, **food:** Applebee's, El Saltillo, KFC/LJ Silver, McDonald's, Red Eye Grill, Sonic, Subway, Waffle House, Wow Cafe, **lodging:** La Quinta, **other:** Ⓗ HOSPITAL, Beauvoir, $General, Harley-Davidson, Home Depot, O'Reilly Parts, to Jeff Davis Shrine, Biloxi Nat Cem |
| 41 | MS 67 N, to Woolmarket, **N gas:** BP, Chevron/dsl, **other:** golf (6mi), **S** Mazalea RV Prk, Parkers Landing RV Prk, Reliable RV Ctr |
| 39.5mm | Biloxi River |
| 38 | Lorraine-Cowan Rd, **N gas:** Exxon/Subway, Kangaroo/dsl, **food:** Capt Al's Cafe, Domino's, McDonald's, Sonic, **S gas:** Pure/dsl, **food:** KFC, **other:** Ⓗ HOSPITAL, Baywood RV Park, Foxes RV Park, to beaches |
| 34b a | US 49, to Gulfport, **N gas:** Chevron/dsl, Exxon, Kangaroo, Texaco/dsl, **food:** Azteca Mexican, |

| 34b a | Continued |
|---|---|
| | Backyard Burger, Barnhill's Buffet, Beef O'Brady's, Burger King, Cane's Chicken, Chick-fil-A, Chili's, ChuckeCheese, CiCi's Pizza, Cracker Barrel, Domino's, Hardee's, KFC, Logan's Roadhouse, O'Charley's, Papa John's, Pizza Hut, Popeye's, Sonic, Starbucks, TGIFriday, Waffle House, Wendy's, Whataburger, **other:** Advance Parts, Barnes&Noble, Belk, Best Buy, Chevrolet/Cadillac, Circuit City, CVS Drug, $General, Goodyear/auto, Goody's, Honda, Office Depot, Old Navy, PetsMart, Rite Aid, Ross, Tire Kingdom, TJ Maxx, USPO, Walgreens, **S gas:** Chevron, Kangaroo/dsl, RaceWay, Shell/dsl, **food:** Applebee's, Arby's/24hr, Burger King, Choung's Garden, Hooters, IHOP, KFC/LJ Silver, Krispy Kreme, Los Tres Amigos, McAlister's Deli, McDonald's, Morelia's Mexican, Sonic, Steve's Marina, Subway, Waffle House, Wendy's, Zaxby's, **lodging:** Best Value, Best Western, Comfort Inn, Day's Inn, Fairfield Inn, Hampton Inn, Holiday Inn, Motel 6, Quality Inn, SunSuites, Value Place, **other:** Ⓗ HOSPITAL, Ford/Lincoln/Mercury, Freightliner, Home Depot, Kia, Michael's, NAPA, Nissan, Prime Outlets/famous brands, Sam's Club, Walmart SuperCtr/gas, transmissions |
| 31 | Canal Rd, to Gulfport, **N gas:** Love's/Arby's/dsl/scales/24hr, **other:** Bayberry RV Park, **S gas:** ✈FLYING J/Conoco/Cookery/dsl/LP/scales/24hr, Shell/McDonald's/dsl/24hr, **food:** Waffle House, Wendy's, **lodging:** Crystal Inn, Econolodge, **other:** Plantation Pines RV Prk |
| 28 | to Long Beach, **S gas:** Chevron/dsl, Shell/dsl, **other:** RV camping, tires |
| 27mm | Wolf River |
| 24 | Menge Ave, **N gas:** Chevron/dsl/scales, **S gas:** Texaco, **other:** A1 RV Park, flea mkt, golf, to beaches |
| 20 | to De Lisle, to Pass Christian, **N gas:** Kin-Mart |
| 16 | Diamondhead, **N gas:** BP/Domino's, Chevron/24hr, **food:** Burger King, Domino's, DQ, Subway, Waffle House, **lodging:** Diamondhead Resort, **other:** Ace Hardware, Choice Foods, **S food:** Pizzazz, **lodging:** motel |
| 15mm | Jourdan River |
| 13 | MS 43, MS 603, to Kiln, Bay St Louis, **N** McLeod SP, **S gas:** Exxon/Subway/dsl, Pure, **lodging:** Traveler's Choice, **other:** Ⓗ HOSPITAL, RV Camping |
| 10mm | **rest area (new)** |
| 2 | MS 607, to Waveland, NASA Test Site, **S Welcome Ctr both lanes, full** ♿ **facilities,** 🕻, 🛆, **litter barrels, RV dump, petwalk, 24hr security,** Buccaneer SP, camping, to beaches |
| 1mm | weigh sta both lanes |
| 0mm | Mississippi/Louisiana state line, Pearl River |

## INTERSTATE 20

| Exit # | Services |
|---|---|
| **I-20 W and I-59 S run together to Meridian.** | |
| 172mm | Mississippi/Alabama state line |
| 170mm | weigh sta both lanes |
| 169 | Kewanee, **S gas:** Kewanee Trkstp/dsl |
| 165 | Toomsuba, **N gas:** Shell/Subway/24hr, Texaco/ChesterFried/dsl, **S gas:** Loves/Arby's/dsl/scales, **other:** KOA (2mi) |

**MS**

## INTERSTATE 20 CONT'D

**164mm** Welcome Ctr wb, full ♿ facilities, 🚻 vending, ⛱ litter barrels, petwalk, RV dump, 24hr security

**160** to Russell, **N gas:** TA/BP/dsl/rest./scales/24hr/@, other: Nanabe RV Camping (1mi) **S gas:** Shell/dsl

**157b a** US 45, to Macon, Quitman

**154b a** MS 19 S, MS 39 N, Meridian, **N gas:** BP/dsl, Pure, Shell, Texaco/Domino's, **food:** Applebee's, Cracker Barrel, Logan's Roadhouse, Penn's Rest., Western Sizzlin, Waffle House, **lodging:** Day's Inn, Drury Inn, Hampton Inn, Hilton Garden, Holiday Inn, Relax Inn, Rodeway Inn, Super 8, **other:** Benchmark RV Park, Cadillac/Pontiac, Chrysler/Jeep/Kia, Hyundai, Lincoln/Mercury, Mitsubishi, U-Haul, **S gas:** Chevron, Texaco, **food:** Chick-fil-A, CiCi's, Crescent City Grill, Garfield's Rest., McAlister's, McDonald's, O'Charley's, Outback Steaks, Popeye's, Red Lobster, Ryan's, Taco Bell, **lodging:** Comfort Inn, Jameson Inn, Microtel, **other:** Belk, Best Buy, BooksAMillion, Dillard's, $Tree, Ethridge RV Ctr, Goody's, Harley-Davidson, JC Penney, Old Navy, PetCo, Ross, Sam's Club/gas, Sears/auto, TJ Maxx, mall, same as 153

**153** MS 145 S, 22nd Ave, Meridian, **N gas:** BP, Shell, **food:** Arby's, Barnhill's Buffet, Burger King, Capt D's, China Buffet, Hardee's, KFC, McDonald's, Pizza Hut, Subway, Wendy's, Western Sizzlin, **lodging:** Relax Inn, Super Inn, **other:** Ⓗ HOSPITAL, Firestone, Ford/Nissan, Fred's Drug, $General, Ford, Saverite Foods, **S gas:** Chevron/dsl, Exxon/dsl, Texaco/dsl, **food:** A&W/LJ Silver, Waffle House, **lodging:** Best Western, Budget 8 Motel, Econolodge, Holiday Inn Express, La Quinta, Motel 6, Quality Inn, Sleep Inn, **other:** Buick, Cadillac/Chevrolet, Chrysler/Jeep, Honda, Suzuki, Lowes Whse, Walmart SuperCtr/gas

**152** 29th Ave, 31st Ave, Meridian, **N gas:** Chevron/ChesterFried/dsl/24hr, **lodging:** Ramada Ltd **S lodging:** Royal Inn

**151** 49th Ave, Valley Rd, **N tires, S gas:** Pilot/Subway/dsl/24hr, **other:** stockyards

**150** US 11 S, MS 19 N, Meridian, **N gas:** Queen City Trkstp/dsl/rest./@, **food:** McDonald's, **other:** RV camping, Okatibbee Lake, **S gas:** Chevron/Stuckey's/Subway/dsl, Shell/dsl **other:** ✈

**130** [149] I-59 S, to Hattiesburg. **I-20 E and I-59 N run together.**

**129** US 80 W, Lost Gap, **S gas:** Spaceway/Grill King/dsl/RV Dump/24hr

**121** Chunky

**119mm** Chunky River

**115** MS 503, Hickory

**109** MS 15, Newton, **N gas:** Shell/Wendy's/dsl/24hr, **food:** Bo-Ro Rest., **lodging:** Thrifty Inn, **other:** lube, **S gas:**

**109** Continued Chevron/dsl/24hr, Newton Jct/dsl, Texaco/dsl, **food:** Hardee's, KFC/Taco Bell, McDonald's, N-Hop Pancakes, Pizza Hut, Sonic, Subway, **lodging:** Day's Inn, **other:** Ⓗ HOSPITAL, Advance Parts, AutoZone, $General, Fred's Drug, Piggly Wiggly, Walmart SuperCtr

**100** US 80, Lake, Lawrence, **N gas:** BP/dsl/rest.

**96** Lake

**95mm** Bienville Nat Forest, Bienville Nat Forest, eastern boundary

## INTERSTATE 20 CONT'D

**E** ↕ **W**

| | |
|---|---|
| **90mm** | rest area eb, full ♿ facilities, 🚻, 🅿, litter barrels, petwalk, RV dump, 24hr security |
| **88** | MS 35, Forest, **N gas:** BP/Subway/dsl, Shell, Texaco/Domino's/dsl, **food:** KFC, McDonald's, Pizza Hut, Popeye's, Taco Bell, Wendy's, **lodging:** Best Value Inn, Comfort Inn, Day's Inn, Holiday Inn Express, **other:** Ⓗ HOSPITAL, Chevrolet/GMC/Pontiac, Honda, Walmart SuperCtr/gas, **S gas:** Chevron/dsl/24hr, **food:** Penn's Rest. |
| **80** | MS 481, Morton |
| **77** | MS 13, Morton, **N gas:** 77 Truck Ctr/dsl, **other:** Ⓗ HOSPITAL, dsl repair, RV camping, to Roosevelt SP |
| **76mm** | Bienville NF, western boundary |
| **75mm** | rest area wb, full ♿ facilities, 🚻, 🅿, litter barrels, petwalk, RV dump, 24hr security |
| **68** | MS 43, Pelahatchie, **N gas:** Chevron/Subway/dsl/24hr, Texaco/dsl/rest./24hr, **other:** RV camping, **S gas:** BP/dsl |
| **59** | US 80, E Brandon, 2 mi **S gas:** Texaco |
| **56** | US 80, Brandon, **N food:** CiCi's, Krystal, McDonald's, Popeye's, Sonny's BBQ, Taco Bell, **lodging:** Microtel, **other:** AutoZone, O'Reilly Parts, **S gas:** BP, Chevron, Exxon, Mac's Gas, Shell/dsl, Texaco, **food:** DQ, Penn's Rest., Sonic, Subway, Waffle House, Wendy's, **lodging:** Day's Inn, Red Roof Inn, **other:** to Ross Barnett Reservoir |
| **54** | Crossgates Blvd, W Brandon, **N gas:** BP, Exxon, Phillips 66, **food:** Applebees, Burger King, China Buffet, Domino's, El Sombrero, Fernando's Mexican, KFC, Little Caesar's, Mazzio's, McDonald's, Papa John's, Pizza Hut, Popeye's, Subway, Waffle House, Wendy's, **lodging:** Ridgeland Inn, **other:** Ⓗ HOSPITAL, Big Lots, Buick/GMC/Pontiac, Chevrolet, CVS Drug, $General, Eckerd, Firestone/auto, Ford, Fred's Drug, GNC, Goodyear/auto, Hancock Fabrics, Kroger, Lincoln/Mercury, Office Depot, Tire Pros, Walmart SuperCtr/gas, **S gas:** Texaco/Domino's, **other:** Home Depot, Honda |
| **52** | MS 475, **N gas:** Chevron, Texaco/dsl, **food:** Waffle House, **lodging:** Quality Inn, Ramada Ltd, Sleep Inn, Super 8, **other:** Peterbilt, to Jackson ✈ |
| **48** | MS 468, Pearl, **N gas:** BP, Shell/dsl, Texaco, **food:** Arby's, Baskin-Robbins, Burger King, Cracker Barrel, Domino's, El Charro's Mexican, Jose's Tamales, KFC, LoneStar Steaks, McDonald's, O'Charley's, Pizza Hut, Popeye's, Ruby Tuesday, Ryan's, Sonic, Starbucks, Subway, Waffle House, Wendy's, **lodging:** Best Western, Comfort Inn, Econolodge, Fairfield Inn, Hampton Inn, Hilton Garden, Holiday Inn Express, Jameson Inn, Motel 6, **other:** CarCare, transmissions, **S gas:** Chevron/dsl/24hr, Huff/dsl/24hr, **lodging:** Candlewood Suites, Country Inn&Suites, Day's Inn, La Quinta, **other:** $General |
| **47b a** | US 49 S, Flowood, **N gas:** ⚡FLYING J/Conoco/CountryMkt/dsl/LP/24hr, Pilot/Krystal/Subway/dsl/24hr, **food:** Western Sizzlin, **lodging:** Airport Inn, Holiday Inn, **other:** Bass Pro Shop, SpeedCo, 2-3 mi **S food:** DQ, Waffle House, **lodging:** Executive Inn, **other:** Freightliner, Kenworth, Truck-Man RV Center, Tires |
| **46** | I-55 N, to Memphis |
| **45b** | US 51, State St, to downtown |
| **45a** | Gallatin St (from wb), to downtown, **N gas:** BP, Petro/dsl/rest./24hr/@, **other:** Blue Beacon, tires/truck repair, |

**BRANDON**

**PEARL**

| | |
|---|---|
| **45a** | Continued vet, **S gas:** Pilot/McDonald's/dsl, **lodging:** Hilltop Inn, **other:** Hyundai, Mitsubishi, Nissan |
| **44** | I-55 S (exits left from wb), to New Orleans |
| **43b a** | Terry Rd, **N gas:** Exxon/dsl, Gasco, **food:** Krystal |
| **42b a** | Ellis Ave, Belvidere, **N gas:** BP, Shell, **food:** Capt D's, McDonald's, Pizza Hut, Popeye's, Rally's, Sonny's BBQ, Wendy's, **lodging:** Day's Inn, Econolodge, Metro Inn, Quality Inn, Ramada, Sleep Inn, Super 8, **other:** Advance Parts, AutoZone, Chrysler/Dodge, Family$, Firestone, KIA, O'Reilly Parts, Radio Shack, Sav-a-Lot Foods, U-Haul, transmissions, zoo, **S gas:** Exxon/dsl, QuickPay, **food:** DQ |
| **41** | I-220 N, US 49 N, to Jackson |
| **40b a** | MS 18 W, Robinson Rd, **N gas:** BP, Exxon/Subway, Shell/dsl, **food:** Arby's, China Buffet, Krystal, Mazzio's, Piccadilly's, Popeye's, **lodging:** Day's Inn, Sleep Inn, **other:** Metro Mall, Office Depot, Sears/auto, USPO, auto repair, **S gas:** Expressway, Mac's, **food:** IHOP, McDonald's, Waffle House, Wendy's, **lodging:** Comfort Inn, **other:** Ⓗ HOSPITAL, $Tree, GNC, Lowes Whse, Radio Shack, Walmart SuperCtr/gas |
| **36** | Springridge Rd, Clinton, **N gas:** Mac's/Burger King, Orbit Gas, Shell, **food:** Capt D's, Chick-fil-A, DQ, KFC, Little Ceasar's, Mazzio's, McAlister's, McDonald's, Sonic, Starbucks, Subway, Taco Bell, Waffle House, Wendy's, Zaxby's, **lodging:** Clinton Inn, Comfort Inn, Day's Inn, **other:** Advance Parts, Home Depot, Kroger, O'Reilly Parts, Radio Shack, Walgreens, Walmart SuperCtr/gas (2mi), **S gas:** Exxon, Texaco/dsl, **food:** Applebee's, Corky's BBQ, Frogs Head Grill, Pizza Hut, Popeye's, Salsa's Mexican, Shoney's, **lodging:** Best Western, Econolodge, Hampton Inn, Holiday Inn Express, Quality Inn, Ramada Ltd, **other:** Curves, Davis Tire, Springridge RV Park, vet |
| **35** | US 80 E, Clinton, **N gas:** Chevron/dsl, Texaco/dsl, **food:** Backyard Burger, Chick-fil-A, McAlister's Deli, **lodging:** Ridgland Inn |
| **34** | Natchez Trace Pkwy |
| **31** | Norrell Rd |
| **27** | Bolton, **N gas:** Chevron, **S gas:** BP/dsl/24hr |
| **19** | MS 22, Edwards, Flora, **N other:** Askew Landing RV Camping (2mi), **S gas:** BP/dsl, Phillips 66 |
| **17mm** | Big Black River |
| **15** | Flowers |
| **11** | Bovina, **N gas:** Texaco/Subway/dsl/24hr, **other:** RV camping |
| **10mm** | weigh sta wb |
| **8mm** | weigh sta eb |
| **6.5mm** | parking area eb |
| **5b a** | US 61, MS 27 S, **N gas:** Chevron, Kangaroo/dsl, **food:** Sonic, **S same as 4a** |
| **4b a** | Clay St, **N gas:** Chevron, Texaco, **food:** KFC, Pizza Hut, **lodging:** Hampton Inn, Motel 6, Quality Inn, Vicksburg Inn, **other:** Ⓗ HOSPITAL, KOA, RV Park, to Vicksburg NP, **S gas:** Texaco/Domino's/dsl, **food:** Bumper's Drive-In, China Buffet, Cracker Barrel, Pizza Inn, McAlister's, Scottish Inn, Waffle House, **lodging:** Beechwood Inn/rest., Comfort Inn, Courtyard, Holiday Inn Express, Jameson Inn, Scottish Inn, **other:** Chrysler/Jeep/Toyota, $General, Lincoln/Mercury, Outlet Mall/famous brands/deli, Toyota, same as 5 |

**JACKSON**

**CLINTON**

**MS**

## INTERSTATE 20 CONT'D

**E W VICKSBURG E W**

**3** Indiana Ave, **N gas:** Texaco/Subway/dsl, **food:** China King, McDonald's, Waffle House, **lodging:** Best Western, Deluxe Inn, **other:** Chevrolet, Chrysler/Dodge/Jeep, Corner Mkt Foods, Ford/Lincoln/Mercury, Honda, Mazda, Rite Aid, **S gas:** BP, **food:** KFC, Goldie's BBQ, **lodging:** Best Inn, **other:** Buick/GMC/Pontiac/Subaru, Family$

**1c** Halls Ferry Rd, **N gas:** Chevron/24hr, Exxon, **food:** Burger King, Sonic, **lodging:** Econolodge, **other:** H HOSPITAL, **S gas:** Kangaroo/dsl, **food:** Capt D's, DQ, Garfield's Rest., Goldie's BBQ, Pizza Hut, Popeye's, Ryan's, Shoney's, Subway, Taco Bell, Taco Casa, TCBY, Wendy's, Whataburger, **lodging:** Day's Inn, Fairfield Inn, Super 8, Wingate Inn, **other:** Advance Parts, Belk, Big Lots, Dillard's, Home Depot, Fred's Drug, JC Penney, Kroger, Walgreens, USPO, mall

**1b** US 61 S, **S gas:** BP, Chevron/Domino's, **food:** McDonald's, **other:** Walmart SuperCtr/Subway, same as 1c

**1a** Washington St, Vicksburg, **N Welcome Ctr both lanes, full ♿ facilities, Ɽ, gas:** Kangaroo/dsl, Shell/Subway/dsl, **lodging:** AmeriStar Hotel, **other:** AmeriStar RV Park, casino, **S food:** Waffle House, **lodging:** La Quinta, Ridgeland Inn

**0mm** Mississippi/Louisiana state line, Mississippi River

## INTERSTATE 22 - (FUTURE)

| Exit # | Services |
|---|---|
| 118mm | Alabama/Mississippi State Line, I-22 (future) |
| 116mm | **Welcome Ctr/Rest Area wb, 🚻, litter barrels, pet-walk, vending, RV dump** |
| 113 | rd 23, Tremont, Smithville |
| 108 | rd 25 N, Belmont, Iuka |
| 107mm | weigh sta, both lanes |

**104** rd 25 S, Fulton, Amory, **N gas:** Shell/cafe/scales/dsl, Woco/dsl, **food:** Burger King, Hardees, Huddle House, McDonald's, Sonic, Subway, **lodging:** Days Inn, **other:** AutoZone, Fred's, O'Reilly Parts, RV camping, Whitten HS, **S gas:** Murphy USA/dsl, **other:** Los Compadres Mexican, Pizza Hut, Wendy's, **other:** Walmart SuperCtr

**104mm** Tombigbee River/Tenn-Tom Waterway

**101** rd 178, rd 363, Peppertown, Mantachie, **N gas:** Exxon, **S gas:** Dorsey Fuel/dsl (2mi)

**97** Fawn Grove Rd

**94** rd 371, Mantachie, Mooreville, **N gas:** Woco/dsl

**90** Auburn Rd, **N gas:** BP/dsl

**87** Veterans Blvd, **N gas:** Shell/Chix Rest/dsl, **food:** Huddle House, **lodging:** Wingate Inn, **other:** E. Presley Campground/Park, **S** Tombigbee SP

**C O R I N T H**

**86** US 45 N, Corinth, **1 exit N gas:** BP, Shell, Texaco, **food:** Abner's Rest., Applebees, Burger King, Chick-fil-A, Chili's, ChuckeCheese, Cracker Barrel, Kyoto Japanese, McDonald's, New China, O'Charley's, Olive Garden, Pizza Hut, Red Lobster, Ryan's, Sonic, Subway, Taco Bell, Wendy's, **lodging:** Baymont Inn, Best Inn, Comfort Inn, Days Inn, Holiday Inn Express, Jameson Inn, Lenny's Subs, **other:** Barnes & Noble, Belk, Best Buy, Books-a-Million, Circuit City, Ford/Lincoln/Mercury, Goody's, Home Depot, JC Penny, Kohl's, Kroger/gas, Lowe's Whse, NAPA, Old Navy, PetsMart, Sam's Club/gas, Sears, Staples, Tuesday Morning, Walmart

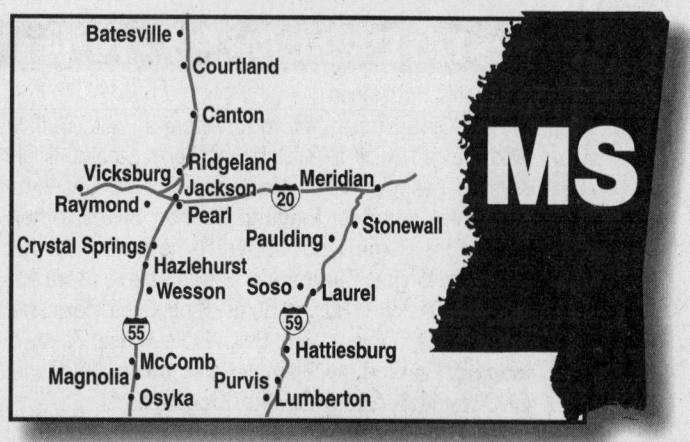

| | |
|---|---|
| 85 | Natchez Trace Pkwy |

**81** rd 178, McCullough Blvd, **S gas:** Exxon/dsl, Shell/dsl, Texaco/dsl, **food:** Old Venice Pizza, Sonic, **lodging:** Super 8, **other:** $General, USPO

**76** rd 9 S, Sherman, Pontotoc, **N gas:** Wild Bill's/dsl, **other:** Sherman RV Ctr

**73** rd 9 N, Blue Springs

**64** rd 15, rd 30 E, Pontotoc, Ripley, **N gas:** BP, Chevron, **food:** George's Rest., **other:** tire repair, USPO, **S gas:** Pilot/Arby's/scales/dsl/24hr, Shell/dsl

**63** New Albany, **N gas:** Dee's Oil/dsl, **food:** Chevrolet/Buick/Pontiac/GMC, Ford, HP

**62mm** Tallahatchie River

**61** rd 30 W, W New Albany, **S gas:** Express, Murphy USA, Shell, **food:** Capt. D's, Huddle House, KFC, McAlisters Deli, McDonald's/playplace, Pizza Hut, Pueblo Mexican, Subway, Taco Bell, Wendy's, Western Sizzlin, **lodging:** Comfort Inn, Hallmarc Inn, **other:** H HOSPITAL, $Tree, Rite Aid, Walgreens, Walmart SuperCtr, to U of MS

**60** Glenfield, **S** U of MS

**55** Myrtle

**48** rd 178, Hickory Flat, **N gas:** Dee's Oil/dsl, **S gas:** BP/rest/dsl/24hr

**41** rd 346, Potts Camp, **S gas:** BP/dsl, **other:** $General, NAPA

**41mm** Tippah River

**37** Lake Center, **N** Chewalla Lake/RV camping

**30** rd 7, rd 4, Holly Springs, Oxford, **N gas:** BP, Exxon, Shell/Chester's/BBQ, **food:** Huddle House, KFC, McDonalds, Panda Buffet, Pizza Hut, Popeye's, Sonic, Subway, Wendy's, **lodging:** Magnolia Inn, **other:** H HOSPITAL, AutoZone, $General, Walldoxey SP/RV camping, **S gas:** Exxon, **lodging:** Days Inn, Le Brooks Inn, **other:** Walmart SuperCtr

**26** W Holly Springs

**21** Red Banks, **N gas:** BP/dsl, Texaco/dsl

**18** Victoria, E Byhalia, **N gas:** BP

**14** rd 309, Byhalia, **N gas:** Exxon, Shell, **lodging:** Best Value

**10** W Byhalia

**6** Bethel Rd, Hacks Crossroad, **N gas:** BP, ✈FLYING J/Country Mkt/dsl/scales/LP/RV dump/24hr, Horizon, **food:** JR's Grill, Tops BBQ, **lodging:** Best Western, Super 8

**6mm** parking area, both lanes

**4** rd 305, Olive Branch, Independence, **N gas:** BP/dsl, Mobil/Huddle House, Shell/Circle K, **food:** Old Style BBQ, Pizza Hut, **lodging:** Holiday Inn Express, **S gas:** BP/Quizno's

**MS**

**E** ↕ **W**

## INTERSTATE 22 CONT'D - FUTURE

| | |
|---|---|
| 3.5mm | weigh sta, both lanes |
| 2 | rd 302, Olive Branch, **N** **food:** Abbay's Rest., Buffalo Wild Wings, Chick-fil-A, Chili's, Colton's Steaks, IHOP, Krystal, Lenny's Subs, McAlisters Deli, O'Charley's, Starbucks, Wendy's, **lodging:** Comfort Suites, **other:** $Tree, Ford, Home Depot, Lowes, Radio Shack, Walmart SuperCtr, **S** **gas:** Chevron/dsl, Shell/Circle K, **food:** Applebees, Backyard Burger, Burger King, Casa Mexicana, McDonald's, Subway, Taco Bell, Waffle House, Zaxby's, **lodging:** Comfort Inn, Hampton Inn, **other:** AutoZone, GNC Nutrition, Goodyear/auto, Kroger/gas |
| 1 | Craft Rd, **N** **lodging:** Candlewood Suites, Holiday Inn, **other:** American RV Ctr, Hyundai, Southaven RV Ctr, Suzuki |
| 0mm | Mississippi/Tennessee state line, I-22 (future) begins/ends. |

## INTERSTATE 55

| Exit # | Services |
|---|---|
| 291.5mm | Mississippi/Tennessee state line |
| 291 | State Line Rd, Southaven, **E** **food:** Exline's Pizza, Interstate BBQ, Little Caesars, Tops BBQ, Waffle House, **lodging:** Comfort Inn, Holiday Inn Express, Quality Inn, Southern Inn, **other:** Family$, Firestone/auto, Goodyear/auto, Kroger, Southaven RV Park, Walgreens, **W** **food:** Capt D's, Checker's, Dales Rest, El Patron Mexican, Lucky China, Mrs Winner's, Sonic, Taco Bell, Wendy's, **other:** Big Lots, Fred's Drug, Rite Aid, Walgreens, USPO, tires |
| 289 | MS 302, to US 51, Horn Lake, **E** **gas:** BP/Circle K, Shell/Circle K, **food:** Backyard Burger, Burger King, Chick-fil-A, Chili's, Coldstone, Danver's, Fazoli's, Firehouse Subs, Fox&Hound, Gordman's, IHOP, Krystal, Huey's Rest., Hunan Buffet, La Hacienda, Logan's Roadhouse, Lonestar Steaks, Longhorn Steaks, McDonald's, O'Charley's, Olive Garden, On-the-Border, Outback Steaks, Qdoba Mexican, Quizno's, Red Lobster, Sonic, Starbucks, Steak'n Shake, Subway, TGIFriday, Wendy's, **lodging:** Comfort Suites, Courtyard, Fairfield Inn, Hampton Inn, Hilton Garden, Residence Inn, **other:** H HOSPITAL, Aldi Foods, Best Buy, BooksAMillion, Chevrolet, Chrysler/Jeep, Circuit City, Dillards, $Tree, Ford, JC Penney, Lowe's Whse, Marshall's, Nissan, Office Depot, Old Navy, PetCo, Pontiac/Buick/GMC, Radio Shack, Sam's Club/gas, Sportsman's Whse, Tuesday Morning, Walmart SuperCtr, World Mkt, mall, **W** **gas:** BP/Circle K, Phillips 66/dsl, Shell/dsl, **food:** Applebee's, Arby's, Country Home Buffet, ChuckeCheese, Cracker Barrel, Hooters, KFC, McDonald's, Mrs Winner's, Papa John's, Pizza Hut, Popeye's, Quizno's, Ryan's, Sekisui Japan, Taco Bell, TX Roadhouse, Waffle House, Wendy's, Zaxby's, **lodging:** Day's Inn, Drury Inn, Motel 6, Sleep Inn, Super 8, **other:** CVS Drug, Family$, Harley Davidson, Home Depot, Kroger, Sav-A-Lot Foods, Target, Walgreens, tires |
| 287 | Church Rd, **E** **gas:** Citgo/dsl, **other:** AutoZone, **W** **gas:** Shell/DQ/dsl, **food:** Boiling Point Seafood, McDonald's, Subway, Taco Bell, Waffle House, **lodging:** Keywest Inn, Magnolia Inn, **other:** Audubon Point RV Park (1mi), El Daze RV Camping (1mi), Southaven RV Ctr |

| | |
|---|---|
| 285mm | weigh sta both lanes |
| 284 | to US 51, Nesbit Rd, **W** **gas:** BP, **food:** Happy Daze Dairybar, **other:** USPO |
| 283 | I-69, Tunica |
| 280 | MS 304, US 51, Hernando, **E** **gas:** Exxon, **food:** Arby's, Backyard Burger, Capt D's, Dominos, Guadalahara Mexican, Huddle House, KFC, Kyoto, Sonic, Steak Escape, Taco Bell, **lodging:** Day's Inn, Hampton Inn, Hernando Inn, Scottish Inn, **other:** $Tree, Goody's, Walmart SuperCtr/gas, Walgreens, repair/tires, **W** **gas:** BP, GasMart, Shell/Circle K/dsl, **food:** Brick Oven Rest., Coleman's BBQ, La Siesta, Lenny's Subs, McDonald's, Mi Pueblo, Papa John's, Pizza Hut, Quizno's, Sonic, Wendy's, **lodging:** Super 8, **other:** AutoZone, Desoto Museum, Kroger/gas, NAPA, Memphis S Camping (2mi), to Arkabutla Lake |
| 279mm | Welcome Ctr sb, full 🚻 facilities, 🅲, 🏚, litter barrels, petwalk, RV dump, 24hr security |
| 276mm | rest area nb, full 🚻 facilities, 🅲, 🏚, litter barrels, petwalk, RV dump, 24hr security |
| 273mm | Coldwater River |
| 271 | MS 306, Coldwater, **W** **gas:** BP, **food:** Subway, **other:** Memphis S RV Park, Lake Arkabutla |
| 265 | MS 4, Senatobia, **W** **gas:** BP/dsl, Exxon, Kangaroo/Stuckey's/Huddle House/dsl/scales/24 hr, Shell, **food:** Backyard Burger, Coleman's BBQ, Domino's, KFC, McDonald's/playplace, New China Buffet, Pizza Hut, Popeye's, Rio Lindo Mexican, Sonic, Subway, Taco Bell, Waffle House, Wendy's, Western Sizzlin, **lodging:** Days Inn, Motel 6, **other:** H HOSPITAL, Buick/Pontiac/GMC, CarQuest, City Drug, Fred's Drug, Kaye Mkt, Pontiac/Buick/GMC, USPO |
| 263 | S Senatobia, new exit |
| 257 | MS 310, Como, **E** **gas:** BP/dsl, **other:** N Sardis Lake, **W** **food:** Windy City Grille (1mi) |
| 252 | MS 315, Sardis, **E** **gas:** Chevron/dsl, Pure/dsl, **food:** McDonald's, Sardis Lake Cafe, **lodging:** Lake Inn, Super 8, **other:** to Kyle SP, Sardis Dam, RV camping, **W** **gas:** Shell/dsl, **food:** Sonic, **lodging:** Happy Days Motel, **other:** H HOSPITAL, $General, Fred's |
| 246 | MS 35, N Batesville, **E** to Sardis Lake, **W** **gas:** Mobil, Shell/dsl |
| 243b a | MS 6, to Batesville, **E** **gas:** BP/dsl, Shell/dsl, **food:** Backyard Burger, Chili's, Mi Pueblo Mexican, Starbucks, **other:** Lowe's Whse, Walmart SuperCtr/dsl, to Sardis Lake, U of MS, **W** **gas:** BP, Chevron/dsl, Exxon/dsl, Phillips 66/dsl, Shell/dsl, **food:** Abner's Rest., Burger King, Cafe Ole, Capt D's, Cracker Barrel, Domino's, Hardee's, Huddle House, KFC, McDonald's, Pizza Hut, Popeye's, Quizno's, Sonic, Subway, Taco Bell, Waffle House, Wendy's, Western Sizzlin, **lodging:** Baymont Inn, Day's Inn, Hampton Inn, Holiday Inn, Ramada Ltd, **other:** H HOSPITAL, Advance Parts, AutoZone, $General, Factory Stores/famous brands, Family$, Fred's Drug, Kroger, O'Reilly Parts, Walgreens, USPO |
| 240mm | rest area both lanes, full 🚻 facilities, 🅲, 🏚, litter barrels, petwalk, RV dump, 24hr security |
| 237 | to US 51, Courtland, **E** **gas:** Pure/dsl |
| 233 | to Enid Dam, **E** to Enid Lake, RV camping, **W** **gas:** Benson's/groceries |

**N** ↕ **S**

**SOUTHAVEN**

**BATESVILLE**

**MS**

Copyright 2009 - The Next Exit®

## INTERSTATE 55 CONT'D

**N ↕ S** **GRENADA** **CANTON**

**227** MS 32, Oakland, **E** to Cossar SP, Sunrise RV Park, **W** gas: Exxon/dsl, Shell/dsl, food: Subway

**220** MS 330, Tillatoba, **E** gas: Conoco/rest./dsl/@

**211** MS 7 N, to Coffeeville, **E** Frog Hollow RV Park, **W** gas: Shell/Chester Fried/dsl

**208** Papermill Rd, **E** Grenada ✈

**206** MS 8, MS 7 S, to Grenada, **E** gas: BP, Exxon/dsl, RaceWay, Shell/dsl, food: Burger King, China Buffet, Cosina Mexican, Domino's, Jake&Rip's Café, La Cabana Mexican, McAlister's Deli, McDonald's, Pizza Hut, Pizza Inn, RagTime Grill, Shoney's, Subway, Taco Bell, Wendy's, Western Sizzlin, lodging: Best Value Inn, Budget Inn, Comfort Inn, Day's Inn, Hampton Inn, Holiday Inn Express, Jameson Inn, Knights Inn, Quaity Inn, Super 8, other: H HOSPITAL, Advance Parts, AutoZone, Chrysler/Dodge, Curves, CVS Drug, $General, Ford/Lincoln/Mercury, GNC, O'Reilly Parts, Radio Shack, USPO, Walmart SuperCtr, to Grenada Lake/RV camping, **W** gas: Exxon/HuddleHouse, food: Waffle house, lodging: Country Inn&Suites, Econolodge, other: Nissan, Toyota/Scion

**204mm** parking area sb, ℂ, litter barrels

**202mm** parking area nb, ℂ, litter barrels

**199** Trout Rd, S Grenada, **E** to camp McCain

**195** MS 404, Duck Hill, **E** to Camp McCain, **W** gas: Conoco/dsl

**185** US 82, Winona, **E** gas: Exxon, Shell/dsl, food: Huddle House, KFC, McDonald's, Sonic, Subway, lodging: Budget Inn, Magnolia Lodge, Relax Inn, Western Inn, other: H HOSPITAL, **W** gas: Pilot/Taco Bell/dsl/24hr/scales/repair

**174** MS 35, MS 430, Vaiden, **E** gas: Chevron/dsl, Down Home/dsl/scales/24hr, Shell, lodging: 35-55 motel, other: NAPA, Vaiden Camping, **W** gas: Exxon/Chesterfried/dsl, other: $General

**173mm** rest area sb, full ♿ facilities, ℂ, ⛱, litter barrels, petwalk, RV dump, 24hr security

**164** to West, **W** gas: West Trkstp/Pure/dsl

**163mm** rest area nb, full ♿ facilities, ℂ, ⛱, litter barrels, petwalk, RV dump, 24hr security

**156** MS 12, Durant, **E** gas: Shell/dsl, lodging: Durant Motel/rest. (3mi), Super 8, **W** H HOSPITAL (7mi)

**150** **E** Holmes Co SP, RV camping

**146** MS 14, Goodman, **W** to Little Red Schoolhouse

**144** MS 17, to Pickens, **E** gas: Texaco/HomePlace Rest./dsl/24hr, **W** gas: BP/dsl/rest./24hr, other: to Little Red Schoolhouse

**139** MS 432, to Pickens

**133** Vaughan, **E** to Casey Jones Museum

**128mm** Big Black River

**124** MS 16, to N Canton

**119** MS 22, to MS 16 E, Canton, **E** gas: BP/dsl, Cappy's/dsl, Exxon, Shell, food: Domin's, El Sombrero Mexican, McDonald's, Pizza Hut, Popeye's, Sonic, Subway, Wendy's, Western Sizzlin, lodging: Comfort Inn, Days Inn, Econolodge, Hampton Inn, Holiday Inn Express, La Quinta, Quality Inn, other: H HOSPITAL, Ford,

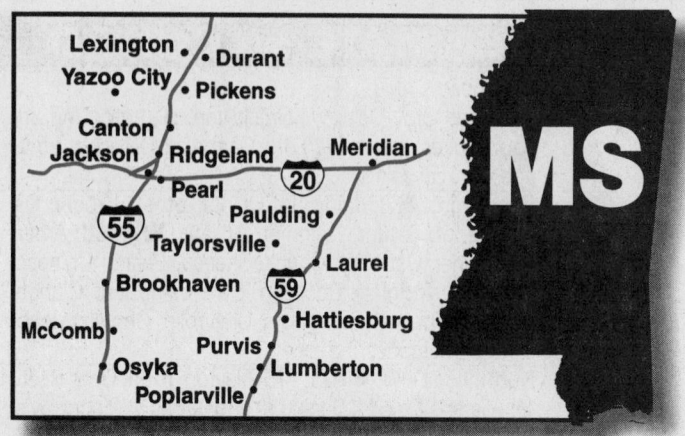

**MADISON** **JACKSON**

**119** Continued
to Ross Barnett Reservoir, **W** gas: Chevron/KFC/dsl, Citgo/dsl, Love's/Arby's/dsl/scales/24hr/@, Texaco/dsl, food: Bumpers Drive-In, 2 Rivers Steaks

**118a b** Nissan Parkway, **E** to Nissan factory

**114a b** Sowell Rd

**112** US 51, Gluckstadt, **E** gas: Exxon/Krystal/dsl, Kangaroo/Subway/dsl, lodging: Super 8, **W** Camper Corral RV Ctr

**108** MS 463, Madison, **E** gas: Shell/dsl, Texaco/Domino's/dsl, food: Alexander's Italian, Anthony Z's, Applebees, Backyard Burger, Burger King, Chick-Fil-A, Chili's, Coldstone, El Potrillo, Haute Pig Café, Lenny's Subs, Starbucks, other: $Tree, Lowe's Whse, Walmart SuperCtr **W** gas: Exxon/KFC/dsl, food: Atlantica Grill, Beef O'brady's, BoneFish Grill, Nagoya Japanese, Papito's Grill, Pizza Inn, Wendy's, lodging: Hilton Garden, other: H HOSPITAL, CVS Drug, Home Depot, Kroger

**105b** Old Agency Rd, **E** gas: Chevron/dsl, other: Honda, Pontiac/Buick/GMC, **W** food: Peppers Cafe, PF Changs, Ruth's Chris Steaks, lodging: Hyatt Place, other: Barnes & Noble, Fresh Mkt Foods

**105a** Natchez Trace Pkwy

**104** I-220, to W Jackson

**103** County Line Rd, **E** gas: BP, Chevron, Exxon/dsl, food: Applebee's, Barnhill's Rest., Bop's Custard, Bulldog Grill, Cane's Chicken, Chick-fil-A, Cozumel Mexican, Garfield's, Grand China, Honey Baked Ham, Huntington's Grill, Jason's Deli, KFC, King Buffet, Krispy Kreme, Macaroni Grill, Mazzio's, Moe's SW Grill, O'Charley's, Popeye's, Quizno's, Shoney's, Starbucks, Subway, Taco Bell, Wendy's, Whataburger, Zaxby's, lodging: Cabot Lodge, Courtyard, Day's Inn, Hilton, Quality Inn, Red Roof Inn, other: Acura, Barnes&Noble, Belk, Best Buy, Cadillac, Circuit City, Dillard's, $Tree, Goodyear, Lowe's Whse, Marshall's, Michael's, Office Depot, Old Navy, Sam's Club, TJ Maxx, Walgreens, Walmart SuperCtr, mall, to Barnett Reservoir, **W** food: Chili's, Olive Garden, Red Lobster, Logan's Roadhouse, Subway, lodging: Comfort Suites, Drury Inn, Motel 6, Studio 6, other: Fred's Drug, Home Depot, Office Depot, PetsMart, Target

**102b** Beasley Rd, Adkins Blvd, **E** gas: Phillips 66, food: Cracker Barrel, LoneStar Steaks, OutBack Steaks, lodging: La Quinta, Super 8, other: Brookshire Food/gas, Chevrolet, Chrysler/Jeep, Ford, Lincoln/Mercury, Nissan, Saturn, Toyota/Scion, **W** gas: Exxon/TCBY, food: McDonald's, lodging: Best Western,

## INTERSTATE 55 CONT'D

**N ↕ S**

**JACKSON**

| Exit | Description |
|---|---|
| 102b | Continued<br>Extended Stay Deluxe, Fairfield Inn, Hampton Inn, In-Town Suites, **other:** Big Lots, Carmax, Mercedes, frontage rds access 102a |
| 102a | Briarwood, **E lodging:** La Quinta, **other:** Kroger, Office Depot, Saturn, Steinmart, UHaul, **W food:** America's Diner, Capt D's, ChuckeCheese, Peking Chinese, Popeye's, **lodging:** Best Inn, Best Value Inn, Clarion, Hampton Inn, **other:** BigLots, Chevrolet, Chrysler/Jeep/Dodge, Mercedes/Porsche |
| 100 | North Side Dr W, **E gas:** BP, Chevron, **food:** Char Rest., McAlister's Deli, McDonald's, Papa John's, Piccadilly's, Pizza Hut, Starbucks, SteakOut, Steam Room Grill, Subway, Wendy's, **lodging:** Extended Stay America, **other:** Audi, BooksAMillion, CVS Drug, Jaguar/Landrover, Kroger/gas, Office Depot, Radio Shack, Steinmart, Tuesday Morning, VW, Walgreens, vet, **W gas:** BP, Exxon/dsl, Shell, **food:** Domino's, Hooters, IHOP, Waffle House, **lodging:** Select Hotel |
| 99 | Meadowbrook Rd, Northside Dr E (from nb) |
| 98c b | MS 25 N, Lakeland Dr, **E gas:** Shell, **lodging:** Parkside Inn, **other:** LaFleur's Bluff SP, museum, **W H** HOSPITAL, ✈ |
| 98a | Woodrow Wilson Dr, downtown |
| 96c | Fortification St, **E lodging:** Residence Inn, **W H** HOSPITAL, Bellhaven College |
| 96b | High St, Jackson, **E other:** BMW, Chevrolet, Infiniti, Lexus, **W gas:** Shell/dsl, Texaco/dsl, **food:** Arby's, Domino's, Farmers Mkt Grill, Popeye's, Shoney's, Taco Bell, Waffle House, Wendy's, Whataburger, **lodging:** Day's Inn, Best Western, Hampton Inn, Holiday Inn Express, Quality Inn, Red Roof Inn, Regency Hotel, **other:** H HOSPITAL, Honda, Subaru/Volvo, museum, st capitol |
| 96a | Pearl St (from nb), Jackson, **W** downtown, access to same as 96b |
| 94 | (46 from nb), I-20 E, to Meridian, US 49 S |
| 45b [I-20] | US 51, State St, to downtown, **N gas:** Petro, **other:** Subaru, Pontiac, Volvo **S gas:** Pilot |
| 45a | Gallatin St (from sb), **N gas:** Petro/dsl, **S gas:** Pilot/McDonald's/dsl/@, **other:** Hyundai/Mazda, Nissan, Toyota |
| 92c | (44 from sb), I-20 W, to Vicksburg, US 49 N |
| 92b | US 51 N, State St, Gallatin St |
| 92a | McDowell Rd, **E gas:** Petro/dsl, Pilot/McDonald's/dsl, **lodging:** Knight's Inn, **W gas:** BP, BJ's, Dixie, Shell, **food:** Waffle House, Wendy's, **lodging:** Super S Inn, **other:** Brookshire's Food/Drug, Rite Aid |
| 90b | Daniel Lake Blvd (from sb), **W gas:** Shell, **other:** Harley-Davidson |
| 90a | Savanna St, **E lodging:** Save Inn, **other:** transmissions, **W gas:** BP, **food:** Bodan's Seafood, **other:** Turning Wheel RV Center |
| 88 | Elton Rd, **W gas:** Chevron, Exxon/ChesterFried/dsl |
| 85 | Byram, **E gas:** Blue Sky, HotSpot/dsl/24hr, **food:** Krystal, Mexican Grill, **lodging:** ValuPlace Hotel, **other:** Swinging Bridge RV Park, **W gas:** Byrem Gas/dsl, Chevron, Exxon/dsl, Texaco/dsl, **food:** Backyard Burger, Capt'n D's, Mazzio's, McAlister's Deli, McDonald's, New China, Pizza Hut, Popeye's, Quizno's, Sonic, Subway, Taco Bell, Waffle House, Wendy's, **lodging:** Day's Inn, **other:** Ace Hardware, AutoZone, Country Creek RV Ctr, $General, Market Place Foods, NAPA, O'Reilly Parts, Super D Drugs, Walgreens, USPO |

**BROOKHAVEN**

**MC COMB**

| Exit | Description |
|---|---|
| 81 | Wynndale Rd, **W gas:** Chevron/dsl |
| 78 | Terry, **E gas:** Texaco/Subway/dsl/24hr, **other:** USPO, **W gas:** Mac's, **other:** $General |
| 72 | MS 27, Crystal Springs, **E gas:** Exxon/Subway/dsl, Phillips 66/dsl, **food:** McDonald's, Popeye's, **other:** Ford/Lincoln/Mercury |
| 68 | to US 51, S Crystal Springs, gas/dsl, **other:** Red Barn Produce, vet |
| 65 | to US 51, Gallman, **E gas:** Stuckey's/gas |
| 61 | MS 28, Hazlehurst, **E gas:** BP, Exxon, Phillips 66/dsl, Pump&Save, **food:** Bumpers Drive Inn, Burger King, Country Catfish, KFC, McDonald's, Sonic, Stark's Rest., Subway, Taco Bell, Wendy's, **lodging:** Best Value, Claridge Inn, Western Inn, **other:** H HOSPITAL, Advance Parts, CVS Drug, $General, Family$, Fred's Drugs, Piggly Wiggly, Supervalu Foods, Walmart SuperCtr |
| 59 | to S Hazlehurst |
| 56 | to Martinsville |
| 54mm | **rest area both lanes, full** 🚻 **facilities,** 📞, 🚻, **litter barrels, petwalk, RV dump, vending, 24hr security** |
| 51 | to Wesson, **E other:** Lake Lincoln SP, **W gas:** Country Jct Trkstp/dsl/rest. |
| 48 | Mt Zion Rd, to Wesson |
| 42 | to US 51, N Brookhaven, **E gas:** Exxon/Subway, Shell/Kasko/scales/dsl, **other:** H HOSPITAL, **W lodging:** Super 8 |
| 40 | to MS 550, Brookhaven, **E gas:** BP/Domino's, Blue Sky, Exxon/Subway, Fleetway, Shell/dsl/24hr, **food:** Bowle BBQ, Burger King, China Buffet, Cracker Barrel, DQ, Hall's BBQ, KFC, Krystal, McDonald's, Mitchell's Steaks, Pizza Hut, Popeye's, Quizno's, Sonic, Taco Bell, Wendy's, Western Sizzlin, **lodging:** Best Value Inn, Comfort Inn, Day's Inn, Lincoln Inn, Hampton Inn, Spanish Inn, **other:** H HOSPITAL, AutoZone, CarQuest, Chevrolet, Chrysler/Dodge/Jeep, Fred's Drugs, Honda, Nissan, O'Reilly Parts, Rite Aid, SaveALot Foods, Super D Drugs, Toyota, Walgreens, Walmart SuperCtr/gas, **W other:** Home Depot |
| 38 | US 84, S Brookhaven, **W gas:** Chevron/dsl/24hr |
| 30 | Bogue Chitto, Norfield, **E gas:** Shell/BogueChitto/dsl, **W other:** Bogue Chitto RV Park |
| 24 | Johnston Station, **E** to Lake Dixie Springs |
| 20b a | US 98 W, to Natchez, Summit, **E gas:** BP/dsl, Shell/dsl, Stop'n Shop/dsl, **W gas:** Exxon/Subway/dsl, Phillips 66/dsl |
| 18 | MS 570, Smithdale Rd, N McComb, **E gas:** BP, **food:** Burger King, China Buffet, McDonald's, Piccadilly's, Ruby Tuesday, **lodging:** Holiday Inn Express, **other:** H HOSPITAL, Belk, JC Penney, Kia, Lowe's Whse, Sears/auto, Walmart SuperCtr/Subway, mall, **W gas:** Chevron/Quizno's/dsl, **food:** Arby's, El Dorado Mexican, Santa Fe Grille, **lodging:** Deerfield Inn, Hampton Inn, Hawthorn Inn, **other:** Ford/Lincoln/Mercury |
| 17 | Delaware Ave, McComb, **E gas:** BP/Subway, Blue Sky Gas, Chevron/dsl, Exxon, Pump & Save, Pure, RaceWay, Shell/dsl, **food:** Backyard BBQ, Burger King, Domino's, Golden Corral, Mexican Grill, McDonald's, New China, Pizza Hut, Pizza Inn, Popeye's, Sonic, Taco Bell, Waffle House, Wendy's, **lodging:** Best Western, Comfort Inn, Executive Inn, National Inn, Super 8, **other:** H HOSPITAL, AutoZone, CVS Drug, $General, Eckerd, Family$, Fred's Drug, Kroger, O'Reilly Parts, Rite Aid, **W lodging:** Day's Inn, **other:** Chrysler/Dodge/Jeep |

## INTERSTATE 55 CONT'D

**N ↕ S**

**15b a** | US 98 E, MS 48 W, McComb, **1 mi E gas:** Exxon/Subway, Pure, Shell, **food:** Church's, Hardee's, KFC, **lodging:** Camellian Motel, **other:** Advance Parts, $General, Family$, tires, vet, **W gas:** BP/dsl

**13** | Fernwood Rd, **W gas:** Conoco/Fernwood/dsl/rest./scales/24hr/@, **lodging:** Fernwood Motel, **other:** golf, to Percy Quin SP

**10** | MS 48, Magnolia, **1 mi E gas:** Exxon, MTS, **food:** Subway, **other:** RV camping

**8** | MS 568, Magnolia, **E** Pike Co Speedway

**4** | Chatawa

**3mm** | Welcome Ctr nb, full ♿ facilities, 📞, 🔁, litter barrels, petwalk, RV dump, 24hr security

**2mm** | weigh station, nb only

**1** | MS 584, Osyka, Gillsburg

**0mm** | Mississippi/Louisiana state line, Mississippi River

## INTERSTATE 59

**N ↕ S**

| Exit # | Services |
|---|---|

**I-59 S and I-20 W run together to Meridian.**

**172mm** | Mississippi/Alabama state line

**170mm** | weigh sta both lanes

**169** | Kewanee, **S gas:** Kewanee Trkstp/dsl

**165** | Toomsuba, **N gas:** Shell/Subway/24hr, Texaco/ChesterFried/dsl, **S gas:** Loves/Arby's/dsl/scales, **other:** KOA (2mi)

**164mm** | Welcome Ctr wb, full ♿ facilities, 📞, vending, 🔁, litter barrels, petwalk, RV dump, 24hr security

**160** | to Russell, **N gas:** TA/BP/dsl/rest./scales/24hr/@, **other:** Nanabe RV Camping (1mi), **S gas:** Shell/dsl

**157b a** | US 45, to Macon, Quitman

**MERIDIAN**

**154b a** | MS 19 S, MS 39 N, Meridian, **N gas:** BP/dsl, Pure, Shell, Texaco/Domino's, **food:** Applebee's, Cracker Barrel, Penn's Rest., Western Sizzlin, Waffle House, **lodging:** Day's Inn, Drury Inn, Hampton Inn, Hilton Garden, Holiday Inn, Relax Inn, Rodeway Inn, Super 8, **other:** Benchmark RV Park, Cadillac/Pontiac, Chrysler/Jeep/Kia, Hyundai, Lincoln/Mercury, Mitsubishi, U-Haul, **S gas:** Chevron, Texaco, **food:** Chick-fil-A, CiCi's, Crescent City Grill, Garfield's Rest., McAlister's, McDonald's, O'Charley's, Outback Steaks, Popeye's, Red Lobster, Ryan's, Taco Bell, **lodging:** Comfort Inn, Jameson Inn, Microtel, **other:** Belk, Best Buy, BooksAMillion, Dillard's, $Tree, Ethridge RV Ctr, Goody's, Harley-Davidson, JC Penney, Old Navy, PetCo, Ross, Sam's Club/gas, Sears/auto, TJ Maxx, mall, same as 153

**153** | MS 145 S, 22nd Ave, Meridian, **N gas:** BP, Shell, **food:** Arby's, Barnhill's Buffet, Burger King, Capt D's, China Buffet, Hardee's, KFC, McDonald's, Pizza Hut, Subway, Wendy's, Western Sizzlin, **lodging:** Relax Inn, Super Inn, **other:** Ⓗ HOSPITAL, Firestone, Ford/Nissan, Fred's Drug, $General, Ford, Saverite Foods, **S gas:** Chevron/dsl, Exxon/dsl, Texaco/dsl, **food:** A&W/LJ Silver, Waffle House, **lodging:** Best Western, Budget 8 Motel, Econolodge, Holiday Inn Express, La Quinta, Motel 6, Quality Inn, Sleep Inn, **other:** Buick, Cadillac/Chevrolet, Chrysler/Jeep, Honda, Suzuki, Lowes Whse, Walmart SuperCtr/gas

**152** | 29th Ave, 31st Ave, Meridian, **N gas:** Chevron/ChesterFried/dsl/24hr, **lodging:** Ramada Ltd, **S lodging:** Royal Inn

**151** | 49th Ave, Valley Rd, **N tires, S gas:** Pilot/Subway/dsl/24hr, **other:** stockyards

**MERIDIAN**

**150** | US 11 S, MS 19 N, Meridian, **N gas:** Queen City Trkstp/dsl/rest./@, **food:** McDonald's, **other:** RV camping, Okatibbee Lake, **S gas:** Chevron/Stuckey's/Subway/dsl, Shell/dsl **other:** ✈

**149mm** | I-59 N and I-20 E run together 22 mi

**142** | to US 11, Savoy, **W** to Dunns Falls

**137** | to N Enterprise, to Stonewall

**134** | MS 513, S Enterprise

**126** | MS 18, to Rose Hill, Pachuta, **E gas:** BP/dsl/24hr

**118** | to Vossburg, Paulding

**113** | MS 528, to Heidelberg, **E gas:** BP/JR's/dsl/24hr, Chevron/dsl, Exxon/Subway/dsl, Shell

**109mm** | parking area sb, litter barrels, no restrooms

**106mm** | parking area nb, litter barrels, no restrooms

**104** | Sandersville

**99** | US 11, **E lodging:** Magnolia Motel, **other:** Sleepy Hollow RV Park (1mi)

**97** | US 84 E, **E gas:** Exxon/dsl/scales, Kangaroo/Subway/dsl/24hr, **food:** Hardee's, Ward's Burgers, **W gas:** BP/dsl, Shell/24hr, **food:** KFC, Vic's Rest.

**96b** | MS 15 S, Cook Ave

**96a** | Masonite Rd, 4th Ave

**95d** | (from nb)

**LAUREL**

**95c** | Beacon St, Laurel, **W gas:** Pump & Save Gas, **food:** Burger King, Church's, McDonald's, Old Mexico, Popeye's, **lodging:** TownHouse Motel, **other:** Expert Tire, Family$, Grocery Depot, JC Penney, USPO, XpertTire

**95b a** | US 84 W, MS 15 N, 16th Ave, Laurel, **0-2 mi W gas:** Exxon/dsl, Pure, Shell, Texaco, **food:** Applebees, Buffet City, Checkers, China Town, Domino's, Fred's, Hardee's, KFC, Laredo Grill, Lenny's Subs, McDonald's, Pizza Hut, Quizno's, Shoney's, Sonic, Subway, Sweet Peppers Deli, Taco Bell, Waffle House, Ward's Burgers, Wendy's, Western Sizzlin, **lodging:** Comfort Suites, Econolodge, Hampton Inn, Holiday Inn Express, Super 8, **other:** Ⓗ HOSPITAL, Advance Parts, AutoZone, BigLots, Chevrolet/Buick/Pontiac, Chrysler/Dodge/Jeep, CVS Drug, $General, $Tree, Ford, Kroger, Lowe's Whse, Office Depot, O'Reilly Parts, Piggly Wiggly, Roses, Toyota, Walgreens, Walmart SuperCtr, Winn-Dixie

**93** | US 11, S Laurel, **W gas:** Exxon/Subway/dsl, Shell/dsl/24hr, Uncle Roy's/dsl, **food:** Hardee's

**90** | US 11, Ellisville Blvd, **E gas:** Texaco/dsl, **food:** Huddle House, **W gas:** Dixie/dsl

**88** | MS 588, MS 29, Ellisville, **E gas:** Chevron/dsl, FastTrak, **food:** Domino's, KFC, McDonald's, Pizza Hut, Subway, **other:** Ellisville Drug, Food Tiger, Family$, NAPA, **W gas:** Exxon/dsl, **lodging:** Best Western

**85** | MS 590, to Ellisville, **W** auto repair

## INTERSTATE 59 CONT'D

| | |
|---|---|
| 80 | to US 11, Moselle, **E** gas: BP/dsl |
| 78 | Sanford Rd |
| 76 | **W** Hattiesburg-Laurel Reg ✈ |
| 73 | Monroe Rd, to Monroe |
| 69 | to Glendale, Eatonville Rd |
| 67b a | US 49, Hattiesburg, **E** gas: BP, Exxon, Kangaroo/dsl, Shell, Texaco, **food:** Arby's, Burger King, Cracker Barrel, DQ, Krystal, McDonald's, Pizza Hut, Waffle House, **lodging:** Budget Inn, Comfort Inn, Econolodge, Howard Johnson, La Quinta, Motel 6, Quality Inn, Ramada, Red Carpet Inn, Regency Inn, Scottish Inn, Sleep Inn, Super 8, **other:** $General, **W** gas: BP/dsl, Chevron, MapleLeaf/dsl, Pure/dsl, Shell/Subway, Stuckey's/dsl, **food:** Sonic, Waffle House, Ward's Burgers, Wendy's, **lodging:** Best Western, Candlewood Suites, Holiday Inn |
| 65b a | US 98 W, Hardy St, Hattiesburg, **E** gas: Exxon, Shell/dsl, Texaco, **food:** Applebee's, Bop's Custard, Buffalo Wild Wings, Cane's Checkers, Chicken, CiCi's, Domino's, IHOP, KFC, La Fiesta Brava, Lenny's Subs, McDonald's, Panino's Italian, Pizza Hut, Quizno's, Smoothie King, Starbucks, Subway, Taco Bell, Ward's Burgers, **lodging:** Courtyard, Executive Inn, Fairfield Inn, Western Motel, **other:** CarQuest, Curves, CVS Drug, Goodyear/auto, Home Depot, Roses, Walgreens, S MS U, vet, **W** gas: BP/dsl, Exxon/Domino's, Kangaroo, Pump & $ave, Shell, **food:** Arby's, Backyard Burger, Burger King, Chick-fil-A, Chili's, China Buffet, ChuckeCheese, Coldstone, FireHouse Subs, Hardee's, Krispy Kreme, Lion's Choice, Logan's Roadhouse, LongHorn Steaks, Mazzio's, McDonald's, McCalisters Deli, Newt's Grill, O'Charley's, Olive Garden, Outback Steaks, Peking Garden, Pepper's Cafe, Pizza Hut, Popeye's, Red Lobster, Ryan's, Starbucks, Stoney's, Subway, Taco Bell, TGIFridays, Waffle House, Ward's Burgers, Wendy's, Zaxby's, **lodging:** Baymont Inn, Comfort Suites, Hampton Inn, Hilton Garden, Microtel, Sun Suites, **other:** H HOSPITAL, Advance Parts, AutoZone, Belk, Best Buy, BooksAMillion, Circuit City, Dillard's, $Tree, Firestone/auto, Gander Mtn, Goodyear/auto, JC Penney, Kohl's, Lincoln/Mercury, Lowe's Whse, Michael's, Nissan, Office Depot, Old Navy, PetsMart, Radio Shack, Rite Aid, Ross, SaveRite Foods, Sam's Club/gas, Sears/auto, Target, TJ Maxx, Walgreens, Walmart SuperCtr, mall |
| 60 | US 11, S Hattiesburg, **E** gas: Shell/dsl, **W** gas: BP/dsl, Kangaroo/Subway/dsl/24hr |
| 59 | US 98 E, to US 49, Lucedale, MS Gulf Coast |
| 56mm | parking area both lanes, litter barrels, no restrooms |
| 51 | rd 589, to Purvis, **W** gas: Chevron/dsl, Pinebelt Oil/dsl, Shell/dsl (2mi), **food:** Pizza Hut (2mi), to Little Black Cr Water Park |
| 48mm | Little Black Creek |
| 41 | MS 13, to Lumberton, **W** gas: Pure, **other:** Bass Pecan Store, $General, to Little Black Cr Water Park |
| 35 | Hillsdale Rd, **E** gas: Pitstop/dsl, **lodging:** to Kings Arrow Ranch, to Lake Hillside Resort |
| 32mm | Wolf River |
| 29 | rd 26, to Poplarville, **W** gas: Kangaroo/dsl (2mi), Pure/dsl, **food:** Burger King (2mi), Hardee's (2mi) |
| 27 | MS 53, to Poplarville, **W** gas: Kangaroo/dsl (2mi), Shell/dsl, **other:** RV Camping (2mi) |

| | |
|---|---|
| 19 | to US 11, Millard |
| 15 | to McNeill, **W** gas: McNeill Trkstop/dsl/rest. |
| 13mm | parking area sb, litter barrels, no restrooms |
| 10 | to US 11, Carriere, **E** gas: Texaco/Huddle House/dsl, **other:** Clearwater RV Camp (5mi), repair/tires |
| 8mm | parking area nb, litter barrels, no restrooms |
| 6 | MS 43 N, N Picayune, **E** food: Marble Slab Creamery, Paul's Pastries, **W** gas: Chevron/dsl, **lodging:** Best Value, **other:** H HOSPITAL, CVS Drug, Winn-Dixie, vet |
| 4 | MS 43 S, to Picayune, **E** gas: RaceTrac, **food:** McDonald's, Ryan's, Wow Cafe, **other:** URGENT CARE, Chevrolet/Pontiac/Buick/Cadillac, Home Depot, Nissan, Sun Roamers RV Park, Walgreens, Walmart SuperCtr/gas, **W** gas: Chevron, Exxon/dsl, K&T/dsl, Shell/dsl, **food:** Burger King, Domino's, El Mariachi, Hardee's, KFC, McDonald's, Papa John's, Pizza Hut, Popeye's, Shoney's, Subway, Taco Bell, Waffle House, Wendy's, **lodging:** Comfort Inn, Day's Inn, Heritage Inn, **other:** H HOSPITAL, Advance Parts, AutoZone, Chrysler/Dodge/Jeep, Curves, $General, Ford/Lincoln/Mercury, Fred's Drug, O'Reilly Parts, Radio Shack, Rite Aid, Winn-Dixie, vet |
| 3mm | Welcome Ctr nb, full ♿ facilities, 📞, vending, 🍴, litter barrels, petwalk, RV dump |
| 1.5mm | weigh sta both lanes |
| 1 | US 11, MS 607, **E** NASA, **W** gas: Chevron/dsl, Shell/dsl |
| 0mm | Mississippi/Louisiana state line, Pearl River. **Exits 11-1 are in Louisiana** |
| 11 | Pearl River Turnaround. Callboxes begin sb. |
| 5b | Honey Island Swamp |
| 5a | LA 41, Pearl River, **E** gas: Chevron |
| 3 | US 11 S, LA 1090, Pearl River, **W** gas: Shell/dsl, **1 mi W** Chevron/dsl/24hr |
| 1.5mm | Welcome Ctr sb, full ♿ facilities, info, 📞, 🍴, litter barrels, petwalk, RV dump |
| 1c b | I-10, E to Bay St Louis, W to New Orleans |
| 1a | I-12 W, to Hammond. I-59 begins/ends on I-10/I-12. |
| | **Exits 1-11 are in Louisiana.** |

## INTERSTATE 220 - JACKSON

| Exit # | Services |
|---|---|
| 11mm | I-220 begins/ends on I-55, exit 104. |
| 9 | Hanging Moss Rd, County Line Rd, **E** gas: BP |
| 8 | Watkins Dr, **E** gas: Shell/Chester Fried, Spur |
| 5b a | US 49 N, Evers Blvd, to Yazoo City, **E** gas: BP, Pump&Save, **food:** KFC, Sonic, **lodging:** Star Motel, Family$, Food Depot, **W** gas: BP, Exxon/Burger King, Shell/Subway/dsl |
| 3 | Industrial Dr, no services |
| 2b a | Clinton Blvd, Capitol St, **E** to Jackson Zoo, **W** gas: RaceWay, Shell, **food:** McDonald's, Popeye's, Sonic, **other:** Family$ |
| 1b a | US 80, **E** food: Bumer's Drive-in, Capt D's, KFC, McDonald's, Pizza Hut, Popeye's, Sonny's BBQ, Taco Bell, Wendy's, **lodging:** Day's Inn, Econolodge, Sleep Inn, Super 8, **W** gas: BP, Exxon/dsl, **food:** Arby's, Krystal, **other:** Belk, Dillard's, Hyundai, Sears/auto |
| 0mm | I-220 begins/ends on I-20, exit 41 |

MS

## INTERSTATE 29

**N ↕ S**

| Exit # | Services |
|---|---|
| 124mm | Missouri/Iowa state line |
| 123mm | Nishnabotna River |
| 121.5mm | weigh sta both lanes |
| 116 | rd A, rd B, to Watson, **W** fireworks |
| 110 | US 136, Rock Port, Phelps City, **E** gas: Shell/dsl, lodging: Rockport Inn, to NW MO St U, **W** gas: BP/dsl/24hr, Phillips 66/Subway/dsl/24hr, food: McDonald's, Trails End Rest., lodging: Super 8, other: KOA, fireworks |
| 109.5mm | Welcome Ctr sb, full ♿ facilities, info, 📞, 🍴, litter barrels, petwalk |
| 107 | MO 111, to Rock Port, **W** motel/RV Park |
| 106.5mm | Rock Creek |
| 102mm | Mill Creek |
| 99 | rd W, Corning |
| 97mm | Tarkio River |
| 92 | US 59, to Fairfax, Craig, **W** gas: Sinclair/dsl |
| 90.5mm | Little Tarkio Creek |
| 86.5mm | Squaw Creek |
| 84 | MO 118, Mound City, **E** gas: Phillips 66/Subway/dsl, Shamrock/dsl, food: Breadeaux Pizza, McDonald's, Quacker's Steaks, lodging: Audrey's Motel, Super 8, other: Dodge/Jeep, $General, Mound City Foods, **W** gas: Shell/dsl/24hr, other: Big Lake SP (12mi) |
| 82mm | rest area both lanes, full ♿ facilities, 📞, 🍴, litter barrels, vending, petwalk |

**S T J O S E P H**

| | |
|---|---|
| 79 | US 159, Rulo, **E** gas: Squaw Creek Trkstp/dsl/rest/RV dump/@, **W** to Big Lake SP (12mi), to Squaw Creek NWR (3mi) |
| 78mm | Kimsey Creek |
| 75 | US 59, to Oregon |
| 67 | US 59 N, to Oregon |
| 66.5mm | Nodaway River |
| 65 | US 59, rd RA, to Fillmore, Savannah, **E** gas: Conoco/dsl, other: antiques |
| 60 | rd K, rd CC, Amazonia, **W** other: Hunt's Fruit Barn, antiques |
| 58.5mm | Hopkins Creek |
| 56b a | I-229 S, US 71 N, US 59 N, to St Joseph, Maryville |
| 55mm | Dillon Creek |
| 53 | US 59, US 71 bus, to St Joseph, Savannah, **E** AOK Camping, fireworks, **W** gas: Phillips 66/dsl |
| 50 | US 169, St Joseph, King City, **1-3 mi W on Belt Hwy...** gas: Conoco, Phillips 66/Domino's, Shell, food: Bob Evans, Cheddar's, Chili's, Chipotle Mexican, Culver's, Famous Dave's, 54th St Grill, Hardee's, LJ Silver, McDonald's, Panda Express, Ryan's, Sonic, Subway, Taco Bell, Wendy's, other: Advance Parts, Border's Books, Home Depot, Kohl's, Lowe's Whse, Michaels, Sam's Club, Target, Tires+, TJ Maxx, Walgreen, Walmart SuperCtr |

Copyright 2009 - The Next Exit®

## INTERSTATE 29 CONT'D

**ST JOSEPH**

**47** MO 6, Frederick Blvd, to Clarksdale, St Joseph, **E** gas: Conoco, **food:** Bandanas BBQ, Country Kitchen, **lodging:** Day's Inn, Drury Inn, **W** gas: Sinclair, Phillips 66/dsl, **food:** Applebee's, Carlos O'Kelly's, Cracker Barrel, Denny's, Dunkin Donuts, Ground Round, Hazel's Coffee, KFC, McDonald's, Perkins/24hr, Pizza Hut, Red Lobster, Russell Stover, Sonic, Subway, Taco Bell, Whiskey Creek Steaks, Village Steaks, **lodging:** Budget Inn, Comfort Suites, Hampton Inn, Motel 6, Ramada Inn, Stoney Creek Inn, Super 8, **other:** H HOSPITAL, BigLots, Chevrolet/Mazda, Dillard's, Ford, Firestone/auto, Goodyear/auto, PriceChopper Foods, Sears, RV camp, **1 mi W on US 169 food:** Arby's, Blimpie, Burger King, Church's, Fazoli's, Ground Round, LJ Silver, Pizza Hut, Rib Crib BBQ, Schlotsky's, Sonic, Starbucks, Taco Bell, **other:** Advance Parts, Aldi Foods, AutoZone, Buick/Pontiac/GMC, Cub Foods, CVS Drug, Eckerd, Food4Less/drugs/24hr, Ford/Lincoln/Mercury, Hastings Books, HyVee Foods, JC Penney, Jo-Ann Fabrics, Office Depot, Radio Shack, U-Haul, Walgreen

**46b a** US 36, to Cameron, St Joseph, **1 mi W on US 169 gas:** BP/dsl, FL, Shell, **food:** Burger King, Godfather's, La Mesa Mexican, Pizza Hut, Taco John's, Wendy's, **other:** $General, Isuzu, Kia, Nissan, QwikLube, Save-a-Lot Foods, Walgreen, Walmart SuperCtr/gas, to MO W St Coll

**44** US 169, to Gower, St Joseph, **E** gas: Phillips 66, Loves/Arby's/dsl/scales/24hr, **food:** Nelly's Mexican, Subway, **lodging:** Best Western, **other:** dsl repair, **W** gas: Shell/dsl/rest/24hr, **food:** DQ, McDonald's, San Jose Steaks, Taco Bell, **other:** Chrysler/Jeep/Dodge, $Tree, Goodyear, Harley-Davidson, Hyundai, Walmart SuperCtr/gas

**43** I-229 N, to St Joseph

**39.5mm** Pigeon Creek

**35** rd DD, Faucett, **W** gas: Farris Trkstp/dsl/motel/rest/24hr/@

**33.5mm** Bee Creek

**30** rd Z, rd H, Dearborn, New Market, **E** gas: Conoco/Subway/dsl/24hr

**29.5mm** Bee Creek

**27mm** **rest area both lanes, full** ♿ **facilities,** 🕻, 🚻, **litter barrels, vending, petwalk**

**25** rd E, rd U, to Camden Point, **E** gas: Phillips 66/dsl/rest.

**24mm** weigh sta both lanes

**20** MO 92, MO 273, to Atchison, Leavenworth, **W** gas: Phillips 66, **other:** to Weston Bend SP

**19.5mm** Platte River

**PLATTE CITY**

**19** rd HH, Platte City, **E** antiques, **W** gas: Casey's, Conoco, Platte City/dsl, **food:** DQ, Red Dragon Chinese, **lodging:** Comfort Inn, Travelodge, **other:** Airport RV Park, Cash Saver Foods, CountryMart Foods, Dodge, CarQuest, USPO, same as 18

**18** MO 92, Platte City, **E** Basswood RV Park (5mi), **W** gas: Casey's, Conoco/KFC, QT/dsl, **food:** Arby's, Burger King, McDonald's, Mr GoodCents Subs, Pizza Shoppe, Rancho Grande Cantina, Sonic, Subway, Taco Bell/Pizza Hut, Waffle House, **lodging:** Best Western, Comfort Inn, Super 8, **other:** Chevrolet/Pontiac/GMC, CVS Drug, Goodyear/auto, Ford, same as 19

**17** I-435 S, to Topeka

**15** Mexico City Ave, **W** lodging: Marriott

**14** I-435 E (from sb), to St Louis

**13** to I-435 E, **E** lodging: Best Western, Clarion, Comfort Suites, Extended Stay America, Fairfield Inn, Holiday Inn, Microtel, Radisson, Sheraton, **W** lodging: Marriott, **other:** KCI ✈

**12** NW 112th St, **E** gas: BP, Conoco/dsl, **lodging:** Day's Inn, Extended Stay America, Day's Inn, Hampton Inn, Hilton, Holiday Inn Express, Microtel, **W** lodging: Econolodge

**10** Tiffany Springs Pkwy, **E** gas: Phillips 66, Shell, **food:** Jade Garden, SmokeBox BBQ, **lodging:** Embassy Suites, Homewood Suites, **W** food: Cracker Barrel, Ruby Tuesday, Waffle House, Wendy's, **lodging:** AmeriSuites, Chase Suites, Courtyard, Drury Inn, Homeswood Suites, Howard Johnson, MainStay Suites, Ramada Inn, Residence Inn, Sleep Inn, **other:** Honda, Lexus, Nissan, Saturn, Toyota, Volvo

**9b a** MO 152, to Liberty, Topeka

**KANSAS CITY**

**8** MO 9, rd T, NW Barry Rd, **E** gas: Valero/dsl, **food:** Applebee's, Boston Mkt, Chili's, Chipotle Mexican, 54th St Grill, Hong's Buffet, Hooters, Kato Japanese, LoneStar Steaks, On the Border, Panda Express, Panera Bread, Pizza Hut/Taco Bell, Starbucks, Subway, Wendy's, Winstead's Rest., **other:** H HOSPITAL, HyVee Foods, Lowe's Whse, Old Navy, SteinMart, Walmart SuperCtr, **W** gas: Phillips 66, QT/dsl, Shell, **food:** Abuelo's Mexican, Hardee's, LJ Silver/A&W, McDonald's, Mimi's Cafe, Minsky's Pizza, Outback Steaks, Rainbow Oriental, Smokehouse BBQ, Sonic, Taco Bueno, **lodging:** Motel 6, Quality Inn, Super 8, **other:** Barnes&Noble, CVS Drug, Tires+

**6** NW 72nd St, Platte Woods, **E** gas: Sinclair/dsl, **W** gas: Phillips 66, **food:** KFC, Papa John's, Tasty Thai, **other:** Sears Grand

**5** MO 45 N, NW 64th St, **W** gas: Shell/dsl, **food:** Goodcents Subs, IHOP, KFC, McDonald's, Nick & Jake's, O'Quigley's Grill, Papa Murphy's, Quizno's, Subway, Thai Place, **other:** CVS Drug, $General, GNC, Goodyear, Radio Shack

**4** NW 56th St (from nb), **W** gas: Phillips 66, same as 5

**3c** rd A (from sb), Riverside, **W** gas: QT, **food:** Argosy Café, Corner Café, MeanGreen's Cafe, Sonic, **lodging:** Skyline Inn, Super 8, **other:** USPO

**3b** I-635 S

**3a** Waukomis Dr, rd AA (from nb)

**2b** US 169 S (from sb), to KC

**2a** US 169 N (from nb), to Smithville

**1e** US 69, Vivion Rd, **E** gas: Shell/dsl, **food:** McDonald's, Steak'n Shake, **other:** Chrysler/Jeep, Chevrolet/Cadillac, Home Depot, Lincoln/Mercury, Mitsubishi, PriceChopper Foods/24hr, **W** gas: Shell, **food:** McDonald's, Subway

**1d** MO 283 S, Oak Tfwy (from sb), **W** gas: Phillips 66, **food:** McDonald's

**1c** Gladstone (from nb), **E** food: Arby's, 54th St Grill, Perkins, Pizza St Buffet, Ryan's, Smokehouse BBQ, Tippen's Café

**1b** I-35 N (from sb), to Des Moines

**1a** Davidson Rd

**8mm** **I-35 N. I-29 and I-35 run together 6 mi. See Missouri Interstate 35, exits 3-8a.**

## INTERSTATE 35

| Exit # | Services |
|---|---|
| 114mm | Missouri/Iowa state line |
| 114 | US 69, to Lamoni, **W gas:** Conoco/dsl/24hr, **other:** RV camping |
| 113.5mm | Zadie Creek |
| 112mm | **MO welcome ctr sb, full (handicapped) facilities, [C], [A], litter barrels, petwalk** |
| 110 | weigh sta both lanes |
| 106 | rd N, Blythedale, **E gas:** Conoco/fireworks, Phillips 66/dsl/café/motel/24hr/@, **food:** DinnerBell Rest., **lodging:** Painted Lady B&B, Eagle's Landing Motel, **other:** dsl repair, **W gas:** Phillips 66/dsl/24hr, **other:** Eagle Ridge RV Park (2mi) |
| 99 | rd A, to Ridgeway, **5 mi W** Eagle RV Camping |
| 94mm | E Fork Big Creek |
| 93 | US 69, Bethany, **W food:** Dos Chiquitas Mexican, **other:** RV Dump |
| 92 | US 136, Bethany, **E gas:** Phillips 66/dsl/24hr, **food:** KFC/Taco Bell, McDonald's, **lodging:** Budget Inn, **W gas:** BP/dsl, Casey's, Kum&Go/Wendy's/dsl, **food:** Country Kitchen, DQ, Subway, Taco Bell, TootToot Rest., **lodging:** Best Western, Super 8, **other:** [H] HOSPITAL, Chevrolet/Buick, Russell Stover, Walmart SuperCtr |
| 90mm | Pole Cat Creek |
| 88 | MO 13, to Bethany, Gallatin, **3 mi W lodging:** Bethany Motel |
| 84 | rds AA, H, to Gilman City, **E** Crowder SP (24mi) |
| 81mm | **rest area both lanes, full [&] facilities, [C], [A], litter barrels, vending, petwalk** |
| 80 | rds B, N, to Coffey |
| 78 | rd C, Pattonsburg, **W gas:** Phillips 66/dsl |
| 74.5mm | Grand River |
| 72 | rd DD |
| 68 | US 69, to Pattonsburg |
| 64 | MO 6, to Maysville, Gallatin |
| 61 | US 69, Winston, Gallatin, **E gas:** Shell/dsl/rest./24hr |
| 54 | US 36, Cameron, **E gas:** BP/rest./dsl/24hr, Cenex/dsl, Shell/Wendy's/dsl/24hr, **food:** McDonald's, Subway, **lodging:** Best Western, Comfort Inn, Crossroads Inn/RV Park, **W gas:** Valero, **food:** Burger King, Dominos, DQ, El Maguey Mexican, Kettle Diner, KFC/Taco Bell, Pizza Hut, Sonic, Subway, **lodging:** Day's Inn, Econolodge, Relax Inn, Super 8, **other:** [H] HOSPITAL, Advance Parts, Ford, Chevrolet/Pontiac/Buick, CountryMart Foods, $General, Ford/Mercury, O'Reilley Parts, Radio Shack, Walmart SuperCtr, W MO Corr Ctr, tires |
| 52 | rd BB, Lp 35, to Cameron, **E other:** [H] HOSPITAL, **W gas:** Casey's, Kum&Go, same as 54 |
| 49mm | Brushy Creek |
| 48.5mm | Shoal Creek |
| 48 | US 69, Cameron, **E** to Wallace SP (2mi), **W gas:** Shamrock, **other:** fireworks |
| 40 | MO 116, Lathrop, **E gas:** Phillips 66/Country Café/dsl, **other:** antiques |
| 34.5mm | **rest area both lanes, full [&] facilities, [C], [A], litter barrels, vending, petwalk** |
| 33 | rd PP, Holt, **E food:** Hilltop Grill, **other:** RV Dump, **W gas:** BP/dsl, Conoco/dsl, **lodging:** American Eagle Inn |
| 30mm | Holt Creek |
| 26 | MO 92, Kearney, **E gas:** Casey's/gas, Phillips 66/dsl, Shell/dsl, **food:** McDonald's, Sonic, **lodging:** Comfort Inn, Day's Inn, Super 8, **other:** CountryMart Foods, CVS Drug, Kramer Hardware, Red Cross Drug, to Watkins Mill SP, **W gas:** Pilot/Taco Bell/dsl/scales/24hr, Platte Clay Fuels, **food:** Arby's, Burger King, Carlitos Mexican, Hunan Garden Chinese, Subway, **lodging:** Best Western, Econolodge, **other:** Chevrolet, Family$, GoodYear/auto, John's Foods, to Smithville Lake |
| 22mm | weigh sta nb, parking area sb |
| 20 | US 69, MO 33, to Excelsior Springs, **E** [H] HOSPITAL |
| 17 | MO 291, rd A, **1 mi E food:** Arby's, CiCi's, LJ Silver, Perkins, Ponderosa, **other:** Chevrolet, CountryMart Foods, Eckerd, Hy-Vee Foods, Liberty RV Ctr, Village Lodge, Walgreen, same as 16, **W gas:** Phillips 66/dsl, QT, **food:** McDonald's, Sonic, Subway, **other:** KCI [✈] |
| 16 | MO 152, Liberty, **E gas:** BP, **food:** Godfather's, Pizza Hut, Planet Sub, Ponderosa, Red Robin, Starbucks, Subway, Texas Roadhouse, Village Inn Rest., Wendy's, **lodging:** Days Inn, Super 8, **other:** [H] HOSPITAL, Chevrolet, Firestone/auto, Ford, Hy-Vee Foods, Lowe's Whse, Sears Grand, Walgreen, **W gas:** BP, Phillips 66/Circle K, **food:** Applebee's, Backyard Burger, Bob Evans, Buffalo Wild Wings, Burger King, Chili's, Corner Cafe, Cracker Barrel, Golden Corral, KFC, LongHorn Steaks, McDonald's, O'Charley's, Panera Bread, Panda Express, Quizno's, Schlotsky's, SmokeStack BBQ, Steak'n Shake, Subway, Taco Bell, Target, Uno Pizzaria, Waffle House, **lodging:** Comfort Suites, Fairfield Inn, Hampton Inn, Holiday Inn Express, **other:** Best Buy, Ford, Home Depot, JC Penney, Jiffy Lube, Kohls, Michael's, NAPA AutoCare, Office Depot, Radio Shack, Target, TJ Maxx, Walmart SuperCtr |
| 14 | US 69 (exits left from sb), Liberty Dr, to Glenaire, Pleasant Valley, **E gas:** Sinclair, Shell, **other:** I-35 RV Ctr, **W gas:** QT/dsl |
| 13 | US 69 (from nb), to Pleasant Valley, **E gas:** Phillips 66/dsl, Shell, Sinclair/24hr, **food:** KFC, McDonald's, **other:** auto repair, **W gas:** QT/dsl |
| 12b a | I-435, to St Louis |
| 11 | US 69 N, Vivion Rd, **E gas:** BP/dsl, Shell/dsl, **food:** Church's, McDonald's, **W gas:** QT, **food:** Sonic, Stroud's Rest. |
| 10 | N Brighton Ave (from nb), **E food:** Church's, McDonald's |
| 9 | MO 269 S, Chouteau Trfwy, **E gas:** Phillips 66, **food:** IHOP, McDonald's, Ming Garden, Outback Steaks, |

Copyright 2009 - The Next Exit®

## INTERSTATE 35 CONT'D

| | |
|---|---|
| **9** | Continued |
| | Papa Murphy's, Popeye's, Subway, Wing Stop, **other:** Food Festival, Harrah's Casino/rest., Radio Shack, Target, **W food:** Wendy's (1mi) |
| **8c** | MO 1, Antioch Rd, **E gas:** 7-11/gas, **food:** Domino's, **lodging:** Best Western, Econolodge, InnTown Inn, **W gas:** Phillips 66, **food:** Catfish Rest., Waffle House, **other:** Walgreen |
| **8b** | I-29 N, US 71 N, KCI ✈ |
| **I-35 S and I-29 S run together 6 mi.** | |
| **8a** | Parvin Rd, **E gas:** BP, Shell, **lodging:** Holiday Inn, **other:** O'Reilly Parts, **W lodging:** Super Inn |
| **6b a** | Armour Rd, **E gas:** Phillips 66/dsl, **food:** Arby's, Burger King, Denny's, McDonald's, **lodging:** Best Value Inn, La Quinta, **other:** H HOSPITAL, repair, to Riverboat Casino, **W gas:** QT, Phillips 66, Shell, **food:** Pizza Hut, Taco Bell, Wendy's, **lodging:** American Inn, Quality Inn, **other:** USPO |
| **5b** | 16th Ave, industrial district |
| **5a** | Levee Rd, Bedford St, industrial district |
| **4.5mm** | Missouri River |
| **4b** | Front St, **E** Isle of Capri Riverboat Casino/rest. |
| **4a** | US 24 E, Independence Ave |
| **3** | I-70 E, US 71 S, to St Louis |
| **2g** | **I-35 N and I-29 N run together 6 mi** |
| **2e** | Oak St, Grand-Walnut St, downtown, **E lodging:** Comfort Inn, **W gas:** Conoco |
| **2d** | Main-Delaware, Wyandotte St, downtown |
| **2a** | I-70 W, to Topeka |
| **2y** | US 169, Broadway, to downtown |
| **2w** | 12th St, Kemper Arena, to downtown |
| **2v** | 14th St, to downtown |
| **2u** | I-70 E, to Broadway, **E food:** Denny's |
| **1d** | 20th St (from sb) |
| **1c b** | 27th St, SW Blvd, W Pennway (from nb), **E gas:** Phillips 66, **other:** H HOSPITAL |
| **1a** | SW Trafficway (from sb) |
| **0mm** | Missouri/Kansas state line |

## INTERSTATE 44

| Exit # | Services |
|---|---|
| **290mm** | I-44 begins/ends on I-55, exit 207 in St Louis. |
| **290a** | I-55 S, to Memphis |
| **290c** | Gravois Ave (from wb), 12th St, **N gas:** Citgo/dsl, **S food:** McDonald's |
| **290b** | 18th St (from eb), downtown |
| **289** | Jefferson Ave, St Louis, **N gas:** Phillip's 66, **food:** Subway, **lodging:** Holiday Inn Express, **S gas:** Conoco, **food:** Lee's Chicken, McDonald's |
| **288** | Grand Blvd, St Louis, **N gas:** BP, **lodging:** Water Tower Inn **other:** H HOSPITAL, **S food:** Jack-in-the-Box, Qdoba Grill |
| **287b a** | Kingshighway, Vandeventer Ave, St Louis, **N gas:** BP, **other:** Jiffy Lube, U-Haul, **S gas:** BP, **other:** Chevrolet, Chrysler/Jeep, Walgreens, to MO Botanical Garden |
| **286** | Hampton Ave, St Louis, **N gas:** CFM, Shell, **food:** Denny's, Jack-in-the-Box, McDonald's, Steak'n Shake, Subway, Taco Bell, **S gas:** Shell, **food:** Burger King, Church's, Hardee's, **lodging:** Holiday Inn, |

| | |
|---|---|
| **286** | Continued |
| | Red Roof Inn, **other:** museums, zoo |
| **285** | SW Ave (from wb, no EZ return) |
| **284b a** | Arsenal St, Jamieson St |
| **283** | Shrewsbury (from wb), some services same as 282 |
| **282** | Laclede Sta Rd, Murdock Ave (from eb), St Louis, **N food:** Imo's Pizza, McDonald's, Starbucks, Subway, **other:** Subaru, vet |
| **280** | Elm Ave, St Louis, **N gas:** BP/repair, **other:** Schnuck's Food/24hr, **S gas:** Shell |
| **279** | (from wb), Berry Rd |
| **278** | Big Bend Rd, St Louis, **N food:** Hardee's, Sonic, **other:** H HOSPITAL, Sam's Club/gas, **S gas:** Mobil/dsl, QT |
| **277b** | US 67, US 61, US 50, Lindbergh Blvd, **N gas:** Shell, **food:** Arby's, Chili's, O'Charley's, Steak&Rice Chinese, Texas Roadhouse, Uno Pizzaria, White Castle, **lodging:** Best Western, **other:** H HOSPITAL, Hancock Fabrics, Harley-Davidson, Lowe's Whse, Office Depot, Target, Walmart SuperCtr, **S gas:** Conoco, Phillips 66, Shell, **food:** Burger King, Denny's, Fuddrucker's, Lion's Choice, Longhorn Steaks, Ruby Tuesday, Steak'n Shake, St Louis Bread, **lodging:** Day's Inn/rest., Hampton Inn, Holiday Inn, Quality Inn, **other:** AutoTire, Home Depot, Marshall's, Old Navy, PetsMart, WorldMkt |
| **277a** | MO 366 E, Watson Rd, access to same as 277b S |
| **276b a** | I-270, N to Chicago, S Memphis |
| **275** | N Highway Dr (from wb), Soccer Pk Rd, **N gas:** Road Ranger/dsl/rest. |
| **274a b** | Bowles Ave, **N gas:** Road Ranger/dsl, **S gas:** BP, Citgo/dsl/24hr, Phillips 66, QT, ZX/dsl, **food:** Bandana's BBQ, Cracker Barrel, Denny's, Krispy Kreme, McDonald's, Plaza Mexican, Quizno's, Sonic, Souper Salad, White Castle, **lodging:** Drury Inn, Econolodge, Fairfield Inn, Holiday Inn Express, Motel 6, PearTree Inn, Stratford Inn, TownePlace Inn, **other:** Goodyear |
| **272** | MO 141, Fenton, Valley Park, **N gas:** Motomart, **S gas:** Mobil, Phillips 66, QT, **food:** Bob Evans, Burger King, Culver's, McDonald's, Ruby Tuesday, Steak'n Shake, Subway, Taco Bell, **lodging:** Drury Inn, Hampton Inn |
| **269** | Antire Rd, Beaumont |
| **266** | Lewis Rd, **N other:** Rte 66 SP, golf |
| **266mm** | Meramec River |
| **265** | Williams Rd (from eb) |
| **264** | MO 109, rd W, Eureka, **N gas:** Phillips 66, **food:** Burger King, Domino's, DQ, KFC, McDonald's, Pizza Hut, Ponderosa, Smokers BBQ, Subway, Taco Bell, Wendy's, White Castle, **lodging:** Day's Inn, **other:** AutoTire, Firestone, NAPA, Schnuck's Foods, to Babler SP, **S gas:** QT, Shell, **other:** Walgreens |
| **261** | Lp 44, to Allenton, **N gas:** Motomart/McDonald's/dsl, **food:** Applebee's, China King, Denny's, KFC, Lion's Choice Rest., Steak'n Shake, **lodging:** Econolodge, Holiday Inn, Super 8, **other:** AutoZone, $Tree, GNC, Radio Shack, Walmart SuperCtr, to Six Flags, same as 264, **S gas:** Shell/dsl, **other:** Ford, KOA |
| **257** | Lp 44, Pacific, **N gas:** Phillips 66, Pilot/dsl/scales/24hr, **food:** Huddle House, **lodging:** Comfort Inn, **S gas:** Mobil/dsl/24hr, Motomart/24hr, BP/dsl, **food:** Hardee's, KFC, McDonald's, Pizza Hut, Taco Bell, **lodging:** Comfort Inn, Holiday Inn Express, Quality Inn, **other:** Buick/Chevrolet, Chrysler/Jeep/Dodge, $General, IGA Foods, NAPA |

## INTERSTATE 44 CONT'D

**E W**

**253** MO 100 E, to Gray Summit, **S** **gas:** Phillips 66, **lodging:** Diamond Motel, Gardenway Inn

**251** MO 100 W, to Washington, **N** **gas:** BP/dsl/24hr, FuelMart/Blimpie/Domino's/dsl/24hr, Mr Fuel/Conoco/dsl/scales, Phillips 66/Burger King/dsl

**247** US 50 W, rd AT, rd O, to Union, **N** **other:** Harley-Davidson, **other:** Pin Oak Creek Camping, flea mkt, **S** to Robertsville SP

**247mm** Bourbeuse River

**242** rd AH, to Hist Rte 66

**240** MO 47, St Clair, **N** **gas:** Phillips 66/Taco Bell/dsl, **food:** Burger King, El Palenque Mexican, **S** **gas:** Mobil/dsl, **food:** Hardee's, McDonald's, Subway, **lodging:** Budget Lodge, Super 8, **other:** $General, IGA Foods

**239** MO 30, rds AB, WW, St Clair, **N** repair, **S** **gas:** BP, Phillips 66

**238mm** weigh sta both lanes

**235mm** **rest area both lanes (both lanes exit left), full** 🚻 **facilities,** 🅲, 🏕, **litter barrels, vending, petwalk**

**230** rds W, Stanton, **N** **lodging:** Stanton Motel, **S** **other:** KOA, Meramec Caverns Camping (3mi)

**226** MO 185 S, Sullivan, **N** **gas:** ⊕*FLYING J*/Conoco/Country Mkt/dsl/LP/scales/24hr/@, **food:** Domino's, **other:** Chrysler/Jeep/Dodge, Ford, **S** **gas:** Phillips 66/Burger King, **food:** Applebee's, Bison Grill, DQ, Hardee's, KFC, McDonald's, Pizza Hut, Steak'n Shake, Subway, **other:** $General, O'Reilly Parts, Walmart SuperCtr, RV Camping, to Meramec SP, same as 225

**225** MO 185 N, rd D, Sullivan, **N** **gas:** Mobil, Phillips 66/dsl, **food:** Domino's, **lodging:** Baymont Inn, Econolodge, Executive Inn, Super 8, **other:** Chrysler/Dodge/Jeep, Ford/Mercury, **S** **gas:** Fas-Trip/dsl/café, Citgo, **food:** Cracker Barrel, Jack-in-the-Box, Lion's Choice, McDonald's, Pizza Hut, Sonic, Subway, **other:** �H HOSPITAL, Aldi Foods, Chevrolet/Buick, Goodyear, same as 226

**218** rds N, C, J, Bourbon, **N** **gas:** Citgo/dsl, **lodging:** Budget Inn, **S** **gas:** Mobil/24hr, **food:** HenHouse Rest., **other:** Suburban RV Ctr, Blue Sprgs Camping (6mi), Riverview Ranch Camping (8mi)

**214** rd H, Leasburg, **N** **gas:** Mobil/dsl, **S** **other:** Ozark Outdoor RV Park, to Onandaga Cave SP (7mi)

**210** rd UU, **S** **food:** MO Hick BBQ, Mt Peasant Winery

**208** MO 19, Cuba, **N** **gas:** Phillips 66, Voss/dsl/rest./24hr/@, **food:** Country Kitchen, Huddle House, Pizza Hut, **lodging:** Best Western, Super 8, **other:** Blue Beacon, **S** **gas:** Casey's, Delano/dsl, Mobil/Taco Bell/24hr, **food:** Burger King, Domino's, Hardee's, Jack-in-the-Box, McDonald's, Sonic, Subway, **lodging:** Holiday Inn Express, Wagon Wheel Motel, **other:** Chevrolet/GMC, $General, Mace Foods, O'Reilly Parts, Walmart/drugs, to Ozark Nat Scenic Riverways

**203** rds F, ZZ, **N** Blue Moon RV Park, **S** Rosati Winery (2mi)

**195** MO 8, MO 68, St James, Maramec Sprg Park, **N** **gas:** Conoco/dsl, Mobil/dsl, Phillips 66/dsl, **food:** John's Café, McDonald's, Pizza Hut, Subway, **lodging:** Econolodge, Economy Inn, **other:** Ford, Goodyear, O'Reilly Parts, St James Winery, **S** **gas:** Delano/dsl, Phillips 66/dsl, **food:** Burger King, **lodging:** Finn's Motel, **other:** CountryMart Foods, Ford

**S U L L I V A N**

**C U B A**

**R O L L A**

**189** rd V, **S** **gas:** Loves/McDonald's/Subway/dsl/scales/24hr

**186** US 63, MO 72, Rolla, **N** **gas:** Sinclair, **food:** Steak'n Shake, **lodging:** Drury Inn, Hampton Inn, Sooter Inn, **other:** Lowe's Whse, Plaza Tires, **S** **gas:** BP, Mobil/dsl, Phillips 66, **food:** Denny's, Donut King, Lee's Chicken, Panera Bread, **lodging:** Budget Motel, **other:** �H HOSPITAL

**185** rd E, to Rolla, **S** **gas:** Phillips 66, **food:** Applebee's, Arby's, DQ, Hardee's/24hr, Subway, Taco Bell, **other:** �H HOSPITAL, UMO at Rolla, st patrol

**184** US 63 S, to Rolla, **N** **lodging:** Comfort Suites, Holiday Inn Express, **S** **gas:** Delano, MotoMart, Rte 66 Gas, **food:** Arby's, Burger King, Domino's, El Rodeo Mexican, Feedlot Rest., Golden Corral, KFC, Kyoto Japanese, Little Caesar's, LJ Silver, Lucky House Chinese, McDonald's, Papa John's, Pizza Hut, Pizza Inn, Shoney's, Sirloin Stockade, Subway, Wendy's, Zeno's Steaks, **lodging:** Best Value, Best Western, Day's Inn, Econolodge, Holiday Inn, Howard Johnson/rest., Western Inn, Wickliffe Inn, **other:** �H HOSPITAL, Chevrolet, Ford/Lincoln/Mercury, Goodyear/auto, transmissions

**179** rds T, C, to Doolittle, Newburg, **S** **gas:** BP/24hr, **food:** Cookin' From Scratch Rest.

**178mm** **rest area both lanes, full** 🚻 **facilities,** 🅲, 🏕, **litter barrels, vending, petwalk**

**176** Sugar Tree Rd, **N** **lodging:** Vernelle's Motel, **S** **other:** Arlington River Resort Camping (2mi)

**172** rd D, Jerome, **N** camping

**169** rd J

**166** to Big Piney

**164mm** Big Piney River

**163** MO 28, to Dixon, **N** **gas:** Road Ranger/Subway/dsl/scales/24hr, **S** **gas:** Conoco, **food:** Country Café, Sweetwater BBQ, **lodging:** Best Western, Day's Inn, Knight's Inn, **other:** GS RV Park

**161b a** rd Y, to Ft Leonard Wood, **N** **gas:** Conoco, Mobil/dsl, **food:** All American Drive-In, Aussie Jack's, Cracker Barrel, Domino's, Jack's Diner, LJ Silver/A&W, Pizza Hut, Popeye's, Ruby Tuesday, Ryan's, Subway, Wendy's, **lodging:** Baymont Inn, Candlewood Suites, Comfort Inn, Fairfield Inn, Hampton Inn, Mainstay Suites, Red Roof Inn, **other:** $Tree, Toyota/Scion, Walmart SuperCtr, **S** **gas:** Cenex/dsl, Conoco, **food:** Arby's, Capt D's, Country Kitchen, El Sombrero, KFC, McDonald's, Papa John's, Taco Bell, Waffle House, **lodging:** Budget Inn, Econolodge, Holiday Inn Express, Microtel, Motel 6, Ramada Inn, **other:** AutoZone, Chrysler/Dodge, $General, Family$, Ford/Lincoln/Mercury/Mazda, NAPA, O'Reilly Parts, Radio Shack

Copyright 2009 - The Next Exit®

## INTERSTATE 44 CONT'D

**E ↕ W**

**159** Lp 44, to Waynesville, St Robert, **N** **food:** DQ, Sonic, **lodging:** Star Motel, Super 8, **other:** IGA Foods, O'Reilly Parts, Covered Wagon RV Park (2mi), **S** **gas:** BP/dsl **food:** Pepper's Rest., **lodging:** Microtel, **other:** Cadillac/Pontiac/GMC, Goodyear/auto

**158mm** Roubidoux Creek

**156** rd H, Waynesville, **N** **gas:** Casey's, Citgo/dsl, Cody's, **food:** Imperial Rest., McDonald's, Subway, **lodging:** Star Motel (1mi), **other:** Chevrolet/Buick, $General, Price Cutter+, vet

**153** MO 17, to Buckhorn, **N** **gas:** Cenex/dsl, **lodging:** Ft Wood Inn, **S** **gas:** Shell/dsl, **other:** Glen Oaks RV Park

**150** MO 7, rd P to Richland, **S** **food:** Joe's Place Steaks

**145** MO 133, rd AB, to Richland, **N** **gas:** Conoco/Oasis/dsl/rest./24hr, **S** camping

**143mm** Gasconade River

**140** rd N, to Stoutland, **S** **gas:** Conoco, **food:** Midway Chinese

**139mm** Bear Creek

**135** rd F, Sleeper

**130** rd MM, **N** **gas:** Cenex, Phillips 66, **food:** Andy's Rest., **lodging:** Best Western, Budget Inn, Munger Moss Inn, **S** **gas:** Kum&Go, **other:** Ⓗ HOSPITAL

**129** MO 5, MO 32, MO 64, to Hartville, Lebanon, **N** **gas:** Kum&Go, **food:** Applebee's, Bamboo Garden, Break-Time, Burger King, Country Kitchen, DQ, KFC, LJ Silver, McDonald's, Papa John's, Pizza Hut, Shoney's, Sonic, Subway, Taco Bell, Taco Hut, Wendy's, Western Sizzlin, **other:** Advance Parts, Aldi Foods, AutoZone, Chevrolet, Ford, IGA Foods, NAPA, O'Reilly Parts, Smitty's Foods, Walgreens, to Bennett Sprgs SP, **S** **gas:** BP, Conoco/dsl, Phillips 66, **food:** Blimpie, Candy's Custard, Capt D's, Domino's, Hardee's, La Mexican Rest., Pizza Hut, **lodging:** Brentwood Motel, **other:** Ⓗ HOSPITAL, $General, FSA/Famous Brands, Goodyear, Lowe's Whse, Walmart SuperCtr, vet, to Lake of the Ozarks

**127** Lp 44, Lebanon, **N** **gas:** Conoco/dsl/rest./scales/24hr, Phillips 66/dsl, Sinclair/dsl, **food:** Dowd's BBQ, Great Wall Chinese, Waffle House, **lodging:** Day's Inn, Econolodge, Hampton Inn, Holiday Inn Express, Rte 66 Inn, Super 8, Travelers Inn, **other:** Cutlery/Walnut Bowl Outlet, Chrysler/Dodge/Jeep, Firestone/auto, Ford/Lincoln/Mercury, **S** **gas:** Phillips 66/dsl, **other:** Buick/Pontiac/GMC/Cadillac, Harley-Davidson, Russell Stover

**123** County Rd, **S** **other:** Happy Trails RV Ctr, KOA

**118** rds C, A, Phillipsburg, **N** **gas:** Conoco/dsl, **S** **gas:** Citgo, **other:** antiques, tourist info

**113** rds J, Y, Conway, **N** **gas:** Phillips 66, **food:** Rockin Chair Café, **lodging:** Budget Inn, **other:** to Den of Metal Arts, **S** **gas:** Sinclair/dsl, **other:** Faircountry Foods, USPO

**111mm** rest area both lanes, full ♿ facilities, 🔌, vending, litter barrels, 🍽 petwalk

**108mm** Bowen Creek

**107** County Rd

**106mm** Niangua River

**100** MO 38, rd W, Marshfield, **N** **gas:** BP, **food:** Subway, **other:** Chevrolet, Ford, Goodyear/auto, Walmart SuperCtr/gas, **S** **gas:** Cenex, Conoco/dsl, Kum&Go/dsl, Mystik, Phillips 66/dsl/24hr, Shell, **food:** Country Kitchen, Dancey's Rest., DQ, El Charro,

**LEBANON**

**100** Continued
KFC/Rib Crib, La Hacienda Mexican, McDonald's, Quizno's, Sonic, Subway, Taco Bell, **lodging:** Holiday Inn Express, **other:** $General, O'Reilly Parts, PriceCutter Foods, RV Express RV Park

**96** rd B, Northview, **N** Paradise RV Park

**89mm** weigh sta both lanes

**88** MO 125, to Fair Grove, Strafford, **N** **gas:** Phillips 66/dsl/rest./scales/24hr, TA/BP/Subway/Taco Bell/dsl/scales/24hr/@, **food:** McDonald's, **other:** Midwest Tire, truckwash, Paradise RV Park (4mi), **S** **gas:** Conoco/dsl, Kum&Go, **food:** Fox's Pizza, **lodging:** Super 8, **other:** Harter House Foods, Strafford RV Park

**84** MO 744, **S** Peterbilt

**82b a** US 65, to Branson, Fedalia, **S** **gas:** Phillips 66/dsl, **food:** Applebee's (2mi), Ryan's (2mi), Waffle House, **lodging:** American Inn, **other:** st patrol, to Table Rock Lake, Bull Shoals Lake

**80b a** rd H to Pleasant Hope, Springfield, **N** **gas:** Conoco/dsl/rest./24hr, Phillips 66/dsl, **food:** Waffle House, **lodging:** Budget Lodge, Microtel, Motel 6, Super 8, **other:** to SWSU, **S** **gas:** Cody's Gas, Conoco/dsl, Phillips 66, QT, **food:** Andy's Rest., Applebee's, Bob Evan's, Braum's, Buckingham Smokehouse, Burger King, Capt D's, Cracker Barrel, Denny's, El Magui Mexican, Fazoli's, Hardee's, Hong Kong Buffet, Jade East Chinese, Krispy Kreme, LJ Silver, McDonald's, Pizza Hut, Pizza Inn, Rib Crib, Ruby Tuesday, Ryan's, Schlotsky's, Shoney's, Sonic, Steak'n Shake, Subway, Taco Bell, Western Sizzlin, Ziggy's Cafe, **lodging:** Best Western, Budget Inn, Candlewood Suites, Comfort Inn, Day's Inn, Drury Inn, Econolodge, Economy Inn, Hampton Inn, Hawthorne Park Inn, Holiday Inn, Krystal Aire Inn, Lamplighter Hotel, La Quinta, Plaza Inn, RainTree Inn, Red Lion Inn, Red Roof Inn, Springfield Inn, **other:** Ⓗ HOSPITAL, Aldi Foods, AutoZone, Cottman Transmissions, K-Mart, O'Reilly Parts, Persell, PriceCutter Foods, U-Haul, Walmart/auto, mall

**77** MO 13, KS Expswy, **N** **lodging:** Interstate Inn, **other:** Lowe's Whse, **S** **gas:** Phillips 66/dsl, QT, **food:** Buffalo Wild Wings, Braum's, CiCi's, Golden Corral, IHOP, Jimmy John's, McAlister's Deli, McDonald's, Panera Bread, Papa John's, Papa Murphys, Pizza Inn, Subway, Taco Bell, Waffle House, Wendy's, **lodging:** Econolodge, **other:** BigLots, Dillon's Foods, $Tree, GNC, Goodyear/auto, O'Reilly Parts, Radio Shack, Staples, Walgreens, Walmart SuperCtr

**75** US 160 W byp, to Willard, Stockton Lake, **S** **gas:** Cody's Gas, Kum&Go, **lodging:** Baymont Inn, Courtyard

**72** MO 266, to Chesnut Expwy, **1-2 mi** **S** **gas:** Casey's, Cody's Gas, **food:** Hardee's, McDonald's, Pizza Hut, Taco Bueno, Waffle House, **lodging:** Best Budget Inn, Ramada Ltd

**70** rds MM, B, **N** antiques, fireworks, **S** **other:** Wilson's Creek Nat Bfd, KOA (1mi)

**69** to US 60, Springfield

**67** rds N, T, Bois D' Arc, to Republic, **S** **lodging:** AmericInn (5mi)

**66mm** Pond Creek

**64.6mm** Dry Branch

**64.5mm** Pickerel Creek

**SPRINGFIELD**

## INTERSTATE 44 CONT'D

E ↑ W

| | |
|---|---|
| **61** | rds K, PP, **N gas:** BP, Cenex/Hoods/dsl/rest./motel/scales/24hr |
| **58** | MO 96, rds O, Z, to Carthage, Halltown, **S gas:** Shell/dsl, **other:** antiques, RV/truck parts |
| **57** | to rd PP (from wb) |
| **56.5mm** | Turnback Creek |
| **56mm** | Goose Creek |
| **52.5mm** | **rest area both lanes, full** ♿ **facilities,** ⓒ, 🚻, **litter barrels, vending, petwalk** |
| **49** | MO 174E, rd CCW, Chesapeake |
| **46** | MO 39, MO 265, Mt Vernon, Aurora, **N gas:** Casey's, Phillips 66/dsl, TA/Conoco/Country Pride/dsl/24hr/@, **food:** Bamboo Garden Chinese, KFC/LJ Silver, Mazzio's, McDonald's, Sonic, Subway, Taco Bell, **lodging:** Super 8, USA Inn, **other:** $General, Family$, O'Reilly Parts, Radio Shack, Summer fresh Foods, **S gas:** BP/dsl/rest., **lodging:** Comfort Inn, **other:** to Table Rock Lake, Stockton Lake |
| **44** | rd H, to Monett, Mt Vernon, **N other:** Mid-America Dental/Hearing |
| **43.5mm** | Spring River |
| **38** | MO 97, to Stotts City, Pierce City, **N** gas/repair, U of MO SW Ctr |
| **33** | MO 97 S, to Pierce City, **S gas:** Sinclair/dsl, **food:** Hungry House Cafe, truck/tire repair |
| **29** | rd U, to La Russell, Sarcoxie, **N** Ozark Village Gifts, WAC RV Park, antiques, **S gas:** Citgo/dsl, Kum&Go, **food:** Nansy Rest. |
| **29mm** | Center Creek |
| **26** | MO 37, to Reeds, Sarcoxie, **N** truck/tire repair, **S** gas |
| **22** | rd 100 N, **N** RV parts, **S gas:** Express |
| **21mm** | Jones Creek |
| **18b a** | US 71 N, MO 59 S, to Carthage, Neosho, **N other:** Coachlight RV Ctr/Camping, **S** Ballard's Camping |
| **15** | MO 66 W, Lp 44 (from wb), Joplin, **N lodging:** Tara Motel |
| **15mm** | Grove Creek |
| **14mm** | Turkey Creek |
| **11b a** | US 71 S, MO 249 N, to Neosho, Ft Smith, **S gas:** ⛟FLYING J/Conoco/Country Mkt/dsl/LP/scales/24hr/@, Speedco, **food:** Applebee's (3mi), **other:** Blue Beacon |
| **8b a** | US 71, to Neosho, Joplin, **N gas:** Citgo, Conoco, Kum&Go/dsl, Phillips 66, **food:** Applebee's, Arby's, Backyard Burger, Bella Pepper's, Bob Evans, Braum's, Burger King, Candlewood Suites, Capt D's, Casa Montez Mexican, Cheddars, CiCi's, Denny's, Golden Corral, Golden Dragon, Great Wall Chinese, IHOP, Jim Bob's Steaks, KFC, King Palace, LJ Silver, Mazzio's, McDonald's, Noodle&Grill, Olive Garden, Outback Steaks, Pizza Hut, Quizno's, Red Hot&Blue Grill, Red Lobster, Rib Crib, Ruby Tuesday, Ryan's, Schlotzky's, Shoney's, Sonic, Steak'n Shake, Subway, Taco Bell, Taco Hut, Timberline Steaks, Waffle House, Wendy's, **lodging:** Baymont Inn, Best Value, Best Western, Comfort Inn, Day's Inn, Drury Inn, Fairfield Inn, Hampton Inn, Hilton Garden, Holiday Inn, Motel 6, Ramada Inn, Residence Inn, Rodesite Inn, Super 8, **other:** Aldi Foods, Books-A-Million, Chrysler/Dodge, Coachlight RV Ctr, $Tree, Firestone, Food4Less/24hr, Ford/Lincoln/Mercury, |

JOPLIN

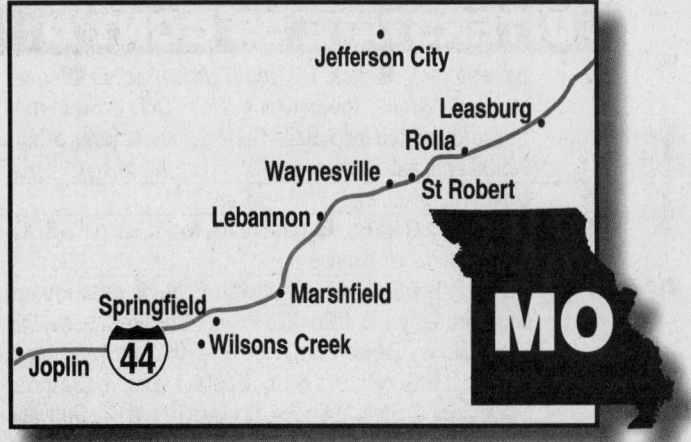

| | |
|---|---|
| **8b a** | Continued Goody's, Hasting's, Home Depot, Hyundai, Jo-Ann Fabrics, Kohl's, Lowe's Whse, Mid-America RV Ctr, Michael's, NAPA, Nissan/Mercedes, Office Depot, O'Reilly Parts, Pennzoil, PetsMart, Sam's Club/gas, Target, Toyota/Scion, VW, Walmart SuperCtr, **S gas:** Casey's, **food:** Cracker Barrel, Fazoli's, **lodging:** Microtel, TownePlace Suites, **other:** Wheelen RV Ctr |
| **6** | MO 86, MO 43 N, to Racine, Joplin, **N gas:** BP, **S** Harley-Davidson |
| **5.5mm** | Shoal Creek |
| **4** | MO 43 to Seneca, **N gas:** Loves/Hardee's/dsl/24hr, **other:** Peterbilt, antiques, **S gas:** Conoco/Subway/dsl, Petro/BP/Iron Skillet/dsl/scales/@, Pilot/Wendy's/dsl/scales/24hr, **food:** McDonald's, **lodging:** Sleep Inn, **other:** IA 80 Truckwash, KOA |
| **3mm** | weigh sta both lanes |
| **2mm** | **Welcome Ctr eb, rest area wb, full** ♿ **facilities,** 🚻, **litter barrels,** ⓒs, **vending** |
| **1** | US 400, US 166W, to Baxter Springs, KS, **N other:** Sandstone Gardens |
| **0mm** | Missouri/Oklahoma state line |

J O P L I N

## INTERSTATE 55

N ↕ S / ST LOUIS

| Exit # | Services |
|---|---|
| **209mm** | Missouri/Illinois state line at St. Louis, Mississippi River |
| **209b** | I-70 W to Kansas City |
| **209a** | to Arch, Busch Stadium |
| **208** | Park Ave, 7th St, **W gas:** BP, **food:** Rally's, Taco Bell, White Castle, **lodging:** Hilton |
| **207c b** | Truman Pkwy, **W** I-44 W, to Tulsa |
| **207a** | Gravois St (from nb), **E gas:** Midwest Petroleum, **W food:** A-1 Chinese Wok, Jack-in-the-Box |
| **206c** | Arsenal St, **E** Anheuser-Busch Tour Ctr, **W gas:** Shell |
| **206b** | Broadway (from nb), |
| **206a** | Potomac St (from nb) |
| **205** | Gasconade, **W** H HOSPITAL |
| **204** | Broadway, **E gas:** Phillips 66/repair, **W gas:** Sinclair/dsl, **food:** Hardee's, McDonald's, Subway, **other:** Radio Shack, Walgreen/24hr |
| **203** | Bates St, Virginia Ave, **W gas:** BP, 7-11 |
| **202c** | Loughborough Ave, **W food:** St Louis Bread Co, Starbucks, **other:** Lowe's Whse, Schnuck's Foods |
| **202b** | Germania (from sb) |
| **202a** | Carondelet (from nb), |
| **201b** | Weber Rd |

## INTERSTATE 55 CONT'D

**N ↕ S**

**ST LOUIS**

| Exit | Description |
|------|-------------|
| **201a** | Bayless Ave, **E gas:** BP, **food:** McDonald's, **W gas:** Mobil, 7-11/gas, **food:** China Wok, DQ, Jack-in-the-Box, Pizza Hut/Taco Bell, Subway, Taco Bell, **other:** Walgreens, auto repair |
| **200** | Union Rd (from sb) |
| **199** | Reavis Barracks Rd, **E gas:** Shell, **food:** Pennie's BBQ, **other:** Hancock Fabrics |
| **197** | US 50, US 61, US 67, Lindbergh Blvd, **E gas:** Phillips 66, **food:** Arby's, Buffalo Wild Wings, ChuckeCheese, Dillard's, Honey Baked Ham, Hooters, KFC, Krispy Kreme, Macaroni Grill, Noodle's & Co, Qdoba Mexican, Quizno's, Station Subs, Steak'n Shake, St Louis Bread Co, Subway, Tucker's Place, **lodging:** Holiday Inn, **other:** Advance Parts, Best Buy, Border's Book, Circuit City, Costco/gas, Dillard's, Discount Tire, Dodge, Ford, Home Depot, JC Penny, Kia, K-Mart, Macy's, Marshall's, NTB, Sears/auto, Tuesday Morning, mall, **W food:** Bob Evans, Casa Gallardo's, Culvers, Denny's, Lenny's Subs, O'Charley's, Ponderosa, **lodging:** Motel 6, Oak Grove Inn, **other:** Aldi Foods, Costco/gas, Ford/Lincoln/Mercury, Honda, Hyundai, Mazda, Office Depot, Saturn, Target |
| **196b** | I-270 W, to Kansas City |
| **196a** | I-255 E, to Chicago |
| **195** | Butler Hill Rd, **E gas:** Phillips 66, **lodging:** Holiday Inn/rest., **other:** Advance Parts, Walgreens, **W gas:** Sinclair, **food:** Burger King, Hardee's, Pizza Hut/Taco Bell, Waffle House, **other:** Schnuck's Foods, tires/repair |
| **193** | Meramec Bottom Rd, **E gas:** Mobil, QT, **food:** Cracker Barrel, **lodging:** Best Western, **other:** Howard RV Ctr |
| **191** | MO 141, Arnold, **E gas:** QT, **food:** Applebee's, Bandana's BBQ, Cici's Pizza, Denny's, Fazoli's, 54th St Grill, Jack-in-the-Box, Jimmy John's, LJ Silver, McDonald's/playplace, Papa John's, Pizza Hut, Steak'n Shake, Super Chinese Buffet, Taco Bell, **lodging:** Drury Inn, Ramada Ltd, **other:** Goodyear, Kohl's, Lions Choice, Napa, O'Reilly Parts, PetCo, Schnuck's Foods, Shop'n Save Foods, Walgreens, Walmart/auto, USPO, mall, **W gas:** Phillips 66/dsl, **food:** Pasta House, **other:** Dierberg's Foods, Lowe's Whse |
| **190** | Richardson Rd, **E gas:** EM/dsl, QT, Shell/dsl, **food:** Culver's, Domino's, DQ, Pizza Hut, Ponderosa, Quizno's, Roly-Poly Sandwiches, Sonic, Taco Bell, White Castle, **other:** Advance Parts, Auto Tire, Firestone, Ford, SavALot Foods, **W gas:** CFM, Phillips 66/dsl, 7-11/gas, Shell/dsl, **food:** Burger King, Happy Wok, Imo's Pizza, McDonald's/playplace, Mr. Goodcents Subs, Ruby Tuesday, Waffle House, **lodging:** Comfort Inn, **other:** Aamco, AutoZone, GNC, Home Depot, Plaza Tire, Radio Shack, Shnuck's Foods/24hr, Target, Walgreens, vet |
| **186** | Imperial, Kimmswick, **E gas:** Mobil, Shell, **food:** Blue Owl (1mi), **other:** auto repair, **W gas:** Phillips 66/Jack-in-the-Box, **food:** Cafe Breve, China Wok, Domino's, Iggy's Mexican, O'aces Grill, Papa John's, Quizno's, Subway, **other:** USPO, to Mastodon SP |
| **185** | rd M, Barnhart, Antonia, **E gas:** EM/gas, **food:** Jenny's Kitchen, **W gas:** EM/gas, 7-11/gas, U-Gas, **other:** Walgreens, **other:** KOA |
| **184.5mm** | weigh sta both lanes |

**PERRYVILLE**

| Exit | Description |
|------|-------------|
| **180** | rd Z, to Hillsboro, Pevely, **E gas:** Mobil/dsl, **food:** BBQ, Burger King, Domino's, Subway, **other:** $General, Queens Foods, **W gas:** Mr Fuel, Phillips 66/McDonald's/scales/dsl, **lodging:** Super 8, **other:** KOA (2mi), auto repair |
| **178** | Herculaneum, **E gas:** QT/Wendy's/scales/dsl, Shell, **food:** Cracker Barrel, DQ, Jack-in-the-Box, **other:** Toyota/Scion, **W** Chevrolet, Ford, Pontiac/Cadillac/Buick |
| **175** | rd A, Festus, **E gas:** Mobil, Phillips 66/dsl, **food:** Arby's, Bob Evans, Burger King, Capt D's, Cici's Pizza, Fazoli's, McDonald's/playplace, Papa John's, Quizno's, Ryan's, Sonic, St. Louis Bread Co, Steak'n Shake, Subway, Taco Bell, Tanglefoot Steaks, White Castle, **lodging:** Drury Inn, Holiday Inn Express, Twin City Motel, **other:** Advance Parts, Aldi Foods, $Tree, Home Depot, Kmart, Radio Shack, Schnuck's Foods, Walgreens, Walmart SuperCtr/gas, **W gas:** Phillips 66/Domino's/dsl, 7-11/dsl, **food:** Hardee's, Ruby Tuesday, Waffle House, **lodging:** Comfort Inn, **other:** Dodge, Lowe's Whse |
| **174b a** | US 67, Lp 55, Festus, Crystal City, **E gas:** Phillips 66/dsl |
| **170** | US 61, **W gas:** BP/dsl/LP |
| **162** | rds DD, OO |
| **160mm** | **rest areas both lanes, full** &#9855; **facilities,** &#127828; **litter barrels,** &#9742;**s, vending, petwalk** |
| **157** | rd Y, Bloomsdale, **E gas:** Phillips 66, **W gas:** Shell/Subway/dsl |
| **154** | rd O |
| **150** | MO 32, rds B, A, to St Genevieve, **E gas:** BP, **food:** DQ, **lodging:** Microtel (4mi), **other:** H HOSPITAL, Hist Site (6mi), **W gas:** Phillips 66/dsl, **other:** Hawn SP (11mi) |
| **143** | rds N, M, Ozora, **W gas:** Ozora Country Store/dsl, Shell/Subway/dsl/@, **lodging:** Budget Inn/rest. |
| **141** | rd Z, St Mary |
| **135** | rd M, Brewer, **E** propane depot |
| **129** | MO 51, to Perryville, **E gas:** MotoMart/McDonald's/dsl, Phillips 66/dsl, **food:** Burger King, KFC, Ponderosa, Taco Bell, **other:** H HOSPITAL, Ford, **W gas:** Rhodes/dsl, **food:** China Buffet, DQ, **lodging:** Comfort Inn, Super 8, Travelodge, **other:** Chevrolet/Pontiac/Buick, Chrysler/Dodge/Jeep, $Tree, KOA (1mi), Walmart SuperCtr |
| **123** | rd B, Biehle, **W gas:** Rhodes/dsl |
| **119mm** | Apple Creek |
| **117** | rd KK, to Appleton, **E food:** Ron's Diner |
| **111** | rd E, Oak Ridge |
| **110mm** | **rest area both lanes, full** &#9855; **facilities,** &#127828; **litter barrels,** &#9742;**s, vending, petwalk** |
| **105** | US 61, Fruitland, **E gas:** BP/dsl, Casey's, Rhodes/dsl, **other:** Trail of Tears SP (11mi), **W gas:** D-Mart, **food:** DQ, Pizza Inn, **lodging:** Drury Inn |
| **102** | E Main St, no facilities |
| **99** | US 61, MO 34, to Jackson, **E other:** Cape RV Park (1mi) |
| **96** | rd K, to Cape Girardeau, **E gas:** BP, **food:** Applebee's (1mi), Blimpie, Bob Evans, Buffalo Wild Wings, Burger King, Cedar St Cafe, Cici's Pizza, Cracker Barrel (1mi), Dexter BBQ, El Acapulco, Great Wall Chinese, Honey Baked Ham, Logan's Roadhouse, O'Charley's, Olive Garden, Panera Bread, Pizza Inn, Popeye's, Red Lobster, Ruby Tuesday, Ryan's, Starbucks, Steak'n Shake, Subway, Taco Bell, TX Roadhouse, **lodging:** Drury Lodge/rest., Holiday Inn Express, PearTree Inn, Victorian Inn, **other:** H HOSPITAL, Barnes&Noble, |

# INTERSTATE 55 CONT'D

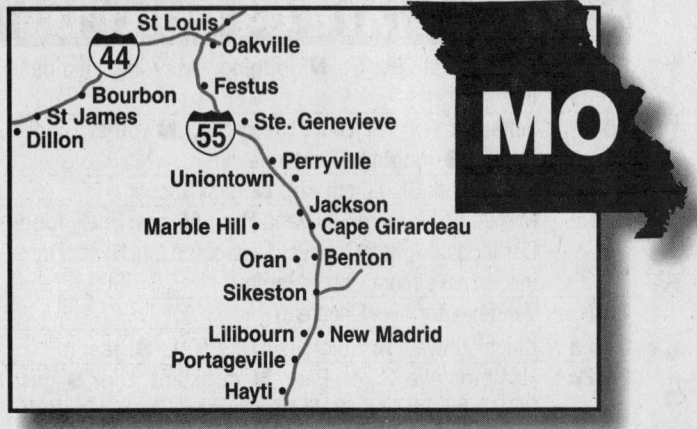

**96** Continued
Best Buy, Big Lots, JC Penney, Macy's, Old Navy, Schnuck's Foods, mall, to SEMSU, **W gas:** Shell/24hr, **food:** McDonald's/playplace, Outback Steaks, Sonic, White Castle, **lodging:** Drury Suites, Hampton Inn, **other:** $Tree, Goody's, Honda, Kohl's, Lowe's Whse, Mazda, Nissan, PetCo, Plaza Tire, Sam's Club, Saturn, Sears Grand, Staples, Target, Toyota, Walmart SuperCtr, USPO

**95** MO 74 E, same as 96

**93a b** MO 74 W, Cape Girardeau, **E lodging:** Townhouse Inn, **other:** diesel repair

**91** rd AB, to Cape Girardeau, **E gas:** Rhodes/dsl, **food:** Huddle House, **other:** Goodyear, Harley-Davidson, RV America, **W** Capetown RV Ctr, ✈

**89** US 61, rds K, M, Scott City, **E gas:** Rhodes, Store 24, **food:** Burger King, Ice Cream Corner, Las Brisas Mexican, Pizza Pro, **other:** $General, Plaza Tires, vet

**80** MO 77, Benton, **W gas:** BP/McDonald's/dsl, Express/dsl, **other:** antiques, winery (8mi)

**69** rd HH, to Sikeston, Miner, **E other:** Peterbilt, **W gas:** Keller Trkstp/dsl (1mi), **other:** RV America, golf

**67** US 60, US 62, Miner, **E gas:** Breaktime/dsl, Express/dsl, **lodging:** Best Western, Holiday Inn Express, Motel 6, **other:** Hinton RV Park, **0-2 mi W gas:** Cenex, Hucks, Jasper's Gas, **food:** Bo's BBQ, Burger King, China Garden, El Tapatio Mexican, Lambert's Rest., McDonald's, Pizza Hut, Pizza Inn, Ruby Tuesday, Sonic, Subway, Taco Bell, Taco John's, Wendy's, **lodging:** Comfort Inn, Country Hearth Inn, Drury Inn, PearTree Inn, Super 8, **other:** H HOSPITAL, AutoZone, Chevrolet/Pontiac/Buick, $General, GMC/Cadillac, Family$, Food Giant, Goodyear/auto, Pennzoil, Sikeston Outlets/famous brands, Walgreen

**66b** US 60 W, to Poplar Bluff, **3 mi W on US 61/62 gas:** BP, Breaktime, Sinclair, **food:** A&W/LJ Silver, Applebee's, Arby's, China Buffet, DQ, El Bracero Mexican, Hardee's, KFC, McDonald's, Sonic, **lodging:** Day's Inn, **other:** Aldi Foods, Chrysler/Dodge/Jeep, $Tree, Ford/Lincoln/Mercury, GNC, Goody's, JC Penny, Lowe's Whse, Mkt Place Foods, O'Reilly Parts, Radio Shack, Walmart SuperCtr

**66a** I-57 E, to Chicago, US 60 W

**59mm** St Johns Bayou

**58** MO 80, Matthews, **E gas:** TA/Taco Bell/scales/dsl24hr/@, **other:** truck repair, **W gas:** ⚙ FLYING J/Conoco/Country Pride/LP/rest./RV dump/dsl/24hr, Loves/Chester Fried/Subway/scales/dsl, **other:** truckwash

**52** rd P, Kewanee, **E gas:** BP/dsl

**49** US 61, US 62, New Madrid

**44** US 61, US 62, Lp 55, New Madrid, **E gas:** Cenex/dsl (1mi), **other:** Relax Inn (2mi), **other:** hist site

**42mm** **Welcome Ctr nb/rest area both lanes, full ♿ facilities, 🍽 litter barrels, ℂ, vending, petwalk**

**40** rd EE, St Jude Rd, Marston, **E gas:** Pilot/Arby's/scales/dsl/24hr, **lodging:** Super 8, **W gas:** BP/dsl, **lodging:** Budget Inn

**32** US 61, MO 162, Portageville, **W gas:** BP/dsl, Casey's, **food:** China King, McDonald's, **lodging:** New Orleans Inn, **other:** dsl repair

**27** rds K, A, BB, to Wardell, **E other:** KOA (2mi)

**19** US 412, MO 84, Hayti, **E gas:** Breaktime/dsl, Pilot/scales/dsl, **food:** McDonald's, KFC/Taco Bell, Pizza Hut, **lodging:** Comfort Inn/rest., Econolodge, **other:** H HOSPITAL, KOA (6mi), **W gas:** BP/dsl, Hayti Trvl Ctr/Subway/dsl, R&P, **food:** Apple Barrel, Chubby's BBQ, Los Portales, Patty Ann's BBQ, **lodging:** Drury Inn, **other:** H HOSPITAL, Fred's Drug, Goodyear/auto, Hay's Foods, repair

**17a** I-155 E, to TN, US 412

**14** rds J, H, U, to Caruthersville, Braggadocio

**10mm** weigh sta nb

**8** MO 164, Steele, **W gas:** BP/Subway/Chester Fried/scales/dsl, **lodging:** Deerfield Inn, **other:** truck repair

**4** rd E, to Holland, Cooter

**3mm** **rest area both lanes, full ♿ facilities, 🍽, litter barrels, ℂ, vending, petwalk**

**1** US 61, rd O, Holland, **W gas:** Shell/dsl/24hr

**0mm** Missouri/Arkansas state line

# INTERSTATE 57

| Exit # | Services |
|---|---|
| **22mm** | Missouri/Illinois state line, Mississippi River |
| **18.5mm** | weigh sta both lanes |
| **12** | US 62, MO 77, Charleston, **E gas:** Cheers/Quiznos/dsl/scales/24hr, **lodging:** Economy Motel, **W gas:** Casey's (1mi), Phillips 66/dsl, **food:** Cotton Inn Rest, **lodging:** Econolodge, **other:** Chrysler/Dodge/Jeep |
| **10** | MO 105, Charleston, **E gas:** BP/Boomland/dsl, Pilot/Subway/dsl/scales/24hr, **food:** Wally's Rest., **other:** Boomland RV Park, **W gas:** Casey's, **food:** China Buffet, DQ, McDonald's, Pizza Hut, **lodging:** Comfort Inn, **other:** Alco, CountryMart Foods, Plaza Tire |
| **4** | rd B, Bertrand |
| **1b a** | I-55, N to St Louis, S to Memphis. **I-57 begins/ends on I-55, exit 66.** |

# INTERSTATE 64

| Exit # | Services |
|---|---|
| **41mm** | Missouri/Illinois state line, Mississippi River |
| **40b a** | Broadway St, to Stadium, to the Arch, **N lodging:** Hilton, Sheraton, stadium, **S other:** Dobb's Tire |
| **40c** | (from wb), I-44 W, I-55 S |
| **39c** | 11th St (exits left), downtown |
| **39b** | 14th St, downtown, **N lodging:** Sheraton, **S gas:** BP |
| **39a** | 21st St, Market St (from wb), **N lodging:** Drury Inn, Hampton Inn |

## INTERSTATE 64 CONT'D

**E ↕ W**

**ST LOUIS**

| | |
|---|---|
| **38d** | Chestnut at 20th St, **N lodging:** Drury Inn, Hampton Inn |
| **38c** | Jefferson Ave, St Louis Union Sta, **N other:** Joplin House, **S lodging:** Residence Inn |
| **38a** | Forest Park Blvd (from wb), **N gas:** Shell |
| **37b a** | Market St, Bernard St, Grand Blvd, **N gas:** Shell, **food:** Del Taco, **lodging:** Courtyard, Hampton Inn, Hyatt, Drury Inn, Adam's Mark Hotel, Marriott |
| **36d** | Vandeventer Ave, Chouteau Ave |
| **36b a** | Kingshighway, **N other:** H HOSPITAL, **S gas:** BP |
| **34d c** | Hampton Ave, Forest Park, **N** museums, zoo, **S gas:** BP, Mobil, Phillips 66, **food:** Courtesy Diner, Hardee's, Imo's Pizza, Jack-in-the-Box, Smokin' Al's BBQ, Steak'n Shake, Subway, Taco Bell, **lodging:** Hampton Inn |
| **34a** | Oakland Ave, **N gas:** BP, **food:** Del Taco, Subway, **other:** H HOSPITAL |
| **33d** | McCausland Ave, **N gas:** BP, **food:** Del Taco |
| **33c** | Bellevue Ave, **N** H HOSPITAL |
| **33b** | Big Bend Blvd |
| **32b a** | Eager Rd, Hanley Rd, **S gas:** Shell, **food:** Lion's Choice, Macaroni Grill, McDonald's, St Louis Bread Co, Subway, **other:** Best Buy, Borders Books, Circuit City, Dierberg's Foods, Home Depot, Target, Whole Foods Mkt |
| **31b a** | I-170 N, **N gas:** Shell, **food:** Burger King, DQ, IHOP, KFC, Steak'n Shake, TGIFriday, Dillard's, **other:** mall, **S gas:** BP, **food:** Macaroni Grill, Subway, **other:** Borders Books, Circuit City, Dierberg's Foods, Goodyear, Target |
| **30** | McKnight Rd |
| **28c** | Clayton Rd (from wb) |
| **28b a** | US 67, US 61, Lindbergh Blvd, **S gas:** BP, **food:** Brio Grill, Fleming's Rest., Schneithouse Rest., Starbucks, **lodging:** Hilton, **other:** Honda, Shnuck's Foods, mall |
| **27** | Spoede Rd |
| **26** | rd JJ, Ballas Rd, **N** H HOSPITAL, **S** H HOSPITAL |
| **25** | I-270, N to Chicago, S to Memphis |
| **24** | Mason Rd, **N lodging:** Courtyard, Marriott, **other:** LDS Temple, hwy patrol |
| **23** | Maryville Centre Dr (from wby), **N lodging:** Courtyard, Marriott |
| **22** | MO 141, **N food:** Regatta Grille, **other:** H HOSPITAL, **S food:** Pizza Hut |
| **21** | Timberlake Manor Pkwy |
| **20** | Chesterfield Pkwy (from wb), same as 19b a |
| **19b a** | MO 340, Chesterfield Pkwy, Olive Blvd, **N gas:** BP, Shell, **food:** Applebee's, Pizzaria Uno, Sheridan's Custard, Taco Bell, Yaya's Cafe, **lodging:** DoubleTree Hotel, Hampton Inn, Homewood Suites, Residence Inn, **other:** USPO, Dobb's Tire, Schnucks Foods, Walgreens, **S gas:** Mobil, **food:** Bahama Breeze Rest., Bacana Cafe, Casa Gallardo's, California Pizza Kitchen, Chili's, Houlihans, Macaroni Grill, PF Chang's, **lodging:** Drury Plaza Hotel, **other:** Borders Books, Dillard's, mall |
| **17** | Boones Crossing, Long Rd, Chesterfield Airport Rd, **1 mi S gas:** Mobil, **food:** Bob Evans, Chick-fil-A, Coldstone Creamery, Cousins Subs, East Coast Pizza, Emperor's Buffet, Fox & Hound, Golden China, Hardee's, Hometown Buffet, IHOP, IMO's Pizza, Joe's Crabshack, Kaldi's Coffe, Lion's Choice, Longhorn Steaks, Matadoe Cafe., McDonald's, Mimi's Cafe, O'Charley's, |

| | |
|---|---|
| **17** | Continued Old Country Buffet, Old Spaghetti Factory, Olive Garden, Original Pancakes, Qdoba Mexican, Quizno's, Red Lobster, Red Robin, SmokeHouse Rest., Sonic, Starbucks, Steak'n Shake, Subway, Taco Bell, **lodging:** Hampton Inn, Hilton Garden, **other:** Best Buy, Circuit City, Dobb's Tire, $Tree, Firestone, Ford, Home Depot, Lowe's Whse, Michael's, PetsMart, Radio Shack, Sam's Club, Target, Walmart Super Ctr/auto, WorldMkt, vet |
| **14** | Chesterfield Airport Rd (from eb), **S gas:** Phillips 66, **lodging:** Comfort Inn |
| **13mm** | I-64 begins/ends, Missouri River |

## INTERSTATE 70

**E ↕ W**

**ST LOUIS**

| Exit # | Services |
|---|---|
| **252mm** | Missouri/Illinois state line, Mississippi River |
| **251a** | I-55 S, to Memphis, to I-44, to downtown/no return |
| **250b** | Memorial Dr, downtown, Stadium, **S gas:** Shell, **food:** McDonald's, **lodging:** Day's Inn |
| **250a** | Arch, Riverfront, **N lodging:** Econolodge, Embassy Suites, **other:** Conv Center, **S lodging:** Drury Inn, Hampton Inn, Radisson, TWA Dome |
| **249c** | 6th St (from eb) |
| **249a** | Madison St, 10th St, **N gas:** Phillips 66/dsl |
| **248b** | St Louis Ave, Branch St |
| **248a** | Salisbury St, McKinley Br, **N** truck repair/24hr, **S gas:** BP, Mobil/dsl |
| **247** | Grand Ave, **N gas:** Phillips 66/dsl, **lodging:** Western Inn, **S lodging:** Economy Inn |
| **246b** | Adelaide Ave |
| **246a** | N Broadway, O'Fallon Park, **N gas:** Mobil/dsl, **other:** Freightliner |
| **245b** | W Florissant |
| **245a** | Shreve Ave, **N** Pillsbury Factory, **S gas:** BP |
| **244b** | Kingshighway, 3/4 mi **S food:** Burger King, McDonald's, Subway |
| **244a** | Bircher Blvd, Union Blvd |
| **243b** | (243c from eb)Bircher Blvd |
| **243a** | Riverview Blvd |
| **243** | Goodfellow Blvd, **N gas:** Shell |
| **242b a** | Jennings Sta Rd, **N gas:** Shell, **S food:** McDonald's, **other:** transmission repair |
| **241b** | Lucas-Hunt Rd, **N gas:** Shell, 3/4 mi **S gas:** Citgo, **food:** Lee's Chicken, McDonald's |
| **241a** | Bermuda Rd, **S gas:** Sinclair, **other:** H HOSPITAL, |
| **240b a** | Florissant Rd, **N gas:** BP/McDonald's, **food:** DQ, Sonic, Taco Bell, **other:** Schnuck's Foods, Walgreen |
| **239** | N Hanley Rd, **N food:** Jack-in-the-Box, **S gas:** Mobil, **food:** McDonald's |
| **238c b** | I-170 N, I-170 S, no return |
| **238a** | **N** Lambert-St Louis ✈, **S lodging:** Renaissance Hotel |
| **237** | Natural Bridge Rd (from eb), **S gas:** BP, Phillips 66, Shell, **food:** ✈ Diner, Arby's, Burger King, Denny's, Jack-in-the-Box, KFC, Pizza Hut, Steak'n Shake, Waffle House, Wendy's, DoubleTree, **lodging:** Best Western, Days Inn, Double Tree, Holiday Inn, Renaissance, Travelodge |
| **236** | Lambert-St Louis ✈, **S gas:** BP, **food:** BBQ, Big Boy, Coco's, Grone Cafeteria, Hardee's, Lombardo's Café Rafferty's Rest., Tiffany's Rest., **lodging:** Best Western, Day's Inn, Drury Inn/rest., Hampton Inn, Hilton Garden, Holiday Inn, Marriott, Motel 6 |
| **235c** | Cypress Rd, rd B W, **N** to ✈ |

MO

## INTERSTATE 70 CONT'D

**E ↕ W**

**235b a** US 67, Lindbergh Blvd, **N gas:** Shell, **lodging:** Executive Intn'l Inn, Holiday Inn/café, Howard Johnson, **S gas:** Shell, **food:** Lion's Choice Rest., Steak'n Shake, TGIFriday, **lodging:** Congress Inn, Embassy Suites, Homestead Studios, Radisson, **other:** Chevrolet, Dillard's, Firestone, JC Penney, Sears/auto, mall

**234** MO 180, St Charles Rock Rd, **N gas:** Phillips 66, Shell, **food:** Applebee's, Casa Gallardo's, Fazoli's, Hardee's, Hatfield's/McCoy's Rest., Jack-in-the-Box, LoneStar Steaks, LJ Silver, McDonald's, Old Country Buffet, Ponderosa, Quizno's, Red Lobster, Shoney's, Steak'n Shake, Taco Bell, Tony Bono's Rest., **lodging:** Economy Inn, **other:** H HOSPITAL, Best Buy, Circuit City, $Tree, GrandPa's Food/drug, Honda, K-Mart, NTB, Office Depot, Sam's Club, Target, Walgreens/24hr, **S** Isuzu

**232** I-270, N to Chicago, S to Memphis

**231b a** Earth City Expwy, **N gas:** Motomart, Phillips 66/Jack-in-the-Box/dsl, **food:** McDonald's, Quizno's, **lodging:** Candlewood Suites, Courtyard, Holiday Inn, Residence Inn, Studio+, **S gas:** Mobil, **food:** Burger King, Dave&Buster's, **lodging:** Holiday Inn Express, Homewood Suites, Wingate Inn, **other:** Harrah's Casino/Hotel, Riverport Ampitheatre

**230mm** Missouri River

**229b a** 5th St, St Charles, **N gas:** BP, Mobil/dsl, **food:** Bellacino's Italian, Buffalo Wild Wings, Denny's, El Tio Pepe, Gordman's, Jack-in-the-Box, KFC, Lee's Chicken, McDonald's, Waffle House, **lodging:** Best Western, Comfort Suites, Quality Inn, **other:** Aldi Foods, Ameristar Casino, Bass Pro Shops, Walgreens/24hr, **S gas:** QT/dsl, **food:** Cracker Barrel, **lodging:** Embassy Suites, Fairfield Inn, **other:** malls

**228** MO 94, to Weldon Springs, St Charles, **N gas:** Phillips 66, ZX Gas/dsl, **food:** Arby's, Chinatown Express, DQ, Imo's Pizza, Papa John's, Steak'n Shake, **other:** Advance Parts, Chevrolet, NAPA, Walgreen, Valvoline, **S gas:** QT, **food:** Chinese Express, ChuckeCheese, Fazoli's, Gingham's Rest., Grappa Grill, Outback Steaks, Pizza Hut, **lodging:** Days Inn, Intown Suites, **other:** Dobb's Tire, vet, access to 227

**227** Zumbehl Rd, **N gas:** ZX Gas, **food:** Culpepper's Grill, **lodging:** Super 8, **other:** Lowe's Whse, SavALot Foods, **S gas:** BP, Mobil, **food:** Applebee's, Bob Evans, Boston Mkt, Capt D's, Chevy's Mexican, Chirco's Grill, CiCi's Pizza, El Mariachi Mexican, Fazoli's, Gingham's Rest., Golden Corral, Great Wall Chinese, Hardee's, Hoho Chinese, Jack-in-the-Box, McCalister's, McDonald's, Quizno's, Subway, Taco Bell/Pizza Hut, Wiliker's Cafe, **lodging:** Days Inn, Red Roof Inn, TownePlace Suites, Travelodge, **other:** BigLots, Dierberg's Foods/24hr, $Tree, GNC, Jiffy Lube, Michael's, NTB, PetsMart, Radio Shack, Sam's Club/gas, Schnuck's Foods/24hr, Walmart/auto, Walgreens, vet, access to 228

**225** Truman Rd, to Cave Springs, **N gas:** BP, Casey's, Shell, ZX Gas, **lodging:** Hampton Inn, Motel 6, **other:** Buick/Pontiac, Cadillac, Kenworth, Mazda, Saturn, Subaru, U-Haul, **S gas:** Conoco, Mobil, QT, **food:** Bandanas BBQ, Big Boy, Burger King, China Wok, Culver's, DQ, Denny's, El Tio Pepe, Hooters, IHOP, Jack-in-the-Box, Longhorn Steaks, Lion's Choice Rest., LJ Silver, McDonald's, O'Charley's, Pasta House, Pizza Hut, Pizza St, Ponderosa, Red Lobster, Steak'n Shake, Subway,

## ST CHARLES

## ST PETERS / O' FALLON

**225** Continued
Taco Bell, Thai Kitchen, White Castle, **lodging:** Holiday Inn Select, **other:** H HOSPITAL, Batteries+, Dodge, Firestone, Home Depot, Kia, Office Depot, Shop'n Save, Target, TJ Maxx

**224** MO 370 E

**222** Mid-Rivers Mall Dr, rd C, St Peters, **N gas:** QT/dsl/24hr, **food:** Burger King, **other:** Chevrolet, Honda, Lincoln/Mercury, Mitsubishi, Toyota/Scion, **S gas:** Mobil, ZX Gas/dsl, **food:** Arby's, Bob Evans, Chili's, China Wok, Domino's, Honey-baked Ham, Jack-in-the-Box, Joe's Crabshack, Macaroni Grill, Max & Erma's, McDonald's/playplace, Olive Garden, Pizza Hut/Taco Bell, Red Robin, Ruby Tuesday, Steak'n Shake, Subway, Wendy's, **lodging:** Drury Inn, Extended Stay America, **other:** Aldi Foods, AutoZone, Barnes&Noble, Best Buy, Big Lots, Borders Books, Circuit City, Costco/gas, Dillard's, Discount Tire, Hancock Fabrics, JC Penney, Marshalls, Nissan/Hyundai/VW, NTB, Sears/auto

**220** MO 79, to Elsberry, **N** Cherokee Lakes Camping (7mi), hardware, **S gas:** BP, Phillips 66/dsl, 7-11/gas, **food:** Hardee's, Jack-in-the-Box, McDonald's/playplace, Quizno's, Sonic, Subway, **other:** Ramada Ltd, **other:** Curves, Dierberg's Foods/drug, O'Reilly Parts, Walgreens

**219** Tru's Rd, **S gas:** QT, **lodging:** Comfort Inn

**217** rds K, M, O'Fallon, **N gas:** BP, **food:** Burger King, Burger King, Jack-in-the-Box, Rally's, Piggy's BBQ, Pizza Hut/Taco Bell, Sonic, Waffle House, **other:** Firestone, Jiffy Lube, Radio Shack, **S gas:** Phillips 66/dsl, QT, ZX Gas, **food:** Applebee's, Arby's, Bob Evans, Chick-fil-A, Domino's, Fazoli's, IHOP, KFC, Krieger's Grill, Lion's Choice Rest., McDonald's/playplace, Pantera's Pizza, Papa John's, Pizza Hut, Red Robin, Stefanina's Pizza, Subway, **other:** Advance Parts, Aldi Foods, Auto Tire, AutoZone, GNC, Home Depot, K-Mart/drugs, Lowe's Whse, Schnuck's Foods, Shop'n Save Foods, TrueValue, Walgreens, Walmart, camping

**216** Bryan Rd, **N lodging:** Super 8, **other:** CarQuest, Ford, Peterbilt, **S gas:** Conoco, Phillips 66/Jack-in-the-Box/dsl, QT, **food:** DQ, Cappuccino's, Mr. Goodcents

**214** Lake St Louis, **N gas:** Q-Stop, **S gas:** Phillips 66/dsl, Shell, **food:** Denny's, El Maguey Mexican, Hardee's, Subway, **lodging:** Day's Inn, **other:** H HOSPITAL, Wharf Drug

**212** rd A, **N lodging:** Economy Inn, Relax Inn, **other:** Freedom RV Ctr, **S gas:** Mobil, **food:** Burger King, Imo's Pizza, **lodging:** Holiday Inn, **other:** Chrysler/Dodge/Jeep

**210b a** US 61, US 40, to I-64 E, **S gas:** Phillips 66/dsl, Shell, **other:** H HOSPITAL

## INTERSTATE 70 CONT'D

**209** rd Z, Church St, New Melle, **N food:** DQ, **S gas:** Phillips 66/dsl

**208** Pearce Blvd, Wentzville Pkwy, Wentzville, **N gas:** QT/dsl, **food:** Applebees, Bob Evans, Culvers, 54th St Grill, Fritz's Custard, Hardee's, Imo's Pizza, Jack-in-the-Box, KFC, Lion's Choice, McDonald's, Mr. Goodcents, Pizza Hut, Qdoba, Queen Buffet, Quizno's, Ruby Tuesday, Sonic, Starbucks, Steak'n Shake/24hr, St Louis Bread, Taco Bell, Waffle House, White Castle, Wing Sta., **other:** H HOSPITAL, AutoZone, Best Buy, Chevrolet/Buick, Curves, Dierberg's Foods, Dobb's Tire, Family$, Home Depot, Kohl's, Lowes Whse., Michael's, Office Depot, PetsMart, Radio Shack, Schnuck's Food, St Louis Bread, Target, Walgreens, Walmart SuperCtr/auto, vet, **S gas:** BP, **food:** Bandana's BBQ, **lodging:** Super 8, **other:** Cottman Transmissions, Thomas RV Ctr

**204mm** weigh sta both lanes

**203** rds W, T, Foristell, **N gas:** TA/Popeye's/Taco Bell/dsl/rest./24hr/@, Mr Fuel/dsl, **lodging:** Best Western, **other:** Freightliner, **S gas:** Phillips 66/dsl, **food:** McDonald's, **other:** dsl repair

**200** rds J, H, F, Wright City, **N gas:** Midwest/dsl, **food:** Ruiz Castillo's Mexican (1mi), **S gas:** Phillips 66, **lodging:** Super 7 Inn, **other:** Economy Foods

**199** (from wb), **N gas:** Shell/McDonald's/dsl, **other:** $General, **S other:** Volvo

**198mm** rest area both lanes, full facilities, litter barrels, petwalk

**193** MO 47, Warrenton, **N gas:** Phillips 66/Subway/dsl, ZX Gas/dsl, **food:** Applebees, Burger King, China House, Dominos, Jack-in-the-Box, McDonald's, Pizza Hut, Sonic, Waffle House, **lodging:** Day's Inn, Holiday Inn Express, Super 8, **other:** Curves, Family$, Ford, Radio Shack, Walmart SuperCtr, **S gas:** BP, Conoco, Phillips 66/dsl, **food:** Hardee's, KFC, Mkt St Grill, Taco Bell, **other:** AutoZone, CarQuest, Chrysler/Dodge/Jeep, Goodyear/auto, Kelly Tire, Napa, Walgreens, **1/2 mi on frontage rd food:** Denny's, Imo's Pizza, **lodging:** AmeriHost, **other:** Chevrolet/Pontiac, Chrysler/Jeep, Ford, Outlet Ctr/famous brands

**188** rds A, B, to Truxton, **S gas:** FLYING J/Conoco/Cookery/dsl/LP/RV Dump/scales/24hr, **lodging:** Budget Inn

**183** rds E, NN, Y, Jonesburg, **1 mi N** Jonesburg Gardens Camping, **S gas:** Phillips 66/dsl, Shell, **other:** USPO

**179** rd F, High Hill, **S lodging:** Budget Motel

**175** MO 19, New Florence, **N gas:** BP/Hardee's/dsl, Shell/dsl/24hr, **food:** Maggie's Café, McDonald's, **lodging:** Best Inn, Clark Plaza Hotel, Day's Inn, **other:** Stone Hill Winery/gifts, auto repair

**170** MO 161, rd J, Danville, **N gas:** Sinclair, **other:** to Graham Cave SP, Kan-Do RV Park, **S** Lazy Day RV Park

**169.5mm** rest area wb, full facilities, vending, litter barrels, petwalk

**168mm** Loutre River

**167mm** rest area eb, full facilities, vending, litter barrels, petwalk

**161** rds D, YY, Williamsburg, **N gas:** Cranes, **food:** Marlene's Cafe, **other:** USPO **S gas:** Conoco/dsl/24hr

**155** rds A, Z, to Calwood, **N** antiques

**148** US 54, Kingdom City, **N gas:** BP, Phillips 66/dsl, **food:** Taco Bell, **other:** MO Tourism Ctr, to Mark Twain Lake,

**148** Continued
**S gas:** Conoco/Subway/scales/dsl, Shell/Gasper's/Arby's/dsl/scales/@, Petro/Mobil/Iron Skillet/dsl/scales/24hr/@, Phillips 66/McDonald's/dsl, **food:** Denny's, **lodging:** Comfort Inn, Day's Inn, Motel 6, Super 8, **other:** Wheeler's Truckwash

**144** rds M, HH, to Hatton, **S other:** fireworks

**137** rds DD, J, to Millersburg, Stephens, **S** antiques, to Little Dixie WA (4mi)

**133** rd Z, to Centralia, **N other:** Loveall's RV

**131** Lake of the Woods Rd, **N gas:** BP, Phillips 66/Subway/dsl, **food:** Georgia Salad Bar, Sonic, **lodging:** Super 8, **other:** Harley Davidson, **S gas:** Conoco/dsl/24hr

**128a** US 63, to Jefferson City, Columbia, **N gas:** BP, QT, **food:** Backyard Burger, Bob Evans, Burger King, China Garden, Casey's Custard, Cracker Barrel, Golden Corral, Hooters, KFC, Lonestar Steaks, McDonald's/playplace, Pizza Hut, Ruby Tuesday, Shakey's Custard, Steak'n Shake, Taco Bell, Wendy's, **lodging:** Comfort Inn, Fairfield Inn, Hampton Inn, Hilton Garden, Residence Inn, Super 8, **other:** Bass Pro Shop, Cottonwood's RV, Home Depot, Menard's, **S gas:** Breaktime/dsl, **food:** Applebees, Chili's, China Chef, CiCi's, Culvers, IHOP, Longhorn Steaks, Quizno's, Sonic, Subway, TGI Friday, **lodging:** Best Western, Candlewood Suites, Country Inn&Suites, Holiday Inn Express, La Quinta, Motel 6, Staybridge Suites, Wingate Inn, **other:** H HOSPITAL, $Tree, Lowes Whse, Patricia's Foods, Sam's Club, Staples, Walmart SuperCtr

**128** Lp 70 (from wb), Columbia, **N food:** Wendy's, **lodging:** Super 8, **S gas:** Conoco/dsl, **food:** Capt D's, **lodging:** Eastwood Motel, **other:** H HOSPITAL, Big O Tire, same as 128a

**127** MO 763, to Moberly, Columbia, **N gas:** Breaktime/dsl, **food:** Waffle House, **lodging:** Travelodge, **other:** Cadillac/Pontiac, Hyundai, Mazda, **S gas:** Midwest, Phillips 66/dsl, **food:** Burger King, DQ, Taco Bell, **lodging:** Super 7 Motel

**126** MO 163, Providence Rd, Columbia, **N food:** Bandanas BBQ, Country Kitchen, **lodging:** Best Value Inn, Quality Inn, Red Roof Inn, **other:** Buick/GMC, CarQuest, Ford, Honda, same as 127, **S gas:** Breaktime/dsl, **food:** Church's, DQ, Hardee's, McDonald's, Pizza Hut, Sonic, Subway, Taco Bell, Wendy's, **other:** H HOSPITAL, Aldi Foods, AutoZone, Best Buy, Chevrolet, Chrysler/Jeep, $General, Lincoln/Mercury, O'Reilly Parts

**125** Lp 70, West Blvd, Columbia, **N lodging:** Comfort Suites, **S gas:** Phillips 66/dsl, Shell, **food:** Chevy's Mexican, Domino's, Fazoli's, Olive Garden, Outback Steaks, **lodging:** Econolodge, **other:** Advance Parts, BMW, Chrysler/Jeep, Firestone/auto, Kia, PriceChopper Foods, Subaru, U-Haul, same as 124

**124** MO 740, rd E, Stadium Blvd, Columbia, **N lodging:** Extended Stay America, **S gas:** BreakTime, Phillips 66, **food:** Applebee's, ChuckeCheese, Hardee's, KFC, Macaroni Grill, McDonald's/playplace, Pizza Hut, Quizno's, Red Lobster, Ruby Tuesday, Steak'n Shake, Subway, Taco Bell, Wendy's, **lodging:** Baymont Inn, Day's Inn, Drury Inn, Holiday Inn Select/rest., Motel 6, **other:** Best Buy, Circuit City, Dillard's, Ford, Isuzu, JC Penney, K-Mart, Michael's, Old Navy, PetCo, Radio Shack, Sears/auto, Target, mall, to U of MO, same as 125

**122mm** Perche Creek

## INTERSTATE 70 CONT'D

**E** ↕ **W**
**B O O N V I L L E**
**C O N C O R D I A**

| Exit | |
|---|---|
| 121 | US 40, rd UU, Midway, **N** gas: Conoco/dsl/rest., Phillips 66, **lodging:** Budget Inn, **other:** Goodyear, Flea Mkt/antiques, **S** golf |
| 117 | rds J, O, to Huntsdale |
| 115 | rd BB, Rocheport, **N** to Katy Tr SP, **S** antiques |
| 114.5mm | Missouri River |
| 111 | MO 98, MO 179, to Wooldridge, Overton, **S** gas: Phillips 66/dsl/repair |
| 106 | MO 87, Bingham Rd, to Boonville, **N** gas: Cenex/dsl, **S** gas: BP |
| 104mm | rest area both lanes, full ♿ facilities, 🚹, 🏕, litter barrels, vending, petwalk |
| 103 | rd B, Main St, Boonville, **N** gas: Breaktime, Phillips 66/dsl, **food:** Breadeaux Pisa, Domino's, KFC/LJ Silver, La Hacienda Mexican, McDonald's, Pizza Hut, Sonic, Subway, Taco Bell, **lodging:** Day's Inn, Super 8, **other:** Ⓗ HOSPITAL, Daves Mkt, Radio Shack, Walmart, to Kay Tr SP, **S** gas: Cenex/dsl, Shell/Bobber Cafe/dsl/24hr, **food:** Shauna Lou's BBQ, **lodging:** QT Inn, **other:** Bobber Lake Camping |
| 101 | US 40, MO 5, to Boonville, **N** gas: Pilot/Wendy's/dsl/24hr, **food:** A&W, Arbys, **lodging:** Comfort Inn, Holiday Inn Express, **other:** Russell Stover Candy, **S** gas: Love's/Hardee's/scales/dsl/24hr, **other:** Chrysler/Dodge/Jeep, to Lake of the Ozarks |
| 98 | MO 41, MO 135, Lamine, **N** to Arrow Rock HS (13mi), tires, **S** gas: Conoco/Dogwood Rest./dsl, Phillips 66/dsl, **other:** repair |
| 93mm | Lamine River |
| 89 | rd K, to Arrow Rock, **N** to Arrow Rock HS |
| 84 | rd J, **N** gas: BP/DQ/Stuckey's, truck repair |
| 78b a | US 65, to Marshall, **N** gas: Conoco/dsl, **other:** Lazy Days RV Park, fireworks, **S** gas: Breaktime/dsl |
| 77mm | Blackwater River |
| 74 | rds YY, **N** gas: Shell/Betty's/dsl/repair/24hr |
| 71 | rds EE, K, to Houstonia |
| 66 | MO 127, Sweet Springs, **N** Ⓗ HOSPITAL, **S** gas: BreakTime/dsl, Casey's, **food:** Apple BBQ, **lodging:** People's Choice Motel, Super 8, **other:** NAPA |
| 65.5mm | Davis Creek |
| 62 | rds VV, Y, Emma |
| 58 | MO 23, Concordia, **N** gas: TA/Pizza Hut/Subway/dsl/scales/24hr/@, **food:** KFC/Taco Bell, McDonald's, **other:** $General, truck wash, **S** gas: Breaktime/dsl, Casey's, Conoco/dsl, Phillips 66 **food:** Biffle's BBQ, Hardee's, Pizza Hut, Sonic, **lodging:** Budget Inn, Day's Inn, Travelodge, **other:** NAPA |
| 57.5mm | rest area both lanes, full ♿ facilities, 🚹, 🏕, litter barrels, vending, petwalk |
| 52 | rd T, Aullville |
| 49 | MO 13, to Higginsville, **N** gas: BP, Pilot/McDonald's/Subway/scales/dsl/24hr, **lodging:** Camelot Inn/rest, **other:** to Whiteman AFB, to Confederate Mem, **S** lodging: Super 8, **other:** Interstate RV Park |
| 45 | rd H, to Mayview |
| 43mm | weigh sta both lanes |
| 41 | rds O, M, to Lexington, Mayview |
| 38 | MO 131 (from wb), Odessa, **S** gas: BP/dsl, Shell, Sinclair, **food:** McDonald's, Pizza Hut, Sonic, Subway, Taco John's, **other:** $General, Radio Shack, camping, same as 37 |
| 37 | MO 131, Odessa, **N** food: Countryside Diner, |

**O D E S S A**
**B L U E  S P R I N G S**

| Exit | |
|---|---|
| 37 | Continued **other:** Country Gardens RV Park/dump, **S** gas: BP/dsl, Shell, Sinclair, **food:** El Camino Real, McDonald's, Pizza Hut, Sonic, Subway, Taco John's, **lodging:** Parkside Inn, **other:** Chrysler/Dodge/Jeep, Ford, O'Reilly Parts, Prime Outlets/famous brands, Patricia's Foods, fireworks, same as 38 |
| 35mm | truck parking both lanes |
| 31 | rds D, Z, to Bates City, Napoleon, **N** other: Bates City RV Camping, **S** gas: BP/dsl, **food:** Bates City BBQ, **other:** fireworks |
| 29.5mm | Horse Shoe Creek |
| 28 | rd HF, Oak Grove, **N** gas: TA/Conoco/Popeye's/Pizza Hut/dsl/scales/24hr/@, **lodging:** Day's Inn, **other:** Blue Beacon, Freightliner, KOA, **S** gas: QT/dsl/24hr, Petro/BP/Blimpie/DQ/Wendy's/scales/dsl/@, **food:** Hardees, KFC/Taco Bell, McDonald's, Pizza Hut, PJ's Rest., Subway, Waffle House, **lodging:** Econolodge, **other:** O'Reilly Parts, Speedco Lube, Walgreens, Walmart SuperCtr |
| 24 | US 40, rds AA, BB, to Buckner, **N** gas: McShop/dsl, Phillips 66/dsl, **lodging:** Comfort Inn, Travelodge, **other:** Lifestyles RV Ctr, **S** gas: Conoco/Subway/dsl/scales/24hr, **food:** Sonic, **other:** Trailside RV Park/Ctr |
| 21 | Adams Dairy Pkwy, **N** lodging: Days Inn, Rodeway Inn, **other:** Nationwide RV Ctr (1mi), **S** gas: Murphy USA, Phillips 66/Burger King/dsl, **food:** Sonic, Taco Bell, TX Roadhouse, **lodging:** Courtyard, **other:** Home Depot, NTB, Walmart Super Ctr |
| 20 | MO 7, Blue Springs, **N** gas: Phillips 66/dsl, Valero/dsl, **food:** Backyard Burger, Blue Moon Cafe, Bob Evans, China One, Dos Amigo's Mexican, Mensky Pizza, Mr. Goodcents, Papa Murphy's, Pizza Shoppe, Pizza St., Quizno's, Rancho Grande, Sonic, Steamin Bean, **lodging:** Comfort Inn, Days Inn, Econolodge, Motel 6, Rodeway Inn, **other:** Ace Hardware, CVS Drug, $General, O'Reilly Parts, PriceChopper Foods, Walgreens, **S** gas: BP/dsl/24hr, QT, Shell, Valero, **food:** Applebee's, Arby's, Bua Thai, Denny's, Godfather's, Jin's Buffet, KFC, LJ Silver, McDonald's, NY Deli, Original Pizza, Sheridan's Custard, Starbucks, Subway, Taco Bueno, Wendy's, Winsteads Cafe, Zarda's BBQ, **lodging:** Hampton Inn, Quality Inn, **other:** Ⓗ HOSPITAL, Advance Parts, AutoZone, Aldi Foods, Chevrolet, $1 Shop, Firestone/auto, Goodyear/auto, NAPA, Office Depot, Radio Shack, Saturn, Winstead's |
| 18 | Woods Chapel Rd, **N** gas: BP, **lodging:** American Inn, Knight's Inn, Super 8, **other:** Harley-Davidson, **S** gas: Conoco/dsl, Phillips 66/dsl, QT, **food:** China Kitchen, |

## INTERSTATE 70 CONT'D

**18** Continued
KFC/Taco Bell, Las Playas Mexican, McDonald's, Pizza Hut, Subway, Waffle House, **other:** Ford, Hyundai, Nissan, same as 20

**17** Little Blue Pkwy, 39th St, **N food:** Applebee's, Buffalo Wild Wings, Chili's, Coldstone Creamery, Fazoli's, Fox & Hound, Hereford House, Jin's Chinese, Joe's Crabshack, Logan's Roadhouse, Macaroni Grill, O'Charley's, On the Border, Sonic, Starbucks, **lodging:** Hilton Garden, **other:** Ⓗ HOSPITAL, Best Buy, Steinmart, World Mkt, mall entrance, **S gas:** QT, **food:** BD Mongolian, Carrabba's, Chipotle, El Maguay Mexican, Hooters, IHOP, Kobe Steaks, Mongolian BBQ, Outback Steaks, Red Robin, Rib Crib, Subway, Wendy's, **lodging:** Comfort Suites, Holiday Inn Express, **other:** Carmax, Costco/gas, Lowe's Whse

**16mm** Little Blue River

**15b** MO 291 N, Independence, **1 exit N on 39th St gas:** Conoco, QT, Phillips 66, 7-11/gas; **food:** Applebee's, Arby's, BBQ, Bob Evans, Burger King, Chevy's Mexican, Chili's, Denny's, 54th St Grill, Fazoli's, Fox&Hound Smokehouse, Hops Grill, KFC, LJ Silver, LoneStar Steaks, Longhorn Steaks, Luby's, McDonald's, Mr GoodCents Subs, Souper Salad, Starbucks, TGIFriday, **lodging:** Fairfield Inn, Residence Inn, **other:** Ⓗ HOSPITAL, Albertson's, Barnes&Noble, Best Buy, Circuit City, Dick's Sports, Dillard's, Jo-Ann Fabrics, Kohl's, Marshall's, NTB, Sam's Club/gas, Sears/auto, Target, Walmart SuperCtr, mall

**15a** I-470 S, MO 291 S, to Lee's Summit

**14** Lee's Summit Rd, **1 mi N food:** Bob Evans, Longhorn Steaks, **S food:** Cracker Barrel, Olive Garden, Ruby Tuesday, Salty Iguana Mexican, Steak'n Shake, **other:** Bass Pro Shops, CVS Drug, Home Depot

**12** Noland Rd, Independence, **N gas:** Conoco, QT, **food:** ChuckeCheese, CiCi's Pizza, Denny's, Hardee's, Mr. Goodcents, Sheridan's Custard, Sonic, **lodging:** Best Western, Super 8, **other:** Advance Parts, CVS Drug, $General, Firestone/auto, Hancock Fabrics, Honda, K-Mart, Office Depot, Walgreens, to Truman Library, **S gas:** Phillips 66, **food:** Arby's, Bandana's BBQ, Burger King, Fuddrucker's, KFC/Taco Bell, Krispy Kreme, Kyoto Steaks, McDonald's, Olive Garden, Pizza Hut, Red Lobster, Ruby Tuesday, Wendy's, **lodging:** American Inn, Crossland Inn, Red Roof Inn, Regency Inn, **other:** Ace Hardware, $Tree, Gordman's, HyVee Foods/gas, Meineke, Pricechopper Foods, U-Haul

**11** US 40, Blue Ridge Blvd, Independence, **N gas:** Conoco, QT, Shell, **food:** A&W/LJ Silver, Sonic, Subway, V's Italiano, **other:** Jiffy Lube, Radio Shack, **S gas:** BP, 7-11, Sinclair, **food:** Applebee's, Big Boy, Church's Chicken, East Buffet, McDonald's, Papa John's, Samurai Steaks, Starbucks, Steak'n Shake, Subway, Taco Bell, **other:** Cadillac, Family$, GNC, Lowes Whse, O'Reilly Parts, Walmart SuperCtr, mall, vet

**10** Sterling Ave (from eb), same as 11

**9** Blue Ridge Cutoff, **N food:** Denny's/24hr, Wendy's, **lodging:** Drury Inn, Sheraton, Sports Stadium Motel, **other:** Ⓗ HOSPITAL, **S gas:** BP/24hr, Conoco/Subway, **food:** Taco Bell, **lodging:** Holiday Inn, **other:** Sports Complex

**8b a** I-435, N to Des Moines, S to Witchita
**7b** Manchester Trafficway
**7mm** Blue River
**7a** US 40 E, 31st St
**6** Van Brunt Blvd, **N gas:** 7-11, **food:** Church's, **S gas:** BP, **food:** McDonald's, Pizza Hut, Subway, Taco Bell, **other:** VA Ⓗ HOSPITAL, Family$, NAPA
**5c** Jackson Ave (from wb)
**5b** 31st St (from eb)
**5a** 27th St (from eb)
**4c** 23rd Ave
**4b** 18th St
**4a** Benton Blvd (from eb), Truman Rd, **N gas:** Super Stop/Wendy's/dsl, **other:** Advance Parts
**3c** Prospect Ave, **N gas:** BP, **food:** Church's, Gate's BBQ, **S food:** McDonald's
**3b** Brooklyn Ave (from eb), **S** same as 3c
**3a** Paseo St, **S gas:** BP, **other:** tires
**2m** US 71 S, downtown
**2l** I-670, to I-35 S
**2j** 11th St, downtown
**2g** I-29/35 N, US 71 N, to Des Moines
**2h** US 24 E, downtown
**2e** MO 9 N, Oak St, **S gas:** Valero, **lodging:** Comfort Inn
**2d** Main St, downtown
**2c** US 169 N, Broadway, **S gas:** Shell, Valero
**2b** Beardsley Rd
**2a** I-35 S, to Wichita
**0mm** Missouri/Kansas state line, Kansas River

## INTERSTATE 270 - ST LOUIS

| Exit # | Services |
|---|---|
| **15b a** | I-55 N to Chicago, S to St Louis. **I-270 begins/ends in Illinois on I-55/I-70, exit 20.** |
| **12** | IL 159, to Collinsville, **1 mi N gas:** Conoco, Phillips 66, **food:** Applebee's, China Rest., DQ, Denny's, Hardee's, Jack-in-the-Box, KFC, Papa John's, Ponderosa, Quizno's **other:** Aldi Foods, Buick/Pontiac/GMC, Chrysler/Dodge/Jeep, Home Depot, Lowes Whse, PetsMart, Radio Shack, Walgreens, Walmart, **S** Ⓗ HOSPITAL |
| **9** | IL 157, to Collinsville, **N food:** Comfort Inn, **S gas:** Phillips 66/24hr, **lodging:** Hampton Inn |
| **7** | I-255, to I-55 S to Memphis |
| **6b a** | IL 111, **N gas:** ⊕FLYING J/Shell/CountryMkt/dsl/scales/24hr, **food:** Hen House Rest., **lodging:** Best Western, **other:** Blue Beacon/scales, Speedco Lube, truck/trailer repair, **S gas:** Mobil/dsl, **food:** Denny's, McDonald's/playplace, La Mexicana Rest., Taco Bell, **lodging:** Day's Inn, Holiday Inn Express, Super 8, **other:** Ⓗ HOSPITAL, to Pontoon Beach |
| **4** | IL 203, Old Alton Rd, to Granite City |
| **3b a** | IL 3, **N** Riverboat Casino, **S gas:** Phillips 66, **food:** Hardee's, Waffle House, **lodging:** Budget Motel, Econolodge, Sun Motel, **other:** KOA, MGM Camping |
| **2mm** | Chain of Rocks Canal |
| **0mm** | Illinois/Missouri state line, Mississippi River, motorist callboxes begin eb |
| **34** | Riverview Dr, to St Louis, **N gas:** Moto Mart, **Welcome Ctr/rest area both lanes, full** ♿ **facilities, info,** ⛽ **litter barrels,** Ⓒ |
| **33** | Lilac Ave, **N** USPO, **S gas:** Phillips 66/Jack-in-the-Box/dsl, QT/dsl/scales/24hr, **food:** Hardee's |
| **32** | Bellefontaine Rd, **N gas:** Mobil, Shell, **food:** |

## INTERSTATE 270 CONT'D - ST LOUIS

**N ↕ S** **ST LOUIS**

| | |
|---|---|
| 32 | Continued<br>China King, McDonald's, Pizza Hut, Steak'n Shake, **lodging:** Economy Inn, Motel 6, **other:** Advance Parts, Firestone, Schnuck's Foods, **S gas:** BP/24hr, **food:** White Castle, **other:** Aldi Foods |
| 31b a | MO 367, **N gas:** BP, QT, **food:** Jack-in-the-Box, McDonalds, Subway, **other:** H HOSPITAL, Chevrolet, $General, Shop'n Save Foods, U-Haul, Walgreens |
| 30b a | Hall's Ferry Rd, rd AC, **N gas:** Mobil/dsl, Phillips 66/dsl, QT/24hr, ZX, **food:** Applebees, Capt. D's, Popeye's, Waffle House, White Castle, **lodging:** Super 8, **other:** Ford/Lincoln/Mercury, **S gas:** BP/dsl, Conoco, Phillips 66, **food:** China Wok, Church's, CiCi's Pizza, Cracker Barrel, IHOP, Steak'n Shake, Subway, **other:** AutoZone, $Buster, Family$, Home Depot, Jo-Ann Fabrics, O'Reilly Parts, Saturn, Shop'n Save Foods |
| 29 | W Florissant Rd, **N food:** Jack-in-the-Box, Lion's Choice, Pasta House, **other:** Dobb's Tire/auto, $General, K-Mart, Firestone, Office Depot, **S gas:** Sinclair, **food:** Arby's, Burger King, Krispy Kreme, Malone's Grill, McDonald's, Pantera's Pizza, Sonic, **other:** Big Lots, Circuit City, $Tree, Mazda, NTB, Radio Shack, Sam's Club/gas, Saturn, Walmart/auto, Walgreens |
| 28 | Elizabeth Ave, Washington St, **N gas:** Sinclair, **food:** Jack-in-the-Box, Jerome's Pizza, Pizza Hut/Taco Bell, Subway, **other:** Chevrolet, Schnuck's Foods/24hr, Walgreens, **S gas:** BP/24hr |
| 27 | New Florissant Rd, rd N, **N gas:** BP, Shell |
| 26b | Graham Rd, N Hanley, **N gas:** 7-11/dsl **food:** Arby's, LJ Silver, Starbucks, **lodging:** Hampton Inn, Red Roof Inn, **other:** H HOSPITAL, **S food:** McDonald's, **lodging:** Day's Inn, **other:** $General, Hancock Fabrics |
| 26a | I-170 S |
| 25b a | US 67, Lindbergh Blvd, **N gas:** BP, Phillips 66, QT, **food:** Bandana's BBQ, Burger King, China Wok, Church's, Del Taco, IHOP, Imo's Pizza, Jack-in-the-Box, McDonald's, Outback Steaks, Papa John's, Pizza Hut/Taco Bell, Pueblo Nuevo Mexican, Quizno's, Rally's, Sonic, Starbucks, Waffle House, Wendy's, **lodging:** Comfort Inn, InTown Suites, La Quinta, Ramada Inn, **other:** AutoZone, Cadillac, Dierberg's Deli, Family$, Firestone/auto, Ford, GNC, Goodyear, NAPA, Nissan, Radio Shack, Sav-a-Lot Foods, Schnuck's Foods, Toyota, Walgreens, **S gas:** 7-11, **food:** Subway, **lodging:** Budget Inn, Econolodge, Extended Stay America, Studio+, **other:** Honda, VW, transmissions, USPO |
| 23 | McDonnell Blvd, **E food:** Denny's, Quizno's, **lodging:** La Quinta, **W gas:** BP, QT, ZX, **food:** Arby's, Jack-in-the-Box, Lion's Choice, McDonald's, Starbucks, Steak'n Shake, **other:** Buick/GMC/Pontiac |
| 22b a | MO 370 W, to MO Bottom Rd |
| 20c | MO 180, St Charles Rock Rd, **E gas:** BP, Phillips 66/dsl, Shell, **food:** Applebees, Casa Gallardo's, Culpepper's Grill, Hometown Buffet, Fazoli's, Jack-in-the-Box, Lonestar Steaks, McDonald's, New China, Ponderosa, Pizza Hut, Quizno's, Red Lobster, St. Louis Bread, Subway, Taco Bell, **lodging:** Economy Inn, **other:** H HOSPITAL, Aldi Foods, AutoZone, Best Buy, $Tree, Honda, K-Mart, Kohl's, Lowes Whse, NTB, Office Depot, PetsMart, Target, Tuesday Morning, Walgreens/24hr, **W gas:** QT, ZX, **food:** Bob Evans, Olive Garden, Waffle House, **lodging:** Econolodge, Motel 6, Red Roof Inn, Super 8 |

| | |
|---|---|
| 20b a | I-70, E to St Louis, W to Kansas City |
| 17 | Dorsett Rd, **E gas:** BP, QT, **food:** BBQ, Syberg's Grill, **lodging:** Best Western, Drury Inn, Hampton Inn, **W gas:** Mobil, Phillips 66, Shell, **food:** Arby's, Denny's, Fuddrucker's, McDonald's, Steak'n Shake, Subway, **lodging:** Baymont Inn |
| 16b a | Page Ave, rd D, MO 364 W, **E gas:** BP, CFM, Citgo/7-11, QT, Sinclair, **food:** Blimpie, Copperfield's Rest., Hardee's, Hooters, Malone's Grill, McDonald's, Stazio's Café, **lodging:** Comfort Inn, Courtyard, DoubleTree, Holiday Inn, Homestead Suites, Red Roof Inn, Residence Inn, Sheraton |
| 14 | MO 340, Olive Blvd, **E gas:** BP, Mobil, **food:** Applebee's, Bristol Cafe, Denny's, Domino's, KFC, McDonald's, Lion's Choice Rest., Pasta House, Steakout, **lodging:** Courtyard, Drury Inn, **other:** H HOSPITAL, BMW/Land Rover/Cadillac, Borders, Chevrolet, Crysler/Jeep, Lexus, **W gas:** Schnucks, **food:** Coldstone Creamery, Culpepper's Café, House of Wong, Subway, TGIFriday, **other:** Dierberg's Foods, Kohl's, Walgreens |
| 13 | rd AB, Ladue Rd |
| 12b a | I-64, US 40, US 61, E to St Louis, W to Wentzville, **E** H HOSPITAL |
| 9 | MO 100, Manchester Rd, **E gas:** BP, **food:** Café America, Houlihan's Rest., IHOP, Lion's Choice Rest., McDonald's, **other:** Famous Barr, Galyan's, Lord&Taylor, Nordstrom's, mall, **W gas:** Phillips 66, Shell, **food:** Applebee's, Casa Gallardo's Mexican, Olive Garden, Red Robin |
| 8 | Dougherty Ferry Rd, **S gas:** Citgo/7-11, Mobil, **food:** McDonald's, **other:** H HOSPITAL |
| 7 | Big Ben Rd, **N** H HOSPITAL |
| 5b a | I-44, US 50, MO 366, E to St Louis, W to Tulsa |
| 3 | MO 30, Gravois Rd, **N gas:** BP, Phillips 66, **food:** Bandana BBQ, Outback Steaks, **lodging:** Day's Inn, Holiday Inn, Quality Inn |
| 2 | MO 21, Tesson Ferry Rd, **N gas:** BP, **food:** Panda Chinese, Pizza Hut, Red Lobster, **lodging:** Holiday Inn, **other:** Acura, AutoZone, Buick, Toyota, **N on Lindbourgh gas:** Phillips 66, **food:** Burger King, Church's, Olive Garden, Quizno's, Taco Bell, TGIFriday, Waffle House, White Castle, **other:** Buick, Saab, Schnuck's Foods, **S gas:** Shell, other Dierberg's Foods |
| 1b a | I-55 N to St Louis, S to Memphis |

## INTERSTATE 435 - KANSAS CITY

| Exit # | Services |
|---|---|
| 83 | I-35, N to KS City, S to Wichita |

**N ↕ S**

**KANSAS CITY**

## INTERSTATE 435 CONT'D - KANSAS CITY

**82** Quivira Rd, Overland Park, **N food:** Burger King, Old Chicago Pizza, Pizza Hut, Ponderosa, Taco Bell, **other:** H HOSPITAL, CVS Drug, **S food:** McDonald's, Subway, Wendy's, **lodging:** Extended Stay America

**81** US 69 S, to Ft Scott

**79** US 169, Metcalf Ave., **N gas:** BP, Shell, **food:** Denny's, Dick Clark's Grill, Hooters, Tippin's Café, **lodging:** Clubhouse Inn, Embassy Suites, Hampton Inn, Red Roof Inn, Super 8, Wyndham Garden, **other:** H HOSPITAL, Chrysler/Dodge, **S food:** KC BBQ, McDonald's, **lodging:** Courtyard, Drury Inn, Marriott, PearTree Inn

**77b a** Nall Ave, Roe Ave, **N gas:** BP, Shell, **food:** DQ, On-the-Border, Panera Bread, Winstead's Grill, **lodging:** Fairfield Inn, **S gas:** BP, **food:** Cactus Grill, McDonald's, Wendy's, **lodging:** AmeriSuites, Courtyard, Hilton Garden, Holiday Inn, Homestead Suites, Sheraton

**75b** State Line Rd, **N gas:** BP, Conoco, **food:** Applebee's, McDonald's, Taco Bell, Waid's Rest., Wendy's, **other:** Buick/Cadillac, Ford, Goodyear, Infiniti, Lexus, Volvo, **S** H HOSPITAL, city park

**75a** Wornall Rd, **N gas:** QT, **food:** Applebees, Coach's Rest., Wendy's, **other:** Chevrolet, Honda, Toyota, VW, **S gas:** BP

**74** Holmes Rd, **S gas:** Phillips 66, **food:** Burger King, Guacamole Grill, Patrikio's Mexican, Subway, **lodging:** Courtyard, Extended Stay America

**73** 103rd St (from sb)

**71b a** I-470, US 71 S, US 50 E

**70** Bannister Rd, **E gas:** Shell, **food:** China Buffet, McDonalds, Wendy's, **other:** K-Mart, **W food:** HomeTown Buffet, KFC/Taco Bell, LJ Silver/A&W, Pizza Hut, **other:** Firestone/auto, Home Depot

**69** 87th St., **E food:** Subway, **lodging:** Day's Inn, Motel 6, Super 8, **other:** Suzuki, **W gas:** BP/dsl, **lodging:** Baymont Inn

**67** Gregory Blvd (same as 66a b), **E gas:** Shell, **food:** Applebee's, Niece's Rest., Wendy's, **other:** Big Lots, $General, PriceChopper Foods, **W** Nature Ctr, IMAX Theatre, zoo

**66a b** MO 350 E, 63rd st, **E gas:** Shell, **food:** Applebee's, Wendy's, **other:** Big Lots, $General, PriceChopper Foods, **W food:** LC's BBQ, **lodging:** Relax Inn

**65** Eastwood Tfwy, **W gas:** Conoco, **food:** KFC, LC's BBQ, McDonald's, Peachtree Buffet, Pizza Hut, **lodging:** Relax Inn

**63c** Raytown Rd, Stadium Dr (nb only), **E lodging:** Day's Inn, Sports Stadium Motel, Villager Lodge, **other:** Sports Complex

**63b a** I-70, W to KC, E to St Louis

**61** MO 78, 1 mi **E** Church's Chicken

**60** MO 12 E, Truman Rd, 12th St, **E gas:** BP/dsl, Shamrock, **W gas:** QT

**59** US 24, Independence Ave, **E gas:** QT, **food:** Hardee's, **other:** to Truman Library, **W other:** CarQuest, Waffle House

**57** Front St, **E gas:** ⊕FLYING J/Conoco/dsl/rest./scales/24hr/@, **other:** Blue Beacon, **W gas:** Phillips 66, QT, **food:** Denny's, KFC, McDonald's, Pizza Hut, Smugglers Rest., Subway, Taco Bell, Waffle House, Wendy's, **lodging:** La Quinta, Park Place Hotel

**56mm** Missouri River

**55b a** MO 210, **E lodging:** Ameristar Hotel/Casino, Red

**KANSAS CITY**

**55b a** Continued
Roof Inn, **other:** Riverboat Casino, Ford/Volvo/GMC/Mercedes Trucks, **W food:** Arby's, Burger King, Denny's

**54** 48th St, Parvin Rd, **E** RV Park, **W gas:** QT, **food:** Alamo Mexican, Golden Buffet, KFC, Mama Jo's BBQ, Ponderosa, Waffle House, Wendy's, **lodging:** Comfort Inn, Crossland Suites, Day's Inn, Fairfield Inn, Hampton Inn, Holiday Inn, Super 8

**52a** US 69, **E gas:** Phillips 66, Shell, Sinclair, **W gas:** Fuel Outlet, **food:** McDonald's, Pizza Hut, Subway, Taco Bell, **other:** CVS Drug, $General, Osco Drug, Sav-A-Lot Foods

**52b** I-35, S to KC

**51** Shoal Creek Dr

**49b a** MO 152 E, to I-35 N, Liberty, **E food:** Applebee's, Bob Evans, Cracker Barrel, 54th St Grill, Longhorn Steaks, Steak'n Shake, **lodging:** Best Western, Comfort Inn, Fairfield Inn, Hampton Inn, Holiday Inn Express, Super 8

**47** NE 96th St

**46** NE 108th St

**45** MO 291, NE Cookingham Ave, **E** to I-35 N

**42** N Woodland Ave

**41b a** US 169, Smithville, **N food:** Burger King, McDonald's, Sonic, **lodging:** Super 8

**40** NW Cookingham, no facilties

**37** NW Skyview Ave, rd C, **N gas:** Shamrock (1mi), **S** golf (3mi)

**36** to I-29 S, to KCI ✈, **N gas:** Shamrock, **S gas:** BP, **lodging:** Best Western, Clarion, Comfort Suites, Fairfield Inn, Hampton Inn, Hilton, Holiday Inn Express, Microtel, Radisson, Wyndham Garden

**31mm** Prairie Creek

**29** rd D, NW 120th St

**24** MO 152, rd N, NW Berry Rd

**22** MO 45, Weston, Parkville

**20mm** Missouri/Kansas state line, Missouri River

**18** KS 5 N, Wolcott Dr, **E** to Wyandotte Co Lake Park

**15b a** Leavenworth Rd, **E** Woodlands Racetrack

**14b a** Parallel Pkwy, **E gas:** QT, **other:** H HOSPITAL

**13b a** US 24, US 40, State Ave, **E food:** Frontier Steaks, **W other:** Cabela's Sporting Goods, KS Race Track

**12b a** I-70, KS Tpk, to Topeka, St Louis

**11** Kansas Ave

**9** KS 32, KS City, Bonner Springs, **W gas:** Phillips 66/dsl

**8b** Woodend Rd, **E** Peterbilt

**8.8mm** Kansas River

**8a** Holliday Dr, to Lake Quivira

**6c** Johnson Dr

**6b a** Shawnee Mission Pkwy, **E gas:** BP/dsl, **food:** Sonic, **other:** museum

**5** Midland Dr, Shawnee Mission Park, **E gas:** Conoco, Shell/Blimpie, **food:** Arizona's Grille, Barley's Brewhaus, Jose Pepper's Grill, Paula&Bill's Ristorante, Wendy's, **lodging:** Hampton Inn

**3** 87th Ave, **E gas:** BP, Phillips 66, Shell, **food:** McDonald's, **other:** NY Burrito, Panera Bread, Sonic, Zarda BBQ, K-Mart, museum

**2** 95th St

**1b** KS 10, to Lawrence

**1a** Lackman Rd, **N gas:** QT, Shell

**0mm** I-435 begins/ends on I-35.

## INTERSTATE 15

**N ↕ S**

**SHELBY**

| Exit # | Services |
|---|---|
| 398mm | Montana/US/Canada Border |
| 397 | Sweetgrass, **W** rest area both lanes, full ♿ facilities, ⛽, litter barrels, petwalk, 🚻 gas: Gastrack, other: Duty Free |
| 394 | ranch access |
| 389 | MT 552, Sunburst, **W** gas/dsl, food: Big D's BBQ, other: Prairie Mkt foods, Sunburst RV Park |
| 385 | Swayze Rd |
| 379 | MT 215, MT 343, to Kevin, Oilmont, **W** food: Four Corners Café |
| 373 | Potter Rd |
| 369 | Bronken Rd |
| 366.5mm | weigh sta sb |
| 364 | Shelby, **E** Lewis&Clark RV Park, **W** ✈ |
| 363 | US 2, to Cut Bank, Shelby, 0-1 mi **E** gas: Cenex, Pilot/Exxon/Subway/dsl/scales/24hr, Sinclair/dsl, food: Dash Drive-In, Dixie Inn Steaks, Pizza Hut, South of the Border, The Griddle, lodging: Comfort Inn, Crossroads Inn, Glacier Motel, O'Haire Motel, other: 🅷 HOSPITAL, Albertson's, CarQuest, Mark's Tire, Parts+, Radio Shack, TrueValue, **W** other: Pamida/drugs, to Glacier NP |
| 361mm | parking area nb |
| 358 | Marias Valley Rd, to Golf Course Rd, **E** camping |
| 357mm | Marias River |
| 352 | Bullhead Rd |
| 348 | rd 44, to Valier, **W** Lake Frances RA (15mi) |
| 345 | MT 366, Ledger Rd, **E** to Tiber Dam (42mi) |
| 339 | Conrad, **W** gas: Cenex/dsl, Dan's Gas/Tires, Exxon/Subway/dsl, MRC/dsl, food: A&W/KFC, Home Cafe, Keg Rest., Main Drive-In, lodging: Northgate Motel, Super 8, other: 🅷 HOSPITAL, Buick/Chevrolet/GMC/Pontiac, IGA Foods, Olson's Drug, Radio Shack, Ford, Pondera RV Park, TrueValue, Westco RV Ctr, vet |
| 335 | Midway Rd, Conrad, **4 mi W** 🅷 HOSPITAL, gas, food, 🚻, lodging, RV camping |

**GREAT FALLS**

| | |
|---|---|
| 328 | MT 365, Brady, **W** gas: Mtn View Co-op/dsl, other: USPO, tires |
| 321 | Collins Rd |
| 319mm | Teton River, rest area both lanes, full ♿ facilities, 🚻, ⛽, litter barrels, petwalk |
| 313 | MT 221, MT 379, Dutton, **W** gas: Cenex/dsl, food: Café Dutton, other: USPO |
| 302 | MT 431, Power |
| 297 | Gordon |
| 290 | US 89 N, rd 200 W, to Choteau, **W** gas: Exxon/dsl, Sinclair/dsl/LP/RV dump, other: USPO |
| 288mm | parking area both lanes |
| 286 | Manchester, **W** livestock auction, same as 290 (2mi) |
| 282 | US 87 N (from sb), weigh sta, **2-3 mi E** gas: Conoco/dsl, Exxon/dsl, food: Arby's, Burger King, McDonald's, Pizza Hut, Subway, Taco Bell, Taco John's, lodging: Day's Inn, other: Albertson's/gas, Checker Parts, $Tree, K-Mart, Sam's Club/gas, ShopKO, Staples, Tire-Rama, Walmart Super Ctr |
| 280 | US 87 N, Central Ave W, Great Falls, **E** gas: Loaf 'N Jug, food: A&W/KFC, Arby's, Double Barrel Diner, Ford's Drive-In, Hardee's, Papa John's, lodging: Alberta Inn, Central Motel, Day's Inn, other: Freightliner, NAPA, U-Haul/LP, Whalen Tire, to Giant Sprgs SP, vet |
| 280mm | Sun River |
| 278 | US 89 S, rd 200 E, 10th Ave, Great Falls, **E** food: Chili's, Classic 50's Diner/casino, Golden Corral, Macaroni Grill, McDonald's Taco Del Mar, Tony Roma's, lodging: Hampton Inn, Hilton Garden, Holiday Inn Express, other: Barnes&Noble, Home Depot, Michael's, Old Navy, PetCo, Smith's Foods, **1-3 mi E** gas: Cenex/dsl, Conoco, Exxon/Subway/dsl, MRC/dsl, Sinclair/dsl, food: Applebee's, Arby's, Best Wok, Big Mouth BBQ, Boston's Pizza, Burger King, Burger Master, China Buffet, China Town, DQ, 4B's Rest., Fuddrucker's, Godfather's, Hardee's, Jaker's Ribs, Jalisco Mexican, JB's Rest., KFC, Ming's Chinese, Monty's Rest., Papa John's, Papa Murphy's, Pizza Hut, PrimeCut Rest., Quizno's, Starbucks, Taco Bell, Taco John's, Taco Treat, Wendy's, lodging: Best Western, Comfort Inn, Extended Stay America, Fairfield Inn, Holiday Inn, La Quinta, Motel 6, |

**MT**

**N** ↕ **S**

**HELENA**

## INTERSTATE 15 CONT'D

**278** Continued
Plaza Inn, Super 8, Townhouse Inn, Western Motel, other: H HOSPITAL, Ace Hardware, Albertson's/gas, Big-O Tire, BMW, Cadillac/Chevrolet/Toyota, Checker Parts, Chrysler/Dodge/Jeep, Dick's RV Park, Discount Drug, $Tree, Firestone/auto, Ford, Hancock Fabrics, Harley Davidson, Hastings Books, Herberger's, Honda, Hyundai, JC Penney, Jo-Ann Crafts, KOA, Lincoln/Mercury, McCollum RVs, NAPA, Nissan, Parts+, Jeep, O'Reilly Parts, Ross, Scheels Sports, Sears/auto, Target, Tire-Rama, Travel Time RV Ctr, Van's Foods, VW, Walgreens, USPO, transmissions, vet, to Malmstrom AFB

**277** Airport Rd, E gas: ⊕FLYING J/Country Mkt./dsl/24, Pilot/Conoco/Subway/dsl/café/casino/scales/24hr, lodging: Crystal Inn W ✈

**275mm** weigh sta nb

**270** MT 330, Ulm, E gas: Conoco/dsl/LP, other: USPO, W to Ulm SP

**256** rd 68, Cascade, 1/2 mi E gas: Sinclair, lodging: Badger Motel/café, other: NAPA, Tom's Foods, USPO

**254** rd 68, Cascade, 1/2 mi E same as 256

**250** local access, no facilites

**247** Hardy Creek, Hardy Creek, W to Tower Rock SP, food, 🏕, RV camping

**246.5mm** Missouri River

**245mm** scenic overlook sb

**244** Canyon Access, 2 mi W camping, food, RV camping, rec area

**240** Dearborn, E RV park

**239mm** rest area both lanes, full 🚻 facilities, 🏕, 🎡 litter barrels, petwalk

**238mm** Stickney Creek

**236mm** Missouri River

**234** Craig, E food: Izaak's Cafe, Trout Shop Café/lodge, other: rec area, boating, camping

**228** US 287 N, to Augusta

**226** MT 434, Wolf Creek, Wolf Creek, E gas: Exxon/dsl, food: Oasis Café, other: MT River Outfitters/lodge/flyshop, camping, W food: Frenchman&Me Café, other: USPO

**222mm** parking area both lanes

**219** Spring Creek, Recreation Rd (from nb), boating, camping

**218mm** Little Prickly Pear Creek

**216** Sieben

**209** E to Gates of the Mtns RA

**205mm** turnout sb

**202mm** weigh sta sb

**200** MT 279, MT 453, Lincoln Rd, W gas: Sinclair/Bob's Mkt/dsl, food: GrubStake Rest., other: Helena Campground (4mi), Lincoln Rd RV Park, to ski area

**HELENA**

**193** Cedar St, Helena, E gas: Conoco, food: Chili's, IHOP, Macaroni Grill, other: Costco, Helena RV Park (5mi), Home Depot, Whalen Tire, W gas: Conoco/dsl, food: Perkins, Wheat Montana/deli, lodging: Wingate Inn, other: NAPA, W on Montana Ave gas: Cenex/dsl, Exxon/dsl, food: Applebee's, Arby's, DQ, Godfather's, Jade Garden Chinese, McDonald's, McKenzie River Pizza, Pizza Hut, Subway, Taco Bell, Taco Del Mar, Taco John's, lodging: Quality Inn, other: Albertson's/24hr,

**HELENA**

**193** Continued
AutoZone, CarQuest, Checker Parts, Chevrolet, $Tree, Hastings Books, Jo-Ann Fabrics, K-Mart, Lowes Whse, Macy's, Murdock's, Office Depot, O'Reilly Parts, Ross, ShopKO, Snyder's Drugs, Target, Tire-Rama, USPO

**192b a** US 12, US 287, Helena, Townsend, E food: Burger King, Pizza Hut, Subway, lodging: Hampton Inn, other: Buick/Cadillac/GMC, Chrysler/Dodge, D&D RV Ctr, Ford/Lincoln/Mercury, Honda, Montana RV Ctr, Toyota, Schwab Tire, Staples, Walmart SuperCtr, st patrol, W gas: Exxon/dsl, Sinclair/24hr, food: A&W/KFC, DQ, JB's Rest, L&D Chinese, McDonald's, Overland Express Rest., Papa John's, Papa Murphy's, Quizno's, Starbucks, Taco John's, Taco Treat, Wendy's, lodging: Comfort Inn, Day's Inn, Fairfield Inn, Guesthouse Inn, Holiday Inn Express, Jorgenson's Inn, Motel 6, Red Lion Inn, Shilo Inn, Super 8, other: H HOSPITAL, AAA, Albertson's/gas, CVS Drug, Dillard's, JC Penney, Safeway/gas, Tire Factory, Walgreens

**190** W H HOSPITAL

**187** 518, Montana City, Clancy, E food: Hugo's Pizza/casino, W gas: Cenex/dsl, food: Jackson Creek Cafe, Montana City Grill, lodging: Elkhorn Inn

**182** Clancy, E RV camping, W food: Chubby's Grill, MT Steaks, other: USPO, to NF,

**178mm** rest area both lanes, full 🚻 facilities, 🏕, 🎡, litter barrels, petwalk

**176** Jefferson City, NF access

**174.5mm** chain up area both lanes

**168mm** chainup area both lanes

**164** rd 69, Boulder, E gas: Exxon/dsl/casino/24hr, food: Gator's Pizza Parlour, Mtn Good Rest., other: L&P Foods, Parts+, USPO, RC RV camping

**161mm** parking area nb

**160** High Ore Rd

**156** Basin, E other: Merry Widow Health Mine/RV camping, W other: Basin Cr Pottery, camping, USPO

**154mm** Boulder River

**151** to Boulder River Rd, Bernice, W camping, picnic area

**148mm** chainup area both lanes

**143.5mm** chainup area both lanes

**138** Elk Park, W other: Sheepshead Picnic Area, wildlife viewing

**134** Woodville

**133mm** continental divide, elev 6368

**130.5mm** scenic overlook sb

**129** I-90 E, to Billings

**I-15 S and I-90 W run together 8 mi**

**BUTTE**

**127** Harrison Ave, Butte, E gas: Conoco/dsl, Exxon/dsl/24hr, Sinclair, food: A&W/KFC, Arby's, Asia Gardens, Burger King, 4B's Rest., Godfather's, McDonald's, McKenzie River Pizza, Perkins, Pizza Hut, Ray's Rest., Silver Bow Pizza, Subway, Taco Bell, Wendy's, lodging: Best Western, Comfort Inn, Copper King, Hampton Inn, Ramada Inn, Super 8, other: American Car Care, Buick/GMC/Pontiac, Checker Parts, Chevrolet, Chrysler/Dodge/Jeep, Ford, Herberger's, Honda, JC Penney, Jo-Ann Crafts, K-Mart, Lincoln/Mercury, O'Reilly Parts, Staples, Subaru, Walmart SuperCtr, Whalen Tire, casinos, W gas: Cenex/dsl, Conoco, food: Denny's, Derby Steaks, Domino's, DQ, El Taco Mexican, Hanging 5 Rest., John's Rest., L&D Chinese, Papa John's,

# INTERSTATE 15 CONT'D

**BUTTE**

**N ↑ S**

| | |
|---|---|
| **127** | Continued<br>Papa Murphy's, Quizno's, Royce's Burgers, Taco John's, **lodging:** Day's Inn, Holiday Inn Express, War Bonnet Inn, **other:** Ace Hardware, Checker Parts, Hastings Books, NAPA, Nissan/Toyota, Safeway |
| **126** | Montana St, Butte, **E gas:** Conoco, Exxon/dsl, **W food:** Chef's Garden Italian, **lodging:** Eddy's Motel, **other:** H HOSPITAL, KOA, Safeway, Schwab Tire |
| **124** | I-115 (from eb), to Butte, City Ctr |
| **123mm** | weigh sta wb |
| **122** | Rocker, **E gas:** Pilot/Conoco/Arby's/McDonald's/Subway/dsl/scales/24hr, **lodging:** Motel 6, **other:** repair, **W gas:** ⊕FLYING J/rest./dsl/LP/24hr, **lodging:** Rocker Inn Motel, **other:** weigh sta eb, RV camping |
| **I-15 N and I-90 E run together 8 mi** | |
| **121** | I-90 W, to Missoula |
| **119** | Silver Bow, Port of MT Transportation Hub |
| **116** | Buxton |
| **112mm** | Continental Divide, elevation 5879 |
| **111** | Feely |
| **109mm** | **rest area both lanes, full 🦽 facilities, 📞, 🪧, litter barrels, petwalk** |
| **102** | rd 43, to Wisdom, Divide, **W food:** Blue Moon Cafe, **other:** to Big Hole Nat Bfd (62mi) |
| **99** | Moose Creek Rd |
| **93** | Melrose, **W food:** Melrose Café/grill/dsl, Hitchin Post Rest., **lodging:** Pioneer Mtn Cabins, **other:** Sportsman Motel/RV Park, Sunrise Flyshop, USPO |
| **85.5mm** | Big Hole River |
| **85** | Glen, **E other:** Willis Sta. RV camping |
| **74** | Apex, Birch Creek |
| **64mm** | Beaverhead River |

**DILLON**

| | |
|---|---|
| **63** | Lp 15, rd 41, Dillon, Twin Bridges, **E gas:** Cenex/dsl/LP, Chevron/JD's Rest./dsl/scales/casino/24hr, Exxon/KFC/dsl/24hr, Phillips 66/dsl, **food:** Grandma's Kitchen, Lions Den, McDonald's, Pizza Hut, Subway, **lodging:** Best Western/rest., Comfort Inn, GuestHouse Inn, Sundowner Motel, Super 8, **other:** H HOSPITAL, CarQuest, Chevrolet/Pontiac/Buick/Cadillac, Ford/Chrysler/Dodge, KOA, O'Reilly Parts, Safeway/drug/gas, Schwab Tire, museum, RV Park, W MT Coll |
| **62** | Lp 15, Dillon, **E food:** DQ, Sparky's Rest., Taco John's, **lodging:** Creston Motel, Flyshop Inn, **other:** H HOSPITAL, KOA, Southside RV Park, to WMT |
| **60mm** | Beaverhead River |
| **59** | MT 278, to Jackson, **W other:** Bannack SP, Countryside RV Park |
| **56** | Barretts, **E** RV camping |
| **52** | Grasshopper Creek |
| **51** | Dalys (from sb, no return) |
| **50mm** | Beaverhead River |
| **46mm** | Beaverhead River |
| **45mm** | Beaverhead River |
| **44** | MT 324, **E food:** Buffalo Lodge, **other:** Armstead RV Park, Beaverhead Flyshop, **W other:** Clark Cyn Reservoir/RA, RV camping |
| **38.5mm** | Red Rock River |
| **37** | Red Rock |
| **34mm** | **parking area both lanes, litter barrels, restrooms** |

| | |
|---|---|
| **29** | Kidd |
| **23** | Dell, **E gas:** Cenex/dsl, **food:** Yesterdays Cafe, **other:** USPO |
| **16.5mm** | weigh sta both lanes |
| **15** | Lima, **E gas:** Exxon/dsl, **food:** Jan's Café, **lodging:** Mtn View Motel/RV Park, **other:** Big Sky tire/auto, USPO, ambulance |
| **9** | Snowline |
| **0** | Monida, **E** 📞, to Red Rock Lakes |
| **0mm** | Monida Pass, elevation 6870, Montana/Idaho state line |

# INTERSTATE 90

**E ↑ W**

| Exit # | Services |
|---|---|
| **559.5mm** | weigh sta both lanes |
| **554.5mm** | Montana/Wyoming state line |
| **549** | Aberdeen |
| **544** | Wyola |
| **530** | MT 463, Lodge Grass, **1 mi S gas:** gas, dsl, food, lodging, 📞 |
| **517.5mm** | Little Bighorn River |
| **514** | Garryowen, **N gas:** Conoco/Subway, **other:** Custer Bfd Museum, **S other:** 7th Ranch RV camp |
| **511.5mm** | Little Bighorn River |
| **510** | US 212 E, **N gas:** Exxon/KFC/dsl/café/gifts, **food:** Crows Nest Café, **other:** H HOSPITAL, to Little Bighorn Bfd, casino, **S other:** Little Bighorn RV Camp/dump |
| **509.5mm** | weigh sta, both lanes exit left |
| **509.3mm** | Little Bighorn River |
| **509** | Crow Agency, **N gas:** Conoco/24hr, **S** to Bighorn Canyon NRA |
| **503** | Dunmore |
| **498mm** | Bighorn River |
| **497** | MT 384, 3rd St, Hardin, **S** H HOSPITAL, Bighorn Cty Museum, **2 mi S lodging:** Western Motel, **other:** Casino Rest./lounge |
| **495** | MT 47, City Ctr, Hardin, **N gas:** Shell/dsl, **food:** Purple Cow Rest., **other:** KOA, **S gas:** Cenex/dsl, Conoco/Subway/dsl/LP/24hr, Exxon/dsl, Sinclair/dsl, **food:** DQ, McDonald's, Pizza Hut, Shawna's Steaks, Taco John's, **lodging:** American Inn, Super 8, Western Motel, **other:** H HOSPITAL, Grand View Camping/RV Park, Sunset Village RV Park, casinos |
| **484** | Toluca |
| **478** | Fly Creek Rd |
| **477mm** | **rest area both lanes, full 🦽 facilities, 📞, 🪧, litter barrels, petwalk** |

**HARDIN**

**MT**

E W BILLINGS BILLINGS

## INTERSTATE 90 CONT'D

| | |
|---|---|
| **469** | Arrow Creek Rd, **N food:** Rock Shop/Cafe |
| **462** | Pryor Creek Rd |
| **456** | I-94 E, to Bismarck, ND |
| **455** | Johnson Lane, **S gas:** Exxon/A&W/Blimpie/dsl/24hr, ⊕**FLYING J**/Conoco/Cookery/dsl/LP/rest./24hr/ scales, **food:** Burger King, DQ, Subway, **lodging:** Holiday Inn Express, **other:** Tour America RV Ctr (1mi) |
| **452** | US 87 N, City Ctr, Billings, **N gas:** Conoco/Arby's/dsl/ LP, Exxon/dsl, **lodging:** Best Western, **other:** American Spirit RV Ctr, Chevrolet, Metra Rv Ctr, transmissions, **2-4 mi N on US 87 gas:** Cenex/dsl, Conoco/dsl, Holiday/dsl, **food:** Applebee's, Arby's, Bugz Rest./casino, Burger King, DQ, Fuddrucker's, Godfather's Pizza, Golden Phoenix, Guadalajara Mexican, KFC, Little Caesar's, MacKenzie River Pizza, Main St Grill, McDonald's, Mongolian Grill, Papa John's, Papa Murphy's, Pizza Hut, Subway, Taco Bell, Taco John's, Wendy's, **lodging:** Country Inn&Suites, Foothills Inn, Heights Motel, **other:** Ace Hardware, Albertson's, Big Lots, CarQuest, Checkers Parts, CVS Drug, O'Reilly Parts, Office Depot, Radio Shack, Schnider's Drug, Target, U-Haul, Walgreens, Walmart SuperCtr, Western Drug, vet, **S gas:** Cenex/ dsl, **other:** RV Capming |
| **451.5mm** | Yellowstone River |
| **450** | MT 3, 27th St, Billings, **N gas:** Conoco/dsl/24hr, Sinclair, **food:** Blondy's Cafe, Pizza Hut, **lodging:** Crowne Plaza, War Bonnet Inn/rest., **other:** Ⓗ HOSPITAL, CarQuest, USPO, **S** KOA, Yellowstone River Camping |
| **447** | S Billings Blvd, **N gas:** Conoco/Subway/dsl/24hr, Holiday, **food:** Burger King, DQ, McDonald's, **lodging:** Best Western/Kelly, Day's Inn, Extended Stay America, Hampton Inn, Sleep Inn, Super 8, Cabela's Sporting Goods, NAPA, **S other:** Billings RV Park (2mi), Freightliner, Kenworth, KOA (2mi), Yellowstone River Campground |
| **446** | King Ave, Billings, **N on King Ave... gas:** Exxon, Conoco/ dsl, Holiday/dsl/LP/RV dump, Sinclair, **food:** Applebee's, Arbys, Burger King, Carrie's Rest., Cactus Creek Steaks, Carino's Italian, City Brew Coffee, Del Taco, Denny's, Dos Machos, Famous Dave's, Fuddrucker's, Gusicks Rest., Hot Mongolian, IHOP, Jade Palace, Olive Garden, Old Chicago, Outback Steaks, Perkins, Pizza Hut, Quizno's, Red Lobster, Taco John's, Taste Of Italy, TX Roadhouse, Wendy's, Wheat Montana, **lodging:** C'Mon Inn, Comfort Inn, Fairfield Inn, Hilton Garden, La Quinta, Quality Inn, Residence Inn, Springhill Suites, Western Executive Inn, **other:** Best Buy, Borders Books, Chevrolet, Chrysler/ Jeep/Kia, Costco/gas, Dodge, Ford, Home Depot, Isuzu, Lowe's Whse, Michael's, Nissan, Office Depot, Old Navy, O'Reilly Parts, PetsMart, Ross, ShopKO, Subaru/Hyundai, Toyota, USPO, Walmart SuperCtr, World Mkt, mall, **N on 24th... gas:** Conoco/dsl, Exxon/Subway, **food:** Buffalo Wild Wings, Golden Corral, Hardee's, Little Caesar's, McDonald's, Taco Bell, Wendy's, **other:** Albertson's/ Osco, Barnes&Noble, Cadillac/GMC/Pontiac, Dillards, JC Penney, K-Mart, Subaru, Tuesday Morning, **S gas:** Conoco/dsl/24hr, **food:** Cracker Barrel, Emporium Rest., **lodging:** Billings Hotel, ClubHouse Inn, Holiday Inn, Kelly Inn, Motel 6, Ramada Ltd, Red Roof Inn, **other:** Volvo/ Mac Trucks, water funpark |

LIVINGSTON

| | |
|---|---|
| **443** | Zoo Dr, to Shiloh Rd, **N gas:** Holiday/dsl, **food:** MT Rib/Chophouse, **lodging:** Hampton Inn, Wingate Inn, **other:** Pierce RV Ctr, Sportsman's Whse, zoo, **S other:** Harley-Davidson, vet |
| **439mm** | weigh sta both lanes |
| **437** | E Laurel, **S gas:** Sinclair/dsl/rest./casino/motel/RV Park/24hr |
| **434** | US 212, US 310, to Red Lodge, Laurel, **N gas:** Cenex/ dsl, Conoco/dsl, Exxon/dsl/24hr, **food:** Burger King, City Brew Coffee, Hardee's, McDonald's, Pizza Hut, Subway, Taco John's, **lodging:** Best Western, Howard Johnson, **other:** Ace Hardware, Chevrolet, CVS Drug, Ford, Jan's Foods, Rapid Tire, Walmart SuperCtr, **S other:** Riverside Park/RV Camping, vet, to Yellowstone NP |
| **433** | Lp 90 (from eb), same as 434 |
| **426** | Park City, **S gas:** Cenex/dsl/café/24hr, KwikStop, **food:** The Other Cafe, **lodging:** CJ's Motel, **other:** auto/tire repair |
| **419mm** | rest area both lanes, full ♿ facilities, Ⓒ, 🚻, litter barrels, petwalk |
| **408** | rd 78, Columbus, **N** Mtn Range RV Park, **S gas:** Conoco, Pilot/Exxon/dsl/24hr, **food:** Apple Village Café/gifts, McDonald's, Stageline Pizza, **lodging:** Big Sky Motel, Super 8, **other:** Ⓗ HOSPITAL, casino, museum, tires/ repair, to Yellowstone |
| **400** | Springtime Rd |
| **398mm** | Yellowstone River |
| **396** | ranch access |
| **392** | Reed Point, **N gas:** Sinclair/dsl, **other:** Old West RV Park, USPO |
| **384** | Bridger Creek Rd |
| **381mm** | rest area both lanes, full ♿ facilities, Ⓒ, 🚻, litter barrels, petwalk |
| **377** | Greycliff, **S other:** Prairie Dog Town SP, KOA |
| **370** | US 191, Big Timber, **1 mi N gas:** Cenex, Sinclair/dsl, **food:** Frosty Freez Diner, **lodging:** Grand Hotel, Lazy J Motel, **other:** Spring Creek RV Ranch (4mi), USPO |
| **369mm** | Boulder River |
| **367** | US 191 N, Big Timber, **N gas:** Exxon/dsl, Conoco/dsl, **food:** Country Skillet, **lodging:** River Valley Inn, Super 8, **other:** CarQuest, Chevrolet, Ford, Spring Creek Camping (3mi), historic site/visitor info |
| **362** | De Hart |
| **354** | MT 563, Springdale |
| **352** | ranch access |
| **350** | East End access |
| **340** | US 89 N, to White Sulphur Sprgs, **S** ✈ ⌖ |
| **343** | Mission Creek Rd, **N** Ft Parker HS |
| **337** | Lp 90, to Livingston, **2 mi N** services |
| **333mm** | Yellowstone River |
| **333** | US 89 S, Livingston, **N gas:** Loaf'n Jug, **food:** Clark's Rest., DQ, Taco John's, **lodging:** Best Western, Livingston Inn, Quality Inn, Rodeway Inn, **other:** Ⓗ HOSPITAL, Ace Hardware, Ford/Lincoln/Mercury, Pamida, Radio Shack, RV Park, Town&Country Foods, Western Drug, **S gas:** Cenex/dsl, Conoco/dsl, Exxon/dsl, **food:** Arby's, Buffalo Jump Steaks, McDonald's, Subway, **lodging:** Comfort Inn, Super 8, **other:** Albertson's, Osen's RV Park, LP, vet, to Yellowstone |
| **330** | Lp 90, Livingston, **1 mi N gas:** Yellowstone Trkstp/dsl/ rest./24hr, **lodging:** Del Mar Motel |
| **326.5mm** | chainup/chain removal area both lanes |
| **324** | ranch access |

## INTERSTATE 90 CONT'D

| | |
|---|---|
| 323mm | chainup/chain removal area wb |
| 322mm | Bridger Mountain Range |
| 321mm | turnouts/hist marker both lanes |
| 319 | Jackson Creek Rd |
| 319mm | chainup area both lanes |
| 316 | Trail Creek Rd |
| 313 | Bear Canyon Rd, **S** other: Bear Canyon Camping |
| 309 | US 191 S, Main St, Bozeman, **N** other: Subaru, Sunrise RV Park, VW, **S** gas: Cenex/dsl, Exxon, food: MT AleWorks, lodging: Blue Sky Motel, Continental Motel; Ranch House Motel, Western Heritage Inn, other: H HOSPITAL, Heeb's Foods, RV service, to Yellowstone, vet |
| 306 | US 191, N 7th, Bozeman, **N** gas: Sinclair, food: McDonald's, lodging: Best Value Inn, Fairfield Inn, Microtel, Ramada Ltd, Super 8, TLC Inn, other: Whalen Tire, RV supplies, ski area, **S** gas: Conoco/Arby's/dsl, Exxon, food: Applebee's, Bar-3 BBQ, Dominos, DQ, Famous Dave's, McDonald's, Papa John's, Santa Fe Red's Cafe, Taco John's, lodging: Best Western, Bozeman/rest., Comfort Inn, Day's Inn, Hampton Inn, Holiday Inn, Royal 7 Inn, other: Big O Tire, CarQuest, Firestone/auto, K-Mart, U-Haul, Van's Foods, Walmart SuperCtr, Museum of the Rockies |
| 305 | MT 412, N 19th Ave, **N** gas: Exxon, lodging: AmericInn, 0-3 mi **S** food: Carino's Italian, IHOP, KFC, MacKenzie River Pizza, Old Chicago Pizza, Outback Steaks, Papa Murphy's, Pizza Hut, Subway, Wendy's, Wheat MT Bakery, lodging: C'mon Inn, Hilton Garden, Residence Inn, Wingate Inn, other: Borders Books, Costco/gas, Ford/Lincoln/Mercury, Home Depot, Lowes Whse, Michaels, Old Navy, Office Depot, PetsMart, Target, Radio Shack, Ross, Smith's, Sportsman's Whse, Staples, UPS, World MKT, USPO, vet, **rest area, full** ♿ **facilities,** ⊞ **litter barrels, petwalk** |
| 298 | MT 291, MT 85, Belgrade, **N** gas: Cenex/dsl, Conoco, Exxon/Subway/dsl, food: Burger King, DQ, McDonald's, Pizza Hut, other: Albertson's/Osco, IGA Foods, NAPA, Radio Shack, Whalen Tire, **S** gas: *FLYING J*/Conoco/dsl/scales/LP, food: Country Kitchen, lodging: Holiday Inn Express, La Quinta, Super 8, other: Harley-Davidson, Interwest Tire, KOA (9mi), TrueValue, truckwash, to Yellowstone NP. |
| 292.5mm | Gallatin River |
| 288 | Manhattan, **N** gas: Conoco/dsl, other: RV camping |
| 283 | Logan, **S** other: Madison Buffalo Jump SP (7mi) |
| 279mm | Madison River |
| 278 | MT 205, rd 2, Three Forks, Trident, **N** Missouri Headwaters SP, **1 mi S** gas: Conoco/dsl, Sinclair/dsl, lodging: Broken Spur Motel, other: camping, ℂ |
| 277.5mm | Jefferson River |
| 274 | US 287, to Helena, Ennis, **N** gas: Sinclair/dsl, food: Wheat MT Bakery/deli, lodgin: Ft 3 Forks Motel, other: KOA (2mi), to Canyon Ferry SP, dsl repair, **S** gas: Pilot/Exxon/Subway/dsl/scales/24hr, other: Camp 3 Forks, Lewis&Clark Caverns SP, to Yellowstone NP |
| 267 | Milligan Canyon Rd |
| 261.5mm | chain-up area |
| 257mm | Boulder River |
| 256 | MT 359, Cardwell, **S** gas: Cardwell/dsl/RV Park, other: to Yellowstone NP, Lewis&Clark Caverns SP, RV camping |
| 249 | rd 55, to rd 69, Whitehall, **S** gas: Exxon/Subway/dsl/24hr, food: A&W/KFC, lodging: Super 8, other: Virginia City NHS, camping, casino |

| | |
|---|---|
| 241 | Pipestone |
| 240.5mm | chainup/chain removal area both lanes |
| 238.5mm | runaway ramp eb |
| 237.5mm | pulloff eb |
| 235mm | **truck parking both lanes, litter barrels, rest rooms** |
| 233 | Homestake, Continental Divide, elev 6393 |
| 230mm | chain-up area both lanes |
| 228 | MT 375, Continental Dr, **S** gas: Conoco/dsl, other: Harley Davidson, 3 Bears Foods |
| 227 | I-15 N, to Helena, Great Falls |
| | **I-90 and I-15 run together 8 mi. See Montana Interstate 15, exits 122-127.** |
| 219 | I-15 S, to Dillon, Idaho Falls |
| 216 | Ramsay |
| 211 | MT 441, Gregson, **3-5 mi S** food, lodging, Fairmont RV Park (Apr-Oct) |
| 210.5mm | parking area wb, Pintlar Scenic route info |
| 208 | rd 1, Pintler Scenic Loop, Georgetown Lake RA, Opportunity, Anaconda, **S** other: H HOSPITAL, gas, food, lodging, RV camp/dump, ski area, **rest area both lanes, full** ♿ **facilities,** ⊞ **litter barrels, petwalk** |
| 201 | Warm Springs, **S** MT ST H HOSPITAL |
| 197 | MT 273, Galen, **S** to MT ST H HOSPITAL |
| 195 | Racetrack, **S** other: dsl repair |
| 187 | Lp 90, Deer Lodge (no wb return), **2 mi S** food: Montey's Subs, lodging: Downtowner Motel, Scharf's Motel/rest., other: H HOSPITAL, KOA (seasonal), Radio Shack, Valley Foods, Old MT Prison, Tow Ford Museum, same as 184 |
| 184 | Deer Lodge, 0-1 mi **S** gas: Exxon/dsl/casino, Conoco/dsl/casino, Sinclair/dsl, food: A&W, Broken Arrow Steaks, Chinese Garden, 4B's Rest., McDonald's, Pizza Hut, lodging: Downtowner Motel, Rodeway Inn, Western Big Sky Inn, other: H HOSPITAL, Indian Cr Camping, Keystone Drug, KOA, Safeway/deli, Schwab Tire, Grant-Kohrs Ranch NHS |
| 179 | Beck Hill Rd |
| 175mm | Little Blackfoot River |
| 175 | US 12 E, Garrison, **N** other: RiverFront RV Park, ℂ, hist site |
| 174 | US 12 E (from eb), **S** food: Ranch House Cafe/RV Park, same as 175 |
| 170 | Phosphate |
| 168mm | **rest area both lanes, full** ♿ **facilities,** ℂ, ⊞ **litter barrels, petwalk, Hist Point** |
| 166 | Gold Creek, **S** other: Camp Mak-A-Dream |
| 162 | Jens |

Left margin (top to bottom): E ↕ W BOZEMAN BELGRADE

Left margin (bottom section): DEER LODGE

Right margin: MT

**MT**

E
↕
W

**M I S S O U L A**

## INTERSTATE 90 CONT'D

**154** to MT 1 (from wb), Drummond, **S** gas: Cenex/dsl, Conoco/dsl/24hr, Sinclair/dsl/24hr, food: TasteeFreeze, Wagon Wheel Café, lodging: Sky Motel, other: Pintler Scenic Lp, Georgetown Lake RA, Goodtime RV Park (3mi)

**153** MT 1 (from eb), **N** other: Garnet Ghost Town, Goodtime RV Park (3mi) **S** same as 154

**150.5mm** weigh sta both lanes

**143mm** rest area both lanes, full ♿ facilities, 🚻, 🏕, litter barrels, petwalk

**138** Bearmouth Area, **N** other: Chalet Bearmouth Camp/rest., to gas, food, lodging

**130** Beavertail Rd, **S** other: to Beavertail Hill SP, rec area, camping (seasonal)

**128mm** parking area both lanes, litter barrels/restrooms

**126** Rock Creek Rd, **S** lodging: Rock Creek Lodge/gas/casino, other: rec area

**120** Clinton, **N** gas: Sinclair/dsl, food: Poor Henry's Café (1mi W in on frtg rd), other: Clinton Market, **S** other: USPO

**113** Turah, **S** Turah RV Park/gas

**109.5mm** Clark Fork, Clark Fork

**109mm** Blackfoot River

**109** MT 200 E, Bonner, **N** gas: Pilot/Exxon/Arby's/Subway/dsl/scales/casino/LP/24hr, Sinclair/dsl, food: River City Grill, other: USPO, banking, hist site

**108.5mm** Clark Fork, Clark Fork

**107** E Missoula, **N** gas: Ole's Mkt/Conoco/diner/dsl/24hr, Sinclair/24hr, food: Reno Cafe lodging: Aspen Motel, other: dsl repair, 2 mi **S** lodging: Holiday Inn Express

**105** US 12 W, Missoula, **S** gas: Cenex/dsl/24hr, Conoco/dsl/24hr, Sinclair/dsl, food: Burger King, Finnegan's, McDonald's, Pizza Hut, Quizno's, Subway, Taco Bell, lodging: Campus Inn, Creekside Inn, DoubleTree, Family Inn, Holiday Inn, Holiday Inn Express, Ponderosa Motel, Thunderbird Motel, other: Ace Hardware, Albertson's, Kingfisher Flyshop, O'Reilly Parts, U of MT, Vietnam Vet's Mem

**104** Orange St, Missoula, **S** gas: Conoco/dsl, food: Pagoda Chinese, Subway, Taco John's lodging: Mountain Valley Inn, Red Lion Inn, other: 🏥 HOSPITAL, Curves, Tire-rama, to City Ctr

**101** US 93 S, Reserve St, **N** gas: Conoco/dsl, food: Cracker Barrel, McKenzie River Pizza, Starbucks, lodging: Best Western, C'Mon Inn, Motel 6, other: ski area, 0-2 mi **S** gas: Cenex/dsl/LP, Conoco/24hr, Exxon/dsl/24hr, Sinclair, food: Arby's, Blue Canyon Rest., Burger King, Carino's, China Bowl, Coldstone Creamery, DQ, Famous Dave's BBQ, Fuddrucker's, Hooters, McDonald's, MT Club rest./casino, Outback Steaks, Perkins, Quizno's, Taco Bell, Taco Time/TCBY, Wendy's, lodging: Courtyard, Econolodge, Hampton Inn, Hilton Garden, La Quinta, Ruby's Inn/rest., Staybridge Suites, Super 8, Travelers Inn, other: Albertson's, Barnes&Noble, Best Buy, Bretz RV/Marine, Chevrolet, Costco/gas, Firestone/auto, Home Depot, KOA, Lowes Whse, Michael's, Old Navy, PetsMart, Radio Shack, Ross, Sportsman's Whse, Staples, Target, TJ Maxx, Walgreens, Walmart SuperCtr, casinos, dsl repair

**99** Airway Blvd, **S** gas: Mobil/dsl/24hr, Sinclair/dsl, lodging: Hawthorn Suites, Wingate Inn, other: Chrysler/Dodge, Harley-Davidson, ✈

**96** US 93 N, MT 200W, Kalispell, **N** gas: Conoco/dsl/rest./scales/24hr/@, lodging: Day's Inn/rest., other: Freightliner, Peterbilt, Jellystone RV Park (1mi), Jim&Mary's RV Park (1mi), to Flathead Lake & Glacier NP, **S** gas: CrossroadsTC/Sinclair/rest/dsl/24hr, lodging: Redwood Lodge, other: Kenworth, RV repair

**92.5mm** inspection sta both lanes

**89** Frenchtown, **S** gas: Conoco/dsl/café/24hr, Sinclair, food: Alcan Grill, other: Frenchtown Drug, USPO, to Frenchtown Pond SP

**85** Huson, **S** gas: Sinclair/café, other: 🚻

**82** Nine Mile Rd, **N** food: Mile House Rest., other: Hist Ranger Sta/info, food, 🚻

**81.5mm** Clark Fork

**80mm** Clark Fork, Clark Fork

**77** MT 507, Petty Creek Rd, Alberton, **S** access to gas, food, lodging, 🚻

**75** Alberton, **S** lodging: River Edge Rest, other: RV camp, casino

**73mm** parking area wb, litter barrels

**72mm** parking area eb, litter barrels

**70** Cyr

**70mm** Clark Fork

**66** Fish Creek Rd

**66mm** Clark Fork

**61** Tarkio

**59mm** Clark Fork

**58mm** rest area both lanes, full ♿ facilities, 🚻, 🏕, litter barrels, petwalk, NF camping (seasonal)

**55** Lozeau, Quartz

**53.5mm** Clark Fork

**49mm** Clark Fork

**47** MT 257, Superior, **N** gas: Cenex/24hr, Conoco/dsl, Sinclair/Durango's Rest., food: Rosie's Rest., lodging: Budget Host, Hilltop Motel, other: 🏥 HOSPITAL, Best Hardware, Family Foods, Mineral Drug, NAPA, TrueValue, USPO, **S** gas: Pilot/Exxon/dsl/casino/24hr, other: Carl's Repair

**45mm** Clark Fork

**43** Dry Creek Rd, **N** NP camping (seasonal)

**37** Sloway Area

**34mm** Clark Fork

**33** MT 135, St Regis, **N** gas: Conoco/dsl/rest./gifts, Exxon, Sinclair, food: Frosty Drive-In, Huckleberry Patch Rest., Jasper's Rest., OK Café/casino, Subway, lodging: Little River Motel, Super 8, other: Nugget Camground, St Regis Campground, USPO, antiques

**30** Two Mile Rd, **S** fishing access

**29mm** fishing access, wb

**26** Ward Creek Rd (from eb)

**25** Drexel

**22** Camels Hump Rd, Henderson, **N** other: camping (seasonal), antiques (1mi)

**18** DeBorgia, **N** food: Billy Big Riggers, O'aces Rest.

**16** Haugan, **N** gas: Exxon/dsl/24hr, lodging: 50,000 Silver $/motel/rest./casino/RV park

**15mm** weigh sta both lanes, exits left from both lanes

**10** Saltese, **N** food: MT Grill, lodging: Mangold's Motel, other: antiques

**10mm** St Regis River

**5** Taft Area, access to Hiawatha Trail

**4.5mm** rest area both lanes, full ♿ facilities, 🏕, litter barrels, petwalk, chainup/removal

## INTERSTATE 90 CONT'D

| | |
|---|---|
| **0** | Lookout Pass, **other:** access to Lookout Pass ski area/lodge, info |
| **0mm** | Montana/Idaho state line, Central/Pacific time zone, Lookout Pass elev 4680 |

## INTERSTATE 94

| Exit # | Services |
|---|---|
| **250mm** | Montana/North Dakota state line |
| **248** | Carlyle Rd |
| **242** | MT 7 (from wb), Wibaux, **S** rest area both lanes, full ♿ facilities, 🚻, 🏕, litter barrels, **gas:** Amsler's/dsl, Cenex/dsl/service, **food:** Tastee Hut, **lodging:** Beaver Creek Inn, **other:** RV camping |
| **241** | MT 261 (from eb), to MT 7, Wibaux, **S** same as 242 |
| **240mm** | weigh sta both lanes |
| **236** | ranch access |
| **231** | Hodges Rd |
| **224** | Griffith Creek, frontage road |
| **222.5mm** | Griffith Creek |
| **215** | MT 335, Glendive, City Ctr, **N** **gas:** Conoco, **food:** C's Family Café, **lodging:** Comfort Inn, Day's Inn, Super 8, Yellowstone River Inn, **other:** Glendive Camping (apr-oct), TrueValue, museum, **S** **gas:** Exxon/dsl, Holiday/gas, Sinclair/dsl/repair, **food:** DQ, Subway, Taco John's, **lodging:** Best Western, Budget Motel, El Centro Motel, **other:** Ⓗ HOSPITAL, to Makoshika SP |
| **215mm** | Yellowstone River |
| **213** | MT 16, to Sidney, Glendive, **N** **gas:** Exxon/dsl, **other:** Green Valley Camping, st patrol, truck tire/repair, **S** **gas:** Cenex, Conoco/dsl, Sinclair/dsl, **food:** Pizza Hut, **lodging:** Parkwood Motel, Riverside Inn, **other:** Albertson's/Osco, Ford, K-Mart, Radio Shack |
| **211** | MT 200S (from wb, no EZ return), to Circle |
| **210** | Lp 94, to rd 200S, W Glendive, **S** **gas:** Cenex, **other:** Buick/Chevrolet/Pontiac, Bumper Parts, Chrysler/Dodge/Jeep, Makoshika SP |
| **206** | Pleasant View Rd |
| **204** | Whoopup Creek Rd |
| **198** | Cracker Box Rd |
| **192** | Bad Route Rd, **S** rest area/weigh sta both lanes, full ♿ facilities, weather info, 🚻, 🏕, litter barrels, camping, petwalk |
| **187mm** | Yellowstone River |
| **185** | MT 340, Fallon, **S** café, 🚻 |
| **184mm** | Fallon Creek |
| **176** | MT 253, Terry, **N** **gas:** Conoco/dsl, **food:** Dizzy Diner, **lodging:** Diamond Motel, Kempton Hotel, **other:** Ⓗ HOSPITAL, Terry RV Oasis |
| **170mm** | Powder River |
| **169** | Powder River Rd |
| **159** | Diamond Ring |
| **148** | Valley Access |
| **141** | US 12 E, Miles City, **N** **other:** RV Camping |
| **138** | MT 58, Miles City, **N** **gas:** Cenex/dsl/24hr, Conoco/dsl, Pilot/Exxon/dsl/24hr, **food:** Bruster's, DQ, 4B's Rest., Gallagher's Rest., KFC, Little Caesar's, McDonald's, Pizza Hut, Subway, Taco John's, Wendy's, **lodging:** Best Western, Econolodge, Motel 6, **other:** Ⓗ HOSPITAL, Ace Hardware, Albertson's/Osco Drug, O'Reilly Parts, Radio Shack, Walmart SuperCtr, casinos, |
| **138** | Continued RV Park, **S** **food:** Hunan Chinese, **lodging:** Comfort Inn, Guesthouse Inn, Holiday Inn Express, Super 8 |
| **137mm** | Tongue River |
| **135** | Lp 94, Miles City, **N** **other:** KOA (April-October) |
| **128** | local access |
| **126** | Moon Creek Rd |
| **117** | Hathaway |
| **114mm** | rest area eb, full ♿ facilities, 🚻, 🏕, litter barrels, petwalk |
| **113mm** | rest area wb, full ♿ facilities, 🚻, 🏕, litter barrels, petwalk, overlook |
| **106** | Butte Creek Rd, to Rosebud, **N** food, 🚻 |
| **103** | MT 446, MT 447, Rosebud Creek Rd, **N** food, 🚻 |
| **98.5mm** | weigh sta both lanes |
| **95** | Forsyth, **N** **gas:** Cenex, Exxon/dsl/24hr, **food:** DQ, **lodging:** Sundowner Motel, **other:** Ⓗ HOSPITAL, Ford, Van's Foods, Yellowstone Drug, to Rosebud RA, **S** camping |
| **93** | US 12 W, Forsyth, **N** **gas:** Cenex, Exxon/dsl/24hr, **food:** Top That Eatery, **lodging:** Rails Inn, Restwell Inn, WestWind Motel, **other:** NAPA, repair/tires, RV camping |
| **87** | MT 39, to Colstrip |
| **82** | Reservation Creek Rd |
| **72** | MT 384, Sarpy Creek Rd |
| **67** | Hysham, **1-2 mi** **N** gas, 🚻, food, lodging |
| **65mm** | rest area both lanes, full ♿ facilities, 🚻, 🏕, litter barrels, petwalk |
| **63** | ranch access |
| **53** | Bighorn, access to 🚻 |
| **52mm** | Bighorn River |
| **49** | MT 47, to Hardin, Custer, **S** **food:** Ft Custer Café, **other:** to Little Bighorn Bfd, camping |
| **47** | Custer, **S** **gas:** Custer Sta./dsl, **food:** Jct City Saloon/café, **other:** Custer Food Mkt, USPO |
| **41.5mm** | rest area wb, full ♿ facilities, 🚻, 🏕, litter barrels, petwalk |
| **38mm** | rest area eb, full ♿ facilities, 🚻, 🏕, litter barrels, petwalk |
| **36** | frontage rd, Waco |
| **23** | Pompeys Pillar, **N** **other:** Pompeys Pillar Nat Landmark |
| **14** | Ballantine, Worden, **S** **food:** Long Branch Café/casino |
| **6** | MT 522, Huntley, **N** gas, 🚻, **food:** Pryor Creek Café |
| **0mm** | I-90, E to Sheridan, W to Billings, I-94 begins/ends on I-90, exit 456. |

Vertical side labels: E, W, GLENDIVE, TERRY, FORSYTH

**NE** E ↕ W

## INTERSTATE 80

| Exit # | Services |
|---|---|
| 455mm | Nebraska/Iowa state line, Missouri River |
| 454 | 13th St, **N gas:** BP/dsl, Infinite, Valero, **food:** Big Horn BBQ, Burger King, McDonald's/playplace, **lodging:** Comfort Inn, **other:** Family$, auto repair, **S food:** King Kong Burgers, **other:** Doorly Zoo, Imax, stadium |
| 453 | 24th St (from eb) |
| 452b | I-480 N, US 75 N, to Henry Ford's Birthplace, Eppley Airfield |
| 452a | US 75 S |
| 451 | 42nd St, **N gas:** BP/dsl, **S gas:** Phillips 66, **food:** Burger King, McDonald's, Taco Bell, **other:** H HOSPITAL, Pitstop Lube |
| 450 | 60th St, **N gas:** Phillips 66, **other:** NAPA, to U of NE Omaha, **S gas:** Omaha 66/dsl, **other:** transmissions |
| 449 | 72nd St, to Ralston, **N gas:** BP, **food:** Burger King, Margarita's Mexican, Perkins, Spezia Italian, **lodging:** Baymont Inn, Comfort Inn, Holiday Inn/rest., Homewood Suites, Howard Johnson, Quality Inn, Super 8, Travelodge, **other:** H HOSPITAL, **S gas:** Cenex/dsl, **food:** Anthony's Steaks |
| 448 | 84th St, **N gas:** BP, Shell, **food:** Arby's, Denny's, Farmhouse Café, Great Wall Chinese, Husker Hounds, McDonald's, Subway, Taco Bell, **lodging:** Econolodge, **other:** Advance Parts, Hancock Fabrics, Mangelson's Crafts, NAPA AutoCare, ShopKO, **S gas:** QT, Shell/dsl, **food:** Wendy's, **other:** Chevrolet, Kia |
| 446 | I-680 N, to Boystown |
| 445 | US 275, NE 92, I thru L St, **N gas:** Cenex, **food:** Austin's Steaks, Wendy's, **lodging:** Clarion, **other:** Buick/Pontiac/GMC, Home Depot, Nelsen's RV Ctr, Sam's Club/gas, Walmart SuperCtr **S food:** Village Inn Rest., **lodging:** Baymont Inn, Best Western, Carlisle Hotel, Comfort Inn, Day's Inn, Econolodge, Hawthorn Suites, Holiday Inn Express, Howard Johnson, La Quinta, Motel 6, Super 8, **other:** Goodyear, NE Beef Co, **S on 108th...gas:** Conoco/dsl, QT/dsl, **food:** Arby's, Burger King, China 1, Godfather's Pizza, Hong Kong Café, LJ Silver, McDonald's, Perkins, Pizza Hut/Taco Bell, Sonic, Subway, Valentino's, Wendy's, **other:** Albertson's, U-Save Drug |
| 444 | Q St, **N gas:** Cenex/dsl |
| 442 | 126th St, Harrison St, **N other:** Chrysler/Jeep/Dodge, Toyota, VW, **S gas:** Phillips 66, **food:** Runza, **lodging:** Embassy Suites, Hampton Inn, ValuePlace Hotel, **other:** Cabela's |
| 440 | NE 50, to Springfield, **N gas:** Phillips 66, Shell/Sapp Bros/Subway/dsl/24hr/@, Woody's/dsl, **food:** Azteca Mexican, Cracker Barrel, Hardee's, McDonald's, Pizza Machine, Quizno's, **lodging:** Ben Franklin Motel, Comfort Inn, Countryside Suites, Days Inn, Quality Inn, Rodeway Inn, **other:** H HOSPITAL, Ford, truckwash, **S gas:** BP/dsl, to Platte River SP |
| 439 | NE 370, to Gretna, **N gas:** Kum&Go/Quizno's, Phillips 66/dsl, **lodging:** Suburban Inn, **S** H HOSPITAL, Volvo Trucks, museum |

**OMAHA**

**LINCOLN**

| | |
|---|---|
| 432 | US 6, NE 31, to Gretna, **N gas:** Sinclair/dsl/rest./24hr, **food:** McDonald's, **lodging:** Super 8, **other:** Curves, Nebraska X-ing/famous brands, **S gas:** ⊘ FLYING J/ Conoco/dsl/LP/rest./24hr, **other:** KOA, to Schramm SP |
| 431mm | rest area wb, full & facilities, info, [ℂ, ▥] litter barrels, petwalk |
| 427mm | Platte River |
| 426 | NE 66, to Southbend, **N** to Mahoney SP, museum |
| 425.5 | rest area eb, full & facilities, [ℂ, ▥] litter barrels, petwalk, vending |
| 420 | NE 63, Greenwood, **N gas:** Cenex/cafe/dsl/scales/24hr, **other:** RV camping, **S gas:** Shell/dsl, **lodging:** Big Inn, **other:** antiques, to Platte River SP, WWII Museum |
| 416mm | weigh sta both lanes |
| 409 | US 6, to E Lincoln, Waverly, **N food:** McDonald's, **S other:** H HOSPITAL |
| 405 | US 77 N, 56th St, Lincoln, **S gas:** Phillips 66, **other:** H HOSPITAL, Freightliner, truck parking, **1 mi S food:** Misty's Rest., **lodging:** Howard Johnson, Travelodge, **other:** antiques |
| 403 | 27th St, Lincoln, **S gas:** Conoco/Wendy's/dsl, Phillips 66/Subway/dsl, **food:** Arby's, Cracker Barrel, DQ, King Kong Burger, Popeye's/Taco Inn, Quizno's, **lodging:** AmericInn, Best Western, Countryside Suites, Settle Inn, Staybridge Suites, ValuePlace Hotel, **other:** BMW, Chevrolet/Pontiac/Cadillac/GMC, Ford/Lincoln/Mercury/Mazda, Lexus, Suzuki, Toyota, **1-3 mi S gas:** Git'N Split, Mobil, Phillips 66/Subway, Shell, **food:** Applebee's, Beacon Hill Rest., Burger King, Carlos O'Kelly's, China Buffet, CiCi's Pizza, Culver's, DaVinci's Italian, Godfather's, Golden Corral, IHOP, McDonald's, Papa John's, Ruby Tuesday, Runza Rest., Schlotsky's, Sonic, Taco Bell, Taco Bueno, Taco John's, Valentino's, Village Inn, **lodging:** Comfort Suites, Country Inn&Suites, Fairfield Inn, Holiday Inn Express, La Quinta, Microtel, Super 8, **other:** AutoZone, Curves, Dodge/Jeep, $Tree, GNC, Haas Tire, Home Depot, HyVee Foods, Menards, Michael's, PetsMart, Radio Shack, Sam's Club/gas, ShopKO, Walmart SuperCtr, to U NE, st fairpark |
| 401b | US 34 W, **S** RV camping |
| 401a | I-180, US 34 E, to 9th St, Lincoln |
| 399 | Lincoln, **N gas:** BP/dsl, Phillips 66, **food:** Baskin-Robbins, McDonald's, Perkins, Quizno's, **lodging:** Airport Inn, Best Value Inn, Comfort Inn, Day's Inn, Hampton Inn, Holiday Inn Express, Horizon Inn, Motel 6, Ramada Inn, Sleep Inn, Quality Inn, **other:** to ✈, **S gas:** Sinclair/dsl, **lodging:** Econolodge, Economy Lodge |
| 397 | US 77 S, to Beatrice |
| 396 | US 6, West O St (from eb), **S gas:** Sinclair/dsl, **lodging:** Super 8, Travelodge, **other:** Lincoln/Mercury |
| 395 | US 6, NW 48th St, **S gas:** Shoemaker's/Shell/dsl, **lodging:** Cobbler Inn, **other:** Harley-Davidson, truck repair |
| 388 | NE 103, to Crete, Pleasant Dale |
| 382 | US 6, Milford |
| 381mm | rest area eb, full & facilities, [ℂ, ▥] litter barrels, petwalk, vending |

## INTERSTATE 80 CONT'D

E→W

**379** NE 15, to Seward, **N** other: Buick/Pontiac/GMC, Ford, 2-3 mi **N** food: McDonald's, lodging: Super 8, other: **H** HOSPITAL, antiques, **S** gas: Shell/dsl,

**375mm** rest area wb, full ♿ facilities, info, 📞, 🎇, litter barrels, petwalk, vending

**373** 80G, Goehner, **N** gas: Sinclair

**369** 80E, Beaver Crossing, **3 mi S** **H** HOSPITAL, food, RV camping

**366** 80F, to Utica

**360** 93B, to Waco, **N** gas: BP/Lori's Kitchen/dsl/24hr, **S** lodging: Double Nickel Camping

**355mm** rest area wb, full ♿ facilities, info, 📞, 🎇, litter barrels, vending, petwalk

**YORK**

**353** US 81, to York, **N** gas: BP/dsl, Byco Fuel, SappBros/Sinclair/Subway/scales/dsl, Shell/dsl, Sinclair, food: Arby's, Burger King, Country Kitchen, Golden Gate Chinese, KFC/Taco Bell, McDonald's, Pizza Hut, Runza, Starbucks, Taco John's, Wendy's, lodging: Comfort Inn, Day's Inn, Hampton Inn, New Victorian Inn, Palmer Inn, Super 8, Yorkshire Motel, other: **H** HOSPITAL, Buick/GMC, Chevrolet/Pontiac, Elms RV Park, Ford, Walmart SuperCtr/Subway, **S** gas: Petro/Phillips 66/Iron Skillet/Pizza Hut/dsl/24hr/@, Shell/dsl/rest./24hr, food: Applebee's, lodging: Camelot Inn, Holiday Inn, other: Blue Beacon, tires/wash/lube

**351mm** rest area eb, full ♿ facilities, info, 📞, 🎇, litter barrels, petwalk, vending

**348** 93E, to Bradshaw

**AURORA**

**342** 93A, Henderson, **N** other: Prarie Oasis Camping, **S** gas: Fuel/dsl, food: Subway, lodging: Grace Inn, other: **H** HOSPITAL

**338** 41D, to Hampton

**332** NE 14, Aurora, **N** gas: Shell/dsl, food: McDonald's (3mi), Pizza Hut (3mi), Subway (2.5), lodging: Budget Host (3mi), Hamilton Motel/rest., other: **H** HOSPITAL, to Plainsman Museum, **S** gas: Love's/Arby's/dsl/scales

**324** 41B, to Giltner

**318** NE 2, to Grand Island, **S** other: KOA

**317mm** rest area wb, full ♿ facilities, info, 📞, 🎇, litter barrels, vending, petwalk

**315mm** rest area eb, full ♿ facilities, info, 📞, 🎇, litter barrels, vending, petwalk

**314mm** Platte River

**314** Locust Street, to Grand Island, (4-6mi) **N** gas: Byco, Casey's, food: LJ Silver, Subway, Tommy's Rest., Wendy's, lodging: Holiday Inn, Howard Johnson, Island Inn Motel, Rodeway Inn, Travelodge, other: Walmart

**312** US 34/281, to Grand Island, **N** gas: Bosselman/Pilot/Sinclair/Max's/Subway/scales/dsl/24hr, Phillips 66, lodging: Motel 6, USA Inn/rest., other: **H** HOSPITAL, Mormon Island RA, to Stuhr Pioneer Museum, **S** gas: Sinclair/Arby's/dsl, lodging: Holiday Inn/rest., Holiday Inn Express, other: Peterbilt, Hastings Museum (15mi)

**305** 40C, to Alda, **N** gas: Sinclair/dsl/scales/24hr, TA/Country Pride/dsl/scales/24hr/@, **S** other: Crane Meadows Nature Ctr/rest area

**300** NE 11, Wood River, **S** gas: Bosselman/Pilot/Sinclair/Grandma Max's/Subway/dsl/24hr/@, lodging: motel/RV park

**291** 10D, Shelton, **N** other: War Axe SRA

**285** 10C, Gibbon, **N** gas: Petro Oasis/dsl, other: Windmill SP, RV camping, **S** lodging: Country Motel

**279** NE 10, to Minden, **N** gas: Shell/dsl, **S** other: Pioneer Village Camping

**275mm** The Great Platte River Road Archway Monument

**KEARNEY**

**272** NE 44, Kearney, **N** gas: BP, Casey's, Cenex/Subway/dsl, Gas Stop, Shell/dsl, Sinclair, Valero, food: Amigo's, Arby's, Burger King, Carlos O'Kelly's, Country Kitchen, DQ, Hunan's Rest., King's Buffet, LJ Silver, McDonald's, Microtel, Old Chicago, Perkins/24hr, Pizza Hut, Quizno's, Red Lobster, Ruby Tuesday, Runza Rest., San Pedro Mexican, Taco Bell, Taco John's, USA Steaks, Wendy's, Whiskey Creek, lodging: AmericInn, Best Western, Comfort Inn, Country Inn&Suites, Day's Inn, 1st Interstate Inn, Hampton Inn, Holiday Inn,

**NE** E ↑↓ W

**LEXINGTON**

## INTERSTATE 80 CONT'D

**272** Continued
Motel 6, Quality Inn, Ramada Inn/rest., Rodeway Inn, Super 8, Western Inn, Wingate Inn, **other:** Ⓗ HOSPITAL, Boogaart's Foods, Buick/Cadillac, Chevrolet, Chrysler/Dodge/Jeep, $General, Pontiac, Goodyear, NAPA, Walmart SuperCtr (3mi), to Archway Mon, U NE Kearney, Museum of NE Art, **S** gas: Valero/dsl, **food:** Grandpa's Steaks, Skeeter's BBQ, **lodging:** 1st Inn Gold, Holiday Inn Express

**271mm** **rest area wb, full** 🅿 **facilities, info,** Ⓒ, ⛽, **litter barrels, petwalk**

**269mm** **rest area eb, full** 🅿 **facilities, info,** Ⓒ, ⛽, **litter barrels, petwalk**

**263** rd 10 b, Odessa, **N** gas: Sapp/Shell/dsl/rest., **other:** UP Rec Area

**257** US 183, Elm Creek, **N** gas: Bosselman/Pilot/Sinclair/Subway/dsl/scales/24hr, **other:** Antique Car Museum, Nebraska Prarie Museum, Nebraska Tire, Sunny Meadows Camping

**248** Overton

**237** US 283, Lexington, **N** gas: Casey's, Cenex/dsl, Conoco/KFC/Taco Bell/dsl, Shell, **food:** Arby's, Burger King, DQ, Hong Kong Buffet, Little Caesar's, McDonald's, Pizza Hut, Sonic, Taquiera Mexican, Wendy's, **lodging:** Comfort Inn, Day's Inn, 1st Interstate Inn, Gable View Inn, Holiday Inn Express, Minute Man Motel, **other:** Ⓗ HOSPITAL, Advance Parts, Chevrolet/Cadillac/Pontiac/Buick, $General, Goodyear/auto, Plum Creek Foods, Walmart SuperCtr/Subway, Military Vehicle Museum, **S** gas: Sinclair/dsl/@, **food:** Kirk's Café, **lodging:** Super 8, to Johnson Lake RA

**231** Darr Rd, **S** truckwash/24hr

**227mm** **rest area both lanes, full** 🅿 **facilities, info,** Ⓒ, ⛽, **litter barrels, vending, petwalk**

**222** NE 21, Cozad, **N** gas: Cenex/dsl, Casey's/dsl, **food:** Burger King, DQ, El Paraiso Mexican, Pizza Hut, PJ's Rest., Runza Rest., South 40 Rest., Subway, **lodging:** Best Value Inn, **other:** Ⓗ HOSPITAL, Alco, Firestone/auto, museum

**211** NE 47, Gothenburg, **N** gas: Shell/dsl/24hr, Sinclair/rest./cafe/dsl, **food:** China Cafe, Lasso Espresso, McDonald's, Mi Ranchito Mexican, Pizza Hut, Randazzle Cafe, Runza Rest., **lodging:** Pony Express Inn, Super 8, Travel Inn, **other:** Ⓗ HOSPITAL, Chevrolet/Buick/Pontiac, Pony Express Sta Museum (1mi), Chevrolet/Pontiac/Buick, NAPA, Pamida, truck permit sta, **S** KOA/Sinclair

**199** Brady, **N** gas: Brady 1 Stop/DQ/dsl

**194mm** **rest area both lanes, full** 🅿 **facilities,** Ⓒ, ⛽, **litter barrels, vending, petwalk**

**190** Maxwell, **N** gas: Sinclair/dsl, **S** other: to Ft McPherson Nat Cemetary, RV camping

**181mm** weigh sta both lanes, Ⓒ

**179** to US 30, N Platte, **N** gas: Sinclair, **lodging:** La

**N PLATTE**

**179** Continued
Quinta, (1mi) Stanford Motel, **other:** RV camping, **S** gas: ⊕FLYING J/Conoco/CountryMkt/dsl/LP/24hr, **other:** truck tire/lube/repair, truckwash

**177** US 83, N Platte, **N** gas: Cenex/dsl, Shell/dsl, Sinclair/McDonald's/dsl, **food:** A&W, Amigo's Rest., Applebee's, Arby's, Burger King, Cold stone Creamery, DQ, Hong Kong Chinese, LJ Silver/Taco Bell, McDonald's, Perkins/24hr, Pizza Hut, Quizno's, Roger's Diner, Ruby Tuesday, Runza Rest., Sonic, Starbucks, Subway, Valentino's, Village Inn Rest., Wendy's, Whiskey Creek Steaks, **lodging:** Best Western, Blue Spruce Motel, Hampton Inn, Hospitality Inn, Motel 6, Oak Tree Inn, Quality Inn, Royal Colonial Inn, Sands Motel, **other:** Hospital, Advance Parts, $General, Goodyear/auto, Harley-Davidson, Holiday TravL Park, Staples, SunMart Foods, U-Save Drug, Walmart SuperCtr/gas/dsl, mall, museum, to Buffalo Bill's Ranch, vet, **S** gas: Cenex, Conoco/Taco Bell/dsl/24hr, Shell/dsl/rest./RV Dump/24hr, **food:** Hunan Chinese, Mi Ranchito, Taco John's, **lodging:** Comfort Inn, Day's Inn, Holiday Inn Express, Ramada Ltd, Super 8, **other:** Cadillac, Chevrolet, Chrysler/Jeep/Dodge, Ford/Lincoln/Mercury, Honda, Menards, Toyota/Mazda, truck permit sta, to Lake Maloney RA, vet

**164** 56C, Hershey, **N** gas: Western/Western Cafe/dsl/24hr/@, **food:** Donna's Cafe, **other:** Rivers Edge Ranch Store

**160mm** **rest area both lanes, full** 🅿 **facilities, info,** Ⓒ, ⛽, **litter barrels, petwalk**

**158** NE 25, Sutherland, **N** lodging: Park Motel (1mi), **S** gas: Sinclair/dsl/24hr, **other:** RV camping

**149mm** Central/Mountain time zone

**145** 51C, Paxton, **N** gas: Shell/dsl/24hr, **lodging:** Day's Inn, other RV camping

**133** 51B, Roscoe

**132mm** **rest area wb, full** 🅿 **facilities, info,** Ⓒ, ⛽, **litter barrels, petwalk**

**OGALLALA**

**126** US 26, NE 61, Ogallala, **N** gas: Cenex/dsl, Sapp/Shell/dsl/24hr, Sinclair, **food:** Arby's, Country Kitchen, McDonald's, Mi Ranchito Mexican, Pizza Hut, Runza Rest., Taco John's, The Star Steaks, Valentino's, **lodging:** Best Western, Day's Inn, Gray Goose Lodge, Holiday Inn Express, **other:** Ⓗ HOSPITAL, Chevrolet/Buick, NAPA, SunMart Foods, TrueValue, U-Save Drug, to Lake McConaughy, **S** gas: Conoco/Subway/dsl, TA/dsl/rest./24hr/scales/@, **food:** DQ, KFC/Taco Bell, Wendy's, **lodging:** Comfort Inn, Econolodge, Super 8, **other:** $General, Corral RV Park, Countryview Camping, Pamida

**124mm** **rest area eb, full** 🅿 **facilities, info,** Ⓒ, ⛽, **litter barrels, petwalk**

**117** 51A, Brule, **N** gas: Sinclair/dsl, **other:** Riverside RV camping

**107** 25B, Big Springs, **N** gas: Big Springs/dsl, Bosselman/Pilot/Sinclair/Grandma Max's/Little Caesar's/Subway/dsl/scales/@, **food:** Sam Bass' Steaks, **lodging:** Motel 6, **other:** truckwash, **S** other: McGreer's Camping

## INTERSTATE 80 CONT'D

| | |
|---|---|
| 102 | I-76 S, to Denver |
| 102mm | S Platte River |
| 101 | US 138, to Julesburg, **S** truck parking |
| 99mm | scenic turnout eb |
| 95 | NE 27, to Julesburg |
| 88mm | **Lodgepole Creek, rest area wb, full** &#9855; **facilities,** &#9742;, &#9985;, **litter barrels, vending, petwalk** |
| 85 | 25A, Chappell, **N gas:** Cenex/dsl, **other:** Creekside RV Park/Camping, USPO, wayside park |
| 82.5mm | **rest area eb, full** &#9855; **facilities,** &#9742;, &#9985;, **litter barrels, vending, petwalk** |
| 76 | 17F, Lodgepole, **1 mi N** gas/dsl, lodging |
| 69 | 17E, to Sunol |
| 61mm | **rest area wb, full** &#9855; **facilities,** &#9742;, &#9985;, **litter barrels, vending, petwalk** |
| 59 | US 385, 17J, Sidney, **N gas:** Conoco/KFC/Taco Bell/TCBY/dsl, Sapp/Shell/dsl/24hr, **food:** Arby's, Buffalo Paint Rest., China 1 Buffet, DQ, McDonald's, Mi Ranchito Mexican, Perkins, Pizza Hut, Taco Bell, Quizno's, Runza Rest., **lodging:** AmericInn, Comfort Inn, Day's Inn, Motel 6, **other:** Cabela's RV Park, Chrysler/Jeep/Dodge, Maddox RV Ctr, Radio Shack, Walmart SuperCtr, RV camping (2mi), golf, truck permit sta, **S gas:** Shamrock, **lodging:** Holiday Inn/rest., **other:** truckwash, auto tire/truck repair |
| 55 | NE 19, to Sterling, Sidney |
| 51.5mm | **rest area/hist marker eb, full** &#9855; **facilities,** &#9742;, &#9985;, **litter barrels, vending, petwalk** |
| 48 | to Brownson |
| 38 | rd 17 b, Potter, **N gas:** Cenex/dsl/LP, **other:** repair |
| 29 | 53A, Dix, 1/2 mi **N** gas, food |
| 25mm | **rest area wb, full** &#9855; **facilities,** &#9742;, &#9985;, **litter barrels, vending, petwalk** |
| 22 | 53E, Kimball, **N lodging:** (1mi)Day's Inn, **other:** Kimball RV Park, golf, **2 mi N lodging:** Days Inn, **food:** DQ, **other:** Family$, NAPA |
| 20 | NE 71, Kimball, **N gas:** Sinclair, **lodging:** 1st Interstate Inn, Super 8, **other:** &#9405; HOSPITAL, Pamida, RV Park, truck permit sta., **1 mi N food:** Pizza Hut, Subway, Taco John's, **lodging:** Days Inn |
| 18mm | parking area eb, litter barrel |
| 10mm | **rest area eb, full** &#9855; **facilities, info,** &#9742;, &#9985;, **litter barrels, petwalk** |
| 8 | 53C, to Bushnell |
| 1 | 53B, Pine Bluffs, **1 mi N** RV camping |
| 0mm | Nebraska/Wyoming state line |

## INTERSTATE 680 - OMAHA

| Exit # | Services |
|---|---|
| 29b a | I-80, W to Omaha, E to Des Moines. I-680 begins/ends on I-80, exit 27. |
| 28 | IA 191, to Neola, Persia |
| 21 | L34, Beebeetown |
| 19mm | **rest area wb, full** &#9855; **facilities, info,** &#9742;, &#9985;, **litter barrels, petwalk** |

| | |
|---|---|
| 16mm | **rest area eb, full** &#9855; **facilities, info,** &#9742;, &#9985;, **litter barrels, petwalk** |
| 15mm | scenic overlook |
| 71 | I-29 N, to Sioux City |
| 66 | Honey Creek, **W gas:** Sinclair/dsl/rest., **food:** Iowa Feed&Grain Co Rest. |
| 3b a | (61 b a from wb) I-29, S to Council Bluffs, IA 988, to Crescent, **E gas:** Phillips 66, **other:** to ski area |
| 1 | County Rd |
| 14mm | Nebraska/Iowa state line, Missouri River, Mormon Bridge |
| 13 | US 75 S, 30th St, Florence, **E gas:** Shell/dsl, **food:** Firehouse Pizza, Zesto Diner, **lodging:** Mormon Trail Motel, **other:** LDS Temple, Mormon Trail Ctr, **W gas:** Sinclair |
| 12 | US 75 N, 48th St, **E gas:** Phillips 66, **food:** Burger King |
| 9 | 72nd St, **E gas:** QuikShop, (1-3 mi) **food:** Famous Dave's BBQ, IHOP, Sonic, Village Inn, **other:** &#9405; HOSPITAL, **W** Cunningham Lake RA |
| 6 | NE 133, Irvington, **E gas:** Conoco/dsl, **food:** Burger King, **other:** Walmart/Subway/drugs |
| 5 | Fort St, **W gas:** KwikShop, Sinclair, **other:** USPO |
| 4 | NE 64, Maple St, **E gas:** BP, **W** Conoco/dsl, Kum&Go, **food:** Burger King, Godfather's Pizza, KFC, La Mesa Mexican, McDonald's, Perkins, Pizza Hut, Runza, Subway, Taco Bell, **lodging:** Comfort Suites, La Quinta, **other:** Bag'n Save, Champion Parts |
| 3 | US 6, Dodge St, **E food:** Macaroni Grill, Panera Bread, PF Chang's, TGIFriday, **lodging:** Hampton Inn, Marriott, **other:** AAA, BMW, Dodge, Ford, Jaguar/Land Rover, JC Penney, Mazda, Whlle Foods Mkt, Von Maur, mall, **W gas:** BP, Phillips 66, **food:** Boston Mkt, Burger King, China buffet, DQ, McDonald's, Starbucks, **lodging:** Best Western, Crowne Plaza Motel, Super 8, **other:** Cadillac, Chevrolet, Costco/gas, Hummer, Nissan/Hyundai, Saturn, Toyota |
| 2 | Pacific St, **E gas:** BP, **lodging:** Regency Lodge |
| 1 | NE 38, W Center Rd, **E gas:** Cenex/dsl, food Blimpie, Don Carmelo's, Don&Millie's Rest., Garden Cafe, **W gas:** Phillips 66, **food:** Burger King, Ozark BBQ, Wendy's |
| 0mm | I-680 begins/ends on I-80, exit 446 |

## INTERSTATE 15

**N** | **S** | **MESQUITE** | **LAS VEGAS**

**LAS VEGAS**

| Exit # | Services |
|---|---|
| 123mm | Nevada/Arizona state line, Pacific/Mountain time zone |
| 122 | Lp 15, Mesquite, **E** NV **Welcome Ctr both lanes, full** ♿ **facilities, petwalk, gas:** Chevron/Subway/dsl/24hr, Shell/DQ, Sinclair/Arby's, **food:** Burger King, Canton Chinese, Golden West Rest./casino, Jack-in-the-Box, Jamba Juice, KFC, Mia's Mexican, Pizza Hut, Rio Virgin Grill, Thunderbird Rest., **lodging:** Best Western, Budget Inn, Desert Palms Motel, Up Town Motel, **other:** Ace Hardware, AutoZone, Big O Tire, CarQuest, El Rancho Mkt, GNC, Great Outdoors RV, NAPA, Radio Shack, Rite Aid, Smith's Foods, USPO, dsl repair, museum, **W gas:** Virgin River/76/dsl/LP/RV park, **food:** McDonald's, **lodging:** Eureka Motel/casino, Mesquite Springs Motel, Virgin River Hotel/casino |
| 120 | Lp 15, Mesquite, Bunkerville, **E gas:** Arco/24hr, Chevron, Shell/dsl, **food:** Carollo's Rest., Jamba Juice, McDonald's, **lodging:** Casablanca Resort/casino/RV Park, Oasis Resort/casino, Peppermill Resort/casino, Players Island Resort/casino, Valley Inn, **other:** USPO, **W lodging:** Falcon Ridge, **other:** Ⓗ HOSPITAL, Ford, Walmart SuperCtr |
| 112 | NV 170, Riverside, Bunkerville |
| 110mm | **truck parking both lanes, litter barrels** |
| 100 | to Carp, Elgin |
| 96mm | **truck parking nb, litter barrels** |
| 93 | NV 169, to Logandale, Overton, **E gas:** Chevron, **lodging:** Best Western (10mi), **other:** Lake Mead NRA, Lost City Museum |
| 91 | NV 168, Glendale, **W gas:** Sinclair/dsl/rest. |
| 90.5mm | Muddy River |
| 90 | NV 168 (from nb), Glendale, Moapa, **W gas, other:** Moapa Indian Reservation, USPO |
| 88 | Hidden Valley |
| 87.5mm | **parking area both lanes, litter barrels** |
| 84 | Byron |
| 80 | Ute |
| 75 | NV 169 E, Valley of Fire SP, Lake Mead NRA, **E gas:** Sinclair/dsl, **other:** casino, fireworks |
| 64 | US 93 N, Great Basin Hwy, to Ely, Great Basin NP |
| 60mm | livestock check sta sb |
| 58 | NV 604, Las Vegas Blvd, to Apex, Nellis AFB, **E other:** Hitchin' Post RV Park (9mi) |
| 54 | Speedway Blvd, Hollywood Blvd, **E gas:** Petro/Mobil/dsl/24hr/@, **other:** Las Vegas Speedway |
| 52 | rd 215 W |
| 50 | Lamb Ave, **E** Hitchin Post RV Park |
| 48 | Craig Rd, **E gas:** Arco, Pilot/DQ/KFC/Pizza Hut/dsl/scales/24hr, Rebel Gas, Shell, Sinclair/Subway/dsl, **food:** Burger King, Jack-in-the-Box, Zapata's Cantina, **lodging:** Best Western (2mi), Hampton Inn, Super 8, **other:** Firestone, to Nellis AFB, **W gas:** Citgo/7-11, **lodging:** Holiday Inn Express, **other:** Freightliner, dsl repair |
| 46 | Cheyenne Ave, **E gas:** Arco/24hr, Chevron, **food:** Hamburger Hut, Speedway Grill, Starbucks, **lodging:** Ramada Inn/casino, **other:** vet, **W gas:** Citgo/7-11, ⓕ *FLYING J*/dsl/LP/rest./24hr/@, Sinclair/Jack-in-the-Box, **food:** Denny's, McDonald's, **lodging:** Comfort Inn, **other:** Blue Beacon, Kenworth, SpeedCo, dsl repair |
| 45 | Lake Mead Blvd, **E gas:** Chevron, 76/dsl, **food:** Arby's, Burger King, Carl's Jr., Jack-in-the-Box, McDonald's, Wendy's, **other:** GNC, PepBoys, Rite Aid, 7-11, **W gas:** Arco, **food:** A&W/LJ Silver |
| 44 | Washington Ave (from sb), **E lodging:** Best Western, casinos |
| 43 | D St (from nb), **E** Best Western, same as 44 |
| 42b a | I-515 to LV, US 95 N to Reno, US 93 S to Phoenix |
| 41b a | NV 159, Charleston Blvd, **E gas:** Arco/dsl, **other:** antiques, 7-11, Smith's Foods, tire/repair, **W gas:** 76, Terrible/dsl/casino, **food:** Carl's Jr, Del Taco, McDonald's, Wendy's, **lodging: other:** Ⓗ HOSPITAL, CVS Drug |
| 40 | Sahara Ave, **E** The Strip, **lodging:** Artisan Hotel, Vagabond Inn, **other:** Big O Tire, LV Conv Ctr, multiple casinos/hotels, **W gas:** Chevron, Rebel Gas, 7-11/gas, **food:** Arby's, Blimpie, Burger King, Carl's Jr, Denny's, In-n-Out, Jose Hoggs Rest, KFC, Landry's Seafood, Macaroni Grill, McDonald's, Pizza Hut, Shilla BBQ, TGI-Friday's, Wendy's, vet, **lodging:** Palace Station Hotel/casino, **other:** Chevrolet, CVS Drug, Food4Less, Home Depot, Liffy Lube, Lexus, Mazda, Mercedes, Mitsubishi, Office Depot, Rite Aid |
| 39 | Spring Mtn Rd (from sb), **E lodging:** Budget Suites, Frontier Hotel, **other:** Mirage, Treasure Island, **W gas:** Arco/24hr, Circle K, United/dsl, **food:** Schlotsky's, **other:** EconoLube/Tune, Discount Tire, Firestone/auto, Goodyear/auto, Lexus, Mercedes, auto/transmission repair |
| 38b a | Dunes Flamingo Rd, **E** The Strip, **lodging:** Bellagio, Caesar's Palace, Flamingo Hilton, Mirage, Monte Carlo, to UNLV, multiple casinos/hotels, **W gas:** Arco/24hr, Chevron, 76/Del Taco, **food:** Burger King, Outback Steaks, Starbucks, Subway, **lodging:** Gold Coast Hotel, Palms Hotel, Rio Hotel, **other:** Terrible Herbst/wash/lube |
| 37 | Tropicana Ave, **E gas:** 76, **food:** Coco's Rest, McDonald's, **lodging:** Bellagio, Excaliber Hotel, Hooters, Mandalay Bay, MGM Grand, Monte Carlo, Motel 6, Tropicana Hotel, **other:** ✈, casinos/hotels, **W gas:** Arco/24hr, Chevron/dsl, 76, Shell/Subway, **food:** Burger King, IHOP, In-n-Out, Jack-in-the-Box, KFC, McDonald's, Taco Bell, Taco's Mexico, Wendy's, **lodging:** Best Western, Budget Suites, Golden Palm, Hampton Inn, La Quinta, Motel 6, Orleans Hotel |
| 36 | Russell Rd, **E lodging:** Mandalay Bay, **other:** casinos, to ✈, **W gas:** Chevron/Herbst/dsl, **lodging:** Courtyard, Fairfield Inn, Holiday Inn Express, Residence Inn |
| 34 | to I-215 E, Las Vegas Blvd, to The Strip, McCarran ✈ |
| 33 | NV 160, to Blue Diamond, Death Valley, **E gas:** Chevron, Citgo/7-11/dsl, **food:** Bootlegger Bistro, Chili's, Canes Rest, Cipotle Mexican, IHOP, La Cosina Mexican, McDonald's, Outback Steaks, Panda Express, Popeyes, Quizno's, Starbucks, Subway, Wienerschnitzel, **lodging:** Budget Suites, Hilton Garden, Microtel, **other:** CVS Drug, Food4Less, Oasis RV Resort, factory outlet/famous brands, **W gas:** Chevron/dsl, TA/Burger King/TacoTime/dsl/LP/scales/24hr/@, Shell, **food:** Bilbo's Grill, Del Taco, Jack-in-the-Box, Subway, **lodging:** Firebird Inn, **other:** Bass ProShops, Kohl's, Office Depot, PetCo, Ross, Silverton Lodge/casino, Target, WorldMkt |
| 31 | Silverado Ranch Blvd, **S lodging:** South Point Hotel/Casino |
| 27 | NV 146, to Henderson, Lake Mead, Hoover Dam, **E gas:** Arco, Chevron, **food:** Jack-in-the-Box, |

## INTERSTATE 15 CONT'D

| | |
|---|---|
| 27 | Continued **2 mi E other:** Camping World, factory outlets |
| 25 | NV 161, Sloan, **1 mi E** Camping World |
| 24mm | bus/truck check sta nb |
| 12 | NV 161, to Goodsprings, Jean, **E** Welcome Ctr nb, **gas:** Mobil/dsl, **other:** Gold Strike Casino/hotel/ Burger King, USPO, sky- diving, **W gas:** Shell/dsl, **other:** Nevada Landing Casino/dsl/24hr, NV Cor- rectional |
| 1 | Primm, **E gas:** Chevron, 76/dsl, **food:** Carl's Jr, Food Ct., McDonald's, Starbucks, **other:** Buffalo Bill's Resort/casino, Primm Val- ley Resort/casino, Prima Donna RV Park, **NV Welcome Ctr**, factory out- lets, **W gas:** Shell/dsl/scales, **lodging:** Whiskey Pete's Hotel/casino/steaks |
| 0mm | Nevada/California state line |

## INTERSTATE 80

| Exit # | Services |
|---|---|
| 411mm | Nevada/Utah state line, Pacific/Mountain time zone |
| 410 | US 93A, to Ely, W Wendover, **S NV Welcome Ctr/info, full ♿ facilities, Ⓒ, gas:** Chevron/24hr, Pilot/Arby's/ dsl/scales/24hr, Shell/dsl, **food:** Burger King, McDon- ald's, Pizza Hut, Subway, **lodging:** Best Value, Day's Inn, Knights Inn, Motel 6, Nugget Hotel/casino, Pep- permill Hotel/casino/RV parking, Rainbow Hotel/ca- sino, Red Garter Hotel/casino, **other:** Best Hardware, Smith's Foods, StateLine RV Park, KOA |
| 407 | Ola, W Wendover |
| 405mm | pacific/central time zone |
| 398 | to Pilot Peak |
| 390mm | Silverzone Pass, Silverzone Pass, elev 5940 |
| 387 | to Shafter |
| 378 | NV 233, to Montello, Oasis, no faciles |
| 376 | to Pequop |
| 373mm | **Pequop Summit, elev 6967, rest area both lanes, 🏕 litter barrels, rest rooms** |
| 365 | to Independence Valley, **N** prison facilities |
| 360 | to Moor |
| 354mm | parking area eb |
| 352b a | US 93, Great Basin Hwy, E Wells, **N gas:** ⊕FLYING J /dsl/café/casino, Shell, **food:** Bella's Diner, Burger King, **lodging:** LoneStar Motel, Motel 6, Rest Inn Motel, Sha- ron Motel, Super 8, **other:** Crossroads RV Park, Four- Way Casino/Rest., Les Schwab, tuckwash, **S gas:** ⊕FLYING J/Conoco/cookery/dsl/scales/LP/casino/ RV Dump/24hr, Love's/McDonalds/dsl/scales/24hr, **other:** Great Basin NP |
| 351 | W Wells, **N gas:** Tesoro/dsl, **lodging:** Wagon Wheel Rest., **other:** Mtn Shadows RV Park, NAPA, |

| | |
|---|---|
| 351 | Continued Stuart's Foods, Well's Hardware, USPO, to Angel Lake RA, **S other:** Angel Lake RV Park |
| 348 | to Beverly Hills, **N** RV camping |
| 343 | to Welcome, Starr Valley, **N** Welcome RV Park, Ⓒ, food |
| 333 | Deeth, Starr Valley |
| 328 | to River Ranch |
| 321 | NV 229, Halleck, Ruby Valley |
| 318mm | N Fork Humboldt River |
| 317 | to Elburz |
| 314 | to Ryndon, Devils Gate, **N gas:** Sinclair/cafe/dsl, **S** RV camping |
| 312mm | check sta both lanes |
| 310 | to Osino, **4 mi S** Valley View RV Park |
| 303 | E Elko, **N gas:** CFN/dsl, Sinclair/Arctic Circle/dsl/24hr, **food:** Wingers, **S gas:** Chevron/24hr, Conoco/dsl, Maverik, Sinclair, Tesoro/dsl, **food:** Burger King, Chef Cheng's Chinese, DQ, JR's Grill, King Buffet, McDon- ald's/playplace, Monkey Sun Chinese, Pizza Barn, |

NV

E

## INTERSTATE 80 CONT'D

| | |
|---|---|
| **303** | **Continued** |
| | Pizza Hut, Ruby Sta. Rest., Subway, Taco Time, Toki Ona Diner, Wendy's, **lodging:** Budget Inn, Comfort Inn, Day's Inn, Econolodge, Elko Inn, High Desert Inn, Hilton Garden, Holiday Inn Express, Holiday Hotel, Microtel, Motel 6, Red Lion Inn/casino, Super 8, Travelodge, **other:** H HOSPITAL, Albertson's, Buick/Cadillac/GMC, Cal Store, Chevrolet/Pontiac, Chrysler/Jeep/Toyota/Honda, Double Dice RV Park, Ford, Gold Country RV Park, Goodyear/auto, Iron Horse RV Park, JC Penney, Lincoln/Mercury, NAPA, Radio Shack, USPO |
| **301** | NV 225, Elko, **N gas:** Maverik, **food:** Arby's, Coffee Mug Rest., Greatwall Chinese, Mattie's Grill, McDonald's/playplace, Papa Murphy's, Port of Subs, RoundTable Pizza, **lodging:** OakTree Inn, Shilo Inn Suites, **other:** GNC, Home Depot, K-Mart, Raley's Foods, True Value, Walmart Super Ctr/auto, **S gas:** Shell, Texaco/dsl/RV park, **food:** Cimarron West Rest., Dominos, Dos Amigos, KFC, Starbucks, Taco Bell, **lodging:** American Inn, Arctic Circle, Centre Motel, Esquire Motel, Key Motel, Manor Inn, Midtown Motel, Rodeway Inn, Stampede Motel, Stockmen's Hotel/casino, Thunderbird Motel, **other:** H HOSPITAL, CarQuest, Checker Parts, CVS Drug, Famliy$, Parts+, Roy's Foods, Smith's Foods/24hr, casino/rest., ✈ |
| **298** | W Elko |
| **292** | to Hunter |
| **285mm** | tunnel |
| **285mm** | Humboldt River |
| **282** | NV 221, E Carlin, **N** prison area |
| **280** | NV 766, Carlin, **N other:** Desert Gold RV Park, dsl repair, **S gas:** Pilot/Subway/dsl/scales/24hr, Texaco/Burger King/dsl, **food:** Chin's Cafe, Pizza Factory, State Café/casino, **lodging:** Cavalier Motel, Comfort Inn, **other:** Ace Hardware, USPO, tires |
| **279** | NV 278 (from eb), to W Carlin, **1 mi S** gas/dsl |
| **271** | to Palisade |
| **270mm** | Emigrant Summit, elev 6114, **truck parking both lanes, litter barrels** |
| **268** | to Emigrant |
| **261** | NV 306, to Beowawe, Crescent Valley |
| **258mm** | **rest area both lanes, full** ♿ **facilities,** 🚻, **litter barrels, petwalk** |
| **257mm** | Humboldt River |
| **254** | to Dunphy |
| **244** | to Argenta |
| **233** | NV 304, to Battle Mountain, **N gas:** Conoco/dsl/24hr, **food:** Mama's Pizza/deli, **lodging:** Comfort Inn, **other:** H HOSPITAL, FoodTown, Royal Harware |
| **231** | NV 305, Battle Mountain, **N gas:** Chevron/dsl/24hr, Quickmart/pizza, **food:** Hide-a-way Steaks, McDonald's, **lodging:** Super 8, **other:** CarQuest, Mills Drug, NAPA, USPO, **1 mi N gas:** ⊕FLYING J/Exxon/Blimpie/dsl/casino/24hr, **food:** El Aguila Mexican, Owl Rest., **lodging:** Big Chief Motel, Nevada Hotel, **other:** H HOSPITAL, NAPA, Tire Factory, True Value |
| **229** | NV 304, W Battle Mountain, **N gas:** ⊕FLYING J/Blimpie/dsl/casino/scales/24hr, Shell/dsl, **lodging:** Battle Mtn. Inn, Big Cheif Motel, **other:** Colt RV camping, NAPA |
| **222** | to Mote |
| **216** | Valmy, **N gas:** Shell/USPO/dsl/24hr, **S rest area both lanes, full** ♿ **facilities,** 🚻, **litter barrels, petwalk, RV dump** |

W
ELKO
CARLIN
BATTLE MTN

| | |
|---|---|
| **212** | to Stonehouse |
| **205** | to Pumpernickel Valley |
| **203** | to Iron Point |
| **200** | Golconda Summit, Golconda Summit, elev 5145, truck parking area both lanes, litter barrels |
| **194** | Golconda, **N food:** Waterhole #1 Cafe, **other:** USPO |
| **187** | to Button Point, **N rest area both lanes, full** ♿ **facilities,** 🚻, **litter barrels, petwalk, RV dump** |
| **180** | NV 794, E Winnemucca Blvd |
| **178** | NV 289, Winnemucca Blvd, Winnemucca, **S gas:** Chevron, Maverik, Sinclair, **food:** Las Margaritas, Rte 66 Grill, **lodging:** Budget Inn, Cozy Motel, Frontier Motel, Scott Motel, Valu Motel, **other:** CarQuest, carwash |
| **176** | US 95 N, Winnemucca, **N gas:** Pacific Pride/dsl, **S gas:** Chevron/dsl/24hr, ⊕FLYING J/Conoco/dsl/LP/rest./RV dump/24hr, Mirastar, Shell/dsl, Texaco, **food:** A&W, Arby's, Burger King, Dos Amigos Mexican, Griddle Rest., Jack-in-the-Box, KFC, LJ Silver, McDonald's/playplace, Pizza Hut, RoundTable Pizza, San Fermin Rest., Sid's Rest., Subway, Taco Time, Twin Wok Chinese, **lodging:** Best Western, Day's Inn, Economy Inn, Holiday Motel, Motel 6, Park Hotel, Pyrenees Motel, Quality Inn, Red Lion Inn/casino, Regency Inn, Santa Fe Inn, Scottish Inn, Super 8, **other:** H HOSPITAL, AutoZone, Ford/Mercury, Freightliner, Kragen Parts, Raley's Foods, Walmart SuperCtr, RV camping, auto/truck repair, casino |
| **173** | W Winnemucca, **N gas:** Pilot/Subway/dsl/scales/24hr, **S** ✈ |
| **168** | to Rose Creek, **S** prison area |
| **158** | to Cosgrave, **S rest area both lanes, full** ♿ **facilities,** 🚻, **litter barrels, petwalk** |
| **151** | Mill City, **N gas:** TA/Subway/Taco Bell/Fork/dsl/casino/24hr/@, **lodging:** Knight's Inn |
| **149** | NV 400, Mill City, **1 mi N gas:** TA/Subway/Taco Bell/Fork/dsl/24hr/@, **lodging:** Knights Inn, **S** Star Point Gen. Sore/RV camping |
| **145** | Imlay |
| **138** | Humboldt |
| **129** | Rye Patch Dam, **N food:** Oasis Pizza, **other:** to Rye Patch SRA, **S gas:** Rye Patch Trkstp/dsl |
| **119** | to Rochester, Oreana |
| **112** | to Coal Canyon, **S** to correctional ctr |
| **107** | E Lovelock (from wb), same as 106 |
| **106** | Main St, Lovelock, **N gas:** Chevron/dsl/LP, PJ's Gas/subs/dsl, Two Stiffs, **food:** Cowpoke Cafe, McDonald's, Pizza Factory, Ricardo's BBQ, **lodging:** Cadillac Inn, Covered Wagon Motel, Royal Inn, Sturgeons Motel/rest., Super 10 Inn, **other:** H HOSPITAL, Ace Hardware, Lazy K Camping, Safeway Foods, city park/playground/restrooms, dsl repair |
| **105** | W Lovelock (from eb), **N gas:** Shell/dsl, Shop'n Go/dsl, **food:** La Cacita Mexican, **lodging:** Lovelock Inn/rest., **other:** H HOSPITAL, Brookwood RV Park, NAPA, museum, same as 106 |
| **93** | to Toulon, **S** ✈ |
| **83** | US 95 S, to Fallon, **S rest area both lanes, full** ♿ **facilities,** 🚻, **litter barrels** |
| **78** | to Jessup |
| **65** | to Hot Springs, Nightingale |
| **48** | US 50A, US 95A, to Fallon, E Fernley, **N gas:** Texaco/dsl, Truck Inn Travel Plaza/dsl/scales/24hr, **other:** RV camping, truckwash, **S gas:** Shell/dsl/24hr, Siverado/dsl, **food:** Bully's Grill, Burger King, Domino's, Jack-in-the-Box, KFC, Louie's China, McDonald's, Pizza |

WINNEMUCCA
LOVELOCK

## INTERSTATE 80 CONT'D

E ↕ W

**48** Continued
Factory, Port Of Subs, Quizno's, Siverado Rest./casino, Starbucks, Subway, Taco Bell, **lodging:** Best Western, Super 8, **other:** AutoZone, Curves, D&D Tires, Kragen Parts, Lowe's Whse, Radio Shack, Scolari's Foods, Walmart SuperCtr, USPO, casinos, to Great Basin NP

**46** US 95A, W Fernley, N **gas:** Love's/Arby's/scales/dsl, S **gas:** Pilot/DQ/Wendy's/dsl/24hr, **food:** Chukars Grill/Casino, **other:** Blue Beacon, SpeedCo

**45mm** Truckee River

**43** to Pyramid Lake, Wadsworth, N **gas:** Pyramid Lake gas/dsl/RV camping

**42mm** rest area wb, full ♿ facilities, 🚻, 🏕, litter barrels, petwalk, wireless internet, check sta eb

**40** Painted Rock

**38** Orchard

**36** Derby Dam

**32** USA Pkwy, Tracy, Clark Station

**28** NV 655, Waltham Way, Patrick

**27mm** scenic view, eb

**25mm** check sta wb

**23** Mustang, N **other:** RV camping, S Chevron/dsl

**22** Lockwood

**21** Vista Blvd, Greg St, Sparks, N **gas:** Chevron/McDonald's, QwikStop, **food:** Del Taco, **lodging:** Fairfield Inn, **other:** H HOSPITAL, S **gas:** Petro/Iron Skillet/dsl/rest./24hr/@, **lodging:** Super 8, **other:** Freightliner, truckwash

**20** Sparks Blvd, Sparks, N **gas:** Shell/dsl/24hr, **food:** Best Buy, Outback Steaks, Subway, **other:** Sheel's Sports, Target, water funpark, S **gas:** Petro/dsl/rest./24hr/@, **lodging:** Super 8

**19** E McCarran Blvd, Sparks, N **gas:** Chevron/dsl, TA/76/dsl/scales/rest./@, Sinclair, Texaco, **food:** Applebee's, Black Bear Diner, Burger King, El Pollo Loco, Hong Kong Kitchen, IHOP, Jack-in-the-Box, KFC, Little Caesars, McDonald's, Pollo Loco, Quizno's, Sizzler, Taco Bell, Wendy's, Wienerschnitzel, **lodging:** Aloha Inn, Sunrise Motel, Windsor Inn, **other:** BigLots, CVS Drug, $Tree, Kragen Parts, Longs Drugs, Pep Boys, Radio Shack, Savemart Foods, Victorian RV Park, S **food:** Denny's, Super Burrito, **lodging:** Holiday Inn, **other:** NAPA Autocare

**18** NV 445, Pyramid Way (from eb), Sparks, N **gas:** 7-11/gas, **food:** In-N-Out, **lodging:** Nugget Courtyard, Silver Club Hotel/casino, S **lodging:** Nugget Hotel/casino

**17** Rock Blvd, Nugget Ave, Sparks, N **gas:** Arco/24hr, Chevron, 76, **lodging:** Victorian Inn, Wagon Train Motel, **other:** Kragen Parts, casinos, S **lodging:** Nugget Hotel/casino

**16** B St, E 4th St, Victorian Ave, N **gas:** Arco/24hr, Texaco, **lodging:** Motel 6, **other:** Rail City Casino, S **gas:** Chevron/repair

**15** US 395, to Carson City, 1 mi N on McCarran Blvd... **gas:** Chevron, Shell/dsl, **food:** Arby's, Burger King, Del Taco, Szechuan Chinese, Sonic, Subway, Taco Bell, TCBY, Wendy's, **other:** Home Depot, Kragen Parts, Ross, Walmart/auto, WinCo Foods, S **food:** Bally's, **lodging:** Hilton/Casino, Holiday Inn, 6 Gun Motel

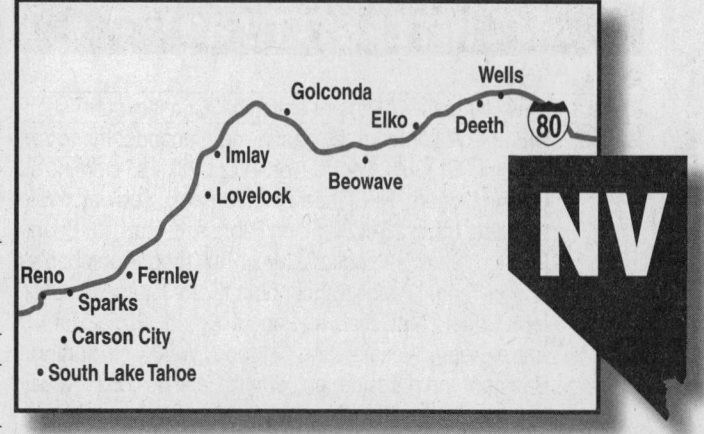

**14** Wells Ave, Reno, N **lodging:** Motel 6, S **gas:** Chevron, Shell, **food:** Carrow's Rest., Denny's, **lodging:** Day's Inn, Econolodge, Super 8, **other:** Goodyear

**13** US 395, Virginia St, Reno, N **gas:** Shell, **food:** JimBoy's Taco's, S **gas:** Shell/dsl, **other:** H HOSPITAL, Circus Circus, NAPA, Walgreens, to downtown hotels/casinos, to UNVReno

**12** Keystone Ave, Reno, N **gas:** Arco/24hr, 76, **food:** Pizza Hut, Rose Garden Asian, Starbucks, **lodging:** Gateway Inn, Motel 6, **other:** CVS Drug, Raley's Foods, 7-11, S **gas:** Chevron, Texaco, **food:** Baskin-Robbins, Burger King, Jack-in-the-Box, KFC, McDonald's, Pizza Baron, Port of Subs, Round Table Pizza, Taco Bell, Wendy's, **other:** Kragen Parts, Meineke, Midas, Radio Shack, Savemart/drug, casinos, RV park

**10** McCarran Blvd, Reno, N **gas:** Arco/24hr, 7-11, **food:** Arby's, Asian Wok, Burger King, Bully's Grill, Carl's Jr, Chili's, Del Taco, DQ, El Pollo Loco, Hacienda Mexican, IHOP, Jack-in-the-Box, KFC, Keva Juice, McDonald's, Papa Murphy's, Pizza+, Port Of Subs, Qdoba, Quizno's, RoundTable Pizza, Starbucks, Subway, Taco Bell, The Chocolate Factory, **other:** Big O Tire, Curves, $Tree, Kohl's, Kragen Parts, PetsMart, Ross, Safeway/dsl, Savemart Foods, Tires+, Walgreens, Walmart Super Ctr, S **gas:** 7-11/gas, **other:** URGENT CARE, Home Depot, vet

**9** Robb Dr, N **gas:** Chevron/dsl, **food:** Bully's Grill, Coldstone, Dominos, Jimmy John's, Moxi's Cafe, Papa John's, Port Of Subs, Starbucks, Subway, Tahoe Burger, **other:** AAA, Longs Drug, Raley's Foods, Scolari's Foods

**8** W 4th St (from eb), Robb Dr, Reno, S RV camping

**7** Mogul

**6.5mm** truck parking/hist marker/scenic view both lanes

**5** to E Verdi (from wb), N Backstop Grill

**4.5mm** scenic view eb

**4** Garson Rd, Boomtown, N **gas:** Chevron/Boomtown Hotel/dsl/casino, **other:** Cabela's, KOA/RV dump

**3.5mm** check sta eb

**3** Verdi (from wb)

**2.5mm** Truckee River

**2** Lp 80, to Verdi, N **gas:** Terribles/Chevron/dsl/24hr, **food:** Jack-in-the-Box, Taco Bell, **lodging:** Gold Ranch Hotel/casino

**0mm** Nevada/California state line

## INTERSTATE 89

| Exit # | Services |
|---|---|
| 61mm | New Hampshire/Vermont state line, Connecticut River |
| 20 (60) | NH 12A, W Lebanon, **E gas:** Irving, Sunoco/24hr, **food:** Benning St Grill, Brick Oven Pizza, Chili's, Domino's, Dunkin Donuts, KFC/Taco Bell, 99 Rest., Subway, Wok Chinese, **other:** GNC, Jo-Ann Fabrics, K-Mart, LL Bean, Rite Aid, Shaw's Foods, TJ Maxx, **W food:** Applebee's, Burger King, D'angelo, Friendly's, Koto Japanese, Lantern Buffet, McDonald's, Panera Bread, Pizza Hut, 7 Barrel Rest., Weathervane Seafood, Wendy's, **lodging:** Baymont Inn, Fireside Inn, **other:** Best Buy, BJ' Whse, Borders Books, CVS Drug, $Tree, Home Depot, JC Penney, PriceChopper Foods, Radio Shack, Sears, Shaw's Foods, Staples, Walgreens, Walmart |
| 19 (58) | US 4, NH 10, W Lebanon, **E gas:** Exxon/dsl/24hr, Shell, **food:** China Station, **other:** AutoZone, Family$, Ford, Harley-Davidson, Honda, NAPA, P&C Foods, **W gas:** Sunoco |
| 57mm | **Welcome Ctr/rest area/weigh sta sb, full** &#9855; **facilities,** &#9993;, &#127869;, **litter barrels, vending, petwalk, weigh sta nb** |
| 18 (56) | NH 120, Lebanon, **E lodging:** Courtyard (3mi), Day's Inn, Residence Inn (2mi), **other:** Buick/Pontiac/GMC, Chevrolet/Cadillac/VW, Dodge/Mazda, Nissan/Jeep/Volvo, Wilson Tire/repair, to Dartmouth Coll, **W gas:** Citgo/dsl, Shell, **other:** H HOSPITAL, U-Haul |
| 17 (54) | US 4, to NH 4A, Enfield, **E food:** Riverside Grill, Shaker Museum, **other:** Northern States Tire |
| 16 (52) | Eastman Hill Rd, **E gas:** Exxon/Subway/dsl/24hr, **W gas:** Mobil/Dunkin Donuts/dsl/24hr, **other:** Whaleback Ski Area |
| 15 (50) | Montcalm |
| 14 (47) | NH 10 (from sb), N Grantham |
| 13 (43) | NH 10, Grantham, **E gas:** Valero/dsl/Gen Store, **W gas:** Irving/Dunkin Donuts/repair, **food:** Pizza Chef |
| 40mm | **rest area nb, full** &#9855; **facilities, info,** &#9993;, &#127869;, **litter barrels, vending, petwalk** |
| 12a (37) | Georges Mills, **W other:** to Sunapee SP, food, &#9993;, lodging, RV camping |
| 12 (34) | NH 11 W, New London, **2 mi E gas:** Exxon/dsl, **food:** McKenna Rest., Peter Christian's Tavern, **lodging:** Maple Hill Country Inn, New London Inn, **other:** H HOSPITAL |
| 11 (31) | NH 11 E, King Hill Rd, New London, **2 mi E lodging:** Fairway Motel, ski area, food, **2 mi W lodging:** Shaker Mtg House B&B |
| 10 (27) | to NH 114, Sutton, **E** to Winslow SP, **1 mi W** lodging, to Wadleigh SB |
| 26mm | **rest area sb, full** &#9855; **facilities, info,** &#9993;, &#127869;, **litter barrels, vending, petwalk** |
| 9 (19) | NH 103, Warner, **E gas:** Citgo/Subway/Pizza Hut, Irving/Dunkin Donuts/dsl/24hr, **food:** Charlie's Pizza (1mi), McDonald's, **other:** Aubuscon Hardware, Mkt-Basket Foods, Rollins SP, **W** to Sunapee SP, ski area |
| 8 (17) | NH 103 (from nb, no EZ return), Warner, **1 mi E** gas, food, museum, to Rollins SP |
| 15mm | Warner River |
| 7 (14) | NH 103, Davisville, **E** camping, **W** Pleasant Lake Camping |
| 12mm | Contoocook River |

| Exit # | Services |
|---|---|
| 6 (10) | NH 127, Contoocook, **1 mi E gas:** Sunoco, **W other:** Elm Brook Park, Sandy Beach Camping (3mi) |
| 5 (8) | US 202 W, NH 9 (exits left from nb), Hopkinton, **W** food, RV camping (seasonal) |
| 4 (7) | NH 103, Hopkinton (from nb, no EZ return), **E** Horse-Shoe Tavern, gas |
| 3 (4) | Stickney Hill Rd (from nb) |
| 2 (2) | NH 13, Clinton St, Concord, **E** H HOSPITAL, food, **W** NH Audubon Ctr |
| 1 (1) | Logging Hill Rd, Bow, **E gas:** Mobil/24hr, **food:** Chen Yang Li Chinese, **lodging:** Hampton Inn |
| 0mm | I-93 N to Concord, S to Manchester, I-89 begins/ends on I-93, 36mm. |

## INTERSTATE 93

| Exit # | Services |
|---|---|
| 2 (11) | I-91, N to St Johnsbury, S to White River Jct. I-93 begins/ends on I-91, exit 19. |
| 1 (8) | VT 18, to US 2, to St Johnsbury, **2 mi E** gas, food, lodging, camping |
| 1mm | **Welcome Ctr nb, full** &#9855; **facilities, info,** &#9993;, &#127869;, **litter barrels, vending, petwalk** |
| 131mm | Vermont/New Hampshire state line. Connecticut River exits 1-2 are in VT., |
| 44 (130) | NH 18, NH 135, **W Welcome Ctr (8am-8pm)/scenic vista both lanes, full** &#9855; **facilities, info,** &#9993;, &#127869;, **litter barrels, petwalk** |
| 43 (125) | NH 135 (from sb), to NH 18, Littleton, **1-2 mi W** H HOSPITAL, same as 42 |
| 42 (124) | US 302 E, NH 10 N, Littleton, **E gas:** Citgo/Quizno's, Gulf, Sunoco/24hr, **food:** Burger King, Cantida de Gerardo, Deluxe Pizza, Dunkin Donuts, Jing Fong Chinese, Littleton Diner, McDonald's, Pizza Hut, Subway, **other:** Parts+, Rite Aid, Walgreens, **W gas:** Mobil, **food:** Applebee's, Asian Garden Chinese, 99 Rest., **lodging:** Continental Inn, Hampton Inn, Littleton Motel, **other:** Aubuchon Hardware, Bond Parts, Buick/Chevrolet/Pontiac, Chrysler/Dodge/Jeep, $Tree, Home Depot, KOA (5mi), Lowes Whse, Shaw's Foods/Osco Drug, Staples, Tire Whse, TJ Maxx, VIP Parts/repair, Walmart/drug, camping |
| 41 (122) | US 302, NH 18, NH 116, Littleton, **E gas:** Irving/dsl/24hr, **lodging:** Eastgate Motel/rest., **W other:** NE Tire |
| 40 (121) | US 302, NH 10 E, Bethlehem, **E lodging:** Adair Country Inn/Rest., **other:** to Mt Washington |
| 39 (119) | NH 116, NH 18 (from sb), N Franconia, Sugar Hill, **W** lodging |
| 38 (117) | NH 116, NH 117, NH 142, NH 18, Sugar Hill, **E food:** Shaw's Rest., **lodging:** Best Western, **W gas:** Mobil, **food:** DutchTreat Rest., Franconia Seafood Dairybar, **lodging:** Franconia Inn (2mi), **other:** Frost Museum, Mac's Mkt, TrueValue, USPO, camping, gifts, info |
| 37 (115) | NH 142, NH 18 (from nb), Franconia, Bethlehem, **E food:** Farmhouse Rest., **lodging:** Cannon Mtn View Motel, Stonybrook Motel |
| 36 (114) | NH 141, to US 3, S Franconia, **W** golf, food, lodging |
| 35 (113) | US 3 N (from nb), to Twin Mtn Lake |
| 112mm | S Franconia, Franconia Notch SP begins sb |
| 34c (111) | NH 18, Echo Beach Ski Area, view area, info |
| 34b | Cannon Mtn Tramway, **W other:** Boise Rock, Old Man Viewing, Lafayette Place Camping |

**NH**

N ↕ S

**W O O D S T O C K**

## INTERSTATE 93 CONT'D

| | |
|---|---|
| **109mm** | trailhead parking |
| **108mm** | Lafayette Place Camping (from sb), trailhead parking |
| **107mm** | The Basin |
| **34a** | US 3, The Flume Gorge, info, camping (seasonal) |
| **104mm** | Franconia Notch SP begins nb |

**33** (103) US 3, N Woodstock, **E gas:** Irving/dsl, **food:** Dad's Rest., Frescolones Pizza, Longhorn Palace Rest., Notchview Country Kitchen, **lodging:** Beacon Resort, Econolodge, Green Village Cottages, Mt Coolidge Motel, Pemi Motel, Profile Motel, Red Doors Motel, Woodward's Resort/Rest., **other:** Indian Head viewing, to Franconia Notch SP, waterpark, **W lodging:** Country Bumpkin Cottages/RV Park, Cozy Cabins, Mt Liberty Motel, White Mtn Motel, **other:** Clark's Trading Post, Cold Springs Camping, Tim's Repair

**32** (101) NH 112, Loon Mtn Rd, N Woodstock, **E gas:** Irving, Mobil, Shell/dsl, **food:** Bill&Bob's Roast Beef, Brittani's Cafe, Cheng Chinese, Dunkin Donuts, Elvio's Pizza, Flapjack's Pancakes, Fratello's Rest., George's Rest., GH Pizza, Gordi's Fish&Steaks, McDonald's, Mr. W's Pancakes, Mtn View Pizza, Nacho's Mexican Grill, Subway, **lodging:** Comfort Inn, Inn Season Resorts, Kancamagu's Lodge, Lincoln Sta. Lodge, Nordic Inn, River Green Hotel, **other:** Aubuchon Hardware, CarQuest, Family$, P&C Foods, Rite Aid, USPO, to North Country Art Ctr, **W gas:** Citgo, Mobil, **food:** Emperial Palace Japanese, Landmark II Rest., Lafayette Dinner Train, Peg's Café, Truant's Rest., **lodging:** Alpine Lodge, Autumn Breeze Motel, Cascade Lodge, Carriage Motel, Woodstock Inn/rest., **other:** NAPA, USPO, candy/fudge/gifts

**31** (97) to NH 175, Tripoli Rd, **E** RV camping (seasonal), **W** KOA (2mi)

**30** (95) US 3, Woodstock, **E food:** Tony's Rest., **lodging:** Jack-O-Lantern Inn/rest., **other:** golf, **W** flea mkt, RV camping (seasonal)

**29** (89) US 3, Thornton, **E** Pemi River RV Park/LP, **W lodging:** Gilcrest Motel

**28** (87) NH 49, Campton, **E gas:** Citgo, Mobil, **food:** Bella Pizza, Dunkin Donuts, **other:** Handy Man Hardware, USPO, to ski area, RV camping, **W gas:** Citgo/dsl, **food:** Sunset Grill, **other:** Branch Brook Camping, Chesley's Glory Sta., Mtn Vista RV Park

**27** (84) Blair Rd, Beebe River, **E food:** Country Cow Rest., **lodging:** Day's Inn, Red Sleigh Condos

**P L Y M O U T H**

**26** (83) US 3, NH 25, NH 3A, Tenney Mtn Hwy, **W** on US 3... **food:** McDonald's, **lodging:** Common Man Inn, Pilgrim Inn, Red Roof Inn, **other:** Ⓗ HOSPITAL

**25** (81) NH 175 (from nb), Plymouth, **W gas:** Irving/dsl, Mobil, **food:** Bro's Pizza, HongKong Garden, Subway, Thai Smile, **other:** Ⓗ HOSPITAL, Chase St Mkt, USPO, to Holderness SchoolSt Coll

**24** (76) US 3, NH 25, Ashland, **E gas:** Gulf, Irving/dsl, Mobil/dsl, **food:** Ashland Pizza, Burger King, Common Man Diner, Dunkin Dounts, John's Cafe, Lucky Dragon Chinese, Village Grill, **lodging:** Lakes Region Inn, **other:**

**24** (76) Continued
AutoValue Parts, Bob's Foods, Jellystone RV Camp (4mi), TrueValue, USPO, repair

**23** (71) NH 104, NH 132, to Mt Washington Valley, New Hampton, **E gas:** Citgo/dsl, Irving/dsl/24hr, **food:** Dunkin Donuts, Quizno's, Rossi Italian, Subway, **other:** New Hampton Parts, info, USPO, **W food:** Homestead Rest. (2mi), **other:** RV Park (2mi), ski area

**22** (62) NH 127, Sanbornton, **1-5 mi W other:** Ⓗ HOSPITAL, gas/dsl, food, Ⓒ

**61mm** rest area sb, full ♿ facilities, info, Ⓒ, 🏕, litter barrels, vending, petwalk

**20** (57) US 3, NH 11, NH 132, NH 140, Tilton, **E gas:** Exxon/Subway/dsl/24hr, Irving/dsl/24hr, **food:**

**N** ↕ **S**

NH

### INTERSTATE 93 CONT'D

**20** (57) Continued
Applebees, Burger King, Chicago Grill, Dunkin Donuts, Green Ginger Chinese, KFC, McDonald's, 99 Rest., Pizzaria Uno, Starbucks, Thai Cuisine, Tilt'n Diner, UpperCrust Pizza, Wendy's, **lodging:** Hampton Inn, Super 8, **other:** BJ's Whse/gas, Home Depot, Tanger Outlet/ famous brands, Shaw's Foods/Osco Drug, Staples, VIP Auto, **W food:** Chili's, Pizza Hut, **other:** Chrysler/ Dodge/Jeep, Ford, Kohl's, Lowes Whse, MktBasket Foods, USPO, Walmart/auto

**56mm** Winnipesaukee River

**19** (55) NH 132 (from nb), Franklin, **W gas:** Exxon, **other:** H HOSPITAL, NH Vet Home, antiques

**51mm** **rest area nb, full** & **facilities,** (, **info,** 🎪, **litter barrels, vending, petwalk**

**18** (49) to NH 132, Canterbury, **E gas:** Sunoco, **other:** to Shaker Village HS

**17** (46) US 4 W, to US 3, NH 132, Boscawen, **4 mi W**...gas

**16** (41) NH 132, E Concord, **E gas:** Mobil/dsl, **other:** Quality Cash Mkt

**15W** (40) US 202 W, to US 3, N Main St, Concord, **W gas:** Citgo, Gulf, Hess, **food:** Domino's, Friendly's, **lodging:** Courtyard/café

**15E** I-393 E, US 4 E, to Portsmouth

**14** (39) NH 9, Loudon Rd, Concord, **E gas:** Shell, **food:** Boston Mkt, Chicago Grill, Family Buffet, Outback Steaks, Panera Bread, **other:** AAA, Ace Hardware, AutoZone, Borders Books, $Tree, GNC, Hannaford Foods, LLBean, Mkt Basket Foods, Radio Shack, Rite Aid, Shaw Foods/24hr, Staples, TJ Maxx, USPO, **1-2 mi E on Loudon Rd...gas:** Irving/Subway, 7-11, Shell/dsl, Sunoco, **food:** Applebee's, Burger King, D'angelo, Dunkin Donuts, Friendly's, Fusion Asian, KFC, LJ Silver/Taco Bell, Longhorn Steaks, McDonald's, Newick's Lobster House, 99 Rest., Olive Garden, PapaGino, Pizza Hut, Ruby Tuesday, Starbucks, TGIFriday, Wendy's, Windmill Rest., **other:** Aamco, Advance Parts, Best Buy, BonTon, Circuit City, Home Depot, JC Penney, Michael's, PetsMart, Sears/auto, Shaw's Foods/Osco Drug, Target, Walgreens, Walmart SuperCtr, **W gas:** Citgo, Gulf/dsl, Hess, **food:** Domino's, Nonni's Rest., Rainbow Buffet, Tea Garden Rest., **lodging:** Holiday Inn, **other:** Pill MktPlace, to state offices, hist sites, museum

**13** (38) to US 3, Manchester St, Concord, **E gas:** Cumberland Farms, Sunoco/dsl/deli, **food:** Beefside Rest., Cat'n Fill Rest., Cityside Grille, Dunkin Donuts, Kaylen's Pizza, Red Blazer Rest., **other:** Buick/GMC/Pontiac, Chrysler, Dodge/ Jeep, Ford/Lincoln, Harley-Davidson, KIA, Mitsubishi/Volvo, Outdoor RV Ctr, Saab, Subaru, **W gas:** Hess, Mobil/ dsl, **food:** Burger King, Common Man Diner, D'angelo's, KFC, McDonald's, **lodging:** Best Western, Comfort Inn, Fairfield Inn, **other:** H HOSPITAL, Aubuchan Hardware, CVS Drug, Firestone, GMC, Goodyear/auto, NAPA

**12N** (37) NH 3A N, S Main, **E gas:** Gulf, Irving/Subway/dsl/24hr, **food:** Dunkin Donuts, **lodging:** Day's Inn, **other:** Ford/ Mazda, Honda, Hyundai, Suzuki, Toyota/Scion, **W other:** H HOSPITAL

**12S** NH 3A S, Bow Junction

**36mm** I-89 N to Lebanon, toll road begins/ends

---

**31mm** rest area both lanes, full & facilities, info, (, vending

**11** (30) NH 3A, to Hooksett, toll plaza, (, **4 mi E gas:** Citgo Trkstp/dsl/rest.

**28mm** I-293 (from sb), Everett Tpk

**10** (27) NH 3A, Hooksett, **E gas:** Irving/Quizno's/dsl, **food:** Subway, Wendy's, **other:** BJ's Whse, Home Depot, Kohl's, Staples, Target, **W gas:** Irving/Dunkin Donuts, Supreme, **food:** Big Cheese Pizza, **other:** Lowes Whse, Walmart

**26mm** Merrimac River

**9N S** (24) US 3, NH 28, Manchester, **W gas:** Manchester/dsl, Sunoco/dsl/24hr, **food:** Amato's Pizza, Burger King, Cheng Du Chinese, D'Angelo's, Happy Garden Chinese, KFC, La Carreta Mexican, Lusia's Italian, PapaGino's, Puritan Rest., Quizno's, Shogun Japanese, Shorty's Mexican, **other:** H HOSPITAL, Chrysler/Dodge/Jeep, Ford/Lincoln/Mercury, Hannaford Foods, KIA, Rite Aid, U-Haul, VIP Parts/service

**8** (23) to NH 28a, Wellington Rd, **W VA** H HOSPITAL, Currier Gallery

**7** (22) NH 101 E, to Portsmouth, Seacoast

**6** (21) Hanover St, Candia Rd, Manchester, **E food:** Dunkin Donuts, Wendy's, **other:** vet, **W gas:** Citgo/dsl, Mobil/ dsl, Shell, **food:** McDonald's, **other:** Goodyear/auto

**19mm** I-293 W, to Manchester, to ✈

**5** (15) NH 28, to N Londonderry, **E gas:** Sunoco/Dunkin Donuts/dsl, **food:** Poor Boy's Diner, **3 mi E gas:** Shell, **food:** Applebee's, Burger King, **other:** Dodge/Jeep, Hannaford Foods, Lincoln/Mercury, NAPA, Sullivan Tire, VIP Parts, Walmart/gas, **W gas:** Shell/dsl, **food:** Subway, **lodging:** Sleep Inn, **other:**

**4** (12) NH 102, Derry, **E gas:** Citgo/dsl, Lukoil, Mobil/24hr, Rte 102 Gas, Shell/24hr, Sunoco/dsl, **food:** Burger King, Cracker Barrel, Derry Rest., **other:** H HOSPITAL, **W gas:** Exxon/dsl, Global, Hess, 7-11, **food:** Domino's, McDonald's, 99 Rest., PapaGino's, Wendy's, **other:** Curves, Ford, Hannaford Foods, Home Depot, Marshall's, Mkt Basket Foods, Radio Shack, Sears Essentials, Shaw's Foods, Staples, TJ Maxx, USPO, VIP Auto, Walgreen

**8mm** weigh sta both lanes

**3** (6) NH 111, Windham, **E gas:** Mobil/McDonald's, **food:** House of Pizza, Windham Rest., **other:** Curves, **W food:** Capri Pizza, Clemm's Bakery, Lobster Tail (3mi), **other:** Castleton Conference Ctr, Osco Drug, Shaw's Foods, USPO

**2** (3) to NH 38, NH 97, Salem, **E lodging:** Red Roof Inn, **W food:** Dunkin Donuts, Margarita's Cafe, **lodging:** Holiday Inn, La Quinta

**1** (2) NH 28, Salem, **E gas:** Citgo/dsl, Exxon, Getty, **food:** Bickfords, Burger King, Chili's, Denny's, Friendly's, McDonald's, 99 Rest., Taco Bell, T-Bones, **lodging:** Park View Inn, **other:** Barnes&Noble, Best Buy, BJ's Whse, DeMoula's Foods, Dodge/Nissan/Toyota, Home Depot, JC Penney, Kohl's, K-Mart, Macy's, Marshall's, MktBasket Foods, NTB, PetCo, Radio Shack, Sears/auto, Shaw's Foods, Staples, Target, TJ Maxx, TownFair Tire, Walgreens, racetrack, mall, vet

**1mm** **Welcome Ctr nb, full** & **facilities, info,** (, 🎪, **litter barrels, vending, petwalk**

**0mm** New Hampshire/Massachusetts

---

**CONCORD**

**CONCORD**

**MANCHESTER**

**DERRY**

**SALEM**

**P O R T S M O U T H**

## INTERSTATE 95

| Exit # | Services |
|---|---|
| 17mm | New Hampshire/Maine state line, Piscataqua River |
| 7 (16) | Market St, Portsmouth, Port Authority, waterfront hist sites, **E lodging:** Sheraton, **W gas:** Gulf, Lukoil, Mobil, **food:** Applebee's, Boston Mkt, Bugaboo Creek Steaks, D'Angelo's, IHOP, Panera Bread, Starbucks, Wendy's, **lodging:** Courtyard, Hampton Inn, Homewood Suites, **other:** Circuit City, Chevrolet, BJ's Whse/gas, K-Mart, Marshall's, MktBasket Foods, PetCo, Rite Aid, Shaw's Foods |
| 6 (15) | Woodbury Ave (from nb), Portsmouth, **E lodging:** Anchorage Inn, Best Inn, **W** same as 7 |
| 5 (14) | US 1, US 4, NH 16, The Circle, Portsmouth, **E gas:** Citgo, Shell/dsl, **food:** Momma D's Rest., **lodging:** Anchorage Inn, Best Inn, Best Western, Fairfield Inn, Holiday Inn, Port Inn, **other:** Ⓗ HOSPITAL, Buick/Cadillac/GMC/Pontiac, Chrysler/Dodge/Toyota, U-Haul, **W gas:** Mobil, **food:** D'Angelo's, Dunkin Donuts, Longhorn Steaks, McDonald's, Pizza Hut, **lodging:** Hampton Inn, Motel 6, Residence Inn, **other:** Barnes&Noble, Best Buy, Ford, Home Depot, Kohl's, Mazda/VW, Michael's, Nissan, Old Navy, Saturn |
| 4 (13.5) | US 4 (exits left from nb), to White Mtns, Spaulding TPK, **E** Ⓗ HOSPITAL, **W** to Pease Int Trade Port |
| 3a (13) | NH 33, Greenland |
| 3b (12) | NH 33, to Portsmouth, **E** Ⓗ HOSPITAL, **W gas:** Sunoco/dsl, TA/dsl/rest./scales/24hr/@, **food:** McDonald's (1mi), **other:** Target, VW |
| 6.5mm | toll plaza |
| 2 (6) | NH 101, to Hampton |
| 4mm | Taylor River |
| 1 (1) | NH 107, to Seabrook, toll rd begins/ends, **E gas:** Getty, Irving/dsl, Prime, Sunoco/Subway/dsl, Xtra, **food:** Applebees, Chili's, Dunkin Donuts, KFC/Taco Bell, McDonald's, 99 rest., PapaGino's, Pizza Hut, Starbucks, Wendy's, **lodging:** Hampshire Inn, Holiday Inn Express, **other:** Ace Hardware, Advance Parts, AutoZone, CVS Drug, Home Depot, Kohl's, Lowes Whse, MktBasket Foods, NTB, Radio Shack, Shaw's Foods, Staples, TJ Maxx, TownFair Tire, Walmart, to Seacoast RA, **W gas:** Citgo, **food:** McGrath's Dining, Sal&Anthony's Pizza, **lodging:** Best Western, **other:** NAPA, Sam's Club, Seabrook Greyhound Pk |
| .5mm | **Welcome Ctr nb, full** ♿ **facilities,** 🚻 **, vending,** 🍽 **litter barrels, petwalk** |
| 0mm | New Hampshire/Massachusetts |

## INTERSTATE 293 - MANCHESTER

**N ↕ S**

| Exit # | Services |
|---|---|
| 8 (9) | I-93, N to Concord, S to Derry. I-293 begins/ends on I-93, 28mm. |
| 7 (6.5) | NH 3A N, Dunbarton Rd (from nb) |
| 6 (6) | Amoskeag Rd, Goffstown, **E gas:** Sunoco, **food:** Harts Rest., **lodging:** Clarion, **W gas:** Shell/dsl, **food:** Dunkin Donuts, **other:** Ⓗ HOSPITAL |
| 5 (5) | Granite St, Manchester, **E lodging:** Radisson, **W gas:** Gulf, 7-11/gas, **food:** Dunkin Donuts, **other:** Ⓗ HOSPITAL, Walgreens, tires |
| 4 (4) | US 3, NH 3A, NH 114A, Queen City Br, **E gas:** 7-11, Mobil/dsl, Sunoco, **lodging:** Emperial Kitchen, **W on** |

**M A N C H E S T E R**

**US 3**

| | |
|---|---|
| 4 | Continued |
| | **gas:** Hess/dsl, Z1 Gas/dsl, **food:** Applebee's, Bickford's, Burger King, Clam King, D'angelo's, DQ, Dunkin Donuts, KC's Rib Shack, KFC, Ling Garden, Little Caesars, McDonald's, Papa John's, Taco Bell, Subway, Wendy's, **lodging:** Comfort Inn, Econolodge, **other:** Goodyear, Hannaford Foods, Radio Shack, Rite Aid, Subaru |
| 3 (3) | NH 101, **W on US 3 food:** Carrabba's, Dunkin Donuts, Outback Steaks, Panera Bread, Papagino's, Quacker's Rest., Sparks Rest., T-Bones Steaks, **lodging:** Quality Inn, **other:** CVS Drug, House Of Cloth, Lowe's, Macy's, Marshalls, Radio Shack, Rite Aid, Stop'n Shop/gas, Staples, Target, VIP Auto, vet, **1-2 mi W lodging:** Country Inn & Suites, Hampton Inn, **food:** Applebees, Bugaboo Creek Steaks |
| 2.5mm | Merrimac River |
| 2 (2) | NH 3A, Brown Ave, **S gas:** Citgo/Subway/dsl, Mobil/dsl, 7-11, **food:** Airport Diner, Dunkin Donuts, McDonald's, **lodging:** Holiday Inn, Super 8, **other:** Manchester ✈ |
| 1 (1) | NH 28, S Willow Rd, **N gas:** Citgo, Mobil/dsl, Sunoco/dsl, **food:** Bickford's, Boston Mkt, Burger King, Cactus Jack's, Chili's, Coldstone Creamery, D'angelo, Friendly's, McDonald's, Panera Bread, PapaGino's, Papa John's, Pizza Hut, Quizno's, Starbucks, Taco Bell, Wendy's, Yee Dynasty Chinese, **lodging:** Fairfield Inn, Holiday Inn Express, Sheraton, **other:** Ⓗ HOSPITAL, AutoZone, Batteries+, Buick/Chevrolet, Circuit City, CVS Drug, $Tree, GMC, Harley-Davidson, Hannaford Foods, Home Depot, Michael's, Osco Drug, PepBoys, PetCo, PetsMart, Pontiac/Cadillac/Mazda, Radio Shack, Sam's Club, Shaw's Foods, Stop'n Shop, Sullivan Tire, TJ Maxx, Town Fair Tire, U-Haul, VW, vet, **S gas:** Shell, **food:** Bertucci's, Chicago Grill, ChuckeCheese, Famous Dave's, FoodCourt, Ground Round, Longhorn Steaks, 99 Rest., Olive Garden, Ruby Tuesday, TGIFriday, **lodging:** Courtyard, TownePlace Suites, **other:** Ⓗ HOSPITAL, Barnes&Noble, Best Buy, Chrysler, Ford, Honda, Hyundai, JC Penney, Lexus, LL Bean, Lowe's, Nissan, Macy's, NTB, Saturn, Sears/auto, Staples, Toyota/Scion, Walmart, mall |
| 0mm | I-93, N to Concord, S to Derry. I-293 begins/ends on I-93. |

**NEWARK** ⬍ **E / W**

**CLINTON**

## INTERSTATE 78

| Exit # | Services |
|---|---|
| 58b a | US 1N, US 9N, NJ Tpk |
| 57 | US 1S, US 9S, **N lodging:** Holiday Inn, Sheraton, **S lodging:** Courtyard, Fairfield Inn, SpringHill Suites, **other:** to Newark ✈ |
| 56 | Clinton Ave (exits left from eb) |
| 55 | Irvington (from wb), **N gas:** Delta, **food:** Wendy's, **other:** H HOSPITAL, Goodyear |
| 54 | Hillside, Irvington (from eb), **N gas:** Delta, **food:** Wendy's, **other:** H HOSPITAL, Goodyear |
| 52 | Garden State Pkwy |
| 50b a | Millburn (from wb), **N gas:** BP, Exxon, Lukoil, **food:** Manny's Wieners, **other:** Best Buy, Firestone/auto, Home Depot Superstore, Lincoln/Mercury, Target, USPO, Whole Foods Mkt. |
| 49b | (from eb), to Maplewood, same as 50b a |
| 48 | to NJ 24, NJ 124, to I-287 N, (exits left from eb), Springfield |
| 48mm | I-78 eb divides into express & local |
| 45 | NJ 527 (from eb), Glenside Ave, Summit |
| 44 | (from eb), to Berkeley Heights, New Providence |
| 43 | to New Providence, Berkley Heights |
| 41 | to Berkeley Heights, Scotch Plains |
| 40 | NJ 531, The Plainfields, **S gas:** Valero (1mi), **food:** Stewart's, **other:** H HOSPITAL |
| 36 | NJ 651, to Warrenville, Basking Ridge, **N gas:** Exxon/service/24hr, **food:** Dunkin Donuts, **other:** A&P, **S gas:** Exxon |
| 33 | NJ 525, to Martinsville, Bernardsville, PGA Golf Museum, **N food:** Ciao Italian, LingLing Chinese, Starbucks, **lodging:** Courtyard, Somerset Hills Inn, **S gas:** Exxon/KwikPik, **food:** Panera Bread |
| 32mm | scenic overlook wb |
| 29 | I-287, to US 202, US 206, I-80, to Morristown, Somerville, **S** H HOSPITAL |
| 26 | NJ 523 spur, to North Branch, Lamington |
| 24 | NJ 523, to NJ 517, to Oldwick, Whitehouse, **2-3 mi S gas:** Exxon/dsl/24hr, Liberty, **food:** McDonald's, Readington Diner |
| 20b a | NJ 639 (from wb), to Cokesbury, Lebanon, **S gas:** Exxon/24hr, Shell/24hr, Sunoco, **food:** Bagelsmith Deli, Dunkin Donuts, Spinning Wheel Diner, **lodging:** Courtyard, **other:** to Round Valley RA |
| 18 | US 22 E, Annandale, Lebanon, **N** H HOSPITAL, same as 17, **S** Honda |
| 17 | NJ 31 S, Clinton, **N gas:** Exxon, Hess/24hr, Valero, **food:** Country Griddle, Dunkin Donuts/Baskin Robbins, Blimpie, McDonald's, **lodging:** Courtyard |
| 16 | NJ 31 N (from eb), Clinton, **N** same as 17 |
| 15 | NJ 173 E, to Pittstown, Clinton, **N gas:** Exxon, Shell/dsl/24hr, **food:** Subway, **lodging:** Holiday Inn Select, **other:** museum, **S food:** Cracker Barrel, Frank's Pizza, Hunan Wok, **lodging:** Hampton Inn, **other:** H HOSPITAL, $Tree, ShopRite Foods, TJMaxx, Walmart/grill |
| 13 | NJ 173 W (from wb), **N food:** Clinton Sta. Diner, same as 12 |
| 12 | NJ 173, to Jutland, Norton, **N gas:** Clinton/dsl, Exxon, Dunkin Donuts/dsl, Pilot/dsl/scales/24hr, **food:** Grand Colonial Rest., **other:** vet, to Spruce Run RA, **S gas:** Shell/dsl, **food:** Bagelsmith Deli, **lodging:** Perryville Inn |
| 11 | NJ 173, West Portal, Pattenburg, **N gas:** Shell/dsl, **food:** Chalet Rest., **other:** st police |
| 8mm | **rest area both lanes,** 🚻, **litter barrels, no restrooms** |
| 7 | NJ 173, to Bloomsbury, West Portal, **N** RV camping, **S gas:** Citgo/dsl/rest./24hr, Country Pride/dsl, Pilot/Subway/dsl/scales/24hr, TA/Buger King/dsl/scales/24hr/@ |
| 6mm | weigh sta both lanes |
| 6 | Warren Glen, Asbury (from eb) |
| 4 | Warren Glen, Stewartsville (from wb) |
| 3 | US 22, NJ 173, to Phillipsburg, **0-2 mi N gas:** Getty/dsl, Hess/dsl, US/dsl/24hr, **food:** Applebee's, Burger King, Friendly's, Key City Diner, McDonald's, Panera Bread, Perkins, Pizza Hut, Ruby Tuesday, Sammy's Drive-in, Taco Bell, **lodging:** Phillipsburg Inn, **other:** H HOSPITAL, BonTon, Circuit City, $Tree, Home Depot, Honda, JC Penney, Kohl's, Lowes Whse, Michael's, Old Navy, ShopRite Foods, Staples, Stop'n Shop, Target, Walmart/auto, **S other:** Chevrolet |
| 0mm | New Jersey/Pennsylvania state line, Delaware River |

## INTERSTATE 80

| Exit # | Services |
|---|---|
| | I-80 begins/ends at G Washington Bridge in Ft Lee, NJ. |
| 73mm | toll plaza eb |
| 72b | US 1 S, US 9, **N food:** Red Oak Rest., **other:** Staples |
| 72a | US 46, NJ 4, **N gas:** BP, Exxon/Subway, Gulf, Hess/Blimpie/dsl, Lukoil, Sunoco, **lodging:** Best Western, Holiday Inn, **S gas:** Lukoil, **lodging:** Courtesy Inn, DoubleTree Inn |
| 71 | Broad Ave, Leonia, Englewood |
| 70b a | NJ 93, Leonia, Teaneck, **N gas:** Marriott, **other:** H HOSPITAL |
| 68b a | I-95, N to New York, S to Philadelphia, to US 46 |
| 67 | to Bogota (from eb) |
| 66 | Hudson St, to Hackensack |
| 65 | Green St, S Hackensack |
| 64b a | NJ 17 S, to US 46 E, Newark, Paramus, **S gas:** BP/24hr, Exxon, **food:** Baskin-Robbins, Dunkin Donuts, Sea Shack Rest., **lodging:** Crowne Plaza, Hilton, **other:** PathMark Foods |
| 63 | NJ 17 N, **N gas:** BP/24hr, Hess/dsl/24hr, Valero, **food:** Boston Mkt, Subway, **other:** H HOSPITAL, CVS Drug, Harley-Davidson, Home Depot, 7-11 |
| 62b a | GS Pkwy, to Saddle Brook, **N gas:** Shell, **lodging:** Marriott, **S lodging:** Wyndham |
| 61 | NJ 507, to Garfield, Elmwood Park, **N** Marcal Paper Co, **S gas:** Sunoco |
| 60 | NJ 20, N to Hawthorne, **N other:** H HOSPITAL, Lowes Whse, Michelin/Cooper Tires |
| 59 | Market St (from wb), to Paterson |
| 58b a | Madison Ave, to Paterson, Clifton, **S** H HOSPITAL |
| 57c | Main St (from wb), to Paterson |
| 57b a | NJ 19 S, to Clifton, downtown Paterson |
| 56b a | Squirrelwood Rd, to Paterson, **S gas:** Lukoil |
| 55b a | Union Blvd (from wb, no EZ return), Totowa, **N gas:** Sunoco/dsl, **S lodging:** Holiday Inn |
| 54 | Minnisink Rd, to Paterson, **S gas:** BP, **other:** Home Depot, JC Penney, Marshall's, Staples, mall |
| 53 | US 46 E, NJ 23 (no eb return), **S gas:** Exxon, Gulf, Sunoco, **food:** Applebee's, Burger King, Dunkin Donuts, Hooters, IHOP, McDonald's, Pizzaria Uno, Red Lobster, |

**E / W**

**PATERSON**

## INTERSTATE 80 CONT'D

**E** ↕ **W**

**53** Continued
Ruby Tuesday, Steak'n Ale, TX Wieners, TGIFriday, Wendy's, **lodging:** Holiday Inn, Ramada Inn, Sheraton, **other:** Borders Books, Costco, Firestone/auto, Ford, Home Depot, Lord&Taylor, Macy's, Nissan, Old Navy, Saturn, Sears/auto, Target, mall

**52** US 46, the Caldwells

**48** to Montville (from wb), Pine Brook

**47b** US 46 W, to Montclair, **N gas:** BP, **lodging:** Holiday Inn, **S gas:** BP, Gulf, Shell, **food:** Dakota Diner/24hr, Dunkin Donuts, McDonald's, Subway

**47a** I-280 E, to The Oranges, Newark

**45** to US 46, Lake Hiawatha, Whippany, **N on US 46...** **gas:** BP, Gulf, Sunoco, **food:** Applebees, Burger King, Chili's, Coldstone Creamery, Eccola Rest., Empire Diner, 5 Guys Burgers, Franco's Pizza, IHOP, Jasper Chinese, Longhorn Steaks, Moe's SW Grill, Outback Steaks, Perkins, Red Lobster, Taco Bell, Wendy's, **lodging:** Budget Inn, Holiday Inn/rest., Howard Johnson, Ramada Ltd, Red Roof Inn, **other:** Cost Cutter Foods, $Tree, Drug Fair, Firestone, K-Mart, PathMark Foods, Pep-Boys, PetCo, Radio Shack, ShopRite Foods, Staples

**43b a** I-287, to US 46, Boonton, Morristown

**42b a** US 202, US 46, to Morris Plains, Parsippany, **N on US 46 gas:** Gulf, Hess, Shell, **food:** Fuddrucker's, McDonald's, TGIFriday, Wendy's, **lodging:** Courtyard, Day's Inn, Embassy Suites, Fairfield Inn, Hampton Inn, **other:** Chrysler/Dodge, Ford, Marshall's, Michael's, Subaru, USPO, same as 39

**39** (from wb) (38 from eb), US 46 E, to NJ 53, Denville, **N on US 46 gas:** Enrite Gas, Gulf/dsl, **food:** Casa Villa Italian, Hunan Taste, Paul's Diner, Wendy's, West Side Diner, **other:** H HOSPITAL, BMW, Chevrolet, Discount Tire, Firestone, PathMark Foods, vet, **S gas:** Shell

**37** NJ 513, to Hibernia, Rockaway, **N gas:** Exxon/dsl, Shell/24hr, **food:** Hibernia Diner, **lodging:** Best Western, Hampton Inn, **S gas:** BP, **other:** H HOSPITAL

**35b a** to Dover, Mount Hope, **S gas:** Exxon/24hr, **food:** Coldstone Creamery, Dunkin Donuts, Fat Burger, La Salsa Mexican, Olive Garden, Peking Garden, Quizno's, Sizzler, **lodging:** Hilton Garden, **other:** H HOSPITAL, Acme Foods, Best Buy, Border's Books, FoodWorks, JC Penney, Lord&Taylor, Macy's, Michael's, Sears/auto, mall

**34b a** NJ 15, to Sparta, Wharton, **N gas:** Exxon/dsl, **food:** McDonald's, Ming Buffet, Subway, **other:** H HOSPITAL, Rite Aid, **S food:** Dunkin Donuts, King's Chinese, Townsquare Diner, **other:** H HOSPITAL, Costco, $Tree, Home Depot, PetsMart, ShopRite Foods, Target, Walmart

**32mm** truck rest area wb

**30** Howard Blvd, to Mt Arlington, **N gas:** Exxon/dsl/24hr, **food:** China City, Cracker Barrel, Davy's Hotdogs,

**30** Continued
IHOP, **lodging:** Courtyard, Holiday Inn Express, **other:** QuickChek Foods

**28** NJ 10, to Ledgewood, Lake Hopatcong, 0-1 mi **S gas:** Delta Gas, Sunoco, **food:** Cliff's Dairy Maid, Dunkin Donuts, KFC, McDonald's, Outback Steaks, Pizza Hut, Red Lobster, Roxbury Diner, Ruby Tuesday, Subway, Taco Bell, TGI Friday, Wendy's, White Castle, **other:** AutoZone, BJ's Whse, CVS Drug, ShopRite Foods, Toyota, Walgreens

**27** US 206 S, NJ 182, to Netcong, Somerville, **N gas:** Valero/dsl, **food:** Perkins, **lodging:** Comfort Inn, Quality Inn, **other:** Ford, **S gas:** Shell/dsl/24hr, **food:** Applebees, Chili's, Longhorn Steaks, Macaroni Grill, McDonald's, Panera Bread, Subway, Wendy's, **lodging:** Extended Stay America, **other:** Lowes Whse, Michael's,

**STANHOPE** · E · W

## INTERSTATE 80 CONT'D

| | |
|---|---|
| 27 | Continued<br>Old Navy, PetsMart, Sam's Club, Staples, TJMaxx, Tuesday Morning, Walmart |
| 26 | US 46 W (from wb, no EZ return), to Budd Lake, **S** **gas:** Shell/dsl, same as 27 |
| 25 | US 206 N, to Newton, Stanhope, 1-2 mi **N** **gas:** Exxon/24hr, Shell/dsl, **food:** Byram Diner, DQ, Dunkin Donuts, Lockwood Tavern, McDonald's, Subway, **lodging:** Extended Stay America, Residence Inn, Wyndham Garden, **other:** CVS Drug, Nissan, Radio Shack, Shop-Rite Foods, STS tires/repair, to Waterloo Village, Int Trade Ctr |
| 23.5mm | Musconetcong River |
| 21mm | **rest area both lanes, NO TRUCKS, scenic overlook (eb), ⛽, 🚻, litter barrels, petwalk** |
| 19 | NJ 517, to Hackettstown, Andover, **N** **gas:** Shell, **other:** RV camping, 1-2 mi **S** **gas:** Shell, **food:** BLD's Rest., Terra Nova Pizza, **lodging:** Panther Valley Inn/rest., **other:** Ⓗ HOSPITAL, 7-11, USPO |
| 12 | NJ 521, to Blairstown, Hope, **N** **food:** Mediterranean Diner, **other:** Harley-Davidson, st police, **S** **gas:** US Gas, **food:** Gio's Pizza, **lodging:** Millrace Pond Inn, **other:** RV camping (5mi), Land of Make Believe, Jenny Jump SF |
| 7mm | **rest area eb, full ♿ facilities, info, ⛽, 🚻, litter barrels, vending, petwalk** |
| 6mm | scenic overlook wb, no trailers |
| 4c | to NJ 94 N (from eb), to Blairstown |
| 4b | to US 46 E, to Buttzville |
| 4a | NJ 94, to US 46 E, to Portland, Columbia, **N** **gas:** TA/BP/Pizza Hut/Taco Bell/dsl/scales/24hr/@, **food:** McDonald's, **other:** RV camping, **S** **gas:** Shell/dsl/24hr |
| 3.5mm | Hainesburg Rd (from wb), accesses services at 4 |
| 2mm | weigh sta eb |
| 1mm | Worthington SF, **S** **rest area both lanes, restrooms, info, 🚻, litter barrels, petwalk** |
| 1 | to Millbrook (from wb), **N** Worthington SF |
| 0mm | New Jersey/Pennsylvania state line, Delaware River |

## INTERSTATE 95

**N · S** · **TRENTON**

| Exit # | Services |
|---|---|
| 124mm | New Jersey/New York state line, Geo Washington Br, Hudson River |
| 123mm | Palisades Pkwy (from sb) |
| 72 (122) | US 1, US 9, US 46, Ft Lee, **E** **gas:** Mobil, Shell, **lodging:** Courtesy Motel, Hilton |
| 71 (121) | Broad Ave, Leonia, Englewood, **E** **gas:** Shell, **W** **gas:** Gulf, **lodging:** Day's Inn, Executive Inn |
| 70 (120) | to NJ 93, Leonia, Teaneck, **W** **lodging:** Marriott |
| 69 (119) | I-80 W (from sb), to Paterson |
| 68 (118) | US 46, Challenger Blvd, Ridgefield Park, **E** **gas:** Exxon, **lodging:** Hampton Inn |
| | **I-95 and NJ Turnpike run together sb. See NJ TPK. exits 7a-18**<br>**I-96 becomes I-295 sb at US 1.** |
| 67b a | US 1, to Trenton, New Brunswick, **E** **gas:** Shell/24hr, **food:** Michael's Diner, **lodging:** Howard Johnson, Sleepy Hollow Motel, **other:** Acura, 0-3 mi **W** **gas:** Gulf, LukOil/dsl, **food:** Applebees, Big Fish Rest., Chevy's Mexican, Chili's, ChuckeCheese, Denny's, Dunkin Donuts, Hooters, Houlihan's Rest., Joe's Crabshack, |

**TRENTON** · N · S

| | |
|---|---|
| 67b a | Continued<br>Macaroni Grill, Olive Garden, On-the-Border, Panera Bread, PF Chang's, Princetonian Diner, Quizno's, Red Lobster, Starbucks, TGIFriday, Wendy's, **lodging:** Clarion, Comfort Inn, Extended Stay America, Hyatt Regency, Red Roof Inn, Residence Inn, **other:** Barnes&Noble, Best Buy, BMW/Mini, Border's Books, Buick/GMC/Pontiac, Chevrolet, Circuit City, GNC, Home Depot, JC Penney, Jo-Ann Fabrics, Kohl's, Lord&Taylor, Lowes Whse, Macy's, Marshall's, Michael's, NTB, Office Depot, Old Navy, PepBoys, PetCo, PetsMart, Porche, Ross, Sam's Club, Sears, Shop Rite Foods, Staples, Suzuki, Target, TJ Maxx, Walmart, Wegman's Foods, Whole Foods Mkt., mall |
| 8b a | NJ 583, NJ 546, to Princeton Pike |
| 7b a | US 206, **W** **gas:** LukOil, **food:** Tasty Subs, TJ's Pizza |
| 5b a | Federal City Rd (sb only) |
| 4b a | NJ 31, to Ewing, Pennington, **E** **gas:** Citgo, Exxon, **food:** Dunkin Donuts, **W** **gas:** LukOil, **other:** ShopRite Foods |
| 3b a | Scotch Rd, **E** **lodging:** Courtyard |
| 2 | NJ 579, to Harbourton, **E** **gas:** LukOil (1mi), **food:** Red Star Pizza, **other:** 7-11, **W** **gas:** BP |
| 1 | NJ 29, to Trenton, 2 mi **W** museum, st police |
| 0mm | New Jersey/Pennsylvania state line, Delaware River |

## NEW JERSEY TURNPIKE

| Exit # | Services |
|---|---|
| 18 (117) | US 46 E, Ft Lee, Hackensack, last exit before toll sb |
| 17 (116) | Lincoln Tunnel |
| 115mm | **Vince Lombardi Service Plaza nb**...Sunoco/dsl, Big Boy, Nathan's, Roy Rogers, TCBY, gifts |
| 114mm | toll plaza, ⛽ |
| 16W (113) | NJ 3, Secaucus, Rutherford, **E** **gas:** Hess, Shell, **lodging:** Hilton, M Plaza Hotel, **W** **lodging:** Sheraton, **other:** Meadowlands |
| 112mm | **Alexander Hamilton Service Area sb**...Sunoco, Roy Rogers, gifts |
| 16E (112) | NJ 3, Secaucus, **E** Lincoln Tunnel |
| 15W (109) | I-280, Newark, The Oranges |
| 15E (107) | US 1, US 9, Newark, Jersey City, **E** Lincoln Tunnel |
| 14c | Holland Tunnel |
| 14b | Jersey City |
| 14a | Bayonne |
| 14 (105) | I-78 W, US 1, US 9, 2 mi **W** **lodging:** Fairfield Inn, Holiday Inn, SpringHill Suites, **other:** ✈ |
| 102mm | **Halsey Service Area**, Sunoco, Roy Rogers, other services in Elizabeth |
| 13a (102) | Elizabeth, **E** **lodging:** Courtyard, Extended Stay America, Residence Inn, **W** **food:** McDonald's, **lodging:** DoubleTree, Econolodge, Hilton, Sheraton, Wyndham Garden, services on US1/US9 |
| 13 (100) | I-278, to Verrazano Narrows Bridge |
| 12 (96) | Carteret, Rahway, **E** **food:** McDonald's, **lodging:** Holiday Inn, **W** **food:** Radisson |
| 93mm | **Cleveland Service Area nb**...**food:** Nathans, Roy Roger's, Starbucks, **T Edison Service Area sb**...**gas:** Sunoco/dsl, **food:** Burger King, Dunkin Donuts, Popeye's, Sbarro's, Starbucks |
| 11 (91) | US 9, Garden State Pkwy, to Woodbridge, **E** **lodging:** Hampton Inn, Homestead Suites, **other:** Home Depot |

Copyright 2009 - The Next Exit®

## NEW JERSEY TURNPIKE CONT'D

**10** (88)   I-287, NJ 514, to Perth Amboy, **E** lodging: Courtyard, **W** gas: Hess/dsl, lodging: Holiday Inn

**9** (83)   US 1, NJ 18, to New Brunswick, E Brunswick, **E** gas: Gulf, Hess/dsl, **food:** Bone Fish Grill, Boston Mkt, Burger King, Carrabbas, Dunkin Donuts, Grand Buffet, KFC, Perkins, Starbucks, **lodging:** Days Inn, Motel 6, **other:** Best Buy, Goodyear/auto, Lowes Whse, Office Depot, PetsMart, Rite Aid, Sam's Club, Shopper's World Foods, Shop Rite Foods, Staples, TJ Maxx, **W** gas: Exxon, **food:** Fuddrucker's, **lodging:** Hilton, Holiday Inn Express, Howard Johnson

**79mm**   **Kilmer Service Area nb...gas:** Sunoco/dsl, **food:** Dick Clark's Grill, Nathan's, Roy Rodgers, Starbucks

**8a** (74)   to Jamesburg, Cranbury, **W** lodging: Courtyard, Crowne Plaza

**72mm**   **Pitcher Service Area sb...gas:** Sunoco/dsl, **food:** Dick Clark's Grill, Nathan's, Roy Rogers, Starbucks

**8** (67)   NJ 33, NJ 571, Hightstown, **E** gas: Exxon/dsl, Hess/dsl, Petro, Shell/Dunkin Donuts, **food:** Prestige Diner, **lodging:** Day's Inn, Holiday Inn, **other:** CVS Drug, vet, **W** lodging: Quality Inn

**7a** (60)   I-195 W to Trenton, E to Neptune

**59mm**   **Richard Stockton Service Area sb...gas:** Sunoco/dsl, **food:** Blimpie, Burger King, Pizza Hut, Starbucks, TCBY, **Woodrow Wilson Service Area nb...gas:** Sunoco, **food:** Roy Rogers

**7** (54)   US 206, to Bordentown, to Ft Dix, McGuire AFB, to I-295, Trenton, **Services W on US 206...gas:** Petro/dsl/rest./24hr/@, Pilot/Wendy's/dsl/@, Sunoco, Valero, WaWa, **food:** Burger King, Denny's, **lodging:** Best Western/rest., Comfort Inn, Day's Inn/rest., Hampton Inn, Ramada Inn, **other:** RV Ctr

**6** (51)   I-276, to Pa Turnpike

**5** (44)   to Mount Holly, Willingboro, **E** gas: US gas/dsl, **food:** Applebees, Cracker Barrel, **lodging:** Hampton Inn, **W** gas: BP, Exxon/dsl, Valero/dsl, **food:** Burger King, China House, ChuckeCheese, Dunkin Donuts, Subway, TGI Friday, Quizno's, **lodging:** Holiday Inn Express, **other:** $Tree, Home Depot, JC Penney, Kohl's, Macy's, Sears/auto, Target, vet

**39mm**   **James Fenimore Cooper Service Area nb...gas:** Sunoco/dsl, **food:** Burger King, Cinabon, Popeye's, Roy Rogers, TCBY, **other:** gifts

**4** (34)   NJ 73, to Philadelphia, Camden, **E** gas: Exxon, LukOil, **food:** Chick-fil-A, Cracker Barrel, Chili's, Denny's, Macaroni Grill, McDonald's, On-the-Border, Sage Rest., TGIFriday, Wendy's, **lodging:** Candlewood Suites, Comfort Inn, Extended Stay America, Hampton Inn, Howard Johnson, Hyatt Place, Rodeway Inn, Staybridge Suites, Wingate Inn, Wyndham Hotel, **other:** BMW, Cadillac, Ford, Lexus, Rite Aid, Saturn, 7-11, Whole Foods Mkt, **1-2 mi W** gas: Exxon, Gulf/dsl, Hess, LukOil/dsl, Shell, **food:** Bob Evans, Burger King, Dunkin Donuts, KFC, Pizza Hut, **lodging:** Courtyard, DoubleTree Motel, Fairfield Inn, Hampton Inn, Marriott, Motel 6, Ramada Inn/rest., Red Roof Inn, Super 8, Track&Turf Motel, **other:** Lincoln/Mercury, Mazda, transmissions, to st aquarium

**30mm**   Walt Whitman Service Area, **Walt Whitman Service Area sb...gas:** Sunoco, **food:** Cinnabon, Roy Rogers, Nathan's, TCBY, **other:** gifts

---

**3** (26)   NJ 168, Atlantic City Expwy, Walt Whitman Br, Camden, Woodbury, **E** gas: Pioneer, 7-11, WaWa, **food:** Luigi's Pizza, Phily Diner, Rita's Ice Cream, Venuto's Pizza, **lodging:** Comfort Inn, Holiday Inn, **other:** Chrysler, CVS Drug, Toyota/Scion, Walgreens, **W** gas: BP, Gulf/repair, Shell/dsl, Valero/dsl, **food:** Burger King, Dunkin Donuts, Pizza Hut, Wendy's, **lodging:** Bellmawr Motel, Econolodge, Howard Johnson, Red Roof Inn, Super 8, **other:** transmissions

**2** (13)   US 322, to Swedesboro, **W** gas: Shell/Dunkin Donuts/dsl

**5mm**   **Barton Service Area sb...gas:** Sunoco, Burger King, Nathan's, Pizza Hut, Starbucks, TCBY, **Fenwick Service Area nb...gas:** Sunoco, **food:** TCBY

**1** (1.2)   Deepwater, **W** gas: Gulf, Pilot/Subway/dsl/scales/24hr/, **lodging:** Comfort Inn, Friendship Motor Inn, Holiday Inn Express, Wellesley Inn

**1mm**   toll road begins/ends

**2** (I-295)   I-295 N divides from toll road, I-295 S converges with toll road

**1** (I-295)   NJ 49, to Pennsville, **E** gas: Exxon, **food:** Burger King, McDonald's, **W** lodging: Seaview Motel

**0mm**   New Jersey/Delaware state line, Delaware River, Delaware Memorial Bridge

## INTERSTATE 195 - NEW JERSEY

| Exit # | Services |
|---|---|
| 36 | Garden State Parkway N. I-195 begins/ends on GS Pkwy, exit 98. |
| 35b a | NJ 34, to Brielle, GS Pkwy S., Pt Pleasant, **0-2 mi S** gas: Exxon/dsl/24hr, Getty, Lukoil/dsl, **food:** Legends Japanese |
| 31b a | NJ 547, NJ 524, to Farmingdale, **N** other: Chevrolet, to Allaire SP |
| 28b a | US 9, to Freehold, Lakewood, **N** gas: Lukoil/dsl, **food:** Ivy League Grill, Stewart's Drive-In, **S** gas: Exxon/24hr, Getty, Gulf, Lukoil, WaWa, **food:** Applebees, Arby's, Boston Mkt, Burger King, Carino's, Chick-fil-A, China Moon, Coldstone Creamery, Domino's, Dunkin Donuts, Longhorn Steaks, Luigi's Pizza, McDonald's, Panera Bread, Pizza Hut, Ruby Tuesday, Starbucks, Taco Bell, **other:** Barnes&Noble, Best Buy, Curves, $Life, Drug Fair, GNC, K-Mart, Kohl's, Lowes Whse, Michael's, Office Depot, PathMark Foods, PepBoys, Radio Shack, Staples, Stop&Shop, Target, TJ Maxx, Walgreens, Walmart, repair, USPO |
| 22 | to Jackson Mills, Georgia, **N** to Turkey Swamp Park, **2 mi S** food: McDonald's, **other:** ShopRite Foods |

## INTERSTATE 195 CONT'D - NEW JERSEY

**NJ**

E ↕ W

| | |
|---|---|
| **21** | NJ 526, NJ 527, to Jackson, Siloam |
| **16** | NJ 537, to Freehold, **N gas:** Remington/dsl/LP, Sunoco, **food:** Dairy Queen, FoodCourt, Gianmarco's Pizza, Java Moon Café, **other:** Ⓗ HOSPITAL, Jackson Outlets/famous brands, **S gas:** Wawa/dsl/24hr, **food:** BelaV Pizzaria, Burger King, Chicken Holiday, Dunkin Donuts, KFC, McDonald's, Rio Grande Mexican, Tommy's Rest., Vinci's Grill, **other:** 6Flags Themepark |
| **11** | NJ 524, Imlaystown, **S** to Horse Park of NJ |
| **8** | NJ 539, Allentown, **S gas:** Shell (1mi), Valero/repair, **food:** American Hero Deli, **other:** Crosswicks HP, vet |
| **7** | NJ 526 (no eb return), Robbinsville, Allentown, **1 mi S food:** La Piazza Ristorante |
| **6** | NJ Tpk, N to NY, S to DE Memorial Br |
| **5b a** | US 130, **N gas:** Delta/dsl, **food:** Domino's, Dunkin Donuts, Rusert's Deli, ShrimpKing Rest., **other:** AAA, Harley-Davidson, vet, **S gas:** GS Fuel/dsl, **food:** Chick-fil-A, Chili's, China Grill, Cracker Barrel, Dairy Queen, Longhorn Steaks, McDonald's, Outback Steaks, Red Robin, Ruby Tuesday, TGI Friday, Wendy's, **lodging:** Hilton Garden, **other:** Barnes&Noble, BJ's Wholesale, GNC, Hamilton Shops/famous brands, Harry's Army Navy, Home Depot, Kohl's, Lowes Whse, Michael's, Old Navy, PetsMart, Ross, ShopRite Foods, Staples, USPO, Walmart/auto, mall, to state aquarium |
| **3b a** | Hamilton Square, Yardville, **N** Ⓗ HOSPITAL |
| **2** | US 206 S, S Broad St, Yardville, **N other:** 7-11, **S gas:** Shell, Valero, **food:** Burger King, Subway, **other:** Acme Foods, CVS Drug, Eckerd, Rite Aid |
| **1b a** | US 206 (eb only), **N food:** Taco Bell, **S other:** ShopRite Foods |
| **0mm** | I-295, I-195 begins/ends. |

## INTERSTATE 287

N ↕ S

| Exit # | Services |
|---|---|
| **68mm** | New Jersey/New York state line |
| **66** | NJ 17 S, Mahwah, **1-3 mi E gas:** Getty, Gulf, Pilot/dsl, Royal, Sunoco, Valero/Subway/dsl, **food:** Boston Mkt, Burger King, Dunkin Donuts, McDonald's, State Line Diner, Wendy's, **lodging:** Best Western, Comfort Suites, Courtyard, Doubletree, Homewood Suites, Holiday Inn Express, Sheraton, Super 8, **other:** Aamco, Chrysler/Jeep, GMC/Pontiac, Home Depot, Hyundai, Mini |
| **59** | NJ 208 S, Franklin Lakes, **W food:** Blimpie, **other:** Super Stop'n Shop Foods |
| **58** | US 202, Oakland, **E gas:** Gulf/dsl, Lukoil, **food:** Dunkin Donuts, Mike's Doghouse, Jr's Pizza, Ruga Rest., **other:** ShopRite Foods, Walgreens, **W gas:** Exxon/24hr |
| **57** | Skyline Dr, Ringwood |
| **55** | NJ 511, Pompton Lakes, **E food:** Frank's Pizza, Quizno's, Wendy's **other:** A&P, **W gas:** Getty/dsl, **food:** Baskin-Robbins, Burger King, Dunkin Donuts, **lodging:** Holiday Inn Express, **other:** Stop'n Shop |
| **53** | NJ 511A, rd 694, Bloomingdale, Pompton Lakes, **E gas:** Sunoco, Valero, **food:** Blimpie, **other:** USPO |
| **52b a** | NJ 23, Riverdale, Wayne, Butler, **0-3 mi E gas:** BP, Lukoil, United/dsl, **food:** Baskin-Robbins, Dunkin Donuts, Friendly's, Fuddrucker's, McDonald's, Pompton Queen Diner, 23 Buffet, **lodging:** Best Western, La Quinta, |

| | |
|---|---|
| **52b a** | Continued **other:** Ⓗ HOSPITAL, A&P, Buick/GMC/Pontiac, Goodyear/auto, Honda, Saturn, TJ Maxx, Toyota/Scion, **W gas:** Getty, Lukoil, **food:** Applebees, Chili's, Ruppert's Rest., Subway, Wendy's, **other:** BJ's Whse, Borders Books, Harley-Davidson, Home Depot, Lowes Whse, Staples, Target, Walmart SuperCtr |
| **47** | US 202, Montville, Lincoln Park, **E gas:** Exxon/24hr, **food:** Harrigan's Rest. |
| **45** | Myrtle Ave, Boonton, **W gas:** Hess, Shell, **food:** Dunkin Donuts, IHOP, McDonald's, Subway, **other:** A&P/24hr, Buick/Chevrolet, Drug Fair |
| **43** | Intervale Rd, to Mountain Lakes, **E gas:** Valero, **W** Dodge |
| **42** | US 46, US 202 (from sb only), **W gas:** Exxon, Shell, Sunoco, **food:** Applebees, Dunkin Donuts, Fuddrucker's, Longhorn Steaks, McDonald's, Subway, Wendy's, **lodging:** Courtyard, Day's Inn, Embassy Suites, Fairfield Inn, Hampton Inn, **other:** Ford, GNC, Marshall's, Michael's, Subaru, USPO |
| **41b a** | I-80, E to New York, W to Delaware Water Gap |
| **40** | NJ 511, Parsippany Rd, to Whippany, **W gas:** BP, Shell/dsl, Woroco Gas, **food:** Fuddrucker's (2mi), Marco's Pizza, Wok's Chinese, Subway, **lodging:** Embassy Suites (1mi) |
| **39b a** | NJ 10, Dover, Whippany, **E gas:** Exxon, Shell, **food:** Bensi Italian, Brookside Diner, Capriccio's Italian, Dunkin Donuts, Melting Pot, Nikko's Japanese, Pancake House, **other:** CVS Drug, PathMark Foods, Tuesday Morning, **W gas:** Lukoil, Raceway, **food:** Atlanta Bread, Chevy's Mexican, Ruth Criss Steak, Subway, Wendy's, **lodging:** Candlewoods Suites, Hilton, Marriott, Red Carpet Inn, Residence Inn, Welsley Motel, **other:** Barnes&Noble, Buick/GMC/Pontiac, GNC, Kohl's, Shoprite, Stop'n Shop |
| **37** | NJ 24 E, Springfield |
| **36b a** | rd 510, Morris Ave, Lafayette |
| **35** | NJ 124, South St, Madison Ave, Morristown, **E food:** Friendly's, **W food:** Brick Oven, Calaloo Cafe, **lodging:** Best Western, **other:** Ⓗ HOSPITAL, Rite Aid, Walgreens |
| **33** | Harter Rd |
| **33mm** | rest area nb, full ♿ facilities, 📞, 🍴, litter barrels, vending, petwalk |
| **30b a** | to US 202, N Maple Ave, Basking Ridge, **E food:** Bamboo Grill, **lodging:** Dolce Resort, **W gas:** Gulf, **food:** Burger King, Friendly's, GrainHouse Rest., **lodging:** Olde Mill Inn/rest. |
| **26b a** | rd 525 S, Mt Airy Rd, Liberty Corner, **3 mi E gas:** Exxon/24hr, **lodging:** Courtyard, Somerset Hotel, **other:** Kwik-Pik Foods |
| **22b a** | US 202, US 206, Pluckemin, Bedminster, **E gas:** Exxon, **food:** Burger King, Golden Chinese, **other:** King's Foods, **W gas:** Shell, **food:** Dunkin Donuts |
| **21b a** | I-78, E to NY, W to PA |
| **17** | US 206 (from sb), Bridgewater, **E other:** Buick, **W gas:** Exxon, Hess, **food:** Chipotle Mexican, Dunkin Donuts, Friendly's, KFC, Lonestar Steaks, Magginos Italian, McDonald's, Red Town Diner, Starbucks, TGIFriday, Wendy's, **lodging:** Marriott, **other:** Best Buy, Bloomingdale's, Borders Books, Lord&Taylor, Macy's, TJ Maxx, mall |
| **14b a** | US 22, to US 202/206, **E gas:** Hess/dsl, **other:** Chevrolet/Lexus, **W food:** Fuddrucker's, Houlihan's, Red Lobster, **lodging:** Day's Inn, **other:** Acura, Buick/Cadillac/Pontiac, Infiniti, Mercedes |

## INTERSTATE 287 CONT'D

**N ↕ S**

**13b a** NJ 28, Bound Brook, **E gas:** BP/24hr, Sunoco, **food:** Amazing Hot Dog, Burger King, Dunkin Donuts, Frank's Pizza, Girasole Rest., Joey's Grill, Rosinas Rest., Subway, **other:** Radio Shack, Rite Aid, 7-11, ShopRite Foods, Walgreens, **W food:** Applebees, Chucke-Cheese, McDonald's, **lodging:** Hilton Garden, **other:** H HOSPITAL, Costco, Home Depot, Marshall's, Michael's, Old Navy, PepBoys, PetsMart, Target

**12** Weston Canal Rd, Manville, **E other:** ShopRite (3mi), USPO, **W food:** SportsTime Rest., **lodging:** Ramada Inn

**10** NJ 527, Easton Ave, New Brunswick, **E lodging:** Crowne Plaza, **W gas:** Exxon, **food:** Burger King (2mi), Dunkin Donuts, McDonald's (2mi), Ruby Tuesday, **lodging:** Courtyard, Holiday Inn, Doubletree, Hampton Inn, Madison Suites, Quality Inn, Staybridge Suites, **other:** H HOSPITAL, Drug Fair, Garden State Exhibit Ctr

**9** NJ 514, River Rd, **W gas:** Delta, **lodging:** Embassy Suites, Radisson

**8.5mm** weigh sta nb

**8** Possumtown Rd, Highland Park

**7** S Randolphville Rd, Piscataway, **E gas:** Lukoil/dsl

**6** Washington Ave, Piscataway, **E gas:** Shell, **W food:** Applebees, Burger King, Friendly's, KFC, McDonald's, TGIFriday, Johnny Carino's, Longhorn Steaks, Panera Bread, Ray's Pizza, Red Lobster, White Castle, **other:** GNC, Lowes Whse, PetCo, ShopRite Foods, same as 5

**5** NJ 529, Stelton Rd, Dunellen, **E gas:** Gulf/dsl, Lukoil, Shell, **food:** Banzai Japanese, KFC, **lodging:** Ramada Ltd., **other:** Home Depot, Stop'n Shop, **W gas:** Exxon, **food:** Baja Fresh, Bennigans, Burger King, Chicago Grill, Dunkin Donuts, Friendly's, Gianni Pizza, IHOP, Fontainbleu Diner, Gabrieles Grill, Grand Buffet, McDonald's, New York Deli, Red Lobster, Red Robin, Quiznos, Starbucks, Taco Bell, Wendy's, **lodging:** Best Western, Motel 6, Hampton Inn, Holiday Inn, **other:** Burlington Coats, $Tree, Kohl's, Lowes Whse, Macy's, Marshall's, PathMark Foods, Pep Boys, Radio Shack, Sears Essentials/auto, Staples, Target, Walmart/auto

**4** Durham Ave (no EZ nb return), S Plainfield, **E gas:** Lukoil, **other:** H HOSPITAL

**3** New Durham Rd (from sb), **E gas:** Shell, **W food:** Dunkin Donuts, **lodging:** Fairfield Inn, Red Roof Inn, **other:** Walgreens

**2b a** NJ 27, Metuchen, New Brunswick, **W gas:** BP, Lukoil, **food:** Dunkin Donuts, **other:** Costco, USPO, Walmart SuperCtr

**1b a** US 1, **1-2 mi N on US 1 gas:** Exxon/dsl, Getty, Gulf, RaceWay/dsl, **food:** Bone Fish Grill, Cheese Burger Paradise, China Cafe, Dunkin Donuts, Famous Dave's BBQ, KFC, Macaroni Grill, McDonald's, Menlo Park Diner, Panera Bread, Polo Tropical, Red Lobster, Ruby Tuesday, TGI Friday, Uno, White Castle, **lodging:** Woodbridge Hotel, **other:** A&P Foods, Best Buy, Goodyear/auto, Macy's, Marshall's, Nordstrom's, Rite Aid, Sears/auto, 7-11, mall, **S gas:** Shell, **food:** Applebees, Boston Mkt, ChuckeCheese, Grand Buffet, McDonald's, Quizno's, **lodging:** Holiday Inn Express, **other:** Astin Martin/Jaguar/Porche, BJ's Whse, BMW, Home Depot, Infiniti, Mercedes, Office Depot, PepBoys, PetCo, Staples, Stop'n Shop Foods

**0mm** I-287 begins/ends on NJ 440, I-95, NJ Tpk.

## INTERSTATE 295

**T R E N T O N**

| Exit # | Services |
|---|---|
| **67b a** | US 1. **I-295 nb becomes I-95 sb at US 1.** See NJ I-95, exit 67b a. |
| **65b a** | Sloan Ave, **E gas:** Exxon, **food:** Burger King, Dunkin Donuts, New China Buffet, Subway, Taco Bell, Uno, **other:** Goodyear/auto, Rizoldi's |
| **64** | NJ 535 N (from sb), to NJ 33 E, same as 63 |
| **63b a** | NJ 33 W, rd 535, Mercerville, Trenton, **E gas:** Hess, Lukoil, Valero, **food:** Applebee's, Boston Mkt, Lobster Dock, McDonald's, Pizza Hut, Popeye's, Subway, Vincent's Pizza, Wendy's, **other:** CVS Drug, Ford, Rite Aid, auto repair, USPO, **W gas:** Exxon/24hr, **food:** Dunkin Donuts, Golden Gate Diner/24hr, Szechuan House, WaWa, **other:** Advance Parts, Family$ |
| **62** | Olden Ave N (from sb, no return), **W gas:** Delta |
| **61b a** | Arena Dr, White Horse Ave, **W gas:** 7-11 |
| **60b a** | I-195, to I-95, **W** to Trenton, **E** to Neptune |
| **58mm** | scenic overlook both lanes |
| **57b a** | US 130, US 206, **E gas:** Petro, Shell/24hr, Valero, **food:** Burger King, Denny's, McDonald's, **lodging:** Best Western, Comfort Inn, Day's Inn, Econolodge, Hampton Inn, **other:** Acme Foods, Blue Beacon, **W lodging:** Candlewood Suites, **other:** st police |
| **56** | US 206 S (from nb, no return), to NJ Tpk, Ft Dix, McGuire AFB, **E gas:** Sunoco, **lodging:** Day's Inn, Holiday Inn Express, same as 57 |
| **52b a** | rd 656, to Columbus, Florence, **E gas:** Petro/dsl/rest./24hr/@, Pilot/Wendy's/dsl/24hr |
| **50mm** | **rest area both lanes, no facilities** |
| **47b a** | NJ 541, to Mount Holly, NJ Tpk, Burlington, **E gas:** BP, Exxon/dsl/24hr, GasWay, Mobil/dsl, **food:** Applebees, Burger King, ChuckeCheese, Cracker Barrel, Dunkin Donuts, FoodCourt, McDonald's, Taco Bell, TGIFriday, **lodging:** Best Western, Econolodge, Hampton Inn, Holiday Inn Express, **other:** Home Depot, Kohl's, Macy's, Sears, Target, mall, vet, **W gas:** Citgo, Exxon, Hess/dsl, **food:** Checker's, Friendly's, Mulligan's Ice Cream, Subway, Wedgewood Farms Rest., Wendy's, **other:** H HOSPITAL, AutoZone, Acme Foods, Curves, Goodyear/auto, K-Mart, Marshall's, WaWa, Walmart/auto |
| **45b a** | to Mt Holly, Willingboro, **W gas:** LukOil, **other:** H HOSPITAL, auto repair |
| **43b a** | rd 636, to Rancocas Woods, Delran, **W gas:** Exxon/24hr, **food:** Carlucci's Rest. |

Copyright 2009 - The Next Exit®

**N** ↕ **S**

**CHERRY HILL**

## INTERSTATE 295

**40b a** NJ 38, to Mount Holly, Moorestown, **W gas:** Shell/Subway/dsl/24hr, **food:** Arby's, Baja Fresh, Burger King, Chick-fil-A, Dunkin Donuts, Panera Bread, Perkin's (3mi), Starbucks, TGIFriday, **lodging:** Quality Inn (4mi), Residence Inn, **other:** H HOSPITAL, Acme Foods/Sav-On, Costco, GNC, Jo-Ann Fabrics, PetsMart, Target, TJ Maxx, U-Haul, Wegman's

**36b a** NJ 73, to NJ Tpk, Tacony Br, Berlin, **E gas:** Exxon, LukOil/dsl, **food:** Bob Evans, Denny's, McDonald's, Sage Rest, Wendy's, **lodging:** Comfort Inn, Courtyard, Fairfield Inn, Hampton Inn, Howard Johnson, Marriott, Red Roof Inn, Rodeway Inn, Super 8, Wingate Inn, **W gas:** Citgo, Exxon, Shell, **food:** Boscov's, Burger King, Chick-fil-A, Chipotle Mexican, Don Pablo, Dunkin Donuts, 5 Guys Burgers, KFC/Taco Bell, McDonald's, Friendly's, Panera Bread, PeiWei Asian, Perkins, Pizza Hut, Uno, Wendy's, **lodging:** Bel-Air Motel, Crossland Suites, Crossroads Inn, Homewood Suites, Motel 6, Quality Inn, Track&Turf Motel, **other:** Acura, AutoZone, Barnes&Noble, Best Buy, Chevrolet, Chrysler, Circuit City, $Tree, Firestone/auto, Ford, Goodyear/auto, Home Depot, Infiniti, K-Mart, Lincoln/Mercury, Lowes Whse, Macy's, Marshall's, NTB, Old Navy, PepBoys, PetsMart, Ross, Sears/auto, ShopRite Foods, mall

**34b a** NJ 70, to Camden, Cherry Hill, **E gas:** BP, Exxon/24hr, Liberty, LukOil, **food:** Big John's Steaks, Burger King, Dunkin Donuts, McDonald's, **lodging:** Extended Stay America, **other:** Curves, Jaguar/Saab, Tires+, **W gas:** Citgo, Exxon, Gulf/dsl, LukOil, **food:** Boston Pizza, Dunkin Donuts, Elephant & Castle, Famous Dave's BBQ, McDonald's, Mirabella Cafe, Pizza Hut, Ponzio's Rest, Steak&Ale, Starbucks, Subway, **lodging:** Best Value Inn, Clarion, Crowne Plaza, **other:** H HOSPITAL, $Tree, Goodyear/auto, Rite Aid, Steinmart, WaWa, vet

**32** NJ 561, to Haddonfield, Voorhees, **3 mi E gas:** LukOil/dsl/24hr, **food:** Applebees, Fuddruckers, Olive Garden, Panera Bread, **lodging:** Hampton Inn, Wingate Inn, **other:** H HOSPITAL, USPO, **W gas:** Pioneer/dsl, Sunoco, **food:** Burger King, Dunkin Donuts, Quizno's, **other:** Curves, Ford, 7-11, vet

**31** Woodcrest Station

**30** Warwick Rd (from sb)

**29b a** US 30, to Berlin, Collingswood, **E gas:** Astro/dsl, Exxon, LukOil, **food:** Arby's, Church's, Dunkin Donuts, Popeye's, Wendy's, **other:** AutoZone, Home Depot, PathMark Foods, PetsMart, Sears Essentials

**28** NJ 168, to NJ Tpk, Belmawr, Mt Ephraim, **E gas:** Citgo, Gulf/repair, Shell/dsl, Valero/dsl, **food:** Burger King, Club Diner, Dunkin Donuts, Wendy's, **lodging:** Bellmawr Motel, Comfort Inn, Econolodge, Holiday Inn, Howard Johnson, Red Roof Inn, Super 8, **other:** CVS Drug, Walgreens, transmissions, **W gas:** BP, Exxon/LP/24hr, Hess, WaWa, **food:** Black Horse Diner, Domino's, Dunkin Donuts, Golden Corral, McDonald's, Subway, **other:** AutoZone, Chrysler/Dodge, Curves, CVS Drug,

**28** Continued
Harley Davidson, Pepboys, Staples, Walgreens, Walmart

**26** I-76, NJ 42, to I-676, Walt Whitman Bridge, Walt Whitman Bridge

**25b a** NJ 47, to Westville, Deptford

**24b a** NJ 45, NJ 551 (no EZ sb return), to Westville, **E gas:** Garden State, **other:** H HOSPITAL, AutoZone, **W other:** Chevrolet, Family$

**23** US 130 N, to National Park

**22** NJ 644, to Red Bank, Woodbury, **E gas:** LukOil, **1 mi W gas:** Crown Point Trkstp/dsl/@, WaWa, **food:** Wendy's

**21** NJ 44 S, Paulsboro, Woodbury, **W food:** WaWa, Wendy's, **lodging:** Westwood Motor Lodge

**20** NJ 643, to NJ 660, to National Park, Thorofare, **E lodging:** Best Western, **W lodging:** Red Bank Inn

**19** NJ 656, to NJ 44, Mantua

**18b a** NJ 667, to NJ 678, Clarksboro, Mt Royal, **E gas:** BP/dsl, TA/Exxon/Buckhorn Rest./dsl/rest./@, **food:** Dunkin Donuts, KFC/Taco Bell, McDonald's, Wendy's, **other:** RV camping

**17** NJ 680, to Mickleton, Gibbstown, **W food:** Burger King, Domino's, **lodging:** Motel 6, **other:** Advance Parts, Family$, GNC, Rite Aid, ShopRite Foods, WaWa

**16b** NJ 551, to Gibbstown, Mickleton

**16a** NJ 653, to Paulsboro, Swedesboro

**15** NJ 607, to Gibbstown

**14** NJ 684, to Repaupo

**13** US 130 S, US 322 W, to Bridgeport (from sb, no return)

**11** US 322 E, to Mullica Hill

**10** Ctr Square Rd, to Swedesboro, **E gas:** WaWa, **food:** Applebees, Dunkin Doughnuts/Baskin Robbins, McDonald's, Subway, Wendy's, **lodging:** Hampton Inn, Holiday Inn Select, **other:** Acme Foods/Sav-On, Rite Aid, **W other:** Camping World RV Supplies/service

**7** to Auburn, Pedricktown

**4** NJ 48, Woodstown, Penns Grove

**3mm** weigh sta nb

**2mm** rest area nb, full ♿ facilities, info, ☎, 🛆, litter barrels, rv dump, vending

**2c** to US 130 (from sb), Deepwater, **E** same as 2b, **W gas:** All-American Plaza/Exxon/Dunkin Donuts/dsl/scales/24hr, ✈FLYING J/CountryMkt/dsl/scales/LP/24hr, **other:** H HOSPITAL

**2b** US 40 E, to NJ Tpk, **E gas:** Gulf, Pilot/Subway/dsl/24hr/@, **lodging:** Comfort Inn, Econolodge, Friendship Motel, Holiday Inn Express, Quality Inn, Wellesley Inn, **W** same as 2c

**2a** US 40 W (from nb), to Delaware Bridge

**1c** NJ 551 S, Hook Rd, to Salem, **E lodging:** White Oaks Motel, **W** H HOSPITAL

**1b** US 130 N (from nb), Penns Grove

**1a** NJ 49 E, to Pennsville, Salem, **E gas:** Exxon/dsl/repair, **food:** Applebees, Burger King, Cracker Barrel, KFC/Taco Bell, McDonald's, **lodging:** Hampton Inn, **other:** Peterbilt, **W gas:** Coastal, **lodging:** Seaview Motel

**0mm** New Jersey/Delaware state line, Delaware River, Delaware Memorial Bridge

NM

---

## INTERSTATE 10

E ↕ W

| Exit # | Services |
|---|---|
| 164.5mm | New Mexico/Texas state line |
| 164mm | **Welcome Ctr wb, full ♿ facilities, 📞, 🎪, litter barrels, petwalk** |
| 162 | NM 404, Anthony, **S** RV camping |
| 160mm | weigh/insp sta wb |
| 155 | NM 227 W, to Vado, **N** Western Sky's RV Park, **S gas:** NTS/dsl/rest./scales/@, Texaco/dsl/rest./24hr, **other:** El Camino Real HS |
| 151 | Mesquite |
| 144 | I-25 N, to Las Cruces |
| 142 | Rd 188, Rd 101, Valley Dr, Las Cruces, **N gas:** Chevron/dsl, **food:** Chilito's Mexican, Dick's Burgers, Steak Company, Whataburger/24hr, **lodging:** Best Western, |

---

**LAS CRUCES**

**142 Continued**
Comfort Inn, Holiday Inn, Holiday Inn Express, Motel 6, Ramada Inn, Super 8, Teakwood Inn, **other:** Ⓗ HOSPITAL, Chevrolet/Cadillac, Dalmont's RV Camping, Ford, Honda, Hyundai, Mazda, Nissan, tires/repair, NMSU, **S gas:** Fina, **other:** USPO

**140** NM 28, to Mesilla, Las Cruces, **N gas:** Phillips 66/dsl, **food:** Applebee's, Blake's Lotaburger, BurgerTime, Cracker Barrel, DQ, McDonald's, Quizno's, Starbucks, **lodging:** Best Western, Hampton Inn, La Quinta, SpringHill Suites, **other:** Radio Shack, Walmart SuperCtr, **N on Valley Dr...gas:** Fina/dsl, **food:** American BBQ, Domino's, Old Town Rest., **other:** Dodge, Toyota, VW, **S food:** Gadsden Purchase Grill, **lodging:** Comfort Inn, **other:** Harley-Davidson, S&H RV Ctr, Siesta RV Park, Sunland RV Ctr

**139** NM 292, Amador Ave, Motel Blvd, Las Cruces, **N gas:** Pilot/Subway/dsl/scales/24hr, TA/Burger King/Pizza Hut/Taco Bell/dsl/rest./24hr/scales/@, **S food:** PitStop Café Mexican, **lodging:** Coachlight Inn/RV Park

## INTERSTATE 10 CONT'D

| | |
|---|---|
| **138mm** | Rio Grande River |
| **135.5mm** | rest area eb, full ♿ facilities, 🌲 litter barrels, pet-walk, scenic view, RV dump |
| **135** | US 70 E, to W Las Cruces, Alamogordo, **1 mi N other:** KOA |
| **132** | **N** to ✈, fairgrounds, **S gas:** Love's/Subway/dsl/24hr |
| **127** | Corralitos Rd, **N gas:** Exxon, **other:** Bowlin's Trading Post, to fairgrounds |
| **120.5mm** | insp sta wb |
| **116** | NM 549 |
| **111mm** | parking area wb, litter barrels |
| **102** | Akela, **N gas:** Exxon/dsl/gifts |
| **85** | East Motel Dr, Deming, **S gas:** Chevron/dsl, Save Gas/dsl, **lodging:** Holiday Inn, La Quinta, Motel 6, **other:** Chrysler/Dodge/Jeep, Dream Catcher RV camping |
| **82b** | Railroad Blvd, Deming, **N gas:** Chevron/dsl, **S gas:** Chevron/dsl, Save Gas, Texaco/dsl, **food:** DQ, KFC, La Fonda Mexican, McDonald's, Wendy's, **lodging:** Best Western, Day's Inn, Grand Motel, Holiday Inn, Mirador Motel, Motel 6, **other:** AutoZone, Big O Tire, Checker Parts, Chevrolet/Pontiac/GMC, $General, $Tree, Ford/Lincoln/Mercury, Firestone, Goodyear, K-Mart, Little RV Park, NAPA, Roadrunner RV Park, Wagon Wheel RV Park, Walmart SuperCtr/Subway, to Rock Hound SP, st police |
| **82a** | US 180, NM 26, NM 11, Deming, **N gas:** Chevron, **food:** Blake's Lotaburger, **S gas:** Exxon, Phillips 66, Shell/dsl, **food:** Burger King, China Rest., Denny's, DQ, K-Bob's, KFC, LJ Silver, Palmas Italian, Pizza Hut, Rancher's Grill, Subway, **lodging:** Grand Motel, **other:** AutoZone, Budget Tire, CarQuest, Radio Shack, museum, tires, to Pancho Villa SP, Rockhound SP |
| **81** | NM 11, W Motel Dr, Deming, **S gas:** Chevron/24hr, Deming TT/dsl/scales, Shamrock/dsl, Shell, **food:** Burger Time, El Camino Real Mexiacan, McDonald's, Sonic, Subway, Taco Bell, **lodging:** Balboa Motel, Best Western, Budget Motel, Comfort Inn, Deming Motel, Deluxe Inn, Executive Motel, Super 8, **other:** Hitchin Post RV Park, to Pancho Villa SP, Rock Hound SP |
| **68** | NM 418, **S gas:** Savoy/dsl/rest./24hr, tires/repair |
| **62** | Gage, **S gas:** Butterfield Station/Exxon/DQ/dsl/RV Park |
| **61mm** | rest area wb, full ♿ facilities, 🌲 litter barrels, vending, petwalk |
| **55** | Quincy |
| **53mm** | rest area eb, full ♿ facilities, 🌲 litter barrels, vending, petwalk |
| **51.5mm** | Continental Divide, elev 4585 |
| **49** | NM 146 S, to Hachita, Antelope Wells |
| **42** | Separ, **S** gas, Bowlin's Continental Divide Gifts, truck/auto repair |
| **34** | NM 113 S, Muir, Playas |
| **29** | no services |
| **24** | US 70, E Motel Dr, Lordsburg, **N gas:** ⊕FLYING J/Country Mkt/dsl/scales/24hr, Pilot/Arby's/dsl/scales/24hr, **lodging:** American Motel, **other:** Range RV Park |
| **23.5mm** | weigh sta both lanes |
| **22** | NM 494, Main St, Lordsburg, **N gas:** Save Gas, **food:** DQ, McDonald's, **lodging:** Comfort Inn, Holiday Motel, **other:** Chevrolet, Family$, Ford, Parts+, Saucito's Foods, **S gas:** Chevron, Save Gas, Shamrock/dsl, **food:** KFC/Taco Bell, Kranberry's Rest., **lodging:** Best Western, Holiday Inn Express, Motel 10, Super 8, **other:** KOA |
| **20b a** | W Motel Dr, Lordsburg, **Visitors Ctr/full** ♿ facilities, |

| | |
|---|---|
| **20b a** | Continued<br>**info, N gas:** Love's/Subway/Godfather's Pizza/Subway/dsl, **lodging:** Day's Inn, **S gas:** Chevron/dsl |
| **15** | to Gary |
| **11** | NM 338 S, to Animas |
| **5** | NM 80 S, to Road Forks, **S gas:** USA/rest./dsl/scales/24hr **lodging:** Desert West Motel/rest., **other:** USPO, fireworks |
| **3** | Steins |
| **0mm** | New Mexico/Arizona state line |

## INTERSTATE 25

| Exit # | Services |
|---|---|
| **460.5mm** | New Mexico/Colorado state line |
| **460** | **E** Cedar Rail Campground, weigh sta sb, Raton Pass Summit, elev 7834 |
| **454** | Lp 25, Raton, **2 mi W gas:** Shell, **lodging:** Budget Host, El Portal Motel, Raton Pass Inn, Robin Hood Motel, **other:** ⊞ HOSPITAL, Buick/Chevrolet/Pontiac, CarQuest, Toyota |
| **452** | NM 72 E, Raton, **E** to Sugarite SP, **W gas:** Conoco, **lodging:** Mesa Vista Motel |
| **451** | US 64 E, US 87 E, Raton, **E gas:** Chevron, Shell/dsl/24hr, **food:** Subway, **other:** Kick Back RV Park, to Capulin Volcano NM, **W info, gas:** Conoco, Loaf'N Jug, Phillips 66, Shell/dsl, **food:** Arby's, All Seasons Rest., DQ, Denny's, K-Bob's, KFC, McDonald's, Pappa's Rest., Pizza Hut, Sonic, **lodging:** Best Western, Comfort Inn, El Kapp Motel, Holiday Classic Motel, Microtel, Motel 6, Sands Motel, Super 8, Texan Motel, Travel Motel, Village Inn Motel, **other:** ⊞ HOSPITAL, K-Mart, NAPA, Visitor's Ctr |
| **450** | Lp 25, Raton, **W gas:** Shamrock/dsl, **lodging:** Holiday Inn Express, Oasis Motel, Robin Hood Motel, Westerner Motel, **other:** ⊞ HOSPITAL, AutoZone, Family$, KOA, SuperSave Foods, vet |
| **446** | US 64 W, to Cimarron, Taos, **4 mi W** NRA Whittington Ctr, camping |
| **440mm** | Canadian River |
| **435** | Tinaja |
| **434.5mm** | rest area both lanes, full ♿ facilities, weather info, 🌲 litter barrels, petwalk |
| **426** | NM 505, Maxwell, **W gas:** LC OneStop/dsl, **other:** USPO, to Maxwell Lakes |
| **419** | NM 58, to Cimarron, **E gas:** Shell/Russell's/Subway/dsl/scales/24hr/@ |
| **414** | US 56, Springer, **E gas:** Conco/dsl, Shell, **lodging:** Oasis Motel |
| **412** | US 56 E, US 412 E, NM 21, NM 468, Springer, **1 mi E gas:** Fina **other:** CarQuest, Ford |
| **404** | NM 569, Colmor, Charette Lakes |
| **393** | Levy |
| **387** | NM 120, to Roy, Wagon Mound, **E gas:** Chevron/dsl, Phillips 66/dsl, truck/tire repair |
| **376mm** | rest area sb, full ♿ facilities, 🔌, 🌲 litter barrels, petwalk, RV camp/dump |
| **374mm** | rest area nb, full ♿ facilities, 🔌, 🌲 litter barrels, petwalk, RV camp/dump |
| **366** | NM 97, NM 161, Watrous, Valmora, **W** Santa Fe Trail, Ft Union NM |
| **364** | NM 97, NM 161, Watrous, Valmora |
| **361** | no services |
| **360mm** | rest area both lanes, litter barrels |
| **356** | Onava |
| **352** | **E** RV camping, **W** ✈ |

## INTERSTATE 25 CONT'D

**LAS VEGAS N↕S**

**347** to NM 518, Las Vegas, **0-2 mi** **W** gas: Pino/dsl/rest., Phillips 66/Burger King, **food:** Arby's, Burger King, Hillcrest Rest., K-Bob's, KFC, McDonald's, Taco Bell, **lodging:** Comfort Inn, Day's Inn, Regal Motel, Super 8, **other:** KOA, Storrie Lake SP

**345** NM 65, NM 104, University Ave, Las Vegas, **E** to Conchas Lake SP, **W** gas: Shell/dsl, **food:** Charlie's Cafe, DQ, KFC, Little Moon Chinese, McDonald's, Subway, Wendy's, **lodging:** Budget Inn, El Fidel, Palamino Motel, Sante Fe Trail Inn, Sunshine Motel, Townhouse Motel, **other:** H HOSPITAL, Firestone, GMC, Hist. Old Town Plaza

**343** to NM 518 N, Las Vegas, **E other:** Garcia Tires, **W** **lodging:** Holiday Inn Express, **0-2 mi** **W** gas: Chevron, Fina, Phillips 66, **food:** McDonald's, Taco Bell, Teresa's Mexican, **lodging:** Thunderbird Motel

**339** US 84 S, to Santa Rosa, Romeroville, **E** KOA, **W** gas: Phillips 66/Subway/dsl

**335** Tecolote

**330** Bernal

**325mm** rest area both lanes, litter barrels, no restrooms

**323** NM 3 S, Villanueva, **E** gas: Sunshine Gas, **food:** La Risa (1mi), **E** to Villanueva SP, Madison Winery (6mi), RV camping

**319** San Juan, San Jose, **W** gas: Pecos River Sta.

**307** NM 63, Rowe, Pecos, **W** Pecos NM, Hist Rte 66, same as 299

**299** NM 50, Glorieta, Pecos, **W** gas: Conoco/dsl (4mi), Shell (6mi), **other:** Glorieta Conf Ctr

**297** Valencia

**294** Apache Canyon, **W other:** KOA, Rancheros Camping (Mar-Nov)

**290** US 285 S, to Lamy, S to Clines Corners, **2 mi** **E food:** Subway, **W other:** KOA, Rancheros Camping (Mar-Nov)

**284** NM 466, Old Pecos Trail, Santa Fe, **W** gas: Chevron/dsl, Sunset Gen Store, **lodging:** to Best Western, Desert Inn, Pecos Trail Inn, The Sands, **other:** H HOSPITAL, museums

**282** US 84, US 285, St Francis Dr, **W** gas: Conoco/Wendy's/dsl, Giant, **food:** Church's

**278** NM 14, Cerrillos Rd, Santa Fe, **0-4 mi** **W** gas: Conoco, Giant, Phillips 66/dsl, Shell, **food:** Adelita's Mexican, Applebee's, Arby's, Blue Corn Cafe, Burger King, China Star, Denny's, Domino's, Flying Tortilla, IHOP, KFC, Lotaburger, McDonald's, Olive Garden, Outback Steaks, Panda Express, Pizza Hut, Quizno's, Lobster, Schlotsky's, Sonic, Starbucks, Taco Bell, Village Inn Rest., Wendy's, **lodging:** Best Western, Budget Host, Comfort Inn, Courtyard, Day's Inn, Econolodge, Fairfield Inn, Hampton Inn, Holiday Inn, Holiday Inn Express, La Quinta, Luxury Inn, Motel 6, Quality Inn, Santa Fe Inn, Super 8, **other:** Albertson's, Best Buy, Big Lots, Buick/Pontiac, Cadillac, Chevrolet/GMC, Chrysler/Jeep/Dodge, Dillard's, Discount Tire, Dodge, Firestone/auto, Ford, Home Depot, Honda, JC Penney, Jo-Ann Fabrics, Kohl's, Michael's, Lowes Whse, Sam's Club/gas, Sears/auto, Staples, Subaru, Target, TJ Maxx, VW, Walgreens, Walmart, Santa Fe Outlets/famous brands

**276b a** NM 599, to NM 14, to Madrid, **E other:** Santa Fe Skies RV Park, **4 mi** **W** gas: Shell, **other:** Sunrise Springs

**271** CR 50F, La Cienega

**269mm** rest area nb, full facilities, litter barrels, petwalk

**SANTA FE**

**267** Waldo Canyon Rd, insp sta.

**264** NM 16, Pueblo, **W** to Cochiti Lake RA

**263mm** Galisteo River

**259** NM 22, to Santo Domingo Pueblo, **W** gas: Phillips 66/cafe/dsl, **other:** to Cochiti Lake RA

**257** Budaghers, **W** Mormon Battalion Mon

**252** San Felipe Pueblo, **E** gas: Phillips 66/dsl, **food:** San Felipe Casino/rest.

**248** Rte 66, Algodones

**242** US 550, NM 44 W, NM 165 E, to Farmington, Aztec, **W** gas: Chevron/dsl, Circle K/gas, Conoco/dsl, Phillips 66/dsl, Shell/Burger King/dsl, **food:** Checkers, Coronado Rest., Denny's, Guang Dong Chinese, KFC, Lotaburger, McDonald's, Papa Murphy's, Pizza Hut, Quizno's, Starbucks, Sonic, Subway, Taco Bell, Twisters, Wendy's, **lodging:** Day's Inn, Holiday Inn Express, Quality Inn, Super 8, **other:** AutoZone, Curves, $General, KOA, Parts+, Walgreens, to Coronado SP

**240** NM 473, to Bernalillo, **W** gas: Chevron, Conoco/dsl, **food:** Abuelito Mexican, Pueblito Mexican, Range Café, **other:** KOA, vet, to Coronado SP

**234** NM 556, Tramway Rd, **E** gas: Shamrock/dsl, **other:** casino, **W** gas: Phillips 66/dsl

**233** Alameda Blvd, **E** gas: Chevron, **food:** Burger King, **lodging:** Comfort Inn, Motel 6, **other:** Audi, Mercedes, Porsche, Toyota, **W** gas: Phillips 66/Circle K/dsl, **food:** Carl's Jr, **lodging:** Holiday Inn Express, Ramada Ltd, **other:** Carmax

**232** Paseo del Norte, **E food:** China Luck, Red Brick Pizza, Starbucks, Subway, Wendy's, **lodging:** Country Inn&Suites, Howard Johnson, **other:** Aloha RV Ctr, AutoZone, Kohl's, Lowe's Whse, Office Depot, Target, Walgreens, **W** gas: Shell/Circle K, **food:** Arby's, **lodging:** Courtyard, Marriott

**231** San Antonio Ave, **E** gas: Fina/7-11, **food:** Cracker Barrel, Denny's, **lodging:** Hilton Garden, Homewood Suites, La Quinta, Quality Suites, **other:** H HOSPITAL, USPO, **W** **lodging:** Crossland Suites, Hampton Inn, La Quinta, **other:** Mazda, VW

**230** San Mateo Blvd, Osuna Rd, Albuquerque, **E** gas: Circle K, Giant/dsl, Phillips 66, Shell, **food:** Applebee's, Arby's, Azuma Grill, Bob's Burgers, Burger King, Chili's, Furrs Buffet, Hooters, KFC, LJ Silver, McDonald's, Olive Garden, Pizza Hut/Taco Bell, Schlotsky's, Sonic, Souper Salad, Starbucks, Subway, SweetTomatoes, Taco Cabana, Teriyaki Chicken, Texas Roadhouse, Village Inn Rest., Wendy's, Wienerschnitzel, **lodging:** Nativo Lodge, **other:** H HOSPITAL, Brake Masters, Buick/Pontiac/GMC,

## INTERSTATE 25 CONT'D

**N** ↕ **S**

**ALBUQUERQUE**

**NM**

**230** Continued
Cadillac, Curves, Firestone/auto, Hummer, Just Brakes, Mercedes, NAPA, Nissan, PepBoys, Subaru/Isuzu, Tires-4-less, Walgreens, Wild Oats Mkt, **W** **gas:** Chevron, Shamrock, **food:** Cajun Kitchen, McDonald's, Oasis Cafe, Whataburger, **lodging:** Studio 6 **other:** Mini/BMW

**229** Jefferson St, **E** **food:** Carrabba's, Landry's Seafood, Outback Steaks, **lodging:** Holiday Inn, **other:** H HOSPITAL, same as 230, **W** **food:** Boston's Pizza, Chama River Rest., Coldstone Creamery, Dickey's BBQ, Food Ct., Fuddrucker's, Jersey Jack's, Mimi's Café, Pappadeaux, PF Chang's, Red Robin, Rockfish Café, Subway, Texas Land&Cattle Steaks, **lodging:** Drury Inn, Residence Inn **other:** Lexus

**228** Montgomery Blvd, **E** **gas:** Chevron/dsl, Conoco/dsl, Fina7/11, **food:** Fiestas Cantina, Lotaburger, **lodging:** Best Western, **other:** H HOSPITAL, Discount Tire, **W** **gas:** Shell, **food:** Arby's, Carls Jr., IHOP, McDonald's, Panda Express, Sonic, Starbucks, Wendy's, **lodging:** InTowne Suites, **other:** Acura, Ford, Costco/gas, Home Depot, Infiniti, Office Depot, PetsMart, Sam's Club/gas, Sportsman's Whse

**227b** Comanche Rd, Griegos Rd, **E** UPS Depot

**227a** Candelaria Rd, Albuquerque, **E** **gas:** Chevron/rest., Circle K, Fina/Subway/dsl, Shell, TA/dsl/24hr/@, **food:** IHOP, Subway, Village Inn Rest., **lodging:** Comfort Inn, Clubhouse Inn, Day's Inn, Fairfield Inn, Hilton, Holiday Inn, Rodeway Inn, Motel 6, Super 8, **W** **gas:** Chevron, **food:** Waffle House, **lodging:** Ambassador Inn, Red Roof Inn, **other:** Volvo

**226b a** I-40, E to Amarillo, W to Flagstaff

**225** Lomas Blvd, **E** **gas:** Chevron/7-11, **food:** JB's, **lodging:** Plaza Inn/rest., **other:** Chevrolet, Dodge, Ford, Saturn **W** **food:** Burger King, **lodging:** Embassy Suites **other:** H HOSPITAL

**224** Lead Ave, Coal Ave, Grand Ave, Central Ave, **E** **lodging:** Crossroads Motel, **other:** H HOSPITAL **W** **gas:** Chevron, **lodging:** Econolodge, Stardust Inn

**223** Chavez Ave, **E** **lodging:** Motel 6, **other:** sports arena

**222b a** Gibson Blvd, **E** **gas:** Phillips 66, **food:** Applebee's, Burger King, Fuddrucker's, Subway, Waffle House, Village Inn Rest., **lodging:** Best Western, Comfort Inn, Country Inn&Suites, Courtyard, Hampton Inn, Hawthorn Suites, Hilton Garden, La Quinta, Quality Suites, Vagabond Inn, **other:** H HOSPITAL, Curves, Kirtland AFB, museum, **W** **gas:** Fina/7-11, **food:** Church's, LotaBurger

**221** Sunport, **E** **lodging:** Holiday Inn Select, Homewood Suites, Hyatt Place, **other:** USPO, ✈

**220** Rio Bravo Blvd, Mountain View, **E** golf, **2 mi** **W** **gas:** Shamrock, **food:** Burger King, Church's, McDonald's, Pizza Hut, Subway, Taco Bell, **other:** Albertson's, Family$, Walgreens

**215** NM 47, **E** **gas:** Conoco/dsl, Phillips 66/dsl, **other:** to Isleta Lakes RA/RV Camping, casino, st police

**214mm** Rio Grande

**213** NM 314, Isleta Blvd, **W** **gas:** Chevron/Subway/dsl/24hr

**209** NM 45, to Isleta Pueblo

**203** NM 6, to Los Lunas, **E** **gas:** Chevron/dsl/24hr, Shamrock, Shell/Wendy's/dsl/24hr, **food:** Benny's, China Buffet, Del Taco, Denny's, McDonald's, Papa John's, Sonic, Starbucks, Village Inn Rest., **lodging:** Day's Inn,

**203** Continued
Las Lumas Inn, **other:** AutoZone, Big O Tire, Chevrolet, Ford, Home Depot, Walgreens, **W** **gas:** Phillips 66/Subway/dsl, **food:** Carl's Jr, Coldstone Creamery, Chili's, KFC, Panda Express, **lodging:** Western Skies Inn, **other:** Discount Tire, Walmart SuperCtr

**B E L E N**

**195** Lp 25, Los Chavez, **1 mi** **E** **food:** KFC, McDonald's, Pizza Hut/Taco Bell, **lodging:** Hub Motel, **other:** Walmart SuperCtr/gas

**191** NM 548, Belen, **1 mi** **E** **gas:** Conoco/dsl, **food:** McDonald's, **lodging:** Super 8, **other:** $General, **W** **food:** Rio Grande Diner, **lodging:** Holiday Inn Express, La Mirada Hotel/RV park

**190** Lp 25, Belen, **1-2 mi** **E** **gas:** Akins/dsl, Conoco/dsl, Phillips 66, **food:** A&W, Arby's, Casa de Pizza, McDonald's, TJ's Mexican, **lodging:** Super 8, **other:** AutoZone, Big O Tire

**175** US 60, Bernardo, **E** Salinas NM, **W** **other:** Kiva RV Park

**174mm** Rio Puerco

**169** **E** La Jolla St Game Refuge, Sevilleta NWR

**167mm** **rest area both lanes, full** 🅰 **facilities,** 🌲 **litter barrels, vending, petwalk**

**166mm** Rio Salado

**165mm** weigh sta/parking area both lanes

**163** San Acacia

**156** Lemitar, **W** Phillis 66/dsl/24hr

**152** Escondida, **W** to st police

**S O C O R R O**

**150** US 60 W, Socorro, **W** **gas:** Chevron, Exxon/dsl, Phillips 66/dsl, Shamrock, **food:** Burger King, China Best, Denny's/24hr, Domino's, El Camino Rest., Healthy Heart Cafe, K-Bob's, KFC, Lotaburger, McDonald's, Pizza Hut, RoadRunner Steaks, Socorro Springs Rest., Sonic, Taco Bell, **lodging:** Best Western, Comfort Inn, Days Inn, Economy Inn, Econolodge, Holiday Inn Express, Howard Johnson, Sands Motel, San Miguel Inn, Super 8, **other:** Ace Hardware, Alco, AutoZone, Brooks Foods, CarQuest, Chevrolet/Pontiac/Buick, Chrysler/Dodge/Jeep, $General, Family$, Ford/Mercury, NAPA, Radio Shack, Smith's Foods, TrueValue, Walmart SuperCtr, to NM Tech

**147** US 60 W, Socorro, **W** **gas:** Chevron/dsl/RV dump, Conoco/LP, Shell/dsl, **food:** Arby's, **lodging:** Motel 6, **other:** H HOSPITAL, Socorro RV Park, to ✈

**139** US 380 E, to San Antonio, **E** gas/food, to Bosque Del Apache NWR

**124** to San Marcial, **E** **other:** to Bosque del Apache NWR, Ft Craig

**115** NM 107, **E** **gas:** Truck Plaza/dsl/rest./24hr, to Camino Real Heritage Ctr

**114mm** **rest areas both lanes, full** 🅰 **facilities,** 🌲 **litter barrels, petwalk, RV parking, vending**

**107mm** Nogal Canyon

**100** Red Rock

**92** Mitchell Point

**90mm** La Canada Alamosa, La Canada Alamosa

**89** NM 181, to Cuchillo, to Monticello, **4 mi** **E**...Monticello RV Park

**83** NM 52, NM 181, to Cuchillo, **3 mi** **E** **food:** Ivory Tusk Inn& Tavern, **lodging:** Elephant Butte Inn/rest., **other:** RV Park, Elephant Lake Butte SP

**82mm** insp sta nb

**79** Lp 25, to Truth or Consequences, **E** **gas:** Chevron/dsl, Circle K, Phillips 66/dsl, **food:** China Buffet, DQ, Denny's,

## INTERSTATE 25 CONT'D

N ↕ S

| | |
|---|---|
| **79** | Continued<br>Hilltop Café, K-Bob's, KFC/Taco Bell, La Cocina Mexican, Los Arcos Steaks, McDonald's, Pizza Hut, Sonic, Subway, **lodging:** Ace Lodge, Comfort Inn, Desert View Motel, Hot Springs Inn, Oasis Motel, Super 8, **other:** Ⓗ HOSPITAL, AutoZone, IGA Foods, NAPA, TrueValue, USPO, Walmart SuperCtr, to Elephant Butte SP |
| **76** | (75 from nb) Lp 25, to Williamsburg, **E gas:** Chevron/24hr, Conoco/dsl, Phillips 66/dsl, Shell/dsl, **food:** Big-A-Burger, **lodging:** Rio Grande Motel, **other:** Alco, Buick/Chevrolet/GMC/Pontiac, Cielo Vista RV Park, Ford, RJ RV Park, Shady Corner RV Park, USPO, auto/tire repair, city park |
| **71** | Las Palomas |
| **63** | NM 152, to Hillsboro, Caballo, **E** Lakeview RV Park/dsl, cliff dwellings |
| **59** | rd 187, Arrey, Derry, **E** to Caballo-Percha SPs |
| **58mm** | Rio Grande |
| **51** | rd 546, to Arrey, Garfield, Derry |
| **41** | NM 26 W, Hatch, **1 mi W gas:** Fina/Subway/dsl, **food:** DQ, **lodging:** Village Plaza Motel, **other:** Franciscan RV Ctr, USPO |
| **35** | NM 140 W, Rincon |
| **32** | Upham |
| **27mm** | scenic view nb, 🏓, litter barrels |
| **26mm** | insp sta nb |
| **23mm** | **rest area both lanes, full** ♿ **facilities,** 🏓 **, litter barrels, vending, petwalk** |
| **19** | Radium Springs, **W** Leasburg SP, Fort Selden St Mon, RV camping |
| **9** | Dona Ana, **W gas:** Circle K/dsl, Chucky's/dsl, Texaco, **food:** Alejandro's Mexican, Lakes Cafe, **other:** Family$, RV camping, USPO |
| **6b a** | US 70, to Alamogordo, Las Cruces, **E gas:** Fina/dsl, Shell, **food:** Coldstone Creamery, IHOP, New China Buffet, Outback Steaks, Papa Johns, Peter Piper Pizza, Pizzaria Uno, Ruby Tuesday, **lodging:** Fairfield Inn, Motel 6, Staybridge Suites, Towneplace Suites, **other:** Ⓗ HOSPITAL, K-Mart, Sam's Club/gas, Saturn, USPO, **W gas:** Chevron, Chucky's/dsl, Shamrock, Shell, **food:** BurgerTime, DQ, Domino's, KFC, Little Caesar's, Lotaburger, McDonald's, Sonic, Spanish Kitchen, Starbucks, Subway, Taco Bell, Whataburger/24hr, **other:** Albertson's, AutoZone, Checker Parts, $General, Family$, Kohl's, Jiffy Lube, Lowe's Whse, Radio Shack, Walgreens, golf, vet |
| **3** | Lohman Ave, Las Cruces, **E gas:** Shell, Valero, **food:** Applebee's, Burger King, Cattle Baron Steaks, Chili's, ChuckeCheese, Farley's Grill, Fidencio's Mexican, Garduno's Mexican, Golden Corral, Jack-in-the-Box, KFC, Pizza Hut, Red Lobster, Risotto's, Sonic, Starbucks, Village Inn Rest., Whataburger, **lodging:** Hotel Encanto, **other:** Albertson's, Barnes&Noble, Dillard's, Discount Tire, Home Depot, JC Penney, Marshalls, PetCo, Ross, Sears/auto, Sportsman's Whse, Target, mall, **W gas:** Western/dsl, **food:** Arby's, Carl's Jr, Casa Luna Pizza, Furr's Buffet, McDonald's, Papa Murphy's, Quizno's, Si Senor, Subway, Taco Bell, Texas Roadhouse, Wendy's, Wienerschnitzel, **lodging:** Hampton Inn, **other:** Best Buy, Big Lots, Hastings Books, Martin Tires, NAPA, Old Navy, PepBoys, PetsMart, Staples, Walgreens, Walmart SuperCtr, vet |
| **1** | University Ave, Las Cruces, **E other:** Ⓗ HOSPITAL, golf, museum, st police, **W gas:** Western/dsl, **food:** |

L A S  C R U C E S

E ↕ W

T U C U M C A R I

| | |
|---|---|
| **1** | Continued<br>DQ, Lorenzo's Italian, McDonald's, **lodging:** Comfort Suites, Ramada Inn, Sleep Inn, Value Place Inn, **other:** $Tree, Jo-Ann Fabrics, NMSU |
| **0mm** | I-25 begins/ends on I-10, exit 144 at Las Cruces. |

## INTERSTATE 40

| Exit # | Services |
|---|---|
| **373.5mm** | New Mexico/Texas state line, Mountain/Central time zone |
| **373mm** | **Welcome Ctr wb, full** ♿ **facilities,** Ⓒ, 🏓 **, litter barrels, petwalk** |
| **369** | NM 93 S, NM 392 N, to Endee |
| **361** | Bard |
| **358mm** | weigh sta both lanes |
| **356** | NM 469, San Jon, **N gas:** Drivers/cafe/dsl/24hr, to Ute Lake SP, **S gas:** Phillips 66/dsl, **lodging:** San Jon Motel |
| **343** | ranch access |
| **339** | NM 278, **N** ✈ |
| **335** | Lp 40, E Tucumcari Blvd, Tucumcari, **N gas:** Conoco, Phillips 66, **food:** Denny's, **lodging:** Comfort Inn, Econolodge, Hampton Inn, Holiday Inn/rest., Howard Johnson, Motel 6, Quality Inn, Super 8, **other:** Empty Saddle RV Park, to Conchas Lake SP, **S gas:** KOA |
| **333** | US 54 E, Tucumcari, **N gas:** ⊕FLYING J/Country Mkt/dsl/LP/scales/RV Dump/24hr, Love's/Arbys/Chester's/Godfather's/scalesdsl, **food:** Deans Rest., Del's Rest., **lodging:** Best Value Inn, **other:** K-Mart, Mtn Rd RV Park, truckwash |
| **332** | NM 209, NM 104, 1st St, Tucumcari, **N gas:** Chevron/Subway/dsl/24hr, Phillips 66, **food:** A&W/LJ Silver, KFC, K-Bob's, McDonald's, Lotaburger, Pizza Hut, Sonic, **lodging:** Best Western, Day's Inn, Microtel, **other:** Ⓗ HOSPITAL, $General, Family$, Lowe's Foods, st police, to Conchas Lake SP |
| **331** | Camino del Coronado, Tucumcari |
| **329** | US 54, US 66 E, W Tucumcari Ave, **N food:** Sonic (2mi), **lodging:** Payless Motel, **other:** Ⓗ HOSPITAL, golf |
| **321** | Palomas, **S gas:** Shell/DQ/Stuckey's/dsl |
| **311** | Montoya |
| **302mm** | **rest area both lanes, full** ♿ **facilities,** Ⓒ, 🏓 **, litter barrels, petwalk, RV dump** |
| **300** | NM 129, Newkirk, **N gas:** Phillips 66/dsl, **other:** to Conchas Lake SP |
| **291** | to Rte 66, Cuervo, **N** Cuervo Gas/repair |
| **284** | no services |
| **277** | US 84 S, to Ft Sumner, **N gas:** Chevron/dsl, **food:** DQ, Denny's, Silver Moon Café, **lodging:** Best Western, Budget Inn, Comfort Inn, Hampton Inn, Holiday Inn Express, |

## INTERSTATE 40 CONT'D

**E** ↕ **W**

**NM**

**S A N T A  R O S A**

**277** Continued
Motel 6, **other:** Ford, KOA, RV/auto repair, **S gas:** Love's/Carl's Jr/dsl/24hr, TA/Shell/Subway/dsl/24hr/@

**275** US 54 W, Santa Rosa, **N gas:** Conoco/Taco Sol, Phillips 66, **food:** KFC/LJ Silver, McDonald's, Rte 66 Rest., **lodging:** Best Western, Day's Inn, La Quinta, Travelodge, **other:** Santa Rosa Camping, **S gas:** Fina, Shell/Circle K/dsl/24hr, **food:** Comet Rest., Joseph's Cantina, Pizza Hut, **lodging:** American Inn, Laloma Motel, Sun'n Sand Motel/rest., Sunset Motel, Super 8, Tower Motel, Western Motel, **other:** H HOSPITAL, CarQuest, Goodyear, NAPA, st police, USPO

**273.5mm** Pecos River

**273** US 54 S, Santa Rosa, **N other:** Santa Rosa Lake SP, **S gas:** Chevron, **food:** Mateo's Rest., **other:** Budget 10 Inn, **other:** NAPA, repair

**267** Colonias, **N gas:** Shell/Stuckey's/dsl/rest./@

**263** San Ignacio

**256** US 84 N, NM 219, to Las Vegas

**252** no services

**251.5mm** rest area both lanes, full ♿ facilities, 🚻, 🅿, litter barrels, petwalk, RV dump

**243** Milagro, **N gas:** Chevron/dsl

**239** no services

**234** **N gas:** Exxon/Flying C/DQ/dsl/gifts, **other:** repair/24hr

**230** NM 3, to Encino, **N other:** to Villanueva SP

**226** no services

**220mm** parking area both lanes, litter barrels

**218b a** US 285, Clines Corners, **N gas:** Shell/Subway/dsl/24hr, **food:** Clines Corners Rest., **S other:** to Carlsbad Caverns NP

**208** Wagon Wheel

**207mm** rest area both lanes, full ♿ facilities, 🅿, litter barrels, petwalk

**203** **N** RV Park

**197** to Rte 66, Moriarty, **S gas:** Lisa's/dsl/rest./@, **other:** auto/RV repair, **1-2 mi S** same as 194, 196

**M O R I A R T Y**

**196** NM 41, Howard Cavasos Blvd, **S gas:** Phillips 66/dsl, 76/Circle K/dsl, Shell, **food:** Lotaburger, SuperChina Buffet, **lodging:** Comfort Inn, Sunset Motel, **other:** Family$, USPO, to Salinas NM (35mi), auto repair

**194** NM 41, Moriarty, **S gas:** Chevron/24hr, Phillips 66/dsl, TA/Pizza Hut/Subway/dsl/24hr/scales/@, **food:** Arby's, KFC/Taco Bell, McDonald's, **lodging:** Day's Inn, Econolodge, Holiday Inn Express, Ponderosa Motel, Super 8, **other:** Alco, Chevrolet/GMC, $General, IGA Foods, Moriarty Foods, RV Ctr

**187** NM 344, Edgewood, **N gas:** Conoco/DQ/dsl, **other:** Walmart SuperCtr, **S gas:** Exxon/dsl, Phillips 66/dsl, **food:** Chili Hills Mexican, China Chef, McDonald's, Pizza Barn, Subway, **other:** AutoZone, $General, Ford, Smith's Foods/gas, Walgreen, USPO, RV Camping

**181** NM 217, Sedillo, **S gas:** Phillips 66/dsl

**178** Zuzax, **S gas:** Chevron/dsl, **other:** Hidden Valley RV Park

**175** NM 337, NM 14, Tijeras, **N food:** Burger Boy (2mi), **other:** to Cibola NF, Turquoise Trail RV Park

**170** Carnuel

**167** Central Ave, to Tramway Blvd, **S gas:** Chevron/24hr, Fina/7-11, Shell, **food:** Canana's Mexican, Carl's Jr., KFC, Lotaburger, McDonald's, Pizza Hut/Taco Bell, Starbucks, Subway, Waffle House, **lodging:** Budget

**167** Continued
Host, Comfort Inn, Day's Inn, Deluxe Inn, Econolodge, Rodeway Inn, Sunset Inn, **other:** $Tree, Enchantment RV Ctr, GNC, Goodyear/U-Haul/auto, Meyer's RV, Raley's Foods, Rocky Mtn RV/marine, Smith's/gas, to Kirtland AFB

**166** Juan Tabo Blvd, **N gas:** Chevron/dsl, Phillips 66/Circle K, **food:** China Star, China King, Dominos, Fedrico's Mexican, Lin's Chinese, McDonald's, Olive Garden, Pizza Hut, Taco Bell, Twisters Diner, Village Inn Rest., Wendy's, Winks Rest, **lodging:** Best Value, Super 8, **other:** Albertson's, Big O Tire, Discount Tire, Hastings Books, Sav-On Drug, transmissions, **S food:** Sonic, Wienerschnitzel, **other:** $General, Holiday RV Ctr, Walgreen, repair

**165** Eubank Blvd, **N gas:** Chevron, MVD/gas, Phillips 66/Circle K, **food:** Applebee's, JB's, Owl Café, Panda Express, Sonic, **lodging:** Best Buy, Day's Inn, Econolodge, Guesthouse Inn, Holiday Inn Express, Howard Johnson, Quality Inn, **other:** Best Buy, Target, **S food:** Bob's Burgers, Boston Mkt, Chili's, Golden Corral, Pizza Hut, Subway, Taco Bell, Twister's Burritos, Wendy's, **other:** Office Depot, PetsMart, Sam's Club/gas, Toyota, Walmart SuperCtr, auto repair/tires

**164** Lomas Blvd, Wyoming Blvd, **N gas:** Circle K, Phillips 66/Subway/dsl, **food:** Dominos, Eloy's Mexican, **other:** H HOSPITAL, vet, **S other:** Ford, Dodge, Honda, Hyundai, Mazda/Kia, Subaru, transmissions, Kirtland AFB

**162b a** Louisiana Blvd, **N food:** Bravo Italian, Buca Italian, Elephant Bar Rest., Fuddrucker's, Garduno's, LePeep, Macaroni Grill, Pei Wei Diner, Japanese Kitchen, Starbucks, Steak&Ale, TGIFriday, **lodging:** Homewood Suites, Hilton Garden, Hyatt Place, Marriott, **other:** Borders Books, Dillard's, JC Penney, Marshall's, Walgreen, **S** atomic museum

**A L B U Q U E R Q U E**

**161b a** San Mateo Blvd, Albuquerque, **N gas:** Conoco, Giant/dsl, Phillips 66/dsl, Shell/A&W, **food:** Arby's, Bob's Burgers, Boston Mkt, Burger King, Carl's Jr., Denny's, Dos Hermano's, KFC, McDonald's, Pizza Hut, Schlotzky's, Starbucks, Subway, Taco Bell, Wendy's, **lodging:** La Quinta, **other:** Circuit City, Office Depot, Old Navy, **S gas:** Chevron/dsl

**160** Carlisle Blvd, Albuquerque, **N gas:** Chevron, Shell, **food:** Applebee's, China Wok, JB's, Lotaburger, McDonald's, Pizza Hut, Range Cafe, Rudy's BBQ, Sonic, Twisters Grill, Village Inn Rest., Whataburger, **lodging:** AmeriSuites, Candlewood Suites, Comfort Inn, Day's Inn, Econolodge, Elegante Hotel, Hampton Inn, Hilton, Motel 6, Park Plaza Hotel, Quality Inn, Residence Inn, Suburban Motel, Super 8, **other:** BMW, Firestone/auto, Goodyear/auto, JC Penney, Smith's Foods, Walgreen, **S gas:** Phillips 66/Subway/dsl, **food:** Burger King, **other:** H HOSPITAL, Wild Oats Mkt

**159b c** I-25, S to Las Cruces, N to Santa Fe

**159a** 2nd St, 4th St, Albuquerque, **N gas:** Chevron/24hr, Love's/Subway/dsl, **food:** Furr's Café, **other:** $Tree, Family$, U-Haul

**158** 6th St, 8th St, 12th St, Albuquerque, **N gas:** Love's/Subway/dsl, **other:** U-Haul, **S gas:** Chevron, **lodging:** Quality Inn

**157b** 12th St (from eb), **N gas:** Fina/Arby's/dsl, **other:** Lowe's Whse, Walgreen

**157a** Rio Grande Blvd, Albuquerque, **N gas:** Valero, **S gas:** Chevron/24hr, Shell, **food:** Starbucks, **lodging:** Best Western/grill, Hotel Albuquerque, **other:** auto repair

Copyright 2009 - The Next Exit®

## INTERSTATE 40 CONT'D

**E** **W**

**ALBUQUERQUE**

| | |
|---|---|
| **156mm** | Rio Grande River |
| **155** | Coors Rd, Albuquerque, **N** **gas:** Chevron/Circle K, Duke City/dsl, Giant Gas/dsl, Valero/dsl/24hr, **food:** Applebee's, Arby's, Chili's, Cracker Barrel, Golden Corral, Great Wall Chinese, IHOP, McDonald's, Panda Express, Papa Murphy's, Quizno's, Royal Buffet, Sonic, Subway, Taco Cabana (1mi), Twisters Burritos, Wendy's, **other:** AutoZone, Brake Masters, Brook's Foods, $Tree, GNC, Goodyear/auto, Home Depot, Jiffy Lube, NAPA, Radio Shack, Staples, Walgreen, Walmart SuperCtr, vet, **S** **gas:** Chevron/24hr, Phillips 66/Circle K/dsl, Shell, **food:** Del Taco, Denny's, Furr's Diner, Lotaburger, Marisco's Mexican, McDonald's, New China, Pizza Hut, Popeye's, Subway, Taco Bell, Village Inn Rest., **lodging:** Comfort Inn, Day's Inn, Hampton Inn, La Quinta, Motel 6, Motel 76, **other:** Checker Parts, Discount Tire, U-Haul |
| **154** | Unser Blvd, **N** **gas:** Valero, **other:** to Petroglyph NM |
| **153** | 98th St, **S** **gas:** ⊕*FLYING J*/Conoco/CountryMkt/dsl/LP/24hr/@, **lodging:** Microtel, **other:** Palasades RV Park |
| **149** | Central Ave, Paseo del Volcan, **N** **other:** American RV Ctr/Camping World, Enchanted Trails RV Camping, Freightliner, to Shooting Range SP, **S** **gas:** Chevron/dsl/24hr, **other:** American RV Park |
| **140.5mm** | Rio Puerco River |
| **140** | Rio Puerco, **S** **gas:** Rte 66 Trvel Ctr/Phillips 66/DQ/Road Runner Cafe/hotel/casino/dsl/rest./@ |
| **131** | To'Hajiilee |
| **126** | NM 6, to Los Lunas |
| **120mm** | Rio San Jose, Rio San Jose |
| **117** | Mesita |
| **114** | NM 124, Laguna, 1/2 mi **N** Conoco/dsl |
| **113.5mm** | scenic view both lanes, litter barrels |
| **108** | Casa Blanca, Paraje, **S** **gas:** Conoco/Casa Blanca/dsl/24hr, **other:** Casa Blanca Mkt, casino |
| **104** | Cubero, Budville |
| **102** | Sky City Rd, Acomita, **N** **gas:** Sky City/McDonald's/hotel/casino/dsl, **food:** Huwak'a Rest., **other:** RV Park/laundry, casino, **S** rest area both lanes, full ♿ facilities, Ⓒ, 🏚, litter barrels, petwalk, Ⓗ HOSPITAL |
| **100** | San Fidel |
| **96** | McCartys |
| **89** | NM 117, to Quemado, **N** **gas:** Skyway/Shell/Subway/dsl/gifts, **S** El Malpais NM |

**GRANTS**

| | |
|---|---|
| **85** | NM 122, NM 547, Grants, **N** **gas:** Chevron/dsl/24hr, Conoco/dsl, Fina, Shell/dsl, **food:** Asian Buffet, Denny's, Lotaburger, Pizza Hut, Subway, Taco Bell, **lodging:** Best Western, Comfort Inn, Day's Inn, Economy Inn/rest., Holiday Inn Express, Motel 6, Sands Motel, South West Motel, Super 8, Travelodge, **other:** Ⓗ HOSPITAL, AutoZone, Checker Parts, Chevrolet/Buick, Chrysler/Jeep/Dodge, $Tree, Walmart SuperCtr, **S** Lavaland RV Park |
| **81b a** | NM 53 S, Grants, **N** **gas:** Chevron, **food:** Domino's, KFC, McDonald's, **other:** Ford/Lincoln/Mercury, NAPA, True Value, USPO, **S** **other:** Blue Spruce RV Park, KOA/Cibola Sands RV Park, El Malpais NM |
| **79** | NM 122, NM 605, Milan, **N** **gas:** Chevron/dsl, Love's/Chester's/Subway/dsl/24hr, **food:** DQ, **lodging:** Crossroads Motel, **other:** Bar-S RV Park, **S** **gas:** Petro/dsl/scales/24hr/@, **other:** Speedco Lube, st police |
| **72** | Bluewater Village, **N** **gas:** Exxon/DQ/dsl |
| **63** | NM 412, Prewitt, **S** to Bluewater SP (7mi) |
| **53** | NM 371, NM 612, Thoreau, **N** **gas:** Red Mtn Mkt&Deli |

**NM**

| | |
|---|---|
| **47** | Continental Divide, 7275 ft, **N** **gas:** Chevron, **other:** Continental Divide Trdg Post, towing/repair, **S** USPO |
| **44** | Coolidge |
| **39** | Refinery, **N** **gas:** Pilot/Subway/Grandma Max's/dsl/24hr/@ |
| **36** | Iyanbito |
| **33** | NM 400, McGaffey, Ft Wingate, **N** **other:** to Red Rock SP, RV camping, museum |
| **26** | E 66th Ave, E Gallup, **N** **gas:** Chevron/Subway/dsl/24hr, **food:** Denny's/24hr, **lodging:** La Quinta, Sleep Inn, **other:** KOA, to Red Rock SP, museum, st police, **S** on Rte 66...**gas:** Conoco/dsl, Fina/dsl, Mustang, Shell/Ortega Gifts, **food:** Burger King, KFC, Lotaburger, McDonald's, Sonic, Wendy's, **lodging:** Best Western, Hacienda Motel, Roadrunner Motel, **other:** Ⓗ HOSPITAL |

**GALLUP**

| | |
|---|---|
| **22** | Montoya Blvd, Gallup, **N** rest area both lanes, full facilities, info, **S** on Rte 66...**gas:** Armco/gas, Chevron, Conoco, Giant Gas, Mustang, Phillips 66, Texaco, **food:** Avalon Rest., Burger King, China Express, Church's, DQ, Earl's Rest., LJ Silver, McDonald's, Papa John's, Pizza Hut, Quizno's, Subway, Taco Bell, Wendy's, **lodging:** El Capitan Motel, El Rancho Motel/rest., Redwood Lodge, **other:** Albertson's, Radio Shack, Walgreen |
| **20** | US 491, to Shiprock, Gallup, **N** **gas:** Giant/dsl, Texaco, **food:** Applebee's, Arby's, Burger King, CA Chinese, Carl's Jr., Church's, Cracker Barrel, DQ, Denny's, Furr's Café, Golden Corral, KFC, King Dragon Chinese, Lotaburger, McDonald's, Pizza Hut, Sizzler, Sonic, Taco Bell, Wendy's, **lodging:** Hampton Inn, Quality Inn, Ramada Ltd, **other:** AutoZone, BigLots, Checker Parts, Chrysler/Dodge/Jeep, Family$, Home Depot, JC Penney, NAPA, Nissan, PepBoys, Radio Shack, Safeway, Walmart SuperCtr, mall, radiators, **S** on Rte 66...**gas:** Shell/dsl, **food:** Chelle's Steaks, Don Diego's Rest., El Dorado Rest., El Sombrero Mexican, Lotaburger, Rte 66 Diner, Sonic, McDonald's, **lodging:** Ambassador Motel, Best Value Inn, Best Western, Day's Inn, Economy Inn, Super 8, **other:** Ⓗ HOSPITAL, Big O Tire, RV camping |

**GALLUP**

| | |
|---|---|
| **16** | NM 118, W Gallup, Mentmore, **N** **gas:** Love's/A&W/Baskin-Robbins/Subway/dsl/24hr, Mataya's/Texaco/dsl/24hr/@, Navajo/dsl/24hr, Phillips 66, TA/Country Pride/dsl/scales/24hr/@, **lodging:** Howard Johnson, **other:** Blue Beacon, dsl repair, **S** **gas:** Best Value/dsl, Chevron/dsl, Conoco, Fina/Allsup's, Shell, **food:** Olympic Kitchen, Ranch Kitchen, Taco Bell, Virgie's Mexican, **lodging:** Best Western, Budget Inn, Comfort Inn, Day's Inn, Econolodge, Gallup Inn, Hampton Inn, Microtel, Motel 6, Red Roof Inn, Travelodge, **other:** USA RV Park |
| **12mm** | inspection/weigh sta eb |
| **8** | to Manuelito |
| **2mm** | Welcome Ctr eb, full ♿ facilities, Ⓒ, 🏚, litter barrels, petwalk |
| **0mm** | New Mexico/Arizona state line |

## INTERSTATE 81

| Exit # | Services |
|---|---|
| **184mm** | US/Canada border, New York state line. I-81 begins/ends. |
| **183.5mm** | US Customs (sb) |
| **52** (183) | Island Rd, to De Wolf Point, last US exit nb, **E** food |
| **51** (180) | Island Rd, to Fineview, Islands Parks, **2-3 mi E food:** Thousand Islands Club, **lodging:** Seaway Island Resort, Torchlite Motel, **other:** Nature Ctr, camping, golf, USPO, **W gas:** Sunoco/dsl |
| **179mm** | St Lawrence River |
| **178.5mm** | **Thousand Islands Toll Bridge Booth, rest area sb, full &#9855; facilities, [⟨, ⊼, litter barrels, petwalk** |
| **50** | NS (178)NY 12, **N** to Alexandria Bay, **gas:** Mobil/dsl, **food:** Kountry Kottage Rest., Subway, **lodging:** Bonnie Castle/rest., Green Acres River Motel, PineHurst Motel, River Edge Hotel, **other:** H HOSPITAL, funpark (seasonal), to Thousand Island Region, **S** to Clayton, **gas:** Mobil, **lodging:** Bridgeview Motel, PJ's Motel, **other: NY Welcome Ctr,** to RV camping |
| **174mm** | **rest area nb, full &#9855; facilities, [⟨, vending, ⊼, litter barrels, petwalk, st police** |
| **49** (171) | NY 411, to Theresa, Indian River Lakes, **E gas:** Mobil/dsl (4mi) |
| **168mm** | parking area sb, ⊼ |
| **161mm** | parking area nb |
| **48** (158) | US 11, NY 37, **1-4 mi E gas:** Mobil/dsl, Nice'n Easy/dsl, Sunoco/dsl, **food:** Arby's, McDonald's, Longway's Diner, **lodging:** Allen's Budget Motel, Hotis Motel, Microtel, Royal Inn, **other:** st police |
| **156.5mm** | **parking area both lanes** |
| **47** (155) | NY 12, Bradley St, Watertown, **E gas:** Nice'n Easy/Subway/dsl, **other:** H HOSPITAL, **W lodging:** Rainbow Motel |
| **154.5mm** | Black River |
| **46** (154) | NY 12F, Coffeen St, Watertown, **E gas:** Mobil, **food:** Cracker Barrel, Shorty's Diner, **other:** URGENT CARE, Home Depot |
| **45** (152) | NY 3, to Arsenal St, Watertown, **E gas:** Mobil, Sunoco, **food:** Applebee's, Arby's, Buffalo Wild Wings, Burger King, China Buffet, Dunkin Donuts, Friendly's, Jreck Subs, KFC, LJ Silver, McDonald's, Panda Buffet, Ponderosa, Quizno's, Ruby Tuesday, Starbucks, Taco Bell, **lodging:** Day's Inn, Econolodge, Hampton Inn, Holiday Inn Express, The Inn, **other:** Advance Parts, Aldi Foods, AutoZone, Big Lots, Chrysler/Dodge/Jeep, $General, $Tree, Jo-Ann Fabrics, Kost Tire, Michael's, PriceChopper Foods/24hr, Radio Shack, Rite Aid, Staples, TJ Maxx, USPO, Walgreens, **W gas:** Fastrac, **food:** Bob Evans, Panera Bread, Pizza Hut, Red Lobster, Subway, Texas Roadhouse, TGI Friday, **lodging:** Ramada Inn, **other:** Best Buy, Borders Books, Ford, Gander Mtn, Hannaford Foods, JC Penney, K-Mart, Kohl's, Lowes Whse, Old Navy, PetCo, Sam's Club, Sears/auto, Target, Walmart, mall, to Sackets Harbor |
| **149mm** | **parking area nb, [⟨** |
| **44** (148) | NY 232, to Watertown Ctr, **3 mi E gas:** Mobil, **lodging:** Best Western |
| **147mm** | **rest area sb, full &#9855; facilities, [⟨, ⊼, litter barrels, vending, petwalk** |

| | |
|---|---|
| **43** (146) | US 11, to Kellogg Hill |
| **42** (144) | NY 177, Adams Center, **E gas:** Nice'n Easy/dsl, **food:** Depot Cafe, **other:** Harley-Davidson, Tucker's Camping |
| **41** (140) | NY 178, Adams, **E gas:** Citgo/dsl, **food:** 2 Bros Pizza, McDonald's, **other:** st police |
| **138mm** | South Sandy Creek |
| **40** (135) | NY 193, to Ellisburg, Pierrepont Manor |
| **134mm** | **parking area, ⊼, both lanes** |
| **39** (133) | Mannsville |
| **38** (131) | US 11, **E lodging:** 81-11 Motel |
| **37** (128) | Lacona, Sandy Creek, **E food:** J&R Diner, **lodging:** Harris Lodge, Lake Effect Inn, **W gas:** Citgo, Sunoco/dsl, **food:** Sandy Creek Diner, **lodging:** Pink House Inn, Salmon River Motel, **other:** Sandy Island Beach SP, USPO |
| **36** (121) | NY 13, Pulaski, **E gas:** Citgo, **food:** Ponderosa, **lodging:** Red Carpet Inn, Scottish Inn, **W gas:** KwikFill, Mobil/dsl, Nice'n Easy/Subway, Sunoco/dsl, **food:** Arby's, Burger King, Dunkin Donuts, Eddy's Place, McDonald's, River House Rest., Stefano's Rest., **lodging:** Super 8, **other:** Aldi Foods, Buick/Chevrolet, Family$, Kinney Drug, NAPA, P&C Foods, Radio Shack, Rite Aid, to Selkirk Shores SP, camping, fish hatchery |
| **35** (118) | to US 11, Tinker Tavern Rd, **W** Grandpa Bob's Animal Park |
| **34** (115) | NY 104, to Mexico, **E gas:** Sunoco/dsl/scales/24hr, **food:** Maple View Rest., **2-12 mi W gas:** Citgo, **lodging:** Cedar Creek, **other:** J&J/Salmon Country/Dowiedale/Jellystone Camping |
| **33** (111) | NY 69, Parish, **E gas:** Sunoco/dsl/24hr, **food:** Grist Mill Rest., **lodging:** E Coast Resort (4mi), **other:** Up Country RV Park (8mi), **W gas:** Citgo, Mobil/dsl, **lodging:** Parish Motel, other:USPO |
| **32** (103) | NY 49, to Central Square, **E gas:** Mobil/dsl, Sunoco/Subway/dsl, **food:** Golly's Rest., **other:** NAPA, **W gas:** Fastrac/gas, Quick Mart, **food:** Burger King, Dunkin Donuts, McDonald's, Quinto's NY Pizza, **lodging:** Town&Country, **other:** Advance Parts, $Tree, Ford, Rite Aid, Walmart SuperCtr, st police |
| **101mm** | **rest area sb, full &#9855; facilities, [⟨, ⊼, litter barrels, vending, petwalk** |
| **31** (99) | to US 11, Brewerton, **E** Oneida Shores Camping, **W gas:** Mobil/dsl, Nice'n Easy, **food:** Brickhouse Cafe, Burger King, Castaway's Cafe, Dunkin Donuts, LinLi's Chinese, Little Caesar's, McDonald's, Subway, **lodging:** BelAir Motel, Brewerton Motel, Holiday Inn Express, **other:** $General, Kinney Drugs, vet |
| **30** (96) | NY 31, to Cicero, **0-1 mi E gas:** Fastrac/dsl, Hess/dsl, KwikFill, **food:** Arby's, Cracker Barrel, Dunkin Donuts, Gino's&Joe's Pizza, McDonald's, **other:** Gander Mtn, Rite Aid, Walgreens, **W gas:** Citgo/dsl, Kwikfill, **food:** Cicero Pizza, Denny's, Frank's Café, Plainville Farms Rest., **other:** Bellair Motel, Brewerton Motel, **other:** RV Ctrs |
| **29** (93) | I-481 S, NY 481, to Oswego, Syracuse, **1 mi W on US 11 gas:** Hess, Mobil/dsl, **food:** Buffalo Wild Wings, Burger King, Denny's, KFC, McDonald's, Moe's SW Grill, Panera Bread, Pizza Hut, Quizno's, Starbucks, Taco Bell, Tully's Rest., Wendy's, **lodging:** Budget Inn, **other:** Advance Parts, Audi/Porsche/VW, Buick/GMC/Pontiac, Burlington Coats, Curves, $Tree, Dunn Tire, Firestone/auto, Goodyear/auto, Home Depot, Hyundai, KIA, Lincoln/Mercury, Lowes Whse, Marshall's, Nissan, |

**N ↕ S**

**NY**

**WATERTOWN**

**PULASKI**

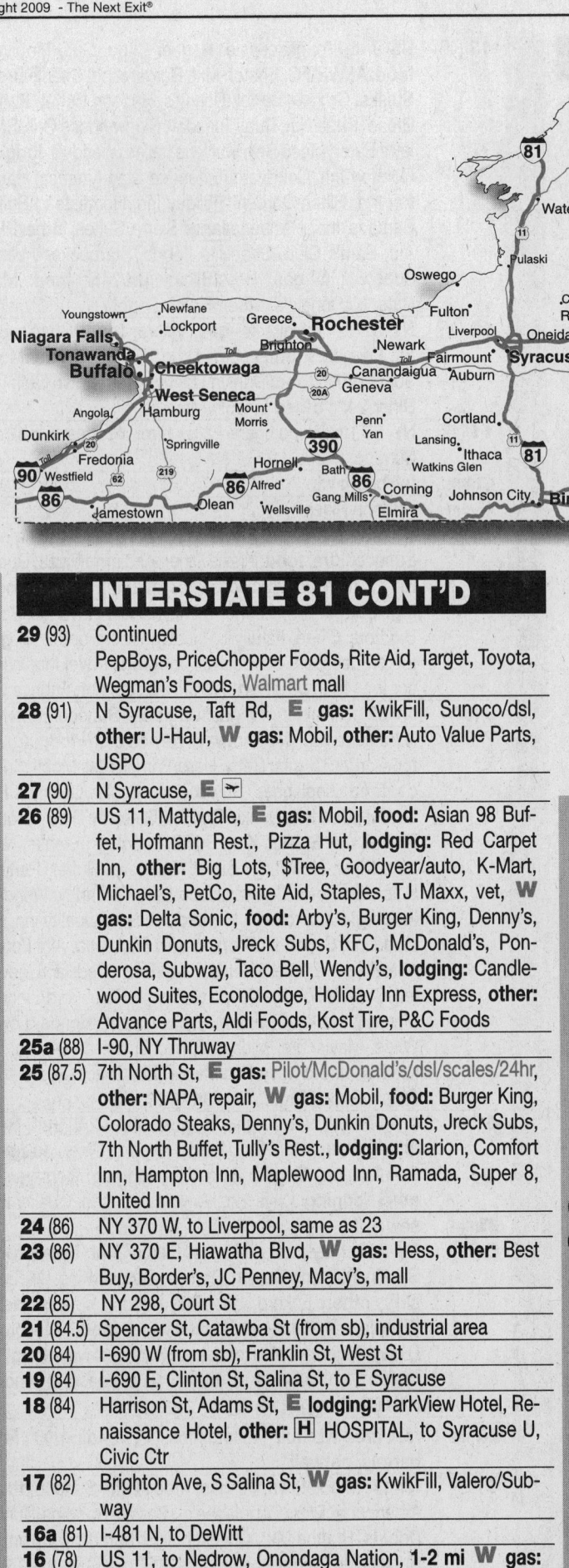

## INTERSTATE 81 CONT'D

**N** ↑ **S**

**S Y R A C U S E**

**29** (93) Continued
PepBoys, PriceChopper Foods, Rite Aid, Target, Toyota, Wegman's Foods, Walmart mall

**28** (91) N Syracuse, Taft Rd, **E gas:** KwikFill, Sunoco/dsl, **other:** U-Haul, **W gas:** Mobil, **other:** Auto Value Parts, USPO

**27** (90) N Syracuse, **E** ✈

**26** (89) US 11, Mattydale, **E gas:** Mobil, **food:** Asian 98 Buffet, Hofmann Rest., Pizza Hut, **lodging:** Red Carpet Inn, **other:** Big Lots, $Tree, Goodyear/auto, K-Mart, Michael's, PetCo, Rite Aid, Staples, TJ Maxx, vet, **W gas:** Delta Sonic, **food:** Arby's, Burger King, Denny's, Dunkin Donuts, Jreck Subs, KFC, McDonald's, Ponderosa, Subway, Taco Bell, Wendy's, **lodging:** Candlewood Suites, Econolodge, Holiday Inn Express, **other:** Advance Parts, Aldi Foods, Kost Tire, P&C Foods

**25a** (88) I-90, NY Thruway

**25** (87.5) 7th North St, **E gas:** Pilot/McDonald's/dsl/scales/24hr, **other:** NAPA, repair, **W gas:** Mobil, **food:** Burger King, Colorado Steaks, Denny's, Dunkin Donuts, Jreck Subs, 7th North Buffet, Tully's Rest., **lodging:** Clarion, Comfort Inn, Hampton Inn, Maplewood Inn, Ramada, Super 8, United Inn

**24** (86) NY 370 W, to Liverpool, same as 23

**23** (86) NY 370 E, Hiawatha Blvd, **W gas:** Hess, **other:** Best Buy, Border's, JC Penney, Macy's, mall

**22** (85) NY 298, Court St

**21** (84.5) Spencer St, Catawba St (from sb), industrial area

**20** (84) I-690 W (from sb), Franklin St, West St

**19** (84) I-690 E, Clinton St, Salina St, to E Syracuse

**18** (84) Harrison St, Adams St, **E lodging:** ParkView Hotel, Renaissance Hotel, **other:** Ⓗ HOSPITAL, to Syracuse U, Civic Ctr

**17** (82) Brighton Ave, S Salina St, **W gas:** KwikFill, Valero/Subway

**16a** (81) I-481 N, to DeWitt

**16** (78) US 11, to Nedrow, Onondaga Nation, **1-2 mi W gas:** Hess, Valero, **food:** McDonald's, Pizza Hut

**15** (73) US 20, La Fayette, **E gas:** Sunoco/dsl/deli, **food:** Old Tymes Rest., **other:** $General, NAPA, USPO, st police, vet, **W food:** McDonald's

**71mm** truck insp sta both lanes, 🚻

**14** (67) NY 80, Tully, **E gas:** Nice'n Easy/deli/dsl, **lodging:** Best Western, **other:** Chevrolet, Kinney Drug, **W food:** Burger King

**13** (63) NY 281, Preble, **E** to Song Mtn Ski Resort

**60mm** rest area/truck insp nb, full ♿ facilities, 🚻, 🅿, litter barrels, vending, petwalk

**12** (53) US 11, NY 281, to Homer, **W gas:** Mobil/dsl/24hr, KwikFill, Valero, **food:** Applebees, Burger King, Doug's Fishfry, Fabio's Italian, Little Italy, Ponderosa, **lodging:** Budget Inn, Country Inn&Suites, **other:** Ⓗ HOSPITAL, to Fillmore Glen SP

**11** (52) NY 13, Cortland, **E food:** Apple Annie's, **lodging:** Comfort Inn, Quality Inn, **W gas:** Mobil/dsl, **food:** Arby's, China Moon, Crown City Rest., Friendly's, Golden Skillet, McDonald's, Subway, Taco Bell, Wendy's, **lodging:** Hampton Inn, Ramada Inn, **other:** Advance Parts, Family$, Jo-Ann Fabrics, Kost Tire, P&C Foods/24hr, camping, museum

**10** (50) US 11, NY 41, to Cortland, McGraw, **W gas:** Citgo/Dunkin Donuts/dsl/cafe, Mobil/Subway/dsl/24hr, Sunoco/dsl, **lodging:** Cortland Motel, Day's Inn, **other:** NAPA

**9** (38) US 11, NY 221, **W gas:** Citgo, Sunoco/XtraMart/dsl/24hr, **food:** NY Pizzaria, **lodging:** 3 Bear Inn/rest., Greek Peak Lodge, **other:** NAPA, Country Hills Camping

**33mm** rest area sb, full ♿ facilities, 🚻, 🅿, litter barrels, vending, petwalk

**C O R T L A N D**

**N ↕ S**

**B I N G H A M T O N**

## INTERSTATE 81 CONT'D

**8 (30)** NY 79, to US 11, NY 26, NY 206 (no EZ return), Whitney Pt, **E gas:** Hess, Kwikfill, Mobil/dsl/24hr, Sunoco, **food:** Aiello's Ristorante, Arby's, McDonald's, Subway, **lodging:** Point Motel, **other:** Chevrolet, $General, Gregg's Mkt, NAPA, Parts+, Radio Shack, Strawberry Valley Farms (3mi), USPO, to Dorchester Park

**7 (21)** US 11, Castle Creek

**6 (16)** US 11, to NY 12, I-88E, Chenango Bridge, **E on US 11 gas:** Citgo/dsl, Exxon, Hess/dsl, **food:** Arby's, Burger King, Denny's, Dunkin Donuts, King Buffet, Pizza Hut, Ponderosa, Subway, Wendy's, **other:** Advance Parts, Curves, CVS Drug, Giant Foods, Kost Tire, Lowes Whse, Radio Shack, Rite Aid, Staples, vet, **W gas:** Diamond Fuel, KwikFill, **food:** Friendly's, McDonald's, Nirchi's Pizza, Spot Diner, Subway, **lodging:** Comfort Inn, Howard Johnson, Motel 6, **other:** $Bazaar, Harley-Davidson, Walgreens

**15mm** I-88 begins eb

**5 (14)** US 11, Front St, **1 mi W gas:** Sunoco, Valero, **food:** Applebees, Coldstone Creamery, Cracker Barrel, KFC/Taco Bell, McDonald's, Quizno's, Starbucks, **lodging:** Comfort Inn, Econolodge, Fairfield Inn, **other:** Cutler Botanical Garden

**4 (13)** NY 17, Binghamton

**3 (12)** Broad Ave, Binghamton, **W gas:** Valero, **food:** KFC, **other:** CVS Drug, Giant Foods

**3 (10)** Industrial Park, same as 2

**2 (8)** US 11, NY 17, **1-2 mi W gas:** Exxon/dsl, Pilot/Wendy's/dsl/scales/24hr/@, TA/dsl/rest./24hr/@, **food:** Arby's, Burger King, McDonald's, Subway, **lodging:** Del Motel

**1 (4)** US 11, NY 7, Kirkwood, **1-2 mi W gas:** Mobil/dsl/24hr, Xtra, **lodging:** Kirkwood Motel, Wright Motel

**2mm** **Welcome ctr nb, full** ♿ **facilities,** 📞, 🎪, **litter barrels, vending, petwalk**

**1mm** weigh sta nb

**0mm** New York/Pennsylvania state line

## INTERSTATE 84

**E ↕ W**

| Exit # | Services |
| --- | --- |
| **71.5mm** | New York/Connecticut state line |
| **21 (68)** | US 6, US 202, NY 121 (from wb), N Salem, same as 20 |
| **20N (67.5)** | US 6, US 202, NY 22, **N gas:** Citgo, Mobil/24hr, Valero, **food:** Bob's Diner, Burger King, McDonald's, **other:** Cadillac/Chevrolet, Curves, Ford, Honda, Subaru |
| **20S** | I-684, to NYC |
| **19 (65)** | NY 312, Carmel, **S food:** Applebee's, Dunkin Donuts, Friendly's, Gaetano's Deli, McDonald's, Sonoma Cafe, Wendy's, **other:** Ⓗ HOSPITAL, Home Depot, Kohl's, Marshall's, Michael's, st police |
| **18 (62)** | NY 311, Lake Carmel, **S** Lake Carmel Gen Store, Lakeview Pizza |
| **17 (59)** | Ludingtonville Rd, **S gas:** Hess/Blimpie/dsl/24hr, Sunoco, **food:** Cutiloo's Rest. (2mi), Gappy's Pizza, Lou's Deli |
| **56mm** | elevation 970 ft |
| **55mm** | **rest area both lanes, full** ♿ **facilities,** 📞, **vending,** 🎪, **litter barrels, petwalk** |
| **16 (53)** | Taconic Parkway, N to Albany, S to New York |
| **15 (51)** | Lime Kiln NY, **3 mi N gas:** Mobil/24hr, **food:** Dunkin Donuts, **lodging:** Royal Inn |

**13 (46)** US 9, to Poughkeepsie, **N gas:** Citgo, Gulf, Mobil/dsl, **food:** A&W/KFC, Boston Mkt, Burger King, Charlie Brown Steaks, Cracker Barrel, Denny's, Hudson Buffet, Panera Bread, Pizza Hut, Ruby Tuesday, Sidewinder's Grill, Stanley's Eatery, Taco Bell, ViaNove Italian, Wendy's, **lodging:** Comfort Inn, Courtyard, Extended Stay America, Hampton Inn, Hilton Garden, Holiday Inn, Homestead Suites, Ramada Inn, Residence Inn, Sierra Suites, **other:** Rite Aid, Sam's Club, ShopRite Foods, Starbucks, Walmart SuperCtr, **S gas:** Hess/Blimpie/dsl/24hr, **food:** Maya Cafe, McDonald's, **other:** Home Depot

**12 (45)** NY 52 E, Fishkill, **N gas:** Valero, **food:** Chan's Buffet, Friendly's, **other:** CVS Drug, $King, **S gas:** Mobil, Sunoco/dsl, **food:** Dunkin Donuts, Hometown Deli, I-84 Diner/24hr, **other:** Lincoln/Mercury

**11 (42)** NY 9D, to Wappingers Falls, **1 mi N gas:** Mobil/dsl, Sunoco

**41mm** toll booth wb

**40mm** Hudson River

**E ↕ W**

**N E W B U R G H**

**10 (39)** US 9W, NY 32, to Newburgh, **N gas:** Citgo, Mobil, Sunoco, Xtra, **food:** Alexis Diner, Andiamo Pizza, Burger King, China King, McDonald's, Pizza Hut, Subway, **lodging:** Budget Inn, Economy Inn, **other:** Advance Parts, Big Lots, $Tree, Family$, PriceChopper Foods, **S gas:** Exxon/dsl, Gulf, Sunoco/dsl, **lodging:** Travel Inn, Windsor Inn (4mi), **other:** Ⓗ HOSPITAL, Jo-Ann Fabrics

**8 (37)** NY 52, to Walden, **N gas:** Citgo/dsl, Sunoco/24hr

**7 (36)** NY 300, to I-87 (NY Thruway), Newburgh, **N lodging:** Hilton Garden, **S gas:** Getty, Hess/Blimpie/dsl, Mobil, Sunoco, **food:** Applebees, Burger King, Chili's, Cosimos Ristorante, Denny's, Dunkin Donuts, Gateway Diner, Ground Round, Jak Steaks, King Buffet, Longhorn Steaks, Neptune Diner, Newburgh Buffet, Old Town Buffet, Perkins, Union Sq Rest., Subway, Taco Bell, TGIFriday, Wendy's, **lodging:** Hampton Inn, Howard Johnson, Quality Inn, Ramada Inn, Super 8, **other:** Adam's Food Mkt, Aldi Foods, AutoZone, Barnes&Noble, BonTon, Cadillac/Chevrolet, Chrysler/Dodge/Jeep, Curves, $Tree, Ford/Lincoln/Mercury, Harley-Davidson, Home Depot, Honda, Lowes Whse, Mavis Tire, Michael's, Midas, Nissan, Kohl's, Office Depot, Old Navy, PetsMart, Radio Shack, Sears/auto, Stop'n Shop, Target, Walmart SuperCtr

**6 (34)** NY 17K, to Newburgh, **N gas:** Mobil/24, Gulf, Pilot/Arby's/dsl/scales/24hr, **food:** Airport Diner, **lodging:** Comfort Inn, **S gas:** Exxon/dsl, **lodging:** Courtyard, **3 mi S lodging:** Days Inn, Howard Johnson, Quality Inn

**33mm** new exit

**5 (29)** NY 208, Maybrook, **N gas:** Exxon/24hr, Mobil, **food:** Baskin-Robbins/Dunkin Donuts, Burger King, McDonald's, **other:** Eckerd, ShopRite Foods, **S gas:** Hess/Blimpie, TA/Pizza Hut/dsl/rest./@, **food:** Maybrook Diner, Renee's Deli, Roadside Rest., Subway, **lodging:** Rodeside Inn, Super 8, **other:** Blue Beacon, Winding Hills Camping

**24mm** **rest area wb, full** ♿ **facilities,** 📞, **vending,** 🎪, **litter barrels, petwalk**

**4 (19)** NY 17, Middletown, **N gas:** Mobil/24hr, Sunoco, **food:** Americana Diner, Applebee's, Baskin-Robbins/Dunkin Donuts, Boston Mkt, Cheeseburger Paradise, Cosimo's Brick Oven, Denny's, Friendly's, KFC, McDonald's, Olive Garden, Perkins, Red Lobster, Ruby Tuesday, Subway,

Copyright 2009 - The Next Exit®

## INTERSTATE 84 CONT'D

**E ↕ W**

**MIDDLETOWN**

**4 (19)** Continued
Taco Bell, Wendy's, **lodging:** Howard Johnson, Middletown Motel, Super 8, **other:** H HOSPITAL, Best Buy, Borders Books, Circuit City, Firestone/auto, Gander Mtn, Hannaford Foods, Home Depot, Honda, JC Penney, Jo-Ann Fabrics, Kohl's, Lowe's Whse, Old Navy, PetCo, PriceChopper Foods, Rite Aid, Sam's Club, Sears/auto, ShopRite Foods, Staples, Stop&Shop Foods, TJ Maxx, U-Haul, mall, vet, Walmart SuperCtr, mall, **S gas:** Citgo/dsl, **food:** Chili's, El Bandido Mexican, Outback Steaks, TGIFriday, **lodging:** Courtyard, Hampton Inn, Holiday Inn, Microtel, **other:** st police

**17mm** rest area eb, full ♿ facilities, 🕻 vending, 🅿 litter barrels, petwalk

**3 (15)** US 6, to Middletown, **N gas:** Citgo/dsl/24hr, Mobil, Valero, **food:** Bradley's Corner Diner, Colonial Diner, Dunkin Donuts, McDonald's, NY Buffet, Perkins, Quinzno's, Subway, Taco Bell, Wendy's, **other:** H HOSPITAL, Acura, Buick/Pontica/GMC, Chevrolet/Isuzu, Mazda, ShopRite Foods, Subaru, **S gas:** Citgo, Sunoco/dsl, **lodging:** Day's Inn, Global Budget Inn, **other:** Chrysler/Jeep, Nissan, Kia, Suzuki, Toyota, USPO, transmissions

**2 (5)** Mountain Rd, **S** Greenville's Deli

**4mm** elevation 1254 ft wb, 1272 ft eb

**3** parking area both lanes

**1 (1)** US 6, NY 23, Port Jervis, **N gas:** Sunoco/dsl, **food:** Arlene&Tom's Diner, Dunkin Donuts/Baskin Robbins, **lodging:** Deerdale Motel, Painted Aprons Motel, **other:** H HOSPITAL, 84 RV Ctr, Ford/Lincoln/Mercury/Jeep, **S gas:** Citgo/dsl, Gulf/dsl, Lukoil, Valero, **food:** Cumberland Farms, DQ, McDonald's, Village Pizza, **lodging:** Comfort Inn, **other:** H HOSPITAL, ShopRite Foods, TJ Maxx, mall

**0mm** New York/Pennsylvania state line, Delaware River

## INTERSTATE 86 - NEW YORK

| Exit # | Services |
|---|---|

**I-86 begins/ends on I-87, exit 16, toll booth**

**E ↕ W**

**131 (379)** NY 17, **N other:** Outlets/famous brands, **S gas:** Exxon/dsl, **food:** Chicago Grill, Chili's, McDonald's, TGIFriday's, **lodging:** American Budget Inn, Hampton Inn, **other:** Home Depot, Kohls, Staples, TJMaxx,

**130a (378)** US 6, Bear Mtn, to West Point (from eb), **S food:** Sonny's Pizza, Outback Steaks, **other:** Best Buy, BJ's Whse, BMW, Home Depot, PetsMart, Target, TJ Maxx, Walmart SuperCtr

**130 (377)** NY 208, Monroe, Washingtonville, **N lodging:** James Motel, Lake Anne Motel, **other:** Chrysler/Dodge/Jeep, Isuzu, st police, **S gas:** Mobil/dsl, Sunoco, Valero, **food:** Burger King, Dunkin Donuts, Monroe Diner, **lodging:** American Budget Inn, **other:** Kohl's, Michael's, ShopRite Foods, Staples

**129 (375)** Museum Village Rd

**128 (374)** rd 51 (only from wb), Oxford Depot

**127 (373)** Greycourt Rd (from wb only), Sugar Loaf, Warwick

**126 (372)** NY 94 (no EZ wb return), Chester, Florida, **N gas:** Mobil, Shell, Sunoco/dsl, **food:** Chester Diner, McDonald's, Wendy's, **lodging:** Holiday Inn Express, **other:** CVS Drug, Radio Shack, Rite Aid, ShopRite Foods, USPO, **S other:** Lowes Whse

**MIDDLETOWN**

**125 (369)** NY 17M E, South St, **S food:** Hacienda Mexican, Pizza Deli, **other:** H HOSPITAL

**124 (368)** NY 17A, NY 207, **N gas:** Exxon/Subway/dsl, Mobil/dsl, **food:** Burger King, Friendly's, Dunkin Donuts, Pizza Hut, **other:** H HOSPITAL, CVS Drug, **S lodging:** Comfort Inn, **other:** Chrysler/Dodge/Jeep, Hyundai

**123** US 6, NY 17M (wb only), Port Jervis

**122a (367)** Fletcher St, Goshen

**122 (364)** rd 67, E Main St, Crystal Run Rd, **N gas:** Mobil, **food:** Chili's, El Bandido Rest., Outback Steaks, TGIFriday's, **lodging:** Courtyard, Hampton Inn, Holiday Inn, Microtel, **S gas:** Citgo/dsl

**121 (363)** I-84, E to Newburgh, W to Port Jervis

**120 (363)** NY 211, **N gas:** Lukoil, Mobil, Sunoco, **food:** Cosimo's Ristorante, Olive Garden, **lodging:** Howard Johnson, Middletown Motel, Super 8, **other:** Best Buy, Gander Mtn, Macy's, Hannaford's Foods, JC Penney, Rite Aid, Sam's Club, Target, **S gas:** Valero, **food:** Americana Diner, Arby's, Boston Mkt, Burger King, Cheeseburger Paradise, Denny's, Dunkin Donuts, Friendly's, KFC, Panera Bread, Pizza Hut, Red Lobster, Subway, Taco Bell, Wendy's, Youyou Chinese, **other:** Aldi Foods, AutoZone, Circuit City, $Tree, Home Depot, Kohl's, Lowes Whse, PriceChopper, Rite Aid, ShopRite Foods, Staples, TJMaxx, U-Haul, Walmart SuperCtr

**119 (360)** NY 309, Pine Bush, **S gas:** Best Gas/dsl

**118a (358)** NY 17M, Fair Oaks

**118 (358)** Circleville, **S gas:** Exxon/dsl, Mobil, **food:** Subway

**116 (355)** NY 17K, Bloomingburg, **S gas:** Citgo/dsl, **food:** Quickway Diner

**114** Wurtsboro, Highview (from wb)

**113 (350)** US 209, Wurtsboro, Ellenville, **N gas:** Mobil/dsl, Stewarts/gas, **food:** Giovanni's Café, Subway, **lodging:** Gold Mtn Chalet, Day's Inn, Valley Brook Motel, **other:** Spring Glen Camping, **S other:** American Family Campground

**112 (347)** Masten Lake, Yankee Lake, **N food:** Potager Diner, **lodging:** Days Inn, ValleyBrook Motel, **other:** Catskill Mtn Ranch Camping, WonderWood Camping, Yankee Lake

**111 (344)** (eb only), Wolf Lake

**110 (343)** Lake Louise Marie, **N food:** Dodge Inn Rest, **lodging:** Rock Hill Lodge

**109 (342)** Rock Hill, Woodridge, **N gas:** Exxon/dsl, **food:** Dutch's Cafe, RockHill Diner, Rock Pizza, **lodging:** Rock Hill Lodge, Rosemond Motel, **other:** Ace Harware, Hilltop Farms Camping, auto repair, **S gas:** Mobil/dsl

**108 (341)** Bridgeville, same as 109

## INTERSTATE 86 CONT'D - NEW YORK

**107** (340) Thompsonville, **S food:** Hana Rest., Old Homestead Diner, **lodging:** Pines Motel, Raleigh Motel, **other:** Chevrolet, Chrysler/Dodge/Jeep, Toyota

**106** (339) (wb only), E. Broadway, **N** Ford/Lincoln/Mercury, **S gas:** Mobil/dsl, **food:** Monitcello Cafe, **lodging:** Super 8 (2 mi), Travel Inn (2mi), **other:** GMC Trucks, Hyundai, tires

**105** (337) NY 42, Monticello, **N gas:** Exxon/dsl, Mobil, Valero, **food:** Bro Bruno's, Blue Horizon Diner, Burger King, Dunkin Donuts, KFC, McDonald's, Subway, **other:** AutoZone, Home Depot, ShopRite Foods, Staples, Walmart SuperCtr, **S gas:** Citgo, Sunoco/dsl, **food:** Pizza Hut, Wendy's, **lodging:** Ramada Ltd, Super 8, **other:** Advance Parts, Family$, NAPA, Rite Aid

**104** (336) NY 17B, Raceway, Monticello, **S gas:** Citgo, Exxon/dsl, **food:** Colosseo Rest., Taco Maker, **lodging:** Best Western, Raceway Motel, Super 8 (2mi), Travel Inn, **other:** Monticello Raceway, Swinging Bridge Camp, Woodstock Camping, ⌖

**103** Rapp Rd (wb only)

**102** (332) Harris, **S other:** Ⓗ HOSPITAL, Swan Lake Camping

**101** (327) Ferndale, Swan Lake, **S gas:** Exxon/dsl

**100** (327) NY 52 E, Liberty, **N gas:** Citgo, Mobil, Sunoco, **food:** Albert's Rest., Burger King, Dunkin Donuts, Grapevine Grill, Last Licks Cafe, McDonald's, Piccolo Italian, Pizza Hut, Subway, Taco Bell, Wendy's, **lodging:** Day's Inn, Howard Johnson, **other:** Ace Hardware, Advance Parts, Curves, ShopRite Foods, USPO, **S gas:** Exxon/dsl, Xtra, **lodging:** Lincoln Motel, **other:** Ford/Lincoln/Mercury, Pontiac/Buick, Southend Parts, Neversink River Camping, Swan Lake Camping, Yogi Bear Camping

**100a** NY 52 W (no wb return), Liberty, **S food:** McCabe's Rest, **other:** st police

**99** (325) NY 52 W, to NY 55, Liberty, **S gas:** Exxon, Sunoco, **lodging:** Catskill Motel

**98** (321) Cooley, Parksville, **N gas:** Mobil, **food:** Charlie's Rest., Dari-King, I-86 Diner, **lodging:** Best Western, **other:** USPO

**97** (319) Morsston

**96** (316) Livingston Manor, **N food:** Tony's Pizza, **lodging:** Econo Motel, **other:** Covered Bridge Camping, Mongaup Pond Camping, **S food:** Tony's Pizza, Puleez Lueez, **lodging:** DeBruce Inn, OZ B&B, Willowemoc Motel

**313mm** rest area eb, full ♿ facilities, 🍴 litter barrels, ⌷, vending, petwalk, truck insp. sta (eb)

**94** (311) NY 206, Roscoe, Lew Beach, **N gas:** Exxon/dsl, Sunoco/dsl, **food:** 1910 Coffeshop, Raimondo's Diner, Roscoe Diner, **lodging:** Reynolds House Motel, Rockland House Motel, Roscoe Motel, Tennanah Lake Motel, **other:** Roscoe Camping, **S gas:** Mobil/dsl, **other:** Beaverkill St Camping (8mi)

**93** (305) to Cooks Falls (from wb)

**92** (303) Horton, Cooks Falls, Colchester, **S gas:** Sunoco/dsl, **food:** Riverside Café/lodge, **other:** Russell Brook Camping

**90** (297) NY 30, East Branch, Downsville, **N gas:** Sunoco, **other:** Beaver-Del Camping, Catskill Mtn Camping, Oxbow Camping, Peaceful Valley Camping, **S lodging:** E Branch Motel

**295mm** rest area wb, full ♿ facilities, 🍴 litter barrels, ⌷, vending, petwalk

**89** (293) Fishs Eddy

**87a** (288) NY 268 (from wb), same as 87

**87** (284) NY 97, to NY 268, to NY 191, Hancock, Cadosia, **S gas:** Getty, Mobil/Subway, Sunoco, **food:** Bluestone Grill, Family Rest., McDonald's, **lodging:** Capra Inn, Colonial Motel, Starlight Lake Inn, **other:** Buick/Chevrolet, Grand Union Foods, NAPA, Parts+, Rite Aid

**276mm** parking area wb, litter barrels

**84** (274) Deposit, **N gas:** Citgo/dsl/24hr, **food:** Grand Stand Rest., Pines Rest., Wendy's, **lodging:** Deposit Motel, Laurel Bank Motel, Scott's Motel, **other:** Family$, QuickWay, st police

**83** (272) Deposit, Oquaga Lake

**82** (270) NY 41, McClure, Sanford, **N other:** Kellystone Park, **S lodging:** Chestnut Inn/rest., Mountain Hollow B&B/diner, **other:** Guestward Camping (3mi)

**265mm** parking area eb, 🍴 litter barrels

**81** (263) E Bosket Rd

**80** (261) Damascus, **N gas:** Exxon/dsl, **other:** Forest Hill Lake Park Camping, auto repair

**79** (259) NY 79, Windsor, **N gas:** Citgo, Sunoco/dsl, **food:** Chip's Pizza, Subway, **other:** Big M Foods, **S food:** Golden Oak Rest., Marian's Pizza, **other:** Lakeside Camping

**78** (256) Dunbar Rd, Occanum

**77** (254) W Windsor, **N gas:** Mobil/dsl, **food:** McDonald's

**76** (251) Haskins Rd, to Foley Rd

**75** (250) I-81 S, to PA (exits left from wb), **N gas:** Exxon/dsl, **food:** Subway, **lodging:** Dell Motel

**72** (244) I-81 N, US 11, Front St, Clinton St, (no wb re-entry), **S food:** McDonald's, **other:** Advance Parts, K-Mart, antiques

**71** (242) Airport Rd, Johnson City, **S gas:** Valero

**70** (241) NY 201, Johnson City, **N gas:** Hess/Blimpie, Valero, **food:** China Buffet, Christy's Grill, Dunkin Donuts, Friendly's, Ground Round, McDonald's, Papa John's, Pizza Hut, Ponderosa, Quizno's, Ruby Tuesday, Taco Bell, **lodging:** Best Western, Hampton Inn, La Quinta, Red Roof Inn, **other:** $Tree, Gander Mtn, Giant Foods, JC Penney, Kost Tire, Macy's, PetCo, Sears/auto, Wegman's Foods, mall, vet, **S** Home Depot

**69** (239) NY 17C

**238mm** Susquehanna River

**68** (237) NY 17C, Old Vestal Rd, (from eb)

**67** (236) NY 26, NY 434, Vestal, Endicott, **S on NY 434...gas:** Hess, Stop'N Gas, Valero/dsl, **food:** A&W/LJ Silver, Arby's, Burger King, California Grill, Chicago Grill, China Wok, Dunkin Donuts, La Vita Bella, McDonald's, Old Country Buffet, Olive Garden, Outback Steaks, Quizno's, Red Lobster, Starbucks, Subway, Taco Bell, TGIFriday, **lodging:** Parkway Motel, Skylark Mote/Diner, Vestal Motel, **other:** Advance Parts, Barnes&Noble, Chevrolet, Chrysler/Jeep/Subaru, Circuit City, CVS Drug, $Tree, Firestone/auto, Ford/Lincoln/Mercury, Giant Foods, JoAnn Fabrics, Kohl's, Kost Tire, Lowe's Whse, Michael's, Nissan, Sam's Club, Subaru, Target, TJ Maxx, Volvo, Walmart SuperCtr, USPO, vet

**66** (231) NY 434, Apalachin, **S gas:** KwikFill, Mobil/dsl, **food:** Blue Dolphin Diner, Dunkin Donuts, McDonald's, Subway, **lodging:** Econolodge, Quality Inn, **other:** Evelyn's Mkt, Red Apple

## INTERSTATE 86 CONT'D - NEW YORK

**E**
**W**

**ELMIRA**

**65** (225) NY 17C, NY 434, Owego, **N gas:** Citgo, Mobil/dsl, **food:** A&W/KFC, Arbys, McDonald's, Panda Wok, Papa John's, Pizza Hut, Subway, Wendy's, **lodging:** Hampton Inn, Holiday Inn Express, Treadway Motel/rest., **other:** $General, Hickories Park Camping, Kost Tire, Medicine Shop Drug, P&C Foods, **S** st police

**64** (223) NY 96, Owego, **N other:** CVS Drug, USPO, **S gas:** Citgo, **other:** auto repair, vet

**222mm** rest area wb, full ♿ **facilities,** 🚻, vending, 🛉 **litter barrels, petwalk**

**63** (218) Lounsberry, **S gas:** Valero/rest./24hr/dsl

**62** (214) NY 282, Nichols, **S gas:** Citgo/Pizza Hut/dsl, **other:** Jim's RV Ctr, Tioga Downs Race Track (2mi)

**212mm** rest area eb, full ♿ **facilities,** 🛉 **litter barrels,** 🚻, **vending, petwalk**

**208mm** Susquehanna River

**61** (206) NY 34, PA 199, Waverly, Sayre, **N other:** $General, Goodyear/gas, **S gas:** Gulf/24hr, Sunoco, **food:** McDonald's, **lodging:** Best Western/rest., **other:** Chevrolet/Buick/Pontiac, Chrysler/Jeep/Dodge, Joe's RV Ctr, Nissan

**60** (204) US 220, to Sayre, Waverly, **N lodging:** O'brien's Inn, **other:** Clark's Foods, **S gas:** Citgo/dsl, Xtra/dsl, **food:** Wendy's (3mi), **lodging:** Hampton Inn, **other:** Advance Parts, Aldi Foods, K-Mart, Rite Aid, Top's Foods

**59a** (202) Wilawana, **S gas:** Sunoco/Subway/dsl

**59** (200) NY 427, Chemung, **N gas:** Dandy/dsl

**58** (195) rd 2, Lowman, Wellsburg, **N food:** W Diner, **lodging:** Red Jacket Motel, **S other:** Gardiner Hill Campsites (4mi)

**56** (190) Jerusalem Hill, **S gas:** Citgo/dsl, KwikFill, Sunoco/Subway, **food:** Hilltop Rest., McDonalds, Pizza Hut, **lodging:** Coachman Motel, Holiday Inn, Mark Twain Motel

**54** (186) NY 13, to Ithaca

**54** I-86 begins ends., **S gas:** Mobil, Sunoco, **food:** Burger King, Dunkin Donuts, Guiseppe's Pizza, LJ Silver, McDonald's, Subway, Wendy's, **lodging:** Motel 6, Red Carpet Inn, **other:** Advance Parts, Family$, K-Mart, Rite Aid, Sav-A-Lot Foods

**53** Horseheads, same as 54

**52b** (184) NY 14, to Watkins Glen, **N food:** Friendly's, **lodging:** Holiday Inn, Knight's Inn, Landmark Inn, **S food:** Denny's

**52a** (183) Commerce Ctr, same as 52b

**51** (182) Chambers Rd, **N gas:** Mobil/Subway/dsl, Sunoco/dsl, **food:** Bon Ton, Chili's, Dunkin Donuts, Friendly's, McDonald's, Olive Garden, Outback Steaks, Red Lobster, Ruby Tuesday, **lodging:** Country Inn&Suites, Hilton Garden, Holiday Inn Express, Knights Inn, **other:** Firestone/auto, JC Penny, Jo-Anne Fabrics, Sears/auto, mall, **S food:** Applebee's, Charlie's Subs, Old Country Buffet, Panera Bread, Taco Bell, TGIFriday, Wendy's, **lodging:** Econolodge, **other:** Barnes&Noble, Best Buy, Buick/Pontiac/GMC, Circuit City, $Tree, Kohl's, Kost Tire, Lowe's Whse, Macy's, Michael's, Nissan, Old Navy, PetCo, PetsMart, Sam's Club, Staples, Subaru, Target, TJ Maxx, Toyota/Scion, Walmart SuperCtr, museum

**50** (180) Kahler Rd, **N** to ✈

**49** (178) Olcott Rd, Canal St, Big Flats, **N** ☛, antiques, **S gas:** Sunoco, **food:** Picnic Pizza, **other:** $General

**48** (171) NY 352, E Corning, **N gas:** Citgo, **food:** Tag's Rest., **lodging:** Budget Inn, Gatehouse Motel

**CORNING**

**47** (174) NY 352, Gibson, Corning, **N lodging:** Radisson Inn, to ⓗ HOSPITAL, Museum of Glass

**46** (171) NY 414, to Watkins Glen, Corning, **5mi N other:** Ferenbaugh Camping, KOA, Watkins Glen Camping, **S gas:** Citgo/dsl, **lodging:** Comfort Inn, Day's Inn, Staybridge Suites, **other:** ⓗ HOSPITAL, museums

**45** (170) NY 352, Corning, **N gas:** Sunoco, **food:** McDonald's, **S gas:** Fastrac, **food:** Bob Evans, Burger King, EnEn Chinese, Friendly's, Subway, Wendy's, **lodging:** Fairfield Inn, **other:** AutoZone, CarQuest, Rite Aid

**44** (168) US 15 S, NY 417 W, Gang Mills

**43** (167) NY 415, Painted Post, **N gas:** Citgo, **food:** Burger King, **other:** AutoValue Parts, $General, Firestone/auto, Jo-Ann Fabrics, **S gas:** Sunoco, **food:** Denny's, **lodging:** Hampton Inn

**167mm** parking area wb, litter barrels

**42** (165) Coopers Plains, **N** st police

**41** (161) rd 333, Campbell, **N other:** Camp Bell Camping (1mi), **S gas:** Sunoco, **other:** Cardinal Campsites (6mi), antiques

**160mm** rest area eb, full ♿ **facilities,** 🛉 **litter barrels,** 🚻, **vending, petwalk**

**40** (156) NY 226, Savona, **N gas:** Mobil/dsl, **food:** Savona Diner, Subway, **other:** Green Acres Camping

**39** (153) NY 415, Bath, **N food:** Chat-a-Whyle Rest. (3mi), **lodging:** Holland American Country Inn, National Hotel, **S other:** Babcock Hollow Camping (2mi)

**BATH**

**38** (150) NY 54, to Hammondsport, Bath, **N gas:** Citgo, KwikFill, Mobil, Sunoco, **food:** Arby's, Burger King, Dunkin Donuts, Ling Chinese, McDonald's/playplace, Pizza Hut, Ponderosa, Subway, **lodging:** Budget Inn, Day's Inn, Microtel, Super 8, VineHurst Inn, **other:** ⓗ HOSPITAL, Advance Parts, AutoValue Parts, Camping World RV Ctr, $General, Family$, Hickory Hill Camping (3mi), K-Mart, Rite Aid, Top's Foods/gas, Walgreens, museum, st police, winery, to Keuka Lake

**147mm** rest area wb, full ♿ **facilities,** 🚻, 🛉, **litter barrels, vending, petwalk**

**37** (146) NY 53, to Prattsburg, Kanona, **S gas:** Pilot/Subway/dsl/scales/@, Sunoco/Smokey's/dsl/scales, **food:** Tally-Ho Rest., **other:** Wagon Wheel Camping, Wilkin's RV Ctr (1mi), USPO

**36** (145) I-390 N, NY 15, to Rochester

**35** (138) Howard, **S** to Lake Demmon RA, 🚻

**34** (130) NY 36, Hornell, Arkport, **0-3 mi S gas:** KwikFill, Sunoco, **food:** Burger King (3mi), China King, Country Kitchen, Dunkin Donuts, Friendly's (3mi), McDonald's, Subway,

**H O R N E L L** ← E | W →

**NY**

**O L E A N**

**S A L A M A N C A**

## INTERSTATE 86 CONT'D - NEW YORK

**34** (130)  Continued
**lodging:** Comfort Inn (3mi), Day's Inn, Econolodge, Sunshine Motel, **other:** Aldi, Chevrolet, Chrysler/Dodge/Jeep, $Tree, Ford, GNC, NAPA, Walmart/auto, Wegman's Foods

**125mm**  scenic overlook eb, litter barrels

**33** (124)  NY 21, to Alfred, Almond, Andover, **S gas:** Mobil, **lodging:** Economy Inn, Saxon Inn Hotel, **other:** Lake Lodge Camping (8mi), Kanakadea Camping

**117mm**  highest elevation on I-86, elev 2110 ft eb, 2080 ft wb

**32** (116)  W Almond

**31** (108)  Angelica, **N gas:** Citgo, **lodging:** Angelica Inn B&B

**30** (104)  NY 19, Belmont, Wellsville, **N** 6-S Camping (3mi), **S gas:** American Trkstp/diner/24hr, **food:** Iron Kettle Rest., **other:** Mothers Piknchikn Camping (6mi)

**101mm**  **rest area eb, full** ♿ **facilities,** 🕿, 🍴, **litter barrels, vending, petwalk**

**29** (99)  NY 275, to Bolivar, Friendship, **S gas:** Mobil, Sunoco, Miller&Brandes Gas, **food:** Subway

**28** (92)  NY 305, Cuba, **N food:** Moonwink's Rest., **lodging:** Econolodge, **other:** $General, Maple Lane RV Park, **S gas:** Sunoco/dsl, Valero/dsl, **food:** McDonald's, **other:** Ⓗ HOSPITAL, Cuba Drug, Giant Foods

**27** (84)  NY 16, NY 446, Hinsdale, **N** food, **S** gas, lodging

**26** (79)  NY 16, Olean, **S gas:** Sunoco, **food:** Burger King, Wendy's, **other:** Ⓗ HOSPITAL

**25** (77)  Buffalo St, Olean, **S gas:** Citgo/dsl, **other:** Ⓗ HOSPITAL, **2 mi S on Constitution...gas:** KwikFill, **food:** Applebee's, Burger King, Dunkin Donuts, Friendly's, McDonald's, Perkins, Pizza Hut, Ponderosa, Quizno's, Tim Horton, **lodging:** Best Western, Comfort Inn, Country Inn, Knight's Inn, Microtel, **other:** Advance Parts, BJ's Whse/gas, $Tree, GNC, Home Depot, Jo-Ann Fabrics, K-Mart, NAPA, Old Navy, Radio Shack, Tops Foods/gas, Walmart, St Bonaventure U

**24** (74)  NY 417, Allegany, **1mi S gas:** Mobil/dsl, **other:** to St Bonaventure U

**73mm**  **rest area wb, full** ♿ **facilities,** 🍴, **litter barrels, petwalk**

**23** (68)  US 219 S, **N gas:** Allegany Jct./Subway/dsl

**66mm**  Allegheny River

**21** (61)  US 219 N, Salamanca, **S food:** Red Garter Rest

**20** (58)  NY 417, NY 353, Salamanca, **N gas:** Antone's Gas, Nafco Quickstop/Burger King/24hr, Seneca OneStop/dsl/24hr, VIP Gas, **food:** McDonald's/24hr, **lodging:** Holiday Inn Express, Westgate Motel, **other:** AutoZone, Rail Museum, Seneca-Iroquis Museum, **S** casino

**19** (54)  **S other:** Allegany SP, Red House Area

**18** (51)  NY 280, **S other:** Allegany SP, Quaker Run Area

**17** (48)  NY 394, Steamburg, **N** gas, **other:** RV camping, **S gas:** M&M/dsl/rest., **other:** camping

**16** (42)  W Main St, Randolph, **N gas:** Mobil/dsl, **food:** R&M Rest., **other:** RV camping

**41mm**  **rest area eb,** 🕿, 🍴, **litter barrel**

**15** (40)  School House Rd

**39mm**  **rest area wb,** 🕿 🍴, **litter barrel**

**14** (36)  US 62, Kennedy, **N gas:** Keystone Gas, **food:** Office Pizza/Subs, **S** RV camping

**32mm**  Cassadaga Creek

**J A M E S T O W N**

**N** ↕ **S**

**P L A T T S B U R G H**

**13** (31)  NY 394, Falconer, **S gas:** Mobil/dsl, Sunoco, **food:** Burger King, McDonald's, Tim Horton, Wendy's, **lodging:** Budget Inn, Red Roof Inn, **other:** CVS Drug, Sugar Creek Stores, Harley-Davidson

**12** (28)  NY 60, Jamestown, **N gas:** KwikFill/deli/dsl, **S gas:** Mobil/McDonald's/dsl, **food:** Bob Evans, **lodging:** Comfort Inn, Hampton Inn, **other:** Ⓗ HOSPITAL, st police

**11** (25)  to NY 430, Jamestown, **S** gas, dsl, food, lodging

**22mm**  **Welcome ctr/rest area eb, full** ♿ **facilities,** 🍴, **litter barrels, petwalk, vending**

**10** (21)  NY 430 W, Bemus Point

**9** (20)  NY 430 E, **N gas:** Mobil, **S** gas, food, lodging

**19mm**  Chautauqua Lake

**8** (18)  NY 394, Mayville, **N gas:** Mobil/dsl, lodging, **other:** RV camping

**7** (15)  Panama

**6** (9)  NY 76, Sherman, **N gas:** Keystone Gas, **food:** Village Pizzeria, **other:** NAPA, Sherman Drug, USPO

**4** (1)  NY 430, Findley Lake, **N lodging:** Holiday Inn Express, Peek'n Peak Motel, **S** gas, food, lodging, **other:** RV camping, to Peek'n Peak Ski Area

**0mm**  New York/Pennsylvania state line. **Exits 3-1 are in PA.**

**3**  PA 89, North East, Wattsburg, **N** gas, food

**1b a**  I-90, W to Erie, E to Buffalo. I-86 begins/ends on I-90, exit 37. I-390 begins/ends on I-86, exit 36.

## INTERSTATE 87

| Exit # | Services |
|---|---|

**176mm**  US/Canada Border, NY state line, I-87 begins/ends.

**43** (175)  US 9, Champlain, **E** World Duty Free, **W gas:** Peterbilt Trkstp/dsl/deli/scales/24hr/@, **other:** repair

**42** (174)  US 11 S, to Rouse's Point, Champlain, **E gas:** Mobil, **food:** J-reck Subs, Pizza+, Subway, **other:** Ace Hardware, Chevrolet/Pontiac (3mi), Kinney Drug, PriceChopper/24hr, Rite Aid, USPO, **W gas:** Exxon/dsl, Mobil/dsl, **food:** McDonald's

**41** (167)  NY 191, Chazy, **E** st police, **W** Miner Institute

**162mm**  **rest area both lanes, full** ♿ **facilities, info,** 🕿, 🍴, **litter barrels, petwalk**

**40** (160)  NY 456, Beekmantown, **E gas:** Mobil/dsl, **lodging:** Pt Auroche Lodge, Stonehelm Motel/café, **W** Twin Ells Camping

**39** (158)  NY 314, Moffitt Rd, Plattsburgh Bay, **E gas:** Mobil/dsl, Stewarts, **food:** A&W, Dunkin Donuts, Gus' Rest., McDonald's, **lodging:** Rip van Winkle Motel, Sundance Inn, Super 8, **other:** Plattsburgh RV Park, **W other:** Shady Oaks Camping, to Adirondacks

**38** (154)  NY 22, NY 374, to Plattsburgh, **E gas:** Mobil/dsl, **food:** Kinney Drug

**37** (153)  NY 3, Plattsburgh, **E gas:** Mobil, Shell, Stewarts, Sunoco, **food:** Burger King, China Buffet, Domino's, Dunkin Donuts, Jade Buffet, KFC, Legends Rest., Mangia Pizza, McDonald's, Michigan's Rest., Papa John's, Perkins, Pizza Hut, Quizno's, Starbucks, Subway, Wendy's, **lodging:** Comfort Inn, Holiday Inn, **other:** Ⓗ HOSPITAL, Aldi Foods, BigLots, Buick/Cadillac/GMC/Pontiac, Family$, Ford, Michael's, PetsMart, Radio Shack, Rite Aid, Sam's Club, Staples, TJ Maxx, Walmart SuperCtr, vet, **W gas:** Exxon, Mobil, Sunoco/J-reck Subs, **food:** Anthony's Rest., Applebee's, Butcher Block Rest., Dunkin Donuts, Friendly's, Ground Round, 99 Rest.,

**P L A T T S B U R G H** N ← → S

## INTERSTATE 87 CONT'D

**37** (153) Continued
Ponderosa, **lodging:** Best Value Inn, Best Western, Day's Inn, Econolodge, La Quinta, Microtel, **other:** Advance Parts, AutoZone, Best Buy, Borders Books, Gander Mtn, Harley-Davidson, Honda, JC Penney, Kinny Drug, K-Mart, Lowes Whse, 1$Store, Prays Mkt, PriceChopper Foods, Sears/auto, Suzuki, Target, vet

**151mm** Saranac River

**36** (150) NY 22, Plattsburgh ✈, **E gas:** Mobil/dsl/24hr, **other:** U-Haul, **W other:** st police

**146mm** truck insp sta nb, rest area nb full ♿ **facilities,** 🅿, **litter barrels,** 🚻 **petwalk**

**35** (144) NY 442, to Port Kent, Peru, **2-8 mi E other:** Iroquois/Ausable Pines Camping, **W gas:** Citgo, Mobil/Subway/Dunkin Donuts/dsl, **food:** Cricket's Rest., McDonald's, **other:** Auchuban Hardware, Grand Union Foods, USPO, repair

**143mm** emergency 🚻 at 2 mi intervals begin sb/end nb

**34** (137) NY 9 N, Ausable Forks, **E gas:** Sunoco/dsl, **food:** Pleasant Corner Rest., Mac's Drive-in, **other:** vet, **W other:** Prays Mkt, Ausable River RV Camping

**136mm** Ausable River

**33** (135) US 9, NY 22, to Willsboro, **E** gas/dsl, food, lodging, RV camping, to Essex Ferry

**125mm** N Boquet River

**32** (124) Lewis, **E other:** RV Camping, **W gas:** Lukoil/dsl, **food:** Trkstp Diner, **other:** RV Camping

**123mm** rest area sb, full ♿ **facilities, info,** 🚻, 🅿, **petwalk, rest area nb, no restrooms**

**120mm** Boquet River

**31** (117) NY 9 N, to Elizabethtown, Westport, **E gas:** Mobil, **lodging:** HillTop Motel, **other:** RV camp/dump, **W other:** Ⓗ HOSPITAL, st police

**111mm** rest area nb only, full ♿ **facilities,** 🚻, 🅿, **litter barrels, vending, petwalk**

**30** (104) US 9, NY 73, Keene Valley

**99mm** rest area both lanes, full ♿ **facilities,** 🚻, 🅿, **litter barrels, petwalk**

**29** (94) N Hudson, **E other:** Jellystone Camping, USPO, **W** Blue Ridge Falls Camping

**28** (88) NY 74 E, to Ticonderoga, Schroon Lake, **E gas:** Getty, Sunoco/dsl, **lodging:** Maple Leaf Motel, Schroon Lake B&B, **other:** RV camp/dump, st police, services on US 9

**83mm** rest area both lanes, full ♿ **facilities,** 🚻, 🅿, **litter barrels, petwalk, vending**

**27** (81) US 9 (from nb, no EZ return), Schroon Lake, to gas/dsl, food, lodging

**26** (78) US 9 (no EZ return), Pottersville, Schroon Lake, **E lodging:** Lee's Corner Motel, **other:** RV Camping, **W gas:** Valero/dsl, **food:** Black Bear Rest.

**25** (73) NY 8, Chestertown, **E gas:** Crossroads Country Store, **W gas:** Mobil/dsl, **other:** RV camping

**24** (67) Bolton Landing, **E** RV camping

**66mm** parking area sb, 🅿, Schroon River

**64mm** parking area nb, 🅿

**23** (58) to US 9, Diamond Point, Warrensburg, **W gas:** Citgo/dsl, Mobil, Stewarts, **food:** Dunkin Donuts, Geroge Henry's Rest., McDonald's, **lodging:** Super 8, **other:** Ford/Mercury, Central Adirondack Tr, RV Camping, ski area

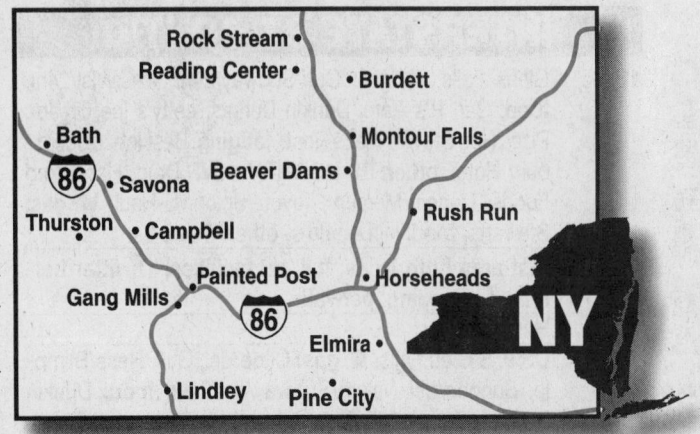

**22** (54) US 9, NY 9 N, to Diamond Pt, Lake George, **E gas:** Citgo, **food:** Boardwalk Rest., KFC, Luigi's Italian, Mario's Italian, Subway, Trattoria Siciliano, **lodging:** Admiral Motel, Balmoral Motel, Blue Moon Motel, Brookside Motel, Heritage Motel, Mohawk Cottages, Oasis Motel, Windsor Lodge, multiple services, **W** parking area both lanes

**21** (53) NY 9 N, Lake Geo, Ft Wm Henry, **E on US 9...gas:** Getty Gas, Stewarts, Sunoco, Valero, **food:** Adirondack Brewery, A&W, Barnsider Smokehouse, Dining Room, Flapjack Pete's, Gino&Tony's, Guiseppe's Pizza, Jasper's Steaks, Kelly's Rest., Lobster Pot, Mama Riso's Italian, McDonald's, Mountaineer Rest., Paolini's, Pizza Hut, Prospect Mt Diner, Quizno's, Smokey Joe's Grill, Sub City, **lodging:** Best Value Inn, Best Western, Comfort Inn, Country Hearth Inn, Econolodge, Ft Henry Inn, Georgian Resort, Hampton Inn, Holiday Inn, Howard Johnson/rest., Lake Crest Hotel, Lake George Inn, Lake Haven Hotel, Lakeview Hotel, Marine Village Resort, Motel Montreal, Nordick's Motel, Park Lane Inn, Ramada Inn, Travelodge, Tiki Motel, Scottish Inn, 7 Dwarf's Motel, Sullivan's Motel, Sundowner Motel, Super 8, Surfside Motel, Villager Motel, Wingate Inn, **other:** Harley-Davidson, King Phillip/Lake George Camping (2mi), Rite Aid, USPO, multiple services, **W gas:** Mobil/dsl/LP, **lodging:** Kathy's Motel

**51mm** Adirondack Park

**20** (49) NY 149, to Ft Ann, **E on US 9... gas:** Mobil/Subway, Sunoco/dsl, **food:** CK's Eatery, Domino's, Frank's Pizza, Leo's Rest., Logjam Rest., Montcalm Rest., Old Post Grill, **lodging:** Comfort Suites, Col. Williams Resort, Day's Inn, Mohican Motel, Rodeway Inn, Rosie's Cabins, Tall Pines Motel, Whipporwill Motel/RV Park, **other:** Carquest, Chevrolet, Ledgeview RV Park (3mi), Factory Outlets/famous brands, st police, **E on US 9S...food:** Johnny Rocket's, **lodging:** Country Inn&Suites, **other:** 6 Flags Funpark

**G L E N S   F A L L S**

**19** (47) NY 254, Glens Falls, **E gas:** Citgo, Getty, Hess, Mobil, Sunoco, **food:** Bon Ton, Burger King, Chicago Pizza, China Town, Dunkin Donuts, Friendly's, LJ Silver, McDonald's, Mr B's Rest., 99 Rest., Olive Garden, Panera Bread, Pizza Hut, Red Lobster, Remington Grill, Silo Rest., Starbucks, Subway, Taco Bell, Wendy's, **lodging:** Alpen Haus, Budget Inn, Econolodge, Quality Inn, Red Roof Inn, Sleep Inn, **other:** Ace Hardware, AutoZone, Firestone/auto, Goodyear, Home Depot, JC Penney, Jo-Ann Fabrics, PriceChopper Foods, Radio Shack, Rite Aid, Sears, Staples, Steve&Barry's, Target, TJ Maxx, Walmart, mall, **W gas:** Mobil, Stewarts, **lodging:** Ramada/rest., st police

**GLENS FALLS · SARATOGA SPRINGS N ↑ S · ALBANY**

## INTERSTATE 87 CONT'D

**18** (45) Glens Falls, **E gas:** Gulf/Subway/24hr, Hess/dsl/24hr, **food:** Carl R's Café, Dunkin Donuts, Lefty's Ice Cream, Pizza Hut, Steve's Place Rest. **lodging:** Best Inn, Queensbury Hotel, **other:** H HOSPITAL, CVS Drug, Hannaford Foods, Lincoln/Mercury, Toyota/Scion, U-Haul, **W gas:** Stewarts, **food:** McDonald's, **other:** Super 8

**43mm** **rest area both lanes, full** & **facilities,** ⊼ **litter barrels,** C **vending, petwalk**

**42mm** Hudson River

**17** (40) US 9, S Glen Falls, **E gas:** Citgo/dsl, Gulf, Hess/Blimpie, Sunoco/dsl, Valero/Subway/dsl/24hr, **food:** Dunkin Donuts, Fitzgerald's Steaks, **lodging:** Budget Inn, Landmark Motel (1mi), Sara-Glen Motel, Town&Country Motel, **other:** Adirondack RV Camp, Jeep, Suzuki, auto repair, transmissions, vet, **W** Moreau Lake SP

**16** (36) Ballard Rd, Wilton, **E other:** Coldbrook Campsites, golf, **W gas:** Mobil, Stewart's, Sunoco/Scotty's Rest./dsl/scales/24hr, **lodging:** Mt View Acres Motel, **other:** Alpin Haus RV Ctr, Ernie's Grocery

**15** (30) NY 50, NY 29, Saratoga Springs, **E gas:** Hess/dsl/24hr, Mobil, **food:** Applebees, BonTon, Burger King, Chicago Grill, Denny's, Dunkin Donuts, FoodCourt, Friendly's, Giavanno's Pizza, Golden Corral, KFC/Taco Bell, McDonald's, Moe's SW Grill, 99 Rest., Panera Bread, Ruby Tuesday, Subway, TGIFriday, Uno Pizzaria, **lodging:** Comfort Inn, **other:** Barnes&Noble, Best Buy, BJ's Whse, Dodge, Ford/Mercury, Hannaford Foods, Home Depot, JC Penney, Lowes Whse, Mazda, Old Navy, PetsMart, PriceChopper Foods, Rite Aid, Sears/auto, Staples, Subaru, Target, TJ Maxx, Toyota/Scion, Walgreens, Walmart SuperCtr, mall, **W lodging:** Residence Inn, **other:** H HOSPITAL

**14** (38) NY 9P, Schuylerville, **2 mi W gas:** Citgo/repair/LP, **lodging:** Holiday Inn, **other:** H HOSPITAL, museum, racetrack

**13** (25) US 9, Saratoga Springs, **E food:** Bentley's Rest., DeLucia's Deli, Saratoga Pizza Place, **lodging:** Budget Inn, Maggiore's Motel, Post Road Lodge, **other:** Nissan, Northway RV, Ballston Spa SP, **W gas:** Mobil, Stewarts, **food:** Big Apple Rest., El Mariachi, Hibachi Grill, PJ's BBQ, **lodging:** Best Western, Design Motel, Hilton Garden (4mi), Roosevelt Inn/rest., Thorobred Motel, Top Hill Hotel

**12** (21) NY 67, Malta, **E gas:** Exxon, **food:** Dunkin Donuts, KFC, Malta Diner, McDonald's, Subway, Taco Bell, Tasty Chinese, **lodging:** Cocca's Motel, Fairfield Inn, Riviera Motel, **other:** CVS Drug, GNC, PriceChopper Foods, Stewarts, Saratoga NHP, st police

**11** (18) Round Lake Rd, Round Lake, **E food:** MyWay Cafe, **W gas:** Citgo/dsl, Sunoco/dsl, **food:** Round Lake Rest., **other:** Rite Aid, Stewarts

**10** (16) Ushers Rd, **E gas:** Hess/dsl, Xtra/dsl, **food:** Ferretti's Rest., **other:** auto repair, **W other:** Stewarts

**14mm** **rest area nb, full** & **facilities, info,** C, ⊼ **litter barrels, vending, petwalk**

**9** (13) NY 146, Clifton Park, **E gas:** Hess/dsl/24hr, USA/gas, **food:** Burger King, Chili's, Cracker Barrel, Pizza Hut, Red Robin, Sam's Pizzaria, Snyder's Rest., **lodging:** Comfort Suites, **other:** Advance Parts, Aldi Foods,

**9** (13) Continued
Goodyear/auto, Home Depot, Kohl's, Lowe's Whse, Michael's, **W gas:** Mobil, Sunoco/dsl, **food:** Applebee's, Denny's, Dunkin Donuts, Friendly's, KFC, McDonald's, Outback Steaks, Quizno's, Ruby Tuesday, Starbucks, Taco Bell, TGIFriday, Wendy's, **lodging:** Best Western, Hampton Inn, **other:** AutoZone, BordersBooks, Chevrolet, CVS Drug, Eckerd, Firestone, Freedom RV Ctr, Hannaford Foods, JC Penney, Jo-Ann Fabrics, K-Mart, Marshall's, PriceChopper Foods, mall, st police

**8a** (12) Grooms Rd, to Waterford, **1-2 mi E on US 9 gas:** Getty, Gulf, **food:** 1/2 Moon Diner, Wendy's, **other:** Walmart SuperCtr

**8** (10) Crescent, Vischer Ferry, **E gas:** Hess/Blimpie/Godfather's/dsl/24hr, **food:** Krause's Rest. (3mi), McDonald's, **W gas:** Citgo, Sunoco/24hr, **food:** Pancho's Mexican, **other:** CVS Drug, Stewarts

**8mm** Mohawk River

**7** (7) NY 7, Troy, **E on US 9N...gas:** Hess/dsl, **food:** Kirker's Steaks, Mr. Subb, **lodging:** Clarion, Hampton Inn, Holiday Inn Express, **other:** Acura, Buick/GMC/Pontiac, Dodge, $General, Firestone, Ford, Lincoln/Mercury, Nissan, Rite Aid, Volvo, **E on US 9S...gas:** Mobil, **food:** Dunkin Donuts, McDonald's, New Panda, Subway, **other:** Firestone, Marshall's

**6** (6) NY 2, to US 9, Schenectady, **E gas:** Getty, Mobil, **food:** Applebee's, BonTon, Boston Mkt, Chicago Grill, Chuck-eCheese, Circle Diner, Dakota Steaks, Domino's, Panera Bread, Red Robin, Starbucks, Wendy's, **lodging:** Cocca's Inn, La Quinta, Travelodge, **other:** CVS Drug, Goodyear/auto, Hannaford Foods, Infiniti, JC Penney, Lowes Whse, PetsMart, PriceChopper Foods, Sam's Club, Staples, Toyota/Scion, VW, Walmart, same as 7, **W gas:** Mobil/24hr, **food:** Carabba's, Fillet 7, Friendly's, Kings Buffet, Ruby Tuesday, Subway, **lodging:** Fairfield Inn, Microtel, Quality Inn, Super 8, **other:** Target, TJ Maxx

**5** (5) NY 155 E, Latham, **E food:** DeeDee's Rest., Philly's Grill, **lodging:** Econolodge, **other:** USPO

**4** (4) NY 155 W, Wolf Rd, **E on Wolf Rd...gas:** Hess/dsl, Sunoco, **food:** Arby's, Capital Buffet, Denny's, Firkin&Fox, Macaroni Grill, Maurice's Sandwiches, McDonald's, Moe's SW Grill, 99 Rest., Old Chicago Grill, Olive Garden, Outback Steaks, Pizza Hut, Real Seafood Co, Red Lobster, Starbucks, Wings&Rings, Wolf Rd Diner, **lodging:** Best Western, Courtyard, Hampton Inn, Holiday Inn, Homewood Suites, Marriott, Red Roof Inn, **other:** Chevrolet, CVS Drug, Ford/Lincoln/Mercury, Hannafords Foods, KIA, **W food:** Koto Japanese, **lodging:** Desmond Hotel, Hotel Indigo, **other:** to Heritage Park

**2** (2) NY 5, Central Ave, **E gas:** Sunoco, **food:** Wendy's, **lodging:** Cocca's Inn, Scottish Inn, Springhill Suites, **other:** Jo-Ann Fabrics, Kost Tire, Macy's, Marshalls, Lowes Whse, PetCo, Sears, Staples, Target, **E on Wolf Rd... gas:** Mobil/Subway/dsl, Sunoco, **food:** Cheesecake Factory, Chili's, Dunkin Donuts, Emperor Chinese, Friendly's, Fuddruckers, Honeybaked Ham, IHOP, LJ Silver/Taco Bell, PF Chang's, **lodging:** Days Inn, Econolodge, **other:** Barnes&Noble, Borders Books, Firestone/auto, Goodyear/auto, LL Bean, Macy's, Steve&Barry's, mall, **W gas:** Exxon, **food:** Butcher Block Grill, Delmonico's Steaks, Domino's, Dunkin Donuts, Empress Diner,

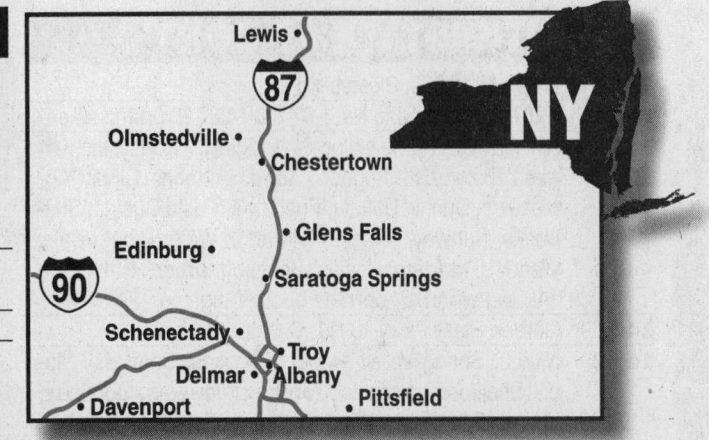

**ALBANY**

**N ↑ ↓ S**

## INTERSTATE 87 CONT'D

**2** (2) Continued
Garcia's Mexican, Mr Subb, Quizno's, Smokey Bones BBQ, Subway, Wendy's, **lodging:** Best Value Inn, Comfort Inn, Howard Johnson, Knights Inn, Quality Inn, Rodeway Inn, Super 8, **other:** Buick/GMC, Krause's Candy, Saturn, Subaru

**1W** (1) **NY State Thruway (from sb), I-87 S to NYC, I-90 W to Buffalo**

**1E** (1) I-90 E (from sb), to Albany, Boston

**1S** (1) to US 20, Western Ave, **W gas:** Mobil, **food:** Burger King, Chicago Grill, Dunkin Donuts, Friendly's, Hana Grill, Ichyban Japanese, McDonald's, Metro 80 Diner, Moe's SW Grill, 99 Rest., Panera Bread, Starbucks, TGIFriday, Wendy's, **lodging:** Holiday Inn Express, **other:** Best Buy, Borders Books, Circuit City, Home Depot, JC Penney, Macy's, Michael's, Old Navy, PetsMart, PriceChopper Foods, Walmart SuperCtr, mall, USPO, vet

**1N** (1) **I-87 N (from nb), to Plattsburgh, NY State Thruway goes west to Buffalo (I-90), S to NYC (I-87), I-87 N to Montreal**

**24** (148) I-90 and I-87 N

**23** (142) I-787, to Albany, US 9 W, **E gas:** Cumberland Farms/Dunkin Donuts/dsl, Mobil/dsl, **lodging:** Comfort Inn, Regency Inn, **other:** transmissions, to Knickerbocker Arena, **W gas:** Stewarts, **lodging:** Econolodge

**139mm** **parking area sb,** [C], [⋒], **litter barrel**

**22** (135) NY 396, to Selkirk

**21a** (134) I-90 E, to MA Tpk, Boston

**127mm** **New Balitmore Travel Plaza both lanes,** Mobil/dsl, Famous Famiglia, Quizno's, Roy Rogers, Starbucks, TCBY, atm, gifts, info, UPS

**21b** (124) US 9 W, NY 81, to Coxsackie, **W gas:** Trvl Plaza/dsl/rest./24hr/@, Sunoco/dsl, **food:** McDonald's (5mi), **lodging:** Best Western, Budget Inn, Holiday Inn Express, Red Carpet Inn, **other:** Boat'n RV Whse, repair, vet

**21** (114) NY 23, Catskill, **E gas:** Mobil, Sunoco/dsl/24hr, **lodging:** Catskill Motel/rest. (2mi), Pelokes Motel (2mi), Quality Inn, **other:** Home Depot, transmissions, to Rip van Winkle Br, **W food:** Anthony's Italian, LogSider Café, **lodging:** Astoria Motel, Budget Inn (3mi), Quality Inn, Rip Van Winkle Motel, **other:** to Hunter Mtn/Windham Ski Areas

**103mm** **Malden Service Area nb,** Mobil/dsl, Carvel Ice Cream, Hotdogs, McDonald's, atm, gifts, [C], **parking area sb**

**20** (102) NY 32, to Saugerties, **E gas:** Citgo, Mobil/dsl, Stewarts, **food:** Dunkin Donuts, Emiliani Italian, Giordano's Pizza, McDonald's, Pizza Star, Starway Café, Subway, **other:** CarQuest, Chrysler/Dodge/Jeep, Curves, CVS Drug, Family$, Grand Union Foods, PriceChopper Foods, vet, **W gas:** Hess/Blimpie/dsl, Sunoco, **food:** Cafe Mezzaluna, Johnny G's Diner, Land&Sea Grill, **lodging:** Comfort Inn, Howard Johnson/rest., **other:** Blue Mtn Campground (5mi), Brookside Campground (10mi), KOA (2mi), Rip Van Winkle Campground (3mi), to Catskills

**99mm** **parking area nb,** [C], [⋒], **litter barrels**

**96mm** **Ulster Travel Plaza sb,** Sunoco/dsl, Nathan's, Roy Rogers, Starbucks, TCBY, atm, gifts, [C]

**19** (91) NY 28, Kingston, **E gas:** Mobil, **food:** Dietz Diner, Friendly's, Olympic Diner, Picnic Pizza, Savona's Pizza,

**NEWBURGH**

**19** (91) Continued
**lodging:** Holiday Inn, Super 8, **other:** Advance Parts, Hannaford Foods, Radio Shack, Walgreens, **W food:** Family Diner, Lorenzo's Pizza, Roudigan's Steaks, **lodging:** Budget 19 Motel, Quality Inn, Skytop Motel/steaks, SuperLodge, **other:** Buick, Camper's Barn RV, Ford, Nissan, access to I-587, US 209

**18** (76) NY 299, to Poughkeepsie, New Paltz, **E gas:** Citgo/dsl, Mobil, **food:** Carribean Cuisine, College Diner/24hr, Village Grill, **lodging:** Econolodge, 87 Motel, Super 8 (5mi), **other:** repair, to Mid-Hudson Br, **W gas:** Sunoco/24hr, **food:** Burger King, Dunkin Donuts, McDonald's, Pasquale's Pizza, Quizno's, Subway, TCBY, **lodging:** Super 8, **other:** Advance Parts, Midas, Radio Shack, Rite Aid, ShopRite Foods, Stop'n Shop, Jellystone (9mi), KOA (10mi), vet

**66mm** **Modena service area sb,** gas: Sunoco/dsl, **food:** Arby's, Carvel's Ice Cream/bakery, Uno Pizzaria, McDonald's, **other:** atm, fax, gifts, UPS

**65mm** **Plattekill Travel Plaza nb,** gas: Sunoco/dsl, **food:** Big Boy, Nathan's, Roy Rogers, **other:** atm, gifts, info

**17** (60) I-84, NY 17K, to Newburgh, **E on NY 300 gas:** Getty, Hess/Blimpie/dsl, Mobil, Sunoco, **food:** Applebees, Burger King, Chili's, Cosimos Ristorante, Denny's, Dunkin Donuts, Gateway Diner, Ground Round, Jak Steaks, King Buffet, Longhorn Steaks, Neptune Diner, Newburgh Buffet, Old Town Buffet, Perkins, Union Sq Rest., Subway, Taco Bell, TGIFriday, Wendy's, **lodging:** Hampton Inn, Howard Johnson, Quality Inn, Ramada Inn, Super 8, **other:** Adam's Food Mkt, Aldi Foods, AutoZone, Barnes&Noble, BonTon, Cadillac/Chevrolet, Chrysler/Dodge/Jeep, Curves, $Tree, Ford/Lincoln/Mercury, Harley-Davidson, Home Depot, Honda, Lowes Whse, Mavis Tire, Michael's, Midas, Nissan, Kohl's, Office Depot, Old Navy, PetsMart, Radio Shack, Sears/auto, Stop'n Shop, Target, Walmart SuperCtr, **W lodging:** Hilton Garden

**16** (45) US 6, NY 17, to West Point, Harriman, **W gas:** Exxon/dsl, **food:** TGIFriday's, **lodging:** American Budget Inn, Hampton Inn, **other:** Buick/Chevrolet, Kohl's, Staples, Walmart SuperCtr (1mi), Woodbury Outlet/famous brands, st police

**34mm** **Ramapo Service Area sb,** gas: Sunoco/dsl/24hr, **food:** McDonald's, **other:** atm

**33mm** **Sloatsburg Travel Plaza nb,** gas: Sunoco/dsl/24hr, **food:** Burger King, Dunkin Donuts, Quizno's, Sbarro's, **other:** atm, gifts, info

## INTERSTATE 87 CONT'D

**15a** (31) NY 17 N, NY 59, Sloatsburg

**15** (30) I-287 S, NY 17 S, to NJ. I-87 S & I-287 E run together.

**14b** (27) Airmont Rd, Montebello, **E lodging:** Holiday Inn, **W gas:** Exxon/dsl, Sunoco, **food:** Airmont Diner, Applebee's, Dunkin Donuts, Friendly's, Pasta Cucina, Starbucks, Subway, Sutter's Mill Rest., Water Wheel Cafe, Wendy's, **lodging:** Howard Johnson, **other:** H HOSPITAL, DrugMart, ShopRite Foods, Walgreens, Walmart

**14a** (23) Garden State Pkwy, to NJ, Chestnut Ridge

**14** (22) NY 59, Spring Valley, Nanuet, **E gas:** Citgo/dsl, Mobil, Shell/dsl, Valero/dsl, **food:** Burger King, Domino's, McDonald's, Planet Wings, **lodging:** Fairfield Inn, **other:** AutoZone, BMW/Ferrari, CarQuest, Michaels, Target, TJ Maxx, **W gas:** Citgo, **food:** ChuckeCheese, Dunkin Donuts/Baskin-Robbins, Great China, KFC, Nanuet Diner, Red Lobster, Starbucks, Taco Bell, White Castle, Wendy's, **lodging:** Day's Inn, Hampton Inn, Hilton Garden, **other:** AutoZone, Barnes&Noble, $Tree, Home Depot, Hyundai, Macy's, Marshalls, PetCo, Sears/auto, Staples, Stop'n Shop Foods, mall

**13** (20) Palisades Pkwy, N to Bear Mtn, S to NJ

**12** (19) NY 303, Palisades Ctr Dr, W Nyack, **E** Saturn, **W gas:** Mobil, **food:** Bravo Italian, Buffalo Wild Wings, Cheesecake Factory, Dunkin Donuts, **lodging:** Nyack Motel, **other:** Barnes&Noble, Best Buy, BJ's Whse, Circuit City, Dave&Buster's, Macy's, Home Depot, JC Penney, Lord&Taylor, Old Navy, Staples, ShopRite Foods, Target, mall

**11** (18) US 9W, to Nyack, **E gas:** Gulf, Shell, **lodging:** Best Western, **W gas:** Discount Fuel, Quality Gas, Shell/dsl, **food:** Dunkin Donuts, McDonald's, Quizno's, **lodging:** Super 8, **other:** H HOSPITAL, J&L Repair/tire

**10** (17) Nyack (from nb), same as 11

**14mm** Tappan Zee Br, Hudson River

**13mm** toll plaza

**9** (12) to US 9, to Tarrytown, **E gas:** Hess, Shell/repair, **other:** Stop&Shop, **W gas:** Mobil, **food:** El Dorado West Diner, **lodging:** Hilton, **other:** Honda/Subaru, Mavis Tire

**8** (11) I-287 E, to Saw Mill Pkwy, White Plains, **E lodging:** Hampton Inn, Marriott

**7a** (10) Saw Mill River Pkwy S, to Saw Mill River SP, Taconic SP

**7** (8) NY 9A (from nb), Ardsley, **W lodging:** Ardsley Acres Motel, **other:** H HOSPITAL

**6mm** Ardsley Travel Plaza nb, Sunoco/dsl, Burger King, Popeye's, TCBY, vending

**5.5mm** toll plaza, ℂ

**6ba** (5) Stew Leonard Dr, to Ridge Hill, **W other:** Costco, Home Depot, Stew Leonard's Farmfresh Foods

**6** (4.5) Tuckahoe Dr, Yonkers, **E gas:** Getty/repair, **food:** Marcellino's Italian, McDonald's, Subway, **lodging:** Tuckahoe Motel, **other:** ShopRite Foods/drug, **W gas:** Gulf, Mobil, **food:** Domino's, Dunkin Donuts, Kim Wei Chinese, Quizno's, Totonno's Italian, **lodging:** Ramada Inn, Regency Hotel

**5** (4.3) NY 100 N (from nb), Central Park Ave, White Plains, **E gas:** Getty, Shell, Sunoco, **food:** Ground Round

**4** (4) Cross Country Pkwy, Mile Sq Rd, **E gas:** Lukoil, **food:** Burger King, **other:** Circuit City, Ford/Lincoln/Mercury/Subaru, Macy's, Sears/auto, TJ Maxx, **W gas:** Getty, Shell/dsl/24hr, **food:** Burger King, **other:** Mavis Tire, to Yonkers Speedway

**3** (3) Mile Square Rd, **E gas:** Stop&Shop, Foods, **other:** GNC, Thriftway Drug, mall, **W gas:** Getty, Shell/24hr

**2** (2) Yonkers Ave (from nb), Westchester Fair, **E gas:** Mobil, **other:** Yonkers Speedway

**1** (1) Hall Place, McLean Ave, **E other:** A&P Foods/Subway

**0mm** New York St Thruway and I-87 N run together to Albany

**14** (11) McLean Ave, **E gas:** Shell, **food:** Dunkin Donuts

**13** (10) E 233rd , NE Tollway, service plaza both lanes/Mobil

**12** (9.5) Hudson Pkwy (from nb), Sawmill Pkwy

**11** (9) Van Cortlandt Pk S

**10** (8.5) W 230th St (from sb), W 240th (from nb), **E gas:** Lukoil, **W gas:** Getty, **other:** H HOSPITAL, Target

**9** (8) W Fordham Rd, **E gas:** BP/dsl, **other:** H HOSPITAL, Toyota

**8** (7) W 179th (from nb), **W** Roberto Clemente SP

**7** (6) I-95, US 1, S to Trenton, NJ, N to New Haven, CT

**6** (5) E 153rd t, River Ave, Stadium Rd, **E other:** Yankee Stadium

**5** (5) E 161st, Macombs Dam Br, **E other:** Yankee Stadium

**3** (3) E 138th St, Madison Ave Br, **E gas:** BP/dsl

**2** (2) Willis Ave, 3rd Ave Br, **E gas:** Mobil/dsl, **W food:** McDonald's

**1** (1) Brook Ave, Hunts Point, **E gas:** BP, Hess

**0mm** I-87 begins/ends on I-278.

## INTERSTATE 88 - NEW YORK

| Exit # | Services |
| --- | --- |

**25a** I-90/NY Thruway. I-88 begins/ends on I-90, exit 25a.

**117mm** toll booth (to enter or exit NY Thruway)

**25** (116) NY 7, to Rotterdam, Schenectady, **S gas:** Citgo/Friendly's/Dunkin Donuts/dsl/24hr, **3 mi S gas:** Gulf, **food:** Burger King, McDonald's, Top's Diner, **lodging:** L&M Motel, Rotterdam Motel, **other:** Frosty Acres Camping

**24** (112) US 20, NY 7, to Duanesburg, **N gas:** Mobil, Stewarts, **food:** Dunkin Donuts, **other:** st police, **S food:** Duanesburg Diner, **other:** USPO

**23** (101) NY 30, to Schoharie, Central Bridge, **N lodging:** Holiday Motel, **other:** Hideaway Camping, Locust Park Camping, **S gas:** Mobil/Subway/dsl, **food:** Dunkin Donuts, **lodging:** Holiday Inn Express, Hyland House B&B (2mi), Parrott House 1870 Inn (4mi), Wedgewood B&B (2mi)

**22** (95) NY 7, NY 145, to Cobleskill, Middleburgh, **2-5 mi N gas:** Hess/dsl, Mobil, **food:** Dunkin Donuts, Pizza Hut, Subway, **lodging:** Colonial CT Motel, Holiday Inn Express, Holiday Motel, Super 8, **other:** H HOSPITAL, Advance Parts, Buick/Chevrolet/GMC/Pontiac, Chrysler/Dodge/Jeep, $General, $Tree, Ford, Howe Caverns Camping, PriceChopper Foods, Walmart SuperCtr to Howe Caverns, **S other:** Twin Oaks Camping, st police

**21** (90) NY 7, NY 10, to Cobleskill, Warnerville, **2-3 mi N gas:** Hess, Mobil/dsl, **food:** Arby's, Burger King, Dairy Deli, KFC/Taco Bell, McDonald's, Pizza Hut, Red Apple Rest., **lodging:** Bast Western, Gables B&B, **other:** H HOSPITAL, Ace Hardware, CarQuest, PriceChopper Foods, Walmart SuperCtr

**20** (87) NY 7, NY 10, to Richmondville, **S gas:** Mobil/dsl/24hr, Sunoco, **food:** Reinhardt's Deli, Sub Express, **lodging:** Rodeway Inn, **other:** USPO

**79mm** rest area wb, full ♿ facilities, ℂ vending, 🪑 litter barrels, petwalk

**19** (76) to NY 7, Worcester, **N gas:** Stewarts, Sunoco/dsl

## INTERSTATE 88 CONT'D - NEW YORK

| | |
|---|---|
| **73mm** | rest area eb, full ♿ facilities, 🚻, vending, 🏕, litter barrels, petwalk |
| **18** (71) | to Schenevus, **N** gas: Citgo, food: Schenevus Rest. |
| **17** (61) | NY 7, to NY 28 N, Colliersville, Cooperstown, **2 mi** **N** gas: Mobil/dsl, food: La Teranella, lodging: Amber Life Motel, Best Western (14mi), Knott's Motel, Redwood Motel, other: to Baseball Hall of Fame |
| **16** (59) | NY 7, to Emmons, **N** food: Arby's, Brooks BBQ, Farmhouse Rest., Morey's Rest., Perrucci's Pizza, Pizza Hut, Sonny's Pizza, lodging: Rainbow Inn, other: PriceChopper Foods, Rite Aid |
| **15** (56) | NY 28, NY 23, Oneonta, **N** gas: Citgo, Hess, KwikFill, food: Friendly's, KFC, lodging: Clarion, Townhouse Inn, other: **H** HOSPITAL, Advance Parts, to Soccer Hall of Fame, **S** gas: Citgo, Hess, food: Applebees, Burger King, Denny's, LJ Silver/Taco Bell, McDonald's, Neptune Diner/24hr, Quizno's, Sabatini's Italian, Subway, Wendy's, lodging: Budget Inn, Christopher's Lodge/rest., Holiday Inn, Sun Lodge, Super 8, other: Aldi Foods, Beaver Spring Camping, BJ's Whse/gas, $Tree, Hannaford Foods, Home Depot, JC Penney, Kost Tire, NAPA, Steve&Barry's, Walmart SuperCtr |
| **14** (55) | Main St (from eb), Oneonta, **N** gas: Citgo, Kwikfill, Stewarts, Sunoco, food: Alfresco's Italian, other: CVS Drug, **S** food: Denny's, McDonald's |
| **13** (53) | NY 205, **1-2 mi** **N** gas: Citgo, Hess, Mobil, food: Burger King, China Buffet King, DQ, Dunkin Donuts, McDonald's, Ponderosa, lodging: Celtic Motel, Hampton Inn, Maple Terrace Motel, Oasis Motor Inn, other: Buick/Cadillac/GMC/Pontiac, Chevrolet, Chrysler/Jeep, Honda, Nissan, Parts+, Rite Aid, to Susquehanna Tr, Gilbert Lake SP (11mi), camping |
| **12** (47) | NY 7, to Otego, **S** gas: Citgo/dsl/cafe, Lukoil |
| **43mm** | rest area wb, full ♿ facilities, 🚻, 🏕, litter barrels, vending, petwalk |
| **11** (40) | NY 357, to Unadilla, Delhi, **N** KOA |
| **39mm** | rest area eb, full ♿ facilities, 🚻, 🏕, litter barrels, vending, petwalk |
| **10** (38) | NY 7, to Unadilla, **2 mi** **N** gas: Apple Gas, lodging: Country Motel (4mi), other: Great American Foods, USPO, st police |
| **9** (33) | NY 8, to Sidney, **N** gas: Citgo/QuickWay/dsl, Hess/dsl, Mobil/dsl, food: China Buffet, McDonald's, Pizza Hut, Subway, lodging: Algonkin Motel, Country Motel, Super 8, other: **H** HOSPITAL, Advance Parts, $General, K-Mart/Little Caesar's, PriceChopper Foods, Tall Pines Camping, USPO |
| **8** (29) | NY 206, to Bainbridge, **N** gas: Citgo, Sunoco/Taco Xtra/dsl/24hr, food: Bob's Family Diner, lodging: Algonkin Motel, other: Chevrolet/GMC/Pontiac, Riverside RV Park, Parts+, USPO, to Oquage Creek Park |
| **7** (22) | NY 41, to Afton, **1-2 mi** **N** gas: Mobil/24hr, Sunoco/dsl Xtra, food: RiverClub Rest., Vincent's Rest., other: Afton Golf/rest., Echo Lake Park, Kellystone Park, Smith-Hale HS |
| **6** (16) | NY 79, to NY 7, Harpursville, Ninevah, **N** food: Gramma's Country Cafe, **S** gas: Citgo/Quickway/dsl, other: USPO, to Nathanial Cole Park |

| | |
|---|---|
| **5** (12) | Martin Hill Rd, to Belden, **N** other: Belden Manor Camping |
| **4** (8) | NY 7, to Sanitaria Springs, **S** gas: Hess/dsl |
| **3** (4) | NY 369, Port Crane, **N** to Chenango Valley SP, **S** gas: Fastrac/dsl, KwikFill |
| **2** (2) | NY 12a W, to Chenango Bridge, **N** gas: Mirabito, other: Red&White Foods, USPO |
| **1** (1) | NY 7 W (no wb return), to Binghamton |
| **0mm** | I-81, N to Syracuse, S to Binghamton. **I-88 begins/ends on I-81.** |

## INTERSTATE 90

| Exit # | Services |
|---|---|
| **B24.5mm** | New York/Massachusetts state line |
| **B3** (B23) | NY 22, to Austerlitz, New Lebanon, W Stockbridge, **N** gas: Citgo/dsl/scales/24hr, food: Lilly's Diner, **S** gas: Sunoco/dsl, lodging: Berkshire Spur Motel, other: Woodland Hills Camp |
| **B18mm** | toll plaza, 🚻 |
| **B2** (B15) | NY 295, Taconic Pkwy, **1-2 mi** **S** gas |
| **B1** (B7) | US 9, NY Thruway W, to I-87, toll booth, 🚻 |
| **12** (20) | US 9, to Hudson, **1-3 mi** **S** gas: Mobil/dsl/24hr (3mi), Sunoco/dsl (3mi), food: McDonald's, lodging: Bel Air Motel (1mi), Blue Spruce Motel (4mi), other: to Van Buren NHS |
| **18.5mm** | rest area wb, full ♿ facilities, 🚻, 🏕, litter barrels, vending, petwalk |
| **11** (15) | US 9, US 20, E Greenbush, Nassau, **N** gas: Citgo/dsl, Hess/dsl, food: BBQ, Dunkin Donuts, other: st police, **S** gas: Mobil (2mi), Stewarts, food: Burger King, Goomba's Pizza, Mercato's, My Place Rest., lodging: Dewitt Motel, Rodeway Inn, other: Chevrolet, Rite Aid, USPO, vet |
| **10** (10) | Miller Rd, to E Greenbush, **S** gas: Mobil/dsl, lodging: Comfort Inn, **1-3 mi** **S** gas: Stewarts, Sunoco, food: Dunkin Donuts, E Greenbush Diner, My Place Rest., Pizza Hut, lodging: Dewitt Motel |
| **9** (9) | US 4, to Rensselaer, Troy, **N** gas: Mobil, food: Applebee's, Ground Round, McDonald's, OffShore Pier Rest., Panera Bread, Starbucks, Subway, lodging: Holiday Inn Express, Residence Inn, other: $Tree, Grand Union Foods, Home Depot, PetsMart, Radio Shack, Staples, Target, Walmart SuperCtr, **S** gas: Stewart's, food: Denny's, Cracker Barrel, other: Fairfield Inn, **1-2 mi** **S** gas: Mobil, food: Dunkin Donuts, Friendly's, Wendy's, lodging: Econolodge |
| **8** (8) | NY 43, Defreestville |

## INTERSTATE 90 CONT'D

**ALBANY** E ↕ W

**7** (7) Washington Ave (from eb), Rensselaer

**6.5mm** Hudson River

**6a** I-787, to Albany

**6** (4.5) US 9, Northern Blvd, to Loudonville, **N gas:** Stewarts, **food:** Mr Subb, Siena Pizza, Ta-Ke Japanese, **lodging:** Red Carpet Inn, **other:** Ⓗ HOSPITAL

**5a** (4) Corporate Woods Blvd

**5** (3.5) Everett Rd, to NY 5, **S gas:** Hess, **food:** Bob&Ron's Fishfry, Chinese Buffet, Friendly's, Gateway Diner, LJ Silver/Taco Bell, Lucky Garden, McDonald's, Popeye's, Quizno's, Subway, **lodging:** Clarion, **other:** Ⓗ HOSPITAL, Aamco, Advance Parts, AutoZone, Chevrolet, Chrysler/Jeep, CVS Drug, Dodge, $Tree, Eckerd, Ford, Hannaford's Foods/24hr, Home Depot, Honda/Nissan, Mazda, Nissan, PepBoys, Pontiac, PriceChopper Foods, Radio Shack, Suzuki, multiple services on NY 5

**4** (3) NY 85 S, to Slingerlands

**3** (2.5) State Offices

**2** (2) Fuller Rd, Washington Ave, **S gas:** Sunoco, **food:** Dunkin Donuts, **lodging:** Courtyard, CrestHill Suites, Extended Stay America, Fairfield Inn, Red Carpet Inn, TownePlace Inn same as 1S

**1N** (1) I-87 N, to Montreal, to Albany ✈

**1S** (1) US 20, Western Ave, **S gas:** Mobil, **food:** Burger King, Chicago Grill, Dunkin Donuts, Friendly's, Hana Grill, Ichyban Japanese, McDonald's, Metro 80 Diner, Moe's SW Grill, 99 Rest., Panera Bread, Starbucks, TGIFriday, Wendy's, **lodging:** Holiday Inn Express, **other:** Best Buy, Borders Books, Circuit City, Home Depot, JC Penney, Macy's, Michael's, Old Navy, PetsMart, PriceChopper Foods, Walmart SuperCtr, mall, USPO, vet

**24** (149) I-87 N to Albany, Montreal, S to NYC

**153mm** **Guilderland Service Area eb**, Mobil/dsl, McDonald's, Mr Subb

**25** (154) I-890, NY 7, NY 146, to Schenectady

**25a** (159) I-88 S, NY 7, to Binghamton

**26** (162) I-890, NY 5 S, Schenectady

**168mm** **Pattersonville Service Area wb**, Mobil/dsl, Big Boy, Quizno's, Roy Rogers, Starbucks, TCBY, atm, fax, gifts, info, UPS

**172mm** **Mohawk Service Area eb**, Mobil/dsl, Breyer's, Fresh Fudge, McDonald's,

**27** (174) NY 30, Amsterdam, **N gas:** Citgo, Mobil/dsl, **lodging:** Super 8/diner/24hr, Valleyview Motel, **1 mi N lodging:** Best Value Inn, **other:** Camping World RV Ctr

**28** (182) NY 30A, Fonda, **N gas:** Citgo/dsl/rest./motel/24hr, Gulf/repair, Lukoil, TA/dsl/rest/motel/scales/24hr/@, **food:** McDonald's, **lodging:** Econolodge, Riverside Motel, **other:** Ⓗ HOSPITAL, st police, truck repair

**184mm** **parking area both lanes,** Ⓒ, **litter barrels**

**29** (194) NY 10, Canajoharie, **N gas:** Gulf, Stewarts, **food:** McDonald's, Pizza Hut, **other:** $General, Rite Aid, **S gas:** Lukoil/dsl, Petro USA/dsl, Sunoco, **food:** Joey D's Seafood, **other:** Chevrolet, NAPA, USPO

**210mm** **Indian Castle Service area eb**...gas: Mobil/dsl, **food:** Hershey's Ice Cream, Roy Rogers, **other:** atm, gifts, UPS. **Iroquois Service Area wb**...gas: Mobil/dsl, Burger King, Dunkin Donuts, gifts, UPS

**UTICA**

**29a** (211) NY 169, to Little Falls, **N lodging:** Best Western, **other:** Ⓗ HOSPITAL, to Herkimer Home

**30** (220) NY 28, to Mohawk, Herkimer, **N gas:** Fastrac/dsl, Mobil/Subway/dsl, Stewarts, **food:** Applebees, Burger King, Denny's, Dunkin Donuts, KFC/Taco Bell, McDonald's, Pizza Hut, Tony's Pizzaria, **lodging:** Budget Motel, Herkimer Inn, **other:** AutoZone, $General, $Tree, Ford/Lincoln/Mercury, Goodyear, K-Mart, Rite Aid, Walmart SuperCtr, vet, **S gas:** Citgo, Fastrac, **other:** Factory Depot, to Cooperstown (Baseball Hall of Fame)

**227mm** **Schuyler Service Area wb**, Mobil/dsl, Breyer's, McDonald's, atm, st police

**31** (233) I-790, NY 8, NY 12, to Utica, **N gas:** Citgo/dsl, Fastrac, **food:** Burger King, Charlie's Pizza, Colozzi's Cafe, Franco's Pizza, Jreck Subs, **other:** Big Lots, BJ's Whse, $Tree, Lowes Whse, PriceChopper Foods, Rite Aid, **1 mi N on frontage rd...food:** Applebees, **other:** BJ's Whse/gas, Lowes Whse, Walmart SuperCtr, **S gas:** Hess/dsl, **food:** Babe's Grill, Delmonico's Steaks, Denny's, Dunkin Donuts, Friendly's, Grand's Pizza, McDonald's, Pizza Hut, Taco Bell, Wendy's, **lodging:** Best Western, Days Inn, Hampton Inn, Happy Journey Motel, Red Roof Inn, Scottish Inn, Super 8

**236mm** I-790 (from eb), to Utica

**237.5mm** Erie Canal

**238mm** Mohawk River

**32** (243) NY 232, Westmoreland, **N lodging:** Quality Inn, Ramada Inn, Red Carpet Inn, **S lodging:** Carriage House Motel, Pinecrest Motel, **1 mi S** gas/dsl

**244mm** **Oneida Service Area eb**, Sunoco/dsl, Burger King, Sbarro's, Starbucks, atm, gifts

**250mm** **parking area eb**, Ⓒ, ⚟, **litter barrel**

**33** (253) NY 365, to Vernon Downs, Verona, **N gas:** SavOn Gas/dsl, **lodging:** Comfort Suites (6mi), Inn at Turning Stone, Quality Inn (9mi), Red Carpet Inn, **S gas:** SavOn Gas/LP/repair, **lodging:** Super 8 (3mi), **other:** Ⓗ HOSPITAL, Turning Stone Casino

**256mm** **parking area wb**, Ⓒ, ⚟, **litter barrel**

**34** (262) NY 13, to Canastota, **S gas:** Mobil/dsl, SavOn/dsl/24hr, **food:** Dunkin Donuts, McDonald's, **lodging:** Days Inn, Graziano Motel/rest., Super 8 (7mi), **other:** Boxing Hall of Fame, Verona Beach SP Camping

**266mm** **Chittenango Service Area wb**, Sunoco/dsl, Dunkin Donuts, Freshen's Treats, Sbarro's, TCBY, atm, gifts

**SYRACUSE**

**34a** (277) I-481, to Syracuse, Chittenango

**35** (279) NY 298, The Circle, Syracuse, **S gas:** Mobil, Valero/dsl, **food:** Burger King, Denny's, Dunkin Donuts, East Wok, Green Onion Rest., Joey's Italian, Jreck Subs, Justin's Grill, McDonald's, Pronto's Pizza, Ruby Tuesday, Starbucks, **lodging:** Candlewood Suites, Comfort Inn, Courtyard, Cresthill Suites, Day's Inn, Doubletree Inn, Embassy Suites, Extended Stay America, Hampton Inn, Hilton Garden, Holiday Inn, John Milton Inn, Microtel, Motel 6, Quality Inn, Ramada Ltd, Red Roof Inn, Residence Inn, Super 8, **other:** Goodyear/auto

**280mm** **Dewitt Service Area eb**, Sunoco/dsl, McDonald's, ice cream

**36** (283) I-81, N to Watertown, S to Binghamton

**37** (284) 7th St, Electronics Pkwy, to Liverpool, **N lodging:** Best Western, **S gas:** Hess/Blimpie/24hr, **food:** KFC/Taco Bell, **lodging:** Holiday Inn, Knight's Inn, **other:** Kinny Drug

Copyright 2009 - The Next Exit®

## INTERSTATE 90 CONT'D

**S Y R A C U S E** **E → W**

**38** (286) NY 57, to Liverpool, Syracuse, **N gas:** Fastrac/dsl, Hess, KwikFill, **food:** Bangkok Thai, Kirby's Rest., Pier 57 Diner, Pizza Hut, Quizno's, Salsarita's Grill, **lodging:** Hampton Inn (7mi), Super 8, **other:** Aldi Foods, $Tree, NAPA, Rite Aid

**39** (290) I-690, NY 690, Syracuse, **N lodging:** Comfort Inn/rest., **other:** Camping World RV Ctr

**292mm** **Warners Service Area wb**, Mobil/dsl/rest., Boston Pizza, Edy's Ice Cream, McDonald's,

**40** (304) NY 34, to Owasco Lake, Weedsport, **N** Riverforest RV Park, **S gas:** Fastrac, KwikFill, Sunoco/dsl, **food:** Arby's, Arnold's Rest., DB's Drive-In, Lin Bo Chinese, Old Erie Diner, **lodging:** Best Western, Day's Inn, Holiday Inn (12mi), **other:** Ace Hardware, Bass Pro Shops (12mi), Big M Foods, $General, Kinney Drug, NAPA

**310mm** **Port Byron Service Area eb**, Mobil/dsl/rest., Edy's Ice Cream, McDonald's, Original Pizza

**318mm** parking area wb, litter barrels, **C**

**41** (320) NY 414, to Cayuga Lake, Waterloo, **S gas:** Nice'n Easy/dsl, Petro/dsl/rest./scales/24hr/@, **food:** MaGee Country Diner, **lodging:** Holiday Inn (4mi), Microtel (4mi), **other:** Cayuga Lake SP, Waterloo Outlets/famous brands (3mi)

**324mm** **Junius Ponds Service Area wb**, Sunoco/dsl, Dunkin Donuts, Roy Rogers

**42** (327) NY 14, to Geneva, Lyons, **N** RV camping, **S gas:** Mobil/dsl/scales, **lodging:** Red Carpet Inn, **other:** Waterloo Outlets/famous brands (3mi), RV Camping, **6 mi S lodging:** Amherst, Best Value Inn, Hampton Inn, Motel 6, Ramada Inn

**337mm** **Clifton Springs Service Area eb**, Sunoco/dsl, Roy Rogers, Sbarro's, Starbucks, atm, gifts

**43** (340) NY 21, to Palmyra, Manchester, **N** Hill Cumorah LDS HS (6mi), **S gas:** Sunoco/dsl/24hr, **food:** Lehigh Valley Rest., McDonald's, **lodging:** Roadside Inn

**44** (347) NY 332, Victor, **S gas:** Getty/Subway/dsl, Mobil/dsl, Sunoco, **food:** Di Pacific's Rest., KFC, King's Wok, McDonald's, **lodging:** Best Value Inn, Budget Inn, Comfort Inn, Econolodge, **other:** CVS Drug, KOA (4mi), casino, st police

**350mm** **Seneca Service Area wb**, **gas:** Mobil/dsl, **food:** Fuddrucker's, Tim Horton, Villa Pizza, **other:** atm, info, **C**

**45** (351) I-490, NY 96, to Rochester, **N gas:** Citgo, **food:** Belini's, Biaggi's Rest., BoneFish Grill, Bonton, Champp's Grill, Chicago Grill, King Buffet, Olive Garden, PF Chang's, TGIFriday, **lodging:** Hampton Inn, **other:** BJ's Whse, Border's Books, Circuit City, K-Mart, Lord&Taylor, Macy's, Michael's, Sears/auto, **S gas:** KwikFill, **food:** Burger King, Charlie's Rest., Chili's, Denny's, Wendy's, **lodging:** Best Western, Holiday Inn Express, Homewood Suites, Microtel, Royal Inn, **other:** Ballantyne RV Ctr, Chevrolet

**353mm** parking area eb, **C**, litter barrels

**46** (362) I-390, to Rochester, **N on NY 253 W gas:** Citgo/dsl, Hess, Sunoco/dsl, **food:** McDonald's, Peppermint's Rest., Tim Horton, Wendy's, **lodging:** Country Inn&Suites, Day's Inn, Fairfield Inn, Microtel, Red Carpet Inn, Red Roof Inn, Super 8 **other:** GMC/Pontiac, Jeep

**366mm** **Scottsville Service Area eb**, **gas:** Mobil/dsl, **food:** Arby's, Tim Horton, Villa Pizza, **other:** atm, info

**376mm** **Ontario Service Area wb**, **gas:** Sunoco/dsl, **food:** Boston Pizza, McDonald's

**R O C H E S T E R**

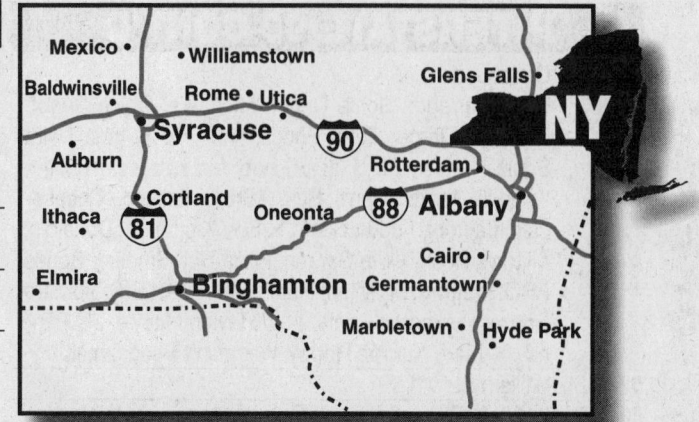

**47** (379) I-490, NY 19, to Rochester, **N** Timberline Camping

**48** (390) NY 98, to Batavia, **N lodging:** Comfort Inn, Hampton Inn, **S gas:** Citgo, **food:** Applebee's, Bob Evans, Peking Buffet, **lodging:** Best Western, Budget Inn, Day's Inn, Holiday Inn, Quality Inn, Ramada Ltd, Super 8, **other:** AutoZone, BJ's Whse, Home Depot, K-Mart, Lowes Whse, PetCo, Target, Walmart SuperCtr

**397mm** Pembroke Service Area eb, **gas:** Sunoco/dsl, **food:** Fuddrucker's, Tim Horton, **other:** atm, gifts, **C**, UPS

**48a** (402) NY 77, Pembroke, **S gas:** ✈FLYING J/dsl/LP/rest./scales/24hr, TA/dsl/rest./scales/24hr/@, **food:** Subway, **lodging:** Econolodge, 6 Flags Motel/RV Park (5mi), **other:** Sleepy Hollow Camping (8mi)

**412mm** **Clarence Service Area wb, full** **&** **facilities, gas:** Sunoco/dsl, **food:** Arby's, Fuddrucker's, Tim Horton, **other:** info, **C**

**49** (417) NY 78, Depew, **1-3 mi N gas:** Mobil, Sunoco, **food:** Applebee's, Arby's, Atlanta Bread, Bonton, Boston Mkt, Buffalo Wild Wings, Burger King, Cracker Barrel, Dave&Buster's, Denny's, Dibella's Subs, Don Pablo, DQ, Fazoli's, Golden Corral, KFC, McDonald's, Mighty Taco, Moe's SW Grill, Old Country Buffet, Panera Bread, Perkins, Picasso's Pizza, Pizza Hut, Pizza Plant, Ponderosa, Protocol Rest., Red Lobster, Roadhouse Grill, Ruby Tuesday, Spilio's Rest., Starbucks, Subway, Taco Bell, TGIFriday, Tim Horton, Tulley's Rest., Wendy's, **lodging:** Clarion, Econolodge, Fairfield Inn, Holiday Inn Express, Microtel, Ramada Ltd, **other:** VET, Acura, Barnes&Noble, Big Lots, BJ's Whse, Buick, Chevrolet, Dodge, $General, Dunn Tire, Eckerd/24hr, Firestone/auto, Ford, Home Depot, Honda, JC Penney, Jo-Ann Fabrics, K-Mart, Lowes Whse, Michael's, NTB, Office Depot, Radio Shack, Saturn, Sears/auto, SteinMart, Target, TJ Maxx, Top's Food/deli, Walmart SuperCtr, Wegman's Foods, mall, **S gas:** Kwikfill, Mobil, **food:** Bob Evans, John&Mary's Cafe, Salvatore's Italian, **lodging:** Garden Place Hotel, Hospitality Inn, Howard Johnson, Red Roof Inn, **other:** Aamco, CarQuest, Top's Foods

**419mm** toll booth

**50** (420) I-290 to Niagara Falls

**50a** (421) Cleveland Dr (from eb)

**51** (422) NY 33 E, Buffalo, **S** ✈, st police

**52** (423) Walden Ave, to Buffalo, **N food:** Applebees, Famous Dave's BBQ, McDonald's, Ruby Tuesday, Starbucks, Subway, TGIFriday, Tim Horton, **lodging:** Hampton Inn, Residence Inn, **other:** Aldi Foods, $Tree, Ford,

**B U F F A L O**

**B U F F A L O**  E ↕ W

**NY**

**D U N K I R K**

## INTERSTATE 90 CONT'D

**52 (423)** Continued
Goodyear/auto, Home Depot, Michael's, Office Depot, PetsMart, Target, Top's Foods, Walmart, **S gas:** Delta Sonic, Jim's Trk Plaza/Sunoco/dsl/rest./scales/24hr, KwikFill, **food:** Alton's Rest., Bravo Italiano, Cheesecake Factory, Fuddrucker's, Krispy Kreme, McDonald's, Milton's Rest., Olive Garden, Pizza Hut, Smokey Bones BBQ, **lodging:** Millenium Hotel, **other:** Best Buy, Borders Books, Burlington Coats, Lord&Taylor, Macy's, JC Penney, K-Mart, Niagara Hobby, Wegman's Foods, mall

**52a (424)** William St

**53 (425)** I-190, to Buffalo, Niagara Falls, **N lodging:** Holiday Inn Express

**54 (428)** NY 400, NY 16, to W Seneca, E Aurora

**55 (430)** US 219, Ridge Rd, Orchard Park, to Rich Stadium, **S gas:** Citgo, Delta Sonic, **food:** Denny's, Ponderosa, Subway, Wendy's, **lodging:** Hampton Inn, **other:** Aldi Foods, Goodyear/auto, Home Depot, K-Mart, Lowes Whse, Tops Foods, Wegman's Foods

**431mm** toll booth

**56 (432)** NY 179, Mile Strip Rd, **N gas:** Choice, Citgo, Sunoco, **food:** Blasdelle Pizza, DiPallo's Rest., Odyssey Rest., Whse Grill, **lodging:** Econolodge, **other:** CarQuest, CVS Drug, repair, **S food:** Applebee's, Bonton, Boston Mkt, ChuckeCheese, Friendly's, McDonald's, Olive Garden, Outback Steaks, Panera Bread, Pizza Hut, Red Lobster, Roadhouse Grill, Ruby Tuesday, Starbucks, Subway, TGIFriday, Wendy's, **lodging:** Clarion, Red Carpet Inn, **other:** Aldi Foods, Barnes&Noble, Best Buy, BJ's Whse, Circuit City, $Tree, Firestone/auto, Home Depot, JC Penney, Jo-Ann Etc, Old Navy, PepBoys, Sears, TJ Maxx, Wegman's Foods, mall

**57 (436)** NY 75, to Hamburg, **N gas:** Mobil/dsl, **food:** Anthony's Diner, Denny's, McDonald's, Wendy's, **lodging:** Comfort Inn, Red Roof Inn, Tallyho Motel, **other:** Chrysler/Dodge/Jeep, Ford, transmissions, **S gas:** Go Gas, Kwikfill/dsl, Stop&Gas, **food:** Arby's, Burger King, Camp Road Diner, Pizza Hut, Subway, **lodging:** Holiday Inn, **other:** AutoZone, Camping World RV Supplies/Service, $General, Goodyear/auto, USPO, vet

**442mm** parking area both lanes, 📞, litter barrels

**57a (445)** to Eden, Angola, 2 mi **N gas:** Sunoco/dsl

**447mm** Angola Service Area both lanes, Sunoco/dsl, Denny's, Ella's Pizza, McDonald's, 📞/fax, gifts

**58 (456)** US 20, NY 5, to Silver Creek, Irving, **N gas:** Citgo, Kwikfill, **food:** Burger King, Millie's Rest., Primo's Rest., Subway, Sunset Grill, Tim Horton, Tom's Rest., **other:** Ⓗ HOSPITAL, to Evangola SP

**59 (468)** NY 60, Fredonia, Dunkirk, **N lodging:** Dunkirk Motel (4mi), **other:** Lake Erie SP (7mi), **S gas:** Country Fair, Kwikfill/dsl, Mobil/dsl, **food:** Applebee's, Arby's, Azteca Mexican, Best Buffet, Bob Evans, Burger King, Denny's, Dunkin Donuts, KFC/Taco Bell, McDonald's, Pizza Hut, Subway, Tim Horton, Wendy's, Wing City Grill, **lodging:** Best Western, Comfort Inn, Day's Inn, **other:** Aldi Foods, AutoZone, $Tree, Ford/Lincoln/Mercury, GNC, Home Depot, NAPA, Radio Shack, Rite Aid, Tops Foods/gas, TJ Maxx, Walmart SuperCtr/gas

**60 (485)** NY 394, Westfield, **N** to Lake Erie SP, camping, **S gas:** Keystone/dsl, **lodging:** Holiday Motel, **other:** Ⓗ HOSPITAL

---

**494mm** toll booth

**61 (495)** Shortman Rd, to Ripley, **N other:** Lakeshore RV Park

**496mm** New York/Pennsylvania state line

## INTERSTATE 95

**N ↕ S**

**N E W Y O R K C I T Y A R E A**

| Exit # | Services |
|---|---|
| **32mm** | New York/Connecticut state line |
| **22 (30)** | Midland Ave (from nb), Port Chester, Rye, **W food:** Subway, **other:** Ⓗ HOSPITAL, Home Depot, Staples |
| **21 (29)** | I-287 W, US 1 N, to White Plains, Port Chester, Tappan Zee |
| **20 (28)** | US 1 S (from nb), Port Chester, **E gas:** Shell, **other:** CVS Drug, Ford, Subaru |
| **19 (27)** | Playland Pkwy, Rye, Harrison |
| **18b (25)** | Mamaroneck Ave, to White Plains, **E gas:** Hess, Shell, **other:** A&P Foods |
| **18a (24)** | Fenimore Rd (from nb), Mamaroneck, **E gas:** Sunoco |
| **17 (20)** | Chatsworth Ave (from nb, no return), Larchmont |
| **19.5mm** | toll plaza |
| **16 (19)** | North Ave, Cedar St, New Rochelle, **E food:** Applebees, Buffalo Wild Wings, **lodging:** Residence Inn, **other:** Toyota, **W** Ⓗ HOSPITAL |
| **15 (16)** | US 1, New Rochelle, The Pelhams, **E gas:** Getty/dsl, PitStop/24hr, **other:** AutoZone, Cadillac, BMW/Jaguar/Lexus/Mercedes, Costco, CVS Drug, Harley-Davidson, Home Depot, NAPA, **W** auto repair |
| **14 (15)** | Hutchinson Pkwy (from sb), to Whitestone Br |
| **13 (16)** | Conner St, to Mt Vernon, **E gas:** Gulf/dsl, **lodging:** Econolodge, **W gas:** BP, **food:** McDonald's, **lodging:** Andrea Motel, **other:** Ⓗ HOSPITAL |
| **12 (15.5)** | Baychester Ave (from nb) |
| **11 (15)** | Bartow Ave, Co-op City Blvd, **E gas:** Mobil, **food:** Applebees, Burger King, Checker's, Dragon City, Little Caesar's, McDonald's, Panera Bread, Popeye's, Red Lobster, **other:** Barnes&Noble, JC Penney, K-Mart, Marshall's, Old Navy, PathMark Foods, Pay Half, Staples, **W gas:** Shell/mart, Sunoco/dsl, **food:** ChuckeCheese, Dunkin Donuts, Eastern Wok, Pizza Hut, Subway, **other:** Circuit City, Home Depot |
| **10 (14.5)** | Gun Hill Rd (from nb), **W lodging:** Pelham Bay Hotel/diner |
| **9 (14)** | Hutchinson Pkwy |
| **8c (13.5)** | Pelham Pkwy W |
| **8b (13)** | Orchard Beach, City Island |
| **8a (12.5)** | Westchester Ave (from sb) |
| **7c (12)** | Pelham Bay Park (from nb), Country Club Rd |
| **7b (11.5)** | E Tremont (from sb), **W other:** Super FoodTown |
| **7a (11)** | I-695 (from sb), to I-295 S, Throgs Neck Br |
| **6b (10.5)** | I-278 W (from sb), I-295 S (from nb) |
| **6a (10)** | I-678 S, Whitestone Bridge |
| **5b (9)** | Castle Hill Ave, **W gas:** Sunoco, **food:** McDonald's, **other:** GNC |
| **5a (8.5)** | Westchester Ave, White Plains Rd |
| **4b (8)** | Bronx River Pkwy, Rosedale Ave, **E gas:** BP, Getty |
| **4a (7)** | I-895 S, Sheridan Expsy |
| **3 (6)** | 3rd Ave, Ⓗ HOSPITAL |
| **2b (5)** | Webster Ave, **E** Ⓗ HOSPITAL |
| **2a (4)** | Jerome Ave, to I-87 |
| **1c (3)** | I-87, Deegan Expswy, to Upstate |
| **1b (2)** | Harlem River Dr |
| **1a (1)** | US 9, NY 9A, H Hudson Pkwy, 178th St, downtown |
| **0mm** | New York/New Jersey state line, Hudson River, Geo Washington Br |

## INTERSTATE 190 - BUFFALO

| Exit # | Services |
|---|---|
| 25.5mm | US/Canada Border, US Customs |
| 25b a | R Moses Pkwy, NY 104, NY 265, Lewiston, **E** H HOSPITAL |
| 24 | NY 31, Witmer Rd, **E** H HOSPITAL, st police |
| 23 | NY 182, Porter Rd, Packard Rd, **E gas:** Sunoco, **food:** Applebees, Burger King, DQ, Mighty Taco, Perkins, Subway, Tim Horton, **other:** Big Lots, CarQuest, Chrysler/Jeep, Firestone/auto, Jo-Ann Fabrics, K-Mart, NAPA, Prime Outlets/famous brands, U-Haul, **W food:** Wendy's, **other:** Aldi Foods, Sam's Club, Walmart/Subway |
| 22 | US 62, Niagara Falls Blvd, **E gas:** Sunoco, **food:** Bob Evans, Burger King, Denny's, Dunkin Donuts, KFC, McDonald's, Pizza Hut, Taco Bell, Wendy's, **lodging:** Budget Host, Caravan Motel, Holiday Motel, Howard Johnson, Knight's Inn, Pelican Motel, Quality Inn, Red Carpet Inn, Super 8, Swiss Cottage Inn, **other:** Advance Parts, Ford, Radio Shack, Rite Aid, Target, Top's Foods/gas, Toyota, **W lodging:** Econolodge, Sunrise Inn, **other:** Home Depot |
| 21a | NY 384, Buffalo Ave, R Moses Pkwy, **W gas:** Getty, **other:** casino, to NY SP, American Falls |
| 21 | La Salle Expswy |
| 20.5mm | Niagara River East, toll booth sb |
| 20b a | Long Rd, **E lodging:** Budget Motel |
| 19 | Whitehaven Rd, **E gas:** Getty, Noco Gas, **food:** McDonald's, Subway, **lodging:** Chateu Motel (2mi), Holiday Inn (4mi), **other:** $Tree, Top's Foods/gas, KOA (1mi), funpark, **W other:** Chevrolet, Toyota/Scion, vet |
| 18b a | NY 324 W, Grand Island Blvd, **E food:** Asian Buffet, Burger King, Tim Horton, Wendy's, **lodging:** Chateu Motel, Grand Suites, **other:** NAPA, **W** Beaver Island SP |
| 17.5mm | Niagara River East, toll booth |
| 17 | NY 266, last free exit nb |
| 16 | I-290 E, to I-90, Albany |
| 15 | NY 324, Kenmore Ave, **E gas:** 7-11, **W other:** U-Haul |
| 14 | Ontario St, **E gas:** KwikFill, **food:** McDonald's, Tim Horton, **other:** Advance Parts, Family$, **W food:** Harry's Grille |
| 13 | (from nb), same as 14 |
| 12 | Amherst St, (from nb), downtown |
| 11 | NY 198, Buffalo, **E gas:** Sunoco |
| 9 | Porter Ave, to Peace Bridge, Ft Erie |
| 8 | NY 266, Niagara St, downtown, **E lodging:** Adam's Mark Hotel |
| 7 | NY 5 W, Church St, Buffalo, downtown |
| 6 | Elm St, **E** H HOSPITAL, downtown, **W** HSBC Arena |
| 5 | Louisiana St, Buffalo, downtown |
| 4 | Smith St, Fillmore Ave, Buffalo, downtown |
| 3 | NY 16, Seneca St, from sb, **W other:** CarQuest |
| 2 | US 62, NY 354, Bailey Ave, Clinton St |
| 1 | Ogden St, **E gas:** Sunoco, **food:** Wendy's, **lodging:** Comfort Inn, Holiday Inn Express, **other:** CVS Drug, Tops Foods, Volvo/GMC Trucks |
| .5mm | toll plaza nb |
| 0mm | I-90. I-190 begins/ends on I-90, exit 53. |

## INTERSTATE 287 - NEW YORK CITY

| Exit # | Services |
|---|---|
| 12 | I-95, N to New Haven, **S to NYC. I-287 begins/ends on I-95, exit 21.** |
| 11 | US 1, Port Chester, Rye, **N gas:** BP, Mobil, Shell/dsl, Sunoco, **food:** Burger King, Domino's, Dunkin Donuts, Mary Anne's Mexican, McDonald's, Port Chester Diner, Subway, Wendy's, **other:** H HOSPITAL, A&P, Goodyear/auto, Kohl's, Nissan, Staples, repair |
| 10 | Bowman Ave, Webb Ave |
| 9N S | Hutchinson Pkwy, Merritt Pkwy, to Whitestone Br |
| 9a | I-684, Brewster |
| 8 | Westchester Ave, to White Plains, **S gas:** Getty, **other:** Nordstrom's, Westchester Mall Place |
| 7 | Taconic Pkwy (from wb), to N White Plains |
| 6 | NY 22, White Plains |
| 5 | NY 100, Hillside Ave, **S gas:** Citgo, Getty, Mobil, **food:** Applebees, Planet Pizza, **other:** Aamco, A&P, K-mart |
| 4 | NY 100A, Hartsdale, **N gas:** Shell, **other:** H HOSPITAL, **S food:** Bamboo Garden Chinese, Burger King, **other:** BMW/Mini, Jaguar, Nissan, Staples, Volvo |
| 3 | Sprain Pkwy, to Taconic Pkwy, NYC |
| 2 | NY 9A, Elmsford, **N gas:** BP, Mobil, Shell, **food:** Dunkin Donuts, KFC/Taco Bell, Subway, **other:** Bridge Auto Parts, Sam's Club, **S gas:** Shell, **food:** Wendy's |
| 1 | NY 119, Tarrytown, **N food:** Ruth's Chris Steaks, **lodging:** Marriott, Sheraton, **S gas:** Exxon/dsl, **food:** El Dorado Diner, **lodging:** Extended Stay America, Hampton Inn |

I-287 runs with I-87 N.

## INTERSTATE 290 - BUFFALO

| Exit # | Services |
|---|---|
| 8 | I-90, NY Thruway, I-290 begins/ends on I-90, exit 50. |
| 7b a | NY 5, Main St, **N gas:** Mobil, Sunoco, **food:** La Nova Pizza/Wings, McDonald's, Pizza Plant, Subway, Tim Horton, Wendy's, **other:** Quality Mkt Foods, Walgreens, **S gas:** Valero, **food:** Sonoma Grille, **lodging:** Amherst Motel, **other:** vet |
| 6 | NY 324, NY 240, **N gas:** Getty, **lodging:** Courtyard, **S gas:** Valero, **food:** China Star, ChuckeCheese, Subway, **other:** Chrysler/Jeep, CVS Drug, Hyundai/Subaru, KIA/Mazda, Lexus, Nissan |
| 5b a | NY 263, to Millersport, **N food:** Houlihan's, **lodging:** Comfort Inn, Marriott, Red Roof Inn, **S gas:** Mobil, **lodging:** Homewood Suites, **other:** Scion/Toyota, VW, Walgreens |

## INTERSTATE 290 CONT'D - BUFFALO

**E W BUFFALO**

| | |
|---|---|
| **4** | I-990, to St U |
| **3b a** | US 62, to Niagara Falls Blvd, **N gas:** Citgo, Valero, **food:** Bob Evans, Dunkin Donuts, Just Pizza, Max's Grill, Pancake House, Ted's Hot Dogs, **lodging:** Blvd Inn, Econolodge, Extended Stay America, Holiday Inn, Knight's Inn, Red Carpet Inn, Sleep Inn, **other:** Buick/GMC/Pontiac, CarQuest, Dodge, Home Depot, Honda, Walmart/auto, vet, **S gas:** Delta Sonic, Mobil, **food:** Applebee's, Arby's, BoneFish Grill, Burger King, Carrabba's, Chili's, Denny's, Dibella's Subs, John's Pizza, McDonald's, Moe's SW Grill, Montana's Grill, Outback Steaks, Panera Bread, Pizza Hut, Starbucks, Subway, Swiss Chalet Grill, TGIFriday, Tim Horton, Tulley's, **lodging:** Days Inn, Royal Inn, **other:** Barnes&Noble, Best Buy, $Tree, Firestone, Goodyear/auto, JC Penney, Jo-Ann Fabrics, Lowes Whse, Macy's, Michael's, PetCo, PetsMart, Sears/auto, Target, mall |
| **2** | NY 425, Colvin Blvd, **N food:** Athena's Rest., KFC, McDonald's, Subway, Texas Roadhouse, Tim Horton, Wendy's, **other:** H HOSPITAL, Big Lots, BJ's Whse/gas, Family$, Gander Mtn, Goodyear/auto, Top's Foods/gas, **S gas:** KwikFill |
| **1b a** | Elmwood Ave, NY 384, NY 265, **N gas:** KwikFill, **food:** John's Pizza/Subs, Sam's Cafe, **lodging:** Microtel, **other:** H HOSPITAL, $Tree, NAPA, Rite Aid, **S gas:** Mobil/dsl, **food:** Arby's |
| **0mm** | I-190. I-290 begins/ends on I-190 in Buffalo. |

## INTERSTATE 390 - ROCHESTER

**N S ROCHESTER**

| Exit # | Services |
|---|---|
| **38mm** | **rest area both lanes, full** &#9855; **facilities,** &#127860; **litter barrels, vending, petwalk** |
| **20a b** (76) | I-490. I-390 begins/ends on I-490 in Rochester |
| **19** (75) | NY 33a, Chili Ave, **N food:** Wishing Well Rest., **S gas:** Sunoco, **food:** Burger King, Pizza Hut, Subway, **lodging:** Motel 6, Quality Inn, **other:** $General |
| **18a b** (74) | NY 204, Brooks Ave, **N lodging:** Holiday Inn, **S lodging:** Fairfield Inn, **other:** &#9992; |
| **17** (73) | NY 383, Scottsville Rd, **W gas:** Sunoco/Subway/dsl |
| **16** (71) | NY 15a, to E Henryetta, **S food:** Basil's Rest., **lodging:** Courtyard, Hampton Inn, **other:** H HOSPITAL |
| **15** (70) | I-590, Rochester |
| **14** (68) | NY 15a, NY 252, **E food:** Domino's, Gray's Cafe, McDonald's, Outback Steaks, Papa John's, Perkins, Tully's Rest., **lodging:** Extended Stay America, **other:** Staples, **W gas:** Mobil/dsl, **food:** Boston Mkt, Dunkin Donuts, Starbucks, Subway, Taco Bell, **lodging:** Best Western, DoubleTree Inn, **other:** Big Lots, Office Depot, Radio Shack, Top's Foods |
| **13** (67) | Hylan Dr., **E food:** Cracker Barrel, **lodging:** Comfort Suites, Homewood Suites, **W gas:** Mobil, **food:** Bonton, Chicago Grill, ChuckeCheese, IHOP, McDonald's, Panera Bread, Ruby Tuesday, Tony Roma's, Wendy's, **other:** Best Buy, BJ's Whse, Border's Books, Circuit City, Gander Mtn, Michael's, Lowes Whse, Pep Boys, Sam's Club/gas, Target, Walmart SuperCtr, Wegman's Foods, mall |
| **12** (66) | I-90. NY Thruway, NY 253, **W gas:** Citgo/dsl, Hess, Sunoco/dsl, **food:** McDonald's, Peppermint's Rest., Tim Horton, Wendy's, **lodging:** Country Inn&Suites, Day's Inn, Fairfield Inn, Microtel, Red Carpet Inn, Red Roof Inn, Super 8 **other:** GMC/Pontiac, Jeep |

| | |
|---|---|
| **11** (62) | NY 15, NY 251, Rush, Scottsville, **2 mi N food:** McDonald's, Tim Horton, Wendy's, **lodging:** Cartwright Inn, Days Inn, Fairfield Inn, Red Roof Inn, RIT Inn |
| **10** (55) | US 20, NY 5, Avon, Lima, **N gas:** Sunoco/dsl, **lodging:** CrestHill Inn, Stratford Inn, **3 mi S gas:** Sugar Creek/dsl, **food:** Avon Cafe, Dutch Hollow Cafe, McDonald's, Tom Wahls Cafe, Subway, **lodging:** Avon Cedar Lodge, **other:** Chrysler/Dodge/Jeep, Ford, Sugar Creek Camping |
| **9mm** | scenic area wb |
| **9** (52) | NY 15, **N gas:** Mobil/dsl, **food:** Dunkin Donuts, Fratelli's Rest., Lakeville Rest., McDonald's, Tee&Gee Cafe, **lodging:** Conesus Motel, **other:** Chevrolet |
| **8** (48) | US 20a, Geneseo, **N food:** Arby's, **lodging:** Oak Valley Inn, **other:** Conesus Camping, **S food:** Denny's, Dunkin Donuts, KFC/Taco Bell, McDonald's, Wendy's, **lodging:** Quality Inn |
| **7** (39) | NY 63, NY 408, Geneseo, **S gas:** Mobil, KwikFill, **food:** Brian's Diner, McDonald's, **lodging:** Alligence B&B, Country Inn, Geneseo Hotel/Rest., Greenway Motel, **other:** Ridge Camping |
| **6** (33) | NY 36, Mt Morris, Sonyea |
| **5** (26) | NY 36, Dansville, **N gas:** KwikFill, Mobil/Subway, **food:** Arby's, Burger King, Dunkin Donuts, HoHo Chinese, McDonald's, Pizza Hut, Subway, **other:** Advance Parts, Chevrolet/Cadillac/Pontiac, CVS Drug, Radio Shack, Rite Aid, Top's Foods/gas, **S gas:** TA/Mobil/Buckhorn Rest./@, **lodging:** Day's Inn |
| **4** (23) | NY 36, Dansville, **N gas:** Sunoco/dsl, **lodging:** Logan's Inn, **other:** H HOSPITAL, Larocca RV Ctr, **S gas:** Skybrook Camping, Stonybrook Park Camping, Sugar Creek Camping, Sunvalley Camping |
| **3** (17) | NY 15, NY 21, Wayland, **N food:** Farmer's Kitchen Rest., **other:** Holiday Hill Campground (7mi), st patrol |
| **2** (11) | NY 415, Cohocton, Naples, **N gas:** Mobil, **ohter:** Tumble Hill Camping (2mi) |
| **1** (2) | NY 415, I-390 begins/ends, Avoca, **N** truck/auto repair, **S gas:** Mobil, **lodging:** Caboose Motel (3mi) |

## INTERSTATE 495 - LONG ISLAND

**E W**

| Exit # | Services |
|---|---|
| I-495 begins/ends on NY 25. | |
| **73** | rd 58, Old Country Road, to Greenport, Orient, **S gas:** Hess/dsl, Exxon, Lukoil, Mobil, **food:** Applebees, Boulder Creek Steaks, Panera Bread, TGI Friday, Taco Bell, Wendy's, **lodging:** Holiday Inn Express, **other:** Best Buy, Borders Books, Chevrolet, CVS Drug, Ford/Lincoln/Mercury, Harley-Davidson, Home Depot, Honda, Michael's, Nissan/Hyundai/Suzuki, PetCo, Tanger/famous brands, Target, Toyota, VW Subaru, Waldbaum's, Walgreens |
| **72** | NY 25, (no ez eb return), Riverhead, Calverton, **N** funpark, **S gas:** Hess, **lodging:** Best Western, **other:** Tanger/famous brands/foodcourt |
| **71** | NY 24, to Hampton Bays (no ez eb return), Calverton, **N gas:** Hess/Subway/dsl |
| **70** | NY 111, to Eastport, Manorville, **S gas:** Citgo/7-11, Mobil, **food:** McDonald's, Michelangelo's Italian, Starbucks, **other:** King Kullen Food/drug |
| **69** | Wading River Rd, Center Moriches, to Wading River |

## INTERSTATE 495 CONT'D - LONG ISLAND

**E**
**W**

**LONG ISLAND**

**68** NY 46, to Shirley, Wading River, **S lodging:** Holiday Inn, golf

**67** Yaphank Ave

**66** NY 101, Sills Rd, Yaphank, **N gas:** Shell/24hr

**65** Horse Block rd, **N food:** Dunkin Donuts/Baskin-Robbins, **other:** Eddy's RV Ctr

**64** NY 112, to Coram, Medford, **N gas:** Getty's, Mobil, **other:** Eckerd, Lowes Whse, Radio Shack, Sam's Club, 7-11, Target, **S gas:** BP, Exxon, Gulf, US/dsl, **lodging:** Comfort Inn, **other:** Aid Parts

**63** NY 83, N Ocean Ave, **N gas:** Hess/dsl, Mobil, **food:** Applebees, Burger King, McDonald's, 7-11, Taco Bell, TGI Fridays, **other:** Hampton Inn, **other:** K-Mart, Stop'n Shop, **S gas:** BP, Exxon, **food:** City Grill, **lodging:** Radisson

**62** rd 97, to Blue Point, Stony Brook, **N gas:** Gulf, **S food:** Charlie Brown's Steaks, Chili's, Wendy's, **lodging:** Residence Inn

**61** rd 19, to Patchogue, Holbrook, **N gas:** Mobil, **S gas:** Exxon/dsl, Hess/dsl, **food:** China 4, Greek Islands Rest, Outback Steaks, Subway, **other:** CVS Drug, 7-11, Waldbaums Foods

**60** Ronkonkoma Ave, **N gas:** Exxon, **S food:** Red Lobster, Smokey Bones BBQ, **lodging:** Courtyard

**59** Ocean Ave, to Oakdale, Ronkonkoma, **S gas:** Citgo/7-11, Exxon, Sunoco, **lodging:** Hilton Garden (1mi)

**58** Old Nichols Rd, Nesconset, **N gas:** Exxon, **food:** Hooters, **lodging:** Marriott, **other:** BJ's Whse, **S gas:** BP

**57** NY 454, Vets Hwy, to Hauppauge, **N gas:** Exxon/dsl, **food:** TGIFriday, **S gas:** Citgo/dsl, Getty's, Gulf/dsl/24hr, Shell, Sunoco, **food:** Dave&Buster's, New Horizon Diner, Subway, **lodging:** Hampton Inn, **other:** Eckerd, Stop&Shop Foods, Radio Shack, TJ Maxx, Walmart

**56** NY 111, Smithtown, Islip, **N gas:** Exxon/Subway/Domino's/dsl, Mobil, **S gas:** Mobil, **food:** Café La Strada, **lodging:** Holiday Inn Express

**55** Central Islip, **N gas:** Mobil, **S gas:** Exxon/dsl

**54** Wicks Rd, **N gas:** BP, **other: lodging:** Sheraton, **S gas:** Mobil

**53** Sunken Meadow Pkwy, to ocean beaches, Bayshore

**52** rd 4, Commack, **N gas:** Mobil/dsl, Shell/repair, **food:** Conca d'Oro Pizza, Ground Round, **lodging:** Hampton Inn, **other:** Costco

**51.5mm** parking area both lanes, 🚻, litter barrels

**51** NY 231, to Northport, Babylon

**50** Bagatelle Rd, to Wyandanch

**49N** NY 110 N, to Huntington, **N lodging:** Marriott

**49S** NY 110 S, to Amityville

**48** Round Swamp Rd, Old Bethpage, **S gas:** Mobil/dsl, **food:** Old Country Pizza/deli, **lodging:** Homewood Suites, Palace Hotel, Sheraton, **other:** USPO

**46** Sunnyside Blvd, Plainview, **N lodging:** Holiday Inn

**45** Manetto Hill Rd, Plainview, Woodbury

**44** NY 135, to Seaford, Syosset

**LONG ISLAND**

**43S** Oyster Bay Rd, to Syosset, Bethpage, **N gas:** Mobil

**42** Northern Pkwy, rd N, Hauppauge

**41** NY 106, NY 107, Hicksville, Oyster Bay, **S gas:** BP, Mobil, Sunoco, **food:** Boston Mkt, Boulder Creek Steaks, Broadway Diner, Burger King, Dunkin Donuts, McDonald's, On the Border, **other:** Circuit City, Goodyear/auto, Sears/auto

**40** NY 25, Mineola, Syosset, **S gas:** BP, Exxon, Hess/dsl, Shell, **food:** A&W, Burger King, Friendly's, IHOP, McDonald's, Wendy's, **lodging:** Howard Johnson, **other:** Home Depot, Kohl's, 7-11, Staples

**39** Glen Cove Rd, **N gas:** Mobil

**38** Northern Pkwy E, Meadowbrook Pkwy, to Jones Beach

**37** Willis Ave, to Roslyn, Mineola, **N gas:** Exxon, Shell, **other:** repair, **S gas:** Gulf,

**36** Searingtown Rd, to Port Washington, **S H HOSPITAL**

**35** Shelter Rock Rd, Manhasset

**34** New Hyde Park Rd

**33** Lakeville Rd, to Great Neck, **N H HOSPITAL**

**32** Little Neck Pkwy, **N food:** pizza

**31** Douglaston Pkwy, **S gas:** BP, **other:** Macy's, USPO, Waldbaum's Foods, mall

**30** E Hampton Blvd, Cross Island Pkwy

**29** Springfield Blvd, **S gas:** Exxon, **food:** Dunkin Donuts, McDonald's

**27** I-295, Clearview Expsy, Throgs Neck, **N gas:** Gulf, 7-11, **food:** Blue Bay Diner, **other:** Rockbottom Drug

**26** Francis Lewis Blvd

**25** Utopia Pkwy, 188th St, **N gas:** Citgo, Gulf, Mobil, Sunoco, **S gas:** Citgo, Mobil, Sunoco, **food:** Arby's, Subway, **other:** Radio Shack, USPO

**24** Kissena Blvd, **N gas:** Exxon/dsl, **food:** Baskin-Robbins, Dunkin Donuts, **S gas:** Mobil

**23** Main St, **N food:** Palace Diner

**22** Grand Central Pkwy, to I-678, College Pt Blvd, **N lodging:** Eden Park Hotel, Paris Suites

**21** 108th St, **N gas:** BP

**19** NY 25, Queens Blvd, Woodhaven Blvd, to Rockaways, **N other:** JC Penney, Macy's, mall, **S gas:** BP, **food:** Applebees, **other:** Circuit City, Marshall's, Old Navy, Sears

**18.5** 69th Ave, Grand Ave (from wb)

**18** Maurice St, **N gas:** Exxon **S gas:** BP, **food:** McDonald's, **other:** dsl repair

**17** 48th St, to I-278, **N lodging:** Holiday Inn Express

**16** I-495 begins/ends in NYC.

Copyright 2009 - The Next Exit®

## INTERSTATE 26

| Exit # | Services |
|---|---|
| 71mm | North Carolina/South Carolina state line |
| 69mm | N Pacolet River |
| 67.5mm | **Welcome Ctr wb, full** ♿ **facilities,** 🚻, 🅿, **litter barrels** |
| 67 | US 74 E, to NC 108, Columbus, Tryon, **N gas:** BP/Burger King/dsl, Texaco, **food:** Cocula Mexican, McDonald's, Subway, Waffle House, Wendy's, **other:** Ⓗ HOSPITAL, Advance Parts, CVS Drug, Family$, Food Lion, **S gas:** Exxon/dsl, Shell, **food:** KFC/Taco Bell, Mtn View Deli, **lodging:** Days Inn, **other:** BiLo, $General |
| 59 | Saluda, **N lodging:** Saluda Motel, **other:** camping, **S gas:** BP/dsl/mart, Texaco/mart, **food:** Schafer's Grill, Subway, **lodging:** B&B, **other:** vet |
| 56mm | Green River |
| 54 | US 25, to Greenville, E Flat Rock, access to Carl Sandburg Home |
| 53.5mm | Eastern Continental Divide, 2130 ft |
| 53 | Upward Rd, Hendersonville, **N gas:** Texaco/dsl, **food:** Waffle House, Zaxby's, **lodging:** Mtn Inn Suites, Mtn Lodge, **other:** Bloomfields Giftshop, **S gas:** Exxon/McDonald's/dsl, Shell/Pizza Inn/dsl, **food:** Cracker Barrel, Subway, **lodging:** Holiday Inn Express, **other:** RV camping, to Carl Sandburg Home |
| 49b a | US 64, Hendersonville, **N gas:** Chevron, Shell/dsl/24hr, Texaco/dsl, **food:** Atlanta Bread Co, Baby Joe's Smokehouse, Chick-fil-A, El Paso Mexican, Golden Corral, Jack-in-the-Box, O'Charley's, Sonic, Waffle House, Zaxby's, **lodging:** Best Western, Hampton Inn, Quality Inn, Ramada Ltd, **other:** Ⓗ HOSPITAL, Advance Parts, CarQuest, $Tree, Ingles, Radio Shack, Sam's Club, Staples, Walmart SuperCtr/gas, World of Clothing, **S gas:** Exxon/dsl/LP, Shell/dsl, **food:** Applebee's, Arby's, Binion's Roadhouse, Bojangles, Burger King, China Sea, Cici's, Denny's, Fatz Café, Hardee's, Honeybaked Ham, KFC, Krispy Kreme, LJ Silver, McDonald's, Outback Steaks, Patron Mexican, Pizza Hut, Subway/TCBY, Taco Bell, Wendy's, **lodging:** Comfort Inn, Day's Inn, Red Roof Inn, **other:** Ⓗ HOSPITAL, Aldi Foods, Belk, BigLots, BiLo Foods, CVS Drug, Home Depot, JC Penney, K-Mart, Lowe's Whse, mall |
| 46mm | weigh sta both lanes, 🚻 |
| 44 | US 25, Fletcher, **N gas:** Exxon/dsl, **food:** Hardee's, Subway, **other:** Ⓗ HOSPITAL, flea mkt campground, vet, **S gas:** Citgo/dsl, Shell/Bojangles/Stuckey's/dsl/scales/24hr, United/dsl, **food:** Burger King, Naples Diner, **other:** Todd's RV/marine, USPO, to Uncle John's |
| 41mm | **rest area both lanes, full** ♿ **facilities,** 🚻, 🅿, **litter barrels, vending** |
| 40 | NC 280, Arden, **N gas:** Exxon/dsl, Shell/Arby's/dsl, **food:** Carrabba's, Chili's, Cracker Barrel, McDonald's, Pizza Hut, Ruby Tuesday, Waffle House, **lodging:** Budget Motel, Comfort Inn, Day's Inn, Econolodge, Hampton Inn, Holiday Inn/rest., **other:** Best Buy, Honda/Acura/Kia, Lowes Whse, Marshall's, Michael's, Ross, Target, World Mkt, **S gas:** BP/dsl, **food:** J&S Cafeteria, Smokehouse BBQ, **lodging:** Fairfield Inn, **other:** Asheville ✈, BMW, Rutledg Lake Camping |
| 37 | NC 146, Skyland, **N gas:** Exxon, Shell/McDonald's/dsl/24hr, **food:** Arby's, Shoney's, Waffle House, **lodging:** Quality Inn, **other:** CVS Drug, **S food:** Riverside Grill |

**E W / HENDERSONVILLE / ARDEN**

**NC**

---

**ASHEVILLE**

| | |
|---|---|
| 34mm | French Broad River |
| 33 | NC 191, Brevard Rd, **N other:** Saturn/Toyota, **2 mi N other:** Asheville Farmers Mkt, Bear Creek RV Camp, **S gas:** Citgo, HotSpot/dsl, **food:** Apollo Bistro, China Garden, Garfield's, Harbor Inn Seafood, LJ Silver, McDonald's, Ryan's, Stoneridge Grill, Taco Bell, Waffle House, **lodging:** Comfort Suites, Country Inn&Suites, Fairfield Inn, Hampton Inn, Holiday Inn Express, Super 8, **other:** Belk, Dillard's, $Tree, Goody's, KIA, K-Mart, Ingles Foods, SuperPetz, mall, to Blue Ridge Pkwy |
| 31b a | I-40, E to Statesville, W to Knoxville |
| 27mm | Hill St |
| 25 | rd 251, to UNCA, **S** Richmond Hill Inn (1mi) |
| 24 | Elk Mtn Rd, Woodfin |
| 23 | Merrimon Ave, N Asheville, **N gas:** BP/dsl, HotSpot, **food:** Bellagio Bistro, **lodging:** Day's Inn, **other:** Food Lion, Tuesday Morning, camping |
| 21 | New Stock Rd, **N gas:** BP, Citgo/dsl, **food:** Pizza Hut, **other:** Ingles/gas, camping |
| 19a b | N US 25, W US 70, Marshall, **N gas:** Shell/dsl, **food:** Arby's, Bojangles, Burger King, KFC, McDonald's, Subway, Waffle House, **other:** Advance Parts, Curves, Kerr Drug, Ingles/gas, Roses, **S gas:** Shell/Huddle House/dsl, **other:** Lowes Whse, Walmart |
| 18 | Weaverville (no EZ return from eb) |
| 17 | to Flat Creek |
| 15 | rd 197, to Jupiter, Barnardsville |
| 13 | Forks of Ivy, **N gas:** BP/dsl, **S gas:** Exxon/dsl |
| 11 | rd 213, to Mars Hill, Marshall, **N tires, S gas:** Chevron/dsl, Exxon//Hardee's/dsl, Shell/Subway/dsl, **food:** Blazerz Steaks, Pizza Roma, Waffle House, Wagon Wheel Rest., **lodging:** Comfort Inn, **other:** Ford, NAPA, Radio Shack |
| 9 | Burnsville, Spruce Pine, to Mt Mitchell SP |
| 7mm | scenic overlook wb, runaway truck ramp eb |
| 6mm | **Welcome Ctr/rest area eb, full** ♿ **facilities** |
| 5.5mm | runaway truck ramp eb |
| 5mm | Buckner Gap, elev. 3370 |
| 3 | to US 23, Wolf Laurel, **N gas:** Exxon, **food:** Little Creek Cafe, **other:** to ski areas |
| 2.5mm | runaway truck ramp |
| 0mm | North Carolina/Tennessee state line |

## INTERSTATE 40

| Exit # | Services |
|---|---|
| 420mm | I-40 begins/ends at Wilmington, **Facilities on US 17, N other:** Ford/Lincoln/Mercury, Land Rover, Hyundai, Home Depot, Nissan, Suzuki, Toyota/Scion, VW, **S gas:** BP, Crown/dsl/24hr, Dodge's Store/dsl, Exxon/dsl/24hr, **food:** Arby's, Bonefish Grill, Buffalo Wings, Carrabba's, Chick-fil-A, Church's Chicken, Cracker Barrel, Hardee's, Hooters, IHOP, McDonald's, O'Charley's, Old Chicago Pizza, Olive Garden, Quizno's, Ruby Tuesday, Sonic, Sticky Fingers Rest., Taco Bell, Waffle House, Whitey's Rest., **lodging:** Best Value, Comfort Suites, Day's Inn, Extended Stay America, Fairview Inn, GreenTree Inn, Holiday Inn, Howard Johnson, Innkeeper, MainStay Suites, Motel 6, Quality Inn, Ramada Inn, Red Roof, Sleep Inn, Super 8, Travelodge, Travel Inn, Wingate Inn, **other:** Advance Parts, AutoZone, BMW, Circuit City, Costco/gas, Food Lion, Marshall's, PetsMart, Radio Shack, Rite Aid, Saab, Saturn, Target, |

**E W**

**NC**

## INTERSTATE 40 CONT'D

**WILMINGTON** E ↕ W

**420mm** Continued

Walmart SuperCtr/gas, **Facilities 2-4 mi S on NC 132**... **gas:** BP, Exxon/dsl, **food:** Applebee's, Bojangles, Burger King, Checker's, Chili's, Cici's Pizza, Domino's, Dragon Garden, Farmhouse Rest., Golden Corral, Hardee's, Honey Baked Ham, KFC, McAlister's Deli, McDonald's, Outback Steaks, Starbucks, Taco Bell, TCBY, Wendy's, **lodging:** Baymont Inn, Comfort Inn, Courtyard, Holiday Inn Express, **other:** Best Buy, Chevrolet, $Tree, Harris-Teeter/24hr, Honda/Acura, Hyundai, K-Mart, Lowe's Foods, Lowe's Whse, PetCo, Pontiac/Buick/GMC/Mercedes, Sam's Club, Staples, TJ Maxx

**420b a** Gordon Rd, NC 132 N, **2 mi N gas:** Kangaroo/dsl, **food:** McDonald's, Smithfield's Chicken/BBQ, Zaxby's, **other:** KOA (4mi), **S gas:** BP/dsl, Kangaroo/dsl, **food:** Carolina BBQ, Subway, **other:** Family$, Lowe's Foods, Rite Aid

**416b a** I-140, US 17, to Topsail Island, New Bern, & Myrtle Beach

**414** to Brunswick Co beaches, Castle Hayne, **S gas:** BP/24hr, Kangaroo, **food:** Hardee's, **other:** CVS Drug, Piggly Wiggly, USPO

**412** NE Cape Fear River

**408** NC 210, **N** Mack/Volvo/International Trucks, **S gas:** CW's Trvl Ctr/cafe/dsl, Exxon/dsl, Hess/Wilco/Wendy's/dsl/24hr, Shell, **food:** Hardee's, Noble Roman's, Sub Express, **other:** Food Lion, to Moore's Creek Nat Bfd/camping

**398** NC 53, Burgaw, **2 mi S food:** Andy's Rest., CW's Cafe, Hardee's, McDonald's, Subway, Wendy's, **lodging:** Burgaw Motel, **other:** H HOSPITAL, camping

**390** to US 117, Wallace

**385** NC 41, Wallace, **N gas:** Exxon, **food:** Mad Boar Rest., **lodging:** Holiday Inn Express, **other:** Lake Leamon Camping

**384** NC 11, Wallace

**380** Rose Hill, **S gas:** BP/dsl (1mi), Pure

**373** NC 903, Magnolia, **N gas:** BP/dsl/24hr., **lodging:** B&B, **other:** H HOSPITAL, Cowan Museum

**369** US 117, Warsaw

**364** NC 24, to NC 50, Clinton, **rest area both lanes, full** 🦽 **facilities,** 🚻, 🏕, **litter barrels, vending, petwalk, N gas:** Wilco/Hess/Arby's/Stuckey's/dsl/24hr, **S gas:** BP/dsl, Crown/24hr, Kangaroo/dsl, Marathon, Sunoco/Bojangles, **food:** KFC, McDonald's, Smithfield's BBQ, Subway, Waffle House, Wendy's, **lodging:** Day's Inn, Holiday Inn Express

**355** NC 403, to US 117, to Goldsboro, Faison, **3 mi N gas:** Pure

**348** Suttontown Rd

**343** US 701, Newton Grove, **1 mi N gas:** Exxon/dsl, to Bentonville Bfd

**341** NC 50, NC 55, to US 13, Newton Grove, **1.5 mi N gas:** Exxon/dsl, **food:** Hardee's, **S gas:** BP/McDonald's, Shell/Subway, **food:** Smithfield BBQ

**334** NC 96, Meadow, **S gas:** BP/dsl (1mi)

**328b a** I-95, N to Smithfield, S to Benson

**325** NC 242, to US 301, to Benson, **S gas:** Citgo/dsl

**324mm** **rest area both lanes, full** 🦽 **facilities,** 🚻, 🏕, **litter barrels, vending, petwalk, no overnight parking**

**319** NC 210, McGee's Crossroads, **N gas:** Citgo/DQ/Papa's Subs & Pizza/dsl, Shell/BBQ/dsl/24hr, **food:** McDonald's, **other:** H HOSPITAL, **S gas:** Mobil/CW's Cafe, **food:** China Star, Italian Pizza/Pasta, KFC/Taco Bell, Subway, Wendy's, **other:** AutoZone, Food Lion, $General

**312** NC 42, to Clayton, Fuquay-Varina, **N gas:** Wilco/Hess/Wendy's/dsl/24hr, Phillips 66/dsl, **food:** Andy's Rest., China King, Cracker Barrel, Golden Corral, Jersey Mike's Subs, Ruby Tuesday, Papa Subs/Pizza, Pizza Inn, Smithfield BBQ, W 42nd St Grill, White Swan BBQ, **lodging:** Holiday Inn Express, Quality Inn, Super 8, ValuePlace, **other:** CarQuest, JustTires, Lowe's Whse, USPO, **S gas:** Exxon/Burger King, BP/Subway/dsl/24hr, Citgo/dsl, Shell/dsl, **food:** Bojangles, DQ, Domino's, Jumbo China, KFC/Taco Bell, Marko's Pizza, McDonald's, Waffle House, **lodging:** Hampton Inn, Sleep Inn, **other:** CVS Drug, Food Lion, vet

**310** I-540, new exit

**306** US 70, to Smithfield, Garner, Goldsboro, **1 mi N gas:** Kangaroo/dsl, Shell/dsl, **S food:** Buffalo Wild Wings, Chili's, Chick-fil-A, Cold Stone Creamery, McDonald's, Moe's SW Grill, New Japan Express, Logan's Roadhouse, Subway, Wendy's, **other:** Best Buy, BJ's Whse/gas, Kohl's, Michaels, PetsMart, Ross, Staples, Target, TJ Maxx

**303** Jones Sausage Rd, Rd, **N gas:** Hess, Shell/dsl, **food:** Bojangles, Burger King, Smithfield BBQ, Sophie's Deli, **S gas:** Hess/dsl

**301** I-440 E, US 64/70 E, to Wilson

**300b a** Rock Quarry Rd, **N other:** Kroger/gas, **S gas:** BP/dsl, Exxon, **food:** Burger King, Subway, **other:** Food Lion, Rite Aid

## INTERSTATE 40 CONT'D

**E** ↕ **W**

**RALEIGH**

**299** Person St, Hammond Rd, Raleigh (no EZ return eb), **1 mi N gas:** Exxon/dsl, **lodging:** King's Motel, **other:** to Shaw U

**298b a** US 401 S, US 70 E, NC 50, **N gas:** Shell, **lodging:** Red Roof Inn, **other:** Parts+, **S gas:** BP, Crown, Exxon/dsl, Hess/Wilco/dsl, Raceway, **food:** Burger King, El Cerro Mexican, Golden Seafood & Chicken, KFC, **lodging:** Sleep Inn, Super 8, **other:** Sam's Club/gas

**297** Lake Wheeler Rd, **N gas:** Exxon, **food:** Subway, **other:** H HOSPITAL, Farmer's Mkt, **S gas:** Citgo

**295** Gorman St, **1 mi N gas:** Exxon/dsl, **food:** Hardee's, McDonald's, Subway, **other:** to NCSU, Reynolds Coliseum, **S gas:** Kangaroo

**293** to I-440, US 1, US 64 W, Raleigh, **.5 mi S gas:** Exxon, Shell, **food:** Chick-fil-A, Cookout, Hardee's, McDonald's, Olive Garden, Pizza Hut, Waffle House, **lodging:** Candlewood Suites, Day's Inn, Red Roof Inn, Motel 6, **other:** Aamco, Borders Books

**291** Cary Towne Blvd, Cary, **1 mi S food:** Burger King, Macaroni Grill, McDonald's, Olive Garden, Ragazzi's, Taco Bell, **other:** Belk, JC Penny

**290** NC 54, Cary, **1 mi N other:** Comfort Suites, **2 mi S gas:** Citgo, Exxon, Shell, **lodging:** Hampton Inn

**289** to I-440, Wade Ave, to Raleigh, **N other:** H HOSPITAL, museum, **S** to fairgrounds

**287** Harrison Ave, Cary, **N** to Wm B Umstead SP, **S gas:** BP, **food:** Bonefish Grill, Burger King, Carolina Cafe, Chick-fil-A, Maggie's Ice Cream, McDonald's, Moe's SW Grill, NY Pizza, Ruth's Chris Steaks, Starbucks, Wendy's, **lodging:** Embassy Suites, Studio+, TownePlace Suites (3mi), **other:** Colony Tire, Jiffy Lube, Sam's Club

**285** Aviation Pkwy, to Morrisville, Raleigh/Durham ✈, **N lodging:** Hilton Garden

**284** Airport Blvd, **N** to RDU ✈, **S gas:** BP/dsl, Mobil, **food:** Bojangles, Cracker Barrel, Hooters, Jersey Mike's Subs, KFC/Taco Bell, Quizno's, Schlotsky's, Texas Steaks, Waffle House, Wendy's, **lodging:** Courtyard, Day's Inn, Extended Stay America, Fairfield Inn, Hampton Inn, Holiday Inn, Holiday Inn Express, Microtel, La Quinta, Residence Inn, Staybridge Suites, **other:** Morrisville Outlets/famous brands/food court

**283** I-540, to US 70, Aviation Pkwy

**282** Page Rd, **S food:** Arbys, Bojangles, McDonald's, Starbucks, **lodging:** Comfort Suites, Sheraton/rest., Sleep Inn, Springhill Suites, Wingate Inn, **other:** World Trade Ctr

**281** Miami Blvd, **N lodging:** Extended Stay Deluxe, Marriott, Wyndham Garden, **S gas:** BP, Shell, **food:** Arby's, Bojangles, Quizno's, Rudino's Grill, Subway, Wendy's, Wok'n Grill, **lodging:** Extended Stay Deluxe, Holiday Inn Express, Homewood Suites, **other:** Atlantic Tire

**280** Davis Dr, **N** to Research Triangle, **S lodging:** Radisson

**279b a** NC 147, Durham Fwy, to Durham, **N** H HOSPITAL

**278** NC 55, to NC 54, World Trade Ctr, Apex, Foreign Trade Zone 93, **N gas:** Circle K/dsl, Citgo, **food:** China 1 Rest., Waffle House, **lodging:** Best Value, Comfort Inn, Doubletree Suites, La Quinta, Red Roof Inn, **S gas:** Crown, Exxon/dsl, Mobil/dsl (1mi), **food:** Arby's, Backyard BBQ, Bojangles, Burger King, Chick-fil-A, Golden Corral, KFC, McDonald's, Mr. Wok, Oh'Brian's,

**CHAPEL HILL**

**278** Continued
Papa John's, Los Paisano's, Pizza Hut, Starbucks, Subway, Taco Bell, Wendy's, **lodging:** Candlewood Suites, Courtyard, Crestwood Inn, Crossland Suites, Homestead Village, Residence Inn, **other:** Aamco, Alltune/Lube, Big-Lots, $Tree, Precision Tune, transmissions/tires

**276** Fayetteville Rd, **N gas:** Circle K/dsl, Exxon/dsl, Phillips 66/dsl, **food:** McDonald's, Quizno's, Ruby Tuesday, Rudino's Pizza, Souper Salad, Subs Etc, TCBY, Waffle House, Wendy's, **other:** Eckerd, GNC, Harris-Teeter, Kroger, Walgreens, to NC Central U, **S food:** Carino's Italian, Chili's, Coldstone Creamery, PF Chang's, Starbucks, Ted's MT Grill, **lodging:** Hilton Garden, **other:** mall, Belks, Best Buy, JC Penney, Macy's, Nordstrom's, Old Navy, Sears/auto

**274** NC 751, to Jordan Lake, **1-2 mi N food:** Burger King, McDonald's, Waffle House, Wendy's, **S gas:** BP, **lodging:** Sheraton

**273** NC 54, to Durham, UNC-Chapel Hill, **N gas:** Shell/dsl, **S gas:** BP/dsl, Citgo, Shell/dsl, **food:** Hardee's, Nantucket Cafe, **lodging:** Best Western (2mi), Hampton Inn, Holiday Inn Express

**270** US 15, US 501, Chapel Hill, Durham, **N gas:** BP, **food:** Bob Evans, Bojangles, Carrabbas, Hank's Rest., Jason's Deli, Outback Steaks, Philly Steaks, Subway, Tripp's Rest., **lodging:** Comfort Inn, Homewood Suites, **other:** H HOSPITALS, Barnes&Noble, Best Buy, Circuit City, $Tree, Home Depot, Kohls, Kroger, Marshall's, Michael's, Old Navy, PetsMart, Saab, Walmart, to Duke U, **S gas:** BP, Exxon, **food:** Applebee's, Golden Corral, Hardee's, La Hacienda Mexican, McDonald's, Subway, Wendy's, **lodging:** Hampton Inn, Holiday Inn, Red Roof Inn, Sheraton, Siena Hotel, **other:** Acura, BMW, Borders Books, Chevrolet, CVS Drug, Lowe's Whse, Saturn, mall

**266** NC 86, to Chapel Hill, **2 mi S gas:** BP, Citgo, Exxon, Wilco/Hess/dsl, **food:** Pop's Pizza, Quizno's, Subway

**263** New Hope Church Rd

**261** Hillsborough, **1.5 mi N gas:** BP, Citgo/dsl, Shell, **food:** Hardee's, KFC/Taco Bell, McDonald's, Subway, Waffle House, Wendy's, **lodging:** Holiday Inn Express, Microtel

**259** I-85 N, to Durham,

**I-40 and I-85 run together 30 mi. See Interstate 85 exits 131-161.**

**44** to US 70

**43** McConnell Rd, **N** Replacements LTD Outlet **S gas:** Exxon/repair,

**41** NC 6, E Lee St, **N gas:** BP/dsl, Phillips 66, **lodging:** Holiday Inn Express, to Coliseum

**39** US 29 N, US 70, US 220 N (from eb), to Reidsville, **N** KOA

**38** US 421 S, to Sanford, **S gas:** Pit Stop, **food:** Arby's, Biscuitville, Burger King, Domino's, Gold Express Pizza, McDonald's, Szechuan Chinese, Subway, Taco Bell, Wendy's, **other:** Advance Parts, CVS Drug, $Max, Food Lion, Hall Tire, Key Food Fresh, Tom's Tire

**37** S Elm St, Eugene St, **N gas:** Citgo/dsl, Crown, **food:** Bojangles, **lodging:** Homestead Lodge, Landmark Inn, **other:** AutoZone, CarQuest, Family$, Food Lion, O'Reilly Parts, **S gas:** BP, Shell/dsl/24hr, **lodging:** Days Inn, Quality Inn, Super 8, **other:** Home Depot

**36b** Randleman Rd, **N gas:** BP, Citgo, Exxon, Solo Gas, **food:** Biscuitville, China Town Express, DQ, KFC, McDonald's, Midori Express, Pizza Hut,

E ↕ W

**G R E E N S B O R O**

## INTERSTATE 40 CONT'D

**36b** Continued
Substation II, Subway, **lodging:** Budget Motel, **other:** Advance Parts, Eckerd, Harley-Davidson, Save-a-Lot Foods, **S gas:** BP, Kangaroo/24hr, **food:** Cookout, Mayflower Seafood, Waffle House, Wendy's

**36a** US 220, US 29, US 70, to I-85 S, Charlotte

**218b a** US 220 S, to I-85 S, Freeman Mill Rd

**217b a** High Point Rd, Greensboro, **N gas:** Exxon/dsl, Shell/dsl, **food:** Akashi Japanese, Arby's, Austin's Grill, Biscuitville, Blue Ribbon, Burger King, Carolina Diner, Chili's, China King, Devereaux Dining, El Paraiso Restorante, Gold India, Ham's Rest., Hooters, La Bamba Mexican, KFC, LoneStar Steaks, Olive Garden, PoFolks, Subway, Taco Bell, **lodging:** Double Tree Inn, Park Lane Hotel, Red Roof Inn, Super 8, Travelodge, **other:** $General, Office Depot, **S gas:** BP, Citgo, Exxon, Texaco, **food:** Bojangles, Burger King, Carrabba's, Chester's Rest., Cookout Café, Darryl's, Krispy Kreme, Kyoto Express, Las Jarochita's, McDonald's, Oh! Brian's, Pizza Inn, Saigon Rest., Smokey Bones, Sonic, Subway, Taco Bell, Tides Seafood, Waffle House, Wendy's, **lodging:** Best Western, Comfort Inn, Day's Inn, Drury Inn, Fairfield Inn, Hampton Inn, Ramada Inn, Residence Inn, Sheraton, **other:** Aamco, Advance Parts, Aldi Foods, AutoZone, Belk, Big Lots, Borders Books, Dillard's, City Tire, Family$, Gander Mtn, JC Penney, Merchant Tire/auto, NAPA, PepBoys, Radio Shack, Roses, Sears/auto, TJ Maxx, Walgreens, World Mkt, mall, vet

**216** NC 6 (from eb, exits left), to Greensboro Coliseum

**214b a** Wendover Ave, **N gas:** Exxon/dsl, Shell/dsl, Sheetz, **food:** Bob Evans, Blimpie, Burger King, Cold Stone Creamery, County BBQ, Jake's Diner, K&W Cafeteria, Mario's Pizza, Moe's SW Grill, Panera Bread, Ruby Tuesday, TCBY, Waffle House, **lodging:** Extended Stay America, Hilton Garden, Holiday Inn Express, Microtel, **other:** Acura, BMW, Celebration Station, Chevrolet, Chrysler, Circuit City, Costco/gas, Dodge, Ford/Isuzu, Goodyear, Honda, Mercedes, Mitsubishi, Nissan, PetCo, Saab/Jaguar, Saturn, Staples, Subaru, Volvo, VW, **S food:** Applebee's, Arby's, Biscuitville, Bojangles, Calabash Seafood, Chick-fil-A, Cracker Barrel, Fuddrucker's, Golden Corral, IHOP/24hr, Imperial Gourmet, Kabuto Japanese, La Hacienda Mexican, Logan's Roadhouse, Longhorn Steaks, McDonald's, O'Charley's, Panda Express, Red Lobster, Schlotsky's, Steak'n Shake, Subway, TGIFriday, Taco Bell, Tripp's Rest., Vilarosa Mexican, Wendy's, **lodging:** AmeriSuites, Best Western, Courtyard, La Quinta, Lodge America, SpringHill Suites, Suburban Lodge, Wingate Inn, **other:** Best Buy, Circuit City, Goodyear, Harris-Teeter, Home Depot, Hummer, Kohl's, K-Mart/gas, Lowe's Whse, Sam's Club/gas, Target, Walmart SuperCtr

**213** Guilford College Rd, Jamestown, **N gas:** BP/dsl, **lodging:** Clarion, **other:** to Guilford Coll, **S gas:** Sheetz, **other:** $Tree, Ferrari/Maserati/Porsche, Hummer, Kohl's, Macy's, Old Navy, Pontiac, Saab, Saturn, Target, vet, same as 214

**212** new exit

**211** Gallimore Dairy Rd, **N other:** Freightliner

**210** NC 68, to High Point, Piedmont Triad, **N gas:** Phillips 66/dsl, **food:** Arby's, **lodging:** Comfort Inn, Day's Inn,

**W I N S T O N • S A L E M**

**210** Continued
Embassy Suites, Fairview Inn, Holiday Inn, Homewood Suites, Sleep Inn, **other:** Ford Trucks, to ✈, **S gas:** Exxon/dsl, **food:** Bojangles, McDonald's, Pizza Hut/Taco Bell, Ruby Tuesday, Shoney's, Subway, **lodging:** Best Value Inn, Best Western, Comfort Suites, Extended Stay America, Fairfield Inn, Hampton Inn, Motel 6, Red Roof Inn

**208** Sandy Ridge Rd, **N gas:** Wilco/Hess/dsl, **other:** Colfax RV Ctr/Camping World, **S gas:** Citgo/dsl, **other:** Farmer's Mkt, Out Of Doors Mart/Airstream

**206** Lp 40 (from wb), to Kernersville, Winston-Salem, downtown

**203** NC 66, to Kernersville, **N gas:** BP, Citgo/McDonald's/dsl, Exxon/Pizza Inn/Subway, **food:** Capt Tom's Seafood, Clark's BBQ, Waffle House, Wendy's, **lodging:** Sleep Inn, **other:** Ford, Merchant Tire/repair, **S gas:** Shell/dsl, **lodging:** Holiday Inn Express

**201** Union Cross Rd, **N gas:** Exxon/dsl, QM, **food:** Blue Naples Pizza, Burger King, China Café, **other:** CVS Drug, Food Lion

**196** US 311 S, to High Point

**195** US 311 N, NC 109, to Thomasville, **S gas:** BP, Wilco/Hess/dsl

**193b a** US 52, NC 8, to Lexington, **S gas:** Hess/dsl, Shell, **food:** Hardee's

**193c** Silas Creek Pkwy (from eb), same as 192

**192** NC 150, to Peters Creek Pkwy, **N gas:** Shell, Wilco/Hess, **food:** Arby's, Bojangles, Burger King, Checker's, China Buffet, Country Roadhouse, Hong Kong Buffet, IHOP, KFC, Little Caesar's, Monterrey Mexican, Old Country Buffet, Perkins, Pizza Hut, Red Lobster, Shoney's, Sonic, Taco Bell, Tokyo Japanese, Wendy's, **lodging:** Comfort Inn (1mi), Innkeeper, Knight's Inn, **other:** Acura/Subaru/Isuzu, Audi, AutoZone, Big Lots, Eckerd, Ford, Hyundai, Kroger, Mazda, NAPA, Office Depot, PharMor Drug, Radio Shack, Suzuki, VW, **S gas:** BP, **food:** Baskin Robbin's, Dunkin Donuts, Libby Hill Seafood, McDonald's, K&W Cafeteria, Wendy's, **lodging:** Holiday Inn Express, **other:** Advance Parts, BiLo, Buick/BMW/Saturn, CVS Drug, Food Lion, Goodyear, Harris Teeter, Honda, K-Mart

**190** Hanes Mall Blvd (from wb, no re-entry), **N food:** Chipotle Mexican, Jimmy John's, McDonald's, O'Charley's, Ruby Tuesday, TGIFriday, Tripp's Rest., **lodging:** Day's Inn, Quality Inn, **other:** H HOSPITAL, Belk, Dillard's, Firestone, JC Penney, Macy's, Marshall's, Sears/auto, mall, same as 189, **S food:** Baja Fresh Grill, Bojangles, Burger King, ChuckeCheese, Lonestar Steaks, Outback Steaks, Starbucks, Subway, **lodging:** Comfort Suites, Fairfield Inn, Microtel, Sleep Inn

## INTERSTATE 40 CONT'D

**E / W — CLEMMONS — MOCKSVILLE**

**189** US 158, Stratford Rd, Hanes Mall Blvd, **N gas:** BP, Exxon, **food:** Bojangles, Chili's, Golden Corral, Kanpai Japanese, McDonald's, Red Lobster, Sagebrush Steaks, Taco Bell, Texas Roadhouse, **lodging:** Courtyard, Fairfield Inn, **other:** H HOSPITAL, Chevrolet, Jo-Ann Fabrics, Macy's, Michael's, NTB, Sears/auto, mall, **S gas:** BP, Shell, **food:** Applebee's, Buffalo Wings, Burger King, Chick-fil-A, Copeland's Grill, Corky's BBQ, Dynasty Buffet, Fuddruckers, Hooters, Jason's Deli, Jimmy's Seafood, KFC/LJ Silver, Little Caesar's, LoneStar Steaks, Longhorn Steaks, Macaroni Grill, Moe's SW Grill, Panera Bread, Qdoba Mexican, Schlotsky's, Subway, **lodging:** Extended Stay America, Hampton Inn, Holiday Inn, La Quinta, Sleep Inn, **other:** Barnes&Noble, Best Buy, Circuit City, Costco/gas, CVS Drug, Discount Tire, Food Lion, Home Depot, Kohl's, Lowe's Whse, Ross, Sam's Club, Target

**188** US 421, to Yadkinville, to WFU (no EZ wb return), Winston-Salem, **1/2mi N** off US 421...**gas:** BP/Amoco, Shell, **food:** Boston Mkt, Burger King, McDonald's, Waffle House, Wendy's, **other:** CVS Drug, $Tree, Kroger, Mercedes, Walmart SuperCtr

**184** to US 421, Clemmons, **N gas:** Mobil, Shell, **food:** Applebees, Bambini Italian, El Jinete Mexican, Grecian Corner, KFC, Marble Slab Creamery, Panera Bread, **lodging:** Holiday Inn Express, **S gas:** BP/dsl, Exxon/dsl, Kangaroo, **food:** Arby's, Biscuitville, Brick Oven Pizza, Burger King, Cozumel Mexican, Cracker Barrel, Dockside Seafood, Domino's, Kimono Japanese, McDonald's, Mi Pueblo Mexican, Pizza Hut, Quizno's, Ruby Tuesday, Sagebrush Steaks, Sonic, Subway, Taco Bell, Waffle House, Wendy's, **lodging:** Holiday Inn, Super 8, Village Inn, **other:** Advance Parts, CarQuest, CVS Drug, $General, Eckerd, K-Mart, Lowe's Foods, Merchant Tire, Parts+, Southern Mkt, Staples, Walgreens, USPO

**182** Bermuda Run (from wb, no re-entry), Tanglewood, **S food:** Chang Thai, Lee's Chinese, Papa John's, **other:** Harris-Teeter

**182mm** Yadkin River

**180** NC 801, Tanglewood, **N food:** Capt's Galley Seafood, Cisson's Rest., Domino's, Subway, **other:** Eckerd, Lowe's Foods, **S gas:** BP/McDonald's/dsl, Deans, Shell, **food:** Bojangles, DQ, Jimmy's Greek, Venezia Italian, Wendy's, **other:** Ace Hardware, CVS Drug, $General, Food Lion, Radio Shack, Walgreens, vet

**177mm** rest areas both lanes, full & facilities, C, vending, A, litter barrels, petwalk

**174** Farmington Rd, **N gas:** Shell/dsl, **other:** antiques, **S other:** Furniture Gallery, vineyards

**170** US 601, Mocksville, **N gas:** Pure/Horn's Rest/DQ/Jersey Mike's/dsl/24hr, **food:** Subway, **other:** RV Superstore, Walmart SuperCtr, **S gas:** BP/dsl, Exxon, Shell/Taco Bell, **food:** Arby's, Bojangles, Burger King, KFC, McDonald's, Pizza Hut, Wendy's, **lodging:** Comfort Inn, HighWay Inn, Quality Inn, **other:** H HOSPITAL, Advance Parts, CVS Drug, $General, Food Lion, Ford/Mercury, Goodyear/auto, Lowe's Whse, USPO, vet

**168** US 64, to Mocksville, **N gas:** Exxon/dsl, **other:** Lake Myers RV Resort (3mi), **S gas:** BP

**162** US 64, Cool Springs, **N other:** Lake Myers RV Resort (5mi), **S gas:** Shell, **other:** Midway RV Park

**STATESVILLE — HICKORY**

**161mm** S Yadkin River

**154** to US 64, Old Mocksville Rd, **N** H HOSPITAL, **S gas:** Citgo/dsl, Rickie's, **food:** Jaybee's Hotdogs

**153** US 64 (from eb), 1/2 mi **S gas:** Citgo/dsl, **lodging:** Hallmark Inn, JB's Hotdogs

**152b a** I-77, S to Charlotte, N to Elkin

**151** US 21, E Statesville, **N gas:** Chevron, Hess/dsl/24hr, PetroExpress, **food:** Applebee's, Bojangles, Burger King, Chick-fil-A, Cracker Barrel, Golden Corral, Hooters, Italian Oven, Jack-in-the-Box, KFC, K&W Cafeteria, Logan's Roadhouse, Lonestar Steaks, McDonald's, Mi Pueblo Café, Pizza Hut/Taco Bell, Pizza Inn, Red Lobster, Ruby Tuesday, Sagebrush Steaks, Schlotsky's, Sorrento Pizza, Wendy's, Zaxby's, **lodging:** Day's Inn, Sleep Inn, **other:** BigLots, Bi-Lo, Chevrolet/Cadillac, Chrysler/Jeep, CVS Drug, Goody's, Home Depot, Lowe's Whse, Staples, Tire Kingdom, Walmart SuperCtr, **S gas:** Exxon, **food:** Lotus Pier Rest., Szechuan Chinese, Waffle House, **lodging:** Econolodge, Holiday Inn Express, Masters Inn, Quality Inn, Super 8, Travelodge, **other:** st patrol

**150** NC 115, Statesville, **N gas:** BP/dsl, Citgo, Shell, **food:** Amalfi's Italian, Little Caesar's, Ol'Bob's BBQ, **other:** CVS Drug, Food Lion, The Family RV Ctr, antiques, museum

**148** US 64, NC 90, W Statesville, **N gas:** Citgo/dsl, Exxon, QP, **food:** Arby's, Boxcar Grille, Burger King, McDonald's, Shike Japanese, Subway, Village Inn Pizza, **lodging:** Economy Inn, **other:** CVS Drug, $General, Ingles Foods

**146** Stamey Farm Rd, **S gas:** Crown/dsl/rest./24hr

**144** Old Mountain Rd, **N gas:** BP, Grand Prix/dsl, **food:** Troy's Rest., **S gas:** BP/dsl, Shell/dsl

**143mm** weigh sta both lanes

**141** Sharon School Rd, **N gas:** Citgo, **other:** antiques

**140mm** Catawba River

**138** Oxford School Rd, to Catawba, **N gas:** Exxon/dsl/24hr

**136mm** rest areas both lanes, full & facilities, C, A, vending, litter barrels, petwalk

**135** Claremont, **S gas:** Shell, **food:** BoxCar Grille, Burger King, Hardee's, Rassie's Subs, **lodging:** Super 8, **other:** $General, Lowe's Foods, Carolina Coach RV Ctr

**133** Rock Barn Rd, **N gas:** Exxon/dsl, **S gas:** Wilco/Hess/Stuckey's/Subway/Godfather's Pizza/dsl/24hr/

**132** to NC 16, Taylorsville, **N gas:** BP, Shell/dsl, **food:** 10th St Rest., **lodging:** Holiday Inn Express

**131** NC 16, Conover, **N gas:** BP/dsl, Shell/dsl, **lodging:** Holiday Inn Express, **other:** Walmart SuperCtr

**130** Old US 70, **N food:** Domino's, Jack-in-the-Box, Subway, **other:** $General, K-Mart, Lowe's Foods, NAPA, **S gas:** Citgo, Pure, Texaco, **food:** Hardee's (1mi), **other:** USPO

**128** US 321, Fairgrove Church Rd, Hickory, **N gas:** BP, Shell, Solo/dsl, **other:** H HOSPITAL, McDonald's, Waffle House, to Catawba Valley Coll, **S gas:** Citgo/dsl, Phillips 66, **food:** Bennitt's Smokehouse, Harbor Inn Seafood, Primo's Tacos, Shoney's, Wendy's, **lodging:** Day's Inn, Ramada Inn, **other:** Chrysler/Jeep/Dodge, GMC/Volvo/Ford

**126** to US 70, NC 155, **S gas:** Citgo, Exxon, Phillips 66, Petro Express, Shell, **food:** Applebee's, Asia Café Buffet, Bob Evans, El Tapatio Mexican, IHOP, Libby Hill Seafood, McDonald's, Melting Pot Rest., O'Charley's, Olive Garden, Taco Bell, Subway, **lodging:** Holiday Inn Express, **other:** Barnes&Noble, Circuit City, $Tree, Goody's, K-Mart, Lowe's Whse, Michael's, Office Depot, Sam's Club, TJ Maxx, Walmart SuperCtr

## INTERSTATE 40 CONT'D

**HICKORY**

**E** ↕ **W**

**MORGANTON**

| | |
|---|---|
| **125** | Hickory, **N** **gas:** Exxon/Subway/dsl/24hr, Raceway, **food:** Bojangles, Bamboo Garden, Golden Corral, Quizno's, Rock-ola Café, Texas Roadhouse, Tripp's Rest., **lodging:** Red Roof Inn, **other:** BMW/Mercedes, Chrysler/Jeep, **S** **gas:** Hess, Servco/24hr, Shell/dsl **food:** Arby's, Atlanta Bread, Buffalo Wild Wings, Butch's BBQ, Chick-fil-A, Chuck-eCheese, China Garden, CiCi's, Cracker Barrel, Firebonz Rest., Fuddrucker's, Hardee's, Hooters, Jack-in-the-Box, J&S Cafeteria, KFC, Kobe Japanese, Krispy Kreme, Long-horn Steaks, Outback Steaks, Panda Express, Quizno's, Red Lobster, Ruby Tuesday, Sagebrush Steaks, Schlotsky's, Waffle House, Wendy's, Zaxby's, **lodging:** Comfort Suites, Courtyard, Fairfield Inn, Hampton Inn, Holiday Inn Select, Jameson Inn, Sleep Inn, **other:** Aldi Foods, Barnes&Noble, Belk, Best Buy, Circuit City, Dillards, $Tree, Food Lion, Ford, Hancock Fabrics, Home Depot, Honda, JC Penney, Kohl's, Lowe's Whse, Mazda, Mitsubishi, Old Navy, Saturn, Sears/auto, Target, Toyota, Volvo, VW/Porsche, mall |
| **123** | US 70/321, to NC 127, Hickory |
| **121** | Long View |
| **119b a** | Hildebran, **N** **gas:** Shell/Subway/dsl, **food:** Hardee's, KFC |
| **118** | Old NC 10, **N** **gas:** Pure, Shell/dsl |
| **116** | Icard, **S** **gas:** Southern Star/dsl/24hr, **food:** Burger King, Granny's Kitchen, McDonald's, **lodging:** Icard Inn/rest. |
| **113** | Connelly Springs, **N** **gas:** Citgo, Southern Star/dsl, **other:** Ⓗ HOSPITAL, CVS Drug, Ford, Hyundai, Valdese Weaver |
| **112** | Mineral Springs Mtn Rd, Valdese |
| **111** | Valdese |
| **107** | NC 114, to Drexel |
| **106** | Bethel Rd, **S** **gas:** Exxon/dsl, **lodging:** Economy Inn |
| **105** | NC 18, Morganton, **N** **gas:** BP, **food:** Abele's Rest., Arby's, Capt D's, Coffeehouse, Fatz Café, Harbor Inn Seafood, McDonald's, Sonic, Uptown BBQ, Wendy's, Western Sizzlin, **lodging:** Hampton Inn, Red Carpet Inn, **other:** Ⓗ HOSPITAL, Pontiac/Cadillac/GMC, White Tire, **S** **gas:** QM/dsl, Texaco, **food:** El Paso Mexican, Sagebrush Steaks, **lodging:** Day's Inn, Holiday Inn/rest., Sleep Inn, to South Mtns SP |
| **104** | Enola Rd, **S** **gas:** Citgo, **food:** Chick-fil-A, Jersey Mike's Subs, **other:** Belk, BigLots, Food Lion, Goody's, Staples, st patrol |
| **103** | US 64, Morganton, **N** **gas:** Citgo, Exxon/dsl/24hr, **food:** Tastee Freez, Village Inn Pizza, **lodging:** Super 8, **S** **gas:** Citgo, Phillips 66/dsl, RaceWay, **food:** Butch's BBQ, Checker's, Denny's, Dragon Chinese, Hardee's, KFC, Subway, Taco Bell, **lodging:** Comfort Inn, **other:** Clarks Tire, Food Lion, Ingles Foods, Lowe's Whse, Radio Shack, Walmart/drugs |
| **100** | Jamestown Rd, **N** **gas:** BP/dsl/24hr, **food:** Waffle Shop, **other:** Chrysler/Jeep, Ford/Mercury, **2 mi N** **food:** KFC, Taco Bell, **lodging:** Eagle Motel |
| **98** | Causby Rd, to Glen Alpine, **S** B&B/food |
| **96** | Kathy Rd |
| **94** | Dysartsville Rd |
| **90** | Nebo, **N** **gas:** Citgo/dsl/rest., **other:** to Lake James SP, **S** **gas:** BP/dsl, **other:** Springs Creek RV Ctr |
| **86** | NC 226, to Spruce Pine, Marion, **N** **gas:** Exxon/dsl, Love's/Subway/Godfather's/dsl/scales, **food:** Hardee's, KFC, **other:** Jellystone RV Park (1mi) |

**ASHEVILLE**

| | |
|---|---|
| **85** | US 221, Marion, **N** **lodging:** Hampton Inn, **other:** to Mt Mitchell SP, **S** **gas:** Shell/dsl/24hr, **food:** Sagebrush Steaks, **lodging:** Day's Inn, Super 8 |
| **83** | Ashworth Rd |
| **82mm** | rest area both lanes, full ♿ facilities, Ⓒ, 🚻, vending, litter barrels, petwalk |
| **81** | Sugar Hill Rd, to Marion, **N** **gas:** BP/dsl, Citgo/dsl, **other:** Ⓗ HOSPITAL, Dodge/Jeep, **S** **gas:** Exxon/dsl/24hr |
| **76mm** | Catawba River |
| **75** | Parker Padgett Rd, **S** **gas:** Stuckey's/DQ/dsl |
| **73** | Old Fort, **N** **gas:** Citgo/dsl, **food:** Hardee's, **lodging:** Bed&Breakfast, **other:** Mtn Gateway Museum, Napa, **S** **gas:** Super Test/dsl, **food:** McDonald's, **other:** Bumper Parts |
| **72** | US 70 (from eb), Old Fort, **N** B&B |
| **71mm** | Pisgah Nat Forest, eastern boundary |
| **67.5mm** | truck rest area eb |
| **66** | Ridgecrest, **N** **lodging:** B&B |
| **65** | (from wb), to Black Mountain, Black Mtn Ctr |
| **64** | NC 9, Black Mountain, **N** **gas:** Exxon, Shell/Subway/24hr, **food:** Pizza Hut, **other:** BiLo/café, Chevrolet, **S** **gas:** Phillips 66, **food:** Denny's, Huddle House, KFC, McDonald's, Taco Bell, Wendy's, **lodging:** Comfort Inn, **other:** Eckerd, Ingles Foods, Radio Shack |
| **63mm** | Swannanoa River |
| **59** | Swannanoa, **N** **gas:** BP/Subway/TCBY, Exxon/dsl, Mystik, **food:** Athens Pizza, Burger King, **other:** Harley-Davidson, Ingles Foods/gas, KOA (2mi), Miles RV Ctr/Park, to Warren Wilson Coll, uspo, **S** **other:** Mama Gertie's Camping |
| **55** | E Asheville, US 70, **N** **gas:** BP, Citgo/Subway, Conoco, **food:** Arby's, Bojangles, Cocula Mexican, Dj's Diner, Waffle House, Zaxby's, **lodging:** B&B, Day's Inn, Holiday Inn, Motel 6, Quality Inn, Super 8, **other:** VA Ⓗ HOSPITAL, Go Groceries, Top's RV park, to Mt Mitchell SP, Folk Art Ctr |
| **53b a** | I-240 W, US 74, to Asheville, Bat Cave, **N** **food:** KFC, J&S Cafeteria, McDonald's, **lodging:** Comfort Inn, **other:** Advance Parts, BiLo, CVS Drug, Eckerd, Hamrick's, **1-2 mi N** on US 74...**gas:** BP, Exxon/dsl, **food:** Applebee's, Burger King, Carrabba's, Chili's, Chick-fil-A, Damon's, IHOP, O'Charley's, Olive Garden, Red Lobster, Subway, Waffle House, **lodging:** Courtyard, Day's Inn, Econolodge, Extended Stay America, Hampton Inn, Ramada Ltd, **other:** Barnes& Noble, Best Buy, Circuit City, Dillard's, Goody's, Home Depot, Ingles Foods, K-Mart, Lowes Whse, Michael's, Office Depot, Radio Shack, Ross, Sears/auto, mall, **S** **gas:** BP/dsl/LP, Phillips 66, **other:** to Blue Ridge Pkwy |

**NC**

## INTERSTATE 40 CONT'D

**ASHEVILLE** E ← → W

| | |
|---|---|
| **51** | US 25A, Sweeten Creek Rd, **1/2 mi** S **food:** Subway |
| **50** | US 25, Asheville, N **gas:** BP, CitiStop, Shell/dsl, **food:** Arby's, Asaka Japanese, Chapala Mexican, Ichiban, Krystal, LJ Silver/A&W, McDonald's, Moe's SW Grill, Subway, Texas Roadhouse, TGIFriday, Wendy's, **lodging:** Baymont Inn, Doubletree Inn, Holiday Inn Express, Howard Johnson, Sleep Inn, **other:** H HOSPITAL, to Biltmore House, S **gas:** Hess, **food:** Atl Bread Co, Huddle House/24hr, Province Rest., **lodging:** Forest Manor Inn |
| **47mm** | French Broad River |
| **47** | NC 191, W Asheville, N **other:** Asheville Speedway, Bear Creek RV Camping, S **gas:** Phillips 66/dsl, **food:** Moose Cafe, **other:** Farmer's Mkt, **2 mi** S **lodging:** Comfort Inn, Country Inn&Suites, Fairfield Inn, Hampton Inn, Holiday Inn Express, Super 8 |
| **46b a** | I-26 & I-240 E, **2 mi** N multiple services from I-240 |
| **44** | US 74, W Asheville, N **gas:** BP, Chevron/dsl, Conoco, Exxon, Hess/dsl, Shell/Substation II/24hr, **food:** Applebee's, Asiana Buffet, Burger King, Cracker Barrel, El Chapala Mexican, Fatz Cafe, Hardees, Kountry Kitchen, Krystal, Los Volcanes Mexican, Pizza Hut, Waffle House, Wendy's, **lodging:** Best Western, Comfort Inn, Red Roof Inn, Sleep Inn, Super 8, Whispering Pines Motel, **other:** CarQuest, Chevrolet, Chrysler/Jeep, CVS Drug, Family$, Ingles Foods, Lowe's Whse, Mercedes/Mazda, S **food:** McDonald's, Shoney's, **lodging:** Budget Motel, Ramada Inn, **other:** BiLo Foods, CVS Drug, Home Depot |
| **41mm** | weigh sta both lanes |
| **37** | E Canton, N **gas:** BP, TA/Buckhorn Rest./dsl/scales/24hr/@, **other:** Goodyear, S **gas:** Exxon/dsl, **lodging:** Day's Inn, Plantation Motel, **other:** KOA |
| **33** | Newfound Rd, to US 74, S gas |
| **31** | Canton, N **food:** Sagebrush Steaks, **lodging:** Econolodge, S **gas:** BP/dsl, Chevron/DQ, Exxon/McDonald's/24hr, Shell/Arby's/dsl, **food:** Burger King, Pizza Hut (2mi), Subway (1mi), Taco Bell, Waffle House, **lodging:** Comfort Inn, **other:** Ingles Foods, Chevrolet/Pontiac/Buick, Ford, RV/truck repair |
| **27** | US 19/23, to Waynesville, Great Smokey Mtn Expswy, **3 mi** S **gas:** Shell/Burger King, **food:** Shoney's, Subway, Taco Bell, **other:** H HOSPITAL, Food Lion, GNC, Lowe's Whse, Walmart/drugs, to WCU (25mi) |
| **24** | NC 209, to Lake Junaluska, N **gas:** Pilot/Subway/dsl/scales/24hr/@, **lodging:** Midway Motel, S **gas:** Texaco/cafe/dsl/24hr |
| **20** | US 276, to Maggie Valley, Lake Junaluska, S **gas:** BP/dsl, Citgo, Exxon/dsl/café, **other:** Creekwood Farm RV Park, Pride RV Resort, Winngray RV Park |
| **16mm** | Pigeon River |
| **15** | Fines Creek |
| **12mm** | Pisgah NF eastern boundary |
| **10mm** | **rest area both lanes, full** ♿ **facilities,** 🕻**, vending,** 🅿**, litter barrels, petwalk** |
| **7** | Harmon Den |
| **4mm** | tunnel both lanes |
| **0mm** | North Carolina/Tennessee state line |

## INTERSTATE 77

N ↑↓ S **ELKIN** **STATESVILLE**

| Exit # | Services |
|---|---|
| **105mm** | North Carolina/Virginia state line |
| **105mm** | **Welcome Ctr sb, full** ♿ **facilities, info,** 🕻**, vending,** 🅿**, litter barrels, petwalk** |
| **103mm** | weigh sta both lanes |
| **101** | I-74 E, to Mt Airy, Winston-Salem, Greensboro, E **lodging:** Hampton Inn, **other:** H HOSPITAL (12mi), |
| **100** | NC 89, to Mt Airy, E **gas:** Brintle's/Citgo/dsl/rest./24hr/@, Exxon/dsl, Marathon/Subway/dsl, **food:** Wagon Wheel Rest., **lodging:** Best Western, Comfort Inn (2mi), **other:** H HOSPITAL (12mi), clothing outlet |
| **93** | to Dobson, Surry, E **gas:** Citgo/dsl/diner, **lodging:** Hampton Inn, Surry Inn, **other:** camping |
| **85** | NC 1138, CC Camp Rd, to Elkin, W **gas:** Exxon/dsl, Shell/Blimpie/Stuckey's/dsl, **1-3 mi** W **gas:** Neighbor's, **food:** Burger King, KFC, McDonald's, **lodging:** Elk Inn |
| **83** | US 21 byp, to Sparta (from nb) |
| **82.5mm** | Yadkin River |
| **82** | NC 67, Elkin, E **gas:** BP/Case Knife Outlet/dsl, Chevron/dsl, **food:** Arby's, Cracker Barrel, Jordan's Rest., **lodging:** Holiday Inn Express, **other:** Holly Ridge Camping (8mi), W **gas:** Exxon/Baskin-Robbins/TCBY/dsl, **food:** Bojangles, Captains Galley, Ham & Eggs Rest, McDonald's, Waffle House, Wendy's, **lodging:** Comfort Inn, Day's Inn, Hampton Inn, Rose's Motel, **other:** AutoValue Parts, Buick/Pontiac/GMC, CarQuest, Curves, D-Rex Drug, Family$, Food Lion, vet |
| **79** | US 21 S, to Arlington, E **gas:** Citgo/Subway/dsl, Shell, **lodging:** Super 8, W **gas:** BP/dsl, **food:** Glenn's BBQ, **lodging:** Best Value Inn |
| **73b a** | US 421, to Winston-Salem (20mi), E **gas:** Shell/Subway/dsl (1mi) |
| **72mm** | **rest area nb, full** ♿ **facilities,** 🕻**, vending,** 🅿**, litter barrels, petwalk** |
| **65** | NC 901, to Union Grove, Harmony, E **other:** Van Hoy Farms Camping, W **gas:** BP/dsl, Shell/Subway/dsl/24hr, **food:** Burger Barn, **lodging:** B&B, **other:** Fiddler's Grove Camping (2mi) |
| **63mm** | **rest area sb, full** ♿ **facilities,** 🕻**, vending,** 🅿**, litter barrels, petwalk** |
| **59** | Tomlin Mill Rd, W **gas:** Citgo/dsl |
| **56.5mm** | S Yadkin River |
| **54** | US 21, to Turnersburg, E **gas:** Citgo, W **gas:** Shell/dsl, **food:** Arby's, **2mi** W **gas:** Chick-fil-A, Dunkin Donuts, Golden Corral, Zaxby's |
| **51b a** | I-40, E to Winston-Salem, W to Hickory |
| **50** | E Broad St, Statesville, E **gas:** BP, Citgo/dsl, Kangaroo/dsl, Shell, **food:** Arby's, Burger King, CiCi's Pizza, Dominos, El Tio's Mexican, IHOP, Jack-in-the-Box, McDonald's, Papa John's, Pizza Hut, Shanghai Buffet, Shoney's, Starbucks, Subway, Wendy's, **lodging:** Brookwood Inn, Red Roof Inn, **other:** Belk, Bi-Lo, $General, Eckerd, JC Penney, JR Outlet, K-Mart, Radio Shack, Sears/auto, USPO, mall |
| **49b a** | US 70, G Bagnal Blvd, to Statesville, E **gas:** BP, Citgo, Circle K, Exxon, **food:** Brewsters, KFC, Waffle House, **lodging:** Best Western, Comfort Inn, Hampton Inn, Holiday Inn/rest., Motel 6, Super 8, **other:** Buick/GMC/Cadillac, Camping World, Dodge, Ford, |

## INTERSTATE 77 CONT'D

**N ↕ S**

**49b a** Continued
Harley-Davidson, Holiday Camper, Honda, Lincoln/Mercury, Nissan, Subaru, Toyota/Scion, **W gas:** Chevron, Citgo, **food:** Carolina BBQ, **lodging:** Best Value Inn, Microtel

**45** to Troutman, Barium Springs, **E** KOA, RV Repair, **W gas:** Chevron/BBQ/dsl

**42** US 21, NC 115, to Troutman, Oswalt, **E gas:** Hess/Wilco/Subway/dsl/scales/24hr/@, **W gas:** Citgo, **other:** to Lake Norman SP, camping

**39mm** rest area both lanes, full ♿ facilities, 📞, 🎪, litter barrels, petwalk, vending

**36** NC 150, Mooresville, **E gas:** Accel/dsl, Exxon, Shell/24hr, **food:** Applebee's, Bob Evans, Cookout Burgers, Denny's, Dominos, FatBoy's Cafe, Jack-in-the-Box, McDonald's, Pizza Hut, Roadhouse Grill, Sonny's BBQ, Taco Bell, Waffle House, Wendy's, **lodging:** Day's Inn, Fairfield Inn, Holiday Inn Express, Ramada Ltd, **other:** Belk, Chevrolet, $Tree, Gander Mtn, GNC, Kohl's, Mazda, Staples, Suzuki, Tuesday Morning, Walmart SuperCtr, **W gas:** BJ's Whse/gas, BP/dsl, Citgo/KrispyKreme/BBQ, Servco, Shell/dsl/24hr, **food:** Arby's, Chick-fil-A, Cracker Barrel, Golden Corral, Hardee's, Hooters, Kyoto Japanese, McDonald's, Monterrey Mexican, Subway, Texas Roadhouse, Velvet Hammer, **lodging:** Hampton Inn, Sleep Inn, Super 8, Wingate Inn, **other:** Food Lion, Lowes Whse, Tire Kingdom, Walgreens

**33** US 21 N, **E food:** Jeffrey's Rest, Legends, McDonald's, Subway, **lodging:** SpringHill Suites, **other:** Ⓗ HOSPITAL, **W gas:** BP/Arby's/Bojangles, Citgo/dsl, **food:** Baskin-Robbins/Dunkin Donuts, Sauza's Mexican, **other:** Food Lion, Woody's Drug, vet

**30** Davidson, **E gas:** Exxon/dsl, **food:** North Harbor Rest., **other:** to Davidson College

**28** US 21 S, NC 73, Cornelius, Lake Norman, **E gas:** BP, Cashion's/dsl, Citgo/24hr, **food:** Acropolis Cafe, **lodging:** Days Inn, Hampton Inn, **other:** NAPA, **W gas:** PetroStop, **food:** Bojangles, Burger King, KFC, Kobe Japanese, McAlister's Deli, McDonald's, Papa John's, Pizza Hut, PJ Gator's, Quizno's, Starbucks, Subway, Taco Bell, Wendy's, **lodging:** Best Western, Econolodge, Microtel, **other:** Chrysler/Jeep, Dodge, Eckerd, Goodyear, Harris-Teeter, SteinMart

**25** NC 73, Concord, Lake Norman, **E gas:** Shell/dsl, Texaco, **food:** Atlanta Bread Co, Burger King, Chick-fil-A, Chili's, Fuddrucker's, IHOP, Longhorn Steaks, McDonald's, O'Charley's, Wendy's, **lodging:** Country Inn&Suites, Hawthorn Suites, Quality Inn, **other:** Home Depot, Kohl's, Lowe's Whse, Old Navy, Target, **W gas:** 76/Circle K/Blimpie/dsl, **food:** Arby's, Best China, Bob Evans, Bojangles, Carrabba's, Cheeseburger Paradise, DQ, Max&Erma's, Outback Steaks, Quiznos, Subway, **lodging:** Candlewood Suites, Courtyard, Sleep Inn, **other:** Food Lion/deli, Walgreens, to Energy Explorium

**23** NC 73, Huntersville, **E gas:** BP, Citgo, Shell/24hr, **food:** Chico's Mexican, Dunkin Donuts-Basin Robbins, Hardee's, Jersey Mike's, Palace of China, Subway, Waffle House, Wendy's, **lodging:** Holiday Inn Express, Red Roof Inn, **other:** $Tree, Eckerd, Food Lion, Ford, Hancock Fabrics, Pontiac/GMC, Radio Shack,

**CHARLOTTE**

**23** Continued
Tuesday Morning, USPO, **W gas:** Shell, **food:** CiCi's Pizza, Friendly's, Pizza Hut, Sekisui, Starbucks, **other:** Ⓗ HOSPITAL, Bi-Lo, CVS Drug, GNC, Harris-Teeter

**19mm** future I-485

**18** Harris Blvd, Reames Rd, **E gas:** BP/Arby's, Shell/dsl, **food:** Bob Evans, Hickory Tavern, Jack-in-the-Box, Lin's Buffet, Quizno's, Waffle House, **lodging:** Comfort Suites, Fairfield Inn, Hilton Garden, Suburban Lodge, **other:** Ⓗ HOSPITAL, to UNCC, Univ Research Park, **W gas:** Chevron, **food:** Chili's, Coldstone Creamery, Firebird Grill, Fox&Hound, Moe's SW Grill, Olive Garden, On-the-Border, Panera bread, Red Robin, TGI Friday, **other:** Belk, Dillard's, Macy's

**16b a** US 21, Sunset Rd, **E gas:** 76/Circle K, **food:** Capt D's, Hardee's, KFC, McDonald's, Subway, Taco Bell, Wendy's, **lodging:** Day's Inn, Super 8, **other:** Winn-Dixie, **W gas:** Citgo/dsl, Shell/dsl/scales/24hr, 76/Circle K, **food:** Bojangles, Bubba's BBQ, Cookout Burgers, Denny's, Dominos, Jack-in-the-Box, Waffle House, **lodging:** Microtel, Sleep Inn, **other:** Advance Parts, Aldi Foods, CVS Drug, RV Ctr

**13b a** I-85, S to Spartanburg, N to Greensboro

**12** La Salle St, **W gas:** Citgo/dsl, Shell/dsl

**11b a** I-277, Brookshire Fwy, NC 16

**10b** Trade St, 5th St (from nb), **E other:** to Discovery Place, **W gas:** Citgo, **food:** Bojangles

**10a** US 21 (from sb), Moorhead St, downtown

**9** I-277, US 74, to US 29, John Belk Fwy, downtown, **E** Ⓗ HOSPITAL, stadium

**8** Remount Rd (from nb, no re-entry)

**7** Clanton Rd, **E gas:** PetroExpress/dsl, **food:** McDonald's, Waffle House, Wendy's, **lodging:** Day's Inn, Econolodge, Super 8, **W gas:** BP, Shell/dsl

**6b a** US 521, Billy Graham Pkwy, **E gas:** BP, Citgo, Shell/dsl, Sunoco, **food:** Azteca Mexican, Bojangles, Capt D's, Carolina Prime Steaks, IHOP, KFC/Pizza Hut, Krispy Kreme, McDonald's, Murphy's Cafe, Shoney's, **lodging:** Best Western, Day's Inn, Howard Johnson, Ramada Ltd, Sheraton, **other:** Walgreens, to Queens Coll, **W gas:** PetroExpress, Shell, **food:** Omaha Steaks, **lodging:** Embassy Suites, Holiday Inn, InTown Suites, Summerfield Suites, La Quinta, Sleep Inn

**5** Tyvola Rd, **E gas:** PetroExpress/dsl, Texaco, **food:** Carolina BBQ, Chili's, China King, Derby Diner, Kiauto Japanese, LoneStar Steaks, McDonald's, Sonny's BBQ, Subway, **lodging:** Candlewood Suites, Comfort Inn,

**N ↕ S**

### INTERSTATE 77 CONT'D

| | |
|---|---|
| 23 | Continued<br>Hilton, Marriott, Quality Inn, Residence Inn, Studio+, **other:** Aldi Foods, Costco/gas, Eckerd, Jaguar, Pontiac/GMC, **W** **lodging:** Extended Stay America, Wingate Inn, **other:** to Coliseum |
| 4 | Nations Ford Rd, **E** **gas:** Citgo, 76/Circle K/24hr, **food:** Caravel Seafood, **lodging:** Budget Inn, Knights Inn, Motel 6, Ramada Ltd., **W** **gas:** Shell/Burger King |
| 3 | Arrowood Rd, to I-485 (from sb), **E** **gas:** Shell, **food:** Bob Evans, Chick-fil-A, Jack-in-the-Box, Japan Express, LJ Silver, McDonald's, Sonic, Starbucks, Wendy's, **lodging:** AmeriSuites, Courtyard, Fairfield Inn, Holiday Inn Express, Mainstay Suites, Staybridge Suites, TownePlace Suites, **W** **food:** Ruby Tuesday, **lodging:** Hampton Inn |
| 2 | I-485 |
| 1.5mm | **Welcome Ctr nb, full** &#9855; **facilities, info,** &#9743;**, vending,** &#127869;**, litter barrels, petwalk** |
| 1 | Westinghouse Blvd, to I-485 (from nb), **E** **gas:** BP/dsl, **food:** Jack-in-the-Box, Subway, Waffle House, **lodging:** Super 8, **W** **gas:** Shell/dsl, **food:** Burger King |
| 0mm | North Carolina/South Carolina state line |

### INTERSTATE 85

**N ↕ S**

| Exit # | Services |
|---|---|
| 234mm | North Carolina/Virginia state line |
| 233 | US 1, to Wise, **E** **gas:** Citgo/Wise/dsl, **food:** Budget Inn |
| 231mm | **Welcome Ctr sb, full** &#9855; **facilities,** &#9743;**,** &#127869;**, litter barrels, petwalk** |
| 229 | Oine Rd, to Norlina, **E** **gas:** BP, **W** rec area |
| 226 | Ridgeway Rd, **W** **other:** to Kerr Lake, to St RA |
| 223 | Manson Rd, **E** **gas:** BP/dsl, **other:** camping, **W** to Kerr Dam |
| 220 | US 1, US 158, Fleming Rd, to Middleburg, **E** **gas:** BP/dsl, **W** **gas:** Exxon/dsl/scales, **lodging:** Chex Motel/rest. |
| 218 | US 1 S (from sb exits left), to Raleigh |
| 217 | Nutbush Bridge, **E** same as 215 on US 158, **W** **gas:** Exxon/dsl, **other:** Kerr Lake RA |
| 215 | US 158 BYP E, Henderson (no EZ return from nb), **E** **gas:** BP, Hess, Shell, Sunoco, **food:** BBQ, Burger King, Golden China, Subway, Waffle Pancakes, **lodging:** Ambassador Inn, Budget Host, Comfort Inn, Scottish Inn, **other:** $General, Food Lion, Goodyear/auto, Roses, services on US 158 |
| 214 | NC 39, Henderson, **E** **gas:** BP, **food:** Andy's Rest., **other:** uspo, **W** **gas:** BP/dsl, Shell/HotStuff Pizza |
| 213 | US 158, Dabney Dr, to Henderson, **E** **gas:** BP, Parade, Shell, **food:** Bamboo Garden, Bojangles, DQ, Denny's, KFC, McDonald's, Papa John's, Pizza Inn, Subway, Wendy's, **other:** CVS Drug, Family$, Food Lion, Goodyear/auto, Radio Shack, Roses, **W** **gas:** BP, Shell, **food:** Chick-fil-A, Golden Corral, Smithfields BBQ, Taco Bell, **lodging:** Holiday Inn Express, **other:** Chevrolet/GMC, Chrysler/Dodge, $Tree, Eckerd, Ford/Lincoln/Mercury, K-Mart, Lowe's Whse, Pontiac, Staples, Tires+ |
| 212 | Ruin Creek Rd, **E** **gas:** Shell/dsl, **food:** Cracker Barrel, Mazatlan Mexican, SiLo Rest., **lodging:** Day's Inn, **W** **gas:** BP/Burger King, **food:** Christoper's Grill, Gary's BBQ, Golden Corral, Pizza Hut, Western Sizzlin, |

| | |
|---|---|
| 212 | Continued<br>**lodging:** Hampton Inn, Jameson Inn, Sleep Inn, **other:** &#9400; HOSPITAL, Belk, Goody's, JC Penney, Walmart SuperCtr, mall |
| 209 | Poplar Creek Rd, **W** Vance-Granville Comm Coll |
| 206 | US 158, Oxford, **E** **gas:** Exxon, **W** **gas:** BP/dsl, **food:** Tony's Rest., **other:** &#9992; |
| 204 | NC 96, Oxford, **E** **gas:** BP/dsl, **lodging:** Best Western, King's Inn, **other:** Honda, Pontiac/Buick/GMC, **W** **gas:** Exxon/DQ/24hr, Hess, Shell/Pizza Hut/24hr, Texaco, **food:** Burger King, Domino's, KFC, McDonald's, 96 Buffet, Subway, Taco Bell, Wendy's, **lodging:** Econolodge, **other:** &#9400; HOSPITAL, $Tree, GNC, Lowe's Foods, Walmart |
| 202 | US 15, Oxford, **2 mi** **W** **lodging:** Crown Motel |
| 199mm | **rest area both lanes, full** &#9855; **facilities,** &#9743;**,** &#127869;**, litter barrels, petwalk** |
| 198mm | Tar River |
| 191 | NC 56, Butner, **E** **gas:** BP/dsl, Hess/dsl, **food:** Bob's BBQ, Bojangles, Burger King, El Rio Mexican, KFC/Taco Bell, McDonald's, Pizza Hut, Stone Crab Landing, Subway, Wendy's, **lodging:** Comfort Inn, **other:** Ace Hardware, Advance Parts, Curves, $General, Eckerd, Food Lion, M&H Tires, vet, to Falls Lake RA, **W** **gas:** Exxon/dsl/24hr, Shell/dsl, **food:** Hardee's, Waffle&Pancake House, **lodging:** Econolodge, Holiday Inn Express, Ramada Ltd, **other:** auto repair |
| 189 | Butner |
| 186b a | US 15, to Creedmoor |
| 185mm | Falls Lake |
| 183 | Redwood Rd |
| 182 | Red Mill Rd, **E** **gas:** Exxon/repair, **other:** Kenworth/Isuzu Trucks |
| 180 | Glenn School Rd |
| 179 | E Club Blvd, **E** **gas:** Exxon |
| 178 | US 70 E, to Raleigh, Falls Lake RA, Research Triangle, RDU &#9992; |
| 177 | Avondale Dr, NC 55, **W** gas Shell, **food:** American Hero, Arby's, Hong Kong Buffet, Los Comales, McDonalds, Pizza Village, **other:** Advance Parts, Big Lots, Jiffy Lube |
| 176b a | Gregson St, US 501 N, **E** **food:** Champps Grill, Tripps Rest., **other:** &#9400; HOSPITAL, Belk, Macy's, Museum of Life&Science, Office Depot, Sears/auto, mall |
| 175 | Guess Rd, **E** **gas:** Citgo/dsl, **food:** Hog Heaven BBQ, **lodging:** Best Value Inn, Holiday Inn Express, Super 8, **other:** Eckerd, **W** **gas:** BP/dsl, Pure, **food:** Bojangles, Honey's Diner/24hr, IHOP, JJ Fish &Chicken, Texas Steaks, Zero's Subs, **lodging:** Red Roof Inn, **other:** CVS Drug, Home Depot, Kroger |
| 174a | Hillandale Rd, **W** **gas:** BP/dsl, **food:** El Corral, Papa's Grill, Sal's Pizza, **lodging:** Courtyard, Hampton Inn, Howard Johnson, **other:** Kerr Drug |
| 174b | US 15 S, US 501 S (from sb), **E** **lodging:** Forest Inn |
| 173 | US 15, US 501, US 70, Colemill Rd, W Durham, **E** **gas:** BP, Exxon/dsl, Shell/Texaco, **food:** Arby's, BBQ, Bojangles, Burger King, Checker's, Chick-fil-a, KFC/Taco Bell, Cracker Barrel, DogHouse Rest., Domino's, Galley Seafood, Italian Garden Rest., McDonald's, Miami Subs, Subway, Taco Bell, Waffle House, Wendy's, **lodging:** Day's Inn, Fairfield Inn, Holiday Inn, Innkeeper, **other:** &#9400; HOSPITAL, Autozone, Dodge/Jeep, Eckerd, Kroger, Rite Aid |

**NC**

**OXFORD BUTNER**

**HENDERSON**

**DURHAM**

## INTERSTATE 85 CONT'D

| | |
|---|---|
| 172 | NC 147 S, to US 15 S, US 501 S (from nb), Durham, from nb |
| 170 | to NC 751, to Duke U (no EZ return from nb), **E lodging:** Best Western/rest., Scottish Inn, **W** to Eno River SP |
| 165 | NC 86, to Chapel Hill, **E gas:** Pure/dsl, **food:** Papa John's, Subway, **other:** $Hut, Home Depot, Walmart SuperCtr, **W gas:** BP/dsl |
| 164 | Hillsborough, **E gas:** BP, Citgo/dsl, **food:** McDonald's, **lodging:** Holiday Inn Express, **W gas:** Exxon/dsl, Shell, **food:** Bojangles, Casa Ibarra Mexican, Domino's, Hardee's, KFC/Taco Bell, Occoneechee Steaks, Pizza Hut, Subway, Waffle House, Wendy's, **lodging:** Microtel, **other:** AutoZone, CarQuest, Chevrolet/Buick, $Tree, Food Lion, Ford, GNC, Goodyear/auto, Lowe's Foods |
| 163 | I-40 E, to Raleigh. **I-85 S and I-40 W run together 38 mi.** |
| 161 | to US 70 E, NC 86 N |
| 160 | to NC 86 N, Efland, **W gas:** Exxon/dsl |
| 158mm | weigh sta both lanes |
| 157 | Buckhorn Rd, **E gas:** BP/dsl, Petro/Mobil/Iron Skillet/dsl/scales/24hr/@, **W gas:** Citgo, Exxon |
| 154 | Mebane, Oaks Rd, **E gas:** Shell/dsl/24hr, Sheetz, **other:** Walmart SuperCtr/gas, **W gas:** BP, Citgo, Shell/dsl/24hr, **food:** Biscuitville, Blue Ribbon Diner, Bojangles, La Fiesta Mexican, McDonald's, Quizno's, Roma Pizza, Waffle House, **lodging:** Budget Inn/rest., **other:** Advance Parts, Autozone, CVS Drug |
| 153 | NC 119, Mebane, **E gas:** BP/KFC/Taco Bell/Pizza Hut, **food:** Cracker Barrel, Hibachi Rest., Jersey Mike's, Ruby Tuesday, Smithfield's BBQ, **lodging:** Hampton Inn, Holiday Inn Express, **other:** Lowe's Whse, **W gas:** Phillips 66/Burger King, **food:** Domino's, La Cocina Mexican, Sonic, Subway, YumYum Chinese, **other:** Curves, CVS Drug, Food Lion, vet |
| 152 | Trollingwood Rd, **E gas:** Pilot/McDonald's/dsl/scales/24hr, **W gas:** Fuel City/dsl |
| 150 | Haw River, to Roxboro, **W gas:** Hess/Wilco/DQ/Wendy's/dsl/scales/24hr/@, ⊛ FLYING J/Cookery/dsl/LP/scales/24hr/@, **lodging:** Best Western, **other:** Blue Beacon |
| 148 | NC 54, Graham, **E gas:** BP/dsl/24hr, Exxon/dsl/24hr, QP, **food:** Waffle House, **lodging:** Comfort Suites, **W food:** MexAm Cafe, **lodging:** Ember's Motel, Travel Inn |
| 147 | NC 87, to Pittsboro, Graham, **E gas:** BP, **food:** Arby's, Bojangles, Burger King, Domino's, Lucky Bamboo, Pizza Hut, Quizno's, Sagebrush Steaks, Sonic, Subway, Wendy's, **other:** Advance Parts, Chevrolet, Curves, Eckerd, Family$, Food Lion, Ford, Jeep, vet, **W gas:** Citgo/dsl, Exxon/dsl, Shell/dsl, **food:** BBQ&Ribs Rest., Biscuitville, Cookout, McDonald's, Taco Bell, **other:** Ⓗ HOSPITAL, CVS Drug, Lowe's Foods, Walgreen |
| 145 | NC 49, Burlington, **E gas:** BP/dsl, Shell/dsl, **food:** Capt D's, Taco Bell, **lodging:** Econolodge, Microtel, Motel 6, **other:** Harley-Davidson, **W gas:** BP/dsl, **food:** Biscuitville, Bojangles, Burger King, China Buffet, Hardee's, KFC, Subway, Waffle House, **lodging:** Best Value Inn, Holiday Inn, La Quinta, Scottish Inn, **other:** Dodge, $General, Eckerd, Food Lion, Radio Shack |
| 143 | NC 62, Burlington, **E gas:** E-Z Stop/dsl, **food:** Bob Evans, Hardee's, Waffle House, Wendy's, to Alamance Bfd, **W gas:** Exxon, 76/Circle K, **food:** Don Pancho's, |

| | |
|---|---|
| 143 | **Continued** K&W Cafeteria, Libby Hill Seafood, **lodging:** Ramada Inn, **other:** Cadillac, Chevrolet, $General, Food Lion, Ford, Home Depot, Mitsubishi, auto repair |
| 141 | to Burlington, **E gas:** BP, Kangaroo, **food:** IHOP, Mayflower Seafood, Outback Steaks, **lodging:** Comfort Inn, Hampton Inn, **W gas:** Phillips 66/dsl, Texaco, **food:** Applebee's, Arby's, Biscuitville, Bojangles, Burger King, Chick-fil-A, Chophouse Grill, Cookout, Cracker Barrel, Crazy Fire Mongolian, Golden Corral, Hooters, KFC, Longhorn Steaks, McDonald's, Namaste Indian Rest., O'Charley's, Panda Express, Panera Bread, Papa John's, Rockola Grill, Ruby Tuesday, Sal's Italian, Starbucks, Steak'n Shake/24hr, Subway, Taco Bell, Wholly Guacamole, **lodging:** Best Western, Country Inn&Suites, Courtyard, Super 8, **other:** Ⓗ HOSPITAL, Belk, Buick/GMC, $Tree, Eckerd, Food Lion, Ford, Honda, K-Mart/gas, Lincoln/Mercury, Lowe's Foods, Mazda, Nissan, JC Penney, Sears/auto, Walmart SuperCtr, mall, to Elon Coll |
| 140 | University Dr, Elon, **W food:** Chick-fil-A, Chili's, Moe's SW Grill, Olive Garden, Red Robin, Starbucks, **other:** Barnes&Noble, Belk, Best Buy, Dillard's, JC Penny, Michael's, Old Navy, PetsMart, Ross, Target |
| 139mm | **rest area both lanes, full** ♿ **facilities,** 🕯, 🅿, **litter barrels, vending** |
| 138 | NC 61, Gibsonville, **W gas:** TA/BP/Burger King/Popeye's/dsl/scales/@, **lodging:** Days Inn |
| 135 | Rock Creek Dairy Rd, **W gas:** Citgo, Exxon, **food:** Bojangles, China 1, Domino's, Guacamole Mexican, Jersey Mike's Subs, McDonald's, **other:** Curves, CVS Drug, Food Lion, Midtown Drug |
| 132 | Mt Hope Church Rd, **E gas:** Citgo/Subway/dsl, **W gas:** Shell/dsl, Wilco/Hess/Wendy's/dsl/24hr, **lodging:** Hampton Inn |
| 131 | to US 70, **I-85 N and I-40 E run together 30 mi.** |
| 129 | Youngsmill Rd, **W lodging:** Holiday Inn Express (3mi) |
| 128 | Alamance Church Rd |
| 126b a | US 421, to Sanford, **E gas:** Exxon/dsl, Kangaroo/dsl |
| 124 | S Elm, Eugene St, **E food:** Bojangles, Cracker Barrel, Starbucks, Subway, Wendy's, **other:** Lowe's Whse, Walmart SuperCtr |
| 122a | US 220, to Greensboro, Asheboro (from sb), access to I-40 |
| 120 | N US 29, E US 70, to I-40 W |
| 119 | Grootnetown Rd, **W gas:** Citgo/dsl |
| 118 | US 29 S, US 70 W, to High Point, Jamestown, **W lodging:** Grandover Resort, **other:** Ⓗ HOSPITAL |

## INTERSTATE 85 CONT'D

**N ↑ S**

**THOMASVILLE**

**NC**

| | |
|---|---|
| **115mm** | Deep River |
| **113** | NC 62, Archdale, **E** gas: Citgo/dsl, **W** gas: BP/dsl, **lodging:** Best Western |
| **111** | US 311, to High Point, Archdale, **E** food: Amici Pizza, Bamboo Garden, Bojangles, Hardee's, Subway, Wendy's, **lodging:** Innkeeper, **other:** Curves, CVS Drug, $General, $City, Food Lion, Lowe's Foods/24hr, **W** gas: Circle K/dsl, Exxon/McDonald's, Marathon/dsl, Shell/dsl, **food:** Biscuitville, Libby Hill Seafood, Spiro's Rest., Waffle House, **lodging:** Comfort Inn, Fairfeild Inn, Hampton Inn, Holiday Inn Express, **other:** H HOSPITAL, USPO, tires |
| **108** | Hopewell Church Rd |
| **106** | Finch Farm Rd, **E** gas: BP/dsl, **W** food: Subway (1mi) |
| **103** | NC 109, to Thomasville, **E** gas: Petro Express, Shell, **food:** Arby's, Cookout Burgers, Elizabeth's Pizza, Taco Bell, **other:** CVS Drug, $Tree, Ingles Foods, K-Mart, Radio Shack, Walmart SuperCtr/gas, **W** gas: Exxon/Subway/dsl, Coastal, RaceWay, Hess/Wilco/dsl, Shell, Sunoco, **food:** BBQ Shack, Biscuitville, Bojangles, Burger King, Captain Tom's, China Garden, Hardee's, Hunan Chinese, KFC, Loflin's Rest., Mazatlan Mexican, McDonald's, Mr Gatti's, Papa John's, Peeble's Rest., Ruby Tuesday, Sonic, Sunrise Grille, Waffle House, Wendy's, **lodging:** Quaility Inn, **other:** Advance Parts, AutoZone, Eckerd, Family$, Food Lion, Mighty$, O'Reilly Parts, Walgreens |
| **102** | Lake Rd, **W** gas: Marathon, Texaco, **lodging:** Day's Inn/rest., Microtel, **other:** H HOSPITAL |
| **100mm** | **rest area both lanes, full** ♿ **facilities,** 🚻 **vending,** 🏞️**, litter barrels, petwalk** |
| **96** | US 64, to Asheboro, Lexington, **E** gas: Exxon/dsl, **W** gas: Chevron/dsl, Citgo (1mi), **food:** Randy's Rest., **lodging:** Quality Inn (4mi), **other:** to Davidson Co Coll, NC Zoo |
| **94** | Old US 64, **E** gas: Shell |
| **91** | NC 8, to Southmont, **E** gas: BP/dsl, Citgo, Shell/dsl, **food:** Biscuit King, Burger King, Christo Rest., Jimmy's BBQ, KFC, McDonald's, Ocean View Seafood, Subway, Wendy's, **lodging:** Comfort Suites, Highway 8 Motel, **other:** Food Lion, High Rock Lake Camping (7mi), Kerr Drug, **W** gas: Exxon/dsl, QM/dsl, **food:** Applebee's, Arby's, Burger King, Cracker Barrel, Golden Corral, Hardee's, King House, Little Caesar's, Pizza Hut (1mi), Stella's Rest., Taco Bell, Zaxby's, **lodging:** Country Hearth Inn, Holiday Inn Express, **other:** H HOSPITAL, Belk, $Tree, GNC, Goody's, Lowe's Whse (1mi), Radio Shack, Walmart SuperCtr (1mi) |
| **88** | Linwood, **W** gas: BP/dsl |
| **87** | US 29, US 70, US 52 (from nb), High Point, **W** other: H HOSPITAL, ✈ |
| **86** | Belmont Rd, **W** gas: Bill's Trkstp/dsl/scales/24hr/@ |
| **85** | Clark Rd, to NC 150 |
| **83** | NC 150 (from nb), to Spencer |
| **82** | US 29, US 70 (from sb), to Spencer |
| **81.5mm** | Yadkin River |
| **81** | Spencer, **E** gas: Exxon, **other:** camping |
| **79** | Spencer Shops SHS, Spencer, E Spencer |
| **76b a** | US 52, to Albemarle, Salisbury, **E** gas: BP, Exxon, RaceTrac/24hr, **food:** Applebee's, Gatti's Pizza, IHOP, LoneStar Steaks, Pancho Villa Mexican, Zaxby's, **lodging:** Day's Inn, Economy Inn, Happy Traveler Inn, |

**SALSBURY**

**CONCORD**

| | |
|---|---|
| **76b a** | Continued
Super 8, **other:** Aldi Foods, Circuit City, CVS Drug, Dodge, $Tree, Eckerd, Food Lion, GNC, Harley-Davidson, Lowe's Whse, Marshall's, Staples, Tire Kingdom, Walgreens, **W** gas: 76/Circke K/dsl, Wilco/Hess/dsl, **food:** Blue Bay Seafood, Bojangles, Burger King, C&H Rest., Capt D's, Chick-fil-A, Christo's Rest., Cookout, Cracker Barrel, Hardee's, Honey Baked Ham, KFC, McDonald's, O'Charley's, Outback Steaks, Pizza Hut, Starbucks, Taco Bell, Tokyo Express, Wendy's, **lodging:** Comfort Suites, **other:** H HOSPITAL, Advance Parts, AutoZone, Family$, Firestone/auto, Goodyear/auto, K-Mart, Office Depot, USPO, Walmart SuperCtr |
| **75** | US 601, Jake Alexander Blvd, **E** food: Arby's, Farmhouse Rest., **lodging:** Travelodge, **other:** Dan Nicholas Park, NAPA, **W** gas: BP, Citgo, Exxon/dsl, Shell/dsl, **food:** Casa Grande, Ichiban Japanese, Ryan's, Sagebrush Steaks, Subway, Waffle House, Wendy's, **lodging:** Best Western, Hampton Inn, Holiday Inn, **other:** Chevrolet/Cadillac, Chrysler/Jeep, Ford, Honda/Kia, Magic Mart, Toyota |
| **74** | Julian Rd |
| **72** | Peach Orchard Rd, **W** ✈ |
| **71** | Peeler Rd, **E** gas: Derrick Trkstp/Shell/CW's Cafe/dsl/24hr/scales, **W** gas: Hess/Wilco/Bojangles/Subway/dsl/scales/24hr, **other:** auto/dsl repair |
| **70** | Webb Rd, **E** flea mkt, **W** st patrol |
| **68** | US 29, US 601, to Rockwell, China Grove, **1 mi W** gas: Gary's BBQ, Hardee's |
| **63** | Kannapolis, **E** gas: Pilot/Subway/dsl/scales, **food:** Waffle House, **lodging:** Best Value |
| **60** | Earnhardt Rd, Copperfield Blvd, **E** gas: Exxon/dsl, BP, **food:** Bob Evans, Bojangles, Cracker Barrel, **lodging:** Hampton Inn, Sleep Inn, **other:** H HOSPITAL, Discount Tire, **W** gas: BP/dsl, **food:** Brewster's, Carino's Italian, Casa Grande Mexican, Dragon Wok, Firehouse Subs, Five Guys Burgers, Logan's Roadhouse, McDonald's, Pizza Pazzo, Ruby Tuesday, Steak & Shake, Subway, Taco Bell, Wendy's, Yamaya Japanese, **lodging:** Holiday Inn Express, **other:** Kohl's, Lowe's Whse, Sam's Club/gas, Walmart SuperCtr, visitor info |
| **59mm** | **rest area both lanes, full** ♿ **facilities,** 🚻 **vending,** 🏞️**, litter barrels, petwalk** |
| **58** | US 29, US 601, Concord, **E** gas: BP, Citgo, Exxon, Petro Express, Shell/dsl, **food:** Applebee's, Burger King, Capt D's, Chick-fil-A, Chili's, El Vallarta Mexican, Fuji Asian, Golden Corral, KFC, Little Caesar's, Longhorn Steaks, Mayflower Seafood, McDonald's, Moe's SW Grill, Mr C's Rest., O'Charley's, Pizza Hut, Starbucks, Subway, Taco Bell, Waffle House, Wendy's, **lodging:** Holiday Inn Express, Howard Johnson, Mayfair Motel, **other:** H HOSPITAL, Belk, Cadillac, Chrysler/Dodge/Jeep, Eckerd, Food Lion, Harris Teeter, JC Penney, Sears/auto, Staples, U-Haul, Walgreen, mall, st patrol, **W** gas: BP, **food:** CiCi's, Bojangles (2mi), Domino's, IHOP, Ryan's, **lodging:** Comfort Inn, Econolodge, Fairfield Inn, Mainstay Suites, Microtel, **other:** $General, Drug Emporium, Eddie's Pizza/funpark, Fred's Store, Hancock Fabrics, Home Depot, vet |
| **55** | NC 73, to Davidson, Concord, **E** gas: Exxon/dsl, Shell, **food:** McDonald's, Waffle House, **W** gas: Shell/Huddle House, 76/Circle K/dsl, World Gas, **lodging:** Day's Inn |

## INTERSTATE 85 CONT'D

**N ↑ S**

**54** Kannapolis Pkwy, George W. Lyle Pkwy, **E gas:** Citgo, **food:** Backyard Burger, China Garden, Noodles & Co, Quizno's, **other:** CVS Drug, FoodLion, Harris Teeter, Walgreen, **W other:** Best Buy, Marshall's, Steinmart, PetsMart, Target

**52** Poplar Tent Rd, **E gas:** Shell/dsl, **food:** R&R BBQ, **other:** to Lowe's Speedway, museum, **W gas:** Accel/dsl, Exxon/24hr

**49** Bruton Smith Blvd, Concord Mills Blvd, **E gas:** BP/McDonalds, Shell/dsl, Texaco, **food:** Arby's, Bob Evans, Bojangles, Carrabbas, ChuckeCheese, Cookout, Cracker Barrel, 5 Guys Burgers, Hooters, KFC/Taco Bell, Quizno's, Jack-in-the-Box, Ruby Tuesday, Sonic, Starbucks, Subway, Sonny's BBQ, TX Land & Cattle, TX Roadhouse, Waffle House, Wendy's, Zaxby's, **lodging:** Comfort Suites, Embassy Suites, Hampton Inn, Holiday Inn Express, Sleep Inn, SpringHill Suites, Suburban Lodge, Wingate Inn, **other:** BJ's Whse/gas, Fleetwood RV camping (1.5mi), Harley-Davidson, Honda, Tom Johnson RV Ctr (1.5mi), Toyota/Scion, to Lowes Motor Speedway, **W gas:** Citgo, Petro Express, **food:** Applebee's, Charanda Mexican, Chick-fil-A, Foster's Grille, Mayflower Seafood, McAlisters Deli, Olive Garden, On-the-Border, Panera Bread, Razzoo's Cafe, Red Lobster, Roadhouse Grill, Ryan's, Steak'n Shake, Sticky Fingers, TGI Friday, **other:** BassPro Shops, BooksAMillion, Circuit City, Discount Tire, $Tree, Concord Mills Mall, Goodyear, PetCo, Radio Shack, Ross, TJ Maxx

**48** I-485, to US 29

**46** Mallard Creek Church Rd, **E gas:** Exxon/24hr, Wilco/dsl (1mi), **other:** Research Park, **W gas:** Petro Express, **food:** Firehouse Subs, Hickory Tavern

**CHARLOTTE**

**45** Harris Blvd, **E gas:** BP, **food:** Applebee's, BBQ, Bojangles, Burger King, Cheddar's, Chili's, Chick-fil-A, IHOP, Logan's Roadhouse, Max&Erma's, McDonald's, Shoney's, Smokey Bones, Taco Bell, TGIFriday, TX Land & Cattle, Waffle House, **lodging:** Comfort Suites (1mi), Courtyard, Drury Inn, Hampton Inn, Hilton, Holiday Inn, Homewood Suites, Residence Inn, Sleep Inn, **other:** H HOSPITAL, Best Buy, Food Lion, GNC, Kohl's, Lowe's Whse, Michael's, Office Depot, Old Navy, Radio Shack, Sam's Club, Walgreen, Walmart/auto, mall, to UNCC, U Research Park, **0-2 mi W gas:** Citgo, Shell, **food:** Longhorn Steaks, Macaroni Grill, McDonald's, Subway, Wendy's, **other:** Food Lion, Rite Aid

**43** to City Blvd

**42** US 29 (nb only)

**41** Sugar Creek Rd, **E gas:** BP, RaceWay, Shell/dsl, **food:** Bojangles, McDonald's, Taco Bell, Wendy's, **lodging:** Best Western, Best Value, Brookwood Inn, Continental Inn, Econolodge, Garden Inn, Microtel, **W gas:** 76/Circle K, **food:** Cookout, Dominic's Cafe, Sugar's Rest., Texas Ranch Steaks, **lodging:** Comfort Inn, Country Hearth Inn, Day's Inn, Ramada Inn, Rodeway Inn, Super 8

**40** Graham St, **E gas:** Exxon/dsl, **lodging:** Budget Inn, **other:** Ford Trucks, UPS, Western Star, **W gas:** Citgo, **other:** Freightliner

**39** Statesville Ave, **gas:** Pilot/Subway/dsl/scales/24hr, **other:** CarQuest, **gas:** Citgo, Shell/dsl, **food:** Bojangles, **other:** Family$

**CHARLOTTE**

**38** I-77, US 21, N to Statesville, S to Columbia

**37** Beatties Ford Rd, **E gas:** Citgo, Phillips 66/dsl, Shell/dsl, **food:** Burger King, KFC/LJ Silver, McDonald's, Subway, Taco Bell, Top's China, **other:** CVS Drug, **W gas:** BP

**36** NC 16, Brookshire Blvd, **E gas:** BP/dsl, **food:** China City, **lodging:** Brookshire Inn, **other:** H HOSPITAL, repair, **W gas:** Exxon, RaceWay, Sunoco, **food:** Bojangles, Burger King, Jack-in-the-Box, Subway

**35** Glenwood Dr, **E lodging:** Knight's Inn, **W gas:** Shell/dsl

**34** NC 27, Freedom Dr, **E gas:** BP/dsl, 76/Circle K, Shell, Walker/gas, **food:** Beauregard's Rest, Bojangles, Capt D's, Freedom Rest., Gilligan's Rest., KFC, McDonald's, Pizza Hut, Subway, Taco Bell, Tung Hoy Chinese, Wendy's, **other:** Advance Parts, K-Mart, Mr Transmission, Rite Aid, Walgreen, U-Haul, **W food:** The Cafe Room, **lodging:** Real Value Inn, **other:** JiffyLube

**33** US 521, Billy Graham Pkwy, **E gas:** 76/Circle K/dsl, Shell, **food:** Bojangles, KFC/Taco Bell, Krystal, McDonald's, Wendy's, **lodging:** Comfort Suites, Day's Inn, Sheraton, Springhill Suites, **other:** to Coliseum, ✈, **W gas:** Exxon/dsl, **food:** Cracker Barrel, Prime Sirloin, Waffle House/24hr, **lodging:** Best Value, La Quinta, Quality Inn, Red Roof

**32** Little Rock Rd, **E gas:** Shell, **food:** Hardee's, Waffle House, **lodging:** Airport Inn, Courtyard, Holiday Inn, **other:** Toyota, **W gas:** Exxon/dsl, **food:** Arby's, Hardee's, Little Rock Deli, Showmar's Rest., Shoney's, Subway, **lodging:** Best Western, Country Inn Suites, Wingate Inn, **other:** Family$, Gerrard Tires, Rite Aid

**30** I-485, to I-77, Pineville

**29** Sam Wilson Rd, **E gas:** BP (1mi), **W gas:** Shell/dsl

**28mm** weigh sta both lanes

**27.5mm** Catawba River

**27** NC 273, Mt Holly, **E gas:** Exxon/dsl, **food:** Arby's, Capt's Seafood, KFC, Niyoshi Japanese, Pizza Hut, Subway, Taco Bell, Waffle House, Wendy's, **other:** Chevrolet, College Park Drug, Family$, Food Lion, Lowe's Whse, NAPA, Radio Shack, Rite Aid, Roses, Walgreen, Walmart SuperCtr, **W gas:** BP/dsl, **lodging:** Holiday Inn Express

**26** **E gas:** BP, Petro Xpress, **food:** Bojangles, Grand Buffet, Hardee's, McDonald's, New China, Papa John's, **lodging:** Hampton Inn, **other:** Advance Parts, Aldi Foods, BiLo, Chrysler/Jeep, Ford, **W** Belmont Abbey Coll

**24mm** South Fork River

**23** NC 7, McAdenville, **W gas:** Exxon/dsl, **food:** Hardee's, Hillbilly's BBQ/Steaks

## INTERSTATE 85 CONT'D

**N ↕ S**

| | |
|---|---|
| **22** | Cramerton, Lowell, **E** **gas:** Hess, Petro Xpress, **food:** Applebee's, Burger King, Chick-fil-A, Dynasty Buffet, Gator's Rest., Hooters, Jack-in-the-Box, Logan's Roadhouse, Moe's SW Grill, Schlotsky's, Shane's Rib Shack, Zaxby's, **other:** Chevrolet/Cadillac, Circuit City, Discount Tire, Honda, Mazda, Kia, Kohl's, Lincoln/Mercury, Misubishi, Nissan, PetsMart, Sam's Club, U-Haul |
| **21** | Cox Rd, **E** **gas:** Exxon, Petro Xpress, **food:** Arby's, Backyard Burger, Chick-fil-A, Chili's, ChuckeCheese, Cookout, Golden Corral, Jackson's Cafeteria, Krispy Kreme, Logan's Roadhouse, Longhorn Steaks, McDonald's, Olive Garden, On-the-Border, Panera Bread, Pizza Inn, Ryan's, Ruby Tuesday, Steak&Shake, Subway, **other:** AAA, Best Buy, BooksAMillion, BiLo/24hr, Dodge, Discount Tire, $Tree, Ford/Lincoln/Mercury, Harley-Davidson, Harris-Teeter/24hr, Home Depot, K-mart, Kohl's, Lowe's Whse, Mazda, Michael's, Nissan, Old Navy, PepBoys, Radio Shack, Ross, Ryan's, Tire Kingdom, Walgreen, Walmart SuperCtr, mall, vet, **W** **gas:** Citgo, **food:** Arby's, IHOP, **lodging:** Super 8, **other:** H HOSPITAL, Harley-Davidson, Rite Aid |
| **20** | NC 279, New Hope Rd, **E** **gas:** Shell, Texaco, **food:** Arby's, Burger King, Capt D's, Checker's, Hong Kong Buffet, McDonald's, Morrison's Cafeteria, O'Charley's, Pizza Hut, Red Lobster, Sake Japanese, Shoney's, Taco Bell, **lodging:** Holiday Inn Express, Ramada Ltd, **other:** Advance Parts, AutoZone, Belk, Dillard's, Firestone/auto, JC Penney, K-Mart, NAPA, Office Depot, Sears/auto, Target, TJ Maxx, mall, **W** **food:** Bojangles, Cracker Barrel, KFC, Outback Steaks, Waffle House, **lodging:** Best Western, Comfort Suites, Courtyard, Fairfield Inn, Hampton Inn, **other:** H HOSPITAL, CarMax |
| **19** | NC 7, E Gastonia, **E** **gas:** Shell |
| **17** | US 321, Gastonia, **E** **gas:** Exxon/dsl/LP, **food:** Los Arcos Mexican, **lodging:** Day's Inn, **other:** Family$, **W** **gas:** Citgo/dsl, Perto Xpress/dsl, **food:** Wendy's, Western Sizzlin, **lodging:** Holiday Inn Express, Microtel, Motel 6 |
| **14** | NC 274, E Bessemer, **E** **food:** Burger King (1mi), McDonald's (1mi), **W** **gas:** BP/Subway, Citgo/dsl, **food:** Bojangles, Waffle House, **lodging:** Express Inn |
| **13** | Edgewood Rd, Bessemer City, **E** to Crowders Mtn SP, **W** **gas:** Exxon/dsl/24hr, **lodging:** Economy Inn |
| **10b a** | US 74 W, US 29, Kings Mtn |
| **8** | NC 161, to Kings Mtn, **E** **lodging:** Holiday Inn Express, **other:** camping, **W** **gas:** BP, **food:** McDonald's, Mi Pueblito Mexican, Taco Bell, Waffle House, Wendy's, **lodging:** Quality Inn, Travelodge, **other:** H HOSPITAL |
| **6mm** | **rest area sb, full** ♿ **facilities,** 🕿, 🍴, **litter barrels, vending, petwalk** |
| **5** | Dixon School Rd, **E** **gas:** Citgo/Subway/dsl, **other:** truck/tire repair |
| **4** | US 29 S (from sb) |
| **2.5mm** | **Welcome Ctr nb, full** ♿ **facilities, info,** 🕿, **vending,** 🍴, **litter barrels, petwalk** |
| **2** | NC 216, Kings Mtn, **E** to Kings Mtn Nat Military Park |
| **0mm** | North Carolina/South Carolina state line |

**GASTONIA**

## INTERSTATE 95

**N ↕ S** **ROANOKE RAPIDS**

| Exit # | Services |
|---|---|
| **181mm** | North Carolina/Virginia state line, **Welcome Ctr sb, full** ♿ **facilities,** 🕿, 🍴, **litter barrels, vending, petwalk** |
| **180** | NC 48, to Gaston, to Lake Gaston, Pleasant Hill, **W** **gas:** Pilot/Subway/dsl/scales/24hr |
| **176** | NC 46, to Garysburg, **W** **gas:** Shell, **food:** Aunt Sarah's, Burger King, **lodging:** Best Western |
| **174mm** | Roanoke River |
| **173** | US 158, Roanoke Rapids, Weldon, **E** **gas:** BP/dsl, Shell/Blimpie, Texaco/dsl, **food:** Ralph's BBQ, Waffle House, **lodging:** Day's Inn, Interstate Inn/RV Park, Orchard Inn, **other:** H HOSPITAL, **W** **gas:** BP/dsl, Exxon/DQ/Stuckey's, RaceWay, Shell, **food:** Applebee's, Arby's, Burger King, Chick-fil-A, Cici's Pizza, Cracker Barrel, Hardee's, J&L Grill, KFC, Little Caesar's, Logan's Roadhouse, Lonestar Steaks, Mayflower Seafood, McDonald's, New China, Pizza Hut, Ruby Tuesday, Ryan's, Starbucks, Subway, Super King Buffet, Texas Steaks, Waffle House, Wendy's, **lodging:** Comfort Suites, Hampton Inn, Jameson Inn, Motel 6, Sleep Inn, **other:** Advance Parts, AutoZone, Belk, Biglots, $General, $Tree, Firestone/auto, Food Lion, Goody's, Harley Davidson, Lowe's Whse, Radio Shack, Rite Aid, Staples, Walgreens, Walmart SuperCtr/gas |
| **171** | NC 125, Roanoke Rapids, **E** **food:** Olive Garden, **W** **gas:** Texaco/dsl, **food:** Chick-fil-A (2mi), Ryan's (2mi), Wendy's (2mi), **lodging:** Hilton Garden, Holiday Inn Express, **other:** Parton Theater, st patrol |
| **168** | NC 903, to Halifax, **E** **gas:** Exxon/Subway/dsl, Shell/Burger King/dsl, **W** **gas:** Oasis/Dunkin Donuts/LP/dsl |
| **160** | NC 561, to Brinkleyville, **E** **gas:** Exxon/24hr, **W** **gas:** Citgo/dsl/rest. |
| **154** | NC 481, to Enfield, 1mi **W** **other:** KOA |
| **152mm** | weigh sta both lanes |
| **150** | NC 33, to Whitakers, **E** golf, **W** **gas:** BP/Subway/DQ/Stuckey's/dsl |
| **145** | NC 4, to US 301, Battleboro, **E** **gas:** BP/dsl, Exxon/DQ, **food:** BBQ, Denny's, 4Seasons, Hardee's, Shoney's, Waffle House, Wendy's, **lodging:** Best Value, Best Western/rest., Budget Inn, Comfort Inn, Day's Inn, Deluxe Inn, Guesthouse Inn, Howard Johnson, Red Carpet Inn, Rodeway Inn |
| **142mm** | **rest area both lanes, full** ♿ **facilities,** 🕿, 🍴, **litter barrels, vending, petwalk** |
| **141** | NC 43, Red Oak, **E** **gas:** BP/dsl, Exxon/dsl/LP, 3mi **food:** Chick-fil-A, Ruby Tuesday, **lodging:** Days Inn (4mi), Quality Inn (4mi), **W** **lodging:** Econolodge |
| **138** | US 64, 1 mi **E** on Winstead **gas:** BP, Exxon, **food:** Cracker Barrel, Gardner's BBQ, Outback Steaks, Texas Steaks, **lodging:** Comfort Inn, Courtyard, Hampton Inn, Holiday Inn, Residence Inn, **other:** H HOSPITAL, Buick/Pontiac/GMC, Harley-Davidson, Honda, to Cape Hatteras Nat Seashore |

## INTERSTATE 95 CONT'D

| | |
|---|---|
| **132** | to NC 58, **E** gas: Pitstop/dsl, **1 mi** **W** gas: BP/dsl |
| **128mm** | Tar River |
| **127** | NC 97, to Stanhope, **E** gas: BP/dsl, other: ✈ |
| **121** | US 264a, Wilson, **E** gas: Citgo/Subway, Eagle Gas, Kangaroo/dsl/LP, Shell, **food:** KFC/LJ Silver, Waffle House, **lodging:** Quality Inn, **other:** H HOSPITAL, **3-4 mi** **E** gas: BP, Exxon, Hess/dsl, **food:** Applebee's, Arby's, Burger King, Chick-fil-A, Chili's, CiCi's, Coldstone Creamery, Denny's, El Tapatio, Golden Corral, Hardee's, Ruby Tuesday, Sonic, Starbucks, Subway, Texas Steaks, Wendy's, **lodging:** Candlewood Suites, Comfort Inn, **other:** H HOSPITAL, Aldi Foods, Belk, BooksAMillion, Chrysler/Jeep/Dodge, $General, Farmfresh Foods, Goody's, Harris-Teeter, Home Depot, Honda, Lowe's Whse, Marshall's, PetsMart, Ross, Staples, Target, Toyota/Scion, Walmart SuperCtr/dsl, **W** gas: BP/dsl, **food:** Bojangles, Burger King, Cracker Barrel, McDonald's, **lodging:** Country Inn Suites, Fairfield Inn, Hampton Inn, Holiday Inn Express, Jameson Inn, Microtel, Sleep Inn, **other:** to Country Doctor Museum |
| **119b a** | US 264, US 117 |
| **116** | NC 42, to Clayton, Wilson, **E** gas: Shell/dsl, other: H HOSPITAL, **W** gas: BP/dsl, **other:** Rock Ridge Camping |
| **107** | US 301, Kenly, **E** gas: BP/dsl, Eagle Gas, Exxon/McDonald's/dsl, Fuel Doc, PitStop/Subway, **food:** Moore's BBQ, Nik's Pizza, Patrick's Rest., **lodging:** Budget Inn, Deluxe Inn, Econolodge, **other:** CarQuest, Food Lion, Ford, Family$, Kinley Tires, Tobacco Museum |
| **106** | Truck Stop Rd, Kenly, **E** gas: ⚡FLYING J/CountryMkt/dsl/LP/scales/24hr, **W** gas: Shell, TA/Wendy's/dsl/24hr/scales/@, Wilco/Hess/Arby's/dsl/scales/24hr/scales, **food:** Waffle House, **lodging:** Day's Inn, Super 8, **other:** Blue Beacon, Speedco Lube, Truck-o-Mat |
| **105.5mm** | Little River |
| **105** | Bagley Rd, Kenly, **E** gas: Big Boys/Shell/Pizza/dsl/scales/24hr |
| **102** | Micro, **W** gas: Shop'N-Go, **food:** Backdoor Cafe, **other:** USPO |
| **101** | Pittman Rd |
| **99mm** | **rest area both lanes, full** ♿ **facilities, vending,** ☕, 🍴, **litter barrels, petwalk, hist marker** |
| **98** | to Selma, **E** other: RVacation |
| **97** | US 70 A, to Pine Level, Selma, **E** gas: Citgo/dsl/24hr, Savannah's Gas/dsl, **food:** Denny's, Southern Buffet, Subway, **lodging:** Holiday Inn Express, **other:** J&R Outlet, **W** gas: BP/dsl, Exxon/dsl/24hr, Shell/dsl, **food:** Bojangles, Carolina Cookout, China Buffet, Golden China, KFC, McDonald's, Shoney's, Waffle House, **lodging:** Comfort Inn, Day's Inn, Hampton Inn, Masters Inn, Quality Inn, Regency Inn, Royal Inn, **other:** H HOSPITAL |
| **95** | US 70, Smithfield, **E** lodging: Log Cabin Motel/rest., Howard Johnson Express, Village Motel, **other:** Ava Gardner Museum, **W** gas: Hess, Shell, Sunoco, |

| | |
|---|---|
| **95** | Continued **food:** Bob Evans, Burger King, Checker's, CiCi's Pizza, Coldstone Creamery, Cracker Barrel, El Sombrero Mexican, Outback Steaks, Ruby Tuesday, Smithfield BBQ (2mi), Texas Steaks, Waffle House, Zaxby's, **lodging:** Best Western, Jameson Inn, Sleep Inn, Super 8, **other:** Harley-Davidson, Carolina Premium Outlets/famous brands |
| **93** | Brogden Rd, Smithfield, **W** gas: BP/dsl, Citgo |
| **91.5mm** | Neuse River |
| **90** | US 301, US 701, to Newton Grove, **E** gas: BP/dsl, Citgo/dsl, **lodging:** Travelers Inn, **other:** KOA, Ronnie's Tires, to Bentonville Bfd, **W** gas: Exxon/dsl, **lodging:** Four Oaks Lodging/RV Park |
| **87** | NC 96, Four Oaks, **W** gas: BP/dsl, **food:** Subway |
| **81b a** | I-40, E to Wilmington, W to Raleigh |
| **79** | NC 50, to NC 27, Benson, Newton Grove, **E** gas: BP/dsl, Citgo, **food:** Waffle House, **lodging:** Dutch Inn, **other:** auto repair, **W** gas: Mobil/McDonald's, Phillips 66/Burger King, Pure, **food:** Charro Mexican, China 8, Domino's, KFC, Pizza Hut, Subway, **lodging:** Day's Inn, **other:** Family$, Food Lion, Kerr Drug |
| **77** | Hodges Chapel Rd, **E** gas: Pilot/Subway/dsl/scales/24hr |
| **75** | Jonesboro Rd, **W** gas: Sadler's/Shell/DQ/Quizno's/dsl/24hr/@, Texaco/Milestone Diner |
| **73** | US 421, NC 55, to Dunn, Clinton, **E** food: Cracker Barrel, Wendy's, **other:** Chrysler/Jeep, Family$, Food Lion, **W** gas: Exxon/dsl, Hess/dsl, Shell, **food:** Bojangles, Burger King, Dairy Freeze, Sagebrush Steaks, Subway, Taco Bell, Triangle Waffle, **lodging:** Econolodge, Hampton Inn, Holiday Inn Express, Jameson Inn, Ramada Inn/rest., **other:** IGA Foods, museum |
| **72** | Pope Rd, **E** lodging: Comfort Inn, Red Carpet Inn, Royal Inn, **W** gas: BP, Pure, **food:** Brass Lantern Steaks, Prime Rib, **lodging:** Budget Inn, Express Inn, **other:** Cadillac/GMC |
| **71** | Longbranch Rd, **E** gas: Citgo/Hardee's/dsl/scales/24hr, **W** to Averasboro Bfd |
| **70** | SR 1811, **E** lodging: Relax Inn |
| **65** | NC 82, Godwin, **W** Children's Home |
| **61** | to Wade, **E** gas: Citgo/dsl, **other:** KOA (1mi), **W** gas: BP/Subway/dsl/24hr |

**WILSON** N↕S

**SELMA**

**DUNN**

**NC**

## INTERSTATE 95 CONT'D

**N** ↑ **S**

**F A Y E T T E V I L L E**

**L U M B E R T O N**

**NC**

| | |
|---|---|
| **58** | US 13, to Newton Grove, I-295 to Fayetteville, **E** **gas:** Eastgate, Shell, **food:** Quizno's, **lodging:** Day's Inn/rest. |
| **56** | Lp 95, to US 301 (from sb), Fayetteville, **W** **gas:** Epco/dsl, Kangaroo/24hr, **lodging:** Budget Inn, **other:** H HOSPITAL, to Ft Bragg, Pope AFB |
| **55** | NC 1832, Murphy Rd, **W** **gas:** Epco/dsl, Kangaroo/24hr, **lodging:** Scottish Inn |
| **52** | NC 24, Fayetteville, **W** **other:** to Ft Bragg, Pope AFB, botanical gardens, museum |
| **49** | NC 53, NC 210, Fayetteville, **E** **gas:** Citgo, Exxon, Kangaroo, Mobil, **food:** Burger King, McDonald's, Pizza Hut, Taco Bell, Waffle House, **lodging:** Deluxe Inn, Motel 6, Quality Inn, **W** **gas:** BP/Subway/dsl, Exxon/dsl, Shell/dsl, **food:** Cracker Barrel, Fuller's BBQ, Ruby Tuesday, Shoney's, **lodging:** Best Western, Comfort Inn, Days Inn, Econolodge, Fairfield Inn, Fayetteville Hotel, Hampton Inn, Holiday Inn, Red Roof Inn, Sleep Inn, Super 8 |
| **48mm** | **rest area both lanes, full** 🚻 **facilities,** 📞, 🍽, **litter barrels, vending, petwalk** |
| **47mm** | Cape Fear River |
| **46b a** | NC 87, to Fayetteville, Elizabethtown, **W** **other:** H HOSPITAL, museum, Civic Ctr, to Agr Expo Ctr |
| **44** | Claude Lee Rd, **W** **other:** Lazy Acres Camping, to ✈ |
| **41** | NC 59, to Hope Mills, Parkton, **E** **gas:** Kangaroo/24hr, **W** **gas:** BP/dsl, **other:** Lake Waldo Camping, Spring Valley RV Park |
| **40** | Lp 95, to US 301 (from nb), to Fayetteville, facilities on US 301 (5-7mi) |
| **33** | US 301, St Pauls, **E** **gas:** BP/dsl/repair/24hr |
| **31** | NC 20, to St Pauls, Raeford, **E** **gas:** BP, Mobil/McDonald's, Pit Row Gas, Shell/Huddle House/dsl/24hr, **food:** Burger King, **lodging:** Day's Inn, **other:** Volvo Trucks, **W** **gas:** Citgo, Exxon/dsl, **other:** FoodLion |
| **25** | US 301, **E** **gas:** BP/dsl |
| **24mm** | weigh sta both lanes |
| **22** | US 301, **E** **gas:** Exxon, Shell/DQ, **food:** Burger King, China Wok, Denny's, Hardee's, Huddle House, John's Rest, Outback Steaks, Quizno's, Ruby Tuesday, Ryan's, San Jose Mexican, Smithfield BBQ, Texas Steaks, Waffle House, Wendy's, Zaxby's, **lodging:** Best Western, Comfort Suites, Hampton Inn, Holiday Inn, Super 8, **other:** Black's Tire, $Tree, Goody's, Lowe's Foods, Lowe's Whse, Office Depot, Walmart SuperCtr, st patrol, **W** **gas:** Circle B, Sun-Do/dsl, Pure/dsl, **other:** Ford/Lincoln/Mercury, Sam's Club/gas |
| **20** | NC 211, to NC 41, Lumberton, **E** **gas:** Citgo, Exxon/dsl, Liberty/dsl, **food:** Arby's, Bojangles, Buger King, Capt D's, Golden City Chinese, Hardee's, KFC, Little Caesar's, McDonald's, River City Grill, Shoney's, Sonic, Subway, Taco Bell, Tokyo Express, Waffle House, **lodging:** Econolodge, Howard Johnson, Quality Inn, **other:** H HOSPITAL, Advance Parts, Belk, CVS Drug, |

| | |
|---|---|
| **20** | Continued Food Lion/deli, JC Penney, K-Mart, Walgreens, **W** **gas:** Shell/dsl, Sun-do/dsl, **food:** Cracker Barrel, Fuller's BBQ Buffet, LungWah Chinese, San Jose Mexican, **lodging:** Best Value Inn, Comfort Inn, Country Inn&Suites, Day's Inn/rest., Econolodge, Fairfield Inn |
| **19** | Carthage Rd, Lumberton, **E** **gas:** BP/dsl, **lodging:** Travelers Inn, **W** **gas:** Circle B, Exxon/dsl, **lodging:** Knight's Inn, Motel 6 |
| **18mm** | Lumber River |
| **17** | NC 72, **E** **gas:** Atkinson's/dsl, BP/dsl, Dobb's/Stuckey's/Wendy's, Go-Gas/dsl, Mobil/dsl, **food:** Burger King, Hardee's, Huddle House, McDonald's, Subway, Waffle House, **lodging:** Budget Inn, Southern Inn, **other:** Advance Parts, AutoZone, Food Lion |
| **14** | US 74, to Laurinburg, Maxton, **W** **gas:** BP/dsl, **other:** Sleepy Bear's RV Camp |
| **13** | US 74, to Wilmington |
| **10** | US 301, to Fairmont |
| **7** | to McDonald, Raynham |
| **5mm** | **Welcome Ctr nb, full** 🚻 **facilities,** 📞, 🍽, **litter barrels, vending, petwalk** |
| **2** | NC 130, to NC 904, Rowland |
| **1b a** | US 301, US 501, Dillon, **E** **gas:** Exxon, Shell, **food:** Hot Tamale Rest., Pedro's Diner, Porky's Truckstp, **lodging:** Budget Motel, South-of-the-Border Motel, **other:** Pedro's Campground, **W** **gas:** Shell/dsl, Sun-Do, **food:** Waffle House, **lodging:** Day's Inn, Super 8 |
| **0mm** | North Carolina/South Carolina state line |

## INTERSTATE 240 - ASHEVILLE

| Exit # | Services |
|---|---|
| **9mm** | I-240 begins/ends on I-40, exit 53b a. |
| **8** | Fairview Rd, **N** **gas:** Shell/Blimpie, **food:** Buddie's Ribs&BBQ, Burger King, J&S Cafeteria, KFC, Little Caesar's, Little Venice, McDonald's, Subway, **lodging:** Best Western, Ramada Inn, **other:** Advance Parts, Bilo Foods, CVS Drug, Hamrick's, Kohl's, PetsMart, Subaru, Walmart SuperCtr **S** **gas:** Citgo, **food:** Pizza Hut, Rezeals Rest., **other:** Aldi Foods, Home Depot |
| **7.5mm** | Swannanoa River |
| **7** | US 70, **N** U-Haul, **S** **gas:** BP, Exxon/dsl, **food:** Applebee's, Bonefish Grill, Burger King, Carrabba's, Cheeseburger Paradise, Chili's, China Palace, Chucke-Cheese, Cornerstone Rest., Cracker Barrel, Don Pablo, DQ, East Buffet, Frank's Pizza, Greenery Rest., Guadalahara Mexican, Ham's Rest., Hooters, IHOP, Joe's Crabshack, Lonestar Steaks, Longhorn Steaks, Mikado, Mtn Ear Inn, O'Charley's, Olive Garden, Outback Steaks, Red Lobster, Ruby's BBQ, Subway, Taco Bell, Waffle House, **lodging:** Best Western, Country Inn&Suites, Courtyard, Day's Inn, Econolodge, Extended Stay America, Hampton Inn, Homewood Suites, InTown Motor Inn, Royal Inn, Spring Hill Suites, **other:** Belk, Best Buy, Books-a-Million, Circuit City, Dillards, $Tree, Firestone, Goody's, |

## INTERSTATE 240 CONT'D - ASHEVILLE

**E ↕ W    ASHEVILLE**

| 7 | Continued |
|---|---|
| | Ingles Foods, K-Mart, Lowe's Whse, Michael's, Office Depot, Radio Shack, Ross, Sears/auto, Target, TJ Maxx, Walgreens |
| 6 | Tunnel Rd (from eb), same as 7 |
| 5b | US 70 E, US 74A, Charlotte St, **N gas:** BP, Pure, **food:** Charlotte St., Fuddruckers, Starbucks, Two Guys Hogi, **lodging:** B&B **S food:** Tripp's Rest., **lodging:** Best Western, Renaissance Motel, Civic Ctr |
| 5a | US 25, Merrymont Ave, **N gas:** Exxon/dsl, Shell, **food:** Bojangles, La Caterina, 3 Pigs BBQ, **other:** Staples |
| 4c | Haywood St (no EZ return to eb), Montford, **S food:** 3 Bros Rest. |
| 4b | Patton Ave (from eb), downtown |
| 4a | US 19 N, US 23 N, US 70 W, to Weaverville |
| 3b | Westgate, **N food:** Jae Thai, **lodging:** Crowne Plaza, **other:** CVS Drug, EarthFare Foods, NTB, Sam's Club/gas |
| 3a | US 19 S, US 23 S, W Asheville, **N gas:** BP, **food:** A&W/LJ Silver, Arby's, Bojangles, Denny's, Green Tea Japanese, KFC, Krispy Kreme, Little Caesar's, McDonald's, New 1 China, Nona Mia Italian, Pizza Hut, Ryan's, Subway, Taco Bell, Vera Cruz Mexican, Wendy's, **other:** Advance Parts, AutoZone, BiLo, Curves, Goodyear/auto, Ingles, Kerr Drug, K-Mart, Radio Shack, Sav-Mor Foods, vet |
| 2 | US 19, US 23, W Asheville, **N other:** B&B Drug, **S gas:** Shell |
| 1c | Amboy Rd (from eb) |
| 1b | NC 191, to I-40 E, Brevard Rd, **S other:** farmers mkt, camping |
| 1a | I-40 W, to Knoxville |
| 0mm | I-240 begins/ends on I-40, exit 46b a. |

## INTERSTATE 440 - RALIEGH

**E ↕ W    RALEIGH**

| Exit # | Services |
|---|---|
| 16 | I-40 |
| 15 | Poole Rd, **W gas:** BP/dsl, Citgo/dsl, **food:** Burger King, McDonald's, Subway KFC/Taco Bell |
| 14 | US 64, to Rocky Mount, limited access hwy |
| 13b a | US 64, US 264 E, New Bern Ave, to Wilson, **2-3 mi E gas:** BP, 76/Circle K, Exxon, Phillips 66 (1mi), Shell/Texaco, Speedway, Circle K, **food:** Arby's, Burger King, Checker's, Hardee's, K&S Cafeteria, Last Catch Grill, McDonald's, Miami Subs, O'Brian's, Papa John's, Pizza Hut, Subway, Taco Bell, Waffle House, Wendy's, **lodging:** Best Western, Holiday Inn Express, Microtel, Red Roof Inn, Super 8, **other:** Firestone/auto, Ford, Hamrick's, K-Mart, Kroger, Food Lion, Radio Shack, RV Ctr, Winn-Dixie, **W H** HOSPITAL |
| 12 | Yonkers Rd, Brentwood Rd |
| 11b a | US 1, US 401, Capital Blvd N, **N gas:** BP, Citgo, Crown Gas, Kangaroo, Shell, **food:** Applebee's (1mi), BBQ, Bojangle's, Buffalo Bro's, Burger King, Carver's Creek, Don Murray's BBQ, Dunkin Donuts, IHOP, |

**R A L E I G H**

| 11b a | Continued |
|---|---|
| | Mayflower Seafood, McDonald's, Outback Steaks, Perkins, Subway, Taco Bell, Vallerta Mexican, Waffle House, Wendy's, **lodging:** Best Western, Comfort Inn, Country Inn, Day's Inn, Econolodge, Holiday Inn, Homestead Suites, Hotel Europa, Lodge America, Sleep Inn, Travelodge, Wingate Inn, **other:** Eckerd, IGA Foods, USPO |
| 10 | Wake Forest Rd, **N food:** Denny's, **food:** Bajama Breze, **lodging:** AmeriSuites, Days Inn, Hilton, **other:** CVS Drug, **S gas:** BP, **food:** A&W/KFC, Applebee's, Bojangles, Jersey Mike's, Melting Pot Rest., Papa John's, Schlotzsky's, Taco Bell, **lodging:** Courtyard, Extended Stay America, Hampton Inn, Residence Inn, **other:** H HOSPITAL, Discount Tire, Staples |
| 8b a | 6 Forks Rd, North Hills, **N gas:** Exxon, **food:** Bonefish Grill, Panera Bread, Starbucks, **lodging:** Comfort Inn, **other:** Dillard's/JC Penney, GNC, Firestone/auto, Kerr Drug, Target, Winn-Dixie |
| 7b a | US 70, NC 50, Glenwood Ave, Crabtree Valley, **N gas:** BP, Exxon, **food:** McDonald's, PF Chang's, Ruby Tuesday, **lodging:** Candlewood Suites, Courtyard, Crabtree Inn, Fairfield Inn, Holiday Inn, La Quinta, Marriott, Motel 6, Residence Inn, Sheraton, **other:** Barnes&Noble, Belk, Goodyear/auto, Macy's, Sears/auto, mall |
| 6 | Ridge Rd (from nb), same as 7 |
| 5 | Lake Boone Tr, **W gas:** Phillips 66, **food:** McDonald's, Subway, Wendy's, **other:** H HOSPITAL, Eckerd, Food Lion |
| 4b a | to I-40 W, Wade Ave, **W** to I-40, RD ✈ |
| 3 | NC 54, Hillsboro St, **E gas:** BP, Citgo, Crowne Gas, Exxon, **food:** Arby's, Bean Sprout Chinese, Quizno's, Snoopy's Hotdogs, Waffle House, **lodging:** Ramada Inn, **other:** to Meredith Coll, to St Mary's |
| 2b a | Western Blvd, **E gas:** Crowne Gas, 76/Circle K, **food:** Domino's, Subway, **other:** to NCSU, Shaw U, **W** K-Mart |
| 1d | Melbourne Rd (from sb) |
| 1c | Jones-Franklin Rd |
| 1b a | I-40. I-440 begins on I-40., **1-2 mi W on Walnut St gas:** Exxon, Shell, **food:** Hardee's, Olive Garden, Pizza Hut, Red Lobster, **lodging:** Best Western, Day's Inn, Motel 6, **other:** Borders Books Michael's, mall |

**NC**

**ND**

N ↑ S

GRAND FORKS

FARGO

## INTERSTATE 29

| Exit # | Services |
|---|---|
| 218mm | North Dakota state line, US/Canada border |
| 217mm | US Customs sb |
| 216mm | historical site nb, tourist info sb |
| 215 | ND 59, rd 55, Pembina, **E gas:** Gastrak/dsl/DutyFree Store, Gastrak/pizza/dsl/scales/24hr, **other:** Pembina State Museum/info |
| 212 | no services |
| 208 | rd 1, to Bathgate |
| 203 | US 81, ND 5, to Hamilton, Cavalier, weigh sta both lanes |
| 200 | no services |
| 196 | rd 3, Bowesmont |
| 193 | no services |
| 191 | rd 11, to St Thomas |
| 187 | ND 66, to Drayton, **E gas:** Cenex/pizza/dsl, Tesoro/dsl, **food:** Andy's Drive Inn, Rte 66 Café, **lodging:** Motel 66, Red River Motel, **other:** USPO, city park |
| 184 | to Drayton, **2 mi E gas:** gas/dsl, **other:** USPO |
| 180 | rd 9 |
| 179mm | **rest area both lanes (both lanes exit left), full** ♿ **facilities,** 🚻, 🏕, **litter barrels, vending, petwalk** |
| 176 | ND 17, to Grafton, **10 mi W** Ⓗ HOSPITAL, gas, food, **lodging:** AmericInn |
| 172 | no services |
| 168 | rd 15, to Minto, Warsaw |
| 164 | no services |
| 161 | ND 54, rd 19, to Ardoch, Oslo |
| 157 | no services |
| 152 | US 81, to Gilby, Manvel, **W gas:** Manvel/dsl/food |
| 145 | US 81 bus, N Washington St, to Grand Forks |
| 141 | US 2, Gateway Dr, Grand Forks, **E gas:** BP/dsl/24hr, Loaf'N Jug/McDonald's/dsl/@, Stamart, Univ. Sta/dsl, **food:** Al's Grill, Burger King, Greatwall Buffet, GreenMill Rest., Northside Cafe, Papa Murphy's, **lodging:** Best Value, Budget Inn, Econolodge, Holiday Inn, Ramada Inn, Select Inn, Super 8, **other:** Advance Parts, Checker Parts, Chrysler/Dodge/Jeep/Toyota, Ford/Lincoln/Mercury, U-Haul, to U of ND, **1 mi E food:** DQ, Domino's, Taco John's, **other:** Ⓗ HOSPITAL, Freightliner, U-Haul, auto repair, **W gas:** Simonson/dsl/café/24hr/@, Stamart/Tesoro/dsl/RV dump/scales/@, **food:** Emerald Grill, Perkins, **lodging:** Settle Inn, **other:** Budget RV Ctr, port of entry/weigh sta, ✈, to AFB |
| 140 | DeMers Ave, **E gas:** BP, **food:** Overtime Grill, Red Pepper Cafe, **lodging:** Hilton Garden, **other:** Ⓗ HOSPITAL, Alerus Ctr, to U of ND |
| 138 | US 81, 32nd Ave S, **E gas:** BP, Holiday/Subway/dsl, Tesoro, **food:** Arby's, Boston's Grill, Buffalo Wild Wings, Burger King, Campbell's Burgers, China Garden, Coldstone's, Culver's, Domino's, DQ, Golden Corral, Grizzly's Steaks, Ground Round, Jimmy John Sandwiches, McDonald's, Papa Murphy's, Pizza Hut, Qdoba Mexican, Quizno's, Red Lobster, Starbucks, Taco Bell, Texas Roadhouse, Village Inn Rest., Wendy's, **lodging:** AmericInn, C'mon Inn, Comfort Inn, Country Inn Suites, Day's Inn, Fairfield Inn, Holiday Inn Express, Lakeview Inn, Roadking Inn, **other:** Best Buy, Cadillac, Chevrolet, Chrysler/Toyota, CVS Drug, $Tree, Ford/Lincoln/Mercury, Honda/Nissan, Hugo's Foods, Hyundai, JC Penney, |

| Exit # | Services |
|---|---|
| 138 | Continued Jo-Ann Fabrics, Kohl's, Lowe's Whse, Marshall Field, Macy's, Mazda, Michael's, Old Navy, PetCo, Sam's Club/gas, Sears/auto, Super 1 Foods, Target, Tires+, TJ Maxx, Walmart SuperCtr, mall, **W gas:** Conoco/Subway/dsl, **other:** Grand Forks Camping |
| 130 | ND 15, rd 81, Thompson, **1 mi W** gas, food |
| 123 | to Reynolds, **E** to Central Valley School |
| 119mm | insp sta, both lanes |
| 118 | to Buxton |
| 111 | ND 200 W, to Cummings, Mayville, **W other:** Big Top Fireworks, to Mayville St U |
| 104 | Hillsboro, **E gas:** Cenex/Burger King/dsl/LP/24hr/@, Tesoro/dsl/24hr, **food:** Country Hearth Rest., **lodging:** Hillsboro Inn, **other:** Ⓗ HOSPITAL, Hillsboro Drug, NAPA, RV park, USPO |
| 100 | ND 200 E, ND 200A, to Blanchard, Halstad |
| 99mm | **rest area both lanes, full** ♿ **facilities,** 🚻, 🏕, **litter barrels, vending, petwalk** |
| 92 | rd 11, Grandin, **E** Co-op/dsl, **W gas:** Stop-n-Shop/dsl |
| 86 | Gardner |
| 79 | Argusville |
| 74.5mm | Sheyenne River |
| 73 | rd 17, rd 22, Harwood, **E gas:** Cenex/pizza/dsl/LP/café/24hr |
| 69 | rd 20 |
| 67 | US 81 bus, 19th Ave N, **E** VA Ⓗ HOSPITAL, Hector Int ✈ |
| 66 | 12th Ave N, **E gas:** Stamart/Tesoro/dsl/24hr/scales, Stop'n Go, **other:** Ⓗ HOSPITAL, to ND St U, **W gas:** Cenex/dsl, **food:** Arby's, **lodging:** Microtel |
| 65 | US 10, Main Ave, W Fargo, **E gas:** Tesoro/dsl/24hr, **food:** Kroll's Diner, **other:** Checker Parts, NAPA, OK Tire, True Value, transmissions, **W gas:** Cenex/Subway/dsl, Simonson/dsl, Stop-n-Go, **food:** Hardee's, O'Kelly's Rest, Outback Steaks, Quizno's, Season Chinese, **lodging:** Best Western, **other:** Aamco, CarQuest, Chevrolet/Buick/Cadillac/Honda, Chrysler/Dodge/Jeep, Cummins dsl, Hyundai, Isuzu/Volvo/GMC, Kenworth, Mac's Hardware, Lincoln/Mercury, Saturn, Subaru, Toyota |
| 64 | 13th Ave, Fargo, **E gas:** Don's, StaMart/dsl, **food:** Acapulco Mexican, Applebees, Arby's, Burger King, DQ, Giant Panda Chinese, GreenMill Rest., Ground Round, Perkins/24hr, Quizno's, Starbucks, Subway, Taco John's, TCBY, Wendy's, **lodging:** AmericInn, Comfort Inn/Suites, Country Inn&Suites, Econolodge, Hampton Inn, Motel 6, Super 8, **other:** Advance Parts, Ace Hardware, CashWise Foods/drug/24hr, CVS Drug, Family$, Goodyear, SunMart Food, Tires+/transmissions, White's Drug, **W gas:** Cenex, Tesoro, **food:** Blimpie, Buffalo Wild Wings, Caribou Coffee, Chili's, Culver's, Denny's, DQ, Fuddrucker's, Grandma's Grill, Grizzly's, Godfather's, Happy Joe's Pizza, Hooters, KFC, Krispy Kreme, Kroll's Diner, LoneStar Steaks, McDonald's, Olive Garden, Paradiso Mexican, Pizza Hut, Red Lobster, Ruby Tuesday, Schlotsky's, Spitfire Grill, Taco Bell, Taco Time, Texas Roadhouse, TGIFriday, TimberLodge Steaks, **lodging:** Comfort Inn, Day's Inn, Fairfield Inn, Holiday Inn Express, Kelly Inn, Ramada Inn, Red River Lodge, Red Roof Inn, Select Inn, **other:** Advance Parts, Barnes&Noble, Best Buy, BigLots, Chevrolet, $Tree, GNC, Hancock Fabrics, Herberger's, Hornbacher's |

## INTERSTATE 29 CONT'D

**N ↕ S FARGO**

| | |
|---|---|
| **64** | Continued<br>Foods, JC Penney, Jo-Ann Crafts, Kohl's, Lowes Whse, Macy's, Menards, Michael's, Office Depot, Old Navy, PetCo, Sam's Club, Savers Foods, Sears/auto, Sportsman's Whse, SunMart Foods, Target, TJ Maxx, Walmart SuperCtr, Walgreens, USPO, mall |
| **63b a** | I-94, W to Bismarck, E to Minneapolis |
| **62** | 32nd Ave S, Fargo, **E** gas: F&F/dsl, Tesoro, **food:** Arby's, Country Kitchen, Culvers, KFC, Little Caesars, Moe's SW Grill, Papa John's, Quizno's, Starbucks, Subway, Taco John's, Village Inn, **other:** H HOSPITAL, Buick/Pontiac/GMC, Ford, Freightliner, JiffyLube, SunMart Foods, **W** gas: ⚑FLYING J/Conoco/dsl/LP/motel/24hr/@, **other:** Goodyear/auto, Peterbilt, PleasureLand RV Ctr |
| **60** | 52nd Ave S, to Fargo, **W other:** Starr Fireworks |
| **56** | to Wild Rice, Horace |
| **54** | rd 16, to Oxbow, Davenport |
| **50** | rd 18, Hickson |
| **48** | ND 46, to Kindred |
| **44** | to Christine, **1 mi E** gas |
| **42** | rd 2, to Walcott |
| **37** | rd 4, to Abercrombie, Colfax, **E** to Ft Abercrombie HS, **3 mi W** gas |
| **31** | rd 8, Galchutt |
| **26** | to Dwight |
| **24mm** | weigh sta both lanes exit left |
| **23b a** | ND 13, to Wahpeton, Mooreton, **10 mi E** H HOSPITAL, ND St Coll of Science |
| **15** | rd 16, to Mantador, Great Bend |
| **8** | ND 11, to Hankinson, Fairmount, **E** gas: Tesoro/dsl, **3 mi W** camping |

**E ↕ W FARGO**

| | |
|---|---|
| **3mm** | Welcome Ctr nb, full ♿ facilities, 🚻, 🏕, litter barrels, petwalk, RV dump |
| **2** | rd 22 |
| **1** | rd 1E, **E** Dakota Magic Casino/Hotel/rest./gas/dsl |
| **0mm** | North Dakota/South Dakota state line |

## INTERSTATE 94

| Exit # | Services |
|---|---|
| **352mm** | North Dakota/Minnesota state line, Red River |
| **351** | US 81, Fargo, **N** gas: Loaf'n Jug, Stop'n Go, Tesoro, **food:** Cousins Subs, Duane's Grill, Great Harvest Breads, Great Wall Chinese, Starbucks, Taco Shop, **other:** H HOSPITAL, Ace Hardware, Hornbacher's Foods, Medicine Shoppe, **S** gas: Clark/dsl, Stop'n Go, Tesoro, **food:** A&W/LJ Silver, Burger King, Gina's Pizza, Happy Joe's Pizza, KFC, McDonald's, N American Steaks, Papa Murphy's, Pepper's Café, Randy's Diner, Subway, Taco Bell, **lodging:** Prairie Rose Inn, Rodeway Inn, **other:** Hyundai/Nissan, K-Mart, USPO |
| **350** | 25th St, Fargo, **N** gas: Stop'n Go, **S** gas: Cenex/dsl, Loaf'n Jug, **food:** Dolittle's Grill, Ruby Tuesday |
| **349b a** | I-29, N to Grand Forks, S to Sioux Falls, facilities **1 mi** N, exit 64 |
| **348** | 45th St, **0-2 mi N**...Visitor Ctr/full facilities, gas: Holiday, Petro/dsl/LP/rest./24hr/@, **food:** Carino's, Culver's, Denny's, IHOP, Little Caesars, McDonald's, Pizza Hut, Qdoba Mexican, Space Alien Rest., Subway, Wendy's, **lodging:** Best Western, C'mon Inn, MainStay Inn, Ramada Inn, Sleep Inn, Staybridge Suites, Wingate Inn, **other:** Blue Beacon, Home Depot, Kohl's, Office Depot, NAPA, Sam's Club, Scheel's Sports, Target, Walmart SuperCtr, **S** gas: Tesoro/DQ/dsl, **food:** Famous Dave's BBQ, Golden Corral, Old Chicago Pizza, Up the Creek Grill, **lodging:** Settle Inn, **other:** Gander Mtn, Red RiverZoo |

## INTERSTATE 94 CONT'D

**FARGO** E ← → W **JAMESTOWN**

| | |
|---|---|
| **346b a** | to Horace, W Fargo, **S** gas: Tesoro/dsl, repair |
| **343** | US 10, Lp 94, W Fargo, **N** gas: Cenex/dsl, **food:** Speedway Steaks, **lodging:** Sunset Motel **other:** Adventure RV Ctr, Harley-Davidson, Pioneer Village |
| **342** | no services |
| **342mm** | weigh sta wb |
| **340** | to Kindred |
| **338** | Mapleton, **N** gas: Petro/dsl |
| **337mm** | truck parking wb, litter barrels |
| **331** | ND 18, to Leonard, Casselton, **N** gas: Tesoro/Subway/dsl, **food:** Capitol Rest., **lodging:** Governors Inn/RV park, **other:** NAPA |
| **328** | to Lynchburg |
| **327mm** | truck parking eb, litter barrels |
| **324** | Wheatland, to Chaffee |
| **322** | Absaraka |
| **320** | to Embden |
| **317** | to Ayr |
| **314** | ND 38, to Alice, Buffalo, **3 mi N** gas, food |
| **310** | no services |
| **307** | to Tower City, **N** gas: Mobil/dsl/café/RV Park/24hr, motel |
| **304mm** | rest area both lanes (both lanes exit left), full facilities, info, litter barrels, vending, petwalk |
| **302** | ND 32, to Fingal, Oriska, **1 mi N** Scotty's Grill |
| **298** | no services |
| **296** | no services |
| **294** | Lp 94, to Kathryn, Valley City, **N** HOSPITAL, camping |
| **292** | Valley City, **N** gas: Tesoro/dsl/café/24hr, **food:** Sabir's Rest., **lodging:** AmericInn, Super 8, Wagon Wheel Inn/rest., **other:** HOSPITAL, to Bald Hill Dam, camping, **S other:** Ft Ransom SP (35mi) |
| **291** | Sheyenne River |
| **290** | Lp 94, Valley City, **N** gas: Tesoro/dsl, **food:** Burger King, Kenny's Rest., Pizza Hut, Roby's Rest., Subway, **other:** HOSPITAL, Chrysler/Dodge/Jeep, Family$, Ford, NAPA, Pamida |
| **288** | ND 1 S, to Oakes, **S** Fort Ransom SP (36 mi) |
| **283** | ND 1 N, to Rogers |
| **281** | to Litchville, Sanborn, **1-2 mi N** gas, food, lodging |
| **276** | Eckelson, **S other:** Prairie Haven Camping/gas/dsl |
| **275mm** | continental divide, elev 1490 |
| **272** | to Urbana |
| **269** | Spiritwood |
| **262** | Bloom, **N** ✈ |
| **260** | Jamestown, **N** gas: Stop'n Go, Tesoro/dsl/café/@, **lodging:** Starlite Motel, **other:** to St HOSPITAL, Buick/Chevrolet Dodge, camping, tires, vet |
| **259mm** | James River |
| **258** | US 281, Jamestown, **N** gas: Super Xpress/TCBY/dsl, Tesoro/dsl, **food:** Arby's, DQ, Hardee's, Little Caesar's, McDonald's, Pizza Ranch, Subway, Taco Bell, **lodging:** Comfort Inn, Day's Inn, Holiday Inn Express, Ranch House Motel, **other:** HOSPITAL, Buffalo Herd/museum, Cadillac/GMC/Pontiac, Chrysler/Toyota, Firestone/auto, NW Tire, O'Reilly Parts, **S** gas: Sinclair/dsl/24hr, **food:** Applebee's, Burger King, Grizzly's Rest., |

**JAMESTOWN** (side bar left bottom)

**JAMESTOWN** / **BISMARCK** (side bar right)

| | |
|---|---|
| **258** | Continued |
| | Hong Kong Buffet, Paradiso Mexican, Perkins, **lodging:** Quality Inn, Super 8, **other:** Ford, Harley-Davidson, JC Penney, K-Mart, Sears, Walmart Super Ctr, mall, USPO, vet |
| **257** | Lp 94 (from eb), to Jamestown, **N** dsl repair |
| **256** | US 52 W, US 281 N, **S other:** Wiest truck/trailer repair, **1 mi S** Jamestown Campground/RV dump |
| **254mm** | rest area both lanes, full facilities, litter barrels, petwalk, vending |
| **251** | Eldridge |
| **248** | no services |
| **245** | no services |
| **242** | Windsor, **1/4 mi N** gas |
| **238** | to Gackle, Cleveland |
| **233** | no services |
| **230** | Medina, **1 mi N** gas: Cenex/dsl/LP, **food:** DairyTreat, **other:** Medina RV Park, USPO, city park |
| **228** | ND 30 S, to Streeter |
| **224mm** | rest area wb, full facilities, litter barrels, vending, petwalk, RV dump |
| **221** | Crystal Springs |
| **221mm** | rest area eb, full facilities, litter barrels, vending, petwalk, RV dump |
| **217** | Pettibone |
| **214** | Tappen, **S** gas/dsl/food |
| **208** | ND 3 S, Dawson, **N** RV camping, **1/2 mi S** gas, food, to Camp Grassick, RV camping |
| **205** | Robinson |
| **200** | ND 3 N, to Tuttle, Steele, **S** gas: Cenex/dsl/24hr, **food:** Lone Steer café, **lodging:** OK Motel, **other:** truckwash |
| **195** | no services |
| **190** | Driscoll, **S** food |
| **182** | US 83 S, ND 14, to Wing, Sterling, **S** gas: Cenex/dsl/24hr, **food:** Darnell's Café, **lodging:** Top's Motel (1mi) |
| **176** | McKenzie |
| **170** | Menoken, **S** to McDowell Dam, RV Park |
| **168mm** | rest area both lanes, full facilities, litter barrels, vending, petwalk |
| **161** | Lp 94, Bismarck Expswy, Bismarck, **N** gas: Cenex/dsl/LP/RV Dump/24hr, Express, **food:** Quizno's, **other:** Dodge/Toyota, **S** gas: Tesoro/Oasis/dsl/rest./24hr, **food:** McDonald's, **lodging:** Ramada Ltd, **other:** Capital RV Ctr, Dakota Zoo, Freightliner, Kenworth, OK Tires, Volvo |
| **159** | US 83, Bismarck, **N** gas: Best Stop/dsl, Simonson/dsl, **food:** Applebee's, Arby's, Burger King, Capt Jack's Rest., China Town, Golden Corral, Hooters, KFC, Kroll's Diner, McDonald's, Paradiso Mexican, Perkins, Quizno's, Red Lobster, Ruby Tuesday, Schlotsky's, Space Alien Grill, Taco Bell, TCBY, Wendy's, **lodging:** AmericInn, Candlewood Suites, Comfort Inn, Country Suites, Fairfield Inn, Hampton Inn, Holiday Inn Express, **other:** Chevrolet, CVS Drug, Dan's Foods, Hancock Fabrics, K-Mart, Menard's, NW Tire, Sears/auto, U-Haul, Walmart Super Ctr/Subway, mall, **S** gas: Conoco/dsl, StaMart/dsl, Tesoro, **food:** DQ, Hardee's, Minerva's Rest., North American Steaks, Pizza Hut, Starbucks, Subway, Taco John's, Woodhouse |

**BISMARCK / MANDAN / HEBRON**

| 159 | Continued |
| | Rest., **lodging:** Best Western, Day's Inn, Kelly Inn, Select Inn, Super 8, **other:**  HOSPITAL, O'Reilly Parts |
| 157 | Divide Ave, Bismarck, **N gas:** Conoco/dsl/LP/24hr, **food:** Carino's, Cracker Barrel, Goodtimes Grill/Taco John's, McDonald's, Quizno's, Texas Roadhouse, Wendy's, **other:** Best Buy, $Tree, Kohls, Lowes Whse, PetsMart, TJ Maxx, **S gas:** Cenex/dsl/LP/RV Dump, **other:** Central Mkt Foods |
| 156mm | Missouri River |
| 156 | I-194, Bismarck Expswy, Bismarck City Ctr, **1/2 mi S** Dakota Zoo |
| 155 | to Lp 94 (exits left from wb), Mandan, City Ctr, same as 153 |
| 153 | ND 6, Mandan Dr, Mandan, **1/2 mi S gas:** Cenex/24hr, StaMart/dsl, Tesoro, **food:** Burger King, DQ, Dakota Farms Rest., Domino's, Hardee's, Pizza Hut, Subway, Taco John's, **lodging:** North Country Inn, **other:** Chevrolet, Goodyear/auto, NW Tire, Parts+, Subaru, Dacotah Centennial Park, Ft Lincoln SP (5mi) |
| 152 | Sunset Dr, Mandan, **N gas:** Conoco, **lodging:** Best Western, **S gas:** Tesoro/RV dump, **other:** H HOSPITAL |
| 152mm | scenic view eb |
| 147 | ND 25, to ND 6, Mandan, **S gas:** Sinclair/Subway/dsl/café/24hr |
| 140 | to Crown Butte |
| 135mm | scenic view wb, litter barrel |
| 134 | to Judson, Sweet Briar Lake |
| 127 | ND 31, to New Salem, **N** Knife River Indian Village (35mi), **S gas:** Cenex/dsl, Tesoro/dsl, **food:** Sunset Cafe, **lodging:** Arrowhead Inn/café, **other:** Farmer's/gas, Food Pride, Gaebe Drug, World's Largest Cow, vet |
| 123 | to Almont |
| 120 | no services |
| 119mm | **rest area both lanes, full** ♿ **facilities,** 📞, 🚻, **litter barrels, petwalk** |
| 117 | no services |
| 113 | no services |
| 110 | ND 49, to Glen Ullin |
| 108 | to Glen Ullin, Lake Tschida, **3 mi S** gas, food, lodging, camping |
| 102 | Hebron, to Glen Ullin, to Lake Tschida, **3 mi S** gas, food, lodging, camping |
| 97 | Hebron, **2 mi N** gas, food, lodging |
| 96.5mm | central/mountain time zone |
| 90 | no services |
| 84 | ND 8, Richardton, **N gas:** Cenex/dsl, **other:** H HOSPITAL, to Assumption Abbey, Schnell RA |
| 78 | to Taylor |
| 72 | to Enchanted Hwy, Gladstone |
| 64 | Dickinson, **S gas:** Tesoro/Tiger Truckstop/dsl/rest./24hr, food; Dakota Diner, **other:** Ford/Lincoln/Mercury, Honda/Toyota, NW Tire, dsl repair |
| 61 | ND 22, Dickinson, **N gas:** Cenex/dsl/LP/24hr, |

**DICKINSON**

| 61 | Continued |
| | Simonson/dsl, **food:** Applebee's, Arby's, Bonanza, Burger King, DQ, El Sombrero Mexican, Happy Joe's Pizza, Papa Murphy's, Sanford's Rest., Taco Bell, Taco John's, Wendy's, **lodging:** AmericInn, Comfort Inn, Days Inn, Holiday Inn Express, **other:** Dan's Foods, Goodyear/auto, Herberger's, JC Penney, K-Mart, NAPA, O'Reilly Parts, TrueValue, Walmart SuperCtr/Subway, White Drug, **S gas:** Cenex/dsl, Conoco/repair, Holiday/dsl/24hr, Tesoro, **food:** A&W/KFC, Country Kitchen, Domino's, King Buffet, McDonald's, Perkins, Subway, **lodging:** Quality Inn, Select Inn, Super 8, Travel Host, **other:** H HOSPITAL, Ace Hardware, museum, visitor info |
| 59 | Lp 94, to Dickinson, **S** to Patterson Lake RA, camping, **3 mi S** services in Dickinson |
| 51 | South Heart |
| 42 | US 85, to Grassy Butte, Belfield, Williston, **N** T Roosevelt NP (52mi), **S** info, **gas:** Conoco/dsl, Tesoro/dsl/24hr, **food:** DQ, **lodging:** Trapper's Inn/rest., **other:** NAPA |
| 36 | Fryburg |
| 32 | T Roosevelt NP, **Painted Canyon Visitors Ctr, N rest area both lanes, full** ♿ **facilities,** 📞, 🚻, **litter barrels, petwalk** |
| 27 | Lp 94, Historic Medora (from wb), T Roosevelt NP |
| 24.5mm | Little Missouri Scenic River |
| 24 | Medora, Historic Medora, Chateau de Mores HS, T Roosevelt NP, **S** visitors ctr |
| 23 | West River Rd (from wb) |
| 22mm | scenic view eb |
| 18 | Buffalo Gap, **N** Buffalo Gap Camping (seasonal), food/lodging |
| 10 | Sentinel Butte, Camel Hump Lake, **S** gas |
| 7 | Home on the Range |
| 1 | ND 16, Beach, **N lodging:** Outpost Motel, **other:** camping, **S gas:** Cenex/dsl/LP/24hr, ⊕**FLYING J**/Country Mkt/dsl/scales/LP/24hr, **lodging:** Buckboard Inn, **other:** H HOSPITAL, **Welcome/Visitor Ctr, full handicapped facilities, litter barrels, petwalk,** 🚻 |
| 1mm | weigh sta both lanes, litter barrel |
| 0mm | North Dakota/Montana state line |

## INTERSTATE 70

| Exit # | Services |
|---|---|
| 225.5mm | Ohio/West Virginia state line, Ohio River |
| 225 | US 250 W, OH 7, Bridgeport, **N gas:** Marathon, Star-Fire, Sunoco/24hr, **food:** KFC, Papa John's, Pizza Hut, Wendy's (1mi), **other:** Advance Parts, AutoZone, Family$, NAPA, **S gas:** Exxon, Gulf, **food:** Domino's |
| 220 | US 40, rd 214, **N gas:** Marathon, Sunoco/dsl, **S gas:** Chevron/dsl, **lodging:** Day's Inn, **other:** vet |
| 219 | I-470 E, to Bel-Aire, Washington PA, new exit |
| 218 | Mall Rd, to US 40, to Blaine, **N gas:** BP, Exxon, **food:** Applebees, Arby's, Buffalo Wild Wings, Burger King, De-Felice Pizza, Denny's, Eat'n Park, King Buffet, Outback Steaks, Red Lobster, Steak'n Shake, Subway, Taco Bell, Undo Italian, Wendy's, W Texas Steaks, **lodging:** Best Value Inn, Econolodge, Hampton Inn, Holiday Inn Express, Red Roof Inn, Super 8, **other:** Aldi Foods, AutoZone, Buick/Cadillac/Chevrolet/Pontiac, Circuit City, $General, $Tree, Kroger, Lowes Whse, Sam's Club, Staples, Stewart's RV Ctr, Walmart SuperCtr, **S food:** Bob Evans, Bonanza, Cracker Barrel, Elder Beerman, Garfield's Rest., KFC/LJ Silver, Longhorn Steaks, McDonald's, Panera Bread, Quizno's, Starbucks, **lodging:** Fairfield Inn, **other:** CVS Drug, Jo-Ann Fabrics, K-Mart, Macy's, NTB, Sears/auto, mall |
| 216 | OH 9, St Clairsville, **N gas:** BP |
| 215 | National Rd, **N gas:** Chevron, **food:** Burger King, Domino's, WenWu Chinese, **other:** NAPA, Riesbeck's Foods, USPO |
| 213 | OH 331, Flushing, **S gas:** BP, Marathon/dsl, Sunoco/dsl, **food:** Subway, **lodging:** Twin Pines Motel |
| 211mm | **rest area both lanes, full** ♿ **facilities,** 🚻 🏞, **litter barrels, petwalk, vending** |
| 208 | OH 149, Morristown, **N gas:** BP/McDonald's/dsl, **food:** Schlepp's Rest., **lodging:** Arrowhead Motel (1mi), **other:** Cannonball Speedway, Ford/Lincoln/Mercury, **S gas:** Chevron/Quizno's/dsl, **other:** Harley-Davidson, Barkcamp SP |
| 204 | US 40 E (from eb, no return), National Rd |
| 202 | OH 800, to Barnesville, **S gas:** 202 Gas/dsl, **other:** Ⓗ HOSPITAL |
| 198 | rd 114, Fairview |
| 193 | OH 513, Middlebourne, **N gas:** BP, FuelMart/dsl, **other:** fireworks |
| 189mm | **rest area eb, full** ♿ **facilities,** 🚻 🏞, **litter barrels, petwalk, vending** |
| 186 | US 40, OH 285, to Old Washington, **N gas:** BP, **S gas:** GoMart/dsl |
| 180b a | I-77 N, to Cleveland, to Salt Fork SP, I-77 S, to Charleston |
| 178 | OH 209, Cambridge, 0-1 mi **N gas:** BP/dsl, Sheetz/dsl, Shell, **food:** Bob Evans, China Village, Cracker Barrel, Denny's, DQ, KFC, McDonald's, Papa John's, Pizza Hut, Ruby Tuesday, Subway, Taco Bell, Wendy's, **lodging:** Best Western, Comfort Inn, Day's Inn, Hampton Inn, Ramada Inn, Super 8, **other:** Ⓗ HOSPITAL, Advance Parts, AutoZone, Big Lots, Buick/Pontiac/GMC/Cadillac, $General, Family$, Mor4Less Foods, **S gas:** Murphy USA, Pilot/Subway/dsl/scales/24hr, **food:** Arby's, Burger King, Great Chinese, Little Caesar's, Talaqueta Mexican, **lodging:** Baymont Inn, **other:** Aldi Foods, $Tree, $Zone, K-Mart/gas, Radio Shack, Spring Valley RV Park (1mi), Walmart SuperCtr |

| | |
|---|---|
| 176 | US 22, US 40, to Cambridge, **N gas:** Sunoco/dsl, **lodging:** Budget Inn, **other:** Western Shop, RV camping, st patrol |
| 173mm | weigh sta both lanes |
| 169 | OH 83, to Cumberland, New Concord, **N gas:** BP, **other:** RV camping, to Muskingum Coll |
| 164 | US 22, US 40, Norwich, **N gas:** BP, **lodging:** Baker's Motel, museum |
| 163mm | **rest area wb, full** ♿ **facilities,** 🚻 🏞, **litter barrels, petwalk, vending** |
| 160 | OH 797, ✈, **N gas:** Love's/Arby's/dsl/scales/24hr, **S gas:** BP, Exxon/Subway/dsl, **food:** Denny's, McDonald's, Wendy's, **lodging:** Best Value Inn, Best Western, Ramada Inn, **other:** st patrol |
| 157 | OH 93, Zanesville, **N gas:** BP, **S gas:** Marathon, Shell/dsl |
| 155 | OH 60, OH 146, Underwood St, Zanesville, **N info, food:** Bob Evans, Olive Garden, Oriental Buffet, Red Lobster, Steak'n Shake, Tumbleweed Grill, **lodging:** Comfort Inn, Fairfield Inn, Hampton Inn, **other:** Ⓗ HOSPITAL, Pick'n Save Foods, **S gas:** Exxon/dsl, **food:** Adornetto Café, Cracker Barrel, Subway, Wendy's, **lodging:** Baymont Inn, Econolodge, **other:** Family$, Rite Aid |
| 154 | 5th St (from eb) |
| 153b | Maple Ave (no EZ return from wb), **N gas:** BP, **food:** Big Boy, DQ, Wendy's, **other:** Ⓗ HOSPITAL, CVS Drug, Family$ |
| 153a | State St, **N gas:** BP/dsl, **other:** Harley-Davidson, to Dillon SP, **S gas:** BP |
| 153mm | Licking River |
| 152 | US 40, National Rd, **N gas:** BP, Exxon/A&W/Blimpie, Starfire, **food:** McDonald's, **lodging:** Super 8 |
| 142 | US 40 (from wb, no EZ return), Gratiot, **N** RV camping |
| 141 | OH 668, US 40 (from eb, no return), to Gratiot, same as 142 |
| 132 | OH 13, to Thornville, Newark, **N** Dawes Arboretum (3mi), **S gas:** BP, Shell, **food:** Subway (2mi), **other:** RV camping |
| 131mm | **rest area both lanes, full** ♿ **facilities,** 🚻 🏞, **litter barrels, petwalk, vending** |
| 129b a | OH 79, to Buckeye Lake, Hebron, **N lodging:** Quality Inn, **S gas:** BP/Duke/dsl/@, Valero, **food:** McDonald's, Pizza Hut/Taco Bell, Subway, Wendy's, **lodging:** Super 8, **other:** CarQuest, IGA Foods, KOA (2mi), Blue Goose Marina (2mi) |
| 126 | OH 37, to Granville, Lancaster, **N gas:** Marathon/dsl/@, Pilot/Chester's/Subway/dsl/scales/24hr, Starfire Express/dsl, **S gas:** Sunoco/dsl, TA/BP/Sbarro's/Popeye's/dsl/scales/24hr/@, **lodging:** Deluxe Inn, Red Roof Inn, **other:** truckwash, KOA (4mi) |
| 122 | OH 158, to Baltimore, Kirkersville, **N lodging:** Rodeway Inn, **S gas:** ⊕FLYING J/CountryMkt/dsl/scales/24hr |
| 118 | OH 310, to Pataskala, **N gas:** BP/McDonald's, Speedway/dsl, Sunoco, **food:** DQ, **S gas:** Duke's/Subway/dsl |
| 112 | OH 256, to Pickerington, Reynoldsburg, **N gas:** BP, Shell/McDonald's, Sunoco/dsl, **food:** Chipotle Mexican, Dynasty Buffet, Logan's Roadhouse, O'Charley's, Panera Bread, Ritter's Custard, Smokey Bones BBQ, TGIFriday's, **lodging:** Country Inn&Suites, Fairfield Inn, **other:** Best Buy, Curves, Gander Mtn, Jo-Ann Fabrics, Marshall's, NTB, Sam's Club/gas, Staples, Target, Tire Discounters, Walgreens, Walmart SuperCtr/gas, **S gas:** Speedway, **food:** Arby's, Bob Evan's, Cracker Barrel, |

## INTERSTATE 70 CONT'D

E
↕
W

**112** Continued
Dragon Chinese, KFC, La Fozata, LJ Silver, Longhorn Steaks, Quizno's, Steak'n Shake, Uno Pizzaria, Wendy's, **lodging:** Best Western, Hampton Inn, Holiday Inn Express, **other:** URGENT CARE, Barnes&Noble, Tuesday Morning

**110** Brice Rd, to Reynoldsburg, **N gas:** Shell, Speedway, Sunoco, **food:** Burger King, Donato's Pizza, Gengi Japanese, Golden China, Max&Erma's, Popeye's, Subway, TeeJaye's Rest., Tim Horton, Treacher's Seafood, Waffle House, **lodging:** Days Inn, Extended Stay America, La Quinta, Red Roof, Super 8, **other:** Big Lots, Goodyear/auto, Home Depot, Midas, **S gas:** BP, Meijer/dsl/24hr, Speedway, **food:** Applebee's, Arby's, Asian Star, Boston Mkt, Chipotle Mexican, El Chico, KFC/Pizza Hut, McDonald's, Ruby Tuesday, Subway, Starbucks, Steak'n Shake, Taco Bell, Waffle House, **lodging:** Comfort Suites,

**110** Continued
Econolodge, Motel 6, **other:** Acura, Advance Parts, Aldi, Circuit City, Farber RV Ctr, Firestone/auto, GNC, Honda, Hyundai, JC Penney, Jo-Ann Fabrics, Kroger/deli, Lowe's Whse, Michael's, NTB, Old Navy, PetCo, Sears/auto, Target, Toyota/Scion, Walgreens, mall

**108b a** I-270 N to Cleveland, access to H HOSPITAL, I-270 S to Cincinnati

**107** OH 317, Hamilton Rd, to Whitehall, **S gas:** Sunoco/dsl, Valero, **food:** Arby's, Bob Evans, Buffalo Wild Wings, Burger King, Capt D's, Dragon Buffet, Eastland Buffet, Ichybon Mexican, McDonald's, Olive Garden, Papa John's, Red Lobster, Steak'n Shake, Taco Bell, **lodging:** Hamilton Hotel, Hampton Inn, Holiday Inn, InTown Suites, Knight's Inn, Residence Inn, **other:** $General, Kohl's, Macy's, Pepboys, Staples

**105a** to Lancaster, 2 mi **N food:** Tat Italian, Wendy's

**105b** US 33, James Rd, Bexley, **N food:** Tat Italian, Wendy's

**E** ↕ **W**

**C O L U M B U S   A R E A**

**OH**

## INTERSTATE 70 CONT'D

| | |
|---|---|
| **103b a** | Livingston Ave, to Capital University, **N gas:** BP, Exxon, Speedway/dsl, **food:** Mr Hero Subs, Peking Chinese, Popeye's, Subway, Taco Bell, Wendy's, **other:** Tuffy, **S gas:** Marathon, Shell, **food:** McDonald's, White Castle/24hr |
| **102** | Kelton Ave, Miller Ave, **S** H HOSPITAL |
| **101a** | I-71 N, to Cleveland |
| **100b** | US 23, to 4th St, downtown |
| **99c** | Rich St, Town St (exits left from eb), **N gas:** Sunoco, **other:** Ford |
| **99b** | OH 315 N, downtown |
| **99a** | I-71 S, to Cincinnati |
| **98b** | Mound St (from wb, no EZ return), **N gas:** Marathon, **S food:** LJ Silver, McDonald's, Rally's |
| **98a** | US 62, OH 3, Central Ave, to Sullivant, access to same as 98b |
| **97** | US 40, W Broad St, **N gas:** Valero, **food:** Arby's, Burger King, KFC, McDonald's, Pizza Hut/Taco Bell, Subway, Tim Horton, Wendy's, White Castle, **lodging:** Knight's Inn, **other:** CVS Drug, U-Haul |
| **96** | I-670 (exits left from eb), to ✈ |
| **95** | Hague Ave (from wb), **S gas:** Sunoco |
| **94** | Wilson Rd, **N gas:** Marathon/Circle K/dsl, Mobil, **S gas:** BP, Pilot/Wendy's/dsl/24hr, Shell/24hr, Speedway/24hr, **food:** McDonald's, Waffle House, White Castle, **lodging:** Econolodge |
| **93b a** | I-270, N to Cleveland, S to Cincinnati |
| **91b a** | to Hilliard, New Rome, **N gas:** GetGo, Meijer/dsl/24hr, Shell, Speedway/dsl, **food:** Applebee's, Arby's, Big Boy, Buffalo Wild Wings, Burger King, Cracker Barrel, Chick-fil-A, Chipotle Mexican, CiCi's Pizza, Culver's, Donato's Pizza, El Vaquero Mexican, Fazoli's, KFC, Golden Chopsticks, McDonald's, Outback Steaks, Perkins, Pizza Hut/Taco Bell, Quizno's, Red Robin, Ruby Tuesday, Salvi's Bistro, Skyline Chili, Subway, Taco Bell, Tim Horton, Texas Roadhouse, White Castle, Wendy's, **lodging:** Best Value, Comfort Suites, Days Inn, Fairfield Inn, Hampton Inn, Hawthorn Inn, Motel 6, Red Roof Inn, Tanglewood Suites, **other:** Discount Tire, Firestone, Ford, Gander Mtn, Giant Eagle Foods/gas, Marshall's, Old Navy, PetsMart, Sam's Club/gas, Radio Shack, Target, Valvoline, Walmart SuperCtr/gas, **S gas:** BP/dsl, Marathon/dsl, **food:** Bob Evans, Handel's Icecream, Steak'n Shake, Wendy's, **lodging:** Best Western, Country Inn&Suites, Microtel |
| **85** | OH 142, to Plain City, W Jefferson, **N other:** Prairie Oaks RV Park, **S other:** Pattele Darby RV Park |
| **80** | OH 29, to Mechanicsburg, **S** hwy patrol |
| **79** | US 42, to London, Plain City, **N gas:** Pilot/Arby's/dsl/scales/24hr, **food:** Waffle House, **other:** truck/auto repair, **S gas:** Sunoco/24hr, Speedway/Subway/dsl/24hr, TA/BP/Popeye's/Pizza Hut/dsl/scales/24hr/@, **food:** McDonald's, Taco Bell, Wendy's, **lodging:** Holiday Inn Express, Knight's Inn, **other:** H HOSPITAL, truckwash |
| **72** | OH 56, to London, Summerford, **N gas:** Marathon/24hr, **4 mi S** H HOSPITAL, lodging |
| **71mm** | **rest area both lanes, full** ♿ **facilities,** 📞, 🚻, **litter barrels, vending, petwalk** |
| **66** | OH 54, to Catawba, South Vienna, **N gas:** FuelMart/dsl, **S gas:** Speedway/dsl, **other:** Crawford RV Park (1mi), Beaver Valley RV Park (3mi) |

**S P R I N G F I E L D**

| | |
|---|---|
| **62** | US 40, Springfield, **N gas:** Rich Gas, **lodging:** Harmony Motel, **other:** antiques, to Buck Creek SP, **S** Beaver Valley Camping |
| **59** | OH 41, to S Charleston, **N other:** H HOSPITAL, Harley-Davidson, st patrol, **S gas:** BP/dsl, Clark/dsl, antiques |
| **54** | OH 72, to Cedarville, Springfield, **N gas:** BP/dsl, Shell, Speedway, Sunoco/dsl/24hr, **food:** A&W/LJ Silver, Arby's, Bob Evans, Cassano's Pizza/subs, Church's, Cracker Barrel, Domino's, El Toro Mexican, Hardee's, KFC, Lee's Chicken, Little Caesar's, McDonald's, Panda Chinese, Rally's, Rudy's Smokehouse, Subway, Wendy's, **lodging:** Comfort Suites, Day's Inn, Hampton Inn, Holiday Inn, Ramada Ltd, Red Roof Inn, Super 8, **other:** H HOSPITAL, Advance Parts, Best Buy RV Ctr, BigLots, Family$, Kroger/deli, Rite Aid, Walgreens, **S gas:** Marathon/dsl, Swifty |
| **52b a** | US 68, to Urbana, Xenia, **S** to John Bryan SP |
| **48** | OH 4 (from wb), to Enon, Donnelsville, **N** Enon RV Camp, **S gas:** Speedway |
| **47** | OH 4 (from eb), to Springfield, **N gas:** Speedway, **other:** RV Camping |
| **44** | I-675 S, Spangler Rd, to Cincinnati |
| **43mm** | Mad River |
| **41b a** | OH 4, OH 235, to Dayton, New Carlisle, **N gas:** BP/dsl, Sunoco/dsl, **food:** KFC/LJ Silver, McDonald's, Wendy's, **other:** Freightliner |
| **38** | OH 201, Brandt Pike, **N gas:** Marathon, Meijer/dsl/E-85, **S gas:** Shell, **food:** Bob Evans, Denny's, Las Piramedes Mexican, McDonald's, Tim Horton, Waffle House, Wendy's, **lodging:** Comfort Inn, Travelodge, **other:** DENTIST, Walmart SuperCtr |
| **36** | OH 202, Huber Heights, **N gas:** Speedway/dsl/24hr, **food:** A&W/KFC, Applebee's, Big Boy, El Toro Mexican, Fazoli's, Ruby Tuesday, Steak'n Shake, Taco Bell, Waffle House, **lodging:** Baymont Inn, Super 8, **other:** Gander Mtn., GNC, Kohl's, Lowe's Whse, Marshall's, Saturn, Target, vet, **S gas:** BP/dsl, Marathon/dsl, **food:** Arby's, Bob Evans, Buffalo Wild Wings, Burger King, Cadillac Jack's Grill, CiCi's Pizza, McDonald's, Skyline Chili, Subway, TGIFriday, TX Roadhouse, White Castle, **lodging:** Days Inn, Hampton Inn, Holiday Inn Express, **other:** CVS Drug, $Tree, K-Mart, Kroger/gas |
| **33b a** | I-75, N to Toledo, S to Dayton |
| **32** | Vandalia, **N** to Dayton Intn'l ✈ |
| **29** | OH 48, to Dayton, Englewood, **N gas:** BP, Speedway, Sunoco, Valero, **food:** Arby's, Big Boy, Bob Evans, Bolt's Cafe, Buffalo Wild Wings, Perkins, Pizza Hut, Penn Sta. Subs, Ponderosa, Skyline Chili, Taco Bell, Tim Horton, Wendy's, Yen Chinese, **lodging:** Best Western, Hampton Inn, Holiday Inn, Motel 6, Super 8, **other:** Advance Parts, Aldi Foods, Family$, O'Reilly Parts, **S gas:** Meijer/dsl/E-85/24hr, **food:** McDonald's, Steak'n Shake, Tumbleweed SW Grill, Waffle House, **lodging:** Comfort Inn, Red Roof Inn, **other:** H HOSPITAL |
| **26** | OH 49 S, **N gas:** Murphy USA, **food:** Bob Evans, La Rosa's Pizzaria, Sonic, Subway, **other:** Radio Shack, Walmart SuperCtr, **S food:** Wendy's |
| **24** | OH 49 N, to Greenville, Clayton, **S gas:** Sunoco/dsl/24hr, **other:** KOA (seasonal) |
| **21** | rd 533, Brookville, **N gas:** GA/Subway, **S gas:** Speedway/dsl, Swifty, **food:** Arby's, Brookville Grill, DQ, K's Rest., KFC/Taco Bell, Lee's Chicken, McDonald's, |

## INTERSTATE 70 CONT'D

| | |
|---|---|
| **21** | Continued<br>Rob's Rest., Waffle House, Wendy's, **lodging:** Day's Inn, Holiday Inn Express, **other:** AAA, Brookville Parts, Chevrolet, Curves, $General, Family$, IGA Foods, Rite Aid |
| **14** | OH 503, to West Alexandria, Lewisburg, **N gas:** Sunoco/Subway/dsl, **food:** Dairy Twist, Grinner's Cafe, **lodging:** Super Inn, **other:** IGA Foods, **S gas:** BP, Valero/dsl |
| **10** | US 127, to Eaton, Greenville, **N gas:** TA/BP/Burger King/Subway/dsl/scales/24hr/@, st patrol, **S gas:** Pilot/Subway/dsl/scales/24hr, **lodging:** Budget Inn |
| **3mm** | Welcome Ctr eb/rest area both lanes, full facilities, vending, litter barrels, petwalk |
| **1** | US 35 E (from eb), to Eaton, New Hope |
| **0mm** | Ohio/Indiana state line, Welcome Arch, weigh sta eb |

## INTERSTATE 71

| Exit # | Services |
|---|---|
| **247b** | I-90 W, I-490 E. I-71 begins/ends on I-90, exit 170 in Cleveland. |
| **247a** | W 14th, Clark Ave |
| **246** | Denison Ave, Jennings Rd (from sb) |
| **245** | US 42, Pearl Rd, **E gas:** BP, Sunoco, **other:** H HOSPITAL, zoo |
| **244** | W 65th, Denison Ave |
| **242b a** | W 130th, to Bellaire Rd, **W gas:** Sunoco, **food:** Burger King (1/2mi) |
| **240** | W 150th, **E gas:** Marathon, Speedway/dsl, **food:** Denny's, **lodging:** Marriott, **W gas:** BP/Subway/dsl, **food:** Burger King, MacKenzie's Grill, Somers Rest., Taco Bell, **lodging:** Holiday Inn, La Quinta |
| **239** | OH 237 S (from sb), **W** to ✈ |
| **238** | I-480, Toledo, Youngstown, **W** ✈ |
| **237** | Snow Rd, Brook Park, **E gas:** BP, Marathon, Shell, **food:** Bob Evans, Goody's Cafe, KFC, McDonald's, Suwaby, **lodging:** Best Western, Holiday Inn Express, Howard Johnson, **other:** AutoZone, Top's Foods, **W** to ✈ |
| **235** | Bagley Rd, **E food:** Bob Evans, **W gas:** BP/dsl, Shell, Speedway, **food:** Burger King, Caribou Coffee, Chipotle Mexican, Damon's, Denny's, Friendly's, McDonald's, Olive Garden, Panera Bread, Perkins, Pizza Hut, Roadhouse Grill, Taco Bell, **lodging:** Comfort Inn, Courtyard, Motel 6, Plaza Motel, Radisson, Ramada Inn, Red Roof Inn, Studio+, TownePlace Suites, **other:** H HOSPITAL, Aldi Foods, Buick, GMC, K-Mart |
| **234** | US 42, Pearl Rd, **E gas:** Sunoco/dsl, **food:** Hunan Chinese, Katherine's Rest., Wendy's, **other:** Audi/Porsche, Honda, Hyundai, Saturn, **W gas:** AP/dsl, **food:** Buffalo Wild Wings, Jennifer's Rest., Mad Cactus Mexican, **lodging:** Day's Inn, Kings Inn, La Siesta Motel, Metrick's Motel, Village Motel, **other:** Circle K, Home Depot, Lowes Whse, Walmart, vet, |
| **233** | I-80 and Ohio Tpk, to Toledo, Youngstown |
| **231** | OH 82, Strongsville, **E gas:** Shell, **lodging:** Holiday Inn, Motel 6, **W gas:** BP/Subway/dsl, Marathon/dsl, Sunoco/dsl, **food:** Applebee's, Buca Italian, Demetrio's Rest., Longhorn Steaks, Macaroni Grill, Panera Bread, Red Lobster, **other:** Borders Books, Dillard's, Giant Eagle Foods, JC Penney, Kohl's, NTB, Sears/auto, Target, mall |

| | |
|---|---|
| **226** | OH 303, Brunswick, **E gas:** Shell/dsl/24hr, **food:** Pizza Hut, **other:** Camping World RV Supplies/service, Chrysler/Jeep/Toyota, **W gas:** BP, GetGo, Marathon/dsl, Sunoco/dsl, **food:** Arby's, Bob Evans, Burger King, CiCi's Pizza, McDonald's, Starbucks, Steak'n Shake, Subway, Taco Bell, Tony Roma's, Wendy's, **lodging:** Howard Johnson, Sleep Inn, **other:** Ford, Giant Eagle Food, K-Mart |
| **225mm** | rest area nb, full facilities, litter barrels, petwalk |
| **224mm** | rest area sb, full facilities, litter barrels, petwalk |
| **222** | OH 3, **W** st patrol |
| **220** | I-271 N, (from nb) to Erie, Pa |
| **218** | OH 18, to Akron, Medina, **E gas:** BP/dsl/24hr, Marathon, Shell/dsl, Sunoco/dsl, **food:** Alexandri's Rest., Blimpie, Burger King, DQ, **lodging:** Best Value, Holiday Inn Express, Super 8, Traveler's Choice, **other:** $General, GMC, KIA, Mitsubishi, **W gas:** Speedway/dsl, **food:** Arby's, Bob Evans, Buffalo Wild Wings, Denny's, McDonald's, Pizza Hut, Waffle House, Wendy's, **lodging:** Hampton Inn, Motel 6, Red Roof Inn, **other:** H HOSPITAL, Aldi Foods, Dodge, Harley-Davidson, Honda, NTB, Pontiac/Buick/Cadillac/GMC |
| **209** | I-76 E, to Akron, US 224, **W gas:** Pilot/Country Kitchen/Subway/dsl/scales/24hr, TA/Burger King/Popeye's/dsl/24hr/@, **food:** Arby's, McDonald's, Starbucks, **lodging:** Super 8, **other:** Blue Beacon, Chippewa Valley Camping (1mi), SpeedCo |
| **204** | OH 83, Burbank, **E gas:** BP/dsl, Duke/dsl, Loves/Hardees/scales/dsl/24hr, **lodging:** Plaza Motel, **W gas:** Pilot/Wendy's/dsl/scales/24hr, **food:** Bob Evans, Burger King, McDonald's, **other:** H HOSPITAL, Buick/Chevrolet/Pontiac, Chrysler/Jeep/Dodge, Lodi Outlets/famous brands |
| **198** | OH 539, W Salem |
| **196** | OH 301 (from nb, no re-entry), W Salem |
| **196mm** | rest area both lanes, full facilities, vending, litter barrels, petwalk |
| **186** | US 250, Ashland, **E gas:** Marathon, **food:** Perkins, Grandpa's Village/cheese/gifts, **other:** Hickory Lakes Camping (7mi), **W gas:** Citgo, Goasis/Pizza Hut/Popeye's/Starbucks/Taco Bell/dsl/rest./24hr, **food:** Bob Evans, Buehler's Rest., Denny's, Donato's Pizza, Jake's Rest., McDonald's, Wendy's, **lodging:** AmeriHost, Day's Inn, Holiday Inn Express, Super 8, **other:** H HOSPITAL, GNC, Home Depot, Walmart SuperCtr, st patrol, to Ashland U |

**MANSFIELD N ↕ S**

## INTERSTATE 71 CONT'D

| | |
|---|---|
| **176** | US 30, to Mansfield, **E** **lodging:** Econolodge, **other:** fireworks |
| **173** | OH 39, to Mansfield |
| **169** | OH 13, Mansfield, **E** **gas:** Marathon/dsl, **food:** Applebee's, Cracker Barrel, HillTop Dairy Bar, Steak'n Shake, Wendy's, **other:** Walmart SuperCtr/Subway/gas, Mohican SP, **lodging:** Best Western, La Quinta, **W** **gas:** Marathon, **food:** Arby's, Bob Evans, Burger King, Cracker Barrel, El Compacino Mexican, Joe's Rest., McDonald's, Taco Bell, **lodging:** Hampton Inn, Super 8, Travelodge, **other:** H HOSPITAL, st patrol |
| **165** | OH 97, to Bellville, **E** **gas:** BP, Speedway/dsl, Shell/dsl, **food:** Burger King, Dutch Heritage Rest., McDonald's, **lodging:** Day's Inn, Comfort Inn, Knight's Inn, Quality Inn, **other:** to Mohican SP, **W** **food:** Dinner Bell Rest., Wendy's |
| **151** | OH 95, to Mt Gilead, **E** **gas:** Duke/BP/dsl/rest./24hr/@, Marathon, **food:** Gathering Rest., McDonald's, Wendy's, **lodging:** Best Western, **other:** st patrol, **W** **gas:** Sunoco/dsl, Shell/dsl, **food:** Leaf Rest., **lodging:** Knight's Inn, **other:** H HOSPITAL, Mt Gilead SP (6mi) |
| **149mm** | truck parking both lanes |
| **140** | OH 61, Mt Gilead, **E** **gas:** Pilot/Arby's/dsl/scales/24hr, **W** **gas:** BP/Taco Bell, Sunoco/Subway, **food:** Ole Farmstead Rest. |
| **131** | US 36, OH 37, to Delaware, **E** **gas:** ⊕ FLYING J/Cookery/dsl/LP/rest./scales/24hr, Pilot/Subway/dsl/scales/24hr, **food:** Burger King, **other:** Harley-Davidson, **W** **gas:** BP/dsl, Shell/Tim Horton, **food:** Arby's, Bob Evans, Cracker Barrel, KFC/LJ Silver, McDonald's, Starbucks, Taco Bell, Waffle House, Wendy's, White Castle, **lodging:** Day's Inn, Hampton Inn, Holiday Inn Express, **other:** H HOSPITAL, Alum Cr SP, Cross Creek Camping (6mi) |
| **129mm** | weigh sta nb |
| **128mm** | **rest area both lanes, full** 🦽 **facilities,** 📞, **vending,** 🍴, **litter barrels, petwalk** |
| **121** | Polaris Pkwy, to Gemini Pl, **E** **gas:** BP, Mobil/24hr, **food:** Bonefish Grill, Buffalo Wild Wings, Canes, Carfagna's, Dynasty Express, McDonald's, Pei Wei Chinese, Quizno's, Skyline Chili, Starbucks, Steak'n Shake, **lodging:** Best Western, Hampton Inn, Wingate Inn, **other:** Mr. Tire, Polaris Ampitheatre, **W** **gas:** BP, Shell/Circle K/Tim Horton/USPO, **food:** Applebee's, Arby's, BJ's Rest., Caribou Coffee, Carrabba's, Charley Subs, Cheese Burger Paradise, Chick-fil-A, Chipotle Mexican, City BBQ, Domino's, Fox's Pizza, Hoggy's Grille, Honey Baked Ham, Hooters, House of Japan, Krispy Kreme, Marcella's Italian, Max&Erma's, Merlot's Rest., MiMi's Cafe, Mitchell Steaks, Noodles & Co., O'Charley's, Olive Garden, Panera Bread, Papa John's, Pizza Hut/Taco Bell, Potbelly, Qdoba Mexican, Quaker Steaks, Red Lobster, Red Robin, Rudedog Grill, Shane's Ribshack, Sonic, Smokey Bones BBQ, Sonic, Starbucks, Subway, TGIFriday, TX Roadhouse, Uncle Chan, Waffle House, Wendy's, **lodging:** Cambria Suites, Candlewood Suites, Comfort Inn, Extended Stay Deluxe, Hilton, Hilton Garden, **other:** Barnes&Noble, Best Buy, Circuit City, Costco/gas, GNC, JC Penney, Jo-Ann Fabrics, Kroger/gas, Lowe's Whse, Macy's, NTB, Old Navy, Sears/auto, Target, Tire Discounters, TJ Maxx, Walmart SuperCtr (3mi), World Mkt, funpark, mall |

**COLUMBUS AREA**

**COLUMBUS AREA**

| | |
|---|---|
| **119b a** | I-270, to Indianapolis, Wheeling |
| **117** | OH 161, to Worthington, **E** **gas:** BP/dsl, Shell, Speedway/dsl, Sunoco, **food:** Burger King, China Dynasty, Chipotle Mexican, KFC, LJ Silver, Max&Erma's, McDonald's, Rally's, Red Lobster, Subway, Super Seafood Buffet, White Castle, **lodging:** Comfort Inn, Day's Inn, Holiday Inn Express, Knight's Inn, Motel 6, **other:** Big Bear Foods, CVS Drug, $General, Staples, Tire Discounters, Walgreens, auto repair, vet, **W** **gas:** Clarion, GetGo, Shell, Speedway/dsl, **food:** Bob Evans, China Jade, McDonald's, Pizza Hut, Skyline Chili, Subway, Tim Horton, Waffle House, Wendy's, **lodging:** Baymont Inn, Best Western, Clarion, Crowne Plaza, Country Inn&Suites, Extended Stay America, Family$, Rodeway Inn, Super 8, Travelodge, **other:** Advance Parts, Chevrolet, Family$, Giant Eagle/gas, Walgreens |
| **116** | Morse Rd, Sinclair Rd, **E** **gas:** BP, Shell, Speedway, **food:** McDonald's, Subway, **lodging:** Howard Johnson, **other:** Buick/Pontiac/GMC, CVS Drug, $General, Ford, Kia, Kohl's, Kroger, PepBoys, Save-a-Lot Foods, **W** **gas:** Sunoco, **food:** La Hacienda Mexican, **lodging:** Best Value Inn, Motel 6, Ramada, **other:** NTB |
| **115** | Cooke Rd |
| **114** | N Broadway, **W** **gas:** Sunoco, **food:** Broadway Mkt Cafe, Subway |
| **113** | Weber Rd, **W** **gas:** Speedway/dsl, **other:** CarQuest, NAPA |
| **112** | Hudson St, **E** **gas:** Marathon, Shell, **food:** Wendy's, **lodging:** Holiday Inn Express, **W** **food:** Big Boy, **other:** Aldi Foods, Lowe's Whse, NTB |
| **111** | 17th Ave, **W** **food:** McDonald's, **lodging:** Comfort Inn, Day's Inn |
| **110b** | 11th Ave |
| **110a** | 5th Ave, **E** **gas:** Sunoco, **food:** White Castle, **W** **gas:** Valero, **food:** Church's, KFC, Popeye's, Rally's, Wendy's, **other:** AutoZone |
| **109a** | I-670 |
| **109b** | OH 3, Cleaveland Ave |
| **109c** | Spring St |
| **108b** | US 40, Broad St, downtown, downtown |
| **108a** | main st |
| **101a** 70 | I-70 E, US 23 N, to Wheeling |
| **100b a** 70 | US 23 S, Front St, High St, downtown |
| **106a** | I-70 W, to Indianapolis |
| **106b** | OH 315 N, Dublin St, Town St |
| **105** | Greenlawn, **W** **gas:** Marathon, **food:** White Castle, **other:** H HOSPITAL |
| **104** | OH 104, Frank Rd |
| **101b a** | I-270, Wheeling, Indianapolis |
| **100** | Stringtown Rd, **E** **gas:** BP, **food:** Bob Evans, Chick-fil-A, Chipotle Mexican, CiCi's Pizza, Coldstone Creamery, DQ, Longhorn Steaks, O'Charley's, Olive Garden, Panda Express, Red Robin, Smokey Bones BBQ, Sonic, Starbucks, Steak'n Shake, White Castle, **lodging:** Best Western, Drury Inn, Hampton Inn, Holiday Inn Express, Hilton Garden, La Quinta, Microtel, Red Roof Inn, **other:** Best Buy, Circuit City, Discount Tire, Home Depot, Michael's, PetsMart, Staples, Target, TJ Maxx, Walmart SuperCtr, **W** **gas:** GetGo, Speedway/dsl, Sunoco/Subway, **food:** Applebee's, Arby's, Burger King, China Bell, Cracker Barrel, Fazoli's, Golden Corral, KFC, |

## INTERSTATE 71 CONT'D

**N ↑ S**

**100** Continued
Mariachi Mexican, McDonald's, Papa John's, Rally's, Ruby Tuesday, Starbucks, Taco Bell, TeeJaye's Rest., Tim Horton, Waffle House, Wendy's, **lodging:** Comfort Inn, Day's Inn, Motel 6, Saver Motel, **other:** Aldi Foods, AutoZone, CVS Drug, Giant Eagle Foods, K-Mart, Kroger/24hr, Radio Shack, Walgreens

**97** OH 665, London-Groveport Rd, **E gas:** Marathon/Circle K, Meijer, Sunoco, **food:** Arby's, McDonald's, Quizno's, Tim Horton/Wendy's, **other:** URGENT CARE, Kroger/gas/E85, to Scioto Downs, **W other:** Eddie's Repair

**94** US 62, OH 3, Orient

**84** OH 56, Mt Sterling, **E gas:** BP/Subway/dsl, Sunoco, **food:** Brewster's Grill, **lodging:** Royal Inn, **other:** to Deer Creek SP (9mi)

**75** OH 38, Bloomingburg, **E** fireworks, **W gas:** Sunoco/dsl

**69** OH 41, OH 734, Jeffersonville, **E gas:** ⭐FLYING J /CountryMkt/dsl/scales/LP/24hr, **other:** H HOSPITAL, Walnut Lake Camping, **W gas:** BP, Shell/Subway, **food:** Arby's, Wendy's, **lodging:** Quality Inn, **other:** Family$

**68mm** **rest area both lanes, full ♿ facilities, v, vending, 🧺, litter barrels, petwalk**

**65** US 35, Washington CH, **E gas:** Shell, TA/BP/Pizza Hut/Popeye's/dsl/scales/24hr/@, **food:** A&W/KFC, Bob Evans, McDonald's/playplace, Taco Bell/LJ Silver, Waffle House, Wendy's, **lodging:** AmeriHost, Hampton Inn, **other:** H HOSPITAL, Prime Outlets/famous brands, **W gas:** Loves/Hardee's/dsl/scales/24hr, **lodging:** Budget Motel, Econolodge

**58** OH 72, to Sabina

**54mm** weigh sta sb

**50** US 68, to Wilmington, **E other:** H HOSPITAL, **W gas:** Pilot/Subway/dsl/scales/24hr, Shell/dsl/24hr, **food:** Max&Erma's, McDonald's, Wendy's, **lodging:** Budget Inn, Holiday Inn, Robert Senter

**49mm** weigh sta nb

**45** OH 73, to Waynesville, **E gas:** BP, **other:** H HOSPITAL, RV Park, **W** Caesar Creek SP (5mi), flea mkt

**36** Wilmington Rd, **E** to Ft Ancient St Mem, RV camping

**35mm** Little Miami River

**34mm** **rest area both lanes, full ♿ facilities, scenic view, ☏, vending, 🧺, litter barrels, petwalk**

**32** OH 123, to Lebanon, Morrow, **E gas:** BP, Valero, **food:** Country Kitchen, **other:** Morgan's RV Park, **3 mi W food:** Bob Evans, Skyline Chili, **lodging:** Knight's Inn

**28** OH 48, S Lebanon, **E lodging:** Countryside Inn (1mi), **W other:** Lebanon Raceway (6mi), hwy patrol

**25** OH 741 N, Kings Mills Rd, **E gas:** Shell/Popeye's, Speedway/dsl, **food:** El Toro Mexican, McDonald's, Ruby Tuesday, Taco Bell, Outback Steaks, **lodging:** Comfort Suites, Great Wolf Lodge, Kings Island Inn, Quality Inn, **other:** Harley-Davidson, **W gas:** BP, Exxon/Subway, **food:** Arby's, Big Boy, Bob Evans, Burger King, DQ, Perkins, Pizza Hut, Skyline Chili, Waffle House, Wendy's, **lodging:** Best Western, Hampton Inn, Microtel, Super 8, **other:** Curves, CVS Drug, GNC, Kroger

**24** Western Row, King's Island Dr (from nb), **E gas:** Sunoco, **lodging:** King's Island, **other:** Jellystone Camping, funpark

**19** US 22, Mason-Montgomery Rd, **E gas:** Meijer/dsl/24hr, Shell, Speedway, Sunoco/24hr, **food:** Arby's, Big Boy, Bob Evans, Boston Mkt, Cracker Barrel, Fazoli's, Fiesta Brava, Fushon Buffet, Golden Corral, Honey-Baked Ham, KFC, McDonald's, Olive Garden, Pizza Hut, Taco Bell, TGIFriday, Wendy's, White Castle, **lodging:** Comfort Inn, Quality Inn, Signature Inn, **other:** AutoZone, Barnes&Noble, Best Buy, Circuit City, Chevrolet, Costco/gas, Firestone/auto, GMC/Buick/Pontiac, Goodyear, Kohl's, Kroger, Lincoln/Mercury, Michael's, Old Navy, Radio Shack, Sam's Club/gas, Saturn, Target, Tires+, Tire Discounters, Toyota, Walgreens, vet, **W gas:** BP/dsl, Marathon/dsl/24hr, Shell, **food:** Abuleo's, Amon's Steaks, Applebee's, Burger King, Carrabba's, Chipotle Mexican, China City, LoneStar Steaks, Macaroni Grill, McAlister's Deli, MiMi's Cafe, Noodles, O'Charley's, Palacio Azteca, Polo Grill, Qdoba Mexican, Red Robin, River City Grill, Steak'n Shake, Skyline Chili, Subway, Tumbleweed Grill, Waffle House, Wendy's, Wild Oats Mkt, **lodging:** AmeriSuites, Best Western, Day's Inn, King's Inn, La Quinta, Marriott, Ramada Ltd, Red Roof Inn, **other:** Bigg's Foods, Border's Books, Home Depot, Lowe's Whse, Staples, Subaru, Walmart Super Ctr

**17b a** I-275, to I-75, OH 32

**15** Pfeiffer Rd, **E H** HOSPITAL, **W gas:** BP, Shell/dsl, Sunoco/dsl/24hr, **food:** Applebee's, Bob Evans, Buffalo Wild Wings, Subway, Watson Bro's Bistro, **lodging:** Courtyard, Crowne Plaza, Embassy Suites, Hampton Inn, Holiday Inn Express, Red Roof Inn, **other:** Office Depot

**14** OH 126, Reagan Hwy, Blue Ash

**12** US 22, OH 3, Montgomery Rd, **E gas:** BP/dsl, Shell/24hr, **food:** Arby's, Bob Evans, Chipotle Mexican, Ember's, Jalapeno Cafe, KFC, LJ Silver, Outback Steaks, Panera Bread, Red Lobster, Ruby Tuesday, Subway, Taco Bell, TGIFriday, Wendy's, **lodging:** Best Western, **other:** Dodge, Firestone, Goodyear, Hyundai, PepBoys, Staples, Tuesday Morning, **W gas:** Chevron, **food:** Cheesecake Factory, IHOP, KFC, Johnny Rocket's, Macaroni Grill, Max&Erma's, McDonald's, Potbelly's, Starbucks, Wendy's, **other:** H HOSPITAL, Barnes&Noble, Dillard's, Firestone/auto, Fresh Mkt Foods, Macy's, Old Navy, Staples, mall

**11** Kenwood Rd, (from nb), **W H** HOSPITAL, same as 12

**10** Stewart Rd (from nb), to Silverton, **W gas:** Marathon/dsl

**9** Redbank Rd, to Fairfax, (no ez sb return), **E gas:** Mobil, Speedway, **other:** BMW

**8** Kennedy Ave, Ridge Ave W, **E gas:** Meijer/dsl, **food:** IHOP, **lodging:** Motel 6, **other:** Circuit City, Dodge,

**C I N C I N N A T I A R E A**

Copyright 2009 - The Next Exit®

## INTERSTATE 71 CONT'D

**N** ↕ **S**

**8** Continued
Sam's Club/gas, Target, **W gas:** Marathon/dsl, Shell/Subway, Speedway, **food:** Denny's, Golden Corral, Gold Star Chili, KFC, LJ Silver, McDonald's, Old Country Buffet, Pizza Hut, Rally's, Taco Bell, White Castle, Wendy's, **other:** Bigg's Foods, Big Lots, Circuit City, Ford, Goodyear, Home Depot, Lowes Whse, Office Depot, Tire Discounter, Walmart, transmissions

**7b a** OH 562, Ridge Ave E, Norwood, **E gas:** BP, **food:** Ponderosa, **other:** AutoZone

**6** Edwards Rd, **E gas:** BP, Shell, Speedway, **food:** Boston Mkt, Buca Italian, Donato's, Don Pablo, Fuddrucker's, GoldStar Chili, J Alexander's Rest., Longhorn Steaks, Max&Erma's, Noodles, PF Chang's, Starbucks, **other:** GNC, SteinMart, **W gas:** Shell

**5** Dana Ave, Montgomery Rd, **W other:** Xavier Univ, Zoo

**3** Taft Rd (from sb), U of Cincinnati

**2** US 42, Reading Rd, Gilbert ave (from sb), **W other:** H HOSPITAL, art museum, ballpark stadium arena, downtown

**1k j** I-471 S

**1d** Main St, downtown

**1c b** Pete Rose Way, Fine St, stadium, downtown

**1a** I-75 N, US 50, to Dayton

**I-71 S and I-75 S run together**

**0mm** Ohio/Kentucky state line, Ohio River

## INTERSTATE 74

**E** ↕ **W**
**CINCINNATI**

| Exit # | Services |
|---|---|
| 20 | I-75 (from eb), N to Dayton, S to Cincinnati, I-74 begins/ends on I-75. |
| 19 | Gilmore St, Spring Grove Ave |
| 18 | US 27 N, Colerain Ave |
| 17 | Montana Ave (from wb), **N gas:** BP |
| 14 | North Bend Rd, Cheviot, **N gas:** Citgo, Speedway/dsl, **food:** DQ, Happy Chinese, McDonald's, Perkins, Skyline Chili, Wendy's, **other:** Sam's Club/gas, Tires+, Walgreen, **S gas:** BP, **food:** Bob Evans, **lodging:** TriStar Motel |
| 11 | Rybolt Rd, Harrison Pike, **S gas:** BP, Meijer/gas, **food:** Angelo's Pizza, Dante's Rest., **lodging:** Imperial House Motel, **other:** Kohl's |
| 9 | I-275 N, to I-75, N to Dayton |
| 8mm | Great Miami River |
| 7 | OH 128, to Hamilton, Cleves, **N gas:** BP/dsl, Marathon/dsl, **food:** BierHaus Rest., Wendy's |
| 5 | I-275 S, to Kentucky |
| 3 | Dry Fork Rd, **N gas:** Citgo, **S gas:** Marathon/dsl, Shell/pizza/dsl |
| 2mm | weigh sta eb |
| 1 | New Haven Rd, to Harrison, **N gas:** BP/dsl, **food:** Buffalo Wild Wings, Cracker Barrel, GoldStar Chili, O'Charley's, Subway, **lodging:** Comfort Inn, **other:** Biggs Foods, Ford, Home Depot, Tires+, **S gas:** Marathon/dsl, Shell/24hr, Speedway/dsl, Sunoco, **food:** A&W/KFC, Arby's, Big Boy, Burger King, DQ, McDonald's, Papa John's, Perkins, Pizza Hut, Skyline Chili, Subway, Taco Bell, Waffle House, Wendy's, White Castle, **lodging:** Holiday Inn Express, Quality Inn, **other:** Advance Parts, AutoZone, Big Lots, CVS Drug, Family$, Firestone, GNC, Goodyear/auto, Jo-Ann Fabrics, K-Mart, Kroger, NAPA, Radio Shack, Walgreens |
| 0mm | Ohio/Indiana state line |

## INTERSTATE 75

**N** ↕ **S**
**TOLEDO**

| Exit # | Services |
|---|---|
| 211mm | Ohio/Michigan state line |
| 210 | OH 184, Alexis Rd, to Raceway Park, **W gas:** BP/dsl/24hr, Meijer/dsl/24hr, Pilot/Subway/dsl/scales/24hr/@, **food:** Arby's, Bob Evans, Burger King, Ground Round, McDonald's, Taco Bell, Wendy's, **lodging:** Comfort Inn, Hampton Inn, **other:** Ford Trucks |
| 210mm | Ottawa River |
| 209 | Ottawa River Rd (from nb), **E gas:** BP, Citgo, Sunoco, **food:** Little Caesar's, Marco's Pizza, **other:** vet, FoodTown, Rite Aid |
| 208 | I-280 S, to I-80/90, to Cleveland |
| 207 | Stickney Ave, Lagrange St, **E gas:** BP, Citgo, Sunoco, **food:** McDonald's, Wendy's, **other:** Family$, K-Mart, Sav-a-Lot Foods |
| 206 | to US 24, Phillips Ave, **W** transmissions |
| 205b | Burdan St, **E H** HOSPITAL, **W** Marathon |
| 205a | to Willys Pkwy, to Jeep Pkwy |
| 204 | I-475 W, to US 23, to Maumee, Ann Arbor |
| 203b | US 24, to Detroit Ave, **W gas:** BP/24hr, **food:** KFC, McDonald's, Rally's, **other:** Rite Aid, Sav-A-Lot Foods, U-Haul |
| 203a | Bancroft St, downtown |
| 202 | Washington St, Collingwood Ave (from sb, no EZ return), **E gas:** BP, **other:** H HOSPITAL, Art Museum, **W food:** McDonald's |
| 201b a | OH 25, Collingwood Ave, **W** Toledo Zoo |
| 200 | South Ave, Kuhlman Dr |
| 200mm | Maumee River |
| 199 | OH 65, Miami St, to Rossford, **E lodging:** Day's Inn |
| 198 | Wales Rd, Oregon Rd, to Northwood, **E gas:** Shell/Subway/dsl/24hr, **food:** Pizza Hut, **lodging:** Baymont Inn, Comfort Inn |
| 197 | Buck Rd, to Rossford, **E gas:** Shell/dsl, **food:** Wendy's, Tim Horton, **W gas:** BP/24hr, Sunoco/dsl, **food:** Denny's, McDonald's, **lodging:** American Inn, Knight's Inn |
| 195 | to I-80/90, OH 795, OH Tpk (toll), Perrysburg, **E gas:** BP/Subway/dsl, **lodging:** Country Inn&Suites, Courtyard, Hampton Inn, **W** Bass Pro Shops |
| 193 | US 20, US 23 S, Perrysburg, **E gas:** BP/dsl/24hr, Meijer, Sunoco, **food:** Arby's, Bob Evans, Burger King, Chili's, Cracker Barrel, Fricker's, Giant Eagle Foods, McDonald's, Panera Bread, Ralphie's, Shanghai Chinese, Subway, Taco Bell, Wendy's, **lodging:** Best Western, Comfort Inn, Day's Inn, Holiday Inn Express, **other:** Belle Tire, Giant Eagle/gas, GNC, Kohl's, K-Mart, Kroger/gas/24hr, KOA (7mi), Lowe's Whse, Michael's, PetsMart, Target, Walgreens, **W gas:** Speedway/dsl, **lodging:** La Quinta, **other:** AutoZone, Harley-Davidson |
| 192 | I-475, US 23 N (exits left from nb), to Maumee, Ann Arbor |
| 187 | OH 582, to Luckey, Haskins |
| 181 | OH 64, OH 105, to Pemberville, Bowling Green, **E gas:** Meijer/dsl/24hr, **lodging:** Holiday Inn Express, **W gas:** BP/Subway/dsl, Speedway, Sunoco/dsl, **food:** Big Boy, Bob Evans, Burger King, Chipotle Mexican, Domino's, El Zarape Mexican, Fricker's Rest., Hunan Buffet, Jimmy John's, McDonald's, Tim Horton, Waffle House, Wendy's, **lodging:** Best Western, Day's Inn, Hampton Inn, Quality Inn, Victory Inn, **other:** H HOSPITAL, Town&Country RV Ctr, to Bowling Green U |

**OH**

## INTERSTATE 75 CONT'D

**N↑↓S**

| | |
|---|---|
| **179** | US 6, to Fremont, Napoleon, **W** museum |
| **179mm** | **rest area both lanes, full ♿ facilities, 🚻, 🏞, litter barrels, vending, petwalk** |
| **175mm** | weigh sta nb |
| **171** | OH 25, Cygnet |
| **168** | Eagleville Rd, Quarry Rd, **E gas:** FuelMart/dsl |
| **167** | OH 18, to Fostoria, North Baltimore, **E gas:** Petro/Mobil/Iron Skillet/dsl/scales/24hr/@, **food:** McDonald's, **other:** Blue Beacon, truck repair, **W gas:** Loves/Arby's/dsl/scales/24hr/@, Sunoco/dsl, **lodging:** Crown Inn, **other:** $General |
| **165mm** | Rocky Ford River |
| **164** | OH 613, to McComb, Fostoria, **E other:** RV Camping, to Van Buren SP, **W gas:** Pilot/Subway/Taco Bell/dsl/scales/24hr |
| **162mm** | weigh sta sb, 🚻 |
| **161** | OH 99, **E gas:** Speedway/dsl, Shell/Subway, **lodging:** Comfort Suites, Holiday Inn Express, **other:** Ford, May RV Ctr, hwy patrol **W** antiques |

**FINDLAY**

| | |
|---|---|
| **159** | US 224, OH 15, Findlay, **E gas:** BP, Speedway/dsl, Swifty, **food:** Archie's Ice Cream, Burger King, Dakota Grill, Dog House Cafe, KFC/LJ Silver, McDonald's, Ming's Great Wall, Pizza Hut, Ponderosa, Ralphie's, Spaghetti Shop, Steak'n Shake, Subway, Taco Bell, Wendy's, **lodging:** Drury Inn, Red Roof Inn, Rodeway Inn, Super 8, **other:** Ⓗ HOSPITAL, **W gas:** Shell/dsl, **food:** Bob Evans, Coldstone Creamery, Cracker Barrel, Denny's, Margarita's Grill, Max&Erma's, Outback Steaks, Tony's Rest., Wings'n Things, Waffle House, **lodging:** Country Inn&Suites, Hampton Inn, Holiday Inn Express, Quality Inn, **other:** Chrysler/Jeep/Dodge, Peterbilt, Walmart SuperCtr/Subway/gas |
| **158** | Blanchard River |
| **157** | OH 12, Findlay, **E gas:** GA/dsl, Marathon/Blimpie/Noble Roman's/dsl, **W food:** Fricker's Rest., **lodging:** Econolodge |
| **156** | US 68, OH 15, to Carey, **E** Ⓗ HOSPITAL |
| **153mm** | **rest area both lanes, full ♿ facilities, 🚻, 🏞, litter barrels, vending, petwalk** |
| **145** | OH 235, to Ada, Mount Cory, **E** TwinLakes Camping |
| **142** | OH 103, to Arlington, Bluffton, **E lodging:** Knight's Inn, **W gas:** BP, Circle K/dsl, **food:** Arby's, Burger King, KFC, McDonald's, Subway, Taco Bell, **lodging:** Comfort Inn, **other:** to Bluffton Coll |
| **140** | Bentley Rd, to Bluffton, **W** Ⓗ HOSPITAL |
| **135** | OH 696, to US 30, to Delphos, Beaverdam, **E gas:** Speedway/dsl/24hr, **W gas:** ✈FLYING J/Cookery/dsl/scales/LP/24hr, Pilot/McDonald's/Subway/dsl/24hr/@, **other:** Blue Beacon, tires, truck repair |
| **134** | Napolean Rd (no nb re-entry), to Beaverdam |
| **130** | Blue Lick Rd, **E lodging:** Best Value |
| **127b a** | OH 81, to Ada, Lima, **W gas:** Marathon/dsl, **food:** Subway, Waffle House, **lodging:** Day's Inn/rest., Econolodge |
| **126mm** | Ottawa River |

**LIMA**

| | |
|---|---|
| **125** | OH 309, OH 117, Lima, **E gas:** BP/dsl, Speedway, **food:** Arby's, Bob Evans, Burger King, Capt D's, China Buffet, Cracker Barrel, Hunan Garden, Little Caesar's, McDonald's, Olive Garden, Pizza Hut, Ponderosa, Ralphie's, Red Lobster, Sedona Grill, Skyline Chili, |

**LIMA**

| | |
|---|---|
| **125** | **Continued** Subway, Taco Bell, Texas Roadhouse, Tumbleweed Grill, Wendy's, **lodging:** Hampton Inn, Holiday Inn, Motel 6, **other:** Ford, K-Mart, PharmX Drug, Ray's Foods, Sam's Club/gas, Walgreens, Walmart SuperCtr, **W gas:** Shell, **food:** Kewbee Hamburger's, Las Cazuelas, **lodging:** Country Inn&Suites, Travelodge, **other:** Ⓗ HOSPITAL, Advance Parts, Curves, $General, Rite Aid, Sav-A-Lot Foods |
| **124** | 4th St, **E** hwy patrol |
| **122** | OH 65, Lima, **E gas:** Speedway/dsl, **W gas:** Shell/dsl/24hr, **other:** Freightliner, GMC, Mack, Volvo |
| **120** | Breese Rd, Ft Shawnee, **W** Harley-Davidson |
| **118** | to Cridersville, **W gas:** Fuelmart/Subway/dsl, Speedway/dsl, **food:** Dixie Ley Diner, **other:** $General |
| **114mm** | **truck parking both directions/no facilities** |
| **113** | OH 67, to Uniopolis, Wapakaneta |
| **111** | Bellefontaine St, Wahpakeneta, **E gas:** TA/Marathon/rest./dsl/scales/@, **lodging:** Knight's Inn, **other:** KOA, **W gas:** BP/dsl, Shell, **food:** Arby's, Bob Evans, Burger King, Capt D's, Comfort Zone, DQ, El Azteca, Groundhog's Cafe, Lucky Steer Rest., McDonald's, Pizza Hut, Taco Bell, Waffle House, Wendy's, **lodging:** Holiday Inn Express, Super 8, Travelodge, **other:** Advance Parts, Aldi Foods, CVS Drug, Family$, Neil Armstrong Museum, Radio Shack, Walmart SuperCtr/gas, st patrol |
| **110** | US 33, to St Marys, Bellefontaine, **E** hwy patrol, KOA |
| **104** | OH 219, **W gas:** Marathon/dsl, Shell/Subway, **lodging:** Budget Host |
| **102** | OH 274, to Jackson Ctr, New Breman, **E** bicycle museum, **W** air stream tours |
| **99** | OH 119, to Minster, Anna, **E gas:** Save a Ton/Apple Valley Café/dsl, **W gas:** GA, Marathon, **food:** Subway, Wendy's, **other:** lube/wash/repair |
| **94** | rd 25A, Sidney |

**SIDNEY**

| | |
|---|---|
| **93** | OH 29, to St Marys, Sidney, **W** Lake Loramie SP, RV camping |
| **92** | OH 47, to Versailles, Sidney, **E gas:** Shell, Speedway/dsl, **food:** Arby's, China Garden, Subway, Wendy's, Winger's, **other:** Ⓗ HOSPITAL, AutoZone, CVS Drug, $General, DM, NAPA, SavALot Foods, Walgreens, **W gas:** Sunoco/dsl, Valero, **food:** A&W/LJ Silver, Applebee's, Bob Evans, Burger King, Cazadores Mexican, Culver's, Highmarks Rest., KFC, McDonald's, Perkins, Pizza Hut, Ponderosa, Quizno's, Rally's, Taco Bell, Waffle House, **lodging:** Comfort Inn, Day's Inn, Econolodge, Holiday Inn/rest., Travel Inn, **other:** Aldi Foods, BigLots, Buick/Pontiac/GMC, Chevrolet, Chrysler/Jeep/Dodge, |

Copyright 2009 - The Next Exit®

## INTERSTATE 75 CONT'D

**SIDNEY N ← S → TROY**

**92** Continued
$Tree, Ford/Lincoln/Mercury, Kelly Tires, Kroger, Lowe's Whse, Menard's, Radio Shack, Staples, Walmart SuperCtr/gas/dsl

**90** Fair Rd, to Sidney, E gas: FuelAmerica, other: repair, W gas: Marathon/DQ/dsl, lodging: Hampton Inn

**88mm** Great Miami River

**83** rd 25A, Piqua, W gas: Marathon/MaidRite Cafe/Noble Roman's/dsl, lodging: Red Carpet Inn, other: Chevrolet, Chrysler/Dodge/Jeep, Sherry RV Ctr, to Piqua Hist Area

**82** US 36, to Urbana, Piqua, E gas: Valero, food: A&W/LJ Silver, Arby's, China East, China Garden, DQ, KFC, Pizza Hut/Taco Bell, Subway, Waffle House, Wendy's, other: BigLots, Home Depot, Goody's, Harley-Davidson, Jo-Ann Fabrics, Walmart SuperCtr, mall, st patrol, W gas: Speedway, food: Bob Evans, Cracker Barrel, FoodCourt, McDonald's, Red Lobster, lodging: Comfort Inn, Knight's Inn, La Quinta, other: Aldi Foods, JC Penney, Sears/auto, mall

**81mm** rest area both lanes, full &#9855; facilities, &#9743;s, &#9809;, litter barrels, vending

**78** rd 25A, E &#9857; HOSPITAL

**74** OH 41, to Covington, Troy, E gas: BP/dsl, food: Al's Pizza, China Garden, McDonald's, Pizza Hut, Subway, other: &#9857; HOSPITAL, Radio Shack, SavALot Foods, to Hobart Arena, W gas: Meijer/dsl/24hr, Shell, Speedway/dsl, food: Applebee's, Big Boy, Bob Evans, Burger King, Culver's, Fazoli's, Friendly's, Highmark's Grill, KFC, Outback Steaks, Quizno's, Ruby Tuesday, Skyline Chili, lodging: Best Inn, Fairfield Inn, Hampton Inn, Holiday Inn Express, Knight's Inn, Residence Inn, other: AutoZone, County Mkt Foods, CVS Drug, Goodyear, Kohl's, Lowe's Whse, Staples, Tire Discounters, Walmart SuperCtr

**73** OH 55, to Ludlow Falls, Troy, E gas: BP, Shell, food: Lincoln Sq Rest., Waffle House, Wendy's, lodging: Best Western, Econolodge, Super 8, other: &#9857; HOSPITAL, $General, Kroger/gas

**69** rd 25A, E gas: BP/Circle K/Subway, Starfire/dsl, other: Arbogast RV Ctr, Buick/Pontiac/GMC, Chrysler/Dodge, Ford

**68** OH 571, to West Milton, Tipp City, E gas: BP/dsl, Shell, Speedway, food: Burger King, Domino's, Fox's Pizza, Ginger Grill, Hickory River Rest., Hong Kong Kitchen, McDonald's, Subway, Taco Bell, other: Ace Hardware, CarQuest, CVS Drug, Family$, FoodTown, Goodyear, Honda, W gas: Speedway/dsl, Valero, food: Arby's, Big Boy, Bob Evans, Tipp' O the Town Rest., Wendy's, lodging: Holiday Inn Express, Travelodge

**64** Northwoods Blvd, E gas: $Tree, Kroger/dsl

**63** US 40, to Donnelsville, Vandalia, E gas: Speedway/dsl, food: Dragon China, Fricker's Rest., W gas: BP/dsl, Shell, Speedway, food: Arby's, Burger King, Domino's, KFC/LJ Silver, McDonald's, Pizza Hut, Rib House, Subway, Taco Bell, Waffle House, Wendy's, lodging: Super 8, other: Goodyear/auto, Rexall Drug, Rite Aid

**61b a** I-70, E to Columbus, W to Indianapolis, to Dayton Int &#9992;

**59** Wyse Rd, Benchwood Rd, E food: El Rancho Grande Mexican, Little York Pizza, Mr. Lee's, lodging: Howard Johnson, Residence Inn, other: Discount Tire, Volvo/BMW/VW, W food: Arby's, Bob Evans,

**DAYTON**

**59** Continued
Cassano's Pizza, Chipotle Mexican, Coldstone Creamery, Cracker Barrel, Don Pablo, Golden Corral, Hooter's, Joe's Crabshack, LoneStar Steaks, Max&Erma's, McDonald's, New Orleans Bistro, O'Charley's, Olive Garden, Outback Steaks, Panera Bread, Pop's Diner, Red Lobster, Ruby Tuesday, Ryan's, Sake Japanese, Skyline Chili, Smokey-Bones BBQ, Steak'n Shake, Tim Horton, lodging: Comfort Inn, Country Inn&Suites, Courtyard, Day's Inn, Drury Inn, Extended Stay America, Fairfield Inn, Hampton Inn, Knight's Inn, Motel 6, Ramada Inn, Red Roof Inn, Rodeway Inn, Villager Lodge, other: Office Depot, Radio Shack, Sam's Club/gas, Walmart SuperCtr

**58** Needmore Rd, to Dayton, E gas: BP/dsl, Shell/McDonald's, food: Big Boy, Hardee's, lodging: Dayton Executive Hotel, other: Goodyear/auto, Tires UnLtd/repair, to AF Museum, W gas: FA, Marathon/dsl, Speedway/dsl, food: A&W/LJ Silver, Church's, Domino's, New Peking, Subway, Tim Horton, Waffle House, Wendy's, other: Advance Parts, Curves, $General, $Tree, Kroger/gas, O'Reilly Parts, Walgreens, USPO, repair/transmissions

**57b** Wagner Ford Rd, Siebenthaler Rd, Dayton, E gas: Sunoco, lodging: Holiday Inn

**57a** Neva Rd

**56** Stanley Ave, Dayton, E gas: Shell, other: truck repair, W gas: Clark, food: Dragon City Chinese, GoldStar Chili, McDonald's, Rally's, Wendy's, lodging: Dayton Motel

**55b a** Keowee St, Dayton, downtown

**54c** OH 4 N, Webster St, to Springfield, downtown

**54mm** Great Miami River

**54b** OH 48, Main St, Dayton, E gas: Chevrolet/Cadillac, W gas: BP, other: &#9857; HOSPITAL

**54a** Grand Ave (from sb), Dayton, downtown

**53b** OH 49, 1st St, Salem Ave, Dayton, downtown

**53a** OH 49, 3rd St, downtown

**52b a** US 35, E to Dayton, W to Eaton

**51** Edwin C Moses Blvd, Nicholas Rd, E lodging: Courtyard, other: &#9857; HOSPITAL, to U of Dayton, W gas: BP/dsl, food: McDonald's, Wendy's, lodging: Econolodge, other: SunWatch Indian Village

**50b a** OH 741, Kettering St, Dryden Rd, E &#9857; HOSPITAL, W gas: Sunoco/Subway/dsl, food: TJ's Rest., lodging: Holiday Inn, Super 8, other: U-haul

**47** Central Ave, W Carrollton, Moraine, E gas: Sunoco, food: Big Boy, Fricker's, Waffle House, other: auto repair, transmissions, W gas: BP, Speedway, food: Drifter's Grill, KFC, McDonald's, Pizza Hut, Taco Bell, Wendy's, other: USPO

**44** OH 725, to Centerville, Miamisburg, E gas: BP/dsl, Shell, Speedway, food: Applebee's, Big Boy, Blimpie, Bone Fish Grill, Bravo Italian, Burger King, Capt D's, Cena Brazilian, Cusina Italian, Dunkin Donuts, Friendly's, Fuddrucker's, Golden Corral, Hardee's, KFC, La Pinata Mexican, Lonestar Steaks, Max&Erma's, McDonald's, O'Charley's, Olive Garden, Panera Bread, PF Chang's, Red Lobster, Rooster's Grill, Rusty Bucket Grill, Sake Japanese, Skyline Chili, Steak'n Shake, Subway, Taco Bell, TGIFriday, Waffle House, Wendy's, lodging: Comfort Suites, Courtyard, Doubletree Suites, Holiday Inn, Homewood Suites, Residence Inn, SpringHill Suites, Studio 6, other: &#9857; HOSPITAL, Aldi Foods,

**N ↕ S**

**M I D D L E T O W N**

## INTERSTATE 75 CONT'D

**44** Continued
Barnes&Noble, Best Buy, Big O Tire, Border's, Circuit City, Cub Foods, Firestone/auto, Goodyear/auto, Home Depot, Honda/Nissan/Mazda, JC Penney, Jo-Ann Fabrics, Kia, Lowe's Whse, Macy's, Michael's, Mitsubishi, Office Depot, PepBoys, PetsMart, Pontiac, Sears/auto, Target, Tire Discounters, TJ Maxx, Toyota, Walmart/SuperCtr, mall, **W gas:** BP, Marathon, Shell, **food:** Bob Evans, LJ Silver, Perkins, Tim Horton, **lodging:** Day's Inn, Knight's Inn, Red Roof Inn, Super 8, **other:** H HOSPITAL, Aamco, Chevrolet, $General, Ford, NAPA

**43** I-675 N, to Columbus

**38** OH 73, Springboro, Franklin, **E gas:** Shell, Speedway, **food:** Applebee's, Arby's, Bob Evans, Burger King, China Buffet, KFC/Taco Bell, LJ Silver, McDonald's, Papa John's, Pizza Hut, Royal Wok, Skyline Chili, Subway, Tim Horton, TomKatz Cafe, Wendy's, **lodging:** Hampton Inn, Holiday Inn Express, **other:** K-Mart, Kroger, Radio Shack, Tire Discounters, **W gas:** Exxon/dsl, Shell, Swifty, **food:** Big Boy, Cazadore's Mexican, Domino's, Gold Star Chili, Lee's Chicken, McDonald's, **lodging:** Econolodge, Knight's Inn, **other:** AutoZone, $General, $Tree, KOI Parts, Marsh Foods, NAPA, Walgreens, Walmart SuperCtr, repair/tires

**36** OH 123, to Lebanon, Franklin, **E gas:** Exxon/Wendy's/dsl/24hr, Pilot/Subway/Pizza Hut/dsl/scales/24hr/@, Shell/scales/dsl, **food:** McDonald's, Waffle House, **lodging:** Quality Inn, **W gas:** Marathon/White Castle/dsl, Sunoco

**32** OH 122, Middletown, **E gas:** Duke, **food:** McDonald's, Waffle House, **lodging:** Best Value, Super 8, Ramada Inn, Red Carpet Inn, **other:** H HOSPITAL, Ford/Mercury/Lincoln, Jeep, **W gas:** Meijer/dsl/24hr, **food:** Applebee's, Arby's, Big Boy, Bob Evans, Cracker Barrel, El Rancho Grande Mexican, Fazoli's, Fricker's, Golden Corral, Golden Dragon, Goldstar Chili, KFC, La Rosa's, LoneStar Steaks, McDonald's, O'Charley's, Olive Garden, Schlotsky's, Sonic, Steak'n Shake, Wendy's, White Castle, **lodging:** Best Western, Drury Inn, Fairfield Inn, Holiday Inn Express, **other:** Aldi Foods, AutoZone, Buick/GMC/Pontiac, Dillard's, Goodyear/auto, K-Mart, Kohl's, Kroger, Lowe's Whse, SavALot, Sears/auto, Staples, Target, Tire Discounters, Walmart/gas, mall

**29** OH 63, to Hamilton, Monroe, **E gas:** Marathon/White-Castle/dsl, Shell/Popeye's/dsl, Stony Ridge Trk Plaza/dsl/scales, **food:** Burger King, GoldStar Chili, Waffle House, Wendy's/Tim Horton, **lodging:** Comfort Inn, **W gas:** Speedway/dsl, Sunoco/dsl, **food:** Froggy Blue's, McDonald's, Sara Jane's Rest., Subway, **lodging:** Hampton Inn, Howard Johnson, **other:** Curves, flea mkt

**27.5mm** rest area both lanes, full 🦽 facilities, info, 🅲, 🎪, litter barrels, vending, petwalk

**24** OH 129 W, to Hamilton, **W** Cinncinati Gardens

**22** Tylersville Rd, to Mason, Hamilton, **E gas:** Marathon, Thornton's/dsl, Sunoco, **food:** Arby's, Bob Evans, BoneFish Grill, Burger King, Caribou Coffee, Carino's Italian, Chick-fil-A, Chipotle Mexican, Chopsticks, Donato's Pizza, Fazoli's, GoldStar Chili, IHOP, KFC, LJ Silver, Longhorn Steaks, McAlister's Deli, McDonald's, Panera Bread, Perkins, Ruby Tuesday, Skyline Chili,

**22** Continued
Soho Japanese, Taco Bell, TGIFriday, Twin Dragon, Waffle House, Wendy's, **lodging:** Econolodge, **other:** H HOSPITAL, BigLots, Firestone, GNC, Home Depot, Kohl's, Kroger, Office Depot, PetsMart, Radio Shack, Target, Tires+, TJ Maxx, Walgreens, **W gas:** Meijer/dsl/24hr, Shell, Speedway/dsl/24hr, **food:** O'Charley's, Steak'n Shake, **lodging:** Wingate Inn, **other:** Aldi Foods, Lowes Whse, Tire Discounters

**21** Cin-Day Rd, **E food:** Big Boy, **lodging:** Holiday Inn Express, **W gas:** Clark, Marathon, Mobil/Subway/dsl, Speedway/dsl, Shell, **food:** Arby's, Casa Tequila Mexican, Domino's, Gunther's Steaks, Papa John's, Waffle House, Wendy's, **lodging:** Knight's Inn, **other:** Ace Hardware, Curves, Pet Mart, Walgreens, Walmart SuperCtr

**19** Union Centre Blvd, to Fairfield, **E food:** Bravo Italian, Champps Rest., Mitchell's Fish Mkt, Original Pancakes, Panera Bread, PF Chang's, Red Robin, Smokey Bones BBQ, Steak'n Shake, **other:** Barnes & Noble, **W gas:** BP/Subway/dsl, Circle K/Marathon, Shell, **food:** Applebee's, Bob Evans, Buffalo Wild Wings, Burger King, Chipotle Mexican, Don Pablo, Max&Erma's, McDonald's, Quizno's, Rafferty's, River City Grille, Skyline Chili, Starbucks, Uno Pizzaria, Wendy's, **lodging:** Comfort Inn, Courtyard, Hampton Inn, Marriott, Staybridge Suites, **other:** Mercedes, Volvo

**16** I-275 to I-71, to I-74

**15** Sharon Rd, to Sharonville, Glendale, **E gas:** Sunoco, Thornton's/dsl, **food:** Big Boy, Bob Evans, Burbank's BBQ, Cracker Barrel, Jim Dandy BBQ, Ruby Tuesday, Skyline Chili, Subway, Waffle House, **lodging:** Baymont Inn, Country Inn& Suites, Drury Inn, Hilton Garden, Holiday Inn Express, La Quinta, Motel 6, Red Roof Inn, Travelodge, **W on Kimper...gas:** Sunoco, **food:** Arby's, Burger King, Chili's, ChuckeCheese, Dos Amigos, IHOP, Long John Silver, Macaroni Grill, McDonald's, Pizza Hut, Taco Bell, Subway, Tokyo Japanese, Vincenzo's, Wendy's, **lodging:** Best Buy, Econolodge, Extended Stay Deluxe, Extended Stay America, Hamilton Hotel, LivInn Suites, Residence Inn, Sheraton, **other:** Costco/gas, Nissan, Target, Walmart SuperCtr

**14** OH 126, to Woodlawn, Evendale, **E** GE Plant, **lodging:** Wingate Inn (3mi), **W gas:** Swifty Gas, **lodging:** Travelodge

**13** Shepherd Lane, to Lincoln Heights, **E** GE Plant, **W food:** Taco Bell, Wendy's, **other:** Advance Parts

**OH**

Copyright 2009 - The Next Exit®

## INTERSTATE 75 CONT'D

**N ↕ S**

| | |
|---|---|
| **12** | Wyoming Ave, Cooper Ave, to Lockland, **W gas:** Marathon, **food:** DQ, Subway |
| **10a** | OH 126, Ronald Reagan Hwy, **E** Chevrolet |
| **10b** | Galbraith Rd (exits left from nb), Arlington Heights |
| **9** | OH 4, OH 561, Paddock Rd, Seymour Ave, **E** to Cincinnati Gardens, **W** fairgrounds |
| **8** | Towne St, Elmwood Pl (from nb) |
| **7** | OH 562, to I-71, Norwood, Cincinnati Gardens |
| **6** | Mitchell Ave, St Bernard, **E gas:** Marathon, Shell, Sunoco, **food:** White Castle, **lodging:** Holiday Inn Express, **other:** Walgreens, to Cincinnati Zoo, to Xavier U, **W gas:** BP/Subway/dsl, **food:** McDonald's, Rally's, **other:** Advance Parts, Chevrolet, Family$, Ford, Honda, Hyundai, Kroger, Tires+ |
| **4** | I-74 W, US 52, US 27 N, to Indianapolis |
| **3** | to US 27 S, US 127 S, Hopple St, U of Cincinnati, **E gas:** BP/Subway/dsl, **food:** Camp Washington Chili, Isador Italian, White Castle, **other:** H HOSPITAL, Family$, **W gas:** Shell, **food:** Wendy's |
| **2b** | Harrison Ave, industrial district, **W gas:** BP, **food:** McDonald's |
| **2a** | Western Ave, Liberty St (from sb) |
| **1g** | Ezzard Charles Dr, **W lodging:** Ramada Inn |
| **1f** | US 50W, Freeman Ave, **W gas:** Sunoco, **food:** Big Boy, Pizza Hut/Taco Bell, Wendy's, White Castle, **lodging:** Ramada Inn, **other:** Ford, NAPA, Pontiac/GMC, USPO |
| **1e** | 7th St (from sb), downtown, **W lodging:** Ramada Inn |
| **1e** | 5th St, downtown, **E gas:** Crowne Plaza, **lodging:** Sheraton |
| **1a** | I-71 N, to Cincinnati, downtown, to stadium |
| **0mm** | Ohio/Kentucky state line, Ohio River |

## INTERSTATE 76

**E ↕ W**

| Exit # | Services |
|---|---|
| | Ohio/Pennsylvania state line |
| | **Exits 232-235 are on the Ohio Turnpike. See Ohio Turnpike exits 232-235** |
| **60mm** | I-76 eb joins Ohio TPK (toll) |
| **57** | to OH 45, Bailey Rd, to Warren |
| **54** | OH 534, to Newton Falls, Lake Milton, **N** RV camping, **S gas:** BP, **other:** to Berlin Lake, camping |
| **52mm** | Lake Milton |
| **48** | OH 225, to Alliance, **N** to W Branch SP, camping, **S** to Berlin Lake |
| **45.5mm** | **rest area both lanes, full** 🅿 **facilities,** 🕻, 🎍, **litter barrels, petwalk** |
| **43** | OH 14, to Alliance, Ravenna, **N** to W Branch SP, **S gas:** Marathon/dsl, **other:** fireworks |
| **38b a** | OH 5, OH 44, to Ravenna, **N gas:** BP, Speedway/dsl, **food:** Acupulco Mexican, Arby's, McDonald's, Wendy's, **other:** H HOSPITAL, **S gas:** Marathon/Circle K/Subway, **food:** Cracker Barrel, **other:** $General, Giant Eagle Foods/drug, auto repair, RV camping |
| **33** | OH 43, to Hartville, Kent, **N gas:** BP/dsl, Sunoco, **food:** Salsita's Mexican, **lodging:** Comfort Inn, Day's Inn, Econolodge, Hampton Inn, Holiday Inn Express, Ramada Inn, Super 8, **other:** to Kent St U, **S gas:** Speedway/dsl, **food:** Giomino's Italian, McDonald's, Wendy's, **other:** RV camping, vet |

**OH**

**A K R O N**

| | |
|---|---|
| **31** | rd 18, Tallmadge, **N food:** Applebee's, Arabica Cafe, Beef O'Brady's, Quizno's, Strickland's Cafe, **other:** $Tree, Lowe's, Walmart SuperCtr/Subway |
| **29** | OH 532, Tallmadge, Mogadore |
| **27** | OH 91, Canton Rd, Gilchrist Rd, **N food:** Bob Evans, **S gas:** Marathon/Subway/dsl, **food:** Hardee's, **lodging:** Best Western, NAPA Truck Parts |
| **26** | OH 18, E Market St, Mogadore Rd, **N gas:** Circle K/dsl, Marathon/dsl, **other:** Goodyear/auto, **S food:** Arby's, McDonald's, Subway, Wendy's, **other:** $General |
| **25b a** | Martha Ave, General St, Brittain, **N gas:** Citgo, **other:** Goodyear World Hdqtrs, Mercedes, Toyota/Scion |
| **24** | Arlington St, Kelly Ave, **N** Goodyear World Hdqtrs |
| **23b** | OH 8, Buchtell Ave, to Cuyahoga, to U of Akron |
| **23a** | I-77 S, to Canton |
| **22b** | Wolf Ledges, Akron, downtown, **S gas:** BP, **food:** McDonald's |
| **22a** | Main St, Broadway, downtown |
| **21c** | OH 59 E, Dart Ave, **N** H HOSPITAL |
| **21b** | Lakeshore St, Bowery St (from eb) |
| **21a** | East Ave (from wb) |
| **20** | I-77 N (from eb), to Cleveland |
| **19** | Battles Ave, Kenmore Blvd |
| **18** | I-277, US 224 E, to Canton, Barberton, interchange |
| **17b a** | OH 619, Wooster Rd, State St, to Barberton, **S gas:** Sunoco/dsl, **other:** H HOSPITAL, NAPA, tires/repair |
| **16** | Barber Rd, **S gas:** Rocky's Gas, **food:** Tomaso's Italian, **other:** Chrysler/Jeep/Suzuki |
| **14** | Cleve-Mass Rd, to Norton, **S gas:** BP, **food:** Charlie's Rest. |
| **13b a** | OH 21, N to Cleveland, S to Massillon |
| **11** | OH 261, Wadsworth, **N gas:** Speedway, **S gas:** GNC Nutrition, Kohl's, Lowe's Whse, MC Sports, PetCo, Target |
| **9** | OH 94, to N Royalton, Wadsworth, **N gas:** Marathon/Circle K, **food:** Applebee's, Arby's, Bob Evans, Burger King, Chinda Express, KFC, Marie's Cafe., McDonald's, Pizza Hut, Ponderosa, Subway, Taco Bell, Wendy's, **lodging:** Holiday Inn Express, Ramada Ltd, **other:** Buehler's Foods, DrugMart, Goodyear/auto, Home Depot, K-Mart, NTB, Radio Shack, Walmart SuperCtr, tires, **S gas:** BP/dsl, Convenient/gas, Marathon, Sunoco, **lodging:** Legacy Inn, **other:** AutoZone, Rite Aid |
| **7** | OH 57, to Rittman, Medina, **N gas:** Marathon/dsl, **other:** H HOSPITAL, ✈ |
| **6mm** | weigh sta both lanes |
| **2** | OH 3, to Medina, Seville, **N gas:** Marathon/Circle K, **food:** DQ, Hardee's, Huddle House, Subway, **lodging:** Comfort Inn, Hawthorn Suites, **other:** Maple Lakes Camping (seasonal), **S gas:** Petro US/dsl, Sunoco, **food:** Acorn Rest., **other:** Curves, Ritzman Drug |
| **1** | I-76 E, to Akron, US 224, **W on US 224 gas:** Pilot/Country Kitchen/Subway/dsl/scales/24hr, TA/Burger King/Popeye's/dsl/24hr/@, **food:** Arby's, McDonald's, **lodging:** Super 8, **other:** Blue Beacon, SpeedCo, Chippewa Valley Camping (1mi), SpeedCo |
| **0mm** | I-76 begins/ends on I-71, exit 209. |

## INTERSTATE 77

| Exit # | Services |
|---|---|
| | I-77 begins/ends on I-90 exit 172, in Cleveland. |
| **163c** | I-90, E to Erie, W to Toledo |
| **163b** | E 9th St, Tower City |

## INTERSTATE 77 CONT'D

| | |
|---|---|
| **162b** | E 22nd St, E 14th St (from nb) |
| **162a** | E 30th St, Woodland Ave, Broadway St (from nb), **W** USPO |
| **161b** | I-490 W, to I-71, E 55th, **E** **H** HOSPITAL |
| **161a** | OH 14 (from nb), Broadway St |
| **160** | Pershing Ave (from nb), **W** **H** HOSPITAL |
| **159b** | Fleet Ave, **E** **gas:** BP/Subway/dsl |
| **159a** | Harvard Ave, Newburgh Heights, **W** **gas:** BP/Subway/dsl/24hr, Marathon |
| **158** | Grant Ave, Cuyahoga Heights |
| **157** | OH 21, OH 17 (from sb), Brecksville Rd |
| **156** | I-480, to Youngstown, Toledo |
| **155** | Rockside Rd, to Independence, **E** **gas:** Shell, Sunoco, **food:** Bob Evans, Bonefish Grill, Chester's, Chipotle Mexican, Del Monico's Steaks, Denny's, McDonald's, Outback Steaks, Red Robin, Shula's Steaks, Wendy's, Zoup, **lodging:** Comfort Inn, Doubletree, Embassy Suites, Holiday Inn, La Quinta, Red Roof Inn, **other:** Lincoln/Mercury, Walgreens, **W** **gas:** BP/dsl, **food:** Applebee's, Damon's, Longhorn Steaks, **lodging:** Courtyard, Hampton Inn, Hyatt Place, Residence Inn, Sheraton |
| **153** | Pleasant Valley Rd, to Independence, 7 Hills |
| **151** | Wallings Rd |
| **149** | OH 82, to Broadview Heights, Brecksville, **1 mi** **E** **gas:** BP, Shell, **food:** McDonald's, Panera Bread, Simons Cafe, Starbucks, **other:** Walgreens, **W** **gas:** BP, **food:** Coco's, Domino's, Mr. Hero, **lodging:** Tallyho Motel, **other:** Curves |
| **147** | to OH 21, Miller Rd (from sb) |
| **146** | I-80/Ohio Tpk, to Youngstown, Toledo |
| **145** | OH 21 (from nb), **E** **gas:** Pilot/Wendy's/dsl/scales, **food:** DQ, Memories Rest., Richfield Rest., Subway, **lodging:** Hampton Inn, Holiday Inn Express, Howard Johnson, Quality Inn, Super 8 |
| **144** | I-271 N, to Erie |
| **143** | OH 176, to I-271 S, **E** to Coliseum, **W** **gas:** Sunoco, **food:** Arabica Café, McDonald's, Panda Chinese, Subway, Teresa's Pizza, **other:** Curves |
| **141mm** | **rest area both lanes, full** ♿ **facilities,** 🚻, 🧺, **litter barrels, vending, petwalk** |
| **138** | Ghent Rd, **2 mi** **E** **lodging:** Hilton, Sheraton, **W** **gas:** Circle K/dsl, **food:** Lanning's Rest., Vaccaro's Italian |
| **137b a** | OH 18, to Fairlawn, Medina, **E** **gas:** BP, Circle K, GetGo, Shell, Speedway, **food:** A Wok, Applebee's, Bob Evans, Boston Mkt, Chili's, Chipotle Mexican, Cracker Barrel, Donato's Pizza, Dynasty Chinese, Fleming's Steaks, Friendly's, Honeybaked Ham, Hyde Park Grill, KFC, LoneStar Steaks, Macaroni Grill, Max&Erma's, McDonald's, Olive Garden, Pad Thai, Quizno's, Red Lobster, Ruby Tuesday, Starbucks, Steak'n Shake, Taco Bell, Wendy's, **lodging:** Courtyard, Hampton Inn, Hilton, Holiday Inn, Quality Inn, Motel 6, Super 8, **other:** Acme Foods, Barnes&Noble, Best Buy, Borders Books, Ford, Dillard's, $Tree, Giant Eagle Foods, Home Depot, Jo-Ann Fabrics, Lowes Whse, Macy's, Michael's, Mr. Tire, Old Navy, PetsMart, Sam's Club, Staples, TJ Maxx, Walmart, World Mkt, **W** **gas:** Sunoco/dsl, **food:** Burger King, Don Pablo, Longhorn Steaks, Outback Steaks, TGIFriday, Tres Patrilios, Wasabi Grill, **lodging:** Best Western, Comfort Inn, Extended Stay America, Radisson, Residence Inn, Studio+ |

| | |
|---|---|
| **136** | OH 21S, to Massillon |
| **135** | Cleveland-Massillon Rd (from nb) |
| **133** | Ridgewood Rd, Miller Rd, **E** **gas:** Circle K/dsl, **food:** Wendy's |
| **132** | White Pond Dr, Mull Ave, **E** Rosarita Cantina, golf |
| **131** | OH 162, Copley Rd, **E** **gas:** Circle K, **other:** SavALot Foods, Walgreens, USPO, **W** **gas:** BP/dsl/24hr, **food:** McDonald's, Pizza Hut |
| **130** | OH 261, Wooster Ave, **E** **gas:** Circle K, Valero, **food:** Ann's Place, Burger King, Church's, New China, Rally's, Subway, White Castle, **other:** Acme Foods, Advance Parts, AutoZone, Family$, **W** **food:** KFC, **other:** Chevrolet, Toyota/Scion, U-Haul |
| **129** | I-76 W, to I-277, to Kenmore Blvd, Barberton |
| **21a** | East Ave (from nb), no facilities, I-77 S and I-76 E run together |
| **21b** | Lakeshore (from sb), to Bowery St |
| **21c** | OH 59 E, Dart Ave, downtown, **E** **H** HOSPITAL |
| **22a** | Main St, Broadway St, downtown, **W** auto parts |
| **22b** | Grant St, Wolf Ledges, **W** **gas:** BP, **food:** McDonald's, **other:** Family$ |
| **125b** | I-76 E, to Youngstown, I-77 and I-76 run together |
| **125a** | OH 8 N, to Cuyahoga Falls, U of Akron |
| **124b** | Lover's Lane, Cole Ave |
| **124a** | Archwood Ave, Firestone Blvd |
| **123b** | OH 764, Wilbeth Rd, **E** to ✈ |
| **123a** | Waterloo Rd, **W** **gas:** Marathon, **other:** Acme Foods |
| **122b a** | I-277, US 224 E, to Barberton, Mogadore |
| **120** | Arlington Rd, to Green, **E** **gas:** Speedway/dsl, **food:** Applebee's, Church's, Denny's, Friendly's, Golden Corral, IHOP, Pizza Hut, Ryan's, Starbucks, Waffle House, White Castle, **lodging:** Comfort Inn, Quality Inn, Red Roof Inn, **other:** $General, Home Depot, Kohl's, Staples, Walmart/auto, **W** **gas:** BP, Speedway, **food:** Bob Evans, Burger King, Lion Garden, Mariachi Mexican, McDonald's, Subway, Taco Bell, TGIFriday, Wendy's, **lodging:** Fairfield Inn, Hampton Inn, **other:** Buick/Pontiac/GMC, Chevrolet, Goodyear/auto, Honda/Mazda, Hyundai, Lexus, Lowes Whse, Nissan, Sirpilla RV Ctr/Camping World, Target |
| **118** | OH 241, to OH 619, Massillon, **E** **gas:** Sheetz, Speedway/dsl, **food:** Gionino's Pizza, Subway, **W** **gas:** BP/Circle K, GetGo, **food:** Arby's, Belgrade Gardens, McDonald's, Menche's Rest., Pancho's Mexican, Quizno's, **lodging:** Cambria Suites, Super 8, **other:** **H** HOSPITAL |
| **113** | Akron-Canton ✈, **2 mi** **W** **lodging:** Hilton Garden, **other:** Clay's RV |

**N ↕ S**

**CANTON**

## INTERSTATE 77 CONT'D

**112** new exit

**111** Portage St, N Canton, **E gas:** Circle K, Marathon, Speedway, Sunoco/dsl, TA/Country Pride/dsl/scales/24hr/@, **food:** Burger King, Cheing's Express, Giesen Haus, KFC, Palambo's Italian, Subway, Sylvester's Italian, **other:** TrueValue, **W gas:** BP/dsl, **food:** Carrabba's, Chuck-eCheese, Coldstone Creamery, Cracker Barrel, Donato's Pizza, Don Pablo, Dunkin Donuts/Baskin-Robbins, Hungry Howie's, IHOP, Longhorn Steaks, Lucky Star Chinese, McDonald's, Pizza Hut, Quizno's, Red Robin, Rockne's Cafe, Samantha's, Starbucks, Taco Bell, Wendy's, **lodging:** Best Western, Microtel, Motel 6, **other:** Best Buy, BJ's Whse, Borders Books, Chevrolet, DrugMart, Gander Mtn, Giant Eagle Foods, GNC, Goodyear/auto, Harley-Davidson, Home Depot, Lowes Whse, Marshall's, Old Navy, Sam's Club/gas, Walmart/Subway/auto

**109b a** Everhard Rd, Whipple Ave, **E gas:** Citgo/Subway, Speedway/dsl, **food:** Burger King, Denny's, Fazoli's, McDonald's, Taco Bell, **lodging:** Comfort Inn, Fairfield Inn, Hampton Inn, Residence Inn, **other:** Ford, Saturn, **W gas:** Marathon, **food:** Applebee's, Arby's, Bob Evans, Bravo Italian, Buffalo Wild Wings, Buffet Dynasty, Chick-fil-A, Chipotle Mexican, Cheeseburger Paradise, CiCi's Pizza, Damon's, Friendly's, HomeTown Buffet, HoneyBaked Ham, Hong Kong Buffet, Logan's Roadhouse, LoneStar Steaks, Macaroni Grill, Manchu Café, Max&Erma's, Mulligan's, Olive Garden, Outback Steaks, Panera Bread, Panini's Grill, Papa Bear's, Penn Sta. Subs, Ponderosa, Red Lobster, Ricky Ly's Chinese, Robek's Grill, Ruby Tuesday, Sahara Grill, Starbucks, Steak'n Shake, TGIFriday, Wendy's, **lodging:** Courtyard, Day's Inn, Holiday Inn, Parke Suites, Red Roof Inn, **other:** Advance Parts, Best Buy, Circuit City, Dillard's, $Tree, Firestone/auto, Goodyear/auto, Jo-Ann Crafts, Kohl's, Macy's, Marc's Foods, Michael's, PetsMart, Radio Shack, Sears/auto, Target, TJ Maxx, World Mkt, mall

**107b a** US 62, OH 687, Fulton Rd, to Alliance, **E** City Park, **W gas:** Circle K, **other:** Pro Football Hall of Fame

**106** 13th St NW, **E H** HOSPITAL

**105b** OH 172, Tuscarawas St, downtown

**105a** 6th St SW (no EZ return from sb), **W food:** Subway, **other:** H HOSPITAL, AutoZone

**104** US 30, US 62, to E Liverpool, Massillon

**103** OH 800 S, **E gas:** Marathon/Subway, Speedway, **food:** Arby's, Taco Bell, Waffle House, **other:** Advance Parts, Firestone

**101** OH 627, to Faircrest St, **E gas:** Gulliver's Trvl Plaza/dsl/rest./scales, Speedway/McDonald's, **food:** Wendy's

**99** Fohl Rd, to Navarre, **W gas:** Sunoco, KOA (4mi)

**93** OH 212, to Zoar, Bolivar, **E gas:** Speedway/Subway, **food:** McDonald's, Pizza Hut, Wendy's, **lodging:** Sleep Inn, **other:** $General, Giant Eagle Foods, NAPA, Zoar Tavern (3mi), vet, to Lake Atwood Region, **W gas:** Marathon/DQ, **other:** KOA

**92mm** weigh sta both lanes

**87** US 250W, to Strasburg, **3 mi E food:** Arby's, **W gas:** Marathon/Quizno's/dsl, **food:** Creekside Cafe, Damon's Pizza, Hardee's, Manor Rest., McDonald's, Subway, **lodging:** Ramada Ltd, Twins Motel

**85mm** rest areas both lanes, full & facilities, info, **C**, ⊼, litter barrels, petwalk

---

**CAMBRIDGE**

**83** OH 39, OH 211, to Sugarcreek, Dover, **E gas:** BP, Speedway/Subway/dsl, **food:** Bob Evans, KFC, McDonald's, Shoney's, Wendy's, **lodging:** Hospitality Inn, **other:** H HOSPITAL, Ford/Chrysler/Dodge/Jeep, Lincoln/Mercury/Nissan, tires, **W gas:** Marathon/DQ, **lodging:** Comfort Inn

**81** US 250, to Uhrichsville, OH 39, New Philadelphia, **E gas:** Marathon, Sheetz/dsl, Speedway, **food:** Burger King, Denny's, El San Jose Mexican, Hog Heaven, LJ Silver, McDonald's, Pizza Hut, Quizno's, Taco Bell, Texas Roadhouse, **lodging:** Hampton Inn, Holiday Inn, Knight's Inn, Motel 6, Schoenbrunn Inn, Super 8, **other:** Advance Parts, Aldi Foods, Big Lots, $General, Walmart SuperCtr, **W gas:** Eagle/dsl/rest./24hr, **other:** Harley-Davidson

**73** OH 751, to rd 21, Stone Creek, **W gas:** Marathon

**65** US 36, Port Washington, Newcomerstown, **W gas:** BP, Duke/dsl/rest., Speedway/Wendy's/24hr, **food:** McDonald's, **lodging:** Hampton Inn, Super 8

**64mm** Tuscarawas River

**54** OH 541, rd 831, to Plainfield, Kimbolton, **W gas:** BP, **food:** Jackie's Rest.

**47** US 22, to Cadiz, Cambridge, **E** to Salt Fork SP (6mi), lodging, RV camping, **W gas:** BP/repair, **other:** H HOSPITAL, to Glass Museum, info

**46b a** US 40, to Old Washington, Cambridge, **W gas:** BP/24hr, Exxon/Wendy's/dsl, Speedway/dsl/24hr, **food:** Burger King, Lee's Rest., LJ Silver, McDonald's, Wally's Pizza, **other:** Riesbeck's Food/deli, SavALot Foods, vet

**44b a** I-70, E to Wheeling, W to Columbus

**41** OH 209, OH 821, Byesville, **W gas:** BP/dsl, Circle K, Starfire, **food:** McDonald's, **other:** Byesville Drug, $General, Family$

**39mm** rest area nb, full & facilities, **C**, ⊼, litter barrels, petwalk, vending

**37** OH 313, Buffalo, **E gas:** BP, Duke, **food:** Coutos Pizza, Donk's BBQ, Subway, **other:** truck repair, to Senecaville Lake

**36mm** rest area sb, full & facilities, **C**, ⊼, litter barrels, petwalk, vending

**28** OH 821, Belle Valley, **E gas:** Sunoco/dsl, **other:** USPO, to Wolf Run SP, RV camping

**25** OH 78, Caldwel, **E gas:** BP, Pilot/Arby's/dsl/scales/24hr, Sunoco/Subway/dsl, **food:** DQ, Lori's Rest., McDonald's, **lodging:** Best Western, **other:** Buick/Chevrolet/Pontiac

**16** OH 821, Macksburg, **E food, other:** antiques

**6** OH 821, to Devola, **E gas:** Exxon, **W gas:** BP/dsl/LP, **other:** H HOSPITAL, RV camping

**3mm** rest area nb, full & facilities, info, **C**, vending, ⊼, litter barrels, petwalk

---

**MARIETTA**

**1** OH 7, to OH 26, Marietta, **E gas:** GoMart/dsl/24hr, **food:** CiCi's, DQ, River City Grill, Ryan's, Subway, **lodging:** Comfort Inn, Econolodge, Holiday Inn, **other:** Aldi Foods, Buick/GMC/Pontiac, Cadillac/Chevrolet, Chrysler/Jeep, Dodge, Ford/Lincoln/Mercury, Harley-Davidson, Lowes Whse, Toyota/Scion, Walmart SuperCtr, **W gas:** BP/dsl, Duke/dsl, GetGo, Marathon/dsl, Speedway/dsl, **food:** Applebees, Arby's, Bob Evan's, Bruster's, Bob Evans, Burger King, Capt D's, China Fun, E Chicago Pizza, Empire Buffet, LJ Silver, McDonald's, Napoli's Pizza, Papa John's, Pizza Hut, Quizno's, Shoney's, Subway, Taco Bell, Tim Horton, Wendy's, **lodging:** Hampton Inn, Microtel, Super 8, **other:** AutoZone, $General, Food4Less, Jo-Ann Crafts, K-Mart, Kroger/24hr, Sav-a-Lot Foods, TrueValue, Walgreens, museum, st patrol

**0mm** Ohio/West Virginia state line, Ohio River

E ↕ W

**Y O U N G S T O W N**

## INTERSTATE 80

| Exit # | Services |
|---|---|
| 237mm | Ohio/Pennsylvania state line |
| 237mm | **Welcome Ctr wb, full** 🚹 **facilities, info,** 📞, 🎁, **litter barrels, vending, petwalk** |
| 234b a | US 62, OH 7, to Sharon, PA, Hubbard, **N gas:** ⊕*FLYING J*/Country Mkt/Magic Dragon Chinese/ dsl/scales/24hr/LP, Shell/dsl/rest./motel/24hr/@, **food:** Arby's, Burger King, McDonald's, Waffle House, **lodging:** Best Western, **other:** Blue Beacon, Homestead RV Ctr., RV camping (2mi), tire/dsl repair, **S gas:** Love's/Chester's/Subway/dls/scales/24hr, **other** Chevrolet |
| 232mm | weigh sta wb |
| 229 | OH 193, Belmont Ave, to Youngstown, **N gas:** GetGo, Speedway/dsl, **food:** Fortune Garden Chinese, Handel's Ice Cream, Knight's Inn, Rotelli Italian, Subway, **lodging:** Hampton Inn, Metroplex Hotel, Super 8, TallyHotel, Travel Inn, **other:** Giant Eagle Foods, **S gas:** BP, Shell, **food:** Arby's, Antone's Italian, Bob Evans, Charley's Subs, Cancun Mexican, Denny's, Golden Hunan Chinese, Ianazone's Pizza, Inner Circle Pizza, Jimmy's Italian, KFC, LJ Silver, McDonald's, Papa John's, Pizza Hut, Subway, Taco Bell, Treacher's, Yougtown Crab Co, Wendy's, Westfork Roadhouse, **lodging:** Days Inn, Quality Inn, **other:** Advance Parts, Aldi Foods, AutoZone, BigLots, Family$, Firestone, Goodyear/auto, Rite Aid, Sav-A-Lot Foods, Walgreens |
| 228 | OH 11, to Warren (exits left from eb), Ashtabula |
| 227 | US 422, Girard, Youngstown, **N gas:** Shell/dsl/24hr, **food:** Burger King, DQ, JibJab Hotdogs, Subway |
| 226 | Salt Springs Rd, to I-680 (from wb), **N gas:** BP/Dunkin Donuts/dsl, Sheetz/24hr, **food:** McDonald's, Waffle House, **other:** vet, **S gas:** Mr Fuel/Piccadilly/dsl/24hr, Petro/dsl/ rest./scales/24hr/@, Pilot/Arby's/scales/dsl/24hr, **other:** Blue Beacon, SpeedCo, dsl repair |
| 224b | I-680 (from eb), to Youngstown |
| 224a | OH 11 S, to Canfield |
| 223 | OH 46, to Niles, **N gas:** Country Fair, Pilot/McDonald's/ scales/dsl/24hr, **food:** Bob Evans, Burger King, IceHouse Rest., Salsita's Mexican, **lodging:** Comfort Inn, Economy Inn, **S gas:** BP/dsl, FuelMart/dsl, Sunoco/Subway, TA/ Counry Pride/dsl/rest./scales/24hr/@, **food:** Arby's, Brudders Grill, Cracker Barrel, DQ, LJ Quaker Steak & Lube, Silver/Taco Bell, Perkins, Starbucks, Wendy's, **lodging:** Best Western, Country Inn & Suites, Econolodge, Fairfield Inn, Hampton Inn, Knight's Inn, Sleep Inn, Super 8, **other:** Blue Beacon, Freightliner/24hr, Harley-Davidson |
| 221mm | Meander Reservoir |
| 219mm | I-80 wb joins Ohio Tpk (toll) |
| | **For I-80 exits 2-218, see Ohio Turnpike.** |

## INTERSTATE 90

E ↕ W

| Exit # | Services |
|---|---|
| 244mm | Ohio/Pennsylvania state line |
| 242mm | **Welcome Ctr/weigh sta wb, full** 🚹 **facilities, info,** 📞, 🎁, **litter barrels, petwalk** |
| 241 | OH 7, to Andover, Conneaut, **N food:** Burger King, McDonald's (2mi), **lodging:** Day's Inn, **other:** 🏥 HOSPITAL, AutoZone, CVS Drug, Evergreen RV Park, K-Mart, **S food:** Beef&Beer Café |

| | |
|---|---|
| 235 | OH 84, OH 193, to Youngstown, N Kingsville, **N gas:** Grab&Go/gas, Marathon/Circle K, **lodging:** Dav-Ed Motel, **other:** Village Green Camping (2mi), **S gas:** Circle K/Subway/dsl, TA/BP/Burger King/dsl/scales/24hr/@, **food:** Kay's Place Diner, **lodging:** Kingsville Motel, **other:** tire repair |
| 228 | OH 11, to Ashtabula, Youngstown, **N** 🏥 HOSPITAL (4mi) |
| 223 | OH 45, to Ashtabula, **N gas:** ⊕*FLYING J*/Shell/Country Mkt/dsl/LP/scales/24hr, **food:** Mr C's Rest., **lodging:** Best Value Inn, Comfort Inn, Holiday Inn Express, Sleep Inn, **other:** Buccaneer Camping, **S gas:** BP, Pilot/Subway/dsl/scales/24hr, SpeedCo, **food:** Burger King, McDonald's, Waffle House, **lodging:** Hampton Inn |
| 218 | OH 534, Geneva, **N gas:** BP, GetGo, **food:** Best Friend's Grill, Chop's Grille, McDonald's, Pizza Hut, Wendy's, **lodging:** Howard Johnson, **other:** 🏥 HOSPITAL, Goodyear/repair, Indian Creek Camping (8mi), to Geneva SP, **S gas:** KwikFill/dsl/rest./scales/24hr, **food:** Quizno's, **other:** Kenisse's Camping |
| 212 | OH 528, to Thompson, Madison, **N food:** McDonald's, **other:** Mentor RV Ctr, **S gas:** Marathon/dsl, **food:** Medvec's Grill, **other:** Heritage Hills Camping (4mi), radiators |
| 205 | Vrooman Rd, 0-1 mi **S gas:** BP/dsl, Marathon/dsl, **food:** Capps Eatery, Subway |
| 200 | OH 44, to Painesville, Chardon, **S gas:** BP/Subway/ dsl, Sunoco/dsl, **food:** Bellacino's, McDonald's, Palmer's Bistro, Red Hawk Grille, Teresa's Pizzaria, Waffle House, **lodging:** Baymont Inn, Renaissance, **other:** 🏥 HOSPITAL, Curves, Reider's Foods, hwy patrol |
| 198mm | **rest area both lanes, full** 🚹 **facilities,** 📞, 🎁, **litter barrels, vending, petwalk** |
| 195 | OH 615, Center St, Kirtland Hills, Mentor, **1-2 mi N gas:** BP, **food:** El Rodeo Mexican, Yours Truly Rest., **lodging:** Best Western |
| 193 | OH 306, to Mentor, Kirtland, **N gas:** BP/Subway, **food:** McDonald's, **lodging:** Motel 6, **S gas:** Marathon, **food:** Burger King, Dino's Rest., Texas Cattle Co, **lodging:** Day's Inn/café, Red Roof Inn, **other:** 🏥 HOSPITAL, Kirtland Temple LDS Historic Site |
| 190 | Express Lane to I-271 (from wb) |
| 189 | OH 91, to Willoughby, Willoughby Hills, **N gas:** BP/ dsl, Shell/24hr, **food:** Bob Evans, Café Europa, Cracker Barrel, Damon's, Eat 'n Park, Peking Chef, Subway, Texas Roadhouse, Wendy's, **lodging:** Courtyard, Motel 6, Travelodge, **other:** 🏥 HOSPITAL, CVS Drug, Walgreens, **N other:** Lexus |

OH

**OH**

E ↕ W

## INTERSTATE 90 CONT'D

| | |
|---|---|
| **188** | I-271 S, to Akron |
| **187** | OH 84, Bishop Rd, to Wickliffe, Willoughby, **S gas:** BP/dsl, Shell, **food:** Baker's Square, Burger King, China King, Manhattan Deli, Mazzio's, McDonald's, Quizno's, Subway, **lodging:** Holiday Inn, **other:** Ⓗ HOSPITAL, Curves, CVS Drug, Chevrolet, Giant Eagle Foods, Marc's Foods, Mazda/VW, NTB, Sam's Club, vet |
| **186** | US 20, Euclid Ave, **N gas:** Sunoco, **food:** Grand Rodeo Mexican, McDonald's, **lodging:** Comfort Inn, **other:** Dodge/Subaru, Ford, Isuzu, radiators, **S gas:** Shell, **food:** Arby's, KFC, Pizza Hut, Popeye's, R-Ribs, Sidewalk Cafe, Taco Bell, **other:** Advance Parts, $General, Firestone/auto, NAPA, SaveAlot Foods |
| **185** | OH 2 E (exits left from eb), to Painesville |
| **184b** | OH 175, E 260th St, **N gas:** Shell/autocare, **S other:** NTB, Ruff's RV Ctr, transmissions, vet |
| **184a** | Babbitt Rd, same as 183 |
| **183** | E 222nd St, **N other:** GMC, **S gas:** BP, Sunoco/dsl/24hr |
| **182b a** | 185 St, 200 St, **N food:** Muldoon's Eatery, **other:** Home Depot, Honda, Hyundai, **S other:** Marathon/dsl, Shell, Speedway |
| **181b a** | E 156th St, **S gas:** BP/24hr |
| **180b a** | E 140th St, E 152nd St |
| **179** | OH 283 E, to Lake Shore Blvd |
| **178** | Eddy Rd, to Bratenahl |
| **177** | University Circle, MLK Dr, **N other:** Cleveland Lake SP, **S other:** Ⓗ HOSPITAL, Rockefeller Park |
| **176** | E 72nd St |
| **175** | E 55th St, Marginal Rds |
| **174b** | OH 2 W, to Lakewood, downtown, Rock&Roll Hall of Fame, Browns Stadium |
| **174a** | Lakeside Ave |
| **173c** | Superior Ave, St Clair Ave, downtown, **N gas:** BP |
| **173b** | Chester Ave, **S gas:** BP |
| **173a** | Prospect Ave (from wb), downtown |
| **172d** | Carnegie Ave, downtown, **S food:** Burger King, **other:** Cadillac |
| **172c b** | E 9th St, **S other:** Ⓗ HOSPITAL, to Cleveland St U |
| **172a** | I-77 S, to Akron |
| **171b a** | US 422, OH 14, Broadway St, Ontario St, **N lodging:** Hilton Garden, **other:** to Browns Stadium |
| **170c b** | I-71 S, to I-490 |
| **170a** | US 42, W 25th St, **S** gas |
| **169** | W 44th St, W 41st St, **N** Ⓗ HOSPITAL |
| **167b a** | OH 10, West Blvd, 98th St, to Lorain Ave, **N** Ⓗ HOSPITAL, **S gas:** BP/dsl, **other:** CVS Drug |
| **166** | W 117th St, **N gas:** BP/dsl, Get Go, Shell, **food:** KFC, Penn Sta. Subs, **other:** Advance Parts, Home Depot, Staples, Target, **S food:** Church's/White Castle |
| **165** | W 140th St, Bunts Rd, Warren Rd, **N other:** Ⓗ HOSPITAL |
| **164** | McKinley Ave, to Lakewood |
| **162** | Hilliard Blvd (from wb), to Westway Blvd, Rocky River, **S gas:** BP, Shell |
| **161** | OH 2, OH 254 (from eb, no EZ return), Detroit Rd, Rocky River |
| **160** | Clague Rd (from wb), **S other:** Ⓗ HOSPITAL, same as 159 |
| **159** | OH 252, Columbia Rd, **N gas:** Speedway, **food:** Carrabba's, Clubhouse Grill, Dave&Buster's, Key West |

CLEVELAND

CLEVELAND

| | |
|---|---|
| **159** | Continued<br>Cafe, Outback Steaks, **lodging:** Courtyard, TownePlace Suites, Super 8, **S gas:** BP, **food:** Houlihan's, KFC, McDonald's, Taco Bell, **other:** Chevrolet, NTB, Rico's Mkt |
| **156** | Crocker Rd, Bassett Rd, Westlake, Bay Village, **N gas:** BP, Shell, **lodging:** Extended Stay Deluxe, Holiday Inn, Red Roof Inn, Residence Inn, **S gas:** Marathon/dsl, **food:** Applebee's, Blake's Seafood, Bob Evans, Cheesecake Factory, Max&Erma's, McDonald's, Subway, TGIFriday, Wendy's, **lodging:** Hampton Inn, **other:** Ⓗ HOSPITAL, Borders Books, CVS Drug, Giant Eagle, GNC, K-Mart, Marc's Foods, Radio Shack, mall |
| **153** | OH 83, Avon Lake, **N gas:** GetGo/dsl, Marathon/Circle K, Speedway, **food:** Bubba's BBQ, Buffalo Wild Wings, Perkins, **other:** Best Buy, Walmart/auto/gas, **S food:** Applebees, Bob Evans, Burger King, Caribou Coffee, CiCi's Pizza, Coldstone Creamery, 5 Guys Burgers, Hot Dog Heaven, IHOP, Moe's SW Grill, Panera Bread, Quizno's, Red Robin, Subway, Wendy's, **other:** Costco/gas, Curves, CVS Drug, GNC, Home Depot, Kohl's, Marshall's, Michael's, Old Navy, Radio Shack, Target, World Mkt |
| **151** | OH 611, Avon, **N gas:** BP/dsl, Pilot/Subway/dsl/24hr, **food:** McDonald's, Dianna's Deli, **lodging:** Fairfield Inn, **other:** Avon RV, Goodyear/repair, Harley Davidson, **S gas:** BJ's Whse/gas, **food:** Mulligan's Grille |
| **148** | OH 254, Sheffield, Avon, **N food:** Quaker Steak, **other:** Dodge, Ford, KIA, Mazda, Mitsubishi, Nissan, **S gas:** BP, GetGo, Speedway, **food:** Arby's, Burger King, Cracker Barrel, Donato's Pizza, KFC, McDonald's, Pizza Hut, Quizno's, Ruby Tuesday, Sedona Grill, Steak'n Shake, Subway, Taco Bell, Wendy's, **other:** Aldi Foods, CVS Drug, $General, Drug Mart, Gander Mtn, Giant Eagle, NTB, Sam's Club/gas |
| **147mm** | Black River |
| **145** | OH 57, to Lorain, I-80/Ohio Tpk E, Elyria, **N food:** Burger King, George's Rest., KFC, **other:** Ⓗ HOSPITAL, U-Haul, **S gas:** BP/McDonald's/dsl, Shell, Speedway **food:** Applebee's, Arby's, Bob Evans, Buffalo Wild Wings, Denny's, Eat'n Park, Fazoli's, Golden Corral, Harry Buffalo, Jumbo Buffet, Olive Garden, Qdoba Mexican, Red Lobster, Subway, TGIFriday's, Tokyo Steaks, Wendy's, **lodging:** Best Western, Comfort Inn, Country Inn&Suites, Econolodge, Holiday Inn, Howard Johnson, Red Roof Inn, Super 8, **other:** Best Buy, Curves, $Tree, Firestone/auto, Home Depot, Honda/Hyundai, JC Penney, Jo-Ann Fabrics, Marc's Foods, Michael's, Lowe's Whse, Macy's, NTB, PetsMart, Radio Shack, Sears/auto, Staples, Target, Walmart/auto |
| **144** | OH 2 W (from wb, no return), to Sandusky, **1 mi** N on Broadway Ave **E gas:** Marathon, Shell/24hr, **food:** McDonald's, **other:** Ⓗ HOSPITAL |
| **143** | I-90 wb joins Ohio Tpk |

**WB exits to Ohio/Indiana state line are on Ohio Turnpike. See Ohio Turnpike exits 142-0.**

## INTERSTATE 270 - COLUMBUS

| Exit # | Services |
|---|---|
| **55** | I-71, to Columbus, Cincinnati |
| **52b a** | US 23, High St, Circleville, **N gas:** Marathon/Circle K, Speedway/dsl, **food:** A&W/KFC, Arby's, Bob Evans, Burger King, China Town, LJ Silver, Los Campero's, |

## INTERSTATE 270 CONT'D - COLUMBUS

**E ↕ W**

**52b a** Continued
McDonald's, Pizza Hut, Ponderosa, Roadhouse Grill, Skyline Chili, Subway, Taco Bell, Tim Horton, Waffle House, Wendy's, White Castle, **lodging:** Kozy Inn, **other:** AutoZone, Curves, $General, Firestone, Kroger/gas, Lowe's, Walgreens, Walmart, **S gas:** BP/dsl, **lodging:** Budget Inn, **other:** Kioto Downs

**49** Alum Creek Dr, **N gas:** Duke/dsl, Sunoco/dsl, **food:** Donato's Pizza, KFC/LJ Silver, Subway, **S gas:** BP/dsl, **food:** Arby's, McDonald's, Taco Bell, Wendy's, **lodging:** Comfort Inn, Sleep Inn

**46b a** US 33, Bexley, Lancaster

**43b a** I-70, E to Cambridge, W to Columbus

**41b a** US 40, **E gas:** BP, Shell, **food:** Bob Evans, Boston Mkt, Hooters, McDonald's, Outback Steaks, Rally's, Steak'n Shake, Texas Roadhouse, **other:** Walgreens, **W gas:** Mobil, Shell, Speedway, **food:** Fuddruckers, Golden Corral, Hunan Chinese, LoneStar Steaks

**39** OH 16, Broad St, **E gas:** Meijer/dsl, Speedway/dsl, **food:** Arby's, Chipotle Grill, Church's, Quizno's, Waffle House, White Castle, **lodging:** Country Inn&Suites, **other:** H HOSPITAL, **W gas:** Shell, **food:** Applebee's, **lodging:** Ramada Inn

**37** OH 317, Hamilton Rd, **E gas:** BP/dsl, Marathon, Speedway/dsl, **food:** Big Boy, Bob Evans, Burger King, Chinese Express, Damon's, Donato's Pizza, Hickory House, KFC, Pizza Hut/Taco Bell, Starbucks, **lodging:** Holiday Inn Express, SpringHill Suites, **other:** Firestone, GNC, Kroger, **2 mi W lodging:** Comfort Suites, Hampton Inn, Hilton Garden

**35b a** I-670W, US 62, **E gas:** Speedway/dsl, **food:** City BBQ, Donato's Pizza, McDonald's, Tim Horton, **other:** CVS Drug, **W** I-670

**33** no services

**32** Morse Rd, **E gas:** Marathon/DM, Speedway/dsl, **food:** Donato's Pizza, **other:** Mazda, Toyota, **W gas:** BP, Mobil/dsl, Shell/Subway, **food:** Applebee's, Champp's Grill, HomeTown Buffet, Kobe Japanese, Logan's Roadhouse, McDonald's, On-the-Border, Pizza Hut/Taco Bell, Steak'n Shake, Wendy's, **lodging:** Extended Stay America, Hampton Inn, **other:** Best Buy, BMW, Cadillac, Carmax, Circuit City, Discount Tire, Jo-Ann Fabrics, Lexus, Lowe's Whse, Macy's, Mercedes, Nordstrom's, NTB, Sam's Club, Target, Walmart SuperCtr, mall

**30** OH 161 E to New Albany, W to Worthington

**29** OH 3, Westerville, **N gas:** BP/dsl, Shell, **food:** Applebee's, Arby's, Chipotle Mexican, McDonald's, Fazoli's, Pizza Hut, Tim Horton, **lodging:** Baymont Inn, Knight's Inn, **other:** CarQuest, Firestone/auto, Kroger, **S gas:** Speedway/dsl, Sunoco/dsl, **food:** Carsoni's Italian, China House, Domino's, Subway, **other:** Aldi Foods, Family$, Midas

**27** OH 710, Cleveland Ave, **N gas:** Speedway, **food:** Subway, Tim Horton, Wendy's, **lodging:** Quality Inn, Ramada Inn, Signature Inn, **other:** CVS Drug, NAPA, Tuffy, **S food:** Bob Evans, McDonald's, O'Charley's, Steak'n Shake, **lodging:** Embassy Suites, **other:** Home Depot

**26** I-71, S to Columbus, N to Cleveland

**23** US 23, Worthington, **N food:** Alexander's, Amazon Grill, Bob Evans, Bravo Italian, Buffalo Wild Wings,

**COLUMBUS**

**OH**

**23** Continued
Champp's Grill, Chipotle Mexican, Columbus Fish Mkt, El Acapulco, Gilbert's Steaks, Lotus Grill, Mitchell's Steaks, Panera Bread, Quizno's, Ruth's Chris Steaks, Starbucks, Sushiko Japanese, Tutt's Italian, **lodging:** AmeriSuites, Courtyard, Days Inn, DoubleTree, Extended Stay America, Motel 6, Homewood Suites, Red Roof Inn, Residence Inn, Sheraton, **S gas:** BP, **food:** Buca Italian, Cosi Grill, Jimmy John's, McDonald's, **lodging:** Econolodge, Holiday Inn

**22** OH 315, **N gas:** Marathon/dsl

**20** Sawmill Rd, **N gas:** BP, Marathon/dsl, **food:** Burger King, McDonald's, Olive Garden, Subway, Taco Bell, Wendy's, **other:** Buick/Pontiac/GMC, CVS Drug, Ford, Hyundai, Lincoln-Mercury, Mazda, NTB, Subaru, Tire Kingdom, **S gas:** Meijer, Shell, Speedway, **food:** Applebee's, Asian Star, Arby's, BajaFresh, Bob Evans, Boston Mkt, Burger King, Charlie's Subs, Chili's, Chipotle Mexican, Cosi Grill, Don Pablo, Golden Corral, HoneyBaked Cafe, Joe's Crabshack, KFC, Krispy Kreme, McDonald's, Mongolian BBQ, Steak'n Shake, Red Lobster, Ruby Tuesday, Ted's MT Grill, **lodging:** Hampton Inn, Quality Inn, Woodfin Suites, **other:** Barnes&Noble, Big Lots, Borders Books, Cadillac/Honda, Circuit City, Discount Tire, $Tree, Firestone, Jo-Ann Fabrics, Kohl's, Lowe's Whse, PetCo, Sam's Club, Staples, SteinMart, Target, Toyota/Scion, Trader Joe's

**17b a** US 33, Dublin-Granville Rd, **E gas:** Marathon, Sunoco, **food:** Bob Evans, Donato's, Max&Erma's, McDonald's, Subway, **lodging:** Best Value Inn, Courtyard, Crowne Plaza, Embassy Suites, Hilton Garden, Red Roof Inn, Residence Inn, **other:** BMW/Mini, CVS Drug, Kroger, Mitsubishi, Mr Tire, USPO

**15** Tuttle Crossing Blvd, **E gas:** BP, Mobil, **food:** Bob Evans, Boston Mkt, Chipotle Mexican, Cozymel's, Longhorn Steaks, Macaroni Grill, McDonald's, PF Chang's, Pizza Hut/Taco Bell, River City Grill, TGIFriday, Wendy's, **lodging:** Drury Inn, Homewood Suites, Hyatt Place, La Quinta, Marriott, **other:** JC Penney, Macy's, Sears/auto, mall, **W gas:** Exxon/Subway/dsl, Shell, **food:** Quizno's, Steak'n Shake, Uno Pizzaria, **lodging:** Staybridge Suites, **other:** Best Buy, NTB, Walmart/auto, World Mkt

**13** Cemetery Rd, Fishinger Rd, **E gas:** Shell/Subway, Speedway, **food:** Burger King, CheeseBurger Paradise, Chili's, Chiotle Mexican, Damon's, Dave&Buster's, Donato's Pizza, KFC, Panera Bread, Quizno's, Skyline Chili, Spaghetti's, TGIFriday, Tropical Bistro, **lodging:**

Copyright 2009 - The Next Exit®

## INTERSTATE 270 CONT'D - COLUMBUS

**E** ↕ **W**

**13** Continued
Comfort Suites, Homewood Suites, **other:** CVS Drug, Home Depot, Lowe's Whse, Radio Shack, Saturn, Staples, Target, Tire Dicounters, **W gas:** BP, Mobil, Speedway, Sunoco, **food:** Bob Evans, Max&Erma's, McDonald's, Tim Horton, Wendy's, **lodging:** Hampton Inn, Motel 6, **other:** Nissan

**10** Roberts Rd, **E gas:** Marathon, Thornton's/dsl, **food:** Subway, Tim Horton, Wendy's, **W gas:** Speedway, **food:** Waffle House, **lodging:** Courtyard, Quality Inn, Royal Inn, **other:** Kroger/gas

**8** I-70, E to Columbus, W to Indianapolis

**7** US 40, Broad St, **E gas:** BP, Speedway, **food:** Bob Evans, Boston Mkt, Burger King, McDonald's, Popeye's, Tee-Jay's, Wendy's, White Castle, **other:** Buick/Pontiac/GMC, Chevrolet, Chrysler/Jeep, Circuit City, Family$, Firestone/auto, Kohl's, NTB, Pepboys, Sears/auto, Staples, Suzuki, Target, Tuffy, **W gas:** GetGo, Speedway/dsl, Thornton's, **food:** A&W/LJ Silver, Arby's, Big Boy, KFC, Papa John's, Waffle House, **lodging:** Holiday Inn Express, Hometown Inn, **other:** H HOSPITAL, CVS Drug, Giant Eagle Foods, Goodyear, Home Depot, Jo-Ann Fabrics

**5** Georgesville, **E gas:** Marathon, Mobil, Sunoco/dsl, **other:** Walmart SuperCtr, **W food:** Applebee's, Arby's, Bob Evans, Buffalo Wild Wings, Chipotle Mexican, DQ, Fazoli's, Fiesta Mariachi, KFC/LJ Silver, LoneStar Steaks, McDonald's, O'Charley's, Red Lobster, Steak'n Shake, Subway, Wendy's, White Castle, **other:** Advance Parts, GNC, Hyundai/Isuzu/Subaru, KIA, Kroger/gas, Lowe's Whse, NTB, Toyota/Scion, VW

**2** US 62, OH 3, Grove City, **N gas:** BP, **S gas:** Shell, Speedway, Sunoco, **food:** Big Boy, Brewster's, Burger King, Domino's, Donato's Pizza, McDonald's, Quizno's, Subway, Tim Horton/Wendy's, Waffle House, **lodging:** Knight's Inn

**0mm** I-71

## INTERSTATE 271 - CLEVELAND

| Exit # | Services |
| --- | --- |
| **39mm** | I-271 begins/ends on I-90, exit 188 |
| **38mm** | I-271/I-480, Express Lanes |
| **36** | Wilson Mills Rd, Highland Hts, Mayfield, **E lodging:** Hilton Garden, **W gas:** BP, Marathon/dsl, **food:** Denny's, Wellington's Rest., **other:** Home Depot, Kohl's, Tuesday Morning |
| **34** | US 322, Mayfield Rd, **E gas:** BP, **food:** TGI Friday, **lodging:** Holiday Inn, **other:** NTB, Walgreens, **W gas:** Shell, Speedway, **food:** Bob Evans, Buca Italian, Burger King, Caribou Coffee, Fat Burger, McDonald's, Panini's Grill, Starbucks, **lodging:** Baymont Inn, **other:** H HOSPITAL, Best Buy, Costco/gas, CVS Drug, Ford, Giant Eagle Foods, Lincoln/Mercury, Marshall's, Midas, Murray's Parts, Old Navy, PetsMart, World Mkt, Walmart vet |
| **32** | Brainerd Rd, Cedar Rd, **E** H HOSPITAL |
| **29** | US 422 W, OH 87, Chagrin Blvd, Harvard Rd, **E gas:** Marathon, Shell, Sunoco, **food:** Bahama Breeze, Bob Evan's, Corky&Lenny's Rest., McDonald's, Olive Garden, Pizza Hut, Red Lobster, Starbucks, Uno Café, Wendy's, |

**N** ↕ **S**

**29** Continued
**lodging:** Courtyard, Extended Stay America, Fairfield Inn, Hampton Inn, Homestead Suites, Super 8, **other:** Saturn, TJ Maxx, Wild Oats Mkt, **W gas:** BP/Subway, Shell, **food:** PF Chang's, Your's Truly, **lodging:** Clarion, Embassy Suites, Hilton, Homewood Suites, **other:** Cadillac, Chrysler/Jeep, NTB

**28b** Harvard Rd, **E food:** Red Robin, **W food:** Abuelo's, Chipotle Mexican, DiBella's Subs, River City Grille, Robek's Cafe, **lodging:** Marriott, **other:** H HOSPITAL

**28a** OH 175, Richmond Rd, Emery Rd, **E gas:** BP, GetGo, Marathon/Circle K/Subway, **food:** Baskin Robbins/Dunkin Donuts, Marianne's Bakery, McDonald's, Quizno's, **W food:** BJ's Whse

**27b** I-480 W

**26** Rockside Rd, **E gas:** Sunoco, **food:** City Diner, **lodging:** Red Roof Inn, **other:** Lowe's Whse

**23** OH 14 W, Forbes Rd, Broadway Ave, **E gas:** Sunoco, **food:** Double Dragon Chinese, McDonald's, Subway, Wendy's, **lodging:** Holiday Inn Express, **other:** Sam's Club/gas, **W gas:** BP, Marathon/Circle K, **other:** H HOSPITAL

**21** I-480 E, OH 14 E (from sb), to Youngstown

**19** OH 82, Macedonia, **E gas:** Speedway, **food:** Papa John's, **W gas:** Sunoco, **food:** Applebee's, Arby's, Caribou Coffee, Chili's, Chipotle Mexican, Golden Corral, KFC, Outback Steaks, Panera Bread, Pizza Hut, Qdoba, Steak'n Shake, Taco Bell, Wendy's, **other:** Best Buy, CVS Drug, $Tree, Giant Eagle Foods, GNC, Home Depot, Kohl's, Lowes Whse, NTB, PetCo, Radio Shack, Target, Walgreens, Walmart/auto

**18** OH 8, Boston Hts, to Akron, **E gas:** BP/Subway/dsl, Speedway, **food:** Bob Evans, Denny's, **lodging:** Country Inn&Suites, Days Inn, Knight's Inn, La Quinta, Motel 6, **W** same as 19

**12** OH 303, Richfield, Peninsula

**10** I-77, to I-80, OH Tpk (from nb), to Akron, Cleveland

**9** I-77 S, OH 176 (from nb), to Richfield

**8mm** **rest area both lanes, full** 🚻 **facilities,** 📞, 🛎, **litter barrels, petwalk**

**3** OH 94, to I-71 N, Wadsworth, N Royalton, **W gas:** Marathon

**0mm** I-271 begins/ends on I-71, exit 220.

**M A C E D O N I A**

## INTERSTATE 275 - CINCINNATI

See Kentucky Interstate 275

## INTERSTATE 280 - TOLEDO

**E** ↕ **W**

| Exit # | Services |
| --- | --- |
| **13** | I-280 begins/ends on exit 13 I-75 |
| **12** | Manhattan Blvd, **E gas:** Sunoco, **W gas:** Sunoco, **food:** Arby's, McDonald's |
| **11** | OH 25 S, Eerie St, **W other:** Convention Ctr, Eerie St Mkt |
| **10mm** | Maumee River |
| **9** | OH 65, Front St, **E gas:** Sunoco, **W gas:** Sunoco |
| **8** | Star Ave, (from sb only) |
| **7** | OH 2, Oregon, **E gas:** Sunoco, **food:** Arby's, Tim Horton, **other:** H HOSPITAL, Ford, K-Mart |

## INTERSTATE 280 CONT'D - TOLEDO

**6** OH 51, Woodville rd, Curtice, **E gas:** BP/dsl, **food:** Bob Evan's, Burger King, **other:** H HOSPITAL, Menard's, **W gas:** Meijer, Speedway/dsl, **food:** Applebees, Arby's, Big Boy, Gino's Pizza, McDonald's, Subway, Taco Bell, **lodging:** Sleep Inn, **other:** Advance Parts, Aldi Foods, $General, $Tree, Jo-Ann Fabrics, Rite Aid, Tires+

**4** Walbridge

**2** OH 795, Perrysburg, **W gas:** Sunoco/Subway/dsl

**1b** Hanley Rd, Latcha Rd, **E gas:** FLYING J/Cookery/dsl/LP/scales/24hr, **lodging:** Crown Inn, Vista Inn, **W gas:** Petro/Mobil/Iron Skillet/dsl/scales/24hr/@, **lodging:** Howard Johnson, Super 8, **other:** Blue Beacon, Speedco

**1a** I-280 begins/ends on Ohio Tpk

## INTERSTATE 475 - TOLEDO

| Exit # | Services |
|---|---|
| 20 | I-75. I-475 begins/ends on I-75, exit 204. |
| 19 | Jackman Rd, Central Ave, **S gas:** Shell, **other:** H HOSPITAL |
| 18b | Douglas Rd (from wb) |
| 18a | OH 51 W, Monroe St |
| 17 | Secor Rd, **N gas:** BP, Shell/dsl, **food:** Applebee's, Bob Evans, Boston Mkt, Burger King, China 1 Buffet, Famous Dave's BBQ, Hooters, KFC, Penn Sta. Subs, Red Lobster, Red Robin, Rudy's Hot Dogs, Tim Horton, **other:** Best Buy, Circuit City, Kroger, Murray's Parts, PharmX Drug, Walgreens, **S gas:** BP, **food:** Big Boy, El Vaquero, McDonald's, Original Pancakes, Pizza Hut, Ponderosa, Popeye's, Taco Bell, Uncle John's Pancakes, **lodging:** Clarion Hotel, Comfort Inn, Red Roof Inn, **other:** Costco/gas, Home Depot, Radio Shack, Sears/auto, Steinmart, U of Toledo |
| 16 | Talmadge Rd (from wb, no return), **N gas:** BP/dsl, Speedway, **food:** Arby's, Panera Bread, **other:** JC Penney, mall |
| 15 | Corey Rd (from eb, no return) |
| 14 | US 23 N, to Ann Arbor |
| 13 | US 20, OH 120, Central Ave, **E gas:** Speedway, Sunoco, **food:** Big Boy, Bob Evans, Magic Wok, McDonald's, Rally's, Wendy's, **other:** BMW, Cadillac, Chrysler/Jeep, Ford, Honda, Kia, Mitsubishi, Nissan, Saturn, Subaru, Toyota/Scion, **W gas:** BP, Shell, Speedway, **other:** Lowes Whse |
| 8b a | OH 2, **E gas:** BP/dsl, **food:** Don Pablo, Texas Roadhouse, **lodging:** Extended Stay America, Knight's Inn, Red Roof Inn, Residence Inn, **other:** H HOSPITAL, Home Depot, Kohl's, Old Navy, to OH Med Coll, **W gas:** BP, Speedway, Sunoco/dsl, **food:** Arby's, Big Boy, Bob Evans, Boston Mkt, Brewhouse Rest., Burger King, Chili's, Empire Chinese, Little Caesar's, Mancino's Pizza, McDonald's, Rally's, Subway, Wendy's, **lodging:** Courtyard, Econolodge, Quality Inn, **other:** Best Buy, Big Lots, Circuit City, Firestone/auto, Kroger, PetsMart, Rite Aid, Sam's Club/gas, Target, **Walmart SuperCtr** |
| 6 | Dussel Dr, Salisbury Rd, to I-80-90/tpk, **E gas:** Barney's/BP, Speedway, **food:** Applebee's, Arby's, Bankok Kitchen, Bluewater Grill, Buffalo Wild Wings, Burger King, Coldstone Creamery, **Cracker Barrel**, Gino's Pizza, Ground Round, Jimmy John's, Longhorn Steaks, Marie's Diner, Max&Erma's, McDonald's, Panera Bread, Wendy's, Subway, Yoko Japanese, **lodging:** Country |

**6 Continued** Inn&Suites, Courtyard, Fairfield Inn, Homewood Suites, Residence Inn, Studio+, Super 8, **W gas:** BP, **food:** Abuelo's, Bob Evans, Briarfield Café, Carraba's, Fox's Pizza, Ground Round, Mancino's Pizza, **lodging:** Baymont Inn, **other:** Churchill's Foods, vet

**4** US 24, to Maumee, Napolean, **N other:** H HOSPITAL, Toledo Zoo

**3mm** Maumee River

**2** OH 25, to Bowling Green, Perrysburg, **N gas:** BP/dsl, Circle K, Shell, **food:** Arby's, Buffalo Wild Wings, Beaner's Coffee, Café Marie, Charlie's Rest., El Vaquero, Gino's Pizza, Hungry Howie, Marco's Pizza, McDonald's, Papa John's, Subway, Wendy's, **other:** Bassett's Mkt Foods, Compounding, Goodyear/auto, Pontiac/GMC, Saab/VW, Toms Tire/repair, Volvo, Young's RV Ctr, **S gas:** Speedway/dsl, **food:** Biaggi's, Bob Evans, Chicago Pizza, Johnny Rockets, Louie's Grill, Maggi's Rest., Max&Erma's, Starbucks, TeaTree Asian, Waffle House, **lodging:** Economy Inn, **other:** Books-a-Million, Tire Man, vet

**0mm** I-475 begins/ends on I-75, exit 192.

## INTERSTATE 480 - CLEVELAND

| Exit # | Services |
|---|---|
| 42 | I-80, PA Tpk, I-480 begins/ends, **0-2mi S gas:** BP, Marathon/Circle K, Sheetz/24hr, Shell, Speedway, **food:** Applebees, Arby's, Baskin Robbins/Dunkin Dounts, Big Boy, Bob Evans, Brown Derby Roadhouse, Buffalo Wild Wings, Burger King, CiCi's Pizza, Denny's, DQ, Eat'n Park, KFC, McDonald's, Mr Hero, New Peking Chinese, Pizza Hut, Quizno's, Rockney's Grill, Ruby Tuesday, Sonic, Steak'n Shake, Taco Bell, Wendy's, Zeppe's Pizza, **lodging:** Best Value Inn, Comfort Inn, Econolodge, Fairfield Inn, Hampton Inn, Holiday Inn Express, Microtel, TownePlace Suites, Wingate Inn, **other:** H HOSPITAL, Aldi Foods, AutoZone, Buick/GMC, Curves, Defer Tire, $General, Giant Eagle, Home Depot, Honda, Hyundai, K-Mart, Lowes Whse, Midas, NAPA, NTB, Save-a-Lot Foods, Staples, Target, U-Haul, Van's Tires, Walgreens, **Walmart SuperCtr**, mall, USPO, vet, to Kent St U |
| 41 | Frost Rd, Hudson-Aurora |
| 37 | OH 91, Solon, Twinsburg, **N food:** Arby's, Pizza Hut, Taco Bell, **other:** Comfort Suites, **other:** Giant Eagle, **S gas:** BP |

## INTERSTATE 480 CONT'D - CLEVELAND

**E / W — YOUNGSTOWN**

**36** OH 82, Aurora, Twinsburg, **N gas:** BP/dsl, Get'n Go, **food:** Burger King, **lodging:** Super 8, **S gas:** Marathon, Bob Evans, Cracker Barrel, Damon's, Donato's Pizza, McDonald's, Wendy's, **lodging:** Hilton Garden

**26** I-271, to Erie, PA

**25a b c** OH 8, OH 43, Northfield Rd, Bedford, **N other:** Harley-Davidson, **S food:** McDonald's, Rally's, White Castle

**23** OH 14, Broadway Ave, **N gas:** Gulf/dsl, **food:** Burger King, KFC

**22** OH 17, Garanger, Maple Hts, Garfield Hts

**21** Transportation Blvd, to E 98th St, **S other:** Giant Eagle Foods, JoAnn Fabrics, Walmart

**20b a** I-77, Cleveland

**17** (eb only) OH 176, Cleveland

**16** OH 94, to OH 176 S, State Rd, **S gas:** BP, Sunoco/dsl, **other:** Kia

**15** US 42, Ridge Rd, **N gas:** BP, **food:** Applebee's, McDonald's, Ponderosa, Starbucks, **other:** Chevrolet, Lowe's Whse, Marc's Foods, TJMaxx, Top's Foods, **S gas:** Speedway, **food:** Arby's, Donato's, **other:** K-Mart, Best Buy

**13** Teideman Rd, Brooklyn, **N gas:** Marathon, **S gas:** BP, Speedway, **food:** Carrabba's, Cracker Barrel, Don Pablo's, Max&Erma's, Panera Bread, Schlotsky's, Steak 'n Shake, TGIFriday's, **lodging:** Extended Stay America, Hampton Inn

**12** W 150th, W 130th, Brookpark, **S gas:** Marathon, Shell, **food:** Arby's, Big Boy, Bob Evans, Thursday's Grill, **lodging:** Day's Inn, Best Value, **other:** Acura, Dodge, Lexus, Tire Kingdom, Toyota

**11** I-71, Cleveland, Columbus

**10** S rd 237, Airport Blvd, (wb only) no services

**9** OH 17, Brookpark Rd, **N lodging:** Hilton Garden, **other:** H HOSPITAL, **S lodging:** Ramada Inn, ✈

**7** (wb only)Clague Rd, to WestLake

**6** OH 252, to N Olmsted, **N gas:** BP, Shell, **food:** Applebee's, Chick-fil-A, Chili's, Harry Buffalo, Lonestar Steaks, Macaroni Grill, Red Lobster, Red Robin, **lodging:** Candlewood Suites, Courtyard, Hampton Inn, Homestead Suites, Radisson, Studio+, **other:** Dillard's, Firestone, JC Penney, Michael's, Sears/auto, Walmart, mall

**3** Stearns Rd, **2 mi S food:** Razzle's Cafe

**2** OH 10, Lorain Rd, to OH Tpk, **N gas:** BP, Marathon, Sheetz/24hr, Speedway/dsl, **food:** Gourme Rest., McDonald's, **lodging:** Motel 6, Super 8, **other:** U-Haul

**0mm** OH 10, to Cleveland, I-480 begins/ends on exit 151, OH Tpk

## OHIO TURNPIKE

| Exit # | Services |
|---|---|
| **241mm** | Ohio/Pennsylvania state line |
| **239mm** | toll plaza, 🅒 |
| **237mm** | Mahoning Valley Travel Plaza eb, Glacier Hills Travel Plaza wb, Valero/dsl/24hr, McDonald's, gifts, 🅒 |
| **234** | I-680 (from wb), to Youngstown |

**232** OH 7, to Boardman, Youngstown, **N gas:** Sheetz/24hr (1mi), **food:** DQ, Rita's Ice Cream, Steamer's Stonewall Tavern, **lodging:** Best Value Inn, Budget Inn, Holiday Inn Express, Quality Inn, **other:** H HOSPITAL, antiques, **S gas:** Pilot/McDonald's/dsl/scales/24hr, **lodging:** Davis Motel, Liberty Inn, **other:** truck repair

**218** I-80 E, to Youngstown. OH Tpk runs with I-76 eb, I-80 wb to Niles, **services S on Mahoning**

**216** Lordstown (from wb), **N** GM Plant

**215** Lordstown (from eb), **N** GM Plant

**210mm** Mahoning River

**209** OH 5, to Warren, **N lodging:** Rodeway Inn, **S gas:** Marathon/dsl, **lodging:** Econolodge, Holiday Inn Express

**197mm** **Portage Service Plaza wb, Bradys Leap Service Plaza eb,** Valero/dsl/24hr, FoodCourt, McDonald's, gifts, 🅒

**193** OH 44, to Ravenna

**192mm** Cuyahoga River

**187** OH 14 S, I-480, to Streetsboro, **0-2 mi S gas:** BP, Marathon/Circle K, Sheetz/24hr, Shell, Speedway, **food:** Applebees, Arby's, Baskin Robbins/Dunkin Dounts, Big Boy, Bob Evans, Brown Derby Roadhouse, Buffalo Wild Wings, Burger King, CiCi's Pizza, Denny's, DQ, Eat'n Park, KFC, McDonald's, Mr Hero, New Peking Chinese, Pizza Hut, Quizno's, Rockney's Grill, Ruby Tuesday, Sonic, Steak'n Shake, Taco Bell, Wendy's, Zeppe's Pizza, **lodging:** Best Value Inn, Comfort Inn, Econolodge, Fairfield Inn, Hampton Inn, Holiday Inn Express, Microtel, TownePlace Suites, Wingate Inn, **other:** H HOSPITAL, Aldi Foods, AutoZone, Buick/GMC, Curves, Defer Tire, $General, Giant Eagle, Home Depot, Honda, Hyundai, K-Mart, Lowes Whse, Midas, NAPA, NTB, Save-a-Lot Foods, Staples, Target, U-Haul, Van's Tires, Walgreens, Walmart SuperCtr, mall, USPO, vet, to Kent St U

**180** OH 8, to I-90 E, **N lodging:** Comfort Inn, Holiday Inn, **other:** Harley-Davidson, **S gas:** BP/dsl, **other:** to Cuyahoga Valley NRA

**177mm** Cuyahoga River

**173** OH 21, to I-77, **N gas:** Pilot/Wendy's/dsl/scales, **lodging:** Holiday Inn Express, Howard Johnson, **S food:** DQ, Memories Rest., Richfield Rest., Subway, **lodging:** Hampton Inn, Quality Inn, Super 8

**170mm** **Towpath Service Plaza eb, Great Lakes Service Plaza wb, gas:** Valero/dsl/24hr, **food:** Burger King, FoodCourt, Panera Bread, Pizza Hut, **other:** gifts, 🅒

**161** US 42, to I-71, Strongsville, **N on US 42...gas:** AP/dsl, **food:** Buffalo Wild Wings, Jennifer's Rest, Mad Cactus Mexican, **lodging:** Day's Inn, Kings Inn, La Siesta Motel, Metrick's Motel, Village Motel, **other:** Circle K, Home Depot, Lowes Whse, Walmart, vet, **S on US 42...food:** Burger King, DQ, J-Bella Rest., KFC, La Volte Grill, Marco's Pizza, Olympia's Cafe, **lodging:** Elmhaven Motel, **other:** Dodge, NAPA, Staples

**152** OH 10, to Oberlin, I-480, Cleveland, **N gas:** BP, Marathon, Sheetz/24hr, Speedway/dsl, **food:** Gourme Rest., McDonald's, **lodging:** Motel 6, Super 8, **other:** U-Haul **S other:** Moore's RV Ctr, drive-in theatre (seasonal)

**151** I-480 E (from eb), to Cleveland, ✈

## OHIO TURNPIKE CONT'D

**LORAIN** E ↕ W

**146mm** Black River

**145** OH 57, to Lorain, to I-90, Elyria, **N food:** Burger King, KFC, George's Rest., **other:** U-Haul, vet, **S gas:** BP/McDonald's/dsl, Shell, Speedway **food:** Applebee's, Arby's, Bob Evans, Buffalo Wild Wings, Denny's, Eat'n Park, Fazoli's, Golden Corral, Harry Buffalo, Jumbo Buffet, Olive Garden, Qdoba Mexican, Red Lobster, Subway, TGIFriday's, Tokyo Steaks, Wendy's, **lodging:** Best Western, Comfort Inn, Country Inn&Suites, Econolodge, Holiday Inn, Howard Johnson, Red Roof Inn, Super 8, **other:** Best Buy, Curves, $Tree, Firestone/auto, Home Depot, Honda/Hyundai, JC Penney, Jo-Ann Fabrics, Marc's Foods, Michael's, Lowe's Whse, Macy's, NTB, PetsMart, Radio Shack, Sears/auto, Staples, Target, Walmart/auto

**142** I-90 (from eb, exits left), OH 2, to W Cleveland

**140** OH 58, Amherst, **0-2 mi N gas:** BP, Speedway, Sunoco/Subway/dsl, food Bob Evans, DQ, **lodging:** Days Inn, Motel 6, **other:** Chevrolet, Chrysler/Dodge, NAPA, Rite Aid, Suzuki, VW, repair, **S other:** Ford

**139mm** **Service Plaza both lanes, gas:** Valero/dsl/24hr, **food:** Burger King, Great Steak, Panera Bread, Popeye's, Starbucks, TCBY, **other:** gifts, C, RV parking

**135** rd 51, Baumhart Rd, to Vermilion

**132mm** Vermilion River

**118** US 250, to Norwalk, Sandusky, **N gas:** BP/Circle K/Dunkin Donuts, Marathon/dsl, **food:** 4Monks Italian, McDonald's, Subway, **lodging:** Comfort Inn, Day's Inn, Hampton Inn, Motel 6, Red Roof Inn, Super 8, **other:** RV Park, to Edison's Birthplace, **S food:** Maw's Place, **lodging:** Colonial Inn, **other:** Chevrolet/Hyundai

**110** OH 4

**100mm** **Service Plaza both lanes, gas:** Valero/dsl/24hr, **food:** Burger King, Cinnabon, Sbarro's, Starbucks, **other:** C

**93mm** Sandusky River

**91** OH 53, to Fremont, Port Clinton, **N lodging:** Day's Inn, **0-1 mi S gas:** BP/Subway/dsl/24hr, **food:** Applebees, Bob Evan's, Burger King, Fricker's, McDonald's, Pizza Hut, Ryan's, Subway, Taco Bell, **lodging:** Comfort Inn (2mi), Delux Inn, Fremont Inn, Hampton Inn, **other:** H HOSPITAL, Aldi Foods, Ford/Lincoln/Mercury, Lowes Whse, Staples, Walmart SuperCtr/gas, Rutherford B. Hayes Library, USPO, vet

**81** OH 51, Elmore, Woodville, Gibsonburg

**80.5mm** Portage River

**77mm** **Service Plaza both lanes, gas:** Valero/dsl/24hr, **food:** Hardee's, Mancino's, C

**71** I-280, OH 420, to Stony Ridge, Toledo, **N gas:** Petro/Mobil/dsl/rest./scales/24hr/@, FLYING J/dsl/rest./scales/24hr/LP, **lodging:** Budget Inn, Crown Inn, Howard Johnson, Super 8, Vista Inn, **other:** Blue Beacon, **S gas:** FuelMart/Subway/dsl/scales, Pilot/dsl/24hr/scales, TA/BP/Burger King/Taco Bell/dsl/scales/24hr/@, **food:** McDonald's, **other:** truckwash

**TOLEDO**

**64** I-75 N, to Toledo, Perrysburg, **S other:** BP/Subway/dsl, **lodging:** Country Inn&Suites, Courtyard, Hampton Inn

**63mm** Maumee River

**59** US 20, to I-475, Maumee, Toledo, **N gas:** BP/dsl, Shell, Speedway/dsl, **food:** Arby's, Bob Evans, McDonald's, Nick's Cafe, Olive Garden, Pizza Hut, Steak'n Shake, Subway, Waffle House, **lodging:** Clarion, Motel 6, **other:** Family$, Goodyear/auto, Jo-Ann Fabrics, K-Mart, Murray's Parts, NAPA, Radio Shack, Rite Aid, Savers, Walgreens, to Toledo Stadium, **S gas:** Speedway/dsl, **food:** Big Boy, Chipotle Mexican, Donato's Pizza, Fazoli's, Fricker's, Friendly's, Jed's BBQ, Red Lobster, Schlotsky's, Taco Bell, **lodging:** Comfort Inn, Day's Inn, Econolodge, Hampton Inn, Holiday Inn, Red Roof Inn, **other:** Chevrolet, Ford, Honda, Meijer, Toyota

**52** OH 2, to Toledo, **S lodging:** Days Inn, **other:** RV/truck repair, ✉

**49mm** **service plaza both lanes, gas:** Valero/dsl/24hr, **food:** Chicago Pizza, Nathan's, gifts/ice cream

**39** OH 109, **S gas:** Country Corral/Valero/Winchesters/dsl/scales/24hr

**34** OH 108, to Wauseon, **S gas:** Shell/Subway/dsl/24hr, **food:** Smith's Rest., **lodging:** Arrowhead Motel, Best Western, Holiday Inn Express, Super 8, **other:** H HOSPITAL, Woods Trucking/repair (1mi), **2 mi S** on US 20A... **gas:** BP/Circle K, Marathon, Valero, **food:** A&W/KFC, Arby's, Burger King, DQ, Grasshopper Rest., McDonald's, Pizza Hut, Subway, Taco Bell, Wendy's, **other:** Ace Hardware, AutoZone, Rite Aid, Walmart SuperCtr/gas

**25** OH 66, Burlington, **N other:** Harrison Lake SP, **3 mi S other:** Sauder Village Museum

**24.5mm** Tiffen River

**13** OH 15, to Bryan, Montpelier, **S gas:** Marathon/dsl, Sunoco, **lodging:** Econolodge, Holiday Inn Express, Rainbow Motel, Ramada Inn, **other:** Hutch's dsl Repair

**11.5mm** St Joseph River

**3mm** toll plaza, C

**2** OH 49, to US 20, **N food:** Burger King, Subway, **other:** info, truck tires

**0mm** Ohio/Indiana state line

## INTERSTATE 35

| Exit # | Services |
|---|---|
| 236mm | Oklahoma/Kansas state line |
| 231 | US 177, Braman, **E** **gas:** Conoco/Grab'n Dash Deli/dsl |
| 230 | Braman Rd |
| 229mm | Chikaskia River |
| 225mm | **Welcome Ctr sb, rest area nb, full** 🔥 **facilities,** 🗑, 🍴, **litter barrels, vending, petwalk, RV dump** |
| 222 | OK 11, to Blackwell, Medford, Alva, Newkirk, **E** **gas:** Conoco/dsl/rest., Shell/dsl, **food:** Braum's, KFC/Taco Bell, Los Potros Mexican, McDonald's, Plains Man Rest., Subway, **lodging:** Best Value Inn, Best Western, Comfort Inn, **other:** H HOSPITAL |
| 218 | Hubbard Rd |
| 216mm | weigh sta both lanes |
| 214 | US 60, to Tonkawa, Lamont, Ponca City, N OK Coll, **W** **gas:** Cenex/dsl, **lodging:** New Western Inn, **other:** Woodland RV Park, tires |
| 213mm | Salt Fork of Arkansas River |
| 211 | Fountain Rd, **E** **gas:** Love's/Chester Fried/Subway/dsl/scales/24hr/RV Dump |
| 209mm | **parking area both lanes, litter barrels** |
| 203 | OK 15, to Marland, Billings, **E** **gas:** Conoco/DQ/dsl/scales/24hr |
| 199mm | Red Rock Creek |
| 195mm | **parking area both lanes, litter barrels** |
| 194b a | US 412, US 64 W, **E** Cimarron Tpk (eb), to Tulsa, **W** to Enid, Phillips U |
| 193 | airport Rd (from nb, no return) |
| 191mm | Black Bear Creek |
| 186 | US 64 E, to Fir St, Perry, **E** **gas:** Mobil/Subway/dsl, **food:** Braum's, McDonald's, Sonic, Taco Mayo, **lodging:** Super 8, **other:** H HOSPITAL, museum, **W** **gas:** Exxon/dsl, **lodging:** Holiday Inn Express, Regency Inn |
| 185 | US 77, to Covington, Perry, **E** **lodging:** American Inn, **W** **gas:** Conoco/dsl/motel/rest./24hr, **other:** RV camping |
| 180 | Orlando Rd |
| 174 | OK 51, to Stillwater, Hennessey, **E** **gas:** Phillips 66/dsl, **lodging:** Fairfield Inn (12mi), Holiday Inn (13mi), Motel 6 (12mi), **other:** Lake Carl Blackwell RV Park, to OSU |
| 173mm | **parking area sb, litter barrels** |
| 171mm | **parking area nb, litter barrels** |
| 170 | Mulhall Rd |
| 166mm | Cimarron River |
| 157 | OK 33, to Cushing, Guthrie, **W** **gas:** K&L/dsl, Love's/Subway/dsl, Shell/dsl, Valero/dsl, **food:** Arby's, Braum's, El Rodeo Mexican, KFC (2mi), Mazzio's, McDonald's (3mi), Pizza Hut, Sonic, The Ribshack, **lodging:** Best Western, Interstate Motel, Sleep Inn, Townhouse Motel (2mi), **other:** H HOSPITAL, OK Terr Museum, Langston U, RV camping |
| 153 | US 77 N (exits left from nb), Guthrie, **W** **food:** McDonald's, **other:** Chrysler/Dodge/Jeep, Ford/Mercury, Pontiac/Buick |
| 151 | Seward Rd, **E** **gas:** Shell/cafe/dsl, **other:** Lazy E Arena (4mi), Pioneer RV park |
| 149mm | weigh sta both lanes |
| 146 | Waterloo Rd, **E** **gas:** Shell/dsl |
| 143 | Covell Rd |
| 142 | Danforth Rd (from nb) |
| 141 | US 77 S, OK 66E, to 2nd St, Edmond, Tulsa, **W** **gas:** Conoco, Phillips 66/dsl, **lodging:** Best Western, Comfort Inn, Fairfield Inn, Hampton Inn, Holiday Inn Express, **other:** H HOSPITAL, vet |
| 140 | SE 15th St, Spring Creek, Arcadia Lake, Edmond Park, **W** **gas:** Phillips 66/Circle K/Subway, **food:** Braum's, **other:** Walmart SuperCtr |
| 139 | SE 33rd St, **W** **lodging:** Sleep Inn |
| 138d | Memorial Rd, **E** **gas:** Shell/dsl, **W** **other:** Enterprise Square USA |
| 138c | Sooner Rd (from sb) |
| 138b | Kilpatrick Tpk |
| 138a | I-44 Tpk E to Tulsa |
| | **I-35 S and I-44 W run together 8 mi.** |
| 137 | NE 122nd St, to OK City, **E** **gas:** Shamrock/dsl, Shell/dsl, **food:** Charly's Rest., IHOP, **lodging:** Sleep Inn, Travelodge, **W** **gas:** ⊕FLYING J/Conoco/CountryMkt/dsl/scales/LP/24hr, Love's/Subway/Godfathers Pizza/dsl/24hr, **food:** Cracker Barrel, McDonald's, Sonic, Waffle House, **lodging:** Comfort Inn, Day's Inn, Economy Inn, Motel 6, Quality Inn, Red Carpet Inn, Super 8, **other:** Abe's RV Park, Frontier City Funpark, Oklahoma Visitors Ctr/info/restrooms |
| 136 | Hefner Rd, **W** **gas:** Conoco/dsl, same as 137 |
| 135 | Britton Rd |
| 134 | Wilshire Blvd, **W** **lodging:** Executive Inn, **other:** Blue Beacon |
| | **I-35 N and I-44 E run together 8 mi** |
| 133 | I-44 W, to Amarillo, **W** st capitol, Cowboy Hall of Fame |
| 132b | NE 63rd St (from nb), 1/2 mi **E** **gas:** Conoco/dsl, **food:** Braum's, **lodging:** Remington Inn |
| 132a | NE 50th St, Remington Pk, **W** **other:** funpark, info, museum, zoo |
| 131 | NE 36th St, **W** **gas:** Phillips 66/dsl/24hr, **other:** 45th Inf Division Museum |
| 130 | US 62 E, NE 23rd St, **E** gas/dsl, **W** to st capitol |
| 129 | NE 10th St, **E** **gas:** Conoco/McDonald's/dsl |
| 128 | I-40 E, to Ft Smith |
| 127 | Eastern Ave, OK City, **W** **gas:** Petro/dsl/rest./Blue Beacon/24hr/@, JR's Trvl Ctr/Wendy's/dsl/scales/24hr/@, Shamrock/dsl, **food:** Waffle House, **lodging:** Brick-Town Hotel, Best Western, Central Plaza Hotel, Econolodge, Quality Inn, **other:** Blue Beacon, Lewis RV Ctr |
| 126a | I-40, W to Amarillo, I-235 N, to st capitol |
| 126b | I-35 S to Dallas |
| 125d | SE 15th St, **E** **gas:** Conoco/dsl |
| 125b | SE 22nd St (from nb) |
| 125a | SE 25th, same as 124b |
| 124b | SE 29th St, **E** **food:** China Queen, Denny's, McDonald's, Sonic, Taco Bell, **lodging:** Days Inn, Plaza Inn, Royal Inn, Super 8, **W** **gas:** Phillips 66, **food:** Mama Lou's Rest., same as 125a |
| 124a | Grand Blvd, **E** **lodging:** Suburban Lodge |
| 123b | SE 44th St, **E** **gas:** Shell, **food:** Dominos, Sonic, **lodging:** Best Value Inn, Courtesy Inn, **W** **food:** Pizza 44, Subway, Taco Mayo, **other:** Bi-4-Less Foods, $General, Family$, SavALot Foods, USPO |
| 123a | SE 51st St, **E** **gas:** Conoco/dsl, **lodging:** Best Value Inn |
| 122b | SE 59th St, **E** **gas:** Phillips 66/dsl, **W** **gas:** Shell, Valero/dsl |

Vertical side labels (left): BLACKWELL, N↕S, OK, GUTHRIE

Vertical side label (right): OKLAHOMA CITY

## INTERSTATE 35 CONT'D

**N↑S** (OKLAHOMA CITY)

**122a** SE 66th St, **E food:** Luby's, McDonald's, Subway, Taco Bell, Texas Roadhouse, Zeke's Rest., **lodging:** Fairfield Inn, Ramada Inn, Residence Inn, **other:** Best Buy, Dillard's, Firestone, JC Penney, Macys, Tires+, mall, **W gas:** 7-11, **food:** Arby's

**121b** US 62 W, I-240 E, no facilites

**121a** SE 82nd St, (from sb), **W lodging:** Baymont Inn

**120** SE 89th St, **E gas:** Valero/dsl/scales, **lodging:** Ford, **W gas:** Love's/Subway/dsl/24hr, **other:** Classic Parts

**119b** N 27th St, **E gas:** Shell/dsl, **W food:** Pickles Rest., **other:** Harley-Davidson

**119a** Shields Blvd (exits left from nb)

**118** N 12th St, **E food:** Mazzio's, **lodging:** Super 8, **W gas:** 7-11, Shell, **food:** A&W/LJ Silver, Arby's, Braum's, DQ, Grandy's, Harry Bear's Grill, KFC, La Fajitas, Mamma Lou's, Mazzio's, McDonald's, Papa John's, Subway, Taco Bell, Wendy's, Western Sizzlin, **lodging:** Best Western, Candlewood Suites, Comfort Inn, **other:** Ace Hardware, AutoZone, Family$

**117** OK 37, S 4th St, **W gas:** Valero, **food:** China Wok, Van BBQ

**116** S 19th St, **E gas:** Conoco, Shell, **food:** Braum's, Capt D's, Carl's Jr, DQ, McDonald's, Popeye's, Sara's Rest., Taco Bell, Waffle House, **lodging:** Microtel, **other:** Firestone/auto, Goodyear/auto, JC Penney, Office Depot, Ross, **W food:** Arby's, Alfredo's Mexican, Applebees, Arby's, Buffalo Wild Wings, Buffet King, Burger King, Earl's Ribs, Freddy's Frozen Custard, Furr's Buffet, IHOP, McAlister's Deli, Panda Express, Quizno's, Sonic, Subway, **lodging:** La Quinta, **other:** Aldi Foods, $Tree, Gordman's, Home Depot, Kohl's, Lowe's Whse, Radio Shack, Russell Stover Candies, Tires+, Walmart SuperCtr/gas

**114** Indian Hill Rd, **E food:** Bill's Fishhouse, Indian Hills Rest., **lodging:** Value Place Hotel, **other:** Guy RV Ctr

**113** US 77 S (from sb, exits left), Norman

**112** Tecumseh Rd, **E other:** Nissan

**110b a** Robinson St, **E food:** Carl's Jr, Sonic, Taco Bell, Teimei Asian Buistro, **lodging:** Day's Inn, Embassy Suites, **other:** H HOSPITAL, Chrysler/Jeep, Circuit City, Ford, GMC/Pontiac, Homeland Foods/drug, Honda, Hyundai, Kohl's, Lincoln/Mercury/Mazda, PetCo, Subaru, Super Target, Tires+, TJ Maxx, Toyota, **W gas:** Conoco/Subway, **food:** Arby's, Braum's, Cafe Escondido, Cracker Barrel, Golden Chef, Outback Steaks, Papa John's, Rib Crib, Saltgrass Steaks, Santa Fe Cattle Co, Waffle House, **lodging:** Comfort Inn, Courtyard, Hilton Garden, Holiday Inn, **other:** Kia/Isuzu

**109** Main St, **E gas:** Phillips 66, Shell, **food:** Arby's, Braum's, CiCi's, Denny's, Golden Corral, JR's Rest., Krispy Kreme, LJ Silver, Panera Bread, Prairie Kitchen,

**NORMAN**

**109** Continued
Subway, Taco Cabana, Waffle House, Wendy's, **lodging:** Days Inn, Econolodge, Guest Inn, Quality Inn, Ramada Inn, Super 8, Thunderbird Lodge, Travelodge, **other:** AutoZone, Best Buy, Cadillac, Chevrolet, Dodge/Jeep, Hastings Books, Lowe's Whse, Nissan, Subaru, Target, Tires+, Walmart SuperCtr/gas, **W gas:** Conoco/Circle K/dsl, **food:** Applebee's, BJ's Brewhouse, Burger King, Don Pablo, Charleston's Rest. Chili's, Marie Callender's, McDonald's, Olive Garden, On the Border, Outback Steaks, Piccadilly's, Red Lobster, Red River Steaks, Rio Cafe, Village Inn Rest., **lodging:** Fairfield Inn, Hampton Inn, La Quinta, **other:** Barnes&Noble, Borders Books, Dillard's, IGA Foods, JC Penney, Kia, Michael's, Old Navy, Saab, Sam's Club, Sears/auto, SteinMart, mall

**108b a** OK 9 E, Norman, **E gas:** Conoco, **food:** Arby's, Braum's, Del Rancho Steaks, Schlotzky's, Taco Bell, **lodging:** Residence Inn, Sooner Legends Inn, **other:** to U of OK, **W food:** Carino's Italian, IHOP, Jasons Deli, Othello's Italian, Red Robin, Souper Salad, **lodging:** Country Inn&Suites, La Quinta, **other:** Home Depot, Michaels, PetsMart, Ross

**107mm** Canadian River

**106** OK 9 W, to Chickasha, **E other:** Casino, **W gas:** Love's/Subway/dsl/24hr, Shell, **food:** McDonald's, Sonic, **other:** casino

**104** OK 74 S, Goldsby, **E other:** Floyd's RV Ctr, **W gas:** Shamrock/dsl, Sinclair/dsl, **food:** Libby's Cafe

**101** Ladd Rd

**98** Johnson Rd, **E gas:** Shamrock/dsl

**95** US 77 (exits left from sb), Purcell, **1-3 mi E gas:** Shell, **food:** Braum's, KFC, Mazzio's, Pizza Hut, Subway, **other:** H HOSPITAL, Ford

**91** OK 74, to OK 39, Maysville, **E gas:** Conoco/dsl, Phillips 66/dsl, **food:** McDonald's, Subway, Taco Mayo, **lodging:** Econolodge, Executive Inn, Ruby's Inn/rest., **other:** Ace Hardware, American RV Park (1mi), Walmart SuperCtr/gas, flea mkt, **W gas:** Shell/dsl

## INTERSTATE 35 CONT'D

| | |
|---|---|
| **86** | OK 59, Wayne, Payne, **E** **other:** American RV Park |
| **79** | OK 145 E, Paoli, **E** **gas:** Phillips 66 |
| **76mm** | Washita River |
| **74** | OK 19, Kimberlin Rd |
| **72** | OK 19, Paul's Valley, **E** **gas:** Conoco/dsl, Valero/dsl/rest./24hr, **food:** Arby's, Braum's, Chicken Express, Denny's, KFC/Taco Bell, Little Ben's Pizza, McDonald's, Punkin's Catfish, Sonic, Subway, Taco Mayo, **lodging:** American Inn, Comfort Inn, Day's Inn, Garden Inn, Relax Inn, **other:** Buick/Pontiac/Cadillac/GMC, Chrysler/Dodge/Jeep, $General, Ford/Lincoln/Mercury, Walmart SuperCtr/gas, **W** **gas:** Love's/Godfather's/dsl/24hr, Phillips 66/dsl/24hr |
| **70** | Airport Rd, **E** **H** HOSPITAL |
| **66** | OK 29, Wynnewood, **W** **gas:** Shell/dsl |
| **64** | OK 17A E, to Wynnewood, **E** GW Exotic Animal Park |
| **60** | Ruppe Rd |
| **59mm** | **rest area both lanes, full** 🚻 **facilities,** Ⓒ, ⛯, **litter barrels, petwalk, RV dump** |
| **55** | OK 7, Davis, **E** **gas:** Conoco, Phillips 66/A&W/dsl/24hr, **other:** Microtel, **other:** casino, to Chickasaw NRA, **W** **other:** Oak Hill RV Park/gas/deli, to Arbuckle Ski Area |
| **54.5mm** | Honey Creek Pass |
| **53mm** | weigh sta both lanes |
| **51** | US 77, Turner Falls, **E** **lodging:** Arbuckle Mtn Motel, Mtnview Inn (3mi), **other:** to Arbuckle Wilderness, RV camping, **W** **gas:** Sinclair/grill, **other:** Botanic Gardens |
| **49mm** | scenic turnout both lanes |
| **47** | US 77, Turner Falls Area |
| **46mm** | scenic turnout both lanes |
| **42** | OK 53 W, Springer, Comanche, **W** **gas:** Exxon/dsl |
| **40** | OK 53 E, Gene Autry, **E** **gas:** Shell/dsl/café/24hr, **food:** Broaster Rest, **other:** Gene Autry Museum (8mi) |
| **33** | OK 142, Ardmore, **E** **gas:** Phillips 66/dsl/24hr, Shamrock, **food:** IHOP, Ponder's Rest., **lodging:** Guest Inn, La Quinta, SpringHill Suites, Super 8, **W** **gas:** ⊘FLYING J/Conoco/Country Mkt/dsl/scales/@ |
| **32** | 12th St, Ardmore, **E** **gas:** Conoco/dsl, Valero, **food:** Braum's, Santa Fe Steaks, Starbucks, Whataburger, **other:** $Tree, Lowe's Whse, PetCo, Walmart, **W** **gas:** Love's/Godfather's/Subway/dsl/24hr/@, **food:** McDonald's, **lodging:** Microtel |
| **31b a** | US 70 W, OK 199 E, Ardmore, **E** **gas:** Shell/dsl, Valero/dsl, **food:** Applebee's, Burger King, Cattle Rustlers, El Chico's, Jack-in-the-Box, KFC, Mazzio's, McDonald's, Pizza Hut, Prairie Kitchen, 2Frogs Grill, **lodging:** Best Western, Comfort Inn, Days Inn, Hampton Inn, Holiday Inn, Motel 6, **other:** AutoZone, Buy4Less/24hr, Honda, O'Reilly Parts, **W** **gas:** Conoco/dsl, **other:** Cadillac, Chrysler/Dodge/Jeep, Ford/Lincoln/Mercury, Mazda, Nissan, Shady Grove RV Park, vet |
| **29** | US 70 E, Ardmore, **E** **lodging:** Economy Inn (1mi), **other:** to Lake Texoma SP, **W** **other:** Hidden Lake RV Park |
| **24** | OK 77 S, **E** **other:** Red River Livestock Mkt, to Lake Murray SP |
| **22.5mm** | Hickory Creek |
| **21** | Oswalt Rd, **W** **gas:** Valero, **other:** KOA |
| **15** | OK 32, Marietta, **E** **gas:** Valero/dsl/24hr, **food:** Carl's Jr, McDonald's, Pizza Hut, Robertson's Sandwiches, Sonic, **lodging:** Lake Country Motel, **other:** **H** HOSPITAL, |

| | |
|---|---|
| **15** | Continued<br>$General, Ford, to Lake Texoma SP, **W** **gas:** Phillips 66/24hr, Shell, **food:** Hickory House BBQ |
| **5** | OK 153, Thackerville, **W** **other:** Shorty's Foods/gas, Red River Ranch RV Park |
| **3.5mm** | **Welcome Ctr nb, full** 🚻 **facilities,** Ⓒ, ⛯, **litter barrels, vending, petwalk** |
| **1** | US 77 N, **E** **gas:** Phillips 66/dsl, **lodging:** Best Western, Mictotel, **other:** Winstar Casino, **W** **other:** Red River RV Resort (3mi) |
| **0mm** | Oklahoma/Texas state line, Red River |

## INTERSTATE 40

| Exit # | Services |
|---|---|
| **331mm** | Oklahoma/Arkansas state line |
| **330** | OK 64D S (from eb), Ft Smith |
| **325** | US 64, Roland, Ft Smith, **N** **gas:** Cherokee Trkstp/Valero/Subway/dsl/scales/24hr, **food:** Four Star Diner, **lodging:** Cherokee Inn, Travelodge, **other:** casino, **S** **gas:** Pilot/Wendy's/dsl/scales/24hr, Shell/dsl/scales, Valero/dsl, **food:** Arby's, El Celaya Mexican, McDonald's, Mazzio's, Sonic, Subway, **lodging:** Interstate Inn, **other:** $General, Marvin's Foods |
| **321** | OK 64b N, Muldrow, **N** **food:** Sonic (1mi), **S** **gas:** Shell/dsl, **food:** Arena Rest, **lodging:** Best Value, **other:** auto/dsl repair |
| **316mm** | **rest area eb, full** 🚻 **facilities, info,** Ⓒ, ⛯, **litter barrels, vending, petwalk, RV dump** |
| **313mm** | **rest area wb, full** 🚻 **facilities, info,** Ⓒ, ⛯, **litter barrels, vending, petwalk, RV dump** |
| **311** | US 64, Sallisaw, **N** **gas:** Cox's/dsl, ED's Trkstp/Phillips 66/diner/dsl, **food:** Hardee's, KFC/Taco Bell, Pizza Hut, Sonic, Taco Mayo, **lodging:** Motel 6, Sallisaw Inn, **other:** **H** HOSPITAL, AutoZone, $General, Fred's Store, **1 mi N food:** Lessley's Café, **other:** to Sallisaw RA, Brushy Lake SP (10mi), Sequoyah's Home (12mi) |
| **308** | US 59, Sallisaw, **N** **gas:** Murphy USA, Phillips 66/dsl, **food:** A&W/LJ Silver, Arby's, Braum's, China Panda, KFC, Mazzio's, McDonald's, Sonic, Subway, Taco Pronto, Western Sizzlin, **lodging:** Best Western, Days Inn, Golden Spur Motel, Super 8, Microtel, **other:** **H** HOSPITAL, $General, Walmart SuperCtr, casino, to Blue Ribbon Downs, **S** **gas:** Shell/dsl, **food:** Ole South Pancakes, **other:** Chevrolet/Buick, Chrysler/Dodge/Jeep, Ford, KOA, to Kerr Lake, truck/tire repair |
| **303** | Dwight Mission Rd, **3 mi N other:** Blue Ribbon Downs |
| **297** | OK 82 N, Vian, **N** **gas:** FL/dsl, **food:** Subway, **lodging:** Siesta Motel, **other:** to Tenkiller Lake RA, USPO, **S** **other:** Sequoia NWR |
| **291** | OK 10 N, to Gore, **N** **other:** Greenleaf SP (10mi), Tenkiller SP (21mi) |
| **290mm** | Arkansas River |
| **287** | OK 100 N, to Webbers Falls, **N** **gas:** Love's/Subway/dsl/24hr, **food:** Charlie's Chicken, Godfather's Pizza, **lodging:** Sleepy Traveler Motel, **other:** parts/tires/repair |
| **286** | Muskogee Tpk, to Muskogee |
| **284** | Ross Rd |
| **283mm** | **parking area both lanes, litter barrels** |
| **278** | US 266, OK 2, Warner, **N** **gas:** Phillips 66/dsl, **food:** Subway, **lodging:** Sleepy Traveler Motel, **other:** Auburn RV Park |

Side margin text: N / S, OK, ARDMORE, E / W, SALLISAW

**E / W**

**INTERSTATE 40 CONT'D**

**270** Texanna Rd, to Porum Landing, **S gas:** Sinclair

**265** US 69 bus, Checotah, **N food:** Pizza Hut, Sonic, **S gas:** R&D/dsl, Shell/dsl **lodging:** Budget Inn, **other:** Chevrolet/Chrysler/Dodge/Jeep

**264b a** US 69, to Eufaula, **1 mi N gas:** ⊛FLYING J/Country Mkt/dsl/LP/scales/RV dump/24hr, Phillips 66/dsl/24hr, **food:** Charlie's Chicken, McDonald's, Simon's Pizza, Subway, **lodging:** Best Value Inn, **other:** $General, O'Reilly Parts, True Value, Walmart SuperCtr, auto repair

**262** to US 266, Lotawatah Rd, **N gas:** Sinclair

**261mm** Lake Eufaula

**259** OK 150, to Fountainhead Rd, **S gas:** Shell/café, **food:** BBQ, **lodging:** Lake Eufaula Inn, **other:** to Lake Eufaula SP

**255** Pierce Rd, **N** KOA

**251mm** rest area both lanes

**247** Tiger Mtn Rd, **S other:** Quilt Barn/antiques

**240b a** US 62 E, US 75 N, Henryetta, **N gas:** Love's/dsl, Phillips 66, Shell, Sinclair, **food:** Arby's, Braum's, KFC, Mazzio's, McDonald's, Sonic, Subway, Taco Mayo, Wilder's Grill, **lodging:** Colonial Motel, Economy Inn, Henryetta Inn/rest., LeBaron Motel, Relax Inn, **other:** Chevrolet, Chrysler/Jeep, Ford, O'Reilly Parts, Walmart, tires, **S** Indian Nation Tpk

**237** US 62, US 75, Henryetta, **N gas:** Shell/dsl/24hr, Short Stop, **food:** Pig Out Palace, **lodging:** Green Country Inn, Trail Motel, **other:** Ⓗ HOSPITAL, Henryetta RV Park (2mi), **S food:** Hungry Traveler Rest., **lodging:** Super 8

**231** US 75 S, to Weleetka, **N gas:** Phillips 66/dsl/café, **food:** Cowpoke's Cafe

**227** Clearview Rd, **S** casino

**221** US 62, OK 27, Okemah, **N gas:** Conoco/dsl, Valero/Subway/dsl/24hr, **food:** Aspen Rest., Mazzio's, Sonic, **lodging:** Day's Inn, **other:** Ⓗ HOSPITAL, Chevrolet, Parts+, **S gas:** Love's/Chester/dsl/24hr, Shell/dsl, **food:** Kellogg's Rest, **other:** truck repair

**217** OK 48, to Bristow, Bearden, **S** gas

**216mm** N Canadian River

**212** OK 56, to Cromwell, Wewoka, **N food:** BBQ, **S gas:** Shell/dsl/cafe, to Seminole Nation Museum

**208mm** Gar Creek

**202mm** Turkey Creek

**200** US 377, OK 99, to Little, Prague, **S gas:** Conoco/dsl/24hr, Love's/Subway/dsl/24hr, Sinclair, **food:** Robertson's Ham Sandwiches, Roundup Rest/RV Park, **lodging:** Best Western

**197mm** rest area both lanes, full ♿ facilities, Ⅽ, ⚏, litter barrels, petwalk

**192** OK 9A, Earlsboro, **S gas:** Shell/dsl, **food:** Biscuit Hill Rest.

**189mm** N Canadian River

**186** OK 18, to Shawnee, **N gas:** Phillips 66, Sinclair, **food:** Denny's, **lodging:** American Inn, Best Value, Day's Inn, La Quinta, Motel 6, Super 8, **S food:** Golden Corral, LJ Silver, Sonic, Van's BBQ, **lodging:** Colonial Inn, **other:** Chevrolet/Cadillac, Chrysler/Jeep, Curves, antique auto museum

**185** OK 3E, Shawnee Mall Dr, to Shawnee, **N gas:** Murphy USA/dsl, **food:** Chili's, Garcia's Mexican, Red Lobster, Santa Fe Steaks, Taco Bueno, Wendy's, **lodging:** Holiday Inn Express, **other:** Dillard's, $Tree, JC Penney, Old Navy, Radio Shack, Sears/auto, Walmart/SuperCtr,

**SHAWNEE**

**185** Continued
mall, **S gas:** Phillips 66/Quizno's/dsl, **food:** Applebee's, Braum's, Charlie's Chicken, CiCi's, Cracker Barrel, Delta Café, Garfield's Rest., IHOP, Mazzio's, McDonald's, Schlotsky's (2mi), Sonic, Starbucks, Subway, Taco Bell, **lodging:** Hampton Inn, **other:** CVS Drug, Lowe's Whse, Staples

**181** US 177, US 270, to Tecumseh, **S lodging:** Budget Inn

**180mm** N Canadian River

**178** OK 102 S, Dale, **N gas:** Firelake/dsl, **other:** casino

**176** OK 102 N, McLoud Rd, **S gas:** Love's/Subway/dsl/24hr, Sinclair, **food:** Curtis Watson Rest.

**172** Newalla Rd, to Harrah

**169** Peebly Rd

**166** Choctaw Rd, to Woods, **N gas:** Love's/Subway/dsl/24hr, **other:** KOA, **S gas:** Phillips 66/dsl, **food:** Sonic, **other:** to Little River SP (11mi)

**165** I-240 W (from wb), to Dallas

**162** Anderson Rd, **N** LP

**159b** Douglas Blvd, **N gas:** Conoco, Shell, **food:** Denny's, LJ Silver, McDonald's, Sonic, Subway, Taco Bell, **other:** Eastland Hills RV Park, **S other:** Tinker AFB, Ⓗ HOSPITAL

**159a** Hruskocy Gate, **N gas:** Shell, **food:** China Grill, **lodging:** Executive Inn, **other:** Chrysler/Dodge, Family$, Firestone/auto, Nissan, U-Haul, same as 157, **S** Gate 7, Tinker AFB

**157c** Eaker Gate, Tinker AFB, same as 159

**157b** Air Depot Blvd, **N gas:** Conoco/dsl, Shell/Circle K, **food:** Applebees, Arby's, Chili's, CiCi's pizza, IHOP, KFC, Logans Roadhouse, Old Chicago Grill, Pizza Inn, Santa Fe Steaks, Schlotsky's, Starbucks, Steak & Shake, Subway, Taco Mayo, **lodging:** Best Western, Super 8, **other:** Best Buy, Chevrolet, Cottman Transmissions, Firestone, JC Penney, Kohl's, Lowe's Whse, Marshall's, O'Reilly Parts, Target, U-Haul, Walgreen, **S** Gate 1, Tinker AFB

**157a** SE 29th St, Midwest City, **N gas:** Conoco/dsl, Shell, **lodging:** Planet Inn, **other:** O'Reilly Parts, **S other:** Ford, Sam's Club/gas

**156b a** Sooner Rd, **N gas:** Conoco/Circle K, **food:** Primo's Rest., Waffle House, **lodging:** Comfort Inn, Hampton Inn, Hawthorn Suites, Holiday Inn Express, La Quinta, Sheraton, Studio 6, **other:** Home Depot, Radio Shack, Walmart SuperCtr/Subway, **S lodging:** Motel 6, **other:** Chevrolet/Pontiac/GMC, Tires+, Toyota

**155b** SE 15th St, Del City, **N gas:** Shell, **other:** Family$, **S food:** Madison's Kitchen, **other:** Mitsubishi

**OK**

**E** ↕ **W**

**OKLAHOMA CITY**

**OK**

**OKLAHOMA CITY**

**OKLAHOMA CITY**

## INTERSTATE 40 CONT'D

**155a** Sunny Lane Rd, Del City, **N** gas: Conoco/dsl, **other:** Hyundai, U-Haul, **S** gas: Shell, **food:** Braum's, Pizza Hut, Sonic

**154** Reno Ave, Scott St, **N** gas: Sinclair, **lodging:** Value Place Motel, **S** gas: Phillips 66/dsl, 7-11/gas

**152** (153 from wb)I-35 N, to Wichita

**127** Eastern Ave (from eb), Okla City, **N** gas: Petro/Mobil/dsl/scales/rest./@, JR's Trvl Crt/Corky's Grill/dsl/24hr, Shamrock, **food:** Waffle House, **lodging:** Econolodge, Quality Inn, **other:** Blue Beacon, Lewis RV Ctr

**151b c** I-35, S to Dallas, I-235 N, to downtown, st capitol

**151a** Lincoln Blvd, **N** gas: Conoco/Subway/Circle K/dsl, **food:** Earl's Rib Palace, Falcon's Pizza, IHOP, Sonic, **lodging:** Renaissance Inn, **other:** Bass Pro Shop, Bricktown Stadium

**150c** Robinson Ave (from wb), OK City, **N** food: Spaghetti Whse, Zio's Italian, **lodging:** Courtyard, Residence Inn, Westin Hotel, **other:** U-Haul, Ford

**150b** Harvey Ave (from eb), downtown, **N** lodging: Courtyard, Renaissance Hotel, Sheraton, Westin Hotel

**150a** Walker Ave (from eb), **N** food: La Luna Mexican, **other:** Ford/Lincoln/Mercury, **S** transmissions

**149b** Classen Blvd (from wb), to downtown, same as 149a

**149a** Western Ave, Reno Ave, **N** gas: Valero/Subway/dsl, **food:** China Queen, McDonald's, Sonic, Taco Bell, **S** gas: Conoco/dsl, Shell, **food:** Sweis Greek Cafe

**148c** Virginia Ave (from wb), to downtown

**148b** Penn Ave (from eb), **N** gas: Shamrock, **S** other: Isuzu/Ryder Trucks

**148a** Agnew Ave, Villa Ave, **N** gas: Phillips 66/dsl

**147c** May Ave

**147b a** I-44, E to Tulsa, W to Lawton

**146** Portland Ave (from eb, no return), **N** gas: Conoco/Subway/dsl, **other:** water funpark

**145** Meridian Ave, OK City, **N** gas: Conoco, Shell/dsl, **food:** Denny's, Louie's Grille, McDonald's, Jin wei Aisan, On the Border, Outback Steaks, Shiki, Shorty Small's Rest., Trapper's Rest., **lodging:** Best Western, Builtmore Hotel, Day's Inn, Extended Stay America, Howard Johnson, Motel 6, Red Roof Inn, Residence Inn, Rodeway Inn, Super 8, Travelers Inn, **other:** Chevrolet, **S** gas: Phillips 66/dsl, Sinclair, **food:** Arby's, Burger King, Charleston Rest., Chili's, Cracker Barrel, Golden Palace Chinese, IHOP, Kona Ranch Steaks, Mazzio's, Panera Bread, Quizno's, Rib Crib, Santa Fe Grill, Sonic, Taco Bueno, Waffle House, Wendy's, Western Sizzlin, Whataburger, Zio's Italian, **lodging:** AmeriSuites, Best Value Inn, Candlewood Suites, Clarion Hotel, Comfort Suites, Courtyard, Embassy Suites, Executive Inn, Governor Suites, Hampton Inn, Hilton Garden, Holiday Inn Express, La Quinta, Meridian Inn, Motel 6, Oak Tree Inn, Ramada Ltd, Regency Inn, Sleep Inn, Wingate Inn

**144** MacArthur Blvd, **N** gas: On-Cue, Shell/dsl, **food:** Applebee's, China 1, Coldstone Creamery, Fire Mtn Steaks, Golden Corral, KFC, McDonald's, Sonic, Starbucks, Taco Bueno, Taco Cabana, Texas Roadhouse, **other:** GNC, Office Depot, PetsMart, Radio Shack, Ross, Walmart SuperCtr, **S** lodging: Green Carpet Inn, Microtel, Super 10 Motel, Travelodge, **other:** Kenworth, Sam's Club/gas

**OKLAHOMA CITY**

**EL RENO**

**143** Rockwell Ave, **N** gas: Shell, **lodging:** Rodeway Inn, **other:** Home Depot, McClain's RV Ctr, Tires+, **S** lodging: Sands Motel/RV Park/LP, **other:** Rockwell RV Park

**142** Council Rd, **N** gas: Shell, Sinclair, **food:** A-1 BBQ, Braum's, McDonald's, Subway, Taco Bell, Wendy's, **lodging:** Best Budget Inn, **other:** Goodyear, **S** gas: TA/Country Pride/dsl/scales/24hr/@, **lodging:** Econolodge, **other:** Council Rd RV Park, IA-80 Truckwash

**140** Morgan Rd, **N** gas: Pilot/McDonald's/dsl/24hr/@, TA/Phillips 66/Popeye's/dsl/24hr/@, **other:** Blue Beacon, **S** gas: ⊕ FLYING J/Conoco/cookery/dsl/LP/scales/24hr/@, Love's/Subway/Ricky's Cafe/dsl/scales/24hr/@, **food:** Sonic, **other:** Speedco

**139** Kilpatrick Tpk

**138** OK 4, to Yukon, Mustang, **N** food: Catcher's Grill, **lodging:** Comfort Inn, Super 7, **other:** Chrysler/Dodge/Jeep, **S** gas: Conoco/dsl, **food:** Burger King, Daylight Doughnuts, Hunan Express, Interurban Grill, KFC, McDonald's, Sonic, Subway, **lodging:** Best Western, **other:** CVS Drug, Homeland Foods, Kottman Transmissions

**137** Cornwell Dr, Czech Hall Rd, **N** Albertson's/Sav-On

**136** OK 92, to Yukon, **N** gas: Murphy USA/dsl, Shell/Circle K, **food:** A&W/LJ Silver, Braum's, Clint's Cafe, KFC, McDonald's, Primo's Italian, Subway, Taco Mayo, Waffle House, Wendy's, Yukon Buffet, **lodging:** Hampton Inn, **other:** AutoZone, Big Lots, Big O Tire, Chevrolet, $General, $Tree, Hancock Fabrics, Hastings Books, Radio Shack, Tuesday Morning, Walmart SuperCtr, **S** food: Alfredo's, Carino's Italian, Chili's, Jimmy's Egg Café, Pizza Hut, Quizno's, Santa Fe Steaks, Starbucks, Taco Bueno, **lodging:** Holiday Inn Express, **other:** H HOSPITAL, Ford, Kohl's, Kwik Kar, Lowe's Whse, PetsMart, Staples, Target, Tires+

**132** Cimarron Rd, **S** ✈

**130** Banner Rd, **N** gas: Shell/dsl/rest.

**129mm** weigh st both lanes

**125** US 81, to El Reno, **N** gas: Conoco, Love's/dsl, **food:** China King, Serapio's Mexican, Taco Mayo, **lodging:** Economy Express, Sands Motel, Super 8, **other:** Chevrolet, Chrysler/Jeep/Dodge, $General, Ford/Lincoln/Mercury, Pontiac/GMC/Buick, **S** truck repair

**123** Country Club Rd, to El Reno, **N** gas: Conoco, Murphy USA/dsl, Shell, Valero, **food:** Arby's, Braum's, Burger King, Carl's Jr, KFC, Little Caesar's, Mazzio's, McDonald's, Pizza Hut, Subway, Taco Bell, **other:** H HOSPITAL, Radio Shack, Walmart SuperCtr, **S** gas: Phillips 66/dsl, **food:** Denny's, MT Mikes Steaks, **lodging:** Best Western/RV Park, Comfort Inn, Day's Inn, Regency Motel

**119** Lp 40, to El Reno

**115** US 270, to Calumet

**111mm** picnic area eb, 🚻, litter barrels

**108** US 281, to Geary, **N** gas: Shell/Subway/dsl/24hr, **other:** KOA/Indian Trading Post, to Roman Nose SP, **S** gas: Love's/Chesterfried/Godfather's Pizza/dsl/@

**105mm** S Canadian River

**104** Methodist Rd

**101** US 281, OK 8, to Hinton, **N** to Roman Nose SP, **S** gas: Loves/Sonic/dsl/scales, **lodging:** Microtel, **other:** Chevrolet, picnic area, to Red Rock Canyon SP

**95** Bethel Rd

**94.5mm** picnic area wb, 🚻, litter barrels

## INTERSTATE 40 CONT'D

| | |
|---|---|
| 88 | OK 58, to Hydro, Carnegie |
| 84 | Airport Rd, **N gas:** Phillips 66/dsl/scales/24hr, **food:** Lucille's Roadhouse, **lodging:** Holiday Inn Express, Travel Inn, **other:** H HOSPITAL, Buick/Pontiac/GMC, Chevrolet/Cadillac, Chrysler/Dodge/Jeep |
| 82 | E Main St, Weatherford, **N gas:** Conoco/dsl, Phillips 66, Shell/Subway/dsl, Sinclair, Valero, **food:** Alfredo's Mexican, Arby's, Braum's, Carl's Jr, Jerry's Rest., KFC/Taco Bell, Mark Rest., Mazzio's, McDonald's, Nita's, Pizza Hut, Sonic, Taco Mayo, T-Bone Steaks, **lodging:** Best Western, Comfort Inn, Scottish Inn, **other:** H HOSPITAL, $General, GNC, O'Reilly Parts, Radio Shack, Walgreens, Walmart, to SW OSU |
| 80 | (80a from eb) W Main St, **N gas:** Shell/dsl, **lodging:** Economy Inn |
| 71 | Custer City Rd, **N gas:** Love's/Subway/dsl/rest., **other:** Cherokee Trading Post |
| 69 | Lp 40 (from wb), to Clinton, **2 mi N food:** DQ, **lodging:** Travel Inn |
| 67.5mm | Washita River |
| 66 | US 183, Clinton, **S gas:** Shell/dsl, **other:** Ford/Lincoln/Mercury, Chrysler/Dodge/Jeep |
| 65a | 10th St, Neptune Dr, Clinton, **N food:** Braum's, China King, Lupita's Mexican, Pizza Hut, **lodging:** Day's Inn, Relax Inn, Super 8, **other:** United Foods, Wink's Campground, **S gas:** Phillips 66/dsl, **lodging:** Clinton Inn |
| 65 | Gary Blvd, Clinton, **N gas:** Conoco, Shell/dsl, **food:** Del Rancho, DQ, Italian Villa, LJ Silver, Mazzio's, McDonald's, MT Mike's, Pancake House, Subway, Taco Mayo, **lodging:** Budget Inn, Hampton Inn, Ramada Inn, Tradewinds Inn, Travelodge, **other:** H HOSPITAL, $General, K-Mart, Rte 66 Museum |
| 62 | Parkersburg Rd, **S** Hargus RV Ctr |
| 61 | Haggard Rd |
| 57 | Stafford Rd |
| 53 | OK 44, Foss, **N** to Foss RA, **S** gas/dsl |
| 50 | Clinton Lake Rd, **N other:** KOA/LP/dsl |
| 47 | Canute, **S gas:** Shell, **lodging:** Sunset Inn |
| 41 | OK 34 (exits left from eb), Elk City, **N gas:** East Side/dsl, Love's/Subway/dsl, Shell, **food:** Home Cooking Rest., **lodging:** Ambassador Inn, Best Western, Economy Express, Motel 6, Red Carpet Inn, Travel Inn, Travelodge, Super 8, **other:** H HOSPITAL, Elk Run RV Park, Rte 66 Museum |
| 40 | E 7th St, Elk City, **N food:** Portobello Grill, same as 41 |
| 38 | OK 6, Elk City, **N gas:** Conoco/dsl, Phillips 66/dsl, **food:** Arby's, Denny's, LJ Silver, McDonald's, Quizno's, Starbucks, Western Sizzlin, **lodging:** Bedford Inn, Best Western (3mi), Day's Inn, **other:** Ace Hardware, Elk Creek RV Park, **S gas:** Phillips 66/dsl, **lodging:** Comfort Inn, Econolodge, Holiday Inn, Ramada Inn, **other:** to Quartz Mtn SP |
| 34 | Merritt Rd |
| 32 | OK 34 S (exits left from eb), Elk City |
| 26 | Cemetery Rd, **S gas:** TA/Taco Bell/Subway/dsl/scales/24hr/@ |
| 25 | Lp 40, Sayre, **N gas:** Shell/dsl, **lodging:** Western Motel (1mi), **other:** H HOSPITAL, Ford |
| 23 | OK 152, Sayre, **S gas:** Shell/dsl |

| | |
|---|---|
| 22.5mm | N Fork Red River |
| 20 | US 283, Sayre, **N gas:** ✈FLYING J/CountryMkt/dsl/LP/RV dump/scales/24hr, **lodging:** AmericInn, **other:** to Washita Bfd Site (25mi) |
| 14 | Hext Rd |
| 13.5mm | check sta both lanes, litter barrels |
| 11 | Lp 40, to Erick, Hext |
| 10mm | Welcome Ctr/rest area both lanes, full ♿ facilities, C, 🛉 litter barrels, petwalk, RV dump |
| 7 | OK 30, Erick, **N lodging:** Comfort Inn, **S gas:** Love's/Subway/dsl/scales, **food:** Simple Simon's Pizza, **lodging:** Days Inn |
| 5 | Lp 40, Honeyfarm Rd |
| 1 | Texola, **S gas:** gas/dsl/rest., **other:** RV camping |
| 0mm | Oklahoma/Texas state line |

## INTERSTATE 44

| Exit # | Services |
|---|---|
| 329mm | Oklahoma/Missouri state line |
| 321mm | Spring River |
| 314mm | **Oklahoma Welcome Ctr, service plaza wb, Phillips 66/dsl** |
| 313 | OK 10, Miami, **N gas:** Citgo/dsl, Conoco, Love's/dsl/24hr, Phillips, **food:** Arby's, McDonald's, Stable's Rest., **lodging:** Best Western/rest., Microtel, Super 8, Townsman Motel/rest., **other:** H HOSPITAL, Miami RV Park, to NE OK A&M Coll, vet, **S other:** Chrysler/Dodge/Jeep, casino |
| 312mm | Neosho River |
| 302 | US 59, US 69, Afton, **S gas:** Conoco, **3 mi S lodging:** Best Western, OK 66 Motel, **other:** Bears Den Resort Camping |
| 299mm | **rest area eb, rest rooms, 🛉, litter barrel** |
| 289 | US 60, Vinita, **N food:** Braum's, McDonald's, Pizza Hut, Simple Simon Pizza, Subway, **lodging:** Holiday Inn Express, **other:** H HOSPITAL, Ace Hardware, Chevrolet, Cooper Tires, $General, Walmart SuperCtr/gas, st patrol |
| 288mm | **service plaza both lanes, Phillips 66/dsl/24hr, McDonald's, C** |
| 286mm | toll plaza |
| 283 | US 69, Big Cabin, **N gas:** Shell/Big Cabin/dsl/rest./scales/24hr/@, **lodging:** Super 8, **S** truck repair |
| 271mm | **picnic eb, 🛉, litter barrel** |
| 269 | OK 28 (from eb, no re-entry), to Adair, Chelsea |
| 269mm | **rest area eb, rest rooms, 🛉, litter barrel** |
| 256mm | **rest area wb, rest rooms, 🛉, litter barrel, C** |
| 255 | OK 20, to Pryor, Claremore, **N gas:** Kum&Go, **food:** Woody's Cafe, **lodging:** Best Western, Clairmore Inn, |

Copyright 2009 - The Next Exit®

## INTERSTATE 44 CONT'D

**E ↕ W**

**OK**

**TULSA**

**255** Continued
Super 8, Travel Inn, **other:** Ⓗ HOSPITAL, Walmart SuperCtr/dsl, to Rogers U, Will Rogers Memorial, museum

**248** to OK 266, Port of Catoosa, **N lodging:** Days Inn

**244mm** Kerr-McClellan Navigation System

**241mm** Will Rogers Tpk begins eb, ends wb, Ⓒ

**241** OK 66 E, to Catoosa

**240b** US 412 E, Choteau

**240a** OK 167 N, 193rd E Ave, **N food:** KFC, McDonald's, Pauline's Buffet, Pizza Hut, Taco Bueno, Taco Mayo, Waffle House, Wendy's, **other:** KOA, O'Reilly Parts, casino, **S gas:** QT, Shell/dsl, **food:** Mazzio's, PortCity Diner, Sonic, Subway, **lodging:** Holiday Inn Express, **other:** Cooper Tires, $General, Family$, Homeland Foods, NAPA, tires/repair

**238** 161st E Ave, **N gas:** Phillips 66/dsl/scales/rest./24hr, truckwash, **S gas:** QT/dsl/scales/24hr, **food:** Arby's, Burger King, **lodging:** Microtel, **other:** I-44 Auto Auction, **OK Welcome Ctr**

**236b** I-244 W, to downtown Tulsa, ✈

**236a** 129th E Ave, **N gas:** ⊕FLYING J/Conoco/dsl/LP/rest./24hr/@, **S food:** McDonald's

**235** E 11th St, Tulsa, **N food:** Big Daddy's BBQ, Mazzio's, Rioberto's Mexican, Sonic, Subway, **lodging:** Executive Inn, Garnett Inn, Motel 6, Super 8, **other:** $General, Drug Whse, O'Reilly Parts, **S gas:** QT, **food:** Braum's, Denny's, Taco Bueno, **lodging:** Econolodge, **other:** Whse Foods

**234b a** US 169, N to Owasso, to ✈, S to Broken Arrow

**233** E 21st St (from wb), **S food:** El Chico, **lodging:** Comfort Suites, **other:** K-Mart, Dean's RV Ctr

**231** (232 from wb) US 64, OK 51, to Muskogee, E 31st St, Memorial Dr, **N gas:** Phillips 66, **food:** CJ's Rest, Country Inn Rest., Whataburger, **lodging:** Best Value, Day's Inn, Delux Inn, Georgetown Plaza Motel, Ramada Inn, Regency Inn, Travelodge, **other:** Homeland Foods, **S gas:** Shell/A&W, **food:** Cracker Barrel, IHOP, McDonald's, Pizza Hut, Village Inn Rest., **lodging:** Best Western, Comfort Inn, Courtyard, Econolodge, Embassy Suites, Extended Stay America, Fairfield Inn, Hampton Inn, Hawthorn Suites, Holiday Inn Express, Park Inn, Quality Inn, Sleep Inn, Studio+, Super 8, **other:** Cavender's Boots, Chevrolet, Chrysler, Nissan

**230** E 41st St, Sheridan Rd, **N gas:** Shell, **food:** Carl's Jr, Desi Wok, El Chico, On-the-Border, Panera Bread, Quizno's, Subway, TGIFriday, Whataburger/24hr, **other:** Barnes&Noble, Circuit City, Dillards, JC Penney, Jo-Ann Fabrics, Michael's, Old Navy, PetsMart, Robertson Tire, Ross, **S lodging:** Heritage Inn, La Quinta, **other:** Best Buy, Home Depot

**229** Yale Ave, Tulsa, **N gas:** Shell, **food:** McDonald's, **other:** Firestone, Foley's, Ross, mall, **S gas:** Phillips 66/dsl, QT/24hr, **food:** Applebee's, Arby's, Braum's,

**229** Continued
Carrabba's, Carino's Italian, Delta Cafe, Denny's, Don Pablo, Outback Steaks, Red Lobster, Steak&Ale, Subway, Taco Bell, Taco Cabana, Village Inn Rest., **lodging:** Baymont Inn, Comfort Inn, Days Inn, Holiday Inn Select, Red Roof Inn, **other:** Ⓗ HOSPITAL, Celebration Sta, Kia, Mazda

**228** Harvard Ave, Tulsa, **N gas:** Shell/dsl, **food:** Johnnie's Charcoal Buffet, NYC Pizza, **lodging:** Best Western, Towers Hotel, Tradewinds Motel, **S food:** Blimpie, Chili's, Chimi's Mexican, LoneStar Steaks, LJ Silver/A&W, Lanna Thai, Marie Callender's, McDonald's, Osaka Steaks, Panera Bread, Papa John's, Perry's Rest., Pizza Hut, Rick's Cafe, Sol's Grill, **lodging:** Holiday Inn Express, Howard Johnson, Ramada Inn, **other:** Albertson's, $Tree, Kelly Tire, K-Mart, SteinMart

**227** Lewis Ave, Tulsa, **S gas:** Phillips 66, Sinclair, **food:** Domino's, El Chico, Goldie's Patio Grill, SteakStuffers USA, **other:** Tires+, Walgreens

**226b** Peoria Ave, Tulsa, **N gas:** QT, **food:** Arby's, Burger St., China Wok, Church's, CiCi's, Mazzio's, KFC, Pizza Hut, Ron's Chili, Taco Bell, Waffle House, **lodging:** Super 8, **other:** Hancock Fabrics, Harley-Davidson, O'Reilly Parts, Radio Shack, Walmart Mkt, **S gas:** Shell, **food:** Braum's, Golden Palace, Kelly's Rest., **other:** AutoZone, $General, Mays Drug

**226a** Riverside Dr (from wb), **S lodging:** Victorian Inn

**225mm** Arkansas River

**225** Elwood Ave, **N other:** Chevrolet, Ford

**224b a** US 75, to Okmulgee, Bartlesville, **N gas:** QT/dsl, **food:** Mazzio's, Subway, **other:** $General, Whse Mkt, **S lodging:** Royal Inn, **other:** RV park

**223c** 33rd W Ave, Tulsa, **N food:** Braum's, Domino's, **S gas:** Citgo, **food:** Rib Crib BBQ

**223b** 51st St (from wb)

**223a** I-244 E, to Tulsa, downtown

**222c** (from wb), **S lodging:** Value Inn

**222b** 55th Place, **N lodging:** Capri Motel, Crystal Motel, **S lodging:** Day's Inn, Economy Inn

**222a** 49th W Ave, Tulsa, **N food:** Carl's Jr, Mama Lou's Rest., Monterey Café, **lodging:** Gateway Motel, Interstate Inn, Motel 6, **other:** BigLots, $General, May's Drug, Piggly Wiggly, Radio Shack, **S gas:** QT/Wendy's/dsl/scales/24hr, **food:** Arby's, McDonald's, Village Inn Rest., Waffle House, **lodging:** Days Inn, Super 8, **other:** Buick/Pontiac/GMC, Peterbilt, Volvo Trucks

**221a** 57th W Ave, (from wb), **S food:** Avalon Steaks, **other:** Buick/Pontiac/GMC

**221mm** Turner Tkp begins wb, ends eb

**218** Creek Tpk E (from eb)

**215** OK 97, to Sand Sprgs, Sapulpa, **S food:** Freddy's, Subway, **lodging:** Super 8, **other:** Ⓗ HOSPITAL

**211** OK 33, to Kellyville, Drumright, Heyburn SP, **S gas:** Shell/dsl

**207mm** service plaza wb, **gas:** Phillips 66/dsl

Copyright 2009 - The Next Exit®

## INTERSTATE 44 CONT'D

E ↕ W

| | |
|---|---|
| **204mm** | picnic area eb, litter barrels,  |
| **197mm** | **service plaza eb, gas:** Phillips 66/dsl/24hr, **food:** McDonald's |
| **196** | OK 48, Bristow, **S lodging:** Carolyn Inn, **other:** H HOSPITAL, Walmart SuperCtr |
| **190mm** | picnic area eb, litter barrels, |
| **182mm** | toll plaza |
| **179** | OK 99, to Drumright, Stroud, **N lodging:** Best Western/rest., **S gas:** Phillips 66/Subway/dsl, **food:** Mazzio's, McDonald's, Sonic, Steak&Eggs Rest., Taco Mayo, **lodging:** Sooner Motel, **other:** H HOSPITAL, auto/tire repair |
| **178mm** | Hoback Plaza both lanes (exits left), **gas:** Phillips 66/dsl, **food:** McDonald's |
| **171mm** | picnic area eb, litter barrels, |
| **167mm** | **service plaza (from eb), S gas:** Phillips 66/dsl |
| **166** | OK 18, to Cushing, Chandler, **N other:** Chrysler/Jeep/Dodge, **S gas:** Phillips 66, **lodging:** Econolodge, Lincoln Motel, **other:** Chandler Tire |
| **166mm** | picnic area wb, , litter barrels, |
| **158** | OK 66, to Wellston, **N gas:** Kum&Go/Subway/dsl/24hr |
| **157** | service plaza (from wb), **N gas:** Phillips 66/McDonald's/dsl, **other:** museum info |
| **138d** | to Memorial Rd, to Enterprise Square |
| **138a** | I-35, I-44 E to Tulsa, Turner Tpk |
| **I-44 and I-35 run together 8 mi. See Interstate 35 exits 137-134.** | |
| **130** | I-35 S, to Dallas, access to facilities on I-35 S |
| **129** | MLK Ave, Remington Park, **N food:** County Line BBQ, **lodging:** Garden Inn, **other:** Cowboy Museum, **S food:** McDonald's, **other:** Family$ |
| **128b** | Kelley Ave, OK City, **N gas:** Conoco, Valero/Subway/dsl, **food:** Sonic |
| **128a** | Lincoln Blvd, st capitol, **S lodging:** Oxford Inn, Whitten Inn |
| **127** | I-235 S, US 77, City Ctr, Broadway St, **1 exit N gas:** Conoco, Phillips 66/dsl, Shell, **lodging:** Best Western, Holiday Inn |
| **126** | Western Ave, **N food:** Camille's Cafe, Deep Fork Rest., Sonic, Flip's Rest. |
| **125c** | NW Expressway (exits left from sb) |
| **125** | Classen Blvd, (exits left from wb), OK City, **N gas:** Shell, **food:** Cheesecake Factory, Chili's, Elephant Bar Rest., Moe's SW Grill, Olive Garden, **other:** Acura, Dillard's, JC Penney, Macy's, Old Navy, Radio Shack, Ross, Walmart SuperCtr, **S food:** IHOP, McDonald's, **lodging:** AmeriSuites, Courtyard, Hawthorn Suites |
| **125a** | OK 3A, Penn Ave, to NW Expswy, **N gas:** Conoco/dsl/24hr, **S gas:** Shell, **food:** Braum's, Coit's Cafe, **lodging:** Habana Inn, **other:** Homeland Foods, |
| **124** | N May, **W gas:** Shell/Subway, **food:** San Marco's Mexican, **lodging:** Comfort Inn, Day's Inn, Super 8, **other:** Dodge, O'Reilly Parts, **S other:** Aamco, Ford, Lowes Whse |
| **123b** | OK 66 W, NW 39th, to Warr Acres, **N gas:** Valero/McDonald's/dsl, **food:** Asian Palace, Carl's Jr, Chinese Buffet, Jimmy's Egg, Los Mariachi's, Quizno's, **lodging:** Carlyle Motel, Hospitality Inn, **other:** $General |

OKLAHOMA CITY

| | |
|---|---|
| **123a** | NW 36th St |
| **122** | NW 23rd St, **N gas:** Conoco/7-11, **food:** Church's, EggRoll King, Taco Mayo, **other:** Tires+, **S gas:** Conoco, **food:** Arby's, Sonic, **other:** Big O Tire, Family$ |
| **121b a** | NW 10th St, **N gas:** Shell, **S gas:** 7-11/gas, Sinclair, **other:** $General, Family$, Whittaker's Foods/24hr, antiques, fairgrounds |
| **120b a** | I-40, W to Amarillo, E to Ft Smith |
| **119** | SW 15th St |
| **118** | OK 152 W, SW 29th St, OK City, **E gas:** 7-11/gas, **food:** A&W/LJ Silver, Burger King, KFC/Taco Bell, La Fiesta Mexican, McDonald's, Sonic, Subway, Taco Bueno, **other:** Advance Parts, AutoZone, $General, $Tree, Grider's Foods/gas, O'Reilly Parts, Walgreen, **W gas:** Shell, **other:** U-Haul, transmissions |
| **117** | SW 44th St, **W** auto repair |
| **116b** | Airport Rd (exits left from nb), **W** ✈ |
| **116a** | SW 59th St, **E gas:** Conoco, **W** Will Rogers ✈ |
| **115** | I-240 E, US 62 E, to Ft Smith |
| **114** | SW 74th St, OK City, **E gas:** TK, Valero, **food:** Braum's, Burger King, Perry's Rest., **lodging:** Cambridge Inn, Ramada Ltd, **other:** $General |
| **113** | SW 89th St, **E gas:** Love's/Subway/dsl/24hr, OG, 7-11/gas, Valero/dsl, **food:** McDonald's, Sonic, Taco Mayo, **other:** H HOSPITAL, CVS Drug |
| **112** | SW 104th St, **E gas:** Valero, **W gas:** Shell/rest./dsl |
| **111** | SW 119th St, **E food:** Sonic, **other:** Walker RV Ctr |
| **110** | OK 37 E, to Moore, **E gas:** Sinclair/dsl, **food:** Sonic |
| **109** | SW 149th St, **E food:** JR's Grill |
| **108mm** | S Canadian River |
| **108** | OK 37 W, to Tuttle, **W gas:** Conoco/Subway/dsl, Phillips 66, **food:** Braum's, Carlito's Mexican, Carl's Jr, Little Caesar's, Mazzio's, McDonald's, New China, Sonic, **other:** $General, O'Reilly Parts, Walmart SuperCtr |
| **107** | US 62 S (no wb return), to Newcastle, **E** casino/gas, **lodging:** Newcastle Motel, **other:** Newcastle RV, Walker RV |
| **99** | H E Bailey Spur, rd 4, to Blanchard, Norman |
| **97mm** | toll booth, |
| **95.5mm** | picnic area wb, , litter barrels |
| **85.5mm** | **service plaza, both lanes exit left**, Phillips 66/dsl, McDonald's |
| **83** | US 62, Chickasha, **W gas:** Jay's/dsl, Valero/dsl, **other:** Indian Museum |

## INTERSTATE 44 CONT'D

**E / W — CHICKASHA / LAWTON**

| | |
|---|---|
| **80** | US 81, Chickasha, **E** **gas:** Conoco/dsl, Phillips 66/dsl, Shell/dsl, **food:** Eduardo's Mexican, Western Sizzlin, **lodging:** Day's Inn, Holiday Inn Express, Royal American Inn, Super 8, **other:** H HOSPITAL, Buick/Chevrolet/Pontiac/Cadillac, Chrysler/Dodge/Jeep, $Tree, Goody's, **W** **gas:** Conoco, Love's, Valero, **food:** Arby's, Braum's, China Moon, Denny's, Domino's, El Rancho Mexican, KFC, LJ Silver, Mazzio's Pizza, McDonald's, Napoli's Rest., New China, Pizza Hut, Quizno's, Sonic, Taco Bell, Taco Mayo, **lodging:** Best Western, Budget Motel, Ranch House Motel, **other:** AutoZone, CVS Drug, Family$, Ford/Lincoln/Mercury, O'Reilly Parts, Radio Shack, Staples, Walmart SuperCtr/Subway/gas |
| **78mm** | toll plaza, 🅒 |
| **63mm** | picnic area wb, 🏕, **litter barrels** |
| **62** | to Cyril (from wb) |
| **60.5mm** | **picnic area eb, tables, litter barrels** |
| **53** | US 277, Elgin, Lake Ellsworth, **E** **gas:** Shamrock, **food:** Goodcents Subs, Sonic, Taco Tico, **W** **gas:** Fina/dsl |
| **46** | US 62 E, US 277, US 281, to Elgin, Apache, Comanche Tribe, last free exit nb |
| **45** | OK 49, to Medicine Park, **W** **gas:** Love's/Subway/dsl/24hr, **food:** Burger King, Sonic, **other:** Whichita NWR |
| **41** | to Ft Sill, Key Gate, **W** Ft Sill Museum |
| **40c** | Gate 2, to Ft Sill |
| **40a** | US 62 W, to Cache, **E** **gas:** Fina/dsl, **W** **lodging:** Super 8 |
| **39b** | US 281 (from sb), **W** **lodging:** Ramada Inn |
| **39a** | US 281, Cache Rd  (exits left from nb), Lawton, **1-3 mi** **W** **gas:** Phillips 66, Valero/dsl, **food:** Applebee's, Braum's, Chili's, Chick-fil-A, Fire Mtn Grill, Golden Corral, KFC, Ryan's, Subway, Wendy's, **lodging:** Baymont Inn, Holiday Inn, Super 8, Super 9 Motel, **other:** $General, U-Haul, transmissions |
| **37** | Gore Blvd, Lawton, **E** **gas:** Conoco, **food:** Braum's, Los Tres Amigos, Sonic, Taco Mayo, Woody's Mexican, **lodging:** Best Western, **other:** Curves, casino, **W** **food:** Arby's (3mi), Cracker Barrel, Mike's Grille, **lodging:** Fairfield Inn, Holiday Inn Express, Ramada Inn (2mi), SpringHill Suites, **other:** Harley-Davidson, Lincoln/Mercury |
| **36a** | OK 7, Lee Blvd, Lawton, **E** **gas:** Phillips 66, **W** **gas:** Fina/dsl/repair, Shamrock/dsl, Suncountry/dsl, Welch/dsl, **food:** Big Chef Rest., KFC/Taco Bell, Leo&Ken's Rest., Popeye's, Salas Mexican, Sonic, **lodging:** Motel 6, **other:** H HOSPITAL, $General, ✈, vet |
| **33** | US 281, 11th St, Lawton, **W** **other:** H HOSPITAL, gas, food, lodging, ✈, to Ft Sill |
| **30** | OK 36, Geronimo |
| **20.5mm** | **Elmer Graham Plaza, both lanes exit left**, Phillips 66/dsl, McDonald's, info |
| **20** | OK 5, to Walters, **E** **food:** BBQ |
| **19.5mm** | toll plaza |
| **5** | US 277 N, US 281, Randlett, last free exit nb, **E** **gas:** Shamrock/dsl |
| **1** | OK 36, to Grandfield |
| **0mm** | Oklahoma/Texas state line, Red River |

## INTERSTATE 240 - OKLAHOMA CITY

**E / W — OKLAHOMA CITY**

| Exit # | Services |
|---|---|
| **16mm** | I-240 begins/ends on I-40. |
| **14** | Anderson Rd, **S** **gas:** Conoco |
| **11b a** | Douglas Blvd, **N** Tinker AFB |
| **9** | Air Depot Blvd |
| **8** | OK 77, Sooner Rd, **N** **gas:** Shell/dsl, **S** **gas:** Phillips 66/Popeye's/dsl, Valero/McDonald's/dsl |
| **7** | Sunnylane Ave, **S** **gas:** Valero/Subway/dsl, **lodging:** Value Place Motel |
| **6** | Bryant Ave |
| **5** | S Eastern Ave |
| **4c** | Pole Rd, **N** **food:** Burger King, Luby's, Taco Bell, TX Roadhouse, **lodging:** Fairfield Inn, Ramada Inn, Residence Inn, **other:** Best Buy, Dillard's, JC Penney, Tires+, Macys, mall |
| **4b a** | I-35, N to OK City, S to Dallas, US 77 S, US 62/77 N |
| **3b** | S Shields, **N** **gas:** Valero/dsl, **other:** Circuit City, Home Depot, **S** **food:** Chili's, **other:** Ford, Lowe's Whse, Nissan, Saturn, Walmart SuperCtr/gas |
| **3a** | S Santa Fe, **S** **gas:** Shell, **food:** Chili's, IHOP, **other:** Buick, Dodge, Chrysler/Jeep, Staples, Lowe's Whse, Walmart SuperCtr |
| **2b** | S Walker Ave, **N** **gas:** Shell/7-11, **food:** Rib Crib, **S** **food:** Carino's, ChuckeCheese, Jimmy's Egg Grill, On-the-Border, Premo's Italian, **other:** Chevrolet, PepBoys |
| **2a** | S Western Ave, **N** **gas:** Conoco, **food:** Burger King, House of Szechwan, Nino's Mexican, Taste of China, **other:** Hyundai, Suzuki, Tires+, **S** **gas:** 7-11/gas, Valero, **food:** A&W/LJ Silver, Arby's, Ashley's Rest./24hr, Grandy's, HomeTown Buffet, KFC, Krispy Kreme, McDonald's, Red Lobster, Steak&Ale, **lodging:** Best Western, Holiday Inn Express, Quality Inn, **other:** Big O Tire, Chevrolet, Honda, Office Depot, Radio Shack |
| **1c** | S Penn Ave, **N** **gas:** Conoco, **food:** Carl's Jr, Denny's, Don Pablo, Golden Corral, Harrigan's Rest., Hooters, Olive Garden, Outback Steaks, Pioneer Pies, Santa Fe Grill, Schlotsky's, **other:** BigLots, Circuit City, GNC, Radio Shack, Michaels, **S** **gas:** Shell/Circle K, **food:** Hunan Buffet, Joe' s Crabshack, Mazzio's, Pancho's Mexican, Papa John's, Subway, Taco Bueno, Wendy's, Western Sizzlin, **other:** $Tree, Hancock Fabrics |
| **1b** | S May Ave, **N** **gas:** 7-11/gas, **food:** Capt D's, Outlaw's BBQ, Taco Bell, Waffle House, **other:** Albertson's, O'Reilly Parts, **S** **gas:** Valero, **food:** Braum's, Burger King, Perry's Rest., **lodging:** Cambridge Inn, Ramada Ltd |
| **1a** | I-44, US 62, I-240 begins ends on I-44. |

Copyright 2009 - The Next Exit®

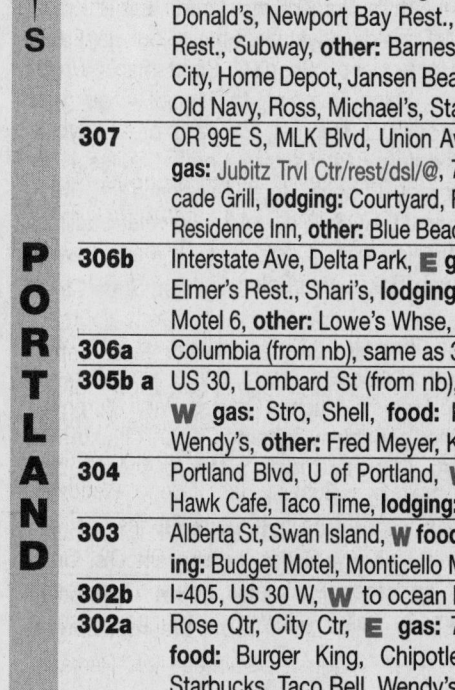

**OR**

## INTERSTATE 5

| Exit # | Services |
|---|---|
| 308.5mm | Oregon/Washington state line, Columbia River |
| 308 | Jansen Beach Dr, **E** gas: Chevron/24hr, **food:** Burger King, Starbucks, Taco Bell, **lodging:** Oxford Suites, Red Lion, **other:** Safeway, **W** food: BJ's Brewery, Bradley's Grill, Denny's, Chang's Mongolian, Hooters, McDonald's, Newport Bay Rest., Original Joe's, Stanford's Rest., Subway, **other:** Barnes&Noble, Best Buy, Circuit City, Home Depot, Jansen Beach RV Park, Office Depot, Old Navy, Ross, Michael's, Staples, Target, mall |
| 307 | OR 99E S, MLK Blvd, Union Ave, Marine Dr (sb only), **E** gas: Jubitz Trvl Ctr/rest/dsl/@, 76/dsl, **food:** Portland Cascade Grill, **lodging:** Courtyard, Fairfield Inn, Portlander Inn, Residence Inn, **other:** Blue Beacon, Expo Ctr, truck repair |
| 306b | Interstate Ave, Delta Park, **E** gas: 76, **food:** Burger King, Elmer's Rest., Shari's, **lodging:** Best Western, Day's Inn, Motel 6, **other:** Lowe's Whse, Portland Meadows |
| 306a | Columbia (from nb), same as 306b |
| 305b a | US 30, Lombard St (from nb), **E** food: Little Caesars, **W** gas: Stro, Shell, **food:** Panda Express, Subway, Wendy's, **other:** Fred Meyer, Knecht's Parts |
| 304 | Portland Blvd, U of Portland, **W** Arco, 76/dsl, **food:** Nite Hawk Cafe, Taco Time, **lodging:** Super Value, Viking Motel |
| 303 | Alberta St, Swan Island, **W** food: Subway, Taco Bell, **lodging:** Budget Motel, Monticello Motel, **E** H HOSPITAL |
| 302b | I-405, US 30 W, **W** to ocean beaches, zoo |
| 302a | Rose Qtr, City Ctr, **E** gas: 76/Circle K/dsl, Shell/dsl, **food:** Burger King, Chipotle Mexican, McDonald's, Starbucks, Taco Bell, Wendy's, **lodging:** Crowne Plaza, **other:** H HOSPITAL, Toyota/Scion, Schwab Tire, 7-11, Walgreens, **W** other: coliseum |

| Exit # | Services |
|---|---|
| 301 | I-84 E, US 30 E, services E off I-84 exits |
| 300 | US 26 E (from sb), Milwaukie Ave, **W** lodging: Hilton, Marriott |
| 299b | I-405 |
| 299a | US 26 E, OR 43 (from nb), City Ctr, to Lake Oswego |
| 297 | Terwilliger Blvd, **W** food: Burger King, KFC, **other:** H HOSPITAL, Fred Meyer, to Lewis and Clark Coll. |
| 296b | Multnomah Blvd |
| 296a | Barbur, **W** gas: Chevron/24hr, Shell, 76/dsl, **food:** Bellagio's Pizza, Original Pancake House, Szechuan Chinese, Subway, Taco Del Mar, **lodging:** Budget Lodge, Capitol Hill Motel, **other:** 7-11, Schwab Tire, vet |
| 295 | Capitol Hwy (from sb), Taylors Ferry Rd (from nb), **E** gas: Shell/dsl, **food:** Juan Colorado Mexican, Koji Japanese, McDonald's, RoundTable Pizza, Starbucks, **lodging:** Hospitality Motel, **E** food: Taco Time, Wendy's |
| 294 | OR 99W, to Tigard, **E** Comfort Suites, **W** gas: Chevron, 76, Shell, **food:** Arby's, Baja Fresh, Banning's Rest., Burger King, Gators Eatery, Hihat Chinese, KFC, Little Caesars, Mazatlan Mexican, McDonald's, Newport Bay Rest., Quizno's, Starbucks, Subway, Taco Bell, **lodging:** Quality Inn, **other:** Americas Tire, Baxter Parts, Costco, Fred Meyer, Petco, Radio Shack, Schwab Tire, U-Haul, Winco Foods, transmissions, vet |
| 293 | Haines St, **W** other: Ford |
| 292 | OR 217, Kruse Way, Lake Oswego, **E** gas: Shell, **food:** Applebee's, Coldstone, Chevy's Mexican, Olive Garden, Quizno's, Stanford's Rest., Stanford's Rest., Starbucks, Taco Del Mar, **lodging:** Crowne Plaza, Hilton Garden, Phoenix Inn, Residence Inn, **other:** AAA, Curves, LDS Temple, **W** lodging: Homestead Suites, **other:** Lowe's Whse |

## INTERSTATE 5 CONT'D

**291** Carman Dr, **W** gas: Chevron, 76/dsl, **food:** Burgerville, Domino's, El Sol De Mexico, Starbucks, Subway, **lodging:** Courtyard, Holiday Inn Express, **other:** Home Depot, Office Depot

**290** Lake Oswego, **E** gas: Chevron, Space Age/dsl/LP, **food:** Arby's, Baja Fresh, Baskin-Robbins, Burger King, Carl's Jr., Fuddruckers, Starbucks, Subway, Taco Bell, Wu's Kitchen, **lodging:** Motel 6, **other:** Safeway Foods, Walgreens, **W** food: California Pizza Kitchen, Claim Jumper Rest., Macaroni Grill, McCormick& Schmick's, PF Changs, Royal Panda, Village Inn Rest., **other:** Borders Books, Whole Foods, Wild Oats Mkt

**289** Tualatin, **E** gas: 76, Shell, **food:** Chipotle Mexican, Famous Dave's, McDonald's, Paera Bread, **other:** Best Buy, GNC Nutrition, Old Navy, PetsMart, Portland RV Park, **W** food: Coldstone, Hayden's Grill, Jack-in-the-Box, Ouback Steaks, Pizza Hut, Quizno's, Samurai Sam's, Schlotzky's, Starbucks, Taco Bell, Thai Bistro, Wendy's, **lodging:** Century Hotel, **other:** H HOSPITAL, Fred Meyer, Hagen's Foods, K-Mart, Michaels, Schuck's Parts, camping

**288** I-205, to Oregon City

**286** Stafford, **E** gas: 76/dsl/24hr, **food:** Booster Juice, Burger King, Moe's SW Grill, Panda Express, PizzaSchmizza, Starbucks, Subway, **lodging:** La Quinta, Super 8, **other:** Costco/gas, Mercedes, Office Depot, PetsMart, Pheasant Ridge RV Resort, Target, **W** gas: Chevron, **food:** Big Town Gyro, **lodging:** Holiday Inn/rest., **other:** Camping World RV Service/supplies, Chevrolet, Dodge, Nissan, Toyota/Scion

**283** Wilsonville, **E** gas: 76/dsl, **food:** Abella Italian, Arby's, Country Grains Cafe., Denny's, Jamba Juice, Juan Colorado Mexican, McDonald's, Papa Murphy's, Quizno's, Red Robin, Shari's/24hr, Starbucks, Subway, Taco Bell, TCBY, Wanker's Café, Wendy's, Wong's Chinese, **lodging:** Best Western, SnoozInn, **other:** Fry's Electronics, GNC, Lamb's Foods, NAPA, Rite Aid, Schwab Tire, USPO, vet, funpark, **W** gas: Baskin-Robbins, Chevron, **food:** Burger King/24hr, Deno's Pizzaria, Domino's, Hunan Kitchen, Sonic, Starbucks, **lodging:** Wilsonville Inn, **other:** Albertson's, 7-11, Walgreens

**282.5mm** Willamette River

**282** Charbonneau District, **E** food: Langdon Farms Rest., **other:** Langdon Farms Golf

**281.5mm** rest area both lanes, full ♿ facilities, 📞 info, 🚻 litter barrels, petwalk, vending, coffee

**278** Donald, **E** gas: Conoco/Circle K/LP/dsl, **other:** Aurora Acres RV Park, **W** gas: Leather's/dsl/@, Shell/CFN/dsl, TA/Country Pride/Popeye's/dsl/scales/24hr/@, **other:** Papa Joe's BBQ, **other:** Speedco Lube, truckwash, to Champoeg SP

**274mm** weigh sta both lanes

**271** OR 214, Woodburn, **E** gas: Arco/24hr, Chevron/24hr, Conoco, 76/repair, **food:** Burger King, Country Cottage Rest., DQ, Denny's, KFC, McDonald's/playplace, Subway, Taco Bell, **lodging:** Best Western, Super 8, **other:** Fairway Drug, Walmart SuperCtr, vet, **W** gas: Shell, **food:** Arby's, Elmer's Rest., Jack-in-the-Box, Quizno's, Starbucks, **lodging:** La Quinta, **other:** Chevrolet,

**271** Continued
Chrysler/Dodge/Jeep, Ford, Outlet/famous brands, Woodburn RV Park, Woodburn Outlets

**263** Brooks, Gervais, **E** gas: 76/LP, **other:** Brooks Mkt/deli, **W** gas: Pilot/Subway/Taco Bell/dsl/LP/scales/24hr, **other:** Chalet Rest., Freightliner, Willamette Mission SP (4mi)

**260b a** OR 99E, Salem Pkwy, Keizer, **2 mi E** camping, **W** food: Jamba Juice, Panda Express, Popeye's, RoundTable Pizza, Starbucks, Subway, Taco Del Mar, **other:** Circuit City, Lowes Whse, Michael's, PetCo, Ross, Staples, Target, World Mkt

**259mm** *45th parallel, halfway between the equator and N Pole*

**258** N Salem, **E** gas: 76/Circle K, **food:** Figaro's Italian, Guesthouse Rest., McDonald's, Original Pancake House, **lodging:** Best Western, Rodeway Inn, **other:** Al's RV Parts, Hwy RV Ctr, Roth's Foods, Trailer RV Park, flea mkt, **W** gas: Chevron, 76/Circle K, Pacific Pride/dsl, Shell/dsl, **food:** Don Pedro Mexican, Jack-in-the-Box, LumYuen Chinese, **lodging:** Budget Lodge, Travelers Inn, **other:** Stuart's Parts, to st capitol

**256** to OR 213, Market St, Salem, **E** gas: Shell, **food:** Alberto's Mexican, Chalet Rest., Denny's, Elmer's, **lodging:** Best Western, Cozzzy Inn, **other:** Fred Meyer/dsl, **E on Lancaster** gas: 76/dsl, **food:** Applebees, Baja Fresh, Blue Willow Rest., Carl's Jr, China Faith, El Mirador Mexican, Jack-in-the-Box, McGrath's Fish House, Olice Garden, Outback, Quizno's, Skipper's, Subway, Taco Bell, **other:** American Tire, Best Buy, BigLots, Macy's, Sears, Schwab Tires, Target, Walgreens, **W** gas: Arco/24hr, Pacific Pride/dsl, Shell/dsl/24hr, Texaco/dsl, **food:** Almost Home Rest., Baskin-Robbins, DQ, McDonald's, Newport Bay Seafood, Pietro's Pizza, Subway, **lodging:** Comfort Inn, Holiday Lodge, Motel 6, Phoenix Inn, Red Lion Hotel, Shilo Inn, Super 8, **other:** Buick/GMC, Jack's IGA, Kia/Mazda/Suzuki, Nissan

**253** OR 22, Salem, Stayton, **E** gas: Chevron/repair, Shell/dsl, 76, **food:** Arby's, Burger King, Carls Jr, Las Polomas Mexican, McDonalds/playplace, Shari's, Subway, **other:** $Tree, Home Depot, ShopKO, Sportsman's Whse, WinCo Foods, Salem Camping, to Detroit RA, **W** gas: Shell/dsl, **food:** DQ, Denny's, Panda Express, Sybil's Omelette, **lodging:** Best Western, Comfort Suites, Holiday Inn Express, Phoenix Hotel, Residence Inn, Travelodge, **other:** H HOSPITAL, AAA, Chevrolet/Cadillac/Subaru, Chrysler/Jeep, Costco/gas, K-Mart, Lowe's Whse, Schwab Tire, Toyota/Scion, Walmart SuperCtr, st police

**252** Kuebler Blvd, **2 mi W on Commercial** gas: Arco/24hr, 76/24hr, **food:** Applebee's, Arby's, Burger King, Jack-in-the-Box, McDonald's, Muchas Gracias, Papa Murphy's, Quizno's, Shari's, Subway, **lodging:** Phoenix Inn, **other:** H HOSPITAL, Circle K, Curves, $Tree, Jo-Anne, Roberson RV Ctr, Schwab Tire, Walmart

**249** to Salem (exits left from nb), **2 mi W** food: Arby's, Burger King, Carl's Jr., King's Buffet, **lodging:** Phoenix Inn

**248** Sunnyside, **E other:** Enchanted Forest Themepark, KOA, Willamette Valley Vineyards, **W** gas: Pacific Pride/dsl

**244** to Jefferson

**243** Ankeny Hill

**242** Talbot Rd

Left margin (reading top to bottom): N ↕ S · WILSONVILLE · OR · SALEM · SALEM

## INTERSTATE 5 CONT'D

**N** ◄► **S ALBANY**

| | |
|---|---|
| **241mm** | rest area both lanes, full ♿ facilities, info, 🚻, 🏕, litter barrels, petwalk |
| **240.5mm** | Santiam River |
| **240** | Hoefer Rd |
| **239** | Dever-Conner, |
| **238** | S Jefferson, Scio |
| **237** | Viewcrest (from sb) |
| **235** | (from nb), Millersburg |
| **234** | OR 99E, Albany, **E** **lodging:** Comfort Suites, Holiday Inn Express, **other:** Harley-Davidson, Knox Butte Camping, RV dump, ✈, **W** **gas:** Chevron, **food:** A&W, Burger King, Carl's Jr., China Buffet, DQ, KFC, McDonald's, Subway, Taco Bell, **lodging:** Best Western/rest., La Quinta, Motel 6, **other:** Ⓗ HOSPITAL, Costco/gas, K-Mart, Kohl's, Nissan, RV repair, to Albany Hist Dist |
| **233** | US 20, Albany, **E** **gas:** Chevron/dsl/LP/24hr, 76/dsl, **food:** Denny's, LumYuen Chinese, **lodging:** Econolodge, Phoenix Inn, Quality Inn, **other:** Chevrolet, Home Depot, Honda, Lassen RV Ctr, RV camping, Toyota/Scion, st police, **W** **gas:** 76/dsl, Shell, **food:** Abby's Pizza, Arby's, Baskin-Robbins, Burgerville, Carl's Jr., Elmer's, Figaro's, Fox Den Pizza, Jack-in-the-Box, Lee's Wok, Los Tequilos Mexican, Original Breakfast Cafe, Sizzler, Skipper's, Starbucks, Taco Time, **lodging:** Valu Inn, **other:** Ⓗ HOSPITAL, Albertson's, Bi-Mart, CarQuest, Chrysler/Dodge/Jeep/Subaru/Hyundai, Fred Meyer/gas/dsl, Jo-Ann Fabrics, Knecht's Parts, NAPA, PetCo, Rite Aid, Schwab Tires, Staples, Subaru, Target, Walgreens |
| **228** | OR 34, to Lebanon, Corvallis, **E** **gas:** Leather's/dsl, 76/dsl/24hr, **food:** Pine Cone Cafe, **other:** Mallard Creek RV Resort, **W** **gas:** Arco/24hr, Chevron/CFN/A&W/dsl, Shell/dsl, **other:** to OSU, KOA (5mi) |
| **222mm** | Butte Creek |
| **216** | OR 228, Halsey, Brownsville, **E** **gas:** Pioneer Villa Trk-Stp/76/Blimpie/dsl/24hr/@, **lodging:** Travelodge, **other:** parts/repair/towing, **W** **gas:** Shell/dsl |
| **209** | to Jct City, Harrisburg, **W** **other:** Diamond Hill RV Park |
| **206mm** | rest area both lanes, full ♿ facilities, info, 🚻, 🏕, litter barrels, petwalk |
| **199** | Coburg, **E** **gas:** Fuel'n Go/dsl, **other:** Premier RV Park, RV Ctr, **W** **gas:** Shell/LP, TA/CFN/Country Pride/Truck'n'Travel Motel/dsl/rest./24hr/@, **other:** Corral RV Ctr, Eugene RV park, Freightliner/GMC, Guaranty RV Ctr, Paradise RV Ctr, Volvo, dsl repair, hist dist |
| **197mm** | McKenzie River |

**S SPRINGFIELD**

| | |
|---|---|
| **195b a** | N Springfield, **E** **gas:** Arco/24hr, Chevron/24hr, 76/Circel K/dsl/24hr, **food:** Applebee's, Cabo Grill, Carl's Jr, China Sun, Ciao Pizza, ChuckeCheese, Denny's, Elmer's Rest., FarMan Chinese, Gateway Chinese, HomeTown Buffet, Howling Coyote, IHOP, Jack-in-the-Box, KFC, McDonald's, Outback Steaks, Quizno's, Roadhouse Grill, Shari's/24hr, Sizzler, Starbucks, Subway, Taco Bell, **lodging:** Best Western, Comfort Suites, Courtyard, Holiday Inn Express, Holiday Inn, Motel 6, Quality Inn, Shilo Inn/rest., Super 8, **other:** Ⓗ HOSPITAL, Best Buy, Circuit City, Kohl's, Michaels, Ross, Sears/auto, Staples, Target, USPO, mall, st police, **W** **food:** Taco Bell, **other:** Costco/gas, Office Depot, PetsMart, ShopKO, to ✈ |

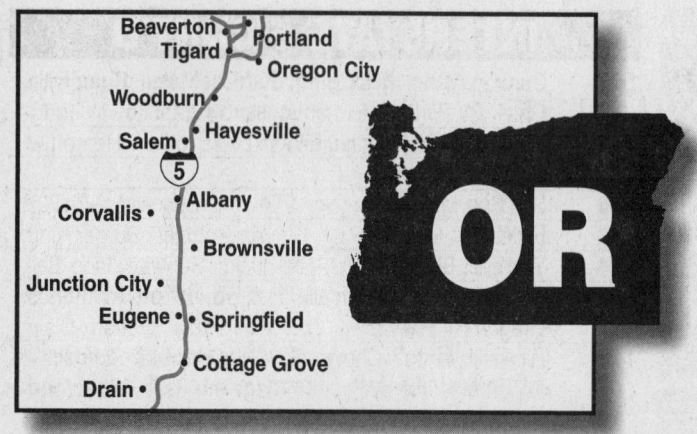

**E EUGENE**

| | |
|---|---|
| **194b a** | OR 126 E, I-105 W, Springfield, Eugene, **1 mi** **W** **gas:** Chevron, 76/repair, **food:** Carl's Jr., PF Chang's, Quizno's, Starbucks, **lodging:** Red Lion Inn, Residence Inn, **other:** Albertson's/gas, Borders Books, Old Navy, Subaru, TJ Maxx, U Of O, mall |
| **193mm** | Willamette River |
| **192** | OR 99 (from nb), to Eugene, **W** **gas:** 76, **food:** Boulevard Grill, House Of Chen, Wendy's, **lodging:** Days Inn, Best Western, Holiday Inn Express, University Inn, **other:** Mkt Of Choice |
| **191** | Glenwood, **W** **gas:** Shell/dsl/LP/24hr, **food:** Denny's, **lodging:** Comfort Suites, Motel 6 |
| **189** | 30th Ave S, Eugene, **E** **gas:** Shell/dsl/LP, **other:** Harley-Davidson, Shamrock RV Park, marine ctr, mobile village, **W** **gas:** 76/dsl |
| **188b** | rd 99 S (nb only), Goshen |
| **188a** | OR 58, to Oakridge, OR 99S, **E** **other:** Deerwood RV Camping, **W** **gas:** Pacific Pride/dsl/rest./24hr, **other:** Big Boy's RV Ctr, tires |
| **186** | to Goshen (from nb) |
| **182** | Creswell, **E** **food:** Subway, **other:** Bi-Mart Foods, Ray's Foods/drug, golf, **W** **gas:** Arco/24hr, 76/dsl, **food:** China Wok, Figaro's Pizza, Hawaiian BBQ, TJ's Rest., **lodging:** Super 8, **other:** Dari Mart, KOA, Knecht's Parts, NAPA, Tire Factory |
| **180mm** | Coast Fork of Willamette River |
| **178mm** | rest area both lanes, full ♿ facilities, 🚻, 🏕, litter barrels, petwalk, coffee |
| **176** | Saginaw |
| **175mm** | Row River |
| **174** | Cottage Grove, **E** **gas:** Chevron/dsl/repair/24hr, Pacific Pride, Shell, **food:** El Paraiso Mexican, Subway, Taco Bell, **lodging:** Village Resort/RV park, **other:** Ⓗ HOSPITAL, Brad's RV Ctr, Chevrolet/Pontiac/Buick/GMC, Chrysler/Dodge/Jeep, Walmart/auto, **W** **gas:** Chevron/dsl/LP, 76/dsl, Shell/dsl, **food:** Arby's, Burger King, Carl's Jr, Figaro's Pizza, KFC, McDonald's/RV parking, Szechuan Chinese, Subway, Torero's Mexican, Vintage Rest./24hr, **lodging:** City Ctr Motel, Comfort Inn, Holiday Inn Express, Relax Inn, **other:** Ⓗ HOSPITAL, Chevrolet, $Tree, Mazda, Shopsmart Foods, Village Green Motel/RV Park |
| **172** | 6th St (no EZ return nb), Cottage Grove Lake, **2 mi** **E** Cottage Grove RV Park |
| **170** | to OR 99, London Rd (nb only), Cottage Grove Lake, **6 mi** **E** Cottage Grove RV Park |

**OR**

## INTERSTATE 5 CONT'D

**N ↑↓ S**

**SUTHERLIN** **OR** **ROSEBURG**

| | |
|---|---|
| **163** | Curtin, Lorane, **E** **lodging:** Stardust Motel, **other:** Pass Creek RV Park, USPO, antiques, **W** **gas:** 76 |
| **162** | OR 38, OR 99 to Drain, Elkton |
| **161** | Anlauf (from nb) |
| **160** | Salt Springs Rd |
| **159** | Elk Creek, Cox Rd |
| **154** | Yoncalla, Elkhead |
| **150** | OR 99, to OR 38, Yoncalla, Red Hill, **W** **other:** Trees of Oregon RV Park |
| **148** | Rice Hill, **E** **gas:** Chevron/LP/24hr, Pacific Pride/dsl, Pilot/Homestead Rest./Subway/dsl/scales/24hr/@, **food:** Peggy's Rest., Ranch Rest., **lodging:** Best Western, Ranch Motel, **other:** Rice Hill RV Park, towing/dsl repair, **W** **food:** K-R Drive-In |
| **146** | Rice Valley |
| **144mm** | **rest area sb, full** ♿ **facilities,** 🚻, 🛻, **litter barrels, petwalk** |
| **143mm** | **rest area nb, full** ♿ **facilities,** 🚻, 🛻, **litter barrels, petwalk** |
| **142** | Metz Hill |
| **140** | OR 99 (from sb), Oakland, **E** **food:** Tolly's Rest., **other:** Oakland Hist Dist |
| **138** | OR 99 (from nb), Oakland, **E** **food:** Tolly's Rest., **other:** Oakland Hist Dist |
| **136** | OR 138W, Sutherlin, **E** **gas:** Chevron/A&W/dsl/24hr, 76/Quizno's/dsl, **food:** Abby's Pizza, Apple Peddler Rest., Burger King, Hong Kong Chinese, McDonald's, Papa Murphy's, Pedotti's Italian, **lodging:** Relax Inn, Sutherlin Inn, Umpqua Regency Inn, **other:** CarQuest, I-5 RV Ctr, **W** **gas:** Shell, **food:** Dakota St Pizza, DQ, Si Casa Flores, Subway, Taco Bell, **other:** Hi-Way Haven RV Camp, Oak Hills RV Park |
| **135** | Wilbur, Sutherlin, **E** **gas:** CFN/dsl, Shell/dsl/LP, muffler repair |
| **130mm** | weigh sta sb, 🚻 |
| **129** | OR 99, Winchester, **E** **gas, food, camping, dsl repair, RV Ctr (1mi)** |
| **129mm** | N Umpqua River |
| **127** | Stewart Pkwy, Edenbower Rd, N Roseburg, **E** **gas:** Shell, **food:** Sheri's Rest., **lodging:** Motel 6, Super 8, **other:** Home Depot, Lowe's Whse, Mt Nebo RV Park, **W** **gas:** Texaco/Taco Maker/dsl, **food:** Applebee's, Coldstone Creamery, Jack-in-the-Box, McDonald's/playplace, Red Robin, Subway, **lodging:** Sleep Inn, **other:** Ⓗ HOSPITAL, Albertson's/gas, Big O Tire, Harley-Davidson, K-Mart, Office Depot, Sherm's Foods, Walmart/auto/drugs, vet |
| **125** | Garden Valley Blvd, Roseburg, **E** **gas:** Texaco, **food:** Brutke's Rest., Casey's Rest., Elmer's, Gilberto's Mexican, Jack-in-the-Box, KFC, Los Dos Amigo's Mexican, McDonald's, Papa Murphy's, Taco Bell, **lodging:** Comfort Inn, Quality Inn, Windmill Inn/rest., **other:** BigLots, GMC, NAPA, Safeway Foods/gas, Toyota, UHaul, Walgreens, transmissions, **W** **gas:** Chevron/dsl, Shell/LP/repair, **food:** Arby's, Burger King, Carl's Jr, Foxden Cafe, IHOP, Quizno's, Rodeo Steaks, RoundTable Pizza, Sizzler, Skippers, Taco Bell, Wendy's, **lodging:** Best Value Inn, Best Western, **other:** Bi-Mart, Fred Meyer, JC Penney, PetCo, Rite Aid, Ross, Sears/auto, Schuck's Parts, Staples, mall |

**ROSEBURG** **CANYONVILLE**

| | |
|---|---|
| **124** | OR 138, Roseburg, City Ctr, **E** **gas:** 76/dsl/24hr, Texaco/dsl, **food:** Chi's Chinese, Denny's, **lodging:** Douglas Co. Inn, Dunes Motel, Holiday Inn Express, Travelodge, **other:** Honda, Mazda, Rite Aid, **W** **gas:** 76/dsl, Shell/dsl, **food:** A&W, Charley's BBQ, Fox's Pizza, Gay 90's Deli, KFC/LJ Silver, Pete's Drive Inn, Subway, Taco Time, **other:** Ⓗ HOSPITAL, Grocery Outlet, Harvard Ave Drug, Hometown Drug |
| **123** | Roseburg, **E** **other:** to Umpqua Park, camping, museum |
| **121** | McLain Ave |
| **120.5mm** | S Umpqua River |
| **120** | OR 99 N (no EZ nb return), Green District, Roseburg, **E** **lodging:** Shady Oaks Motel, **W** **other:** Do It Hardware, auto repair |
| **119** | OR 99 S, OR 42 W, Winston, **E** **other:** Ingraham Dist., **W** **gas:** Chevron/A&W/dsl/24hr, Love's/Arby's/dsl/scales/LP/24hr, Shell/dsl, **food:** Coyote Jack's Grill, Fox's Pizza, McDonald's, Papa Murphy's, Subway, **other:** Ray's Foods, UPS, Western Star RV Park |
| **113** | Clarks Branch Rd, Round Prairie, **W** **lodging:** Quikstop Motel, **other:** On the River RV Park (2mi), Quikstop Mkt, dsl repair |
| **112.5mm** | S Umpqua River, S Umpqua River |
| **112** | OR 99, OR 42, Dillard, **E** **other:** Rivers West RV park, **rest area nb, full** ♿ **facilities,** 🚻, 🛻, **litter barrels, petwalk** |
| **111mm** | **rest area sb, full** ♿ **facilities,** 🚻, 🛻, **litter barrels, petwalk, weigh sta nb** |
| **110** | Boomer Hill Rd |
| **108** | Myrtle Creek, **E** **food:** DQ, Golf Course Cafe, Myrtle Creek Cafe, **other:** Myrtle Creek RV Park |
| **106** | Weaver Rd |
| **103** | Tri City, Myrtle Creek, **E** **other:** Tri-City RV Park, **W** **gas:** Chevron/A&W/dsl/24hr, Pacific Pride, **food:** McDonald's |
| **102** | Gazley Rd, **E** Surprise Valley RV Park (1mi) |
| **101.5mm** | S Umpqua River, S Umpqua River |
| **101** | Riddle, Stanton Park, **W** camping |
| **99** | Canyonville, **E** **gas:** Penny Pincher, **food:** Burger King, El Paraiso, **lodging:** Riverside Motel, 7 Feathers Hotel/casino, Valley View Motel, **other:** Canyon Mkt, **W** **gas:** 7 Feathers Trkstp/dsl/24/café/@, **food:** Creekside Rest., **lodging:** Best Western, **other:** 7 Feathers RV Resort |
| **98** | OR 99, Canyonville, Days Creek, **E** **gas:** 76/dsl, Shell/dsl/24hr, **food:** Canyon Cafe, El Pariso Mexican, FeedLot Rest., Ken's Cafe, Sarafino's Italian, **lodging:** Leisure Inn, **other:** NAPA, Ray's Foods, **W** **other:** Bill's Tire/repair, museum |
| **95** | Canyon Creek |
| **90mm** | Canyon Creek Pass, Canyon Creek Pass, elev 2020 |
| **88** | Azalea |
| **86** | Barton Rd, Quine's Creek, **E** gas/dsl/LP, **other:** Heaven on Earth Rest./rest., Meadow Wood RV Park (3mi) |
| **83** | Barton Rd (from nb), **E** **other:** Meadow Wood RV Park |
| **82mm** | **rest area both lanes, full** ♿ **facilities,** 🚻, 🛻, **litter barrels, petwalk** |
| **80** | Glendale, **W** **gas:** Country Jct./LP, **food:** Village Inn Rest. |
| **79.5mm** | Stage Road Pass, elev 1830 |
| **78** | Speaker Rd |

## INTERSTATE 5 CONT'D

**76** Wolf Creek, **W** gas: Pacific Pride/dsl, 76/deli/dsl, Texaco/dsl/24hr, food: Wolf Creek Inn Rest., other: Creekside RV park, auto repair

**74mm** Smith Hill Summit, elev 1730

**71** Sunny Valley, **E** lodging: Sunny Valley Motel, other: Covered Bridge Store/gas, **W** other: Sunny Valley RV Park

**69mm** Sexton Mtn Pass, elev 1960

**66** Hugo, **E** other: Joe Creek Waterfalls RV Camping

**63mm** rest area both lanes, full ♿ facilities, ℂ, info, ♨, litter barrels, vending, petwalk

**61** Merlin, **W** gas: Shell/dsl, other: Almeda RV Park, Beaver Creek RV Resort (2mi), OR RV Ctr, Ray's Foods, Rouge Valley RV Ctr, repair

**58** OR 99, to US 199, Grants Pass, **W** gas: CFN/dsl, Chevron, 76/dsl/RV dump, Shell/dsl/repair, Texaco/dsl, TownePump Gas, food: Burger King, Carl's Jr, China Hut, Della's Rest., DQ, Denny's, Hart's Cafe, Jack-in-the-Box, McDonald's, Muchas Gracias Mexican, Papa Murphy's, Pizza Hut, Sizzler, Subway, Taco Bell, Tubby's Rest., Wendy's, lodging: Best Way Inn, Comfort Inn, La Quinta, Motel 6, Royal Vue Motel, Shilo Inn, Sunset Inn, Super 8, SweetBreeze Inn, Travelodge, other: Ⓗ HOSPITAL, AutoZone, Chevrolet/Honda, Chrysler/Dodge/Jeep, Curves, $Tree, Jack's RV Resort, Radio Shack, Ray's Foods, Rouge Valley RV Park, Schwab Tire, st police, towing

**55** US 199, Redwood Hwy, E Grants Pass, **W** gas: Arco/24hr, CFN/dsl, food: Applebee's, Abby's Pizza, Arby's, Elmer's, Iguana Grill, McDonald's, Quizno's, Shari's/24hr, Si Casa Flores Mexican, Subway, Taco Bell, lodging: Best Western, Holiday Inn Express, other: Ⓗ HOSPITAL, Albertson's/gas, Big Lots, Big O Tire, $Tree, Fred Meyer/gas/dsl, Grocery Outlet, JC Penney, Moon Mnt. PetCo, RV Park, Rite Aid, RiverPark RV Park, Schuck's Parts, Siskiyou RV Ctr, Staples, Walmart SuperCtr

**48** Rogue River, **E** gas: Chevron/dsl, food: Abby's Pizza, Aunt Betty's, Baci's Pizza, Homestead Rest., Tarasco Mexican, other: Ace Hardware, Curves, NAPA, Rogue River Drug, Rogue River RA, **W** food: Karen's Kitchen, Mkt Basket Deli, lodging: Best Western, other: Chinook Winds RV Park, Bridgeview RV Park, Whispering Pines RV Park, visitors ctr/info

**45b** **W** other: Valley of the Rogue SP/rest area both lanes, full (handicapped) facilities, ℂ, ♨, litter barrels, petwalk, camping

**45mm** Rogue River

**45a** OR 99, Savage Rapids Dam, **E** other: Cypress Grove RV Park

**43** OR 99, OR 234, to Crater Lake, Gold Hill, **E** food: Rhino's Grill, lodging: B&B, Lazy Acres Motel/RV Park

**40** OR 99, OR 234, Gold Hill, **E** food: Gold Hill Auto Ctr/gas, Patti's Kitchen, other: to Shady Cove Trail, KOA, Lazy Acres Motel/RV Park, Running Salmon RV Park, **W** Dardanell's RV Ctr/gas, Dardanell's Trailer Park

**35** OR 99, Blackwell Rd, Central Point, 2-4 mi **W** gas, food, lodging, st police, Jacksonville Nat Hist Landmark

**33** Central Point, **E** gas: Chevron, Pilot/Subway/Taco Bell/dsl/scales/24hr, food: Burger King, KFC, Quizno's, Shari's, Sonic, lodging: Candlewood Suites (2mi), Courtyard (2mi), Fairfield Inn, Holiday Inn Express, Super 8, other: RV Ctr, funpark, **W** gas: 76/Circle K/dsl, Shell/dsl/24hr, food: Abby's Pizza, Mazatlan Grill, McDonald's, other: Albertson's, USPO

**30** OR 62, to Crater Lake, Medford, **E** gas: Chevron, Witham Trkstp/76/rest./dsl/24hr/@, food: Burger King, Carl's Jr., Del Taco, Elmer's, IHOP, Marie Callender's, McDonald's, Olive Garden, Outback Steaks, Panda Express, Papa John's, Pizza Hut, Quizno's, Red Robin, Schlotsky's, Si Casa Mexican, Sizzler, Sonic, Starbucks, Subway, Taco Bell, Taco Delite, Thai Bistro, Wendy's, lodging: Comfort Inn, Hampton Inn, Motel 6, Quality Inn, Ramada, Rogue Regency Hotel, Shilo Inn, other: Ace Hardware, Barnes&Noble, BigLots, BiMart Foods, Circuit City, Costco/gas, $Tree, Ford/Lincoln/Mercury, Fred Meyer, Food4Less, Jo-Ann, Lowe's Whse, Mercedes, Michael's, Old Navy, Radio Shack, Ross, Safeway, Sears/auto, Schwab Tire, Sportsman's Whse, Triple A RV, USPO, Walmart, st police, **W** gas: Chevron/dsl, 76/dsl, Shell/dsl, food: KFC, King Wah Chinese, Red Lobster, Wendy's, other: Ⓗ HOSPITAL, CarQuest, JC Penney, Kohl's, Macy's, Target, Toyota/Scion, mall

**27** Barnett Rd, Medford, **E** food: Blackbear Diner, DQ, lodging: Best Western, Day's Inn/rest., Homewood Suites, Motel 6, Travelodge, other: Ⓗ HOSPITAL, AAA, **W** gas: Chevron/24hr, 76/Circle K, Shell/dsl/24hr, food: Abby's Pizza, Arby's, Burger King, Carl's Jr, HomeTown Buffet, Jack-in-the-Box, KFC, Kim's Chinese, McDonald's, McGrath's FishHouse, Pizza Hut, Quizno's, Rooster's Rest., Senor Sam's Mexican, Shari's, Starbucks, Subway, Taco Bell, Wendy's, lodging: Capri Motel, Comfort Inn, Holiday Inn Express, Residence Inn, Royal Crest Motel, Springhill Suites, TownePlace Suites, other: Ford/Mercury/Lincoln, Fred Meyer, Grocery Outlet, Harry&David's, Office Depot, Radio Shack, Saturn, Schwab Tires, Shucks Parts, Staples, Toyota, Walgreens, WinCo Foods

**24** Phoenix, **E** gas: Petro/Iron Skillet/dsl/rest./scales/RV dump/24hr/@, lodging: PearTree Motel/rest./RV park, Super 8, other: Home Depot, Peterbilt/GMC, **W** gas:

## INTERSTATE 5 CONT'D

| N ↕ S | | |
|---|---|---|

**24** Continued
76/Circle K/dsl, **food:** Angelo's Pizza, Annie's Cafe, Jack-in-the-Box, McDonald's, Sicasa Flores Mexican, **lodging:** Bavarian Inn, **other:** Curves, Ray's Foods, Holiday RV Park, vet

**22mm** **rest area sb, full** ♿ **facilities,** 🚻, ⛽, **litter barrels, vending, petwalk**

**21** Talent, **W gas:** Chevron/dsl, **food:** Avalon Grill, Figaro's Italian, **lodging:** GoodNight Inn, **other:** American RV Resort, Walmart/auto, repair

**19** Valley View Rd, Ashland, **W gas:** Pacific Pride/dsl, 76/dsl, Shell/dsl/LP, **food:** Burger King, El Tapatio Mexican, **lodging:** Econolodge, La Quinta, **other:** Chevrolet, Ford

**18mm** weigh sta both lanes

**14** OR 66, to Klamath Falls, Ashland, **E gas:** Chevron, 76/dsl/LP, Shell/dsl, **food:** Miguel's, OakTree Rest., **lodging:** Best Western, Holiday Inn Express, Relax Inn, Windmill Inn, **other:** Emigrant Lake Camping (3mi), Glenyan RV Park (3mi), KOA (3mi), Nat Hist Museum, **W gas:** Arco/24hr, Texaco, **food:** Apple Bakery, Arrieo Mexican, Subway, Taco Bell, Wendy's, Wild Goose Cafe, Yuan yuan Chinese, **lodging:** Knight's Inn/rest., Super 8, **other:** Albertson's, Bi-Mart, Radio Shack, Rite Aid, Schwab Tire

**11.5mm** chainup area

**11** OR 99, Siskiyou Blvd (nb only, no return), **services 2-4 mi W**

**6** to Mt Ashland, **E lodging:** Callahan's Siskiyou Lodge/rest., **other:** 🚻, ski area

**4mm** Siskiyou Summit, elev 4310, brake check both lanes

**1** to Siskiyou Summit (from nb, no return)

**0mm** Oregon/California state line

**ASHLAND**

## INTERSTATE 84

| Exit # | Services |
|---|---|
| **378mm** | Oregon/Idaho state line, Snake River |
| **377.5mm** | **Welcome Ctr wb, full** ♿ **facilities, info,** 🚻, ⛽, **litter barrels, vending, petwalk** |

**376b a** US 30, to US 20/26, Ontario, Payette, **N gas:** Chevron/dsl, **food:** A&W/KFC, Burger King, Coldstone Creamery, China Buffet, Country Kitchen, DQ, Denny's, Domino's, McDonald's, Primo's Pizza, Quizno's, Taco Del Mar, Taco Time, Wingers, **lodging:** Best Western, Colonial Inn, Holiday Inn, Motel 6, Sleep Inn, Super 8, **other:** Chrysler/Dodge/Jeep, Home Depot, K-Mart, Radio Shack, Staples, Toyota, Walmart SuperCtr, st police, **S gas:** Pilot/Arby's/dsl/scales/24hr, Shell/dsl, **food:** DJ's, Domino's, Far East Chinese, Ogawa's Japanese, Rusty's Steaks, Sizzler, Subway, Taco Bell, Wendy's, **lodging:** Economy Inn, OR Trail Motel, Rodeway Inn, Stockman's Motel, **other:** Ⓗ HOSPITAL, Commercial Tire, NAPA, Schwab Tire, U-Haul, RV repair, 4 Wheeler Museum

**374** US 30, OR 201, to Ontario, **N** to Ontario SP, **S gas:** Shell/dsl, **lodging:** Budget Inn, **other:** Ⓗ HOSPITAL

**E ↕ W** **ONTARIO**

---

| **373.5mm** | Malheur River |
|---|---|
| **371** | Stanton Blvd, **2 mi S** to correctional institution |
| **362** | Moores Hollow Rd |
| **356** | OR 201, to Weiser, ID, **3 mi N** Catfish Junction RV Park, Oasis RV Park |
| **354.5mm** | weigh sta eb |

**353** US 30, to Huntington, **N** weigh sta wb, **gas:** Joy Travel Plaza/dsl/rest./motel/@, **other:** to Farewell Bend SP, truck repair, RV camping, info

| **351mm** | Pacific/Mountain time zone |
|---|---|

**345** US 30, Lime, Huntington, **1 mi N** gas, food, lodging, to Snake River Area, Van Ornum BFD

| **342** | Lime (from eb) |
|---|---|
| **340** | Rye Valley |
| **338** | Lookout Mountain, **N other:** OR Trail RV Park |
| **337mm** | Burnt River |

**335** to Weatherby, **N rest area both lanes, full** ♿ **facilities, Oregon Trail Info,** ⛽, **litter barrels, vending, petwalk**

| **330** | Plano Rd, to Cement Plant Rd, **S** cement plant |
|---|---|
| **329mm** | pulloff eb |
| **327** | Durkee, **N gas:** Co-op/dsl/LP/café |
| **325mm** | Pritchard Creek |
| **321mm** | Alder Creek |
| **317** | to Pleasant Valley (from wb) |
| **315** | to Pleasant Valley (from wb) |
| **313** | to Pleasant Valley (from eb) |

**306** US 30, Baker, **2-3 mi S gas:** Chevron/dsl, **food:** DQ, **lodging:** Baker City Motel, Bridge Street Hotel, Budget Inn, OR Tr Motel/rest., **other:** Ⓗ HOSPITAL, to st police, same as 304

**304** OR 7, Baker, **N gas:** Chevron/dsl, **lodging:** Super 8, Welcome Inn, **S gas:** Shell/Blimpie/dsl/24hr, Sinclair/dsl/rest./scales/24hr, **food:** Arceo's Mexican, DQ, Fong's Chinese, Golden Crown, McDonald's, Papa Murphy's, Pizza Hut, Subway, Sumpter Jct Rest., Taco Time, **lodging:** Best Western, Budget Inn, Eldorado Inn, Rodeway Inn, Western Motel, **other:** Ⓗ HOSPITAL, Albertson's/gas, Bi-Mart Foods, CarQuest, $Tree, Ford/Lincoln/Mercury, Mtn View RV Park (3mi), Rite Aid, Safeway Foods, museum, transmissions, to hist dist

**302** OR 86 E to Richland, **S other:** Ⓗ HOSPITAL, OR Tr RV Park/LP

| **298** | OR 203, to Medical Springs |
|---|---|
| **297mm** | Baldock Slough |

**295mm** **rest area both lanes, full** ♿ **facilities, info,** 🚻, ⛽, **litter barrels, vending, petwalk**

| **289mm** | Powder River |
|---|---|
| **287.5mm** | *45th parallel halfway between the equator and north pole* |
| **286mm** | N Powder River |

**285** US 30, OR 237, North Powder, **N gas:** Cenex/dsl/café, **lodging:** Powder River Motel, **S other:** to Anthony Lakes, ski area

| **284mm** | Wolf Creek |
|---|---|
| **283** | Wolf Creek Lane |

**BAKER**

## INTERSTATE 84 CONT'D

| E | | |
|---|---|---|
| **278** | Clover Creek | |
| **273** | Frontage Rd | |
| **270** | Ladd Creek Rd (from eb, no return) | |

**W**

**L A G R A N D E**

**269mm** rest area both lanes, full ♿ facilities, info, 🕐, 🏞, litter barrels, vending, petwalk

**268** Foothill Rd

**265** OR 203, LaGrande, **N** other: Eagles Hot Lake RV Park, ✈, **S** gas: Chevron (2mi), ⊕ *FLYING J*/Shell/dsl/rest./scales/24hr, food: SmokeHouse Rest. (2mi)

**261** OR 82, LaGrande, **N** gas: Chevron/dsl, Shell/dsl, **food:** Denny's, Pizza Hut, Quizno's, Starbucks, Taco Bell, **lodging:** LaGrande Inn, other: Chrysler/Dodge/Jeep, Ford/Lincoln/Mercury, Grocery Outlet, Thunder RV Ctr, Walmart Super Ctr, st police, **S** gas: 76/Subway/dsl, Texaco/dsl, food: Bear Mtn. Pizza, China Buffet, Cinco de Mayo Mexican, DQ, KFC, La Fiesta Mexican, McDonald's, Moi's Dynasty, Papa Murphy's, Smokehouse Rest., Taco Time, Wendy's, **lodging:** All American Inn, Best Western, Moon Motel, Royal Motel, Sandman Inn, Super 8, Travelodge, other: ♓ HOSPITAL, Albertson's, $Tree, Kottman Transmissions, Rite Aid, Safeway/gas, Schuck's Parts, Schwab Tire, vet, E OR U, Wallowa Lake

**260mm** Grande Ronde River

**259** US 30 E (from eb), to La Grande, **1-2 mi S** gas: Chevron, Shell, **food:** Burger King, **lodging:** All-American Motel, Greenwell Motel/rest., Royal Motel, **other:** Safeway/gas, same as 261

**257** Perry (from wb)

**256.5mm** weigh sta eb

**256** Perry (from eb)

**255mm** Grande Ronde River

**254mm** scenic wayside

**252** OR 244, to Starkey, Lehman Springs, **S** other: Hilgard SP, camping, chainup area

**251mm** Wallowa-Whitman NF, eastern boundary

**248** Spring Creek Rd, to Kamela, **3 mi N** Oregon Trail Visitors Park

**246mm** Wallowa-Whitman NF, western boundary

**243** Summit Rd, Mt Emily Rd, to Kamela, Oregon Trail info, **2 mi N** other: Emily Summit SP

**241mm** Summit of the Blue Mtns, elev 4193

**238** Meacham, **1 mi N** food, other: Oregon Trail info

**234** Meacham, **S** other: Emigrant Sprs SP, RV camping

**231.5mm** Umatilla Indian Reservation, eastern boundary

**228mm** **Deadman Pass, Oregon Trail info, rest area both lanes, full ♿ facilities, 🕐 (wb), 🏞, litter barrel, petwalk, vending, RV Dump (wb)**

**227mm** weigh sta wb, brake check area

**224** Poverty Flats Rd, Old Emigrant Hill Rd, to Emigrant Springs SP

**223mm** wb viewpoint, no restrooms

**221.5mm** eb viewpoint, no restrooms

**220mm** wb runaway truck ramp

**P E N D L E T O N**

**216** Mission, McKay Creek, **N** gas: Arrowhead Trkstp/Pacific Pride/dsl/24hr, food: Cody's Rest., other: Wildhorse Casino/RV Park

**213** US 30 (from wb), Pendleton, **3-5 mi N** gas: Chevron/dsl, Shell, lodging: Travelers Inn, other: ♓ HOSPITAL, Pendleton NHD

**212mm** Umatilla Indian Reservation western boundary

**210** OR 11, Pendleton, **N** other: ♓ HOSPITAL, museum, **S** gas: Chevron/dsl, Shell/dsl/LP, food: Shari's/24hr, lodging: Best Western, Holiday Inn Express, Motel 6, Red Lion Inn/rest., Super 8, other: Mtn View RV Park, st police

**209** US 395, Pendleton, **N** food: A&W/Taco Bell, Jack-in-the-Box, KFC, Pizza, lodging: B&B, Oxford Suites, Travelodge, Travelers Inn, other: Curves, Rite Aid, Safeway/dsl, Walmart SuperCtr/Subway, **S** gas: 76/dsl, food: Abby's Pizza, Arby's, Burger King, Denny's, McDonald's, Rooster's Rest, Starbucks, Subway, Wendy's, lodging: Econolodge, other: Chevrolet/Pontiac/Buick, Honda, Schwab Tire, Thompson RV Ctr

**208mm** Umatilla River

**207** US 30, W Pendleton, **N** gas: Shell/dsl/LP, other: Lookout RV Park

**202** Barnhart Rd, to Stage Gulch, **N** Woodpecker Truck Repair, **S** lodging: Rodeo Inn, other: Oregon Trail info

**199** Stage Coach Rd, Yoakum Rd

**198** Lorenzen Rd, McClintock Rd, **N** other: trailer/reefer repair

**193** Echo Rd, to Echo, Oregon Trail Site

**188** US 395 N, Hermiston, **N** gas: Chevron/dsl (1mi), Pilot/Subway/McDonald's/dsl/24hr/RV park/@, **5 mi N** food: Denny's/24hr, Jack-in-the-Box, McDonald's, Shari's/24hr, lodging: Best Western, Economy Inn, Oak Tree Inn, Oxford Suites, other: ♓ HOSPITAL, **S** other: Henrietta RV Park (1mi), Echo HS

**187mm** rest area both lanes, full ♿ facilities, 🕐, info, 🏞, litter barrels, petwalk

**182** OR 207, to Hermiston, **N** other: Space Age/A&W/dsl/24hr, lodging: Comfort Inn

**180** Westland Rd, to Hermiston, McNary Dam, **N** trailer repair, **S** gas: Shell/Western Express/dsl/24hr

**179** I-82 W, to Umatilla, Kennewick, WA

**177** Umatilla Army Depot

## INTERSTATE 84 CONT'D

| | |
|---|---|
| **171** | Paterson Ferry Rd, to Paterson |
| **168** | US 730, to Irrigon, **8 mi N other:** Green Acres RV Park, Oregon Trail info |
| **165** | Port of Morrow, **S gas:** Pacific Pride/dsl |
| **164** | Boardman, **N gas:** Chevron/dsl, Shell/dsl, **food:** C&D Drive-In, Leonard's Cafe, **lodging:** Dodge City Motel, Riverview Motel, **other:** USPO, Boardman RV/Marina Park, **S gas:** Shell/dsl, **lodging:** Econolodge, **lodging:** NAPA Repair/parts, Family Foods, Oregon Trail Library, tires |
| **161mm** | **rest area both lanes, full ♿ facilities, 🚻, 🅿, litter barrels, vending, petwalk** |
| **159** | Tower Rd |
| **151** | Threemile Canyon |
| **147** | OR 74, to Ione, Blue Mtn Scenic Byway, Heppner, Oregon Trail Site |
| **137** | OR 19, Arlington, **S gas:** Shell/dsl, **food:** Happy Canyon Cafe, Pheasant Grill, Village Inn, **other:** Ace Hardware, Thrifty Foods, Columbia River RV Park (1mi), city park |
| **136.5mm** | view point wb, 🅿, litter barrels |
| **131** | Woelpern Rd (from eb, no return) |
| **129** | Blalock Canyon, Lewis&Clark Trail |
| **123** | Philippi Canyon, Lewis&Clark Trail |
| **114.5mm** | John Day River |
| **114** | **S** LePage Park |
| **112** | **parking area, both lanes, litter barrels, N John Day Dam** |
| **109** | Rufus, **N** John Day Visitor Ctr, **S gas:** Pacific Pride/dsl, Shell/dsl, **food:** Bob's T-Bone, Frosty's Café, Hi-Mkt Deli, Larry's Rest., **lodging:** Hillview Hotel, Tyee Motel, **other:** Ed's RV camping |
| **109** | Rufus, **N** John Day Visitor Ctr, **S gas:** Shell/dsl, **food:** Bob's T-Bone, **lodging:** Rufus Inn, Tyee Motel, **other:** RV camping |
| **104** | US 97, Biggs, **N other:** Des Chutes Park Bridge, **S gas:** Exxon, 76/Circle K/dsl/24hr, Pilot/McDonald's/dsl/scales/24hr, Linda's/Shell/Subway/rest./dsl, **lodging:** Biggs Motel/café, Dinty's Motel, Travelodge, **other:** Maryhill Museum, dsl repair |
| **100mm** | Deschutes River, Columbia River Gorge Scenic Area |
| **97** | OR 206, Celilo, **N other:** Celilo SP, restrooms, **S other:** Deschutes SP, Indian Village |
| **92** | pullout, eb |
| **88** | **N** to The Dalles Dam |
| **87** | US 30, US 197, to Dufur, **N gas:** Chevron, 76/dsl/24hr, **food:** McDonald's, Portage Grill, **lodging:** Comfort Inn, Shilo Inn/rest., **other:** Columbia Hills RV Park, Lone Pine RV Park, st police, **S food:** Big Jim's Drive-In, **lodging:** Riverview Inn, **other:** Schwab Tire |
| **85** | The Dalles, **N Riverfront Park, restrooms,** 🅲 🅿, **litter barrels, playground, marina, S gas:** Chevron, 76/dsl, **food:** BurgervilleUSA, RoadStop Rest., **lodging:** Best Western, Oregon Motel, **other:** Ⓗ HOSPITAL, Fast Auto Repair, Lincoln/Mercury/Toyota, NAPA, camping, USPO, to Nat Hist Dist |

| | |
|---|---|
| **83** | (84 from wb) W The Dalles, **N food:** Casa El Mirador, Orient Café, Windseeker Rest., **other:** NAPA, Tire Factory, **S gas:** Chevron, Exxon, Shell/dsl, **food:** Arby's, Burger King, Denny's, Ixtapa Mexican, McDonald's, Papa Murphy's, Skipper's, Subway, Taco Bell, Taco Time, **lodging:** Best Western, Cousin's Inn/rest., Motel 6, Shilo Inn, Tillicum Inn, Super 8, **other:** Ⓗ HOSPITAL, Albertson's, Buick/Pontiac/GMC, Chevrolet, Chrysler/Dodge, $Tree, Ford, Fred Meyer, Grocery Outlet, Jo-Ann Fabrics, K-Mart, PetCo, Radio Shack, Rite Aid, Safeway, Schuck's Parts, Staples, Subaru, Walgreens |
| **82** | Chenowith Area, **S gas:** Astro/dsl/24hr, **food:** Spooky's Café, **other:** Bi-Mart Foods, Columbia Discovery Ctr, Home Depot, museum, same as 83 |
| **76** | Rowena, **N other:** Mayer SP, Lewis & Clark info, windsurfing |
| **73mm** | **Memaloose SP, rest area both lanes, full ♿ facilities, 🅿, litter barrels, 🅲, petwalk, RV dump, camping** |
| **69** | US 30, Mosier, **S food:** Goodriver Rest. **other:** USPO |
| **66mm** | **N** Koberg Beach SP, **rest area wb, full facilities, 🅿, litter barrels** |
| **64** | US 30, OR 35, to White Salmon, Hood River, **N gas:** Chevron, Shell/24hr, **food:** McDonald's, Riverside Grill, Starbucks, **lodging:** Best Western, **other:** marina, museum, st police |
| **63** | Hood River, City Ctr, **N gas:** 76/dsl, **other:** Visitor Ctr, **S food:** Annz Cafe, Gorge Grill, Pietro's Pizza, Sage's Cafe, Taco Del Mar, **lodging:** Hood River Hotel/rest., **other:** Ⓗ HOSPITAL, USPO, same as 64 |
| **62** | US 30, Westcliff Dr, W Hood River, **N food:** Charburger, **lodging:** Columbia Gorge Hotel, Vagabond Lodge, **S gas:** Chevron/dsl/LP, 76/dsl, **food:** Domino's, DQ, Egg Harbor Cafe, HoHo Rest., McDonald's, Quizno's, Red Carpet Cafe, Starbucks, Subway, Taco Bell, **lodging:** Comfort Suites, Prater's Motel, Riverview Lodge, Stonehedge Inn, **other:** Ⓗ HOSPITAL, Cascade Mkt, Chevrolet/Pontiac/Buick/GMC, Oil Can Henry's, Rite Aid, Safeway, Schwab Tire, Walmart |
| **61mm** | pulloff wb |
| **60** | service rd wb (no return) |
| **58** | Mitchell Point Overlook (from eb) |
| **56** | **N other:** Viento SP, RV camping, 🅲 |
| **55** | Starvation Peak Tr Head (from eb), restrooms |
| **54mm** | weigh sta wb |
| **51** | Wyeth, **S** camping |
| **49mm** | pulloff eb |
| **47** | Forest Lane, Hermon Creek (from wb), camping |
| **45mm** | weigh sta eb |
| **44** | US 30, to Cascade Locks, **1-4 mi N gas:** CFN, Chevron/LP, Shell/dsl, **food:** Charburger, Salmon Row Cafe, **lodging:** Best Western, Bridge of the Gods Motel, Cascade Motel, Econolodge, **other:** to Bridge of the Gods, Stern Wheeler RV Park |
| **41** | Eagle Creek RA (from eb), to fish hatchery |
| **40** | **N other:** Bonneville Dam NHS, info, to fish hatchery |

*Side tabs: E ↕ W, RUFUS, OR, THE DALLES, HOOD RIVER*

## INTERSTATE 84 CONT'D

**E ↕ W**

**37** Warrendale (from wb)

**35** Historic Hwy, Multnomah Falls, **S other:** Ainsworth SP, scenic loop highway, waterfall area, Fishery RV Park 31 Multnomah Falls (exits left from both lanes), **S lodging:** Multnomah Falls Lodge/Rest. (hist site), camping

**31** Multnomah Falls (exits left from both lanes), **S** Multnomah Falls Lodge/Rest. (hist site), camping

**30** **S** Benson SRA (from eb)

**29** Dalton Point (from wb)

**28** to Bridal Veil (7 mi return from eb)

**25** **N** Rooster Rock SP

**23mm** viewpoint wb, hist marker

**22** Corbett, **2 mi S gas:** Corbett Mkt, **lodging:** Vista House, **other:** Crown Point RV Camping

**19mm** Columbia River Gorge scenic area

**18** Lewis&Clark SP, to Oxbow SP, lodging, food, RV camping

**17.5mm** Sandy River

**17** Marine Dr, Troutdale, **N food:** Wendy's, **lodging:** Holiday Inn Express, **S gas:** Chevron/24hr, *FLYING J*/Conoco/Roadside Diner/dsl/LP/scales/24hr/@, TA/Arco/Buckhorn Rest./Popeye's/Subway/dsl/scales/24hr/@, Shell/dsl, **food:** Arby's, McDonald's, Shari's/24hr, Taco Bell, Troutdale Diner, **lodging:** Best Value Inn, Comfort Inn, Motel 6, **other:** Premium Outlets/famous brands, Sandy Riverfront RV Resort

**16** 238th Dr, Fairview, **N gas:** Arco/dsl/24hr, **food:** Jack-in-the-Box, Quizno's, Taco Del Mar, Yazzie's Grill, **lodging:** Travelodge, **other:** Olinger RV Ctr, Walmart SuperCtr, **S gas:** Chevron, **lodging:** Best Western, **other:** H HOSPITAL

**14** 207th Ave, Fairview, **N gas:** Shell/dsl, **food:** GinSun Chinese, **other:** American Dream RV Ctr, Portland RV Park, Rolling Hills RV Park, auto repair

**13** 181st Ave, Gresham, **N gas:** CFN, Chevron, **lodging:** Hampton Inn, **S gas:** 76/Circle K, **food:** Burger King, Jung's Chinese, McDonald's, Shari's/24hr, Wendy's, Xavier's, **lodging:** Comfort Suites, Extended Stay America, Hawthorn Suites, Quality Inn, Sheraton, Sleep Inn, Super 8, **other:** Candy Basket Chocolates, Safeway, 7-11, auto repair, vet

**10** 122nd Ave (from eb)

**9** I-205, S to Salem, N to Seattle, to ✈, (to 102nd Ave from eb)

**8** I-205 N (from eb), **N** to ✈

**7** Halsey St (from eb), Gateway Dist

**6** I-205 S (from eb)

**5** OR 213, to 82nd Ave (eb only), **N lodging:** Capri Motel, Day's Inn, Motel Cabana, **1-3 mi N gas:** 76, Shell, 7-11, **food:** Arby's, Burgerville, Domino's, Pizza Hut, Wendy's, **lodging:** Quality Inn, Shilo Inn, **S food:** Elmer's Rest., Taco Bell, **lodging:** Comfort Inn, Microtel, **other:** NAPA

**46** 8th Ave (from eb), to Halsey Ave

**PORTLAND** (side tab)

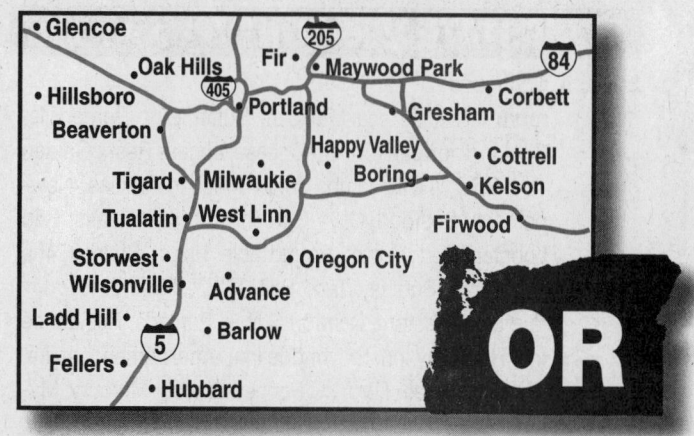

**35** 8th Ave (from eb), **S gas:** KC, Shell, **other:** H HOSPITAL, Fred Meyer

**24** 3rd Ave, 39th Ave, Halsey St, **N gas:** Chevron, 76, Shell, **food:** Baja Fresh, Burger King, McDonald's, Subway, Winchell's, **lodging:** Banfield Motel, Rodeway Inn, **other:** Rite Aid, **S other:** H HOSPITAL, Buick/Pontiac, Jeep, same as 1

**13** 3rd Ave, Lloyd Blvd (eb only), **N gas:** 76, Pacific Pride/dsl, Shell/dsl, **food:** Burger King, Domino's, **lodging:** Banfield Motel, Best Western, Holiday Inn, Red Lion Inn, Residence Inn, **other:** JC Penney, Rite Aid, **S food:** Pizza Hut, **other:** Buick

**1** to downtown (wb only)

**0mm** I-84 begins/ends on I-5, exit 301.

## INTERSTATE 205 - PORTLAND

| Exit # | Services |
|---|---|
| **37mm** | I-205 begins/ends on I-5. Exits 36-27 are in Washington. |

**36** NE 134th St (from nb), **E gas:** Arco, 7-11, 76, TrailMart/dsl, **food:** Applebee's, Billygan's Roadhouse, Booster Juice, Burger King, Burgerville, Jack-in-the-Box, McDonald's, Muchas Gracias, Panda Express, Round Table Pizza, Starbucks, Subway, Taco Bell, Taco Del Mar, **lodging:** Comfort Inn, Holiday Inn Express, Olympia Motel, Red Lion, Salmon Creek Inn, Shilo Inn, **other:** H HOSPITAL, Albertson's/gas, Long's Drugs, Safeway/gas, Zupan's Mkt, 99 RV Park, to Portland ✈, **W gas:** Shell, **food:** Baskin-Robbins, Coldstone, El Tapatio, Papa Murphy's, PizzaSchmitzza, Quizno's, Starbucks, The Great Impasta, **lodging:** La Quinta, **other:** Fred Meyer

**32** NE 83rd St, Andreson Rd, Battle Ground, **W gas:** Shell/dsl/24hr, **food:** Burger King, Emporor Chinese, Krispy Kreme, Panda Express, Starbucks, Subway, Wendy's, Wienerschnitzel, **other:** Costco/gas, Home Depot

**30c b a** WA 500, Orchards, Vancouver, **E gas:** 76, Shell/24hr, **food:** ABC Buffet, Applebee's, Burger King, Burgerville, DQ, Imperial Palace, McDonald's, Papa Murphy's, Starbucks, Subway, Wendy's, **other:** Jo-Ann Crafts, Office Depot, PetCo, Sportsman's Whse, Toyota, Tuesday Morning, Walgreens, **W gas:** Chevron/24hr, Shell/dsl,

**N ↕ S PORTLAND AREA** (side tab)

## INTERSTATE 205 CONT'D - PORTLAND

**N ↕ S**

**PORTLAND AREA**

**OR**

**30c b a** Continued

**food:** A&W, Azteca Mexican, Buffet City, Burgerville, Chevy's Mexican, ChuckeCheese, Elmer's Rest., Golden Tent BBQ, IHOP, Jamba Juice, Muchas Gracias, Newport Bay Seafood, Olive Garden, Outback Steaks, Red Lobster, Red Robin, RoundTable Pizza, Shari's/24hr, Starbucks, Subway, Taco Bell, TCBY, TGIFriday, **lodging:** Best Western, Comfort Suites, Ramada, Residence Inn, Rodeway Inn, Staybridge Inn, **other:** Americas Tire, Big Lots, $Tree, Ford, JC Penney, Lincoln/Mercury, Macy's, Old Navy, Ross, Sears/auto, Saturn, Target, VW, mall, RV park

**28** Mill Plain Rd, **E gas:** Chevron/24hr, 76/Circle K, Shell/dsl, **food:** Baskin-Robbins, Burger King, Burgerville, DQ, Elmer's Rest., Irishtown Grill, Kings Buffet, McDonald's, Muchas Gracias Mexican, Pizza Hut, Quizno's, Shari's, Starbucks, Taco Bell, **lodging:** Best Western, Extended Stay America, Motel 6, **other:** $Tree, Fred Meyer, PetCo, Schuck's Parts, Schwab Tire, 7-11, **W gas:** Arco/24hr, 76, 7-11, **food:** Arby's, Jack-in-the-Box, Subway, Taco Del Mar, **other:** H HOSPITAL, Chevrolet, Walmart SuperCtr, Walgreens, auto/tire repair, vet, transmissions

**27** WA 14, Vancouver, Camas, Columbia River Gorge

**25mm** Oregon/Washington state line. Columbia River. **Exits 27-36 are in Washington.**

**24** 122nd Ave, **E food:** Burger King, China Wok, Coffee-House, Jack-in-the-Box, McDonald's, Shari's, Subway, **lodging:** Comfort Suites, Courtyard, Fairfield Inn, Hilton Garden, Holiday Inn Express, La Quinta, Shilo Inn/rest., Silver Cloud Inn, SpringHill Suites, Staybridge Suites, Super 8, **other:** Best Buy, Home Depot, **W lodging:** Hampton Inn, Sheraton/rest.

**23b a** US 30 byp, Columbia Blvd, **E gas:** Leather's Fuel/dsl, Shell/dsl, **food:** Bill's Steaks, Elmer's Rest., **lodging:** Best Western, Econolodge, Carolina Motel, Red Lion Hotel, Roadway Inn, **other:** H HOSPITAL, **W gas:** Shell, **lodging:** Holiday Inn, Radisson, Ramada Inn, **other:** camping

**22** I-84 E, US 30 E, to The Dalles

**21b** I-84 W, US 30 W, to Portland

**21a** Glisan St, **E gas:** 76, **food:** Szechuan Chinese, **E on NE 102nd St gas:** Arco, Applebee's, Carl's Jr, Izzy's Pizza, Quizno's, Circuit City, McDonald's, Rubio's, **other:** Fred Meyer, Office Depot, Ross, WinCo Foods, mall

**20** Stark St, Washington St, **E food:** Acapulco Mexican, Arby's, Baja Fresh, Burger King, Denny's, Elmer's Rest., Hooters, Izzy's Pizza, Newport Bay Café, Old Chicago Pizza, Old Country Kitchen, Olive Garden, Panda Express, Village Inn, **lodging:** Chesnut Tree Inn, Holiday Inn Express, **other:** Cottman Transmissions, Home Depot, Target, mall, **W food:** ChuckeCheese, McDonald's, Stark St Pizza, Taco Bell, **lodging:** Rodeway Inn, **other:** 7-11

**PORTLAND AREA**

**19** US 26, Division St, **E gas:** Space Age/dsl, **other:** H HOSPITAL, **W gas:** Chevron/24hr, 76, Shell/dsl, **food:** Carl's Jr, Izzy's Pizza, McDonald's, Sizzler, Subway, Wendy's, **other:** Best Value Inn

**17** Foster Rd, **1 mi W gas:** Chevron, 76, Shell, **food:** Arby's, Burger King, IHOP, McDonald's, Wendy's, **lodging:** Econolodge, Home Depot, **other:** U-Haul

**16** Johnson Creek Blvd, **W gas:** 76, **food:** Applebee's, Burger King, Carl's Jr, Denny's, Fuddrucker's, Hometown Buffet, McDonald's, Old Chicago Pizza, Outback Steaks, Papa Joe's, Ron's Café, Starbucks, Subway, Taco Bell, **other:** Best Buy, Fred Meyer/gas, Home Depot, RV Ctrs, Schuck's Parts, Walgreens

**14** Sunnyside Rd, **E food:** A&W/KFC, Baja FreshMex, Burger King, Domino's, Izzy's Pizza, KFC, Quizno's, Starbucks, Subway, Thai House, Wendy's, **lodging:** Best Western, Day's Inn, **other:** H HOSPITAL, Office Depot, **W gas:** 76/LP/24hr, Texaco/dsl/24hr, **food:** Chevy's Mexican, Chili's, Claim Jumper, Macaroni Grill, McDonald's, Old Spaghetti Factory, Olive Garden, Red Robin, Stanford's Rest., Sweet Tomatoes, Taco Time, **lodging:** Courtyard, Monarch Hotel/rest., **other:** America Tire, Barnes&Noble, JC Penney, Macy's, Nordstroms, Old Navy, PetCo, Sears/auto, Target, World Mkt, mall

**13** OR 224, to Milwaukie, **W** K-Mart, Lowe's Whse

**12** OR 213, to Milwaukie, **E gas:** Chevron/24hr, Pacific Pride, Shell, **food:** Denny's, Elmer's, KFC, McDonald's, Taco Bell/24hr, Wendy's, **lodging:** Clackamas Inn, Hampton Inn, **other:** Fred Meyer, 7-11, **W lodging:** Comfort Suites

**11** 82nd Dr, Gladstone, **W gas:** Arco/24hr, Chevron, **food:** McDonald's, **lodging:** Oxford Suites, **other:** Harley-Davidson, Safeway

**10** OR 213, Park Place, **E gas:** 76/Pacific Pride/dsl, **other:** H HOSPITAL, Home Depot, to Oregon Trail Ctr

**99** OR 99E, Oregon City, **E gas:** 76, **food:** KFC, **other:** H HOSPITAL, Subaru, **W food:** La Hacienda Mexican, McDonald's, Shari's, Starbucks, Subway, Thai Rest., **lodging:** Rivershore Hotel, **other:** Coastal Ranch Store, $Tree, Firestone/auto, Michael's, Rite Aid

**8.5mm** Willamette River

**8** OR 43, W Linn, Lake Oswego, **E gas:** 76, **other:** museum, **W gas:** Shell/dsl/24hr

**7mm** viewpoint nb, hist marker

**6** 10th St, W Linn St, **E gas:** Chevron/LP, 76, **food:** Ixtapa Mexican, McDonald's, Shari's/24hr, West Linn Cafe, **other:** Oil Can Henry's, Schwab Tire, vet, **W food:** Bugatti's Pizza, Jack-in-the-Box, Subway, **other:** Albertson's

**4mm** Tualatin River

**3** Stafford Rd, Lake Oswego, **W food:** Corner Saloon, **other:** H HOSPITAL

**0mm** I-205 begins/ends on I-5, exit 288.

## INTERSTATE 70

**E ↕ W · BREEZEWOOD**

| Exit # | Services |
|---|---|
| **171mm** | Pennsylvania/Maryland state line, **Welcome Ctr wb, full (handicapped) facilities, info,** 📞, **vending,** 🍴, **litter barrels, petwalk** |
| **168** | US 522 N, Warfordsburg, **N gas:** Exxon/dsl **S** fireworks |
| **163** | PA 731 S, Amaranth |
| **156** | PA 643, Town Hill, **N lodging:** Day's Inn, **other:** NAPA |
| **153mm** | **rest area eb, full** 🦽 **facilities,** 📞, 🍴, **litter barrels, vending, petwalk** |
| **151** | PA 915, Crystal Spring, **N food:** CornerStone Family Rest., **other:** auto repair, **S other:** Country Store/USPO |
| **149** | US 30 W, to Everett, S Breezewood (no immediate wb return), **3 mi S food:** McDonald's, **lodging:** Penn Aire Motel, Redwood Motel, Wildwood Motel |
| **147** | US 30, Breezewood, **Services on US 30...gas:** BP/dsl, Citgo, Exxon/dsl, Mobil/dsl/24hr, Sheetz/24hr, Shell, Sunoco/dsl/café, TA/dsl/rest./24hr/@, Texaco/Subway, **food:** Arby's, Big John's Buffet, Bob Evans, Burger King, DQ, Denny's, Domino's, Family House Rest., Hardee's, KFC, McDonald's, Perkins, Pizza Hut, Taco Bell, Wendy's, **lodging:** Best Western, Breezewood Motel, Comfort Inn/rest., Econolodge, Holiday Inn Express, Penn Aire Motel, Quality Inn, Ramada Inn, Wiltshire Motel, **other:** museum |
| | **I-70 and I-76/PA Turnpike run together 71 mi. For I-70 and I-76/PA TPK exits 146-75 see Pennsylvania Interstate 76/PA TPK.** |
| **57** | I-70 W, US 119, PA 66 (toll), New Stanton, **N gas:** Exxon, Sheetz, **food:** Bob Evans, Eat'n Park, KFC, McDonald's, Pagano's Rest., Pizza Hut, Quizno's, Subway, Szechuan Wok, Wendy's, **lodging:** Budget Inn, Comfort Inn, Day's Inn, Fairfield Inn, Howard Johnson, Quality Inn, Super 8, **S gas:** BP/7-11/dsl, Sunoco/24hr, **food:** Cracker Barrel, La Tavola Risorante, TJ's Rest., **other:** USPO |
| **54** | Madison, **N** KOA, truck repair |
| **53** | Yukon |
| **51b a** | PA 31, West Newton |
| **49** | Smithton, **N gas:** Citgo/dsl/rest./scales/@, *FLYING J*/Country Mkt/dsl/scales/LP/24hr/@ |
| **46b a** | PA 51, Pittsburgh, **N gas:** BP/dsl, **food:** Burger King, **lodging:** Comfort Inn, **other:** Buick/Cadillac/Chevrolet/Kia/Pontiac, Harley-Davidson, **S gas:** GetGo/dsl/24hr, **lodging:** Holiday Inn, Knotty Pine Motel, Relax Inn |
| **44** | Arnold City |
| **43b a** | (43 from eb) PA 201, Fayette City, **S gas:** Exxon/24hr, **food:** A&W/LJ Silver, Burger King, China 88 Buffet, Denny's, Eat'n Park, Hoss' Rest., KFC, Little Bamboo, McDonald's, Pizza Hut, Quizno's, Sonny's Grille, Starbucks, Subway, Wendy's, **lodging:** Hampton Inn, **other:** Advance Parts, Aldi Foods, Big Lots, Curves, CVS Drug, $General, $Tree, Giant Eagle Foods, GNC, Jo-Ann Fabrics, K-Mart, Lowes Whse, Radio Shack, Rite Aid, Staples, Walmart SuperCtr |
| **42a** | Monessen |
| **42** | **N** Belle Vernon, **S gas:** BP/7-11/McDonald's, Sunoco/dsl, **food:** DQ |
| **41** | PA 906, Belle Vernon |
| **40mm** | Monongahela River |
| **40** | PA 88, Charleroi, **N gas:** BP, Gulf, Sunoco, **food:** McDonald's, **other:** H HOSPITAL, Sav-a-Lot Foods, Valley Tire |
| **39** | Speers, **N food:** Loraine's Rest., **S gas:** Exxon |
| **37b a** | PA 43 |
| **36** | Lover (from wb, no re-entry) |
| **35** | PA 481, Centerville |
| **32b a** | PA 917, Bentleyville, **S gas:** BP/dsl, Pilot/DQ/Subway/dsl/scales/24hr, **food:** Burger King, CJ's Cafe, King Rest., McDonald's, **lodging:** Best Western, Holiday Inn Express, **other:** Advance Parts, Blue Beacon, $General, Ford, Giant Eagle Foods, Rite Aid |

**F A Y E T T E C I T Y**

## INTERSTATE 70 CONT'D

| | |
|---|---|
| 31 | to PA 136, Kammerer, **N** lodging: Carlton Motel, **food:** Carlton Kitchen |
| 27 | Dunningsville, **S** lodging: Avalon Motel |
| 25 | PA 519, to Eighty Four, **S** gas: BP/7-11 Diner/dsl/24hr, Sunoco/dsl |
| 21 | I-79 S, to Waynesburg. **I-70 W and I-79 N run together 3.5 mi.** |
| 20 | PA 136, Beau St, **S** to Washington & Jefferson Coll |
| 19b a | US 19, Murtland Ave, **N** food: Applebee's, Arby's, Bruster's, Cracker Barrel, Krispy Kreme, Max&Erma's, McDonald's, Outback Steaks, Panera Bread, Ponderosa, Quizno's, Red Lobster, Red Robin, Starbucks, Subway, TX Roadhouse, TGIFriday, **lodging:** Springhill Suites, **other:** Aldi Foods, $Tree, Giant Eagle Foods, GNC, Honda, Hyundai, JC Penney, Kohl's, Lowes Whse, Mercedes, Michael's, Nissan, PetCo, PetsMart, Radio Shack, Sam's Club/gas, Sav-a-Lot Foods, Target, Toyota, Walmart SuperCtr, vet, **S** gas: BP/dsl, Exxon, Sunoco, Valero, **food:** A&W/LJ Silver, Bob Evans, CiCi's Pizza, Eat'n Park/24hr, Evergreen Chinese, KFC, Old Mexico, Papa John's, Pizza Hut, **lodging:** Hampton Inn, Motel 6, **other:** H HOSPITAL, Big Lots, Buick/Cadillac/GMC, Firestone/auto, Home Depot, Jo-Ann Fabrics, Rite Aid, Staples, Subaru, mall |
| 18 | **I-79 N, to Pittsburgh. I-70 E and I-79 S run together 3.5 mi.** |
| 17 | PA 18, Jefferson Ave, Washington, **N** gas: GetGo, **food:** DQ, McDonald's, **other:** Family$, Rite Aid, **S** gas: Co-Go's/dsl, Sunoco, **food:** Burger King, Domino's, 4Star Pizza, Little Caesars, Subway, **other:** Advance Parts |
| 16 | Jessop Place, Jessop Place, **N** gas: Citgo, **S** auto/truck repair |
| 15 | US 40, Chesnut St, Washington, **N** food: USA Steaks, **other:** Food Land, **S** gas: BP, Sunoco/dsl, Valero, **food:** Bob Evans, Denny's, Garfield's Rest., LJ Silver, McDonald's, Pizza Hut, Taco Bell, Wendy's, **lodging:** Comfort Suites, Day's Inn, Econolodge, Ramada Inn, Red Roof Inn, The Inn, **other:** Gander Mtn, Macy's, Rite Aid, Sears/auto, mall |
| 11 | PA 221, Taylorstown, **N** gas: BP/dsl, **other:** truck repair |
| 6 | to US 40, PA 231, Claysville, **N** gas: Exxon, **S** gas: Petro/King's/Sbarro's/Subway/scales/24hr@ |
| 5mm | **Welcome Ctr/weigh sta eb, full ♿facilities, ⓒ, vending, ▦, litter barrels, petwalk** |
| 1 | W Alexander |
| 0mm | Pennsylvania/West Virginia state line |

## INTERSTATE 76

| Exit # | Services |
|---|---|
| 354mm | Pennsylvania/New Jersey state line, Delaware River, Walt Whitman Bridge |
| 351 | Front St, I-95 (from wb), **N** to Trenton, **S** to Chester |
| 350 | Packer Ave, 7th St, to I-95 (from eb), **S** lodging: Holiday Inn, **other:** to sports complex |
| 349 | to I-95, PA 611, Broad St |
| 348 | PA 291, W to Chester, **S** lodging: Ramada Inn |
| 347a | to I-95 S |
| 347b | Passyunk Ave, Oregon Ave, **S** other: sports complex |
| 346c | 28th St, Vare Ave, Mifflin St (from wb) |
| 346b | Grays Ferry Ave, University Ave, civic center, **N** food: McDonald's, PathMark Foods, **other:** Radio Shack, |

| | |
|---|---|
| 346b | Continued **S gas:** BP/24hr, Hess |
| 346a | South St |
| 345 | 30th St, Market St, downtown |
| 344 | I-676 E, US 30 E, to Philadelphia (no return from eb) |
| 343 | Spring Garden St, Haverford |
| 342 | US 13, US 30 W, Girard Ave, Philadelphia Zoo, E Fairmount Park |
| 341 | Montgomery Dr, W River Dr, W Fairmount Park, W Fairmount Park |
| 340b | US 1 N, Roosevelt Blvd, to Philadelphia |
| 339 | US 1 S, **S** lodging: Adams Mark Hotel, Holiday Inn |
| 340a | Lincoln Dr, Kelly Dr, to Germantown |
| 338 | Belmont Ave, Green Lane, **N** other: CVS Drug, **S** gas: Sunoco/24hr, **food:** WaWa |
| 337 | Hollow Rd (from wb), Gladwyne |
| 332 | PA 23 (from wb), Conshohocken, **N** lodging: Marriott |
| 331b a | I-476, PA 28 (from eb), to Chester, Conshohocken |
| 330 | PA 320, Gulph Mills, **S** to Villanova U |
| 328 | US 202 N, to King of Prussia, **N** gas: Exxon/dsl, Mobil, WaWa, **food:** Charlie's Place Rest., Dunkin Donuts, Friendly's, Sizzler, TGIFriday, Uno Pizzaria, **lodging:** Econolodge, Holiday Inn, Howard Johnson, McIntosh Inn, **other:** JC Penney, Macy's, Sears/auto, Thrift Drug, mall, **S** George Washington Lodge |
| 327 | US 202 S, Goddard Blvd, to Valley Forge, Valley Forge Park, Valley Forge Park |
| 326 | I-76 wb becomes I-76/PA Tpk to Ohio |

**For I-76 westbound to Ohio, see I-76/PA Turnpike.**

## INTERSTATE 76/TURNPIKE

| Exit # | Services |
|---|---|
| | PA Tpk runs wb as I-276. |
| 359 | Pennsylvania/New Jersey state line, Delaware River Bridge, I-276 continues to NJ, connecting with NJ TPK |
| 358 | US 13, Delaware Valley, **N** gas: BP, WaWa, **food:** Dallas Diner, **lodging:** Comfort Inn, Day's Inn, Ramada Inn, **other:** auto repair, 7-11, U-Haul, vet, **S** gas: LukOil/dsl, Sunoco/dsl, Valero, **food:** Burger King, Gigi's Pizza, Golden Eagle Diner, Italian Family Pizza, **lodging:** Villager Lodge, **other:** Buick, $General, Mr. Transmission |
| 352mm | **Neshaminy Service Plaza, wb...Welcome Ctr,** gas: Sunoco/dsl/24hr, **food:** Burger King, Nathan's, **other:** Starbucks, **eb...gas:** Sunoco/dsl, **food:** Breyer's, Hot-Dog Co, McDonald's, Nathan's |
| 351 | US 1, to I-95, to Philadelphia, **N** food: Bob Evans, Chick-fil-A, Cracker Barrel, Longhorn Steaks, On The Border, 99, Red Robin, Ruby Tuesday, Starbucks, Wendy's, **lodging:** Courtyard, Hampton Inn, Holiday Inn Select, **other:** Buick/Pontiac/Saturn/GMC, Home Depot, Lowes Whse, Macy's, Sears/auto, Target, Walmart, mall, **S** gas: Exxon/Subway, LukOil, Sunoco/dsl, **food:** Dunkin Donuts, **lodging:** Comfort Inn, Howard Johnson, Knight's Inn, Neshaminy Inn, Radisson, Red Roof Inn, Sunrise Inn, **other:** Toyota/Scion |
| 343 | PA 611, Willow Grove, **N** gas: Shell, **food:** Carrabba's, **lodging:** Candlewood Suites (5mi), Courtyard, **other:** H HOSPITAL, **S** gas: Hess/dsl, Shell, Sunoco, **food:** Bonefish Grill, China Garden, Domino's, Dunkin Donuts, Friendly's, McDonald's, Nino's Pizza, Ooka Japanese, Starbucks, Williamson Rest., **lodging:** Hampton Inn, |

## INTERSTATE 76/TURNPIKE CONT'D

**E**
↕
**W**

**343** Continued
**other:** Audi/Infiniti, Best Buy, PepBoys, 7-11, Staples, repair, transmissions

**340** VA Dr, EZ tagholder only, no trucks, no return eb (New Exit)

**339** PA 309, Ft Washington, **N gas:** Gulf, LukOil/dsl, **food:** Dunkin Donuts, Friendly's, Subway, **lodging:** Best Western, Hilton Garden, Holiday Inn, **other:** BMW, Mercedes, Volvo, WaWa

**334** PA Tpk NE Extension, I-476 S to Philadelphia, N to Allentown

**333** Germantown Pike, to Norristown, **N gas:** LukOil/dsl, Sunoco/Dunkin Donuts, **food:** California Pizza Kitchen, Houlihan's, PF Chang's, Red Stone Grill, Starbucks, **lodging:** Courtyard, DoubleTree, Extended Stay America, SpringHill Suites, **other:** H HOSPITAL, Boscov's, Macy's, **S gas:** LukOil

**328mm King of Prussia Service Plaza wb**...Sunoco/dsl/24hr, Breyer's, McDonald's

**PA Tpk runs eb as I-276, wb as I-76.**

**326** I-76 E, to US 202, I-476, Valley Forge, **N gas:** Shell, **food:** Burger King, Cracker Barrel, Hooters, Hoss' Rest., **lodging:** MainStay Suites, Radisson, Sleep Inn, **S gas:** Exxon, LukOil, Shell, Sunoco, WaWa, **food:** American Grill, California Pizza Kitchen, Cheesecake Factory, Chili's, Denny's, Houlihan's, Lone Star Steaks, Maggiano's, McDonald's, Red Lobster, Ruth's Chriss Steaks, Sullivan Steaks, **lodging:** Best Western, Comfort Inn, Hampton Inn, Holiday Inn Express, McIntosh Inn, Motel 6, **other:** Borders Books, Best Buy, Costco, Crate&Barrel, Home Depot, JC Penney, Macy's, Neiman Marcus, Nordstrom, Sears/auto, Walmart SuperCtr, mall

**325mm Valley Forge Service Plaza eb**...gas: Sunoco/dsl/24hr, **food:** Burger King, Nathan's, Starbucks, TCBY, gifts

**312** PA 100, to Downingtown, Pottstown, **N gas:** Valero, **other:** CarSense, Harley-Davidson, **S gas:** Sunoco/dsl/24hr, WaWa, **food:** Hoss' Rest, Isaac's Rest, Quizno's, Red Robin, Starbucks, Uno, **lodging:** Comfort Suites, Extended Stay America, Fairfield Inn, Hampton Inn, Holiday Inn Express, Inn at Chester Springs, Residence Inn, **other:** H HOSPITAL

**305mm Camiel Service Plaza wb**...Sunoco/dsl/24hr, Mrs Fields, Roy Rogers, Sbarro's, Starbucks, TCBY, gifts

**298** I-176, PA 10, to Reading, Morgantown, **N lodging:** Economy Lodge, Heritage Motel/rest., **other:** H HOSPITAL, Walmart SuperCtr, **S gas:** Exxon, Sheetz, **food:** McDonald's, **lodging:** Holiday Inn, **other:** Chevrolet, Rite Aid

**290mm Bowmansville Service Plaza eb**...gas: Sunoco/dsl/24hr, **food:** Big Boy, Pizza Hut, Starbucks, Taco Bell, TCBY, **other:** gifts

**286** US 322, PA 272, to Reading, Ephrata, **N gas:** Citgo/dsl, Turkey Hill, **food:** Bejing Chef, Park Place Diner, Subway, Zia Maria Italian, **lodging:** Black Horse Lodge/rest., Knights Inn, Penn Amish Motel, **other:** Antiques Galore, Dutch Cousins Camping, **S gas:** Turkey Hill, **food:** Dunkin Donuts, **lodging:** Econo Lodge, Holiday Inn, Red Carpet Inn

**266** PA 72, to Lebanon, Lancaster, **N gas:** Hess/Blimpie/dsl, Sunoco, **food:** Farmer's Hope Inn Rest, **lodging:** Holiday Inn Express (17 mi), Red Carpet Inn, Rodeway

**266** Continued
Inn, **other:** Harley-Davidson, NAPA, **S food:** Hitz Mkt/deli, **lodging:** Hampton Inn, **other:** H HOSPITAL, Mt Hope Winery, Pinch Pond Camping

**259mm Lawn Service Plaza wb**...gas: Sunoco/dsl/24hr, **food:** Burger King, Hershey's Ice Cream, Starbucks, Uno, **other:** RV dump

**250mm Highspire Service Plaza eb**...gas: Sunoco/dsl/24hr, **food:** Sbarro's

**247** I-283, PA 283, to Harrisburg, Harrisburg East, Hershey, **N gas:** Exxon/dsl, Sunoco, **food:** Bob Evans, Capitol Diner, Eat'n Park, McDonald's, Taco Bell, Wendy's, **lodging:** Best Western, Courtyard, Day's Inn, EconoLodge, Holiday Inn Express, Howard Johnson, La Quinta, Red Roof Inn, Rodeway Inn, Sheraton, Super 8, Travelodge, Wingate Inn, Wyndham, **other:** Harrisburg East Camping, JC Penney, Kia, Target

**246mm Susquehannah River**

**242** I-83, Harrisburg West, **N gas:** BP, Hess/Dunkin Donuts, **food:** Bob Evans, Doc Holliday's Rest, Eat'n Park, McDonald's, Pizza Hut, **lodging:** Best Western, Comfort Inn, Holiday Inn, Motel 6, Quality Inn, Rodeway Inn, Travel Inn, **other:** vet, **S lodging:** Days Inn, Keystone Inn

**236** US 15, to Gettysburg, Gettysburg Pike, Harrisburg, **N gas:** BP/dsl, Exxon, **food:** Isaac's Rest, McDonald's, Papa John's, Peppermill Rest, Subway, **lodging:** Comort Inn, Country Inn&Suites, Courtyard, EconoLodge, Hampton Inn/rest., Holiday Inn, Homewood Suites, **other:** H HOSPITAL, U-haul, vet, **S gas:** Sheetz/24hr, **food:** Arby's, Burger King, Cracker Barrel, Quizno's, Wendy's, **lodging:** Best Western, Wingate Inn, **other:** Giant Food/gas/24hr, GNC, Rite Aid

**226** US 11, to I-81, to Harrisburg, Carlisle, **N gas:** BP, Petro/dsl/24hr/@, 🚛 FLYING J/dsl/LP/rest./24hr/scales, Pilot/Wendy's/dsl/24hr, Shell/dsl/scales, Sunoco, Universal/dsl, **food:** Arby's, Bob Evans, Carelli's Subs, Country Club Diner, Country Oven Rest, Dunkin Donuts, Ember's Steaks, McDonald's, Middlesex Diner/24hr, Waffle House, **lodging:** Best Inn, EconoLodge, Hampton Inn, Holiday Inn, Hotel Carlisle, Howard Johnson, Quality Inn, Ramada Ltd, Residence Inn, Rodeway Inn, Super 8, Travelodge, **other:** H HOSPITAL, Blue Beacon, **S gas:** Rutter's, Sheetz/24hr, Turkey Hill, **food:** Hoss' Rest., **lodging:** Best Western, Motel 6, **other:** H HOSPITAL, U-haul, vet

**H A R R I S B U R G**

**PA**

## INTERSTATE 76/ TURNPIKE CONT'D

**E ↕ W**

**BREEZEWOOD**

**219mm** Plainfield Service Plaza eb...**gas:** Sunoco/dsl/24hr, **food:** Hershey's Ice Cream, Roy Rogers, **other:** gifts

**203mm** Blue Mtn Service Plaza wb...**gas:** Sunoco/dsl/24hr, **food:** Nathan's, Hershy's Ice Cream, Roy Rogers, Uno

**201** PA 997, to Shippensburg, Blue Mountain, **S lodging:** Johnnie's Motel/rest., Kenmar Motel

**199mm** Blue Mountain Tunnel

**197mm** Kittatinny Tunnel

**189** PA 75, Willow Hill, **S lodging:** Willow Hill Motel/rest.

**187mm** Tuscarora Tunnel

**180** US 522, Ft Littleton, **N gas:** BP/dsl, Noname/dsl, **food:** The Family Rest., **lodging:** Downes Motel, **other:** H HOSPITAL, st police

**172mm** Sideling Hill Service Plaza both lanes **S**...**gas:** Sunoco/dsl/24hr, **food:** Burger King, Famiglia Pizza, Hershey's Ice Cream, Popeye's, Starbucks, **other:** gifts

**161** US 30, Breezewood, **Services on US 30**...**gas:** TA/Gateway Rest/dsl/rest./24hr/@, BP/dsl, Exxon/dsl, Petro/Blue Beacon, Sheetz/24hr, Shell/Blimpie, Sunoco/dsl/café, Valero/dsl, **food:** Bob Evans, DQ, Denny's, Domino's, Family House Rest., Hardee's, KFC, McDonald's, Perkins, Pizza Hut, Quizno's, Starbucks, Subway, Taco Bell, Wendy's, **lodging:** Best Western, Breezewood Motel, Holiday Inn Express, Howard Johnson, Penn Aire Motel, Quality Inn, Ramada Inn, Village Motel, Wiltshire Motel, **other:** Radio Shack, camping, museum, truck/tire repair

**161mm** I-70 W and I-76/PA Turnpike W run together

**150mm** roadside park wb

**148mm** Midway Service Plaza both lanes, Sunoco/dsl/24hr, Hershey's Ice Cream, KFC, Quizno's, Sbarro's, Starbucks, gifts

**146** US 220, to I-99, Bedford, **N gas:** BP/dsl, Pacific Pride, Sheetz/dsl, **food:** Arena Rest., Denny's, Ed's Steaks, Hoss' Rest., LJ Silver, McDonald's, Pizza Hut, Subway, Wendy's, **lodging:** Best Western, Budget Host, Hillcrest Motel, Holiday Inn Express, Quality Inn, Relax Inn, Super 8, **other:** to Shawnee SP (10mi), Blue Knob SP (15mi), **S lodging:** Hampton Inn

**142mm** parking area wb

**123mm** Allegheny Tunnel

**112mm** Somerset Service Plaza both lanes, eb...Sunoco/dsl/24hr, **food:** Chili's, Famiglia Pizza, Hershey's Ice Cream, Quizno's, Roy Rogers, Starbucks, **other:** gifts

**110** PA 601, to US 219, Somerset, **N gas:** KwikFill/dsl, Sheetz/24hr, **food:** Hog Father's BBQ, Hoss' Rest., King's Rest., Pizza Hut, **lodging:** $ Inn, Economy Inn, **other:** Advance Parts, Chrysler/Jeep, Ford, tires, **S gas:** Somerset TravelCtr/dsl/@, Turkey Hill, **food:** Arby's, Bruster's Ice Cream, DQ, Donut Connection, Eat'n Park, KFC, LJ Silver, Maggie Mae's Café, McDonald's, Pine Grill, Ruby Tuesday, Starbucks, Subway, Summit Diner, Wendy's, **lodging:** Best Western, Budget Host, Budget Inn, Day's Inn, Hampton Inn, Holiday Inn, Knight's Inn, Quality Inn, Super 8, **other:** Dodge, Harley-Davidson

**91** PA 711, Donegal, **N food:** Tall Cedars Rest., **S gas:** BP/McDonald's, Exxon/Subway/dsl, Sunoco/dsl, **food:** DQ, Ladle's Rest., **lodging:** Day's Inn, **other:** camping, golf

**78mm** service plaza wb...**gas:** Sunoco/dsl/24hr, **food:** Quizno's, Starbucks, Uno

---

I-70 E runs with I-76/PA Turnpike eb.

**PITTSBURGH**

**75** I-70 W, US 119, PA 66 (toll), New Stanton, **N gas:** Exxon, Sheetz, **food:** Bob Evans, Eat'n Park, KFC, McDonald's, Pagano's Rest., Pizza Hut, Quizno's, Subway, Szechuan Wok, Wendy's, **lodging:** Budget Inn, Comfort Inn, Day's Inn, Fairfield Inn, Howard Johnson, Quality Inn, Super 8, **S gas:** BP/7-11/dsl, Sunoco/24hr, **food:** Cracker Barrel, La Tavola Risorante, TJ's Rest., **other:** USPO

**74.6mm** Hemphill Service Plaza eb...**gas:** Sunoco/dsl/24hr, **food:** Breyer's, McDonald's, **other:** atm

**67** US 30, to Greensburg, Irwin, **N gas:** BP/dsl, Sheetz/24hr, **other:** H HOSPITAL, Ford, tires, vet, **S gas:** Marathon/7-11, Sunoco/24hr, **food:** Arby's, Bob Evans, Burger King, CiCi's Pizza, Denny's, DQ, Dunkin Donuts, Eat'n Park, KFC, LJ Silver, Los Campesinos Mexican, McDonald's, Panera Bread, Pizza Hut, Subway, Taco Bell, Teddy's Rest., Wendy's, **lodging:** Conley Inn, Holiday Inn Express, **other:** Advance Parts, Aldi Foods, CarQuest, $Tree, Giant Eagle Foods/24hr, GNC, Kohl's, Radio Shack, Rite Aid, Target

**61mm** parking area eb

**57** I-376, US 22, to Pittsburgh, Monroeville, **S gas:** Citgo/dsl, Exxon, Sheetz, Sunoco, **food:** A&W/LJ Silver, Arby's, Baskin-Robbins, Bob Evan's, Chick-fil-A, China Palace, ChuckeCheese, CiCi's Pizza, Damon's, Denny's, Golden Corral, Honeybaked Ham, Max&Erma's, McDonald's, Olive Garden, Outback Steaks, Panera Bread, Park Diner, Pizza Hut, Primanti Bro's, Quizno's, Red Lobster, Starbucks, Taco Bell, TGIFridays, Wendy's, **lodging:** Comfort Suites, Courtyard, Day's Inn, Extended Stay America, Hampton Inn, Holiday Inn, Radisson Inn, Red Roof Inn, Springhill Suites, **other:** H HOSPITAL, Aamco, Big Lots, Border's Books, Firestone/auto, Honda, Jaguar/Land Rover, Jo-Ann Fabrics, Marshall's, Michael's, Lowes Whse, NTB, Office Depot, Old Navy, PetCo, Pet Land, Radio Shack, Rite Aid, Saturn, to Three Rivers Stadium

**49mm** Oakmont Service Plaza eb...Sunoco/dsl/24hr, FoodCourt, ♿, litter barrels, phone

**48.5mm** Allegheny River

**48** PA 28, to Pittsburgh, Allegheny Valley, New Kensington, **N gas:** Shell/24hr, Sunoco, **food:** Pizza Hut, Subway, **other:** CarQuest, Rite Aid, **S gas:** Exxon/dsl, GetGo, **food:** Bob Evans, Bruster's, Denny's, Gino Bro's Pizza, KFC, King's Rest., McDonald's, Ponderosa, Primanti Bro's, Subway, Taco Bell, Wendy's, **lodging:** Comfort Inn, Day's Inn, Holiday Inn Express, Super 8, Valley Motel, **other:** Advance Parts, Ford, Target

**41mm** parking area/call box eb

**39** PA 8, to Pittsburgh, Butler Valley, 0-1 mi **N gas:** Exxon/7-11/dsl, GetGo, Sheetz/24hr, Sunoco, **food:** Applebees, Atria's Rest., Bruno's Pizza, Buffalo Wild Wings, Eat'n Park, King's Rest., Max&Erma's, McDonald's, Sonic, Starbucks, Taco Bell, Wendy's, **lodging:** Comfort Inn, Pittsburgh N Motel/rest, **other:** Advance Parts, Curves, Dodge, $Tree, Giant Eagle Foods, GNC, Kohl's, Lowes Whse, Rite Aid, Shop'n Save Foods, Target, TJ Maxx, Walmart/auto/drugs, **S gas:** BP, Sunoco/dsl, **food:** Arby's, Brusters, Burger King, China Bistro, KFC, McDonald's, Pasquales Pizza, Panera Bread, Pizza Hut, Subway, Vocelli Pizza, Wendy's, **other:** H HOSPITAL, AutoZone, Firestone/auto, Goodyear/auto, Home Depot, Mr. Tire, Radio Shack, Rite Aid, USPO

## INTERSTATE 76/TURNPIKE CONT'D

**PITTSBURGH** E ↕ W

| | |
|---|---|
| 31mm | Toll Plaza wb |
| 28 | to I-79, to Cranberry, Pittsburgh, **N gas:** BP/dsl, Exxon/dsl/24hr, GetGo, Sheetz/24hr, Sunoco/24hr, **food:** A&W/LJ Silver, Alladin's Eatery, Arby's, Bob Evans, Boston Mkt, Box's Pizza, Bravo Italian, Burger King, CiCi's Pizza, Denny's, DQ, Dunkin Donuts, Eat'n Park, Hartner's Rest., HotDog Shoppe, Ichiban Steakhouse, King's Rest., Krispy Kreme, LoneStar Steaks, Max&Erma's, McDonald's, Montecello's Grill, Panera Bread, Papa John's, Perkins, Pizzaroma, Primanti Bro's, Subway, TCBY, Wendy's, **lodging:** Comfort Inn, Fairfield Inn, Hampton Inn, Holiday Inn Express, Hyatt Place, Motel 6, Oak Leaf Motel, Red Roof Inn, Residence Inn, Sheraton, Super 8, **other:** Barnes&Noble, Best Buy, CarQuest, Costco/gas, Curves, GNC, Giant Eagle, Goodyear/auto, Home Depot, Jo-Ann Fabrics, Kuhn's Foods, Michael's, Old Navy, PepBoys, PetCo, Radio Shack, Rite Aid, Toyota/Scion, Walgreens, Walmart SuperCtr, mall, transmissions, USPO, vet |
| 23.5mm | pulloff eb |
| 22mm | **Zelienople Service Plaza eb...Welcome Ctr, gas:** Sunoco/dsl/24hr, **food:** FoodCourt, **other:** crafts, gifts |
| 17mm | parking area eb |
| 13.4mm | parking area eb |
| 13mm | Beaver River |
| 13 | PA 8, to Ellwood City, Beaver Valley, **N gas:** Al's Corner, **food:** Subway, **lodging:** Alpine Inn, Beaver Falls Motel, HillTop Motel, Holiday Inn, Lark Motel, **other:** H HOSPITAL, **S lodging:** Super 8 |
| 10 | PA 60 (toll), to New Castle, Pittsburgh, **S** services (6mi), to ✈ |
| 6mm | pulloff eb |
| 2mm | pulloff eb |
| 1mm | toll plaza eb, 📞, call boxes located at **1 mi** intervals |
| 0mm | Pennsylvania/Ohio state line |

## INTERSTATE 78

E ↕ W

| Exit # | Services |
|---|---|
| 77 | Pennsylvania/New Jersey state line, Delaware River |
| 76mm | **Welcome Ctr wb, full ♿ facilities, 📞, vending, 🍴 litter barrels, petwalk, toll booth wb** |
| 75 | to PA 611, Easton, **N gas:** TurkeyHill/dsl, **food:** McDonald's (1mi), **lodging:** Quality Inn, **other:** Crayola Factory, **S gas:** Exxon |
| 71 | PA 33, to Stroudsburg, **1 mi N on Freemansburg Ave... food:** Frank's Pizza, JJ Wong's, Panera Bread, Ruby Tuesday, Texas Roadhouse, TGIFriday, **lodging:** Courtyard, **other:** Barnes&Noble, Circuit City, Lowes Whse, Michael's, Pet Supplies+, Staples |
| 67 | PA 412, Hellertown, **N gas:** TurkeyHill/gas, **lodging:** Comfort Suites (3mi), **food:** Wendy's, **other:** H HOSPITAL, Chevrolet, **S gas:** Citgo, Exxon/dsl, Lukoil, Sunoco, **food:** McDonald's, Rocco's Pizza, Rita's Shakes, Vassi's Drive-In, Waffle House, **lodging:** Holiday Inn Express, **other:** CVS Drug, Firestone, 7-11, repair |
| 60b a | PA 309 S, Quakertown |
| 59 | to PA 145 (from eb), Summit Lawn |
| 58 | Emaus St (from wb), **S gas:** Gulf, Sunoco |
| 57 | Lehigh St, **N gas:** Hess/dsl, WaWa, **food:** Arby's, Dragon Pond Chinese, IHOP, Palumbo Pizza, Queen City |

**ALLENTOWN**

| | |
|---|---|
| 57 | Continued Diner, Subway, Willy Joe's Rest., **lodging:** Day's Inn, **other:** BigLots, CVS Drug, $Tree, Family$, Home Depot, Dodge/Kia/Isuzu, Lincoln/Mercury, Radio Shack, Redner's Whse, Shop Fair Foods, VW, Whse Mkt Foods, **S gas:** Lukoil, Pipeline/dsl, Sunoco, TurkeyHill/gas, **food:** Bob Evans, Brass Rail Rest., Domino's, Dunkin Donuts, Dynasty Chinese, Friendly's, Japanese Steaks, McDonald's, Papa John's, Perkins, Pizza Hut/Taco Bell, Rossi's Pizza, Subway, Wendy's, **other:** Acura, Audi/Mercedes/Porsche, BonTon, Buick/GMC/Jeep/Saturn, Chevrolet/Saab, Chrysler, Ford, Honda, Hyundai, Lehigh Tire, Mazda, Mitsubishi, PetCo, Staples, SteinMart, Volvo |
| 55 | PA 29, Cedar Crest Blvd, **S** H HOSPITAL |
| 54 | US 222, Hamilton Blvd, **N gas:** Hess, **food:** Baskin-Robbins, Boston Mkt, Burger King, Cali Burrito, Carrabba's, Friendly's, Ice Cream World, King George Rest., Mango's Rest., McDonald's, Perkins, Subway, Teppan Steaks, TGIFriday, Wendy's, **lodging:** Comfort Suites/rest., Holiday Inn Express, Howard Johnson, **other:** Aamco, Dorney Funpark, Dorneyville Drug, King's Food/drug, Office Depot, Rite Aid, **S gas:** Sunoco, WaWa/gas, **food:** Dunkin Donuts, Pizza Hut, **lodging:** Wingate Inn, **other:** Queen City Tire, Subaru |
| 53 | PA 309 (wb only) |
| 51 | to I-476, US 22 E, PA 33 N (eb only), Whitehall |
| 49b a | PA 100, Fogelsville, **N food:** Arby's, Cracker Barrel, LJ Silver, Panda&Fish Chinese, Pizza Hut, **lodging:** Comfort Inn, Hawthorn Inn, **other:** Curves, KOA, Rite Aid, STS Tire/repair, **S gas:** Shell, Sunoco/24hr, WaWa, **food:** Boston's Grill, Burger King, Damon's, Starlite Diner, Taco Bell, Yocco's Hotdogs, **lodging:** Hampton Inn, Hilton Garden, Holiday Inn, Sleep Inn, Staybridge Suites, **other:** Clover Hill Winery, Toyota/Scion, st police |
| 45 | PA 863, to Lynnport, **N gas:** Exxon/Subway/dsl, Sunoco/dsl, **other:** New Smithfield Diner, **S lodging:** Super 8 |
| 40 | PA 737, Krumsville, **N other:** Pine Hill Campground, Robin Hill RV Park (4mi), **S gas:** Shell/dsl, **lodging:** Skyview Rest. |
| 35 | PA 143, Lenhartsville, **3 mi S** Robin Hill Park |
| 30 | Hamburg, **S food:** Hamburg Mkt |
| 29b a | PA 61, to Reading, Pottsville, **N gas:** Shell/dsl, **food:** Baskin Robbins/Dunkin Donuts, Burger King, Campfire Rest., Cracker Barrel, LJ Silver/Taco Bell, McDonald's, Pappy T's, Pizza Hut, Wendy's, **lodging:** Microtel, **other:** Cabela's Outdoor, Harley-Davidson (8mi), Toyota/Scion, st police, **S other:** Boat'n RV Ctr RV (4mi) |

**E ⇅ W**    **N ↕ S**    **ERIE**    **PA**

**MEADVILLE**

## INTERSTATE 78 CONT'D

| | |
|---|---|
| 23 | Shartlesville, **N gas:** Love's/McDonald's/Subway/dsl/scales/24hr, **other:** Appalachian Campsites, **S food:** Blue Mtn Family Rest., **lodging:** Haag's Motel/rest., **other:** Dutch Haus/gifts, antiques, camping, USPO |
| 19 | PA 183, Strausstown, **N gas:** Lukoil, **S gas:** Power/dsl, **food:** C&C Pizza |
| 17 | PA 419, Rehrersburg, **N gas:** Best/dsl, truck/tire repair |
| 16 | Midway, **N gas:** Exxon/dsl, Sunoco/dsl, **food:** Midway Diner, **lodging:** Comfort Inn, **S** auto/truck repair |
| 15 | Grimes |
| 13 | PA 501, Bethel, **N gas:** Shell/dsl/24hr, **S gas:** Exxon/dsl |
| 10 | PA 645, Frystown, **S gas:** All-American Trkstp/rest./dsl/24hr/@, Gulf/dsl/24hr |
| 6 | (8 from wb, US 22) PA 343, Fredricksburg, **1 mi S gas:** Pacific Pride/dsl, Redner's Whse/mkt, **food:** Esther's Rest., **other:** KOA (5mi) |
| 1 | I-81. I-78 begins/ends on I-81, exit 89. |

## INTERSTATE 79

| Exit # | Services |
|---|---|
| 183b a | PA 5, 12th St, Erie, **E gas:** Shell, **other:** H HOSPITAL, **W gas:** Country Fair, Sunoco, **food:** Applebee's, Backyard Burger, Bob Evans, Eat'n Park/24hr, Hibachi Japanese, KFC, McDonald's, Panera Bread, Serafini's Italian, Taco Bell, Tim Horton, Wendy's, **lodging:** Comfort Inn (2mi), **other:** Advance Parts, Aldi Foods, Big Lots, CVS Drug, $General, Dunn Tire, Giant Eagle Foods, GNC, NAPA, Rite Aid, Tires-4-Less, Tuesday Morning, U-HAUL, vet, to Presque Isle SP |
| 182 | US 20, 26th St, **E gas:** KwikFill, **food:** Subway, **other:** H HOSPITAL, CVS Drug, Family$, Tops Foods/gas/24hr, **W gas:** Country Fair, GetGo, **food:** Arby's, Burger King, LJ Silver, McDonald's, Super Buffet, Tim Horton, Vocelli's Pizza, **other:** Aamco, AutoZone, $General, Ford, Giant Eagle, K-Mart, Radio Shack, TrueValue, Volvo, vet |
| 180 | US 19, to Kearsarge, **E food:** Arby's, Buffalo Wild Wings, Coldstone Cramery, Fox&Hound, KFC, Max&Erma's, Olive Garden, Outback Steaks, Ponderosa, Red Lobster, Roadhouse Grill, Smokey Bones BBQ, Starbucks, Subway, Wendy's, **lodging:** Fairfield Inn, Homewood Suites, SpringHill Suites, TownePlace Suites, **other:** H HOSPITAL, Audi/Cadillac, Barnes&Noble, Borders Books, Chrysler/Jeep, Gander Mtn, JC Penney, Macy's, Michael's, Office Depot, Old Navy, PetCo, Sears/auto, TJ Maxx, Toyota/Scion, mall, **W gas:** Country Fair, **other:** camping |
| 178b a | I-90, E to Buffalo, W to Cleveland |
| 174 | to McKean, **E** access to gas/dsl, **W** camping |
| 166 | US 6N, to Edinboro, **E gas:** Citgo, Sheetz, **food:** Burger King (3mi), McDonald's (3mi), Perkins (2mi), Subway, Wendy's, **lodging:** Comfort Suites, Edinboro Inn, **other:** $Tree, Walmart SuperCtr, vet, **W** camping |
| 163mm | **rest area both lanes, full ♿ facilities, C, vending, litter barrels, petwalk** |
| 154 | PA 198, to Saegertown, Conneautville |
| 147b a | US 6, US 322, to Meadville, **E gas:** All American Gas/wash, Country Fair, GetGo, Sheetz/dsl/24hr, **food:** Applebee's, Chovy's Italian, Cracker Barrel, DQ, Hoss' Rest., KFC, Perkins, Pizza Hut, Steak&Shake, Super Buffet, **lodging:** Best Value, Day's Inn/rest., Holiday Inn |

| | |
|---|---|
| 147b a | Continued   Express, **other:** H HOSPITAL, Advance Parts, Giant Eagle/24hr, Home Depot, Radio Shack, **W gas:** Sheetz, **food:** King's Rest./24hr, McDonald's, Ponderosa, Red Lobster, Subway, Yuen's Garden, **lodging:** Quality Inn, **other:** Aldi Foods, AutoZone, Buick/Pontiac/Cadillac/GMC, Chevrolet, $Tree, K-Mart, Staples, Toyota/Scion, Walmart SuperCtr, to Pymatuning SP, st police |
| 141 | PA 285, to Geneva, **E** to Erie NWR (20mi), **W food:** Aunt Bee's Rest./dsl |
| 135mm | **rest area/weigh sta both lanes, full ♿ facilities, C, vending, litter barrels, petwalk** |
| 130 | PA 358, to Sandy Lake, **W other:** H HOSPITAL (13mi), to Goddard SP |
| 121 | US 62, to Mercer, **E other:** Valley Tire, **W gas:** Sunoco/dsl, **other:** st police |
| 116b a | I-80, E to Clarion, W to Sharon |
| 113 | PA 208, PA 258, to Grove City, **E gas:** BP, Country Fair/dsl/24hr, **other:** H HOSPITAL, **W gas:** KwikFill/Subway, Sheetz/24hr, **food:** Eat'n Park/24hr, Elephant&Castle Rest., Hoss's Rest., King's Rest., McDonald's, Wendy's, **lodging:** Best Western, Comfort Inn, Hampton Inn, Holiday Inn Express, Microtel, Super 8, **other:** KOA (3mi), Prime Outlets/famous brands, tires |
| 110mm | **rest area sb, full ♿ facilities, C, vending, litter barrels, petwalk** |
| 107mm | **rest area nb, full ♿ facilities, C, vending, litter barrels, petwalk** |
| 105 | PA 108, to Slippery Rock, **E gas:** QuickStop/dsl, **food:** DQ, **lodging:** Evening Star Motel/rest., **other:** Slippery Rock Camping, to Slippery Rock U |
| 99 | US 422, to New Castle, **E** to Moraine SP, **W gas:** Pilot/Subway/McDonald's/dsl/scales/24hr, **other:** Coopers Lake Camping to Rose Point Camping |
| 96 | PA 488, Portersville, **E** Bear Run Camping, Moraine SP, **W food:** Brown's Country Kitchen, McConnell's Mill SP (3mi), gas/dsl |
| 88 | (87 from nb), to US 19, PA 68, (no ez return), Zelienople, **W gas:** Exxon, **food:** Bruster's, Thompson's Rest |
| 85 | (83 from nb), PA 528 (no quick return), to Evans City, **W other:** Buick/Pontiac |
| 80mm | parking area both lanes |
| 78 | (76 from nb, exits left from nb), US 19, PA 228, to Mars, **access to I-76, PA TPK, E gas:** Citgo/7-11, **food:** Applebees, Chick-fil-A, DiBella's Subs, McDonald's, Moe's SW Grill, Olive Garden, On-the-Border, Quizno's, Red Robin, Smokey Bones BBQ, Subway, Taipei Chinese, **lodging:** Marriott, **other:** H HOSPITAL, Kohl's, Lowes Whse, PetsMart, Staples, Target, TJ Maxx, **W on US 19...gas:** BP/dsl, Exxon/dsl/24hr, GetGo, Sheetz/24hr, Sunoco/24hr, **food:** A&W/LJ Silver, Alladin's Eatery, Arby's, Bob Evans, Boston Mkt, Box's Pizza, Bravo Italian, Burger King, CiCi's Pizza, Denny's, DQ, Dunkin Donuts, Eat'n Park, Hartner's Rest., HotDog Shoppe, Ichiban Steakhouse, King's Rest., Krispy Kreme, LoneStar Steaks, Max&Erma's, McDonald's, Montecello's Grill, Panera Bread, Papa John's, Perkins, Pizzaroma, Primanti Bro's, Subway, TCBY, Wendy's, **lodging:** Comfort Inn, Fairfield Inn, Hampton Inn, Holiday Inn Express, Hyatt Place, Motel 6, Oak Leaf Motel, Red Roof Inn, Residence Inn, Sheraton, Super 8, **other:** Barnes&Noble, |

## INTERSTATE 79 CONT'D

N ↕ S

| | |
|---|---|
| **78** | Continued<br>Best Buy, CarQuest, Costco/gas, Curves, GNC, Giant Eagle, Goodyear/auto, Home Depot, Jo-Ann Fabrics, Kuhn's Foods, Michael's, Old Navy, PepBoys, PetCo, Radio Shack, Rite Aid, Toyota/Scion, Walgreens, Walmart SuperCtr, mall, transmissions, USPO, vet |
| **77** | I-76/Tpk, to Youngstown **E** food: Quizno's |
| **75** | US 19 S (from nb), to Warrendale, services along US 19 |
| **73** | PA 910, to Wexford, **E** gas: BP/24hr, food: Eat'n Park, King's Family Rest./24hr, Starbucks, lodging: Best Inn, other: **W** gas: Exxon/dsl/24hr, food: Carmody's Rest. |
| **72** | I-279 S (from sb), to Pittsburgh |
| **68** | Mt Nebo Rd, **W** H HOSPITAL, gas |
| **66** | to PA 65, Emsworth |
| **65** | to PA 51, Coraopolis, Neville Island, **E** gas: Gulf, lodging: Fairfield Inn, other: Penske Trucks, **W** food: Subway |
| **64.5mm** | Ohio River |
| **64** | PA 51 (from nb), to Coraopolis, McKees Rocks |
| **60b a** | PA 60, Crafton, **E** gas: Exxon/dsl/24hr, food: King's Rest./24hr, Primanti Bros, lodging: Carefree Inn, Comfort Inn, Econolodge, Motel 6, Pittsburgh Motel, other: H HOSPITAL, **W** gas: BP/Subway/dsl (1mi), food: Juliano's Rest. |
| **59b** | US 22 W, US 30 (from nb), **W** ✈ |
| **59a** | I-279 N, to Pittsburgh |
| **57** | to Carnegie, **1-3 mi E** gas: BP, Exxon, food: LJ Silver, McDonald's, lodging: Ford, Lowes Whse, Radio Shack, Shop'n Save, Walgreens, Walmart, mall |
| **55** | PA 50, to Heidelberg, **E on PA 50**...gas: Sunoco, food: Arby's, Bob Evans, ChuckeCheese, CiCi's Pizza, Damon's, DQ, Eat'n Park, KFC, King's Rest., Pizza Hut, Firestone/auto, Starbucks, Taco Bell, Wendy's, other: Big Lots, $Discount, Giant Eagle Foods, GNC, Home Depot, Jo-Ann Fabrics, K-Mart/Little Caesar's, Mr Tire, TJ Maxx, Tuesday Morning |
| **54** | PA 50, to Bridgeville, **E** gas: BP/dsl, Exxon/dsl, food: Burger King, King's Rest./24hr, McDonald's, lodging: Holiday Inn Express, other: H HOSPITAL, Chevrolet, Dodge, NAPA, Rite Aid, USPO, **W** gas: Sunoco, lodging: Knight's Inn |
| **50mm** | rest area/weigh sta both lanes, full 🚻 facilities, 🅲, vending, ⛲ litter barrels, petwalk |
| **48** | South Pointe, **W** food: Jackson's Rest., Subway, lodging: Hilton Garden |
| **45** | to PA 980, Canonsburg, **E** gas: Sheetz, **W** gas: BP/24hr, Citgo, food: KFC/Taco Bell, LJ Silver, McDonald's, Papa John's, Pizza Hut, Quizno's, Starbucks, Subway, Wendy's, lodging: Super 8, other: Advance Parts, Walgreens |
| **43** | PA 519, Houston, **E** gas: BP/dsl, **W** gas: Sunoco/24hr, other: Freightliner |
| **41** | Race Track Rd, **E** gas: Exxon, food: Brick Oven Pizza, Buger King, McDonald's, Waffle House, Wendy's, lodging: Comfort Inn, Hampton Inn, Holiday Inn, **W** gas: BP/dsl, lodging: Candlewood Suites, other: Trolley Museum |
| **40** | Meadow Lands (from nb, no re-entry), **W** other: Trolley Museum (3mi), golf, racetrack |
| **38** | I-70 W, to Wheeling |
| **19b a** | (I-77), US 19, Murtland Ave, **N** food: Applebee's, Arby's, Bruster's, Cracker Barrel, Krispy Kreme, Max&Erma's, McDonald's, Outback Steaks, Panera Bread, |

WASHINGTON

| | |
|---|---|
| **19b a** | Continued<br>Ponderosa, Quizno's, Red Lobster, Red Robin, Starbucks, Subway, TX Roadhouse, TGIFriday, lodging: Springhill Suites, other: Aldi Foods, $Tree, Giant Eagle Foods, GNC, Honda, Hyundai, JC Penney, Kohl's, Lowes Whse, Mercedes, Michael's, Nissan, PetCo, PetsMart, Radio Shack, Sam's Club/gas, Sav-a-Lot Foods, Target, Toyota, Walmart SuperCtr, vet, **S** gas: BP/dsl, Exxon, Sunoco, Valero, food: A&W/LJ Silver, Bob Evans, CiCi's Pizza, Eat'n Park/24hr, Evergreen Chinese, KFC, Old Mexico, Papa John's, Pizza Hut, lodging: Hampton Inn, Motel 6, other: H HOSPITAL, Big Lots, Buick/Cadillac/GMC, Firestone/auto, Home Depot, Jo-Ann Fabrics, Rite Aid, Staples, Subaru, mall |
| **20** | (I-77) PA 136, to Beau St, **S** to Washington&Jefferson Coll |
| **34** | I-70 E, to Greensburg |
| **33** | US 40, to Laboratory, **W** other: KOA |
| **31mm** | parking area/weigh sta sb |
| **30** | US 19, to Amity, **W** gas: Exxon/Subway/dsl |
| **23** | to Marianna, Prosperity |
| **19** | PA 221, to US 19, Ruff Creek, **W** gas: BP/dsl |
| **14** | PA 21, to Waynesburg, **E** gas: Sunoco, food: Bob Evans, lodging: Comfort Inn, other: Walmart SuperCtr, visitor info, **W** gas: BP/dsl/24hr, Exxon/dsl, GetGo, Marathon, 7-11, Sheetz, food: Burger King, DQ, Golden Wok, Hardee's, KFC, Little Caesar's, McDonald's, Scotty's Pizza, Subway, Vocelli Pizza, Wendy's, lodging: Econolodge, Super 8, other: H HOSPITAL, Advance Parts, Aldi Foods, AutoZone, Big Lots, Buick/GMC/Pontiac, Cadillac/Chevrolet/Subaru, Chrysler/Dodge/Jeep, CVS Drug, $General, Giant Eagle Foods, Family$, Radio Shack, Rite Aid, Walgreens, st police |
| **7** | to Kirby |
| **6mm** | Welcome Ctr/weigh sta nb, full 🚻 facilities, 🅲, ⛲, litter barrels, vending, petwalk |
| **1** | Mount Morris, **E** gas: Citgo/dsl/rest./scales, other: Honda/Mazda, **W** gas: BP/dsl, Marathon, other: Mt Morris Campground |
| **0mm** | Pennsylvania/West Virginia state line |

## INTERSTATE 80

E ↕ W

| Exit # | Services |
|---|---|
| **311mm** | Pennsylvania/New Jersey state line, Delaware River |
| **310.5** | toll booth wb, phone |
| **310** | PA 611, Delaware Water Gap, **S Welcome Ctr/rest area, full services, info**...gas: BP, Gulf/repair, food: Doughboys Pizza, Water Gap Diner |

**STROUDSBURG** E ↕ W

## INTERSTATE 80 CONT'D

**309** US 209 N, PA 447, to Marshalls Creek, **N gas:** Exxon/dsl/24hr, Gulf, **food:** Blue Tequila Mexican, DQ, Wendy's (2mi), **lodging:** Shannon Motel, **other:** H HOSPITAL

**308** East Stroudsburg, **N gas:** Exxon, **other:** H HOSPITAL, WaWa, vet, **1 mi N food:** Arby's, Burger King, China King, Friendly's, McDonald's, **other:** Goodyear/auto, K-Mart, NAPA, Radio Shack, ShopRite Foods, Walmart SuperCtr, Weis Foods, **S food:** JR's Grill, **lodging:** Budget Motel, Super 8

**307** PA 191, Broad St, **N lodging:** Hampton Inn, **other:** H HOSPITAL, **S gas:** Sunoco, **food:** Compton's, **lodging:** Budget Host

**306** Dreher Ave (from wb, no EZ return), **N gas:** Wawa

**305** US 209, Main St, **N gas:** Gulf, Shell, **food:** Perkins/24hr, **lodging:** Quality Inn, **S gas:** Exxon/24hr, **lodging:** Alpines Motel

**304** US 209, to PA 33, 9th St (from wb), same as 303

**303** 9th St, (from eb), **N gas:** Lukoil, **food:** Arby's, Boston Mkt, Burger King, Dunkin Donuts, Fulay Chinese, Garfield's Rest., McDonald's, Panera Bread, Pizza Hut, Ruby Tuesday, Starbucks, TX Roadhouse, **other:** Best Buy, Border's Books, Cadillac, Chevrolet, CVS Drug, $Tree, JC Penney, Nissan, Old Navy, PetsMart

**302** PA 611, to Bartonsville, **N gas:** Exxon/dsl, **food:** Chili's, Lee's Rest., Longhorn Steaks, McDonald's (3mi), Ponderosa (3mi), Red Robin, Subway (2mi), **lodging:** Comfort Inn, Howard Johnson, Knight's Inn, **other:** Goodyear, Kohl's, Lowes Whse

**299** PA 715, Tannersville, **N gas:** BP, Shell, **lodging:** Ramada Ltd, **other:** The Crossing Factory Outlet/famous brands, **1-4 mi N food:** Barley Creek Brewing, Friendly's, Subway, Wendy's, **lodging:** Chateau Inn/rest., Knight's Inn, Super 8, **other:** camping, **S gas:** Sunoco/24hr, **food:** Tannersville Diner, **lodging:** Day's Inn, Summit Resort, **other:** to Camelback Ski Area, to Big Pocono SP

**298** PA 611 (from wb), to Scotrun, **N gas:** Shell, Sunoco/dsl, **food:** Anthony's Steaks, Plaza Deli, **lodging:** Scotrun Diner/motel, **other:** to Mt Pocono

**295mm** rest area eb, full ♿ facilities, 🕿, 🍴, litter barrels, vending, petwalk

**293** I-380 N, to Scranton, (exits left from eb)

**284** PA 115, to Wilkes-Barre, Blakeslee, **N gas:** WaWa (1mi), **lodging:** Best Western, Blakeslee Inn (2mi), **other:** Fern Ridge Camping, st police, **S gas:** Exxon/dsl, **other:** to Pocono Raceway

**277** PA 940, to PA Tpk (I-476), to Pocono, Lake Harmony, Allentown, **N gas:** WaWa, **food:** A&W/LJ Silver, Arby's, Denny's, Gino's Pizza, McDonald's, **lodging:** Comfort Inn, CountryPlace Inn, Day's Inn, Ramada Inn, Split Rock Resort

**274** PA 534, **N gas:** Hickory Run/Valero/dsl/rest./scales/24hr, Sunoco/Subway/dsl/24hr, **other:** towing/repair, **S other:** to Hickory Run SP (6mi)

**273mm** Lehigh River

**273** PA 940, PA 437, to Freeland, White Haven, **N gas:** BP, Exxon, **S food:** Powerhouse Eatery, **other:** Sandy Valley Campground

**270mm** rest area eb, full ♿ facilities, info, 🕿, 🍴, litter barrels, vending, petwalk

**BLOOMSBURG**

**262** PA 309, to Hazleton, Mountain Top, **N gas:** BP, **food:** Mary's Rest., Stagecoach Rest., Wendy's, **lodging:** Econolodge, **other:** Hazelton Campground, **S lodging:** Holiday Inn Express, **other:** st police

**260b a** I-81, N to Wilkes-Barre, S to Harrisburg

**256** PA 93, to Nescopeck, Conyngham, **N gas:** Pilot/Subway/dsl/scales/24hr, Sunoco/repair, **lodging:** Lookout Motel, **S food:** Tom's Kitchen (2mi), **lodging:** Best Value Inn, Hampton Inn (4mi), **other:** H HOSPITAL, towing/truck repair

**251mm** Nescopeck River

**246mm** rest area/weigh sta both lanes, full ♿ facilities, weather info, 🕿, 🍴, litter barrels, vending, petwalk

**242** PA 339, to Mainville, Mifflinville, **N gas:** Loves/Arby's/dsl/24hr, **food:** McDonald's, **lodging:** Super 8/rest., **S gas:** Citgo/dsl/repair, **lodging:** Best Western

**241mm** Susquehanna River

**241b a** US 11, to Berwick, Lime Ridge, Bloomsburg, **N lodging:** Red Maple Inn (2mi), **other:** H HOSPITAL, **S gas:** Exxon, **food:** Kemler's Rest., **lodging:** Budget Host, **2-5 mi S gas:** Sheetz/dsl/24hr, **food:** Applebee's, Arby's, Burger King, China Queen, Domino's, Dunkin Donuts, McDonald's, Morris Rest., New China Buffet, Pizza Hut, Playa Cancun, Subway, Taco Bell, Terrapins Cantina, Wendy's, **other:** Ace Hardware, Advance Parts, Bardo's Tires, Big-Lots, Bloomsburg RV Ctr, Buick/GMC/Pontiac, Cadillac/Chevrolet, CVS Drug, $Tree, Ford/Honda, Giant Foods/gas, Kost Tire, Rite Aid, Staples, U-Haul, Weis Foods/gas

**236** PA 487, to Bloomsburg, Lightstreet, **S gas:** Sunoco/24hr, **food:** Denny's/24hr, **lodging:** Hampton Inn, Tennytown Motel (2mi), Turkey Hill Inn, **other:** H HOSPITAL, to Bloomsburg U

**232** PA 42, Buckhorn, **N gas:** Exxon, TA/BP/Subway/dsl/scales/24hr/@, **food:** Burger King, Charlie Brown's Steaks, Cracker Barrel, KFC, Perkins, Quaker Steak&Lube, Ruby Tuesday, Wendy's, **lodging:** Econolodge, Holiday Inn Express, **other:** Home Depot, JC Penney, Sears, mall, **S food:** Gourmet Buffet, Panera Bread, **other:** $Tree, Indian Head camping (3mi), Lowes Whse, Office Depot, Walmart SuperCtr

**224** PA 54, to Danville, **N gas:** Shell/Subway/dsl/24hr, Sunoco, **food:** Country Kitchen, **lodging:** Quality Inn, **S food:** Friendly's, McDonald's, Mom's Dutch Kitchen, **lodging:** Best Western, Day's Inn, Hampton Inn, Key Motel, Red Roof Inn, **other:** H HOSPITAL

**219mm** rest area both lanes, full ♿ facilities, info, 🕿, 🍴, litter barrels, vending, petwalk

**215** PA 254, Limestonevill, **N gas:** Milton 32 Trkstp/dsl/rest./24hr, **S gas:** Petro/Shell/Iron Skillet/Subway/dsl/rest./24hr/@

**212b a** I-180 W, PA 147 S, to Muncy, Williamsport, **S gas:** Sunoco/24hr (1mi)

**210.5mm** Susquehanna River

**210b a** US 15, to Williamsport, Lewisburg, **S gas:** Citgo, **food:** Bonanza, **lodging:** Comfort Inn, Holiday Inn Express, **other:** H HOSPITAL, KOA (5mi)

**199** Mile Run Rd

**194mm** rest area/weigh sta both lanes, full ♿ facilities, 🕿, 🍴, litter barrels, vending, petwalk

**192** PA 880, to Jersey Shore, **N gas:** Citgo/dsl/24hr, **food:** Pit-Stop Rest., **S gas:** BP/dsl, **other:** H HOSPITAL, towing/truck repair

## INTERSTATE 80 CONT'D

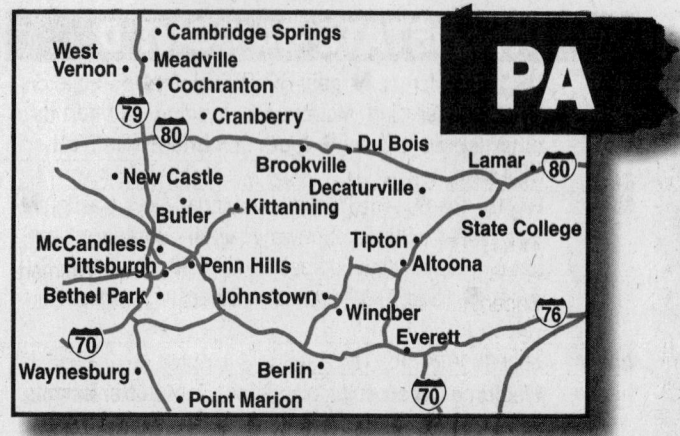

**185** PA 477, Loganton, **N gas:** BP, **other:** camping, **S food:** Twilight Diner, RV Winter SP (12mi)

**178** US 220, Lock Haven, **5 mi N gas:** KwikFill/dsl, Sheetz, **food:** Ruby Tuesday, Subway, **other:** Advance Parts, K-Mart, Lowes Whse, Walmart SuperCtr

**173** PA 64, Lamar, **N gas:** Pilot/Subway/dsl/scales/24hr, **food:** Cottage Rest., McDonald's, Perkins, **lodging:** Comfort Inn/rest., Hampton Inn, **S gas:** Citgo, ⊕FLYING J/Shell/Country Mkt/dsl/LP/scales, TA/Country Pride/Subway/dsl/scales/24hr/@, **food:** DQ, **other:** auto repair

**161** PA 26, US 220 S, to Bellafonte, **S other:** KOA, to PSU

**158** US 220 S, PA 150, to Altoona, Milesburg, **N gas:** BP/Subway, Bestway/dsl/rest./motel/24hr/@, Citgo/dsl, TA/dsl/scales/24hr/@, **food:** Buckhorn Rest., McDonald's, **lodging:** Holiday Inn, **S** st police

**147** PA 144, to Snow Shoe, **N gas:** Citgo/dsl/24hr, Exxon/dsl/repair/24hr, **food:** Snow Shoe Sandwich Shop, Subway, **other:** Hall's Foods, repair

**146mm** rest area both lanes, full ♿ facilities, 🅲, 🏚, litter barrels, vending, petwalk

**138mm** Moshanna River

**133** PA 53, to Philipsburg, Kylertown, **N gas:** KwikFill/motel/dsl/scales, Sunoco/LP, **food:** Roadhouse Rest., **other:** USPO, dsl repair, Black Moshannon SP (9mi), **S other:** Ⓗ HOSPITAL

**123** PA 970, to Shawville, Woodland, **S gas:** BP/dsl (1mi), Pacific Pride/dsl, **food:** Gio's BBQ (2mi), **other:** st police

**120mm** Susquehanna River, W Branch

**120** PA 879, Clearfield, **N gas:** Sapp Bros/dsl/rest./24hr/2, **lodging:** Econolodge, **S gas:** BP, Sheetz/24hr, Snappy's Gas, **food:** Arby's, Burger King, Dunkin Donuts, Dutch Pantry, KFC/Pizza Hut/Taco Bell, McDonald's, **lodging:** Comfort Inn, Day's Inn, Hampton Inn, Holiday Inn Express, Super 8, **other:** Ⓗ HOSPITAL, Lowes Whse, Walmart SuperCtr/Subway/gas

**111mm** highest point on I-80 east of Mississippi River, 2250 ft

**111** PA 153, to Penfield, **N** to Parker Dam, to SB Elliot SP, **S** Ⓗ HOSPITAL

**101** PA 255, Du Bois, **N gas:** Snappy's/24hr, **other:** camping, **S other:** Ⓗ HOSPITAL, st police, **1-2 mi S gas:** Sheetz/dsl/24hr, **food:** A&W/LJ Silver, Arby's, Bruster's, Burger King, Eat'n Park/24hr, Italian Oven, McDonald's, Maxwell St Rest., Perkins/24hr, Ponderosa, Red Lobster, Ruby Tuesday, Subway, Taco Bell, Valley Dairy Rest., Wendy's, **lodging:** Best Western, Hampton Inn, **other:** Big Lots, BiLo Foods, BonTon, $Tree, Goodyear/auto, JC Penney, Jo-Ann Fabrics, K-Mart, Lowes Whse, Old Navy, Rite Aid, Ross, Sears, Shop'n Save Foods, Staples, Walmart/drugs, mall

**97** US 219, to Brockway, Du Bois, **S gas:** Pilot/Arby's/dsl/24hr, Sheetz/dsl/24hr, **food:** Dutch Pantry Rest., **lodging:** Clarion, Holiday Inn Express, **other:** Ⓗ HOSPITAL, Freightliner, st police, **2 mi S food:** Hoss' Rest., Pizza Hut, **lodging:** Best Western, **other:** Advance Parts

**90** **N gas:** Du Bois Regional ✈

**87.5mm** rest area both lanes, full ♿ facilities, 🅲, 🏚, litter barrels, vending, petwalk

**86** PA 830, to Reynoldsville

**81** PA 28, to Brookville, to Hazen, **S** to Brookville, hist dist (2mi)

**78** PA 36, to Sigel, Brookville, **N gas:** ⊕FLYING J/Country Mkt/dsl/scales/LP/24hr, TA/BP/Taco Bell/dsl/scales/24hr/@, **food:** DQ, KFC, McDonald's, Pizza Hut, **lodging:** Howard Johnson, Super 8, **other:** NAPA, to Cook Forest SP, **S gas:** Country Fair/24hr, Sheetz, Sunoco, **food:** Arby's, Burger King, Plyler's Buffet, Subway, **lodging:** Budget Host, Day's Inn, Holiday Inn Express, Quality Inn, **other:** Chrysler/Dodge/Jeep, Family$

**73** PA 949, Corsica, **N other:** to Clear Creek SP, **S** USPO

**70** US 322, to Strattanville

**64** PA 66 S, to New Bethlehem, Clarion, **N** to Clarion U

**62** PA 68, to Clarion, **N gas:** BP/24hr, KwikFill/dsl, **food:** A&W/LJ Silver, Arby's, Eat'n Park, Hunan King, McDonald's, Perkins/24hr, Pizza Hut, RRR Roadhouse, Subway, Taco Bell, **lodging:** Comfort Inn, Hampton Inn, Holiday Inn/rest., Microtel, Quality Inn, Super 8, **other:** Ⓗ HOSPITAL, Advance Parts, Aldi Foods, $Tree, JC Penney, K-Mart, Radio Shack, Staples, Walmart SuperCtr, mall

**61mm** Clarion River

**60** PA 66 N, to Shippenville, **N gas:** Citgo, **other:** to Cook Forest SP, camping

**56mm** parking area/weigh sta both lanes

**53** to PA 338, to Knox, **N gas:** Satterlee Gas/dsl, **food:** BJ's Eatery, **other:** Countryside Crafts/Quilts, Wolf's Camping Resort, **S other:** Good Tire Service

**45** PA 478, to St Petersburg, Emlenton, **4 mi S other:** Golf Hall of Fame

**44.5mm** Allegheny River

**42** PA 38, to Emlenton, **N gas:** Exxon/Subway/dsl/24hr, Roady's Trkstp/dsl/rest./scales/24hr, **lodging:** Deluxe Motel, **other:** Gaslight RV Park, truck/RV repair

**35** PA 308, to Clintonville

**30.5mm** rest area both lanes, full ♿ facilities, 🅲, 🏚, litter barrels, vending, petwalk

**29** PA 8, to Franklin, Barkeyville, **N food:** Arby's, Burger King, King's Rest., **lodging:** Comfort Inn, Super 8, **other:** Freightliner, **S gas:** Citgo/dsl/24hr, KwikFill/dsl/scales//24hr, TA/BP/Subway/dsl/scales/24hr/@, **other:** to Slippery Rock U

**24** PA 173, to Grove City, Sandy Lake, **S other:** Ⓗ HOSPITAL, Grove City Coll, Wendell August Forge/gifts (3mi), truck repair

**19b a** I-79, **N** to Erie, **S** to Pittsburgh

## INTERSTATE 80 CONT'D

**N ↕ S**

| | |
|---|---|
| **15** | US 19, to Mercer, **N gas:** BP, PP/dsl, **food:** Charlie B's Rest., Burger King, McDonald's, **lodging:** Comfort Inn, **other:** st police, **2 mi S food:** Iron Bridge Rest., **other:** KOA (4mi) |
| **4b a** | PA 18, PA 60, to Sharon-Hermitage, New Castle, **N gas:** Sheetz, Sunoco/Subway/dsl/24hr, **lodging:** Comfort Inn, Holiday Inn Express, Quality Inn, Radisson, Super 8, **S food:** DQ, MiddleSex Diner/24hr, **other:** Auto Value Parts |
| **2.5mm** | Shenango River |
| **1mm** | Welcome Ctr eb, full ♿ facilities, 🚻, 🛉, litter barrels, vending, petwalk |
| **0mm** | Pennsylvania/Ohio state line |

## INTERSTATE 81

**N ↕ S**

| Exit # | Services |
|---|---|
| **233mm** | Pennsylvania/New York state line |
| **232mm** | Welcome Ctr/weigh sta sb, full ♿ facilities, 🚻, 🛉, litter barrels, petwalk |
| **230** | PA 171, Great Bend, **E gas:** Valero/24hr, **W gas:** Exxon/Arby's/dsl/24hr, Sunoco/dsl, **food:** Burger King, Dobb's Country Kitchen, Dunkin Donuts, McDonald's, Subway, **lodging:** Colonial Brick Motel, **other:** Big M Foods, Ford, Reddon's Drugs, Rob's Mkt |
| **223** | PA 492, New Milford, **W gas:** Gulf/dsl, Sunoco, Valero/24hr, **food:** Blue Ridge Motel, Green Gables Rest. |
| **219** | PA 848, to Gibson, **W gas:** Exxon/McDonald's/dsl/24hr, ✈FLYING J/Shell/Country Mkt/dsl/scales/24hr, **lodging:** Holiday Inn Express, st police |
| **217** | PA 547, Harford, **E gas:** Exxon/Subway/dsl/24hr, Getty's/dsl/rest./24hr |
| **211** | PA 92, Lenox, **E** Elk Mtn Ski Area, Shady Rest Camping (3mi), **W gas:** Lukoil/dsl/24hr, Shell/dsl, **food:** Bingham's Rest., Mamasita's Mexican, **other:** Lenox Drug |
| **209mm** | rest area sb, full ♿ facilities, 🚻, 🛉, litter barrel, vending, petwalk |
| **206** | PA 374, to Glenwood, Lenoxville, **E** to Elk Mountain Ski Resort |
| **203mm** | rest area nb, full ♿ facilities, 🚻, 🛉, litter barrels, vending, petwalk |
| **202** | PA 107, to Fleetville, Tompkinsville |
| **201** | PA 438, East Benton, **W gas:** Duchniks/dsl/repair |
| **199** | PA 524, Scott, **E gas:** BP/dsl, **W gas:** Exxon/Subway, **lodging:** Motel 81, **other:** to Lackawanna SP |
| **197** | PA 632, Waverly, **E other:** Mr Z's Foods, Rite Aid, **W gas:** Sunoco/24hr, **food:** Doc's Deli/24hr |
| **194** | US 6, US 11, to I-476/PA Tpk, Clarks Summit, **W gas:** Shell/dsl, Sheetz/24hr, Sunoco/dsl, **food:** Burger King, Damon's, Dino&Francesco's, Domino's, Dunkin Donuts, Euro Cafe, Friendly's, Krispy Kreme, Kyoto, McDonald's, New Century Chinese, Pizza Hut, Quizno's, Starbucks, Subway, Taco Bell, Waffle House, Wendy's, **lodging:** Comfort Inn, Econolodge, Hampton Inn, Nichols Village Inn, Ramada Inn, **other:** Advance Parts, $Bazaar, Kost Tire, Radio Shack, Rite Aid, Weis Foods |
| **191b a** | US 6, US 11, to Carbondale, **E gas:** Shell/dsl, Sheetz/dsl, **food:** A&W/LJ Silver, Applebees, Arby's, Burger King, Chicago Grill, China Wok, ChuckeCheese, |

**THROOP**

**SCRANTON**

| | |
|---|---|
| **191b a** | **Continued** Denny's, Don Pablo, Eastern Buffet, 5 Guys Cafe, Fresno's, La Tonalateca, McDonald's, Old Country Buffet, Olive Garden, Perkins, Pizza Hut, Red Lobster, Red Robin, Ruby Tuesday, Smokey Bones BBQ, Subway, TCBY, TX Roadhouse, TGIFriday, **lodging:** Days Inn, **other:** Aldi Foods, Borders Books, Firestone/auto, Harley-Davidson, Home Depot, Hyundai, JC Penney, Jo-Ann Crafts, K-Mart, Kohl's, Macy's, Marshall's, Michael's, PepBoys, PetsMart, Radio Shack, Sears/auto, Target, TJ Maxx, Walmart SuperCtr, William's Tires, mall, **W other:** to Anthracite Museum |
| **190** | Main Ave, Dickson City, **E food:** Charlie Brown's Steaks, Wendy's, **lodging:** Fairfield Inn, Residence Inn, **other:** Best Buy, Gander Mtn, Lowes Whse, Sam's Club/gas, Staples, **W other:** Toyota/Scion |
| **188** | PA 347, Throop, **E gas:** Sheetz/24hr, Sunoco/dsl, **food:** China World Buffet, McDonald's, Quizno's, Wendy's, **lodging:** Day's Inn, Sleep Inn, Super 8, **other:** Advance Parts, Big Lots, Kost Tire, PriceChopper Foods, st police, **W gas:** Exxon, **food:** Burger King, Dunkin Donuts, Friendly's, New China Star, Subway |
| **187** | to I-84, I-380, US 6 (no return from nb) |
| **186** | PA 435, Drinker St (from nb), **E gas:** Valero, **lodging:** Holiday Inn, **W gas:** Exxon |
| **185** | Central Scranton Expwy (exits left from nb), **W H** HOSPITAL |
| **184** | to PA 307, River St, **W gas:** Citgo, Lukoil, Shell, USA/Subway/dsl, **food:** Dunkin Donuts, **lodging:** Clarion, **other: H** HOSPITAL, Curves, CVS Drug, $Tree, Gerrity Foods |
| **182** | Davis St, Montage Mtn Rd, **E gas:** Exxon, **food:** Mugg's Rest., Ruby Tuesday, Stadium Club Rest., **lodging:** Comfort Suites, Courtyard, Hampton Inn, **W gas:** Sunoco, **food:** Dunkin Donuts, Waffle House, Wendy's, **other:** CVS Drug, USPO |
| **180** | to US 11, PA 502, to Moosic, (exits left from nb), **W gas:** BP/Subway/dsl/24hr |
| **178b a** | to US 11, Avoca, **E lodging:** Holiday Inn Express, **W gas:** Petro/Sunoco/dsl/rest./24hr/@ |
| **175b a** | PA 315 S, to I-476, Dupont, **E gas:** Exxon, Sunoco/24hr, **food:** Arby's, McDonald's, Perkins, **lodging:** Knight's Inn, Super 8, **other:** Chevrolet, **W gas:** Getty/repair, Pilot/Wendy's/dsl/scales/24hr, **lodging:** Quality Inn, **other:** Walmart |
| **170b a** | PA 115, PA 309, Wilkes-Barre, **E gas:** Exxon/Subway/dsl, Sunoco/dsl, **lodging:** Best Western, **other:** to Pocono Downs, **W gas:** BP, Sunoco/24hr, **food:** Burger King, Denny's, Friendly's, LJ Silver, Lonestar Steaks, McDonald's, Pizza Hut, Ruby Tuesday, TGIFriday, **lodging:** Day's Inn, Extended Stay Deluxe, Holiday Inn, Red Roof Inn, **other: H** HOSPITAL, BonTon, Chevrolet, Goodyear, Land Rover/Mercedes, Macy's, Sears/auto, mall |
| **168** | Highland Park Blvd, Wilkes-Barre, **W gas:** Sheetz/24hr, Sunoco, **food:** Applebees, Bob Evans, Chili's, Chuck-eCheese, Cracker Barrel, Grotto Pizza, Ground Round, King's Buffet, Logan's Roadhouse, McDonald's, Olive Garden, Outback Steaks, Panera Bread, Quizno's, Red Robin, Smokey Bones BBQ, Subway, Starbucks, Wendy's, **lodging:** Best Western, Days Inn, Hilton Garden, Ramada Inn, **other:** Barnes&Noble, Best Buy, BonTon, Circuit City, Firestone, JC Penney, Kohl's, Kost Tire, |

**PA**

## INTERSTATE 81 CONT'D

**N** ↕ **S**

**HAZLETON** (vertical)

| | |
|---|---|
| **168** | Continued<br>Lowes Whse, Macy's, Marshall's, Michael's, Office Depot, Old Navy, PetCo, Ross, Sam's Club/gas, Staples, Target, TJ Maxx, Walmart SuperCtr, Wegman's Foods |
| **165b a** | PA 309 S, Wilkes-Barre, **W gas:** BP/dsl, Gulf, **food:** Dunkin Donuts, Mark II Rest., McDonald's, Perkins, Taco Bell, **lodging:** Comfort Inn, Econolodge, **other:** Advance Parts, K-Mart, Rite Aid |
| **164** | PA 29, to Nanticoke, Ashley |
| **159** | Nuangola, **W gas:** BP/cafe/24hr |
| **157mm** | rest area/weigh sta sb, full ♿ facilities, vending, 🅲, 🚻, litter barrels, petwalk |
| **156mm** | rest area/weigh sta nb, full ♿ facilities, vending, 🅲, 🚻, litter barrels, petwalk |
| **155** | to Dorrance, **E gas:** Sunoco/dsl/24hr, **lodging:** Econolodge (2mi), **W gas:** Blue Ridge Plaza/dsl |
| **151b a** | I-80, E to Mountaintop, W to Bloomsburg |
| **145** | PA 93, W Hazleton, **E gas:** Exxon, Sunoco/dsl/24hr, Turkey-Hill, **food:** Bonanza, Damon's, Friendly's, Ground Round, McDonald's, Perkins, Pizza Hut, Taco Bell, Wendy's, **lodging:** Best Western (2mi), Comfort Inn, Fairfield Inn, Forest Hill Inn, Ramada Inn (2mi), **other:** Ⓗ HOSPITAL, Aldi Foods, Buick/Cadillac/GMC/Pontiac, Chrysler/Dodge/Jeep, $Tree, JC Penney, K-Mart, Mazda, st police, **W food:** Top of the 80's, **lodging:** Candlewood Suites, Hampton Inn |
| **143** | PA 924, to Hazleton, **W gas:** Exxon/dsl, Shell, Turkey-Hill, **food:** Subway, **lodging:** Residence Inn |
| **141** | PA 424, S Hazleton Beltway |
| **138** | PA 309, to McAdoo, **2 mi E lodging:** Pines Motel |
| **134** | to Delano |
| **132mm** | parking area/weigh sta both lanes |
| **131b a** | PA 54, Mahanoy City, **E other:** to Tuscarora/Locust Lake SP, **W gas:** Exxon, Shell/dsl |
| **124b a** | PA 61, to Frackville, **E food:** China Palace, Cracker Barrel, McDonald's, **lodging:** Holiday Inn Express, **other:** Big Lots, BonTon, K-Mart, Sears/auto, mall, **W gas:** Exxon, Hess, **food:** Anthony's Pizza, Dutch Kitchen, Subway, **lodging:** Econolodge, Granny's Motel, Rodeway Inn, **other:** Ⓗ HOSPITAL, Rite Aid, st police |
| **119** | High Ridge Park Rd, to Gordon, **E lodging:** Country Inn&Suites, **other:** Ⓗ HOSPITAL |
| **116** | PA 901, to Minersville, **E food:** 901 Rest. |
| **112** | PA 25, to Hegins, **W** camping |
| **107** | US 209, to Tremont |
| **104** | PA 125, Ravine, **E gas:** Exxon/Pizza Hut/Quizno's/dsl/24hr, **other:** Echo Valley Campgrd |
| **100** | PA 443, to Pine Grove, **E gas:** Exxon/dsl, **food:** Arby's, McDonald's, **lodging:** Comfort Inn, Econolodge, **W gas:** Shell/DQ/Subway/dsl/scales/24hr, Sunoco/dsl/24hr, **food:** Gooseberry Farms Rest., **lodging:** Hampton Inn, **other:** KOA (5mi) |
| **90** | PA 72, to Lebanon, **E gas:** Exxon/Subway, Hess/Blimpie/dsl, Love's/McDonald's/dsl/scales/24hr, **food:** DQ/Sbarro's, Wendy's, **lodging:** Best Western, Day's Inn, **other:** KOA (5mi), Lickdale Camping, st police, **W lodging:** Quality Inn |
| **89** | I-78 E, to Allentown |
| **85b a** | PA 934, to Annville, **2 mi W gas:** LukOil/dsl/24hr, **food:** Funck's Rest., **other:** to IndianTown Gap Nat Cem |

**HARRISBURG** (vertical)

| | |
|---|---|
| **80** | PA 743, Grantville, **E gas:** LukOil/dsl, **lodging:** Days Inn, Hampton Inn, **W gas:** Exxon/dsl, **food:** Winnner's Circle, **lodging:** Comfort Suites, Holiday Inn, **other:** camping, racetrack |
| **79mm** | rest area/weigh sta both lanes, full ♿ facilities, 🅲, vending, 🚻, litter barrels, petwalk |
| **77** | PA 39, to Hershey, **E gas:** Exxon/dsl, Pilot/Pizza Hut/dsl/scales/24hr, Valero, **lodging:** Country Hearth Inn, Country Inn&Suites, Howard Johnson, Scottish Inn, **other:** to Hershey Attractions, st police, **W gas:** Citgo/Subway/dsl, TA/dsl/scales/24hr/@, Wilco/Hess/Perkins/Stuckey's/dsl/24hr/@, **food:** McDonald's, **lodging:** Comfort Inn, Daystop, **other:** Goodyear |
| **72** | to US 22, Linglestown, **E gas:** Hess/dsl, Sunoco/dsl, **food:** Burger King, McDonald's, **lodging:** Holiday Inn Express, Quality Inn, **other:** Advance Parts, CVS Drug, Harley-Davidson, Jo-Ann Fabrics, Karn's Foods, Toyota/Scion, U-haul, **W food:** Country Oven Rest., **lodging:** Best Western, MainStay Suites, **other:** Ace Hardware |
| **70** | I-83 S, to York, ✈ |
| **69** | Progress Ave, **E gas:** 7-11, **food:** Cracker Barrel, Damon's, Macaroni Grill, Moe's SW Grill, Starbucks, **other:** Maggie Moo's, Susquehanna Shoppes, st police, **W gas:** Turkey Hill, **food:** Arby's, Steak House, YP Rest., **lodging:** Capital Plaza Inn, Red Roof Inn |
| **67b a** | US 22, US 322 W, PA 230, Cameron St, to Lewistown |
| **66** | Front St, **E** HOSPITAL, **W gas:** Exxon, Sunoco, **food:** Jade Buffet, McDonald's, Pizza Hut, Taco Bell, Wendy's, **lodging:** Day's Inn, Super 8 |
| **65** | US 11/15, to Enola, **1 mi E gas:** Sunoco/dsl/24hr, Tom's, **food:** Al's Pizza, China Taste, DQ, Dunkin Donuts, McDonald's, Subway, Summerdale Diner, Wendy's, **lodging:** Quality Inn, **other:** Advance Parts, $Tree, Fischer Parts, K-Mart, Radio Shack, Rite Aid |
| **61** | PA 944, to Wertzville |
| **59** | PA 581, to US 11, I-83, Harrisburg, **3 mi E food:** Bob Evans, Burger King, Friendly's, McDonald's, Wendy's, **lodging:** Comfort Inn, Hampton Inn, Holiday Inn |
| **57** | PA 114, to Mechanicsburg, **1-2 mi E food:** Arby's, Isaac's Rest., McDonald's, Pizza Hut, Red Robin, Taco Bell, **lodging:** Ramada Ltd |
| **52b a** | US 11, to I-76/PA Tpk, Middlesex, **E gas:** Exxon/Taco Bell/24hr, Sheetz/24hr, **food:** Hoss' Rest., **lodging:** Motel 6, **other:** Ⓗ HOSPITAL, Chrysler/Jeep, U-Haul, **W gas:** BP, Petro/dsl/24hr/@, ⊕ **FLYING J**/dsl/LP/rest./24hr/@, Pilot/Wendy's/dsl/24hr, |

## INTERSTATE 81 CONT'D

**N** ↕ **S**

**CARLISLE**

**52b a** Continued
Shell/dsl/scales, Sunoco, Universal/dsl, **food:** Arby's, Bob Evans, Carelli's Subs, Country Club Diner, Country Oven Rest, McDonald's, Middlesex Diner/24hr, Waffle House, **lodging:** Best Western, Hampton Inn, Holiday Inn, Howard Johnson, Quality Inn, Ramada Ltd, Rodeway Inn, Super 8, Travelodge, **other:** H HOSPITAL, Blue Beacon

**49** PA 74 (no EZ sb return) , **E food:** Red Robin, Starbucks, **other:** Kohl's, Michael's, Old Navy, PetsMart, Target, **W gas:** Citgo, **food:** Burger King, McDonald's, same as 48

**48** PA 74, York St (no EZ nb return) , **E food:** Coldstone Creamery, Red Robin, Starbucks, **other:** Aldi Foods, $Tree, Kohl's, Michael's, Old Navy, PetsMart, Rite Aid, Target, **W gas:** Gulf, Hess, KwikFill, **other:** Ford, **1 mi W food:** Burger King, McDonald's, Pizza Hut, Quizno's, Taco Bell, **other:** BonTon, CVS Drug, Lowes Whse, Radio Shack, Weis Foods

**47** PA 34, Hanover St, **E food:** Cracker Barrel, **lodging:** Sleep Inn, **W gas:** Gulf, **food:** Al's Pizza, Applebees, Bruster's, Chili's, Palace China, Panera Bread, Papa John's, Subway, Super Buffet, **other:** CVS Drug, Home Depot, Rite Aid, Ross, TJ Maxx, Walmart

**45** College St, **E gas:** BP/dsl, **food:** Alfredo Pizza, Arby's, Bonanza, Friendly's, Great Wall Chinese, McDonald's, **lodging:** Day's Inn, Super 8, **other:** K-Mart, Nell's Foods, Staples, tires, **W** HOSPITAL

**44** PA 465, to Plainfield, **E lodging:** Fairfield Inn, **other:** st police, **W gas:** Sheetz/24hr, **food:** Subway

**38mm** **rest area both lanes, full** ♿ **facilities,** 🕻, 🏕, **litter barrels, petwalk**

**37** PA 233, to Newville, **E** Pine Grove Furnace SP, **W** Col Denning SP

**29** PA 174, King St, **E gas:** Shippensburg TP/dsl/scales/24hr, **lodging:** Budget Host, **W gas:** Rutter's/dsl, **food:** Burger King, China House, Little Caesar's, McDonald's (2mi), Subway, Wendy's, **lodging:** Best Western, **other:** Ford, K-Mart, Walmart SuperCtr

**24** PA 696, Fayette St, **W gas:** Exxon/dsl, Pacific Pride

**20** PA 997, Scotland, **E gas:** Exxon/dsl, **food:** McDonald's, **lodging:** Comfort Inn, Super 8, **other:** Gander Mtn, JC Penney, Sears/auto, mall, **W gas:** BP/dsl, Sunoco/24hr, **lodging:** Sleep Inn

**17** Walker Rd, **W gas:** Sheetz/24hr, **food:** Bruster's, Fox's Pizza, Fuddrucker's, Jerry's Subs, Moe's SW Grill, Panera Bread, Quizno's, Red Robin, TGIFriday, **lodging:** Country Inn&Suites, **other:** Circuit City, Ford, Giant Foods/gas, Kohl's, Michael's, PetsMart, Staples, Target

**CHAMBERSBURG**

**16** US 30, to Chambersburg, **E gas:** Exxon, Fuel Ctr, Sheetz/24hr, **food:** Arby's, Best Way Pizza, Bro's Pizza, Chris's Country Kitchen, Hoss's Rest., KFC, Meadow's Custard, Montezuma Mexican, Perkins, Popeye's, Quizno's, Rita's Ice Cream, Ryan's, Waffle House, Wendy's, **lodging:** Days Inn, **other:** Aldi Foods, Curves, $Tree, Harley-Davidson, Jo-Ann Fabrics, Lowes Whse, Nissan/Toyota/Scion, Radio Shack, Walmart SuperCtr/Subway, st police, vet, **W gas:** Hess/dsl, **food:** Burger King, Copper Kettle, Hardee's, LJ Silver, McDonald's, Pizza Hut, Ponderosa, Ruby Tuesday, Starbucks, Taco Bell, **lodging:** Best Western, Country Inn&Suites, Sheraton,

**16** Continued
Travelodge, **other:** H HOSPITAL, Advance Parts, Auto-Zone, Lincoln/Mercury, Walgreens

**14** PA 316, Wayne Ave, **E food:** Bob Evans, Cracker Barrel, **lodging:** Fairfield Inn, Hampton Inn, Red Carpet Inn, **W gas:** BP, KwikFill, Sheetz, **food:** Applebee's, Arby's, China Wok, Dakota Steaks, Denny's, Mario's, Montezuma Mexican, New China, Papa John's, Pizza Hut, Quizno's, Red Lobster, Subway, Wendy's, **lodging:** Econolodge, Holiday Inn Express, Quality Inn, **other:** CVS Drug, $Tree, Giant Foods/gas, GNC, K-Mart, Staples, Weis Foods

**12mm** weigh sta sb

**10** PA 914, Marion

**7mm** weigh sta nb

**5** PA 16, Greencastle, **E gas:** TA/BP/dsl/rest./scales/24hr/@, Sunoco/grill/dsl, **food:** Arby's, McDonald's, Subway, **lodging:** Econolodge, Rodeway Inn, **other:** Whitetail Ski Resort, **W gas:** Exxon/dsl, **lodging:** Castle Green Motel/rest.

**3** US 11, **E gas:** Exxon, **food:** Bro's Pizza, **lodging:** Comfort Inn

**2mm** **Welcome Ctr nb, full** ♿ **facilities,** 🕻, 🏕, **litter barrels, vending, petwalk**

**1** PA 163, Mason-Dixon Rd, **W lodging:** Knight's Inn, **other:** Keystone RV Ctr

**0mm** Pennsylvania/Maryland state line, Mason-Dixon Line

## INTERSTATE 83

| Exit # | Services |
|---|---|
| **51b a** | I-83 begins/ends on I-81, exit 70. |

**50b a** US 22, Jonestown Rd, Harrisburg, **E gas:** Hess/dsl, Sunoco/dsl, USA, **food:** Applebees, Arby's, Atlanta Bread, Chef Wong's, Cold Stone Creamery, Colonial Park Diner, Domino's, El Rodeo Mexican, Gander Mountain, Gilligan's Grill, Hong Kong City, LJ Silver, McDonald's, Old Country Buffet, Olive Garden, Pizza Hut, Red Lobster, Red Robin, Starbucks, Subway, Taco Bell, Tonino's Pizza, Vocelli's Pizza, Wendy's, **other:** Aamco, Advance Parts, Best Buy, BonTon, Borders Books, Boscov's, Chevrolet, Circuit City, Coscto/gas, CVS Drug, Ford, Giant Foods, Goodyear/auto, Home Depot, K-Mart, Kohl's, Marshall's, Michael's, NAPA, NTB, Old Navy, PepBoys, PetCo, Radio Shack, Ross, Sears/auto, Super Petz, Target, Tires+, U-haul, Weis Foods, William's Tires/repair, mall, **W gas:** Capital, **food:** Dairy Queen, Dunkin Donuts, Friendly's, Gabriella's Italian, KFC, Roberto's Pizza, **other:** Rite Aid

**N** ↕ **S**

**HARRISBURG**

**48** Union Deposit Rd, **E gas:** Sunoco, **food:** Arby's, Burger King, Dunkin Donuts, Evergreen Chinese, Panera Bread, **lodging:** Hampton Inn, Sheraton, **other:** H HOSPITAL, Giant Foods, Rite Aid, Staples, mall, **W gas:** BP, **food:** Charlie Brown Steaks, ChuckeCheese, Great Wall Chinese, McDonald's, New China, OutBack Steaks, Rita's Ice Cream, Ruby Tuesday, Starbucks, Subway, Texas Roadhouse, TGIFriday, Waffle House, Wendy's, **lodging:** Country Inn&Suites, Fairfield Inn, Holiday Inn Express, **other:** Big Lots, Curves, $Tree, Hancock Fabrics, Lowes Whse, PriceRight Foods, Radio Shack, Tuesday Morning, Weis Foods

**47** (46b from nb), US 322 E, to Hershey, Derry St, **E...gas:** Hess Gas, **food:** Papa John's, **other:** Home Depot, PetsMart

## INTERSTATE 83 CONT'D

| | |
|---|---|
| **46a b** | I-283 S, to I-76/PA Tpk, **services off I-283 E gas:** Exxon/dsl, Sunoco, **food:** Bob Evans, Capitol Diner, Doc Holliday's Steaks, Domino's, Eat'n Park, McDonald's, Waffle House, **lodging:** Courtyard, EconoLodge, Holiday Inn, Howard Johnson, La Quinta, Red Roof Inn, Sheraton, Super 8, Travelodge, Wyndham, **other:** Buick, JC Penney, LandRover, Target, VW/Audi, **W gas:** Sunoco, **food:** Taco Bell, Wendy's, **lodging:** Best Western, Day's Inn, |
| **45** | Paxton St, **E gas:** Sheetz/dsl, **food:** Applebees, Burger King, Dunkin Donuts, Fuddrucker's, Isaac's Rest., Pizza Hut, Ruby Tuesday, Starbucks, Wendy's, **lodging:** Hilton Garden, Homewood Suites, Towneplace Suites, **other:** Bass Pro Shops, Barnes&Noble, JC Penney, Macy's, Mazda/Subaru/Toyota, Nissan, mall |
| **44b** | 17th St, 19th St, **E gas:** Sunoco, **food:** Bankok Thai Cuisine, Benihana Japanese, Dunkin Donuts, Hardee's, **other:** Advance Parts, AutoZone, Buick/GMC/Pontiac, Firestone/auto, Honda, Hyundai/Suzuki, Nissan, Pontiac, Tires+ |
| **44a** | PA 230, 13th St, Harrisburg, downtown, **W other:** Chevrolet, Saturn |
| **43** | 2nd St, Harrisburg, downtown, st capitol, **W lodging:** Crowne Plaza, Hilton, **other:** H HOSPITAL |
| **42.5mm** | Susquehanna River |
| **42** | Lemoyne |
| **41b** | Highland Park, **E gas:** Hess, Turkey Hill, **food:** Burger King, KFC, **E gas:** Sunoco, **food:** Ciao Pizza, **other:** Ace Hardware, Family$, Weis Foods |
| **41a** | US 15, PA 581 W, to Gettysburg |
| **40b** | New Cumberland, **W gas:** BP/dsl, **food:** JoJo's Pizza, McDonald's, New China, Sidoti's Italian, Subway, **other:** CVS Drug, $General |
| **40a** | Limekiln Rd, to Lewisberry, **E gas:** BP, Tom's, **food:** Bob Evans, Doc Holliday's Rest., Eat'n Park, McDonald's, Pizza Hut, **lodging:** Comfort Inn, Holiday Inn, Quality Inn, Rodeway Inn, **W gas:** Hess, **lodging:** Best Western, Motel 6, Travel Inn, **other:** vet |
| **39b** | I-76/PA Tpk |
| **39a** | PA 114, Lewisberry Rd, **E lodging:** Day's Inn, Keystone Inn, Red Carpet Inn |
| **38** | Reesers Summit |
| **36** | PA 262, Fishing Creek, **E gas:** Hess, **food:** Bruster's, Culhane's Steaks, Mamma's Pizza, **other:** CVS Drug, **W gas:** Citgo/dsl |
| **35** | PA 177, Lewisberry, **E food:** Hillside Café, **W gas:** Exxon, **food:** Francescos, Summit Rest., **lodging:** Alpine Inn |
| **34mm** | parking area/weigh sta sb |
| **34** | Valley Green (from nb), same as 33 |
| **33** | PA 392, Yocumtown, **E gas:** Hess/dsl, Rutter's, **food:** Alice's Rest., Burger King, Maple Donuts, McDonald's, NewBerry Diner, New China Buffet, 2 Bro's Pizza, **lodging:** Super 8, **other:** Family$, Radio Shack, Rite Aid, SuperFresh Food |
| **33mm** | parking area/weigh sta nb |
| **32** | PA 382, Newberrytown, **E gas:** Rutter's/Pizza Hut/dsl/24hr, **W gas:** Exxon/dsl |
| **28** | PA 295, Strinestown, **W gas:** Rutter's/24hr, **food:** 83 Diner, Wendy's |
| **24** | PA 238, Emigsville, **W gas:** Tom's, **food:** 4 Bro's Rest. |

| | |
|---|---|
| **22** | PA 181, N George St, **E gas:** Rutter's, **lodging:** Comfort Inn, Homewood Suites, **W** same as 21b |
| **21b a** | US 30, Arsenal Rd, to York, **E food:** Round-the-Clock, San Carlo's Rest., **lodging:** Day's Inn, Motel 6, Sheraton, **other:** Buick/GMC/Pontiac, **W gas:** Citgo, Rutter's/dsl, **food:** Arby's, Bob Evan's, Burger King, China Kitchen, Damon's, Denny's, DQ, El Rodeo Mexican, 5 Guys Burgers, Friendly's, Hardee's, Hooters, KFC, Logan's Roadhouse, LJ Silver, McDonald's, Nautilus Diner, Old Country Buffet, Olive Garden, Panera Bread, Pizza Hut, Popeye's, Quizno's, RipTide Seafood, Rita's Ice Cream, Ruby Tuesday, Smokey Bones BBQ, Subway, Taco Bell, TGIFriday, Wendy's, **lodging:** Best Western, Red Roof Inn, Super 8, Wingate Inn, **other:** Acura, Advance Parts, AutoZone, BJ's Whse, BMW, BonTon, Cadillac/Chevrolet, CVS Drug, Dodge, $General, Giant Foods/gas, Harley-Davidson, Lowes Whse, Macy's, NTB, Office Depot, Old Navy, PepBoys, PetsMart, Radio Shack, Ross, Staples, Subaru, TJ Maxx, Walmart SuperCtr, Weis Foods/gas, transmissions |
| **19** | PA 462, Market St, **E gas:** Hess, **food:** Applebees, Arby's, ChuckeCheese, Coldstone Creamery, DQ, Fuddruckers, Outback Steaks, Papa John's, Perkins, Rita's Ice Cream, Taco Bell, Tokyo Diner, Wendy's, **lodging:** Quality Inn, **other:** H HOSPITAL, Advance Parts, Aldi Foods, $General, $Tree, Giant Foods, Home Depot, Lowes Whse, Nissan, NTB, Sam's Club, Saturn, Walgreens, Walmart SuperCtr, Weis Foods |
| **18** | PA 124, Mt Rose Ave, Prospect St, **E gas:** Pacific Pride, Rutters, **food:** Al Dente Italian, Burger King, 5 Guys, Nino's Pizza, Pizza Hut, Sweet House Chinese, Uncle Nick's Diner, **lodging:** Budget Host, **other:** Curves, K-Mart, Nello Tire |
| **16b a** | PA 74, Queen St, **E gas:** Tom's, **food:** Baskin-Robbins/Dunkin Donuts, Bella's Italian, China Buffet, Cracker Barrel, Isaac's Rest., Ruby Tuesday, **lodging:** Country Inn&Suites, **other:** Giant Foods/gas, Lincoln/Mercury, **W gas:** LukOil, Sheetz, **food:** Infinito's Pizza, McDonald's, Pizza Hut/Taco Bell, Quizno's, S Yorke Diner, Subway, **other:** BonTon, CVS Drug, $General, $Tree, Jo-Ann Fabrics, Price Rite Foods, Tuesday Morning, Walgreens |
| **15** | S George St, I-83 spur into York, **W** H HOSPITAL |
| **14** | PA 182, Leader Heights, **E food:** Domino's, First Wok, Subway, **other:** vet, **W gas:** Rutter's/Pizza Hut, **food:** McDonald's, **lodging:** Holiday Inn Express, **other:** Rite Aid |
| **10** | PA 214, Loganville, **W food:** Elsie's Rest., Mamma's Pizza, **lodging:** Midway Motel, **other:** TrueValue, st police |
| **8** | PA 216, Glen Rock, **E lodging:** Rocky Ridge Motel, **W other:** Amish Farmers Mkt (2mi) |

## INTERSTATE 83 CONT'D

**4**   PA 851, Shrewsbury, **E**   **gas:** Tom's/dsl/24hr, **food:** Cracker Barrel, Ruby Tuesday, **lodging:** Hampton Inn, **other:** Home Depot, TrueValue, **W gas:** Exxon/dsl/24hr, **food:** Arby's, Chick-fil-A, Coachlight Rest., Emerald Garden Chinese, KFC/Taco Bell, McDonald's, Quizno's, Rita's Ice Cream, Starbucks, Subway, Szechuan Chinese, Wendy's, **other:** Advance Parts, Curves, $Tree, Giant Foods, GNC, Radio Shack, Sauble's Foods, Walmart SuperCtr

**2mm**   **Welcome Ctr nb, full** ♿ **facilities,** 📞**, vending,** 🏕 **litter barrels, petwalk**

**0mm**   Pennsylvania/Maryland state line

## INTERSTATE 84

| Exit # | Services |
|---|---|
| 54mm | Pennsylvania/New York state line, Delaware River |

**53**   US 6, PA 209, Matamoras, **N Welcome Ctr/both lanes, full** ♿ **facilities,** 📞**, vending,** 🏕 **litter barrels, petwalk, gas:** Exxon, Gulf, Go24/Taco Palace, Turkey Hill, **food:** Apple Grill, Stewart's Drive-Inn, **lodging:** Apple Valley Motel, **other:** AutoZone, PriceChopper Foods, Tri-State Camping, **S gas:** Mobil/dsl, **food:** McDonald's, Perkins, Roma Pizza, Subway, Wendy's, **lodging:** Best Western, Scottish Inn, **other:** Eckerd, Grand Union Foods, Home Depot, K-Mart, Lowes Whse, Staples, Walmart/SuperCtr, Riverbeach Camping

**46**   US 6, to Milford, **N gas:** Mobil/24hr, **2 mi S gas:** Citgo/dsl/24hr, Sunoco/dsl, **food:** Apple Valley Rest., **lodging:** Black Walnut B&B, Cliff Park Inn, Sherelyn Motel, Red Carpet Inn

**34**   PA 739, to Lords Valley, Dingmans Ferry, **S gas:** Mobil, Sunoco/Taco Xtra/dsl, **food:** Bruno's Pizza, China Dynasty, McDonald's, **other:** Curves, Family$, Mr Z's Foods, Rite Aid, USPO

**30**   PA 402, to Blooming Grove, **N** st police, to Lake Wallenpaupack

**26**   PA 390, to Tafton, **N** Exxon/dsl, to Lake Wallenpaupack, **S other:** to Promised Land SP

**26mm**   **rest area/weigh sta both lanes, full** ♿ **facilities,** 📞**, vending,** 🏕 **litter barrels, petwalk**

**20**   PA 507, Greentown, **N gas:** Exxon/dsl, Mobil/Sbway, **food:** John's Italian, **other:** Animal Park (5mi)

**17**   PA 191, to Newfoundland, Hamlin, **N gas:** Exxon/24hr, Howe's 84/dsl/24hr, **food:** Twin Rocks Rest., **lodging:** Comfort Inn/rest.

**8**   PA 247, PA 348, Mt Cobb, **N gas:** Gulf/dsl/24hr, **other:** golf, **S gas:** Mobil/dsl/24hr

**4**   I-380 S, to Mount Pocono

**2**   PA 435 S, to Elmhurst

**1**   Tigue St, **N lodging:** Holiday Inn, **S gas:** Mobil

**0mm**   I-84 begins/ends on I-81, exit 54.

## INTERSTATE 90

| Exit # | Services |
|---|---|
| 46mm | Pennsylvania/New York state line, **Welcome Ctr/weigh sta wb, full** ♿ **facilities,** 📞**, vending,** 🏕 **litter barrels, petwalk** |

**45**   US 20, to State Line, **N gas:** KwikFill/dsl/scales, **food:** McDonald's, **S gas:** BP/Subway/dsl, **lodging:** Red Carpet Inn, **other:** Niagara Falls Info, fireworks

**41**   PA 89, North East, **N gas:** Shell, **lodging:** Holiday Inn Express, Super 8, Vineyard B&B, **S** camping, winery

**37**   I-86 E, to Jamestown

**35**   PA 531, to Harborcreek, **N gas:** TA/BP/dsl/rest./scales/24hr/@, **food:** Pizza Hut, Subway, **lodging:** Rodeway Inn, **other:** Blue Beacon, dsl repair

**32**   PA 430, PA 290, to Wesleyville, **N gas:** Country Fair, st police, **S other:** camping

**29**   PA 8, to Hammett, **N gas:** Country Fair, **food:** Wendy's, **other:** Ⓗ HOSPITAL, **S lodging:** Travelodge, **other:** Peterbilt, dsl repair

**27**   PA 97, State St, Waterford, **N gas:** Country Fair/dsl/24hr, Kwikfill, **food:** Arby's, Barbato's Italian, Doc Holiday's Grill, McDonald's, **lodging:** Day's Inn, La Quinta, Red Roof Inn, Tallyho Inn, **other:** Ⓗ HOSPITAL, **S gas:** Pilot/Subway/dsl/scales/24hr, Shell/dsl, **lodging:** Quality Inn, Super 8, **other:** casino

**24**   US 19, Peach St, to Waterford, **N gas:** Country Fair, Delta Sonic, KwikFill, **food:** Applebee's, Bruster's, Burger King, Chick-fil-A, China Garden, ChuckeCheese, Cracker Barrel, Damon's, Eat'n Park, Golden Corral, Longhorn Steaks, McDonald's, Old Country Buffet, Panera Bread, Quaker Steak&Lube, Safari Grill, Steak'n Shake, Taco Bell, Texas Roadhouse, TGI Friday, Torero's Mexican, **lodging:** Courtyard, Hilton Garden, **other:** Ⓗ HOSPITAL, Advance Parts, Best Buy, Circuit City, Country Fair/deli, $Tree, Giant Eagle, Home Depot, Jo-Ann Fabrics, K-Mart, Kohl's, Lowes Whse, Marshall's, PetsMart, Sam's Club/gas, Staples, Target, VW, Walmart/auto, Wegman's Foods, **S gas:** BP, Country Fair, Shell/dsl, **food:** Bob Evans, Boston's Rest., **lodging:** Comfort Inn, Country Inn&Suites, Econolodge, Hampton Inn, Holiday Inn Express, Microtel, Residence Inn, **other:** waterpark

**22b a**   I-79, N to Erie, S to Pittsburgh, **3-5 mi N** services in Erie

**18**   PA 832, Sterrettania, **N gas:** Marathon/dsl/24hr, **food:** Burger King, **other:** Hill's Family Camping, to Presque Isle SP, **S lodging:** Quality Inn

**16**   PA 98, to Franklin Center, Fairview, **S other:** Follys Camping (2mi), Mar-Da-Jo-Dy Camping (5mi)

**9**   PA 18, to Girard, Platea, **N other:** Gulf/dsl repair, st police, **S lodging:** Green Roof Inn (2mi)

**6**   PA 215, to Albion, E Springfield, **N lodging, S gas:** Sunoco, lodging, repair

**3**   US 6N, to Cherry Hill, West Springfield, **N** lodging on US 20, **S gas:** BP/dsl/rest./scales/24hr

**2.5mm**   **Welcome Ctr/weigh sta eb, full** ♿ **facilities, info,** 📞**,** 🏕**, litter barrels, vending, petwalk**

**0mm**   Pennsylvania/Ohio state line

## INTERSTATE 95

| Exit # | Services |
|---|---|
| 51mm | Pennsylvania/New Jersey state line, Delaware River |

**51**   PA 32, to New Hope, **W** Washington Crossing Hist Park

**49mm**   **Welcome Ctr sb, full** ♿ **facilities, vending,** 📞**,** 🏕**, litter barrels, petwalk**

**49**   PA 332, to Yardley, Newtown, **W food:** Dunkin Donuts, **lodging:** Hampton Inn, **other:** Ⓗ HOSPITAL, to Tyler SP

**46b a**   US 1 to I-276, PA TPK, Langhorne, Oxford Valley, **E** Ⓗ HOSPITAL

## INTERSTATE 95 CONT'D

**44** US 1, PA 413, to Penndel, Levittown, **E gas:** Shell/dsl/24hr, **food:** Blue Fountain Diner, Cheeseburger Paradise, ChuckeCheese, Dunkin Donuts, Friendly's, Great American Diner, Hong Kong Pearl, Langhorn Ale House, Ming's Asian, Olive Garden, Panera Bread, Quizno's, Red Lobster, Ruby Tuesday, Subway, Tennessee BBQ, Wendy's, **other:** H HOSPITAL, Acura, Border's Books, Chrysler, Circuit City, Dodge, $Tree, Firestone/auto, Ford, Goodyear/auto, Harley Davidson, Honda, Hyundai/Suzuki, Jeep, Kia, K-Mart, Lincoln/Mercury, Lowes Whse, Marshalls, Mazda/Subaru, NTB, Office Depot, Sam's Club, Staples, Subaru, Target, TJ Maxx, VW/Volvo, Redner's Whse Mkt, **W gas:** LukOil, **food:** Denny's, McDonald's, **other:** Toyota/Scion, U-Haul

**40** PA 413, I-276, to Bristol Bridge, Burlington, **E gas:** Hess/dsl, **food:** Fish Factory Rest., Golden Eagle Diner/24hr, Pizza Hut, **other:** H HOSPITAL, Chevrolet, Walmart

**37** PA 132, to Street Rd, **W gas:** BP/dsl/24hr, Shell, Sunoco/dsl, **food:** Burger King, China Sun Buffet, Golden Corral, IHOP, KFC, McDonald's, Sonic, Tx Roadhouse, Wendy's, **other:** $Tree, Firestone, GNC, K-Mart, PepBoys, Radio Shack, Sav-a-Lot, 7-11, U-haul, WaWa

**35** PA 63, to US 13, Woodhaven Rd, Bristol Park, **W gas:** Liberty, **food:** Bob Evan's, Dunkin Donuts, Old Haven Pizza, Rita's Ice Cream, **lodging:** Hampton Inn, **other:** H HOSPITAL, Acme Foods, Hancock Fabrics, Home Depot, WaWa, **1 mi W gas:** BP, Exxon, LukOil, Sunoco/dsl, **food:** Arby's, Boston Mkt, Bugaboo Creek Steaks, Dave & Buster's, Dynasty Rest., International Buffet, KFC, McDonald's, Pizza Hut, Ruby Tuesday, Subway, Taco Bell, Uno, Wendy's, **other:** Big Lots, JC Penney, Marshall's, NTB, Sam's Club, Sears/auto, Steve&Barry's, SuperFresh Foods, Tires+, Walmart, mall

**32** Academy Rd, **W other:** H HOSPITAL, K-Mart

**30** PA 73, Cottman Ave, **W gas:** Sunoco

**27** Bridge St, **W gas:** BP, Exxon, LukOil, 7-11, **food:** Dunkin Donuts, **other:** H HOSPITAL, Rite Aid

**26** to NJ 90, Betsy Ross Brdg, **W gas:** BP, Hess, Sunoco/dsl, **food:** Applebees, Burger King, KFC, McDonald's, Wendy's, **other:** Home Depot, ShopRite Foods, Target

**25** Allegheny Ave, **W gas:** Sunoco, **other:** H HOSPITAL, WaWa

**23** Lehigh Ave, Girard Ave, **W gas:** Exxon, **food:** Applebees, Arby's, Cold Stone, Dunkin Donuts, Pizza Hut, Rita's Ice Cream, **other:** H HOSPITAL, AutoZone, CVS Drug, Family$, GNC, PepBoys, Radio Shack, Rite Aid, WaWa

**22** I-676, US 30, to Central Philadelphia, Independence Hall

**20** Columbus Blvd, Penns Landing, **E gas:** BP, LukOil, Sunoco, Xpress, **food:** Burger King, Boston Mkt, Dave&Buster's, ChartHouse Rest., ChuckeCheese, Enginehouse Rest, Grand King Buffet, Hooters, McDonald's, **lodging:** Comfort Inn, Hyatt Hotel (1mi), **other:** Best Buy, Home Depot, Lowes Whse, Marshall's, PepBoys, SavALot Foods, ShopRite Foods, Staples, Target, Walmart, WaWa

**19** I-76 E, to Walt Whitman Bridge, **W on Oregon Ave... gas:** Shell, **food:** Burger King, Church's Chicken, McDonald's, Subway, Wendy's, **lodging:** Holiday Inn, **other:** Aldi, K-Mart, to stadium

**17** PA 611, to Broad St, Pattison Ave, **W other:** H HOSPITAL, to Naval Shipyard, to stadium

**15mm** Schuykill River

**15** Enterprise Ave, Island Ave (from sb)

**14** Bartram Ave, Essington Ave (from sb)

**13** PA 291, to I-76 W (from nb), to Central Philadelphia, **E gas:** Exxon/dsl, **lodging:** Day's Inn, 4Points Sheraton, Guest Quarters, Hilton, Renaissance Inn, Residence Inn, Sheraton Suites, Westin Suites

**12** **E** Philadelphia Intl ✈, services same as 10

**10** PA 29, Bartrom Ave, (from nb), Cargo City, **E lodging:** Marriott, Renaissance Hotel, **W lodging:** Courtyard, Hampton Inn, Embassy Suites, Extended Stay America, Fairfield Inn, Microtel, Studio+

**9b a** PA 420, to Essington, Prospect Park, **E gas:** Sunoco/dsl, Valero/dsl, **food:** Denny's, Lehmans Rest., Philly Diner, **lodging:** Comfort Inn, Holiday Inn, Motel 6, Ramada Inn, Red Roof Inn, **other:** USPO, WaWa

**8** to Chester Waterfront, Ridley Park, **W on US 13...food:** Stargate Diner

**7** I-476 N, to Plymouth, Meeting

**6** PA 352, PA 320, to Edgmont Ave, **1 mi E on US 13... food:** McDonald's, Popeye's, **other:** Radio Shack, Walmart/Subway, **W lodging:** Days Inn

**5** Kerlin St (from nb) , **E gas:** BP, Gulf

**4** US 322 E, to NJ, to Barry Bridge, **W lodging:** Highland Motel

**3** (from nb, no EZ return) US 322 W, Highland Ave, **E gas:** Sunoco/dsl/24hr, **other:** Ford/Lincoln/Mercury, Goodyear

**2** PA 452, to US 322, Market St, **E gas:** LukOil, **W gas:** Exxon, **food:** McDonald's, Subway

**1** Chichester Ave, **E gas:** Sunoco, **W gas:** BP

**0mm** Pennsylvania/Delaware state line, **Welcome Ctr/weigh sta nb, full** ♿ **facilities,** 🚻, 🏞, **litter barrels, petwalk**

## INTERSTATE 99

| Exit # | Services |
|---|---|
| 67 | PA 322 **E gas:** Exxon |
| I-99 beings/ends on US 322 at St college | |
| 61 | US 322 W, Port Matilda, **E gas:** Best, **food:** Brother's Pizza, Subway, **lodging:** Port Matilda Hotel, **other:** USPO |
| 52 | PA 350, **E gas:** BP/Subway |
| 48 | PA 453, Tyrone, **W gas:** Choice, **food:** Burger King, **other:** H HOSPITAL, Rite Aid |

## INTERSTATE 99 CONT'D

**N ↕ S**

**ALTOONA**

**45** Tipton, Grazierville, **W food:** Pizza Hut (2mi), Sammy's BBQ, **other:** H HOSPITAL, DelGrosso's Funpark

**41** PA 865 N, Bellwood, **E** Ft Roberdeau HS, **W gas:** Martin Gen Store/dsl, Sheetz/dsl, **other:** DelGrosso's Funpark

**39** PA 764 S, Pinecroft, **W** Oak Spring Winery

**33** 17th St, Altoona, **E** same as 32, **W gas:** Sheetz/24hr, **food:** Hoss' Rest., Subway (2mi), **other:** Lowes Whse, Railroader Museum, U-haul

**32** PA 36, Frankstown Rd, Altoona, **E gas:** GetGo, **food:** Chili's, Panera Bread, **other:** Barnes&Noble, Best Buy, Boscov's, Giant Eagle Foods, GNC, Home Depot, Kohl's, Michael's, PetCo, Ross, Staples, Canoe Cr SP, **W gas:** BP, Sheetz, **food:** ChuckeCheese, Dunkin Donuts, Hong-Kong Buffet, McDonald's, Olive Garden, Papa John's, Perkins, Pizza Hut, Red Lobster, Subway, Uno, Wendy's, **lodging:** EconoLodge, Holiday Inn Express, Quality Inn, Super 8, **other:** H HOSPITAL, AutoZone, Cadillac, CVS Drug, Dodge, $Tree, Jo-Ann Fabrics, NAPA, Nissan, Rite Aid, Sav-a-Lot, Walgreens, USPO

**31** Plank Rd, Altoona, **E food:** Cici's Pizza, Friendly's, Hoss' Rest., Jethro's Rest., King's Rest., Krispy Kreme, Outback Steaks, Ruby Tuesday, TGIFriday, **lodging:** Comfort Inn, Ramada Inn, **other:** Circuit City, Firestone/auto, Radio Shack, Sam's Club/gas, Target, TJ Maxx, Walmart SuperCtr, st police, **W gas:** BP/Subway, **food:** Applebees, Arby's, Burger King, Cracker Barrel, Denny's, Eat'n Park, Hooters, KFC, Little Ceasars, LJ Silver, Ponderosa, Taco Bell, **lodging:** Hampton Inn, Motel 6, **other:** Advance Parts, BigLots, $General, Giant Eagle Foods, JC Penney, K-Mart, Macy's, PharMor, Sears/auto, Weis Foods

**28** US 22, to Ebensburg, Holidaysburg

**23** PA 36, PA 164, Roaring Spring, Portage, **E gas:** GetGo/dsl, Sheetz/24hr, Turkey Hill, **food:** Backyard Burger, **other:** H HOSPITAL, Walmart SuperCtr, truck repair

**15** Claysburg, King, **W food:** Subway, gas

**10** to Imler, **W** gas, food, Blue Knob SP (8mi)

**7** PA 869, Osterburg, St Clairsville, **W** gas, food, Blue Knob SP

**3** PA 56, Johnstown, Cessna, **E other:** truck parts

**1** I-70/76. I-99 begins/ends on US 220., **E gas:** BP/dsl, Pacific Pride, Sheetz/dsl, **food:** Arena Rest., Denny's, Ed's Steaks, Hoss' Rest, LJ Silver, McDonald's, Pizza Hut, Subway, Wendy's, **lodging:** Best Western, Budget Host, Hampton Inn, Hillcrest Motel, Holiday Inn Express, Quality Inn, Relax Inn, Super 8

## INTERSTATE 476

**E ↕ W**

| Exit # | Services |
|---|---|
| 131 | US 11, US 6. I-476 begins/ends on I-81, services same as I-81, exit 194. |
| 122 | Keyser Ave, Old Forge, Taylor |
| 121mm | toll plaza |
| 115 | I-81, PA 315, Wyoming Valley, Pittston, **W gas:** Mobil, Pilot/Wendy's/dsl/scales/24hr, Sunoco, **food:** Arby's, |

**PA**

**PHILADELPHIA**

**115** Continued McDonald's, Perkins, **lodging:** Knight's Inn, Ramada Inn, **other:** Chevrolet

**112mm** toll plaza

**105** PA 115, Wilkes-Barre, Bear Creek, **E gas:** BP, Exxon, PSC

**97mm** parking areas both lanes

**95** I-80, PA 940, Pocono, Hazleton, **W gas:** BP/24hr, Texaco, WaWa, **food:** A&W/LJ Silver, Arby's, Denny's, Gino's Pizza, McDonald's, **lodging:** Comfort Inn, CountryPlace Inn, Day's Inn, Ramada Inn, Split Rock Resort

**90mm** parking area sb

**86mm** **Hickory Run Service Plaza both lanes...gas:** Sunoco/dsl, **food:** Breyer's, McDonald's, hot dogs

**74** US 209, Mahoning Valley, Lehighton, Stroudsburg, **W gas:** Shell/Subway/dsl, **food:** Trainer's Inn Rest., **lodging:** Country Inn&Suites, Hampton Inn

**71mm** Lehigh Tunnel

**56** I-78, US 22, PA 309, Lehigh Valley, **E gas:** Gulf, **food:** Dunkin Donuts, Quizno's, Red Robin, Trivet Diner, Wendy's, **lodging:** Comfort Inn, Day's Inn, McIntosh Inn, **other:** BMW, CVS Drug, Infiniti, Jaguar, K-Mart, Land Rover, Staples, **W on US 22...gas:** Mobil, Sunoco, **food:** Chris Rest., Parma Pizza, **lodging:** Best Western, **other:** CVS Drug

**56mm** **Allentown Service Plaza both lanes...gas:** Sunoco/dsl, **food:** Big Boy, Hershey's Ice Cream, Pizza Hut, Roy Rogers

**44** PA 663, Quakertown, Pottstown, **E gas:** BP, Mobil/dsl, **food:** Avanti Grill, Faraco's Pizza, **lodging:** Best Western (3mi), Comfort Suites, Hampton Inn, Holiday Inn Express, Rodeway Inn, **other:** H HOSPITAL

**37mm** parking area sb

**31** PA 63, Lansdale, **E gas:** Exxon, Lukoil, WaWa **food:** Bones Grill, **lodging:** Best Western, Courtyard, Lansdale Motel, Residence Inn, **other:** H HOSPITAL

**20** Germantown Pike W, to I-276 W, PA Tpk W

**19** Germantown Pike E

**18b a** (18 from sb), Conshohocken, Norristown, **E gas:** Lukoil, Sunoco, **food:** Baja Fresh, Burger King, Domino's, LoneStar Steaks, Maria's Pizza, McDonald's, Outback Steaks, Salad Works, Starbucks, **other:** Eckerd, Genuradi's Foods, Marshall's, **E on Chemical rd...food:** Cracker Barrel, Ruby Tuesday, **lodging:** Hampton Inn, **other:** Barnes&Noble, Best Buy, Giant Foods, Lowes Whse, Office Depot, PetsMart, Ross, Target, **W food:** Papa John's, Uno Pizzaria, Wendy's, **other:** BJ's Whse, Circuit City, Ford, Home Depot, Honda, Michael's, Nissan, Toyota

**16b a** (16 from sb), I-76, PA 23, to Philadelpia, Valley Forge

**13** US 30, **E gas:** Shell, **food:** Campus Pizza, Winger's, **other:** H HOSPITAL, Fresh Grocer, Radnor Drugs, Staples, USPO, Villanova Hardware, to Villanova U

**9** PA 3, Broomall, Upper Darby, **E food:** Barnaby's Rest., **other:** H HOSPITAL, PathMark Foods, carwash

**5** US 1, Lima, Springfield, **E food:** Mesa Mexican, Salad Central, **other:** Circuit City, Jo-Ann Fabrics, Marshall's, Old Navy

**3** Baltimore Pike, Media, Swarthmore, **E** H HOSPITAL, Swarthmore Coll

**1** McDade Blvd, **E gas:** Exxon, **food:** Dunkin Donuts, KFC, McDonald's

**0mm** I-476 begins/ends on I-95, exit 7.

## INTERSTATE 95

| Exit # | Services |
|---|---|
| **43mm** | Rhode Island/Massachusetts state line |
| **30** (42) | East St, to Central Falls, **E** **food:** Dunkin Donuts, Subway |
| **29** (41) | US 1, Cottage St, **W** **food:** d'Angelo's, **other:** Firestone |
| **28** (40) | RI 114, School St, **E** **gas:** Sunoco, **other:** H HOSPITAL, Tire Pro, to hist dist |
| **27** (39) | US 1, RI 15, Pawtucket, **W** **gas:** Shell/repair, Sunoco/dsl/24hr, **food:** Burger King, Dunkin Donuts, Ground Round, **lodging:** Comfort Inn, **other:** H HOSPITAL |
| **26** (38) | RI 122, Lonsdale Ave (from nb) , **E other:** U-Haul |
| **25** (37) | US 1, RI 126, N Main St, Providence, **E** **gas:** Hess, Shell, **food:** Chili's, Dunkin Donuts, Gregg Rest., Subway, **other:** HOSPITAL, PepBoys, Rite Aid, Shaw's Foods, Walgreens, **W** **gas:** Gulf/dsl, Hess, **food:** Burger King, Chelo's Italian, **other:** AAA, Aamco |
| **24** (36.5) | Branch Ave, Providence, downtown, **W** **gas:** Mobil, **food:** Wendy's, **other:** Stop&Shop Foods, Walmart |
| **23** (36) | RI 146, RI 7, Providence, **E** **gas:** Mobil/dsl, **lodging:** Marriott, **other:** HOSPITAL, **W** USPO |
| **22** (35.5) | US 6, RI 10, Providence, **E** **food:** Cheesecake Factory, Dave&Buster's, **other:** JC Penney, Macy's, Nordstrom's, mall |
| **21** (35) | Broadway St, Providence, **E lodging:** Hilton |
| **20** (34.5) | I-195, to E Providence, Cape Cod |
| **19** (34) | Eddy St, Allens Ave, to US 1 (from sb) , **W** **food:** Wendy's, Dunkin Donuts, H HOSPITAL |
| **18** (33.5) | US 1A, Thurbers Ave, **W** **gas:** Shell, **food:** Burger King, **other:** HOSPITAL |
| **17** (33) | US 1 (from sb) Elmwood Ave, **W other:** Cadillac, Tires Whse |
| **16** (32.5) | RI 10, Cranston, **W** Williams Zoo/park |
| **15** (32) | Jefferson Blvd, **E** **gas:** Getty/dsl, Mobil, **food:** Bickford's, Bugaboo Steaks, Dunkin Donuts, **lodging:** Courtyard, Fairfield Inn, Motel 6, **W other:** Colony RV Ctr/Ford Trucks, Ryder |
| **14** (31) | RI 37, Post Rd, to US 1, **W** **gas:** Shell, Sunoco **food:** Burger King, Krispy Kreme, **other:** HOSPITAL, CVS Drug, Lincoln/Mercury |
| **13** (30) | 1 mi **E** TF Green Airport, **gas:** Exxon, Shell, **food:** Chelo's Grill, Legal Seafood, **lodging:** Best Western, Comfort Inn, Hampton Inn, Hilton Garden, Holiday Inn Express, Homestead Suites, Homewood Suites, MainStay Suites, Quality Suites, Radisson, Residence Inn |
| **12b** (29) | RI 2, I-295 N (from sb) |
| **12a** | RI 113 E, to Warwick, **E** **gas:** Shell/Dunkin Donuts/dsl, **lodging:** Crowne Plaza Hotel, **other:** Lowes Whse, **W** **gas:** Sunoco, **food:** ChuckeCheese, Wendy's, other Kohl's, Sears/auto, Walmart/Subway, mall |
| **11** (29) | I-295 N (exits left from nb), to Woonsocket |
| **10b a** (28) | RI 117, to Warwick, **W** HOSPITAL |
| **9** (25) | RI 4 S, E Greenwich |
| **8b a** (24) | RI 2, E Greenwich, **E** **gas:** Shell/dsl, **food:** China Buffet, Coldstone Creamery, Dunkin Donuts, McDonald's, Outback Steaks, Panera Bread, Ruby Tuesday, TX Roadhouse, **lodging:** Extended Stay America, **other:** Dave's Mkt, Walgreens, **0-2 mi W** **gas:** Citgo, Sunoco/dsl, **food:** Applebee's, Boston Mkt, Denny's, KFC, Olive Garden, PapaGino's, Smokey Bones, Starbucks, TGI Friday, Wendy's, **lodging:** Comfort Suites, SpringHill Suites, **other:** Acura/BMW, Aldi Foods, Arlington RV Ctr, Barnes & Noble, Best Buy, Boston Mkt, GNC, Goodyear/auto, Honda/Volvo, Hyundai, |

## INTERSTATE 95 CONT'D

**8b a** Continued
Jo-Ann Fabrics, Lexus/Infiniti, Lowe's Whse, Mazda/Hyundai, Mercedes, Michael's, Mitsubishi, Nissan, Pep-Boys, Pontiac/GMC/VW, Radio Shack, Sam's Club, Saturn, Shaw's Foods, Stop&Shop Foods, mall

**7** (21) to Coventry, **E gas:** Mobil/dsl, **W food:** Applebee's, Chen's Buffet, Cilantro Mexican, Cracker Barrel, Denny's, Dunkin Donuts, Honeydew Doughnuts, Quizno's, Subway, Wendy's, **lodging:** Fairfield Inn, Hampton Inn, Residence Inn, **other:** BJ's Whse/gas, CVS Drug, Home Depot, Walmart SuperCtr, auto repair

**6a** (20) Hopkins Hill Rd, **W food:** Dunkin Donuts, **other:** park&ride

**6** (18) RI 3, to Coventry, **W gas:** Getty/dsl, Shell/dsl/24hr, Sunoco/dsl/repair, **food:** Dunkin Donuts, Gentleman Farmer Diner, Tim Horton, Venus Pizza, **lodging:** Best Western, Super 8, **other:** Curves, True Value

**5b a** (15) RI 102, **W gas:** R.I.'s Only Trkstp/dsl/scales/24hr, **lodging:** Classic Motor Lodge

**10mm** rest area/weigh sta both lanes

**4** (9) RI 3, to RI 165 (from nb), Arcadia, **W** Arcadia SP, camping

**3b a** (7) RI 138 E, to Kingston, Wyoming, **E food:** Dunkin Donuts, McDonald's, Tim Horton, Wendy's, **other:** VET, Rite Aid, Stop&Shop Food/gas, **W gas:** Gulf, Hess, Mobil, **food:** Subway, Village Pizza, Woodriver Inn Rest., **lodging:** 95 Motel & Grill, Sun Valley Inn/rest., **other:** Curves, CVS Drug, Family$, NAPA, USPO

**6mm** Welcome Ctr nb, full facilities, litter barrels, vending, petwalk

**2** (4) Hopkinton

**1** (1) RI 3, to Hopkinton, Westerly, **E other:** H HOSPITAL, to Misquamicut SP, RV camping, beaches

**0mm** Rhode Island/Connecticut state line, motorist callboxes begin nb/end sb

## INTERSTATE 295 - PROVIDENCE

**Exit #** Services

**2b a** (4) I-95, N to Boston, S to Providence. I-295 begins/ends on I-95, exit 4 in MA. Exits 2-1 are in MA.

**1b a** (2) US 1, **E food:** Chicago Grill, ChuckeCheese, Friendly's, Hearth'n Kettle, Longhorn Steaks, 99 Rest., Panera Bread, Papagino's Italian, TGIFriday, **other:** Best Buy, BJ's Whse, Borders, Circuit City, CVS Drug, $Tree, GMC/Pontiac, Jo-Anne, Lowe's Whse, Marshalls, Michael's, Office Depot, Old Navy, PetsMart, Sears/auto, Staples, Stop&Shop, Target, TJMaxx, Town fair Tire, Walmart, mall, **W gas:** Emerald/dsl, Gulf, Shell/Tim Horton, **food:** Applebee's, Dunkin Donuts, **lodging:** Holiday Inn Express, Pineapple Inn, Super 8, **other:** Nissan, Toyota

**0mm** Rhode Island/Massachusetts state line. Exits 1-2 are in MA.

**11** (24) RI 114, to Cumberland, **E gas:** Shell/dsl, Sunoco, **food:** Dunkin Donuts, Honeydew Donuts, **other:** CVS Drug, Dave's Foods, **W food:** J's Deli, Saki's Pizza/subs,

**11** (24) Continued
**other:** Tedeschi Foods, Diamond Hill Mkt, Diamond Hill SP

**10** (21) RI 122, **E gas:** Gulf, Lukoil/dsl, **food:** Burger King, Dunkin Donuts, Jacky's Rest., Jim's Deli, McDonald's, Ronzio Pizza, **W food:** Chicken Power, Curves, Fortune House Chinese, Subway, **other:** Ace Hardware, CVS Drug, Rite Aid, Seabra Foods

**20mm** Blackstone River

**19.5mm** weigh sta/rest area (full facilities) both lanes

**9b a** (19) RI 146, Woonsocket, Lincoln, **2 mi W gas:** Sunoco, Valero/dsl, **food:** Dunkin Donuts, **lodging:** Traveler's Motel, **other:** Chrysler, Honda, Subaru

**8b a** (16) RI 7, N Smithfield, **E food:** Euro Rest., **W gas:** 7-11/gas, Shell, **food:** Dunkin Donuts, House of Pizza, Parentes Rest., Roost House Rest., **lodging:** Comfort Suites, Hampton Inn, Quality Inn, **other:** Smith-Appleby House

**7b a** (13) US 44, Centerdale, **E gas:** Hess, Mobil, **food:** Isabella's Deli, Orlando Rest., **other:** H HOSPITAL, Advance Parts, NAPA, CarQuest, 4 Seasons RV Ctr, auto repair, **W gas:** Citgo, Exxon/dsl, Mobil, Shell, **food:** A&W, Applebee's, Burger King, Chelo's Grill, Chicago Grill, Chili's, D'angelo's, Dominos, Dunkin Donuts, KFC/Taco Bell, McDonald's, Panera Bread, PapaGino's, Subway, Tin-Tsin Chinese, Wendy's, **other:** Barnes&Noble, Curves, CVS Drug, Home Depot, Kohl's, Michael's, Old Navy, Radio Shack, Rite Aid, Staple's, Stop&Shop Foods, Target, TJ Maxx, to Powder Mill Ledges WR

**6b c** (10) US 6, to Providence, **E gas:** Mobil, 7-11, Shell, **food:** Atwood Grill, Burger King, China Jade, Dunkin Donuts, KFC, McDonald's, Ruby Tuesday, Subway, Wendy's, **other:** AutoZone, Chevrolet/Buick, CVS Drug, General Tire, Home Depot, Honda, Kia, Office Depot, PetsMart, Pontiac/GMC, Saab, Shaw's Foods, Stop&Shop, USPO

**6a** (9) US 6 E Expswy, **E food:** McDonald's, Ruby Tuesday, Subway, **other:** Home Depot, PetsMart

**5** (8) RI Resource Recovery Industrial Park

**4** (7) RI 14, Plainfield Pk, **W gas:** Mobil/dsl/24hr, **food:** Dunkin Donuts

**3b a** (4) rd 37, Phenix Ave, **E** TF Green Airport

**2** (2) RI 2 S, to Warwick, **E food:** Chicago Grill, Longhorn Steaks, **other:** JC Penney, Macy's, Marshalls, Walgreens, mall, **W gas:** Citgo, Mobil, Sunoco, **food:** Burger King, Chili's, Chipotle Mexican, ChuckeCheese, Dunkin Donuts, HomeTown Buffet, McDonald's/playplace, Olive Garden, On-the-Border, Panera Bread, Starbucks, Taco Bell, Tim Horton, Tuesday Morning, Subway, Wendy's, **other:** Barnes&Noble, Best Buy, Dodge/Subaru, Home Depot, Jaguar, Kohl's, Price Rite Foods, PetsMart, Rite Aid, Sam's Club, Sears/auto, Staples, Subaru, Target, TJMaxx, TownFair Tire, Walmart, mall

**1** (1) RI 113 W, to W Warwick, same as 2

**0mm** I-295 begins/ends on I-95, exit 11.

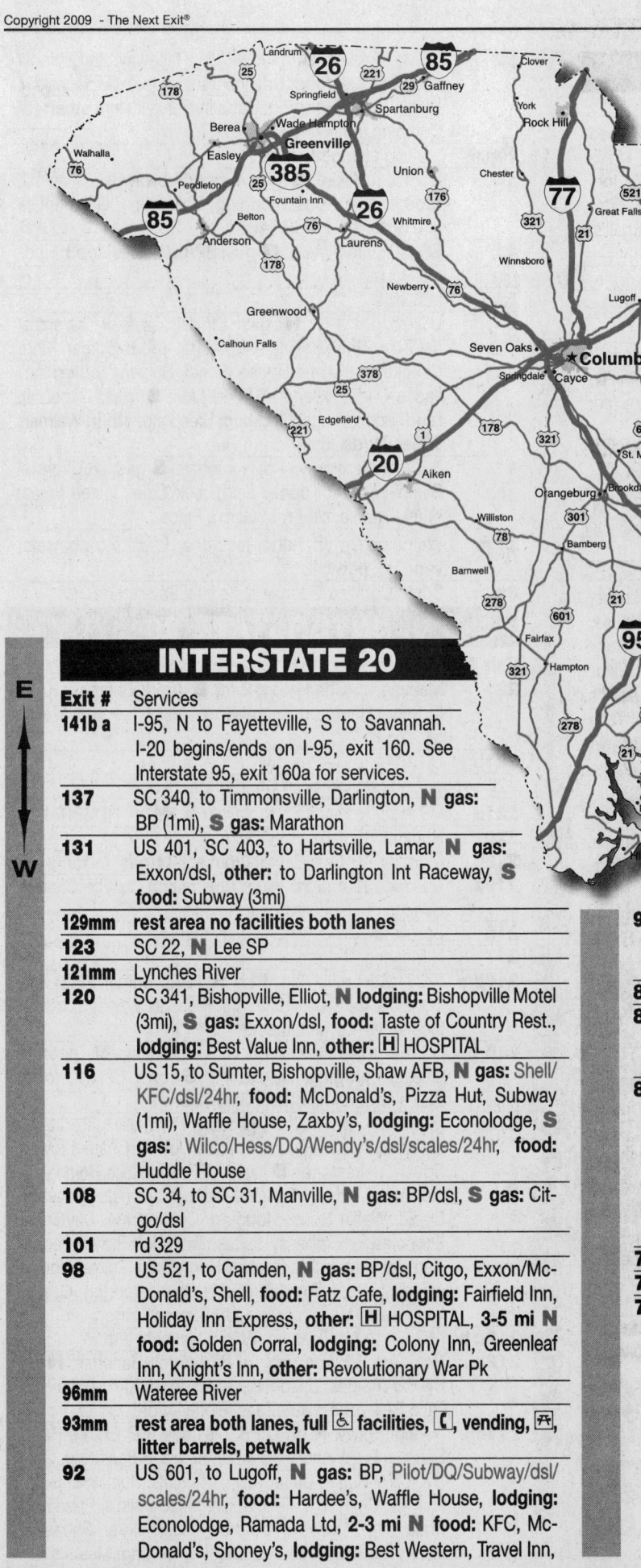

E
↑
↓
W

## INTERSTATE 20

| Exit # | Services |
|---|---|
| 141b a | I-95, N to Fayetteville, S to Savannah. I-20 begins/ends on I-95, exit 160. See Interstate 95, exit 160a for services. |
| 137 | SC 340, to Timmonsville, Darlington, N gas: BP (1mi), S gas: Marathon |
| 131 | US 401, SC 403, to Hartsville, Lamar, N gas: Exxon/dsl, other: to Darlington Int Raceway, S food: Subway (3mi) |
| 129mm | rest area no facilities both lanes |
| 123 | SC 22, N Lee SP |
| 121mm | Lynches River |
| 120 | SC 341, Bishopville, Elliot, N lodging: Bishopville Motel (3mi), S gas: Exxon/dsl, food: Taste of Country Rest., lodging: Best Value Inn, other: H HOSPITAL |
| 116 | US 15, to Sumter, Bishopville, Shaw AFB, N gas: Shell/KFC/dsl/24hr, food: McDonald's, Pizza Hut, Subway (1mi), Waffle House, Zaxby's, lodging: Econolodge, S gas: Wilco/Hess/DQ/Wendy's/dsl/scales/24hr, food: Huddle House |
| 108 | SC 34, to SC 31, Manville, N gas: BP/dsl, S gas: Citgo/dsl |
| 101 | rd 329 |
| 98 | US 521, to Camden, N gas: BP/dsl, Citgo, Exxon/McDonald's, Shell, food: Fatz Cafe, lodging: Fairfield Inn, Holiday Inn Express, other: H HOSPITAL, 3-5 mi N food: Golden Corral, lodging: Colony Inn, Greenleaf Inn, Knight's Inn, other: Revolutionary War Pk |
| 96mm | Wateree River |
| 93mm | rest area both lanes, full ♿ facilities, 📞 vending, 🍴, litter barrels, petwalk |
| 92 | US 601, to Lugoff, N gas: BP, Pilot/DQ/Subway/dsl/scales/24hr, food: Hardee's, Waffle House, lodging: Econolodge, Ramada Ltd, 2-3 mi N food: KFC, McDonald's, Shoney's, lodging: Best Western, Travel Inn, |

| 92 | Continued other: Ace Hardware, Chrysler/Dodge/Jeep, Ford/Lincoln/Mercury, Toyota, S Camden RV Park (1mi) |
|---|---|
| 87 | SC 47, to Elgin, N gas: BP/dsl, Shell/dsl |
| 82 | SC 53, to Pontiac, N gas: Shell, loding: Value Place Hotel, other: Harley-Davison, Pontiac, S other: Clothing World Outlet |
| 80 | Clemson Rd, N gas: Exxon/dsl, 76/Circle K, Shell/Bojangles/dsl, food: Brick Oven Pizza, China Garden, Coldstone Creamery, D's Rest, Groucho's Deli, Maurice's BBQ, McDonald's, Santa Fe Mexican, Sumo Japanese, Waffle House, Zaxby's, lodging: Hampton Inn, Holiday Inn Express, other: CVS Drug, S food: Wendy's, other: Chevrolet, Hyundai |
| 76b | Alpine Rd, to Ft Jackson, N Sesquicentennial SP |
| 76a | (76 from eb), I-77, N to Charlotte, S to Charleston |
| 74 | US 1, Two Notch Rd, to Ft Jackson, N gas: Kangaroo, Mobil/dsl, Shell/Circle K, food: Arby's, Burger King, Chili's, Fazoli's, Hooters, Hops Grill, IHOP, Lizard's Thicket, Outback Steaks, Ryan's, Texas Roadhouse, Waffle House, lodging: AmeriSuites, Best Western, Baymont Inn, Comfort Inn, Fairfield Inn, Hampton Inn, Holiday Inn, InTown Suites, Jameson Suites, La Quinta, Microtel, Motel 6, Quality Inn, Ramada Inn, Red Roof Inn, Travelodge, Wingate Inn, other: Home Depot, USPO, U-Haul, to Sesquicentennial SP, S gas: Hess/dsl, Exxon, Shell/dsl, food: Applebees, Bojangles, |

SC

E
W
COLUMBIA

## INTERSTATE 20 CONT'D

| | |
|---|---|
| **74** | Continued<br>Capt D's, Church's, Crabhouse, Hardees, Honeybaked Ham, Longhorn Steaks, McDonald's, Monterrey Mexican, Schlotzky's, Splendid China, **lodging:** Day's Inn, **other:** Advance Parts, Best Buy, Dillard's, Family$, Firestone/auto, K-Mart, Lowes Whse, Macy's, Marshall's, NAPA, Sears/auto, Staples, mall |
| **73b** | SC 277 N, to I-77 N |
| **73a** | SC 277 S, to Columbia, **S** Ⓗ HOSPITAL |
| **72** | SC 555, Farrow Rd |
| **71** | US 21, N Main, to Blythewood, Columbia, **N gas:** BP/dsl, TravelPlaza/Pizza Hut/Subway/dsl/scales/24hr/@, Save-a-Ton/dsl, **food:** McDonald's, **lodging:** Day's Inn, **other:** truckwash, tires, **S gas:** Shell |
| **70** | US 321, Fairfield Rd, **S gas:** Exxon, ⊕FLYING J/Conoco/Hardee's/dsl/LP/24hr/@, **lodging:** Super 8 |
| **68** | SC 215, Monticello Rd, to Jenkinsville, **N gas:** Exxon/dsl, Shell, **S gas:** Shell/dsl, **food:** Big Daddy's Café |
| **66mm** | Broad River |
| **65** | US 176, Broad River Rd, to Columbia, **N gas:** Exxon, 76/Circle K, **food:** Applebee's, Bojangles, Chop Stix Chinese, Monterrey Mexican, Rush's Rest., Subway, Waffle House, **lodging:** Economy Inn, **other:** Aamco, **S gas:** Hess/Godfather's Pizza, RaceWay, **food:** Arby's, Capt Tom's, Chic-fil-A, Church's, Dunkin Donuts, Hooters, KFC, Lizard's Thicket, McDonald's, Pizza Hut, Sandy's HotDogs, Taco Bell, Wendy's, **lodging:** American Inn, Best Inn, InTown Suites, Ramada Ltd, Royal Inn, **other:** Advance Parts, Belk, CVS Drug, Family$, PepBoys, Rite Aid, mall |
| **64b a** | I-26, US 76, E to Columbia, W to Greenville, Spartanburg |
| **63** | Bush River Rd, **N gas:** BP, 76/Circle K/dsl, **food:** Burger King, Cracker Barrel, Real Mexican, Subway, **lodging:** Travelodge, **other:** CVS Drug, Hamrick's, **S gas:** Citgo, **food:** El Chico, Fuddrucker's, Waffle House, **lodging:** Best Western, Courtyard, Knight's Inn, Radisson, Sleep Inn, **other:** Walmart SuperCtr |
| **61** | US 378, W Colombia, **N gas:** Exxon/Hardees, **food:** Chili's, **lodging:** Wingate Inn, **S gas:** BP/dsl/24hr, **food:** Waffle House |
| **58** | US 1, W Columbia, **N gas:** Exxon, Shell/Subway/dsl, **food:** Waffle House, **0-2 mi S gas:** BP, **food:** Burger King, KFC, McDonald's, San Jose Mexican, **lodging:** Value Place Inn, **other:** Barnyard RV Park, to ✈ |
| **55** | SC 6, to Lexington, **N gas:** Shell, **food:** Hardee's, **lodging:** Hampton Inn (2mi), **other:** CarQuest, John's RV Ctr, **S gas:** BP/dsl, Citgo, Kangaroo/DQ/dsl, **food:** Bojangles, Great Wall Chinese, Maurice's BBQ, McDonald's, Subway, Waffle House, Wendy's, **lodging:** Ramada Ltd, **other:** CVS Drug, Piggly Wiggly |
| **52.5mm** | weigh sta wb |
| **51** | SC 204, to Gilbert, **N gas:** Exxon/dsl, Shell/Stuckey's/Subway/dsl/24hr, **food:** Burger King, **S gas:** Mobil/dsl, **other:** $General |
| **44** | SC 34, to Gilbert, **N gas:** BP/dsl, 44Trkstp/dsl/rest./24hr |
| **39** | US 178, to Batesburg, **N gas:** Exxon/dsl, **food:** Hillview Rest. **S gas:** BP/dsl/24hr, |
| **35.5mm** | weigh sta eb |
| **33** | SC 39, to Wagener, **N gas:** El Cheapo/dsl, **S gas:** BP/Huddle House/dsl/scales |
| **29** | SC 49 |

SC

COLUMBIA

| | |
|---|---|
| **22** | US 1, to Aiken, **S gas:** BP/dsl, Raceway, 76/Circle K/dsl, Shell/dsl, **food:** Baynham's, Hardee's, McDonald's, Waffle House, **lodging:** Day's Inn, Quality Inn, **other:** RV Camping (5mi), to USC Aiken |
| **20mm** | parking area both lanes |
| **18** | SC 19, to Aiken, **S gas:** Exxon/Subway/dsl, Shell/dsl, **food:** Waffle House, **lodging:** Deluxe Inn, Guesthouse Inn, **other:** Ⓗ HOSPITAL |
| **11** | SC 144, Graniteville, **N gas:** BP/dsl/scales, **food:** Huddle House |
| **6mm** | new exit |
| **5** | US 25, SC 121, **N gas:** BP/dsl, Circle K/DQ/pizza/dsl/24hr, Shell/Bojangles/dsl/24hr, **food:** Burger King, Checker's, Huddle House, Sonic, Subway, **other:** Advance Parts, $General, Food Lion, **S gas:** Citgo/dsl, **food:** Waffle House, **lodging:** Sleep Inn, **other:** Walmart Super Ctr/dsl (5mi) |
| **1** | SC 230, Martintown Rd, N Augusta, **S gas:** 76/Circle K/Blimpie/dsl/24hr, **food:** Fox Creek Cafe, Tastee Freez, Waffle House, **other:** to Garn's Place |
| **.5mm** | Welcome Ctr eb, full ♿ facilities, [C], [☂], litter barrels, vending, petwalk |
| **0mm** | South Carolina/Georgia state line, Savannah River |

## INTERSTATE 26

E
W
CHARLESTON

| Exit # | Services |
|---|---|
| **221** | Meeting St, Charleston, **2 mi E food:** Church's, KFC, **lodging:** Hampton Inn, **other:** Visitors Ctr, Family$, Piggly Wiggly |
| **221b** | US 17 N, to Georgetown |
| **I-26 begins/ends on US 17 in Charleston, SC.** | |
| **221a** | US 17 S, to Kings St, to Savannah, **N** Ⓗ HOSPITAL |
| **220** | Romney St (from wb) |
| **219b** | Morrison Dr, East Bay St (from eb), **N gas:** Exxon |
| **219a** | Rutledge Ave (from eb, no EZ return), to The Citadel, College of Charleston |
| **218** | Spruill Ave (from wb), N Charleston |
| **217** | N Meeting St (from eb) |
| **216b a** | SC 7, Cosgrove Ave, **1 mi S food:** Burger King, McDonald's, S&S Cafeteria, SunFire Grill, Wendy's, **other:** to Charles Towne Landing |
| **215** | SC 642, Dorchester Rd, N Charleston, **N gas:** El Cheapo, **lodging:** Deluxe Inn, **S gas:** BP/dsl, **food:** Alex's Rest./24hr, **other:** Best Value Inn |
| **213b a** | Montague Ave, Mall Dr, **N food:** Piccadilly's, Red Lobster, **lodging:** Courtyard, Sheraton, **other:** Charles Towne Square, Firestone, **S gas:** BP/dsl, Hess/Bojangles/dsl, Mobil, **food:** Kamille's Cafe, McDonald's, Panera Bread, Waffle House, **lodging:** Comfort Inn, Day's Inn, Econolodge, Embassy Suites, Extended Stay America, Hampton Inn, Hilton Garden, HomePlace Suites, Homewood Suites, InTown Suites, N Charleston Inn, Quality Inn, Residence Inn, Sleep Inn, Super 8, **other:** vet |
| **212c b** | I-526, E to Mt Pleasant, W to Savannah, airport |
| **212a** | Remount Rd (from wb, no EZ return), Hanahan, **N on US 52/78...gas:** Exxon, Hess/dsl, **food:** KFC, Pizza Hut/Taco Bell, **other:** AutoZone, Dodge, Ford |
| **211b a** | Aviation Pkwy, **N on US 52/78...gas:** BP, Exxon, Hess, Sunoco, **food:** Andolini's Pizza, Arby's, Burger King, Capt D's, C&W Buffet, China Town, Church's, Domino's, Golden River Chinese, Hilliard's Rest., McDonald's, Pizza Hut, Pizza Inn, Popeye's, Quizno's, Schlotsky's, Shoney's, Sonic, Subway, Taco Bell, Zaxby's, **lodging:** Masters |

E ↕ W

NORTH CHARLESTON

## INTERSTATE 26 CONT'D

| | |
|---|---|
| **211b a** | Continued |
| | Inn, Radisson, **other:** Batteries+, Big Lots, $General, $Tree, Goodyear, PepBoys, Radio Shack, Super Pets, U-Haul, USPO, **S gas:** Citgo/dsl, **food:** Waffle House, **lodging:** Budget Inn, Howard Johnson, Palace Inn |
| **209** | Ashley Phosphate Rd, to US 52, **N gas:** Exxon, Kangaroo, **food:** Applebee's, Carraba's, Chick-fil-A, China Buffet, ChuckeCheese, Denny's, Fazoli's, Hardee's, Hooters, Jason's Deli, Larry's Subs, Longhorn Steaks, Moe's SW Grill, Noisy Oyster Grill, O'Charley's, Olive Garden, Outback Steaks, Perkins, Pizza Hut, Ryan's, Smokey Bones BBQ, Starbucks, Sticky Fingers Rest., Subway, Taco Bell, Thai Rest., Waffle House, Wendy's, Wild Wing Cafe, **lodging:** Candlewood Suites, Country Hearth Inn, Country Inn&Suites, Holiday Inn Express, Ramada Inn, Red Roof Inn, Residence Inn, Studio+, Suburban Lodge, **other:** HOSPTIAL, Barnes&Noble, Best Buy, BooksAMillion, Cicuit City, Dillard's, Firestone/auto, Hancock Fabrics, Home Depot, JC Penney, Lowe's Whse, Marshall's, Michael's, Nissan, Office Depot, Old Navy, Ross, Sears/auto, Target, Tire Kingdom, Toyota, Walmart SuperCtr, mall, **S gas:** BP, Hess, RaceWay, **food:** Bojangles, Cracker Barrel, Domino's, IHOP, McDonald's, Ruby Tuesday, Waffle House, **lodging:** Best Western, Hampton Inn, InTown Suites, La Quinta, Motel 6, Quality Inn, Relax Inn, Sleep Inn, Value Place Inn |
| **209a** | to US 52 (from wb), to Goose Creek, Moncks Corner |
| **205b a** | US 78, to Summerville, **N gas:** BP, Hess/dsl, **food:** Arby's, Atl Bread Co, Bruster's, Dunkin Donuts, Sonic, Subway, Waffle House, Wendy's, Zaxby's, **lodging:** Fairfield Inn, Wingate Inn, **other:** H HOSPITAL, Dentist, Kerr Drug, Charleston Southern U, **S gas:** Sunoco, **food:** KFC, **other:** KOA |
| **204mm** | rest area eb, full 🅰 facilities, vending, ℂ, 🏕, litter barrels, petwalk |
| **203** | College Park Rd, Ladson, **N gas:** BP, Sunoco, **food:** McDonald's, Waffle House, **lodging:** Best Western, Day's Inn, **2 mi S other:** KOA (2mi) |
| **202mm** | rest area wb, full 🅰 facilities, vending, ℂ, 🏕, litter barrels, petwalk |
| **199b a** | US 17 A, to Moncks Corner, Summerville, **N gas:** BP, Hess/dsl, Pilot/McDonald's/dsl/24hr, Shell, Texaco/dsl, **food:** KFC, Pizza Hut, Subway, **other:** Advance Parts, AutoZone, BiLo, Buick/GMC/Pontiac, $General, Family$, vet, **S gas:** Shell, **food:** Applebee's, Atlanta Bread, Bojangles, Burger King, Coldstone Creamery, Domino's, Fazoli's, Hardee's, IHOP, La Hacienda, Logan's Roadhouse, McAlisters, Deli, Moe's SW Grill, O'Charleys, Papa John's, Perkins/24hr, Ryan's, Shoney's, Waffle House, Zaxby's, **lodging:** Comfort Suites, Country Inn&Suites, Econolodge, Hampton Inn, Holiday Inn Express, Sleep Inn, **other:** Best Buy, Belk, Chevrolet, Chrysler/Jeep, GNC, Home Depot, Kohl's, Lowe's Whse, PetsMart, Radio Shack, Staples, Superpetz, Target, Tire Kingdom, TJ Maxx, Walmart SuperCtr, Walgreens |
| **194** | SC 16, to Jedburg, access to Foreign Trade Zone 21 |
| **187** | SC 27, to Ridgeville, St George, **N gas:** Shell, **S gas:** BP/dsl, **10 mi S other:** Francis Beidler Forest |
| **177** | SC 453, to Holly Hill, Harleyville, **S gas:** Shell/dsl/LP |
| **174mm** | weigh sta both lanes |
| **172b a** | US 15, to Santee, St George, **S gas:** Horizon/Subway/dsl/scales/24hr |

| | |
|---|---|
| **169b a** | I-95, N to Florence, S to Savannah |
| **165** | SC 210, to Bowman, **N gas:** Exxon/dsl, **S gas:** BP/dsl/rest. |
| **159** | SC 36, to Bowman, **N gas:** Li'l Cricket/Stuckey's, Pilot/McDonald's/dsl/scales/@ |
| **154b a** | US 301, to Santee, Orangeburg, **N lodging:** Days Inn, **S gas:** Exxon/dsl, Loves/Subway/dsl/scales/24hr, Shell, **food:** Waffle House |
| **152mm** | rest area wb, full 🅰 facilities, vending, ℂ, 🏕, litter barrels, petwalk |
| **150mm** | rest area eb, full 🅰 facilities, vending, ℂ, 🏕, litter barrels, petwalk |
| **149** | SC 33, to Cameron, to SC State Coll, Orangeburg, Claflin Coll |
| **145b a** | US 601, to Orangeburg, St Matthews, **S gas:** BP/24hr, Exxon, Shell, Sunoco/dsl, **food:** Burger King, Cracker Barrel, Fatz Café, Hardee's, KFC, McDonald's, Mediterranean Grill, Ruby Tuesday, Subway, Waffle House, Zaxby's, **lodging:** Best Western, Carolina Lodge, Comfort Inn, Country Inn&Suites, Fairfield Inn, Hampton Inn, Holiday Inn Express, Howard Johnson, Sleep Inn, Southern Lodge, Traveler's Inn, **other:** H HOSPITAL, **other:** Cadillac/Chevrolet, Chrysler/Dodge, Nissan, Toyota/Scion |
| **139** | SC 22, to St Matthews, **S gas:** Horizon, Li'l Cricket, Wilco/Hess/Arby's/dsl/scales/24hr, **other:** Sweetwater Lake Camping (2.5mi) |
| **136** | SC 6, to North, Swansea, **N gas:** Exxon/dsl/LP/rest./24hr |
| **129** | US 21, **N gas:** Shell/grill/dsl |
| **125** | SC 31, to Gaston, **N other:** Sandy Run Store/gas, Wolfe's Truck/trailer repair |
| **123mm** | rest area both lanes, full 🅰 facilities, vending, ℂ, 🏕, litter barrels, petwalk |
| **119** | US 176, US 21, to Dixiana, **S gas:** BP/Subway/dsl, Exxon/Stuckey's/dsl |
| **116** | I-77 N, to Charlotte, US 76, US 378, to Ft Jackson |
| **115** | US 176, US 21, US 321, to Cayce, **N gas:** BP, Raceway/24hr, Texaco, **food:** Waffle House, **other:** Advance Parts, Bi-Lo, $General, Harley-Davidson, **S gas:** Pilot/DQ/Wendy's/dsl/scales/24hr, Shell, **food:** Bojangles, Great China, Hardee's, McDonald's, Subway, **lodging:** Country Hearth Inn, **other:** Firestone, Piggly Wiggly |
| **113** | SC 302, Cayce, **N gas:** Exxon, Mobil/Burger King, Sunoco, **food:** Waffle House, **lodging:** Airport Inn, Cambridge Plaza, Knight's Inn, Masters Inn, **other:** O'Reilly Parts, **S gas:** BP, Raceway, Shell/Circle K, **food:** Lizard's Thicket, Shoney's, Subway, Waffle House/24hr, **lodging:** Carolina Lodge, Comfort Inn, Country Inn& Suites, Sleep Inn, Travelers Inn, **other:** NAPA, ✈ |

SC

**E** ↕ **W COLUMBIA**

## INTERSTATE 26 CONT'D

**111b a** US 1, to W Columbia, **N gas:** Raceway/dsl, Shell/Circle K, **food:** Domino's, Dragon City Chinese, Hardee's, Maurice's BBQ, Ruby Tuesday, Sonic, Subway, TCBY, Waffle House, Zaxby's, **lodging:** Holiday Inn, Quality Inn, **other:** BiLo Foods, $General, $Tree, GNC, Goody's, Kroger, Pet Supplies+, Walgreens, Walmart SuperCtr/gas, to USC, **S gas:** Hess, **food:** Applebee's, Popeye's, Wendy's, **other:** Aldi Foods, Big Lots, Family$, Lowe's Whse, U-Haul

**110** US 378, to W Columbia, Lexington, **N food:** Burger King, Grecian Garden, Lizard's Thicket, Maurice's BBQ, McDonald's, Rush's Rest., Subway, Waffle House, **lodging:** Best Value Inn, Day's Inn, Hampton Inn, Holiday Inn, **other:** CVS Drug, Food Lion, Rite Aid, U-Haul, **S gas:** Li'l Cricket/dsl, 76/Circle K, **food:** Atlanta Bread, Bojangles, Pizza Hut, **lodging:** Executive Inn, SpringHill Suites, **other:** H HOSPITAL

**108b a** I-126 to Columbia, Bush River Rd, **N gas:** Shell/dsl, **food:** Blimpie, Capt D's, Chick-fil-A, Hardee's, Peking Palace, Ruby Tuesday, Schlotsky's, Shoney's, Super China, Wendy's, Zaxby's, **lodging:** Day's Inn, Scottish Inn, Villager Lodge, Western Inn, **other:** Advance Parts, Belk, $General, Firestone/auto, K-Mart, Office Depot, Rite Aid, mall, **S gas:** City Gas, RaceWay, Sunoco/dsl, **food:** Cracker Barrel, Fuddrucker's, Villa Italian, Waffle House, **lodging:** Best Inn, Courtyard, Knight's Inn, Radisson, Sleep Inn, **other:** Walmart SuperCtr, multiple services **1-3 mi N off I-126, Greystone Blvd**...**N gas:** BP, Exxon, **food:** Waffle House, **lodging:** Embassy Suites, Extended Stay America, Homewood Suites, Residence Inn, Studio+, **other:** Chrysler/Jeep, Dodge, Ford, Honda, Hyundai, KIA, Lincoln/Mercury, Mazda, **S** Riverbanks Zoo

**107b a** I-20, E to Florence, W to Augusta

**106b a** St Andrews Rd, **N gas:** Exxon/dsl, **food:** Chic-fil-A, ChuckeCheese, IHOP, Papa John's, Sonic, Top China Buffet, **lodging:** Motel 6, **other:** BiLo Foods, Buick/GMC/POntiac, Camping World RV Ctr, CVS Drug, $General, Infiniti, Jaguar, Kroger/deli, Nissan, Walgreen, **S gas:** BP/dsl, Hess/dsl, Shell, **food:** Domino's, King Buffet, Maurice's BBQ, McDonald's, Pizza Hut, Steak Out, Thai Lotus, Waffle House, Zaxby's, **lodging:** Ecocnolodge, Red Roof Inn, **other:** $General, Food Lion, Tire Kingdom

**104** Piney Grove Rd, **N gas:** Sunoco/dsl, **food:** Hardee's, San Jose Mexican, Waffle House, **lodging:** Quiality Inn, **other:** Sportsman's Whse, RV/Marine Ctr, **S gas:** Exxon/dsl, Shell, **lodging:** Comfort Suites, Microtel, **other:** Carmax, Land Rover

**103** Harbison Blvd, **N food:** Applebee's, Hooters, Hops Grill, Wendy's, **lodging:** Hampton Inn, **other:** Chevrolet, Home Depot, Hummer, Lowe's Whse, funpark, **S gas:** BP/24hr, Hess/dsl, Shell, **food:** Alehouse, Bailey's Grill, Blimpie, Bojangles, BoneFish Grill, Bruster's, Carrabba's, Chili's, Chick-fil-A, Coldstone, Copper River Grill, D's Rest., Denny's, Fazoli's, 5 Guys Pizza, Inyabi, LongHorn Steaks, Macaroni Grill, McAlister's, McDonald's, Monterrey Mexican, O'Charley's, Olive Garden, Outback Steaks, Panera Bread, Popeye's, Quizno's, Ruby Tuesday, Rush's Rest., Ryan's, Shoney's, Sonic, Sticky Fingers, Subway, Super Buffet, Texas Roadhouse, Tokyo Grill, Tsunami Steaks, Yamato Japanese, **lodging:** Comfort Suites, Country Inn&Suites, Fairfield Inn, Hilton Garden, Holiday Inn Express, InTown Suites,

**COLUMBIA**

**103** Continued
TownePlace Suites, Wingate Inn, **other:** Barnes& Noble, Belk, Best Buy, BooksAMillion, Circuit City, Dillard's, $Tree, Goodyear, Goody's, Hancock Fabrics, Kohl's, Marshall's, Michael's, Midas, Old Navy, PetsMart, Publix, Rite Aid, Ross, Sam's Club/gas, Saturn, Sears/auto, Target, Tire Kingdom, TJ Maxx, Walmart SuperCtr, mall

**102** SC 60, Ballentine, Irmo, **N food:** Cracker Barrel, **lodging:** Extended Stay America, Hyatt Place, **S gas:** 76/Circle K, Shell, SKS, **food:** Arby's, Atlanta Bread, Bellacino's Pizza, Maurice's BBQ, Moe's SW Grill, New China, Papa John's, Quizno's, TCBY, Zaxby's, **other:** CVS Drug, Jiffy Lube, tires, same as 103

**101b a** US 76, US 176, to N Columbia, **1/2 mi N gas:** Exxon/Subway/dsl, **food:** China House, Fatz Café, Zorba's, **other:** AutoZone, $General, Food Lion, Publix, Rite Aid, Walgreen, **S gas:** BP, Mobil, **food:** Burger King, Oyster House Grill, Waffle House, **other:** Toyota/Scion

**97** US 176, to Ballentine, Peak, **N other:** Food Lion, Woodsmoke Camping, **S gas:** Exxon/dsl

**94mm** weigh sta wb, phones

**91** SC 48, to Chapin, **S gas:** BP/dsl, Exxon/Taco Bell/Blimpie/dsl, Shell/dsl, **food:** Hardee's (3mi), McDonald's, Subway (2mi), Waffle House, **other:** to Dreher Island SP

**85** SC 202, Little Mountain, Pomaria, **S** to Dreher Island SP

**82** SC 773, to Prosperity, Pomaria, **N gas:** BP/Subway/dsl/24hr/@, **other:** Flea Mkt Campground

**81mm** weigh sta eb

**76** SC 219, to Pomaria, Newberry, **2 mi S gas:** BP, MurphyUSA, **food:** Burger King, Wendy's, **lodging:** Hampton Inn, Holiday Inn Express, **other:** Walmart SuperCtr/gas, to Newberry Opera House

**74** SC 34, to Newberry, **N gas:** BP, Shell/dsl/24hr, **food:** Bill&Fran's Café, **lodging:** Best Western/rest., **S gas:** Texaco, **food:** Arby's, Capt D's, Hardee's (2mi), McDonald's (2mi), Waffle House, **lodging:** Comfort Inn (2mi), Day's Inn, Economy Inn (2mi), Holiday Inn Express (2mi), **other:** H HOSPITAL, to NinetySix HS

**72** SC 121, to Newberry, **S gas:** Citgo/dsl/@, **other:** H HOSPITAL, to Newberry Coll

**66** SC 32, to Jalapa

**63.5mm** rest area both lanes, full ♿ facilities, 📞 vending, 🛆 litter barrels, petwalk

**60** SC 66, to Joanna, **S gas:** Chevron, **food:** Carolina Country Kitchen, **other:** Magnolia Camping

**54** SC 72, to Clinton, **N gas:** BP, **S gas:** Citgo/dsl/24hr, **food:** Fatz Cafe, **lodging:** Hampton Inn, **other:** H HOSPITAL, to Presbyterian Coll, Thornwell Home

**52** SC 56, to Clinton, **N gas:** Pilot/Subway/dsl/24hr/@, **food:** Blue Ocean Rest., McDonald's, Waffle House, **lodging:** Comfort Inn, **S gas:** Citgo/dsl, **food:** Hardee's, Waffle House, Wendy's, **lodging:** Clinton Hotel, Day's Inn, Travelers Inn (2mi), **other:** H HOSPITAL

**51** I-385, to Greenville (from wb)

**45.5mm** Enoree River

**44** SC 49, to Cross Anchor, Union

**41** SC 92, to Enoree, **N gas:** Valero

**38** SC 146, to Woodruff, **N gas:** Hot Spot/Shell/Hardee's/dsl/24hr/@, **food:** Big Country Rest./lounge

**35** SC 50, to Woodruff, **S gas:** BP/dsl/rest./24hr, **other:** H HOSPITAL

**SC**

## INTERSTATE 26 CONT'D

**E ↕ W**

**S P A R T A N B U R G**

| | |
|---|---|
| **33mm** | S Tyger River |
| **32mm** | N Tyger River |
| **28** | US 221, to Spartanburg, **N gas:** Citgo/AuntM's/dsl/24hr, Shell/Subway/dsl/24hr, **food:** Burger King, Hardee's, Waffle House, Walnut Grove Seafood Rest., **other:** Ⓗ HOSPITAL, Pine Ridge Camping (3mi), to Walnut Grove Plantation |
| **22** | SC 296, Reidville Rd, to Spartanburg, **N gas:** BP/dsl, Exxon, **food:** Arby's, BBQ, Capri's Italian, Fuddrucker's (1mi), Hong Kong Express, Little Caesar's, McDonald's, Outback Steaks, Ryan's, Waffle House, Zaxby's, **other:** Advance Parts, Rite Aid, to Croft SP, **S gas:** BP/dsl, **food:** Burger King, Denny's, Domino's, Hardee's, Subway, TCBY, Waffle House/24hr, **lodging:** Sleep Inn, Southern Suites, Super 8, **other:** Abbot Farms/fruit, BiLo, BMW, CVS Drug, Eckerd, Harris-Teeter, Saturn, Toyota, Walgreen |
| **21b a** | US 29, to Spartanburg, **N gas:** BP, **food:** Bojangles, Burger King, Chick-fil-A, ChuckeCheese, CiCi's, City Range Grill, Corona Mexican, DQ, Fuji's, Golden Corral, Hardee's, Hooters, Jack-in-the-Box, Japanese Rest., LJ Silver/A&W, McAlister's Deli, Moe's SW Grill, O'Charley's, Olive Garden, Pizza Hut, Red Lobster, Ruby Tuesday, Ryan's, Schlotzsky's, Substation II, Subway, Wendy's, **lodging:** Hampton Inn, Holiday Inn Express, **other:** Barnes&Noble, Belk, Best Buy, Circuit City, Costco/gas, Dillard's, Discount Tire, $General, Firestone/auto, Goodyear, Home Depot, JC Penney, Lowe's Whse, Michael's, Office Depot, Old Navy, Rite Aid, Ross, Sears/auto, Walmart SuperCtr, mall, USPO, **S gas:** Citgo/dsl/cafe, Sphinx Gas, **food:** Applebee's, Blimpie, IHOP, McDonald's, Piccadilly's, Pizza Inn, Prime Sirloin, Shogun Japanese, Taco Bell, Taste of Thai, Waffle House, **other:** Advance Parts, CarQuest, $Tree, Ingles Foods/gas, Kohl's, Sam's Club/gas, Target, TrueValue |
| **19b a** | Lp I-85, Spartanburg, **N food:** Cracker Barrel, **lodging:** Country Hearth Inn, Radisson, Ramada Inn, Residence Inn, **S lodging:** Bradford Inn, **other:** Lowes Whse, Walmart SuperCtr |
| **18b a** | I-85, N to Charlotte, S to Greenville |
| **17** | New Cut Rd, **S gas:** Chevron/dsl, Sunoco/dsl, **food:** Burger King, Fatz Café, McDonald's, Waffle House, **lodging:** Day's Inn, Econolodge, Howard Johnson Express, Quality Inn |
| **16** | John Dodd Rd, to Wellford, **N gas:** Citgo/Aunt M's/dsl, **other:** Camping World RV Ctr, **S** Cunningham RV Park (2mi) |
| **15** | US 176, to Inman, **N gas:** Breakers, Racetrac (2mi), 76/Circle K/dsl, **food:** Waffle House, **other:** Ⓗ HOSPITAL, **S gas:** Mystik/dsl, **food:** Taco Bell (2mi) |
| **10** | SC 292, to Inman, **N gas:** Shell/Subway/dsl/24hr |
| **7.5mm** | Lake William C. Bowman |
| **5** | SC 11, Foothills Scenic Dr, Chesnee, Campobello, **N gas:** Kangaroo/Aunt M's Café/dsl/scales, **S gas:** Li'l Cricket |
| **3mm** | Welcome Ctr eb, full ♿ facilities, info, Ⓒ, 🅿, litter barrels, vending, petwalk |
| **1** | SC 14, to Landrum, **S gas:** BP/Burger King/dsl, HotSpot/gas (2mi), **food:** Bojangles, China Cafe, Pizza Hut (1mi), Subway, **other:** BiLo Foods, $General, Ingles/café/gas/24hr, vet |
| **0mm** | South Carolina/North Carolina state line |

## INTERSTATE 77

**N ↕ S**

**R O C K H I L L**

| **Exit #** | Services |
|---|---|
| **91mm** | South Carolina/North Carolina state line |
| **90** | US 21, Carowinds Blvd, **E gas:** PetroExpress, Red Rocket/fireworks, **food:** Bojangles, **other:** Ⓗ HOSPITAL, RV camping (4mi), **W gas:** Citgo, Exxon/café, 76/Circle K/Wendy's/dsl, **food:** Cracker Barrel, El Cancun Mexican, KFC, Papa Pino's, Shoney's, Wendy's, **lodging:** Best Western, Comfort Inn, Holiday Inn Express, Motel 6, Plaza Motel, Sleep Inn, **other:** Carowinds Funpark, Carolina Pottery/outlet mall/famous brands |
| **89.5mm** | Welcome Ctr sb, full ♿ facilities, info, Ⓒ, vending, 🅿, litter barrels, petwalk/weigh sta nb |
| **88** | Gold Hill Rd, to Pineville, **W gas:** Exxon/dsl, Gate Gas (2mi), Shell/dsl, **food:** Bojangles (2mi), **other:** Chrysler/Jeep/Dodge, Ford/Hyundai, KOA |
| **85** | SC 160, Ft Mill, Tega Cay, **E gas:** Exxon, **food:** Subway, **other:** Bi-Lo, The Drug Store, **W gas:** BP/dsl, Circle K, **food:** Backyard Burger, Beef O'Brady's, Bojangles (3mi), Burger King, Papa John's, Pizza Hut, Starbucks, Wendy's, **other:** CVS Drug, Harris-Teeter, Lowes Whse, Walgreens |
| **84.5mm** | weigh sta sb |
| **83** | SC 49, Sutton Rd, **W gas:** Loves/Chester/Godfathers/dsl/scales/24hr |
| **82.5mm** | Catawba River |
| **82c** | US 21, SC 161, Rock Hill, Ft Mill, **E gas:** Exxon, Phillips 66, **food:** IHOP, Sonny's BBQ, Steak'n Shake, Zaxby's, **other:** Home Depot, PetsMart, museum, **W gas:** Exxon, Phillips 66, Shell, Valero, **food:** CiCi's Pizza, Hooters, Outback Steaks, Starbucks, **lodging:** Courtyard, Ramada/rest., **other:** Ⓗ HOSPITAL, Aldi Foods, Toyota, U-Haul |
| **82b a** | **E gas:** Exxon, **other:** Conference Ctr, **W gas:** Citgo, RaceWay, **food:** Arby's, Bojangles, Burger King, Capt's Galley, Chick-fil-A, Denny's, Firebonez, Jack-in-the-Box, Little Caesar's, Marco's Pizza, McDonald's, Penn Sta., Pizza Hut, Sakura Japanese, Shoney's, Subway, Taco Bell, Toyo Grill, Waffle House, Wendy's, **lodging:** Best Value Inn, Country Inn&Suites, Days Inn, Econolodge, Howard Johnson, Microtel, Quality Inn, Regency Inn, Super 8, **other:** Aamco, Advance Parts, Bi-Lo, Chevrolet/Cadillac, $General, Family$, Firestone, NAPA, Nissan, Office Depot, O'Reilly Parts, PepBoys, Winn-Dixie |
| **79** | SC 122, Dave Lyle Blvd, to Rock Hill, **E gas:** BP, **food:** Applebee's, Chick-fil-A, Cracker Barrel, DQ, Hardee's, Longhorn Steaks, Lucky Buffet, O'Charley's, Ryan's, Ruby Tuesday, **lodging:** Hampton Inn, Wingate Inn, **other:** Belk, Discount Tire, Food Lion, Goody's, Honda, JC Penney, |

**SC**

**ROCK HILL N ↕ S**

## INTERSTATE 77 CONT'D

| | |
|---|---|
| **79** | Continued |
| | Kohl's, Lowe's Whse, Sears/auto, Staples, Tire Kingdom, Walmart SuperCtr/drugs/gas/24hr, mall, **W** **gas:** Citgo, **food:** Bob Evans, Chili's, Dunkin Donuts, Jack-in-the-Box, McCallister's Deli, McDonalds, Midtown Rest., Olive Garden, Panera Bread, Quizno's, Stagebrush Steaks, Subway, Taco Bell, Wendy's, **lodging:** Hillside Inn, Hilton Garden, **other:** Best Buy, Books-a-Million, Ford, Lincoln/Mercury, Michael's, Ross, Target, TJ Maxx, visitor ctr |
| **77** | US 21, SC 5, to Rock Hill, **E** **gas:** BP/Subway/dsl, Citgo/dsl, Cone/dsl/24hr, **other:** to Andrew Jackson SP (12mi) **W** **gas:** Exxon/dsl, Pride/dsl/scales, **food:** KFC, McDonald's, Subway, Waffle House, **other:** to Winthrop Coll |
| **75** | Porter Rd, **E** **gas:** Citgo, Texaco |
| **73** | SC 901, to Rock Hill, York, **E** **gas:** Exxon/dsl, ⊕*FLYING J*/CountryMkt/dsl/scales/LP/24hr/@, **W** HOSPITAL |
| **66mm** | **rest area both lanes, full** ♿ **facilities,** 🚻, 🏤, **litter barrels, vending, petwalk** |
| **65** | SC 9, to Chester, Lancaster, **E** **gas:** BP/24hr, Liberty/Subway/dsl, Petro Engery/dsl, **food:** Subway, Waffle House, **lodging:** Day's Inn, Econolodge, Relax Inn, **other:** Chevrolet/Ponitac/Buick, Dodge/Jeep, IGA Foods/gas, **W** **gas:** Exxon/dsl, **food:** Burger King, Country Omelette/24hr, Front Porch Cafe, KFC, McDonald's, **lodging:** Comfort Inn, Rodeway Inn, Super 8, **other:** H HOSPITAL |
| **62** | SC 56, to Fort Lawn, Richburg |
| **55** | SC 97, to Chester, Great Falls, **E** **gas:** Exxon/dsl, **W** HOSPITAL |
| **48** | SC 200, to Great Falls, **E** **gas:** Shell/Grand Central Rest./dsl/@, **W** **gas:** Wilco/Hess/DQ/Wendy's |
| **46** | SC 20, to White Oak |
| **41** | SC 41, to Winnsboro, **E** to Lake Wateree SP |
| **34** | SC 34, to Winnsboro, Ridgeway, **E** **gas:** AM,PM/dsl/24hr, **lodging:** Ridgeway Motel (1mi), **other:** camping (1mi), **W** **gas:** Exxon/Blimpie/dsl, **food:** Lois's Cafe, Waffle House, **lodging:** Day's Inn (6mi), Ramada Ltd. |
| **32** | Peach Rd, Ridgeway |
| **27** | Blythewood Rd, **E** **gas:** BP/dsl, Exxon/Bojangles/dsl/24hr, **food:** Hardee's, McDonald's, Pizza Hut/KFC, Southern Pig BBQ, Subway, Waffle House, Wendy's, WG's Wings, **lodging:** Comfort Inn, Holiday Inn Express, **other:** Curves, $General, IGA Foods, **W** **other:** Food Lion, Groucho's Deli |
| **24** | US 21, to Wilson Blvd., **E** **gas:** BP, Shell/Subway/dsl, **food:** Myer's BBQ |
| **22** | Killian Rd |
| **19** | SC 555, Farrow Rd, **E** **gas:** BP, **food:** Bojangles, Cracker Barrel, Wendy's, **lodging:** Courtyard, Residence Inn, **other:** H HOSPITAL, Longs Drug, **W** **gas:** Shell/dsl, **food:** Waffle House, **other:** SC Archives |
| **18** | to SC 277, to I-20 W (from sb), Columbia |
| **17** | US 1, Two Notch Rd, **E** **gas:** BP, Kangaroo, Shell/Circle K, **food:** Arby's, Burger King, Hops Grill, Outback Steaks, Ryan's, Texas Roadhouse, **lodging:** AmeriSuites, Best Western, Baymont Inn, Fairfield Inn, Holiday Inn, InTown Suites, La Quinta, Quality Inn, Red Roof Inn, Travelodge, Wingate Inn, **other:** Home Depot, USPO, U-Haul, to Sesquicentennial SP, **W** **gas:** Hess/Godfather's Pizza, Mobil, RaceWay, **food:** Capt Tom's, Chic-fil-A, Chili's, Church's, Dunkin Donuts, Fazoli's, Hooters, IHOP, KFC, Lizard's Thicket, McDonald's, Pizza Hut, Sandy's Hot |

**COLUMBIA**

| | |
|---|---|
| **17** | Continued |
| | Dogs, Taco Bell, Waffle House, Wendy's, **lodging:** American Inn, Best Inn, Comfort Inn, Hampton Inn, Jameson Suites, Microtel, Motel 6, Ramada Ltd, Royal Inn, **other:** Advance Parts, Belk, CVS Drug, Family$, PepBoys, Rite Aid, mall |
| **16b a** | I-20, W to Augusta, E to Florence, Alpine Rd |
| **15b a** | SC 12, to Percival Rd, **W** **gas:** El Cheapo/gas, Shell, 1/2 mi **W** **gas:** Exxon |
| **13** | Decker Blvd (from nb) , **W** **gas:** El Cheapo |
| **12** | Forest Blvd, Thurmond Blvd, **E** to Ft Jackson, **W** **gas:** BP/dsl, 76/dsl, Shell/dsl/24hr, **food:** Bojangles, Chick-fil-A, Fatz Café, Golden Corral, Hardee's, McDonald's, RedBone Rest., Steak&Ale, Subway, Wendy's, **lodging:** Extended Stay America, Marlboro Inn, Super 8, **other:** H HOSPITAL, $Tree, Sam's Club/gas, Walmart SuperCtr, museum |
| **10** | SC 760, Jackson Blvd, **E** to Ft Jackson, **2 mi W** **gas:** BP, **food:** Applebee's, Bojangles, Burger King, Maurices BBQ, Ruby Tuesday, Subway, **lodging:** Econolodge, Liberty Inn |
| **9b a** | US 76, US 378, to Sumter, Columbia, **E** **gas:** BP, Citgo, Hess/dsl, Sunoco/dsl, United, **food:** Arby's, Capt D's, Chick-fil-A, Domino's, KFC, Maurice's BBQ, McDonald's, Pizza Hut, Popeye's, Ruby Tuesday, Rush's Rest., Ryan's, Shoney's, Subway, Taco Bell, Waffle House, Zaxby's, **lodging:** Best Western, Candlewood Suites, Comfort Inn, Country Inn&Suites, Day's Inn, Hampton Inn, Holiday Inn Express, La Quinta, Quality Inn, Sleep Inn, **other:** Advance Parts, Aldi Foods, $Tree, Family$, Firestone/auto, Food Lion, Goodyear/auto, Interstate Batteries, Lowes Whse, NAPA, Piggly Wiggly, Pontiac/GMC, Radio Shack, Sears, Tire Kingdom, U-Haul, USPO, Walgreens, Walmart SuperCtr/gas/auto, **W** **gas:** Shell, **food:** CiCi's, Hardee's, Sonic, Wendy's, **lodging:** Best Value Inn, Economy Inn, **other:** H HOSPITAL, BigLots, $General, Fred's Store, Jo-Ann Fabrics, Rite Aid, Sav-a-Lot Foods, Target |
| **6b a** | Shop Rd, **W** to USC Coliseum, fairgrounds |
| **5** | SC 48, Bluff Rd, **1 mi E...gas:** 76, **W** **gas:** Shell/Burger King/dsl, **food:** Bojangles (2mi) |
| **3mm** | Congaree River |
| **2** | Saxe Gotha Rd |
| **1** | US 21, US 176, US 321 (from sb), Cayce, **W** accesses same as SC I-26, exit 115. |
| **0mm** | I-77 begins/ends on I-26, |

**N ↕ S**

## INTERSTATE 85

| Exit # | Services |
|---|---|
| **106.5mm** | South Carolina/North Carolina state line |
| **106** | US 29, to Grover, **E** **gas:** BP/dsl, **W** **gas:** Exxon/dsl, Hickory Point/gas, Wilco/Hess/DQ/Wendy's/dsl/scales/24hr |
| **104** | SC 99, **E** **gas:** Mr. Waffle/dsl/rest./scales/24hr/@ |
| **103mm** | **Welcome Ctr sb, full** ♿ **facilities, info,** 🚻, 🏤, **litter barrels, vending, petwalk** |
| **102** | SC 198, to Earl, **E** **gas:** BP/dsl, Shell/gas, **food:** Hardee's, **W** **gas:** Citgo/dsl, ⊕*FLYING J*/Cookery/dsl/scales/LP/rest./24hr/@, **food:** McDonald's, Waffle House |
| **100mm** | Buffalo Creek |
| **100** | SC 5, to Blacksburg, Shelby, **W** **gas:** Sunoco/Subway/dsl/scales/24hr, Texaco/dsl |
| **98** | Frontage Rd (from nb) , **E** **food:** Broad River Café |
| **97mm** | Broad River |

**SC**

N S ← → GAFFNEY

## INTERSTATE 85 CONT'D

| | |
|---|---|
| **96** | SC 18, **W gas:** Kangaroo/Krystal/dsl, Sunoco/dsl |
| **95** | SC 18, to Gaffney, **E gas:** Kangaroo/Aunt M's Rest/dsl, Mr Petro/dsl, **food:** Mr Waffle, **other:** H HOSPITAL, Suzuki, to Limestone Coll |
| **92** | SC 11, to Gaffney, **E gas:** Citgo, Fastpoint, **food:** Applebee's, Blue Bay Seafood, Bojangles, Bruster's, Burger King, Chinese Buffet, Daddy Joe's BBQ, Domino's, KFC, McDonald's, Pizza Hut, Ruby Tuesday, Ryan's, Sagebrush Steaks, Sonic, Subway, Super China, Taco Bell, Waffle House, Wendy's, Zaxby's, **lodging:** Jameson Inn, Super 8, **other:** Advance Parts, Belk, BigLots, BiLo, $Tree, Eckerd, Ingles Foods, Lowe's Whse, Radio Shack, Walgreen, Walmart SuperCtr/gas, USPO, to Limestone Coll, **W gas:** Texaco/dsl, **lodging:** Homestead Lodge, Quality Inn, **other:** to The Peach, Foothills Scenic Hwy |
| **90** | SC 105, SC 42, to Gaffney, **E gas:** BP/DQ/dsl, Pilot/Arby's/dsl/scales/24hr, **food:** Bronco Mexican, Clock Rest., Starbucks, Subway, Waffle House, **lodging:** Holiday Inn Express, Roof Inn, **W gas:** Citgo/Burger King, Texaco, **food:** Cracker Barrel, FoodCourt, La Fogata Mexican, Outback Steaks, **lodging:** Hampton Inn, **other:** Hamrick's, Prime Outlets/famous brands, fruit stand |
| **89mm** | **rest area both lanes, full** 🚹 **facilities,** 🕿, 🅿, **litter barrels, vending, petwalk** |
| **87** | SC 39, **E other:** Pinecone Camping (1.5mi) , **W other:** Rug Outlet, fruit stand/peaches/fireworks |
| **83** | SC 110, **E gas:** Hot Spot/dsl, **other:** NAPA, fruit stand, truck repair, **W gas:** Auto Trkstp/Mr Waffle/dsl/24hr/@, **other:** to Cowpens Bfd, fruitstand |
| **82** | Frontage Rd (from nb) |
| **80.5mm** | Pacolet River |
| **80** | SC 57, to Gossett, **E gas:** Hot Spot/dsl |
| **78** | US 221, Chesnee, **E gas:** Citgo/dsl, **food:** Hardee's, **lodging:** Motel 6, **other:** fruit stand, **W gas:** BP, RaceWay/dsl, Sunoco/Burger King/dsl, **food:** Arby's, Bojangles, McDonald's, Subway, Waffle House, Wendy's, **lodging:** Hampton Inn, Holiday Inn Express, **other:** Advance Parts, $General, Harley-Davidson, Ingles Foods |
| **77** | Lp 85, Spartanburg, services along Lp 85 exits E |
| **75** | SC 9, Spartanburg, **E food:** Denny's, **lodging:** Fairfield Inn, **1-3 mi E on Lp 85...gas:** Exxon, **lodging:** Best Western, Comfort Inn, **W gas:** BP/Burger King/dsl, Pure, RaceWay, **food:** Bruster's Ice Cream, Capri's Italian, Copper River Grill, Fatz Café, LJ Silver, McDonald's, Pizza Hut, Pizza Inn, Ron's BBQ, Waffle House, Zaxby's, **lodging:** Days Inn, Comfort Inn, **other:** CVS Drug, Ingles/gas, USPO |
| **72** | US 176, to I-585, **E food:** Steak&Ale, **other:** to USCS, Wofford/Converse Coll, **W gas:** BP, RaceWay, **food:** Waffle House, **other:** Masters RV Ctr |
| **70b a** | I-26, E to Columbia, W to Asheville |
| **69** | Lp 85, SC 41 (from nb), to Fairforest |
| **68** | SC 129, to Greer |
| **67mm** | N Tyger River |
| **66** | US 29, to Lyman, Wellford |
| **63** | SC 290, to Duncan, **E gas:** Citgo/dsl, 76/Circle K, Spinx/DQ/dsl, **food:** A&W/KFC, Burger King, Clock Rest., Denny's, Jack-in-the-Box, Paisanos Italian, Pizza Inn, Taco Bell, Thai Cuisine, Waffle House, Zaxby's, **lodging:** Hampton Inn, Jameson Inn, Microtel, **other:** Curves, **W gas:** Phillips 66, Pilot/Wendy's/dsl/scales/24hr, |

S P A R T A N B U R G

| | |
|---|---|
| **63** | Continued TA/BP/DQ/rest./dsl/scales/24hr/@, **food:** Arby's, BBQ, Bojangles, Hardee's, McDonald's, Waffle House, **lodging:** Comfort Inn, Day's Inn, Holiday Inn Express, Quality Inn, Travelodge, **other:** Sonny's RV Ctr, Speedco Lube |
| **62.5mm** | S Tyger River |
| **60** | SC 101, to Greer, **E gas:** Grand/dsl, Lil' Cricket/gas, Sunoco, **food:** Senor Garcia's Mexican, Subway, Theo's Rest, **W gas:** Exxon/Burger King, **food:** Waffle House, **lodging:** Super 8 |
| **58** | Brockman-McClimon Rd |
| **57** | **W other:** Greenville-Spartanburg Airport |
| **56** | SC 14, to Greer, **E gas:** Citgo/dsl, **W gas:** Spinx/DQ/dsl, **other:** H HOSPITAL, Goodyear, Outdoor World RV Ctr |
| **55mm** | Enoree River |
| **54** | Pelham Rd, **E gas:** BP/dsl, **food:** Burger King, Corona Mexican, Waffle House, **lodging:** Best Western, **W gas:** BP/dsl, Spinx, **food:** Atlanta Bread Co, Bojangles, Burtollos Pizza, California Dreaming Rest., Chick-fil-A, China Wok, Chophouse 47, Chops Cajun, Happy China, Hardee's, Jack-in-the-Box, Joe's Crabshack, Logan's Roadhouse, Macaroni Grill, Mayflower Seafood, McDonald's, On the Border, Ruby Tuesday, Schlotsky's, Starbucks, Stax Omega Buffet, Subway, Wendy's, **lodging:** Best Western, Courtyard, Extended Stay America, Fairfield Inn, Hampton Inn, Holiday Inn Express, Marriott, Microtel, Residence Inn, Wingate Inn, **other:** BiLo/24hr, CVS Drug, Goodyear/auto, Ingles, Radio Shack, Walgreen |
| **52mm** | weigh sta nb |
| **51** | I-385, SC 146, Woodruff Rd, **E gas:** Blue Jay/dsl, **food:** Bluefire Grill, Bob Evan's, Burger King, Cracker Barrel, Fatz Café, Fuddrucker's, IHOP, Lieus Bistro, Midori's Rest., Mimi's Cafe, Monterrey Mexican, Panera Bread, PF Chang, Quizno's, Red Robin, Sticky Fingers, TCBY, Waffle House, **lodging:** Drury Inn, Hampton Inn, **other:** Barnes&Noble, Best Buy, BiLo, Circuit City, Goodyear/auto, Hamrick's Outlet, Lowe's Whse, PetsMart, Ross, Sams Club, Whole Foods Mkt, funpark, vet, **W gas:** BP, RaceWay/24hr, **food:** Blimpie, Capri's Italian, Carrabba's, Flatrock Grille, Jack-in-the-Box, McDonald's, Ruby Tuesday, TGIFriday, Waffle House, **lodging:** Crowne Plaza, Comfort Inn, Day's Inn, Embassy Suites, Fairfield Inn, Holiday Inn Express, La Quinta, Marriott (3mi), Microtel, **other:** BJ's Whse/gas, Costco/gas, Firestone/auto, Goody's, Home Depot, Lowe's Whse, Old Navy, Target, mall |
| **48b a** | US 276, Greenville, **E food:** Waffle House, **lodging:** Red Roof Inn, **other:** CarMax, **W gas:** BP, Exxon/dsl, |

G R E E N V I L L E

SC

## INTERSTATE 85 CONT'D

| | |
|---|---|
| **48b a** | Continued |
| | Murphy USA, Sunoco, **food:** Arby's, Bailey's Grille, Bojangles, Burger King, Hooters, Jack-in-the-Box, KFC, McDonalds, Olive Garden, Ryan's, Subway, Taco Bell/Pizza Hut, Zaxby's, **lodging:** Best Inn, Day's Inn, Embassy Suites, **other:** Acura/Honda, Advance Parts, AutoZone, Bi-Lo, BMW/Mini, BooksAMillion, Buick, Chrysler/Jeep, Dodge, $General, Ford, Kia, Lexus, Lincoln/Mercury, Marshall's, Mazda, Mercedes, Michael's, Nissan, Office Depot, Pepboys, PetsMart, Pontiac/GMC, Saab, SteinMart, Suzuki, Toyota, Volvo, VW/Audi/Porsche |
| **46c** | rd 291, Pleasantburg Rd, Mauldin Rd, **W gas:** BP, Citgo/dsl, Spinx, **food:** Jack-in-the-Box, Subway, **lodging:** Quality Inn, Value Place, **other:** Aamco, Advance Parts, BiLo/gas, CVS Drug, Home Depot, Tire Kingdom |
| **46b a** | US 25 bus, Augusta Rd, **E gas:** Mike&Jack, Spinx, Sunoco, **food:** Burger King, Waffle House, **lodging:** Camelot Inn, Holiday Inn, Motel 6, Southern Suites, **W food:** Big Papa's Grill, **lodging:** Economy Inn, Traveler's Inn, **other:** Home Depot |
| **44** | US 25, White Horse Rd, **E gas:** Spinx/Subway/dsl, **W gas:** Citgo/McDonald's, RaceWay, **food:** Waffle House, **other:** H HOSPITAL, Freightliner |
| **44a** | SC 20 (from sb), to Piedmont |
| **42** | I-185 toll, US 29, to Greenville, **W** H HOSPITAL |
| **40** | SC 153, to Easley, **E gas:** Breakers/dsl, **food:** Waffle House, **W gas:** BP, Citgo/dsl, RaceWay, **food:** Arby's, Bojangles, Burger King, Cracker Barrel, El Soreno Mexican, Hardee's, Huddle House, KFC, McDonald's, Pizza Hut/Taco Bell, Sonny BBQ, Sonic, Subway, Zaxby's, **lodging:** Executive Inn, Super 8, **other:** Advance Parts, BiLo, Eckerd |
| **39** | SC 143, to Piedmont, **W gas:** Shell/dsl, **other:** Ace Hardware, antiques |
| **35** | SC 86, to Easley, Piedmont, **E gas:** Pilot/McDonald's/dsl/scales/24hr, **food:** Hardee's (1.5mi), Las Margaritas, Subway (1.5mi), **W gas:** BP/grill/dsl |
| **34** | US 29 (from sb), to Williamston |
| **32** | SC 8, to Pelzer, Easley, **E gas:** Shell/dsl |
| **27** | SC 81, to Anderson, **E gas:** BP/dsl, Exxon, Pumper's Gas/dsl, **food:** Arby's, KFC/Pizza Hut, McDonald's, Waffle House, **lodging:** Holiday Inn Express, **other:** H HOSPITAL, **W gas:** Travel Ctr/DQ/dsl/scales/24hr, **food:** Charlie's Wings |
| **23mm** | rest area sb, full [&] facilities, [C], vending, [⊞] litter barrels, petwalk |
| **21** | US 178, to Anderson, **E gas:** Shell/dsl, **2 mi E food:** Applebee's, Chick-fil-a, Fazoli's, O'Charley's, Ruby Tuesday, **lodging:** La Quinta, Mainstay Suites, Quality Inn, Super 8, **other:** Publix/deli |
| **19b a** | US 76, SC 28, to Anderson, **E gas:** Exxon/dsl, **food:** Charlie T's Wings, Fuddruckers, Hardee's, **lodging:** Day's Inn, Hilton Garden, Royal American Motel, **other:** Aldi Food, Buick/GMC, Chrysler, Publix, Russell Stover, **1 mi E gas:** BP/dsl, Shell, **food:** Chick-fil-A, Chili's, Grand China, Jack-in-the-Box, Longhorn Steaks, O'Charley's, Olive Garden, Panera Bread, Sonny BBQ, TX Roadhouse, Zaxby's, **lodging:** Best Value Inn, **other:** Aldi Foods, Best Buy, Curves, Ford, GNC, Harley-Davidson, Honda, KIA, K-Mart, Mazda, Old Navy, O'Reilley Parts, Ross, Sam's Club, Target, |

| | |
|---|---|
| **19b a** | Continued |
| | Walmart SuperCtr, vet, **W gas:** HotSpot/McDonald's, RaceWay/dsl/24hr, **food:** Buffalo's Café, Cracker Barrel, Fats Cafe, Hooters, Outback Steaks, Subway, Waffle House, Wendy's, Wild Wing Cafe, **lodging:** Comfort Suites, Country Inn Suites, Fairfield Inn, Hampton Inn, Holiday Inn Express, Jameson Inn, **other:** to Clemson U |
| **18mm** | rest area nb, full [&] facilities, [C], vending, [⊞], litter barrels, petwalk |
| **15mm** | Lake Hartwell |
| **14** | SC 187, to Clemson, Anderson, **E gas:** FuelClub/dsl/24hr/@, **food:** Huddle House/24hr, **other:** KOA (1mi) , **W gas:** BP/dsl, **food:** Famous Pizza Grill, **lodging:** Budget Inn, **other:** to Clem Research Pk |
| **12mm** | Seneca River, Lake Hartwell |
| **11** | SC 24, SC 243, to Townville, **E gas:** Exxon/dsl, Sunoco/dsl/24hr, **food:** Subway, **other:** Savannah River Scenic Hwy, **W gas:** Shell/dsl, **food:** Circle's Cafe, TCBY, **other:** GS RV Park (3mi) |
| **9mm** | weigh sta nb |
| **4** | SC 243, to SC 24, **E gas:** Exxon, Mobil/dsl/LP/rest./scales/24hr, **W gas:** Marathon/Russell's Gen. Store |
| **2** | SC 59, to Fair Play, **W** fireworks |
| **1** | SC 11, to Walhalla, **W food:** Gazebo Rest., **other:** fireworks, to Lake Hartwell SP |
| **.5mm** | Welcome Ctr nb, full [&] facilities, info, [C], [⊞], litter barrels, vending, petwalk |
| **0mm** | South Carolina/Georgia state line, Lake Hartwell, Tagaloo River |

## INTERSTATE 95

| Exit # | Services |
|---|---|
| **198mm** | South Carolina/North Carolina state line |
| **196mm** | Welcome Ctr sb, full [&] facilities, info, [C], vending, [⊞], litter barrels, petwalk |
| **195mm** | Little Pee Dee River |
| **193** | SC 9, SC 57, to N Myrtle Beach, Dillon, **E gas:** BP/24hr, Exxon, Mobil, Sunoco/dsl, **food:** Bojangles, Burger King, Fiesta Tapatia, Huddle House, Shoney's, Subway, Waffle House, Wendy's, Zaxby's, **lodging:** Best Value Inn, Comfort Inn, Deluxe Inn, Hampton Inn, Holiday Inn Express, Knights Inn, Ramada Ltd, **other:** H HOSPITAL, Bi-Lo Foods, CVS Drug, $General, Food Lion, Walmart, **W gas:** BP/dsl, **lodging:** Econolodge, Super 8 |
| **190** | SC 34, to Dillon, **E gas:** BP/Stuckey's/DQ, **other:** repair |
| **181** | SC 38, Oak Grove, **E gas:** BP/Subway/dsl/24hr, ⊕ FLYING J /Cookery/dsl/LP/scales/24hr/@, Shell/McDonald's/dsl/24hr, **W gas:** Wilco/Hess/DQ/Wendy's/dsl/scales/24hr, **lodging:** Best Western, **other:** auto/truck repair |
| **175mm** | Pee Dee River |
| **172mm** | rest area both lanes, full [&] facilities, [C], [⊞], vending, litter barrels, petwalk |
| **170** | SC 327, **E gas:** BP, Pilot/Wendy's/dsl/scales/24hr, **food:** McDonald's, **lodging:** Holiday Inn Express, **other:** to Myrtle Beach, Missile Museum, **W gas:** Citgo/dsl |
| **169** | TV Rd, to Florence, **E other:** KOA (1mi), Peterbilt, dsl repair, **W gas:** BP, Petro/Shell/Pizza Hut/dsl/rest./24hr/@, **lodging:** Best Value Inn, **other:** Blue Beacon |
| **164** | US 52, to Darlington, Florence, **E gas:** Citgo/dsl, Exxon/Pizza Hut/dsl, RaceWay/24hr, Shell, **food:** Arby's, Cracker Barrel, Denny's, Hardee's, Huddle House, Longhorn Steaks, McDonald's, Olive Garden, Quincy's, |

*(Left margin vertical text: N ↑ S, ANDERSON, SC)*

*(Right margin vertical text: ANDERSON, N ↑ S, DILLON)*

## INTERSTATE 95 CONT'D

**N**
**S**
**FLORENCE**

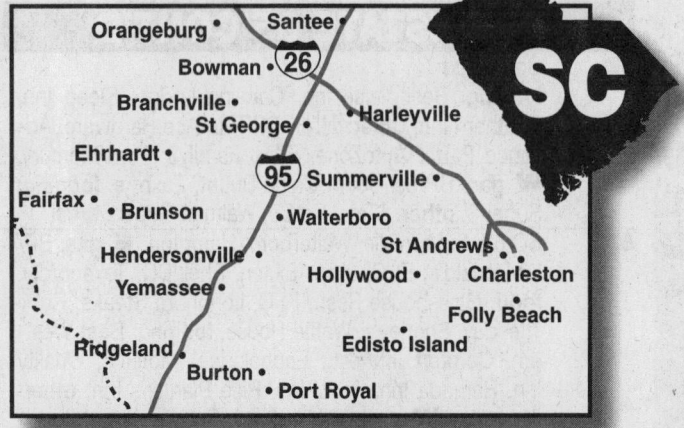

**164** Continued
Quizno's, Red Lobster, Ruby Tuesday, Waffle House, Wendy's, Western Sizzlin, **lodging:** Best Western, Comfort Inn, Courtyard, Econolodge, Holiday Inn, Knight's Inn, Motel 6, Red Roof Inn, Suburban Lodge, Super 8, **other:** H HOSPITAL, Best Buy, Chrysler/Jeep, $Tree, Home Depot, Kohl's, Lowes Whse, Pontiac/Buick, Sam's Club, Walmart, **W gas:** Hess/dsl, TA/BP/Popeye's/dsl, Pilot/Subway/Taco Bell/dsl, **food:** Arby's, Bojangles, Burger King, Fatz Café, KFC, Shoney's, Zaxby's, **lodging:** Country Inn&Suites, Day's Inn, Hampton Inn, Microtel, Ramada Inn, Sleep Inn, Thunderbird Inn, Travel House Inn, Wingate Inn, **other:** to Darlington Raceway

**160b** I-20 W, to Columbia

**160a** Lp 20, to Florence, **E gas:** Shell/dsl, **food:** Arby's, Bruster's Ice Cream, Burger King, Chick-fil-A, ChuckeCheese, Huddle House, IHOP, Morrison's Cafeteria, Outback Steaks, Pizza Hut, Red Lobster, Ruby Tuesday, Shoney's, Waffle House, Western Sizzlin, **lodging:** Courtyard, Fairfield Inn, Hampton Inn, Hilton Garden, Holiday Inn Express, Red Roof Inn, SpringHill Suites, **other:** Advance Parts, Belk, Best Buy, Chevrolet, $Tree, Goody's, JC Penney, Lowes Whse, Sam's Club, Sears/auto, Target, Walmart/drugs, mall

**157** US 76, Timmonsville, Florence, **E gas:** BP/dsl, Exxon/McDonald's/dsl, Kangaroo/dsl, Phillips 66, **food:** Shooky's Diner, Swamp Fox Diner, Waffle House, **lodging:** Day's Inn, Howard Johnson Express, **W gas:** Sunoco, **lodging:** Ramada, Tree Room Inn/rest., Swamp Fox Camping (1mi)

**153** Honda Way, **W** Honda Plant

**150** SC 403, to Sardis, **E gas:** BP/dsl, **lodging:** Budget Inn, **W gas:** Exxon/dsl

**147mm** Lynches River

**146** SC 341, to Lynchburg, Olanta, **E lodging:** Relax Inn

**141** SC 53, SC 58, to Shiloh, **E gas:** Exxon/dsl, **other:** Don-Mar RV Ctr, to Woods Bay SP, **W gas:** Shell

**139mm** **rest area both lanes, full** ♿ **facilities,** 📞**, vending,** 🍽, **litter barrels, petwalk**

**135** US 378, to Sumter, Turbeville, **E gas:** BP, Citgo/dsl/24hr, **food:** Compass Rest., **lodging:** Day's Inn, Knight's Inn, **W gas:** Exxon/dsl, **other:** Pineland Golf Course

**132** SC 527, to Sardinia, Kingstree

**130mm** Black River

**122** US 521, to Alcolu, Manning, **W gas:** Exxon/dsl, **food:** MD Fried Chicken (2mi)

**119** SC 261, to Paxville, Manning, **0-1 mi E gas:** Mobil, Shell/24hr, TA/BP/Popeye's/Pizza Hut/dsl/scales/24hr/@, **food:** Arby's, Burger King, Huddle House, KFC, Mariachi's Mexican, Shoney's, Sonic, Subway, Waffle House, Wendy's, Yucatan Mexican, Zaxby's, **lodging:** Best Western, Comfort Inn, Hampton Inn, Holiday Inn Express, Ramada Inn, **other:** H HOSPITAL, AutoZone, Chrysler/Jeep/Dodge, Campers Paradise RV Park, CVS Drug, $General, Ford, Goodyear/auto, Radio Shack, Southern Holiday RV Ctr, Walmart SuperCtr/gas, **W gas:** Horizon/dsl, Paxville/24hr, **lodging:** Super 8, **other:** auto repair

**115** US 301, to Summerton, Manning, **W gas:** Shell/dsl/24hr, **food:** Georgio's Greek, **lodging:** Econolodge

**SANTEE**

**108** SC 102, Summerton, **E gas:** BP/DQ/Stuckey's, Citgo/dsl, **other:** TawCaw RV Park (6m) , **W lodging:** Best Inn, Day's Inn, Deluxe Inn, Knight's Inn

**102** US 15, US 301 N, to Santee, **E gas:** StopSpot/dsl, **lodging:** Santee Resort/Motel, **other:** Bigwater RV Camping, Santee Lakes Camping, **W gas:** Shell/dsl, **other:** to Santee NWR

**100mm** Lake Marion

**99mm** **rest area both lanes, full** ♿ **facilities,** 📞**, info, vending,** 🍽**, litter barrels, petwalk**

**98** SC 6, to Eutawville, Santee, **E gas:** BP/Bojangles, Chevron/LP, Citgo, Mobil, **food:** Coaster's Seafood, Huddle House, KFC, La Fogata Mexican, LT's Rest., Pizza Hut, Shoney's, Subway, Theo's Rest., **lodging:** Best Western, Hampton Inn, Howard Johnson, Ramada, Super 8, Travelodge, **other:** $General, Piggly Wiggly, Russell Stover Candy, Santee Outlets/famous brands, **W gas:** Citgo, Exxon, Hess/dsl, Horizon/Noble Roman's/dsl/24hr, Shell/dsl, **food:** Burger King, Cracker Barrel, Maurice's BBQ, McDonald's, Peking Chinese, Tastee Rest., Waffle House, Wendy's, **lodging:** Baymont Inn, Budget Motel, Clark Inn/rest., Country Inn&Suites, Holiday Inn, Lake Marion Inn, Mansion Park Motel, Quality Inn, **other:** CarQuest, CVS Drug, Family$, Food Lion, USPO, to Santee SP (3mi)

**97** US 301 S (from sb, no return), to Orangeburg

**93** US 15, to Santee, Holly Hill

**90** US 176, to Cameron, Holly Hill, **W gas:** Exxon/dsl

**86b a** I-26, W to Columbia, E to Charleston

**82** US 178, to Bowman, Harleyville, **E gas:** BP, Wilco/Hess/Stuckey's/Wendy's/DQ/dsl/scales/24hr, **lodging:** Peachtree Inn, **other:** antiques, **W gas:** Shell/dsl, **other:** tires/truck repair

**77** US 78, to Bamberg, St George, **E gas:** Exxon/KFC, Monoco, Shell/Subway/TCBY, **food:** Georgio's Rest., Hardee's, McDonald's, Pizza Hut, Skynyrd's Grill, Waffle House, **lodging:** Best Value Inn, Comfort Inn/RV Park, Quality Inn, **other:** Chevrolet/Pontiac/GMC, Family$, Ford, Jolly Acres RV Park, Ried's Foods, USPO, **W gas:** BP, Shell/Taco Bell/dsl, **food:** Huddle House, **lodging:** Country Hearth Inn, Day's Inn, Super 8

**68** SC 61, Canadys, **E gas:** BP, El Cheapo/scales, Shell/Subway/dsl, **other:** truck lube/repair, to Colleton SP (3mi)

**62** SC 34

**57** SC 64, Walterboro, **E gas:** BP/Subway/TCBY/dsl/24hr, Horizon, Shell/DQ, Mobil/dsl, Sunoco/dsl, **food:** Arby's, Burger King, Capt D's, Huddle House, KFC, McDonald's, Olde House Café, Waffle House, Wendy's,

**SC**

**W A L T E R B O R O   N ↕ S   H A R D E E V I L L E**

## INTERSTATE 95 CONT'D

| | |
|---|---|
| 57 | Continued |
| | **lodging:** Best Value Inn, Carolina Lodge, Sleep Inn, Southern Inn, **other:** H HOSPITAL, Ace Hardware, Advance Parts, AutoZone, BiLo, Family$, Ford/Mercury, **W gas:** BP/dsl, **food:** China Buffet, Zaxby's, **lodging:** Super 8, **other:** $Tree, PetCo, Walmart SuperCtr/dsl |
| 53 | SC 63, to Varnville, Walterboro, Hampton, **E gas:** BP/McDonald's, El Cheapo, Exxon, Shell/DQ, Texaco/dsl, **food:** Glasshouse Rest., KFC, Longhorn Steaks, Ruby Tuesday, Shoney's, Waffle House, **lodging:** Best Western, Comfort Inn/rest., Econolodge, Motel 6, Quality Inn, Ramada Inn, Royal Inn, Rice Planter's Inn, **other:** fireworks, **W gas:** BP/dsl, **food:** Cracker Barrel, **lodging:** Day's Inn, Deluxe Inn, Hampton Inn, Holiday Inn Express, Microtel, **other:** Green Acres Camping |
| 47mm | **rest area both lanes, full ♿ facilities, 🕿, vending, ⛲, litter barrels, petwalk** |
| 42 | US 21, to Yemassee, Beaufort |
| 40mm | Combahee River |
| 38 | SC 68, to Hampton, Yemassee, **E gas:** Chevron, **other:** Family$, **W gas:** BP/Subway/TCBY, Exxon/dsl, Shell/dsl, **food:** Courtney Bay Seafood, J's Rest., **lodging:** Palmetto Lodge/rest., Super 8 |
| 33 | US 17 N, to Beaufort, **E gas:** BP/dsl, Exxon/McDonald's, Shell, Texaco/TCBY/Subway, **food:** Denny's, Waffle House, Wendy's, **lodging:** Best Western, Budget Inn, Hampton Inn, Holiday Inn Express, Knight's Inn, **other:** Confederate Railroad Museum, KOA, Oaks RV Camping |
| 30.5mm | Tullifinny River |
| 29mm | Coosawhatchie River |
| 28 | SC 462, to Coosawhatchie, Hilton Head, Bluffton, **W gas:** Chevron/dsl, Citgo, Exxon/Chester Fried/dsl |
| 22 | US 17, Ridgeland, **W gas:** Sunoco, **lodging:** Plantation Inn, **other:** H HOSPITAL |
| 21 | SC 336, to Hilton Head, Ridgeland, **E food:** Wendy's, **other:** Boat'n RV Ctr, **W gas:** BP/dsl, Chevron/dsl/24hr, Citgo, Exxon, **food:** Bella Pizza, Burger King, Hong Kong Chinese, Huddle House, Jasper's Porch, KFC, Subway, Waffle House, **lodging:** Carolina Lodge, Comfort Inn/rest., Days Inn, Quality Inn, **other:** H HOSPITAL, Curves, $General, Harvey's Foods, Rite Aid |
| 18 | SC 13, to US 17, US 278, to Switzerland, Granville, Ridgeland |
| 17mm | parking area both lanes, commercial vehicles only |
| 8 | US 278, to Bluffton, Hardeeville, **E gas:** BP/Huddle House/Wendy's/dsl/scales, Exxon, Kangaroo/McDonald's, **other:** H HOSPITAL, **W gas:** Chevron/Noble Roman/TCBY/Subway/dsl, Mobil/Kangaroo/dsl, **lodging:** Holiday Inn Express, Motel 6 |
| 5 | US 17, US 321, to Savannah, Hardeeville, **E gas:** Chevron/dsl, Exxon/Blimpie, Shell/24hr, **food:** Mi Tierrita Mexican, Waffle House, **lodging:** Day's Inn, Economy Inn, Sleep Inn, **other:** fireworks, to Savannah NWR, **W gas:** BP/dsl, Citgo, Exxon, Sunoco/dsl, **food:** Burger King, Los 3 Garcia's, New China Rest., Shoney's, Wendy's, **lodging:** Clean Stay USA, Comfort Inn, Country Hearth Inn, Deluxe Inn, Econolodge, Knight's Inn, Quality Inn, Super 8, **other:** $General, NAPA |
| 4.5mm | **Welcome Ctr nb, full ♿ facilities, info, 🕿, ⛲, litter barrels, vending, petwalk** |
| 4mm | weigh sta both lanes |
| 0mm | South Carolina/Georgia state line, Savannah River |

**N ↕ S   G R E E N V I L L E**

## INTERSTATE 385 - GREENVILLE

| Exit # | Services |
|---|---|
| 42 | US 276, Stone Ave, to Travelers Rest., to Greenville Zoo, **E other:** CarQuest, **W gas:** Spinx, **1-2 mi W** multiple services on US 276, I-385 begins/ends on US 276. |
| 40b a | SC 291, Pleasantburg Dr, **E gas:** Sunoco, **food:** Jack-in-the-Box, Little Caesar's, Olive Tree, Pizza Hut, S&S Cafeteria, Sonic, Steak&Ale, Subway, Taco Casa, Wendy's, **other:** CVS Drug, Walgreens, to BJU, Furman U, **W gas:** Citg/dsl, **food:** Domino's, Krispy Kreme, **lodging:** Quality Inn, Sleep Inn, **other:** transmissions |
| 39 | Haywood Rd, **E gas:** BP, Exxon/dsl, **food:** Domino's, LongHorn Steaks, Outback Steaks, Tony's Pizzaria, **lodging:** AmeriSuites, Courtyard, GuestHouse Suites, Hawthorn Inn, Hilton, La Quinta, Quality Inn, Residence Inn, **other:** Firestone, TJ Maxx, **W gas:** Crown, Shell, Texaco, **food:** Arby's, Applebee's, Blackeyed Pea, Buffalo's Café, Burger King, Chili's, ChuckeCheese, CityRange Steaks, Don Pablo, Hardee's, Italian Mkt/grill, Jack-in-the-Box, Jason's Deli, Kanpai Tokyo, O'Charley's, Ruby Tuesday, Senor Wrap's, Starbucks, Steak'n Shake, Waffle House, Wendy's, **lodging:** Hampton Inn, Studio+, **other:** Barnes&Noble, Belk, Circuit City, Dillard's, Discount Tire, Goodyear, Harley-Davidson, JC Penney, LensCrafters, Macy's, NTB, Sears/auto, mall |
| 37 | Roper Mtn Rd, **E other:** BiLo Foods, **W gas:** Amoco, BP/dsl, Exxon/Pantry, RaceTrac, **food:** Atl Bread Co, Backyard Burger, Burger King, Capri's Italian, Cracker Barrel, Fazoli's, LoneStar Steaks, McDonald's, Miyabi Japanese, Rafferty's, Remington's Rest., Waffle House, **lodging:** Day's Inn, Crowne Plaza, Embassy Suites, Fairfield Inn, Holiday Inn Select, La Quinta, Travelodge, **other:** BJ's Whse, Goody's, Home Depot, Lowe's Whse, Old Navy, Target, mall |
| 36b a | I-85, N to Charlotte, S to Atlanta |
| 35 | SC 146, Woodruff Rd, **E gas:** Spinx, **food:** Applebee's, AZ Steaks, Bojangles, Bone Fish Grill, Boston Pizzaria, Brewster's, Burger King, Chick-fil-A, Chili's, Fazoli's, Grand Buffet, Hardee's, Jersey Mike's Subs, KFC, King Buffet, McAlister's Deli, Moe's SW Grill, Perkins, Ryan's, Sonic, Starbucks, Subway, Taco Bell, Topper's Rest., Waffle House, Wendy's, Zaxby's, **other:** Ace Hardware, Aldi Foods, BiLo Foods, Discount Tire, $Tree, Eckerd, Kohl's, Publix, Radio Shack, Sam's Club/gas, Staples, Tire Kingdom, USPO, Walmart SuperCtr, **W gas:** Blue Jay/dsl, **food:** Bob Evan's, Burger King, Fatz Café, Fuddrucker's, IHOP, Lieus Bistro, Midori's Rest., Mimi's Cafe, Monterey Mexican, Red Robin, Sticky Fingers, TCBY, Waffle House, **lodging:** Drury Inn, Hampton Inn, **other:** Barnes& Noble, Goodyear/auto, Hamrick's Outlet, Lowe's Whse, funpark |
| 34 | Butler Rd, Mauldin, **E gas:** Exxon, **food:** Arby's, **other:** CVS Drug, **W gas:** Phillips 66, **lodging:** Super 8 (3mi) |
| 33 | Bridges Rd, Mauldin |
| 31 | I-185 toll, SC 417, to Laurens Rd, **E gas:** BP, **food:** Hardee's, Jack in the Box, **other:** H HOSPITAL, **S food:** A&W, LJSilver, **lodging:** Masters Inn |
| 30 | I-185 toll, US 276, Standing Springs Rd |
| 29 | Georgia Rd, to Simpsonville |
| 27 | Fairview Rd, to Simpsonville, **E gas:** Pumper's, **food:** Carolina Rest., CoachHouse rest., Hardee's, Little Ceasar's, McDonald's, Milano Pizzaria, New China Buffet, Subway, **lodging:** Palmetto Inn, **other:** H HOSPITAL, Advance Parts, AutoZone, Chevrolet, $General, Rite Aid, |

**SC**

## INTERSTATE 385 CONT'D - GREENVILLE

**N / S SIMPSONVILLE / E / W CHARLESTON**

| | |
|---|---|
| 27 | Continued **W gas:** BP, Exxon, **food:** Applebee's, Arby's, AZ Steaks, Beef o'Brady's, Brewster's, Burger King, Chic-fil-A, Cracker Barrel, Dragon Den Chinese, Hungry Howie's, Jack in the Box, Jersey Mike's, KFC, McDonalds, O'Charley's, Pizza Hut, Quizno's, Ruby Tuesday, Ryan's, Starbucks, Taco Bell, Tequila's Mexican, Waffle House, Wendy's, **lodging:** Comfort Inn, Day's Inn, Hampton Inn, Holiday Inn Express, **other:** Belk, BiLo, CVS Drug, $Tree, GNC, Ingles, Goodyear/auto, Home Depot, Kohl's, Lowe's Whse, Panera Bread, Publix, Ross, Target, Tire Kingdom, TJ Maxx, Walgreen, Walmart SuperCtr/gas, USPO |
| 26 | Harrison Bridge Rd (from sb) |
| 24 | Fairview St, **E gas:** Phillips 66, **food:** Hardee's, Waffle House, **other:** carwash |
| 23 | SC 418, to Fountain Inn, Fork Shoals, **E gas:** Exxon/Subway/dsl/24hr |
| 22 | SC 14 W, Old Laurens Rd, to Fountain Inn |
| 19 | SC 14 E, to Gray Court, Owings |
| 16 | SC 101, to Woodruff, Gray Court |
| 10 | SC 23, to Ora |
| 9 | US 221, to Laurens, Enoree, **E gas:** Exxon/Sub Express/dsl/24hr, **food:** Hunts Bros. Pizza, Waffle House, **lodging:** Budget Lodge, **W** Walmart Dist Ctr, **lodging:** Travel Inn (2mi) |
| 6mm | rest area both lanes (both lanes exit left), full ♿ facilities, 🚻, vending, 🍴 litter barrels, petwalk |
| 5 | SC 49, to Laurens, Union |
| 2 | SC 308, to Clinton, Ora, **W other:** Ⓗ HOSPITAL, to Presbyterian Coll in Clinton |
| 0mm | I-26 S to Columbia, I-385 begins/ends on I-26 at 52mm. |

## INTERSTATE 526 - CHARLESTON

| Exit # | Services |
|---|---|
| 33mm | I-526 begins/ends. |
| 32 | US 17, **0-1 mi N gas:** Hess/dsl, Shell, **food:** Benito's Pizza, Burger King, Chili's, IHOP, LongHorn Steaks, Mama Fu's Asian, On The Border, Starbucks, TGIFriday, **lodging:** Courtyard, **other:** Advance Parts, Barnes&Noble, Belk, Chevrolet, CVS Drug, Firestone, Lowes Whse, Midas, Old Navy, Rite Aid, Tire Kingdom, TrueValue, Walgreens, **0-1 mi S gas:** Exxon/Dunkin Donuts, Mobil, Shell/Circle K, Sunoco, **food:** Applebees, Arby's, Chick-fil-A, Cici's, Domino's, Hardee's, Huddle House, KFC, La Hacienda Mexicana, McDonald's, Outback Steaks, Papa John's, Sticky Fingers, Subway, Wendy's, Zeus Grill, **lodging:** Best Western, Day's Inn, Extended Stay America, Hampton Inn, Holiday Inn, Masters Inn, Quality Inn, Red Roof Inn, River Inn, **other:** Aamco, Bi-Lo, Cadillac, Circuit City, $General, Ford, Harris Teeter, Jiffy Lube, K-Mart, Marshall's, Office Depot, Radio Shack, Staples, TJ Maxx, USPO, VW, Walmart, Whole Foods Mkt, vet |
| 30 | Long Point Rd, **N gas:** BP, Exxon, **food:** Bamboo Garden, Beef'o Brady's, McAlister's, Moe's SW Grill, Sonic, Starbucks, Subway, Waffle House, Wendy's, **other:** CVS Drug, Food Lion, Harris Teeter Foods, PetsMart, Ross, Steinmart, Charles Pinckney NHS |
| 26mm | Wando River |
| 24 | Daniel Island, **S gas:** Texaco, **food:** Dragon Palace, Lana's Mexican, Queen Anne's Steaks/seafood, Subway, |

**CHARLESTON**

| | |
|---|---|
| 24 | Continued **lodging:** Hampton Inn, **other:** Publix |
| 23b a | Clements Ferry Rd |
| 21mm | Cooper River |
| 20 | Virginia Ave (from eb), **S gas:** Hess Depot |
| 19 | N Rhett Ave, **N gas:** Hess, Kangaroo/Subway/dsl, **food:** Hardee's, **other:** Family$, Food Lion, Rite Aid, **S gas:** BP |
| 18b a | US 52, US 78, Rivers Ave, **N gas:** BP/dsl, Hess, Kangaroo/dsl, **food:** KFC, Peking Gourmet, Pizza Hut/Taco Bell, **other:** AutoZone, Dodge, Family$, Ford, H&L Foods, auto repair, **S gas:** Exxon |
| 17b a | I-26, E to Charleston, W to Columbia |
| 16 | Montague Ave, Airport Rd, **S gas:** Sunoco, **food:** Chili's, La Hacienda, Panera Bread, Quizno's, Starbucks, Wendy's, **lodging:** Comfort Inn, Embassy Suites, Extended Stay America, Hilton Garden, Holiday Inn, Homewood Suites, Quality Inn, Residence Inn, Wingate Inn, **other:** Sam's Club, Staples, Tanger Outlet/famous brands, Walmart SuperCtr |
| 15 | SC 642, Dorchester Rd, Paramount Dr, **N gas:** BP, **food:** Pizza Roma (1mi), Wendy's (1mi), **S gas:** Citgo/dsl, Sunoco, **food:** Burger King, Checker's, Domino's, East Bay Deli, Huddle House, Pizza Hut, **lodging:** Airport Inn, **other:** Bi-Lo Foods, CVS Drug, Family$, Food Lion, Harley-Davidson, U-Haul |
| 14 | Leeds Ave, **S lodging:** Value Place Inn, **other:** Ⓗ HOSPITAL, boat marina |
| 13mm | Ashley River |
| 11b a | SC 61, Ashley River Rd, **N food:** Chick-fil-A, McDonald's, O'Charley's, Subway, **other:** Ⓗ HOSPITAL, Food Lion, Home Depot, Lowes Whse, Rite Aid |
| 10 | US 17, SC 7, **services from US 17, E gas:** BP, **food:** Alex's Rest., Burger King, Capt D's, Checker's, CiCi's, Dunkin Donuts, 5 Guys Burgers, Hopsing's, IHOP, McDonald's, Messengers BBQ, Pizza Hut, Red Lobster, Ruby Tuesday, Shoney's, Taco Bell, **lodging:** Best Western, Holiday Inn Express, Motel 6, Sleep Inn, **other:** Buick/GMC/Pontiac, Chevrolet, Dillards, Ford, Honda, Hyundai, Jaguar, Kerr Drug, K-Mart, Mazda, Mini, Mitsubishi, Nissan, Dodge, Pepboys, Piggly Wiggly, Sears/auto, Tire Kingdom, vet, **W gas:** Exxon, Hess, Shell/Circle K, **food:** Halligan's Rest., Hardees, Subway, Waffle House, **lodging:** Econolodge, Hampton Inn, InTown Suites, **other:** Acura, Audi, Advance Parts, Carmax, Chrysler/Jeep, Costco/gas, CVS Drug, Family$, Food Lion, KIA, Subaru, Toyota |

**I-526 begins/ends on US 17.**

## INTERSTATE 29

**N ↕ S**

**WATERTOWN**

| Exit # | Services |
|---|---|
| 253mm | South Dakota/North Dakota state line |
| 251mm | **Welcome Ctr sb, full** 🚻 **facilities, info,** 🕿 🏕, **litter barrels, petwalk** |
| 246 | SD 127, to Rosholt, New Effington, **3 mi** W gas, food, RV camping, Sica Hollow SP (24mi) |
| 242 | no services |
| 235mm | weigh sta sb |
| 232 | SD 10, Sisseton, E **gas:** Dakota Connection/dsl/casino/24hr, **food:** Crossroads Cafe, **1-3 mi** W **gas:** Alco, BP/dsl, Cenex/dsl, Sinclair/dsl, **food:** Cottage Rest, DQ, Pizza Hut, Subway, Taco John's, **lodging:** Holiday Motel, I-29 Motel, Super 8, Viking Motel, **other:** Camp Dakotah, Chevrolet, Family$, NAPA Parts, SuperValu Foods/gas, to Roy Lake SP (25mi), Ft Sisseton SP (35mi) |
| 224 | Peever, Sioux Tribal Hqtrs, E **gas:** Cenex/dsl, W Pickerel Lake (16mi) |
| 213 | SD 15, to Wilmot, **rest area both lanes, full** 🚻 **facilities,** 🕿 🏕, **litter barrels, petwalk, RV dump,** st patrol, **7 mi** E gas, food, to Hartford Beach SP (17mi) |
| 207 | US 12, Summit, E **gas:** Conoco/dsl/24hr, W Blue Dog Fish Hatchery (15mi), Waubay NWR (19mi) |
| 201 | to Twin Brooks |
| 193 | SD 20, to South Shore, Stockholm |
| 185 | to Waverly, **4 mi** W **other:** Dakota Sioux Casino/rest. |
| 180 | US 81 S, to Watertown, **5 mi** W **gas:** Conoco, **other:** H HOSPITAL, Bramble Park Zoo, airport |
| 177 | US 212, Watertown, E **gas:** BP/Subway/Grainery Cafe/dsl/24hr, **lodging:** Holiday Inn Express, **other:** Truckers QuikLube, tires, W **gas:** Shell/dsl, **food:** Applebees, Culvers, Hunter's Rest., McDonald's, Starbucks, **lodging:** Comfort Inn, Country Inn Suites, Day's Inn, **other:** H HOSPITAL, $Tree, Redlin Art Ctr, Walmart SuperCtr, **1-2 mi** W **gas:** BP/dsl, Cenex/dsl, Conoco/dsl, **food:** Arby's, Burger King, China Buffet, Domino's Pizza, DQ, Dragon Wall Chinese, Godfather's, Herberger's, Little Caesar's, Papa John's, Papa Murphy's, Perkins, Pizza Hut, Quizno's, Senor Max's Mexican, Subway/TCBY, Taco John's, **lodging:** Drake Hotel, Travelers Inn, **other:** Advance Parts, Buick/Nissan, Chrysler/Dodge/Jeep, EconoFoods, Firestone/auto, Ford/Lincoln/Mercury, Goodyear/auto, Herberger's, Hy-Vee Foods, JC Penney, Jo-Ann Fabrics, K-Mart, NAPA Parts, Nissan, Osco Drug, Pronto Parts, ShopKO, Target, Tires+, Walgreen, mall, to Sandy Shore RA (10mi) |
| 164 | SD 22, to Castlewood, Clear Lake, **9 mi** E **gas:** Cenex/dsl, **other:** H HOSPITAL |
| 161mm | **rest area both lanes, full** 🚻 **facilities,** 🕿 🏕, **litter barrels, vending, petwalk, RV dump** |
| 157 | to Brandt |
| 150 | SD 28, SD 15 N, to Toronto, **7 mi** W gas, food, lodging, **24 mi** W Lake Poinsett RA, SD Amateur Baseball Hall of Fame |
| 140 | SD 30, to White, Bruce, W Oakwood Lakes SP (12mi) |
| 133 | US 14 byp, Brookings, W to SD St U, museums, Laura Ingalls Wilder Home, E tires |
| 132 | US 14, Lp 29, Brookings, E **gas:** Cenex/Burger King/dsl, **food:** Applebee's, **lodging:** Fairfield Inn, Holiday Inn Express, Super 8, W **gas:** BP, **food:** Burger King, DQ, Guadalajara Mexican, KFC, King's Wok, McDonald's, Papa John's, Papa Murphy's, Perkins, Pizza Ranch, |

**SIOUX FALLS**

| | |
|---|---|
| 132 | Continued Subway, Z'Kota Grill, **lodging:** Comfort Inn, Days Inn, Staurolite Inn, **other:** H HOSPITAL, Advance Parts, Big O Tire, CarQuest, Chevrolet/Pontiac/Buick/Cadillac, Lowe's Whse, Radio Shack, Walmart SuperCtr, city park |
| 127 | SD 324, to Elkton, Sinai |
| 124mm | Big Sioux River |
| 121 | to Nunda, Ward, E **rest area both lanes, full** 🚻 **facilities,** 🕿 🏕, **litter barrels, vending, petwalk, RV dump,** st patrol, W food, RV camping |
| 114 | SD 32, to Flandreau, **7 mi** E **gas:** Cenex, **food:** Subway, **lodging:** Sioux River Motel/RV park, **other:** Santee Tribal Hqtrs |
| 109 | SD 34, to Madison, Colman, W **gas:** BP/dsl/rest., Shell/dsl/rest., **20 mi** W **other:** to Lake Herman SP, Dakota St U, museum |
| 104 | to Trent, Chester |
| 103mm | **parking area both lanes** |
| 98 | SD 115 S, Dell Rapids, E Chevrolet/Pontiac, **3 mi** E **gas:** Kum&Go, Shell, **food:** Pizza Ranch, **lodging:** Bilmar Inn, **other:** H HOSPITAL |
| 94 | SD 114, to Baltic, E **gas:** flea mkt **10 mi** E **other:** to EROS Data Ctr, US Geological Survey |
| 86 | to Renner, Crooks |
| 84b a | I-90, W to Rapid City, E to Albert Lea |
| 83 | SD 38 W, 60th St, E **gas:** ⊕FLYING J/Country Mkt/dsl/24hr/scales/@, **lodging:** Quality Suites, **other:** Freightliner Trucks, Harley-Davidson, Northview Campers, repair, W **other:** fireworks |
| 82 | Benson Rd |
| 81 | SD 38 E, Russell St, Sioux Falls, E **gas:** BP/24hr, Citgo, Food'n Fuel, **food:** Burger King, Country Kitchen, Roll'n Pin Rest., **lodging:** Arena Motel, Best Western, Brimark Inn, Kelly Inn, Motel 6, Oaks Hotel, Ramada Inn, Ramkota/rest., Sheraton, Sleep Inn, Super 8, **other:** Schaap's RV Ctr, auto repair, st patrol |
| 80 | Madison St, E fairgrounds |
| 79 | SD 42, 12th St, E **gas:** BP/24hr, Cenex, F&F, **food:** Burger King, Burger Time, Godfather's, Golden Harvest Chinese, KFC, McDonald's, Pizza Hut, Subway, Taco Bell, Taco John's, Tomacelli's Pizza, Wendy's, **lodging:** Nite's Inn (1mi), Ramada Ltd, **other:** H HOSPITAL, Ace Hardware, BMW/Toyota, Chevrolet, $General, Jack's Campers, JiffyLube, K-Mart, Lewis Drug, Saturn, Toyota/Scion, Walgreen, city park, to Great Plains Zoo/museum, W **gas:** Cenex/dsl, Citgo, Phillips 66/dsl, **food:** Z'Kota Grille, **lodging:** Westwick Motel, **other:** Tower RV Park, to USS SD Battleship Mem |
| 78 | 26th St, Empire St, E **gas:** Phillips 66/dsl, **food:** Carino's Italian, Coldstone Creamery, Chevy's Mexican, Chuck-eCheese, Cracker Barrel, Culver's, Domino's, KFC, Michael's Steaks, Outback Steaks, Rookie's Grill, Ruby Tuesday, Rue 41 Cafe, Sonic, **lodging:** Clubhouse Suites, Hampton Inn, Holiday Inn Express, StayBridge Suites, **other:** Home Depot, Michael's, Sam's Club/gas, USPO, World Mkt, W **food:** DQ, Oscar's Coffee, Papa John's, Quizno's, Referee Grill, Starbucks, **lodging:** TownePlace Suites, **other:** Hy-Vee Foods/gas, Lowes Whse |
| 77 | 41st St, Sioux Falls, E **gas:** BP/24hr, Sinclair/dsl, SA/dsl, Shell, **food:** Arby's, Burger King, Carlos O'Kelly's,'s, Champp's Grill, Chili's, China Express, Fry'n Pan Rest., |

## INTERSTATE 29 CONT'D

**N ↕ S SIOUX FALLS E ↕ W**

**77** Continued

Fuddrucker's, Ground Round, HuHot Mongolian, KFC, Krispy Kreme, La Fiesta Mexican, LoneStar Steaks, McDonald's, Old Chicago Pizza, Olive Garden, Pancake House, Papa Murphy's, Perkins, Pizza Hut, Pizza Inn, Qdoba Mexican, Quizno's, Red Lobster, Schlotsky's, Starbucks, Subway, Szechwan Chinese, Taco Bell, Taco John's, Texas Roadhouse, TimberLodge Steaks, Valentino's Rest., Wendy's, **lodging:** Best Western Empire, Comfort Suites, Fairfield Inn, Microtel, Radisson, Residence Inn, Rodeway Inn, Super 8, **other:** Advance Parts, Barnes&Noble, Batteries+, Best Buy, Big O Tire, Checker Parts, Chrysler/Jeep/Mazda, Curves, Ford/Lincoln/Mercury, Goodyear/auto, Hancock Fabrics, Hyundai/Nissan, JC Penney, JiffyLube, Macy's, Old Navy, PetCo, Radio Shack, Sears/auto, ShopKO, Target, Tires+, Toyota, Village Automotive, Walgreen, Walmart SuperCtr, VW, Younkers, mall, **W gas:** Citgo, Shell/dsl, **food:** Burger King, Denucci's Pizza, Godfather's, IHOP, Little Caesars, Peking Chinese, Perkins/24hr, Subway, **lodging:** AmericInn, Baymont Inn, Day's Inn, Red Roof Inn, **other:** Lewis Drug, USPO

**75** I-229 E, to I-90 E

**73** Tea, **E gas:** Larry's Trkstp/dsl/café, **1.5mi W** Red Barn Camping

**71** to Harrisburg, Lennox, **W** RV camping

**68** to Lennox, Parker

**64** SD 44, Worthing, **W other:** Chevrolet/Pontiac/Buick, Great Plains RV Ctr

**62** US 18 E, to Canton, **E gas:** Shell/pizza/dsl, **lodging:** motel/RV park, **W** repair

**59** US 18 W, to Davis, Hurley

**56** to Fairview, **E** to Newton Hills SP (12mi)

**53** to Viborg

**50** to Centerville, Hudson

**47** SD 46, to Irene, Beresford, **E gas:** Casey's, Conoco/Burger King/dsl, Sinclair/dsl, **food:** Emily's Café, Stone Hearth Cafe, Subway, **lodging:** Crossroads Motel, Super 8, **other:** Chevrolet, Fiesta Foods, Windmill Camping,

**47** Continued

repair, **W gas:** Cenex/cafe/dsl/24hr, **other:** Radio Shack

**42** to Alcester, Wakonda

**41mm** truck check (from sb)

**38** to Volin, **E** to Union Grove SP (3mi)

**31** SD 48, to Akron, Spink

**26** SD 50, to Vermillion, **E** Welcome Ctr/rest area both lanes, full ♿ facilities, info, 🅲, 🏕, litter barrels, petwalk, RV dump, **W gas:** Conoco/dsl/cafe/24hr, 6-7 mi **W gas:** Casey's/gas, Phillips 66, **food:** Burger King, Pizza Hut, Subway, Taco John's, **lodging:** Comfort Inn, Holiday Inn, Prairie Inn, Super 8, Westside Inn, **other:** Ⓗ HOSPITAL, Hy-Vee Foods, to U of SD, to Lewis & Clark RA

**18** Lp 29, to Burbank, Elk Point, **E gas:** BP/dsl, Casey's, **food:** Cody's Rest., **lodging:** HomeTowne Inn

**15** to Elk Point, 1 mi **E** gas, food, lodging, **W** fireworks

**13mm** weigh sta nb, parking area sb

**9** SD 105, Jefferson, **E gas:** BP/Choice Cut Rest./dsl

**4** McCook, 1 mi **W other:** KOA (seasonal), Adams Homestead/nature preserve

**2** N Sioux City, **E gas:** Cenex, Goode/dsl/rest/casino, **food:** Glass Palace Rest. (1mi), McDonald's, Taco John's, **other:** USPO, fireworks, **W gas:** Casey's/gas, Freeway Express/Chester Fried, **lodging:** Comfort Inn, Hampton Inn, Red Carpet Inn, Super 8, **other:** KOA, to Sodrac Dogtrack

**1** **E other:** Dakota Dunes Golf Resort, **W gas:** Phillips 66/dsl, **food:** Graham's Grill, **lodging:** Country Inn Suites

**0mm** South Dakota/Iowa state line, Big Sioux River

## INTERSTATE 90

| Exit # | Services |
|---|---|
| **412.5mm** | South Dakota/Minnesota state line |
| **412mm** | Welcome Ctr wb/rest area eb, full ♿ facilities, info, 🅲, 🏕, litter barrels, petwalk, RV dump (wb), weigh sta both lanes |

## INTERSTATE 90 CONT'D

| | |
|---|---|
| **410** | Valley Springs, **N** Palisades SP (7mi), **S** Beaver Creek Nature Area, gas, food |
| **406** | SD 11, Brandon, Corson, **S** Palisades SP (10mi), **S** **gas:** BP/dsl, Shell, Sinclair/McDonald's/dsl, **food:** Brandon Steaks, Dominos, DQ, Pizza Ranch, Subway, Taco John's, Tailgater's Grill, **lodging:** Comfort Inn, Holiday Inn Express, **other:** Lewis Drug, Sunshine Foods, True Value, to Big Sioux RA (2mi) |
| **402** | EROS Data Ctr, **N other:** fireworks, Jellystone RV Park, tires |
| **400** | I-229 S |
| **399** | SD 115, Cliff Ave, Sioux Falls, **N gas:** TC's Minimart/dsl, **other:** Spader RV Ctr, KOA, **S gas:** BP, Holiday/dsl, Pilot/Grandma Max's Rest./Subway/dsl/24hr/@, Shell, **food:** Arby's, Burger King, McDonald's, Perkins, Rocco's Italian, Taco Bell, Taco John's, **lodging:** Cloud Nine Motel, Comfort Inn, Day's Inn, Super 8, **other:** H HOSPITAL, Blue Beacon, Graham Tire, Kenworth, Peterbilt, Volvo |
| **398mm** | Big Sioux River |
| **396b a** | I-29, N to Brookings, S to Sioux City |
| **390** | SD 38, Hartford, **N other:** Camp Dakota RV Park, Goos RV Ctr, **S gas:** Cowboy Town/dsl |
| **387** | rd 17, Hartford, **N gas:** Phillips 66/dsl, **food:** Pizza Ranch |
| **379** | SD 19, Humboldt, **N gas:** Mobil/dsl, Shell/Town&Country Store/dsl (1mi), **food:** Main Cafe (1mi), **other:** USPO |
| **375mm** | E Vermillion River |
| **374** | to SD 38, Montrose, 5 mi **S other:** Battle Creek Res., Lake Vermillion RA, RV camping |
| **368** | Canistota, 4 mi **S lodging:** Best Western |
| **364** | US 81, to Yankton, Salem, 4 mi **N gas:** Cenex, Sinclair, **lodging:** Home Motel, **other:** Camp America |
| **363.5mm** | W Vermillion River |
| **363mm** | **rest area both lanes, full** &#x267F; **facilities,** [, &#x1F6BB;, **litter barrels, vending, petwalk, RV dump, st patrol** |
| **357** | to Bridgewater, Canova |
| **353** | Spencer, Emery, **S gas:** FuelMart/Subway/dsl/casino/24hr |
| **352mm** | Wolf Creek |
| **350** | SD 25, Emery, Farmer, **N** to DeSmet, Home of Laura Ingalls Wilder |
| **344** | SD 262, to Fulton, Alexandria, **S gas:** Shell/dsl, **food:** Joe's Cafe |
| **337mm** | **parking area both lanes** |
| **335** | Riverside Rd, **N** KOA (1mi) |
| **334.5mm** | James River |
| **332** | SD 37 S, to Parkston, Mitchell, **N gas:** BP/24hr, Cenex/dsl, Conoco, Phillips 66, Pilot/Shell/Subway/dsl/scales/24hr, **food:** Arby's, Bonanza, Burger King, Country Kitchen, DQ, Kinder's Cafe, McDonald's, Perkins, Pizza Hut, Pizza Ranch, Twin Dragon Chinese, **lodging:** AmericInn, Best Western, Quality Inn, Day's Inn, Super 8, Thunderbird Motel, **other:** H HOSPITAL, Advance Parts, Big K-Mart, R&R RV Park, Rondee's Campground, Walgreens, transmissions, **1-2 mi N other:** to Corn Palace, Museum of Pioneer Life, **S gas:** Shell/Godfather's/Taco Bell/dsl/24hr, **food:** Culver's, KFC, Quizno's, Ruby Tuesday, **lodging:** Comfort Inn, Hampton Inn, Kelly Inn, **other:** Cabela's, $Tree, Radio Shack, Walmart SuperCtr/gas |
| **330** | SD 37 N, Mitchell, **N gas:** Cenex/dsl/24hr, Shell/dsl, Sinclair, **food:** DQ, **lodging:** Anthony Motel, Econolodge, |

| | |
|---|---|
| **330** | Continued Holiday Inn/rest., Motel 6, Siesta Motel, **other:** H HOSPITAL, County Fair Foods, Jack's Campers/RV ctr., Mr. Tire, to Corn Palace, museum, transmissions, weigh sta, **S other:** Dakota RV Park |
| **325** | Betts Rd, **S** Famil-e-Fun Camping |
| **319** | Mt Vernon, 1 mi **N gas:** Cenex, Sinclair/dsl |
| **310** | US 281, to Stickney, **S gas:** Sinclair/Deli Depot/dsl/24hr, **other:** to Ft Randall Dam |
| **308** | Lp 90, to Plankinton, **N gas:** Cenex, Sinclair/Al's Cafe/dsl, **food:** Golden Pheasant, **lodging:** Cabin Fever Motel/RV Park, Smart Choice Inn, **other:** Gordy's Camping, USPO, repair |
| **301.5mm** | **rest area both lanes, full** &#x267F; **facilities,** [, &#x1F6BB;, **litter barrels, RV dump** |
| **296** | White Lake, 1 mi **N gas:** A-Z Gas, Cenex/dsl, **lodging:** A-Z Motel, **other:** USPO |
| **294mm** | Platte Creek |
| **293mm** | **parking area both lanes** |
| **289** | SD 45 S, to Platte, **S other:** to Snake Cr/Platte Cr RA (25mi) |
| **284** | SD 45 N, Kimball, **N gas:** BP/tires, Phillips 66/dsl/24hr, **food:** Ditty's Diner, Frosty King Drive-In, **lodging:** Dakota Winds Motel, Super 8, **other:** Parkway Campground, repair/tires, **S other:** tractor museum |
| **272** | SD 50, Pukwana, 2 mi **N** gas, food, lodging, **S other:** Snake/Platte Creek Rec Areas (25mi) |
| **265** | SD 50, Chamberlain, **N gas:** BP/DQ/dsl, **lodging:** AmericInn, **S gas:** SA/dsl, **other:** Happy Camper Campground |
| **264mm** | **rest area both lanes, full** &#x267F; **facilities, scenic view, info,** [, &#x1F6BB;, **litter barrels** |
| **263** | Chamberlain, **N** gas: Sinclair/dsl, **food:** Casey's Café, McDonald's, Pizza Hut, Subway (1mi), Taco John's, **lodging:** Best Western (1mi), Bel Aire Motel (1mi), Riverview Inn, Super 8, **other:** Crow Creek Sioux Tribal Hqtrs |
| **262mm** | Missouri River |
| **260** | SD 50, Oacoma, **N gas:** BP/Arby's/dsl, Conoco/dsl, Shell/dsl, **lodging:** Al's Oasis/Motel/Campgroung/cafe/mkt, Cedar Shore Motel (3mi), Comfort Inn, Day's Inn, Holiday Inn Express, **other:** Chevrolet/Buick/Pontiac, Hi&Dri Camping, Old West Museum |
| **251** | SD 47, to Winner, Gregory |
| **248** | SD 47, Reliance, **N** gas: BP/dsl (1mi), Cenex (1mi), **other:** Sioux Tribal Hqtrs, to Big Bend RA |
| **241** | to Lyman |
| **235** | SD 273, Kennebec, **N gas:** Conoco/dsl, **food:** Pony Express Café, **lodging:** Budget Host, Kings Inn, **other:** KOA |
| **226** | US 183 S, Presho, **N gas:** Conoco/dsl, Sinclair/dsl, **lodging:** Coachlight Inn, Hutch's Motel/café/RV Park, Sweeney's B&B, **other:** New Frontier RV park, museum, repair |
| **225** | lp 90, Presho, same as 226 |
| **221mm** | **rest area wb, full** &#x267F; **facilities, info,** [, &#x1F6BB;, **litter barrels, RV dump, petwalk** |
| **220** | no services |
| **218mm** | **rest area eb, full** &#x267F; **facilities, info,** [, &#x1F6BB;, **litter barrels, RV dump, petwalk** |
| **214** | Vivian |
| **212** | US 83 N, SD 53, to Pierre, **N gas:** Sinclair/dsl, **food:** Vivian Jct Rest., **other:** H HOSPITAL (34mi) |
| **208** | no services |
| **201** | Draper, **N gas:** Farmer's Oil/Cafe |

Side markers: E W SIOUX FALLS MITCHELL (left); CHAMBERLAIN (right); SC

Copyright 2009 - The Next Exit®

## INTERSTATE 90 CONT'D

**SD**

| | |
|---|---|
| 194mm | parking area both lanes |
| 192 | US 83 S, Murdo, **N gas:** BP/dsl, HHH/Shell/dsl, Kwik-mart/dsl, Sinclair/dsl, **food:** Murdo Drive-In, Star Rest., The Diner, **lodging:** American Inn, Anchor Inn, Best Western, Day's Inn, Iversen Inn, Landmark Country Inn, Sioux Motel, Super 8, **other:** American RV Park/camping, Murdo Foods, Super Value Foods, auto museum, USPO, **S lodging:** Country Inn, **other:** to Rosebud |
| 191 | Murdo, **N** access to same as 192 |
| 188mm | parking area both lanes, litter barrels |
| 183 | Okaton, **S** gas, Ghost Town |
| 177 | no services |
| 175mm | central/mountain timezone |
| 172 | to Cedar Butte |
| 170 | SD 63 N, to Midland, **N gas:** Shell, **other:** 1880's Town, KOA |
| 167mm | rest area wb, full [&] facilities, [C], [A], litter barrels, RV dump, petwalk |
| 165mm | rest area eb, full [&] facilities, [C], [A], litter barrels, RV dump, petwalk |
| 163 | SD 63, Belvidere, **S gas:** BP/dsl/café, Sinclair/dsl |
| 152 | Lp 90, Kadoka, **N gas:** Conoco/dsl/rest./24hr, **S other:** Badlands Petrified Gardens, camping |
| 150 | SD 73 S, Kadoka, **N lodging:** Dakota Inn/rest., **S gas:** BP, Conoco/dsl, **food:** H&H Rest., Happy Chef, **lodging:** Best Value, Best Western, Budget Host, Ponderosa Motel/RV park, Wagon Wheel Motel, **other:** Kadoka Kampground, to Buffalo Nat Grasslands, repair |
| 143 | SD 73 N, to Philip, **15 mi N** [H] HOSPITAL |
| 138mm | scenic overlook wb |
| 131 | SD 240, **S gas:** BP, **lodging:** Badlands Inn/Best Value (9mi), Cedar Pass Lodge/rest. (9mi), **other:** Circle 10 Camping, Prairie Home NHS, KOA (11mi), to Badlands NP |
| 129.5mm | scenic overlook eb |
| 127 | no services |
| 121 | Bigfoot Rd |
| 116 | 239th St |
| 112 | US 14 E, to Philip |
| 110 | SD 240, Wall, **N gas:** BP/dsl, Exxon, Phillips 66/Subway, **food:** Cactus Café, DQ, Elkton House Rest., Red Rock Rest., Subway, Wall Drug Rest., **lodging:** Anne's Motel, Best Value Inn, Best Western, Day's Inn, Econolodge, Fountain Hotel, Motel 6, Sunshine Inn, Super 8, The Wall Motel, Welsh Motel, **other:** NAPA, Ace Hardware, NAPA, Wall Drug/gifts/rest., The Arrow Campground, Wounded Knee Museum, **S** to Badlands NP, RV camping |
| 109 | W 4th Ave, Wall, **1-2 mi N** access to same as 110 |
| 107 | Cedar Butte Rd |
| 101 | rd T-504, Jensen Rd, to Schell Ranch |
| 100mm | rest area both lanes, full [&] facilities, info, [C], [A], litter barrels, RV dump, vending, petwalk |
| 99.5mm | Cheyenne River |
| 98 | Wasta, **N gas:** BP/dsl, **lodging:** Redwood Motel, **other:** Sunrise Campgrnd |
| 90 | 173rd Ave, to Owanka |
| 88 | 171st Ave (from eb, no re-entry) |
| 84 | 167th Ave, rd 497, **N** Olde Glory Fireworks |
| 78 | 161st Ave, New Underwood, **1/2 mi S gas:** Sinclair, **lodging:** Jake's Motel, **other:** Boondocks Camping, Steve's General Store/gas/motel/rest |

| | |
|---|---|
| 69mm | parking area both lanes |
| 67 | to Box Elder, Ellsworth AFB, **N gas:** Loaf'n Jug, **other:** museum |
| 63 | (eb only), to Box Elder, Ellsworth AFB |
| 61 | Elk Vale Rd, **N gas:** ⊕ FLYING J/Conoco/CountryMkt/dsl/LP/RV dump/24hr/scales/@, **S gas:** BP, Mobil/dsl, **food:** Ardy's, McDonalds, **lodging:** Fairfield Inn, La Quinta, **other:** I-90 RV Ctr, KOA (seasonal) (3mi), transmissions |
| 60 | Lp 90, to Mt Rushmore, Rapid City, **1-3 mi S food:** KFC, LJ Silver, **lodging:** Holiday Inn Express, Stardust Motel, **other:** [H] HOSPITAL, Nat Coll of Mines/Geology |
| 59 | La Crosse St, Rapid City, **N gas:** BP/24hr, Phillips 66, **food:** Boston's Rest, Burger King/TCBY, Denny's, Fuddrucker's, Minerva's Rest., Outback Steaks, TGIFriday, **lodging:** Best Value, Best Western, Country Inn Suites, Econolodge, Grand Stay Hotel, Holiday Inn Express, Super 8, **other:** Sears/auto, Old Navy, PetsMart, mall, st patrol, **S gas:** Cenex/dsl, Exxon/24hr, **food:** ChuckeCheese, Golden Corral, McDonald's, Mongolian Grill, MillStone Rest., Perkins/24hr, Schlotsky's, Subway, **lodging:** AmericInn, Comfort Inn, Dakota Pines Motel, Day's Inn, Fair Value Inn, Foothills Inn, Grand Gateway Hotel, Hampton Inn, Microtel, Motel 6, Quality Inn, Thrifty Motel, **other:** Sam's Club/gas, Walgreens, Walmart SuperCtr/gas |
| 58 | Haines Ave, Rapid City, **N gas:** Conoco, **food:** Applebee's, Chili's, Hardee's, Herburger's, IHOP, Olive Garden, Red Lobster, **lodging:** Best Value, Grand Stay Motel, **other:** $Discount, Best Buy, Borders, Hancock Fabrics, Herbergers, JC Penney, Kohl's, Lowe's Whse, Target, Tires+, to Rushmore Mall, **S gas:** Loaf'n Jug, **food:** ChuckeCheese, Taco John's, Wendy's, **other:** [H] HOSPITAL, ShopKO, same as 59 |
| 57 | I-190, US 16, to Rapid City, to Mt Rushmore, **1 mi S on North St...gas:** Conoco, Exxon, **lodging:** Holiday Inn, Howard Johnson, Radisson, Starbucks, **other:** Ace Hardware, Albertson's/Osco Drug |
| 55 | Deadwood Ave, **N other:** Dakota RV Ctr, Harley-Davidson/cafe, Lazy JD Camp (6mi), **S gas:** Pilot/Sinclair/Subway/dsl/scale/24hr/@, **food:** A&W (2mi), Culver's (3mi), Wendy's (3mi), Windmill Rest., **lodging:** Best Western, Sun Inn (3mi), **other:** Black Hills Dogtrack, Chevrolet, dsl repair |
| 51 | Black Hawk Rd, **N other:** Three Flags Camping (1mi), **S food:** Cenex, Culver's, **lodging:** Family Inn, **other:** USPO |

MURDO E W KADOKA WALL WASTA

RAPID CITY

## INTERSTATE 90 CONT'D

**E ↕ W**

**STURGIS**

**SPEARFISH**

**SD**

| | |
|---|---|
| **48** | Stagebarn Canyon Rd, **N other:** RV camping, **S gas:** C-Store/gas, Sinclair/Haggar's Mkt/food, **food:** Rookies Rest., **lodging:** Ramada, **other:** Mid-States RV Ctr, auto repair |
| **46** | Piedmont Rd, Elk Creek Rd, **N** Elk Creek Resort/Camping, **other:** to Petrified Forest, **lodging:** Elk Creek Resort, **other:** to Petrified Forest, camping, **S gas:** Conoco/dsl, **other:** Sacora Camping/Grill |
| **44** | Bethlehem Rd, **S other:** Bethlehem RV Park (2mi), Jack's RV Ctr (2mi), Historic Food |
| **42mm** | **rest area both lanes, full [♿] facilities, info, [C], [🚻], litter barrels, RV dump, petwalk, vending** |
| **40** | Tilford, **S** Behtlehem Rd RV Park (2mi), Clifford Gulch RV Park |
| **39mm** | weigh sta eb |
| **37** | Pleasant Valley Rd, **N other:** Elkview Camp, **S other:** Bulldog Camping, Rush-No-More Camping |
| **34** | **S other:** Black Hills Nat Cemetary, Katmandu Camping, No Name RV Park, Suzie's RV Camping |
| **32** | SD 79, Sturgis, **N gas:** BP, Conoco, Exxon/dsl, **food:** Country Kitchen, Jambonz Rest., Phil-Town Rest., Taco John's, **lodging:** Best Western, StarLite Motel, **other:** [H] HOSPITAL, Ford/Lincoln/Mercury, Grocery Mart, Rodney RV Park, to Bear Butte SP |
| **30** | US 14A W, SD 34E, to Deadwood, Sturgis, **N gas:** Cenex/dsl, Fresh Start, **food:** Pizza Hut, Pony Express Cafe, McDonald's, Pizza Hut, **other:** CarQuest, Famliy$, Mr Tire, O'Reilly Parts, Pamida/drug, Radio Shack, Day's End Camping, **S gas:** Conoco/dsl, RanchMart, **food:** Burger King, DQ, Pizza Ranch, Subway, **lodging:** AmericInn (11mi), Holiday Inn (11mi), Day's Inn, Super 8/rest., **other:** Chevrolet |
| **23** | SD 34 W, to Belle Fourche, Whitewood, **N other:** Northern Hills RV Ctr, **S gas:** Arpil's/dsl, BP, **food:** Shea's Diner, **lodging:** Iron Horse Inn, Tony's Motel, Whitewood Rest., **other:** USPO |
| **17** | US 85 S, to Deadwood, **9-12 mi S in Deadwood...food:** Cadillac Jack's Diner, 4Aces Buffet, Pizza Hut, Silverado Café, **lodging:** AmericInn, Elkridge Motel, Franklin Motel, Holiday Inn Express, Mineral Dance Motel, Super 8, Deadwood Gulch Resort, **other:** KOA, Whistler Gultch Camping, Winner's Casino |
| **14** | US 14A, Spearfish Canyon, **N food:** Applebee's, **lodging:** Comfort Suites, Fairfield Inn, Holiday Inn/rest., Quality Inn, **other:** Walmart SuperCtr, **S gas:** BP/dsl, **food:** KFC/LJ Silver, Perkins, Pizza Ranch, **lodging:** All American Inn, Howard Johnson, Super 8, **other:** Ace Hardware, Ford/Lincoln/Mercury, K-Mart, auto museum |
| **12** | Jackson Blvd, Spearfish, **S gas:** BP, Conoco/dsl, Loaf'n Jug, **food:** Arby's, Domino's, Millstone Rest., Papa Murphy's, Pizza Hut, Quizno's, Subway, **lodging:** Best Western, Travelodge, **other:** [H] HOSPITAL, CarQuest, Black Hills St U, fish hatchery, same as 10 |
| **10** | US 85 N, to Belle Fourche, **S food:** Burger King, Cedar House Rest., DQ, Golden Dragon Chinese, McDonald's, Subway, Taco Bell, **lodging:** Best Western, Day's Inn, |

| | |
|---|---|
| **10** | Continued |
| | Travelodge, **other:** [H] HOSPITAL, Bob's Drug, Cadillac/GMC, Chevrolet/Buick/Cadillac, Jeep, Jo's Camping, KOA, Safeway/drug/gas, USPO, Valley Corner Store, same as 12 |
| **8** | McGuigan rd, W Spearfish, **S** KOA (1mi) |
| **2** | **1 mi N** McNenny St Fish Hatchery |
| **1mm** | **Welcome Ctr eb, full [♿] facilities, info, [C], [🚻], litter barrels, RV dump, petwalk** |
| **0mm** | South Dakota/Wyoming state line |

## INTERSTATE 229 - SIOUX FALLS

**N ↕ S**

**SIOUX FALLS**

| Exit # | Services |
|---|---|
| **10b a** | I-90 E and W. I-229 begins/ends on I-90, exit 400. |
| **9** | Benson Rd, **W gas:** BP/pizza, **gas:** Marlin's Rest., **other:** Ford Trucks, Western Star |
| **7.5mm** | Big Sioux River |
| **7** | Rice St, **E** winter sports, **W** to stockyards |
| **6** | SD 38, 10th St, **E gas:** Mobil, Sinclair, **food:** A&W, Applebee's, Arby's, Boston's Rest., Denny's, DQ, Domino's, Fryn' Pan Rest., KFC, Pizza Hut, Quizno's, Ruby Tuesday, Taco Bell, Tomacelli's Italian, **lodging:** Super 8, **other:** AutoZone, Family$, Hy-Vee Foods, K-Mart, Pronto Parts, ShopKO, Sunshine Foods, Valvoline, USPO, **W gas:** Cone's Gas, Get'n Go/dsl, Phillips 66/dsl/mart, Shell, **food:** Burger King/TCBY, BurgerTime, Godfather's, Little Caesar's, McDonald's, Pizza Inn, Puerto Vallarta, Stake-Out, Subway, Taco John's, Z'Kota Grille, **lodging:** Rushmore Motel, **other:** Jiffy Lube, Lewis Drug, vet |
| **5.5mm** | Big Sioux River |
| **5** | 26th St, **E gas:** Shell/dsl, **food:** Cherry Creek Grill, Dario's Pizza, McDonald's, SaiGon Panda, **other:** city park, **W other:** [H] HOSPITAL |
| **4** | Cliff Ave, **E gas:** Get'n Go, **food:** China Star, **other:** Curves, Lewis Drug, Sunshine Foods, Walgreens, city park |
| **3** | SD 115, Lp 229, Minnesota Ave, **E** city park, **1 mi W gas:** BP, Sinclair, **food:** Burger King, Camilles Cafe, Culver's, Famous Dave's BBQ, Golden Bowl Chinese, Little Caesar's, McDonald's, Subway, Z'kota Grille, **other:** Ace hardware, Dodge, $Tree, GMC/Buick, Hy-Vee Foods/gas, Kia, Lewis Drug, Mitsubishi/Toyota, Staples, vet |
| **2** | Western Ave, **E gas:** Shell/dsl, **food:** Bracco Cafe, DQ, Izzy's Cafe, Nucci, Scooters Coffee, **W gas:** Cenex/dsl, Gas Stop, **food:** Burger King, Champp's Café, China Buffet, Huhot Mongolian, La Fiesta Mexican, Lonestar Steaks, Papa Murphy's, Pizza Hut, Qdoba Mexican, Quizno's, Redrossa Pizza, Valentino's Italian, **other:** Checker Parts, Curves, Goodyear/auto, Hancock Fabrics, Radio Shack |
| **1.5mm** | Big Sioux River |
| **1c** | Louise Ave, **E lodging:** Homewood Suites, **other:** [H] HOSPITAL, **W gas:** BP, Phillips 66/dsl, **food:** Applebee's, Burger King, Culvers, McDonald's, Wendy's, **lodging:** Honda/Mercedes, mall |
| **1b a** | I-29 N and S. I-229 begins/ends on I-29, exit 75. |

## INTERSTATE 24

E ↕ W

**CHATTANOOGA**

| Exit # | Services |
|---|---|
| **185b a** | I-75, N to Knoxville, S to Atlanta. I-24 begins/ends on I-75, exit 2 in Chattanooga. |
| **184** | Moore Rd, **S food:** Chef Lin Buffet, Provino's Italian, **other:** $Tree, Radio Shack, Sears Essentials/auto |
| **183** | (183a from wb), Belvoir Ave, Germantown Rd |
| **181a** | US 41 S, to East Ridge (from eb), **S food:** Westside Grill, King's Lodge, **other:** Ford Trucks |
| **181** | Fourth Ave, to TN Temple U, Chattanooga, **N gas:** Citgo/dsl, Exxon/dsl, Hi-Tech Fuel, Stop'n Save, **food:** Bojangles, Burger King, Capt D's, Central Park, Hardee's, Krystal/24hr, Subway, Waffle House, **lodging:** Villager Lodge, **other:** BiLo, $General, Family$, Goodyear, Mr Transmission, O'Reilly Parts, repair, vet, **S gas:** Citgo |
| **180b a** | US 27 S, TN 8, Rossville Blvd, **N other:** U-Haul, to Chickamauga, UT Chatt, **S gas:** Exxon, RaceWay/dsl/24hr, **lodging:** Hamilton Inn, **other:** NTB |
| **178** | US 27 N, Market St, to Lookout Mtn, Chattanooga, **N gas:** BP/dsl, Citgo, **lodging:** Day's Inn, La Quinta, Marriott, Ramada Inn, Staybridge Suites, **other:** Ford, Nissan, U-Haul, to Chattanooga ChooChoo, **S food:** KFC, **lodging:** Comfort Suites, Hampton Inn, Motel 6 |
| **175** | Browns Ferry Rd, to Lookout Mtn, **N gas:** BP, Exxon/dsl, **food:** China Gourmet, **lodging:** Best Value Inn, **other:** CVS Drug, $General, Food Lion, **S gas:** Conoco/dsl, Shell/dsl, **food:** Hardee's, McDonald's, **lodging:** Comfort Inn, Econolodge, Quality Inn |
| **174** | US 11, US 41, US 64, Lookout Valley, **N food:** Waffle House, **lodging:** Day's Inn, **other:** Racoon Mtn Camping (1mi), **S gas:** BP/dsl/24hr, Kangaroo, **food:** Cracker Barrel, New China, Taco Bell, Waffle House, Wendy's, **lodging:** Baymont Inn, Best Western, Budget Motel, Country Inn&Suites, Hampton Inn, Holiday Inn Express, Knight's Inn, Ramada Ltd, Super 8, **other:** Ace Hardware, Lookout Valley Camping, Walmart SuperCtr, st patrol |
| **172mm** | **rest area eb, full** ♿ **facilities,** 🚻, 🅿️, **litter barrels, vending, petwalk** |
| **171mm** | Tennessee/Georgia state line |
| **169** | GA 299, to US 11, **N gas:** Exxon/dsl/24hr, **S gas,** BP/Momma's Chicken/dsl/24hr/@, Pilot/Subway/dsl/scales/24hr, RaceWay/24hr, **food:** Pappy's BBQ, **other:** repair |
| **167** | I-59 S, to Birmingham |
| **167mm** | Tennessee/Georgia state line, *Central/Eastern time zone* |
| **161** | TN 156, to Haletown, New Hope, **N gas:** BP/dsl (1mi), **other:** Hales RV Park, **S gas:** Chevron/fireworks, **other:** On The Lake Camping |
| **160mm** | Tennessee River/Nickajack Lake |

**MONTEAGLE** **MANCHESTER**

| Exit # | Services |
|---|---|
| **159mm** | Welcome Ctr wb/rest area eb, full ♿ facilities, 🚻, vending, 🅿️, litter barrels, petwalk |
| **158** | US 41, TN 27, Nickajack Dam, **S gas:** BP/dsl/fireworks, **other:** Shellmound Camping (2.5mi) |
| **155** | TN 28, Jasper, **N gas:** BP/dsl (1mi), Exxon/dsl, **food:** Dairy Queen (1mi), Hardee's, Western Sizzlin, **lodging:** Acuff Country Inn, **S gas:** BP/Quizno's/dsl, **other:** 🅷 HOSPITAL |
| **152** | US 41, US 64, US 72, Kimball, S Pittsburg, **N gas:** BP/fireworks, RaceWay, Shell/dsl, **food:** A&W/LJ Silver, Arby's, China Buffet, Cracker Barrel, Domino's, KFC, Krystal, McDonald's, Mi Jacal Mexican, Pizza Hut, Shoney's, Subway, Taco Bell, Waffle House, Wendy's, **lodging:** Best Value, Comfort Inn, Country Hearth Inn, Holiday Inn Express, **other:** 🅷 HOSPITAL, Chevrolet/Pontiac/Buick, $Tree, Goody's, Lowe's Whse, Radio Shack, Walmart SuperCtr, to Russell Cave NM, **3 mi S other:** Lodge Cast Iron |
| **143** | Martin Springs Rd, **N gas:** Chevron/dsl/fireworks |
| **135** | US 41 N, Monteagle, **N gas:** Citgo/dsl/rest./24hr, Mystik/dsl, **food:** Shan Chinese, Smok'n B's BBQ, **other:** S Cumberland RV Park, USPO, **S** Day's Inn |
| **134** | US 64, US 41A, to Sewanee, Monteagle, **N gas:** BP/McDonald's, Papa Ron's Grill, **lodging:** American Eagle Inn, **other:** Monteagle Winery, to S Cumberland SP, **S gas:** Citgo, Shell/dsl, **food:** Hardee's, Monteagle Diner, Pizza Hut, Smokehouse BBQ, Subway, Waffle House, **lodging:** Best Western, Regency Inn, **other:** $General, Fred's Drugs, Piggly Wiggly, to U of The South |
| **133mm** | **rest area both lanes, full** ♿ **facilities,** 🚻, 🅿️, **litter barrels, vending, petwalk** |
| **128mm** | Elk River |
| **127** | US 64, TN 50, to Winchester, Pelham, **N gas:** BP, Phillips 66, Texaco/Stuckey's, **S gas:** Exxon/dsl, **other:** to Tims Ford SP/RV camping |
| **119mm** | trucks only parking area both lanes |
| **117** | to Tullahoma, USAF Arnold Ctr, UT Space Institute |
| **116mm** | weigh sta both lanes |
| **114** | US 41, Manchester, **N gas:** BP/24 Truckers/scales/dsl, Marathon, Shell/dsl, **food:** Domino's, Huddle House, O'Charley's, Panda Express, Starbucks, **lodging:** Comfort Inn, Holiday Inn Express, Ramada Ltd, Scottish Inn, Super 8, **other:** Country Cabin Camping, Dollar Stop, Home Depot, KOA, Nissan, Toyota, Truck/tire repair, Walmart SuperCtr/gas, museum, **S gas:** Citgo, Kangaroo, RaceWay, **food:** Arby's, Burger King, Capt D's, KFC, Krystal, McDonald's/playplace, Pizza Hut, Shoney's, Subway, Taco Bell, Waffle House, Wendy's, **lodging:** Country Inn Suites, Day's Inn, Royal Inn, **other:** |

TN

**MANCHESTER E ← W → MURFREESBORO**

## INTERSTATE 24 CONT'D

**114** Continued
Advance Parts, AutoZone, Chevrolet, Curves, Family$, Ford/Lincoln/Mercury, Fred's Drug, Goodyear, Napa, O'Reilly Parts, Russell Stover, USPO, carwash

**111** TN 55, Manchester, **N gas:** BP/dsl, Citgo/dsl/24hr, Co-op gas/dsl, **other:** to Rock Island SP, **S gas:** BP, **food:** Hardee's, J&G Pizza/Steaks, Sonic, **other:** H HOSPITAL, to Jack Daniels Dist HS, Old Stone Fort

**110** TN 53, Manchester, **N gas:** BP, Kangaroo, Shell/dsl, **food:** Coconut Bay Cafe, Cracker Barrel, D Crockett's Roadhouse, Emma's Rest., Oak Rest., **lodging:** Ambassador Inn, Economy Inn, Hampton Inn, **S gas:** Shell/dsl/24hr, **food:** Los 3 Amigos Mexican, Waffle House, **other:** H HOSPITAL, U-Haul

**110mm** Duck River

**105** US 41, **N gas:** BP/dsl/24hr, Shell/dsl, **food:** RanchHouse Rest., **S** tire/repair, to Normandy Dam, Dickle HS

**97** TN 64, to Shelbyville, Beechgrove, **N other:** auto parts/repair, **S gas:** Citgo

**89** Buchanan Rd, **N gas:** Love's/McDonald's/scales/dsl, Texaco/Outpost Rest/dsl, **S gas:** Shell/dsl/rest./24hr, **food:** Huddle House, **other:** A&L RV Ctr

**84** Joe B. Jackson Pkwy

**81** US 231, Murfreesboro, **N gas:** BP/dsl/24hr, Exxon, RaceWay/24hr, Shell, **food:** Cracker Barrel, King's Table Rest., Krystal, Parthenon Steaks, Shanghai Chinese, Shoney's, Waffle House/24hr, Wendy's, **lodging:** Best Value, Knight's Inn, Quality Inn, Ramada Ltd, Regal Inn, Scottish Inn, **other:** H HOSPITAL, Dodge, Honda, Mazda, **S gas:** Citgo/24hr, Kangaroo, Mapco/dsl/24hr, Phillips 66/dsl/24hr/@, Pilot/Arbys/scales/dsl/24hr, **food:** La Siesta Mexican, McDonald's/playplace, Pizza Hut/Taco Bell, Quizno's, Sonic, Subway, Waffle House, Zaxby's, **lodging:** Howard Johnson, Safari Inn, Vista Inn, **other:** Gateway Tire, Rite Aid, Toyota/Scion

**80** New Salem Hwy, rd 99, **S food:** Domino's

**78** TN 96, to Franklin, Murfreesboro, **N gas:** BP, Citgo, Phillips 66/Church's/White Castle/dsl, Shell/Jack-in-the-Box, Texaco/24hr, **food:** Arby's, Applebee's, Bellacino's Pizza, Bonefish Grill, Buffalo Wild Wings, Chick-fil-A, Chucke-Cheese, Coconut Bay Cafe, Cracker Barrel, Fazoli's, IHOP, Jason's Deli, Jim'n Nick's BBQ, KFC, McDonald's, Olive Garden, Outback Steaks, Panera Bread, Quizno's, Red Lobster, Red Robin, Ryan's, Santa Fe Steaks, Starbucks, Steak'n Shake, Subway, TGI Friday's, The Chophouse, Waffle House, Wendy's, Zaxby's, **lodging:** Baymont Inn, Best Western, Comfort Inn, Country Inn Suites, Day's Inn, DoubleTree, Econolodge, Fairfield Inn, Hampton Inn, Holiday Inn, Microtel, Motel 6, Red Roof Inn, Sleep Inn, Super 8, Wingate Inn, **other:** Aldi Foods, Belk, BooksAMillion, Dillard's, Discount Tire, Goody's, Home Depot, JC Penney, Lowe's Whse, Marshall's, Michael's, Old Navy, PetsMart, Ross, Sears/auto, Staples, Target, TJ Maxx, Walmart SuperCtr/gas, mall, to Stones River Bfd, **S gas:** BP/dsl/24hr, Chevron/24hr, Kangaroo/dsl, **food:** Corky's BBQ, China Garden, Hardee's, Las Palmas, McDonald's, O'Charley's, Papa Murphy's, Pizza Hut, Sonic, Subway, Taco Bell, Waffle House, **other:** AutoZone, $General, Kohl's, Kroger, Old Time Pottery, Sam's Club/gas, Walgreen

**NASHVILLE**

**76** Manson Pike, Medical Center Pkwy, **N other:** H HOSPITAL, to Stones River Nat. Bfd

**74b a** TN 840, to Lebanon, Franklin

**70** TN 102, Lee Victory Pkwy, Almaville Rd, to Smyrna, **N gas:** Shell/dsl/scales, **S gas:** BP, Kangaroo/Quizno's/dsl, Mapco, **food:** McDonald's, Legends Steaks, Ringalino's, Sonic, **lodging:** Deerfield Inn, **other:** $General, Tennessee Expo

**66** TN 266, Sam Ridley Pkwy, to Smyrna, **N gas:** Citgo/dsl/24hr, Shell/dsl, **food:** Arby's, A&W/LJ Silver, Blue Coast Burrito, Catfish House, Chili's, Famous Dave's, Hickory Falls Cafe, Jim'n Nick's BBQ, Logan's Roadhouse, Papa John's, Sonic, Starbucks, Subway, Wendy's, **other:** CVS Drug, Kohl's, Kroger/gas, PetsMart, Publix, Staples, Target, Nashville I-24 Camping (3mi), **S food:** Cracker Barrel, O'Charley's, Ruby Tuesday, **lodging:** Fairfield Inn, Hampton Inn, Hilton Garden, Sleep Inn, **other:** I-24 Expo

**64** Waldron Rd, to La Vergne, **N gas:** Kangaroo, Kwik Sak, Pilot/Subway/dsl/24hr/scales, **food:** Arby's, Hardee's, Krystal/24hr, McDonald's, Waffle House, **lodging:** Comfort Inn, Holiday Inn Express, Super 8, **other:** Music City Camping (3mi), RV service, **S gas:** Mapco/dsl/24hr, **lodging:** Motel

**62** TN 171, Old Hickory Blvd, **N gas:** Chevron, Citgo/Subway, Shell/dsl/24hr, TA/BP/Burger King/Popeye's/dsl/24hr/scales/@, **food:** El Arroyo Mexican, Waffle House, **lodging:** Best Western

**60** Hickory Hollow Pkwy, **N gas:** BP, Mapco, Shell, **food:** Applebee's, Arby's, Bailey's Grill, Burger King, Chuck-eCheese, Cracker Barrel, KFC, Logan's Roadhouse, McDonald's/Playplace, O'Charley's, Outback Steaks, Pizza Hut, Red Lobster, Starbucks, Subway, Taco Bell, TGIFriday, Wendy's, **lodging:** Country Inn Suites, Hampton Inn, Holiday Inn, **other:** Best Buy, Chevrolet, Circuit City, Dillard's, Dodge, $Tree, Firestone/auto, Kroger/gas, Macey's, Mazda, NTB, Office Depot, Rite Aid, Sears, mall, transmissions, **S gas:** BP/dsl, Shell, **food:** Camino Royale Mexican, Casa Fiesta Mexican, Evergreen Chinese, IHOP, Olive Garden, Shoney's, Steak'n Shake, Waffle House/24hr, **lodging:** Knight's Inn, Super 8, Vista Inn, **other:** Acura, Goodyear/auto, Home Depot, KIA, Target

**59** TN 254, Bell Rd, same as 60

**57** Haywood Lane, **N gas:** Kwik Sak, Marathon, **food:** Hardee's, Pizza Hut, **other:** CarQuest, $General, Food Lion, Walgreen, **S gas:** Kangaroo, Shell

**56** TN 255, Harding Place, **N gas:** Chevron/dsl, Exxon, Mapco, Shell/dsl/24hr, **food:** Applebee's, KFC, McDonald's, Mikado Japanese, Pizza Hut/Taco Bell, Waffle House, Wendy's, **lodging:** Executive Inn, Knight's Inn, Motel 6, Stay Lodge, Thrifty Inn, **other:** Sam's Club/gas, **S gas:** Mapco, Shell, **food:** Burger King, Fiesta Mexican, Hooters, Jack-in-the-Box, **lodging:** Best Value Inn, Motel 6, **other:** H HOSPITAL

**54b a** TN 155, Briley Pkwy, to Opryland

**53** I-440 W, to Memphis

**52** US 41, Murfreesboro Rd, **N gas:** Shell, Texaco, **food:** Jack-in-the-Box, Piccadilly's, Pizza Hut, Taco Bell, Waffle House, **lodging:** Day's Inn, Economy Inn, Econolodge, Executive Inn, Holiday Inn Express, Howard Johnson, Quality Inn, Ramada Inn, Rodeway Inn, Scottish Inn, Sunrise Inn, **other:** CarQuest, Office Depot, **S other:** Chevrolet, Dodge

**TN**

### INTERSTATE 24 CONT'D

**E** ↕ **W**

**NASHVILLE**

| | |
|---|---|
| **52b a** | I-40, E to Knoxville, W to Memphis |
| **I-24 and I-40 run together 2 mi. See Interstate 40 exits 212-213.** | |
| **50b** | I-40 W |
| **48** | James Robertson Pkwy, **N gas:** Citgo, Shell, **S gas:** Exxon, TA/Subway/dsl/24hr/@, **food:** Shoney's, **lodging:** Ramada Ltd, Stadium Inn, **other:** Titan Stadium, st capitol |
| **47a** | US 31E |
| **47** | N 1st St, Jefferson St, **N gas:** Express/dsl, **S gas:** Mystic Gas, **lodging:** Day's Inn, Knight's Inn, **other:** U-Haul |
| **I-24 and I-65 run together. See Interstate 65 exit 87 b a.** | |
| **87b a** | US 431, Trinity Lane, **N gas:** Citgo, Pilot/Subway/scales/dsl, **food:** Krystal, White Castle, **lodging:** Cumberland Inn, Delux Inn, **S gas:** Chevron, Express, Exxon, **food:** Jack-in-the-Box, Jack's BBQ, McDonald's, Subway, Taco Bell, Waffle House, **lodging:** Best Value Inn, Comfort Inn, Day's Inn, Econolodge, Howard Johnson, Liberty Inn, Quality Inn, Travelodge, **other:** Family$, to American Bapt Coll |
| **44b a** | I-65, N to Louisville, S to Nashville |
| **43** | TN 155, Briley Pkwy, Brick Church Pike |
| **40** | TN 45, Old Hickory Blvd, **N gas:** Citgo/dsl, Shell/Subway/dsl, Phillips 66/dsl/24hr, **food:** Country Kitchen, Jack-in-the-Box (3mi), Hot Wings, **lodging:** Super 8 |
| **35** | US 431, to Joelton, Springfield, **S gas:** BP/Subway/dsl/24hr, Shell, **food:** Family Rest., Mazatlan Mexican, McDonald's, Subway, **lodging:** Day's Inn, **other:** Curves, Family$, OK Camping |
| **31** | TN 249, New Hope Rd, **N gas:** Shell/Taco Tico, **S gas:** BP/dsl, Citgo/dsl/24hr, **food:** Sullivan's Rest. |
| **24** | TN 49, to Springfield, Ashland City, **N gas:** BP, Express/dsl/24hr, Phillips 66/dsl/24hr, **other:** ⒽHOSPITAL, **S gas:** Horizon/Wendy's, Shell/dsl, **food:** Sonic, Subway, **other:** $General, Hill Foods |
| **19** | TN 256, Maxey Rd, to Adams, **N gas:** BP/dsl, **S gas:** Shell/deli/dsl/24hr |
| **11** | TN 76, to Adams, Clarksville, **N gas:** Shell/dsl/24hr, **S gas:** BP/dsl/24hr, Marathon, **food:** Don Poncho Mexican, Homeplace Rest., McDonald's, Waffle House, **lodging:** Comfort Inn, Day's Inn, Holiday Inn Express, Quality Inn, Super 8, **other:** ⒽHOSPITAL |
| **9mm** | Red River |
| **8** | TN 237, Rossview Rd, **S** Dunbar Cave SP |
| **4** | US 79, to Clarksville, Ft Campbell, **N gas:** BP/dsl/24hr, **food:** Cracker Barrel, **other:** Sam's Club/gas, Spring Creek Camping (2mi), Clarksville RV Ctr, **S gas:** BP/dsl/24hr, Citgo/dsl, Shell/dsl, **food:** Applebee's, Arby's, Burger King, Capt D's, 's, ChuckeCheese, Church's/White Castle, DQ, Golden Bowl Buffet, Golden Corral, Golden Rule BBQ, IHOP, KFC, Krystal, Logan's Roadhouse, LJ Silver, Longhorn Steaks, McDonald's, O'Charley's, Old Chicago Pizza, Olive Garden, Outback Steaks, Ponderosa, Quizno's, Rafferty's, Red Lobster, Ryan's, Shogun Japanese, Shoney's, Starbucks, Steak'n Shake, Taco Bell, Waffle House, Wendy's, **lodging:** Best Value, Best Western, Candlewood Suites, Comfort Inn, Country Inn Suites, Day's Inn, Econolodge, Guesthouse Inn, Hampton Inn, Holiday Inn, Microtel, Ramada Ltd, Red Roof Inn, Royal Inn, Super 8, Wingate Inn, **other:** ⒽHOSPITAL, Advance Parts, Belk, Best Buy, |

**CLARKSVILLE**

| | |
|---|---|
| **4** | **Continued** BooksAMillion, Borders Books, Goodyear/auto, Hancock Fabrics, JC Penny, Kohl's, K-Mart, Lowe's Whse, Office Depot, PetsMart, Sears/auto, Target, TJ Maxx, U-Haul, Walmart SuperCtr/gas, mall, winery, to Austin Peay St U, to Land Between the Lakes |
| **1** | TN 48, to Clarksville, Trenton, **N gas:** Shell/dsl, **other:** Clarksville RV Camping, antiques, **S gas:** BP, Mystic, **food:** Rib Dr. BBQ, Sonic, **other:** $General |
| **.5mm** | Welcome Ctr eb, full ♿ facilities, 🕯, vending, ⛽, litter barrels, petwalk |
| **0mm** | Tennessee/Kentucky state line |

### INTERSTATE 26

**E** ↕ **W**

**ERWIN**

| Exit # | Services |
|---|---|
| **54.5mm** | Tennessee/North Carolina state line |
| **54mm** | runaway truck ramp wb |
| **52mm** | scenic overlook eb (no trucks) |
| **50** | Flagpond Rd |
| **47.5mm** | scenic overlook wb (no trucks) |
| **46** | Clear Branch Rd |
| **44mm** | S Indian Creek |
| **43** | US 19 W, rd 352, Temple Hill Rd, **N gas:** Exxon (2mi) |
| **42mm** | S Indian Creek |
| **40** | Jackson-Love Hwy, Erwin, Jonesborough, **N gas:** Appco Gas/A&W/LJ Silver, **lodging:** Holiday Inn Express, **other:** ⒽHOSPITAL, Nolichucky Gorge Camping (2mi) |
| **37** | TN 81, rd 107, Erwin, Jonesborough, **N gas:** Shell/dsl/24hr, **food:** Huddle House/24hr, McDonald's, Sonic, **other:** ⒽHOSPITAL, NAPA, Walgreens, **S lodging:** Super 8, **other:** River Park Camping (5mi) |
| **36** | Main St, Erwin, **N gas:** Appco/dsl, BP/24hr, **food:** Backwoods BBQ, El Azteca, Hardee's, KFC, Little Caesar's, Pizza Hut, Subway, Wendy's, **other:** Advance Parts, $General, Firestone, Rite Aid, White's Foods |
| **34** | Tinker Rd, **N other:** Walmart SuperCtr |
| **32** | rd 173, Unicoi Rd, to Cherokee NF, **N gas:** Volco Gas, **food:** Maple Grove Café, **S** Woodsmoke Camping |
| **27** | rd 359 N, Okolona Rd, **N gas:** BP, **food:** Kozy Kitchen, **lodging:** Budget Inn (3mi) |
| **24** | US 321, TN 67, Elizabethton, **N gas:** Shell/dsl, **food:** Schlotsky's, **S gas:** BP/dsl, **food:** Arby's, Burger King, Little Caesars, LJ Silver, Subway, **lodging:** Comfort Inn, Carnegie Hotel, **other:** Advance Parts, CVS Drug, Food City/gas, White's Foods, to ETSU, Roan Mtn SP |
| **23** | rd 91, Market St, **N food:** McDonald's, **S other:** museum |

**TN**

## INTERSTATE 26 CONT'D

**22** rd 400, Unaka Ave, Watauga Ave

**20b a** US 11 E, US 19 N, to Roan St, **N** **gas:** Citgo, **food:** Arby's, DQ, El Chico, El Matador, Harbor House Seafood, Hardee's, Peerless Rest., Perkins, Pizza Hut, Sonic, **lodging:** Best Western, Holiday Inn, LJ Silver, Ramada Ltd, Super 8, **other:** Acura, Advance Parts, AutoZone, Big Lots, Ford, Honda, Mazda, Saturn, Tuesday Morning, repair, **S** **food:** Applebees, Bailey's Grill, Carino's Italian, Fazoli's, Hooters, KFC, Lonestar Steaks, McDonald's, O'Charley's, Olive Garden, Red Lobster, Ruby Tuesday, Ryan's, Salsarito's, Shoney's, Smokey Bones BBQ, Starbucks, Subway, Taco Bell, TCBY, Texas Roadhouse, Zaxby's, **lodging:** Day's Inn, Econolodge, Quality Inn, Red Roof Inn, **other:** Books-a-Million, CVS Drug, $General, $Tree, Hancock Fabrics, Sears/auto, Target, TJ Maxx, Walgreens

**19** TN 381, to St of Franklin Rd, to Bristol, **N** **gas:** Appco/ McDonald's, **food:** El Chico Mexican, Golden Corral, Honeybaked Ham, Logan's Roadhouse, Quizno's, Outback Steaks, Subway, **lodging:** Comfort Suites, **other:** Big Lots, Radio Shack, VW, Walmart SuperCtr/gas, **S** **gas:** Exxon (2mi), **food:** Atlanta Bread, Barbarito's, Carrabba's, Cheddar's, Chick-fil-A, Chili's, China Chef, ChuckeCheese, CiCi's, Fuddruckers, IHOP, Panera Bread, Stir Fry Cafe, Wendy's, **lodging:** Hampton Inn (2mi), Sleep Inn, **other:** Barnes&Noble, Best Buy, Circuit City, Home Depot, K-Mart, Kohl's, Lowe's Whse, Natural Foods Mkt, Old Navy, Ross, Sam's Club/gas, Steinmart, vet

**17** Boone St, **N** **gas:** BP, **food:** Beef'o Brady's, Bob Evan's, Buck's Pizza, Burger King, Kemosabe's BBQ, **other:** Ingles Foods, **S** **gas:** Appco, Shell, **food:** Cracker Barrel, Domino's, El Matador Mexican, Waffle House, Wendy's, **lodging:** Jameson Inn, Value Place, **other:** Wilson Drugs

**13** rd 77, Bobby Hicks Hwy, **N** **gas:** BP, Shell, **food:** China Luck, DQ, McDonald's, Papa John's, Pizza Hut, Subway, Taco Bell, Yong Asian, **other:** Advance Parts, General, Firestone, Food City/gas, Rite Aid, Walgreens, White's Foods, USPO, **S** **gas:** Appco

**10** Eastern Star Rd

**8b a** I-81, to Bristol, Knoxville

**6** rd 37, Rock Springs Rd, **S** **gas:** Citgo

**4** TN 93, Wilcox Dr, **N** **gas:** BP/Subway, Shell/dsl, **food:** Burger King, Damon's, Hardee's, La Carreta Mexican, McDonald's, Pizza Hut, Wendy's, **lodging:** Hampton Inn, Holiday Inn Express, Jameson Inn, **other:** Cave's Drug, $General, White's Foods, **S** **gas:** BP, Exxon/Arby's/dsl

**3** Meadowview Pkwy, **N** **lodging:** Marriott

**1** West Stone Dr, **N** **gas:** Shell, Valero/dsl, **food:** Little Caesar's, Molcajete's Mexican, **lodging:** Days Inn, Super 8, **other:** H HOSPITAL, Walgreens, **S** **gas:** BP, **food:** Bojangles, Fatz Cafe, Sonic, Subway, **other:** $Tree, Lowe's Whse, Walmart SuperCtr/gas

**0mm** I-26 begins/ends on US 23.

## INTERSTATE 40

| Exit # | Services |
| --- | --- |
| 451mm | Tennessee/North Carolina state line |
| 451 | Waterville Rd |

**447** Hartford Rd, **N** **gas:** Citgo/dsl, **S** **gas:** BP/towing, **food:** Bean Trees Cafe, **other:** Shauan's Riverside RV Park, whitewater rafting

**446mm** Welcome Ctr wb, full & facilities, C, vending, 🛋, litter barrels, petwalk, NO TRUCKS

**443** Foothills Pkwy, to Gatlinburg, Great Smoky Mtns NP, **S** camping

**443mm** Pigeon River

**440** US 321, to Wilton Spgs Rd, Gatlinburg, **N** **gas:** Sunoco/ dsl/rest./repair, **S** **gas:** BP, **other:** Arrow Creek Camping (14mi), CrazyHorse Camping (12mi), Jellystone Camping (12mi)

**439mm** Pigeon River

**435** US 321, to Gatlinburg, Newport, **N** **gas:** Exxon/dsl/24hr, Shell, **food:** Arby's, Burger King, Hardee's, KFC, La Carreta Mexican, McDonald's, Pizza Hut, Pizza+, SageBrush Steaks, Shoney's, Subway, Taco Bell, **lodging:** Motel 6, Parkway Inn, **other:** H HOSPITAL, Town&Country Drug, **S** **gas:** BP/TCBY, **food:** Cracker Barrel, Papa John's, Quizno's, Ryan's, Ruby Tuesday, Waffle House/24hr, Wendy's, **lodging:** Best Western, Family Inn, Holiday Inn, **other:** $General, Goody's, Lowe's, Save-A-Lot, Walmart SuperCtr/gas

**432b a** US 70, US 411, US 25W, to Newport, **N** **gas:** BP, Exxon/ dsl/24hr, TimeOut Travel Ctr/Huddle House/dsl, Phillips 66, **food:** Lois' Country Kitchen, Sonic, **lodging:** Budget Motel, Comfort Inn, Relax Inn, **other:** Chevrolet/Pontiac/ Buick, Chrysler/Jeep/Dodge, Ford/Mercury, KOA, TMC Camping, **S** **gas:** BP, Citgo/24hr, Texaco/dsl, Shell, **lodging:** Family Inn/rest.

**426mm** rest area wb, full & facilities, C, vending, 🛋, litter barrels, petwalk

**425mm** French Broad River

**424** TN 113, Dandridge, **N** **gas:** BP/dsl

**421** I-81 N, to Bristol

**420mm** rest area eb, full & facilities, C, vending, 🛋, litter barrels, petwalk

**417** TN 92, Dandridge, **N** **gas:** BP, Pilot/Subway/dsl/ scales/24hr/@, **food:** Capt's Galley, Hardee's, McDonald's, Perkins, Ruby Tuesday, **lodging:** Econolodge, **S** **gas:** Shell/Wendy's/dsl, Texaco/KFC/dsl, Weigel's, **food:** LJ Silver/Taco Bell, Shoney's, Waffle House, **lodging:** Comfort Inn, Holiday Inn Express, Jefferson Inn, Super 8, **other:** Advance Parts

**415** US 25W, US 70, to Dandridge, **S** **gas:** Dadu/dsl **food:** Sonic (3mi)

**412** Deep Sprgs Rd, to Douglas Dam, **N** **gas:** Love's/Chester Fried/Subway/dsl, **S** **gas:** TR Trkstp/Chevron/dsl/ rest/scales/24hr

**407** TN 66, to Sevierville, Pigeon Forge, Gatlinburg, **N** **gas:** Citgo/Huddle House/dsl, **food:** Chophouse, Cracker Barrel, McDonald's, **lodging:** Hampton Inn, Motel 6, **other:** Bass Pro Shops, KOA, **S** **gas:** BP/DQ, Exxon/ Subway/dsl, Shell/Krystal/dsl, **food:** FlapJack's, Wendy's, **lodging:** Best Western, Comfort Suites, Day's Inn, Quality Inn, Ramada Ltd, **other:** Russel Stover, RV Camping, TN RV Ctr, USPO, flea mkt, **3-10 mi** **S** multiple services/outlets

**402** Midway Rd

**398** Strawberry Plains Pk, **N** **gas:** BP/dsl, Exxon/Pizza Hut/ dsl, Shell, **food:** McDonald's, Outback Steaks, Ruby Tuesday, Waffle House, Wendy's, **lodging:** Baymont Inn, Comfort Inn, Country Inn&Suites, Econolodge, Hampton Inn, Holiday Inn Express, Ramada Ltd,

## INTERSTATE 40 CONT'D

**E ↑↓ W**

**398** Continued
Super 8, **other:** TN RV Camping World, **S gas:** Pilot/Subway/dsl/scales/24hr, Weigel's, **food:** Arby's, Burger King, Cracker Barrel, Golden Wok Chinese, KFC, Krystal, Puleo's Grille, Starbucks, Taco Bell, **lodging:** Best Western, Comfort Suites, Fairfield Inn, La Quinta, Motel 6

**395mm** Holston River

**394** US 70, US 11E, US 25W, Asheville Hwy, **N gas:** Marathon, Mobil/dsl, Pilot, **food:** Subway, Wendy's, **lodging:** Gateway, Sunbeam Motel (2mi), **other:** Advance Parts, AutoZone, $General, Food Lion, city park, **S gas:** Exxon, Shell/dsl, **food:** Waffle House/24hr, **lodging:** Day's Inn, **other:** CVS Drug, Kroger/gas, Walgreens, vet

**393** I-640 W, to I-75 N

**392** US 11W, Rutledge Pike, **N gas:** Shell/dsl, **other:** $General, U-Haul, repair, tires, **S gas:** BP, **food:** Buddy's BBQ, Hardee's, Shoney's, **lodging:** Family Inn, **other:** NAPA, Sav-a-Lot Foods, transmissions, to Knoxville Zoo

**K N O X V I L L E**

**390** Cherry St, Knoxville, **N gas:** Marathon/dsl, Top Fuel Mart, Weigel's/Subway, **food:** Happy Garden Chinese, **lodging:** Red Carpet Inn, **other:** tires, **1 mi S gas:** Exxon, **food:** Arby's, KFC, McDonald's, Subway, Taco Bell, WishBone's Wings, **lodging:** Regency Inn, **other:** Advance Parts, Family$, O'Reilly Parts, Walgreens

**389** US 441 N, Broadway, 5th Ave, **1/2 mi N gas:** BP, Conoco, Star, **food:** Burger King, Capt D's, KFC, Krystal, SteakOut, Subway, Taco Bell, Wendy's, **other:** CVS Drug, $General, Family$, Firestone, Kroger/deli/24hr, Radio Shack, Tires+, USPO, Walgreens/24hr, transmissions

**388** US 441 S (exits left from wb), downtown, **S lodging:** Hilton, Holiday Inn, Crowne Plaza, **other:** to Smokey Mtns, to U of TN

**387b** TN 62, 17th St, **N gas:** Pilot/dsl, **lodging:** Best Inn, **other:** $General

**387a** I-275 N, to Lexington

**386b a** US 129, University Ave, to UT, **N** Food City/gas

**385** I-75 N, I-640 E

**I-40 W and I-75 S run together 17 mi.**

**383** Papermill Rd, **N lodging:** Holiday Inn/rest., **S gas:** BP, Citgo, Spur Gas, **food:** Applebee's (1mi), Burger King, China Buffet, Darryl's, Dunkin Donuts, IHOP, Longhorn Steaks, McDonald's, Morrison's Cafeteria, Pizza Hut, Regas Café, Ruby Tuesday, Showbiz Pizza, Taco Bell, Taco Rancho Mexican, Waffle House, Western Sizzlin, **lodging:** Econolodge, Howard Johnson, Super 8, **other:** Buick/GMC, Firestone, same as 380

**380** US 11, US 70, West Hills, **S gas:** BP, Citgo, Conoco, Pilot, Shell, Texaco/dsl, Weigel's, **food:** Amerigo's Italian, Applebee's, Arby's, Chick-fil-A, Chili's, China Buffet, Firehouse Subs, Hardee's, Honeybaked Ham, Hooters, IHOP, KFC, Macaroni Grill, Margarita's, Mr Gatti's, Mr Gatti's, O'Charley's, Olive Garden, Oscar's Rest., Papa John's, Petro's Chili, PF Chang's, Pizza Hut, PlumTree Chinese, Qdoba Mexican, Red Lobster, Schlotsky's, Sawyer's Chicken, Starbucks, Subway, Taco Bell, Texas Roadhouse, Wendy's, Wishbone Wings, Zaxby's, **lodging:** Comfort Hotel, Extended Stay America, Howard Johnson, Quality Inn, Super 8, **other:** Barnes&Noble, Belk, BiLo Foods, Borders Books, Dillard's, $General,

**380** Continued
Food Lion, Goody's, JC Penney, K-Mart, Kohl's, NTB, Office Depot, Old Navy, O'Reilly Parts, Pet Supplies+, Ross, Sears, Staples, TJ Maxx, U-Haul, Walgreens, mall, st patrol, **1 mi S on Kingston Pike...gas:** Citgo/7-11, **food:** Morrison's Cafeteria, Central Park, Little Caesar's, **lodging:** Family Inn, **other:** Office Depot, Radio Shack

**379** Bridgewater Rd, **N gas:** Exxon/Subway, Shell, **food:** McDonald's, Pizza Hut/Taco Bell, **lodging:** Red Carpet Inn, **other:** Sam's Club, Walmart SuperCtr, **S gas:** BP/dsl, Pilot/dsl, Texaco/dsl, **food:** Burger King, ChuckeCheese, Cici's, Don Pablo, Logan's Roadhouse, Mrs Winners, Old Country Buffet, Omelette House, Ryan's, Shoney's, Sonic, Steak Escape, Wendy's, **lodging:** Family Inn, Holiday Inn, Scottish Inn, **other:** AutoZone, BooksAMillion, Buy4Less Foods, Cadillac, Firestone/auto, Ford, Dodge, GMC, Goodyear, Isuzu, Mitsubishi, Nissan, Saab, SuperX Drug, transmissions

**K N O X V I L L E**

**378** Cedar Bluff Rd, **N gas:** Pilot/Taco Bell, Shell, Texaco, Weigel's, **food:** Arby's, Burger King, Cracker Barrel, Dunkin Donuts, KFC, Little Caesar's, LJ Silver, McDonald's, Papa John's, Pizza Hut, Starbucks, Subway, Waffle House, Wendy's, **lodging:** Budget Inn, Econolodge, Hampton Inn, Holiday Inn, Ramada Inn, Sleep Inn, **other:** H HOSPITAL, Food Lion, Walgreen, **S gas:** Exxon, **food:** Applebee's, Bob Evans, Carrabba's, Corky's Ribs/BBQ, Denny's, Fazoli's, Famous Dave's BBQ, Firehouse Subs, Friendly's, Fuddrucker's, Grady's Grill, IHOP, Outback Steaks, Pulio's Grill, Rafferty's, Rubio's Grill, **lodging:** Best Western, Clubhouse Inn, Comfort Inn, Courtyard, Extended Stay America, Guesthouse Suites, Hilton Garden, Jameson Inn, La Quinta, Microtel, Red Roof Inn, Residence Inn, Signature Inn, **other:** Best Buy, Celebration Sta, Chevrolet, Chrysler, Circuit City, Ford, Goody's, Jo-Ann Fabrics, Kia, Lowes Whse, Michael's, Saturn, Staples, Walgreens

**376** I-140 E, TN 162 N, to Maryville, **N** to Oak Ridge Museum

**374** TN 131, Lovell Rd, **N gas:** BP, Shell/dsl, TA/dsl/rest./24hr/@, **food:** McDonald's, Taco Bell, Waffle House, **lodging:** Best Western, Knight's Inn, La Quinta, Travelodge, Vista Inn, **other:** Harley-Davidson, Passport RV Ctr, **S gas:** Citgo, Pilot/Wendy's/dsl/24hr/@, Speedway, **food:** Arby's, Carino's, Chick-fil-A, Chili's, Connor's, Krystal, McDonald's, Mimi's, Olive Garden, Ruby Tuesday, Shoney's, Steak&Shake, Texas Roadhouse, **lodging:** Candlewood Suites, Day's Inn/rest., Homewood Suites, Motel 6, Springhill Suites, **other:** Belk,

**TN**

## INTERSTATE 40 CONT'D

**E ↕ W**

**374** Continued
CarMax, Goody's, Honda, Land Rover, Lexus, Mercedes, Target, Toyota, Walmart SuperCtr

**373** Campbell Sta Rd, **N** gas: Shell/dsl, Marathon/dsl **lodging:** Comfort Suites, Country Inn&Suites, Ramada Ltd, Super 8, **other:** Buddy Gregg RV Ctr, **S** gas: BP, Pilot, Weigel's, **food:** Cracker Barrel, Gridiron Burgers, Hardee's, Little Bangkok, Wild Wing Cafe, Yellow Mushroom, **lodging:** Baymont Inn, Holiday Inn Express, **other:** Gander Mtn

**372mm** weigh sta both lanes

**369** Watt Rd, **N** gas: ✈FLYING J/Conoco/dsl/LP/scales/RV dump/24hr, Speedco, **S** gas: Exxon/dsl, Petro/Mobil/dsl/24hr/@, TA/BP/Burger King/Pizza Hut/dsl/24hr/@, **other:** Blue Beacon

**I-40 E and I-75 N run together 17 mi.**

**368** I-75 and I-40

**364** US 321, TN 95, Lenoir City, Oak Ridge, **N** gas: Melton Hill Mkt/gas, **other:** Crosseyed Cricket Camping (2mi), **4-5 mi S** food: KFC, Krystal, Ruby Tuesday, **lodging:** Comfort Inn, Days Inn, Econolodge, Ramada Ltd

**363mm** parking area wb, [C], litter barrel

**361mm** new exit

**360** Buttermilk Rd, **N** Soaring Eagle RV Park

**356** TN 58 N, Gallaher Rd, to Oak Ridge, **N** gas: BP/dsl, Weigels/dsl, **food:** Huddle House, **lodging:** Day's Inn, Kingston Inn, **other:** 4 Seasons Camping, **S** gas: Citgo/dsl (1mi)

**355** Lawnville Rd, **N** gas: Pilot/dsl

**352** TN 58 S, Kingston, **N** lodging: Knight's Inn, **other:** NAPA, **S** gas: Exxon/dsl, RaceWay, Shell, **food:** Hardee's, McDonald's, Pizza Hut, Sonic, Subway, Taco Bell, **lodging:** Comfort Inn, **other:** Family$, Marina RV Park, to Watts Bar Lake, Piggly Wiggly, USPO

**351mm** Clinch River

**350** US 70, Midtown, **S** other: Kroger/Starbucks, Lowe's Whse, Patterson RV Supplies, Walgreen

**347** US 27, Harriman, **N** gas: Phillips 66/Subway/dsl, Shell, **food:** Hardee's, KFC, Los Primos Mexican, LJ Silver, McDonald's, Pizza Hut, Ruby Tuesday, Taco Bell, Wendy's, **lodging:** Best Western, **other:** to Frozen Head SP, Big S Fork NRA, **S** gas: BP, Exxon, Shell/Krystal/dsl/24hr, **food:** Cancun Mexican, Cracker Barrel, Shoney's, **lodging:** Caney Creek Inn, Holiday Inn Express, Super 8, **2-3 mi S** food: Capt D's, Domino's, Sonic, **other:** [H] HOSPITAL, Goody's, Radio Shack, Walmart SuperCtr/gas

**340** TN 299 N, Airport Rd

**339.5mm** *eastern/central time zone line, eastern/central time zone line*

**338** TN 299 S, Westel Rd, **N** gas: BP/dsl, **S** gas: Shell/dsl, **other:** Lighthouse RV Park

**336mm** parking area/weigh sta eb, litter barrel

**329** US 70, Crab Orchard, **N** gas: BP/dsl, Liberty/dsl, **other:** KOA (4mi), **S** other: Cumberland Trails SP, Wilson SP

**327mm** rest area wb, full [♿] facilities, [C], [⊞], litter barrels, petwalk, vending

**324mm** rest area eb, full [♿] facilities, [C], [⊞], litter barrels, petwalk, vending

**322** TN 101, Peavine Rd, Crossville, **N** gas: BP/Bean Pot Rest., Exxon/dsl, Phillips 66, **food:** Hardee's, McDonald's, **lodging:** Holiday Inn Express, **other:** Deer Run

**H A R R I M A N**

**TN**

---

**322** Continued
Resort, KOA Camping, Roam-Roost RV Campground, to Fairfield Glade Resort, **S** gas: Texaco/dsl, **food:** Cancun Mexican, Taco Bell, **lodging:** Comfort Suites, Super 8, **other:** [H] HOSPITAL, Tennessee RV Ctr, Cumberland Mtn SP

**320** TN 298, Crossville, **N** antiques, golf, winery, **S** gas: BP/DQ/Pizza Hut/dsl, Shell/24hr, **food:** Big Boy's BBQ, Genesis Grill, Krystal (2mi), Wendy's (2mi), **other:** [H] HOSPITAL, Factory Outlet/famous brands, Save-A-Lot Foods, antiques, auto repair

**318mm** Obed River

**317** US 127, Crossville, **N** gas: BP/dsl, Exxon/Subway/dsl/24hr, Horizon, Shell/dsl, **food:** Huddle House, Shoneys, **lodging:** Best Western, La Quinta, Ramada Inn, **0-2 mi S** gas: BP, Chevron, Citgo, Jiffy Gas, Phillips 66/dsl, Sunoco, **food:** Arby's, Burger King, Cancun Mexican, Cracker Barrel, Dickie's BBQ, La Costa Mexican, McDonalds, Papa Johns, Ruby Tuesday, Ryan's, Sonic, Taco Bell, TCBY, Vegas Steaks, Waffle House, Zaxby's, **lodging:** Best Value, Days Inn, Heritage Inn, **other:** [H] HOSPITAL, Chevrolet/Cadillac/Buick/Pontiac/GMC, Chrysler/Dodge/Jeep, $Tree, GNC, Goodys, Lowe's Whse, Staples, Walmart SuperCtr/gas, Walgreen, tires, to Cumberland SP

**311** Plateau Rd, **N** gas: Citgo/dsl, **food:** Papa Lorenzo's Pizza, **S** gas: BP/dsl, Exxon

**306mm** parking area/weigh sta wb, litter barrels

**301** US 70 N, TN 84, Monterey, **N** gas: Phillips 66, Shell, **food:** Burger King, Cup N' Saucer Rest., DQ, Subway

**300** US 70, Monterey, **N** gas: Citgo/dsl, **food:** Hardee's

**291mm** Falling Water River

**290** US 70, Cookeville, **N** gas: BP (1mi), **S** gas: Citgo, **lodging:** Alpine Suites

**288** TN 111, to Livingston, Cookeville, Sparta, **N** Cordell SP, **S** gas: Citgo/dsl, Mid Tenn Trkstp/Phillips 66/Subway/dsl/24hr/@, **food:** Huddle House, **lodging:** Knight's Inn

**287** TN 136, Cookeville, **N** gas: BP/TCBY, Chevron/dsl, Citgo, Exxon, Shell/dsl, **food:** Applebee's, Arby's, Burger King, Capt D's, Cheddars, Chick-fil-A, Chili's, China Star, Cracker Barrel, DQ, Fazoli's, Golden Corral, IHOP, Jack-in-the-Box, King Buffet, Krystal, LJ Silver, Logan's Roadhouse, Longhorn Steaks, McDonald's, Mr Gatti's, New China, Nick's Rest., O'Charley's, Outback Steaks, Pizza Hut, Puleo's Grill, Quizno's, Red Lobster, Ryan's, Shoney's, Sonic, Steak'n Shake, Subway, Taco Bell, Waffle House, Wendy's, **lodging:** Best Value, Best Western, Comfort Inn, Comfort Suites, Day's Inn, Garden Hotel, Hampton Inn, Super 8, **other:** Auto Value Parts, BigLots, Cadillac/Honda, CVS Drug, $Tree, Firestone/auto, Goody's, Harley-Davidson, JC Penney, Kroger/gas, Lowe's Whse, Radio Shack, Toyota, U-haul, Walmart SuperCtr/gas, mall, st patrol, transmissions, **S** gas: Exxon/dsl, Marathon/dsl, Pilot/dsl, **food:** CJ's Wings, KFC, Waffle House, **lodging:** Baymont Inn, Country Hearth Inn, Country Inn Suites, Holiday Inn Express, **other:** Dodge, Sam's Club/gas

**286** TN 135, Burgess Falls Rd, **N** gas: BP, Exxon, RaceWay/dsl, Shell/dsl, **food:** Applebee's, Arby's, Chick-fil-A, El Palenque Mexican, Hardee's, Steak'n Shake, Thai Cuisine, Toot's, Waffle House, **lodging:** KeyWest Inn, **other:** [H] HOSPITAL, Chrysler/Jeep, GMC, Goodyear, Kia/Mitsubishi, Mazda, Middle TN RV Ctr, Nissan, Toyota, U-Haul, to TTU, **S** gas: Citgo/dsl, **lodging:** Star Motor Inn/rest.

**C O O K E V I L L E**

## INTERSTATE 40 CONT'D

E
W

L
E
B
A
N
O
N

| 280 | TN 56 N, Baxter, **N gas:** Loves/McDonalds/Subway/dsl/24hr, Shell/dsl (1mi), **food:** Wagonwheel Rest. (1mi), **other:** Camp Discovery (2mi), Twin Lakes RV Park (2mi) |
| 276 | Old Baxter Rd, **S gas:** Citgo/dsl, **other:** fireworks |
| 273 | TN 56 S, to Smithville, **S gas:** BP/dsl, Phillips 66, **food:** Rose Garden Rest., **lodging:** Lakeside Inn, Timber Ridge Inn |
| 268 | TN 96, Buffalo Valley Rd, **S** to Edgar Evins SP |
| 267mm | Caney Fork River |
| 267mm | **rest area both lanes, full ♿ facilities, info, [C], [🏠], litter barrels, petwalk, vending** |
| 266mm | Caney Fork River |
| 263mm | Caney Fork River |
| 258 | TN 53, Gordonsville, **N gas:** Exxon/KFC/Taco Bell, Shell/dsl, **food:** McDonald's, Timberloft Café, Waffle House, **lodging:** Comfort Inn, **other:** to Cordell Hull Dam, **S gas:** KeyStop/dsl, **food:** Cornerstone Cafe, **other:** $General |
| 254 | TN 141, to Alexandria |
| 252mm | **parking area/weigh sta both lanes, [🏠], litter barrels** |
| 245 | Linwood Rd, **N gas:** BP/dsl |
| 239 | US 70, Lebanon, **N gas:** Citgo/dsl, RaceWay, **S gas:** Phillips 66/Uncle Pete's/dsl/rest/scales |
| 238 | US 231, Lebanon, **N gas:** Exxon, Mapco, Shell, **food:** Applebee's, Arby's, Cici's Pizza, Cracker Barrel, Demo's Steaks, Hardee's, Jack-in-the-Box, KFC, King Buffet, McDonald's, Mrs Winner's, Pizza Hut, Ponderosa, Ryan's, Shoney's, Subway, Taco Bell, Waffle House, Wendy's, White Castle, Zaxby's **lodging:** Best Value, Best Western, Comfort Inn, Executive Inn, Hampton Inn, Holiday Inn Express, **other:** [H] HOSPITAL, Aldi Foods, $Tree, Goody's, Lowe's Whse, Walmart SuperCtr, **S gas:** Citgo/dsl, Pilot/Subway/dsl/24hr/scales, **food:** O'Charley's, Sonic, **lodging:** Comfort Suites, Country Inn Suites, Day's Inn, Knight's Inn, Super 8, **other:** Prime Outlets/famous brands, flea mkt, to Cedars of Lebanon SP, RV camping |
| 236 | S Hartmann Dr, **N gas:** Mapco, Shell, **food:** Chili's, Outback Steaks, **other:** [H] HOSPITAL, Home Depot, **2 mi N food:** Ruby Tuesday |
| 235 | TN 840 W, to Murfreesboro |
| 232 | TN 109, to Gallatin, **N gas:** Citgo, Mapco, Shell/McDonald's/dsl/24hr, **food:** Bellacino's Pizza, Brewster's Grille, Sonic, Subway, Waffle House, Wendy's, **lodging:** Sleep Inn, Value Place Inn, **2 mi S other:** Countryside Resort Camping |
| 226mm | truck sta, eb only |
| 229 | new exit |
| 226 | TN 171, Mt Juliet Rd, **N gas:** BP/McDonald's/dsl, Citgo, Exxon/dsl, Mapco/dsl, Shell/dsl/24hr, **food:** Arby's, Capt D's, **S gas:** Mapco/dsl, **food:** Chick-fil-A, Cracker Barrel, Logan's Roadhouse, O'Charly's, Olive Garden, Panera Bread, Red Robin, Ruby Tuesday, Steak&Shake, Taco Bell, Waffle House, **lodging:** Hampton Inn, Microtel, Quality Inn, **other:** Belk, Best Buy, BooksAMillion, Curves, JC Penney, JoAnne Fabrics, Kroger, Old Navy, PetsMart, Ross, Target, TJ Maxx, to Long Hunter SP |
| 221 | TN 45 N, Old Hickory Blvd, to The Hermitage, **N gas:** Express/dsl, RaceWay, Shell/24hr, **food:** Applebee's, DQ, IHOP, Jack-in-the-Box, O'Charley's, Outback, Subway, Taki Japanese, Waffle House, **lodging:** Best Inn, |

N
A
S
H
V
I
L
L
E

| 221 | Continued Comfort Inn, Motel 6, Suburban Lodge, Super 8, Vista Hotel, **other:** [H] HOSPITAL, CVS Drug, Kroger, Walgreen, **S gas:** Phillips 66/White Castle, Shell/McDonald's, Texaco |
| 219 | Stewart's Ferry Pike, **N gas:** Mapco, **S gas:** Mapco, Shell/dsl, **food:** China King, Cracker Barrel, Hacienda Mexican, Sal's Pizza, Waffle House, **lodging:** Best Value Inn, Best Western, Country Inn Suites, Day's Inn, Family Inn, Sleep Inn, **other:** $General, FoodLion, vet |
| 216 | (216 c from eb) TN 255, Donaldson Pk, **N gas:** BP/dsl, Citgo, Mapco, RaceWay, Shell/Subway/dsl/24hr, **food:** Arby's, Backyard Burger, BBQ, Burger King, Darfon's, Domino's, Don Chile's, KFC, McDonald's, New China, Papa John's, Pizza Hut/Taco Bell, Ruby Tuesday, Shoney's, Subway, Waffle House, Wendy's, **lodging:** Country Inn Suites, Drury Inn, Fairfield Inn, Hampton Inn, Holiday Inn Express, La Quinta, Radisson, Springhill Suites, Super 8, Wingate Inn, **other:** Advance Parts, K-Mart, Walgreens |
| 216b a | (from eb), **S** Nashville Intn'l Airport |
| 215b a | TN 155, Briley Pkwy, to Opryland, **N on Elm Hill...gas:** Citgo, Mapco, **food:** Jack-in-the-Box, Waffle House, **lodging:** Alexis Inn, Comfort Suites, Courtyard, Embassy Suites, Extended Stay, Hampton Inn, Hilton Garden, Holiday Inn Select, Homestead Suites, Hotel Preston, La Quinta, Marriott, Residence Inn, Studio+, **2 mi N on Lebanon Pike...food:** Capt D's, **other:** to Camping World RV Service, KOA, **S gas:** Phillips 66, **food:** Mazatlan Mexican, Panda House, Subway |
| 213b | I-24 W |
| 213a | I-24 E/I-440, E to Chattanooga |
| 213 | US 41 (from wb no return), to Spence Lane, **N other:** Kenworth, **S gas:** Shell, Texaco, **food:** Denny's, Waffle House, **lodging:** Day's Inn, Holiday Inn Express, Rodeway Inn, Sunrise Inn, Super 8, same as 212 |
| 212 | Fessler's Lane (from eb, no return), **N other:** Freightliner, Harley-Davidson, **S gas:** Express/dsl, Shell/dsl, **food:** Burger King, Krystal, McDonald's, Mrs Winners, Sonic, Wendy's, **lodging:** Best Value, same as 213 |
| 211mm | Cumberland River |
| 211b | I-24 W |
| 211a | I-24E, I-40 W |
| 210c | US 31 S, US 41A, 2nd Ave, 4th Ave, **N lodging:** Hilton, Sheraton, Stouffer Hotel, **S** museum |
| 210b a | I-65 S, to Birmingham |

**NASHVILLE** E ↕ W / **DICKSON**

### INTERSTATE 40 CONT'D

**209b a** US 70 S, Charlotte Ave, Nashville, **N gas:** Exxon, **food:** McDonald's, **lodging:** Sheraton, **other:** Chrysler/Jeep, Nissan, Country Music Hall of Fame, Conv Ctr, transmissions, **S gas:** Exxon, **food:** Burger King, Krystal, Subway, White Castle, **lodging:** Comfort Inn, Guesthouse Inn, **other:** Chevrolet, Lincoln/Mercury, Pontiac/GMC, Subaru, Toyota

**208b a** I-65, N to Louisville, S to Birmingham

**207** 28th Ave, Jefferson St, Nashville, **N gas:** Citgo, Phillips 66, **food:** Subway, Wendy's, Wing Zone, **other:** H HOSPITAL, Family$, to TN St U

**206** I-440 E, to Knoxville

**205** 46th Ave, W Nashville, **N other:** Harley-Davidson, **S gas:** Mapco, Shell, **food:** McDonald's, Mrs. Winners

**204** TN 155, Briley Pkwy, **S gas:** Citgo, **food:** Burger King, China Buffet, Church's/White Castle, 5 De Maio, Domino's, Jack-in-the-Box, KFC, Krystal, Las Palmas, Papa John's, Shoney's, Subway, Waffle House, **lodging:** Baymont Inn, Best Western, Comfort Inn, Days Inn, **other:** CarQuest, CVS Drug, Firestone/auto, Ford, Kroger/gas, NTB, O'Reilly Parts, Sav-a-lot Foods, Walgreen

**201b a** US 70, Charlotte Pike, **N gas:** Exxon, Shell/dsl/24hr, **food:** Bojangles, China Buffet, Cracker Barrel, Jim 'N Nick's BBQ, Krystal, Subway, Super China, Waffle House, **lodging:** Super 8, **other:** $Tree, GNC, Lowe's Whse, Radio Shack, Walmart SuperCtr, **S gas:** BP, Mapco, Shell, **food:** Arby's, McDonald's, Pizza Hut, Taco Bell, **other:** Best Buy, Books-A-Million, BigLots, Costco/gas, Firestone/auto, Marshall's, Old Navy, PetsMart, Ross, Staples, Target, Uhaul, World Mkt

**199** rd 251, Old Hickory Blvd, **N gas:** Shell, **S gas:** BP, Mapco, **food:** Sonic, Waffle House, **other:** Sam's Club/gas

**196** US 70, to Bellevue, Newsom Sta, **N gas:** Mapco, **food:** Shoney's, **S gas:** BP, Mapco/dsl, Shell/dsl/24hr, **food:** Applebee's, Arby's, Baskin-Robbins, Jack-in-the-Box, O'Charley's, Pizza Hut, Quizno's, Sir Pizza, Sonic, Subway, Taco Bell, Waffle House, Wendy's, **lodging:** Hampton Inn, Microtel, **other:** Circuit City, $Tree, Firestone/auto, Home Depot, Macey's, Michael's, Old Navy, Petco, Publix, Sears/auto, Staples, USPO, Walgreen/24hr

**195mm** Harpeth River

**192** McCrory Lane, to Pegram, **N gas:** Eddie's Mkt, **4 mi S food:** Loveless Cafe, **other:** Natchez Trace Pkwy

**190mm** Harpeth River

**188mm** Harpeth River

**188** rd 249, Kingston Springs, **N gas:** BP, Mapco/dsl, Shell/Arby's, **food:** McDonald's/playplace, Sonic, Subway, **lodging:** Best Western, Mid-Town Inn, Relax Inn, Scottish Inn, **other:** USPO, **S gas:** Petro/Chevron/Iron Skillet/Pizza Hut/Quick Skillet/dsl/showers/scales/24hr/@, **other:** vet

**182** TN 96, to Dickson, Fairview, **N gas:** Express Fuel, **lodging:** Best Value, Fairview Inn, **other:** M Bell SP (16mi), **S gas:** ◈FLYING J/Conoco/Cookery/Country Mkt/dsl/LP/scales/24hr/@, Horizon/Backyard Burger/dsl, **lodging:** Deerfield Inn

**175** TN 840

**172** TN 46, to Dickson, **N gas:** Citgo/Subway, Exxon, Pilot/Wendy's/dsl/scales/24hr, Shell, **food:** Arby's, Cracker Barrel, McDonald's, Ruby Tuesday, Sandilly's Grill,

---

**DICKSON** / **JACKSON**

**172** Continued
Subway, Waffle House/24hr, Wang's China, **lodging:** Best Western, Comfort Inn, Econolodge, Hampton Inn, Motel 6, Quality Inn, South-Aire, Super 8, **other:** H HOSPITAL, Chevrolet, Dickson RV Park, truck repair, to M Bell SP, **S gas:** Phillips 66, Shell, **food:** O'Charley's, Sonic, **lodging:** Day's Inn, Holiday Inn Express, Ramada

**170** rest area both lanes, full & facilities, ᴄ, 🕿, litter barrels, vending, petwalk

**166mm** Piney River

**163** rd 48, to Dickson, **N gas:** Phillips 66/dsl, **other:** tire repair, **S gas:** Shell, **other:** Pinewood Camping (7mi), Tanbark Camping

**152** rd 230, Bucksnort, **N gas:** Citgo, **food:** Rudy's Rest., **lodging:** Travel Inn

**149mm** Duck River

**148** rd 50, Barren Hollow Rd, to Turney Center

**143** TN 13, to Linden, Waverly, **N gas:** BP, Pilot/Arby's/scales/dsl/24hr, Shell, **food:** Las Fuentes Mexican, Loretta's Kitchen, McDonald's, Mustang BBQ, Subway, **lodging:** Best Western, Day's Inn, Holiday Inn Express, Knight's Inn, **other:** KOA, tires, **S gas:** Exxon/dsl, **lodging:** Budget Motel, Southside Motel/rest.

**141mm** Buffalo River

**137** Cuba Landing, **N other:** TN River RV Park, **S food:** Cuba Landing Rest./gas

**133mm** Tennessee River

**133** rd 191, Birdsong Rd, **N lodging:** Lakeside RV Resort/marina (9mi), **S** Good Sam RV Park

**131mm** rest area both lanes, full & facilities, ᴄ, vending, 🕿, litter barrels, petwalk

**126** US 641, TN 69, to Camden, **N gas:** Exxon/Subway/TCBY/dsl, Phillips 66/North 40/dsl/rest., Shell/dsl, **other:** tire/truck repair, to NB Forrest SP, **S gas:** BP/dsl, Shell/dsl, **lodging:** Day's Inn/rest., **other:** H HOSPITAL

**116** rd 114, **S other:** to Natchez Trace SP, RV camping

**110mm** Big Sandy River

**108** TN 22, to Lexington, Parkers Crossroads, **N gas:** BP/McDonald's/24hr/dsl, Citgo/dsl/24hr, Phillips 66/dsl, **food:** Bailey's Rest., DQ, Subway, **lodging:** Knight's Inn, **other:** USPO, city park, **S gas:** Exxon, **lodging:** Best Value, **other:** H HOSPITAL, RV camping, to Shiloh Nat Bfd (51mi)

**103mm** parking area/truck sta eb, litter barrels, ᴄ

**102mm** parking area/truck sta wb, litter barrels

**101** rd 104, **N gas:** Conoco/101 TP/rest/dsl/24hr, **other:** golf (3mi)

**93** rd 152, Law Rd, **N gas:** Phillips 66/dsl/deli/24hr, **S gas:** Global Fuel/cafe

**87** US 70, US 412, Jackson, **N gas:** Coastal/dsl, **S gas:** BP/dsl, Love's/Hardee's/scales/dsl/24hr

**85** Christmasville Rd, to Jackson, **N gas:** BP/dsl, Exxon/dsl/24hr, Pilot/Denny's/dsl/scales/24hrs, **food:** Guthery's, Lenny's Subs, Los Portales, Reggi BBQ, Sparky's Grill, **lodging:** Howard Johnson Express, **other:** $General, **S gas:** Horizon, Shell (1mi), **food:** Baskin-Robbins, Sonic

**83** Campbell St, **N gas:** Exxon/Old Madina Mkt/dsl **S lodging:** Courtyard, Hampton Inn

JACKSON

E ↑ W

JACKSON

## INTERSTATE 40 CONT'D

**82b a** US 45, Jackson, **N gas:** BP, Exxon, **food:** Cracker Barrel, **lodging:** Knight's Inn, Microtel, **other:** Batteries+, Smallwoods RV Ctr (4mi) **S gas:** BP, Clark Gas/dsl, Exxon, RaceWay, **food:** Barley's Cafe, Burger King, Capt D's, Catfish Galley, ChuckeCheese, DQ, Jumbo Buffet, KFC, Krystal, LJ Silver, McDonald's/playplace, Papa John's, Pizza Hut, Pizza Inn, Popeye's, Shoney's, Sonic, Subway, Taco Bell, Wendy's, **lodging:** Executive Inn, La Quinta, Ramada Ltd, Super 8, **other:** Advance Parts, AutoZone, BigLots, CarQuest, $General, Firestone/auto, Goodyear/auto, Kroger/24hr, Macy's, Office Depot, Radio Shack, Sears/auto, TJ Maxx, WaldenBooks, mall, vet

**80b a** US 45 Byp, Jackson, **N food:** Backyard Burger, Baskin-Robbins, Buffalo Wings, Chili's, Chick-fil-A, China Pan, Corky's BBQ, Fazoli's, Honey Baked Ham, IHOP, Jason's Deli, KFC, Lenny's Subs, Moe's SW Grill, LoneStar Steaks, Longhorn Steaks, Olive Garden, Peking Chinese, Perkins, Popeye's, Schlotsky's, Starbucks, Steak'n Shake, TGI Friday, Wendy's, Zaxby's, **lodging:** Baymont Inn, Comfort Inn, Country Inn Suites, Jameson Inn, Red Roof Inn, **other:** Best Buy, Firestone/auto, Home Depot, Kohl's, Lowe's Whse, Marshalls, Nissan, PetsMart, Ross, Sam's Club/gas, Saturn, Walmart SuperCtr/gas, **1 mi N on 45 BP...food:** Arby's, Burger King, China Pan, Los Portales, LJ Silver, McDonald's, Outback Steaks, Red Robin, Ruby Tuesday, other Books-A-Million, Cadillac/Chevrolet, Gateway Tires, Steinmart, Target, **S gas:** BP/Circle K, Phillips 66/dsl, **food:** Barnhill's Buffet, Burger King, Dunkin Donuts, El Chico's, Logan's Roadhouse, Madison's Rest., McDonald's, Mrs Winner's, O'Charley's, Old Hickory Steakhouse, Red Bones Rest., Subway, Waffle House, **lodging:** Best Western, Casey Jones Motel, Day's Inn, DoubleTree, Econolodge, Guesthouse Inn, Holiday Inn, Motel 6, Old Hickory Inn, Quality Inn, **other:** Ⓗ HOSPITAL, $General, Hancock Fabrics, Harley-Davidson, King Tires, K-Mart, Toyota/Scion, Tuesday Morning, to Pinson Mounds SP, Chickasaw SP

**79** US 412, Jackson, **N other:** Gander Mtn., **S gas:** BP/dsl, Exxon, Horizon/Baskin-Robbins/dsl, Phillips 66, **lodging:** Day's Inn, **other:** Jackson RV Park

**78mm** Forked Deer River

**76** rd 223 S, **S other:** McKellar-Sites ✈, Whispering Pines RV Park

**74** Lower Brownsville Rd

**73mm** **rest area both lanes, full** ♿ **facilities, info,** 🕿, 🍴, **litter barrels, vending, petwalk**

**68** rd 138, Providence Rd, **N gas:** BP/dsl, **lodging:** Ole South Inn, **S gas:** TA/Citgo/Subway/dsl/scales/rest./24hr/@, Valero/dsl, **other:** Joy-O RV Park

**66** US 70, to Brownsville, **N other:** Ft Pillow SHP (51mi) **S gas:** Exxon/dsl, **lodging:** Motel 6

**60** rd 19, Mercer Rd

**56** TN 76, to Brownsville, **N gas:** BP, Shell/dsl/24hr, **food:** DQ, KFC, McDonald's/playplace, Pizza Hut/Taco Bell,

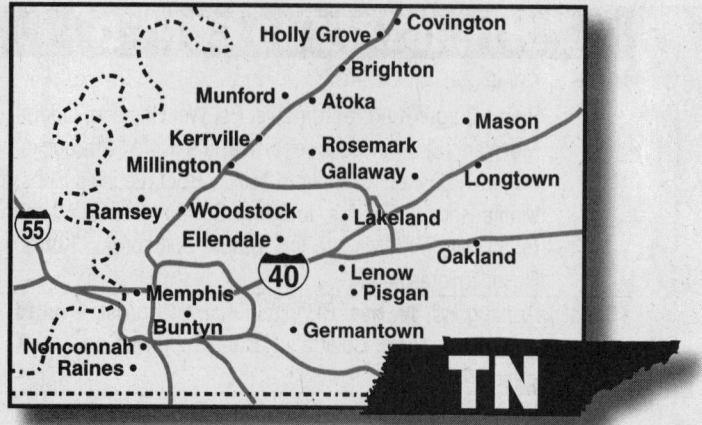

**56** Continued
**lodging:** Best Value, Day's Inn, Econolodge, Hotel O'Bannon, **S gas:** Exxon/Huddle House/dsl/24hr

**55mm** Hatchie River

**52** TN 76, rd 179, Koko Rd, to Whiteville

**50mm** weigh sta both lanes, phone

**47** TN 179, to Stanton, Dancyville, **S gas:** Exit 47 Trkstp/dsl

**42** TN 222, to Stanton, **N lodging:** Best Value, **S gas:** Exxon/dsl, Pilot/Chester's/Subway/dsl/scales/24hr, **lodging:** Deerfield Inn

**35** TN 59, to Somerville, **S gas:** BP/dsl/scales, **food:** Longtown Rest.

**29.5mm** Loosahatchie River

**25** TN 205, Airline Rd, to Arlington, **N gas:** Shell/Chester's/dsl, **S gas:** Horizon/Backyard Burger/dsl, **other:** vistor ctr

**24** TN 385, rd 204, to Arlington, Millington, Collierville

**20** Canada Rd, Lakeland, **N gas:** BP/McDonald's, Shell, **food:** Cracker Barrel, Waffle House, **lodging:** Day's Inn/rest., Relax Inn, Super 8, **S gas:** Exxon/Subway/dsl, **other:** Factory Outlet/famous brands/food court, Memphis East Campground, Old Time Pottery

**18** US 64, to Bartlett, **N gas:** Shell/Circle K/Burger King, **food:** Abuelo's, American Cafe, Bob Evans, Buffalo Wings, Dyer's Cafe, El Porton, Firebird's Grill, Hooters, McCalisters Deli, O'Charley's, Olive Garden, Steak'n Shake, TGI Friday, TX Roadhouse, **lodging:** Best Western, Fairfield Inn, SpringHill Suites, **other:** Best Western, Firestone, Goodyear/auto, Hummer, Lowe's Whse, Pontiac/GMC, Sam's Club/gas, Walmart SuperCtr, same as 16, **S gas:** BP/Circle K, Citgo/dsl, 76/Circle K, **food:** Backyard Burger, KFC, Lenny's Subs, Pizza Pro, **other:** Kroger, Schnuck's/gas, Walgreen, Zaxby's

**16b a** TN 177, to Germantown, **N gas:** BP, Shell/Circle K, **food:** Alexander's Rest., Arby's, Bahama Breeze, Burger King, Casa Mexicana, Chili's, Chick-fil-A, Colton's Steaks, IHOP, J. Alexander's, Joe's Crabshack, Logan's Roadhouse, Macaroni Grill, McDonald's/playplace, Old Navy, Onthe-Border, Red Lobster, Taco Bell, Waffle House, Wendy's, **lodging:** Extended Stay Deluxe, Hampton Suites, Hyatt Place, **other:** Barnes&Noble, Best Buy, Chevrolet, Chrysler/Dodge, Circuit City, Dillard's, Ford, Home Depot, Honda, Infinity, JC Penney, Macey's, Michael's, Nissan, Office Depot, Old Navy, Sears/auto, Target, TJ Maxx, Walgreen, World Mkt, mall, **S gas:** Shell, **food:** Abbay's

Copyright 2009 - The Next Exit®

## INTERSTATE 40 CONT'D

**16b a** Continued
Rest., Burger King, Gordman's, Pei Wei Chinese, Qdoba Mexican, Shogun Japanese, Newk's Cafe, Starbucks, Howard's Doughnut's, Jim'n Nick's BBQ, Lenny's Subs, Waffle House, Wendy's, **lodging:** Comfort Suites, Microtel, Quality Inn, Wingate Inn, **other:** Costco/gas, Kohl's, Ross, Toyota/Scion

**15b a** Appling Rd, **N** gas: BP/Circle K, Horizon/dsl, **1 mi N** gas: Shell, **food:** Coletta's Italian, Suburban Lodge, **S** gas: BP

**14** Whitten Rd, **N** gas: Citgo/dsl, Mapco, Shell/Burger King, **food:** Sidecar Café, **other:** Harley-Davidson, **S** gas: BP, Shell/Backyard Burger/dsl, **lodging:** Travelers Inn, **other:** Walgreens

**12** Sycamore View Rd, **N** gas: Citgo/dsl, Texaco/dsl, **food:** Cajun Catfish Co., Capt D's, Church's, Cracker Barrel, IHOP, Krystal, McDonald's, Mrs Winner's, Perkins, Ruby Tuesday, Shoney's, Sonic, Taco Bell, Waffle House, **lodging:** Baymont Inn, Drury Inn, Econolodge, Extended Stay America, Memphis Plaza, Ramada Ltd, Red Roof Inn, **other:** AutoZone, $General, Fred's Drug, Walgreens, vet, **S** gas: BP/Circle K/dsl, Citgo, Exxon, Mapco, **food:** Beijing Chinese, Burger King, Playita Mexican, Popeye's, Subway, Tops BBQ, Wendy's, **lodging:** Best Western, Comfort Inn, Day's Inn, Fairfield Inn, La Quinta, Memphis Inn, Motel 6, Quality Inn, Super 8, **other:** Bass Pro Shop, Parts+

**10.5mm** Wolf River

**10b a** (from wb) I-240 W around Memphis, I-40 E to Nashville

**12c** (from eb) I-240 W, to Jackson, I-40 E to Nashville

**12b** Sam Cooper Blvd (from eb)

**12a** US 64/70/79, Summer Ave, **N** gas: Mapco/dsl, Shell, **food:** Waffle House, **lodging:** Guest Inn, **other:** Ford, U-Haul, mall, **S** gas: Exxon, **food:** Arby's, Great China, McDonald's, Wendy's, **other:** Curves, $Tree, Firestone/auto, Fred's Drug, Goodyear/auto, Piggly Wiggly, Sav-a-Lot Foods

**10** TN 204, Covington Pike, **N** gas: BP, **food:** McDonald's, Wendy's, **other:** Audi/VW, Buick, Chevrolet, Crysler/Jeep/Dodge, Honda, Hyundai, Isuzu/Mazda, Kia, Mazda, Mitsubishi, Nissan, Pontiac/GMC, Sam's Club, Subaru, Suzuki, SuperLo Food/gas, Volvo

**8b a** TN 14, Jackson Ave, **N** gas: Citgo/dsl, Shell, **lodging:** Day's Inn, Sleep Inn, **other:** Raleigh Tire, vet, **S** gas: Citgo/dsl, Mapco, **other:** AutoZone, Family$, O'Reilly Parts, transmissions

**6** Warford Rd

**5** Hollywood St, **N** gas: BP, Mapco, **food:** Burger King, Mother's Rest., **other:** Walgreens, **S** other: Memphis Zoo

**3** Watkins St, **N** gas: BP, Chevron, Texaco/dsl, **other:** Family$, U-Haul

**2a** rd 300, to US 51 N, Millington, **N** other: Meeman-Shelby SP

**2** Smith Ave, Chelsea Ave, **N** gas: Citgo, **S** gas: BP

**1g f** TN 14, Jackson Ave, **S** gas: Mapco

**1e** I-240 E

**1d c b** US 51, Danny Thomas Blvd, **N** gas: Exxon, **food:** KFC, Wendy's, **other:** Ronald McDonald House, St Jude Research Ctr

**1a** 2nd St (from wb), downtown, **S** lodging: Holiday Inn, Marriott, Sheraton, Wyndham Garden, **other:** Conv Ctr

**1** Riverside Dr, Front St (from eb), Memphis, **S** lodging: Comfort Inn, **other:** Conv Ctr, Riverfront

**0mm** Tennessee/Arkansas state line, Mississippi River

## INTERSTATE 55

| Exit # | Services |
|---|---|
| **13mm** | Tennessee/Arkansas state line, Mississippi River |
| **12c** | Delaware St, Memphis, **W** lodging: Super 8 |
| **12b** | Riverside Dr, downtown Memphis, **E** TN Welcome Ctr |
| **12a** | E Crump Blvd (from nb) , **E** gas: BP, **other:** museum |
| **11** | McLemore Ave, Presidents Island, industrial area |
| **10** | S Parkway, **1/2 mi E** gas: BP/dsl |
| **9** | Mallory Ave, industrial area |
| **8** | Horn Lake Rd (from sb) |
| **7** | US 61, 3rd St, **E** gas: BP, Exxon/mart, **food:** Church's, Interstate BBQ, Taco Bell, **other:** AutoZone, Family$, Walgreens, **W** gas: MapCo, PitStop, **food:** KFC, McDonald's, Subway, **lodging:** Rest Inn, **other:** Fuller SP, Indian Museum |
| **6b a** | I-240 |
| **5b** | US 51 S, Elvis Presley Blvd, to Graceland, **W** gas: BP, Citgo/dsl, Exxon, Phillips 66, **food:** Capt D's, Checker's, China Buffet, Kettle Rest., KFC, Peking Chinese, Picadilly's, Taco Bell, **lodging:** American Inn, Day's Inn, Graceland Inn, Heartbreak Hotel, Scottish Inn, Value Place Inn, **other:** Ⓗ HOSPITAL, Advance Parts, D&N RV Ctr, Dodge's Store, Harley-Davidson, Presley RV Ctr, Walgreens, transmissions, to Graceland |
| **5a** | Brooks Rd, **E** gas: BP, Exxon, MapCo, **food:** Popeye's, **lodging:** Airport Inn, Best Value Inn, Budget Lodge, Clarion, Quality Inn, **other:** Freightliner, Peterbilt, Toyota |
| **3mm** | **Welcome Ctr nb, full ♿ facilities, 🕿, vending, 🛏, litter barrels, petwalk** |
| **2b a** | TN 175, Shelby Dr, Whitehaven, **E** gas: BP/dsl, Citgo/Subway, Exxon, Shell/dsl, Texaco, **lodging:** Colonial Inn, **W** gas: BP, Citgo, **food:** Burger King, CK's Coffee, Dixie Queen, IHOP, McDonald's, Piccadilly, Popeye's, **other:** Family$, Goodyear/auto, Macy's, Sav-a-Lot Foods, Schnuck's Foods, Sears, U-Haul, Walgreens |
| **0mm** | Tennessee/Mississippi state line |

## INTERSTATE 65

| Exit # | Services |
|---|---|
| **121.5mm** | Tennessee/Kentucky state line |
| **121mm** | **Welcome Ctr sb, full ♿ facilities, 🕿 🛏, litter barrels, vending, petwalk** |
| **119mm** | weigh sta both lanes |
| **117** | TN 52, Portland, **E** gas: BP/Quizno's/Godfather's/dsl, Shell/dsl/fireworks, **other:** Ⓗ HOSPITAL, **W** gas: BP/dsl, **lodging:** Budget Host, **other:** fireworks |
| **116mm** | Red River |

## INTERSTATE 65 CONT'D

**N ↕ S**

**113mm**  Red River

**112**  TN 25, Cross Plains, **E gas:** BP/dsl, **food:** Biggs Chicken, Sad Sam's Deli, **other:** Bledsoe SP, antiques, fireworks **W gas:** Mapco/dsl, Shell/dsl

**108**  TN 76, White House, **E gas:** Nervous Charlie's/dsl, Shell, **food:** A&W/KFC, Cracker Barrel, DQ, Hardee's, McDonald's, Mr Wok, Sonic, Subway, Taco Bell, Waffle House, Wendy's, **lodging:** Comfort Inn, Hampton Inn, Holiday Inn Express, Quality Inn, **other:** Ace Hardware, Kroger/gas, O'Reilly Parts, Rite Aid, Walmart SuperCtr/Subway, Walgreens, USPO, park/playground, **W gas:** BP, **food:** Stop 30 BBQ, **lodging:** Day's Inn

**104**  rd 257, Bethel Rd, **E gas:** BP/rest./dsl, **W gas:** Shell, **other:** Owl's Roost Camping

**98**  US 31 W, Millersville, **E gas:** Citgo/dsl, RaceWay, Shell/dsl, **food:** Subway, Waffle House, **other:** $General, **W gas:** BP/dsl, **lodging:** Economy Inn, **other:** Nashville Country Camping

**97**  rd 174, Long Hollow Pike, **E gas:** BP/dsl, Exxon, Mapco, **food:** Arby's, Capt D's, Cracker Barrel, Domino's, Kabuto Japanese, KFC, McDonald's, Quizno's, Shoney's, Subway, Waffle House, Wendy's, **lodging:** Best Western, Days Inn, Executive Inn, Hampton Inn, Quality Inn, Red Roof Inn, **other:** K-Mart, Kroger, **W gas:** Shell/dsl, **food:** Hardee's, Jack-in-the-Box, Krystal/24hr, Poncho Villa Grill, Sonic, Stroud's BBQ, **lodging:** Holiday Inn Express, Motel 6, **other:** Rite Aid, Walgreens, vet

**96**  Rivergate Pky, **E gas:** Citgo/dsl, Shell, **food:** Dougie Ray's Grill, El Chico, Hooters, Fuji Steaks, Honey-Baked Ham, Las Cibolas Mexican, Las Palmas Mexican, McDonald's, Mrs Winner's, O'Charley's, Pizza Hut, Subway, Waffle House, Wendy's, **lodging:** Best Value Inn, Comfort Suites, Rodeway Inn, Parkway Hotel, **other:** H HOSPITAL, Best One Tires, Cadillac, Dillard's, Goodyear, Macy's, NTB, JC Penney, Sears/auto, mall, **E on Gallatin...food:** Arby's, Bar-B-Cutie, Burger King, Calhoun's Cafe, Cici's Pizza, Checker's, Chick-fil-A, Chili's, Chuck-eCheese, Fafari's Rest., Fazoli's, IHOP, Krispy Kreme, LJ Silver/A&W, Logan's Roadhouse, Longhorn Steaks, Hometown Buffet, Olive Garden, Outback Steaks, Panera Bread, Pizza Hut, Popeye's, Rafferty's, Red Lobster, Starbucks, Steak'n Shake, TGI Friday, Taco Bell, **other:** AAA, Best Buy, BooksAMillion, CarMax, Chevrolet, Chrysler/Jeep, Circuit City, CVS Drug, Discount Tire, Firestone, Goody's, Goodyear/auto, Harley-Davidson, Home Depot, Honda, Jo-Ann's Etc., Lincoln/Mercury, Macy's, Marshall's, Michael's, Nissan, Office Depot, Old Navy, PepBoys, PetsMart, Sam's Club/gas, SuperPetz, Target, TJ Maxx, VW, Walgreens, Walmart/drugs, **W gas:** Chevron, Volunteer

**95**  TN 386, Vietnam Veterans Blvd (from nb)

**92**  rd 45, Old Hickory Blvd, **E other:** H HOSPITAL, to Old Hickory Dam

**90b**  TN 155 E, Briley Pkwy, **E** to Opreyland

**90a**  US 31W, US 41, Dickerson Pike, **E gas:** Exxon, Express/dsl, Shell, **food:** Arby's, Burger King, Capt D's, China King, Domino's, Gyros, Jay's Rest., KFC, Lee's Chicken, McDonald's, Mrs Winner's, Pizza Hut, Subway, Taco Bell, Waffle House, Wendy's, **lodging:** Day's Inn, Econolodge, Sleep Inn, Super 8, **other:** Advance Parts, AutoZone, Camping World RV Supply, CVS Drug, Family$, KOA, Kroger, Walgreens

**88b a**  I-24, W to Clarksville, E to Nashville

**87b a**  US 431, Trinity Lane, **E gas:** Citgo, Pilot/Subway/scales/dsl, **food:** Krystal, White Castle, **lodging:** Cumberland Inn, **W gas:** Chevron, Express, Exxon, **food:** Jack-in-the-Box, Jack's BBQ, McDonald's, Subway, Taco Bell, Waffle House, **lodging:** Best Value Inn, Comfort Inn, Day's Inn, Econolodge, Howard Johnson, Liberty Inn, Quality Inn, Travelodge, **other:** Family$, to American Bapt Coll

**86**  I-24 E, to I-40 E, to Memphis

**86mm**  Cumberland River

**85**  US 41A, 8th Ave, **E gas:** Citgo, **other:** tires, to st capitol, **W gas:** Exxon, **food:** Arby's, McDonald's, Pizza Hut, Starbucks, Subway, Taco Bell, Wendy's, **lodging:** Millennium Motel, Springhill Suites, **other:** Cadillac/Honda, Saab

**84b a**  I-40, E to Knoxville, W to Memphis

**209 [I-40]**  US 70, Charlotte Ave, Church St, **E food:** McDonald's, **other:** Nissan, **W gas:** Exxon, **food:** Burger King, Krystal, Subway, White Castle, **lodging:** Comfort Inn, **other:** Chevrolet/Pontiac/GMC, Chrysler/Jeep, Firestone, Isuzu/Subaru

**82b a**  I-40, W to Memphis, E to Nashville

**81**  Wedgewood Ave, **W gas:** BP, Exxon, Shell, **food:** Burger King, Krystal, McDonald's, Mrs Winner's, **other:** $General, $Tree, Kroger, U-Haul, Walgreens

**80**  I-440, to Memphis, Knoxville

**79**  Armory Dr, **E on Powell...gas:** Citgo, Shell, **food:** Applebee's, Rafferty's, Subway, Wendy's, **other:** Chiropractor, CarMax, Home Depot, Michael's, Ross, Staples, mall

**78b a**  rd 255, Harding Place, **E gas:** Express, Marathon, Shell, **food:** Cracker Barrel, Mama Mia's Italian, Sub House, Waffle House, **lodging:** La Quinta, Red Roof Inn, Traveler's Rest Hist Home, **other:** CVS Drug

**74**  TN 254, Old Hickory Blvd, to Brentwood, **E food:** Capt D's, Coldstone, LongHorn Steaks, Panera Bread, Qdoba Mexican, Shoney's, Waffle House,

## INTERSTATE 65 CONT'D

**74** Continued
lodging: Best Western, Holiday Inn, Hyatt Place, Steeplechase Inn, other: GNC, Target, **W** gas: BP, Exxon, Shell/dsl, food: Brentwood Grille, Chick-fil-A, Corky's BBQ, Mazatlan Mexican, McAlister's Deli, McDonald's, Mrs Winner's, O'Charley's, Papa John's, Pizza Hut, Ruby Tuesday, Starbucks, Wendy's, lodging: Courtyard, Extended Stay America, Hampton Inn, Hilton Suites, Homestead Suites, Studio+, other: Border Books, CVS Drug, Fresh Mkt Foods, Harris-Teeter, Kroger, Office Depot, Rite Aid, SteinMart, TJ Maxx, USPO, Walgreens

**71** TN 253, Concord Rd, to Brentwood

**69** rd 441, Moores Lane, Galleria Blvd, **E** gas: MapCo/dsl, Shell, food: Amerigo's Grill, Cozymel's, Domino's, Outback Steaks, Shogun Japanese, Saltgrass Steaks, Sonic, Starbucks, lodging: Hyatt Place, Red Roof Inn, Wingate Inn, other: Acura/Lexus, CVS Drug, Home Depot/gas, Michael's, PetsMart, Publix, Walgreens, vet, **W** gas: BP, Shell/dsl, food: Backyard Burger, Buca Italian, Chili's, Famous Dave's, J Alexander's Rest., Logan's Roadhouse, Macaroni Grill, McDonald's, Pizza Hut/Taco Bell, Red Lobster, Schlotsky's, Stoney River Steaks, Subway, lodging: Sleep Inn, other: Barnes&Noble, Belk, Best Buy, Costco/gas, Dillard's, $Tree, JC Penney, Old Navy, Ross, Sears/auto, Target, Whole Foods Mkt, mall

**68b a** Cool Springs Blvd, **E** food: Mexicani Grill, lodging: Embassy Suites, Marriott, **W** gas: Exxon, Shell, food: A&W, Atl Bread, Baja Fresh, BoneFish Grill, Carrabba's, Chicken Fingers, ChuckeCheese, Genghis Grill, Golden Corral, Jack-in-the-Box, Jason's Deli, KFC, McAlister's Deli, McDonald's, Ming Chinese, Moe's SW Grill, Omikoshi Japanese, Papa John's, PF Chang's, Ruby Tuesday, Starbucks, TGIFriday, Wendy's, lodging: Country Inn & Suites, Hampton Inn, other: Acura, Borders Books, Circuit City, Harley-Davidson, Harris-Teeter, Home Depot, Jo-Ann Fabrics, Kohl's, Kroger, Lowe's Whse, Marshall's, Office Depot, Sam's Club, Saturn, Staples, Walgreens, Walmart SuperCtr, to Galleria Mall

**67** McEwen Dr

**65** TN 96, to Murfreesboro, Franklin, **E** gas: Mapco, Shell, food: Cracker Barrel, Steak'n Shake, lodging: Best Value Inn, Comfort Inn, Day's Inn, Holiday Inn Express, La Quinta, other: Buick/Pontiac/GMC/Kia, Chevrolet, Food Lion, Honda/Volvo, Walgreens, **W** gas: BP/dsl, Mapco/dsl, Shell/dsl, food: Arby's, Backyard Burger, CiCi's, Hardee's, Jack-in-the-Box, KFC, McDonald's, O'Charley's, Papa John's, Pizza Hut, Shoney's, Starbucks, Subway, Taco Bell, Waffle House, Wendy's, lodging: Best Western, Quality Inn, other: Big Lots, CVS Drug, $General, Ford/Mercury, Goody's, Home Depot, Kroger, K-Mart, Rite Aid, SteinMart, Toyota, USPO, to Confederate Cem at Franklin, vet

**64mm** Harpeth River

**61** TN 248, Peytonsville Rd, to Spring Hill, **E** gas: TA/BP/dsl/rest./scales/24hr/@, **W** gas: Mapco/24hr, Shell/dsl, other: Goose Creek Inn/rest.

**59b a** TN 840

**58mm** W Harpeth River

**53** TN 396, Saturn Pkwy, Spring Hill, Columbia, TN Scenic Pkwy

**48mm** truck insp/weigh sta nb, litter barrels

**46** US 412, TN 99, to Columbia, Chapel Hill, **E** gas: Loves/Arbys/dsl/scales/24hr, Texaco/dsl, **W** gas: BP, Citgo/dsl, Horizon/dsl, TJ's/Burger King, food: Cracker Barrel, Waffle House, Wendy's, lodging: Best Value Inn, Comfort Inn, Hampton Inn, Holiday Inn Express, Relax Inn, other: H HOSPITAL

**40.5mm** Duck River

**37** TN 50, to Columbia, Lewisburg, **E** other: H HOSPITAL, TN Walking Horse HQ, **W** gas: Shell/dsl, other: to Polk Home

**32** rd 373, to Lewisburg, Mooresville, **E** gas: Exxon/dsl

**27** rd 129, to Lynnville, Cornersville, **E** other: Texas T Camping

**25mm** parking area sb, litter barrels

**24mm** parking area nb, litter barrels

**22** US 31A, to Pulaski, **E** gas: Tennesseean Trkst/BP/TN Rest./dsl/rest./scales/24hr/@, food: McDonald's, Subway, lodging: Econolodge, **W** gas: Pilot/dsl/scales, Shell/dsl/24hr

**14** US 64, to Pulaski, **E** gas: BP/dsl, Shell/dsl, food: Sarge's Shack Rest., lodging: Super 8, other: TN Valley RV Park, to Jack Daniels Distillery, **W** H HOSPTIAL, to David Crockett SP

**6** rd 273, Bryson, **E** gas: Phillips 66/dsl/rest., lodging: Best Value Inn, other: dsl repair, **W** gas: Marathon (2mi)

**4mm** Elk River

**3mm** Welcome Ctr nb, full ♿ facilities, info, ©, ☎, litter barrels, petwalk

**1** US 31, rd 7, Ardmore, **E** gas: Chevron/dsl/24hr, Exxon/Chicken Express/dsl, **1-2 mi E** gas: Shell/repair, food: DQ, Hardee's, McDonald's, Subway

**0mm** Tennessee/Alabama state line

## INTERSTATE 75

| Exit # | Services |
|---|---|
| 161.5mm | Tennessee/Kentucky state line |

**161mm** Welcome Ctr sb, full ♿ facilities, ©, vending, ☎, litter barrels, petwalk

**160** US 25W, Jellico, **E** gas: BP, Exxon/dsl, food: El Charito, KFC, lodging: Jellico Motel, **W** gas: BP/Wendy's, Shell/Arby's/dsl, food: Hardee's, Subway, lodging: Best Value Inn, Day's Inn/rest., other: H HOSPITAL, camping, fireworks, to Indian Mtn SP

**156** Rarity Mtn rd

**144** Stinking Creek Rd

**141** TN 63, to Royal Blue, **E** gas: Shell/Stuckey's/24hr, food: Perkins, **W** gas: Shell/Stuckey's/dsl, Pilot/Subway/dsl/24hr, lodging: Comfort Inn, other: fireworks, to Big South Fork NRA

**134** US 25W, TN 63, Caryville, **E** gas: Shell/24hr, food: Loui's Rest., Waffle House/24hr, lodging: Econolodge, Family Inn, Hampton Inn, Super 8, Thacker Christmas Inn, other: H HOSPITAL, to Cove Lake SP, **W** gas: BP, food: Shoney's, Scotty's Hamburgers, lodging: Budget Host

## INTERSTATE 75 CONT'D

**N**
↕
**S**

**130mm**   weigh sta both lanes, 🚻

**129**   US 25W S, Lake City, **W gas:** BP/Sonic, Citgo, Exxon/Subway/dsl/24hr, Shell, **food:** Cracker Barrel, KFC/Taco Bell, McDonald's, **lodging:** Day's Inn, Blue Haven Motel, Lake City Motel, Lamb's Inn/rest., **other:** $General, same as 128

**128**   US 441, to Lake City, **E gas:** BP, Sunoco, **other:** Mountain Lake Marina (4mi) , **W gas:** Exxon/dsl/24hr, Mystik, Shell, **food:** Cottage Rest., La Fiesta, Subway, **lodging:** Blue Haven Motel, Lake City Motel, Lamb's Inn, **other:** Advance Parts, $General, antique cars, to Norris Dam SP, same as 129

**126mm**   Clinch River

**122**   TN 61, Bethel, Norris, **E gas:** Shell, **food:** Shoney's, **other:** Fox Inn Camping, antiques, museum, **W gas:** BP, Exxon/Burger King/Subway/dsl/24hr, Get'n Go, Phillips 66, **food:** Arby's, Golden Girls Rest., Hardee's, Harrison's Grill, Krystal/24hr, McDonald's, Waffle House, Wendy's, Zaxby's, **lodging:** Best Western, Country Inn&Suites, Holiday Inn Express, Norris Inn, Super 8, **other:** Ford, Big Pine Ridge SP

**117**   TN 170, Racoon Valley Rd, **E gas:** BP/dsl, Pilot/dsl/scales/24hr, **W lodging:** Valley Inn/camping, **other:** Escapee's RV Park

**112**   TN 131, Emory Rd, to Powell, **E gas:** BP/Buddy's BBQ/dsl, Chevron, Pilot/DQ/Taco Bell/dsl/24hr/@, **food:** Aubrey's Rest., McDonald's, KFC, Krystal, Ruby Tuesday, Steak'n Shake, Subway, Wendy's, Zaxby's, **lodging:** Country Inn&Suites, Holiday Inn Express, **other:** CVS Drug, Family$, Ingles, Toyota, **W gas:** Exxon/24hr, Shell/dsl/24hr, Weigel's, **food:** Hardee's, Shoney's, Waffle House/24hr, **lodging:** Comfort Inn

**B**
**E**
**T**
**H**
**E**
**L**

**110**   Callahan Dr, **E gas:** Weigel's, **lodging:** Knight's Inn, Quality Inn/rest., **other:** Honda, **W gas:** BP, **food:** Burger King (2mi), Chick-fil-A, Chili's (2mi), Golden Corral (2mi), McDonald's, Ruby Tuesday (2mi), Wendy's (2mi), **lodging:** Scottish Inn, **other:** GMC/Volvo, Mac Trucks

**K**
**N**
**O**
**X**
**V**
**I**
**L**
**L**
**E**

**108**   Merchant Dr, **E gas:** BP/dsl, Citgo/dsl, Pilot/dsl, Shell/dsl, **food:** Applebee's, Cracker Barrel, El Chico's, Highway Host, Hooter's, Logan's Roadhouse, O'Charley's, Pizza Hut, Starbucks, Sonic, Puelo's Grill, Ramsey's Rest., Ryan's, Waffle House, **lodging:** Best Western, Comfort Inn, Day's Inn, Econolodge, Hampton Inn, Sleep Inn, **other:** Ingles, Valvoline, **W gas:** Citgo, Exxon/Godfather's, Pilot/Conoco, Shell, **food:** Arby's, Burger King, Cancun Mexican, Capt D's, Darryl's Rest., Great American Steaks, IHOP, Mandarin House, McDonald's, Outback Steaks, Pizza Inn, Quaker Steak, Red Lobster, Subway, Waffle House/24hr, **lodging:** Best Value, Clarion Inn, Econolodge, Motel 6, Super 8, **other:** Food Lion, Walgreens

**107**   I-640 & I-75

**3b** [I-640]   US 25W, **N gas:** Amoco, BP, Texaco/dsl, **food:** Hardee's, KFC, Krystal, LJ Silver, Mr Gatti's, Pizza Hut, Quincy's, Taco Bell, Wendy's, **other:** Chevrolet, CVS Drug, Firestone, Ford, K-Mart, Kroger, transmissions, same as 108

**1** [I-640]   TN 62, Western Ave, **N gas:** Cargo/dsl, RaceTrac, Shell/dsl, **food:** Central Park, Golden Corral, KFC, LJ Silver, McDonald's, Mixon's Deli, Ruby Tuesday, Shoney's, Subway, Taco Bell, Wendy's, **other:** CVS Drug, Kroger, Walgreen, **S gas:** BP, **food:** Dad's Donuts, Domino's, Hardee's, Krystal, **other:** Advance Parts, USPO

**I-75 and I-40 run together 17 mi. See Interstate 40, exits 369 through 385.**

**84 b a** [368]   I-40, W to Nashville, E to Knoxville

**81**   US 321, TN 95, to Lenoir City, **E gas:** BP/Buddy's BBQ/TCBY/dsl, Exxon/Subway/dsl, Mobil, Shell, Texaco/dsl, **food:** Aubrey's Rest., Burger King (1mi), Capt D's, Chili's, China Buffet, Cracker Barrel, Dinner Bell Rest., KFC, McDonald's, Monterrey Mexican, Quizno's, Shoney's, Tokyo Express, Waffle House, Zaxby's, **lodging:** Days Inn, Hampton Inn, Holiday Inn Express, King's Inn/rest., **other:** $Tree, Goody's, Home Depot, Radio Shack, Walmart SuperCtr/gas, Great Smokies NP, Ft Loudon Dam, **W gas:** Citgo/dsl, Shell/dsl, **food:** Krystal, Ruby Tuesday, **lodging:** Comfort Inn, Econolodge, Ramada Ltd, **other:** Chevrolet, Crosseyed Cricket Camping, Pontiac/Buick/GMC, tires

**76**   rd 324, Sugar Limb Rd, **W** to TN Valley Winery

**74mm**   Tennessee River

**72**   TN 72, to Loudon, **E gas:** BP/McDonald's, Shell/Wendy's, **food:** Log Cabin BBQ, **lodging:** Country Inn&Suites, Super 8, **other:** to Ft Loudon SP, **W gas:** Citgo, **food:** Over the Hill Grill, **lodging:** Best Value Inn, **other:** Express Camping

**68**   rd 323, to Philadelphia, **E gas:** BP/dsl, **food:** cheese factory/store (2mi)

**62**   rd 322, Oakland Rd, to Sweetwater, **E food:** Dinner Bell Rest., **W other:** KOA

**S**
**W**
**E**
**E**
**T**
**W**
**A**
**T**
**E**
**R**

**60**   TN 68, Sweetwater, **E gas:** RaceWay, Shell/dsl, **food:** Bradley's BBQ, Burger King, McDonald's, Wendy's, **lodging:** Best Value Inn, Comfort Inn, Day's Inn, Knights Inn, **other:** Ⓗ HOSPITAL, to Lost Sea Underground Lake, **W gas:** BP/dsl, Marathon, Kangaroo/dsl, **lodging:** Best Western, Magnuson Hotel, Quality Inn, **other:** flea mkt, to Watts Bar Dam, tires/repair

**56**   rd 309, Niota, **E gas:** BP/dsl/rest./scales/24hr/@, **other:** TN Country Camping, **W** tires

**52**   rd 305, Mt Verd Rd, to Athens, **E gas:** Citgo, **food:** Subway, **other:** Overniter RV Park, **W gas:** BP, **lodging:** Travelodge

TN

**ATHENS N ↑ S CLEVELAND**

**TN**

## INTERSTATE 75 CONT'D

**49** TN 30, to Athens, **E** gas: BP, Marathon, Kangaroo, RaceWay, Shell/dsl/24hr, **food:** Applebee's, Burger King, Hardee's, KFC, Krystal, MexiWing, Monterrey Mexican, Ruby Tuesday, Shoney's, Subway, Waffle House, Wendy's, **lodging:** Day's Inn, Econolodge, Hampton Inn, Holiday Inn Express, Homestead Inn, Motel 6, Super 8, **other:** H HOSPITAL, Athens I-75 Camping, Russell Stover, to TN Wesleyan Coll, **W** gas: Shell, **food:** Cracker Barrel, **lodging:** Homestead Inn, **other:** Jeep

**42** TN 39, Riceville RD, **E** gas: Citgo/dsl, **lodging:** Relax Inn, Rice Inn (2mi)

**36** TN 163, to Calhoun, **E** food: Hardee's (3mi), **other:** Hiwassee/Ocoee River SP

**35mm** Hiwassee River

**33** rd 308, to Charleston, **E** 33 Camping, gas, **W** gas: Love's/McDonald's/Subway/dsl/scales/24hr, Shell/dsl/rest./24hr

**27** Paul Huff Pkwy, **1 mi E** gas: Phillips 66, **food:** Applebee's, Capt D's, Chili's, CiCi's, DQ, Fazoli's, Golden Corral, IHOP, McDonald's, O'Charley's, Outback Steaks, Panera Bread, Quizno's, Ryan's, Sonic, Steak'n Shake/24hr, Taco Bell, **lodging:** Jameson Inn, **other:** AutoZone, Belk, Buick/Pontiac, CVS Drug, $Tree, Food Lion, Goodyear/auto, Goody's, Home Depot, JC Penney, K-Mart, Lowe's Whse, PetCo, Rite Aid, Sears, Staples, TJ Maxx, Walmart SuperCtr/gas, mall, **W** gas: Exxon, Shell/Subway, Texaco, **food:** Denny's/24hr, Hardee's, Waffle House, Wendy's, **lodging:** Classic Suites, Hampton Inn, Quality Inn, Ramada Ltd, Royal Inn, Super 8, **other:** BooksAmillion, Kohls, Target

**25** TN 60, Cleveland, **E** gas: Chevron, RaceWay, Shell/dsl, Texaco, **food:** Bojangle's, Burger King, Cracker Barrel, Hardee's, McDonald's, Old Fort Rest., Schlotsky's, Sonic, Waffle House, Wendy's, Zaxby's, **lodging:** Best Inn, Colonial Inn, Day's Inn, Douglas Inn, Economy Inn, Fairfield Inn, Howard Johnson, Knight's Inn, Travel Inn, **other:** H HOSPITAL, to Lee Coll, **W** gas: Shell, **lodging:** Baymont Inn, Holiday Inn, Wingate Inn

**23mm** truck/weigh sta nb

**20** US 64 byp, to Cleveland, **1-4 mi E** gas: Exxon, FuelMart, Shell, **food:** Hardee's, McDonald's, Subway, Taco Bell, **lodging:** Whitewater Lodge, **other:** Chrysler/Jeep/Dodge, Honda, Toyota, **W** gas: Exxon/dsl/24hr, Horizon/DQ/Pizza Hut/dsl/24hr, **other:** KOA (1mi), fireworks

**16mm** scenic view sb

**13mm** truck/weigh sta, litter barrels sb

**11** US 11 N, US 64 E, Ooltewah, **E** gas: BP, RaceWay, Shell, **food:** Arby's, Bojangles, Burger King, Cracker Barrel, Capt D's, Hardee's, Little Ceasars, McDonald's, Subway, Taco Bell, Wendy's, Zaxby's, **other:** BiLo, Curves, O'Reilly Parts, Walgreens, Walmart SuperCtr, **W** gas: BP/Quizno's/dsl, **food:** Krystal, **lodging:** Super 8, **other:** Publix, to Harrison Bay SP

**CHATANOOGA**

**9** no services

**7b a** US 11, US 64, Lee Hwy, **E** gas: Exxon, **W** gas: Shell, **food:** City Cafe, Waffle House, **lodging:** Best Inn, Best Value Inn, Best Western/rest., Comfort Inn, Econolodge, Motel 6, **other:** Harley-Davidson, Jaguar/Land Rover/Porsche

**5** Shallowford Rd, **E** food: Alexander's, Arby's, CiCi's, DQ, Famous Dave's, Krystal, Logan's Roadhouse, Macaroni Grill, McAlister's Deli, McDonald's, Smokey Bones BBQ, Starbucks, Steak'n Shake/24hr, Souper Salad, Taco Bell, **lodging:** Courtyard, Quality Inn, Wingate Inn, **other:** Barnes&Noble, Best Buy, BooksAMillion, Circuit City, Firestone/auto, Ford, FreshMkt Foods, Home Depot, Lowe's Whse, Office Depot, Old Navy, PetsMart, SteinMart, Walgreens, Walmart SuperCtr, World Mkt, **W** gas: BP, Citgo, Shell, **food:** Applebee's, Blimpie, Cracker Barrel, Fazoli's, GlenGene Deli, McDonald's, O'Ace's Grill, O'Charley's, Papa John's, Sonic, Subway, Texas Roadhouse, Waffle House, Wendy's, **lodging:** Comfort Inn, Country Inn&Suites, Fairfield Inn, Guesthouse Inn, Hampton Inn, Hilton Garden, Holiday Inn, Homewood Suites, Knights Inn, La Quinta, MainStay Suites, Microtel, Ramada Ltd, Red Roof Inn, Sleep Inn, Staybridge Suites, **other:** H HOSPITAL, BiLo, Goodyear, U of TN/Chatt, same as 4a

**4a** (from nb) Hamilton Place Blvd, **E** food: Abuelo's, Acropolis, Big River Grill, BoneFish Grill, Carraba's, DQ, El Mason, Fox&Hound Grill, Golden Corral, Jason's Deli, Moe's SW Grill, Olive Garden, Outback Steaks, Panera Bread, PF Chang's, Piccadilly's, Red Lobster, Ruby Tuesday, Shogun Japanese, Starbucks, Sticky Fingers BBQ, Kampai Of Tokyo, **lodging:** InTown Suites, **other:** Belk, Dillard's, Firestone, Goody's, JC Penney, Kohl's, Marshall's, Michael's, Ross, Sears/auto, Staples, Target, TJ Maxx, mall, same as 5

**4** TN 153, Chickamauga Dam Rd

**3b a** TN 320, Brainerd Rd, **E** gas: BP, **food:** Baskin Robbins, Subway, **W** other: BMW

**2** I-24 W, to I-59, to Chattanooga, Lookout Mtn

**1.5mm** Welcome Ctr nb, full ♿ facilities, 🚻 vending, 🎁 litter barrels, petwalk

**1b a** US 41, Ringgold Rd, to Chattanooga, **E** gas: BP, Texaco, **lodging:** Best Value Inn, Comfort Inn, Crown Inn, Econolodge, Howard Johnson, Ramada Ltd, **other:** BiLo Foods, Camping World RV Ctr/Shipp's RV Ctr/park, Family$, **W** gas: Conoco/dsl, Shell/dsl, **food:** A&W/LJ Silver, Arby's, Burger King, Central Park Burger, Cracker Barrel, Hardee's, Krystal, McDonald's, PortoFino Italian, Shoney's, Taco Bell, Teriyaki House, Uncle Bud's Catfish, Waffle House, Wally's Rest., **lodging:** Best Inn, Day's Inn, Holiday Inn Express, Super 8, Superior Creek Lodge, Waverly Motel, **other:** Holiday Travel Park, U-Haul

**0mm** Tennessee/Georgia state line

## INTERSTATE 81

| Exit # | Services |
|---|---|
| 75mm | Tennessee/Virginia state line, **Welcome Ctr sb, full** ♿ **facilities, info,** 🕿, **vending,** 🚻, **litter barrels, petwalk** |
| 74b a | US 11W, to Bristol, Kingsport, **E lodging:** Day's Inn, Hampton Inn, **other:** Ⓗ HOSPITAL, **W gas:** Valero, **lodging:** Best Western, Bristol Inn |
| 69 | TN 394, to Blountville, **E gas:** BP/Subway/dsl, **food:** Arby's, Burger King (1mi), McDonald's, **other:** Advance Parts, Bristol Int Speedway, Lakeview RV Park (8mi) |
| 66 | TN 126, to Kingsport, Blountville, **E gas:** BP/dsl, **W gas:** Chevron/24hr, **food:** McDonald's, **other:** Carolina Pottery |
| 63 | rd 357, Tri-City Airport, **E gas:** BP/Taco Bell/Krystal/dsl, Shell/Subway/dsl/24hr, **food:** Cracker Barrel, Wendy's, **lodging:** La Quinta, Sleep Inn, **W gas:** Citgo/dsl, **lodging:** Red Carpet Inn, **other:** KOA, Rocky Top Camping |
| 60mm | Holston River |
| 59 | rd 36, to Johnson City, Kingsport, **E gas:** Citgo/dsl, **lodging:** Super 8, **W gas:** BP/LP, Shell/dsl, Sunoco, Zoomerz, **food:** Arby's, Domino's, Hardee's, HotDog Hut, La Carreta Mexican, Little Caesar's, McDonald's, Pal's Drive-Thru, Perkins, Pizza Hut, Sonic, Steak House, Subway, The Shack BBQ, **lodging:** Best Western, Comfort Inn, **other:** Advance Parts, CVS Drug, $General, $Tree, Firestone/auto, Food City/gas, Ingles/deli, Walgreens, USPO, to Warrior's Path SP |
| 57b a | I-26 |
| 56 | Tri-Cities Crossing |
| 50 | TN 93, Fall Branch, **W other:** auto auction, st patrol |
| 44 | Jearoldstown Rd, **E gas:** Marathon |
| 41mm | **rest area sb, full** ♿ **facilities,** 🕿, **vending,** 🚻, **litter barrels, petwalk** |
| 38mm | **rest area nb, full** ♿ **facilities,** 🕿, **vending,** 🚻, **litter barrels, petwalk** |
| 36 | rd 172, to Baileyton, **E gas:** Pilot/Subway/dsl/scales, **W gas:** BP/dsl/24hr, Shell/Subway/dsl/24hr, TA/Country Pride/dsl/scales/24hr/@, **food:** Pizza+, **lodging:** 36 Motel, **other:** Baileyton Camp (2mi), Family$ |
| 30 | TN 70, to Greeneville, **E gas:** Exxon/DQ/Stuckey's/dsl |
| 23 | US 11E, to Greeneville, **E gas:** BP/Wendy's, Mobil/Subway, **other:** to Andrew Johnson HS, Crockett SP, **W gas:** Exxon/dsl, Phillips 66/dsl/rest./scales, **food:** McDonald's, Taco Bell, Tony's BBQ, **lodging:** Best Western, Super 8 |
| 21mm | weigh sta sb |
| 15 | rd 340, Fish Hatchery Rd |
| 12 | TN 160, to Morristown, **E gas:** Phillips 66, **W gas:** Shell/dsl, **lodging:** Days Inn (6mi), Hampton Inn (12mi), Motel 6 (6mi), **other:** to Crockett Tavern HS |
| 8 | US 25E, to Morristown, **E gas:** Shell/dsl/repair, **food:** Sonic (2mi), **lodging:** Twin Pines Motel (3mi), **W gas:** BP/dsl, **food:** Cracker Barrel, Hardee's, **lodging:** Holiday Inn/rest., Parkway Inn, Super 8, **other:** to Cumberland Gap NHP |
| 4 | rd 341, White Pine, **E gas:** Pilot/McDonald's/dsl/ |

| 4 | Continued scales/24hr/@, **lodging:** Crown Inn, **W gas:** Wilco/Hess/Wendy's/dsl/scales/24hr/@, **food:** Huddle House/24hr, **lodging:** Day's Inn, **other:** to Panther Cr SP |
|---|---|
| 2.5mm | **rest area sb, full** ♿ **facilities,** 🕿, 🚻, **litter barrels, vending, petwalk** |
| 1b a | I-40, E to Asheville, W to Knoxville. I-81 begins/ends on I-40, exit 421. |

## INTERSTATE 640 - KNOXVILLE

| Exit # | Services |
|---|---|
| 9mm | I-640 begins/ends on I-40, exit 393. |
| 8 | Millertown Pike, Mall Rd N, **N gas:** Exxon/DQ/24hr, Shell, **food:** Applebee's, Burger King, Don Pablos, KFC, Krystal, McDonald's, Piccadilly's, Pizza Inn, Proffit's, Ruby Tuesday, Taco Bell, Texas Roadhouse, Wendy's, **other:** Circuit City, Dillard's, JC Penney, Kohl's, Sam's Club, Sears/auto, Target, Walmart SuperCtr/gas, mall, **S gas:** Shell, **food:** Cracker Barrel, Little Caesars, O'Charley's, Subway, **other:** Food Lion, Home Depot, Lowe's Whse, PepBoys |
| 6 | US 441, to Broadway, **N gas:** BP, Chevron, Citgo, Conoco, Phillips 66, Pilot/dsl, **food:** Arby's, Austin's Steaks, Cancun Mexican, Chop House, CiCi's, Fazoli's, Hardee's, Krispy Kreme, Larry's Subs, LJ Silver, McDonald's, Papa John's, Ruby Tuesday, Sonic, Subway, Taco Bell, **lodging:** Best Western, **other:** Advance Parts, AutoZone, Batteries+, BigLots, CVS Drug, $General, Firestone, Food City/gas, Goodyear, Kroger/24hr, NAPA, Target, Walgreen, **S gas:** Conoco, **food:** Buddy's BBQ, Sam's Rest., Shoney's, **other:** BiLo Foods, CVS Drug, Food Lion, Home Depot, K-Mart, NAPA, Office Depot, transmissions |
| 3a | I-75 N to Lexington, I-275 S to Knoxville |
| 3b | US 25W, Clinton Hwy, **N on US 25...other:** Chevrolet, Dodge, Ford, Nissan, services on frontage rds |
| 1 | TN 62, Western Ave, **N gas:** Exxon/dsl, RaceTrac, Texaco/dsl, **food:** Central Park, KFC, LJ Silver, McDonald's, Ruby Tuesday, Shoney's, Sonic, Subway, Taco Bell, Wendy's, **other:** CVS Drug, Kroger, Walgreen, **S gas:** BP, **food:** Hardee's, Krystal, **other:** Advance Parts, O'Reilly Parts, USPO |
| 0mm | I-640 begins/ends on I-40, exit 385. |

BRISTOL JOHNSON CITY

N ↕ S

KNOXVILLE

TN

## INTERSTATE 10

| Exit # | Services |
|---|---|
| **880.5mm** | Texas/Louisiana state line, Sabine River |
| **880** | Sabine River Turnaround, RV camping |
| **879mm** | **Welcome Ctr wb, full** 🚻 **facilities,** 📞, 🌲, **litter barrels, vending, petwalk** |
| **878** | US 90, Orange, **N gas:** Mobil/dsl, **other:** airboat rides, **S other:** Western Store |
| **877** | TX 87, 16th St, Orange, **N gas:** Chevron, Shamrock, **food:** Pizza Hut, Subway, **other:** Ace Hardware, Buick/Pontiac/Toyota, $General, Eckerd, MktBasket/deli, Radio Shack, **S gas:** Exxon, Shell/dsl, Valero, **food:** Burger King, Casa Ole, Church's, DQ, Jack-in-the-Box, McDonald's, Popeye's, Sonic, Taco Bell, **other:** Buick/Pontiac, Cadillac/GMC, CVS Drug, HEB Foods, Kroger, Modica Tires, O'Reilly Parts, Toyota, Walgreens |
| **876** | Adams Bayou, frontage rd, Adams Bayou, **N food:** Gary's Café, Waffle House, **lodging:** Best Western, Best Value Inn, Executive Inn, Motel 6, Ramada Inn, Quality Inn, Super 8, **other:** Pontiac/Buik/GMC, Toyota, **S gas:** Chevron/dsl, **lodging:** Holiday Inn Express, same as 877 |
| **875** | FM 3247, MLK Dr, **N food:** Richard's Grill, **S other:** 🏥 HOSPITAL, Chrysler/Dodge/Jeep |
| **874** | US 90, Womack Rd, to Orange, **S** 🏥 HOSPITAL |
| **873** | TX 62, TX 73, to Bridge City, **N gas:** Exxon/dsl/24hr, ⊕FLYING J/Conoco/Cookery/dsl/LP/scales/24hr, **other:** Oakleaf Park RV Park, tires/repair, **S gas:** Pilot/Subway/Wendy's/dsl/scales/24hr, Shell/Church's/dsl, Valero, **food:** Jack-in-the-Box, McDonald's, Sonic, Waffle House, Whataburger |
| **870** | FM 1136 |
| **869** | FM 1442 (from wb), to Bridge City, **S** Lloyd's RV Ctr |
| **868.5mm** | **rest areas both lanes, full** 🚻 **facilities, vending,** 🌲, **litter barrels** |
| **867** | frontage rd (from eb) |
| **865** | Doty Rd (from wb), frontage rd |
| **864** | FM 1132, FM 1135, **N food:** Burr's BBQ, **lodging:** Budget Inn |
| **862c** | Timberlane Dr (from eb) |
| **862b** | Old Hwy (from wb) |
| **862a** | Railroad Ave |
| **861d** | TX 12, Deweyville |
| **861c** | Denver St, **N gas:** Conoco/dsl |
| **861b** | Lamar St (from wb), **N gas:** Conoco/dsl |
| **861a** | FM 105, Vidor, **N gas:** Chevron/dsl, Shell, Valero, **food:** Casa Ole, Church's, DQ, Domino's, Jack-in-the-Box, McDonald's, Ming's Buffet, Navrosky's, Popeye's, Senor Toro, Waffle House, **other:** Ace Hardware, AutoZone, Curves, CVS Drug, Mktbasket Foods, O'Reilly Parts, Radio Shack, Walgreens, Walmart, **S gas:** Exxon/dsl, Texaco, **food:** Burger King, Great Wall Chinese, KFC, Pizza Hut, Sonic, Subway, Taco Bell, Whataburger, **lodging:** La Quinta, **other:** $General, Family$, auto repair, tires |
| **860b a** | Dewitt Rd, frontage rd, W Vidor |
| **859** | Bonner Turnaround (from eb), Asher Turnaround (from wb), **N other:** Boomtown RV Park, **S gas:** Chevron/dsl/24hr |
| **858** | Rose City |
| **856** | Old Hwy 90 (from eb), Rose City |
| **855b** | Magnolia St (from wb) |
| **855a** | US 90 bus, to downtown, Port of Beaumont |
| **854** | ML King Pkwy, Beaumont, **N gas:** Conoco, **food:** Texas Brotha, **S gas:** Exxon, Shamrock/dsl, **food:** McDonald's |
| **853b** | 11th St, **N food:** Cafe Del Rio, Red Lobster, Rocky's Roadhouse, Waffle House, **lodging:** Best Value Inn, Days Inn, Holiday Inn, Red Carpet Inn, Sleep Inn, Super 8, Travel Inn, **other:** MktBasket, **S gas:** Texaco/dsl, Fina, **food:** Checker's, Chula Vista Mexican, Luby's, **lodging:** Howard Johnson, Interstate Inn, **other:** 🏥 HOSPITAL |
| **853a** | US 69 N, to Lufkin |
| **852** | Harrison Ave, Calder Ave, Beaumont, **N gas:** Shell/dsl, Valero, **food:** Casa Ole Mexican, Chili's, Olive Garden, Willie Ray's BBQ, **S gas:** Chevron, **food:** Church's, McDonald's, **lodging:** Econolodge, La Quinta, **other:** 🏥 HOSPITAL, Chevrolet, transmissions |
| **851** | US 90, College St, **N gas:** Exxon/dsl, RaceWay, **food:** Acapulco Mexican, Carrabba's, China Border, Floyd's Cajun Cafe, Golden Corral, Hooters, Outback Steaks, Tokyo Japanese, Waffle House, **lodging:** Best Western, Comfort Inn, Travelodge, **other:** Advance Parts, AutoZone, Harley-Davidson, O'Reilly Parts, Pennzoil, **S gas:** Exxon, Mobil, Shell, Texaco, **food:** Baytown Seafood, China Hut, DQ, IHOP, Jack-in-the-Box, KFC, Pizza Hut, Quizno's, Sonic, Taco Bell, Taste Of China, Wendy's, Whataburger, **lodging:** Courtyard, Econolodge, Economy Inn, Elegante Motel, Fairfield Inn, Motel 6, **other:** 🏥 HOSPITAL, CVS Drug, Discount Tire, Dodge, Firestone/auto, Ford/Lincoln/Mercury, GMC/Cadillac, Honda, Jeep, MktBasket Foods, Mazda, Mercedes, Mitsubishi, Nissan, NTB, Office Depot, Sam's Club/gas, U-Haul, Volvo, Walgreens |
| **850** | wb only, same as 851 |
| **849** | US 69 S, Washington Blvd, to Port Arthur, ✈ |
| **848** | Walden Rd, **N gas:** Shell, **food:** Pappadeaux Seafood, Sonic, **lodging:** Holiday Inn/rest., La Quinta, **other:** USPO, **S gas:** Petro/Mobil/dsl/scales/24hr/@, Shell, **food:** Carino's Italian, Cheddar's, Cracker Barrel, Jack-in-the-Box, Joe's Crabshack, Waffle House, **lodging:** Candlewood Suites, Hilton Garden, Knight's Inn, Super 8, **other:** Blue Beacon |
| **847** | Brooks Rd (from wb), **S other:** Gulf Coast RV Resort |
| **845** | FM 364, Major Dr (from eb), same as 847 |
| **843** | Smith Rd |
| **838** | FM 365, Fannett, **N gas:** Bar-H Store/gas/BBQ |
| **837.5mm** | **picnic areas both lanes,** 🌲, **litter barrels,** 🚻 **accessible** |
| **833** | Hamshire Rd |
| **829** | FM 1663, Winnie, **N gas:** Exxon/dsl, Shell/dsl/24hr, Texaco/Burger King/dsl, **food:** McDonald's, Taco Bell, Whataburger/24hr, **lodging:** Holiday Inn Express, **other:** RV Park, **S gas:** Chevron/dsl, Mobil/Subway/dsl/scales/24hr, **food:** Al-T Seafood, Hunan Chinese, Jack-in-the-Box, Pizza Inn, Waffle House, **lodging:** Best Western, Motel 6, Quality Inn, Winnie Inn/RV Park, **other:** 🏥 HOSPITAL, Chevrolet, Chrysler/Jeep/Dodge, Ford |
| **828** | TX 73, TX 124 (from eb), to Winnie, **S** 🏥 HOSPITAL, same as 829 |
| **827** | FM 1406 |
| **822** | FM 1410 |
| **819** | Jenkins Rd, **S gas:** Texaco/Stuckey's |
| **817** | FM 1724 |
| **815mm** | check sta both lanes |

ORANGE E W VIDOR

TX

BEAUMONT WINNIE

## INTERSTATE 10 CONT'D

**E ↕ W**

| | |
|---|---|
| **813** | TX 61 (from wb), Hankamer, **N gas:** Shell/dsl, **lodging:** Best Value Inn, **S gas:** Exxon/dsl, **food:** McDonald's, same as 812 |
| **812** | TX 61, Hankamer, **S gas:** Exxon/dsl, **food:** DJ's Diner |
| **811** | Turtle Bayou Turnaround, **S gas:** Gator Jct/dsl, **other:** Ford, Turtle Bayou RV Park |
| **810** | FM 563, to Anahuac, Liberty, **S gas:** Chevron/Blimpie/dsl, Shell/Jack-in-the-Box/dsl, **other:** Ford |
| **807** | to Wallisville, **S other:** Heritage Park |
| **806** | frontage rd (from eb), turnaround |
| **805.5mm** | Trinity River |
| **804mm** | Old, Lost Rivers |
| **803** | FM 565, Cove, Old River-Winfrey, **N other:** Paradise Cove RV Park, **S gas:** Valero/dsl |
| **800** | FM 3180, **N gas:** Exxon/dsl |
| **797** | TX 146, to Baytown, **N gas:** Chevron, Conoco/Subway/dsl/scales, Shell/dsl, **food:** DQ, Iguana Joe's, McDonald's, Waffle House, **lodging:** Crystal Inn, Motel 6, Super 8, Value Inn/RV Park, **other:** L&R RV Park, **S gas:** Exxon, Texaco/Popeye's/dsl, RaceWay/dsl, **food:** Baytown Seafood, Jack-in-the-Box, Sonic, **other:** H HOSPITAL, KOA (1mi), RV Service, vet |
| **796** | frontage rd, **N gas:** Chevron/Phillips/Chemical Refinery |
| **795** | Sjolander Rd |
| **793** | N Main St, **S gas:** Citgo/KFC/dsl/24hr |
| **792** | Garth Rd, **N gas:** Chevron/24hr, **food:** Burger King, Cracker Barrel, Denny's, Jack-in-the-Box, Red Lobster, Richard's Cajun, Sonic, Starbucks, Waffle House, Whataburger/24hr, **lodging:** Best Western, Comfort Inn, Hampton Inn, La Quinta, **other:** Chrysler/Jeep, Hyundai, Lincoln/Mercury, Nissan, Toyota, **S gas:** RaceWay, |

**B A Y T O W N**

| | |
|---|---|
| **792** | Continued |
| | Shell/dsl, **food:** Carino's Italian, Chili's, Chinese Buffet, McDonald's, Outback Steaks, Pizza Hut/Taco Bell, Popeye's, Subway, Tortuga Mexican, Wendy's, **lodging:** Sleep Inn, **other:** H HOSPITAL, Chevrolet, $General, Ford, JC Penney, Kohl's, Marshall's, Sears/auto, Tuesday Morning, Vaughn RV Ctr, mall |
| **791** | John Martin Rd, same as 792 |
| **790** | Ellis School Rd, **N lodging:** Super 8 |
| **789** | Thompson Rd, **N gas:** Pilot/McDonald's/dsl, Valero/dsl, **other:** Buick/Pontiac/GMC, **S gas:** ⊕ FLYING J /CountryMkt/dsl/scales/24hr/@, TA/SpeedCo Lube/dsl/rest./24hr/scales/@, **other:** Blue Beacon, truck repair |
| **788.5mm** | rest area eb, full ♿ facilities, ☏, 🛉, litter barrels, petwalk |
| **788** | sp 330 (from eb), to Baytown |
| **787** | sp 330, Crosby-Lynchburg Rd, to Highlands, **N gas:** Texaco/Domino's/dsl, **food:** Jack-in-the-Box (2mi) Subway (1mi), Village Pizza (1mi), **other:** RV Camping (1mi), **S gas:** Phillips 66/dsl, **other:** to San Jacinto SP, camping |
| **786.5mm** | San Jacinto River |

## INTERSTATE 10 CONT'D

**E ↑↓ W**

**786** Monmouth Dr

**785** Magnolia Ave, to Channelview, **N** gas: Shell/dsl, **S** gas: Phillips/dsl, same as 784

**784** Cedar Lane, Bayou Dr, **N** gas: Valero/dsl, **lodging:** Budget Lodge, Knight's Inn

**783** Sheldon Rd, **N** gas: Shell, Texaco/dsl, Valero, **food:** Burger King, Church's, Jack-in-the-Box, KFC, Pizza Hut, Pizza Inn, Popeye's, Sonic, Subway, Taco Bell, Whataburger, **lodging:** Best Western, Day's Inn, Super 8, Travelodge, **other:** Advance Parts, AutoZone, DiscountTire, CVS Drug, Family$, FoodFair, Garland's Foods, Goodyear/auto, Radio Shack, USPO, **S** food: Capt D's, Hilda's Mexican, McDonald's, Quizno's, Wendy's, **lodging:** Leisure Inn, **other:** RV Service

**782** Dell-Dale Ave, **N** gas: Exxon, **lodging:** Best Value Inn, Dell-Dale Motel, Economy Inn, I-10 Motel, **other:** [H] HOSPITAL, **N** gas: Texaco/dsl

**781b** Market St, **N** food: Brewsky's, **lodging:** Holiday Inn, **other:** [H] HOSPITAL

**781a** TX 8, Sam Houston Pkwy

**780** (779a from wb) Uvalde Rd, Freeport St, **N** gas: Chevron/dsl, Mobil, Texaco, **food:** China Dragon, IHOP, Jack-in-the-Box, KFC, Sonic, Subway, Taco Bell, Taco Cabana, **other:** [H] HOSPITAL, Ace Hardware, $Tree, Office Depot, **S** food: Baytown Seafood, Whataburger, Wing's Inn, **other:** Circuit City, Home Depot, Sam's Club/gas, U-Haul, Walmart/auto

**779b** **N** gas: Chevron, **lodging:** Interstate Motel

**778b** Normandy St, **N** gas: Shell/Jack-in-the-Box, **food:** Golden Corral, **S** gas: Citgo, **food:** Cafe KO, **lodging:** Scottish Inn

**778a** FM 526, Federal Rd, Pasadena, **N** gas: Shell, **food:** Burger King, Casa Ole Mexican, Golden River Chinese, Jack-in-the-Box, KFC/Taco Bell, Luby's, Pizza Hut, Popeye's, Subway, Wendy's, **lodging:** Comfort Inn, **other:** CVS Drug, Discount Tire, Fiesta Foods, HEB Foods, Kroger/gas, Target, **S** gas: Shell, Valero, **food:** Chili's, Joe's Crabshack, McDonald's, Pappa's Seafood, Sonic, **lodging:** Holiday Inn Express, Super 8, **other:** Auto-Zone, Discount Tire, Family$, O'Reilly Parts

**776b** John Ralston Rd, Holland Ave, **N** gas: Chevron, **food:** Papacito's Cantina, Steak Kountry, **lodging:** Best Western, La Quinta, Palace Inn, Regency Inn, **other:** Kroger/deli/24hr, NTB, Walgreens, **S** same as 778

**776a** Mercury Dr, **N** gas: Conoco, Texaco, **food:** Aranda's Mexican, Burger King, E China Rest., McDonald's, **lodging:** Best Western, Day's Inn, Hampton Inn, Premier Inn, Quality Inn, **S** gas: Shell/dsl, Valero

**775b a** I-610

**774** Gellhorn (from eb) Blvd, Anheuser-Busch Brewery

**773b** McCarty St, **N** gas: Mobil/dsl, Shell

**773a** US 90A, N Wayside Dr, **N** gas: Exxon, Mystik, **food:** Jack-in-the-Box, Whataburger/24hr, **S** gas: Chevron, Shell, Texaco, **food:** Church's, **other:** NAPA, dsl repair

**772** Kress St, Lathrop St, **N** gas: Conoco, Exxon, **S** food: Burger King, Seafood Rest.

**771b** Lockwood Dr, **N** gas: Chevron/dsl, **food:** McDonald's, Subway, **other:** Family$, Fiesta Foods, **S** gas: Shell/dsl, **lodging:** Palace Inn

**771a** Waco St

**770c** US 59 N

**770b** Jenson St, Meadow St, Gregg St

**770a** US 59 S, to Victoria

**769c** McKee St, Hardy St, Nance St, downtown

**769a** Smith St (from wb), to downtown

**768b a** I-45, N to Dallas, S to Galveston

**767b** Taylor St

**767a** Studemont Dr, Yale St, Heights Blvd, **N** food: Subway, **S** gas: Shell/dsl, **other:** Target

**766** (from wb), Heights Blvd, Yale St, same as 767a

**765b** N Durham Dr, N Shepherd Dr, **N** food: Wendy's, **lodging:** Howard Johnson, **other:** vet, **S** gas: Valero/dsl

**765a** TC Jester Blvd, **N** food: Wendy's, **S** gas: Exxon/dsl, Texaco/dsl

**764** Westcott St, Washington Ave, Katy Rd, **N** food: Denny's, **lodging:** Comfort Inn, **S** gas: Chevron, **food:** IHOP

**763** I-610

**762** Silber Rd, Post Oak Rd, **N** food: Cafe Adobe, Red Robin, Wings & More, **other:** Dodge, **S** gas: Shell, **food:** Jack-in-the-Box, **lodging:** Best Western, Holiday Inn, Ramada Inn, **other:** Chevrolet, NTB, carwash

**761b** Antoine Rd, **N** food: Hunan Chinese, **S** gas: Exxon, Shell, **food:** Blue Oyster Grill, McDonald's, Papa John's, Whataburger/24hr, **lodging:** Wellesley Inn, **other:** NTB

**761a** Wirt Rd, Chimney Rock Rd, **N** food: Capt Penny's Seafood, **S** gas: Chevron, Exxon/TCBY, Shell, **food:** Mc-Donald's, Steak&Ale

**760** Bingle Rd, Voss Rd, **N** Home Depot, **S** gas: Citgo, Mobil, Shell, **food:** Goode Co BBQ, Marie Callender, Mason Jar Rest., Pappy's Café, Redwood Grill, SaltGrass Steaks, Sweet Tomatos, TX BBQ, **other:** [H] HOSPITAL

**759** Campbell Rd (from wb), same as 758b

**758b** Blalock Rd, Campbell Rd, **N** food: Ciro's Italian, Sonic, **other:** Adam's Automotive, Fiesta Foods, LubeStop, Mail It, cleaners, **S** gas: Chevron/McDonald's/dsl, Exxon, Texaco, **other:** [H] HOSPITAL, Kroger, Walgreen

**758a** Bunker Hill Rd, **N** gas: Exxon, **food:** CiCi's, **other:** Best Buy, Costco/gas, Lowe's Whse, Michael's, PepBoys, Radio Shack, **S** gas: Texaco/dsl, Circle K, **food:** Charlie's Burgers, Guadalajara Mexican, Quizno's, Subway, **lodging:** Day's Inn, Howard Johnson, Super 8, **other:** Ford, Goodyear/auto, Marshall's, Nissan, Ross, Target

**757** Gessner Rd, **N** gas: Exxon, **food:** BBQ, Chili's, Cici's, DQ, McDonald's, Murphy's Deli, Schlotsky's, Taco Bell, Tuesday Morning, Wendy's, Whataburger/24hr, **other:** BrakeCheck, Eckerd, Home Depot, Honda, Kroger, NAPA, Radio Shack, Sam's Club/gas, U-Haul, Walmart, **S** gas: Shell, **food:** Fuddrucker's, Jack-in-the-Box, Jason's Deli, Macaroni Grill, Olive Garden, Pappasito's, Papadeaux Seafood, Taste of TX Rest., **lodging:** Radisson, Sheraton, **other:** [H] HOSPITAL, Circuit City, Cost+, Dillards, Foley's, Ford, Goodyear, Macys, Office Depot, Sears/auto, Target, World Mkt, mall

**756** TX 8, Sam Houston Tollway

**755** Willcrest Rd, **N** other: Discount Tire, Kia, Mazda, NTB, **S** gas: Citgo/dsl, Exxon/McDonald's/24hr, Texaco, **food:** Carabbas, China View, Denny's, IHOP, Steak&Ale, Taco Cabana, **lodging:** Extended Stay America, Hampton Inn, La Quinta, Radisson

**HOUSTON**

**TX**

## INTERSTATE 10 CONT'D

E ↕ W

**HOUSTON**

**754** Kirkwood Rd, **N other:** Lexus, Lincoln/Mercury, Saturn, Toyota, same as 753b, **S gas:** Chevron/dsl, Shell/24hr, **food:** Carrabba's, IHOP/24hr, Kingfish Mkt, Mesa Grill, Original Pasta Co, Subway, Taco Cabana, **lodging:** Extended Stay America, Hampton Inn, **other:** Chevrolet, Discount Tire, Subaru

**753b** Dairy-Ashford Rd, **N other:** Buick, Chrysler/Dodge, Infiniti, Lexus, Nissan, Toyota, Volvo, **S gas:** Exxon/TCBY/dsl, Shamrock, **food:** Beck's Prime Rest., Subway, TX Cattle Steaks, Whataburger, **lodging:** Courtyard, Guesthouse Inn, Holiday Inn Express, **other:** Audi/Porsche, Cadillac, Mitsubishi, Pontiac/GMC/Suzuki

**753a** Eldridge Pkwy, **N gas:** Conoco/dsl, **lodging:** Omni Hotel, **S gas:** Valero

**751** TX 6, to Addicks, **N gas:** Shell, **food:** Cattlegard Rest., Waffle House, **lodging:** Crowne Plaza, Drury Inn, Red Roof Inn, Studio 6, **other:** Sam's Club/gas, **S gas:** Exxon, Chevron, Conoco/dsl, Texaco/dsl, **food:** Blimpie, DQ, Denny's/24hr, El Yucatan Mexican, Jack-in-the-Box, Wendy's, **lodging:** Baymont Inn, Bradford Home-Suites, Fairfield Inn, La Quinta, Motel 6, Super 8, Townplace Suites, **other:** Acura, BMW, USPO, carwash

**748** Barker-Cypress Rd, **N gas:** Texaco, **food:** Subway, **S food:** Cracker Barrel, Lulu's Buffet, **lodging:** Fairfield Inn, **lodging:** TownePlace Inn, **other:** Chrysler/Jeep, Dodge, Hoover RV Ctr, Hyundai, Subaru, VW

**747** Fry Rd, **N gas:** Chevron, Phillips 66, Shamrock/dsl, Shell/24hr, **food:** Applebee's, Bennigans, Burger King, Church's, DQ, Denny's, Godfather's, McDonald's, Panda Express, Pizza Hut, Sonic, Souper Salad, Subway, Taco Bell, Victor's Mexican, Waffle House, Whataburger, **other:** Best Buy, Goodyear, HEB Food/gas, Home Depot, Kohl's, Ross, Sam's Club/gas, Walgreen, Walmart Super Ctr/gas, **S gas:** Chevron, Citgo, Shell, **food:** Baskin-Robbins, Boston Mkt, Capt Tom's Seafood, El Chico, Fazoli's, IHOP, Jack-in-the-Box, Ninfa's Café, Omar's Mexican, Orient Express, Outback Steaks, Quizno's, Wendy's, **other:** Albertson's, Ford, Lowe's Whse, NTB, PetsMart, Radio Shack, Target, Uhaul

**HOUSTON**

**745** Mason Rd, **S gas:** Chevron/24hr, Exxon/24hr, Shamrock, Shell/24hr, **food:** Babin's Seafood, BBQ, Black-eyed Pea, Burger King, Carino's Italian, Carrabba's, Chick-fil-A, Chili's, CiCi's, DQ, Fuzzy's Pizza, Hartz Chicken, Jack-in-the-Box, Jason's Deli, KFC, Landry's Seafood, Little Caesar's, LJ Silver, Luby's, McDonald's, Monterey Mexican, Papa John's, Pizza Hut, Popeye's, SaltGrass Steaks, Schlotsky's, SpagEddie's, Subway, Taco Bell, Taco Cabana, Taquiera Mexican, TCBY, Whataburger/24hr, **lodging:** Comfort Inn, Hampton Inn, Holiday Inn, Sleep Inn, Super 8, **other:** CarQuest, Discount Tire, Dodge, Eckerd, Firestone/auto, Goodyear/auto, HEB Food/gas, K-Mart, Kroger, Randall's Food, Walgreen, transmissions

**743** TX 99, Grand Pkwy, Peek Rd, **N other:** JC Penny, **S gas:** Shell/dsl, **food:** A&W, Popeye's, Taquirea Arrandas, **lodging:** Best Western, Comfort Inn, Holiday Inn Express, La Quinta, Super 8, **other:** Chevrolet, Isuzu, Kia, Kroger

**741** (742 from wb) Katy-Fort Bend County Rd, Pin Oak Rd, **S gas:** Chevron, Mobil/dsl/24hr, **food:** ChuckeCheese,

**741 Continued** Fuddruckers, Jack-in-the-Box, Red Lobster, TGIFriday, **lodging:** SpringHill Suites, **other:** H HOSPITAL, BassPro Shops, Chrysler/Jeep, Discount Tire, Katy Mills Outlet/famous brands, Outdoor World, Walmart SuperCtr

**740** FM 1463, **N food:** McDonald's, Sonic, **other:** RV World of TX, Yamaha, **S gas:** Chevron, **food:** RainForest Café, **other:** Books-A-Million, Pyle RV Ctr

**737** Pederson Rd, **N gas:** Loves/Arby's/dsl/scales/24hr, **S other:** Camping World RV Super Ctr, Holiday World RV Ctr

**732** FM 359, to Brookshire, **N gas:** Exxon/dsl, ⊕ FLYING J /CountryMkt/dsl/scales/24hr/@, Shell, **food:** Orlando's Pizza, **lodging:** Executive Inn, **other:** KOA, **S gas:** Chevron/dsl, Citgo/dsl, Exxon/Burger King/dsl/24hr, **food:** Jack-in-the-Box, **lodging:** La Quinta, **other:** Ford Trucks, truckwash

**731** FM 1489, to Koomey Rd, **N gas:** Exxon/dsl, **food:** Ernesto's Mexican, **lodging:** Carefree Inn, **other:** RV Park

**730mm** **picnic areas (both lanes exit left)**, 🏞, **litter barrels**

**729** Peach Ridge Rd, Donigan Rd (730 from wb)

**726** Chew Rd (from eb), **S** golf

**725** Mlcak Rd (from wb)

**724mm** check sta wb

**723** FM 1458, to San Felipe, **N gas:** Exxon/Subway/dsl/scales/24hr, **other:** to Stephen F Austin SP (3mi), **S other:** Goodyear/auto

**721** (from wb) US 90, **N gas:** Shell/dsl, **other:** Ford, **S other:** Sealy Mall

**720a** Outlet Ctr Dr, **N gas:** Shell/dsl, **S** to Sealy Mall

**720** TX 36, to Sealy, **N gas:** Shell/dsl, **food:** DQ, Hartz Chicken, McDonald's, Sonic, Tony's Rest., **other:** Chevrolet/Pontiac/Buick/GMC, Jones RV Ctr, Walgreen, **S gas:** Chevron/dsl/24hr, Mobil/dsl, Shell/dsl/24hr, **food:** Hinze's BBQ, Hunan Chinese, Jack-in-the-Box, KFC/Taco Bell, Omar's Mexican, Pizza Hut, Subway, Whataburger/24hr, **lodging:** Best Western, Holiday Inn Express, Rodeway Inn, **other:** Chrysler/Dodge/Jeep, Radio Shack, Walmart SuperCtr/gas

**SEALY**

**718** US 90 (from eb), to Sealy

**716** Pyka Rd, **N gas:** Exxon/dsl/rest./showers/24hr/@

**713** Beckendorff Rd

**709** FM 2761, Bernardo Rd

**704** FM 949, **N** Happy Oaks RV Park (3mi)

**701mm** no services

**699** FM 102, to Eagle Lake, **N other:** Happy Oaks RV Park, antiques, **S other:** Eagle Lake SP (14mi)

**E**
↕
**W**

**C O L U M B U S**

## INTERSTATE 10 CONT'D

| | |
|---|---|
| **698** | Alleyton Rd, **N** food: Mikeska's BBQ, **S** gas: Shell/Taco Bell/BBQ/dsl, other: Chrysler/Jeep/Dodge, Ford |
| **697mm** | Little Colorado River |
| **696** | TX 71, Columbus, **N** gas: Chevron/dsl/24hr, Shell/dsl, food: DQ, Denny's, Guadalajara Mexican, Jack-in-the-Box, Pizza Hut, Schobel's Rest., Whataburger, lodging: Columbus Inn, Holiday Inn Express, other: H HOSPITAL, AutoZone, Buick/Chevrolet, HEB Foods, Radio Shack, Walmart/drugs, **S** gas: Citgo/Church's/dsl, Valero/dsl, food: McDonald's, Nancy's Steaks, Sonic, Subway, lodging: Country Hearth Inn |
| **695** | TX 71 (from wb), to La Grange |
| **693** | FM 2434, to Glidden |
| **692mm** | rest areas both lanes, full & facilities, vending, C, ⊞, litter barrels, RV dump, petwalk |
| **689** | US 90, to Hattermann Lane, **N** Motorcoach RV Park |
| **682** | FM 155, to Wiemar, **N** gas: Exxon/dsl, Shell/BBQ/dsl, Texaco, food: DQ, Subway/Texas Burger, lodging: Czech Inn, other: H HOSPITAL, $General, Tire Pro, **S** other: Buick/Chevrolet |
| **678mm** | E Navidad River |
| **677** | US 90, **N** food: Casa deCortez Mexican |
| **674** | US 77, Schulenburg, **N** gas: Chevron/dsl, Exxon/dsl, food: McDonald's, lodging: Executive Inn, Oak Ridge Motel/rest., other: Ford, **S** gas: Exxon, Shell/dsl, Valero/Subway, food: DQ, Frank's Rest., Guadalajara Mexican, Oak Ridge Smokehouse, Whataburger, lodging: Holiday Inn Express, other: $General, Schulenberg RV Park |
| **672mm** | W Navidad River |
| **668** | FM 2238, to Engle |
| **661** | TX 95, FM 609, to Flatonia, **N** food: Joel's, BBQ, San Jose Mexican, **S** gas: Exxon/24hr, Shell/McDonald's/Grumpy's Rest./motel, Valero, food: DQ, Robert's Steaks, lodging: Carefree Inn, other: NAPA |
| **658mm** | picnic areas both lanes, ⊞, litter barrels |
| **653** | US 90, Waelder, **N** gas: Shell/dsl/cafe |
| **649** | TX 97, to Waelder |
| **642** | TX 304, to Gonzales |
| **637** | FM 794, to Harwood |
| **632** | US 90/183, to Gonzales, **N** gas: Love's/Subway/dsl/scales/24hr, lodging: Coachway Inn (2mi), **S** gas: Shell/Buc-ee's/dsl, other: to Palmetto SP, camping |
| **630mm** | San Marcos River |
| **628** | TX 80, to Luling, **N** gas: Exxon (2mi), Valero/Church's/dsl/24hr, food: DQ (2mi), other: H HOSPITAL, Riverbend RV Park |
| **625** | Darst Field Rd |
| **624.5mm** | Smith Creek |
| **620** | FM 1104 |
| **619mm** | rest area both lanes, full & facitlities, C, ⊞, petwalk |
| **617** | FM 2438, to Kingsbury |
| **616mm** | truck weigh sta both lanes |
| **614.5mm** | Mill Creek |
| **612** | US 90 |
| **611mm** | Geronimo Creek |
| **610** | TX 123, to San Marcos, **N** gas: Exxon/dsl, Chevron/Subway/dsl, Shamrock/dsl, food: Chili's, IHOP, Los Cucos Mexican, R&B Steaks, lodging: Comfort Inn, |

**TX**

| | |
|---|---|
| **610** | Continued Hampton Inn, Holiday Inn, other: tires, **S** gas: Valero/dsl, food: Taco Cabana, other: H HOSPITAL, River Shade RV |
| **609** | TX 123, Austin St, **S** gas: Mobil/dsl, other: Chevrolet, Home Depot |
| **607** | TX 46, FM 78, to New Braunfels, **N** gas: Texaco/Jack-in-the-Box/dsl, lodging: Alamo Inn, **S** gas: Chevron/dsl, Exxon/DQ/dsl, food: Dixie Grill, Hong Kong Chinese, Kettle, McDonald's, Soilitas Mexican, Whataburger/24hr, lodging: Best Western, La Quinta, Super 8, other: Chrysler/Dodge/Jeep |
| **605** | FM 464, **N** other: Twin Palms RV Park |
| **605mm** | Guadalupe River |
| **604** | FM 725, to Lake McQueeney, **N** other: America RV Ctr, D&A RV Resort, Explore USA RV Ctr |
| **603** | US 90 E, US 90A, to Seguin, **N** other: Explorer USA RV Sales |
| **601** | FM 775, to New Berlin, **N** gas: Mobil/Subway/dsl/scales/24hr |
| **600** | Schwab Rd |
| **599** | FM 465, to Marion |
| **599mm** | Santa Clara Creek |
| **597** | Santa Clara Rd, **N** auto racetrack |
| **595** | Zuehl Rd |
| **594mm** | Cibolo Creek |
| **593** | FM 2538, Trainer Hale Rd, **S** gas: Exxon/dsl/rest./24hr, Texaco/dsl |
| **593mm** | Woman Hollering Creek |
| **591** | FM 1518, to Schertz, **N** gas/dsl/repair |
| **589** | Pfeil Rd, Graytown Rd |
| **589mm** | Salatrillo Creek |
| **587** | LP 1604, Randolph AFB, to Universal City |
| **585.5mm** | Escondido Creek |
| **585** | FM 1516, to Converse, **N** gas: Shell/Church's/dsl/motel/scales, **S** other: Peterbilt/GMC/Freightliner |
| **585mm** | Martinez Creek |
| **583** | Foster Rd, **N** gas: ⊕FLYING J/Conoco/Cookery/dsl/LP/scales/24hr/@, Valero/Subway/dsl/24hr, food: Jack-in-the-Box/24hr, lodging: La Quinta, other: Speedco Lube, Charlie's, Truckwash, **S** gas: TA/Chevron/Burger King/Pizza Hut/Popeye's/dsl/24hr/@ |
| **582.5mm** | Rosillo Creek |
| **582** | Ackerman Rd, Kirby, **N** gas: Pilot/Subway/dsl/scales/24hr, other: Blue Beacon, **S** gas: Petro/Mobil/dsl/scales/24hr/@, KFC/Taco Bell, Pizza Hut, food: Wendy's, lodging: Relay Station Motel, other: Petrolube, truckwash |
| **581** | I-410 |
| **580** | LP 13, WW White Rd, **N** gas: Chevron, Fina/dsl, food: Frijoles Rest., Wendy's, lodging: Motel 6, Red Roof Inn, Rodeway Inn, other: Ford/Volvo Trucks, RV camping, tires, **S** gas: Exxon/A&W/dsl, food: Bill Miller BBQ, McDonald's, Mexican Rest., Popeye's, Pizza Hut, Sandrita's Mexican, Sonic, Subway, lodging: Econolodge, Quality Inn, Rosepark Inn, Super 8, other: Ford/Freightliner, Volvo Trucks, tires |
| **579** | Houston St, **N** gas: Valero/dsl, lodging: Best Value Inn, **S** gas: Chevron, lodging: Day's Inn, Passport Inn |
| **578** | Pecan Valley Dr, ML King Dr, **N** gas |
| **577** | US 87 S, to Roland Ave, **S** food: Whataburger/24hr, lodging: Super 8 |

**K I R B Y**

## INTERSTATE 10 CONT'D

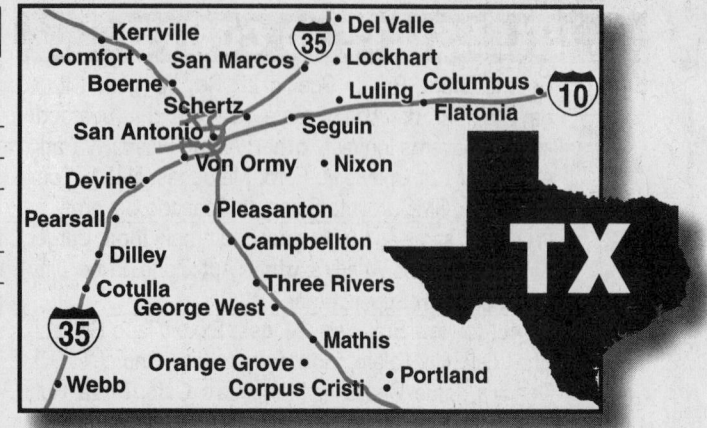

| | |
|---|---|
| **576** | New Braunfels Ave, Gevers St, **S gas:** Fina, Valero, **food:** McDonald's |
| **575** | Pine St, Hackberry St, **S food:** Little Red Barn Steaks |
| **574** | I-37, US 281 |
| **573** | Probandt St, **N food:** Jack-in-the-Box, Miller's BBQ, **S gas:** Valero, **other:** to SA Missions HS, tires |
| **572** | **I-10 and I-35 run together 3 miles** |
| **155b** | Durango Blvd, downtown, **E lodging:** Best Western, Comfort Suites, Courtyard, Fairfield Inn, Holiday Inn, La Quinta, Ramada Ltd, Residence Inn, Woodfield Suites, **other:** H HOSPITAL, **W food:** McDonald's, **lodging:** Microtel, Motel 6, Radisson |
| **155a** | South Alamo St, **E gas:** Exxon, Shell, **food:** Church's, Eddie's Drive Thru, McDonald's, Piedra's Negras, Pizza Hut, Wendy's, **lodging:** Comfort Inn, Day's Inn, Ramada Ltd, **other:** USPO, **W gas:** Conoco, **lodging:** Microtel |
| **154b** | S Laredo St, Ceballos St, same as 155b |
| **154a** | Nogalitos St |
| **153** | I-10 E, US 90 W, US 87, to Kelly AFB, Lackland AFB |
| **570** | **I-10 and I-35 run together 3 miles** |
| **569c** | Santa Rosa St, downtown, to Our Lady of the Lake U |
| **568** | spur 421, Culebra Ave, Bandera Ave, **S** to St Marys U |
| **567** | Lp 345, Fredericksburg Rd (from eb upper level accesses I-35 S, I-10 E, US 87 S, lower level accesses I-35 N) |
| **566b** | Hildebrand Ave, Fulton Ave, **S gas:** Exxon, 7-11, **lodging:** Galaxy Motel |
| **566a** | Fresno Dr, **N gas:** Exxon, Valero, **food:** McDonald's, Subway, Whataburger |
| **565c** | (from wb), access to same as 565 a b, **S gas:** Shell, **food:** Guadalahara Mexican, Starbucks, **lodging:** La Quinta |
| **565b** | Vance Jackson Rd, **N food:** Miller's BBQ, **lodging:** Econolodge, Quality Inn, **other:** Walmart SuperCtr, **S gas:** Shell, **lodging:** La Quinta |
| **565a** | Crossroads Blvd, Balcone's Heights, **N gas:** Exxon, Shell/dsl, **food:** Denny's, Whataburger, **lodging:** Comfort Suites, Rodeway Inn, **S food:** Dave&Buster's, El Pollo Loco, McDonald's, **lodging:** Sumner Suites, Super 8, **other:** Firestone/auto, Mazda, RV Ctr, Target, Toyota, mall, transmissions |
| **564b a** | I-410, services off of I-410 W, Fredericksburg Rd |
| **563** | Callaghan Rd, **N gas:** Mobil, Valero, **food:** Las Palapas Mexican, Subway, **lodging:** Embassy Suites, Marriott, **other:** Chiropractor, $General, Ford, Lexus, Mazda, Sun Harvest Foods, Toyota, **S gas:** Exxon, **food:** Mamacita's Rest., **other:** Lowe's Whse |
| **561** | Wurzbach Rd, **N gas:** Mobil/dsl, **food:** Bolo's Grille, County Line BBQ, Fuddrucker's, Golden Corral, Honeybaked Ham, Jason's Deli, Pappasito's Cantina, Popeye's, Quizno's, Sea Island Shrimphouse, Starbucks, Taste Of China, TX Land&Cattle, Wasabi Grill, **lodging:** AmeriSuites, Homewood Suites, Knight's Inn, Omni Hotel, Staybridge Suites, Studio+, **other:** BigLots, Ford, HEB Food/gas, Eckerd/24hr, Toyota, **S gas:** Shell/dsl, **food:** Alamo Café, Arby's, Benihana, Chester's Burgers, China Sea, Church's, Denny's, El Taco Tote, IHOP, Jack-in-the-Box, Jim's Rest., Luby's, McDonald's, Pizza Hut, Sombrero Rosa Café, Taco Bell, Taco Cabana, |

| | |
|---|---|
| **561** | Continued<br>Tony Roma, Village Inn, Wendy's, **lodging:** Baymont Inn, Best Western, Candlewood Suites, Drury Inn, Hawthorn Suites, Holiday Inn Express, Motel 6, Residence Inn, Sleep Inn, **other:** CarMax |
| **560b** | frontage rd (from eb), **N food:** Water St Seafood, **other:** Chrysler/Jeep, Kia, Nissan |
| **560a** | Huebner Rd, **N food:** Champp's, La Madeline, Macaroni Grill, On the Border, SaltGrass Steaks, **other:** Borders, Old Navy, Ross, **S gas:** Chevron, Exxon, **food:** Burger King, Cracker Barrel, Jim's Rest., **lodging:** AmeriSuites, Day's Inn, Hampton Inn, Homestead Village, **other:** Cadillac/Hummer |
| **559** | Lp 335, US 87, Fredericksburg Rd, **N food:** Outback Steaks, Pearl Inn, **other:** Buick/GMC, Land Rover, **S gas:** Texaco, **food:** Krispy Kreme, **lodging:** Days Inn, Studio 6 |
| **558** | De Zavala Rd, **N gas:** Chevron, Exxon/dsl, Shell/Subway, **food:** Burger King, Carrabba's, Chili's, Joe's Crabshack, KFC/Taco Bell, Logan's Roadhouse, McDonald's, Sonic, Taco Cabana, **lodging:** Best Western, Econolodge, Super 8, **other:** Barnes&Noble, Chevrolet, HEB Food/gas, Home Depot, Hyundai, Marshall's, PetsMart, Target, **S food:** A&W, CiCi's, IHOP, LJ Silver, Matamros, Quizno's, Schlotsky's, TGIFriday, Whataburger, Zio's Italian, **other:** Buick, Discount Tire, Sam's Club, Walmart SuperCtr |
| **557** | Spur 53, Univ of TX at San Antonio, **N other:** Jaguar/Mazerati/Ferrari, **lodging:** Howard Johnson, **S lodging:** La Quinta, **other:** Costco/gas, Honda |
| **556b** | frontage rd |
| **556a** | to Anderson Lp, **S lodging:** Comfort Inn, **other:** to Seaworld |
| **555** | La Quintera Pkwy, **S food:** Olive Garden, **lodging:** Motel 6, **other:** to La Cantera Pkwy |
| **554** | Camp Bullis Rd, **N gas:** Citgo, **food:** Chick-fil-A, Mimi's Cafe, TGI Friday, **other:** Bass Pro Shop, Best Buy, JC Penney, Lowe's Whse, Old Navy, Ross, Russell Park, Target, WorldMkt, **S gas:** Shell, **lodging:** Rodeway Inn, Motel 6 (2mi) |
| **551** | Boerne Stage Rd (from wb), to Leon Springs, **N gas:** Shamrock/dsl, **food:** Leon Springs Grill, McDonald's, Sonic, **S food:** Las Palapas Mexican, Longhorns Rest., Pappa Nacho's, Quizno's, Starbucks, **other:** GNC, HEB Foods/gas |
| **550** | FM 3351, Ralph Fair Rd, **N gas:** Exxon/dsl, Valero/dsl, **S gas:** Shell/Domino's/dsl |
| **546** | Fair Oaks Pkwy, Tarpon Dr, **S other:** American Dream RV Ctr, Harley-Davidson, **S gas:** Chevron/dsl/café, Exxon/dsl/café, **other:** Chrysler/Jeep, Explore USA RV Ctr (1mi), Harley-Davidson, Hoover RV Ctr |

TX

## INTERSTATE 10 CONT'D

**543** Boerne Stage Rd, to Scenic LP Rd, **N gas:** Citgo/dsl/24hr, **food:** Alamo Café, Copeland's Seafood/steaks, Caverns Inn/rest., **other:** Alamo Fiesta RV Park, Ancira RV Ctr, Chevrolet, Ford, Mercedes, NAPA, Pontiac/Buick/GMC, Toyota/Scion, to Cascade Caverns

**542** (from wb), same as 540 **N gas:** Shamrock, **food:** Burger King, El Matador, Wendy's, **other:** AutoZone, $Tree, Jiffy Lube, Walmart SuperCtr/gas

**540** TX 46, to New Braunfels, **N gas:** Exxon/Taco Bell/dsl, Shell/dsl/24hr, Valero, **food:** Burger King, Church's, DQ, Denny's, Little Caesar's, Margarita's Café, Pizza Hut, Quizno's, Shanghai Chinese, Sonic, Taco Cabana, Wendy's, **lodging:** Best Western, Holiday Inn Express, Key to the Hills Motel, **other:** HEB Food/gas, Radio Shack, Walgreens, **S food:** Chili's, Starbucks, Whataburger, **other:** Home Depot

**539** Johns Rd, **N lodging:** La Quinta, **S gas:** Valero/dsl/LP

**538mm** Cibolo Creek

**538** Ranger Creek Rd

**537** US 87, to Boerne

**533** FM 289, Welfare, **N food:** Po-Po Family Rest., **other:** Top of the Hill RV Park (1mi)

**532mm** Little Joshua Creek

**531mm** picnic area wb, 🏕, **litter barrels**

**530mm** Big Joshua Creek

**529.5mm** picnic area eb, 🏕, **litter barrels**

**527** FM 1621 (from wb), to Waring

**526.5mm** Holiday Creek

**524** TX 27, FM 1621, to Waring, **N** vet, **S gas:** Chevron/dsl, Shell/24hr

**523.5mm** Guadalupe River

**523** US 87 N, to Comfort, **N gas:** Chevron/McDonald's/dsl, **S gas:** Exxon/dsl/24hr, **food:** DQ, **lodging:** Executive Inn, **other:** $General, USA RV Park

**521.5mm** Comfort Creek

**520** FM 1341, to Cypress Creek Rd

**515mm** Cypress Creek

**514mm** rest areas both lanes, full ♿ facilities, vending, 📞, 🏕, **litter barrels, petwalk, playground, wireless internet**

**508** TX 16, Kerrville, **N gas:** Exxon/dsl, **other:** Chevrolet/Pontiac/Buick/Cadillac, RV camping, **0-2 mi S gas:** Chevron/Subway/dsl, Exxon, Shell/McDonald's/dsl/24hr, T&C, Valero/dsl, **food:** Acapulco Mexican, Bamboo Asian, Cracker Barrel, DQ, Denny's, IHOP, KFC, Jack-in-the-Box, Luby's, McDonald's, Roma's Italian, Santo Coyote, Schlotsky's, Sonic, Tabas Mexican, Taco Bell, Taco Casa, Valentino's Italian, **lodging:** Best Value Inn, Budget Inn, Comfort Inn, Day's Inn, Econolodge, Hampton Inn, Holiday Inn Express, La Quinta, Motel 6, Whitten Inn, Yo Ranch Hotel, **other:** Ⓗ HOSPITAL, Advance Parts, Big Lots, $Tree, Hastings Books, Home Depot, Kerrville RV Ctr, Lowe's Whse, O'Reilly Parts, Walgreens, vet

**505** FM 783, to Kerrville, **S gas:** Exxon/dsl, **3 mi S on TX 27...** gas: Shell, **lodging:** Inn of the Hills, **food:** Billy Gene's, Cafe Riverstone, Chili's, CiCi's Pizza, Culver's, DQ, La Four Seafood, Lakehouse Rest., Mamcita's, McDonald's, Pizza Hut, Quizno's, Starbucks, Sonic, Subway, Taco Casa, Wendy's, Whataburger, **other:** AutoZone, CVS Drug, Discount Tire, HEB Foods, Walmart SuperCtr

**503.5mm** scenic views both lanes, litter barrels

**501** FM 1338, **N other:** Buckhorn RV Resort, **S other:** KOA (2mi)

**497mm** picnic area both lanes, 🏕, **litter barrels**

**492** FM 479, **S** Lone Oak Store

**490** TX 41

**488** TX 27, to Ingram, Mountain Home

**484** Midway Rd

**477** US 290, to Fredericksburg

**476.5mm** service rd eb

**472** Old Segovia Rd

**465** FM 2169, to Segovia, **S gas:** Phillips 66/dsl/rest., **lodging:** Econolodge/RV park

**464.5mm** Johnson Fork Creek

**462** US 83 S, to Uvalde

**461mm** picnic area eb, 🏕, **litter barrels**

**460** (from wb), to Junction

**459mm** picnic area wb, 🏕, **litter barrels**

**457** FM 2169, to Junction, **N gas:** Shell/dsl, **S lodging:** Day's Inn/rest., **other:** RV camping, S. Llano River SP

**456.5mm** Llano River

**456** US 83/377, Junction, **N gas:** Chevron/dsl, Conoco/dsl, Valero/McDonald's/dsl/24hr, **food:** Cooper's BBQ, JR's Rest., Tia Nina Mexican, **lodging:** Best Value Inn, **S gas:** Exxon, Fina/dsl, Shell/dsl, **food:** DQ, Issac Rest., La Familia Mexican, Lum's BBQ, Sonic, **lodging:** Best Western, Hills Motel, Lazy T, Legends Inn, Rodeway Inn, **other:** Ⓗ HOSPITAL, KOA (.5mi), Food Basket Foods, TrueValue, to S Llano River SP

**452.5mm** Bear Creek

**451** RM 2291, to Cleo Rd

**448mm** North Creek

**445** RM 1674, **S** camping

**444.5mm** Stark Creek

**442mm** Copperas Creek

**442** RM 1674, to Ft McKavett, **N** to Ft McKavett SHC

**439mm** N Llano River

**438** Lp 291 (from wb), to Roosevelt, same as 437

**437** Lp 291 (from eb, no EZ return), to Roosevelt, **1 mi N gas:** Simon Bros Mercantile/dsl, **other:** USPO

**429** RM 3130, to Harrell

**423mm** parking area both lanes, litter barrels

**420** RM 3130, to Baker Rd

**412** Allison Rd, RM 3130

**404** RM 3130, RM 864, **N** to Ft McKavett St HS, **3 mi S gas:** TC/dsl, **lodging:** Best Value Inn, Holiday Host Motel, **other:** Ⓗ HOSPITAL

**400** US 277, Sonora, **N gas:** Shell/dsl, **food:** Sutton Co Steaks, **lodging:** Day's Inn, **other:** vet, **S gas:** Chevron/dsl, Exxon/dsl/24hr, Fina/dsl, T&C/dsl, **food:** Country Cookin Café, DQ, La Mexicana Rest., Pizza Hut, Sonic, **lodging:** Best Value Inn, Best Western, Comfort Inn, **other:** Alco, Family$, Parts+

**399** (from eb) LP 467, Sonora, **S gas:** Chevron/dsl, Fina/24hr, Phillips 66, Exxon/dsl, **food:** DQ, **lodging:** Day's Inn, **other:** Ⓗ HOSPITAL, RV camping

**394mm** rest area both lanes, full ♿ facilities, 📞, 🏕, **litter barrel, petwalk, RV dump**

**392** RM 1989, Caverns of Sonora Rd, **8 mi S other:** Caverns of Sonora Camping, phone

**388** RM 1312 (from wb)

*Side markers:* E / W — KERRVILLE — TX — JUNCTION — SONORA

## INTERSTATE 10 CONT'D

**OZONA** → **E** / **W**

| | |
|---|---|
| **381** | RM 1312 (from eb) |
| **372** | Taylor Box Rd, **N gas:** Chevron/Circle Bar/dsl/rest./24hr, **lodging:** Super 8/RV Park, **other:** auto museum |
| **368** | LP 466, **N** same as 365 & 363 |
| **365** | TX 163, Ozona, **N gas:** Chevron/dsl, Exxon, Texaco/dsl/café, T&C/Country Cookin Cafe/Godfather's/dsl, **food:** Café NextDoor, DQ, Sonic, Subway, **lodging:** Best Value, Best Western, Economy Inn/RV Park, **other:** H HOSPITAL, $General, NAPA, to David Crockett Mon, **N gas:** Chevron, **food:** El Chato |
| **363** | Lp 466, to Ozona |
| **361** | RM 2083, Pandale Rd |
| **357mm** | Eureka Draw |
| **351mm** | Howard Draw |
| **350** | FM 2398, to Howard Draw |
| **349mm** | parking area wb, litter barrels |
| **346mm** | parking area eb, litter barrels |
| **343** | TX 290 W, **S** Ft. Lancaster Historic Site |
| **337** | Live Oak Rd |
| **336.5mm** | Live Oak Creek |
| **328** | River Rd, Sheffield, **S gas:** Fina/dsl |
| **327.5mm** | Pecos River |
| **325** | TX 290, TX 349, to Iraan, Sheffield, **N** H HOSPITAL |
| **320** | frontage rd |
| **314** | frontage rd |
| **309mm** | **rest area both lanes, full** ♿ **facilities,** 🚻, 🅿, **litter barrels, petwalk, wireless internet** |
| **307** | US 190, FM 305, to Iraan, **N** H HOSPITAL |
| **298** | RM 2886 |
| **294** | FM 11, Bakersfield, **N gas:** Exxon, **S gas:** Chevron/dsl/café, **other:** 🚻 |
| **288** | Ligon Rd, **N** many windmills |
| **285** | McKenzie Rd, **S other:** Domaine Cordier Ste Genevieve Winery |
| **279mm** | picnic area eb, 🅿, litter barrels |
| **277** | FM 2023 |
| **273** | US 67/385, to McCamey, **N other:** picnic area wb, 🅿, litter barrels |
| **272** | University Rd |
| **264** | Warnock Rd, **N other:** KOA/BBQ/cafe |
| **261** | US 290 W, US 385 S, **N gas:** Exxon/TCBY/dsl, **S gas:** T&C, **lodging:** Econolodge, **food:** DQ, Pizza Hut, Sonic, Subway, **other:** H HOSPITAL, RV camping |

**FT STOCKTON**

| | |
|---|---|
| **259b a** | (259 from eb) TX 18, FM 1053, Ft Stockton, **N gas:** Apache Fuel Ctr/dsl, Exxon, Fina/dsl, Shell/Burger King/dsl, **other:** I-10 RV Park |
| **257** | US 285, to Pecos, Ft Stockton, **N other:** Comanche Land RV Park, golf, **S gas:** Chevron/T&C/dsl, Exxon/dsl/rest., Shell, Valero/dsl, **food:** IHOP, KFC/Taco Bell, McDonald's, Pizza Hut, Pizza Pro, Sonic, Steak House, Subway, **lodging:** Day's Inn, Hampton Inn, Holiday Inn Express, Knight's Inn/Atrium West, La Quinta, Motel 6, Town&Country Motel, **other:** Ace Hardware, AutoZone, Chevrolet/Pontiac/Buick, $General, Ford/Lincoln/Mercury, Goodyear/auto, Mktbasket Foods, Walmart, tires/repair |
| **256** | to US 385 S, Ft Stockton, **1 mi S gas:** Shell/dsl, Valero/dsl, **food:** Alpine Rest., DQ, K-Bob's Steaks, KFC, Sonic, Subway, **lodging:** Best Western, Comfort Inn, Econolodge, Motel 6, Sleep Inn, Super 8, **other:** H HOSPITAL, Ford, to Ft Stockton Hist Dist, Big Bend NP |

| | |
|---|---|
| **253** | FM 2037, to Belding |
| **248** | US 67, FM 1776, to Alpine, **S** to Big Bend NP |
| **246** | Firestone |
| **241** | Kennedy Rd |
| **235** | Mendel Rd |
| **233mm** | **rest area both lanes, full** ♿ **facilities,** 🚻, 🅿, **litter barrels, petwalk** |
| **229** | Hovey Rd |
| **222** | Hoefs Rd |
| **214** | (from wb), FM 2448 |
| **212** | TX 17, FM 2448, to Pecos, **N** picnic area, litter barrels, **S gas:** Fina/dsl/café, RV Camping |
| **209** | TX 17, **S other:** to Davis Mtn SP, Ft Davis NHS |
| **206** | FM 2903, to Balmorhea, **S other:** to Balmorhea SP |
| **192** | FM 3078, to Toyahvale, **S other:** to Balmorhea SP |
| **188** | Giffin Rd |
| **187** | I-20, to Ft Worth, Dallas |
| **186** | I-10, E to San Antonio (from wb) |
| **185mm** | **picnic area both lanes,** 🅿, **litter barrels** |
| **184** | Springhills |
| **181** | Cherry Creek Rd, **S gas:** Chevron/24hr |
| **176** | TX 118, FM 2424, to Kent, **N gas:** Chevron/dsl, **S other:** to McDonald Observatory, Davis Mtn SP, Ft Davis |
| **173** | Hurd's Draw Rd |
| **166** | Boracho Sta |
| **159** | Plateau, **N gas:** Exxon/dsl/rest./24hr |
| **153** | Michigan Flat |
| **146** | Wild Horse Rd |
| **146mm** | weigh sta wb |
| **145mm** | **rest area both lanes, full** ♿ **facilities,** 🅿, **litter barrels, petwalk** |

**VAN HORN**

| | |
|---|---|
| **140b** | Ross Dr, Van Horn, **N gas:** Chevron, Exxon/dsl, Love's/Subway/dsl/24hr, **lodging:** Comfort Inn, Day's Inn/rest., Desert Inn, Sands Motel/rest., **other:** El Campo RV Park, **S other:** Mountain View RV Park/dump |
| **140a** | US 90, TX 54, Van Horn Dr, **N gas:** Phillips 66, Shell/dsl, **food:** Village Inn, **other:** H HOSPITAL, $General, NAPA, Radio Shack, USPO, **S gas:** Exxon, Pilot/Wendy's/dsl/scales/24hr, **food:** Papa's Café, **other:** KOA, RV Dump |
| **138** | Lp 10, to Van Horn, **N food:** Chuey's Rest., DQ, Pizza Hut, **lodging:** Best Western, Budget Inn, Econolodge, Economy Inn, Knights Inn, Motel 6, Ramada Ltd, **other:** Eagles Nest RV Park, Goodyear, IGA Foods, Pueblo Foods, USPO, auto/dsl repair, **S gas:** Chevron/dsl/24hr, **food:** McDonald's, **lodging:** Hampton Inn, Holiday Inn Express, Super 8, **other:** tires/repair |

**TX**

## INTERSTATE 10 CONT'D

| | |
|---|---|
| **137mm** | parking area eb |
| **136mm** | scenic overlook wb, 🏞, litter barrels |
| **135mm** | *Mountain/Central time zone line* |
| **133** | (from wb) frontage rd |
| **129** | to Hot Wells, Allamore |
| **108** | to Sierra Blanca (from wb), same as 107 |
| **107** | FM 1111, Sierra Blanca Ave, **N gas:** Exxon/dsl/24hr, **food:** Michael's Rest., **other:** Sierra Blanca RV Park, truck/tire repair, USPO, to Hueco Tanks SP, **S gas:** Chevron, **food:** La Familia, **other:** Stagecoach Trading Post |
| **105** | (106 from wb) Lp 10, Sierra Blanca, same as 107 |
| **102.5mm** | insp sta eb |
| **99** | Lasca Rd, **N other:** picnic area both lanes, 🏞, **litter barrels, no restrooms** |
| **98mm** | **picnic area eb, 🏞, litter barrels, no restrooms** |
| **95** | frontage rd (from eb) |
| **87** | FM 34, **S gas:** Driver's Travel Mart/dsl/rest./24hr |
| **85** | Esperanza Rd |
| **81** | FM 2217 |
| **78** | TX 20 W, to McNary |
| **77mm** | truck parking area wb |
| **72** | spur 148, to Ft Hancock, **S gas:** Shell/dsl, **food:** Angie's Rest., **other:** Ford Hancock Motel |
| **68** | Acala Rd |
| **55** | Tornillo |
| **51mm** | **rest area both lanes, full ♿ facilities, 🏞, litter tables, petwalk** |
| **49** | FM 793, Fabens, **S gas:** Exxon, **lodging:** Fabens Inn/Cafe, **other:** S&S Foods, **1 mi S food:** Church's, McDonald's, Subway, **food:** Charlie Bigg's, **other:** Family$ |
| **42** | FM 1110, to Clint, **S gas:** Exxon/dsl, **lodging:** Cotton Valley Motel/RV Park/rest./dump |
| **37** | FM 1281, Horizon Blvd, **N gas:** Flying J/Bonito's Rest./scales/@, Love's/Chester Fried/Subway/dsl/scales/24hr/@, **lodging:** Americana Inn, **other:** Freightliner **S gas:** Petro/Mobil/Blimpie/dsl/scales/24hr/@, **food:** McDonald's, **lodging:** Deluxe Inn, **other:** Blue Beacon |
| **35** | Eastlake Blvd. |
| **34** | TX 375, Americas Ave, **N gas:** Chevron/dsl/24hr, Exxon, Shamrock/dsl, **lodging:** Microtel, Value Place, **other:** GMC, Mission RV Camping, Peterbilt, **S other:** RV camping, El Paso Museum of Hist |
| **32** | FM 659, Zaragosa Rd, **N gas:** Chevron/dsl, **food:** Arby's, Barrigos, BJ's Grill, Cheddar's, Furr's Buffet, Great American Steaks, IHOP, Krispy Kreme, LJ Silver/Taco Bell, Logan's Roadhouse, Macaroni Grill, Outback Steaks, Peiwei Asian, Peter Piper Pizza, San Francisco Oven, Starbucks, Whataburger/24hr, **lodging:** Holiday Inn Express, Red Roof Inn, **other:** Chevrolet, Circuit City, Discount Tire, Kohl's, Lowe's Whse, Michael's, Nissan, Office Depot, World Mkt, **S gas:** Fina/7-11, Shamrock/dsl, **food:** Howah Chinese |
| **30** | Lee Trevino Dr, **N gas:** Exxon, **food:** Chili's, Jack-in-the-Box, Taco Cabana, Whataburger, **lodging:** La Quinta, Red Roof Inn, Studio 6, **other:** Discount Tire, Firestone, Ford, Isuzu, Home Depot, Lexus, NTB, Sears/auto, Toyota, mall, **S gas:** Valero/24hr, **lodging:** Ramada, **other:** Chrysler/Jeep/Dodge, Nissan, Harley-Davidson, Hyundai |

| | |
|---|---|
| **29** | Lomaland Dr, **N food:** Denny's, **lodging:** AmeriSuites, **S gas:** Fina/7-11, **food:** Julio's Café, **lodging:** HomeGate Studios, Ramada, Westar Suites, **other:** Harley-Davidson |
| **28b** | Yarbrough Dr, El Paso, **N gas:** Chevron/24hr, Shell, **food:** Beijing Chinese, Burger King, Grandy's, Hong Kong Buffet, LJ Silver, McDonald's, Quizno's, Sonic, Subway, Texas Roadhouse, Wendy's, Whataburger, Wienerschnitzel, Wyatt's Cafeteria, **lodging:** Days Inn, **other:** Marshall's, PepBoys, Radio Shack, Ross, Walmart SuperCtr/gas, **S gas:** Shamrock/24hr, **food:** Applebee's, LaMalenche Café, Lin's Buffet, Pizza Hut, Rudy's BBQ, Shangri-La, **lodging:** Comfort Inn, InTown Suites, Suburban Lodge |
| **28a** | FM 2316, McRae Blvd, **N gas:** Chevron/24hr, **food:** ChuckeCheese, Jack-in-the-Box, KFC, Pizza Hut, Red Barrel Grill, Taco Bell, **lodging:** La Quinta, **other:** Ⓗ HOSPITAL, Barnes&Noble, Best Buy, BigLots, Firestone/auto, Goodyear/auto, Jo-Ann Fabrics, K-Mart, Michael's, Office Depot, Walgreens, **S gas:** Circle K, Shamrock, **food:** Fuddrucker's, **lodging:** Comfort Inn, La Quinta, **other:** Hyundai/Saturn |
| **27** | Hunter Dr, Viscount Blvd, **N gas:** Fina/7-11, Valero, **food:** Carrow's Rest., Grand China Buffet, K-Bob's, Red Lobster, Taco Bell, **lodging:** La Quinta, **other:** Barnes&Noble, Best Buy, Firestone, **S gas:** Exxon/Subway/dsl, Shell, **food:** Whataburger/24hr, **other:** Family$, Food City |
| **26** | Hawkins Blvd, El Paso, **N gas:** Chevron, Shamrock, Shell, **food:** Arby's, Burger King, Country Kitchen, DQ, Golden Corral, IHOP, Landry's Seafood, Luby's, Olive Garden, Red Lobster, Taco Cabana, Wyatt's Cafeteria, **lodging:** Howard Johnson, **other:** Circuit City, Dillard's, JC Penney, Office Depot, Pennzoil, Sam's Club/gas, Sears/auto, Walmart SuperCtr/gas, **S gas:** Shamrock/dsl, **food:** China King, Hooters, McDonald's, Village Inn Rest., **lodging:** Best Western, **other:** Tony Lama Boots |
| **25** | Airway Blvd, El Paso Airport, **N gas:** Valero, Shell/dsl/24hr, Phillips 66, Western, **food:** Jack-in-the-Box, Whataburger, **lodging:** Courtyard, Hampton Inn, Holiday Inn, Radisson, Residence Inn, **other:** VW/Volvo/Mercedes, **S gas:** Chevron/dsl/rest./24hr, **lodging:** Homewood Suites, **other:** Goodyear/auto, Subaru |
| **24b** | Geronimo Dr, **N gas:** Chevron/24hr, **food:** Steak&Ale, Taco Cabana, **other:** Dillard's, Office Depot, Target, Walgreens, mall, **S gas:** Circle K/gas, Fina/7-11, Phillips 66, **food:** Senses De Brazil, Bombay Bicycle Club, Denny's, **lodging:** AmeriSuites, Embassy Suites, La Quinta |
| **24a** | Trowbridge Dr, **N gas:** Fina, Thunderbird Gas, **food:** Alexandrio's Mexican, Luby's, McDonald's, Steak&Ale, Whataburger, **lodging:** Budget Inn, **other:** Chiropractor, Ford, Nissan, Toyota |
| **23b** | US 62/180, to Paisano Dr, **N food:** Jack-in-the-Box, McDonald's, **other:** Ford, U-Haul, to Carlsbad |
| **23a** | Raynolds St, **S food:** Arby's, **lodging:** Motel 6, Super 8, **other:** Ⓗ HOSPITAL |
| **22b** | US 54, Patriot Fwy |
| **22a** | Copia St, El Paso, **N gas:** Valero, **food:** KFC |
| **21** | Piedras St, El Paso, **N gas:** Exxon, **food:** Burger King, McDonald's, **other:** Family$ |
| **20** | Dallas St, Cotton St, **N gas:** Valero, **food:** Church's, Subway |
| **19** | TX 20, El Paso, downtown, **N gas:** Chevron, **S gas:** Texaco, **food:** Burger King, **lodging:** Holiday Inn Express, Travelodge |

EL PASO

TX

## INTERSTATE 10 CONT'D

| | |
|---|---|
| **E** ↕ **W** | |
| **18b** | Franklin Ave, Porfirio Diaz St |
| **18a** | Schuster Ave, **N** Sun Bowl, **S** to UTEP |
| **16** | Executive Ctr Blvd, **N gas:** Valero/24hr, **food:** Burger King, **lodging:** Howard Johnson, **other:** Ford |
| **13b a** | US 85, Paisano Dr, to Sunland Park Dr, **N gas:** Valero/24hr, **food:** Barriga's Café, Carino's Italian, ChuckeCheese, Grand China, Great American Steaks, IHOP, Olive Garden, PF Chang's, Red Lobster, Sonic, Whataburger/24hr, **other:** Barnes&Noble, Best Buy, Circuit City, Dillard's, JC Penney, Office Depot, PetsMart, Sears/auto, Target, mall, **S gas:** Shamrock/dsl/24hr, Shell, **food:** La Malinche Mexican, McDonald's, Sonic, Subway, **lodging:** Best Western, Comfort Suites, Holiday Inn, Sleep Inn, Studio+, **other:** GMC/Pontiac/Buick, Sunland Park RaceTrack |
| **12** | Resler Dr (from wb) |
| **11** | TX 20, to Mesa St, Sunland Park, **N gas:** Chevron/dsl/24hr, Circle K/gas, Phillips 66, Valero/dsl/24hr, **food:** Carrow's/24hr, Chili's, CiCi's, Cracker Barrel, Denny's, Famous Dave's, Golden Corral, Jaxon's Rest/brewery, K-Bob's, LJ Silver/A&W, Papa John's, Popeye's, Rancher's Grill, Red Lobster, Souper Salad, Subway, Taco Bell, Taco Tote, Tony Roma, Wienerschnitzel, Wendy's, Whataburger, **lodging:** Baymont Inn, Comfort Suites, La Quinta, Red Roof Inn, **other:** Albertson's, BigLots, Checker Parts, Fabric Whse, Firestone/auto, Goodyear/auto, Home Depot, PepBoys, SteinMart, Walmart SuperCtr, **S gas:** Chevron/dsl/24hr, Valero/dsl/24hr, **food:** Ay Caramba Mexican, Burger King, Church's, Golden China, Hudson's Grill, Jack-in-the-Box, KFC, Leo's Mexican, Luby's, McDonald's, Peter Piper Pizza, Pizza Hut, Subway, Taco Cabana, Village Inn Rest., **lodging:** Best Value Inn, Day's Inn, Extended Stay America, Motel 6, Travelodge, **other:** AutoZone, Big 8 Foods, Furr's Foods, Hobby Lobby, Martin Tires, Radio Shack, Sam's Club/gas, Walgreen |
| **9** | Redd Rd, **N food:** Applebee's, Burger King, Double Dave's Pizza, Pizza Hut, Starbucks, **other:** Albertson's/gas, Checker Parts, Ford, Kohl's, Lowe's Whse, **S gas:** Circle K/gas, **other:** Chevrolet, Honda |
| **8** | Artcraft Rd, **S gas:** Shell/dsl, **food:** Carl's Jr, Rudy's BBQ, **lodging:** Hampton Inn, Holiday Inn Express, Microtel |
| **6** | Lp 375, to Canutillo, **N gas:** Shell/Taco Bell/dsl, **other:** to Trans Mountain Rd, Franklin Mtns SP, **S gas:** Shorty's/Subway/dsl, **other:** El Paso Shops/Famous Brands, RV camping |
| **5mm** | truck check sta eb |
| **2** | Westway, Vinton, **N gas:** Petro/Mobil/Blimpie/dsl/scales/24hr/@, **other:** American RV Center, Camping World (1mi), PetroLube/tires, **S gas:** gas/24hr, **other:** Volvo/Mac, truck repair |
| **1mm** | Welcome Ctr eb, full ♿ facilities, info, Ⓒ, 🍴, litter barrels, petwalk, weigh sta wb |
| **0** | FM 1905, Anthony, **N gas:** ✈FLYING J/Conoco/dsl/LP/24hr/@, **lodging:** Super 8, rest area wb, full ♿ facilities, 🍴, litter barrels, **S gas:** Fina/7-11/dsl, Piggy Bank/Burger King/dsl/24hr, Pilot/Subway/Wendy's/dsl/24hr/@, **food:** Great American Steaks, **lodging:** Best Western, **other:** Big 8 Foods, $General, truckwash |
| **0mm** | Texas/New Mexico state line |

## INTERSTATE 20

| Exit # | Services |
|---|---|
| **636mm** | Texas/Louisiana state line |
| **635.5mm** | Welcome Ctr wb/parking area eb, full ♿ facilities, Ⓒ, 🍴, litter barrels, petwalk |
| **635** | TX 9, TX 156, to Waskom, **N gas:** Chevron/Burger King/dsl, Exxon/dsl, **food:** DQ, Jim's BBQ, **other:** Family$, USPO |
| **633** | US 80, FM 9, FM 134, to Waskom, **N gas:** Texaco, **food:** Catfish Village Rest., **S other:** Miss Ellie's RV Park |
| **628** | to US 80, to frontage rd |
| **624** | FM 2199, to Scottsville |
| **620** | FM 31, to Elysian Fields |
| **617** | US 59, Marshall, **0-2 mi N gas:** Exxon/dsl, Texaco/24hr, **food:** Applebee's, Burger King, Cafe Italia, Catfish Express, Golden Corral, Gucci's Pizza, IHOP, LJ Silver, McDonald's, Pizza Hut, Sonic, Subway, Taco Bell, Waffle House, Wendy's, Whataburger, **lodging:** Best Western, Comfort Suites, Fairfield Inn, Hampton Inn, La Quinta, Quality Inn, **other:** Buick/GMC/Pontiac, Cadillac/Chevrolet, Chrysler/Dodge/Jeep, Ford/Lincoln/Mercury, Toyota/Scion, Country Pines RV Park (8mi), **S gas:** Chevron/dsl, Pony Express/rest./dsl, Valero/dsl, **food:** Hungri Maverick Rest., **lodging:** Econolodge, Guest Inn, Holiday Inn Express, Motel 6, Super 8 |
| **614** | TX 43, to Marshall, **S** to Martin Creek Lake SP |
| **610** | FM 3251 |
| **608mm** | rest area both lanes, full ♿ facilities, Ⓒ, vending, 🍴, litter barrels |
| **604** | FM 450, Hallsville, **N gas:** Shamrock/dsl, **other:** 450 Hitchin' Post RV Park, to Lake O' the Pines |
| **600mm** | Mason Creek |
| **599** | FM 968, Longview, **N lodging:** Comfort Suites, Fairfield Inn (8mi), Wingate Inn (8mi), **other:** Kenworth Trucks, **S gas:** Chevron/Natl TrkStp/Quizno's/dsl/scales/@, Exxon/dsl, **other:** Goodyear, truck repair |
| **596** | US 259 N, TX 149, to Lake O' Pines, **N gas:** Exxon/Grandy's/dsl, **food:** Burger King, Whataburger, **lodging:** Comfort Suites, Microtel, Super 8, **other:** Ⓗ HOSPITAL, **S gas:** Valero/dsl, **lodging:** Holiday Inn Express, **other:** to Martin Lake SP |
| **595b a** | TX 322, Estes Pkwy, **N gas:** Exxon, EZ Mart, Texaco/dsl/24hr, **food:** Jack-in-the-Box, McDonald's, Pizza Hut, Waffle House, **lodging:** Best Value Inn, Day's Inn, Express Inn, Guest Inn, La Quinta, **S gas:** Fina/dsl, Mobil, **food:** KFC/Taco Bell, **lodging:** Baymont Inn, Hampton Inn, Motel 6, **other:** Walmart SuperCtr/gas |

EL PASO / EL PASO

MARSHALL

TX

**E ↕ W**

## INTERSTATE 20 CONT'D

| | |
|---|---|
| **593mm** | Sabine River |
| **591** | FM 2087, FM 2011 |
| **589b a** | US 259, TX 31, Kilgore (exits left from both lanes), **1-3 mi S food:** Kilgore Café, **lodging:** Budget Inn, Comfort Inn, Day's Inn, Holiday Inn Express, Homewood Suites, Ramada Inn, **S other:** E Texas Oil Museum |
| **587** | TX 42, Kilgore, **N gas:** Valero, **food:** Bodacious BBQ, **S gas:** Exxon/dsl, **other:** E TX Oil Museum, **3 mi S other:** Walmart SuperCtr |
| **583** | TX 135, to Kilgore, Overton, **N gas:** Exxon/dsl, **other:** Shallow Creek RV Resort |
| **582** | FM 3053, Liberty City, **N gas:** Chevron/Whataburger/dsl, Exxon/Subway/dsl, **food:** Bob's BBQ, DQ, Java House, Soda Shoppe, Sonic |
| **579** | Joy-Wright Mtn Rd |
| **575** | Barber Rd |
| **574mm** | picnic area both lanes, 🏕, litter barrels, ♿ accessible |
| **571b** | FM 757, Omen Rd, to Starrville |
| **571a** | US 271, to Gladewater, Tyler, **S gas:** Shell/Sonic/Texas Smokehouse/dsl/scales/24hr |
| **567** | TX 155, **N gas:** Valero/dsl/24hr, **S lodging:** Day's Inn, **other:** H HOSPITAL |
| **565** | FM 2015, to Driskill-Lake Rd |
| **562** | FM 14, **N food:** Bodacious BBQ, **other:** Northgate RV Park, to Tyler SP |
| **560** | Lavender Rd |
| **557** | Jim Hogg Rd, **N gas:** Shell |
| **556** | US 69, to Tyler, **N gas:** RaceWay, Shamrock/dsl, **food:** Burger King, Chili's, Domino's, Eastern Buffet, KFC\LJ Silver, Juanita's Mexicans, McDonald's, Pizza Inn, Posado's Cafe, Sonic, Subway, Taco Bell, Texas BBQ, **lodging:** Best Western, Comfort Suites, Day's Inn, Hampton Inn, La Quinta, **other:** Ace Hardware, Curves, Lowes Whse, Walmart SuperCtr/gas, vet, **S gas:** Chevron, Exxon, **food:** Cracker Barrel, DQ, Wendy's, **lodging:** Best Value Inn |
| **554** | Harvey Rd, **S other:** Yellow Rose RV Park |
| **552** | FM 849, **N gas:** Shell, **food:** La Valleta Italian |
| **548** | TX 110, to Grand Saline, **N gas:** Exxon/dsl, **S gas:** Valero/dsl |
| **546mm** | check sta eb |
| **544** | Willow Branch Rd, **N gas:** Conoco/dsl/rest., **other:** Willow Branch RV Park |
| **540** | FM 314, to Van, **N gas:** Love's/Carl's Jr/dsl/24hr, **food:** DQ, **lodging:** Van Inn |
| **538mm** | rest area both lanes, full ♿ facilities, 🔌, vending, 🏕, litter barrels, petwalk |
| **537** | FM 773, FM 16 |
| **536** | Tank Farm Rd |
| **533** | Oakland Rd, to Colfax, **N gas:** Shamrock/dsl/rest. |
| **530** | FM 1255, **N other:** RV Camping |
| **528** | FM 17, to Grand Saline |
| **527** | TX 19, **N gas:** Texaco/dsl/24hr, **food:** Burger King, Whataburger/24hr, **lodging:** Comfort Inn, Luxury Suites, Super 8, **S gas:** Chevron/dsl/24hr, Circle K/dsl/24hr, Shell/Subway/dsl, **food:** DQ, Dairy Palace, Juanita's Mexican, KFC/Taco Bell, McDonald's, Senorita's Mexican, **lodging:** Best Western, Day's Inn, **other:** Chrysler/Dodge/Jeep, Ford/Mercury, Mule Creek Ranch RV Resort, to First Monday SP, LP |

**CANTON**

**TERRELL**

| | |
|---|---|
| **526** | FM 859, to Edgewood |
| **523** | TX 64, to Canton |
| **521** | Myrtle Springs Rd, **N** trailer sales, **S other:** Marshall's RV Ctr, RV camp/dump, U-Haul |
| **519** | Turner-Hayden Rd, **S** Canton RV Park |
| **516** | FM 47, to Wills Point, **N** to Lake Tawakoni, **S gas:** Shamrock/24hr, **food:** Robertson's Café/gas, **lodging:** Interstate Motel |
| **512** | FM 2965, Hiram-Wills Point Rd |
| **512mm** | weigh sta both lanes |
| **509** | Hiram Rd, **S gas:** Phillips 66/dsl/café |
| **506** | FM 429, FM 2728, College Mound Rd, **S** Blue Bonnet Ridge RV Park |
| **503** | Wilson Rd, **S gas:** TA/Shell/Country Fair/Pizza Hut/Subway/dsl/LP/24hr/@ |
| **501** | TX 34, to Terrell, **N gas:** Chevron/24hr, Exxon/dsl, **food:** Capt D's, Schlotsky's, Sonic, Starbucks, Waffle House, **lodging:** Best Value Inn, Best Western, Comfort Inn, Day's Inn, La Quinta, Motel 6, **other:** H HOSPITAL, Home Depot, **S gas:** Circle K, Valero/dsl/24hr, **food:** Applebee's, Carmona's Cantina, IHOP, McDonald's, Wendy's, **lodging:** Holiday Inn Express, Super 8, **other:** Tanger Outlet/famous brands |
| **499b** | Rose Hill Rd, to Terrell |
| **499a** | to US 80, W to Dallas, same as 498 |
| **498** | FM 148, to Terrell, **N gas:** Exxon/Denny's/Subway/dsl, Shell/dsl |
| **493** | FM 1641, **S gas:** Exxon/Pizza Inn/Sonic/dsl |
| **491** | FM 2932, Helms Tr, to Forney, **N gas:** Shell/Subway/dsl |
| **490** | FM 741, to Forney |
| **487** | FM 740, to Forney, **S** Forney RV park |
| **483** | Lawson Rd, Lasater Rd |
| **482** | Belt Line Rd, to Lasater, **S gas:** Shell/KFC/Pizza Hut/Subway, **other:** RV park |
| **481** | Seagoville Rd, **N gas:** Valero/dsl, Shell/Church's, **lodging:** La Quinta, **S food:** Lindy's Rest. |
| **480** | I-635, N to Mesquite |
| **479b a** | US 175, **S gas:** Shell/dsl |
| **477** | St Augustine Rd, **S gas:** Shell/dsl, **food:** Sonic |
| **476** | Dowdy Ferry Rd |
| **474** | TX 310 N, Central Expsy |
| **473b a** | JJ Lemmon Rd, I-45 N to Dallas, S to Houston |
| **472** | Bonnie View Rd, **N gas:** ✈FLYING J/Conoco/dsl/LP/rest./24hr/@, Shell, **food:** Jack-in-the-Box, **lodging:** Ramada Ltd, **other:** Blue Beacon, Speedco Lube, **S gas:** TA/Exxon/Burger King/Taco Bell/dsl/scales/24hr/@ |
| **470** | TX 342, Lancaster Rd, **N gas:** Chevron, USA/Texaco/Popeye's/dsl/scales/24hr, **food:** Big Bruce's BBQ, **S gas:** Pilot/Wendy's/dsl/24hr, Shell, **food:** McDonald's, Sonic, Subway, Taco Bell/LJ Silver, Whataburger, William's Chicken, **lodging:** Day's Inn |
| **468** | Houston School Rd, **S gas:** Exxon/dsl, **food:** Whataburger |
| **467b a** | I-35E, N to Dallas, S to Waco, **1 mi N** off of I-35E, **gas:** Shell, **food:** McDonald's |
| **466** | S Polk St, **N gas:** Exxon, Texaco, **food:** DQ, Sonic, Subway, **S gas:** Love's/Carl's Jr/dsl/scales/24hr |
| **465** | Wheatland/S Hampton Rds, **N gas:** Shell/dsl, **S gas:** Chevron/McDonald's, RaceWay, **food:** Arby's, Cheddar's, Jack-in-the-Box, Popeye's, Sonic, Spring Creek BBQ, Taco Bell, Wendy's, **lodging:** Comfort Inn, Super 8, **other:** H HOSPITAL, Buick/GMC/Pontiac, |

**DALLAS**

**TX**

## INTERSTATE 20 CONT'D

**E** ↕ **W**
**D A L L A S**

**465** Continued
Home Depot, Honda, Hyundai, Lincoln/Mercury, Lowes Whse, Mazda, PetsMart, Sam's Club/gas, Saturn, Walmart SuperCtr

**464b a** US 67, Love Fwy

**463** Camp Wisdom Rd, **N gas:** Chevron/McDonald's, Exxon, TA, **food:** Catfish King Rest., Denny's, Taco Bell/LJ Silver, Taco Cabana, **lodging:** Best Value Inn, Holiday Inn, Lexington Suites, Motel 6, Ramada Inn, Royal Inn, Suburban Lodge, **other:** Chief Parts, Chrysler/Jeep, Ford, Nissan, Tuesday Morning, **S gas:** Citgo, **food:** Blimpie, Burger King, Jack-in-the-Box, McDonald's, Olive Garden, Owens Rest., Red Lobster, Subway, Wendy's, **other:** Advance Parts, Best Buy, K-Mart, NTB, PepBoys, Pontiac, Target, Toyota

**462b a** Duncanville Rd (no EZ wb return), **S gas:** Exxon, Shell/dsl, **food:** Arby's, KFC, Mr Gatti's, Whataburger, **lodging:** Hilton Garden, Motel 6, **other:** Goodyear, Kroger, Radio Shack

**461** Cedar Ridge Rd

**460** TX 408

**458** Mt Creek Pkwy

**457** FM 1382, to Grand Prairie, **N gas:** Shell/dsl, Valero/dsl, **food:** Waffle House, **S gas:** RaceTrac, **food:** Jack-in-the-Box, **other:** to Joe Pool Lake

**456** Carrier Pkwy, to Corn Valley Rd, **N food:** Chick-fil-A, Don Pablo, Taco Cabana, Whataburger, **other:** Home Depot, Kohl's, Radio Shack, Target, **S gas:** Shell, **food:** Boston Mkt, Chapp's Cafe, Cheddar's, Chili's, Denny's, IHOP, McDonald's, Spring Creek BBQ, Subway, **lodging:** Holiday Inn Express, **other:** Albertson's/gas, CVS Drug, Walgreens, vet

**D A L L A S**

**454** Great Southwest Pkwy, **N gas:** Chevron/24hr, Conoco/dsl, **food:** Beto's, Carino's Italian, China Dragon, ChuckeCheese, KFC, McDonald's, Taco Bell, Taco Bueno, Texas Roadhouse, Waffle House, Wendy's, Wienerschnitzel, **lodging:** Heritage Inn, La Quinta, Quality Inn, **other:** H HOSPITAL, Harley-Davidson, **S gas:** 7-11, Shell/Subway/dsl, Valero/dsl, **food:** Applebee's, Arby's, Buffalo Wild Wings, Burger King, Schlotzsky's, Sonic, **lodging:** Comfort Inn, Super 8, **other:** Discount Tire, Dodge, $Tree, Kroger, Office Depot, PetsMart, Sam's Club, Walgreens, Walmart SuperCtr, to Joe Pool Lake

**453b a** TX 360

**452** Frontage Rd

**451** Collins St, New York Ave, **N gas:** Mobil, RaceTrac, **food:** Jack-in-the-Box, Pizza Hut, **other:** Acura, Chrysler/Jeep, Kia/Mazda/VW, Saturn, **S gas:** QT, Shamrock, Shell, **food:** Chicken Express, McDonald's, Sonic, Taco Bueno, **lodging:** Hampton Inn, **other:** Buick/GMC/Pontiac, Lincoln/Mercury, Nissan

**450** Matlock Rd, **N gas:** Citgo/7-11, Fina/dsl, **food:** BJ's Brewhouse, Bravo Italian, Genghis Grill, IHOP, Mercado Juarez Café, PF Changs, Rio Bravo, Spaghetti Whse, Wendy's, **lodging:** Quality Inn, **other:** H HOSPITAL, Border's, Jo-Ann Fabrics, Lowes Whse, Michael's, Old Navy, PetsMart, Staples, **S gas:** Citgo/7-11, Shamrock, Shell, **food:** Joe's Pizza, **other:** Fry's Electronics, NTB

**D A L L A S**

**449** FM 157, Cooper St, **N gas:** Mobil, Shell, 7-11, Texaco, **food:** Abuelo's Mexican, Atlanta Bread, Blackeyed Pea, Cheesecake Factory, Chili's, China Café, CiCi's, Corner Bakery, Don Pablo, Golden Corral, Grandy's, Hong Kong Cafe, Jason's Deli, KFC, McDonald's, On-the-Border, Outback Steaks, Razzoo's Cajun Café, Red Lobster, Rock Fish Grill, Salt Grass Steaks, Schlotsky's, Souper Salad, Spaghetti Whse, Starbucks, Thai Cuisine, Wendy's, Whataburger, **lodging:** Best Western, Days Inn, Holiday Inn Express, Homestead Village, La Quinta, Studio 6, **other:** Barnes&Noble, Best Buy, Circuit City, Dillard's, Discount Tire, Hancock Fabrics, Hyundai, JC Penney, Office Depot, PetCo, Sears/auto, Subaru, Target, TJ Maxx, mall, **S gas:** Chevron, Conoco, Shell, **food:** Applebee's, Arby's, Boston Mkt, Burger King, Burger St, Chick-fil-A, Denny's, El Fenix Mexican, LJ Silver, Luby's, Macaroni Grill, McDonald's, Olive Garden, Panda Express, Popeye's, Ryan's, Sonic, Subway, Taco Bueno, TGIFriday, **lodging:** InTown Suites, **other:** Acura, Ford, GMC, Home Depot, Honda, Hyundai, Isuzu, Kia, K-Mart, Kroger, Pontiac, Ross, Walmart SuperCtr

**448** Bowen Rd, **N gas:** QT, RaceTrac, Shell/24hr, **food:** Cracker Barrel, **S gas:** Shell

**447** Kelly-Elliott Rd, Park Springs Blvd, **N gas:** Lonestar Express, 7-11, **S gas:** Exxon, Fina/Blimpie, **other:** camping

**445** Green Oaks Blvd, **N gas:** Conoco, Shell, **food:** Arby's, Boston Mkt, Burger King, Grandy's, Hooters, Jack-in-the-Box, KFC, Koltr's BBQ, Mac's Grill, Pizza Hut, Pizza Inn, Schlotsky's, Taco Bell, Taco Cabana, Taipan Chinese, Whataburger, **other:** Albertson's, Eckerd/24hr, Minyard/gas/food, Office Depot, **S gas:** Chevron/24hr, Citgo/7-11, Shamrock, **food:** Cheddar's, IHOP, Fazoli's, Khaki's, McDonald's, Pancho's Mexican, Panda Express, Sonic, Steak&Ale, Taco Bueno, Waffle House, **other:** AutoZone, Discount Tire, $General, O'Reilly Parts

**444** US 287 S, to Waxahatchie

**443** Bowman Springs Rd (from wb)

**442b a** I-820 to Ft Worth, US 287 bus, **N gas:** Valero, **lodging:** Great Western Inn, Super 8, **S gas:** Chevron

**441** Anglin Dr, Hartman Lane, **N gas:** Valero/dsl, **lodging:** Super 8, **S gas:** Conoco/dsl

**440b** Forest Hill Dr, **N gas:** Value Place Inn, **S gas:** Chevron/24hr, Conoco, Shell/dsl, **food:** Braum's, Capt D's, CiCi's, DQ, Denny's, Domino's, Jack-in-the-Box, Luby's, McDonald's, Sonic, Starbucks, Subway, **lodging:** Comfort Inn, **other:** AutoZone, CVS Drug, Discount Tire, $General, $Tree, Super 1 Foods, Walgreens

**D A L L A S / F T W O R T H**

## INTERSTATE 20 CONT'D

E ↕ W

**440a** Wichita St, **N** **gas:** Chevron/dsl, **food:** #1 Chinese, Taco Casa, Wendy's, **S** **gas:** Texaco, Valero, **food:** Braum's, Chicken Express, Denny's, Domino's, McDonald's, Pizza Hut, Schlotzsky's, Taco Bueno, Whataburger, **lodging:** Comfort Inn

**439** Campus Dr, **N** **other:** Ford, Chrysler/Jeep, **S** **other:** Sam's Club/gas

**438** Oak Grove Rd, 1 mi **N** **gas:** Shell, **food:** Burger King, Denny's, Jack-in-the box, McDonald's, Whataburger, **lodging:** Day's Inn, **S** **gas:** Valero

**437** I-35W, N to Ft Worth, S to Waco

**436b** Hemphill St, **N** **gas:** Shell/dsl, **S** **other:** Chevrolet

**436a** FM 731 (from eb), to Crowley Ave, **N** **gas:** Valero, **other:** $General, Sav-a-Lot Foods, **S** **gas:** Conoco/dsl, **food:** DQ, Pizza Hut/Taco Bell, Subway

**435** McCart St, **N** **gas:** Shell, Shamrock, **S** **gas:** Mobil

**434b** Trail Lakes Dr, **S** **gas:** Shell, **food:** Sonic, Starbucks, **other:** CVS Drug

**434a** Granbury rd, **S** **food:** Pancho's Mexican, Wendy's, **other:** JoAnn Fabrics

**433** Hulen St, **N** **gas:** Shell/dsl, **food:** ChuckeCheese, Grady's Grill, Hooters, Olive Garden, Souper Salad, Subway, TGI-Friday, **lodging:** TownePlace Suites, **other:** Albertson's, Circuit City, Home Depot, Office Depot, PetsMart, TJ Maxx, **S** **gas:** Valero, **food:** Denny's, Jack-in-the-Box, McDonald's, Red Lobster, Taco Bell, **lodging:** Hampton Inn, **other:** Borders, Dillards, Macy's, Ross, mall

**431** (432 from wb), TX 183, Bryant-Irvin Rd, **N** **food:** Chipotle Mexican, Genghis Grill, Mimi's Café, On-the-Border, Taste of Asia, **other:** Best Buy, Kohls, Lowes Whse, Sam's Club/gas, **S** **gas:** Chevron/24hr, Exxon, QT, Shell, Texaco, **food:** Blackeyed Pea, Chicken Express, Chick-fil-A, Cousin's BBQ, Fuddruckers, IHOP, Outback Steaks, Quizno's, Razzoo's Cajun, Rio Mambo, SaltGrass Steaks, Schlotzsky's, Sonic, Starbucks, Subway, **lodging:** AmeriSuites, Extended Stay America, Holiday Inn Express, Hyatt Place, La Quinta, **other:** Ⓗ HOSPITAL, Buick, Costco/gas, Ford, Goodyear/auto, Lexus, Mazda, PetCo, Saturn, Suzuki, Staples, Target, Tom Thumb/gas, Walgreens, transmissions/repair

**430mm** Clear Fork Trinity River

**429b** Winscott Rd, **N** **gas:** Circle K/dsl **food:** Cracker Barrel, **lodging:** Best Western, Comfort Suites

**429a** US 377, to Granbury, **S** **gas:** RaceTrac/24hr, Valero, **food:** Arby's, Burger King, Chicken Express, Domino's, DQ, Jack-in-the-Box, KFC/Taco Bell, McDonald's, Sonic, Starbucks, Waffle House, Whataburger/24hr, **lodging:** Motel 6, **other:** Albertson's, AutoZone, $General, Walgreens

**428** I-820, N around Ft Worth

**426** RM 2871, Chapin School Rd

**425** Markum Ranch Rd

**421** I-30 E (from eb), to Ft Worth

**420** FM 1187, Aledo, Farmer, parking, **S** **other:** Cowtown RV Camping

**419mm** weigh sta eb

**418** Ranch House Rd, Willow Park, Willow Park, **N** **gas:** Exxon, Shell/dsl, **food:** Los Vaqueros, Pizza Hut, Sonic, Subway, Taco Texas, Whataburger, **S** **gas:** Shell/ChickenExpress/dsl, **food:** Domino's, McDonald's, **lodging:** Ramada Inn, **other:** Brookshire Foods, Funtime RV Park (1mi)

**417mm** weigh sta wb

**415** FM 5, Mikus Rd, Annetta, **S** **gas:** Shell/dsl, **other:** 415 RV Ctr

**413** (414 from wb), US 180 W, Lake Shore Dr, **N** **gas:** RaceTrac, Texaco/dsl, Valero, **food:** DQ, Sonic, **other:** Buick/GMC/Pontiac, Cadillac/Chevrolet, Ford, Jeep, Lincoln/Mercury, Nissan, Toyota/Scion, Walmart SuperCtr/Subway/dsl/24hr, **S** **gas:** Chevron/dsl, Valero

**410** Bankhead Hwy, **S** **gas:** Loves/Subway/dsl/24hr

**409** FM 2552 N, Clear Lake Rd, **N** **gas:** Petro/Mobil/dsl/rest./24hr/@, **food:** David Beard's Catfish, Jack-in-the-Box, **lodging:** Best Western, Sleepgo, **other:** Ⓗ HOSPITAL, Blue Beacon, **S** **gas:** Shell/dsl

**408** TX 171, FM 1884, FM 51, Tin Top Rd, Weatherford, **N** **gas:** Exxon/Pizza Inn/24hr, Mobil, **food:** Applebee's, Baker's Ribs, Braum's, Chicken Express, China Garden, Cotton Patch Cafe, Dickey's BBQ, Golden Corral, IHOP, LJ Silver, Logan's Roadhouse, McDonald's, MT Rest., Schlotsky's, Starbucks, Subway, Taco Bell, Taco Bueno, Wendy's, Whataburger, **lodging:** La Quinta, Sleep Inn, Super 8, **other:** AutoZone, Belk, Discount Tire, $Tree, Home Depot, JC Penney, Kroger, Walmart SuperCtr/gas, **S** **gas:** Exxon/Subway/dsl, Shell/Burger King/dsl/24hr, **food:** Chick-fil-A, Chili's, Coldstone Creamery, Cracker Barrel, On-the-Border, Waffle House, **lodging:** Comfort Suites, Hampton Inn, Holiday Inn Express, Motel 6, Super Value Inn, **other:** Best Buy, GNC, Kohls, Lowes Whse, NTB, Ross, Target

**407** Tin Top Rd (from eb), **S** **other:** Serenity Ranch RV Park, same as 408

**406** Old Dennis Rd, **N** **gas:** Conoco/dsl/24hr, **food:** Chuck Wagon Rest., **lodging:** Quest Inn, **S** **gas:** Pilot/Wendy's/dsl/scales/24hr, **lodging:** Econolodge, Quality 1 Motel, **other:** Rip Griffin Repair

**402** (403 from wb), TX 312, to Weatherford

**397** FM 1189, to Brock, **N** **gas:** Valero/dsl, **S** **tires**

**394** FM 113, to Millsap, **N** **other:** Hillbilly Haven RV Park

**393mm** Brazos River

**391** Gilbert Pit Rd

**390mm** rest area both lanes, full ♿ facilities, 🕿, vending, 🚻, litter barrels, petwalk

**386** US 281, to Mineral Wells, **N** **gas:** Shell/Subway/dsl

**380** FM 4, Santo, **S** **food:** Sunday Creek BBQ, **other:** Windmill Acres RV Park

**376** Blue Flat Rd, Panama Rd

**373** TX 193, Gordon

**370** TX 108 S, FM 919, Gordon, **N** **gas:** Texaco/Bar-B/dsl/rest., **S** **gas:** Exxon/dsl, **other:** Cactus Rose RV Park, Longhorn Inn/Country Store

**367** TX 108 N, Mingus, **N** **food:** Smoke Stack Café, **other:** Thurber Sta, **S** **food:** NY Hill Rest.

**364mm** Palo Pinto Creek

**363** Tudor Rd, **picnic area**, 🚻, **litter barrels**

**362mm** Bear Creek, **picnic area both lanes**, 🚻, **litter barrels**

**361** TX 16, to Strawn

**358** (from wb), frontage rd

**356mm** Russell Creek

**354** Lp 254, Ranger

**351** (352 from wb), College Blvd

**349** FM 2461, Ranger, **N** **gas:** Love's/Godfather's/Subway/dsl/scales/24hr, **food:** DQ, **lodging:** Best Value Inn, Relax Inn (2mi), **other:** RL RV Park, **S** **gas:** Shell/dsl, repair

**W E A T H E R F O R D**

**TX**

## INTERSTATE 20 CONT'D

**E ↕ W**

| | |
|---|---|
| 347 | FM 3363 (from wb), Olden, **S other:** TX Steak Exchange |
| 345 | FM 3363 (from eb), Olden, **S food:** Texas Steakhouse |
| 343 | TX 112, FM 570, Eastland, Lake Leon, **N gas:** Conoco/dsl, Fina/7-11/Subway, Shell, **food:** Chicken Express, DQ, McDonald's, Pizza Inn, Sonic, Starbucks, Taco Bell, **lodging:** La Quinta, Super 8/RV park, **other:** AutoZone, Buick/Cadillac/Chevrolet, Chrysler/Dodge/Jeep, Curves, $General, Ford/Mercury, GMC/Pontiac, O'Reilly Parts, Walmart/SuperCtr/dsl/24hr, **S gas:** Exxon/dsl/24hr, **food:** Pulido's Mexican, **lodging:** Budget Host, Ramada Inn |
| 340 | TX 6, Eastland, **N gas:** Chevron/dsl, **other:** H HOSPITAL, **S gas:** Shell/dsl |
| 337 | spur 490, **N other:** The Wild Country RV Park |
| 332 | US 183, Cisco, **N gas:** Exxon, **food:** Cow Pokes, DQ, Pizza Heaven, Sonic, Subway, **lodging:** Executive Inn, Knight's Inn, **S gas:** Fina/dsl |
| 330 | TX 206, Cisco, **N lodging:** Best Value Inn, **other:** H HOSPITAL |
| 329mm | picnic area wb, tables, litter barrels, ♿ accessible |
| 327mm | picnic area eb, tables, litter barrels, ♿ accessible |
| 324 | Scranton Rd |
| 322 | Cooper Creek Rd |
| 320 | FM 880 N, FM 2945 N, to Moran |
| 319 | FM 880 S, Putnam, **N gas:** gas/dsl/café, **other:** USPO |
| 316 | Brushy Creek Rd |
| 313 | FM 2228 |
| 310 | Finley Rd |
| 308 | Lp 20, Baird |
| 307 | US 283, Clyde, **N food:** DQ, **lodging:** Baird Motel/RV park/dump, **S gas:** Conoco/dsl, **food:** Robertson's Café |
| 306 | FM 2047, Baird, **N other:** Chevrolet/GMC/Pontiac, Chrysler/Dodge/Jeep, Hanner RV Ctr |
| 303 | Union Hill Rd |
| 301 | FM 604, Cherry Lane, **N gas:** Exxon/Subway/dsl, **food:** Sonic, Whataburger/24hr, **S gas:** Fina/7-11/dsl/café, Shell/dsl/24hr, **food:** DQ, **other:** Family$ |
| 300 | FM 604 N, Clyde, **N other:** Chrysler/Dodge/Jeep, **S gas:** Conoco/dsl, **other:** White's RV Park/dump |
| 299 | FM 1707, Hays Rd |
| 297 | FM 603, Eula Rd |
| 296.5mm | rest area both lanes, full ♿ facilities, 📞, 🅿, litter barrels, petwalk |
| 294 | Buck Creek Rd, **N** RV Dump, **S** West TX RV Ctr |
| 292b | Elmdale Rd |
| 292a | Lp 20 (exits left from wb) |
| 290 | TX 36, Lp 322, **S** ✈, zoo |
| 288 | TX 351, **N gas:** Fina/7-11/Subway/dsl, **food:** Chili's, Cracker Barrel, DQ, Skillet's Café, **lodging:** Comfort Suites, Day's Inn, Executive Inn, Holiday Inn Express, Quality Inn, Whitten Inn, **other:** $Tree, Lowes Whse, Walmart SuperCtr/gas, **S lodging:** Super 8, **other:** H HOSPITAL |
| 286c | FM 600, Abilene, **N gas:** Exxon/dsl, Fina/dsl, **food:** Denny's/24hr, **lodging:** Best Western, Hampton Inn, La Quinta, **S gas:** Fina/7-11/dsl, **other:** Russell Stover's Candies |
| 286 | US 83, Pine St, Abilene, **S gas:** Fina, **lodging:** Budget Host, **other:** H HOSPITAL |
| 285 | Old Anson Rd, **N gas:** Exxon/dsl, **lodging:** Travel Inn, **S gas:** Exxon/dsl |

**ABILENE**

| | |
|---|---|
| 283a | US 277 S, US 83 (exits left from wb) |
| 282 | FM 3438, Shirley Rd, **S lodging:** Motel 6, **other:** KOA |
| 280 | Fulwiler Rd, to dyess air force base |
| 279 | US 84 E, to Abilene, **1-3 mi S** access to facilities |
| 278 | Lp 20, **N gas:** Conoco/dsl/24hr, **other:** dsl repair, **S gas:** Conoco/dsl/rest./scales/@, **other:** Mac Trucks/Volvo |
| 277 | FM 707, Tye, **N gas:** FLYING J/Shell/Country Mkt/dsl/LP/24hr/@, **other:** Tiey RV Park, **S gas:** Fina/7-11/dsl |
| 274 | Wells Lane |
| 272 | Wimberly Rd |
| 270 | FM 1235, Merkel, **N gas:** Conoco/dsl, Shell/dsl/café/24hr |
| 269 | FM 126, **N food:** Subway, **lodging:** Scottish Inn, **S gas:** Fina/dsl/rest./24hr, Shell, **food:** DQ, Skeet's BBQ |
| 267 | Lp 20, Merkel, **1mi S** access to gas, food, lodging |
| 266 | Derstine Rd |
| 264 | Noodle Dome Rd |
| 263 | Lp 20, Trent |
| 262 | FM 1085, **S gas:** Fina/7-11/dsl/24hr |
| 261 | Lp 20, Trent |
| 259 | Sylvester Rd |
| 258 | White Flat Rd, oil wells |
| 257mm | rest area both lanes, full ♿ facilities, 📞, vending, 🅿, litter barrels, petwalk |
| 256 | Stink Creek Rd |
| 255 | Adrian Rd |
| 251 | Eskota Rd |
| 249 | FM 1856 |
| 247 | TX 70 N, Sweetwater |
| 246 | Alabama Ave, Sweetwater |
| 245 | Arizona Ave (from wb), same as 244 |
| 244 | TX 70 S, Sweetwater, **N gas:** Chevron/dsl, Fina/dsl/24hr, **food:** Domino's, DQ, McDonald's, Subway, Wendy's, **lodging:** Best Western, La Quinta, Motel 6, **other:** H HOSPITAL, AutoZone, Ford/Mercury, Health Mart Drugs, Walmart SuperCtr/gas, **S gas:** Chevron, Shell, **food:** Buck's BBQ, Golden Chick, Great Wall, Schlotsky's, Taco Bell, **lodging:** Days Inn, Holiday Inn Express, Ranch House Motel/rest., Super 8, **other:** Buick/Cadillac/Chevrolet/Pontiac, K-Mart, |
| 243 | Hillsdale Rd, Robert Lee St, **N other:** Bewley's Service |
| 242 | Hopkins Rd, **S gas:** TA/Conoco/Pizza Hut/dsl/scales/24hr/@, **other:** Rolling Plains RV Park, truck/tire repair |
| 241 | Lp 20, Sweetwater, **N** gas, food, lodging, **S** RV camping |
| 240 | Lp 170, **N** ✈, camping |
| 239 | May Rd |
| 238b a | US 84 W, Blackland Rd |

## INTERSTATE 20 CONT'D

**E** ↕ **W**

| | |
|---|---|
| 237 | Cemetery Rd |
| 236 | FM 608, Roscoe, **N gas:** Shell, TC/Country Cookin/dsl, **other:** NAPA |
| 235 | to US 84, Roscoe, **S other:** Travel Stop/rest./truck repair/dsl |
| 230 | FM 1230, many wind turbines |
| 229mm | **picnic area wb, 🏕, litter barrels, ♿ accessible** |
| 228mm | **picnic area eb, 🏕, litter barrels, ♿ accessible** |
| 227 | Narrell Rd |
| 226b | Lp 20 (from wb), Loraine |
| 226a | FM 644 N, Wimberly Rd |
| 225 | FM 644 S, **1 mi S** access to gas, food |
| 224 | Lp 20, to Loraine, **1 mi S** gas, food |
| 223 | Lucas Rd, **S other:** 223 RV Park |
| 221 | Lasky Rd |
| 220 | FM 1899 |
| 219 | Lp 20, Country Club Rd, Colorado City |
| 217 | TX 208 S |
| 216 | TX 208 N, **N gas:** Chevron/Subway/dsl, **food:** DQ, **lodging:** Day's Inn, **S gas:** TC/Country Cookin/dsl, **food:** China Star, Pizza Hut, Sonic, **lodging:** American Inn, **other:** Ⓗ HOSPITAL, Alco, Health Mart Drugs, Parts+ |
| 215 | FM 3525, Rogers Rd, **2 mi S** access to gas, food |
| 214.5mm | Colorado River |
| 213 | Lp 20, Enderly Rd, Colorado City |
| 212 | FM 1229 |
| 211mm | FM 1229, Morgan Creek |
| 210 | FM 2836, **S gas:** Just Stop/dsl, **other:** to Lake Colorado City SP, picnic area, camping |
| 209 | Dorn Rd |
| 207 | Lp 20, Westbrook |
| 206 | FM 670, to Westbrook |
| 204mm | **rest area wb, full ♿ facilities, 📞, 🏕, litter barrels, petwalk** |
| 200 | Conaway Rd |
| 199 | Latan Rd |
| 195 | frontage rd (from eb) |
| 194a | E Howard Field Rd |
| 192 | FM 821, many oil wells |
| 191mm | **rest area eb, full ♿ facilities, 📞, 🏕, litter barrels, petwalk** |
| 190 | Snyder Field Rd |
| 189 | McGregor Rd |
| 188 | FM 820, Coahoma, **N gas:** TC/Country Cookin/dsl, **food:** DQ, **other:** USPO |
| 186 | Salem Rd, Sand Springs |
| 184 | Moss Lake Rd, Sand Springs, **N gas:** Fina/dsl, **S** RV camping |
| 182 | Midway Rd |
| 181b | Refinery Rd, **N gas:** Fina Refinery |
| 181a | FM 700, **N** ✈, RV camping, **2 mi S** Ⓗ HOSPITAL |
| 179 | US 80, Big Spring, **S gas:** Fina/7-11, **food:** Denny's, **lodging:** Camlot Inn, Comfort Inn, Quality Inn, **other:** $General, Buick/Cadillac/Chevrolet |
| 178 | TX 350, Big Spring, **N gas:** Shell/dsl, **S other:** truck repair |
| 177 | US 87, Big Spring, **N gas:** Exxon/dsl, TA/Popeye's/Subway/dsl/scales/24hr/@, **food:** Texas Cajun Cafe, **lodging:** Advantage Inn, Motel 6, Whitten Inn, **S gas:** Chevron/dsl, Fina/dsl, **food:** Casa Blanca Mexican, DQ, **lodging:** Best Western, Holiday Inn Express |

**B I G   S P R I N G**

**TX**

| | |
|---|---|
| 176 | TX 176, Andrews |
| 174 | Lp 20 E, Big Springs, **S gas:** Shell/dsl, **other:** Ⓗ HOSPITAL, ✈ |
| 172 | Cauble Rd |
| 171 | Moore Field Rd |
| 169 | FM 2599 |
| 168mm | **picnic area both lanes, 🏕, litter barrels** |
| 165 | FM 818 |
| 158 | Lp 20 W, to Stanton, **N** RV camping |
| 156 | TX 137, Lamesa, **S gas:** Phillips 66/Country Cookin/Subway/dsl/24hr, **food:** Sonic |
| 154 | US 80, Stanton, **2 mi S** access to gas, food, lodging |
| 151 | FM 829 (from wb) |
| 144 | Loop 250, **2-3 mi N** facilities in Midland |
| 143mm | frontage rd (from eb) |
| 142mm | **picnic area both lanes, 🏕, litter barrels, hist marker** |
| 140 | FM 307 (from eb) |
| 138 | TX 158, FM 715, Greenwood, **N gas:** Shell/dsl, United/dsl, **food:** KD's BBQ, Whataburger/24hr, **S gas:** TC/Subway/dsl |
| 137 | Old Lamesa Rd |
| 136 | TX 349, Midland, **N gas:** Fina/dsl, **food:** Domino's, DQ, Gatty's Pizza, IHOP, Little Caesar's, McAlister's Deli, Sonic, Starbucks, **lodging:** Comfort Inn, West Texas Inn, **other:** Advance Parts, AutoZone, $Tree, Family$, McAlister's Deli, Petroleum Museum, Walmart SuperCtr/gas, tires, **S gas:** Exxon/Burger King/dsl, Daves Gas/NAPA, TC/Country Cookin |
| 134 | Midkiff Rd, **0-1 mi** (Wall St) **N gas:** Chevron/Subway/dsl, Fina/7-11, Exxon/dsl, **food:** Denny's, DQ, **lodging:** Best Value Inn, Clarion, Day's Inn, Executive Inn, La Quinta, Motel 6, Super 8, **other:** Ⓗ HOSPITAL, Bo's RV Ctr, Casey's Camper, Chevrolet, Chrysler/Jeep, Honda, Ford, Mercedes/Volvo, Midland RV Park, Nissan, Toyota |
| 131 | TX 158, Midland, **N lodging:** Travelodge, **other:** Midland RV Park |
| 126 | FM 1788, **N gas:** Chevron/dsl, Pilot/McDonald's/dsl, Warfield/Texaco/Subway/dsl/scales/@, **other:** Western Auto, museum, airport |
| 121 | Lp 338, Odessa, **0-3 mi** (TX 191) **N gas:** Chevron/dsl, Fina/7-11, **food:** Carino's, Chili's, Fazoli's, Logan's Roadhouse, McDonald's, Pizza Hut, Quizno's, Rosa's Cafe, Schlotzsky's, Whataburger, **lodging:** Day's Inn, Elegante Hotel, Fairfield Inn, Grand Hotel, Hampton Inn, Holiday Inn, La Quinta, Marriott, Motel 6, **other:** Albertson's, Buick/GMC/Pontiac, Circuit City, Home Depot, Sears/auto, Sam's Club/gas, Staples, Target, Walmart SuperCtr, U of TX Permian Basin |
| 120 | JBS Pkwy, new exit |
| 118 | FM 3503, Grandview Ave, **N gas:** Fina/dsl, **other:** Freightliner/Peterbilt, |
| 116 | US 385, Craine, Andrews, **N gas:** Chevron, **food:** DQ, **lodging:** Best Western, Delux Inn, Villa West Inn, **other:** Ⓗ HOSPITAL, **S gas:** Fina/dsl, Shell/dsl, **lodging:** Motel 6, **other:** city park |
| 115 | FM 1882, **N gas:** TC/Country Cookin/dsl, **S gas:** Love's/McDonald's/Subway/dsl/scales/24hr |
| 113 | TX 302, Odessa |
| 112 | FM 1936, Odessa |
| 108 | Moss Ave, Meteor Crater |
| 104 | FM 866, Meteor Crater Rd |
| 103.5mm | weigh sta wb/parking area eb, litter barrels |

**M I D L A N D**

**O D E S S A**

Copyright 2009 - The Next Exit®

## INTERSTATE 20 CONT'D

**MONAHANS**

| | |
|---|---|
| 101 | FM 1601, Penwell |
| 93 | FM 1053 |
| 86 | TX 41, **N** Monahans Sandhills SP, camping |
| 83 | US 80, Monahans, **2 mi N** other: H HOSPITAL, RV camping |
| 80 | TX 18, Monahans, **N** gas: Chevron/dsl/24hr, **food:** Bar-H Steaks, DQ, Great Wall Buffet, McDonald's, Pappy's BBQ, Pizza Hut, Sonic, **other:** H HOSPITAL, Alco Discount, CarQuest, $General, Family$, Kwik Lube, Lowe's Foods, RV Park, **S** gas: Fina/dsl/24hr, Kent Gas, TC/Subway/dsl, **lodging:** Best Value Inn, Best Western, Texan Inn, **other:** Buick/Chevrolet/GMC/Pontiac, Chrysler/Dodge/Jeep |
| 79 | Lp 464, Monahans |
| 76 | US 80, Monahans, **2 mi N** other: to Million Barrel Museum, RV camping |
| 73 | FM 1219, Wickett, **N** gas: Shell/Allsup's, **S** gas: Texaco/Subway/dsl/24hr |
| 70 | TX 65 |
| 69.5mm | **rest area both lanes, full** ♿ **facilities,** ℂ, 🍴, **litter barrels, petwalk** |
| 66 | FM 1927, to Pyote |
| 58 | frontage rd, multiple oil wells |
| 52 | Lp 20 W, to Barstow |
| 49 | FM 516, to Barstow |
| 48mm | Pecos River |
| 44 | Collie Rd |
| 42 | US 285, Pecos, **N** gas: Chevron/24hr, Fina, ⊘ *FLYING J* /Conoco/dsl/scales/24hr/@, Shell/dsl, Valero, **food:** DQ, El Rodeo Mexican, Panda House, Pizza Hut, **lodging:** Motel 6, Quality Inn, OakTree Inn, **other:** AutoZone, Walmart/24hr, museum, tire repair |
| 40 | Country Club Dr, **N** st patrol, **S** gas: Chevron/Subway, **lodging:** Best Western/rest., **other:** Chevrolet, RV camping, municipal park |
| 39 | TX 17, Pecos, **S** other: Chevrolet/Buick |
| 37 | Lp 20 E, **2 mi N food:** Sonic |
| 33 | FM 869 |
| 29 | Shaw Rd, **S** to TX AM Ag Sta |
| 25mm | **picnic area both lanes,** 🍴, **litter barrels,** ♿ **accessible** |
| 22 | FM 2903, to Toyah |
| 13 | McAlpine Rd |
| 7 | Johnson Rd |
| 3 | Stocks Rd |
| 0mm | I-20 begins/ends on I-10, 187mm. |

**E ↕ W**

**PECOS**

## INTERSTATE 27

**N ↕ S**

| Exit # | Services |
|---|---|
| | **I-27 begins/ends on I-40, exit 70 in Amarillo.** |
| 123b | I-40, W to Albuquerque, E to OK City |
| 123a | 26th Ave, **E** gas: Fina, **W** food: DJ Burgers, La Campana Mexican |
| 122c | from sb only |
| 122b | 34th Ave, Tyler St, **E** gas: Conoco, Shell, Valero, **food:** Sonic |
| 122a | FM 1541, Washington St, Parker St, Moss Lane, **W** food: Hungry Howie's |
| 121b | Hawthorne Dr, Austin St, **E** lodging: Amarillo Motel, **other:** Honda Motorcycles, **W** other: Scottie's Transmissions |

**AMARILLO**

| | |
|---|---|
| 121a | Georgia St, **E** gas: Phillips 66/dsl, **food:** BBQ, Waffle House, **other:** Buick/Pontiac/GMC, Honda, Mazda, Nissan, Sizemore RV, Subaru, Toyota, Walmart SuperCtr/gas |
| 120b | 45th Ave, **E** gas: Fina, **food:** Waffle House, **other:** repair, **W** gas: Exxon, Valero, **food:** Abuelo's Mexican, Burger King (.5mi), Gatti's Pizza, Grand Burger, McDonald's, Whataburger, **other:** Advance Parts, BMW, Dodge, $General, Drug Emporium |
| 120a | Republic Ave |
| 119b | Western St, 58th Ave, **E** gas: Phillips 66, **food:** Sonic, **other:** $General, **W** gas: Shell/dsl, Valero, **food:** Arby's, Braum's, LJ Silver, Ming Palace Chinese, Pizza Hut, Wendy's, **other:** Aamco, Stout RV Ctr, U-Haul, USPO |
| 119a | W Hillside |
| 117 | Bell St, Arden Rd, **E** other: transmissions, **W** gas: Shell/24hr, **food:** Burger Palace, LJ Silver, Popeye's, Sonic, **other:** $General |
| 116 | Lp 335, Hollywood Rd, **E** gas: Love's/Subway/dsl/24hr, Phillips 66/dsl, **food:** McDonald's, Waffle House, Whataburger, **lodging:** Comfort Suites, Day's Inn, **W** other: H HOSPITAL (8mi) |
| 115 | Sundown Lane |
| 113 | McCormick Rd, **E** other: Ford, **W** other: Family Camping Ctr |
| 112 | FM 2219, **E** other: Stater's RV Ctr |
| 111 | Rockwell Rd, **E** other: Chevrolet, **W** other: Buick/GMC/Pontiac |
| 110 | (from sb) US 87 S, US 60 W, Canyon |
| 109 | Buffalo Stadium Rd, **W** stadium |
| 108 | FM 3331, Hunsley Rd |
| 106 | TX 217, to Palo Duro Cyn SP, Canyon, **E** other: Palo Duro RV Park, RV camping, **W** lodging: Holiday Inn Express (2mi), **other:** Plains Museum, to WTA&M |
| 103 | FM 1541 N, Cemetery Rd |
| 99 | Hungate Rd |
| 98mm | **parking area both lanes, litter barrels** |
| 96 | Dowlen Rd |
| 94 | FM 285, to Wayside |
| 92 | Haley Rd |
| 90 | FM 1075, Happy, **W** gas/dsl |
| 88b a | US 87 N, FM 1881, Happy, same as 90 |
| 83 | FM 2698 |
| 82 | FM 214 |
| 77 | US 87, Tulia, **1-2 mi E** gas: Phillips 66, **food:** Pizza Hut, Sonic, **lodging:** Lasso Inn, **other:** H HOSPITAL, Ford, ✈ |

**TX**

## INTERSTATE 27 CONT'D

| | |
|---|---|
| **75** | NW 6th St, Tulia, **1 mi E gas:** Phillips 66, Shell, **food:** DQ, Pizza Hut, Sonic, **lodging:** Lasso Motel, **W** same as 74 |
| **74** | TX 86, Tulia, **E lodging:** Lasso Motel, **other:** H HOSPITAL, **W gas:** Rip Griffin/Phillips 66/Subway/Chester's/dsl/scales/24hr/@, **lodging:** Select Inn |
| **70mm** | **parking area both lanes, litter barrels** |
| **68** | FM 928 |
| **63** | FM 145, Kress, **1 mi E** gas/dsl, food, phone |
| **61** | US 87, County Rd |
| **56** | FM 788 |
| **54** | FM 3183, to Plainview, **W** truck service |
| **53** | Lp 27, Plainview, **E other:** H HOSPITAL, access to gas, camping, food, lodging |
| **51** | Quincy St |
| **50** | TX 194, Plainview, **E gas:** Phillips 66, **other:** H HOSPITAL, to Wayland Bapt U |
| **49** | US 70, Plainview, **E gas:** Allstar Fuel/dsl, Conoco, Fina/dsl, Valero/dsl, Shell/dsl, **food:** Alfredo Italian, Carlito's Mexican, China Dragon, Cotton Patch Café, Domino's, Far East Chinese, Furr's Café, Kettle, Leal's Mexican, LJ Silver/A&W, Pizza Hut, Sonic, Thai Taste, Tokyo Steaks, **lodging:** Best Western, Comfort Suites, Day's Inn, **other:** Beall's, Buick/Pontiac/Cadillac/GMC, Chrysler/Jeep, $Tree, Ford/Lincoln/Mercury/Toyota, GNC, Hastings Books, NAPA, O'Reilly Parts, Pinnell Drug, Radio Shack, United Foods, **W gas:** Chevron, Phillips 66/dsl, 76, **food:** Burger King, Chicken Express, Chili's, IHOP, Little Mexico, McDonald's, New China, Quizno's, Sonic, Starbucks, Subway, Taco Bell, Wendy's, **lodging:** Best Value, Holiday Inn Express, **other:** JC Penney, Walmart SuperCtr/gas |
| **45** | Lp 27, to Plainview |
| **43** | FM 2337 |
| **41** | County Rd |
| **38** | Main St |
| **37** | FM 1914, Cleveland St, **E gas:** Co-op, **food:** Sylvia's Cafe, **W** H HOSPITAL |
| **36** | FM 1424, Hale Center |
| **32** | FM 37 W |
| **31** | FM 37 E |
| **29mm** | **rest area both lanes, full** ♿ **facilities,** 🕿 🚻**, litter barrels, petwalk, tornado shelter** |
| **27** | County Rd |
| **24** | FM 54, **W** RV park/dump |
| **22** | Lp 369, Abernathy, **W** Filling Sta Cafe/dsl |
| **21** | FM 597, Main St, Abernathy, **W gas:** Conoco/dsl, **food:** DQ, Shady's BBQ, **other:** $General, USPO |
| **20** | Abernathy (from nb) |
| **17** | County Rd 53 |
| **15** | Lp 461, to New Deal, same as 14 |
| **14** | FM 1729, **E gas:** Fina/rest./dsl/scales/24hr |
| **13** | Lp 461, to New Deal |
| **12** | access rd (from nb) |
| **11** | FM 1294, Shallowater |
| **10** | Keuka St, **E other:** DHL, Fed Ex |
| **9** | Airport Rd, **E** ✈, **W other:** Lubbock RV Park/LP/dump |
| **8** | FM 2641, Regis St |
| **7** | Yucca Lane, **E** Pharr RV Ctr |
| **6b a** | Lp 289, Ave Q, Lubbock, **E other:** Pharr RV |

| | |
|---|---|
| **5** | B. Holly Ave, Municipal Dr, **E other:** Mackenzie Park |
| **4** | US 82, US 87, 4th St, to Crosbyton, **W gas:** ⊕ FLYING J/CountryMkt/dsl/24hr/@, **other:** to TTU |
| **3** | US 62, TX 114, 19th St |
| **2** | 34th St, **E gas:** Phillips 66, **food:** Pete's Drive Inn, **W food:** Simple Simon's Pizza, **other:** AutoZone, Hall Drug, I-27 RV Ctr |
| **1c** | 50th St, **E gas:** Fina, **food:** El Jalapeno Café, Prince Castle, **W gas:** Bolton Fuel, Conoco, Valero, **food:** Bryan's Steaks, Burger King, China Star, Church's, DQ, Domino's, Grand Buffet, KFC, LJ Silver/A&W, McDonald's, Pinocchio's Pizza, Pizza Hut/Taco Bell, Subway, Taco Villa, Whataburger, Wienerschnitzel, **lodging:** Howard Johnson, **other:** Chrysler/Jeep, $General, O'Reilly Parts, United Food/drug/gas, USPO, Walgreen, Woody Tire |
| **1b** | US 84, **E lodging:** Circus Inn, Day's Inn, **W lodging:** Best Western, Comfort Inn, Holiday Inn Express, Motel 6, Quality Inn, Ramada, Super 8, Value Place |
| **1a** | Lp 289 |
| **1** | 82nd St, **W gas:** Phillips 66 |

**I-27 begins/ends on US 87 at 82nd St in S Lubbock.**

## INTERSTATE 30

| Exit # | Services |
|---|---|
| **223mm** | Texas/Arkansas state line |
| **223b a** | US 59, US 71, State Line Ave, Texarkana, **N gas:** Citgo/dsl, EZ Mart, Mobil, Shell, Speedway, **food:** Cajun Harbor, Denny's, IHOP, Pizza Inn, Red Lobster, Waffle House, **lodging:** Best Western, Budget Host, Clarion, Comfort Suites, Holiday Inn, Hampton Inn, Holiday Inn Express, La Quinta, Quality Inn, Sheraton, Super 8, **other:** Firestone/Auto, KOA, tires, **S gas:** Exxon, RaceWay, Shell, State Line Gas, **food:** Arby's, Backyard Burger, Baskin-Robbins, Burger King, Cattleman's Steaks, China King, Colima's Mexican, El Chico, KFC, La Carreta Mexican, Little Caesars, LJ Silver, Mandarin House, McDonald's, Papa John's, Pizza Hut, Pizza Inn, Popeye's, Quizno's, Schlotsky's, Subway, Taco Bell, Taco Tico, Wendy's, Whataburger/24hr, **lodging:** Ambassador Inn, Best Value, Best Western, Comfort Inn, Day's Inn, Econolodge, Economy Inn, Executive Inn, Express Inn, Knight's Inn, La Quinta, Motel 6, **other:** Albertson's, AutoZone, Chevrolet/Buick, Jeep, Radio Shack, Suzuki, Walmart SuperCtr, Walgreen |
| **223mm** | **Welcome Ctr wb, full** ♿ **facilities, info,** 🕿 🚻**, litter barrels, vending, petwalk** |
| **222** | TX 93, FM 1397, Summerhill Rd, **N gas:** Shell, Valero/Subway/dsl, **food:** Amigo Juan's, Applebee's, McDonald's, Shogun Japanese, Waffle House, **lodging:** Motel 6, **other:** Ford/Freightliner, Goodyear/auto, Honda, **S gas:** Shell/24hr, **food:** Bryce's Rest., **other:** Buick/Pontiac/GMC, Curves, Ford, Mazda/Nissan/GMC, Mercedes |
| **220b** | FM 559, Richmond Rd, **N gas:** Chevron, Exxon, Shell, **food:** Buffalo Wild Wings, Burger King, Carino's Italian, Cracker Barrel, Chick-fil-a, Cici's Pizza, DQ, Domino's, Jumbo Chinese, Little Caesars, McAlister's Deli, On-the-Border, Pizza Hut, Popeye's, Randy's BBQ, Red Lobster, Ruby Tuesday, Sonic, Starbucks, Taco Bell, Ta-Molly's Mexican, Texas Roadhouse, Wendy's, **lodging:** Comfort Suites, Courtyard, TownePlace Suites, **other:** Best Buy, Chevrolet, Discount Tire, $Tree, Gander Mtn, |

**TX** (vertical tab, left margin)

**N / S  PLAINVIEW**

**E / W  TEXARKANA**

## INTERSTATE 30 CONT'D

**E ↕ W**

**N E W B O S T O N**

**220b** Continued
Home Depot, Hyundai, Kohls, Old Navy, PetsMart, Sam's Club/gas, Staples, Super 1 Food/gas, Target, TJ Maxx, **S gas:** Valero/dsl, **food:** Arby's, Chili's, ChuckeCheese, El Chico, Golden Corral, Grandy's, Lee's Chinese, Luby's, McDonald's, Olive Garden, Outback Steaks, Quizno's, Subway/Baskin-Robbins, **lodging:** Hampton Inn, **other:** AutoZone, Albertson's, Books-A-Million, Buick/Pontiac/GMC, Cavender's Boots, Dillard's, JC Penney, Jeep, Mazda, Michael's, Office Depot, Ross, Saturn, Sears/auto, Walgreen, mall

**220a** US 59 S, Texarkana, **S gas:** Exxon/Wendy's, **food:** DQ, Subway, **other:** Lowe's Whse, Radio Shack, Walmart SuperCtr/gas, mall

**218** FM 989, Nash, **N gas:** Road Runner/dsl, **food:** Dixie Diner, **other:** McKinnon RV Ctr, **S gas:** Exxon/Burger King/dsl, **other:** Peterbilt/GMC, to Lake Patman

**213** FM 2253, Leary, **N other:** Palma RV Ctr

**212** spur 74, Lone Star Army Ammo Plant, **S gas:** Shell

**208** FM 560, Hooks, **N gas:** Texaco/dsl/24hr, **food:** Old Farm Mkt/BBQ, **other:** Hooks Camper Ctr., **S gas:** Texaco/Subway/dsl/scales/24hr, **food:** DQ, Sonic, Tastee-House Rest., **other:** Family$, tires

**206** TX 86, **S other:** Red River Army Depot

**201** TX 8, New Boston, **N gas:** Shell/dsl, Valero, **food:** Pitt Grill, **lodging:** Tex Inn, **other:** Chevrolet, Chrysler/Jeep/Dodge, **S gas:** Shell, **food:** Catfish King, Church's, DQ, KFC/Taco Bell, McDonald's, Nana's Diner, Pizza Hut, Randy's BBQ, Sonic, **lodging:** Best Western, Bostonian Inn, Holiday Inn Express, **other:** H HOSPITAL, Brookshire's Foods/gas, Curves, CVS Drug, Ford/Mercury, Walmart SuperCtr/gas, RV park

**199** US 82, DeKalb, **1/2 mi N gas:** Shell

**198** TX 98, **1/2 mi N gas:** Shell

**193mm** Anderson Creek

**192** FM 990, **N gas:** FuelStop/Culpeppers Rest/dsl

**191mm** rest area both lanes, full ♿ facilities, 📞, 🍴, litter barrels, vending, petwalk

**186** FM 561

**181mm** Sulphur River

**178** US 259, to DeKalb, Omaha

**174mm** White Oak Creek

**170** FM 1993

**165** FM 1001, **S gas:** Exxon/dsl

**M T  P L E A S A N T**

**162b a** US 271, FM 1402, FM 2152, Mt Pleasant, **N gas:** Exxon/dsl/24hr, **food:** Applebee's, Blalock BBQ, Pitt Grill, **lodging:** Holiday Inn Express, Super 8, **other:** KOA, **S gas:** Shell/dsl, Valero/Subway/dsl, **food:** Burger King, DQ, Luigi's Italian, McDonald's, **lodging:** Best Western/rest., **other:** H HOSPITAL, Chevrolet/Cadillac, Family$, vet

**160** US 271, FM 1734, Mt Pleasant, **N gas:** BP/dsl, **food:** Senorita's Mexican, **other:** Buick/Pontiac/GMC (1mi), Lowe's Whse, Toyota, **S gas:** Exxon/dsl, Shell/dsl, **food:** El Chico, Western Sizzlin, **lodging:** Comfort Inn, Day's Inn, Executive Inn

**158mm** weigh sta both lanes

**156** frontage rd

**153** spur 185, to Winfield, Millers Cove, **N gas:** BP/dsl, Chevron, Winfield Trkstp/dsl/café, **other:** dsl repair, **S gas:** Shamrock/dsl

**150** Ripley Rd, **N other:** Lowe's Distribution

**147** spur 423, **N gas:** Love's/Subway/dsl/scales/24hr, **lodging:** American Inn, Economy Inn

**146** TX 37, Mt Vernon, **N gas:** Shell/dsl, **other:** H HOSPITAL, **S gas:** Exxon/dsl, Fina/dsl/24hr, **food:** Burger King, DQ, Mt Vernon Cafe, **lodging:** Super 8, **other:** to Lake Bob Sandlin SP, auto repair

**143** rest area both lanes, full ♿ facilities, 📞, 🍴, litter barrels, vending, petwalk

**142** County Line Rd (from eb)

**141** FM 900, Saltillo Rd

**136** FM 269, Weaver Rd

**135** US 67 N

**131** FM 69

**127** US 67, Lp 301, **N lodging:** Budget Inn, Comfort Inn, Days Inn, Holiday Inn, **other:** H HOSPITAL, **S gas:** Shell, **food:** Burton's Rest./24hr, **lodging:** Best Western

**126** FM 1870, College St, **S gas:** Exxon, **food:** Burton's Rest./24hr, **lodging:** Best Western, **other:** Firestone/auto, same as 127

**125** Bill Bradford Rd, same as 124

**124** TX 11, TX 154, Sulphur Springs, **N gas:** Chevron/dsl, Exxon/Quizno's/A&W, **food:** BBQ, Broadway Buffet, Chicken Express, Domino's, John's Diner, KFC, La Familia Mexican, Peddlar's Pizza, Pitt Grill, Pizza Hut, Popeye's, San Rimo Italian, Sonic, Subway, TaMolly's Mexican, **lodging:** Holiday Inn Express, Royal Inn, **other:** H HOSPITAL, AutoZone, Brookshire's Food/gas, Cadillac, Chevrolet/Buick/GMC, Chrysler/Jeep, Curves, CVS Drug, $General, Family$, Ford, FSA Outlet/famous brands, Nissan, O'Reilly Parts, USPO, **S gas:** Exxon/dsl, Shell, **food:** Braum's, Burger King, Chili's, Dominos, Furr's Rest., Jack-in-the-Box, K-Bob's Steaks, McDonald's, Pizza Inn, Taco Bell/LJ Silver, Whataburger, **lodging:** Holiday King Motel, **other:** Discount Tire, Eckerd, Fred's Drug, Lowe's Whse, Radio Shack, Walmart SuperCtr/gas (1mi), factory outlet

**123** FM 2297, League St, **N gas:** Chevron/dsl, Shell

**122** TX 19, to Emory, **N gas:** Chevron, **other:** H HOSPITAL, **S gas:** Phillips 66/dsl/rest./24hr, Pilot/Arby's/dsl/scales/24hr/@, **other:** Shady Lake RV Park (2mi), to Cooper Lake

**120** US 67 bus

**116** FM 2653, Brashear Rd

**112** FM 499 (from wb)

**110** FM 275, Cumby, **N gas:** Phillips 66, **S gas:** Shell/24hr

**S U L P H U R  S P R I N G S**

**TX**

## INTERSTATE 30 CONT'D

**E** ↕ **W**

**GREENVILLE**

**TX**

**DALLAS**

| | |
|---|---|
| 104 | FM 513, FM 2649, Campbell, **S** to Lake Tawakoni |
| 101 | TX 24, TX 50, FM 1737, to Commerce, **N gas:** Valero/dsl, **other:** to E TX St U |
| 97 | Lamar St, **N gas:** Exxon/dsl, **lodging:** Budget Inn, Dream Lodge Motel |
| 96 | Lp 302 |
| 95 | Division St, **S other:** H HOSPITAL, Puddin Hill Fruit Cakes |
| 94b | US 69, US 380, Greenville, **N gas:** Valero/dsl, **food:** Ninja's Grill, Senorita's Mexican, **lodging:** American Inn, Best Western, Royal Inn, **other:** Hyundai, **S gas:** Exxon, Fina/dsl, **food:** Arby's, Burger King, Catfish Cove Rest., McDonald's, **lodging:** Econolodge, Economy Inn, Motel 6, Quality Inn, Super 8 |
| 94a | US 69, US 380, Greenville, **N food:** Old Whiskers Buffet, **S gas:** Valero, **other:** Chrysler/Dodge/Jeep, Nissan |
| 93b a | US 67, TX 34 N, **N gas:** Chevron, Exxon, **food:** Applebee's, Chick-fil-A, Chicken Express, CiCi's, Grandy's, IHOP, Jack-in-the-Box, KFC, LJ Silver/A&W, Pizza Hut, Popeye's, Royal Drive-In, Ryan's, Schlotsky's, Sonic, Soulman's Texmex, Starbucks, Steak Angus, Subway, Taco Bell, Taco Bueno, TCBY, Tony's Italian, Wendy's, Whataburger/24hr, **lodging:** Hampton Inn, **other:** H HOSPITAL, Ace Hardware, Belk, BigLots, Brookshire's Foods, Buick/Pontiac, Cadillac, Goody's, JC Penney, Lowes Whse, O'Reilly Parts, Staples, USPO, Walgreen, mall, **S gas:** Exxon/dsl/24hr, Valero/dsl, **food:** Chili's, Cracker Barrel, Dickey's BBQ, Eastrock Buffet, Paesano Italian, Red Lobster, Tamolly's Mexican, **lodging:** Holiday Inn Express, La Quinta, **other:** $Tree, Ford/Lincoln/Mercury, Home Depot, Mitsubishi, Radio Shack, RV Ctr, Walmart SuperCtr/gas |
| 90mm | Farber Creek |
| 89 | FM 1570, **S lodging:** Luxury Inn |
| 89mm | E Caddo Creek |
| 87 | FM 1903, **N gas:** Chevron/Pizza Inn/dsl, **other:** fireworks, **S gas:** Exxon/Pancake House/dsl, Pilot/McDonald's/dsl/scales/24hr, **other:** tire repair |
| 87mm | Elm Creek |
| 85 | FM 36, Caddo Mills, **N** KOA |
| 85mm | W Caddo Creek |
| 83 | FM 1565 N, **N gas:** Exxon/dsl |
| 79 | FM 2642, **N** Budget RV Ctr |
| 77b | FM 35, Royse City, **N gas:** Exxon/dsl, Texaco/Subway/dsl/scales/24hr/@, **food:** Soulman's BBQ, **other:** Family$ |
| 77a | TX 548, Royse City, **N gas:** Shell/dsl, **food:** Jack-in-the-Box, McDonald's, **lodging:** Sun Royse Inn, **other:** tires, **S gas:** Exxon/KFC/Quizno's, **food:** Sonic, **other:** Royce City Hardware, auto repair |
| 73 | FM 551, Fate |
| 70 | FM 549, **S gas:** Love's/Carl's Jr./dsl/scales/24hr |
| 69 | (from wb), frontage rd, **N** Super 8 |
| 68 | TX 205, to Rock Wall, **N gas:** RaceWay, Shell, **food:** Braum's, DQ, Jowilly's Grill, KFC, Luigi's Italian, Pizza Hut, Pizza Inn, Subway, Whataburger, **lodging:** Holiday Inn Express, Super 8, Value Place, **other:** Chevrolet, Dodge, Ford/Mercury, **S gas:** TA/Burger King/Starbucks/dsl/rest./24hr/scales/@, Valero/dsl |
| 67 | FM 740, Ridge Rd, **N gas:** Chevron, Mobil, Shell, **food:** Arby's, Burger King, Carrabba's, Culver's, Dominos, |

| | |
|---|---|
| 67 | Continued Grandy's, IHOP, McDonald's, Schlotsky's, Steak&Shake, Waffle House, Wendy's, **other:** Goodyear/auto, Kwik Kar Lube, Walmart SuperCtr, cleaners, **S gas:** Chevron, Exxon/Pizza Inn, Shamrock/dsl, Shell, **food:** Applebee's, Bahama Buck's Ice Cream, Blackeyed Pea, Buffalo Wild Wings, Carino's Italian, Chick-fil-A, Chili's, ChuckeCheese, CiCi's Pizza, El Chico, Jack-in-the-Box, McDonald's, On-the-Border, Sonic, Starbucks, Subway, Taco Bell/Pizza Hut, TCBY, TGIFriday's, **lodging:** Country Inn Suites, **other:** Albertson's, BestBuy, Circuit City, Discount Tire, $Tree, Eckerd, GNC, Home Depot, Kohl's, Lowe's Whse, Michael's, Old Navy, PetCo, Radio Shack, Ross, Staples, SteinMart, Target, Walgreen, to Lake Tawakoni, vet |
| 67a | Horizon Rd, Village Dr, **N gas:** Shamrock, **food:** Café Express, RanchHouse Rest., Saltgrass Steaks, Culpeper Cattle Steaks, **lodging:** Hilton Garden |
| 66mm | Ray Hubbard Reservoir |
| 64 | Dalrock Rd, Rowlett, **N gas:** Exxon, Valero/dsl, **lodging:** Comfort Suites, **other:** H HOSPITAL, Express Drug |
| 63mm | Ray Hubbard Reservoir |
| 62 | Bass Pro Rd, **N lodging:** Best Western, **other:** to Hubbard RA, **S gas:** Shell, **other:** Bass Pro Shop |
| 61 | Zion Rd (from wb), **N gas:** Conoco/dsl, Texaco, **lodging:** Jack-in-the-Box, **lodging:** Discovery Inn |
| 60b | Bobtown Rd (eb only), **N gas:** Shell **food:** Jack-in-the-Box |
| 60a | Rose Hill Dr |
| 59 | Beltline Rd, Garland, **N gas:** Conoco, QT, 7-11/gas, **food:** Chili's, Denny's, India Morning, KFC, LJ Silver, McDonald's, QT, Starbucks, Subway, Taco Bell/Pizza Hut, Taco Casa, Taco Cabana, Tuesday Morning, Whataburger, Wendy's, **other:** Albertson's, $General, GNC, Radio Shack, Walgreen, Walmart SuperCtr, **S gas:** Shell/dsl, **food:** Baker's Ribs, Buffet King, Burger King, DQ, Grandy's, Sonic, Waffle House, Williams Chicken, **lodging:** Day's Inn, I-30 Inn, Motel 6, **other:** Kroger |
| 58 | Northwest Dr, **N gas:** Shell, Valero/dsl, **other:** Nissan, **S gas:** Fina, **food:** Jack-in-the-Box, **other:** Lowe's Whse |
| 56c b | I-635 S-N |
| 56a | Galloway Ave, Gus Thomasson Dr (from eb), **N food:** KFC, **S food:** Celebration Sta, Checker's, Circuit City, Grandy's, Hooters, Kroger, Olive Garden, Outback Steaks, Posades Cafe, Red Lobster, Steak&Ale, TGIFriday, Luby's, On-the-Border, Subway, Wendy's, **lodging:** Courtyard, Crossland Suites, Delux Inn, Fairfield Inn, **other:** H HOSPITAL, BigLots, Nichols RV Ctr, other multiple services, Bigtown Mall |
| 55 | Motley Dr, **N gas:** Shell/dsl, **food:** Castillo Mexican, **lodging:** Astro Inn, Executive Inn, **S gas:** Chevron, **food:** Mesquite Grill, **lodging:** Microtel, **other:** H HOSPITAL, Dodge, to Eastfield Coll |
| 54 | Big Town Blvd, **N gas:** Valero/dsl, **lodging:** Mesquite Inn, **S other:** Affordable RV Ctr |
| 53b | US 80 E (from eb), to Terrell, **N** Toyota |
| 53a | Lp 12, **N lodging:** Lamplighter Motel, Super 8, **other:** Chevrolet, **S food:** CiCi's, Taco Cabana, Whataburger, **lodging:** Holiday Inn Express, **other:** $Tree, Ford, Sam's Club, Staples, Walmart SuperCtr/gas |
| 51 | (52 a from wb), Highland Rd, **N gas:** Exxon, **food:** Country China, Denny's, Kettle, Luby's, McDonald's, |

## INTERSTATE 30 CONT'D

**E ← → W** **D A L L A S**

| | |
|---|---|
| **51** | Continued |
| | Owen's Rest., **lodging:** La Quinta, **S gas:** RaceWay, Shell/dsl, **food:** Burger King, Capt D's, Furr's Dining, Grandy's, KFC, Pizza Hut, Popeye's, Taco Bell, Wendy's, **lodging:** Exel Inn, Howard Johnson, Motel 6, Super 7 Inn, **other:** AutoZone, CVS Drug |
| **50b a** | Ferguson Rd, **N gas:** Texaco, **S other:** Brake-O, U-Haul |
| **49b** | Dolphin Rd, Lawnview Ave, Samuell Ave, **N lodging:** Best Value Inn |
| **49a** | Winslow St, **N gas:** Circle K/gas, Shell/dsl/repair, **food:** McDonald's, **S gas:** Shell/24hr |
| **48b** | TX 78, E Grand, **S** fairpark, arboretum |
| **48a** | Carroll Ave, Central Ave, Peak St, Haskell Ave, **N gas:** Valero, **other:** H HOSPITAL, tires, **S gas:** Fina, **food:** Joe's Burgers |
| **47** | 2nd Ave, **S food:** McDonald's, **other:** Cotton Bowl, fairpark |
| **46b** | I-45, US 75, to Houston |
| **46a** | Central Expswy, downtown |
| **45** | I-35E, N to Denton, to Commerce St, Lamar St, Griffin St, **S gas:** Fina, **food:** McDonald's, **lodging:** Ramada Inn |
| **44b** | I-35E S, Industrial Blvd |
| **44a** | I-35E N, Beckley Ave (from eb) |
| **43b a** | Sylvan Ave (from wb), **N gas:** Shell/Quizno's/dsl, **other:** H HOSPITAL, Family$, USPO/24hr |
| **42** | Hampton Rd N, **1 mi N food:** Burger King, KFC/Taco Bell |
| **41** | Hampton Rd S (no EZ eb return), **N gas:** Mobil, **S gas:** Exxon, Shell, **food:** Jack-in-the-Box, DQ, Luby's, Wendy's, **other:** AutoZone, Goodyear/auto, O'Reilly Parts |
| **39** | Cockrell Hill Rd |
| **38** | Lp 12, **N gas:** Exxon, **food:** Burger King |
| **36** | MacArthur Blvd, **S other:** U-Haul |
| **34** | Belt Line Rd, **N gas:** Chevron, **lodging:** Day's Inn, Motel 6, Ramada Ltd, **other:** Ford, Ripley's Museum, **S gas:** Shell/Subway, Valero, **food:** DQ, McDonald's |
| **32** | NW 19th, **N gas:** Valero, **S gas:** Mobil, **food:** Denny's, McDonald's, Pizza Hut, Taco Bell, Whataburger, **lodging:** La Quinta |
| **30** | TX 360, Six Flags Dr, Arlington Stadium, **N gas:** Shell, **food:** Grand Buffet, Ninfa's Café, Saltgrass Steaks, TrailDust Steaks, Candlewood Suites, **lodging:** Day's Inn, Fairfield Inn, Flagship Inn, Hilton, Park Inn, Radisson Suites, **other:** Studio+, Super 8, Wingate Inn, **S gas:** Shell/dsl, Valero, **food:** Denny's, Jack-in-the-Box, Luby's, McDonald's, Owen's Rest., Steak&Ale, **lodging:** Baymont Inn, La Quinta, **other:** Dillard's, JC Penney, K-Mart, Sears/auto, Six Flags Funpark, mall |
| **29** | Ball Park Way, **N gas:** Chevron, **food:** Frijoles Café, Grady's Grill, Macaroni Grill, TrailDust Steaks, **lodging:** Fairfield Inn, **other:** Toyota, **S gas:** Fina/dsl, **food:** On-the-Border, Texas Steaks, **lodging:** Howard Johnson, Marriott, Stadium Inn, Wyndham Hotel, **other:** Six Flags Funpark |
| **28b** | TX 157, Nolan Ryan Expswy, **N gas:** Mobil, **food:** Waffle House, **lodging:** Country Inn Suites, **S food:** Chili's, Cozymel's, Harrigan's Grill, Joe's Crabshack, Landry's Seafood, Olive Garden, Pappadeaux Seafood, **lodging:** Courtyard, Day's Inn, **other:** Wyndham Garden, **other:** Barnes&Noble, SteinMart, TX Stadium |
| **28a** | FM 157, Collins St, **N food:** Whataburger, **other:** H HOSPITAL, Dodge, **S food:** Pappasito's Cantina, **other:** Home Depot |

**F T W O R T H**

| | |
|---|---|
| **27** | Lamar Blvd, Cooper St, **N gas:** Mobil, **food:** Jack-in-the-Box, **other:** CVS Drug, Kroger, **S gas:** 7-11, Shell, **food:** Burger King, Denny's |
| **26** | Fielder Rd, **S other:** to Six Flags (from eb) |
| **25mm** | Village Creek |
| **24** | Eastchase Pkwy, **N food:** Jack-in-the-Box, **other:** Car-Max, Sam's Club/gas, Walmart SuperCtr, **S gas:** Chevron, Shell/dsl, **food:** IHOP, McDonald's, Whataburger, **other:** Office Depot, Old Navy, Ross, Target |
| **23** | Cooks Lane, **S gas:** Mobil |
| **21c** | Bridgewood Dr, **N gas:** Mobil, Shell, **food:** Luby's, Wendy's, **other:** Discount Tire, Home Depot, Kroger, U-Haul, **S gas:** Shell/dsl/24hr, Valero, **food:** Burger King, McDonald's, Pizza Hut, Taco Bueno, Whataburger/24hr |
| **21b a** | I-820 |
| **19** | Brentwood Stair Rd (from eb), **N gas:** Chevron, Shell/dsl, **food:** Chuy's Mexican, Steak&Ale, **other:** Kroger, **S gas:** Shell |
| **18** | Oakland Blvd, **N gas:** Phillips 66, Shell/dsl, **food:** Burger King, Taco Bell, Waffle House, **lodging:** Motel 6 |
| **16c** | Beach St, **S gas:** 7-11, **lodging:** Ambassador Hotel, Best Western |
| **16b a** | Riverside Dr (from wb), **S lodging:** Great Western Inn |
| **15b a** | I-35W N to Denton, S to Waco |
| **14b** | Jones St, Commerce St, Ft Worth, downtown |
| **14a** | TX 199, Henderson St, Ft Worth, downtown |
| **13b** | Summit Ave, downtown |
| **13a** | 8th Ave, downtown |
| **12d** | Forest Park Blvd, **N food:** Pappadeaux Café, Pappasito's, **S other:** H HOSPITAL |
| **12b** | Rosedale St |
| **12a** | University Dr, City Parks, **S lodging:** SpringHill Suites |
| **11** | Montgomery St, **S gas:** Shell/dsl, **food:** Whataburger, **other:** visitor info |
| **10** | Hulen St, Ft Worth, **S food:** Chick-fil-A, Coldstone, Micocina, **other:** Borders Books, WorldMkt |
| **9b** | US 377, Camp Bowie Blvd, Horne St, **N food:** Uncle Julio's Mexican, **S gas:** Exxon, Fina, 7-11/gas, Shell, Texaco/dsl, **food:** Jack-in-the-Box, Mexican Inn, Pizza Hut/Taco Bell, Szechuan Chinese, Subway, Taco Bueno, Wendy's |
| **9a** | Bryant-Irvin Rd, **S gas:** Shell, same as 9b |
| **8b** | Ridgmar, Ridglea, **N gas:** Valero/dsl |
| **8a** | TX 183, Green Oaks Rd, **N food:** Applebee's, Chili's, Don Pablo, Grand Buffet, Jack-in-the-Box, Olive Garden, Quizno's, Starbucks, Taco Bueno, |

## INTERSTATE 30 CONT'D

**8a** Continued
lodging: Courtyard, other: Albertson's, Best Buy, $Tree, Dillard's, Firestone/auto, JC Penney, Macy's, Neiman Marcus, NTB, Office Depot, Old Navy, PetsMart, Ross, Sam's Club/gas, Sears/auto, U-Haul, Walmart SuperCtr, **S** food: Tommy's Burgers, lodging: Comfort Suites, Green Oaks Hotel, Hampton Inn

**7b a** Cherry Lane, TX 183, spur 341, to Green Oaks Rd, **N** gas: Conoco, Shell, Valero, food: ChuckeCheese, IHOP/24hr, Luby's, Popeye's, Ryan's, Subway, Taco Bell, Wendy's, lodging: Days Inn, La Quinta, Super 8, other: Big Lots, Ford, Home Depot, O'Reilly Parts, U-Haul, Walmart/auto, **S** lodging: Hampton Inn, Holiday Inn Express, Quality Inn, other: Dodge, Mitsubishi, Nissan, Target

**6** Las Vegas Trail, **N** gas: Chevron/24hr, food: McDonald's, Waffle House, lodging: Day's Inn, other: Acura, Lincoln/Mercury, vet, **S** gas: Shell/dsl, Texaco, Valero/dsl, food: Pancake House, lodging: Best Budget Suites, Comfort Inn, Courtesy Inn, Motel 6, other: AutoZone, Kia

**5b c** I-820 S and N

**5a** Alemeda St (from eb, no EZ return)

**3** RM 2871, Chapel Creek Blvd

**2** spur 580 E

**1b** Linkcrest Dr, **S** gas: Chevron/dsl, Mobil/dsl

**0mm** I-20 W. I-30 begins/ends on I-20, exit 421.

## INTERSTATE 35

| Exit # | Services |
|---|---|
| **504mm** | Texas/Oklahoma state line, Red River |
| **504** | frontage rd, access to Texas Welcome Ctr |
| **503mm** | parking area both lanes |
| **502** | Welcome Ctr sb, full ♿ facilities, TX Tourist Bureau/info, 📞 🎁, litter barrels, wireless internet |

**501** FM 1202, Prime Outlets Blvd, **E** other: Chrysler/Dodge/Jeep, Ford/Mercury, **W** gas: Conoco/dsl/café, food: Applebee's, Cracker Barrel, lodging: Hampton Inn, La Quinta, other: Prime Outlets/famous brands, Western Outfitter, Harper's Steaks, RV camping

**500** FM 372, Gainesville, **W** gas: Hitchin' Post/Shell/dsl

**498b a** US 82, to Wichita Falls, Gainesville, Sherman, **E** gas: Exxon, Phillips 66/dsl, Shell/dsl, Valero/dsl, food: Catfish Louie's, CiCi's, Subway, Whatburger/24hr, lodging: Bed&Bath Inn, Budget Host, Comfort Inn, Delux Inn, Super 8, 12 Oaks Inn, other: Ⓗ HOSPITAL, Firestone, **W** gas: Exxon/dsl, lodging: Comfort Suites, Day's Inn, Fairfield Inn, Rodeway Inn

**497** frontage rd, **W** gas: Valero/dsl

**496b** TX 51, FM 51, California St, Gainesville, **E** gas: Chevron, Conoco/dsl, food: Arby's, Braum's, IHOP, McDonald's, Starbucks, Taco Bell, Taco Casa, Sonic, Wendy's, lodging: Holiday Inn Express, Quality Inn, other: Cadillac, Dodge, Goodyear/auto, Mkt Place Foods, N Central TX Coll, **W** food: Chili's

**496a** to Weaver St

**496mm** Elm Fork of the Trinity River

**495** frontage rd

**494** FM 1306

**492mm** picnic area sb, 🎁, litter barrels

**491** Spring Creek Rd

**490mm** picnic area nb, 🎁, litter barrels

**489** (488 from nb) FM 1307, to Hockley Creek Rd

**487** FM 922, Valley View, **W** gas: Chevron/dsl/24hr, food: Big Fatty's BBQ, DQ, other: USPO

**486** Fm 1307, **W** gas: Texaco/dsl, lodging: Valley View Inn

**485** frontage rd (from sb)

**483** FM 3002, Lone Oak Rd, **E** Shell/Subway/dsl, other: Roberts Lake SP

**482** Chisam Rd

**481** View Rd, **W** other: TX Sundown Ranch RV Park

**480** Lois Rd, **E** other: Walmart Dist Ctr

**479** Belz Rd, Sanger, same as 478

**478** FM 455, to Pilot Pt, Bolivar, **E** gas: QuikTrack, Shell, food: DQ, Migualito's Mexican, Sonic, Subway, lodging: Sanger Inn, other: USPO, **W** gas: Chevron/24hr, Fuel 4 TX/Chicken Express/dsl, food: Jack-in-the-Box, McDonald's, other: Chevrolet, Family$, IGA Foods, Kwikar Lube, O'Reilly Parts, RV Park, Ray Roberts Lake and SP

**477** Keaton Rd, **E** food: Smokey's BBQ, **W** gas: Shamrock/dsl, other: RV Ctr

**475b** Rector Rd

**475a** FM 156, to Krum

**474** Cowling rd (from nb)

**473** FM 3163, Milam Rd, **E** gas: Love's/Subway/dsl/24hr

**472** Ganzer Rd, **W** RV Sales

**471** US 77, FM 1173, Lp 282, to Denton, Krum, **E** gas: TA/Pizza Hut/Taco Bell/dsl/scales/24hr/@, food: Good Eats Café, other: Ⓗ HOSPITAL, **W** gas: Fina/dsl/café/scales/24hr, Texaco/dsl/scales/24hr/@, other: Foster's Western Shop, to Camping World RV Supply, Fun Time RV Ctr

**470** Lp 288, same services as 469 from sb

**469** US 380, University Dr, to Decatur, McKinney, **E** gas: Chevron/Subway, RaceTrac, food: Braum's, ChinaTown Café, Cracker Barrel, Luigi's Pizza, McDonald's, lodging: Best Western, Fairfield Inn, other: Albertson's/drugs, Office Depot, Toyota, **W** gas: Conoco/dsl, Shell/dsl, Valero, food: DQ, Denny's, Sonic, Waffle House, lodging: Exel Inn, Howard Johnson, Motel 6, Value Place Hotel, other: Ⓗ HOSPITAL, Camping World RV Supply, to TX Woman's U

**468** FM 1515, Airport Rd, W Oak St, **E** Ⓗ HOSPITAL

**467** I-35W, S to Ft Worth

I-35 divides into E and W sb, converges into I-35 nb. See Texas I-35 W.

**466b** Ave D, **E** gas: Exxon/dsl, food: Central Grill, Chicken Express, IHOP, McDonald's, NY Sub Hub, Pancho's Mexican, Taco Cabana, lodging: Comfort Suites, other: $General, Sack'n Save Foods, to NTSU

**466a** McCormick St, **E** gas: Phillips 66, Shell/dsl, lodging: Royal Inn, **W** gas: Fina/dsl/U-Haul

**465b** US 377, Ft Worth Dr, **E** gas: RaceTrac, Valero, food: Michael's Kitchen, Taco Bueno, Whataburger/24hr, lodging: La Quinta, **W** gas: Conoco, QuickTrack, food: Outback Steaks, Sonic, lodging: Day's Inn

**465a** FM 2181, Teasley Ln, **E** gas: 7-11, food: Applebee's, Braum's, Carino's, ChuckeCheese, Hooters, KFC, Little Caesar's, Pizza Hut, lodging: Hampton Inn, Holiday Inn, Quality Inn, other: Brookshires Foods, bank, **W** gas: Exxon, Shell, food: Rudy's BBQ/gas, lodging: Best Value Inn, Super 8

**464** US 77, Pennsylvania Dr, Denton, same as 463

## INTERSTATE 35 CONT'D

**N ↑↓ S**

**463** Lp 288, to McKinney, **E gas:** RaceTrac, **food:** Arby's, Burger King, Chick-fil-A, Colter's BBQ, Grandy's, Jason's Deli, KFC/Taco Bell, McAlister's Deli, Pizza Hut, On-the-Border, Sonic, Starbucks, Texas Roadhouse, Wendy's, Wienerschnitzel, **other:** Barnes&Noble, Big Lots, Burlington Coats, Circuit City, Dillards, Discount Tire, $Tree, Hastings Books, Home Depot, JC Penney, Kroger, Macy's, Office Depot, Old Navy, Ross, Sears/auto, Staples, PetCo, **W gas:** Chevron/dsl, **food:** Blackeyed Pea, Chili's, Jack-in-the-Box, Luby's, Red Lobster, Red Pepper's Rest., Schlotsky's, **other:** Albertson's, vet, same as 464

**462** State School Rd, Mayhill Rd, **E gas:** QT, Texaco/dsl, **food:** Dickey's BBQ, Olive Garden, **other:** H HOSPITAL, Hyundai, **W gas:** Chevron, Exxon/café, **food:** Shogun Japanese, Sonic, **other:** Albertsons, Buick/Pontiac/GMC, Cadillac, Chevrolet, Dodge, Honda, Toyota/Scion

**461** Sandy Shores Rd, Post Oak Dr, **E other:** Ford, McClain RV Ctr, **W other:** Chrysler/Jeep/Kia, Lincoln/Mercury/Mazda, Nissan

**460** Corinth Pkwy, **E gas:** Chevron/dsl/repair, **other:** McClain RV Ctr, camping, **W other:** Harley-Davidson

**459** frontage rd, **W other:** Destiny RV Resort

**458** FM 2181, Swisher Rd, **E gas:** Circle K, **lodging:** Best Western, **other:** O'Reilly Parts, **W gas:** Chevron/McDonald's, Exxon, **food:** Burger King, Chick-fil-A, IHOP, Jack-in-the-Box, JC China, KFC/Pizza Hut/Taco Bell, McDonald's, Quizno's, Starbucks, Subway, Wendy's, Whataburger, **other:** Albertson's, AutoZone, Discount Tire, GNC, Radio Shack, Walmart SuperCtr/gas

**457b** Denton Rd, Hundley Dr, Lake Dallas, **E gas:** Shell, **food:** Chili's, Hickory Creek BBQ, Subway, TX L&C Steaks, vet

**457a** Hundley Dr (from nb), Lake Dallas

**456** Highland Village

**456mm** Lewisville Lake

**454b** Garden Ridge Blvd, **W gas:** Fuel 4 TX, **other:** city park

**454a** FM 407, Justin, **E gas:** Valero, **food:** BBQ, **W gas:** QT, Texaco, **food:** McDonald's

**453** Valley Ridge Blvd, **E other:** Ford, **W gas:** Chevron, **food:** Burger King, Subway, **other:** Home Depot, Kohl's, Lowes Whse, Staples

**452** FM 1171, to Flower Mound, **E food:** IHOP, Taco Bueno, **lodging:** Days Inn, **other:** H HOSPITAL, **W gas:** Chevron, Exxon/dsl, Shell, **food:** Burger King, Chick-fil-A, Chipotle Mexican, CiCi's Pizza, Golden Corral, Grandy's, Panda Express, Taco Bell, Whataburger/24hr, **other:** Sam's Club/gas, Staples, U-Haul, Walmart SuperCtr same as 451

**451** Fox Ave, **E gas:** Shell/dsl, **food:** Braum's, **W gas:** Chevron/24hr, Conoco/dsl, QuickTrack Gas, **food:** Cracker Barrel, El Chico, **lodging:** Econolodge, Hampton Inn, **other:** transmissions, VW

**450** TX 121, Lewisville, **E gas:** Citgo/7-11, RaceTrac, **food:** China Dragon, Owens Rest., Sugarbaby's BBQ, **lodging:** Ramada Ltd, Rodeway Inn, **other:** Chevrolet/Subaru, Dodge, **W gas:** Chevron, Conoco/dsl, 7-11, Texaco/dsl, **food:** Burger King, Chili's, Church's, IHOP, KFC, LJ Silver, McDonald's, Pancho's Mexican, Pizza Hut, Subway, Taco Bell, Waffle House, Whataburger/24hr, **lodging:** Best Value Inn, Crossroads Inn, Super 8, **other:** Chief Parts, Eckerd, Firestone/auto, Food Lion, KIA, Kroger, Mitsubishi, Nissan, Saturn, Toyota, transmissions

**LEWISVILLE**

**449** Corporate Drive, **E gas:** Conoco, **food:** China Dragon, Hooters, On-the-Border, **lodging:** Extended Stay America, Hearthside Inn, Motel 6, **other:** Cavender's Boots, Honda, Ross, Target, **W gas:** Texaco, **food:** Chili's, **lodging:** Best Western, La Quinta, Sun Suites, **other:** Honda, Kia, NTB, Saturn

**448b a** FM 3040, Round Grove Rd, **E gas:** 7-11, **food:** Abuelo's Mexican, Cane's, Jack-in-the-Box, Joe's Crabshack, Mimi's Cafe, Olive Garden, Peiwei Chinese, **lodging:** Homewood Suites, **other:** Circuit City, Honda, Ross, Target, **W gas:** Exxon, **food:** Applebee's, BJ's Grill, Buffalo Wild Wings, Cantina Laredo, Carino's Italian, Chick-fil-A, Chipotle Mexican, Denny's, Don Pablo, Logan's Roadhouse, Macaroni Grill, McDonald's, Outback Steaks, Red Lobster, Schlotsky's, Sonic, Spring Creek BBQ, Steak'n Shake, Taco Bueno, Taco Cabana, TGIFriday, Tony Roma, Wendy's, **lodging:** Comfort Suites, Country Inn&Suites, Courtyard, Fairfield Inn, Hilton Garden, Holiday Inn Express, Old Country Inn, **other:** Barnes&Noble, Best Buy, Circuit City, Costco/gas, Dillard's, Discount Tire, JC Penney, Macy's, Marshall's, Michael's, Office Depot, Old Navy, Sears/auto, Target, mall

**446** Frankford Rd, **E gas:** RaceTrac, **food:** La Hacienda Ranch Grill, **other:** Buick/GMC/Pontiac, Volvo

**445b** Pres Geo Bush Tpk

**444** Whitlock Lane, Sandy Lake Rd, **E gas:** Shell, **food:** Pizza Pasta, **lodging:** Rodeway Inn, **other:** RV camping, **W food:** McDonald's, Starbucks, **lodging:** Delux Inn, **other:** Harley-Davidson

**443** Belt Line Rd, Crosby Rd, **E gas:** RaceTrac, **other:** Ford, Hyundai, NTB, **W gas:** Shell, **other:** U-Haul

**442** Valwood Pkwy, **E gas:** Chevron/Subway, **food:** El Chico, Grandy's, Jack-in-the-Box, Redline Burgers, Taco Bueno, Waffle House, **lodging:** Comfort Inn, Guest Inn, LoneStar Inn, Royal Inn, **W gas:** Fina/dsl, **other:** transmissions

**441** Valley View Lane, **W gas:** Mobil, Shell, **food:** Michael's Rest., **lodging:** Best Value Inn, Day's Inn, Econolodge, La Quinta

**440b** I-635 E

**440c** I-635 W, to DFW ✈

**439** Royal Lane, **E gas:** Fina, Shell, **food:** McDonald's, Wendy's, Whataburger/24hr, **other:** Daewoo, **W gas:** Chevron, Conoco, **food:** Jack-in-the-Box

**438** Walnut Hill Lane, **E gas:** Chevron, Shell, Valero, **food:** Burger King, Church's, Dave&Buster's, Denny's, Porter House Steaks, Trail Dust Steaks, Wild Turkey Grill, **lodging:** Comfort Inn, Hampton Inn, Quality Inn, **other:** Isuzu, **W gas:** Chevron, Shell/dsl, **other:** RV Ctr

**LEWISVILLE** (left margin)

**TX**

## INTERSTATE 35 CONT'D

**N ↕ S DALLAS**

**437** Manana Rd (from nb), same as 438

**436** TX 348, to DFW, Irving, **E gas:** Exxon/dsl, Shell, **food:** IHOP, Luby's, Waffle House, **lodging:** Courtyard, Days Inn, Elegante Hotel, Holiday Inn Express, La Quinta, Springhill Suites, Studio 6, Suburban Lodge, **W gas:** Fina, Mobil, Shell, **food:** Chili's, Don Pablo, Ghengis Grill, Jack-in-the-Box, Jason's Deli, Joe's Crabshack, McDonald's, Olive Garden, Outback Steaks, Papadeaux Seafood, Pappasito's Mexican, Red Lobster, Taco Bell/ Pizza Hut, Tony Roma's, TX L&C, Wendy's, Wing House, **lodging:** Budget Lodge, Century Inn

**435** Harry Hines Blvd (from nb) , **E gas:** RaceTrac, **food:** Arby's, **other:** U-Haul, same as 436

**434b** Regal Row, **E gas:** Texaco/Grandy's, **food:** Denny's, Whataburger/24hr, **lodging:** Econolodge, **W lodging:** Ramada Inn

**434a** Empire, Central, **E gas:** Chevron/McDonald's, **food:** Sonic, Tony's Grill, Wendy's, **lodging:** Budget Suites, Candlewood Suites, InTown Suites, Wingate Inn, **other:** Office Depot, **W gas:** Texaco, **food:** Burger King, Pizza Hut/Taco Bell, Schlotsky's

**433b** Mockingbird Lane, Love Field Airport, **E gas:** Shell, **food:** Jack-in-the-Box, **lodging:** Budget Suites, Comfort Inn, Crowne Plaza, InTown Suites, Sheraton, Radisson, Residence Inn

**433a** (432b from sb) TX 356, Commonwealth Dr, **W lodging:** Delux Inn

**432a** Inwood Rd, **E gas:** Exxon, **other:** H HOSPITAL, Chevrolet, **W gas:** Texaco/Subway/dsl, Shell, **food:** Whataburger/24hr, **lodging:** Embassy Suites, Homewood Suites

**431** Motor St, **E gas:** Chevron, **food:** Denny's, **other:** H HOSPITAL, **W gas:** Shell, **food:** Pepe's Grill, **lodging:** Marriott Suites

**430c** Wycliff Ave, **E food:** JoJo's Rest., **lodging:** Holiday Inn, Renaissance Hotel, **other:** Intn'l Apparel Mart, **W lodging:** Hilton Anatole, Hilton Garden

**430b** Mkt Ctr Blvd, **E other:** World Trade Ctr, **W gas:** Shell, **food:** Denny's, **lodging:** Courtyard, Fairfield Inn, Ramada Inn, Sheraton, Wilson World Hotel, Wyndham Garden

**430a** Oak Lawn Ave, **E lodging:** Holiday Inn, **W gas:** Shell, Texaco/dsl, **food:** Denny's, Medieval Times Rest., **other:** to Merchandise Mart

**429c** HiLine Ave (from nb)

**429b** Continental Ave, Commerce St W, downtown, **E food:** Hooters, **W gas:** Exxon, Shell, **food:** McDonald's

**429a** to I-45, US 75, to Houston

**428e** Commerce St E, Reunion Blvd, Dallas, downtown

**428d** I-30 W, to Ft Worth

**428a** I-30 E, to I-45 S

**428b** Industrial Blvd, **E gas:** Chevron, **W gas:** Fina, Kwik-Stop/dsl, Shamrock

**427b** I-30 E

**427a** Colorado Blvd, **E** H HOSPITAL

**426c** Jefferson Ave, **E gas:** Shell/dsl

**426b** TX 180 W, 8th St, **E gas:** Shell/dsl

**426a** Ewing Ave, **E food:** McDonald's, Popeye's

**425c** Marsalis Ave, **E lodging:** Dallas Inn, **W gas:** Chevron, Valero

**DALLAS**

**425b** Beckley Ave, 12th St, sb only, **W gas:** Shell, Valero, **food:** Wendy's

**425a** Zang Blvd, same as 425b

**424** Illinois Ave, **E gas:** Chevron, **food:** William's Chicken, **other:** H HOSPITAL, **W gas:** Exxon, **food:** Jack-in-the-Box, Pancake House, Sonic, Taco Bell, **other:** Kroger, Ross, Walgreens

**423b** Saner Ave

**423a** (422b from nb) US 67 S, Kiest Blvd, **W gas:** Shell/repair, **food:** McDonald's, Subway, Taco Del Mar, **lodging:** Dallas Inn

**421b** Ann Arbor St

**421a** Lp 12E W, **E gas:** RaceWay, **lodging:** Delux Inn

**420** Laureland, **W gas:** Conoco, Texaco, **lodging:** Linfield Inn

**419** Camp Wisdom Rd, **E gas:** Exxon, **lodging:** Oak Cliff Inn, **W gas:** Chevron, Shell/24hr, **food:** McDonald's, **lodging:** Suncrest Inn, **other:** U-Haul

**418c** Danieldale Rd (from sb)

**418b** I-635/I-20 E, to Shreveport

**418a** I-20 W, to Ft Worth

**417** Wheatland Rd (from nb)

**416** Wintergreen Rd, **E other:** repair, **W gas:** Citgo/7-11, **food:** Cracker Barrel, Golden Corral, Waffle House, **lodging:** Holiday Inn Express, Red Roof Inn

**415** Pleasant Run Rd, **E gas:** Chevron/24hr, RaceTrac, Shell/Blimpie/dsl, **food:** Bienvenidos Mexican, Evergreen Buffet, Subway, Waffle House, **lodging:** Great Western Inn, Royal Inn, Spanish Trails Motel, Super 8, **other:** Chrysler/Jeep, PepBoys, transmissions, **W gas:** Chevron, Exxon, **food:** Burger King, El Chico, Golden Corral, KFC, LJ Silver, Luby's, McDonald's, On the Border, Outback Steaks, Pizza Inn, Taco Bueno, Wendy's, **lodging:** Best Western, **other:** H HOSPITAL, Chevrolet, Discount Tire, Ford, Kroger, K-Mart, Office Depot, Ross

**414** FM 1382, Desoto Rd, Belt Line Rd, **E food:** Chili's, Whataburger, **other:** Walmart SuperCtr/gas

**413** Parkerville Rd, **W gas:** Exxon/Subway, **other:** U-Haul

**412** Bear Creek Rd, **W gas:** Shell/dsl, **food:** Bubba's BBQ, Jack-in-the-Box, Whataburger, **other:** HiHo RV Park, transmissions

**411** FM 664, Ovilla Rd, **E gas:** Exxon/TCBY/24hr, RaceTrac/24hr, **food:** LJ Silver/Taco Bell, McDonald's, Whataburger, **lodging:** Comfort Inn, **other:** Brookshire's Foods, CVS Drug, **W gas:** Exxon/Subway, Shamrock

**410** Red Oak Rd, **E gas:** Citgo/dsl, Nock's/Shell/Pizza Inn/ Subway/dsl, **food:** Denny's, Merryland Chinese, **lodging:** Day's Inn, **W other:** Hilltop Travel Trailers

**408** US 77, TX 342, to Red Oak, **E golf**

**406** Sterrett Rd, **E fireworks**

**405** FM 387, **E gas:** Phillips 66/dsl

**404** Lofland Rd, industrial area

**403** US 287, to Ft Worth, **E food:** Jack-in-the-Box, McDonald's, Taco Bell, Waffle House, **lodging:** Hampton Inn, **other:** Chevrolet/Cadillac, Jeep, **W other:** Buick/Pontiac/GMC, Chrysler/Dodge, Ford/Mercury

**401b** US 287 bus, Waxahatchie, **E lodging:** Best Western, Super 8

**401a** Brookside Rd, **E lodging:** Best Value Inn, Days Inn

**399b** FM 1446

**399a** FM 66, FM 876, Maypearl, **E lodging:** Texas Inn, **W gas:** Chevron/dsl, StarMart/dsl/24hr

## INTERSTATE 35 CONT'D

N ↕ S

**H I L L S B O R O**

| | |
|---|---|
| **397** | to US 77, to Waxahachie |
| **393mm** | rest area both lanes, full ♿ facilities, 📞, 🎪, litter barrels, vending, petwalk |
| **391** | FM 329, Forreston Rd |
| **386** | TX 34, Italy, **E** gas: Shell/dsl, food: DQ, Smokehouse BBQ, Sonic, other: $General, **W** gas: Exxon/Grandy's/Mcdonald's/Subway/Pizza Inn/dsl, lodging: Italy Inn, other: truckwash |
| **384** | Derrs Chapel Rd |
| **381** | FM 566, Milford Rd |
| **377** | FM 934 |
| **374** | FM 2959, Carl's Corner, **W** gas: Carl's Trkstp/dsl/rest. |
| **371** | I-35 W. I-35 divides into E and W nb, converges sb, See Texas I-35 W. |
| **370** | US 77 N, FM 579, Hillsboro |
| **368b** | FM 286, **E** food: LoneStar Café, Taco Bell, Wendy's, lodging: Hampton Inn, Super 8, other: Prime Outlets/famous brands, **W** gas: Exxon/Domino's, Valero/dsl, food: Braum's, Domino's, DQ, El Conquistador Mexican, El Taco Jalisco, McDonald's, Pizza Hut, lodging: Best Western, Comfort Inn, other: Ⓗ HOSPITAL |
| **368a** | TX 22, TX 171, to Whitney, **E** gas: 7-11, Love's/Subway/Pizza Hut/dsl/scales/24hr/@, food: Arby's, Blackeyed Pea, Burger King, IHOP, Merryland Chinese, McDonald's, Starbucks, Taco Bell, lodging: Day's Inn, Holiday Inn Express, Motel 6, Super 8, **W** gas: Chevron, Exxon, Mobil, Shell/dsl, food: Chicken Express, Jack-in-the-Box, KFC, Schlotsky's, Whataburger/24hr, lodging: Thunderbird Motel/rest., other: Buick/Pontiac/GMC, Chevrolet/Cadillac, Chrysler/Dodge/Jeep, Ford/Mercury, Walmart SuperCtr/gas |
| **367** | Old Bynum Rd (from nb) |
| **364b** | TX 81 N, to Hillsboro (exits left from nb) |
| **364a** | FM 310, **E** gas: Exxon/dsl, **W** gas: Fina/diese/24hr, food: Up In Smoke BBQ |
| **362** | Chatt Rd |
| **359** | FM 1304, **W** gas: Mobil/Subway/dsl/24hr, other: antiques |
| **358** | FM 1242 E, Abbott, **E** gas: Exxon, food: Smokin' Cafe |
| **356** | Co Rd 3102 |
| **355** | County Line Rd, **E** food: Yianni's Rest, other: KOA |
| **354** | Marable St, **E** other: KOA |
| **353** | FM 2114, West, **E** gas: Chevron, Fina/dsl, Shell/Czech Bakery, food: Bush's Chicken, Subway, DQ, other: Ford, **W** gas: Exxon, Texaco, lodging: Czech Inn, other: Chevrolet |
| **351** | FM 1858 |
| **349** | Wiggins Rd |
| **347** | FM 3149, Tours Rd |
| **346** | Ross Rd, **E** gas: Shell/dsl/24hr, **W** gas: Exxon/dsl/24hr, other: I-35 RV Park, antiques |
| **345** | Old Dallas Rd, **E** antiques, **W** other: I-35 RV Park |
| **343** | FM 308, Elm Mott, **E** gas: Exxon/DQ, Fina/dsl, Shell/Jct Cafe/dsl/scales/24hr, **W** gas: Chevron/dsl/24hr, food: BBQ, Heitmiller Steaks |
| **342b** | US 77 bus, **W** RV Park |
| **342a** | FM 2417, Crest Dr, **W** gas: Valero/dsl, food: Bush's Chicken, DQ, lodging: Everyday Inn, other: Family$, auto repair |
| **341** | Craven Ave, Lacy Lakeview, **E** gas: Chevron, **W** gas: BP/dsl, Shell/pizza |

**W A C O**

| | |
|---|---|
| **340** | Myers Lane (from nb) |
| **339** | to TX 6 S, FM 3051, Lake Waco, **E** gas: Valero/dsl, food: Beall's Rest, Casa Ole,'s, Domino's, El Conquistador, Jack-in-the-Box, Luby's, Little Caesars, Pizza Hut, Popeye's, Sonic, Subway, Wendy's, Whataburger/24hr, lodging: Country Inn Suites, other: Advance Parts, $General, HEB/gas, Home Depot, Radio Shack, Sam's Club, Walmart SuperCtr/gas, **W** gas: Chevron, Citgo, Shell, food: Burger King, Cracker Barrel, KFC, McDonald's, Papa John's, Starbucks, lodging: Fairfield Inn, Hampton Inn, Hawthorn Inn, Knight's Inn, other: to ✈ |
| **338b** | Behrens Circle (from nb) , **E** food: Jack-in-the-Box, Sonic, same as 339, **W** food: Cracker Barrel, gas: Shell/dsl/LP, lodging: Comfort Inn, Country Inn, Day's Inn, Delta Inn, Hawthorn Inn, Hampton Inn, Knight's Inn, Motel 6, other: Eckerd |
| **337** | (338a from nb) US 84, to TX 31, Waco Dr, **E** food: ChopStix, lodging: Value Place Suites, other: AutoZone, Family$, HEB Food/gas, Sam's Club/gas, **W** gas: Texaco, other: Ⓗ HOSPITAL |
| **335c** | Lake Brazos Dr, MLK Blvd, **E** food: Summer Palace Chinese, lodging: Holiday Inn, RiverPlace Inn/café, **W** food: Doc's Riverfront Rest., lodging: Travel Inn, Victorian Inn, other: Ⓗ HOSPITAL |
| **335mm** | Brazos River |
| **335b** | FM 434, University Parks Dr, **E** food: China Grill, IHOP, Jim's Rest., Quizno's, Thai Cuisine, lodging: Best Western, other: Baylor U, **W** food: Arby's, Jack-in-the-Box, lodging: Clarion, Lexington Inn, Residence Inn |
| **335a** | 4th St, 5th St, **E** gas: Exxon/Subway/TCBY/dsl, Shell/dsl, food: China Grill, Denny's, IHOP, Lupito's Mexican, Pizza Hut, lodging: Best Western, La Quinta, other: Baylor U, **W** gas: BP, Shamrock, food: Fazoli's, LJ Silver, McDonald's, Taco Bell, Taco Cabana, Wendy's, Whataburger/24hr, lodging: Clarion, other: to Baylor U |
| **334b** | US 77 S, 17th St, 18th St, **E** gas: BP, Chevron, Shell/dsl, food: Burger King, Fazolies, Popeye's, Schlotsky's, Vitek's BBQ, Wendy's, Whataburger, lodging: Budget Inn, Comfort Inn, Econolodge, Super 8, other: Harley-Davidson, **W** gas: Phillips 66/dsl, Shell, food: Mexico Lindo, Renee's Rest., Taquiera Mexican, other: Ⓗ HOSPITAL |
| **333a** | Lp 396, Valley Mills Dr, **E** gas: Chevron, food: Denny's, El Chico, Elite Café, Rudy's BBQ, TX Roadhouse, Trujillo's Mexican, lodging: Astro Motel, Comfort Suites, La Quinta, Motel 6, other: Isuzu/Mazda, Suzuki, **W** gas: Valero, food: Bush's Chicken, Church's Chicken, DQ, Jack-in-the-Box, Papa John's, Sonic, |

**TX**

**N ↑ ↓ S**

**TX**

**TEMPLE**

## INTERSTATE 35 CONT'D

| | | |
|---|---|---|
| **333a** | Continued | Taco Bueno, **lodging:** Comfort Inn, **other:** Eckerd, Jeep, Lincoln/Mercury, Volvo/Freightliner |
| **331** | New Rd, **E gas:** Chevron/dsl, **lodging:** New Road Inn, Relax Inn, Rodeway Inn, **W gas:** ⊕*FLYING J*/CountryMkt/dsl/scales/24hr/@, **food:** Hooters, IHOP, **lodging:** Quality Inn, **other:** Harley Davidson | |
| **330** | Lp 340, TX 6, **W food:** Camille's Cafe, Logan's Roadhouse, Smokey Bones BBQ, **other:** Belk, Best Buy, Books-A-Million, Kohl's, Ross, Old Navy, **2 mi W food:** Chick-fil-A, Luby's, McDonald's, Outback Steaks, TGI-Friday, Wienerschnitzel, **lodging:** Extended Stay America, Fairfield Inn, **other:** Ford, Honda, Lowe's Whse, Toyota, Walmart SuperCtr | |
| **328** | FM 2063, FM 2113, Moody, **E gas:** Pilot/Subway/Wendy's/dsl/scales/24hr/@, **food:** McDonald's, **W gas:** Shell/24hr, Valero/dsl, lodging Sleep Inn | |
| **325** | FM 3148, Moonlight Dr, **W gas:** Conoco/dsl, **other:** Walkabout RV Ctr | |
| **323** | FM 2837 (from sb), Lorena, **W gas:** Brookshire Bros/gas, **food:** Pizza House | |
| **322** | Lorena, **E gas:** Phillips 66/dsl, **food:** Baytown Seafood, **W gas:** Chevron/dsl, **food:** Bush's Chicken, Ruthy's Mexican, **other:** $General | |
| **319** | Woodlawn Rd | |
| **318b a** | Bruceville, **E gas:** Conoco/dsl, **other: picnic area both lanes, litter barrels,** ⛽ | |
| **315** | TX 7, FM 107, Eddy, **1 mi E** RV Park, **W gas:** BP, Shell/Subway/dsl/24hr, **other:** Family$, to Mother Neff SP | |
| **314** | Old Blevins Rd | |
| **311** | Big Elm Rd, **E** fireworks | |
| **308** | FM 935, Troy, **E gas:** Shell, **other:** Troy Foods, **W gas:** Exxon, **other:** All-American RV Ctr | |
| **306** | FM 1237, Pendleton, **W gas:** Love's/Subway/dsl/24hr, **other:** Temple RV Park | |
| **305** | Berger Rd, **W gas:** Exxon/dsl/scales/24hr, **lodging:** Sharon Jean's Rest, **other:** Lucky's RV Park, Temple RV Park, repair | |
| **304** | Lp 363, Dodgen Loop, **W gas:** Shell/Wendy's/dsl, Valero/dsl/24hr | |
| **303** | spur 290, N 3rd St, Temple, **E gas:** S-2 Gas, **lodging:** Texas Inn, **W lodging:** Continental Inn | |
| **302** | Nugent Ave, **E gas:** Exxon/dsl, **lodging:** Comfort Suites, Econolodge, Holiday Inn Express, Red Roof Inn, **W gas:** BP/dsl, Chevron, **food:** Denny's, **lodging:** Best Western, Day's Inn, Motel 6, Stratford House Inn, Travelodge, **other:** Ford/Lincoln/Mercury, Harley Davidson | |
| **301** | TX 53, FM 2305, Adams Ave, **E gas:** Valero, **food:** Arby's, Chick-fil-A, Gatti's Rest., Jim's Rest., KFC, LJ Silver, McDonald's, Pizza Hut, Starbucks, Subway, Taco Bell, Wendy's, Whataburger, **lodging:** La Quinta, **other:** Ⓗ HOSPITAL, Advance Parts, Ford, **W food:** Catfish Shack, **lodging:** Best Western, **other:** Chrysler/Jeep, $General, Lincoln/Mercury, Harley-Davidson, Jeep | |
| **300** | Ave H, 49th-57th Sts, **E gas:** Shell, **food:** Las Casas Mexican, **W gas:** Shell | |
| **299** | US 190 E, TX 36, **E gas:** Shell, Texaco/dsl, **food:** Golden Corral, Jack-in-the-Box, Luby's, Phillip's Steakhouse, **lodging:** Best Value, Budget Inn, Regency Inn, | |
| **299** | Continued | **other:** Ⓗ HOSPITAL, Ancira RV Ctr, Chevrolet/Toyota, Dodge, K-Mart, Saturn, Subaru, **W food:** Chili's, Best Buy, Burger King, Chili's, Home Depot, IHOP, McDonald's, Target |
| **298** | nb only, to frontage rd, **E lodging:** Residence Inn, **other:** Subaru | |
| **297** | FM 817, Midway Dr, **E gas:** Phillips 66, **food:** Taquiera Mexican, **lodging:** Holiday Inn, Super 8/rest., **other:** BMW, Nissan, Saab, Volvo, **W gas:** Valero, **other:** Buick/Pontiac/GMC, Fed Ex, Suzuki, VW | |
| **294b** | FM 93, 6th Ave, **E gas:** Shell/dsl, **food:** McDonald's, **other:** Chevrolet, Toyota, **W food:** Buger King, Great SW Rest., Pizza Hut, Subway, Whataburger, **lodging:** Ramada Ltd, River Forest Inn, **other:** U of Mary Hardin Baylor | |
| **294a** | Central Ave, **W gas:** Shell/dsl, **food:** BBQ, Burger King, Bobby's Burgers, Great SW Rest., Jalisco's Mexican, Pizza Hut, Sonic, Whataburger, **lodging:** Ramada Ltd, **other:** AutoZone, Goodyear | |
| **293b** | TX 317, FM 436, Main St | |
| **293a** | US 190 W, to Killeen, Ft Hood | |
| **292** | Lp 121 (same as 293a) , **E gas:** Valero/dsl/rest./24hr, **lodging:** Budget Host, **W gas:** Mobil/dsl/24hr, **lodging:** La Quinta, **other:** Ford, auto/tire repair | |
| **290** | Shanklin Rd | |
| **289** | Tahuaya Rd, **E other:** Hi-Way Parts | |
| **287** | Amity Rd | |
| **286** | FM 2484, **E lodging:** Holiday Inn Express, **W** to Stillhouse Hollow Lake | |
| **285** | FM 2268, Salado, **E gas:** Conoco/Brookshire Foods, **food:** Subway, **lodging:** Holiday Inn Express, **W gas:** Chevron, **food:** Cowboys BBQ, Robertson's Rest., Sonic | |
| **284** | Stagecoach Rd, **E gas:** Exxon/Burger King, **food:** Arbys, DQ, Roy T's Subway, Subway, **W gas:** Texaco/dsl, **food:** DQ, **lodging:** Super 8 | |
| **283** | FM 2268, FM 2843, to Holland, Salado, **E lodging:** Stagecoach Inn | |
| **282** | FM 2115, **E gas:** Valero/dsl, **other:** RV camping | |
| **281mm** | **rest area both lanes, full** ♿ **facilities,** 📞, 🚻, **litter barrels, vending, petwalk, RV dump** | |
| **280** | Prairie Dell | |
| **279** | Hill Rd, **W other:** RV Park | |
| **277** | Yankee Rd | |
| **275** | FM 487, to Florence, Jarrell, **E gas:** Exxon/dsl, Shamrock/dsl/scales, Shell, **food:** Burger King, Denny's, **W gas:** Shell, **other:** USPO | |
| **271** | Theon Rd, **E gas:** Explore USA RV Ctr, **W gas:** Shell/Subway/dsl/24hr | |
| **268** | fm 972 (fom nb), Walburg, **E other:** Crestview RV Ctr | |
| **266** | TX 195, **E gas:** Mobil/dsl | |
| **265** | toll 130, to Austin, new exit | |
| **264** | Lp 35, Georgetown | |
| **262** | RM 2338, Lake Georgetown, **E food:** KFC, Luby's, McDonald's, Quizno's, Sonic, Subway, **lodging:** Holiday Inn Express, **other:** Albertson's, Eckerd, Parts+, Radio Shack, **W gas:** Phillips 66, Texaco, **food:** Chuck Wagon Café, DQ, Popeye's, Taco Bueno, Wendy's, Whataburger/24hr, **lodging:** Day's Inn, La Quinta | |
| **261** | TX 69, Georgetown, **E gas:** Shell/dsl, **food:** Applebee's, Burger King, Chili's, KFC/Taco Bell, Schlotsky's, **lodging:** Comfort Suites, Holiday Inn Express, | |

## INTERSTATE 35 CONT'D

**G E O R G E T O W N   N**

**↕**

**S**

**R O U N D   R O C K**

**261** Continued
**other:** HEB Foods, same as 262, **W food:** Village Inn, Wendy's, **other:** Best Buy, Home Depot, Kohl's, PetsMart, Target, TJ Maxx, Walmart SuperCtr, antiques

**260** RM 2243, Leander, **E other:** H HOSPITAL, USPO, **W gas:** Chevron, Exxon, **food:** Jack-in-the-Box, **lodging:** Quality Inn

**259** Lp 35, **W other:** RV Outlet Ctr, to Interspace Caverns

**257** Westinghouse Rd, **E other:** Chevrolet/Buick, Chrysler/Dodge/Jeep, Ford, Kia, Mazda, Mitsubishi, VW

**256** RM 1431, Chandler Rd, **E other:** Round Rock Outlet, Hummer, Mazda, JC Penny, Volvo

**254** FM 3406, Round Rock, **E gas:** Chevron, Citgo/7-11, Texaco, **food:** Arby's, Castaways Seafood, Fuddruckers, Gatti's Pizza, Giovanni's Italian, McDonald's, Schlotsky's, Sonic, **other:** Firestone, GMC/Pontiac, Honda, Pennzoil, Toyota, **W gas:** Phillips 66/24hr, **food:** Carino's Italian, China One, Chuy's Mexican, Cracker Barrel, Denny's, Golden Corral, Mesa Rosa Mexican, Rudy's BBQ, SaltGrass Steaks, **lodging:** AmeriSuites, Courtyard, Hilton Garden, Holiday Inn, La Quinta, Red Roof Inn, SpringHill Suites, Super 8, **other:** Nissan

**253b** US 79, to Taylor, **E gas:** Chevron, **food:** Arby's, Baskin-Robbins, DQ, Famous Sam's Café, Fuddrucker's, KFC, LoneStar Café, LJ Silver, Sirloin Stockade, **other:** H HOSPITAL, AutoZone, HEB/deli, **W gas:** Exxon/dsl, Shell/dsl/24hr, **food:** BBQ, IHOP, K-Bob's Rest., Taco Bell, Thundercloud Subs, **lodging:** Country Inn Suites, La Quinta, Red Roof Inn, Sleep Inn, Value Place Motel, **other:** Eckerd, USPO

**253a** Frontage Rd, **E gas:** Shell, **food:** Arby's, Beal's Cafe, Castaway's Seafood/steaks, DQ, Damon's, KFC, Taco Bell, **lodging:** Best Western, Wingate Inn, **W food:** La Marguarita, Mr Gatti, Popeye's, Taco Bell, **lodging:** Ramada Ltd, **other:** CVS Drug, USPO

**252b a** RM 620, **E gas:** Shell/dsl/24hr, **lodging:** Candlewood Suites, Crossland Suites, Extended Stay America, **other:** bank, **W gas:** BP, Phillips 66, **food:** Grandy's, Little Caesar's, McDonald's, Starbucks, **lodging:** Comfort Suites, Staybridge Suites, **other:** mall

**251** Lp 35, Round Rock, **E food:** Cici's Pizza, Outback Steaks, Whataburger, **lodging:** Residence Inn, **other:** Aamco, Advance Parts, BigLots, Brake Check, Diahatsu, $General, transmissions, **W gas:** Exxon, Shell, **food:** Burger King, Jack-in-the-Box, Luby's, Peter Piper Pizza, Taco Cabana, **lodging:** Day's Inn, **other:** Albertson's, Hastings Books, NTB, Walgreen

**250** FM 1325, **E gas:** Chevron, Mobil/dsl, **food:** Applebee's, Chick-fil-A, Chili's, El Chico, Jason's Deli, Joe's Crabshack, Macaroni Grill, McDonald's, Subway, **lodging:** Hampton Inn, **other:** Best Buy, Discount Tire, Goodyear/auto, Home Depot, Michael's, PetsMart, Ross, Steinmart, Target, Walmart SuperCtr, **W gas:** Shell, **food:** Antonio's Cantina, Fast Eddie's Rest, Hooters, Krispy Kreme, Olive Garden, Starbucks, **lodging:** Baymont Inn, Extended Stay America, **other:** Barnes&Noble, Circuit City, Kohl's, Lowe's Whse, Marshall's, Office Depot, Old Navy, PetCo, Sam's Club/gas

**248** Grand Ave Pkwy, **E gas:** Texaco/Subway/dsl, **food:** Cheddar's, Fish Daddy's Grill, Jack-in-the-Box, Posado's Mexican, Taco Cabana, TX Roadhouse, **other:** Firestone, **W gas:** Chevron/McDonald's, **other:** Goodyear/auto

**247** FM 1825, Pflugerville, **E gas:** RaceTrac, **food:** Jack-in-the-Box, Sonic, Taco Cabana, Wendy's, **other:** Firestone/auto, HEB Foods, cinema, **W gas:** Exxon, Shell/Church's, **food:** BBQ, IHOP, KFC, Miller's BBQ, Whataburger, **lodging:** Holiday Inn Express, Quality Suites, **other:** Goodyear/auto

**246** Howard Lane, **E gas:** Citgo, Shell/dsl, **food:** Arby's, Baby Acapulco, McDonald's, Subway, Wings'n More, **other:** Home Depot, Kohl's, NTB, **W gas:** Valero/dsl

**245** FM 734, Parmer Lane, to Yager Lane (244 from nb), **E food:** Carino's, Chick-fil-A, Chili's, Golden Wok, Schlotzsky's, Subway, **other:** HEB Food/gas, JC Penny, Kohl's, PetsMart, Radio Shack, Ross, Sears Grand, Target, **W gas:** Citgo/7-11, Exxon, **food:** Red Robin, Starbucks, Village Inn, **lodging:** Residence Inn, SpringHill Suites, **other:** CarMax, Lowe's Whse, Walmart SuperCtr/gas

**243** Braker Lane, **E gas:** Valero, **food:** Jack-in-the-Box, Whataburger/24hr, **other:** Harley-Davidson, U-Haul, **W gas:** Shell/dsl, **lodging:** Austin Motel, **other:** vet

**241** Rundberg Lane, **E gas:** Exxon, **food:** Golden Corral, Jack-in-the-Box, Mr Gatti's, Old San Francisco Steaks, **lodging:** Extended Stay America, Ramada Inn, **other:** Albertson's, Chevrolet, $General, U-Haul, Walmart SuperCtr, **W gas:** Chevron, Conoco, Shell, **food:** Sonic, **lodging:** Austin Suites, Budget Inn, Holiday Inn Express, Home-Style Inn, Motel 6, Red Roof Inn, Super 8, Travelodge, Wingate Inn

**240a** US 183, Lockhart, **E gas:** Exxon, **food:** DQ, Jack-in-the-Box, Old San Francisco Steaks, **lodging:** Day's Inn, Ramada Inn, Wellesley Inn, **other:** Chevrolet, **W gas:** Chevron/dsl/24hr, Texaco/dsl, **lodging:** Motel 6, Red Roof Inn, Super 8, Travelodge Suites, Wingate Inn

**239** St John's Ave, **E gas:** Shell, **food:** Chili's, Fuddruckers, Japon Japanese, Jim's Rest., Owen's Rest., Pappadeaux, Pappasito's Mexican, Steak&Egg, Sushi Japan, **lodging:** Crowne Plaza, Budget Host, Day's Inn, DoubleTree, Drury Inn, Hampton Inn, Red Lion Hotel, Studio 6, **other:** Dodge, Home Depot, Volvo, Walmart SuperCtr, **W gas:** Conoco/dsl, Exxon, **food:** Antonio's TexMex, Applebee's, Carrabba's, Denny's, Quizno's, **lodging:** AmeriSuites, Comfort Inn, Country Inn Suites, Baymont Inn, Holiday Inn Express, La Quinta, Sheraton, Sumner Suites, **other:** Office Depot

**TX**

**N ↕ S**

**AUSTIN**

### INTERSTATE 35 CONT'D

**238b** US 290 E, RM 222, same as 238a, frontage rds connect several exits

**238a** 51st St, **E gas:** Exxon, Chevron, Phillips 66, Shell, **food:** Burger King, Chili's, Dixie's Roadhouse, El Torito, Fuddrucker's, Grandy's, LJ Silver, McDonald's, Pappasito's, Sonic, Subway, Texas Steaks, Whataburger, **lodging:** Doubletree Hotel, Drury Inn, Econolodge, Embassy Suites, Holiday Inn, Homestead Village, Red Lion Hotel, Studio 6 Suites, **other:** Advance Parts, $Tree, Firestone, FoodLand, Jo-Ann Crafts, Ross, Target, Volvo, Walgreen, **W gas:** Shell, **food:** Baby Acapulco, Bombay Bicycle Club, Capt's Seafood, Carrabba's, IHOP, India Cuisine, Outback Steaks, Quizno's, **lodging:** Courtyard, Drury Inn, Fairfield Inn, Hilton, La Quinta, Motel 6, Quality Inn, Ramada Ltd, Rodeway Inn, Super 8, **other:** Dillard's, Ford, Office Depot

**237b** 51st St, same as 238a

**237a** Airport Blvd, **E food:** BBQ, **W food:** Jack-in-the-Box, Wendy's, GNC, Goodyear, **other:** Best Buy, HEB Foods, Marshall's, Old Navy, PetCo, Sears/auto

**upper level is I-35 thru, lower level accesses downtown**

**236b** 39th St, **E gas:** Chevron, **food:** Subway, **other:** Fiesta Foods, HiLo Parts, O'Reilly Parts, U-Haul, **W gas:** Shell/dsl, **other:** Tune&Lube, tires, to U of TX

**236a** 26th-32nd Sts, **E food:** Subway, **lodging:** Day's Inn, **W lodging:** Rodeway Inn, **other:** H HOSPITAL

**235b** Manor Rd, same as 236a, **E food:** Denny's, **lodging:** Double Tree, **W lodging:** Rodeway Inn, **other:** U of TX, st capitol

**235a** MLK, 15th St, **W** H HOSPITAL

**upper level is I-35 thru, lower level accesses downtown**

**234c** 11th St, 12th St, downtown, **E gas:** Chevron, Shell, **food:** Wendy's, **lodging:** DoubleTree Hotel, Super 8, **other:** CVS Drug, Eckerd, **W gas:** Exxon, Mobil, Shell, **food:** Wendy's, **lodging:** Crowne Plaza, Marriott, Hilton Garden Inn, Hilton Garden Inn, Omni Motel, Radisson, Sheraton, **other:** H HOSPITAL, museum, st capitol

**234b** 8th-3rd St, **W food:** IHOP

**234a** Cesar Chavez St, Holly St, downtown

**233** Riverside Dr, Town Lake, **E gas:** Citgo, **lodging:** Extended Stay America, **W gas:** Chevron/dsl, **lodging:** Holiday Inn

**232mm** Little Colorado River

**232b** Woodland Ave

**232a** Oltorf St, **E gas:** Shell/dsl, **food:** Kettle, La Taraza Grill, Luby's, **lodging:** Best Value Inn, Country Garden Inn, Exel Inn, La Quinta, Motel 6, Suburban Lodge, **W gas:** Chevron, Exxon, **food:** Denny's, Starbucks, **lodging:** Clarion, Quality Inn

**231** Woodward St, **E gas:** Shell/dsl, **food:** Country Kitchen, **lodging:** Wyndham Garden, same as 232, **W other:** Home Depot

**230b a** US 290 W, TX 71, Ben White Blvd, St Elmo Rd, **E gas:** Shell, **food:** Domino's, Jim's Rest., McDonald's, Sigon Kitchen, Subway, Western Choice Steaks, **lodging:** Best Western, Comfort Suites, Courtyard, Fairfield Inn, Hampton Inn, Marriott, Omni Hotel, Red Roof Inn, Residence Inn, SpringHill Suites, **other:** Acura, Sam's Club/gas, **W food:** Burger King, Furr's Cafeteria, IHOP,

**230b a** Continued
Pizza Hut, Taco Cabana, **lodging:** Candlewood Suites, Day's Inn, Hawthorn Suites, La Quinta, **other:** H HOSPITAL, BMW, Dodge/Jeep, Ford, GMC, Honda, Hyundai, Kia, Lincoln/Mercury, Mazda, NTB, Nissan, Pontiac/Cadillac/Mazda, Suzuki/Kia, Toyota

**229** Stassney Lane, **W food:** Chili's, Logan's Roadhouse, Macaroni Grill, Rockfish Grill, Texas Cattle Co Steaks, **other:** Albertson's/gas, Fiesta Foods, Lowe's Whse

**228** Wm Cannon Drive, **E gas:** Exxon, **food:** Applebee's, McDonald's, Taco Bell, **other:** Brake Check, Chrysler, Discount Tire, HEB Foods, Hyundai/Subaru, Mitsubishi, Nissan, Radio Shack, Target, **W gas:** Shell/dsl, **food:** Burger King, Gatti's Pizza, KFC, LJ Silver, Peter Piper Pizza, Taco Cabana, Whataburger/24hr, Wendy's, **other:** Advance Parts, BigLots, Chevrolet, CVS Drug, $General, Firestone

**227** Slaughter Lane, Lp 275, S Congress, **E gas:** Shell/dsl, **food:** IHOP, **other:** Home Depot, Lone Star RV Resort, U-Haul, **W gas:** Texaco, Valero/dsl, **food:** Chili's, Miller BBQ, Sonic, Starbucks, Steak&Shake, Subway, Jack-in-the-Box, TGIFriday's, TX Roadhouse, Whataburger, **other:** PetsMart, Walmart SuperCtr/gas

**226** Slaughter Creek Overpass

**225** FM 1626, Onion Creek Pkwy, **E gas:** Shell, Texaco, **other:** Harley-Davidson

**224** frontage rd (from nb)

**223** FM 1327

**221** Lp 4, Buda, **E gas:** Chevron/McDonald's, Shell/dsl, **lodging:** Best Value, Interstate Inn, **other:** Allstar RV Ctr, Ford, Marshall's RV Ctr, **W gas:** Chevron/24hr, Shell, **food:** Chili's, Cracker Barrel, Jack-in-the-Box, Sonic, Subway, **other:** Cabela's, HEB Food/gas, Radio Shack, Walmart SuperCtr

**220** FM 2001, Niederwald, **E gas:** Texaco, **other:** Camper Clinic RV Ctr, **W other:** Crestview RV Ctr/Park

**217** Lp 4, Buda, **E gas:** Conoco/dsl/24hr, **W gas:** Exxon/dsl, Valero/Pizza Hut/dsl, **food:** Burger King, **lodging:** Best Western, **other:** Home Depot

**215** Bunton Overpass, **E gas:** Exxon/KFC/LJ Silver, **W** HEB Foods/gas

**213** FM 150, Kyle, **E gas:** Valero/dsl, **food:** DQ, Karen's Kountry Kitchen, **other:** AutoZone, Goodyear/auto, **W gas:** Conoco, Texaco

**211mm** weigh sta sta nb

**210** Yarrington Rd, **E** Hyundai, **W other:** Plum Creek RV Resort

**209mm** truck check sta sb

**208mm** Blanco River

**208** Frontage Rd, Blanco River Rd

**206** Lp 82, Aquarena Springs Rd, **E gas:** Conoco, Valero, **other:** San Marcos RV Park, **W gas:** Exxon/dsl, Phillips 66/dsl, Shell, Texaco, **food:** Jim's Rest., Pancake House, Popeye's, Sonic, **lodging:** Best Value, Comfort Inn, La Quinta, Motel 6, Quality Inn, Ramada Ltd, Rodeway Inn, Stratford Inn, Super 8, University Inn, **other:** to SW TX U, RV camping

**205** TX 80, TX 142, Bastrop, **E gas:** Chevron, Conoco, Exxon, RaceWay, Shell/dsl, Valero, **food:** Arby's, DQ, Fazolies, Jason's Deli, Subway, Taste of China, **lodging:** Executive Inn, **other:** AutoZone, CVS Drug, $General,

**SAN MARCUS**

**TX**

**SAN MARCUS**

**N ↕ S**

**NEW BRAUNFELS**

## INTERSTATE 35 CONT'D

**205** Continued
Eckerd, Hastings Books, Walmart SuperCtr, **W** gas: Chevron, Circle K/gas/24hr, Valero, **food:** A&W/LJ Silver, Applebee's, Burger King, Church's, CiCi's, IHOP, KFC, Logan's Roadhouse, LJ Silver, Logan's Roadhouse, McDonald's, MT Mike's, Pizza Hut, Taco Cabana, Wendy's, **lodging:** Best Western, Budget Inn, Day's Inn, Gateway Inn, Microtel, ParkSide Inn, Red Roof Inn, Rodeway Inn, **other:** Best Buy, Brake Check, HEB Foods/gas, JC Penney, Office Depot, Target, Walgreen

**204mm** San Marcos River

**204b** CM Allen Pkwy, **W** gas: Chevron, Conoco/dsl, Shell/dsl, **food:** Chinese Buffet, DQ, Red Robin, Sonic, **lodging:** Best Western, Econolodge

**204a** Lp 82, TX 123, to Seguin, **E** gas: Conoco, Valero, **food:** Burger King, Carino's, Chili's, FasTaco, Golden Corral, Luby's, McDonald's, Red Lobster, Whataburger/24hr, **lodging:** Comfort Suites, Holiday Inn Express, **other:** Ⓗ HOSPITAL, Chevrolet/Buick, Ford/Mercury, Jeep/Chrysler, transmissions

**202** FM 3407, Wonder World Dr, **E** gas: Exxon, Shell/Church's, **food:** Jack-in-the-Box, Pitt BBQ, Taco Bueno, Wienerschnitzel, **other:** Ⓗ HOSPITAL, Discount Tire, Lowe's Whse, Marshalls, PetsMart, Ross, Sams Club/gas, **W** gas: Valero/dsl, **food:** BBQ, **other:** Chrysler/Dodge, transmissions

**201** McCarty Lane, **E** other: Discount Tire, **W** other: Chrysler/Dodge, Nissan

**200** Centerpoint Rd, **E** food: Cracker Barrel, Food Court, LoneStar Café, Outback Steaks, Subway, Taco Bell, Wendy's, **other:** Cavender's Boots, Old Navy, Prime Outlets/famous brands, Tanger Outlet/famous brands, **W** gas: Valero/dsl, **food:** McDonald's, Quizno's, Starbucks, Whataburger/24hr, **lodging:** AmeriHost, **other:** Honda

**199** Posey Rd, **E** other: Tanger Outlets/famous brands, Toyota/Scion, same as 200

**196** FM 1106, York Creek Rd

**195** Watson Lane, Old Bastrop Rd, **E** fireworks

**193** Conrads Rd, Kohlenberg Rd, **E** Roman Holiday RV Ctr, **W** gas: TA/Country Fare Rest/Popeye's/Subway/dsl/scales/24hr/@, **food:** Coconut's Rest.

**191** FM 306, FM 483, Canyon Lake, **E** gas: Conoco/Quizno's/dsl, Texaco, **other:** I-35 RV Camping, Walmart Dist Ctr, **W** gas: Chevron, Exxon/dsl, **food:** Burger King, GristMill Rest., **other:** Camping World RV Supply/SW RV Ctr, transmissions

**190c** Post Rd

**190b** Lp 35 S, New Braunfels, **W** gas/dsl, **food:** Capparelli's Italian, **lodging:** Hawthorn Inn

**190a** frontage rd, **E** gas: Shell, **other:** Discount Tire, Home Depot, **W** gas: McDonald's, **food:** Wendy's, **lodging:** Best Western, Comfort Suites, Motel 6, Quality Inn

**189** TX 46, Seguin, **E** gas: Conoco/dsl, Exxon, Shell/dsl, **food:** Chili's, Luby's, Olive Garden, Oma's Haus Rest., Village Inn, **lodging:** Best Value, La Quinta, Oakwood Inn, Stratford House, Super 8, **other:** Circuit City, Discount Tire, Home Depot, K-Mart, Kohl's, Office Depot, **W** gas: Chevron/24hr, Texaco, **food:** Applebee's, IHOP, McDonald's, New Braunfels Smokehouse, Pizza Hut,

**189** Continued
Skillet's Rest., Taco Bell, Taco Cabana, Wendy's, **lodging:** Best Western, Comfort Suites, Day's Inn, Hampton Inn, Holiday Inn, Motel 6, Rodeway Inn, Quality Inn, Sleep Inn, **other:** Ⓗ HOSPITAL, Walgreen

**188** Frontage Rd, **W** food: Mamacita's Rest., Ryan's, **other:** Hastings Books

**188mm** Guadalupe River

**187** FM 725, Lake McQueeny Rd, **E** gas: Chevron/24hr, **food:** Arby's, Burger King, China Kitchen, CiCi's, Guadalajara Mexican, LJ Silver/A&W, Subway, Whataburger/24hr, **other:** Aamco, BigLots, Family$, Ford/Lincoln/Mercury, Jeep, Radio Shack, **W** gas: Exxon/dsl, Shell/dsl, **food:** Adobe Café, DQ, Jack-in-the-Box, Rally's, Steaks to Go, **lodging:** Budget Host, Budget Inn, Faust Hotel, **other:** Ⓗ HOSPITAL, CVS Drug, NAPA AutoCare, River Ranch RV Resort, transmissions

**186** Walnut Ave, **E** gas: Exxon/Subway, Valero, **food:** Chick-fil-A, McDonald's, Popeye's, Schlotsky's, Taco Bell, **lodging:** Red Roof Inn, **other:** Chevrolet, Lowes Whse, Walmart SuperCtr/gas/auto, **W** gas: Shell/dsl, **food:** KFC, Mr Gatti's, Papa John's, Shanghai Chinese, Starbucks, **other:** AutoZone, Brake Check, $Tree, GNC, HEB Foods/deli/gas, Radio Shack, Ross, Target, U-Haul, Walgreen

**185** FM 1044

**184** FM 482, Lp 337, Ruekle Rd, **E** gas: Shell/Blimpie/dsl, **other:** Buick/Pontiac/GMC, Kia, Mazda, **W** Suzuki

**183** Solms Rd, **W** gas: Exxon

**182** Engel Rd, **E** other: Stamann RV Ctr

**180** Schwab Rd

**179mm** rest area both lanes, full ♿ facilities, 🅲, 🅿, litter barrels, vending, petwalk, RV Dump

**178** FM 1103, Cibolo Rd, Hubertus Rd, **E** gas: Shell/dsl

**177** FM 482, FM 2252, **E** Stone Creek RV Park

**176** Weiderstein Rd, same as 175

**175** FM 3009, Natural Bridge, **E** gas: Valero, **food:** Chili's, La Pasadita Mexican, McDonald's, Miller's BBQ, Schlotsky's, Sonic, Taco Cabana, **lodging:** Hampton Inn, **other:** HEB Food/gas, Radio Shack, **W** gas: Valero/Subway/dsl, Shell/dsl, **food:** Arby's, Denny's, Jack-in-the-Box, KFC/Taco Bell/Pizza Hut, Starbucks, Wendy's, **lodging:** Atrium Inn, Country Inn, **other:** Factory Shoestore, Walmart SuperCtr/gas

**174b** Schertz Pkwy, **E** gas: Shell

**174a** FM 1518, Selma, **E** gas: Phillips 66/dsl, **food:** Ruddy's BBQ, **other:** Honda/Mitsubishi, Saturn, **W** other: Crestview RV Ctr

## INTERSTATE 35 CONT'D

**N ↕ S**

**173** Old Austin Rd, Olympia Pkwy, **E** **food:** Chick-fil-A, Chili's, Freddy's Custard, Hooters, Macaroni Grill, Red Robin, Sea Island Srimp, Subway, TGIFriday's, **lodging:** Holiday Inn Express, **other:** Best Buy, Borders Books, Costco/gas, Home Depot, Old Navy, Ross, Target, WorldMkt, **W** **other:** Retama Park RaceTrack

**172** TX 218, Anderson Lp, P Booker Rd, **E** **food:** Buffalo Wild Wings, Coldstone Creamery, IHOP, Outback Steaks, Texas Roadhouse, Village Inn, **lodging:** Comfort Inn, Value Place, **other:** Ford, Nissan, Home Depot, Hyundai, Kohls, Target, to Randolph AFB, **W** **food:** Camino Ranch Steak, **other:** to SeaWorld

**171** Topperwein Rd, same as 170

**170** Judson Rd, to Converse, **E** **food:** Denny's, India Cuisine, Kettle, Subway, Whataburger/24hr, **lodging:** Best Value, La Quinta, **other:** H HOSPITAL, Chevrolet, Chrysler, Ford, Hyundai, Nissan, Pontiac/GMC, Toyota, **W** **gas:** Exxon, **lodging:** Best Western, **other:** Kia, Mazda, Sam's Club/gas, Subaru

**169** O'Conner Rd, Wurzbach Pkwy, **E** **gas:** Exxon/dsl, **food:** McDonald's, Quizno's, Subway, Taco Cabana, **other:** Chrysler/Jeep, Lowe's Whse, Walgreen, **W** **gas:** Shell/dsl, Valero, **food:** Jack-in-the-Box, Jim's Rest., Mi Casa Mexican, Sonic, **lodging:** Holiday Inn Express, **other:** Mazda

**168** Weidner Rd, **E** **gas:** Citgo/dsl, **lodging:** Day's Inn, Comfort Suites, **W** **gas:** Chevron, **lodging:** Budget Host, Quality Inn, Park Inn, Super 8, **other:** Harley-Davidson, Volvo

**167b** Thousand Oaks Dr, Starlight Terrace, **E** **gas:** Valero/dsl, **other:** Suzuki, **W** **lodging:** Park Inn

**167a** Randolph Blvd, **E** **other:** TravelTown TX RV Ctr, **W** **lodging:** Best Western, Comfort Inn, Continental Inn, Day's Inn, Howard Johnson, Motel 6, RoadWay Inn, Ruby Inn, **other:** Suzuki

**166** I-410 W, Lp 368 S, **W** **other:** to Sea World

**165** FM 1976, Walzem Rd, **E** **gas:** Chevron, Shell, Valero/dsl, **food:** Applebee's, ChuckeCheese, Church's, IHOP, Jack-in-the-Box, Las Palapas Mexican, LJ Silver, Luby's, McDonald's, Marie Callendar's, Olive Garden, Pizza Hut, Red Lobster, Shoneys, Starbucks, Subway, Taco Bell, Taco Cabana, Wendy's, Whataburger, **lodging:** Hampton Inn, Peartree Inn, **other:** AutoZone, CarQuest, Cavender's Boots, Circuit City, Dillard's, Discount Tire, Firestone/auto, Home Depot, Michael's, PepBoys, Radio Shack, Target, Walmart SuperCtr, **W** **gas:** Mobil, **food:** Sonic, **other:** NTB

**164b** Eisenhauer Rd, **E** **gas:** Exxon/dsl, **lodging:** Hawthorn Suites, Value Place Hotel, **other:** $General, Hancock Fabrics

**164a** Rittiman Rd, **E** **gas:** Exxon, Shell/dsl, Valero/dsl, **food:** Burger King, Church's, Cracker Barrel, Denny's, Guadalajara Mexican, Jack-in-the-Box, McDonald's, Rally's, Taco Cabana, Whataburger/24hr, **lodging:** Best Value, Best Western, Comfort Suites, Halmark Inn, La Quinta, Motel 6, Rittiman Inn, Super 8, **other:** Cummins dsl Repair, **W** **gas:** Chevron/dsl, Valero, **food:** Miller's BBQ, Popeye's, Sonic, Wendy's

**163** I-410 S (162 from nb, exits left from sb)

**161** Binz-Engleman Rd (from nb), same as 160

**160** Splashtown Dr, **E** **gas:** Valero/Subway/dsl/24hr, **lodging:** Delux Inn, **W** **food:** Grady's BBQ, **lodging:** Best Value, Day's Inn, Holiday Inn/rest., Microtel, Super 8, Travelodge

**159b** Walters St, **E** **food:** McDonald's, **W** **lodging:** Econolodge, **other:** to Ft Sam Houston

**159a** New Braunfels Ave, **E** **gas:** Shell/dsl, Texaco/Burger King, **W** **gas:** Chevron, Valero/dsl/24hr, **food:** Sonic, **lodging:** Antonian Suites, Ramada Suites, **other:** to Ft Sam Houston

**158c** N Alamo St, Broadway

**158b** I-37 S, US 281 S, to Corpus Christi

**158a** US 281 N (from sb), to Johnson City

**157b a** Brooklyn Ave, Lexington Ave, N Flores, downtown, **E** **lodging:** Super 8, **other:** H HOSPITAL, **W** **food:** Luby's

**156** I-10 W, US 87, to El Paso

**155b** Durango Blvd, downtown, **E** **lodging:** Best Western, Courtyard, Fairfield Inn, Holiday Inn, La Quinta, Residence Inn, Woodfield Suites, **other:** H HOSPITAL, **W** **food:** McDonald's, **lodging:** Motel 6, Radisson

**155a** South Alamo St, **E** **gas:** Exxon, Shell, **food:** Church's, Denny's, McDonald's, Piedras Negras Mexican, Pizza Hut, Wendy's, **lodging:** Best Western, Comfort Inn, Day's Inn, Holiday Inn, La Quinta, Ramada Ltd, Residence Inn, **other:** USPO, **W** **gas:** Conoco, **lodging:** Microtel

**154b** S Laredo St, Ceballos St, same as 155b

**154a** Nogalitos St

**153** I-10 E, US 90 W, US 87, to Kelly AFB, Lackland AFB

**152b** Malone Ave, Theo Ave, **E** **food:** Taco Cabana/24hr, **W** **gas:** Shamrock, Shell

**152a** Division Ave, **E** **gas:** Chevron, **food:** Miller's BBQ, Whataburger/24hr, **lodging:** Quality Inn, **W** **food:** Sonic, **other:** transmissions

**151** Southcross Blvd, **E** **gas:** Exxon, Shell, **W** **gas:** Shell/dsl, **food:** Taquiera Mexican

**150b** Lp 13, Military Dr, **E** **gas:** Chevron, Texaco, **food:** Applebees, Denny's, KFC, Pizza Hut, Taco Cabana, **lodging:** La Quinta, **other:** AutoZone, Brake Check, Discount Tire, U-Haul, **W** **gas:** Exxon, Mobil, **food:** Chili's, China Buffet, Hungry Farmer Rest, Jack-in-the-Box, KFC, LJ Silver, Luby's, McDonald's, Mr Gatti, Panda Express, Pizza Hut, Wendy's, Whataburger, **other:** Best Buy, $Tree, Firestone/auto, HEB Foods, Home Depot, JC Penney, Office Depot, Old Navy, Sears/auto, Target, Walgreen, mall

**150a** Zarzamora St (149 fom sb), same as 150b

**149** Hutchins Blvd (from sb), **E** **gas:** Valero/dsl, **lodging:** Motel 6, **other:** H HOSPITAL, **W** **other:** Chevrolet, Ford, Kia

**148b** Palo Alto Rd, **W** **gas:** Valero

**148a** TX 16 S, spur 422 (exits left from sb), Poteet, **E** **gas:** Chevron, **W** **gas:** Phillips 66, **other:** $General, NAPA

**147** Somerset Rd, **E** **gas:** Shell/dsl, **W** **other:** Dodge, Ford Trucks

**146** Cassin Rd (from nb)

**145b** Lp 353 N

**145a** I-410, TX 16

**144** Fischer Rd, **E** **gas:** Valero/Subway/dsl/24hr, **lodging:** D&D Motel, **other:** Speedlube, RV camping, **W** **gas:** Love's/Carl's Jr/dsl/24hr

**142** Medina River Turnaround (from nb)

**141** Benton City Rd, Von Ormy, **W** **gas:** Shell/dsl/Parador Café

**140** Anderson Lp, 1604, **E** **gas:** Exxon/Burger King/dsl/24hr, **W** **gas:** Valero/Church's/Pizza Hut/dsl/scales/24hr, **other:** Alamo River RV Resort, to Sea World

**SAN ANTONIO**

**TX**

## INTERSTATE 35 CONT'D

N ↕ S

| | |
|---|---|
| 139 | Kinney Rd |
| 137 | Shepherd Rd, **E** truck repair, **W** gas/dsl, dsl repair |
| 135 | Luckey Rd |
| 133 | TX 132 S (from sb), Lytle, same as 131 |
| 131 | FM 3175, FM 2790, Benton City Rd, **E** other: NAPA, **W** gas: Conoco/dsl/24hr, food: DQ, McDonald's, Miller's BBQ, Sonic, Topis Mexican, Willie's Cafe, lodging: Day's Inn, other: $General, HEB Food/gas |
| 129mm | rest area both lanes, full 🚹 facilities, 🅲, 🏕, litter barrels, vending, petwalk |
| 127 | FM 471, Natalia |
| 124 | FM 463, Bigfoot Rd, **E** Ford |
| 122 | TX 173, Devine, **E** gas: Exxon/dsl, food: Panco Villa Mexican, other: Chevrolet, Chrysler/Jeep/Dodge, **W** gas: Chevron/McDonald's/Subway/dsl, food: CCC Steaks, DQ (2mi), Pizza Inn, Sonic, lodging: Country Corner Inn, Curves |
| 121 | TX 132 N, Devine, **E** other: Gusville RV Park |
| 118.5mm | weigh sta both lanes |
| 114 | FM 462, Bigfoot |
| 111 | US 57, to Eagle Pass, **W** gas: Valero/dsl |
| 104 | Lp 35, 3 mi **E** gas: Valero, food: McDonald's, Sonic, lodging: Executive Inn, other: 🅷 HOSPITAL |
| 101 | FM 140, Pearsall, **E** gas: Chevron/dsl, food: Cowpokes BBQ, lodging: Best Western, Rio Frio Motel, Royal Inn, other: 🅷 HOSPITAL, GMC, **W** gas: Exxon/Subway/dsl/24hr |
| 99 | FM 1581, to Divot, Pearsall |
| 93mm | parking/🏕 both lanes, litter barrels, handicapped accessible |
| 91 | FM 1583, Derby |
| 90mm | Frio River |
| 86 | Lp 35, Dilley |
| 85 | FM 117, **E** food: Garcia Café/motel, lodging: Relax Inn, **W** gas: Exxon, food: DQ, lodging: Safari Motel, Sona Inn, other: RV Park |
| 84 | TX 85, Dilley, **E** food: Millie's Mexican, other: 🅷 HOSPITAL, Chevrolet/Pontiac, Super S Foods/dsl, **W** gas: Shell/Church's/dsl/24hr, Valero/dsl/24hr, lodging: Executive Inn |
| 82 | County Line Rd, to Dilley |
| 77 | FM 469, Millett |
| 74 | Gardendale |
| 69 | 68 from nb, Lp 35, Cotulla, **E** Super S Food/gas |
| 67 | FM 468, to Big Wells, **E** gas: Exxon/Wendy's/dsl/24hr, Conoco/Country Store/rest., Valero/Pollo Grande/dsl/24hr, food: DQ, lodging: Executive Inn, Village Inn, other: tire repair, **W** gas: Chevron/McDonald's/dsl/scales/24hr |
| 65 | Lp 35, Cotulla |
| 63 | Elm Creek Interchange |
| 59mm | parking/🏕 both lanes, litter barrels, 🚹 accessible |
| 56 | FM 133, Artesia Wells |
| 48 | Caiman Creek Interchange |
| 39 | TX 44, Encinal, **E** gas: Love's/Subway/Chester Fried/dsl/scales/24hr |
| 38 | TX 44 (from nb), Encinal |
| 32 | San Roman Interchange |
| 29mm | inspection sta nb |
| 27 | Callaghan Interchange |

| | |
|---|---|
| 24 | 255 toll, Camino Colombia toll rd, to Monterrey |
| 22 | Webb Interchange |
| 18 | US 83 N, to Carrizo Springs, **E** TX **Travel Info Ctr (8am-5pm)** /rest area, full facilities, 🏕, litter barrels, petwalk, wireless internet, **W** RV Camping |
| 14mm | parking area, sb |
| 13 | Uniroyal Interchange, **E** gas: Pilot/McDonald's/Subway/dsl/scales/24hr/@, other: Blue Beacon, **W** gas: ⊕FLYING J/CountryMkt/dsl/scales/24hr/@, TA/Burger King/dsl/scales/24hr/@ |
| 10 | Port Laredo Carriers Dr (from nb) |
| 9 | Industrial Blvd, to Bob Bullock Lp (from sb only) |
| 9 | Industrial Blvd, to Bob Bullock Lp (from sb only) |
| 8b | Lp 20 W, to Solidarity Bridge |
| 8a | Lp 20 W, to to World Trade Bridge, Milo |
| 7 | Shilo Dr, Las Cruces Dr, sb only |
| 4 | FM 1472, Del Mar Blvd, **E** gas: Chevron/repair, Exxon/dsl, food: Applebee's, Burger King, Carino's Italian, CiCi's, DQ, IHOP, Jack-in-the-Box, Las Asadas Mexican, Lin's Chinese, McDonald's, Quizno's, Whataburger, lodging: Extended Stay America, Hampton Inn, Residence Inn, other: Albertson's, Best Buy, HEB Foods, Honda, Lowe's Whse, Marshall's, Old Navy, Radio Shack, Target, **W** gas: Shell/dsl, food: Golden Corral, lodging: Day's Inn, Executive House Motel, Motel 6, other: Harley Davidson |
| 3b | Mann Rd, **E** food: Krispy Kreme, Lin's Chinese, Logan's Roadhouse, Luby's, Olive Garden, Sirloin Stockade, lodging: Residence Inn, other: Buick, Dillard's, Foley's, Ford/Lincoln/Mercury, Honda, Lowes Whse, Mazda, Pontiac/Cadillac/GMC, Sears/auto, Toyota, mall, **W** food: Chili's, Golden Corral, Outback Steaks, Pancake House, Subway, Taco Palenque, lodging: Days Inn, Family Garden Inn, Fiesta Inn, La Hacienda Motel, Motel 6, Springhill Suites, other: $General, Home Depot, Michael's, Office Depot, Ross, Walmart/auto |
| 3a | San Bernardo Ave, **E** gas: Shell/dsl, food: Chick-fil-A, Emperor Chinese, Fuddrucker's, LJ Silver, Logan's Roadhouse, Luby's, Peter Piper Pizza, Red Lobster, lodging: Fairfield Inn, other: HEB Foods, K-Mart, NAPA, PepBoys, Sears/auto, SteinMart, mall, **W** gas: Chevron, food: Burger King, Coyote Creek Rest., DQ, Dunkin Donuts, Hacienda Mexican, Kettle, McDonald's, Pizza Hut, Popeye's, Taco Bell, Taco Palenque, Tori Cafe, Wendy's, Whataburger, lodging: Best Western, Fiesta Inn, Gateway Inn, Monterey Inn, Motel 6, Red Roof Inn, other: Gonzales Auto Parts, Goodyear/auto, Radio Shack, Sam's Club |

PEARSALL

LAREDO

TX

## INTERSTATE 35 CONT'D

**N ↕ S**

**2** US 59, Saunders Rd, **E gas:** Conoco, Gas USA, Shell, **food:** Jack-in-the-Box, **other:** Ⓗ HOSPITAL, **W gas:** Chevron/dsl/24hr, Conoco, Exxon/Burger King/dsl, Shell, Valero, **food:** Church's, Denny's, Popeye's, Pizza Hut, **lodging:** Civic Ctr Inn, Courtyard, El Cortez Motel, Executive Inn, Holiday Inn, La Quinta, Mayan Inn, **other:** Advance Parts, AutoZone, Mexico Insurance, Ramirez Tire

**1b** Park St, to Sanchez St, **W gas:** Conoco/dsl, **food:** KFC, La Mexicana Rest., Pizza Hut, Popeye's

**1a** Victoria St, Scott St, Washington St, **E gas:** Exxon, Shell, Valero, **W gas:** Chevron, Exxon/24hr, **food:** KFC, Mariachi Express, McDonald's, Wendy's, **other:** Firestone/auto, Goodyear/auto, transmissions

I-35 begins/ends in Laredo at Victoria St...access to multiple services

## INTERSTATE 35W CONT'D

| Exit # | Services |
|---|---|
| **N ↕ S** | |
| **I-35** | W begins/ends on I-35, exit 467. |
| **85b** | W Oak St, **E** Ⓗ HOSPITAL |
| **85a** | I-35E S |
| **84** | FM 1515, Bonnie Brae St, **E** Ⓗ HOSPITAL |
| **82** | FM 2449, to Ponder |
| **79** | Crawford Rd |
| **76** | FM 407, to Justin, Argyle, **W gas:** Phillips 66/dsl/24hr, **other:** Corral City RV Park, Paradise Foods |
| **76mm** | **picnic area both lanes, litter barrels,** 🚻 |
| **74** | FM 1171, to Lewisville |
| **72** | Dale Earnhardt Way, **E** same as 70, **W** TX Motor Speedway |
| **70** | TX 114, to Dallas, Bridgeport, **E gas:** 7-11, Shell/A&W/LJ Silver/dsl, **food:** Waffle House/24hr, **lodging:** Comfort Suites, Sleep Inn, **other:** to DFW ✈, **W lodging:** Doral Hotel, **other:** TX Motor Speedway |
| **68** | Eagle Pkwy, **W** ✈ |
| **67** | Alliance Blvd, **W other:** to Alliance Airport, FedEx |
| **66** | to Westport Pkwy, Keller-Haslet Rd, **E lodging:** Hampton Inn, Residence Inn, **W gas:** Mobil/Wendy's/dsl, **food:** Bryan's BBQ, Schlotsky's, Snooty Pig, Subway, Taco Bueno, **other:** USPO |
| **65** | TX 170 E, **E gas:** Pilot/McDonald's/dsl/24hr/@, **food:** IHOP, **other:** Cabela's/cafe |
| **64** | Golden Triangle Blvd, to Keller-Hicks Blvd, **E other:** Chrysler/Jeep/Dodge |
| **63** | Heritage Trace, **E food:** Cheddar's, **other:** JC Penney |
| **61** | North Tarrant Pkwy |
| **60** | US 287 N, US 81 N, to Decatur |
| **59** | Basswood (sb only) , **E gas:** Chevron/Jack-in-the-Box/dsl, **food:** Sonic, **other:** Home Depot |
| **58** | Western Ctr Blvd, **E gas:** 7-11, Shell, **food:** Blackeyed Pea, Braum's, Chili's, Denny's, Domino's, Dublin Square Rest., Macaroni Grill, On-the-Border, Posados Cafe, Quizno's, SaltGrass Steaks, Shady Oak BBQ, Wendy's, Zio's Italian, **lodging:** Best Western, Residence Inn, **other:** Kauffman Tire, **W food:** Boston's, Joe's Crabshack, Starbucks, Waffle House, Whataburger, **lodging:** Holiday Inn Express |
| **57b a** | I-820 E&W |
| **56b** | Melody Hills |
| **56a** | Meacham Blvd, **E gas:** Shell, **lodging:** Comfort Inn, Hilton Garden, La Quinta, **W gas:** Texaco/dsl, **food:** Cracker Barrel, McDonald's, Subway, **lodging:** Baymont Inn, Radisson, Super 8, **other:** USPO |
| **55** | Pleasantdale Ave (from nb) |
| **54c** | 33rd St, Long Ave (from nb) , **W gas:** Conoco/dsl, Valero/dsl, **lodging:** Motel 6 |
| **54b a** | TX 183 W, Papurt St, **W gas:** QuikStop/dsl, **lodging:** Classic Inn |
| **53** | North Side Dr, Yucca Dr, **E gas:** Shell/dsl, **W food:** Mercado Juarez Café, **lodging:** Country Inn&Suites |
| **53mm** | Trinity River |
| **52e** | Carver St (from nb) |
| **52d** | Pharr St |
| **52b** | US 377N, Belknap |
| **52a** | US 377 N, TX 121, to DFW |
| **51a** | I-31 E, to Avalene (from nb), downtown Ft Worth |
| **50c a** | I-30 W, E to Dallas |
| **50b** | TX 180 E (from nb) |
| **49b** | Rosedale St, **W** Ⓗ HOSPITAL |
| **49a** | Allen Ave, **E gas:** Chevron, **W** Ⓗ HOSPITAL |
| **48b** | Morningside Ave (from sb), same as 48a |
| **48a** | Berry St, **E gas:** Chevron/McDonald's, **food:** Texas Style Rest., **other:** Autozone, Sack'n Save Foods, **W gas:** RaceTrac, **other:** U-Haul |
| **47** | Ripy St, **E other:** transmissions, **W lodging:** Astro Inn |
| **46b** | Seminary Dr, **E gas:** RaceWay, **food:** Empress Cafe, Grandy's, Golden Corral, Jack-in-the-Box, Sonic, Subway, Taco Cabana, Whataburger, **lodging:** Day's Inn, Delux Inn, Regency Inn, Super 7 Inn, **other:** NAPA, **W gas:** Shell, **food:** Denny's, **other:** Dillard's, Dodge, $General, Firestone/auto, JC Penney, Sears |
| **46a** | Felix St (from nb) , **E gas:** Fina, **food:** Los Cantaritos Mexican **lodging:** Best Value Inn, **W food:** McDonald's, **other:** Carnival Foods, Family$ |
| **45b a** | I-20, E to Dallas, W to Abilene |
| **44** | Altamesa, **E lodging:** Radisson, **W food:** Rig Steaks, Waffle House, **lodging:** Baymont Inn, Best Western, Comfort Suites, La Quinta, Motel 6, South Lp Inn |
| **43** | Sycamore School Rd, **W gas** Exxon, QT/dsl, Shell, **food:** Chicken Express, Jack-in-the-Box, Whataburger, **other:** $General, Home Depot, Radio Shack, RV Ctr |
| **41** | Risinger Rd, **W other:** Camping World RV Service/Supplies, McClain's RV Ctr |
| **40** | Garden Acres Dr, **E gas:** Love's/Subway/dsl/scales/24hr, **lodging:** Microtel, **other:** Ⓗ HOSPITAL, Happy Camper RV Ctr, **W other:** Sun Time RV Ctr |
| **39** | FM 1187, McAlister Rd, **E** Ⓗ HOSPITAL, **W gas:** Citgo/dsl, Shamrock/dsl/24hr, **food:** Taco Bell, Waffle House, **lodging:** Howard Johnson |
| **38** | Alsbury Blvd, **E gas:** Chevron/24hr, Mobil/dsl, **food:** Chili's, Country Steaks, Cracker Barrel, IHOP, McDonald's, Mexican Inn Cafe, On the Border, Outback Steaks, Spring Creek BBQ, Tai-Pan Chinese, **lodging:** Holiday Inn Express, Super 8, **other:** Discount Tire, Ford, Lowe's Whse, **W gas:** Shell/24hr, **food:** Applebees, Arby's, Buffalo Wild Wings, Burger King, Chick-fil-A, Coldstone Creamery, Logan's Roadhouse, Olive Garden, Quizno's, Red Lobster, Sonic, Taco Cabana, Wendy's, **other:** Albertson's, Best Buy, Borders Books, Chevrolet, JC Penney, Kohl's, K-Mart, Michael's, Old Navy, PetsMart, Ross, Staples |

TX

## INTERSTATE 35W CONT'D

| | |
|---|---|
| **37** | TX 174, Wilshire Blvd, to Cleburne, **W** Walmart Super Ctr (2mi), from sb, same as 36 |
| **36** | FM 3391, TX 174S, Burleson, **E** **gas:** Citgo/dsl, Mobil, **food:** Miranda's Cantina, Sonic, Waffle House, **lodging:** Comfort Suites, Day's Inn, **W** **gas:** Chevron, **other:** $General |
| **34** | Briaroaks Rd (from sb) , **W** RV camping |
| **33mm** | **rest area sb, full ♿ facilities, ⎗, ⛱, litter barrels** |
| **32** | Bethesda Rd, **E** **gas:** Valero, **food:** Milana's Rest., **lodging:** 5 Star Inn, **other:** RV Ranch Park, **W** **other:** Buffalo Ridge RV Park, Mockingbird Hill RV Park |
| **31mm** | **rest area nb, full ♿ facilities, ⎗, ⛱, litter barrels** |
| **30** | FM 917, Mansfield, **E** **gas:** Shell/Sonic/dsl, **W** **gas:** Shell/dsl, **food:** RanchHouse Rest., **other:** Smith's RV Ctr |
| **27** | rd 604, Rd 707, **E** **other:** Ancira RV Ctr |
| **26b a** | US 67, Cleburne, **E** **gas:** Chevron, Exxon/Subway/24hr, Shell, **food:** Chicken Express, KFC, McDonald's, Pizza Hut, Sonic, Waffle House, Whataburger, **lodging:** Super 8, **other:** Brookshire Foods, Doc's RV Camping, Family$, Motor Home Specialist, Parts+, Walmart SuperCtr |
| **24** | FM 3136, FM 1706, Alvarado, **E** **gas:** Conoco/dsl, Shell/Grandy's/dsl/24hr, **food:** Alvarado House Rest. |
| **21** | rd 107, to Greenfield |
| **17** | FM 2258 |
| **16** | TX 81 S, Rd 201, Grandview |
| **15** | FM 916, Maypearl, **W** **gas:** Chevron/dsl, Mobil/Subway |
| **12** | FM 67 |
| **8** | FM 66, Itasca, **E** **gas:** Valero/dsl/café/24hr, **W** **gas:** gas/dsl, **food:** DQ, **other:** Ford, ⛱, **litter barrels** |
| **7** | FM 934, **E** ⛱, **litter barrels**, **W** **gas:** Exxon, **food:** Golden Chick Cafe |
| **3** | FM 2959, **E** to Hillsboro Airport |

**I-35W begins/ends on I-35, 371mm.**

## INTERSTATE 37

| Exit # | Services |
|---|---|
| **142b a** | I-35 S to Laredo, N to Austin. I-37 begins/ends on I-35 in San Antonio. |
| **141c** | Brooklyn Ave, Nolan St (from sb), downtown |
| **141b** | Houston St, **E** **lodging:** Red Roof Inn, **other:** tires, **W** **food:** Denny's, **lodging:** Crockett Hotel, Day's Inn, Hampton Inn, Holiday Inn, Hyatt Hotel, Marriott, La Quinta, Residence Inn, **other:** to The Alamo |
| **141a** | Commerce St, downtown, **W** **food:** Dennys, **lodging:** La Quinta, Marriott, **other:** Macey's |
| **140b** | Durango Blvd, downtown, **E** **food:** Bill Miller BBQ, **other:** to Alamo Dome |
| **140a** | Carolina St, Florida St, **E** **gas:** Citgo |
| **139** | I-10 W, US 87, US 90, to Houston, **W** **other:** to Sea World |
| **138c** | Fair Ave, Hackberry St, **E** **food:** Jack-in-the-Box, KFC, Popeye's, Taco Bell, Tapatia Mexian, Whataburger/24hr, **other:** Brake Check, Family$, Home Depot, **W** **gas:** Exxon, Shell |
| **138b** | E New Braunfels Ave (from sb) , **E** **food:** Chick-fil-A, Hong Kong Buffet, Jim's Rest., Luby's, McDonald's, Taco Cabana, Pizza Hut, Wendy's, **other:** mall, **W** **gas:** Exxon |

| | |
|---|---|
| **138a** | Southcross Blvd, W New Braunfels Ave, **E** **gas:** McDonald's, Taco Cabana, Wendy's, **W** **gas:** Exxon, **food:** Burger King, Sonic |
| **137** | Hot Wells Blvd, **W** **food:** IHOP, **lodging:** Motel 6, Super 8 |
| **136** | Pecan Valley Dr, **E** **gas:** Citgo/dsl, **food:** KFC/Taco Bell, Pizza Hut, **lodging:** La Quinta, Pecan Valley Inn, **other:** AutoZone, O'Reilly Parts, **W** HOSPITAL |
| **135** | Military Dr, Lp 13, **E** **gas:** Shell, Valero, **food:** Jack-in-the-Box, **lodging:** Best Western, **other:** Mission Trail RV park, **W** **gas:** Valero/Subway/dsl, **food:** Buffalo Wild Wings, Burger King, Carino's Italian, Chick-fil-A, Chili's, El Taco Tote, Little Caesars, LJ Silver/A&W, Panda Express, Peter Piper Pizza, Starbucks, Subway, Village Inn Rest, Whataburger/24hr, **lodging:** La Quinta, **other:** Advance Parts, Best Buy, BigLots, Discount Tire, $Tree, Hancock Fabrics, HEB Food/gas, Home Depot, Office Depot, PetCo, Radio Shack, Ross, Target, Walgreen, Walmart SuperCtr, to Brooks AFB |
| **133** | I-410, US 281 S |
| **132** | US 181 S, to Floresville, **E** **gas:** Fina/dsl, Shell |
| **130** | Donop Rd, Southton Rd, **E** **gas:** Valero/dsl/RV dump, **food:** Braunig Lake Café, Tom's Burgers, **lodging:** Comfort Inn, **other:** Braunig Lake RV Resort, **W** **gas:** Shell/dsl, **other:** car/truckwash |
| **127** | San Antonio River Turnaround (from nb), Braunig Lake |
| **127mm** | San Antonio River |
| **125** | FM 1604, Anderson Lp, **E** **gas:** Conoco/dsl/24hr, **food:** Burger King, **W** **gas:** Citgo/dsl, Exxon/dsl, **food:** Bill Miller BBQ, Whataburger |
| **122** | Priest Rd, Mathis Rd |
| **120** | Hardy Rd |
| **117** | FM 536 |
| **113** | FM 3006 |
| **112mm** | **picnic area both lanes, handicapped accessible, ⛱, litter barrels** |
| **109** | TX 97, to Floresville, **E** **gas:** Chevron/dsl/rest., **other:** Chrysler/Dodge/Jeep |
| **106** | Coughran Rd |
| **104** | spur 199, Leal Rd, to Pleasanton (no immediate sb return), same as 103 |
| **103** | US 281 N, Leal Rd, to Pleasanton, **E** **gas:** Valero/dsl, **food:** DQ, K&K Cafe, **lodging:** Kuntry Inn |
| **98** | TX 541, McCoy |
| **92** | US 281A, Campbellton, **2 mi** **W** **gas:** Kuntry Korner gas, **food:** Stetson's Cafe |
| **88** | FM 1099, to FM 791, Campbellton |

## INTERSTATE 37 CONT'D

**N ↕ S**

| | |
|---|---|
| 83 | FM 99, Whitsett, Peggy, **E gas:** Shell/dsl, **food:** cafe, **W gas:** Chevron/dsl |
| 82mm | **rest area sb, full ♿ facilities, ☎ ⛱, litter barrels** |
| 78mm | **rest area nb, full ♿ facilities, ☎ ⛱, litter barrels** |
| 76 | US 281A, FM 2049, Whitsett |
| 75mm | truck weigh sta sb |
| 74mm | truck weigh sta nb |
| 72 | US 281 S, Three Rivers, **4 mi W gas:** Valero, **food:** DQ, Subway, **lodging:** Best Western, Econolodge, **other:** to Rio Grande Valley |
| 69 | TX 72, Three Rivers, **W gas:** Valero/dsl/café/24hr, **other:** tires, to Choke Canyon SP |
| 65 | FM 1358, Oakville, **E food:** Van's BBQ, **W gas:** Oakville Mercantile/gas |
| 59 | FM 799 |
| 56 | US 59, George West, **E gas:** Valero/dsl/24hr, **W gas:** Shell/Subway/24hr, Valero/Burger King/dsl/24hr, **other:** Rockin'N RV Park |
| 51 | Hailey Ranch Rd |
| 47 | FM 3024, FM 534, Swinney Switch Rd, **W other:** Mikes Mkt/gas (1mi), to KOA (4mi) |
| 44mm | parking area sb |
| 42mm | parking area nb |
| 40 | FM 888 |
| 36 | TX 359, to Skidmore, Mathis, **W gas:** Valero/dsl (1mi), Shell/McDonald's/dsl, Texaco/Subway/dsl, **food:** Pizza Hut, **lodging:** Best Western, **other:** Lake Corpus Christi SRA |
| 34 | TX 359 W, **E other:** Adventure TX RV Ctr, **W gas:** Valero/dsl, **lodging:** Pizza Hut, **other:** Ford, to Lake Corpus Christi SP |
| 31 | TX 188, to Sinton, Rockport |
| 22 | TX 234, FM 796, to Odem, Edroy |
| 20b | Cooper Rd |
| 19.5mm | **picnic area both lanes, ♿ accessible, ⛱, litter barrels** |
| 17 | US 77 N, to Victoria |
| 16 | LaBonte Park, **W info, ⛱, litter barrels** |
| 15 | Sharpsburg Rd (from sb), Redbird Ln |
| 14 | US 77 S, Redbird Ln, to Kingsville, Robstown, **1 mi W on FM 624...gas:** Valero/Burger King/dsl, Shell, **food:** BBQ, Chili's, CiCi's, Denny's, Good'n Crisp Chicken, K-Bob's, Miller's BBQ, Pizza Hut, Popeye's, Quizno's, Sonic, Subway, Whataburger/24hr, Wienerschnitzel, **lodging:** Comfort Inn, **other:** Ⓗ HOSPITAL, Beall's, CVS Drug, Firestone/auto, Home Depot, Radio Shack, Walmart SuperCtr |
| 13b | Sharpsburg Rd (from nb) |
| 13a | FM 1694, Callicoatte Rd, Leopard St |
| 11b | FM 24, Violet Rd, Hart Rd, **E food:** Chicken Shack, Roadhouse Cafe, **lodging:** La Quinta, **W gas:** Exxon/Circle K/dsl, Valero/dsl, **food:** DQ, Domino's, KFC/LJ Silver, McDonald's, Schlotsky's, Sonic, Subway, Taco Bell, Whataburger/24hr, **lodging:** Hampton Inn, **other:** AutoZone, Family$, HEB Food/gas, O'Reilly Parts, Walgreen |
| 11a | McKinzie Rd, **E gas:** Shell, **lodging:** La Quinta, **W gas:** Valero/dsl |
| 10 | Carbon Plant Rd |
| 9 | FM 2292, Up River Rd, Rand Morgan Rd, **W gas:** Valero/dsl, **food:** Whataburger/24hr |

**CORPUS CHRISTI**

**E ↕ W SHAMROCK**

| | |
|---|---|
| 7 | Suntide Rd, Tuloso Rd, Clarkwood Rd, **W other:** Freightliner Trucks |
| 6 | Southern Minerals Rd, **E gas:** refinery |
| 5 | Corn Products Rd, Valero Way, **E other:** Kenworth, **W gas:** PetroFleet, **food:** Jalisco Rest., **lodging:** Best Value, Red Carpet Inn, Super 8, Travelodge |
| 4b | Lantana St, McBride Lane (from sb), **W lodging:** Airport Inn, Motel 6 |
| 4a | TX 358, to Padre Island, **W gas:** Shell/dsl, **lodging:** Drury Inn, Holiday Inn, Quality Inn, **other:** Walmart Super Ctr (6mi) |
| 3b | McBride Lane (from nb), **W lodging:** Ramada Ltd, **other:** Greyhound Raceway |
| 3a | Navigation Blvd, **E gas:** Valero/dsl, **lodging:** Rodeway Inn, **W gas:** Exxon/dsl, **food:** Denny's, **lodging:** Best Western, Day's Inn, Hampton Inn, La Quinta, **other:** CarQuest |
| 2 | Up River Rd, **E refinery |
| 1e | Lawrence Dr, Nueces Bay Blvd, **W gas:** Valero, **food:** Church's, **lodging:** Red Roof Inn, **other:** Aamco, HEB Foods, Firestone, USPO |
| 1d | Port Ave (from sb), **W gas:** Coastal, Shell, **food:** Vick's Burgers, **lodging:** Comfort Inn, **other:** Radio Shack, Port of Corpus Christi |
| 1c | US 181, TX 286, Shoreline Blvd, Corpus Christi, **W Ⓗ HOSPITAL** |
| 1b | Brownlee St (from nb) |
| 1a | Buffalo St (from sb), **1 mi W on Shoreline... E gas:** Valero/dsl, **food:** Burger King, Joes Crabshack, Landry's Seafood, Subway, Whataburger, **lodging:** Bayfront Inn, Best Western, Super 8, **other:** USPO, I-37 begins/ends on US 181 in Corpus Christi. |

## INTERSTATE 40

| Exit # | Services |
|---|---|
| 177mm | Texas/Oklahoma state line |
| 176 | spur 30 (from eb), to Texola |
| 175mm | **picnic area wb, ⛱, litter barrels** |
| 173mm | **picnic area eb, ⛱, litter barrels** |
| 169 | FM 1802, Carbon Black Rd |
| 167 | FM 2168, Daberry Rd, **N gas:** Valero/dsl, **other:** RV Park |
| 165mm | check sta wb |
| 164 | Lp 40 (from wb), to Shamrock, **1 mi S lodging:** Budget Inn, **other:** Ⓗ HOSPITAL, museum |
| 163 | US 83, to Wheeler, Shamrock, **N gas:** Chevron/Pizza Hut/Taco Bell/dsl, Conoco/dsl, **food:** Mitchell's Rest., **lodging:** Best Western, Irish Inn/rest., **other:** Ace Hardware, mall, **S gas:** Phillips 66/Subway/24hr, Valero/dsl, **food:** DQ, McDonald's, **lodging:** Budget Host, Econolodge, Sleep Inn, Western Motel |
| 161 | Lp 40, Rte 66 (from eb), to Shamrock, **S gas:** Chevron |
| 157 | FM 1547, Lela, **1 mi S other:** RV Camping |
| 152 | FM 453, Pakan Rd |
| 150mm | **picnic area wb, ⛱, litter barrels** |
| 149mm | **picnic area eb, ⛱, litter barrels** |
| 148 | FM 1443, Kellerville Rd |
| 146 | County Line Rd |
| 143 | Lp 40 (from wb), to McLean, to gas |
| 142 | TX 273, FM 3143, to McLean, **N gas:** Shell, **food:** Red River Steaks, **lodging:** Cactus Inn, **other:** RV Camping |
| 141 | Rte 66 (from eb), McLean, same as 142 |

**TX**

# TEXAS 465

## INTERSTATE 40 CONT'D

**E** ↕ **W**

| | |
|---|---|
| **135** | FM 291, Rte 66, Alanreed, **S gas:** Conoco/motel/café/RV park, **other:** USPO |
| **132** | Johnson Ranch Rd, ranch access |
| **131mm** | rest area wb, full ♿ facilities, 🚻, ⛱, litter barrels, petwalk |
| **129mm** | rest area eb, full ♿ facilities, 🚻, ⛱, littler barrels, petwalk |
| **128** | FM 2477, to Lake McClellan, **N other:** Lake McClellan RA/RV dump |
| **124** | TX 70 S, to Clarendon, **S** camping |
| **121** | TX 70 N, to Pampa |
| **114** | Lp 40, Groom |
| **113** | FM 2300, Groom, **S gas:** Texaco/dsl, **food:** DQ, **lodging:** Chalet Inn |
| **112** | FM 295, Groom, **S other:** Biggest Cross, **1 mi S** gas |
| **110** | Lp 40, Rte 66 |
| **109** | FM 294 |
| **108mm** | parking area wb, litter barrels |
| **106mm** | parking area eb, ⛱, litter barrels |
| **105** | FM 2880, grain silo |
| **98** | TX 207 S (from wb), to Claude |
| **96** | TX 207 N, to Panhandle, **N gas:** Love's/Subway/dsl/24hr, **S lodging:** Budget Host, Conway Inn/cafe |
| **89** | FM 2161, to Rte 66 |
| **87** | FM 2373 |
| **87mm** | picnic areas both lanes, litter barrels |
| **85** | Amarillo Blvd, Durrett Rd, access to camping |
| **81** | FM 1912, **N gas:** Phillips 66/dsl, **S gas:** Valero/Am Best/dsl/rest./scales/24hr/@, Country Fresh Rest. |
| **80** | FM 228, **N other:** AOK RV Park |
| **78** | US 287 S (from eb), FM 1258, Pullman Rd, same as 77 |
| **77** | FM 1258, Pullman Rd, **N gas:** USA Travel Plaza/Arby's/dsl/scales/24hr, **S other:** Custom RV Ctr |
| **76** | spur 468, **N gas:** ⊛FLYING J/Conoco/dsl/LP/rest./LP/RV dump/scales/24hr, Shell/dsl, **lodging:** Holiday Inn Express, **other:** GMC/Volvo/Mack Trucks, tourist info, **S gas:** Speedco |
| **75** | Lp 335, Lakeside Rd, **N gas:** Pilot/McDonald's/dsl/rest./24hr/@, **food:** Waffle House, **lodging:** Airport Plaza Hotel, Best Value Inn, Quality Inn, Super 8, **other:** UPS, Peterbilt Trucks, KOA (2mi), **S gas:** Petro/Mobil/dsl/rest./@, **other:** Blue Beacon |
| **74** | Whitaker Rd, **N lodging:** Big Texan Inn/café, **other:** RV camping, **S gas:** Love's/Subway/dsl/@, TA/Exxon/FoodCourt/dsl/24hr/@, **lodging:** Budget Inn, **other:** Blue Beacon |
| **73** | Eastern St, Bolton Ave, Amarillo, **N gas:** Shell/dsl, Valero/dsl, **food:** Stockman's Rest., **lodging:** Motel 6, Red Roof Inn, Value Place, **S gas:** Chevron/dsl, **lodging:** Best Western, Motel 6, **other:** Ford Trucks |
| **72b** | Grand St, Amarillo, **N gas:** Shell, **food:** Henk's BBQ, KFC, **lodging:** Motel 6, Travelodge, Value Inn, **other:** Family$, O'Reilly Parts, U-Haul, **S gas:** Exxon, Murphy USA, Phillips 66, **food:** Braum's, Chicken Express, McDonald's, Pizza Hut, Sonic, Subway, Taco Cabana, Taco Villa, Whataburger, **lodging:** Motel 6, **other:** Advance Parts, AutoZone, Big Lots, $General, Walmart SuperCtr, same as 73 |

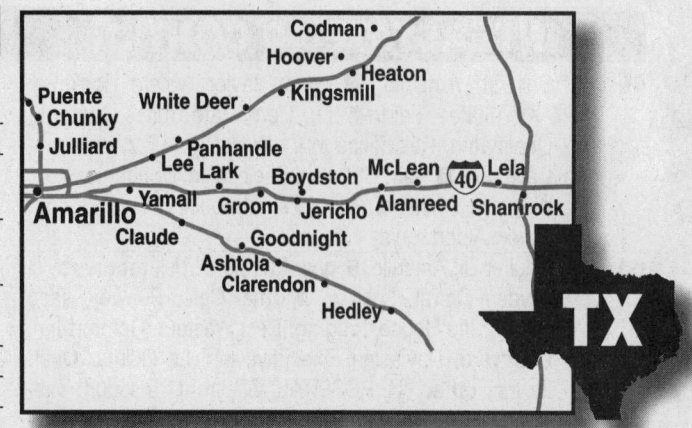

| | |
|---|---|
| **72a** | Nelson St, **N food:** Cracker Barrel, KFC, **lodging:** Ashmore Inn, Budget Host, Econolodge, La Kiva Hotel, Ramada Inn, Sleep Inn, Super 8, Travelodge, **other:** Qtrhorse Museum, **S gas:** Chevron, Shell/dsl, **lodging:** Camelot Inn, **other:** Chevrolet |
| **71** | Ross St, Osage St, Amarillo, **N gas:** Conoco/dsl, Shell/dsl, **food:** Burger King, El Tapatio's Mexican, IHOP, Longhorn Diner, LJ Silver, McDonald's, Popeye's, Schlotsky's, Subway, **lodging:** Coachlight Inn, Comfort Inn, Day's Inn, Holiday Inn, Microtel, **S gas:** Valero, **food:** Arby's, Denny's, Fiesta Grande Mexican, Sonic, Taco Bell, Wendy's, **lodging:** Hampton Inn, Howard Johnson, La Quinta, Ramada Ltd, **other:** Chevrolet, Ford, Hyundai, Sam's Club/gas, USPO |
| **70** | I-27 S, US 60 W, US 87, US 287, to Canyon, Lubbock, **N other:** Goodyear/auto, bank |
| **69b** | Washington St, Amarillo, **N other:** **S gas:** Phillips 66, Shell, **food:** DQ, Subway, **other:** CVS Drug |
| **69a** | Crockett St, access to same as 68b |
| **68b** | Georgia St, **N gas:** Shell/Subway, **food:** Schlotzky's, TGI-Friday, **lodging:** Ambassador Hotel, **S gas:** Phillips 66, **food:** Burger King, Denny's, Furr's Café, LJ Silver, Moe's SW Grille, Red Lobster, Taco Villa, TX Roadhouse, Western Sizzlin, Whataburger, **lodging:** Baymont Inn, Comfort Suites, Econolodge, Holiday Inn Express, Motel 6, Quality Inn, Travelodge, **other:** Ⓗ HOSPITAL, Cadillac, Chrysler/Dodge, Discount Tire, Hastings Books, Home Depot, K-Mart, Mitsubishi, Office Depot, Radio Shack, Saturn |
| **68a** | Julian Blvd, Paramount Blvd, **N gas:** Chevron, Shell, **food:** Arby's, Chili's, Macaroni Joe's, Nick's Rest., Pancho's Mexican, Pizza Hut, Schlotzsky's, Wendy's, **lodging:** Harley Hotel, same as 67, **S gas:** Valero, **food:** Caboose Diner, Cactus Grill, Cajun Magic, Calico Country Café, El Chico, Godfather's, Kabuki's Japanese Steaks, LJ Silver, New China, Orient Express, Peking Rest., Pizza Planet, Popeye's, Ruby Tequila's Mexican, Steak&Ale, **other:** Pennzoil |
| **67** | Western St, Amarillo, **N gas:** Phillips 66, Shell, **food:** Beef Rigger Rest., Bourbon St. Cafe, Braum's, Burger King, Chili's, Cty Line BBQ, Legends Grill, Marie Callender's, McDonald's, Pancho's Mexican, Rosa's Cafe, Sonic, Subway, Taco Bell, **S gas:** Phillips 66, **food:** Blue Sky Rest., Catfish Shack, DQ, IHOP, Furr's Café, Gary's BBQ, IHOP, Olive Garden, Taco Cabana, Vince's Pizza, Waffle House, Wienerschnitzel, **lodging:** Baymont Inn, Holiday Inn Express, **other:** Discount Tire, NAPA, O'Reilly Parts, Radio Shack, same 68 |

**A M A R I L L O**

**TX**

## INTERSTATE 40 CONT'D

**66** Bell St, Amarillo, **N gas:** Taylor, Valero, **lodging:** AmeriSuites, Fairfield Inn, HomeGate Suites, Motel 6, Quality Inn, Residence Inn, **other:** Big A Parts, Harley-Davidson, **S gas:** Chevron, Shell, **food:** Doughnut Stop, King & I Chinese, Popeye's, Starbucks, Taco Bueno, **other:** Albertson's

**65** Coulter Dr, Amarillo, **N gas:** Phillips 66/dsl, **food:** Arby's, Golden Corral, Luby's, My Thai Café, Subway, Taco Bell, Waffle House, **lodging:** Best Western, Comfort Inn, Courtyard, Day's Inn, Executive Inn, La Quinta, Quality Inn, **other:** H HOSPITAL, Chevrolet, Discount Tire, Dodge, Firestone/auto, Nissan, **S gas:** Chevron/KFC, Shell, **food:** BBQ, Braum's, ChinaStar, ChuckeCheese, CiCi's, Hoffbrau Steaks, Jason's Deli, McDonald's, Outback Steaks, Pizza Hut, Santa Fe Rest., Sonic, Subway, Taco Villa, TCBY, Wendy's, Whataburger, Wienerschnitzel, **lodging:** Hampton Inn, 5th Season Inn, **other:** Best Buy, Goodyear/auto, IGA Foods, Lowe's Whse, Sears/auto

**64** Soncy Rd, to Pal Duro Cyn, **N food:** Carino's Italian, Furr's Buffet, Joe's Crabshack, Red Robin, Lin's Chinese, Logan's Roadhouse, **lodging:** Comfort Inn, Country Inn&Suites, Drury Inn, Extended Stay America, Hilton Garden, Homewood Suites, **other:** Discount Tire, Gander Mtn, **S gas:** Valero/dsl/24hr, **food:** Applebee's, DQ, Fazoli's, Hooters, Legends Steaks, McDonald's, On-the-Border, Ruby Tuesday, Starbucks, Subway, Zookini's Grill, **other:** Barnes&Noble, Best Buy, Circuit City, Dillard's, Ford, Home Depot, K-Mart, Kohl's, Mazda, Old Navy, Ross, Sears, Target, World Mkt, mall

**62b** Lp 40, Amarillo Blvd, **N** Gander Mtn.

**62a** Hope Rd, Helium Rd, **S other:** RV camping, antiques

**60** Arnot Rd, **S gas:** Love's/Subway/dsl, **other:** Oasis RV Resort/dump

**57** RM 2381, to Bushland, **N** grain silos, **S gas:** Shell/dsl, **food:** Original Fried Pie Place, **other:** USPO, RV camping/dump (1mi)

**55mm** parking area wb, litter barrels

**54** Adkisson Rd

**53.5mm** **parking area eb, litter barrels**

**49** (50 from wb) FM 809, to Wildorado, **S gas:** Phillips 66/dsl, **lodging:** Royal Inn

**42** Everett Rd

**37** Lp 40 W, to Vega, **1 mi N lodging:** Bonanza Motel, **other:** Walnut RV Park, same as 36

**36** US 385, Vega, **N gas:** Conoco/dsl/24hr, **food:** DQ, **lodging:** Best Western, Comfort Inn, **other:** CarQuest, **S gas:** Shell/dsl

**35** to Rte 66, to Vega, **N lodging:** Best Western, **lodging:** Bonanza Motel (1mi), **other:** Walnut RV Park (1mi), same as 36

**32mm** **picnic area both lanes, litter barrels**

**28** to Rte 66, Landergin

**22** TX 214, to Adrian, **N lodging:** Fabulous 40's Motel, **S gas:** Phillips 66/dsl/café, **other:** Tommy's Foods

**18** FM 2858, Gruhlkey Rd, **S gas:** Shell/Stuckey's/rest./dsl

**15** Ivy Rd

**13mm** **picnic area both lanes, ⛽, litter barrels**

**5.5mm** turnout

**0** Lp 40, to Glenrio

**0mm** Texas/New Mexico state line, *Central/Mountain time zone*

## INTERSTATE 44

| Exit # | Services |
|---|---|
| 15mm | Texas/Oklahoma state line, Red River |
| 14 | Lp 267, E 3rd St, **W other:** Burk RV Park |
| 13 | Glendale St, **W food:** Subway, **other:** Beall's, Family$, Sav-A-Lot Foods, Walmart |
| 12 | Burkburnett, **E lodging:** Hampton Inn, **W gas:** Fina/7-11, **food:** Braum's, Feedlot Rest., Lite Pan Asian, Mazzio's, McDonald's, Whataburger/24hr, **other:** CarQuest, Chevrolet/Pontiac, Ford |
| 11 | FM 3429, Daniels Rd |
| 9mm | picnic area both lanes, ⛽, litter barrels, petwalk |
| 7 | East Rd |
| 6 | Bacon Switch Rd |
| 5a | FM 3492, Missile Rd, **E food:** El Mejicano Rest., Hunan Chinese, Pizza Hut, **other:** st patrol, **W gas:** Exxon/dsl |
| 5 | Access Rd |
| 4 | City Loop St |
| 3c | FM 890, **W food:** Cracker Barrel, KFC/Taco Bell, Subway, **other:** Walmart SuperCtr/gas, vet |
| 3b | sp 325, Sheppard AFB |
| 3a | US 287 N, to Amarillo, **W gas:** Shell, **food:** Carl's Jr, **lodging:** Ramada Ltd |
| 2 | Maurine St, **E gas:** Fina/7-11/dsl, Shell/dsl, **lodging:** Best Value Inn, Comfort Inn, Motel 6, Quality Inn, **other:** Chevrolet, Mazda, **W gas:** Fina/7-11, **food:** China Star, Denny's, El Chico, LJ Silver, Whataburger/24hr, **lodging:** Best Western, Candlewood Suites, La Quinta, Super 8, Travelers Inn |
| 1d | US 287 bus, Lp 370, **W gas:** Conoco/dsl, **lodging:** Travelodge |
| 1c | Texas Tourist Bureau, **E gas:** $Saver, **W lodging:** The Inn |
| 1b | Scotland Park (from nb) |
| 1a | US 277 S, to Abilene |
| 0mm | I-44 begins/ends in Witchita Falls, **1-2 mi S in Wichita Falls**...**gas:** Valero, **food:** Arby's, Burger King, Carl's Jr, IHOP, McDonald's, Popeye's, Subway, **lodging:** Econolodge, Holiday Inn, Howard Johnson, Knights Inn, **other:** H HOSPITAL |

## INTERSTATE 45

| Exit # | Services |
|---|---|
| 286 | to I-35 E, to Denton. I-45 begins/ends in Dallas. |
| 285 | Bryan St E, US 75 N |
| 284b a | I-30, W to Ft Worth, E to Texarkana, access to H HOSPITAL |
| 283b | Pennsylvania Ave, to MLK Blvd, **E gas:** Shamrock, **W food:** KFC/Taco Bell |
| 283a | Lamar St |
| 281 | Overton St (from sb) , **W gas:** Chevron |
| 280 | Illinois Ave, Linfield St, **E lodging:** Star Motel, **W gas:** Shell/dsl |
| 279b a | Lp 12 |
| 277 | Simpson Stuart Rd, **W other:** to Paul Quinn Coll |
| 276b a | I-20, W to Ft Worth, E to Shreveport |
| 275 | TX 310 N (from nb, no re-entry) |
| 274 | Dowdy Ferry Rd, Hutchins, **E gas:** Exxon/Subway, Shell/dsl, **lodging:** Gold Inn, **W food:** DQ, Jack-in-the-Box |
| 273 | Wintergreen Rd |

(Left margin, top to bottom: **AMARILLO** | **E** ↕ **W** | **VEGA** | TX)

(Center margin, top to bottom: **E** ↕ **W** | **WICHITA FALLS** | **N** ↕ **S** | **DALLAS**)

**N**
**S**
**D A L L A S**

## INTERSTATE 45 CONT'D

| 272 | Fulghum Rd, **E** gas: Love's/Carl's Jr/dsl/scales/24hr, **W** weigh sta, both lanes |
|---|---|
| 271 | Pleasant Run Rd |
| 270 | Belt Line Rd, to Wilmer, **E** gas: Shell/dsl, Texaco/Pizza Inn/dsl, **W** gas: Exxon/Sonic/dsl, Shell/Church's/Subway/dsl, **other:** $General |
| 269 | Mars Rd |
| 268 | Malloy Bridge Rd |
| 267 | Frontage Rd |
| 266 | FM 660, **W** gas: Shamrock/dsl, **food:** DQ |
| 265 | Lp 45, Ferris, nb only |
| 263a b | Lp 561 |
| 262 | frontage rd |
| 260 | Lp 45 |
| 259 | FM 813, FM 878, Jefferson St, **W** other: Goodyear |
| 258 | Lp 45, Palmer, **E** gas: Exxon/Subway/dsl/scales/24hr, **other:** golf, **W** gas: Mobil/dsl/Quizno's/24hr, **lodging:** Palmer Motel |
| 255 | FM 879, Garrett, **E** gas: Exxon/dsl, **W** gas: Chevron/dsl |
| 253 | Lp 45, **W** gas: Shell/Subway/dsl, **lodging:** Geneva Inn (2mi) |
| 251b | TX 34, Ennis, **E** gas: Fina/dsl, Shell/dsl, **food:** Bubba's BBQ, McDonald's, **lodging:** Best Western, Day's Inn, Holiday Inn Express, **other:** Ford, **W** gas: Chevron/dsl, Exxon/dsl/24hr, **food:** Arby's, Braum's, Burger King, Chili's, Corral Buffet, Denny's, DQ, Domino's, Golden Corral, IHOP, Jack-in-the-Box, KFC, Sonic, Starbucks, Subway, Taco Bell/Pizza Hut, Taco Cabana, Waffle House, Wall Chinese Café, Wendy's, Whataburger/24hr, **lodging:** Ennis Inn, Quality Inn, **other:** Ⓗ HOSPITAL, AutoZone, Chevrolet/Pontiac, Chrysler/Dodge, $Tree, Ford/Mercury, Pennzoil, Pontiac/Buick, Radio Shack, Walmart SuperCtr/gas, RV camping |
| 251a | Creechville Rd, FM 1181, **W** Ⓗ HOSPITAL |
| 249 | FM 85, Ennis, **E** lodging: Budget Inn, **W** gas: Exxon/Subway, **other:** Blue Beacon, **other:** repair |
| 247 | US 287 N, to Waxahatchie |
| 246 | FM 1183, Alma, **W** gas: Chevron |
| 244 | FM 1182 |
| 243 | Frontage Rd |
| 242 | Rice |
| 239 | FM 1126, **W** gas: Phillips 66 |
| 238 | FM 1603, **E** gas: Fina/dsl/24hr, **other:** Casita RV Trailers |
| 237 | Frontage Rd |
| 235b | Lp I-45 (from sb), to Corsicana |
| 235a | Frontage Rd |
| 232 | Roane Rd, E 5th Ave |
| 231 | TX 31, Corsicana, **E** gas: gas/dsl, **food:** Jack-in-the-Box, **lodging:** Best Western, Colonial Inn, **other:** Chevrolet/Cadillac/Pontiac/Buick, **W** gas: Chevron, Exxon/Subway/dsl, **food:** Bill's Fried Chicken, DQ, McDonald's, **lodging:** Comfort Inn, **other:** Ⓗ HOSPITAL, Chrysler/Dodge/Jeep, Ford/Lincoln/Mercury, to Navarro Coll |
| 229 | US 287, Palestine, **E** gas: Exxon/Wendy's/dsl, Shell/dsl/24hr, **food:** Chili's, Russell Stover Candies, Sonic, **lodging:** Hampton Inn, Holiday Inn, **other:** Gander Mtn, Home Depot, VF Outlet/famous brands, **W** food: Cancun Mexican, Waffle House, **lodging:** Corsicana Inn, Motel 6, Royal Inn, Travelers Inn |

**F A I R F I E L D**

| 228b | Lp 45 (exits left from nb), Corsicana, **2 mi W** services in Corsicana |
|---|---|
| 228a | 15th St, Corsicana |
| 225 | FM 739, Angus, **E** gas: Conoco/dsl, Exxon/dsl, **other:** to Chambers Reservoir, RV park, **W** gas: Citgo/dsl, **other:** Camper Depot |
| 221 | Frontage Rd |
| 220 | Frontage Rd |
| 219b | Frontage Rd |
| 219a | TX 14 (from sb), to Mexia, Richland, **W** gas: Shell |
| 218 | FM 1394 (from nb), Richland, **W** gas: Shell |
| 217mm | rest area both lanes, full ♿ facilities, 📞, 🍴, litter barrels, vending, petwalk |
| 213 | TX 75 S, FM 246, to Wortham, **W** gas: Texaco/dsl |
| 211 | FM 80, to Streetman, Kirvin |
| 206 | FM 833 |
| 198 | FM 27, to Wortham, **E** gas: Shell/BBQ, **food:** Gilberto's Mexican, **lodging:** La Quinta, **other:** HOSPITAL, Cedar Grove RV Park (3mi), **W** gas: Exxon, Love's/Burger King/dsl/24hr/scales, **lodging:** Budget Inn, **other:** Deer Crossing RV Park (1mi) |
| 197 | US 84, Fairfield, **E** gas: Chevron, Exxon, Shell/dsl, **food:** DQ, Jack-in-the-Box, McDonald's, Ponte's Diner, Sam's Rest., Sonic, Subway/Texas Burger, **lodging:** Day's Inn, Holiday Inn Express, Super 8, **other:** Brookshire Foods/gas, Chevrolet, Chrysler/Jeep/Dodge, Fred's Store, **W** gas: Shell/dsl, Texaco/dsl, **food:** Dalia's Mexican, I-45 Rest., KFC/Taco Bell, Pizza Hut, Sammy's Rest., **lodging:** Best Value, Regency Inn, **other:** Ace Hardware, Ford/Mercury |
| 189 | TX 179, to Teague, **E** gas: Exxon/dsl/cafe, Citgo/dsl/cafe |
| 187mm | picnic area both lanes, 🍴, litter barrels |
| 180 | TX 164, to Groesbeck |
| 178 | US 79, Buffalo, **E** gas: Conoco, Gilliam's/dsl, Shell/dsl, **food:** Subway/Texas Burger, **other:** Brookshire Foods/gas, Family$, **W** gas: Exxon/Church's/Pizza Inn/dsl/scales, Mobil/dsl, Shamrock/dsl/24hr, **food:** Dickey's BBQ, DQ, Longhorn BBQ, Pitt Grill/24hr, Rainbow Rest., Rancho Mexican, Sonic, **lodging:** Best Western, Comfort Inn, Economy Inn |
| 175mm | Bliss Creek |
| 166mm | weigh sta sb |
| 164 | TX 7, Centerville, **E** gas: Chevron, Shell/Woody's BBQ/dsl, **food:** Country Cousins Café, Texas Burger/Subway, **lodging:** Day's Inn, **W** gas: Exxon/24hr, Shell/Woody's BBQ/dsl, **food:** DQ, Jack-in-the-Box, Roble's Mexican |

TX

## INTERSTATE 45 CONT'D

**160mm** picnic area sb, tables, litter barrels, hist marker, ♿ accessible

**159mm** Boggy Creek

**156** FM 977, to Leona, **W gas:** Exxon/dsl

**155mm** picnic area nb, ⛱, litter barrels, ♿ accessible

**152** TX OSR, to Normangee, **W gas:** Chevron/dsl, **other:** Yellow Rose RV Park/café

**146** TX 75

**142** US 190, TX 21, Madisonville, **E gas:** Exxon/BBQ/dsl, **food:** Robel's Mexican, **lodging:** Best Western, Carefree Inn, **W gas:** Chevron/Church's, Exxon, Shell/Subway/24hr, **food:** China Café, Jack-in-the-Box, Lakeside Rest., McDonald's, Pizza Hut, Sonic, Texas Burger, **lodging:** Budget Motel, Western Lodge, **other:** Ⓗ HOSPITAL, Toyota

**136** spur 67, **E** Home on the Range RV camping/LP (3mi)

**132** FM 2989

**124mm** rest area both lanes, full ♿ facilities, 🕻, ⛱, litter barrels, vending, petwalk

**123** FM 1696

**118** TX 75, **E gas:** Shell/Hitchin Post/dsl/24hr/@, **other:** Texas Prison Museum, truckwash, **W gas:** Pilot/Wendy's/dsl/scales/24hr/@, **food:** Rodeo Mexican

**116** US 190, TX 30, **E gas:** Valero/dsl, **food:** Bandera Grill, Church's, El Chico, Mr Gatti's, Golden Corral, Imperial Garden Chinese, Jct Steaks, McDonald's, Popeye's, Sonic, The Jct Rest., Whataburger/24hr, **lodging:** Comfort Inn, Econolodge, La Quinta, Motel 6, **other:** Ⓗ HOSPITAL, AutoZone, Brookshire Foods/gas, CVS Drug, &General, Firestone/auto, Hastings Books, Nissan, O'Reilly Parts, Jeep/Dodge, Pontiac/Buick/GMC, Walgreen, vet, **W gas:** Exxon/dsl, Chevron/24hr, Shell/24hr, **food:** Bob Luby's Seafood, Burger King, Chili's, CiCi's, Denny's, Grand Buffet, IHOP, Jack-in-the-Box, KFC, Pizza Hut, Schlotzsky's, Starbucks, Subway, Taco Bell, **lodging:** Holiday Inn Express, **other:** Chrysler/Jeep/Dodge, Discount Tire, $Tree, GNC, Home Depot, JC Penney, Kroger, Office Depot, Radio Shack, Walmart SuperCtr/gas

**114** FM 1374, **E gas:** Exxon/dsl, Shell, **food:** DQ, Margaritas Rest., **lodging:** Gateway Inn, Super 8, **other:** Ford/Lincoln/Mercury, **W gas:** Chevron, Citgo/dsl, Shamrock/dsl, **food:** Country Inn Steaks, **lodging:** Quality Inn, Sam Houston Inn, **other:** Ⓗ HOSPITAL

**113** TX 19 (from nb), Huntsville, **E food:** Catfish Palace Rest. (2mi)

**112** TX 75, **E gas:** Citgo,**food:** Jack-in-the-Box, Wendy's, **lodging:** Baker Motel, **other:** Houston Statue, to Sam Houston St U, museum

**109** Park 40, **W other:** to Huntsville SP

**105mm** picnic area both lanes, ⛱, litter barrels

**103** FM 1374/1375 (from sb), to New Waverly, **W gas:** Mystick Gas (1mi)

**102** FM 1374/1375, TX 150 (from nb), to New Waverly, **E gas:** Shell/Subway/dsl (1mi), **W food:** Waverly Rest.

**101mm** weigh sta nb

**98** TX 75, Danville Rd, Shepard Hill Rd, **E other:** Convenience RV Park/repair

**94** (95 from nb) FM 1097, Longstreet Rd, to Willis, **E food:** Jack-in-the-Box, Mr Gatti, Quizno's, Sonic, **other:** AutoZone, $General, Kroger/gas, **W gas:** Chevron/Popeye's, Shell/Taco Bell/dsl/24hr, **food:** Bubba Leone's Pizza, McDonald's, Subway, **lodging:** Best Western

**92** FM 830, Seven Coves Dr, **W other:** Omega Farms RV Park, RV Park on the Lake (3mi), Thousand Trails Resort

**91** League Line Rd, **E gas:** Chevron/McDonald's, **food:** McDonald's, Subway, Waffle House, Wendy's, **lodging:** Comfort Inn, La Quinta, Supreme Inn, **other:** Conroe Outlets/famous brands, **W gas:** Citgo, Shell/Jack-in-the-Box, **food:** Cracker Barrel

**90** FM 3083, Teas Nursery Rd, Montgomery Co Park, **E gas:** Exxon/dsl, **food:** Applebees, Buffalo Wild Wings, **other:** Kohls, Old Navy, PetsMart, Ross, TJ Maxx, convention center (4mi)

**88** Lp 336, to Cleveland, Navasota, **E gas:** Mobil/dsl, Shell/24hr, Valero/dsl, **food:** Arby's, Burger King, Chili's, China Delight, Denny's, Domino's, Los Cucos Mexican, LJ Silver/A&W, Margarita's Mexican, McDonald's, Papa John's, Pizza Hut, Quizno's, Sonic, Subway, TX Roadhouse, Whataburger, **lodging:** Holiday Inn Express, **other:** Buick/Pontiac, CVS Drug, Discount Tire, $Tree, GNC, Goodyear/auto, HEB Foods/gas, Just Brakes, Kroger/gas, Michael's, Walgreen, **W gas:** Chevron/24hr, **food:** Casa Ole Mexican, El Bosque Mexican, Ryan's, Tuesday Morning, KFC, **other:** Goody's, GNC, Hancock Fabrics, JC Penney, Lowe's Whse, 99¢ Store, PetCo, Radio Shack, PetCo, Sam's Club/gas, Walmart SuperCtr

**87** TX 105, Conroe, **E gas:** Shamrock, **food:** Burger King, CiCi's, Imperial Garden Chinese, Jack-in-the-Box, Kettle, Luther's BBQ, McDonald's, Outback Steaks, Steak&Ale, Taco Bell, Tast of China, **other:** Ⓗ HOSPITAL, BigLots, CVS Drug, Eckerd/24hr, Firestone/auto, Hyundai, Kia, Kroger, NTB, Suzuki, **W gas:** Exxon/TCBY, **food:** Chick-fil-A, Golden Corral, Luby's, Panera Bread, Starbucks, Subway, **other:** Best Buy, Buick/GMC/Isuzu, Hastings Books, Home Depot, Office Depot, Radio Shack, Target

**85** FM 2854, Gladstell St, **E gas:** Citgo/dsl, **lodging:** Motel 6, **other:** Ⓗ HOSPITAL, Ford/Mercury, Honda, Mitsubishi, Nissan, **W gas:** Shamrock, Shell/dsl, **food:** IHOP, **lodging:** Baymont Inn, Day's Inn, **other:** Cadillac, Chrysler/Jeep/Dodge, Ford/Mercury, Fun Country RV Ctr, Mazda, Toyota/Scion

**84** TX 75 N, Frazier St, **E gas:** Chevron, Conoco/dsl, **lodging:** Corporate Inn, Holiday Inn, Ramada Ltd, **other:** U-Haul, **W gas:** Shell, **food:** China Buffet, IHOP, Pizza Hut, Taco Cabana, Waffle House, **lodging:** Baymont Inn, **other:** Ⓗ HOSPITAL, Albertson's, Discount Tire, K-Mart, Kroger

**83** Crighton Rd, Camp Strake Rd

**82** River Plantation Dr

**82mm** San Jacinto River

**81** FM 1488, to Hempstead, Magnolia, **E gas:** Citgo/dsl, **W gas:** Shamrock, **other:** CamperLand RV Ctr

**80** Needham Rd (from sb)

**79** TX 242, Needham, **E gas:** Shell, **food:** Mama Juanita's Mexican, McDonald's, Quizno's, **other:** Woodland Lakes RV Resort (2mi), **W gas:** Chevron, **food:** Burger King, ChuckeCheese, Dominos, Fazoli's, Popeye's, Sonic, Subway, Taco Cabana, Wendy's, Whataburger/24hr,

HUNTSVILLE

CONROE

TX

N S

## INTERSTATE 45 CONT'D

**N ↑ S**

**79** Continued
Willie's Grill, Wings & More, **lodging:** Country Inn Suites, Fairfield Inn, **other:** Ⓗ HOSPITAL, BMW/Mini, Firestone/auto, Kohl's, Lowe's, Walgreen, Walmart SuperCtr/gas

**78** Needham Rd (from sb), Tamina Rd, access to same as 77

**77** Woodlands Pkwy, Robinson, Chateau Woods, **E gas:** Conoco/dsl, **food:** Babin's Steaks, Buca italian, Chuy's, Hooters, Lupe Tortilla, Pancho's Mexican, Pappadeaux Rest., Pizza Hut, Red Lobster, Red Robin, Saltgrass Steaks, Tom's Steaks, **lodging:** Budget Inn, **other:** Discount Tire, Home Depot, Jo-Ann Fabrics, Michael's, NTB, Office Depot, Old Navy, Sam's Club, SteinMart, Walgreen, **W gas:** Mobil, Shamrock, Shell, Texaco, Valero, **food:** Blackeyed Pea, Chili's, Denny's, Guadalajara Mexican, Kirby's Steakhouse, Landry's Seafood, Luby's, Macaroni Grill, Outback Steaks, Pancho's Mexican, Red Lobster, **lodging:** Best Value, Comfort Inn, Day's Inn, Drury Inn, Hampton Inn, Homewood Suites, La Quinta, Marriott, Spring Inn, **other:** Ⓗ HOSPITAL, Best Buy, Dillard's, Marshall's, Ross, Target, World Mkt, mall

**76** Research Forest Dr, Tamina Rd, **E gas:** Chevron/dsl, Coastal/lube, Shamrock, Stop'n Go, Texaco, **food:** Casa Elena Mexican, LJ Silver, Pappa's BBQ, **other:** Food Basket, Firestone, **W gas:** Shell, **food:** Carrabba's, Denny's, El Chico, IHOP, Jack-in-the-Box, Kyoto Japanese, Macaroni Grill, Olive Garden, TGIFriday's, Tortuga Mexican, **lodging:** Crossland Suites, Courtyard, Residence Inn, **other:** Circuit City, Goodyear/auto, JC Penny, Sears/auto, Woodlands Mall

**73** Rayford Rd, Sawdust Rd, **E gas:** Conoco, Shell, Valero, **food:** Dry Dock Rest, Jack-in-the-Box, LJ Silver, McDonald's, Popeye's, Sonic, Taqueria Arandas, Thomas BBQ, **lodging:** Hawthorn Suites, Holiday Inn Express, **other:** AutoZone, Firestone, Just Brakes, O'Reilly Parts, **W gas:** Mobil/dsl, Shell, Texaco, **food:** Carrabba's, Grandy's, IHOP, India Cuisine, Kyoto Japanese, Sam's Rest., Subway, Taipei Chinese, Tortuga, Woodland Chinese, **lodging:** Extended Stay America, Red Roof Inn, Super 8, **other:** Discount Tire, Eckerd, Goodyear/auto, Harley-Davidson, HEB Foods, Kroger

**72a** Spring Crossing Dr, **W gas:** Texaco/dsl

**72b** to Hardy Toll Rd from sb

**70b** Spring-Stuebner Rd, **E** Vaughn RV Ctr

**70a** FM 2920, to Tomball, **E gas:** Exxon, **food:** El Palenque Mexican, McDonald's, Pizza Hut, Wendy's, **other:** BigLots, $General, Kroger, Radio Shack, Vaughn's RV Ctr, Walgreen, transmissions, **W gas:** Chevron, RaceWay, Texaco, **food:** Burger King, Taco Bell, Whataburger/24hr, **lodging:** Travelodge, **other:** Ford, U-Haul

**68** Holzwarth Rd, Cypress Wood Dr, **E gas:** Shell, Texaco/dsl, **food:** Arby's, Burger King, Chick-fil-A, Gander Mtn., Hartz Chicken, Pizza Hut/Taco Bell, Quizno's, Sonic, Taco Cabana, Wendy's, Whataburger, **other:** Albertson's, $Tree, Gander Mtn, GNC, Kohl's, Kroger, Lincoln/Mercury, Michael's, Radio Shack, Ross, Toyota/Scion, Walmart SuperCtr, **W gas:** Chevron/24hr, **food:** Denny's, Jack-in-the-Box, Pizza Hut, Starbucks, Popeye's, **lodging:** Day's Inn, Motel 6, **other:** Best Buy, Ford, Home Depot, Lowe's Whse, Office Depot, Target, Texan RV Ctr, Walgreen

**HOUSTON**

**66** FM 1960, to Addicks, **E gas:** Chevron, RaceTrac, Shell, **food:** Jack-in-the-Box, Sonic, TX Roadhouse, Waffle House, **lodging:** Best Value, Day's Inn, Holiday Inn, Ramada Inn, **other:** Acura, BMW, Chevrolet, Honda, Mercedes, Mistubishi, PetsMart, Radio Shack, **W gas:** Exxon, Shell/dsl/24hr, Texaco/dsl, **food:** Cici's Pizza, Coney Island, Grandy's, Hooters, Ixtapa Mexican, Jack-in-the-Box, Jojo's Rest., Luby's, McDonald's, Outback Steaks, Pizza Hut, Popeye's, Red Lobster, Steak&Ale, Subway, Taco Bell, **lodging:** Baymont Inn, Comfort Suites, Fairfield Inn, Hampton Inn, Motel 6, **other:** GolfSmith, Infiniti, Jaguar/LandRover, Lexus, NTB, Saturn, mall

**64** Richey Rd, **E gas:** Texaco/Church's, **food:** Atchafalaya River Café, China Bear, Pappasito's Cantina, **lodging:** Holiday Inn, Lexington Suites, **other:** Cadillac, Carmax, Discount Tire, Nissan, Sam's Club, **W gas:** ⊕ *FLYING J*/Conoco/Country Mkt/dsl/24hr/scales/@, **food:** Cracker Barrel, House of Creole, Jack-in-the-Box, Joe's Crabshack, Lupe Tortilla, SaltGrass Steaks, Whataburger, Zio's Italian, **other:** Jones RV Ctr, U-Haul

**63** Airtex Dr, **E gas:** Texaco, Valero, **other:** Acura, Cadillac, LoneStar RV Ctr, Nissan, **W food:** Cracker Barrel, Jack-in-the-Box, McDonald's, Whataburger, **lodging:** Best Western, Guesthouse Suites, SunSuites, **other:** Celebration Sta

**62** Rankin Rd, Kuykendahl, **W gas:** Chevron/McDonald's, Shell, **food:** Luby's, **lodging:** Studio+, SunSuites, **other:** BMW, Buick/Subaru, Hummer, Hyundai, Kia/GMC/Pontiac, Mercedes, Mitsubishi, Saab, Suzuki, Volvo, VW

**61** Greens Rd, **E food:** Whataburger, **lodging:** Day's Inn, Marriott, Wyndham Hotel, **other:** Circuit City, Dillard's, Foley's, JC Penney, mall, **W food:** Burger King, Luby's, **lodging:** Baymont Inn, Comfort Inn, **other:** Kroger, Office Depot, Target

**60c** Beltway E

**60b** TX 8, **E lodging:** La Quinta, Marriott, **other:** Dillard's, Sears/auto, mall, **W food:** Marco's Mexican

**60a** TX 525, **E gas:** Exxon, Shamrock, Shell, Texaco, **food:** Burger King, Champ's Rest., China Border, Denny's/24hr, Furr's Cafeteria, LJ Silver/A&W, Mambo Seafood, Moon Palace Chinese, Mucho Mexico, Pizza Hut, Pizza Inn, Steak&Ale, **other:** Firestone/auto, Honda, Randall's Foods, Walgreen, **W food:** Gordito's Mexican, Pappa's Rest., Quizno's, Wendy's, **lodging:** Best Value Inn, **other:** Best Buy, Discount Tire, Dodge, GNC, Home Depot, Pontiac/GMC, Radio Shack, NTB, Walmart SuperCtr

**TX**

## INTERSTATE 45 CONT'D

**N ↕ S HOUSTON**

**59**   FM 525, West Rd, **E gas:** Exxon, Shell, **food:** McDonald's, Pizza Hut, Wendy's, Wings & More, **other:** Fiesta Foods, **W gas:** Exxon, Shell, **food:** Panda Express, Pizza Inn, Sonic, Subway, Taco Bell, Taco Cabana, Taquiera Arrandas, **lodging:** Best Western, GreenChase Inn, Holiday Inn Express, La Quinta, Ramada Ltd, **other:** CVS Drug, Family$, Fry's Electronics, K-Mart, Lincoln/Mercury, PepBoys

**57**   TX 249, Gulf Bank Rd, Tomball, **E gas:** Conoco, Exxon/dsl, Mobil/dsl, **other:** Discount Tire, Kroger, **W gas:** Shell, **food:** KFC, Pizza Inn, Sonic, **lodging:** American Inn, La Quinta, **other:** Chevrolet, Chrysler/Jeep, CVS Drug, Eckerd, Family$, Ford, Mazda, Saturn

**56**   Canino Rd, **E lodging:** Taj Inn, **W gas:** Shell, **food:** Denny's, Luby's, **lodging:** Gulfwind Motel, Passport Inn, **other:** Ford, Isuzu, Nissan, Toyota, Walgreen

**55b a**   Little York Rd, Parker Rd, **E gas:** Chevron, Exxon, Shell, Texaco, **food:** Schlotsky's, Whataburger, **lodging:** Olympic Motel, **other:** H HOSPITAL, FoodTown, Goodyear, **W gas:** Chevron/24hr, Shell, **food:** Capt D's, Denny's, Hartz Chicken, Jack-in-the-Box, KFC, LJ Silver, McDonald's, Popeye's, **lodging:** Best Value Inn, Econolodge, Symphony Inn, Town Inn, **other:** Family$, Walgreen

**54**   Tidwell Rd, **E gas:** Exxon, **food:** Pancho's Mexican, Pizza Inn, Subway, Taco Cabana, Thomas BBQ, **other:** BigLots, CVS Drug, Eckerd, Jo-Ann Fabrics, Radio Shack, **W lodging:** Guest Motel, Southwind Motel, **other:** U-Haul

**53**   Airline Dr, **E gas:** Chevron, Conoco, **other:** Discount Tire, Fiesta Foods/drug, **W food:** Little Mexico, Whataburger, same as 52

**52**   Crosstimbers Rd, **E gas:** Shell, Texaco/dsl, **food:** Burger King, CiCi's, IHOP, James Coney Island, McDonald's, Pancho's Mexican, Pappas BBQ, Taco Bell, Taco Cabana, Wendy's, **other:** Discount Tire, Fiesta Foods, Firestone, mall, **W gas:** Chevron/dsl, Citgo, **food:** Little Mexico Rest., Wendy's, Whataburger/24hr, **lodging:** Howard Johnson, Luxury Inn, Palace Inn, Super 8, Texan Inn, **other:** Coach USA RV Ctr, U-Haul

**51**   I-610

**50b**   Calvacade St, Link Rd, **E gas:** Exxon, Shell, **W lodging:** Astro Inn

**50a**   Patton St, **E gas:** Chevron/24hr, **lodging:** Classic Inn, Luxury Inn, **W gas:** Shell/dsl/24hr

**49b**   N Main St, Houston Ave, **E gas:** Citgo, **food:** Casa Grande Mexican, **lodging:** Best Value, Luxury Inn, **W gas:** Exxon/dsl, **food:** KFC, McDonald's, Whataburger/24hr, **other:** Auto Supply

**48b a**   I-10, E to Beaumont, W to San Antonio

**47d**   Dallas St, Pierce St (from sb) , **E other:** H HOSPITAL

**47c**   McKinney St (from sb, exits left)

**47b**   Houston Ave, Memorial Dr, downtown, **W lodging:** Double Tree Hotel

**47a**   Allen Pkwy (exits left from sb)

**46b a**   US 59, N to Cleveland, S to Victoria, **E gas:** Chevron, **food:** BBQ, **W gas:** Texaco, **food:** McDonald's, Taco Bell, **other:** BMW

**45b a**   South St, Scott St, Houston, **E gas:** Shell, **other:** Firestone, to TSU

**44**   Cullen Blvd, Houston, **E gas:** Valero/dsl, to U of Houston

**43b**   Telephone Rd, Houston, **E food:** Luby's

**43a**   Tellepsen St, **E food:** Luby's, **lodging:** Day's Inn, **W other:** U of Houston

**41b**   US 90A, Broad St, S Wayside Dr, **E gas:** Phillips 66, **food:** La Terraza, **lodging:** Day's Inn, Red Carpet Inn, **W gas:** Chevron, Exxon, Mobil, **food:** Jack-in-the-Box, McDonald's, Monterrey Mexican, Subway, Taquiera Mexican, Wings and More, **other:** $Tree, K-Mart, Sellars Foods

**41a**   Woodridge Dr, **E gas:** Shell, **food:** Bonnie's Seafood, Denny's, McDonald's, Pappa's Seafood House, Schlotsky's, **W gas:** Citgo, **food:** BoneBreak BBQ, IHOP, Pappas BBQ, Sonic, Subway, Whataburger, Wendy's, **other:** Chevrolet/Buick, Dillard's, HEB Food/gas, Home Depot, Lowe's Whse, Marshall's, Office Depot, Old Navy, Radio Shack, Ross, mall

**40c**   I-610 W

**40b**   I-610 E, to Pasadena, **E food:** Bennigan's

**40a**   Frontage Rd (from nb)

**39**   Park Place Blvd, Broadway Blvd, **E gas:** Shell, **W food:** Kelley's Rest., Los Campos, **other:** Chevrolet, Dodge, Family$

**38b**   Howard Dr, Bellfort Dr (from sb) , **E gas:** Shell, **food:** Jack-in-the-Box, Wendy's, **W gas:** Citgo, **food:** Chilo's Seafood, **lodging:** Camelot Inn, Mustang Inn, Palace Inn, Passport Inn, **other:** HEB Food/gas, PepBoys

**38**   TX 3, Monroe Rd, **E gas:** Chevron, Shell, Valero, **food:** DQ, Jack-in-the-Box, Luther's BBQ, Ninfa, Wendy's, **other:** Firestone, NTB, U-Haul, **W gas:** Chevron/dsl, Texaco/dsl, **food:** Luby's, Manny's Seafood, Pappa's BBQ, **lodging:** Best Western, Holiday Inn Express, Quality Inn, Smile Inn, **other:** Firestone, Kottman Transmissions, Radio Shack, Suzuki, U-Haul

**36**   College Ave, Airport Blvd, **E gas:** Shamrock, Shell, **food:** DQ, Waffle House, **lodging:** Best Value, Day's Inn, Fairfield Inn, Rodeway Inn, **other:** RV Ctr, **W gas:** Exxon, Mobil, Shell, Valero, **food:** Church's Chicken, Denny's, Taco Cabana, **lodging:** AmeriSuites, Baymont Inn, Comfort Inn, Country Inn, Courtyard, Drury Inn, Hampton Inn, Holiday Inn Express, La Quinta, Marriott/Damon's, Motel 6, Red Roof Inn, Regency Inn, SpringHill Suites, Super 8, Travel Inn, **other:** Discount Tire

**35**   Edgebrook Dr, **E gas:** Chevron, Exxon, RaceTrac, **food:** Burger King, Aranda's Bakery, Jack-in-the-Box, KFC,

## INTERSTATE 45 CONT'D

**N ↑ S**

**35**  Continued
Popeye's, Subway, Taco Bell, Taquiera Arrandas, Waffle House, **lodging:** Airport Inn, **other:** Eckerd, Family$, Fiesta Foods, Firestone, Office Depot, Terry Vaugn's RV Ctr, Walgreens, **W gas:** Exxon, Shell, Circle K, **food:** James Coney Island, KFC, LJ Silver, McDonald's, Pizza Hut, Whataburger, **other:** Academy Sports, Honda, NTB

**34**  S Shaver Rd, **E gas:** Conoco, RaceWay, **food:** McDonald's, **lodging:** Island Suites, **other:** Acura, Honda, Kia, Pontiac/GMC, Saturn, Toyota, Vaughn's RV Ctr, **W gas:** Chevron/24hr, Exxon, Mobil, **food:** Arby's, Burger King, Pancho's Mexican, Wendy's, **lodging:** Scottish Inn, **other:** Best Buy, Circuit City, Discount Tire, $Tree, Honda, Jo-Ann Fabrics, Macy's, Nissan, NTB, Target, Walmart SuperCtr/gas

**33**  Fuqua St, **E gas:** Shamrock, **food:** Chili's, Fuddrucker's, Las Haciendas, Luby's, Olive Garden, Schlotzky's, TGI-Friday, **lodging:** Studio 6, Sun Suites, **other:** Chrysler/Jeep, Dodge, Ford, Honda, Hyundai, Isuzu, Lincoln/Mercury, **W food:** Blackeyed Pea, Boston Mkt, Bouderaux's Cajun Kitchen, Casa Mexican, Casa Ole, CiCi's Pizza, Fox&Hound, Golden Corral, Gringo's Mexican, IHOP, Joe's Crabshack, Outback Steaks, Steak&Ale, Subway, Taco Cabana, Taco Bell, TX Cattle Steaks, Whataburger, **other:** BigLots, CarMax, Chevrolet, Firestone, JC Penney, Kroger, Macy's, Old Navy, Radio Shack, Ross, Sam's Club, Subaru, Tire Station, mall

**32**  Sam Houston Tollway

**31**  FM 2553, Scarsdale Blvd, **W gas:** Shell, **other:** Chevrolet, Mitsubishi

**30**  FM 1959, Dixie Farm Rd, Ellington Field, **E gas:** Shell/dsl, **food:** Subway, **lodging:** Howard Johnson, **other:** H HOSPITAL, Dodge, Infiniti, **W gas:** RaceWay, Shell/dsl, **food:** McDonald's, Popeye's, **lodging:** Palace Inn, **other:** Lonestar RV, VW

**29**  FM 2351, Clear Lake City Blvd, to Clear Lake RA, Friendswood

**27**  El Dorado Blvd, **E gas:** Shell, **food:** DQ, **W food:** Sonic, Texas Roadhouse, Whataburger, **other:** Cadillac, Hummer, Kohl's, Lexus, Radio Shack, Sam's Club/gas, Walmart SuperCtr

**26**  Bay Area Blvd, **E food:** Red Lobster, TGI Friday's, **other:** H HOSPITAL, Barnes&Noble, Lowe's Whse, Michael's, Old Navy, Oshman's Sports, Steinmart, to Houston Space Ctr, **W gas:** Shell, **food:** Chick-fil-A, Denny's/24hr, McDonald's, Olive Garden, **lodging:** Best Western, **other:** Circuit City, Dillard's, Macy's, Office Depot, Sears/auto, Target, U of Houston, mall

**25**  FM 528, NASA rd 1, **E gas:** Conoco, Shamrock, Texaco, **food:** Cheddar's, Chili's, Hooters, IHOP, Las Haciendas Mexican, Pappasito's Cantina, Saltgrass Steaks, Waffle House, Vito's, **lodging:** Best Western, Comfort

**25**  Continued
Suites, La Quinta, Motel 6, **other:** H HOSPITAL, Audi, Best Buy, Big Lots, Fry's Electronics, Home Depot, Honda, Mazda, Volvo, **W food:** Hot Wok Chinese, Pappa's, Subway, **other:** Fiesta Foods, Radio Shack, Tuesday Morning

**23**  FM 518, League City, **E gas:** RaceWay, Shell/dsl, **food:** Applebee's, Burger King, Jack-in-the-Box, KFC, Little Caesar's, Pepper's Beef, Sonic, Subway, Sudie's Seafood, **other:** Academy Sports, BMW, Eckerd, Just Brakes, Kroger, Mercedes, Walgreens, **W gas:** Chevron, Exxon/24hr, Mobil, **food:** Cracker Barrel, Hartz Chicken, McDonald's, Taco Bell, Waffle House, Wendy's, **lodging:** Super 8, **other:** Discount Tire, Space Ctr RV Park, U-Haul

**22**  Calder Dr, Brittany Bay Blvd, **E other:** Nissan, Toyota, camping, **W other:** Holiday World RV Ctr

**20**  FM 646, Santa Fe, Bacliff, **E food:** Denny's, Panda Express, Whataburger, **other:** Best Buy, Home Depot, JC Penney, Lowes Whse, Radio Shack, Walmart Super Ctr, **W gas:** Valero/dsl, **food:** Chili's, Subway, Taco Cabana, **other:** HEB Foods/gas, Kohl's, PetCo

**19**  FM 517, Dickinson Rd, Hughes Rd, **E food:** Jack-in-the-Box, Monterey Mexico, Pizza Inn, **other:** Adventure Out RV Park, Buick/Pontiac/GMC/Subaru, CVS Drug, Family$, Food King, Radio Shack, **W gas:** Mobil, Shell/dsl, **food:** Burger King, Dickenson's Seafood, Heartbreak Grill, KFC, McDonald's, Pizza Hut, Sonic, Subway, Taco Bell, Wendy's, Whataburger/24hr, **lodging:** Day's Inn, El Rancho Motel, **other:** Ford, Kroger, Subaru, Target, Walgreens

**17**  Holland Rd, **W** to Gulf Greyhound Park

**16**  FM 1764 E (from sb), Texas City, same as 15

**15**  FM 2004, FM 1764, Hitchcock, **E gas:** Shell, **food:** Gringo's Cafe, Jack-in-the-Box, Olive Garden, Popeye's, Ryan's, Uncle Chan's, **lodging:** Best Western, Fairfield Inn, Hampton Inn, Holiday Inn Express, **other:** H HOSPITAL, Chevrolet/Toyota/RV Ctr, Dillard's, JC Penney, Lowe's Whse, Macy's, Sam's Club/gas, Sears/auto, mall, **W gas:** Mobil/Subway, Shell, **food:** IHOP, Sonic, Waffle House, Wendy's, Whataburger, **lodging:** Super 8, **other:** Chevrolet/RV Ctr, Gulf Greyhound Park, Radio Shack, Toyota/Scion, Walmart SuperCtr/gas

L E A G U E   C I T Y

## INTERSTATE 45 CONT'D

**13** Century Blvd, Delany Rd, **E gas:** Valero, **W food:** Acupulco Mexican, **lodging:** Super 8, Travelodge, **other:** VF Factory Outlet/famous brands

**12** FM 1765, La Marque, **E gas:** Chevron/24hr, **food:** Domino's, Jack-in-the-Box, Kelley's Rest., Sonic

**11** Vauthier Rd

**10** **E gas:** Valero, **food:** McDonald's, **W gas:** Shell/dsl, **other:** Oasis RV Park

**9** Frontage Rd (from sb)

**8** Frontage Rd (from nb)

**7c** Frontage Rd

**7b** TX 146, TX 6 (exits left from nb), Texas City, **W gas:** EZ Mart

**7a** TX 146, TX 3

**6** Frontage Rd (from sb)

**5** Frontage Rd

**4** Frontage Rd, Village of Tiki Island, **W gas:** Valero **other:** public boat ramp

**4mm** West Galveston Bay

**1c** TX 275, FM 188 (from nb), Port Ind Blvd, Teichman Rd, Port of Galveston, **E gas:** Exxon, Mobil/dsl, Valero, **lodging:** Howard Johnson, Motel 6, **other:** Chevrolet, Chrysler/Dodge/Jeep, Ford, Honda, Mazda, Mitsubishi, Nissan, Toyota/Scion

**1b** 71st St (from sb) , **E gas:** EZ Mart/gas, same as 1c

**1a** TX 342, 61st St, to W Beach, **E gas:** Chevron, **other:** GNC, Home Depot, NTB, Target, **W gas:** RaceWay, **food:** Church's, McDonald's, Taco Bell, **lodging:** Day's Inn, **other:** Big Lots, Chevrolet/Pontiac/Buick/Cadillac, Chrysler/Jeep, Family$, Honda, O'Reilly Parts, U-Haul, USPO, **1-2 mi W gas:** Chevron/dsl, Exxon/dsl, Valero, **food:** China Island, CiCi's Pizza, Happy Buddah, Jack-in-the-Box, KFC, Little Caesar's, Luby's, Mario's Italian, McDonald's, Papa John's, Pizza Hut, Popeye's, Quizno's, Starbucks, Subway, Taco Cabana, Waffle House, Whataburger, **lodging:** Baymont Inn, Beachcomber Inn, Best Value Inn, Quality Inn, Super 8, **other:** Curves, CVS Drug, Firestone/auto, Hastings Books, HEB Foods, Office Depot, Randall's Food/gas, Ross, Walgreens

I-45 begins/ends on TX 87 in Galveston.

## INTERSTATE 410 - SAN ANTONIO

| Exit # | Services |
| --- | --- |
| **53** | I-35, S to Laredo, N to San Antonio |
| **51** | FM 2790, Somerset Rd |
| **49** | TX 16 S, spur 422, **N gas:** Chevron, **food:** Church's Chicken, Subway, **other:** H HOSPITAL, to Palo Alto Coll, **S gas:** Shamrock |
| **48** | Zarzamora St |
| **46** | Moursund Blvd |
| **44** | US 281 S, spur 536, Roosevelt Ave, **N gas:** Shell/dsl, **other:** dsl repair, RV camping |

**43** Espada Rd (from eb)

**42** spur 122, S Presa Rd, to San Antonio Missions Hist Park, **S gas:** Whiteside/dsl

**41** I-37, US 281 N

**39** spur 117, WW White Rd

**37** Southcross Blvd, Sinclair Rd, Sulphur Sprs Rd, **N H** HOSPITAL

**35** US 87, Rigsby Ave, **E gas:** Exxon/TacoMaker, Shamrock/dsl, **food:** Denny's, Jack-in-the-Box, McDonald's, Taco Bell, **other:** Radio Shack, Walmart SuperCtr/gas, **W gas:** Chevron, **food:** Barnacle Bill's Seafood, BBQ, Pizza Hut, Sonic, Subway, Taco Cabana, Whataburger, **lodging:** Day's Inn, **other:** Aamco, Advance Parts

**34** FM 1346, E Houston St, **W gas:** Chevron, Shamrock, **food:** McDonald's, Wendy's, **lodging:** Comfort Inn, Motel 6

**33** I-10 E, US 90 E, to Houston, I-10 W, US 90 W, to San Antonio

**32** Dietrich Rd (from sb), FM 78 (from nb), to Kirby

**31b** Lp 13, WW White Rd

**31a** FM 78, Kirby

**30** Binz-Engleman, Space Center Dr (from nb)

**I-410 and I-35 run together 7 mi. See Interstate 35, exits 161 thru 165.**

**27** I-35, N to Austin, S to San Antonio

**26** Lp 368 S, Alamo Heights

**25b** FM 2252, Perrin-Beitel Rd, **N gas:** Chevron/dsl, Mobil, Shamrock, **food:** Denny's, KFC/Taco Bell, Quizno's, Schlotsky's, Taco Bell, Taco Cabana, Wendy's, Wienerschnitzel, **lodging:** Comfort Inn, Econolodge, Welsley Inn, **S food:** Jim's Rest.

**25a** Starcrest Dr, **N gas:** Texaco, **food:** Jack-in-the-Box, Los Patios Mexican, **lodging:** Hawthorn Inn, HillCoutry Inn, **other:** H HOSPITAL, Toyota

**24** Harry Wurzbach Hwy, **N food:** Taco Cabana, **S food:** BBQ Sta., **other:**

**23** Nacogdoches Rd, **N food:** BBQ, Church's, IHOP, Jack-in-the-Box, Mamma's Cafe, Pizza Hut, Schlotsky's, Sonic, Taco Cabana, Wendy's, **lodging:** Club Hotel, **S gas:** Exxon, **other:** Audi/VW, Volvo

**22** Broadway St, **N gas:** Shell/dsl, **food:** Crystal Steaks, Las Palapas, Luby's, McDonald's, Oceans Seafood Grill, **lodging:** Courtyard, Radisson, Ramada Inn, **other:** Firestone, **S gas:** Citgo, Shamrock, **food:** Chesters Hamburgers, Jim's Rest., Quizno's, Whataburger, **lodging:** Residence Inn, TownHouse Motel, **other:** Infiniti, Jiffy Lube

**21** US 281 S, Airport Rd, Jones Maltsberger Rd, **N food:** Applebee's, Smokey Onion, **lodging:** Drury Suites, Hampton Inn, Holiday Inn Select, PearTree Inn, **S gas:** Texaco/dsl, **food:** Pappadeaux, Red Lobster, Texas Land&Cattle, **lodging:** Courtyard, Day's Inn, Fairfield Inn, La Quinta, Renaissance Hotel, Staybridge Suites, **other:** Hyundai/Kia, Mitsubishi, Subaru, Target, Walmart

N ↕ S

SAN ANTONIO

SAN ANTONIO

## INTERSTATE 410 - SAN ANTONIO

**20** TX 537, **N food:** Arby's, Jason's Deli, Subway, TGI-Friday, **lodging:** DoubleTree Hotel, Hilton, **other:** Barnes&Noble, Best Buy, Chevrolet, Circuit City, Honda, Lincoln/Mercury, Marshall's, Mazda, Ross, **S food:** Arby's, El Pollo Loco, Luby's, McDonald's, Taco Cabana, Texas Cattle Co., **other:** Dillard's, Dodge, Macy's, Saks 5th, Sears/auto, mall

**19b** FM 1535, FM 2696, Military Hwy, **N food:** Crown Buffet, Guajillos Mexican, Souper Salad, **S food:** Denny's, Jim's Rest.

**19a** Honeysuckle Lane, Castle Hills

**17b** (from wb), **S gas:** Shell, **food:** DQ, Dunkin Donuts, Subway, **other:** Firestone, HEB Foods/gas

**17** Vance Jackson Rd, **N gas:** Mobil, Phillips 66, Shamrock, **food:** Burger King, Jack-in-the-Box, KFC, McDonald's, Steak&Ale, Sonic, Taco Cabana, Tom's Ribs, Whataburger, **lodging:** Embassy Suites, Marriott, **other:** Aamco, CarQuest, Discount Tire, Target, Tire Sta, transmissions, **S gas:** Exxon, **food:** Subway, **other:** U-Haul

**16b a** I-10 E, US 87 S, to San Antonio, I-10 W, to El Paso, US 87 N

**15** Lp 345, Fredericksburg Rd, **E gas:** Shell, **food:** Church's, Dave&Buster's, Jack-in-the-Box, Jim's Rest., Kettle, Luby's, N China Rest., Taquiera Mexican, **lodging:** AmeriSuites, Best Value Inn, Comfort Suites, SpringHill Suites, **other:** BMW, Target, **W gas:** Mobil, **lodging:** Holiday Inn, **other:** K-Mart

**14** Callaghan Rd, Babcock Ln, **E gas:** Chevron, Exxon, Shamrock, **food:** Marie Callender's, Popeye's, **lodging:** Comfort Inn, Hampton Inn, Super 8, Travelodge Suites, **other:** GMC/Pontiac, **W gas:** Conoco, **food:** Burger King, Chili's, ChopSticks Chinese, Cook's Steaks, Ding-How Chinese, El Chico, Golden Corral, HomeTown Buffet, Joe's Crabshack, Landry's Seafood, Paulo Italian, Pizza Hut, Quizno's, Red Lobster, Wendy's, Whataburger, **other:** H HOSPITAL, Cavander's Boots, Home Depot, Sam's Club, Walmart SuperCtr

**13b** Rolling Ridge Dr, **W food:** Jack-in-the-Box, KFC, Las Palapas Mexican, same as 14

**13a** TX 16 N, Bandera Rd, Evers Rd, Leon Valley, **E food:** Outback Steaks, **other:** Albertson's, Audi, HEB Foods, Office Depot, Old Navy, Saturn, Toyota, U-Haul, **W gas:** Exxon, Shamrock, Shell, **food:** Applebee's, BBQ, IHOP, Jack-in-the-Box, Jason's Deli, Jim's Rest., KFC, Luby's, McDonald's, Olive Garden, Schlotsky's, Taco Cabana, **lodging:** Super 8, **other:** Aamco, Best Buy, BigLots, Chevrolet, Circuit City, Dillard's, Eckerd, Honda, Marshall's, NTB

**11** Ingram Rd, **E gas:** Shell/dsl, **food:** Calloway's Rest., Fazoli's, KFC/Taco Bell, Krispy Kreme, Pepe's, Texas Roadhouse, **lodging:** Day's Inn, Econolodge, Holiday Inn Express, Red Roof Inn, **other:** Aamco, BrakeCheck,

**11 Continued**
 **W food:** Applebee's, Burger King, ChuckeCheese, Denny's, Jack-in-the-Box, Jason's Deli, Olive Garden, Subway, Whataburger, **lodging:** Best Western, Super 8, **other:** Barnes&Noble, Best Buy, Dillard's, $Tree, Firestone, JC Penney, Michael's, Ross, Sears/auto, mall

**10** FM 3487, Culebra Rd, **E food:** Barnacle Bill's Seafood, BBQ, Denny's, McDonald's, Wendy's, **lodging:** La Quinta, Ramada Ltd, **other:** Chrysler/Dodge/Jeep, Mazda/Nissan, to St Mary's U, **W gas:** Phillips 66, RaceTrac, Shamrock, **food:** Blimpie, Fuddrucker's, **lodging:** InTown Inn, **other:** Firestone/auto, Ford

**9b a** TX 151, **W gas:** Chili's, **food:** Carino's Italian, Cracker Barrel, **lodging:** Quality Inn, **other:** Home Depot, Lowe's Whse, Walmart SuperCtr/gas, to Sea World

**7** (8 from sb) Marbach Dr, **E gas:** Exxon, **food:** IHOP, McDonald's, **other:** PepBoys, **W gas:** Chevron/dsl, Texaco/dieel, **food:** Acadiena Café, Burger King, Golden Wok, Jack-in-the-Box, Jim's Rest., KFC, LJ Silver, Luby's, McDonald's, Mr Gatti's, Pancho's Mexican, Peter Piper Pizza, Pizza Hut, Red Lobster, Sonic, Subway, Taco Bell, Taco Cabana, Whataburger/24hr, **other:** Advance Parts, BigLots, Discount Tire, $General, $Tree, Eckerd, Firestone/auto, HEB Food, Target

**6** US 90, to Lackland AFB, **E lodging:** Country Inn Motel, **other:** Explore USA RV Ctr, **W gas:** Shamrock, Shell/dsl, **food:** Andrea's Mexican, **lodging:** Motel 6, Super 8

**4** Valley Hi Dr, to Del Rio, San Antonio, **E gas:** Mobil, Phillips 66/dsl, Shamrock, **food:** Church's Chicken, McDonald's, Pizza Hut, Sonic, **other:** AutoZone, HEB Food/gas, Radio Shack, **W** to Lackland AFB

**3b a** Ray Ellison Dr, Medina Base, **W gas:** Shamrock/Subway

**2** FM 2536, Old Pearsall Rd, **E gas:** Shamrock/dsl, Shell/dsl, **food:** BBQ, Mexico Taqueria, McDonald's, Sonic

**1** Frontage Rd

## INTERSTATE 610 - HOUSTON

| Exit # | Services |
|---|---|
| 38c a | TX 288 N, downtown, access to zoo |
| 37 | Scott St, **N gas:** Citgo, Valero |
| 36 | FM 865, Cullen Blvd, **N lodging:** Crystal Inn, **S gas:** |

TX

## INTERSTATE 610 CONT'D - HOUSTON

**N ↕ S HOUSTON HOUSTON**

| | |
|---|---|
| **36** | Continued<br>Chevron/McDonald's, Mobil, Shamrock, Shell, **food:** Timmy Chan, **lodging:** Crown Inn, Cullen Inn |
| **35** | Calais Rd, Crestmont St, MLK Blvd, **N** **gas:** Exxon, Shamrock, **food:** Burger King |
| **34** | S Wayside Dr, Long Dr, **N** **gas:** Chevron, Phillips 66, Shell, **food:** Church's, Wendy's, **other:** Fiesta Foods, **S** **gas:** Valero, Shell |
| **33** | Woodridge Dr, Telephone Rd, **N** **gas:** Shell/dsl, **food:** IHOP, KFC/Taco Bell, McDonald's, Papa John's, Wendy's, **lodging:** South Lp Inn, **other:** Lowe's Whse, Old Navy, **S** **gas:** Texaco, **food:** BBQ, Burger King, KFC, Piccadilly's Cafeteria, Spanky's Pizza, Whataburger, **other:** Dodge, Ford, mall |
| **32b a** | I-45, S to Galveston, N to Houston, to ✈ |
| **31** | Broadway Blvd, **S** **gas:** Shamrock/dsl, Texaco/dsl |
| **30c b** | TX 225, to Pasadena, San Jacinto Mon |
| **29** | Port of Houston Main Entrance |
| **28** | Clinton Dr, to Galina Park |
| **27** | Turning Basin Dr, industrial area |
| **26b** | Market St |
| **26a** | I-10 E, to Beaumont, I-10 W, to downtown |
| **24b** | Wallisville Rd, **E** **gas:** Mobil/dsl, Phillips 66, **food:** McDonald's |
| **24** | US 90 E, **E** **gas:** Chevron, Luv's/Arby's/dsl, Phillips 66, **food:** Luby's, Wendy's, **W** **gas:** Citgo |
| **23b** | N Wayside, **E** **gas:** Shamrock |
| **23a** | Kirkpatrick Blvd |
| **22** | Homestead Rd, Kelley St, **N** **gas:** Shell/dsl, **food:** Whataburger, **lodging:** Super 8 |
| **21** | Lockwood Dr, **N** **gas:** Chevron/McDonald's, Shell, **food:** Chan Chinese, Church's, Popeye's, **other:** Popeye's, Family$, **S** HOSPITAL |
| **20a b** | US 59, to downtown, to downtown |
| **19b** | Hardy Toll Rd |
| **18** | Irvington Blvd, Fulton St, **N** **gas:** Chevron, **S** **gas:** Shell/dsl |
| **17b c** | I-45, N to Dallas, S to Houston |
| **17a** | (eb only) Airline Dr, **S** **gas:** Shell, **food:** Jack-in-the-Box, **lodging:** Western Inn |
| **16** | Yale St, N Main St, Shamrock, **N** **gas:** Exxon, **other:** Harley Davidson, **S** **gas:** Mobil, Shell, **food:** Burger King, Church's Chicken, KFC/Pizza Hut/Taco Bell, **lodging:** Western Inn |
| **15** | TX 261, N Shepherd Dr, **N** **food:** Sonic, Taco Cabana, **S** **gas:** Chevron, Shell, Texaco/dsl, **food:** Wendy's, Whataburger, **other:** Home Depot, PepBoys |
| **14** | Ella Blvd, **N** **gas:** Exxon, Shell/24hr, Texaco, **food:** A&W, Blimpie, Burger King, Jack-in-the-Box, KFC, LJ Silver, McDonald's, Popeye's, Taco Bell, **S** **gas:** Shell, **food:** BBQ, **other:** Ⓗ HOSPITAL, Lowe's Whse |

**HOUSTON HOUSTON HOUSTON**

| | |
|---|---|
| **13c** | TC Jester Blvd, **N** **gas:** Chevron, Mobil, Shell, **food:** Atchafalaya Kitchen, Denny's, Golden Gate Chinese, Juanita's Mexican, Luisitos Mexican, Po' Boys Sandwiches, **lodging:** Courtyard, SpringHill Suites, **S** **gas:** Phillips 66 |
| **13b a** | US 290 |
| **12** | W 18th St, **N** **food:** CiCi's, **lodging:** Sheraton, **other:** JC Penney, mall, **S** **food:** Whataburger |
| **11** | I-10, W to San Antonio, E to downtown Houston |
| **10** | Woodway Dr, Memorial Dr, **E** **gas:** Shamrock, **food:** Steak'n Egg, **W** **gas:** Exxon, Shell, **food:** Shug's Rest. |
| **9b** | Post Oak Blvd, **E** **lodging:** Drury Inn, La Quinta, **W** **food:** Champp's Rest., McCormick&Schmick's Café |
| **9a** | San Felipe Rd, Westheimer Rd, FM 1093, **E** **gas:** Mobil, Shell, **lodging:** Courtyard, Hampton Inn, La Quinta, **other:** Circuit City, CVS Drug, NTB, Target, **W** **gas:** Shell, **food:** Champ's Rest., Luke's Burgers, **lodging:** Crowne Plaza Hotel, HomeStead Suites, Marriott, Sheraton, **other:** Best Buy, Dillard's, Nieman-Marcus |
| **8a** | US 59, Richmond Ave, **E** **lodging:** Holiday Inn, Extended Stay America, **other:** CVS Drug, **W** **gas:** Shell, **other:** Dillards, |
| **7** | Bissonet St, West Park Dr, Fournace Place, **E** **food:** Beudreax's Kitchen, **lodging:** Candlewood Suites, **other:** Home Depot, **W** **gas:** Shell/dsl/repair |
| **6** | Bellaire Blvd |
| **5b** | Evergreen St |
| **5a** | Beechnut St, **E** **gas:** Chevron, **food:** Boston Mkt, IHOP, Lowe's Whse, McDonald's, Outback Steaks, **other:** bank, **W** **gas:** Citgo, Shell, **food:** Escalante Mexican Grill, James Coney Island, Saltgrass Steaks, Smoothie King, **other:** Borders Books, GNC, Marshall's, mall |
| **4a** | S Post Oak Rd, Brasswood, **E** **gas:** Citgo, **food:** Outback Steaks, **lodging:** Day's Inn, **W** **other:** Target, Walmart |
| **3** | Stella Link Rd, **N** **gas:** Chevron, **food:** Jack-in-the-Box, **other:** Discount Tire, Food City, Radio Shack, **S** **gas:** Exxon, Phillips 66/dsl, Shell |
| **2** | US 90A, **N** **gas:** Chevron, Conoco, Shamrock, **food:** Arby's, Burger King, Church's, Denny's/24hr, KFC, McDonald's, Shoney's, Taco Bell, Wendy's, **lodging:** Grand Plaza Hotel, Howard Johnson, Villa Motel, **other:** CVS Drug, Discount Tire, Ford, Honda, Walgreen, **S** **gas:** Chevron, Shell, **food:** Golden Corral, Pizza Hut/Taco Bell, Whataburger/24hr, **lodging:** CareFree Inn, La Quinta, Motel 6, Super 8, **other:** Chevrolet, Firestone, Mazda, Nissan, Toyota, U-Haul, to Buffalo Speedway |
| **1c** | Kirby Dr (from eb), **N** **food:** Shell, **food:** Burger King, **lodging:** Radisson, **S** **food:** Joe's Crabshack, Pappadeaux Seafood, Pappasito's Cantina, **other:** Cavender's Boots, NTB, Pontiac/GMC, Sam's Club, Toyota |
| **1b a** | FM 521, Almeda St, Fannin St, **N** **gas:** Chevron, Shell, **food:** Burger King, **lodging:** Scottish Inn, **other:** Astro Arena, **S** **gas:** Shell, **food:** McDonald's, **other:** Aamco, to Six Flags |

TX

## INTERSTATE 15

| Exit # | Services |
|---|---|
| **400.5mm** | Utah/Idaho state line |
| **398** | Portage |
| **392** | UT 13 S, Plymouth, **E** gas: Sinclair/Subway/dsl |
| **385** | UT 30 E, to Riverside, Fielding, 1 mi **E** gas: Sinclair/Riverside Grill/dsl |
| **381** | Tremonton, Garland, 2 mi **E** other: **H** HOSPITAL, gas, food, lodging |
| **379** | I-84 W, to Boise |
| **376** | UT 13, to Tremonton, **E** gas: Texaco/Arby's/dsl/24hr, **2-3 mi E food:** Arctic Circle, Crossroads Rest., El Parral Mexican, JC'S Diner, Subway, Taco Time, **lodging:** Marble Motel, Sandman Motel |
| **372** | UT 240, to UT 13, to rec area, Honeyville, **E** other: Crystal Hot Springs Camping |
| **370mm** | rest area sb, full ⬥ facilities, info, **C**, **A**, litter barrels, vending, petwalk |
| **365** | UT 13, Brigham City, **W** other: to Golden Spike NHS |
| **363** | Forest St, Brigham City, **W** other: Bear River Bird Refuge |
| **362** | US 91, to US 89, Brigham City, Logan, **E** gas: Chevron/dsl, ⊕**FLYING J**/dsl/rest./24hr, 7-11/gas, Sinclair, **food:** Arby's, Beto's Mexican, Burger King, Donna's Rest., Hunan Chinese, KFC/Taco Bell, Little Caesar's, McDonald's, Old Grist Mill Bread, Pizza Hut, Pizza Press, Sonic, Subway, Taco Time, Wendy's, Wingers, **lodging:** Bushnell Motel, Crystal Inn, Galaxie Motel, Howard Johnson Express, **other:** **H** HOSPITAL, AutoZone, Checker Parts, Chevrolet/Buick/Cadillac/Pontiac, Chrysler/Dodge/Jeep, $Tree, Golden Spike RV Park, KOA, Smith's, Radio Shack, ShopKO, Walmart SuperCtr/Mirastar//24hr, RV camping, to Yellowstone NP via US 89, **W** gas: ⊕**FLYING J**/Crt St Grill/dsl/24hr, **lodging:** Days Inn |
| **361mm** | rest area nb, full ⬥ facilities, **C**, **A**, litter barrels, vending, petwalk |
| **359** | Port of Entry both lanes |
| **357** | UT 315, to Willard, Perry, **E** gas: ⊕**FLYING J**/Country Mkt/Pepperoni's/dsl/LP, **other:** KOA (2mi) |
| **351** | UT 126, to US 89, to Utah's Fruit Way, Willard Bay, **W** other: Smith & Edwards hardware |
| **349** | UT 134, N Ogden, Farr West, **E** gas: Exxon/Wendy's, Maverik, 7-11, **food:** Arby's, Domino's, Jumbo Burger, McDonald's, Melina's Mexican, Subway, **other:** Kwik Lube, **W** gas: Conoco/dsl |
| **346** | to Harrisville, **W** gas: Chevron/dsl, Cal Store, dsl repair |
| **344** | UT 39, 12th St, Ogden, **E** gas: Chevron, Phillips 66, Shell/dsl, **lodging:** Best Western/rest., 1-2 mi **E** gas: |
| **344** | Continued Chevron, **food:** Denny's, KFC, McDonald's, Sizzler, Village Inn Rest., **lodging:** Motel 6, **other:** to Ogden Canyon RA, **W** gas: Pilot/DQ/Subway/Taco Bell/dsl/24hr, **food:** Iron Pan Bistro, **lodging:** Sleep Inn, Western Inn |
| **343** | UT 104, 21st St, Ogden, **E** gas: Chevron/Arby's/dsl, ⊕**FLYING J**/Conoco/dsl/LP/24hr, Phillips 66/dsl, **food:** Cactus Red's Rest., McDonalds, Outlaw Rest., **lodging:** Best Western, Comfort Suites, Holiday Inn Express, ValuePlace Inn, **other:** Justus RV Ctr, RV Repair, **W** gas: Texaco, **lodging:** Super 8, **other:** Century RV Park |
| **342** | (from nb), UT 53, 24th St, Ogden, **E** gas: Sinclair/dsl |
| **341b a** | UT 79 W, 31st St, Ogden, **1-2 mi E** on Wall St...gas: 7-11, **food:** Arby's, Golden Corral, JJ North's Buffet, Sizzler, **lodging:** Day's Inn, Hampton Inn, Marriott, **other:** **H** HOSPITAL, Dillard's, Chevrolet, Ford/Lincoln/Mercury, RV Ctr, mall, to Weber St U, **W** ✈ |
| **340** | I-84 E (from sb), to Cheyenne, Wyo |
| **339** | UT 26 (from nb), to I-84 E, Riverdale Rd, **E** gas: Conoco/dsl, Sinclair, **food:** Applebee's, Arby's, Boston Mkt, Carl's Jr, Chili's, La Salsa Mexican, McDonald's, **lodging:** Motel 6, **other:** Chrysler/Jeep, Circuit City, Harley-Davidson, Home Depot, Honda/Nissan, Isuzu, Jo-Ann Fabrics, Lincoln/Mercury/Toyota/Kia, Mazda, |

UT

**N ↑ ↓ S**

**L A Y T O N**

**S A L T L A K E**

**UT**

## INTERSTATE 15 CONT'D

**339** Continued
Mitsubishi, Pontiac/Buick/GMC, Sam's Club/gas, Saturn, Target, Toyota, Walmart SuperCtr, Wilderness RV

**338** UT 97, Roy, Sunset, **E other:** Air Force Museum, **W gas:** Exxon/dsl, Phillips 66, 7-11, Sinclair, **food:** Arby's, Arctic Circle, Blimpie, Burger King, Central Park, DQ, KFC, McDonald's, Panda Express, Pizza Hut, Ponderosa, Sonic, Subway, Taco Bell, Village Inn Rest., Wendy's, **lodging:** Quality Inn, Motel 6, **other:** AutoZone, BrakeWorks, Checker Parts, Citte RV Ctr, Discount Tire, Early Tires, Firestone, Goodyear, Radio Shack, RiteAid, Schwab Tires, Smith's/gas, Walgeen, transmissions

**335** UT 103, Clearfield, **E** Hill AFB, **W gas:** Chevron, Conoco, PetroMart, 7-11, Texaco, Circle K, **food:** Arby's, Carl's Jr, KFC, McDonald's, Skipper's, Subway, Taco Bell, Winger's, **lodging:** Days Inn, The Cottage Inn, **other:** Big O Tire, Sierra RV Ctr

**334** UT 193, Clearfield, to Hill AFB, **E gas:** Chevron, Maverik, **W gas:** Chevron/dsl, **food:** Wendy's

**332** UT 108, Syracuse, **E gas:** Chevron, Phillips 66/dsl, Circle K, **food:** Applebee's, Carl's Jr., Cracker Barrel, Famous Dave's, Golden Corral, JB's, Marie Callender's, Outback Steaks, Quizno's, Red Robin, TimberLodge Steaks, **lodging:** Courtyard, Fairfield Inn, Hampton Inn, Hilton Garden, Holiday Inn Express, La Quinta, TownePlace Suites, **other:** Barnes&Noble, Lowe's Whse, Office Depot, Old Navy, Target, **W gas:** Conoco, 7-11, **food:** Arby's, McDonald's, **other:** H HOSPITAL, to Antelope Island

**331** UT 232, UT 126, Layton, **E gas:** Mobil, Phillips 66, Texaco, **food:** Denny's, Garcia's, McDonald's, Olive Garden, Red Lobster, Sizzler, Training Table Rest., Wendy's, **lodging:** Comfort Inn, Hilton Garden, **other:** JC Penney, mall, to Hill AFB S Gate, **W gas:** ⊛FLYING J, **food:** Blimpie, Burger King, China Buffet, ChuckeCheese, IHOP, KFC, Krispy Kreme, LoneStar Steaks, McGrath's FishHouse, Taco Bell, **other:** Batteries+, Chevrolet, Discount Tire, Dodge, Home Depot, NTB, Jeep, Pontiac/Cadillac/GMC, Ream's Foods, Sam's Club/gas, ShopKO, Staples, Walmart SuperCtr

**330** to UT 126 (from nb), Layton, **E food:** Little Orient Chinese, **other:** repair, **W gas:** Texaco, **other:** Jensen's RV

**328** UT 273, Kaysville, **E gas:** Chevron/McDonald's, Citgo/7-11, Phillips 66/dsl, Sinclair, **food:** Arby's, Cutler's Sandwiches, DQ, Joanie's Rest., Gandolfo's, KFC, Subway, Taco Maker, Taco Time, Wendy's, Winger's, **other:** Albertson's, Checker Parts, Schwab Tire, Walgreens, **W other:** Camping World/Jensen RV Ctt

**325mm** parking area both lanes

**325** UT 225, Lagoon Dr, Farmington (from sb) , **E food:** Subway, **other:** funpark, camping

**324** US 89 N, UT 225, Legacy Pkwy (from sb), **1 mi E gas:** Conoco/Smith's Foods/dsl, Maverik/gas, **food:** Arby's, Burger King, Little Caesar's, Subway, **other:** Aunt Pam's, Goodyear/auto, RV Park, to I-84

**322** UT 227 (from nb), Lagoon Dr, to Farmington, **E food:** Subway, **other:** Lagoon Funpark/RV Park

**319** Centerville, **E gas:** Chevron/dsl, Phillips 66/dsl, **food:** Arby's, Arctic Circle, Burger King, Carl's Jr, Chili's, DQ,

**319** Continued
Del Taco, Fusion of Asia, Gandolfo's, IHOP, Jake's Shakes, LoneStar Steaks, McDonald's, Subway, Taco Bell, TacoMaker, Wendy's, **other:** Albertson's, Big O Tire, Checker Parts, Curves, Home Depot, Kohl's, Land Rover, Radio Shack, Schwab Tire, Target/foods, Walmart SuperCtr, **W other:** RV Ctr

**317** US 89 S (exits left from sb), UT 131, 500W,, S Bountiful, **E gas:** Chevron/24hr, Exxon/dsl, Phillips 66/dsl, Sinclair/dsl, **food:** Alicia's Rest., Starbucks, **lodging:** Country Inn Suites, **other:** Office Depot, Parts+, PetCo, Goodyear, Jiffy Lube, tires

**316** UT 68, 500 S, W Bountiful, Woods Cross, **E gas:** Exxon, Texaco, **food:** Applebee's, Blimpie, Burger King, Carl's Jr, Christopher's Steaks, ChuckaRama, Coldstone, Del Taco, HogiYogi, KFC, La Frontera Mexican, McDonald's, Panda Express, Pizza Hut, Rinny's Rest., Sizzler, Subway, SuCasa Mexican, Taco Bell, Winger's, **other:** H HOSPITAL, Albertson's, AutoZone, Barnes&Noble, Big O Tire, Checker Parts, Costco/gas, Firestone/auto, Michael's, Radio Shack, Ross, ShopKO, TJ Maxx, Walgreens, **W gas:** Phillips 66/A&W/dsl, **lodging:** InTown Suites

**315** 26th S, N Salt Lake, **E gas:** Chevron/dsl, Sinclair, Tesoro, **food:** Apollo Burger, Arby's, Atlantis Burger, Empire Chinese, McDonald's, Subway, Taco Time, Village Inn, Wendy's, **lodging:** Best Western, Comfort Inn, **other:** Ace Hardware, Chevrolet/Pontiac/Buick/Kia, Discount Tire, Dodge, Ford/Lincoln/Mercury, Honda, K-Mart, Mazda, Mitsubishi, Nissan, Schwab Tire, Smith's Foods, Toyota, Tunex, U-Haul, **W gas:** Conoco, **food:** Denny's, Lorena's Mexican, **lodging:** Hampton Inn, Motel 6, **other:** Goodyear

**314** Center St, Cudahy Lane (from sb), N Salt Lake, **E gas**

**313** I-215 W (from sb), to ✈

**312** US 89 S, to Beck St, N Salt Lake

**311** 2300 N

**310** 900 W, **W food:** Tia Maria's Mexican, **lodging:** Regal Inn, Salt City Motel, **other:** 7-11, Self's conv/rest.

**309** 600 N, **E other:** H HOSPITAL, LDS Temple, downtown, to UT State FairPark

**308** I-80 W, to Reno, ✈

**307** 400 S, downtown

**306** 600 S, SLC City Ctr, **1 mi E gas:** Chevron, Phillips 66/dsl, Circle K, **food:** Burger King, DQ, Denny's, McDonald's, Wendy's, **lodging:** Embassy Suites, Hampton Inn, Little America, Motel 6, Quality Inn, Ramada Inn, Residence Inn, Super 8, **other:** Ford, Toyota, to Temple Square, LDS Church Offices

**305c-a** 1300 S, 2100 S UT 201 W, West Valley, **E gas:** Phillips 66, Texaco, **food:** Atlantis Burgers, Carl's Jr, McDonald's, Wienerschnitzel, **other:** Costco/gas, Home Depot, PetsMart, U-Haul, Walmart SuperCtr, **W gas:** ⊛FLYING J /Conoco/dsl/LP/rest./24hr, **food:** Wendy's, **other:** Best Buy, Blue Beacon, Cadillac, Chevrolet, $Tree, Ford, Goodyear, Hummer, Mitsubishi, Napa, Office Depot

**304** I-80 E, to Denver, Cheyenne

**303** UT 171, 3300 S, S Salt Lake, **E gas:** Citgo/7-11, Phillips 66, **food:** Apollo Diner, Burger King, McDonald's, Taco Bell, **lodging:** Bonneville Inn, Day's Inn, Roadrunner Motel, **W gas:** Maverik/gas, **other:** Sam's Club/gas, GMC

## INTERSTATE 15 CONT'D

**N ↕ S**

**301** UT 266, 4500 S, Murray, Kearns, **E food:** McDonald's, **other:** UpTown Tire, **W gas:** Chevron, Conoco, Shell/dsl, Sinclair/Burger King/dsl, Texaco, **food:** Burger King, Denny's, Wendy's, **lodging:** Fairfield Inn, Hampton Inn, Holiday Inn Express, Quality Inn, **other:** InterMtn RV Ctr, Lowe's Whse

**300** UT 173, 5300 S, Murray, Kearns, **E** ⊞ HOSPITAL, **W gas:** Chevron, Conoco, Sinclair, 7-11, **food:** KFC, Schlotsky's, **lodging:** Reston Hotel, **other:** Smith's Foods, FunDome, Jenson's RV Ctr

**298** I-215 E and W

**297** UT 48, 7200 S, Midvale, **E gas:** Chevron, Conoco, Phillips 66, Sinclair, Texaco/LP, **food:** Chili's, Denny's, John's Place, KFC, McDonald's, Midvale Mining Café, Sizzler, South Seas Café, Taco Bell, Village Inn Rest., **lodging:** Best Western, Day's Inn, Discovery Inn/café, Executive Inn, La Quinta, Motel 6, Rodeway Inn, Sandman Inn, Super 8, **other:** Cadillac/Buick, carwash, to Brighton, Solitude Ski Areas, Walgreens, **W gas:** Sinclair/Subway/dsl

**S A N D Y**

**295** UT 209, 9000 S, Sandy, **E gas:** Chevron, Sinclair, **food:** Arby's, Burger King, Fuddrucker's, Hardee's, Johanna's Kitchen, Schlotzky's, Sconecutter's Rest., Sweet Tomato, **lodging:** Comfort Inn, Majestic Rockies Motel, **other:** Discount Tire, Early Tires, Firestone, Ford, NAPA, to Snowbird, Alta Ski Areas, **W gas:** Maverik, Tesoro, **food:** KFC, Village Inn **other:** ⊞ HOSPITAL, Aamco

**293** 106th S, Sandy, S Jordan, **E gas:** Conoco, Phillips 66, Tesoro, **food:** Bennett's BBQ, Carver's Prime Rib, Chili's, Eat a Burger, HomeTown Buffet, Jim's Rest., Johanna's Rest., Subway, TGIFriday, Village Inn, Wendy's, **lodging:** Best Western, Courtyard, Extended Stay America, Hampton Inn, Hilton Garden, Marriott, Residence Inn, TownePlace Suites, **other:** Best Buy, Chevrolet, Chrysler/Jeep, Costco/gas, Dillard's, Goodyear, Honda, JC Penney, Nissan, Target, Toyota, mall, **W food:** Denny's, **lodging:** Country Inn Suites, Sleep Inn, Super 8, **other:** Buick/GMC/Pontiac, CarMax, VW, Walmart SuperCtr

**D R A P E R**

**291** UT 71, 12300 S, Draper, Riverton, **E gas:** Chevron, ⊕FLYING J/dsl, **food:** Arby's, Arctic Circle, Café Rio Mexican, Carl's Jr, Del Taco, Fazoli's, Guadalahonky's Mexican, Jamba Juice, KFC, McDonald's, Panda Express, Pizza Hut, Quizno's, Ruby Tuesday, Sonic, Teriyaki Express, Wendy's, Wienerschnitzel, Wingers Diner, **lodging:** Comfort Inn, Fairfield Inn, Ramada Ltd, **other:** Brown RV, Camping World RV Supplies (1mi), Discount Tire, Goodyear/auto, Greenbax, Kohl's, Mountain Shadows Camping, Smith's Foods, FSA Outlets/famous brands **W gas** Phillips 66, **other:** Walmart SuperCtr

**289** Bangerter Hwy, **W gas** Exxon, 7-11, **food:** Quizno's

**288** UT 140, Bluffdale, **E gas:** Chevron/dsl, **other:** Kohl's, Camping World RV Supplies (2mi), Quality RV Ctr, **W gas:** Common Sense/gas, 7-11, **other:** st prison

**284** UT 92, to Alpine, Highland, **E other:** Cabela's, **W gas:** Chevron/Iceberg Café/dsl, Maverik/dsl, **lodging:** Hampton Inn, **other:** Lone Peak RV Ctr, Thanksgiving Point/café, to Timpanogas Cave

**282** US 89 S, 12th W, to UT 73, Lehi, **W gas:** Chevron

**279** UT 73, to Lehi, **E gas:** Texaco/dsl, **food:** Applebee's, 1 Man Band Diner, **lodging:** Motel 6, **other:** Lowe's

**279** Continued
Whse, **W gas:** Chevron/dsl/24hr, Phillips 66/Wendy's/24hr, **food:** Arctic Circle, Dutch Oven Rest., KFC/Pizza Hut, McDonald's, Papa Murphy's, Subway, Tepenyki Japanese, Wingers, **lodging:** Best Western, Comfort Inn, Day's Inn, Super 8, **other:** Albertson's, Big O Tire, Checker Parts, GNC, Dave's Chiropractic, USPO, museum

**278** Main St, American Fork, **E gas:** Phillips 66/dsl/24hr, Texaco, **food:** Chili's, Cobblestone Pizza, Del Taco, Ottavio's Italian, Pier 49, Sonic, Wendy's, **other:** ⊞ HOSPITAL, Chevrolet, Chrysler/Dodge/Jeep, $Tree, Home Depot, K-Mart, Kohl's, Old Navy, Smith's Foods, Subaru/Suzuki, Target, Walmart SuperCtr

**276** 5th E, Pleasant Grove, **E gas:** Conoco/Blimpie, **food:** Carl's Jr, Denny's, McDonald's, Taco Bell, **lodging:** Quality Inn, **other:** Stewart's RV Ctr, **1-2 mi E gas:** Circle K, Phillips 66, Texaco, **food:** Arby's, Del Taco, Golden Corral, Hardee's, KFC, Subway, Wendy's, **other:** ⊞ HOSPITAL, American Camping, Chevrolet, **W other:** Buick/GMC/Pontiac, Ford, Land Rover

**275** Pleasant Grove, **E food:** Bajio Grill, Panda Express, Sonic, Wienerschnitzel, **other:** BMW, Macey's Foods

**273** Orem, Lindon, **E gas:** Exxon/dsl, Holiday, **food:** Costa Vida Mexican, Del Taco, **other:** Discount Tire, Home Depot, Lexus, Mercedes, Schwab Tire, **W gas:** Sinclair/dsl

**O R E M**

**272** UT 52, to US 189, 8th N, Orem, **E gas:** Maverik, Phillips 66, **lodging:** La Quinta, **1 mi E food:** Arby's, DQ, Denny's, Sonic, **other:** to Sundance RA

**271** Center St, Orem, **E gas:** Conoco, 7-11, **other:** ⊞ HOSPITAL, funpark, **1-2 mi E food:** Burger King, Hardee's, KFC, Panda Express, Taco Bell, Wendy's, **W gas:** Tesoro, **food:** La Casita Blanca Mexican, **lodging:** Econolodge, **other:** LP

**269** UT 265, 12th St S, University Pkwy, , **E gas:** Texaco/Wendy's/dsl/24hr, Sinclair, **food:** IHOP, Krispy Kreme, McDonald's, McGrath's FishHouse, Subway, **lodging:** Comfort Inn, Hampton Inn, La Quinta, **other:** Ford, JiffyLube, Mazda, Saturn, Walmart SuperCtr, **1-3 mi E gas:** Chevron, **food:** Applebee's, Arby's, Carrabba's, Chili's, Fuddrucker's, Golden Corral, Noodles & Co., Outback Steaks, Pizza Hut, Sizzler, Village Inn, **lodging:** Best Western, Courtyard, **other:** Barnes&Noble, Circuit City, Honda, JC Penney, JoAnn Fabrics, Lowe's Whse, Mitsubishi, Nissan, Office Depot, Old Navy, Ross, Subaru, TJ Maxx, mall, to BYU, many services on US 89, **W gas:** Chevron

## INTERSTATE 15 CONT'D

**265b a** UT 114, Center St, Provo, **E gas:** Conoco, Phillips 66, Shell, Sinclair/dsl, 7-11, **other:** H HOSPITAL, Firestone/auto, auto repair, **1 mi E lodging:** Marriott, Travelers Inn, Travelodge, **other:** Albertson's, Checker Parts, Firestone, **W gas:** Chevron, Shell, **lodging:** Econolodge, **other:** KOA, Lakeside RV, to Utah Lake SP

**263** US 189 N, University Ave, Provo, **E gas:** Chevron/24hr, Conoco/dsl, Maverik, Sinclair, **food:** A&W/KFC, Arby's, Burger King, ChuckaRama, Fazoli's, Hogi Yogi, McDonald's, Papa Murphy's, Ruby River Steaks, Sizzler, Taco Bell, Taco Time, Village Inn Rest., Wendy's, **lodging:** Best Western, Colony Inn, Fairfield Inn, Hampton Inn, La Quinta, Motel 6, National 9 Inn, Sleep Inn, Super 8, **other:** Curves, Dillard's, GoodEarth Foods, Home Depot, JC Penney, K-Mart, Les Schwab, NAPA, Sam's Club/gas, Sears/auto, Staples, Silver Fox RV Camping, mall, to BYU, **1 mi E food:** Los Three Amigos Mexican, **lodging:** Best Western, Hotel Roberts, Safari Motel, Western Inn, **other:** CarQuest, VW/Audi, auto repair

**261** UT 75, Springville, **E gas:** ⊕FLYING J/dsl/rest./scales/24hr/scales, Maverik, **food:** McDonald's (1mi), **lodging:** Best Western, **other:** E Bay RV Park, RestStop

**260** UT 77, Springville, Mapleton, **E gas:** Phillips 66/Quizno's/dsl, **food:** Del Taco, DQ, IHOP, Mongolian Grill, Pizza Hut, Quizno's, Wendy's, **other:** Big O Tire, JiffyLube, Walmart SuperCtr, **W gas:** Sinclair/Arby's/dsl, **food:** Cracker Barrel, **lodging:** Day's Inn, **other:** Quality RV Ctr

**258** US 89 S, US 6 E (from sb), to Price, **E gas:** Chevron/dsl, Phillips 66, Texaco, **food:** Arby's, Burger King, Carl's Jr, KFC, McDonald's, Papa Murphy's, Subway, Taco Bell, Wendy's, Winger's, **lodging:** Holiday Inn Express, Western Inn, **other:** Albertson's/gas, Checker Parts, Fakler's Tire, K-Mart, Radio Shack, RV Ctr

**257** US 6 E, UT 156, Spanish Fork, **E gas:** Chevron, Phillips 66, Sinclair, Tesoro, Texaco/dsl/LP, **food:** Amber Rest., Arby's, Bajio Grill, Burger King, China Wok, Hogi Yogi, Italian Place, KFC, Little Caesar's, McDonald's, One Man Band Diner, Pizza Factory, Sonic, Subway, Taco Bell, Taco Time, Wendy's, **other:** Albertsons, Big O Tire, Cal Store, $Tree, Jo-Anne Fabrics, K-Mart, Macey's Foods, ShopKO, USPO, transmissions, **W gas:** Conoco/dsl, **other:** Chevrolet, Chrysler/Jeep, Ford, RV Ctr

**253** UT 164, to Spanish Fork

**250** UT 115, Payson, **E gas:** Chevron/dsl, ⊕FLYING J/Cookery/dsl/LP/rest./scales/24hr, **food:** McDonald's, Subway, **lodging:** Comfort Inn, **other:** H HOSPITAL, Checker Parts, Payson Foods, RiteAid, Mt Nebo Loop, dsl repair

**248** Payson, Salem, **E gas:** Chevron, Sinclair/Arby's/dsl, **food:** Tsing Tao Asian, Hunan City, Pizza Hut, Subway, **other:** $Tree, Walmart SuperCtr, **W gas:** Phillips 66/Wendy's/dsl

**244** US 6 W, Santaquin, **E other:** Tire Factory, TrueValue, **W gas:** Chevron/dsl, Conoco/dsl, Sinclair, **food:** Family Tree Rest., One Man Band Diner, Santa Queen Burgers, Subway, Taco Time, **other:** Family$, Ford, Main St Mkt, Nat Hist Area, USPO, auto/tire care

**242** to S Santaquin, **W** Chevron/dsl

**233** UT 54, Mona

**228** UT 28, to Nephi, **2-4 mi W** services

**225** UT 132, Nephi, **E gas:** Tesoro/dsl/LP, **food:** Salt Creek Steaks, Taco Time, One Man Band Rest., **other:** Burn's Bros RV Park (5mi), **W gas:** Chevron/Arby's/dsl, Phillips 66/Wendy's/dsl, **lodging:** Economy Inn, **other:** H HOSPITAL, Big O Tire

**222** UT 28, to I-70, Nephi, **E gas:** Chevron/dsl, Sinclair/Hogi Yogi/scales/dsl/24hr, Texaco/dsl/24hr, **food:** Burger King, Mickelson's Rest., Subway, **lodging:** Motel 6, Roberta's Cove Motel, Super 8, **other:** dsl repair, **W gas:** ⊕FLYING J/Cookery/dsl/LP/scales/24hr, **food:** Lisa's Country Kitchen, **lodging:** Best Western, Safari Motel, **other:** H HOSPITAL, Hi-Country RV Park

**207** to US 89, Mills

**202** Yuba Lake, ⟨⟩, access to boating, camping, rec facilities

**188** US 50 E, to I-70, Scipio, **E gas:** Sinclair/Subway/dsl, Texaco, **lodging:** Super 8, **W gas:** Chevron/DQ/dsl/rest stop

**184** ranch exit

**178** US 50, to Delta, **W gas:** ⟨⟩, to Great Basin NP

**174** to US 50, Holden, to great Basin NP

**167** Lp 15, Fillmore, **0-3 mi E gas:** Chevron/dsl, Shell, Sinclair/dsl, **food:** 5 Buck Pizza, Old Frontier Steaks, **lodging:** Best Western/rest., **other:** H HOSPITAL, CarQuest, Goodyear, KOA, WagonsWest RV Park, **W gas:** Chevron/Subway/rest stop, Texaco/dsl, **food:** Carl's Jr

**163** Lp 15, to UT 100, Fillmore, **E gas:** Chevron/Arby's/dsl/24hr, Maverik, **lodging:** Apple Creek Inn, **other:** H HOSPITAL, KOA, **W gas:** Texaco/Burger King, **lodging:** motel

**158** UT 133, Meadow, **E gas:** Chevron/dsl, Shell/dsl

**153mm** view area sb

**151mm** view area nb

**146** Kanosh, **2 mi E** gas, chainup area

**138** ranch exit

**135** Cove Fort Hist Site, **E gas:** Chevron/Subway, **other:** rest stop

**132** I-70 E, to Denver, Capitol Reef NP, Fremont Indian SP

**129** Sulphurdale, chainup area

**125** ranch exit

**120** Manderfield, chainup area nb

**112** to UT 21, Beaver, Manderfield, **E gas:** Chevron, Sinclair/dsl, Conoco/dsl, **food:** Arby's, Arshel's Café, Hunan Chinese, McDonald's, Paradise Canyon Grill, Subway, **lodging:** Best Western, Country Inn, Day's Inn, Rodeway Inn, **other:** H HOSPITAL, Family$, KOA (1mi), auto repair, **W gas:** ⊕FLYING J/cafe/dsl/24hr/scales, **food:** Wendy's, **lodging:** Eagle's Landing Hotel, Super 8, **other:** to Great Basin NP

**109** to UT 21, Beaver, **E gas:** Phillips 66/dsl, Shell/Burger King/dsl/24hr, **lodging:** Best Western, Comfort Inn, **other:** H HOSPITAL, Cache Valley Cheese, Camper Land RV Park, Mike's Foodtown, NAPA, auto repair, **W gas:** Chevron/DQ/dsl/24hr, **food:** KanKun Mexican, Timberline Rest., **lodging:** Quality Inn, **other:** RV park, truckwash, to Great Basin NP

**100** ranch exit

**95** UT 20, to US 89, to Panguitch, Bryce Canyon NP

**88mm** **rest area both lanes, full** ⟨⟩ **facilities,** ⟨⟩, ⟨⟩, **litter barrel, petwalk, hist site**

**82** UT 271, Paragonah

**78** UT 141, **1 mi E gas:** Chevron/dsl, Maverik, **lodging:** Day's Inn, **other:** ski areas, **W gas:** TA/Subway/Taco Bell/LP/dsl/scales/24hr/@

## INTERSTATE 15 CONT'D

CEDAR CITY N ↕ S

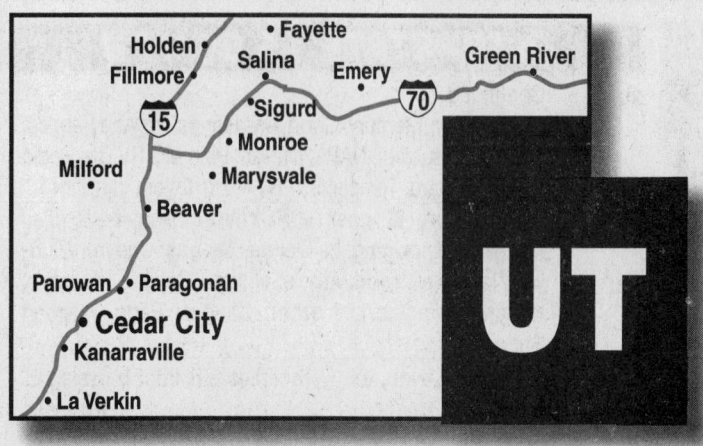

**75** UT 143, **2 mi** E **lodging:** Day's Inn, **other:** to Brian Head/Cedar Breaks Ski Resorts

**71** Summit

**62** UT 130, Cedar City, E **gas:** Loves/Carl's Jr/Subway/dsl/scales/24hr, Phillips 66/dsl, **food:** Arctic Circle, Godfather's Pizza, **other:** Country Aire RV Park, KOA (2mi), st patrol, W **gas:** Maverik/dsl, Shell/dsl/24hr/dsl repair, **lodging:** Travelodge

**59** UT 56, Cedar City, **0-2 mi** E **gas:** FoodMart/dsl, Maverik, Phillip 66/LP/dsl, Tesoro, **food:** A&W/KFC, Arby's, Bahio, Burger King, Denny's, Godfather's, Great Harvest Bread Co., IHOP, Little Caesars, McDonald's/playplace, Papa Murphy's, Pizza Factory, Sizzler, Taco Bell, Wendy's, **lodging:** Abbey Inn, Best Western, Econolodge, Quality Inn, Stratford Hotel, Super 7, **other:** Chevrolet/Buick, $Tree, Goodyear/auto, Lin's Mkt, NAPA, Tire Co., USPO, W **gas:** Maverik, Sinclair/dsl, **food:** Bard's Cafe, Subway, **lodging:** Crystal Inn, Motel 6, Super 8

**57** Lp 15, to UT 14, Cedar City, **0-2 mi** E **gas:** Chevron/repair/24hr, Phillips 66/dsl, Shell, Sinclair/dsl, **food:** DQ, Domino's, Hogi Yogi, Pizza Hut, Subway, **lodging:** Comfort Inn, Days Inn, Holiday Inn Express, Knights Inn, Rodeway Inn, SpringHill Suites, **other:** H HOSPITAL, Albertson's, AutoZone, Beall's, Big O Tire, CAL Ranch, Checker Parts, Country Aire RV Park, Family$, KOA, Main 57 Tire, NAPA Auto Care, Smith's Food/gas/24hr, Staples, to Cedar Breaks, Navajo Lake, Bryce Cyn, Duck Crk, W **gas:** Chevron/dsl, **food:** Applebee's, Chili's, Costa Vida, Del Taco, Lupita's Mexican, Ninja Japanese, Panda Express, Quizno's, Starbucks, Subway, Winger's, **lodging:** Hampton Inn, **other:** GNC, Home Depot, Jiffy Lube, Radio Shack, Tunex, Walgreens, Walmart SuperCtr/gas

**51** Kanarraville, Hamilton Ft

**44mm** **rest area both lanes, full** ♿ **facilities,** 🚻, 🏕, **litter barrels, petwalk, hist site**

**42** New Harmony, Kanarraville, W **gas:** Texaco/dsl

**40** to Kolob Canyon, E **other:** Zion's NP, tourist info/phone, scenic drive

**36** ranch exit

**33** ranch exit

**31** Pintura

**30** Browse

**27** UT 17, Toquerville, E **other:** to Zion NP, to Grand Cayon, to Lake Powell

**23** Leeds, Silver Reef (from sb), **3 mi** E **other:** Leed's RV Park/gas, hist site, museum

**22** Leeds, Silver Reef (from nb), same as 23

**16** UT 9, to Hurricane, E **gas:** Shell/Arby's/dsl, **lodging:** Holiday Inn Express, **other:** Harley-Davidson, Walmart Dist Ctr, **10 mi** E **gas:** Chevron, Shell, **food:** Calydascope Cafe, Coral Canyon Grille, **lodging:** Comfort Inn, Motel 6, Travelodge, **other:** to Zion NP, Grand Canyon, Lake Powell, RV Camping

**13** Washington Pkwy

**10** Middleton Dr, Washington, E **gas:** Phillips 66/dsl, Sinclair, **food:** Arby's, Arctic Circle, Bajio Cafe, Burger King, Del Taco, Honeybaked Ham, IHOP, In-n-Out, Jack-in-the-Box, Jimmy John's, Little Caesars, Lucky Buffet,

ST GEORGE

**10** Continued
Noble Romans, Ruby Tuesday, Sonic, Steak&Seafood, Subway, Texas Roadhouse, Toro Moro Mexican, Wendy's, **lodging:** Country Inn&Suites, Red Cliffs Inn, **other:** AAA, Albertson's/Sav-On, AutoZone, Barnes&Noble, Best Buy, Big Lots, Checker Parts, Costco/gas, Dillard's, Discount Tire, Home Depot, Kohl's, JC Penney, Jiffy Lube, PetCo, Sears/auto, Sportsman's Whse, Tunex, Walmart SuperCtr/gas, mall, W **gas:** Chevron/dsl/LP, Texaco/24hr, **other:** auto repair

**8** St George Blvd, St George, E **gas:** Chevron/Subway/dsl, Freddy's/dsl, Texaco, **food:** Applebee's, Arby's, Carl's Jr, Chili's, ChuckaRama, Coldstone Creamery, Don Jose Mexican, Famous Dave's BBQ, Fazoli's, Golden Corral, Mongolian BBQ, Outback Steaks, Pachanga's, Panda Express, Papa John's, Quizno's, Red Lobster, Ruby River Steaks, Sharky's Mexican, Starbucks, Village Inn Rest., Winger's, **lodging:** Best Inn, Courtyard, Hampton Inn, Ramada Inn, **other:** H HOSPITAL, Harmon's Foods, Lowe's Whse, Michael's, Old Navy, Ross, Staples, Sunrise Tire, Target, TJ Maxx, Zion Factory Stores/famous brands, same as 10, W **gas:** Chevron, Maverik/gas, Sinclair/Domino's/LP/dsl, Shell, Texaco/dsl, **food:** A&W/KFC, Burger King, Cafe Rio, China King, Denny's, Ernesto's Mexican, McDonald's, Panda Garden, Pizza Hut, Taco Bell, Taco Time, Wendy's, Wienerschnitzel, **lodging:** Best Western, Comfort Inn, Coronada Inn, Day's Inn, Econolodge, GuestHouse Inn, Howard Johnson, Motel 6, Rodeway Inn, Sands Motel, SunTime Inn, Travelodge, **other:** Big O Tire, Checker Parts, Desert Coach RV Ctr, Honda Motorcycles, Kauffman Transmissions, NAPA, Rite Aid, St Geo RV, to LDS Temple

**6** UT 18, Bluff St, St George, E **gas:** Chevron/dsl/24hr, Texaco/dsl/24hr, **food:** Cracker Barrel, Jack-in-the-Box, Subway, **lodging:** Ambassador Inn, Comfort Inn, Fairfield Inn, Hilton Garden, **other:** Buick/Pontiac/GMC, Firestone/auto, Hyundai, Saturn, U-Haul, W **gas:** Shell, Texaco, **food:** Arby's, Bluffs Rest., Burger King, Claimjumper Steaks, DQ, Denny's, JB's, McDonald's, Palms Rest., Pancho&Lefty's Mexican, Pier 49, Pizza Hut, San Francisco Pizza, Tony Roma, **lodging:** Best Western, Budget Inn, Claridge Inn, Comfort Suites, Crystal Inn, Holiday Inn, Howard Johnson, Quality Inn, Ridgeview Inn, South Lodge Inn, Super 8, **other:** H HOSPITAL, Albertson's, AutoZone, Big O Tire, Chevrolet/Cadillac, Chrysler/Dodge/Jeep,

UT

## INTERSTATE 15 CONT'D

| | |
|---|---|
| 6 | Continued<br>Ford/Lincoln/Mercury, Goodyear, Honda, Jo-Ann Fabrics, Mazda, Mitsubishi, NAPA, Nissan, Painter's RV Ctr, Radio Shack, Subaru, TempleView RV Park, Toyota, funpark |
| 4 | Bloomington, **E gas:** ⊕*FLYING J*/Burger King/dsl/scales/24hr, **lodging:** La Quinta, **W gas:** Chevron/Subway/Taco Bell, **food:** Arby's, Hungry Howie's, Wendy's, **lodging:** Wingate Inn, **other:** Checker Parts, Walmart SuperCtr/dsl |
| 2 | **Welcome Ctr nb, full** ♿ **facilities,** 🛆 **litter barrels,** 📞, **petwalk** |
| 1 | Port of Entry/weigh sta both lanes |
| 0mm | Utah/Arizona state line |

## INTERSTATE 70

| Exit # | Services |
|---|---|
| 232mm | Utah/Colorado state line |
| 228mm | **view area wb, litter barrels** |
| 227 | Westwater |
| 221 | ranch exit |
| 214 | to Cisco |
| 204 | UT 128, to Cisco |
| 193 | Yellowcat Ranch Exit |
| 190mm | **Welcome Ctr wb, full** ♿ **facilities, vending, info,** 🛆, **litter barrels** |
| 187 | Thompson Springs, **N gas:** Shell/dsl, **other:** café, camping, lodging |
| 182 | US 191 S, Crescent Jct, to Moab, **S** to Arches/Canyonlands NP |
| 181mm | **rest area eb, full** ♿ **facilities, scenic view,** 🛆, **litter barrels** |
| 175 | ranch exit |
| 164 | UT 19, Green River, **1-3 mi N gas:** Phillis 66/Burger King/dsl, Silver Eagle/Blimpie/dsl, Westwinds Trkstp/Sinclair/rest/dsl/scales/24hr, **food:** Tamarisk Rest., **lodging:** Best Western, Bookcliff Lodge, Comfort Inn, Holiday Inn Express, Motel 6, Super 8, Ramada Ltd, **other:** KOA, Powell River Museum, tires/repair, same as 160 |
| 160 | UT 19, Green River, **0-2 mi N gas:** Chevron/Subway/dsl, Conoco/Arby's/dsl, **food:** Ben's Cafe, Chowhound, **lodging:** Budget Inn, Sleepy Hollow Motel, Ray's Hotel, Robbers Roost, **other:** AG Mkt, Green River SP, NAPA/repair, Shady Acres RV Park, USPO, city park, same as 164 |
| 157 | US 6 W, US 191 N, to Price, Salt Lake |
| 147 | UT 24 W, to Hanksville, to Capitol Reef, Lake Powell |
| 144mm | **rest area wb, restrooms** ♿, **litter barrels** |
| 141.5mm | runaway truck ramp eb |
| 140mm | **rest area both lanes, view area, restrooms** ♿, **litter barrels** |
| 139mm | runaway truck ramp eb |
| 136mm | brake test area eb |
| 129 | ranch exit |
| 120mm | **rest area both lanes, restrooms** ♿, **litter barrels** |
| 114 | to Moore, **N rest area both lanes, restrooms** ♿, **litter barrels** |
| 105 | ranch exit |
| 102mm | **rest area both lanes, restrooms** ♿, **litter barrels** |

| | |
|---|---|
| 91 | ranch exit |
| 89 | UT 10 N, UT 72, to Emery, Price, **12 mi N** gas, **S** to Capitol Reef NP |
| 84mm | **S rest area both lanes, full** ♿ **facilities, litter barrels, petwalk** |
| 72 | ranch exit |
| 61 | Gooseberry Rd |
| 56 | US 89 N, to Salina, US 50 W, to Delta, **0-1 mi N gas:** Conoco/dsl, Phillips 66/dsl, Sinclair/Burger King/dsl, **food:** Denny's, El Mexicano Mexican, Mom's Cafe, Subway, **lodging:** Best Western, Rodeway Inn, Super 8, **other:** Barrett Foods, Butch Cassidy RV Camp, NAPA, auto repair, radiators, ***NEXT SERVICES 108 MI EB*** |
| 48 | UT 24, to US 50, Sigurd, Aurora, **1-2 mi S** gas, food, to Fishlake NF, Capitol Reef NP |
| 40 | Lp 70, Richfield, **0-2 mi S gas:** Chevron, ⊕*FLYING J*/Pepperoni's/dsl/LP/rest./24hr, Maverik, Shell, Sinclair, Texaco/dsl, **food:** Arby's, Chuckwagon Steaks, JB's Rest., McDonald's, South China Rest., Subway, Taco Time, **lodging:** Appletree Inn, Best Western, Budget Host, Day's Inn/rest., Quality Inn, Super 8, Travelodge, **other:** Ⓗ HOSPITAL, Albertson's/drug, Big O Tire, Chevrolet, Buick/Pontiac/Cadillac/GMC, Family$, Ideal Dairy, KOA, Lin's Mkt, NAPA, USPO, RV/truck repair |
| 37 | Lp 70, Richfield, **S gas:** Phillips 66/Wendy's/dsl, **food:** KFC/Taco Bell, Papa Murphy's, Wingers, **lodging:** Comfort Inn, Fairfield Inn, Hampton Inn, **other:** Home Depot, **1-2 mi S gas:** Conoco/dsl/Munchie's RV Park, Texaco/Burger King/dsl, **food:** Lotsa Motsa Pizza, McDonald's, Pizza Hut, Subway, **lodging:** Days Inn, Quality Inn, Romanico Inn, **other:** Ace Hardware, Albertson's, Big Kmart, Checker Parts, Chevrolet, $Tree, Ford/Mercury, Home Depot, K-Mart, KOA, Walmart SuperCtr, to Fish Lake/Capitol Reef Parks, st patrol |
| 31 | Elsinore, Monroe, **S gas:** Silver Eagle/gas |
| 25 | UT 118, Joseph, Monroe, **S gas:** Flying U Country Store/dsl, **other:** RV park |
| 23 | US 89 S, to Panguitch, Bryce Canyon |
| 17 | **N other:** Fremont Indian Museum, info, 📞, camping |
| 13mm | brake test area eb |
| 8 | Ranch Exit |
| 3mm | Western Boundary Fishlake NF |
| 1 | Historic Cove Fort, **N gas:** Chevron (2mi) |
| 0mm | I-15, N to SLC, S to St George. I-70 begins/ends on I-15, exit 132. |

## INTERSTATE 80

| Exit # | Services |
|---|---|
| 197mm | Utah/Wyoming state line |
| 193 | Wahsatch |
| 189 | ranch exit |
| 185 | Castle Rock |
| 182mm | Port of Entry/weigh sta wb |
| 180 | Emery (from wb) |
| 170 | **Welcome Ctr wb/rest area eb, full** ♿ **facilities,** 📞, **vending,** 🛆, **litter barrels, petwalk, RV dump** |
| 169 | Echo, **1 mi N** gas/dsl, food, lodging |
| 168 | I-84 W, to Ogden, I-80 E, to Cheyenne |
| 166 | view area both lanes, litter barrels |

## INTERSTATE 80 CONT'D

| | |
|---|---|
| **164** | Coalville, **N** **gas:** Phillips 66/dsl/mart, **lodging:** Best Western, **other:** Holiday Hills RV Camp/LP, Camper-World RV Park, **S** **gas:** Chevron/dsl, Sinclair, **other:** Griffith's Foods, NAPA, USPO, to Echo Res RA |
| **155** | UT 32 S, Wanship, **N** **food:** Spring Chicken Café, **S** **gas:** Sinclair/dsl, **other:** to Rockport SP |
| **150** | toll gate promontory |
| **146b a** | US 40 E, to Heber, Provo, **N** **gas:** Sinclair/Blimpie/dsl, **S** **other:** Home Depot |
| **145** | UT 224, Kimball Jct, to Park City, **N** **other:** Chevrolet, Ford/Mercury, RV camping, **S** **gas:** Chevron, **food:** Arby's, Bajio Grill, Coldstone Creamery, Gandalfo's Deli, Ghidottis Italian, Loco Lizard Cantina, McDonald's, Panda Express, Quizno's, Starbucks, Subway, Ruby Tuesday, Taco Bell, Wendy's, Wild Oats Cafe, Wingers, **lodging:** Best Western, Hampton Inn, Holiday Inn Express, **other:** GNC, Smith's Foods, USPO, Walmart, Outlet Mall/famous brands, RV camping, to ski areas |
| **144mm** | view area eb |
| **141** | ranch exit, **N** **gas:** Phillips 66/Blimpie, **food:** Pizza Hut, **other:** to Jeremy Ranch, **S** **food:** Booster Juice, Cafe Sabor, Oh Shucks Grill, **other:** Albertson's, camping, ski area |
| **140** | Parley's Summit, **S** **gas:** Sinclair/dsl, **food:** No Worries Café |
| **137** | Lamb's Canyon |
| **134** | UT 65, Emigration Canyon, East Canyon, Mountaindale RA |
| **133** | utility exit (from eb) |
| **132** | ranch exit |
| **131** | (from eb) Quarry |
| **130** | I-215 S (from wb) |
| **129** | UT 186 W, Foothill Dr, Parley's Way, **N** **H** HOSPITAL |
| **128** | I-215 S (from eb) |
| **127** | UT 195, 23rd E St, to Holladay |
| **126** | UT 181, 13th E St, to Sugar House, **N** **gas:** Chevron, Texaco, **food:** Olive Garden, Red Lobster, Sizzler, Training Table Rest., Wendy's, **other:** ShopKO |
| **125** | UT 71, 7th E St, **gas:** Texaco, **other:** Firestone, **N** **food:** McDonald's |
| **124** | US 89, S State St, **N** **gas:** Citgo/7-11, Chevron, Texaco/dsl, **food:** Burger King, Skipper's, Taco Bell, Uncle Sid's Rest., Wendy's, Woody's Drive-In, **other:** Buick, Chrysler/Jeep, Discount Tire, Dodge, Honda, Jeep, Suzuki, transmissions, **S** **food:** KFC, Pizza Hut, **lodging:** Ramada Inn |
| **123mm** | I-15, N to Ogden, S to Provo |
| **I-80 and I-15 run together approx 4 mi. See Interstate 15 exits 308-310.** | |
| **121** | 600 S, to City Ctr |
| **120** | I-15 N, to Ogden |
| **118** | UT 68, Redwood Rd, to N Temple, **1 mi** **N** **on N Temple...gas:** Chevron/Subway/dsl, Maverik, Pilot/Arby's/dsl/scales/24hr, Tesoro, **food:** A&W/KFC, Burger King, Carls Jr, Denny's, Taco Bell, Wendy's, **lodging:** Airport Inn, Candlewood Suites, Comfort Suites, Day's Inn, Holiday Inn Express, Motel 6, Quality Inn, Radisson, Utah St Fairpark, **S** HOSPITAL |
| **117** | I-215, N to Ogden, S to Provo |
| **115b a** | 40th W, W Valley Fwy, **N** to Salt Lake ✈ |
| **114** | Wright Bros Dr (from wb), **N** same as 113 |

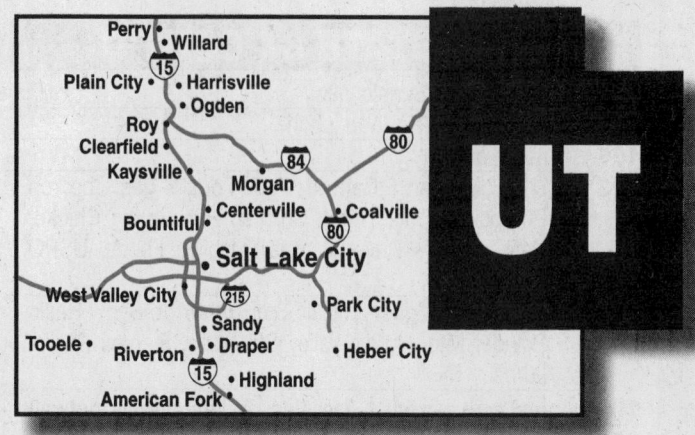

| | |
|---|---|
| **113** | 5600 W (from eb), **N** **gas:** Phillips 66/mart, **food:** Perkins, Pizza Hut, Subway, **lodging:** Best Western, Comfort Inn, Courtyard, Fairfield Inn, Hampton Inn, Hilton, Holiday Inn, La Quinta, Microtel, Residence Inn, Super 8 |
| **111** | 7200 W, **N** visitor ctr |
| **104** | UT 202, Saltair Dr, to Magna, **N** **other:** Great Salt Lake SP, beaches |
| **102** | UT 201 (from eb), to Magna |
| **101mm** | view area wb |
| **99** | UT 36, to Tooele, **S** **gas:** Chevron/Subway, ✈ FLYING J/Conoco/Country Mkt/dsl/scales/LP/24hr, TA/Burger King/Taco Bell/dsl/rest./scales/24hr/@, Shell/dsl, Speedco, **food:** McDonald's, **lodging:** Oquirrh Motel/RV Park, **other:** **H** HOSPITAL, Blue Beacon, Mamie's Place |
| **88** | to Grantsville |
| **84** | UT 138, to Grantsville, Tooele |
| **77** | UT 196, to Rowley, Dugway |
| **70** | to Delle, **S** **gas:** Delle/Sinclair/dsl/café/24hr |
| **62** | to Lakeside, Eagle Range, military area |
| **56** | to Aragonite |
| **55mm** | **rest area both lanes, full ♿ facilities, 📞, 🏕, litter barrels, petwalk, vending** |
| **49** | to Clive |
| **41** | Knolls |
| **26mm** | architectural point of interest |
| **10mm** | **rest area both lanes, full ♿ facilities, 📞, 🏕, litter barrels, vending, petwalk, observation area** |
| **4** | Bonneville Speedway, **N** **gas:** Sinclair/dsl/café/24hr |
| **3mm** | Port of Entry, weigh sta both lanes |
| **2** | UT 58 (no EZ wb return), Wendover, **S** **gas:** Sinclair/dsl, Shell/dsl, **food:** Quizno's, Subway, Taco Poblano, **lodging:** Best Western, Bonneville Inn, Day's Inn, Econolodge, Knight's Inn, Motel 6, Nugget Hotel/casino, Western Ridge Motel, **other:** CarQuest, Family$, Fred's Foods, Bonneville Speedway Museum, Montego Bay, Stateline Inn/casino, RV park, USPO, auto repair |
| **0mm** | Utah/Nevada state line, *Mountain/Pacific time zone* |

## INTERSTATE 84

| Exit # | Services |
|---|---|
| **120** | I-84 begins/ends on I-80, exit 168 near Echo, Utah. |
| **115** | to Henefer, Echo, **1/2 mi** **S** **other:** USPO, to E Canyon RA, **1/2 mi** **S** **other:** USPO, to E Canyon RA |
| **112** | Henefer, **S** gas, food, lodging |
| **111** | Croydon |

## INTERSTATE 84 CONT'D

| | |
|---|---|
| **111mm** | Devil's Slide Scenic View |
| **108** | Taggart, **N** gas, food, phone |
| **106** | ranch exit |
| **103** | UT 66, Morgan, E Canyon RA, **N** Ford, **S gas:** Chevron, Phillips 66, Shell, **food:** Chicken Hut, Spring Chicken Café, Steph's Drive-In, **other:** Jubilee Foods, USPO, city park |
| **96** | Peterson, **N gas:** Sinclair (3mi), **other:** to Snow Basin, Powder Mtn, Nordic Valley Ski Areas, **S gas:** Phillips 66/dsl |
| **94mm** | rest area wb, full ♿ facilities, 🛉 litter barrels, petwalk |
| **92** | UT 167 (from eb), to Huntsville, **N gas:** Sinclair/dsl (2mi), **other:** trout farm (1mi), to ski areas |
| **91mm** | rest area eb, full ♿ facilities, 🛉 litter barrels, petwalk |
| **87b a** | US 89, to Layton, Ogden, Hill AFB, **N food:** McDonald's (2mi), **1/2 mi S gas:** Shell |
| **85** | S Weber, Uintah |
| **81** | to I-15 S, UT 26, Riverdale Rd, **N gas:** Conoco/dsl, Sinclair, **food:** Applebee's, Boston Mkt, Carl's Jr, Chili's, La Salsa Mexican, McDonald's, **other:** Chrysler/Jeep, Circuit City, Harley-Davidson, Home Depot, Honda/Nissan, Isuzu, Lincoln/Mercury/Toyota/Kia, Lowe's Whse, Mazda, Mitsubishi, PepBoys, Pontiac/Buick/GMC, Sam's Club/gas, Target, Walmart SuperCtr, Wilderness RV, **S food:** McDonald's, **lodging:** Motel 6 |
| **I-84 and I-15 run together. See Interstate 15 exits 341-376** ||
| **41** | I-15 N to Pocatello |
| **40** | UT 102, Tremonton, Bothwell, **N gas:** Chevron/Quizno's/dsl/wash/24hr, Sinclair/Burger King/dsl/scales/@, **food:** Denny's/24hr, McDonald's, Wendy's, **lodging:** Hampton Inn, Western Inn, **other:** H HOSPITAL (4mi), Jack's RV Ctr, truck/tire repair, **1 mi N gas:** Maverik, Phillips 66/dsl, Tesoro, **lodging:** Marble Motel, **other:** Alco, **S other:** to Golden Spike NM, tires/repair |
| **39** | to Garland, Bothwell, **N** H HOSPITAL |
| **32** | ranch exit |
| **26** | UT 83 S, to Howell |
| **24** | to Valley |
| **20** | to Blue Creek |
| **17** | ranch exit |
| **16** | to Hansel Valley |
| **12** | ranch exit |
| **7** | Snowville, **N gas:** Chevron/Subway/dsl, ⊕FLYING J/Pepperoni's/dsl/LP/24hr, **food:** Mollie's Café, Ranch House Diner, **lodging:** Outsiders Inn, **other:** Lotti Dell RV camping |
| **5** | UT 30, to Park Valley |
| **0mm** | Utah/Idaho state line |

## INTERSTATE 215 - SALT LAKE

| Exit # | Services |
|---|---|
| **29** | I-215 begins/ends on I-15. |
| **28** | UT 68, Redwood Rd, **W gas:** ⊕FLYING J/dsl/rest./mart/24hr/@, Maverik/24hr, **food:** Subway, **other:** BMW (motorcycles) |
| **26** | Legacy Pkwy |
| **25** | 22nd N |
| **23** | 7th N, **E gas:** Exxon, Maverik, Pilot/Arbys/dsl/ |

| | |
|---|---|
| **23** | Continued scales/24hr (1.5 mi), **food:** Arby's, KFC, McDonald's, Taco Bell, Wendy's, **lodging:** Motel 6, **W lodging:** Airport Inn, Baymont Inn, Candlewood Suites, Comfort Suites, Holiday Inn Express, Radisson |
| **22b a** | I-80, W to Wendover, E to Cheyenne |
| **21** | California Ave, **E gas:** Chevron/dsl, Sapp Bros/Sinclair/Burger King/dsl/@, **food:** Great American Diner, Subway, **other:** Goodyear |
| **20b a** | UT 201, W to Magna, 21st S, **W other:** Goodyear, Kenworth |
| **18** | UT 171, 3500 S, W Valley, **E gas:** Sinclair, **food:** Applebee's, Chili's, Costa Vida Mexican, Cowloon Moon, Cracker Barrel, Denny's, IHOP, Training Table, **lodging:** Baymont Inn, Country Inn Suites, Crystal Inn, Extended Stay America, La Quinta, Ruby Tuesday, Sleep Inn, **other:** H HOSPITAL, PepBoys, **W food:** Apollo Burger, **other:** Big O Tire, Firestone, JC Penney, Macy's, Staples |
| **15** | UT 266, 47th S, **E gas:** Conoco/dsl, **food:** Dee's Rest., KFC, Pizza Hut, Taco Time, Taco Bell, Village Inn, Wendy's, **other:** Albertson's, Goodyear/auto, Marie Callender's, Rite Aid, Walgreens, **W gas:** Chevron, **food:** Arby's |
| **13** | UT 68, Redwood Rd, **E gas:** Chevron, Tesoro, **food:** Applebee's, Apollo Burger, Arby's, Bajio Grill, Burger King, Carl's Jr, Golden China, Great Harvest Bread, Honey Baked Ham, McDonald's/playplace, Old Spaghetti Factory, Panda Express, Papa John's, Souper Salad, Starbucks, Subway, TX Roadhouse, Tuesday Morning, **lodging:** Homestead Suites, **other:** $Tree, Harmon's, Jo-Ann Fabrics, PetsMart, Radio Shack, Ross, ShopKO, Walmart SuperCtr/auto |
| **12** | I-15, N to SLC, S to Provo |
| **11** | same as 10 (from eb), same as 10 (from eb) |
| **10** | UT 280 E, **E other:** Sam's Club, **W food:** Applebee's, Arby's, Hooters, Jason's Deli, La Salsa Mexican, Macaroni Grill, Olive Garden, Red Lobster, Taco Bell, Wendy's, Village Inn, **other:** H HOSPITAL |
| **9** | Union Park Ave, **E food:** Black Angus, Carl's Jr, Chili's, Denny's, Famous Dave's BBQ, LaSalsa Mexican, Marie Callender's, Outback Steaks, Sweet Tomato, Tony Roma, **lodging:** Best Western, Crystal Inn, Extended Stay America, Homewood Suites, **other:** Albertson's, Barnes&Noble, Circuit City, Home Depot, Old Navy, Ross, Smith's Foods, Target, Walmart/auto, **W gas:** Tesoro, **lodging:** Crystal Inn, Motel 6, Super 8 |
| **8** | UT 152, 2000 E, **E gas:** Chevron, **food:** KFC, Panda Express, Taco Bell, **W food:** Wendy's |
| **6** | 6200 S, **E food:** Loco Lizards Café, Mikado Café, Quizno's, **other:** Alta, Brighton, Snowbird, Solitude/ski areas |
| **5** | UT 266, 45th S, Holladay, **W gas:** Tesoro |
| **4** | 39th S, **E gas:** Chevron, Sinclair, **food:** Barbacoa Grill, Rocky Mtn Pizza, **other:** Ace Hardware, Dan's Foods, **W** H HOSPITAL |
| **3** | 33rd S, Wasatch, **W gas:** Tesoro, **food:** Burger King, KFC, McDonald's, Taco Bell, Wendy's |
| **2** | I-80 W |
| **I-215 begins/ends on I-80, exit 130.** ||

**SALT LAKE CITY**

## INTERSTATE 89

N ↑↓ S

ST ALBANS

| Exit # | Services |
|---|---|
| **130mm** | I-89 Begins/Ends, US/Canada Border, Vermont state line |
| **129.5mm** | rest area sb, full (handicapped) facilities, [phone], [picnic], litter barrels, petwalk |
| **22** (129) | US 7 S, Highgate Springs, **E** other: DutyFree, **3 mi E gas:** Mobil/dsl |
| **129mm** | Latitude 45 N, midway between N Pole and Equator |
| **128mm** | Rock River |
| **21** (123) | US 7, VT 78, Swanton, **E gas:** Exxon/dsl/24hr, **W gas:** Mobil/dsl, Shell, Sunoco/dsl, **food:** Dunkin Donuts, Jacob's Rest., McDonald's, **other:** Grand Union Foods, NAPA |
| **20** (118) | US 7, VT 207, St Albans, **W gas:** Mobil/dsl Shell/dsl, **food:** Burger King, Dunkin Donuts, KFC/Taco Bell, McDonald's, Oriental Kitchen, Panda China, Pizza Hut, Wendy's, **other:** [H] HOSPITAL, Advance Parts, Aubuchon Hardware, Chevrolet, Ford, Hannaford Foods, Kinney Drug, PriceChopper Foods, Radio Shack, Sears, Staples |
| **19** (114) | US 7, VT 36, VT 104, St Albans, **W gas:** Exxon/dsl, Mobil/dsl, **lodging:** La Quinta, **other:** [H] HOSPITAL, st police, vet |
| **111mm** | rest area both lanes, full [wheelchair] facilities, info, [phone], [picnic], litter barrels, vending, petwalk |
| **18** (107) | US 7, VT 104A, Georgia Ctr, **E gas:** Citgo, Mobil/dsl, Shell, **food:** GA Farmhouse Rest., **other:** GA Auto Parts, Homestead RV Park, USPO, repair |
| **17** (98) | US 2, US 7, Lake Champlain Islands, **E gas:** Exxon, Mobil, **other:** camping (4mi), **W other:** to NY Ferry, camping (6mi) |
| **96mm** | weigh sta both lanes |
| **16** (92) | US 7, US 2, Winooski, **E gas:** Mobil, **food:** Friendly's, T-Bones Rest., **lodging:** Hampton Inn, **other:** CostCo, Osco Drug, Shaw's Foods, **W gas:** Citgo, GoGo Gas, Shell/dsl, **food:** Burger King, Jr's Italian, Libby's Diner, McDonald's, Subway, **lodging:** Motel 6, Quality Inn |
| **15** (91) | VT 15 (from nb no return), Winooski, **E lodging:** Day's Inn, Handys Extended Stay Suites, **W gas:** Exxon, Mobil, **other:** USPO |
| **90mm** | Winooski River |

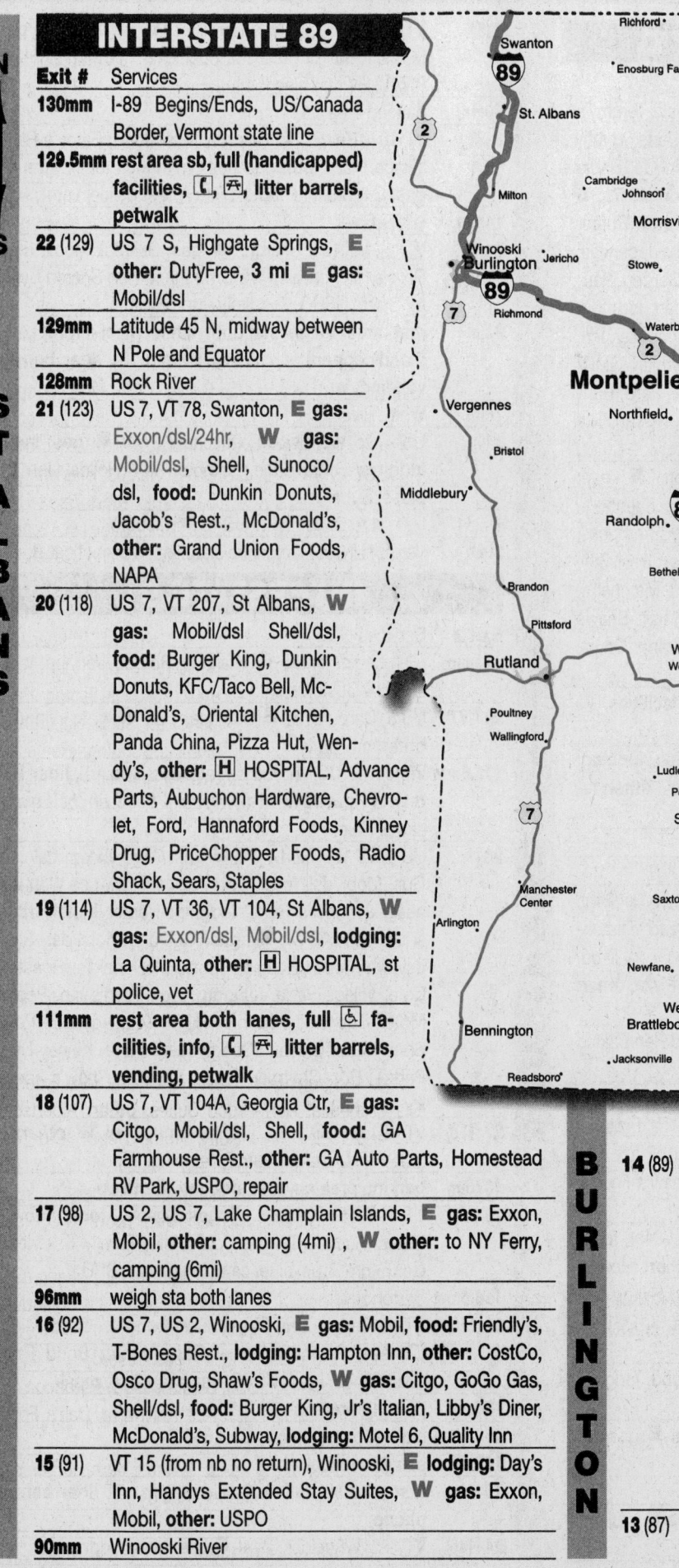

BURLINGTON

| | |
|---|---|
| **14** (89) | US 2, Burlington, **E gas:** Citgo/repair, Exxon, Gulf, Maverick, Mobil, Shell/dsl, **food:** Al's Cafe, Applebee's, Burger King, CheeseTraders, Dunkin Donuts, Friendly's, Kohl's, Leonardo's Pizza, Marco's Pizza, McDonald's, Moe's SW Grill, Nothing but Noodles, Outback Steaks, Quizno's, Starbucks, Zachary's Pizza, **lodging:** Anchorage Inn, Best Western, Comfort Inn, DoubleTree Hotel, Hawthorn Suites, Holiday Inn, La Quinta, SwissHost Motel, **other:** Barnes&Noble, BonTon, Grand Union Foods, JC Penney, Kohl's, Natural Foods Mkt, Sears/auto, mall, USPO, **W gas:** Exxon, Mobil, **lodging:** Sheraton, **other:** [H] HOSPITAL, Advance Parts, Michael's, PetCo, Staples |
| **13** (87) | I-189, to US 7, Burlington, **2 mi W on US 7... N gas:** Citgo, Shell, **food:** Blimpe, China Express, |

VT

## INTERSTATE 89 CONT'D

**13** (87) Continued
Dunkin Donuts, KFC, Starbucks, TGIFriday, Tommy's Grill, **lodging:** Liberty Inn, **other:** Bond Parts, Hyundai/Subaru, Kinney Drug, PriceChopper Foods, Radio Shack, Shaws Foods, TJ Maxx, **2 mi** W on US 7... S **gas:** Exxon, Gulf, Mobil, Sunoco, Shell, **food:** Burger King, Chicago Grill, Denny's, Friendly's, Koto Japanese, Lakeview House Rest., McDonald's, Olive Garden, Pauline's Cafe, Pizza Hut, Quizno's, Zen Garden, **lodging:** Comfort Suites, Holiday Inn Express, Rodeway Inn, **other:** Advance Parts, Audi/VW, Buick/Cadilac/GMC/Pontiac, Chevrolet, Chrysler/Saturn, Dodge, Ford, Hannaford Foods, Jeep, K-Mart, Lowes Whse, Nissan, Tire Whse, Toyota/Scion, vet

**12** (84) VT 2A, to US 2, to Essex Jct, Williston, E **gas:** Mobil/24hr, Sunoco/dsl/24hr, **food:** Chili's, Friendly's, Longhorn Steaks, 99 Rest., Ponderosa, Starbucks, **lodging:** Fairfield, TownePlace Suites, **other:** Best Buy, Circuit City, Hannaford Foods, Home Depot, Marshall's, Natural Provisions Mkt, Osco Drug, PetsMart, Shaws Foods, Staples, Walmart, st police, W **lodging:** Courtyard, Residence Inn

**82mm** rest area both lanes (7am-11pm) , full ♿ facilities, 🚻, 🅿, litter barrels, vending, petwalk, WiFi

**11** (79) US 2, to VT 117, Richmond, E **gas:** Citgo, **lodging:** Checkered House Motel, Kitchen Table Rest., **other:** repair, W **gas:** Mobil

**67mm** parking area/weigh sta sb
**66mm** parking area/weigh sta nb

**10** (64) VT 100, to US 2, Waterbury, E **gas:** Exxon/dsl/24hr, Mobil/dsl/24hr, **lodging:** Best Western/rest, Thatcher Brook Inn/rest., **other:** Shaws Foods/Osco Drug, TrueValue, W **gas:** Citgo, **food:** Zachary's Pizza, **other:** USPO

**9** (59) US 2, to VT 100B, Middlesex, W **food:** Red Hen Baking Co, **other:** museum, st police

**8** (53) US 2, Montpelier, **1 mi** E **gas:** CF/gas, Citgo, Exxon/dsl, Gulf/dsl, Mobil, Sunoco/repair, **food:** La Pizzaria, Sarducci's Rest., Subway, **lodging:** Capitol Plaza Hotel, Montpelier Inn, **other:** Bond Parts, Shaw's Foods, camping (6mi), to VT Coll

**7** (50) VT 62, to US 302, Barre, E **gas:** Mobil/dsl/24hr, **food:** Applebee's, **lodging:** Comfort Suites, **other:** Honda, Shaw's Foods, Staples, **1 mi** E **lodging:** Hilltop Inn, **other:** 🏥 HOSPITAL, Cadillac/GMC/Toyota, JC Penney, Jo-Ann Fabrics, camping (7mi)

**6** (47) VT 63, to VT 14, S Barre, **4 mi** E gas, food, lodging, camping, info

**5** (43) VT 64, to VT 12, VT 14, Williamstown, **6 mi** E gas/dsl, food, lodging, camping, W to Norwich U

**41mm** highest elevation on I-89, 1752 ft

**34.5mm** rest area/weigh sta both lanes (11am-9pm) , full ♿ facilities, info, 🚻, litter barrels, petwalk

---

**4** (31) VT 66, Randolph, E **other:** RV camping (1mi) , W **gas:** Mobil, **food:** McDonald's, lodging (3mi), **other:** 🏥 HOSPITAL, RV camping (5mi)

**30mm** parking area

**3** (22) VT 107, Bethel, E **gas:** Shell/dsl, **food:** Eaton's Rest., Village Pizza, **other:** to Jos Smith Mon (8mi), **1 mi** W **gas:** Citgo/dsl/LP, **other:** Rite Aid, st police, vet

**14mm** White River

**2** (13) VT 14, VT 132, Sharon, W **gas:** Gulf/dsl, Mobil, **food:** Dixie's Kitchen, Sandy's Drive Inn, **other:** Sharon Country Store, USPO, Jos Smith Mon (6mi)

**9mm** rest area/weigh sta both lanes (7am-11pm) , full (handicapped) facilities, 🚻, info, 🅿, litter barrels, vending, wi-fi

**7mm** White River

**1** (4) US 4, to Woodstock, Quechee, **3 mi** E **gas:** Irving, **lodging:** Econolodge, Hampton Inn, Holiday Inn Express, Super 8

**1mm** I-91, N to St Johnsbury, S to Brattleboro

**0mm** Vermont/New Hampshire state line, Connecticut River

## INTERSTATE 91

| Exit # | Services |
| --- | --- |
| **178mm** | I-91 begins/ends, US/Canada Border, Vermont state line, US Customs |
| **29** (177) | US 5, Derby Line, E Dutyfree, **1 mi** W **gas:** Irving/dsl, **other:** city park |
| **176.5mm** | Welcome Ctr sb, full ♿ facilities, info, 🅿, litter barrels, 🚻, petwalk, wi-fi, *Midpoint between the Equator and N Pole* |
| **28** (172) | US 5, VT 105, Derby Ctr, E **gas:** Citgo, Exxon/dsl/24hr, Gulf, Mobil/dsl, **food:** Cow Palace Rest., Lee Wah Chinese, Jennifer's Rest., **lodging:** Border Motel, **other:** st police, USPO, W **gas:** Gulf/dsl, Mobil/dsl, Shell/dsl/24hr, **food:** Hoagie's Pizza, McDonald's, Roaster's Cafe, Village Pizza, **lodging:** Lady Pearl's Inn, Pepin's Motel, Super 8, **other:** 🏥 HOSPITAL, Advance Parts, Bond Parts, Chrysler/Dodge/Jeep, $Tree, Kinney Drug, Parts+, PriceChopper Foods, Rite Aid, Shaw's Foods, RV camping, st police |
| **27** (170) | VT 191, to US 5, VT 105, Newport, **3 mi** W **other:** 🏥 HOSPITAL, Border Patrol, camping, info |
| **167mm** | parking area nb, rest area/weigh sta sb |
| **26** (161) | US 5, VT 58, Orleans, E **gas:** Sunoco, **food:** Subway, **other:** Austin's Drugs, Cole's Mkt, Family $, Orleans Gen Store, TrueValue, camping (8mi), USPO |
| **156.5mm** | Barton River |
| **25** (156) | VT 16, Barton, **1 mi** E **gas:** Gulf, Irving/dsl, **food:** Ming's Chinese, Parson's Corner Rest., **other:** Bond Parts, C&C Foods, Ford, USPO, camping (2mi), repair |
| **154mm** | parking area nb |
| **150.5mm** | highest elevation on I-91, 1856 ft |
| **143mm** | scenic overlook nb |
| **141mm** | rest area sb, full ♿ facilities, info, 🅿, litter barrels, phone |
| **24** (140) | VT 122, Wheelock, **2 mi** E gas, food, lodging |

*(left margin: N↕S, MONTPELIER, VT)*
*(right margin: N↕S, DERBY CTR)*

## INTERSTATE 91 CONT'D

**JOHNSBURY N ↕ S**

**23 (137)** US 5, to VT 114, Lyndonville, **E** **gas:** Gulf/dsl, Mobil/ Dunkin Donuts, **food:** Hoagie Pizza, McDonald's, **lodging:** Colonnade Inn, **other:** Ace Hardware, NAPA, Kinney Drug, Rite Aid, White Mkt Foods, **W** **lodging:** Lyndon Motel

**22 (132)** to US 5, St Johnsbury, **1-2 mi** **E** **gas:** Citgo/dsl/LP, **food:** KFC/Taco Bell, Kham's Cuisine, Pizza Hut, **other:** H HOSPITAL, Aubuchon Hardware, Bond Parts, Buick/ GMC/Pontiac, Kinney Drug, PriceChopper Foods, repair, **3 mi** **E** on US 5...**gas:** Irving, **other:** Firestone, JC Penney, Radio Shack, Sears

**21 (131)** US 2, to VT 15, St Johnsbury, **1-2 mi** **E** services

**20 (129)** US 5, to US 2, St Johnsbury, **E** **gas:** Irving/dsl, Mobil, Shell/dsl, **food:** Anthony's Diner, Dunkin Donuts, East Garden Chinese, McDonald's, Subway, **other:** Family$, Kevin's Repair, Rite Aid, **W** **lodging:** Comfort Inn, **other:** st police

**19 (128)** I-93 S to Littleton NH

**122mm** scenic view nb

**18 (121)** to US 5, Barnet, **E** **other:** camping (5mi) , **W** **other:** camping (5mi)

**115mm** **rest area sb**

**114mm** **rest area nb**

**17 (110)** US 302, to US 5, Wells River, NH, **E** **food:** Warner's Rest., **other:** camping (10mi), RV Ctr, **W** **gas:** P&H Trkstp/dsl/rest./scales/24hr, **other:** H HOSPITAL (5mi), camping (9mi)

**100mm** **nb rest area, full** ♿ **facilities,** C **, info,** ⊞ **, litter barrels, petwalk, sb parking area/weigh sta**

**16 (98)** VT 25, to US 5, Bradford, **E** **gas:** Mobil/dsl/LP/café, **food:** Hungry Bear Rest., **lodging:** Bradford Motel, **other:** Kinney Drug, NAPA, P&C Foods, Pierson Farm Mkt, **W** st police

**15 (92)** Fairlee, **E** **gas:** Citgo/dsl, Gulf, Mobil/deli, Shell/dsl/LP, **food:** Subway, Your Place Rest., **other:** USPO, camping, golf

**14 (84)** VT 113, to US 5, Thetford, **1 mi** **E** **other:** food, camping, **W** **other:** camping

**WHITE RIVER JCT**

**13 (75)** US 5, VT 10a, Hanover, NH, **E** **other:** H HOSPITAL, camping, to Dartmouth, **W** Subaru

**12 (72)** US 5, White River Jct, Wilder, **E** **gas:** Gulf/dsl/24hr, Mobil

**11 (71)** US 5, White River Jct, **E** **gas:** Exxon/Subway/dsl, Mobil, **food:** China Moon Cafe, Crossroads Café, McDonald's, **lodging:** Comfort Inn, Regency Inn, **other:** Ford/Lincoln/ Mercury, Hyundai, Jct Mktplace, Saturn, Toyota, USPO, **W** **gas:** Citgo, Irving/Dunkin Donuts, Lukoil, **lodging:** Comfort Suites, Econolodge, Hampton Inn, Holiday Inn Express, Super 8, **other:** H HOSPITAL, Nissan, Saab

**10N (70)** I-89 N, to Montpelier

**10S** I-89 S, to NH, airport

**68mm** rest area/weigh sta both lanes (7am-11pm) , full ♿ facilities, ⊞ litter barrels, C vending, petwalk

**9 (60)** US 5, VT 12, Hartland, **E** H HOSPITAL, **W** **gas:** Mobil (1mi), info

**8 (51)** US 5, VT 12, VT 131, Ascutney, **E** **gas:** Citgo/dsl, Gulf/ dsl, Irving, Sunoco/Dunkin Donuts/dsl, **food:** Mr. G's Rest., RedBarn Cafe, **lodging:** Yankee Village Motel, **other:** H HOSPITAL, USPO

**7 (42)** US 5, VT 106, VT 11, Springfield, **W** **gas:** Irving/scales/ dsl/24hr, **lodging:** Holiday Inn Express, **other:** H HOSPITAL (5mi), camping

**39mm** parking area both lanes

**6 (34)** US 5, VT 103, to Bellows Falls, Rockingham, **E** **gas:** Shell/dsl, **food:** Leslie's Rest., **lodging:** Every Day Inn, **W** **gas:** Sunoco/dsl/24hr, **other:** st police (6mi)

**5 (29)** VT 121, to US 5, to Bellows Falls, Westminster, **3 mi** **E** gas, food, C, lodging

**24mm** parking area both lanes

**22mm** weigh sta sb

**20mm** parking area nb

**4 (18)** US 5, Putney, **E** **lodging:** Putney Inn/rest., **W** **gas:** Sunoco/dsl/LP/24hr, **other:** camping (3mi)

**BRATTLEBORO**

**3 (11)** US 5, VT 9 E, Brattleboro, **E** **gas:** Agway/dsl, Citgo, Mobil, Sunoco, **food:** Bickford's, China Buffet, Dunkin Donuts, Friendly's, KFC, McDonald's, 99 Rest., Pizza Hut, Steak-out Rest, Wendy's, **lodging:** Best Inn, Colonial Motel, Hampton Inn, Holiday Inn Express, Motel 6, Red Roof Inn, Super 8, **other:** Advance Parts, Chrysler/ Dodge/Jeep, Consumer Parts, $Tree, Ford/Mercury, GNC, Hannaford Foods, NAPA, Pontiac/Buick/GMC, Radio Shack, Rite Aid, Staples, Subaru, True Value, U-Haul, USPO

**2 (9)** VT 9 W, to rd 30, Brattleboro, **E** **gas:** Sunoco, **W** **gas:** Shell, **food:** Country Deli, VT Country Deli, **other:** to Marlboro Coll, st police

**1 (7)** US 5, Brattleboro, **E** **gas:** Getty, Gulf/dsl, Irving/dsl, Planet/Dunkin Donuts, Shell/Subway/dsl, Sunoco, **food:** Burger King, Millenium Pizzaria, Quizno's, VT Inn Pizza, **lodging:** Econolodge, **other:** H HOSPITAL, PriceChopper Foods, Rite Aid, Walgreens, to Ft Dummer SP

**6mm** **Welcome Ctr nb, full** ♿ **facilities, info,** C **,** ⊞ **, litter barrels, vending, petwalk, playground**

**0mm** Vermont/Massachusetts state line

## INTERSTATE 93

**See New Hampshire Interstate 93.**

VT

## INTERSTATE 64

**E ← → W**

**N O R F O L K**

| Exit # | Services |
|---|---|
| **299b a** | I-264 E, to Portsmouth. I-64 begins/ends on I-264. |
| **297** | US 13, US 460, Military Hwy, **N gas:** 7-11/gas |
| **296b a** | US 17, to Portsmouth, **N gas:** 7-11/gas, **S gas:** BP |
| **294mm** | S Br Elizabeth River |
| **292** | VA 190, to VA 104 (from eb, no EZ return), Dominion Blvd, **S gas:** BP, Shell, **food:** Burger King, Hardee's, **other:** Family$, Food Lion, Rite Aid |
| **291b a** | I-464 N, VA 104 S, to Elizabeth City, Outer Banks, same services as 292 |
| **290b a** | VA 168, Battlefield Blvd, to Nag's Head, Manteo, **N other:** K-mart, Merchant's Auto Ctr, **S gas:** BP/dsl/24hr, 7-11, Shell/Blimpie, **food:** Applebee's, Burger King, Carrabba's, Chick-fil-A, ChuckeCheese, Dunkin Donuts, Firehouse Subs, Five Guys Burgers, Golden Corral, Grand China Buffet, Hardee's, Honey Glazed Ham, Silver Diner, Starbucks, Texas Steakhouse, TGIFriday's, Waffle House, Wendy's, Woodchick's BBQ, **lodging:** Day's Inn, Hampton Inn, Savannah Suites, Super 8, **other:** $Tree, Home Depot, Kohl's, Lowe's Whse, Sam's Club/gas, Walgreens, Walmart SuperCtr, USPO, vet |
| **289b a** | Greenbrier Pkwy, **N gas:** BP, Citgo, 7-11/gas, Wawa, **food:** Burger King, Crazywing Cantina, Taco Bell, Subway, Wendy's, **lodging:** Cedar Tree Inn, Extended Stay, Hampton Inn, InTown Suites, Marriott, Red Roof Inn, Staybridge Suites, TownePlace Suites, Wingate Inn, **other:** Acura, BMW, Chevrolet, Cloth World, Dodge, Ford, Honda, Hyundai, Isuzu, Macy's, Mitsubishi, Pontiac, Subaru, Toyota/Acura, Volvo, U-Haul, auto repai/transmissions, vet, **S food:** Boston Mkt, Coldstone Creamery, Fazoli's, Fuddruckers, Jason's Deli, Joe's Crabshack, LoneStar Café, McDonald's, Old Country Buffet, Olive Garden, Panera Bread, Paradocks Grill, Ruby Tuesday, Smokey Bones BBQ, Starbucks, **lodging:** Aloha Hotel, Comfort Suites, Courtyard, Extended Stay America, Fairfield Inn, Hilton Garden, Homewood Suites, Residence Inn, Springhill Suites, Sun Suites, **other:** Barnes&Noble, Best Buy, Circuit City, Dillard's, $General, Food Lion, Harris Teeter, Macy's, Marshall's, Michael's, Office Depot, Old Navy, Ross, Sears/auto, Steinmart, Target, TJ Maxx, mall |
| **286b a** | Indian River Rd, **N gas:** BP/dsl, Hess/dsl, RaceCo/dsl, Shell, Texaco, **food:** Hardee's, **S gas:** Sunoco/dsl, **food:** Capt D's, Shoney's, Top's China, Waffle House, **lodging:** Founder's Inn, **other:** 7-11 |
| **285** | E Branch Elizabeth River |
| **284a** | I-264, to Norfolk, to VA Beach (exits left from eb) |
| **284b** | Newtown Rd |
| **282** | US 13, Northampton Blvd, **N lodging:** Quality Inn, Sleep Inn, **other:** to Chesapeake Bay Br Tunnel |
| **281** | VA 165, Military Hwy (no EZ eb return), **N gas:** Shell/dsl/24hr, **lodging:** Econolodge, **other:** Aamco, **S food:** Max&Erma's, **lodging:** Hampton Inn, Hilton, Holiday Inn Select, Ramada, Residence Inn, **other:** Firestone/auto |
| **279** | Norview Ave, **N gas:** Shell, **food:** Golden Corral, Pizza Hut, Wendy's, **other:** $General, Food Lion, K-Mart/gas, to ✈ & botanical garden |
| **278** | VA 194 S (no EZ return) |
| **277b a** | VA 168, to Tidewater Dr, **N gas:** 7-11, **food:** Hardee's, **S gas:** BP |

**H A M P T O N**

| Exit # | Services |
|---|---|
| **276c** | to US 460 W, VA 165, Little Creek Rd, wb only, **N gas:** Flag Gas, **S gas:** BP, Shell, **food:** McDonald's, KFC, Old Virginia Ham, Subway, Taco Bell, Wendy's, **other:** AutoZone, $Tree, Farm Fresh, Kroger, Rite Aid, Walgreens |
| **276b a** | I-564 to Naval Base |
| **274** | Bay Ave (from wb), to Naval Air Sta |
| **273** | US 60, 4th View St, Oceanview, **N gas:** BP/dsl/24hr, **lodging:** Econolodge, **other:** Oceanview Boathouse/Pier, **S other:** to Norfolk Visitors Ctr, info |
| **272** | W Ocean View Ave, **N food:** Willoughby's Seafood, **S food:** Sunset Grill |
| **270mm** | Chesapeake Bay Tunnel |
| **269mm** | weigh sta eb |
| **268** | VA 169 E, to Buckroe Beach, Ft Monroe, **N gas:** Citgo, **food:** Hardee's, McDonald's, **other:** to VA Ctr |
| **267** | US 60, to VA 143, Settlers Ldg Rd, **S food:** Burger King, Golden City Chinese, **other:** H HOSPITAL, to Hampton U |
| **265c** | (from eb), **N other:** Armistead Ave, to Langley AFB |
| **265b a** | VA 134, VA 167, to La Salle Ave, **N gas:** Citgo, RaceWay, **lodging:** Super 8, **other:** Home Depot, **S gas:** BP, **food:** McDonald's, KFC/Taco Bell, **other:** H HOSPITAL, Advance Parts, Family$ |
| **264** | I-664, to Newport News, Suffolk |
| **263b a** | US 258, VA 134, Mercury Blvd, to James River Br, **N gas:** BP, Shell, **food:** Applebee's, Blimpie, Boston Mkt, Burger King, Chick-fil-A, Chili's, Denny's, Dunkin Donuts, Golden Corral, Hooters, IHOP, KFC, McDonald's, New Garden Buffet, Olive Garden, Outback Steaks, Pizza Hut, Quizno's, Rally's, Red Lobster, Rockola Café, Schlotzsky's, Steak&Ale, Taco Bell, Waffle House, Wendy's, **lodging:** Clarion, Comfort Inn, Courtyard, Day's Inn, Embassy Suites, Fairfield Inn, Holiday Inn, Quality Inn, Red Roof Inn, **other:** Chevrolet/Mazda, Chrysler/Jeep, $Tree, Ford, Goodyear/auto, JC Penney, Jo-Anne, Macy's, Mazda, NAPA, Office Depot, Target, U-Haul, Volvo, USPO, Walmart SuperCtr, **S gas:** BJ's Whse, Citgo/dsl, Miller's Gas, **food:** Cracker Barrel, Lone Star Steaks, Pizza Hut, Sonic, Texas Steaks, Waffle House, **lodging:** Best Western, Econolodge, Hampton Bay Suites, Hilton Garden, Interstate Inn, La Quinta, Savannah Suites, Springhill Suites, **other:** Advance Parts, BassPro Shop, BigLots, $General, Firestone/auto, Lowe's Whse, PepBoys, Radio Shack, Toyota |
| **262** | VA 134, Magruder Blvd (from wb, no EZ return), **N gas:** Exxon, 7-11/gas, **other:** Dodge/Acura |
| **261b a** | Center Pkwy, to Hampton Roads, **S gas:** Shell, Zooms, **food:** Azteca Mexican, ChuckeCheese, McDonald's, Peking Chinese, Pizza Hut/Taco Bell, Ruby Tuesday, Subway, **other:** BooksAMillion, $Tree, FarmFresh Foods, FoodLion, Rite Aid, TJMaxx |
| **258b a** | US 17, J Clyde Morris Blvd, **N gas:** BP, Shell/dsl, **food:** Chatfield's Grill, Domino's, New China, Waffle House, **lodging:** BudgetLodge, Country Inn & Suites, Holiday Inn, Host Inn, PointPlaza Hotel, Super 8, **other:** Advance Parts, Food Lion, 7-11/24hr, **S gas:** BP, Citgo/dsl/24hr, WaWa, **food:** Angelo's Steaks, Burger King, DQ, KFC, Starbucks, Subway, Taco Bell/KFC, Vinny's Pizza, **lodging:** Motel 6, Omni Hotel/rest., **other:** H HOSPITAL, BMW/Honda, $Tree, Radio Shack, museum |
| **256b a** | Victory Blvd, Oyster Point Rd, **N gas:** BP, Citgo/Kangaroo/dsl, **food:** Arby's, Blimpie, Burger King, Chicago Pizza, Chick-fil-A, Fuddrucker's, Hardee's, Pizza Hut, |

**VA**

# INTERSTATE 64

| | |
|---|---|

**256b a** Continued
Starbucks, Subway, TX Roadhouse, **lodging:** Candle-Wood Suites, Courtyard, Hampton Inn, Hilton Garden, Staybridge Suites, TownePlace, **other:** $Tree, K-Mart, Kroger, **S lodging:** Crestwood Suites, Mariott, Sleep Inn

**255b a** VA 143, to Jefferson Ave, **N gas:** Shell/dsl **food:** Castle Italian, Chilli's, FarmFresh Foods, Red City Buffet, Red Lobster, Smokey Bones BBQ, Golden Corral, Hooters, McDonald's, Moe's SW Grill, Olive Garden, Panera Bread, Silver Diner, Tuesday Morning, **lodging:** Comfort Suites, Travelodge (2mi), **other:** H HOSPITAL, Acura, Buick/Cadillac/GMC, FarmFresh Foods/deli, Home Depot, Kohl's, Lowe's Whse, Ross, PetCo, Sam's Club/gas, Saturn, Walmart SuperCtr, Saturn, TJ Maxx, airport, **S gas:** BP, Citgo/dsl, Exxon/dsl, 7-11, **food:** Applebee's, Bailey's Grill, Buffalo Wild Wings, Burger King, Carrabba's, Cheddar's, Cheeseburger Paradise, Chick-fil-A, Cracker Barrel, Don Pablo, KFC, McDonald's/playpalce, Outback Steaks, Red Robin, Samurai, Starbucks, Subway, TGIFriday's, Waffle House, Wendy's, **lodging:** Best Western, Comfort Inn, Courtyard, Day's Inn, Econolodge, Hampton Inn, Microtel, Residence Inn, Studio+, **other:** Barnes&Noble, Best Buy, Belk, Borders Book, Circuit City, Costco/gas, Dillard's, JC Penny, Macy's, NTB, PetsMart, Sears/auto, Target, World Mkt, mall

**250b a** to US Army Trans Museum, **N gas:** BP/dsl, Dodge's Gas, Exxon/dsl, 7-11/gas, Sunoco, **food:** China Dragon, Hardee's, **other:** B&L Auto Repair, $Green, Newport News Campground/Park (1mi), to Yorktown Victory Ctr, vet, **S gas:** RaceTrac, **food:** McDonald's, Taco Bell, Wendy's, **lodging:** Ft Eustis Inn, Holiday Inn Express, Mulberry Inn, TDY Inn

**247** VA 143, to VA 238 (no EZ return wb), **N gas:** Citgo, 7-11/gas, **other:** to Yorktown, **S other:** to Jamestown Settlement

**243** VA 143, to Williamsburg, exits left from wb, **S** same as 242a

**242b a** VA 199, to US 60, to Williamsburg, **N lodging:** Day's Hotel/rest., **other:** Best Buy, JC Penny, Kohl's, Target, water funpark, to Yorktown NHS, **1 mi S gas:**

**242b a** Continued
7-11/gas, **food:** Starbucks, Subway, Wendy's, Burger King, LJ Silver, McDonald's, Wendy's, **lodging:** Country Inn & Suites, Courtyard, Marriott/rest., Quality Inn, Rodeway Inn, **other:** 1st Settlers Camping, to William&Mary Coll, Busch Gardens, to Jamestown NHS

**238** VA 143, to Colonial Williamsburg, Camp Peary, **2-3 mi S** on US 60...**gas:** 7-11/gas, Shell, Texaco, Zooms, **food:** Chicago Grill, Cracker Barrel, DQ, Golden Corral, Hooter's, IHOP, McDonald's, Mirabella's Pizza, Pizza Hut, Sal's Rest., The Gazebo Pancakes, **lodging:** Comfort Inn, Country Inn & Suites, Day's Inn, Econolodge, Embassy Suites, Fairfield Inn, Hampton Inn, Holiday Inn/rest., Homewood Suites, La Quinta, Quality Inn/rest., Ramada, Sleep Inn, Travelodge, **other:** H HOSPITAL, Anvil Camping (4mi), K-Mart

**234** VA 646, to Lightfoot, **1-2 mi N other:** KOA, **2-3 mi S gas:** BP/dsl, Exxon/dsl, Shell/dsl, **food:** Burger King, Chick-fil-A, Hardee's, IHOP, KFC, McDonald's, Pierce's BBQ, Sonic, Starbucks, Subway, **lodging:** Day's Inn, Greatwolf Lodge, Quality Inn, **other:** Ford/Lincoln/Mercury, Go-Carts+, Home Depot, Lowe's Whse, PetCo, Pottery Camping (3mi), Radio Shack, Ross, Ukrops Foods, Walmart SuperCtr

**231b a** VA 607, to Norge, Croaker, **N gas:** 7-11/gas, **other:** to York River SP, **1-2 mi S** on US 60...**gas:** Shell/dsl, **food:** FarmFresh Deli/gas, Candle Light Rest., Wendy's, **lodging:** Econolodge, **other:** American Heritage RV Park, Dodge, Doll Factory, Honda, Hyundai, vet

**227** VA 30, to US 60, to West Point, Toano, **S gas:** BP/dsl, Shell/Stuckey's/dsl, **food:** Big South Rest., McDonald's

**220** VA 33 E, to West Point, **N gas:** Exxon/dsl

**214** VA 155, to New Kent, Providence Forge, **S gas:** Exxon/DQ/dsl, **food:** Antonio's Pizza, Tops China, **other:** Colonial Downs Racetrack, Rockahock Camping (8mi)

**213mm** **rest area both lanes, full** [symbol] **facilities,** [symbol]**, vending,** [symbol]**, litter barrels, petwalk**

**211** VA 106, to Talleysville, to James River Plantations, **S gas:** Pilot/Subway/dsl/scales/24hr

**205** VA 33, VA 249, to US 60, Bottoms Bridge, Quinton, **N gas:** Exxon/dsl, Valero, **food:** Pearl City Chinese, Subway, **other:** Food Lion, Rite Aid, USPO,

## INTERSTATE 64 CONT'D

**E** ↕ **W**

**RICHMOND**

**205** Continued
**S gas:** FasMart, Shell/dsl, **food:** McDonald's, Prima Pizza, **lodging:** Star Motel (3mi)

**204mm** Chickahominy River

**203mm** weigh sta both lanes

**200** I-295, N to Washington, S to Rocky Mount, to US 60

**197b a** VA 156, Airport Dr, to Highland Springs, **N gas:** 7-11/gas, Shell/dsl, Valero, **food:** Domino's, Hardee's, Subway, Tops China, **other:** Advance Parts, CVS Drug, Farmers Foods, **S gas:** BP, Citgo/dsl, East Coast/dsl, 7-11/gas, Wawa, **food:** Arby's, Aunt Sarah's, Burger King, Chicago Pizza, Pizza Hut, Waffle House, **lodging:** Best Value, Clarion, Courtyard, Day's Inn, Econolodge, Hampton Inn, Hilton Garden, Holiday Inn, Homewood Suites, Microtel, Motel 6, Red Roof Inn, Super 8, Wingate Inn, **other:** to ✈

**195** Laburnum Ave, **N gas:** Chevron, Shell, **other:** repair, **S gas:** BP/24hr, Exxon, 7-11/gas, **food:** Applebee's, Burger King, Capt D's, Chick-fil-A, Chinese Buffet, Cici's Pizza, Firehouse Subs, Hardee's, KFC, Longhorn Steaks, McDonald's, Papa John's, Qdoba Mexican, Red Lobster, Starbucks, Steak&Shake, Subway, Taco Bell, TGIFriday, Wendy's, **lodging:** Airport Inn, Hyatt, Wyndham Garden, **other:** Books-A-Million, CarQuest, Circuit City, CVS Drug, $Tree, Ford, JC Penney, Kroger, Lowe's, PetsMart, Radio Shack, Sam's Club/gas, Target, Ukrops Foods, Walgreens

**193b a** VA 33, Nine Mile Rd, **N gas:** Exxon/Subway, **food:** McDonald's (2mi), **S** Ⓗ HOSPITAL

**192** US 360, to Mechanicsville, **N gas:** Chevron, Citgo/dsl, **food:** McDonald's, **S gas:** BP, Citgo, **food:** Church's

**190** I-95 S, to Petersburg, 5th St, **N other:** Richmond Nat Bfd Park, **S lodging:** Marriott, **other:** st capitol, coliseum.

**I-64 W and I-95 N run together. See Virginia Interstate 95, exits 76-78.**

**187** I-95 N (exits left from eb), to Washington.

**186** I-195, to Powhite Pkwy, from wb, Richmond

**185b a** US 33, Staples Mill Rd, Dickens Rd

**183c** from wb, US 250 W, Broad St, Glenside Dr N, same as exit 183

**183** US 250, Broad St E, Glenside Dr S., **N gas:** Chevron, **food:** Bob Evans, Buffalo Wild Wings, Famous Dave's, Olive Garden, TGIFriday, Waffle House, **lodging:** Best Western, Embassy Suites, **other:** Dodge, Honda, Hyundai, K-Mart, Volvo, same as 181, **S other:** Ⓗ HOSPITAL, to U of Richmond

**181b a** Parham Rd, **2 mi N on Broad...gas:** BP/24hr, Citgo, Exxon, Hess, Sheetz/dsl, Shell, Wawa, **food:** Burger King, Casa Grande Mexican, Chick-fil-A, ChuckeCheese, Friendly's, Fuddruckers, Gyros & Subs, Hardee's, Hooters, KFC, LoneStar Steaks, McDonald's, Outback Steaks, Piccadilly's, Pizza Hut, Red Hot&Blue BBQ, Red Lobster, Sarah's Kitchen, Shoney's, Starbucks, Superking Buffet, Wendy's, **lodging:** Extended Stay America, Quality Inn, Suburban Lodge, Super 8, **other:** Ⓗ HOSPITAL, Acura, BigLots, BooksAMillion, CVS Drug, $General, Ford/Lincoln/Mercury, Hancock Fabrics, Honda/Mitsubishi, Infiniti, Lowe's, Lincoln/Mercury, Mazda/BMW, Mercedes, Napa, PepBoys, Saturn, Subaru, Staples, TJ Maxx, Toyota, Walgreens, Ukrops Foods, transmissions, tires

**RICHMOND**

**180** Gaskins Rd, **N gas:** BP/24hr, East Coast, Shell/dsl, **food:** Cracker Barrel, Starbucks, **lodging:** Courtyard, Fairfield Inn, Holiday Inn Express, Residence Inn, Springhill Suites, Studio+, **other:** Goodyear, Kroger, **N on Broad... food:** Applebee's, Arby's, Boston Mkt, Burger King, Golden Corral, IHOP, KFC, McDonald's, O'Charley's, Pizza Hut, Qdoba Mexican, Ruby Tuesday's, Subway, Taco Bell, Tripp's Rest., Wendy's, **other:** BMW/Mini, Borders Books, Cadillac, Chrysler/Jeep, Costso/gas, Circuit City, Costco, $Tree, Goodyear/auto, Lowe's Whse, Michael's, Office Depot, Sam's Club, VW, mall

**178b a** US 250, Short Pump, **N gas:** Citgo, Exxon/dsl, 7-11, **food:** Capitol Ale House, Chipotle Mexican, DQ, Firehouse Subs, Five Guys Burgers, Leonardo's Pizza, Moe's SW Grill, Panera Bread, Starbucks, **lodging:** Comfort Suites, Courtyard, Hampton Inn, Hilton Garden, Hyatt Place, **other:** CarMax, Firestone/auto, Ford, Hagen Daaz, **1 mi S gas:** BP, Citgo, 7-11/gas, Shell, Valero, **food:** Arby's, Bertucci's, Burger King, Cheesecake Factory, Chick-fil-A, Chilli's, Chipotle Mexican, Kanpai, KFC, Longhorn Steaks, McDonald's/playplace, Mexico Rest., Red Robin, Taco Bell, TGIFriday, Wendy's, **lodging:** Candlewood Suites, **other:** Barnes&Noble, Best Buy, CarQuest, Chevrolet/Pontiac/GMC, Goodyear/auto, Home Depot, Kohl's, Kroger, Lowe's Whse, Nissan, Nordstrom, PetCo, Target, Ukrop's Foods, Walmart SuperCtr, World Mkt

**177** I-295, to I-95 N to Washington, to Norfolk, VA Beach, Williamsburg

**175** VA 288

**173** VA 623, to Rockville, Manakin, **S gas:** Citgo/dsl, Valero, **food:** Manakin Grill, **other:** $General, Food Lion

**169mm** **rest area both lanes, full** ♿ **facilities, vending,** 📞, 🚻, **litter barrels, petwalk**

**167** VA 617, to Goochland, Oilville, **N gas:** Exxon/dsl, **S gas:** BP/Bullets/dsl/24hr

**159** US 522, to Goochland, Gum Spring, **N gas:** Exxon/dsl, **S gas:** BP/DQ/dsl, Citgo

**152** VA 629, Hadensville, **S gas:** BP (1mi)

**148** VA 605, Shannon Hill

**143** VA 208, to Louisa, Ferncliff, **7 mi N other:** Small Country Camping, **S gas:** Citgo/dsl, Exxon/dsl

**136** US 15, to Gordonsville, Zion Crossroads, **S lodging:** Best Western, **other:** Lowe's, **S gas:** BP/McDonald's/dsl/24hr, Citgo/Blimpie/dsl, Exxon/Burger King/dsl, **food:** Crescent Rest.

**129** VA 616, Keswick, Boyd Tavern, **S gas:** Citgo

**124** US 250, to Shadwell, **2 mi N gas:** BP, Exxon, Liberty, **food:** Applebees, Aunt Sarah's, Burger King, Guadalajara Mexican, McDonald's, Ponderosa, Quizno's, Starbucks, Taco Bell, Topeka's Steaks, Wendy's, **lodging:** Hilton Garden, Town&Country Motel, White House Motel, **other:** Ⓗ HOSPITAL, Audi, CarMax, Ford, Giant Foods, Kia, Rite Aid, **S lodging:** Comfort Inn

**123mm** Rivanna River

**121** VA 20, to Charlottesville, Scottsville, **N gas:** BP/Blimpie/dsl, **other:** Ⓗ HOSPITAL, **S other:** KOA (10mi), to Monticello

**120** VA 631, 5th St, to Charlottesville, **N gas:** Exxon/dsl, Shell, **food:** Amigo's Mexican, Burger King, Domino's, Hardee's, Jade Garden, McDonald's, Pizza Hut/Taco Bell, Waffle House, Wendy's, **lodging:**

**VA**

## INTERSTATE 64 CONT'D

| | |
|---|---|
| **120** | Continued<br>Hampton Inn (2mi), Holiday Inn, Omni Hotel (2mi), Sleep Inn, **other:** CVS Drug, Family$, Food Lion |
| **118b a** | US 29, to Lynchburg, Charlottesville, **1-4 mi N gas:** BP, Citgo/dsl, Exxon, Shell, **food:** Blimpie, Hardee's, Subway, **lodging:** Best Western, Boar's Head Inn, Budget Inn, Comfort Inn, Econolodge, **other:** H HOSPITAL, UVA |
| **114** | VA 637, to Ivy |
| **113mm** | **rest area wb, full** & **facilities,** C, **vending,** 🛇, **litter barrels, petwalk** |
| **111mm** | Mechum River |
| **108mm** | Stockton Creek |
| **107** | US 250, Crozet, **1 mi N gas:** Exxon, Shell/dsl, **1 mi S other:** Misty Mtn Camping |
| **105mm** | **rest area eb, full** & **facilities,** C, **vending,** 🛇, **litter barrels, petwalk** |
| **104mm** | scenic area eb, litter barrels, no truck or buses |
| **100mm** | **scenic area eb, litter barrels, hist marker, no trucks or buses** |
| **99** | US 250, to Waynesboro, Afton, **N lodging:** Colony Motel, **other:** to Shenandoah NP, Skyline Drive, ski area, to Blue Ridge Pkwy, **S lodging:** Afton Inn |
| **96** | VA 622, to Lyndhurst, Waynesboro, **3 mi N gas:** Shell, **food:** Tastee Freez **lodging:** Quality Inn, **other:** Waynesboro Camping |
| **95mm** | South River |
| **94** | US 340, to Stuarts Draft, Waynesboro, **N gas:** Exxon/dsl, 7-11/dsl, **food:** Applebee's, Arby's, Burger King, Cracker Barrel, Fosters Grille, Giovanni's Pizza, Jack's Rest., KFC, Quizno's, Ruby Tuesday, Shoney's, Sonic, South River Rest., Taco Bell (1mi), Starbucks, Wendy's, **lodging:** Best Western, Comfort Inn, Day's Inn, Holiday Inn Express, Residence Inn, Super 8, **other:** H HOSPITAL, Home Depot, Lowe's, Martin's Food/Drug, Radio Shack, Waynesboro N 340 Camping (9mi), Walmart SuperCtr, **S gas:** Shell/dsl, **other:** Kohl's, PetsMart, Ross, Target, Waynesboro Outlet Village, museum |
| **91** | Va 608, to Stuarts Draft, Fishersville, **N gas:** Shell/Dunkin Donuts/dsl, **food:** Subway, **lodging:** Hampton Inn, **other:** H HOSPITAL, **S gas:** Exxon/McDonald's, Sheetz/dsl, **other:** Shenadoah Acres Camping (8mi), Walnut Hills Camping (9mi) |
| **89mm** | Christians Creek |
| **87** | I-81, N to Harrisonburg, S to Roanoke |
| | **I-64 and I-81 run together 20 miles. See Interstate 81 exits 195-220.** |
| **56** | I-81, S to Roanoke, N to Harrisburg |
| **55** | US 11, to VA 39, **N gas:** Exxon, **food:** Burger King, Crystal Chinese, Naples Pizza, Ruby Tuesday, Waffle House, **lodging:** Best Western, Sleep Inn, Super 8, Wingate Inn, **other:** $Tree, Radio Shack, Stonewall Jackson Museum, Lowe's, Walmart SuperCtr, **S gas:** BP/DQ, Texaco/Subway, **food:** Country Cookin', Redwood Rest., **lodging:** Country Inn & Suites, Econolodge, Holiday Inn Express |
| **50** | US 60, VA 623, to Lexington, **3 mi S lodging:** Day's Inn |
| **43** | VA 780, to Goshen |
| **35** | VA 269, VA 850, Longdale Furnace |
| **33mm** | **truck rest area eb** |
| **29** | VA 269, VA 850, **S gas:** Citgo/dsl/rest. |
| **27** | US 60 W, US 220 S, VA 629, Clifton Forge, **N other:** to Douthat SP, **S gas:** BP, Citgo/dsl, Exxon, **food:** Pizza Hut, **other:** Alleghany Highlands Arts/crafts |

| | |
|---|---|
| **24** | US 60, US 220, Clifton Forge, **1 mi S gas:** Shell/dsl, **food:** DQ, Hardee's |
| **21** | to VA 696, Low Moor, **S gas:** Exxon, **food:** Quizno's, **other:** H HOSPITAL |
| **16** | US 60 W, US 220 N, to Hot Springs, Covington, **N gas:** BP, Exxon, Shell, Texaco, **food:** Belly-up Cafe, Cucci's, Starbucks, Western Sizzlin, **lodging:** Best Value Inn, Best Western, Holiday Inn Express, Pinhurst Hotel, **other:** to ski area, **S food:** McDonald's, **lodging:** Compare Inn, **other:** K-Mart |
| **14** | VA 154, to Hot Springs, Covington, **N gas:** Exxon/Arby's, Sunoco, **food:** Hong Kong Chinese, KFC, Little Caesar's, LJ Silver, Subway, Wendy's, **lodging:** Budget Motel, **other:** Advance Parts, AutoZone, CVS Drug, Family$, Food Lion, **S food:** Applebee's, China House, Mama Pizza, **other:** $Tree, Walmart SuperCtr |
| **10** | US 60 E, VA 159 S, Callaghan, **S gas:** Marathon/dsl/LP |
| **7** | VA 661 |
| **2.5mm** | **Welcome Ctr eb, full** & **facilities,** C, 🛇, **litter barrels, petwalk** |
| **1** | Jerry's Run Trail, **N** to Allegheny Trail |
| **0mm** | Virginia/West Virginia state line |

## INTERSTATE 66

| Exit # | Services |
|---|---|
| **77mm** | Independence Ave, to Lincoln Mem. I-66 begins/ends in Washington, DC. |
| **76mm** | Potomac River, T Roosevelt Memorial Bridge |
| **75** | US 50 W (from eb), to Arlington Blvd, G Wash Pkwy, I-395, US 1, **S** Iwo Jima Mon |
| **73** | US 29, Lee Hwy, Key Bridge, to Rosslyn, **N lodging:** Marriott, **S lodging:** Holiday Inn |
| **72** | to US 29, Lee Hwy, Spout Run Pkwy (from eb, no EZ return), **N gas:** Shell, **lodging:** Virginia Inn, **S food:** Starbucks, Tarbouch Grill, **other:** CVS Drug, Starbucks, Giant Foods, Rite Aid |
| **71** | VA 120, Glebe Rd (no EZ return from wb), **N** HOSPITAL, **S gas:** Sunoco, **food:** Booeymonger Grill, IHOP, Melting Pot, PF Chang's, **lodging:** Comfort Inn, Holiday Inn |
| **69** | US 29, Sycamore St, Falls Church, **N gas:** Exxon, **S lodging:** Econolodge |
| **68** | Westmoreland St (from eb), same as 69 |
| **67** | to I-495 N (from wb), to Baltimore, Dulles Airport |
| **66** | VA 7, Leesburg Pike, to Tysons Corner, Falls Church, **N gas:** Exxon, Sunoco, **food:** China King, Honeybaked Ham, Jason's Deli, Ledo's Pizza, Olive Garden (2mi), |

*(left margin, top to bottom)* E ↕ W

*(left margin)* LEXINGTON

*(center margin, top to bottom)* COVINGTON

*(center margin)* E ↕ W DC AREA

*(bottom right)* VA

E ↕ W

M A N A S S A S

## INTERSTATE 66 CONT'D

**66** Continued
Starbucks, Tara Thai, **other:** Whole Foods Mkt, **S gas:** Citgo, **food:** Chicken Out, LJ Silver, McDonald's, Starbucks, Taco Bell, **other:** Giant Foods, GNC, Volvo, vet

**64b a** I-495 S, to Richmond

**62** VA 243, Nutley St, to Vienna, **S gas:** Chevron, **other:** CVS Drug, Michael's, Safeway Foods, **1 mi S on Lee Hwy...gas:** Citgo, Shell, Sunoco/dsl, **food:** Dunkin Donuts, IHOP/24hr, McDonald's, Up-Town Grill, **lodging:** Econolodge, **other:** Advance Parts, Harley-Davidson, Home Depot, Jeep, Radio Shack, Saturn, 7-11, Subaru,

**60** VA 123, to Fairfax, **S gas:** Exxon, Shell/24hr, Sunoco, **food:** Denny's, Fuddrucker's, Hooters, KFC, Outback Steaks, Red Lobster, 29 Diner, **lodging:** Best Western, **other:** Chevrolet, Chrysler, CVS Drug, Goodyear, Honda, Hyundai, Mazda, NAPA, Rite Aid, Toyota/Scion, to George Mason U

**57a b** US 50, to Dulles Airport, **N food:** Cheesecake Factory, **lodging:** Extended Stay America, Marriott, **other:** Macy's, JC Penney, Lord&Taylor, Macy's, Sears/auto, mall, access to same as 55, **S gas:** Shell/dsl, **food:** McDonald's, Ruby Tuesday, Wendy's, **lodging:** Candlewood Suites, Comfort Inn/rest., Courtyard, **other:** Goodyear/auto, K-Mart, Giant Foods, NRA Museum

**55** Fairfax Co Pkwy, to US 29, **N** 4 Lakes Mall, **gas:** Exxon, Sunoco, **food:** Applebees, Blue Iguana Café, Burger King, Cantina Italiana, Cooker Rest., Joe's Crabshack, Logan's Roadhouse, Malibu Grill, Olive Garden, Pizza Hut/Taco Bell, Red Robin, Sakura Japanese, Starbucks, Wendy's, **lodging:** Hyatt Hotel, Residence Inn, **other:** H HOSPITAL, Best Buy, BJ's Whse, Bloom's Foods, GNC, Kohl's, Michael's, PetsMart, Radio Shack, Target, Walmart, Whole Foods Mkt, World Mkt

**53b a** VA 28, to Centreville, Dulles Airport, Manassas Museum, **S** same as 52

**52** US 29, to Bull Run Park, Centreville, **N gas:** Mobil, **other:** Bull Run Park/RV Dump, Goodyear/auto, **S gas:** Exxon, Sunoco, **food:** Austin Grill, Carrabba's, Domino's, Panda Express, Quizno's, Red Rock King Grille, Ruby Tuesday, Wendy's, **other:** SpringHill Suites, **other:** CVS Drug, Giant Foods, Grand Mart, Jo-Ann Fabrics, Shoppers Foods, same as 53

**49mm** **rest area both lanes, full & facilities, Ⓒ, ⚠, litter barrels, petwalk**

**47b a** VA 234, to Manassas, **N gas:** Shell/dsl, **food:** Cracker Barrel, 5 Guys Burgers, Golden Corral, Jerry's Subs, Uno Pizzaria, Wendy's, **lodging:** Country Inn&Suites, Courtyard, Fairfield Inn, Sheraton, **other:** Borders, Kohl's, Old Navy, Manassas Nat Bfd, **S gas:** BP, Exxon, Hess, RaceWay/dsl/24hr, Shell/repair, 7-11, Sunoco/24hr, **food:** Arby's, Backyard Grill, Baja Fresh, Bob Evans, Burger King, Casa Chimayo, Checker's, Chili's, China Jade, Chipotle Mexican, Coldstone Creamery, Denny's, Domino's, Don Pablo's, El Tolteca, Foster's Grill, Great American Buffet, Hooters, KFC, Logan's Roadhouse, McDonald's, Olive Garden, Panera Bread, Papa John's, Pizza Hut, Popeye's, Potbelly's, Red Hot&Blue BBQ, Red Lobster, Ruby Tuesday, Shoney's, Starbucks, Subway, Taco Bell, TGIFriday, Wendy's,

**47b a** Continued
Wok'n Roll, **lodging:** Best Western, Comfort Suites, Hampton Inn, Holiday Inn, Quality Inn, Red Roof Inn, Residence Inn, Super 8, **other:** Aamco, Advance Parts, AutoZone, Barnes&Noble, Best Buy, Bottom$ Foods, Buick/GMC/Pontiac, Burlington Coats, Camping World RV Service/supples/Reines RV Ctr, Circuit City, Costco/gas, CVS Drug, Chevrolet, Family$, Giant Foods, Macy's, Home Depot, Honda, JC Penney, Jo-Ann Fabrics, K-Mart, Lowes Whse, Marshall's, Merchant Auto Ctr, Michael's, NTB, Office Depot, PepBoys, PetCo, Ross, Saturn, Sears/auto, Shopper's Foods, Staples, Target, Toyota, Tuesday Morning, U-Haul, Walmart, vet

**44** VA 234, Manassas

**43b a** US 29, to Warrenton, Gainesville, **N gas:** WaWa, **S gas:** 7-11, Sunoco, **food:** Burger King, Chick-fil-A, Chili's, Coldstone Creamery, Domino's, 5 Guys Burgers, Joe's Italian/pizza, KFC/Pizza Hut/Taco Bell, McDonald's, Mimi's Cafe, Papa Johns, PeiWei, Qdoba, Steakmaster's Grill, Subway, Wendy's, **lodging** Hampton Inn, **other:** Best Buy, Giant Foods/drug, GNC, Goodyear/auto, Lowes Whse, PetsMart, Target/foods, Walgreens, World Mkt

**40** US 15, Haymarket, **N other:** Greenville Farm Camping, **S gas:** Sheetz/dsl/24hr, **food:** Guiseppe's Italian, McDonald's, Papa John's, Subway, **other:** Bloom Foods, Home Depot, Safeway Foods

**31** VA 245, to Old Tavern, **1 mi N gas:** BP/dsl

**28** US 17 S, Marshall, **N gas:** BP/McDonald's/dsl, 7-11, **food:** Anthony's Pizza, Foster's Grille, Great Wall Chinese, Subway, **other:** H HOSPITAL, Bloom Foods, Radio Shack, vet

**27** VA 55 E, VA 647, Marshall, **1 mi N gas:** Chevron/dsl/LP, Citgo, **food:** Marshall Diner, **other:** IGA Foods

**23** US 17 N, VA 55, Delaplane (no eb re-entry)

**20mm** Goose Creek

**18** VA 688, Markham

**13** VA 79, to VA 55, Linden, Front Royal, **S gas:** Exxon/dsl/24hr, Shell, **food:** Applehouse Rest., **other:** to Shenandoah NP, Skyline Drive

**11mm** Manassas Run

**7mm** Shenandoah River

**6** US 340, US 522, to Winchester, Front Royal, **N gas:** Quarle's/Bullet's/dsl, 7-11, **food:** Applebees, Checkers, Cracker Barrel, Ledo's Pizza, Los Potrollo's, Panda Express, Quizno's, Starbucks, TGIFriday, **other:** Buick/GMC/Pontiac, Ford, GNC, Lowes Whse, Staples, Target, Walmart SuperCtr, **S gas:** Exxon/Dunkin Donuts, 7-11, Shell, **food:** McDonald's, **lodging:** Hampton Inn, **other:** Southfork Camping (2mi)

**1b a** I-81, N to Winchester, S to Roanoke

**0mm** I-66 begins/ends on I-81, exit 300.

## INTERSTATE 77

N ↕ S

| Exit # | Services |
|---|---|
| 67mm | Virginia/West Virginia state line, East River Mtn |
| 66 | VA 598, to East River Mtn |
| 64 | US 52, VA 61, to Rocky Gap |
| 62 | VA 606, to South Gap |
| 62mm | **Welcome Ctr sb, full & facilities, info, Ⓒ, vending, ⚠, litter barrels, petwalk** |

VA

Copyright 2009 - The Next Exit®

## INTERSTATE 77 CONT'D

**N↕S**

**W Y T H R V I L L E**

| | |
|---|---|
| **60mm** | rest area nb, full ♿ facilities, 🚻, vending, 🅿️, litter barrels, petwalk |
| **58** | US 52, to Bastian, **E gas:** BP/dsl, **food:** Front Porch Cafe, **W gas:** Citgo/dsl, Exxon/dsl |
| **56mm** | runaway ramp nb |
| **52** | US 52, VA 42, Bland, **E gas:** Citgo, **food:** Subway, **other:** $General, **W gas:** Shell/DQ/dsl, **food:** Log Cabin Rest., **lodging:** Big Walker Motel |
| **51.5mm** | weigh sta both lanes |
| **48mm** | Big Walker Mtn |
| **47** | VA 717, 6 mi **W other:** to Deer Trail Park/NF Camping |
| **41** | VA 610, Peppers Ferry, Wytheville, **E food:** Sagebrush Steaks, **lodging:** Best Western, Sleep Inn, Super 8, **W gas:** Kangaroo/dsl/scales/24hr, TA/Country Pride/Popeye's/Subway/Taco Bell/dsl/scales/24hr/@, **food:** Southern Diner, **lodging:** Comfort Suites, Country Inn&Suites, Fairfield Inn, Hampton Inn, Ramada Inn |
| **40** | I-81 S, to Bristol, US 52 N |
| **I-77 and I-81 run together 9 mi. See Interstae 81, exits 73-80.** | |
| **73** | US 11 S, Wytheville, **W gas:** BP, Kangaroo, **food:** Applebees, Bob Evan's, Cracker Barrel, DQ, El Puerto, Hardee's, Kimono Japanese, LJ Silver, Ocean Bay Rest., Peking Rest., Shoney's, Sonic, Waffle House, Wendy's, **lodging:** Budget Host, Day's Inn, Econolodge, La Quinta, Motel 6, Quality Inn, Red Carpet Inn, Travelodge, **other:** Ⓗ HOSPITAL, AutoZone, Buick/Cadillac/Chevrolet/Pontiac, CVS Drug, Food Lion, Ford, Goodyear/auto, Harley-Davidson, K-Mart, Nissan |
| **77** | Service Rd, **E gas:** Exxon/dsl, Wilco/Hess/Arby's/DQ/dsl/scales/24hr, **other:** Truck'o Mat, st police, **W gas:** Citgo/Subway/dsl/24hr, ✈FLYING J/Cookery/dsl/LP/RV Dump/24hr/@, Wilco/Hess/dsl, **food:** Burger King, **other:** KOA |
| **80** | US 52 S, VA 121 N, to Ft Chiswell, **E gas:** BP, Citgo/Kangaroo/dsl, **food:** McDonald's, **lodging:** Comfort Inn, **other:** Speedco, **W gas:** BP/Burger King/dsl, ✈FLYING J/Cookery/dsl/scales/24hr/@, **food:** Wendy's, **lodging:** Hampton Inn, Super 8, **other:** Blue Beacon, Ft Chiswell Outlets/famous brands, GS Camping, NAPA |
| **I-77 and I-81 run together 9 mi. See Interstae 81, exits 73-80.** | |
| **32** | I-81 N, to Roanoke |
| **26mm** | New River |
| **24** | VA 69, to Poplar Camp, **E gas:** Pure/gas, **other:** to Shot Tower SP, New River Trail Info Ctr, **W gas:** Citgo/dsl |
| **19** | VA 620, 🚬 |
| **14** | US 58, US 221, to Hillsville, Galax, **E gas:** Citgo/Subway, **food:** Peking Palace, **lodging:** Red Carpet Inn, **other:** Ⓗ HOSPITAL, **W gas:** BP/24hr, Cockerham's Trkstp/dsl/24hr, Exxon/DQ/dsl, Marathon, Shell, **food:** Countryside Rest., McDonald's, Pizza Inn/TCBY, Shoney's, Wendy's, **lodging:** Best Western, Comfort Inn, Hampton Inn, Holiday Inn Express, Super 8, **other:** Carrollwood Camping (1mi) |
| **8** | VA 148, VA 775, to Fancy Gap, **E gas:** Chevron (2mi), Citgo/dsl, **lodging:** Lakeview Motel/rest., Mountaintop Motel/rest., **other:** Fox Trail Camping, Utt's Camping, to Blue Ridge Pkwy, **W gas:** BP, Kangaroo/dsl, **lodging:** Countryview Inn, Day's Inn |
| **6.5mm** | runaway truck ramp sb |
| **4.5mm** | runaway truck ramp sb |

---

[Map of Virginia showing Winchester area with locations: Hayfield, Nain, Opequon, Winchester, Kemstown, Stephens Fort, Stephens City, Middletown, Tulip, Paris, Strasburg, Rockland, Happy Creek, Belle Meade, Harmony, Woodstock, Linden, Markham, Morgantown, Bowmans, Bentonville, Hawkinstown, Flint Hill, Shenandoah Caverns. Highways 81 and 66 shown. VA]

| | |
|---|---|
| **3mm** | runaway truck ramp sb |
| **1** | VA 620 |
| **.5mm** | Welcome Ctr nb, full ♿ facilities, info, 🚻, 🅿️, litter barrels, petwalk |
| **0mm** | Virginia/North Carolina state line |

## INTERSTATE 81

**N↕S**

**W I N C H E S T E R**

| Exit # | Services |
|---|---|
| **324mm** | Virginia/West Virginia state line |
| **323** | rd 669, to US 11, Whitehall, **E gas:** Exxon, **W gas:** ✈FLYING J/Country Mkt/dsl/LP/scales/24hr |
| **321** | rd 672, Clearbrook, **E gas:** Citgo/dsl, **food:** Olde Stone Rest. |
| **320mm** | Welcome Ctr sb, full ♿ facilities, 🚻, vending, 🅿️, litter barrels, petwalk |
| **317** | US 11, Stephenson, **E food:** Arby's, Daily Grind, Subway, **other:** Lowes Whse, Target, **W gas:** Exxon/dsl, Liberty/Blimpie/dsl, Sheetz/dsl/24hr, Sunoco/dsl, **food:** Burger King, Denny's, Godfather's Pizza, McDonald's, Pizza Hut/Taco Bell, Tastee Freez, **lodging:** Comfort Inn, Econolodge, Holiday Inn Express (3mi), **other:** Ⓗ HOSPITAL, Candy Hill Camping |
| **315** | VA 7, Winchester, **E gas:** Exxon, Sheetz/24hr, **food:** Foster's Grille, Ledo's Pizza, Maggie Moo's, Quizno's, Sonic, Starbucks, **other:** Curves, Dodge, $Tree, Martin's Foods, PetCo, **W gas:** Chevron/dsl, Exxon/Subway, Liberty/dsl, Shell/dsl, **food:** Arby's, Baskin-Robbins/Dunkin Donuts, Camino Real Mexican, Chian Town, 5 Guys Burgers, George's Pizza, KFC, LJ Silver, McDonald's, Pizza Hut, Wendy's, **lodging:** Hampton Inn, Shoney's Inn/rest., **other:** AutoZone, CVS Drug, Food Lion, TrueValue |
| **314mm** | Abrams Creek |
| **313** | US 17/50/522, Winchester, **E gas:** BP/dsl, Citgo, Exxon/Subway, Shell/dsl, **food:** Cracker Barrel, Golden Corral, IHOP, Los Tolteco's Mexican, TX Steaks, Waffle House, **lodging:** Candlewood Suites, Holiday Inn, Fairfield Inn, Red Roof Inn, Sleep Inn, Super 8, Travelodge, **other:** Big Lots, Costco/gas, Food Lion, Jo-Ann Fabrics, Nissan, vet, **W gas:** Sheetz/24hr, **food:** Bob Evans, Chick-fil-A, Chili's, China Jade, Chipotle Mexican, CiCi's, Glory Days Grill, KFC, McDonald's, Olive Garden, Panera Bread, Perkin's, Pizza Hut/Taco Bell, Quizno's, Rancho Mexican, Red Lobster, Ruby Tuesday, TGIFriday, Subway, Waffle House, Wendy's, **lodging:** Best Western, Hampton Inn, Hilton Garden, Wingate Inn, **other:** Belk, BooksAMillion, Border's, Circuit City, $Tree, Home Depot, Food Lion, JC Penney, K-Mart, Kohl's, |

**VA**

**N** ↕ **S**

## INTERSTATE 81 CONT'D

**313** Continued
Lowes Whse, Martin's Foods, Michael's, PepBoys, PetsMart, Old Navy, Ross, Sears/auto, Staples, Target, Walgreens, Walmart SuperCtr, mall, to Shenandoah U

**310** VA 37, to US 50W, **W gas:** Sunoco, **food:** Bo's Express, Daily Grind, McDonald's, Outback Steaks, Popeye's, **lodging:** Best Value Inn, Country Inn&Suites, Days Inn, Royal Inn, **other:** H HOSPITAL, Bloom Foods, Camping World, Carquest, CVS Drug, Gander Mtn, Honda, Suzuki, VW

**307** VA 277, Stephens City, **E gas:** CB's, 7-11, Shell/Subway/dsl, **food:** Arby's, Burger King, Butcher Block Cafe, Daily Grind, KFC/Taco Bell, McDonald's, Pizza Hut, Roma Italian, Waffle House, Wendy's, **lodging:** Comfort Inn, Holiday Inn Express, **other:** Advance Parts, Curves, $General, Food Lion, Martin's Foods/gas, McCoy's Dairy Barn, Rite Aid, vet, **W gas:** Exxon/Dunkin Donuts, Sheetz/24hr

**304mm** weigh sta both lanes

**302** rd 627, Middletown, **E gas:** Exxon/dsl, **W gas:** Liberty/dsl, 7-11, **lodging:** Super 8, Wayside Inn/rest., **other:** to Wayside Theatre

**300** I-66 E, to Washington, Shenandoah NP, Skyline Dr

**298** US 11, Strasburg, **E gas:** BP/dsl, Exxon/dsl/LP, **food:** Arby's, Burger King, Castiglia Italian, Ciro's Pizza, Denny's, Great Wall Buffet, McDonald's, Rancho Viejo Mexican, **lodging:** Fairfield Inn, Hotel Strasburg/rest., Ramada Inn, **other:** Family$, Food Lion, Rite Aid, vet, **W other:** Battle of Cedar Grove Camping, to Belle Grove Plantation

**296** US 48, VA 55, Strasburg, **E other:** to Hupp's Hill Bfd Museum

**291** rd 651, Toms Brook, **E lodging:** Budget Inn, **W gas:** Love's/Arby's/dsl/scales/24hr/@, Wilco/Hess/DQ/dsl/scales/24hr, **food:** Milestone Rest., **other:** truckwash

**283** VA 42, Woodstock, **E gas:** Liberty/7-11, Sheetz, Shell, **food:** Arby's, Dunkin Donuts, Hardee's, KFC, McDonald's, Pizza Hut, Ponderosa, Taco Bell, Wendy's, **lodging:** Budget Host, Comfort Inn, Holiday Inn Express, **other:** H HOSPITAL, CVS Drug, Food Lion, Radio Shack, Rite Aid, to Massanutten Military Academy, **W gas:** Exxon/dsl/24hr, Sunoco, **food:** China Wok, Cracker Barrel, Domino's, Subway, **other:** Curves, $Tree, Lowes Whse, Walmart SuperCtr

**279** VA 185, RD 675, Edinburg, **E gas:** BP/dsl, Exxon/dsl, Shell/dsl/24hr, **food:** Subway, **other:** Ace Hardware, Creekside Camping (2mi)

**277** VA 614, Bowmans Crossing

**273** VA 292, RD 703, Mt Jackson, **E gas:** Exxon/dsl, Liberty/Blimpie/dsl/scales/24hr, 7-11, Sheetz/Wendy's/dsl/scales/24hr, **food:** Burger King, China King, Denny's, Godfather's, **lodging:** Super 8, **other:** Curves, $General, Food Lion/24hr, USPO, to Mt Jackson Hist Dist

**269** rd 730, to Shenandoah Caverns, **E gas:** Chevron/dsl

**269mm** N Fork Shenandoah River

**264** US 211, New Market, **E gas:** BP/Blimpie/dsl, Chevron/dsl, Exxon/dsl, Shell/dsl, Texaco, **food:** Appleseed's Rest., Burger King, Godfather's, McDonald's, Publik House Rest., Southern Kitchen, **lodging:** Budget Inn, Quality Inn, Shenvalee Motel/rest., **other:** NAPA, Rancho Camping, to Shenandoah NP Skyline Dr, **W gas:** 7-11, **lodging:** Day's Inn, **other:** to New Market Bfd

**HARRISONBURG**

**262mm** rest area both lanes, full ♿ facilities, 📞 vending, 🎁, litter barrels, petwalk

**257** US 11, VA 259, to Broadway, **E gas:** Liberty/Burger King/Blimpie/Godfather's/dsl, **3-5 mi E other:** KOA, Endless Caverns Camping

**251** US 11, Harrisonburg, **W gas:** Exxon/dsl, **lodging:** Economy Inn

**247b a** US 33, Harrisonburg, **E gas:** BP/Blimpie/dsl, Citgo/dsl, Royal, Sheetz, **food:** Applebees, Bob Evans, Bruster's, Chili's, CiCi's Pizza, Domino's, El Charro Mexican, 5 Buys Burgers, Golden Corral, Great Wok, Heavenly Ham, IHOP, Jess' Lunch, LJ Silver, O'Charley's, Outback Steaks, Panera Bread, Quizno's, Red Lobster, Ruby Tuesday, Shoney's, Smokin Pig, Taco Bell, TX Steaks, Waffle House, Wendy's, **lodging:** Best Western, Candlewood Suites, Comfort Inn, Courtyard, Econolodge, Hampton Inn, Holiday Inn, Jameson Inn, Motel 6, Sleep Inn, **other:** Barnes&Noble, Belk, Books-a-Million, Circuit City, $Tree, Firestone/auto, Home Depot, JC Penney, K-Mart, Kohl's, Kroger, Lowes Whse, Martin's Foods/gas, Michael's, Nissan, Office Depot, Old Navy, PepBoys, PetsMart, Ross, Saturn, Staples, Target, TJ Maxx, Walmart SuperCtr/gas, to Shenandoah NP, Skyline Dr, mall, **W gas:** Chevron/dsl, Exxon/dsl, Royal, Sheetz, Texaco, **food:** Arby's, China Inn, Ciro's Italian, Dragon Palace, Dunkin Donuts, Golden China, Hardee's, KFC, Kyoto, La Italia, Little Caesar's, McDonald's, Papa John's, Pizza Hut, Sam's Hotdogs, Subway, **other:** H HOSPITAL, Advance Parts, Big Lots, CVS Drug, Food Lion

**245** VA 659, Port Republic Rd, **E gas:** Exxon/Subway/dsl, Liberty/dsl, Neighbor's, Texaco, **lodging:** Day's Inn, **W other:** H HOSPITAL, to James Madison U

**243** US 11, to Harrisonburg, **W gas:** BP/dsl, Exxon/dsl, Harrisonburg Travel Ctr/diner/dsl/scales, Liberty, 7-11, Sheetz, **food:** Burger King, China Gourmet, Cracker Barrel, Dunkin Donuts, McDonald's, Pizza Hut, Subway, Taco Bell, Waffle House, **lodging:** Country Inn&Suites, Hampton Inn, Holiday Inn Express, Ramada Inn, Red Carpet Inn, Super 8, **other:** Advance Parts, AutoZone, BMW, Buick/GMC/Pontiac, Chrysler, Ford, Honda, Hyundai, Kia, Lincoln/Mercury, Subaru, Toyota

**240** VA 257, RD 682, Mount Crawford, **1-3 mi W gas:** Exxon/dsl, **food:** Burger King, Mrs. Rowe's, **lodging:** Village Inn

**235** VA 256, Weyers Cave, **E gas:** Texaco/dsl, **W gas:** BP/Subway/dsl, Exxon/dsl **other:** Freightliner, antiques, to Grand Caverns

**232mm** rest area both lanes, full ♿ facilities, 📞 vending, 🎁, litter barrels, petwalk

**227** rd 612, Verona, **E gas:** BP/Subway/dsl, **food:** Waffle Inn, **W gas:** Citgo/Wendy's/dsl, Exxon, Shell, **food:** Burger King, Ciro's Pizza, Dunkin Donuts, Hardee's, McDonald's, **lodging:** Knight's Inn, **other:** Food Lion, Good Sam RV Park (3mi), Rite Aid, antiques

**225** VA 275, Woodrow Wilson Pkwy, **E lodging:** Quality Inn, **W lodging:** Day's Inn, Holiday Inn/rest.

**222** US 250, Staunton, **E gas:** BP, Texaco/dsl, **food:** Cracker Barrel, McDonald's, Mrs Rowe's Rest., Shoney's, TX Steaks, **lodging:** Best Western, Guesthouse Inn, Sleep Inn, **W gas:** Hess, Sheetz, **food:** Burger King, Chili's, Dunkin Donuts, 5 Guys Burgers, Quizno's, Starbucks, Waffle House, **lodging:** Comfort Inn, Econolodge, Microtel, Super 8, **other:** AutoZone, Lowes Whse,

**VA**

Copyright 2009 - The Next Exit®

## INTERSTATE 81 CONT'D

N ↑↓ S

**222** Continued
Martin's Foods/gas, TireMart, Toyota/sSion, Walmart SuperCtr, American Frontier Culture Museum

**221** I-64 E, to Charlottesville, Skyline Dr, Shenandoah NP

**220** VA 262, to US 11, Staunton, **1 mi** **W** **gas:** BP, Citgo, Exxon, Shell, **food:** Applebee's, Arby's, Burger King, Country Cookin', KFC, McDonald's, Red Lobster, **lodging:** Budget Inn, Hampton Inn, **other:** Advance Parts, Belk, Books A Million, Buick/Pontiac/GMC, Chrysler, CVS Drug, $Tree, Ford/Lincoln/Mercury, Harley-Davidson, Honda, Hyundai, JC Penney, Jeep/Dodge, Merchant's Tire/auto, Nissan, Rule RV Ctr, VW

**217** rd 654, to Mint Spring, Stuarts Draft, **E** **gas:** BP/Subway/dsl, Exxon/dsl, **lodging:** Day's Inn, **W** **gas:** Citgo/Stuckey's/dsl/24hr, Liberty, **lodging:** Relax Inn, Walnut Hill Camping (3mi)

**213b a** US 11, US 340, Greenville, **E** **gas:** BP/Subway, Pilot/Arby's/scales/dsl/24hr, Shell, **food:** Edelweiss Rest., **lodging:** Budget Host

**205** rd 606, Raphine, **E** **gas:** Exxon/Burger King, Smiley's/BBQ/dsl/24hr, Whites/dsl/24hr/motel/@, **W** **gas:** Wilco/Hess/Wendy's/dsl/scales/24hr, **lodging:** Day's Inn/rest. **other:** Koogler RV Ctr

**200** rd 710, Fairfield, **E** **gas:** BP/McDonald's/dsl/24hr, Texaco, **W** **gas:** Exxon/Subway/dsl, Shell/dsl

**199mm** rest area sb, full ♿ facilities, 📞 vending, 🍽 litter barrels, petwalk

**195** US 11, Lee Hwy, **E** **lodging:** Maple Hall Lodging/dining, **W** **gas:** Citgo/dsl/24hr, Shell/dsl, **food:** Aunt Sarah's, **lodging:** Best Value, Days Inn, Howard Johnson/rest., **other:** Lee-Hi Camping

**191** I-64 W (exits left from nb), US 60, to Charleston

**188b a** US 60, to Lexington, Buena Vista, **3-5 mi** **E** **gas:** BP, Exxon, **food:** Hardee's, KFC, LJ Silver, McDonald's, Pizza Hut, Taco Bell, Wendy's, **lodging:** Budget Inn, Buena Vista Inn, **other:** Ⓗ HOSPITAL, to Glen Maury Park, to Stonewall Jackson Home, Marshall Museum, to Blue Ridge Pkwy, **W** **gas:** Exxon/dsl/24hr, **lodging:** Day's Inn, Hampton Inn, **other:** to Washington&Lee U, VMI

**180** US 11, Natural Bridge, **E** **gas:** Shell/dsl, **lodging:** Relax Inn, **other:** Cave Mtn NF, **W** **gas:** Shell/dsl, **food:** Pink Cadillac Diner, **lodging:** Budget Inn, **other:** KOA, (180a exits left from sb)

**175** US 11 N, to Glasgow, Natural Bridge, **E** **gas:** Exxon, **lodging:** Natural Bridge Hotel/rest., **other:** to James River RA, Jellystone Camping

**168** VA 614, US 11, Arcadia, **E** **gas:** Shell, **food:** Mtn View Rest., **lodging:** Wattstull Inn, **other:** Middle Creek Camping (6mi), **2 mi** **W** **gas:** Exxon, **food:** Burger King, Mtn View Rest

**167** US 11 (from sb), Buchanan

**162** US 11, Buchanan, **E** **gas:** Exxon/dsl, **other:** to BR Pkwy, **W** **gas:** Texaco/Subway/24hr

**158mm** rest area sb, full ♿ facilities, 📞 vending, 🍽 litter barrels, petwalk

**156** rd 640, to US 11, **E** **gas:** Exxon/Brugh's Mill/dsl

**150** US 11/220, to Fincastle, **E** **gas:** Citgo/dsl/24hr, Dodge's/dsl, Pilot/Subway/dsl/24hr, TA/dsl/@, **food:** Country Cookin', Cracker Barrel, Hardee's, McDonald's,

LEXINGTON

ROANOKE SALEM

**150** Continued
Shoney's, Taco Bell, Waffle House, **lodging:** Comfort Inn, Holiday Inn Express, Red Roof Inn, Travelodge, **other:** Berglund RV Ctr, CVS Drug, $General, truckwash, **W** **gas:** BP/dsl, Exxon/dsl/24hr, **food:** Bojangles, Pizza Hut, Rancho Viejo Mexican, Wendy's, **lodging:** Howard Johnson, Super 8, **other:** Curves, Kroger/gas, vet

**149mm** weigh sta both lanes

**146** VA 115, Cloverdale, **E** **gas:** Exxon, Shell/dsl, **food:** Anthony's Diner, Burger King, El Rodeo Mexican, Hardees, McDonald's, Subway, **lodging:** Country Inn&Suites, Day's Inn/rest., Fairfield Inn, Hampton Inn, **other:** Camping World, CVS Drug, Gander Mtn

**143** I-581, US 220, to Roanoke, Blue Ridge Pkwy (exits left from sb), **1 mi** **E** **gas:** Sheetz, **food:** El Toreo, Subway, Waffle House, **lodging:** Hampton Inn, Holiday Inn, Knights Inn, Quality Inn, Super 8, **2-3 mi E** on Hershberger...**gas:** BP, Exxon, Shell, **food:** Abuelo's Mexican, Applebees, Buffalo Wild Wings, Carrabba's, Chick-fil-A, Flat Rock Grille, Hardee's, IHOP, Logan's Roadhouse, O'Charley's, Olive Garden, Panera Bread, Red Palace Chinese, Ruby Tuesday, Shaker's, Smokey Bones BBQ, Starbucks, Subway, TX Steaks, TGIFriday, **lodging:** Best Western, Comfort Inn, Courtyard, Extended Stay America, Holiday Inn, Howard Johnson, Hyatt Place, MainStay Suites, Residence Inn, **other:** Barnes&Noble, Belk, Circuit City, JC Penney, Macy's, Old Navy, Sears/auto, Target, U-Haul, Walmart SuperCtr/gas, mall

**141** VA 419, Salem, **E** **gas:** BP, Liberty/Burger King, Valero, **food:** Hardee's, Country Cookin' Rest., McDonald's, **lodging:** Econolodge, Holiday Inn Express, La Quinta, Quality Inn, **other:** Ⓗ HOSPITAL, Chevrolet, Kroger/gas, **W** **gas:** BP/dsl, Citgo

**140** VA 311, Salem, **1 mi** **E** **food:** Mac&Bob's Cafe, **1 mi** **W** **food:** Hanging Rock Grill/golf

**137** VA 112, VA 619, Salem, **E** **gas:** BP, Chevron, Citgo, Exxon/dsl, Go-Mart, Liberty, Sheetz/24hr, **food:** Anthony's Cafe, Applebees, Arby's, Bojangles, Burger King, China Wok, Denny's, Dickey's BBQ, Dynasty Buffet, El Rodeo Mexican, Firehouse Subs, Hardee's, K&W Cafeteria, KFC, LJ Silver, Mamma Maria Italian, McDonald's, Omelette Shoppe, Pizza Hut, Quizno's, Shoney's, Sonic, Starbucks, Subway, Taco Bell, Tokyo Express, Wendy's, **lodging:** Comfort Inn, Econolodge, Super 8, **other:** Aamco, Advance Parts, AutoZone, BigLots, $General, Tree, Food Lion, Goodyear, Goody's, K-Mart, Kroger, Merchant's Tire, Mitsubishi, Snyder's RV, Walgreens, Walmart SuperCtr, **W** **lodging:** Holiday Inn, Howard Johnson

## INTERSTATE 81 CONT'D

**N ↕ S**

**132** VA 647, to Dixie Caverns, **E gas:** Citgo, Shell, **lodging:** Budget Host, **other:** Dixie Caverns Camping, st police

**129mm** rest area nb, full ♿ facilities, 📞, vending, ⛱ litter barrels, petwalk

**128** US 11, VA 603, Ironto, **E gas:** Texaco, **W gas:** Exxon/Dixie's/Subway/dsl/24hr

**118c b a** US 11/460, Christiansburg, **E gas:** Shell/dsl, **food:** Denny's, Cracker Barrel, **lodging:** Day's Inn, Fairfield Inn, Holiday Inn Express, Quality Inn, Super 8, **other:** Harley-Davidson, **W gas:** BP, Exxon/dsl, RaceWay, Shell, **food:** Country Cookin, Hardee's, McDonald's, Pizza Hut, Ruby Tuesday, Subway, Waffle House, Wendy's, **lodging:** Econolodge, Knight's Inn, **other:** H HOSPITAL, Advance Parts, Chevrolet/Subaru, Chrysler/Dodge, Ford, Honda, Hyundai, KIA, Subaru, Toyota, to VA Tech

**114** VA 8, Christiansburg, 0-1 mi **W gas:** Citgo, Sunoco, **food:** Anthony's Cafe, Burger King, Macado's Rest., Pizza Inn, **lodging:** Budget Inn, **other:** $General, repair

**109** VA 177, VA 600, **E other:** H HOSPITAL, 0-2 mi **W gas:** BP/dsl, Marathon, **lodging:** Best Western, Comfort Inn, La Quinta, Super 8

**107mm** rest area both lanes, full ♿ facilities, 📞, vending, ⛱ litter barrels, petwalk

**105** VA 232, RD 605, to Radford, **W gas:** Citgo (2mi), **lodging:** Executive Motel (4mi), **other:** museum

**101** rd 660, to Claytor Lake SP, **E lodging:** Claytor Lake Inn, Sleep Inn, **W gas:** Citgo/DQ/dsl, Shell/Omelette Shoppe/Taco Bell/dsl/scales/@

**98** VA 100 N, to Dublin, **E gas:** Exxon/Subway/dsl, **food:** Bojangles, Shoney's, **lodging:** Comfort Inn, Hampton Inn, Holiday Inn Express, **W gas:** Liberty/Blimpie/dsl, Marathon, **food:** Arby's, Burger King, Fatz Cafe, McDonald's, Subway, Wendy's, **lodging:** Super 8, **other:** H HOSPITAL, Walmart SuperCtr, to Wilderness Rd Museum

**94b a** VA 99 N, to Pulaski, **E lodging:** Day's Inn, 0-2 mi **W gas:** Exxon, **food:** Domino's, LJ Silver, Pizza Hut, **other:** H HOSPITAL, $General, Sav-a-Lot Foods

**92** rd 658, to Draper, **E gas:** BP, **other:** to New River Trail SP

**89b a** US 11 N, VA 100, to Pulaski

**86** rd 618, Service Rd, **W gas:** Sunoco/Appletree Rest./dsl, **other:** repair

**84** rd 619, to Grahams Forge, **W gas:** Kangaroo/DQ/dsl/24hr, Love's/Chester Fried/Subway/dsl/scales/24hr, **lodging:** Fox Mtn Inn, Trail Motel

**81** I-77 S, to Charlotte, to Blue Ridge Pkwy. **I-81 S and I-77 N run together 9 mi.,** Galax

**80** US 52 S, VA 121 N, to Ft Chiswell, **E gas:** BP/Burger King/dsl, ⊕FLYING J/Cookery/dsl/scales/24hr/@, **food:** Wendy's, **lodging:** Hampton Inn, Super 8, **other:** Blue Beacon, Ft Chiswell Outlets/famous brands, GS Camping, NAPA, **W gas:** BP, Citgo/Kangaroo/dsl, **food:** McDonald's, **lodging:** Comfort Inn, **other:** Speedco

**77** Service Rd, **E gas:** Citgo/Subway/dsl/24hr, ⊕FLYING J/Cookery/dsl/LP/RV Dump/24hr/@, Wilco/Hess/dsl, **food:** Burger King, **other:** KOA, **W gas:** Exxon/dsl, Wilco/Hess/Arby's/DQ/dsl/scales/24hr, **other:** Truck'o Mat, st police

**73** US 11 S, Wytheville, **E gas:** BP, Kangaroo, **food:** Applebees, Bob Evan's, Cracker Barrel, DQ, El Puerto, Hardee's, Kimono Japanese, LJ Silver,

**WYTHEVILLE**

**73** Continued
Ocean Bay Rest., Peking Rest., Shoney's, Sonic, Waffle House, Wendy's, **lodging:** Budget Host, Day's Inn, Econolodge, La Quinta, Motel 6, Quality Inn, Red Carpet Inn, Travelodge, **other:** H HOSPITAL, AutoZone, Buick/Cadillac/Chevrolet/Pontiac, CVS Drug, Food Lion, Ford, Goodyear/auto, Harley-Davidson, K-Mart, Nissan

**I-81 N and I-77 S run together 9 mi**

**72** I-77 N, to Bluefield, 1 mi **N**, I-77 exit 41 **E food:** Sagebrush Steaks, **lodging:** Best Western, Sleep Inn, Super 8, **W gas:** Kangaroo/dsl/24hr, TA/Country Pride/Popeye's/Subway/Taco Bell/dsl/scales/24hr/@, **food:** Southern Diner, **lodging:** Comfort Suites, Country Inn&Suites, Fairfield Inn, Hampton Inn, Ramada/rest.

**70** US 21/52, Wytheville, **E gas:** BP/dsl, Exxon, Sheetz, **food:** Arby's, China Wok, KFC/Taco Bell, Little Caesar's, McDonald's, Ruby Tuesday, Starbucks, Subway, Wendy's, **other:** H HOSPITAL, $Tree, Food Lion, Goody's, IGA Foods, Lowes Whse, Old Navy, Radio Shack, Walmart SuperCtr, **W gas:** Kangaroo, **lodging:** Comfort Inn

**67** US 11 (from nb, no re-entry), to Wytheville

**61mm** rest area nb, full ♿ facilities, 📞, vending, ⛱ litter barrels, petwalk, NO TRUCKS

**60** VA 90, Rural Retreat, **E gas:** Chevron/dsl, **food:** El Ranchero, McDonald's, Subway, **other:** to Rural Retreat Lake, camping

**54** rd 683, to Groseclose, **E gas:** Shell/dsl, **food:** The Barn Rest., **lodging:** Relax Inn, **other:** Settler's Museum

**53.5mm** rest area sb, full ♿ facilities, 📞, vending, ⛱ litter barrels, petwalk

**50** US 11, Atkins, **W gas:** Citgo/Subway/dsl/24hr, Exxon/Pizza+, **food:** Atkins Diner, **lodging:** Comfort Inn

**47** US 11, to Marion, **W gas:** BP/Subway, Chevron/dsl/24hr, **food:** Arby's, KFC/Taco Bell, Little Caesar's, LJ Silver, McDonald's, Pizza Hut, Puerto Mexican, Sonic, Wendy's, **lodging:** Best Western/rest., Econolodge, VA House Inn, **other:** H HOSPITAL, Advance Parts, AutoZone, Buick/Chevrolet/GMC/Pontiac, Chrysler/Dodge/Jeep, CVS Drug, $General, Family$, Food City, Food Lion, Ford, Ingles, Marion Drug, O'Reilly Parts, Radio Shack, Rite Aid, Walgreens, Walmart, to Hungry Mother SP (4mi)

**45** VA 16, Marion, **E gas:** Valero, **food:** AppleTree Rest., **other:** to Grayson Highlands SP, Mt Rogers NRA, **W gas:** BP, Chevron, **food:** Hardee's, **other:** NAPA, USPO

**44** US 11, Marion, **W gas:** Marathon/dsl

**39** US 11, RD 645, Seven Mile Ford, **E lodging:** Budget Inn/rest., **W other:** Interstate Camping/food

**35** rd 107, Chilhowie, **E food:** Hardees, **lodging:** Knight's Inn, **W gas:** Chevron, Gas'n Go, Exxon/dsl, Rouse Fuel, **food:** McDonald's, Subway, TasteeFreez, **lodging:** Budget Inn (1mi), **other:** Curves, $General, Food City, NAPA

**32** US 11, to Chilhowie, **E other:** Greenway Creek RV Park

**29** VA 91, to Damascus, Glade Spring, **E gas:** Marathon/Subway/dsl, Petro/dsl/rest./24hr/@, Valero, **food:** Giardino's Italian, Pizza+, Wendy's, **lodging:** Swiss Inn, Travel Inn, **other:** $General, Peterbilt, **W gas:** Chevron/dsl/24hr, Coastal, Exxon

**26** VA 737, Emory, **W food:** Emory Crossing Deli, **other:** to Emory&Henry Coll

**24** VA 80, Meadowview Rd, **W** auto repair

**22** VA 704, Enterprise Rd

**MARION**

**VA**

## INTERSTATE 81 CONT'D

**A B I N G D O N**

**N ↑ S**

| | |
|---|---|
| **19** | US 11/58, to Abingdon, **E gas:** Shell/Subway/dsl, **food:** Pizza+, **other:** vet, to Mt Rogers NRA, **W gas:** Chevron/dsl/24hr, Exxon/dsl, **food:** Burger King, Cracker Barrel, DaVinci's Cafe, Harbor House Seafood, Huddle House, Wendy's, **lodging:** Alpine Motel, Days Inn, Holiday Inn Express, Quality Inn |
| **17** | US 58A, VA 75, Abingdon, **E food:** Domino's, LJ Silver, **lodging:** Hampton Inn, **other:** Mr Transmission, **W gas:** Chevron, Exxon, Gas'n Go, **food:** Arby's, China Wok, Hardee's, KFC, Los Arcos Mexican, McDonald's, Papa John's, Pizza Hut, Shoney's, Taco Bell, Tuscan Grill, Wendy's, **lodging:** Martha Washington Inn, Super 8, **other:** H HOSPITAL, Advance Parts, $General, Food City, GNC, Kroger, K-Mart, Medicine Shoppe, Radio Shack |
| **14** | US 19, VA 140, Abingdon, **W gas:** Chevron/dsl/24hr, Exxon, Shell/dsl, **food:** McDonald's, Milano's Italian, Pizza Inn, Subway, **lodging:** Comfort Inn, **other:** CarQuest, Ford/Lincoln/Mercury, Riverside Camping (10mi) |
| **13.5mm** | **TRUCKERS ONLY rest area nb, full ♿ facilities, 🚻, vending, 🎪 litter barrels** |
| **13** | VA 611, to Lee Hwy, **W gas:** Shell/dsl, **other:** Kenworth, Mack |
| **10** | US 11/19, Lee Hwy, **W gas:** Appco, BP/dsl, Chevron, **lodging:** Beacon Inn, Deluxe Inn, Evergreen Inn, Red Carpet Inn, Skyland Inn |
| **7** | Old Airport Rd, **E gas:** Shell/dsl, **food:** Bojangles, Cracker Barrel, Sonic, **lodging:** La Quinta, **W gas:** BP/dsl, Conoco/dsl, Marathon, **food:** Chili's, Chop's Rest., Damon's, Domino's, El Patio Mexican, Fazoli's, Golden Corral, IHOP, Kobe Japanese, Logan's Roadhouse, Los Arco's, O'Charley's, Outback Steaks, Perkins, Pizza Hut, Red Lobster, Ruby Tuesday, Starbucks, Subway, Taco Bell, Wendy's, **lodging:** Courtyard, Holiday Inn, Microtel, Motel 6, **other:** Advance Parts, Best Buy, Curves, $Tree, $General, Home Depot, Lowes Whse, Office Depot, Old Navy, PetsMart, Ross, Sam's Club/gas, Target, Walmart SuperCtr, Sugar Hollow Camping |
| **5** | US 11/19, Lee Hwy, **E gas:** Shell, **food:** Arby's, Burger King, Hardee's, KFC, LJ Silver, McDonald's, Shoney's, **lodging:** Budget Inn, Super 8, **other:** Family$, Food Lion, Harley-Davidson, USPO, **W gas:** Exxon, **lodging:** Comfort Inn, **other:** Blevins Tire, Buick/Pontiac, Lee Hwy Camping |
| **3** | I-381 S, to Bristol, **1 mi E gas:** Chevron, Exxon/dsl, **food:** Arby's, Krystal, Ryan's |
| **1b a** | US 58/421, Bristol, **1 mi E gas:** Appco, Chevron, Citgo, Shell, **food:** Burger King, Capt D's, Chick-fil-A, KFC, Lighthouse Cafe, LJ Silver, McDonald's, Pizza Hut, Sonic, Subway, Taco Bell, Wendy's, **lodging:** Howard Johnson, Knight's Inn, **other:** H HOSPITAL, Belk, Chrysler/Jeep, CVS Drug, Dodge, Family$, Goody's, K-Mart, Kroger, Sears/auto, Toyota/Scion, Walgreens, mall |
| **0mm** | **Virginia®/Tennessee state line, Welcome Ctr nb, full ♿ facilities, info, 🚻, vending, 🎪 litter barrels, petwalk, NO TRUCKS** |

**B R I S T O L**

## INTERSTATE 85

**P E T E R S B U R G**

**N ↑ S**

| Exit # | Services |
|---|---|
| 69mm | I-85 begins/ends on I-95. |
| 69 | US 301, Wythe St, Washington St, Petersburg, **W lodging:** Regency Inn |
| 68 | I-95 S, US 460 E, to Norfolk, Crater Rd, **E** H HOSPITAL, **3/4 mi E gas:** Exxon/dsl, RaceTrac/dsl, Shell, **food:** Hardee's, **lodging:** California Inn, **other:** to Petersburg Nat Bfd |
| 65 | Squirrel Level Rd, **E other:** to Richard Bland Coll, **W gas:** BP |
| 63b a | US 1, to Petersburg, **E gas:** Chubby's, Exxon/dsl/24hr, Shell/Burger King, **food:** Hardee's, Waffle House, **lodging:** Holiday Inn Express, **W gas:** BP, **food:** McDonald's |
| 61 | US 460, to Blackstone, **E gas:** EastCoast/Subway/dsl/LP, **food:** Huddle House, **lodging:** Day's Inn (3mi), **W gas:** Shell/dsl, Valero (1mi), **other:** ✈ |
| 55mm | **rest area both lanes, full ♿ facilities, 🚻, 🎪, litter barrels, vending, petwalk** |
| 53 | VA 703, Dinwiddie, **W gas:** Exxon/dsl, **food:** HomePlace Rest. (3mi), Rumorz Cafe, **other:** to 5 Forks Nat Bfd |
| 52mm | Stony Creek |
| 48 | VA 650, DeWitt |
| 42 | VA 40, McKenney, **W gas:** Citgo, Exxon, **other:** auto repair, **1.5 mi W lodging:** Economy Inn |
| 40mm | Nottoway River |
| 39 | VA 712, to Rawlings, **E other:** VA Battlerama, **W gas:** Chevron/Davis/dsl/24hr, Citgo/dsl, **lodging:** Nottoway Motel/rest. |
| 34 | VA 630, Warfield, **W gas:** Exxon/dsl |
| 32mm | **rest area both lanes, full ♿ facilities, 🚻, 🎪, litter barrels, vending, petwalk** |
| 28 | US 1, Alberta, **W gas:** Exxon |
| 27 | VA 46, to Lawrenceville, **E other:** to St Paul's Coll |
| 24 | VA 644, to Meredithville |
| 22mm | weigh sta both lanes |
| 20mm | Meherrin River |
| 15 | US 1, to South Hill, **E gas:** Citgo/deli, **W gas:** Valero, **food:** Kahill's Diner, Rumorz |
| 12 | US 58, VA 47, to South Hill, **E gas:** RaceWay, Shell/dsl, **food:** Applebee's, Arby's, Bojangles, Domino's, Taste of Italy, **lodging:** Hampton Inn, Holiday Inn Express, Super 8, **other:** $Tree, Walmart SuperCtr, **W gas:** Citgo, Exxon/dsl, Kangaroo/dsl, Petrol, **food:** Brian's Steaks, Burger King, Cracker Barrel, Denny's, Down Home Buffet, Hardee's, KFC/Taco Bell, McDonald's, New China, Pizza Hut, Subway, Wendy's, **lodging:** Best Value Inn, Comfort Inn, |

VA

**N ↑↓ S**

## INTERSTATE 85

| | |
|---|---|
| 12 | Continued<br>Crossroads Inn, **other:** Ⓗ HOSPITAL, CVS Drug, $General, Food Lion, Goodyear/auto, Home Depot, Roses |
| 4 | VA 903, to Bracey, Lake Gaston, **E gas:** BP/DQ/Subway/dsl, Exxon/Simmon's/dsl/rest./scales/24hr/@, **other:** Americamps Camping (5mi) , **W gas:** Shell/Pizza Hut/Quizno's, **food:** Memphis Grill, **lodging:** Lake Gaston Inn |
| 3mm | Lake Gaston |
| 1mm | Welcome Ctr nb, full 🚻 facilities, 🅲, 🅿, 🅲, litter barrels, vending, petwalk |
| 0mm | Virginia/North Carolina state line |

## INTERSTATE 95

**N ↑ S**

**DC AREA**

| Exit # | Services |
|---|---|
| 178mm | Virginia/Maryland state line, Potomac River, W Wilson Mem Br |
| 177c b a | US 1, to Alexandria, Ft Belvoir, **E food:** Great American Steak Buffet, **lodging:** Budget Host, Hampton Inn, **other:** Chevrolet, Chrysler/Jeep, Dodge, **W gas:** Hess, Liberty/repair |
| 176b a | VA 241, Telegraph Rd, **E gas:** Hess/dsl, **W lodging:** Courtyard, Holiday Inn |
| 174 | Eisenhower Ave Connector, to Alexandria |
| 173 | rd 613, Van Dorn St, to Franconia, **E lodging:** Comfort Inn, **1 mi W gas:** Exxon, Shell, **food:** Dunkin Donuts, Jerry's Subs, McDonald's, Papa John's, Quizno's, Red Lobster, **other:** Aamco, Giant Foods, NTB |
| 170a | I-495 N, I-495 & I-95 N run together to MD, to Rockville |
| 170b | I-395 N, to Washington |
| 169b a | rd 644, Springfield, Franconia, **E food:** Family Diner, Starbucks, Subway, TGIFriday's, **lodging:** Best Western, Courtyard, Extended Stay America, Hampton Inn, Hilton, **other:** Ⓗ HOSPITAL, Barnes&Noble, Best Buy, CVS Drug, Firestone/auto, Ford, Home Depot, JC Penney, Macy's, Michael's, Old Navy, PetsMart, Staples, Target, mall, **W gas:** BP, Mobil, Shell, Sunoco, **food:** Chipotle Mexican, Deliah's Grill, Domino's, Dunkin Donuts, KFC, McDonald's, Outback Steaks, Quizno's, Starbucks, Subway, Tokyo Japanese, **lodging:** Holiday Inn Express, Red Roof Inn, **other:** CVS Drug, Diahatsu, Giant Foods, Goodyear/auto, K-Mart, Mr. Tire, Toyota/Scion, vet |
| 167 | VA 617, Backlick Rd (from sb) , **W gas:** InterFuel/dsl, **other:** Chevrolet |
| 166b a | VA 7100, Newington, to Ft Belvoir, **E gas:** Exxon/dsl, **W gas:** Exxon, **food:** McDonald's |
| 163 | VA 642, Lorton, **E gas:** Shell/24hr, **W gas:** Shell, **food:** Antoneli's Pizza, Burger King, McDonald's, **lodging:** Comfort Inn |
| 161 | US 1 S (exits left from sb), to Ft Belvoir, Mt Vernon, Woodlawn Plantation, Gunston Hall, **1 mi E gas:** BP, Exxon, Shell, Sunoco, **food:** Denny's, DixieBones BBQ, Dunkin Donuts, McDonald's, Taco Bell, **lodging:** Econolodge, Hampton Inn, Quality Inn, Rodeway Inn, VA Inn, **other:** Aldi Foods |
| 160.5mm | Occoquan River |
| 160b a | VA 123 N, Woodbridge, Occoquan, **E odging:** Comfort Inn, Econolodge, Hampton Inn, Quality Inn, **other:** Aldi Foods, GNC, Radio Shack, **W gas:** BP, Exxon/dsl, Shell, **food:** KFC, McDonald's, VA Grill, Wendy's, **other:** 7-11, same as 161 |

**DUMFRIES**

| | |
|---|---|
| 158b a | VA 3000, Prince William Pkwy, Woodbridge, **W gas:** Exxon, Shell, 7-11, Sunoco, WaWa, **food:** Chick-fil-A, Chipotle Mexican, ChuckeCheese, Coldstone Creamery, Famous Dave's BBQ, Fuddrucker's, Hooter's, Macaroni Grill, Old Country Buffet, On-the-Border, Red Lobster, Smokey Bones BBQ, Taco Bell, TGIFriday, UNO, Wendy's, **lodging:** Country Inn&Suites, Courtyard, Fairfield Inn, Holiday Inn Express, Residence Inn, Sleep Inn, **other:** Best Buy, Border's Books, $Tree, Lowes Whse, Michael's, Office Depot, PetsMart, Sam's Club/gas, Shopper's Foods, Target, Walmart SuperCtr/Subway |
| 156 | VA 784, Potomac Mills, **E gas:** Exxon, Wawa/gas, **food:** Checkers, McDonald's, Taco Bell, **other:** Ⓗ HOSPITAL, Hyundai, Kia, Lincoln/Mercury, Mazda, Mitsubishi, Nissan, Radio Shack, Safeway, Trak Auto, to Leesylvania SP, **W gas:** Chevron, Exxon, Shell, Sunoco, Texaco, **food:** Bamboo Buffet, Bob Evans, Burger King, Chili's, Denny's, Domino's, DQ, El Charro Mexican, Guapo's, Jerry's Subs, McDonald's, Olive Garden, Outback Steaks, Popeye's, Silver Diner, Subway, Wendy's, **lodging:** Best Western, Wytestone Suites, **other:** Book-a-Million, Circuit City, Costco/gas, Family$, Firestone/auto, Jo-Ann Fabrics, K-Mart, Marshall's, Michael's, NAPA, Nordstrom's, NTB, Potomic Mills Outlets/Famous Brands, Staples, TJ Maxx, U-Haul, **rest area both lanes, full** 🚻 **facilities,** 🅲, **vending,** 🅿, **litter barrels, petwalk, NO TRUCKS** |
| 154mm | truck rest area/weigh sta both lanes |
| 152 | VA 234, Dumfries, to Manassas, **E gas:** BP/dsl/24hr, Chevron/service, Shell/dsl, **food:** Golden Corral, KFC, McDonald's, Subway, Taco Bell, **lodging:** Sleep Inn, Super 8, **other:** NAPA Autocare, Weems-Botts Museum, **W gas:** Exxon/Blimpie, 7-11, Shell, **food:** Cracker Barrel, MontClair Rest., Tiziano Italian, Waffle House, **lodging:** Comfort Inn, Day's Inn, Econolodge, Hampton Inn, Holiday Inn, Holiday Inn Express, **other:** Prince William Camping |
| 150 | VA 619, Quantico, to Triangle, **E gas:** Exxon, Shell/dsl, 7-11, **food:** Burger King, Dunkin Donuts, McDonald's, Wendy's, **lodging:** Best Value Inn, Ramada Inn, **other:** auto repair, to Marine Corps Base, **W** Prince William Forest Park |
| 148 | to Quantico, **2 mi E gas:** Texaco/dsl, **lodging:** Spring Lake Motel, **other:** to Marine Corps Base |
| 143b a | to US 1, VA 610, Aquia, **E gas:** BP, Exxon, Shell/dsl/24hr, **food:** Carlos O'Kelly's, DQ, DaVanzo's Italian, KFC, Kingstreet BBQ, McDonald's, Pizza Hut, Ruby Tuesday, Shoney's, Vocelli's Pizza, Wendy's, **lodging:** Best Western, Day's Inn, Hampton Inn, **other:** Tires+, **W gas:** BP/dsl, Exxon, 7-11/dsl, WaWa, **food:** Applebees, Bob Evans, Burger King, Chick-fil-A, China Wok, Dunkin Donuts, 5 Guys Burgers, Golden Corral, Hardee's, IHOP, Jerry's Subs, Kobe Japanese, Maggie Moo's, Moe's SW Grill, Outback Steaks, Pancho Villa, Panera Bread, Popeye's, Ruby Tuesday, Starbucks, Taco Bell, Wendy's, **lodging:** Comfort Inn, Country Inn, Holiday Inn Express, Super 8, Wingate Inn, **other:** AutoZone, Best Buy, Border's Books, CVS Drug, $General, $Tree, Giant Foods, Home Depot, Kohl's, Lowes Whse, Michael's, PetsMart, Ross, Shopper's Foods, Staples, Target, TJ Maxx, Toyota, Walmart/auto, Aquia Pines Camping |
| 140 | VA 630, Stafford, **E gas:** 7-11, Sunoco, Valero, **food:** McDonald's, **lodging:** Bradshaw Motel (3mi) , **W gas:** BP/dsl, Shell/dsl |

**VA**

## INTERSTATE 95

**N** ↑↓ **S**

**F R E D E R I C K S B U R G**

**137mm** Potomac Creek

**136** rd 8900, Centreport, **W** ✈

**133b a** US 17 N, to Warrenton, **E** **gas:** Exxon/dsl, Texaco, **food:** Arby's, **lodging:** Howard Johnson Express, Motel 6, **other:** CarQuest, 7-11, **W** **gas:** BP/dsl, EastCoast/Subway/dsl, Shell/dsl, **food:** Burger King, Foster's Grille, Hardee's, McDonald's, Perkin's, Pizza Hut, Ponderosa, Taco Bell, Waffle House, Wendy's, **lodging:** Best Inn, Comfort Inn, Country Inn&Suites, Day's Inn, Holiday Inn, Quality Inn, Sleep Inn, Super 8, Travelodge, Wingate Inn, **other:** Advance Parts, Blue Beacon, Honda, PetsMart, Target

**132.5mm** Rappahannock River

**132mm** rest area sb, full ♿ facilities, 🚻, 🌲, litter barrels, petwalk, vending

**130b a** VA 3, to Fredericksburg, **E** **gas:** BP/dsl/24hr, Shell, Texaco, Wawa/24hr, **food:** Arby's, Bob Evans, Carlos O'Kelly's, Chesapeake, Friendly's, KFC, King Buffet, Mexico Lindo, Mkt St Buffet, Popeye's, Shoney's, Starbucks, Subway, TCBY, Vinny's Pizza, Wendy's, **lodging:** Best Western, Quality Inn, **other:** Ⓗ HOSPITAL, Batteries+, BigLots, $King, Hancock Fabrics, Home Depot, PepBoys, Radio Shack, Staples, U-Haul, **W** **gas:** BP, Chevron, Exxon/dsl/24hr, Shell, Sheetz, Valero, Wawa/24hr, **food:** A&W/LJ Silver, Applebees, Arby's, Asia Bistro, Aunt Sarah's, Baja Fresh, BoneFish Grill, Boston Mkt, Buffalo Wild Wings, Burger King, Caribou Coffee, Carrabba's, Checker's, Cheeseburger Paradise, Chick-fil-A, Chili's, China Jade, ChuckeCheese, CiCi's Pizza, Cracker Barrel, Denny's, Dunkin Donuts, El Paso Mexican, 5 Guy's Burgers, Firehouse Subs, Fuddrucker's, Great Steak, IHOP, Joe's Crabshack, Krispy Kreme, Ledo Pizza, Logan's Roadhouse, McDonald's, Melting Pot, Noodles&Co, NY Diner, O'Charley's, Old Country Buffet, Olive Garden, Outback Steaks, Pancho Villa, Panda Express, Panera Bread, Piccadilly, Pizza Hut, Popeye's, Qdoba, Quizno's, Red Lobster, Red Hot&Blue BBQ, Ruby Tuesday, Ryan's, Santa Fe Grill, Smokey Bones BBQ, Starbucks, Subway, Taco Bell, TGIFriday, Tia's TexMex, TX Steaks, Waffle House, **lodging:** Best Western, Hampton Inn, Hilton Garden, Homewood Suites, Ramada Inn, Super 8, **other:** Advance Parts, AutoZone, Belk, Best Buy, BJ's Whse, Borders Books, Circuit City, Costco, CVS Drug, $Tree, Gander Mtn, Giant Foods, GNC, Macy's, JC Penney, Kohl's, K-Mart, Lowes Whse, Macy's, Merchants Tire, Michaels, NTB, Office Depot, Old Navy, PetsMart, Ross, Sears/auto, Shopper's Foods, Target, Walmart SuperCtr/gas, mall

**126** US 1, US 17 S, to Fredericksburg, **E** **gas:** BP, Chevron, Citgo, Exxon, Shell/dsl, **food:** Arby's, Bates Grill, Denny's, DQ, Friendly's, Hardee's, Hooters, McDonald's, Pizza Hut, Ruby Tuesday, Subway, Taco Bell, Waffle House, **lodging:** Country Inn&Suites, Day's Inn/rest., Econolodge, Fairfield Inn, Hampton Inn, Heritage Inn, Ramada Inn, Super 8, TownePlace Inn, **other:** Advance Parts, Aldi Foods, AutoZone, BMW, Buick/GMC/Pontiac, Cadillac, CVS Drug, Dodge, Goodyear/auto, Honda/Nissan, Little Tires, Rite Aid, Subaru, **W** **gas:** Exxon, Sunoco/dsl, WaWa, **food:** Applebees, Bob Evans, Burger King, Chick-fil-A, Chili's, China Jade, Chipotle Mexican, Coldstone Creamery, Cracker Barrel, El Charro Mexican, Famous Dave's BBQ,

**126** Continued
Firehouse Subs, 5 Guys Burgers, Foster's Grill, Golden China, KFC, Lenny's Subs, Longhorn Steaks, McDonald's, Mimi's Cafe, Moe's SW Grill, Noodles&Co, Panera Bread, Papa John's, Pollo Campero, Red Robin, UNO, Starbucks, Sonic, Subway, Wendy's, **lodging:** Comfort Inn, Sleep Inn, WyteStone Suites, **other:** Best Buy, Carmax, CVS Drug, $Plus, Kohl's, Lowes Whse, Marshall's, PetsMart, Rite Aid, Ross, Target, Walmart SuperCtr, World Mkt, USPO

**118** VA 606, to Thornburg, **E** **gas:** Shell/dsl, **other:** Safford RV Ctr, to Stonewall Jackson Shrine, **W** **gas:** Citgo/dsl, Exxon, Shell/DQ, Valero, **food:** Angela's Rest., Burger King, McDonald's, Subway, **lodging:** Holiday Inn Express, Lamplighter Motel, Quality Inn, **other:** KOA (7mi), to Lake Anna SP

**110** VA 639, to Ladysmith, **E** **gas:** Citgo, Shell/dsl, **W** **gas:** Citgo/dsl, Exxon/dsl, **food:** Domino's, Guiseppe's Rest., Subway, VA BBQ, **other:** Express Tire/repair, Family$, Food Lion

**108mm** rest area both lanes, full ♿ facilities, vending, 🚻, 🌲, litter barrels, petwalk

**104** VA 207, to US 301, Bowling Green, **E** **gas:** Chevron, Exxon/dsl, Mr Fuel/dsl, Petro/dsl/rest./24hr/@, Pilot/Subway/DQ/dsl/24hr, Shell/dsl, Valero/dsl, **food:** McDonald's, Wendy's, **lodging:** Howard Johnson, Super 8, **other:** Blue Beacon, Russell Stover Candies, SpeedCo, to Ft AP Hill, **W** **gas:** Exxon/dsl, ⊕FLYING J/Country Mkt/dsl/scales/24hr, **food:** Aunt Sarah's, Waffle House, **lodging:** Comfort Inn, Day's Inn/rest., Econolodge, Quality Inn, Travelodge, **other:** USPO

**98** VA 30, Doswell, **E** to King's Dominion Funpark, **gas:** All American Plaza/dsl, Exxon, 7-11, **food:** Burger King, Denny's, Subway, **lodging:** Best Western, Comfort Suites, Day's Inn, Econolodge, **other:** All American Camping, King's Dominion Camping, truckwash

**92** VA 54, Ashland, **E** **gas:** Sunoco, **W** **gas:** BP, TA/dsl/rest./@, Citgo/dsl, EastCoast/Blimpie/Krispy Kreme/dsl, Exxon/Subway, Shell/dsl, **food:** Applebees, Arby's, Burger King, Capt D's, Cracker Barrel, DQ, Hardee's, KFC/LJ Silver, McDonald's, New China Buffet, Perkin's, Pizza Hut, Ponderosa, Ruby Tuesday, Starbucks, Taco Bell, Waffle House, Wendy's, **lodging:** Day's Inn, Econolodge, Hampton Inn, Holiday Inn Express, Howard Johnson, Motel 6, Quality Inn, Ramada Inn, Sleep Inn, Super 8, Travelodge, **other:** Advance Parts, AutoZone, Buick/Pontiac, CarQuest, CVS Drug, Family$, Food Lion, Rite Aid, Tuesday Morning, Ukrop's Foods

## INTERSTATE 95 CONT'D

**N ↑ ↓ S**

**89**    VA 802, to Lewistown Rd, **E gas:** Shell, TA/Pizza Hut/ Popeye's/dsl/café/24hr/@, **other:** Americamps RV Camp, **W lodging:** Cadillac Motel, **other:** Bass Pro Shops, Kosmo Village Camping, Rolling Hills RV Ctr

**86b a**    VA 656, Elmont, to Atlee, **E gas:** Sheetz, Valero, **food:** Burger King, McDonald's, Waffle House, **other:** CVS Drug, **W food:** CiCi'S Pizza, Jade Chinese, **other:** Gander Mtn, Home Depot, **W on US 1...gas:** 7-11, Shell/dsl, **food:** Applebees, Arby's, Buffalo Wild Wings, Burger King, Chick-fil-A, Chili's, Chipotle Mexican, Chophouse, Famous Dave's BBQ, McDonald's, O'Charley's, Panera Bread, Papa John's, Pizzaro, Quizno's, Red Robin, Ruby Tuesday, Shoney's, Subway, TX Roadhouse, Vinny's Grill, Wendy's, **lodging:** Candlewood Suites, Comfort Suites, Courtyard, Hampton Inn, SpringHill Suites, **other:** Barnes&Noble, Best Buy, Circuit City, Dillard's, Firestone/auto, Goodyear/auto, Home Depot, JC Penney, Macy's, Merchant's Tire, Michael's, Old Navy, PetsMart, Sears/auto, Target, Tire America, Ukrop's Foods, Walgreens, mall

**84b a**    I-295 W, to I-64, to Norfolk

**83b a**    VA 73, Parham Rd, **W gas:** EC/dsl, Exxon/DQ, 7-11, Shell/dsl, **food:** Aunt Sarah's, Burger King, El Paso Mexican, Hardee's, KFC, McDonald's, Papa Lou's, River City Diner, Starbucks, Subway, Waffle House, Wendy's, **lodging:** Econolodge, Holiday Inn, Knight's Inn, Sleep Inn, **other:** BigLots, CVS Drug, Family$, Food Lion, Kroger, Lowes Whse, Walmart SuperCtr

**82**    US 301, Chamberlayne Ave, **E gas:** Exxon/dsl, Sunoco, Texaco, WaWa, **food:** Friendly's, McDonald's, Subway, **lodging:** Days Inn, Super 8, **other:** Food Lion

**81**    US 1, Chamberlayne Ave (from nb), same as 82

**80**    Hermitage Rd, Lakeside Ave (from nb, no return) , **W gas:** EC/Subway, **other:** Goodyear/auto, Ginter Botanical Gardens

**79**    I-64 W, to Charlottesville, I-195 S, to U of Richmond

**78**    Boulevard (no EZ nb return) , **E gas:** BP, **lodging:** Holiday Inn, **W gas:** Citgo/dsl, **food:** Bill's BBQ, **other:** H HOSPITAL, to VA HS, stadium

**76**    Chamberlayne Ave, Belvidere, **E other:** H HOSPITAL, VA Union U

**75**    I-64 E, VA Beach, to Norfolk, airport

**74c**    US 33, US 250 W, to Broad St, **W other:** H HOSPITAL, st capitol, Museum of the Confederacy

**74b**    Franklin St, **E other:** Richmond Nat Bfd Park

**74a**    I-195 N, to Powhite Expswy, downtown

**73.5mm**    James River

**73**    Maury St, to US 60, US 360, industrial area

**69**    VA 161, Bells Rd, **E** Port of Richmond, **W gas:** Exxon/dsl/24hr, Shell/dsl, **food:** McDonald's, Subway, **lodging:** Candlewood Suites, Hampton Inn, Ramada Inn, Red Roof Inn

**67b a**    VA 895 (toll E), VA 150, to Chippenham Pkwy, Falling Creek, **W gas:** Raceway

**64**    VA 613, to Willis Rd, **E gas:** BP, Exxon, **lodging:** Best Value Inn, Econolodge, **other:** Drewry's Bluff Bfd, **W gas:** Chubby's, Citgo, 7-11, Shell/dsl, Sunoco, **food:**

**R I C H M O N D** *(vertical label)*

---

**C H E S T E R** *(vertical label)*

**64**    Continued
Burger King, Hank's BBQ, McDonald's, Subway, **lodging:** Country Inn&Suites, Economy House Motel, La Quinta, Sleep Inn, VIP Inn, **other:** flea mkt

**62**    VA 288 N, to Chesterfield, Powhite Pkwy, to ✈

**61b a**    VA 10, Chester, **E gas:** Raceway, **food:** Don Jose Mexican, Hardee's, **lodging:** Comfort Inn, Courtyard, Hampton Inn, Holiday Inn Express, Homewood Suites, Quality Inn, **other:** H HOSPITAL, to James River Plantations, City Point NHS, Petersburg NBF, **W gas:** BP, EC/dsl, Exxon/dsl, 7-11, Texaco, **food:** Applebees, Burger King, Capt D's, Chili's, CiCi's, Cracker Barrel, Denny's, 5 Guys Burgers, Friendly's, Hardees, Hooter's, IHOP, KFC, McDonald's, O'Charley's, Panera Bread, Pizza Hut, Shoney's, Subway, Taco Bell, UNO, Waffle House, Wendy's, **lodging:** Clarion, Country Inn&Suites, Day's Inn, Fairfield Inn, Super 8, **other:** Aamco, Chevrolet, CVS Drug, $General, $Tree, Food Lion, Home Depot, K-Mart, Kohl's, Lowes Whse, NAPA, PetCo, Rite Aid, Target, Tuesday Morning, Ukrops Foods, to Pocahontas SP

**58**    VA 746, to Ruffinmill Rd, **E other:** Honda, Hyundai, Toyota/Scion, **W gas:** Exxon, **food:** Dunkin Donuts, Subway, **lodging:** Candlewood Suites

**54**    VA 144, Temple Ave, Hopewell, to Ft Lee, **E gas:** BP/24hr, Exxon, Sheetz, Shell, **food:** Applebees, Arby's, Buffalo Wild Wings, Burger King, CicC's Pizza, El Caporal Mexican, 5 Guys Burgers, Golden Corral, Great China, LoneStar Steaks, McDonald's, Olive Garden, Outback Steaks, Panera Bread, Picadilly's, Pizza Hut, Quizno's, Red Lobster, Ruby Tuesday, Starbucks, Subway, Taco Bell, Wendy's, **lodging:** Comfort Suites, Hampton Inn, Hilton Garden, Holiday Inn, **other:** Best Buy, Books-a-Million, Chevrolet/Cadillac/Buick/Nissan, Circuit City, Dillard's, $Tree, Macy's, Home Depot, JC Penney, Jo-Ann Fabrics, KIA, K-Mart, Macy's, Marshall's, Merchant's Tire, Michael's, Nissan, PetsMart, Sam's Club/gas, Sears/auto, Staples, Target, Walmart SuperCtr, mall, **W gas:** Kangaroo, **food:** DQ, Hardee's, Waffle House, **other:** U-Haul, to VSU

**53**    S Park Blvd (from nb) , **E** same as 54

**52.5mm**    Appomattox River

**52**    Washington St, Wythe St, **E gas:** Exxon/dsl, Valero, **food:** Jade Garden, **lodging:** Best Value Inn, Knight's Inn, Red Carpet Inn, Royal Inn, Super 8, Travelodge, **other:** Petersburg Nat Bfd, **W gas:** Liberty, **lodging:** Ramada Inn, Rodeway Inn, **other:** H HOSPITAL

**51**    I-85 S, to South Hill, US 460 W

**50d**    Wythe St, (from nb), same as 52

**50b c**    **E gas:** 7-11, **lodging:** Knight's Inn

**50a**    US 301, US 460 E, to Crater Rd, County Dr, **E gas:** BP, Citgo, RaceWay, **food:** Hardee's, McDonald's, **lodging:** Armada Inn, California Inn, Knight's Inn, Quality Inn, **other:** H HOSPITAL

**48b a**    Wagner Rd, **W on Crater Rd...gas food:** Capt D's, KFC, Pizza Hut, Taste of China, Taco Bell, **other:** Curves, CVS Drug, $Tree, $General, Lincoln/Mercury, Pepboys, Radio Shack, Ukrops Foods, Walgreens, Walmart SuperCtr, vet

**P E T E R S B U R G** *(vertical label)*

**VA** *(corner tab)*

## INTERSTATE 95 CONT'D

N ↕ S

| | |
|---|---|
| 47 | VA 629, to Rives Rd, **W gas:** Citgo, Texaco/dsl, **lodging:** Heritage Motel, **1-2 mi W food:** Arby's, Burger King, Mad Italian, McDonald's, Pizza Hut, Subway, Taco Bell, **lodging:** Crater Inn, LaSalle Motel, **other:** Softball Hall of Fame Museum, same as 48 on US 301 |
| 46 | I-295 N (exits left from sb), to Washington |
| 45 | US 301, **E gas:** Shell/dsl, **W gas:** Exxon, **food:** Lighthouse Rest., Nanny's BBQ, Steven-Kent Rest., **lodging:** Best Western, Comfort Inn, Day's Inn/rest., Hampton Inn, Holiday Inn Express, Quality Inn |
| 41 | US 301, VA 35, VA 156, **E gas:** Chevron/dsl, **lodging:** Econolodge, **other:** South 40 camp resort, **W lodging:** Knight's Inn, Traveler's Inn |
| 40mm | weigh sta both lanes |
| 37 | US 301, Carson, **W gas:** BP/dsl, Shell/dsl |
| 36mm | **rest area nb, full** ♿ **facilities,** 📞**, vending,** 🍴**, litter barrel, petwalk** |
| 33 | VA 602, **W gas:** Chevron/dsl, Davis/Exxon/Subway/Starbucks/dsl/scales/24hr, **food:** Burger King, Denny's/24hr, **lodging:** Hampton Inn, Sleep Inn |
| 31 | VA 40, Stony Creek, to Waverly, **W gas:** Shell/dsl/24hr, Sunoco, **food:** Tastee Hut |
| 24 | VA 645 |
| 20 | VA 631, Jarratt, **W gas:** Exxon/Blimpie/Pizza Hut/dsl/24hr, Race-in/dsl, **other:** Ford |
| 17 | US 301, **1 mi E lodging:** Knight's Inn, Reste Motel, **other:** Jellystone Park Camping |
| 13 | VA 614, to Emporia, **E gas:** Shell/dsl |
| 12 | US 301 (from nb) |
| 11b a | US 58, Emporia, to South Hill, **E gas:** BP/DQ/Subway/dsl, Citgo/Burger King, Exxon/LJ Silver/Stuckey's, Texaco, **food:** Applebee's, Arby's, Cracker Barrel, Hardee's, KFC, McDonald's, Pizza Hut, Wendy's, **lodging:** Country Inn & Suites, Fairfield Inn, Holiday Inn, US Inn, **other:** Ⓗ HOSPITAL, Advance Parts, CVS Drug, $Tree, Family$, Food Lion, NAPA, Radio Shack, Rite Aid, Walmart SuperCtr, **W gas:** Exxon, Petrol, Race-In/dsl, Shell/Sadler/dsl/rest./scales/24hr/@, **food:** Bojangles, Pueblo Viejo, Quizno's, Shoney's, Starbucks, **lodging:** Best Western, Day's Inn, Hampton Inn, Holiday Inn Express, Quality Inn, Sleep Inn |
| 8 | US 301, **E gas:** BP/Simmon's/dsl/rest./scales/24hr, Exxon, **lodging:** Red Carpet Inn, Super 8, **other:** truck repair |
| 4 | VA 629, to Skippers, **E gas:** Loves/McDonald's/dsl/scales/24hr, **W gas:** Shell/dsl, **lodging:** Econolodge, **other:** Cattail Creek Camping (2mi) |
| 3.5mm | Fountain's Creek |
| .5mm | **Welcome Ctr nb, full** ♿ **facilities,** 📞**, vending,** 🍴**, litter barrels, petwalk** |
| 0mm | Virginia/North Carolina state line |

E ↕ M P O R I A (left margin label)

## INTERSTATE 264 - NORFOLK

| Exit # | Services |
|---|---|
| 23mm | I-264 begins/ends, BP, Shell, convention ctr |
| 22 | Birdneck Rd, I-264 begins/ends, **S food:** McDonald's/playplace, **lodging:** DoubleTree Hotel, **other:** museum |

E ↕ W

| | |
|---|---|
| 21 | VA Beach Blvd, First Colonial Rd, **N gas:** BP, Shell, **food:** Applebee's, Burger King, McDonald's, Outback Steaks, Taco Bell, Target, Wendy's, Virginian Steaks, **other:** Borders Books, K-Mart, **S other:** 7-11, NAPA |
| 20 | US 58 E, to VA Beach Blvd (eb only), **N food:** Capt. George's Seafood, China Moon, Hardee's, Ruby Tuesday, Tuesday Morning, **other:** Family$, Food Lion, Lincoln/Mercury, Lowe's Whse, 7-11, TJ Maxx |
| 19 | Lynnhaven Pkwy, **N gas:** 7-11, Wawa, **food:** Mauie Wowie, Moe's SW Grill, Quizno's, Subway, **other:** Audi, Ford, Jaguar, PepBoys, Porsche, VW, **S food:** McDonald's |
| 18 | Rosemont, **N gas:** BJ's Whse, Exxon, **food:** Bonefish Grill, Burger King, Denny's, Hardee's, KFC, LJ Silver, McDonald's, Mi Casita Mexican, Papa John's, Taco Bell, Wendy's, **lodging:** Econolodge, Nissan, Radio Shack, **other:** Food Lion, Harris Teeter, Home Depot, Honda, Kroger, Merchant's Tire/Auto, Rite Aid, Sam's Club/gas, Walgreens, **S gas:** Hess/dsl, Shell, Wawa, **food:** Four Seasons Chinese, **other:** Chrysler/Dodge |
| 17.5mm | wb only, inspection sta |
| 17a b | Independance Blvd, **N gas:** Exxon, **food:** Fuddruckers, Macaroni Grill, Max & Erma's, McDonald's, Smokey Bones BBQ, Starbucks, Taco Bell, Tripps Rest., Wendy's, Village Inn, **lodging:** Crowne Plaza, Extended Stay, Motel 6, **other:** Best Buy, Circuit City, Sears/auto, **S gas:** BP, Exxon, 7-11/gas, Wawa, **food:** Arby's, Azteca Mexican, Golden Corral, Hardee's, KFC, Quizno's, Starbucks, Wing Zone, **lodging:** InTown Suites, **other:** $General, Food Lion, Mazda, Rite Aid |
| 16 | Witchduck |
| 15a b | Newtown Rd, **N gas:** Citgo, Crown Royal, **food:** Domino's, McDonald's, Wendy's, **lodging:** Homewood Suites, TownePlace Suites, **S gas:** BP, Shell, **food:** Denny's, Ruby Tuesday, **lodging:** Courtyard, Hampton Inn, Holiday Inn, La Quinta, Red Roof Inn, SpringHill Suites, **other:** Rite Aid, 7-11 |
| 14b a | I-64. US 13, to Military Hwy |
| 13 | US 13, Military Hwy, **N gas:** Shell, **food:** Arbys, Great Steak, Lonestar Steaks, Mihogar Mexican, Piccadilly, Schlotzky's, **lodging:** Best Value, Day's Inn, Econolodge, Motel 6, Ramada Ltd, **other:** Firestone/auto, JC Penny, Ross, Sears/auto, |
| 12 | Ballentine Blvd, **N other:** Ⓗ HOSPITAL, Norfolk SU |

VA

## INTERSTATE 264 CONT'D - NORFOLK

**11b a** US 460, VA 166/168, Brambleton Ave, Campostello Rd, **N gas:** 7-11/gas, Shell

**10** Tidewater Dr, City Hall Ave, downtown

**9** St Paul's Blvd, Waterside Dr, to Harbor Park Stadium

**8** I-464 S, to Chesapeake

**7.5mm** tunnel

**7b a** VA 141, Effingham St, Crawford St, **N gas:** 7-11, **food:** Hardees, **other:** Naval H HOSPITAL, **S other:** Shipyard

**6.5mm** weigh sta eb

**6** Des Moines Ave (from eb)

**5** US 17, Frederick Blvd, Midtown Tunnel, **N** HOSPITAL, **S gas:** BP, **other:** Harley-Davidson

**4** VA 337, Portsmouth Blvd

**3** Victory Blvd, **N gas:** Exxon, 7-11/gas, Wawa, **food:** Capt D's, DQ, Domino's, McDonald's, Pizza Hut, Ruby Tuesday, Wendy's, **other:** AutoZone, BigLots, $Tree, FarmFresh Food/drug, Ford, Lowe's Whse, PepBoys, Radio Shack, **S gas:** Valero/dsl

**2b a** Greenwood Dr

**0mm** I-264 begins/ends on I-64, exit 299.

## INTERSTATE 295 - RICHMOND

| Exit # | Services |
|---|---|

**53b a** I-64, W to Charlottesville, E to Richmond, to US 250, I-295 begins/ends.

**51b a** Nuckols Rd, **1 mi N gas:** Miller's Gas/dsl, Valero, **food:** Bottoms Up Pizza, Bruster's, Cheeburger, Chen's Chinese, McDonald's, Nonna's Pizzaria, Salsarita's Cantina, Smoothie Cafe, Starbucks, Subway, **other:** CVS Drug, Food Lion, Walgreens, vet, **S gas:** Exxon, **food:** Capital Alehouse, Mkt Cafe, **other:** USPO

**49b a** US 33, Richmond, **1 mi S food:** Carbel's Ice Cream, Quizno's, **other:** Ukrop's Foods

**45b a** Woodman Rd, **1-2 mi S gas:** 7-11, Valero, Little Caesar's, **other:** CVS Drug, $General, Meadow Farm Museum

**43** I-95, US 1, N to Washington, S to Richmond (exits left from nb), **N on US 1...gas:** 7-11, Shell/dsl, **food:** Applebees, Arby's, Buffalo Wild Wings, Burger King, Chick-fil-A, Chili's, Chipotle Mexican, Chophouse, Famous Dave's BBQ, McDonald's, O'Charley's, Panera Bread, Papa John's, Pizzaro, Quizno's, Red Robin, Ruby Tuesday, Shoney's, Subway, TX Roadhouse, Vinny's Grill, Wendy's, **lodging:** Candlewood Suites, Comfort Suites, Courtyard, Hampton Inn, SpringHill Suites, **other:** Barnes&Noble, Best Buy, Circuit City, Dillard's, Firestone/auto, Goodyear/auto, Home Depot, JC Penney, Macy's, Merchant's Tire, Michael's, Old Navy, PetsMart, Sears/auto, Target, Tire America, Ukrop's Foods, Walgreens, mall, **1-2 mi S gas:** Exxon, EC/dsl, 7-11, Shell, WaWa/dsl, **food:** Aunt Sarah's, Burger King, El Paso Mexican, Hardee's, McDonald's, Subway, Waffle House, Wendy's, **lodging:** Broadway Motel, Cavalier Motel, Econolodge, GuestHouse Inn,

**43** Continued
Howard Johnson, Knight's Inn, **other:** Aamco, Food Lion, Firestone, Lowes Whse, Rite Aid, Walmart SuperCtr

**41b a** US 301, VA 2, **E gas:** BP/dsl, Valero, **food:** Burger King, McDonald's, Subway, **W gas:** Exxon/dsl, **food:** Friendly's, **lodging:** Holiday Inn, Super 8, Travelodge

**38b a** VA 627, Pole Green Rd, **E gas:** BP/Miller's Mkt/dsl, Exxon (1mi), 7-11, **food:** Bruster's, Chen's Rest., Coffee Lane, Mimmo's Rest., Nacho Mamas, Subway, **other:** Curves, Food Lion, vet, **W gas:** 7-11, Valero

**37b a** US 360, **1 mi E gas:** Shell/dsl, Texaco, **food:** Applebees, Arby's, Buffalo Wild Wings, Chick-fil-A, Cracker Barrel, IHOP, KFC, McDonald's, Moe's SW Grill, Noodles&Co, Outback Steaks, Panera Bread, Ruby Tuesday, Starbucks, Super Buffet, Taco Bell, Waffle House, Wendy's, **lodging:** Hampton Inn, Holiday Inn Express, **other:** Best Buy, BJ's Whse/Gas, $General, $Tree, GNC, Home Depot, Kohl's, Marshall's, PetsMart, Radio Shack, Target, Ukrops Foods, Walmart SuperCtr, **W gas:** 7-11, Sunoco, Valero, **other:** to Mechanicsville

**34b a** VA 615, Creighton Rd, **E gas:** 7-11, Valero

**31b a** VA 156, **E gas:** Citgo/dsl, **other:** to Cold Harbor Bfd

**28** I-64, to US 60, **W other:** museum

**25** rd 895 W (toll), to Richmond, **E gas:** Shell, Valero, **food:** Dunkin Donuts

**22b a** VA 5, Charles City, **E gas:** Exxon/dsl, **food:** DQ, **other:** Shirley Plantation, **W gas:** Valero/dsl, **food:** Portabella's Cafe, **other:** Food Lion, Richmond Nat Bfd

**18mm** James River

**15b a** VA 10, Hopewell, **E gas:** BP/dsl, **food:** Burger King, **lodging:** Evergreen Motel (3mi), **other:** H HOSPITAL, James River Plantations, **W gas:** EC/Subway/dsl, Exxon/dsl, Sheetz, WaWa, **food:** Chen's Rest., McDonald's, River's Bend Cafe, Wendy's, **lodging:** Hyatt Place, **other:** Curves, CVS Drug, Food Lion, 7-11, vet

**13mm** Appomattox River

**9b a** VA 36, Hopewell, **E gas:** Chevron, Petrol, WaWa, **food:** Bojangles, El Nopal Mexican, Hardees, Hong Kong's Rest., Huddle House, KFC, Little Caesar's, Rosa's Italian, **lodging:** Best Western, Econolodge, Fairfield Inn, Stayover Suites, **other:** Advance Parts, AutoZone, Family$, Walgreens, vet, **W gas:** BP/dsl/24hr, Shell, Valero, **food:** Burger King, Denny's, DQ, Dunkin Donuts, McDonald's, Papa John's, Pizza Hut, Ruby Tuesday, Shoney's, Subway, Taco Bell, Waffle House, Wendy's, **lodging:** Candlewood Suites, Comfort Inn, Hampton Inn, Quality Inn, **other:** Chevrolet, $General, Family$, Food Lion, Rite Aid, U-Haul, US Army Museum, to Petersburg NBF

**5.5mm** Blackwater Swamp

**3b a** US 460, Petersburg, to Norfolk, **E gas:** EC/dsl, Hess, Texaco, **food:** Prince George BBQ, Subway, Wendy's, **1-2 mi W gas:** BP/dsl, **food:** Hardee's, McDonald's

**1** I-95, N to Petersburg, S to Emporium, I-295 begins/ends.

MECHANICSVILLE

HOPEWELL

VA

**N ↑↓ S**

**DC AREA**

## INTERSTATE 495 - DC

| Exit # | Services |
|---|---|
| 27 | I-95, N to Baltimore, S to Richmond. I-495 & I-95 S run together. |
| 28b a | MD 650, New Hampshire Ave, **N** gas: Citgo, Exxon/dsl, Shell/repair, **food:** Domino's, Quizno's, Starbucks, Urban BBQ, **other:** CVS Drug, Radio Shack, Safeway, 7-11 |
| 29b a | MD 193, University Blvd |
| 30b a | US 29, Colesville, **N** gas: BP, Getty, Shell, **food:** McDonald's, Subway, **other:** CVS Drug, Safeway, 7-11/Jerry's Subs |
| 31b a | MD 97, Georgia Ave, Silver Springs, **N** gas: H HOSPITAL, **S** gas: CG Gas, Chevron, Exxon/dsl, Shell, **food:** Domino's, Mayflower Chinese, **other:** CVS Drug, Snider's Foods, Staples |
| 33 | MD 185, Connecticut Ave, **N other:** LDS Temple, **S** gas: Citgo/repair, Liberty, Sunoco, **food:** Chevy Chase Foods |
| 34 | MD 355, Wisconsin Ave, Bethesda |
| 35 | (from wb), I-270 |
| 36 | MD 187, Old Georgetown Rd, **S other:** H HOSPITAL |
| 38 | I-270, to Frederick |
| 39 | MD 190, River Rd, Washington, Potomac |
| 40 | Cabin John Pkwy, Glen Echo (from sb), no trucks |
| 41 | Clara Barton Pkwy, Carderock, Great Falls, no trucks |
| 42mm | **Potomac River, Virginia/Maryland state line. Exits 41-27 are in Maryland.** |
| 43 | G Washington Mem Pkwy, no trucks |
| 44 | VA 193, Langley |
| 45b a | VA 267 W (toll), to I-66 E, to Dulles Airport |
| 46b a | VA 123, Chain Bridge Rd, **W lodging:** Hilton |
| 47b a | VA 7, Leesburg Pike, Tysons Corner, Falls Church, **E lodging:** Westin, **W** gas: BP/dsl, Exxon, Shell, **food:** Chili's, McDonald's, NY Deli, Olive Garden, On-the-Border, Panera Bread, Pizza Hut, Starbucks, Wendy's, **lodging:** Best Western, Courtyard, Marriott, **other:** Best Buy, Borders Books, Chevrolet/Chrysler, Ford, Marshall's, Merchant's Tire, PetCo, Staples, Subaru, mall |
| 49c b a | I-66 (exits left from both lanes), to Manassas, Front Royal |
| 50b a | US 50, Arlington Blvd, Fairfax, Arlington, **E lodging:** Marriott, **E** gas: Shell, Sunoco, **food:** Chevy's Mexican, KFC, McDonald's, Panda Express, Panera Bread, Wendy's, **lodging:** Residence Inn, **other:** H HOSPITAL, CVS Drug |
| 51 | VA 657, Gallows Rd, **W** gas: Exxon, **other:** H HOSPITAL, 7-11 |
| 52b a | VA 236, Little River Tpk, Fairfax, **N** gas: Citgo, Sunoco/repair, **food:** La Fondita, McDonald's, Wendy's, **other:** 7-11 |
| 54b a | VA 620, Braddock Rd, Ctr for the Arts, Geo Mason U, **S** gas: Sunoco, **food:** DQ, **other:** NTB, Rite Aid, Safeway |
| 56c b a | I-95 S, I-395 N, I-95 N. I-495 & I-95 N run together. |

## INTERSTATE 664 - PORTSMOUTH

**N ↑↓ S**

**PORTSMOUTH**

| Exit # | Services |
|---|---|
| 15b a | I-64 th Chesapeake, I-264 E to Portsmouth & Norfolk., I-664 begins/ends on I-64, exit 299. |
| 13b a | US 13, US 58, US 460, Military Hwy, **E** gas: Shell/dsl, **lodging:** Econolodge |
| 12 | VA 663, Dock Landing Rd |
| 11b a | VA 337, Portsmouth Blvd, **E** gas: BP, 7-11, Shell/dsl, **food:** Applebees, Arby's, Backyard Burger, Burger King, Chick-fil-A, ChuckeCheese, Fazoli's, KFC, McDonald's, Outback Steaks, Pizza Hut, Red Lobster, Red Robin, Taco Bell, **lodging:** Hampton Inn, Holiday Inn Express, Springhill Suites, **other:** AutoZone, Dodge, $Tree, Home Depot, JC Penny, K-Mart, Michael's, PetsMart, Sears/auto |
| 10 | VA 659, Pughsville Rd, **E** gas: 7-11, Shell, **food:** IHOP, McDonald's |
| 9b a | US 17, US 164, **E** gas: Hess, 7-11, Wa Wa, **food:** Captain D's, DQ, Dunkin Donuts, Sonic, **lodging:** Budget Lodge, Hampton Inn, Sleep Inn, Super 8, **other:** H HOSPITAL, Chevrolet, Farm Fresh Foods, Honda, Nissan, tires, **W** to James River Br, museum |
| 8b a | VA 135, College Dr, **E** gas: 7-11, Shell/Burger King, **food:** Applebees, Firehouse Subs, McDonald's, Panchero's Mexican, Ruby Tuesday, Subway, Wendy's, **other:** FoodLion, Kohl's, Radio Shack, Staples, Walmart SuperCtr, **W food:** Riverstone Chophouse, **lodging:** Courtyard, TownePlace Suites |
| 11.5mm | insp sta nb |
| 9mm | James River |
| 8mm | tunnel |
| 7 | Terminal Ave |
| 6 | 25th St, 26th St, **E** gas: 7-11, **food:** McDonald's |
| 5 | US 60 W, 35th St, Jefferson Ave, **E** gas: Citgo, **food:** Church's, Pizza Palace |
| 4 | Chesnut Ave, Roanoke Ave |
| 3 | Aberdeen Rd, **E** gas: Zooms/dsl, **W food:** Hardee's, McDonald's, Wendy's |
| 2 | Powhatan Pkwy, **E** gas: 7-11, **1-2 mi W** gas: BJ's Whse, **food:** Coldstone Creamery, Cracker Barrel, Joe's Crabshack, Lonstar Steaks, McFadden's Rest., **lodging:** Hilton Garden, **other:** Bass Pro Shop, Lowe's Whse |
| 1b a | I-64, W to Richmond, E to Norfolk. I-664 begins/ends on I-64. |

VA

## INTERSTATE 5

| Exit # | Services |
|---|---|

**BLAINE N ↑ S**

**277mm** USA/Canada Border, Washington state line, customs

**276** WA 548 S, Blaine, **E gas:** Shell/dsl, Texaco/dsl, USA/dsl/24hr, **food:** Big Al's Diner, **other:** Duty Free, to Peace Arch SP, **W gas:** Chevron/repair, **food:** Chada Thai, Pizza Factory, Seaside Bakery, Subway, **lodging:** Anchor Inn, Bayside Motel, Cottage by the Bay B&B, International Motel/cafe, Sunset Inn, **other:** Coast to Coast Hardware, NAPA

**275** WA 543 N (from nb, no return), truck customs, **E gas:** Chevron/dsl, Exxon/dsl, Shell/dsl, **food:** Burger King, **other:** Ace Hardware, CostCutter Foods, $Tree, Rite Aid, vet

**274** Peace Portal Drive (from nb, no return), Blaine, **W gas:** Shell, **other:** Semi-ah-moo Resort, camping

**270** Birch Bay, Lynden, **W gas:** Shell/Domino's/Subway/dsl/24hr, **food:** Bob's Burgers, Jack-in-the-Box, **lodging:** Semi-ah-moo Resort, **other:** Birch Bay Outlet/famous brands, Curves, Lighthouse RV Park (5mi), Mkt Foods, vet

**269mm** **Welcome Ctr sb, full 🚹 facilities, info, 📞, 🍴, litter barrels, petwalk, vending**

**267mm** **rest area nb, full 🚹 facilities, info, 📞, 🍴, litter barrels, petwalk, vending**

**266** WA 548 N, Grandview Rd, Custer, **W gas:** Arco/24hr, **other:** Birch Bay SP

**263** Portal Way, **E gas:** Pacific Pride/dsl, Shell/dsl, **other:** AA RV Park, Cedars RV Park

**263mm** Nooksack River

**262** Main St, Ferndale, **E gas:** 76/dsl, Texaco/dsl, **food:** Denny's, McDonald's, Subway, **lodging:** Super 8, **other:** RV Park, TDS Tires, **W gas:** Gull/dsl, 76, Shell/Domino's/dsl, **food:** Asian Bistro, Bob's Burgers, DQ, Quizno's, Sonic, **lodging:** Scottish Lodge, **other:** Costcutter Foods, Haggen's Foods, NAPA, Schwab Tire, Walgreens, vet

**260** Slater Rd, Lummi Island, **E gas:** Arco/24hr, **other:** El Monte RV Ctr, antiques, **4 mi W gas:** 76, Shell/dsl, **lodging:** Silver Reef Hotel/Casino, **other:** Lummi Ind Res

**258** Bakerview Rd, **E food:** Magic Dragon, Subway, **other:** Fred Meyer/gas, **W gas:** Arco/24hr, 76, **food:** Mykono's Greek Rest., **lodging:** Hampton Inn, Shamrock Motel, **other:** Bellingham RV Park, airport, st patrol

**257** Northwest Ave, **E other:** Cadillac/Chevrolet

**256b** Bellis Fair Mall Pkwy, **E other:** Sears, Target, mall

**256a** WA 539 N, Meridian St, **E gas:** Meridian, Shell/dsl, Super Gas, **food:** Arby's, Burger King, China Palace, Coldstone Creamery, Denny's, Kowloon Garden, Lorenzo's Italian, McHale's Rest., Olive Garden, Pad Thai, Quizno's, Red Robin, Shari's/24hr, Starbucks, Subway, Taco Bell, Taco Del Mar, Taco Time, Wendy's, **lodging:** Best Western, Comfort Inn, Holiday Inn Express La Quinta, Quality Inn, **other:** AAA, Barnes&Noble, Best Buy, Circuit City, Costco/gas, Costcutter Foods, $Tree, Home Depot, JC Penney, Macy's, Michael's, Nordstrom's, Office Depot, PetCo, Rite Aid, Ross, Safeway, Schuck's Parts, Schwab Tire, Sears, Target, TJ Maxx, U-haul, Walgreens, Walmart/auto, mall, st patrol, to Nooksack Ind Res, **W food:** Eleni's Rest., **lodging:** Econolodge, Rodeway Inn

**BELLINGHAM**

**255** WA 542 E, Sunset Dr, Bellingham, **E gas:** Chevron/dsl/24hr, 76, Shell/Subway/Domino's/dsl, **food:** A&W/KFC, Applebees, Domino's, Hawaii BBQ, Jack-in-the-Box, Panda Express, RoundTable Pizza, Taco Bell, **other:** Costcutter Foods, Jo-Ann Fabrics, K-Mart, Lowes Whse, Tuesday Morning, Walgreens, USPO, to Mt Baker, **W other:** 🏥 HOSPITAL

**254** Iowa St, State St, Bellingham, **E gas:** 76, Valero, **other:** Audi/VW, Honda, Hyundai, Mercedes, Kia, Nissan, Toyota/Scion, Vacation Land RV Ctr, Volvo, **W gas:** Chevron/24hr, Shell, **food:** DQ, McDonald's, Skipper's Rest., Subway, **other:** Chrysler/Dodge, Ford/Lincoln/Mercury, NAPA, Schuck's Parts, Subaru, repair

**253** Lakeway Dr, Bellingham, **E food:** Burger Me, Lychee Buffet, Little Caesar's, Papa Murphy's, Port of Subs, Sol de Mexico, Subway, **lodging:** Best Western, Guesthouse Inn, **other:** Costcutter Foods, Discount Tire, Fred Meyer, Radio Shack, 7-11, **W** same as 252

**252** Samish Way, Bellingham, **E lodging:** Evergreen Motel, **other:** same as 253, **W gas:** Chevron, Mobil, 76, Shell/dsl/24hr, **food:** Arby's, Diego's Mexican, 5 Columns Steaks, IHOP, McDonald's, Pizza Hut, Pizza Pipeline, Popeye's, Quizno's, Starbucks, Taco Time, Thai Cuisine, Wendy's, **lodging:** Bay City Motel, Cascade Inn, Coachman Inn, Days Inn, Mac's Motel, Motel 6, Travelodge, Villa Inn, **other:** Haggen Foods, Rite Aid

**250** WA 11 S, Chuckanut Dr, Bellingham, Fairhaven Hist Dist, **W gas:** Arco, Chevron/repair, **other:** Food Pavilion, Larrabee SP, to Alaska Ferry, vet

**246** N Lake Samish, **W gas:** Shell/dsl, **other:** Lake Padden RA, RV camping

**242** Nulle Rd, S Lake Samish

**240** Alger, **E gas:** Shell/dsl/LP/RV dump, **food:** Alger Grille, **lodging:** Whispering Firs Motel/RV Parking

**238mm** **rest area both lanes, full 🚹 facilities, 📞, 🍴, litter barrels, vending, petwalk**

**236** Bow Hill Rd, **E** Skagit Hotel Casino/rest./dsl/LP

**235mm** weigh sta sb

**234mm** Samish River

**232** Cook Rd, Sedro-Woolley, **E gas:** 76/Subway/dsl, Shell/dsl, **food:** Bob's Burgers, Jack-in-the-Box, **lodging:** Fairfield Inn, **other:** 🏥 HOSPITAL, KOA

**231** WA 11 N, Chuckanut Dr, **E other:** Camping World RV Ctr, Kia, st patrol, **W** to Larrabee SP (14mi)

**230** WA 20, Burlington, **E gas:** Shell/dsl, **food:** Burger King, Cascade Brewery Rest., China Wok, El Cazador, Jack-in-the-Box, Krispy Kreme, Outback Steaks, Pizza Factory, Red Robin, Subway, **lodging:** Cocusa Motel, Sterling Motel, **other:** 🏥 HOSPITAL, Fred Meyer, Haggen Foods, JC Penney, Macy's, Schwab Tire, Sears/auto, 7-11, Target, mall, transmissions, to N Cascades NP, **W food:** McDonald's, **lodging:** Holiday Inn Express, Mark II Motel, **other:** Harley-Davidson, Hyundai, to San Juan Ferry

**BURLINGTON**

**229** George Hopper Rd, **E gas:** Arco/24hr, USA/dsl, **food:** Jamba Juice, McDonald's, Olive Garden, Sakura Japanese, Shari's, Starbucks, Subway, Taco Del Mar, Wendy's, **lodging:** Hampton Inn, **other:** Best Buy, Costco/gas, Costcutter Foods, Discount Tire, Home Depot, K-Mart, Kohl's, NAPA, Old Navy, PetsMart, Outlet Shops/famous brands, Ross, Saturn, See's Candies, Sportsman's Whse, **W other:** Buick/Pontiac, Cadillac, Chrysler/Jeep/Dodge, Ford, Mazda/Honda, Nissan, Toyota/Scion, Subaru, VW, RV Ctr

<table>
</table>

**INTERSTATE 5 CONT'D**

**M T V E R N O N**  **N ↕ S**

**228mm** Skagit River

**227** WA 538 E, College Way, Mt Vernon, **E gas:** 76, **food:** A&W, Big Scoop Rest., Denny's, Jack-in-the-Box, KFC, La Hacienda, Pizza Hut/Taco Bell, Quizno's, Round Table Pizza, Skipper's, Taco Time, **lodging:** Best Western, Day's Inn, West Winds Motel, **other:** Ace Hardware, AutoZone, Buick/Cadillac/GMC, $Plus, $Tree, Goodyear/auto, Jo-Ann Fabrics, Office Depot, PetCo, Rite Aid, Safeway/gas, Schuck's Parts, ValueVillage Foods, Walmart/auto, **W gas:** FuelExpress/24hr, Shell/dsl, **food:** Arby's, Burger King, Cranberry Tree Rest., DQ, Forks&Knives Steaks, Fortune Chinese, Royal Fork Buffet, **lodging:** Best Western, Quality Inn, Tulip Inn, **other:** Chevrolet, Lowes Whse

**226** WA 536 W, Kincaid St, City Ctr, **E** H HOSPITAL, **W food:** Old Towne Grainery Rest., Skagit River Brewing Co, **other:** NAPA, Red Apple Foods, Valley RV Ctr, RV camping, antiques

**225** Anderson Rd, **E gas:** Fuel Express, 76/dsl, **other:** Lifestyles RV Ctr, **other:** transmissions, **W gas:** Truck City Trkstp/dsl, Valero, **food:** Long Haul Cafe, **other:** Freightliner, Pulsbo RV Ctr, Valley RV Ctr

**224** WA 99 S (from nb, no return), S Mt Vernon, **E** gas/dsl, food

**221** WA 534 E, Conway, Lake McMurray, **E gas:** Shell/dsl/24hr, **W gas:** 76/dsl, Texaco/dsl, **food:** Conway Deli, **lodging:** Channel Lodge/Rest. (11mi), **other:** Blake's RV Park/marina (6mi)

**218** Starbird Rd, **W lodging:** Hillside Motel

**215** 300th NW, **W gas:** Interstate/dsl

**214mm** weigh sta nb

**212** WA 532 W, Stanwood, Bryant, **W gas:** 76/dsl, Shell/dsl, **other:** Camano Island SP (19mi)

**210** 236th NE, **E other:** Casino

**209mm** Stillaguamish River

**208** WA 530, Silvana, Arlington, **E gas:** Chevron/24hr, 76/Circle K, Shell, Tesoro, **food:** Denny's, O'Brien Turkeyhouse, **lodging:** Arlington Motel, **other:** H HOSPITAL, to N Cascades Hwy, **W gas:** 76/dsl

**207mm** rest area both lanes, full facilities, litter barrels, coffee, vending, RV dump, petwalk

**206** WA 531, Lakewood, **E gas:** Arco/24hr, Shell/24hr, 7-11, **food:** Alfy's Pizza, Baskin-Robbins, Buzz Inn Steaks, Domino's, Jack-in-the-Box, KFC, La Corona Mexican, McDonald's, Olympia Pizza, Quizno's, Starbucks, Subway, Taco Del Mar, Taco Time, Wienerscnitzel, Wendy's, **lodging:** Hawthorn Suites, Smokey Point Motel, **other:** Buick/GMC/Pontiac, Chrysler/Dodge/Jeep, $Plus, Harley Davidson, Lowes Whse, Rite Aid, Safeway/gas/24hr, Schuck's Parts, **W gas:** Chevron/24hr, **food:** Bajio, Boston's Rest., IHOP, Jamba Juice, Paradise Grill, Pizza Hut, Red Robin, Taco Bell, Village Rest., **other:** Best Buy, Costco/gas, Discount Tire, Marshall's, Michael's, Office Depot, PetCo, Target, to Wenburg SP

**202** 116th NE, **E gas:** 76/dsl, Shell/dsl, Texaco, **food:** Carl's Jr, Magic Dragon Chinese, Starbucks, Subway, Taco Bell, **other:** Albertson's, Kohl's, PetCo, Rite Aid, Ross, WinCo Foods, **W gas:** Donna's Trkstp/Gull/dsl/scales/24hr/@, **food:** McDonald's, **other:** Seattle Premium Outlets/famous brands, st patrol

**200** 88th St NE, Quil Ceda Way, **E gas:** 7-11, 76, Shell/dsl/LP, **food:** Applebees, Neapolis Rest., Quizno's, Starbucks, **lodging:** Holiday Inn Express, **other:** Haggen's Foods/24hr, **W food:** Bob's Burgers, Port of Subs, Taco Del Mar, **other:** Home Depot, Walmart/SuperCtr/gas, casino

**199** WA 528 E, Marysville, Tulalip, **E gas:** Arco/24hr, Chevron/24hr, 76, Shell/dsl, **food:** Burger King, Don's Rest./24hr, DQ, Jack-in-the-Box, Jumbo Buffet, Las Margaritas Mexican, **lodging:** Village Motel/Rest., **other:** Albertson's, Big O Tire, JC Penney, Rite Aid,

Copyright 2009 - The Next Exit®

## INTERSTATE 5 CONT'D

**N ↕ S**

**EVERETTE**

**SEATTLE**

**199** Continued
Schuck's Parts, Staples, **W gas:** 76, **food:** Arby's, McDonald's, Taco Time, Wendy's, **lodging:** Best Western/rest., Comfort Inn, **other:** Chevrolet/Subaru, Robinson RV Ctr, to Tulalip Indian Res

**198** Port of Everett (from sb), Steamboat Slough, st patrol

**195mm** Snohomish River

**195** Port of Everett (from nb), Marine View Dr

**194** US 2 E, Everett Ave, City Ctr, **W gas:** Shell/dsl, **other:** Schwab Tire

**193** WA 529, Pacific Ave (from nb) , **W gas:** Chevron, 76, **food:** Denny's, **lodging:** Best Western, Holiday Inn, Marina Village Inn (3mi), Travelodge, **other:** Ⓗ HOSPITAL, Lowes Whse

**192** Broadway, to Evergreen Way, City Ctr, **W gas:** Arco/24hr, Chevron, 76, Shell, Texaco, **food:** Alfy's Pizza, Buzz Inn Steaks, IHOP, Iver's Seafood, Jack-in-the-Box, McDonald's, O'Donnell's Café, Starbucks, Subway, Taco Bell, **lodging:** Days Inn, ravelodge, **other:** Ford

**189** WA 526 W, WA 527, Everett Mall Way, Everett, **E gas:** Arco/24hr, Chevron, Shell/dsl, **food:** Alfy's Pizza, Burger King, Buzz Inn Steaks, McDonald's, Subway, Wendy's, **lodging:** Travelodge, **other:** Costco/gas, vet, **W gas:** Shell, **lodging:** Days Inn, Extended Stay America, Motel 6, **other:** Goodyear/auto, Macy's, mall

**188mm** rest area/weigh sta sb, full ♿ facilities, info, Ⓒ, 🅿, litter barrels, coffee, RV dump

**186** WA 96, 128th SW, **E gas:** 76, Shell/dsl/24hr, Texaco, **food:** O'Donnells Rest., **lodging:** Quality Inn, **other:** Lakeside RV Park, Silver Lake RV Park, **W gas:** Arco/24hr, Chevron/24hr, 7-11, Shell, **food:** A&W/KFC, Acropolis Pizza, DQ, Denny's, McDonald's, Ming Dynasty, Mitzel's Kitchen, Papa John's, Pizza Hut, Skipper's, Starbucks, Taco Bell, Taco Time, **lodging:** Holiday Inn Express, La Quinta, Motel 6, **other:** Albertson's/Sav-on, $Tree, Goodyear/auto, Maple RV Park, transmissions

**183** 164th SW, **E gas:** Arco, Shell/dsl/24hr, **food:** Jack-in-the-Box/24hr, Panda Express, Quizno's, Starbucks, Subway, Taco Del Mar, Taco Time, **other:** Curves, Radio Shack, Walgreens, Walmart, **W gas:** Shell/dsl

**182** WA 525, Alderwood Mall Blvd, to Alderwood Mall, **E** I-405 S, to Bellevue, **W gas:** Arco/24hr, **food:** Keg Steaks/seafood, Panera Bread, PF Chang's, Red Robin, Subway, TCBY, **lodging:** Residence Inn, **other:** Border's Books, JC Penney, Kohl's, Macy's, Marshall's, Michael's, Nordstrom's, Sears/auto, Target, Evans Tire

**181** 44th Ave W, to WA 524, Lynnwood, **E gas:** Arco, 76, Shell, **food:** Little Caesar's, McDonald's, Old Spaghetti Factory, Papa Murphy's, Wok Inn, **lodging:** Embassy Suites, Extended Stay America, Hampton Inn, **other:** Albertson's, Barnes&Noble, Best Buy, Circuit City, Land Rover, Lowes Whse, Old Navy, PetCo, Staples, **W gas:** Arco, Chevron/24hr, 76/dsl, Shell/repair, **food:** Alfy's Pizza, Applebees, Arby's, Azteca Mexican, Barbara's Cafe, Black Angus, Buca Italian, Chevy's Mexican, Chipotle Mexican, Denny's, IHOP, Jack-in-the-Box, KFC, McDonald's, Old Country Buffet, Olive Garden, Panda Express, Red Lobster, Rock Grill, Starbucks, Subway, Taco Bell, Taco Del Mar, Taco Time, Tony Roma's, Wendy's,

**SEATTLE**

**SEATTLE**

**181** Continued
**lodging:** Best Western, Comfort Inn, Courtyard, Holiday Inn Express, La Quinta, **other:** AAA, Firestone/auto, Fred Meyer, Goodyear/auto, Grocery Outlet, Radio Shack, Schwab Tire, 7-11, mall, USPO, vet

**179** 220th SW, Mountlake Terrace, Mountlake Terrace, **W gas:** Shell/dsl, **food:** Azteca Mexican, Port of Subs, Subway, **other:** Ⓗ HOSPITAL, Curves, vet

**178** 236th St SW (from nb), Mountlake Terrace

**177** WA 104, Edmonds, **E gas:** Chevron/24hr, Shell/dsl, **food:** Canyons Rest., McDonald's, Starbucks, Subway, **lodging:** Studio 6, **other:** Office Depot, RiteAid, Schuck's Parts, Thriftway Foods, **1-2 mi W on WA 99**... **gas:** 76/dsl, **food:** A&W, Arby's, Barlee's Rest., Denny's, KFC, Scott's Grill, Starbucks, **lodging:** Day's Inn, **other:** Costco, Discount Tire, GNC, Home Depot, Nissan, PetCo, Radio Shack, VW

**176** NE 175th St, Aurora Ave N, to Shoreline

**175** WA 523, NE 145th, 5th Ave NE

**174** NE 130th, Roosevelt Way

**173** 1st Ave NE, Northgate Way, **E gas:** 76, **food:** Azteca Mexican, California Pizza Kitchen, Chipotle Mexican, Macaroni Grill, Marie Calender's, Panera Bread, Quizno's, Ram Rest., Stanford's Rest., Super Buffet, Taco Del Mar, **other:** Barnes&Noble, Best Buy, Curves, Discount Tire, JC Penney, Macys, Nordstrom's, Ross, Target, mall, **W gas:** 76, Shell/dsl, **food:** Arby's, McDonald's, Pizza Xpress, Saffron Grill, Starbucks, **lodging:** Hotel Nexus, **other:** 7-11

**172** N 85th, Aurora Ave

**171** WA 522, Lake City Way, Bothell

**170** (nb only) Ravenna Blvd, **E gas:** Shell/dsl

**169** NE 45th, NE 50th, **E gas:** 76, Shell, **food:** Subway, **other:** Ⓗ HOSPITAL, PetCo, U of WA, **W other:** to Seattle Pacific U, zoo

**168b** WA 520, to Bellevue

**168a** Lakeview Blvd, downtown

**167** Mercer St (exits left from nb), Fairview Ave, Seattle Ctr, **W gas:** Shell, **lodging:** Silver Cloud Inn

**166** Olive Way, Stewart St, **E other:** Ⓗ HOSPITAL, **W lodging:** SpringHill Suites, **other:** Honda

**165a** Seneca St (exits left from nb), James St, **E other:** Ⓗ HOSPITAL

**165b** Union St, **E lodging:** Homewood Suites, **W food:** Ruth's Chris Steaks, **lodging:** Renaissance Inn

**164b** 4th Ave S, to Kingdome, downtown

**164a** I-90 E, to Spokane, downtown

**163** 6th Ave, S Spokane St, W Seattle Br, Columbian Way, **1 mi W on 4th Ave**...**gas:** Arco, **food:** Arby's, Burger King/24hr, Denny's, McDonald's, Subway, Taco Bell, **other:** Sears, auto repair, transmissions

**162** Corson Ave, Michigan St (exits left from nb), same as 161

**161** Swift Ave, Albro Place, **W gas:** Shell/dsl, **food:** Starbucks, Thai Rest., **lodging:** Georgetown Inn

**158** Pacific Hwy S, E Marginal Way, **W gas:** Chevron, **other:** NAPA

**157** ML King Way

**156** WA 539 N, Interurban Ave (no EZ return to sb), Tukwila, **E gas:** Pacific Pride/dsl, **food:** Gordon's Rest., **W gas:** 76/dsl, Shell/dsl, **food:** Emerald Green, Jack-in-the-Box, Quizno's, Starbucks, **lodging:** Day's Inn, **other:** Harley-Davidson

## INTERSTATE 5 CONT'D

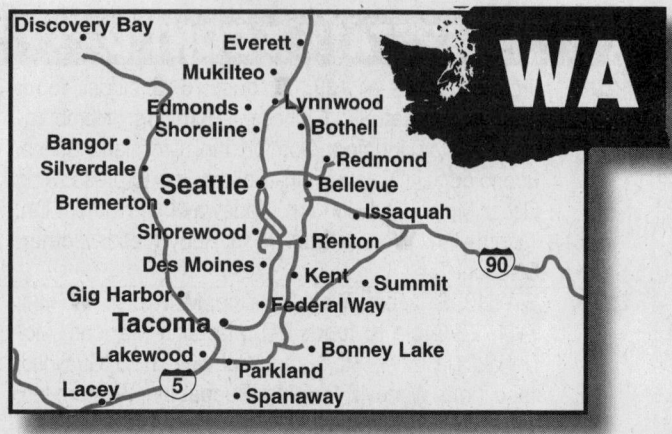

**N** ↕ **S**

**SEATTLE**

| | |
|---|---|
| **154b** | WA 518, Burien, **W** **lodging:** Extended Stay America |
| **154a** | I-405, N to Bellevue |
| **153** | S Center Pkwy, (from nb) , **E** **gas:** Chevron/dsl, **food:** Applebees, Azteca Mexican, Bahama Breeze, Cheesecake Factory, Chipotle Mexican, Claim Jumper, Famous Dave's, IHOP, Jamba Juice, Johnny Rockets Cafe, Newport Bay Rest., Olive Garden, Outback Steaks, Panda Express, Rainforest Cafe, Red Robin, Sizzler, Starbucks, Stanford's Rest, Taco Del Mar, Thai Rest., Zoopa, **lodging:** Courtyard, DoubleTree Inn, **other:** Acura, Best Buy, Borders, Jo-Ann Fabrics, Kohl's, Macy's, Marshall's, Nordstrom, Old Navy, PetCo, Sears/auto, Schwab Tire, Ross, Target, World Mkt, mall |
| **152** | S 188th, Orillia Rd, **W** **gas:** 76/dsl, **lodging:** Motel 6, **other:** to ✈ |
| **151** | S 200th, Military Rd, **E** **gas:** Shell/dsl, **lodging:** Motel 6, **W** **gas:** Chevron, 7-11, 76, **food:** Burger Teriyaki, Herfy's Burgers, IHOP, **lodging:** Best Value, Best Western, Days Inn, Comfort Inn, Econolodge, Fairfield Inn, Hampton Inn, Holiday Inn Express, Quality Inn, Skyway Inn, Sleep Inn, Super 8, **other:** NAPA, Uhaul |
| **149** | WA 516, to Kent, Des Moines, **E** **lodging:** Century Motel, **other:** Poulsbo RV Ctr, **W** **gas:** Shell/dsl/24hr, **food:** Burger King, McDonald's, Midway Doughnuts, Pizza Hut, Subway, Taco Bell, **lodging:** Garden Suites, Kings Arms Motel, New Best Inn, **other:** $Tree, Radio Shack, Walgreens, USPO, to Saltwater SP |
| **147** | S 272nd, **E** **gas:** 76/Circle K, **W** on Pacific Hwy...**gas:** Arco/24hr, Shell/dsl, **food:** Fox Hollow Coffee, Jack-in-the-Box, La Cabana Grill, McDonald's, Quizno's, Subway, Taco Bell, Thai 3, **other:** Ace Hardware, AutoZone, Bartell Drug, Rite Aid, Safeway/24hr |
| **143** | S 320th, Federal Way, **W** **gas:** Arco/24hr, 76/Circle K, Shell/dsl/24hr, **food:** Applebee's, Arby's, Azteca Mexican, Black Angus, Black Bear Diner, Blimpie, Chipotle Mexican, Church's, Denny's, Grand Buffet, Great Harvest Bread, Herfy's Burgers, Jasmine Mongolian, Marie Callender, McDonald's, McGrath's Fishouse, Mongolian Grill, Old Country Buffet, Outback Steaks, Panda Express, Panera Bread, Qdoba Mexican, Quizno's, Red Lobster, Red Robin, Starbucks, Subway, Taco Bell, Taco Del Mar, Taco Time, Torero's Mexican, Taco Bell, Tokyo Japanese Steaks, Tony Roma, Torero's Mexican, Village Inn, Wendy's, **lodging:** Best Western, Comfort Inn, Courtyard, Extended Stay America, **other:** Barnes & Noble, Best Buy, Big Lots, Borders Books, Discount Tire, Jo-Ann Fabrics, K-Mart, Long's Drugs, Macy's, Michaels, PetCo, PetsMart, Radio Shack, Rite Aid, Ross, Safeway/24hr, Sears/auto, Shuck's Parts, Target, TJ Maxx, Top Foods, mall, to Dash Point SP |
| **142b a** | WA 18 E, S 348th, Enchanted Pkwy, **E** **other:** funpark, **W** **gas:** Chevron, Shell/dsl, **food:** Arby's, Burger King, DQ, Del Taco, Denny's, Fatburger, Jack-in-the-Box, Jamba Juice, Jimmy Mac's Roadhouse, KFC, LJ Silver, McDonald's, Olive Garden, Panda Express, Popeye's, Puerta Vallarta, Quizno's, RoundTable Pizza, Shari's, Starbucks, Taco Bell, Taco Del Mar, Time Out Grill, **lodging:** Days Inn, Quality Inn, Super 8, **other:** H HOSPITAL, Chevrolet Circuit City, Costco/gas, Home Depot, Lowe's Whse, NAPA, Office Depot, Schwab Tire, Walmart SuperCtr |

**TACOMA**

| | |
|---|---|
| **140mm** | weigh sta, both lanes. Rest area, nb, full ♿ facilities, litter barrels, ☏ petwalk, RV dump |
| **137** | WA 99, Fife, Milton, **E** **gas:** Arco/24hr, Chevron/dsl/24hr, 76/dsl, Shell/24hr, **food:** DQ, Johnny's Rest., **lodging:** Motel 6, **other:** Acura, Cadillac, Hummer, Infinity, Saab, **W** **gas:** 76/Circle K, **food:** Arby's, Baskin-Robbins, Denny's, Herfy Burgers, KFC/A&W, McDonald's, Mitzel's Kitchen, Pizza Hut/Taco Bell, Poodle Dog, Quizno's, Starbucks, Subway, Taco Del Mar, Taco Time, **lodging:** Emerald Guesthouse Inn, Queen Motel, EQC Motel/casino, Fife Motel, Kings Motel, Quality Inn, **other:** Camping World RV Ctr, Great American RV Ctr, Holiday RV Ctr, Infinity, NAPA, Schwab Tire, Shuck's Parts, Western Motorcoach RV Ctr, Volvo |
| **136b a** | Port of Tacoma, **E** **gas:** CFN/dsl, **other:** Costco, Great American RV Ctr, Honda, Mercedes, Mini/BMW, Peterbilt, Tacoma RV Ctr, **W** **gas:** Chevron, ◈FLYING J/dsl/LP/rest./24hr, Gull/dsl, Shell/dsl, **food:** Jack-in-the-Box, Subway, **lodging:** Best Inn, Day's Inn, Econolodge, Extended Stay America, Howard Johnson, Sunshine Motel, Travelodge, **other:** Goodyear/biodsl, Harley-Davidson, Land Rover/Jaguar/Lexus, Nissan, Volvo |
| **135** | Bay St, Puyallup, **E** **gas:** Shell, **other:** Majestic RV Park (4mi) , **W** **gas:** Arco/24hr, **lodging:** La Quinta, **other:** to Tacoma Dome |
| **134** | Portland Ave (from nb), same as 135 |
| **133** | WA 7, I-705, City Ctr, **W** **lodging:** Best Western, Courtyard, Hotel Murano, **other:** Tacoma Dome, museum |
| **132** | WA 16 W, S 38th, Gig Harbor, to Bremerton, **W** **gas:** Tesoro, **food:** Adriatic Grill, BJ's Rest., Jamba Juice, Jimmy John's, Krispy Kreme, Quizno's, Red Robin, Subway, TGIFriday, Wendy's, **other:** Best Buy, Borders, Circuit City, Costco/gas, Diahatsu, $Tree, Firestone/auto, Ford, Hyundai, JC Penney, Jo-Ann's, Macy's, Michael's, Nordstrom, Petco, Ross, Sears/auto, Toyota, mall, to Pt Defiance Pk/Zoo, mall |
| **130** | S 56th, Tacoma Mall Blvd, **W** **gas:** Shell, **food:** Axteca Mexican, ChuckeCheese, Jack-in-the-Box, Subway, Wingers, **lodging:** Extended Stay America |
| **129** | S 72nd, S 84th, **E** **gas:** Chevron/24hr, Valero, **food:** Burger King, DQ, Denny's, Elmer's Rest., Famous Dave's, IHOP, Mongolian Grill, Olive Garden, Popeye's, Red Lobster, RoundTable Pizza, Shari's, Starbucks, **lodging:** Motel 6, Shilo Inn, **other:** Lowe's Whse, MegaFoods, **W** **food:** Hooters, **lodging:** Day's Inn, **other:** Home Depot, to Steilacoom Lake |

Copyright 2009 - The Next Exit®

## INTERSTATE 5 CONT'D

**N ↕ S**

**NISQUALLY**

| | |
|---|---|
| **128** | (from nb) same as 129, **E** **gas:** 76, Shell/dsl, **food:** Denny's, Greatwall Chinese, Herman's Hamburgers, Subway, **lodging:** Comfort Inn, Crossland Suites, Econolodge, Hampton Inn, Holiday Inn Express, King Oscar Motel, Red Lion Inn, Rodeway Inn, Rothem Inn, Tacoma Inn, **W** **gas:** Shell, **food:** Ruby Tuesday, **other:** Discount Tire |
| **127** | WA 512, S Tacoma Way, Puyallup, Mt Ranier, **W** **gas:** 7-11, 76/Circle K, **food:** DQ, Mazatlan Mexican, McDonald's, Sizzler, Starbucks, Subway, Taco Guaynas, Taco Time, Wendy's, **lodging:** Budget Inn, Western Inn, Vagabond Motel, **other:** Schuck's Parts, transmissions |
| **125** | to McChord AFB, Lakewood, **W** **gas:** 76/Circle K/dsl, Shell/dsl, **food:** A&W/KFC, Black Angus, Church's, Denny's, Pizza Hut, Wendy's, **lodging:** La Quinta, **other:** H HOSPITAL, Aamco, Ford, 7-11, U-Haul, mall, vet |
| **124** | Gravelly Lake Dr, **W** **gas:** Arco/repair, 76/24hr, **food:** El Toro Mexican, **other:** CarQuest, same as 125 |
| **123** | Thorne Lane, Tillicum Lane |
| **122** | Camp Murray, **E** **other:** H HOSPITAL, **W** **gas:** Chevron/repair, **food:** Baskin-Robbins, Domino's, Gertie's Grill, Happy Wok, KFC, McDonald's, Papa John's, Subway, Taco Bell, Teriyaki House, **other:** AutoZone, 7-11 |
| **120** | Ft Lewis, **E** **other:** Ft Lewis Military Museum |
| **119** | Du Pont Rd, Steilacoom, **E** to Ft Lewis, **W** **gas:** Chevron, 76, **food:** Jack-in-the-Box, Starbucks, Subway |
| **118** | Center Dr, **W** **food:** Bruceski's Pizza, Domino's, Farrelli's Pizza, Harbor Rock Grill, Jack-in-the-Box, Koko's Wok, Pegasus Cafe, Quizno's, Subway, Super Buffet, Viva Mexico, **lodging:** GuestHouse Inn, Liberty Inn |
| **117mm** | weigh sta nb |
| **116** | Mounts Rd, Old Nisqually, **E** Blue Camas Buffet (8mi) |
| **115mm** | Nisqually River |
| **114** | Nisqually, **E** **gas:** Chevron/repair, Exxon/dsl, Shell/dsl/LP, Texaco (1mi), **food:** Nisqually Grill, Norma's Burgers, Shipwreck Café, **other:** Nisqually RV Park, River Bend RV Park (3mi) |
| **111** | WA 510 E, Marvin Rd, to Yelm, **E** **gas:** Chevron/24hr, 76/Circle K, Shell/dsl, **food:** Burger King, Coldstone, Hawk's Prairie Rest./casino, Jamba Juice, McDonald's, Panda Express, Panera Bread, Papa Murphy's, Puerto Vallarta, Quizno's, RoundTable Pizza, Ruby Tuesday, Starbucks, Taco Del Mar, **lodging:** King Oscar Motel, **other:** Best Buy, Big Lots, Costco/gas, $Tree, Harley Davidson, Home Depot, Radio Shack, Rite Aid, Safeway/gas/24hr, Schuck's Parts, Schwab Tire, Sportsman's Whse, Walgreens, Walmart SuperCtr/Subway, **W** **gas:** Pacific Pride/dsl, **food:** Mayan Mexican, **other:** Cabela's, Tolmie SP (5mi), RV camping |
| **109** | Martin Way, Sleator-Kenny Rd, **E** **food:** Main Chinese Buffet, Pizza Hut/Taco Bell, The Rock Pizza, **other:** Discount Tire, ShopKO, Top Food/24hr, **W** **gas:** 76/Circle K, Shell/dsl/24hr, **food:** Casa Mia Rest., Denny's, El Serape Mexican, IHOP, Mandarin House, Red Lobster, Shari's Rest./24hr, Subway, **lodging:** AmeriTel, Comfort Inn, Quality Inn, La Quinta, Super 8, **other:** H HOSPITAL, Tire Factory, NAPA |
| **108** | Sleater-Kinney Rd, **E** **gas:** Shell/dsl, **food:** Applebee's, Arby's, McDonald's/playplace, Wendy's, |

**OLYMPIA**

**CENTRALIA**

| | |
|---|---|
| **108** | Continued **other:** $Tree, Firestone/auto, Fred Meyer, Kohl's, Marshall's, Michael's, Office Depot, PetsMart, Radio Shack, Rite Aid, Sears/auto, Target, **W** **gas:** Arco, Shell, **food:** Casa Mia, Coldstone, El Sarape Mexican, Jack-in-the-Box, Subway, Vietnamese Rest., **lodging:** AmeriTel Inn, **other:** H HOSPITAL, K-Mart, Lowes Whse, Safeway/gas, Tire Factory, same as 109 |
| **107** | Pacific Ave, **E** **gas:** Shell/dsl, **food:** Izzy's Pizza, Shari's, Sizzler, Subway, Taco Time, **other:** Albertson's/Sav-on, Home Depot, Ross, mall, vet, **W** **other:** Columbus RV Ctr, Ford |
| **105** | St Capitol, **W** **gas:** Chevron/24hr, Shell/Subway/dsl/24hr, **lodging:** Quality Inn, **other:** to St Capitol |
| **104** | US 101 N, W Olympia, to Aberdeen, **W** **gas:** Arco, Chevron, 7-11, Shell/dsl, **food:** Jack-in-the-Box, **lodging:** Extended Stay America, Red Lion Motel, **other:** H HOSPITAL, to Capitol Mall |
| **103** | 2nd Ave |
| **102** | Trosper Rd, Black Lake, **E** **gas:** Shell/dsl/24hr, **food:** Arby's, Brewery City Pizza, Burger King, Cattin's Rest./24hr, El Sarape Mexican, Happy Teriyaki, Jack-in-the-Box, KFC, McDonald's, Starbucks, Subway, Taco Bell, Taco Time, **lodging:** Best Western, Motel 6, **other:** Ace Hardware, Curves, $Store, Goodyear/auto, Schuck's Parts, **W** **gas:** Chevron/24hr, 76/Circle K, **food:** Nickelby's Rest., Panda Express, Quizno's, Starbucks, The Brick Rest., **other:** Albertson's/gas, Alderbrook RV Park, AutoZone, Costco/gas, Fred Meyer, GNC, Home Depot, MegaFoods/24hr, Radio Shack |
| **101** | Airdustrial Way, **E** **gas:** Chevron, Shell, **food:** DQ (1mi), Inferno Pizza, Quizno's, Teriyaki Wok, **lodging:** Comfort Inn, GuestHouse Inn, Olympia Camping, USPO |
| **99** | WA 121 S, 93rd Ave, Scott Lake, **E** **gas:** Pilot/McDonald's/Subway/dsl/scales, **other:** American Heritage Camping, **W** **gas:** Shell/Deanna's Rest./rest/dsl/LP, **lodging:** Restover Motel |
| **95** | WA 121, Littlerock, **3 mi** **E** **other:** Millersylvania SP, RV camping, **W** **food:** Farmboy Drive-In |
| **93.5mm** | rest area sb, full ♿ facilities, info, 🚻, 🔀, litter barrels, vending, coffee, petwalk |
| **91mm** | rest area nb, full ♿ facilities, info, 🚻, 🔀, litter barrels, vending, coffee, petwalk |
| **88** | US 12, Rochester, **E** **other:** RV Service, **W** **gas:** Arco/24hr, CFN, 76/dsl, Shell/dsl/LP/repair, **food:** DQ, Little Red Barn Rest., Lucky Eagle Casino/café, Quizno's, The Grill, **lodging:** Great Wolf Lodge, **other:** Curves, Outback RV Park (2mi) |
| **82** | Harrison Ave, Factory Outlet Way, Centralia, **E** **gas:** Arco/24hr, Shell/dsl, **food:** Burger King, Burgerville, Casa Ramos Mexican, DQ, Panda Chinese, Peking House Chinese, Pizza Hut, Quizno's, Thai Dish, Wendy's, **lodging:** Econolodge, Ferryman's Inn, King Oscar Motel, **other:** H HOSPITAL, VF/famous brands, **W** **gas:** Chevron, Shell, Texaco/Circle K, **food:** Arby's, Bill & Bea's, Country Cousin Rest., Denny's, Dominos, Jack-in-the-Box, McDonald's, Papa Murphy's, Starbucks, Subway, Taco Bell, **lodging:** Motel 6, **other:** Centralia Outlets, GNC, Midway RV Park, Outlet Mall/famous brands, Rite Aid, Safeway/gas, Schuck's Parts, Schwab Tire |
| **82mm** | Skookumchuck River |

## INTERSTATE 5 CONT'D

N ↕ S

| | |
|---|---|
| **81** | WA 507, Mellen St, **E** **gas:** Chevron, Shell, **food:** PJ's Rest., Subway, **lodging:** Empress Inn, Pepper Tree Motel/RV Park/dump, Travel Inn, **W** **H** HOSPITAL |
| **79** | Chamber Way, **E** **gas:** Shell/dsl/24hr, **food:** Jalisco Mexican, **other:** Ford, Goodyear/auto, museum, vistor info, **W** **gas:** Texaco/Burger King/dsl/LP, **food:** Applebees, McDonald's, Roobucks Pizza, Starbucks, Subway, Taco Del Mar, Wendy's, **other:** $Tree, GNC, Grocery Outlet, Home Depot, K-Mart/Little Caesar's, Michael's, Quizno's, Radio Shack, Scion/Toyota, Walgreens, Walmart SuperCtr, st patrol |
| **77** | WA 6 W, Chehalis, **E** **gas:** Cenex/dsl, 76/dsl, **food:** Dairy Bar, **other:** NAPA, Schwab Tire, **W** **other:** Rainbow Falls SP (16mi), museum, truck parts |
| **76** | 13th St, **E** **gas:** Arco/24hr, Chevron, Texaco, **food:** Denny's, Jack-in-the-Box, Kit Carson Rest., South Pacific Bistro, Subway, **lodging:** Best Western, Chehalis Inn, Relax Inn, **other:** Baydo's RV Ctr, I-5 RV Ctr, Safeway, Uhlmann RV Ctr/RV dump, **W** RV park/dump |
| **73** | new exit, **W** Poulsbo RV Ctr |
| **72** | Rush Rd, Napavine, **E** **gas:** Shell/dsl/scales, **food:** Burger King, McDonald's, Subway, **other:** Dave's RV Ctr, RV park, **W** **gas:** Chevron/FoodCourt/dsl/24hr, Shell/dsl |
| **72mm** | Newaukum River |
| **71** | WA 508 E, Onalaska, Napavine, **E** **gas:** 76/dsl/KC Truck Parts |
| **68** | US 12 E, Morton, **E** **gas:** Arco/24hr, **food:** Spiffy's Rest./24hr, **other:** to Lewis&Clark SP, Mt Ranier NP, **W** **gas:** 76/dsl/rest./24hr, **food:** Jammer's Rest. |
| **63** | WA 505, Winlock, **E** **other:** RV park (3mi), **W** **gas:** Shell/Cruisin' Cafe/dsl/LP |
| **60** | Vader Rd, Toledo |
| **59** | WA 506 W, Vader, **E** **gas:** Shell/dsl, **food:** Beesley's Cafe, **W** **gas:** Chevron/Subway/dsl/24hr, **food:** Country House Rest. |
| **59mm** | Cowlitz River |
| **57** | Barnes Dr, Jackson Hwy, **E** **other:** R&R Tires, **W** **gas:** GeeCee's/dsl/scales/café/24hr/@, **other:** repair, RV camping |
| **55mm** | **rest area both lanes, full ♿ facilities, 🚻, 🎪, litter barrels, vending, petwalk** |
| **52** | Toutle Park Rd, **E** **other:** Paradise Cove RV Park/general store |
| **50mm** | Toutle River |
| **49** | WA 504 E, Castle Rock, **E** **gas:** Shell/dsl, Texaco/dsl/LP, **food:** Burger King, C&L Burgers, El Compadre Mexican, 49er Diner, Papa Pete's Pizza, RoseTree Rest., Subway, **lodging:** Mt St Helens Motel, 7 West Motel, Silver Lake Motel/resort, Timberland Inn, **other:** Seaquest SP (5mi) |
| **48** | Huntington Ave, **W** **food:** Hattie's Rest., **other:** RV dump |
| **46** | Pleasant Hill Rd, **E** **other:** RV Park |
| **44mm** | weigh sta sb, phone |
| **42** | Ostrander Rd |
| **40** | to WA 4, Kelso-Longview |
| **39** | WA 4, Kelso, to Longview, **E** **gas:** Arco/24hr, Shell, **food:** Denny's, Hilander Rest., McDonald's, Shari's/24hr, Subway, Taco Time, **other:** Brook Hollow RV Park, **lodging:** Motel 6, Red Lion Motel, Super 8, **other:** Rite Aid, **W** **food:** Azteca Mexican, Burger King, ChuckeCheese, DQ, Izzy's Pizza, Red Lobster, Starbucks, Taco Bell, **lodging:** Comfort Inn, GuestHouse Inn, |

K E L S O

| | |
|---|---|
| **39** | Continued **other:** JC Penney, Macys, Safeway/drug/gas, Sears/auto, Target, mall, museum |
| **36** | WA 432 W, to WA 433, US 30, Kelso, **E** **other:** U-Neek RV Ctr, **1-3 mi** **W** **other:** Toyota/Scion |
| **32** | Kalama River Rd, **E** **food:** Fireside Café, **other:** Camp Kalama RV Park/gifts |
| **31mm** | Kalama River |
| **30** | Kalama, **E** **gas:** Chevron, Texaco, **food:** Burger Bar, Columbia Rest., Lucky Dragon Chinese, Playa Azul Mexican, Subway, **lodging:** Columbia Motel, Kalama River Inn, **other:** USPO, antiques, **W** **gas:** Spirit/gas, **other:** RV camping |
| **27** | Todd Rd, Port of Kalama, **E** **gas:** Shell/dsl/café/24hr |
| **22** | Dike Access Rd, **E** **other:** Tire Factory, transmissions, **W** **gas:** CFN/dsl/24hr, **other:** Columbia Riverfront |
| **21** | WA 503 E, Woodland, **E** **gas:** Arco/24hr, Chevron, Pacific Pride, Shell/LP/dsl, **food:** Burgerville, Casa Tapatia, Figaro's, Gilliano's, Mali Thai, McDonald's, OakTree Rest., Rosie's Rest., Subway, **lodging:** Best Western, Cedar's Inn, Lewis River Inn, **other:** Ace Hardware, Hi-School Drug, Radio Shack, Safeway, Oil Can Henry's, Woodland Shores RV Park, **W** **gas:** Astro, Shell, **food:** Guadalahara Mexican, McDonald's, Papa Murphy's, Quizno's, Starbucks, Subway, **lodging:** Hansen's Motel, Lakeside Motel, Scandia Motel, **other:** Chevrolet, NAPA, Safeway/gas, Uhaul, repair |
| **20mm** | N Fork Lewis River |
| **18mm** | E Fork Lewis River |
| **16** | NW 319th St, La Center, **E** **gas:** Shell/dsl/24hr, **food:** Twin Dragons Rest., **other:** Paradise Point SP, Tri-Mountain Golf/rest. |
| **15mm** | weigh sta nb |
| **14** | WA 501 W, NW 269th St, **E** **gas:** Arco/24hr, 76/Circle K/dsl, **food:** Country Café, Papa Pete's Pizza, Subway, **other:** to Battleground Lake SP (14mi), Big Fir RV Park (4mi), Ridgefield WR, Tri-Mountain RV Park, **W** **gas:** Chevron/dsl |
| **13mm** | **rest area sb, full ♿ facilities, info, 🚻, 🎪, litter barrels, vending, petwalk, RV dump** |
| **11** | WA 502, Battleground, **rest area nb, full ♿ facilities, info, 🚻, 🎪, litter barrels, vending, petwalk, RV dump** |
| **9** | NE 179th St, **E** **food:** Jollie's Rest./24hr, **other:** Poulsbo RV, **W** **gas:** Chevron/dsl, **other:** RV Park |
| **7** | I-205 S (from sb), to I-84, WA 14, NE 134th St, **E** **gas:** Arco, 7-11, 76, TrailMart/dsl, **food:** Applebee's, |

W O O D L A N D

Copyright 2009 - The Next Exit®

**N ↕ S**

**VANCOUVER**

## INTERSTATE 5 CONT'D

| | |
|---|---|
| 7 | Continued<br>Billygan's Roadhouse, Booster Juice, Burger King, Burgerville, Jack-in-the-Box, McDonald's, Muchas Gracias, Panda Express, Round Table Pizza, Starbucks, Subway, Taco Bell, Taco Del Mar, **lodging:** Comfort Inn, Holiday Inn Express, Olympia Motel, Red Lion, Salmon Creek Inn, **other:** H HOSPITAL, Albertson's/gas, Long's Drugs, Safeway/gas, Zupan's Mkt, 99 RV Park, to Portland Airport, **W gas:** Shell, **food:** Baskin-Robbins, Coldstone, El Tapatio, Papa Murphy's, PizzaSchmitzza, Quizno's, Starbucks, The Great Impasta, **lodging:** La Quinta, **other:** Fred Meyer |
| 5 | NE 99th St, **E gas:** 7-11, **food:** Burgerville, Carl's Jr, Del Taco, Domino's, Fat Dave's Rest., Quizno's, **other:** Harley-Davidson, Nissan/Kia, Walgreens, Walmart/Subway, Winco Foods/gas/24hr, **W gas:** Arco/24hr, Chevron/24hr, **food:** Applebee's, Bortolemi's Pizza, McDonald's, Papa John's, Primo's Subs, Subway, Taco Del Mar, **other:** $Tree, Kohl's, Office Depot, PetCo, Target |
| 4 | NE 78th St, Hazel Dell, **E gas:** 76, 7-11, **food:** Baja Fresh, Burger King, Don Pedro Mexican, Dragon Buffet, KFC, McDonald's, Pizza Hut, PeachTree Rest., Skipper's, Smokey's Pizza, Steakburger, Subway, Taco Bell, **lodging:** Quality Inn, **other:** Aamco, CarQuest, Cost-Less Parts, Firestone, Fred Meyer, Dodge, Ford, Mazda, Nissan, Radio Shack, Save A Lot Foods, Schuck's Parts, Tire Factory, U-Haul, **W gas:** Shell/dsl/LP, **food:** Jack-in-the-Box, Nick & Willy's Pizza, Panda Express, RoundTable Pizza, Starbucks, Tully's Coffee, Wendy's, **other:** PetsMart, Ross, Safeway, Tuesday Morning |
| 3 | NE Hwy 99, Main St, Hazel Dell, **E gas:** 7-11, **food:** Muchas Gracias Mexican, Pizza Hut, Skippers, **other:** H HOSPITAL, Schwab Tire, **W gas:** 76/dsl, **other:** Safeway, transmissions |
| 2 | WA 500 E, 39th St, to Orchards |
| 1d | E 4th, Plain Blvd W, to WA 501, Port of Vancouver |
| 1c | Mill Plain Blvd, City Ctr, **W gas:** Chevron, **food:** Black Angus, Cattle Co Rest., Burgerville, Denny's, **lodging:** Shilo Inn, **other:** Ford, Lincoln/Mercury, Pontiac/Cadillac/GMC, Jeep, Mitsubishi, Suzuki, Clark Coll, st patrol |
| 1b | 6th St, **E food:** Joe's Crabshack, **W lodging:** Econolodge, Hilton, Red Lion |
| 1a | WA 14 E, to Camas, **E** H HOSPITAL, **W lodging:** Red Lion |
| 0mm | Washington/Oregon state line, Columbia River |

## INTERSTATE 82

**E ↕ W**

| Exit # | Services |
|---|---|
| 11mm | I-82 Oregon begins/ends on I-84, exit 179. |
| 10 | Westland Rd, **E other:** to Umatilla Army Depot, **other:** H HOSPITAL |
| 5 | Power Line Rd |
| 1.5mm | Umatilla River |
| 1 | US 395/730, Umatilla, **E food:** Jack-in-the-Box (5mi), **lodging:** Best Western (8mi), Desert Inn/rest. (2mi), **other:** Hatrock Camping (8mi), to McNary Dam, **W gas:** Shell/Crossroads Trkstp/dsl/rest./24hr, Tesoro/Subway/dsl, **lodging:** Tillicum Motel, Umatilla Inn, **other:** Red Apple Mkt, USPO, st police, **Welcome Ctr, weigh sta** |

**KENNEWICK**

| | |
|---|---|
| 132mm | Washington/Oregon state line, Columbia River |
| 131 | WA 14 W, Plymouth, **N other:** RV camping, to McNary Dam |
| 130mm | weigh sta wb |
| 122 | Coffin Rd |
| 114 | Locust Grove Rd |
| 113 | US 395 N, to I-182, Kennewick, Pasco, **2-4 mi N gas:** Chevron, Exxon, Tesoro/dsl, **food:** A&W/KFC, Azteca Mexican, Burger King, Carl's Jr, DQ, Denny's, Jack-in-the-Box, Little Ceasar's, McDonald's, Taco Bell, Panda Express, Papa Murphy's, Starbucks, Subway, Taco Del Mar, **lodging:** Best Western, Day's Inn, EconoLodge, La Quinta, Wingate Inn, **other:** $Tree, Fiesta Foods, Fred Meyer, GNC, Harley-Davidson, Hastings Books, Home Depot, PetCo, Radio Shack, Rite Aid, Safeway/food/gas, Traveland RV Ctr, Walgreens, Walmart SuperCtr/gas, st patrol |
| 109 | Badger Rd, W Kennewick, **N gas:** Shell/Subway/dsl/24hr, **food:** Chico's Tacos, **3 mi N lodging:** Guesthouse Suites, Quality Inn, Red Lion Inn, Super 8 |
| 104 | Dallas Rd, **3 mi N gas:** Conoco/dsl/24hr |
| 102 | I-182, US 12 E, to US 395, Spokane, H HOSPITAL, services in Richland, Pasco |
| 96 | WA 224, Benton City, **N gas:** Conoco/cafe/dsl/24hr, **other:** Beach RV Park |
| 93 | Yakitat Rd |
| 88 | Gibbon Rd |
| 82 | WA 22, WA 221, Mabton, **S gas:** Conoco, **2 mi S food:** Blue Goose Rest., **lodging:** Prosser Motel, **other:** H HOSPITAL, to WA St U Research, to Wine Tasting Facilities, museum |
| 82mm | Yakima River |
| 80 | Gap Rd, **S gas:** Chevron, Pacific Pride, Shell/dsl/scales, **food:** Blue Goose Rest., Burger King, El Rancho Alegre, KFC/Taco Bell, McDonald's, Starbucks, Subway, **lodging:** Barn Motel/RV Park/rest., Best Western, Prosser Motel, **other:** H HOSPITAL, Ford/Mercury, Wine Country RV Park, vet, **rest area both lanes, full 🚹 facilities, 🄲, 🚻, litter barrels, rv dump** |
| 76mm | weigh sta eb |
| 75 | County Line Rd, Grandview, **S gas:** Cenex/dsl, Conoco/dsl/24hr (1mi), **1 mi S...lodging: other:** Safeway Food & Drug/gas, same as 73 |
| 73 | Stover Rd, Wine Country Rd, Grandview, **S gas:** Chevron/Subway/dsl, Conoco/dsl/24hr, **food:** DQ, Eli&Kathy's Breakfast, New Hong Kong, 10-4 Café, Subway, **lodging:** Apple Valley Motel, Grandview Motel, **other:** Chrystler/Jeep/Dodge, Grandview Market, RV park/dump, Safeway, Schwab Tire, auto repair |
| 69 | WA 241, to Sunnyside, **N gas:** Arco/dsl/24hr, Shell/TacoMaker/dsl/scales/24hr, **food:** A&W, Arby's, Burger King, China Buffet, China Grove, DQ, El Charrito Mexican, KFC, Little Ceasar's, McDonald's, Papa Murphy's, Pizza Hut, Subway, Taco Bell, **lodging:** Best Western, Rodeway Inn, **other:** Buick/Chevrolet/Nissan, $Tree, Fiesta Foods, GNC, JC Penney, Radio Shack, Rite Aid, Schuck's Parts, Walmart SuperCtr/gas |
| 67 | Sunnyside, Port of Sunnyside, **N gas:** Chevron/CFN/dsl, Conoco/dsl/E85, **food:** Jack-in-the-Box, **other:** H HOSPITAL, BiMart Foods, **S other:** DariGold Cheese |
| 63 | Outlook, Sunnyside, **3 mi N food:** Burger Ranch, Snipe's Rest., **lodging:** Country Inn, Sunnyside B&B, Travel Inn, **other:** RV camping |

## INTERSTATE 82 CONT'D

E ↕ W

Y A K I M A

| 58 | WA 223 S, to Granger, S gas: Chevron/dsl, Conoco/dsl |
|---|---|
| 54 | Division Rd, Yakima Valley Hwy, to Zillah, S other: Teapot Dome NHS |
| 52 | Zillah, Toppenish, N gas: Chevron/dsl, 76/dsl, Shell/dsl/24hr, food: El Porton Mexican, McDonald's, Pizza Hut, Subway, lodging: Comfort Inn |
| 50 | WA 22 E, to US 97 S, Toppenish, 3-4 mi S food: Legends Buffet/casino, McDonald's, lodging: Best Western Toppenish other: H HOSPITAL, Murals Museum, RV Park, to Yakima Nation Cultural Ctr |
| 44 | Wapato, N gas: Shell/dsl |
| 40 | Thorp Rd, Parker Rd, Yakima Valley Hwy, N other: Sagelands Vineyard/Winery, S other: Windy Point Vineyard |
| 39mm | Yakima River |
| 38 | Union Gap (from wb), 1 mi S food: Peppermint Stick Drive-In, other: gas, lodging, museum |
| 37 | US 97 (from eb), 1 mi S gas: Shell |
| 36 | Valley Mall Blvd, Yakima, S gas: Arco/dsl/24hr, Cenex/dsl, Shell/Gearjammer/dsl/Subway/scales/24hr/@, food: A&W/KFC, Cold Stone Creamery, Denny's/24hr, El Porton Mexican, IHOP, McDonald's, Miner's Drive-In, Old Country Buffet, Old Town Station Rest., Outback Steaks, SeaGalley Rest., Shari's, Skipper's, Starbucks, Taco Bell, lodging: Quality Inn, Super 8, other: Best Buy, Border's Books, Canopy RV Ctr, Gap Autoparts, Lowes Whse, Office Depot, Old Navy, Macy's, Rite Aid, Ross, Sears/auto, ShopKO, Tire Factory, TJ Maxx, dsl/repair, mall, st patrol |
| 34 | WA 24 E, Nob Hill Blvd, Yakima, N other: K-Mart, Sportsman SP, KOA, dsl/repair, International, S gas: Arco/24hr, Chevron/dsl/24hr, CFN/dsl, 7-11, Time/dsl, food: Arby's, McDonald's, other: H HOSPITAL, 19th Hole RV Park, Fiesta Foods, Freightliner, Peterbuilt, Shuck's Parts, GMC/Volvo/trucks, museum |
| 33 | Yakima Ave, Yakima, N gas: Chevron/dsl, Shell/Chester's/dsl, food: Burger King, El Mirador Mexican, lodging: Oxford Inn&Suites, other: Chevrolet, GMC/Honda, Hyundai, Mazda, Walmart SuperCtr/McDonald's, S gas: Arco/24hr, 7-11, food: Asian Express, DQ, Pizza Hut, Taco Bell, lodging: Cedars Motel, Fairfield Inn, Hilton Garden, Holiday Inn Express, Howard Johnson, Ledgestone Hotel, Red Lion Motel, other: Schwab Tire, Target, mall |
| 31b a | US 12 W, N 1st St, to Naches, S gas: Arco/dsl/24hr, Shell, food: Arctic Circle, Black Angus Steaks, El Sieta Marie's Mexican, Golden Moon Chinese, Jack-in-the-Box, Peking Palace, Red Apple Rest., Red Lobster, Smokin' Bones BBQ, Subway, Waffle's Cafe, Wendy's, lodging: All Star Motel, Best Western, Day's Inn, Clarion, Econolodge, Economy Inn, Motel 6, Quality Inn, Ramada Inn, Red Apple Motel, Sun Country Inn, Tourist Motel, Yakima Inn, other: Harley-Davidson, Nendel's, Trailer Inns RV park |
| 30 | WA 823 N, Rest Haven Rd, to Selah |
| 29 | E Selah Rd, N other: fruits/antiques |
| 26 | WA 821 N, to WA 823, Canyon Rd, N gas: Shell/dsl/Noble Romans |
| 24mm | rest area eb, full & facilities, 🅿 litter barrels, RV dump |

| 23mm | Selah Creek |
|---|---|
| 22mm | rest area wb, full & facilities, 🅿 litter barrels, RV dump |
| 21mm | S Umptanum Ridge, 2265 elev |
| 19mm | Burbank Creek |
| 17mm | N Umptanum Ridge, 2315 elev |
| 15mm | Lmuma Creek |
| 11 | Military Area, Military Area |
| 8mm | view point both lanes, Manastash Ridge, 2672 elev |
| 3 | WA 821 S, Thrall Rd |
| 0mm | I-90, E to Spokane, W to Seattle. I-82 begins/ends on I-90, exit 110. |

## INTERSTATE 90

E ↕ W

V E R A D A L E

| Exit # | Services |
|---|---|
| 300mm | Washington/Idaho state line, Spokane River |
| 299 | State Line, Port of Entry, N Welcome Ctr/rest area both lanes, weigh sta, full & facilities, 🅲 🅿 litter barrels, petwalk, N gas: Shell, other: Cabela's |
| 296 | Otis Orchards, Liberty Lakes, N gas: Shell/dsl, food: HomePlate Grill, lodging: Best Western, other: Buick/GMC/Pontiac, Hummer, Kia, Porsche, S gas: Cenex/dsl, Chevron/LP, food: Carl's Jr, Domino's, Great Harvest Bread, McDonald's, Papa Murphy's, Pizza Hut, Quizno's, Starbucks, Subway, Taco Bell, Taco Time, lodging: Cedar's Inn, other: Albertson's/Sav-On, Alton's Tire, Curves, GNC, Home Depot, RNR RV Ctr, Safeway/gas, Walgreens, vet |
| 294 | Sprague Ave (from wb, no EZ return), S other: North Country RV/marine, Nut Factory, auto repair |
| 293 | Barker Rd, Greenacres, N gas: Conoco/dsl, food: Roadside Grill, Wendy's, other: Freedom RV Ctr, S gas: Exxon/Subway/dsl/24hr, Shell/dsl/24hr, other: NW RV Ctr, repair |
| 291b | Sullivan Rd, Veradale, N food: Arby's, Hooters, Krispy Kreme, Outback Steaks, lodging: Oxford Suites, Residence Inn, other: Barnes&Noble, Best Buy, Circuit City, Staples, mall, S gas: Cenex, Chevron, 76, Shell/dsl, Tesoro, food: A&W, Bruchi's Rest., DQ, Jack-in-the-Box, KFC, McDonald's, Mongolian BBQ, Noodle Express, Panda Express, Pizza Hut, Quizno's, Round Table Pizza, Schlotsky's, Shari's/24hr, Starbucks, Subway, Taco Bell, Wendy's, lodging: Mirabeau Park Hotel, Ramada Inn, other: Ace Hardware, $Tree, Fred Meyer/gas, Hancock Fabrics, Hastings Books, Kohl's, Lowes Whse, Michael's, NAPA, PetCo, PetsMart, Ross, Schwab Tires, Walgreens, Walmart SuperCtr/auto, Yoke's Foods, USPO |

Copyright 2009 - The Next Exit®

## INTERSTATE 90 CONT'D

**291a** Evergreen Rd, **N food:** Black Angus, Boston's Rest, Honey Baked Ham, IHOP, Red Robin, TGIFriday, Wingers, **other:** JC Penney, Macy's, Old Navy, Sportsman's Whse, Sears/auto, TJ Maxx, mall, **S gas:** Shell

**289** WA 27 S, Pines Rd, Opportunity, **N gas:** 7-11, **food:** Old Matthews Rest., **S gas:** Cenex, Holiday, Shell/dsl, **food:** Applebees, DQ, Jack-in-the-Box, Old Country Buffet, Quizno's, **lodging:** Pheasant Hill Inn, **other:** Ⓗ HOSPITAL, Jo-Ann Fabrics, Walgreens, repair

**287** Argonne Rd, Millwood, **N gas:** Holiday/dsl **food:** Burger King, Denny's, Domino's, DQ, Jack-in-the-Box, Longhorn BBQ, Marie Callender's, McDonald's, Panda Express, Papa Murphy's, Pizza Hut, Starbucks, Subway, Taco Time, Tasty House Chinese, Wendy's, **lodging:** Motel 6, Super 8, **other:** Albertson's/gas, Yoke's Foods, Savon, Schuck's Parts, Walgreens, $ Tree, **S gas:** Cenex/dsl, Shell, **food:** Casa de Oro Mexican, Perkins, Starbucks, **lodging:** Holiday Inn Express, Quality Inn, **other:** Curves, Rite Aid/24hr, Safeway

**286** Broadway Ave, **N gas:** Chevron, ✦FLYING J/Conoco/Rest./dsl/LP/scales/24hr/@, **food:** Zip's Burgers, Goodyear, **lodging:** Rodeway Inn, **Other:** International Trucks, Volvo, Kenworth, Peterbuilt, Schwab Tire, TDS Tires, **S Other:** 7-11

**285** Sprague Ave, **N food:** Dragon Garden Rest, IHOP, Jack-in-the-Box, McDonald's, Subway, Wendy's, **lodging:** ParkLane Motel, **other:** Costco/gas, Grocery Outlet, Freightliner, Home Depot, K-Mart, Lowes Whse, Radio Shack, Schuck's Parts, **S gas:** Conoco, **food:** Puerta Vallarta Mexican, Starbucks, Taco Time, Zip's Burger, **other:** Alton's Tire, Chrysler, Dodge, Nissan/Saab, Trailer Inn RV Park, transmissions, vet

**284** Havana St (from eb, no EZ return), **N food:** Jack-in-the-Box, McDonald's

**283b** Freya St, Thor St, **N gas:** Tesoro/dsl/24hr, **food:** Jack-in-the-Box, McDonald's, Wolf Lodge Steaks, **S gas:** Conoco/dsl, **Other:** Fred Myer

**283a** Altamont St, **S gas:** Cenex

**282b** 2nd Ave, **N gas:** Shell, **lodging:** Comfort Inn, **other:** Office Depot

**282a** WA 290 E, Trent Ave, Hamilton St, **N gas:** Shell/dsl, **lodging:** Comfort Inn, **other:** Office Depot

**281** US 2, US 395, to Colville, **N gas:** 7-11, Shell/repair, Tesoro/dsl, **food:** Arby's, Dick's Hamburgers, Franky Doodles Rest., Jack-in-the-Box, Starbucks, Taco Time, **lodging:** Day's Inn, Howard Johnson, **other:** Firestone/auto, Ford, Schwab Tire, U-haul, **S lodging:** Quality Inn, **other:** Ⓗ HOSPITAL

**280b** Lincoln St, **N gas:** Chevron, Conoco/dsl, Shell, **food:** Carl's Jr, Domino's, Jack-in-the-Box, McDonald's, Molly's Rest., Taco Bell, Taste of Asia, Zip's Burgers, **lodging:** Ramada Inn, Rodeway Inn, Tradewinds Motel, **other:** Honda, Saturn, Scion/Toyota, Tire Factory, **S** Ⓗ HOSPITAL

**280a** downtown, **N gas:** Chevron/McDonald's/dsl, Conoco/dsl, Fuel USA, **food:** Arctic Circle, Frank's Diner, Pizza Hut, Subway, **lodging:** Select Inn, **other:** AAA, Jaguar, Land Rover, Lexus

**279** US 195 S, Pullman, to Colfax

**277b a** US 2 W (no ez wb return), to Grand Coulee Dam, Fairchild AFB, **N lodging:** Econolodge, Hampton Inn, Motel 6, Ramada Inn, Spokanne House, Travelodge, West Wynn Motel

**276** Geiger Blvd, **N gas:** ✦FLYING J/dsl/LP/24hr, **food:** Denny's, Subway, **lodging:** Airway Express Inn, Best Western, **other:** USPO, st patrol, **S gas:** Shell/dsl/LP, **other:** Hideaway RV Park

**272** WA 902, Medical Lake, **N gas:** Shell/dsl, **other:** Overland Sta/RV Park, **S gas:** Petro/dsl/rest./24hr/@, **food:** Iron Skillet, Subway, **lodging:** Super 8, **other:** Freightliner, Ponderosa Falls RV Resort, truck repair

**270** WA 904, Cheney, Four Lakes, **S gas:** Exxon, **lodging:** Willow Springs Motel (6mi), **other:** Peaceful Pines RV Park, Ford, E WA U

**264** WA 902, Salnave Rd, to Cheney, Medical Lake, **2 mi N** camping

**257** WA 904, Tyler, to Cheney, **S other:** Tyler Store/RV Park, to Columbia Plateau Trail SP

**254** Fishtrap, **S other:** Fishtrap RV camping/tents

**245** WA 23, Sprague, **S gas:** Chevron/dsl, **food:** Viking Drive-In, **lodging:**, Sprague Motel, **other:** 4 Seasons RV Park (6mi), Sprague Lake Resort/RV Park

**242mm** rest area both lanes, full ♿ facilities, 🕿, 🍴, litter barrels, tourist/weather info, petwalk, RV dump (eb)

**231** Tokio, **S** weigh sta both lanes, **gas:** Exxon/Templin's Café/dsl, **other:** RV Park

**226** Schoessler Rd

**221** WA 261 S, Ritzville, City Ctr, **N gas:** Conoco/dsl, Chevron/McDonald's, Shell/Subway/dsl, **food:** Circle T Rest., Killian's Kitchen, Perkins, Sharon's Drive-in, Starbucks, Whisperin Palms, Zip's Rest., **lodging:** Best Value Inn, Best Western, The Cottage/RV Park, Empire Motel, La Quinta/RV Park, Top Hat Motel, **other:** Ⓗ HOSPITAL, Cow Creek Merchantile, hist dist

**220** to US 395 S, Ritzville, **N gas:** Pacific Pride, Texaco/Jake's Rest/dsl, **lodging:** Top Hat Motel, **other:** Chrysler/Dodge/Jeep, Harvest Foods, NAPA, Schwab Tires, st patrol

**215** Paha, Packard

**206** WA 21, Odessa, to Lind

**199mm** rest area both lanes, full ♿ facilities, 🕿, 🍴, litter barrels, vending, RV dump, petwalk

**196** Deal Rd, to Schrag

**188** U Rd, to Warden, Ruff

**184** Q Rd

**182** O Rd, to Wheeler

**179** WA 17, Moses Lake, **N gas:** Conoco/dsl, Ernie's Trkstp/Chevron/dsl/café/24hr, Exxon/Subway, 76/dsl, Shell/dsl, **food:** Arby's, Burger King, DQ, Denny's, McDonald's, Shari's Rest./24hr, Starbucks, Taco Bell, **lodging:** Comfort Suites, Holiday Inn Express, Moses Lake Inn, Ramada Inn, Shilo Inn/rest./24hr, **other:** Ⓗ HOSPITAL, Buick/Chevrolet/Pontiac, Chrysler/Dodge/Jeep Lowes Whse, Toyota, vet, **1 mi N food:** DQ, Subway, **lodging:** El Rancho Motel, **other:** $tree, Ford, Honda, Nissan, Sun Country RV Park, USPO, **S other:** I-90 RV, Mardon RV Park (15mi), Willows RV Park (2mi), Potholes SP (22mi)

**177mm** Moses Lake

**176** WA 171, Moses Lake, **1 mi N gas:** Cenex/dsl, Chevron/dsl, Conoco, Exxon/dsl, 76/dsl, Shell/dsl, **food:** El Rodeo Mexican, Paradise Rest., Perkins/24hr,

## INTERSTATE 90 CONT'D

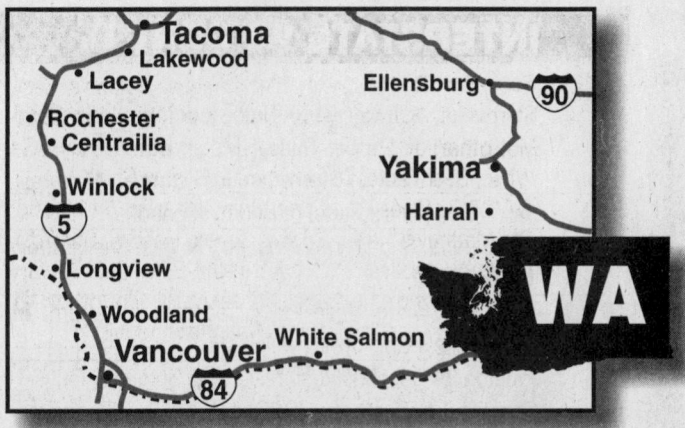

**E ← → W SPOKANE**

| | |
|---|---|
| **176** | Continued<br>Subway, Taco Del Mar, **lodging:** Best Western/rest., Interstate Inn, Motel 6, Oasis Motel, Super 8, **other:** H HOSPITAL, AAA RV Park, Ace Hardware, Harvest Foods, Lake Front RV Park, OK Tires, auto repair, transmissions, vet, **S lodging:** Lakeshore Motel |
| **175** | Westshore Dr (from wb), **N other:** Moses Lake SP, to Mae Valley, **S other:** st patrol |
| **174** | Mae Valley, **N other:** Suncrest Resort/RV, **S gas:** Conoco/dsl, **other:** Pier RV Park, st patrol |
| **169** | Hiawatha Rd |
| **164** | Dodson Rd, **N other:** Sunbasin RV park/camp (1mi) |
| **162mm** | **rest area wb, full** ♿ **facilities,** 🚻, 🏞, **litter barrels, petwalk, RV dump** |
| **161mm** | **rest area eb, full** ♿ **facilities,** 🚻, 🏞, **litter barrels, petwalk, RV dump** |
| **154** | Adams Rd |
| **151** | WA 281 N, to Quincy, **N gas:** Shell/dsl/pizza/subs, **other:** H HOSPITAL (12mi), Shady Grove RV park |
| **149** | WA 281 S, George, **N** HOSPITAL (12mi), **S gas:** Cenex/dsl, 76/Subway/dsl, **other:** RV camp |
| **143** | Silica Rd, to The Gorge Ampitheatre |
| **139mm** | Wild Horses Mon, scenic view both lanes |
| **137** | WA 26 E, to WA 243, Othello, Richland |
| **137mm** | Columbia River |
| **136** | Huntzinger Rd, Vantage, **N gas:** Shell, Texaco/dsl, **food:** Blustry's Burger Drive-in, Harvest Room Rest., **lodging:** Motel Vantage, **other:** Riverstone Resort RV park, Vantage Gen. Store, to Ginkgo/Wanapum SP (3mi), auto repair, **4 mi S other:** Gettys Cove RV Park |
| **126mm** | Ryegrass, elev 2535, **rest area both lanes, full** ♿ **facilities,** 🚻, 🏞, **litter barrels, petwalk** |
| **115** | Kittitas, **N gas:** Shell/dsl/LP/24hr, **other:** Olmstead Place SP |
| **110** | I-82 E, US 97 S, to Yakima |

**E L L E N S B U R G**

| | |
|---|---|
| **109** | Canyon Rd, Ellensburg, **N gas:** Astro/dsl, Chevron/24hr, Circle K, Eagle/dsl, 76, Shell/24hr, **food:** Arby's, Baskin Robbins, Burger King, Fiesta Mexican, Golden Dragon Chinese, KFC, Los Cabos Mexican, McDonald's, Papa Murphy's, Quizno's, RanchHouse Rest., Roadhouse Grill, Subway, Taco Bell, Taco Del Mar, Wendy's, Yuan Chinese, **lodging:** Best Western, Comfort Inn, Goose Creek Inn, Holiday Inn Express, Quality Inn, Super 8, **other:** H HOSPITAL, AutoZone, CarQuest, Chevrolet, Fred Meyer, NAPA, Radio Shack, Rite Aid, Schwab Tire, Super 1 Food/24hr, TrueValue, vet, **S gas:** ⊕FLYING J /Sak's/dsl/scales/LP/24hr, **food:** Buzz Inn Steaks, **lodging:** Days Inn/RV park |
| **106** | US 97 N, to Wenatchie, **N gas:** Chevron, Conoco/dsl, Pilot/Subway/dsl/24hr, 76/dsl, **food:** DQ, Perkins, **lodging:** Hampton Inn, Harold's Motel (2mi), I-90 Inn, **other:** Buick/Pontiac/GMC, Canopy Country RV Ctr, Chrystler/Jeep, Truck/RV Wash, **S other:** KOA, st patrol |
| **101** | Thorp Hwy, **N gas:** Arco, **other:** antiques/fruits/vegetables |
| **93** | Elk Heights Rd, Taneum Creek |
| **92.5mm** | Elk Heights, elev 2359 |
| **89mm** | Indian John Hill, elev 2141, **rest area both lanes, full** ♿ **facilities,** 🚻, 🏞, **litter barrels, RV dump, petwalk, vending** |

**C L E E L U M**

| | |
|---|---|
| **85** | WA 970, WA 903, to Wenatchie, **N gas:** Gas Save, 76/dsl, Shell/dsl/24hr, **food:** Cottage Café/24hr, DQ, Giant Burger, Home Stead Rest., McKean's Drive-In, **lodging:** Aster Inn, Cascade Mtn Inn, Chalet Motel, Cle Elum Motel, Traveler's Inn, **other:** vet |
| **84** | Cle Elum (from eb, return at 85), **N gas:** Chevron/dsl, Pacific Pride/dsl, Shell/Subway/dsl, **food:** Burger King, Cle Elum Bakery, DQ, El Caporal Mexican, Mama Vallones, Quizno's, Sahara Pizza, Spaconi's Rest., Sunset Café, Taco Del Mar, **lodging:** Timber Lodge Motel, Stewart Lodge, **other:** H HOSPITAL, Cle Elum Drug, NAPA, Radio Shack, Safeway/gas, Trailer Corral RV Park, museum |
| **81mm** | Cle Elum River |
| **80** | Roslyn, Salmon la Sac |
| **80mm** | weigh sta both lanes, phone |
| **78** | Golf Course Rd, **S other:** Sun Country Golf/RV Park |
| **74** | W Nelson Siding Rd |
| **71** | Easton, **S gas:** CB's Store/dsl/LP, **other:** USPO, John Wayne Tr, Iron Horse SP |
| **71mm** | Yakima River |
| **70** | Lake Easton SP, **N gas:** Shell/RV Town/dsl/café, **food:** Mtn High Burger, **other:** Silver Ridge Ranch RV Park, repair, **S other:** Lake Easton SP |
| **63** | Cabin Creek Rd |
| **62** | Stampede Pass, elev 3750, to Lake Kachess, camping both lanes |
| **56mm** | parking area, eb (.5mi) |
| **54** | Hyak, Gold Creek, **S** Ski Area |
| **53** | Snoqualmie Pass, elev 3022, info, **S gas:** Chevron, **food:** Family Pancake House, **lodging:** Summit Lodge, **other:** to rec areas |
| **52** | W Summit (from eb), same as 53 |
| **47** | Tinkham Rd, Denny Creek, Asahel Curtis, **N other:** chain area, **S other:** RV camping/dump |
| **45** | USFS Rd 9030, **N other:** to Lookout Point Rd |
| **42** | Tinkham Rd |
| **38** | **N other:** fire training ctr |
| **35mm** | S Fork Snoqualmie River |
| **34** | 468th Ave SE, Edgewick Rd, **N gas:** 76/BBQ/dsl, Shell/Subway/dsl/24hr, TA/dsl only/rest./@, **food:** Ken's Rest., **lodging:** Edgewick Inn, **other:** NW RV Park |
| **32** | 436th Ave SE, North Bend Ranger Sta, **1 mi N** gas, food, lodging |
| **31** | WA 202 W, North Bend, Snoqualmie, **N gas:** Chevron/dsl, Shell/dsl, **food:** Arby's, Blimpie, Burger King, Los Cabos, McDonald's, Mongolian Grill, Papa Murphy's, |

Copyright 2009 - The Next Exit®

## INTERSTATE 90 CONT'D

**E → W**

**ISSAQUAH**

| | |
|---|---|
| 31 | Continued Starbucks, Subway, Taco Time, **lodging:** North Bend Motel, Sallish Lodge, Sunset Motel, **other:** H HOSPITAL, NorthBend Stores/famous brands, Safeway/deli/24hr, Shuck's Parts, museum, st patrol |
| 27 | North Bend, Snoqualmie (from eb), **N gas:** Shell, **other:** H HOSPITAL |
| 25 | WA 18 W, Snoqualmie Pkwy, Tacoma, to Auburn, **N food:** Mike's Grill, **other:** weigh sta |
| 22 | Preston, **N gas:** Shell/dsl/24hr, **food:** Burgers& Teriyaki, Sherm's BBQ, **other:** USPO, LP, NAPA, Snoqualmie River RV Park (4mi), **S other:** Blue Sky RV Park |
| 20 | High Point Way |
| 18 | E Sunset Way, Issaquah, **S gas:** Shell (1mi), **food:** Flying Pie Pizza, Front St Mkt, Issaquah Brewhouse, Jack's Grill, Korean Grill, Mandarin Garden, Shanghai Garden Chinese, Stan's BBQ |
| 17 | E Sammamish Rd, Front St, Issaquah, **N gas:** Chevron, 76, **food:** Coho Café, Coldstone Creamery, Fatburger, Jamba Juice, Krispy Kreme, McDonald's, Qdoba Mexican, Papa John's, Pallino Pasta, Starbucks, **other:** Fred Meyer, Home Depot, Walgreens, **S gas:** Chevron/24hr, Shell, **food:** Boehms Chocolates, Domino's, Extreme Pizza, La Costa Mexican, Las Margaritas, Pogacha Rest., **other:** Big O Tire, U-Haul, transmissions |
| 15 | WA 900, Issaquah, Renton, **N gas:** Arco/24hr, **food:** Cocina Cocina, IHOP, Ochar Thai, Red Robin, Tully's Coffee, **lodging:** Holiday Inn, Motel 6, **other:** Barnes&Noble, Costco/gas, Lowes Whse, Michael's, Office Depot, PetsMart, Trader Joe's, to Lk Sammamish SP, vet, **S gas:** Shell, **food:** Baskin-Robbins, Burger King, Chipotle Mexican, Denny's, Georgio's Subs, Issaquah Cafe, Jack-in-the-Box, Jamba Juice, KFC/Taco Bell, Lombardi's Italian, McDonald's, O'Ginger Bistro, Papa Murphy's, RoundTable Pizza, Starbucks, Subway, Taco Time, **lodging:** Hilton Garden, **other:** Chevrolet, Firestone/auto, Ford, GNC, PetCo, QFC Foods, Rite Aid, Ross, Safeway Foods, Schuck's Parts, Target, USPO |
| 13 | SE Newport Way, W Lake Sammamish |
| 11 | SE 150th, 156th, 161st, Bellevue, **N** LDS Temple, **gas:** Shell, **food:** DQ, Greenwood Mandarin Chinese, Lil' Jon's Rest., McDonald's, Starbucks, Subway, Tulley's Coffee, **lodging:** Day's Inn, Embassy Suites, Silver Cloud Inn, **other:** Ford, 7-11, Subaru/VW, Safeway, Toyota, **S gas:** 76, Standard, Shell/dsl/24hr, **food:** Baskin-Robbins, Domino's, Outback Steaks, Pizza Hut, **lodging:** Homestead Suites, **other:** Albertson's, Honda, Larkspur Landing, Rite Aid, Schuck's Parts |
| 10 | I-405, N to Bellevue, S to Renton, services located off I-405 S, exit 10 |
| 9 | Bellevue Way |
| 8 | E Mercer Way, Mercer Island |
| 7c | 80th Ave SE (exits left from wb) |
| 7b a | SE 76th Ave, 77th Ave, Island Crest Way, Mercer Island, **S gas:** Chevron, 76/repair, Shell/dsl/repair, |

| | |
|---|---|
| 7b a | Continued **food:** McDonald's, Starbucks, Subway, Thai Rest., Tully's Coffee, **lodging:** Travelodge, **other:** Island Foods, TrueValue, Walgreens |
| 6 | W Mercer Way (from eb), same as 7 |
| 5mm | Lake Washington |
| 3b a | Ranier Ave, Seattle, downtown, **N gas:** Shell/dsl, **other:** vet |
| 2c b | I-5, N to Vancouver, S to Tacoma |
| 2a | 4th Ave S, to King Dome |

I-90 begins/ends on I-5 at exit 164.

## INTERSTATE 182 - RICHLAND

**E → W**

**RICHLAND**

| Exit # | Services |
|---|---|
| 14b a | US 395 N, WA 397 S, OR Ave, **N gas:** ⊕*FLYING J* dsl/scales/24hr, King City/Shell/rest/dsl/@, **food:** Burger King, Subway, **lodging:** Knight's Inn, **other:** Goodyear, Peterbilt, **S lodging:** Motel 6, **I-182 begins/ends on US 395 N.** |
| 13 | N 4th Ave, Cty Ctr, **N gas:** CFN/dsl, **lodging:** Airport Motel, Starlite Motel, **S gas:** 76/dsl/24hr, **other:** H HOSPITAL, RV park, museum |
| 12b | N 20th Ave, **N lodging:** Best Western, Red Lion Inn |
| 12a | US 395 S, Court St, **S on** Court St. **gas:** Conoco, Exxon/Jack-in-the-Box, Shell, Tesoro, Texaco, **food:** A&W/KFC, Baskin Robbins, Burger King, DQ, Francisco's Rest., Little Ceasar's, McDonald's, Pizza Hut, Quizno's, Round Table Pizza, Subway, Super China Buffet, Taco Bell, Wendy's, **other:** Albertson's/gas, AutoZone, Cadillac/Chevrolet/Pontiac, Chief RV Ctr, Ford, Nissan, Rite Aid, Sav-a-Lot Foods, Subaru, U-haul, Walgreens |
| 9 | rd 68, Trac, **N gas:** Shell, Tesoro, **food:** Antonio's Pizza, Applebees, Arby's, Bruchi's & Figaro's Pizza, Cousin's Rest., Eatza Pizza Buffet, Emperial Buffet, Fiesta Mexican, IHOP, King China Buffet, Jack-in-the-Box, McDonald's, Nick n Willy's Pizza, Panda Express, Pier 39 Seafood, Quizno's, Sonic, Starbucks, Subway, Taco Bell, Teriyaki Grill, **lodging:** Holiday Inn Express, **other:** Lowes Whse, Walgreens, Walmart Super Ctr, Yokes Foods |
| 7 | Broadmoor Blvd, **N lodging:** Sleep Inn, **other:** Broadmoor Outlet Mall/famous brands, GNC, **S other:** Broadmoor RV Ctr, Sandy Heights RV Park |
| 6.5mm | Columbia River |
| 5b a | WA 240 E, Geo Washington Way, to Kennewick, **N food:** Applebees, Jack In the Box, Starbucks, **lodging:** Courtyard, Day's Inn, Economy Inn, Hampton Inn, Red Lion, Royal Hotel, Shilo Inn, **other:** $Tree, Winco Foods/gas |
| 4 | WA 240 W, **N gas:** Conoco/dsl, **food:** McDonald's, Rancho Boninto, **other:** Fred Meyer/gas |
| 3.5mm | Yakima River |
| 3 | Keene Rd, Queensgate, **N gas:** Shell, **food:** A&W/KFC, Burger King, El Rancho Alegre, LJ Silver, McDonald's, Panda Express, Starbucks, Subway, Taco Bell, **other:** Home Depot, PetCo, Target, Walmart Super Ctr/auto/gas, **S other:** RV Park (3mi) |
| 0mm | I-182 begins/ends on I-82, exit 102. |

## INTERSTATE 405 - SEATTLE

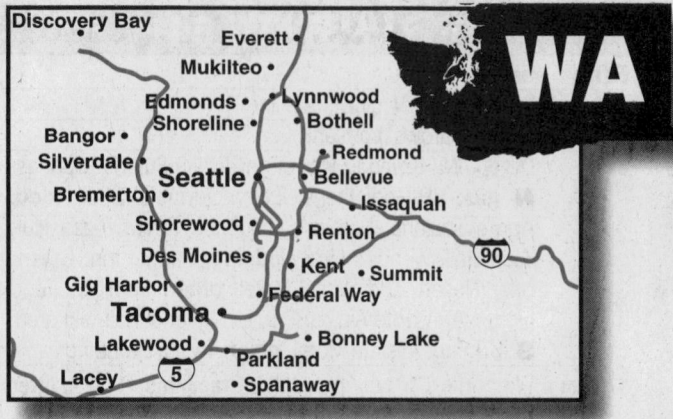

| Exit # | Services |
|---|---|
| 30 | I-5, N to Canada, S to Seattle, I-405 begins/ends on I-5, exit 182. |
| 26 | WA 527, Bothell, Mill Creek, **E** **food:** Canyon's Rest., McDonald's, Thai-Rama, **other:** Lake Pleasant RV Park, **W** **gas:** Shell/dsl **food:** Applebees, Arby's, Bamboo House, Bonefish Grill, Crystal Creek Cafe, Denny's, Fortune Cookie Chinese, Grazie Ristorante, Imperial Wok, Jack-in-the-Box, Mongolian Grill, Outback Steaks, Papa Murphy's, Qdoba Mexican, Quizno's, Subway, Taco Bell, Taco Time, Tully's Coffee, Wendy's, **lodging:** Comfort Inn, Extended Stay America, Holiday Inn Express, **other:** Albertson's, Bartell Drug, Curves, Goodyear/auto, QFC Foods, Radio Shack, Rite Aid, 7-11 |
| 24 | NE 195th St, Beardslee Blvd, **E** **gas:** Shell/Quizno's/dsl, **food:** Teryaki Etc, **lodging:** Country Inn&Suites, Residence Inn |
| 23b | WA 522 W, Bothell |
| 23a | WA 522 E, to WA 202, Woodinville, Monroe |
| 22 | NE 160th St, **E** **gas:** Chevron, Shell/dsl/24hr, **food:** Denice's Cafe |
| 20 | NE 124th St, **E** **gas:** Shell/dsl/24hr, **food:** Denny's, Georgio's Subs, Pizza Hut, Santa Fe Mexican, Shari's, Zaburo's Grill, **lodging:** Baymont Inn, Comfort Inn, Motel 6, **other:** H HOSPITAL, Big O Tire, Chrysler/Dodge/Jeep, Discount Tire, Firestone, Infiniti, Radio Shack, Rite Aid, Ross, Schucks Parts, Schwab Tire, Toyota/Scion, mall, **W** **gas:** Arco/24hr, 76, **food:** Azteca Mexican, Burger King, Domino's, Hunan Wok, McDonald's, Romio's Pizza, Olive Garden, Starbucks, Subway, Taco Time, Wendy's, **lodging:** Courtyard, **other:** Buick/GMC/Pontiac, Fred Meyer, GNC, QFC Foods/24hr |
| 18 | WA 908, Kirkland, Redmond, **E** **gas:** Arco/dsl, Chevron/24hr, 7-11, 76/Circle K, Shell/dsl, **food:** Garlic Jim's, McDonald's, Outback Steaks, Starbucks, Subway, Valhalla Grill, **other:** Chevrolet, Costco, Hancock Fabrics, Honda, Mazda, Nissan, PetCo, Safeway Foods, Schuck's Parts, 7-11, Tuesday Morning, U-Haul, Walgreens, **W** **gas:** Chevron, Shell, **food:** Acropolis Pizza, Cafe Creek, Crab Cracker, Papa John's, Subway, TGI-Friday, Wendy's, **other:** QFC Foods, Tire Factory, vet |
| 17 | NE 70th Pl |
| 14b a | WA 520, Seattle, Redmond |
| 13b | NE 8th St, **E** **gas:** Chevron/dsl, Shell/dsl, **food:** Denny's, **lodging:** Coast Hotel, Extended Stay America, **other:** H HOSPITAL, Best Buy, Buick/Pontiac, Ford, Home Depot, Hummer, Larry's Mkt, Lincoln/Mercury, Mercedes, Whole Foods Mkt, **W** **food:** Starbucks, Subway, **lodging:** Courtyard, Hyatt |
| 13a | NE 4th St, **E** **lodging:** Extended Stay America, **other:** Ford, Lexus, **W** **lodging:** Best Western, Doubletree Hotel, Hilton, Ramada Ltd., Red Lion/Bellevue Inn, Sheraton |
| 12 | SE 8th St, **W** **lodging:** Residence Inn |
| 11 | I-90, E to Spokane, W to Seattle |
| 10 | Cold Creek Pkwy, Factoria, **E on Factoria Blvd...gas:** Chevron, 76/Circle K, **food:** Applebees, Burger King, Coldstone Creamery, Jamba Juice, KFC, Keg Steaks, McDonald's, Old Country Buffet, Peking Wok, Quizno's, Red Robin, Romio's Pizza, Sideline Grill, Starbucks, Subway, Taco Bell, Taco Time, Torero's Mexican, **other:** Old Navy, PetCo, QFC Foods, Rite Aid, Safeway, Schuck's Parts, 7-11, Target, mall, vet |
| 9 | 112th Ave SE, Newcastle, phone |
| 7 | NE 44th St, **E** **food:** Denny's/24hr, McDonald's, Subway, **lodging:** Econolodge |
| 6 | NE 30th St, **E** **gas:** Arco/24hr, **W** **gas:** Chevron/24hr, Shell, **other:** 7-11 |
| 5 | WA 900 E, Park Ave N, Sunset Blvd NE, **W** **other:** Fry's Electronics |
| 4 | WA 169 S, Wa 900 W, Renton, **E** **food:** Shari's, **lodging:** Quality Inn, **other:** Aqua Barn Ranch Camping, **W** **food:** Burger King, Stir Rest., **lodging:** Renton Inn, **other:** 7-11, |
| 2 | WA 167, Rainier Ave, to Auburn, **E** **lodging:** Hilton Garden, Larkspur Landing, SpringHill Suites, TownePlace Suites, H HOSPITAL, **W** **gas:** Chevron, 76/dsl, Shell, USA/dsl, **food:** A&W/KFC, Applebees, Arby's, Baskin-Robbins, Georgio's Subs, IHOP, Jack-in-the-Box, Jimmy Mack's, King Buffet, Mazatlan Mexican, McDonald's, PanAsia, Panda Express, Papa Murphy's, Pizza Hut, Popeye's, Qdoba Mexican, Starbucks, Subway, Taco Bell, Taco Time, Torero's Mexican, Wendy's, Yankee Grill, **lodging:** Holiday Inn, **other:** Aamco, Buick/Cadillac/GMC/Pontiac, Chevrolet, Chrysler/Jeep, Discount Tire, Dodge, Ford, Fred Meyer, Firestone/auto, Honda/Hyundai/Kia/Mazda, Isuzu, Radio Shack, Rite Aid, Safeway/gas, Sam's Club/gas, Schuck's Parts, Schwab Tire, Subaru, Toyota/Scion, Walgreens, Walmart/auto, vet |
| 1 | WA 181 S, Tukwila, **E** **gas:** Chevron/dsl, 76/dsl, Shell/dsl, **food:** Barnaby's Rest., Jack-in-the-Box, McDonald's, Sushi & Grill, Taco Bell, Teriyaki Wok, Wendy's, **lodging:** Best Western, Courtyard, Embassy Suites, Hampton Inn, Homestead Suites, Residence Inn, **other:** 7-11, mall, **W** **gas:** Shell, **lodging:** Comfort Suites, Homewood Suites, **other:** fun center |
| 0mm | I-5, N to Seattle, S to Tacoma, WA 518 W. I-405 begins/ends on I-5, exit 154. |

**WV**

E

↕

W

## INTERSTATE 64

| Exit # | Services |
|---|---|
| 184mm | West Virginia/Virginia state line |
| 183 | VA 311, Crows (from eb) |
| 181 | US 60, WV 92 (no ez wb return), White Sulphur Springs, **N gas:** BP/Godfather's, Exxon/Quizno's, Shell, **food:** April's Pizzaria, Hardee's, Legends Rest., Pizza Hut, Taco Bell, Wendy's (4mi), **lodging:** Budget Inn, Greenbrier Resort, Old White Motel, **other:** Family$, Food Lion, NAPA, Rite Aid, USPO, to Midland Trail, ski area, **S lodging:** Allstate Motel, **other:** Twilite Camping |
| 179mm | Welcome Ctr wb, info, full ♿ facilities, 🚻, 🅿, litter barrels, petwalk |
| 175 | US 60, WV 92, Caldwell, **N gas:** Chevron/dsl/24hr, Exxon, Shell/Subway/dsl, **food:** Granny's House Rest., Greenbrier's Mountainaire Rest., McDonald's, Wendy's, **lodging:** Village Motel, **other:** $General, **S other:** Greenbrier SF, camping |
| 173mm | Greenbrier River |
| 169 | US 219, Lewisburg, Hist Dist, **N gas:** Shell, **food:** Blackwell's Rest., **lodging:** Relax Inn, **S gas:** Exxon/dsl, Gomart, Shell, **food:** Applebee's, Arby's, Bob Evans, Hardee's, Ruby Tuesday, Shoney's, Subway, Western Sizzlin, **lodging:** Brier Inn, Econolodge, Hampton Inn, Holiday Inn Express, Super 8, **other:** Ⓗ HOSPITAL, Chevrolet, Ford, Lowe's Whse, Walmart SuperCtr/gas |
| 161 | WV 12, Alta, **S gas:** Alta Sta/cafe, Exxon, **other:** Greenbrier River Camping (14mi) |
| 156 | US 60, Midland Trail, Sam Black Church, **N gas:** Citgo, Exxon/dsl, Shell/dsl, **food:** Linda's Rest. |
| 150 | Dawson, **S gas:** Exxon, **food:** Cheddar's Cafe, **lodging:** Dawson Inn, **other:** RV camping |
| 147mm | runaway truck ramp wb |
| 143 | WV 20, Green Sulphur Springs, **N gas:** Liberty/dsl |
| 139 | WV 20, Sandstone, Hinton, **S gas:** Citgo/dsl, **other:** Blue Stone SP (16mi), Richmond Store, to Pipestem Resort Park (25 mi), USPO |
| 138mm | New River |
| 133 | WV 27, Bragg Rd, Sandstone Mtn (Elev. 2765), mandatory truck stop eb, **S** RV camping |
| 129 | WV 9, Shady Spring, **N other:** to Grandview SP, **S gas:** Exxon/dsl, Shell/dsl, **food:** Subway, **other:** Little Beaver SP |
| 125 | WV 307, Airport Rd, Beaver, **N gas:** Shell/dsl, **food:** Biscuit World, **lodging:** Sleep Inn, **S gas:** BP/dsl, Exxon, GoMart/gas, **food:** Hardee's, KFC, LJ Silver, McDonald's, Pizza Hut, **lodging:** Glade Spgs Resort, Patriot Motel |
| 124 | US 19, E Beckley, 0-2 mi **N gas:** BP, Exxon, GoMart/gas, **food:** Capt D's, Huddle House, **lodging:** Microtel, **other:** last exit before toll rd wb |
| 121 | I-77 S, to Bluefield |
| | **I-64 and I-77 run together 61 mi. See Interstate 77, exits 42 through 100.** |
| 59 | I-77 N (from eb), to I-79 |
| 58c | US 60, Washington St, **N gas:** Exxon, GoMart/gas, **food:** Arby's, **other:** Lincoln/Mercury, **S food:** LJ Silver, Shoney's, **lodging:** Embassy Suites, Hampton Inn, Holiday Inn Express, Marriott, **other:** Ⓗ HOSPITAL, civic ctr, mall |
| 58b | US 119 N (from eb), Charleston, downtown |
| 58a | US 119 S, WV 61, MacCorkle Ave, **S food:** Steak&Ale |

C
H
A
R
L
E
S
T
O
N

| | |
|---|---|
| 56 | Montrose Dr, **N gas:** Chevron, Exxon/dsl, Speedway, **food:** Hardee's, Los Agaves Mexican, **lodging:** Microtel, Ramada Inn, Wingate Inn, **other:** Advance Parts, Chevrolet, Chrysler, Dodge, Hyundai, Kia, NAPA, Rite Aid, Toyota, VW |
| 55 | Kanawha Tpk |
| 54 | US 60, MacCorkle Ave, **N food:** Burger King, Subway, **other:** Kroger/gas, **S gas:** Citgo, **food:** Bob Evans, KFC, LJ Silver, McDonald's, Pizza Hut, Schlotsky's, Taco Bell, Wendy's, **other:** Ⓗ HOSPITAL, Aamco, Harley-Davidson, Honda, Mazda/Mitsubishi |
| 53 | Roxalana Rd, to Dunbar, **S gas:** GoMart/gas, **food:** BiscuitWorld, Capt D's, Gino's Pizza, McDonald's, Shoney's, Subway, Wendy's, **lodging:** Super 8, Travelodge, **other:** Advance Parts, Aldi, CarQuest, CVS Drug, Family$, Jo-Ann Fabrics, Kroger, NTB, Radio Shack |
| 50 | VW 25, Institute, **S gas:** GoMart/gas |
| 47b a | WV 622, Goff Mtn Rd, **N gas:** Chevron/24hr, Exxon, GoMart, Speedway/dsl, **food:** BiscuitWorld, Bob Evans, Capt D's, Domino's, Gino's Pizza, McDonald's, Papa John's, Pizza Hut, Rice Bowl, Subway, Taco Bell, Tim Horton, Wendy's, **lodging:** Motel 6, **other:** Advance Parts, Curves, Kroger/gas, Rite Aid, **S food:** Arby's, Burger King, Coco's Chinese, Cracker Barrel, Fazoli's, La Roca Mexican, Subway, TGIFriday, **lodging:** Comfort Inn, Sleep Inn, **other:** $Tree, Freightliner, Goody's, Lowe's Whse, Radio Shack, Staples, Walmart SuperCtr |
| 45 | WV 25, Nitro, **N gas:** Pilot/Arby's/dsl/scales/24hr, **other:** Chevrolet, **S gas:** Exxon/dsl, GoMart, Speedway/dsl, **food:** BiscuitWorld, Checker's, DQ, Gino's Pizza, McDonald's, Subway, Wendy's, **lodging:** Econolodge, **other:** Chevrolet |
| 44.3mm | Kanawha River |
| 44 | US 35, St Albans, **S gas:** Chevron/dsl, **other:** 7-11 |
| 41 | Scott Depot, **S food:** DQ |
| 39 | WV 34, Winfield, **N gas:** BP/Arby's, GoMart/dsl, **food:** Applebee's, Bob Evans, Hardee's, Taste of Asia, **lodging:** Day's Inn, Holiday Inn Express, Red Roof Inn, **other:** Advance Parts, Big Lots, $General, GNC, Home Depot, Radio Shack, USPO, **S gas:** Exxon/7-11/dsl, GoMart/gas, TA/dsl/rest./scales/24hr/@, **food:** Biscuit World, Burger King, Capt D's, China Chef, Gino's Pizza, KFC, McDonald's, Monty's Pizza, Papa John's, Schlotzsky's, Shoney's, Subway, Taco Bell, TCBY, Wendy's, **lodging:** Hampton Inn, **other:** AutoZone, K-Mart, Kroger, NAPA, Rite Aid |
| 38mm | weigh sta both lanes |
| 35mm | rest area both lanes, full ♿ facilities, 🚻, vending, 🅿, litter barrels, petwalk |
| 34 | WV 19, Hurricane, **N food:** KFC, **other:** Chevrolet, Chrysler/Jeep/Dodge, Ford, Mountain State RV Ctr, Saturn, Walmart SuperCtr, **S gas:** Exxon/7-11, GoMart, **food:** BiscuitWorld/Gino's Pizza, Little Caesar's, McDonald's, Mi Pueblito, Pizza Hut, Subway, **lodging:** Super 8, **other:** Rite Aid, vet |
| 28 | US 60, Milton, 1-3 mi **S gas:** Chevron/dsl, Exxon, GoMart, Rich Gas, **food:** Biscuit World, DQ, Gino's Pizza, McDonald's, Pizza Hut, Subway, Wendy's, **other:** Advance Parts, $General, Family$, Foodland, Jim's Camping (2mi), KOA (3mi), NAPA, Rite Aid, Sav-A-Lot foods, USPO |
| 20 | US 60, Mall Rd, Barboursville, **N food:** Applebee's, Arby's, Bob Evans, Burger King, Chick-fil-A, Chili's, |

## INTERSTATE 64 CONT'D

E
↑
↓
W

**20** Continued
Cici's Pizza, IHOP, Logan's Roadhouse, McDonald's, Olive Garden, Panera Bread, Ruby Tuesday, Wendy's, **lodging:** Comfort Inn, **other:** Best Buy, Borders Books, Circuit City, Drug Emporium, Elder-Berman, Firestone/auto, Goody's, JC Penney, Jo-Ann Fabrics, Kohl's, Lowe's Whse, Macy's, Michael's, NTB, Sears/auto, mall, Walmart SuperCtr, **S gas:** BP, **food:** Cracker Barrel, Famous Dave's BBQ, Outback Steaks, Sam's Hotdogs, Sonic, Steak&Shake, Subway, Taco Bell, TCBY, **lodging:** Best Western, Comfort Inn, Hampton Inn, Holiday Inn, **other:** KOA, Toyota

**18** US 60, to WV 2, Barboursville, **N food:** Bellacino's, O'Charley's, Starbucks, **other:** $Tree, Home Depot, Marshall's, Office Depot, PetsMart, Target, **S gas:** Chevron/7-11, **food:** Hardee's, Hooters, Papa John's, Pizza Hut, **lodging:** Comfort Suites, **other:** Kia, Kroger/gas, Rite Aid

**15** US 60, 29th St E, **N gas:** GoMart/dsl, Speedway/dsl, **food:** Arby's, Biscuit World, Gino's Pizza, Pizza Hut, Subway, Wendy's, Waffle House, **other:** H HOSPITAL, BigLots, Curves, $General, Sav-a-Lot Foods,

**15** Continued
Walmart SuperCtr/McDonald's, st police, **S gas:** Exxon, **food:** Fazoli's, Golden Corral, KFC, Little Caesar's, McDonald's, Penn Sta., Shoney's, Taco Bell, **lodging:** Day's Inn, Red Roof Inn, **other:** Chrysler/Jeep, CVS Drug, Nissan/Mitsubishi, Pontiac/Cadillac/GMC/Buick, Subaru

**11** WV 10, Hal Greer Blvd, **0-2 mi N gas:** BP, Go-Mart, Marathon, **food:** Arby's, Bob Evan's, Frostop Drive-In, Gino's Pizza, KFC, McDonald's, Wendy's, **lodging:** Holiday Inn, Ramada Ltd, Super 8, **other:** H HOSPITAL, Rite Aid, **S other:** Beech Fork SP (8mi)

**10mm** Welcome Ctr eb, full ♿ facilities, 📞, vending, 🏕 litter barrels, petwalk

**8** WV 152 S, WV 527 N, **S gas:** Speedway, **food:** DQ

**6** US 52 N, W Huntington, Chesapeake, **N gas:** Marathon, Speedway/24hr, **food:** Pizza Hut, **other:** H HOSPITAL, AutoZone, BigLots, $General, Family$, Sav-A-Lot Foods

**1** US 52 S, Kenova, **1-3 mi N gas:** Chevron/dsl, Exxon, Speedway, **food:** Burger King, Evaroni's Pizza, Gino's Pizza, Little Caesar's, McDonald's, Pizza Hut, Stewart's Hotdogs, **lodging:** Hollywood Motel, **other:** Advance Parts, Sav-A-Lot

**0mm** West Virginia/Kentucky state line, Big Sandy River

H
U
N
T
I
N
G
T
O
N

**WV**

## INTERSTATE 68

| Exit # | Services |
|---|---|
| 32mm | West Virginia/Maryland state line |
| 31mm | **Welcome Ctr wb, full ♿ facilities, 🛝 litter barrels, 📞 vending, petwalk** |
| 29 | rd 5, Hazelton Rd, **N gas:** Sunoco/dsl, **lodging:** Microtel (1mi), **S other:** Big Bear Camping (3mi), Pine Hill RV Camp (4mi) |
| 23 | WV 26, Bruceton Mills, **N gas:** BP/Subway/dsl/24hr, Sunoco/Little Sandy's Rest./dsl/24hr, **food:** Twila's Rest., **lodging:** Maple Leaf Motel, **other:** Family$, Hostetler's Store, USPO, antiques |
| 18mm | Laurel Run |
| 17mm | runaway truck ramp eb |
| 16mm | weigh sta wb |
| 15 | WV 73, WV 12, Coopers Rock, **N other:** Chestnut Ridge SF, Sand Springs Camping (2mi) |
| 12mm | runaway truck ramp wb |
| 10 | WV 857, Fairchance Rd, Cheat Lake, **N gas:** BP/Little Ceasar's/TCBY/dsl/24hr, Exxon/dsl, **food:** China Kitchen, Pizza'n Pasta, Subway, USPO, **lodging:** Lakeview Resort, **S food:** Burger King, Dimitri's Steaks |
| 9mm | Cheat Lake |
| 7 | rd 705, Pierpont Rd, **N gas:** BP/Little Ceasar's/Subway/TCBY, Exxon/Taco Bell/dsl, **food:** Bob Evans, Fujiyama Steaks, Heavenly Ham, IHOP, Outback Steaks, Ruby Tuesday, Wendy's, **lodging:** Euro Suites, Holiday Inn Express, Super 8, **other:** Ⓗ HOSPITAL, BooksAMillion, Family$, GNC, Harley-Davidson, Lowes Whse, Michael's, Shop'n Save Foods, to WVU Stadium, **S gas:** Crestpoint, **food:** Fox's Pizza Den |
| 4 | rd 7, to Sabraton, **N gas:** BP/Subway/dsl, Exxon/24hr, Sheetz/dsl/24hr, **food:** Arby's, Burger King, Hardee's, Hero Hut, KFC, LJ Silver, McDonald's, Pizza Hut, Wendy's, **lodging:** SpringHill Suites, **other:** Advance Parts, CVS Drug, $General, Family$, Ford/Lincoln/Mercury, Kroger/gas, Sav-a-Lot Foods, USPO, **S gas:** Allstar/dsl, Pacific Pride/dsl |
| 3mm | Decker's Creek |
| 1 | US 119, Morgantown, **N gas:** Go-Mart/dsl, **lodging:** Comfort Inn, Ramada Inn/rest., **other:** tires, **S food:** Subway, **other:** $Tree, Walmart SuperCtr, to Tygart L SP |
| 0mm | I-79, N to Pittsburgh, S to Clarksburg. I-68 begins/ends on I-79, exit 148. |

## INTERSTATE 70

| Exit # | Services |
|---|---|
| 14mm | West Virginia/Pennsylvania state line |
| 13.5mm | **Welcome Ctr wb, full ♿ facilities, 📞 vending, 🛝 litter barrels, petwalk** |
| 11 | WV 41, Dallas Pike, **N gas:** TA/dsl/rest./@, **lodging:** Comfort Inn, **S gas:** AM Best/Country Kitchen/Taco Joe/CK Burger/dsl/scales/24hr, Exxon, Mobil/DQ/dsl, **lodging:** Holiday Inn Express, **other:** RV camping |
| 10 | rd 65, to Cabela Dr, **N food:** Applebee's, Bob Evans, Cheddar's, Coldstone Creamery, Cracker Barrel, Eat'n Park, McDonald's, Olive Garden, Panera Bread, Quizno's, Wendy's, **other:** Best Buy, Books-a-Million, Cabela's, JC Penney, Kohl's, Michael's, Old Navy, PetCo, Russel Stover Candies, Target, TJ Maxx, Walmart SuperCtr |
| 5 | US 40, WV 88 S, Tridelphia, **N gas:** Marathon, **food:** Christopher's Café, Hoss' Rest., Pizza Hut, Subway, |

| | |
|---|---|
| 5 | Continued<br>Wendy's, **lodging:** Super 8, **other:** Chrysler/Dodge/Jeep, Family$, Riesbeck's Foods, vet, **S gas:** Exxon/dsl, Mobil, **food:** Arby's, Domino's, DQ, McDonald's, Silver Chopsticks, Undo's Rest., **other:** Advance Parts, Rite Aid, museum |
| 5a | I-470 W, to Columbus |
| 4 | WV 88 N (from eb), Elm Grove, same as 5 |
| 3.5mm | weigh sta wb |
| 2b | Washington Ave, **N gas:** Exxon, **food:** Greco's Rest., **other:** Kroger/gas, **S food:** Figaretti's Italian, **other:** Ⓗ HOSPITAL |
| 2a | rd 88 N, to Oglebay Park, **N gas:** Exxon, Sheetz, **food:** Bob Evans, Hardee's, LJ Silver, Papa John's, Perkins, Subway, Super Buffet, Tim Horton's, TJ's Rest., **lodging:** Hampton Inn, Springhill Suites, **other:** Advance Parts, CVS Drug, Kroger/gas, NTB, Radio Shack |
| 1b | US 250 S, WV 2 S, S Wheeling |
| 1mm | tunnel |
| 1a | US 40 E, WV 2 N, Main St, downtown, **S lodging:** Wheeling Inn |
| 0 | US 40 W, Zane St, Wheeling Island, **N gas:** Exxon/dsl, **food:** Burger King, KFC |
| 0mm | West Virginia/Ohio state line, Ohio River |

## INTERSTATE 77

| Exit # | Services |
|---|---|
| 186mm | West Virginia/Ohio state line, Ohio River |
| 185 | WV 14, WV 31, Williamstown, **W gas:** GoMart, 7-11/gas (1mi), **food:** Dutch Pantry, Subway (1mi), **lodging:** Day's Inn, **other:** Glass Factory Tours, **WV Welcome Ctr/rest area, full facilities, info, 🛝 litter barrels** |
| 179 | WV 2 N, WV 68 S, to Waverly, **E gas:** Exxon, **other:** airport, **W gas:** BP, Chevron (3mi), **food:** Burger King, Hardee's (3mi), **lodging:** Red Carpet Inn, **other:** Ⓗ HOSPITAL |
| 176 | US 50, 7th St, Parkersburg, **E** to North Bend SP, **W gas:** BP, GoMart, 7-11, **food:** Bob Evans, Burger King, Domino's, DQ, LJ Silver, McDonald's, Mountaineer Rest./24hr, Omelette Shoppe, Wendy's, **lodging:** Econolodge, Knight's Inn, Red Roof Inn, Travelodge, **other:** Advance Parts, CVS Drug, Family$, Ford, Hyundai, Kroger/dsl, Lincoln/Mercury, Mercedes, NAPA, Rite Aid, Toyota, to Blennerhassett Hist Park, vet |
| 174 | WV 47, Staunton Ave, **1 mi E gas:** FinishLine Gas, **food:** Subway, **W gas:** Citgo/dsl |
| 174mm | Little Kanawha River |
| 173 | WV 95, Camden Ave, **E gas:** Marathon/dsl, **1-4 mi W gas:** BP, **food:** Hardee's, **lodging:** Blennerhassett Hotel, **other:** Ⓗ HOSPITAL |
| 170 | WV 14, Mineral Wells, **E gas:** BP/dsl/repair/24hr, Chevron, FinishLine Gas, Parkersburg Trkstp/dsl/scales/24hr, Liberty Trkstp/dsl/24hr, **food:** McDonald's, Subway, Taco Bell, Wendy's, **lodging:** Comfort Suites, Hampton Inn, **other:** USPO, **W food:** Cracker Barrel, **lodging:** AmeriHost, Holiday Inn Express, Microtel |
| 169mm | weigh sta both lanes, 📞 |
| 166mm | **rest area both lanes, full ♿ facilities, 📞, 🛝 litter barrels, vending, petwalk, RV dump** |
| 161 | WV 21, Rockport, **W gas:** Marathon |
| 154 | WV 1, Medina Rd |

**WV**

N
↑
↓
S

## INTERSTATE 77 CONT'D

**146**  WV 2 S, Silverton, Ravenswood, **E other:** Ruby Lake Camping (4mi) , **W gas:** BP/dsl, Exxon/24hr, Marathon/dsl/24hr, **food:** DQ, Gino's Pizza, McDonald's (3mi), Wendy's (3mi), Subway (4mi), **lodging:** Scottish Inn

**138**  US 33, Ripley, **E gas:** BP/dsl/24hr, Exxon/24hr, Marathon/dsl, **food:** Arby's, KFC, LJ Silver, McDonald's, Pizza Hut, Taco Bell, Wendy's, **lodging:** McCoy's Inn, Super 8, **other:** Family$, Kroger, NAPA, Rite Aid, Sav-a-Lot Foods, Walmart SuperCtr/Subway, vet, **W gas:** Exxon/dsl/24hr, **food:** Bob Evan's, Ponderosa, Shoney's, Subway, **lodging:** Holiday Inn Express, **other:** H HOSPITAL

**132**  WV 21, Fairplain, **E gas:** BP/7-11/dsl, GoMart/dsl, **food:** Burger King, Fratello's Italian, Village Pizza, **other:** Curves, $General, Ford/Lincoln, Statts Mills RV Park (6mi) , **W gas:** Loves/Subway/dsl/scales/24hr

**124**  WV 34, Kenna, **E gas:** Exxon

**119**  WV 21, Goldtown, same as 116

**116**  WV 21, Haines Branch Rd, Sissonville, **4 mi E other:** Rippling Waters Camping

**114**  WV 622, Pocatalico Rd, **E gas:** BP/dsl, **other:** FasChek Foods/drug, Tom's Hardware

**111**  WV 29, Tuppers Creek Rd, **W gas:** BP/Subway/dsl, **food:** Gino's (2mi), Tudor's Biscuit World, Wendy's (2mi)

**106**  WV 27, Edens Fork Rd, **W gas:** Chevron/dsl/country store, **lodging:** Sunset Motel (3mi)

**104**  I-79 N, to Clarksburg

**102**  US 119 N, Westmoreland Rd, **E gas:** BP/7-11/24hr, GoMart/24hr, **food:** Hardee's/24hr, **lodging:** Parsley Motel

**101**  I-64, E to Beckley, W to Huntington

**100**  Broad St, Capitol St, **W food:** Charleston House Rest., **lodging:** Fairfield Inn, Holiday Inn, Marriott, Super 8, **other:** H HOSPITAL, CVS Drug, Family$, GMC, Honda Motorcycles, JC Penney, Kroger

**99**  WV 114, Capitol St, **E** ⬚, **W gas:** Exxon, Domino's, **food:** KFC/Taco Bell, McDonald's, Wendy's, **other:** to museum, st capitol

**98**  35th St Bridge (from sb) , **W food:** KFC/Taco Bell, McDonald's, Steak Escape, Shoney's, Subway, Taco Bell, Wendy's, **other:** H HOSPITAL, Rite Aid, to U of Charleston

**97**  US 60 W (from nb), Kanawha Blvd

**96**  US 60 E, Midland Trail, Belle, **W food:** Biscuit World, Gino's, **lodging:** Budget Host

**96mm**  W Va Turnpike begins/ends

**95.5mm**  Kanawha River

**95**  WV 61, to MacCorkle Ave, **E gas:** BP/Subway/dsl, GoMart/dsl/24hr, **food:** Bob Evans, IHOP, Lonestar Steaks, McDonald's, TX Steaks, Wendy's, **lodging:** Comfort Suites, Country Inn&Suites, Day's Inn, Knight's Inn, Motel 6, Red Roof Inn, **other:** Advance Parts, AutoZone, K-Mart, **W gas:** Ashland/Blimpie/24hr, Chevron/7-11, Exxon/dsl/24hr, GoMart/24hr, **food:** Applebee's, Arby's, Burger King, Capt D's, Cracker Barrel, Hooters, La Carreta Mexican, Pizza Hut/Taco Bell, Southern Kitchen/24hr, **other:** Drug Emporium, Foodland, Kroger/gas, Lowe's Whse, mall

**89**  WV 61, WV 94, to Marmet, **E gas:** Exxon/Subway/dsl/24hr, GoMart, Sunoco, **food:** BiscuitWorld, Gino's Pizza, Hardee's, LJ Silver, Sam's Hotdogs, Wendy's, **other:** Family$, Ford (1mi), Kroger/deli, NAPA, Rite Aid

C
H
A
R
L
E
S
T
O
N

**85**  US 60, WV 61, East Bank, **E gas:** GoMart/dsl/24hr, **food:** Gino's Pizza, McDonald's, Shoney's, **other:** Chevrolet, $General, Kroger, tire repair, USPO

**82.5mm**  toll booth

**79**  Cabin Creek Rd, Sharon

**74**  WV 83, Paint Creek Rd

**72mm**  Morton Service Area eb, **gas:** Exxon/dsl, **food:** Burger King, KFC, Pizza Hut, Starbucks, TCBY, atm

**69mm**  **rest area wb, full** ♿ **facilities,** ⬚, ⬚, **litter barrels**

**66**  WV 15, to Mahan, **1/2 mi W gas:** Sunoco/dsl/24hr

**60**  WV 612, to Mossy, Oak Hill, **1/2 mi E gas:** Exxon/dsl/repair/24hr, **other:** RV camping

**56.5mm**  toll plaza, phone

**54**  rd 2, rd 23, Pax, **E gas:** BP

**48**  US 19, N Beckley, **1-4 mi E on US 19/WV 16...gas:** Exxon/Subway, **food:** Bob Evans, Burger King, Chick-fil-A, Chilli's, Garfield's Rest., Hardee's, Logan's Roadhouse, LoneStar Steaks, LJ Silver, McDonald's, Peking Buffet, Ryan's, Starbucks, Taco Bell, Wendy's, **lodging:** Days Inn, **other:** Advance Parts, Acura, AutoZone, Belk, Buick, Chevrolet/Cadillac, CVS Drug, $General, $Tree, Food Lion, JC Penny, Honda, Hyundai, Kohl's, Lowe's, Nissan, Radio Shack, Rite Aid, Sam's Club, Sears, Staples, Subaru/Kia, Toyota, Turning Wheel RV Ctr, U-Haul, Walmart SuperCtr/gas

**45mm**  **Tamarack Service Area both lanes, W gas:** Exxon/dsl, **food:** Burger King, Quizno's, Sbarro's, Starbucks, TCBY, **other:** gifts

B
E
C
K
L
E
Y

**44**  WV 3, Beckley, **E gas:** Chevron/dsl, Exxon, Shell/Hardee's/24hr, **food:** Applebee's, Campestre Mexican, DQ, Hibachi Japanese, Hooters, IHOP, McDonald's, Omelette Shoppe, Outback Steaks, Pizza Hut, **lodging:** Econolodge, Best Western, Courtyard, Fairfield Inn, Howard Johnson, Quality Inn/rest., Super 8, **other:** CVS Drug, Kroger/gas, Outback Steaks, Rite Aid, Tires, **W gas:** BP/Subway/dsl, GoMart/dsl, **food:** Bob Evans, Cracker Barrel, Ruby Tuesday, Texas Roadhouse, Wendy's, **lodging:** Country Inn&Suites, Hampton Inn, Holiday Inn, Microtel, Park Inn

**42**  WV 16, WV 97, to Mabscott, **2 mi E food:** BiscuitWorld, **lodging:** Budget Inn, **other:** H HOSPITAL, **W gas:** BP/dsl, GoMart, **food:** Godfather's, Subway, **other:** AutoValue Parts, Walmart/SuperCtr, USPO

**40**  I-64 E, to Lewisburg

**30mm**  toll booth, ⬚

**28**  WV 48, to Ghent, **E gas:** BP, Exxon/dsl, Marathon/dsl, **food:** Subway, **lodging:** Glade Springs Resort (1mi),

WV

N ↕ S

**PRINCETON**

## INTERSTATE 77 CONT'D

| 28 | Continued |
| | Appalachian Resort Inn (12mi), **other:** to ski area, **W** **lodging:** Econolodge |
| 26.5mm | Flat Top Mtn, elevation 3252 |
| 20 | US 19, to Camp Creek, **E** **gas:** Exxon/dsl, **W** **other:** Camp Creek SP/RV camping |
| 18.5mm | scenic overlook/parking area/weigh sta sb, Bluestone River |
| 17mm | **Bluestone Service Area/weigh sta nb, full &#9855; facilities, scenic view, 🏕 area,** Exxon/dsl, Blimpie, Starbucks, TCBY, atm/fax |
| 14 | WV 20, Athens Rd, **E** **gas:** Citgo, **other:** Pipestem Resort SP |
| 9mm | WV Turnpike begins/ends |
| 9 | US 460, Princeton, Pearisburg, **E** Welcome Ctr, **food:** Outback Steaks, Ryan's, **other:** $Tree, Radio Shack, Walmart SuperCtr, **W** **gas:** BP/dsl, Chevron/dsl/24hr, Exxon/dsl/24hr, Marathon/Subway/dsl, **food:** Applebee's, Bob Evans, Burger King, Capt D's, Chili's, Cracker Barrel, DQ, Hardee's, McDonald's, Omelette Spot, Shoney's, Taco Bell, Texas Roadhouse, Wendy's, **lodging:** Budget Inn, Comfort Inn, Day's Inn, Hampton Inn, Holiday Inn Express, Ramada Ltd, Sleep Inn, Super 8, Turnpike Motel, **other:** &#9851; HOSPITAL, Hyundai, K-Mart, Lowes Whse |
| 7 | WV 27, Ingleside Rd (from nb, no re-entry) |
| 5 | WV 112 (from sb, no re-entry), to Ingleside |
| 3mm | East River |
| 1 | US 52 N, to Bluefield, **4 mi** **W** **food:** LJ Silver, Wendy's, **lodging:** Brier Motel, Econolodge, Highlander Motel, Holiday Inn/rest., Knight's Inn, Ramada Inn, **other:** &#9851; HOSPITAL |
| 0mm | West Virginia/Virginia state line, East River Mtn |

## INTERSTATE 79

N ↕ S

**MORGANTOWN**

| Exit # | Services |
| 160mm | West Virginia/Pennsylvania state line |
| 159 | **Welcome Ctr sb, full &#9855; facilities, info, 🏕 litter barrels, 📞, vending, petwalk** |
| 155 | US 19, WV 7, **0-3 mi** **E** **gas:** GetGo, Sheetz, **food:** Burger King, Cheddars, Chili's, Cracker Barrel, Eat'n Park, EverGreen Buffet, Golden Corral, LJ Silver, Longhorn Steaks, McDonald's, Olive Garden, Shoney's, Wendy's, **lodging:** Fairfield Inn, Hampton Inn, Holiday Inn, **other:** &#9851; HOSPITAL, Barnes&Noble, Best Buy, CVS Drug, $Tree, Giant Eagle Foods, Goody's, Old Navy, PetCo, Sam's Club, Target, TJ Maxx, Walmart SuperCtr, to WVU |
| 152 | US 19, to Morgantown, **E** **gas:** BP/dsl, Exxon, **food:** Arby's, China Wok, McDonald's, Pizza Hut, Subway, Taco Bell, **lodging:** Econolodge, **other:** Advance Parts, Big Lots, KIA, Shop'n Save Foods, **W** **food:** Bob Evans, Burger King, Garfield's Rest., **lodging:** Microtel, **other:** Belk, JC Penney, K-Mart, Lowes Whse, Sears/auto, mall |
| 150mm | Monongahela River |
| 148 | I-68 E, to Cumberland, MD, **1 mi** **E** **gas:** Exxon/dsl/24hr, **lodging:** Regatta Grill, **lodging:** Comfort Inn, Morgantown Motel, Ramada Inn |
| 146 | WV 77, to Goshen Rd |
| 141mm | weigh sta both lanes |

**C L A R K S B U R G**

| 139 | WV 33, E Fairmont, **E** **gas:** Chevron, **W** **gas:** Exxon/24hr, K&T/BP/dsl, **other:** RV camping, tires, vet, to Prickett's FT SP |
| 137 | WV 310, to Fairmont, **E** **gas:** BP, Exxon/dsl/24hr, **food:** Subway, **lodging:** Holiday Inn, **other:** to Valley Falls SP, vet, **W** **gas:** Chevron, **food:** Domino's, KFC, McDonald's, Wendy's, **other:** &#9851; HOSPITAL |
| 136 | new exit |
| 135 | WV 64, Pleasant Valley Rd |
| 133 | Kingmont Rd, **E** **gas:** BP/Subway/dsl, **food:** Cracker Barrel, **lodging:** Super 8, **W** **gas:** Chevron/dsl/24hr, King/dsl, **food:** DJ's Diner, **lodging:** Comfort Inn |
| 132 | US 250, S Fairmont, **E** **gas:** Chevron, **food:** Applebees, Arby's, Bob Evans, Colasessano's Italian, Dragon Buffet, Dutchman's Daughter, Hardee's, Hunan Rest., McDonald's, Subway, Taco Bell, **lodging:** Day's Inn, Fairfield Inn, Red Roof Inn, **other:** Ace Hardware, Advance Parts, Chrysler/Dodge/Jeep, $General, GNC, Sav-a-Lot Foods, Shop'n Save, Walmart SuperCtr, mall, to Tygart Lake SP, **W** **gas:** Exxon/dsl/24hr, GoMart/dsl/24hr, Sunoco, **lodging:** Country Club Motel (4mi), **other:** &#9851; HOSPITAL, Buick/GMC/Pontiac, Ford/Lincoln/Mercury, Toyota/Scion, Trailer City RV Ctr |
| 125 | WV 131, Saltwell Rd, to Shinnston, **E** **food:** Oliverio's Rest. (4mi), **W** **gas:** Exxon/Subway/dsl/24hr |
| 124 | rd 279, Jerry Dove Dr, **E** **gas:** Exxon, **food:** Buffalo Wild Wings, **lodging:** Microtel, Wingate Inn |
| 123mm | **rest area both lanes, full &#9855; facilities, info, 📞, 🏕, litter barrels, vending, petwalk, RV dump** |
| 121 | WV 24, Meadowbrook Rd, **E** **gas:** GoMart/24hr, Sheetz, **food:** Bob Evans, Gino's Pizza, Subway, **lodging:** Hampton Inn, **other:** Hyundai/Subaru, **W** **gas:** Exxon/dsl, **food:** Burger King, Garfield's Rest., Outback Steaks, **lodging:** Super 8, **other:** Honda, JC Penney, Jo-Ann Fabrics, NTB, Old Navy, Sears/auto, Target, mall |
| 119 | US 50, to Clarksburg, **E** **gas:** Exxon/dsl, GoMart/gas, **food:** A&W/LJ Silver, CiCi's Pizza, Denny's, Eat'n Park, Grand China, KFC, Las Trancas, Little Caesar's, Maxey's Rest., McDonald's, Panera Bread, Pizza Hut, Quizno's, Shogun Japanese, Starbucks, Taco Bell, TX Roadhouse, USA Steaks, Wendy's, **lodging:** Comfort Inn, Day's Inn, Holiday Inn, Knight's Inn, Sleep Inn, Sutton Inn, **other:** &#9851; HOSPITAL, Advance Parts, Big Lots, Chevrolet, GNC, Home Depot, K-Mart, Kohl's, Kroger/gas/24hr, Lowes Whse, Nissan, Radio Shack, Sam's Club/gas, USPO |
| 117 | WV 58, to Anmoore, **E** **gas:** BP/dsl, **food:** Applebee's, Arby's, Ruby Tuesday, Ryan's, Subway, **other:** Hilton Garden, **other:** Aldi Foods, Circuit City, $Tree, Goody's, Walmart SuperCtr |
| 115 | WV 20, Nutter Fort, to Stonewood, **E** **gas:** BP/7-11/dsl, Chevron, Exxon/dsl, **food:** **other:** Stonewood Bulk Foods, **W** **lodging:** Greenbrier Motel (5mi) |
| 110 | Lost Creek, **E** **gas:** BP/dsl |
| 105 | WV 7, to Jane Lew, **E** **gas:** Chevron/dsl/rest., I-79 Trk-stp/dsl/rest., **lodging:** Plantation Inn, **W** **gas:** GoMart, **other:** glass factory tours |
| 99 | US 33, US 119, to Weston, **E** **gas:** Fuel Ctr, Sheetz/24hr, **food:** Burger King, Gino's Pizza, McDonald's, Peking Buffet, Steer Steakhouse, Subway, **lodging:** Comfort Inn/rest., Hampton Inn (9mi), Holiday Inn Express, Super 8, **other:** Advance Parts, Family$, GNC, Kroger, |

## INTERSTATE 79 CONT'D

**N ↑ S**

**CHARLESTON**

| | |
|---|---|
| **99** | Continued |
| | Radio Shack, Walmart, **W** gas: Chevron, Rich Gas, food: Domino's, Fox's Den Pizza, Hardee's, KFC, LJ Silver, Pizza Hut, Wendy's, other: **H** HOSPITAL, $General, Ford, NAPA, Sav-a-Lot, Twin Lakes Camper Sales, to Canaan Valley Resort, Blackwater Falls |
| **96** | WV 30, to S Weston, **E** other: Broken Wheel Camping, to S Jackson Lake SP |
| **91** | US 19, to Roanoke, **E** gas: Marathon, food: Stillwaters Rest, other: Whisper Mtn Camping, to S Jackson Lake SP |
| **85mm** | **rest area both lanes, full** ♿ **facilities, info,** ⛱, **litter barrels,** 🕿, **vending, petwalk, RV dump** |
| **79.5mm** | Little Kanawha River |
| **79** | WV 5, Burnsville, **E** gas: Exxon/24hr, lodging: 79 Motel/rest., other: NAPA, **W** gas: GoMart, food: Gino's Pizza, other: Cedar Cr SP |
| **78mm** | Saltlick Creek |
| **67** | WV 4, to Flatwoods, **E** gas: BP/Arby's//dsl, Chevron/dsl, Exxon/dsl, Go-Mart/dsl, food: KFC/Taco Bell, McDonald's, Subway, Waffle Hut, lodging: Day's Inn, Sutton Lake Motel, other: Buick/Chevrolet, to Sutton Lake RA, antiques, camping, **W** gas: Sunoco/motel/dsl, food: China Buffet, Shoney's, Wendy's, other: Bulk Foods, Flatwood Factory Stores |
| **62** | WV 4, Gassaway, to Sutton, **E** food: Century Rest. (2mi), lodging: Elk Motel, **W** gas: GoMart, food: Giovanni's Pizza, LJ Silver, Pizza Hut, lodging: Microtel, other: **H** HOSPITAL, Chrysler/Dodge/Jeep, CVS Drug, Ford, Kroger/deli, Super$ |
| **57** | US 19 S, to Beckley |
| **52mm** | Elk River |
| **51** | WV 4, to Frametown, **E** antiques |
| **49mm** | **rest area both lanes, full** ♿ **facilities,** ⛱, 🕿, **litter barrels, vending, petwalk, RV dump** |
| **46** | WV 11, Servia Rd |
| **40** | WV 16, to Big Otter, **E** gas: GoMart/dsl, **W** gas: Exxon/dsl |
| **34** | WV 36, to Wallback, **10 mi E** food: Gino's Diner, BiscuitWorld |
| **25** | WV 29, to Amma, **E** gas: Exxon/dsl |
| **19** | US 119, VW 53, to Clendenin, **E** gas: BP/dsl/24hr, food: BiscuitWorld, Gino's Diner, other: Shafer's Superstop |
| **9** | WV 43, to Elkview, **E** gas: GoMart/dsl, food: Burger King, **W** gas: Exxon/Arby's/dsl, Speedway/dsl/24hr, food: Bob Evans, McDonald's, Pizza Hut, Ponderosa, Subway, lodging: Country Inn&Suites, other: Advance Parts, CVS Drug, $Tree, K-Mart, Kroger, Radio Shack |
| **5** | WV 114, to Big Chimney, **1 mi E** gas: Exxon, food: Hardee's/24hr, other: Rite Aid, Smith's Foods |
| **1** | US 119, Mink Shoals, **E** food: Harding's Family Rest., lodging: Sleep Inn |
| **0** | I-77, S to Charleston, N to Parkersburg. I-79 begins/ends on I-77, exit 104. |

## INTERSTATE 81

| Exit # | Services |
|---|---|
| **26mm** | West Virginia/Maryland state line, Potomac River |
| **25mm** | **Welcome Ctr sb, full** ♿ **facilities, info,** 🕿, ⛱, **litter barrels, petwalk** |

**N ↑ S**

**MARTINSBURG**

| | |
|---|---|
| **23** | US 11, Marlowe, Falling Waters, **1 mi E** other: Falling Waters Camping, **W** gas: BP/dsl, 7-11, other: Outdoor Express RV Ctr |
| **20** | WV 901, Spring Mills Rd, **E** food: Barney's Rest., China Spring, McDonald's, Pizza Montese, Subway, Tokyo Cafe, lodging: Econolodge, other: Walmart SuperCtr, **W** gas: Shell/dsl, food: Domino's, lodging: Holiday Inn Express |
| **19mm** | rest area sb |
| **16** | WV 9, N Queen St, Berkeley Springs, **E** gas: BP, Citgo, Exxon/Subway/dsl, Sheetz/24hr, food: Arby's, Casa Gonzales Mexican, China King, Domino's, Hoss's, KFC, LJ Silver, McDonald's, Popeye's, Thai Hut, Waffle House, lodging: Comfort Inn, Knight's Inn, Super 8, Rodeway Inn, other: Advance Parts, AutoZone, CVS Drug, Food Lion, **W** gas: Citgo, Shell/dsl |
| **14** | rd 13, Dry Run Rd, **E** other: **H** HOSPITAL, **W** other: Butler's Farm Mkt (1mi) |
| **13** | rd 15, Kings St, Martinsburg, **E** gas: BP/Subway/dsl, Sheetz/24hr, food: Applebees, Arkena's Cafe, Buffalo Wild Wings, Burger King, Cracker Barrel, Jerry's Subs, Kobe Japanese, Las Trancas, Outback Steaks, Pizza Hut, Shoney's, Wendy's, lodging: Day's Inn, Holiday Inn/rest., other: **H** HOSPITAL, Chevrolet/Toyota/Scion, Tanger/famous brands, Walmart SuperCtr, same as 12 |
| **12** | WV 45, Winchester Ave, **E** gas: Citgo/dsl, Sheetz/24hr, Shell/dsl, food: Arby's, Bob Evans, Chick-fil-A, China City Buffet, McDonald's, Papa John's, Quizno's, Ryan's, Ruby Tuesday, Taco Bell, TX Steaks, Waffle House, Wendy's, lodging: Comfort Suites, Economy Inn, Hampton Inn, Kristalite Inn, Relax Inn, other: Advance Parts, AutoZone, BonTon, Food Lion, JC Penney, K-mart/Little Caesar's, Lowes Whse, Martin's Foods/gas, Sears/auto, mall, same as 13 |
| **8** | rd 32, Tablers Sta Rd, **2 mi E** lodging: Pikeside Motel, **W** other: Orr's Farm Mkt |
| **5** | WV 51, Inwood, to Charles Town, **E** gas: Exxon, Liberty, 7-11, Sheetz, Shell/dsl, food: Burger King, DQ, KFC, McDonald's, Pizza Hut, Pizza Oven, Subway, Waffle House, lodging: Hampton Inn, other: CVS Drug, Family$, Food Lion, NAPA, **W** other: Lazy-A Camping (9mi) |
| **2mm** | **Welcome Ctr/weigh sta nb, full** ♿ **facilities, info,** 🕿, **vending,** ⛱, **litter barrels, petwalk** |
| **0mm** | West Virginia/Virginia state line |

**WI**

**N ↑ S**

**W A U S A U**

## INTERSTATE 39

| Exit # | Services |
|---|---|
| 211 | US 51, rd K, Merrill, **2 mi W gas:** Cenex, **food:** Chip's Burgers, Hardee's, Pizza Hut, **other:** ✈ |
| 210mm | Prairie River |
| 208 | WI 64, WI 70, Merrill, **W food:** Taco Bell, **W gas:** Mobil/dsl, Shell/dsl, **food:** Frazier's Grille, McDonald's, Subway, Taco Bell, Three's Company Rest., **lodging:** Americinn, Pine Ridge Inn, Super 8, **other:** Ⓗ HOSPITAL, Chrysler/Dodge/Jeep, $Tree, Piggly Wiggly, Walmart, to Council Grounds SP |
| 206mm | Wisconsin River |
| 205 | US 51, rd Q, Merrill, **E gas:** BP/dsl/rest./24hr, Hwy 51 TrkStp, **other:** Buick/Cadillac/Chevrolet/Pontiac |
| 197 | rd WW, to Brokaw, **W gas:** Citgo/dsl |
| 194 | US 51, rd U, rd K, Wausau, **E gas:** F&F/dsl, KwikTrip/gas, **food:** McDonald's, Taco Bell, **other:** Toyota/Scion, **E food:** BP, **food:** Arby's, **other:** Ford/Mercedes, KIA, Saturn |
| 193 | Bridge St, **E food:** Culvers, Quizno's, **lodging:** Plaza Hotel, **W** Ⓗ HOSPITAL |
| 192 | WI 29 W, WI 52 E, Wausau, to Chippewa Falls, same as 191 |
| 191 | Sherman St, **E gas:** BP, **food:** Annie's Rest., Applebee's, Buffalo Wild Wings, Coldstone Creamery, Cousins Subs, Herford&Hops, Figaro's Pizza, Hong Kong Buffet, Hudson's Grill, Little Caesar's, McDonald's, Subway, **lodging:** Country Inn&Suites, Courtyard, Hampton Inn, La Quinta, Super 8, **other:** Ⓗ HOSPITAL, **W food:** Burger King, Hardee's, 2510 Deli, **other:** Audi/Nissan/VW, County Mkt Foods, Home Depot, Honda, Menard's |
| 190mm | Rib River |
| 190 | rd NN, **E gas:** Mobil/Burger King, **food:** Krumbee's Bakery, **lodging:** Howard Johnson, **W gas:** The Store/Subway/dsl, **lodging:** Best Western, **other:** Rib Mtn Ski Area, st patrol |
| 188 | rd N, **E gas:** BP/dsl/scales/24hr, Phillips 66/dsl, **food:** El Tapatio, Fazoli's, Hong Kong Buffet, McDonald's, Starbucks, Subway, Texas Roadhouse, Wendy's, **lodging:** Country Inn&Suites (1mi), Day's Inn, **other:** Aldi, Barnes&Noble, Best Buy, Chevrolet, GNC, Gordman's, Jo-Ann Fabrics, King's RV Ctr, Kohl's, Nissan, PetCo, Peterbilt, Radio Shack, Sam's Club, TJ Maxx, Tires+, Volvo, VW, Walmart SuperCtr, **W other:** Rib Mtn SP |
| 187mm | I-39 begins/ends. Freeway continues N as US 51. |
| 187 | WI 29 E, to Green Bay |
| 186mm | Wisconsin River |
| 185 | US 51, **E gas:** Cenex, **food:** Arby's, Culver's, Denny's, Green Mill Rest., Subway, Tony Roma's, **lodging:** Candlewood Suites, Cedar Creek Lodge, Comfort Inn, Holiday Inn, Rodeway Inn, Stoney Creek Inn, **other:** Cedar Creek Factory Stores/famous brands, Gander Mtn, Harley Davidson, Pick'n Save Foods, mall, visitor ctr |
| 183mm | **sb, restroom facilities, drinking water,** 🏕 |
| 181 | Maple Ridge Rd, **W** Kenworth |
| 179 | WI 153, Mosinee, **W gas:** BP/Subway/dsl, KwikTrip, Shell/dsl/24hr, **food:** McDonald's, StageStop Rest., Subway, **lodging:** Super 8 |
| 178mm | **nb, restroom facilities, drinking water,** 🏕 |
| 175 | WI 34, Knowlton, to WI Rapids, **1 mi W other:** Mullins Cheese Factory |
| 171 | rd DB, Knowlton, **E** camping, **W other:** to gas, food, lodging |
| 165 | rd X, **E** gas, food, camping |
| 163 | Casimir Rd |

**S T E V E N S P O I N T**

**P O R T A G E**

| | |
|---|---|
| 161 | US 51, Stevens Point, **W gas:** BP, KwikTrip/24hr, Quik Mart/dsl, Shell, The Store, **food:** China Wok, Coldstone Creamery, Hardee's, KFC, McDonald's, Noodles&Co, Olympia Rest., Papa John's, Perkins, Pizza Hut, Red Apple Rest., Rococo's Pizza, Starbucks, Subway, Taco Bell, Topper's Pizza, **lodging:** Best Value Inn, Comfort Suites, Country Inn&Suites, Point Motel, Ramada Inn, Stay Inn, **other:** Buick/Pontiac, $Deals, $Tree, Jeep, K-Mart, Radio Shack |
| 159 | WI 66, Stevens Point, **W gas:** KwikTrip/dsl, **other:** Chrysler/Dodge/Plymouth, Ford, GMC, Honda, Nissan |
| 158 | US 10, Stevens Point, **E gas:** F&F/dsl, Mobil/dsl/24hr, **food:** Applebee's, Arby's, Culver's, DQ, El Mezcal Mexican, Fazoli's, Grazie's Italian, Hong Kong Buffet, McDonald's, Rudy's Grill, Subway, Taco Bell, Wendy's, **lodging:** Fairfield Inn, Holiday Inn, Holiday Inn Express, **other:** Aldi, Copp's Foods, Frank's Hardware, Hancock Fabrics, Staples, Target, vet, **W gas:** BP/24hr, **food:** Hilltop Grill, **lodging:** La Quinta, Royale Inn |
| 156 | rd HH, Whiting, **E gas:** The Store/dsl, **food:** Charcoal Grill, Chili's, Cousin's Subs, Golden Corral, Hudson's Grill, McDonald's, Starbucks, Subway, **other:** Best Buy, GNC, Kohl's, Lowes Whse, Michael's, PetCo, Walmart SuperCtr |
| 153 | rd B, Plover, **W gas:** BP, Mobil/dsl, **food:** Bamboo House, Burger King, Cousins Subs, Elder Beerman, IHOP, Lupuna, Taco Bell, **lodging:** AmericInn, Comfort Inn, Hampton Inn, **other:** Copp's Foods, $Tree, Menard's, ShopKo, Toyota/Scion, vet |
| 151 | WI 54, to Waupaca, **E gas:** Shell/Arby's/dsl/scales/24hr, **food:** 4Star Family Rest., Shooter's Rest., **lodging:** Elizabeth Inn/Conv Ctr, **other:** tires/repair |
| 143 | rd W, Bancroft, to WI Rapids, **E gas:** Citgo/dsl |
| 139 | rd D, Almond |
| 136 | WI 73, Plainfield, to WI Rapids, **E gas:** BP/dsl, **food:** Hooligan's Grill, **W gas:** Phillips 66/Subway/dsl |
| 131 | rd V, Hancock, **E gas:** Citgo, **food:** Country Kettle |
| 127mm | weigh sta both lanes (exits left) |
| 124 | WI 21, Coloma, **E gas:** Mobil/A&W/dsl, **lodging:** Mecan Inn, **other:** camping, **W gas:** BP/dsl |
| 120mm | **rest area sb, full** ♿ **facilities,** ☏, 🏕, **vending, litter barrels, petwalk** |
| 118mm | **rest area nb, full** ♿ **facilities,** ☏, 🏕, **vending, litter barrels, petwalk** |
| 113 | rd E, rd J, Westfield, **W gas:** BP/Burger King, Marathon, Mobil/dsl, **food:** McDonald's, Subway, **lodging:** Pioneer Motel/rest., **other:** Danny's Campers, Family$ |
| 106 | WI 82 W, WI 23 E, Oxford, **E lodging:** Crossroads Motel, **W gas:** Citgo/dsl |
| 104 | (from nb, no EZ return) rd D, Packwaukee |
| 100 | WI 23 W, rd P, Endeavor, **E gas:** BP/dsl |
| 92 | US 51 S, Portage, **E gas:** KwikTrip/dsl, Mobil, **food:** Culver's, Dino's Rest., Jimmy John's, KFC, La Tolteca Mexican, McDonald's, Subway, Taco Bell, Wendy's, World Buffet, **lodging:** Best Western, Ridge Motel, Super 8, **other:** Ⓗ HOSPITAL, Ace Hardware, AutoZone, Chrysler/Dodge/Jeep, Curves, $Tree, Ford/Lincoln/Mercury, GNC, K-Mart, Pierce's Foods, Radio Shack, Staples, Walgreens, Walmart SuperCtr |
| 89b a | WI 16, to WI 127, Portage, **E food:** Hitching Post Eatery |
| 88.5mm | Wisconsin River |
| 87 | WI 33, Portage, **W** ski area |
| 86mm | Baraboo River |
| 85 | Cascade Mt Rd |
| 84 | I-39, I-90 & I-94 run together sb. |

Copyright 2009 - The Next Exit®

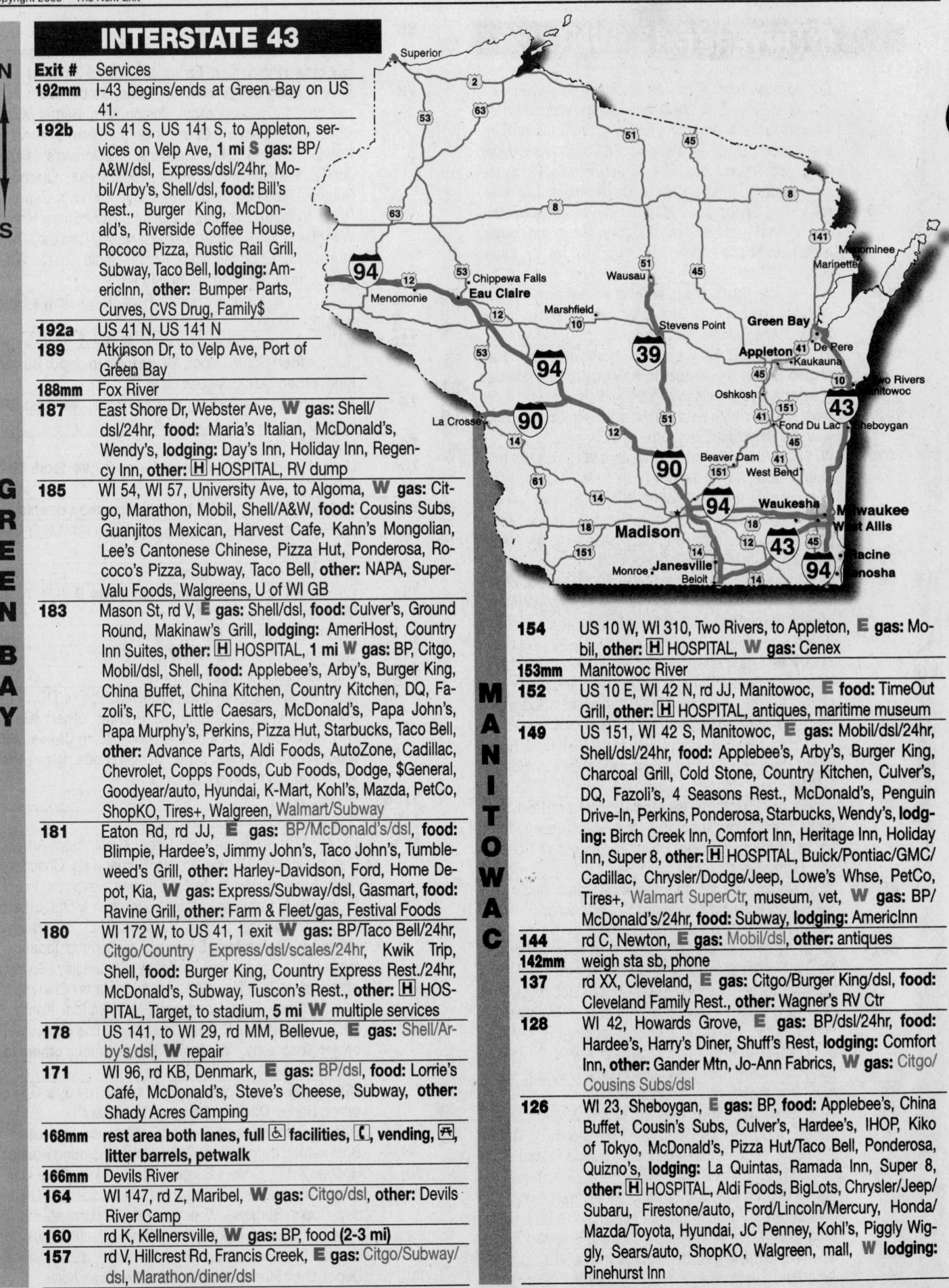

## INTERSTATE 43

**N** ↕ **S**

**GREEN BAY**

| Exit # | Services |
|---|---|
| 192mm | I-43 begins/ends at Green Bay on US 41. |
| 192b | US 41 S, US 141 S, to Appleton, services on Velp Ave, **1 mi S gas:** BP/A&W/dsl, Express/dsl/24hr, Mobil/Arby's, Shell/dsl, **food:** Bill's Rest., Burger King, McDonald's, Riverside Coffee House, Rococo Pizza, Rustic Rail Grill, Subway, Taco Bell, **lodging:** AmericInn, **other:** Bumper Parts, Curves, CVS Drug, Family$ |
| 192a | US 41 N, US 141 N |
| 189 | Atkinson Dr, to Velp Ave, Port of Green Bay |
| 188mm | Fox River |
| 187 | East Shore Dr, Webster Ave, **W gas:** Shell/dsl/24hr, **food:** Maria's Italian, McDonald's, Wendy's, **lodging:** Day's Inn, Holiday Inn, Regency Inn, **other:** H HOSPITAL, RV dump |
| 185 | WI 54, WI 57, University Ave, to Algoma, **W gas:** Citgo, Marathon, Mobil, Shell/A&W, **food:** Cousins Subs, Guanjitos Mexican, Harvest Cafe, Kahn's Mongolian, Lee's Cantonese Chinese, Pizza Hut, Ponderosa, Rococo's Pizza, Subway, Taco Bell, **other:** NAPA, SuperValu Foods, Walgreens, U of WI GB |
| 183 | Mason St, rd V, **E gas:** Shell/dsl, **food:** Culver's, Ground Round, Makinaw's Grill, **lodging:** AmeriHost, Country Inn Suites, **other:** H HOSPITAL, **1 mi W gas:** BP, Citgo, Mobil/dsl, Shell, **food:** Applebee's, Arby's, Burger King, China Buffet, China Kitchen, Country Kitchen, DQ, Fazoli's, KFC, Little Caesars, McDonald's, Papa John's, Papa Murphy's, Perkins, Pizza Hut, Starbucks, Taco Bell, **other:** Advance Parts, Aldi Foods, AutoZone, Cadillac, Chevrolet, Copps Foods, Cub Foods, Dodge, $General, Goodyear/auto, Hyundai, K-Mart, Kohl's, Mazda, PetCo, ShopKO, Tires+, Walgreen, Walmart/Subway |
| 181 | Eaton Rd, rd JJ, **E gas:** BP/McDonald's/dsl, **food:** Blimpie, Hardee's, Jimmy John's, Taco John's, Tumbleweed's Grill, **other:** Harley-Davidson, Ford, Home Depot, Kia, **W gas:** Express/Subway/dsl, Gasmart, **food:** Ravine Grill, **other:** Farm & Fleet/gas, Festival Foods |
| 180 | WI 172 W, to US 41, 1 exit **W gas:** BP/Taco Bell/24hr, Citgo/Country Express/dsl/scales/24hr, Kwik Trip, Shell, **food:** Burger King, Country Express Rest./24hr, McDonald's, Subway, Tuscon's Rest., **other:** H HOSPITAL, Target, to stadium, **5 mi W** multiple services |
| 178 | US 141, to WI 29, rd MM, Bellevue, **E gas:** Shell/Arby's/dsl, **W** repair |
| 171 | WI 96, rd KB, Denmark, **E gas:** BP/dsl, **food:** Lorrie's Café, McDonald's, Steve's Cheese, Subway, **other:** Shady Acres Camping |
| 168mm | rest area both lanes, full ♿ facilities, 📞, vending, ⛱, litter barrels, petwalk |
| 166mm | Devils River |
| 164 | WI 147, rd Z, Maribel, **W gas:** Citgo/dsl, **other:** Devils River Camp |
| 160 | rd K, Kellnersville, **W gas:** BP, food **(2-3 mi)** |
| 157 | rd V, Hillcrest Rd, Francis Creek, **E gas:** Citgo/Subway/dsl, Marathon/diner/dsl |

**MANITOWOC**

| Exit # | Services |
|---|---|
| 154 | US 10 W, WI 310, Two Rivers, to Appleton, **E gas:** Mobil, **other:** H HOSPITAL, **W gas:** Cenex |
| 153mm | Manitowoc River |
| 152 | US 10 E, WI 42 N, rd JJ, Manitowoc, **E food:** TimeOut Grill, **other:** H HOSPITAL, antiques, maritime museum |
| 149 | US 151, WI 42 S, Manitowoc, **E gas:** Mobil/dsl/24hr, Shell/dsl/24hr, **food:** Applebee's, Arby's, Burger King, Charcoal Grill, Cold Stone, Country Kitchen, Culver's, DQ, Fazoli's, 4 Seasons Rest., McDonald's, Penguin Drive-In, Perkins, Ponderosa, Starbucks, Wendy's, **lodging:** Birch Creek Inn, Comfort Inn, Heritage Inn, Holiday Inn, Super 8, **other:** H HOSPITAL, Buick/Pontiac/GMC/Cadillac, Chrysler/Dodge/Jeep, Lowe's Whse, PetCo, Tires+, Walmart SuperCtr, museum, vet, **W gas:** BP/McDonald's/24hr, **food:** Subway, **lodging:** AmericInn |
| 144 | rd C, Newton, **E gas:** Mobil/dsl, **other:** antiques |
| 142mm | weigh sta sb, phone |
| 137 | rd XX, Cleveland, **E gas:** Citgo/Burger King/dsl, **food:** Cleveland Family Rest., **other:** Wagner's RV Ctr |
| 128 | WI 42, Howards Grove, **E gas:** BP/dsl/24hr, **food:** Hardee's, Harry's Diner, Shuff's Rest., **lodging:** Comfort Inn, **other:** Gander Mtn, Jo-Ann Fabrics, **W gas:** Citgo/Cousins Subs/dsl |
| 126 | WI 23, Sheboygan, **E gas:** BP, **food:** Applebee's, China Buffet, Cousin's Subs, Culver's, Hardee's, IHOP, Kiko of Tokyo, McDonald's, Pizza Hut/Taco Bell, Ponderosa, Quizno's, **lodging:** La Quintas, Ramada Inn, Super 8, **other:** H HOSPITAL, Aldi Foods, BigLots, Chrysler/Jeep/Subaru, Firestone/auto, Ford/Lincoln/Mercury, Honda/Mazda/Toyota, Hyundai, JC Penney, Kohl's, Piggly Wiggly, Sears/auto, ShopKO, Walgreen, mall, **W lodging:** Pinehurst Inn |

## INTERSTATE 43 CONT'D

**123** WI 28, rd A, Sheboygan, **E gas:** Citgo/dsl/24hr, Mobil/McDonald's/dsl, **food:** Cold Stone, Jimmy John's, Perkins, Starbucks, Taco Bell, Wendy's, **lodging:** AmericInn, Holiday Inn Express, **other:** Harley-Davidson/Cruisers Burgers, Walmart SuperCtr, **W food:** Arby's, Century Buffet, Chili's, **other:** Best Buy, $Tree, Elder-Berman, Home Depot, Michael's, PetsMart, Radio Shack, Target, TJ Maxx

**120** rds OK, V, Sheboygan, **E gas:** Citgo/dsl, **food:** Handlebar Rest., Judi's Rest., **lodging:** Sleep Inn, **other:** Nissan, to Kohler-Andrae SP, camping, **1 mi W other:** Horn's RV Ctr

**116** rd AA, Foster Rd, Oostburg, **W food:** Pizza Ranch, Subway

**113** WI 32 N, rd LL, Cedar Grove, **W gas:** Citgo/dsl/repair, **food:** Country Grove Rest., **lodging:** Lakeview Motel

**107** rd D, Belgium, **E lodging:** Lake Church Inn, **other:** Harrington Beach SP, **W gas:** BP/DQ/dsl/24hr, How-Dea Trkstp/dsl/scales, Mobil/McDonald's/dsl/24hr, **food:** Bic's Place, Curly's Rest., Hobo's Korner Kitchen, Subway, **lodging:** AmericInn, **other:** NAPA

**100** WI 32 S, WI 84 W, Port Washington, **E gas:** Citgo/dsl, Mobil, **food:** Arby's, Luigi's Italian, McDonald's, Pizza Hut, Subway, **lodging:** Country Inn Suites, Holiday Inn, **other:** Allen-Edmonds Shoes, Goodyear/auto, Sentry Foods, True Value, **W lodging:** Nisleit's Country Rest.

**97** (from nb, exits left), WI 57, Fredonia

**96** WI 33, to Saukville, **E gas:** Mobil/dsl/24hr, **food:** Beanie's, Culver's, LJ Silver/KFC, **lodging:** Best Western, **other:** Buick/Pontiac/Cadillac, Dodge, Ford/Lincoln, Pick'n Save Foods, Piggly Wiggly, Walgreens, Walmart/drug, **W gas:** Exxon/McDonald's, **food:** Bubblet's Rest., DQ, Foster St Rest., Lam's Chinese, Papa Murphy's, Quizno's, Subway, Taco Bell, **lodging:** Super 8

**93** WI 32 N, WI 57 S, Grafton, **1-2 mi E gas:** Citgo, **food:** Dairy House Rest., Mamma Mia's Cafe, Pied Piper Rest., Smith Bros Fish (4mi), **lodging:** Best Western, Holiday Inn, **W food:** Flannery's Cafe

**92** WI 60, rd Q, Grafton, **E food:** GhostTown Rest., **W gas:** Citgo/DQ/dsl, **food:** Charcoal Grill, Quizno's, Starbucks, Subway, **lodging:** Baymont Inn, **other:** Costco/gas, Home Depot, Target

**89** rd C, Cedarburg, **W gas:** Mobil/dsl, **food:** Cedar Crk Settlement Café (6mi), **lodging:** StageCoach Inn, Washington House Inn, **other:** H HOSPITAL

**85** WI 57 S, WI 167 W, Mequon Rd, **W gas:** Citgo/dsl, Mobil/24hr, Sendik's, Shell, **food:** Casa Grande Mexican, Caribou Coffee, Chancery Rest., Cousins Subs, Culver's, DQ, Hong Palace Chinese, Jimmy John's, McDonald's, Panera Bread, Starbucks, Subway, **lodging:** Best Western, Chalet Motel, **other:** Ace Harware, Kohl's, Office Depot, Pick'n Save Foods, Sendik's Foods, Walgreen, vet

**83** rd W, Port Washington Rd (from nb only)

**82b a** WI 32 S, WI 100, Brown Deer Rd, **E gas:** BP/24hr, Sendik's/dsl, **food:** Benji's Deli, Coldstone Creamery, Cousins Subs, La Paisa Mexican, McDonald's, Noodles & Company, Outback Steaks, Pizza Hut, Qdoba Mexican, Spring Garden Chinese, Subway, **other:** Best Buy, Borders Books, CVS Drug, Kohl's Foods, Land's Inlet, Osco Drug, Walgreens, **W lodging:** Courtyard, Sheraton

**80** Good Hope Rd, **E gas:** BP, **food:** Jimmy John's, Samurai Japanese, Stonecreek Coffee, King's Wok, Willy's Pizza,

**80** Continued
**lodging:** Manchester East Hotel, Radisson, Residence Inn, **other:** Pick'n Save Foods, to Cardinal Stritch U

**78** Silver Spring Dr, **E gas:** BP, Citgo, Mobil, **food:** Applebee's, BD's Mongolian, Boston Mkt, Burger King, Cheesecake Factory, Cousin's Subs, Denny's, Ground Round, Kopps, Little Caesar's, McDonald's, Papa John's, Panera Bread, Perkins, Pizza Hut, Quizno's, Subway, Taco Bell, Tumbleweed Grill, Wendy's, Zappa's Rest., **lodging:** Exel Inn, La Quinta, NorthShore Motel, Woodfield Suites, **other:** Barnes&Noble, Cadillac, Firestone/auto, Goodyear/auto, Kohl's, Radio Shack, Walgreens, mall, **W other** H HOSPITAL

**77b a** (from nb) , **E food:** Anchorage Rest., **food:** Solly's Grill, **lodging:** Hilton

**76b a** WI 57, WI 190, Green Bay Ave, **E food:** Anchorage Rest., **other:** Home Depot, **W gas:** Citgo, **food:** Burger King, **other:** Buick, Jaguar/Volvo

**75** Atkinson Ave, Keefe Ave, **E gas:** Mobil, **W gas:** BP, Citgo/dsl

**74** Locust St

**73c** North Ave (rom sb) , **E food:** Wendy's, **W food:** McDonald's

**73a** WI 145 E, 4th St (exits left from sb), Broadway, downtown

**72c** Wells St, **E lodging:** Hilton, **other:** H HOSPITAL, Civic Ctr, museum

**72b** (from sb), I-94 W, to madison

**72a** (310c from nb, exits left from sb), I-794 E, I-94 W to Madison, to Lakefront, downtown

**311** WI 59, National Ave, 6th St, downtown

**312a** Lapham Blvd, Mitchell St, **W gas:** Citgo

**312b** (from nb), Becher St, Lincoln Ave

**314a** Holt Ave, **E gas:** Andy's/dsl, **food:** Applebee's, DQ, Jimmy John's, Quizno's, Starbucks, Subway, **other:** $General, Home Depot, Pick'n Save Foods, **E on Chase...W food:** Arby's, Wendy's, **other:** Sentry Foods, Target, **W** HOSPITAL, to Alverno Coll

**314b** Howard Ave

**10b** (316 from sb), I-94 S to Chicago, ✈

**9b a** US 41, 27th St, **E gas:** BP, Citgo, Mobil, **food:** Arby's, Baskin-Robbins/Dunkin Donuts, Burger King, Chancery Rest., Famous Dave's, JanBo Chinese, Pizza Hut, Rusty Skillet Rest., Subway, **lodging:** Suburban Motel, **other:** AutoZone, Dodge, K-Mart, Target, USPO, Walgreens, **W food:** Boston Mkt, Denny's, Los Burritos Tapatios, McDonald's, Taco Bell, **lodging:** Hospitality Suites, **other:** H HOSPITAL, AAA, Advance Parts, Chevrolet, Chrysler/Jeep, Ford, Goodyear, GMC/Hyundai, Kohl's

**8a** WI 36, Loomis Rd, **E gas:** Citgo, **food:** Los Mariachi's, **other:** Walgreens, **W food:** George Webb, **other:** to Alverno Coll

**7** 60th St, **E gas:** Speedway/dsl, **food:** Wendy's Grille, **other:** Harley-Davidson, **W gas:** Speedway

**5b** 76th St (from sb, no EZ return) , **E food:** Applebee's, Boston Mkt, Burger King, George Webb, Ground Round, Hooters, KFC, Kopp's Burgers, McDonald's, Olive Garden, Outback Steaks, Pizza Hut, Red Lobster, TGIFriday, Top's Burgers, Wendy's, **other:** Barnes&Noble, Best Buy, Borders Books, BreadSmith, Circuit City, Cub Foods, Firestone/auto, Goodyear/auto, Isuzu, Office Depot, SteinMart, Valvoline, **W other:** Trak Auto

MILWAUKEE

MILWAUKEE

WI

Copyright 2009 - The Next Exit®

## INTERSTATE 43 CONT'D

**5a** WI 24 W, Forest Home Ave, **E** gas: Citgo, other: Boerner Botanical Gardens

**61** (4 from sb), I-894/US 45 N, I-43/US 45 S

**60** US 45 S, WI 100, 108th St (exits left from sb) , **E** gas: BP, Citgo, Mobil, food: A&W, Amore Italian, Balisteri Italian, Chili Pepper Rest., Open Flame Rest., Pizza Hut, Taco Bell, Wendy's, other: AutoZone, Curves, Tuesday Morning, vet, **W** gas: Phillips 66, food: Forum Rest., McDonald's, Omega Custard, Organ Piper Pizza, other: Aldi Foods, Badger Transmissions, Goodyear, Mr P Tire, Walgreens, Walmart/drug, vet

**59** WI 100, Layton Ave (from nb, exits left), Hales Corner, same as 60

**57** Moorland Rd, **E** gas: Mobil/dsl, food: Applebee's, TX Roadhouse, lodging: La Quinta, **W** gas: Mobil/24hr, Speedway/dsl/24hr, food: Buffalo Wild Wings, Micocina Mexican, Quizno's, Taco Bell, Tumbleweed Grill, lodging: Baymont Inn, Best Western, Country Inn Suites, other: Michael's, Sportsman's Whse, Target

**54** rd Y, Racine Ave, **1-2 mi E** gas: Citgo/dsl, KwikTrip, other: Culver's, Cousins Subs, McDonald's

**50** WI 164, Big Bend, **W** gas: Citgo/dsl, food: Coach House Grill, Long Neck's Rest, McDonald's

**44mm** Fox River

**43** WI 83, Mukwonago, **E** gas: BP/dsl, other: Home Depot, Walmart SuperCtr, **W** gas: Citgo, Shell, food: Antigua Real Cafe, Boneyard Grill, Dominos, DQ, Mario's, Taco Bell, lodging: Sleep Inn

**38** WI 20, East Troy, **W** gas: BP, Road Ranger/Subway/dsl/24hr, Shell/McDonald's, food: Burger King, other: CarQuest, Chrysler/Dodge

**36** WI 120, East Troy, **E** lodging: Alpine Valley Resort, **W** lodging: Country Inn Suites

**33** Bowers Rd, **E** to Alpine Valley Music Theatre

**32mm** rest area both lanes, full ♿ facilities, 📞, 🍴, litter barrels, vending, petwalk

**29** WI 11, Elkhorn, fairgrounds

**27b a** US 12, to Lake Geneva, **E** 🅷 HOSPITAL

**25** WI 67, Elkhorn, **E** gas: BP/dsl, lodging: AmericInn, other: Chevrolet/Buick/GMC, Chrysler/Dodge/Jeep, **W** gas: Speedway/dsl/24hr, food: Burger King, lodging: Thomas Inn, other: Dehaan Auto/RV Ctr

**21** WI 50, Delavan, **E** gas: Shell/dsl/24hr, food: Chili's, China One, Culvers, Domino's, Panera Bread, Papa Murphy's, Quizno's, Starbucks, Subway, Yoshi Japanese, other: Aldi Foods, Greyhound DogTrack, Kohl's, Lowe's Whse, Radio Shack, Staples, Walmart SuperCtr, **W** gas: Mobil/24hr, food: Cousins Subs, KFC, McDonald's, Perkins, Pizza Hut, Subway, Taco Bell, Wendy's, lodging: Comfort Suites, Econolodge, Super 8, other: Chevrolet/Cadillac, $Tree, Ford/Lincoln/Mercury, GNC, Pick'n Save, Piggly Wiggly, ShopKO, Walgreens

**17** rd X, Delavan, Darien, **W** gas: BP

**15** US 14, Darien, **E** gas: Citgo/dsl, food: West Wind Diner

**6** WI 140, Clinton, **E** gas: BP, Citgo, food: Subway, other: Ford

*(left margin, top to bottom)* N ↕ S     D E L A V A N

**2** rd X, Hart Rd, **E** food: Butterfly Fine Dining

**1b a** I-90, E to Chicago, W to Madison, **S** gas: BP, Exxon/Subway/dsl, Shell, Pilot/DQ/Taco Bell/dsl/24hr/@, Speedway/dsl, food: Applebee's, Arby's, Asia Buffet, Burger King, Cousins Subs, Country Kitchen, Culver's, DQ, Fazoli's, McDonald's, Papa Murphy's, Perkins, Wendy's, lodging: Beloit Inn, Comfort Inn, Econolodge, Fairfield Inn, Holiday Inn Express, Super 8, other: Buick/Pontiac, Chevrolet/Cadillac/Nissan, Radio Shack, Staples, Tires +, Walmart SuperCtr

I-43 begins/ends on I-90, exit 185 in Beloit.

## INTERSTATE 90

| Exit # | Services |
|---|---|
| 187mm | I-90 & I-39 run together nb., Wisconsin/Illinois state line |
| 187mm | **Welcome Ctr wb, full ♿ facilities, info, 📞, 🍴, litter barrels, vending, petwalk** |
| 185b | I-43 N, to Milwaukee |

**185a** WI 81, Beloit, **S** gas: BP, Exxon/Subway/dsl, Mobil/McDonald's/dsl, Pilot/Taco Bell/dsl/scales/24hr, Shell, Speedway/dsl, food: Applebee's, Arby's, Asia Buffet, Atl Bread, Burger King, Cousins Subs, Country Kitchen, Culver's, Papa Murphy's, Wendy's, lodging: Best Value, Comfort Inn, Econolodge, Fairfield Inn, Holiday Inn Express, other: Aldi Foods, Buick/Pontiac, Chevrolet/Cadillac, Radio Shack, Staples, Tires+, Walmart SuperCtr

**183** Shopiere Rd, rd S, to Shopiere, **S** gas: Rollette/dsl/24hr, other: 🅷 HOSPITAL, camping

**181mm** weigh sta, wb

**177** WI 351, Janesville, **S** gas: BP, KwikTrip, food: El Jardin Mexican, Cursing Stone Grill, other: to Blackhawk Tec Coll, Rock Co Airport

**175b a** WI 11, Janesville, to Delavan, **N** gas: BP/Subway/dsl/24hr, food: Denny's, lodging: Baymont Inn, **S** gas: BP, food: DQ, Hardee's, lodging: Lannon Stone Motel

**171c b** US 14, WI 26, Janesville, **N** gas: TA/Mobil/Wendy's/dsl/scales, food: Damon's, Fuddruckers, IHOP, Old Country Buffet, Starbucks, Subway, TX Roadhouse, lodging: Holiday Inn Express, Microtel, other: Best Buy, Gander Mtn, GNC, Home Depot, Michael's, Old Navy, PetCo, Staples, Tires+, TJ Maxx, **S** gas: Kwik Trip/dsl/24hr, food: Applebee's, Arby's, Asia Buffet, Big Boy, Burger King, CK Grill, Cousins Subs, Culver's, El Chipala Mexican, Famous Dave's, Fazoli's, Ground Round, Hardee's, Hooters, KFC, Little Caesars, Milio's Cafe, McDonald's, Noodle's & Co., Olive Garden, Papa Murphy's,

*(middle margin, top to bottom)* E ↕ W   B E L O I T   J A N E S V I L L E

Copyright 2009 - The Next Exit®

**WI** E ↕ W

**MADISON**

## INTERSTATE 90 CONT'D

**171c b** Continued
Peking Chinese, Perkins, Pizza Hut, Prime Quarter Steaks, Red Robin, Shakey's Pizza, Taco Bell, World Buffet, **lodging:** Select Inn, **other:** H HOSPITAL, Aldi Foods, F&F, Ford/Lincoln/Mercury, Harley-Davidson, Hyundai, JC Penney, Kohl's, K-Mart, Mazda, Mercedes, Sears/auto, ShopKO, Target, VW, Woodman Foods/gas, mall

**171a** N **gas:** Phillips 66/dsl, **food:** Cracker Barrel, Best Western/rest., Hampton Inn, Motel 6, Hampton Inn, **other:** Chrysler/Jeep/Dodge, Sam's Club, Walmart SuperCtr, S same as 171c b

**168mm** rest area eb, full & facilities, C, A, litter barrels, vending, petwalk

**163.5mm** Rock River

**163** WI 59, Edgerton, to Milton, N **gas:** Mobil/Subway/dsl, Shell/Taco John's, **food:** Cousins Subs, Culver's, McDonald's, Red Apple Rest., WI Cheese Store, **lodging:** Comfort Inn, **other:** marina, S **gas:** BP

**160** US 51S, WI 73, WI 106, Oaklawn Academy, to Deerfield, N **other:** Hickory Hills Camping, S **gas:** BP/dsl/scales/24hr/@, KwikTrip, **food:** Ray's Rest., Subway, Winchester Rest., **lodging:** Towne Edge Motel, **other:** H HOSPITAL, Janesville RV Ctr

**156** US 51N, to Stoughton, S **lodging:** Coachman's Inn/rest., H HOSPITAL

**148mm** weigh sta wb

**147** rd N, Cottage Grove, to Stoughton, S **gas:** BP/Arby's/24hr, Road Ranger/Subway/dsl, **other:** Lake Kegonsa SP, fireworks

**146mm** weigh sta eb

**142b a** (142a exits left from wb) US 12, US 18, Madison, to Cambridge, N **gas:** Mobil/dsl, **food:** Subway, **lodging:** Best Value, Wingate Inn, **other:** Harley-Davidson, S **gas:** Cenex/dsl, Mobil/dsl, Phillips 66/Arby's/dsl, Shell/dsl, **food:** Denny's, Quizno's, Wendy's, **lodging:** Day's Inn, Rodeway Inn, **other:** H HOSPITAL, UWI

**138a** I-94, E to Milwaukee, W to La Crosse, **I-90 W and I-94 W run together for 93 miles, (exits left from EB)**

**138b** WI 30, Madison, S 🛩

**135c b** US 151, Madison, N **gas:** BP, **food:** Cheesehaus, Happy Wok, Subway, **lodging:** Courtyard, Staybridge Suites, Woodfield Suites, **other:** Buick, Chevrolet, Chrysler/Dodge, Ford, Isuzu, Kia, Nissan, Toyota

**135a** US 151, Madison, S **gas:** BP, **food:** Chicago Grill, **lodging:** Holiday Inn, Grand Stay Suites, La Quinta, Staybridge Suites, **other:** Buick, Chevrolet, Chrysler, Ford/Lincoln/Mercury, Toyota, S **gas:** BP/24hr, Shell, **food:** Applebee's, Arby's, Carlos O'Kelly's, Chili's, Country Kitchen, Cracker Barrel, Denny's, Hardee's, IHOP, KFC, McDonald's, Noodles & Co., Old Country Buffet, Olive Garden, Outback Steaks, Panera Bread, Perkins, Potbelly's Rest., Pizza Hut, Red Lobster, Red Robin, Rocky's Pizza, Subway, Takumi Japanese, TGIFriday, Tumbleweed Grill, TX Roadhouse, Wendy's, **lodging:** Best Western, Comfort Inn, Courtyard, Crowne Plaza Hotel/rest., Econolodge, Excel Inn, Hampton Inn, Microtel, Motel 6, Red Roof Inn, Residence Inn, Select Inn, Super 8, **other:** Barnes & Noble, Best Buy, Circuit City, $Tree, Firestone/auto, Gander Mtn, Home Depot,

**MADISON**

**135a** Continued
JC Penney, Jo-Ann Fabrics, Kohl's, Marshall's, Office Depot, Old Navy, PetsMart, Sears, ShopKO, Tuesday Morning, mall, st patrol, vet

**132** US 51, Madison, De Forest, N **gas:** Shell/Pinecone Rest/dsl/24hr, **food:** Cousin's Subs, **other:** Camping World RV Ctr, Gander Mtn, S **gas:** TA/Mobil/Subway/Taco Bell/dsl/scales/24hr/@, **lodging:** Economy Motel, **other:** Goodyear, Peterbilt, Freightliner/GMC/Volvo/White, WI RV World, camping

**131** WI 19, Waunakee, N **gas:** Kwik Trip, Mobil, Speedway/dsl, **food:** A&W, McDonald's, Rodeside Grill, **lodging:** Day's Inn, Super 8, **other:** Mousehouse Cheesehaus, Kenworth Trucks, Truckwash, S **lodging:** Country Inn Suites (4mi)

**126** rd V, De Forest, to Dane, N **gas:** BP, Phillips 66/Arby's/dsl, **food:** Burger King, Culver's, DeForest Rest., McDonald's, Subway, **lodging:** Holiday Inn Express, **other:** Cheese Chalet, KOA, S **gas:** Exxon/dsl, **lodging:** Comfort Inn

**119** WI 60, Arlington, to Lodi, S **gas:** Mobil/Cousins Subs/dsl, **food:** A&W, Rococo's Pizza, **lodging:** Best Western, **other:** Interstate RV Ctr

**115** rd CS, Poynette, to Lake Wisconsin, N **gas:** BP/dsl, **food:** McDonald's, Subway, **other:** Smokey Hollow Camping, dsl truck/trailer repair, motel, trout fishing

**113mm** rest area both lanes, full & facilities, C, A, litter barrels, vending, petwalk

**111mm** Wisconsin River

**108b a** I-39 N, WI 78, to US 51 N, Portage, N **other:** H HOSPITAL, to WI Dells, S **gas:** BP, Petro/DQ/Subway/dsl/24hr/@, **lodging:** Comfort Suites, Day's Inn, Devil's Head Resort/Conv Ctr, **other:** Blue Beacon

**106mm** Baraboo River

**106** WI 33, Portage, N **other:** H HOSPITAL, S **gas:** BP, **other:** Kamp Dakota, SkyHigh Camping, to Cascade Mtn Ski Area, Devil's Lake SP, Circus World Museum, Wayside Park

**92** US 12, to Baraboo, N **gas:** BP/dsl, Exxon, Mobil/dsl/24hr, Sinclair/Subway/dsl, **food:** Buffalo Phil's Grille, Burger King, Cracker Barrel, Culver's, Damon's, Danny's Diner, Denny's, Dominos, Field's Steaks, McDonald's, Monk's Grill, Ponderosa, Sarento's Rest., Wintergreen Grill, Uno Pizzaria, **lodging:** Alakai Hotel, Great Wolf Lodge, Country Squire Motel, Grand Marquis Inn, Holiday Inn Express, Kalahari Resort, Lake Delton Hotel, Ramada Ltd., Wilderness Hotel, Wintergreen Hotel/grill, **other:** Broadway Theater, Kalahari Conv Ctr, Mkt Sq Cheese, Sundara Resort, Tanger Outlets Famous Brands, WI Cheese, museum, S **lodging:** Motel 6, **other:** H HOSPITAL, Scenic Traveler RV Ctr, Jellystone Camping, Red Oak Camping, Mirror Lake SP

**89** WI 23, Lake Delton, N **gas:** Phillips 66, Shell/dsl, **food:** Brathouse Grill, Denny's Diner, Howie's Rest., KFC, Los Primos, Moosejaw Pizza, **lodging:** Econolodge, Hilton Garden, Kings Inn, Malibu Inn, Olympia Motel, **other:** Crystal Grand Music Theatre, Springbrook Camping, Jellystone Camping, USPO, S **food:** McDonald's, Northwoods Grill, **other:** Home Depot, Kohls, Walmart SuperCtr/Subway, Country Roads RV Park, Wannabee Campground

## INTERSTATE 90 CONT'D

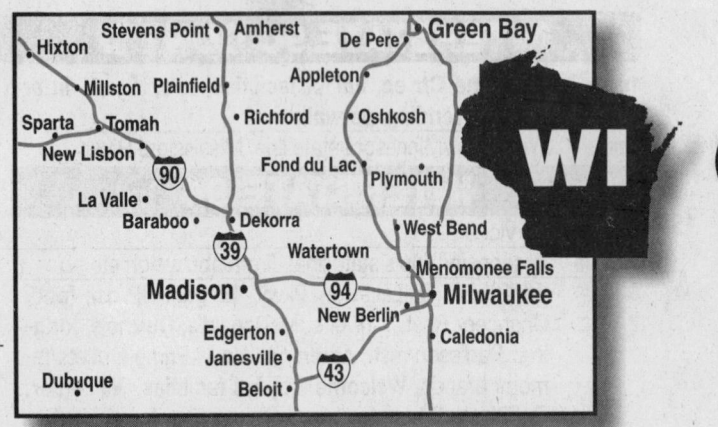

E
W

**87**   WI 13, Wisconsin Dells, **N** gas: BP/dsl, Mobil/Arby's/dsl, Shell, **food:** Applebee's, Bunyan's Rest., Burger King, Cold Stone, Country Kitchen, Denny's, Green Mill Rest., IHOP, McDonald's, Mexican Rose Rest., Outlaw Steakhouse, Perkins, Quizno's, Starbucks, Taco Bell, Wendy's, **lodging:** AmericInn, Best Western, Comfort Inn, Day's Inn, Howard Johnson, Polynesian Hotel, Super 8, **other:** KOA, Sherwood Forest Camping, Tepee Park Camping, Walgreens, golf, waterpark, info

**85**   US 12, WI 16, Wisconsin Dells, **0-3 mi N food:** Crabby's Seafood, Starbucks, **lodging:** Days Inn, Mayflower Motel, **other:** to Rocky Arbor SP, American World RV Park/Hotel, KOA, Rocky Arbor SP, Sherwood Forest Camping, Standing Rock Camping, **S** gas: BP, **food:** Piccadilly's, **lodging:** Arrowhead Camping, Edge-O-the-Dell RV Camping, Summer Breeze Resort

**79**   rd HH, Lyndon Sta, **S** gas: BP/Subway/dsl/24hr

**76mm**   **rest area wb, full** ♿ **facilities,** 🚻, ⛐, **litter barrels, vending, petwalk**

**74mm**   **rest area eb, full** ♿ **facilities,** 🚻, ⛐, **litter barrels, vending, petwalk**

**69**   WI 82, Mauston, **N** gas: Mauston TP/Taco Bell/24hr, Pilot/Wendy's/dsl/scales/24hr, Shell/24hr, **food:** Country Kitchen, **lodging:** Best Western Oasis, Country Inn, Super 8, **other:** to Buckhorn SP, **S** gas: KwikTrip/BP/scales/dsl, Marathon, Mobil, **food:** CJ's Italian, Culver's, Garden Valley Rest., McDonald's, Pizza Hut, Roman Castle Rest., Subway, **lodging:** Best Value Inn, **other:** HOSPITAL, Buckhorn SP, Family$, K-Mart, Pick'n Save, Walgreens

**61**   WI 80, New Lisbon, to Necedah, **N** gas: Mobil/A&W/Subway/dsl/@, New Lisbon Trkstp/dsl/24hr/@, **lodging:** Edge O' the Wood Motel, Travelers Inn, **other:** Buckhorn SP, Chrysler/Jeep, Ford, fireworks, **S** gas: KwikTrip/24hr, **other:** Barnes Foods, True Value, Elroy-Sparta ST Tr

**55**   rd C, Camp Douglas, **N** other: wayside, to Camp Williams, Volk Field, **S** gas: BP/dsl, Mobil/Subway/dsl, **food:** German Haus Rest., **lodging:** German Haus Rest., K&K Motel, **other:** to Mill Bluff SP

**51mm**   weigh sta eb

**48**   rd PP, Oakdale, **N** gas: Road Ranger/Subway/dsl/scales/24hr, **other:** Granger's Camping, KOA, Mill Bluff SP, truck/car wash, antiques, **S** gas: Love's/Hardee's/dsl/scales/24hr, **other:** Mill Bluff SP

**47.5mm**   weigh sta wb

**45**   I-94 W, to St Paul, **I-90 E and I-94 E run together for 93 miles**

**43**   US 12, WI 16, Tomah, **N** gas: BP, KwikTrip/dsl/24hr, **food:** Burnstadt's Café, DQ, Embers Rest., European Café, **lodging:** Daybreak Inn, **other:** Ⓗ HOSPITAL, vet

**41**   WI 131, Tomah, to Wilton, **N** gas: Mobil/dsl, KwikTrip/dsl (24hr), **food:** Burnstadts Cafe, **lodging:** Brentwood Motel, Daybreak Inn, **other:** VA MED CTR, **S** st patrol

**28**   WI 16, Sparta, Ft McCoy, **N** gas: BP, Kwiktrip/dsl, **lodging:** Best Western, **other:** Ⓗ HOSPITAL

**25**   WI 27, Sparta, to Melvina, **N** gas: Cenex/dsl, KwikTrip, Phillips 66/Taco Bell, Shell/dsl, **food:** Burger King, Country Kitchen, Culver's, DQ, KFC, McDonald's,

T O M A H

**25**   Continued
Pizza Hut, Subway, **lodging:** Best Nights Inn, Country Inn, Super 8, **other:** Ⓗ HOSPITAL, Ace Hardware, Chevrolet/Buick/Pontiac, Family$, Ford/Mercury, Piggly Wiggly, Walgreen, Walmart SuperCtr (2mi, WI 16), **S** camping

**22mm**   **rest area wb, full** ♿ **facilities,** 🚻, ⛐, **litter barrels, vending, petwalk**

**20mm**   **rest area eb, full** ♿ **facilities,** 🚻, ⛐, **litter barrels, vending, petwalk**

**15**   WI 162, Bangor, to Coon Valley, **N** gas, **S** other: Chevrolet

**12**   rd C, W Salem, **N** gas: Cenex/cafe/dsl/24hr, **other:** Coulee Region RV Ctr, NAPA, Neshonoc Camping, **S** gas: BP/Quizno's/dsl, **lodging:** AmericInn

**10mm**   weigh sta eb

**5**   WI 16, La Crosse, **N** food: Cold Stone Creamery, Manny's Mexican, Outback Steaks, Quizno's, **lodging:** Baymont Inn, Hampton Inn, Microtel, **other:** $Tree, Freightliner, Gander Mtn, Walmart SuprCtr/Subway, Woodman's Foods/gas/lube, Aldi Foods, Home Depot, **S** gas: Kwik Trip/dsl/24hr, **food:** Carlos O'Kelly's,'s, ChuckeCheese, Culver's, Fazoli's, Jimmy John's, McDonald's, Hong Kong Buffet, Old Country Buffet, Olive Garden, Perkins, Starbucks, TGIFriday, **lodging:** Holiday Inn Express, Stony Creek Inn, **other:** Ⓗ HOSPITAL, Barnes&Noble, Best Buy, Goodyear/auto, F&F, JC Penney, Kohl's, Macy's, Marshall Field, Michael's, Sears/auto, ShopKO, Target, mall

**4**   US 53 N, WI 16, to WI 157, La Crosse, **N** other: Harley-Davidson, **S** gas: Kwik Trip/gas, TO, **food:** Applebee's, Bakers Square, Burger King,'s, Famous Dave's BBQ, Panera Bread, Papa Murphy's, Red Lobster, Rococo's Pizza, Subway, Taco Bell, Wendy's, **lodging:** Comfort Inn, Day's Inn, **other:** Ⓗ HOSPITAL, Barnes & Noble, Curves, Festival Food/24hr, GNC, Goodyear/auto, K-Mart, Macy's, Office Depot, PetCo, Sam's Club, Tires+, TJ Maxx, SuperLube, La Crosse River St Trail

**3**   US 53 S, WI 35, to La Crosse, **S** gas: Kwik Trip, **food:** Burger King, Coney Island, Edwardo's Pizza, Hardee's, KFC, La Crosse Rest., McDonald's, North Country Steaks, Perkins, Pizza Hut, Subway, **lodging:** Best Value, Best Western, Brookstone Inn, Econolodge, Exel Inn, Settle Inn, Super 8, **other:** Curves, ShopKo/drug, U-Haul, Walgreens, to Great River St Trail, Viterbo Coll

**2.5mm**   Black River

**2**   rd B, French Island, **N** other: ✈, **S** gas: BP/dsl, Kwik Trip, **lodging:** Day's Inn/rest.

L A C R O S S E

**WI**

E ↕ W

K E N O S H A

## INTERSTATE 90 CONT'D

| | |
|---|---|
| **1mm** | **Welcome Ctr eb, full** 🚻 **facilities, info,** 📞, 🏕, **litter barrels, vending, petwalk** |
| **0mm** | Wisconsin/Minnesota state line, Mississippi River |

## INTERSTATE 94

| Exit # | Services |
|---|---|
| **349mm** | Wisconsin/Illinois state line, (from nb), weigh sta nb |
| **347** | WI 165, rd Q, Lakeview Pkwy, **E gas:** BP/dsl, **food:** Chancery Rest., Culver's, McDonald's, Quizno's, **lodging:** Radisson/rest., **other:** Old Navy, Prime Outlets/famous brands, **Welcome Ctr, full facilities, W other:** GolfShack Whse |
| **345** | rd C, **E gas:** Phillips 66/dsl |
| **345mm** | Des Plaines River |
| **344** | WI 50, Lake Geneva, to Kenosha, **E food:** Citgo/dsl, Shell, Woodman's/gas, **food:** Buffalo Wild Wings, Nick&Willy's Pizza, Noodles&Co, Perkins, Pizza Hut, Quizno's, Starbucks, Texas Roadhouse, White Castle, **lodging:** La Quinta, Super 8, **other:** 🏥 HOSPITAL, Best Buy, Gander Mtn, Walgreens, **W gas:** BP/Subway, Speedway/dsl, **food:** Arby's, Birchwood Grill, Cracker Barrel, KFC, McDonald's, Pheonix Rest., Taco Bell, Wendy's, **lodging:** Best Western, Country Inn&Suites, Day's Inn, Value Inn, **other:** BMW, BratStop Cheese Store, Carmax, Chevrolet, Toyota/Scion |
| **342** | WI 158, to Kenosha, **E** Harley-Davidson, **W** antiques |
| **340** | WI 142, rd S, to Kenosha, **E gas:** Mobil/dsl, **other:** 🏥 HOSPITAL, **W food:** Mars Cheese Castle Rest., Star-Bar Rest., **lodging:** Oasis Inn, **other:** to Bong RA |
| **339** | rd E, **E gas:** Marathon/dsl/24hr |
| **337** | County Line Rd, rd KR, **E other:** to Great Lakes Dragaway, **W food:** Apple Holler Rest. |
| **335** | WI 11, Burlington, to Racine |
| **333** | US 20, Waterford, to Racine, **E gas:** KwikTrip/dsl/24hr, Shell/Cousins Subs/dsl, **food:** Burger King, McDonald's, **lodging:** Holiday Inn Express, Ramada Ltd, **other:** 🏥 HOSPITAL, **W gas:** Citgo/Wendy's/dsl/24hr, Petro/Mobil/Iron Skillet/dsl/scales/@, **food:** Culver's, Spokes Rest., Subway, **lodging:** Grandview Inn, **other:** Burlington RV Ctr |
| **329** | rd K, Thompsonville, to Racine, **E gas:** Pilot/Arby's/dsl/scales/24hr, **W gas:** Mobil/A&W |
| **328mm** | weigh sta eb |
| **327** | rd G, **W other:** Black Jack's Fireworks |
| **326** | 7 Mile Rd, **E gas:** BP/24hr, **other:** Jellystone Park, **W gas:** Mobil/24hr, antiques |
| **325** | US 41 N (from wb), to 27th St |
| **322** | WI 100, to Ryan Rd, **E food:** McDonald's, Wendy's, Wild Wild Burgers, **other:** Goodyear/Cummins dsl, **W gas:** ◆FLYING J/Country Mkt/dsl/scales/24hr, Mobil, Pilot/Subway/dsl/LP/scales/24hr, Shell/A&W/KFC/dsl, **food:** Arby's, Cousins Subs, Perkins, Starbucks, Yen Hwa Chinese, **other:** Blue Beacon, Freightliner/repair, Pick'n Save, Walgreens |
| **320** | rd BB, Rawson Ave, **E gas:** BP/24hr, Mobil, **food:** Applebee's, Burger King, **lodging:** La Quinta |
| **319** | rd ZZ, College Ave, **E gas:** Shell/Subway, Speedway/dsl, **food:** Branded Steer Rest., Houlihan's, McDonald's, **lodging:** Comfort Suites, Country Inn&Suites, |

| | |
|---|---|
| **319** | Continued<br>Econolodge, Hampton Inn, Holiday Inn Express, MainStay Suites, Radisson, Red Roof Inn, **W gas:** BP/24hr, Citgo/dsl |
| **318** | WI 119 |
| **317** | Layton Ave, **E gas:** Andy's/dsl, Clark, **food:** Burger King, Culver's, IHOP, J-Roberts Porterhouse Steaks, Martino's Rest., Prime Qtr Steaks, Wendy's, **other:** Checker Parts, **W food:** Spring Garden Rest., **lodging:** Howard Johnson |
| **316** | I-43 S, I-894 W ( I-94 exits left from eb), to Beloit |
| **314b** | Howard Ave, to Milwaukee, **W** to Alverno Coll |
| **314a** | Holt Ave, **E gas:** Andy's/dsl, **food:** Applebee's, DQ, Jimmy John's, Quizno's, Starbucks, Subway, **other:** $General, Home Depot, Pick'n Save Foods, **E on Chase... W food:** Arby's, Wendy's, **other:** Sentry Foods, Target, **W** 🏥 HOSPITAL |
| **312b a** | Becher St, Mitchell St, Lapham Blvd, **W gas:** BP, Citgo/dsl |
| **311** | WI 59, National Ave, 6th St, downtown |
| **310a** | 13th St (from eb), **E** 🏥 HOSPITAL |
| **310b** | I-43 N, to Green Bay |
| **310c** | I-794 E, **E lodging:** Hilton, Holiday Inn, **other:** to downtown and Lake Michigan Port of Entry |
| **309b** | 26th St, 22nd St, Clybourn St, St Paul Ave, **N other:** 🏥 HOSPITAL, to Marquette U |
| **309a** | 35th St, **N gas:** BP, Speedway, **other:** 🏥 HOSPITAL |
| **308c b** | US 41 |
| **308a** | VA Ctr, **N other:** Miller Brewing, **S other:** County Stadium |
| **307b** | 68th-70th St, Hawley Rd |
| **307a** | **N** 68th St, **N other:** Valvoline |
| **306** | WI 181, to 84th St, **N** 🏥 HOSPITAL, **S other:** Olympic Training Facility |
| **305b** | US 45 N, to Fond du Lac, **N** 🏥 HOSPITAL |
| **305a** | I-894 S, US 45 S, to Chicago, to ✈ |
| **304b a** | WI 100, **N gas:** Mobil, OP, Shell/dsl, **food:** Cousins Subs, Edwardo's Pizza, Ghengis Khan Mongolian, Honeybaked Cafe, Jimmy John's, Moe's Irish Grill, Pony Rest., Qdoba Mexican, Starbucks, Taco Bell, **lodging:** 40 Winks Inn, Super 8, **other:** 🏥 HOSPITAL, zoo, **S gas:** MiniMart/dsl, Mobil, Speedway/dsl, **food:** DQ, Fazoli's, McDonald's, Wendy's, **other:** Checker Parts, U-Haul, Walgreens |
| **301b a** | Moorland Rd, **N gas:** BP, **food:** Bakers Square, Bravo Italiano, Chicago Grill, Claim Jumper Rest., Fleming's Rest., Houlihan's, McDonald's, Mitchell's Fish Mkt, **lodging:** Sheraton, **other:** Ace Hardware, Barnes&Noble, JC Penney, Office Depot, PetCo, Sears/auto, Walgreens, mall, vet, **N on US 18...gas:** Mobil, **food:** Caribou Coffee, Chili's, Fuddrucker's, Noodles&Co, Old Country Buffet, Pedro's Mexican, Starbucks, TGI Fridays, **lodging:** Courtyard, Towneplace Suites, **other:** Circuit City, Fresh Mkt Foods, Goodyear/auto, Jo-Ann Fabrics, Michael's, Office Depot, PetCo, TJ Maxx, World Mkt, **S food:** Champp's Grill, Charcoal Grill, Maxwell's Rest., Panera Bread, Outback Steaks, **lodging:** Best Western Midway, Brookfield Suites, Country Inn&Suites, Midway Motel, Residence Inn, **other:** Pick'n Save Foods, Walgreens, golf |

**E** ↕ **W**

**WAUKESHA**

## INTERSTATE 94 CONT'D

**297** US 18, rd JJ, Blue Mound Rd, Barker Rd, **N gas:** BP/24hr, Mobil, **food:** Applebee's, Charhouse, ChuckeCheese, Heavenly Ham, KFC, Kopp's Cafe, Krispy Kreme, McDonald's, Melting Pot, Perkins, Subway, **lodging:** Hampton Inn, Homestead Suites, La Quinta, Motel 6, Quality Inn, **other:** Acura, Advance Parts, Best Buy, Lexus/Mazda/VW, Menard's, **S gas:** F&F/dsl, PDQ Gas, **food:** Arby's, Cousin's Subs, Famous Dave's BBQ, McDonald's, Milio's, Oscar's Cafe, Papa John's, Starbucks, Taco Bell, Texas Roadhouse, Topper's Pizza, Wendy's, **lodging:** Extended Stay America Ramada Ltd, **other:** Cadillac/GMC, Carmax, Firestone, Ford/Lincoln/Mercury, Gander Mtn, Home Depot, Infiniti, KIA, Kohl's, Mercedes, Sam's Club, Target, Tires+, Walgreens, st patrol

**295** WI 164, Waukesha, **N gas:** KwikTrip/gas, **food:** Jimmy John's, **lodging:** Marriott, **S other:** Ⓗ HOSPITAL, to Carroll Coll

**294** rd J, to Waukesha, **N gas:** Mobil, **food:** Machine Shed Rest., Thunder Bay Grille, **lodging:** Comfort Suites, Radisson, **S other:** Expo Ctr, Peterbilt

**293c** WI 16 W, Pewaukee (from wb), **N other:** GE Plant

**293b a** rd T, Wausheka, Pewaukee, **S gas:** Mobil, KwikTrip, **food:** Canyon City Wood Grill, Cousins Subs, Culver's, Denny's, Fazoli's, Great Northern BBQ, McDonald's, Mr. Wok, Peking House, Qdoba Mexican, Quizno's, Rococo's Pizza, Spring City Rest., Subway, Taco Amigo, Weissgerber's Gasthaus Rest., **lodging:** Best Western, **other:** Central Mkt Foods, CVS Drug, $Tree, Firestone/auto, GNC, Jo-Ann Fabrics, Office Depot, Osco Drug, Pick'n Save Foods, Radio Shack, Walgreens

**291** rd G, **N lodging:** Country Springs Inn

**290** rd SS

**287** WI 83, Hartland, to Wales, **N food:** Applebees, 5 Guys Burgers, Hardee's, McDonald's, Noodles&Co, Panera Bread, Perkins, Qdoba, Starbucks, Water St Brewery/rest., **lodging:** Holiday Inn Express, **other:** Amish Barn Gifts, Best Buy, GNC, Kohl's, Marshall's, Radio Shack, Sentry Foods, Walgreens, **S gas:** BP/dsl/24hr, PDQ/dsl/24hr, **food:** Burger King, Delafield Bewhaus, DQ, Rococo's Pizza, Subway, **lodging:** La Quinta, **other:** Ace Hardware, Home Depot, PetCo, Target, Walmart/drugs, vet

**285** rd C, Delafield, **N gas:** BP, Mobil/deli, **lodging:** Delafield Hotel, **other:** to St John's Military Academy, **S other:** to Kettle Moraine SF

**283** rd P, to Sawyer Rd (from wb)

**282** WI 67, Dousman, to Oconomowoc, **N gas:** BP, KwikTrip, **food:** Chili's, Culver's, Pizza Hut, Quizno's, Rococo's Pizza, Schlotsky's, Subway, **lodging:** Hilton Garden, Olympia Resort, **other:** Ⓗ HOSPITAL, Aldi Foods, K-Mart, Pick'n Save, **S other:** Ⓗ HOSPITAL, Harley-Davidson, vet, to Kettle Moraine SF (8mi), Old World WI HS (13mi)

**277** Willow Glen Rd (from eb, no return)

**275** rd F, Ixonia, to Sullivan, **N gas:** BP/dsl, **other:** Concord Gen Store, **S** camping

**267** WI 26, Johnson Creek, to Watertown, **N gas:** BP/McDonald's/dsl, Shell/dsl/rest./scales/24hr, **food:** Arby's, Hwy Harry's Cafe, **lodging:** Comfort Suites, Day's Inn,

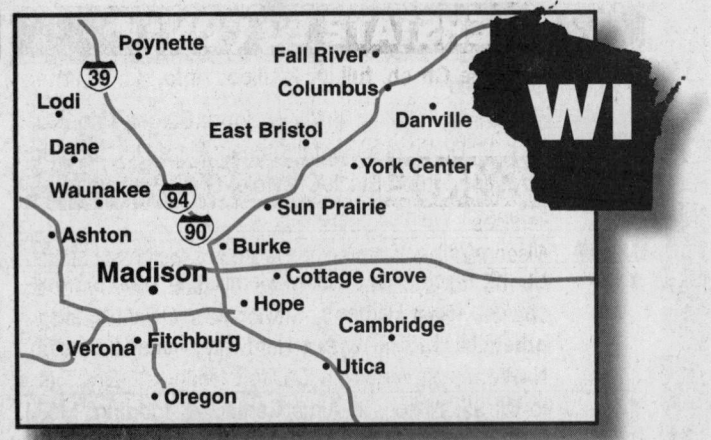

**MADISON** **TOMAH**

**267** Continued
**other:** Goodyear/auto, Johnson Creek Outlet Ctr/famous brands, Old Navy, **S gas:** KwikTrip/dsl, **food:** Culver's, Subway, **other:** Ⓗ HOSPITAL, Kohl's, Menard's, to Aztalan SP

**266mm** Rock River

**264mm** rest area wb, full ♿ facilities, ☏, ⛱, litter barrels, vending, petwalk

**263mm** Crawfish River

**261mm** rest area eb, full ♿ facilities, ☏, ⛱, litter barrels, vending, petwalk

**259** WI 89, Lake Mills, to Waterloo, **N gas:** Citgo/dsl/24hr, **lodging:** Best Value Inn, **other:** truck repair, **S gas:** BP/dsl/24hr, KwikTrip/dsl/24hr, **food:** McDonald's, Pizza Pit, Subway, **lodging:** Pyramid Motel/RV park, **other:** Buick/Cadillac/Chevrolet, Country Campers RV Ctr, Walgreens, urgent care, to Aztalan SP

**250** WI 73, Deerfield, to Marshall

**244** rd n, Sun Prairie, Cottage Grove, **N gas:** Citgo/dsl, **S gas:** Shell, **food:** Arby's, Subway

**240** I-90 E.

**I-94 and I-90 run together 93 miles. See Interstate 90 exits 48-138**

**147** I-90 W, to La Crosse **143** US 12, WI 21, Tomah, **N gas:** Mobil/dsl, **food:** A&W/LJ Silver, Four Star Rest., Perkins, **lodging:** AmericInn, Holiday Inn, Microtel, Super 8, **other:** Humbird Cheese/gifts, **S gas:** BP, KwikTrip/dsl/rest./scales/24hr, **food:** China Buffet, Culver's, Ground Round, KFC, McDonald's, Pizza Hut, Quizno's, Subway, Taco Bell, **lodging:** Comfort Inn, Cranberry Suites, Econolodge, **other:** Ⓗ HOSPITAL, Advance Parts, Aldi Foods, $Tree, U-Haul, Walmart SuperCtr, to Ft McCoy (9mi), **S on US 12...food:** Burger King, **other:** Ace Hardware, Buick/Chevrolet, Chrysler/Dodge/Jeep, Curves, Firestone/auto, Ford/Lincoln/Mercury, Radio Shack

**135** rd EW, Warrens, **N gas:** BP, **lodging:** 3 Bears Resort, **other:** Jellystone Camping, **S food:** Bog Rest.

**128** rd O, Millston, **N other:** Black River SF, camping, **S gas:** Cenex/dsl, **other:** USPO

**123mm** rest area/scenic view both lanes, full ♿ facilities, ☏, ⛱, litter barrels, vending, petwalk

**116** WI 54, **N gas:** Cenex/Subway/Taco Johns/dsl/LP, **food:** Perkins, **lodging:** Best Western Arrowhead/rest., Holiday Inn Express, Super 8, **other:** Black River RA, Parkland Camp, casino, **S gas:** ✦FLYING J/Cookery/

## INTERSTATE 94 CONT'D

**E** ↕ **W**

**WI**

**116** Continued
dsl/24hr/@, KwikTrip/dsl/rest., **food:** Burger King, Culvers, McDonald's, Oriental Kitchen, Pizza Hut, **lodging:** Day's Inn, **other:** Buick/Chevrolet/GMC/Pontiac, $Tree, $General, Walmart SuperCtr

**115mm** Black River

**115** US 12, Black River Falls, to Merrillan, **S gas:** BP, Holiday/dsl, **food:** Hardee's, KFC, Subway, Sunrise Rest., **other:** H HOSPITAL, Ace Hardware, Harley-Davidson, NAPA

**105** to WI 95, Hixton, to Alma Center, **N lodging:** Motel 95/campground, **other:** KOA (3mi), **S gas:** Cenex/dsl, Clark/dsl/rest./24hr, **other:** city park

**98** WI 121, Northfield, Pigeon Falls, to Alma Center, **S gas:** Cenex/dsl, **food:** DeeDee's Diner, Jackie's Café

**88** US 10, Osseo, to Fairchild, **N gas:** BP/DQ, Mobil/dsl, Shell/Elderberry's/dsl/scales, **food:** Hardee's, Moe's Diner, **lodging:** 10-7 Inn, Super 8, **other:** Chevrolet, Ford, Stony Cr RV Park, **S gas:** Speedway/dsl, **food:** McDonald's, Subway, Taco John's, **lodging:** Osseo Inn, **other:** H HOSPITAL, Family$

**81** rd HH, rd KK, Foster, **S gas:** BP/dsl/LP, **food:** Foster Cheesehaus

**70** US 53, Eau Claire, **N** off Golf Rd...**gas:** Mobil/dsl, **food:** A&W, Applebee's, Bakers Square, Bear Creek Grille, Buffalo Wild Wings, Burracho's, Coldstone Creamery, Fazoli's, Jade Garden, McDonald's, Nanny's Grill, Noodles&Co, Olive Garden, Outback Steaks, Panera Bread, Texas Roadhouse, TGIFriday, **lodging:** Country Inn&Suites, Grandstay, Heartland Inn, **other:** Aldi Foods, Best Buy, Borders Books, Gander Mtn, JC Penney, Kohl's, Macy's, Menard's, Michael's, Office Depot, PetCo, Sam's Club, Scheel's Sports, Sears/auto, Target, TJ Maxx, Younker's, Walmart SuperCtr, mall, **S other:** Gander Mtn, st police

**68** WI 93, to Eleva, **N gas:** BP, Holiday, KwikTrip, **food:** Burger King, DQ, Red Robin, **lodging:** Econolodge, **other:** Chrysler/Dodge, Family$, Firestone/auto, Goodyear/auto, Jeep, NAPA, Nissan, Saturn, Subaru, USPO, transmission, same as 70, **S gas:** BP, **other:** Audi/VW, Buick/Cadillac/GMC/Hyundai/Pontiac, Ford/Lincoln/Mercury

**65** WI 37, WI 85, Eau Claire, to Mondovi, **N gas:** BP, **food:** Arby's, Green Mill Rest., Hardee's, Mancino's Rest., McDonald's, Randy's Rest., Red Lobster, Starbucks, Subway, Taco Bell, Wendy's, **lodging:** Best Western, Comfort Inn, Day's Inn/rest., Hampton Inn, Highlander Inn, Holiday Inn/rest., Quality Inn, Super 8, **other:** H HOSPITAL, Castle Foods, Mazda/Toyota, Radio Shack, ShopKo, Walgreens

**64mm** Chippewa River

**59** to US 12, rd EE, to Eau Claire, **N gas:** BP/Burger King/dsl/24hr, Holiday/Subway/dsl/24hr, **food:** Embers Rest., McDonald's, **lodging:** AmericInn, Day's Inn, Super 8, **other:** H HOSPITAL, Freightliner, Mack/Volvo Trucks, Peterbilt, auto repair/towing, **S** US RV Ctr, trailer repair

**E A U   C L A I R E**

---

**M E N O M O N I E**

**52** US 12, WI 29, WI 40, Elk Mound, to Chippewa Falls, **S gas:** U-Fuel/pizza

**49mm** weigh sta wb

**45** rd B, Menomonie, **N gas:** Cenex/dsl/rest./scales, **S gas:** KwikTrip/Subway/dsl/scales/24hr, **food:** Country Kitchen, Culver's, **lodging:** Comfort Inn, **other:** H HOSPITAL, AOK RV Ctr, Kenworth, Walmart Dist Ctr

**44mm** Red Cedar River

**43mm** **rest areas both lanes, full** ♿ **facilities,** 📞 🚻, **litter barrels, vending, petwalk, weather info**

**41** WI 25, Menomonie, **N gas:** Cenex, **food:** Applebee's, Burracho's, China Buffet, Pizza Hut, Quizno's, Subway, **other:** H HOSPITAL, Aldi Foods, $Tree, Radio Shack, Walmart SuperCtr, Edgewater Camping, GS Camping, **S gas:** F&F/dsl, Holiday, SA/dsl, **food:** Arby's, Green Mill Rest., Kernel Rest., KFC, McDonald's, Perkins, Taco Bell, Taco John's, Wendy's, **lodging:** AmericInn, Country Inn&Suites, Motel 6, Super 8, **other:** Advance Parts, Chevrolet, Chrysler/Jeep, Ford, K-Mart, NAPA, O'Reilly Parts, Walgreens, to Red Cedar St Tr

**32** rd Q, to Knapp

**28** WI 128, Wilson, Elmwood, to Glenwood City, **N gas:** KwikTrip/dsl/rest./24hr, **S other:** Eau Galle RA, camping, dsl repair

**24** rd B, to Baldwin, **N gas:** BP, **food:** Wild Wood Rest., **lodging:** Woodville Motel, **S other:** Eau Galle RA, camping

**19** US 63, Baldwin, to Ellsworth, **N gas:** Freedom/dsl, KwikTrip/Subway/dsl, **food:** A&W, DQ, Hardee's, McDonald's, **lodging:** AmericInn, **other:** H HOSPITAL, **S gas:** Mobil/rest./dsl, **lodging:** Super 8

**16** rd T, Hammond

**10** WI 65, Roberts, to New Richmond

**8mm** weigh sta eb

**4** US 12, rd U, Somerset, **N gas:** BP/dsl, TA/Country Pride/dsl/rest./24hr/@, **food:** Rich's Eatery, **lodging:** Best Value Inn, **other:** vet, to Willow River SP, **S other:** Curves

**3** WI 35, to River Falls, U of WI River Falls

**2** rd F, Carmichael Rd, Hudson, **N gas:** BP/repair, Freedom/dsl, Holiday, **food:** Applebee's, Caribou Coffee, Cousin's Subs, Culver's, Domino's, KFC, Fiesta Mexicana, Papa Murphy's, Taco John's, **lodging:** Royal Inn, **other:** Family Fresh Foods, GNC, Radio Shack, Target, TrueValue, **S Welcome Ctr both lanes, full** ♿ **facilities,** 📞 🚻, **litter barrel, info, petwalk, gas:** F&F/dsl, Holiday, KwikTrip/dsl, **food:** Arby's, Buffalo Wild Wings, Burger King, Chipotle Mexican, Coldstone Creamery, Country Kitchen, Denny's, Green Mill Rest., McDonald's, Pizza Hut, Perkins, Starbucks, Subway, Taco Bell, Wendy's, **lodging:** Best Western, Comfort Inn, Fairfield Inn, Holiday Inn Express, Super 8, **other:** H HOSPITAL, Checker Parts, Chevrolet/GMC/Pontiac, Chrysler/Dodge/Jeep, County Mkt Foods, Ford/Mercury, Home Depot, Menard's, NAPA, Tires+, Walmart, USPO, to Kinnickinnic SP

**1** WI 35 N, Hudson, **1 mi N gas:** Freedom/dsl, Holiday, **food:** DQ

**0mm** Wisconsin/Minnesota state line, St Croix River

**H U D S O N**

WY

## INTERSTATE 25

**BUFFALO**

N ↕ S

| Exit # | Services |
|---|---|
| 300 | I-90, E to Gillette, W to Billings. I-25 begins/ends on I-90, exit 56. |
| 299 | US 16, Buffalo, **E** gas: Exxon/dsl, Johnson Cty/dsl, Shell/dsl/24hr, **food:** Winchester Steaks, **lodging:** Comfort Inn, Motel 6, **other:** Deer Park Camping, KOA, NAPA, **W** gas: Bighorn/dsl/24hr, Cenex/dsl/rest./24hr, **food:** Bozeman Tr Steaks, Dash Inn Rest., Hardee's, Hoot'n Howl Rest., McDonald's, Pizza Hut, Sub Shop, Subway, Taco John's, **lodging:** Best Western Crossroads, Horsemen's Inn, Rodeway Inn, Wyo Motel, Super 8, **other:** ⊞ HOSPITAL, Ace Hardware, Family$, Indian RV Camp |
| 298 | US 87, Buffalo, **W** gas: Kum-N-Go, Sinclair/dsl/pizza, **other:** Nat Hist Dist Info |
| 291 | Trabing Rd |
| 280 | Middle Fork Rd |
| 274mm | parking area both lanes, litter barrels |
| 265 | Reno Rd |
| 254 | Kaycee, **E** gas: Exxon/dsl, **food:** Country Inn Diner, **other:** Kaycee Gen. Store, NAPA Repair, Powder River RV Park, USPO, museum, **W** rest area both lanes, full 🚻 facilities, 🅲, 🅿, litter barrels, petwalk, gas: Sinclair/dsl/LP/motel, **other:** KC RV Park |
| 249 | TTT Rd |
| 246 | Powder River Rd |
| 235 | Tisdale Mtn Rd |
| 227 | WY 387 N, Midwest, Edgerton |
| 223 | no services |
| 219mm | parking area both lanes, litter barrels |
| 216 | Ranch Rd |
| 210 | Horse Ranch Creek Rd, Midwest, Edgerton |
| 197 | Ormsby Rd |
| 191 | Wardwell Rd, to Bar Nunn, **W** gas: Minimart/dsl, **other:** KOA |
| 189 | US 20, US 26 W, to Shoshone, Port of Entry, airport |
| 188b | WY 220, Poplar St, **E** food: El Jarro Mexican, JB's, Poor Boy's Steaks, Sideline BBQ, **lodging:** Best Western, Hampton Inn, Hilton Garden, Motel 6, Quality Inn, Ramada, **W** gas: Exxon, **food:** Burger King, Casper's Rest., DQ, **other:** Harley-Davidson, to Ft Casper HS |
| 188a | Center St, Casper, **E** gas: Conoco/dsl, Shell/dsl, **food:** Taco John's, **lodging:** National 9 Inn, Ramada, **W** food: Platte River Rest., Subway, **lodging:** Day's Inn, Parkway Plaza Motel, **other:** USPO |
| 187 | McKinley St, Casper, **E** gas: Loaf'n Jug/dsl, **lodging:** Ranch House Motel, **other:** repair/transmissons |
| 186 | US 20, US 26, US 87, Yellowstone St, **E** other: Audi/VW, dsl repair, **W** gas: Exxon, **other:** ⊞ HOSPITAL, Checker Parts, Chevrolet/Subaru, Toyota |
| 185 | WY 258, Wyoming Blvd, E Casper, **E** gas: Kum&Go/dsl, Loaf'n Jug/dsl, **food:** Applebee's, IHOP, |

**CASPER**

**WY**

N ↕ S

## INTERSTATE 25 CONT'D

**185** Continued
Outback Steaks, **lodging:** C'mon Inn, Comfort Inn, Shilo Inn, Super 8, **other:** KOA (1mi), Smith RV Ctr, **W** **gas:** Exxon/dsl, ⊕*FLYING J*/Conoco/Cookery/dsl/LP/scales/24hr, **food:** Arby's, Burger King, DQ, Hardee's, HomeTowne Buffet, KFC/LJ Silver, McDonald's/playplace, Mongolian Grill, Old Chicago Grill, Perkins, Pizza Hut, Red Lobster, South Sea Chinese Rest., Sanford's Cafe, Starbucks, Taco Bell, Taco John's, Village Inn Rest., Wendy's, **lodging:** Coutyard, 1st Interstate Motel, Holiday Inn Express, **other:** AutoZone, Home Depot, JC Penney, K-Mart, PetCo, Plains Tire, Red Lobster, Safeway Foods, Sam's Club/gas, Sears/auto, Sportsman's Warehouse, Staples, Target, Village Inn, Walgreens, Walmart SuperCtr, to Oregon Tr, mall

**182** WY 253, Brooks Rd, Hat Six Rd, **E** **gas:** Sinclair/Chesterfried/dsl, **food:** Lou's Rest., **lodging:** Sleep Inn, **other:** to Wilkins SP, **W** **food:** Firerock Rest., **lodging:** Holiday Inn, Mainstay Suites, **other:** H HOSPITAL, Buick/Cadillac/Pontiac/GMC, Menard's, Rendezvous RV Ctr

**171mm** parking area both lanes, litter barrels

**165** Glenrock, **2 mi** **E** **gas:** Sinclair/dsl, **lodging:** Higgins Hotel, **other:** Deer Creek Village RV Camping (apr-nov)

**160** US 87, US 20, US 26, E Glenrock, **E** **other:** to Johnston Power Plant

**156** Bixby Rd

**154** Barber Rd

**153mm** parking area both lanes, litter barrels

**151** Natural Bridge

**150** Inez Rd

**146** La Prele Rd

**140** WY 59, Douglas, **E** **gas:** Conoco/Subway/dsl, Maverik/dsl, **food:** Arby's, La Costa Mexican, McDonald's, Taco John's, **lodging:** Best Western, Holiday Inn Express, Super 8, **other:** H HOSPITAL, Buick/Chevrolet/GMC/Pontiac, KOA, Lone Tree RV Park, Pioneer Museum, WY St Fair

**135** US 20, US 26, US 87, Douglas, **E** **gas:** Sinclair/dsl/rest., **lodging:** Alpine Inn, 1st Interstate Inn, **other:** H HOSPITAL, auto repair, **1-2 mi** **E** **gas:** Sinclair, **food:** Four Seasons Chinese, Hoggie's Rest., KFC/Taco Bell, Plains Trading Post Rest., Village Inn Rest., **lodging:** Plains Motel, **other:** Ace Hardware, Chrysler/Dodge/Jeep, Family$, Ford/Mercury, Pamida, Safeway

**129mm** parking area both lanes

**126** US 18, US 20 E, Orin, **E** Orin Jct **Rest Area** both lanes, **full** ♿ **facilities,** 🅲, 🛈, **litter barrels, petwalk, RV dump, gas:** Sinclair/Orin Jct Trkstp/dsl/café

**125mm** N Platte River

**111** Glendo, **E** **gas:** Sinclair/dsl, **food:** Glendo Marina Café, **lodging:** Howard's Motel, **other:** to Glendo SP, Glendo Lakeside RV camping

**104** to Middle Bear

**100** Cassa Rd

**94** El Rancho Rd

**92** US 26 E, Dwyer, **E** **rest area** both lanes, **full** ♿ **facilities,** 🛈, **litter barrel, petwalk,** RV dump to Guernsey SP, Ft Laramie NHS

---

**DOUGLAS**

---

**87** Johnson Rd

**84** Laramie River Rd

**84mm** Laramie River

**80** US 87, Laramie Power Sta, Wheatland, Laramie Power Sta, **E** **gas:** Sinclair/A&W/dsl/24hr, **food:** Pizza Hut, **lodging:** Best Western, Super 8, **other:** CarQuest, Chevrolet/Pontiac/Buick/Cadillac, Chrysler/Dodge/Jeep, Family$, Ford/Mercury, Pamida/drug, Safeway, Arrowhead RV Park, same as 78

**78** US 87, Wheatland, **E** **gas:** Cenex/dsl, Loaf'n Jug/dsl, Maverik/dsl, Shell/dsl, **food:** Arby's, Burger King, Subway, Taco John's, Wheatland Rest., **lodging:** Motel 6, Vimbo's Motel/rest., Wyo Motel, **other:** H HOSPITAL, **W** **gas:** Exxon/dsl, Pitstop/dsl, **other:** Radio Shack, Mtn. View RV Park

**73** WY 34 W, to Laramie

**70** Bordeaux Rd

**68** Antelope Rd

**66** Hunton Rd

**65.5mm** parking area both lanes, litter barrels

**65** Slater Rd

**64mm** Richeau Creek

**57** TY Basin Rd, Chugwater

**54** Lp 25, Chugwater, **E** **gas:** Sinclair/dsl, **lodging:** Buffalo Lodge/Grill, **other:** RV camping, **rest area both lanes, full** ♿ **facilities,** 🅲, 🛈, **litter barrels, petwalk, RV dump**

**47** Bear Creek Rd

**39** Little Bear Community

**36mm** Little Bear Creek

**34** Nimmo Rd

**33mm** Horse Creek

**29** Whitaker Rd

**25** ranch exit

**21** Ridley Rd

**17** US 85 N, to Torrington, **W** **food:** Little Bear Rest. (2mi)

**16** WY 211, Horse Creek Rd

**13** Vandehei Ave, **E** **gas:** Loaf'n Jug/Subway, **food:** Silvermine Subs, **W** **gas:** Shamrock/dsl

**12** Central Ave, Cheyenne, **E** **gas:** Exxon, **lodging:** Rodeway Inn, **other:** H HOSPITAL, Frontier Days Park, museum, **E on Dellrang...food:** Applebee's, McDonald's, **lodging:** Fairfield Inn

**11b** Warren AFB, Gate 1, Randall Ave, **E** **other:** to WY St Capitol, museum

**10b d** Warren AFB, Gate 2, Missile Dr, WY 210, HappyJack Rd, **W** **other:** to Curt Gowdy SP

**9** US 30, W Lincolnway, Cheyenne, **E** **gas:** Crossroads/Exxon/dsl, **food:** Comfort Inn, Country Kitchen, Denny's, Outback Steaks, Village Inn Rest., **lodging:** Candlewood Suites, Day's Inn, Express Inn, Hampton Inn, Holiday Inn Express, La Quinta, Microtel, Motel 6, Ramada Inn, Super 8, **other:** Cadillac, Chevrolet, Ford/Lincoln/Mercury, Home Depot, Honda, Hyundai, Nissan, Saturn, Subaru, Toyota, **W** **gas:** Little America/Sinclair/dsl/rest./motel/@

---

**WHEATLAND**

**CHEYENNE**

**WY**

## INTERSTATE 25 CONT'D

| | |
|---|---|
| **8d b** | I-80, E to Omaha, W to Laramie |
| **7** | WY 212, College Dr, **E** gas: Love's/Wendy's/dsl/scales/24hr/@, Shamrock/Subway/dsl/24hr, **food:** Arby's, **other:** A-B RV Park (2mi), Bailey Tire, Truck Repair, **W** WY Info Ctr/rest area both lanes, full  facilities, [, litter barrels, petwalk, gas: ✈ *FLYING J*/Conoco/dsl/LP/scales/rest./24hr/@, **food:** McDonald's, **lodging:** Comfort Inn |
| **6.5mm** | Port of Entry, nb |
| **2** | Terry Ranch Rd, **2 mi E** Terry Bison Ranch RV camping |
| **0mm** | Wyoming/Colorado state line |

## INTERSTATE 80

| Exit # | Services |
|---|---|
| **402mm** | Wyoming/Nebraska State line |
| **401** | WY 215, Pine Bluffs, **N** gas: Cenex/A&W/dsl/24hr/@, Conoco/Subway/dsl, Race Track/rest./dsl, Sinclair/dsl, **food:** Uncle Fred's Rest., **lodging:** Gator's Motel, **other:** NAPA, USPO, Pine Bluff RV Park, **S Welcome Ctr/rest area both lanes, full  facilities, info, [, playground, nature trail, litter barrels, petwalk** |
| **391** | Egbert |
| **386** | WY 213, WY 214, Burns, **N** Antelope Trkstp/dsl/cafe |
| **377** | WY 217, Hillsdale, **N** gas: TA/Burger King/Taco Bell/dsl/motel/scales/24hr/@, **other:** Wyo RV Camping |
| **372mm** | Port of Entry wb, truck insp |
| **370** | US 30 W, Archer, **N** gas: Sapp/dsl/T-Joe's Rest./24hr/@, **other:** fireworks, repair, RV park |
| **367** | Campstool Rd, **N** gas Pilot/dsl/scales/24hr, **lodging:** Sleep Inn, **other:** KOA (seasonal), **S other:** to Wyoming Hereford Ranch |
| **364** | WY 212, to E Lincolnway, Cheyenne, **1 mi N on Lincolnway...gas:** Loaf'n Jug/Subway, Valero, **food:** IHOP, McDonald's, Papa John's, Perkins, Pizza Hut, Shari's Rest., Taco Bell, Wendy's, **other:** H HOSPITAL, AutoZone, BigLots, Checker Parts, $Tree, Econo Foods, Harley-Davidson, Sierra Trading Post, **S other:** AB Camping (4mi), Peterbilt |
| **362** | US 85, I-180, to Central Ave, Cheyenne, Greeley, **1 mi N on Dell Range Rd...gas:** Kum&Go/dsl, Sinclair/dsl, Spirit Gas, **food:** Arby's, Carls' Jr., Hacienda Mexican, **other:** CarQuest, dsl repair, museum, st capitol, **S** gas: Exxon/Domino's/dsl, Shamrock/dsl, **food:** Burger King, GoodTimes Grill/Taco John's, Little Caesar's, Sonic, Subway, **lodging:** Holiday Inn, Roundup Motel, SpringHill Suites, **other:** H HOSPITAL, Family$, Safeway/gas, RV camping, transmissions |
| **359c a** | I-25, US 87, N to Casper, S to Denver |
| **358** | US 30, W Lincolnway, Cheyenne, **N** gas: Exxon/dsl/24hr, Little America/Sinclair/dsl/motel/@, **food:** Denny's, Outback Steaks, Pizza Inn, **lodging:** Village Inn, Day's Inn, Econolodge, Express Inn, Hampton Inn, Hitching Post Inn, Holiday Inn Express, La Quinta, Luxury Inn, Motel 6, Super 8, **other:** H HOSPITAL, Chevrolet, Home Depot, Honda |
| **357** | Wy 222, Roundtop Rd |
| **348** | Otto Rd |

| | |
|---|---|
| **345** | Warren Rd, **N** truck parking |
| **344mm** | no services |
| **343.5mm** | no services |
| **342** | Harriman Rd |
| **341mm** | **parking area both lanes** |
| **339** | Remount Rd |
| **335** | Buford, **N** fireworks, **S** gas: Buford Trading Post/Cenex/dsl/24hr |
| **333mm** | point of interest, parking area both lanes |
| **329** | Vedeauwoo Rd, **S** to Ames Monument, Nat Forest RA |
| **323** | WY 210, Happy Jack Rd, **N** rest area both lanes, full  facilities, [, litter barrels, petwalk, Lincoln Monument, elev. 8640, to Curt Gowdy SP |
| **322mm** | chain up area both lanes |
| **316** | US 30 W, Grand Ave, Laramie, **1-2 mi N** gas: Conoco/dsl, Loaf'N Jug, **food:** Applebee's, Arby's, Bailey's Rest., Burger King, Godfather's Pizza, McDonald's, Papa Murphy's, Sonic, Subway, Taco Bell, Taco John's, Village Inn, Wendy's, Winger's, **lodging:** AmericInn, Comfort Inn, Hampton Inn, Hilton Garden, Holiday Inn, **other:** H HOSPITAL, Albertson's/gas, Chevrolet/Cadillac/Buick/Pontiac, $Tree, Ford/Lincoln/Mercury, Goodyear, Grease Monkey, Staples, Toyota, Walmart SuperCtr, conf. ctr |
| **313** | US 287, to 3rd St, Laramie, Port of Entry, **N** gas: Loaf'N Jug, Conoco/dsl, Exxon, Phillips 66/dsl, Shell/dsl, **food:** Burger King, Chuck Wagon Rest., Great Wall Chinese, **lodging:** 1st Inn Gold, Laramie Inn/rest., Motel 8, Sunset Inn, **other:** H HOSPITAL, Honda/Nissan/Isuzu, Laramie Plains Museum, NAPA, **S lodging:** Motel 6, Ramada Inn |
| **312mm** | Laramie River |
| **311** | WY 130, WY 230, Snowy Range Rd, Laramie, **S** gas: Conoco/dsl, Phillips 66/dsl, Sinclair/dsl/LP, **food:** McDonald's, Subway, **lodging:** Best Value Inn, Howard Johnson, to Snowy Range Ski Area, WY Terr Park |
| **310** | Curtis St, Laramie, **N** gas: Pilot/Wendy's/dsl/24hr/@, Shamrock/café/dsl, **lodging:** Best Western, Day's Inn, Econolodge, Quality Inn, Super 8, **other:** H HOSPITAL, Goodyear/service/towing, KOA, **1 mi N on 3rd...food:** Pizza Hut, Shari's Rest., **other:** Checker Parts, Family$, Hastings, Jeep/Subaru, K-Mart, Safeway Foods, **S** gas: Petro/Iron Skillet/dsl/scales/24hr/@, Blue Beacon, **lodging:** Baymont Inn, Fairfield Inn |
| **307mm** | parking area both lanes, litter barrels |
| **297** | WY 12, Herrick Lane |

**WY**

E ↕ W

## INTERSTATE 80 CONT'D

**RAWLINS**

| Exit | Description |
|------|-------------|
| 290 | Quealy Dome Rd |
| 279 | Cooper Cove Rd |
| 272mm | Rock Creek |
| 272 | WY 13, to Arlington, **N** gas, RV camping |
| 267 | Wagonhound Rd, **S** rest area both lanes, full ♿ facilities, 🚻, 🏕, litter barrels, petwalk |
| 262mm | parking area both lanes |
| 260 | CR 402 |
| 259mm | Medicine Bow River, E Fork |
| 257mm | Medicine Bow River |
| 255 | WY 72, Elk Mtn, to Hanna, **N gas:** Conoco/dsl, |
| 238 | Peterson Rd |
| 235 | US 30/87, WY 130, **N gas:** Shell/dsl/café |
| 229mm | N Platte River |
| 228 | Ft Steele HS, **N** rest area both lanes, full ♿ facilities, 🚻, 🏕, litter barrels, petwalk |
| 221 | E Sinclair, **N gas:** Phillips 66/dsl/rest./24hr, **other:** to Seminoe SP, camping |
| 219 | W Sinclair, **N other:** to Seminoe SP, camping |
| 215 | Cedar St, Rawlins, **N gas:** City Mkt, Conoco/dsl, Phillips 66/dsl, Shell/KFC/Taco Bell, Sinclair, **food:** McDonald's, Pizza Hut, Subway, Taco John's, **lodging:** Comfort Inn, Day's Inn, 1st Choice Inn, Hampton Inn, Holiday Inn Express, Quality Inn, OakTree Inn, The Key Motel, **other:** Alco, Buick/Chevrolet/Pontiac/GMC, CarQuest, Checker Parts, Chrysler/Dodge/Jeep, City Mkt Food/gas, Pamida, TDS Tire, museum, Frontier Prison NHS, to Yellowstone/Teton NP |
| 214 | Higley Blvd, Rawlins, **N lodging:** Microtel, **other:** KOA, **S gas:** TA/Shell/Subway/dsl/24hr/@, **lodging:** Best Value Inn |
| 211 | WY 789, to US 287 N, Spruce St, Rawlins, **N gas:** Conoco/dsl, Exxon/dsl, Phillips 66, Sinclair/dsl, **food:** Cappy's Rest., Golden 8 Chinese, **lodging:** Best Western, Budget Inn, Econolodge, Express Inn, Ideal Motel, La Bella, Super 8, Sunset Motel, Travelodge, **other:** H HOSPITAL, Family$, RV World, V1/LP, Western Hills Camping, **1 mi N lodging:** Economy Inn, **other:** Ford/Lincoln/Mercury |
| 209 | Johnson Rd, **N gas:** ✈FLYING J/dsl/LP/rest./scales/24hr/@ |
| 206 | Hadsell Rd (no return) |
| 205.5mm | continental divide, elev 7000 |
| 204 | Knobs Rd |
| 201 | Daley Rd |
| 196 | Riner Rd |
| 190mm | parking area wb, litter barrels |
| 189mm | parking area eb, 🏕, litter barrels |
| 187 | WY 789, Creston, Baggs Rd |
| 184 | Continental Divide Rd |
| 173 | Wamsutter, **N gas:** Loves/Chester Fried/Subway/dsl/24hr/@, Sinclair/dsl/LP/@, **S gas:** Conoco/dsl/repair/café/24hr, Phillips 66/dsl/@, **food:** Broadway Café, **lodging:** Wamsutter Motel |
| 170 | Rasmussen Rd |
| 168 | Frewen Rd |

**ROCK SPRINGS**

| Exit | Description |
|------|-------------|
| 166 | Booster Rd |
| 165 | Red Desert |
| 158 | Tipton Rd, continental divide, elev 6930 |
| 156 | GL Rd |
| 154 | BLM Rd |
| 152 | Bar X Rd |
| 150 | Table Rock Rd |
| 146 | Patrick Draw Rd |
| 144mm | rest area both lanes, full ♿ facilities, 🚻, 🏕, litter barrels, petwalk |
| 143mm | parking area both lanes, litter barrels |
| 142 | Bitter Creek Rd |
| 139 | Red Hill Rd |
| 136 | Black Butte Rd |
| 133mm | parking area both lanes |
| 130 | Point of Rocks, **N gas:** Conoco/dsl |
| 122 | WY 371, to Superior |
| 111 | Airport Rd, Baxter Rd, **S** ✈ |
| 107 | Pilot Butte Ave, Rock Springs, **S gas:** Mobil/dsl/lodging, Phillips 66/dsl, **lodging:** Sands Inn/cafe, Springs Motel |
| 104 | US 191 N, Elk St, Rock Springs, **N gas:** Exxon, ✈FLYING J/Conoco/dsl/LP/rest./24hr, Kum&Go/gas, Phillips 66/dsl, Sinclair, Texaco/Burger King/dsl, **food:** Fiesta Guadalajara Mexican, McDonald's, Renegade Rest., Santa Fe Trail Rest., Taco Time, **lodging:** Best Western, Econolodge/rest., **other:** Buick/Pontiac/GMC, Great Western RV, Jeep, truck repair, to Teton/Yellowstone Nat Parks via US 191, **S gas:** Exxon/dsl, **lodging:** Day's Inn |
| 103 | College Dr, Rock Springs, **S gas:** Loaf'n Jug/dsl/24hr, **food:** Domino's **other:** H HOSPITAL, W WY Coll |
| 102 | WY 430, Dewar Dr, Rock Springs, **N gas:** Exxon, Loaf'N Jug, Sinclair/dsl, **food:** Applebee's, China King, KFC/LJ Silver, Taco Time, **lodging:** Best Value Inn, Comfort Inn La Quinta, Motel 6, The Inn, **other:** Chevrolet/Cadillac, Chrysler/Dodge/Subaru, $Tree, Harley-Davidson, Home Depot, K-Mart, JC Penney, Smith's Foods, **S gas:** Kum&Go, Loaf'N Jug, Mobil, **food:** Arby's, Bonsai Chinese, Burger King, Golden Corral, IHOP, JB's, McDonald's, Pizza Hut, Quizno's, Sonic, Starbucks, Subway, Taco Bell, Village Inn Rest., Wendy's, Wingers, **lodging:** Hampton Inn, Holiday Inn, Homewood Suites, Motel 8, Quality Inn, Super 8, Wingate Inn, **other:** H HOSPITAL, Albertson's, AutoZone, Big O Tire, Checker Parts, Curves, Hastings Books, NAPA, Radio Shack, Walgreens, Walmart SuperCtr/gas |

**GREEN RIVER**

| Exit | Description |
|------|-------------|
| 99 | US 191 S, E Flaming Gorge Rd, **N other:** KOA (1mi), **S gas:** Sinclair/dsl/rest./24hr/@, **food:** Ted's Rest., **other:** fireworks, transmissions |
| 94mm | Kissing Rock |
| 91 | US 30, to WY 530, Green River, **S gas:** Gasamat, Loaf'N Jug/gas **food:** Arctic Circle, Buckaroo's Rest., China Garden, Don Pedro's Mexican, McDonald's, Pizza Hut, Subway, Taco John's, Taco Time, **lodging:** Coachman Inn, Mustang Inn, Super 8, Western Motel, **other:** Expedition NHS, to Flaming Gorge NRA, same as 89 |
| 89 | US 30, Green River, **N lodging:** Hampton Inn, **S gas:** Exxon, Sinclair/dsl, **food:** Don Pedro's, McDonald's, Penny's Diner, Pizza Hut, Taco Time, **lodging:** OakTree Inn, Super 8, Western Inn, **other:** Adam's RV Service, NAPA, Tex's RV Camp, to Flaming Gorge NRA |

## INTERSTATE 80 CONT'D

| | |
|---|---|
| 87.5mm | Green River |
| 85 | Covered Wagon Rd, **S other:** Adams RV parts/service, Tex's Travel Camp |
| 83 | WY 372, La Barge Rd, **N** to Fontenelle Dam |
| 78 | (from wb) |
| 77mm | Blacks Fork River |
| 72 | Westvaco Rd |
| 71mm | parking area both lanes |
| 68 | Little America, **N gas:** Sinclair/Little America Hotel/rest./dsl/24hr@, **other:** RV camping |
| 66 | US 30 W, to Teton, Yellowstone, Fossil Butte NM, Kemmerer |
| 61 | Cedar Mt Rd, to Granger |
| 60mm | parking area both lanes, litter barrels |
| 54mm | parking area eb, litter barrels |
| 53 | Church Butte Rd |
| 49mm | parking area wb, litter barrels |
| 48 | Lp 80, Lyman, Ft Bridger, Hist Ft Bridger |
| 45mm | Blacks Fork River |
| 41 | WY 413, Lyman, **N gas:** Gas'n Go/dsl/cafe/@, **S rest area both lanes, full ♿ facilities, 🚻, 🏕, litter barrels, petwalk, food:** Taco Time, **other:** Gateway Inn (2mi), KOA (1mi) |
| 39 | WY 412, WY 414, to Carter, Mountain View |
| 34 | Lp 80, to Ft Bridger, **S gas:** Phillips 66, **lodging:** Wagon Wheel Motel, **other:** Ft Bridger RV Camp, Ft Bridger NHS, to Flaming Gorge NRA |
| 33.5mm | parking area eb, litter barrels |
| 33 | Union Rd |
| 30 | Bigelow Rd, **N gas:** TA/Tesoro/Burger King/Taco Bell/Fork In the Road/dsl/scales/24hr/@, **S** fireworks |
| 28 | French Rd |
| 28mm | French Rd, parking area both lanes |
| 24 | Leroy Rd |
| 23 | Bar Hat Rd |
| 21 | Coal Rd |
| 18 | US 189 N, to Kemmerer, to Nat Parks, Fossil Butte NM |
| 15 | Guild Rd (from eb) |
| 14mm | **parking area both lanes** |
| 13 | Divide Rd |
| 10 | Painter Rd, to Eagle Rock Ski Area, to Eagle Rock Ski Area |
| 6 | US 189, Bear River Dr, Evanston, **N gas:** Pilot/Subway/dsl/scales/24hr, Sinclair/dsl, **food:** Bear Town Rest., Don Pedro Mexican, **lodging:** Best Value Inn, Holiday Inn Express, Motel 6, Prairie Inn, Vagabond Motel, **other:** Bear River RV Park, CarQuest, Freeway Tire, Ford/Mercury, Goodyear, KC's RV Ctr, Tire Factory, Wyo Downs Racetrack, **S Welcome Ctr both lanes, full ♿ facilities, 🚻, 🏕, litter barrels, petwalk, RV dump (seasonal), playground,** Bear River SP |
| 5 | WY 89, Evanston, **N gas:** Chevron/Taco Time/dsl, Maverik/dsl, Sinclair/LP, **food:** Arby's, DragonWall Chinese, McDonald's, Papa Murphy's, Shakey's Pizza, Sonic, Starbucks, Subway, Wendy's, **lodging:** Best Value Inn, **other:** H HOSPITAL, AutoZone, Chevrolet/Buick, Family$, Jiffy Lube, Jubilee foods/gas, Murdoch's, NAPA, Radio Shack, Walmart SuperCtr, **S** WY St H HOSPITAL |

| | |
|---|---|
| 3 | US 189, Harrison Dr, Evanston, **N gas:** Chevron/dsl, ✈FLYING J/dsl/rest./scales/24hr/@, Gasamat, Sinclair, **food:** JB's, Legal Tender, Lotty's Rest., Taco Time, Wally's Burgers, **lodging:** Best Western/rest., Comfort Inn, Day's Inn, Economy Inn, HighCountry Inn, HillCrest Motel, Holiday Inn Express, Howard Johnson, The Lodge, Weston Inn, **other:** Automotive+, Chrysler/Jeep, GMC/Pontiac/Cadillac, USPO, **S food:** KFC/Taco Bell, **other:** H HOSPITAL, fireworks |
| .5mm | Port of Entry eb, weigh sta wb |
| 0mm | Wyoming/Utah state line |

## INTERSTATE 90

| Exit # | Services |
|---|---|
| 207mm | Wyoming/South Dakota state line |
| 205 | Beulah, **N gas:** Conoco/Buffalo Jump/dsl/LP, **lodging:** The Mill, **other:** Sand Creek Camping, USPO, Ranch A NHP (5mi) |
| 204.5mm | Sand Creek |
| 199 | WY 111, to Aladdin, to Vore Buffalo Jump NHP |
| 191 | Moskee Rd |
| 189 | US 14 W, Sundance, **N gas:** BP/dsl/24hr, **food:** Aro Rest. (2mi), Subway (2mi), **lodging:** Bear Lodge, Best Western, Budget Host Arrowhead, **other:** H HOSPITAL, Mt View Camping, to Devil's Tower NM, museum, **S rest area both lanes, full ♿ facilities, info, 🚻, 🏕, litter barrels, playground, petwalk, RV dump,** port of entry/weigh sta |
| 187 | WY 585, Sundance, **N gas:** BP/dsl, Fresh Start/dsl, **food:** Subway, **lodging:** Best Western, Decker's Motel, Pineview Motel, Rodeway Inn, Sundance Mtn Inn, **other:** Decker's Foods |
| 185 | to WY 116, to Sundance, **S gas:** Conoco/dsl/service, **food:** ARO Rest., Subway, **lodging:** Bear Lodge, Best Western, Budget Host, **other:** Mt View Camping, to Devil's Tower |
| 178 | Coal Divide Rd |
| 177mm | parking area both lanes, litter barrels |
| 172 | Inyan Kara Rd |
| 171mm | parking area both lanes, litter barrels |
| 165 | Pine Ridge Rd, to Pine Haven, **N** to Keyhole SP |
| 163mm | parking area both lanes, litter barrels |
| 160 | Wind Creek Rd |
| 154 | US 14, US 16, **S gas:** Conoco/dsl, **food:** Donna's Diner, Subway, Taco Time, **lodging:** Cozy Motel, Moorcourt Motel, Wyo Motel, **other:** Dihl's Foods, USPO, museum, city park |

**WY**

E ↑ W

GILLETTE

SHERIDAN

## INTERSTATE 90 CONT'D

| | |
|---|---|
| **153** | US 16 E, US 14, W Moorcroft, **N rest area both lanes, full &#9855; facilities, &#128227;, &#127983;, litter barrels, petwalk** |
| **152mm** | Belle Fourche River |
| **141** | Rozet |
| **138mm** | **parking area both lanes** |
| **132** | Wyodak Rd |
| **129** | Garner Lake Rd, **S other:** Harley-Davidson, High Plains Camping, WY Marine/RV ctr, auto repair |
| **128** | US 14, US 16, Gillette, Port of Entry, **N gas:** Cenex, Conoco, Maverik/dsl, **food:** Mona's American/Mexican, Taco John's, Village Inn Rest., **lodging:** Howard Johnson, National 9 Inn, Smart Choice Inn, **other:** Crazy Woman Camping (2mi), East Side RV Ctr., **S other:** High Plains Camping |
| **126** | WY 59, Gillette, **N gas:** Cenex/dsl, Conoco, **food:** Hardee's, Maria's Mexican, McDonald's, Papa John's, Pokey's BBQ, Prime Rib Rest., Starbucks, Subway, **lodging:** Best Value, Rolling Hills Motel, **other:** Radio Shack, Smith's Foods, Tire Factory, city park, **S gas:** Exxon, &#9884;FLYING J/dsl/rest./24hr, Loaf'n Jug, **food:** A&W/LJ Silver, Applebee's, Arby's, Burger King, DQ, Goodtimes Grill/Taco John's, Golden Corral, KFC, Papa Murphy's, Perkins/24hr, Pizza Hut, Popeye's, Quizno's, Taco Bell, Wendy's, **lodging:** Clarion, Comfort Inn, Day's Inn, Fairfield Inn, Holiday Inn Express, Wingate Inn, **other:** Ace Hardware, Albertson's, Checker Parts, Chrysler/Dodge/Jeep, GNC, Goodyear/auto, Home Depot, K-Mart, Office Depot, O'Reilly Parts, Osco Drug, Tire-O-Rama, Walgreens, Walmart SuperCtr, city park, RV dump |
| **124** | WY 50, Gillette, **N gas:** Conoco/dsl/24hr, Shell/Burger King/dsl, **food:** Granny's Kitchen, Hong Kong Rest., Pizza Hut, Subway, **lodging:** Best Western/rest., Budget Inn, Comfort Inn, Hampton Inn, Motel 6, Super 8, **other:** &#72; HOSPITAL, Don's Foods, **S gas:** Cenex/dsl, **other:** Bighorn Tire, Chevrolet/Cadillac/Buick |
| **116** | Force Rd |
| **113** | Wild Horse Creek Rd |
| **110mm** | **parking area both lanes** |
| **106** | Kingsbury Rd |
| **102** | Barber Creek Rd |
| **91** | Dead Horse Creek Rd |
| **89mm** | Powder River |
| **88** | Powder River Rd, **N gas:** Exit 88 Fuel/dsl, Powder River Trvl Plaza/dsl/camping, **rest area both lanes, full &#9855; facilities, &#128227;, &#127983;, litter barrels, petwalk** |
| **82** | Indian Creek Rd |
| **77** | Schoonover Rd |
| **73.5mm** | Crazy Woman Creek |
| **73** | Crazy Woman Creek Rd |
| **69** | Dry Creek Rd |
| **68.5mm** | parking area both lanes, litter barrels |
| **65** | Red Hills Rd, Tipperary Rd |
| **60mm** | parking area both lanes, litter barrels |
| **58** | US 16, to Ucross, Buffalo, **S gas:** Cenex/dsl/rest./24hr, Exxon/dsl, **other:** Bighorn Tire, **1-3 mi S gas:** Johnson |

| | |
|---|---|
| **58** | Continued<br>Cty/dsl, Shell/dsl/24hr, **food:** Bozeman Tr Steaks, Dash Inn Rest., Hardee's, Hoot'n Howl Rest., McDonald's, Pizza Hut, Sub Shop, Subway, Taco John's, Winchester Steaks, **lodging:** Best Western Crossroads, Comfort Inn, Horsemen's Inn, Motel 6, Rodeway Inn, Super 8, Wyo Motel, **other:** &#72; HOSPITAL, Ace Hardware, Deer Park Camping, Family$, Indian RV Camp, KOA, NAPA, Nat Hist Dist |
| **56b** | I-25 S, US 87 S, to Buffalo |
| **56a** | 25 Bus, 90 Bus, to Buffalo, services 2 mi south |
| **53** | Rock Creek Rd |
| **51** | Lake DeSmet, **1 mi N** Lake Stop gas, Lake Stop Motel, Lake Desmet RV park |
| **47** | Shell Creek Rd |
| **44** | US 87 N, Piney Creek Rd, to Story, Banner, **N other:** Ft Phil Kearney, museum, **5 mi S** Wagon Box Rest., Wagon Box Cabins |
| **39mm** | scenic turnout wb, litter barrel |
| **37** | Prairie Dog Creek Rd, to Story |
| **33** | Meade Creek Rd, to Big Horn |
| **31mm** | **parking area eb, litter barrel** |
| **25** | US 14 E, Sheridan, **N lodging:** Comfort Inn, **other:** Big Sky RV Ctr, **S gas:** Exxon/dsl, Holiday, Loaf'n Jug/dsl, Maverik, **food:** Arby's, Burger King, Golden China, JB's, Los Agaves, Ole's Pizza, Perkins/24hr, Starbucks, Subway, Taco Bell, Taco John's, Wendy's, **lodging:** Day's Inn, Holiday Inn, Mill Inn, Parkway Motel, **other:** Ace hardware, Albertson's/Osco Drug, Checker Parts, $Tree, Firestone, Ford/Lincoln/Mercury, Goodyear, Home Depot, NAPA, O'Reilly Parts, Pontiac/Cadillac, Safeway Foods, Toyota, Walgreens, Walmart SuperCtr, Whse Mkt Foods, mall, to Hist Dist, Sheridan Coll |
| **23** | WY 336, 5th St, Sheridan, **N gas:** Rock Stop/Subway/dsl, **lodging:** Wingate Inn, **rest area both lanes, full &#9855; facilities, info, &#128227;, &#127983;, litter barrels, petwalk, RV dump, 1-2 mi S gas:** Cenex, Holiday/dsl, **food:** DQ, Pablo's Mexican, Quizno's, Rid & Chophouse, **lodging:** Alamo Motel, Best Value, Best Western, Hampton Inn, Motel 6, Sheridan Inn, **other:** &#72; HOSPITAL, Honda, Main St Drub, Peter D's RV Sheradon Cty Museum, park, radiators |
| **20** | Main St, Sheridan, **S gas:** Conoco, Exxon/dsl/scales/24hr, Shell/dsl, **food:** Country Kitchen, McDonald's, Pizza Hut, **lodging:** Aspen Inn, Budget Host, Super Save Motel, Trails End Motel, Stage Stop Motel, Sundown Motel, Super 8, **other:** &#72; HOSPITAL, K-Mart, KOA |
| **16** | to Decker, Montana, port of entry |
| **15mm** | Tongue River |
| **14** | Acme Rd |
| **9** | US 14 W, Ranchester, **1 mi S gas:** Big Country Oil/dsl, **other:** Western Motel, **other:** Foothills Campground, Lazy R campground, to Yellowstone, Teton NPs, Conner Bfd NHS, Ski Area |
| **1** | Parkman |
| **0mm** | Wyoming/Montana state line |

# Assist A Fellow Traveler with...

Published annually,

## the Next EXIT®

provides the best

## USA Interstate Highway Information available.
## Use this form to order another copy of the Next EXIT®
## for yourself or someone special.

Please send _____ copies of the Next Exit® to the address below.

I've enclosed my check or money order for $20.95 US/$23.95 Canadian per copy.

Name:_____

Address: _____ Apt./Suite # _____

City: _____ State: _____ Zip: _____

## THREE EASY ORDER OPTIONS:

**1. MAIL ORDER FORM TO:**
the Next EXIT®, Inc.
PO Box 888
Garden City, Utah 84028

**2. ORDER ON THE WEB AT:**
www.theNextExit.com

**3. Give Us A Call & Use Your Charge Card**
1-800-NEX-EXIT or 1-800-639-3948

**the Next EXIT® is Available Online at: www.theNextExit.com**